Rock Island Public Library
401 - 19th Street
Rock Island, IL 61201-8143

W9-DFQ-912

FADE TO
BLACK

DATE DUE

GAYLORD   #3522PI   Printed in USA

FADE TO
BLACK

A BOOK OF
FILM
OBITUARIES

PAUL DONNELLEY

OMNIBUS PRESS
London/New York/Paris/Sydney/Copenhagen/Madrid/Tokyo

Text © Paul Donnelley
This edition copyright © 2010 Omnibus Press
(A Division of Music Sales Limited)

Cover designed by Fresh Lemon

ISBN: 978.1.84938.246.5
Order Number: OP53295

The Author hereby asserts his right to be identified as the author of
this work in accordance with Sections 77 to 78 of the Copyright,
Designs and Patents Act 1988.

All rights reserved. No part of this book may be reproduced in any
form or by any electronic or mechanical means, including information
storage or retrieval systems, without permission in writing from the
publisher, except by a reviewer who may quote brief passages.

Exclusive Distributors:
Music Sales Limited,
14/15 Berners Street,
London, W1T 3LJ.

Music Sales Corporation,
257 Park Avenue South,
New York, NY 10010, USA.

Macmillan Distribution Services,
56 Parkwest Drive,
Derrimut, Vic 3030,
Australia.

Every effort has been made to trace the copyright holders of the
photographs in this book but one or two were unreachable. We would
be grateful if the photographers concerned would contact us.

Typeset by Galleon Typesetting, Ipswich.
Printed in Great Britain by MPG Books Ltd, Bodmin, Cornwall

A catalogue record for this book is available from the British Library.

Visit Omnibus Press on the web at www.omnibuspress.com

In memory of my Mum and Dad . . .

He first took me to "the pictures" when I
was little – she was probably grateful for the
couple hours of peace and quiet.

And for Karima with whom I rediscovered my
love of sitting in the dark with a bunch of
strangers watching a big screen.

Foreword by Michael Winner

You know you're heading for an entry in *Fade To Black* when the chairman of the company you're doing commercials for says, "If you drop dead, do you still want us to play your esure ads?" "Absolutely, Peter," I said, "there are more dead people on TV than live ones when you consider all those old movies and repeats that are running." "Write me a letter confirming it," Peter Wood said. He was right. Why pay a fortune for commercials and the twit who stars in them falls off the log and you can't use them any more? I like the idea of haunting the world with my presence when I'm gone. "Calm down dear, it's only a corpse."

I hope Paul Donnelley who puts this highly entertaining and informative book together will scrape the barrel of tabloid turnings-over I've suffered and rumours of everything from my being gay (untrue) to my being totally mad (true) in order to fill the pages with jolly reading material. I read very few books. The only books I've read in the last three years are *Fade To Black* and *Walter The Farting Dog*. *Walter* which headed *The Sunday Times* bestseller list for children's books. My fiancée gave it to me. Obviously trying to tell me something.

As *Fade To Black* gets bigger with every edition (the sharp-eyed will notice even my Foreword has got longer) I wonder when it will have to be in two then three and then 106 volumes. One thing is for sure: Hollywood people keep dying. Some, if not most of them, die before they expire. That's why it's so important to have a record of what they did and didn't do and where the poor souls ended up. *Fade To Black* is marvellously scurrilous. I was employing, as one of my assistants, the ex-girlfriend of Christopher Reeve, the lady with whom he had children. I said, assuming she knew (and I only "knew" because I read it here) "I didn't know Christopher was gay." She said, "He wasn't." I said, "Well it says so in *Fade To Black*, Gae. Maybe they know something you didn't." I wish I hadn't said it really. She was terribly upset. I note *Fade To Black* says one of my best friends in showbusiness, Burt Lancaster took sex where he could, with men or women. I never saw any sign of the gay bit in the 25 years I knew Burt. But in one major biography a woman writer said he'd been with Rock Hudson to a gay party with 167 US Marines. I wish Burt had been alive. I can imagine the phone call – "Did you see what that cocksucker said? She said I'd been to a party with 167 Marines. Fucking bitch. There were 171 of them." I have these conversations with dead people all the time.

I'll tell you a story about another of my best friends, Oliver Reed. He was indeed, as this book says, buried in Ireland near his favourite pub. In a field behind it, actually. I wept at the church service. Then the hearse drove through little Irish villages. The locals stood at the roadside crossing themselves. It was very moving. We finally got to this pub and walked down a rutted alleyway at the side to get to the field behind. I was with Oliver's first wife Kate, a beautiful Irish lady who was still very lovely. Everyone was saying, "What an enchanting place. Look at those elm trees, the peace, the tranquillity. What a marvellous place Oliver chose to be buried." Kate said to me, "What a shit-hole. Full of fucking flies and cow shit, only Oliver could have wanted to be buried in a crap-hole like this." I had another of my imaginary phone calls to Oliver the next day. "Oliver," I said, "this is what Kate said at your funeral yesterday . . ." I can hear Oliver's response now. In that very quiet voice (he was the most marvellous person) Oliver said, "Did she really, Michael? Kate always had a great sense of humour." Oh dear, I could do stories about dead stars enough to fill an entire volume of *Fade To Black*. I'm a bit pissed off they didn't put my famous quote about Brando (another marvellous, kind, witty person) in his obituary, at least not in the edition I read. I said, with total truth, "Before Brando actors acted. After Brando actors behaved." What do I want them to say about me? List all my achievements and boost them magnificently. As a summation of Michael Winner: "He cheered people up. He made them laugh." What more could anyone want? As for my tombstone inscription: "I will return."

PS: I'm with Michael Caine and Joan Collins. Joan said, "I was in The Ivy last night. There was no one there that I knew." Michael Caine said, "That's cos they're all dead." Not in The Ivy any more – in this book.

FURTHER READING: *Winner Takes All* – Michael Winner (London: Robson Books, 2004); *Michael Winner's Fat Pig Diet* – Michael Winner (London: JR Books, 2007): *Winner's Dinners The Restaurant and Hotel Guide* – Michael Winner (London: JR Books, 2009)

Introduction to the Tenth Anniversary Edition (2010)

Is it really ten years since the first edition of this book came out? In that time the book has doubled in size and we have lost a number of giants of the film industry including Marlon Brando, Charles Bronson, Katharine Hepburn, Charlton Heston, Bob Hope and Paul Newman to name but half a dozen.

Perhaps it might be fitting here to explain the idea behind the book, in modern parlance "the mission statement" if you like. *Fade To Black* was never intended to be a comprehensive guide to everyone who has ever made a film – it could never be. If that were the case, it would need to be several dozen volumes and even then I would probably omit someone's favourite. I hope it does feature the *major* people in front of and behind the camera but for many of them there is already a plethora of literature available. If you just want to browse filmographies with little or no biographical information, then may I recommend *Halliwell's Who's Who In The Movies* (formerly *Halliwell's Filmgoer's Companion*). *Fade To Black* is and was intended to provide an overview of the life and career of filmdom's most interesting personalities. The length of a personality's entry in the book, however, should in no way be construed as to my opinion of their import in cinematic history, merely what I find most interesting about them. I don't know of any other film reference book that includes full dates (where known) and places for births, deaths and marriages plus for some entries, the dates of film releases or premières as well as real names and wealth at death.

Entries are constantly revised, usually enlarged, and none are deleted or reduced in size. The beauty of the book, if I do say so myself, is that it can never be out of date, only incomplete as people die around the cut-off date for inclusion. If they are big or interesting enough, they nearly always get into the next edition.

A favourite of many readers (so they tell me) is the "quiz" or snippets of information that whets their appetite before the real meat of the book begins in a few pages. So, to avoid disappointment, here are this edition's questions:

> Who was described by a critic as "a Clark Gable who had been left out in the sun too long"?
> Which actress twice married her late husband's barber?
> Who was the first man to kiss Mary Pickford on screen?
> Which heartthrob played a gay cyclist and then appeared in the soap *Home And Away* before stardom beckoned?
> Who was sacked from Warner Bros for sleeping with Jack L. Warner's wife?

If you have any comments on the book – bouquets and brickbats – I would be pleased to hear from you, either c/o of the publishers or via my website.

Paul Donnelley
2009
www.pauldonnelley.com

Introduction to the First Edition (2000)

On a Saturday afternoon about a year ago I was browsing in a well-known book shop when I spotted *The Encyclopædia Of Rock Obituaries*. I bought a copy that day little realising that I would write and compile the companion volume which you now hold in your hands. On the Monday I sat down and wrote to the publishers suggesting this book. Within a fortnight of my approach, a contract was drawn up and I began work in earnest on this volume. How could I know what a mammoth task I had set myself? Firstly, I drew up an initial list of entrants. Then I thought of more people and more people. Eventually I had to stop, or the present book would never have been finished. I have searched through literally thousands of sources checking, double checking and triple checking facts. It would take a book almost as long again to list just some of my sources. Many so-called reliable reference works disagree about even some fundamental data so I have had to make a decision about which is the most accurate. If you can prove any errors, I'd love to hear from you. Where possible, a bibliography is amended to each entry for readers who want to learn more about a particular personality.

Readers will notice that in numerous cases I have listed, for the sake of completeness, the actual addresses where stars were born, married, died or buried. Many of these buildings are still standing and should the reader wish to visit any of them they should remember these are often in private hands and the current owners may not welcome unsolicited visits. Please show the same respect you would expect from visitors to your own home.

I believe the people I have chosen are representative of all genres in Hollywood. This volume contains actors, actresses, producers, directors, moguls, gossip columnists, animals, lawyers and even Sid Grauman, the man outside whose famous Chinese Theatre are enshrined hundreds of celebrity foot- and handprints. Some entries are disproportionately longer than others. This is in no way a reflection on the abilities of the subject or their importance in filmdom. It's just some people have more interesting stories than others and, since there are several film books already around, I believe it is only right to concentrate on fascinating tales rather than regurgitate bare facts. Some readers may feel I have overly concentrated on the dark side of stardom. But I believe that it is the foibles and very human failings of people that make them so fascinating.

For example, can you name the following celebrities?

- The first Oscar winner to cry when picking up the statuette?
- The German singer who, after the death of her first husband, married three alcoholic homosexuals?
- The Western star who formed his own private army?
- The actor whose wife was suspected of being a German spy and was bugged by the FBI?
- The first actor to refuse to shave his chest?

- The actress who, upon catching her husband in bed with another woman, shouted that if he could have mistresses, so could she?
- The actress who died of a heart attack aged 31 while bending over to tie a shoelace?

Yes, I am a film buff – I still recall some of the earliest films I saw at the pictures, in the days when if you missed the beginning you just stayed in your seat and the film would begin again almost immediately – but I am also a people buff. I love fascinating, interesting people. However, if there are any film personalities you think should have been included, then please write telling me why c/o the publishers or direct via email at filmobits@hotmail.com. I think Hollywood, Elstree and this book deserve a second volume.

Paul Donnelley
June 1, 2000
(The 74th anniversary of
Marilyn Monroe's birth)

Acknowledgments

My initial note of gratitude goes to all the people who have bought the various editions of *Fade To Black*. Without them, I would be writing obituaries that no one reads.

Thanks as always go to Chris Charlesworth and the team at Omnibus for their support of this book.

My friend Jeremy Beadle, sadly, isn't around to read this edition of *Fade To Black*, a book he always enthusiastically supported in public and private. He is much missed.

Thanks also to Michael Winner and his continued generous interest in the book as well as the enlarged foreword.

And to: David K. Frasier, Barry A. Kemelhor, Scott Michaels, Mitchell Symons, Shannon Whirry, Anthony Wynn, Jennifer Young.

I would also like to thank all those who have written to me offering information or suggestions for new entries. In particular, I am grateful to Jean Brinson, Berwick Coates and L.K. O'Drudy.

Finally, in an unusual step, I would like to pay tribute to two of my readers who are not around to see this edition. They were both the parents of friends. Marji Shaffer, the mother of Jeremy Beadle, named this book as her favourite and considering how well-read Marji was, that is quite an honour. She kept it by her bedside so she could dip it into before she went to sleep. Marji was a terrific lady and I enjoyed the times we spent chatting over dinner at Jeremy's. I never had the pleasure of meeting Eric North, the father of my friend Erika, who died in 2008. Erika told me how much he liked *Fade To Black* and when they gathered as a family to watch a film he would read aloud the entries of the stars of that film. May they both rest in peace.

A

Aaliyah

Born January 16, 1979
Died August 25, 2001

Hopes dashed. Born in Brooklyn, New York and raised from the age of five in Detroit, Michigan 5'7½", Aaliyah Dana Haughton was a promising R&B singer and actress whose life was cut tragically short. At the age of 14 she released her first album *Nothing But A Number* from which she released the hit singles 'Back And Forth' and 'Try Again' which earned her a Grammy nomination. She graduated from the Detroit High School for the Fine and Performing Arts. She made her film début in the hip-hop kung fu film *Romeo Must Die* (premièred March 20, 2000) playing Trish O'Day (for which she also wrote and sang some of the songs) and followed that with *Queen Of The Damned* (released February 10, 2002) as Queen Akasha. On August 30, 1994 she married the singer R. Kelly but the marriage was annulled on February 7, 1995 because she was only 15 at the time. Supposedly her album title is a reference to the marriage. In 2000 she said, "I don't know what's going to happen in the next five or ten years. At some point I'd like to have a family and settle down, but I don't see that happening for a long time because I love [performing]. This is my life, my world."
CAUSE: Aaliyah died in an aeroplane crash. She had been filming a video for the song 'Rock The Boat' in the Bahamas and was flying back to Opa-Locka, Florida when her overcrowded Cessna 404 crashed into Marsh Harbour, Abaco Island about two hundred feet after take-off. Aaliyah, pilot Luis Morales III, hairstylist Eric Forman, Anthony Dodd, minder Scott Gallin, video producer Douglas Kratz, stylist Christopher Maldonado, and Blackground Records employees Keith Wallace and Gina Smith were all killed. Aaliyah's funeral was held on Friday August 31, 2001 and she was buried in a private alcove in Crypt 3, Unit 4, Tier CC, Rosewood Mausoleum, Ferncliff Cemetery and Mausoleum, Hartsdale, Westchester County, New York. In 2002 her song 'More Than A Woman' topped the UK charts. She was only 22.

Angela Aames

Born February 27, 1956
Died November 27, 1988

Tragic beauty. Born in Pierre, South Dakota, Angela Aames, like many before her, began acting in school plays. After graduating from the University of South Dakota she moved to Hollywood in 1978 in search of fame and fortune. She made her film début playing a nude Little Bo Peep in the film *Fairy Tales* (1978). Next was the teen flick *H.O.T.S.* (1979) in which she portrayed Linda 'Boom-Boom' Bang, baring her breasts in several scenes. In the early Eighties she landed a job on Los Angeles' Channel 11 as their 'Bedtime Movie Girl' presenting the films wearing skimpy outfits. Many of her film parts relied on her bosomy appearance and she doffed her duds in several movies. Her other films included a topless appearance in *All The Marbles* (1981) as Louise, *Scarface* (1983), *Bachelor Party* (1984) as Mrs Klupner, a nude scene in *The Lost Empire* (1985) as Heather McClure, a topless appearance in *Basic Training* (1985) as Cheryl and *Chopping Mall* (1986) as Miss Vanders. She also appeared on a number of TV shows, including *Cheers*, *The Fall Guy*, *Alice* and *Night Court*. Her last role was as Penny, a fitness instructor on *The Dom DeLuise Show* in 1987, a year before her untimely death. She was married to

but separated from Mark Haughland and was living with a female room-mate, Rasa Banja.
CAUSE: Heart disease. Aames was found dead on the bedroom floor of a house in West Hills, San Fernando Valley. At her inquest the coroner said her death was the result of a deterioration of the heart muscle, possibly caused by a virus. However, a friend believed "she died of heart failure brought on in part by diet pills she popped to stay Hollywood thin." "Angela had trouble staying slim," the friend revealed, "and she needed to stay that way if she was going to get another acting job. She was always up and down in weight, and like a lot of actors, she depended heavily on diet pills to kill her appetite." Her mother, Lillian Tlustos, raged, "Angela was obsessed with being a movie star and it killed her. She lived for Hollywood and Hollywood killed her. I know she would have been alive if she hadn't gone there." Her room-mate Banja revealed, "She had been sick but everyone thought it was just the flu. It's tragic because Angela seemed like such a strong person – the kind you expect to take Hollywood by storm." She was just 32 years old.

John Aasen
Born March 5, 1890
Died August 1, 1938
Giant amongst men. Born in Minneapolis, Minnesota, the son of Kristi Danielsen (b. Numedal, Norway 1868, d. Sheyenne, North Dakota 1902), his father's identity remains a mystery. Norwegian-born Aasen stood 7′2″ (claims that he was 8′9″ are fanciful at best) and so not surprisingly worked for a time as a circus giant. He even played a circus giant in *Growing Pains* (1928). His cinematic appearances were playing Colosso opposite Harold Lloyd in Hal Roach's *Why Worry?* (1923), *Long Fliv The King* (1926), *The Sting Of Stings* (1927), *Two Flaming Youths* (1927), *Legionnaires In*

Paris (1927) as Shorty, with Laurel & Hardy in *Should Married Men Go Home?* (1928) in which he played a giant golfer, *Freaks* (1932), *Charlie Chan At The Circus* (1936) and *Bengal Tiger* (1936).
CAUSE: Like many of extreme growth, Aasen suffered from poor health. He died in Mendocino, California aged 48.

Abbott & Costello
(WILLIAM ALEXANDER ABBOTT)
Born October 2, 1895
Died April 24, 1974
(LOUIS FRANCIS CRISTILLO)
Born March 6, 1906
Died March 3, 1959
The poor man's Laurel & Hardy. Unlike Stan and Ollie, tall, thin Bud Abbott and short (5′5″), fat Lou Costello were never great friends and Costello, for a time, wanted his name to come first in their billing. (Universal Studios refused to countenance the change to Costello & Abbott.) He also insisted on, and got, 60% of the money earned by the pair. Both had hair loss problems, as producer Sheldon Leonard revealed: "Bud wore a toupée and Lou used to blacken his scalp because his hair was very thin – unlike the rest of him." Bud Abbott was born in Asbury Park, New Jersey, the son of the Lutheran Harry Abbott, Sr, a publicity man for Barnum & Bailey's Circus, and Jewish Rae Fisher, a bareback rider for the same outfit. Not long after their son's birth the Abbotts left the circus and moved to Coney Island where Harry Abbott set about organising the first burlesque touring circuit. In 1911 young Bud became an assistant treasurer of the Casino Burlesque theatre in Brooklyn where he was to meet dancer Betty Smith (née Jenny Mae Pratt). They married in Alexandria, Virginia, on September 17, 1918, and had a very happy marriage. They adopted two children – Frank James in 1944, and Rae Victoria five years later. Abbott would often watch acts from the wings critiquing them

until his wife could stand it no more and insisted he give it a go himself. She became the comedian to his straight man – as Bud & Betty Abbott – but quickly found herself pushed to one side after a number of other successful comics expressed an interest in standing at Bud's side. In 1936 he was partnering Harry Evanson at the Eltinge Theater on New York's West 42nd Street. Also on the bill was another double act – Joe Lyons and Lou Costello. It wasn't the first time the two men had met (that date is lost in the mists of time) but it was the first time they were able to become properly acquainted. Lou Costello was born at 14 Madison Street, Paterson, New Jersey, the younger son of three children. The family originally hailed from Caserta, Italy, and Costello's grandfather was the local chief of police; one of his aunts joined a closed order. His father, Sebastian Cristillo, considered the priesthood at one point, but instead chose to emigrate to New Jersey in 1898. From the age of four Lou wanted to go into show business and bunked off school to go to the pictures, much to his father's annoyance. Lou's admiration for Charlie Chaplin encouraged him to become a comedian rather than a straight actor. In fact, one Halloween he won a prize for his impersonation of Chaplin. Like many entertainers before and since, Lou didn't excel academically at school, although he was skilled at baseball, basketball and boxing. He would often find himself in detention, having to write "I'm a bad boy" over and over on the blackboard. It was a phrase that would return later in his life as a performer. In 1927 he set out for Hollywood, hitchhiking along the way. Arriving in Tinseltown, Lou landed a job as a general handyman at MGM, sleeping in cars until he had enough money to rent a flat. When he did find somewhere he lived on bread and jam for a month so he could afford to have the gas and electricity switched on. His first appearance before the cameras was as a stunt double for Dolores Del Rio in *Trails Of '98* (1928) after the real stuntman failed to show. He appeared in several other films before being advised to go to New York and learn his trade, advice he followed. However, his money ran out in St Joseph, Missouri, and he landed a job as a comic at a burlesque theatre paying $16 a week. After a year he headed for New York, by now calling himself Lou Costello. He began working burlesque theatres in New York and met a Glasgow-born dancer called Anne Battler whom he married in Boston on January 30, 1934. Like the Abbotts, the Costellos were to have a very happy marriage. They were to have four children: Patricia Ann 'Paddy' (b. Providence, Rhode Island, September 28, 1936); Carole Lou (b. Providence, Rhode Island, December 23, 1939); Louis Francis Jr, known as 'Butch' (b. Los Angeles, California, November 6, 1942, d. November 4, 1943 in a drowning accident) and Christine (b. Los Angeles, California, August 15, 1947). Abbott and Costello began working the burlesque circuit until the theatres were all closed on May 3, 1937, by order of New York Mayor LaGuardia who felt the houses gave the Big Apple a bad name. Moving to the Apollo Theater on 42nd Street, the pair perfected some of their most famous routines, including 'Crazy House', 'The Lemon Bit' and, best known of all, 'Who's On First'. In 1938 the duo began appearing on radio turning a ten-minute guest spot on the *Kate Smith Show* into a regular appearance for the next 18 months. When they left the show, Abbott & Costello were raking in $1,250 per week. In 1941 they landed their own show. Hollywood took note and MGM offered no less than $20,000 for a couple of guest slots in the big musicals. Costello refused, not wanting to play second fiddle to established names. While MGM decided whether or not to increase their offer, Universal jumped in and paid the pair $35,000 for what was to become their first feature, *One Night In The Tropics* (1940). The score for the film was written by Jerome Kern, who objected violently to the casting, but the final say was not his. The film starred Allan Jones and Nancy Kelly but it was Abbott & Costello who stole the movie. (Years later, Jones was furious when he saw a marquee advertising "Abbott & Costello in *One Night In The Tropics*".) It was the duo's second film, *Buck Privates* (1941), that established them as stars – it also grossed over $10 million at the box office, the biggest return Universal had then seen. Universal signed them to a seven-year contract making four films a year on $50,000 per movie plus 10 per cent of the profits. In their first year, Abbott & Costello banked a cool $1 million. *Buck Privates* had the twosome enlist in the army and is generally regarded to be their best film. It was filmed in 20 days and cost $180,000 to make. (A sequel, *Buck Privates Come Home*, was made in 1947.) In 1942 Costello fell ill with rheumatic fever, necessitating a nine-month lay-off. On set, Costello laughed and joked with the crew while Abbott retired, alone, to his dressing room. He drank heavily and suffered from epilepsy. If an attack started when the pair were on stage, Costello would thump Abbott hard in the stomach in an attempt to stop the epilepsy. (Unknowing audiences laughed at what they presumed to be a slapstick routine.) Following the accidental death of his baby son (for which he held his wife responsible) those closest to Costello detected a change in him. The war years saw most of the pair's best work, such as *In The Navy* (1941), *Hold That Ghost* (1941) and *Pardon My Sarong* (1942) although their rivalry continued to simmer just below the surface. (Interestingly, around this time they took out an insurance policy in

case any member of the audience died laughing.) In 1945 they split up for the first time, over the fact that Abbott hired a maid formerly employed by the Costello family. Eventually, their manager, Eddie Sherman, reunited the pair after explaining that they would be sued for millions. Costello begrudgingly agreed to reform the partnership but for a very long time afterwards he only spoke to Abbott in front of the cameras. When Abbott bought a house, Costello bought a larger one and when Abbott had a swimming pool installed, Costello's was exactly one foot longer and one foot wider. Both men were to run into problems over tax in later years, having been given poor financial advice when younger. The two became friendly again when Costello founded the Lou Costello, Jr Youth Foundation. In the late Forties and Fifties Abbott & Costello began making films for different studios and starring opposite established actors, many best known for their horror roles, *viz*: Boris Karloff (*Abbott & Costello Meet The Killer, Boris Karloff* [1949], *Abbott & Costello Meet Dr Jekyll & Mr Hyde* [1953]), Charles Laughton (*Abbott & Costello Meet Captain Kidd* [1952]), Lon Chaney, Jr and Bela Lugosi (*Abbott & Costello Meet Frankenstein* [1948]), the Keystone Kops (*Abbott & Costello Meet The Keystone Kops* [1955]) and Marie Windsor (*Abbott & Costello Meet The Mummy* [1955]). On February 9, 1950, the McCarthy witch hunt for communists – real or imagined – began. Costello, a fervent Republican all his life, publicly supported the Wisconsin senator, believing there was a communist plot to take over the motion picture industry. He took petitions around the studios asking everyone he met to sign to confirm they were not communists or fellow travellers. John Grant, Abbott & Costello's scriptwriter, refused to sign and never worked with them again. On December 5, 1952, the first episode of

The Abbott & Costello Show aired, going on to become one of the most successful syndicated television shows in American history, despite being panned by the critics. Over two years, the boys made 52 episodes. On July 14, 1957, they finally split, Costello by now fed up by what he saw as the lack of recognition for comedians. He wanted to try more dramatic parts. It was said he was also disturbed by Abbott's increasingly heavy drinking. Costello went on to make one more film *The Thirty Foot Bride Of Candy Rock* (1958) which bombed but, fortunately, wasn't released until after his death. He made two appearances on television in dramatic roles. Following Costello's death Abbott was pursued by the Internal Revenue Service to the tune of $750,000. He sold his home and his wife sold her furs and jewellery to help with his financial problems; moreover, Abbott also gave up his right to the profits of Abbott & Costello films. He even begged fans to donate 50¢ each to help him out, a plea that fell on mostly deaf ears. Another partnership, with pallid Costello imitator Candy Candido, failed to win him work and he suffered a stroke in 1964 that paralysed the left side of his body, though he recovered sufficiently to provide the vocals for Abbott & Costello cartoons. In 1972 he broke his hip and spent the rest of his life in a wheelchair. He once said of his former partner: "I never understood Lou. I never knew why he broke us up so suddenly." To the public Abbott was polite and always ready with an autograph. Loyally, if not strictly accurately, he insisted: "We never had any arguments. Lou was the greatest." In 1991 the duo were honoured in America with a commemorative stamp. Nine years later, in April 2000, FBI files were released that revealed that both men had been the subject of a ten-year Bureau investigation over allegations they were involved in "suspicious dealings with mobsters and prostitutes" and that both were regular customers of hardcore pornography, regularly buying "specially filmed loops from a ring of obscene motion picture operators in Hollywood".

CAUSE: Bud Abbott died of cancer, plagued by strokes and hip and leg fractures, at his home in Woodland Hills, California, aged 78. His ashes were scattered at sea. Lou Costello died of a heart attack in Doctors Hospital, Beverly Hills, three days before his 53rd birthday. He was buried, alongside his son, in Crypt B1 Block 354 of the Main Mausoleum of Calvary Cemetery, 4201 Whittier Boulevard, Los Angeles 90023. Bud Abbott was one of the pallbearers.

FURTHER READING: *Lou's On First* – Chris Costello with Raymond Strait (New York: St Martin's Press, 1981).

Dorothy Abbott
Born December 16, 1920
Died December 15, 1968
Tragic wannabe. Born in Kansas City, Missouri, the daughter of Helen M. and William V. Abbott, young Dorothy was spotted in a nightclub and offered a $150-a-week contract by Paramount. She appeared, often uncredited, in 20 films including *A Virgin In Hollywood* (1948) as Dorothy Sloan, *Night Has A Thousand Eyes* (1948), *Take Me Out To The Ball Game* (1949), *My Favorite Spy* (1951), *Rebel Without A Cause* (1955) as a nurse, *Gunfight At The O.K. Corral* (1957) and *That Touch Of Mink* (1962). She also appeared in *Dragnet* playing Sergeant Joe Friday's girlfriend. In 1950 she won three beauty contest titles: Miss Wilshire Club, Miss Los Angeles Transit and Miss Oil Cans. In 1951 she made $175 per week by dancing in the show *Aaron Slick From Punkin Crick*. As acting work dried up, she turned her hand to being an estate agent. "She bought for a song a nice house that had to be moved because of the new Hollywood freeway. She fixed up the house on a Hollywood lot and now leases it for a pretty penny,"

reported one gossip column. In 1949 she married policeman Rudy Diaz (b. October 16, 1918 as Adolph Diaz, d. Los Angeles, California, December 5, 2006) but they separated and in 1964 he was seen squiring Ann Sothern about town. He got a taste for the bright lights because in November 1967 he resigned from the police force after 21 years and became an actor. Abbott and Diaz divorced in June 1968.

CAUSE: In a fit of depression over the break-up of her marriage and lack of career success, she killed herself in Los Angeles, California. She was a little short of her 48th birthday. She was interred in lot 2939, Valley Lawn at Rose Hills Memorial Park, Whittier, California.

Gypsy Abbott
Born January 31, 1895
Died July 25, 1952
Silent comedienne. Born in Atlanta, Georgia, Gypsy Abbott began her career on stage aged eight and appeared with legends of the American theatre Minnie Maddern Fiske and Nat Goodwin. Work in vaudeville and repertory preceded her first films for Balboa Amusement Productions, an early film company that was operational between 1913 and April 1918 and run by H.M. Horkheimer and his brother Elwood. Abbott later moved to Mutual where she appeared opposite Crane Wilbur. In 1916 she became the face of Mutual's *Vogue* comedies. Her films included: *The Key To Yesterday* (1914) as Mrs Marston, *The Man Who Could Not Lose* (1914) as Melissa, *Beulah* (1915), *Who Pays?* (1915), *Vengeance Is Mine!* (1916) as Marion Grey Loring, *For Ten Thousand Bucks* (1916), *Some Liars* (1916), *Bungling Bill's Dress Suit* (1916), *Her Luckless Scheme* (1916), *Going To The Dogs* (1916), *Rolling To Ruin* (1916), *Paste And Politics* (1916), *A Touch Of High Life* (1916), *Her Painted Pedigree* (1916), *Bungling Bill's Bow-Wow*

(1916), *Lost, Strayed Or Stolen* (1916), *With Or Without* (1916), *The Wicked City* (1916), *Shot In the Fracas* (1916), *Jealous Jolts* (1916), *A Lislebank* (1917), *A Circus Cyclone* (1917), *The Musical Marvel* (1917), *The Butcher's Nightmare* (1917), *A Studio Stampede* (1917), *His Bogus Boast* (1917), *He Looked Crooked* (1917) and *Lorelei Of The Sea* (1917) as Sea Lorelei. She was married to the 6', Oscar-nominated director Henry King (b. Christiansburg, Virginia, January 24, 1886, d. Toluca Lake, California, June 29, 1982 of a heart attack).
CAUSE: She died in Hollywood aged 57.

John Abbott
Born July 5, 1905
Died May 24, 1996
Reliable actor. Born in London, Abbott wanted to be an actor from early on, practising 'faces' in the mirror, but initially studied art, becoming a commercial artist. A fortuitous illness (affecting someone else) propelled Abbott into performing in an amateur production, where he was spotted by Dame Sybil Thorndike who declared: "Now *there's* a man who knows how to make an entrance." Six years later, in 1936, he joined the Old Vic at the invitation of Tyrone Guthrie. The following year he made his film début in *Mademoiselle Docteur* (1937) opposite Claire Luce and Erich von Stroheim. He followed that up with *The Return Of The Scarlet Pimpernel* (1938), *This Man Is News* (1939) and *The Saint In London* (1939) as Count Stephen Duni. He made his first appearance on television in June 1937 in the BBC play *The Harmfulness Of Tobacco*. He spent the first year of World War II working in the British Embassy in Stockholm. Travelling via the Soviet Union to Canada he went to New York on holiday. On his last day in the States he landed a role in *The Shanghai Gesture* (1941) and stayed in America thereafter. He appeared in over 60 films, including

Joan Of Paris (1942) playing an English spy, *Mrs Miniver* (1942) as Fred, *Anna And The King Of Siam* (1946) as Phya Phrom, *Humoresque* (1946) as Rozner, *Madame Bovary* (1949) as Mayor Tuvache, *Omar Khayyam* (1957) as Yusuf, *Gigi* (1958) as Manuel, *Who's Minding The Store?* (1963) as Roberts and *The Greatest Story Ever Told* (1964) as Aben but believed his best work was as Frederic Fairlie in *The Woman In White* (1948). In 1950 playwright Tennessee Williams wrote the one-act play *Auto-Da-Fé* for Abbott.

CAUSE: Natural causes. He died in Los Angeles, California, aged 90.

Alfred Abel

Born March 12, 1879
Died December 12, 1937

'The Lewis Stone of German pictures', Alfred Abel was born in Leipzig, Germany. He worked in a number of jobs, including forest warden, designer and bank clerk, before he was discovered by Asta Nilsen and cast in *Eine Venezianische Nacht* (1913) playing Anselmus Aselmeyer. He was highly regarded in Germany in the years between the wars and also turned his hand to directing. He appeared in over 100 films, including *Sodoms Ende* (1913), *Die Geschichte Der Stillen Mühle* (1914), *Peter Lump* (1916), *Lola Montez* (1918), *Die Dame, Der Teufel Und Die Probiermamsell* (1918), *Eine Junge Dame Aus Guter Familie* (1919), *Sappho* (1921), *Die Große Und Die Kleine Welt* (1921), *Dr Mabuse, Der Spieler* (1922) as Graf Told, *Der Bankraub Unter Den Linden* (1925), *Metropolis* (1927) as John Fredersen, *Rasputins Liebesabenteuer* (1928) and *Und Du Mein Schatz Fährst Mit* (1937) as William Liners.

CAUSE: He died of natural causes in Berlin, Germany, aged 58.

Walter Abel

Born June 6, 1898
Died March 26, 1987

Suave, moustachioed leading man.

Born in St Paul, Minnesota, Abel's family disapproved of but did not discourage his early acting ambitions. Arriving in New York City in 1916 he appeared in a number of silent pictures and in vaudeville while studying at the American Academy of Dramatic Art. He made his first professional appearance at the Manhattan Opera House on December 20, 1919, as Second Lieutenant Vincent Moretti in *Forbidden*. Playwright Eugene O'Neill sponsored Abel in two of his plays and ten years later, on June 3, 1929, he made his début on the London stage as Michael Jeffrey in *Coquette* at the Apollo Theatre. In 1926 he married harpist Marietta Bitter and was widowed in 1978. He appeared in over 50 films including *The North Wind's Malice* (1920) as Tom, *The Three Musketeers* (1935) as D'Artagnan, *The Witness Chair* (1936) as James Trent, *The Lady Consents* (1936) as Stanley Ashton, *Fury* (1936) as the District Attorney, *Men With Wings* (1938) as Nick Ranson, *Who Killed Aunt Maggie?* (1940) as Dr George Benedict, *Michael Shayne, Private Detective* (1940) as Elliott Thomas, *Hold Back The Dawn* (1941) as Inspector Hammock, *Star Spangled Rhythm* (1942) as B.G. DeSoto, *Holiday Inn* as Danny Reed (1942), *Mr Skeffington* (1942) as George Trellis, *The Kid From Brooklyn* (1946) as Gabby Sloan, *That Lady In Ermine* (1948) as Major Horvath, *The Indian Fighter* (1955) as Captain Trask, *Raintree County* (1957) as T.D. Shawnessy, *Silent Night, Bloody Night* (1974) as the mayor and *Grace Quigley* (1984) as Homer Morrison. In June 1949 he appeared as Claudius in *Hamlet* at Elsinore. He was known for his beautifully modulated voice and was a regular on television from 1944. He rarely socialised with his co-stars saying, "Either they're dead, or they believe I am."

CAUSE: He died in Essex, Connecticut, of a heart attack, aged 88.

John Abineri

Born May 18, 1928
Died June 29, 2000
Steady second lead. Born in London, 5'10" Abineri trained at the Old Vic theatre school. He was a regular on television appearing as Chingachgook in the BBC drama series *The Last Of The Mohicans* (January 17, 1971–March 7, 1971), a role he reprised two years later in *Hawkeye, The Pathfinder* (November 18, 1973–December 16, 1973). Among his films were *Dead Man's Chest* (1965) as Arthur, *Funeral In Berlin* (1966) as Rukel, *The McKenzie Break* (1970) as Hauptman Kranz, *Diamonds Are Forever* (1971) as an airline rep, *Pope Joan* (1972) as a Church official, *The Godfather: Part III* (1991) as Hamilton Banker, *Giorgino* (1994) as Dr Jodel and *The Window Bed* (1999) as Jack. He also guested on *Bergerac, Blake's 7, Red Dwarf, Callan* and *Dr Who.*
CAUSE: Abineri died aged 72 of motor neurone disease.

Jean Acker

Born October 23, 1893
Died August 16, 1978
Mrs Rudolph Valentino the First. Born in Trenton, New Jersey, the petite, hazel-eyed brunette began acting aged 18. She met Valentino at a party on Sunset Boulevard on November 2, 1919. At the time she had very short hair, wore a man's suit, a shirt and tie and sensible shoes. She was very friendly with Alla Nazimova (as was Mrs Rudolph Valentino the Second), one of Hollywood's most notorious lesbians. At the time, Acker had already appeared in a couple of films – *The $5,000,000 Counterfeiting Plot* (1914) as Helen Long and *Are You A Mason?* (1915) – but had not reached any kind of stardom. She was paid $200 a week by Metro. At the party, Acker offered Valentino a cocktail, which he at first refused. Insistent, she refused to take no for an answer – in anything. Three days later, they were married at the home of Joseph Engle, Metro Films' treasurer on Hollywood Boulevard and Mariposa Hollywood. For their honeymoon they headed back to Acker's room at the Hollywood Hotel, 6811 Hollywood Boulevard. However, they spent the wedding night apart after she locked him out of her room and told him that she did not love him. Unsurprisingly, the marriage was never consummated. On December 6, newspapers carried the story of their separation. Acker remained close to Valentino and it was with her that he spent his final days, although he repaid her for the honeymoon débâcle by leaving her just $1 in his will. He even wore a silver slave bracelet she had given him (despite reports to the contrary, it was not a gift from second wife Natacha Rambova or his 'fiancée' Pola Negri). On November 23, 1921, they faced each other in the divorce court and their divorce was finalised in Valentino's favour on January 10, 1922. However, the separation cost him $12,000, a sum lent by Jesse Lasky. The dissolution came not long after the release of *The Sheik* (1922) and despite Acker's testimony that Valentino had punched her and knocked her down, their separation did him no harm whatsoever. Acker appeared in around 30 films in all and was often billed as Mrs Rudolph Valentino or Jean Acker Valentino (even as late as 1952). Her movies included *An Arabian Knight* (1920) as Zorah, *Brewster's Millions* (1921) as Barbara Drew, *Her Own Money* (1922) as Ruth Alden, *Good Girls Go To Paris* (1939), *My Favorite Wife* (1940), *Spellbound* (1945) and *Something To Live For* (1952). Two of her films had rather revealing titles, making one wonder whether she was deliberately cast as an in-joke by the studios who would have been more than aware of her sexual preferences. In 1920 she played Ethel in *Help Wanted – Male*; 15 years later she appeared in *No More Ladies.*

CAUSE: Natural causes. She died in Los Angeles, California, aged 84.

Art Acord

Born April 17, 1890
Died January 4, 1931

Early cowboy hero. Arthemus Ward Acord, half-Ute, was born in Stillwater in the Indian Territory, now modern-day Oklahoma. The short and stocky Acord was a real-life cowboy before he became a cinematic one. He worked in Dick Stanley's Wild West Show and then in 1909 landed a job as a stuntman with the Bison Film Company. He began appearing in his own right (occasionally billed as Buck Parvin [a character based on himself that he played in Cecil B. DeMille's *The Squaw Man*] or Art Accord) in films such as *The Two Brothers* (1910), *The White Medicine Man* (1911), *George Warrington's Escape* (1911), *Buck Parvin In The Movies* (1914), *When Fiddler Came To Big Horn* (1915), *Buck's Lady Friend* (1915), *A Cattle Queen's Romance* (1915), and *A Cowboy's Sweetheart* (1915) before World War I interrupted his career. After heroic service in France, where he won the Croix de Guerre, he returned to the States and became a cowboy hero once again, this time for Universal Studios. His films included *The Cowpuncher's Comeback* (1921), *Unmasked* (1922), *In The Days Of Buffalo Bill* (1922), *Fighting For Justice* (1924) as Bullets Bernard, *The Wild Girl* (1925) as Billy Woodruff, *Two Gun O'Brien* (1928) and *Fighters Of The Saddle* (1929) as Dick Weatherby. His career ended with the advent of sound and he fell from grace in a spectacular way. He became an alcoholic, fighting with anyone who upset him. He broke Victor Fleming's nose after the future director of *Gone With The Wind* (1939) suggested Acord was not a real Native American. He was jailed for bootlegging, and worked as a miner in Mexico where he went broke gambling. Rather than undergo vocal training to get work, he decided publicity was the key and staged a fake kidnapping with the help of some Mexican friends. It was not successful. He was married twice. Both his wives – Edythe Sterling and Louise Lorraine (1901–1981), his co-star in *The Oregon Trail* (1923) – were actresses.

CAUSE: He died by his own hand in the Palacio Hotel in Chihuahua, Mexico, from cyanide poisoning, aged 40. His body lay unclaimed for a week. He is buried in Forest Lawn Memorial-Parks in Glendale, California.

Rodolfo Acosta

Born July 29, 1920
Died November 7, 1974

Moustachioed Mexican baddie. Born in Chihuahua, Mexico, Rudy Acosta was a star in films in his native land. His movies included *Rosenda* (1948) and *Salón México* (1949) as Paco before he was signed to Universal. His subsequent films (usually with him playing a villain) included: *Pancho Villa Returns* (1950) as Martin Corona, *Yankee Buccaneer* (1952) as Poulini, *Wings Of The Hawk* (1953) as Arturo Torres, *Drum Beat* (1954) as Scarface Charlie, *The Tijuana Story* (1957), the real life story of one man's fight against drugs, in which he played Manuel Acosta Mesa, *The Greatest Story Ever Told* (1965), *The Sons Of Katie Elder* (1965) as Bondie Adams, *Return Of The Seven* (1966) as Lopez and *The Magnificent Seven Ride!* (1972) as Juan De Toro. On the small screen he regularly played in cowboy series, including *Cade's County*, *Bonanza*, *Laredo*, *The Big Valley*, *Death Valley Days*, *The Virginian*, *Rawhide*, *Cheyenne* and a two-year stint on *The High Chaparral* as Vaquero. He fathered five children.

CAUSE: He died of cancer in Woodland Hills, California, aged 54.

Eddie Acuff

Born June 3, 1903
Died December 17, 1956

Stalwart. Although Acuff never

achieved stardom he was rarely out of work, appearing in over 180 films. His best-known role was probably that of the postman in the 'Blondie' series but he also appeared in several other serials and B pictures. He can be seen in, among many others, *Here Comes The Navy* (1934), *I Found Stella Parish* (1935) as Dimmy, *The Case Of The Velvet Claws* (1936) as Spudsy Drake, *The Law In Her Hands* (1936) as Eddie O'Malley, *Love Is On The Air* (1937) as Dunk Glover, *Law Of The Underworld* (1938) as Bill, *Society Smugglers* (1939), *Rough Riders' Round-up* (1939) as Tommy Ward, *The Mysterious Miss X* (1939), *Days Of Jesse James* (1939), *Blondie Meets The Boss* (1939), *The Green Hornet Strikes Again* (1940) as Lowery, *Dr Kildare's Crisis* (1940) as Clifford Genet, *Dr Kildare Goes Home* (1940) as Clifford Genet, *Charlie Chan In Panama* (1940), *The Texas Rangers Ride Again* (1940), *The People vs. Dr Kildare* (1941) as Clifford Genet, *Dr Kildare's Wedding Day* (1941) as Clifford Genet, *Dr Kildare's Victory* (1941) as Clifford Genet, *Blondie Goes Latin* (1941), *High Sierra* (1941), *Dr Gillespie's New Assistant* (1942) as Clifford Genet, *Blondie For Victory* (1942), *Yankee Doodle Dandy* (1942), *Leave It To Blondie* (1945), *Life With Blondie* (1946), *Buck Privates Come Home* (1947), *Blondie's Holiday* (1947), *Blondie's Big Moment* (1947), *Blondie's Anniversary* (1947), *Blondie In The Dough* (1947), *The Secret Life Of Walter Mitty* (1947), *Blondie's Secret* (1948), *Blondie's Reward* (1948), *Blondie's Big Deal* (1949) and *The Milkman* (1950).
CAUSE: He died in Hollywood, California, aged 53, from a heart attack.

Janice Adair

(BEATRICE DUFFY)
Born 1904
Died November 11, 1996
Promise unfulfilled. Born in Morpeth, Northumberland, 5'3" Janice Adair was unusual among early screen stars in that she had no stage training or bit-part work as an extra before becoming a film actress. Her first film was *Streets Of London* (1929) and she went on to appear in *The Informer* (1929) as Bessie, *To What Red Hell* (1929) as Madge Barton, *The Rocket Bus* (1929) as Joan, *Red Aces* (1929), *Such Is The Law* (1930) as Marjorie Majoribanks, *Deadlock* (1931) as Joan Whitelaw, *Contraband Love* (1931) as Janice Machin, *Lloyd Of The C.I.D.* (1932) as Dion Brooks, *The Silver Greyhound* (1932) as Ira Laennic, *Lucky Ladies* (1932) as Pearl, *The Acting Business* (1933), *Nine Forty-Five* (1934) as Molly Clayton and *Flood Tide* (1935) as Betty Buckett. She married film editor Alfred Wallace Roome (b. London, December 22, 1908, d. Gerrards Cross, Buckinghamshire, November 19, 1997) in 1929 and by him had a son and a daughter. He edited 14 *Carry On . . .* films.
CAUSE: She died aged 91 at Gerrards Cross, Buckinghamshire from natural causes.

Jean Adair

Born June 13, 1873
Died May 11, 1953
Gentility personified. Born in Hamilton, Ontario, Canada, Jean Adair spent most of her professional life on the stage. She only made six films but created a stir as Martha Brewster, one of the murderous aunts, in *Arsenic And Old Lace* (1944). Her other films were *In The Name Of The Law* (1922), *Advice To The Lovelorn* (1933) as Mrs Prentiss, *Living In A Big Way* (1947) as Abigail Morgan, *Something In The Wind* (1947) as Aunt Mary Collins and *The Naked City* (1948).
CAUSE: She died of natural causes in New York aged 79.

Robert Adair

Born January 3, 1900
Died August 10, 1954
Posh American. Born in San Francisco, California, 6'1" Adair was educated at Harrow before making his film début in

Raffles (1925). He also appeared often on the American stage. His other films included *Journey's End* (1930) as Captain Hardy, *King Of The Jungle* (1933) as John C. Knolls, a court officer in *The Kiss Before The Mirror* (1933), *The Invisible Man* (1933), a policeman in *The Mystery Of Mr X* (1934), a barman in *Riptide* (1934), *Where Sinners Meet* (1934) as Jacob, *Treasure Island* (1934) as Tom the sailor, *Great Expectations* (1934) as Sergeant, a policeman in *Limehouse Blues* (1934), *Father Brown, Detective* (1935), *Bride Of Frankenstein* (1935), *The Farmer Takes A Wife* (1935), a hotel clerk in *Top Hat* (1935), *The Girl Who Came Back* (1935) as Charles Matthews, a sergeant in *The Last Outpost* (1935), a prisoner in *Peter Ibbetson* (1935), *Sylvia Scarlett* (1935), *Brilliant Marriage* (1936) as Thorne, a sentry in *Sons O'Guns* (1936), *Empty Saddles* (1936) as Biggers, *The Ticket Of Leave Man* (1937) as Hawkshaw, *Bulldog Drummond Escapes* (1937) as Woolsey, the first guard in *The Prince And The Pauper* (1937), *What A Man!* (1938) as Lord Bromwich, *The Face At The Window* (1939) as Inspector Gouffert, *Jamaica Inn* (1939) as Captain Murray, *Noose* (1948) as Sergeant Brooks, *The Gambler And The Lady* (1952) as Engles, *Eight O'Clock Walk* (1952) as Albert Pettigrew, *Scotland Yard Inspector* (1952) as John, *There Was A Young Lady* (1953) as Basher, *Park Plaza 605* (1953) as Baron von Henschel, *Meet Mr Callaghan* (1954) and *Gilbert Harding Speaking Of Murder* (1954).
CAUSE: He died in London aged 54 of natural causes.

Ronald Adam, OBE
Born December 31, 1896
Died March 27, 1979
Officer material. Born in Worcestershire, Adam came from a theatrical family (his father was the actor Blake Adams and his mother the actress Mona Robin) but after University College School he trained to be a chartered accountant. He gave up that steady profession to work in one that was far riskier, albeit probably less boring. In 1914 he joined the Middlesex Regiment at the outbreak of war, becoming a pilot with the Royal Flying Corps. He ended up in a prisoner of war camp. In 1924 he worked as a theatre manager and later producer, working on over 150 productions. He made his film début in *Strange Boarders* (1938) playing Barstow and followed that up with *The Drum* (1938) as Major Gregoff, *Too Dangerous To Live* (1939), *The Foreman Went To France* (1942) as Sir Charles Fawcett and *Meet Maxwell Archer* (1942) as Nicolides. In 1939 he had re-enlisted in the RAF and served as a Wing Commander. Returning to acting he appeared in numerous films, usually in an official or commanding role. He made his Broadway début on December 19, 1951, at the Ziegfeld Theater in *Antony And Cleopatra*. His other films included: *Christopher Columbus* (1949) as Talavera, *The Bad Lord Byron* (1949) playing a judge, *Shadow Of The Past* (1950) playing a solicitor, *Seven Days To Noon* (1950) as Prime Minister Arthur Lytton, *The Lavender Hill Mob* (1951) as Turner, *Captain Horatio Hornblower* (1951) as Admiral Macartney, *Circumstantial Evidence* (1954) as Sir William Harrison, *Reach For The Sky* (1956) as Air Vice-Marshal Leigh-Mallory, *Lust For Life* (1956) as Commissioner De Smet and *Carlton-Browne Of The F.O.* (1959) as Sir John Farthing. He was married twice. His first wife was Tanzi Cutava Barozzi and his second Allyne Dorothy Franks. He had two children: David (b. 1926) and Jane (b. 1922).
CAUSE: He died of natural causes in London, aged 82.

Abigail 'Tommye' Adams
Born January 11, 1922
Found dead February 13, 1955
Good-time girl. Born in South

Carolina, Abigail 'Tommye' Adams was a beautiful girl who saw making movies as a way to live a pleasant life. Her only problem was that she preferred the pleasant life to making movies. She appeared in a number of low-budget Westerns and other B pictures, including *Moonlight Masquerade* (1942) as Miss Mink, *Old Acquaintance* (1943), *Colorado Serenade* (1946) as Lola, the title role in *Mary Lou* (1947), *Copacabana* (1947) and the receptionist in *Trapped By Boston Blackie* (1948). She married (January 22, 1942) and had the marriage annulled (autumn 1942) actor Lyle Talbot (1902–1996) and had an 11-year relationship with Fox producer George Jessel as well as numerous other lovers. In December 1947 her dog, Albert, saved her from death when she fell asleep in bed while holding a lit cigarette. In 1950 she attempted suicide by slashing her wrists but was saved by a hospital intern. On December 12, 1954, she was arrested for being drunk and disorderly along with actors Broderick Crawford and Myron McCormick in West Los Angeles. When the police arrived Adams was barefoot, and she told them that she was 37 and her name was Terra Hall. All three were released on $20 bond each. Later that month, she denied that she had been drunk: "I'm no playgirl. I was cold sober when I was arrested. We had been sitting around a friend's kitchen, reciting Shakespearean sonnets and reading T. S. Eliot poems." She turned to drink and drugs when her longed-for stardom didn't arrive. On February 11, 1955 she attended the Santa Anita races with George Jessel and the next night, went clubbing with a chemist shop owner called Max Marks. When she didn't answer her phone the next morning, Mr Marks was concerned. CAUSE: She committed suicide by a drugs overdose. Her body was discovered full of Seconal and ethynyl in a sleazy room on Sunset Strip in Hollywood. When Jessel learned of her death, he collapsed. "She had a rather frustrated life," he said later, "but of course you don't know why people do those things. She used to take a lot of pills for insomnia." She was just a month past her 33rd birthday. On February 16, 1955 the coroner declared her death accidental. Two days later, she was interred in lot 104, section 4A of Evergreen Cemetery, 4426 Central Avenue, Charleston, North Carolina 28215.

Claire Adams
Born September 24, 1898
Died September 25, 1978
Silent star. Claire Adams was born in Winnipeg, Manitoba, Canada, and entered the film world in 1918. Her brother, Gerald Drayson Adams, was a screenwriter. Among her 50-plus movies were *A Misfit Earl* (1919) as Phyllis Burton, *The Great Lover* (1920) as Ethel, *Riders Of The Dawn* (1920) as Lenore Anderson, *Man Of The Forest* (1921) as Helen Raynor, *When Romance Rides* (1922) as Lucy Bostil, *Golden Dreams* (1922) as Mercedes McDonald, *Brass Commandments* (1923) as Ellen Bosworth, *Legally Dead* (1923) as Minnie O'Reilly, *Daddies* (1924) as Bobette Audrey, *Honor Among Men* (1924) as Patricia Carson, *The Kiss Barrier* (1925) as Marion Weston, *The Lunatic* (1927) and *Married Alive* (1927) as Viola Helmesley Duxbury. Following the death of her first husband she married Australian sportsman Donald MacKimmon in 1938 and retired to Australia.
CAUSE: She died in Melbourne, Australia, aged 80 years and one day, from natural causes.

Ernie Adams
Born June 18, 1885
Died November 26, 1947
Perennial cowboy. Born in San Francisco, California, the short, stocky Adams was also credited in films as

Ernest S. Adams, Ernest Adams and Ernie S. Adams. Irrespective of the credit on screen, his output was phenomenal. Between 1919 and his death he appeared in more than 260 films. They included *The Beloved Brute* (1924) as Swink Tuckson, *The Pony Express* (1925), *Hair Trigger Baxter* (1926) as Shorty Hillis, *Nevada* (1927) as Cash Burridge, *The Gay Defender* (1927) as Bart Hamby, *Stool Pigeon* (1928) as Dropper, *The Virginian* (1929), *Dance, Fools, Dance* (1931), *Merrily We Go To Hell* (1932), *She Done Him Wrong* (1933), *It Happened One Night* (1934), *Hopalong Cassidy Returns* (1936) as Benson, *Hopalong Rides Again* (1937) as Keno, *Flash Gordon Conquers The Universe* (1940), *Alias Boston Blackie* (1942) as Pop, *The Man Who Came To Dinner* (1942) as Haggerty, *Brenda Starr, Reporter* (1945) as Charlie, *Son Of Zorro* (1947) as Judge Hyde, *Dick Tracy Meets Gruesome* (1947) and *The Secret Life Of Walter Mitty* (1947).
CAUSE: He died of natural causes in Hollywood, California, aged 62.

Jimmie Adams

Born October 4, 1888
Died December 19, 1933
Cheekie chappie. Born in Paterson, New Jersey, James B. Adams began his career in Educational & Christie Film Company's Mermaid comedies before he moved on to appear in the Hall Room Boys series replacing Harry McCoy. By 1924 he was back at Educational where he spent much of his remaining career apart from stints at Pathé and PDC. His films included: *A Jungle Gentleman* (1919), *A Village Venus* (1919), *Chasing Her Future* (1919), *African Lions And American Beauties* (1919), *The Good Ship Rock'n'Rye* (1919), *Weak Hearts And Wild Lions* (1919), *A Baby Doll Bandit* (1920), *Over The Transom* (1920), *Movie Hero* (1920), *Kismet* (1920) as Chamberlain, *A Fresh Start* (1921), *Bang!* (1921), *Better Late Than Never*

(1922), *Beware Of Blondes* (1922), *Breaking Into Jail* (1922), *Crash* (1922), *Bumps* (1923), *Broke* (1923), *Aggravating Poppa* (1924), a painter in *Triumph* (1924), *Hold Your Breath* (1924) as a beauty salon owner, *Hotel Hysteria* (1924), *Stop Flirting* (1925) as Count Spinagio, *Be Careful* (1925), *Whoa, Emma!* (1926), *Chase Yourself* (1926), *Her Man O' War* (1926) as Shorty Flynn, *Beauty A La Mud* (1926), *For Sadie's Sake* (1926), *Break Away* (1927), *Swiss Movements* (1927), *Meet The Folks* (1927) as James Pettingill, *The Farmer's Daughter* (1928) as Cicero Hopkins, *Goofy Ghosts* (1928), *The Office Scandal* (1929) as Delaney, *The Grand Parade* (1930) as Jones, *High Cs* (1930), *Rough Seas* (1931), *The Tabasco Kid* (1932), *Arabian Tights* (1933), *Sherman Said It* (1933), *Midsummer Mush* (1933) and *Luncheon At Twelve* (1933).
CAUSE: Adams died aged 45 in Glendale, California, of a heart attack.

Nick Adams

(NICHOLAS ALOYSIUS ADAMSCHOCK)
Born July 10, 1931
Died February 5, 1968
The poor man's James Dean. Born in Nanticoke, Pennsylvania, the son of a Lithuanian miner, he was raised in New Jersey. The chillingly ambitious Nick Adams hitchhiked to Hollywood when he was 18, determined to make his mark on the movie capital. "Some men bet on horses and dogs. I gambled on myself," he would tell interviewers. At first his gamble didn't pay off and in 1952 he joined the Coast Guard. However, on leave he would return to Tinseltown and badger producers and directors for work. His persistence landed him a role in a Betty Hutton musical *Somebody Loves Me* (1952), but his first major part was playing Reber in *Mister Roberts* (1955). On leaving the Coast Guard, Adams was cast in *Rebel Without A Cause* (1955) as Moose. Following the death of James Dean, Adams was brought back to the studio

by director George Stevens and dubbed some of Dean's dialogue. In 1956 Adams befriended Elvis Presley, who was visiting Hollywood to film his first feature, *Love Me Tender*. Presley, a Dean fan, took to Adams, who in turn introduced Elvis to Natalie Wood (with whom Adams had an affair). Both Adams and Wood visited Elvis in Memphis but the friendship was discouraged by Presley's manager, Colonel Tom Parker, who thought that Adams might be a bad influence or that he might, at the very least, put unwelcome ideas into Elvis' head. From October 4, 1959, until September 12, 1962, he played Johnny Yuma in the ABC television series *The Rebel*, so named to cash in on Adams' association with Dean. When *The Rebel* was cancelled Adams played a journalist in *Saints And Sinners*. The following year he played Ben Brown, a man wrongly accused of murder, in *Twilight Of Honor* (1963). He lobbied hard for an Oscar (spending $8,000 on advertisements in trade papers) and gave interviews to anyone who wanted one, talking himself up. He was nominated as Best Supporting Actor but lost out to Melvyn Douglas for *Hud* (1963) at the ceremony held at the Santa Monica Civic Auditorium on April 13, 1964. Anticipating that he would receive the award, Adams and his wife had turned up one and a half hours before the show began. Reporter Sidney Skolsky wrote: "I was fascinated by the face of Nick Adams. Nick looked like Instant Murder. I never believed I'd want to give Nick a prize, but really, he should be given an Oscar for his Portrait of a Loser. I'll say this for him, his face and emotions were honest." After that disappointment, Adams found work hard to come by. He was further distraught by the break-up of his marriage to actress Carol Nugent and her new boyfriend's habit of punishing his two children, Allyson and Jeb Stuart, for supposed misbehaviour. A court awarded him custody, allowing the mother limited access but only alone. He appeared in low-budget fare such as *Frankenstein Conquers The World* (1964), *Die, Monster, Die!* (1965) as Stephen Reinhart, *Monster Zero* (1966), *Fever Heat* (1967) as Ace Jones, and *Mission Mars* (1968) as Nick Grant, one of the first American astronauts on the moon. CAUSE: Suicide or accident? The death of 36-year-old Nick Adams is still something of a mystery. His lawyer and friend, Erwin Roeder, had a dinner date with Adams on February 6, but the actor never arrived. Going to Adams' house at 2126 El Robles Lane in Beverly Hills the next night he found his car garaged. Roeder broke into the house and found Adams dead in his bedroom, leaning against a wall, his eyes wide open. Adams had died of a drug overdose but police found no drug paraphernalia and nothing to suggest his death was the result of anything other than natural causes. The coroner Dr Thomas Noguchi's report stated that Adams died instantly from paraldehyde, a drug prescribed for alcoholics, and promazine intoxication. The cause of death on the death certificate is listed as "Accident; Suicide; Undetermined". Adams is buried in Saints Cyril & Methodius Cemetery, 706 North Warren Street, Berwick, Pennsylvania 18603.

Stanley Adams

Born April 7, 1915
Died April 27, 1977
Sturdy actor. Adams appeared in over 50 films and was a regular face on television. Among his movies were *The Atomic Kid* (1954) as Wildcat Hooper, *Calling Homicide* (1956) as Peter von Elda, *Hell Ship Mutiny* (1957), *Hell Bound* (1957) as Herbert Fay, Jr, *North By Northwest* (1959) as Lieutenant Harding, *Studs Lonigan* (1960), *Breakfast At Tiffany's* (1961) as Rusty Trawler, *Ship Of Fools* (1965) as Hutten and *Everything You Always Wanted To Know About Sex* (1972). On

television he played Cyrano Jones in a memorable episode of *Star Trek* ('The Trouble With Tribbles') and also appeared in *Kolchak: The Night Stalker, Gilligan's Island, Lost In Space, Gunsmoke, Laredo, Wagon Trail, Perry Mason, The Twilight Zone* and *Rawhide*. CAUSE: He shot himself in Santa Monica, California, aged 62.

Stella Adams

Born April 24, 1883
Died September 17, 1961
Early star. Born in Sherman, Texas, she began her career with the company Nestor in the early days of the motion picture industry. The majority of her work was in silent films – she made no movies between 1917 and 1927 and she retired in 1936 at the age of 53. Her films included: *In The Sultan's Power* (1909), *The Passing Parade* (1912) as G.A.R. bazaar worker, *The Lucky Loser* (1912) as Lily Worthing, *The Lady Barber Of Roaring Gulch* (1912) as Mrs Allen, *To The Brave Belong The Fair* (1913) as Alice's mother, *Four Queens And A Jack* (1913) as the girl's mother, *When His Courage Failed* (1913) as the club president, *The Tale Of A Hat* (1913) as Mother Gray, *The Power Of Heredity* (1913) as Mrs Del Mar, *The Girls And Dad* (1913) as Jennie, *When Cupid Won* (1913) as Jenny Simpkins, *The Girl Ranchers* (1913), *Under Western Skies* (1913), *Hawkeye's Great Capture* (1913), *A Man Of The People* (1913), *His Wife's Burglar* (1913), *The Prairie Trail* (1913), *The Golden Princess Mine* (1913) as the young prospector's mother, *War Of The Cattle Range* (1913), *Her Friend, The Butler* (1913), *A Woman's Way* (1913), *Teaching Dad A Lesson* (1913), *The God Of Girzah* (1913), *The Unhappy Pair* (1913), *A Tale Of The West* (1913), *When Ursus Threw The Bull* (1914), *Cupid's Close Shave* (1914), *Twixt Love And Flour* (1914), *His Royal Pants* (1914), *Scooped By A Hencoop* (1914), *She Was Only A Working Girl* (1914), *What A Baby Did* (1914), *Those Persistent Old Maids* (1914), *The Wrong Miss Wright* (1914), *When The Girls Joined The Force* (1914), *Her Husbands* (1914), *Could You Blame Her?* (1914), *When Eddie Went To The Front* (1914), *Way Of Life* (1914), *When Bess Got It Wrong* (1914), *For The Good Of The Cause* (1915), *A Maid By Proxy* (1915), *All Aboard* (1915), *The Heart Of Sampson* (1915), *When He Proposed* (1915), *A Coat's A Coat* (1915), *His Wife's Husband* (1915), *It Happened On Friday* (1915), *All In The Same Boat* (1915), *Her Friend, The Milkman* (1915), *Almost A King* (1915), *Following Father's Footsteps* (1915), *With Father's Help* (1915), *Behind The Screen* (1915), *A One Cylinder Courtship* (1915), *Those Kids And Cupid* (1915), *Father's Lucky Escape* (1915), *A Looney Love Affair* (1915), *Wanted: A Leading Lady* (1915), *Keeping It Dark* (1915), *Where The Heather Blooms* (1915) as Mary's mother, *Love And A Savage* (1915), *Her Steady Carfare* (1916), *When Aunt Matilda Fell* (1916), *Mingling Spirits* (1916), *Mixed Kids* (1916), *Her Friend, The Doctor* (1916), *Cupid Trims His Lordship* (1916), *He Almost Eloped* (1916), *A Leap Year Tangle* (1916), *Eddie's Night Out* (1916), *The Newlyweds' Mix-Up* (1916), *Her Hero Maid* (1916), *Never Lie To Your Wife* (1916), *The Janitor's Busy Day* (1916), *Good Night, Nurse* (1916), *Twixt Love And The Iceman* (1916), *What Could The Poor Girl Do?* (1916), *The Browns See The Fair* (1916), *Double Crossing The Dean* (1916), *By The Sad Sea Waves* (1916), *Dad's Masterpiece* (1916), *Cupid's Uppercut* (1916), *Almost A Scandal* (1917), *A Bold, Bad Knight* (1917), *Keeping In Trim* (1927), *Society Breaks* (1927), *Passing The Joneses* (1927), *Showing Off* (1927), *Horse Play* (1928), *Meet The Count* (1928), *Start Something* (1928), *Indoor Golf* (1928), *Her Only Husband* (1928), *A Big Bluff* (1928), *A Full House* (1928), *Reel Life* (1928), *McGinnis Vs Jones* (1928), *Me, Gangster* (1928) as

Lizzie Williams, *Polished Ivory* (1930), *Prize Puppies* (1930) as a landlady, *College Cuties* (1930), *Bachelor Mother* (1932) as Mrs Smith, *Sister To Judas* (1932) as Mrs Frayne, *The Vampire Bat* (1933) as Georgiana, *Whirlwind* (1933), *Sing, Sinner, Sing* (1933), *Whom The Gods Destroy* (1934) as the Newfoundland Woman, *The Tonto Kid* (1934) as a landlady and *Theodora Goes Wild* (1936) as a townswoman.

CAUSE: She died at the Motion Picture & TV Hospital Country Home, 23388 Mulholland Drive, Woodland Hills, California.

Al Adamson

Born July 25, 1929
Died August 2, 1995
Gore machine. Albert Victor Adamson, Jr was born in Hollywood, California, the son of silent Western star-turned-director Denver Dixon (1901–1972) a.k.a. Art Mix. After an unsuccessful acting career in other people's forgettable films, Adamson turned to writing, producing and directing and also appearing in his own forgettable films. He wrote, directed, produced and appeared (using the pseudonym Lyle Felisse) as Vito in *Psycho A Go-Go* ([1965], later [1969] re-released with added scenes and re-released again shortly thereafter with the new title of *Blood Of Ghastly Horror* [1971]) and *Horror Of The Blood Monsters* (1970). He produced and directed *Blood Of Dracula's Castle* (1967) starring John Carradine as George the butler, *Hell's Bloody Devils* (1967) starring Carradine, Broderick Crawford and Scott Brady, *Five Bloody Graves* (1969) starring Carradine, Brady and *Dallas'* Jim Davis, *Satan's Sadists* (1969) starring Russ Tamblyn and Regina Carrol (a nightclub singer and Adamson's real-life wife), *Dracula vs. Frankenstein* (1969, 1971) starring J. Carrol Naish, Lon Chaney, Jr, Tamblyn and Carrol, *Brain Of Blood* (1971) with Carrol, *Angels' Wild Women* (1972) with Carrol as Margo

and a Diana Ross-lookalike with a 48" bust, *Jessi's Girls* (1975), *Black Heat* (1976) and *Cinderella 2000* (1977), and directed such fare as *The Female Bunch* (1969) starring Lon Chaney, Jr, Tamblyn and Carrol and filmed on mass murderer Charles Manson's ranch, *I Spit On Your Corpse* (1974) starring porn star Georgina Spelvin, *Blazing Stewardesses* (1974) again starring Carrol, *Death Dimension* (1978), *Naughty Stewardesses* (1978), *Sunset Cove* (1978) with John Carradine and *Doctor Dracula* (1981). Many of his films, which were gorefests or overtly sexual, featured respected actors (such as John Carradine, Lon Chaney, Jr, Broderick Crawford and Scott Brady) who didn't quite know when to quit.

CAUSE: Adamson was murdered aged 65 at his home on Avenue 49 in Indio, California, about 150 miles south-east of Los Angeles. Adamson's body was stuffed into a hole where his whirlpool bath had been, covered in four tons of cement and then tiled over. A warrant was issued for the arrest of his handyman, 46-year-old Fred Fulford, who had been living at the house since October 1994 while remodelling it. The builder had fled to Florida a week before Adamson's body was found on August 2, 1995 and avoided extradition to California until 1996. A preliminary hearing took place in July of that year and Fulford indicated that he wanted to conduct his own defence but later relented and took counsel, Robert Hurley. At his trial, which opened in October 1999, Fulford was accused of hitting Adamson over the head with a heavy object, a charge he denied. Adamson's brother, Kenneth, testified that the film director had told him that Fulford was stealing from him and had run up $4,000 in telephone calls. On November 9, taking the stand Fulford admitted perjury, theft and forgery but denied killing Adamson. He claimed that he had an arrangement with the director that the house would be sold and they would split the profits. However, the jury disagreed and after less than two hours' deliberation on November 17 they found Fulford guilty of first degree murder. On March 3, 2000 he was sentenced to 25 years in prison.

Peter Adamson

Born February 16, 1930
Died January 17, 2002
Paedophile soap star. For almost twenty-three years (February 1961– August 1983) Peter Adamson played the role of rough diamond Len Fairclough in *Coronation Street*. In his £500-a-week time in Britain's most famous thoroughfare Len was elected to the local council, romanced Elsie Tanner and Bet Lynch, bought the Kabin, was suspected of murder, married Rita Littlewood, was beaten up by Fred Gee and was finally killed in a car crash on the way home after visiting his secret mistress. Peter Adamson led an equally eventful life. An alcoholic, he was arrested for drink driving and attempted suicide three times before giving up booze in February 1973. Ten years later to the month, he was suspended by Granada TV for six weeks for selling a series of backstage articles to a tabloid. On April 23, during his suspension, he was arrested at Haslingden, Lancashire, and accused of molesting two 8-year-old girls in a swimming pool where he worked as a part-time instructor teaching young kids to swim. Adamson hired top lawyer George Carman, Q.C. to defend him. Carman had previously engineered the acquittal of Jeremy Thorpe, M.P. on conspiracy to murder charges and would also later ensure Ken Dodd's acquittal on tax avoidance charges. Adamson's trial began at Burnley Crown Court in July 1983. One of his alleged victims reputedly considered suicide asking her mother if she would die if she jumped off a roof. However, after just eight days Adamson was acquitted of all charges on July 26 after the four-woman, eight-man jury deliberated for just 36 minutes. His legal costs were estimated at £120,000 and to recoup some of the outlay he sold more stories to *The Sun*. Unsurprisingly, he was not allowed back to the *Street* and claimed, "It gives me the chance to prove that I'm capable of doing things other than soap opera." He toured in a play in Canada. Work, however, began to dry up. On September 26, 1984, Jean Adamson, his arthritis-suffering wife, died aged 55. In June 1988 he was signed to appear in a play featuring children but just before it opened Adamson pulled out admitting he had been guilty of the assault five years previously. In a startlingly frank and often bizarre interview he admitted, "I am bloody fascinated by paedophiliacs [*sic*] . . . If you think I am a paedophile – Okay, print it. But also print that I would willingly fuck my lovely little granddaughter who is only six months old . . . If you think I am a paedophile – Okay, I love old women too." Adamson said he sometimes thought he was partly gay. "I think I am possibly one of the few people in the world to admit to being 35 per cent homosexual. I will kiss a man but I have never engaged in the act of buggery. That is abhorrent to me." In 1985 55-year-old Adamson began drinking again. Six years later, in August 1991, he went bankrupt with debts of £33,000. As with many soap stars he spent much of the time playing just the one role but Adamson did find time to appear outside of Weatherfield. He was in the film *Take Her By Surprise* (1967) playing Korba. Before Len Fairclough he was in the television series *Knight Errant Limited* (1959) and *Skyport* (1959).
CAUSE: Adamson died aged 71 of stomach cancer at Lincoln County Hospital, Lincoln. He left £5,000 in his will to his elder son, Michael (b. 1954). His ashes were left to his other child, Greg (b. 1962).

Dawn Addams

Born September 21, 1930
Died May 7, 1985
Unspectacular glamourpuss. Born in Felixstowe, Suffolk, the daughter of test pilot Captain James Ramage Addams and Ethel Mary Hickie. Her stepmother was actress Arlene Judge (1912–1974), who was married and divorced seven times. Her sixth marriage was to her former brother-in-law Bob Topping, who was to marry Lana Turner. The 5'6" Dawn Addams auditioned for the film *National Velvet* (1944) but lost out to another pretty dark-haired, dark-eyed girl by the name of Elizabeth Taylor. Educated at 14 schools in England, India and America and at RADA, she made her West End début as Amy Spettigue in a production of *Charley's Aunt* on December 22, 1949, at the Piccadilly Theatre. She went to Hollywood seeking stardom in 1950. The following year she appeared in *Night Into Morning* as Dottie Phelps and followed that up with a bit part in *Singin' In The Rain* (1952), *The Robe* (1953) as Junia, *Return To Treasure Island* (1954) as Jamesina Hawkins, *Khyber Patrol* (1954) as Diana Rivington, *Riders To The Stars* (1954) as Susan Manners, *A King In New York* (1957) as Ann Kay, *I Battellieri Del Volga* (1958), *Geheimaktion Schwarze Kapelle* (1959), *The Two Faces Of Dr Jekyll* (1960) as Kitty Jekyll, *Follow That Man* (1961) as Janet Clark, *Come Fly With Me* (1965), *The Vampire Lovers* (1970) and *The Vault Of Horror* (1973) as Inez. In 1954 she married Prince Vittorio Massimo and, on January 10, 1955, gave birth to their son Prince Stefano. Although they were not divorced until 1971 they separated in 1958. A seven-year custody battle for the boy ensued, which was eventually won by his father. Following her marriage to former journalist James White, Addams retired from acting. CAUSE: She died in London aged 54 from cancer.

Jay Adler

Born September 26?, 1896
Died September 23, 1978
Character brother. Born in New York, Jay was one of six children of the Yiddish stage and screen actor Jacob Pavlovich Adler (b. Odessa, Russia, February 12, 1855, d. New York, April 1, 1926) and Sarah Heine (d. 1953). Jay Adler's birthdate is in doubt because although every published source and, indeed, the Social Security Index, lists the above date, his gravestone states that he was born on August 14, 1896. His siblings were Luther, Stella, Julia, Florence, Frances and Charles (d. New York, June 22, 1955). He also had a half-sister, the thrice-married Celia Feinman Adler (b. 1891, d. The Bronx, New York, January 31, 1979), from his father's marriage to the stage actress Dinah Shtettin. Adler began his career in the theatre appearing in both Yiddish and English productions before he made his film début in *Penrod And His Twin Brother* (1938) playing Johnson. His other movies included: *No Time To Marry* (1938) as Hess, *Three Secrets* (1950) as the city editor, *Cry Danger* (1951) as Williams, *The Mob* (1951) as Russell, *Scandal Sheet* (1952) as Bailey, *The Bad And The Beautiful* (1952) as Mr Z, *My Six Convicts* (1952) as Steve Kopac, *Dreamboat* (1952) as desk clerk, *Assignment: Paris* (1952) as Henry, *The Prisoner Of Zenda* (1952) as a customs officer, *The Turning Point* (1952) as Sammy, *My Pal Gus* (1952) as Van Every, *The Juggler* (1953) as Papa Sander, *Vice Squad* (1953) as Frankie Pierce, *99 River Street* (1953) as Christopher, *The Long Wait* (1954) as Joe the bellhop, *Down Three Dark Streets* (1954) as Uncle Max Martell, *The Big Combo* (1955) as Sam Hill, *Murder Is My Beat* (1955) as Barman, *Love Me Or Leave Me* (1955) as Orry, *Lucy Gallant* (1955) as Sam, *Illegal* (1955) as Joseph Carter, *Man With The Gun* (1955) as Cal, *Runaway Daughters* (1956) as Mr Rubeck, *The Killing*

(1956) as Leo, *The Catered Affair*
(1956) as Sam Leiter, *Lust For Life*
(1956) as Waiter, *Hell On Devil's Island*
(1957) as Toto, *Crime Of Passion*
(1957) as Mr Nalence, *Sweet Smell Of Success* (1957) as Manny Davis, *The Brothers Karamazov* (1958) as Pawnbroker, *Seven Guns To Mesa* (1958) as Ben Avery, *Saddle The Wind* (1958) as Hank, *Curse Of The Undead* (1959) as Barman, *The Story On Page One* (1960) as Lauber, *All The Fine Young Cannibals* (1960) as Sammy, *Dime With A Halo* (1963) as Mr Lewis, *Who's Been Sleeping In My Bed?* (1963), *The Family Jewels* (1965) as Mr Lyman, *Brother, Cry For Me* (1970), *Grave Of The Vampire* (1972) as Old Zack, *Bummer!* (1972) as Sid Rosen and *Macon County Line* (1974) as the impound yard worker. He was also a regular on television, appearing in numerous programmes such as *Richard Diamond, Private Detective, Have Gun – Will Travel, The Untouchables, 77 Sunset Strip, Wanted: Dead Or Alive, The Barbara Stanwyck Show, The Detectives Starring Robert Taylor, The Twilight Zone, The Fugitive, Ben Casey* and *Perry Mason*.
CAUSE: He died in Woodland Hills, California, after a long illness three days before his 82nd birthday.

Larry Adler

Born February 10, 1914
Died August 7, 2001
Mouth organist. Lawrence Cecil Adler was born in Baltimore, Maryland, the son of the plumber Louis Adler and Sadie Hack. The family had emigrated from Russia and their original name was Zelakovitch. Adler began piano lessons at six and was the youngest cantor at the Baltimore synagogue at the age of 10. He was educated at Baltimore City College and then the Peabody Conservatory of Music but was asked to leave after he performed a rendition of 'Yes, We Have No Bananas' at a recital instead of Grieg's waltz in A minor. In 1927 he won the

Maryland harmonica championship and ran away to New York to find work as a professional musician. He landed a job as an interval turn touring American picture houses for $100 a week. He met and befriended many celebrities in his work and made his first film *Operator 13* in 1934. The impresario Sir C.B. Cochran hired Adler for a London tour and he became the talk of the town. He played Constantine Dan in the film *St Martin's Lane* (1938) which starred Charles Laughton and Vivien Leigh. During the Second World War he entertained the troops in western Europe and the Middle East. In 1943 he made his début at Carnegie Hall. At the end of the war he played 'The Battle Hymn Of The Republic' on the balcony of Hitler's former chancellery in Berlin and 'Rhapsody In Blue' at the Nuremberg stadium. Not long after, his life and career in America crashed when Joseph McCarthy and the House Un-American Activities Committee (HUAC) called him a communist. In 1949 he moved to England where his career flourished once more. Four years later, he wrote the score for the film *Genevieve*. In lieu of a fee Adler received 2.5 per cent of the royalties which later added up to around £250,000. *Genevieve*'s American distributors insisted that Adler's name be excised from the credits because of his continuing refusal to co-operate with McCarthy. When the music was nominated for and won an Oscar, the Academy of Motion Picture Arts and Sciences gave the credit to the music's conductor, Muir Matheson. Adler wrote music for more films including *The Hellions* (1961), *The Great Chase* (1962), *The Hook* (1963), *King And Country* (1964) and *A High Wind In Jamaica* (1965). He married the model Eileen Walser on April 11, 1938 and had a son, Peter, and two daughters by her. They divorced in 1961 and on January 1, 1969, he married Sally Cline. They divorced in 1977 having had one daughter. He went on to have a ten-year relationship with the biographer Lady Selina Shirley Hastings, daughter of Francis John Clarence Westenra Plantagenet Hastings (b. March 5, 1945), 16th Earl of Huntingdon (d. 1990).

CAUSE: Larry Adler was plagued by ill-health in the latter years of his life, having suffered a number of strokes. He died of pneumonia at St Thomas' Hospital, Lambeth, London. He was 87. He left just under £208,000.

Luther Adler

Born May 4, 1903
Died December 8, 1984
Heavy brother. Born in New York, one of six children of Jacob P. Adler. [*For full family details see under Jay Adler.*] Luther Adler was a heavily built man which usually meant he played only villains. Oddly for a Jew, he played Hitler twice in *The Magic Face* (1951) and *The Desert Fox: The Story Of Rommel* (1951). His other films included: *Lancer Spy* (1937) as Schratt, *Cornered* (1945) as Marcel Jarnac, *Saigon* (1948) as Lieutenant Keon, *The Loves Of Carmen* (1948) as Dancaire, *Wake Of The Red Witch* (1948) as Mayrant Ruysdaal Sidneye, *South Sea Sinner* (1949) as Cognac, *House Of Strangers* (1949) as Joe Monetti, *Under My Skin* (1950) as Louis Bork, *D.O.A.* (1950) as Majak, *Kiss Tomorrow Goodbye* (1950) as Keith 'Cherokee' Mandon, *M* (1951) as Dan Langley, *The Tall Texan* (1953) as Josh Tinnen, *The Miami Story* (1954) as Tony Brill, *Crashout* (1955) as Pete Mendoza, *The Girl In The Red Velvet Swing* (1955) as Delphin Delmas, *Hoodlum Empire* (1952) as Nick Mansani, *Hot Blood* (1956) as Marco Torino, *The Last Angry Man* (1959) as Dr Max Vogel, *The Three Sisters* (1966) as Chebutykin, *Cast A Giant Shadow* (1966) as Jacob Zion, *The Brotherhood* (1969) as Dominick Bertolo, *Crazy Joe* (1974) as Falco, *Murph The Surf* (1975) as Max

'The Eye', *The Man In The Glass Booth* (1975) as the presiding judge, *Voyage Of The Damned* (1976) as Professor Weiler, *Mean Johnny Barrows* (1976) and *Absence Of Malice* (1981) as Uncle Santos Malderone. Adler also appeared on television, usually in crime series such as *Hawaii Five-O*, *The Untouchables* and *Naked City*. Twice married, his wives were Sylvia Sidney (in London on August 10, 1938 as her second husband; their son, Jacob known as Jody, was born in New York City on October 22, 1939. She filed for divorce in Los Angeles on January 11, 1946 citing mental cruelty) and Julia Roche.

CAUSE: He died, aged 81, in Kutztown, Pennsylvania, of natural causes.

Stella Adler

Born February 10, 1901
Died December 21, 1992
Stage sister. Born in New York, one of six children of the actor Jacob P. Adler. [*For full family details see under Jay Adler.*] Stella made her acting début in 1906 in *Broken Hearts* at her father's theatre, The Grand, in New York and appeared regularly in his company for many years after. She once said, "I don't know what's the matter with young actresses these days – they're only interested in Chekhov. When I was starting out actresses were only interested in diamonds." She gave her first performance on the London stage in 1919 at the Pavilion Theatre, Mile End, playing Naomi in *Elisha Ben Avia*. She studied under her father, Maria Ouspenskaya and Richard Boleslavsky at the American Laboratory Theater and under Konstantin Stanislavsky in Europe. She became an acting teacher in 1940 at the Dramatic Workshop of the New School for Social Research and opened the Stella Adler Conservatory of Acting in New York in 1949. Her students included Alvin Ailey, Warren Beatty, Marlon Brando, James Coburn, Kevin Costner, Robert

De Niro, Benicio Del Toro, Teri Garr,
Harvey Keitel, Cloris Leachman, Karl
Malden, Bette Midler, Matthew
Modine, Sydney Pollack, Anthony
Quinn, John Ritter, Jerome Robbins,
Diana Ross, Martin Sheen, Elaine
Stritch, Henry Winkler and Shelley
Winters. Her film appearances were
sparse although she desperately wanted
to become a movie star. She made her
début (under the name Stella Ardler to
avoid anti-Semitism) in the romantic
screwball comedy *Love On Toast*
(1937), directed by E. A. Dupont,
playing Linda Craven. (Apparently,
studio heads suggested in all
seriousness that she change her name
to Beverly Wilshire.) She was also in
W.S. Van Dyke II's *Shadow Of The
Thin Man* (1941) as Claire Porter and
Elliott Nugent's *My Girl Tisa* (1948) as
Mrs Faludi. In 1943 she became
associate producer at Metro Studios. In
February 1951 she celebrated her 50th
birthday with a party attended by many
notables and her mother. Mrs Adler
was asked her age and replied that she
was 62. The guest was puzzled and
pointed out that Stella was 50. "That's
her problem," retorted her mother.
Stella Adler was married three times.
Her first husband was Horace
Eleascheff by whom she had one
daughter, Ellen. In 1943 she married
Harold Clurman but that ended in
divorce. He was constantly unfaithful
to her and at a party she stood on a
table and asked all her lovers to form a
circle around her. "You see, Harold,"
she told her husband, "you have your
girls but I have my men." Her third
husband was Mitchell Wilson, the
novelist and scientist, and they were
together until his death from a heart
attack on February 26, 1973.
CAUSE: When she was in her early
eighties, Stella Adler fell and broke her
hip. The doctors who fitted the
replacement did a poor job and she
struggled to walk for the rest of her life.
She died, aged 91, of heart failure in
Los Angeles, California.

Renée Adorée
(JEANNE DE LA FONTE)
Born September 30, 1898
Died October 5, 1933
La petite fille. Born in a circus tent in
Lille, France, the 5'1" daughter of an
English clown and a French horse
rider, she followed in her mother's
saddle steps and aged ten became a
bareback rider in the ring. After a stint
as a dancer at the Folies Bergères the
blue-eyed brunette moved to
Hollywood to become a film star. She
appeared in over 40 films but faded
from the public eye through ill-health
and the arrival of the talkies. Her
movies included *Made In Heaven*
(1921) as Miss Lowry starring opposite
Tom Moore (whom she married on
February 12, 1921), *West Of Chicago*
(1922) as Della Moore, *Monte Cristo*
(1922) as Eugénie Danglars, *Women
Who Give* (1924) as Becky Keeler,
Defying The Law (1924) as Lucia
Brescia, *Exchange Of Wives* (1925) as
Elise Moran, *Exquisite Sinner* (1926),
Mr Wu (1927) as Nang Ping with Lon
Chaney, *His Glorious Night* (1929) and
Call Of The Flesh (1930) as Lola. It was
her performance as Mélisande with
John Gilbert in *The Big Parade* (1925)
that brought her the stardom she
craved. The film told the tale of a
young couple in love; he is sent off to
war and she fears for his safety. Luck is
on their side and he returns home to
continue their passion. Adorée's sexiest
role was as Suzette in *Man And Maid*
(1925), a film written by Elinor Glyn
(who labelled Clara Bow "The It
Girl".) Following her divorce from
Moore in October 1924 she was
engaged twice. She married agent
William Sherman Gill in Los Angeles
on June 28, 1927 but that marriage was
also destined to end in the divorce
courts – on February 2, 1929, after Gill
testified his wife had a ferocious
temper.
CAUSE: In 1930 Adorée discovered she
had tuberculosis and moved to Arizona
in a bid to overcome it. However, she

missed her life in Tinseltown and returned in early 1933. She died in Tujunga, California, a week after her 35th birthday. She is buried in crypt 19, Abbey of the Psalms Foyer in Hollywood Memorial Park, 6000 Santa Monica Boulevard, Hollywood, Los Angeles 90038.

Iris Adrian
(IRIS ADRIAN HOFSTADTER)
Born May 29, 1912
Died September 17, 1994
Blonde wisecracker. Born in Los Angeles, California, her father's death from the flu epidemic of 1918 meant that Iris Adrian had to leave school at the end of the eighth grade. She won a competition for having a perfect back in 1929 and landed a job as a chorus girl in a revue at the Paramount Theater in Hollywood. After a couple of shows she was spotted by impresario Florenz Ziegfeld, who cast her in *Ziegfeld Follies Of 1931*. That led to work in a restaurant theatre in New York where she honed her comedic skills. She made about 100 films, including *Paramount On Parade* (1930), *Gay Deception* (1935), *Gold Diggers Of 1937* (1936) as Verna, *Go West* (1940), *Road To Zanzibar* (1941), *Million Dollar Kid* (1944) as Marcie Cortland, *Shake Hands With Murder* (1944) as Patsy Brent, *Boston Blackie's Rendezvous* (1945) as Martha, *The Paleface* (1948) as Pepper, *Mighty Joe Young* (1949), *G.I. Jane* (1951) as Lieutenant Adrian and *My Favorite Spy* (1951) as Lola although out of her 120+ films, her best roles were probably in *Roxie Hart* (1942) in which she played the killer Two-Gun Gertie, and as the stripper in *The Trouble With Women* (1947). She appeared often on television in *The Jack Benny Show* and featured as Dottie in the short-lived *The Ted Knight Show* (1978). She married former American football player Fido Murphy but never had children. She didn't consider her colleagues as suitable for romance. "I never went with actors.

Basically, they're bums who got lucky in the looks department. Very vain. It would be like dating another dame."
CAUSE: She died aged 82 as a result of an earthquake in Hollywood, California.

Max Adrian
(MAX BOR)
Born November 1, 1903
Died January 19, 1973
Camp and fruity. Born in Enniskillen, County Fermanagh, Ireland, Max Adrian was educated at Portora Royal School in Enniskillen. He was 22 when he made his stage début appearing in the chorus of *Katja The Dancer* at the Gaiety Theatre, Douglas, on the Isle of Man in August 1926. He made his London début in December 1927 at the Globe Theatre and made his first film seven years later in *The Primrose Path*. He was a touch too camp for stardom on the silver screen and spent much of his career in the theatre. Nevertheless, he appeared in many films including *The Primrose Path* (a remake of the 1925 film – as Julian Leigh) (1934), *A Touch Of The Moon* (1936) as Francis Leverton, a salesman in *To Catch A Thief* (1936), *Nothing Like Publicity* (1936) as Bob Wharncliffe, *The Happy Family* (1936) as Noel Hutt, *When The Devil Was Well* (1937) as David, *Macushla* (1937) as Kerry Muldoon, *Why Pick On Me?* (1938) as Jack Mills, *Merely Mr Hawkins* (1938) as Mr Fletcher, *Kipps* (1941) as Chester Coote, *Penn Of Pennsylvania* (1942) as Elton, *The Young Mr Pitt* (1942) as Sheridan, *Talk About Jacqueline* (1942) as Lionel, *The Chronicle History Of King Henry The Fifth With His Battle At Agincourt in France* (1944) as The Dauphin, Charles VII, *Quel Bandito Sono Io* (1949) as Catoni, *Pool Of London* (1951) as Charlie Vernon, an aide in *The Pickwick Papers* (1952), *Uncle Vanya* (1963) as Professor Serebryskov, *Dr Terror's House Of Horrors* (1965) as Dr Blake, *The Deadly Affair* (1966) as

adviser, *The Terrornauts* (1967) as Dr Henry Shore, *The Devils* (1971) as Ibert, *The Boy Friend* (1971) as Mr Max/Lord Hubert Brockhurst and *The Music Lovers* (1971) as Nicholas Rubinstein. A sufferer from asthma, Adrian collapsed on the first day of rehearsals for *The Boy Friend* and the insurance company insisted that director Ken Russell drop him. Russell refused but put Adrian in a wheelchair and had him sing "to playback . . . [so] if he pegs out halfway through, we'll go on filming in long shot and no one will be any the wiser." Adrian also appeared as Senator Ludicrus Sextus in the television sitcom *Up Pompeii*.
CAUSE: He died in Wilford, aged 69, of natural causes.

John Agar

Born January 31, 1921
Died April 7, 2002
The first Mr Shirley Temple. 6'2" John George Agar, Jr was born in Chicago, Illinois. His father, a former star athlete and the head of the family meat-packing business, died in 1935 and John's mother, Lillian, opened an exclusive boutique that soon gained a wealthy clientele. In 1942 Agar joined the air force where he served as a sergeant at the Fourth Air Force base in Ephrata. One day while visiting Ann Gallery, the daughter of his mother's friend ZaSu Pitts, Agar briefly met her next door neighbour Shirley Temple. After a hesitant start and a few double dates, they became secretly engaged. Agar proposed at traffic lights on Sunset Boulevard by an old age people's home and a petrol station. Agar accompanied her to a party at the home of David O. Selznick where he fell into conversation with the producer who asked if the airforceman might be interested in an acting career. Once he was discharged Agar was put under contract by Selznick. Meanwhile, his relationship with Temple flourished and, fearful of an overseas posting, they married on September 19, 1945 in the Wilshire Methodist Church on Wilshire Boulevard. Their 10-day honeymoon was spent in Santa Barbara although on arrival at the hotel they discovered that the honeymoon suite had been given to another couple. The couple announced that they would live on his salary – $150 a week – and put hers into trust and they moved into a small home. In fact, it had been the doll's house on Shirley Temple's parents' estate. He made his film début – opposite his wife – in *Fort Apache* (1948) as 2nd Lieutenant Michael Shannon O'Rourke. However, like many men with more successful wives Agar found it difficult to cope being labelled "Mr Shirley Temple" and he began drinking. He became an alcoholic and he and Shirley Temple divorced on December 6, 1949, becoming final on December 5, 1950. His career flourished but that did not stop his drinking. By 1951 he had served 60 days' prison time for drink-related offences. On May 17 of that year a judge refused to marry Agar to Loretta Barnett Combs, the fashion model who was to be his second wife, until he had drunk enough black coffee to sober up. In 1953 he was arrested twice in the same day and was sentenced to four months in prison. His films up to that time included *I Married A Communist* (1949) as Don Lowry, *Adventure In Baltimore* (1949) as Tom Wade, *She Wore A Yellow Ribbon* (1949) as Lieutenant Flint Cohill, *Sands Of Iwo Jima* (1949) as Private First Class Peter Conway, *Breakthrough* (1950) as Lieutenant Joe Mallory, *The Magic Carpet* (1951) as Ramoth, *Along The Great Divide* (1951) as Billy Shear, *Woman Of The North Country* (1952) as David Powell, *Man Of Conflict* (1953) as Ray Compton and *Shield For Murder* (1954) as Detective Sergeant Mark Brewster. After that he began to make low-budget horror and sci-fi films with the occasional big picture in between. They included *Tarantula* (1955) as Dr Matt Hastings, *Revenge Of The Creature*

(1955) as Professor Clete Ferguson, *The Mole People* (1956) as Dr Roger Bentley, *Ride A Violent Mile* (1957) as Jeff Dunning, *Joe Butterfly* (1957) as Sergeant Dick Mason, *The Brain From Planet Arous* (1957) as Steve March, *Daughter Of Dr Jekyll* (1957) as George Hastings, *Jet Attack* (1958) as Captain Tom Arnett, *Attack Of The Puppet People* (1958) as Bob Westley, *Raymie* (1960) as Ike, *Hand Of Death* (1962) as Alex Marsh, *Journey To The Seventh Planet* (1962) as Captain Don Graham, *Law Of The Lawless* (1964) as Pete Stone, *Zontar The Thing From Venus* (1966) as Dr Curt Taylor, *Curse Of The Swamp Creature* (1966) as Barry Rogers, *Women Of The Prehistoric Planet* (1966) as Dr Farrell, *Johnny Reno* (1966) as Ed Tomkins, *Waco* (1966) as George Gates, *Chisum* (1970) as Amos Patton, *Big Jake* (1971) as Bert Ryan, *King Kong* (1976) as a public official, *Miracle Mile* (1989) as Ivan Peters and *The Pandora Directive* (1996) as Thomas Malloy. Agar once said: "I never made a movie that pleased me, but living has given me more dimension than I had then. I simply wasn't ready when it was handed to me. Yes, I'd really like another shot at it." He adopted two sons, Martin David (b. 1957) and John George III (b. 1964), from his second marriage but had no contact with Linda Susan (b. Santa Monica Hospital, January 30, 1948), his daughter from his marriage to Shirley Temple. "I know that Shirley and I are now grandparents. That is because it was in the news. I was not invited to the wedding. We are not in touch."
CAUSE: Agar died aged 81 of emphysema in Los Angeles, California.

Robert Agnew

Born June 4, 1899
Died November 8, 1983
Silent star. Born in Dayton, Kentucky, Agnew was one of the leading juvenile stars of the early cinema. His career began on the stage and quickly moved to the silver screen. He retired a few years after the advent of sound and worked as an assistant director at Warner Bros. His films included: *The Sporting Duchess* (1920) as Dick Hammond, *The Valley Of Doubt* (1920) as Tommy, *The Frisky Mrs Johnson* (1920) as Lal Birkenread, *The Sin That Was His* (1920), *The Sign On The Door* (1921) as Alan Churchill, *The Highest Law* (1921) as Bobby Goodwin, *Passion Flower* (1921) as Faustino Eusebio, *The Wonderful Thing* (1921) as Laurence Mannerby, *Who Are My Parents?* (1922) as Bob Hale, *Pawn Ticket 210* (1922) as Chick Saxe, *Kick In* (1922) as Jerry Brandon, *A Dangerous Adventure* (1922) as Jimmy Morrison, *Without Fear* (1922) as Walter Hamilton, *Clarence* (1922) as Bobby Wheeler, *A Dangerous Game* (1922) as John Kelley, *Three Who Paid* (1923) as Hal Sinclair, *Trimmed In Scarlet* (1923) as David Peirce, *Prodigal Daughters* (1923) as Lester Hodge, *Only 38* (1923) as Bob Stanley, *Bluebeard's Eighth Wife* (1923) as Albert de Marceau, *The Marriage Maker* (1923) as Cyril Overton, *The Spanish Dancer* (1923) as Juan, *Woman-Proof* (1923) as Dick Rockwood, *Love's Whirlpool* (1924) as Larry, *Those Who Dance* (1924) as Matt Carney, *Wine Of Youth* (1924) as Bobby, *Broken Barriers* (1924) as Bobbie Durland, *Wine* (1924) as Harry van Alstyne, *Troubles Of A Bride* (1924) as Robert Wallace, *Gold Heels* (1924) as Boots, a young officer in *The Denial* (1925), *Private Affairs* (1925) as Fred Henley, *The Man Without A Conscience* (1925) as James Warren, *Lost: A Wife* (1925) as Dick, *Tessie* (1925) as Roddy Wells, *Steppin' Out* (1925) as Henry Brodman, Jr, *The Great Love* (1925) as Dr Lawrence Tibbits, *Racing Blood* (1926) as James Fleming, *Wild Oats Lane* (1926) as the boy, *Fourth Commandment* (1926) as Sonny, *The Taxi Mystery* (1926) as Harry Canby, *Unknown Treasures* (1926) as Bob Ramsey, *Dancing Days* (1926) as

Gerald Hedman, *Wandering Girls* (1927) as Jerry Arnold, *Quarantined Rivals* (1927) as Bruce Farney, *Snowbound* (1927) as Peter Foley, *Heart Of Salome* (1927) as Redfern, *She's My Baby* (1927) as Bobby Horton, *Down The Stretch* (1927) as Marty Kruger, *The Prince Of Headwaiters* (1927) as Elliott Cable, *Slightly Used* (1927) as Donald Woodward, *The College Hero* (1927) as Bob Cantfield, *The Heart Of Broadway* (1928) as Billy Winters, *The Midnight Taxi* (1928) as Jack Madison, *Hold The Baby* (1930), *Woman Racket* (1930) as Rags, *French Kisses* (1930), *Mind Your Business* (1930) as Tommy Seymour, *Extravagance* (1930) as Billy, *The Naughty Flirt* (1931) as Wilbur Fairchild, *The Love Bargain* (1931), *Gold Diggers Of 1933* (1933), *Business Is A Pleasure* (1934) and *Little Man, What Now?* (1934). Agnew married three times: to Susanne Sheldon, Elaine Titus Fearon and Bettina von Hutton by whom he had his only child.
CAUSE: He died of kidney failure in Palm Springs, California.

Brian Aherne

Born May 2, 1902
Died February 10, 1986
Mr Dapper. Born at The Pleasaunce, in King's Norton, Worcestershire, William Brian de Lacy Aherne didn't make his stage début as a babe in arms, unlike so many other thespians. He was a more mature three-year-old when he began to tread the boards. Aherne studied at the Italia Conti stage school and then Malvern College. He began to study architecture but having failed to land a job designing buildings, he decided to give acting a try "until something better comes along". He wowed audiences on the London stage (he made his first appearance in *Where The Rainbow Ends* at the Garrick Theatre on December 26, 1913) before travelling to Broadway where he received accolades as Robert Browning in *The Barretts Of Wimpole Street* (the show opened on February 9, 1931, at the Empire) opposite Katharine Cornell. Aherne made his film début in *The Eleventh Commandment* (1924), a silent film. His first major Hollywood role was playing a sculptor opposite Marlene Dietrich in *Song Of Songs* (1933). It was a flop. Dietrich asked him at the start of the shoot: "Why do you, an important actor from Broadway, come here to make this silly picture? I have to do it . . . But you! Are you crazy?" Aherne was too shy to tell Dietrich the real reason: he fancied her. Aherne was never to really make his presence felt on the big screen although he gave creditable performances in movies such as *The Fountain* (1934), *Captain Fury* (1939), *Juarez* (1939) (which won him an Oscar nomination as Emperor Maximilian), *My Son, My Son* (1940) and *A Night To Remember* (1943). The pipe-smoking Aherne, who was exceptionally careful when it came to money, was very aware of his looks – he was tall (6'3½"), handsome and blond. His *Juarez* co-star Bette Davis once complained that during one scene he was ignoring her and looking in the mirror over her shoulder. He once remarked, "I have never taken acting very seriously" adding (in 1969), "I have never advertised in trade papers, as many actors do. But if I did, I suppose my ad would read: '(William) Brian de Lacy Aherne, professionally known as Brian Aherne, having signally failed to find a proper job in life, is still available in show business. Not arrogant or difficult any more. Has wardrobe. Will travel.'" Hmmm. Aloof and cool, he was married twice. His first wife was actress Joan Fontaine (he had previously dated her sister, Olivia de Havilland). They married on August 19, 1939, in Del Monte, California, and were divorced on June 5, 1944, three years after their estrangement due to his "extreme cruelty". He later commented: "My

marriage to Joan Fontaine roughly coincided with World War II. It even began the same year. Enough said?" Problems were undoubtedly exacerbated by the fact that Fontaine suffered from a cystic condition that made intercourse painful. On January 27, 1946, in Steven's Landing, New York, he married Eleanor de Liagre Labrot. They were together 42 years. Aherne wrote a memoir of his close friend George Sanders. Aherne's brother, Patrick (b. King's Norton, Worcestershire, January 6, 1901, d. Woodland Hills, California, September 30, 1970, of cancer) was also an actor with over 30 films under his belt. He was married to the actress Renee Houston.
CAUSE: He died in Venice, Florida aged 83, from heart failure.

Philip Ahn
(PIL LIP AHN)
Born March 29, 1905
Died February 28, 1978
Inscrutable Oriental. Born in Los Angeles of Korean parentage, his father was a diplomat. Ahn was educated at the University of Southern California and made his first performance in a film in 1935. He became extremely busy playing all sorts of Orientals – Chinese, Japanese and Korean, in over 100 films. To television audiences he is best known for his continuing role as Master Kan in the series *Kung Fu* (1972–1975). Among his films were *A Scream In The Night* (1935) as Wu Ting, *Klondike Annie* (1936) as Wing, *Tex Rides With The Boy Scouts* (1937) as Sing Fung, *Thank You, Mr Moto* (1937) as Prince Chung, *Daughter Of Shanghai* (1937) as Kim Lee, *Charlie Chan In Honolulu* (1939) as Wing Foo, *Drums Of Fu Manchu* (1940) as Dowlah-Rao, *China's Little Devils* (1945), *Boston Blackie's Chinese Venture* (1949) as Wong Chung Shee, *Halls Of Montezuma* (1950) as Nomura, *Around The World In 80 Days* (1956)

and *Thoroughly Modern Millie* (1967) as Tee. His brother Philson Ahn was also an actor.
CAUSE: He died of lung cancer in Los Angeles aged 72.

Henry Ainley
Born August 21, 1879
Died October 31, 1945
The Master's granddad. Born in Morley, Leeds, Yorkshire, the son of Richard Ainley, Henry Hinchcliffe Ainley began his professional career as an accountant. He began acting on the stage making his first London appearance at the Lyceum in 1900 before becoming an early movie star. His films included: *Henry VIII* (1911) as Buckingham, *She Stoops To Conquer* (1914) as Marlow, *Called Back* (1914) as Gilbert Vaughan, *A Bachelor's Love Story* (1914) as Henry Norman, *Sweet Lavender* (1915) as Dick Phenyl, *The Prisoner Of Zenda* (1915) as Rudolph Rassendyll, the French officer in *The Outrage* (1915), *A Man Of His Word* (1915), *The Great Adventure* (1915) as Liam Carve, *Brother Officers* (1915) as John Hinds, *Sowing The Wind* (1916), *The Marriage Of William Ashe* (1916), *The Manxman* (1916), *Iris* (1916) as Maldonado and *Rupert Of Hentzau* (1916) as Rudolph Rassendyll. The First World War interrupted his career and from 1916 until 1919 he served as a lieutenant with the Royal Garrison Artillery. After being demobbed, he appeared in *Quinneys* (1919), *Build Thy House* (1920) as Arthur Burnaby, *The Prince And The Beggarmaid* (1921) as Prince Olaf, *Money* (1921) as Alfred, *Evelyn The Royal Oak* (1923) as Oliver Cromwell, *Sally Bishop* (1924) as John Traill, *The First Mrs Fraser* (1932) as James Fraser, the narrator of the prologue in *The Good Companions* (1933) and *As You Like It* (1936) as the exiled duke. It seems likely that in 1936–1937 Ainley had a homosexual affair with Laurence Olivier just as Olivier was about to leave Jill Esmond for Vivien Leigh. Ainley married twice.

His first wife was Suzanne Sheldon, an American whom he married in 1903. She died in 1924. His second trip to the altar was with Elaine Fearon. He had one son and one daughter. His son was the actor Richard Ainley (b. Stanmore, Middlesex, December 22, 1910, d. London, May 18, 1967) who appeared with his father in *As You Like It* and married three times. His son was the actor Anthony Ainley (b. London, August 20, 1932, d. Harrow, Middlesex, May 3, 2004) who played the Master on the television series *Doctor Who* for nine years.
CAUSE: He died in London aged 65.

Spottiswoode Aitken

Born April 16, 1868
Died February 26, 1933
Prodigious thespian. Frank Spottiswoode Aitken was born in Edinburgh, Scotland, and after a long stage career travelled to America where he found employment – and lots of it – in the fledgling film industry. He often worked with D.W. Griffith, and appeared in more than 100 films including: *Her Humble Ministry* (1911), *The Battle* (1911), *The Sands Of Dee* (1912), *Once Was Enough* (1912), *A Guilty Conscience* (1913), *What's In A Name?* (1913), *She Must Elope* (1913), *Auntie's Affinity* (1913) as the cook, *Pete Joins The Force* (1913), *The Old Maid* (1914), *Liberty Belles* (1914), *The Availing Prayer* (1914), *The Angel Of Contention* (1914), *Home, Sweet Home* (1914) as Mary's father, the uncle in *The Avenging Conscience: Thou Shalt Not Kill* (1914), *The Birth Of A Nation* (1915) as Dr Cameron, *A Temperance Lesson* (1915) as John Hammond, a lawyer in *The Outcast* (1915), a soothsayer in *The Outlaw's Revenge* (1915), *Captain Macklin* (1915) as General Laquerre, *Her Shattered Idol* (1915) as Colonel Nutt, *Acquitted* (1916) as Charles Ryder, *The Price Of Power* (1916), *The Flying Torpedo* (1916) as Bartholomew Thompson, *Macbeth* (1916) as Duncan, *An Innocent Magdalene* (1916) as Colonel Raleigh, the father of Brown Eyes in *Intolerance* (1916), a judge in *The Old Folks At Home* (1916), grandfather in *The Wharf Rat* (1916), *The Americano* (1916) as Presidente de Castalar, a judge in *Stage Struck* (1917), *A Woman's Awakening* (1917) as Judge Cotter, *Cheerful Givers* (1917) as Reverend John Deady, *Souls Triumphant* (1917) as Josiah Vale, *Her Country's Call* (1917) as Dr Downie, *Melissa Of The Hills* (1917) as Jethro Stark, *Charity Castle* (1917) as Lucius Garrett, *Southern Pride* (1917) as Father Mort, *A Game Of Wits* (1917) as Silas Stone, *Beauty And The Rogue* (1918) as Benjamin Wilson, *The Mating Of Marcella* (1918) as Jose Duranzo, *How Could You, Jean?* (1918) as Rufus Bonner, *In Judgment Of . . .* (1918) as Mr Manners, *The Cruise Of The Make-Believes* (1918) as Simon Quarle, *The Thunderbolt* (1919) as Allan Pomeroy, *Jane Goes A'Wooing* (1919) as David Lyman, *The Secret Garden* (1919) as Archibald Craven, *Who Cares?* (1919) as Mr Ludlow, *Fighting Through* (1919) as Colonel DuBrey Carter, *The Wicked Darling* (1919) as Fadem, *Captain Kidd, Jr* (1919) as Angus MacTavish, *The White Heather* (1919) as James Hume, *Caleb Piper's Girl* (1919) as Caleb Piper, *An Innocent Adventuress* (1919) as Meekton, *Hay Foot, Straw Foot* (1919) as Thaddeus Briggs, *Evangeline* (1919) as Benedict Bellefontaine, the king in *Rough-Riding Romance* (1919), *The Broken Commandments* (1919) as Mr Banard, *Her Kingdom Of Dreams* (1919) as David Rutledge, *Bonnie Bonnie Lassie* (1919) as Jeremiah Wishart, *A Woman Of Pleasure* (1919) as Wilberforce Pace, the father in *Dangerous Love* (1920), *Witch's Gold* (1920), *The White Circle* (1920) as Bernard Huddlestone, *Nomads Of The North* (1920) as Old Roland, *Reputation* (1921) as Karl, *The Unknown Wife* (1921) as Henry Wilburton, *At The End Of The World* (1921), *Beyond*

(1921) as Rufus Southerne, *One Wonderful Night* (1922) as a minister, *Merry-Go-Round* (1922) as Minister of War/Gisella's father, *The Price Of Youth* (1922) as Gregory Monmouth, *The White Messenger* (1922), *Man Of Courage* (1922) as Stephen Gregory, *The Trap* (1922) as The Factor, *Monte Cristo* (1922) as Abbé Faria, *The Snowshoe Trail* (1922) as Herbert Lounsbury, *Manslaughter* (1922), *The Young Rajah* (1922) as Caleb, *A Dangerous Game* (1922) as Edward Peebles, *The Love Pirate* (1923) as Cyrus Revere, *Around The World In Eighteen Days* (1923), *Six Days* (1923) as Père Jerome, *Pioneer's Gold* (1924), *Triumph* (1924) as Torrini, *Lure Of The Yukon* (1924) as Sourdough McCraig, *The Fire Patrol* (1924) as Captain John Ferguson, *Gerald Cranston's Lady* (1924) as Ephraim Brewster, *Those Who Dare* (1924) as Thorne Wetherell, *The Coast Patrol* (1925) as Capt. Slocum, *The Eagle* (1925) as Dubrovsky's father, *Accused* (1925) as Eagle Eye, the father in *The Power Of The Weak* (1926), *The Two-Gun Man* (1926) as Dad Randall and *Roaring Fires* (1927) as Calvert Carter. Following his retirement from acting, he took to writing and created *God's Great Wilderness* (1927).
CAUSE: He died in Los Angeles, California, aged 64.

Muriel Aked
Born November 9, 1887
Died March 21, 1955
Cinematic spinster. Born in Bingley, Yorkshire, she took great pleasure in her portrayals of misery guts and shockable spinsters. Her films included *A Sister To Assist 'Er* (1922, 1931, 1939, 1948), *Rome Express* (1932), *Yes, Madam* (1933) as Mrs Peabody, *Friday The Thirteenth* (1933) as Miss Twigg, *Autumn Crocus* (1934) as Miss Mayne, *Can You Hear Me, Mother?* (1935) as Mother, *Mother, Don't Rush Me* (1936) as Amy Andrews, *Mr Stringfellow Says No* (1937) as Mrs Piper, *The Life And*

Death Of Colonel Blimp (1943) as Aunt Margaret Hamilton, *The Blue Lamp* (1950) as Mrs Waterboume and *The Story Of Gilbert And Sullivan* (1953) as Queen Victoria.
CAUSE: She died in Settle, Yorkshire, aged 67.

Luis Alberni
Born October 4, 1886
Died December 23, 1962
Talented polyglot. Born in Barcelona, Spain, Alberni was educated at the University of Madrid where he studied drama. His interest in acting started at university and he began to appear in numerous plays including Shakespeare. In 1914 he moved to America to appear in Spanish versions of American films. However, he was so popular that he was persuaded to stay. Twice married, he had two sons, Luis and Carlos, by his first wife. His second marriage was to Wanda Kay Wilson. Fluent in seven languages, 5'7" Alberni was also a talented artist and a gourmet chef. His films included: *Children Of The Ghetto* (1915) as Pincus, *The Madonna Of The Slums* (1919), *39 East* (1920) as Count Gionelli, *Little Italy* (1921) as Ricci, *The Man From Beyond* (1922) as Captain of the Barkentine 68, *The Bright Shawl* (1923) as Vincente Escobar, *The Valley Of Lost Souls* (1923) as Jacques, *Second Youth* (1924), *The Cheerful Fraud* (1927), *The Battle Of Paris* (1929), *The Santa Fe Trail* (1930) as Juan Castinado, *Strange Birds* (1930), *One Heavenly Night* (1931), *Svengali* (1931) as Gecko, *Sweepstakes* (1931), *Movie Town* (1931), *Children Of Dreams* (1931), *The Last Flight* (1931), *I Like Your Nerve* (1931) as Sao Pedro waiter, *Side Show* (1931) as The Great Santini, *The Tip-Off* (1931) as Scarno, *The Mad Genius* (1931) as Sergei Bankieff, *Men In Her Life* (1931) as Anton, *Manhattan Parade* (1932) as Vassiloff, *Cock Of The Air* (1932) as Captain Tonnino, *High Pressure* (1932) as Colombo, *Stop That Run* (1932),

Hombres De Mi Vida (1932) as Gaston, *The Cohens And Kellys In Hollywood* (1932) as Bladimir Petrosky, an anarchist in *Rule 'Em And Weep* (1932), *The Woman In Room 13* (1932) as Tonelli, *First In War* (1932), *Weekend Marriage* (1932) as Louis, *Crooner* (1932) as Tamborini, *Two Against The World* (1932), *A Parisian Romance* (1932) as Pascal, *Guilty Or Not Guilty* (1932) as Pete, *The Big Stampede* (1932) as Sonora Joe, *Trouble In Paradise* (1932), *The Conquerors* (1932), *The Bride's Bereavement* (1932), a photographer's assistant in *Rasputin And The Empress* (1932), a consul in *Hypnotized* (1932), *Girl In The Tonneau* (1932), *Artist's Muddles* (1933) as Pietro Cellini, *Topaze* (1933) as Dr Bomb, *Child Of Manhattan* (1933) as Bustamente, *Men Must Fight* (1933) as Soto, *The California Trail* (1933) as Commandant Emilio Quierra, *Trick For Trick* (1933) as Metzger, *The Sphinx* (1933) as Luigi Baccigalupi, *When Ladies Meet* (1933) as Pierre, *I Love That Man* (1933) as Angelo, *The Man From Monterey* (1933) as Felipe Guadalupe Constacio Delgado Santa Cruz de la Verranca, *The Last Trail* (1933), *Sherman Said It* (1933), *Stage Mother* (1933) as Hors d'Oeuvres waiter, *Menu* (1933) as the Master Chef, *The Chief* (1933), *Goodbye Love* (1933) as Tony, the second taxi driver in *Havana Widows* (1933), *If I Were Free* (1933 – although his scenes were deleted before the film went on general release), *Above The Clouds* (1933) as the owner of the speakeasy, *California Weather* (1933), *By Candlelight* (1933), *Flying Down To Rio* (1933) as the Rio casino manager, *Lady Killer* (1933), *La Ciudad De Cartón* (1934), *When Do We Eat?* (1934) as Rigo, *Glamour* (1934) as Monsieur Paul, *I Believed In You* (1934) as Giacomo, *The Black Cat* (1934) as a train steward (although again his scenes were deleted before release), *Strictly Dynamite* (1934) as a barber, *Stingaree* (1934), *La Buenaventura* (1934) as Fresco, *I Surrender Dear* (1934) as Marquis, *The Count Of Monte Cristo* (1934) as Jacopo, *One Night Of Love* (1934) as Giovanni, *When Strangers Meet* (1934) as Nick, *The Captain Hates The Sea* (1934) as Juan Gilboa, *Caravane* (1934) as the gypsy chieftain, *The Gilded Lily* (1935) as Nate, *The Good Fairy* (1935) as the barber, *The Winning Ticket* (1935) as Tony, *Roberta* (1935) as Alexander Petrovitch Moskovich Voyda, *Asegure A Su Mujer* (1935), *Public Opinion* (1935) as Caparini, *Let's Live Tonight* (1935) as Mario Weems, *Goin' To Town* (1935) as Señor Vitola, *In Caliente* (1935) as the magistrate, *Ticket Or Leave It* (1935), *Love Me Forever* (1935) as Luigi, *Manhattan Moon* (1935) as Luigi, *The Gay Deception* (1935) as Ernest, *Thunder In The Night* (1935) as a taxi driver (although once again his scenes were deleted and he was replaced by Herman Bing), *Metropolitan* (1935) as Ugo Pizzi, *Bad Boy* (1935) as Tony, *Music Is Magic* (1935) as Señor Castellano, *Colleen* (1936) as Carlo, *Dancing Pirate* (1936) as Pamfilo, *Ticket To Paradise* (1936) as Dr Munson, *Anthony Adverse* (1936) as Tony Guiseppe, *Follow Your Heart* (1936) as Tony, *Hats Off* (1936) as Rosero, *When You're In Love* (1937) as Luis Perugini, *Two Wise Maids* (1937) as Guili, *The King And The Chorus Girl* (1937) as Gaston, *Sing And Be Happy* (1937) as Posini, *Easy Living* (1937) as Mr Louis Louis, *Madame X* (1937) as Scipio, *The Great Garrick* (1937) as Luis Basset, *Under Suspicion* (1937) as Luigi, *Manhattan Merry-Go-Round* (1937) as Martinetti, *Love On Toast* (1937) as Joe Piso, *Hitting A New High* (1937) as Luis Marlo, a reporter in *I'll Give A Million* (1938), *The Great Man Votes* (1939) as Manos, *Let Freedom Ring* (1939) (uncredited) as Tony, *Naughty But Nice* (1939) as Stanislaus Pysinski, *The Housekeeper's Daughter* (1939) as Veroni, *The Amazing Mr Williams* (1939) as Rinaldo, *High School* (1940) as Signor Cicero,

Twincuplets (1940), *Enemy Agent* (1940) as A. Calteroni, *The Lone Wolf Meets A Lady* (1940) as N. Pappakontous, *Scatterbrain* (1940) as Professor DeLemma, *Public Deb No. 1* (1940) as Frontenac, *The Lady Eve* (1941) as Emile, *That Hamilton Woman* (1941) as the king of Naples, *Road To Zanzibar* (1941) as the native booth proprietor, *They Met In Argentina* (1941) as Don Luis Jose Alfonso Frutos y Murphy, an inventor in *She Knew All The Answers* (1941), *San Antonio Rose* (1941) as Nick Ferris, *They Met In Bombay* (1941) as Maître d'hôtel, *World Premiere* (1941) as Signor Scaletti, *Babes On Broadway* (1941) as Nick, *Obliging Young Lady* (1942) as Riccardi, *I Married An Angel* (1942) as Jean Frederique, *Mexican Spitfire's Elephant* (1942) as Luigi, *Two Weeks To Live* (1943) as Van Dyke, *My Son, The Hero* (1943) as Tony, *Submarine Base* (1943) as Mr Styx, *The Man From Down Under* (1943) as Dino, *Here Comes Kelly* (1943) as Nick, *You're A Lucky Fellow, Mr Smith* (1943) as Goreni, *Nearly Eighteen* (1943) as Gus, *Here Comes Elmer* (1943) as Dr Zichy, a café manager in *Harvest Melody* (1943), *Men On Her Mind* (1944) as Alberti Verdi, *A Voice In The Wind* (1944) as a barman, *Henry Aldrich Plays Cupid* (1944) as Tony, a restaurant owner in *It Happened Tomorrow* (1944), *Machine Gun Mama* (1944) as Ignacio, *Abbott & Costello In Society* (1944) as Luigi, *Rainbow Island* (1944) as Jerry, a prison guard in *The Conspirators* (1944), *When The Lights Go On Again* (1944), another prison guard in *I Was A Criminal* (1945), *Wonder Man* (1945), *A Bell For Adano* (1945) as Cacopardo, *Hit The Hay* (1945) as the French professor, *In Fast Company* (1946) as Tony, *Double Rhythm* (1946), *The Road To Hollywood* (1946) as the Marquis, the barman in *When Willie Comes Marching Home* (1950), *Captain Carey, U.S.A.* (1950) as Sandro, *What Price Glory* (1952) as the great uncle and *The Ten Commandments* (1956) as Old Hebrew.

CAUSE: Alberni died aged 76 in Hollywood, California. He is buried in Pierce Brothers Valhalla Memorial Park, 10621 Victory Boulevard, Burbank, California 91606.

Hans Albers
Born September 22, 1891
Died July 24, 1960
German leading man. Born in Hamburg, the youngest son of six children, to William Philipp Albers, a master butcher, and his wife Johanna Dorothea, Hans Philipp August Albers began working as a teacher in 1907 but secretly took acting lessons. In 1911 he failed an audition to join a theatre company and began work in a Frankfurt silk factory. However, he was spotted by theatre manager Arthur Hellmer and made his stage début on September 20, 1911 in Frankfurt. In 1913 Albers began to take on major roles in the Altona and Thalia Theatres. In 1915 he was called up to serve in the German army during the First World War but was invalided out two years later with a wounded leg. While recovering from his injuries he resumed his theatrical career on the Berlin stage. When the war ended Albers found himself without regular work and concentrated on the theatre. His first success was as a light comedian before turning to more dramatic roles and then, as he aged, character parts. In 1925 Albers began a relationship with the half-Jewish actress Hansi Burg (d. 1975) and in 1928 he received acclaim for his work on the play *The Criminals* in the Berlin Theatre. He had also by this time made innumerable silent films and is probably best known to British audiences for his role as Mazeppa in *Der Blaue Engel* (1930) opposite Marlene Dietrich. He reached the apogee of his stage career in 1931 with the play *Liliom*. His most successful film to that time as a leading man was *F.P.1 Antwortet Nicht* (1932) in which

he played Ellissen. He also sang 'The Flier Song' in the movie and it became a popular hit. In 1938, Hansi Burg fled into exile in Switzerland to escape the Nazis while Albers stayed behind. Five years later, Albers starred in *Münchhausen*, an early German colour film that was intended to be the movie that showed Hitler's Germany could compete with Hollywood in terms of producing lavish spectacles. During the filming of his next movie *Große Freiheit Nr 7* (1944), for which he was paid DM460,000 to play Hannes Kroeger, Albers came under pressure from German propaganda minister Joseph Goebbels who disapproved of the content as well as the bombs falling on Hamburg. Albers turned to the bottle to cope. During one scene the director Helmut Kaeutner asked Albers to remove his hat but the actor refused, "I can't. I forgot to put my toupee on today." Following the end of the Second World War, Albers returned to the theatre and reprised his role in *Liliom* at the Hebbel Theatre in Berlin. In 1946 Hansi Burg returned to Germany and they resumed their relationship. His first post-war film was . . . *Und Uber Uns Der Himmel* (1947) in which he played Hans Richter but mostly his career after the Second World War was a disappointment. In 1958 he spoke out against the rearmament of West Germany. His films include: *Jahreszeiten Des Lebens* (1915), *Das Spitzentuch Der Fürstin Wolkowska* (1917), *Rauschgold* (1917), *Rache Des Gefallenen* (1917), *Die Prinzessin Von Urbino* (1918), *Irrwege Der Liebe* (1918), *Der Fluch Des Nuri* (1918), *Baroneßchen Auf Strafurlaub* (1918), *Taumel* (1919), *Madeleine* (1919), *Lola Montez 2* (1919), *Taschendiebe* (1920), *Die Marquise Von O.* (1920), *Schieber* (1921), *Die Große Und Die Kleine Welt* (1921), *Der Fürst* (1921), *Der Falschspieler* (1921), *Der Böse Geist* (1922), *Der Falsche Dimitri* (1922), *Versunkene Welten* (1922), *Der Tiger Des*

Zirkus Farini (1922), *Söhne Der Nacht* (1922), *Menschenopfer* (1922), *Lydia Sanin* (1922), *Die Geliebte Des Königs* (1922), *Fräulein Raffke* (1923), *Inge Larsen* (1923), *Das Schöne Abenteuer* (1924), *Das Testament Des Joe Sivers* (1924), *Ein Sommernachtstraum* (1924) as Demetrius, *Guillotine* (1924), *Gehetzte Menschen* (1924), *Auf Befehl Der Pompadour* (1924), *Luxusweibchen* (1925), *Halbseide* (1925), *Vorderhaus Und Hinterhaus* (1925), *Die Venus Von Montmartre* (1925), *Der Mann Aus Dem Jenseits* (1925), *Der König Und Das Kleine Mädchen* (1925), *Die Gesunkenen* (1925), *Deutsche Herzen Am Deutschen Rhein* (1925), *Der Bankraub Unter Den Linden* (1925), *Athleten* (1925), *Mein Freund Der Chauffeur* (1926), *Der Prinz Und Die Tänzerin* (1926), *Wir Sind Vom K.U.K. Infanterie-Regiment* (1926) as Oberleutnant Ahrens, *Ich Hatt' Einen Kameraden* (1926), *Versunkene Flotte* (1926), *Der Soldat Der Marie* (1926), *Seeschlacht Beim Skagerrak* (1926), *Schatz, Mach' Kasse* (1926), *Der Lachende Ehemann* (1926), *Jagd Auf Menschen* (1926), *Husarenliebe* (1926), *Die Frau Die Nicht Nein Sagen Kann* (1926), *Die Drei Mannequins* (1926), *An Der Schönen Blauen Donau* (1926), *Eine Dubarry Von Heute* (1927) as Toinette's first lover, *Bara En Danserska* (1927), *Primanerliebe* (1927), *En Perfekt Gentleman* (1927) as Jacques Renard, *Eine Kleine Freundin Braucht Jeder Mann* (1927), *Der Größte Gauner Des Jahrhunderts* (1927), *Der Goldene Abgrund* (1927) as Baron Armand, *Die Dollarprinzessin Und Ihre Sechs Freier* (1927), *Frauenarzt, Dr Schäfer* (1928), *Ein Tag Film* (1928) as Hilfsregisseur, *Saxophon-Susi* (1928), *Dornenweg Einer Fürstin* (1928), *Weib In Flammen* (1928), *Rasputins Liebesabenteuer* (1928) as Offizier, *Prinzessin Olala* (1928) as René Chichotte's friend, *Asphalt* (1929) as Ein Dieb, *Mascottchen* (1929) as Antoine, *Vererbte Triebe* (1929), *Der Rote Kreis* (1929), *Die Nacht Gehört Uns* (1929) as Harry Bredow, *Möblierte Zimmer* (1929), *Ja,*

*Ja, Die Frauen Sind Meine Schwache
Seite* (1929), *Drei Machen Ihr Glück*
(1929), *Der Greifer* (1930) as Sergeant
Harry Cross, *Hans In Allen Gassen*
(1930) as Hans Steindecker, *Bomben
Auf Monte Carlo* (1931) as Craddock,
Der Draufgänger (1931) as Hans Röder,
Drei Tage Liebe (1931) as Franz, *Der
Sieger* (1932) as Hans Kühnert, *Monte
Carlo Madness* (1932) as Captain
Erickson, *Quick* (1932) as Quick, *Der
Weiße Dämon* (1932) as Heini
Gildemeister, *Flüchtlinge* (1933) as
Arneth, *Heut Kommt's Drauf An* (1933)
as Hannes Eckmann, *Ein Gewisser Herr
Gran* (1933) as Ein Gewisser Herr
Gran, *Gold* (1934) as Werner Holk,
Peer Gynt (1934) as Peer Gynt, *Varieté*
(1935) as Pierre, *Henker, Frauen Und
Soldaten* (1935) as Rittmeister
Michael von Prack/General Alexej
Alexandrowitsch von Prack,
Savoy-Hotel 217 (1936) as Andrei
Volodkin, *Unter Heißem Himmel* (1936)
as Captain Kellersperg, *Der Mann, Der
Sherlock Holmes War* (1937) as Morris
Flint alias Sherlock Holmes, *Die Gelbe
Flagge* (1937) as Peter Diercksen,
Fahrendes Volk (1938) as Fernand,
Sergeant Berry (1938) as Sergeant
Mecki Berry alias Mecki Brown, *Wasser
Für Canitoga* (1939) as Oliver, *Ein
Mann Auf Abwegen* (1939) as Percival
Pattersson Montstuart, *Trenck, Der
Pandur* (1940) as Trenck, *Carl Peters*
(1941) as Dr Carl Peters, *Shiva Und
Die Galgenblume* (1945), *Föhn* (1950)
as Dr Johannes Jensen, *Vom Teufel
Gejagt* (1950) as Dr Blank, *Blaubart*
(1951) as Was weisst du denn schon
von mir, *Nachts Auf Den Straßen*
(1952) as Heinrich Schlueter, *Käpt'n
Bay-Bay* (1953) as Käpt'n Bay-Bay,
Jonny Rettet Nebrador (1953) as
General Jonny Oronta, *An Jedem Finger
Zehn* (1954) as a singer, *Auf Der
Reeperbahn Nachts Um Halb Eins*
(1954) as Hannes Wedderkamp, *Der
Letzte Mann* (1955) as Karl Knesebeck,
Vor Sonnenuntergang (1956) as
Generaldirektor Clausen, *Das Herz Von
St Pauli* (1957) as Käpt'n Jonny Jensen,

Der Tolle Bomberg (1957) as Rittmeister
Baron Gisbert von Bomberg, *I
Fidanzati Della Morte* (1957), *Der
Mann Im Strom* (1958) as Paul
Hinrichs, *Dreizehn Alte Esel* (1958) as
Josef Krapp and *Der Greifer* (1958) as
Otto Friedrich Dennert.
CAUSE: In February 1960 Albers
became sick in Vienna with flu and was
committed to hospital. In April he
returned to his country home on Lake
Starnberger. While filming *Kein Engel
Ist So Rein* (1960) in which he plays Dr
Zilinsky, he fell ill suffering from heavy
internal bleeding. He died in a
sanatorium in Kempfenhausen,
Bavaria, Germany. He was buried in
Ohlsdorfer cemetery in Hamburg on
July 29, 1960 in a ceremony attended
by Hansi Burg, three of his sisters, Max
Schmeling and Paul Verhoeven. Curt
Jurgens sent a wreath.

Eddie Albert

(EDWARD ALBERT HEIMBERGER)
Born April 22, 1906
Died May 26, 2005
The star's best friend. Born at 11.30am
at Rock Island, Illinois, the illegitimate
son of estate agent Frank Daniel
Heimberger and Julia M. Jones, 5'11"
Albert was educated at the University
of Minnesota and then became the
daring young man on the flying
trapeze. In 1933 he co-hosted the
popular radio show *The Honeymooners –
Grace And Eddie Show*. In June 1936 he
featured in an early television
experiment by RCA/NBC in New York.
That year he starred in the original
Broadway production of *Brother Rat* –
alongside Ronald Reagan and Wayne
Morris – about cadets at the Virginia
Military Institute. Warner Bros offered
him a contract in 1936. Two years later
he made his film debut in *Brother Rat*
opposite Reagan and Jane Wyman,
reprising his Broadway role as cadet
Bing Edwards, a part he also played in
the sequel *Brother Rat And A Baby*
(1938). He played the male lead in a
number of films including: *On Your*

Toes (1939), *An Angel From Texas* (1940), *The Great Mr Nobody* (1941) and *Ladies' Day* (1943). He had support roles in *Out Of The Fog* (1941), *Eagle Squadron* (1942) and *Bombardier* (1943). His other films at the time include: *Four Wives* (1939) as Dr Clint Forrest, *My Love Came Back* (1940), William Dieterle's *A Dispatch From Reuter's* (released October 19, 1940) as Max Wagner, *Four Mothers* (1941) reprising his role as Dr Clint Forrest, *The Wagons Roll At Night* (1941), *Thieves Fall Out* (1941) and *Treat 'Em Rough* (1942) as the boxer Panama Kid. Albert was supposedly sacked from Warners after he had an affair with Jack L. Warner's wife. Before the outbreak of the Second World War, Albert worked for US Military Intelligence and on September 9, 1942, he joined the navy. He was discharged the following year to become a lieutenant in the US Naval Reserve. He saw action at the Battle of Tarawa in November 1943 and was awarded the Bronze Star for rescuing 47 marines and helping to rescue 30 more while under heavy enemy fire. In 1956 he played Captain Erskine Caldwell, a cowardly soldier, in Robert Aldrich's *Attack!*, a reel character who was the antithesis of his real character. In 1944 he was assigned to the navy's training films department. After the war, he formed Eddie Albert Productions, a company that made educational films for children and documentaries for companies. Returning to Hollywood he appeared in *Strange Voyage* (1946), *Rendezvous With Annie* (1946), *The Perfect Marriage* (1947), *Hit Parade Of 1947* (1947), *Smash-Up: The Story Of A Woman* (1947), *Time Out Of Mind* (1947), *The Dude Goes West* (1948), *You Gotta Stay Happy* (1948), *Every Girl Should Be Married* (1948), *The Fuller Brush Girl* (1950) opposite Lucille Ball, *You're In The Navy Now* (1951), *Meet Me After The Show* (1951), *Actors And Sin* (1952), *Carrie* (1952), *Roman Holiday* (1953) as

Irving Radovich for which he was nominated for a Best Supporting Actor Oscar, *The Girl Rush* (1955), *Oklahoma!* (1955), *I'll Cry Tomorrow* (1955), *The Teahouse Of The August Moon* (1956), *The Sun Also Rises* (1957), *The Joker Is Wild* (1957), *Orders To Kill* (1958), *The Roots Of Heaven* (1958), *The Gun Runners* (1958), *Beloved Infidel* (1959), *The Young Doctors* (1961), *Madison Avenue* (1962), *The Longest Day* (1962), *Who's Got The Action?* (1962), *The Two Little Bears* (1963), *Miracle Of The White Stallions* (1963), *Captain Newman, M.D.* (1963), *The Party's Over* (1965) and *7 Women* (1966). He said, "I took everything they could throw at me, pictures like *The Dude Goes West* and *The Fuller Brush Girl*. I worked myself back up, but I never wanted to be a star. I was aiming to play the star's best friend." In the mid-Sixties he finally turned to television having turned down lead roles in *My Three Sons* (1960) and *Mister Ed* (1961) to concentrate on the big screen. In 1965 he was cast as big city lawyer turned gentleman farmer Oliver Wendell Douglas in the sitcom *Green Acres* opposite Eva Gabor, who is noticed elsewhere in this book. "The comedy is like *The Pickwick Papers*, or *Gulliver's Travels*, or Voltaire. It's so far out that it becomes truth, deep truth," he said. "Everyone gets tired of the rat race. Everyone would like to chuck it all and grow some carrots. It's basic. Sign me. I knew it would be successful. Had to be. It's about the atavistic urge, and people have been getting a charge out of that ever since Aristophanes wrote about the plebs and the city folk." The show was cancelled in 1971, much to Albert's annoyance. The following year he returned to the cinema and appeared in *The Heartbreak Kid* (released December 17, 1972) opposite Charles Grodin, Cybill Shepherd and Jeannie Berlin. Albert played Shepherd's overly protective father, Mr Corcoran, in the film, which garnered him his second Best Supporting Actor nomination. In 1975 he signed a new contract with Universal Television and starred with Robert Wagner in the crime drama *Switch*. The show lasted three series. Albert continued to appear in films including: *The Longest Yard* (1974), *McQ* (1974), *The Take* (1974), *Escape To Witch Mountain* (1975), *The Devil's Rain* (1975), *Whiffs* (1975), *Hustle* (1975), *Moving Violation* (1976), *Birch Interval* (1977), *Border Cop* (1979), *The Concorde: Airport '79* (1979), *How To Beat The High Co$t Of Living* (1980), *Foolin' Around* (1980), *Yesterday* (1981), *Take This Job And Shove It* (1981), *The Act* (1982), *Yes, Giorgio* (1982), *Dreamscape* (1984), *Head Office* (1985), *Turnaround* (1987), *Brenda Starr* (1989), *The Big Picture* (1989) and in 1990 reprised his role as Oliver Wendell Douglas in the TV movie *Return To Green Acres* (1990) and was a regular on the small screen in such programmes as *Falcon Crest*, *Murder, She Wrote*, *Columbo* and the daytime soap *General Hospital* as Jack Boland. On December 5, 1945 he married the Mexican actress Margo (b. Mexico City, Mexico May 10, 1917 as María Marguerita Guadalupe Teresa Estela Bolado Castilla y O'Donnell d. Pacific Palisades, California July 17, 1985 from a brain tumour): they had two children, the actor Edward Albert (b. Los Angeles, California February 20, 1951 as Edward Laurence Heimberger d. Malibu, California September 22, 2006 of lung cancer) and an adopted daughter Maria. "I don't really care how I am remembered as long as I bring happiness and joy to people," he said. "What's the most important thing in the world? It's love, and I look at that as an energy, not a sentiment." CAUSE: Alzheimer's disease affected his last years but Albert kept as active as he could. He died of pneumonia at his home in Pacific Palisades, California, aged 99. He was buried at Westwood Village Memorial Park Cemetery in Los Angeles, California, next to his wife.

Frank Albertson

Born February 2, 1909
Died February 29, 1964
Wisecracker. Born in Fergus Falls, Minnesota, 5'9" Albertson was educated in Puyallup, Washington and Hollywood. He made his film début shortly after joining the industry as a prop boy in 1922. Albertson, no relation to Jack, never quite attained stardom and played quick-witted roles as policemen or taxi-drivers. He was rarely out of work in the Twenties and Thirties. His films included: *The Covered Wagon* (1923), *The Farmer's Daughter* (1928) as Allan Boardman Jr, *Prep And Pep* (1928) as Bunk Hill, *Blue Skies* (1929) as Richard Lewis, *Words And Music* (1929) as Skeet Mulroy, *Salute* (1929) as Midshipman Albert Edward Price, *Men Without Women* (1930) as Ensign Albert Edward Price, *The Big Party* (1930) as Jack Hunter, *Son Of The Gods* (1930) as Kicker, *Spring Is Here* (1930) as Stacy Haden, *Born Reckless* (1930) as Frank Sheldon, *So This Is London* (1930) as Junior Draper, *Wild Company* (1930) as Larry Grayson, *Just Imagine* (1930) as RT-42, *A Connecticut Yankee* (1931) as Clarence, *Big Business Girl* (1931) as Johnny Saunders, *Traveling Husbands* (1931) as Barry Greene, *The Brat* (1931) as Stephen Forester, *The Tiger's Son* (1931), *Way Back Home* (1932) as David Clark, *Racing Youth* (1932) as Teddy, *Blue Huddle* (1932) as Larry Wilson, *Who, Me?* (1932), *Airmail* (1932) as Tommy Bogan, *Boys Will Be Boys* (1932), *The Lost Special* (1932) as Tom Hood, *Billion Dollar Scandal* (1933) as Babe Partos, *Should Crooners Marry?* (1933), *The Cohens And Kellys In Trouble* (1933) as Bob Graham, *Room Mates* (1933), *Ann Carver's Profession* (1933) as Jim Thompson, *Dangerous Crossroads* (1933), *Midshipman Jack* (1933) as Russell Burns, *'Tis Spring* (1933), *Ever In My Heart* (1933) as Sam Archer, *Rainbow Over Broadway* (1933) as Don Hayes, *King For A Night* (1933) as Dick,

Love Detectives (1934), *The Last Gentleman* (1934) as Allan, *Stars In The Making* (1934), *The Life Of Vergie Winters* (1934) as Ranny Truesdale, a publicist in *Hollywood Hoodlum* (1934), *Tripping Through The Tropics* (1934) as Jack, *Bachelor Of Arts* (1934) as Pete Illings, *Enter Madame* (1935) as John Fitzgerald, *Doubting Thomas* (1935) as Jimmy Brown, *Alice Adams* (1935) as Walter Adams, *Personal Maid's Secret* (1935) as Kent Fletcher, *Waterfront Lady* (1935) as Ronny Hillyer a.k.a. Bill, *East Of Java* (1935) as Larry, *Kind Lady* (1935) as Peter Santard, *Ah, Wilderness!* (1935) as Arthur Miller, *The Farmer In The Dell* (1936) as Davy Davenport, *Fury* (1936) as Charlie Wilson, a young trooper in *The Plainsman* (1937), *Navy Blue And Gold* (1937) as Weeks, *Hold That Kiss* (1938) as Steven Evans, *The Magician's Daughter* (1938) as Bob Wilson, *Mother Carey's Chickens* (1938) as Tom Hamilton, Jr, *Fugitives For A Night* (1938) as Matt Ryan, *Room Service* (1938) as Leo Davis, *Spring Madness* (1938) as Hat Hatton, *The Shining Hour* (1938) as Benny Collins, *Bachelor Mother* (1939) as Freddie Miller, *Framed* (1940) as Henry T. 'Hank' Parker, *The Ghost Comes Home* (1940) as Ernest, *Dr Christian Meets The Women* (1940) as Bill Ferris, *When The Daltons Rode* (1940) as Emmett Dalton, *Behind The News* (1940) as Jeff Flavin, *Ellery Queen's Penthouse Mystery* (1941) as Sanders, *Man Made Monster* (1941) as Mark Adams, *Father Steps Out* (1941) as Jimmy Dugan, *Citadel Of Crime* (1941) as Jim Rogers, *Burma Convoy* (1941) as Mike Weldon, *Flying Cadets* (1941) as Bob Ames, *Louisiana Purchase* (1941) as Robert Davis, Jr, *Man From Headquarters* (1942) as Larry Doyle, *Shepherd Of The Ozarks* (1942) as Jimmy Maloney, *Junior G-Men Of The Air* (1942) as Jerry Markham, *Wake Island* (1942) as Johnny Rudd, *City Of Silent Men* (1942) as Gil Davis, *Underground Agent* (1942) as Johnny Davis, *Silent Witness* (1943) as Bruce Strong, *Keep 'Em Slugging* (1943) as Frank, *Here Comes Elmer* (1943) as Joe Maxwell, *Mystery Broadcast* (1943) as Michael Jerome, *O, My Darling Clementine* (1943) as Dan Franklin, *Rosie The Riveter* (1944) as Charlie Doran, *And The Angels Sing* (1944) as Oliver, *Arson Squad* (1945) as Tom Mitchell, *How Doooo You Do!!!* (1945) as Tom Brandon, *Gay Blades* (1946) as Frankie Dowell, *They Made Me A Killer* (1946) as Al, *It's A Wonderful Life* (1946) as Sam Wainwright, *How Do You Do* (1946), *Ginger* (1947) as Barney O'Hara, *Killer Dill* (1947) as William T. Allen, *The Hucksters* (1947) as Max Herman, *Shed No Tears* (1948) as Hutton, *Girl On The Run* (1953) as Hank, *Nightfall* (1957) as Dr Edward Gurston, *The Enemy Below* (1957) as Lieutenant Crain, *The Last Hurrah* (1958) as Jack Mangan, *Psycho* (1960) as Tom Cassidy, *Don't Knock The Twist* (1962) as Herb Walcott, a gambler in *Papa's Delicate Condition* (1963), *Bye Bye Birdie* (1963) as Sam and *Johnny Cool* (1963) as Bill Blakely. In 1931 he married Virginia Shelley but that ended in divorce and he was remarried to Grace Gillern.

CAUSE: He died in Santa Monica, California, 27 days after his 55th birthday.

Jack Albertson
Born June 16, 1907
Died November 25, 1981
Dependable second lead. Born in Malden, Massachusetts, Albertson began his professional life in vaudeville and burlesque before moving on to the legitimate stage. He began making films in 1937 and won an Oscar for *The Subject Was Roses* (1968) in which he played John Cleary. He also played Grandpa Bucket in *Willy Wonka And The Chocolate Factory* (1971) and in later life appeared in the hit TV show *Chico And The Man* for which he won an Emmy.

CAUSE: He died of cancer aged 74 in Hollywood.

Mabel Albertson

Born July 24, 1901
Died September 28, 1982
Wise and witty mum. The elder sister of Jack Albertson, Mabel was born in Lynn, Massachusetts, and although she worked regularly on big and little screens, she never eclipsed her brother's fame. Her cinematic work began with *Gang War* (1928) and included: the widow in *Mutiny On The Blackhawk* (1939), *My Pal Gus* (1952) as Mrs Frisbee, *She's Back On Broadway* (1953) as Velma Trumbull, *So This Is Love* (1953) as Mary Garden, *About Mrs Leslie* (1954) as Mrs Sims, *Black Widow* (1954) as Sylvia, *Ma And Pa Kettle At Waikiki* (1955) as Tess Andrews, *The Cobweb* (1955) as Regina Mitchell-Smyth, *Ransom!* (1956) as Mrs Partridge, a society reporter in *Forever, Darling* (1956), *Four Girls In Town* (1957) as Mrs Conway, *Man Afraid* (1957) as Maggie, *The Female Animal* (1958) as Irma Jones, *The Long, Hot Summer* (1958) as Mrs Stewart, *Home Before Dark* (1958) as Inez Winthrop, *The Hangman* (1959), *Don't Give Up The Ship* (1959) as Mrs Trabert, *The Gazebo* (1959) as Mrs Chandler, *All The Fine Young Cannibals* (1960) as Mrs McDowall, *All In A Night's Work* (1961) as Mrs Kingsley, *Period Of Adjustment* (1962) as Mrs Alice McGill, *A Fine Madness* (1966) as the chairman, *Barefoot In The Park* (1967) as Aunt Harriet, *On A Clear Day You Can See Forever* (1970) as Mrs Hatch and *What's Up, Doc?* (1972) as Mrs Van Hoskins.
CAUSE: She died from Alzheimer's disease aged 81 in Santa Monica, California.

Hardie Albright

(HARDIE ALBRECHT)
Born December 16, 1903
Died December 7, 1975
Blond, blue-eyed leading man. Born in Charleroi, Pennsylvania, 5'10" Hardie Albright was the son of vaudevillians and he made his stage début aged six in their act. After studying drama at Carnegie Tech and the Arts Institute in Chicago, he joined Eve Le Gallienne's repertory theatre. His first performance on the Great White Way came in 1926. Hardie appeared in many Broadway plays before making his film début in 1931. Appearing in more than 50 films, he retired from acting in 1948, and became a drama instructor at UCLA, where he wrote several books on acting and directing. Perhaps his biggest claim to fame is that he provided the voice for the adolescent Bambi in the 1942 film. His films included: *Young Sinners* (1931) as Gene Gibson, *Hush Money* (1931) as Stuart Elliot, *Skyline* (1931) as John Breen, *Heartbreak* (1931) as Count Carl Walden, *So Big!* (1932) as Dirk De Jong, *The Purchase Price* (1932) as Don Leslie, *Jewel Robbery* (1932) as Paul, *This Sporting Age* (1932) as Johnny Raeburn, *A Successful Calamity* (1932) as George Struthers, *The Crash* (1932) as Arthur Pringle, *The Cabin In The Cotton* (1932) as Roland Neal, *Three On A Match* (1932) as Phil, *20,000 Years In Sing Sing* (1932), *The Match King* (1932) as Erik Borg, *The Working Man* (1933) as Benny Burnett, *The Song Of Songs* (1933) as Von Prell, *Three-Cornered Moon* (1933) as Ronald, *The House On 56th Street* (1933) as Henry Burgess, *The Ninth Guest* (1934) as Henry Abbott, *Nana* (1934), *White Heat* (1934) as Chandler Morris, *Beggar's Holiday* (1934), *The Scarlet Letter* (1934) as Arthur Dimmesdale, *Two Heads On A Pillow* (1934) as Dave Talbot, *Crimson Romance* (1934) as Hugo, *The Silver Streak* (1934) as Allen Dexter, *Sing Sing Nights* (1934) as Howard Trude, *Women Must Dress* (1935) as David, *Champagne For Breakfast* (1935) as Bob Bentley, *Calm Yourself* (1935) as Bobby Kent, *Ladies Love Danger* (1935) as Phil Morton, *Red Salute* (1935) as Arner, *Granny Get Your Gun* (1940) as Philip Westcott, *Ski Patrol* (1940) as Tyko Gallen, *Carolina Moon* (1940) as Henry Wheeler, *Flight From Destiny*

(1940) as Ferrers, *Marry The Boss's Daughter* (1941) as Putnam Palmer, *Bachelor Daddy* (1941) as Ethelbert, *Men Of The Timberland* (1941) as Dudley, *Navy Blues* (1941), *Captains Of The Clouds* (1942) as Kingsley, *The Mad Doctor Of Market Street* (1942) as William Saunders, a police detective in *Saboteur* (1942), a chauffeur in *Lady In A Jam* (1942), *The Pride Of The Yankees* (1942) as Van Tuyl, *The Loves Of Edgar Allan Poe* (1942) as Shelton, *Mom And Dad* (1945) as Carl Blackburn, an exploitative sex documentary, *Army Wives* (1945) as Verne, *The Jade Mask* (1945) as Walter Meeker, *Sunset In El Dorado* (1945) as Cecil Phelps/Cyril Earle, *Captain Tugboat Annie* (1945) as Johnny Webb and *Angel On My Shoulder* (1946) as Smiley Williams. He was married twice, firstly (from 1934 until 1940) to Martha Sleeper. His second wife was the comedian Arnita Wallace (b. 1924, d. Mission Viejo, California, June 11, 1985 in her sleep), by whom he had his only child, Victoria.
CAUSE: Albright died of congestive heart failure in Mission Viejo, California. He was 71.

Robert Alda

(ALPHONSO GIUSEPPE GIOVANNI ROBERTO D'ABRUZZO)
Born February 26, 1914
Died May 3, 1986
Cinematic pop. To the cinema audiences of the Forties and Fifties actors such as Robert Alda and Kirk Douglas were stars in their own right. To the cinema audiences of the Seventies they are predominantly known for their famous offspring. Born in New York, Alphonso D'Abruzzo, the son of Anthony D'Abruzzo, an immigrant hairdresser, dropped out of New York University because of the Great Depression. In 1933 he first appeared on stage at the RKO in New York in vaudeville in an act called Charlie Ahearn And His Millionaires. From

1935 until 1940 he toured in burlesque. He first appeared on radio in 1934 and television three years later. He made his cinematic début playing composer George Gershwin in *Rhapsody In Blue* (1945) but that was to be the pinnacle of his movie career. His other films include *Cloak And Dagger* (1946), *Tarzan And The Slave Girl* (1950), *Imitation Of Life* (1959), *Cleopatra's Daughter* (1963), *Cagliostro* (1974), *I Will, I Will . . . For Now* (1976) and *The Big Rip Off* (1978). He was more successful on stage having made his legitimate Broadway début on November 24, 1950, at the 46th Street Theater playing Sky Masterson in *Guys & Dolls*, a performance that would win him a Tony. In the Sixties he emigrated to Rome and worked there steadily for the next 20 years. In September 1932 he married beauty contest winner Joan Brown and their only child, a son, Alfonso Jr, who went on to become better known as Alan Alda, was born on January 28, 1936, in New York City. Following his divorce in Las Vegas on November 24, 1957, Alda married Italian actress Flora Marino and their son, Antony, was born in 1957.
CAUSE: Alda died in Los Angeles aged 72 following a stroke suffered in 1984.

Robert Aldrich

Born August 9, 1918
Died December 5, 1983
Independent director. Born in Cranston, Rhode Island, Aldrich never intended to enter show business. At the University of Virginia he studied law and economics. In 1941 he landed a job at RKO in a menial capacity before working his way up to becoming a second assistant director, production manager and associate producer. He learned his trade on films such as *Joan Of Paris* (1942), *Rookies In Burma* (1943), *Adventures Of A Rookie* (1944), *The Story Of G.I. Joe* (1945), *The Strange Love Of Martha Ivers* (1946), *The Private Affairs Of Bel Ami* (1947), *Force Of Evil* (1948) and *Abbott & Costello Meet Captain Kidd* (1952). In

the early Fifties he began working in television writing and directing various series. He turned to directing feature films in 1953 with movies such as *Apache* (1954), *World For Ransom* (1954) and *The Big Knife* (1955) which he also produced. That year he set up his own production company, the Associates and Aldrich, to allow himself more autonomy in his work. On October 25, 1955 *The Big Knife*, starring Jack Palance, Ida Lupino, Shelley Winters and Rod Steiger, opened at the Hollywood Paramount. It was a look at the dark side of Tinseltown and was universally loathed by certain sections of the Hollywood community who labelled it "a gross misrepresentation of the motion picture industry". Aldrich's first major cinematic coup was persuading arch rivals Bette Davis and Joan Crawford to star as the Hudson sisters, Blanche and Jane, in *Whatever Happened To Baby Jane?* (1962). At the press conference to announce the film the two ageing movie queens jostled each other to get a better picture vantage and Davis only agreed to make the film after Aldrich assured her he had never had sex with Crawford. Aldrich commented: "A director is a ringmaster, a psychiatrist and a referee." The film was shot in just three weeks and was a smash, recouping its outlay (less than $1 million) in eleven days and eventually taking $9 million at the box office. Aldrich later commented, "Joan and Bette were perfect pros on the set of *Whatever Happened To Baby Jane?* until 6pm. Then I'd get a call from Joan asking, 'Did you see what that bitch did to me today?' A couple of minutes later Bette would call and ask, 'What did that bitch call you about?' First one and then the other. I could count on it every night." Despite their antipathy both women signed for the follow-up *Hush . . . Hush, Sweet Charlotte* (1964) but Crawford dropped out to be replaced by Olivia De Havilland. In 1966 Aldrich made the war film *The Dirty Dozen,* which was another smash, and followed that up with two lesbian-themed movies *The Killing Of Sister George* (1968) and *The Legend Of Lylah Clare* (1969). Of his star in the second he commented, "Kim Novak has been seriously hurt by men. Unlike Marilyn [Monroe], she survived. But her pain has also survived, and she no longer trusts men, particularly if they want to become or seem to be getting intimate. So I have to remain fatherly and detached when guiding her through her roles. In *The Legend Of Lylah Clare* she plays two roles, two actresses, one of them a late star, a legend in the Dietrich-Garbo persona who is sapphic. I have no trouble ignoring Kim's beauty because I just think of her as being sapphic, like Lylah." In 1977 he made *The Choirboys*, lambasted as one of the worst police films ever made. By that time Aldrich was already ill.

CAUSE: He died aged 65 in Los Angeles from kidney failure. As he lay dying he was visited by actor Richard Jaeckel who asked Aldrich if there was anything he needed. "Yeah, a good script," came the reply.

Kay Aldridge

Born July 9, 1917
Died January 12, 1995
Serial queen. Katharine Gratten Aldridge was born in Tallahassee, Florida, and was raised in the home of two spinsters after her mother was widowed at a young age. On leaving school she landed herself a clerical job in Baltimore, Maryland. In 1935, laid up in bed with a broken leg (the result of a horse riding accident), her story was featured in a local paper. A copy of the feature was sent to a New York modelling agent who signed her up. Two years later, film producer Walter Wanger (1894–1968) employed "the ten most photographed girls in the world" to appear in his film *Vogues Of 1938* (1937). Of the ten models Aldridge was the only one to express an

interest in Hollywood. When she went up for the role of Scarlett O'Hara she was coached by Henry Fonda. She appeared as the second lead in *Hotel For Women* (1939) (credited as Katharine Aldridge) as Melinda Craig after she was replaced by Linda Darnell. She went on to appear in over 20 films including *Here I Am A Stranger* (1939) as Lillian Bennett, *Yesterday's Heroes* (1940), *Shooting High* (1940) as Evelyn Trent, *Girl In 313* (1940) as Sarah Sorrell, *Girl From Avenue A* (1940) as Lucy, *Free, Blonde And 21* (1940) as Adelaide, *You're In The Army Now* (1941), *Sailor's Lady* (1940) as Georgine, *Down Argentine Way* (1940) as Helen Carson, *Golden Hoofs* (1941) as Cornelia Hunt, *Dead Men Tell* (1941) as Laura Thursday, *Navy Blues* (1941) and *Louisiana Purchase* (1941) as Louisiana Belle. It was her casting as Nyoka Gordon in *The Perils Of Nyoka* (1942) that assured her place in serial history. It ran to 15 episodes and was re-released as *Nyoka And The Tigermen* in 1952 and *Nyoka And The Lost Secrets Of Hippocrates* 14 years after that. She retired from the screen after playing Wilhelmina Hammond in *The Man Who Walked Alone* (1945) and Claudia Moore in *The Phantom Of 42nd Street* (1945) at the insistence of her much older first husband, Arthur Cameron, whom she married on St Valentine's Day 1945. They had four children, two of each, before separating in 1954. Two years later, Aldridge married painter Richard Derby Tucker and lived happily with him until his death in 1979. A third trip up the aisle in 1982 ended when her husband died eight months later.
CAUSE: She died in Rockport, Maine, of a heart attack aged 77.

Grigori Aleksandrov

(GRIGORI VASSILEYEVICH MARMONENKO)
Born January 23, 1903
Died December 16, 1984
Soviet cineaste. Born in Ekaterinburg,

Russia, Aleksandrov began his theatrical career on the stage before becoming assistant to Sergei Eisenstein and starring in his masterpieces such as *Strike* (1924), *Battleship Potemkin* (1925) and *October* (1927). He and Eisenstein later travelled to America on a fact-finding mission for *Que Viva Mexico!* (1931). Back in the Soviet Union, Aleksandrov directed his first film *Jazz Comedy* (1934), a musical that inspired a new wave in Soviet cinema. His last film was *Skvorets I Lira* (1973). His first wife was the actress Anna Sten.
CAUSE: He died in Moscow, Soviet Union, aged 81 of natural causes.

Ben Alexander

Born May 26, 1911
Died July 5, 1969
Joe Friday's partner. Nicholas Benton Alexander was born in Goldfield, Nevada, and began his career as a child star in *Each Pearl A Tear* (1916) in which he played Cupid. He was educated at Hollywood High School in between films, followed by a degree at the University of California. He began as a child star then made the transition to juvenile lead. These included: *The Little American* (1917) as Bobby Moore, *The Lady Of The Dugout* (1918) as the lady's son, *The Heart Of Rachael* (1918) as Jim, *Little Orphan Annie* (1918) as an orphan, *The Turn In The Road* (1919) as Bob, *The White Heather* (1919) as Donald Cameron, *Josselyn's Wife* (1919) as Tommy Josselyn, *The Hushed Hour* (1919) as Gondy, *The Mayor Of Filbert* (1919) as Carroll, *Tangled Threads* (1919) as 'Sonny Boy' Wayne, *The Better Wife* (1919) as Little Dick, *The Family Honor* (1920) as Little Ben Tucker, *Through Eyes Of Men* (1920) as Little Billy, *Penrod And Sam* (1923) as Penrod Schofield, *Jealous Husbands* (1923) as Bobbie, *Boy Of Mine* (1923) as Bill Latimer, *A Self-Made Failure* (1924) as Sonny, *Flaming Love* (1925) as Benny Keene, *Pampered Youth* (1925) as George

Minafer, *The Shining Adventure* (1925) as Benny and *The Highbinders* (1926) as Roy Marshall. He successfully made the move to talkies from silent films and struck an early note as Franz Kemmerich, the tragic amputee, in *All Quiet On The Western Front* (1930). During the rest of the decade he made around four films a year but none of them set the screen alight and he moved to radio where he hosted quiz and chat shows and appeared in sitcoms. Alexander later became an advertising executive with Foote, Cone & Belding, and made just three films in the Forties and Fifties. With the advent of television he moved to the small screen and hosted and produced his own short-lived talent show *Party Time At Club Roma* from October 14, 1950 until January 6, 1951. Two years later, another opportunity arose when Alexander became Officer Frank Smith on the police show *Dragnet* playing Sergeant Joe Friday's genial but permanently worried partner. He played the part until 1959. In 1960 he became a regular guest on the primetime quiz show *Take A Good Look*. In 1966 he landed the part of kindly but fussy Desk Sergeant Dan Briggs on the Broderick Crawford series *Felony Squad*, a role that lasted until his death.

CAUSE: He died of natural causes aged 58 in Hollywood, California. He was cremated and his ashes were interred in Maui Cemetery, Wailuku, Hawaii.

Frank 'Fatty' Alexander

Born May 25, 1879
Died September 8, 1937
Huge star. Born in Olympia, Washington, Alexander joined Keystone in 1913 and was a support act rather than ever becoming a major star like Fatty Arbuckle. The 5'8" Alexander weighed in at 25 stone resulting in his nicknames 'Fatty' and the more ironic if less accurate 'Tiny'. He was one-third of the trio known as A Ton of Fun. On October 24, 1925, Film Box Office announced that they were to produce a series of comedies starring "the three fattest men on the screen" to be produced by Joe Rock. The series lasted until 1928. The other men were Hilliard 'Fat' Karr and 'Kewpie' Ross and the films were *Three Wise Goofs* (1925), *On The Links* (1925), *All Tied Up* (1925), *Tailoring* (1925), *In The Air* (1926), *A Beauty Parlor* (1926), *Three Of A Kind* (1926), *Wedding Daze* (1926), *Backfire* (1926), *Oh, What A Night!* (1926), *The Vulgar Yachtsman* (1926), *Three Fleshy Devils* (1926), *Honeymoon Feet* (1926), *The Heavy Parade* (1926), *Heavy Fullbacks* (1926), *What Price Dough* (1927), *Campus Romeos* (1927), *Wanderers Of The Waistline* (1927), *Old Tin Sides* (1927), *3 Missing Links* (1927), *All Alike* (1928) and *Big Berthas* (1928). Alexander's other films included: *When Ambrose Dared Walrus* (1915) as a fireman, *Bath Tub Perils* (1916), *Social Pirates* (1917), *Melting Millions* (1917) as Bailey, *By The Sad Sea Waves* (1917), a bather in *Rainbow Island* (1917), *Bathing Beauties And Big Boobs* (1918) as Fat, a café owner in *Huns And Hyphens* (1918), *Bears And Bad Men* (1918) as Paw Slawson, *Pluck And Plotters* (1918), *Dull Care* (1919) as the chief of police, *Traps And Tangles* (1919), *The Grocery Clerk* (1920) as Big Ben, *The Stage Hand* (1920) as the stage manager, *The Rent Collector* (1921) as a thug, *The Bakery* (1921) as the bakery owner, *The Fall Guy* (1921) as the sheriff, *The Bell Hop* (1921) as a government official, *The Sawmill* (1922) as the mill owner, *The Show* (1922) as a ballet dancer, *Cyclone Jones* (1923) as Fatty Wirthing, *Her Boy Friend* (1924) as Slim Chance, *Kid Speed* (1924) as Mr Avery DuPoys, *Wizard Of Oz* (1925) as Uncle Henry/Prince of Whales, a hotel guest in *Hop To It!* (1925), a cook in *S.O.S. Perils Of The Sea* (1925), *The Perfect Clown* (1925) as Tiny Tott, *Assorted Nuts* (1926), *Play Safe* (1927),

Madame Q (1929), the fat lodger in *The Shrimp* (1930), the fat man in the audience in *Catch As Catch Can* (1931), *The Kickoff* (1931*)*, *The Bargain Of The Century* (1933) and *The Barber Shop* (1933). Alexander appeared with another cinematic fat man Oliver Hardy in thirteen films: *Dull Care* (1919), *The Stage Hand* (1920), *The Rent Collector* (1921), *The Bakery* (1921), *The Fall Guy* (1921), *The Bell Hop* (1921), *The Sawmill* (1922), *The Show* (1922), *Her Boy Friend* (1924), *Kid Speed* (1924), *Wizard Of Oz* (1925) (Hardy played The Tin Man), *Hop To It!* (1925) and *The Perfect Clown* (1925).
CAUSE: Alexander died in Los Angeles, California, aged 58.

Ross Alexander
(ROSS SMITH)
Born July 27, 1907
Died January 2, 1937
Leading man. Brooklyn-born 6'1¼" Alexander began appearing on stage aged 16 and was signed by Warner Bros in the early Thirties. Groomed for stardom, he never reached the dizzy heights of contemporaries such as Clark Gable and Errol Flynn. He appeared in less than 20 films, including *The Wiser Sex* (1932) as Jimmy O'Neill, *Flirtation Walk* (1934) as Oskie, *Gentlemen Are Born* (1934) as Tom Martin, *A Midsummer Night's Dream* (1935) as Demetrius, *Maybe It's Love* (1935) as Rims O'Neil, *Captain Blood* (1935) as Jeremy Pitt, *China Clipper* (1936) as Tom Collins and the posthumously released *Ready Willing And Able* (1937) as Barry Granville. He married twice – to actress Aleta Friele (1907–1935) on February 23, 1934, and co-star Anne Nagel (1912–1966) on September 16, 1936. On December 7, 1935, his first wife, a successful Broadway actress, killed herself at 7357 Woodrow Wilson Drive in the Hollywood Hills. She was distraught at her own lack of success in Hollywood and believed her husband

to be philandering. Thirteen months later, he, too, was dead.
CAUSE: Deeply in debt, Alexander shot himself, aged 29, at 17221 Ventura Boulevard, Los Angeles. He used the same rifle his first wife had used to kill herself. He is buried in Forest Lawn Memorial-Parks, 1712 South Glendale Avenue, Glendale, California 91209. Warner Bros later signed Ronald Reagan as a replacement for Alexander because they had similar voices and mannerisms.

Alexandre of Paris
(LOUIS ALEXANDRE RAIMON)
Born 1923
Died January 12, 2008
Coiffurist to the stars. Born in Saint-Tropez, Var, Provence-Alpes-Côte d'Azur, France, Alexandre began his hairdressing career in Cannes in 1938. Among his clientele were Audrey Hepburn, Maria Callas, Greta Garbo, the Duchess of Windsor, Lauren Bacall, Liza Minnelli, Shirley Maclaine and Jackie Kennedy. His best-known cinematic work was working with Elizabeth Taylor's distinctive hair-do for *Cleopatra* (1963) and he did her hair on several more films and television dramas. Jean Cocteau designed the logo for Alexandre's first Paris salon.
CAUSE: He died aged 85 from natural causes in Saint-Tropez, Var, Provence-Alpes-Côte d'Azur, France.

Elizabeth Allan
Born April 9, 1908
Died July 27, 1990
Blonde, blue-eyed Brit. Skegness, Lincolnshire-born Allan was educated at the Quaker School in Darlington, and began her career at the Old Vic appearing in various Shakespearean plays. She then went into rep before making her film début in *Alibi* (1931) in which she played Ursula Browne. Her mentor was Herbert Marshall and she signed a contract with MGM that expired in 1938. Her films included:

Michael And Mary (1931) as Romo, *The Rosary* (1931) as Vera Mannering, *Down Our Street* (1931) as Maisie Collins, *Chin Chin Chinaman* (1931) as the Countess, *Black Coffee* (1931) as Barbara Amory, *Service For Ladies* (1932) as Sylvia Robertson, *The Lodger* (1932) as Daisy Bunting, *Insult* (1932) as Pola Dubois, *The Chinese Puzzle* (1932) as Naomi Melsham, *No Marriage Ties* (1933) as Peggy Wilson, *Ace Of Aces* (1933) as Nancy Adams, *The Shadow* (1933) as Sonia Bryant, *The Mystery Of Mr X* (1934) as Jane Frensham, *The Lost Chord* (1934) as Joan Elton, *The Personal History, Adventures, Experience, And Observation Of David Copperfield, The Younger* (1935) as Mrs (Clara) Copperfield, *Mark Of The Vampire* (1935) as Irena Borotyn, *A Tale Of Two Cities* (1935) as Lucie Manette, *A Woman Rebels* (1936) as Flora Anne Thistlewaite, *Camille* (1936) as Nichette, *Slave Ship* (1937) as Nancy Marlowe, *The Girl Who Forgot* (1940) as Leonora Barradine, *Inquest* (1940) as Margaret Hamilton, *The Great Mr Handel* (1942) as Mrs Cibber, *Went The Day Well?* (1942) as Peggy Pryde, *He Snoops To Conquer* (1944) as Jane Strawbridge, *That Dangerous Age* (1949) as Lady Sybil, *No Highway* (1951) as Shirley Scott, *Folly To Be Wise* (1953) as Angela Prout, *Twice Upon A Time* (1953) as Carol-Anne Bailey, *The Heart Of The Matter* (1953) as Louise Scobie, *Front Page Story* (1954) as Susan Grant, *The Brain Machine* (1956) as Dr Phillipa Roberts and *Grip Of The Strangler* (1958) as Barbara Rankin. On June 6, 1932, 5′6″ Allan married her manager Wilfred J. O'Bryen and theirs was a happy marriage that lasted until his death in 1977.
CAUSE: She died aged 82 of natural causes in Hove, East Sussex.

Marc Allégret
Born December 22, 1900
Died November 3, 1973
Gay nepotistic toyboy. Allégret was born in Basle, Switzerland, the son of a French pastor. Aged 16 he became the lover of his 47-year-old adoptive uncle, writer André Gide. Allégret's father had been best man at Gide's wedding; Gide wrote *Les Faux-Monnayeurs* specifically for his toyboy. Allégret also had an affair with Jean Cocteau. Allégret's films included *Fanny* (1932) his first directorial success, *Les Beaux Yeux* (1935), *Blanche Fury* (1947), *Blackmailed* (1951), *Avec André Gide* (1952), *L'Amante Di Paride* (1953) and *L'Amant De Lady Chatterley* (1955) among others. In 1947 he went to England where he made three films and later employed Roger Vadim for ten years. His brother Yves (1907–1986) was also a director.
CAUSE: Died of natural causes, aged 72.

Adrianne Allen
Born February 7, 1907
Died September 14, 1993
Matriarch. The daughter of Charles D. Allen and Ethel Mapleston, 5′4″ Manchester-born Adrianne Allen was educated in France and Germany before studying for the stage at RADA. She began her career on June 9, 1926, playing Nina Vansittart in Noël Coward's *Easy Virtue* where she met Raymond Massey. She became his second wife on November 12, 1929, and they had two children – the actors Daniel and Anna. Raymond Massey got her a job in Coward's *The Rat Trap*. On November 2, 1931, she made her Broadway début as Doris Lea in *Cynara* and was spotted by a Paramount scout and quickly signed to a contract. She had made her first film *Loose Ends* (1930) playing Brenda Fallon. Her other films included: *The Woman Between* (1931) as Lady Pamela, *The Stronger Sex* (1931) as Mary Thorpe, *Black Coffee* (1931) as Lucia Amory, *Merrily We Go To Hell* (1932) as Claire Hempstead, *The Night Of June 13th* (1932) as Elna Curry, *The Morals Of*

Marcus (1935) as Judith, *The October Man* (1947) as Joyce Carden, *Bond Street* (1947) as Mrs Taverner, *Vote For Huggett* (1949) as Mrs Hall, *The Final Test* (1953) as Aunt Ethel and *Meet Mr Malcolm* (1954) as Mrs Durant. On July 6, 1939, she and Massey were divorced. Her case was handled by the lawyer William Whitney who, with his wife Dorothy, would socialise with the Masseys. Not long after the Massey divorce, the Whitneys also separated. In a situation worthy of the television programme *Wife Swap*, Adrianne then married William Whitney while his ex-wife married Adrianne's ex-husband. In the Fifties, the Whitneys moved to Glion-sur-Montreux, Switzerland, where they lived happily until his death in 1973.

CAUSE: Adrianne Allen died aged 86 of cancer in Glion-sur-Montreux.

Chesney Allen

Born April 5, 1894
Died November 13, 1982

Crazy gangster. Born in Brighton, the son of a successful master builder, Allen worked in a solicitor's office before he began amusing audiences on stage from 1919. He teamed up with Bud Flanagan to make people laugh and they became members of the Crazy Gang in 1931. Ill-health forced his retirement in 1945 but he outlived the other Gang members, becoming their agent. Among his films were *A Fire Has Been Arranged* (1935), *Underneath The Arches* (1937), *Okay For Sound* (1937)★, *Alf's Button Afloat* (1938)★, *The Frozen Limits* (1939)★, *Gasbags* (1940)★, *We'll Smile Again* (1942), *Dreaming* (1944), *Life Is A Circus* (1958)★ and *Dunkirk* (1958). (Those with the Crazy Gang are marked with an asterisk.) In 1922 he married Aleta Turner in Bradford.

CAUSE: Allen suffered badly from arthritis. He died aged 88, the last surviving member of the Crazy Gang, leaving £92,978 in his will.

Fred Allen

(JOHN FLORENCE SULLIVAN)
Born May 31, 1894
Died March 17, 1956

Failed radio comedian. Born in Cambridge, Massachusetts, Fred Allen never made the transition to either big or small screens despite excellent backing and big budgets. He made a few films including *Thanks A Million* (1935) as Ned Allen, *Sally, Irene And Mary* (1938) as Gabriel 'Gabby' Green, *It's In The Bag!* (1945) as Fred Floogle and two Marilyn Monroe movies – *O. Henry's Full House* (1952) as Sam and *We're Not Married!* (1952) as Steve Gladwyn.

CAUSE: Heart attack. He died in New York, New York, aged 61. He is buried in the Cemetery of the Gate of Heaven, Stevens Avenue, Hawthorne, New York 10532.

Gracie Allen

Born July 26, 1902
Died August 27, 1964

Ditzy comedienne. Born in San Francisco, California, the daughter of an entertainer, 5' Grace Ethel Cecile Rosalie Allen was scarred for life on her left shoulder and arm aged 18 months when she was scalded with hot tea. While still a child she was hit in the eyes by glass from a smashed lamp leaving her with one blue and one green eye. She made her début aged three, appearing with her father. She left her Catholic school at 14 to join her family on stage but found it not to her liking and trained to become a secretary. In 1922 she heard the comedy team of George Burns and William Lorraine was splitting and that Lorraine was looking for a new partner. Mistaking Burns for Lorraine she asked if she could join the team. He didn't tell her of her mistake for three days by which time they had gelled perfectly. So perfectly that on January 7, 1926, in Cleveland, Ohio, they were married. (In the following decade they adopted two children, Sandra Jean in 1934 and

Ronald John in 1935.) In the Twenties they were one of America's most popular double acts and by the Thirties they had a number one radio show. Allen appeared in several films, often playing herself or someone with a very similar name. They included: *Lambchops* (1929) as herself, *Pulling A Bone* (1931) as Gracie, *Fit To Be Tied* (1931) as herself, *100% Service* (1931) as herself, *Oh, My Operation* (1932) as Nurse Allen, *We're Not Dressing* (1934) as Gracie, *The Gracie Allen Murder Case* (1939) as Gracie Allen and *Two Girls And A Sailor* (1944) as herself. In 1958, in poor health, she retired from show business.

CAUSE: While lying in bed watching a Spencer Tracy film she suffered an angina attack. She was taken to Cedars of Lebanon Hospital, 1831 Fountain Avenue, Los Angeles, where she died of a heart attack (acute myocardial infarction and arteriosclerotic heart disease) aged 62 at 11.55pm. Gracie Allen is buried in the Freedom Hall Mausoleum of the Forest Lawn Memorial-Parks, 1712, South Glendale Avenue, Glendale, California 91209. Jack Benny read the eulogy at the funeral and 1,300 people attended. Despite the fact that Allen was Catholic, the ceremony was an Episcopalian one. George Burns wanted to be buried alongside his wife but as he was Jewish he would not be allowed in Catholic consecrated ground. Episcopalian was the closest he could get.

Phyllis Allen

Born November 25, 1861
Died March 26, 1938
Domineering housewife. Born in Staten Island, New York, like many of her contemporaries Allen began her career in vaudeville and entered films towards the end of the Edwardian era. Her early work was at the Selig and Keystone Studios. She worked alongside many of the era's big names including Fatty Arbuckle and Charlie Chaplin although her physical bulk meant that she was usually cast in the role of a domineering spouse rather than a romantic leading lady. She appeared in *Tillie's Punctured Romance* (1914) as a prison matron/restaurant patron. The movie was America's first feature-length comedy and starred Marie Dressler (her début film), Charlie Chaplin and Mabel Normand. Her films included: *On His Wedding Day* (1913), *Those Good Old Days* (1913), *The Riot* (1913), *Fatty At San Diego* (1913), *Murphy's I.O.U.* (1913), a dancer in *Caught In A Cabaret* (1914), *A Busy Day* (1914) as the other woman, *Caught In Tights* (1914), *The Rounders* (1914) as Charlie's wife, *His Trysting Place* (1914) as Ambrose's wife, *Dough And Dynamite* (1914) as a customer, *Gentlemen Of Nerve* (1914) as his wife, *Cursed By His Beauty* (1914), *Fatty's Jonah Day* (1914), *Getting Acquainted* (1914) as his wife, *Ambrose's First Falsehood* (1914), *The Property Man* (1914) as Hamlene Fat, *Hello, Mabel* (1914) as the woman in the hall, *A Fatal Sweet Tooth* (1914), *Her Winning Punch* (1915), *Ambrose's Sour Grapes* (1915) as a party guest, *That Little Band Of Gold* (1915), *Gussle Rivals Jonah* (1915) as Mrs Gussle, *Gussle's Day Of Rest* (1915) as Mrs Gussle, *A Submarine Pirate* (1915) as an awkward guest, *A Night In The Show* (1915) as a lady in the audience, *Hogan's Wild Oats* (1915), *Gussle Tied To Trouble* (1915), *Gussle's Wayward Path* (1915), *Gussle's Backward Way* (1915) – the latter three as Mrs Gussle, *Giddy, Gay, And Ticklish* (1915), *Fickle Fatty's Fall* (1915), *A Movie Star* (1916) as his real wife, *The Judge* (1916), *The Adventurer* (1917) as a governess, *Monkey Stuff* (1919), *Her First Flame* (1920) as Minnie Fish, *White Youth* (1920) as Madame Le Moyne, *Pay Day* (1922) as his wife and *The Pilgrim* (1923) as a member of the congregation.

CAUSE: She died in Los Angeles, California, aged 76.

Rex Allen

Born December 31, 1920
Died December 17, 1999
Western star. Born in Wilcox, Arizona, Allen first came to prominence on the radio in the Forties before finding B-movie fame in Western pictures such as *The Arizona Cowboy* (1949) and *The Hills Of Oklahoma* (1950) in which he first rode his famous mount, Koko the Wonder Horse. In 1958 he starred in the television series *Frontier Doctor*. He also narrated over 80 Walt Disney films. His son, Rex Jr (b. Chicago, Illinois, August 23, 1947), was the only one of his four children to follow him into the business.
CAUSE: He died after being run over by his own car in Tucson, Arizona. His caretaker was driving the vehicle and police believe she didn't know her boss was behind her when she reversed.

Robert 'Tex' Allen

(IRVING THEODORE BAEHR)
Born March 28, 1906
Died October 9, 1998
The Texas Ranger. Born in Mount Vernon, New York, 5'11" Bob Allen was educated at Dartmouth College where, in 1926, he made his début in front of the cameras as a stuntman in Richard Arlen's *The Quarterback*. (However, *Halliwell* has him appearing in *Mr Potter Of Texas* four years earlier.) At university he excelled in polo and boxing and upon graduation in 1929 joined a bank that collapsed in the Great Depression. He later worked as a commercial airline pilot although that business also failed. Some sources claim that Allen modelled for a time. He appeared in the Marx Brothers' *Animal Crackers* (1930) as a house party guest. In 1931 Warner Bros signed him to a contract and he appeared in *Party Husband* (1931), *Night Nurse* (1931) as a party guest and *The Reckless Hour* (1931) but he failed to make an impact and turned to the stage. In 1934, the year he married his first wife, he took another shot at films

and joined Columbia. He appeared in *The Social Register* (1934), *The Captain Hates The Sea* (1934), *Broadway Bill* (1934) as a journalist, *Menace* (1934) as Andrew Forsythe, *Jealousy* (1934) as Jim Rainey, *I'm A Father* (1935), *Death Flies East* (1935) as Baker, *I'll Love You Always* (1935) as Joe, *Party Wire* (1935) as Roy Daniels, *Air Hawks* (1935) as Bill 'Okay' Lewis, *Love Me Forever* (1935) as Philip Cameron, *The Black Room* (1935) as Lieutenant Albert Lussan, *Guard That Girl* (1935) as Larry Donovan, *Crime And Punishment* (1935) as Dmitri, *White Lies* (1935) as Arthur Bradford, *Lady Of Secrets* (1936) as Richard Terrance, *Pride Of The Marines* (1936) as Larry Allen, *Craig's Wife* (1936) as Gene Fredericks, *Let's Get Married* (1937) as Charles and *Hold 'Em Navy* (1937) as a midshipman. He worked with Tim McCoy on three westerns: *Law Beyond The Range* (1935) as Johnny Kane, *The Revenge Rider* (1935) as Chad Harmon and *Fighting Shadows* (1935) as Bob Rutledge. When McCoy left the studio, Allen took over the reins and appeared in the Texas Ranger series of B movies that were directed by Spencer G. Bennett. The first was *The Unknown Ranger* (1936) and that was followed by *Rio Grande Ranger* (1936), *Ranger Courage* (1937), *Law Of The Ranger* (1937), *Reckless Ranger* (1937) and *The Rangers Step In* (1937). The series ended when Allen moved to 20th Century Fox for meatier roles. He appeared as a doctor in *Penitentiary* (1938), *The Big Broadcast Of 1938* (1938) as a petrol pump attendant, *Gateway* (1938), *Keep Smiling* (1938) as Stanley Harper, *Meet The Girls* (1938) as Charles Tucker, *Up The River* (1938) as Ray Douglas, *Fighting Thoroughbreds* (1939) as Greg Bogart, *Tail Spin* (1939) as Charlie, *Everybody's Baby* (1939) as Dick Lane, *Winter Carnival* (1939) as Rocky Morgan, *Winner Take All* (1939) as Tom Walker and *City Of Chance* (1940) as Fred Walcott, after which he returned to the

theatre for a quarter of a century. He returned to the big screen in 1965 playing a Philadelphia judge in *Dirtymouth* (1965), a low-budget biopic of Lenny Bruce, the comedian. He was to make just four more films: *Terror In The City* (1966) as Brill's father, *Naked Evil* (1966), *Hells Angels On Wheels* (1967) as Dr Carstairs and *Raiders Of The Living Dead* (1986) as Dr Carstairs. Married twice, his first wife (in 1934) was Evelyn Pierce (b. Del Rio, Texas, February 5, 1908, d. Oyster Bay, Long Island, New York, August 9, 1960) by whom he had two children, Katherine and Theodore who became a doctor. In 1964 he married, secondly, to Frances Cookman.
CAUSE: Allen died in Oyster Bay, Long Island, New York, aged 92 of cancer and a collapsed lung.

Ronald Allen

Born December 16, 1930
Died June 18, 1991
Soap star. For sixteen years Ronnie Allen played motel manager David Hunter on the television soap *Crossroads* until he was unceremoniously sacked. It had been his third stint on a soap, having played magazine editor Ian Harman on *Compact* and football manager Mark Wilson on *United!* Born in Reading, Berkshire, Allen trained at RADA where he won the John Gielgud Scholarship. He joined Salisbury Rep and then the Old Vic where he appeared in *Henry V* with Richard Burton. He was signed to a two-year contract by 20th Century Fox but never really made it in Hollywood. Allen also appeared in the films *A Night To Remember* (1958) as Mr Clarke, *A Circle Of Deception* (1961) as Abelson, *Cleopatra* (1963), *The Projected Man* (1967) as Chris Mitchell, *Hell Boats* (1970) as Commander Ashurst, R.N., *The Fiend* (1971) as Paul, *The Supergrass* (1985) as Commander Robertson and *Eat The Rich* (1987) as Commander Fortune. He was signed to appear in the American soap *Generations* but was

unable to get a work permit and returned to Britain. A homosexual, he lived in London with his long-term boyfriend, Brian Hankins, until Hankins' death from cancer in 1979 whereupon Allen surprised almost everyone who knew him by moving in with his *Crossroads* co-star Sue Lloyd. They married six weeks before his death.
CAUSE: He died of lung cancer in Reading, Berkshire, at the age of 60.

Theresa Allen

Born October 17, 1908
Died May 18, 1997
Early retiree. Born in Indianapolis, Indiana, 5'3" Theresa Allen began her career by winning a Miss Personality contest which gained her a stage contract in a Lupino Lane revue. In 1925, she moved to the silent screen and was a double for Colleen Moore in *Twinkletoes* (1927) who also taught her how to dance for that film. Theresa Allen found that the cinema was not for her and she retired aged 22 with just a few films under her belt. For the rest of her life she worked as an estate agent. Her films included: *The Dance Of Life* (1929), *Happy Days* (1930), *The Vagabond King* (1930), *The Golden Calf* (1930), *Sweet Kitty Bellairs* (1930) and *Scarlet Pages* (1930).
CAUSE: She died aged 88 of an aortic aneurysm in Newport Beach, California.

Sara Allgood

Born October 15, 1879
Died September 13, 1950
Irish character. Born in Dublin, Ireland, she toured with William George Fay before a long and successful career as one of the founders of the Abbey Theatre in 1904. It was at the Abbey that she created the role of Juno in Sean O'Casey's *Juno And The Paycock*, a part she reprised in the Alfred Hitchcock cinematic version (1930). Hitchcock may not have been overly complimentary about actors but

Sara Allgood was not his greatest fan either – she called him a "cheap, second-rate director". When she moved to Hollywood she gave up stage acting. She mostly played mothers in Tinseltown. She became an American citizen in 1945. Her films included *Just Peggy* (1918) as Peggy, *To What Red Hell* (1929), *Blackmail* (1929) as Mrs White, *The World, The Flesh, The Devil* (1932) as Emme Stanger, *The Fortunate Fool* (1933) as Rose, *Lily Of Killarney* (1934) as Mrs O'Connor, *Irish Hearts* (1934) as Mrs Gogarthy, *Riders To The Sea* (1935) as Maurya, *Peg Of Old Drury* (1935) as an Irish woman, *The Passing Of The Third Floor Back* (1935) as Mrs de Hooley, *Lazybones* (1935) as Bridget, *Southern Roses* (1936) as Miss Florence, *Sabotage* (1936) as a customer in the bird shop, *Pot Luck* (1936) as Mrs Kelly, *It's Love Again* (1936) as Mrs Hopkins, *Kathleen Mavourneen* (1937) as Mary Ellen O'Dwyer, *Storm In A Teacup* (1937) as Honoria Hegarty, *The Sky's The Limit* (1938) as Mrs O'Reilly, *The Londonderry Air* (1938), *On The Night Of The Fire* (1939) as a charwoman, *That Hamilton Woman* (1941) as Mrs Cadogan-Lyon, *Dr Jekyll And Mr Hyde* (1941) as Mrs Higgins, *Lydia* (1941) as Johnny's Mother, *How Green Was My Valley* (1941) as Mrs Beth Morgan, *Roxie Hart* (1942) as Mrs Morton, *This Above All* (1942) as a tea room waitress, *It Happened In Flatbush* (1942) as Mrs 'Mac' McAvoy, *The War Against Mrs Hadley* (1942) as Mrs Michael Fitzpatrick, *Life Begins At Eight-Thirty* (1942) as Alma Lothian, *City Without Men* (1943) as Maria Barton, *The Lodger* (1944) as Ellen, *Jane Eyre* (1944) as Bessie, *Between Two Worlds* (1944) as Mrs Midget, *The Keys Of The Kingdom* (1944) as Sister Martha, *The Strange Affair Of Uncle Harry* (1945) as Nona, *Kitty* (1945) as Old Meg, *Cluny Brown* (1946) as Mrs Maile, *The Spiral Staircase* (1946) as Nurse Barker, *Ivy* (1947) as Martha Huntley, *The Fabulous Dorseys* (1947)

as Mrs Dorsey, *Mother Wore Tights* (1947) as Grandmother McKinley, *My Wild Irish Rose* (1947) as Mrs Brennan, *Mourning Becomes Electra* (1947) as Landlady, *One Touch Of Venus* (1948) as Mrs Gogarty, *The Girl From Manhattan* (1948) as Mrs Beeler, *Challenge To Lassie* (1949) as Mrs MacFarland, *Sierra* (1950) as Mrs Jonas and *Cheaper By The Dozen* (1950) as Mrs Monahan. Sara Allgood was nominated for a Best Supporting Actress Oscar for her performance in *How Green Was My Valley* but lost out to Mary Astor. In 1916 she married Gerald Henson, the actor, and had one daughter who died in the influenza epidemic of 1917. Henson himself died the following year. She did not remarry.

CAUSE: She died aged 70 of a combination of Bright's disease and a heart attack in the Motion Picture Country House and Hospital, 23450 Calabasas Road, Woodland Hills, California.

Claud Allister

(WILLIAM CLAUD MICHAEL PALMER)
Born October 3, 1888
Died July 26, 1970
Amiable silly ass. The son of a general, Allister was born in London and educated at Felstead. He began life as a stockbroker's clerk but decided that that life was not glamorous enough and opted for a stage career. His long nose, weak chin and posh voice meant that he was often cast as a silly ass. 5'10" Allister made his film début in *The Trial Of Mary Dugan* (1929) playing Henry Plaisted but found a measure of fame as Algy Longworth, Bulldog Drummond's buffoonish sidekick in three films in the long-running film series: *Bulldog Drummond* (1929), *The Return Of Bulldog Drummond* (1934) and *Bulldog Drummond At Bay* (1937) although in *Arrest Bulldog Drummond* (1939) he played Sir Basil Leghorne. His other films included: *Charming Sinners* (1929) as Gregson, *Three Live*

Ghosts (1929) as Spoofy, *Such Men Are Dangerous* (1930) as Fred Wyndham, *Ladies Love Brutes* (1930) as Tailor, *The Florodora Girl* (1930) as Rumblesham, *Monte Carlo* (1930) as Prince Otto Von Seibenheim, *Reaching For The Moon* (1930) as Sir Horace Partington Chelmsford, *Meet The Wife* (1931) as Victor Staunton, *Platinum Blonde* (1931) as Dawson, *The Sea Ghost* (1931) as Percy Atwater, *The Return Of Raffles* (1932) as Bunny, *The Midshipmaid* (1932) as Chinley, *The Private Life Of Henry VIII* (1933) as Cornell, *Sleeping Car* (1933) as Baron Delande, *The Medicine Man* (1933) as the Honourable Freddie Wiltshire, *The Private Life Of Don Juan* (1934) as The Duke, *The Dark Angel* (1935) as Lawrence Bidley, *Captain Fury* (1939) as Suco, *Lillian Russell* (1940) as Arthur Sullivan, *Charley's Aunt* (1941), *A Yank In The R.A.F.* (1941), *Never Give A Sucker An Even Break* (1941), *Kiss The Bride Goodbye* (1945) as Adolphus Pickering, *The Wind In The Willows* (1949) as Rat, *Kiss Me Kate* (1953) as Paul and *The Black Shield Of Falworth* (1954) as Sir George. He was married twice, to Gwen Dowling and Barbara Fay. CAUSE: Claud Allister retired in 1955. He died aged 81 in Santa Barbara, California, and is buried in Westwood Village Memorial Park, 1218 Glendon Avenue, Los Angeles, California. His death was due to cancer.

June Allyson

(ELEANOR GEISMAN)
Born October 7, 1917
Died July 8, 2006
Hometown girl. Born in the Bronx, New York June Allyson was the daughter of an alcoholic caretaker who left her mother in April 1918. It resulted in their move from their Bronx tenement on 143rd Street to her grandparents' apartment near Pelham Bay and was to be the first of many upheavals in her young life. The only constant was her grandmother. "Her

arms around me [were] the most precious thing in my life and my protection against the world," she wrote in her autobiography. In 1925 she was injured and a friend killed when a tree fell on them, resulting in four years in a steel back brace. Physical exercise strengthened her and she entered talent shows while at Theodore Roosevelt High School. She made her first short film in 1937 in New York and adopted the name June (after the month) and Allyson (at a friend's suggestion). She landed a job in a Broadway show *Sing Out The News*, which opened at the Music Box Theatre on September 24, 1938 and ran for 105 performances. For the next five years she was a regular in various shows on the Great White Way until she sang the Gershwin tune "Treat Me Rough" in *Girl Crazy* (1943) after which she found regular work in films despite Louis B. Mayer wanting to drop her because he didn't like her husky voice. During the filming of *Meet The People* (1944) she fell in love with co-star Dick Powell and they were married on August 19, 1945. Mayer was a reluctant stand-in to give the bride away. Allyson and Powell adopted a daughter, Pammie (b. June 18, 1948), on August 10, 1948. Their son, Richard Keith, was born on Christmas Eve 1950. In 1944 5'1½" Allyson had taken her first starring role as Patsy Deyo in *Two Girls And A Sailor* (1944), co-starring Van Johnson. Allyson's next film, *Music For Millions* (1944), was lauded by the *New York Post*'s film critic Irene Thirer. Allyson's other films included: *The Secret Heart* (1946) as Penny Addams, *Two Sisters From Boston* (1946), *High Barbaree* (1947) as Nancy Frazer which reteamed her with Van Johnson, *Good News* (1947) as Connie Lane, *The Bride Goes Wild* (1948) as Martha Terryton, *The Three Musketeers* (1948) as Constance, *Little Women* (1949) as Jo, *The Stratton Story* (1949) as Ethel, *The Reformer And The Redhead* (1950) as Kathy Maguire, *Right Cross* (1950) as Pat O'Malley, *Too Young To Kiss* (1951) as Cynthia Potter for which she won a Best Actress Golden Globe, *The Girl In White* (1952) as Dr Emily Dunning, *Battle Circus* (1953) as Lieutenant Ruth McGara, *Remains To Be Seen* (1953) as Jody Revere, *The Glenn Miller Story* (1954) as Helen Berger Miller and *Executive Suite* (1954) as Mary Blemond Walling, the last two opposite Jimmy Stewart. In 1953 she left MGM after making two dozen films in ten years. "The only parental authority I had was the studio," she said. "When I left the studio I was already married and had two children, but I felt as sad as a child leaving home for the first time." In 1954 she received the top box office award from *Photoplay*. She and Powell separated in 1961 but did not finalise their divorce. He died aged 58 at their Los Angeles home on January 2, 1963 and she coped by hitting the bottle. In 1959 she began to host the television show *The DuPont Show With June Allyson*, which lasted for two years. Like many of her ilk, she began appearing in guest slots on the small screen. These included *Burke's Law* (both in its original run in 1963 and when it returned in 1995), *Vega$*, *The Incredible Hulk*, *House Calls*, *Simon & Simon*, *The Love Boat*, *Hart To Hart*, *Murder, She Wrote*, *Crazy Like A Fox* and *Airwolf*. She married her husband's barber Glenn Maxwell on October 12, 1963 but the couple divorced on April 20, 1965; she claimed that he had hit her and called her names in front of her children. They remarried on April 1, 1966 but redivorced on March 17, 1970. On October 30, 1976 Allyson married dentist and bitpart actor David Prince Ashrow. In 1997 she founded the June Allyson Foundation for research into incontinence. Of herself and her career she said, "I have big teeth. I lisp. My eyes disappear when I smile. My voice is funny . . . [perhaps that is why] women identify with me.

And while men desire Cyd Charisse, they'd take me home to meet mum. Women never had to fear me. I could never be the other woman and men saw me as the wife they'd want, always having dinner ready, never complaining, always being there."
CAUSE: Allyson died of pulmonary respiratory failure and acute bronchitis at Ojai, California. She was 89.
FURTHER READING: *June Allyson* – June Allyson with Frances Spatz Leighton (New York: Berkley Books, 1983).

Néstor Almendros

(NESTOR ALMENDROS CUYAS)
Born October 30, 1930
Died March 4, 1992
New Wave-ist. Cinematographer and director Almendros, born in Barcelona, Spain, was educated at the University of Cuba where he read literature and philosophy. On graduating he moved to New York to study editing and cinematography at the Big Apple's City College. In the Sixties he moved again, this time to Paris where he was at the forefront of the New Wave movement. On April 9, 1979, he won an Oscar for *Days Of Heaven* (1978) and worked on *Kramer vs. Kramer* (1979), *The Blue Lagoon* (1980), *Sophie's Choice* (1982), *Pauline At The Beach* (1983), *Heartburn* (1986) and *Billy Bathgate* (1991). Four years before his death, he returned to Cuba and made a documentary on Fidel Castro's poor human rights record.
CAUSE: A homosexual, he died in New York aged 61 from AIDS.

Don Alvarado

(JOSE PAIGE)
Born November 4, 1904
Died March 31, 1967
Valentino clone. Born in Albuquerque, New Mexico, Alvarado's father intended for the boy to become a sheep farmer. However, he decided a career on the silver screen would be more exciting than counting sheep and ran away from home aged 17 to make his way to Hollywood. In Tinseltown he

befriended Gilbert Roland and came to the attention of Jack Warner. Warner supposedly thought of the stage name while driving down Alvarado Street in Los Angeles. He got work in several films thanks to his swarthy good looks. His films included: *The Wife Who Wasn't Wanted* (1925) as Theo, *The Night Cry* (1926) as Pedro, *The Loves Of Carmen* (1927) as Jose, *Breakfast At Sunrise* (1927) as Lussan, *The Bridge Of San Luis Rey* (1929) as Manuel, *Captain Thunder* (1930) as Juan Sebastian, *Beau Ideal* (1931) as Ramon Gonzales and *The Devil Is A Woman* (1935) as Morenito. By this time 5'11" Alvarado had married Ann Boyar and become a father to daughter Joy (b. November 9, 1924). After six years of marriage Ann fell in love with Jack Warner in 1930. They married in 1936 after his parents had died. The advent of the talkies ruined Alvarado's acting career and he moved behind the cameras as an assistant director. He ended his life as the manager of an 80,000 acre cattle ranch owned by his ex-wife and Jack Warner.
CAUSE: He died aged 62 in Hollywood, California, from cancer.

Kirk Alyn

(JOHN FEGGO, JR)
Born October 8, 1910
Died March 14, 1999
The first superhero. Kirk Alyn was born in Oxford, New Jersey. Like many entertainers, he began in vaudeville and as a chorus boy on Broadway. He began to make small supporting appearances in low-budget fare. Remarkably in his first film *Private Lessons* (1934) in which he played John Humphries he was credited as Jack Fago. It was in 1948 that he achieved stardom as the first Superman, a role he played for two years. However, when the film serial ended he was unable to maintain his stardom and eventually retired to Arizona. One of his last films was playing Lois Lane's father in the 1978 version of *Superman*.

In 1942 he married Virginia O'Brien. They divorced in 1955. His films included *Rooftop Frolics* (1937), *You Were Never Lovelier* (1942) as a suitor, *The Man From The Rio Grande* (1943) as Tom Traynor, *Is Everybody Happy?* (1943) as Thew, *Overland Mail Robbery* (1943) as Tom Hartley, *Pistol Packin' Mama* (1943) as J. Leslie Burton, III, a pilot in *Four Jills in a Jeep* (1944), *Goodnight, Sweetheart* (1944), *Forty Thieves* (1944) as Jerry Doyle, *Call Of The Rockies* (1944) as Ned Crane, *Daughter Of Don Q* (1946) as Cliff Roberts, *Little Miss Broadway* (1947) as Detective Mel O'Brien, *Sweet Genevieve* (1947) as Doctor Wright, *The Three Musketeers* (1948) as Aramis' friend, *Federal Agents Versus Underworld, Inc.* (1949) as Inspector David Worth, *Radar Patrol Versus Spy King* (1950) as Chris Calvert, *Atom Man Versus Superman* (1950) as Superman/Clark Kent, *Blackhawk: Fearless Champion Of Freedom* (1952) as Blackhawk and *Scalps* (1983) as Professor Machen.
CAUSE: Alyn died aged 88 of natural causes in Woodlands, Texas.

Don Ameche

(DOMINIC FELIX AMICI)
Born May 31, 1904
Died December 6, 1993
Dapper comedian. Born in Kenosha, Wisconsin, one of eight children of an Italian publican, he was educated at the University of Wisconsin where he read law. He also appeared in the university's theatre and went on to work in radio. Having failed his first screen test, he made it in his second and made his first film in 1935 (*Clive Of India* [1935]). Ameche subsequently became one of the most popular stars at Twentieth Century-Fox and the highest paid ($7,500 a week). With a voice described by some as "butterscotch baritone", he appeared in over 70 films, often opposite Alice Faye. In the Fifties his film work began to wane and he took to Broadway instead. His career was revived playing

the artful and conniving Mortimer Duke in the Wall Street comedy *Trading Places* (1983). Hollywood ignored him when it came to the Academy Awards for many years until he finally won a Best Supporting Actor Oscar as Art Selwyn in Ron Howard's *Cocoon* (1985), making him the oldest ever winner. Among his other films were *One In A Million* (1936) as Bob Harris, *Ladies In Love* (1936) as Dr Rudi Imre, *Love Under Fire* (1937) as Tracy Egan, *Love Is News* (1937) as Marty Canavan, *You Can't Have Everything* (1937) as George Macrae, *Alexander's Ragtime Band* (1938) as Charlie Dwyer, the title role in *The Story Of Alexander Graham Bell* (1939), *The Three Musketeers* (1939) as D'Artagnan, *Hollywood Cavalcade* (1939) as Michael Linnett Connors, *Down Argentine Way* (1940) as Ricardo Quintan, *Moon Over Miami* (1941) as Phil O'Neil, *Heaven Can Wait* (1943) as Henry Van Cleve, *Picture Mommy Dead* (1966) as Edward Shelley, *Suppose They Gave A War And Nobody Came?* (1970) as Colonel Flanders, *Harry And The Hendersons* (1987) as Doctor Wallace Wrightwood, *Cocoon: The Return* (1988) as Art Selwyn and *Corrina, Corrina* (1994) as Grandpa Harry. At one time he was a heavy gambler, losing almost one million dollars on the horses. On November 26, 1932, he married dietitian Honore Prendergast. They had four sons Dominic Felix (b. 1933), Ronald John (b. 1936), Thomas Anthony (b. 1940) and Lawrence Michael (b. 1941) and adopted two daughters, Barbara and Cornelia. Within the family they are known as Donnie, Ronnie, Tommie, Lonnie, Bonnie and Connie.
CAUSE: He died in Arizona of prostate cancer aged 89.

Adrienne Ames

(ADRIENNE RUTH MACCLURE)
Born August 3, 1907
Died May 31, 1947
Beautiful B-leading lady. Born in Fort Worth, Texas, 5'5" Adrienne Ames was one of four boys and three daughters of Samuel Hugh MacClure (b. 1871, d. August 1928, after falling from the third floor) a chief engineer at the Baker Hotel, Texas, and Flora Parthenia. Her sister Doris died when she was just one year old. Her younger sister was the actress Gladys MacClure (b. Fort Worth, Texas, August 5, 1914, d. San Francisco, California, November 26, 1933 aged 29 in a car crash that left four dead). Adrienne studied literature at Columbia University and art at the Metropolitan Museum of Modern Art. She made her screen début as a stand-in for Pola Negri on *Hotel Imperial* (1927) and then in a small part in *Sally* (1929). In 1931 after a Hawaiian holiday with her second husband, Adrienne stopped off in California where she was spotted by a Paramount scout who, captivated by her beauty, offered Adrienne a contract without a screen test. Her films included: *The Road To Reno* (1931), *24 Hours* (1931) as Ruby Wintryingham, *Girls About Town* (1931) as Anne, *Working Girls* (1931), *Husband's Holiday* (1931) as Myrtle, *Two Kinds Of Women* (1932) as Jean, *Sinners In The Sun* (1932) as Claire Kinkaid, *Merrily We Go To Hell* (1932), *Guilty As Hell* (1932) as Vera Marsh, *The Death Kiss* (1932) as Marcia Lane, *From Hell To Heaven* (1933) as Joan Burt, *Broadway Bad* (1933) as Aileen, *A Bedtime Story* (1933) as Paulette, *Disgraced!* (1933) as Julia Thorndyke, *The Avenger* (1933) as Ruth Knowles, *George White's Scandals* (1934) as Barbara Loraine, *You're Telling Me!* (1934) as Princess Lescaboura, a girl in the audience in *The Old Fashioned Way* (1934), *Abdul The Damned* (1935) as Therese Alder, *Gigolette* (1935) as Kay Parrish, *Black Sheep* (1935) as Mrs Millicent Bath, *Woman Wanted* (1935) as Betty Randolph, *Ladies Love Danger* (1935) as Adele Michel, *Harmony Lane* (1935) as Jane McDowell, *La Fiesta De Santa Barbara* (1935) as herself, *City*

Girl (1938) as Vivian Ross, *Fugitives For A Night* (1938) as Eileen Baker, *Slander House* (1938) as Helen Smith, *Panama Patrol* (1939) as Lia Maing and *The Zero Hour* (1939) as Susan. Her scenes in her last film, *I Take This Woman* (1940), in which she played Lola Estermonte, were deleted before release. In 1941 she retired from films and landed a job as a wireless commentator on WHN, a New York-based radio station. From 1942 until 1945 she was active in the war effort, raising funds. The lure of acting proved too great and in the summer of 1946 she appeared in repertory in Clinton, Connecticut and Norwich, Rhode Island. Adrienne Ames was married three times: to the Texas oilman Deward Truax (from 1923 until 1925) by whom she had a daughter Barbara (b. 1924); in 1929 to the millionaire broker, later film producer Stephen Ames (b. New York, December 18, 1898, d. April 22, 1955). When he was away, Ames allowed the actor Bruce Cabot to squire her around town. On September 15, 1933 she moved to Reno to enable her to get a divorce from Stephen Ames to allow her to marry Bruce Cabot. The divorce became final on October 30, 1933. The following day she married Cabot at the Carlsbad, New Mexico, home of his mother. She learned of her sister's death on her honeymoon with Cabot. The marriage was fraught and they separated. Adrienne moved to New York but Cabot followed her to try to salvage their relationship. In July 1936 Cabot persuaded her not to divorce him but it was only a brief respite. On March 4, 1937, Adrienne again went to court and applied for a divorce, citing Cabot's unreasonable behaviour such as smashing up furniture during drunken sprees. On April 6, 1937, the divorce was granted and she was awarded alimony of $125 a week plus 20 per cent of any salary he might earn. Cabot resisted paying and on October 27, 1939, Adrienne went back to court to apply for back maintenance pay.

CAUSE: She died of cancer at her home, 25 Sutton Place South, in New York City. She was 39. Her funeral was held on June 2, 1947, in New York. Two days later, her body was flown back to Texas and a second ceremony was held at the Robertson-Mueller-Harper funeral home before her burial in the family plot in Oakwood Cemetery, Fort Worth, next to her sister who had been interred on December 7, 1933.

Leon Ames

(LEON WYCOFF)
Born January 20, 1902
Died October 12, 1993
Dependable dad. Born in Portland, Indiana, Leon Ames was in regular stage employment in the Twenties before trying his hand in Hollywood. In 1931 he made a screen test for Universal opposite a promising young actress called Bette Davis. He appeared under his real name in *Murders In The Rue Morgue* (1932) before deciding that he preferred the stage. However, he decided to give films a second chance and by the late Thirties was a regular on screen. He appeared in over 100 films, including *Calling All Marines* (1939), *Meet Me In St Louis* (1944) his favourite role even though his singing was dubbed, *Thirty Seconds Over Tokyo* (1944), *Son Of Lassie* (1945), *The Postman Always Rings Twice* (1946), *Little Women* (1949), *Peyton Place* (1957) and *Tora! Tora! Tora!* (1970). One of the founding members (in 1933) of the Screen Actors Guild, Ames believed that none of his films were particularly worthy. He also appeared as a regular on the television series *Life With Father* (1953–1955), *Father Of The Bride* (1961–1962) and *Mr Ed* (1963–1965). Following his retirement, he lived on the Ford car dealership he had the foresight to buy. He was financially tight: "Don't lend your friends money, or they won't stay your friends. Unhappily, we don't

choose our relatives. So don't lend your relatives money – they'll still be your relatives . . . And if you are a celebrity, your friends *and* relatives will interpret the word 'loan' to mean 'give'." He married actress Christine Gossett on June 25, 1938, and they had a son, Leon Jr, in 1944, and a daughter, Shelley, in 1941.

CAUSE: He died aged 91 following a stroke.

Gene Anderson

Born March 28, 1931
Died May 5, 1965

Tragic actress. Born in London, Anderson studied at the Central School of Dramatic Art. Married to actor Edward Judd (b. Shanghai, October 4, 1932), she died without ever fulfilling her potential. She appeared in less than a dozen films before her untimely death. Her body of work included: *Flannelfoot* (1952) as Rene Wexford, *The Intruder* (1954) as June Maple, *Double Cross* (1956), *The Long Haul* (1957) as Connie Miller, *Yangtse Incident* (1957) as Ruth Worth, *The Day The Earth Caught Fire* (1961) as May and *The Break* (1963) as Jean Tredegar.

CAUSE: She died in London aged 34 from a cerebral haemorrhage.

Gilbert M. 'Broncho Billy' Anderson

Born March 21, 1882
Died January 20, 1971

The world's first movie star. Born in Little Rock, Arkansas, he began his working life as a travelling salesman before becoming a model in New York then landing a job on the film *The Messenger Boy's Mistake* (1902). In 1903 he played several roles in an Edwin S. Porter short film, *The Great Train Robbery*, which made film history. He was intended to play one of the villains but was so useless on a horse he was demoted to extra work. Nonetheless, in February 1907 he was one of the first film stars to create his own production company, Essanay (named after Anderson and his partner George K. Spoor). That year he starred in and directed the first of over 400 films starring himself in his cowboy guise of Broncho Billy Anderson, *The Bandit Makes Good*. Oddly, one of the remarkable things about the films was their lack of continuity. He might marry in one picture and be a bachelor in the next, dead in one and fighting fit in the next. It didn't seem to worry his audiences, as he became the first Western hero and a multi-millionaire in the process, modifying the spelling of his stage name to 'Bronco' along the way. Among his many, many movies were *Raffles, An American Cracksman* (1905) as Raffles, *Ten Nights In A Barroom* (1909), *Shanghaied* (1909), *A Westerner's Way* (1910), *A Western Woman's Way* (1910), *A Western Maid* (1910), *Western Chivalry* (1910), *The Girl From The Triple X* (1910), *Broncho Billy's Redemption* (1910) as Broncho Billy, *Spike Shannon's Last Fight* (1911), *The Outlaw's Deputy* (1911), *The Outlaw's Samaritan* (1911), *The Outlaw And The Child* (1911), *Mustang Pete's Love Affair* (1911), *Broncho Billy's Christmas Dinner* (1911), *Broncho Billy's Adventure* (1911), *The Reward For Broncho Billy* (1912), *Broncho Billy's Promise* (1912), *Broncho Billy's Outwitted* (1912), *Broncho Billy's Mexican Wife* (1912), *Broncho Billy's Heart* (1912), *Alkali Ike Beats Broncho Billy* (1912), *The Making Of Broncho Billy* (1913), *Broncho Billy's Way* (1913), *Broncho Billy's Ward* (1913), *Broncho Billy's Squareness* (1913), *Broncho Billy's Sister* (1913), *Broncho Billy's Secret* (1913), *Broncho Billy's Last Deed* (1913), *Broncho Billy's Gun Play* (1913), *Broncho Billy's Gratefulness* (1913), *Broncho Billy's First Arrest* (1913), *Broncho Billy's Christmas Deed* (1913), *Broncho Billy And The Outlaw's Mother* (1913), *Broncho Billy's Sermon* (1914), *Broncho Billy's Bible* (1914), *Broncho Billy's Protégé* (1915) and hundreds more. Although he retired from acting in 1916, it would be 41 years before he was honoured with a special Oscar. He was Stan Laurel's first producer and mentor and introduced Laurel & Hardy in the film *The Lucky Dog*. Made between November 17–29, 1919, it wasn't released until 1922. Anderson signed Charlie Chaplin to his company and away from Mack Sennett in 1915 but the Little Tramp only stayed a year. CAUSE: He died aged 88 in South Pasadena, California, and was cremated at the Chapel of Pines Crematory, 1605, South Catalina, Los Angeles 90006.

Jean Anderson

Born December 12, 1907
Died April 1, 2001
Versatile matriarch. Born in Eastbourne, East Sussex, of Scottish parentage, Mary Jean Heriot Anderson was the second of five children raised in Guildford, Surrey. Her childhood ambitions were to entertain but as a musician not an actress. She wanted to be a concert violinist and indeed played with the Guildford Orchestra under the conductorship of Claud Powell, whose son she would later marry. Anderson realised that she did not have the temperament for the platform and in 1926 she enrolled at RADA where she studied for two years. Her first professional role was appearing in a 50-week tour of *Many Waters* alongside her fellow RADA student Robert Morley. A follow-up, *Out All Night*, a farce, closed in Glasgow leaving the company with their train fares back to London but no wages. Resolute, Anderson landed a job working in Cambridge where she met Peter Powell. They married in 1934 in between the morning rehearsal of *The Nelson Touch* and the evening performance of *The Circle*. Their honeymoon was on the Sunday and lasted one day. They had one daughter, Aude, named after a character in *The Unknown Warrior* played by Anderson and directed by Powell. (The couple

was divorced in 1949. Anderson never remarried.) In 1936 she moved to Ireland for three years appearing at the Gate Theatre, Dublin, returning at the outbreak of war to make sandwiches for the Players' Theatre Club, a music hall venue for soldiers, actors and politicians to meet and chat. Its director was the actor Leonard Sachs and when he was called up, Anderson took over. After the war Anderson began appearing on television and in films, making her début in *The Mark Of Cain* (1947). From February 6, 1951 and again from March 3, 1957, she played the mother in an eight-part production of *The Railway Children*. Her film and television career prospered and she appeared in *The Romantic Age* (1949), *The Franchise Affair* (1950) as Miss Tuff, *White Corridors* (1951) as Sister Gater, *The Brave Don't Cry* (1952) as Mrs Sloan, *Johnny On The Run* (1953) as Mrs MacIntyre, *Lease Of Life* (1954) as Miss Calthorp, *A Town Like Alice* (1956) as Miss Horsefall, *Lucky Jim* (1957) as Mrs Welch, *The Barretts Of Wimpole Street* (1957) as Wilson, *Robbery Under Arms* (1957) as Ma Marston, *Heart Of A Child* (1958) as Maria, *SOS Pacific* (1959) as Miss Shaw, *Solomon And Sheba* (1959) as Takyan, *Spare The Rod* (1961) as Mrs Pond, *Lisa* (1962) as Mrs Jongman, *Waltz Of The Toreadors* (1962) as Agnes, *The Three Lives Of Thomasina* (1963) as Mrs MacKenzie, *Silent Playground* (1964) as Mrs Lacey, *Half A Sixpence* (1967) as Lady Botting, *The Night Digger* (1971) as Mrs McMurtrey, *The Lady Vanishes* (1979) as Baroness Kisling and *Screamtime* (1983) as Mildred. On March 10, 1972, she became the matriarch Mary Hammond in the trucking soap *The Brothers*. The show made Anderson a household name in the United Kingdom and throughout Europe but not in America where its portrayal of trade unions was thought likely to offend the powerful Teamsters union.

Years later, Anderson would live in the same road as Richard Easton who played Brian in the series. Shopkeepers would tell Anderson that they had just served her son. In the Eighties Anderson played Lady Jocelyn Holbrook in three series of the Second World War Japanese prisoner of war drama *Tenko*. "Jocelyn's a scruffy character who wears a tattered grey dress. I was bored with being elegant. Ever since *The Brothers*, I've been cast as a grand lady in the theatre. This time I'm an aristocrat with a Cambridge degree but not a bit nice to hear. I'm a bit of a women's lib character and I think I can be forgiven a few bloodys." She also played Ruth, Lady Fermoy in the television movie of Andrew Morton's best-selling biography *Diana: Her True Story* (1993). Her real passion was horse racing and she would often sit in the Green room reading the racing pages. When she appeared on *This Is Your Life* all the invitees turned up, a rare occurrence in a back-biting business. CAUSE: Jean Anderson died aged 93 in Edenhall, Cumbria, of natural causes.

Dame Judith Anderson

(FRANCES MARGARET ANDERSON)
Born February 10, 1898
Died January 3, 1992
Icily imperious Australian. Born in Adelaide, South Australia, one of four children of James Anderson-Anderson, Anderson took the stage name Judith and became famous on Broadway (arriving in America in 1918, having made her stage début in Australia three years earlier in *A Royal Divorce* at the Theatre Royal, Sydney) occasionally making a foray to Hollywood. In September 1934 she appeared as Lila in the play *Divided By Three* with Hedda Hopper, causing one critic to comment, "Judith may never find someone manlier than herself to act with or engage." She played Gertrude to John Gielgud's Hamlet on Broadway to great acclaim in October 1936 and

the following year (from November 26, 1937) played Lady Macbeth opposite Laurence Olivier at the Old Vic. She made her first feature film in 1933 as Ruby Darling in *Blood Money*, and went on to appear in *Forty Little Mothers* (1940) as Madame Madeline Granville, *Lady Scarface* (1941) as Slade, *Kings Row* (1942) as Mrs Harriet Gordon, *Edge Of Darkness* (1942) as Gerd Blarnesen, *Laura* (1944) as Anne Treadwell, *And Then There Were None* (1945) as Emily Brent (who comments on the murder of the butler: "Very stupid to kill the only servant in the house. Now we don't even know where to find the marmalade"), *The Ten Commandments* (1956) as Memnet, *Cat On A Hot Tin Roof* (1958) as Big Mama, *A Man Called Horse* (1970) as Buffalo Cow Head and a high priestess in *Star Trek III: The Search For Spock* (1984). She said of herself, "I have not a very serene temperament", and confirmed this with her chilly performances. She was nominated for an Oscar for her portrayal of the malignant Mrs Danvers in Hitchcock's *Rebecca* (1940). After one particularly good performance of *Medea* (1947) Claire Trevor went backstage to congratulate Anderson. "I simply can't find the words to tell you how superb you were," she enthused. Anderson's response was succinct: "Try." A (very) closeted lesbian, she nonetheless married twice. Her first husband (they married on May 18, 1937, in Kingman, Arizona) was Benjamin Harrison Lehman. They were divorced on August 23, 1939. Seven years later, on July 11, 1946, she married theatre producer Luther Greene. They divorced on June 26, 1951. Unsurprisingly, there were no children from either match. "I wouldn't come out in a million years. Why should I? I owe nothing! I don't owe anyone any explanations, and I won't join up with anything. Ever. They never gave me anything, and I certainly don't need them. I live my own life, and good luck to them, but leave me alone! Everybody, just leave me alone!" In 1984 she began appearing as matriarch Minx Lockridge in the short-lived soap opera *Santa Barbara* (her adoptive home town from 1950) at a salary of $5,000 per week.

CAUSE: She died in Santa Barbara, California, aged 93, from pneumonia.

Lindsay Anderson

Born April 17, 1923
Died August 30, 1994

Self-professed anarchist. Lindsay Gordon Anderson was born in King Lodge, Bangalore, India, the second of the three sons of Major-General Alexander Vass Anderson, CB, CMG, MBE (b. North India, November 17, 1895, d. St Martin, Jersey, Channel Islands, October 17, 1963) and his first wife (in 1918) Estelle Bell, née Gasson (b. Queenstown, South Africa, 1898, d. March 20, 1973) whom he does not mention in his *Who's Who* entry. He also omits any mention of his sons. Anderson's parents separated in 1926 and his mother settled in England with her two eldest sons, Murray and Lindsay. In September 1932 Estelle Anderson returned to India for a brief reconciliation with her husband, resulting in a third son, Alexander Vass, after she returned to England, but in 1935 the couple divorced. A year later she married Major Cuthbert Sleigh (so close to the Andersons that the two elder boys called him 'Uncle Father'), and moved with her three sons to his house in Camberley, Surrey. Anderson was educated at St Ronan's preparatory school in West Worthing, Sussex (where he was something of a rebel) and Cheltenham College. In 1941 he won a scholarship in classical studies to Wadham College, Oxford, but he was drafted into the 60th King's Royal Rifles and thence to the army intelligence corps in 1943. After six months of military training, he worked as a cryptanalyst at the Wireless Experimental Centre in Delhi for the rest of the Second World War. In July 1945 he celebrated the Labour Party's landslide victory in the general election by persuading a couple of colleagues to join him in raising the red flag over the officers' mess. On January 10, 1947, he saw John Ford's *My Darling Clementine* (1946) and in December of that year he co-founded (with Karel Reisz and Tony Richardson) the film magazine *Sequence*. When the magazine floundered after 14 issues in 1951 Anderson began to produce documentaries with a social theme. He won an Oscar for his film about the deaf, *Thursday's Children* (1954). He was a leading figure in the Free Cinema movement, launched in 1956 to further the beliefs of *Sequence*. It aimed to push the British film industry into what they saw as a more realistic not to say controversial direction. He made his first feature film *This Sporting Life* (1963) from David Storey's first novel. The film gave a break to Irish actor Richard Harris. Anderson's other films included *If . . .* (1968), *O Lucky Man!* (1973), the satire *Britannia Hospital* (1982), which starred Malcolm McDowell and *The Whales Of August* (1987). In 1942 Anderson noted in his diary, "It seems I am homosexual. It really is rather awful and I suppose I shall never get rid of it." Yet by June 4, 1945, he was questioning whether he was indeed "irredeemably homosexual". It seemed that Lindsay Anderson, like Frankie Howerd, did not like being gay. *If . . .* was filmed at Cheltenham College and won the Palme d'Or at the 1969 Cannes Film Festival. For many years, film students debated the movie changing from colour to black and white. Anderson later confessed the real reason – he had run out of money and could only afford monochrome film.

CAUSE: In 1992 5'6" Anderson developed arrhythmia. He died aged 71 after suffering a fatal heart attack while on holiday near Angoulême in the South of France. He was cremated in

Périgord, France, on September 5, 1994. He left £633,397.
FURTHER READING: *Mainly About Lindsay Anderson* – Gavin Lambert (London: Faber & Faber, 2000); *The Diaries* – Paul Sutton (London: Methuen, 2004).

Gwili Andre

(GURLI ANDRESEN)
Born February 4, 1908
Died February 5, 1959
"America's most beautiful model". Blonde and beautiful, 5'6" Andre worked as a fashion model in Europe and New York before moving to Hollywood in 1932 to try and become a film star. David O. Selznick signed her to RKO and she appeared in *Roar Of The Dragon* (1932) opposite Richard Dix, *Secrets Of The French Police* (1932) and *No Other Woman* (1933) opposite Irene Dunne. However the critics were cruel and her seventh and last film was a bitpart role in *The Falcon's Brother* in 1942. She was married to chess champion Stanislaws Miotkowski and real estate agent William Dallas Cross, Jr but both ended in divorce. As her career faltered she turned to alcohol.
CAUSE: On the day after her 51st birthday alone in her apartment at 2109-B Ocean Front, Venice, California, she committed suicide by self-immolation. She surrounded herself with all her publicity material, set fire to it and allowed the flames to "burn her to a crisp".

Dana Andrews

Born January 1, 1909
Died December 17, 1992
Always the hero. Carver Dana Andrews was born in Collins, Mississippi, the son of baptist minister Charles Forrest Andrews, and was educated at Sam Houston State College, Texas. (His brother is the actor Steve Forrest.) Originally an accountant at Gulf Oil by profession, he studied at the Pasadena Playhouse (while working as a petrol pump attendant) at 39 South El Molino Avenue, Pasadena, first appearing on stage there in June 1935 playing the Frenchman in *Cymbeline*. Signed by Samuel Goldwyn on March 14, 1939, he made his film début in *Lucky Cisco Kid* (1940) as Sergeant Dunn and went on to appear in over 80 films. His most notable roles were playing Donald Martin in *The Ox-Bow Incident* (1943) and detective Mark McPherson in *Laura* (1944). His other films included *Kit Carson* (1940) as Captain John C. Fremont, *Belle Starr* (1941) as Major Thomas Grail, *Wing And A Prayer* (1944) as Lieutenant Commander Edward Moulton, *Fallen Angel* (1945) as Eric Stanton, *My Foolish Heart* (1949) as Walt Dreiser, *Elephant Walk* (1954) as Dick Carver, *Battle Of The Bulge* (1965) as Colonel Pritchard, *Johnny Reno* (1966) as Johnny Reno, *Airport 1975* (1974) as Scott Freeman, *The Last Tycoon* (1976) as Red Ridingwood and *Prince Jack* (1984) as the Cardinal. Away from the screen he developed a drink problem. On December 29, 1956, he was arrested for drink-driving in North Hollywood when his car went into the back of another; he was fined. On January 4, 1968, he was hospitalised after fracturing his skull after falling in his hotel bathroom. In 1972 he began appearing in television ads for Alcoholics Anonymous, announcing: "I'm Dana Andrews, and I'm an alcoholic. I don't drink any more, but I used to – all the time." Combating alcoholism, he fell victim to Alzheimer's disease towards the end of his life. He was married twice. His first wife (they married on December 31, 1932) was Janet Murray, who died in 1935. Their son, David Murray, was born in 1933 and died in 1964. Andrews married for the second time to actress Mary Todd (on November 17, 1939) and they had three children: Stephen (b. 1944), Catherine (b. 1948), and Susan (b. 1949). Mary Andrews filed for divorce on May 28, 1968, but later withdrew the suit.

CAUSE: He died in Los Alamitos, California, aged 83, from pneumonia.

Harry Andrews, CBE
Born November 10, 1910
Died March 7, 1989
Gruff and bluff. Harry Stewart Fleetwood Andrews was born at St Mary's, Pembury Road, Tonbridge, Kent, the son of Henry Arthur Andrews, a Scottish doctor, and Amy Diana Frances Horner. He was educated at Tonbridge School and at Wrekin College, Shropshire. Before making his stage début at the Liverpool Playhouse in September 1933, playing John in *The Long Christmas Dinner*, he contemplated a life in the police force or on the cricket pitch. Eighteen months later, on March 26, 1935, he made his West End début at the St James's Theatre, again playing a character called John in *Worse Things Happen At Sea*. Andrews was spotted and sponsored by Sir John Gielgud, appearing as Tybalt in Gielgud's and Laurence Olivier's production of *Romeo & Juliet* in 1935. Andrews appeared in the appropriately named *He Was Born Gay* in June 1937 at the Lyric Theatre. Enlisting in the Royal Artillery, 15th Scottish Division, during the war (October 1939 until October 1945), he became an acting major. He joined the Royal Shakespeare Company on being demobbed. In 1952 he moved into films but didn't achieve stardom, possibly because he refused one studio's kind offer of plastic surgery on his sticking-out ears. He appeared in more than 80 films, making his début as the Scots sergeant major in *The Red Beret* (1953). His other works included Hector in *Helen Of Troy* (1956), Darius in *Alexander The Great* (1956), *Moby Dick* (1956) as Stubb, *St Joan* (1957) as John de Stogumber, *Ice Cold In Alex* (1958) as MSM Tom Pugh, *633 Squadron* (1964) as Air Vice-Marshal Davis, *The Hill* (1965) as Regimental Sergeant Major Bert Wilson, *The Charge Of The Light Brigade* (1968) as

Lord Lucan, *The Night They Raided Minsky's* (1968) as Jacob Schpitendavel, *Entertaining Mr Sloane* (1970) as Ed, *Wuthering Heights* (1970) as Mr Earnshaw, *Nicholas And Alexandra* (1971) as Grand Duke Nicholas, *Death On The Nile* (1978) as Barnstable, the second elder in *Superman* (1978) and *SOS Titanic* (1979) as Captain Edward John Smith. In 1966 he was appointed a CBE. A homosexual, he never married but lived with long-term boyfriend, the actor Basil Hoskins.
CAUSE: He died aged 78 at his home, Church Farm Oasts, Salehurst, Sussex of bronchitis and emphysema and a viral infection complicated by asthma. He left £257,093.

Heather Angel
Born February 9, 1909
Died December 13, 1986
Miss Nearly. 5'2" Heather Grace Angel was born in Oxford, the daughter of a chemistry professor, and began her career on the stage, making her début at the Old Vic in 1926. She travelled to the West Coast of America to try her hand in the talkies that were still in their infancy. She landed a bit part in *Bulldog Drummond* (1929) but stardom was to elude her and she would not make another film for two years. She returned to the silver screen in *Night In Montmartre* (1931) playing the lead female part Annette Lefevre. That same year she appeared in *City Of Song* (1931) as Carmela and then landed the role of Beryl in *The Hound Of The Baskervilles* (1932). Regular celluloid work may have escaped her in the Twenties but in the Thirties she was rarely off the screen although not in big budget films. She screen-tested for the role of Melanie in *Gone With The Wind* (1939) but lost out to Olivia de Havilland. In 1937 she landed the part of Phyllis Clavering in *Bulldog Drummond Escapes* and stayed with the series, appearing in *Bulldog Drummond In Africa* (1938), *Bulldog Drummond's Secret Police* (1939), *Arrest Bulldog*

Drummond (1939), until the final film *Bulldog Drummond's Bride* (1939). Her subsequent career was restricted to supporting roles. In her final work she played Harry S Truman's mother-in-law in the mini-series *Backstairs At The White House* (1979). She was thrice married. Her first husband was the 6'4" actor Henry Wilcoxon (b. Dominica, West Indies, September 8, 1905, d. Los Angeles, California, March 6, 1984 from heart failure and cancer), then came another actor, 6' Ralph Forbes (b. London, September 30, 1902 as Ralph Taylor, d. The Bronx, New York, March 31, 1951) from August 29, 1934 until their divorce in 1937 and finally the director Robert B. Sinclair (b. Toledo, Ohio, May 24, 1905) on April 15, 1944 until his murder by a prowler on January 4, 1970. Her films included: *Self Made Lady* (1932) as Sookey, *Men Of Steel* (1932) as Ann Ford, a girl in *Frail Women* (1932), *Bill, The Conqueror* (1932) as Rosemary Lannick, *After Office Hours* (1932) as Pat, *Pilgrimage* (1933) as Suzanne, *Charlie Chan's Greatest Case* (1933) as Carlotte Eagan, *Berkeley Square* (1933) as Helen Pettigrew, *Early To Bed* (1933) as Grete, *Orient Express* (1934) as Coral Musker, *Murder In Trinidad* (1934) as Joan Cassell, *Romance In The Rain* (1934) as Cynthia Brown, *Springtime For Henry* (1934) as Miss Smith, *Mystery Of Edwin Drood* (1935) as Rosa Bud, *It Happened In New York* (1935) as Chris Edwards, *The Informer* (1935) as Mary McPhillip, *The Headline Woman* (1935) as Myrna Van Buren, *The Three Musketeers* (1935) as Constance, *The Perfect Gentleman* (1935) as Evelyn Alden, *The Last Of The Mohicans* (1936) as Cora Munro, *Daniel Boone* (1936) as Virginia Randolph, *The Bold Caballero* (1936) as Lady Isabella Palma, *Western Gold* (1937) as Jeannie Thatcher, *Portia On Trial* (1937) as Elizabeth Manners, *The Duke Comes Back* (1937) as Susan Corbin Foster, *Army Girl* (1938) as

Mrs Bradley, *Undercover Doctor* (1939) as Cynthia Weld, *Half A Sinner* (1940) as Anne Gladden, *Pride And Prejudice* (1940) as Kitty Bennet, *Kitty Foyle: The Natural History Of A Woman* (1940), *Shadows On The Stairs* (1941) as Sylvia Armitage, a street girl in *That Hamilton Woman* (1941), *Singapore Woman* (1941) as Frieda, *Suspicion* (1941) as Ethel, *The Undying Monster* (1942) as Helga Hammond, *Time To Kill* (1943) as Myrle Davis, *Cry "Havoc"* (1943) as Andra West, *Lifeboat* (1944) in the memorable role of Mrs Higgins, the woman with the dead baby, *In The Meantime, Darling* (1944) as Mrs Nelson, *The Saxon Charm* (1948) as Vivian Saxon, the voice of Alice's sister in *Alice In Wonderland* (1951), the voice of Mrs Darling in *Peter Pan* (1953) and *The Premature Burial* (1962) as Kate Carrell.

CAUSE: She died of cancer in Santa Monica, California, aged 77.

Pier Angeli

(ANNA MARIA PIERANGELI)
Born June 19, 1932
Died September 10, 1971
Fragile but unstable beauty. Born 20 minutes before her twin sister, Marisa Pavan, in Cagliari, Sardinia, the family moved to Rome where, aged 15, she was raped by an American G.I. Discovered by film director Leonide Moguy, the green-eyed Pier appeared in a number of Italian films – including *Domani E Troppo Tardi/Tomorrow Is Too Late* (1949) as Mirella and *Domani E Un Altro Giorno* (1950) – before flying to Hollywood to appear in the lead role of Fred Zinnemann's *Teresa* (1951). It was said that Angeli was so shy she passed out during her first screen kiss. The film's success assured her stay and she went on to star opposite Paul Newman in *The Silver Chalice* (1954) as Deborra. While making that movie she met, and some say fell in love with, James Dean, who was making *East Of Eden* (1955). It was not her first

Hollywood romance. She had loved many others including Kirk Douglas, John Drew Barrymore and Eddie Fisher. Even today opinions are divided on whether Dean and Pier ever actually had sex. "He always had uncertain relations with girlfriends," said Elia Kazan. Her mother violently disapproved of Dean because of his bad behaviour and this caused numerous arguments between the couple. The devoutly Catholic Enrica Pierangeli got her way and, on October 4, 1954, 5'2" Pier announced her engagement to singer Vic Damone. The wedding, at St Timothy's Church at Beverly Glen and Pico on November 24, 1954, was attended by Debbie Reynolds, Ann Miller and Dean Martin. For many years a rumour has circulated that Dean watched the event from across the street, sitting on his motorbike. It has never been established exactly why Angeli split from Dean. They were seeing each other a fortnight before the wedding, although it seems he saw her as a casual fling while she believed the romance to be something altogether more serious. They were never to meet again. At the Cedars of Lebanon Hospital on August 21, 1955, Angeli gave birth to Perry Rocco Luigi Damone, named for singer Perry Como. Two months later, Dean was killed in a car crash. Angeli herself had several physical mishaps during this period. On February 25, 1955, she broke her pelvis during a turbulent plane flight; two years later, she received $45,000 in compensation. In January 1956 she broke her ankle after falling down the steps of her Bel Air home. Eleven months later, she suffered a miscarriage. In August 1957 Angeli and Damone separated and in November 1958 she filed for divorce, claiming Damone was jealous, cruel and had beaten her. The divorce was granted on December 18, 1958. Over the course of the next seven years both made claims and counterclaims and fought for custody of their son. In 1965

Angeli was granted custody. Among her films in this period were *Somebody Up There Likes Me* (1956) as Norma, *Port Afrique* (1956) as Ynez, *S.O.S. Pacific* (1960) as Teresa, *The Last Days Of Sodom And Gomorrah* (1963) as Ildith and *Battle Of The Bulge* (1965) as Louise. In London on St Valentine's Day 1962 she had married bandleader Armando Trovajoli and gave birth to his son, Howard Andrea, on January 8, 1963. They divorced in 1966, with Angeli later claiming that Dean was the only man she had ever truly loved. Her career took a turn for the worse and she appeared in a number of films she previously wouldn't have touched with a barge pole. Her last films were sexploitation flicks including the X-rated *Addio, Alexandra* (1968), *Nelle Pieghe Della Carne/In The Folds Of The Flesh*, (1969) as Falesse/Ester in which she bared her breasts and *Octaman* (1971) before she returned to Hollywood broke and hoping for a chance to appear in *The Godfather*. It was not to be.
CAUSE: She died of a massive self-inflicted overdose of phenobarbital at the home she shared with her drama coach, 355 South McCarty Drive, Beverly Hills, aged 39. She once told a friend: "I'm so afraid to get old – for me, being 40 is the beginning of old age . . . Love is now behind me, love died in a Porsche."

Tony Anholt
Born January 19, 1941
Died July 26, 2002
Off-screen Lothario. Born in Singapore of Anglo-Dutch heritage, 5'10" Tony Anholt had a peripatetic childhood, moving to Australia and South Africa before settling in Britain. His father, a prisoner on the Burmese railway, died in 1944 and Tony's mother remarried in 1949. Leaving school at 18, he became variously a tea taster, a Latin and English teacher at a Surrey prep school, a travel courier and an insurance salesman. Around this time

he met his first wife, Sheila. The couple married in 1964 and moved to Spain where they taught before moving to Paris where they followed a similar profession. Although comfortable in his job, Anholt longed to act and he landed a job at the Leas Pavilion in Folkestone where he appeared in 26 plays in 27 weeks. In 1969 he made his West End début playing Larry in *Boys In The Band* at the Wyndham Theatre. He was a regular on television appearing in *Space 1999* as Tony Verdeschi and causing waves off-screen as Charles Frere in *Howard's Way*. Anholt had a reputation as something of a Lothario and in 1986 he left his wife for his beautiful co-star Tracey Joanne Childs (b. Chiswick, west London, May 30, 1963). They married on July 1, 1990 but divorced in 1998.

CAUSE: Anholt died aged 61 in London of a brain tumour. He was survived by his actor son Christien (b. 1971).

Annabella

(SUZANNE GEORGETTE CHARPENTIER)
Born July 14, 1904
Died September 18, 1996
The one who 'stole' Ty. Born in Paris she moved with her family to La Varenne-Saint-Hilaire when she was four. The blonde daughter of a magazine editor and publisher, she came to fame marrying heartthrob Tyrone Power. Taking her stage name from an Edgar Allan Poe poem *Annabelle Lee*, she appeared in a number of French films including *Napoléon* (1926) as Violine and *La Bacarolle D'Amour* (1928) before being discovered by director René Clair who put her in movies such as *Le Million* (1931) and *Un Soir De Raffle* (1931). She went to Hollywood and appeared in French versions of American films. (The accepted standard at the time was to make the same movie on the same set and with the same script but in a different language and with a different cast.) Learning English, she moved to London and appeared in a number of films including *Wings Of The Morning* (1937), the first British film in Technicolor, again coming to the attention of Hollywood. She also appeared on Broadway but following her interlocutory divorce from Power in 1948 made one French film (*Dernier Amour* [1949]) and one Spanish (*Don Juan* [1950]) and retired. Prior to Power she had married (and was widowed by) French writer Albert Sorré by whom, in 1930, she had a daughter, Anne. The latter was adopted by Tyrone Power and took his name. She married (1954) and divorced (1968) actor Oskar Werner and taught deaf children in North Hampton, Long Island, New York. On October 4, 1934, Annabella married French actor Jean Murat (1888–1968). She and Power fell in love in 1938 while making *Suez* (1938) (she played Toni and was third billed after his Ferdinand de Lesseps) and were married on St George's Day 1939 at her home on St Pierre Road, Bel Air. Actor Don Ameche was best man and Pat Peterson (Mrs Charles Boyer) was maid of honour. Producer Darryl F. Zanuck had done everything in his power to prevent the match, believing it would harm his star's box-office draw if he was married. As it turned out, it was Annabella's career that was wrecked. She and Power remained on excellent terms following their January 24, 1949, divorce.

CAUSE: She died aged 92 in Neuilly-sur-Seine, France, of a heart attack.

Ken Annakin, OBE

Born August 10, 1914
Died April 22, 2009
Comedic director. Kenneth Cooper Annakin was born in Beverley, Yorkshire, an only child who was not close to his parents. He left school early and landed a job as an income tax clerk in Hull. He did not enjoy the work and when he won £100 on the Derby he used the money to emigrate to New Zealand, Australia and America. On his

return to England he found work as an insurance salesman before turning his selling talents to cars and then became a journalist. He joined the Royal Air Force as a flight mechanic but was injured during the Blitz on Liverpool. His career as a cameraman began on RAF training films and he later directed war propaganda films. His first feature film was *Holiday Camp* (1947) for the Rank Organisation, a comedy about the working-class Huggett family. He would work on three more Huggett films over the next few years. He directed the comedy *Miranda* (1948), which starred Glynis Johns as a mermaid caught by a doctor on a fishing trip – her tail reappears whenever she gets wet – and sequences for *Quartet* (1948) and *Trio* (1950), based on short stories by Somerset Maugham. In 1952 he filmed one of the first live-action Disney movies *Story Of Robin Hood And His Merrie Men* and for the same studio, also made *Swiss Family Robinson* (1960) with John Mills, Dorothy McGuire and James MacArthur. Shot on the island of Tobago, Disney's nephew, Roy Disney, considered it one of the greatest family adventure films of all time. According to his daughter, Deborah Peters, Annakin's favourite own film was *Across The Bridge* (1957) in which Rod Steiger was a Wall Street conman who hid in Mexico using the identity of a man he had killed. Five years later, Annakin was one of the three credited directors of *The Longest Day*, the Second World War epic about D-Day. It had an all-star cast led by Henry Fonda, John Wayne, Robert Mitchum, Rod Steiger, Sean Connery and Peter Lawford. He was responsible for the scenes involving British and French troops. In 1965 he directed *Battle Of The Bulge* with Henry Fonda. That same year he made *Those Magnificent Men In Their Flying Machines, or How I Flew From London To Paris In 25 Hours 11 Minutes*, the screenplay for which (co-written with Jack Davies) earned

him an Oscar nomination. His other films included *The Fast Lady* (1963), *The Biggest Bundle Of Them All* (1968), a heist film starring Robert Wagner, *Monte Carlo Or Bust* (1969), *Those Daring Young Men In Their Jaunty Jalopies* (1969), *The Call Of The Wild* (1972), which starred Charlton Heston, and *The Pirate Movie* (1982), an adaptation of *The Pirates Of Penzance* starring Kristy McNichol and Christopher Atkins.
CAUSE: Annakin suffered a heart attack and stroke within a day of each other in February 2009. He died at his home in Beverly Hills, California. He was 94. He died on the same day as Jack Cardiff, his cinematographer on the 1979 film *The Fifth Musketeer*, who is noticed elsewhere in this book.

Colleen Applegate
Born May 24, 1963
Died March 23, 1984
Suicide blonde. Born in Farmington, Minnesota, Colleen Applegate was a gorgeous girl who made her living appearing in pornographic movies. She lost her virginity aged 16 and left her home town with boyfriend Mike Marcel, having tried to kill herself with pills while still in high school. She made her first porn film, *Maximum #4*, in 1983. However, unlike others in the industry she never really enjoyed performing on screen. While working in porn she underwent an abortion, contracted herpes and moved in with drug dealer Jake Erlich. Among her films (many made under the name Shauna Grant) were *All American Bad Girls #2: In Heat* (1983), *Candy's Bedtime Story* (1983), *Centerfold Celebrities #2* (1983), *Centerfold Celebrities #3* (1983), *Feels Like Silk* (1983), *Swedish Erotica Superstar #4: Shauna Grant* (1983) and several posthumously released compilation tapes.
CAUSE: She died by her own hand aged 20. On March 22, 1984, she shot herself in the right temple with a .22

calibre rifle and lay on a life support system for 24 hours before doctors decided she was brain dead.

Andrew Arbuckle
Born September 5, 1884
Died September 21, 1938
Fatty's cousin. Little is known of Andrew Arbuckle, apart from him sharing a surname and a weight problem with his cousin, Fatty. Some sources list his date of birth as 1887 (the same as Fatty) while at least one gives his year of death as 1931 and another as 1939. This particular Arbuckle, who weighed almost 24 stone, was born in Galveston, Texas, and began his career in vaudeville. He was discovered by the producer William H. Ince and became one of the silent screen's most prominent character actors. With the advent of sound he retired, but returned to the screen in the Thirties to play bit parts. His brother was the actor Macklyn Arbuckle (b. San Antonio, Texas, July 9, 1866, d. Waddington, New York, April 1, 1931 from a brain haemorrhage). In October 1915, he married Blanche Duquesne. His films included: *Graft* (1915), *The Red Circle* (1915), *Little Mary Sunshine* (1916) as Bob's Father, *The Matrimonial Martyr* (1916) as Professor Stanley, *A Lucky Leap* (1916), *Big Tremaine* (1916) as Samuel Leavitt, *Happiness* (1917) as Nicodemus, *Should She Obey?* (1917) as Uncle John, *Peggy Leads The Way* (1917) as H.E. Manners, *Naughty, Naughty!* (1918) as Adam Miller, *His Own Home Town* (1918) as Reverend John Duncan, a clergyman in *Denny From Ireland* (1918), *A Romance Of Happy Valley* (1919), *The Spider And The Rose* (1923), *The Love Hunger* (1919) as Bob Clinton, *The Hoodlum* (1919) as Pat O'Shaughnessy, *A White Man's Chance* (1919) as Valentino, *Darling Mine* (1920), *Unseen Forces* (1920) as Mr Leslie, *Mother O' Mine* (1921) as Henry Godfrey, *The Light In The Clearing* (1921) as Horace

Dunkelberg, *The Deuce Of Spades* (1922) as Fat Ed, *Caught Bluffing* (1922) as Ham Thomas, *Saved By Radio* (1922) as Pat, *Name The Man* (1924) as Vondy, *The Dangerous Coward* (1924) as David McGuinn, *The Fighting Boob* (1926) as Old Man Hawksby and *The Dark Angel* (1935) as Mr Gallop.
CAUSE: Arbuckle died just over a fortnight after his 54th birthday in Los Angeles, California.

Roscoe Conkling 'Fatty' Arbuckle
Born March 24, 1887
Died June 29, 1933
Wronged heavyweight. Today the name of Fatty Arbuckle is known only as the participant in one of Hollywood's earliest scandals. Yet, though Fatty was cleared of any malfeasance, still the smear hangs over him. It should all have been so different. Arbuckle was born, three days prematurely, in Smith Center, Kansas, weighing a hefty 14 pounds. Despite his father being an ardent Democrat, the new-born child was named for a right-wing Republican. When Roscoe was two, the family emigrated to Santa Ana, California. The boy was regularly beaten by his father, often for no apparent reason. (Some believe it was because he suspected Roscoe was not sired by him, but this is extremely unlikely given the devout Baptist background of his wife.) Still a teenager, Roscoe began to earn a good living as a singer in San Francisco. By this time he weighed over 15st, but it was mainly muscle. Following the earthquake of April 18, 1906, he travelled to Portland, Oregon, where he joined a vaudeville troupe led by Leon Errol earning $25 a week, half what he had been on in Frisco. In 1909 he started at the Selig Polyscope Company, where he worked under the direction of Francis Boggs, regarded by many as potentially as great a director as D.W. Griffith. (Boggs would be

murdered by a deranged Japanese gardener in November 1911.) In April 1913 he signed for Mack Sennett's studio, Keystone (originally as a Keystone Kop, earning $3 a day) and became known as 'Fatty', a nickname he despised, reminding reporters, "I have a name, you know." On July 17, 1913, *A Noise From The Deep* was released, in which Mabel Normand delivered the first recorded custard pie-in-the-face gag to Arbuckle. Despite his bulk, Roscoe was surprisingly agile and was the only Kop never to hurt himself during stunt work. He was also ambidextrous, able to throw two pies at once and in different directions. In his first 12 months with Sennett, Arbuckle made anywhere between 50 and 100 films (the exact figure can never be known because many of them are no longer extant) and was the studio's biggest money earner. On August 1, 1916, the 19-stone star, who was the first American actor to endorse cigarettes, was persuaded to join a Paramount subsidiary called the Comique Film Corporation. He was given complete artistic control of his work and was paid $1,000 a day; he was also given a Rolls-Royce as a signing present. Remarkably, no formal contract was ever signed. (Less than a year after Arbuckle's departure Keystone Studios crumbled.) Arbuckle and mogul Joseph M. Schenck had a meal and simply shook hands on the deal. He quickly became one of America's most popular stars in films such as *For The Love Of Mabel* (1913), *Fatty's Day Off* (1913), *Fatty's Flirtation* (1913), *Mabel And Fatty's Married Life* (1913) and *His Wedding Night* (1917). He became very conscious of his family appeal and toned down or cut gags that he felt were too risqué. On August 6, 1908, he had married an actress called Minta Durfee (b. Los Angeles, California, 1890, d. Motion Picture Country House and Hospital, Woodland Hills, California, September 9, 1975) at the Byde-A-While Hotel in Long Beach, California, but Arbuckle was quite puritanical and it was a week before the marriage was consummated. He also insisted on turning the lights out before sex. To keep up with the demand for his films, Fatty often filmed three pictures simultaneously. On Labor Day 1916 Arbuckle underwent a painful operation to drain a carbuncle on his leg. To ease the pain he was given heroin. As a result he lost over 6st in weight and leant heavily on two walking sticks, which were always hidden from public view. In early 1917 he went on a month-long trip to publicise his new contract. Despite the widely repeated story in Kenneth Anger's scabrous *Hollywood Babylon*, Fatty didn't take part in an orgy at Mishawum Manor in Woburn, Massachusetts at the end of the tour on March 7, 1917. However, others, including Paramount Presidents Adolph Zukor, Hiram Abrams and Walter Greene and Vice President Jesse Lasky, did enjoy the pleasures of champagne, chicken legs and 15 whores. Arbuckle was even unable to make love to his wife because of the pain in his leg. That year also saw the first splintering of Arbuckle's marriage. He moved into his club and lived separately from his wife, although they occasionally met and had sex. Arbuckle didn't have a sex life outside his marriages. He was refused permission to join the army after America's declaration of war against Germany on April 6, 1917, because he was too fat. In 1919 Zukor negotiated to buy the rights to Arbuckle's next 22 films, unheard of for a comedian. The new contract raised his earnings to $3,000 a day! Arbuckle bought a new house at 649 West Adams Boulevard, Los Angeles, for $250,000. Its previous occupants included Theda Bara and Alla Nazimova. (The cellar of the house was stocked with alcohol, making it a very popular venue after January 16, 1920, and the passing of the 18th Amendment.) A second house was purchased at 1621 East Ocean Avenue, close to Long Beach. The contract wasn't officially signed until January 1921. To celebrate the new contract and the Labor Day (September 5) Holiday that year, Arbuckle held a party at San Francisco's swanky St Francis Hotel, booking rooms 1219–1221. At the time he had six full-length films playing in the cinemas of New York and Los Angeles, plus 27 two-reelers. This was at the height of Prohibition, when America in its wisdom banned alcohol. No such restriction existed in Arbuckle's rooms, where bootleg gin and whisky flowed, well, like water. One visitor was the illegitimate, clap-infested, 26-year-old starlet Virginia Rappé (née Rapp). Rappé had undergone five abortions between the ages of 14 and 16. At 17 she became pregnant by John Sample, a 40-year-old sculptor, and had the baby (a daughter born in 1910) fostered. She later became an artist's nude model. It was also claimed that she was a prostitute, hooked into 'white slavery' that involved several studios. According to Arbuckle's wife, "She was sweet enough, naïve. But had no morals whatsoever. She'd sleep with any man who asked her. In fact, Mack Sennett had to shut the studio down twice because of her . . . because she was spreading lice and some sort of venereal disease. She was a sad case." In 1918 Rappé was named "Best Dressed Girl In Pictures" but by the time of the party she had not worked for two years and was living on, and with, director Henry Pathé Lehrman, a man to whom she referred optimistically as her fiancé. She was also pregnant at the time and begged Arbuckle for money ($2,000) for an (illegal) abortion. He had been sympathetic to her plight, but suggested she talk to her boyfriend, a recommendation Rappé greeted with horror, leading the comedian to believe

that Lehrman was not the baby's father. At the party she went into the bathroom in the suite Arbuckle had hired (1219). Determined to change into his street clothes, the pyjama-clad corpulent comic went to his room and found her vomiting. After giving her two glasses of water, he carried her to the single bed and went to clean up the mess. (Arbuckle was something of a cleanliness freak, regularly taking three baths a day.) Returning from the bathroom, he discovered Rappé had fallen off the bed onto the floor where she lay groaning. He put her back on the bed, where she vomited over herself. Fatty went to find Rappé's friend Bambina Maude Delmont. With showgirl Zey Prevon, they went to comfort Rappé who was sitting on the bed, fully clothed. A few minutes later she screamed, "I'm hurt! I'm dying. I know I'm dying" and began tearing at her clothes. Arbuckle's director friend, Fred Fischbach, at the suggestion of Prevon turned the now naked Rappé upside down then placed her in a bath of ice cold water. Next she was given bicarbonate of soda, which she promptly threw up, and then ice was applied to her body by the drunken guests. At Roscoe's insistence the hotel manager was summoned. Roscoe wrapped Rappé in a dressing gown and carried her to room 1227. Then the party continued. A doctor examined Rappé and found her to be uninjured, only drunk, a diagnosis confirmed by Delmont, who wanted to be left in peace. The hotel detective, George Glennon, looked in on the two women and concurred there was nothing serious amiss. However, Bambina Maude Delmont was a woman with an eye for the easy chance and a fast buck; she was also a bigamist, a professional co-respondent and had a long police record. When her friend was examined by the house doctor, Virginia Rappé was in pain and Delmont told the doctor she had been attacked by Arbuckle, something that Rappé denied. The doctor left and Delmont went back to the party, where she stripped naked. Arbuckle called George Glennon, asking for Delmont to be removed. The next day Delmont finally showed some concern for her friend and summoned another doctor. Furious at her ejection from the party, and what she saw as her rejection from Arbuckle's life, she began telling anyone who would listen that Arbuckle had attacked Rappé. She then contacted two lawyers, sending them identical telegrams: "We have Roscoe Arbuckle in a hole here. Chance to make some money out of him." She went to the authorities and accused Arbuckle of abusing and raping Rappé, who died in Wakefield Sanatorium, 114 Walnut Street, San Francisco on September 9, 1921, at 1.30pm and was buried in Hollywood Memorial Cemetery. (Delmont would not be called as a witness because her statements were so contradictory, mainly because she was lying through her teeth.) A scapegoat had to be found both for Virginia Rappé's death and for the 'moral guardians' of society to bring the film industry to heel, and poor Fatty was it. Two days later, he was arrested for the murder of Rappé. His films were blacklisted by the Hays Office and women's groups called for his head. On September 28 he was released from jail on $5,000 bail. The local D.A. put Arbuckle in the dock three times, although the charges were reduced to rape and manslaughter. His first trial began before Judge Harold Louderback on November 14, 1921, and ended, after 44 hours' deliberation, on December 4, with a hung jury (10–2 for acquittal). On February 3, 1922, a second jury also hung, but this time 9–3 for conviction. On April 12 Arbuckle's third trial, which began on March 13, ended in his acquittal after just five minutes in the jury room. That five minutes had been spent composing a statement. The foreman of the jury read it to the court: "Acquittal is not

enough for Roscoe Arbuckle. We feel a great injustice has been done to him. We feel also that it was only our plain duty to give him this exoneration, under the evidence, for there was not the slightest proof adduced to connect him in any way with the commission of a crime. He was manly throughout the case, and told a straightforward story on the witness stand, which we all believed. The happening at the hotel was an unfortunate affair for which Arbuckle, so the evidence shows, was in no way responsible. We wish him success, and hope the American people will take the judgment of 14 men and women who have sat listening for 31 days to evidence, that Roscoe Arbuckle is entirely innocent and free from all blame." Rappé had been suffering from bladder infections and a 'running abscess' that ultimately caused her death. However, it was too late to save Arbuckle's career. The cost of defending himself was put at $750,000. Six days after the end of the case, censor-in-chief Will Hays temporarily banned Arbuckle from making films. His studio withdrew his pictures. The ban was to last until December 20. Pathetically, Arbuckle pleaded, "Just let me work . . . I think I can entertain and gladden the people that see me. All I want is that. If I do get back it will be grand. If I don't, well okay." In January 1923 he began work again, on a film called *Handy Andy*. However, he soon moved behind the cameras to direct under the pseudonym William Goodrich (his father's two Christian names). For the next nine years, he directed films, ran a nightclub and appeared on stage to pay off his debts. His wife divorced him on January 27, 1925. He married actress Doris Deane (b. Butte, Montana 1899 as Doris Dibble, d. Los Angeles, March 1974) four months later on May 16. Divorced again in August 1928, he married, for the third time, on June 21, 1932, in Erie, Pennsylvania. The bride this time was actress Addie Oakley Dukes

McPhail. In 1932 he appeared in a 'talkie' and signed a contract for six more only to die after a celebratory meal with just one in the can.

CAUSE: He died of angina pectoris and coronary sclerosis at Park Central Hotel, 55th St and 7th Avenue, New York, N.Y. at 2.15am aged 46. He was cremated.

FURTHER READING: *The Day The Laughter Stopped* – David Yallop (London: Hodder & Stoughton 1976); *Fatty* – Andy Edmonds (London: Macdonald 1991).

Army Archerd

Born January 13, 1919
Died September 8, 2009

"The town crier of Hollywood". For 47 years from 1958 Army Archerd would greet attendees at the Oscars, often spending weeks boning up on information about nominees – he even learned sign language so he could converse with Marlee Matlin the year she was a nominee. Armand Archerd was probably born in the Bronx but his family moved west and in 1941 he got a job in the post room at Paramount. He joined the US navy at the outbreak of war where he served with Herman Wouk who would write *The Caine Mutiny Court Martial*. On demob Archerd met Associated Press reporter and future showbiz biographer Bob Thomas (b. January 26, 1922) and the two men opened the AP bureau in the *Hollywood Citizen News* on Wilcox Avenue on October 18, 1945. Archerd's beat included nightclubs such as the Mocambo and Ciro's. On April 27, 1953 he wrote his first column for *Daily Variety* as replacement for Sheilah Graham. He would work there until almost his death. His reputation was such that even actors who were normally reticent to speak to the press spoke on the record to Archerd. However, Greta Garbo avoided his entreaties for an interview. In 1984 he was given a star on Hollywood's Walk of Fame, in front of Mann's Chinese Theater. The following year, on July 23, 1985, he was the first reporter to write about Rock Hudson's battle with AIDS. "The whispering campaign on Rock Hudson can and should stop. He has flown to Paris for further help. The Institute Pasteur has been very active in research on Acquired Immune Deficiency Syndrome. Hudson's dramatic weight loss was made evident to the national press last week when he winged to Carmel to help longtime friend Doris Day launch her new pet series. His illness was no secret to close Hollywood friends, but its true nature was divulged to very, very few. Doctors warn that the dread disease is going to reach catastrophic proportions in all communities if a cure is not soon found," he wrote. Hudson's handlers tried to discredit Archerd but his story was on the money. In 1995 the Jewish Archerd forced Michael Jackson to change the anti-Semitic lyrics of the song 'They Don't Care About Us'. In 1999 Archerd was critical of the honorary Oscar that was given to director Elia Kazan. Archerd wrote his last column for *Variety* on September 1, 2005. In 1944 he married Joan and had two children, a son Evan and a daughter, Amanda Falk, who died in 2008 after running a marathon. The marriage ended in divorce and he married actress Selma Fenning (b. Newark, New Jersey February 26, 1925) on November 15, 1969.

CAUSE: Archerd died aged 90 (like so many denizens of Hollywood, he was not averse to knocking a few years off his age) in Los Angeles. He collapsed at his home on the afternoon of September 7 and was taken to Ronald Reagan UCLA Medical Center where he died the next day at 2pm. He had been suffering from a rare form of mesothelioma cancer since 2004, thought to be the result of his exposure to asbestos in the navy during the Second World War.

Eve Arden

(EUNICE QUEDENS)
Born April 30, 1908
Died November 12, 1990
Queen of the caustic crack. Born in Mill Valley, California, the daughter of a one-time actress, Eve Arden was educated at Mill Valley Grammar School and Tamalpais High School. Like many, she began her career on the stage, joining the Henry Duffy Stock Company at San Francisco's Alcazar Theater for 18 months. On January 4, 1934, she made her first appearance on Broadway at the Winter Garden in *The Ziegfeld Follies*. She had made her film début as Maisie in *Song Of Love* (1929), credited under her real name, Eunice Quedens, and went on to appear in almost 60 movies. She took the name 'Eve Arden' after seeing the names 'Evening In Paris' and 'Elizabeth Arden' on the make-up counter in a shop. Her early films included *Oh Doctor* (1937) as Shirley Truman, *Stage Door* (1937) as Eve (the film that originally made her. She wore a live cat as a fur and her lines were written during shooting), *Cocoanut Grove* (1938) as Sophie De Lemma, *Eternally Yours* (1939) as Gloria, *Big Town Czar* (1939) as Susan Warren, *No, No, Nanette* (1940) as Winnie, *Comrade X* (1940) as Jane Wilson, *She Knew All The Answers* (1941) as Sally Long and *Obliging Young Lady* (1941) as 'Space' O'Shea. It was for her portrayal of Ida in *Mildred Pierce* (1945) that she was nominated for an Oscar. Arden was confident enough in her abilities to play unsympathetic roles, including Paula in *The Unfaithful* (1947) and Olive Lashbrooke in *The Voice Of The Turtle* (1947). She opined: "If you're confident before you attain fame, then you're okay. Don't care *too* much what people think . . . If you're not happy or not confident before you're known, then no amount of fame or money will bestow instant happiness or self-confidence." In 1948 she began appearing as schoolteacher Connie

Brooks in the radio show *Our Miss Brooks* before it transferred to television on October 3, 1952. On February 11, 1954, she won an Emmy for her work and spent much of the Fifties appearing on the small screen, including *The Eve Arden Show*. She made the occasional foray into films in the Fifties, Sixties, Seventies and Eighties, including *We're Not Married!* (1952) as Katie Woodruff, *Anatomy Of A Murder* (1959) as Maida, *Sergeant Deadhead* (1965) as Lieutenant Charlotte Kinsey, *Grease* (1978) as Principal McGee, *Pandemonium* (1982) as Warden June and *Grease 2* (1982), reprising her role as Principal McGee. In June 1939 she married literary agent Edward Bergen and adopted a daughter, Liza, in 1944. Three years later, on July 27, 1947, they divorced. Single parent Arden adopted a second daughter, Connie, also in 1947. In August 1951 she married actor Brooks West (1915–1984) and in the summer of 1952 adopted Duncan Paris. Their son, Douglas Brooks, was born in September 1953. The couple was happily married for 32 years until West's death on February 7, 1984. It was Arden who told Joan Crawford how to go about adopting children. CAUSE: She died of cardiac arrest and arteriosclerotic heart disease aged 82 at her home, 9066 St Ives Drive, Los Angeles, California 90069. She was cremated and her ashes buried at Westwood Memorial Park, 1218 Glendon Avenue, Los Angeles, California 90024 on November 15, 1990.

Richard Arlen

(CORNELIUS RICHARD VAN MATTIMORE)
Born September 1, 1898
Died March 28, 1976
One of the first. Born in Charlottesville, Virginia, after the University of Pennsylvania, 5'11" Arlen began his career as a pilot with the Royal Canadian Flying Corps and then

became a messenger working for a film laboratory. After a lucky escape in a car accident he came to the attention of Hollywood and he was signed by Paramount Pictures as an extra. His role as the volatile and tragic pilot David Armstrong in *Wings* (1927) won him rave reviews. It also won the film the first Best Picture Oscar, the only silent feature ever to do so. Arlen was never to achieve such dizzy heights again but became a steady, if unexciting, support player. His films included *Sally In Our Alley* (1927) as Jimmie Adams, *Under The Tonto Rim* 1928) as Edd Denmeade, *Manhattan Cocktail* (1928) as Fred Tilden, *Thunderbolt* (1929) as Bob Morgan, *The Virginian* (1929) as Steve, *Dangerous Paradise* (1930) as Heyst, *The Santa Fe Trail* (1930) as Stan Hollister, *Three-Cornered Moon* (1933) as Dr Alan Stevens, *Alice In Wonderland* (1933) as the Cheshire Cat, *Mutiny On The Blackhawk* (1939) as Captain Robert Lawrence, *Mutiny In The Arctic* (1941) as Dick Barclay, *Wildcat* (1942) as Johnny Maverick, *Buffalo Bill Rides Again* (1947) as Buffalo Bill Cody, *Sex And The College Girl* (1964), *Apache Uprising* (1966) as Captain Gannon and *Won Ton Ton, The Dog Who Saved Hollywood* (1976). He married Ruth Austin in 1923 and had a daughter, Rosemarie. His second wife was his *Wings* co-star Jobyna Ralston (b. November 24, 1902, d. January 22, 1967) on January 28, 1927 at the Mission Inn, Riverside, California. Their son, Richard Ralston Mattimore, was born in Los Angeles on May 18, 1933. The couple was divorced in Los Angeles on September 5, 1945. His third wife was Margaret Kinsella. CAUSE: He died of emphysema aged 77 in North Hollywood, California.

Arletty

(ARLETTE-LÉONIE MARIE JULIE BATHIAT)
Born May 15, 1898
Died July 24, 1992
Latecomer. Born in Courbevoie,

Hauts-de-Seine, France, the daughter of a miner, Arlette-Léonie left school aged 13 to work in a munitions factory. She went on to become a model (for Matisse and Braque) and chorus girl. Following the death of her lover in World War I, she became a devout pacifist. She came to cinema relatively late. She was in her early thirties when she first appeared in front of the cameras and knocking 40 when she played the prostitute Raymonde in Marcel Carné's *Hôtel Du Nord* (1938). Her name was made playing the courtesan Garance in Carné's *Les Enfants Du Paradis* (1945). However, her star was soured when it was revealed she had slept with a German Luftwaffe officer during the Second World War. "My heart is French but my arse is international," she was reputed to have said in mitigation. Her head was shaved and she spent four months in Fresnes prison for collaboration following her trial in Algiers in 1944. In December of that year she was placed under house arrest for two years and was forbidden from working for three years. An accident in 1963 gradually wrecked her eyesight (she went blind in 1966) and her last film was *Les Petits Matins* (1962). CAUSE: She died in Paris aged 94 from natural causes.

George Arliss

(GEORGE AUGUSTUS ANDREWS)
Born April 10, 1868
Died February 5, 1946
'The first gentleman of the talking screen.' Born in London, the son of a printer and publisher, he first appeared on stage at the Elephant and Castle Theatre in September 1886. In 1901 he went to America with Mrs Patrick Campbell and played to great acclaim. He made his film début in *The Devil* (1921) playing Dr Muller and followed that up with his portrayal of the dandy Prime Minister, *Disraeli* (1921), a role he had played on stage. His co-star was his wife, Florence Montgomery Arliss

(b. 1871, d. March 11, 1950), and he reprised the part in a talkie version in 1929, a film that won him a Best Actor Oscar, although he didn't turn up to collect his statuette in person. He was on holiday in France but knew he had won because the Academy had asked him to pose for celebratory pictures on November 3, 1930, two days before the prize-giving. He tended to play great men on stage and reprise them on film and his roles included the leads in *Alexander Hamilton* (1931) and *Voltaire* (1933), the Duke of Wellington in *The Iron Duke* (1934) and the title role in *Cardinal Richelieu* (1935). He was nominated for another Best Actor Oscar for *The Green Goddess* (1930), a remake of his 1923 film. His contract at Warner Bros stipulated that he did not have to work after 4.30pm. The 5'9" Arliss retired from movie making in 1937 when his wife (whom he married at Harrow Weald on September 16, 1899) went blind. Contrary to several reference books, the director Leslie Arliss was not their son.
CAUSE: He died in London aged 77 of a bronchial ailment. He left an estate valued at £136,000.

Pedro Armendáriz

(PEDRO GREGORIO ARMENDÁRIZ HASTINGS)
Born May 9, 1912
Died June 18, 1963
Mr Swarthy. Born in Churubusco, Mexico, the son of a Mexican man and an American woman (who both died in 1921), the family moved to Laredo, Texas. Armendáriz was educated at the Polytechnic Institute of San Luis Obispo, California, where he read journalism and business studies. Back in Mexico City, he found work as a tourist guide, insurance salesman and on the railways. Bizarrely, his big break came when director Miguel Zacarias spotted him declaiming Hamlet's "To be or not to be" soliloquy to a tourist. He rapidly became a massive star in Mexico and was much in demand

north of the border as well. Among his films were *Rosario* (1936), *María Elena* (1936) as Eduardo, *El Indio* (1939), *Simón Bolívar* (1940), *Ni Sangre, Ni Arena* (1941), *Guadalajara* (1943) as Pedro, *María Candelaria* (1944) as Lorenzo Rafael, *Enamorada* (1946) as General José Juan Reyes, *Fort Apache* (1948) as Sergeant Beaufort, *Three Godfathers* (1948) as 'Pete' Pedro Roca Fuerte, *Vuelve Pancho Villa* (1950) as Pancho Villa, *Lucrèce Borgia* (1953) as César Borgia, *The Big Boodle* (1957) as Colonel Mastegui and *Captain Sinbad* (1963) as El Kerim. One film he would regret making was *The Conqueror* (1956) in which he played Jamuga. The film starred his close friend John Wayne as an unintentionally hilarious Genghis Khan. During filming his horse stumbled and threw Armendáriz, who broke his jaw. The long-term consequences were to be even more horrific. He married Carmelita Bohr on June 19, 1938, and their son is the actor Pedro Armendáriz, Jr.
CAUSE: He had been diagnosed with cancer some time after working on the Howard Hughes film *The Conqueror* (1956) – in fact, an inordinately large number (around half) of cast and crew were stricken with the disease. The movie had been shot in St George, Utah, near the site of atom bomb tests. At the start of 1963 Armendáriz was diagnosed with lymph cancer and his scenes as Karim Bey in the Bond film *From Russia With Love* (1964) were completed at breakneck speed. In June 1963, 51-year-old Armendáriz was admitted to Los Angeles' UCLA Medical Center with neck cancer. On the 18th he shot himself through the heart with a gun he had brought with him to the hospital.

Billy Armstrong

Born January 14, 1891
Died March 1, 1924
Bristolian comedian. Armstrong was among the first English comedians to travel to America with Fred Karno and

in 1915 signed with the Essanay Studios. He appeared in *The Bank* (1915) and *By The Sea* (1915). At the end of the year he joined Cub Comedies where he starred in *The Twin Trunk Mystery* (1916). He then joined Mack Sennett to appear in *Black Eyes And Blue* (1916). He also worked with Oliver Hardy and Harry Langdon. He was married to the actress Marion Parker who died in November 1920. CAUSE: Armstrong died aged 33 in Sunland, California.

Desi Arnaz
(DESIDERIO ALBERTO ARNAZ Y DE ACHA III)
Born March 2, 1917
Died December 2, 1986
Mr Lucy. Born in Santiago, Cuba, the scion of a wealthy family Arnaz arrived in America aged 16 and broke because of the Battista revolution in Cuba. He was a talented musician and soon had his own band. In 1940 he made his film début in *Too Many Girls* (1940) and also married his co-star Lucille Ball. He was to make only ten films but gained immortality as the male lead of the *I Love Lucy* television show and co-founder of the Desilu Studios. CAUSE: He died in Del Mar, California, aged 69, of lung cancer. He was cremated.

Peter Arne
(PETER ALBRECHT)
Born September 29, 1918
Died August 1, 1983
Suavey. Peter Arne was one of those rare actors who never really made it to stardom although he was rarely short of work. Born in Kuala Lumpur, Arne began his acting career in the theatre in 1937. During World War II he became a fighter pilot and was shot down over the Channel. As he swam ashore he was greeted with shouts from scores of people on the shore who had watched the dogfight. Thinking they were lauding him as a hero, he was later horrified to find out the crowd were

trying to warn him that he was swimming through a minefield. After the war Peter Arne appeared in more than 50 films, including *Ice Cold In Alex* (1957), *Khartoum* (1966), *Chitty Chitty Bang Bang* (1968), *Straw Dogs* (1971), *Antony & Cleopatra* (1972), *Return Of The Pink Panther* (1975) and *Victor/Victoria* (1982). On television he worked on *The Avengers, Man In A Suitcase, The Saint, To Serve Them All My Days* and *Secret Army*. Like many actors Peter Arne was a homosexual and, like many homosexuals, he was a witty raconteur much in demand at society parties. However, Arne was ashamed of his sexuality and sought to hide it. He dared not venture to gay clubs lest he be recognised and publicly exposed. In order to find sexual partners Arne would dress as a tramp and hang around the arches of London's Charing Cross and Victoria Embankment. If he met some vagrant who took his fancy he would invite the man to his home, offer him a bath and a meal and then suggest sex. Arne's flat in Hans Place, Knightsbridge, was decorated with art deco glassware and other antiques, a subject on which he was well versed.
CAUSE: On July 29, 1983, Arne made himself up, donned his tramp's rags and set out for Victoria Embankment. There he met Tom Jackson, a 24-year-old Nottingham man and, discovering he was homeless, Arne took Jackson to Hans Place. There the vagrant took a bath and ate a meal but Arne made no sexual approaches. The next night Arne stayed in with Jackson and the two men chatted. Again, Arne did not make any advances. On July 31 Arne made his move and Jackson allowed himself to be seduced. The next day Jackson went to sign on and gave Arne's flat as his address. Arne had recently achieved one of his dearest ambitions, to appear in *Dr Who*. That morning, after going to the dole office himself, Arne went for costume fittings. He had arranged to meet Jackson at the

flat at 2pm. Arne returned to the flat early – at 12.30. Sometime during the next 80 minutes Peter Arne was murdered. At 1.50pm neighbours heard what was later described as "a commotion" although none of them thought to go and investigate. Jackson arrived back at 2pm and rang the doorbell but was unable to elicit a reply. He waited outside, occasionally going to a telephone and ringing Arne's number. Just before 4pm a maid from an upstairs flat discovered a bloodstained log in the communal hall and summoned the police. Jackson was still waiting outside when the police arrived and he was arrested. Forty-eight hours later, he was released. Police discovered Arne's bloody, beaten body just inside the door of his flat. He had been savagely attacked with a log from his own fireplace. The flat was not ransacked and none of Arne's valuable antiques were missing. Police assumed that Arne had been murdered by a former boyfriend. Three days later, the body of one of Arne's ex-boyfriends, 32-year-old Giuseppe Perusi, was found floating in the Thames. It is only supposition – Arne's murder is still unsolved – but a theory holds that Arne was murdered by Perusi after a sex act and then the Italian committed suicide. Another theory has it that Arne's interest in antiques had led him to be unwittingly caught in an international smuggling operation that led to the deaths of a Milanese cocaine dealer and Jeanette May, an Englishwoman who disappeared in Italy in 1980. Whoever killed him robbed the acting profession of a fine professional, society of a witty raconteur and Peter Arne of his most treasured ambition and his life. A waste.

Cecile Arnold
(CECILE LAVAL ARNOUX)
Born April 1891
Died 1931
Keystone supporting actor. Born in New York to a French father and American mother she worked alongside Charlie Chaplin, although a claim that she also worked with Fatty Arbuckle cannot be substantiated. She made her début in *Such A Cook* (1914) and the following year she began to appear in Keystone films but her career came to an end in 1917 after she holidayed in Honolulu. She then travelled to China where she met her future husband, a British banker. A son was later born in America but she preferred to live in the Far East.
CAUSE: She died of the flu while visiting Hong Kong. She was 40.

Dorothy Arnold
(DOROTHY ARNOLDINE OLSON)
Born November 21, 1917
Died November 13, 1984
The first Mrs Joe DiMaggio. It must be bad enough to lose your husband to another woman, but when the other woman is Marilyn Monroe it must be doubly distressing. Born in Duluth, Minnesota, her father worked for the local railway and she had three sisters. 5'5" Dorothy Arnold was an athletic blonde who wanted to become a big star. She appeared in a few productions at Denfield High School in Duluth and when she left education at the age of 15 she joined a travelling theatre troupe. Yet a life on the road was not the glamorous show business life she expected and she returned home but her ambitions remained undiminished. By the age of 17, she was living in New York, eking out an existence as a singer. Spotted by a talent scout she was signed to Universal Pictures on a small retainer. She was to tell reporters that she fell in love with 6'2" Joe DiMaggio (b. Martinez, California, November 25, 1914) in August 1937 on the set of *Manhattan Merry-Go-Round* (1937) "before I even knew who he was". However, many close to her believe she knew exactly who the world's biggest baseball star was and set her cap at him, knowing

that an association with him would help with her own cinematic ambitions. Dorothy announced their betrothal on April 25, 1939, at a press conference where reporters noticed the absence of a ring on the third finger of her left hand. She explained, "Oh, I haven't got a ring or anything. It's just understood between Joe and me. We'll get married this summer and go on holiday after the baseball season." In fact, although DiMaggio had popped the question, he had not even thought about a date let alone a honeymoon and knew nothing of the announcement. He confirmed the engagement but denied that he would be married that summer. To Dorothy's disappointment Universal did not capitalise on her fame or rather her boyfriend's fame by putting her in big pictures. She played a barmaid in *The Storm* (1938), a secretary in *Secrets Of A Nurse* (1938), both films starring Edmund Lowe. She played the lead, Jean Drew, in *The Phantom Creeps* (1939) but it did not set the box office alight and no print remains. She appeared in *Risky Business* (1939), *Gambling Ship* (1939), *Pirates Of The Skies* (1939) and *You Can't Cheat An Honest Man* (1939) but did not receive on-screen billing in any of them. A Universal executive commented, "She isn't anybody special. To tell you the truth, we doubt if she ever will be." Dorothy made four more films in that momentous year of 1939: *The Family Next Door*, *The House Of Fear*, *Unexpected Father* and *Hero For A Day*. On Sunday, November 19, 1939, two days before her 22nd birthday and after she had converted to Catholicism, she married DiMaggio at the Church of St Peter and St Paul in San Francisco. Huge crowds thronged the streets around the church to see the sporting hero and his bride. The mayor placed plain-clothes policemen among the congregation to ensure their safety and the church doors were locked early resulting in Vince DiMaggio almost missing his brother's wedding. The

ceremony began 30 minutes behind schedule. The guests ate and quaffed $1,500 worth of food and drink at the reception. However, DiMaggio had been used to being pampered by his mother and five sisters and expected his new wife to be subordinate to his whims and his career. Dorothy insisted they move to New York whereas he preferred San Francisco. In New York he preferred nights out with the boys to nights in with his wife. Like many couples on the verge of splitting, the DiMaggios thought that perhaps a baby might bring them closer together. Their only child, Joseph Paul DiMaggio, Jr was born on October 23, 1941, in San Francisco. Within a year Dorothy had moved to Reno, Nevada, with her young son to establish residency rights and file for divorce. On January 13, 1943, the couple attempted a reconciliation and on February 17, DiMaggio joined the military (he was discharged on September 14, 1945, having never fired a shot in anger). On October 11, 1943, Dorothy filed for divorce in Los Angeles, charging her husband with cruelty. The marriage ended in 1944 but DiMaggio carried a torch for his ex-wife. That torch was extinguished two years later when she married New York stockbroker, George Schubert. That same year DiMaggio had a poor season and his team mates put it down to him pining for his ex-wife. In 1950 the Schuberts were divorced and Dorothy spent that Christmas with her son and Joe DiMaggio in a ski chalet in Reno. In 1951, Dorothy told gossip columnist Hedda Hopper that "just between us, I am thinking of getting back with Joe". On December 2, 1951, DiMaggio announced his retirement from professional baseball. But the possible reconciliation was scuppered when DiMaggio met the world's greatest sex symbol of all time. Their first date was at a restaurant called The Villa Nova on Sunset Boulevard in March, 1952. When DiMaggio's romance with

Marilyn Monroe became serious, Arnold began to badmouth him to the media claiming that he was a bad father who was exposing his son to unsuitable people and places. However, naturally, she insisted that she was only speaking out for everyone's benefit and not, heaven forbid, because she was a woman scorned. DiMaggio hit back by claiming that his ex-wife was spending some of the child support payments on herself. The matter could only be settled in court and on October 16, 1952, Judge Elmer Doyle in Los Angeles found for DiMaggio and even told Dorothy she had been foolish to divorce the ball player eight years earlier. DiMaggio married Monroe on January 14, 1954, at San Francisco Town Hall but the match was punctuated with violence and the couple separated after nine months. Dorothy married again (to Gary Peck) and in 1957 made another film *Lizzie* but her career and her life in the spotlight were over. Joe DiMaggio outlived his first wife by 15 years, dying of lung cancer in Hollywood, Florida, on March 8, 1999. Joe Jr married Sue Adams, an attractive divorcée with two daughters, but the couple divorced in 1974 after Joe became involved with drugs and beat up his wife. In 1976 a car accident resulted in surgery to remove a blood clot from his brain. The operation saved his life but left him short-tempered. He found it difficult to live in his father's shadow and the two men were estranged at the elder DiMaggio's death, not least due to the younger DiMaggio's continued closeness to Monroe after Joe Sr fell out with her. DiMaggio Sr left his son just a $20,000 annual trust while leaving the two girls he regarded as his granddaughters much more. Five months after his father died, Joe DiMaggio Jr died on August 6, 1999 in a hospital in Antioch, northern California. A hospital spokesman ascribed the death to natural causes. CAUSE: She died in Palm Springs eight days before her 67th birthday. She had been suffering from cancer.

Jean Arthur
(GLADYS GEORGIANNA GREENE)
Born October 17, 1900
Died June 19, 1991
Reclusive star. Jean Arthur guarded her privacy so well she made Greta Garbo look like the life and soul of the party. Like Garbo, she, too, was lesbian. Born in Plattsburgh, upstate New York, about 20 miles south of the American-Canadian border, the brown-haired, blue-eyed daughter of a photographer, Arthur grew up in Manhattan. A stint as a teenage model led the 5'2" Arthur to film work and an appearance in *Somebody Lied* (1923) and John Ford's *Cameo Kirby* (1923) as Ann Playdell. Arthur appeared in over 20 silent films, including *The Temple Of Venus* (1923), *Case Dismissed* (1924), *Wine Of Youth* (1924), *Biff Bang Buddy* (1924) as Bonnie Norton, *Bringin' Home The Bacon* (1924) as Nancy Norton, *The Drug Store Cowboy* (1925) as Jean, *Thundering Through* (1925) as Ruth Burroughs and *Born To Battle* (1926) as Eunice Morgan, but never seemed to show any real star potential. In 1927 she signed to Paramount, where she began an affair with producer David O. Selznick. She appeared in *Warming Up* (1928) as Mary Post, *Brotherly Love* (1928) as Mary, *Sins Of The Fathers* (1928) as Mary Spengler, *The Mysterious Dr Fu Manchu* (1929) as Lia Eltham, *The Greene Murder Case* (1929) as Ada Greene, *Halfway To Heaven* (1929) as Greta Nelson and *The Return Of Dr Fu Manchu* (1930) reprising her portrayal of Lia Eltham. In 1928 she married photographer Julian Anker but the marriage lasted just one day – it was annulled when Arthur claimed her studio contract forbade any match. In April 1931 she was dropped by Paramount and returned to the stage. On June 11, 1932, she married singer (later producer) Frank Ross, Jr. They

divorced on March 14, 1949. (Ross then married Joan Caulfield who, by a bizarre coincidence, died on the same day as Jean Arthur.) Later (1933) she signed with Columbia and appeared in *Whirlpool* (1934) as Sandra Morrison, *The Defense Rests* (1934) as Joan Hayes, *If You Could Only Cook* (1935) as Joan Hawthorne, Frank Capra's *Mr Deeds Goes To Town* (1936) as Babe Bennett, Cecil B. DeMille's *The Plainsman* (1936) as Calamity Jane, *History Is Made At Night* (1937) as Irene Vail and Capra's *Mr Smith Goes To Washington* (1939) as Clarissa Saunders. Capra admitted she was his favourite actress but said of her: "You can't get her in front of the camera without her crying, whining, vomiting, all that shit she does. But when she does get in front of the camera, and you turn on the lights – wow! All of that disappears and out comes a strong-minded woman. Then, when she finished the scene, she runs back to the dressing room and hides." She also had a reputation for being difficult with her co-stars and insisted her face was only ever shot from the right side. "I am not an adult. Except when I am actually working on the set, I have all the inhibitions and shyness of the bashful, backward child." On December 17, 1938, she screen-tested, unsuccessfully, for the part of Scarlett O'Hara in *Gone With The Wind* (1939). During the early war years she appeared in *Arizona* (1940) as Phoebe Titus, *The Devil And Miss Jones* (1941) as Mary Jones, *The Talk Of The Town* (1942) as Nora Shelley, *The More The Merrier* (1943) as Connie Milligan, for which she was nominated for a Best Supporting Actress Oscar (losing out to Jennifer Jones for *The Song Of Bernadette* [1943]), and *The Impatient Years* (1944) as Janice Anderson before jettisoning Hollywood for a second time. When her contract with Columbia ended she ran through the streets yelling, "I'm free! I'm free!" She returned to the stage and made just two more films before leaving Hollywood

for good. She was Phoebe Frost in Billy Wilder's *A Foreign Affair* (1948) and Marian Starrett in George Stevens' *Shane* (1953). From September 12 until December 5, 1966, she appeared on television in the CBS sitcom *The Jean Arthur Show* playing Patricia Marshall, the best defence lawyer in town. She never returned to the big screen and rarely talked about her previous life. "I hated [Hollywood] – not the work, but the lack of privacy, those terrible prying fan magazine writers and all the surrounding exploitation." When asked by one television station for an interview, she replied, "Quite frankly, I'd rather have my throat slit." She taught drama at Vassar from 1968 until 1972 and other colleges.
CAUSE: In 1989 she suffered a stroke that invalided her. She died in Carmel Convalescent Hospital, Carmel, California, of heart failure aged 90. No funeral service was held, at her own request, and she was cremated. Her ashes were sprinkled at sea off Point Lobos, California.

Johnny Arthur

(JOHN LENNOX ARTHUR WILLIAMS)
Born May 20, 1883
Died New Year's Eve, 1951
Whiny comic. Born in Scottsdale, Philadelphia, 5'8" Johnny Arthur began his career in the theatre playing opposite Lou Tellegen before he moved to the silver screen where he was best known for his appearances in the 'Tuxedo' comedies made by Educational in the Twenties. He later appeared as a harassed father in Hal Roach's *Our Gang* series. He also had a role in the first of the Crosby-Hope *Road To . . .* films.
CAUSE: Arthur died of heart disease in Woodland Hills, California. He was 68.

Dorothy Arzner

Born January 3, 1897
Died October 1, 1979
The premier female director. Born,

appropriately enough, in San Francisco the daughter of the owner of the Hoffman Café in Hollywood. It was patronised by Charlie Chaplin, D.W. Griffith, Hal Roach, Mack Sennett and Erich Von Stroheim. Arzner was educated at Westlake School for Girls and then attended, but never graduated from, the University of Southern California, where she studied medicine. During World War I she drove ambulances and then worked in newspapers. She landed a job as a typist at Paramount in 1919 and worked her way up to cutter, editor (in one year she edited 32 films, including *Blood And Sand* [1922] starring Rudolph Valentino) and assistant director before becoming a director. She was only allowed to direct after continually threatening to resign. Her films included *Get Your Man* (1927) starring Clara Bow, *Cocktail* (1928) the first talkie directed by a woman, *The Wild Party* (1929) also starring Clara Bow, *Sarah And Son* (1930) with Ruth Chatterton and *Merrily We Go To Hell* (1932) starring Frederic March and Sylvia Sidney. She had a clause in her contract stating that she would not have to attend meetings on arch philanderer Harry Cohn's yacht. Arzner left Paramount to work in the freelance sector, directing Katharine Hepburn in *Christopher Strong* (1933) and Joan Crawford in *The Bride Wore Red* (1937). The first woman elected to the Directors' Guild of America (an organisation she helped to found in 1936), Arzner retired early (1943) of her own volition ("The true reason I retired from Hollywood may forever remain a secret, and I'd rather it does," she said in a 1978 interview) and taught at the University of California at Los Angeles. One of her students was Francis Ford Coppola. "When you direct, you're learning. When you're a teacher, you impart learning. This helps me feel more serene," she once said. "Directing, I always had people at my back. In the classroom, I have

people in front of me, bright, eager pupils . . . The press can't trivialise teaching. With motion pictures, they tried to reduce your accomplishments to what star you worked with . . . I didn't want to be known just for making Clara Bow a star." She also directed over 50 Pepsi Cola advertisements for her friend Joan Crawford. Arzner, who stood 5'4", was a lesbian. Gay director George Cukor commented: "She was too tough for Hollywood. Most of her movies were hits, which is a track record Hollywood loves. But she didn't modify her ways or looks or manner. As a woman directing movies, she was looked on by most as a freak. And as *that* kind of woman, they found her less and less acceptable. They didn't want her inside their golden boys' club." Arzner moved in an almost exclusively sapphic circle that included her lover Alla Nazimova and Dolly Wilde (niece of Oscar, the only member of the family to sleep with women, it was jested).
CAUSE: She died of natural causes aged 82 in La Quinta, California.

Dame Peggy Ashcroft
Born December 22, 1907
Died June 14, 1991
Theatrical *grande dame*. Born in Croydon as Edith Margaret Emily Ashcroft, the second child of land agent William Worsley Ashcroft, she was educated at Woodford School, Croydon (the town's Ashcroft Theatre was named after her in 1962) and the Central School of Dramatic Arts. There she studied under Elsie Fogerty and earned a Diploma in Dramatic Art from the University of London. On May 22, 1926, she made her stage début playing Margaret in J. M. Barrie's *Dear Brutus* and a year later made her first appearance in London as Bessie in Joseph Conrad's *One Day More* at the Playroom Six. She rarely stopped working (except through choice or ill-health) until her death, on stage, in films and on television. Sir

John Gielgud admiringly said of her: "She can be enchantingly feminine yet turn and play monstrous, villainous people, parts you wouldn't think her right for." In May 1930 she caused a sensation playing Desdemona opposite Paul Robeson in *Othello* at the Savoy Theatre. She was asked by one journalist if she minded kissing a 'coloured' man. She told the hack it was a 'privilege' to work with a 'great artist' like Robeson; the journalist can have little suspected that the leading man and lady were in the throes of a passionate affair that resulted in the beginning of the end of Ashcroft's first marriage. She made her first foray into films in 1933 playing Olalla Quintana in *The Wandering Jew* and followed that up with just 15 movies including *The 39 Steps* (1935) as Mrs Crofter, *Rhodes Of Africa* (1936) as Anna Carpenter, *The Nun's Story* (1958) as Mother Mathilde, *Three Into Two Won't Go* (1969) as Belle, *Sunday, Bloody Sunday* (1971) as Mrs Greville, *A Passage To India* (1985) as Mrs Moore, a role that won her a Best Supporting Actress Oscar (although she was in bed with the flu at the time and didn't attend the ceremony), *Madame Sousatzka* (1989) and *She's Been Away* (1989) as Lillian Huckle. She also shone on television in 1984 as Barbie Batchelor in Granada TV's *The Jewel In The Crown*. In 1956 Ashcroft became a Dame Commander of the British Empire. She recalled: "When they asked Judith Anderson how becoming a dame had changed her life, she said she found she wore gloves more often . . . I'm surprised she takes it so lightly – it's a great honour, though I still don't like the word 'dame' when it's pronounced by an American." Ashcroft, a Labour party and CND supporter (Binkie Beaumont nicknamed her 'The Red Dame'), was a private individual who much preferred to let her work speak for itself. A journalist once asked her to imagine speaking to the public at a tea table. "But I wouldn't have the public to tea," was her response. Ashcroft married three times. Her first husband was publisher (Sir) Rupert Hart-Davis, whom she married on December 23, 1929, at Saviour's Church, Chelsea. They divorced in the summer of 1933. Five months later, she married theatre producer Theodore Komisarjevsky (b. Venice, May 23, 1882, d. Darien, Connecticut, April 17, 1954). He left her for a young American dancer and the couple was divorced in London on June 15, 1937. Her third and final husband was barrister Jeremy Hutchinson (now Baron Hutchinson of Lullington, QC), whom she married on September 14, 1940, at Marylebone Registry Office. On June 14, 1941, she gave birth to daughter Eliza and at Welbeck Street, London, on May 3, 1946, to son Nicholas, now a stage director. In December 1965 they were divorced on the grounds of adultery.

CAUSE: Towards the end of her life Peggy Ashcroft suffered from depression, perhaps exacerbated by a rift with her daughter. On May 23, 1991, she suffered a severe stroke and was admitted to the Royal Free Hospital, north London, in a coma. She never regained consciousness and died there, aged 83. Shortly before her death she had sold (for £1.1 million to publisher Tom Maschler) the house (Manor Lodge, 40 Frognall Lane, Hampstead, London NW3) she lived in for 40 years and moved to a small flat in Belsize Park (Flat 14, 9–11 Belsize Grove, London NW3). Her funeral was a private affair. Bizarrely, no record exists of her will. It was thought she left £900,000 although to whom is an enduring mystery.

FURTHER READING: *Peggy Ashcroft* – Michael Billington (London: John Murray, 1988); *The Secret Woman: A Life Of Peggy Ashcroft* – Garry O'Connor (London: Weidenfeld & Nicolson, 1997).

Ted Ashley

(THEODORE ASSOFSKY)
Born August 3, 1922
Died August 24, 2002
The new Warner brother. It was the business and cultural acumen of Ted Ashley that made Warner Bros the place to work during the Seventies. Born in Brooklyn, Ashley left school at 15 and joined the William Morris Agency. By night he studied business administration and later started his own agency, the Ashley Famous Agency, with clients such as Perry Como, Arthur Miller and Tennessee Williams. The agency was also responsible for television series such as *Mission: Impossible, Tarzan* and *Get Smart*. In 1969 Ashley became chief executive of Warner Bros and within weeks had sacked 17 of the 21 executives. It was due to Ashley that *Roots*, Alex Haley's fictionalised version of his family's struggle to escape slavery, was made. His successes on the big screen included *A Clockwork Orange* (1971), *The Exorcist* (1973), *Blazing Saddles* (1974) and *Superman* (1978). Ashley avoided giving interviews, didn't mix with the people he made stars and spent his time reading material that he thought would make good films. He was married with four daughters.
CAUSE: He died aged 80 of acute leukaemia.

Arthur Askey, CBE

Born June 6, 1900
Died November 16, 1982
Big-hearted Arthur. Born at 29 Moses Street, Liverpool, Arthur Bowden Askey was a diminutive (5'3") Scouser who could do it all – sing, dance, and tell jokes. As a boy, he sang in the church choir and was chosen to perform a solo when the Archbishops of Canterbury and York visited Liverpool Cathedral. One year the family holidayed in Rhyl, North Wales, where a pierrot troupe, The Jovial Sisters, performed daily on the sands. Young Arthur went along to the performances religiously and by the

end of the vacation knew the act verbatim. At 16 he began his working life as a clerk at Liverpool education offices, earning £10 per month. With the outbreak of war he sang to entertain the troops, most often solo although occasionally he duetted with Tommy Handley. In June 1918 he became a private in the Welch Regiment but was demobilised almost immediately at the end of hostilities in November. He returned to his desk at the education office until 1924 when he made his professional début in the Song Salad touring concert party from the Electric Theatre, Colchester. He was paid £6 10s. a week for the 30-week engagement. He moved into radio in 1932, though it wasn't until *Band Waggon* six years later that he became a massive star. First broadcast on January 5, 1938, the show was not an immediate success and the original commission of 12 shows was cut to six. After show four Askey said that if he was the 'resident comedian' he should live on the premises and so he and sidekick Richard Murdoch were installed in an imaginary flat at the top of Broadcasting House with a goat called Lewis and Lucy and Basil, two pigeons. For a period, a camel called Hector even lived with the motley crew. The goat was introduced because it was thought too far to go down seven floors just to collect the milk. This led to the joke: "A goat in the flat? What about the smell?" "Oh, he'll get used to it." By show six, *Band Waggon* was so successful that the run was extended to 18 weeks. It spawned a number of catch-phrases, including Askey's "I thank you", pronounced "Aye-thang-yu", which he picked up from a London bus conductor; "Doesn't it make you want to spit" (BBC Director-General Sir John [later Lord] Reith hated this 'vulgar' expression and told Askey not to include it but he [Askey] was so popular he ignored the directive and used the phrase all the more frequently);

"Here and now, before your very eyes" and "Oh, don't be filthy". It was BBC policy to refuse to credit the writers because they wanted listeners to believe Askey and Murdoch made it all up. The show finished when Murdoch was drafted into the Air Force. Askey made his film début two years before the outbreak of hostilities in *Calling All Stars* (1937) and followed that up with *Band Waggon* (1939), *Charley's Big-Hearted Aunt* (1940), *The Ghost Train* (1941), *I Thank You* (1941), *Back Room Boy* (1942), *King Arthur Was A Gentleman* (1942), *The Nose Has It* (1942), *Miss London Limited* (1943), *Bees In Paradise* (1944), *The Love Match* (1954), *Ramsbottom Rides Again* (1956), *Make Mine A Million* (1958), *Friends And Neighbours* (1959), *The Alf Garnett Saga* (1972) and *End Of Term* (1977). Askey had moved into television following WWII and had a new series every year from 1953. In 1954 he co-starred with David Nixon in *Hello Playmates*, written by Bob Monkhouse and Denis Goodwin. Askey was equally famous for his silly songs 'The Seagull', 'The Worm' and, the best known, 'The Bee'. He featured in a remarkable ten Royal Variety Performances – 1946, 1948, 1952, 1954, 1955, 1957, 1968, 1972, 1978 and 1980 – and remains one of the few people to have been featured twice on *This Is Your Life*.
CAUSE: His health began to fail rapidly after his 80th birthday. He suffered muscular difficulties in his legs which eventually resulted in double amputation. He died at St Thomas' Hospital, London, aged 82. He left £283,867 in his will.
FURTHER READING: *Before Your Very Eyes* – Arthur Askey (London: The Woburn Press, 1975).

Hon. Anthony Asquith

Born November 9, 1902
Died February 20, 1968
'Puffin'. The youngest child of British Prime Minister Herbert Henry Asquith, he was born in London and educated at Summer Fields, Oxford, Winchester and Balliol College, Oxford. Despite an early love of music he decided his ambitions lay in the cinema and founded the Film Society in London in 1925. He studied film under Mary Pickford and Douglas Fairbanks and, returning to London, began to direct. Unlike his contemporaries, Asquith's career was spent in England. His forte was producing cinematic versions of West End plays, including *The Way To The Stars* (1945), *The Winslow Boy* (1948) and *The Browning Version* (1951), all based on Terence Rattigan's works. In 1937 he was invited to become president of the Association of Cinematographic Technicians, a position he held until his death. Dominated by his mother, he was unmarried and, some believe, homosexual. He spent his weekends serving burly lorry drivers in a greasy spoon café in Catterick, North Yorkshire. One of the most bizarre rumours about Asquith is that he was the infamous 'Man In The Mask' at an orgy known as the 'Feast of the Peacocks' held in December 1961 at Hyde Park Square in London by notorious prostitute Mariella Novotny. The mystery man was whipped by the guests as they entered and then ordered to hide under a table out of sight. In her unpublished memoirs, *The Government Chief Whip (Retired)*, Novotny identifies the masochist as "Lord Asquith". 'Lord' was a nickname given to Asquith by crews on his films. Novotny's husband, Hod Dibben, refused to deny that Asquith was the man as he had done when other candidates were suggested. It seems likely that Asquith was, indeed, the mysterious 'Man In The Mask'.
CAUSE: He was involved in a car crash in December 1963 and was never fully well again. He died in London of cancer aged 65 and was buried in All

Saints' churchyard in Sutton Courtenay, Berkshire. He left £64,231.

Fred Astaire

(FREDERIC AUSTERLITZ, JR)
Born May 10, 1899
Died June 22, 1987
Mr Twinkletoes. Born on South 10th Street in Omaha, Nebraska, Astaire and his sister, Adèle, worked in vaudeville (and were once replaced by a dog act) before making their Broadway début on November 28, 1917, at the 44th Street Roof Theater in *Over The Top*. They became the toast of London society in the Twenties. The show, *Stop Flirting*, ran for 418 performances at the Shaftesbury Theatre from May 30, 1923. On March 5, 1932, Adèle retired and two months later, on May 9, she married Lord Frederick Cavendish. Fred and Adèle had made their movie débuts as uncredited extras in a 1915 short, *Fanchon The Cricket*, starring Mary Pickford. In January 1933, 5'9" Astaire was given a proper screen test by RKO. It wasn't good: "Can't act. Slightly bald. Also dances." Studio boss David O. Selznick reported, "I am a little uncertain about the man, but I feel, in spite of his enormous ears and bad chin line, that his charm is so tremendous that it comes through even in this wretched test." His first major role was playing himself in MGM's *Dancing Lady* (1933) starring Joan Crawford, Clark Gable and Franchot Tone. However, it was the next film, Thornton Freeland's *Flying Down To Rio* (1933) for RKO, co-starring Dolores Del Rio, Gene Raymond and Ginger Rogers, that established Astaire as a star. He spent hours on set practising his steps. "Choreography for the camera requires 80% brain work and 20% footwork," he once remarked. Novelist Graham Greene commented: "He is the nearest thing we are ever likely to get to a human Mickey Mouse." However, choreographer Hermes Pan, who worked out many of Astaire's routines, observed, somewhat disparagingly: "Fred Astaire was almost as concerned with his toupee looking right as he was with perfecting each dance number." *The Gay Divorcée* (1934), *Roberta* (1935) and *Top Hat* (1935) (during which he broke a dozen canes) began the teaming with Ginger Rogers, a coupling that was so successful RKO insured his legs for $1 million and paid him a percentage of the profits. However, Astaire was not certain about the partnership. "I did not go into pictures with the thought of becoming a team," he said on the suggestion he should work with Ginger Rogers. Altogether, they appeared together in ten films. Look out for one of those films – *Swing Time* (1936). In it, Astaire puts a lighted pipe in his pocket. On July 12, 1933, he married divorced mother-of-one Phyllis Potter in Brooklyn. She had a speech impediment and called him 'Fwed'. They were happily married for 21 years and had two children: Fred Jr (b. Good Samaritan Hospital, Los Angeles, January 21, 1936) and Phyllis Ava (b. Los Angeles, March 28, 1942). Astaire danced so energetically during the making of *Holiday Inn* (1942) that he lost a stone in weight. In 1949 he was awarded a special Oscar in recognition of his contribution to film. Following Phyllis' death from lung cancer, aged 46, at 10am on September 13, 1954, Astaire lived with his mother, Ann, until she too died, aged 97, on July 26, 1975. Five years later, on June 24, 1980, Astaire married jockey Robyn Caroline Smith (b. San Francisco, August 14, 1942, as Melody Dawn Constance Palm), five months younger than his daughter. In 1959 Astaire, who watched what he ate and rarely touched alcohol, had begun appearing in dramatic films, beginning with the part of Julian Osborne in *On The Beach*, co-starring Gregory Peck, Ava Gardner and Anthony Perkins. Astaire was nominated for a Best Supporting Actor Oscar for his performance as Harlee Claiborn in *The Towering Inferno*

(1974). Away from the screen he was fascinated by crime, so much so that he often toured with police patrols. In 1981 the American Film Institute bestowed its lifetime achievement award on him. It is for his dancing that Fred Astaire will always be known. As Russian ballet dancer Mikhail Baryshnikov said: "No dancer can watch Fred Astaire and not know we should all have been in a different business."

CAUSE: Astaire died of pneumonia aged 88 in Century City Hospital, Los Angeles, ten days after he was admitted (under the name Fred Giles) with respiratory problems. Astaire's will, written on January 16, 1986, directed that there be no memorial service. He is buried, with sister Adèle and first wife Phyllis, in Oakwood Memorial Park, 22601 Lassen, Chatsworth, California 91311.

FURTHER READING: *Astaire: The Man, The Dancer* – Bob Thomas (New York: St Martin's Press, 1984); *Astaire: The Biography* – Tim Satchell (London: Arrow, 1988).

Gertrude Astor

Born November 9, 1887
Died November 9, 1977
Blonde bombshell. Born in Lakeland, Ohio, Gertrude Astor was the first actress to sign a contract with Universal in 1915. She worked with Harry Langdon, Gloria Swanson, Laurel & Hardy and Hal Roach. Her films included: *Laughing Ladies* (1925), *Stagestruck* (1925) with Swanson, *Tell 'Em Nothing* (1926), *Oh! What A Man!* (1927), *The Cat And The Canary* (1927), *Come Clean* (1931) with Laurel & Hardy, *Misbehaving Husbands* (1940), *Around The World In 80 Days* (1956) and *The Man Who Shot Liberty Valance* (1962). She often portrayed gold-diggers and socialites. Off-screen she was regarded as one of Hollywood's best-dressed citizens.

CAUSE: She died on her 90th birthday of a stroke.

Mary Astor

(LUCILLE VASCONELLES LANGHANKE)
Born May 3, 1906
Died September 25, 1987
Purple diarist. Born in Quincy, Illinois, the only child of Otto Langhanke, an ambitious (ambitious for his daughter, anyway) German immigrant father and Helen Vasconelles, his American-Portuguese wife, Mary Astor is probably better known for her scandalous private life than for any films she made. She was a beauty queen as a 14-year-old teenager and made her film début in *The Scarecrow* (1920). Despite failing a screen test for D.W. Griffith, the 5'6" Astor went on to appear in over 120 films, even though she hated Hollywood. "I was never totally involved in movies. I was making my father's dream come true," she once admitted. Her final appearance was in Robert Aldrich's *Hush . . . Hush, Sweet Charlotte* (1964) playing Mrs Jewel Mayhew. Her big break came playing Lady Margery Alvanley opposite her lover John Barrymore's *Beau Brummel* (1924) for which she was paid $1,100 a week; Barrymore took her virginity when she was 17. She also played Adriana della Varnese opposite him in *Don Juan* (1926) and appeared in *The Rough Riders* (1927) as Dolly and *Dressed To Kill* (1928) as Jeanne. On February 23, 1928, she married Kenneth Neil Hawks (b. Goschen, Indiana, August 12, 1898), brother of director Howard. He was killed in a plane crash at Point Vincente, California, on January 2, 1930. "My marriage to Ken Hawks had rainbows around it," she later lamented. "He had values that have become extinct." She subsequently flung herself into her work, appearing in *Ladies Love Brutes* (1930) as Mimi Howell, *Those We Love* (1932) as May Ballard and *Red Dust* (1932) as Barbara Willis, a refined married lady who is entranced by mean, moody Dennis Carson (Clark Gable). On March 20, 1934, she was sued for support by her

parents but the judgement went against them on May 1. She turned down an RKO contract and starred in *I Am A Thief* (1935) as Odette Mauclair, *Trapped By Television* (1936) as Bobby Blake, *Dodsworth* (1936) as Edith Cortright, plus *And So They Were Married* (1936) as Edith Farnham. Following Kenneth Hawks' death she went under the care of Dr Franklyn Thorpe (b. Denver, Colorado, June 29, 1892, d. Los Angeles, California February 12, 1977) and they were married on June 29, 1931, in Yuma, Arizona. Their daughter, Marylyn Haoli, was born in Honolulu, Hawaii, on June 15, 1932. In 1933 Astor travelled to New York on holiday and met writer George S. Kaufman. Astor was possessed of a fearsome sexual appetite but so was the weedy-looking Kaufman and they began an affair that continued after Astor returned to the West Coast. On April 12, 1935, Thorpe was granted a divorce from his wife and sued for custody of their daughter. Astor countersued on July 15, and discovered that her diary (normally kept in her underwear drawer) was missing. The court case made for lurid newspaper reading (even though the judge excluded the diary from evidence, Thorpe's lawyers leaked selected excerpts to the press) when it was revealed the diary contained explicit passages detailing Astor and Kaufman's lovemaking. One entry read: ". . . remarkable staying power . . . We played kneesies during the first two acts, my hand wasn't in my own lap during the third . . . It's been years since I felt up a man in public, but I just got carried away . . . His powers of recuperation are amazing, and we made love all night . . . we shared our fourth climax at dawn . . . Was any woman ever happier? It seems that George is just hard all the time . . . I don't see how he does it, he is perfect . . . he tore out of his pajamas and I was never undressed by someone so fast in my life . . . Ah,

desert night – with George's body plunging into mine, naked under the stars." The child's nurse reported that she had seen Dr Thorpe in bed with a starlet who wore only red toenail polish and also that three Busby Berkeley babes had slept in his bed. Where was the doctor at this time, asked the lawyer. "He was right in there in his bed, too," the nurse responded. The judge awarded the house to Astor and ordered that the daughter spend six months with each parent. He further ordered that the diary be burned. The scandal did not affect Astor's career (only her health caused by her alcoholism and a suicide attempt) and she went on to star in *There's Always A Woman* (1938) as Lola Fraser, *The Great Lie* (1941) as Sandra Kovac (for which Astor won a Best Supporting Actress Academy Award) and gave a sterling performance opposite Humphrey Bogart in *The Maltese Falcon* (1941) as Brigid O'Shaughnessy. Four years earlier, on February 18, 1937, again in Yuma, Arizona, she had married for the third time to Manuel Martinez de Campo (who changed his name to Michael Field; b. Mexico City, November 14, 1913, d. London, February 16, 1969), seven years her junior. Their son, Anthony Paul, was born on June 5, 1939. The couple was divorced on December 14, 1942. As she grew older, Astor played maternal roles during a seven-year contract at MGM. She played Judy Garland's mother (Mrs Anna Smith) in *Meet Me In St Louis* (1944) and the mother of Elizabeth Taylor, June Allyson, Margaret O'Brien and Janet Leigh (Marmee March) in *Little Women* (1949). She became even more disillusioned with Hollywood over time, and found her vocation instead as a writer, producing five novels. On December 24, 1945, she married Chicagoan stockbroker Thomas Wheelock but that marriage was no more successful than her previous attempts at matrimony and they divorced in 1955.

CAUSE: She suffered a stroke in the Eighties and was in poor health for some time before her death, aged 81, at the Motion Picture Country Home, 23450 Calabasas Road, Woodland Hills, California, from a heart attack. She was buried in plot N-L523-5 of Holy Cross Cemetery, 5835 West Slauson Avenue, Culver City, California 90230.

Lionel Atwill

Born March 1, 1885
Died April 22, 1946
'Pinky'. Lionel Alfred William Atwill was born in Croydon, Surrey, educated at Mercer's School in London and began his professional career on October 31, 1904, taking a small role in *The Walls Of Jericho* at the Garrick Theatre, moving to Broadway in the Twenties. In 1913 he married the actress Phyllis Relph by whom he had a son, John Anthony Atwill (who joined the RAF and was killed in action in 1941), but they divorced in 1919. Four years earlier, in 1915, he had toured America with Lillie Langtry who had been the mistress of King Edward VII when he was Prince of Wales. Atwill stayed on after the tour and appeared with Billie Burke (Mrs Florenz Ziegfeld) in *The Lodger*, a play about Jack the Ripper, in New York. He made his film début in *Eve's Daughter* (1918) playing Courtenay Urquhart. It was to be the start of a long career in which he played mainly villains including the fiendish Professor James Moriarty, Holmes' nemesis, in *Sherlock Holmes And The Secret Weapon* (1942). Atwill had previously appeared as James Mortimer in *The Hound Of The Baskervilles* (1939), Basil Rathbone's first outing as the legendary sleuth, and also appeared with Rathbone in *Captain Blood* (1935) as Colonel Bishop, *Son Of Frankenstein* (see below) and *The Sun Never Sets* (1939) as Dr Hugo Zurof. Atwill's forte was

horror and he appeared in several films within that genre including: *The Vampire Bat* (1933) as Dr Otto von Niemann, a film that was the biggest hit for Majestic Studios, in which Atwill starred opposite Fay Wray, *The Sphinx* (1933) as Jerome Breen, *Murders In The Zoo* (1933) as jealous zookeeper Eric Gorman who sews his wife's lover's mouth shut and leaves him to starve to death in the jungle before throwing another victim into the crocodile pit; *Mark Of The Vampire* (1935) as Inspector Neumann in MGM's version of the Dracula story; with Lionel Barrymore in *Son Of Frankenstein* (1939) as Inspector Krogh in which Boris Karloff played the monster for the last time; *The Ghost Of Frankenstein* (1942) as Dr Theodor Bohmer, *Frankenstein Meets The Wolf Man* (1943) as the mayor of Vasaria; Universal's first all-star 'monsterfest' *House Of Frankenstein* (1944) as Inspector Arnz in which Boris Karloff played the mad scientist, John Carradine played Dracula and Lon Chaney, Jr as the Wolfman, and *House Of Dracula* (1945) as Inspector Holtz, the last outing for Universal's monsters. Of his cinematic appearance, Atwill once said, "One side of my face is gentle and kind, incapable of anything but love of my fellow man. The other profile is cruel and predatory and evil, incapable of anything but lusts and dark passions. It all depends which side of my face is turned to you – or the camera. It all depends on which side faces the moon at the ebb of the tide." His eyes were described as "Satanic neons" in Warner's *Doctor X* (1932) in which he played Dr Jerry Xavier. Atwill played Ivan Igor, a mad sculptor who murders people and then displays them in his own collection in *Mystery Of The Wax Museum* (1933). One of the earliest colour films, it is, oddly, often shown on television in black and white. In 1920 Atwill married again, this time to another actress Poppy Wyndham (b. 1893 as the Hon. Elsie Mackay,

d. March 14, 1928 when her aeroplane crashed into the sea). Shortly before her death, Atwill and private detectives that he had hired discovered her in flagrante at 59 West 68th Street, New York, with Atwill's protégé Max Montesole. Atwill filed for divorce. In 1930 he married Henrietta Louise Cromwell Brook MacArthur, who had been the first wife of the decorated soldier General Douglas MacArthur. Atwill and his third wife divorced on June 18, 1943. His other films included: *For Sale* (1918), *The Marriage Price* (1919) as Kenneth Gordon, *The Eternal Mother* (1920) as Howard Hollister, *The Highest Bidder* (1921) as Lester, *Silent Witness* (1932) as the perjurer Sir Austin Howard, *I Am A Fugitive From A Chain Gang* (1932) and *20,000 Years In Sing Sing* (1932) both as the off-screen narrator of the trailer, *The Secret Of Madame Blanche* (1933) as Aubrey St John, *The Song Of Songs* (1933) as Baron von Merzbach, *Secret Of The Blue Room* (1933) as Robert von Helldorf, *The Solitaire Man* (1933) as Inspector Wallace, *Nana* (1934) as Colonel Andre Muffat, *Beggars In Ermine* (1934) as John 'Flint' Dawson a.k.a. John Daniels, *Stamboul Quest* (1934) as Herr Von Sturm, *One More River* (1934) as Brough, *The Age Of Innocence* (1934) as Julius Beaufort, *The Firebird* (1934) as John Pointer, *The Man Who Reclaimed His Head* (1934) as Henry Dumont, *The Devil Is A Woman* (1935) as Captain Don Pasqual 'Pasqualito' Costelar, *The Murder Man* (1935) as Captain Cole, *Rendezvous* (1935) as Major William Brennan, *Lady Of Secrets* (1936) as Mr Whittaker, *Till We Meet Again* (1936) as Ludwig, *Absolute Quiet* (1936) as Gerald 'G.A.' Axton, *The High Command* (1936) as Major General Sir John Sangye, VC, the prosecutor in *The Road Back* (1937), *The Last Train From Madrid* (1937) as Colonel Vigo, *Lancer Spy* (1937) as Colonel Fenwick, *The Wrong Road* (1937) as Mike Roberts, *The Great Garrick* (1937) as Monsieur

Beaumarchais, *Three Comrades* (1938) as Franz Breuer, *The Great Waltz* (1938) as Count Anton Hohenfried, *The Gorilla* (1939) as Walter Stevens, *The Three Musketeers* (1939) as De Rochefort, *Johnny Apollo* (1940) as Jim McLaughlin, *Mr Moto Takes A Vacation* (1939) as Professor Hildebrand, *The Secret Of Dr Kildare* (1939) as Paul Messenger, *Balalaika* (1939) as Professor Marakov, *The Mad Empress* (1939) as Bazaine, *Charlie Chan In Panama* (1940) as Cliveden Compton, *Girl In 313* (1940) as Russell Woodruff, *Charlie Chan's Murder Cruise* (1940) as Dr Suderman, *The Great Profile* (1940) as Dr Bruce, *Boom Town* (1940) as Mr Harry Compton, *Man Made Monster* (1941) as Dr Paul Rigas, *The Mad Doctor Of Market Street* (1942) as Dr Ralph Benson posing as Graham, *To Be Or Not To Be* (1942) as Rawitch, *The Strange Case Of Doctor Rx* (1942) as Dr Fish, *Junior G-Men Of The Air* (1942) as the Baron, *Pardon My Sarong* (1942) as Dr Varnoff, *Cairo* (1942) as the German, *Night Monster* (1942) as Dr King, *Captain America* (1944) as Dr Cyrus Maldor, *Lady In The Death House* (1944) as Finch, *Raiders Of Ghost City* (1944) as Erich von Rugen, *Secrets Of Scotland Yard* (1944) as Waterlow, *Fog Island* (1945) as Alec Ritchfield, *Crime, Inc.* (1945) as Pat Coyle and *Genius At Work* (1946) as the murderer Latimer Marsh/The Cobra. Atwill was seen as the epitome of the cultured Englishman in Hollywood – he often spent his pay packets buying Old Masters. However, he had a darker side. James Whale, the director, had found a house in Pacific Palisades that he thought would be suitable for Atwill and his society wife, a descendant of Oliver Cromwell. And so it proved. The marriage to all outward appearances was a happy one. The couple often enjoyed threesomes with both men and women but eventually Mrs Atwill grew tired of the sex games and in 1939 she left her husband, moving to Washington, D.C.

where she hosted a radio programme. Meanwhile, free from marital shackles, Atwill hosted orgies at his house at 13515 d'Este Drive, on the edge of the Santa Monica canyon. He did insist that his guests had regular check-ups to ensure that they were free of venereal disease. In December 1940, Atwill threw a Christmas party that would bring his sexual edifice crashing to the ground. Atwill dressed as Father Christmas to greet his guests and planned everything down to the last detail, well almost everything – he should have checked his guest list with rather more care. The orgy was due to start at a given signal – a note on the piano played by a blind pianist who would then play *The Blue Danube* – after dinner. One of the guests was a 16-year-old from Hibbing, Minnesota, known only as Sylvia who was pregnant but had had great plans for stardom. The music began to play and guests' clothes began to come off. After the event Sylvia wrote to her parents in Hibbing and requested a large sum of money. Her father was suspicious and called the police. Social services picked up Sylvia and told a Grand Jury in 1941 that during the orgy two adult entertainment films had been shown at Atwill's – *The Plumber And The Girl* and *The Daisy Chain*. Atwill denied not only showing the films but also owning anything of that genre. The jury chose to believe the suave actor rather than the pregnant teen. Sylvia went back to Minnesota and was never heard from again. A year later, one of the other guests fell on hard times and decided that he had saved Atwill. While on a chain gang for writing rubber cheques he wrote to the Grand Jury offering to tell the full story of the orgy and the films. Atwill was recalled to the stand but on advice from his learned friends refused to testify. After talking to a friendly judge Atwill returned to court and admitted that he did own some pornographic films but they had been rented for a friend in the Royal

Canadian Mounted Police and that he (Atwill) had never seen them and was out playing tennis when they were shown. The 1942 jury did not believe him and he was indicted on a charge of perjury. On August 12, he was charged on a second count of perjury. At the trial in September, Atwill confessed that he had lied but only to save the reputations of his friends. On October 15, 1942, he was sentenced to five years probation and ordered to visit the LAPD Vice Department weekly. The sentence meant that Atwill did not work for seven months as studios were reluctant to hire someone in breach of the Hays Code. On April 23, 1943, Atwill went to the judge who had sentenced him and pleaded for mercy which the judge was happy to agree to. Atwill still found Hollywood work impossible to come by and moved to New York where he hoped to revive his career on the Great White Way. It was a forlorn hope and he returned to Hollywood. But there he was ignored by the major studios and ended working in bit parts and for small companies. It was an ignominious end to a glorious career.

CAUSE: On July 7, 1944 Atwill married Mary Paula Pritter by whom he had a son, Lionel Anthony Guile. Atwill died of pneumonia in Pacific Palisades six months after the birth of his son while making *Lost City Of The Jungle* (1946) in which he played Sir Eric Hazarias. His scenes were completed by a double. Atwill was cremated and his ashes interred in the Chapel of the Pines Cemetery, 1605 South Catalina, Los Angeles, California.

Maxine Audley

(MAXINE HECHT)
Born April 29, 1923
Died July 23, 1992
Dark-haired beauty. Born in London, the daughter of Henry Julius Hecht and the opera singer Katharine Arkandy, Maxine Audley was trained at the Tamara Daykharhanova Stage School

in New York and London's Mask Theatre School. She made her stage début at the Open Air Theatre in *A Midsummer Night's Dream* on July 27, 1940. From 1940 until 1942 she appeared in rep and then from 1943 until 1945 was engaged in war work. Three years later, she made her first film *Anna Karenina* (1948) and went on to appear in *The Pleasure Garden* (1952) as Lady Ennui, *The Sleeping Tiger* (1954) as Carol, *The Barretts Of Wimpole Street* (1957) as Arabel, *The Prince And The Showgirl* (1957) as Lady Sunningdale, *A King In New York* (1957) as Queen Irene, *Dunkirk* (1958) as Diana Foreman, *The Vikings* (1958) as Enid, *Our Man In Havana* (1959) as Teresa, *Bluebeard's Ten Honeymoons* (1960) as Cynthia, *Peeping Tom* (1960) as Mrs Stephens, *Hell Is A City* (1960) as Julia Martineau, *The Trials Of Oscar Wilde* (1960) as Ada Leverson, *Petticoat Pirates* (1961) as the superintendent, *The Man At The Carlton Tower* (1961) as Lydia Daney, *Ein Toter Secht Seinen Mörder* (1962) as Marion Fane, *Ricochet* (1963) as Yvonne Phipps, *A Jolly Bad Fellow* (1964) as Clarinda Bowles-Ottery, *Never Mention Murder* (1964) as Liz Teasdale, *The Battle Of The Villa Fiorita* (1965) as Charmian, *The Agony And The Ecstasy* (1965), *Payment In Kind* (1967), *Here We Go Round The Mulberry Bush* (1967) as Mrs Beauchamp, *House Of Cards* (1968) as Matilde Rosier, *Sinful Davey* (1969) as the Duchess of Argyll, *Frankenstein Must Be Destroyed* (1969) as Ella Brandt, *The Looking Glass War* (1969) as Mrs LeClerc and *Running Scared* (1972) as Mrs Betancourt. Her final acting job on television was playing Mrs Marlow, the suspect's mother, in *Prime Suspect* (1991), and on Radio 4 reading Elinor Glyn's novel *Three Weeks* (1992). Four times married, her first husband was Leonard Cassini, her second was Andrew Broughton, her third was Frederick Granville and her fourth Leo Maguire. All the marriages except the last ended in divorce.

CAUSE: Her husband found her collapsed in the bathroom of their London home, calling for help after suffering a heart attack. She died in hospital an hour later. She was 69.

Mischa Auer
(MIKHAIL SEMYONOVICH UNSKOVSKY)
Born November 17, 1905
Died March 5, 1967
Mad Russian. Born in St Petersburg, Russia, the grandson of violinist Leopold Auer, his father was killed in the Russo-Japanese War and his mother died of typhoid. In 1920 he emigrated to New York where his grandfather took him under his wing. 6'2" Auer made his Broadway debut on February 24, 1925 in a bitpart in Henrik Ibsen's *The Wild Duck*. Beginning with Frank Tuttle's *Something Always Happens* (1928) Auer appeared in more than 150 films including *East Side Of Heaven* (1939) as Nicky, *Arsène Lupin* (1932), *One Hundred Men And A Girl* (1937), Frank Capra's *You Can't Take It With You* (1938), Walter Wanger's *Vogues Of 1938*, *Destry Rides Again* (1939), *Cracked Nuts* (1941) as Boris Kabikoff, *Hold That Ghost* (1941) as Gregory, *Sing Another Chorus* (1941) as Stanislaus, *Hellzapoppin'* (1941) as Pepi, *Twin Beds* (1942) as Nicolai Cherupin, *Brewster's Millions* (1945) as Mikhail Mikhailovich, *Sentimental Journey* (1946) as Gregory Petrovich Rogozhin, *Sofia* (1948) as Ali Imagu, *Mr Arkadin* (1955), *Frou-Frou* (1955) as Grand-Duc Alexis, *Tabarin* (1958) as Boris, *Sacrée Jeunesse* (1958) as Professeur Koranoff, *The King's Breakfast* (1963), *Cleopazza* (1964) as Produttore Strombic, *Drop Dead Darling* (1966) as Romeo and his last film *Per Amore . . . Per Magia . . .* (1967) as Magrebì. In 1936, Auer was cast as Alice Brady's protégé Carlo in the classic screwball comedy *My Man Godfrey*, for which he was nominated for the Academy Award for Best Supporting Actor, the first occasion on

which a supporting Oscar was awarded. He said, "That one role made a comedian out of me. I haven't been anything else since. It's paid off very well. Do you wonder that I am flattered when people say I am mad?" Auer married four times, and had three children. In 1931 he married Norma Tillman by whom he had two children, Anthony and Zoe. They divorced in 1940. On December 4, 1941 he married Joyce Hunter and divorced in 1950. On May 5, 1950 he married Susanne Kalish by whom he had a child. In 1965 he married Elise Souls Lee.

CAUSE: Auer suffered a heart attack in 1957 but recovered sufficiently to return to work. Suffering from cardiovascular disease, Auer had a second coronary and died in Rome, aged 61. He was buried in lot 51, section X at Prospect Hill Cemetery, Gloversville, New York.

Albert Austin
Born December 13, 1881
Died August 17, 1953
Brummy comic. Born in Birmingham the lean and lugubrious Austin travelled to America on Fred Karno's 1912–1913 tour and stayed. He spent two years in rep in Denver before signing a contract with Charlie Chaplin's company at Mutual in 1916, where he was the only player to appear alongside Chaplin in all 12 Mutual comedies. He worked alongside him as friend, advisor and assistant director until 1931. He is not mentioned in Chaplin's autobiography despite their long friendship. He spent the last 11 years of his life as a security guard for Warner Bros. His brother William is noted below.
CAUSE: He died aged 71 in North Hollywood.

Gene Austin
(EUGENE LUCAS)
Born June 24, 1900
Died January 24, 1972
Singing cowboy. Born in Gainesville, Texas, singer-songwriter Austin was educated at Baltimore University, Maryland and served his country on a Mexican Punitive Mission in 1916 during the First World War. He appeared in vaudeville from 1923 and in 1925 joined ASCAP. He wrote songs alone and with others and was the first performer to get a certified million seller for his record 'My Blue Heaven', recorded in December 1927. In 1928 he achieved another million seller with 'Ramona'. Austin made his film début in *Sadie McKee* (1934), an early Joan Crawford vehicle. He also appeared in *Gift Of The Gab* (1934), *Belle Of The Nineties* (1934), *Klondike Annie* (1936), *Songs And Saddles* (1938), *My Little Chickadee* (1940) and *Moon Over Las Vegas* (1944). His daughter is the former actress Charlotte Austin (b. Charlotte, North Carolina, November 2, 1933).
CAUSE: Austin died aged 72 of cancer in Palm Springs, California.

William Austin
Born June 12, 1884
Died June 15, 1975
Silly ass. Born in Georgetown, British Guyana where his father owned a sugar plantation, 6'1" William Crosby Piercy Austin was said to be the younger brother of Albert (see above). He travelled widely on business but when he came to America he became an actor and worked in various stock companies for three years. He signed a five-year contract with Paramount and appeared in Clara Bow's *It* (1927) and with the Marx Brothers in *Duck Soup* (1933). He was most often to be seen playing monocled silly asses on screen.
CAUSE: He died three days after his 91st birthday in Newport Beach, California.

Gene Autry
Born September 29, 1907
Died October 2, 1998
'Oklahoma's Yodelin' Cowboy' was actually born near Tioga Springs, Texas, as Orvon Gene Autry although

he grew up on a ranch in Ravia, Oklahoma. On leaving school Autry began working as a cowboy and then a telegrapher for the Frisco Railroad in Sapulpa, Oklahoma. Aged 21 he began appearing on the radio station KCVOO-Tulsa, from 1929 until 1930 when he started making records for the American Record Corporation (ARC) and Victor. That led to the *National Barn Dance* show on WLS-Chicago where he met Smiley Burnette, who was to become his movie partner. Seeing his potential ARC, who also owned Republic Pictures (then called Mascot Pictures), put him in films. Autry performed two songs in the Ken Maynard Western *In Old Santa Fé* (1934) before moving in front of the cameras in his own right for the 13-episode serial *The Phantom Empire* (1934). In 1935 he starred in *Tumblin' Tumbleweeds*, which cost $18,000 to make and took $1 million at the box office. In 1938 he staged a walkout over pay, returning to Republic Films on December 4 after they agreed to pay him $10,000 per film. Always a popular box-office draw, Autry appeared in over 100 films, achieving first place as Most Popular Western Star between 1937 and 1942. He always played a chaste character and if he had to kiss the girl it was always done in the last reel – even then the camera would focus on his horse. He was also a non-smoking teetotaller on screen and refused to hit anyone shorter or weaker than himself. On July 26, 1942, he was sworn in as a member of the US Army Air Corps and gained not a little personal publicity by doing it live on his radio show, *Melody Ranch*. He served for three years. Back on screen he continued to make films for Republic until June 26, 1947, when he finally left the company to move to Columbia. Perhaps realising that television was where it was at, in April 1947 Autry had become the first major movie star to announce he was to appear in a TV series. His final film was *Last Of The Pony Riders* (1953). He wrote over 200 songs and sold over 30 million records, including million sellers *That Silver Haired Daddy Of Mine* (1939, over 5 million copies sold), *South Of The Border* (1939), *Here Comes Santa Claus* (1947), *Peter Cottontail* (1949), *Rudolph The Red-Nosed Reindeer* (1949, over 12 million copies sold) and *Frosty The Snowman* (1950). In 1950 he became the first cowboy to be named as one of the Ten Best Dressed Men in America. It was Autry who started the fad for C&W singers to wear Western apparel and in 1969 he was elected to the Country Music Hall of Fame. He is equally famous for the horse he rode, Champion the chestnut stallion. The horse was bought for $1,000 because it looked exactly the same as the first horse Autry ever rode on screen. That horse was called Tony Jr (real name Lindy) and appeared alongside Tom Mix. Autry was one of the richest stars in Hollywood, worth well over $200 million. He owned several record companies, two television stations, a TV and film production company (they made the series *Champion The Wonder Horse*), the Los Angeles (later California) Angels baseball club and had interests in real estate and oil. In 1980 he was named as the eighth richest man in California by the *Los Angeles Times*. "We made over 100 Westerns together. At the end of each picture Gene would ride off into the sunset," quipped his TV sidekick Pat Buttram, "now he owns it." Autry married twice. On April 1, 1932, he married Ina Mae Spivey. They had 48 happy years together until her death in Palm Springs, California on May 20, 1980. On July 19, 1981, Autry married bank vice-president Jacqueline Ellam, 35 years his junior, at the First United Methodist Church in Burbank, California.

CAUSE: He died in Studio City, California, of cancer three days after his 91st birthday.

Charles Avery

(CHARLES AVERY BRADFORD)
Born May 28, 1873
Died July 23, 1926
Charlie Chaplin's dresser. Born in
Chicago, Avery was one of the original
seven Keystone Kops. He later became
a director but Hollywood legend has
him as one of the contributors to
Charlie Chaplin's tramp ensemble.
Apparently, Chaplin took Fatty
Arbuckle's huge trousers and Avery's
tiny jacket but Chaplin claims to have
originated the costume himself "on the
way to wardrobe".
CAUSE: Avery committed suicide aged
53 in Los Angeles, California.

Tex Avery

Born February 26, 1908
Died August 26, 1980
Bugs Bunny's dad. Born in Taylor,
Texas, Frederick Bean Avery was a
descendant of Daniel Boone and Judge
Roy Bean, "the law west of the Pecos",
although his grandmother warned him
against revealing the family connection:
"Don't ever mention you are kin to
Roy Bean. He's a no-good skunk."
Avery was educated at North Dallas
High School, graduating in 1927 and
after a summer course at the Chicago
Art Institute and a failed attempt to
launch a newspaper cartoon, he moved
to California two years later landing a
job working at a harbour. In 1929, he
began work at the Walter Lantz Studios
as an animator and in 1930, worked on
Aesop's Fables. In 1935 he joined
Warner Bros. where he was employed
on the Merry Melodies and Loony
Tunes series. He was one of the
creators of Bugs Bunny and also coined
the phrase "What's up, doc?" He often
interrupted the action in his cartoons
with a question – for example, a chase
scene would stop and the words
"Exciting, isn't it?" would appear on
screen. In 1942 he moved to MGM
and the first cartoon he directed was
The Blitz Wolf, a version of *The Three
Little Pigs* in which Hitler is the Big Bad

Wolf. He next created Droopy the dog.
Interestingly for someone who relied on
the visual, Avery was blind in his left
eye and had no depth of vision. In
1954 Avery returned briefly to Lantz
but began working on advertisements
in 1955. Lantz said, "The thing about
Avery is that he can write a cartoon, lay
it out, time it, do the whole thing
himself." He also created Lucky Ducky
and Chilly Willy the penguin. Although
several of his films were nominated,
Tex Avery never won an Oscar. His
work included: *Towne Hall Follies*
(1935), *Quail Hunt* (1935), *Gold
Diggers Of '49* (1936), *The Blow Out*
(1936), *Plane Dippy* (1936), *I'd Love
To Take Orders From You* (1936), *Page
Miss Glory* (1936), *I Love To Singa*
(1936), *Porky The Rain-Maker* (1936),
The Village Smithy (1936), *Milk And
Money* (1936), *Don't Look Now* (1936),
Porky The Wrestler (1937), *Picador
Porky* (1937), *I Only Have Eyes For You*
(1937), *Porky's Duck Hunt* (1937),
Uncle Tom's Bungalow (1937), *Ain't We
Got Fun* (1937), *Porky's Garden* (1937),
I Wanna Be A Sailor (1937), *Egghead
Rides Again* (1937), *A Sunbonnet Blue*
(1937), *Little Red Walking Hood*
(1937), *Daffy Duck And Egghead*
(1938), *The Sneezing Weasel* (1938),
The Penguin Parade (1938), *The Isle Of
Pingo Pongo* (1938), *A Feud There Was*
(1938), *Johnny Smith And
Poker-Huntas* (1938), *Daffy Duck In
Hollywood* (1938), *Cinderella Meets Fella*
(1938), *The Mice Will Play* (1938),
Hamateur Night (1939), *A Day At The
Zoo* (1939), *Thugs With Dirty Mugs*
(1939), *Believe It Or Else* (1939),
Dangerous Dan McFoo (1939),
Detouring America (1939), *Land Of The
Midnight Fun* (1939), *Fresh Fish*
(1939), *Screwball Football* (1939*),* *The
Early Worm Gets The Bird* (1940), *Cross
Country Detours* (1940), *The Bear's Tale*
(1940), *A Gander At Mother Goose*
(1940), *Circus Today* (1940), *A Wild
Hare* (1940), *Ceiling Hero* (1940),
Wacky Wildlife (1940), *Of Fox And
Hounds* (1940), *Holiday Highlights*

(1940), *The Haunted Mouse* (1941), *The Crackpot Quail* (1941), *Tortoise Beats Hare* (1941), *Porky's Preview* (1941), *Hollywood Steps Out* (1941), *The Heckling Hare* (1941), *Aviation Vacation* (1941), *Speaking Of Animals Down On The Farm* (1941), *All This And Rabbit* Stew (1941), *The Bug Parade* (1941), *Speaking Of Animals In The Zoo* (1941), *The Cagey Canary* (1941), *Aloha Hooey* (1942), *Crazy Cruise* (1942), *The Early Bird Dood It!* (1942), *Dumb-Hounded* (1943), *Red Hot Riding Hood* (1943), *Who Killed Who?* (1943*)*, *One Ham's Family* (1943), *What's Buzzin' Buzzard?* (1943), *Screwball Squirrel* (1944), *Batty Baseball* (1944), *Happy-Go-Nutty* (1944*)*, *Big Heel-Watha* (1944), *The Screwy Truant* (1945), *Jerky Turkey* (1945), *The Shooting Of Dan McGoo* (1945), *Swing Shift Cinderella* (1945), *Wild And Woolfy* (1945), *Lonesome Lenny* (1946), *The Hick Chick* (1946), *Northwest Hounded Police* (1946), *Henpecked Hoboes* (1946), *Hound Hunters* (1947), *Red Hot Rangers* (1947), *Uncle Tom's Cabaña* (1947), *Slap Happy Lion* (1947), *King-Size Canary* (1947), *What Price Fleadom* (1948), *Little 'Tinker* (1948), *Half-Pint Pygmy* (1948*)*, *The Cat That Hated People* (1948), *Bad Luck Blackie* (1949), *Señor Droopy* (1949), *The House Of Tomorrow* (1949), *Doggone Tired* (1949), *Wags To Riches* (1949), *Little Rural Riding Hood* (1949), *Out-Foxed* (1949), *The Counterfeit Cat* (1949), *Ventriloquist Cat* (1950), *The Cuckoo Clock* (1950), *Garden Gopher* (1950), *The Chump Champ* (1950), *The Peachy Cobbler* (1950), *Cock-A-Doodle Dog* (1951), *Daredevil Droopy* (1951), *Droopy's Good Deed* (1951), *Symphony In Slang* (1951), *Car Of Tomorrow* (1951), *Droopy's Double Trouble* (1951), *Magical Maestro* (1952), *One Cab's Family* (1952), *Rock-A-Bye Bear* (1952), *Little Johnny Jet* (1952), *T.V. Of Tomorrow* (1953), *The Three Little Pups* (1953), *Drag-A-Long Droopy* (1954), *Billy Boy* (1954), *Homesteader Droopy* (1954), *Farm Of Tomorrow* (1954), *The Flea Circus* (1954), *Dixieland Droopy* (1954), *I'm Cold* (1954), *Crazy Mixed Up Pup* (1954), *The Legend Of Rockabye Point* (1955), *Field And Scream* (1955), *Sh-h-h-h-h* (1955), *The First Bad Man* (1955), *Deputy Droopy* (1955), *Cellbound* (1955), *Millionaire Droopy* (1956) and *Cat's Meow* (1957).

CAUSE: He died of lung cancer in Burbank, California, aged 72.

George Axelrod
Born June 9, 1922
Died June 21, 2003
Hollywood's highest-paid scriptwriter. George Axelrod was born in 1922 – "a great year for writers and drunks" he was to say – and grew up in New York. He spent his teenage years reading voraciously "to make up for my lack of formal education" and hanging around outside theatres. During the Second World War he served with the US Army Signal Corps and once demobbed he began to write for television and radio, notably *Midnight In Manhattan* and the *Grand Ole Opry* on the wireless and *Celebrity Time* for television. In 1947 he turned his hand to fiction and wrote the novel *Beggar's Choice*, which he followed five years later with *Blackmailer*. In 1948, he began to concentrate mainly on film and television. On November 20, 1952, *The Seven Year Itch* opened at the Fulton Theater on Broadway and ran for 1,141 performances. Starring Tom Ewell and Vanessa Brown, it was the story of a publishing executive who began to have adulterous thoughts when his wife left him alone in New York for the summer. When the play arrived at the Aldwych Theatre in London on May 14, 1953, the *Daily Telegraph*'s theatre critic said that the play was "highly ingenious, with plenty of amusing quirks", but felt that the play was actually trite. The play was made into a film with Ewell and Marilyn Monroe in 1955. That year

Axelrod's disjointed Hollywood satire *Will Success Spoil Rock Hunter?* opened at the Belasco Theater on October 13, 1955 starring Orson Bean, Martin Gabel, Walter Matthau and Jayne Mansfield. It ran for 444 performances. It was made into a film starring Tony Randall and Mansfield in 1957. In 1954 he wrote his first film *Phffft!* which starred Judy Holliday and Jack Lemmon. Two years later, in 1956, Axelrod wrote the screenplay for William Inge's 1955 play *Bus Stop* which starred Kim Stanley as Cherie in the theatre and Marilyn Monroe on screen. On December 16, 1959, *Goodbye Charlie* had its stage première at the Lyceum Theatre and starred Lauren Bacall and Sydney Chaplin (it was filmed in 1964 with Debbie Reynolds and Tony Curtis). Axelrod moved to Hollywood but tired of its phoniness and moved his family to England where they lived in Chester Square, London (minus a crate of expensive paintings and silver which fell into the Atlantic en route). The Axelrods stayed in London for almost a decade but George wrote little in that period. His best work was undoubtedly in the Fifties and early Sixties but increasing sexual freedom in the latter half of that decade began to lessen his appeal. One of his greatest successes was *Breakfast At Tiffany's*, drawn from Truman Capote's novella, which has been enormously popular since its release in 1961, thanks to Audrey Hepburn's performance in the lead role. He made another film with Hepburn two years later, *Paris When It Sizzles*. *The Manchurian Candidate* (1962), John Frankenheimer's film of Richard Condon's Cold War thriller, was a flop when it was first released. It was withdrawn by its leading man, Frank Sinatra, who owned the copyright, after President John F. Kennedy's assassination in 1963, but when it was re-released 20 years later, the film was hailed as a masterpiece. In 1965, on the release of *How To Murder Your Wife*, starring Jack Lemmon and Terry-Thomas, Axelrod said, "The American male is the only member of the animal kingdom that has consistently permitted itself to be bullied, coddled, mothered, tyrannised and in general made to feel like a feeble-minded idiot by the female of the species." "In my experience," he told another interviewer, "there are five things which make a man sexually attractive to a woman: power, money, energy and the ability to make her laugh." Asked about the fifth, he replied, "If you think I'm going to tell you that, you must be crazy." Axelrod's other film scripts included *The Secret Life Of An American Wife* (1968), *The Lady Vanishes* (1979), Frankenheimer's *The Holcroft Covenant* (1982) and *The Fourth Protocol* (1987). He married Gloria Washburn in 1942. They had two sons but divorced in 1954; that year he was remarried to the actress Joan Stanton (b. 1923), who died on September 13, 2001, in Los Angeles. They had a daughter, the actress Nina Axelrod. A stepson, Jonathan Axelrod (b. New York, July 9, 1949), also became a scriptwriter and producer. CAUSE: Axelrod died in Los Angeles, aged 81, of heart failure.

Sir Felix Aylmer, OBE

(FELIX EDWARD AYLMER-JONES)
Born February 21, 1889
Died September 6, 1979
Fruity-voiced thesp. If not for Kenneth Williams impersonating Aylmer in films and chat shows the old actor might be completely forgotten. Felix Aylmer was born at Alexander House in Corsham, Wiltshire, the second of five sons (one of whom died as a child) and one daughter of Lieutenant-Colonel (Thomas) Edward Aylmer-Jones and Lilian Cookworthy. He was educated at Magdalen College School and Exeter College, Oxford where he studied mathematical moderations and physics. At university he dabbled with the Oxford University Dramatic Society

and much to his parents' displeasure he decided on a theatrical career. He made his stage début in 1911 not long after his 22nd birthday playing the Italian in *Cook's Man* at the Coliseum Theatre. He subsequently worked with Fred Terry and Sir Herbert Beerbohm Tree before joining the Birmingham Repertory Company in 1913. From 1914 until 1918 he served with the Royal Navy Volunteer Reserve.

Unlike many actors Aylmer did not appreciate the Bard. "I am a bit of an anti-Shakespearean. I acknowledge his greatness, of course – but, you know, Shakespeare has done so much harm to actors. He has been responsible for so much work that is artificial and unreal." He claimed to prefer film-making, saying that it required a greater skill than stage work. He made his film début in *Escape* (1930) as the governor and went on to appear in, among many others, *The World, The Flesh, The Devil* (1932) as Sir Henderson Trent, *The Shadow* (1933) as Sir Richard Bryant, the coroner in *The Ghost Camera* (1933), *Whispering Tongues* (1934) as Superintendent Fulton, *The Iron Duke* (1934) as Lord Uxbridge, *Doctor's Orders* (1934) as Sir Daniel Summerfield, *The Price Of A Song* (1935) as Graham, *She Shall Have Music* (1935) as Donald Black, *Old Roses* (1935) as Lord Sandelbury, *Hello, Sweetheart* (1935) as Peabody, *Checkmate* (1935) as Henry Nicholls, *The Ace Of Spades* (1935) as Lord Yardleigh, *Tudor Rose* (1936) as Edward Seymour, Michael Powell's *Her Last Affaire* (1936) as Lord Carnforth, *Seven Sinners* (1936) as Sir Charles Webber, *As You Like It* (1936) as Duke Frederick, *Sensation* (1936) as Lord Bouverie, *Royal Eagle* (1936) as Windridge, *Man In The Mirror* (1936) as the Earl of Wigan, *The Improper Duchess* (1936) as Count Seidel, *The Frog* (1936) as John Bennett, the police commissioner in *Dusty Ermine* (1936), *Dreaming Lips* (1937) as Sir Robert Blaker, *Action For Slander* (1937) as Sir Eustace Cunninghame, *The Vicar Of Bray* (1937) as Earl of Brendon, *The Mill On The Floss* (1937) as Mr Wakem, *The Live Wire* (1937) as Wilton, *The Citadel* (1938) as Mr Boon, *I've Got A Horse* (1938) as Lovatt, *Break The News* (1938) as Sir George Bickory, *Just Like A Woman* (1939) as Sir Robert Hummel, *Young Man's Fancy* (1940) as Sir Caleb Crowther, *Spies Of The Air* (1940) as Colonel Cairns, *Night Train To Munich* (1940) as Dr John Fredericks, *Charley's Big-Hearted Aunt* (1940) as Henry Crawley, *The Briggs Family* (1940) as Mr Sand, *The Case Of The Frightened Lady* (1940) as Dr Lester Charles Amersham, *The Ghost Of St Michael's* (1941) as Dr Winter, *The Saint's Vacation* (1941) as Charles Leighton, *Spellbound* (1941) as Mr Morton, *Major Barbara* (1941) as James, *Kipps* (1941), *I Thank You* (1941) as Henry Potter, *South American George* (1941) as Mr Appleby, *Hi Gang!* (1941) as Lord Amersham, *The Seventh Survivor* (1941) as Sir Elmer Norton, *The Black Sheep Of Whitehall* (1942) as Crabtree, *Uncensored* (1942) as Colonel von Hohenstein, *Sabotage At Sea* (1942) as John Dighton, *Thursday's Child* (1943) as Mr Keith, *Escape To Danger* (1943) as Sir Alfred Horton, *The Demi-Paradise* (1943) as Mr Runalow, the lead in *Mr Emmanuel* (1944), *English Without Tears* (1944) as Mr Spaggot, *The Wicked Lady* (1945) as Hogarth, the first nobleman in *Caesar And Cleopatra* (1945), *The Years Between* (1946) as Sir Ernest Foster, *The Magic Bow* (1946) as Signor Fazzini, *The Laughing Lady* (1946) as Sir Felix Mountroyal, *A Man About The House* (1947) as Richard Sanctuary, *The October Man* (1947) as Dr Martin, *Green Fingers* (1947) as Daniel Booth, *The Ghosts Of Berkeley Square* (1947) as Colonel H. 'Bulldog' Kelsoe, *Hamlet* (1948) as Polonius, *The Calendar* (1948) as Lord Forlingham, *Quartet* (1949) as Maryin, *Edward, My Son* (1949) as Mr Hanray, *Prince Of*

Foxes (1949) as Count Marc Antonio Verano, *She Shall Have Murder* (1950) as Mr Playfair, *Quo Vadis* (1951) as Plautius, *No Highway* (1951) as Sir Philip, *The House In The Square* (1951) as Sir William, *Ivanhoe* (1952) as Isaac of York, *The Man Who Watched The Trains Go By* (1953) as Mr Merkemans, *The Master Of Ballantrae* (1953) as Lord Durrisdeer, *Knights Of The Round Table* (1953) as Merlin, *The Love Lottery* (1954) as Winant, *The Angel Who Pawned Her Harp* (1954) as Joshua Webman, *Anastasia* (1956) as the chamberlain, *Saint Joan* (1957) as the inquisitor, *I Accuse!* (1958) as Edgar Demange, *The Doctor's Dilemma* (1958) as Sir Patrick Cullen, *Separate Tables* (1958) as Mr Fowler, *The Two-Headed Spy* (1958) as Cornaz, *The Mummy* (1959) as Stephen Banning, *Exodus* (1960) as Dr Lieberman, *Never Take Sweets From A Stranger* (1960) as Clarence Olderberry, Sr, *From The Terrace* (1960) as James Duncan MacHardie, *The Hands Of Orlac* (1961) as Dr Francis Cochrane, *The Road To Hong Kong* (1962) as Grand Lama and *Masquerade* (1965) as Henrickson. He played Queen Victoria's libidinous prime minister Lord Palmerston three times on screen in *Victoria The Great* (1937), *Sixty Glorious Years* (1938) and *The Lady With A Lamp* (1951). He also played the ineffectual Lord North in *The Young Mr Pitt* (1942) and Lord Melbourne in the television film *Victoria Regina* (1961). He began appearing on television as early as 1938 and was a regular on the small screen. His last major role on television was playing Father Anselm, the Prior of Mountacres Priory, in the sitcom *Oh Brother!* (September 13, 1968– February 27, 1970) and in a couple of episodes of its successor *Oh Father!* He played bishops or other clergymen in *Kate Plus Ten* (1938), *The Life And Death Of Colonel Blimp* (1943), *The Chronicle History Or King Henry The Fifth With His Battell Fought At Agincourt In France* (1944) as

Archbishop of Canterbury, *The Way To The Stars* (1945) as Reverend Charles Moss, *The Man Within* (1947) as a priest, *Christopher Columbus* (1949) as Father Perez, *The Running Man* (1963) as a parson, *Becket* (1964) as Theobald of Bec, Archbishop of Canterbury, and lawyers in *The Temporary Widow* (1930), *Home, Sweet Home* (1933) as Robert Wilding, KC, *My Old Dutch* (1934) as a judge, *Girl In The News* (1941), *Once A Crook* (1941), *Your Witness* (1950) as a British judge, *The Boys* (1962) as a judge, *The Chalk Garden* (1964) as Judge McWhirrey, *Decline And Fall . . . Of A Birdwatcher* (1968) as the judge and *Hostile Witness* (1968) as Justice Osborne. He was president of the actors' union Equity for 20 years from 1949. He was made OBE in the 1950 Birthday Honours List and received his knighthood in the 1965 Birthday Honours List. He wrote two books about Dickens – *Dickens Incognito* (1959) in which he theorised (incorrectly) that the writer had a child by his mistress Ellen Ternan and *The Drood Case* (1964) about Dickens' final, unfinished work. He was married to the actor Cecily Byrne (b. Nottingham, July 31, 1889, d. Sussex, June 30, 1975). They had two sons, David and Ian, who both predeceased him and one daughter, Jennifer. David Aylmer (b. Hampstead, London, 1933, d. London, July 20, 1964 by his own hand) was an actor.

CAUSE: He retired to his Surrey home, 6 Painshill House, Cobham, Surrey, following a stroke. He died in a Sussex nursing home aged 90.

Agnes Ayres

(AGNES EYRE HENKEL)
Born April 4, 1896
Died Christmas Day, 1940
Twenties leading lady. Born in Carbondale, Illinois, she made her film début in *The Masked Wrestler* (1914) and went on to appear in more than 80 films. She is best known for appearing

opposite Rudolph Valentino in *The Sheik* (1921) as Lady Diana Mayo, *The Son Of The Sheik* (1926) as Diana and in Cecil B. DeMille's *The Ten Commandments* (1923). Her career ended in 1929 with the advent of talkies although she did appear in bit parts in five films in 1936 and 1937. 5'3" Agnes Ayres was married twice, to the producer Manuel Reachi (b. 1900, d. April 26, 1955) by whom she had one child, and to Frank P. Schuker. CAUSE: She died of a cerebral haemorrhage in Los Angeles, California. She was 44.

Lew Ayres

Born December 28, 1908
Died December 30, 1996
Actor with a conscience. Lewis Frederick Ayres III was born in Minneapolis, Minnesota, the scion of a musical family. His parents separated when he was 14 and he went to live in San Diego, California, with his mother. When he left Lake Harriett High School in Minneapolis, he studied medicine at the University of Arizona. Ayres formed a band and toured for a while before hooking up with Henry 'Hank' Halstead. At a tea dance working with Ray West's Cocoanut Grove Orchestra, he was spotted by Paul Bern (later Jean Harlow's husband), an executive with Pathé, who signed him up on a six-month contract. In that time he made just one film, *The Sophomore* (1929), before moving to MGM where he starred opposite Garbo in *The Kiss* (1929). It was the lead role as Paul Baumer, the patriotic German soldier in Lewis Milestone's *All Quiet On The Western Front* (1930), that made the 5'11" Ayres a star and also instilled pacifist views in him, beliefs that were to be sorely tested. The famous hand reaching out for a butterfly in the film is not Ayres'; it belongs to Lewis Milestone. Bizarrely, the film was banned in the Fatherland for being anti-German and in Poland for being pro-German. During the Thirties Ayres appeared in mainly disappointing B films, such as *Common Clay* (1930), *My Weakness* (1933), *State Fair* (1933) and *Holiday* (1938) before making the nine-part *Dr Kildare* series (1938–1942) opposite Lionel Barrymore. However, none matched up to *All Quiet . . .* On America's belated intervention in World War II, Ayres, a devout Quaker, was one of the first stars to be called up. In March 1942 he declared himself a conscientious objector and refused to go. MGM were bombarded with thousands of letters calling him a traitor and a coward, but Ayres stuck to his guns. He worked as an assistant to a chaplain and a doctor during the conflict in battle areas. Following the cessation of hostilities, his welcome back was lukewarm. It is often said Hollywood will forgive anything except failure and Ayres proved his mettle in *The Dark Mirror* (1946) and *Johnny Belinda* (1948), which garnered him a Best Actor nomination for his portrayal of Dr Robert Richardson, the medic who befriends a deaf mute. In 1955 he made *Altars Of The East*, a documentary about religion and two years later he was appointed to a three-year term with UNESCO. Just when it seemed he was destined for a quiet retirement, Ayres appeared in *Battle For The Planet Of The Apes* (1973), *Damien – Omen II* (1978), *Battlestar Galactica* (1979) and the pilot of *Hawaii Five-O*, which aired on September 20, 1968, playing the governor. Ayres married three times. He wed Lola Lane in Las Vegas, Nevada, on September 15, 1931, and was divorced in Los Angeles two years later on February 3, 1933. On November 14, 1934, in the Little Church of the Flowers in Glendale, California, he married Ginger Rogers (Janet Gaynor and Mary Brian were the bridesmaids) but that union ended acrimoniously in 1936; they divorced on March 13, 1940. Ayres said of the match: "Ginger Rogers was married to

her career and to that mother of hers. I interfered with both relationships. They were stronger or more important to Ginger than I was. It was fine while it lasted, except I often felt like an interloper. When it ended, I felt a bit sad and a lot relieved." Single for almost 30 years, he married English-born Diana Hall on February 7, 1964. His only child, a son called Justin Bret, was born on December 27, 1968.

CAUSE: Ayres died in his sleep two days after his 88th birthday, in Los Angeles.

B

Steven Bach

Born April 29, 1938
Died March 25, 2009
Fall guy. Born in Pocatello, Idaho, Bach was educated at high school in Boise, the Sorbonne and Northwestern University from where he graduated in 1961 with a degree in French and English. He taught American literature at New Trier High School in Winnetka, Illinois (the home town of Rock Hudson) before moving to Los Angeles in 1966 where he earned a doctorate in film at the University of Southern California, writing a dissertation on the films of Josef von Sternberg. He worked with the producer Gabriel Katzka for the next ten years as a story editor on theatrical and film projects. In 1978 he was appointed vice president and head of international production at United Artists. However, Bach's lasting infamy rests with his association with the mega flop *Heaven's Gate* (1980), Michael Cimino's sprawling historical drama about range wars in Wyoming in the 1890s. The film ran for three and a half hours – and ended up costing $36 million, five times the budget of an average studio film at the time. The critics were merciless. Roger Ebert wrote, "If the film was formless at four hours, it was insipid at 140 minutes. At either length it is so incompetently photographed and edited that there are times when we are not even sure which character we are looking at." The public's curiosity was not piqued. "It is as if somebody called every household in the country and said, 'There will be a curse on your family if you go see this picture,'" one United Artists executive said. Bach was sacked but got his revenge with a book about the film

Final Cut: Dreams And Disaster In The Making Of Heaven's Gate, published in 1985. United Artists was sold to MGM while the film was being shown at the Cannes Film Festival. Bach turned to writing and teaching at Columbia University and then film and literature at Bennington College. He was the author of three well-received biographies *Marlene Dietrich: Life And Legend* (1992), *Dazzler: The Life And Times Of Moss Hart* (2001) and *Leni: The Life And Work Of Leni Riefenstahl* (2007). Bach shared his life with his boyfriend, Werner Rohr.
CAUSE: Bach died aged 70 of cancer at his home in Arlington, Vermont.

Jim Backus

Born February 25, 1913
Died July 3, 1989
The voice of Mr Magoo. James Gilmore Backus was born in Cleveland, Ohio, and educated at the American Academy of Dramatic Arts. As with many performers, he appeared in vaudeville and on the radio before progressing to movies. His voice meant he was destined to play character parts instead of leads but he also branched out on television as Judge Bradley Stevens on *I Married Joan* (1952–1955), the pompous Thurston Howell III in *Gilligan's Island* (1964–1967) and, of course, the voice of myopic Quincy Magoo. One of his dramatic film roles was as James Dean's father in *Rebel Without A Cause* (1955). Among his other films were *The Pied Piper* (1942), *The Great Lover* (1949), *Don't Bother To Knock* (1952), *Meet Me In Las Vegas* (1956), a sheriff in *Macabre* (1960), a drunk pilot in *It's A Mad Mad Mad Mad World* (1963), *Myra Breckinridge* (1970), *Pete's Dragon* (1977) and *C.H.O.M.P.S.* (1979). He was married to actress Henriette 'Henny' Kay and up to his death they lived at 10914 Bellagio Road, Bel-Air. One of their neighbours was Alfred Hitchcock.
CAUSE: He was diagnosed with

Parkinson's disease some time before his death. On June 13, 1989, he was admitted to St. John's Hospital, Santa Monica because he had contracted pneumonia. For the two weeks leading up to his death he and wife Henny wrote two humorous books about living with Parkinson's. He died of complications from the disease aged 76. He was buried in Westwood Village Memorial Park, 1218 Glendon Avenue, Los Angeles 90024.

Olga Baclanova

Born August 19, 1896
Died September 6, 1974
'The Russian Tigress'. Born in Moscow, one of six children of Vladimir Baklanoff and his wife Alexandra, 5'4" Olga Baclanova graduated from the Cherniavsky Institute in Moscow and in 1912 aged 16 she enrolled in the Moscow Arts Theatre. She left the theatre in 1918 four years after she began making films. Her early work included: *Simfoniya Lyubvi E Smerti* (1914), *Kugda Zvuchat Struni Serdtza* (1914), *Velikij Magaraz* (1915), *Zagrobnaya Skitalitsa* (1915), the title role in *Zhenshchina Vampir* (1915), *Lyubov Pod Maskoi* (1915), *Tot, Kto Poluchayet Poshchechini* (1916), *Tsvety Zapozdalye* (1917) as Maruska and *Khleb* (1918), a pro-communist propaganda vehicle. In 1925 she toured America for eight months and when the theatre company returned to the Soviet Union she defected. She was spotted by Hollywood studios while playing the part of the nun in *The Miracle* in Los Angeles. Her Tinseltown début was a bit part in United Artists' *The Dove* (1927). In 1928 she made several films – *The Czarina's Secret*, *The Man Who Laughs* as Duchess Josiana opposite Conrad Veidt, *Three Sinners* as Baroness Hilda Brings, *Street Of Sin* as Annie, *Forgotten Faces* as Lilly Harlow, *The Docks Of New York* as Lou and *Avalanche* as Grace Stillwell – and her career was in the ascendancy. But then as the talkies became ever more

popular she was reduced to supporting roles because of her stage mannerisms (not because of her accent as is generally supposed). She appeared in *The Wolf Of Wall Street* (1929) as Olga, *A Dangerous Woman* (1929) as Tania Gregory, *The Man I Love* (1929) as Sonia Barondoff, *Cheer Up And Smile* (1930) as Yvonne, *Are You There?* (1930) as Countess Helenka and *The Great Lover* (1931) as Savarova. It was her next film that brought notoriety to all concerned and the film was banned in Britain for many years. In MGM's *Freaks* (opened on July 8, 1932), directed by Tod Browning at a cost of $311,000, Baclanova played Cleopatra, a trapeze artist who married a wealthy midget for his money. The film featured many deformed and disabled people who had previously been exhibited in sideshows for the public amusement. Studio head Louis B. Mayer was appalled and the film was withdrawn before being reissued with the title *Nature's Mistakes*. After *Freaks* Baclanova made just four more films before retiring from the screen – *Downstairs* (1932) as Baroness Eloise von Burgen, *Billion Dollar Scandal* (1933) as Anna, *Telephone Blues* (1935) and *Claudia* (1943) as Madame Daruschka. For ten years from 1933 she appeared in a number of Broadway shows and then toured America. She made her West End début in 1936 in *Going Places*. She later became a radio announcer before permanent retirement. She refused to travel to England because her dog would have to go into quarantine. When the animal died, she put its corpse into one of her drawers rather than bury it. She was married three times. Her first husband (in 1922) was Vladimir Zoppi by whom she had one child. They divorced on February 23, 1929. On March 5, 1929 she married the actor Nicholas Soussanin (b. Yalta, Russia, January 16, 1889, d. New York, April 27, 1975 of a heart attack) and had another child. Their marriage was dissolved in

1939, the year she married the film distributor Richard Davis.
CAUSE: After years of poor health, she died in Vevey, Switzerland.

Lloyd Bacon

Born December 4, 1889
Died November 15, 1955
Multi-talent. Born in San Jose, California, 5'10" Lloyd Francis Bacon intended to become a lawyer rather than an actor like his father, Frank (b. Marysville, California, January 16, 1864, d. Chicago, Illinois, November 19, 1922) and mother Jane Jennie Weidman. But the lure of the greasepaint was too much and he entered show business. Lloyd made his film début in 1914 and the following year joined Essanay where he worked with Charlie Chaplin. He appeared with the Little Tramp in *The Floorwalker* (1916) but then his career was interrupted by the First World War. Demobbed in 1919 he signed for Triangle but two years later moved behind the cameras as a director. He worked for Mack Sennett, Universal and Warner Bros. His films included *The Singing Fool* (1928) with Al Jolson, *Moby Dick* (1930), *The Picture Snatcher* (1933) with James Cagney, *Wonder Bar* (1934) again with Al Jolson, *42nd Street* (1933), *Footlight Parade* (1933), *Devil Dogs Of The Air* (1935), *Gold Diggers Of 1937* (1937), *A Slight Case Of Murder* (1938) with Edward G. Robinson, *The Oklahoma Kid* (1939), *Give My Regards To Broadway* (1948) and *The French Line* (1954). He was married to Margaret Adele Lowdermilk. Another brother, the 6' tall Irving (b. St Joseph, Missouri, September 6, 1893, d. Hollywood, California, February 5, 1965) also became an actor and appeared in more than 400 films between 1915 (*A Favorite Fool*) and 1958 (*Fort Massacre*).
CAUSE: He died aged 65 of a cerebral haemorrhage in Burbank, California.

Angela Baddeley, CBE

(MADELEINE AGGIE CLINTON-BADDELEY)
Born July 4, 1900
Died February 22, 1976
Overshadowed sibling. Born at 64 Pretoria Road, West Ham, London, one of the four daughters of journalist William Herman Clinton-Baddeley and his wife, Louise Rosalie Bourdin, she was a descendant of Sir Henry Clinton, the British general who captured New York during the American War of Independence. Educated privately, the elder sister of Hermione Baddeley made her stage début at the Old Vic on November 22, 1915, aged 15 (not 11 as many reference books have it) in *Richard III* playing the little Duke of York. It was on the stage that she predominantly worked and she excelled as Jenny Diver in the long-running revival (June 5, 1920–1923) of John Gay's *The Beggar's Opera* at The Lyric, Hammersmith. She had a versatility that annoyed some critics and delighted others. James Agate once commented that she could be "an ingénue without being a ninny". She was one of Emlyn Williams' favourite actresses in the Thirties and Forties. She was acclaimed for her portrayal of Olivia Grayne in his macabre *Night Must Fall* on May 31, 1935 at the Duchess Theatre. This part took her to her American stage début at the Barrymore Theater in New York on September 28, 1936. She joined the Old Vic company in the late Forties. Her films were *The Speckled Band* (1931) which starred Raymond Massey as Sherlock Holmes, *The Ghost Train* (1931), written by *Dad's Army*'s Arnold Ridley (Private Godfrey), *Arms And The Man* (1932), *The Citadel* (1938) and *Tom Jones* (1963). It was for her portrayal of the cook Mrs Bridges in *Upstairs Downstairs* (1971–1975) that she became known to TV audiences. She married twice. Her first husband (in 1921) was director Stephen Kerr Thomas by whom she had a daughter.

He left her on the day that her sister, Hermione, married for the first time. Husband number two (on July 8, 1929) was the bisexual actor-director Glencairn Alexander Byam Shaw, CBE (b. December 13, 1904, d. Goring-on-Thames, April 29, 1986) by whom she had a son and a daughter. He numbered Siegfried Sassoon among his lovers and had an affair with Rachel Kempson, Lady Redgrave.

CAUSE: Appearing in Stephen Sondheim's *A Little Night Music* in the West End she caught a cold that turned to bronchitis and then pneumonia. She went to convalesce in a nursing home and seemed to be making progress but died suddenly at Grayshott Hall, Grayshott, Hampshire, near Haslemere. She was 75. Survived by her husband, she left £56,781.

Hermione Baddeley
(HERMIONE YOULANDA RUBY CLINTON-BADDELEY)
Born November 13, 1906
Died August 19, 1986
Blowsy sophisticate. Born in Broseley, Shropshire, the youngest of four daughters and educated privately, she appeared on the stage from the age of eight. She later became celebrated for her performances in revues. For a time following her first marriage she retired from performing but returned to the
. stage with her sister in *The Greeks Have A Word For It* at the Duke of York's Theatre in November 1934. She made her movie début in *A Daughter In Revolt* (1926) and appeared in numerous films including *Kipps* (1941), *Brighton Rock* (1947) as Ida Arnold, *Passport To Pimlico* (1949), *Tom Brown's Schooldays* (1951), *The Pickwick Papers* (1952), *Room At The Top* (1958) for which she was nominated for an Oscar, *Mary Poppins* (1964), *The Unsinkable Molly Brown* (1964), *Harlow* (1965), and *The Happiest Millionaire* (1967). In April 1928 she married the Hon. David Tennant at the Henrietta Street

Registry Office just off the Strand. She was an hour late for the wedding, believing she was getting hitched at midday instead of the 11am the office was booked for. Even then things didn't go to plan. The registrar disappeared and the couple eventually married at 12.30pm. They had one son, David (b. 1930), and one daughter, Pauline, born before their marriage. They divorced in 1939. Her second husband was Captain J. H. 'Dozey' Willis, MC, whom she married in 1941 at Caxton Hall, Westminster, London. It was not an auspicious match. Most of the wedding presents were stolen at the reception and Baddeley admitted that she never loved her husband. They divorced in 1946. She never remarried but had several affairs, including one with the much younger Laurence Harvey. An animal lover, she dedicated her autobiography to her dog.

CAUSE: She died of a stroke in the Cedars-Sinai Hospital Medical Center, 8700 Beverly Boulevard, Los Angeles, aged 79.

FURTHER READING: *The Unsinkable Hermione Baddeley: An Autobiography* – Hermione Baddeley (London: William Collins, 1984).

Alan Badel
Born September 11, 1923
Died March 19, 1982
Second string. Born in Rusholme, Manchester, the son of Auguste Firman Joseph Badel and Elizabeth Olive Durose, Alan Badel was educated at Burnage High School in Manchester before attending RADA (1939–1941) where he was a Bancroft Gold medallist. He made his stage début in August 1940 as George in *The Black Eye* and first appeared in London a year later on August 18, 1941 at the Mercury Theatre playing Pierrot in *L'Enfant Prodigue*. From 1942 until his demob in April 1947 he served with the Parachute Regiment, 6th Airborne

Division. During his service he performed with the army play unit in various roles. In 1942 he married Yvonne Owen and their daughter Sarah (b. London, March 30,1943) became an actor and appeared nude in television series *The History Man* (1981). He made his film début in *The Stranger Left No Card* (1952) as John Smith and also appeared in *Salome* (1953) as John the Baptist, *Will Any Gentleman . . .?* (1953) as The Great Mendoza, *Magic Fire* (1956) as Richard Wagner, *This Sporting Life* (1963) as Weaver, *Children Of The Damned* (1963) as Dr David Neville, *Bitter Harvest* (1963) as Karl Denny, *Arabesque* (1966) as Beshraavi, *Otley* (1968) as Sir Alex Hadrian, *Where's Jack?* (1969) as the Lord Chancellor, *The Adventurers* (1970) as President Rojo, *The Day Of The Jackal* (1973) as the minister, *Luther* (1973) as Thomas De Vio, *Telefon* (1977) as Colonel Malchenko, *Force 10 From Navarone* (1978) as Major Petrovich, a barrister in *The Medusa Touch* (1978), *Agatha* (1979) as Lord Brackenbury, *The Riddle Of The Sands* (1979) as Dollmann and *Nijinsky* (1980) as Baron de Gunzburg. Badel once appeared in a play with John Gielgud and at one stage Gielgud was to be found in the opposite wing from which he was to enter with Badel. When another cast member queried Gielgud's behaviour, he was shushed with the words, "I am just hiding from that awful Alan Badel."
CAUSE: He died in Chichester, Sussex, aged 59 from a heart attack.

Clarence Badger

Born June 8, 1880
Died June 17, 1964
Respected director. A former stage actor and journalist, San Francisco-born Badger became a screenwriter and then a director at Triangle-Keystone in 1915. Among his films was *The Danger Girl* (1915) which starred Gloria Swanson. In 1920 he moved to the Goldwyn studios but maintained his freelance status, also working for First National, Metro and Paramount. His films included: *Potash And Perlmutter* (1923), *Painted People* (1924) starring Colleen Moore, *Miss Brewster's Millions* (1926), *It* (1927) starring Clara Bow, *Man Power* (1927), *She's A Sheik* (1927), *Kiss In A Taxi* (1927), *The Fifty-Fifty Girl* (1928), *No, No, Nanette* (1928), *The Hot Heiress* (1931), *When Strangers Marry* (1933) and *Rangle River* (1939). Badger's rosy red cheeks led to Clara Bow nicknaming him 'Santa' during the filming of *It*. He told the actor Louise Brooks, "When I start to direct [Clara], I get mad because she's doing all these things. And then I run them and they're wonderful." Badger found the best way to work was to "set up the camera, explain the scene to [Clara] and just let her go." It seemed to work because Bow rated Badger and Victor Fleming as her favourite directors. In 1940 he retired and emigrated to Australia. On July 16, 1903, he married Lillian Schoene and they had one son, Clarence, Jr (b. California, March 8, 1904, d. Los Angeles, California, April 21, 1992).
CAUSE: Badger died in New South Wales, Australia, nine days after his 84th birthday.

Max Baer

Born February 11, 1909
Died November 21, 1959
'The Livermore Larruper'. Born in Omaha, Nebraska, 6'2" Maximilian Adelbert Baer was the son of a California cattle slaughterer. His younger brother was the boxer Buddy Baer (b. Denver, Colorado, June 11, 1915, d. Martinez, California, July 18, 1986). Max began professional boxing on May 16, 1929 and went on to become world heavyweight champion in Long Island on June 14, 1934 when he beat reigning champion Primo Carnera, putting him down 11 times in 11 rounds. During the fight Baer

laughed and joked constantly but when he tried the same tactics the following year on June 13, 1935 against James Braddock, he was beaten on points. Baer held the title for 364 days. Determined to regain his title, Baer trained hard but was beaten by Joe Louis in four rounds. He never recovered from the embarrassing defeat. Baer turned to show business and made his début in *The Prizefighter And The Lady* (1933) as Steve Morgan. He went on to appear in *Kids On The Cuff* (1935), *Over She Goes* (1938) as Silas Morner, *The Navy Comes Through* (1942) as Coxswain G. Berringer, *The McGuerins From Brooklyn* (1942) as Professor Samson, *Ladies' Day* (1943) as Hippo Jones, *Buckskin Frontier* (1943) as Tiny, *Africa Screams* (1949) as Grappler McCoy, *Bride For Sale* (1949) as Litka, *Two Knights From Brooklyn* (1949) as Mr Samson, *Riding High* (1950) as Bertie, *Two Roaming Champs* (1950), *Wine, Women And Bong* (1951), *Skipalong Rosenbloom* (1951) as Butcher Baer, *The Champ Steps Out* (1951), *Rootin' Tootin' Tenderfeet* (1952) as Max, *The Harder They Fall* (1956) as Buddy Brannen, *Utah Blaine* (1957) as Gus Ortmann and *Once Upon A Horse . . .* (1958) as Ben. Baer was inducted into the World Boxing Hall of Fame in 1984 and into the International Boxing Hall of Fame in 1995. He was married twice, firstly to the actor Dorothy Dunbar (b. Colorado Springs, May 28, 1902, d. Seattle, Washington, October 23, 1992) – she was married seven times – and then to Mary Ellen Sullivan. His son Max Baer, Jr, (b. Oakland, California, December 4, 1937) is best known as Jethro Bodine in the original *Beverly Hillbillies* television series. CAUSE: Max Baer died aged 50 from a heart attack.

Robin Bailey

Born October 5, 1919
Died January 14, 1999
Robin Bailey was born in Hucknall,

Nottingham, the son of George Henry Bailey and Thirza Ann Mettam. After school at Mellish, he joined the Post Office but found the lure of the stage too great and in 1938 he joined Nottingham Theatre Royal. He served in the Army from 1940 until 1944. He made his London stage début on March 26, 1947 at the Piccadilly Theatre as Ludovico in *Othello*. The previous year he began making films appearing in *School For Secrets* (1946). His other films included: *Private Angelo* (1949) as Simon Telfer, *Portrait Of Clare* (1950) as Dudley Wilburn, *His Excellency* (1952) as Charles, *Gift Horse* (1952) as Lieutenant Michael Grant, *Single-Handed* (1953) as Commander John Stafford, *Another Time, Another Place* (1958) as Captain Barnes, *The Diplomatic Corpse* (1958) as Mike Billings, *The Mouse On The Moon* (1963), *Catch Us If You Can* (1965) as Guy, *Commuter Husbands* (1973) as Dennis, *Sins With Our Permission* (1980) as Dr Perry, *If You Go Down In The Woods Today* (1981) as the Chief Constable, *Screamtime* (1983) as Jack, *Jane And The Lost City* (1987) as the colonel and *Number 27* (1988) as Dr Maurice Barwick. On the small screen he was best known for his roles in comedies. He played Uncle Mort in Alan Tinniswood's *I Didn't Know You Cared* (August 27, 1975–June 26, 1979). He appeared in the sketch show *Took And Co* (August 7–September 18, 1977). He was the star of *Sorry, I'm A Stranger Here Myself* (June 15, 1981–May 18, 1982) playing the librarian Henry Nunn. Following the death of Arthur Lowe on April 15, 1982 he took over the lead in *Potter* for the third series which ran on BBC1 from July 17 until August 28, 1983. On the drama front he appeared in *Rumpole Of The Bailey* (1978) as Judge Graves, *Charters & Caldicott* (1985) as Charters, *Dalziel And Pascoe: An Autumn Shroud* (1996) as Hereward Fielding and *A Dance To The Music Of Time* (1997) as Uncle Alfred Tolland.

He married Patricia Weekes and fathered three sons, Nicholas, Simon and Justin.
CAUSE: Robin Bailey died aged 79 in London from respiratory failure.

Fay Bainter

Born December 7, 1891
Died April 16, 1968
Always mom. Born in Los Angeles, Fay Bainter didn't enter films until an age when many actresses regard their best work as being behind them. She made her first stage appearance aged six and her Broadway début aged 20 on January 22, 1912, at Daly's Theater as Celine Marinter in *The Rose Of Panama* but was 42 before she made her way in front of a movie camera in *This Side Of Heaven* (1934). Four years later, she became the first actor ever to be nominated for Best Actress (*White Banners* [1938]) and Best Supporting Actress (*Jezebel* [1938] as Aunt Belle) Oscars in the same year. She won for *Jezebel* but lost the other nomination. It was this that forced the Academy to change its rules regarding nominees. In her other films she played strong maternal parts. Her work included *Young Tom Edison* (1940), *Our Town* (1940), *The Secret Life Of Walter Mitty* (1947) and *The Children's Hour* (1962) which earned her another Oscar nod.
CAUSE: She died aged 76 of natural causes in Los Angeles.

Bob Baker

(LELAND T. WEED)
Born November 8, 1901
Died August 30, 1975
B-movie singing cowboy. Born in Forest City, Iowa, Baker was a real cowboy before becoming a *reel* one, joining a cattle ranch in Colorado while he was still a teenager. His next career move involved working as a singer on the radio before joining the *National Barn Dance* wireless show. In 1936 he successfully auditioned for Universal who were looking to cash in on the singing cowboy craze. He made

his first film *Courage Of The West* as Jack Saunders for Universal in 1937 and went on to make a dozen films at the studio – *The Singing Outlaw* as Scrap Gordon (1937), *The Black Bandit* as Bob Ramsay/Don Ramsay, *Border Wolves* as Rusty Reynolds, *Ghost Town Riders* as Bob Martin, *Guilty Trails* as Bob Higgins, *The Last Stand* as Tip Douglas posing as the Laredo Kid, *The Outlaw Express* as Captain Bob Bradley, *Prairie Justice* as US Marshal Bob Randall, a.k.a. Bob Smith, *Western Trails* as Bob Mason (all 1938), *Honor Of The West* as Sheriff Bob Barrett and *The Phantom Stage* as Bob Carson (both 1939) – before he was dropped from leading man status. He next appeared in six films in the Frontier Marshall series alongside Johnny Mack Brown and Fuzzy Knight: *Desperate Trails* (1939) as Clem Waters, *Oklahoma Frontier* (1939) as Tom Rankin, *Chip Of The Flying U* (1939) as Dusty, *West Of Carson City* (1940) as Nevada, *Riders Of Pasco Basin* (1940) as Bruce Moore and *Bad Man From Red Butte* (1940) as Gabriel Hornsby. He also appeared in Edward Killy's *Along The Rio Grande* (1941) as the jailer Deputy Bob, *Arizona Bound* (1941) as Marshal Bat Madison, Abbott & Costello's *Ride 'Em Cowboy* (1942) as the ranch cowhand driving a bus and *Overland Mail* (1942) as Bill Cody. In 1943 he joined Monogram Pictures where he appeared in *Wild Horse Stampede* (1943) as Marshal Bob Tyler, part of the Trail Blazer series with Hoot Gibson and Ken Maynard. In 1943 Baker retired from film-making. His last two films, released after his retirement, were uncredited bit-parts in *Oklahoma Raiders* (1944) and *Mystery Man* (1944). He served in the Korean War and later became a policeman in Arizona.
CAUSE: In 1969 he suffered several coronaries and his health was never the same. He died aged 73 of an embolism in Veterans Hospital, Prescott, Arizona.

Eddie Baker

Born November 17, 1897
Died February 4, 1968

Real life private dick. Born in Davis, West Virginia and educated in Washington, DC, Edwin King Baker's career began in his father's repertory company and in 1913 he became a prop boy at Biograph. Baker appeared in comedies, working three times with Laurel & Hardy, where he often played a detective or a sheriff. His size (he was 6′1″) meant he was often cast as a thug but equally he played policemen. He was the first secretary/treasurer of the Screen Actors' Guild but when he left show business he became a real life detective.

CAUSE: He died in Hollywood, California, of emphysema. He was 70.

Hylda Baker

Born February 4, 1905
Died May 1, 1986

Malapropist extraordinaire. Born, with a cawl (which was probably the reason she was very superstitious), at 23 Ashworth Street, Farnworth, Lancashire, the eldest of seven children, she made her stage début aged ten at the Opera House, Tunbridge Wells. She toured music halls regularly but it wasn't until she hit 50 that she became known to a wider audience via TV's *The Good Old Days*. With her stooge Cynthia (actually a man in drag) towering over her, the 4′10½″ actress had audiences doubled up. She was a star in the Granada TV sitcom *Nearest & Dearest*. The series began on August 15, 1968, and was created by Vince Powell (b. Miles Platting, Manchester, August 6, 1928 as Vincent Joseph Smith, d. Guildford, Surrey July 13, 2009) and his partner Harry Driver (b. Manchester, May 13, 1931, d. November 25, 1973 from polio complications) who would also create *Bless This House*, *Love Thy Neighbour*, *Mike & Bernie*, *For The Love Of Ada* and *Never Mind The Quality, Feel The Width*. *Nearest & Dearest* was

the story of Eli and Nellie Pledge, an unmarried brother and sister who had been bequeathed their father's pickle factory in his will. The humour came mostly from the insults traded by the two – "You knock-kneed knackered old nosebag" and "You big girl's blouse" – and Nellie's malapropisms: "How dare you? Calling your own sister a trombone!" and "You remind me of that song from *The Sound Of Music*." "Which one? 'My Favourite Things'?" "No. Idleswine!" Other characters included the inept handy man Stan and Nellie's cousin Lilly Tattershall and her husband Walter who was perennially troubled by his internal waterworks – "Has 'e been?" *Nearest & Dearest* ran for four years, during which 45 episodes were made. The bickering on screen between the two characters was as nothing compared to the off-screen fireworks. Jimmy Jewel and Hylda Baker loathed each other with a passion. Each believed the other was given funnier lines and strove to top them. Both refused to appear when the other was featured on *This Is Your Life*. It was a relief to both when the series ended, but long-term happiness was to elude Hylda Baker. Her next series was called *Not On Your Nellie* and saw her installed as Nellie Pickersgill, a pub landlady. When that series finished she gradually disappeared from the public view. She made just five films. She played Aunt Ada, a backstreet abortionist, in *Saturday Night And Sunday Morning* (1960) and appeared in *She Knows You Know* (1961), Winny in *Up The Junction* (1967), Mrs Sowerberry in *Oliver!* (1968) and the film version of *Nearest & Dearest* (1972) in which she reprised her role as Nellie Pledge. She married divorcé Ben Pearson on January 12, 1929. She miscarried their first child and the second, third and fourth were ectopic pregnancies. The couple divorced in 1933. Hylda Baker remained an extremely superstitious person throughout her life.

CAUSE: In the Eighties she began to suffer from mental problems. On June 6, 1981 she went into Brinsworth House, the Entertainment Artists' Benevolent Home in Twickenham. In December 1982, she was institutionalised in Horton Hospital, a psychiatric centre, in Epsom. She died there aged 81 from bronchial pneumonia and was cremated in Twickenham. She left less than £40,000 in her will.
FURTHER READING: *She Knows You Know! The Remarkable Story Of Hylda Baker* – Jean Fergusson (Derby: Breedon Books, 1997).

Kenny Baker

Born September 30, 1912
Died August 10, 1985
Boyish singer. Kenneth Laurence Baker was born in Monrovia, California, and came to prominence as the singer on Jack Benny's radio shows in the Thirties. When he left in 1939 to concentrate on films, he was replaced by Dennis Day. Baker appeared in *College Rhythm* (1934), *George White's 1935 Scandals* (1935), *Metropolitan* (1935), *King Of Burlesque* (1935) as Arthur, *The King And The Chorus Girl* (1937) as the Folies Bergère soloist, *A Day At The Races* (1937), *Mr Dodd Takes The Air* (1937) as Claude Dodd, *52nd Street* (1937) as Benjamin Zamarelli, *The Goldwyn Follies* (1938) as Danny Beecher, *The Mikado* (1939) as Nanki-Poo, *At The Circus* (1939) as Jeff Wilson, *Hit Parade Of 1941* (1940) as David Farraday, *Silver Skates* (1943) as Danny, *Doughboys In Ireland* (1943) as Danny O'Keefe, *The Harvey Girls* (1946) as Terry O'Halloran and *Calendar Girl* (1947) as Byron Jones. He starred with Mary Martin in the original Broadway production of Kurt Weill and Ogden Nash's *One Touch Of Venus* before retiring in the Fifties to become a Christian Science practitioner.
CAUSE: He died in Solvang, California of a heart attack.

Sir Stanley Baker

Born February 28, 1928
Died June 28, 1976
He-man hero. Born at 32 Albany Street in Ferndale, a village in the Rhondda, South Wales, William Stanley Baker was the third of three children of John Henry Baker and Elizabeth Louisa Lock. John Baker had lost a leg in a mining accident in 1917, and found it hard to gain full-time employment so the family lived in poverty. Baker greatly resented the charity that was given to his family. Like his contemporary and life-long friend Richard Burton, Baker was taken under the wing of a paternal schoolmaster, Glynne Morse. Teaching at Ferndale secondary school, English master Morse wrote plays for his pupils. It was said that Morse was struck by Baker's "satanic" stage presence and accompanied the boy to Cardiff where he auditioned at the age of thirteen for the film producer Sir Michael Balcon. Baker made his film début aged 14 in Balcon's Ealing war drama *Under Cover* (1942) playing the patriot Peter. Baker began his professional stage career by understudying Richard Burton in Emlyn Williams' play *The Druid's Rest* (1943). In 1944 Morse took Baker to audition for Sir Barry Jackson at the Birmingham Repertory where he stayed for two years before being called up for the army (1946–1948). Among his roles at Birmingham was that of Hector Malone in a production of George Bernard Shaw's *Man And Superman* (1945) directed by a young Peter Brook, in which a then unknown Paul Scofield played John Tanner. It seemed that Baker was destined to appear as the villain in any number of Fifties melodramas, such was his demeanour. He appeared in *All Over The Town* (1949) as Barnes, *Obsession* (1949), *Your Witness* (1950) as Sergeant Bannoch, *Lilli Marlene* (1950) as Evans, *The Rossiter Case* (1951) as Joe, a reporter in *Whispering Smith Hits London* (1951), *Home To Danger*

(1951) as Willie Dougan and the milkman in *Cloudburst* (1951). In *Captain Horatio Hornblower* (1951), which starred Gregory Peck, Baker played Mr Harrison, the testy bosun and showed that he could act as well as look menacing. In Charles Frend's *The Cruel Sea* (1953), an epic war film also made at Ealing Studios in the summer and autumn of 1952, he was cast as Bennett, the bullying first lieutenant. Lockhart, the character played by Donald Sinden, represented Nicholas Montserrat, the author of the autobiographical novel on which the film was based. *The Cruel Sea* was produced by Leslie Norman, father of former BBC film critic Barry Norman and written by Eric Ambler. It was the first of several major action movies in which Baker played a hard-bitten hero or a determined villain. These included: *The Red Beret* (1953) as Breton, *The Tell-Tale Heart* (1953) as Edgar Allan Poe, *The Good Die Young* (1954) as Mike Morgan, *Knights Of The Round Table* (1953) as the villainous Sir Modred, *Hell Below Zero* (1954) as Erik Bland, *Beautiful Stranger* (1954) as Louis Galt, *Richard III* (1955) as Henry, Earl of Richmond, *Helen Of Troy* (1956) as the wily Achilles, *Alexander The Great* (1956) as Attalus, *A Hill In Korea* (1956) as Corporal Ryker, *Child In The House* (1956) as Stephen Lorimer, *Checkpoint* (1956) as O'Donovan, *Hell Drivers* (1957) as Tom Yately, *Campbell's Kingdom* (1957) as Owen Morgan, *Violent Playground* (1958) as Sergeant Truman, *Sea Fury* (1958) as Abel Hewson, *The Angry Hills* (1959) as Conrad Heisler, *Yesterday's Enemy* (1959) as Captain Langford, *Jet Storm* (1959) as Captain Bardow and *Hell Is A City* (1960) as Inspector Martineau. In 1961 he co-starred with Gregory Peck in what became the most successful war film up to that time – J. Lee Thompson's *The Guns Of Navarone*. The film was shot between March and November of 1960 on

location on the island of Rhodes and at Shepperton Studios. Baker played Private 'Butcher' Brown in an all-star cast that included David Niven, Anthony Quinn, Anthony Quayle, Richard Harris and James Robertson-Justice. Two years earlier, Baker had made *Blind Date* (1959) as Inspector Morgan. It was his first collaboration with the American film director Joseph Losey, who, after being blacklisted in Hollywood by Senator Joe McCarthy's House Un-American Activities Committee, had come to live in Britain. Their next film together was *The Criminal* (1960) in which Baker played the unscrupulous gangster Johnny Bannion. In the early Sixties, Baker went into partnership with the Canadian director Cy Endfield, another refugee from Hollywood, to co-produce the film *Zulu* (1964), the true-life story of the defence of Rorke's Drift on January 22, 1879 by the South Wales Borderers. The film was shot on location in Natal from May to July 1963. Four thousand real Zulus were used as extras but they were mystified by what they had to do until Baker showed them an old Gene Autry film. Baker played the tough commanding officer of the besieged garrison, Lieutenant John Rouse Merriott Chard (b. Boxhill, near Plymouth, Devon, December 21, 1847, d. Hatch Beauchamp, Somerset, November 1, 1897 of cancer of the tongue). Michael Caine was his cavalier second-in-command, Lieutenant Gonville Bromhead (b. Versailles, France, August 29, 1845, d. Camp Dabhaura, Allahabad, India, February 9, 1891 of enteric fever). Both Chard and Bromhead were gazetted VCs on May 2, 1879 for their bravery at Rorke's Drift. Nine other VCs were awarded that day. In 1972 Baker bought Chard's VC and campaign medal at auction for £2,700. *Zulu* grossed more than $12 million through its sales worldwide, eight times its original investment and Baker became a wealthy and successful film producer overnight with his own company, Diamond Films. However, other films that he produced, including *Sands Of The Kalahari* (1965) in which Baker played the reluctant hero Mike Bain, were not so successful. In *Eva* (1962) and *Accident* (1967) Losey cast Baker against type as a bogus writer and a university don with startling success. In 1968 Baker and Richard Burton were invited to become directors of the newly formed independent television company Harlech Television (HTV). Baker returned to playing villainous roles as the gangster Paul Clifton in *Robbery* (1967) and the corrupt thief-taker Jonathan Wild in *Where's Jack?* (1969), both of which he also produced. Baker also played television roles, appearing in *The Taming Of The Shrew* (1952) as Petruchio, *The Creature* (1955) as Tom Friend, *Jane Eyre* (from February 24, 1956) as Mr Rochester, *A Fear Of Strangers* (1964) as Chief Inspector Tom Dyke, *Who Has Seen The Wind?* (1965) as Janos, *The Tormentors* (1966) as John Ellis, *Code Name: Heraclitus* (1967) as Frank G. Wheatley, *The Changeling* (1974) as De Flores, *Who Killed Lamb?* (1974), *Robinson Crusoe* (1974) as Robinson Crusoe, *Graceless Go I* (1974) as the drunken psychiatrist and *How Green Was My Valley* (from December 29, 1975) as Gwilym Morgan, a part he based on his father. His other films included: *Eva* (1962) as Tyvian Jones, *Sodom And Gomorrah* (1962) as Astaroth, *A Prize Of Arms* (1962) as Turpin, *The Man Who Finally Died* (1962) as Joe Newman, *In The French Style* (1963) as Walter Beddoes, *Dingaka* (1965) as Tom Davis, *La Ragazza Con La Pistola* (1968) as Dr Osborne, *The Italian Job* (1969) which he also produced, *The Last Grenade* (1970) as Major Harry Grigsby, *The Games* (1970) as Bill Oliver, *Perfect Friday* (1970) as Mr Graham opposite a topless Ursula Andress, *Una Lucertola Con La Pelle Di Donna* (1971) as

Inspector Corvin, *Popsy Pop* (1971) as Inspector Silva, *Innocent Bystanders* (1972) as John Craig, *Zorro* (1975) as Colonel Huerta and *Pepita Jiménez* (1975) as Pedro de Vargas. Baker also produced *The Other People* (1968) and *Colosseum And Juicy Lucy* (1970). During the Fifties Baker became one of Britain's highest-paid actors but, unlike Richard Burton, Baker spurned the international jet set. He remained insular and quick to lose his temper. Humourless, stubborn and old-fashioned, Baker was not a typical actor. He wore his toupeed hair short and nearly always dressed in a conservative suit. A socialist, he accepted a knighthood from his friend Harold Wilson shortly before his death but Baker's socialism was more of the Bollinger Bolshevik variety. On October 21, 1950, he married the actress Ellen Rose Martin who had been introduced to him by Richard Burton. The Bakers had four children, Glyn, Sally, Martin, and Adam. He owned and lived, while in London, in Alembic House, 93 Albert Embankment, London SE1, where the disgraced peer Jeffrey Archer has a flat. CAUSE: In the mid-Seventies Baker began to make plans for a sequel to *Zulu*. In January 1976 Baker threw a party and showed a guest his hand. Baker pointed out that his fingers had become suddenly stubby. The guest told him that meant he had cancer or a heart problem. The following month Baker underwent surgery to remove a cancerous tumour from his lung. The procedure appeared to have resolved the problem and Baker underwent an intense course of chemotherapy. Unfortunately, the cancer had not cleared up and Baker moved to his home in Marbella, Spain for the good weather. However, the bright sun meant that he had to wear a vest and long johns all the time because he was susceptible to skin cancers. Baker spent his time dining out when he could summon the strength and moaning at his wife. By early June the cancer had spread to his hip and he returned to London for treatment. Returning to Spain, he suffered a relapse and he was so weak he could not untie his pyjama cord. An oncology specialist travelled to Spain and told Baker that he must return to London where the facilities were much better. Before arrangements could be made for the trip Baker died aged 48 in Residencia Sanitaria Carlos Haya, a hospital in Malaga, close to his second home. He was worth £421,823 at death. His ashes were scattered in Ferndale.

Sir Michael Balcon

Born May 19, 1896
Died October 17, 1977
Ealing's inventor. Michael Elias Balcon was born at 116 Summer Lane, Edgbaston, Birmingham, the youngest son and fourth of five children of Louis Balcon (c.1858–1946), a Jewish-Lithuanian salesman and Laura Greenberg (c.1863–1934). Balcon described his childhood as "respectable but impoverished". In 1907 he won a scholarship to George Dixon Grammar School in Birmingham. He left school in 1913 because of family hardships and went to work as a jeweller's apprentice. Balcon was turned down for military service in 1914 because of a problem with his left eye. Instead, in 1915 he joined the Dunlop Rubber Company's plant at Aston Cross and eventually became personal assistant to the managing director. At the end of hostilities he formed a film company with Victor Savile, Victory Motion Pictures. Their backer was Oscar Deutsch, a rich scrap-metal dealer who later founded the Odeon cinema chain. It was a modest success and in 1923 they produced their first film *Woman To Woman* starring Betty Compson and directed by Graham Cutts. Balcon and Cutts went on to form Gainsborough Pictures in Poole Street, Islington, London N1, the former home of

Famous Players–Lasky (later to become Paramount). One of the earliest films was *The Pleasure Garden* (1925) directed by a newcomer called Alfred Hitchcock. Early Gainsborough pictures often featured Ivor Novello including *The Rat* (1925), directed by Graham Cutts, and Alfred Hitchcock's *The Lodger* (1926). In 1928 Gainsborough was relaunched as a public company. In 1931 Balcon took charge at Gaumont-British Picture Corporation, Gaumont's Lime Grove Studios in Shepherd's Bush. Later that year he suffered a nervous breakdown. Balcon presided over a number of worthy films over the next five years including *The Good Companions* (1932), *The Constant Nymph* (1933), *The Ghoul* (1933) starring Boris Karloff, *Evergreen* (1934) starring Jessie Matthews, Hitchcock's *The Thirty-Nine Steps* (1935) and *Rhodes Of Africa* (1936). He also found a home for many Jews fleeing from Nazi persecution in Germany. He even made a film *Jew Süss* (1934) subtly criticising the anti-Semitism. Conrad Veidt escaped through Balcon's direct intervention. Though Gaumont and Gainsborough productions generally did well in Britain, they rarely found much favour in the USA. In November 1936 he moved to MGM-British at Denham but his experience was an unhappy one and he produced just one film, *A Yank At Oxford* (1938) starring Robert Taylor and Vivien Leigh. After 18 months he replaced Basil Dean at Ealing Studios, a company whose name he was to make internationally known. He made many George Formby movies which were popular with the public but Balcon himself liked neither the films nor their star. During the Second World War he produced a number of military films. *The Next Of Kin* (1942) was a vivid dramatisation of the slogan "Careless talk costs lives" and infuriated Churchill, but was released at the insistence of the War Office. Other similar films included *The*

Foreman Went To France (1942), *Went The Day Well?* (1942), *Nine Men* (1943), and *San Demetrio London* (1944). In 1944 Balcon arranged a deal with the Rank Organisation to distribute Ealing films. In the aftermath of the war he made a number of comedies that have stood the test of time including *Hue And Cry* (1947), *Whisky Galore* (1948), *Kind Hearts And Coronets* (1949), *Passport To Pimlico* (1949), *The Lavender Hill Mob* (1951), *The Man In The White Suit* (1951) and *The Ladykillers* (1955). He also excelled in drama with *Dead Of Night* (1945), *Nicholas Nickleby* (1947), *Scott Of The Antarctic* (1948), *Saraband For Dead Lovers* (1949), *Where No Vultures Fly* (1951) and *Mandy* (1952). He was responsible for bringing PC George Dixon (later to find fame in Dock Green) to the big screen in *The Blue Lamp* (1949) (although Dixon is killed 21 minutes into the film). In 1948 Balcon became Sir Michael. Balcon presided over the studios like a benevolent despot, bestowing his favours on promising young men (rarely women). Monja Danischewsky, Ealing's press officer, referred to Ealing as "Mr Balcon's Academy for Young Gentlemen". At meetings if he was overruled, he quipped, "Well, if you fellows feel so strongly, on my head be it." Balcon's politics were left of centre although he lived a moderate but comfortable life. He said, "I have never owned a yacht, a racehorse or even a swimming pool. Neither do I smoke cigars." When J. Arthur Rank stepped down from the day-to-day running of his company Balcon found himself dealing with John Davis, the managing director. Davis was not a fan of Balcon's films. In 1955 Ealing Studios was sold to the BBC and Balcon and his team, now Ealing Films, moved to Borehamwood. Four years later, the last Ealing film was made and he formed Bryanston Films. The studio produced *Saturday Night And Sunday Morning* (1960) and *Tom Jones* (1963)

and Balcon became a director of Border Television. In 1964 he became chairman of British Lion. Two years later, he resigned and became chairman of the British Film Institute production board, funding low-budget experimental work. On April 10, 1924 he married Aileen Freda Leatherman, MBE (b. Middlesex, 1905, d. February 1988) and fathered a son, Jonathan (b. 1931), and a daughter, Jill Angela Henriette (b. 1924). She became the second wife of poet Cecil Day-Lewis (1904–1972) on April 27, 1951 at Kensington Register Office, and their son is actor Daniel Day-Lewis. CAUSE: He died of natural causes at his home, Upper Parrock, Hartfield, East Sussex, aged 81. He left £272,880. He was cremated and his ashes were buried at Upper Parrock.

Betty Balfour
Born March 27, 1903
Died November 4, 1977
'Queen of Happiness'. Born in London 5'3" Betty Balfour made her stage début at the Wood Green Empire Theatre in 1914 and established herself as one of the most popular stars in British films of the Twenties. Her most notable role was as Squibs Hopkins in the Gaumont/Welsh-Pearson series which included *Squibs* (1921), *Squibs Wins The Calcutta Sweep* (1922), *Squibs MP* (1922), *Squibs's Honeymoon* (1924) and *Squibs* (1935, a remake as a talkie). With the advent of talkies, she became a successful supporting player. CAUSE: She died in Weybridge, Surrey, aged 74.

Lucille Ball
Born August 6, 1911
Died April 26, 1989
Ditzy redhead. Born in Jamestown, New York, Lucille Ball spent 20 years appearing on the radio and making movies before finding real fame in television. Attempting to enter show business in the Twenties she was told she was too skinny, too shy and had no

future. Ball, who had been sacked as a soda jerk because she forgot to put the banana in a banana split, was told by Robert Milton of New York's prestigious John Murray Anderson/ Robert Milton School Of The Theater And Dance: "Try another profession. Any other." Undeterred she went to Hollywood anyway and found herself film roles, albeit small ones. In 1934 she appeared in eleven films and at one time she was promoted as "the new Harlow"! Her films included *Roman Scandals* (1933), *Nana* (1934), *Kid Millions* (1934), *Top Hat* (1935) as a flower shop assistant, *Chatterbox* (1936), *Don't Tell The Wife* (1937), *Stagedoor* (1937) as Judy Canfield, *The Affairs Of Annabel* (1938), *Annabel Takes A Tour* (1938), *The Marines Fly High* (1940), *Too Many Girls* (1940), *A Girl, A Guy And A Gob* (1941), *Meet The People* (1944), *Abbott & Costello In Hollywood* (1945), *Lover Come Back* (1946), *Fancy Pants* (1950), *The Long Long Trailer* (1954), *Yours Mine And Ours* (1968) and *Mame* (1974). On November 30, 1940, in Greenwich, Connecticut, she married Cuban bandleader Desi Arnaz (b. Santiago, March 2, 1917, as Desiderio Arnaz y de Acha III, d. Del Mar, California, December 2, 1986). Their daughter, Lucie Desirée, was born on July 17, 1951, but they created television history on January 19, 1953, when Lucy gave birth to their son, Desi Jr, in real life and simultaneously on screen. They founded their own studio, Desilu, which would make many TV series, including *Star Trek*. The couple divorced in Santa Monica on May 4, 1960, and the following year, on November 19, 1961, Lucy married comedian Gary Morton (b. New York, December 19, 1924, d. Eisenhower Memorial Hospital, 39000 Bob Hope Drive, Palm Springs, California, March 30, 1999 at 2.15pm from respiratory failure and advanced lung cancer) with whom she remained happy to the end. It was her show *I Love Lucy* (which

began on October 15, 1951, and lasted until September 24, 1961) that really endeared her to the American public. During one episode of the show, Ball donned a clown's outfit complete with bulbous red nose. Co-star William Holden got rather too close with a lighted cigarette and set fire to the proboscis. Ball only saved herself from permanent damage by plunging the smouldering nose in a cup of coffee. Said fellow comedienne Phyllis Diller: "Lucille Ball was a control freak. Had to be in charge of everything. Never saw a woman who took her comedy so seriously." The Emmy Awards are the prestigious accolades bestowed by the American television industry on itself. On May 19, 1975, 5′6″ Ball stepped to the podium to present the gong for Outstanding Comedy Series. As she picked up the envelope to read the nominations she let out a plaintive cry that she had forgotten to bring her spectacles. The audience tittered, thinking this was part of a gag. It was no joke – TV's Lucy was virtually blind without them and kept mumbling, "I'm really in trouble" before some kind soul lent her a pair of glasses and she was able to announce that *The Mary Tyler Moore Show* had triumphed. Her daughter revealed: "One of my mother's favourite things to do, when a small group of people were involved in some ordinary conversation, was to wait until one of them left the room and as soon as she returned, blurt out convincingly, 'Here she is now! Why don'tcha tell her to her face?!!'"

CAUSE: In May 1988 she suffered a heart attack and was in poor health thereafter. Her last public appearance was at the 61st Academy Awards on March 29, 1989. At home (1000 North Roxbury Drive, Beverly Hills 90210) on April 18, 1989, she began experiencing chest pains. Husband Morton called for an ambulance but she refused to go to hospital until she had made up her face. At Cedars-Sinai Medical Center, 8700 Beverly

Boulevard, she underwent eight hours of heart surgery. She received an aorta from a 27-year-old male victim of a motorcycle crash. Fourteen hours after her operation she awoke and her first words to Morton were: "How's the dog doing?" She seemed to be on the road to recovery when the aorta burst. She died at 5.47am from acute rupture of the abdominal aorta. Her funeral was a private affair. Lucy was cremated, and her ashes buried in the Columbarium of Radiant Dawn, at Forest Lawn-Hollywood Hills, 6300 Forest Lawn Drive, Los Angeles 90068.
FURTHER READING: *Lucy: The Real Life Of Lucille Ball* – Charles Higham (New York: St Martin's Press, 1987); *The 'I Love Lucy' Book* – Bart Andrews (New York: Doubleday, 1989).

Suzan Ball

Born February 3, 1933
Died August 5, 1955
'The New Cinderella Girl of 1952'. Born in Jamestown, New York, Susan Ball was a second cousin of Lucille of that ilk. Her mother enrolled her in a modelling school to teach her to walk properly. She was already 5'7" at school and had begun to slouch. At school she harboured ambitions to be a singer and when she was 15, landed an audition on Richard Arlen's television show. That led to three years as the singer with Mel Baker's Orchestra. However, Ball dreamed of a movie career. When her parents moved to Santa Maria for her mother's health, Susan stayed in Hollywood and landed a bit part in *Aladdin And His Lamp* (1952). She also decided to alter the spelling of her Christian name to the more exotic Suzan. She landed a screen test at Universal-International and so impressed Sophie Rosenstein (second wife of Gig Young) that she was offered a four-month contract, which she signed on October 24, 1951. She appeared in *The World In His Arms* (1952) and played Lottie, a mistress in *Untamed Frontier* (1952). She had a

brief fling with Scott Brady and double dated with Shelley Winters. Her next film was *Yankee Buccaneer* (1952) in which she played Countess Donna Margarita, a Spanish noblewoman, opposite Jeff Chandler and Brady. *Variety* commented, "Suzan Ball, with little to do but look beautiful, does that most successfully." She signed for the powerful William Morris Agency and appeared in *City Beneath The Sea* (1953) as Venita, during which time she fell deeply for co-star Anthony Quinn. They were lovers for a year despite Quinn's marriage (to Cecil B. DeMille's daughter) and the potential harm to brunette Ball's career. *Modern Screen* magazine named her as one of the 15 most promising newcomers. During filming of *East Of Sumatra* (1953) – she played Minyora – she injured her right leg. Again she starred opposite Quinn and Chandler. When she was promoting the film she was involved in a minor car accident and banged her knee but thought nothing of it at the time. Back in Hollywood she dumped Quinn and began seeing actor Richard Long (b. Chicago, Illinois December 17, 1927, d. December 22, 1974, of a heart attack) and he moved into her home at 1025 Moorpark Avenue, Los Angeles. *War Arrow* (1953) placed her opposite Maureen O'Hara and the seemingly ubiquitous Jeff Chandler. More seriously, by this time she had developed tumours on her leg and was unable to walk without crutches. She was told by two doctors that amputation was the only solution. At home shortly thereafter, she slipped and broke her leg. In hospital doctors removed the cancerous part of her leg and took a bone graft from her hip. At first it seemed as if the operation had been a success. But then it was discovered that the disease was still present and amputation became the only course of action. In December 1953 Ball and Long became engaged. On January 12, 1954, she underwent

the operation at Orchard Grove Sanatorium, having told Long the night before that she did not expect to marry him. "I love her, not her legs," retorted Long. Three months later, on an artificial leg, she married Long at the El Montecito Presbyterian Church, Santa Barbara. It was April 11, 1954. Among the guests were Jeff Chandler, Tony Curtis, Rock Hudson, David Janssen, Janet Leigh, Hugh O'Brian and 100 others. Despite opposition from on high, director George Sherman cast her as Black Shawl opposite Victor Mature in *Chief Crazy Horse* (1955). During filming she lost over a stone in weight. On finishing, she and Richard Long began a successful nightclub tour. Not long after, while rehearsing a television show, she collapsed and in hospital it was discovered that the cancer, thought to be gone, had spread to her lungs. She only had weeks to live, but was not told the awful truth. The cat was let out of the bag by her mother who asked for various possessions so she could distribute them to the family. Long threw her out. Suzan Ball once said: "I felt no pity for myself, nor have I any feeling of regret. Sometimes I pondered, 'Why has this thing happened to me?' But it was never in terms of a complaint, I sought a real answer. It is not an easy one to find, and perhaps I never will know."
CAUSE: She died aged 22 of cancer at City Of Hope Hospital. Universal-International met all her expenses. Her last word was "Tony", a reference to her former lover Anthony Quinn. Her funeral was held in the Eventide section of Forest Lawn Memorial-Parks, 1712 South Glendale Avenue, Glendale, California 91209.

Smith Ballew

Born January 21, 1902
Died May 2, 1984
Singing cowboy. Born in Palestine, Texas, the son of William Y. and May Ballew, 6'5" Sykes 'Smith' Ballew was educated at Sherman High School,

Austin College and then the University of Texas from 1920 until 1922. He formed a band called Jimmie's Joys, first playing the banjo and then as vocalist. In March 1925, he formed the Texajazzers and, four years later, the Smith Ballew Orchestra. He landed a job as a singer on the wireless before moving into vaudeville with his band Smith Ballew and the Sons of the Sage. In 1929 he began his recording career with Okeh Records of Chicago and worked with the Dorsey brothers and Duke Ellington among many others. The following year he had a residency at White's restaurant in New York. In the early Thirties, Glenn Miller played trombone in Ballew's orchestra. From 1933 until 1934 he was the voice of John Wayne in Monogram's Singing Sandy movies. In 1936 he made his début proper in Palm Springs as Slim. Ballew went on to appear in *Racing Lady* (1937) as Steven Wendall, *Western Gold* (1937) as Bill Gibson, *Roll Along, Cowboy* (1937) as Randy Porter, *Hawaiian Buckaroo* (1938) as Jeff Howard, *Panamint's Bad Man* (1938) as Larry Kimball alias John Smith, *Gaucho Serenade* (1940) as Buck Benson, *The Man Who Walked Alone* (1945) as Alvin Bailey, *Drifting Along* (1946) as band singer Smith, *Under Arizona Skies* (1946) in which he appeared with his band, *Tex Granger, Midnight Rider Of The Plains* (1948) as 'Marshal' Blaze Talbot, *The Mutineers* (1949) as Beasly, *Gun Cargo* (1949) as a singing sailor, *I Killed Geronimo* (1950) as Lieutenant Furness and the captain in *The Red Badge Of Courage* (1951). In *Rawhide* (1938), in which he played Larry Kimball, Ballew starred opposite Lou Gehrig, the baseball star, who became more famous for his battle against motor neurone disease, known in America as Lou Gehrig's disease. That same year Ballew appeared on the list of Top 10 movie cowboys but then his star suddenly waned. Although he carried on making films he concentrated on his singing. During the Second World War Ballew worked in the aircraft industry and in 1952 he moved to Fort Worth, Texas. In 1924 he married Justine Vera (d. 1960) by whom he had a daughter. In 1960 he was remarried to Mary Ruth Clark (d. 1972).

CAUSE: He died in Longview, Texas, aged 82, and was buried in Section 26, Lot 38 of Laurel Land Memorial Park, Tarrant County, Fort Worth.

Martin Balsam

Born November 4, 1914
Died February 13, 1996

Methodologist. Born in New York City, 5'7" Martin Henry Balsam was a practitioner of Method acting and made his film début in *On The Waterfront* (1954) going on to appear in several major films, including the part of the jury foreman in *12 Angry Men* (1957), *Al Capone* (1959), Detective Milton Arbogast in *Psycho* (1960), *Breakfast At Tiffany's* (1961) as O.J. Berman, Mark Dutton in *Cape Fear* (1962), *The Carpetbaggers* (1965) as Bernard B. Norman, *Harlow* (1965), Arnold Burns in *A Thousand Clowns* (1965), a performance that won him a Best Supporting Actor Oscar, *Catch-22* (1970), Admiral Kimmel in *Tora! Tora! Tora!* (1970), *The Anderson Tapes* (1971), *The Man* (1972), *The Taking Of Pelham One Two Three* (1974), *Murder On The Orient Express* (1974) as Bianchi, *All The President's Men* (1976) as Howard Simons, *St Elmo's Fire* (1985), *Death Wish 3* (1985) and as a judge in Martin Scorsese's re-make of *Cape Fear* (1991). Balsam said his biggest disappointment was being passed over as HAL in Kubrick's *2001* (1968). He had recorded his lines when the eccentric director had second thoughts and decided he wanted a more sinister tone. Balsam was married three times. Firstly to Pearl L Somer (1952–1954), then to Joyce Van Patten (1959–1962) by whom he had a daughter, Talia (b. New York, January 1, 1960) and finally to Irene Miller from 1963 by whom he had two children.

CAUSE: He died of a heart attack in Rome, Italy. He was 81.

Anne Bancroft

(ANNA MARIA LOUISA ITALIANO)
Born September 17, 1931
Died June 6, 2005

Mrs Robinson. Born in The Bronx, New York, the daughter of Michael Italiano, a dress pattern maker, and Mildred DiNapoli, she was educated at Christopher Columbus High School and went on to the American Academy of Dramatic Arts, the Actors Studio, and the American Film Institute's Directing Workshop for Women at UCLA. She originally called herself Anne Marno before becoming Anne Bancroft for her film debut as Lyn Lesley in *Don't Bother To Knock* (1952). As she began her film career the Hollywood studio system was coming to an end so after being offered poor roles, she returned to New York. In 1958 she made her Broadway debut as Gittel Mosca opposite Henry Fonda in *Two For The Seesaw* and won the Tony Award for Best Performance by a Featured Actress in a Play. She won another Tony for playing Annie Sullivan in *The Miracle Worker* (1960). When the film version was made in 1962 she reprised her role and won the Best Actress Oscar, which Joan Crawford accepted on her behalf. She also won the BAFTA Award for Best Foreign Actress. Bancroft won an Emmy for *Annie: The Women In The Life Of A Man*, making Bancroft one of the few actors to win an Emmy, Oscar and Tony. Perhaps her best known role was as the seductress Mrs Robinson in *The Graduate* (1967) who beds her daughter's best friend played by Dustin Hoffman. In fact, Bancroft was not the first choice for the role – Patricia Neal, Doris Day and Jeanne Moreau all turned it down. Oddly, the "older" woman of the film was only six years older than her seductee. In 1980 5'6½" Bancroft wrote, directed and starred in *Fatso* (1980) opposite Dom DeLuise.

The following year she turned down the role of Joan Crawford in *Mommie Dearest* and that of Aurora Greenway in *Terms Of Endearment* to appear in the remake of *To Be Or Not To Be* (1983). Her other films included: *Tonight We Sing* (1953) as Emma Hurok, *Gorilla At Large* (1954) as Laverne Miller, *Demetrius And The Gladiators* (1954) as Paula, *New York Confidential* (1955) as Kathy Lupo, *The Naked Street* (1955) as Rosalie Regalzyk, *The Last Frontier* (1955) as Corinna Marston, *Nightfall* (1957) as Marie Gardner, *The Girl In Black Stockings* (1957) as Beth Dixon, *The Pumpkin Eater* (1964) as Jo Armitage for which she was nominated for a Best Actress Academy Award and won the BAFTA Award for Best Foreign Actress and the Golden Globe Award for Best Actress, *The Slender Thread* (1965) as Inga Dyson, *Young Winston* (1972) as Lady Randolph Churchill for which she was nominated for the BAFTA Award for Best Actress in a Leading Role, *The Prisoner Of Second Avenue* (1975) as Edna Edison which resulted in another nomination for the BAFTA Award for Best Actress in a Leading Role, *The Turning Point* (1977) as Emma Jacklin and was nominated for Academy Award for Best Actress, BAFTA Award for Best Actress in a Leading Role and Golden Globe Award for Best Actress, *The Elephant Man* (1980) as Mrs Kendal, *84 Charing Cross Road* (1987) as Helene Hanff winning a BAFTA Best Actress award, *Torch Song Trilogy* (1988) as Ma Beckoff, *Bert Rigby, You're A Fool* (1989) as Meredith Perlestein and *G.I. Jane* (1997) as Senator Lillian DeHaven. In Britain Bancroft is probably best remembered for her monosyllabic performance on Terry Wogan's television chat show in 1987. She walked on to the set counting to herself and the show went downhill from there. Wogan called her performance completely unprofessional. Bancroft was married twice. On July 1, 1953 she wed building contractor Martin May – they divorced on February 13, 1957. There were no children. In 1961 she met Mel Brooks and bizarrely went to see her psychiatrist to tell him to finish the therapy because she had met the man she wanted to marry. Bancroft and Brooks married on August 5, 1964, at the Manhattan Marriage Bureau near New York City Hall. She said, "When [Mel] told his Jewish mother he was marrying an Italian girl, she said, 'Bring her over. I'll be in the kitchen – with my head in the oven'." They had one son, Maximilian Michael, born in New York on May 22, 1972.
CAUSE: Bancroft, 73, died of uterine cancer at Mount Sinai Hospital in New York City. She was buried in lot 6, section 180 at Kensico Cemetery in Valhalla, Westchester County, New York, near her father.

George Bancroft
Born September 30, 1882
Died October 2, 1956
Heavy. Born in Philadelphia, it seemed as if 6'2" Bancroft was set for a career far removed from the frippery of showbusiness when he graduated as a commissioned officer from the United States Naval Academy at Annapolis. The call of the stage was greater than the call of the sea, and, after a stint as a theatre manager and minstrel, he became a straight actor. He began appearing in films in 1921 and made his Broadway debut in 1923. Tall and dark, he usually played baddies. He appeared alongside Wallace Beery in James Cruze's *The Pony Express* (1925) in which Bancroft played the villainous Jack Slade. Paramount Pictures took a second look at him and began casting him in leads. The culmination of this was his casting as Thunderbolt Jim Lang, a death row convict in Sing Sing in Josef von Sternberg's *Thunderbolt* (1929). The role won Bancroft a Best Actor nomination. As his star rose, so did his ego and demands. In one film he was shot but refused to die despite

the director's instructions, "One bullet can't kill Bancroft!" he explained. As he aged he moved into character roles: he was the newspaper editor MacWade in *Mr Deeds Goes To Town* (1936) and perhaps most memorably Marshal Curly Wilcox in John Ford's *Stagecoach* (1939). Three years later, he retired to become a rancher. His films included: *The Journey's End* (1921) as The Ironworker, *The Prodigal Judge* (1922) as Cavendish, *Driven* (1923) as Lem Tolliver, *Teeth* (1924) as Dan Angus, *The Rainbow Trail* (1925) as Jake Willets, *The Splendid Road* (1925) as Buck Lockwell, *The Enchanted Hill* (1926) as Ira Todd, *Sea Horses* (1926) as Cochran, *The Runaway* (1926) as Lesher Skidmore, *White Gold* (1927) as Sam Randall, *Tell It To Sweeney* (1927) as Cannonball Casey, *The Rough Riders* (1927) as Happy Joe, *The Showdown* (1928) as Cardan, *The Dragnet* (1928) as Two-Gun Nolan, *The Mighty* (1929) as Blake Greeson, *Ladies Love Brutes* (1930) as Joe Forziati, *Derelict* (1930) as Bill Rafferty, *Scandal Sheet* (1931) as Mark Flint, *Rich Man's Folly* (1931) as Brock Trumbull, *World And The Flesh* (1932) as Kylenko, *Blood Money* (1933) as Bill Bailey, *Elmer And Elsie* (1934) as Elmer Beebe, *Hell-Ship Morgan* (1936) as Captain Ira "Hell-Ship" Morgan, *Wedding Present* (1936) as Stagg, *A Doctor's Diary* (1937) as Dr Clem Driscoll, *John Meade's Woman* (1937) as Tim Mathews, *Racketeers In Exile* (1937) as William Waldo, *Submarine Patrol* (1938) as Captain Leeds, *Angels With Dirty Faces* (1938) as Mac Keefer, *Each Dawn I Die* (1939) as John Armstrong, *Young Tom Edison* (1940) as Samuel Edison, *When The Daltons Rode* (1940) as Caleb Winters, *North West Mounted Police* (1940) as Jacques Corbeau, *Little Men* (1940) as Major Burdle, *Texas* (1941) as Windy Miller, *Syncopation* (1942) as Steve Porter and *Whistling In Dixie* (1942) as Sheriff Claude Stagg. He was married twice, firstly to Edna Brothers and then to Octavia Broske by whom he had a daughter, Georgette. CAUSE: Bancroft died in Santa Monica, California and is buried at Woodlawn Memorial Cemetery. He was 74.

Tallulah Bankhead
Born January 31, 1902
Died December 12, 1968
Husky-voiced good-time girl. Born in Courthouse Square, Huntsville, Alabama, 5'3" Tallulah Brockman Bankhead's father was Speaker of the House of Representatives from 1936 until 1940. Her mother died aged 21 of blood poisoning, just over three weeks after Tallulah was born. There is some evidence to suggest that Tallulah was actually born on February 12, 1902 but that her birthday was changed to January 31 because that was her parent's second (and last) wedding anniversary. She was educated at Mary Baldwin's School, Staunton, Virginia, the Convent of The Holy Cross, Washington DC and Fairmount School for Girls, also in the capital. When she was 15 she won a beauty contest and that launched her career. She made her stage début aged 16 at the Bijou Theater, New York, on March 15, 1918, playing Gladys Sinclair in *Squab Farm*. A year later, in May 1919, she appeared in *Foot Loose* at the Greenwich Village Theater playing Rose de Brissac. She made her West End stage début on February 15, 1923, at the Wyndham Theatre playing Maxine in *The Dancers*. Over the course of the next seven years Tallulah was a regular in high society and appeared in two films *His House In Order* (1928) and *A Woman's Law* (1928). Back in her homeland Paramount signed her to a long-term contract in 1931 but it was really her stage work in which she shone although critics did laud her performance in Hitchcock's *Lifeboat* (1944). She also pleased the male members of the cast and crew because she eschewed underwear and had to climb a ladder to get into the boat, which was floating in a tank. On

December 22, 1936, she screen-tested for the role of Scarlett O'Hara in *Gone With The Wind* (1939). Her other films included *Who Loved Him Best?* (1918), *The Devil And The Deep* (1932) (she later commented, "Dahling, the main reason I accepted [the part] was to fuck that divine Gary Cooper!"), *A Royal Scandal* (1945) and *Fanatic* (1965). Tallulah was well known for her caustic comments and quips about her co-stars. Of Bette Davis she once remarked, "Don't think I don't know who's been spreading gossip about me and my temperament out there in Hollywood, where that film was made – All About Me [*All About Eve*]. And after all those nice things I've said about that hag. When I get hold of her I'll tear out every hair of her moustache." Actress Patsy Kelly remarked: "Tallulah never beat about the bush – she'd gossip about you in front of your back!" Donald Sutherland added: "I did a movie with Miss Bankhead in England. One day, she wandered into my dressing room completely nude. I couldn't help staring, and she said, 'What's the matter, dahling? Haven't you ever seen a blonde before?' " Ethel Merman remembered: "Tallulah went into a public ladies' room and discovered there was no toilet tissue. She looked underneath the booth and said to the lady in the next stall, 'I beg your pardon, do you happen to have any toilet tissue in there?' The lady said no. So Tallulah said, 'Well, dahling, do you have two fives for a ten?' " A bisexual, she also dabbled in drugs: "Daddy always warned me about men and alcohol, but he never said a thing about women and cocaine!"; "Dahling, of course cocaine isn't habit-forming, and I should know: I've been using it for 20 years." Patsy Kelly again: "Tallulah told me that one time she was relaxing with a lady friend, listening to a waltz or some old-fashioned music like that. And her friend sighed, 'Oh Tallulah, do you remember the minuet?' And

Tallulah said, 'Dahling, I can't even remember the men I *slept* with.' " She married actor John Emery (b. 1905, d. November 16, 1964) in Jasper, Alabama, on August 31, 1937. On June 13, 1941, she received a divorce on the grounds of his "mental cruelty". Among her (long) list of lovers were John Barrymore, Robert Benchley, Marlon Brando, Yul Brynner, Douglas Fairbanks, Jr, Billie Holiday, Libby Holman, Patsy Kelly, Bea Lillie, Frederic March, Hattie McDaniel, Burgess Meredith, Robert Montgomery, Edward R. Murrow, Robert Ryan, Dame Sybil Thorndike and Johnny Weissmuller. There were scores more. However, Tallulah wasn't to everyone's taste. Mrs Patrick Campbell said, "Tallulah is always skating on thin ice. Everyone wants to be there when it breaks."
CAUSE: In early December 1968 she contracted Asian flu during an epidemic that swept through New York. She was hospitalised at St Luke's and sank into a coma when pneumonia set in. She was 66. Tallulah was buried in Rock Hall, Maryland, leaving over $2 million in her will.
FURTHER READING: *Miss Tallulah Bankhead* – Lee Israel (London: W.H. Allen, 1972); *Tallulah – Darling Of The Gods: An Intimate Portrait* – Kieran Tunney (London: Secker & Warburg, 1972); *Tallulah Bankhead: A Scandalous Life* – David Bret (London: Robson Books, 1996).

Leslie Banks, CBE

Born June 9, 1890
Died April 21, 1952
Taciturn thespian. Leslie James Banks was born in West Derby, Liverpool, Lancashire, the son of George Banks, a general merchant, and Emily Dalby. He won a classical scholarship to Trinity College, Glenalmond, and then went on to Keble College, Oxford, again as a classical scholar. He made his stage professional début in 1911 at Brechin town hall as Old Gobbo in *The

Merchant Of Venice with the company of Frank Benson. Banks made his West End début at the Vaudeville in May 1914, in H.V. Esmond's *The Dangerous Age*. Serving with the Essex regiment he was facially disfigured by injuries suffered in the First World War. However, this was turned to his advantage when he became a star in middle age. He made his first film *Experience* in 1921. His other films included: *The Most Dangerous Game* (1932) as Count Zaroff, *I Am Suzanne* (1933) as Adolpe 'Baron' Herring, *Strange Evidence* (1933) as Francis Relf, *The Fire Raisers* (1934) as Jim Bronson, *Red Ensign* (1934) as David Barr, *The Man Who Knew Too Much* (1934) as Bob Lawrence, *Sanders Of The River* (1935) as Commissioner R.G. 'Lord Sandy' Sanders, *The Night Of The Party* (1935) as Sir John Holland, *The Tunnel* (1935) as Frederick 'Robbie' Robbins, *Three Maxims* (1936) as Mac, *Debt Of Honour* (1936) as Major Jimmie Stanton, *Fire Over England* (1937) as Robin, the Earl of Leicester, *Wings Of The Morning* (1937) as Lord Clontarf, *Farewell Again* (1937) as Colonel Harry Blair, *Jamaica Inn* (1939) as Joss Merlyn, *Sons Of The Sea* (1939) as Captain Hyde, *21 Days* (1940) as Keith Durrant, *The Arsenal Stadium Mystery* (1940) as Inspector Anthony Slade, *The Big Blockade* (1940) as Taylor, *Dead Man's Shoes* (1940) as Roger de Vetheuil, *Busman's Honeymoon* (1940) as Inspector Andrew Kirk, *The Door With Seven Locks* (1940) as Dr Manetta, *Neutral Port* (1940) as George Carter, *Cottage To Let* (1941) as John Barrington, *Give Us More Ships* (1941), *Ships With Wings* (1942) as Vice Admiral David Wetherby, *Went The Day Well?* (1942) as Oliver Wilsford, *The Chronicle History Or King Henry The Fifth With His Battell Fought At Agincourt In France* (1944) as Chorus, *Mrs Fitzherbert* (1947) as Charles Fox, *The Small Back Room* (1949) as Colonel A.K. Holland and *Your Witness* (1950) as Colonel Roger

Summerfield. His penultimate film was *Madeleine* (1949) in which he played the respected architect James Smith. *Madeleine* was based on a Glaswegian *cause célèbre*. In 1855 Madeleine Smith (b. March 29, 1835, d. April 12, 1928) began an affair with a 34-year-old packing clerk from Jersey called Pierre Emile L'Angelier. The pair consummated their love in June 1856 but the social mores of the time prevented their relationship becoming overt. James Smith discovered the assignations and forbade his daughter from seeing her lover. Another suitor arrived and L'Angelier became jealous and threatened to send her love letters to her father. In February 1857 he fell ill and died on March 23. An autopsy revealed 82 grains of arsenic in his body. On March 31 when her *billets-doux* were discovered Madeleine was arrested and charged with his murder. In court L'Angelier was painted as a seducer and blackmailer. On July 9 the jury returned the peculiarly Scottish verdict of "Not proven", i.e. we think you did it, but the Crown has not proved the case. She emigrated to America where she died. Leslie Banks also appeared in an early television production of *Cyrano De Bergerac* (1938) in the lead role. In 1915 Banks married Gwendoline Haldane, daughter of Edwin Thomas Unwin. They had three daughters, one of whom is the actor Evangeline Banks who married the actor Tenniel Evans (b. Nairobi, Kenya, May 17, 1926). They have a son, Matthew, and a daughter, Serena, who are both in the profession.
CAUSE: Leslie Banks died at his home, 27 South Terrace, Kensington, London of a stroke after a long illness. He was 61. He left £19,094 14s. 4d.

Monty Banks

(MARIO BIANCHI)
Born July 18, 1897
Died January 7, 1950
Multifaceted performer. Despite the

fact that he was an Italian, Monty Banks was actually born in Nice, France. The 5'5" Banks began as an actor before branching out into directing, writing and producing. His early films as an actor included *The Purple Mask* (1916), *Aired In Court* (1917), a crook in *His Hidden Talent* (1917), *Too Much Johnson* (1919) as Leon Dathis, *Hero'n'Everything* (1920), *Don't Park Here* (1920), *Bride And Gloom* (1921), *A Bedroom Scandal* (1921), *The South Bound Limited* (1923), *Paging Love* (1923), *Boy In Blue* (1924), the groom in *Wedding Bells* (1924), *Pay Or Move* (1924) as Monty, *Racing Luck* (1924) as Mario, *The Golf Bug* (1924) as Monty, *Keep Smiling* (1925) as the boy, which he also wrote and produced, *Atta Boy* (1926) as Monty Milde, *Play Safe* (1927) as the boy, which he also wrote and was executive producer, *Horse Shoes* (1927) as Monty Milde which he also wrote and was executive producer, *Flying Luck* (1927) as the boy, which he also wrote and produced, *Chasing Choo Choos* (1927) as the boy which he also wrote and was executive producer, *A Perfect Gentleman* (1928) as Monty Brooks, *Adam's Apple* (1928) as Monty Adams, *Week-End Wives* (1929) as Max Ammon, *Atlantic* (1929) as Dandy, *The Compulsory Husband* (1930) as Monty, which he also directed, *The Wife's Family* (1931) which he also directed, a convict in *Tonight's The Night: Pass It On* (1932) which he also directed, *Old Soldiers Never Die* (1932) which he also directed and produced, *Not So Quiet On The Western Front* (1932) which he also directed, *Money For Nothing* (1932) which he also directed, a taxi driver in *You Made Me Love You* (1933), *The Church Mouse* (1934) as Harry Blump, *The Girl In Possession* (1934) as Caruso, *So You Won't Talk* (1935) as Tony, which he also directed, *No Limit* (1935) which he also directed and *Man Of The Moment* (1935) as a doctor and which he also

directed. In 1935 he was hired to beef up the films of (Dame) Gracie Fields. The quality improved. He directed. The films included *Queen Of Hearts* (1936), *Keep Smiling* (1937), *We're Going To Be Rich* (1938) and *Shipyard Sally* (1939) in which he also appeared. Banks and Fields also began an affair that was complicated by the fact that she was married to someone else. In 1940 that became the least of their problems. As an Italian, Banks could be interned and to escape this fate he and Gracie Fields fled to America taking £34,000 with them. They married in March 1940 and were together until his death ten years later. His first wife was Gladys Frazin. There were no children from either marriage.

CAUSE: He died in Arona, Italy from a heart attack. He was 52.

Vilma Bánky

(VILMA LONCHIT)
Born January 9, 1898
Died March 18, 1991
The Hungarian Rhapsody. Born in Nagyrodog, near Budapest, blonde 5'6" Bánky was educated at Zugloi High School and then Zugloi College. She was spotted by Samuel Goldwyn when he was on a trip to Europe in 1924. She had already appeared in 13 films, including *Im Letzen Augenblick* (1920), *Veszélyben A Pokol* (1921), *Tavaszi Szerelem* (1921), *Galathea* (1921), *Schattenkinder Des Glücks* (1922), *Kauft Mariett-Aktien* (1922), *Der Zirkuskönig* (1924) and *Das Bildnis* (1925) and was well known in her native land. Her first American film was playing Kitty Vane in *The Dark Angel* (1925), starring opposite Ronald Colman. It was a smash. According to one author she spoke Hungarian during the love scene and Colman chatted about cricket. Her next two films paired her with Rudolph Valentino in *The Eagle* (1925) as Mascha Troekouroff and *Son Of The Sheik* (1926) as Yasmin. Again, both

were smashes. Bánky was again cast with Colman in the title role of *The Winning Of Barbara Worth* (1926), *The Night Of Love* (1927) as Princess Marie, *The Magic Flame* (1927) as Bianca and *Two Lovers* (1928) as Donna Leonora de Vargas. When Bánky married actor Rod LaRocque on June 26, 1927, at the Roman Catholic Church of the Good Shepherd in Beverly Hills, it was a star-studded affair. She was given away by Samuel Goldwyn, Cecil B. DeMille was best man and Louella O. Parsons was matron of honour. The ushers were Donald Crisp, Harold Lloyd and Jack Holt and the bridesmaids included Mrs Samuel Goldwyn and Constance Talmadge. They remained married until LaRocque's death in 1969. The couple only made one professional appearance together, in the touring play *The Cherries Are Ripe* (1930–1931). Her grasp of English was limited and her verbal gaffes became known as 'Bánkyisms'. Her accent would have made the transition to sound pictures difficult and she was sacked by Goldwyn on April 1, 1930. After her career as an actress was over, she and her husband sold real estate, making millions in the process. Rumours have long circulated that Bánky's and LaRocque's marriage was a lavender one. Perhaps tellingly, screenwriter Frances Marion said the two happiest couples in Hollywood she knew were the LaRocques and former actor William Haines and his boyfriend Jimmy Shields.
CAUSE: She died of cardiorespiratory arrest, aged 93.

Ian Bannen

Born June 29, 1928
Died November 3, 1999
Scots wa'hey. Ian Edmund Bannen was born in Airdrie, Lanarkshire, and was educated at Ratcliffe College, Leicestershire. On leaving school he joined the army and became a corporal. A devout Roman Catholic, at one time

he thought about becoming a monk but instead chose to worship alcohol, along with his close friends Peter O'Toole and Richard Burton. He gave up booze when stricken with hepatitis. His first appearance on stage came in the summer of 1947 at the Gate Theatre, Dublin. In March 1955 he first appeared on the small screen, five years after his big screen début. Among his films were *Private's Progress* (1956), *Carlton Browne Of The F.O.* (1958), *The Flight Of The Phoenix* (1965) for which he was nominated for an Oscar, *The Sweeney* (1976), *Gandhi* (1982), *Gorky Park* (1983), *Defence Of The Realm* (1985), *Hope And Glory* (1987) as Grandfather George, *Braveheart* (1995) and the critically acclaimed *Waking Ned Devine* (1998), the story of an Irishman's determination to claim a major lottery jackpot for his village after the real winner passed away. Bannen was given the opportunity to star in a new police series being made in America in the late Sixties. He turned it down because he didn't want to spend much time in California. Little did he know that the series would actually be filmed in the beautiful state of Hawaii. Jack Lord went on to play Steve McGarrett in *Hawaii Five-O* for 12 years and became a multi-millionaire as a result. Bannen did not marry until he was 48 when he wed Marilyn Salisbury, 17 years after they first met.
CAUSE: He was killed in a car crash near Loch Ness aged 71.

Jim Bannon

Born April 9, 1911
Died July 28, 1984
Athletic actor. Born in Kansas City, Missouri, James Shorttel Bannon excelled as an athlete at Rockhurst College and then, on graduation, became an athletics commentator on KCKN in Kansas and later KMOX, St Louis. In 1938 he landed in California and began work on the radio announcing such programmes as *The*

Joe Penner Show (1939–1940), *Stars Over Hollywood* (early Forties), *The Great Gildersleeve* (1941–1942), *The Adventures Of Nero Wolfe* (1943–1944), and *The Eddie Bracken Show* (1945–1946), getting bit parts in films and in the early Forties he worked as a movie stuntman. In 1945, Columbia Pictures made a film of the radio series *I Love A Mystery* and Bannon was cast as Detective Jack Packard, a role he reprised in *The Devil's Mask* (1946) and *The Unknown* (1946). Two years later, he starred as Sergeant Christopher Royal in the Republic serial *Dangers Of The Canadian Mounted* which ran for 12 episodes. In 1949 he became the fourth actor (after Don Barry, Wild Bill Elliott and Allan 'Rocky' Lane) to star in the Red Ryder cowboy series made by Eagle Lion Productions. The films were *Ride, Ryder, Ride* (1949), *Roll, Thunder, Roll* (1949), *The Fighting Redhead* (1950) and *The Cowboy And The Prizefighter* (1950). The series ended with the encroachment of television. From September 30, 1955 until February 3, 1956, he played Uncle Sandy North on the television series *Champion The Wonder Horse* which was produced by Gene Autry. In Sea Cliff, San Francisco, in August 1938, Bannon married the actress Bea Benaderet (b. New York, New York, April 4, 1906, d. October 13, 1968) who provided the voice of Betty Rubble in *The Flintstones*. Their son Jack (b. Los Angeles, California, June 14, 1940) became an actor appearing in the television series *Lou Grant*. A daughter, Margaret Benaderet Bannon, was born in March 1947. Bea Benaderet filed for divorce in September 1950. Bannon's other films included: *Soul Of A Monster* (1944) as Dr Roger Vance, *Sergeant Mike* (1944) as Patrick Henry, *The Missing Juror* (1944) as Joe Keats, *Tonight And Every Night* (1945) as *Life* photographer, *The Gay Senorita* (1945) as Phil, *Out Of The Depths* (1945) as Captain Faversham, *Renegades* (1946)

as Cash Dembrow, *Johnny O'Clock* (1947) as Chuck Blayden, *The Thirteenth Hour* (1947) as Jerry Mason, *Framed* (1947) as Jack Woodworth, *The Corpse Came C.O.D.* (1947) as Detective Mark Wilson, *T-Men* (1947) as Lindsay, *The Man From Colorado* (1948) as Nagel, *Trail To Laredo* (1948) as Dan Parks, *Frontier Revenge* (1948) as Brant, *Miraculous Journey* (1948) as Nick, *Daughter Of The Jungle* (1949) as Kenneth Richards, *Jiggs And Maggie Out West* (1950) as Snake Bite, *Kill The Umpire* (1951) as Dusty, *Sierra Passage* (1951) as Jud Yorke, *Ridin' The Outlaw Trail* (1951) as Ace Donley, *Wanted: Dead Or Alive* (1951) as Marshal Jim Bannon, *Canyon Raiders* (1951) as Jim Bannon, *Nevada Badmen* (1951) as Jim Bannon, an outlaw in *The Texas Rangers* (1951), *Stagecoach Driver* (1951) as Jim Bannon, *Unknown World* (1951) as Andy Ostergaard, *Lawless Cowboys* (1951) as Jim Bannon, *Rodeo* (1952) as Bat Gorman, *Phantom From Space* (1953) as Desk Sergeant Jim, *The Great Jesse James Raid* (1953) as Bob Ford, *Jack Slade* (1953) as Farnsworth, *War Arrow* (1953) as Captain Roger G. Corwin, a soldier in *The Command* (1954), a pilot in *Chicago Confidential* (1957), *They Came To Cordura* (1959) as Captain Paltz, *Inside The Mafia* (1959) as Louie, *40 Pounds Of Trouble* (1962) as The Westerner, *A Gathering Of Eagles* (1963) as Colonel Morse, a forest ranger in *Man's Favorite Sport?* (1964) and a policeman in *Good Neighbor Sam* (1964).

CAUSE: Bannon retired to Plano, Texas, but returned to California where he died aged 73 in Ojai. He was cremated.

Theda Bara

(THEODOSIA BURR GOODMAN)
Born July 20, 1885
Died April 7, 1955
The original vamp. Born in Cincinnati, Ohio, the daughter of a Polish-Jewish tailor, she was named for Aaron Burr's tragic daughter. In July 1917 all of the

immediate family legally changed the name to Bara. She attended the University of Cincinnati from 1903 until 1905, making her one of the few (if not the only) early actresses to be college educated. Her early theatrical career has proved almost impossible to trace. In 1914 she was cast as a vampire in *A Fool There Was* (1915) and the public immediately took to her. When producers Fox realised that she was the one people wanted to see not the supposed star, Edward Jose, they signed her to a long-term contract. Over the next four years she made almost 40 films for Fox, including *The Devil's Daughter* (1915) as La Gioconda, *The Two Orphans* (1915) as Henriette, *Sin* (1915) as Rosa, *Carmen* (1915) as Carmen, *The Galley Slave* (1915) as Francesca Brabaut, *Destruction* (1915) as Fernade, *The Serpent* (1916) as Vania Lazar, *The Eternal Sappho* (1916) as Laura Bruffins, *Her Double Life* (1916) as Mary Doone, *Romeo And Juliet* (1916) as Juliet, *The Vixen* (1916) as Elsie Drummond, *The Rose Of Blood* (1917) as Lisza Tapenka, *The Darling Of Paris* (1917) as Esmaralda, *The Tiger Woman* (1917) as Princess Petrovitch, *Her Greatest Love* (1917) as Hazel, *Camille* (1917) as Marguerite Gauthier, *Cleopatra* (1917) as Cleopatra (the first film to be shot in California as opposed to Jersey City or Fort Lee, New Jersey. It was also subject to calls for a ban, owing to Bara's skimpy clothing. The film took over $1 million at the box office), *Madame Du Barry* (1917) as Jeanne Vaubernier, *When A Woman Sins* (1918) as Lilian Marchard/Poppea, *The She Devil* (1918) as Lorette, *Salome* (1918) as Salome and *When Men Desire* (1919) as Marie Lohr. At her peak Bara was paid $4,000 a week, but after *Cleopatra* it all seemed to go downhill. Of her portrayal as a vamp she confessed: "The popular idea of a wicked woman is a dark and midnight beauty . . . a rolling eye and an undraped figure was all the public required of a vampire." Sex and mystery sells, so two enterprising spin doctors allowed the public to 'learn' that Bara had been born in an oasis under the shadow of the sphinx; that 'Bara' was 'Arab' backwards and 'Theda' was an anagram of 'death'. Newspapers began running her picture captioned "Is This The Wickedest Face In The World?" Other stories circulated that she was the reincarnation of historical villainesses such as Delilah and Lucrezia Borgia. It was all harmless nonsense. Thanks to Bara, make-up became fashionable and the word 'vamp' was added to the dictionary, although she preferred the fuller 'vampire'. Not everyone liked her. Said one Bette Davis: "She was divinely, hysterically, insanely malevolent." Gradually, the truth about her background seeped out. Theda Bara was no more an Arab than most of her audience. She had never been to Egypt; the only camels she knew were the brand of cigarettes that went by that name. She was by no stretch of the imagination a man-eating vamp, living as she did at home with her parents in New York's West End Avenue. Her preferred fare was cabbage, corned beef and sausages. Following the end of her contract, she left Fox but found work difficult to come by. In June 1921 she married Charles J. Brabin (b. Liverpool, April 17, 1883, d. November 3, 1957) who had been responsible for directing her last Fox movie. She made the unsuccessful *The Unchastened Woman* (1925) as Caroline Knollys before her last cinematic role in the Hal Roach comedy *Madame Mystery* (1926) playing Madame Mystery, a character not too dissimilar to her vamp creation. She had a happy retirement.

CAUSE: She died in California Lutheran Hospital, Los Angeles, of abdominal cancer, aged 69. She was cremated and her ashes placed in the left wall of the Columbarian of Memory of the Great Mausoleum of Forest Lawn

Memorial-Parks, 1712 South Glendale Avenue, Glendale, California 91209.

Lynn Bari
(MARJORIE SCHUYLER FISHER)
Born December 18, 1913
Died November 20, 1989
The other woman, described by one critic as "Claudette Colbert with biceps" and another as "the Paulette Goddard of the B feature". Born in Roanoke, Virginia, the stepdaughter of a minister, Reverend Robert Bitzer, Lynn Bari moved to Hollywood with her family when she was ten. In 1933 she saw a newspaper advertisement requesting tall chorus girls (she was 5'7"), applied and landed a job in the Joan Crawford flick *Dancing Lady*. She landed a contract at 20th Century Fox where she worked for 12 years and appeared in B films such as *Spring Tonic* (1935), *Redheads On Parade* (1935), *Show Them No Mercy!* (1935), *The Man Who Broke The Bank At Monte Carlo* (1935), *Ladies Love Danger* (1935), *King Of Burlesque* (1935), *Doubting Thomas* (1935), *Curly Top* (1935), *Charlie Chan In Paris* (1935), *The Great Hotel Murder* (1935), *Charlie Chan In Shanghai* (1935), *The Great Ziegfeld* (1936), *Lancer Spy* (1937) as Miss Fenwick, *Rebecca Of Sunnybrook Farm* (1938), *Mr Moto's Gamble* (1938) as Penny Kendall, *News Is Made At Night* (1939) as Maxine Thomas, *Charlie Chan In City Of Darkness* (1939) as Marie Dubon and *Charter Pilot* (1940) as Marge Duncan before being cast as Encarnación in *Blood And Sand* (1941). After one more A film, *The Magnificent Dope* (1942) as Claire Harris, she went back to low-budget movies such as *Shock* (1946) as Elaine Jordan, *Nocturne* (1946) as Frances Ransom, *Home, Sweet Homicide* (1946) as Marian Carstairs, *The Spiritualist* (1948) as Christine Faber, *On The Loose* (1951) as Alice Bradley, *Francis Joins The WACS* (1954) as Major Louise Simpson and *Abbott & Costello Meet The Keystone Kops* (1955) as Leota Van Cleef. Altogether she appeared in over 130 films. During World War II Bari was the GI's second favourite pin-up, after Betty Grable. Usually she would be cast as a gun-toting moll or a husband stealer. She loathed guns, was actively bisexual and married three times. Her first husband, Walter Kane, was a 'sort of talent scout' for Howard Hughes. They married in 1938 between the main course and dessert at Hollywood's Lamaze restaurant. She ran out of the eatery to find a judge who would perform the ceremony and found one more used to dealing with traffic violations. After a very 'tempestuous marriage' they divorced on November 26, 1943. Two days later, she married former test pilot Sid Luft (who would go on to marry Judy Garland) and divorced him acrimoniously seven years later on December 26, 1950. Their son, John Michael, was born in 1948. Following the divorce, custody of the boy was awarded to Luft and Garland, a decision later reversed by another court. Just hours after Luft married the pregnant Garland on June 8, 1952, he was sued by Bari for additional child support. Superior Court Judge Burke doubled the child support from $200. From 1955 until July 26, 1972, Bari was married to Beverly Hills shrink Dr Nathan Rickles.
CAUSE: Heart attack. She died in Santa Barbara, California, aged 75.

Eric Barker
Born February 20, 1912
Died June 1, 1990
Supporting comedian. Eric Leslie Barker was born in Thornton Heath, Surrey, and made his theatre début in rep in 1930. He appeared in films, television and radio as well as the theatre. His radio series *Just Fancy* was a huge hit. He appeared in more than 30 movies including: *Blue Murder At St Trinian's* (1958) as Culpepper-Brown, *Carry On Sergeant* (1958) as Captain Potts, *Carry On Constable* (1959) as

Inspector Mills, *Dentist In The Chair* (1960), *The Pure Hell Of St Trinian's* (1958) as Culpepper-Brown, a doctor in *On The Beat* (1962), *Carry On Spying* (1964) as The Chief, *Those Magnificent Men In Their Flying Machines* (1965) as a French postman, *There's A Girl In My Soup* (1970) and *Carry On Emmannuelle* (1978) as an ancient general. *Carry On Cruising* (1962) was based on an Eric Barker story. Barker won a BAFTA Best Newcomer Award (aged 45!) for *Brothers In Law* (1957) in which he played Alec Blair. He also wrote three novels, a collection of short stories and his autobiography. He was married to the actor Pearl Hackney (b. Burton-on-Trent, October 28, 1916) by whom he had a daughter.
CAUSE: He died aged 78 in Faversham, Kent.

Lex Barker

Born May 8, 1919
Died May 11, 1973
Jekyll & Hyde? Born in Rye, New York, 6'4" Alexander Crichlow Barker, Jr, the son of a socially prominent family, went to Princeton University but left after two years to become an actor. His first film was *Doll Face* (1945) and he went on to appear as a builder in *Mr Blandings Builds His Dream House* (1948) and five Tarzan films (he was the tenth actor to play the lord of the jungle, replacing Johnny Weissmuller, but quit because Tarzan never had much to say) beginning with *Tarzan's Magic Fountain* (1949), *Tarzan And The Slave Girl* (1950), *Tarzan's Peril* (1951), *Tarzan's Savage Fury* (1952) and finishing with *Tarzan And The She-Devil* (1953). In keeping with the Lord of the Jungle's familiar appearance, Barker shaved his body hair throughout his life. After 1958 linguist Barker worked mostly in Italy and Germany appearing in *La Dolce Vita* (1960). In 1966 he won Germany's Bambi Award for Best

Foreign Actor. By all accounts he was not an especially nice man. "Twice I've gotten into loud quarrels with alleged fans who said I *owed* them an autograph. Never again. You can't reason with such dumbbells . . . If, in return for my salary, I go to work, do my job and then also perform mandated publicity, how am I left owing anybody anything? By what logic?" He was married five times. His first wife was socialite Constance Thurlow; they married on January 27, 1942, in Manhattan. They had a son, Alexander III 'Zan' (b. 1948) and a daughter Lynn (b. 1944), but were divorced in Los Angeles on November 16, 1950, on the grounds of Barker's alleged cruelty towards her. Wife number two, as of April 1951, was actress Arlene Dahl. They married at the Central Presbyterian Church in New York. Less than two years later, on October 15, 1952, the couple was divorced. Barker had once referred to Dahl as "a hick from Minnesota". The divorce was finalised on November 13, 1953. Meanwhile, two months earlier on September 8, 1953, Barker had married (as her fourth husband) Lana Turner in Turin's sixteenth-century city hall. On October 6, 1956, she miscarried their baby at St John's Hospital. Eight months later, on June 28, 1957, Turner filed for divorce, citing Barker's "cruel and inhuman conduct". Barker blamed Turner's daughter, Cheryl, for the breakdown of the marriage: "The girl told a story to her mother. I denied it was true. But Lana always had one great fault – to believe her daughter first, although knowing she was full of complexes and accustomed to lie." Cheryl was not a bad girl, said Barker "but certainly very strange." Lana Turner's biographers, writing in 1972 a year before Barker's death, never revealed what story Cheryl had told her mother. It is this. For three years Barker systematically raped and abused Cheryl. He began by exposing himself and masturbating in front of her before progressing to full sex. The abuse began when Cheryl was just ten years old. She also began menstruating at that age; a doctor examined the girl and confirmed she had been damaged internally. When Turner heard about Barker's behaviour she held a gun on him and gave him 20 minutes to pack and get out of the house. On March 14, 1959, in Lucerne, he married for the fourth time. Wife number four was Swiss drama student Irene Labhart. Their son, Christopher, was born in 1960. On October 23, 1962, Labhart died of a heart attack in Rome, aged 32. In Geneva on March 6, 1965, Barker took his fifth wife. She was Miss Spain of 1961, Maria del Carmen Cervera, and they were together until his death. Wife number three, Lana Turner commented, "When I call my ex-husband anal, people think I'm being intellectual or Freudian. But merely I'm using a polite word for what he really is, deep down . . . "

CAUSE: He died of a heart attack on Lexington Avenue near 61st Street in New York three days after his 54th birthday. When she was told, Lana Turner remarked: "What took him so long?"

Binnie Barnes

(GITELLE ENOYCE GERTRUDE MAUDE BARNES)
Born March 25, 1903
Died July 27, 1998
The one with the withering look. Born in Finsbury Park, north London, the daughter of a policeman, 5′5″ Barnes was one of 17 children. Her first paid appointment was as a milkmaid, then a nurse, a draper's shop assistant and finally a dance hostess before she saw and was captivated by Tex McLeod's rope spinning act. The two teamed up and toured South America for a year before Barnes branched out on her own as 'Texas Binnie' Barnes. She amazed audiences by her dexterity with a rope

and tales of the Wild West – a place she had never visited. In 1929 she began her legitimate stage career but it was the role of Fanny in Noël Coward's *Cavalcade* that assured her of stardom. She went to New York aboard the *Queen Mary* to make the film version but, after the briefest of stays in the Big Apple, caught the same ship home. She was cast as Katherine Howard (the one who was beheaded for treason) opposite Charles Laughton's monarch in *The Private Life Of Henry VIII* (1933). She starred opposite Douglas Fairbanks in *The Private Life Of Don Juan* (1934) as the maid Rosita, and made 26 two-reel comedies with Lupino Lane before returning to America to fulfil her contractual obligations. Over the next two decades she appeared in *The Lady Is Willing* (1934) as Helene Dupont, *Diamond Jim* (1935) as Lillian Russell, *Sutter's Gold* (1936) as Countess Elizabeth Bartoffski, *The Last Of The Mohicans* (1938) as Alice Munro, *The Adventures Of Marco Polo* (1938) as Nazama, *Daytime Wife* (1939) as Blanche, *Man About Town* (1939) as Lady Arlington, *The Three Musketeers* (1939) as Milady De Winter, *I Married An Angel* (1942) as Peggy, *The Hour Before The Dawn* (1944) as May Heatherton and *The Decameron Nights* (1953) as Countess of Florence/Nerina/ the old witch. A devout Roman Catholic, in 1931 Barnes married art dealer Samuel Joseph; they were to divorce five years later. In 1940 she married sports commentator Mike Frankovitch and they adopted twin sons and a daughter. In 1941 she was in the news after threatening to sue Columbia Pictures over a picture of her in scanty black underwear in *This Thing Called Love*. Barnes claimed she had been promised she would be seen in silhouette only. Unfortunately, her complaint led to even more unwanted publicity when the picture was printed in the press. She was widowed in 1992. CAUSE: Natural causes. She died at her Beverly Hills home aged 95.

Patrick Barr

Born February 13, 1908
Died August 29, 1985
Stalwart. Born in Akola, India the son
of a judge, Patrick Barr was educated at
Radley and Trinity College, Oxford.
An engineer, he made his stage début
in rep in 1932 and in the West End in
1936. His career encompassed all three
media. He was a regular on television
in Britain in the Fifties. His films
included: *Robin Hood* (1951) as King
Richard I, *Singlehanded* (1953), *St Joan*
(1957) as Captain La Hire, *The Longest
Day* (1962) as Group Captain J.N.
Stagg, *Billy Liar* (1963) as Inspector
MacDonald, *House Of Whipcord* (1974)
as Justice Bailey and *Octopussy* (1983)
as the British ambassador. He was
married with a daughter.
CAUSE: He died in London, aged 74.

Jean-Louis Barrault

Born September 8, 1910
Died January 22, 1994
Stage director. Born in Vésinet, France,
Barrault made his stage début in
Volpone in 1931. It was in the theatre
that he achieved his greatest success
although he made a number of notable
films including *Drôle De Drame* (1937),
Les Enfants Du Paradis (1945) and *The
Longest Day* (1962) as Father Louis
Roulland. He was married to the actor
Madeleine Renaud (b. Paris, France,
February 21, 1900, d. Paris, France,
September 23, 1994) from 1940 until
his death. The actor Marie-Christine
Barrault was his niece.
CAUSE: Barrault died aged 83 in Paris,
France, of a heart attack.

Majel Barrett

(MAJEL LEIGH HUDEC)
Born February 23, 1932
Died December 18, 2008
Mrs Star Trek. Born in Cleveland,
Ohio, she began acting when she was
10, enrolling in an acting workshop.
However it was a career in law that was
her original aim but she dropped out
after a year, hoping to become a legal

clerk. After failing her contract law
exam, she relocated to New York
where she became an actress. She went
west and appeared in a number of
small roles in films including *Black
Orchid* (1958), *As Young As We Are*
(1958) and *The Buccaneer* (1958)
before deciding that her future lay on
the small screen. She appeared in
shows including *The Untouchables* and
Bonanza. After meeting Lucille Ball at
an acting class, she signed a contract
with Desilu, the company ran by Ball
and her husband Desi Arnaz. In 1964
Barrett appeared in a television show
called *The Lieutenant*, produced by
Gene Roddenberry. Later that year she
co-starred in *The Cage*, the pilot for
Roddenberry's new sci-fi programme
Star Trek. NBC who were
commissioning the series were not
keen on a female second-in-command
for the space ship so they told
Roddenberry to make another pilot
without her. When the show was
commissioned, Roddenberry cast her
as Nurse Christine Chapel, changed
her name (to Majel Barrett) and put
her in a blonde wig. Barrett and
Leonard Nimoy (who got the role as
second-in-command) were the only
two actors to appear in both the first
and last episodes of the original *Star
Trek* series. She said, "I never
particularly cared for Christine. [She]
only comes into heat once every seven
years. Let's face it, this broad's a real
loser." Barrett also provided the voice
for the ship's computer in the
programmes and films and supplied
several voices in the cartoon version of
the show. She also appeared in *Star
Trek: The Next Generation* as the
Betazoid Ambassador Lwaxana Troi
and played the same role in several
episodes of *Star Trek: Deep Space Nine*.
She appeared in the films *A Guide For
The Married Man* (1967), *Westworld*
(1973) and *The Domino Principle*
(1977). Shortly before her death she
voiced again the ship's computer for
J.J. Abrams's *Star Trek* (released

May 8, 2009). Barrett married Roddenberry in a Shinto-Buddhist wedding on August 6, 1969. However, his divorce was not final so they had a civil ceremony on December 29, 1969. CAUSE: Barrett died aged 76 at 12.27am on December 18, 2008 of leukaemia. Her son, Rod, was by her side. She was diagnosed with the disease six months before her death. In 2010 the ashes of Barrett and Roddenberry will be launched into space aboard a rocket. Barrett arranged the tribute in 1997, six years after her husband's death.

Wendy Barrie

(MARGUERITE WENDY JENKINS)
Born April 18, 1912
Died February 2, 1978
Gangster's moll. Wendy Barrie was born in Hong Kong, the daughter of an English barrister, who practised in China. Educated in England and Switzerland she was named after the heroine in *Peter Pan* so she took author J.M. Barrie's surname when she began her professional career. She worked in a beauty parlour before becoming a secretary and finally, at 19, an actor. She made her film début in *Where Is This Lady?* (1932) as Lucie Kleiner and went on to appear in nine more films – *Threads* (1932) as Olive Wynn, *Collision* (1932) as Joyce, *The Callbox Mystery* (1932) as Iris Banner, *The Barton Mystery* (1932) as Phyllis Grey, *It's A Boy* (1933) as Mary Bogle, *The House Of Trent* (1933) as Angela, *Cash* (1933) as Lilian Gilbert, *The Acting Business* (1933) as Joyce and *Wedding Rehearsal* (1933) as Lady Mary Rose – before Sir Alexander Korda signed her to play Jane Seymour in *The Private Life Of Henry VIII* (1933), starring Charles Laughton in the title role for which he won an Oscar. Her performance led to a contract in Hollywood for Paramount in 1935 (until 1943). She was Beryl Stapleton in the first Sherlock Holmes-Dr Watson outing for Basil Rathbone and Nigel Bruce, *The Hound*

Of The Baskervilles (1939). She appeared in many films (usually B pictures) and was three times – each with different character names – George Sanders' leading lady in *The Saint* series: *The Saint Strikes Back* (1939) as Val Travers, *The Saint Takes Over* (1940) as Ruth Summers and *The Saint In Palm Springs* (1941) as Elna Johnson. She also appeared with Sanders in the first two of the Falcon series – *The Gay Falcon* (1941) and *A Date With The Falcon* (1941) but this time played the same character – Helen Reed. Wendy Barrie fell in love in the Forties but as women are wont to do, she fell in love with the wrong man. Her relationship put paid to her Hollywood career. Benjamin Siegel – no one with any sense called him 'Bugsy' to his face – was not the type of boyfriend a girl could take home to dinner with her parents. Seven years her senior, Siegel (born on February 28, 1905 – some sources say 1906 – in Brooklyn, the second of five children) was a Prohibition bootlegger, a rapist, a kidnapper, a white slaver, an illegal bookmaker, a hijacker, an extortionist, a drugs trafficker and a murderer (12 confessed killings) – apart from that, an upstanding citizen. Despite Warren Beatty's sanitised filmic portrayal, Siegel was a cold-hearted killer and definitely not a man to be crossed. He first came to the attention of the police on January 3, 1926, a month short of his 21st birthday, when he was arrested for rape. The woman dropped the charge and Siegel walked free. He was later to say, "The wench called me up . . . and told me I was a little bit brutal with her – but that when she thought about it later, she admitted I had given her the best lay of her life." In 1927 he married Estelle and in 1930 their first daughter, Millicent, was born, followed two years later by Barbara. A wife and young family did not prevent Siegel playing the field and he became friendly with a number of women including prostitutes, socialites like Countess Dorothy Dendice Taylor diFrasso, good-time girls like Virginia Hill and actors like Ketti Gallion, Wendy Barrie and Marie 'The Body' McDonald. The latter two women disliked each other and whenever McDonald saw Barrie she flew into a temper. Once at the Flamingo hotel and casino she punched her in the face, nearly dislocating her jaw. Not long after the Flamingo opened in 1947 Siegel installed Barrie, McDonald, Hill and diFrasso in separate suites. He was shot to death on June 20, 1947, while sitting in Virginia Hill's Beverly Hills mansion at 810 North Linden Drive. 5'5" Wendy fled to New York and a career on Broadway. Her other films were: *Without You* (1934) as Molly Bannister, *There Goes Susie* (1934) as Madeleine Sarteaux, *Murder At The Inn* (1934) as Angela, *The Man I Want* (1934) as Marion Round, *Give Her A Ring* (1934) as Karen Svenson, *Freedom Of The Seas* (1934) as Phyllis Harcourt, *It's A Small World* (1935) as Jane Dale, *College Scandal* (1935) as Julie Fresnel, *The Big Broadcast Of 1936* (1935) as Sue, *A Feather In Her Hat* (1935) as Pauline Anders, *Millions In The Air* (1935) as Marion Keller, *What Price Vengeance?* (1936) as Polly Moore, *Love On A Bet* (1936) as Paula Gilbert, *Speed* (1936) as Jane Mitchell, *Ticket To Paradise* (1936) as Jane, *Under Your Spell* (1936) as Cynthia Drexel, *Breezing Home* (1937) as Floria, *Wings Over Honolulu* (1937) as Lauralee Curtis, *Dead End* (1937) as Kay Burton, *A Girl With Ideas* (1937) as Mary Morton, *Prescription For Romance* (1937) as Valerie Wilson, *Pacific Liner* (1938) as Nurse Ann Grayson, *I Am The Law* (1938) as Frankie Ballou, *Newsboys' Home* (1938) as Gwen Dutton, *Five Came Back* (1939) as Alice Melbourne, *The Witness Vanishes* (1939) as Joan Marplay, *Day-Time Wife* (1939) as Kitty Frazier, *Women In War* (1940) as Pamela Starr, *Cross-Country Romance* (1940) as Diane North, *Who Killed Aunt Maggie?* (1940) as Sally

Ambler, *Men Against The Sky* (1940) as Kay Mercedes, *Repent At Leisure* (1941) as Emily Bladwin, *Public Enemies* (1941) as Bonnie Parker, *Eyes Of The Underworld* (1943) as Betty Standing, *Forever And A Day* (1943) as Edith Trimble-Pomfret, *Follies Girl* (1943) as Anne Merriday and *Submarine Alert* (1943) as Ann Patterson. In her last film, *It Should Happen To You* (1954), she played herself as a chat show host.
CAUSE: Wendy Barrie died in Englewood, New Jersey, aged 65, after a long illness.

Don Barry
(DONALD BARRY DEACOSTA)
Born January 11, 1912
Died July 17, 1980
Red. Born in Houston, Texas, Barry was trained at the Texas School of Mines and began appearing in repertory productions. He made his film début as a student in Cecil B. De Mille's *This Day And Age* (1933). He took a break from the screen until 1936 when he reappeared in *Night Waitress* (1936) as Mario Rigo and then was in *When's Your Birthday?* (1937) as Marty. His films included: *The Woman I Love* (1937) as Michel, *The Last Gangster* (1937) as Billy Ernst, *Sinners In Paradise* (1938) as Jessup and the Dr Kildare series – *Young Dr Kildare* (1938) as Dr Collins, *Calling Dr Kildare* (1939) as Intern Collins and *The Secret Of Dr Kildare* (1939) as Collins. In 1939 he was signed to Republic Pictures and began to appear in the westerns that would make his name. In 1940 he appeared in the Red Ryder serial that gave him his nickname 'Red'. Over the course of five years he appeared in 29 Westerns: *One Man's Law* (1940) as Jack Summers, *The Tulsa Kid* (1940) as Tom Benton, *Frontier Vengeance* (1940) as Jim Sanders, *Texas Terrors* (1940) as Bob Millbourne, *Ghost Valley Raiders* (1940) as Tim Brandon, *Wyoming Wildcat* (1941) as Bill Gannon, *The*

Phantom Cowboy (1941) as Jim Lawrence, *Two Gun Sheriff* (1941) as The Sundown Kid, *Desert Bandit* (1941) as Bob Crandall, *Kansas Cyclone* (1941) as Jim Randall, *The Apache Kid* (1941) as Pete Dawson, *Death Valley Outlaws* (1941) as Johnny Edwards, *A Missouri Outlaw* (1941) as Cliff Dixon, *Arizona Terrors* (1942) as Jim Bradley, *Stagecoach Express* (1942) as Dave Gregory, *Jesse James, Jr* (1942) as Johnny Barrett, *The Cyclone Kid* (1942) as Johnny Dawson/Cyclone Kid, *The Sombrero Kid* (1942) as Jerry Holden, *Outlaws Of Pine Ridge* (1942) as Chips Barrett, *The Sundown Kid* (1942) as Red Tracy, *Dead Man's Gulch* (1943) as Tennessee Colby, *Carson City Cyclone* (1943) as Gilbert Phalen, *Days Of Old Cheyenne* (1943) as Clint Ross, *Fugitive From Sonora* (1943) as Dave Winters/Keeno Phillips, *Black Hills Express* (1943) as Lon Walker, *The Man From The Rio Grande* (1943) as Lee Grant, *Canyon City* (1943) as Terry Reynolds, *California Joe* (1943) as Lieutenant Joe Weldon and *Outlaws Of Santa Fe* (1944) as Bob Conroy/Bob Hackett. Barry began to feel that his talents were being wasted on westerns and he made the move to "more demanding roles" but still he returned to his stetson because that was what the fans wanted. He was in *The Dalton Gang* (1949) as Larry West, *Red Desert* (1949) as the Pecos Kid, *I Shot Billy The Kid* (1950) as Billy The Kid, *Gunfire* (1950) as Frank James and Bat Fenton, *Train To Tombstone* (1950) as Len Howard and *Border Rangers* (1950) as Bob Standish. In 1951 he moved to the small screen but returned with the self-financed *Jesse James's Women* (1954) as Jesse James. He was now only cast in bit parts, something that dented his ego. He appeared in *Gun Duel In Durango* (1957) as Larry, *Frankenstein - 1970* (1958) as Douglas Row, *Andy Hardy Comes Home* (1958) as Councilman Fitzgerald, *Ocean's Eleven* (1960) as McCoy, *Walk On The Wild Side* (1962) as Dockery, *The Carpetbaggers* (1964), *Apache Uprising* (1966) as Henry Belden, *Bandolero!* (1968) as Jack Hawkins, *Shalako* (1968) as Buffalo and *Rio Lobo* (1970) as Feeny. In 1970 he announced that he wanted to make another western and asked fans to send in loans to finance the project. It never came to fruition. Married three times including once to the actor Peggy Stewart (b. West Palm Beach, Florida, June 5, 1923) from 1940 until 1944, the short Barry was something of a ladies' man. He had affairs with many Hollywood beauties including Linda Darnell, Joan Crawford and Ann Sheridan. On November 4, 1955 he created headlines when his girlfriend, Jill Jarmyn, caught him in flagrante with his co-star Susan Hayward. The two women began a fist fight.
CAUSE: By the summer of 1980 Barry was separated from his wife but was trying to patch things up. On July 17 police were called to his North Hollywood home during a domestic. After calming things down the policemen returned to their patrol car only for Barry to run after them wielding a .38 calibre revolver. In a split second he put the gun to his head and pulled the trigger. He was pronounced dead at 10pm at Riverside Hospital.

Diana Barrymore

(DIANA BLANCHE BLYTH)
Born March 3, 1921
Died January 25, 1960
Regularly soused actress. Born in New York, New York, Diana Barrymore was the daughter of John Barrymore by his second wife, the actress-turned-authoress Blanche Oelrichs (who called herself Michael Strange and dressed as a man). She was somewhat of a middling actress but a spectacular drunk. Playwright Tennessee Williams said, "She had great talent but no control, like an engine running away." Thrice married, she called her autobiography *Too Much, Too Soon.*

She once attempted to kill herself by downing 27 sleeping tablets and a bottle of whisky and was arrested on more than one occasion for shoplifting and being drunk and disorderly. Such was her lack of professionalism, she made only very few films: *Eagle Squadron* (1942), *Between Us Girls* (1942), *Nightmare* (1942), *Frontier Badmen* (1943), *Fired Wife* (1943) and *Ladies Courageous* (1944).
CAUSE: She died in New York of an overdose of whisky and sleeping pills aged 38. She was buried in Division 20 of Woodlawn Cemetery, 233rd Street & Webster Avenue, The Bronx, New York 10470.

Ethel Barrymore
(ETHEL MAE BLYTH)
Born August 15, 1879
Died June 18, 1959
The First Lady of American Theatre. Born at Ninth Street, Philadelphia, Pennsylvania, she made her stage début aged 15. Unlike her siblings, she was not overly keen on Hollywood and after making films would hurry back to her beloved Broadway. "I have always belonged to the theatre," she stated and claimed never to have seen any of her films. A Broadway theatre was named after her. She appeared alongside both her brothers in the movie *Rasputin And The Empress* (1932). Lionel was the mad monk, John played Prince Paul Chegodieff and Ethel was the Tsarina Alexandra. In 1944, after a ten-year absence from the big screen, she won a Best Supporting Actress Oscar for *None But The Lonely Heart*, playing Cary Grant's mother, Ma Mott. Among her other films (including 15 silents) were *The Awakening Of Helena Ritchie* (1916) as Helena Ritchie, *The Greatest Power* (1917) as Miriam Monroe, *The Lifted Veil* (1917) as Clorinda Gildersleeve, *The Divorcee* (1919) as Lady Frederick Berolles, *The Spiral Staircase* (1946) as Mrs Warren, *The Paradine Case* (1947) as Lady Sophie Horfield, *That Midnight Kiss* (1949) as

Abigail Trent Budell, *Just For You* (1952) as Alida De Bronkhart and *Young At Heart* (1954) as Aunt Jessie Tuttle. Ethel married Russell Greenwood Colt (b. 1882, d. 1960) on March 14, 1909, in the rectory of the Roman Catholic Church of the Most Precious Blood in Hyde Park, Massachusetts. They had three children: actor Samuel Peabody Colt (b. November 29, 1909) actress Ethel Barrymore Colt (b. April 30, 1912, d. May 22, 1977); and actor John Drew Colt (b. September 9, 1913, d. 1975). Ethel and Colt were divorced in Providence, Rhode Island, on July 5, 1923. Bizarrely, her hobby was boxing. She never missed a Joe Louis fight and had an enormous collection of boxing prints.
CAUSE: She died of a heart condition aged 79 in Beverly Hills, California, having spent the last 18 months of her life bedridden. She was buried in Crypt 3F, Block 60 of the Main Mausoleum of Calvary Cemetery, 4201 Whittier Boulevard, Los Angeles 90023.

John Barrymore
(JOHN SIDNEY BLYTH)
Born February 15, 1882
Died May 29, 1942
'The Great Profile'. Part of the legendary acting family, 5'8" Barrymore, born at 2008 Columbia Avenue, Philadelphia, Pennsylvania, would not allow his right side to be photographed. The family Bible lists his birth date as February 15 although his birth certificate records the event as occurring on St Valentine's Day. Barrymore was the youngest son of the respected thespian Maurice Barrymore (b. Fort Agra, Amritsar, India, September, 1839, d. Bellevue Hospital, Amityville, New York, March 26, 1905). His father died hopelessly insane (due to syphilis) and alcoholic. Barrymore was tortured with the fear he would end his days the same way. There was a hitch at Maurice's funeral and the coffin had to be raised again.

Just before it was lowered for a second time, Lionel nudged his brother John and whispered, "How like father – a curtain call." The following year John, who preferred drinking to working, was appearing in San Francisco when the famous earthquake struck on April 18. He was supposedly in bed at the time. "It takes an earthquake to get Jack out of bed, a flood to make him wash and the United States army to put him to work," quipped brother Lionel. Barrymore made his film début in 1913 and among his films were *An American Citizen* (1914) as Beresford Kruger, *Are You A Mason?* (1915) as Frank Perry, *The Incorrigible Dukane* (1915) as James Dukane, *Nearly A King* (1916) as Jack Merriwell, Prince of Bulwana, *Raffles, The Amateur Cracksman* (1917) as A.J. Raffles, *Dr Jekyll And Mr Hyde* (1920) as Dr Henry Jekyll/Mr Edward Hyde (performed the change without make-up), *Sherlock Holmes* (1922) as Sherlock Holmes, *Beau Brummel* (1924) as Gordon Bryon 'Beau' Brummel, *Don Juan* (1926) as Don Jose de Marana/Don Juan de Marana (during the film he kissed 191 times – an average of once every 53 seconds!), *Rasputin And The Empress* (1932) as Prince Paul Chegodieff, *Grand Hotel* (1932) as Baron Felix von Geigern, *Dinner At Eight* (1933) as Larry Renault, *Counsellor-At-Law* (1933) as George Simon (during the filming he was so drunk he fluffed his lines 56 times and shooting was abandoned for the day. Next morning Barrymore was word perfect), *Romeo And Juliet* (1936) as Mercutio, *Bulldog Drummond's Revenge* (1937), *Bulldog Drummond Comes Back* (1937), *Bulldog Drummond's Peril* (1938) all as Colonel J.A. Nielson, *Marie Antoinette* (1938) as King Louis XV, *The Great Profile* (1940) as Evans Garrick and *The Invisible Woman* (1940) as Professor Gibbs. In 1931 he was paid $460,000 for his film work. Barrymore was equally at home on stage. He claimed his one regret was not being able to sit in a theatre and watch himself act. One obviously poor woman arrived at the stage door one day and let it be known that sexual favours would be on offer if Barrymore helped her. After they coupled, Barrymore presented her with two tickets for the next day's matinée. The woman looked at the pieces of paper. "No, no," she wailed. "Bread! Bread for my children!" Replied the somewhat insensitive actor, "Madam, you want bread – go fuck a baker." On another occasion he was responsible for hiring the actresses to carry the body of Ophelia in a production of *Hamlet*. Barrymore felt that they didn't look quite right and asked if they could attempt to look more like the virgins they were supposed to be rather than the chorus girls they actually were. Said one, "My dear Mr Barrymore, we are extras, not character actresses." In 1932 he was caught using a ladies' toilet. "Excuse me," said the woman who caught him, "this is for ladies." Barrymore thrust his penis in her direction, saying, "So, madam, is this." That same year he was involved in a car crash and broke his hip. With one exception (in 1936) he never drove again. In an attempt to dry out he went on a cruise but managed to drink everything he could lay his hands on including mouthwash, perfume, kerosene and spirit of camphor. He even sent an SOS for booze to a passing ship. He kept a pet vulture named Maloney which he fed on rotten meat scavenged from neighbours' dustbins in the early hours of the morning. Barrymore was married four times. Wife number one was the actor Katherine Corri Harris (b. 1892, d. New York, May 2, 1927) who he married on September 1, 1910 at St Xavier's Catholic Church in New York. They divorced on December 6, 1916. The second Mrs John Barrymore was another actor (later author) Blanche Marie Louise Oelrichs (b. New York, October 1, 1890, d. Boston, Massachusetts, November 5, 1950).

They married at the Ritz-Carlton Hotel, New York, on August 5, 1920 and had one daughter, Diana, who is noticed above. They divorced in Kingston, New York, on November 19, 1928. She became an author using the *nom de plume* Michael Strange. Number three, on November 24, 1928 in Beverly Hills, was attractive blonde actor Dolores Costello (b. Pittsburgh, Pennsylvania, September 17, 1903, d. Fallbrook, California, March 1, 1979 of emphysema). Before their divorce on October 9, 1935 they had two children: Dolores Ethel Blyth Barrymore (b. April 8, 1930) and John Blyth Barrymore, who is noticed below. His final wife was Elaine Barrie (b. New York, July 16, 1915 as Elaine Jacobs, d. New York, March 1, 2003), nearly thirty-five years his junior, whom he first met when she interviewed him for her school magazine! They married on November 8, 1936 in Yuma, Arizona and divorced on November 26, 1940. CAUSE: At the time of his death (in Hollywood Presbyterian Hospital, California, ten days after collapsing during rehearsals for a radio show) from pneumonia and cirrhosis of the liver, he was severely in debt and had just 60¢ in his pockets. His funeral on June 2, 1942 was attended by more than 2,000 people and his pallbearers included W.C. Fields (another drunk), and Louis B. Mayer. His third wife and children were not among the mourners. He was buried in Cavalry Cemetery in Los Angeles alongside his sister-in-law Irene Fenwick Barrymore. In 1980 his corpse was disinterred, cremated and reburied in the Barrymore family grave in Mount Vernon, Philadelphia. His grave in Calvary Cemetery still bears the legend "Good Night, Sweet Prince".

FURTHER READING: *Good Night, Sweet Prince* – Gene Fowler (New York: The Viking Press, 1944); *Damned In Paradise: The Life Of John Barrymore* – John Kobler (New York: Atheneum, 1977).

John Drew Barrymore

(JOHN BLYTH BARRYMORE, JR)
Born June 4, 1932
Died November 29, 2004
Son of the Great Profile. With legendary hard drinker John Barrymore as your father, life was never going to be easy. John Drew Barrymore was born at 3.42pm in Beverly Hills, California, the son of John Barrymore and Dolores Costello. His sister Dolores Ethel Blyth Barrymore had been born two years earlier on April 8, 1930. To be outshone by a parent must rankle but to be outshone by a parent and a child must be doubly galling and yet that is the situation that John Drew found himself in. He never lived up to his father's name or his uncle Lionel's or his aunt Ethel's but he did share his father's predilection for hard living and reckless drinking. Barrymore père left his wife when Barrymore fils was just three and he claimed to remember seeing his father only once. In a failed attempt to stop him following the family acting tradition Dolores Costello sent her son to St John's Military Academy in Wisconsin, from where, at the age of 13, he and his cousin, Dirk Drew Davenport, successfully joined the US Navy, both claiming to be 17 years old. When he reached 17 John Drew decided to become an actor. His famous name ensured that he was thrown in at the deep end and given leading man roles but twice backed out before the first night. Aunt Ethel was furious at what she saw as the besmirching of the family name. He made his film début in a B-movie western *The Sundowners* (1950) as Jeff Cloud. John Drew was haunted by his family history. "I don't mind if my acting is compared to him," Barrymore once said of his father. "The trouble is that people expect me to live like him." Sadly, he did. He made several films in the Fifties under the name John Barrymore, Jr, including *High Lonesome* (1950) as Cooncat, *Quebec* (1951) as Mark Douglas, *The Big Night* (1951) as George La Main,

Thunderbirds (1952) as Private Tom McCreery and *While The City Sleeps* (1956) as Robert Manners but drink and drugs began to dominate Barrymore's life. In 1958 he changed his name to John Drew Barrymore and his career was briefly revived with his performances in *High School Confidential!* (1958) as J.I. Coleridge, *Never Love A Stranger* (1958) as Francis 'Frankie' Kane and *Night Of The Quarter Moon* (1959) as Roderic 'Chuck' Nelson. In 1960 he moved to Italy and appeared in a series of awful films. In 1962, he was arrested in Rome for fighting in the street. Over the next two decades Barrymore alternated between prison and occasional acting jobs on television and in films. Towards the end of his life he became increasingly reclusive and estranged from his family. In 2003, wheelchair bound, he appeared at a Los Angeles court hearing to determine who should act as his guardian. He was married three times. His first marriage on December 23, 1952 was to the actor Cara Williams (b. Brooklyn, New York, June 29, 1925) by whom he had one son, the actor John Blyth Barrymore (b. May 15, 1954). The couple was divorced in 1959. On October 28, 1960 he married Gaby Palazzolo. Their daughter Blythe was born in 1962. The couple divorced in 1964. His third marriage was to Ildiko Jaid Mako (b. Brannenburg, West Germany, May 8, 1946) although no one seems to know when they were married. When they met he had just been arrested for the fourth time for possession of marijuana. With her he had the actor Drew (b. Culver City, California, February 22, 1975 weighing 6lb 5oz). In her autobiography he was depicted as a menacing figure, showing up only to abuse his daughter and former wife and ask for money.

CAUSE: John Drew Barrymore died aged 72 in Los Angeles, California, after suffering from bone cancer. Daughter Drew paid for his medical bills for the last two years of his life.

Lionel Barrymore
(LIONEL HERBERT BLYTH)
Born April 28, 1878
Died November 15, 1954
Crusty old man. The eldest of Maurice's children, 6' Barrymore was born at 119 North Nine Street, Philadelphia, Pennsylvania, and was educated at Gilmore School, London, St Vincent's Academy, New York, and Seton Hall, New Jersey. Like his siblings he took to the stage and made his début in Kansas City at the age of sixteen, playing Thomas the coachman in a touring production of Sheridan's *The Rivals* which also featured his grandmother as Mrs Malaprop. In 1900 he made his Broadway début in the play *Sag Harbor* but his career was not as successful as his siblings and in 1909 he made the transition to Hollywood when he joined the Biograph Studio. He gave up the stage completely in 1925. Among his early films were *The Battle* (1911), *The Miser's Heart* (1911), *Friends* (1912), *So Near, Yet So Far* (1912), *The One She Loved* (1912), *The Painted Lady* (1912), *Gold And Glitter* (1912), *The Vengeance Of Galora* (1913) and many more. It was in 1923 that he finally forsook the theatre and spent the following 27 years working for MGM (the longest ever contract). He claimed in later years that while directing the melodrama *Madame X* (1929) he invented the boom mike, but some have disputed this. Barrymore directed fellow actor John Gilbert's first talkie *His Glorious Night* (1929), generally regarded as one of the worst talkie débuts of all time. Barrymore was also responsible for Clark Gable's stardom. It was he who persuaded *wunderkind* Irving Thalberg of Gable's potential despite Thalberg's misgivings about the size of Gable's ears. Barrymore played character roles rather than leading parts but was rarely without work. "In any actors' hall of fame," said Frank Capra, "Lionel Barrymore's name deserves top billing among the immortals, yet he

was the humblest, most co-operative actor I have ever known." Barrymore won a Best Actor Oscar for his performance in *A Free Soul* (1931), as Stephen Ashe, a drunken lawyer who defended his daughter against a murder charge so passionately that he collapsed and died during his summation to the jury. He also impressed in *Sadie Thompson* (1928) as Davidson, *Mata Hari* (1931) as General Serge Shubin, *Rasputin And The Empress* (1932) as Rasputin (the only occasion on which Ethel, John, and Lionel Barrymore worked together), *Grand Hotel* (1932) as Otto Kringelein (in which he appeared with brother John), *Treasure Island* (1934) as Billy Bones, *David Copperfield* (1935) as Dan Peggotty, *Camille* (1937) as Monsieur Duval, *Captains Courageous* (1937) as Captain Disko Troop, *Young Dr Kildare* (1938), *Calling Dr Kildare* (1939), *The Secret Of Dr Kildare* (1939), *Dr Kildare's Strange Case* (1940), *Dr Kildare's Crisis* (1940), *Dr Kildare Goes Home* (1940), *The People Vs. Dr Kildare* (1941), *Dr Kildare's Wedding Day* (1941), *Dr Kildare's Victory* (1941), *Dr Gillespie's New Assistant* (1942), *Calling Dr Gillespie* (1942), *Dr Gillespie's Criminal Case* (1943), *Three Men In White* (1944), *Between Two Women* (1944), *Dark Delusion* (1947) all as the kind-but-cranky Dr Leonard Barry Gillespie (played in a wheelchair or behind a desk because of his crippling arthritis caused when a drawing board fell on him in 1936, breaking his hip). The pain stopped him playing Scrooge in *A Christmas Carol* (1937) (Reginald Owen was cast instead). Barrymore told one reporter: "L.B. [Mayer] gets me $400-worth of cocaine a day to ease my pain. I don't know where he gets it. And I don't care. But I bless him every time it puts me to sleep." He also starred in *Duel In The Sun* (1946) as Senator McCanles, *It's A Wonderful Life* (1946) as Mr Potter, *Key Largo* (1948) as James Temple and *Right Cross* (1950) as Sean O'Malley.

Barrymore also found time to write a novel, *Mr Cantonwine*, compose a symphony and paint pictures. He married twice. His first wife (on June 19, 1904 at St Xavier's Catholic Church in New York) was the actor Doris Rankin (b. 1880, d. Washington, DC 1946) who was the sister of his uncle. They had two daughters: Ethel (b. 1909, d. 1910) and Mary (b. 1916, d. 1917). They divorced in New York City on December 21, 1922. His second wife (July 16, 1923 in Rome) was divorced actress Irene Fenwick (b. Chicago, Illinois, September 5, 1887 as Irene Frizzel) who died in Beverly Hills of *anorexia nervosa* on Christmas Eve 1936 aged 49. It was her second marriage and she had previously been the lover of his brother John. Director George Cukor said: "Irene treated Lionel with cruelty, almost sadistically. Lionel worshipped her, then her memory, until the day he died." CAUSE: He died in Valley Hospital, Van Nuys, California, from a heart attack several hours before he was due to appear on *The Hallmark Theatre* radio show. He was 76. He was buried on November 23, 1954 in Block 352 of the Main Mausoleum of Calvary Cemetery, 4201 Whittier Boulevard, Los Angeles 90023. The sole beneficiary in his will (worth $25,000) was the woman who had helped to look after him in old age.

Judith Barsi
Born June 6, 1978
Died July 27, 1988
Promising young actress. Judith Eva Barsi was the daughter of Hungarians Jozsef Barsi and Maria Benko. As with many mothers Maria wanted to be an actress and she enjoyed the new found fame she achieved through her daughter. Discovered at an ice rink, Judith looked as if she could be one of the few adorable moppets that populate so many Hollywood films to become a successful adult actress. Father Jozsef was not a pleasant man. When Judith

went to the Bahamas to film *Jaws The Revenge* (1987) he held a knife to his daughter's throat and told her, "If you decide not to come back, I will cut your throat." By 1988, Judith was earning $100,000 a year. The Barsis bought a three bedroomed house at 22100, Michale Street, Canoga Park, California. Not long after they moved in Jozsef erected a fence around the property. Judith appeared in *Eye Of The Tiger* (1986) and *Slamdance* (1987) but the chance for adulthood, never mind adult stardom, was never to be hers. Maria would constantly complain to anyone who would listen that Jozsef abused them – verbally and physically – and threatened to murder them and burn the house down. People tried to intervene, but to no avail. When Judith started showing outward signs of odd behaviour (she plucked her own eyebrows out and de-whiskered a cat), it was recommended that she see a psychiatrist. When Judith told of the abuse at home, Maria was advised to call the authorities. She did but still not much was done. Jozsef agreed to a divorce and Maria told them that everything was under control. Sadly, it wasn't. One of the television films Judith was in was called *Fatal Vision* (1984) about a little girl murdered by her father.

CAUSE: At around 8.30 in the morning of July 27, 1988, a neighbour heard a shot come from the Barsi house and then saw smoke billowing out. She called the emergency services. Judith had been sleeping in her nightgown in her canopied bed, just a few feet from the pink television set that her father bought her as an apology for pulling her around by the hair. She was mercifully asleep when he shot her in the head. Maria heard the shot and came running, still in her own nightgown. He blew her brains out in the hallway. Jozsef then walked into the garage and turned the gun on himself. Despite the original press reports, repeated in the first edition of this book, Judith's corpse was not dowsed in petrol and set afire. A picture exists, seen by the present author, that shows a remarkably clean bullet wound in the right side of her lower skull, untouched by fire.

Lionel Bart
(LIONEL BEGLEITER)
Born August 1, 1930
Died April 3, 1999
Sixties songsmith. Born in Mother Levy's Maternity Home, 24 Underwood Road, London E1, the youngest of eleven children (seven lived to maturity), the son of Morris Begleiter and Yetta Darumstundler, who hailed from Galicia. Morris was a master tailor and all his children followed him into the business except the youngest. For a time he worked as a silkscreen printer and was by his own admission expelled from St Martin's School of Art for mischievousness. However, it was in the theatre that Bart made his name and, for a time, his money, despite the fact that he could neither read nor write music. After National Service in the RAF he joined the Communist Party and in 1952 produced a cabaret for the International Youth Centre, another leftist organisation. On June 30, 1960, his musical *Oliver!* opened at the New Theatre. Rex Harrison, Sid James and Peter Sellers all turned down the part of Fagin before Ron Moody was cast, a role he was to play in the film version eight years later. Michael Caine auditioned for the part of Bill Sikes but was unsuccessful and reportedly cried for days afterwards. Barry Humphries played the undertaker Mr Sowerberry and almost 40 years later when the show was revived at the London Palladium he played Fagin. The show was a huge success (although at the time not with critics) but it did not bring Bart long-term happiness. He took to wearing a Stetson to hide his baldness and had a rhinoplasty ("He cut off his nose to spite his race"). Another musical, *Twang!!*, was a

disaster but Bart used his own money to prop it up. On February 16, 1971, he was arrested at his London Reece Mews home on charges of drug possession and later fined £50 with £10 costs. Just over a year later, on February 29, 1972, he went bankrupt. He also became an alcoholic. Bart had 45 godchildren and 35 nephews and nieces. Oddly, he sent them presents on his birthday. A homosexual, Bart never married but counted Rudolph Nureyev among his lovers. He was linked in the press 'romantically' with both Judy Garland and Alma Cogan, one an icon with a huge gay following, the other one of the most popular female singers of the early Sixties who died a virgin and proposed marriage to him on *This Is Your Life*. Among the songs he wrote or co-wrote were 'The Ballad Of The Liver Birds', 'From Russia With Love', 'A Handful Of Songs', 'Happiness', 'Happy Endings', 'Little White Bull', 'Livin' Doll', 'Maggie May' (the tale of a Liverpudlian lady of easy virtue, as opposed to the Rod Stewart classic), 'Rock With The Caveman', 'Tommy The Toreador' and 'Who's This Geezer Hitler?'. His stage play *Lock Up Your Daughters* was also filmed in 1969. CAUSE: In the 1970s he permanently damaged his liver downing three bottles of vodka a day. He joined Alcoholics Anonymous but later fell victim to diabetes. He was 68 when he died in Hammersmith Hospital, west London. He left £1,299,856. FURTHER READING: *Bart! The Unauthorised Life & Times, Ins And Outs, Ups And Downs Of Lionel Bart –* David Roper (London: Pavilion, 1994).

Richard Barthelmess

Born May 9, 1895
Died August 17, 1963
Social animal. Richard Semler Barthelmess was born in New York City, the son of actress Caroline Harris and worked in the theatre during school holidays. The 5′9″ actor began his movie career in 1916, appearing in films such as *War Brides* (1916) as Arno, *Just A Song At Twilight* (1916) as George Turner, *Gloria's Romance* (1916), *The Moral Code* (1917), *The Eternal Sin* (1917) as Gennaro and *The Valentine Girl* (1917) as Robert Wentworth. He began appearing alongside Marguerite Clark (b. February 22, 1883, d. September 25, 1940, from pneumonia), the major rival of Mary Pickford. He then began playing opposite the Gish sisters and was taken under the wing of D.W. Griffith appearing alongside Lillian in *Broken Blossoms* (1919) as Cheng Huan. The tale of a young Chinaman who befriended a down and out, it was the film that launched Barthelmess to stardom. Dorothy Gish said that Barthelmess' face was the "most beautiful of any man who ever went before a camera." At the première of *Broken Blossoms* he met Ziegfeld girl Mary Hay and they were married on June 18, 1920, at the Church of the Heavenly Rest in New York. That year they appeared together in *Way Down East*. In *Tol'able David* (1921) he played David Kinemon, a Virginia mountain boy whose mission in life was to get the post through. The film was such a success that he was able to form Inspiration Pictures on the back of it. He reprised his film *Just A Song At Twilight* (1922), playing George Turner again. In 1923 his daughter Mary was born. He subsequently starred in *The Seventh Day* (1922) as John Alden, Jr, *Fury* (1923) as Boy Leyton, *The Bright Shawl* (1923) as Charles Abbott, *The Fighting Blade* (1923) as Karl Van Kerstenbroock, *Twenty-One* (1923) as Julian McCullough and *The Enchanted Cottage* (1924) in which he portrayed Oliver Bashforth, a World War I veteran who eschews pretty women to find happiness in the arms of a plain woman. In 1925 he and Mary Hay separated, divorcing in Paris on December 29, 1926. That same year he also closed down Inspiration Pictures

and signed a three-year deal with First National Pictures. His salary at the time was a whopping $375,000 per annum. His first film for his new employers was the story of a prize-fighting boxer, *The Patent Leather Kid* (1927). Then came *The Drop Kick* (1927) as Jack Hamill and *The Noose* (1928) as Nickie Elkins, a man imprisoned for a homicide he did not commit. In 1927 Barthelmess served on a committee that formulated plans for a series of awards to be given to the film industry. The committee evolved into the dramatic sounding Academy of Motion Pictures, Arts & Sciences. In 1928 he married Jessica Stewart Sargent, a match that was to last until his death. At the first Oscars Barthelmess was nominated for both *The Patent Leather Kid* and *The Noose*. He failed to win either nomination. His first talkie was *Weary River* (1929) in which he portrayed Jerry Larrabee, a bootlegger who had been framed for a crime he didn't commit. Then he appeared in *Drag* (1929) as David Carroll, *Young Nowheres* (1929) as Albert 'Binky' Whalen, *Son Of The Gods* (1930) as Sam Lee, *The Dawn Patrol* (1930) as Dick Courtney, *The Finger Points* (1931) as Breckenridge Lee, *The Last Flight* (1931) as Cary Lockwood, *Alias The Doctor* (1932) as Karl Muller, *The Cabin In The Cotton* (1932) as Marvin Blake, *Heroes For Sale* (1933) as Thomas Holmes, *Central Airport* (1933) as Jim Blaine, *Midnight Alibi* (1934) as Lance McGowan, *Massacre* (1934) as Joe Thunderhorse and *Four Hours To Kill!* (1935) as Tony Mako, after which he began to work as a freelance. He quickly lost interest in film-making, appearing sporadically until his retirement in 1942. One of his best-known last roles was playing the cowardly Bat MacPherson in *Only Angels Have Wings* (1939). His 81st and final film was *The Spoilers* (1942) playing Bronco Kid Farrell. In 1942 he joined the US Navy as a lieutenant

commander. Following demob, he became a New York socialite and landowner.

CAUSE: He died of throat cancer in Southampton, New York, aged 68. He left over $1 million.

Freddie Bartholomew
(FREDERICK LLEWELLYN)
Born March 28, 1924
Died January 23, 1992

Irritatingly cissified child star. Born in London, the son of a civil servant who lost a leg in World War I, Bartholomew epitomised the perfect English kid. Consequently, he was loathed by children and adored by their mothers and other female relatives. He was raised by his grandparents in Warminster but it was his spinster aunt Millicent Bartholomew (who gave him her name) who recognised his acting ability and gave him elocution lessons to flatten out his London vowels. He made his film début in *Fascination* (1931) and at the age of 10 was given a contract by MGM at $175 a week to appear in *David Copperfield* (1935) as the young David Copperfield. When money comes in the door, common sense and family loyalty go out of the window and so it was with Freddie B. His parents, who virtually gave him away when he was small, went to America to ask the courts for custody of their son plus, of course, a percentage of his earnings. Aunt Millie countersued and won custody but at a price. His salary was divided, with 10% going to his parents, 10% to Aunt Millie, 5% to his sisters (!) and the rest being put in trust for him. The court battles raged throughout most of the Thirties, almost overshadowing his career. He appeared in films such as *Professional Soldier* (1936) as King Peter, *Lloyds Of London* (1936) as young Jonathan Blake, *Little Lord Fauntleroy* (1936) as Cedric Erroll, *The Devil Is A Sissy* (1936) as Claude Pierce, *Captains Courageous* (1937) as Harvey Cheyne, *Kidnapped* (1938) as

David Balfour, *Lord Jeff* (1938) as Geoffrey Braemer, *Two Bright Boys* (1939) as David Harrington, *Tom Brown's School Days* (1940) as East, *Swiss Family Robinson* (1940) as Jack Robinson, *Naval Academy* (1941) as Steve Kendall, *A Yank At Eton* (1942) as Peter Carlton and *Cadets On Parade* (1942) as Freddie Hewlett by which time he had attained his majority and become an American citizen. He also joined the air force. In 1946 he married Maely Danielle who was eight years older than him. They had a daughter but the marriage didn't last and in 1953 he married Aileen Paul. His last film was *St Benny The Dip* (1951) in which he played Reverend Wilbur. Following his retirement from films he began a second career in advertising. CAUSE: He died in Sarasota, Florida, from emphysema and heart failure, aged 67.

Albert Bassermann

Born September 7, 1867
Died May 15, 1952
Teutonic thespian. Born in Mannheim, Germany, Bassermann (sometimes his surname was spelled Basserman in credits) is probably best known for playing the kidnapped diplomat Van Meer in Alfred Hitchcock's *Foreign Correspondent* (1940) and the murder scene amidst the rain and the umbrellas. The role had him nominated for a Best Supporting Actor Oscar although he did not win, losing out to Walter Brennan in *The Westerner* (1940). It was a long way from the start of his acting career, which began in his hometown in 1887. Moving to Berlin in 1891 he worked at various theatres before joining Max Reinhardt at the Deutsches Theatre. An early actor in films, he played Professor Osterode in *Der Letzte Tag* (1913) and the lawyer Dr Hallers in Max Mack's *Der Andere* (1913, *The Other*). In January 1933 Adolf Hitler became German chancellor and Bassermann, like many Jews, fled Germany fearful of their future. He settled in America in 1938 although his English was limited. He learned his lines phonetically helped by his wife, Elsa, whom he had married in 1908. His films included *Der König* (1913) as Provinzschauspieler, *Urteil Des Arztes* (1914) as Dr Erwin Hofmüller, *Du Sollst Keine Anderen Götter Haben* (1917), *Dr Schotte* (1918), *Eine Schwache Stunde* (1919), *Die Duplizität Der Ereignisse* (1920), *Die Stimme* (1920), *Die Söhne Des Grafen Dossy* (1920), *Masken* (1920), *Die Nächte Des Cornelis Brouwer* (1921) as Cornelis Brouwer, *Der Frauenarzt* (1921) as Dr Wolfgang Holländer, *Brennendes Land* (1921), *Frauenopfer* (1922) as Graf, *Lucrezia Borgia* (1922) as Pope Alexander VI, *Erdgeist* (1923) as Dr Schoen, *Christoph Columbus* (1923) as Columbus, *Helena* (1924) as Aisakos, *Der Herr Generaldirektor* (1925) as Generaldirektor Herbert Heidenberg, *Die Mühle Von Sanssouci* (1926) as Adjudant Buddenbrock, *Fräulein Else* (1929) as Dr Alfred Thalhof, *Dreyfus* (1930) as Colonel Picquart, *Voruntersuchung* (1931) as Dr Konrad Bienert, *Kadetten* (1931) as General von Seddin, *Knute Rockne All American* (1940) as Father Julius Nieuwland, *A Dispatch From Reuter's* (1940) as Franz Geller, *Escape* (1940) as Dr Arthur Henning, *Moon Over Burma* (1940) as Basil Renner, *A Woman's Face* (1941) as Consul Magnus Barring, *New Wine* (1941) as Ludwig van Beethoven, *The Shanghai Gesture* (1941) as Van Elst, *Fly-By-Night* (1942) as Dr Storm, *Invisible Agent* (1942) as Arnold Schmidt, *Desperate Journey* (1942) as Dr Mather, *The Moon And Sixpence* (1942) as Dr Coutras, *Once Upon A Honeymoon* (1942) as General Borelski, *Reunion In France* (1942) as General Hugo Schroeder, *Good Luck, Mr Yates* (1943) as Dr Carl Hesser, *Madame Curie* (1943) as Professor Jean Perot, *Since You Went Away* (1944) as Dr Sigmund Gottlieb Golden, *I Was A Criminal* (1945) as Wilhelm Voight,

Rhapsody In Blue (1945) as Professor Franck, *The Searching Wind* (1946) as Count von Stammer, *The Private Affairs Of Bel Ami* (1947) as Jacques Rival, *Escape Me Never* (1947) as Professor Heinrich and *The Red Shoes* (1948) as Ratov.
CAUSE: Bassermann died aged 84 from a heart attack while flying from New York to Zurich. He was buried in Mannheim.

Amelia Batchelor
Born February 2, 1908
Died April 15, 2002
Miss Columbia. You will almost certainly have never heard of Frances Amelia Batchelor but I guarantee that you will have seen her more times than almost any actress. Amelia Batchelor was the second model for Lady Liberty, the actress who holds the torch in the Columbia Films logo. She posed for the picture in 1936 and earned just $25. She also had uncredited roles in five films including *Kid Millions* (1934) and *The Wizard Of Oz* (premièred August 19, 1939).
CAUSE: She died of natural causes, aged 98, in Santa Monica, California.

Sir Alan Bates, CBE
Born February 17, 1934
Died December 27, 2003
Leading 'red brick actor'. Alan Arthur Bates was born in a nursing home in 1934 at Allestree, Derbyshire, the eldest of three sons (his two brothers are artists) of Harold Arthur Bates, (b. May 4, 1898, d. December 1976), a cellist who worked as an insurance salesman, and Florence Mary Wheatcroft (b. November 12, 1904, d. Derbyshire January 26, 1999), a pianist who had studied in Paris. Bates was educated at the Herbert Strutt Grammar School, Belper, where he acted in school plays. Aged 11, he was taken to the Derby Little Theatre Club by his mother. John Osborne and John Dexter were the leading actors at the time and Bates formed a friendship with the nine years older homosexual Dexter that worried Bates' father. After national service in the RAF, he trained for the stage at RADA, where he gained the Forbes-Robertson Award. His fellow students included Peter Bowles, Richard Briers, Albert Finney and Peter O'Toole. He made his stage début in 1955 in Coventry with *You And Your Wife*. In April 1956, 5'11" Bates made his London début in *The Mulberry Bush* for the English Stage Company in its first repertory season at the Royal Court Theatre. His third play for the company (on May 8, 1956) was John Osborne's *Look Back In Anger* in which Bates played Cliff, the quiet, sympathetic friend of Jimmy Porter. The part took him to Moscow, to Broadway and on a tour of America. He made the part his own, just as Kenneth Haigh was the only true Jimmy Porter, however many players succeeded them in the roles. That year Bates met and began an affair with 5'10" actor Peter Wyngarde (b. Marseille, Bouches-du-Rhône, France, August 23, 1925) – they lived together at 1 Earls Terrace, Kensington, London and the relationship lasted for ten years. It ended bitterly. One day Bates said, "I think I should get married." Wyngarde said years later, "I thought we had a really important and mutually beneficial relationship. We seemed to share the same romantic ideas – that we would be like the Oliviers. I would direct plays for him to act in, and we would have a wonderful joint career together. [But the marriage idea] was the end of our dream." When Bates returned to London he played Edmund, the younger, tubercular brother, in Eugene O'Neill's *Long Day's Journey Into Night* (at the Edinburgh Festival from September 8, 1958 and at the Globe in London from September 24, 1958) for which he was awarded the Clarence Derwent Award as the year's

most promising actor in the West End. Two years later on April 17, 1960, he created another stir as the menacing, fast-talking Mick in Harold Pinter's *The Caretaker*, another role he had the right to call his own. Of the stage role he opined, "It was an unforgettable piece of good fortune, the only play I have ever done in which I have not for one second thought, 'Oh God, I've got to do this again next week.' It was a sheer joy to play all the time." Bates made his first film in 1956 playing an uncredited King Lear in *It's Never Too Late*. Four years later, in 1960, he played Frank Rice, Archie's son, opposite Laurence Olivier in *The Entertainer*. He followed this as the murderous tramp in Bryan Forbes' *Whistle Down The Wind* (1961), the working-class hero Victor Arthur Brown in John Schlesinger's *A Kind Of Loving* (1962), recreating his stage role as Mick in *The Caretaker* (1963), as the quiet adulterer Stephen in Carol Reed's *The Running Man* (1963), as the attractively contemptible upstart Jimmy Brewster in Clive Donner's *Nothing But The Best* (1964), as Basil, an inhibited Englishman embarrassed by his virility in Michael Cacoyannis' *Zorba The Greek* (1964), *Once Upon A Tractor* (1965), as Jos Jones the lover who realises he has chosen the wrong girl in Silvio Narizzano's *Georgy Girl* (1966), as Private Charles Plumpick in *Le Roi De Coeur* (1966), and as Gabriel Oak in *Far From The Madding Crowd* (1967). He won an Oscar nomination for his portrayal of Yakov Bok the suffering victim of prejudice in *The Fixer* (1968). One reviewer wrote, "Alan Bates' bare posterior, known to us from *Georgy Girl* and *King Of Hearts*, makes another timely appearance here, thus becoming one of the most exposed arses in cinematic annals." The buttocks and much more were bared in his next film – Ken Russell's adaptation of D.H. Lawrence's

Women In Love (1969) in which Bates, as Rupert Birkin, wrestled naked in front of a fire with Oliver Reed. Both men were reticent to perform in the nude scene worrying about how they would measure up to each other. One night they went to a pub and got drunk and then went to the toilets together where cautiously they eyed each other up. Upon seeing that they were of nearly identical dimensions, they agreed to the scene. His next cinematic works included: *Three Sisters* (1970) as Colonel Vershinin, *The Go-Between* (1970) as Ted Burgess, *A Day In The Death Of Joe Egg* (1972) as Bri, *Story Of A Love Story* (1973) as Harry, *Royal Flash* (1975) as Rudi Von Sternberg, *In Celebration* (1975) as Andrew Shaw, *Butley* (1976) as Ben Butley, *An Unmarried Woman* (1978) as Saul, *The Shout* (1978) as Crossley, *The Rose* (1979) as Rudge Campbell, *Nijinsky* (1980) as Sergei Diaghilev, *Quartet* (1981) as H.J. Heidler, *Very Like A Whale* (1981) as Sir Jock Mellor, *Rece Do Góry* (1981) as Wikto, *Britannia Hospital* (1982) as Macready, *The Return Of The Soldier* (1982) as Chris Baldry, Michael Winner's *The Wicked Lady* (1983) as Jerry Jackson, *Duet For One* (1986) as David Cornwallis, *A Prayer For The Dying* (1987) as Jack Meehan, *We Think The World Of You* (1988) as Frank Meadows, *Force Majeure* (1989) as Malcolm Forrest, *Mister Frost* (1990) as Felix Detweiler, *Docteur M.* (1990) as Dr Marsfeldt/Guru, *Hamlet* (1990) as Claudius, *Unnatural Pursuits* (1991) as Hamish Partt, *Shuttlecock* (1991) as James Prentis, *Secret Friends* (1991) as John, *Silent Tongue* (1994) as Eamon McCree, *The Grotesque* (1995) as Sir Hugo Coal, *Gosford Park* (2001) as Mr Jennings the butler, *The Mothman Prophecies* (2002) as Alexander Leek, *The Sum Of All Fears* (2002) as Dressler, *Evelyn* (2002) as Tom Connolly, *Hollywood North* (2003) as Michael Baytes and *The Statement* (2003) as Armand

Bertier. Bates was equally prolific in later years on the small screen, appearing in several TV movies and series. He was the playwright John Mortimer in *A Voyage Round My Father* (1982), Mortimer's dramatisation of his father's blindness, and John Malcolm/Major Pollock in *Separate Tables* (1983). In 1984, he won a BAFTA Best Television Actor Award for playing the homosexual spy Guy Burgess in Alan Bennett's television film *An Englishman Abroad* (1983). Bates also played King Henry VIII in *The Prince And The Pauper* (2000) and was King George VI in *Bertie And Elizabeth* (2002). Following Wyngarde, Bates's next boyfriend (in 1967) was a young actor called Paul Taylor (b. Lancashire 1947). "Alan taught me a great deal, and we had a very intense and loving sexual relationship," said Taylor. "One evening, Alan came home and he said very quickly and simply, 'I'm going to have to ask you to leave, as I'm going to be married'. I was taken completely by surprise." On May 9, 1970 at Bradbourne, Derbyshire, Bates married the actress Valerie June 'Victoria' Ward (b. London, January 20, 1940) whom he had met in New York in 1962. On November 12, 1970, at First Maternity Hospital, Nottingham, they had twin sons Benedick Arthur and Tristan. While Ben lived a fulfilling life, his brother began taking drugs and running with a louche crowd. On January 13, 1990, 19-year-old Tristan Bates was found dead of a drug overdose in a public lavatory at Ajiro Park, Tokyo, Japan. As the years went on, Victoria Bates descended into madness: she refused to put the heating on and did not let her sons see doctors or dentists. Clothes remained unwashed, the fridge contained rotting food, and she would cook only beans or cabbage. On June 22, 1992 she was found dead in a Sardinian hotel from a suspected heart attack, following the wasting disease

cachexia. "Her body is in a chronic state of deterioration," said the pathologist while a friend commented that she looked like "a photo of a starving African child". During his marriage Bates had numerous gay affairs. His lovers included Ian Charleson who was to die of AIDS, actor Nickolas Grace (Bates ended the relationship with the words, "It's been very nice to have known you. I'm sure I'll see you around in London" to Grace's horror. The younger man said, "I told him labels didn't matter, but that we must be who we are but he just could not accept that. Alan was at ease as long as he pretended – and he insisted on pretending – that our relationship was not what it was, and was not disclosed to or evident to others"), artist Gerard Hastings (b. 1960), and he had a two-year affair with the ice skater John Curry. Although they split, Bates cared for his ex-boyfriend when Curry was diagnosed with AIDS. On April 15, 1994 Curry, then 44, suffered a heart attack and died in the arms of Bates. He began a relationship with the actress Angharad Rees who had also lost a child early – her son Linford Cazenove had been killed in a car crash on September 10, 1999, aged 25. It was her doubts that stopped a wedding going ahead and Bates returned to work with a vengeance. Actress Joanna Pettet stepped into the breech. He was made a Commander of the British Empire in 1995 and awarded a knighthood in the New Year's Honours List in 2003. Reports circulate that Princess Margaret had blocked his gong after he spurned her advances.

CAUSE: On October 9, 2002 Bates underwent hip replacement surgery at King Edward VII Hospital in London. In January 2003 he was diagnosed with inoperable pancreatic cancer. Bates died at the London Clinic, 20 Devonshire Place, London, W1 aged 69, his son by his side.

FURTHER READING: *Otherwise Engaged: The Life Of Alan Bates* – Donald Spoto (London: Hutchinson, 2007).

Ralph Bates

Born February 12, 1940
Died March 27, 1991
Hammer horror star. Born in Bristol, Bates made his stage début in 1963 at the Gate Theatre, Dublin, and joined various repertory companies. He appeared in several Hammer films including *Horror Of Frankenstein* (1970), *Lust For A Vampire* (1970) and *Dr Jekyll & Sister Hyde* (1971). On television he appeared in *Poldark* but gained more fame as John Lacey, the cuckolded teacher who joins a lonely hearts club, in the hit BBC sitcom *Dear John*. His wife, Virginia Wetherill, and daughter, Daisy, are also actresses. CAUSE: Bates died of cancer aged 51. *Dear John* was cancelled by the BBC when it was discovered it was cheaper to buy an American version. Bates' family blamed the stress of losing his job for the cancer that killed him.

Greg Bautzer

Born April 3, 1911
Died October 26, 1987
The real-life Arnie Becker. Raised in San Pedro, Gregson Bautzer was "tall and husky, with soulful dark eyes, a tanned complexion and a flashy smile" – perfect for his profession, that of a lawyer who plied his trade with some of Hollywood's most glamorous leading ladies. One day his life story will make a great book and film. Bautzer attended the University of Southern California Law School and, after war service in the navy, he began a law practice with Bentley Ryan. In 1937 he was dating blonde bombshell Lana Turner, who lost her virginity to him. Of the latter, Turner has said, "I was awkward. I had no idea how to move or what to do. The act itself hurt like hell, and I must confess I didn't enjoy it at all. I didn't even know what an orgasm was. But I loved being close to Greg." Not long afterwards he took up with Joan Crawford after she called Lana to her house and asked her to finish with Bautzer. That affair quickly fizzled out and he moved on to romances with Merle Oberon and Sonja Henie. By 1946 he was ready for a rematch with Crawford but she ignored his calls. He travelled down to where she was staying in Palm Springs and booked into the same hotel, La Quinta, where he continued his wooing. Eventually, his persistence paid off and they began seeing each other. She presented him with a black convertible Cadillac as a token of her love and, no doubt, lust. As well as womanising, Bautzer liked boozing (often until he couldn't stand) and gambling, usually together. One night after a heavy session he ended up wrecking a mailbox and lamppost on Wilshire Boulevard and his drink-driving resulted in front page coverage. Crawford was horrified by the adverse publicity and dumped him. He retaliated by seeing old flame Merle Oberon and Crawford went off with Steve Crane, who was previously married to Lana Turner . . . whose first love had been Bautzer. A week later, Bautzer and Crawford were once again an item. Crawford liked rough sex and Bautzer was only too happy to oblige. On one occasion he went too far and blacked her eye – but she didn't seem to mind. He related, "I still have four scars on my face which she put there. She could throw a cocktail glass across the room and hit you in the face, two times out of three." In 1946 Bautzer lost several front teeth in a fight with cowboy actor Don 'Red' Barry (b. Houston, Texas, January 11, 1911, as Donald Barry d'Acosta, d. North Hollywood, California, July 17, 1980, by his own hand) defending the honour of Crawford. That was probably more than she ever did to defend it herself, although she did pay for his reconstructive dentistry. In February 1947 he had lunch two days

on the trot with Rita Hayworth, so Crawford was seen out with English actor Peter Shaw (who went on to marry Angela Lansbury). Shaw even went so far as to discuss marriage to Crawford with gossip columnist Hedda Hopper. However, in March 1947 Crawford was back with Bautzer. Their on-off affair was to last for ten years. He said, "A night with Joan was better than a year with ten others." One time Bautzer fell asleep in Joan's private cinema and she insisted all the guests left him there, locking the door. The next morning Bautzer woke up, cooked himself some breakfast in the small diner attached, broke a window to get out and went home. A furious Crawford later rang him: "How dare you leave my home without washing the dishes?" she raged. On another occasion he irritated Joan when playing baseball with her son Christopher. She had told the boy to throw right-handed and call Bautzer 'Uncle Greg'. When she saw the boy doing neither she reprimanded first him and then Bautzer. The lawyer apologised, but Crawford wanted more. "If you're really sorry, you'll kneel in front of me." Bautzer thought she was joking, but Crawford was deadly serious. "I'm not kidding. If you were truly sorry, you'd kneel. Franchot [Tone] always did." Bautzer refused but later asked Tone if Joan had told him the truth. He replied that she had. Through Crawford Bautzer enlarged his client base. He represented Ingrid Bergman, John Garfield, Joseph Schenck, Jerry Wald, Jane Wyman and Ginger Rogers. In October 1949 Crawford and Bautzer attended an event in honour of Prince Bernhard of the Netherlands. At the party Bautzer danced with Ginger Rogers all night, to Joan's fury. Her revenge was swift. Driving home at 1.30am that night, she stopped the car and asked Bautzer to check the right rear tyre. As soon as he got out of the vehicle she drove off, leaving him stranded. He walked the three miles home to the Bel-Air hotel and this time did not call Crawford to make up as he had done so often in the past. Instead, he began seeing Ginger Rogers. By January 1951 he was dating Jane Wyman, recently separated from Ronald Reagan. He also squired 5'2" blonde actress Terry Moore, who may have been married to Howard Hughes, for whom Bautzer was personal attorney. When the bashful billionaire saw Elizabeth Taylor, he decided he wanted her. He sent Bautzer to Taylor with a proposal of marriage and an incentive payment of $1 million. (Hughes never got to bed Taylor.) Later that year, Bautzer was back with Crawford. During one row he tore off a pair of diamond cufflinks (worth $10,000) that she gave him and in her temper she flushed them down the toilet. Realising the folly of her actions she forbade anyone to use any of the conveniences until a plumber could be called. He charged her $500 for retrieving them. On the way home, Bautzer wrote off the black Cadillac Crawford had given him. In autumn 1952 they co-hosted a special party for Noël Coward, who commented of Bautzer: "Too many teeth." Following another fight Crawford turned up unexpectedly at his law office on Hollywood Boulevard demanding to see her lover. Bautzer had instructed his secretary to tell Crawford he was out. The movie star ignored the amanuensis and burst into the office. She looked under his desk, in his cupboards, behind the curtains and even in his private lavatory. No Bautzer. She stormed out, puzzling the secretary, who knew that Bautzer was in there somewhere. She found him on a narrow window ledge 12 storeys up. Single past 40, Bautzer finally made a trip up the altar and married British actress Dana Wynter (b. 1927).

CAUSE: He died of a heart attack aged 76. He was buried in Westwood Village Memorial Park, 1218 Glendon Avenue, Los Angeles 90024.

Anne Baxter

Born May 7, 1923
Died December 12, 1985

Posh actress. Many stars have rags-to-riches stories. Anne Baxter had a riches-to-riches story. She was born in Michigan City, Indiana, the granddaughter of architect Frank Lloyd Wright and the only child of Kenneth Stuart Baxter, a top-flight executive in the Seagram Distillery company. It was seeing Helen Hayes that made the 10-year-old Anne Baxter decide an actor's life was for her. She attended Theodora Irvine's School of the Theater, where she studied under Madame Maria Ouspenskaya. She made her Broadway début on September 17, 1936, at the Henry Miller Theater as Elizabeth Winthrop in *Seen But Not Heard*. When she was 16 Baxter screen-tested for the role of Rebecca in the film of the same name, losing out to Joan Fontaine. However, bosses at Fox were so impressed by her that they offered her a contract. Baxter stayed there for 13 years but made her film début on loan out to MGM in Wallace Beery's *20 Mule Team* (1940) playing Joan Johnson. By the time she graduated from Los Angeles High School in 1941 she had appeared in substantive roles in four films. Her other movies included *The Great Profile* (1940) as Mary Maxwell, *Swamp Water* (1941) as Julie, *Charley's Aunt* (1941) as Amy Spettigue, *The Pied Piper* (1942) as Nicole Rougeron, *The Magnificent Ambersons* (1942) as Lucy Morgan, *Five Graves To Cairo* (1943) as Mouche, *Crash Dive* (1943) as Jean Hewlett and *Sunday Dinner For A Soldier* (1944) playing Tessa Osborne. It was during the shoot for the latter that she met actor John Hodiak (b. Pittsburgh, Pennsylvania, April 16, 1914, d. Tarzana, California, October 19, 1955 from a coronary thrombosis) and they married at her parents' home in Burlinghame, California, on July 7,1946. Their daughter, Katrina, was born on July 9,

1951. They were divorced in Los Angeles on January 27, 1953. During their marriage Baxter appeared in the two films that were to garner her Oscar nominations. She won a Best Supporting Actress Academy Award for her portrayal of the alcoholic Sophie in *The Razor's Edge* (1946). Up to that time Fox chief Darryl F. Zanuck believed Baxter was only suitable for mousy parts, such as that of a librarian. Fashion guru Mr Blackwell commented, "Her hair looks as if someone ran a brush through it and then thought 'Oh the hell with it'." She appeared in *Blaze Of Noon* (1947) as Lucille Stewart, *Yellow Sky* (1948) as Mike, *The Walls Of Jericho* (1948) as Julia Norman, *Homecoming* (1948) as Penny Johnson, *A Ticket To Tomahawk* (1950) as Kit Dodge, Jr, and Eve Harrington in *All About Eve* (1950), which earned her a Best Actress nomination. (Strangely, years later she replaced Lauren Bacall in the musical version, *Applause*, and played Margo Channing, the Bette Davis role. Later still, when Davis was forced to drop out of the TV soap *Hotel* through illness, Baxter took the lead.) Her career post-*Eve* was disappointing. She appeared in *O. Henry's Full House* (1952) as Joanna (the third time she and Marilyn Monroe appeared in the same film), *My Wife's Best Friend* (1952) as Virginia Mason, *Bedevilled* (1955) as Monica Johnson, *One Desire* (1955) as Tacey Cromwell, *Three Violent People* (1956) as Lorna Hunter Saunders, *The Ten Commandments* (1956) as Nefretiri and *Cimarron* (1960) as Dixie Lee. She married land developer Randolph Galt on February 18, 1960, in Honolulu. They had two daughters: Melissa (b. October 5, 1961) and Maginal (b. March 11, 1963). The first three years of the marriage were spent in the Australian bush, but it became too much for Baxter and she was divorced on the grounds of irreconcilable differences on January 29, 1970. By this time she was appearing more and more on the small screen and less and less on the big one. On January 30, 1977, she married the much older Wall Street banker David Klee. He died ten months later in New York City on October 15, 1977, aged 70.

CAUSE: Baxter died following a brain haemorrhage in New York aged 62.

Warner Baxter
Born March 29, 1889
Died May 7, 1951

Prolific diva. Born in Columbus, Ohio, 5'11" Warner Leroy Baxter moved to San Francisco in 1898 with his widowed mother. Following the April 18, 1906 earthquake the family lived in a tent for a fortnight. He became part-owner of a garage before he took to the stage in 1910 and then Hollywood. He appeared in numerous forgettable silents including *All Woman* (1918), *Lombardi, Ltd* (1919), *Sheltered Daughters* (1921) as Pep Mullins, *The Love Charm* (1921) as Thomas Morgan, *First Love* (1921) as Donald Halliday, *Cheated Hearts* (1921) as Tom Gordon, *Her Own Money* (1922) as Lew Alden, *The Girl In His Room* (1922) as Kirk Waring, *A Girl's Desire* (1922) as Jones/Lord Dysart, *If I Were Queen* (1922) as Vladimir, *The Ninety And Nine* (1922) as Tom Silverton/Phil Bradbury, *St Elmo* (1923) as Murray Hammond, *Blow Your Own Horn* (1923) as Jack Dunbar, *In Search Of A Thrill* (1923) as Adrian Torrens, *Alimony* (1924) as Jimmy Mason, *His Forgotten Wife* (1924) as Donald Allen/John Rolfe, *Those Who Dance* (1924) as Bob Kane, *The Female* (1924) as Colonel Valentia, *Christine Of The Hungry Heart* (1924) as Stuart Knight, *The Garden Of Weeds* (1924) as Douglas Crawford, *The Golden Bed* (1925) as Bunny O'Neill, *The Air Mail* (1925) as Russ Kane, *The Awful Truth* (1925) as Norman Slatterley, *Welcome Home* (1925) as Fred Prouty, *Rugged Water* (1925) as Calvin Horner, *A Son Of His Father* (1925) as Big Boy

Morgan, *The Best People* (1925) as Henry Morgan, *The Runaway* (1926) as Wade Murrell, *Mannequin* (1926) as John Herrick, *Miss Brewster's Millions* (1926) as Thomas B. Hancock, Jr, *Aloma Of The South Seas* (1926) as Nuitane, *Mismates* (1926) as Ted Carroll, *The Great Gatsby* (1926) as Jay Gatsby, *The Telephone Girl* (1927) as Matthew Standish, *Drums Of The Desert* (1927) as John Curry, *The Coward* (1927) as Clinton Philbrook and *Singed* (1927) as Royce Wingate. For *In Old Arizona* (1929), he became known for playing the Cisco Kid, a performance that won him a Best Actor Oscar on April 30, 1930 – beating off the talents of George Bancroft, Chester Morris, Paul Muni and Lewis Stone. The occasion overwhelmed Baxter and he forgot his "thank you" speech. His win was all the more remarkable because Baxter was not even supposed to be in the film. *In Old Arizona* was the first Western talkie and the original star and director was intended to be Raoul Walsh but while driving back from the location in Utah a jackrabbit jumped through his windscreen and blinded him in his right eye. Walsh pulled out and was replaced in front of the camera by Baxter and behind by Irving Cummings. *In Old Arizona*, based on a short story by O. Henry, was also unusual in that a third of the film was shot indoors because of difficulties with portable sound equipment. Baxter reprised his role as the Cisco Kid in *The Arizona Kid* (1930), *The Slippery Pearls* (1931), *The Cisco Kid* (1931) and *Return Of The Cisco Kid* (1939). As in modern times an Oscar win increased the pay packet of an actor and Baxter became one of the highest paid stars of the Thirties, earning $284,000 a year. Baxter was also, in modern parlance, a diva – his on-screen persona was a mask for his unpleasant, argumentative personality. He guarded his privacy as enthusiastically as Garbo. Following his performance as Adam Stoddard opposite Ingrid Bergman in Gregory Ratoff's frankly awful *Adam Had Four Sons* (1941) he suffered a nervous breakdown and took almost three years to recover. He spent much of that time in the South Seas hunting buried pirate treasure but came home without any booty. He returned to the screen in the 10-film Columbia series *Crime Doctor* based on Max Marcin's successful wireless series. Baxter played amnesia victim and former gang leader Phil Morgan who becomes Robert Ordway, America's leading criminal psychologist. The films were *Crime Doctor* (1943), *Crime Doctor's Strangest Case* (1943), *Shadows In The Night* (1944), *The Crime Doctor's Courage* (1945), *Crime Doctor's Warning* (1945), *Crime Doctor's Man Hunt* (1946), *Just Before Dawn* (1946), *The Millerson Case* (1947), *Crime Doctor's Gamble* (1947) and *The Crime Doctor's Diary* (1949). It was a light load requiring just eight weeks of work a year. His other films included: *Three Sinners* (1928) as James Harris, *A Woman's Way* (1928) as Tony, *The Tragedy Of Youth* (1928) as Frank Gordon, *Ramona* (1928) as Alessandro, *Danger Street* (1928) as Rolly Sigsby, *Craig's Wife* (1928) as Walter Craig, *West Of Zanzibar* (1928) as Doc, *Linda* (1929) as Dr Paul Randall, *Thru Different Eyes* (1929) as Jack Winfield, *The Far Call* (1929), *Behind That Curtain* (1929) as Colonel John Beetham, *Romance Of The Rio Grande* (1929) as Pablo Wharton Cameron, *Such Men Are Dangerous* (1930) as Ludwig Kranz, *Renegades* (1930) as Deucalion, *Doctors' Wives* (1931) as Dr Judson Penning, *Daddy Long Legs* (1931) as Jervis Pendleton, *Their Mad Moment* (1931) as Esteban Cristera, *The Squaw Man* (1931) as James Wingate, *Surrender* (1931) as Sergeant Dumaine, *Amateur Daddy* (1932) as Jim Gladden, *Man About Town* (1932) as Stephen Morrow, *Six Hours To Live* (1932) as Captain Paul Onslow, *42nd Street* (1933) as Julian Marsh, *Dangerously Yours* (1933) as Andrew Burke, *I Loved You Wednesday* (1933) as Philip Fletcher, *Paddy The Next Best Thing* (1933) as Lawrence Blake, *Penthouse* (1933) as Jackson Durant, *As Husbands Go* (1934) as Charles Lingard, *Stand Up And Cheer!* (1934) as Lawrence Cromwell, *Such Women Are Dangerous* (1934) as Michael Shawn, *Grand Canary* (1934) as Dr Harvey Leith, *Broadway Bill* (1934) as Dan Brooks, *Hell In The Heavens* (1934) as Lieutenant Steve Warner, *King Of Burlesque* (1935) as Kerry Bolton, *One More Spring* (1935) as Jaret Otkar, *Under The Pampas Moon* (1935) as Cesar Campo, *White Hunter* (1936) as Captain Clark Rutledge, *The Prisoner Of Shark Island* (1936) as Dr Samuel Mudd, *The Robin Hood Of El Dorado* (1936) as Joaquin Murrieta, *The Road To Glory* (1936) as Captain Paul La Roche, *To Mary – With Love* (1936) as Jack Wallace, *Vogues Of 1938* (1937) as George Curson, *Slave Ship* (1937) as Jim Lovett, *Wife, Doctor And Nurse* (1937) as Dr Judd Lewis, *Kidnapped* (1938) as Alan Breck, *I'll Give A Million* (1938) as Tony Newlander, *Wife, Husband And Friend* (1939) as Leonard Borland, *Barricade* (1939) as Hank Topping, *Earthbound* (1940) as Nick Desborough, *Lady In The Dark* (1944) as Kendall Nesbitt, *The Gentleman From Nowhere* (1948) as Earl Donovan/Robert Ashton, *The Devil's Henchmen* (1949) as Jess Arno, *Prison Warden* (1949) as Warden Victor Burnell and *State Penitentiary* (1950) as Roger Manners. He married Viola Caldwell in 1909 but they separated after just seven months. On January 29, 1918, he married the actor Winifred Bryson who was his leading lady in *The Awful Truth* (1925).

CAUSE: Warner Baxter suffered from arthritis and had a lobotomy to ease his pain. He contracted pneumonia following surgery and died in Beverly Hills, California, aged 62. He was buried in Westwood Cemetery, Glendale, California.

Sir Cecil Beaton

Born January 14, 1904
Died January 18, 1980

Jack of all trades. Born at 21 Langland
Gardens, Hampstead, north London,
at 11.30am the eldest of four children
of a timber merchant, Cecil Walter
Hardy Beaton was a photographer who
was much in demand during five
decades of the twentieth century.
Educated at Harrow and St John's
College, Cambridge, he was the official
photographer at the wedding of the
Duke of Windsor to Mrs Simpson on
June 3, 1937. Also in the Thirties he
began working in the theatre, designing
revues for Sir C.B. Cochran. After
World War II he created designs for
opera, ballet, film and the theatre. In
1948 he worked on the films *An Ideal
Husband* and *Anna Karenina*. Eight
years later, he designed the costumes
for *My Fair Lady*. Two years after
that he won the first of his two Oscars
for *Gigi* (1958), followed up by the
film version of *My Fair Lady* (1964).
He never married. Although
predominantly homosexual, Beaton
had a four-month affair with actress
Greta Garbo at the end of 1947 and
beginning of 1948 and even proposed
marriage to her.

CAUSE: In July 1974 while taking a
bath at his home at 8 Pelham Place,
south-west London, Beaton suffered a
stroke. The embolism robbed him of
the use of his right hand and his ability
to remember people's names. He once
referred to Queen Elizabeth the Queen
Mother as "that friend whose daughter
does an important job". Beaton was
taken to the London Clinic before
returning to Pelham Place and then to
Reddish House, Broadchalke,
Wiltshire, a house he had purchased
on June 21, 1947 for £10,000. In
October 1975, Pelham Place was sold.
Beaton was to say four years after the
stroke, "I thought I had had it. I
thought I'd never recover." But
recover he did and he fought his way
back to health, teaching himself to
paint and write with his left hand. He
died at Reddish House and was buried
in All Saints Church, Broadchalke, on
January 23, 1980. Beaton left
£597,757. Reddish House was sold in
June 1980.

FURTHER READING: *Cecil Beaton The
Authorised Biography* – Hugo Vickers
(London: Weidenfeld & Nicolson,
1985); *The Unexpurgated Beaton* –
Introduction by Hugo Vickers
(London: Weidenfeld & Nicolson,
2002).

Norman Beaton

Born October 31, 1934
Died December 13, 1994

West Indian stalwart. Norman Lugard
Beaton was born in Georgetown,
British Guiana, the son of William
Solomon Beaton (d. 1983), civil
servant, and his wife, Ada, née
Mackintosh (d. 1962). He was
educated at St Stephen's School and
Queen's College, Georgetown, and
later became deputy headmaster at the
Government Teachers' Training
College. In 1958 he became calypso
champion of British Guiana and
released 24 records with his own group
Four Bees. That same year he also
married one of his backing singers
Gloria Moshette and they had a son,
Jayme (b. British Guiana 1958), and a
daughter, Kim (b. British Guiana
1960). In 1960 Beaton emigrated to
Britain where he was later joined by his
wife and children. A third child, Jeremy
(b. 1962), was born in England.
Beaton became a teacher in Liverpool
and began acting and directing. He
played leading roles at the Old Vic, the
National Theatre and the Royal Court
Theatre. His reputation grew steadily.
In 1974 he started the Black Theatre of
Brixton. He was named Best Film
Actor by the Variety Club of Great
Britain for his performance in *Black Joy*
(1977), the first coloured British actor
to be honoured with a film award.
Among his most memorable television
successes were *The Fosters* (April 9,

1976–July 9, 1977), *Black Christmas* (1977), *Empire Road* (1978–1979), *Nice* (1984), *Big George Is Dead* (1987), *Little Napoleons* (1993) and *Desmond's* (January 5, 1989–December 19, 1994) in which he played barber Desmond Ambrose. Beaton's marriage ended in divorce. In 1969 he had a third son, William, by Jane Atto, with whom he briefly ran a London restaurant. In 1976 he married Leah Garady, who adopted the children of his first marriage; but this marriage too ended in divorce. From 1978 until his death he lived with Jane Cash.

CAUSE: Beaton died aged 60 in his native country after collapsing in a friend's arms. He left £203,086.

Edmond Beauchamp

Born March 3, 1900
Died June 3, 1985
French lead. Born in Montpellier, Hérault, Languedoc-Rousillon, France, Edmond Beauchamp was one of his country's stalwart actors. Grey-haired and aquiline of feature, he was often known just by his surname. His films included *Madame Bovary* (1933) as Binet, *Le Crime De Monsieur Lange* (1936) as a priest in the train, *Feu!* (1937), *Werther* (1938), *La Marseillaise* (1938) as a priest, *Louise* (1939) as Le Philosophe, *Un Seul Amour* (1943), *Le Bossu* (1944), *Le Visiteur* (1946), *Le Diable Au Corps* (1946) as the wine steward, *Les Jeux Sont Faits* (1947), *L'Armoire Volante* (1948) as Le Commissaire, *Meurtres* (1950) as Le Gossec, *Le Passe-Muraille* (1951) as Arturo, *Marie-Antoinette Reine De France* (1955) as Comte de Luxembourg, *Futures Vedettes* (1955) as Elise's father, *Le Maître Du Pérou* (1958), *Le Bossu* (1959) as Don Miguel, *Le Beau Serge* (1959) as Glomaud, *Le Petit Professeur* (1959) as the grandfather, *Un Nommé La Rocca* (1961) and *The Hotshots* (1968). To English viewers he was best known as the grandfather, César, in the television series *Belle Et Sébastien*, the tale of an orphaned boy and his large white dog set in the Pyrenees. The 13 25-minute episodes were transmitted by the BBC between October 2 and Boxing Day 1967.

CAUSE: Edmond Beauchamp died exactly three months past his 85th birthday in Saint-Brieuc, Côtes d'Armor, Bretagne, France.

Harold Beaudine

Born November 29, 1894
Died May 9, 1949
Directorial brother. Born in New York, Harold was the younger brother of William Beaudine and began his career as prop boy at Biograph's New York studio. He studied hard and became an assistant director before he moved to California to continue his career. His more than 30 films included: *In Dutch* (1922), *Nerve Tonic* (1924), *For Sadie's Sake* (1926) and *College Racket* (1931).

CAUSE: He died of cancer in Sawtelle, California, aged 54.

William Beaudine

Born January 15, 1892
Died March 18, 1970
'One-Shot' Beaudine. Born in New York, Beaudine was educated at Morris High School. He began in show business in 1904 as a prop man and general handyman for D.W. Griffith. He spent six years learning his trade before becoming a director in 1915. For seven years he honed his craft on shorts such as *Punch The Clock* (1922) and *Strictly Modern* (1922) before progressing to feature films in 1922. When told that one of his Monogram shorts was behind schedule, he commented in amazement, "You mean someone out there is actually waiting to see this?" He was adept at directing children but could also handle stars such as Mary Pickford in *Little Annie Rooney* (1925) and *Sparrows* (1926). He worked on hundreds of films in different genres usually low to medium budget fare. He

directed Will Hay in *Hey! Hey! USA!* (1938) while working in England during a three-year spell. He was in the chair for many of the Bowery Boys films but was at the centre of controversy in 1944 when he directed a sex education film *Mom And Dad* which showed an actual birth. The film was not released until 1957 because of numerous court cases. 6'1" Beaudine also worked on many television programmes as has his son, William, Jr (b. Hollywood, California, April 28, 1921). He had four children by his wife, Marguerite Fleischer.

CAUSE: At the time of his death in Canoga Park, California, aged 78, Beaudine was Hollywood's oldest active director.

Hugh Beaumont

Born February 16, 1909
Died May 14, 1982
TV dad. Probably best known for his role as Ward Cleaver on the popular TV sitcom *Leave It To Beaver* (1957–1963), Eugene Hugh Beaumont was born in Lawrence, Kansas. He was educated at the University of Chattanooga and the University of Southern California. Like Lew Ayres, Beaumont, a devout Methodist, was a conscientious objector during World War II. Among his 60-plus films were *South Of Panama* (1941) as Paul, *Northwest Rangers* (1942) as Warren, *Mexican Spitfire's Blessed Event* (1943) as Mr Sharpe, *There's Something About A Soldier* (1944) as Lieutenant Martin, *Objective Burma!* (1945) as Captain Hennessey, *The Blue Dahlia* (1946) as George Copeland, *Murder Is My Business* (1946) as Michael Shayne, *Larceny In Her Heart* (1946) as Michael Shayne, *Blonde For A Day* (1946) as Michael Shayne, *Too Many Winners* (1947) as Michael Shayne, *Three On A Ticket* (1947) as Michael Shayne, *The Counterfeiters* (1948) as Philip Drake, *Savage Drums* (1951) as Bill Fenton, *Mr Belvedere Rings The Bell* (1952) as a policeman and *The Mole People* (1957) as Dr Jud Bellamin. He was divorced,

with two sons. Like many typecast TV actors, Beaumont disliked *Leave It To Beaver* although he appreciated the hefty pay packets and handy residuals.

CAUSE: He suffered a stroke in 1972 and died of a heart attack in Munich, West Germany, aged 73.

James Beck

Born February 21, 1929
Died August 6, 1973
TV wideboy. To millions of TV fans Jimmy Beck will be forever associated with Private Joe Walker, the cockney spiv, in the highly popular BBC sitcom *Dad's Army*. Born in Islington, north London, his father was often unemployed and his mother made artificial flowers. He worked as a commercial artist before being called up for the war. On demob, he tried his hand as an actor and worked successfully in rep. When he married his wife Kay, they needed some extra money so they took in a lodger. That lodger was Jean Alexander, immortal as *Coronation Street*'s Hilda Ogden. He played Joe Walker on television and in the 1971 film version until his untimely death.

CAUSE: He died aged 44 of a burst pancreas.

Thomas Beck

Born December 29, 1909
Died September 23, 1995
Bland leading man. Born in New York City, 6' Beck was raised in Baltimore, where his father ran the Maryland Workshop for the Blind. He was educated at Johns Hopkins University, where he appeared in college plays and also with the University Players. His Players contemporaries included Henry Fonda, Josh Logan, James Stewart and Margaret Sullavan. After failing to find engineering work because of the Depression, Beck turned to the stage instead and appeared in the play *Mademoiselle* (1932) on Broadway. While appearing in *Her Majesty The Widow* (1934), he was spotted by a Fox

Films talent scout and signed up. He made his movie début in *Hell In The Heavens* (1934) opposite Conchita Montenegro, who was referred to as 'the poor man's Lupe Velez'. He also appeared in *Lottery Lover* (1934), *Life Begins At Forty* (1935) as Joe Abercrombie, *Music Is Magic* (1935) as Tony Bennet, *My Marriage* (1935) as Roger Tyler, *Charlie Chan In Paris* (1935) as Victor Descartes, *Charlie Chan In Egypt* (1935) as Tom Evans, *Crack-Up* (1936) as Joe Randall, *Every Saturday Night* (1936) as Clark Newall, *White Fang* (1936) as Hal Burgess, *Charlie Chan At The Race Track* (1936) as Bruce Rogers, *Think Fast, Mr Moto* (1937) as Bob Hitchings, *Thank You, Mr Moto* (1937) as Tom Nelson, *Heidi* (1937) as the priest opposite Shirley Temple, *Charlie Chan At The Opera* (1937) as Phil Childers and *I Stand Accused* (1939) as Paul. He became disillusioned when passed over for leading roles and not given the raises stipulated in his contract. He left filmdom on Labor Day 1939 and the following year enlisted in the army. Five years later, he was demobbed as a major. He appeared in *Temper The Wind* (1946) on Broadway, but was unemployed after the play closed. He again gave up on acting and became an advertising salesman and then an art director with the same New York agency. In 1965 he became an estate agent and retired 21 years later following the death of his boyfriend.
CAUSE: He died in Miami Shores, Florida, of Alzheimer's disease and heart ailments, aged 85.

Richard Beckinsale
Born July 6, 1947
Died March 19, 1979
Comedy great. If ever a performer was cut down in his prime, that performer was Richard Beckinsale. With two hit television series – *Porridge* and *Rising Damp* – under his belt, it looked as if he had a very long and very promising

future in show business. Born in Nottingham, he had a number of jobs, including inspecting iron pipes in a factory, before auditioning for RADA. He was accepted at the second attempt. He said, "When I decided to become an actor, it wasn't actually to make money or to make a living. I wanted to be an actor because I wanted to act. I've always had this desire to communicate a great kind of beauty to other people, like a vicar or priest does, to transport people to the world where I live. I just appreciate living on earth at an artistic level. There's a great deal of satisfaction in living this way. It's like love, I suppose. There are no words for it, apart from love – to give people love, to teach people love. I think it is probably the main driving force in my life." His first TV job was in March 1969 as PC Wilcox arresting Ena Sharples in *Coronation Street*. That led to *The Lovers*, starring opposite Paula Wilcox, on the big and little screens (1970–1971 on television and a film version, released in May 1973). From September 2, 1974 until he quit on May 27, 1977 Beckinsale appeared in the sitcom *Rising Damp* as the perpetually lazy and randy medical student Alan Moore. He was equally popular as con Lennie Godber in *Porridge* and its sequel *Going Straight*. The film version of *Porridge* was released on August 12, 1979. In 1965 Beckinsale married Margaret Bradley in a small ceremony at Highbury Vale Register Office. They had one daughter, 5'8" Samantha Jane (b. London July 23, 1966), before their 1971 divorce. On July 26, 1973 actress Judy Loe gave birth to Kathryn Bailey Beckinsale. As Kate Beckinsale, the 5'7" thespian became a success in Hollywood. Beckinsale and Loe finally married in 1977.
CAUSE: Beckinsale began making another comedy called *Bloomers* but complained of feeling tired and then admitted that he had blacked out during the filming of the first episode.

He was also ill during the filming of *Bloody Kids* (1979) but because he was so young no one thought to take it seriously. Some time on the night of March 19, 1979 Beckinsale suffered a massive heart attack in his sleep and died alone at his home in Sunningdale, Berkshire. He was 31. He was cremated at Bracknell, Berkshire before his ashes were buried at Mortlake Cemetery, Richmond.

FURTHER READING: *The Richard Beckinsale Story* – David Clayton (Stroud: The History Press, 2008)

Don Beddoe

Born July 1, 1891
Died January 19, 1991
Permanently startled. The son of Welsh parents (his father sang at the coronation of George V), Donald T. Beddoe was born in Pittsburgh, Pennsylvania. At the University of Cincinnati he studied business, even though he freely admitted he had no interest in the subject. His mother introduced him to the gay impresario Stuart Walker and Beddoe appeared in five Walker productions. His first Broadway appearance was on September 20, 1929, at the Royale Theater in *Nigger Rich*, which starred Spencer Tracy. He also appeared with James Cagney, Katharine Hepburn and Joan Blondell but while Hollywood beckoned them all, Beddoe remained on the Great White Way and the London stage. Harry Cohn happened to see Beddoe in a production of *The Night Of January 16* (which opened at the Ambassador Theater on September 16, 1935) and signed him to a contract. Beddoe claimed to have been in 73 Cohn productions (175 or so movies in all) but the most memorable were *Missing Daughters* (1939) as Al Farrow, *Mandrake The Magician* (1939) as Frank Raymond, *Konga, The Wild Stallion* (1939) as Martin, *Good Girls Go to Paris* (1939) as Burton, *Golden Boy* (1939) as Borneo, *My Son Is Guilty* (1939) as Duke Mason, *This Thing Called Love* (1940) as Tom Hawland, *Military Academy* (1940) as Marty Lewis, *Island Of Doomed Men* (1940) as Brand, *The Face Behind The Mask* (1941) as Jim O'Hara, *Unholy Partners* (1941) as Mike Reynolds, *Sabotage Squad* (1942) as Chief Hanley, *Harvard, Here I Come!* (1942) as Hypo McGonigle and the police chief in *The Talk Of The Town* (1942). He also was in a number of B pictures and serials including *Flying G-Men* (1939) as W. S. Hamilton, *Blondie Meets The Boss* (1939) as Marvin Williams, *Charlie Chan's Murder Cruise* (1940) as James Ross, *Blondie On A Budget* (1940) as Marvin Williams, *Abbott & Costello's Buck Privates Come Home* (1947) as Mr Roberts and *Francis Goes To The Races* (1951) as Dr Quimby. In the Fifties he graduated to main features including *Cyrano de Bergerac* (1950) as The Meddler, *Carrie* (1952), *Don't Bother To Knock* (1952) as Mr Ballew, *A Star Is Born* (1954), *The Night Of The Hunter* (1955) as Walt Spoon, *Tarzan's Hidden Jungle* (1955) and *Pillow Talk* (1959) as Mr Walters. In 1970, after playing Dr Littlefield in *How Do I Love Thee?* (1970) he retired from acting to care for his sick wife. They travelled frequently and were in the Canary Islands when she died. In 1974 he remarried. His wife was the travel agent who had booked the last cruise he had taken with his first wife. She also had something of a show business background herself. Her name was Joyce Matthews and she had twice married and divorced both comedian Milton Berle (1941 [divorced October 1947] and June 16, 1949 [divorced March 1950]) and impresario Billy Rose (June 1956 [divorced July 1959] and December 1961 [divorced 1963]). Of his career, Beddoe revealed candidly: "I knew from the very outset that I'd never get a part or hold an audience with my looks, so I learned to act . . . Acting was all I really liked about the profession. I got along well with everyone I worked with but was

never really friendly with anyone of them." He also appeared in several TV shows including *Maverick*, *Alfred Hitchcock Presents: The Cuckoo Clock*, *Laramie*, *Rawhide*, *Petticoat Junction*, *Bewitched*, *F Troop* and *Little House On The Prairie*.

CAUSE: He died of natural causes shortly before his 100th birthday.

Noah Beery

Born January 17, 1884
Died April 1, 1946
Screen heavy. The middle acting Beery brother was born in Kansas City, Missouri, and started his movie career in 1917, having been on the stage for almost two decades. He was best known as a villain and the advent of sound films added to his menace. Probably his best-known film was *Beau Geste* (1926) in which he played Lejaune. Married just once, he and his wife were separated for the last 18 years of his life.

CAUSE: Beery died of a heart attack in Beverly Hills, aged 62.

Noah Beery, Jr

Born August 10, 1913
Died November 1, 1994
Carrying on the family tradition. Born in New York, Beery appeared in a number of his father's films when still young. He then enrolled in a military academy but subsequently decided acting, not soldiering, was for him. He made dozens of films, usually as the hero's friend, including: *The Call Of The Savage* (1935), *Ace Drummond* (1936), *Only Angels Have Wings* (1939), *Sergeant York* (1941), *Gung Ho* (1941), *Red River* (1948), *The Story Of Will Rogers* (1952), *Inherit The Wind* (1960) and *Heaven With A Gun* (1969). To the Seventies television audience he was best known as Rocky, James Garner's interfering dad, in *The Rockford Files*. He married the daughter of cinematic cowboy Buck Jones.

CAUSE: Beery died aged 81 of natural causes.

Wallace Beery

Born April 1, 1885
Died April 15, 1949
Menacing funny guy. Born in Kansas City, Missouri, Beery was the younger brother of William C. Beery (b. Clay County, Missouri, 1879, d. Beverly Hills, California, December 25, 1949) and Noah Beery and uncle of Noah Beery, Jr, actors three. His first paid employment lacked a certain glamour – he cleaned train engines. A step up was his next job, when he joined Ringling Bros Circus in 1902 as an elephant trainer. His film career began in 1914 in Chicago with Essanay. At the company he met and married Gloria Swanson. She came to her wedding bed on her 19th birthday (March 29, 1917) a virgin, but left it in a damaged condition. Swanson had expected that her licence to marry would be, as she put it, her "ticket to heaven". Instead, she was "brutalised in pitch blackness by a man who whispered filth in my ear while he ripped me almost in two." After the act, when 6′1″ bridegroom Beery finally went to sleep, Swanson spent the remainder of her wedding night huddled on the bathroom floor, swathed in towels, trying to staunch her bleeding and ease her pain. By the morning she climbed into bed beside her husband, still racked with pain. He woke Swanson with a kiss and then dressed and shaved before kissing her goodbye. She pretended to be sleeping both times. On December 13, 1918, Beery received a divorce on the grounds of desertion. Meanwhile, Beery appeared in a number of Keystone comedies and then came up with the idea of a character that was humorous with just a touch of menace. It was this character that led to stardom. In 1930 he was nominated for Best Actor Oscar for playing Machine Gun Butch Schmidt in *The Big House* (1930). Among his many other films were: *The Plum Tree* (1914), *Fable Of The Bush League Lover Who Failed To Qualify* (1914), *Cactus Nell* (1917), *The*

Four Horsemen Of The Apocalypse
(1921), *The Last Of The Mohicans*
(1921), *Robin Hood* (1922), *Patsy*
(1923), *Richard The Lion-Hearted*
(1923), *The Drums Of Jeopardy* (1923),
Another Man's Wife (1924), *The Pony
Express* (1925), *The Champ* (1931) as
Andy Purcell, a part that won him a
Best Actor Oscar and *Grand Hotel*
(1932). His last film was *Big Jack*
(1949). Beery was not an easy actor to
work with. For a start he refused to
rehearse, he changed his lines at the
last minute and continually tried to
upstage his fellow pros. In 1930 he
married Rita Gilman.
CAUSE: Beery died of a heart attack in
Beverly Hills, a fortnight after his 64th
birthday.

David Begelman

Born August 26, 1921
Died August 8, 1995
Big con. In 1973 New York-born
Begelman was headhunted to be
President of Columbia Studios. He was
credited with saving the studio from
bankruptcy with box-office hits such as
Shampoo (1975) and *The Deep* (1977).
His annual salary was said to be
$250,000, with another $150,000 in
perks. However, by 1976 he was deep
in financial trouble. His prolific
gambling ensured that his expenditure
always exceeded his income. On
February 25, 1977, the actor Cliff
Robertson was informed by the
accounts department that on
September 2, 1976, he had received a
cheque for $10,000 for services
rendered. Robertson was puzzled
because he had not worked for the
studio recently and so was not owed
any money. Investigating further, he
discovered the cheque had been signed
and banked by Begelman. Robertson
knew all about *omerta* – Hollywood's
code of silence that could result in his
blacklisting if he broke it. Still, he
informed the police and FBI of the
discrepancy, though nothing was done.
Robertson waited a while before going

public and eventually Begelman
confessed he had forged the signature.
Robertson was blacklisted from the
industry for four years for blowing the
whistle. On October 3, 1977,
Begelman confessed to the board of
Columbia Pictures that he had
embezzled over $84,000 from the
company by forging $61,000 in
cheques and fiddling his expenses to
the tune of $23,000. He was ordered to
pay back the money and to take a
six-week leave of absence. Begelman
was also evaluated by a psychiatrist,
who reported that his behaviour was
due to a "temporary period of
self-destructive behaviour" and that
now he was "completely cured". All of
this occurred before Robertson went
public about the cheque. Meanwhile,
Begelman had been responsible for
another hit, *Close Encounters Of The
Third Kind* (1977). His expertise had
made the studio around $100 million
and they did not want that kind of
talent to go to waste. It was only when
Robertson publicly revealed what had
happened that Begelman resigned as
President on February 9, 1978. The
company then offered him a lucrative
three-year $1.5 million deal as an
independent producer. Begelman was
charged with fraud and theft and
pleaded *nolo contendere* (no contest). He
was fined $5,000 and placed on
probation for three years. In December
1978 he once again became President
of Columbia Pictures. In the second
week of February 1979, after a public
outcry, he resigned and accepted a job
as an independent producer, but with
the same salary. On June 27, 1979, his
felonious crime was reduced to a
misdemeanour when he appeared
before the Burbank Municipal Court.
The charges against him were dropped,
as were the remaining two years of his
probation. In December of the same
year he was appointed President of
MGM. It was not the first time that
Begelman, who at one time was
married to Lana Wood, had been

involved in financial irregularities. In the Sixties he had been Judy Garland's agent. Between May and October 1962 Begelman had cashed 13 cheques ranging from $500 to $6,000 totalling $35,714. Part of a quantity of money paid to blackmailers had also mysteriously ended up in Begelman's bank account and a car due to Garland for an appearance on *The Jack Paar Show* also turned up registered to Begelman. On January 30, 1964, Sid Luft, Garland's then-husband, sued Begelman and his partner, claiming that they had defrauded Garland of $450,000, also asking for $1 million punitive and exemplary damages. On March 15, 1967, Garland filed suit against Begelman and his partner claiming financial mismanagement. CAUSE: Suicide. He was 73 years old.

Rex Bell
(GEORGE FRANCIS BELDHAM)
Born October 16, 1903
Died July 4, 1962
Mr 'It'. Born in Chicago, Illinois, Bell was one of two sons of a horse trader who moved his family to Hollywood when he came down with a bronchial complaint caused by the stench of newly slaughtered livestock. Bell was educated at Hollywood High School and at weekends he caddied for the actor Wallace Reid. Still at school he organised a charity rodeo with fellow pupil Joel McCrea. In 1924 his father died and Bell became a truck driver to support his mother and brother, Hodson. He was discovered while delivering to Fox and offered a contract. The honest Bell confessed that he could not act but Fox countered that if he could ride he could work as a stuntman, so for four years that is how Bell earned a living. He made a few nondescript films including *The Cowboy Kid* (1928), *Wild West Romance* (1928) as Phil O'Malley, *Taking A Chance* (1928) as Joe Courtney before John Ford hired him to appear in *Salute* (released

September 1, 1929) alongside Marion Morrison who was to become his life-long friend, known to the world as John Wayne. In 1929 he met the fast-living Brooklynite Clara Bow while both were filming *True To The Navy* (released May 25, 1930). Bell was smitten by Clara and the two married on December 3, 1931 in Las Vegas. They had two sons: 6'5" Rex Larbow 'Tony' (b. Santa Monica Hospital, December 16, 1934) and 5'9" George Francis Robert (b. June 14, 1938) and one miscarriage in between. In 1931 Bell appeared in one episode of the serial *Battling With Buffalo Bill* and was signed to Monogram where he made eight films between 1932 and 1933. They were *Broadway To Cheyenne* (released September 10, 1932), *The Man From Arizona* (October 21, 1932), *Lucky Larrigan* (December 1, 1932), *Crashin' Broadway* (December 30, 1932), *Diamond Trail* (April 25, 1933), *The Fugitive* (July 15, 1933), *Rainbow Ranch* (July 25, 1933) and *The Fighting Texan* (July 26, 1933). He made half a dozen films for the Alexander brothers – Max and Art – who ran Poverty Row studios such as Beacon, Normandy and Colony. The films were *Too Much Beef* (released June 6, 1936), *West Of Nevada* (July 21, 1936), *The Idaho Kid* (August 6, 1936), *Men Of The Plains* (September 29, 1936), *Law And Lead* (November 11, 1936) and *Stormy Trails* (December 23, 1936). For Paramount, he played Virgil Earp in *Tombstone – The Town Too Tough To Die* (June 13, 1942). In 1942 he announced his retirement. In the Forties Rex and Clara drifted apart and they separated in 1950. Bell became interested in Republican politics and in 1944 he stood for congress but was defeated. From 1954 until 1962 he was Lieutenant-Governor of Nevada. CAUSE: On June 18, 1962, as he announced his candidacy for state governor, Rex Bell died of a heart attack, aged 58. He was pronounced dead at the Sunrise Hospital and was buried in Forest Lawn Memorial Park, Los Angeles, California.

Ralph Bellamy

Born June 17, 1904
Died November 29, 1991
'The man who never got the girl'. Born in Chicago, Illinois, 6'1½" Bellamy ran away from home aged 16 to join a troupe of actors who travelled the length and breadth of America performing Shakespeare. Over the next decade he worked with 15 different outfits before making his film début in the mob movie *The Secret Six* (1931), two years after his initial Broadway appearance, and went on to appear in over 100 films, although he never fully attained stardom. He did receive one Oscar nod playing one of Irene Dunne's suitors in *The Awful Truth* (1937). He also received acclaim for his portrayal of polio-stricken Franklin Delano Roosevelt in *Sunrise At Campobello* (1960). In the Thirties and Forties he regularly played detectives, firstly as Inspector Trent beginning with *Before Midnight* (1933) and then as New York consulting detective Ellery Queen, starting with *Ellery Queen, Master Detective* (1940). After World War II he concentrated more on television, but he is probably best known to the cinematic under-40s audience for his portrayal of the manipulative Randolph Duke opposite Don Ameche, Eddie Murphy and Dan Aykroyd in John Landis' *Trading Places* (1983), his 100th motion picture. In 1986 he was awarded an honorary Oscar "for his unique artistry and his distinguished service to the profession of acting." He was fêted for his stage work, picking up a Tony award, and was also one of the founders of the Screen Actors' Guild. On December 28, 1927, Bellamy married Alice Delbridge; he fathered one daughter before their Detroit divorce in June of 1931. A month later on July 6, 1931, in Reno, Nevada, he married actress Catherine Willard. They adopted a son, also called Willard, in the latter part of the decade. On August 6, 1945 (the day the atom bomb was dropped on Hiroshima), Mr & Mrs Bellamy were divorced in Reno on grounds of his mental cruelty. Later that month he married for the third time. The new Mrs Bellamy was Ethel M. Smith. Two years later, on November 24, 1947, they were divorced because of her desertion. Bellamy's fourth and final marriage was to Alice Murphy on November 27, 1949.
CAUSE: He died in Los Angeles aged 87 of natural causes.

John Belushi

Born January 24, 1949
Died March 5, 1982
Brash comic. John Adam Belushi came, saw and died of a drug overdose before his cinematic stardom could be assured. Born in Wheaton, Illinois, the eldest boy in a family of four and the son of an Albanian émigré, his younger brother, Jim (b. June 15, 1954), has also achieved a measure of fame in acting. After university Belushi began appearing in local theatre productions and landed a job in the off-Broadway show *National Lampoon's Lemmings*, which opened on January 25, 1973. This led to a gig on *Saturday Night Live* (beginning on October 11, 1975), the seminal comedy show. Belushi stayed with the show for four years, becoming one of its most popular performers. One of his routines with co-star Dan Aykroyd featured two siblings, the Blues Brothers. On December 31, 1976, he married long-time girlfriend Judy Jacklin in Colorado. In 1978 Belushi signed to appear as Bluto in John Landis' *National Lampoon's Animal House*, which was a box-office success. The following year he left *Saturday Night Live* to concentrate on films. It was at this time that his drug habit began to spiral out of control. Much of his *Saturday Night Live* salary had gone to feed his need for cocaine.

He appeared in films such as *1941* (1979) and *Neighbors* (1981) which were flops. *The Blues Brothers* (1980), slated by the critics and ignored at the time by the public, although it was later to become a cult classic, did little to help him regain his self-confidence. Belushi, 5'8" and nearly 16st, decided the way forward was to write and produce his own movies. His last project was a script called *Noble Rot*. Paramount Pictures passed on the option.

CAUSE: Following the rejection of his idea, Belushi flew alone to Hollywood and on March 1, 1982, booked into bungalow B#3 of the Chateau Marmont Hotel, 8221 Sunset Boulevard. He visited a friend and borrowed $5 for breakfast and asked if he could get him some heroin. That afternoon he was introduced to heroin addict Cathy Evelyn Smith (b. Ontario, Canada, April 25, 1947). Smith had earned a living as a backing singer for Gordon Lightfoot (and also been his lover) and was on probation. Over the next three days Belushi and Smith consumed vast quantities of drugs. On the night of March 4, Belushi went out partying with friends. He drank alcohol heavily and returned to his bungalow with Smith in tow. Back in his rooms, Belushi continued to drink and snorted cocaine. The next morning Belushi had visitors: his friends Robin Williams and *Saturday Night Live* writer Nelson Lyon stopped by briefly. Belushi had been up all night flying and began shivering as dawn approached. To try and warm himself he went for a shower. He increased the heating and slumped in bed around 8am. Around 60 minutes later, Smith heard Belushi gasping and went into his bedroom. After Belushi reassured her that he was fine, Smith returned to the living room and Belushi went back to sleep. At 10.15am Smith checked on Belushi, who looked peaceful. She went out in his car to get some food for breakfast, taking some drug paraphernalia with her. At midday

Belushi's personal trainer William Wallace called by to see him and found the actor quiet. Too quiet. Wallace checked the naked actor's pulse. There was none. Wallace asked the receptionist to get a doctor and John Belushi was officially pronounced dead at 12.45pm. His death certificate states he died of acute cocaine and heroin intoxication. However, not all was as it seemed. In March 1983 a grand jury was convened to look into the behaviour of Cathy Evelyn Smith at the time Belushi died. It was alleged she had injected Belushi with the fatal overdose of drugs. She admitted as much to the *National Enquirer* for $15,000, something that got her committed for trial in June 1986. Before that could take place she pleaded guilty on June 10, 1986, to involuntary manslaughter to avoid a second degree murder charge. She was sentenced to three years in prison in September 1986. Originally, the Los Angeles Police Department had announced Belushi had died of natural causes. 'Coroner to the Stars' Dr Thomas T. Noguchi (the basis for TV's *Quincy, M.E.*) performed the autopsy: Medical Examiner's Case #82-3036. Noguchi announced death had occurred some time between 10.15am and 12.45pm yet Smith said she last injected Belushi at 3.30am. Drug overdose deaths usually occur within two hours of ingestion. So did Belushi or someone else inject him later that day, or was his death due to a heart attack? He was very overweight, but Noguchi ruled this out as a contributing factor: "If he had been in the best of health, the combination of heroin and cocaine would have killed anyone." The coroner noted two dozen needle marks on Belushi's arms, some less than a day old. His good friend Dan Aykroyd and his widow both claim that Belushi hated needles. John Belushi was buried in Abel's Hill Cemetery, Chilmark, Massachusetts, on March 10, 1982. The following day a memorial service was held at the Cathedral of St John Divine in Manhattan. Belushi's 22-page will, written on March 23, 1979, left everything to his wife. In May 1983 Belushi's corpse was disinterred because his grave was regularly being despoiled. He was reburied in an unmarked grave eleven feet to the north of his previous resting place. His wooden coffin gave way during the operation and a copper casket replaced it. Also, a boulder bearing the legend BELUSHI was moved to the cemetery entrance. In an interview not long before his death Belushi had said, "I'm going to die young. I just can't stop destroying myself."

FURTHER READING: *Wired: The Short Life And Fast Times Of John Belushi* – Bob Woodward (London: Faber & Faber, 1989).

William Bendix

Born January 14, 1906
Died December 14, 1964
Gravel-voiced all-rounder. Born in New York City, Bendix was the son of the conductor of the New York Metropolitan Opera Orchestra who wanted his son to be a violinist. Bendix was more concerned with a career in baseball, earning a one-month trial with the New York Giants. Love knocked his sporting career on the head when he married childhood sweetheart Therese in 1928. To provide for his wife he worked in a greengrocer's in Orange, New Jersey. The Depression the following year forced the shop's closure, so Bendix invented a theatrical background for himself and landed a job at the New Jersey Federal Theater. He spent two years with the company gaining experience and decided to try Broadway. His first six plays all flopped but the seventh was good enough to win him a part in *Woman Of The Year* (1942), which starred Katharine Hepburn and Spencer Tracy. Success came very quickly for Bendix, who was nominated for a Best Supporting Actor

Oscar for his performance as soldier Aloysius 'Smacksie' Randall in *Wake Island* (1942). He never actually served in the military because he had chronic asthma. He spent the next ten years of his life working at Paramount, where he turned his hand to playing nice guys and not too few hated ones.
CAUSE: He died of complications from lobar pneumonia aged 58 in Los Angeles.

Alma Bennett

Born April 9, 1904
Died September 16, 1958
Leading lady. Born in Seattle, Washington, 5'4″ Alma Bennett was a star of the silent screen who appeared in many different genres. She appeared with Ben Turpin and Harry Langdon in comedies, plus Westerns and Cecil B. DeMille's dramas. She was married to Harry Spingler.
CAUSE: She died aged 54 in Los Angeles, California.

Barbara Bennett

Born August 13, 1906
Died August 8, 1958
Damaged goods. Born in Palisades, New Jersey, she was beset with mental problems, as was her only daughter. She married for the first time in St Patrick's Cathedral, New York on January 28, 1929. Her husband was the singer Morton Downey (b. Wallingford, Connecticut, November 14, 1901, d. Palm Beach, Florida October 25, 1985 of the effects of a stroke) and they had four children: 5'8½″ loudmouth TV personality (Sean) Morton Downey, Jr (b. New York, December 8, 1932, d. Los Angeles, California March 12, 2001 of lung cancer and respiratory problems); Lorelle Downey (b. New York, November 18, 1934, as Lesley Ann Downey. She was a potential Olympic athlete but was given to violent outbursts. One of the first mental patients to undergo a prefrontal lobotomy, she died on March 18, 1977); Anthony Downey (b. New

York, 1935); and Kevin Downey (b. New York, August 13, 1938). Divorced from Downey in 1941, Bennett married actor Addison Randall in Los Angeles on St Valentine's Day, 1942. He died on July 16, 1954, after falling from his horse during filming in Canoga Park, California. Her final marriage was to Canadian writer Laurent Suprenant. Barbara appeared in a few films, including *Black Jack* (1927) as Nancy Blake, *Syncopation* (1929) as Fleurette, *Mother's Boy* (1929) as Beatrix Townleigh and *Love Among The Millionaires* (1930) as Virginia Hamilton.
CAUSE: She died of a heart attack aged 51 in Montreal, Canada.

Belle Bennett

Born April 22, 1891
Died November 4, 1932
Circus star. Belle Bennett was born in Milaca, Minnesota (or possibly in Milcoon Rapids, Iowa) and began her career as a child performer in the circus before entering films. She appeared in *The Reckoning Day* (1915), *Jerry In The Movies* (1916), *Not My Sister* (1916), *Ashes Of Hope* (1917) as Gonda, *The Lonely Woman* (1918) as Martha Sellers, *A Soul In Trust* (1919) as Courtney Maitland and *Monkey Shines* (1920). Although she was relatively young, she appeared older than her years and so was often cast as mothers in films such as *The Fourth Commandment* (1926) playing Virginia, Henry King's *Stella Dallas* (1926) playing Stella Dallas, John Ford's *Mother Machree* (1928) in the title role, *My Lady's Past* (1929) and *Courage* (1930) as Mary Colbrook. She also appeared on stage to great acclaim opposite Tyrone Power, Sr. Belle Bennett was married three times. Her husbands were Jack Oaker, William Macey and, from 1924 until her death, the director Fred Windemere (b. Muscatine, Iowa, April 15, 1892, d. Newport Beach, California, March 18, 1970).

CAUSE: She died aged 41 in Los Angeles, California.

Constance Bennett

Born October 22, 1904
Died July 24, 1965
Diva. Blonde and beautiful, 5'4" Constance Campbell was the eldest of the Bennett sisters. Although she and Joan were best known for their cinematic work, they came from a long line of theatrical actors. Their grandmother, Rosabel Wood, was a dancer and, by all accounts, not someone to be trifled with. Her youngest daughter, Adrienne, married handsome divorced actor Richard Bennett on November 8, 1903. He was famous for his mellifluous speaking voice and was to later appear with Constance in a film (*Bought* [1931]). He was to father three daughters – Constance, Barbara and Joan – before his divorce in 1925. Born in Deacon's Mills, Indiana, on May 21, 1873, he died of a heart attack in Los Angeles on October 21, 1944. New York-born Constance was educated at Miss Shandor's School, Mrs Merrill's School and Mademoiselle Balsan's Finishing School in Paris. She married Chester Hirst Moorhead, an 18-year-old law student on June 6, 1921, in Greenwich, Connecticut, when she was 16 years old. At the time her mother was preparing her coming out party. The newlyweds were refused a honeymoon by her irate parents, who sent her off to Europe and had the marriage annulled on January 17, 1923. After five minor films Constance made her first major film, *Cytherea* (1924), playing Annette Sherman. She went on to make a name for herself in sophisticated comedies such as *What Price Hollywood* (1932) as Mary Evans, *Lady With A Past* (1932) as Venice Muir, *The Affairs Of Cellini* (1934) as Duchess of Florence, *Ladies In Love* (1936) as Yoli Haydn, *Topper* (1937) as Marion Kerby, *Merrily We Live* (1938) as Jerry Kilbourne and *Two-Faced Woman* (1941) as Griselda

Vaughn. She eventually made 57 films. The highest paid star ($30,000 a week) in Hollywood for a brief period at the start of the Thirties, she thought of acting as a means to support an extravagant lifestyle rather than as a career: "Hollywood is pretty painful, even in small doses," she once complained. David Niven commented: "She seemed to me the quintessence of a movie star. Everything about her shone – her burnished head, her jewels, her famous smile, her lovely long legs, and the highly publicised fact that she pulled down 30,000 bucks a week." Supposedly, her high wages so concerned the government that it introduced new tax legislation aimed specifically at Hollywood. In 1940 she made her stage début in Noël Coward's *Easy Virtue*. In the Fifties she virtually retired from the big screen, preferring to concentrate on-stage work. Away from the screen she was litigious, an expert poker player, a proficient skier and a media loather. In the Sixties she founded her own cosmetic company. She married five times. Her first husband was to commit suicide on December 12, 1945, aged 42. Her second husband was big game hunter, Philip Morgan Plant, the stepson of the fabulously wealthy Commodore Morton F. Plant. They married on November 3, 1925, in the lobby of the Pickford Arms Hotel, Greenwich, Connecticut. The Justice of the Peace who performed the ceremony had also conducted Constance's first wedding. (Plant's mother later went on to marry Colonel William Hayward, father of the theatrical producer Leland Hayward. On November 15, 1936, Hayward married the actress Margaret Sullavan, who had previously been married to Henry Fonda and had two daughters and a son. One of the daughters, Brooke, author of the best-selling book *Haywire*, married Dennis Hopper in 1961 and the son, film producer William, married the beautiful British actress Fiona Lewis in 1978.) Their

son, Peter Bennett Plant, was born at the Royal Free Hospital, London on January 3, 1929, although his paternity has long been in dispute. Philip Plant never recognised the boy as his son. Eleven months later, in Paris on November 14, 1929, Plant and Constance were divorced. She received a settlement of $500,000. On November 22, 1931, she married Henri, Marquis de la Falaise de la Coudraye in Beverly Hills. He had formerly been married to Gloria Swanson. Oddly, in November 1932 the press reported that Constance was trying to adopt a three-year-old English boy, Dennis A. Armstrong. The boy had been born on January 21, 1929, 18 days after Peter Plant's birth. Gossips wondered if Peter Bennett Plant and Dennis A. Armstrong were the same boy. Or was he the illegitimate son of Constance's cousin? The question has never been satisfactorily answered. The de la Falaise de la Coudrayes were divorced on November 14, 1940, in Reno, Nevada. On April 20, 1941, Constance married actor Gilbert Roland in Yuma, Arizona. She later commented that he "was a wonderful husband. In one room of the house . . ." They had two daughters. The eldest, Rolinda, was born three years before the marriage (while Constance was still married to Henri, Marquis de la Falaise de la Coudraye) in New York City on April 21, 1938. The younger, Christina Gyl Consuelo known simply as Gyl, was born on December 9, 1941. She became an actress, appearing in films such as *Day Of The Locust* (1976) and *Body Heat* (1982). The Rolands divorced on June 20, 1946. Two days later, in Riverside, California, Constance married for the fifth and final time. Her last husband was Brigadier-General John Theron Coulter and she subsequently took on the organisation of entertainments for troops serving overseas in such places as Berlin. They were together at her death.

CAUSE: She died in Fort Dix Hospital, New Jersey of a cerebral haemorrhage. In recognition of her work with the army she was buried in Section 3, Lot 2231-A, Grid P-13 of Arlington National Cemetery, Arlington, Virginia.

Harold Bennett
Born November 17, 1898
Died September 15, 1981
Forever old. Although he was an old man Harold Bennett specialised in playing even older men such as the elderly Mr Blewitt in *Dad's Army*, too old even for the Home Guard. Born in Hastings, East Sussex, he left school at the age of 12 and became an assistant in a jeweller's shop and later taught English at the Working Men's College in London. After service in the army in the First World War, he hired a coach and arranged a sightseeing tour of the battlefields. He began acting as an amateur later turning professional and touring with Donald Wolfit. When Bennett's wife died in the Thirties he gave up acting and worked as a draughtsman for an electric light company to support his three children. He retired in 1964 and turned his hand to acting once more finding fame as an old-age pensioner. He played an old man in *Vote, Vote, Vote for Nigel Barton* (1965), an old photographer in *Games That Lovers Play* (1970), appeared in *Au Pair Girls* (1972) as Lord Tryke, *The Ups And Downs Of A Handyman* (1975) as Gasper but it was his portrayal of decrepit but lecherous Young Mr Grace in the sitcom and film (1977) *Are You Being Served?* for which he was most famous.
CAUSE: He died aged 82 in London from a heart attack.

Jill Bennett
Born December 24, 1929
Died October 5, 1990
Confused actress. Nora Noel Jill Bennett was born in Penang, Malaya, the only child of (James) Randle

Bennett, a rubber plantation owner, and Nora Adeline Beckett. In 1939 she and her mother fled to England but her father was captured by the Japanese and held prisoner for five years. In England Jill attended various boarding schools but was expelled at 14 and the following year decided to become an actress. From 1944 until 1946 she studied at RADA and made her stage début in 1947 in *Now Barabbas* at Bolton's Theatre. In 1949 she began an affair with Godfrey Tearle, despite the fact that he was more than forty years older than her, that lasted until his death nine years later. In 1962 she married Willis Hall, the playwright but they divorced in 1965. Three years later she married (as his fourth wife) John Osborne. That marriage lasted nine years and during that time she suffered two miscarriages. Osborne also wrote a play, *Time Present*, based on her relationship with Tearle. She made her film début playing a murder victim in *The Long Dark Hall* (1951) and then appeared in *Moulin Rouge* (1952). Her other films included *Hell Below Zero* (1954) as Captain Gerda Peterson, *Aunt Clara* (1954) as Julie, *Lust For Life* (1956) as Willemien, *The Extra Day* (1956) as Susan, *The Skull* (1965) as Jane Maitland, *The Charge Of The Light Brigade* (1968) as Mrs Fanny Duberly, *Inadmissible Evidence* (1968) as Liz, *Julius Caesar* (1970) as Calpurnia, *I Want What I Want* (1972) as Margaret Stevenson, *The Old Curiosity Shop* (1975) as Sally Brass, *Full Circle* (1977) as Lily Lofting, *For Your Eyes Only* (1981) as Jacoba Brink, *Britannia Hospital* (1982) as Dr MacMillan, *Lady Jane* (1986) as Mrs Ellen, *Hawks* (1988) as Vivian Bancroft and *The Sheltering Sky* (1990) as Mrs Lyle. However, she was terribly insecure and believed that her relationships with men were failures.
CAUSE: In September 1990 she attempted suicide. The following month, on October 5, 1990, she took an overdose of sleeping pills at her

home, 23 Gloucester Walk, Kensington, London. She was 60.

Joan Bennett

Born February 27, 1910
Died December 7, 1990
Brunette bombshell. Born in Palisades, New Jersey, 5'5" Joan Geraldine was the youngest of the three Bennett sisters. She was educated at St Margaret's School, Waterbury, Connecticut. Like Constance, Joan also married early. On September 15, 1926, aged 16, she married John Fox, a theatrical producer, in Chelsea. She met him on a boat when she was travelling to attend L'Ermitage finishing school in Versailles. They lived at 22 Carlyle Square, London SW3 (now the home of TV personality Sir David Frost). Their daughter, Adrienne Ralston (later Diana), was born on February 20, 1928. Later that year, she and Fox divorced. A few bit parts on stage and film followed, such as *The Valley Of Decision* (1915), *The Eternal City* (1923) as Page and *Power* (1928), before she played opposite her father in *Jarnegan* (1929) at the Longacre Theatre and was spotted by Hollywood. Her first major acting part was playing Phyllis Benton opposite Ronald Colman in *Bulldog Drummond* (1929). In 1931 she signed a two-year contract at Fox Films, which paid her $2,000 a week, compared to sister Constance's $30,000. She starred in several films, such as *Disraeli* (1929) as Lady Clarissa Pevensey, *Puttin' On The Ritz* (1930) as Dolores Fenton, *Moby Dick* (1930) as Faith Mapple, *Doctors' Wives* (1931) as Nina Wyndram, *She Wanted A Millionaire* (1932) as Jane Miller, *Careless Lady* (1932) as Sally Brown, *The Man Who Broke The Bank At Monte Carlo* (1935) as Helen Berkeley, *Mississippi* (1935) as Lucy Rumford and a number of 'worthy' films including *Little Women* (1934) as Amy March and *Private Worlds* (1935) as Sally MacGregor. However, none of these roles shot her to stardom. On

March 12, 1932, she married for the second time. Her new husband was the screenwriter Gene Markey (1895–1978). (He was to later marry Hedy Lamarr and Myrna Loy.) Their daughter, Melinda, arrived on February 27, 1934. They were divorced in 1937. Film producer Walter Wanger (1894–1968) saw a potential in her and cast her as Kay Kerrigan in *Trade Winds* (1939) in which she wore a brunette wig. It was such a success that she dyed her blonde hair brown. The following year, on January 12, 1940, she married Wanger. They were to have two daughters: Stephanie, born on June 26, 1943, and Shelley, born on Independence Day, 1948. She made several films during her marriage, including *Son Of Monte Cristo* (1940) as Grand Duchess Zona, *Nob Hill* (1945) as Harriet Carruthers, *Scarlet Street* (1946) as Kitty March, *The Woman In The Window* (1944) as Alice Reed, *Father Of The Bride* (1950) as Ellie Banks, *Father's Little Dividend* (1951) reprising her role and *We're No Angels* (1955) as Amelie Ducotel. Although she was more at ease with the media than sister Constance, she, too, kept her distance. She later revealed that on St Valentine's Day, 1950, "I had a live skunk shipped to [gossip writer Hedda Hopper's] house. Later she wrote that she named it Joan. A columnist always got the last word." Bennett had also taken a full-page advertisement in the *Hollywood Reporter* that day to ridicule Hopper. However an incident in her off-screen life was to propel her to the front pages of the press in a way that she could never have envisaged. On December 13, 1951, a jealous Wanger, convinced she was having an affair with her agent Jennings Lang and, catching his wife having an innocent lunch with Lang, shot him in the groin. On April 22, 1952, Wanger was sentenced to four months in prison. Despite this, the couple remained married until 1965. Her fourth and final husband was the

former film critic David Wilde, whom she married on St Valentine's Day, 1974. Towards the end of her life she rarely watched new films because she was offended by the bad language in them. "I've certainly used most of those words – still do now and then – but not in a picture," she stated. She wasn't impressed by the newcomers either. "The heyday of the Hollywood blonde is over. Before, there was Harlow and Lana and Marilyn. Now, being blonde has nothing at all to do with being sexy. There's silly, giddy Goldie Hawn or chunky Kathleen Turner, who's twice the woman – literally – that Lauren Bacall was, or Meryl Streep, who can act Polish or Australian but she sure as hell can't act blonde."
CAUSE: Died in New York, New York, of a heart attack, aged 80.

Jack Benny
(BENJAMIN KUBELSKY)
Born February 14, 1894
Died December 26, 1974
The meanest '39-year-old' in Hollywood. Born in Mercy Hospital, Chicago, Illinois, Benny was the son of a publican. He was presented with his first violin (a half-sized model costing $50) when he was six years old. Like many children Benny loved to play but hated practising his instrument. When he left school he hired himself out at weddings, bar mitzvahs and the like at $1.50 a pop. Originally, he called himself Ben Benny but when another entertainer, then much more successful, called Ben Bernie objected, young Kubelsky became Jack Benny. Benny's mother died when he was 23 but his father lived to see his success and on his retirement to Miami Beach (paid for by Benny) he would hand out pictures of his famous son to strangers, whether they wanted them or not. As with many entertainers, Benny, who was plagued by insecurity throughout his life, got his start in show business in vaudeville before progressing to the radio (regularly from 1932), films and

television, where *The Jack Benny Show* played on CBS from October 28, 1950, until September 1964, when it transferred to NBC for one series. Benny was known for his mincing walk, his hand-to-cheek gesture, his vanity about his supposed age of 39 and his meanness. "When Jack Benny has a party not only do you bring your own Scotch, you bring your own rocks," George Burns quipped and another friend, Bob Hope, added: "They asked Jack Benny if he would do something for the Actors' Orphanage so he shot both his parents and moved in." Among his films (in which he often played himself) were *Medicine Man* (1930) as Dr John Harvey, *Taxi Tangle* (1931) as himself, *Transatlantic Merry-Go-Round* (1934) as Chad Denby, *It's In The Air* (1935) as Calvin Churchill, *Broadway Melody Of 1936* (1935) as Bert Keeler, *The Big Broadcast Of 1937* (1936) as Jack Carson, *Artists & Models* (1937) as Mac Brewster, *Artists And Models Abroad* (1938) as Buck Boswell, *Charley's Aunt* (1941) as Babbs Babberley, *To Be Or Not To Be* (1942) as Josef Tura, *George Washington Slept Here* (1942) as Bill Fuller, *The Great Lover* (1949), *Gypsy* (1962) and *It's A Mad Mad Mad Mad World* (1963). Benny married underwear seller Sadie Marks, aka Mary Livingstone (whom he met on a blind date), in Waukegan's only hotel on January 14, 1927. In 1934 they adopted a six-week-old girl named Joan Naomi. In his act Benny was to say: "Mary and I have been married for 47 years, and not once have we ever had an argument serious enough to mention the word 'divorce' . . . 'murder' yes, but 'divorce' never."
CAUSE: In October 1974 Benny was stricken with a numbness in his hand when he picked up his violin. An examination showed nothing amiss, although he then began to suffer from stomach pains. On December 20, Mrs Benny rang her husband's agent, Irving Fein, and told him that cancer of the pancreas had been diagnosed and he

was given around a fortnight to live but that Benny had been kept in the dark about the nature of his illness. Just six days later, Benny died at 11.26pm at his Holmby Hills home. He was buried in Hillside Memorial Cemetery, Culver City, California on December 29, 1974. Over 3,000 people attended the service. Among the ten pallbearers were Milton Berle, Gregory Peck, Frank Sinatra and Billy Wilder. His estate was worth over $4 million. In his will, written exactly six months before his death, he dictated that if anyone challenged the document and lost they would be entitled to just $1. Benny's violin, manufactured in Paris in 1845, was auctioned in 1997 and raised $84,300.

FURTHER READING: *Jack Benny: An Intimate Biography* – Irving A. Fein (New York: G.P. Putnam's Sons, 1976).

Berry Berenson

Born April 14, 1948
Died September 11, 2001
Long-suffering wife. Berinthia Berenson was born in New York City and had a distinguished pedigree. Her elder sister was the actress and model Marisa Berenson (b. New York February 15, 1947); their grandmother was the fashion designer Elsa Schiaparelli and their great-uncle was Bernard Berenson, the art historian and expert on the Italian Renaissance. Berry was educated in Switzerland, Italy, France and England. She fell in love with the actor Anthony Perkins when she was 12 years old and saw him in *Phaedra* (1961). Berry became a fashion photographer and wore jeans and pearls as her "uniform". In November 1972, after meeting Perkins at a party and confessing her pubescent crush, she interviewed him for Andy Warhol's magazine *Interview*. Despite Perkins' homosexuality, they began an affair and soon she was pregnant. On August 9, 1973, Berry the bride three months gone, barefoot and carrying a

bouquet of wild flowers, was married to confirmed bachelor Tony Perkins in Wellfleet, near Cape Cod, Massachusetts. Their son, Osgood Robert, was born on February 2, 1974. He now acts. A second son, Elvis, was born two years and one week later on February 9, 1976. Berry denied knowing that her husband was homosexual but this seems unlikely since she grew up in a milieu in which homosexuality flourished. Jennifer Lee, the actress who was married to Richard Pryor, remembered, "She knew everybody in fashion and was very comfortable in the mix of gay men." She fell for gay photographer Robert Mapplethorpe's assistant and lover. Another friend confirmed, "Berry had a definite penchant for homosexual men, which was kind of odd." Berry made her film début playing Barbara Curry, the wife of a construction worker (Perkins) in *Remember My Name* (1978), a thriller by Alan Rudolph. She also appeared in *Winter Kills* (1979) playing a morgue attendant and *Cat People* (1982) as Sandra, as well as a receptionist in the television mini-series *Scruples* (1980). She also appeared in episodes of various television shows such as *Cheers* and *Friends*. On March 27, 1990 their world was shattered when the *National Enquirer* reported that Perkins had the deadly disease AIDS. Although his homosexuality was an open secret in Hollywood, Perkins had hidden it from the public since becoming famous in 1956. He had never been tested for the disease and decided to sue the tabloid until his wife suggested he go for a test to ensure their case was watertight. The Perkinses were shocked when the story proved to be deadly accurate and he was indeed stricken with the HIV virus. On September 12, 1992 Anthony Perkins died of AIDS at the age of 60. Following her husband's death, Berry continued to raise her family, acted on television and returned to work as a photographer.

CAUSE: Berry Berenson Perkins was murdered aged 53 on a bright September morning in 2001 when the American Airlines Flight 11 aeroplane she was flying on was hijacked by Moslem fanatics and deliberately crashed into the north tower of the World Trade Center in New York. She had been returning to her California home after a holiday in Cape Cod.

Ingrid Bergman
Born August 29, 1915
Died August 29, 1982
Swedish scandalite. Although a fine and gifted actress it seemed likely that at one stage 5′9″ Ingrid Bergman's career would be virtually overshadowed by her stormy private life. Born at 3 Strandvägen in Stockholm, she was named after Sweden's then two-year-old princess. Her mother, Frieda Adler, died aged 33 on January 19, 1918, when Ingrid was just two. Her father, Julius, succumbed to stomach cancer on July 29, 1929, leaving Ingrid an orphan at 13. She studied at the Royal Dramatic Theatre School (other pupils included Garbo, Max Von Sydow, Mai Zetterling and Viveca Lindfors) and soon began making films. Her first was an uncredited role in *Landskamp* (1932) before a major part in *Munkbrogreven* (1934) as Elsa Edlund. She became the protégée and lover (her first) of actor-director Edvin Adolphson, a married man and at 41 more than twice her age. After using him she became involved with 6′2″ dentist Petter Aron Lindstrom (b. Stöde, Sweden, March 1, 1907). They were married in Stöde, Sweden, at 4pm on July 10, 1937, and had one daughter, Friedel Pia (b. Stockholm, Sweden, September 20, 1938). Bergman's films included *Valborgsmässoafton* (1935) as Lena Bergström, *Swedenhielms* (1935) as Astrid, *På Solsidan* (1936) as Eva Bergh and *Dollar* (1938) as Julia Balzar. Associates of producer David O. Selznick saw Bergman's film *Intermezzo*

(1936) in which she portrayed Anita Hoffman and told him about the lead actress. When he saw the film for himself he was impressed and offered her the chance to work in America. He also suggested she Anglicise her name to Berryman as well as have plastic surgery on her eyebrows and teeth. At this time Bergman was also working in Nazi Germany (a fact Selznick was understandably desperate to hide) in films such as *Die Ver Gellen* (1938) and was much admired by Joseph Goebbels. In Berlin she had no compunction about giving the Nazi salute, although she declared herself apolitical. She eventually decided to further her career in America rather than Germany and flew to the land of the free leaving her husband to look after their daughter. It was a wise career choice. However, in America she rarely worked for Selznick, who loaned her out to various studios. Her first American film was a remake of *Intermezzo* called *Intermezzo: A Love Story* (1939) co-starring Leslie Howard. She appeared in a number of films, including *Dr Jekyll And Mr Hyde* (1941) as Ivy Peterson, *Rage In Heaven* (1941) as Stella Bergen and *Adam Had Four Sons* (1941) as Emilie Gallatin, before Michael Curtiz cast her on April 20, 1942, as Ilsa Lund Laszlo in *Casablanca* (1942), the film that was to make her an international star. The original choice for the lead female role was Hedy Lamarr, but that changed after Curtiz saw Bergman. Filming began on May 25, 1942, and lasted until July. The movie was shot at Van Nuys Airport and on the Warner Bros lot and was something of a mishmash. The 'sides' (pages of the script) given to the cast had been written sometimes only minutes beforehand and the film was shot in the order it appears on screen as opposed to the usual procedure, i.e. shoot all scenes with the same set together, irrespective of where they fit in the finished film. Off-set Humphrey Bogart was constantly accused by his third wife (Mayo Methot) of having an affair with Bergman. He never did and, if anything, she was intimidated by him. He was four inches shorter than her and wore wooden blocks strapped to his shoes to make the two of them appear the same height in front of the camera. The film's last scene (at the airport) was shot on Stage 21 at Warners with fog created by machines; many of the aeroplanes in the background were, in reality, small models. The film was rush-released on November 27, 1942, to coincide with the Allied capture of Casablanca. (Bogart never said, "Play it again, Sam." The line "Play it, Sam. Play 'As Time Goes By'" was actually spoken by Bergman. Anyway, pianist Dooley Wilson couldn't actually play the piano [he was a drummer] and mimed to Elliot Carpenter's playing. The song was almost cut but had to be included because of continuity. Bergman had restyled her hair for her next part in *For Whom The Bell Tolls* [1943] and vital scenes could not be re-shot without the song.) *Casablanca* went on to win three Oscars. Bergman's next films were *For Whom The Bell Tolls* (1943) as María, which won her her first Oscar nomination, *Gaslight* (1944) as Paula Alquist, a role that gave Bergman her first Academy Award, *Saratoga Trunk* (1945) as Clio Dulaine, *The Bells Of St. Mary's* (1945) as Sister Benedict and another Oscar nomination, Hitchcock's *Spellbound* (1945) as Dr Constance Peterson and *Notorious* (1946) as Alicia Huberman, *Arch Of Triumph* (1948) as Joan Madou and the lead in *Joan Of Arc* (1948), which was her fourth Oscar nod. Bergman had been portrayed to the public as a "normal, healthy, non-neurotic career woman, devoid of scandal and with an idyllic home life". That was all to change in the late Forties. On September 23, 1948, she had written to a friend: "Over the weekend I'll meet Roberto Rossellini. I look forward to it so much." That

meeting was to light a spark that would shock Hollywood and, ultimately, the world. At the time, Rossellini was involved in a tempestuous relationship (which had begun in 1939) with the fiery Italian actress Anna Magnani. Bergman had recently played Joan of Arc and the characteristics of the French saint were gradually ascribed to the actress, who was occasionally referred to in the press as 'Saint Ingrid'. The truth was very different. Bergman was a woman of voracious sexual appetites ("She'd do it with doorknobs," said Alfred Hitchcock) and often had several lovers on the go simultaneously. One morning, not long after the end of their honeymoon, she told Lindstrom: "I'd like to make love to one man of each race." The world was shocked when she began an affair with Rossellini who, ladies' man though he undoubtedly was, was plump with tiny hands and feet, a beaked nose, thinning hair and reeked of talcum powder and perfume. In the spring of 1949 Bergman flew off to make a film with Rossellini. Petter Lindstrom remained at their Hollywood home, 1220 Benedict Canyon Drive. After seeing his wife off at the airport Lindstrom returned home to discover she had removed nearly all her wardrobe as well as her precious collection of press cuttings and photo albums. Lindstrom then realised that his wife had not only flown out of the country – she had also flown out of their marriage. The couple stayed at a former monastery where, in a fit of pique, Anna Magnani had once thrown a plate of spaghetti in Rossellini's face. It was an ironic setting – a former monastery where celibacy was a way of life – to start properly the affair that would cause Ingrid Bergman to be ostracised from Hollywood for many years. The affair caused the film they were due to make, *Stromboli*, to be delayed for almost a week. Rossellini's myriad other affairs had merely been distractions but his love for Ingrid threatened to ruin his film-making. Said his cousin, Renzo Avanzo, "The family disapproved but not from a moral point of view. Nobody gave a damn about that. We disapproved because we knew, with her, he was through making the kind of films he should be making . . . They were enamoured with the idea of what they could do together artistically . . . and it was a lousy idea." If Rossellini's family disapproved because of the fear that it would ruin Rossellini's career, the rest of the world, it seemed, disapproved because the affair was, to their eyes, shameful. Telegrams began to arrive from Hollywood. Joseph Breen, head of the motion picture capital's all-powerful Production Code Administration, cabled Ingrid with the warning "These stories may very well destroy your career." Studio boss Walter Wanger added, "Do not fool yourself by thinking that what you're doing is of such courageous proportions or so artistic to excuse what ordinary people believe." Despite having written to Lindstrom asking for a divorce, Ingrid still had much to discuss with him and so she arranged to meet him on neutral ground. Messina in Sicily was chosen and Ingrid arrived with Rossellini, who was determined to show Lindstrom that he was now the man in Ingrid's life. Lindstrom would have none of this and pushed Ingrid into a hotel room locking Rossellini outside. The Italian went into a jealous frenzy and even called the police. However, they decided it was a domestic matter and left the participants to sort things out between themselves. Rossellini jumped into his sports car and began racing around the hotel. Recalled Ingrid: "He never stopped all night long, hour after hour. It was a nightmare." Things became worse for Ingrid on December 11, 1949 when the *Los Angeles Herald Examiner* broke the news that Ingrid was pregnant with Rossellini's child. The condemnation of Ingrid, which had previously been

fierce, now became vicious. She even found herself condemned by the Vatican. Gossip columnist Louella O. Parsons, however, drew comparison between Ingrid and historical figures. "Few women in history or men either," wrote Parsons, "have made the sacrifice the Swedish star has for love. Mary, Queen of Scots, gave up her throne because of her love for the Earl of Bothwell. Lady Hamilton, beautiful queen of English society, gave up her position in the London social world to bear a child out of wedlock to Lord Nelson . . . King Edward VIII renounced his throne to marry the woman he loved." Parsons' story had an impact as dramatic as the journalist had hoped. It knocked President Truman's announcement of the development of the hydrogen bomb off the front pages. People were horrified still by the Swede who was thumbing her nose at the sexual mores of the country that had made her a star. On February 2, 1950, Ingrid gave birth to Robertino Rossellini in the Villa Margherita Clinic, Rome. The press tried to speak to the mother but Ingrid gave no interviews and Rossellini went so far as to punch an American reporter who he felt had gone too far in the interests of getting his story. One enterprising hack had a pregnant wife and he enlisted her help in obtaining pictures of Ingrid's newest offspring. The wife booked into the same clinic with a suitcase but when the nuns discovered that the holdall actually contained a selection of cameras rather than swaddling clothes the woman was asked to leave. Twelve days after the birth Ingrid left the clinic at 4am. The nuns did not like patients checking out in the middle of the night and they chased after the proud parents. Joining in the scramble was the motley collection of press photographers. A car chase ensued and the *paparazzi* would have finally clicked their shutters on Ingrid and the baby as she rushed into her home, had it not been for one of

Rossellini's friends blocking off the road with his car. Ingrid's divorce did not become final until February 9 (in Mexico, where divorces were easier to obtain, and not at all in the United States) so she could not officially be registered as the baby's mother. (Lindstrom had begun to drag his feet over the divorce; in any case, the divorce legally didn't have to become final in the United States.) Probably the most famous infant in the world that year, Robertino's birth certificate, incredibly, reads "Father: Roberto Rossellini. Mother: Unknown." On March 14, Ingrid and Rossellini were denounced on the floor of the US Senate. Ingrid was described as a "cheap, chiselling female . . . a powerful influence for evil" and Rossellini found himself lambasted as "the vile and unspeakable Rossellini who sets an all-time low in shameless exploitation and disregard for good public morals." The film on which they had been working, *Stromboli*, opened on February 15. One might have expected to see nuns and priests and other clerics picketing the film. In fact, only ten people turned up to the Broadway opening. The public was vastly outnumbered by the press. The film was a commercial disaster both in Europe and in the States. It was described by *The New York Times* as "incredibly feeble, inarticulate, uninspiring and painfully banal." Meanwhile, Ingrid received thousands of letters, many in support of her, although she did receive at least one death threat. As so often in these matters, the public and press gradually lost interest in the scandal and by the end of March Ingrid could look out from her Rome apartment without seeing hordes of reporters waiting for her. Ingrid's friends begged her to go to Mexico and marry Roberto but she refused and decided to marry by proxy. An attorney representing her and one for Rossellini flew to Mexico City where in Juarez at 10.30am on May 24,

1950, Ingrid Bergman and Roberto Rossellini were married. At the same time in Rome Ingrid decided to exchange private vows with the man she loved in a small church. It was early evening in Rome as Ingrid waited for her husband-to-be to return from a day's filming. She waited and she waited and she waited. The church had long shut its doors by the time Rossellini turned up. The Italian found another church and there he and Ingrid held hands, knelt and repeated the vows. As a wedding gift Rossellini gave Ingrid a gold charm bracelet with a small policeman's whistle. The honeymoon was spent on Capri. More controversy followed when it was revealed that Bergman's American divorce did not become final until November 1, 1950. Gradually, as people realised that Bergman and Rossellini's love was not just a brief fling, the couple became accepted. America was still, however, very wary of Ingrid. The birth of her twins (Isabella Fiorella Elettra Giovanna weighing 7lb 3oz, Isotta Ingrid Frieda Giuliana weighing 8lb 5oz) in Rome on June 18, 1952, went some of the way to assuaging her 'guilt'. However, the odd piece of hate mail still occasionally arrived. Ingrid later told her friend Kenneth Williams that the British people had been very kind to her during her troubles and she had always time to stop and chat to a British fan. However, the marriage to Rossellini was destined not to last and they separated on November 7, 1959. The scandalous match that wrecked two marriages and brought three people into the world was over. By contrast, thirty-eight years after her mother's elopement, Isabella Rossellini, herself twice married (once to Martin Scorsese), began an affair with another film director, David Lynch. The affair elicited virtually no adverse press comment. Still Ingrid was 'exiled' from the States for some years. Then she was chosen to play the lead in a film

about the life of the youngest daughter of Tsar Nicholas II, *Anastasia* (1956), or rather the faker Anna Anderson, who claimed to be the Grand Duchess. Her performance won her a second Oscar and she had an affair with co-star Yul Brynner. Chat show host Ed Sullivan asked his audience to vote as to whether Bergman should be allowed on his show. The vote was close, but favoured the 'no's. It appeared that not all of America had forgiven the 'loose woman'. Her films became fewer. She won the role of missionary Gladys Aylward in *The Inn Of The Sixth Happiness* (1958) after Audrey Hepburn rejected the part. Bergman also appeared in *Indiscreet* (1958) as Anne Kalman, *The Yellow Rolls-Royce* (1965) as Gerda Millett, *Cactus Flower* (1969) as Stephanie Dickinson, *Murder On The Orient Express* (1974) as Greta Ohlsson, winning her third and final Academy Award and a BAFTA, *Autumn Sonata* (1978) another Oscar nomination and her final role (in a TV movie), which won her numerous plaudits, *A Woman Called Golda* (1982) as Golda Meir. Bergman married for the third time at Caxton Hall Register Office, London, at 11.15am on December 21, 1958. Her new husband was the divorcé Lars Reinhold Schmidt (b. 11 June 1917). They were divorced in 1975.
CAUSE: In November 1973 while lying in bed in her flat in Mount Street, Mayfair, Bergman discovered a lump in her left breast. In May 1974 she was advised by her doctor to go into hospital for a biopsy but she demurred, flying instead to New York to see her first grandson. She saw a doctor there who also insisted she enter hospital. Again, she refused. Finally, on June 15, 1974, she was admitted to the London clinic where she underwent the mastectomy of her left breast. A lump grew in a lymph node under her arm and it was removed in 1977. However, it was malignant. In July 1978 her right breast was also removed in an operation at the Harley Street Clinic

and she began undergoing radiation therapy. Not long afterwards she bought a new home at Flat 4, 9 Cheyne Gardens, London SW3. The film company that made *A Woman Called Golda* were unable to get insurance to cover the film because of Ingrid's illness. Ingrid spent her last Christmas in Choisel, France. Cancer had rendered her right arm useless and she learned to write with her left hand. In June 1982 she flew to New York to celebrate her twins' 30th birthday. On July 3 she returned to London. Later that summer she flew to Sweden to say goodbye to her homeland. On August 21, 1982, she collapsed getting out of the bath; the disease had spread to her spine. To ease her pain she was given heroin. Eight days later, her right lung collapsed and only the top third of her left was still working. Cancer claimed her in her London home that afternoon. It was her 67th birthday. "I have no regrets," she reflected. "I wouldn't have lived my life the way I did if I was going to worry about what people were going to say."
FURTHER READING: *Ingrid Bergman* – Curtis F. Brown (London: Star Books, 1973); *Ingrid Bergman: My Story* – Ingrid Bergman and Alan Burgess (London: Michael Joseph, 1980); *As Time Goes By: The Life Of Ingrid Bergman* – Laurence Leamer (New York: Harper & Row, 1986); *Notorious: The Life Of Ingrid Bergman* – Donald Spoto (New York: HarperCollins, 1997).

Elisabeth Bergner

Born August 22, 1897
Died May 12, 1986
Star with a heart. Born in Vienna (according to *Who's Who* and *Who's Who In The Theatre*, although both wrongly give her year of birth as 1900; the usually reliable Katz has her birthplace as Drohobycz), the daughter of Emil Bergner and Anna Rosa Wagner began acting professionally in the autumn of 1919 at the City Theatre,

Zurich. She began to work regularly in Germany and Switzerland as well as her home town of Vienna. She worked under Max Reinhardt, playing Katherine in *The Taming Of The Shrew*, and Rosalind in *As You Like It* among many other parts in the Twenties. Her international reputation was made on stage when she appeared as St Joan in Shaw's play of the same name. Her first appearance on an English stage came at the Opera House, Manchester on November 21, 1933, playing Gemma Jones in *Escape Me Never* under the direction of Sir C.B. Cochran. Ten years earlier, she had made her film début in *Der Evangelimann* (1923). It was for her reprise of the character of Gemma Jones that she was nominated for an Oscar in 1935. She moved to Britain (becoming naturalised in 1938) to escape the Nazis and lived at Virginia Water, Surrey. During World War II she took in evacuated children including, for a time, the mother of the present author. She married director Dr Paul Czinner (b. Budapest 1890, d. 1972) and among her films were *Nju* (1925), *Der Grieger Von Florenz* (1926), *The Loves Of Ariane* (1931), *Catherine The Great* (1934), *Dreaming Lips* (1938), *Cry Of The Banshee* (1970) and *Der Füssganger* (1973). The character of Margo Channing in the short story *The Wisdom Of Eve*, which appeared in *Cosmopolitan* in May 1946 and which later became the basis for *All About Eve* (1950), was based on Elisabeth Bergner.
CAUSE: She died aged 88 in London after a long illness. She was cremated at Golders Green Crematorium.

Busby Berkeley

(WILLIAM BERKELEY ENOS)
Born November 29, 1895
Died March 14, 1976
Choreographer extraordinaire. Born in Los Angeles, he was educated at Mohegan Lake Military Academy in New York before making his real stage début during a tour of *The Man Who Came Back* in 1917. (He had previously appeared as a child in a production of *A Doll's House* in which his mother, 'Queen Gertrude', appeared alongside her great friend, the lesbian Alla Nazimova.) Two years later he was on Broadway appearing in *Irene* playing Madame Lucy opposite Irene Dunne at the Vanderbilt Theater. He was nicknamed 'Busby' after Amy Busby, a *fin de siècle* Broadway actress. He moved into movies, choreographing *Whoopee* (1930) at the behest of Samuel Goldwyn and then went on to work on *Palmy Days* (1931), *Roman Scandals* (1933), which featured nude girls, and *42nd Street* (1933) (for Warner Bros. It was his undoubted genius that saved the company from going under, yet he had never had a day's dance lesson in his life), *Gold Diggers Of 1933* (1933), *Footlight Parade* (1933), *Dames* (1934), *Gold Diggers Of 1935* (1935), *Stage Struck* (1935), *Gold Diggers Of 1937* (1936), *Gold Diggers In Paris* (1938), *Men Are Such Fools* (1938), *Babes In Arms* (1939), *Bitter Sweet* (1940), *Strike Up The Band* (1940), *Girl Crazy* (1943), *Take Me Out To The Ball Game* (1949) starring Frank Sinatra and Gene Kelly, *Call Me Mister* (1951), *Million Dollar Mermaid* (1952) starring Esther Williams and many more. Away from the screen, however, Berkeley was a mixed-up individual with, some suspect, a mother complex. He bought a mansion in Beverly Hills for mum and allowed her to indulge her whim of collecting expensive antiques. On September 8, 1935, he drank too deeply and too often at a party to celebrate the end of *In Caliente* (1935). On the drive home he lost control of his car and ended up smashing into two cars coming in the opposite direction. Three people in the second car were killed and Berkeley was charged with second-degree murder. Warner Bros were furious – he was supposed to be directing films for them, after all! Schedules were changed so the films were shot at night and Berkeley could be in court during the day. Originally, he

was wheeled into court on a stretcher. His brief was the famed Hollywood lawyer Jerry Giesler. The legal eagle produced witnesses who stated that Berkeley had not been drunk when he left the party. Coincidentally, or perhaps not, all the witnesses – Glenda Farrell, Pat O'Brien and Mervyn Leroy – were contracted to Warner Bros. Berkeley's mother sat with him in court, holding his hand. The first jury was locked. The second voted 7–5 for acquittal and it was at his third trial on September 25, 1936, that he got off. He settled a civil suit for $95,000. Berkeley certainly had an eye for the ladies (and occasionally the boys), and not just professionally. He gave breaks to Lucille Ball, Virginia Bruce, Paulette Goddard, Betty Grable, Veronica Lake and Carole Landis. Landis' husband, Irving Wheeler, launched a $250,000 alienation of affection suit against Berkeley in 1938 that was subsequently thrown out by the court. Berkeley's mother died in June 1946 and not long after he slashed his wrists and throat. Discovered by his Japanese house boy he was admitted to the psychiatric ward of Los Angeles General Hospital. He was there for six weeks, during which time he lost almost 5st in weight. When he was released on July 18, 1946, he had just $650 to his name. He was helped by his old boss Jack Warner but now Berkeley was fighting a battle with alcohol. He directed his last film in 1962, 14 years before his death. He was married five times: to actress Esther Muir (b. 1895, d. August 1995), Myra Steffens, Marge Pemberton, actress Merna Kennedy (b. September 7, 1908, d. December 20, 1944), actress Claire James and Etta Dunn.
CAUSE: He died aged 81 of natural causes in Palm Springs.

Milton Berle
(MENDEL BERLINGER)
Born July 12, 1908
Died March 27, 2002
'The thief of bad gags'. Berle was born in New York, the fourth son of five children of Moses, a painter, and store detective Sarah (d. May 31, 1954) Berlinger. His siblings were Phil (b. 1901), Francis (b. 1904), Jack (b. 1905) and Rosalind (b. 1913). He was schooled at New York Professional Children's School and took to the stage at the age of 5. By the age of 6 he was entering "Charlie Chaplin contests" and usually won. Aged 12, he changed his name from Berlinger to the more manageable Berle. In November 1920 he lost his virginity to a dancer in the Broadway show, *Florodora*, in which he was appearing. She saw him gawping at her and invited him into her dressing room. The entire performance lasted just seconds. "One second her hand was undoing my buttons, the next she had me inside her – and from what I know now, there was room in there for the entire Sextet." He worked in nightclubs and theatres before moving to radio in 1934. He had made his film début in *The Perils Of Pauline* (1914) aged 6. He was also in *Birthright* (1920), *The Mark Of Zorro* (1920) and *Ruth Of The Range* (1923). Claims that Berle was the first person to appear on television, in an experimental broadcast in New York City in 1928 can be discounted. His other films included *Poppin' The Cork* (1933) as Elmer Brown, *New Faces Of 1937* (1937) as Wallington Wedge, *Radio City Revels* (1938) as Teddy Jordan, *Tall, Dark And Handsome* (1941) as Frosty, *Sun Valley Serenade* (1941) as Jerome K. 'Nifty' Allen, *Rise And Shine* (1941) as Seabiscuit, *Whispering Ghosts* (1942) as H.H. Van Buren, *A Gentleman At Heart* (1942) as Lucky Cullen, *Over My Dead Body* (1943) as Jason Cordry, *Margin For Error* (1943) as Moe Finkelstein and *Always Leave Them Laughing* (1949) as Kip Cooper. In the late Forties, Fifties and much of the Sixties 5'10" Berle concentrated on television. He was the star of *The Milton Berle Show* on NBC from June 8, 1948 until 1959. A similar show was revived on

ABC from September 1966 until January 6, 1967 but it was destroyed in the ratings by *The Man From U.N.C.L.E.* and was dropped. In 1960 Berle made a cameo appearance as himself in the Marilyn Monroe–Yves Montand feature *Let's Make Love* in which he tried to make Jean-Marc Clément funny. He was also in *It's A Mad Mad Mad Mad World* (1963) as J. Russell Finch, *The Loved One* (1965) as Mr Kenton, *Don't Worry, We'll Think Of A Title* (1966) as himself, *Who's Minding The Mint?* (1967) as Luther Burton, a film director in *Where Angels Go, Trouble Follows* (1968), *For Singles Only* (1968) as Mr Parker, *Can Hieronymus Merkin Ever Forget Mercy Humppe and Find True Happiness?* (1969) as Goodtime Eddie Filth, *Seven In Darkness* (1969) (TV) as Sam Fuller, *Lepke* (1975) as Mr Meyer, a blind man in *Won Ton Ton, The Dog Who Saved Hollywood* (1976), *The Muppet Movie* (1979) as Mad Man Mooney, *Broadway Danny Rose* (1984) as himself, *Pee-Wee's Big Adventure* (1985) as himself, *Going Overboard* (1989) as himself, a hotel clerk in *Driving Me Crazy* (1991) and *Let Me In, I Hear Laughter* (1999) as himself. Rivalry existed between Berle and several comics. Groucho Marx once told Berle, "You're not funny," only for Berle to reply, "Everything I know, I stole from you, Grouch." Marx had the last line. "Then you didn't listen." As well as his performing career Berle was known in Hollywood for his apparently enormous penis. Betty Grable commented: "They say the two best hung men in Hollywood are Forrest Tucker and Milton Berle. What a shame. It's never the handsome ones. The bigger they are, the homelier." In January 1992 when Berle was 83, a 24-year-old woman saw him in a restaurant. He signalled her to come over to his table, and greeted her with "You have such beautiful breasts. I'd love to put my head between them." She said thank you before Berle continued, "I have something big and beautiful, too. Here, have a feel," and proceeded to force her hand into his crotch. She gave him her phone number and two days later he called her for a date. Berle sent a stretch limo, complete with a bottle of champagne inside, to pick her up. She recounted: "I barely got through the front door [of his house] before he attacked me. He pulled me to him and we kissed. Then he stepped back, and took his pants off and I got the shock of my life. Here was a man in his eighties standing stark naked before me and he was huge! It must've been over a foot long and sent shivers of fear up my spine. And, to my horror, he forced me to give him oral sex. But Milton didn't get excited. Then he joined me down on the floor and we tried to make love, but it was just a total bust." Berle married 5'5" former showgirl Joyce Matthews (b. New York, December 6, 1919, d. Laguna Beach, California, January 17, 1999) in 1941 and they adopted a daughter, Victoria Melanie. They divorced in Reno, Nevada, in October 1947. On June 16, 1949 they remarried and in 1950 they re-divorced. In New York on December 9, 1953 Berle married press agent Ruth Cosgrove. They adopted a son, William, in 1962. Cosgrove died in April 1989. In 1992, Berle married Lorna Adams. He also had affairs, some by his own unsubstantiated admission, with Lucille Ball, Veronica Lake, Lana Turner, Marilyn Monroe (during, he claimed, the 1948 filming of *Ladies Of The Chorus* although it may be that Berle actually slept with the burlesque performer Dixie Evans and later mistook her for Marilyn), Theda Bara, Ann Sheridan and Nancy Reagan. In 1995 Berle was accused of ruining a 33-year-old bellman's sex life by grabbing his crotch and squeezing. The bellman at the Taj Mahal Hotel in Atlantic City says that he told Uncle Miltie, "You look terrific for your age," which may have irritated him because of the mention of his age. He said Berle then "lunged for his crotch and squeezed" necessitating later hospital visits. Berle fought the suit, saying: "I'm nearly 88-years-old. I have better things to do in my life than go around grabbing some guy's crotch. Hell, at my age, I'm lucky if I can find my own crotch."

CAUSE: In December 1998 Berle suffered a stroke which left him with severe eye problems. His estranged son Bill said, "I haven't spoken to him in years. And now that I know he had a stroke, I don't intend to call him." On April 3, 2001, tests at Cedars-Sinai revealed that Berle was suffering from colon cancer. Doctors decided not to operate. His wife Lorna stated, "It's a small tumour in his colon. He isn't scheduled for any surgery, but that could always change. He is in no pain." He died of colon cancer in his sleep at 2.45pm, on Wednesday, March 27, 2002 and was cremated and his ashes interred in Hillside Memorial Park, 6001 West Centinela Avenue, Los Angeles 90045. The cemetery was obviously expecting a throng of friends, admirers and fans to attend the service. Around 150 chairs were set up outside the chapel complete with loud speakers to hear the memorials and a heavy security presence. Sadly, when the service began only four of the chairs were occupied. Eulogies were delivered by Norm Crosby, Red Buttons, Connie Stevens, Don Rickles, Jan Murray, Larry Gelbart and Richard Moll (best known as Bull from *Night Court* and Berle's son-in-law). Ed Begley arrived late and had to sit outside with the "ordinary people".

Paul Bern
(PAUL LEVY)
Born December 3, 1889
Died Labor Day (September 5) 1932
Suicidal executive? The name of Paul Bern would be all but forgotten but for his marriage to Thirties sex symbol

Jean Harlow and for the strange manner of his death. Bern was born in Wandsbek, Germany the son of Julius Levy and Henrietta Hirsh. The family emigrated to America in 1899 and settled first in Newark, New Jersey, then at 3781 Third Avenue in New York. He became an actor, studying at the American Academy of Dramatic Arts. In 1911 he moved in with one of his fellow students, 5'3" Dorothy Millette (b. Indianapolis 1886). They were together for ten years (until she was hospitalised) and right up to his death, Bern paid her bills and living expenses, $350 per month. In 1920 he landed a job writing for the Samuel Goldwyn Company. He moved from studio to studio before finally making his mark in 1923. Over the next two years he directed five silent films for Paramount. In 1929 he became production supervisor at MGM. Bern was a modest, cultured gentleman who shunned the false hilarity and the hectic revelry of Hollywood and ignored the glittering parties that were so fashionable in those early golden years of Tinseltown. In early 1930 Bern met blonde bombshell Jean Harlow and championed her cause (unsuccessfully) to Irving Thalberg. He may have not been successful professionally but he triumphed personally; Harlow and Bern were married on July 2, 1932, at her mother's home. The news shocked Hollywood. No one had realised the intensity of their relationship. On the surface, the match seemed strange, perhaps ludicrous. Harlow was the epitome of everything glamorous, the embodiment of the Hollywood girl. Bern was exactly the opposite. Marriage between the two seemed improbable at best, disastrous at worst. Additionally, there was the untrue allegation that Bern was impotent. It was reported that Adela Rogers St. John, the famed Hollywood writer, had gone to see Jean after her engagement and learned Bern hadn't told her about himself. "Then it's true," Harlow allegedly burst out, and began to cry. "But Paul loves me, for my mind, my spirit, my companionship, for me. He's paid me the highest compliment I've ever had. No man has ever loved me before for what's best in me." Two months later he was dead. It was eleven years to the day since the Fatty Arbuckle scandal had enveloped Hollywood.

CAUSE: Bern died from a bullet in the brain at 9820 Easton Drive, Beverly Hills. His death was officially classed as suicide, and was as unexpected as it was shocking. Those closest to Paul and Jean couldn't, wouldn't believe it. True, the couple had been seen to argue occasionally. Perhaps more than might be expected in two people after a mere eight weeks of marriage. There were no signs of depression in Bern. He'd been coming to the studio daily, putting in long hours on work (as well as a screenwriter, Bern had worked as a production executive and a director) that required tremendous concentration on detail. He could hardly have continued functioning if his despondency were so deep. Yet, it was widely presumed, he must have been secretly distraught; it seemed like a clear-cut case of suicide. The entire movie industry was taken by surprise, stunned by the tragic news. Harlow was visiting her mother at 1353 Club View Drive, Beverly Hills, at the time. When she heard about her husband's death, she collapsed in tears, locked herself in a bedroom and, inconsolable with grief, refused to talk to anyone. The corpse was found by the chauffeur-cum-butler, John Herman Carmichael. He entered the master bedroom on the morning of September 6, to ask if Bern was ready for breakfast, and instead found his employer lying on the floor – between the bed and dresser, in a sea of blood – and promptly fainted. A .38 calibre gun, serial number 572972, was in Bern's hand. On the table next to the bed was a note written in what authorities assured all was Bern's hand. It was scribbled in a green Morocco-bound notebook, and stated, rather cryptically:

Dearest Dear:

Unfortuately [sic] *this is the only way to make good the frightful wrong I have done you and to wipe out my abject humiliation. I Love you. Paul*

A postscript added: *You understand that last night was* [sic] *only a comedy.* Chief of Detectives Joe Taylor questioned Harlow about what her husband meant by the note. "I don't know," she replied. "I cannot by the wildest stretch of the imagination imagine what Paul meant in that note he left." "Did he ever talk of suicide to you?" the detective asked. "He has often talked of suicide," Harlow said, "but never with himself in mind, that I know of." As is the case in every police inquiry, rumours rapidly gained currency. One of them had Jean and Paul quarrelling violently the night before he shot himself to death. "That is absolutely not so," maintained Harlow. "There were no bad feelings between us." Butler John Carmichael confirmed this. The note Bern left was interpreted thus by Jean's stepfather, Marino Bello: "He was apologising to Jean for his suicide. If you marry a girl and soon afterward kill yourself, that is something to apologise for." Dr Edward Brant Jones, Bern's personal doctor, gave public assurances he would supply his patient's clinical records in confidence to Coroner Frank A. Nance, and that they would show it was "impossible that any other person was involved in his death". The suggestion that someone else might have had a hand in Bern's death came from a curious piece of testimony that went unexplained. Housekeeper Winifred Carmichael told authorities that on Sunday night – the night before Bern's body was found – she heard a car pull out of the driveway and roar away at high speed. The driver of the car was Dorothy Millette and she and

Bern had argued violently. This revelation touched off reports that Bern was murdered. However, the inquest was held on September 8, 1932, at the Price-Daniel Mortuary, and the official finding was that Bern's death was suicide, brought on by melancholia that apparently evolved from depression and overwork. And that was how it stayed for 50 years until Bern's friend, screenwriter Samuel Marx, decided to investigate. By this time all the principle players in the saga were dead, and any influence they may have had was no more. Marx's investigation produced circumstantial evidence that uncovered many of the fictions that had built up around Paul Bern. Apparently, Harlow and Bern did argue the night before he died but their disagreement was about where they lived – Harlow wanted to move – not his inability to consummate their match. The 'suicide' note was, indeed, written by Paul Bern and not a forgery. On September 6, 1932, Dorothy Millette left her San Francisco hotel room and boarded the *Delta King*, an overnight ferry to Sacramento. When police searched her room they discovered numerous fan magazines about the wedding of Bern and Harlow plus letters written by Bern to Millette severing their relationship for good. On the dresser was blotting paper, on which was imprinted a single word, reversed: "Justification". On September 14, Millette's body was found. Her death (on September 7, 1932), like Bern's, was adjudged a suicide. On the fateful night she had visited Bern who was worried she might declare herself Mrs Bern and thus make him a bigamist. That would undoubtedly have ruined Harlow's career. At first all seemed to go well. They sat by the pool and drank champagne, then Millette suggested they go for a swim. Bern agreed and that was when the arguments began. She stripped off her bathing costume and offered herself to him. He spurned her advances and went to the pool

house to get changed. He slipped out of his trunks and stood there naked about to wrap himself in a dressing gown. Bern kept two guns in his bedroom and within seconds Millette was standing nude beside him pressing herself against him and, tragically, pressing one of his guns against his temple. She fired, killing Bern instantly. The powerful publicity machine at MGM swung into operation to protect its star from a murder scandal. According to Marx, following Louis B. Mayer's orders, Bern's body was moved to the bedroom, the gun wiped with oil to remove fingerprints and placed in the director's hand. Mayer initially also removed the note that Bern had written to Harlow from his notebook by the bed, but was then persuaded to replace it – after all, it could serve suitably as a cryptic suicide note. Another theory has Bern killing himself fearful of the shame Dorothy Millette could bring him and Jean Harlow. Millette then committed suicide when she learned of Bern's death. Whatever the truth, Jean Harlow was compassionate in the aftermath of events. She paid for Millette's funeral and the headstone, which was engraved "Dorothy Millette Bern 1886–1932". Harlow gave her in death something that Dorothy Millette never had in life – Paul Bern's name.
FURTHER READING: *Deadly Illusions: Who Killed Jean Harlow's Husband? –* Samuel Marx & Joyce Vanderveen (London: Century, 1991).

Bibi Besch
Born February 1, 1940
Died September 7, 1996
Handy supporter. Born in Vienna, Austria, the daughter of Gusti Huber, Bibiana Besch was raised in Westchester County, New York, and worked in television for more than twenty years before finally being nominated for an Emmy. She received one Best Supporting Actress Emmy

nomination for *Doing Time On Maple Drive* (1992) and another in 1993 for Guest Actress on *Northern Exposure*. She made her film début in *Distance* (1975) as Joanne and regularly commuted between the big and small screens. She appeared in *The Pack* (1977) as Marge, *Hardcore* (1979) as Mary, *Meteor* (1979) as Helen Bradley, *The Lonely Lady* (1983) as Veronica Randall, *Date With An Angel* (1987) as Grace Sanders, *Who's That Girl?* (1987) as Mrs Worthington, *Kill Me Again* (1989) as Jack's secretary, *Steel Magnolias* (1989) as Belle Marmillion, *Tremors* (1990) as Megan, *Betsy's Wedding* (1990) as Nancy Lovell, *Lonely Hearts* (1991) as Maria Wilson and *My Family* (1995) as Mrs Gillespie. On the small screen she also appeared in *Ellery Queen*, *Police Woman*, *The Rockford Files*, *Charlie's Angels*, *How The West Was Won*, *Hart To Hart*, *Cagney & Lacey*, *Scarecrow And Mrs King*, *Remington Steele*, *Who's The Boss?*, *Dynasty*, *Highway To Heaven*, *L.A. Law*, *Family Ties*, *Murder, She Wrote*, *The Golden Girls*, *Coach*, *Dr Quinn*, *Medicine Woman*, *ER* and *Melrose Place*. Her daughter is the actress Samantha Mathis (b. Brooklyn, New York May 12, 1970).

CAUSE: Bibi Besch died of metastasised breast cancer in Los Angeles, California aged 56. She died one day before *Star Trek*'s 30th anniversary, having played Dr Carol Marcus in *Star Trek: The Wrath Of Khan* (1982).

Lyle Bettger

Born February 13, 1915
Died September 24, 2003
Fifties baddie. Born in Philadelphia, Pennsylvania, the son of the St Louis Cardinals' third baseman Franklin Bettger, Lyle S. Bettger was the caricature of the cinematic villain. In 1935 he enrolled in the American Academy of Dramatic Arts in New York City and graduated two years later. After a period on Broadway he

was signed by Paramount. In his first film *No Man Of Her Own* (1949) he played Stephen Morley who menaced Barbara Stanwyck and when he got her pregnant bought her a train ticket to go away. The train crashed and she assumed the identity of a dead passenger but he found her and threatened to blackmail her. In his next outing, *Union Station* (1950), he was Joe Beacon who kidnapped the blind daughter of a millionaire. In Cecil B. DeMille's circus epic *The Greatest Show On Earth* (released January 2, 1952), Bettger played the elephant trainer Klaus who was insanely jealous of his partner in the act, Gloria Grahame. He played Johnny Buff, a baddie, in *Denver And Rio Grande* (1952) and as Stephen Cook he caused *The Great Sioux Uprising* (1953) by stealing ponies from the Indians and selling them to the army. He was Audie Murphy's enemy in *Destry* (1954) as Phil Decker and *Drums Across The River* (1954) as Frank Walker. He was behind another Red Indian rebellion in *The Lone Ranger* (1955) as Reece Kilgore, when he broke a treaty so he could look for silver in a sacred mountain. In John Sturges' *Gunfight At The OK Corral* (premièred on May 30, 1957), Bettger played Ike Clanton, the crooked rancher. He was Clay Bell, Alan Ladd's nemesis, in *Guns Of The Timberland* (which opened in New York on February 1, 1960). Bettger was not always the villain of the piece. He played Frank Colloni in *Carnival Story* (1954), "a cheap and unattractive production," according to Halliwell, which was, in Bettger's own words, "the first and only time in my recollection that I'm not the bad guy in a feature picture". As the Sixties progressed the popularity of Westerns in the cinema declined so Bettger moved to the small screen where he plied his villainous trade in shows such as *Bonanza*, *Gunsmoke* and *Rawhide*. He played special investigator Sam Larsen in the NBC crime series *The*

Court Of Last Resort (October 4,
1957–April 1958). In 1969, after
playing Joe Fletcher in an episode of
Hawaii Five-O, Bettger, his wife, Mary
Boyd, and their three children moved
to the Aloha State. Bettger appeared in
the series several times in differing roles
until 1978. In 1979 Bettger retired,
commenting on his career, "On the
whole, I enjoyed playing the villains,
they're usually a better role in most
cases than the leading man."
CAUSE: He died aged 88 in Atascadero,
San Luis Obispo County, California.

Billy Bevan
(WILLIAM BEVAN HARRIS)
Born September 29, 1887
Died November 26, 1957
Moustachioed comic. Born in Orange,
New South Wales, Australia, he was
educated at the University of Sydney
and then joined the Pollard Opera
Company. In 1917 he began making
films as a supporting player. For nine
years from 1920 he appeared in more
than 70 two-reel Mack Sennett
comedies. He also appeared in the
Tired Businessman series of comedies.
Bevan predominantly played
philanderers alongside pretty girls in
the heady days before the Hays Office.
He was known for a thick moustache
reminiscent of Glenn Hughes (the
leather man) of Village People.
Towards the end of his Sennett career
he did appear clean-shaven. He was
virtually unrecognisable without the
'tache. His films included playing a
policeman in *On Patrol* (1922),
Wall Street Blues (1924) as an office
caretaker, *Fight Night* (1926),
From Rags To Britches (1926) as a
department store manager, *Circus
Today* (1926) as a clown, *A Sea-Dog's
Tale* (1926) as a shipwreck victim and
Ice Cold Cocos (1926). This last film
saw him cast as an ice delivery man
who has to negotiate a long flight of
steps à la Laurel & Hardy in *The Music
Box* (1932). In his last films, despite
being Australian, he was usually cast as

a cockney. He retired in 1952. He was
married to the actor Leona Roberts
(b. Illinois, July 14, 1881 as Leona
Doty, d. Santa Monica, California,
January 30, 1954).
CAUSE: He died in Escondido,
California. He was 70.

Charles Bickford
Born January 1, 1891
Died November 9, 1967
Red-headed rebel. 6′1″ Charles
Ambrose Bickford was born in
Cambridge, Massachusetts, the fifth of
seven children, and was something of a
menace as a small boy. He later
described himself as "pure devil" and
legend has it that at nine he was tried
and acquitted for attempted murder
after shooting a man who ran over his
dog. Bickford later worked as a
lumberjack, investment promoter,
wheat harvester, brewery lorry driver,
carnival barker and sparring partner for
James J. Corbett before he briefly ran
his own pest control business. He
joined a burlesque in San Francisco
and spent the next 12 years touring
America. His star rose when Cecil B.
DeMille saw Bickford on Broadway in
Outside Looking In and offered him the
starring role in *Dynamite* (released
on December 13, 1929). He signed
a contract with MGM but was
blacklisted after he told studio head
Louis B. Mayer to "go fuck yourself".
He earned his living working in the
docks before he was allowed back in
front of the cameras and was offered a
contract at 20th Century Fox.
Unluckily he was mauled by a lion
while filming *East Of Java* (1935)
before he signed. His neck was badly
scarred and Fox dropped him. No
longer able to be a leading man, he
turned to character work and received
three Best Supporting Actor Oscar
nominations for his performance as
Peyramale in *The Song Of Bernadette*
(released Christmas Day, 1943), *The
Farmer's Daughter* (March 25, 1947) as
Joseph Clancy and *Johnny Belinda*

(September 14, 1948) as Black McDonald. He became very rich – not through his films but through wise investments. Unlike many stars Charles Bickford kept his own counsel and rarely revealed too much to anyone – friend, fan or press. He married Beatrice Loring in 1919 and had two children by her: a son, Rex, born in 1921 and a daughter, Doris, born in 1920. None are mentioned in his 1965 autobiography *Bulls, Balls, Bicycles & Actors*.

CAUSE: He died, aged 76, in Los Angeles, California, from a blood infection and was buried at Woodlawn Cemetery, Santa Monica, California.

John Bindon

Born October 4, 1943
Died October 10, 1993

"Fists for hire". London-born John Dennis Arthur Bindon, nick-named Biffo, was a thug who found a measure of success as an actor. The son of a London taxi driver, Bindon had what he described as a miserable childhood – his mother kept him under the kitchen table. He once admitted, "I've had this overwhelming urge to smash things up ever since I was a kid." Aged 11, he was charged with malicious damage and six years later was sent to Borstal for possessing live ammunition. He was functionally illiterate. He began acting after being spotted in a pub by director Ken Loach who cast him as Tom, the wife-beater, in *Poor Cow* (1967). 6'2" Bindon once cut the arm off a man who had upset him. In 1968 he met Vicki Hodge (b. 17 October, 1946, the daughter of baronet Sir John Rowland Hodge, MBE), a model and soft-porn actress. Other flings included Profumo scandalite Christine Keeler (b. Staines, Middlesex, February 22, 1942), Bunny girl Serena Williams, the very busty singer Dana Gillespie (b. Woking, Surrey, March 30, 1949) and rock star wife Angie Bowie (b. Cyprus, 25 September, 1949) at whose house he took part in orgies. In 1968 Bindon

won an award for bravery from the Royal Humane Society for saving a man drowning in the Thames. What the press didn't report was that it was Bindon who had thrown him in the river in the first place. The two men had been fighting and Bindon had pushed him in. He only dived in when he saw a policeman approaching. In the early Seventies Bindon earned £2,000 from acting and £10,000 (around £100,000 in 2002) from the protection rackets he ran in and around Chelsea and Fulham, south-west London. Bindon was proud of his apparently huge penis and was known for exposing himself. When Lord Longford was conducting his enquiry into pornography Bindon flashed at him outside the Chelsea Potter public house on the King's Road. His party piece was to balance five (or was it three or six?) half pint glasses on his erect penis. In 1972 he was introduced to Princess Margaret (1930–2002) on Mustique, and took great delight in showing her his trick. Bindon also claimed that he and the princess had had an affair. "On a scale of one to ten I would give her a nine for technique and a bloody great 15 for enthusiasm. I thought I was a goer but if I'd have let her she'd have had me at it all bloody night." In 1976 Bindon went bankrupt over unpaid taxes. A year later he was doing security work for Led Zeppelin and was involved in their notorious thuggery incident backstage after a concert in San Francisco. On November 21, 1978 a cocaine deal went disastrously wrong at the Ranelagh Yacht Club, a Fulham drinking den at 74 Station Approach, London, SW6, and a gangster and police informer named Johnny Darke, 32, was killed, stabbed nine times. Bindon was stabbed, his heart was nicked in the fight. Bindon's friend, Lennie Osborne dragged the semi-conscious Bindon away from the Ranelagh. Bindon's girlfriend, Hodge and his sister, Geraldine, helped to dispose of his bloodstained clothes and other evidence. Leaning on Hodge, the heavily bleeding Bindon made his way to Heathrow, and he and 'Hodgey' flew Aer Lingus to Dublin, Ireland, intending to stay at an IRA safe house to avoid an investigation by the police. After four days Bindon was taken to St Vincent's hospital where a priest administered the Last Rites. A life on the run wasn't what Bindon wanted so he gave himself up to Detective Chief Inspector George Mould and was charged with murdering Johnny Darke. On remand in Brixton Vicki Hodge took the drug Mandrax to Bindon. At his trial at the Old Bailey the prosecution alleged that Bindon had been paid £10,000 to kill Darke. The defence claimed that Bindon had gone to help a man who had been stabbed in the face by Darke. The actor Bob Hoskins appeared as a character witness for Bindon and told the court that Bindon's nick-name came from the comic character Biffo the Bear not as a result of his propensity for hitting people. On November 13, 1979, after twelve hours' deliberation, Bindon was acquitted on grounds of self-defence. The judge, Mr Justice Mars-Jones, said that he believed the truth of what had happened had not been told in his courtroom. Bindon's life took a downward turn after the case. He would often use his fists on Vicki Hodge but was careful never to mark her face. In pubs Bindon would often get down on all fours and bang the floor shouting, "What's it like down there, Darkey?" In 1982, a year after he and Hodge split, he pleaded guilty to using a piece of pavement as an offensive weapon against a "short and weedy" man who had bumped into him while Bindon was celebrating his birthday. Bindon was fined £100. The following year, he was again declared bankrupt. In 1984 he appealed successfully against a conviction on September 18, 1984 for threatening an off-duty detective constable in a Kensington restaurant with a carving knife. In 1985 he was charged with possessing an offensive weapon and then cleared of threatening to firebomb the home of a mother of three. His other films included *Performance* (1970) as Moody, Sid Fletcher in *Get Carter* (1971), Coulter in *Man In The Wilderness* (1971), *The Mackintosh Man* (1973) as Buster, a groom in *Love Thy Neighbour* (1973), *No Sex Please, We're British* (1973) as Pete, *Dead Cert* (1974) as Walter, a soldier in *Barry Lyndon* (1974) and *Quadrophenia* (1979) where, in a case of life imitating art, he played Harry, a drug dealer. He also often played villains in television cop shows like *The Sweeney*, *Hazell* and *Softly, Softly Task Force*. Bindon was known for deliberately fluffing his lines so that filming would be delayed and he would get paid overtime. He never married but had a daughter, Kelly (b. 1963) by Sheila Davies.

CAUSE: Bindon spent his final years living alone and on the dole in his flat in Chesham Mews, Belgravia. He died of bronchopneumonia caused by AIDS, a week after his 50th birthday.

Betsy Blair

(ELIZABETH WINIFRED BOGER)
Born December 11, 1923
Died March 13, 2009
Left-wing thespian. Born in Cliffside Park, New Jersey, she worked as a tap dancer in an amateur show that toured New Jersey when she was 11 and later worked for the John Robert Powers modelling agency. In 1940, at 16, she won a scholarship to Sarah Lawrence College, but before she enrolled she auditioned for the chorus line in Billy Rose's Diamond Horseshoe, a Times Square, Manhattan nightclub that employed 28-year-old Gene Kelly as a choreographer. They married in 1941. That year she also took the female lead in William Saroyan's Broadway play *The Beautiful People* and then the couple moved to Hollywood to launch Kelly's film career. Blair did not appear in films until later that decade and

featured in *The Guilt Of Janet Ames* (1947), *Another Part Of The Forest* (1948), *The Snake Pit* (1948) and *Kind Lady* (1951). She did not take to Hollywood and began to follow liberal causes associating with the Joint Anti-Fascist Refugee Committee, the Sleepy Lagoon Committee, the Civil Rights Congress, the National Association for the Advancement of Colored People and the Independent Progressive Party. She even tried to join the Communist Party but was turned down because of her marriage to the high-profile Kelly. In New York when she was 16 she had attended a weekly Marxist study group and in Hollywood the FBI put her under surveillance. She was to later write that her ideals "had always been American, not Russian" and her "battles and contribution – small as it may have been – were against racism, for strong unions, for the rights of women; to put it simply, for democracy". Her views caused her work to dry up and she almost lost the role as Clara Snyder in *Marty* (1955) because of them. After three readings for the part, producer Harold Hecht telephoned her and asked her to write a letter that would "clear" her of left-wing association. Hecht told her that she didn't have to "name names" – at least not names that hadn't already been exposed.So determined was she to play the part she agreed to write a letter she later described as "like a schoolgirl essay for civics class . . . [I] went on about freedom of speech and the American Constitution and the secret ballot . . . both Harold Hecht and I knew it wouldn't pass muster. It didn't come near what the Un-American Activities Committee wanted – no, demanded." In the end Kelly asked studio head Dore Schary "to do something" to help his wife or he would go on strike. Schary, "called the American Legion in Washington right there and then in front of Gene, and he vouched for me. And so I was in *Marty*," recalled Blair.

The role of the shy schoolteacher who meets Ernest Borgnine's lonely Bronx butcher at the Stardust Ballroom earned an Academy Award nomination as Best Supporting Actress. (It also won as Best Film as well as Oscars for screenwriter Paddy Chayefsky, director Delbert Mann and Borgnine but Jo Van Fleet beat Blair for *East Of Eden*.) *Los Angeles Times* film critic Edwin Schallert wrote, "[Blair] shines right along with [Borgnine] as the gentle and understanding wallflower whom he meets in the dance hall, and with whom he finds deep and mutual understanding, because he seems to be such a bull in a china shop himself." In 1956 she left Kelly and moved to Paris, later settling in London. "How could I have left Gene, this wonderful man, after 16 years of marriage?" Blair said in 2003. "This perfect husband, father, friend, protector, provider, hard worker. I loved and admired him as a brilliant actor and dancer as well as a good, good man! To this day, I can't explain it. It had nothing to do with sex. It was freedom." The couple divorced in 1957. In 1963 she married Karel Reisz and they were together until his death in 2002. She studied for a degree in speech therapy from the Central School of Speech and Drama in London.

CAUSE: Blair died aged 85 of cancer in a hospital in London.

FURTHER READING: *The Memory Of All That: Love And Politics In New York, Hollywood, And Paris* – Betsy Blair (New York: Alfred A. Knopf, 2003)

Amanda Blake

(BEVERLY LOUISE NEILL)
Born February 20, 1927
Died August 16, 1989
TV Queen. Amanda Blake did not appear in as many films as she perhaps could have done. Born in Buffalo, New York, she began acting while still at school. In 1949 she signed with MGM, making four films: *Duchess Of Idaho* (1950), *Lili* (1953), *A Star Is Born*

(1954) and *High Society* (1956). However, for almost twenty years (1955–1974) she reigned supreme as Miss Kitty on the television series *Gunsmoke*. Blake was married five times, the last time to a bisexual estate agent who effectively sentenced her to death. CAUSE: In 1974 she underwent an operation for cancer of the tongue, having smoked 40 a day for as long as she could remember. Amanda Blake died aged 62 from AIDS at 7.15pm at Mercy General Hospital, Sacramento.

Mel Blanc

Born May 30, 1908
Died July 10, 1989
The Voice. In the course of his career, San Francisco-born Melvin Jerome Blanc's voice appeared in over 3,000 films. He provided the cartoon voices for, amongst others, Bugs Bunny, Daffy Duck, Porky Pig, Barney Rubble, the Road Runner, Sylvester and Tweety Pie. His birthdate in Katz appears as June 30, 1892.
CAUSE: He died of natural causes aged 81, or possibly 97, in Los Angeles.

Sally Blane

(ELIZABETH JANE YOUNG)
Born July 11, 1910
Died August 27, 1997
Loretta Young's big sister. Sally Blane was born Elizabeth Jane Young in Salida, Colorado, almost on a train. One of five children, the family split in 1915 and Sally and her siblings moved to Hollywood. All the Young children landed work as extras – Blane was the first to be cast in featured roles. In the first of her 70-plus films she portrayed a nymph in *Sirens Of The Sea* (1917) and was also in *The Sheik* (1921), playing an Arab child. Aged 14, she was spotted dancing by director Wesley Ruggles and cast in the *Collegian* series. Soon afterwards, she signed a contract with Paramount and was placed in *Rolled Stockings* (1927). Even though she was a well-paid starlet, she still cadged lifts off her male co-stars

because her stage mother wouldn't allow any of her children to buy a car. In the Twenties and early Thirties she appeared in *Dead Man's Curve* (1928) as Ethel Hume, *Horseman Of The Plains* (1928) as Dawn O'Day, *Fools For Luck* (1928) as Louise Hunter, *The Vanishing Pioneer* (1928) as June Shelby, *Tanned Legs* (1929) as Janet Reynolds, *Eyes Of The Underworld* (1929) as Florence Hueston, *Vagabond Lover* (1929) as Jean, *Once A Sinner* (1930) as Hope Patterson, *Little Accident* (1930) as Isabel, *X Marks The Spot* (1931) as Sue, *Probation* (1932) as Janet Holman, *Forbidden Company* (1932) as Janet Blake, *Local Bad Man* (1932) as Marian Meade, *Pride Of The Legion* (1932) as Peggy, and Alice in *I Am A Fugitive From A Chain Gang* (1932) (she was due to play Helen Vinson until she was nixed by Mrs Paul Muni) before moving to low-budget studios Chesterfield and Artclass where she starred in B pictures such as *Trick For Trick* (1933) as Constance Russell, *Half A Sinner* (1934) as Phyllis, *City Limits* (1934) as Helen Matthews, *No More Women* (1934) as Helen Young, *The Great Hospital Mystery* (1937) as Ann Smith and *Charlie Chan At Treasure Island* (1939) as Stella Essex. As her sister's star soared, Blane's waned. "She had more drive than the rest of us," she said of her sister. "Loretta was always really ambitious. She would turn down parts that I would have given anything to have played, but she never realised how much I wanted them. But while Loretta was concentrating on her career, I had all the beaux." In 1937 she married director Norman Foster (who had gone out with sister Loretta) and spent time raising their son and daughter. She was widowed in 1976. Her youngest sister, Georgianne, married actor Ricardo Montalban. Of her career, 5'4½" Blane said, "I never felt I was photogenic. People ask if I watch my old movies on television. I don't. I never liked a single thing I did."

CAUSE She died of natural causes in Los Angeles, California aged 87.

Billy Bletcher

Born September 24, 1894
Died January 5, 1979
Busy comedian. Born in Lancaster, Pennsylvania, Billy Bletcher was a much in-demand comedian. He entered films in 1913 with Vitagraph and was still working 53 years later. At the company's New York studio he also trained to be an assistant director. After a brief flirtation with another company (Vim) Bletcher returned to Vitagraph and when the organisation announced it was opening a second office on the West Coast he was one of the first to volunteer. Bletcher spent a couple of years working with Mack Sennett. He appeared in *A Roman Scandal* (1919) which starred Colleen Moore. That same year he made his first feature film *The Love Hunger*. From 1920 he appeared in two comedic series – Gayety Comedies and Spotlight Comedies. In the Twenties Bletcher worked for Fox, Christie and Educational. As well as comedies he also featured in Westerns. He worked for Hal Roach and appeared with Laurel & Hardy in *Babes In Toyland* (1934) and *The Big Noise* (1944). He also provided the voice of the Big Bad Wolf in Disney's *The Three Little Pigs* (1933). He was married to the actress Arlyn Roberts (b. New York, March 20, 1893 as Arline Harriet Roberts, d. Los Angeles, California, July 3, 1992, aged 99, of cardiac arrest).
CAUSE: He died in Los Angeles, California, aged 84.

Joan Blondell

Born August 30, 1909
Died December 25, 1979
Wisecracker. New York-born 5'4" Rose Joan Blondell was an actress and one-time wife of actor Dick Powell (September 19, 1936–July 14, 1944) and flamboyant impresario Michael (*Around The World In 80 Days*) Todd (July 4, 1947–June 8, 1950). As a teenager Blondell won a beauty contest and used the title to get to New York where she appeared on Broadway with James Cagney in *Penny Arcade*. That won them both contracts in Hollywood, where she made a name for herself as a wisecracking, loose woman – on screen that is – in the Thirties. She received an Oscar nomination for *The Blue Veil* (1951) and matured into a woman of certain standing – on screen that is. Among her last films was *Grease* (1978).
CAUSE: She died in Santa Monica, California, aged 70, from leukaemia.

Sergei Bodrov, Jr

Born December 27, 1971
Died September 20, 2002
Rising Russian star. Born in Moscow, Bodrov's father, Sergei Sr, was also a film-maker. The younger Bodrov graduated from Moscow State University in 1993 with a degree in history and combined work and study to achieve an MA in 1998. In 1996 he made his acting début in his father's film *The Prisoner Of The Mountains* playing Vania Zhilin alongside Oleg Menshikov, the country's leading film star. The professional and the amateur worked well together and won awards for their work on the film. Bodrov landed the presenting role on *Vzgliad* (*View*), a chat show on ORT, Russia's first television channel. It was a job he held for three years until 1999. In *Brother* (1997) and *Brother 2* (2000) Bodrov played Danila Bagrov, a soldier in the Chechen war who returns home to St Petersburg and rescues his brother from the Chechen Mafia by killing large numbers of them. When he gave up his television career Bodrov moved behind the cameras to become a film director. His first film *Sisters* (2001) won awards for the best début film in Russia. He also appeared, again playing a soldier, in *War* (2002). He

was married with two children.
CAUSE: Bodrov and his film crew had
travelled to Karmadon Gorge in the
north Caucasus to make his second
film *The Messenger*. Waiting for their
transport to take them away, Bodrov
and the entire crew, young actors from
Moscow and Vladikavkas, were killed
when a glacier slid down the gorge and
buried them all alive under a mass of
ice and mud. Bodrov was 30.

Sir Dirk Bogarde

(DEREK NIVEN VAN DEN BOGAERDE)
Born Easter Monday (March 28), 1921
Died May 8, 1999
Suave Englishman. Born in West
Hampstead, London, the Catholic
eldest son of three children of Ulric
Gontron Jules Van Den Bogaerde (b.
Walsall Road, Perry Bar, Birmingham,
June 14, 1892, d. Cherry Tree Cottage,
Sussex, 1972), the first art editor of *The
Times*, and Margaret Niven (b. 1898,
d. Sussex, March 29, 1980 of heart
failure), a former actress. Young Derek
worked as a commercial artist to fund
his acting lessons. He made his stage
début on January 15, 1940 in a play
ironically entitled *When We Are Married*
and written by J.B. Priestley. His career
was interrupted by the war and he
served in the Army (Queen's Royal
Regiment) from May 8, 1941. He
served in Europe and the Far East until
September 5, 1946. He reappeared on
stage in February 1947 and entered
films properly the following year. He
was signed to a contract by Rank on
June 7, 1947 and played heavy dramas,
light comedies and everything in
between. However, when he started at
Rank he was told his head was too
small, he was too thin and his neck
"wasn't right". Little wonder he lacked
confidence and covered this by being
arrogant, rude and often drunk. In his
first film he was credited as 'Birk
Gocart' in *Esther Walters* (1948) in
which he played William Latch and
which began shooting on September 6,
1947. Bogarde had appeared in two bit

parts earlier including one as an extra
in the George Formby comedy *Come
On George* (1939) and the other as a
radio operator in *Dancing With Crime*
(1947). He was acclaimed for his
performance as Melville Farr, a gay
lawyer, in Basil Dearden's *Victim*
(1961) and won large audiences for his
Doctor . . . films including *Doctor In The
House* (1954), *Doctor At Sea* (1955),
Doctor At Large (1956) and *Doctor In
Distress* (1963) all as Simon Sparrow.
His other films included *The Blue Lamp*
(1950) as Tom Riley in which he shot
and killed PC George Dixon, *Cast A
Dark Shadow* (1955) as Edward Bare,
A Tale Of Two Cities (1958) as Sydney
Carton, *Darling* (1965) as Robert Gold,
a part that won him a BAFTA, *Modesty
Blaise* (1966) as Gabriel, *Oh! What A
Lovely War* (1969) as Stephen, *Death
In Venice* (1971) as Gustav Von
Aschenbach, *The Night Porter* (1974)
playing a former Nazi concentration
camp guard, *A Bridge Too Far* (1977)
as Lieutenant-General Frederick 'Boy'
Browning and *Despair* (1978) as
Hermann Hermann after which he
seemed to retire from the screen. He
returned in 1990 with *Daddy Nostalgie*
playing Daddy. He attracted a huge
female following and had to have his
flies sewn up when he ventured out on
publicity junkets. He left England in
1968 for a rambling farmhouse in the
South of France, returning twenty
years later to live in a Spartan flat near
Sloane Square. One of the biggest
puzzles concerning Bogarde was his sex
life. Was he gay? Bisexual? Asexual? In
his memoirs he tells of being seduced
as a boy by a Mr Dodd, losing his
virginity to a female rapist and his
affairs with Kay Kendall and Judy
Garland who once stabbed him
because he wouldn't kiss her. Although
Bogarde never married, he claimed he
wasn't homosexual although few
people believed him. Bogarde grew up
at a time when homosexuality was
illegal. The actor Helena Bonham
Carter, who worked with Bogarde on

one of his last TV films, believed that he could not come out because, if he did, he would have found it impossible to cope with the sorrow at not having done so sooner. Bogarde would even tell people that his live-in companion, Tony Forwood (b. Melcombe Regis, Dorset, October 3, 1915 as Ernest Lytton Langton Forwood), the ex-husband of Glynis Johns, was actively anti-homosexual. The two men met in 1940 in Amersham. Their *affaire propre* began in late 1946 and on May 26, 1948, a month before his divorce became final, Forwood moved into Bogarde's home at 44 Chester Row, Belgravia, London SW1. The two men would live together for forty years. In 1986 the gay chat show host Russell Harty interviewed Bogarde for a Yorkshire Television programme. During the course of the show Bogarde asked Forwood how it was going, to be told that he was going over the same material. Bogarde told Harty to "Throw me some interesting questions. Be provocative, and I'll answer." Harty tried to get Bogarde to open up fully about Forwood but without success – "I'm still in the shell and you haven't cracked it yet, honey." His move back to England that same year and the selling of their home Le Haut Clermont, Châteauneuf de Grasse for £275,000 was necessitated by Forwood being diagnosed with Parkinson's disease. With Bogarde holding his hand, he died aged 72 in St Stephen's Hospital, London, at 2.15am on May 18, 1988, after almost fifty years together. The cause of death was cancer of the liver. Bogarde was knighted in the 1992 New Year's Honours List, the year in which he received a lifetime achievement award from the British Academy. Director Joseph Losey recalled the actor he knew: "Dirk Bogarde is a fine actor. His problem is breaking through his own coldness and emotional hostility to his softer, guarded emotions. I may reasonably say that he is the least

friendly or outgoing actor I've ever worked with." For himself, 5′8″ Bogarde was as determined to protect his privacy in death as well as in life. As he completed each volume of his autobiography, he destroyed the original material on which it was based. Interviewed by Lynn Barber, he told her, "I don't care if I'm remembered or not. It doesn't matter on your gravestone, does it? It doesn't matter a bugger . . . I have said that in my will: no funeral, no memorial, just forget me."

CAUSE: Bogarde suffered a minor stroke on November 16, 1987 which left him partially paralysed. He recovered, although it left him with a slight limp. He dyed his hair towards the end of his life. Bogarde became vice-president of the Voluntary Euthanasia Society in 1991. In 1994 he suffered from shingles. On September 18, 1996, he was admitted to King Edward VII Hospital for an angioplasty. He was recovering from the surgery when he suffered another stroke which left him confined to a wheelchair. He was discharged on December 19. Sir Dirk Bogarde died at midday of a heart attack in his flat at 2 Cadogan Gardens, Chelsea, London, aged 78. On May 13, 1999, he was cremated at St Marylebone Crematorium. The only attendees were Bogarde's nephew, Brock, and chauffeur, Bob Pearson. His ashes were scattered at his former home, Le Haut Clermont, Châteauneuf de Grasse. In his will he left £859,000 and two Picassos.

FURTHER READING: *A Postillion Struck By Lightning* – Dirk Bogarde (London: Chatto & Windus, 1977); *Snakes And Ladders* – Dirk Bogarde (London: Chatto & Windus, 1978); *An Orderly Man* – Dirk Bogarde (London: Chatto & Windus, 1983); *Backcloth* – Dirk Bogarde (London: Viking, 1986); *Dirk Bogarde The Authorised Biography* – John Coldstream (London: Weidenfeld & Nicolson, 2004).

Humphrey Bogart

Born December 25, 1899
Died January 14, 1957

Tough guy. Humphrey DeForest Bogart was born at 245 West 103rd Street in New York City weighing 8lb 7oz. His true birthday is one of the most contentious of all film stars, even in a profession where the truth is rarely admitted. No birth certificate exists to confirm the date. His widow, Lauren Bacall, stated emphatically on her 1988 TV show *Bacall On Bogart*: "Despite what you may have heard or read, Bogie *was* born on Christmas Day." His authorised biographer concurs, but then the introduction to that book was written by Lauren Bacall. His death certificate also states December 25, 1899, as his birthday. Before he became a star Bogart's birthday was given as January 23, 1899, and this date appears in several editions of the *Motion Picture Almanac*. Following the success of *The Petrified Forest* (1936), Warner Bros changed his birthday to December 25, 1900. This date appears in the *Motion Picture Almanac* from its 1937/8 edition. Bogie later modified the year to 1899. There was no reason for the pre-1937 date to be disputed. Why would Bogart lie about his birthday *before* he was famous? There the matter seemed to rest until his most recent biographer discovered a cutting from *The Ontario County Times* from January 10, 1900. It reads: "Born: at New York, Dec 25, 1899, to Mr and Mrs. Belmont DeForest Bogart, a son." Bogart was raised in a large brownstone in Manhattan. His father was a morphine-addicted GP and his mother an artist under her maiden name Maud Humphrey. He had two sisters: Frances, known as Pat (b. October 25, 1901, d. October 1982), and Catherine Elizabeth, known as Kay (b. 1903, d. New York City, 1937, of peritonitis caused by a ruptured appendix). A sketch of the young Humphrey by his mother was used as an image of the ideal baby to promote Mellin's baby food. In 1909 he went to Trinity School on New York's 91st Street and eight years later, in September 1917, he enrolled in Phillips Academy in Andover, Massachusetts, where his father had been educated. Eight months later he was expelled because he didn't apply himself to studying – not, as his studio would have it, because he was an inveterate practical joker. On May 28, 1918, he joined the navy and spent two years in the North Atlantic. He claimed that the scar on his lip was as the result of enemy action but the war was over before Bogart had finished basic training. One explanation is that it occurred when he was escorting a prisoner who tried to escape by smacking him in the mouth with the handcuffs he was wearing. Another story has it caused by a bar room brawl. On leaving the navy on June 20, 1919, he drifted through various jobs before landing a position with a touring company. It was there that he met his first wife. Bogie married actress Helen Menken (b. New York December 12, 1901, d. The Lambs, 128 West 44th Street, New York City, 27 March 1966 from a heart attack) on May 20, 1926 at her home in the Gramercy Park Hotel, 52 Gramercy Park, by which time he was established as an actor. Pastor John Kent of St Ann's Church For Deaf Mutes conducted the ceremony. The clergyman was deaf as were the bride's parents. Stuart Rose, who was Bogie's best man and brother-in-law, described the ceremony as "macabre, almost obscene". In the marriage register bride and groom both listed their age as 26 – she was actually 24. The couple began to argue as soon as they had said "I do" although, in fact, Menken signed the words rather than speak them. There was no honeymoon and she took to her bed alone on the wedding night. Bogart told Rose that he thought he had made a big mistake. Helen Menken Bogart opened at the Empire Theatre, New York City in *The Captive*, based on

Marcel Proust's novel and the first Broadway play to deal with the subject of lesbianism, on September 29, 1926. Among her co-stars was Basil Rathbone and on February 9, 1927 the cast were arrested by vice officers after the performance. A plea bargain was arrived at and the producers and cast agreed to drop the play from Broadway in return for no obscenity charges being filed. Arrested the same day were the producers and casts of *Sex*, the Mae West vehicle, and *The Virgin Man*. On January 26, 1927 Bogart opened at the Actors' Theatre as Rims O'Neil in *Saturday's Children* and had a brief affair with cast member Ruth Gordon. Bogart appeared briefly in *Baby Mine* with Fatty Arbuckle but the play closed after a fortnight. When he was asked to appear in a Chicago, Illinois production of *Saturday's Children*, he asked his wife to accompany him but she declined and they divorced on November 18, 1927. Rumours long circulated that the titian-haired first Mrs Bogart was not averse to sharing her bed with women and had had affairs with Greta Garbo, Louise Brooks and Tallulah Bankhead. Two years earlier he had met Louise Brooks. She recalled: "My first impression was of a slim boy with charming manners, who was unusually quiet for an actor. His handsome face was made extraordinary by a most beautiful mouth. It was very full, rosy, and perfectly modelled – perfectly, that is, except that, to make it completely fascinating, at one corner of his upper lip a scarred, quilted piece hung down in a tiny scallop. It was taken for granted that he got punched in the mouth at some speakeasy. When Humphrey went into films, a surgeon sewed up the scallop, and only a small scar remained. Photographically, it was an improvement, but I missed this endearing disfigurement." In 1924 he had a screen test for Fox and was promised a part in *The Man Who Came Back* (1924) but the role went to the established Charles Farrell instead. At 24 Hopkins Street, the home of the bride's mother in Hartford, Connecticut, on April 3, 1928, he married for the second time. The new Mrs Bogart was short, blonde actress Mary Philips (b. New London, Connecticut, January 23, 1901, d. St John's Hospital, Santa Monica, California, April 22, 1975 from lung and brain cancer). Mary Bogart was torn between Bogart and his close friend, actor and designer Kenneth MacKenna (1899–1962). Usually, the two men shared women and it was normally MacKenna who got there first. It was different with Mary Philips – she married Bogart but only after MacKenna had proposed. Then to be fair, when she and Bogart divorced in 1938 she married MacKenna in August of that year. It had all begun rather unconventionally – when the Bogarts returned from a fortnight's honeymoon, she spent their first night back in bed with MacKenna while Bogart, lonely, rang his ex-wife and slept with her. It was to be the start of an affair that would run the entirety of his marriage with Mary Philips. They divorced in 1938. Bogie finally entered films in the Twenties, appearing in *The Dancing Town* (1928), *Broadway's Like That* (1930), *Up The River* (1930) as ex-con Steve, *A Devil With Women* (1930) as wealthy Tom Standish, *Love Affair* (1932) as aviator Jim Leonard and others before *The Petrified Forest* made his name. The latter saw Bogart in the role of Duke Mantee, a killer based not too loosely on John Dillinger; it was a part he had played on Broadway. Bogart had been signed to a seven-year contract by Warner Bros in November 1935 and he made two dozen films during the mid-to-late Thirties, including *China Clipper* (1936) as pilot Hap Stuart, *Black Legion* (1936) as killer Frank Taylor, *Marked Woman* (1937) as District Attorney David Graham, *Kid Galahad* (1937) as boxing manager Turkey

Morgan, *Swing Your Lady* (1938) as Ed Hatch (Bogart regarded this as his worst film), *Men Are Such Fools* (1938) as advertising executive Harry Galleon, *The Amazing Dr Clitterhouse* (1938) as hoodlum 'Rocks' Valentine, *Angels With Dirty Faces* (1938) as hoodlum James Frazier and *The Roaring Twenties* (1939) as George Hally, before two of his most famous roles established his stardom. He was suspended 12 times by Warner Bros for refusing to appear in certain films. However, he was second choice for both *The Maltese Falcon* (1941) in which he played Dashiell Hammett's hero Sam Spade, and *High Sierra* (1941) in which he was gangster Roy 'Mad Dog' Earle. George Raft turned down both roles. *Casablanca* (1942) consolidated his position in the pantheon of film gods and he was nominated for a Best Actor Oscar, losing out to Paul Lukas for *Watch On The Rhine* (1942). Bogie was a keen chess player. He played on set, by phone and even had it written into the opening scene of *Casablanca*. He never said "Play it again Sam" in the film. The line "Play it, Sam. Play 'As Time Goes By' " was actually spoken by Ingrid Bergman. In Beverly Hills on August 20, 1938, Bogart had married for the third time to busty blonde Broadway actress Mayo June Methot Morgan (b. Portland, Oregon, April 3, 1904, d. Holladay Park Hospital, Portland, Oregon, June 9, 1951, of acute alcoholism), a highly strung woman who had been married twice before herself and was convinced he would have an affair with Ingrid Bergman. (He didn't.) In 1942 he met wigmaker Verita Thompson (b. Nogales, Arizona 1918 d. Louisiana February 1, 2008) during a party to promote *Casablanca* and began an affair that lasted 15 years. Bogie appeared in *To Have And Have Not* (1944) as Harry Morgan during which (in March 1944) he met the future fourth Mrs Bogart, Lauren Bacall (b. New York September 16, 1924) known to her friends as Betty. It was in this film, a re-run of the *Casablanca* story, that Bacall utters the immortal words to Bogart: "You know you don't have to act with me, Steve. You don't have to say anything and you don't have to do anything. Not a thing. Oh, maybe just whistle. You know how to whistle don't you, Steve? Just put your lips together and blow." When he married her on Malabar Farm in Ohio on May 21, 1945, eleven days after his third divorce, he cried throughout the whole ceremony. They had one son: Stephen Humphrey (b. Cedars Of Lebanon Hospital, Los Angeles, January 6, 1949, at 11.22pm, weighing 6lb 6oz) and one daughter, Leslie Howard (b. Cedars Of Lebanon Hospital, Los Angeles, August 23, 1952, weighing 6lb 5oz). Bogie and Bacall also appeared in *The Big Sleep* (1946). He was Raymond Chandler's ace private eye Philip Marlowe; she played Vivian Rutledge. The film was actually made between October 10, 1944, and January 13, 1945. It ran 34 days over its 42-day schedule, due in no small part to Bogie's domestic troubles with Mayo Methot and director Howard Hawks' insistence on rewriting the script as they went along. Bogart appeared in two major John Huston pictures, *The Treasure Of The Sierra Madre* (1948) as Fred C. Dobbs and *Key Largo* (1948) as ex-soldier Frank McCloud. In *Tokyo Joe* (1949) Bogart played Joe Barrett, a bar owner in the Japanese capital who becomes a fighter pilot at the outbreak of war. Another Bogie blockbuster was *The African Queen* (1951) based on C.S. Forester's 1935 novel. John Huston tried to make the film in the Forties with Bogart and Bette Davis but her acrimonious row with the studio kiboshed that plan. Finally, Huston and Sam Spiegel got the project off the ground and the company flew to the Belgian Congo in May 1951 for two months' filming followed by a further six weeks in London. Bogie plays

Charlie Allnut, a rough, hard-drinking riverboat captain in 1914 German East Africa. It was a portrayal that won him his only Oscar (on March 20, 1952). His co-star was Katharine Hepburn who, unlike Bogart, enjoyed her time in the jungles. (By the way, the leeches on Bogart's body were not real. They were made of rubber.) *Beat The Devil* (1954) again teamed Bogie with John Huston. He played fortune hunter Billy Dannreuther, but the film flopped at the box office. On February 7, 1953, while filming in Italy, Bogart and Huston were involved in a car crash that injured Bogart's mouth, necessitating a week off work. In *The Caine Mutiny* (1954) Bogie plays Lieutenant Commander Philip Francis Queeg, a naval officer who believes that everything should be done by the book; it won him another Oscar nomination. Not everyone liked him. The film's producer Stanley Kramer said to him: "I have to be up early to make sure the set is ready for prematurely balding and ageing actors like you." His remaining films included *The Barefoot Contessa* (1954) as Hollywood director Harry Dawes, *We're No Angels* (1955) as escaped convict Joseph and his 75th and last film, *The Harder They Fall* (1956), in which he played Eddie Willis, an unemployed sportswriter. In 1947 Bogie had become increasingly political, leading a march on October 26 to protest about the communist witch hunts. He had been a Republican until Bacall persuaded him to see the error of his ways. He was also short. He stood just 5'8½" and wore special devices on his shoes to make himself look taller as well as a wig to hide his receding hairline. Bogart was also supposed to have popularised the line "Tennis, anyone?" He denied ever saying it, either on film or in real life, but he did coin the phrase "Louis, I think this is the beginning of a beautiful friendship."

CAUSE: On February 29, 1956, Bogart was admitted to Good Samaritan Hospital, Los Angeles. The following day he underwent a nine-hour operation for cancer of the oesophagus. Newspaper reports did not mention the word cancer but later that year stories began to proliferate about the truth behind his failing health. On November 26 he was admitted to St John's Hospital, Santa Monica. He stayed for anti-cancer treatment for five days. In early January 1957 he greeted guests in his pyjamas and dressing gown, a cigarette in one hand and a Martini in the other. Almost a fortnight later, he died at his home, 232 South Mapleton Drive, Los Angeles, at 2.25am, aged 57. On January 17, 1957, he was cremated at Forest Lawn Memorial-Park's Crematory, 1712 South Glendale Avenue, Glendale, California 91209. The next day at All Saints Episcopal Church, Santa Monica Boulevard, Los Angeles, over 3,000 people attended a memorial service, including Marlene Dietrich, Samuel Goldwyn, Danny Kaye, Swifty Lazar, David Niven, Gregory Peck and Dick Powell. John Huston delivered the eulogy: "In each of the fountains at Versailles there is a pike, which keeps all the carp active, otherwise they would grow over fat and die. Bogie took rare delight in performing a similar duty in the fountains of Hollywood. Yet his victims seldom bore him any malice, and when they did, not for long . . . We have no reason to feel any sorrow for him – only for ourselves for having lost him. He is quite irreplaceable." Bogart had wanted his ashes sprinkled on the Pacific from his 55-foot yacht *Santana*. However, this was illegal, so the remains were kept at Forest Lawn. His estate was worth over $1 million. On July 31, 1997, a commemorative stamp was issued in Bogart's honour by the American post office.

FURTHER READING: *Bogie: The Authorised Biography* – Joe Hyams (London: Mayflower, 1973); *Bogie And*

Me: A Love Story – Verita Thompson with Donald Shepherd (New York: Pinnacle, 1982); *Humphrey Bogart* – Allan Eyles (London: Sphere, 1990); *Bogart* – A.M. Sperber & Eric Lax (London: Weidenfeld & Nicolson, 1997). *The Secret Life Of Humphrey Bogart: The Early Years 1899–1931* – Darwin Porter (New York: Georgia Literary Association, 2003).

Eddie Boland
Born December 27, 1883
Died February 3, 1935
Silent star. Born and educated in San Francisco, 5'7" Boland worked as an accountant before becoming an actor in 1907. Six years later, he joined Carl Laemmle's Imp company. In the Twenties he worked for Hal Roach appearing with Harold Lloyd in *The Kid Brother* (1927) as Flash Farrell. His other films included: *The Brotherhood Of Man* (1912), *Sheridan's Pride* (1914), *Jane's Lovers* (1914), *Refugees* (1915), *Fares, Please!* (1915), *No Soup* (1915), *When A Wife Worries* (1916), *Alias Aladdin* (1920), *The Chink* (1921), *Oliver Twist* (1922) as Toby Crackit, *City Girl* (1930) and *Flying Down To Rio* (1933). On May 28, 1921, he married the actress Jean Hope.
CAUSE: He died in Santa Monica, California, aged 51 of a heart attack.

John Boles
Born October 27, 1895
Died February 27, 1969
Versatility personified. Born in Greenville, Texas, 6' John Love Boles, Jr was educated at the University of Texas, graduating in 1917. A pacifist, he nonetheless joined General Pershing's American Expeditionary Forces and later became a spy in Belgium. Boles was the ideal Thirties romantic lead – handsome, dark, and slim with a cleft chin and a trim moustache. He made his first film playing John Brant in *The Sixth Commandment* (1924). He was also Uriah in *So This Is Marriage* (1924) and Lieutenant Shaw in *Excuse Me* (1925). Then Hollywood legend took over and, reportedly, it was Gloria Swanson that saw him singing and dancing on Broadway in *Kitty's Kisses* and signed him to a personal contract. The story has it that he then made his début with Swanson in *Loves Of Sunya* (1927) as Paul Judson. He also appeared with Swanson in *Music In The Air* (1934). In *Back Street* (1932) and *Only Yesterday* (1933) he played respectively Walter Saxel and James Stanton Emerson who were in love with other men's wives and was so convincing that many assumed he was using personal knowledge. He wasn't. In 1917 he married his college sweetheart Marcelita Dobbs by whom he had two daughters, Frances Marcelita and Janet. He actually disliked the roles, having a strong moral code. He became extremely rich through shrewd investments.
CAUSE: John Boles died, aged 73, in San Angelo, Texas from a heart attack. He was buried in the Sanctuary of Serenity of Westwood Memorial Park, Los Angeles County, California.

Ray Bolger
(RAYMOND WALLACE BULCAO)
Born January 10, 1904
Died January 15, 1987
The Scarecrow. Born in Dorchester, Massachusetts, the son of James Edward Bolger and Anne Wallace, Roman Catholic Bolger was raised in an Irish-Jewish neighbourhood and educated at Dorchester High School. After various amateur productions he made his professional début in Boston in 1922 appearing with the Bob Ott Musical Comedy repertory company. He stayed with them for two years when he moved to vaudeville where he was one half of a team called Sanford and Bolger. He also appeared in several Broadway shows as a singer, dancer and comedian. He made his film début in *Carrie Of The Chorus* (1924) but it

would be 12 years before he returned to the screen. In 1935 he signed to make one film at MGM for $20,000 a week for seven weeks. On April 11, 1936, he signed a long-term contract with MGM worth $3,000 a week. He played himself in *The Great Ziegfeld* (1936), the biopic of Florenz Ziegfeld. This was followed by *Rosalie* (1937) in which he played Bill Delroy opposite Eleanor Powell. *Sweethearts* (1938) was his first singing and dancing role and he played opposite Jeanette MacDonald. It was his "wooden shoes" number that brought him to the attention of MGM's bigwigs and in March 1938 he was called into the office of Mervyn Le Roy and told he was to play the part of the Tin Man in *The Wizard Of Oz* (1939). His response was less than enthusiastic. He wanted to be in the film but wanted the role of the Scarecrow which he eventually got. In fact, Bolger quickly realised that he was not cut out for film stardom and a month after *The Wizard Of Oz* he asked to be released from his contract. He later signed for RKO where he made *Sunny* (1941) as Bunny Billings and *Four Jacks And A Jill* (1942) as Nifty. In 1946 he was reunited with Judy Garland at MGM in *The Harvey Girls* (1946) where he played Chris Maule. After a few more films he returned to the theatre where he felt more at home. He won the 1948–49 Tony Award, as well as two Donaldson Awards. On October 8, 1953 he began his own television sitcom *Where's Raymond?* (later changed to *The Ray Bolger Show*) which ran until June 10, 1955. Neither incarnation was very successful. His other films included *Look For The Silver Lining* (1949) as Jack Donahue, *April In Paris* (1952) as S. Winthrop Putnam, *Babes In Toyland* (1961) as Barnaby, *The Daydreamer* (1966) as The Pieman, *The Runner Stumbles* (1979) as Monsignor Nicholson and *Just You And Me, Kid* (1979) as Tom. Bolger's greatest success came in *Where's Charley* (1952) in which he played Charley Wykeham, a role he was to repeat on Broadway and on tour for four years. In 1976 at the age of 72 Bolger spent an hour dancing every morning to keep his joints supple. In 1980 he was elected to the Theatre Hall of Fame. On July 9, 1929, he married Gwendolyn Rickard. They were still together at his death.

CAUSE: Bolger died five days after his 83rd birthday in Los Angeles, California, from cancer. He is buried in the Mausoleum, Crypt F2, Block 35 at Holy Cross Cemetery, Culver City, California.

Beulah Bondi

(BEULAH BONDY)
Born May 3, 1888
Died January 11, 1981
Perennially the old woman. Born in Chicago, Illinois, Bondi made her stage début aged seven in the title role of *Little Lord Fauntleroy*. Three years later, she won a gold medal for her acting. Signed up for a repertory company she earned $25 a week for two years before launching out on her own. She studied at a Catholic college in Montreal, achieving her Bachelor of Arts degree before gaining her Masters at the University of Valparaiso. She first appeared on Broadway in 1925 in *One Of The Family* and later (1929) appeared in the original production of *Street Scene*. Two years later, she was signed to recreate her role in the movie version. She was to return to Broadway only four more times. Bondi never signed a studio contract, which meant she dictated her own conditions and wages – $500 a week, even in 1931. She made 63 films including *Arrowsmith* (1931) as Mrs Tozer, *Rain* (1932) as Mrs Davidson, *Ready for Love* (1934) as Mrs Burke, *Finishing School* (1934) as Miss Van Alstyn, *The Case Against Mrs. Ames* (1936) as Mrs Livinston Ames, *Trail Of The Lonesome Pine* (1936) as Melissa, *The Gorgeous Hussy* (1936) as Rachel Jackson, for which she was Oscar-nominated,

Vivacious Lady (1938) as Mrs Martha Morgan, *Of Human Hearts* (1938) as Mary Wilkins, which again garnered an Oscar nomination, *Mr Smith Goes To Washington* (1939) as Ma Smith, *One Foot In Heaven* (1941) as Mrs Lydia Sandow, *Our Hearts Were Young And Gay* (1944) as Miss Horn, *The Southerner* (1945) as Granny Tucker, *It's A Wonderful Life* (1946) as Ma Bailey, *High Conquest* (1947) as Clara Kingsley, *So Dear To My Heart* (1949) as Granny Kincaid, *A Summer Place* (1959) as Mrs Hamilton Humble, *Tammy Tell Me True* (1961) as Mrs Call and her last appearance reprising Mrs Call in *Tammy And The Doctor* (1963). Her two major disappointments were, she claimed, not failing winning the Oscars but being replaced (by May Robson) in *The Adventures Of Tom Sawyer* (1938) and (by Jane Darwell) in *The Grapes Of Wrath* (1940). She only occasionally appeared on television but won an Emmy for a performance in *The Waltons* in 1977. She was unmarried.
CAUSE: She died in Hollywood from injuries caused when she fell over her cat. She was 92.

Margaret Booth

Born January 16, 1898
Died October 28, 2002
Female techie. Born in Los Angeles, California, her elder brother, (William) Elmer (b. Los Angeles, California, December 9, 1882), a promising actor for D.W. Griffith at Biograph, was killed in Los Angeles on June 16, 1915 when the director Tod Browning drove his car into a freight train on a foggy night. To help the family Margaret Booth was given a job by Griffith as a patcher or film joiner. It was difficult, often tedious, work. Her next job was working for Louis B. Mayer at the Mission Road Studios which also housed the Selig Jungle Zoo. "I once went into the vault to get some film and there was a monkey jumping around," she recalled. "At night a trainer used to take one of those big apes for a walk around our lot. It scared me to death." Respite came when Mayer merged his company with Metro and Sam Goldwyn and Miss Booth (almost no one called her Margaret) moved to Culver City. She stayed behind after all the other workers had left and began to leaf through the discarded rushes. She would cut them together and after a time director John M. Stahl, Mayer's favourite, began to look at her work. "Sometimes he'd take a whole sequence that I had cut and put it in the picture. Then gradually, I got round to making his first cut – and that's how I got to be an editor." Still, in those days before Moviola (introduced in 1924), the work was by hand and painstaking. Booth was fanatical in guarding her privacy and in this regard was seen as a kindred spirit by Greta Garbo. She cut Garbo's film *Mysterious Lady* (1928) and was always allowed on Garbo's closed sets. When Stahl left MGM he asked Booth to go with him but she refused because "MGM was like a home to me". She worked closely with Irving Thalberg and admired his courage. "He knew when something was wrong [and went] in and face[d] it. That's a weakness of today. People do not want to face issues. They want to wait and think it will right itself and it never does." In the Thirties she was editing films like *The Barretts Of Wimpole Street* (1934), *Mutiny On The Bounty* (1935) for which she was nominated for an Oscar and *Romeo And Juliet* (1936). Following Thalberg's death Booth became a supervising editor and never went back to the cutting room. She worked from the projection theatre. Booth spent 30 years at MGM and was feared by many. In the late Sixties she joined Rastar, Ray Stark's company and in 1977 she was awarded an honorary Oscar. Late in life, she opined, "I was pretty difficult at the start, wasn't I?" No one disagreed.

CAUSE: She died in Los Angeles aged 104 of complications following a stroke.

Sam Bottoms
Born October 17, 1955
Died December 16, 2008
Brotherly act. Samuel John Bottoms was born in Santa Barbara, California, the third of four acting brothers. Timothy and Joseph were older and Ben was younger. Sam Bottoms made his film debut by accident. In 1971 when he was 15 he went from his home in Santa Barbara to visit his brother Timothy in Archer City, Texas on the set of *The Last Picture Show* (1971). He was sitting on a street corner drinking a can of Dr Pepper with his brother where the director Peter Bogdanovich spotted him and cast him as Billy, the backward boy who sweeps the streets of the dusty Texas town. 5'11" Bottoms went on to appear in more than 30 films including *Class of '44* (1973) as Marty, *Zandy's Bride* (1974) as Mel Allan, *The Outlaw Josey Wales* (1976) as Jamie, *Up From The Depths* (1979) as Greg Oliver, *Bronco Billy* (1980) as Leonard James, *Prime Risk* (1985) as Bill Yeoman, *Hunter's Blood* (1987) as David Rand, Francis Ford Coppola's *Gardens Of Stone* (1987) as Lieutenant Webber, *After School* (1988) as Father Michael McCarren, *Ragin' Cajun* (1991) as Legs, *Dolly Dearest* (1992) as Elliot Wade, *The Trust* (1993) as James Baker, *Sugar Hill* (1994) as Oliver Thompson, *Joseph's Gift* (1998) as Robert Keller, *The Unsaid* (2001) as Joseph Caffey, *Shadow Fury* (2001) as Mitchell Madsen, *True Files* (2002) as Alex Lomax, *Looking Through Lillian* (2002) as Gene, *Seabiscuit* (2003) as Mr Blodget, *Havoc* (2005) as Lieutenant Maris, *Shopgirl* (2005) as Dan Buttersfield, *Winter Passing* (2005) as Brian, *SherryBaby* (2006) as Bob Swanson Sr and *Finishing the Game: The Search For A New Bruce Lee* (2007) as Martey Kurtainbaum. He was probably most famous for playing Lance Johnson, the surfer turned Vietnam patrol-boat gunner in Francis Ford Coppola's *Apocalypse Now* (1979). Bottoms recalled, "Francis is a great general, he's a General Patton, a General Sherman, a great leader. I was his loyal soldier. I would have done anything he asked. I did, and I'm surprised that I came out of it alive." For his part Coppola said, "He was a handsome, tall young man and very sweet-natured and seemed to be right for that part. He, Larry Fishburne and Fred Forrest were like a young family almost to me [during filming], and they went through thick and thin uncomplainingly. We all admired them. Sam was an especially likable, beautiful young man. He was quiet and undemanding and always anxious to help and had a nice smile." On April 27, 1980 Bottoms married Susan Arnold who was an apprentice film editor on *Apocalypse Now* and fathered two daughters, Clara and Io. The marriage ended in divorce and on September 21, 2002 he married Laura Condé Bickford, an Oscar-nominated film producer.
CAUSE: Bottoms died aged 53 from a brain tumour at his home in Los Angeles.

Chili Bouchier
(DOROTHY IRENE BOUCHER)
Born September 12, 1909
Died September 9, 1999
The British 'It Girl'. Chili (after the song 'I Love My Chili Bom-Bom') Bouchier was born in London and first worked in Harrods, although she was sacked "for allowing myself to be seduced by a senior member of staff". Unusually for an entertainer of the early twentieth century, Bouchier appeared in films before she appeared on the stage. In 1927 she made her foray into films with *A Woman In Pawn*. By the time of her retirement she had appeared in over 60 movies including *Shooting Stars* (1928) in which she played a bathing beauty with

an inordinate number of close-ups, *Dawn* (1928), *Chick* (1928) playing a vamp, *You Know What Sailors Are* (1928), *Brown Sugar* (1931) as Ninon de Veaux, *Carnival* (1931) as Simonetta Steno, *Summer Lightning* (1933) as Sue Brown, *To Be A Lady* (1934) as Diana Whitcombe, *Get Off My Foot* (1935), *Mr Cohen Takes A Walk* (1935), *The Ghost Goes West* (1936) as Cleopatra, *Faithful* (1936) as Pamela Carson, *Mayfair Melody* (1937) as Carmen, *Mr Satan* (1938) as Jacqueline Manet, *The Mind Of Mr Reeder* (1939) as Elsa Weford, *The Case Of Charles Peace* (1948) as Katherine Dyson, *Old Mother Riley's New Venture* (1949) as Cora and *Dead Lucky* (1960) as Mrs. Winston. On September 8, 1930, she appeared as Phyllis in *Open Your Eyes* at the Piccadilly Theatre and was rarely off the stage for the rest of her life. In 1933 she lost the part of Nell Gwyn to Anna Neagle, who was the lover of the director. She was married to Harry Milton, her co-star in *Chick*, in June 1929. They divorced in 1936 after his affair with Jessie Matthews, and Bouchier sank into depression. A relationship with band leader Teddy Joyce that lasted until his death in 1940 did not help, because he was insanely jealous. Bouchier was the first British actress that Hollywood took an active interest in, although Jack Warner was ultimately unable to find a suitable vehicle for her and she returned to London. In 1946 she married actor Peter de Greef (b. 1921); they divorced in 1955. Her third marriage was in 1977 to Australian film director Bluey Hill (d. 1986), 23 years after they moved in together.
CAUSE: She died aged 89 in her London council flat of natural causes.

Clara Bow

Born July 29, 1905
Died September 27, 1965
The original 'It Girl'. Born at 697, Bergen St, Brooklyn, New York, Clara Gordon Bow, the definitive flapper of the Twenties, was the daughter of Robert Bow (1875–1959), a sexually aggressive waiter (who was himself one of 13 children), and Sarah Gordon Bow, an asexual, epileptic, schizophrenic, semi-invalid. Clara was the third daughter born to the Bows: the first two died within days of birth and the first girl's body was dumped in a skip. Clara, also not expected to live, was delivered by her insane maternal grandmother. Presuming death would take her, neither parent bothered to register her birth and so no certificate exists. When Clara was a year old her grandmother was committed to a lunatic asylum and died a year afterwards. Her grandfather moved in and doted on his granddaughter, though this was to provide only a brief spell of happiness for the young Clara. On January 21, 1909, he died following an apoplectic fit suffered in front of the little girl. Afterwards, Clara's mother told her that she wished Clara had died instead of her grandfather. Bow's parents were dirt poor and she was teased mercilessly at infants school, P.S. 111, because of a slight stammer and because she wore her mother's cast-offs: "I was the worst looking kid on the street". In 1918, to avoid the flu epidemic, Robert Bow briefly moved his family to Coney Island. Clara left school, P.S. 98, aged 13 and began working firstly as a hot dog bun slicer and then as a doctor's receptionist. She left when it was revealed that the doctor was in fact an illegal abortionist. In January 1921 she entered a Fame & Fortune Contest in *Motion Picture* magazine, though she did not tell her parents. On September 2 she was given a screen test. Seven days later, she was asked back for another test. Over the next couple of months she was given more tests until just she and one other girl remained. At home Clara finally told her mother what she had been doing over the previous months and Sarah Bow was furious. However, the effect of her mother's anger was

negligible because Clara had won the contest. She made her film début as Virginia Gardener in *Beyond The Rainbow* (1922), although all her scenes were excised before the film's release. (When she became a star they were restored.) Returning home one night after shooting, Clara went to bed only to awake and find her mother standing over her, butcher's knife in hand, threatening to slit her daughter's throat. Sarah Bow then fainted and would have no recollection of her actions afterwards. Later, when the film was finished, she again tried to murder her daughter, chasing her around the apartment brandishing a knife. Clara fled to Coney Island until her father rescued her and brought her back to their home. On February 24, 1922, Sarah Bow was committed to the same asylum her mother had been sent to in 1906. Released in October, she was recommitted on New Year's Eve 1922 and declared terminally insane. She died there aged 43 on January 5, 1923. Back at home, the sexually aggressive Robert Bow was now left alone with his vivacious 16-year-old daughter, who cooked his meals and cleaned his house because she loved him. He returned this love by raping her. Meanwhile, director Elmore Clifford had seen Clara's picture in January 1922's edition of *Motion Picture Classic* and cast her as Dot Morgan in the low-budget *Down To The Sea In Ships* (1922). She played a girl who disguised herself as a boy in order to go to sea. The film received positive reviews and Bow signed to Preferred Pictures in 1923. It was run by B.P. Schulberg. The 5'3½" Clara appeared in a number of steady but unspectacular movies, including *Enemies Of Women* (1923), *Maytime* (1923) as Alice Tremaine, *The Daring Years* (1923) as Mary, *Grit* (1924) as Orchid McGonigle, *Black Oxen* (1924) as Janet Ogelthorpe (after which Schulberg quadrupled her salary to $200 a week), *Poisoned Paradise* (1924)

as Margot LeBlanc, *Daughters Of Pleasure* (1924) as Lila Millas, *Wine* (1924) as bootlegger's daughter Angela Warriner, *Empty Hearts* (1924) as Rosalie, *This Woman* (1924) as Aline Sturdevant (credited in *The New York Times* as "Clare Bow"), *My Lady's Lips* (1925) as Lola Lombard, *Parisian Love* (1925) as Marie, *Eve's Lover* (1925) as Rena DArcy, *Lawful Cheaters* (1925) as Molly Burns, *Free To Love* (1925) as Marie Anthony and *My Lady Of Whims* (1926) as flapper heiress Prudence Severn. Following the release of *The Plastic Age* (1925) in which she portrayed sexy student Cynthia Day, Bow was labelled "the hottest jazz baby in films". While working at Preferred she rented a three-bedroomed bungalow at 7576 Hollywood Boulevard. One bedroom was for Clara and then-boyfriend Artie Jacobson, one for her father and the final one was for her dog! In early November 1925 her contract was transferred to Adolph Zukor's Paramount Pictures at Vine Street, Hollywood, when that company bought out Preferred. Her first film at the new studio was *Dancing Mothers* (1926) playing flapper Kittens Westcourt. *Mantrap* (1926), directed by her lover Victor Fleming, received great reviews. After filming she moved to 261 West Canyon Drive and continued her affairs with Fleming and fiancé Gilbert Roland. In August 1926 she signed a five-year contract with Paramount. That same year her name was to be linked with numerous men, one of whom claimed he had attempted suicide after a one-night stand with Clara. According to a secretary at Paramount: "She took [actor] Larry Gray home with her and when he came out, he could barely stand up." On September 16, 1926, during the filming of *Wings* [1927] in which she played Mary Preston, Clara announced her engagement to Victor Fleming. (Despite rumours, she did not have an affair with co-star Richard Arlen. He married the second female lead Jobyna

Ralston at the completion of shooting.) Clara also, very briefly, reveals her breasts in the film. Look out for the scene one hour and twenty-two minutes into the film. Her name was made when she was dubbed the "It Girl" (from the film *It* (1927) in which she played the part of shop assistant Betty Lou Spence) by author Elinor Glyn (for a $50,000 fee from Paramount). In private Bow referred to Glyn as "that shithead" and when asked exactly what 'It' was replied, "I ain't exactly sure." In November 1926 she began an affair with Gary Cooper and on December 2 she broke off her engagement to Victor Fleming. She told her friend Esther Ralston: "He's so sweet t'me. He always lets me take my dog in the tub when he gives me a bath every mornin'." To Hedda Hopper she was more graphic: "He's hung like a horse and can go all night." However, she continued to see Fleming on the quiet. Clara's star was in the ascendant (she was top female box-office star in 1928 and 1929, yet her studio charged her 25¢ for every photograph she asked for) and she had a new home 512, North Bedford Drive, Beverly Hills. The house has become infamous because it was supposedly the scene for one of Hollywood's most enduring legends. If Kenneth Anger, writing in *Hollywood Babylon*, is to be believed (and he isn't) in 1927 Clara had sex at the house with the entire University of Southern California Trojans football team, the so-called 'Thundering Herd', including the future John Wayne. She certainly let the squad of college football players scrimmage on her front lawn and attend teetotal parties at her house (along with Joan Crawford and Lina Basquette) but entertaining though the orgy rumour undoubtedly is, it simply isn't true. On February 13, 1928, she underwent an appendectomy and it made front-page news. In May 1928 she received 33,727 fan letters, many addressed simply to "The It Girl, Hollywood, USA". However, dramatic though the events had been thus far, Clara Bow's life was to become yet more complicated. On September 22, 1928, her father married her best friend, Tui Lorraine. What Clara didn't know, although virtually everyone else in Tinseltown did, was that Tui was in love with another Bow . . . Clara herself. In the parlance of the day, Tui "was on the lavender side." Robert Bow was soon up to his old tricks again, sleeping with wannabe actresses with the enticing promise of an introduction to Clara and, who knows, possible stardom. With her lesbian lover, Tui discovered her new husband in flagrante delicto and was quickly divorced on the grounds of mental cruelty. However, the split from Robert Bow also meant a split from his daughter, the real object of Tui's passion; they never saw each other again. Clara's next romantic entanglement was with the married Dr William Earl Pearson. It was against Bow's moral code to consort with a married man, but the attraction proved too strong. It was also costly. When Pearson's wife filed for divorce in October 1928 Paramount gave her $30,000 – i.e. three of Clara's $10,000 film bonuses – if she kept Clara's name out of the divorce. Paramount also withheld a $26,000 trust fund set up for Clara when she signed her contract. The films continued. Clara appeared in *Rough House Rosie* (1927) as Rosie O'Reilly (the film cost $225,000 to make and made over $1 million), *Hula* (1927) as heiress Hula Calhoun (directed by Victor Fleming, it signalled the end of her affair with Gary Cooper: "Poor Gary. The biggest cock in Hollywood an' no ass t'push it with."), *Red Hair* (1928) as Bubbles McCoy, *Ladies Of The Mob* (1928) as Yvonne, *The Fleet's In* (1928) as Trixie Deane, *The Wild Party* (1929) as student Stella Ames (Clara's first talkie, it began filming on January 2, 1929, the month she received an astonishing 45,000 fan letters), *Dangerous Curves*

(1929) as bareback rider Pat Delaney, *Love Among The Millionaires* (1930) as Pepper Whipple, *True To The Navy* (1930) as Ruby Nolan, *Her Wedding Night* (1930) as randy film star Norma Martin, and *No Limit* (1931) as Helen 'Bunny' O'Day. And then it was all over. As quickly as Clara Bow rose to become a star she came down to earth with a mighty bump. Clara was not the most popular person in Hollywood – she had made no attempt to disguise her working-class background and never sought to lose her impenetrably thick Brooklyn accent. She was regularly excluded from celebrity functions and when her friend Joan Crawford took up with Douglas Fairbanks, Jr, and was invited to the best social events, she dropped Clara like a hot potato. Other women didn't like her because of her open sexuality (it was also revealed that she menstruated fortnightly) and men were scared of her or wanted to bed her but without anyone else knowing. Around this time Bow met beautiful, bleached blonde Daisy DeVoe (b. Kentucky, 1904, as Daisy DeBoe) and they quickly became friends. DeVoe worked as a hairdresser at Paramount from 1924 although the two women didn't meet until 1927. Following the débâcle of the Pearson divorce, Daisy became Clara's personal secretary. In quick succession Daisy fired Clara's business manager, evicted her cousin and banned her father from access to Clara's bank account. Clara suffered from chronic insomnia (like Marilyn Monroe) and planned to retire once her contract had expired. The problem was money – she didn't have enough to stop working. Daisy sprang into action. In May 1929 she opened a savings account for Clara with $16,000, arranging to add 50% of her weekly salary. Another account was opened for everyday use and Daisy 'paid' Clara a 'wage' of $75 per week. When Clara began an affair with Broadway singer Harry Richman (b. Cincinnati, Ohio,

August 10, 1895, as Harry Reichman, d. Burbank, California, November 3, 1972), her friends were unimpressed. Louise Brooks called him "A ham who exploited her" while Daisy DeVoe labelled him "a scumbag. He used Clara for his fame." The press was outraged at the couple's scandalous behaviour and more so when Richman returned to New York and she moved into his Beechhurst, Long Island, mansion. Back in Hollywood, the tryst almost ended when he caught her visiting old flame Gary Cooper. Instead, Richman wound up giving her a $5,000 engagement ring. On November 20, 1929, at Sylvan Lodge Hospital, Clara was operated on and one of her ovaries was removed. The studio announced she had suffered post-appendectomy problems. Others suspected a breakdown while still others believed she had aborted Richman's child. The last theory was easily disprovable. Richman was sterile. Shortly afterwards, Clara began two-timing Richman again. Her new lover was Guinn 'Big Boy' Williams, a former rodeo star. After a trip to New York to see Richman she returned to California and met the man who was to become her husband. Rex Bell (b. Chicago, Illinois, October 16, 1903, as George Beldam, d. Las Vegas, Nevada, July 4, 1962, from a heart attack) worked as a stunt man at Fox for four years. Then he was cast with Marion Morrison in John Ford's *Salute* (1929). His name was changed to the more Western-sounding Rex Bell and Morrison's was changed to John Wayne. The two men became firm friends. Bell was smitten by Clara and she rather liked him. She dumped Big Boy and gave Richman the cold shoulder. However, Daisy DeVoe didn't like the newcomer in Clara's life. In June 1930 Richman asked for his engagement ring back after Clara flew to Dallas, Texas, to ask Elizabeth Pearson to return her $30,000. Mrs Pearson says she never received the money. It seems likely her husband took the cash. The feud between Rex and Daisy grew more bitter. Overhearing a conversation one day in which Bell said he should manage Clara's affairs, Daisy took the cheque book and locked it in her safety deposit box. Rex discovered it and told Clara Daisy was stealing from her. He had all the locks on the North Bedford Drive house changed and barred Daisy's admission. When Daisy was fired, Clara's savings account contained $249,000. Daisy asked for $125,000 severance pay, threatening to reveal certain things to the press that she knew would wreck Clara's career. Next day she recanted, but by then it was too late. Rex Bell accused her of blackmail and called the police. The police opened the safety deposit box and discovered the cheque book and some jewellery. On November 6, 1930, Daisy was arrested and charged with theft. She countersued for wrongful arrest and asked Clara for $5,000 damages. A Grand Jury was convened and on November 25, 1930, they indicted Daisy on 37 counts of grand theft, based on the number of cheque stubs Daisy had written to herself on Clara's account. Daisy's defence that she paid for everything because Clara did not carry money and then reimbursed herself was not believed. It was almost certainly true, however. *People vs. DeVoe* opened on January 13, 1931, at Los Angeles County Courthouse. Daisy smeared her former best friend in the courtroom. Clara was often drunk. Clara threatened to murder Daisy. Clara was promiscuous (this one was true, but not by today's standards). Clara blackmailed her father. When it was Clara's turn to testify she could so easily have flung dirt at Daisy. Daisy's father was in prison. Her boyfriend was the Chinese cameraman James Wong Howe – miscegenation was highly discouraged at the time and that revelation would have wrecked Howe's career and won the case for Clara.

However, Clara kept her counsel over those matters. She broke down in the witness box but received no sympathy from Daisy. On January 23, 1931, DeVoe was found not guilty on 34 counts but guilty on one. Even then Clara wrote to the District Attorney, begging him to ask the judge for mercy. He didn't show any and Daisy was sent down for 18 months. The damage to Clara's career had been done. On March 28, the *Coast Reporter* ran the first of four articles that defamed Bow in no uncertain terms. They claimed that she slept with any man who took her fancy, including a cousin. If men were unavailable, she allegedly bedded women and was reported to have indulged in a threesome with two Mexican whores; if there were no women around she reportedly had sex with animals. The articles also alleged that Clara had a serious gambling problem, was an alcoholic and drug addict. No journalist had the guts to sign his name to the exposé (although on July 31, 1931, the editor was jailed for eight years for distributing obscene material through the post). Bow's mental health began to suffer and on June 8, Paramount announced her contract had been terminated. (Production chief B.P. Schulberg had already given Bow's dressing room to his new protégée and lover, Sylvia Sidney.) Clara made two more films, *Call Her Savage* (1932) as Texas heiress Nasa 'Dynamite' Springer and *Hoopla* (1933) as dancer Lou but they were not successful and she retired to raise a family. She had married Rex Bell in Las Vegas on December 3, 1931. They had two sons: 6'5" Rex Larbow 'Tony' (b. Santa Monica Hospital, December 16, 1934) and 5'9" George Francis Robert (b. June 14, 1938); Clara had one miscarriage in-between. On September 3, 1937, Clara opened the "It Café", a restaurant at 1637 Vine Street, Hollywood. It was not a roaring success and closed after less than a month. In the Forties Rex and Clara drifted apart. He became interested in Republican politics. From 1954 until 1963 he was Lieutenant-Governor of Nevada. In 1943 she attempted suicide. Following the death of her favourite actress Marilyn Monroe, Clara said in a comment that said much about her own experiences: "Being a sex symbol is a heavy load to carry, especially when one is very tired, hurt and bewildered."

CAUSE: Bow and Bell separated in 1950, the year after she was diagnosed schizophrenic, and she moved to Los Angeles, renting a two-bedroomed bungalow at 12214 Aneta Street. She was looked after by a trained nurse, although when her sons came to stay she showed no outward signs of mental illness. With the nurse she would keep abreast of new films via drive-in cinemas. Her favourites were Marilyn Monroe and Marlon Brando. Former lovers Gilbert Roland and, for a time, Harry Richman visited. In 1961 Clara became a grandmother. The following year she made her first public appearance in 15 years at the funeral of Rex Bell. He left her nothing in his will; everything went to his lover and two sons. Clara's privacy was protected by her mostly Japanese neighbours. When fans or tourists came a-calling, they would pretend not to understand English. Clara Bow died of a heart attack at 12.07am in her Los Angeles home. She was 60 years old. She was buried next to her husband in Forest Lawn Memorial-Park's Freedom Mausoleum, Arlington Road, Glendale, California 91209. She planned her own funeral, even determining her make-up and coffin lining which would be "either satin or silk . . . preferably in apricot or eggshell." Many of Clara's films were destroyed or neglected. Silent film buffs still hope many will turn up in some long-lost archive. However, they are not optimistic.

FURTHER READING: *Clara Bow: Runnin'* *Wild* – David Stenn (New York: Doubleday, 1988).

Charley Bowers
Born 1889
Died November 26, 1946
'Bricolo'. Born in Cresco, Iowa, Charles R. Bowers got his start in show business supposedly at the tender age of six when he was kidnapped by circus performers. He developed a high wire act and also began designing and drawing the publicity material. He began acting in rep before becoming a cartoonist for the *Chicago Tribune And Star*. In 1916 he went into business with the illustrator Raoul Barré but within two years he had taken over. He co-wrote and co-directed 12 live animation Whirlwind Comedies with H.L. Muller. He drew more than 100 cartoons in 1926 including the *Mutt & Jeff* series for Pathé-Freres. That year he developed a photographic process, revolutionary for the time, by which he could incorporate incredible special effects into his films. In 1926 and 1927 he made 12 comedies for R-C Pictures. In 1928 he made another six for Educational. He played an eccentric or ne'er-do-well and based his character on Charlie Chaplin, Buster Keaton and Harry Langdon. In later years he wrote and illustrated children's books and when he fell ill he trained his wife, Winifred Leyton, to take his place. Bricolo was how he was known in France.

CAUSE: He died, aged 57, in Paterson, New Jersey, after a long illness.

Cliff Bowes
Born November 14, 1894
Died July 6, 1929
Silent funnyman. Born in Colorado, Clifford W. Bowes came to prominence with his own series of comedies for Educational usually playing an accident-prone husband. He appeared in almost 50 films including: *Cactus Nell* (1917), *Are Waitresses Safe?* (1917), *Good Little Brownie* (1920), *Up*

In Mary's Attic (1920), *Back Stage* (1921), *Should Stepmothers Trifle?* (1921), *Between Showers* (1923), *Wrecks* (1923), *West Is West* (1923), *Out Bound* (1924) as Matthew, *Fun's Fun* (1925), *Brotherly Love* (1926) and *Ship Shape* (1926).
CAUSE: Unknown.

Betty Box, OBE
Born September 25, 1915
Died January 15, 1999
Rank's First Lady. Betty Evelyn Box was born at 283 Beckenham Road, Beckenham, Kent, the youngest of the five children of Frank Edward Box (d. 1939) and Eva Annie Dowling. Her eldest brother was the film producer Sydney Box (b. Beckenham, Kent, April 29, 1907, d. Perth, May 25, 1983). She went to Balgowan Primary School, Sydenham, Bromley Road Elementary School, Beckenham, and the Girls' Elementary School, Beckenham. On leaving full-time education she trained as a commercial artist, and in the early Thirties flirted with left-wing politics and joined the Young Communists. Three days after the outbreak of the Second World War, she married a car mechanic called Victor Albert Langfeld Taylor but they were divorced four years later. She joined Verity Films at the behest of her brother and contributed to more than 200 documentaries. She moved to Gainsborough in 1946 and made a dozen films there including *Miranda* (1948) and *Here Come The Huggetts* (1948). On Christmas Eve 1948 she married the film producer Peter Rogers and the following year she met the director Ralph Thomas and formed a partnership for the Rank Organisation at Pinewood that lasted from 1949 to 1979. The films were so successful she was nicknamed 'Betty Box Office'. On a train one day she was reading Richard Gordon's novel *Doctor In The House* and realised its film potential. The 1954 version became one of the biggest hits of the decade. It led to six sequels.

She was offered the first James Bond film but did not think that she was the right person for the project and declined. In 1958 Box was awarded the OBE for her services to the film industry. Ironically, following the gong her films began to lose some commercial viability. Her last films included the sex comedies *The Love Ban* (1970), *Percy* (1971) and *Percy's Progress* (1974).
CAUSE: She died of cancer at her home, The Oaks, Manor Lane, Gerrards Cross, Buckinghamshire. Her autobiography, *Lifting The Lid*, was published posthumously in 2000. She left £2,811,251 gross; £2,775,011 net.

Bill Boyd
Born September 29, 1910
Died December 7, 1977
The cowboy rambler. Boyd, who was born in Fannin County, Texas, is perhaps better known for his singing than the half dozen films he made in 1942 for PRC. He had been a regular performer with his younger brother, Jim (b. Fannin County, Texas, September 28, 1914), on the wireless from 1926. He was given his own show on WRR-Dallas in 1932 and in 1934 began recording for Bluebird. PRC decided that they needed a singing cowboy and teamed Boyd with Art Davis and Lee Powell for a short series of pictures. As was normal for this genre, Boyd, Davis and Powell all played a character with the same name as themselves. The films were *Texas Manhunt* (1942), *Raiders Of The West* (1942) for which he contributed a song, *Rolling Down The Great Divide* (1942) for which he wrote a number of songs, *Tumbleweed Trail* (1942) for which he also wrote a number of songs, *Prairie Pals* (1942) and *Along The Sundown Trail* (1942). He had two Top 10 hits on *Billboard*'s country chart in the mid-Forties: 'Shame On You' which reached number four in 1945 and 'New Steel Guitar Rag' which

peaked at number five the following year. Bill Boyd retired from the music business in 1950.

CAUSE: Boyd died, aged 67, at his ranch in Dallas, Texas.

William Boyd
Born June 5, 1895
Died September 12, 1972
Western hero. Born in Hendrysburg, Ohio, William Lawrence Boyd is one of those actors known just for one role (one that he began playing at the age of 40) even though he had been making films since 1915. The role, of course, was that hero of the West, Hopalong Cassidy, a character created by pulp writer Clarence E. Mulford. Cassidy, called Hopalong because of a slight limp, was a teetotal, non-smoker who didn't swear and would never draw his gun in anger. He was also the only goodie to wear black, made even more dramatic by Boyd's prematurely white hair. The actor was often cast by Cecil B. DeMille but it looked as if his career might be over when in 1933 another actor called William Boyd was involved in an unsavoury incident and this William Boyd's picture appeared in the newspapers. Boyd was released by RKO and took to drinking heavily to drown his sorrow at the injustice of it all. A sturdy 6', Boyd began playing Hopalong in 1935 and went on to portray him in 66 films, making himself a small fortune in the process. He was married four times and to four actresses: Ruth Miller (from 1921 until 1924; their son, his only child, died aged 9 months), Elinor Fair (married Santa Ana, California January 13, 1926, divorced 1930; she was born in Richmond, Virginia, on December 21, 1903, and died in Seattle, Washington on April 26, 1957), 5'3" Dorothy Sebastian (married 1930, divorced May 29, 1936; she was born in Birmingham, Alabama, on April 26, 1903, and died in Hollywood on April 8, 1957) and from June 5, 1937, until his death to blonde Grace Bradley.

CAUSE: He died aged 74 in South Coast Community Hospital, Laguna Beach, California, the result of a combination of Parkinson's disease and congestive heart failure. When he tried to join the army to fight in World War I, he was turned down because of a heart problem. He was buried in the Sanctuary of Sacred Promise at Forest Lawn Memorial-Parks, 1712 Glendale Avenue, Glendale, California 91209.

Charles Boyer
Born August 28, 1899
Died August 26, 1978
Gallic charmer. Boyer was born weighing 2.2kg, an only child, in Figeac, France. His father sold farm machinery and died before Charles was ten. After studying at the Sorbonne and the Paris Conservatory, Boyer made his stage début in *Les Jardins Des Marcie* in 1920 in the French capital. That same year the 5'9" Boyer made his first film, *L'Homme Du Large*, followed by *Chantelouve* (1921), *L'Esclave* (1923) and *Le Grillon Du Foyer* (1923), but he didn't become a success in the cinema of his native land so he travelled to America where he made French versions of American films. His film début Stateside came in *The Magnificent Lie* (1931). He appeared in two English language films, *The Man From Yesterday* (1932) opposite Claudette Colbert and *Red-Headed Woman* (1932) with Jean Harlow before disappointedly returning to France. Back at home he threw himself into films and plays before getting the call to return to the land of the free where he was promoted as 'the new Valentino' at Fox Studios. The appellation didn't quite stick, perhaps because he was bald (he wore a toupee on screen) and pot-bellied. He moved to other studios, appearing as a doctor in *Private Worlds* (1935) again opposite Claudette Colbert, as Napoleon in *Conquest* (1937) with Greta Garbo, as thief Pépé Le Moko in *Algiers* (1938)

playing with Hedy Lamarr and in *Gaslight* (1944) alongside Ingrid Bergman. The last three films all won him Oscar nominations. *Algiers* was Lamarr's first American film and it made her a star and launched a new fashion with her white turban. Boyer wasn't impressed; he moaned that she couldn't act. One of the most famous cinematic sayings is linked to the film, but Boyer never actually said, "Come wiz me to ze Casbah." On St Valentine's Day 1934, he eloped to Yuma, Arizona, and married actress Pat Paterson (b. Bradford, Yorkshire, April 7, 1911), 22 days after they met. A son, Michael Charles, was born on December 9, 1943. Theirs was a supremely happy marriage. During World War II Boyer worked with other stars to raise money for the Allies. In 1942 he was presented with a special Oscar for "his progressive cultural achievement in establishing the French Research Foundation in Los Angeles as a source of reference for the Hollywood motion picture industry." In 1961 he was again nominated for an Oscar for his role in *Fanny* and spent much of the Sixties on either Broadway or the West End stage. On September 23, 1965, his son, believing himself a loser, committed suicide in his Coldwater Canyon home, 1861 Heather Court, with a .38 calibre revolver. The memorial service was attended by only family and close friends including actors Van Heflin and Gig Young, himself to die in similar circumstances. The Boyers never came to terms with their only child's premature death. They sold their Californian home and rarely returned to the state. Charles Boyer's 47th and last American film was *A Matter Of Time* (1976) with Liza Minnelli.
CAUSE: In the Seventies Boyer went for a health check-up and suggested his wife did the same. Pat Boyer was diagnosed with inoperable colon and liver cancer and was given a year to live. Boyer kept this from her and the couple moved to Paradise Valley, Scottsdale, Arizona, for what she believed was *his* health. Boyer read constantly to his wife as she became sicker. On August 24, 1978, at 3am, she died aged 67 of the disease as Boyer held her hand. Boyer was grief-stricken and two days later he took an overdose of Seconal. He died in hospital in Phoenix. He was buried next to his wife and son in Holy Cross Cemetery & Mausoleum, 5835 West Slauson Avenue, Culver City, California 90230 on what would have been his 79th birthday.
FURTHER READING: *Charles Boyer: The Reluctant Lover* – Larry Swindell (New York: Doubleday, 1983).

Alice Brady

Born November 2, 1892
Died October 28, 1939
Cinematic mother. Born in New York, the daughter of producer William Aloysius Brady (b. San Francisco, California, June 19, 1863, d. New York, January 6, 1950) and Rose Marie René who died in 1896 when Alice was three. She was educated in a convent school in Madison, New Jersey and at the New England Conservatory of Music where she trained to become an opera singer. With her father working in the business it was no surprise that Alice entered the world of entertainment, although he actively discouraged her ambitions. She made her Broadway début in a minor role in his 1910 production of *The Mikado*, appeared under an assumed name in *The Balkan Princess* the following year, and in 1912, using her real name, she won wide acclaim in *Little Women*. She moved into films in 1914 with *As Ye Sow*, playing Dora Leland. Before Mary Pickford overtook her, Brady was the highest paid film actress in Hollywood and also maintained her stage career. She appeared in almost 80 films, many for her father's company, over 25 years. Her early films included: *The Gilded Cage* (1914) as Princess

Honore, *La Bohème* (1916) as Mimi,
Betsy Ross (1917) as Betsy Griscom and
Woman And Wife (1918) as Jane Eyre.
In 1918 she returned to Broadway in
the play *Forever After* and enjoyed great
successes in *Zander The Great* (1923),
Old Mama (1925), *The Bride Of The
Lamb* (1926), Eugene O'Neill's
Mourning Becomes Electra (with Alla
Nazimova – 13 years older – playing
her daughter!) (1931), *Mademoiselle*
(1932) and many more plays. She
made no films between 1923 and 1933,
returning to appear in *When Ladies
Meet* (released June 23, 1933) as
Bridgie Drake. Her later films included
The Gay Divorcee (October 12, 1934)
as Aunt Hortense, *Gold Diggers Of 1935*
(March 15, 1935), *Three Smart Girls*
(1936) as Mrs Lyons, *Go West Young
Man* (November 13, 1936) as Mrs
Struthers, *One Hundred Men And A
Girl* (September 5, 1937) as Mrs Frost
and her last film *Young Mr Lincoln*
(May 30, 1939) as Abigail Clay. She
was twice nominated for a Best
Supporting Actress Oscar – for *My
Man Godfrey* (September 6, 1936) as
Angelica Bullock and *In Old Chicago*
(January 6, 1938) as Tyrone Power's
mother Molly O'Leary, for which she
won. She was unable to attend the
ceremony because she had broken an
ankle on March 10, 1938 at the
Biltmore Bowl in LA's Biltmore Hotel.
An unknown man walked up and
accepted the award on her behalf. After
the show, he and the golden statuette
were never seen again. On March 22
the Academy presented Brady with a
replacement trophy. In 1919 she
married the actor James L. Crane
(b. Rantoul, Illinois, August 9, 1889,
d. San Gabriel, June 2, 1968) and by
him had a son, Donald, but they
divorced in 1922.
CAUSE: Alice Brady died of cancer,
aged 46, in New York. She was buried
next to the kerb in plot Gibeon 57,
of Sleepy Hollow Cemetery in
Westchester County, Tarrytown, New
York.

Wilfrid Brambell
Born March 22, 1912
Died January 18, 1985
'Dirty old man'. Henry Wilfrid
Brambell was born at 6 Edenvale Road,
Rathgar, County Dublin, one of at least
two sons of Henry Lytton Brambell, a
cashier at the Guinness brewery, and
his wife, Edith Marks (b. *circa* 1879),
who was an opera singer. He made his
first appearance on stage in November
1914 entertaining the troops in the
First World War. After attending
Kingstown Grammar School, he
became a journalist for *The Irish Times*
before turning part-time to the Abbey
Theatre in Dublin where he was paid
ten shillings a week. Deciding he
preferred the roar of the crowd to the
clack of the typewriter, he left
journalism and began acting full-time
at the Gate Theatre, also in Dublin.
During the Second World War he
performed with ENSA. He appeared in
several plays and pantomimes including
making his Broadway début in the
musical *Kelly* which opened at the
Broadhurst Theater on February 6,
1965. It was the true-life story of Steve
Brodie who may or may not have
jumped off the Brooklyn Bridge in the
1880s. Among those who rejected the
title role were Richard Harris, Gene
Kelly and Frank Gorshin (later to find
fame as The Riddler in *Batman*). Anita
Gillette was signed to play the leading
female part. (Like Gorshin she, too,
would find fame on TV, as Dr Emily
Hanover, wife of *Quincy, M.E.*) Like
many shows the reviews were terrible.
One read, "Ella Logan was written
out of *Kelly* before it reached the
Broadhurst Theater Saturday night.
Congratulations Miss Logan." The
show closed the same night. Brambell
found lasting fame as the "dirty old
man" Albert Steptoe in the hit sitcom
Steptoe And Son, about father and son
rag and bone men. The series ran from
June 14, 1962 until December 26,
1974 and also spawned a couple of
unsuccessful film versions, *Steptoe And*

Son (1972) and *Steptoe And Son Ride Again* (1974). To play the dishevelled Albert, Brambell wore a special set of worn-down, blackened false teeth that he kept in a glass of gin and tonic. Brambell also appeared in *The Thirty-Nine Steps* (1935), *Another Shore* (1948), *Dry Rot* (1956) as a tar man, *What A Whopper!* (1961) as a postman, *Flame In The Streets* (1961), *The Boys* (1962) as Robert Brewer, *In Search Of The Castaways* (1962) as Bill Gaye, *The Three Lives Of Thomasina* (1963) as Willie Bannock, *A Hard Day's Night* (1964) playing John McCartney, Paul's grandfather, a train guard on *Where The Bullets Fly* (1966), *Witchfinder General* (1968), *Carry On Again Doctor* (1969) as Mr Pullen, *Holiday On The Buses* (1974) as Bert Thompson, who romances Stan's mum, *The Adventures Of Picasso* (1978) as Alice B. Toklas and Uncle Jocelyn in *The Island Of Adventure* (1978). In 1955 he divorced his wife of seven years, Molly Josephine, after she became pregnant by their lodger, Roderick Fisher, and gave birth to a son, Michael. She apparently died in 1956. He claimed that he forsook sex for ten years after that. However, on November 22, 1962 he was arrested outside a public lavatory on Shepherd's Bush Green in London for importuning for immoral purposes. At his trial in December Brambell denied he was gay (although his homosexuality was well known to the police and in show business) and claimed that he was drunk at a BBC cocktail party and decided to walk a quarter of a mile to find a taxi to take him home to Acton. He visited two lavatories in quick succession because he was "extremely fuddled" and "it was necessary". Luckily for him, the magistrates believed his feeble defence and he received a conditional discharge and was ordered to pay 25 guineas in costs. From 1969 until his death he lived with Yussof Ben mat Saman. CAUSE: Wilfrid Brambell died of cancer in Westminster Hospital, London. He

was 72. He left his flat in Pimlico and his entire £170,720 fortune, apart from three rings which went to his brother James, to his Chinese boyfriend, Yussof Saman.

Marlon Brando
Born April 3, 1924
Died July 1, 2004
The mumbler. A tight, white T-shirt may not have kick-started Marlon Brando, Jr's career but it certainly typified his early cinematic image – ironically, at the end of his life he would have needed several T-shirts to cover his enormous bulk. Born just before midnight in Omaha Maternity Hospital, Nebraska, Marlon Brando, Jr, was the youngest of three children and the only son of Marlon Brando (b. January 11, 1895, d. July 18, 1965), a notorious philanderer and manufacturer of chemical feedstuffs and insecticides, and an alcoholic mother, Dorothy, known as Dodie, Pennebaker Myers (b. Grand Island, Nebraska, January 20, 1897, d. Huntington Memorial Hospital, March 31, 1954 with Marlon holding her hand). His parents married on June 22, 1918. As a boy, Brando was nicknamed 'Bud' while his sister Jocelyn became 'Tiddy' (b. San Francisco, California, November 18, 1919, m. Dan Hanmer) and Frances 'Fran' or 'Franny' (b. September 1922, m. Richard Loving, d. April 2, 1994). In 1927 the family moved to 1026 South Second Street, a larger house in a nicer part of town, but his childhood was blighted by his father's indifference and his mother's drinking. "He enjoyed telling me I couldn't do anything right. He had a habit of telling me I would never amount to anything," recalled Brando in his autobiography, *Songs My Mother Taught Me* (1994). Brando's favourite place to be was the monkey house at the local zoo where young Bud spent many hours watching the apes. His mother had founded the Omaha Community Playhouse not

long before Bud was born and she starred in many of the productions and on occasion roped her husband in to tread the boards. Jocelyn Brando was to complain that her mother's involvement with the theatre meant that she became a virtual surrogate mother to Franny and Bud. An assistant director at the Playhouse was later to become well known in his own right. Henry Fonda repaid Dodie Brando's kindness by recommending Jocelyn for the only female part in the Broadway play *Mister Roberts* in which he starred. In 1930 the family moved to 1044 Judson Avenue, Evanston, Illinois, when Marlon, Sr. landed a new job. Bud began to attend Lincoln School on the corner of Main and Forest and the family moved to 524 Sheridan Square. A classmate of Brando's was Wally Cox and they began a close friendship that would last – apart from a 14-year gap from the ages of eight until 22 – until Cox's death. In 1936 after discovering another woman's lipstick on her husband's underwear, Dodie Brando drank herself into a temper and attacked her husband. In 1938 Brando had his first date with a plain girl. His grandmother was to tell Truman Capote, "Ah, Bud. He always went for the ugly ones." By this time he had become fat so his father bought him a set of dumbbells and insisted that Bud train daily. Brando was also becoming an unruly pupil so Marlon, Sr. decided to send him, in September 1941, to his own alma mater, Shattuck Military Academy in Faribault, Minnesota. At the strictly disciplined school, which he hated, Brando honed his 5′8″ physique to 11 stone 2lbs. He joined the Crack Squad, a precision drill team which his father had been a member of in 1916. It was one of the few times that Brando, Sr. appreciated his son. Bud was to ruin the appreciation by pretending to be lame to get out of the Crack Squad and then compounding his misdemeanour by bunking off. He

was expelled. Bud also joined the Shattuck Players. To compound his father's disappointment at Bud being expelled from military school, he was also rated 4F at his draft medical. Brando was to later claim that he had psychologically outwitted the medic who examined him, although his rating may have had to do with an American football injury. Brando began work as a labourer for the Tile Drainage and Construction Company in Libertyville, Illinois, but digging ditches was not for him and, aged 19 at the end of May 1943, he headed to New York where Jocelyn was already enjoying a measure of success. Their father did not approve, describing acting as a profession for "faggots or fairies". Brother and sister shared an apartment in Patchin Place in Greenwich Village and he began seeing a dark-haired girl called Cecilia d'Artuniaga Webb. To support himself Brando worked as a lemonade seller on Fifth Avenue and a lift attendant in Best's department store. Then he enrolled at the Dramatic Workshop of the New School for Social Research (founded 1940) under the direction of the veteran director, Erwin Piscator. Other students would include Harry Belafonte, Tony Curtis, Ben Gazzara, Walter Matthau, Rod Steiger, Elaine Stritch, Shelley Winters and the playwright Tennessee Williams. Brando also studied under Stella Adler, a leading teacher of the Method school of acting; she became a formative influence. She later said, "I taught him nothing. I opened possibilities of thinking, feeling, experience, and I opened the doors that he walked right through. He never needed me after that . . . He lives the life of an actor 24 hours a day. If he is talking to you, he will absorb everything about you, your smile, the way your teeth grow. His style is the perfect marriage of intuition and intelligence." On October 29, 1943, Brando began appearing in Dramatic Workshop productions and his first was Shaw's *St Joan*. Thus began a steady stream of work that only let up briefly for Christmas. On February 2, 1944, her birthday, he dated Elaine Stritch who had fallen madly in love with Brando at first sight. He took the devoutly Catholic, still virgin Stritch to a library, then to a synagogue, a Presbyterian church, then to Russian and Greek Orthodox ones before a Greenwich Village restaurant, where she drank so much she couldn't eat anything, before finishing the night at a seedy nightclub. They returned to Brando's apartment where he allowed Stritch to play with his cat while he changed into pyjamas. With this she fled and rushed back to the convent where she was living, an hour after curfew. When Elaine told Mother Superior what had happened, she was advised to "say a prayer to Our Lady and she'll straighten you out". In March and April 1944, Brando's wilful, independent streak resurfaced and he missed 17 performances in 34 days. In spite of his lack of application, Brando was signed to the MCA agency and on October 19, 1944 he made his début in *I Remember Mama*. For a joke, he had told the programme writer that he had been born in Calcutta and left when he was six months old – thus an early Brando myth was born. Most of the critics ignored Brando although Robert Garland of *The New York Journal-American* described him as "charming". Again the inability to concentrate on anything for long periods of time affected Brando's performances. To avoid what he saw as the tedium of doing the same play over and over again, he developed a habit that would last for the rest of his life of rearranging his lines or walking across the stage when least expected. Naturally, this angered older members of the cast. Brando played a trick on his co-star Oscar Homolka on stage, by replacing the sugar that he was to put in his coffee with salt. Homolka spat out the confection and did not speak to

him for several months. On March 2, 1946, at the Belasco Theater, he opened in *Truckline Café*. Brando played Sage McCrae, a Second World War veteran who murders his unfaithful wife, Tory. Karl Malden was also in the cast and Elia Kazan, who had wanted Burgess Meredith for the part of Sage because he did not rate Brando, directed the play. Although the audiences enjoyed the work and were wowed by Brando's performance the critics did not share their enthusiasm and the play closed a week later. Next came Bernard Shaw's *Candida*, as Marchbanks, a play that even his father flew to New York for the opening night on April 3, 1946. His performance in *A Flag Is Born* (about the birth of Israel) was directed by Luther Adler and starred Paul Muni. It opened on September 5, 1946. Around this time Brando renewed his friendship with Wally Cox, his boyhood chum. Brando had become bulkier thanks to his weightlifting and Cox was of slight build. Brando became his friend, confidant, bodyguard and lover. Hollywood historian Kenneth Anger spent years tracking down a photograph purporting to show Brando administering oral sex to Cox. Brando's friend Carlo Fiore (b. Brooklyn, New York, June 19, 1919, d. Veteran's Memorial Hospital, Westwood, Los Angeles, August 11, 1978, aged 59 from drink and drug abuses) described an occasion when Brando grabbed hold of his penis and claimed that he had thought he was in bed with a woman. Brando appeared opposite Tallulah Bankhead in *The Eagle Has Two Heads* but regretted it ever after. She insisted on "auditioning" him and tried to seduce him but her age and bad breath from smoking and drinking put him off. Undeterred she again attempted a seduction in his dressing room during rehearsals. On opening night she made her third assault on the Brando body and was rebuffed for the third time. He then irritated her by regularly breaking wind outside her dressing room. He asked his agent to get him out of the play and, when his wish was granted, Tallulah put it around that Brando was unprofessional and untalented. The role that was to make Brando's name, that of Stanley Kowalski in *A Streetcar Named Desire* almost escaped him – the producers originally wanted John Garfield for the Broadway production. He turned it down when the producers refused his demands: to be allowed to leave the production at any time to make a film, a guarantee that he would have the role in any movie version and a commitment to the stage for only a few months. Next in the frame was Burt Lancaster but Hal Wallis refused to release him. The director, Elia Kazan, was not enthusiastic about Brando but agreed to let him read. That was the least of his problems. At the time, to preserve his privacy Brando did not have a phone at home and used the payphone in the lobby of his building. When he finally read, Kazan thought Brando would make an interesting Stanley Kowalski and sent him to the author Tennessee Williams. It took Brando three days to reach Williams' Cape Cod home from New York and when he finally arrived the playwright was furious at being kept waiting. But when he saw Brando the part was finally cast. He even loaned Brando the $20 train fare back to New York. During rehearsals Brando began dating the sexy and then slim Shelley Winters. The play, which had originally been called *The Poker Night*, opened on December 3, 1947 with Brando playing opposite Jessica Tandy. His fee was $550 a week. Theatrical history was made that night – usually actors enunciated their lines clearly. Brando deliberately slurred his words. It was an innovative approach that was to set the tone for the whole of the next decade and the audience gave Brando a standing ovation. Despite a plethora of film offers Brando had no intention of moving to the West Coast. Nor did he

wish to play the celeb game, eschewing press interviews and refusing requests for pictures. He also lived in a dingy room on 52nd Street and shared a filthy bathroom with the other residents. His only indulgence was a gramophone on which he constantly played Gene Krupa records loudly. Eventually, the lure of Tinseltown became too great. In July 1950, under Fred Zinnemann's direction, Brando made his screen début in *The Men* playing a paraplegic war veteran, a role to which he brought an astonishing physical force. To prepare for the part, he spent six weeks observing real casualties at the Veterans' Hospital in Van Nuys, California. He either spent the day in bed or wheeled himself around in a wheelchair. He spent time with the paraplegics in bars in his wheelchair. Then he reprised on the screen his powerful performance in *A Streetcar Named Desire* (1951) opposite Vivien Leigh. Filmed between August 14 and mid-October 1950, the film required 68 rewrites from the stage version to appease the various censorious bodies. Blanche's nymphomania was toned down and mentions of her first husband's homosexuality excised. Brando and Lady Olivier did not get on at first. She was ill with tuberculosis and retired early, sometimes at only 9pm. He was irritated by her habit of saying "Good morning" or "Good afternoon" the first time she saw him and her constant "pleases" and "thank yous". One day he turned on her, "Why are you so fucking polite?" Gradually, he softened towards her and she adopted some of his acting skills to give one of the best performances of her career. Elia Kazan wrote about his portrayal of the animally magnetic, uncouth, slobbish Kowalski, "If there is a better performance by a man in the history of film in America, I don't know what it is." Brando suffered during filming – Karl Malden playing Mitch accidentally dislocated Brando's right shoulder in one scene when he pushed him under a shower. Brando also hurt his knees begging Stella Kowalski (Kim Hunter) not to leave him. His performance received his first (of eight) Academy Award nominations, although he lost out to Humphrey Bogart for *The African Queen* when Greer Garson announced the winner. Of the top four acting awards Brando was the only *Streetcar* star to miss out. On March 20, 1952 co-stars Vivien Leigh (Best Actress), Karl Malden (Best Supporting Actor) and Kim Hunter (Best Supporting Actress) all went home from the RKO Pantages Theater in Hollywood clutching Oscars. That same year Brando acquired a pet racoon called Russell, named for a boyhood friend of Wally Cox. Everyone apart from Brando hated the animal which was decidedly un-housetrained and would leave its mess everywhere in Brando's home. When the creature crawled onto the window ledge and hung by its claws every one of Brando's friends hoped Russell would fall to his death. Instead Brando summoned the fire brigade to rescue the animal. Wally Cox also moved in with Brando and the pair would spend the weekends cheating at Monopoly. Brando was a Mexican revolutionary in *Viva Zapata!* (1952), despite the opposition of studio chief Darryl F. Zanuck who disliked Brando's mumbling. Zanuck favoured Tyrone Power or Anthony Quinn for the role but director Elia Kazan stood firm. Zanuck even sent Kazan a telegram stating: "I DON'T UNDERSTAND A GODDAMNED THING THE SON OF A BITCH SAYS. CAN'T YOU STOP HIM FROM MUMBLING?" Eventually, Zanuck relented and Brando received $100,000 to play Zapata. Ever the perfectionist Brando grew a thick bushy moustache for the part only to have it trimmed to more manageable proportions at the studio's insistence. Quinn was to play Brando's brother but the two did not gel. Remembered Quinn, "I didn't feel totally comfortable with Marlon. Our

egos just didn't jibe." Mumbling, jibing or not, Brando received his second Oscar nod and his second defeat, losing to Gary Cooper in *High Noon*. In the summer of 1952 Wally Cox moved out, unable to stand Russell the racoon any longer. Brando then played Johnny, the leader of a gang of motorcyclists in *The Wild One* (1953) which was considered so powerful and inflammatory that the film was banned in Britain for 15 years. It is remembered especially for an exchange in which Brando, asked what he is rebelling against, replies, "Whaddaya got?" The film was shot in just 24 days over the summer of 1953 and Brando improvised some of the scenes despite the director's initial reluctance to let him. Brando and co-star Lee Marvin (who played Chino) did not get on and by the end of the shoot had nicknames for each other – Marlow Brandy and Lee Moron. *The Wild One* was not a box office smash but it did have a cultural influence, with many youths of the time adopting a Brando style. The film was based on a true story when the small Californian municipality of Hollister was taken over on July 4, 1947 by 4,000 bikers, who vandalised the entire town. In fact, the film was such a disappointment that Brando seriously talked of retirement. He claimed that the farm in Nebraska he had invested his money in would yield more than enough income for him to survive on, but it was a financial disaster. In July 1953 Brando toured in the Shavian play *Arms And The Man*, beginning at the Theater-by-the Sea in Matunuck, Rhode Island. The tour was not a great success – most of the company were Brando's friends and they lacked much of the finesse needed to handle Shaw's work. Still, it gave Brando a respite from the flop that was *The Wild One*. Shakespeare was the next to get the Brando treatment. He played Mark Antony in Joseph L. Mankiewicz's *Julius Caesar* (1953) opposite James Mason (Brutus) and John Gielgud

(Cassius). Gielgud remembered that Brando heeded his solicited advice on the delivery of the great Forum speeches "in every particular", and noted Brando's collection of tape-recordings by the great American classical actors John Barrymore and Maurice Evans, which he used to improve his diction. However, it would be Brando's first and last meeting with the Bard. Oscar nod number three and the third consecutive defeat losing out to William Holden for *Stalag 17* came with *Julius Caesar*. In his first half dozen films, culminating in *On The Waterfront* (1954) as Terry Malloy, the inarticulate, gum-chewing longshoreman who gradually learns where his true loyalties lie, for which he finally won an Oscar, Brando was consistently superb. The celebrated taxi scene in which he berates his brother (Rod Steiger) for robbing him of the chance to become a boxing champion – "I coulda been a contender" – remains a classic. However, when it was Steiger's turn to deliver his lines Brando went home early leaving Steiger to talk to a wall, a slight it took Steiger more than 40 years to forgive. It is no coincidence that three of the best Brando films were directed by Elia Kazan, himself a leading figure at the Actors Studio. Had Brando maintained the quality of these films it is indisputable that he would have become the greatest actor on film. It was not to be. *On The Waterfront* was to be the apex of his career, setting standards that he would never quite recapture, even in the best of the films that followed. It was the first time that an actor had been nominated for Best Actor four years running. Brando had told everyone he knew that he would send a taxi driver to collect the statuette if he won. It was therefore a surprise when he turned up in a natty tuxedo to present the Oscar for Best Director (to Kazan) and accept his award from a bald Bette Davis wearing a jewelled skullcap. She had shaved her head to play Queen Elizabeth I. Ironically, Darryl F. Zanuck was not keen to make the film, "Who the hell gives a shit about labour unions?" he yelled at Elia Kazan. The film is unusual in that it has several links to the rabidly anti-communist McCarthy hearings. It was directed by Kazan who named names before the House Un-American Activities Committee (Arthur Miller refused to write the screenplay because of his disgust at Kazan's actions); it was written by another informer Budd Schulberg and it co-starred Lee J. Cobb who had also blabbed about who was a communist or had sympathies, naming Lloyd Bridges and Sam Jaffe. The film was shot between November 17, 1953 and January 1954 in Hoboken, New Jersey. Many of the major characters in the film were based on real people. Terry Malloy (Brando) was based on Anthony De Vincenzo, a whistle-blowing docker; Roman Catholic priest John M. Corridan was the basis for Father Barry (Karl Malden) and Johnny Friendly (Lee J. Cobb) was the gangster Anthony Anastasio (b. Italy 1906, d. 1963 of natural causes), the brother of Albert Anastasia who was known as the Lord High Executioner. Anastasia was one of the Mafia's most ruthless killers who personally killed more than 50 people but as head of Murder, Inc. was responsible for hundreds if not thousands of killings. He was murdered as he had his hair cut in a Manhattan hotel. 'Tough Tony' ran the Brooklyn docks through his vice-presidency of the International Longshoreman's Association. The mob still held sway in those days so the set was heavy with police guarding the production to ensure no "accidents" occurred. Brando never spoke out against the Un-American Activities Committee even though its work affected the careers of a number of his friends. Brando disliked *On The Waterfront* when he saw it and refused to give press interviews until the studio forced him. He told UP and AP, "I am fed up with the whole picture . . . The first time I saw *Waterfront* in a projection room I thought it was terrible." Brando's feelings may have been a crisis of conscience for appearing in a film made by informers. After he finally won the Oscar (on March 30, 1955) every studio wanted a piece of Brando and Fox signed him to star in the epic *The Egyptian* which would be directed by Michael Curtiz. Brando's co-star was to be Bella Darvi who was Zanuck's mistress and a woman with a penchant for alcohol and gambling. She later became a lesbian and committed suicide. She is noticed elsewhere in this book. As he read the script Brando realised that the film would be an enormous flop and sought to extricate himself from it. Fox sued him for $2 million. In March 1954, Dodie Brando's health finally gave way and she died on the last day of the month. Only her husband, son, two daughters and sister, Betty Lindemeyer, attended her funeral. Brando's lawyers worked behind the scenes with Fox and as with all these scenarios it was a case of quid pro quo. Fox dropped the suit when Brando agreed to make *Desiree* (1954) for them. He was to play Napoleon – a better part but in an equally dire script. Brando later admitted that he "let the make-up do the work" much to the annoyance of the director, Henry Koster. "Brando couldn't play Napoleon," he said. Koster said that Brando made it very obvious that he was in the film under the strongest protest. Cameron Mitchell who played Joseph Bonaparte, remarked, "Marlon didn't give a damn. He was fucking 20th Century Fox. He would walk onto the set and go from chalk mark to chalk mark without the slightest show of interest. He flubbed and fumbled and fluffed his way through everything." Merle Oberon, who was playing the Empress Josephine, was dismayed and

furious by Brando's antics. He would ruin scenes by scratching his nose, his crotch or his buttocks. Haile Selassie, the Emperor of Ethiopia, visited the set and was introduced to "Napoleon". Selassie had a chest full of medals whereas Brando had a solitary gong pinned to his tunic. Brando said, "You won more battles than I did." Selassie was not amused. The studio publicity department worked overtime to stop the bad behaviour from reaching the ears of the press. The film was a box office success, not because it was any good but because of Brando's appeal. On October 29, a Bandol, Nice, newspaper published the announcement of Brando's engagement to Jossane Mariani-Bérenger, a children's nanny and the daughter of a fisherman. The press swarmed to Bandol and, for once, Brando cooperated with them happily posing for pictures. Then Brando cooled the relationship when he discovered that Jossane had posed nude for eight paintings. He went on a trip with his gay lover Christian Marquand while Jossane appeared on an American television show for a fee of $1,000 and said that she hoped she and Brando would be married in June of the following year. But the couple split when Brando began to see other women including a black cabaret dancer and the entertainer Rita Moreno. Brando's next film was *Guys And Dolls* (1955) in which he played opposite Frank Sinatra. Brando was keen to work with Ol' Blue Eyes but Sinatra did not share his enthusiasm. He was still annoyed at being passed over for the lead role in *On The Waterfront* (indeed, he had sued producer Sam Spiegel for breach of contract) and he also wanted to play Skye Masterson, the part given to Brando. Their working styles were also different. Brando liked to consider each scene carefully while Sinatra was very much a one-take man. This difference was much in evidence when the two men came to film their first scene. The script called for Sinatra to eat cheesecake while Brando delivered his lines. Brando could not get it right and one take followed another until eight were in the can. The mercurial Sinatra lost his temper, threw the confection across the set, slammed his fork into the table and screamed at director Joseph L. Mankiewicz, "These fuckin' New York actors. How much cake do you think I can eat?" The Chairman of the Board stormed off to his dressing room and it took all of Mankiewicz's diplomatic skills to persuade him to return. Sinatra completed the day's filming but hated every second of it. Over the next fortnight both men were at daggers drawn and Brando constantly criticised Sinatra's singing. Brando again disliked the finished product but in the end the film was a commercial success. He later said of Sinatra, "He's the kind of guy that, when he dies, he's going to heaven and give God a bad time for making him bald." In 1955 Brando made a documentary about hunger and deprivation in southeast Asia for UNESCO. That same year in November he met the woman who was to become his first wife in the Paramount commissary. Anna Kashfi claimed that she was born illegitimately in Calcutta, India on September 30, 1934, the daughter of Devi Kashfi, an architect, and Selma Ghose. When she was 18 she enrolled, she alleged, at the London School of Economics but left when she fell in love with an Italian. She became a model and was then discovered by Paramount Pictures. They eventually went out and in December of that year finally went to bed. They were watching television when Brando picked her up and carried her to his bedroom. As she lay in his arms she asked if he was going to rape her and Brando said that rape was just "assault with a friendly weapon". The sex, she revealed, was "a well-rehearsed, polished performance, selfish, without

warmth or naturalness . . . Physically, Marlon is not well appointed. He screens that deficiency by undue devotion to his sex organ. 'My noble tool,' he characterised it with some puffery." For a time Brando was faithful to her but never wooed her. If he awoke feeling randy, he would drive to her home and when she opened the door would carry her to the bedroom. After his passion was sated, he would get up and leave without saying goodnight. Brando's next film project was *The Teahouse Of The August Moon* (1956) which was one of his favourite plays, having seen it four times on Broadway. Brando became one of the first Hollywood stars powerful enough to be able to select his own director and he chose Daniel Mann for the project. He flew to Tokyo, Japan, on April 3, 1956 to begin filming with co-stars Glenn Ford and Louis Calhern. In the Japanese capital Brando was lonely without Anna Kashfi and even the geisha girls could not cheer him. Calhern and Brando renewed their friendship which had begun when they appeared in *Julius Caesar*. Calhern confessed that he was unhappy because he had a new, much younger girlfriend but was unable to satisfy her sexually. Brando did his best to comfort his friend but on May 12, Calhern died of a coronary. Glenn Ford brought a priest and insisted on holding a wake despite Calhern's atheism. Brando's next film, *Sayonara* (1957), in which he was a Southern Air Force officer involved in an inter-racial love affair in occupied Japan, allowed him to return to the country that he had grown to love. It also meant he was thousands of miles from Kashfi, the woman he loved, but that didn't seem to deter him. It would be a pattern he would repeat in subsequent relationships much to the annoyance of the women involved. Brando disliked the film's director Joshua Logan but agreed to work with him because Logan had given Jocelyn a job on *Mister Roberts*. While the company was filming, the writer Truman Capote arrived to profile Brando for *The New Yorker*. Capote employed an old journalistic trick to get Brando to open up – he got him drunk. Brando confessed more details than he should about his mother's alcoholism, insulted Josh Logan and *Sayonara*, revealed that James Dean had tried to "get close" to him and was generally more open than he would normally be. The piece appeared on October 27, 1957 and 20 years later when it appeared in a collection of his work Capote described Brando as "a wounded young man who is a genius, but not markedly intelligent". In his next work, *The Young Lions* (1958), Brando played Christian Diestl, a nasty Nazi. Filmed in Europe Brando began an affair with the model and actress France Nuyen (b. Marseilles, July 31, 1934 as France Nguyen Vannga). The relationship was terminated when another actress knocked an urn of boiling water into Brando's lap, scalding his genitals. *The Young Lions* was a critical and commercial success. In September 1957, Brando and the by-now-pregnant Kashfi decided to get married. The ceremony took place on October 11 at the Eagle Rock home of Brando's aunt Betty Lindemeyer but was not without incident. Brando's father was not invited. In June 1958, Brando, Sr married again to Anna Parramore, a woman younger than his son, and Brando was pointedly not invited. Brando's honeymoon was spent with the Western writer Louis L'Amour and his wife. At breakfast Brando would entertain his new wife by stubbing out lit cigarettes on his hands. Then another bombshell followed. A factory worker called William Patrick O'Callaghan claimed that Anna was not Indian as she had claimed but English. He knew that she was born in Calcutta because he had been working on the railways there and that her real

name was Joan O'Callaghan. MGM revealed that her pay packets were made out in the name of Joanna O'Callaghan and immigration authorities said that was the name she used when she arrived in the States. She told Brando she had used the name to avoid the quotas that were placed on Indians entering America. The Brandos became the top of every party must-have list because everyone wanted to meet the mysterious "Indian woman" that the Oscar winner had married. The couple argued and Brando resumed his affair with France Nuyen. On May 11, 1958, at 7.30pm in Cedars of Lebanon Hospital, Hollywood, Anna Kashfi Brando gave birth to a 7lb 10oz blond, blue-eyed boy who was named Christian Devi after Christian Marquand, Brando's gay lover, and her reputed father. The mother did not approve of the naming of her son as Christian and to this day has never addressed him as such. Brando and Kashfi also argued over whether the boy should be circumcised. She was in favour, he against. "I've never been circumcised and my noble tool has performed its duties through thick and thin without fail," he said. Brando did not play the devoted husband and when his son was a few weeks old he turned up at home with France Nuyen on his arm. Kashfi was shocked and more so when Nuyen went to the fridge and casually helped herself to a mango. She retired to her bedroom in tears and told Brando that Nuyen had 30 seconds to get out of the house. In September 1958, the Brandos' maid, Sako, drowned in their pool. Brando was away in New York with France Nuyen and when the news was brought to him he was told that it was his wife who had drowned. Kashfi remembers that when Brando came home he stared at her with disappointment in his eyes. That day she left Brando, taking their son with her, and hired a lawyer. In 1961 he made his only film as a director – the

Western *One-Eyed Jacks*, originally intended for Stanley Kubrick and called *The Authentic Death Of Hendry Jones*. Brando also took the lead role as a bandit. Though it opened to mixed reviews, it was an intensely personal picture, in which Brando's relationship with a surrogate father ('Dad' Longworth, played by Karl Malden) plainly echoed elements from his own life. Paramount cut it and tampered with the ending, but the brooding atmosphere survived and the film broke new ground for a Western in being set extensively on the Californian coast against a background of crashing waves. Brando had an affair with his leading lady Pina Pellicer. She was to become another person involved directly or indirectly with Brando who would commit suicide. She is noted elsewhere in this book. Towards the end of shooting *One-Eyed Jacks* Anna Kashfi filed for divorce, which was granted on April 22, 1959. Before *One-Eyed Jacks* was released Brando made *The Fugitive Kind* (1960). It was yet another film with which Brando was unhappy. He continued his romance with France Nuyen and the couple went to extraordinary lengths to hide from the press. False noses, make-up, wigs, false names and faux accents were all the order of the day. However, Nuyen commented, "He wasn't so much afraid of the press. He just wanted an excuse to be a little boy and dress up and be someone else and see how long he could fool everybody." Brando decided to visit Haiti because he thought no one would know him there. They left New York in the now obligatory disguises and once on the aeroplane Brando told her, "We did it. Not a soul in Haiti will know who we are anyway." Imagine his disappointment when they got off the flight to be greeted by a brass band and a huge sign bearing the legend, "Welcome Marlon Brando". The affair fizzled out when Brando became involved with a beautiful actress called

Barbara Luna. But on June 4, 1960, during a battle over custody of Christian, Brando married Movita Castenada, a Roman Catholic Mexican who had been an extra in the original version of *Mutiny On The Bounty* (1935) and who Brando had wooed some years earlier. In October 1960, she gave birth to Brando's son Sergio (after Christian Marquand's brother but known by his nickname Miko) who was to become a bodyguard to eccentric pop star Michael Jackson. (The marriage was later annulled on the grounds that she had been married to an Irish boxer at the time of her wedding to Brando.) Brando was not in a good mood when he went for preliminary talks about his new film which was to be a big budget production and a bigger flop. *Mutiny On The Bounty* (1962) cost $19 million, changed director in mid-course and returned only $9 million after 12 different endings were shot in a desperate search for a way to wrap it up. Brando took the role of lead mutineer Fletcher Christian, played by Clark Gable in the original, while Trevor Howard took over from Charles Laughton as Captain William Bligh. Brando was paid $500,000 plus percentages and overages and was given provisional script approval. Carol Reed was hired as director while Eric Ambler was given the task of writing the script. He began work in December 1959 but it soon became obvious that his script was not up to scratch and a new one was commissioned in July 1960 from John Gay. That version was jettisoned and more scripts were written by William Driscoll, Borden Chase, and finally Howard Clewes and Charles Lederer. The final tally of writing costs amounted to $237,000, more than a million dollars today. The boat that was to represent the Bounty was built in Nova Scotia at a cost of $750,000. On November 28, 1960, Brando arrived in Tahiti to begin work and was much smitten with the islands almost immediately. For once Brando was not a recognised star and the local Polynesian girls were very attracted to any man with white skin and had very little in the way of morals compared to the American women Brando was used to. Many of the crew had affairs with local women. Brando was (almost) on his best behaviour and was rarely late on set, such was the respect he had for Carol Reed. Brando began an affair with a Chinese-Polynesian dancer, Tarita Teriipaia, who was then involved with a Danish chef but finished with him for Brando. Tarita played Fletcher Christian's girlfriend in the film and Brando spent much time with her going through her lines. In January 1961 Carol Reed fell ill with gallstones and heat stroke. The weather turned bad and Brando began to display the eccentricities for which he was famous. The company flew home and MGM asked for a completion date for the film. Reggie Callow, the assistant director, proffered 139 days but the studio demanded 100. When Reed said that he could not accede to that request he was sacked. Lewis Milestone, then 70, was hired to finish the film. He had no time for method acting and soon he and Brando were at loggerheads. Filming continued at the MGM lot until April 22, 1961, when the company returned to Tahiti. Brando was late on set nearly every day and fell ill often, as did many of the crew. On July 25, 1961, tragedy struck when a Tahitian extra was killed and several others injured in a freak accident. Brando and co-star Richard Harris did not get on. One scene called for Brando to strike Harris but for some inexplicable reason he could not bring himself to do it and barely tapped Harris. After three takes, Harris shouted, "Why the fuck don't you kiss me and be done with it?" In October, the film closed down again while Lewis Milestone and the studio decided on the ending. In July 1962, George Seaton came on board to direct. When

it came to film Fletcher Christian's death scene Brando asked for 200lbs of ice and lay almost naked on it until he began to shiver violently. The cameras began rolling but Brando could not remember his lines. Eventually, his lines were written on Tarita's forehead. The scene may have been dramatic but it also put Brando in bed for several days and once again the production closed down. Amazingly, the film received an Academy Award nomination for Best Picture among seven nods. It lost out to David Lean's *Lawrence Of Arabia*. The studio chiefs held Brando personally responsible for the on-set delays and budget over-runs that scuppered the picture and his influence in Tinseltown was weakened. For the rest of the Sixties, with the exception of *Reflections In A Golden Eye* (1967), directed by John Huston from a Carson McCullers novel, Brando was unable to find a worthy role. Film followed film – *The Ugly American* (1963) in which he had difficulty remembering his lines, also featured Jocelyn Brando; *Bedtime Story* (1964) as Freddy Benson, a con man, mimic and seducer; *The Saboteur: Codename Morituri* (1965); and *Southwest To Sonora* (1966) – without making waves. Even *A Countess From Hong Kong* (1967), Charlie Chaplin's last film, was a disaster. Intended as a sophisticated comedy and originally written in the Thirties by Chaplin for his then wife Paulette Goddard, Brando played a diplomat opposite Sophia Loren. It stank and they did not get on. During a love scene, he ungallantly asked her, "Did you know that you have hairs up your nostrils?" *Candy* (1968), an example of mainstream porn with Brando in only one scene as an Indian guru, was the low point of his career. *The Night Of The Following Day* (1969) was relegated to the second half of a double bill. During the filming of *The Ugly American* Brando had become involved with a woman named Marie Cui who he had met in Manila on the way to film *Teahouse Of The August Moon*. She became pregnant in June 1962 but Brando was not convinced the child was his. Nevertheless Cui sued Brando for child support for the daughter, Maya Gabriella, who was born on February 27, 1963 in Manila. Brando's lawyers claimed that he was not the child's father and Brando was vindicated by blood tests. Cui still claimed that he was the father. Also in 1963, Brando became heavily involved with the civil rights movement. On December 7, 1964 Anna Kashfi attempted to commit suicide with a drugs overdose. While she was taken to UCLA Medical Center Brando took his son to his Mulholland Drive home. He had to film scenes for *The Saboteur: Codename Morituri* and Kashfi discharged herself from the hospital and broke into Brando's home armed with a loaded gun. Taking her son, she hid out at the Bel Air Sands Hotel. Brando arrived with his lawyer, two private detectives and a policeman. A hysterical Kashfi attacked several members of the hotel staff and was arrested. A custody hearing was held in February 1965 and Christian was placed in the custody of his aunt and uncle, Franny and Dick Loving in Illinois. Five months later, a judge returned full custody of the boy to Anna Kashfi. The Seventies began with little respite for Brando. *Queimada* (1970), made in Italy for Gillo Pontecorvo, was better but little seen abroad; while *The Nightcomers* (1971), made in England for Michael Winner paired Brando, as Peter Quint, with Stephanie Beacham as Miss Jessel, and was a prequel to Henry James' *The Turn Of The Screw*. By now Brando had had a daughter, Rebecca (b. September 1966), by Movita Castenada, and a son, Simon Teihotu (b. May 30, 1963) then a daughter, Tarita Zumi Cheyenne (b. February 20, 1970), by Tarita Teriipaia, and the financial strain of supporting his brood was telling. By 1972 Brando was virtually unemployable, and it took all of Francis Ford Coppola's persuasion to win Paramount's approval to cast him in *The Godfather*. The novel by Mario Puzo about the Corleone crime family had become the fastest-selling paperback novel at that time. He sold the rights to Paramount for $12,500 against a possible $50,000 payday. Puzo read in a newspaper that television comic Danny Thomas was being considered for the role of Don Corleone and was horrified. He rang Brando and begged him to take the part but Brando was totally uninterested. Coppola believed that only Brando or Laurence Olivier could do the role justice. Olivier was ill and, thus, uninsurable. Brando it was. At first the studio wanted nothing to do with him, one executive declaring, "He's dead in this business. Worse than dead, he's a vampire." Paramount had suffered some major recent losses – *Darling Lili* and *Paint Your Wagon*, to name but two – and didn't want to risk another flop. Eventually they agreed that Coppola could screen test Brando (his first since 1946). For it, he stuffed his cheeks with tissue paper, rubbed boot-polish in his hair, smoked, ate Italian sausage, gestured feebly with his hands and jutted out his chin. The effect was instant. "The guy's terrific," said one of those who viewed the test. "Who is he?" Word got around Hollywood and almost every name actor wanted to be in *The Godfather*. The fat, 46-year-old Rod Steiger wanted to play slim, 25-year-old Michael Corleone. Al Pacino eventually took the part. In 1971 the studio producer Albert S. Ruddy made a deal with the youngest Mafioso Joe Colombo (b. June 16, 1914, d. May 23, 1978, seven years after an assassination attempt left him in a persistent vegetative state) that the mob would not interrupt shooting on the film. In return the film would not use the words "Mafia" or "la cosa nostra". They are used in the sequel, however.

Coppola was to say, "I've had so many complaints about the horse's head. There were 30 or so people killed in the film but everyone said, 'You killed a living animal to get the horse's head?' Not I. The horse was killed by the dog food companies to feed your little poodles." Frank Sinatra, no stranger to mob ties himself, was said to hate the portrayal of crooner Johnny Fontaine (Al Martino, after Vic Damone turned down the part) and associates were unwise to mention the film in the presence of Ol' Blue Eyes. James Caan spent so much time researching his role as Sonny Corleone with real-life hoods that the FBI put him under surveillance thinking that he was a new "made" guy. Brando based his godfather on Frank Costello (b. Laurapoli, Calabria, Italy, January 26, 1891 as Francesco Castiglia, d. February 18, 1973), the "Prime Minister of the Underworld", although he had to redub some of his lines when he was even more unintelligible than usual. Filming was watched by genuine Mafia members and they were not impressed by the way that the actors held their guns "like flowers". The film, which was shot between March and July 1971, premièred on March 14, 1972, in New York but Brando was absent. His performance as Don Vito Corleone for which he was paid $50,000 plus deferments earned him his second Oscar. However, he declined to accept it, nor did he accept a New York Film Critics Award or a Foreign Press Golden Globe. Brando sent a telegram criticising the government for its treatment of blacks and Red Indians, imperialist foreign policy and curtailment of press freedom. The Oscar ceremony was held on March 27, 1973 at the Dorothy Chandler Pavilion and *The Godfather* had received 11 nominations. Brando sent an aspiring actress named Sacheen Littlefeather to the ceremony to refuse on his behalf. When telecast producer Howard W. Koch saw Littlefeather, he said, "My God, Marlon Brando sent the Indians to get us." With his co-presenter Liv Ullman, Roger Moore announced that Brando had won. Littlefeather ran to the stage and announced that she could not read the long (15 pages!) speech prepared by Brando because of the time limitation (Koch had promised her 45 seconds and "if you go one second over I'll have you bodily removed from [the] stage. I promise you I'm not afraid to do that"). She refused to take possession of the statuette. She made a brief speech to a mixture of boos and claps but was met with silence as she left the stage. Some of the other winners and presenters made comments about Brando's decision, much to his annoyance. It was then revealed that Sacheen Littlefeather was really Maria Cruz and had been Miss American Vampire 1970. Chief Dan George claimed that Littlefeather's speech was ten years too late. Brando's career revival was brief but consolidated in Bernardo Bertolucci's *Last Tango In Paris* (1972). Bertolucci originally didn't want Brando or Maria Schneider – he preferred Jean-Louis Trintignant as Paul and Dominique Sanda and then Catherine Deneuve for the role of the anonymous French girl. Bertolucci described his star as "an angel of a man, a monster of an actor". Brando was no more complimentary about his director: "I don't think Bertolucci knew what the film was about. I didn't either. He went around telling everyone it was about his prick." Brando's performance as an ageing American, who commits a series of indecent acts in an unfurnished apartment with Jeanne (Schneider) won respect although he may have been responsible for the decline in sales of butter. Some time after filming (which took place in Paris between February 12 and April 1972) Schneider commented, "When I read *Last Tango In Paris*, I didn't see anything that worried me. I was 20. I didn't want to be a star, much less a scandalous actress – simply to be in cinema. Later, I realised I'd been completely manipulated by Bertolucci and Brando. People insulted me in the street. In restaurants, waiters would bring me butter with a funny smile." Brando refused to wear make-up for the part. In an industry where actors often have affairs, Schneider confessed that she felt no sexual attraction for her co-star at all. Much of the film had been improvised before the cameras and Brando had his lines pinned to Schneider's bare buttocks. The film was banned in Italy because of a scene in which Schneider appears to put her fingers into Brando's back passage and another in which he has anal sex with her. Released on December 15, 1972, by the time the film opened in New York on February 1, 1973, it had taken more than $100,000 in advance bookings. Hollywood offered Bertolucci the chance to make *Last Tango In Paris 2* but he declined, pointing out that Brando's character had died at the end of the original. No problem, said the studio, we will say he went to a hospital and recovered. Brando's later work in the decade consisted largely of cameos. In *The Missouri Breaks* (1975) he had a small role but equal billing with Jack Nicholson. Cast as a "Regulator" hired to bring Nicholson's outlaw to book, he camped up the production, playing one scene in a gingham dress and a granny cap. For *Superman* (1978) he was paid an unprecedented $3.7 million for just one scene as Superman's father on Planet Krypton. In *The Formula* (1980) he had three scenes but co-star billing with George C. Scott. Of both stars, the director Steve Shagan said, "I sensed a loss of purpose, a feeling that they didn't want to work any more and had come to think of acting as playing with choo-choo trains." Brando, never the most enthusiastic advocate of film acting, began to lose what little interest he had and concentrated on his other passion, eating. Movies, he said, he

made only for the money. "Acting is an empty and useless profession." He went into virtual voluntary retirement on his very own South Sea island (Teti'aroa, an atoll 30 miles north of Tahiti he bought from an elderly Englishwoman for £2 million in 1963). In the late Eighties, Brando returned to the cinema after a long absence, but the films were no better. *The Freshman* (1989) was an inferior comic retread of his work in *The Godfather*, and in 1992 he played Torquemada in *Christopher Columbus – The Discovery*, the feebler of two weak movies made to celebrate the 400th anniversary of Columbus' first landing in America. Such was his bulk that when he did return to the screen in his later years it was hard for him to play anything other than sedentary roles. Hence the South African lawyer he played in Euzhan Palcy's *A Dry White Season* (1989) and the psychiatrist in *Don Juan De Marco* (1995). In 1996 he appeared in a remake of *The Island Of Dr Moreau*. An Irish comedy, *Divine Rapture*, with Brando as a Roman Catholic priest, was abandoned in 1995 after two weeks' shooting. In 1999 he appeared in a film called *Free Money*, a comedy made exclusively for the Sky Premier television channel in Britain. Marlon Brando's private life was always public, and he took care to make it so. "Like the vast majority of men," he said, "I've had several homosexual experiences and I'm not remotely ashamed of it." "I went to bed with them because I thought I was doing them a favour," he reasoned. At a London party in the Sixties, to which he turned up drunk, Brando invited his host, the critic Kenneth Tynan, to accompany him to the bathroom. There he dared him, as a proof of friendship, to kiss him full on the lips. Tynan, eyebrows raised, assented. Brando had told the actor Cameron Mitchell, his co-star in *Desiree*, that he was "trisexual", which must have caused some head scratching in 1954.

His last years were overshadowed by tragedy. On May 16, 1990, Christian shot and killed his pregnant sister Cheyenne's boyfriend of four years, 6'5" Dag Drollet (b. Tahiti, 1963), in Mulholland Drive. Although the full circumstances will probably never be known, Brando, who had a $500-a-day cocaine habit, was sentenced to ten years in jail for manslaughter. Photographs showed Drollet was shot from half an inch away by a single .45 calibre bullet in the left side of his face as he sat down. In his left hand barefoot Drollet clutched a Bic lighter, a tobacco pouch and a packet of cigarette papers while next to his right hand lay the TV remote control, yet Brando claimed the gun went off during a struggle. Shortly beforehand Cheyenne, a regular user of pot, tranquillisers, LSD, PCP (Angel Dust) and crack cocaine who underwent psychiatric treatment in April 1990 at a Tahitian military hospital, had told him that Drollet regularly beat her. On June 26, Cheyenne gave birth to an allegedly drug-addicted son, Tuki, who weighed 6lb 3oz. She was said to have once boasted, "I am the most beautiful girl in Polynesia, the most intelligent and also the richest because of my father." On July 2, Jacques-Denis Drollet (b. 1922) filed a civil suit in Tahiti, charging Cheyenne with murder and complicity in murder. Doctors looking after Cheyenne had removed all sharp instruments. In a deposition Cheyenne said that Christian Brando had repeatedly said that he wanted to kill Drollet. Shortly afterwards, a $100,000,000 wrongful death suit was filed against Christian and Marlon Brando by Drollet's father and stepfather, Albert LeCaill. On January 3, 1991, the prosecutor accepted an offer of Brando pleading guilty to a lesser charge of voluntary manslaughter. Shirley Cumpanas, Christian's former lover, posed nude for $15,000 for *Penthouse* and set up a 1-900-number to sell the sex secrets of their affair. She gave Elvis Presley a blowjob while married to her first husband and left husband number two for Brando. Joycelyne Lew, who had her breasts cosmetically enlarged, another of Christian's lovers, sold her story to the tabloids. She said, "He used to worry about his physique and whether he could satisfy me . . . but, believe me, he could." Brando's former wife was later arrested for prostitution. In 1989, after her father refused to allow her to visit him on the set of *The Freshman*, Cheyenne drove her jeep into a ditch at 100mph. She required months of reconstructive plastic surgery and attempted suicide four times before finally succeeding by hanging herself in her Panaouila, Tahiti home on April 16, 1995. Previous attempts included a drugs overdose on Halloween 1990 and, three days later, trying to hang herself from a tree with a dog lead. Her third unsuccessful attempt was another overdose when her brother was sentenced to ten years in prison (later reduced) while the fourth came in 1994. A curious feature about Brando's career was the number of films that called for him to be beaten up or otherwise physically abused. In *On The Waterfront* and *The Wild One* he was beaten to a pulp; in *The Fugitive Kind* he was castrated; in *Apocalypse Now* (1979) in which he played Colonel Walter E. Kurtz he was felled like an ox; and in *One-Eyed Jacks*, he had his trigger finger smashed by a vindictive lawman. Freud would have had a field day. His last significant role was as Max in Frank Oz's tortuous 2001 gangster movie *The Score*, with Robert De Niro and Edward Norton – who apparently took on the film just so that he could see his name on the same poster as Brando. Marlon Brando once famously opined that "the only thing an actor owes his public is not to bore them." In an interview in 1956 with the *Observer* he commented, "An actor's a guy who if you ain't talking about him ain't listening." Not everyone was enamoured of Brando. Edward Dmytryk said, "Montgomery Clift was an exceptionally bright man who liked to pretend he wasn't, unlike Brando who likes to pretend he's bright whereas, in fact, he isn't really." Michael Winner opined, "He was the most tolerable, wonderful, witty companion and a marvellous human being. Claims that he wasted his talent are total rubbish. He was the most marvellous screen actor ever. He was a great actor . . . but he didn't like acting." Anthony Hopkins agreed, "Whether the film is good or bad Brando is always compulsive viewing, like Sydney Greenstreet, the vulgarian of all time, or Peter Lorre, or Bette Davis daring to do Baby Jane." Director Josh Logan concurred, "Marlon's the most exciting person I've met since Garbo. A genius. But I don't know what he's like. I don't know anything about him." However, in summation, it is hard to disagree with James Mason's opinion that "Brando made such a mess of his career."

CAUSE: Morbidly obese, Brando died in a hospital in Los Angeles, aged 80. The cause of death was given as lung failure. Brando had suffered from pneumonia, an illness that left him wheelchair-bound and breathing through an oxygen mask. Brando did nothing to help his battles with his weight: he had been spotted raiding the ice-cream freezer at a supermarket after his nurses chained his refrigerator door shut. Jocelyn Brando said, "There will be no service of any kind. If someone wants to do something that's their business. But Marlon would have hated it." She told *Fox News* that she was shocked by the suddenness of her brother's death. "He'd been on oxygen for about a year. He had pulmonary thrombosis. He went in [to hospital] to get a couple of things looked at and he just took off." Brando left behind an estate worth $21.6 million according to his will. True to his secretive life, he cut at least two heirs out of his will and revealed the names of two previously unknown children among his 10 surviving offspring, including three by his maid, Christina Ruiz. Details in his will show that Brando had an income of $500,000 a year. The core of his financial assets consisted of a hilltop estate on Los Angeles' Mulholland Drive, reportedly worth up to $10 million, and his Tahitian atoll, Teti'aroa, his private retreat. Brando ordered his assets, including around $8.6 million in real estate and $3 million in other property, said to include paintings, sketches and rare scripts, to be transferred to what the will refers to as a "living trust". The will did not state who would inherit. Christian Brando married artist Deborah Presley on October 16, 2004 in Las Vegas, Nevada. She claims that she is Elvis Presley's daughter. On January 10, 2005 he was charged with two counts of spousal abuse. He pleaded guilty and was sentenced to three years' probation and two months of drug and alcohol treatment. The couple divorced in June 2005. Six months later, she sued him in Los Angeles County Superior Court claiming that he had been violent towards her, raped her and threatened to smother her with a pillow and cut her 13-year-old daughter "into a million pieces". A settlement was reached in February 2007. He died at Hollywood Presbyterian Medical Center from pneumonia on the morning of January 26, 2008. He was 49 and had been hospitalised for fifteen days prior to his death. Brando was buried on February 17, 2008 at the Kalama Oddfellows Cemetery in Kalama, Washington.

FURTHER READING: *Bud: The Brando I Knew* – Carlo Fiore (New York: Dell, 1975); *Brando: Portrait Of The Rebel As An Artist* – Bob Thomas (London: Star Books, 1975); *Marlon Brando* – René Jordan (London: Star Books, 1976); *Brando: The Unauthorised Biography* – Charles Higham (New York: Signet,

1988); *Brando* – Peter Manso (London: Weidenfeld & Nicolson, 1994); Brando Unzipped – Darwin Porter (New York: Blood Moon, 2005); *Somebody: The Reckless Life And Remarkable Career Of Marlon Brando* – Stefan Kanfer (London: Faber & Faber, 2008).

Irving Brecher
Born January 17, 1914
Died November 17, 2008
The Wicked Wit of the West. Irving Brecher was born in the Bronx and got his break in showbusiness selling jokes to columnists Walter Winchell and Ed Sullivan while he worked as an usher in a cinema on 57th Street in Manhattan. With a small success, he and a friend, Al Schwartz, advertised their comedy-writing services in *Variety*. At the time (early 1930s) Milton Berle was notorious for stealing other people's material ("The Thief Of Bad Gags") so Brecher and Schwartz advertised their wares as "Berle-proof gags, so bad not even Milton will steal them". Their first customer was Milton Berle who paid them $50 for a page of one-liners. Brecher became Berle's writer when the comedian presented *The Gillette Original Community Sing* in 1936 and the following year scripted *New Faces Of 1937* starring Milton Berle. He was an uncredited contributor to the comedy scenes of *The Wizard Of Oz* (1939) and was signed to a contract by producer-director Mervyn LeRoy at MGM where he wrote the screenplays for the Marx Brothers' *At The Circus* (1939) and *Go West* (1940) – the only man to write two Marx Brothers films by himself – and shared an Oscar nomination for the screenplay to *Meet Me In St Louis* (1944). His other screenwriting credits include *Shadow Of The Thin Man* (1941), *Du Barry Was A Lady* (1943), *Best Foot Forward* (1943), *Yolanda And The Thief* (1945), *Ziegfeld Follies* (1946), *Summer Holiday* (1948), *Somebody Loves Me* (1952, which he also directed), *Cry For Happy* (1961) and *Bye Bye Birdie* (1963). In the 1940s Brecher created, wrote and produced the radio series *The Life Of Riley* starring William Bendix. He also wrote, produced and directed a film version of *The Life Of Riley* (1949) in which Bendix reprised his radio role. Brecher was married twice. Eve Bennett, his first wife, by whom he had two children, died in 1981. He married again in 1983 to Norma. Brecher said that Groucho Marx was the easiest star to write for. "I'm a complainer, a dissenter and a put-downer. He was my alter ego. I liked the anarchism."
CAUSE: Brecher died aged 94 at Cedars-Sinai Medical Center, Los Angeles, California, of natural causes. His autobiography was published posthumously.
FURTHER READING: *The Wicked Wit Of The West: The Last Great Golden-Age Screenwriter Shares The Hilarity And Heartaches Of Working With Groucho, Garland, Gleason, Burns, Berle, Benny And Many More* – Irving Brecher as told to Hank Rosenfield (New Jersey: Ben Yehuda Press, 2009).

Walter Brennan
Born July 25, 1894
Died September 21, 1974
Lovable old man. Walter Andrew Brennan, born in Swampscott, Massachusetts, was a precocious child. He left home at 11 and by the age of 15 he had a degree in engineering. However, instead of putting his knowledge to practical use he joined a vaudeville troupe before serving in France with the 101st Field Artillery. Demobbed, he worked variously digging ditches, in a bank and as an estate agent before landing his first film job as an extra in 1923. He became firm friends with another extra, Frank Cooper, who later changed his first name to Gary. Brennan worked as stuntman, having his teeth knocked out in the process, which stood him in good stead for the rest of his career, playing lovable old codgers in almost 200 films. He once confessed: "I never

wanted anything out of this business except a good living. Never wanted to be a star – just wanted to be good at what I was doing." He succeeded, probably beyond his wildest dreams. He was the first actor to get a hat trick of Best Supporting Actor Oscars. The first was for *Come And Get It* (1936) in which he played Swedish lumberjack Swan Bostrom. Next was *Kentucky* (1938), playing Peter Goodwin and he gained his third playing Judge Roy Bean in *The Westerner* (1940). He was nominated a fourth time for *Sergeant York* (1941) but lost out to Donald Crisp for *How Green Was My Valley* (1941). His other films included *The Mystery Of Edwin Drood* (1935), *Seven Keys To Baldpate* (1935), *Banjo On My Knee* (1936) as Newt Holley, *When Love Is Young* (1937) as Uncle Hugo, *Mother Carey's Chickens* (1938) as Mr Popham, *The Adventures Of Tom Sawyer* (1938) as Muff Potter, *Stanley And Livingstone* (1939) as Jeff Slocum, *They Shall Have Music* (1939) as Professor Lawson, *Northwest Passage* (1940) as Hunk Marriner, *The Pride Of The Yankees* (1942) as Sam Blake and *To Have And Have Not* (1944) as Eddie. The wealthy owner of two ranches, a hotel and a cinema, Brennan married childhood sweetheart Ruth Welles in 1920 and they were still together at his death.
CAUSE: He died in Oxnard, California, from emphysema, aged 80.

Bernard Bresslaw

Born February 25, 1934
Died June 11, 1993
He only arsked. The (mostly) lovable lug of the *Carry On* . . . films was born in Stepney, London, weighing 10lb 4oz. "I am the son of a poor East End tailor's cutter," he told one interviewer. His ambition to become an actor was born at an early age but the Jewish Bresslaw was convinced his height (6'7") would count against him. He won a scholarship to RADA, where he won the coveted Emile Littler prize for most promising actor. His first big break came as the dopey Sergeant 'Popeye' Popplewell in the Granada sitcom *The Army Game* (1957–1958) a role that paid him £750 a week. His catch phrase "I only arsked" soon caught on with the public. He even got into the pop charts with the unlikely 'Mad Passionate Love' making number 6 in 1958. However, it was the *Carry On*s that made him instantly recognisable. He appeared in 14 between 1965 and 1975, ranging from *Carry On Cowboy* (1965), in which he played Red Indian Little Heap, through the Boris Karloff-like butler Sockett in *Carry On Screaming* (1966), the romantic Ken Biddle in *Carry On Doctor* (1967), the bloodthirsty Burpa Bunghit Din in *Carry On Up The Khyber* (1968), the randy but shy Bernie Lugg in *Carry On Camping* (1969), the fearsomely jealous wrestler Gripper Burke in *Carry On Loving* (1970), incompetent thief Ernie Bragg in *Carry On Matron* (1971) to his last appearance as Arthur Upmore in *Carry On Behind* (1975). His other films included *Up Pompeii* (1970), *One Of Our Dinosaurs Is Missing* (1976) and *Krull* (1983). Bresslaw was an avid reader. He and his wife Liz had three sons.
CAUSE: In the Eighties he began to lose his sight and at one stage was nearly blind for five months; an operation in 1990 at Moorfields Eye Hospital restored his sight. A tireless worker, he collapsed in 1992 and his health was compromised. Bresslaw was about to play Grumio in *The Taming Of The Shrew* in Regents Park when he suffered a massive heart attack. He was taken to University College Hospital where he died, aged 59.

Monte Brice

Born July 12, 1891
Died November 8, 1962
Multi-talent. Born in New York, Monte Brice was educated at Columbia University where he read mining and

engineering. He became sales manager at the Texas Oil Company's office in Manhattan. He longed to get into show business so for a time he was a businessman, actor, director, playwright, and also wrote songs ('The Daughter Of Rosie O'Grady' being one of his better known efforts). He made his first film in 1912 and then, disillusioned, left the business, returning five years later to make a few more films but concentrating on a career as a screenwriter. His films included *Hands Up!* (released January 1926) starring Raymond Griffiths, *Behind The Front* (1926) with Wallace Beery, *Miss Brewster's Millions* (1926), *The Fleet's In* (1928), *Merry Go Round Of 1938* (1937), *You're A Sweetheart* (1937), *Mexican Spitfire Sees A Ghost* (1942), *Joan Of Ozark* (1942), *Genius At Work* (1946) and *Variety Girl* (1947). He also directed *Casey At The Bat* (1927), directed *The Golf Specialist* (1930), W.C. Fields' first sound film, *Street Singer* (1932), *The Hold-Up* (1933), *The Radio Murder Mystery* (1933), *My Pal The Prince* (1933), *Beauty On Broadway* (1933), *Boswell Sisters* (1933) and *Sweet Surrender* (1935). Brice later became a joke writer for Bob Hope.
CAUSE: He died in London, aged 71, of a heart attack.

Lloyd Bridges

Born January 15, 1913
Died March 10, 1998
Hardworking support actor. Despite never being nominated for an Oscar, Lloyd Vernet Bridges, Jr was a regular in films for over 60 years. Born in San Leandro, California, he worked in various repertory theatres before making his Broadway début in 1939. He made his first film, *Freshman Love*, in 1936 but it wasn't until he signed for Columbia in 1941 that he worked regularly on the big screen. He was usually cast as a thug and it was only when he left Columbia that he began to play a wider range of characters. In the Fifties he testified before the House Un-American Activities Committee and admitted that he had been a member of the Communist Party. His films included: *The Royal Mounted Patrol* (1941) as Hap Andrews, *Shut My Big Mouth* (1942) as Skinny, *Riders Of The Northland* (1942) as Alex, *Flight Lieutenant* (1942) as Bill Robinson, *Blondie Goes To College* (1942) as Ben Dixon, *Alias Boston Blackie* (1942) as the bus driver, *Passport To Suez* (1943) as Fritz, *Sahara* (1943) as Fred Clarkson, *Louisiana Hayride* (1944) as Montague Price, *Secret Agent X-9* (1945) as Secret Agent X-9, *Abilene Town* (1946) as Henry Dreiser, *Ramrod* (1947) as Red Cates, *Unconquered* (1947) as Lieutenant Hutchins, *Red Canyon* (1949) as Virgil Cordt, *Calamity Jane And Sam Bass* (1949) as Joel Collins, *Trapped* (1949) as Tris Stewart, *Colt .45* (1950) as Paul Donovan, *Little Big Horn* (1951) as Captain Phillip Donlin, *Last Of The Comanches* (1952) as Jim Starbuck, *High Noon* (1952) as Harvey Pell, *Plymouth Adventure* (1952) as Coppin, *Third Party Risk* (1955) as Philip Graham, *Apache Woman* (1955) as Rex Moffett, *Wetbacks* (1956) as Jim Benson, *Daring Game* (1968) as Vic Powers, *The Fifth Musketeer* (1979) as Aramis, *Airplane!* (1980) as McCroskey, *Airplane II: The Sequel* (1982) as McCroskey, *Weekend Warriors* (1986) as Colonel Archer, *Cousins* (1989) as Vince, *Joe Versus The Volcano* (1990) as Samuel Harvey Graynamore, *Hot Shots!* (1991) as Admiral Benson, *Honey, I Blew Up The Kid* (1992) as Clifford Sterling, *Hot Shots! Part Deux* (1993) as President Thomas 'Tug' Benson, *Blown Away* (1994) as Max O'Bannon and *Jane Austen's Mafia* (1998) as Vincenzo Cortino. His sons Beau (b. Los Angeles, California, December 9, 1941 as Lloyd Vernet Bridges, III) and Jeff (b. Los Angeles, California, December 4, 1949) and grandchildren: Casey (b. 1969), Jordan (b. 1975),

Dylan (b. 1984) and Emily (b. 1987) are all actors.

CAUSE: He died of natural causes, aged 85, in Los Angeles, California.

Albert R. 'Cubby' Broccoli

Born April 5, 1909
Died June 27, 1996

James Bond's cinematic dad. Born in New York City, Albert Romolo 'Cubby' Broccoli was introduced to films by his cousin the seedy Pat DeCicca (then married to Thelma Todd). He became a salesman selling make-up until landing a job as a dogsbody on *The Outlaw* (1943). A few more films followed but Broccoli felt frustrated and so he moved to England in 1951 and set up Warwick Pictures with Irving Allen, a fellow *emigré*. Their first effort was *The Red Beret* (1953) starring Alan Ladd. In 1956 Harry Saltzman bought the rights to Ian Fleming's suave secret agent and offered Broccoli the chance to film them. However, in 1960 Warwick Films closed down following a series of disagreements between Allen and Broccoli. In June 1961 Broccoli and Saltzman made a deal on the options to the Bond books. They formed a company, Eon Productions (Eon stands for "Everything Or Nothing"). Broccoli approached Columbia Pictures with the project, but a minion there commented that James Bond was the poor man's Mike Hammer. He was quickly proved wrong: the first Bond film, *Dr No* (1962), was a mammoth success and Broccoli was made. Apart from one film (*Chitty Chitty Bang Bang* [1968]) he concentrated all his efforts on 007. Yes, in case you were wondering, he is related to the vegetable. His ancestors crossed the cauliflower with the rabe to form broccoli. He was married twice. His first wife died of cancer, leaving him with two children. On June 20, 1959, he married Dana and their daughter, Barbara, was born in 1960.

CAUSE: He died in Beverly Hills,

California, as the result of heart problems, on June 27, 1996.

Dana Broccoli

(DANA NATOL)
Born January 3, 1922
Died February 29, 2004

James Bond's protector. Born in New York, she decided to become an actress at an early age and began studying at Cecil Clovelly's Academy of Dramatic Arts, at Carnegie Hall. While there she met her first husband, Lewis Wilson, who was the first actor to play Batman (b. New York, January 28, 1920, d. San Francisco, California, August 9, 2000). In 1943, she gave birth to a son, Michael G., and three years later the family moved to California where Dana Wilson and her husband joined the Pasadena Playhouse. In 1950 she made her first film appearing as Jane in *Once A Thief*. The following year she played Queen Bonga Bonga in *Wild Women*. Her only other screen appearance was as a tourist in St Mark's Square in *Moonraker* (1979). When she left her husband she became a screenwriter in Beverly Hills. At a party in 1959, she met the widower Cubby Broccoli. Twelve years earlier, Broccoli had had a job selling Christmas trees on a street corner and was particularly struck by a beautiful young woman who had bought one of the trees and for whom he had built a stand to hold it. The beautiful woman was Dana Wilson. Both remembered the incident and believed that fate had brought them together. They married on June 20, 1959, in Las Vegas with Cary Grant as the best man and then moved to London. On June 18, 1960, their daughter Barbara was born. The following year Broccoli and the Canadian producer Harry Saltzman created a film company to put Ian Fleming's James Bond novels on the silver screen. Helped by his shrewd and glamorous wife, the New Yorker struck up an unlikely friendship with Fleming, an Old Etonian who had a marked

disdain for Hollywood. "I found him a lovely man," Dana Broccoli recalled years later, "charming and intelligent." It was Dana who decided that the unknown Sean Connery was the right man to play 007 in *Dr No* (1962), the first of the Bond films. "One day," Dana Broccoli later recalled, "Cubby called me and said, 'Could you come down and look at this Disney leprechaun film, *Darby O'Gill And The Little People*, at the Goldwyn Studios? I don't know if this Sean Connery guy has any sex appeal.' I saw that face and the way he moved and talked, and I said, 'Cubby, he's fabulous!' He was just perfect, he had star material right there." However, Connery and the Broccolis were to have several fallings-out. In 1966 Connery gave an interview in which he mentioned "fat-slob producers living off the backs of lean actors". Eighteen years later, Connery issued a lawsuit against Broccoli demanding more royalties from the Bond films. The actor eventually abandoned the dispute after settling for merchandising rights. In 1996 Connery did not attend Broccoli's memorial service. "I don't have to understand Sean," she said in 2000, "and he doesn't need my understanding; he's doing very well without my understanding." Dana Broccoli was not someone to cross. She recalled, "I'm half-Irish and half-Italian. I'm just bloody-minded." "Dana," Cubby wrote in his autobiography, "takes no prisoners. She does not have the gift of forgiveness." Dana Broccoli also published two novels, *Scenario For Murder* and *Florinda*. She adapted the latter for the musical, *La Cava*, which was staged in London in 2000.
CAUSE: She died, aged 82, of cancer in Los Angeles, California.

Helen Broderick

Born August 11, 1891
Died September 25, 1959
Deadpan comedienne. Born in Philadelphia, Pennsylvania, to parents who were light opera stars and who discouraged her from entering show business. She was to later forbid her only child from the business – he ignored her. Despite their opposition she became a chorus girl when she was 14 and then joined the Ziegfeld Follies. With her husband, Lester Crawford (b. Massachusetts, Christmas Day, 1882, d. Los Angeles, California, November 24, 1962 – their only child being the actor Broderick Crawford) she formed a double act "Crawford & Broderick – Songs, Dances, Funny Sayings". She appeared in numerous Broadway shows: in the chorus for *Ziegfeld Follies Of 1907* (July 8, 1907–November 10, 1907), *Algeria* (August 31, 1908– October 10, 1908), *The Honeymoon Express* (opened February 6, 1913), *Nifties Of 1923* (September 25, 1923), *The Wild Westcotts* (December 24, 1923), *Puzzles Of 1925* (February 2, 1925), *Mama Loves Papa* (February 22, 1926), *Oh, Please* (December 17, 1926) as Emma Bliss, *Fifty Million Frenchmen* (November 27, 1929–July 5, 1930 at The Lyric Theatre which ran for 254 performances), *The Band Wagon* (opened June 3, 1931 at the New Amsterdam Theatre and ran for 260 performances), *Earl Carroll's Vanities* (September 27, 1932– December 10, 1932) and *As Thousands Cheer* (September 30, 1933–September 8, 1934 at the Music Box Theatre which ran for 400 performances). She is said to have made her film début in *High Speed* (1924) but was definitely in *For Art's Sake* (1930) and *Nile Green* (1930). She wrote screenplays for two films, *High Speed* (1924) and *The Mystery Club* (1926). Her other films included *Cold Turkey* (1931), *Court Plastered* (1931), *Fifty Million Frenchmen* (1931) as Violet, *The Spirits Of 76th Street* (1931), *Top Hat* (1935) as Madge Hardwick, *To Beat The Band* (1935) as Freeda McCrary, *Love On A Bet* (1936) as Aunt Charlotte, *Murder On A Bridle Path* (1936) as Hildegarde

Withers, *The Bride Walks Out* (1936) as
Mattie Dodson, *Swing Time* (1936) as
Mabel Anderson, *Smartest Girl In Town*
(1936) as Gwen Mayen, *We're On The
Jury* (1937) as Agnes Dean, *Meet The
Missus* (1937) as Emma Foster, *The
Life Of The Party* (1937) as Pauline,
She's Got Everything (1937) as Aunt
Jane Carter, *The Road To Reno* (1938)
as Aunt Minerva, *Radio City Revels*
(1938) as Gertie Shaw, *The Rage Of
Paris* (1938) as Gloria, *Service De Luxe*
(1938) as Pearl, *Stand Up And Fight*
(1939) as Aunt Amanda Griffith,
Naughty But Nice (1939) as Aunt
Martha Hogan, *Honeymoon In Bali*
(1939) as Lorna Smith, *The Captain Is
A Lady* (1940) as Nancy Crocker, *No,
No, Nanette* (1940) as Mrs Smith,
Virginia (1941) as Theo Clairmont,
Nice Girl? (1941) as Cora Foster,
Father Takes A Wife (1941) as Aunt
Julie, *Chip Off The Old Block* (1944) as
Glory Marlow, Sr, *Her Primitive Man*
(1944) as Mrs Winthrop, *Three Is A
Family* (1944) as Irma, *Love, Honor
And Goodbye* (1945) as Mary Riley and
Because Of Him (1946) as Nora.
CAUSE: She died in Beverly Hills,
California, aged 68. She was buried in
Ferndale Cemetery, Johnstown, Fulton
County, New York.

Charles Bronson

(CHARLES DENNIS BUCHINSKI)
Born November 3, 1921?
Died August 30, 2003
Screen tough guy. Bronson was born in
Ehrenfeld, Pennsylvania, one of fifteen
children of a Lithuanian immigrant
coalminer. Two of Bronson's brothers
were born handicapped – one had a
hunchback and one a heart condition
and his eldest sister was born dumb.
Most sources list the year above as
Bronson's date of birth but in 1971
during the filming of *Chato's Land* his
then wife Jill Ireland told Michael
Winner, with whom she had had a
relationship in the 1950s that Bronson
was, in fact, eight years older than the
official date. After leaving school,

Bronson followed his father down the
pit until the Second World War
eventually intervened. Using the GI
Bill that helped so many servicemen,
Bronson began to study art and then
joined the Pasadena Playhouse in
California. A teacher recommended
Bronson to director Henry Hathaway
who cast him in *You're In The Navy
Now* (released February 23, 1951) as
Wascylewski. Bronson found regular
unbilled work after that but was
unnoticed until cast as Vincent Price's
malicious assistant Igor in the 3-D
thriller *House Of Wax* (released
April 25, 1953). Bronson began to
receive good notices from critics for
Vera Cruz (released Christmas Day
1954) as Pittsburgh, *Target Zero*
(released November 15, 1955) as
Sergeant Vince Gaspari and *Run Of
The Arrow* (released September 5,
1957) as Blue Buffalo, one describing
him as "a Clark Gable who had been
left out in the sun too long". Roger
Corman, the independent director,
gave Bronson the lead role in his
low-budget gangster flick *Machine-Gun
Kelly* (released May 1958) which lead
to the actor's own TV show *Man With
A Camera* (1958). The role that he
hoped would make him internationally
famous was half Irish/half Mexican
gunslinger Bernardo O'Reilly in John
Sturges's *The Magnificent Seven*
(released October 23, 1960) for which
he was paid $50,000. However,
although the film was a success it did
not bring Bronson stardom. Sturges
again hired Bronson for the Second
World War big budget epic *The Great
Escape* (released July 4, 1963) in which
he played Danny Velinski. Two years
later, Bronson was back in uniform
in *Battle Of The Bulge* (released
December 16, 1965) as Wolenski and
again after another two years had
passed alongside Lee Marvin and
Ernest Borgnine in *The Dirty Dozen*
(released June 15, 1967; premièred in
England September 23, 1967) as
Joseph Wladislaw. The role that brought

him further attention was as villain
Henry Fonda's nemesis 'Harmonica'
(a role originally offered to Clint
Eastwood and James Coburn) in Sergio
Leone's cult spaghetti western, the
legendary *C'era Una Volta Il West* –
a.k.a. *Once Upon A Time In The West*
(1968; released in the US 1969).
Bronson was by any stretch of the
imagination a minimalist actor, a
style that appealed to European
audiences and he appeared in several
action-oriented films including *La
Bataille De San Sebastian* (1968) as
Teclo, *Le Passager De La Pluie* (1970)
as Dobbs and *Soleil Rouge* (1971) as
Link alongside Japanese actor Toshirô
Mifune who had appeared in *The Seven
Samurai* (1954), the film that inspired
The Magnificent Seven. Back in the
States Bronson appeared in *The Valachi
Papers* (released November 3, 1972) as
Mafia stool pigeon Joseph Valachi and
the revenge western *Chato's Land*
(released May 25, 1972) as Apache
half-breed Pardon Chato in his first
collaboration with Michael Winner.
Bronson acceped the role because: "I
wanted to play an Indian as an Indian
should be played realistically on the
screen [and] I wanted to give a good,
clean-cut and fair identification."
Author David Downing described the
film as "one of the most powerful
Westerns of the post-war era . . . and
Winner must take credit for that". It
began a friendship and partnership with
Winner that saw them make half a
dozen films together. They made *The
Mechanic* (released November 17,
1972) with Bronson as aging hitman
Arthur Bishop, the actor's first
Hollywood film in nearly five years,
and *The Stone Killer* (released August 8,
1973) as Detective Lou Torrey. In
1972 Bronson and Sean Connery
shared the title of the world's most
loved film star in a poll by Reuters,
which took in 60 countries. However,
he did not let his popularity temper his
views. That same year he announced,
"If any of the things that these

Women's Libbers want were to come
about I would leave America
immediately. Women are not equal –
never could be." Bronson then played
Vince Majestyk, a Colorado melon
farmer-done-wrong in Richard
Fleischer's *Mr Majestyk* (released
July 17, 1974) before resuming his
partnership with Winner. Their next
collaboration, *Death Wish*, would
become one of the most successful
films of the 1970s and one of the most
notorious. Bronson played architect
Paul Kersey whose life is changed when
thugs break into his apartment and kill
his wife Joanna (Hope Lange) and rape
the couple's daughter, Carol Toby
(Kathleen Tolan). America at the time
was beset by street violence and
audiences flocked to see *Death Wish*
(released July 24, 1974), which became
one of the country's two most popular
films that year. In New York cinemas
crowds cheered every time a mugger
was murdered. A story has it that when
Bronson and Winner were discussing
their next film the director said, "The
best script I've got is *Death Wish*. It's
about a man whose wife and daughter
are mugged and he goes out and shoots
muggers." "I'd like to do that," said
Bronson. "The film?" asked Winner.
Bronson responded, "No . . . shoot
muggers." There are eleven murders in
the film and Paul Kersey commits ten.
Jeff Goldblum makes his cinematic
debut. Critics were divided over the
film. Vincent Canby of *The New York
Times* called it "a despicable movie,
one that raises complex questions in
order to offer bigoted, frivolous,
oversimplified answers". Bronson was
not unduly concerned, "We don't
make movies for critics, since they
don't pay to see them anyhow." *Death
Wish* spawned four sequels and in 1987
Bronson said, "I think they provide
satisfaction for people who are
victimised by crime and look in vain
for authorities to protect them. But I
don't think people try to imitate that
kind of thing." Bronson appeared in

Breakout (released May 22, 1975) as Nick Colton and then alongside his *Magnificent Seven* co-star James Coburn in *Hard Times* (released October 8, 1975) as Chaney. He starred with wife Jill Ireland in the western *Breakheart Pass* (released May 5, 1976) written by Alistair MacLean based on his own novel. Bronson's final films included: *From Noon Till Three* (1976) as Graham, Don Siegel's Cold War thriller *Telefon* (1977) as Major Grigori Borzov, *Caboblanco* (1980) as Gifford Hoyt, *Death Hunt* (1981) as Albert Johnson, *Death Wish II* (1982) as Paul Kersey, *10 To Midnight* (1983) as Leo Kessler, *Death Wish 3* (1985) as Paul Kersey, *Assassination* (1987) as Jay Killion, *Death Wish 4: The Crackdown* (1987) as Paul Kersey, *The Indian Runner* (1991) as Mr Roberts and *Death Wish V: The Face Of Death* (1994) as Paul Kersey. On September 30, 1949 Bronson married Harriet Tendler by whom he had two children Anthony (b. February 19, 1961) and Suzanne (b. February 27, 1955) before their divorce. He married the actress Jill Ireland on October 5, 1968 and they had a daughter Zuleika (b. Los Angeles, California August 4, 1971). Her son, Jason, died of a drugs overdose in 1989 and Jill Ireland passed away the following year from breast cancer. On December 22, 1998 he married Kim Weeks.
CAUSE: Bronson suffered from ill health in his last years. He retired from acting in 1998 after undergoing hip replacement surgery. He was diagnosed with Alzheimer's disease in 2000. He died of pneumonia at Cedars-Sinai Medical Center with his wife at his bedside. He is buried at Brownsville Cemetery, West Windsor, Windsor County, Vermont.
FURTHER READING: *Charles Bronson Superstar* – Steven Whitney (London: Coronet Books, 1980); *Charles Bronson* – David Downing (London: Star Books, 1984).

Clive Brook
(CLIFFORD HARDMAN BROOK)
Born June 1, 1887
Died November 17, 1974
The son of an opera singer, 5'11" Brook was born in London. His father wanted the boy to become a lawyer and to this end he was sent to Dulwich College. However, aged 15, he had to leave after the family's fortunes dived. He moved to a polytechnic to study elocution and became so proficient that he became a teacher to earn some pin money. Upon graduation he became a journalist and joined the army in September 1914. He was demobbed with the rank of major at the end of the war to end all wars, and decided to give acting a shot. His first appearance in London was at the St Martin's Theatre in *Just Like Judy* on February 11, 1920. On October 2 of that year he married co-star Charlotte Elizabeth Mildred Evelyn. He fathered a son, Lyndon (b. 1926) who became a playwright, and a daughter, the actress Faith Brook (b. York, February 16, 1922). Around this time he began to appear in silent films such as *Debt Of Honour* (1918) and *The Royal Oak* (1923). When the latter was seen in Hollywood, Brook was offered contracts by no less than three studios. He began with Thomas Ince before moving briefly to Warner Bros. In 1926 he moved again, this time to Paramount where he stayed for eight years. Adolph Zukor described Brook as being like the Rock of Gibraltar, a description the actor loathed. Brook soon tired of only playing cads or gentlemen, yet was continually cast in those roles. Among his films were the title role in *The Sheik* (1922), *A Tale Of Two Cities* (1922) as Sidney Carton, *Through Fire And Water* (1923) as John Dryden, *Woman To Woman* (1924) as David Compos/ Davis Anson-Pond, *Christine Of The Hungry Heart* (1924) as Dr Alan Monteagle, *When Love Grows Cold* (1925) as Jerry Benson, *Seven Sinners* (1925) as Jerry Winters, *You Never Know Women* (1926) as

Norodin, *For Alimony Only* (1926) as Peter Williams, *Underworld* (1927) as 'Rolls-Royce', Sir John Marlay in *Interference* (1928) which was Paramount's first talkie, *Four Feathers* (1929) as Lieutenant Durrance, *The Return Of Sherlock Holmes* (1929) as the great detective, *Scandal Sheet* (1931) as Noel Adams, *Shanghai Express* (1932) as Captain Donald Harvey, *Sherlock Holmes* (1932) again in the title role, *Gallant Lady* (1933) as Dan Pritchard, and *Cavalcade* (1933) as Robert Marryot. In 1936 he returned to England permanently after a short time with RKO. He was worried by threats to kidnap his children. He appeared regularly in films, television and on the stage in his native land and ended his days in a spacious flat at 95 Eaton Square, London SW1. Although he wrote his autobiography, he was unable to find a publisher for it.
CAUSE: He died in London.

Tyler Brooke

(VICTOR HUGO DE BIERE)
Born June 6, 1886
Died March 2, 1943
'The best dressed leading man of Broadway'. Born in New York, 5'8" Brooke studied commercial law before working in banking for many years. Commerce's loss was show business' gain because Brooke threw in his "boring" job and began appearing in musical comedies in theatres. He was signed by Hal Roach in 1925 and often appeared in his comedies, playing lounge lizards in films such as *Moonlight And Noses* (1925), *Wandering Papas* (1925), *Should Husbands Pay?* (1926) and *Wise Guys Prefer Brunettes* (1926), the last two starring Laurel & Hardy's regular foil James Finlayson, *Raggedy Rose* (1926) starring Mabel Normand, *On The Front Page* (1926) starring Stan Laurel (Brooke played the playboy son of a tough newspaper editor), *Love Me Tonight* (1932), *Hallelujah, I'm A Bum* (1933) starring

Al Jolson, *Belle Of The Nineties* (1934) with Mae West, *Reckless* (filmed between December 6, 1934 and February 23, 1935 and released by MGM on April 17, 1935) starring Jean Harlow in her musical début which lost $125,000, *In Old Chicago* (1938) and the film that introduced Abbott & Costello, *One Night In The Tropics* (1940). In March 1929 Brooke sued Oliver Hardy for $109,570, alleging that Hardy "hit him with a billiard cue and broke his arm" at a pool hall at Sycamore Avenue and Cahuenga in Los Angeles. The outcome of the lawsuit is not known. Tyler Brooke was married to the exotically named La Runa Walcott.
CAUSE: Brooke committed suicide in his car by carbon monoxide poisoning. He was 56.

Louise Brooks

Born November 14, 1906
Died August 8, 1985
Lulu. Born in Cherryvale, Kansas, 5'2" Mary Louise Brooks, the daughter of a lawyer, began her entertainment career as a dancer with Ziegfeld Follies before making the transition to films as a bit part player. She appeared in *The American Venus* (1926) as Miss Bayport, *A Social Celebrity* (1926) as Kitty Laverne, *It's The Old Army Game* (1926) as Mildred Marshall, *Love 'Em And Leave 'Em* (1926) as Janie Walsh, *Just Another Blonde* (1926) as Diana O'Sullivan, *Rolled Stockings* (1927) as Carol Fleming, and *The City Gone Wild* (1927) as Snuggles Joy before really making her mark in *A Girl In Every Port* (1928) as Marie. Her reputation as a sex symbol was further enhanced by *Beggars Of Life* (1928) in which she played Nancy, a girl who disguised herself as a boy. The pinnacle of her career came playing the amoral Lulu in G.W. Pabst's *Die Büchse Der Pandora* (1929). Millions of women rushed to their hairdresser to copy her famously bobbed style. Then things steadily

began to go wrong. Her next two films were *The Canary Murder Case* (1929) as Margaret Odell and *Das Tagebuch Einer Verlorenen* (1929) as Thymiane. Brooks was a strong-willed woman, much ahead of her time. She was bright, beautiful, sexy and promiscuous ("Love is a publicity stunt, and making love – after the first curious raptures – is only another petulant way to pass the time waiting for the studio to call"; "I don't think I ever loved the men I knew. It's a very strange thing. I've noticed that very often the men who were the best in bed were the men I cared least about. The men who were the worst in bed were the men I liked the most") none of which went down too well in Thirties Hollywood. Writer Anita Loos said, "Her favourite form of exercise was walking off a movie set, which she did with the insouciance of a little girl playing hopscotch." A battle with Harry Cohn ensued which the mogul won and he took great pleasure in humiliating the actress. He made her work as an uncredited ballet dancer in the Grace Moore musical *When You're In Love* (1937). The following year Brooks made her last film, *Overland Stage Raiders* (1938), and promptly retired from the screen. She worked as a nightclub entertainer for a while then became a $40 a week shop assistant at Saks Fifth Avenue before slipping into a reclusive lifestyle. She was twice married. From July 21, 1926, to June 20, 1928, she was the wife of director Edward Sutherland (b. London, January 5, 1895, d. 1974) and from October 10, 1933, she was married to Deering Davis, who made farming equipment. They separated six months after the wedding but didn't get around to getting a divorce until February 10, 1938.
CAUSE: Brooks suffered from emphysema and arthritis but died of a heart attack in Rochester, New York. She was 78 years old. She is buried at Holy Sepulchre Cemetery, Rochester, New York.

Joe E. Brown
Born July 28, 1892
Died July 6, 1973
Big-mouthed comedian. Joseph Evan Brown was born in Holgate, Ohio, and ran away from home aged nine to join the circus. He was the youngest of the Marvellous Ashtons, an aerial acrobatic troupe. When the Ashtons went their separate ways in 1906, 5'7" Brown became a semi-pro baseball player, almost making the first team of the Pittsburgh Pirates. (When he signed a contract with Warner he insisted that the company maintained a team for him among its employees.) Back in showbiz, he joined the Bell-Prevost Trio but that ended when he broke a leg. He became a straight actor for a while but returned to his comic roots in the Twenties. His first hit film was controversial. *Hold Everything* (1930) was based on a Broadway play starring Bert Lahr who paid for an ad in *Variety* claiming that Brown had stolen his mannerisms. Brown was very popular during the Depression and was among the Top 10 Moneymakers in 1932, 1935 and 1936. In 1915 he married Kathryn McGraw (1892–1977) and had two sons and two daughters. On October 8, 1936, his oldest son, Don Evan, was killed in a plane crash. That night, unsurprisingly, the show did not go on. His other son Joe L. became general manager of the Pittsburgh Pirates. During the Second World War and the Korean War Brown worked tirelessly to raise money and entertain the troops. He is now mostly forgotten except for one role – that of Osgood Fielding III in the hilarious *Some Like It Hot* (released March 29, 1959). Osgood is wooing Daphne, little realising that "she" is really Jerry. Daphne explains the reasons why they cannot be married: "For years I've lived with a saxophone player." "I forgive you." "We can never have children." "We can adopt some." "You don't understand – I'm a man!" and the final deadpan response, "Well, nobody's perfect."

CAUSE: Joe E. Brown died, aged 80, after a long illness in Brentwood, California. He was buried in the Sunrise Slope, south of the Great Mausoleum, Forest Lawn, Glendale, California.

Johnny Mack Brown

Born September 1, 1904
Died November 14, 1974
'Dothan Antelope'. Born in Dothan, Alabama, the great-great-grandson of a Red Indian princess, 6'1" Johnny Mack Brown was the second of six sons of John Henry Brown and Hattie McGillivray who owned the local clothes shop. His siblings were Harry, Tolbert, William Wallace, Fred, Louise, Elsa, Doris and David. He graduated from Dothan High School in 1922 and after a gap year enrolled at the University of Alabama in 1924 and, two years later, was discovered by Erich von Stroheim when Brown led his team to glory in the Rose Bowl American football competition. They beat the Washington Huskies 20-19, despite losing 12-0 at half time. Signed to MGM, he made his début in the film *Slide, Kelly, Slide* (1927) – a film about baseball which starred William Haines. His next film was *The Bugle Call* (1927) which starred Jackie Coogan. Brown appeared with some of Hollywood's most glamorous ladies. He worked with Marian Davies in *The Fair Co-Ed* (1927) in which he played Bob, and worked with Greta Garbo three times. The first film *The Divine Woman*, in which Brown played Jean Lery, was made on a budget of $267,000, and released on January 14, 1928. On July 28, 1928, he began filming as David Furness in *A Woman Of Affairs* based on Michael Arlen's novel *The Green Hat*. Allocated a budget of $383,000, the film co-starred John Gilbert, Lewis Stone, Douglas Fairbanks, Jr and Dorothy Sebastian. The film wrapped on September 11 and was released on December 29, 1928. On April 15, 1929, filming began on *The Single Standard* (1929) in which Brown played Tommy Hewlett, Garbo's on-screen husband. Based on the novel by Adela Rogers St John, the romantic drama starred Nils Asther, Dorothy Sebastian and a bit part for Joel McCrea. *The Single Standard* cost $336,000 and was premièred at New York's Capitol Theater on July 27, 1929. Brown starred with Joan Crawford in the silent *Our Dancing Daughters* (released October 8, 1928) playing Ben Blaine. The film also featured Dorothy Sebastian and Nils Asther. Leonard Maltin, the critic, described the film as "one of the best Jazz Age silents, with [an] absurdly melodramatic story". Brown played Steve Crandall in Norma Shearer's last silent film *A Lady Of Chance* (1928). The 'Flapper Age' melodrama *Coquette* (released March 30, 1929) was Mary Pickford's first talkie and it won her an Oscar. Brown played Michael Jeffery. It soon became apparent that his dashing good looks could only get him so far and he was fast becoming just another pretty face. His slow drawl did not help his box office appeal. A Stetson and a horse would save his career. In 1930 he made his first Western, *Montana Moon* (released April 14, 1930) playing Larry Kerrigan, which coincidentally starred Joan Crawford. He would go on to appear in almost 200 Westerns. Between 1930 and 1936 he alternated between Westerns and straight films before plumping to stay in the saddle. His early films included: *Mockery* (1927), *After Midnight* (1927), *Soft Living* (1928) as Stockney Webb, *Square Crooks* (1928) as Larry Scott, *The Play Girl* (1928) as Bradley Lane, *Annapolis* (1928) as Bill, *The Valiant* (1929) as Robert Ward, *Jazz Heaven* (1929) as Barry Holmes, *Great Day* (1930), *Undertow* (1930) as Paul Whalen and *Hurricane* (1930) as Dan. His next film would be the one that would make him a Western star. King Vidor was due to make a film of the life of the outlaw William H. Bonney,

better known to history as Billy the Kid. Vidor did not want to hire Brown but in the end he acquiesced and *Billy The Kid* (released October 1930) was a hit. If Brown thought his stardom was assured at MGM he was soon to be disabused of the notion. He left MGM and although he worked regularly it was to be for smaller studios like Mascot, Monogram, Supreme and Republic. In 1943 he began filming as US Marshal 'Nevada Jack' McKenzie in the Rough Riders series for Monogram. The films were *The Stranger From Pecos* (1943), *Six Gun Gospel* (1943), *Outlaws Of Stampede Pass* (1943), *The Texas Kid* (1943), *The Ghost Rider* (1943), *Raiders Of The Border* (1944), *Partners Of The Trail* (1944), *Law Men* (1944), *Range Law* (1944), *West Of The Rio Grande* (1944), *Land Of The Outlaws* (1944), *Law Of The Valley* (1944), *Ghost Guns* (1944), *The Navajo Trail* (1945), *Gun Smoke* (1945), *Stranger From Santa Fe* (1945), *The Lost Trail* (1945), *Frontier Feud* (1945), *Border Bandits* (1946) and *The Haunted Mine* (1946). From 1946 he played characters whose names were a variation of his own – Johnny Macklin, Johnny Mackey, Johnny Mack, and just plain Johnny: *Gentleman From Texas* (1946), *Trailing Danger* (1947), *Land Of The Lawless* (1947), *The Law Comes To Gunsight* (1947), *Code Of The Saddle* (1947), *Flashing Guns* (1947), *Crossed Trails* (1948), *Frontier Agent* (1948), *Triggerman* (1948), *Gunning For Justice* (1948), *Hidden Danger* (1948), *Law Of The West* (1949), *Trail's End* (1949), *West Of El Dorado* (1949), *Western Renegades* (1949), *Over The Border* (1950), *Six Gun Mesa* (1950), *Law Of The Panhandle* (1950), *Colorado Ambush* (1951), *Man From The Black Hills* (1952) and *Dead Man's Trail* (1952). He was Johnny Mack Brown in *Back Trail* (1948), *The Fighting Ranger* (1948), *Sheriff Of Medicine Bow* (1948), *Range Justice* (1949), *West Of Wyoming* (1950), *Man From Sonora* (1951),

Blazing Bullets (1951), *Oklahoma Justice* (1951), *Whistling Hills* (1951), *Texas Lawmen* (1951), *Texas City* (1952) and *Canyon Ambush* (1952). Between 1940 and 1950 he was never out of the Top 10 in *Motion Picture Herald*'s annual ranking. His highest position was fifth in 1943, sixth in 1940, 1942, 1944 and 1945, seventh in 1941 and 1946 and eighth in 1947, 1948, 1949 and 1950. His other films included *The Great Meadow* (1931) as Berk Jarvis, *The Secret Six* (released April 18, 1931) as Hank Rogers, *The Last Flight* (1931) as William 'Bill' Talbot, *Lasca Of The Rio Grande* (1931) as Miles Kincaid, *Hollywood Halfbacks* (1931), *Flames* (1932) as Charlie, *The Vanishing Frontier* (1932) as Kirby Tornell, *70,000 Witnesses* (1932) as Wally Clark, *Malay Nights* (1932), *Fighting With Kit Carson* (1933) as Kit Carson, *Saturday's Millions* (1933) as Alan Barry, *Female* (released November 11, 1933) as George P. Cooper, *Son Of A Sailor* (1933) as Duke, *Three On A Honeymoon* (1934) as Chuck Wells, *Missouri Nightingale* (1934) as Jim Warren, *Marrying Widows* (1934) as The Husband, *Cross Streets* (1934) as Adam Blythe, *Belle Of The Nineties* (released September 21, 1934) as Brooks Claybourne, *Against The Law* (1934) as Steve Wayne, *Rustlers Of Red Dog* (1935) as Jack Wood, *Branded A Coward* (1935) as Johnny Hume/Billy Hume, *Between Men* (1935) as Johnny Wellington, Jr, *Courageous Avenger* (1935) as Kirk Baxter, *Valley Of The Lawless* (1936) as Bruce Reynolds, *Desert Phantom* (1936) as Billy Donovan, *Rogue Of The Range* (1936) as Dan Doran, *Everyman's Law* (1936) as Dog Town Kid, *The Crooked Trail* (1936) as Jim Blake, *Under Cover Man* (1936) as Steve McLain, *The Gambling Terror* (1937) as Jeff Hayes, *Trail Of Vengeance* (1937) as Kenneth Dude Ramsey, *Lawless Land* (1937) as Ranger Jeff Hayden, *Bar-Z Bad Men* (1937) as Jim Waters, *Guns In The*

Dark (1937) as Johnny Darrell, A Lawman Is Born (1937) as Tom Mitchell, Wild West Days (1937) as Kentucky Wade, Boothill Brigade (1937) as Lon Cardigan, Born To The West (1937) as Tom Fillmore, Wells Fargo (1937) as Talbot Carter, Flaming Frontiers (1938) as Tex Houston, The Oregon Trail (1939) as Jeff Scott, Desperate Trails (1939) as Steve Hayden, Oklahoma Frontier (1939) as Jeff McLeod, Chip Of The Flying U (1939) as 'Chip' Bennett, West Of Carson City (1940) as Jim Bannister, Boss Of Bullion City (1940) as Tom Bryant, Riders Of Pasco Basin (1940) as Lee Jamison, Bad Man From Red Butte (1940) as Gil Brady/Buck Halliday, Son Of Roaring Dan (1940) as Jim Reardon, Ragtime Cowboy Joe (1940) as Steve Logan, Law And Order (1940) as Bill Ralston, Pony Post (1940) as Cal Sheridan, Bury Me Not On The Lone Prairie (1941) as Joe Henderson, Law Of The Range (1941) as Steve Howard, Rawhide Rangers (1941) as Brand Calhoun, Man From Montana (1941) as Sheriff Bob Dawson, The Masked Rider (1941) as Larry Prescott, Arizona Cyclone (1941) as Tom Baxter, Fighting Bill Fargo (1941) as Bill Fargo, Stagecoach Buckaroo (1942) as Steve, Ride 'Em Cowboy (1942) as Alabam Brewster, The Silver Bullet (1942) as Silver Jim Donovan, Boss Of Hangtown Mesa (1942) as Steve Collins, Deep In The Heart Of Texas (1942) as Jim Mallory, Little Joe, The Wrangler (1942) as Neal Wallace, The Old Chisholm Trail (1942) as Dusty Gardner, Tenting Tonight On The Old Camp Ground (1943) as Wade Benson, Cheyenne Roundup (1943) as Buck Brandon/Gils Brandon, Raiders Of San Joaquin (1943) as Rocky Morgan, Forever Yours (1945) as Major Tex O'Connor, Flame Of The West (1945) as Dr John Poole, Drifting Along (1946) as Steve Garner, Under Arizona Skies (1946) as Dusty Smith, Trigger Fingers (1946) as Sam 'Hurricane' Benton, Shadows On The Range (1946) as Steve Mason, Silver

Range (1946) as Johnny Bronton, Raiders Of The South (1947) as Captain Johnny Brownell, Valley Of Fear (1947) as Johnny Williams, Prairie Express (1947) as Johnny Hudson, Gun Talk (1947) as Johnny McVey, Overland Trails (1948) as Johnny Murdock, Western Feud! (1949) as Jim McPhail, Stampede (1949) as Sheriff Aaron Ball, Outlaw Gold (1950) as Dave Willis, Short Grass (1950) as Sheriff Keown and Montana Desperado (1951) as Dave Borden. Brown retired in 1953. He made a brief comeback in the mid-Sixties playing Enkoff in Requiem For A Gunfighter (1965), The Bounty Killer (1965) as Sheriff Green and Apache Uprising (released New Year's Day, 1966) as Sheriff Ben Hall. He was married to Connie Foster by whom he had a son, Lachlan (known as Locky) and three daughters, Cynthia, Jane Harriet (b. 1929) and Sally. In 1957 he was inducted into the College Football Hall of Fame and on New Year's Day, 2001 into the Rose Bowl Hall of Fame. CAUSE: Johnny Mack Brown suffered financial hardship in his later years and was forced to sell his Beverly Hills home. He died from heart failure, aged 70, in Woodland Hills, California. He was buried in the Court of Freedom, Columbarium of Heavenly Peace, at Forest Lawn, Glendale, California. His daughter, Jane Harriet Brown was interred with him in 1997.

Coral Browne

(CORAL EDITH BROWN)
Born July 23, 1913
Died May 29, 1991
Wicked wit. Coral Browne (she added the e for dramatic purposes) was born in Melbourne, Australia, the only child of Leslie Clarence Brown, a restaurateur, and Victoria Elizabeth Bennett. She was educated at the Claremont Ladies' College and then went to an art school where she studied costume design. In 1931 she made her stage début in Loyalties when an actress fell ill. Despite her parents' reservations

about her stage career, her father gave her £50 for her 21st birthday to travel to London. His only proviso was that she returned home if she had not made a success of herself when the money ran out. The £50 went long before she made her name but she began a number of liaisons with men who kept her. She made her film début in *Line Engaged* (1935) playing Doreen and made eight films in five years including the George Formby vehicle *Let George Do It* (1940) in which she portrayed Iris. In 1941 she played Maggie Cutler in *The Man Who Came To Dinner* opposite Robert Morley. At the time she had an affair with Jack Buchanan. She didn't make another film until 1946 but after one more film in 1947 she disappeared from the screen until 1954 when she appeared in *Beautiful Stranger*. On June 26, 1950 she married the bisexual actor and agent Philip Westrope Pearman (b. 1910, d. 1964). In 1951, she joined the Old Vic company to play first Emilia to Douglas Campbell's Othello, and then Regan to Donald Wolfit's King Lear. In 1956 she was Lady Macbeth, and Gertrude to Michael Redgrave's Hamlet, both at the Old Vic. She toured Moscow with the play and met the spy Guy Burgess, who had been Redgrave's lover at Cambridge. The meeting became the subject of Alan Bennett's television play *An Englishman Abroad* (1983). In 1958 she was bitchy Vera Charles in *Auntie Mame* and the cynical Meg in *The Roman Spring Of Mrs Stone*, three years later. She made half a dozen more films in the Sixties including *The Night Of The Generals* (1967) as Eleanore von Seidlitz-Gabler and *The Killing Of Sister George* as Mercy Croft, the lesbian BBC administrator. In 1964 Philip Pearman died and Browne began a long affair with the actor Michael Hordern. In 1973 she met Vincent Price while making *Theatre Of Blood* and they married on October 24, 1974. They decided to live in London and went to

buy a bed. They were told that there would be a five-week delay. Browne pointed to her corpse-like husband and quipped, "Five weeks? Have you seen Mr Price?" The couple decamped to California but she was not happy there. Her last film was *Dreamchild* (1985), a version of the Lewis Carroll book. CAUSE: She died of breast cancer in Los Angeles. She was 77. A Thanksgiving Mass was held in London's Church of the Immaculate Conception, Farm Street on September 5, 1991.

Tod Browning
Born July 12, 1880
Died October 6, 1962
'The Edgar Allan Poe of the cinema'. Born in Louisville, Kentucky, the son of Lydia J. and Charles Avery Browning, Charles Albert Browning was educated at Louisville Male High School but at 16 joined a travelling circus, the Manhattan Fair and Carnival Company. He served as an emcee introducing the sideshow freaks, a job he would never forget and later introduce into his films. At 18 he became a jockey but yearned for show business and became a singer-dancer in shows on the Ohio and Missouri rivers. In 1905 he formed a comedy contortion act – Lizard & Coon – with Roy C. Jones. Five years later, he joined a vaudeville-burlesque troupe, World of Mirth, where he became the principal comedian. In 1913 he arrived in Los Angeles and met the vaudevillian Charlie Murray who was working for Mack Sennett. With Murray's encouragement, Browning appeared in his first film, *Scenting A Terrible Crime* (released October, 1913 by Biograph). The same month that his début film was released, Browning moved with D.W. Griffith to Mutual where he starred in a series of short comedies for Komic (1914–1915). He also directed 25 comedies for Reliance-Majestic and was a set changer for *Atta Boy's Last Race* (1916) which starred Dorothy

Gish. He worked as an assistant for D.W. Griffith and appeared in several roles in *Intolerance* (1916). In 1917 he made his first feature film, *Jim Bludso*, starring Wilfred Lucas and Kate Taggart for Fine Arts and in 1917 moved to Metro Pictures where he directed five suspense melodramas. After the First World War Browning signed for Universal Pictures where he emerged as a first-rate director with a taste for low-life characters. However, by 1923, his alcoholism severely impacted on his work. It was two years before he recovered and he went to see his old boss Irving Thalberg about work. Browning directed Lon Chaney in *The Unholy Three* (made in 1925 on a budget of $103,000, it made $704,000), the first of eight grotesque fantasies by the two men for MGM: *The Black Bird* (1926), *The Road To Mandalay* (1926), *London After Midnight* (1927), *The Unknown* (1927), *The Big City* (1928), *West Of Zanzibar* (1928) and *Where East Is East* (1929). Browning directed *Dracula* (released February 14, 1931) for Universal, intending Lon Chaney to play the title role. When Chaney died, Browning cast Bela Lugosi in the film which cost $355,000 to make. The following year, for $311,000, Browning made the film for MGM for which he is best remembered. *Freaks* (released July 9, 1932) was the story of a circus in which the "normal" characters are cruel, greedy and venal while the "freaks" are loyal and selfless. The film was a financial flop and banned for many years. It also irritated Louis B. Mayer and caused a rift between the two. In the last seven years before his retirement in 1939, Browning made just four films – his last film being *Miracles For Sale* (1939). In 1906 he married Amy Louise Stevens but they divorced in 1910. On June 9, 1911, he married Alice L. Houghton Wilson (d. May 12, 1944) whom he had met when they were both in World of Mirth. There were no children.

CAUSE: In 1944 Tod Browning became one of the few people to read his own obituary when *Variety* prematurely killed him off. Following his wife's death Browning lived a solitary life, dying of cancer in Santa Monica, California.

Frank Brownlee
Born October 11, 1874
Died February 10, 1948
Silent support. Born in Dallas, Texas, Brownlee was an early supporting actor in Hal Roach comedies. He made more than 100 films and worked, often uncredited, in many different cinematic genres from comedy to cowboys, to crime to romances. He worked on Charley Chase's *Be Your Age* (1926) as Mr Blaylock and *Bigger And Better Blondes* (1927). He appeared with Laurel & Hardy in *With Love And Hisses* (filmed March 1927, released August 28, 1927) as Major General Rohrer, *Sailors Beware* (filmed April 1927, released September 25, 1927) as Captain Bull, *The 2nd Hundred Years* (filmed June 1927, released October 8, 1927) as a prison warder, *Do Detectives Think?* (filmed May 1927, released November 20, 1927) as the detective agency boss, *Pack Up Your Troubles* (filmed May–June 1, 1932, released September 23, 1932) as the drill sergeant and *The Midnight Patrol* (filmed June 24–July 6, 1933, released August 3, 1933) as Police Chief Ramsbottom. Other comedies included *Country Fair* (1941) and *Ice-Capades Revue* (1942) as Mr Sawyer. His early films included: *The Fireman And The Girl* (1914), *She Left Without Her Trunks* (1916), *Sold For Marriage* (1916) as Nicholas, *Intolerance* (1916) as the Girl's brother and *The Call Of The Past* (1916). He appeared in Westerns such as *The Half-Breed* (1916) as Winslow Wynn, *Brass Buttons* (1919) as Terence Callahan, *Desert Gold* (1919) as Jonas Warren, *Riders Of The Dawn* (1920) as Glidden, *Tombstone Canyon* (1932) as Alf Sykes, *Terror Trail* (1933) as Sheriff Judell,

Tumbling Tumbleweeds (1935) as
Cattleman, *The Desert Trail* (1935) as
the Sheriff of Rattlesnake Gulch, a
doctor in *Trail Of The Vigilantes*
(1940), *Three Faces West* (1940) as
Bill, *Arizona* (1940) as Weaver, *Riders
Of Death Valley* (1941) as Slim,
The Apache Kid (1941) as Harry
Castleman, *A Missouri Outlaw* (1941)
as Dairyman Jensen, *Arizona Terrors*
(1942) as Henry Adams, a rancher in
Man From Cheyenne (1942), *Denny
Stagecoach Buckaroo* (1942) as Higgins,
a Council member in *Jesse James, Jr*
(1942), *Romance On The Range* (1942)
as a member of the lynch mob, *In Old
California* (1942) as a man on the
street, *Sons Of The Pioneers* (1942) as a
hired hand, *The Sombrero Kid* (1942) as
Mayor Lem Barnett, *Shadows On The
Sage* (1942) as Johnson and *Dead
Man's Gulch* (1943) as Stevens. He was
in sci-fi films including *Mysterious
Doctor Satan* (1940) as Panamint Pete,
war films including *Me Und Gott*
(1918) as The Butler/August Weber,
and dramas such as *Mentioned In
Confidence* (1917) as Mr Leigh, *The
Martinache Marriage* (1917) as Roscoe
Vandercourt, *The Mysterious Mrs
Musslewhite* (1917) as Dr Woodman,
Wild Sumac (1917) as Lupin, *The Best
Man* (1917) as Captain Hale, *The Ship
Of Doom* (1917) as 'Sundown'
Shattuck, *Her Moment* (1918) as Victor
Dravich, *The Return Of Mary* (1918) as
John Graham, *The Vanity Pool* (1918)
as Jarvis Flint, *Girl From Nowhere*
(1919) as Klondyke Jim, *Paid In
Advance* (1919) as a gold dust barker,
The Valley Of Tomorrow (1920) as Fang
Morgan and *Gallant Lady* (1942) as
Luke Walker. He was in crime/mystery
films including *The Phantom Shotgun*
(1917) as Hamilton Forbes, *The
Inspirations Of Harry Larrabee* (1917) as
Batonyi, *The Mysterious Mr Tiller*
(1917) as Ramon Mordant, *The Double
Standard* (1917) as Editor George
Ferguson, *$5,000 Reward* (1918) as
Ackley, *The Empty Cab* (1918) as Big
Ed, *The Lincoln Highwayman* (1919) as

Captain Claver, *Boston Blackie* (1923)
as Warden Benton and *Lucky Devils*
(1941) as the farmer. He appeared in
adventure films including *The Little
Pirate* (1917) as John Baird, *June
Madness* (1917), *Miss Adventure* (1919)
as Bog Nichols, *The Brute Breaker*
(1919) as Norres and *South Of Tahiti*
(1941) as the harbour master.
CAUSE: He died in Los Angeles,
California, aged 73.

Nigel Bruce
Born September 4, 1895
Died October 8, 1953
Forever Dr Watson. Despite being the
epitome of the English gentleman,
William Nigel Ernle Bruce was born in
Ensenada, Mexico, while his parents
were on holiday. (Coincidentally, that
other "Englishman" and Bruce's dear
friend, Basil Rathbone, was born in
South Africa.) Bruce's father was
Sir William Waller Bruce, 10th Bt.
(1856–1912) and his mother Angelica
Mary (d. 1917), the daughter of
General George Selby, an officer in the
Royal Artillery. Bruce was educated at
The Grange, Stevenage, and Abingdon
School and was training to be a
stockbroker when the First World War
broke out. He joined the Honourable
Artillery Company but was badly
wounded. He rose to be a captain in
the Somerset light infantry's home
battalion, but his injuries caused him to
be invalided out of the service. Back in
civvy street he became a much in
demand actor, making his stage début
in 1920. He made his first (of nearly
80) films – the British silent film *Red
Aces* – in 1929. He moved permanently
to America five years later and became
a leading member of the English raj in
Tinseltown. It was for his portrayal of
the bumbling Dr John Watson in the
Sherlock Holmes films that he will
always be remembered. They were *The
Hound Of The Baskervilles* (1939), *The
Adventures Of Sherlock Holmes* (1939),
Sherlock Holmes And The Voice Of Terror
(1942), *Sherlock Holmes And The Secret*

Weapon (1942), *Sherlock Holmes Faces Death* (1943), *Sherlock Holmes In Washington* (1943), *The Pearl Of Death* (1944), *The Spider Woman* (1944), *The Scarlet Claw* (1944), *The House Of Fear* (1945), *The Woman In Green* (1945), *Pursuit To Algiers* (1945), *Terror By Night* (1946) and *Dressed To Kill* (1946). The first two films were made by 20th Century Fox but they dropped the films in 1940. Universal picked up the baton and set the stories in a contemporary era so that Holmes and Watson could fight the Germans. Bruce and Rathbone also played the sleuthing duo in more than 200 wireless programmes between 1938 and 1945. His other films included playing the Prince of Wales in *The Scarlet Pimpernel* (1934), *Treasure Island* (1934) as Squire Trelawney, *She* (1935) as Professor Holly, Joseph Sedley in *Becky Sharp* (1935), RKO's version of *Vanity Fair* which was the first feature to be filmed in three-strip Technicolor, *The Charge Of The Light Brigade* (1936) as Sir Benjamin Warrenton, *Suez* (1937) as Sir Malcolm Cameron, *A Dispatch From Reuter's* (1940) as Sir Randolph Persham, Hitchcock's *Rebecca* (1940) and *Suspicion* (1941), *Frenchman's Creek* (1944) as Lord Godolphin, *Dragonwyck* (1946), Charlie Chaplin's *Limelight* (1952) as Postant, the 3-D jungle adventure *Bwana Devil* (1952) as Dr Angus McLean and the posthumously released *World For Ransom* (1954) as Governor Coutts. On May 19, 1921, he married the actress Violet Campbell (b. Hertfordshire, April 24, 1892 as Violet Mary Pauline Shelton, d. London, January 3, 1970) and had two daughters, Pauline and Jennifer. CAUSE: Preparing to be reunited with Basil Rathbone on the stage, Nigel Bruce died aged 58 of a heart attack in St John's Hospital, Santa Monica, California. He was cremated at the Chapel of the Pines crematorium, Los Angeles.

Yul Brynner
(YUL BRYNER)
Born July 11, 1920
Died October 10, 1985
Egotistical baldy. Yul Brynner was a man known for just three roles: King Mongkut in *The King & I* (1956) and the gunslingers Chris in *The Magnificent Seven* (1960) and the robot in *Westworld* (1973) yet he maintained an air of mystery about much of his life. Until his son told the real story many speculated that Brynner may have been five years older than the date given above and it was thought he was born on Sakalin Island off Siberia. He refused to confirm or deny it, saying, "Just call me a nice clean-cut Mongolian boy," adding, "People don't know my real self and they're not about to find out." He was actually born in Vladivostok and moved to Paris in 1934 so that his elder sister could have a chance of a singing career. Brynner spoke French when discussing fashion or the arts but always used English for business. He began in show business on June 15, 1935, as a singer and guitarist in a gypsy orchestra. Always keen for a physical challenge he became a trapeze artist for two years at the Cirque d'Hiver, playing the part of a sad clown who made dreadful errors but saved himself just before he hit the ground. One day he failed to save himself and spent seven months in a plaster cast. In 1941 he travelled to America and began studying with Michael Chekhov, with whom Marilyn Monroe would also study. The following year he began to earn a living strumming his guitar in New York nightclubs and at private parties. When work was scarce he earned his money as a nude model. Brynner married actress Virginia Gilmore on September 6, 1944, and his only son, Rock, was born on December 23, 1946. Brynner made his film début in 1949, appearing in the little-known *Port Of New York*. It was to be another seven years before he stepped in front of the cameras again.

On February 26, 1951, Brynner took the part at the Shubert Theater in New Haven, Connecticut, that was to bring him international fame and an Oscar – the monarch in Rodgers & Hammerstein's *The King & I*. He played the role for three years on Broadway, though when the film version came to be made he originally wanted to direct and for Marlon Brando to play the lead. Eventually he was persuaded to take the lead part himself. Dinah Shore wanted the role of Mrs Anna but Brynner held out for Deborah Kerr. He also shaved his head for the part, a look he adopted for the rest of his life. The major rival for his Oscar nomination was Kirk Douglas in *Lust For Life* (1956) but he also received fierce competition from Laurence Olivier for *Richard III* (1955), Rock Hudson for *Giant* (1956) and, with the Academy's liking for sentiment, the late James Dean, also for *Giant*. Brynner's hand was considerably strengthened by strong performances as Pharaoh Rameses in *The Ten Commandments* (1956), the con man in *Anastasia* (1956) and by winning the coveted role of Dmitri in *The Brothers Kamarazov* (1958). Within a year Brynner had shot into the Top 10 Box-Office Draws list. *Redbook* called him "The most exciting male on the screen since Rudolph Valentino" and over a dozen teenage boys were suspended from an Iowa school for having their heads shaved à la Yul. When asked why he thought he had been so successful, Brynner replied: "I'm not of the can-kicking, shovel-carrying, ear-scratching torn T-shirt school of acting. There are very few real men in the movies these days. Yet being a real man is the most important quality an actor can offer on the screen." Brynner was never to be nominated again, although he did present three Oscars to other winners. In 1960 he was divorced by Virginia Gilmore and five days later, on March 31, 1960, he married Doris Kleiner. (They had a daughter in 1962.) In the spring of that year he was cast as Chris, the leader of a group of cowboy mercenaries, in *The Magnificent Seven*, a Westernized version of Akira Kurosawa's *The Seven Samurai* (1954). Playing Vin opposite Brynner was Steve McQueen. Both men had enormous egos (Brynner once compared his to an "average-sized aircraft carrier") and Brynner constantly complained that the more experienced McQueen was scene stealing using little nuances, such as fiddling with his hat. McQueen denied the accusation but Brynner even went as far as hiring someone to watch what McQueen did with his hat! Brynner kept himself busy for the rest of the decade with a variety of films such as *Taras Bulba* (1962), *Invitation To A Gunfighter* (1964), *Cast A Giant Shadow* (1966) and *Villa Rides* (1968). In 1971 he was divorced for the second time. On September 23, 1971, he married Jacqueline DeCroisset and the couple adopted two Vietnamese orphans. In 1973 he appeared in the Michael Crichton-written-and-directed *Westworld* about a theme park for rich playboys staffed by robots. Brynner plays a robot cowboy that goes berserk and starts killing the customers. Three years later, he made the sequel, *Futureworld*. It was to be his penultimate film, although he continued to tour the world in the role of the King that he had made his own. In 1983 he was divorced for the third time and in April married Kathy Lee (née Kathy Yam Choo), a dancer 37 years his junior, on his final tour of *The King & I*.

CAUSE: Cancer. Brynner smoked three to five packets of Gauloise cigarettes a day from 15 until he was 50. On the day in 1983 that he played the King for the 4,000th time, he discovered that he had inoperable lung cancer. After radiation treatment Brynner announced in January 1984 that he had beaten the disease. The following month he set off on what was billed as

"The Final Tour", which would be succeeded by four months on Broadway. The cancer spread to his spine but Brynner was loath to miss any performances because he had bought the rights to the play in a deal that meant he had to reimburse sold tickets at any show in which he did not appear. He made his 4,633rd and final appearance as the King on June 30, 1985. On September 2 he suffered a stroke and pneumonia set in, followed by meningitis. He died in New York with his wife, son and daughter at his side. Brynner had recorded a TV advertisement warning against the dangers of smoking. It was shown only after his death. His first wife, Virginia, committed suicide on Good Friday (March 28) 1986.

FURTHER READING: *Yul: The Man Who Would Be King*, Rock Brynner (New York: Simon & Schuster 1989).

Elsa Buchanan

(ELSIE WINIFRED BUCHANAN TINKER)
Born December 22, 1908
Died January 17, 2004
'The girl with the largest eyes and the smallest waist in Hollywood.' Born in London, the daughter of a civil servant, 5'3" Buchanan made her stage début aged three at the Palace Theatre during a performance attended by Queen Mary. Educated at Clapham High School, she danced in wartime charity performances, then studied at RADA before becoming a member of Edward Stirling's company at the English Playhouse in Paris for 15 months. The then Elsie Tinker impressed the local critics in *Hindle Wakes* and *Hay Fever* and became the only Englishwoman to win a place at the training school for the Academie Française. On her return to England, she joined the Plymouth repertory company to appear in *The Angel Of The House* and *The Marsdens*, before joining Marie Tempest's Passing Brompton Road Company at the Criterion in Kingsway. In 1934, Elsa Buchanan, as she had now become,

travelled to Hollywood, where a touring company needed someone to play a leading part in the satire *I Am So Sorry*. It was an eventful time: there was an earthquake, after which she was cut off from her friends for three days with only 10 cents in her pocket and she was involved in a car crash. She attracted attention for her performance as Lord Byron's humiliated wife in *Bitter Harvest*. Unable to take up further offers until her contract was fulfilled, it was not long before her blonde good looks brought the photographers running. She modelled ball gowns and linen shorts, and frolicked in the sea at Malibu. A regular in the gossip columns, she failed to translate the publicity into steady work. In 1934, she appeared as Daphne in *Riptide* and followed that with *Charlie Chan In London* (1934) in which she played the maid, Alice Perkins. Her accent changes between Cockney and Irish because the producers could not make up their minds which they wanted. Nothing if not flexible, she then appeared in *The Mystery Of Edwin Drood* (1935) as Mrs Tisher, a schoolmarm, and in *Becky Sharpe* (1935) as a schoolgirl. She worked on *Little Lord Fauntleroy* (1936), as Susan the parlour maid with Freddie Bartholomew and Sir C. Aubrey Smith (who recalled appearing on stage with her when she was five), and in *Here's To Romance* (1935) as Enid, *I Found Stella Parish* (1935), *Lloyd's Of London* (1936) as a servant, *Trouble For Two* (1936), *The Thirteenth Chair* (1937) as Miss Stanby, and *Call It A Day* (1937) as Vera the maid, as well as many other films for which she often never even earned a credit. After two years she returned home for a holiday, and immediately won a job as a chatty nurse in the Teddington production *From A Dark Stairway*. But Hollywood was losing its attraction, and she had caught the fancy of a merchant navy officer, Noll Charlton, who had proposed to her several times when his ship visited California. She finally accepted at a ball for King George VI's coronation. They married in 1938 and had a son. They were together until his death in 1966. During the Second World War Elsa did some advertisements for the Women's Land Army and then, claiming to be 22 instead of 32, she joined the Women's Auxiliary Air Force as a clerk. She arrived at Fighter Command's 11 Group at Uxbridge just as the Battle of Britain began, and became a plotter in the ops room. As the pressure eased, she set about organising a weekly variety concert and writing a skit, *Alice in WAAFland*, about a WAAF enrolment centre. When the Luftwaffe abandoned its campaign, Elsa was commissioned as section officer and sent to Bomber Command at RAF Finningley. She joined the publicity staff at the Air Ministry, which led to her last film appearance in *They Flew Alone*, which starred Anna Neagle as the pilot Amy Johnson. Elsa Buchanan was shown with 50 airwomen under her command back in the ops room at Uxbridge. The final part of her wartime career was spent with Coastal Command before she was invalided out in 1944. When her husband was demobbed, he worked for Iraq Petroleum in Qatar, and then at Tripoli, where his family joined him. Following his retirement in 1962, they moved to the Isle of Man. After his death four years later, Elsa moved to Childswickham, Worcestershire, where she lived in a Georgian farmhouse, owned a Pyrenean mountain dog, and became a keen Scrabble player and a devotee of the *Daily Telegraph* quick crossword. Elsa Buchanan did not miss show business, though she once took her son to see *Charlie Girl* in London, where Anna Neagle told him that, while she had always been a showgirl, his mother had been an actress. CAUSE: Shortly before her death, Elsa Buchanan watched a DVD of the film *Gosford Park*. The plot concerns a

house party in the Thirties at which an American producer spends much of his time discussing the casting for *Charlie Chan In London*. At the end of *Gosford Park*, he offers the movie-obsessed blonde maid a lift to London, and the clear chance that she will get the part originally played by Elsa Buchanan. The original died at Childswickham, near Evesham, Worcestershire, aged 95, from natural causes.

Jack Buchanan

Born April 2, 1890
Died October 20, 1957
Mr Suave. Born in Helensburgh, near Glasgow, Scotland, the son of an auctioneer 6'2" Walter John Buchanan seemed to spend his entire cinematic working life in top hat and tails. At school he veered towards the law but his heart was never there. When Buchanan made his music hall début in 1911 he was so appallingly bad that the audience booed him and began to throw things. Fearing for his safety the management quickly brought down the curtain. Rather too quickly. It hit Buchanan on the head and made him see stars. The catcalls and jeers turned to sympathetic laughter and thereafter the management paid him £1 a week to do the routine twice nightly. Among his films (the vast majority of which were made in Britain) were *Auld Lang Syne* (1917), *The Audacious Mr Squire* (1923), *Bulldog Drummond's Third Round* (1925), *Brewster's Millions* (1935), *Bulldog Sees It Through* (1940), *As Long As They're Happy* (1953) and *The Band Waggon* (1953) opposite his American equivalent, Fred Astaire. Buchanan was a generous, loyal man and it was his efforts that saw the building of the Leicester Square Theatre, as well as being involved in the early days of television. He was married twice – firstly, on November 25, 1915 to Drageva Sava and then on January 14, 1949 to Susan Bassett. There were no children from either match.

CAUSE: He died aged 67 in the Middlesex Hospital, London. His ashes were scattered on Southampton Water. He left £24,489 12s 9d.

Horst Buchholz

Born December 4, 1933
Died March 3, 2003

The Magnificent German. There have been comparatively few German cowboys but Horst Buchholz achieved fame as one of them. Born in the predominantly proletarian Prenzlauer Berg district of Berlin, the son of a shoemaker, he was evacuated during the Second World War to the countryside. When his father was killed, Buchholz left a Bavarian children's home and went back to Berlin where he left school to study acting. In the cinema he was first employed dubbing foreign language films but he caught the eye of the French director Julien Duvivier while he was performing in a play at the Berlin Schiller Theatre. Horst first appeared on stage at the age of 15 in a Berlin production of *Emil And The Detectives*. His early show business work was on radio and he had a flare for languages – he spoke English, French, German, Spanish, Russian and Italian. In his native land he became a brooding James Dean figure in films such as *Die Halbstarken* (1956) in which he played Freddy Borchert. His early films included: *Die Spur Führt Nach Berlin* (1952) as Junger mann am funkturm, *Marianne De Ma Jeunesse* (1954) as a student, *Himmel Ohne Sterne* (1955) as Mischa Bjelkin for which he won a Silver German Film Award, *Robinson Soll Nicht Sterben* (1957) as Tom, *Bekenntnisse Des Hochstaplers Felix Krull* (1957) as Felix Krull, *Herrscher Ohne Krone* (1957), *Monpti* (1957) as King Christian, *Ein Stück Vom Himmel* (1957) as Cabrio-Fahrer, *Endstation Liebe* (1957) as Mecky Berger, *Nasser Asphalt* (1958), *Auferstehung* (1958) as Nechljudoff, *Tiger Bay* (1959) as

Korchinsky opposite Hayley Mills and *Das Totenschiff* (1959) as Philip Gale. But it was his performance as the hot-headed Chico in *The Magnificent Seven* (1960) that gained him international fame. Although not the star of the film, Buchholz commanded attention in the role which Toshiro Mifune had made famous in the Japanese original as the youngest of the seven mercenaries hired to defend a Mexican town from bandits. James Coburn, who played another of the Magnificent Seven, certainly thought so. He felt that the director, John Sturges, had become besotted with Buchholz: "John was enamoured . . . He shot a lot of film of Horst. I thought he missed there, but that was the one place. I think everybody else was cast quite well." Buchholz also did himself no favours by retaining the German name that young American teenagers (his natural audience) would have found hard to pronounce. Two years earlier, on December 7, 1958, he had married the actress Myriam Bru (b. Paris, France, April 20, 1932), by whom he had one son, Christopher (b. January 9, 1962) and one daughter, Beatrice. Following *The Magnificent Seven* he failed to capitalise on his success and although he made several films, he was never again able to capture the public's attention. His post-*Seven* work included: *Fanny* (1961) as Marius, Billy Wilder's *One, Two, Three* (1961) as Otto Ludwig Piffl, an East Berlin communist who secretly marries the daughter of a West Berlin Coca-Cola executive played by James Cagney, *Nine Hours To Rama* (1963) as Naturam Godse, *Estambul 65* (1965) as Tony Maecenas, *Marco The Magnificent* (1965) as Marco Polo, *Cervantes* (1966) as Miguel de Cervantes, *Johnny Banco* (1967) as Johnny Banco, *Come, Quando, Perché* (1968) as Alberto, *L'Astragale* (1968) as Julien, *Le Sauveur* (1971), *La Colomba Non Deve Volare* (1971), *The Great Waltz* (1972) as Johann Strauss,

Jr, . . . *aber Jonny!* (1973) as Jonny
Pittsville, *Ein Safe Voll Blut* (1974) as
Mark Kalvin, *Frauenstation* (1976) as
Dr Schumann, *Dead Of Night* (1977),
Da Dunkerque Alla Vittoria (1979) as
Jurgen Dietrich, *Avalanche Express*
(1979) as Scholten, *Aphrodite* (1982) as
Harry Laird, *Wenn Ich Mich Fürchte*
(1984) for which he won a Gold
German Film Award, *Code Name:
Emerald* (1985) as Walter Hoffman,
I Skrzypce Przestaly Grac (1988) as
Dymitr, *Touch And Die* (1991) as
Limey, *Aces: Iron Eagle III* (1992) as
Leichman, *In Weiter Ferne, So Nah!*
(1993) as Tony Baker, Roberto
Benigni's *La Vita è Bella* a.k.a. *Life Is
Beautiful* (1997) as Dr Lessing and
*Detective Lovelorn Und Die Rache Des
Pharao* (2002) as Professor
Svedenborg. He was also the voice of
the emperor of China in the German
version of *Mulan* (1998).
CAUSE: Buchholz died in Berlin's
Charite Hospital, aged 69. He had
been recovering from a broken
thighbone when he died of pneumonia
in the intensive care unit. Buchholz had
been in and out of hospital in his last
few months.

George Bunny
Born July 13, 1867
Died April 16, 1952
The replacement. The younger brother
of John Bunny, whom he resembled,
5'7" George was born in New York and
signed by Vitagraph as a replacement
following John's premature death.
However, his films did not prove as
successful as those of his brother and
he was later signed to Samuel Goldwyn.
George Bunny's films included *"If
Only" Jim* (1921), *Danger Ahead*
(1921), *The Lost World* (1925), *Thrilling
Youth* (1926), *The Love Mart* (1928)
and *The Locked Door* (1929). He made
almost 50 films but much of his later
work was limited to bit parts. He was
married to Anna McCade.
CAUSE: He died in Hollywood,
California, aged 84, from a heart attack.

John Bunny
Born September 21, 1863
Died April 26, 1915
America's first comedy film star. Born
in New York, the son of a sailor from
Penzance, Cornwall, Bunny senior was
the last of seven generations of his
family to have gone to sea with the
Royal Navy. John Bunny decided that
a life on the ocean waves was not the
life for him so he became a shop
assistant but found serving customers
boring so he formed a minstrel troupe
and toured America. A large, affable
man he appeared in musicals,
comedies and straight work. Realising
that films were the future, he travelled
to New York at the end of 1910
where, according to one story, he
offered his services free to Vitagraph.
Keen to hire him, Vitagraph bosses J.
Stuart Blackton and Albert E. Smith
could not match the money he was
earning on stage. His films included
Jack Fat And Jim Slim At Coney Island
(released December 1910), *He Who
Laughs Last* (December 1910), *Doctor
Cupid* (January 1911), *The New
Stenographer* (February 1911), *The
Wooing Of Winnifred* (April 1911) in
which he played Maurice Costello's
butler, *The Troublesome Secretaries*
(1911), *Vanity Fair* (December 1911),
A Cure For Pokeritis (February 1912),
Mr Bolter's Infatuation (March 1912),
The Troublesome Stepdaughters (July
1912), *Bachelor Buttons* (October
1912), *Bunny All At Sea* (October
1912), *Bunny At The Derby* (October
1912), *Michael McShane, Matchmaker*
(November 1912), *Cork And Vicinity*
(December 1912), *Doctor Bridget*
(December 1912), *And His Wife Came
Back* (January 1913), *Blarney Stone*
(March 1913), *When The Press Speaks*
(August 1913) and *Bunny's Little
Brother* (December 5, 1914).
CAUSE: In late 1914, Bunny went on
tour with his own show, *Bunny In
Funnyland*, but the strain proved too
much for him and he fell ill. Although
Vitagraph were keen for him to make

more films, his health did not permit it. He died, aged 51, from Bright's disease.

Luis Buñuel

(LUIS BUÑUEL PORTOLÉS)
Born February 22, 1900
Died July 29, 1983
The father of cinematic Surrealism. Born in Calanda, Spain, and raised by Jesuits, Buñuel moved to Madrid to study religion. He befriended Salvador Dalí and Federico García Lorca. His name and reputation was made with just one 17-minute long film, *Un Chien Andalou* (1928), which he wrote, directed, produced, edited and appeared in. The film was partly financed by his mother and received creative input from Dalí. He was lauded by Surrealists for the film, which includes a scene of an eyeball being sliced. He left Spain after the 1936 Civil War and moved to America and then Mexico, becoming a citizen in 1948. He spent the Fifties making cheap films. In 1961 Generalissimo Franco asked Buñuel to come back to Spain but insteaad he made the film *Viridiana* (1961) which was banned in his home country because it was considered blasphemous. His film *Belle De Jour* (1966) with Catherine Deneuve playing a housewife who works as a prostitute by day was lauded and he won an Oscar nomination for *The Discreet Charm Of The Bourgeoisie* (1972). He married Jeanne Rucar in 1925.
CAUSE: He died in Mexico City from cirrhosis of the liver, aged 83.

Victor Buono

Born February 3, 1938
Died January 1, 1982
Sixties' Sydney Greenstreet. Born in San Diego, the son of Victor Francis Buono (b. Orgeon, May 28, 1907, d. San Diego, California, May 17, 1981) and Myrtle Belle Keller (b. Washington, October 19, 1909, d. San Diego, California, August 27, 1979), and the grandson of vaudevillian Myrtle Glied

(b. California April 18, 1886, d. San Diego, California December 9, 1969), 6'3" Charles Victor Buono's star blazed briefly and was just as quickly extinguished. He had intended to become a doctor but the lure of the stage was too much. In 1959 he was offered a screen test and began to appear regularly on television. He appeared uncredited in two films – including *The Guns Of Navarone* (1961) – before director Robert Aldrich cast him as Edwin Flagg in the psychological horror movie *Whatever Happened To Baby Jane?* (premièred October 26, 1962) with Bette Davis and Joan Crawford. Buono was nominated for a Best Supporting Actor Oscar but things could have been so different. Bette Davis was not happy with Aldrich's hiring of Buono for the film and tried to get him sacked but Aldrich stood resolute. After the first scenes were in the can Davis strode up to Buono and said, "I confess that before we began, I did not care for Bob's choice of you, and I tried to persuade him not to use you. He was right and I was wrong. I hope you will accept my apology, because you are absolutely marvellous." His other films included *Robin And The Seven Hoods* (1964), *Hush . . . Hush, Sweet Charlotte* (1965), *The Greatest Story Ever Told* (1965), *Young Dillinger* (1965), *Beneath The Planet Of The Apes* (1970) and *The Man With Bogart's Face* (1980). He was also memorable as the villainous King Tut in *Batman*. Buono, a homosexual, who weighed 22st, never married. He once commented: "I've heard or read about actors being asked the immortal question 'Why have you never married?' They answer with the immortal excuse 'I just haven't found the right girl.' Because I'm on the hefty side, no one's asked me yet. If they do, that's the answer I'll give. After all if it's good enough for Monty Clift and Sal Mineo . . ."
CAUSE: He died aged 43 in Apple Valley, California, a premature death brought about by his chronic obesity.

Helen Burgess

Born April 26, 1916
Died April 7, 1937
Young tragedy. Discovered by Cecil B. DeMille in the studio commissary, Burgess made her début in his *The Plainsman* (released November 16, 1936) as Buffalo Bill's wife, Louisa Cody. It was a promising start and she appeared in *King Of Gamblers* (1937) as Jackie Nolan and *A Doctor's Diary* (1937) as Ruth Hanlon.
CAUSE In early 1937 she eloped with musician Herbert Rutherford and began to film *Night Of Mystery* (released May 21, 1937) in which she played Ada Greene. During filming she came down with a heavy cold that turned into lobar pneumonia. She died in Beverly Hills, California, aged 20. The studio, Paramount, decided to carry on filming and used a double for Helen's scenes. Her marriage was annulled on the grounds of non-consummation. She was buried in Forest Lawn Memorial Park in Glendale, California.

Paul Burke

Born July 21, 1926
Died September 13, 2009
Second lead. Born in New Orleans, Louisiana, the son of Marty Burke, a boxer turned restaurateur and nightclub owner who had once fought the heavyweight champion Gene Tunney, Burke said that watching the sad people in his father's club gave him a sense of purpose. "I stayed up late watching the barflies, the brawlers. I listened to the stories of wasted lives, I watched the effect of wasted lives. It gave me a strong feeling of urgency about my own life." He studied at the Pasadena Playhouse before making his film debut in the Betty Grable musical *Call Me Mister* (1951) playing a soldier. Burke appeared regularly on television as well as films but he became well known for playing Detective Adam Flint from 1960 to 1963 in the police show *Naked City* for which he received two Emmy nominations. Each week the narrator ended the programme with the clichéd, "There are eight million stories in the Naked City. This has been one of them". In 1984 he took over the role of C.C. Capwell in the soap opera *Santa Barbara*. In 1967 he played Lyon Burke in *Valley Of The Dolls* and the following year was a policeman who chased the upmarket art thief played by Steve McQueen in *The Thomas Crown Affair*. Burke retired to Palm Springs in the early 1990s, his last part was in the film *The Fool* (1990). "Acting is more exciting than living, more electric, more immediate than living," he said. "That's because life is full of random elements. In acting, you select, you choose the elements. This selection allows you to get to the essence of the character, the essence of an experience." He was married twice and had three children by his first wife.
CAUSE: Burke died aged 83 at his home in Palm Springs, California. He had leukaemia and non-Hodgkins lymphoma.

Bobby Burns

Born September 1, 1878
Died January 16, 1966
Comedy support. Born in Philadelphia, Pennsylvania, the diminutive Robert P. Burns began acting in rep before moving into vaudeville. He began making films in 1908 for Selig. He formed a partnership with Walter Stull as Pokes & Jabbs in the Wizard films and then in Vim comedies from 1915. He appeared in seven Laurel & Hardy films and later supported The Three Stooges. He made more than 120 films and directed a dozen more.
CAUSE: He died in Los Angeles, California, aged 87.

George Burns

(NATHAN BIRNBAUM)
Born January 20, 1896
Died March 9, 1996
Centenarian comedian. Born in New

York's Lower East Side, he began his career in vaudeville in 1903 as a member of a children's singing quartet. In 1910, aged 14, he adopted the prop that was to stay with him for the rest of his life – the cigar. It was after he married Gracie Allen (on January 7, 1926) that his star really began to shine. They were a massive hit on the radio and then on television. When Allen retired through ill-health in 1958, Burns carried on as a solo performer. Following the cancellation of his sitcom *Wendy And Me* in 1965 he faded from view. The death of Jack Benny was a lucky break for Burns, who was given the role of Al Lewis intended for Benny in *The Sunshine Boys* (1975). He won a Best Supporting Actor Oscar for his performance. In 1985 he hosted *The George Burns Comedy Week*. He once quipped, "People think all I do is stand up and tell a few jokes. The jokes are easy. It's the standing up that's hard." CAUSE: In July 1994 Burns fell in his bath and hit his head. His health was never the same afterwards. In December 1995 he caught influenza after attending a Christmas party at the Frank Sinatras. He died at his home, 720 North Maple Drive, in Beverly Hills 90210, where Gracie Allen had died 32 years earlier. The house was used as the façade in *The George Burns And Gracie Allen Show* from October 12, 1950, until September 22, 1958. Burns, a couple of months after his 100th birthday, died at 10am from cardiorespiratory failure, congestive heart failure and coronary artery disease. His funeral was held on March 12, 1996, at the Wee Kirk O' the Heather Chapel, Forest Lawn Memorial-Parks, 1712 South Glendale Avenue, Glendale, California 91209. According to his butler, Daniel Dhoore, Burns was interred in his best dark blue suit, light blue shirt and red tie. Dhoore said: "We put three cigars in his pocket, put on his toupee, put on his watch that Gracie gave him, his ring, and in his pocket, his keys and his wallet with ten $100 bills, a five and three ones – so wherever he went to play bridge he'd have enough money." He was buried in the Freedom Mausoleum next to his wife.

Raymond Burr
Born May 21, 1917
Died September 12, 1993
Defender of right. It's rare for an actor to have two characters so closely identified with him that the public accepts both equally. Such was the case with Raymond William Stacy Burr, who was born in New Westminster, British Columbia. He spent part of his formative years in China. Following his parents' divorce he was raised by his mother and grandparents; it is believed by many psychologists that the presence of a dominating mother can affect a boy's sexuality. To support his mother and siblings Burr took a variety of jobs including working as a rancher in Roswell, New Mexico, as a deputy sheriff, selling photographs and even as a nightclub singer. He joined the Navy in World War II and was wounded (shot in the stomach) in Okinawa and shipped home. Burr made his film début in *San Quentin* (1946) playing Jeff Torrance. He went on to appear in over 90 films including *Without Reservations* (1946) as Paul Gill, *Desperate* (1947) as Walt Radak, *Walk A Crooked Mile* (1948) as Krebs, *Ruthless* (1948) as Pete Vendig, *Raw Deal* (1948) as Rick Coyle, *Red Light* (1949) as Nick Cherney, *Love Happy* (1950) as Alphonse Zoto, *M* (1951) as Pottsy, *A Place In The Sun* (1951) as Frank Marlowe, *His Kind Of Woman* (1951) as Nick Ferraro, *Meet Danny Wilson* (1952) as Nick Driscoll, *Tarzan And The She-Devil* (1953) as Vargo, *Fort Algiers* (1953) as Amir, *Casanova's Big Night* (1954) as Bragadin, *Godzilla, King Of The Monsters!* (1956) as Steve Martin and *Affair In Havana* (1957) as Mallabee. However, in the last 30 years of his life he was known for playing two upholders of law and order, lawyer

Perry Mason (from September 21, 1957, until 1993) and paralysed former San Francisco police chief Robert T. Ironside in *A Man Called Ironside* (from September 14, 1967, until January 16, 1975). Perry Mason never lost a case and this irritated one fan, causing Burr to respond, "But madam, you only see the cases I try on Saturdays." In his entries in biographical dictionaries, 6′2″ Burr claimed he had married three times. Sadly, for the Mrs Burrs they had an unfortunate propensity for dying – or so their supposed husband claimed. Burr's first wife, English actress Annette Sutherland, allegedly died in the same plane crash that killed Leslie Howard. Their son, Michael, was reported to have died of leukaemia ten years later aged 12. Burr divorced his second wife, Isabella Ward, while the third, Laura Andrine Morgan, reportedly died in 1955. In reality Burr made up his first and third weddings and his son. Playwright Emlyn Williams commented, "He uses the same trick a lot of Latin American actors, singers and writers use – he invents wives and offspring for himself so people will believe him heterosexual." In fact, Burr lived with his lover of 31 years, the 12-years-younger Robert Benevides, whom he 'married' in a gay ceremony in 1963, on a 40-acre ranch in Heraldsburg, northern California. The couple was known as Mr & Mrs Benevides, since Burr preferred to be the 'woman' in the relationship. A friend of the couple said that Burr didn't "like women and preferred not to have them around."
CAUSE: He died of kidney cancer at his home at 8.40pm on September 12, 1993. He was 76. The actor left his entire $32-million fortune to the Portuguese-born Robert Benevides.

Richard Burton

(RICHARD WALTER JENKINS)
Born November 10, 1925
Died August 5, 1984
The Voice of the Valleys. Richard

Walter Jenkins was born at 2 Dan-y-Bont, Pontrhydyen, Wales, weighing a remarkable 12lb. His father, who bore the same name, was 49 and just 5′3″; his mother, Edith Thomas, was 42 when Richard was born, the twelfth out of thirteen children. His mother died following the birth of her final child, Graham, in 1927 "of puerperal fever". His sister Cissie raised Richard until he was 17, when he moved in (on March 1, 1943, at 6 Connaught Street, Port Talbot) with a gay schoolteacher by the name of Philip Burton (b. November 30, 1904). The latter took an interest in young Jenkins, who later took his mentor's name. Thanks to Burton's tutelage the boy won a scholarship to Exeter College, Oxford, in April 1944. The previous year, in November 1943, he had made his tentative first stage appearance at the Royal Court Theatre, Liverpool playing Glan in *Druid's Rest*. The war burst into his studies and from 1944 until 1947 he served with the RAF. In 1948 he made his film début playing Gareth in *The Last Days Of Dolwyn* (1948). On the set he met an actress by the name of Sybil Williams (b. 1929) and they were married at 8.45am at Kensington Registry Office on February 5, 1949. They had two daughters, the actress Kate (b. Switzerland, September 11, 1957) and Jessica (b. Switzerland, 1959) who was autistic. In 1949 in London and in 1950 on Broadway, the 5′11″ Burton appeared in *The Lady's Not For Burning* to critical acclaim. In 1952 he made his first film in America, *My Cousin Rachel*, playing Philip Ashley, a role that won him the first of his seven Academy Award nominations. The following year he was nominated in the Best Actor category for his portrayal of Marcellus Gallio in *The Robe* (1953). It would be ten years later on the set of *Cleopatra* (1963), where he played Mark Antony, that Richard Burton's stature changed from that of a respected actor to gossip column fodder. He fell in love with the star of the film, Elizabeth Taylor, thus launching an avalanche of newspaper stories that would not abate for over 20 years. Acting legend Laurence Olivier told him, "Make up your mind, Richard Burton. A household word or a great actor." It seems he chose the former by embarking on his reckless affair with Taylor. Some have said that Burton would have eclipsed Olivier as the greatest actor of the Twentieth Century had he not met Taylor. He initiated divorce proceedings against Sybil so he could be free to marry Taylor. However, there was a problem. At the time Taylor was married to singer Eddie Fisher who had commented, "Who could take that scruffy, arrogant buffoon seriously?" It was a serious mistake. Burton was divorced on December 16, 1963, and he and Taylor were married on March 15, 1964, on the eighth floor of the Ritz-Carlton Hotel in Montreal, Canada. Prior to the wedding Fisher's godfather, mobster Frank Costello, asked him if he wanted Burton taken care of. Fisher didn't because he, too, had been having an affair with Burton. On the wedding night Burton and Taylor "sat and talked and giggled and cried until seven in the morning." Taylor said at the time, "I'm so happy you can't believe it . . . I love him enough to stand by him, no matter what he might do and I would want." Burton opined, "I did not tame Elizabeth; she came, she saw and then I conquered." Professionally, Burton provided the voice-over for Stanley Baker and Cy Enfield's *Zulu* (1964) but following his marriage producers queued to hire him and Taylor as a pair, offering telephone number salaries as inducements. They appeared together in *The V.I.P.s* (1963), *The Sandpiper* (1965), *Who's Afraid Of Virginia Woolf?* (1966), *Doctor Faustus* (1967), *The Comedians* (1967) and *Boom* (1968). His other films included *The Longest Day* (1962) as Flight

Officer David Campbell, *Becket* (1964) as Thomas à Becket (which saw him nominated for another Best Actor Oscar; appearing with Peter O'Toole the two serious drinkers made a pact not to drink for ten days: each man lasted just five), *The Night Of The Iguana* (1964) as The Reverend T. Lawrence Shannon, the lead in *Hamlet* (1964), *What's New, Pussycat?* (1965) (an uncredited cameo role in which he played a man in the bar, something of an in-joke reference to O'Toole's and his own fondness for drink), *The Spy Who Came In From The Cold* (1965) as Alec Leamas (winning yet another Best Actor Oscar nomination), *Anne Of The Thousand Days* (1969) as King Henry VIII (and his sixth nomination), *The Assassination Of Trotsky* (1972) as Leon Trotsky, *Under Milk Wood* (1973), *Equus* (1977) as Dr Martin Dysart (his seventh and last Oscar nomination), *Exorcist II: The Heretic* (1977) as Father Lamont, *The Wild Geese* (1978) as Colonel Allen Faulkner, *Absolution* (1981) as Father Goddard, which saw him playing opposite a naked Tatum O'Neal, and his last film, released posthumously, *Nineteen Eighty-Four* (1984) as O'Brien. But Burton's private life fascinated as much if not more than his professional one. As a token of his love for Taylor, Burton bought her the 69.42 carat Cartier-Burton diamond which cost him a cool $1,050,000. He also splashed out on the most expensive mink coat in the world (a snip at $125,000), the 33.9 carat Krupp diamond (a bargain at $350,000), the Ping-Pong diamond ($38,000), La Peregrina pearl ($37,000), a $93,000 emerald and a sapphire brooch valued at $65,000. They had no children together, but adopted a daughter, Maria. In 1974, talking about a possible marriage split between them, Burton said, "Elizabeth and I have been through too much to watch our marriage go up in flames. There is too much love going for us ever to

divorce." Soon after (June 26, 1974) they divorced but on October 10, 1975, they remarried in a mud hut in Botswana. However, the passion was spent and nine months later, on July 30, 1976, they divorced for the second and last time. Taylor did not see Burton through rose-tinted spectacles. She once said, "Richard Burton is so discriminating that he won't go to see a play with anybody in it but himself." Just over three weeks after his divorce from Taylor, Burton married Suzy Hunt, the ex-wife of Formula 1 champion James Hunt, in Arlington, Virginia. Seven years later, they too divorced. On July 3, 1983, he married freelance secretary Sally Hay (b. January 18, 1948) in a Las Vegas hotel, during a run of *Private Lives* in which he starred opposite Elizabeth Taylor. Despite his lady-killing reputation, Burton admitted he had homosexual tendencies and that he drowned them out by drinking excessively. Third wife Suzy Hunt believed she was marrying "a drunk and a roaring madman" but commented that she finished with "a little goody two-shoes". He was also, on occasion, prone to engaging mouth before brain, as at a benefit for haemophilia in which Burton told the audience that he had been a "bleeder" all his life. He had no illusions about himself, admitting he had made some dire films because of the money. He was paid $327,600 for *Cleopatra*, $462,000 for *The Night Of The Iguana* and $1 million for *The Sandpiper*. He summed up his life thus: "I rather like my reputation: that of a spoiled genius from the Welsh gutter, a drunk, a womaniser. It's rather an attractive image."
CAUSE: Touring America in the musical *Camelot* in 1981, Burton was left partially paralysed by a trapped nerve in his spine. In his final year he suffered from arthritis, back pains and the slight epilepsy which had factored in much of his life became worse. In

his last week he worked on scripts for *Wild Geese II* and *The Quiet American* at his home in Céligny, on a lake north of Geneva, Switzerland. On August 3, 1984, he got drunk in a local café and suffered a hangover and headache the next day. The following morning his wife was unable to wake him and he was taken to a hospital in Nyon then to Geneva where he died that afternoon of a cerebral haemorrhage aged 58. His wife and daughter, Kate, were by his side. He was buried in Céligny. Elizabeth Taylor did not attend his funeral. Burton left £692,456 in England and £3,500,000 overseas.
FURTHER READING: *Richard Burton: His Intimate Story* – Ruth Waterbury (London: Mayflower-Dell, 1965); *Rich: The Life Of Richard Burton* – Melvyn Bragg (London: Hodder & Stoughton, 1988).

Mae Busch

Born January 20, 1891
Died April 19, 1946
Comedy foil. Born in Melbourne, Australia, Mae Busch appeared on stage and in vaudeville before she began making films with her début coming in *The Agitator* (1912). She went on to become a Mack Sennett Bathing Beauty and took many major roles in silent pictures. Busch got work through the good offices of Mabel Normand but she repaid her by ending Normand's romance with Sennett. They were caught together although Sennett insisted that it was a joke that misfired. An on-set injury ended her career at Keystone so she signed to Fox. After meeting Erich von Stroheim she was cast in *The Devil's Passkey* (1919) and then appeared in *The Christian* (1923) as Glory Quayle and *The Unholy Three* (1925). Her career was virtually wrecked following an argument with MGM after which she suffered a nervous breakdown. She was rescued by Hal Roach who cast her in *Love 'Em And Weep* (filmed in January 1927,

released June 12, 1927). She received top billing over Stan Laurel, James Finlayson and Oliver Hardy who played Judge Chigger. Roach had recognised her comedic talents and cast her in 14 Laurel & Hardy films, most notably playing Ollie's wife in *Sons Of The Desert* (shot between October 2–October 23, 1933, released December 29, 1933) and Charlie Hall's wife in *Them Thar Hills* (filmed June 11–20, 1934, released July 21, 1934) and *Tit For Tat* (filmed December 10–20, 1934, released January 5, 1935).
CAUSE: She died in Woodland Hills, California, after a long illness.

Frank Butler

Born December 28, 1890
Died June 10, 1967
Multi-talent. Born in Oxford, 6'0½" Butler made his home and career in America where he starred in his own film series. He appeared in Hal Roach's *Tol'able Romeo* (released December 1925), *No Man's Law* (1927), and *Seeing The World* (1927) with Stan Laurel and he directed Laurel & Hardy in *Flying Elephants* (filmed May 1927, released February 12, 1928) which also starred James Finlayson. In the mid-Thirties Butler became the head of Hal Roach's scenario department and later wrote the Crosby-Hope-Lamour comedies *Road To Singapore* (1940), *Road To Zanzibar* (1941) and *Road To Morocco* (1942) for which he was nominated for an Oscar. That same year he was also nominated for *Wake Island* (1942). He finally won an Academy Award on March 15, 1945, at Grauman's Chinese Theater for Leo McCarey's multi-award winning *Going My Way* (1944) starring Bing Crosby. His competitors that year were *Double Indemnity*, *Gaslight*, *Laura* and *Meet Me In St Louis*. He was married to Ethel Virginia Chapman.
CAUSE: He died in Oceanside, Long Island, New York, aged 76 on the same day as Spencer Tracy. Ironically, it had been Tracy's film *Woman Of The Year* that prevented Butler winning an Oscar for *Wake Island* and *Road To Morocco* on March 4, 1943.

Merritt Butrick

Born September 3, 1959
Died March 17, 1989
Young blood. Born in Gainesville, Florida, 6'1" Merritt R. Butrick was raised in Mill Valley near San Francisco and attended the California Institute of Arts, where instructors told him that he did not have the talent to become an actor so he left. He appeared in the second *Star Trek* spin-off *Star Trek: The Wrath Of Khan* (released June 4, 1982) playing Dr David Marcus, a role he reprised in *Star Trek III: The Search For Spock* (1984). His other films included *Zapped!* (1982) as Gary Cooter, *Head Office* (released January 3, 1985) as John Hudson, *Shy People* (released December, 1988) as Mike, *Death Spa* (1988) as David Avery and was Richie in *Fright Night Part II* (released May 19, 1989). Of his career, he said, "I'm part of a legend. I gave what I had to give at the right time and place for my own personal gratification. I look at my résumé at this point and it reminds me of how well I've done in the few years I've done it. What I'm working on in my career is longevity and not instant success. I haven't particularly found the leading man image that I have yet to give, but I certainly explored certain aspects of him. Hopefully, I'll look in the mirror someday and he'll be there." Sadly, it was not to be.
CAUSE: On March 10, 1989 Butrick, suffering from pneumonia, underwent a lumbar puncture to relieve the cranial pressure on his brain. He died a week later at 9.50pm on St Patrick's Day, 1989 at his home, Apartment 1, 7728 Hollywood Boulevard, Hollywood, California 90046, of toxoplasma of the brain caused by AIDS. Toxoplasmosis infection is only a danger to developing foetuses and to people with AIDS. He was 29.

Red Buttons

(AARON CHWATT)
Born February 5, 1919
Died July 13, 2006
Small comic. Born to Polish Jewish immigrants on Manhattan's Lower East Side, 5'6" Buttons learned his trade in hotels in the Catskill Mountains before making his Broadway debut in 1942 in *Vickie*, a farce. Conscripted in 1943 he joined an army entertainment unit and appeared as Whitey in *Winged Victory* on the Great White Way from November 1943 until May 1944. He reprised the role in the 1944 film version. He entertained US troops in Europe in 1945. In 1948 he joined the National Theatre in Lower Manhattan. On television in October 1951 he appeared in an episode of the drama series *Suspense* about Joe E. Lewis, who had his throat cut by the Mafia during Prohibition. *The Red Buttons Show* was launched in October 1952. His other films included: *Sayonara* (1957) as Airman Joe Kelly for which he won a Best Supporting Actor Oscar, *Imitation General* (1958) as Corporal Chan Derby, *The Big Circus* (1959) as Randy Sherman, *Hatari!* (1962) as Pockets, *The Longest Day* (1962) as Private John Steele, *A Ticklish Affair* (1963) as Uncle Cy, *Your Cheatin' Heart* (1964) as Shorty Younger, *Harlow* (1965) as Arthur Landau, a sailor in *They Shoot Horses, Don't They?* (1969), *The Poseidon Adventure* (1972) as Martin, *Gable And Lombard* (1976) as Ivan Cooper, *Viva Knievel!* (1977) as Ben Andrews, *C.H.O.M.P.S.* (1979) as Bracken and *When Time Ran Out . . .* (1980) as Francis Fendly. He was married three times: in 1947 he married 5'7", 35-21-34 actress Roxanne Arlen (b. Detroit, Michigan January 10, 1931, d. London, February 22, 1989) but the marriage ended in divorce in 1951. On December 8, 1949 he married Helayne McNorton and that, too, ended in divorce. On January 27, 1964 he married Alicia Pratt (d. March 2001) by whom he had a son and a daughter, Adam and Amy.
CAUSE: Red Buttons (the name under which he is listed on the Social Security Index) died at his home in Century City, California of vascular disease. He was 87.

Spring Byington

Born October 17, 1886
Died September 7, 1971
America's favourite screen mother-in-law. Spring Dell Byington was born in Denver, Colorado, the daughter of Professor Edwin Lee Byington (1852–1891) and Helene Maud Cleghorn (d. 1907). The couple had another daughter, Helene Kimball Byington (b. Colorado September 4, 1890). When Professor Byington died, his widow sent their daughters to her parents, Arthur and Charlotte Cleghorn, at Port Hope, Ontario, and she moved to Boston where she enrolled at the Boston University School of Medicine and graduated in 1896. 5'3" Spring Byington began acting while still at North High School and after her mother's death moved to New York to pursue an acting career. She began travelling with repertory companies and on a tour of South America met and married Roy Chandler, a Broadway stage manager. They had two daughters – Phyllis (b. 1916) and Lois (b. 1918) – before their divorce after four years. Back in America she left her daughters with friends so she could concentrate on her career. She made her Broadway debut in George S. Kaufman and Marc Connelly's *Beggar On Horseback*, which opened on February 12, 1924 and ran for six months. She spent much of the next eleven years treading the boards. In 1931 she made her first film, a short film titled *Papa's Slay Ride*. Two years she made her first major film playing Marmee March, the mother of Katharine Hepburn, Joan Bennett, Jean Parker and Frances Dee in *Little*

Women (1933). It began her career of playing wise mothers on screen. She was the mother in a series of seventeen films about the Jones Family in the Thirties beginning with *Every Saturday Night* (1936) and ending with *On Their Own* (1940). Her other films included: *Werewolf Of London* (1935) as Miss Ettie Coombes, *Mutiny On The Bounty* (1935) as Mrs Byam, *Dodsworth* (1936) as Matey Pearson, *The Charge Of The Light Brigade* (1936) as Lady Octavia Warrenton, *The Buccaneer* (1938) as Dolley Madison, *The Adventures Of Tom Sawyer* (1938) as Widow Douglas, *Jezebel* (1938) as Mrs Kendrick, *The Devil And Miss Jones* (1941) as Elizabeth Ellis, *Meet John Doe* (1941) as Mrs Mitchell, *When Ladies Meet* (1941) as Bridget Drake, *Roxie Hart* (1942) as Mary Sunshine, *Heaven Can Wait* (1943) as Bertha Van Cleve, *I'll Be Seeing You* (1944) as Mrs Marshall, *A Letter For Evie* (1946) as Mrs McPherson, *It Had To Be You* (1947) as Mrs Stafford, *Louisa* (1950) as Louisa Norton, *According To Mrs Hoyle* (1951) as Mrs Hoyle, *Angels In The Outfield* (1951) as Sister Edwitha and *Please Don't Eat The Daisies* (1960) as Suzie Robinson, the mother of Doris Day's character. She was nominated for a Best Supporting Actress Oscar for her performance as Penny Sycamore in *You Can't Take It With You* (1938) but lost out to Fay Bainter for *Jezebel*, a movie in which Byington also appeared. She played Lily Ruskin in 111 episodes of the television sitcom *December Bride* from October 4, 1954 until 1959. In 1961 she began a two-year stint on the Western series *Laramie*. For a time she lived on Cordell Drive, off North Doheny Drive, Los Angeles, with the actress Marjorie Main. Their affair was in full bloom during the filming of *Little Women*.
CAUSE: She died of cancer at Hollywood, California. Byington was 84. She donated her body to medical science.

Ralph Byrd
Born April 22, 1909
Died August 18, 1952
Forever Dick Tracy. Born in Dayton, Ohio Byrd became best known for playing the comic strip detective Dick Tracy on screen in serials (from 1937 for Republic Pictures), films and television. The first serial was *Dick Tracy* (1937) and it spawned three sequels *Dick Tracy Returns*, *Dick Tracy's G-Men* and *Dick Tracy Versus Crime Inc.* In 1945 RKO Radio Pictures made a feature film, *Dick Tracy*, but the fans did not like them because Morgan Conway took the title role. Byrd made two films *Dick Tracy's Dilemma* (1947) and *Dick Tracy Meets Gruesome* (1947) with Boris Karloff in the role of Gruesome. In 1936 Byrd married Virginia Carroll who is noticed elsewhere in this book.
CAUSE: Byrd died of a heart attack at Tarzana, California, aged just 43.

Marion Byron
(MIRIAM BILENKIN)
Born March 16, 1911
Died July 5, 1985
'Peanuts'. Born in Dayton, Ohio, Marion Byron followed her elder sister, Betty Byron, into show business after leaving school. She appeared in numerous stage shows before turning to film in 1926, starring with Buster Keaton in *Steamboat Bill, Jr* (1928). Hal Roach decided that he wanted a female Laurel & Hardy so he teamed Byron with Anita Garvin. They made three films together – *A Pair Of Tights* (1928), *Feed 'Em And Weep* (1928) and *Going Ga-Ga* (1929) – before she left Roach. She went on to appear in *Broadway Babies* (1929) as Florine Chanler, *So Long, Letty* (1929) as Ruth Davis, *His Captive Woman* (1929) as Baby Myers, *The Forward Pass* (1929) as Mazie and *Golden Dawn* (1930) as Joanna. In 1932 she married the screenwriter Lou Breslow and six years later, in 1938, she retired.
CAUSE: She died in Santa Monica, California, aged 74.

C

Sebastian Cabot

Born July 6, 1918
Died August 22, 1977
Heavy. Born in London, Charles
Sebastian Thomas Cabot left school
aged 14 and worked in a number of
jobs before turning his hand to acting.
He played heavies (in more ways than
one), buffoons and likeable characters,
usually with a beard. Among his films
were *Othello* (1946), *Dual Alibi* (1947),
Old Mother Riley's New Adventure
(1949), *Dick Barton Strikes Back*
(1949), *Old Mother Riley, Headmistress*
(1950), *Old Mother Riley's Jungle
Treasure* (1951), *Ivanhoe* (1952) and
the voice of Bagheera the panther in
The Jungle Book (1967).
CAUSE: Cabot died from a stroke aged
59 at his home 10891 Deep Cove
Road, North Saanich, British Columbia.
He was buried in Westwood Village
Memorial Park, 1218 Glendon
Avenue, Los Angeles 90024.

Susan Cabot

Born July 9, 1927
Died December 10, 1986
Tragic beauty. Born in Boston,
Massachusetts, brunette Susan Cabot
was one of those beautiful women who
were there simply to adorn movies
rather than being in any real way
central to the plot. She was often
placed in clothes more usually found in
a harem, which showed off her petite
but glorious figure. She appeared in
films such as *On The Isle Of Samoa*
(1950) as Moana, *Tomahawk* (1951) as
Monahseetah, *Flame Of Araby* (1951)
as Clio, *Son Of Ali Baba* (1952) as
Tala, *The Battle At Apache Pass* (1952)
as Nono, *Ride Clear Of Diablo* (1954)
as Laurie Kenyon, *Sorority Girl* (1957)
as Sabra Tanner, *The Saga Of The*
*Viking Women And Their Voyage To The
Waters Of The Great Sea Serpent* (1958)
as Enger, *Fort Massacre* (1958) as Piute
Girl and her final film *The Wasp
Woman* (1960) as Janice Starlin. In
1959 the press began writing of her
love affair with King Hussein of Jordan.
The romance lasted over a year but
ultimately came to nought. Having
retired from films to marry and raise a
family she began to work with various
charities. Towards the end of her life
she began to suffer from mental
problems and became somewhat
reclusive, letting her once glorious
home go to rack and ruin.
CAUSE: She was bludgeoned to death
aged 59 by her dwarf student son,
22-year-old Timothy Scott Roman, in
her Encino, California, home.

James Cagney

Born July 17, 1899
Died Easter Sunday (March 30) 1986
Little tough guy. Born in New York
City, the son of an Irish barman and a
half-Norwegian, half-Irish mother,
James Francis Cagney, Jr began as a
waiter, worked in a pool room and as a
drag queen before becoming a
thespian. In November 1918 his father
died aged 41, officially of flu though he
had been drinking himself steadily into
the grave for years. On March 25,
1919, James' actress sister Jeanne
Carolyn Cagney was born. (She would
appear in several plays, films and TV
shows before her death on December
7, 1984.) In 1920 Jimmy joined the
chorus of a Broadway show and earned
his spurs touring for five years before
returning to the Great White Way to
play leading roles. On March 28, 1922,
he married Frances Willard Vernon
(b. Fairfield, Iowa 1904) whom he
nicknamed Bill. (They adopted two
children: James, III [d. 1984] and
Cathleen, known as Casey.) Cagney's
first film was the 55-minute *Sinner's
Holiday* (1930) for Warner Bros. He
was so nervous during shooting that he
almost threw up every time he had to

film a scene, but he made himself perform. The *New York Times* paid tribute to the performance: "The most impressive acting is done by James Cagney in the role of Harry Delano. His fretful tenseness during the closing scenes is conveyed with sincerity." The film was a competent feature in which Cagney played a cry-baby mother's boy who was a killer on the sideline but the bosses liked what they saw and offered him an extension on his three-week contract (for another three weeks) and then a seven-year contract at $400 a week. To capitalise on his baby-faced appearance, Warner Bros knocked five years off 5′6½″ Cagney's age, claiming he was born in 1904. Director Lewis Milestone wanted him to appear in *The Front Page* (1931) but Howard Hughes nixed the idea, describing Cagney as "a little runt". Despite Hughes' animus, Cagney was a star by his fifth film. He played Tom Powers in *The Public Enemy* (1931). Shot in just 26 days in February and March 1931 for just $150,000, *The Public Enemy* and *Little Caesar* (1931) were the two films that really kick-started the popularity of gangster films. The former tells the story of two guttersnipes who become hoodlums and then return to their roots. Until two days before shooting Cagney was slated to play the part of the good guy, probably because up till then he was regarded as primarily a song and dance man. Warner Bros' head of production, Darryl F. Zanuck, claimed that gangster movies were dead but director William Wellman promised him "the toughest, the most violent, realistic picture you ever did see." In fact, only eight people are killed and none on screen. The most memorable scene in the film is one in which Powers (Cagney) pushes half a grapefruit into the face of Kitty (Mae Clarke). There are various explanations concerning how the scene came to be. Both Cagney and Clarke claim it was a practical joke on the crew to see how they would react. Neither expected it to

remain in the final cut. Forever after, Cagney was always offered half a grapefruit when he went to a restaurant – and usually ate them. Despite appearing in 90 films, Clarke was henceforth known as 'The Grapefruit Girl' and claimed the advertising industry missed a trick by not hiring her to promote the fruit. In a fight scene Donald Cook smacked Cagney full in the mouth instead of pulling his punch, breaking one of Cagney's teeth. When the ground crumbles around Cagney's feet, you are seeing real bullets disintegrate the pavement; the practice of using blanks didn't originate for some years. The character of Tom Powers was supposedly based on the gangster Dion 'Deanie' O'Bannion (b. Aurora, Illinois, July 8, 1892, k. 738 North State Street, Chicago, Illinois, November 10, 1924, one of the most vicious killers of the Prohibition Era; he was murdered in the flower shop he owned by three of Al Capone's henchmen) and two thugs Cagney had known on the Lower East Side. Cagney was worried that he might be typecast as a villain and even wrote to his mother, reminding her it was all play-acting. It was too late, but Cagney managed to show his versatility playing Bottom in *A Midsummer Night's Dream* (1935) and George M. Cohan in *Yankee Doodle Dandy* (1942), which won him a Best Actor Oscar. Rosemary de Camp played Cagney's mother in the latter; in fact, she was eleven years younger than him. It's ironic that Cagney plays Cohan because although Cohan may have been a great songwriter, like many he was less than brilliant at spotting talent. He once turned down the young Cagney, who auditioned for him, and later had Clark Gable sacked from his 1929 play *Gambling*. Cagney would reprise his performance as Cohan in *The Seven Little Foys* (1955). In 1942 Cagney formed Cagney Productions with his younger brother, William (b. New York City, March 26, 1904, d. January 3,

1988) a former actor who went on to produce some of Jimmy's films. Among his other films were *Footlight Parade* (1933) as Chester Kent, *Jimmy The Gent* (1934) as Jimmy Corrigan, *Here Comes The Navy* (1934) as Chester J. O'Conner, *Devil Dogs Of The Air* (1935) as Timmy O'Toole, *'G' Men* (1935) as James 'Brick' Davis, *The Irish In Us* (1935) as Danny O'Hara, *Mutiny On The Bounty* (1935), *The Roaring Twenties* (1939) as Eddie Bartlett, *Each Dawn I Die* (1939) as Frank Ross, *The Bride Came C.O.D.* (1941) as Steve Collins and *Blood On The Sun* (1945) as Nick Condon. His performance as William 'Rocky' Sullivan in *Angels With Dirty Faces* (1938) earned him a nomination for Best Actor Oscar but it was also criticised for not being realistic enough. Once again the bullets used were live ammunition and for one scene where the police shot at him while he was holed up in a building Cagney had sensibly refused to stand in the window. Lucky for him that he did because one bullet passed through the place where his head would have been! Critics also moaned that he had been able to hold off the entire New York Police Department without once reloading his gun. Cagney took note and in his next film, *The Oklahoma Kid* (1939), made sure he never fired more than six bullets in any one scene. During the Second World War Cagney and several other celebrities toured America to raise money for the war effort. One of the thespians on the trip was the beautiful Merle Oberon who was determined to seduce Cagney. She flashed her shapely legs at him but he managed to avoid her advances until one day she bribed a porter to let her into his couchette. She lay naked under the sheets and when Cagney arrived she made her move. Having been without sex for some time, he relented but after a few minutes she cried out, "Oooh, Jimmy Cagney's fucking me." At that he

stopped, withdrew and getting up, got dressed. She asked him what he was doing and Cagney apologised, "This is my fault. I guess I'm not the type."He felt ashamed and guilty at betraying Willie. They remained friends but she didn't flash her legs at him again and he avoided being alone with her. He won another Best Actor nomination for playing racketeer Martin 'The Gimp' Snyder in *Love Me Or Leave Me* (1955). Cagney retired from film-making in the Sixties because he said the fun had gone out of it. However, in 1981 he returned to the cameras to play police commissioner Rheinlander Waldo in *Ragtime*, despite diabetes, poor circulation, the after-effects of several strokes and sundry other health problems.
CAUSE: Cagney died of cardiac arrest at his home, Verney Farms, in Stanfordville, 30 miles west of Poughkeepsie, New York, aged 86.
FURTHER READING: *Cagney: The Authorised Biography* – Doug Warren with James Cagney (New York: St Martin's Press, 1986)); *Cagney* – John McCabe (London: Aurum, 1998).

Louis Calhern

(CARL HENRY VOGT)
Born February 19, 1895
Died May 12, 1956
Flexible fiend. Born in New York City, Calhern was a tall, romantic lead in the Twenties who blossomed into a moustachioed, masterful character actor. He was acclaimed for his portrayal of Justice Oliver Wendell Holmes in *The Magnificent Yankee* (1950), for which he was nominated for an Oscar, the criminal mastermind Alonzo Emmerich in *The Asphalt Jungle* (1950) and Buffalo Bill in *Annie Get Your Gun* (1950). His other films included: *What's Worth While* (1921) as 'Squire' Elton, his first film, *Stolen Heaven* (1931) as Steve, *The Road To Singapore* (1931) as Dr George March, *Blonde Crazy* (1931) as Dapper Dan Barker, *They Call It Sin* (1932) as

Ford Humphries, *20,000 Years In Sing Sing* (1933) as Joe Finn, *Woman Accused* (1933) as Leo Young, *Strictly Personal* (1933) as Magruder, *Diplomaniacs* (1933) as Winklereid, *Duck Soup* (1933) as Ambassador Trentino, *Sweet Adeline* (1934) as Major James Day, *The Count Of Monte Cristo* (1934) as Raymond de Villefort, Jr, *Woman Wanted* (1935) as Smiley, *The Life Of Emile Zola* (1937) as Major Dort, *Fast Company* (1938) as Elias Z. Bannerman, *Dr Ehrlich's Magic Bullet* (1940) as Brockdorf, *Heaven Can Wait* (1943) as Randolph Van Cleve, *The Bridge Of San Luis Rey* (1944) as The Viceroy, *Notorious* (1946) as Paul Prescott, *The Red Pony* (1949) as Grandfather, *Two Weeks With Love* (1950) as Horatio Robinson, *Nancy Goes To Rio* (1950) as Gregory Elliott, *We're Not Married* (1952) in which he played Freddie Melrose, *The Prisoner Of Zenda* (1952) as Colonel Zapt, *The Bad And The Beautiful* (1952) as the narrator, *Julius Caesar* (1953) in the title role, *The Blackboard Jungle* (1955) as Jim Murdock and *Forever Darling* (1956) as Charles Y. Bewell, his last film. He was married and divorced four times. His first wife was actress-writer Ilka Chase. They married in June 1926 but divorced in February 1927 on account of his adultery. On September 17, 1927, he married actress Julia Hoyt at Norton Presbyterian Church, Darien, Connecticut. They were divorced in Reno, Nevada, on August 6, 1932. On April 20, 1933, in Los Angeles, he married actress Natalie Schaefer. Following their divorce he married actress Marianne Stewart in Plainfield, New Jersey, on November 25, 1946. The couple was divorced in Juarez, Mexico, on July 19, 1955.
CAUSE: Calhern died of a heart attack in Tokyo while filming *The Teahouse Of The August Moon*. He was buried in Hollywood Memorial Park, 6000 Santa Monica Boulevard, Hollywood, California 90038.

Rory Calhoun
(FRANCIS TIMOTHY DURGIN)
Born August 8, 1922
Died April 28, 1999
The scapegoat. Rory Calhoun was born in Los Angeles and worked as a lumberjack, miner, cowboy and park ranger. An opportune meeting with Alan Ladd turned him on to acting and after changing his name from Frank McCown (his stepfather's name) he quickly made a small name for himself as a tough guy in a number of Westerns. It looked as if major stardom beckoned Calhoun, but then it all went wrong. Various stories have done the rounds about Calhoun's fall from grace and so myth has probably replaced fact by now. The story goes that scandal rag *Confidential* had become very successful at exposing the secrets of Hollywood stars and had discovered Hollywood's best kept open secret: that Rock Hudson, the celluloid lady-killer was, in fact, a friend of Dorothy. The magazine threatened to run the story, which would have wrecked Hudson's career. As a compromise, the studio offered a scapegoat to save the more valuable Hudson. That scapegoat, as the tale has it, was Calhoun. On April 23, 1940, Calhoun had been arrested in Salt Lake City, Utah, and charged with second-degree burglary and taking a stolen car across state lines. He was sent to juvenile hall in El Reno, Oklahoma. Some reference books give Calhoun's birthday as 1918 but if that is correct he would have been 21 when arrested and too old for juvenile hall. In borstal a priest, Father Donald Kanaly, attempted to befriend the delinquent but was spurned and Calhoun tried to escape. He was put in solitary confinement for a fortnight. Father Kanaly didn't give up hope and finally put him on the path to the straight and narrow. On August 8, 1943, Calhoun was released. It may have been coincidental that Calhoun's record was released (in a May 1955 issue of *Confidential*) at the time of

Hudson's possible exposure, but it certainly wrecked Calhoun's chance of major stardom. (Just to 'confirm' his heterosexuality, Hudson married his gay agent's secretary four months later.) Among Calhoun's films were: *Sunday Dinner For A Soldier* (1944), *Something For The Boys* (1944), *That Hagen Girl* (1947) as Ken Freneau, *Miraculous Journey* (1948) as Larry, *Sand* (1949) as Chick Palmer, *A Ticket To Tomahawk* (1950) as Dakota, *With A Song In My Heart* (1952) as John Burn, *Way Of A Gaucho* (1952) as Martin, *How To Marry A Millionaire* (1953) as Eben, *River Of No Return* (1954) as Harry Weston, *Ain't Misbehavin'* (1955) as Kenneth Post, *Marco Polo* (1961) as Marco Polo, *Operación Dalila* (1967) as Rory, *Won Ton Ton, The Dog Who Saved Hollywood* (1976) as Philip Hart, *Hell Comes To Frogtown* (1987) as Looney Tunes and *Roller Blade Warriors: Taken By Force* (1989) as Old Turkel. On August 29, 1948, he married singer Lita Baron. They had three daughters: Cindy Frances (b. 1957), Tami Elizabeth (b. 1960) and Lorri Marie (b.1961). The couple was divorced in July 1970. On April 20, 1971, he married Australian journalist Sue Rhodes Boswell. A daughter, Rorye, was born that same year.

CAUSE: Calhoun died aged 76 from the effects of diabetes and emphysema in Los Angeles.

Phyllis Calvert

(PHYLLIS BICKLE)
Born February 18, 1915
Died October 8, 2002
'Million pound girl'. Born in Chelsea, south-west London, she was the daughter of Frederick Bickle, a blacksmith, and Anne Williams. The young Phyllis Bickle trained as a dancer until an injury forced her to change to drama. She was educated in London at the Margaret Morris School (where her strong cockney accent was replaced by a more pleasing vocal attitude) and the

French Institute. She made her stage début in Walter de la Mare's *Crossings* on November 19, 1925 at the Lyric, Hammersmith, as Dame Ellen Terry was making her last appearance. She made her film début in a silent picture called *The Land Of Heart's Desire* (1927) but never officially admitted to any film earlier than 1939. By then she had been in *School For Stars* (1935), *Inspector Hornleigh* (1938) as Mrs Wilkinson and *Two Days To Live* (1939). She made her West End début in 1939 in *A Woman's Privilege* at Kingsway. Appearing in Max Catto's *Punch Without Judy* at the Q Theatre, she met her future husband, Peter Murray-Hill, an actor, publisher and part-time police constable. At the outbreak of war she returned to Gainsborough Studios at Shepherd's Bush and worked with Arthur Askey in *Charley's Big-Hearted Aunt* (1940), a frolicsome version of the old standard *Charley's Aunt* as Betty Forsythe and in films with Will Fyffe and George Formby in *Let George Do It* (1940) as Mary Wilson. She also appeared in Carol Reed's *Kipps* (1941) as Anne Pornick and in Anthony Asquith's *The Young Mr Pitt* (1942) as Eleanor Eden. Her tremulous lower lip and liquid brown eyes meant that the success of *The Man In Grey* (1943) as Clarissa Richmond, *Fanny By Gaslight* (1944) as Fanny, *Madonna Of The Seven Moons* (1944) as Maddalena Labardi (in the film she and co-star Stewart Granger broke censorship rules of the time by taking their feet off the floor during a love scene although she later rather ruined the image by revealing that his breath had "smelt of sardines") and *They Were Sisters* (1945) as Lucy Moore gave her the box office pull of Greer Garson and Bette Davis. She won plaudits as Christine Garland, the mother of the deaf girl in *Mandy* (1952). By the Sixties she was making fewer films including *Child In The House* (1956) as Evelyn Acheson, *The Young And The Guilty* (1958) as Mrs

Connor and *Oscar Wilde* (1960) as
Constance Wilde and playing more
regularly in the West End. Her many
television appearances included *Cover
Her Face* (1985), *All Passion Spent*
(1986) and the plays *Death Of A Heart*
(1985), *Across The Lake* (1988), *The
Memoirs Of Sherlock Holmes* (1994) and
Midsomer Murders (1997). She came out
of retirement to appear in the feature
film *Mrs Dalloway* (1997), starring
Vanessa Redgrave. "Some people love
sitting in a chair," she said, reflecting on
her long career. "That's my idea of
dull." Her husband Peter Murray-Hill
died in 1957; they had a son and a
daughter. "My acting," she said in 1995,
"has improved with age. I can't look at
any of my old films – I was frightful."
CAUSE: She died aged 87 of natural
causes.

Rod Cameron

(NATHAN RODERICK COX)
Born December 7, 1910
Died December 21, 1983
Rangy puncher. Born in Calgary,
Alberta, Canada, 6′5″ Cameron
worked on a building site and then as a
lorry driver and skin diving instructor
before making the move to films in
1939. He worked as a stand-in for Fred
MacMurray. His first film was *Heritage
Of The Desert* (1939) and although he
never achieved A-list stardom he was a
regular in B pictures. In 1943 he
appeared as secret service agent Rex
Bennett for Republic Pictures in *Secret
Service In Darkest Africa* (1943) and
G-men Vs. The Black Dragon (1943)
before reprising the role on television
more than 20 years later in *Black
Dragon Of Manzanar* (1966) and *The
Baron's African War* (1966). In 1944
and 1945 he appeared in six Westerns
for Universal. They were *Boss Of
Boomtown* (1944) as Steve Hazard,
Trigger Trail (1944) as Clint Farrel,
Riders Of The Santa Fe (1944) as Matt
Conway, *The Old Texas Trail* (1944) as
Jim Wiley, *Beyond The Pecos* (1945) as
Lew Remington and *Renegades Of The*

Rio Grande (1945) as Buck Emerson.
In 1945 he landed the starring role as
Jim Steed opposite Yvonne De Carlo in
Salome, Where She Danced (1945) but it
never led anywhere and soon Cameron
was back in B Westerns. His films
included *The Old Maid* (1939) as a
man, *The Quarterback* (1940) as Tex,
Rangers Of Fortune (1940) as Shelby
henchman, *Christmas In July* (1940) as
Dick, *North West Mounted Police* (1940)
as Corporal Underhill, *Life With Henry*
(1941) as Bill Van Dusen, *The Monster
And The Girl* (1941) as Sam Daniels, *I
Wanted Wings* (1941) as the voice on
the loudspeaker, *The Parson Of
Panamint* (1941) as Porter, *Buy Me
That Town* (1941) as Gerard, a sailor in
Nothing But The Truth (1941), *Henry
Aldrich For President* (1941) as Ed
Calkins, *Night Of January 16th* (1941)
as District Attorney's Assistant, *No
Hands On The Clock* (1941) as Tom
Reed, *Among The Living* (1941) as
Eddie, a pilot in *Pacific Blackout*
(1941), a sailor in *The Fleet's In* (1942),
The Remarkable Andrew (1942) as Jesse
James, *True To The Army* (1942) as
Private O'Toole, *Priorities On Parade*
(1942) as the stage manager, *Wake
Island* (1942) as Captain Pete Lewis,
The Forest Rangers (1942) as Jim
Lawrence, *Star Spangled Rhythm*
(1942) as Petty Officer, *Commandos
Strike At Dawn* (1942) as Pastor, *No
Time For Love* (1943) as Taylor,
Honeymoon Lodge (1943) as Big Boy
Carson, *The Good Fellows* (1943), *The
Kansan* (1943) as Kelso, *Riding High*
(1943) as Sam Welch, *Gung Ho!*
(1943) as Rube Tedrow, *Mrs
Parkington* (1944) as Al Swann, *Swing
Out, Sister* (1945) as Geoffrey, *Frontier
Gal* (1945) as Johnny Hart, *The
Runaround* (1946) as Eddie J. Kildane,
Pirates Of Monterey (1947) as Phillip
Kent, *River Lady* (1948) as Dan
Corrigan, *Panhandle* (1948) as John
Sands, *The Plunderers* (1948) as John
Drum, *Belle Starr's Daughter* (1948) as
Bob 'Bitter Creek' Yauntis, *Strike It
Rich* (1949) as Duke Massey, *Stampede*

(1949) as Mike McCall, *Brimstone*
(1949) as Johnny Tremaine, *Stage To Tucson* (1950) as Grif Holbrook, *Dakota Lil* (1950) as Harve Logan a.k.a. Kid Curry, *Short Grass* (1950) as Steve Lewellyn, *Oh! Susanna* (1951) as Captain Webb Calhoun, *Cavalry Scout* (1951) as Kirby Frye, *The Sea Hornet* (1951) as Gunner McNeil, *Fort Osage* (1952) as Tom Clay, *Wagons West* (1952) as Jeff Curtis, *The Jungle* (1952) as Steve Bentley, *Woman Of The North Country* (1952) as Kyle Ramlo, *Ride The Man Down* (1952) as Will Ballard, *San Antone* (1953) as Carl Miller, *The Steel Lady* (1953) as Mike Monahan, *Southwest Passage* (1954) as Edward Beale, *Hell's Outpost* (1954) as Tully Gibbs, *Passport To Treason* (1955) as Mike O'Kelly, *Santa Fe Passage* (1955) as Jess Griswold, *Double Jeopardy* (1955) as Marc Hill, *Headline Hunters* (1955) as Hugh Woodruff, *The Fighting Chance* (1955) as Bill Binyon, *Yaqui Drums* (1956) as Webb Dunham, *Spoilers Of The Forest* (1957) as Boyd Caldwell, *Escapement* (1958) as Jeff Keenan, *The Man Who Died Twice* (1958) as William 'Bill' Brennon, *The Gun Hawk* (1963) as Sheriff Ben Corey, *Le Pistole Non Discutono* (1964) as Pat Garrett, *Il Piombo E La Carne* (1965) as Nathaniel Masters, *Requiem For A Gunfighter* (1965) as Dave McCloud, *The Bounty Killer* (1965) as Johnny Liam, *Winnetou Und Sein Freund Old Firehand* (1966) as Old Firehand, *Evel Knievel* (1971) as Charlie Knesson, *The Last Movie* (1971) as Pat Garrett, *Psychic Killer* (1975) as Dr Commanger, *Jessi's Girls* (1975) as Rufe and *Love And The Midnight Auto Supply* (1977) as Sheriff Dawson. He also starred in three television series. *City Detective* was syndicated from the autumn of 1953 until 1955 and starred Cameron as Detective Lieutenant Bart Grant. The show was not actually set in one city and Grant travelled widely solving crimes wherever he went. Not everyone was impressed. *TV Guide* once commented, "Most of his acting is in his fists." Produced from 1956 until 1959 with the first of 104 episodes released in January 1957 Cameron's second syndicated television series, *State Trooper*, had him playing Rod Blake, the chief investigator for the Nevada State Police. The pilot, *Killer On Horseback*, had been broadcast by NBC in February 1956 but was not considered saleable enough so the show was released only in syndication. Cameron's third show was *Coronado 9*, syndicated in 1959, in which he played Dan Adams. Oddly, in 1960, he divorced his wife of 10 years, Angela, and married her mother, Dorothy. CAUSE: Rod Cameron died of cancer in Gainesville, Georgia. He was a fortnight past his 73rd birthday.

Gerald Campion
Born April 23, 1921
Died July 9, 2002
Yaroo! Forever Bunter. Gerald Theron Campion was born in the Bloomsbury district of London, the son of Cyril Campion (1893–1961), the scriptwriter. One of his godparents was Sir Gerald du Maurier. Educated at University College School, Hampstead, he went to RADA aged 15. At the age of 16 he was cast as Billy Bunter in a film but the company went bust and the production was never made. At the outbreak of the Second World War, he joined up and served as a wireless operator with the RAF in Kenya. On demob he went back to acting, but he also began a separate life as a club owner. In 1950 he opened The Buckstone, a theatrical club opposite the stage door of the Haymarket Theatre. Once he was furious to discover that a visiting artist had doodled on one of the tablecloths; Campion threw it away, only to discover later that the vandal was Pietro Annigoni. Six years later, Campion started The Key Club – to which each member had his own key – in Dean Street. This was followed by

Gerry's, in Shaftesbury Avenue, whose members included Michael Caine, Keith Waterhouse, Tony Hancock and Graham Hill. It is as *Billy Bunter,* the Fat Owl of the Remove of Greyfriars School that Gerald Campion is best remembered. When the show first aired on February 19, 1952 with the episode *The Siege Of The Remove*, Campion, far from being a teenage schoolboy, was a 29-year-old father of two. He was also not especially overweight. Campion, who stood 5'5", weighed 11st 12lb, having recently been dieting. "He simply isn't fat enough in the tummy," the producer of the series, Joy Harrington, said. Campion later claimed that, to regain weight, he had gorged himself on home-made jam tarts. The rest was padding which also protected Campion from the regular beatings that Bunter received. *Billy Bunter* was screened twice, once for the children and once for their parents. Campion was simultaneously running his own club and later claimed that he could only cope with the schedule by taking amphetamines. The first reviews for the show, which was broadcast at 5.40pm for younger viewers and then again at 8pm for the more mature, were not good. The *Daily Sketch* said the show was "dull, dated, boring" but children loved it. The programme ran for 120 episodes and ended in 1961 and Bunter suffered at the hands of the sadistic Mr Quelch (the first was played by Kynaston Reeves; "Bend over, you wretched boy") and his own schoolmates who included Michael Crawford, David Hemmings, Anthony Valentine and Melvyn Hayes. The show finished following the death of Bunter's prolific creator Frank Richards (who was born Charles St John Hamilton at 15 Oak Street in Middlesex on August 8, 1876 and died on Christmas Eve 1961 at his home, Kingsgate in Kent, and who entered *The Guinness Book Of Records* as the world's most prolific writer with a weekly output of 80,000 words and a lifetime total estimated at 75,000,000. Compilers Norris and Ross McWhirter commented drily, "He enjoyed the advantage . . . of being unmarried.") who also wrote all the television scripts. The programme made Campion one of television's earliest celebrities. He didn't always enjoy the attention: "Sweet shops were the worst," he moaned later. "I'd be in them and blokes would manhandle their kids round to face me, and point at me and shout: 'Look there – that's Billy Bunter!' " However, Campion was not so put off playing the Fat Owl that he didn't try to resurrect the show himself and sent scripts to the BBC. One featured Bunter in a cooking pot and being force fed garlic by cannibals. The corporation did not reply. His professional life post-Bunter was not as successful. His films included *Carry On Sergeant* (1958) as Andy Calloway, the first of the series but he wasn't retained for the series, a fireman in *Those Magnificent Men In Their Flying Machines* (1965), *Half A Sixpence* (1967) and *Chitty Chitty Bang Bang* (1968). He also appeared in television series such as *Minder, Dr Who* and *Sherlock Holmes*. Away from acting, Campion became an expert on French cuisine and opened a number of establishments in the south-east including Froops, in north London, Bassetts, in Tunbridge Wells, and The Woodman's Arms Auberge, a hotel/restaurant at Hastingleigh in Kent which he ran with his second wife Suzie. He once said, "I suppose it is fitting that the man who played Billy Bunter should end up in the Good Food Guide." He was twice married, firstly in 1947 to Jean Symond by whom he had one son and two daughters, Anthony, Anthea and Angelica and, secondly, in 1972 to Suzie Marks, a former dancer at Gerry's. In 1991 they retired to France. CAUSE: Campion died aged 81 of heart problems in St Hilaire Clinic, Agen, France.

John Candy

Born October 31, 1950
Died March 6, 1994
Funny fatman. John Franklin Candy
was born in Toronto, Canada. He
began acting in school and continued
while training to become a journalist at
the Centennial Community College.
He changed tack and joined the
Second City comedy troupe, appearing
with them on television. On September
25, 1983, he won an Emmy for
Outstanding Writing In A Variety Or
Musical Program for his work with
them. Weighing a whopping 26st, his
films included: *Hercules In New York*
(1970), *It Seemed Like A Good Idea At
The Time* (1975) as Kopek, *Find The
Lady* (1976) as Kopek, *1941* (1979) as
Private Foley, *The Blues Brothers* (1980)
as Burton Mercer, *Stripes* (1981) as Ox,
Splash (1984) as Freddie Bauer,
Summer Rental (1985) as Jack Chester,
Sesame Street Presents Follow That Bird
(1985) as state trooper, *Brewster's
Millions* (1985) as Spike Nolan, *Little
Shop Of Horrors* (1986) as Wink
Wilkinson, *Spaceballs* (1987) as Barf,
Planes, Trains And Automobiles (1987)
as Del Griffith, *Uncle Buck* (1989) as
Buck Russell, *Who's Harry Crumb?*
(1989) as Harry Crumb, *Home Alone*
(1990) as Gus Polinski, *Only The
Lonely* (1991) as Danny, *JFK* (1991) as
Dean Andrews and *Cool Runnings*
(1993) as Irwin Blitzer. He was
married with two children.
CAUSE: Candy was in Durango,
Mexico, almost one hundred miles
north-west of Mexico City, filming the
movie *Wagons East* at the time of his
death. He was staying in room 128 of
the Camino del Perque hotel. The
room contained a king-sized bed with a
large crucifix over it. On March 5,
1994, the cast and crew worked long
hours, only stopping at 10pm. Candy
decided he was hungry (he had often
said eating was his hobby) and ate
spaghetti. Around 11pm he went for a
shower and then to bed. At 8am the
next morning his bodyguard, Gustavo

Populus, called to wake him up but
received no reply. A quarter of an hour
later he let himself into the room.
Candy, wearing a long red and black
nightshirt, was lying half in and
half out of the bed. He was cold. A
doctor was called who pronounced
death, from a mammoth heart attack,
had occurred at 7.30am. No autopsy
was performed, at the specific request
of Candy's widow, Rosemary. His
funeral took place on March 9 at St
Martin of the Tours Church,
Brentwood, California. The eulogy was
delivered by Dan Aykroyd and the
mourners included Jim Belushi, Chevy
Chase, Tom Hanks, Ed Harris, Rick
Moranis, Bill Murray, Rhea Perlman,
Martin Short and George Wendt.
Candy was buried at Holy Cross
Cemetery & Mausoleum, 5835 West
Slauson Avenue, Culver City,
California 90230.

Esma Cannon

Born December 3, 1892
Died October 18, 1972
Diminutive character actress. Born in
Australia, Esma Cannon became one of
the best-known faces, if not names, in
British comedy films of the Fifties and
Sixties, but also appeared in several
dramatic roles playing an interfering
spinster or some such character.
Emigrating to Britain in the Thirties
she appeared on the stage before
making the transition to films in 1937.
Her movies included *The £5 Man*
(1937) as Lucy, *It's In The Air* (1938),
Poison Pen (1939) as Mrs Warren, *I
Met A Murderer* (1939), *The Young Mr
Pitt* (1941), *Asking For Trouble* (1942)
as Ada, *English Without Tears* (1944) as
Queenie, *Here Come The Huggetts*
(1948), *The Huggetts Abroad* (1949) as
Brown Owl, *Fools Rush In* (1949) as
Mrs Atkins, *Trouble In Store* (1953),
The Dam Busters (1954), *Three Men In
A Boat* (1956), *Jack The Ripper* (1959)
as Nelly, *I'm All Right Jack* (1959) as
Spencer, *Expresso Bongo* (1959), *Carry
On Constable* (1960) as the deaf old

dear helped across the road by Kenneth Williams, *Doctor In Love* (1961), *Carry On Regardless* (1961) as Miss Cooling, *Carry On Cruising* (1962) as Bridget Madderley and *Carry On Cabby* (1963) as Flo Sims. Esma Cannon was also well known on television, appearing in shows such as *The Rag Trade* playing Little Lil. She retired in 1963.
CAUSE: She died aged 79 of natural causes.

Eddie Cantor
(EDWARD ISRAEL ISKOWITZ)
Born January 31, 1892
Died October 10, 1964
Better on radio. Born in New York, New York, the son of Russian immigrants who died when he was young, 5'8" Cantor began working as a pro at 14. He became a singing waiter at Coney Island and then moved into vaudeville and burlesque. He made his film début as himself in *A Few Moments With Eddie Cantor* (1924) and his acting début proper two years later as Samuel 'Kid' Boots in *Kid Boots* (1926). His subsequent films included *Glorifying The American Girl* (1929), *Insurance* (1930) as Sidney B. Swieback, *Getting A Ticket* (1930), *Whoopee!* (1930) as Henry Williams (Samuel Goldwyn's first musical and the first to contain dances choreographed by Busby Berkeley), *Palmy Days* (1931) as Eddie Simpson, *Roman Scandals* (1933) as Eddie, *Kid Millions* (1934) as Edward Grant Wilson, Jr, *Ali Baba Goes To Town* (1937) as Al Babson and *If You Knew Susie* (1948) as Sam Parker. It has to be said that none of his films was especially satisfactory, although he was very successful. In Thirties America radio shows were prominently sponsored by various companies. One of the most popular radio shows was *Eddie Cantor's Chase And Sanborn Hour* on NBC. It was estimated that half of America tuned in on Sunday nights to listen to the show. One night the announcer Jimmy Wallington said that

lexicographer Samuel Johnson drank 24 cups of coffee every day and would have drunk more if he could have bought the products made by Chase and Sanborn. The NBC switchboard was jammed by better informed listeners who knew Johnson actually drank tea. A biopic was made of his life starring Keefe Brasselle. *The Eddie Cantor Story* (1953) features a scene set in 1904, yet Eddie sings 'Meet Me Tonight In Dreamland' which wouldn't be written for another five years. In 1952 Cantor went into semi-retirement following a heart attack and four years later was presented with a special Oscar. He married Ida Tobias on June 9, 1914, in New York City. He had five daughters: Marjorie (b. March 31, 1915, d. May 17, 1959, of cancer), Natalie (b. April 27, 1916), Edna (b. June 10, 1919), Marilyn (b. September 16, 1921) and Janet (b. October 8, 1927). Ida died of a heart attack on August 8, 1962. The song 'Ida Sweet As Apple Cider' was inspired by her.
CAUSE: Cantor died in Beverly Hills, California, aged 72 from a heart attack.

Truman Capote
(TRUMAN STRECKFUS PERSONS)
Born September 30, 1924
Died August 25, 1984
Social gadfly. Born in Touro Infirmary, New Orleans, Louisiana, Truman Garcia Capote (as he became after taking his stepfather's name) was a short, alcoholic, drug-addicted, gossipy socialite and author whose name was made internationally famous in January 1966 when his book *In Cold Blood* was published. It was a fictionalised account of the murders of four members of the Clutter family by Richard E. Hickok and Perry E. Smith at River Valley Farm, Holcombe, Kansas on November 15, 1959. The two men were hanged in Lansing Prison, Kansas, on April 14, 1965. It was filmed in 1967, starring Robert Blake. Capote's previous work,

Breakfast At Tiffany's (1958), had also been made into a successful film. His other books included *A Christmas Memory* (1966), *The Thanksgiving Visitor* (1968), *Music For Chameleons* (1980), *One Christmas* (1983) and, posthumously, *Answered Prayers: The Unfinished Novel* (1987). On November 28, 1966, he threw one of the most famous parties of modern times, the Black & White Ball, "an international list for the guillotine", at Manhattan's Plaza Hotel Grand Ballroom, Fifth Avenue at 59th Street. The event only cost him around $16,000 and he was able to recoup part of that on tax deductibles. Capote turned to interviewing and elicited remarkable confessions from the people he spoke to, often to their later chagrin. One such subject was Marlon Brando who confessed his numerous homosexual affairs. "The little bastard spent half the night telling me his problems," moaned Brando. "I figured the least I could do was tell him a few of mine." CAUSE: Capote died of a drug overdose in Los Angeles, but whether it was deliberate or accidental no one knows. He was 59.
FURTHER READING: *Capote A Biography* – Gerald Clarke (London: Cardinal, 1988)

Frank Capra, OBE, DSM

Born May 18, 1897
Died September 3, 1991
Director of the common man. Born in Bisacquino, Sicily, one of seven (some sources say fourteen) children of farmers Salvatore Capra and Rosaria Nicolosi, the family left for America aboard the ship Germania on May 10, 1903. It was an unpleasant voyage: "There [was] no ventilation, and it stank like hell. It [was] the most degrading place you could ever be. It was awful, awful. It seemed to always be storming, raining like hell and very windy, with these big long rolling Atlantic waves. Everybody was sick, vomiting. God, they were sick. And the

poor kids were always crying." The ship docked on May 23 and the Capras left for California, arriving in Los Angeles on June 3, 1903. Francesco Rosario Capra began at the Castelar Elementary School on September 14, 1903 and graduated from high school on January 27, 1915. He was the only Capra child to attend higher education – he read for a degree in chemical engineering, graduating on September 15, 1918. During the First World War he served as an artillery instructor, enisting on October 18. On demob two months later, he was unable to find work as an engineer so he took to selling door-to-door. He worked as an extra on John Ford's film *The Outcasts Of Poker Flat* (1919). In 1920 Capra took American citizenship. In 1922 he directed his first film, *Fultah Fisher's Boarding House*, having persuaded Walter Montague, a San Franciscan filmmaker, to let him direct shorts. He was paid $75-a-week for his work. He moved to Hollywood in 1923 to work, writing jokes for Hal Roach and the Our Gang comedies. Six months later in January 1924, 5'7" Capra landed a job as a joke writer for Harry Langdon who was so impressed he hired Capra to direct his subsequent films: *The Strong Man* (1926) and *Long Pants* (released March 1927). Capra and Langdon began to argue about who was responsible for the success of the films, each men believing that he was the one. Of Langdon Capra commented, "It is the principal of the brick: If there was a rule for writing Langdon material, it was this: his only ally was God. Harry Langdon might be saved by a brick falling on a cop, but it was verboten that he in any way motivated the bricks fall." Capra returned to New York but his one effort, *For The Love Of Mike* (1927) his first film with Claudette Colbert, flopped so he returned to the Mack Sennett Studio as a writer. In October 1927, Harry Cohn's Columbia Pictures hired Capra to work at his Poverty Row

Studio. Capra had complete control over the films but was paid just $1,000 each. It did not augur well when Cohn wanted to sack Capra just three days into his first production, *That Certain Thing* (1928). Watching the rushes, Cohn did not understand why Capra had shot everything in long shot on the first day, in medium shot on the second day and close-ups on the third day. Capra explained, "I did it that way for time. It was so easy to be better than the other directors, because they were all dopes. They would shoot a long shot, then they would have to change the setup to shoot a medium shot, then they would take their close-ups. Then they would come back and start over again. You lose time, you see, moving the cameras and the big goddamn lights. I said, 'I'll get all the long shots on that first set first, then all the medium shots, and then the close-ups.' I wouldn't shoot the whole scene each way unless it was necessary. If I knew that part of it was going to play in long shot, I wouldn't shoot that part in close-up. But the trick was not to move nine times, just to move three times. This saved a day, maybe two days." Cohn decided to perservere with Capra and was later pleased that he did. Capra found his metier, social comedies with sexually forthright actresses like Barbara Stanwyck who was cast, eventually, in *Ladies Of Leisure* (1930) and Jean Harlow in *Platinum Blonde* (1931). *Lady For A Day* (1933), which cost $300,000, became the first Columbia film to be nominated for a Best Film Oscar and Capra was nominated for Best Director. Capra's *The Bitter Tea Of General Yen* (1933), an erotic melodrama set in China, received critical acclaim but was a box office flop. On March 16, 1934 Capra attended the Oscars held at the Fiesta Room of the Ambassador Hotel in Los Angeles, hosted by Will Rogers who presented all the awards. Rather than announcing the nominees, Rogers

would open the envelope, announce the winner and then after the victor had made a speech, Rogers would then read out the other nominees and ask for a round of applause. It had a catastrophic effect when he came to announce Best Director. Rogers opened the envelope and said, "Well, well, well. What do you know? I've watched this young man for a long time. Saw him come up from the bottom, and I mean the bottom. It couldn't have happened to a nicer guy. Come on up and get it, Frank!" Ecstatic, Capra began making his way to the dais: "The spotlight searched around trying to find me. 'Over here!' I waved. Then it suddenly swept away from me – and picked up a flustered man standing on the other side of the dance floor – Frank Lloyd!" The winner was indeed Lloyd for *Cavalcade* (1933). As Capra stood bereft and alone on the dance floor, a man yelled, "Down in front." Capra turned and began the "longest, saddest, most shattering walk in my life. I wished I could have crawled under the rug like a miserable worm. When I slumped in my chair I felt like one. All of my friends at the table were crying." Capra went home and drank himself unconscious. He vowed that "if ever [the Academy] did vote me one [an Oscar], I would never, never, *never* show up to accept it." The next year Capra did show up when nominated and winning for *It Happened One Night* (1934) starring Clark Gable and Claudette Colbert – the first of his three wins. The film transformed Gable and Colbert into sex symbols. The following year Capra was beset by appendicitis and peritonitis. During his recuperation he claimed that he had a vision in which he was told to use his "God-given talents for His purpose". After that Capra dropped all sexual innuendoes and sensuality from his films. Thereafter, his films focused on the innate goodness of mankind. Capra made some of the best, most memorable "feelgood" movies anyone in Hollywood has produced. They included: *Mr Deeds Goes To Town* (1936) starring Gary Cooper and Jean Arthur (for which Capra won an Oscar), the Oscar nominated *Mr Smith Goes To Washington* (1939) starring James Stewart and Claude Rains, *You Can't Take It With You* (1938) which won Oscars for Best Film and Best Director and the Oscar nominated *It's A Wonderful Life* (1946) starring James Stewart and Henry Travers. The latter was one of only two films – the other being *State Of The Union* (1948) – made for Liberty Films, the company Capra formed in Hollywood with Samuel J. Briskin, William Wyler and George Stevens, with the express intention of making movies for "a better America". In 1949 Liberty Films went broke and merged with Paramount. Capra found it difficult to get work afterwards and journalists derisively called his genre of films "Capracorn". In 1959 Capra went into business with Frank Sinatra to film the comedy *A Hole In The Head* (released July 15, 1959), his first colour film. The public loved the film as much as the critics loathed it and the song 'High Hopes' won an Oscar. The following year it was adopted as the campaign anthem for Senator John F. Kennedy's successful run for the presidency. Capra's last feature film was *Pocketful Of Miracles* (1961), a flop remake of *Lady For A Day*. Capra retired in 1966 and moved to La Quinta, California. Arguably his best-known film, *It's A Wonderful Life* did not achieve any real measure of success until 1974 when its copyright expired and it began to be shown on television. The RKO film had originally been a vehicle for Cary Grant and Jean Arthur was intended to play the Donna Reed part. The film was also colourised against the director's express wishes. During the Second World War Capra was head of the Army Pictorial Service for which he was awarded the Distinguished Service

Medal and an honorary OBE. On November 25, 1923, Capra married actress Helen Edith Howell but the marriage fell to pieces when she discovered that she had a life-threatening ectopic pregnancy that had to be terminated. He coped by becoming a workaholic while she turned to booze. They split in April 1927 and divorced two days after Christmas 1928. In the summer of 1929, he was introduced to a young widow, Lucille Rayburn Warner (b. Oakland, California, April 23, 1903) whom he married on July 1, 1932. They had four children: Frank, Jr (see below), Tom (b. February 12 1941), Lulu (b. September 16, 1937) and John (b. April 12, 1935, d. August 23, 1938). Mrs Capra died on July 1, 1984 after which Capra became a recluse. He admitted "I made some mistakes in drama. I thought drama was when the actors cried. But drama is when the audience cries."

CAUSE: He died in La Quinta, California, of a heart attack in his sleep. He was 94-years-old. He was buried in block 77, unit 8, lot 289 of Coachella Valley Public Cemetery, 82-925 Avenue 52, Coachella, California CA92236.

Frank Capra, Jr
Born March 20, 1934
Died December 19, 2007
Son didn't shine. It is always difficult to follow in the footsteps of a cinematic giant and Frank Capra (see above), Jr's life was no different so he left Hollywood and moved to Wilmington, North Carolina and became the president of EUE/Screen Gems Studios in the largest motion picture studio east of Tinseltown. Frank Warner Capra was born in Los Angeles, the eldest of three children of Frank Capra and his second wife Lucille Rayburn Warner and was educated at the California Institute of Technology and Pomona College where he obtained a degree in geology. He decided to become a filmmaker but unlike his father, chose

to make films that documented government research on torpedoes and helicopters conducted by the Hughes Tool Company rather than Hollywood blockbusters. Capra Jr. enlisted in the US Army's film unit, the Signal Corps, and spent three years stationed in New Jersey. On demob he worked on television shows including *Dennis The Menace, Gunsmoke, The Rifleman* and *Wanted: Dead Or Alive* before progressing to become an assistant director and then a film producer on *Escape From The Planet Of The Apes* (1971), *Play It Again, Sam* (1972), *Conquest Of The Planet Of The Apes* (1972), *Tom Sawyer* (1973), *Battle For The Planet Of The Apes* (1973), *Billy Jack Goes To Washington* (1977), *The Black Marble* (1980), *An Eye For An Eye* (1981) and *Firestarter* (1984). It was in pre-production for *Firestarter* in 1983 that Capra was sent by producer Dino De Laurentis to Wilmington to find an antebellum mansion to burn. Both were so taken by the area that they decided to found a studio there. Frank Capra Jr was married twice; firstly, to Priscilla A. Pearson by whom he had two sons, Frank III (b. July 16, 1959) and Jonathan (the marriage ended in divorce); and, then to Debra Lewis by whom he had a daughter, Christina (b. December 7, 1972). CAUSE: Capra died of prostate cancer in a Philadelphia hospital. He was 73.

Capucine

(GERMAINE LEFEBVRE)
Born January 6, 1931
Died March 17, 1990
Glacial actress. Born in Toulon, France, the daughter of an industrialist, she became a fashion model on leaving school and married, very briefly, by the time she was 20. She renamed herself Capucine (pronounced Kap-oo-seen), the French word for nasturtium, her favourite flower. She revealed "I hated my real name. In France it's as common as Gladys" and made her film début in 1949 in *Les Rendez-Vous De*

Juillet, following this up with *Bertrand Coeur De Lion* (1950), but it would be another five years before her next screen appearance, in *Frou-Frou* (1955), and then another five years before she went to America. Because of her height (5'7") and exotic grey-eyed look she was immediately hailed as 'the new Garbo'. (Perhaps her sexuality had something to do with the comparison.) Her first film in America, *Song Without End* (1960) playing Princess Carolyne, was cruelly dubbed by wags as 'Without End'. It was a biopic of the rampantly heterosexual composer Franz Liszt, who was played by Dirk Bogarde (!). Gay director George Cukor also had a hand in the production. He opined: "She didn't have much range. Capucine was a Look. Bacall and others were launched as a Look. However, Capucine was rather wooden on screen and inhibited. She posed . . . Movies were her passport and her means, but she put more energy into her life, into travelling and living it up on both continents in-between film assignments. That's just what they were to her." Capucine's cause was taken up by agent-turned-producer Charles K. Feldman. Although the media painted the couple as an item, there was no romance between them. In 1962 she appeared as Hallie in *Walk On The Wild Side* with Anne Baxter, Jane Fonda, Barbara Stanwyck and Laurence Harvey. The film revolved around a love triangle – Harvey, Stanwyck and Capucine. The Lithuanian-born Harvey was not impressed by his love interest. He told her: "Kissing you is like kissing the side of a beer bottle." Her most prominent part was in *The Pink Panther* (1963) as Simone, the wife of the bumbling Inspector Clouseau. For a time William Holden left his wife for Capucine and they appeared together in *The Lion* (1962) and *The Seventh Dawn* (1964) with Capucine playing Dhana. (Holden left her $50,000 in his will.) In an interview, when asked whether the affair was ever consummated, the predominantly lesbian Capucine replied: "He desired me more than I desired him. I have had romantic or sexual liaisons with women, and one or two with men . . . it happened . . . because I was so strongly attracted." She reprised her Mme Clouseau role in *Trail Of The Pink Panther* (1982) and *Curse Of The Pink Panther* (1984) but began to suffer from loneliness and depression as parts dried up. Her other films included: *What's New, Pussycat?* (1965) as Renee Lefebvre, *Fräulein Doktor* (1969) as Dr Saforet, *Satyricon* (1969) as Trifena, *Ciao, Federico!* (1970), *Soleil Rouge* (1971) as Pepita, *Per Amore* (1976), *Ritratto Di Borghesia In Nero* (1977) as Amalia Mazzarini, *Jaguar Lives!* (1979) as Zina Vanacore, *Balles Perdues* (1982) as Madam Teufminn and *I Miei Primi Quarant'Anni* (1987) as Massimiliano. CAUSE: She died by her own hand, jumping from the eighth-floor window of her Swiss attic home. She was 59.

Jack Cardiff OBE

Born September 18, 1914
Died April 22, 2009
Technicolor pioneer. Jack Cardiff was born in Great Yarmouth, Norfolk, the son of vaudeville performers and made his stage debut at an early age and was only four when he made his first film *My Son, My Son* in 1918. In a later movie, he played a boy who dies after being run over and it took three days to film his death. It was a dreadful experience for his parents since his elder brother had died in infancy. Ten years later, Cardiff had moved behind the camera to work on the crew of the last big British silent movie *The Informer* (1929). In 1935 he worked as a camera operator on René Clair's *The Ghost Goes West*. The following year, Cardiff was working at Denham Studios in London and was hired by Technicolor after impressing them with his knowedge of lighting in the paintings of his favorite old masters.

Cardiff was the camera operator on the 1937 romantic drama *Wings Of The Morning*, which starred Henry Fonda and was the first Technicolor film made in Britain. He worked on Michael Powell and Emeric Pressburger's *The Life And Death Of Colonel Blimp* (1943), a film Churchill said was unpatriotic. Cardiff's reputation was assured when Powell invited Cardiff to be the cinematographer on his and Pressburger's wartime fantasy drama *A Matter Of Life And Death* (1946) that starred David Niven as a wartime pilot who, after being killed in a crash, is overlooked by the heavenly messengers sent to collect him. He is given another chance after a celestial trial hears he has fallen in love with Kim Hunter, an American wireless operator. It was Cardiff's first feature film as a cinematographer. *A Matter Of Life And Death* was chosen as the first Royal Film performance and consolidated Cardiff's place with Powell and Pressburger's Archers production team. During his career Cardiff worked with directors such as Alfred Hitchcock, John Huston and King Vidor and stars such as Humphrey Bogart, Marilyn Monroe and Ava Gardner. Bogart approached him the first time they worked together and told him, "Cardiff, see this face? I got all these lines and wrinkles – that's character. I don't want you to soften anything . . ." Cardiff remembered, "I said, 'Well, Bogie, you got me beat because there's too much debauchery there.' And he laughed and said, 'Right, put down that sissy drink,' which was a beer, 'and let's have a real one.'" Powell described Cardiff as "the greatest colour cameraman in the world". Among his films were *The Red Shoes* (1948), *Under Capricorn* (1949), *The Black Rose* (1950), *The African Queen* (1951), *Pandora And The Flying Dutchman* (1951), *The Magic Box* (1952), *The Barefoot Contessa* (1954), *The Prince And The Showgirl* (1957 – he said "[Marilyn] Monroe was a manic depressive. Olivier should have got an Oscar for his patience"), *The Vikings* (1958), *Young Cassidy* (1965, on which he took over direction from John Ford), *Ride A Wild Pony* (1976), *Death On The Nile* (1978), *Conan The Destroyer* (1984), *Rambo: First Blood Part II* (1984) and *Tai Pan* (1986). Cardiff won an Oscar for his work on the drama *Black Narcissus* (1947), the Powell-Pressburger film starring Deborah Kerr about a group of nuns who establish a remote mission in the Himalayas. He was also Oscar nominated for *War And Peace* (1957) and *Fanny* (1962). He directed *Sons And Lovers* (1961), which starred Trevor Howard, Dean Stockwell, Mary Ure and Wendy Hiller and it won him an Oscar nomination for best director. In 2001, Cardiff received an honorary Academy Award, the first awarded to a cinematographer for artistic achievement rather than technical merit. Cardiff was married three times. CAUSE: Cardiff died of age-related causes at his home in Ely, Cambridgeshire. He was 94.

Harry Carey
Born January 16, 1878
Died September 21, 1947
Early superstar. Born in The Bronx, New York, Henry DeWitt Carey II joined Biograph Pictures in 1909 (first film *Bill Sharkey's Last Game* [1909]) and appeared in many films produced by D.W. Griffith before finding his true vocation as the star of early Westerns with John Ford. They worked together on 26 films including *A Knight Of The Range* (1916), *Cheyenne's Pal* (1917), *The Soul Herder* (1917), *Straight Shooting* (1917) (the first John Ford feature), *The Secret Man* (1917), *A Marked Man* (1917), *Bucking Broadway* (1917), *Wild Women* (1918), *Thieves' Gold* (1918), *Three Mounted Men* (1918), *Roped* (1919), *Bare Fists* (1919), *Riders Of Vengeance* (1919), *Ace Of The Saddle* (1919), *Marked Men* (1919) and *Aces Wild* (1937). More

often than not he would play a cowboy called Cheyenne Harry Henderson. As well as acting, 6' Carey also wrote, directed and produced. He was nominated for an Oscar for his performance as the President of the Senate in Frank Capra's *Mr Smith Goes To Washington* (1939). He married actress Olive Fuller Golden (b. January 31, 1896, d. March 13, 1988) in 1920 and their son, Harry Carey, Jr (b. Saugus, California May 16, 1921), was also in the business.
CAUSE: Harry Carey, who appeared in over 230 films, died in Brentwood, California, of coronary thrombosis and cancer. He was 69 years old. The John Ford film *The Three Godfathers* (1949) was dedicated "To the memory of Harry Carey – bright star of the early western sky".

Jeanne Carmen
Born August 4, 1930
Died December 20, 2007
Femme fantasistique. Jeanne Laverne Carmen was just one of a million girls with little acting talent who arrived in Hollywood hoping for a screen career – and she would have remained anonymous had it not been for her claims of being a close friend of Marilyn Monroe. 36-26-36 Carmen was born in Paragould, Arkansas and began picking cotton in fields before running away when she was 13 after her mother forbade her to enter a beauty contest. Arriving in New York, she landed a job as a dancer in a Broadway show called *Burlesque* with comic Bert Lahr. She became a model posing for men's magazines like *Carnival*, *Dare*, *Glance*, *Pose* and *Titter* and then a trickshot golfer. In her twenties, she moved to Hollywood and appeared in a number of low budget films including *Striporama* (released October 2, 1953) as Venus Beauty, *The Three Outlaws* (released May 13, 1956) as Serelda, *War Drums* (released March 21, 1957) as Yellow Moon, *A Merry Mix-up* (released March 28, 1957) as

Mary, *Untamed Youth* (released July 19, 1957) as Lillibet, *Portland Exposé* (released August 11, 1957) as Iris, *Too Much, Too Soon* (released April 17, 1958) as Tassles and *The Monster Of Piedras Blancas* (1959) as Lucy. In Hollywood she claimed to have had affairs with, among others, Clark Gable, Errol Flynn, Frank Sinatra and Elvis Presley. She parlayed a non-friendship with Monroe into a second career giving interviews to credulous writers telling of her "closeness" to Monroe even though no pictures exist of the two women together nor did any of Carmen's details appear in Monroe's address books and none of Marilyn's friends had ever heard of her. She further alleged that she was told to leave town by the gangster Johnny Rosselli after Monroe's death. 5'6½" Carmen was married and divorced three times and had three children Melinda Belli, Kellee Jade Campo and Brandon James. "Everything I've done, I think I did at the right time," she recalled. "And it turned out great. Maybe a few marriages I could have done without. As for my career, it absolutely happened the way it was supposed to happen. A door opened and I was a pin-up. I'm as happy as a pig in a pond."
CAUSE: Jeane Carmen died from lymphoma at her home in Turtle Ridge, Orange County, California, where she had lived since 1978. She was 77. Her only son, Brandon James, said, "It was very peaceful – she just went to sleep. I was holding her hand when it happened."

Martine Carol
(MARYSE LOUISE MOURER)
Born May 16, 1920
Died February 6, 1967
Femme fatale. Born in Saint-Mande, France, she was the premier European love goddess of the Fifties. Blonde and beautiful she usually portrayed loose women in even looser clothing, encouraged by her husband (he was the director Christian-Jaque [b. 1904, d. 1994]). She played Martine in *Le Désir Et L'Amour* (1951), Minouche in *Adorables Créatures* (1952), Edmee in *Les Belles De Nuit* (1952), the leads in *Lucrèce Borgia* (1953), *Nana* (1955) and *Lola Montès* (1955). She attempted to break into Hollywood with disastrous results. Her only major film was *Around The World In 80 Days* (1956) and even then she only played a tourist. Her star was quickly eclipsed by the younger Brigitte Bardot and Jeanne Moreau, who took her mantle. CAUSE: She died aged 46 of a heart attack in Monte Carlo, Monaco.

Johnny Carpenter
(JASPER CARPENTER)
Born June 25, 1914
Died February 27, 2003
Charitable cowboy. If there was money to be saved, corners to be cut, Johnny Carpenter was the man to do it. Born in the small Ozark mountain town of Debinsville, Arkansas, the son of a butcher, Carpenter learned to ride while still a child. He was educated at the University of Arkansas and showed such sporting promise that he was set to play for the Chicago White Sox in 1936 when, during spring practice, he was run over by a car in a hit and run accident. He suffered a broken back, internal injuries and broke his left leg in seven places. He was in a body cast for 119 days and lost his chance at a baseball career. It took him eight years to recover fully and he used that time to perfect his horse riding and shooting skills. In the early Forties he travelled to Hollywood with his brother, Frank 'Red' Carpenter. It is believed that his first film was a bit part in *Thundering Trails* (1943) with the 3 Mesquiteers at Republic, although some insist that he had appeared as a concessionaire in *Dante's Inferno* (1935). Carpenter became a stuntman and rode the Grand National course for Mickey Rooney in *National Velvet* (1944). He didn't star in a film until *Badman's*

Gold in 1951 and his work never progressed above B-picture rating. In the mid-Fifties he wrote, produced and starred in four Westerns that made his name among aficionados of that genre – *Son Of The Renegade* (1953), Yakima Canutt's *The Lawless Rider* (1954), *Outlaw Treasure* (1955) and Richard Talmadge's *I Killed Wild Bill Hickok* (1956). For reasons unknown, on the last two, Carpenter listed himself as writer/producer but billed himself when acting as John Forbes. Away from the screen Carpenter was a tireless worker for handicapped children. He said that he had made a deal with God in 1936 that if He allowed him to walk again, he would spend his time helping the disabled. He opened a ranch called Heaven On Earth in the mid-Forties in Glendale, California, and had ranches in different locations until he was evicted in January 1994 to make way for a housing development. Thousands of children from Los Angeles schools and groups such as the United Cerebral Palsy/Spastic Children's Foundation were greeted at the gates by Johnny as they spent the day touring the Western town set and riding horseback, with Carpenter's help if need be. Johnny's motto, emblazoned on a sign at the ramshackle ranch, read, "The service we render to others is really the rent we pay for our room on this earth. Dedicated free forever to the handicapped." In 1982 he said, "The Bible says, 'As you sow, so shall ye reap.' Well, I've reaped two-hundredfold. I've gotten more satisfaction out of this ranch than anything else I've ever done. Everything I own is on my back. Yet because of the ranch, I can get up every morning and walk down the street like a king. If I get to Heaven, it'll be on the coat-tails of these kids."
CAUSE: Johnny Carpenter died in a Burbank nursing home, aged 88. He had been suffering from cancer. Johnny was buried at Forest Lawn Cemetery, Forest Lawn Drive, Los Angeles.

Allan Carr
(ALLAN SOLOMON)
Born May 27, 1937
Died June 26, 1999
Tubby extrovert. Born in Chicago, Illinois, the flamboyant movie producer Allan Carr's career was made with just one film – the megahit *Grease* (1978), which he wrote and co-produced. Two years later, that career was virtually wrecked with another musical. Carr stood out in a world of eccentrics in Tinseltown. He wore multi-coloured caftans that would have put Demis Roussos to shame, and would often turn up to a swanky event dressed in a full-length mink coat, training shoes and little else. Unsurprisingly, or perhaps not, he never married. In 1979 he attended a pop concert given by Village People, the incredibly successful disco group, who had begun as an idea in a Moroccan-born music producer's head in a gay disco called the Anvil in New York's Greenwich Village in the mid-70s. Jacques Morali, for that was the producer's name, spotted clerk Felipé Rose dancing dressed as a Red Indian. Morali immediately saw the potential for a group to appeal to homosexual men. He advertised for "gay singers and dancers, very good-looking and with mustaches [*sic*]" and from the response put together Village People. To Morali's amazement the group appealed to straight people and teenage girls as well as his targeted audience. Soon Village People were a world-wide phenomenon, scoring massive international hits such as 'Y.M.C.A.' (number 1 in the UK, number 2 in the US), 'In The Navy', 'Go West' and 'Can't Stop The Music'. Carr was so impressed by what he saw at the gig he decided to star the group in his next film – to be called *Discoland: Where The Music Never Stops*. He hired a young actor called Steve Guttenberg to play Morali (renamed Jack Morell) and described him to the press as "a Jewish John Travolta". "A teenaged

Tennessee Williams" called Bronte Woodward was commissioned to write the film. Carr approached his *Grease* star Olivia Newton-John, but balked at her demand for $1 million to appear. His second choice was the beautiful 39-24-35 Valerie Perrine and, as her love interest, he chose Olympic decathlete Bruce Jenner, whom he labelled "the Bob Redford of the Eighties". Directing her first movie was Nancy Walker who was well known for her role as the housekeeper Mildred in *McMillan & Wife*. "I'll say I'm lucky! My first movie, and it's a big-budget musical! It's got everything . . . the Village People, hit songs, male nudity, Valerie Perrine and her cleavage, Bruce Jenner and his legs . . . My producer thinks it will be another *Grease*!" was her opinion. Unfortunately, by the time the film was released in the summer of 1980, under the new title *Can't Stop The Music*, the Village People bubble had burst and the film was an unmitigated disaster . . . except, strangely, in Australia, where it was a smash and broke box-office records wherever it played. Elsewhere, however, straight audiences didn't take it seriously and the group's original core fans – the gay community – hated the film because it had been "heterosexualised". All the Village Persons were assigned girlfriends. Carr commented, "You don't spend $20m to make a minority movie." *Newsweek* sniped, "The first all-singing, all-dancing horror film . . . chilling . . . a celebration of greed, narcissism, unbridled ambition and the triumph of mediocrity . . . If this is the movie musical event of the Eighties, we've got nine grim years ahead." Carr took his stars on the publicity junket to promote the film but one by one they all found other pressing engagements until only Guttenberg and June Havoc appeared with the producer. Carr was undeterred and set out to make *Grease 2* (1982). Without the catchy songs of the original and without Travolta,

Newton-John *et al*, it, too, was a flop. You can't keep a good man down though, and two years later Allan Carr was back with his last two movies, *Cloak And Dagger* (1984) and *Where The Boys Are '84* (1984). The first was about an imaginative boy (played by Henry Thomas) who plays spying games with a fantasy friend only to get caught up in a real-life espionage situation; it was a success. Sadly not so the second film, a remake of the 1960 hit version that starred Dolores Hart, George Hamilton, Yvette Mimieux, Jim Hutton and Connie Francis. The remake cast the beautiful Lisa Hartman and Judy Garland's lesser-known daughter Lorna Luft. It bombed. Like many fat people who struggle to maintain a happy exterior while fighting raging demons within, Carr was unhappy about his size. In a desperate bid to lose weight he once had his jaws wired shut. It didn't work. He pulled out the wires with pliers. CAUSE: He died of cancer in Beverly Hills, California aged 62, not the 57 he would have people believe.

David Carradine
(JOHN ARTHUR CARRADINE)
Born December 8, 1936
Found dead June 4, 2009
Eccentric star. The son of John Carradine (see below) David Carradine appeared in more than 100 films but it was as the Shaolin monk Kwai Chang Caine in the television series *Kung Fu* that he achieved international fame. Born in Hollywood Carradine, who was said to have had English, Irish, German, Spanish, Italian, Ukrainian and Cherokee blood, began truanting from school when he was 13 and spent time in a borstal and various foster homes. Pulling himself together, he studied music theory and composition at what is now called San Francisco State University where he first became interested in acting and signed for a Shakespearean repertory company. He planned to play Hamlet on Broadway,

an ambition that was never realised. He also worked as a commercial artist and was for a time in the army. He made his film debut in 1964 playing Cal Dodge in *Taggart*, having made his first appearance on television the year before. In 1965 he appeared on Broadway as the Inca chief Atahualpa in Peter Shaffer's *Royal Hunt Of The Sun*. He took the title role in the television series *Shane* in 1966 and was a regular in Westerns on the small screen. He played "Big" Bill Shelly in Martin Scorsese's first film, *Boxcar Bertha* (released June 14, 1972), where he met the actress Barbara Hershey who was to become his girlfriend. His father also appeared in the film. Carradine and Hershey were together for three years and on October 6, 1972 they had a son that they gave the hippyish name Free – the boy later changed his name to Tom. 1972 also saw the first of 60 episodes of *Kung Fu*. "How I got the *Kung Fu* part amazes me to this day. I arrived for the audition barefooted with my head shaved and accompanied by my dog. To be sure I've never made any secret about my growing my own pot and smoking it. I've been in court on marijuana charges too, though I was not convicted. I'll admit to other unsavoury things about myself too. I have a record of thieving, I was a ring-leader of a teenage crime gang. I was expelled from school. I was court martialled three times in the army . . . and even if that's all behind me now, I still don't please a lot of people by the way I live with my girlfriend and have a kid without bothering to get married." In the show Master Po (Keye Luke) is murdered by the nephew of the Emperor of China, in retaliation Caine kills the nephew and to avoid death flees to America where he searches for his half-brother. He became interested in the martial art and believed himself to be an expert, a view not shared by everyone: "David Carradine is about as good a martial artist as I am an actor,"

said Chuck Norris tartly. After *Kung Fu*, 6′1″ Carradine appeared in *Death Race 2000* (1975) and was nominated for a Golden Globe for his portrayal of Woody Guthrie in *Bound For Glory* (1976). The following year he was in Ingmar Bergman's *The Serpent's Egg* (1977). With his half-brothers Keith and Robert he played in Walter Hill's *The Long Riders* (1980) taking the part of Cole Younger. After that his star rather waned although he received another Golden Globe nomination for the TV mini-series *North And South* (1985–86). He reprised the role of Kwai Chang Caine in *Kung Fu: The Movie* (1986) and the TV series *Kung Fu: The Legend Continues* (1993–97). "Every day," he said of the role, which won him several Emmys, "at least six people will come up to me and say 'Your show changed my life'." In 1989 he spent 48 hours in jail for drink driving. His star was re-polished when Quentin Tarantino cast him in the title role of *Kill Bill* (2003 and 2004), which earned him a Golden Globe nomination as best supporting actor. The role lead to commercial opportunities and Carradine became the face of Yellowbook telephone directories and Lipton tea. David Carradine was married five times. His first marriage, on December 29, 1960, to Donna Lee Becht, by whom he had a daughter, Calista (born Virginia April 1962), ended in 1968, and he married, secondly, Linda Gilbert on February 2, 1977. They had a daughter, Kansas (b. at Los Angeles, California April 19, 1978). This marriage ended in 1983, and on December 4, 1988 he married actress (Patricia) Gail Jensen (b. October 5, 1949, Sanger, California). On February 20, 1998, he married his fourth wife, actress Marina Anderson (b. Burbank, California October 5, 1952), but this was dissolved on December 12, 2001. On Boxing Day 2004, David Carradine married Annie Bierman at a ceremony in the Malibu home of Michael Madsen performed by

Carradine's lawyer, and a long-time friend of his fifth bride. Carradine realised that he had never really fitted into the Hollywood milieu. "I'm like a renegade and that rubs people wrong," he said.

CAUSE: In 2004, Carradine confessed to contemplating suicide often. "Why would you be afraid of death? It would be an inconvenience. I have a lot of undone things and it's bound to get in the way. But, no, it doesn't scare me at all," he said. "Look, there was a period in my life when I had a single action Colt .45, loaded, in my desk drawer. And every night I'd take it out and think about blowing my head off. And then decide not to and go on with my life. Put it back in the drawer and open up the laptop and continue writing my autobiography or whatever. But it was just to see. And then I remember one time sitting in the window of the third or fourth floor of the Plaza Hotel for about an hour thinking about just tipping off. And that was at a time when I was having more fun than you could imagine. I just thought, 'Who the fuck cares, man? Why don't I just split?' Of course I didn't, so there you go." In the end death came in a bizarre way, not altogether dissimilar from the death of pop star Michael Hutchence. While filming *Stretch* in Bangkok Carradine's naked body was found by a maid at 11.30am in the wardrobe of suite 352 in the luxury five-star Swissitel Nai Lert Park Hotel on Wireless Road, four days after he had checked in. The hotel, next to the British Embassy in Bangkok is famous for its penis shrine, a tribute to penis power. Carradine had used cords from curtains to bind his hands, neck and penis and seemed to die from erotic auto-asphyxiation that had gone wrong. "There was a rope tied around his neck and another rope tied to his genitals, and the two ropes were tied together and they hung in the closet," said Lieutenant General Worapong Siewpreecha. "Under these circumstances we cannot be sure that he committed suicide but he may have died from masturbation." Police Commander Somprasong Yenthuam said, "We have checked the CCTV and nobody else came in and out of his room. The room was also in perfect order. Nothing else seems to have been touched. There was some money lying around on a table and a bottle of drinking water and some water in a glass. His body has been taken to Chulalongkorn Hospital for a forensic examination but we expect they will find he died of asphyxiation." Forensic pathologist Dr Michael Baden concluded that the Kung Fu star had indeed died from asphyxiation. The way the body was bound allowed him to rule out suicide. "He didn't die of natural causes, and he didn't die of suicidal causes. That leaves some kind of accidental death." Two days after Carradine's corpse was found, the tabloid *Thai Rath* published a picture of his body on its front page. Unsurprisingly, the family were horrified. Keith Carradine said in a statement that the family was "profoundly disturbed by the release in Thailand of photographs taken at the scene of David Carradine's death . . . The family wants it understood that any persons, publications or media outlets will be fully prosecuted for invasion of privacy and causing severe emotional distress if the photos are published." Ten days after his death, Carradine's funeral took place at the Hall of Liberty at Forest Lawn-Hollywood Hills, a 400-acre cemetery next to Griffith Park in Los Angeles.

FURTHER READING: *Endless Highway –* David Carradine (Boston: Tuttle Publications, 1995).

John Carradine

(RICHMOND REED CARRADINE)
Born February 5, 1906
Died November 27, 1988
Cinematic villain. Born in Greenwich

Village, New York City, the son of a lawyer who wrote poetry and a surgeon, 6'1¼" Carradine was educated at the Episcopal Academy and the Graphic Art School, both in Philadelphia. He first trod the boards in 1925 at the St Charles Theater in New Orleans but after a little while he became a portrait painter before being hired by Cecil B. DeMille as a designer. He made his film début in 1928 (using the name John Peter Richmond; he became John Carradine in 1935 after signing a contract with Fox) appearing in innumerable films, many unworthy of his talent, particularly those of Al Adamson. Among his 200+ films, made over 60 years, were: *Tol'able David* (1930) as Buzzard, *Forgotten Commandments* (1932), *The Invisible Man* (1933), *Cleopatra* (1934), *She Gets Her Man* (1935), *The Man Who Broke The Bank At Monte Carlo* (1935), *Cardinal Richelieu* (1935), *Bride Of Frankenstein* (1935), *Alias Mary Dow* (1935), *Clive Of India* (1935), *White Fang* (1936) as Beauty Smith, *Dimples* (1936) as Richards, *Daniel Boone* (1936) as Simon Girty, *Mary Of Scotland* (1936) as David Rizzio, *The Garden Of Allah* (1936), *Thank You, Mr Moto* (1937) as Periera, *Nancy Steele Is Missing!* (1937) as Harry Wilkins, *Laughing At Trouble* (1937) as Deputy Sheriff Alec Brady, *Ali Baba Goes To Town* (1937) as Ishak, *Captains Courageous* (1937) as Long Jack, *Of Human Hearts* (1938) as Abraham Lincoln, *Kidnapped* (1938) as Gordon, *Alexander's Ragtime Band* (1938), *Stagecoach* (1939) as Mr Hatfield, *Drums Along The Mohawk* (1939) as Caldwell, *Jesse James* (1939) as Bob Ford, *Mr Moto's Last Warning* (1939) as Danforth aka Richard Burke, *The Hound Of The Baskervilles* (1939) as Barryman, *Brigham Young – Frontiersman* (1940) as Porter Rockwell, *The Grapes Of Wrath* (1940) as Reverend Jim Casey, *The Return Of Frank James* (1940) as Bob Ford, *Northwest Rangers* (1942) as Martin Caswell, *Son Of Fury* (1942) as Caleb Green, *Hitler's Madman* (1943) as Reinhardt Heydrich, *The Adventures Of Mark Twain* (1944) as Bret Harte, *House Of Frankenstein* (1944) as Dracula, *The Ten Commandments* (1956) as Aaron, *Around The World In 80 Days* (1956) as Colonel Proctor Stamp, *Half Human: The Story Of The Abominable Snowman* (1957) as Dr John Rayburn, *Tarzan The Magnificent* (1960) as villainous Abel Banton determined to rescue his son from Tarzan and justice, *The Adventures Of Huckleberry Finn* (1960), *The Man Who Shot Liberty Valance* (1962) as Major Cassius Starbuckle, *Cheyenne Autumn* (1964) as Major Jeff Blair, *Psycho A Go-Go* (1965) as Dr Varnard, *House Of The Black Death* (1965) as Andre Dessard, *Night Train To Mundo Fine* (1966), *Billy The Kid vs. Dracula* (1966) as Count Dracula, *Blood Of Dracula's Castle* (1967) as George, *Autopsia De Un Fantasma* (1967) as Satan, *The Mummy And The Curse Of The Jackals* (1969), *Astro-Zombies* (1969) as Dr DeMarco, *Horror Of The Blood Monsters* (1970) as Dr Rynning, *Five Bloody Graves* (1970) as Boone Hawkins, *Blood Legacy* (1971) as Christopher Dean, *Blood Of Ghastly Horror* (1972) as Dr Van Ard, *Terror In The Wax Museum* (1973) as Claude Dupree, *Silent Night, Bloody Night* (1973) as Charlie Towman, *Won Ton Ton, The Dog Who Saved Hollywood* (1976), *Mary, Mary, Bloody Mary* (1976) as Mary's dad, *Satan's Cheerleaders* (1977), *Vampire Hookers* (1979) as John Peter Richmond, *Satan's Mistress* (1981) as Father Stratten, *Peggy Sue Got Married* (1986) as Leo and *Bikini Drive-In* (1995). In 1944 he was jailed for a week for failing to pay alimony to his first wife. He did not neglect his stage work, appearing as Jonathan Brewster in *Arsenic And Old Lace* (October 1946), Brutus in *Julius Caesar* (1951), Sir Robert Morton in *The Winslow Boy* (1951), Mephistopheles in *Doctor*

Faustus (January 1955), Lycus in *A Funny Thing Happened On The Way To The Forum* (1966) a part he played on tour for nearly two years, Fagin in *Oliver!* (1970) and Jeeter Lester in *Tobacco Road* (1973). Away from the stage and screen Carradine would walk along the streets declaiming Shakespeare and was something of an eccentric loner, a trait picked up by his son, David. He was married four times. The first Mrs Carradine was Ardanelle McCool Cosner, whom he married on December 31, 1935. Carradine adopted his wife's son, actor Bruce (b. Los Angeles, California April 10, 1933) and the couple had another son John Arthur who is noticed above under his professional name David Carradine. The couple was divorced on March 14, 1944; wife number two was Sonia Henius (b. Milwaukee, Wisconsin May 18, 1921, d. Los Angeles, California September 24, 2004) and they married on August 13, 1944. They had three sons: architect Christopher John (b. 1947) and actors Keith (b. San Mateo, California, August 8, 1949, he is the father of actress Martha Plimpton) and Robert (b. Los Angeles, California, March 24, 1954). That marriage ended in divorce on March 6, 1957; the third wife (on August 30, 1957) was Doris Irving Rich (b. Canada May 3, 1919) who died in a blaze on May 18, 1971 at Oxnard, California, and the final Emily Cisneros on July 3, 1975. They divorced before Carradine's death. CAUSE: Carradine died of natural causes in Milan, Italy, aged 81. His last words were, "Milan: What a beautiful place to die."

Madeleine Carroll

(MARIE-MADELEINE BERNADETTE O'CARROLL)
Born February 26, 1906
Died October 2, 1987
Icy blonde. Born in West Bromwich in the West Midlands, blonde, 5'5" Carroll was one of Britain's most popular early film stars. After studying French at the University of Birmingham she became a schoolteacher in Hove, East Sussex, but she saved £20 and, giving up the security of that profession, she travelled to London where agents fought to sign her. Her first film was *The Guns Of Loos* (1928) in which she played Diana Cheswick, quickly followed by *The First Born* (1928) playing Lady Madeleine Boycott and *What Money Can Buy* (1928) as Rhoda Pearson. She travelled west to Hollywood in the mid-Thirties and appeared in John Ford's *The World Moves On* (1934) but it was her acting in two Hitchcock thrillers that secured her status. She was a sexy Pamela in *The 39 Steps* (1935) and the scene in which she and Richard Hannay (Robert Donat) are handcuffed together remains one of the most memorable in cinema history. Hitchcock was a notorious and sometimes cruel practical joker. He handcuffed Carroll and Donat together not long after they first met and then disappeared for the rest of the day, taking the only key with him. He said at the time that he'd done it to see how they got on together, but later confessed that his major enjoyment was wondering how they would answer the calls of nature! Carroll's other Hitchcockian film was *Secret Agent* (1936), in which she took the part of Elsa Carrington. She was memorable in *The Prisoner Of Zenda* (1937) as Princess Flavia playing opposite Ronald Colman and had the title role in the Bob Hope comedy *My Favorite Blonde* (1942) as Karen Bentley. In 1942 her sister was killed in the Blitz and she returned to London to help with war work, specifically the Red Cross. She stayed for the duration and afterwards discovered that her heart was no longer in acting. She made just three more films: *White Cradle Inn* (1946) as Magda, *An Innocent Affair* (1948) as Paula Doane and *The Fan* (1949) as Mrs Erlynne. She worked for UNESCO, occasionally venturing onto

the stage or television. Carroll married four times. Her first husband was Captain Philip Astley. They were married on August 25, 1931, and were divorced on December 12, 1939. Number two was Sterling Hayden in Peterboro, New Hampshire, on St Valentine's Day 1942; they were together until May 8, 1946. The third trip up the aisle was taken with French film producer Henri Lavorel, on July 13, 1946. They divorced in 1949 and Carroll's final marriage was to Andrew Heiskell, the publisher of the magazine *Life*. They married on September 1, 1950 and were together until their divorce on January 22, 1965, in Litchfield, Connecticut. They had one daughter: Anne-Madeleine (b. 1952, d. 1983).

CAUSE: She died in Marbella, Spain, aged 81, after a long illness.

Virginia Carroll

(VIRGINIA BROBERG)
Born December 2, 1913
Died July 23, 2009
B-lead. Born in Los Angeles, she was educated at Hollywood High School where her classmates included Walter Stickel who became a political aide to President George Bush. On leaving school he worked as a model in Bullocks, a department store on Wilshire Boulevard. One day shopping for a present for his wife, RKO producer Pandro S. Berman spotted 5'5" Carroll and cast her in *Roberta* (1935), starring Fred Astaire and Ginger Rogers. She impressed enough to be offered a contract at the studio and joined the chorus in *George White's Scandals*, and made her Western feature debut opposite Jack La Rue in *A Tenderfoot Goes West* (1936). In the 1940s she played opposite most of the cinematic cowboys including Gene Autry and Roy Rogers. She played opposite Don "Red" Barry in *The Phantom Cowboy* (1941), as Margarita Valdez, the female lead in *The Masked Rider* (1941) and played Lucy Wade in

Prairie Gunsmoke (1942), with Tex Ritter. She also appeared in non B-Westerns including: *Waterloo Bridge* (1940), *Pot O' Gold* (1941), *G-Men Vs The Black Dragon* (1943), *The Crimson Ghost* (1946), *GI War Brides* (1946), *That's My Girl* (1947) and Martha Kent in *Superman* (1948). She also appeared in several television shows before her retirement in 1959. Of her screen work, she said, "Hollywood's minor studios were apt at churning out countless low-budget features and serials during the 1930s, and whereas the cowboy stars were held in high esteem by a generation of juveniles, their sweethearts attracted very little attention. We were pretty much eye candy for the fathers who came to accompany their sons." She was married twice. In 1936 she married Ralph Byrd who played Dick Tracy on television and in films. They had one daughter, Carroll. Byrd died on August 18, 1952 from a heart attack. In 1957 she married Lloyd J. McLean (b. Idaho August 29, 1906), a projectionist at 20th Century Fox and they were together until his death on February 11, 1969.

CAUSE: Virginia Carroll died aged 95 from natural causes at Santa Barbara, California.

Sunset Carson

(WINIFRED MAURICE HARRISON)
Born November 12, 1918?
Died May 1, 1990
The mystery cowboy. 6'6" Sunset Carson was born probably in Gracemont, Caddo County, Oklahoma, the son of Maurice Greely Harrison (b. Georgia, 1897) and Azalee Belle 'Dot' McAdams Harrison (b. Texas, 1898). The Harrisons had six children and one, Dale, appeared with Carson in some films. The year of Sunset Carson's birth is a subject of some dispute. No birth certificate exists and Carson seems to have been educated at the Zsa Zsa Gabor school of numeracy. On June 30, 1937, he

filled in a social security application and gave his birthday as November 12, 1918 and his place of birth as Plainview, Texas. His death certificate states he was born in 1926 in Texas. The family Bible says that he came into the world on November 12, 1920, in Gracemont, Caddo County, Oklahoma. His driver's licence showed his birthplace as Plainview, Texas and birthdate as November 12, 1927. A family friend claimed that "Sunset was born in 1924". A census of April 1, 1930 gives his age as 9 and his birthplace as Oklahoma. Whatever the truth of his birth, the family apparently moved to Plainview, Texas, when he was eight or nine years old. Carson claimed that his father was a rodeo performer in the Tom Mix Circus but again this is open to question. In 1941 and 1942, Carson was named All Around Champion Cowboy of South America and he claimed that Tom Mix suggested he try film acting. Presumably Mix suggested this when Carson's father worked for him and not when Carson was All Around Champion Cowboy of South America, Mix being dead by that time. Carson made his début in *Stage Door Canteen* (1943) playing Tex, using the name Michael Harrison – presumably because Winifred Harrison didn't sound too macho a name for a cowboy. The following year he was signed to Republic Studios and his name was changed to Sunset Carson, supposedly after studio president Herbert Yates saw a car dealership called Sunset Boulevard Cars. He used the name Sonny 'Sunset' Carson for the first time in the film *Call Of The Rockies* (released July 14, 1944) in which he co-starred with Harry Woods, Ellen Hall and Kirk Alyn. From then on he was just Sunset Carson in *Bordertown Patrol* (released August 11, 1944), *Code Of The Prairie* (released October 6, 1944), the Western comedy *Firebrands Of Arizona* (released December 1, 1944), Yakima Canutt's *Sheriff Of*

Cimarron (released February 28, 1945) the first film in which he topped the bill, *Santa Fe Saddlemates* (released June 2, 1945), *Bells Of Rosarita* (1945) which co-starred Roy Rogers and Dale Evans, *Oregon Trail* (released July 14, 1945), *Bandits Of The Badlands* (released September 14, 1945), *Rough Riders Of Cheyenne* (released November 1, 1945), *The Cherokee Flash* (released December 13, 1945), *Days Of Buffalo Bill* (released February 8, 1946) which despite its title had nothing to do with Bill Cody, *Alias Billy The Kid* (released April 17, 1946) like its predecessor had nothing to do with the name in the title, *The El Paso Kid* (released May 22, 1946), *Red River Renegades* (released July 23, 1946) and his last outing for Republic, *Rio Grande Raiders* (released September 9, 1946). Carson would endure a two-year absence from the screen before he was signed by Astor Pictures, also known as Yucca Productions, for more low budget Western fare. His first effort for that studio was *Fighting Mustang* (released February 10, 1948). That was followed by *Deadline* (released March 12, 1948) and *Sunset Carson Rides Again* (released September 10, 1948). He made *Rio Grande* (1949) and his final "Sunset Carson" film, *Battling Marshall* (released January 15, 1950 although it was actually filmed in 1947), for other studios. It would be 22 years before Carson was seen again on the big screen, playing the lead in *The Marshal Of Windy Hollow* (1972). Five years later, he played Sheriff Deese in *Seabo* and his last film was playing a character called Sunset in the low-budget sci-fi flick *Alien Outlaw* (1985). Carson was married four times. On August 22, 1938, in Yuma, Arizona he married Canadian-born Patricia Eleanor Hussey by whom he had one daughter, Ann Caleen Harrison (b. Vallejo, California, March 29, 1940). He married secondly around 1947 to Betty Jo Price (d. 1993), by whom he had a son, Michael (b. 1948, killed in a tractor accident on his farm in Autauga County, Alabama, November 16, 2003). On August 15, 1969, he married Margaret J. Nesbitt, by whom he had a son and daughter. On June 17, 1989, he married Jean J. Davis.

CAUSE: He died in Reno, Nevada, aged 71 or 69 or 54 or 53. He was buried at Highland Memorial Gardens, Madison County, Tennessee.

John Paddy Carstairs

(NELSON JOHN KEYS)
Born May 11, 1910
Died December 12, 1970
Comedy director. John Paddy Carstairs was born at 1 St Stephen's Mansions, Smith Square, London, the eldest of four sons of the actor and comic Nelson Waite (Bunch) Keys (b. London, April 7, 1886, d. April 26, 1939 of a heart attack) and the actor Hazel Eileen Saqui (b. Dublin). Another son was the producer Anthony Nelson Keys (b. 1911, d. Richmond, Surrey, March 19, 1985). Carstairs was educated at Alleyn Court preparatory school, Westcliff-on-Sea, Essex, and Repton (from 1924) where he excelled as a lightweight boxer and, with the aid of the headmaster, the Reverend Geoffrey Fisher, later Archbishop of Canterbury, he formed a cinema club. He produced a film about public school life, *The Hero Of St Jim's*, which attracted the attention of the gentlemen of the fourth estate. Buoyed by the success he forsook Cambridge University and became an apprentice to Herbert Wilcox, a friend of his father. A name change came to avoid cashing in on his father's fame. Wilcox taught him editing, screenwriting and camera angles and in 1929 Carstairs went to America for a year. On his return he worked for two years as Basil Dean's assistant director but Dean disliked Carstairs who had adopted an American accent and loud clothes. He made his first film *Paris Plane* (1933) but it flopped and it was four years

before he was allowed to try again. Back in Hollywood he landed a six-month contract with MGM as a scenario writer. On his return to England he was involved in a serious car crash after which he directed *Night Ride* (1937). *Incident In Shanghai* (1938) starring Patrick Barr was the first film he wrote and directed. In 1939 he made *The Saint In London* with George Sanders in the title role of Simon Templar. During the Second World War he made short films for the Ministry of Information and joined the Royal Navy's air photography section. His film *Spare A Copper* (1940), a comedy set in Merseyside, starred George Formby and took £130,000 at the box office. After the cessation of hostilities he resumed directing comedies and worked with (Sir) Norman Wisdom on the successful Rank films *Trouble In Store* (filmed in the summer of 1953, previewed at the Gaumont Cinema in Camden Town, November 25, 1953), *One Good Turn* (1954), *Man Of The Moment* (1955), *Up In The World* (1956), *Just My Luck* (1957) and *The Square Peg* (1958), although Carstairs and Wisdom did not always see eye to eye. He directed Tommy Steele in the musical *Tommy The Toreador* (1959). He also wrote more than 30 books, both fiction and non-fiction, and was a talented artist in a variety of genres.

CAUSE: He died aged 60 of heart failure at Kingston Hospital, Kingston upon Thames, and was cremated at the Kingston crematorium. He was survived by his wife, Molly. He left £7,123.

Katrin Cartlidge

Born May 15, 1961
Died September 7, 2002
Intense actress. Born in London, one of two daughters and a son of Bobbi and Derek Cartlidge, and schooled at Parliament Hill School for Girls in Hampstead, where she suffered from undiagnosed dyslexia, Katrin Cartlidge

began her career at the Royal Court Theatre where she was a dresser to Jill Bennett in the number one dressing room. She was picked by Peter Gill to appear in *Apart From George* at the National Theatre although her first stage appearance was naked at the Riverside Studios in the early Eighties. She also worked as a life model at the Slade School of Fine Art. In 1982 she was signed to play Lucy Collins in the Channel 4 soap opera *Brookside* and stayed in the close for six years until 1988. She made her film début playing Doris in *Sacred Hearts* (1985) but it was her portrayal of Sophie, a lost soul, in Mike Leigh's *Naked* (1993) that brought her to public attention. Her scenes, some topless, with David Thewlis were disturbing but at the same time compulsive. Playing Hannah in *Career Girls* (1997) saw her win the *Evening Standard* Best Cinema Actress Award and going topless probably didn't harm either. Cartlidge often played in films that were not commercial because she enjoyed pushing the boundaries with new often untried directors. She also appeared in *Before The Rain* (1994) as Anne in which she also bared her breasts, *Breaking The Waves* (1996) as Dodo McNeill, the title role in *Claire Dolan* (1998) and *From Hell* (2001) as Annie Chapman. She once said, "I actually love getting older. I hated my twenties, I couldn't wait to be 30. I'm really looking forward to turning 40, if I get there . . . I think the older you get, the more you find life interesting . . . So roll on, I can't wait."
CAUSE: Cartlidge died aged 41 of complications from pneumonia and septicaemia.

Peggy Cass

Born May 21, 1924
Died March 8, 1999
Talkaholic. Boston-born Cass was intended (by her family) to be a secretary but her desire to be on the stage was too strong and she made her

professional début in 1945 on an Australian tour. Four years later, she made her first appearance on Broadway in *Touch And Go* but it was her performance as Agnes Gooch in *Auntie Mame* that won her a Tony and a Best Supporting Actress Oscar nomination. Her film appearances were infrequent as she seemed to prefer chat shows on the small screen. Her movies included *If It's Tuesday This Must Be Belgium* (1969) and *Age Of Consent* (1969), which starred James Mason and a naked Helen Mirren.
CAUSE: She died of heart failure aged 74.

John Cassavetes

Born December 9, 1929
Died February 3, 1989
Influential all-rounder. Born in New York City, the son of a Greek immigrant, Cassavetes worked as an actor, writer, director, producer and film editor. He made his first appearance before the cameras in *Fourteen Hours* (1951) but Cassavetes never quite seemed to attain the megastardom his talent deserved. Perhaps he didn't want it badly enough. His performance as Victor Franko in *The Dirty Dozen* (1967) earned him a Best Supporting Actor Oscar nomination. He was equally memorable as Guy Woodhouse in the horror flick about devil worship *Rosemary's Baby* (1968). Cassavetes was at times an obsessive loner. Perhaps most tellingly he made a film called *I'm Almost Not Crazy: John Cassavetes – The Man And His Work* in 1984. Many of his films co-starred his wife Gena Rowlands (they married on March 19, 1958) and his dear friend Peter Falk. He appeared in one and directed two episodes of *Columbo* in the early Seventies. He had three children: the arrogant Nick (b. New York City, 1959) who acts in low-budget, straight-to-video films, Alexandra (b. 1965) and Zoe (b. 1970).
CAUSE: Cassavetes died in Los Angeles,

California, of cirrhosis of the liver. He was 59. He was buried in Westwood Village Memorial Park, 1218 Glendon Avenue, Los Angeles 90024. His will was brief and to the point: "I leave all and everything I own to my beloved wife Gena Rowlands Cassavetes. I leave nothing to anyone else, whomsoever, they may be. I owe no one any debt or obligation, other than usual and ordinary bills. No one has done me a special service that I feel obligated to."

Jack Cassidy

Born March 5, 1927
Died December 12, 1976
Desperately cruel thespian. John Edward Joseph Cassidy was born in New York, the son of an Irish father and a German mother. After giving up his dream of becoming a priest, he made his Broadway début aged 15 as a chorus boy in the Ethel Merman musical *Something For The Boys* and became a musical star throughout the Fifties and Sixties, often appearing with second wife Shirley Jones. He did not appear in too many films, preferring the smell of the greasepaint and innumerable television shows. He won an Emmy and a Tony. His films included Irving Wallace's *The Chapman Report* (1962) as Ted Dyson, *Cockeyed Cowboys Of Calico County* (1970) as Roger Hand and *W.C. Fields And Me* (1976) as John Barrymore. His first wife was actress Evelyn Ward (b. West Orange, New Jersey) and their son David (b. New York City, April 12, 1950) became a teeny heartthrob in the Seventies. Jack Cassidy married Shirley Jones (b. Smithtown, Pennsylvania, March 31, 1934) in Cambridge, Massachusetts, on August 5, 1956. Their son Shaun Paul (b. Los Angeles, September 27, 1958) became a singer and actor, appearing as one of *The Hardy Boys*. The other sons were Patrick (b. January 4, 1962) and Ryan (b. February 23, 1966). The couple was divorced in 1975. Cassidy was bisexual and one of his lovers was the handicapped composer Cole Porter. Cassidy would take great pleasure in sadistically teasing the musicologist. He would take out his penis and offer it to Porter but as soon as Porter got close enough on his crippled legs (he broke them falling from a horse) to perform oral sex, Cassidy would move away. CAUSE: At around 5am on December 12, 1976, following a party the night before, Cassidy fell asleep on the living room settee of his penthouse flat at 1221 North Kings Road, West Hollywood. Cassidy was smoking a cigarette and it dropped from his hand onto the material. Within minutes the whole building, which he owned, was ablaze. It took five fire tenders to put out the flames and the other one hundred residents of 1221 had to be evacuated. One corpse was found but was burned beyond recognition. Cassidy's car was missing from the garage and hope was raised in the family that someone else had died in the conflagration. Their hopes were dashed when a friend returned the car and later dental records identified the body as that of Cassidy. What was left of him was cremated three days later.

Ted Cassidy

Born July 31, 1932
Died January 16, 1979
Lurch. Theodore Crawford Cassidy was born in Pittsburgh and was raised in Philippi, Pennsylvania. Neither parent stood taller than 5'8" but Ted grew to be 6'9". Unsurprisingly, he became a successful basketball player but ultimately preferred acting to sport. After graduating with a degree in speech and drama from Stetson University, De Land, Florida, Cassidy decided to pursue his acting dream, despite offers to join two bands as a vocalist. He married his college sweetheart, Margaret Helen Jesse, and the couple had two children, Sean and Lynn Cameron, but things didn't work out and the couple divorced. Probably

because of his huge size, Ted Cassidy was not as extrovert as many other actors. His best-known part was as the butler Lurch in the ABC sitcom *The Addams Family*. He also terrified younger viewers as Injun Joe in an NBC production of *The New Adventures Of Huckleberry Finn*. His films included: *Trigger Law* (1944), *Butch Cassidy And The Sundance Kid* (1969) as Harvey Logan, *Poor Pretty Eddy* (1973) as Keno, *The Harrad Experiment* (1973), which he co-wrote and which features a nude Don Johnson and Bruno Kirby, and *The Last Remake Of Beau Geste* (1977). His friend John Astin said that Cassidy was concerned that his height and look made jobs difficult to come by. He wanted to play serious parts but was cast in junk roles, such as playing Bigfoot in an episode of *The Six Million Dollar Man*. He was horrified when people began to mistake him for 7'2" Richard Kiel, who played Jaws in *The Spy Who Loved Me* (1977). "There was a point when I was ready to get out of the business because of that – because he's not an actor. He does his best, but if that's acting I'm a bricklayer . . . It was awful. That's the big, dumb brute character again and I will not be known as that dumb brute."
CAUSE: In late December 1978 Cassidy underwent open-heart surgery in St Vincent's Hospital, 2131 West 3rd Street, Los Angeles to remove a non-malignant tumour from his left atrium ventricle. The operation seemed to be a success and Cassidy was sent home, 21858 De La Luz, Los Angeles, California 91364. However, all was not well and he was readmitted to St Vincent's on January 16, 1979, and suffered a cardiac arrest. He died at twelve minutes to two in the afternoon. He was cremated at Forest Lawn on January 20, 1979, and the ashes were buried in his back garden. Mrs Cassidy soon moved, leaving the urn behind. Someone has Lurch in their garden without realising it.

Roy Castle

Born August 31, 1932
Died September 2, 1994
All-round entertainer. Born in Holmfirth Infirmary, Yorkshire, an only child (he shared a bedroom with his parents until he was 16) Roy Castle began his career as music hall was on its deathbed. He was stooge to comedian Jimmy James for two years but was probably best known for his 22-year stint as presenter of BBC Television's *Record Breakers*. His film appearances were rare and probably his best-known part was that of Captain Keene (a role that Jim Dale would normally have played) in *Carry On Up The Khyber* (1968). Another appearance came in *Dr Who & The Daleks* (1966) but it is for his ability to play almost any musical instrument (he was especially noted for his trumpet playing) and his prodigious tap-dancing skills that Castle will be remembered.
CAUSE: Despite having never smoked a cigarette in his life, he died at his home, "Bearwood", 21 South Park View, Gerrard's Cross, Buckinghamshire, of lung cancer contracted through passive smoking having worked for years in smoky jazz clubs. He was two days past his 62nd birthday. He left £582,199.
FURTHER READING: *Now And Then: An Autobiography* – Roy Castle (London: Robson Books, 1994).

Walter Catlett

Born February 4, 1889
Died November 14, 1960
Mr Fusspot. Born in San Francisco, California, 5'10½" Catlett was educated at St Ignatius College and began his acting career in vaudeville and in theatre, even performing in opera for a time. He was best known for his owlish glasses and his voice. Sturdy at first, he would crumble under the slightest stress. He appeared in *Second Youth* (1924), which was his début, *The Front Page* (1931), *A Tale Of Two Cities* (1935), *Mr Deeds Goes To Town* (1936) as Morrow, *Bringing Up*

Baby (1938), *Li'l Abner* (1940), *Pinocchio* (1940) as the voice of J. Worthington Foulfellow, *Yankee Doodle Dandy* (1942), *The Boy With Green Hair* (1948) as the King, *The Inspector General* (1949), *Davy Crockett And The River Pirates* (1956) as Colonel Plug, *Friendly Persuasion* (1956) as Professor Waldo Quigley and his final film *Beau James* (1957) as Al Smith.
CAUSE: He died aged 71 from a stroke in Woodland Hills, California.

Marilyn Chambers
(MARILYN ANN BRIGGS)
Born April 22, 1952
Died April 12, 2009
Soap star who got dirty. Born the youngest of three children, at Providence, Rhode Island and raised in Westport, Connecticut, she began her acting and modelling career while still in her teens. She appeared in advertisements for shampoo and other products and she appeared in a bitpart in *The Owl And The Pussycat* (1970) (using the pseudonym Evelyn Lang) but her life changed when, working as an exotic dancer in San Francisco, she applied for what she claimed she thought would be a major film role. It turned out to be a porn film called *Behind The Green Door* (released August 1972) and she played the starring role of Gloria Saunders. She later said, "Back then in my naive brain I was thinking that something like *Behind The Green Door* had never been done before and the way our sexual revolution was travelling I really thought it was going to be a stepping stone which would further my acting career." By accident one of her modelling pictures (cuddling a laughing, nappy-clad baby) appeared on a box of Ivory Snow soap powder and Procter & Gamble, whose products were claimed to be "100% pure", quickly withdrew the boxes from the shops. She then appeared in the hardcore films *Resurrection Of Eve* (1973) and *Inside Marilyn Chambers*

(1975) before forsaking porn to pursue other interests. In 1977 she appeared in the non-porn film *Rabid* and played in a one-woman show but the lure of the explicit was too much for her and she returned to adult films in 1980 in *Insatiable*. She said, "The adult films have been a total pleasure. They were like getting paid to live out my greatest fantasies. The rest of the stuff . . . sometimes got to be a real grind. There will always be a stigma on people who do adult films. It's unfortunate that that's the way society has made it." 5'7" Chambers was married three times. Her first husband was Doug Chapin whom she divorced in 1974. That year on December 5, she married Chuck Traynor (b. August 21, 1937 d. Chatsworth, California July 22, 2002 of a heart attack) who had also been married to Linda Lovelace. Her third husband was Tom Taylor by whom she had her only child, McKenna Marie Taylor (b. Riverside California May 13, 1991). In 2004 35C-26-35 Chambers ran for Vice President of the USA on the Personal Choice Party ticket. Charles Jay topped the ticket and they made it onto one state ballot in 2004 – Utah – and received 946 votes. Chambers admitted that she didn't expect to win. "That would be lovely," she said. "But I can't picture myself in the White House. Our country is not that progressive."
CAUSE: On April 12, 2009, Chambers was found dead in her home in Santa Clarita, California by her daughter. Cause of death was attributed to a cerebral haemorrhage and aneurysm related to heart disease. She was 56.

Jeff Chandler
(IRA GROSSEL)
Born December 15, 1918
Died June 17, 1961
Tough guy with a secret. Jeff Chandler's reputation as a Hollywood he-man was shattered in the autumn of 1999 by his former girlfriend and co-star Esther Williams when she

revealed that the 6'5" hunk had been a transvestite. Such matters were a far cry from the rough area of Brooklyn where the actor was born. Deserted by his father, Ira Grossel became involved in the restaurant business early on. Growing up in a dominantly female household, young Ira began wearing women's clothes as a small boy; it became a compunction he never grew out of. After high school and a brief spell in the catering industry he joined the Feagin School of Dramatic Art, becoming a stagehand and then an actor. However, Pearl Harbor stopped him progressing too far in the profession. He served in the army, rising to the rank of first lieutenant, and after World War II developed a crush on Esther Williams after seeing her in *Easy To Wed* (1945). The male lead in the film was Van Johnson who played a character called Bill Chandler. Because Bill Chandler got the girl, Gossel changed his name to Jeff Chandler. Despite the name change, Chandler remained exceptionally proud of his Jewish heritage. He made his first post-war foray into show business in radio dramas before making his film début in *Johnny O'Clock* (1947). On October 13, 1946, he married actress Marjorie Hoshelle in Los Angeles and fathered two daughters, Jamie and Dana. The couple divorced on April 15, 1954, but reconciled before the decree absolute; they were finally divorced in 1960. Signed to Universal on an exclusive seven-year contract, the prematurely grey Chandler began appearing in Westerns, usually playing Native American Indians and, in 1950, was nominated for an Oscar for his portrayal of the Apache chief Cochise in *Broken Arrow* (1950). It was a part he was to play on two more occasions – *The Battle At Apache Pass* (1952) and *Taza, Son Of Cochise* (1954) (playing Rock Hudson's dad). In 1954 he became a singer, signing a contract with Decca Records. Three years later,

he appeared in Las Vegas. Separated from his wife, Chandler began an affair with Esther Williams during the filming of *Raw Wind In Eden* (1958) after which he revealed his secret, much to Williams' disgust; his transvestitism stopped her becoming his second wife. From the mid-Fifties Chandler's career rather faltered, perhaps because of his earlier Red Indian typecasting. He appeared in a number of truly awful films, earning his living using his looks rather than his undoubted talent. CAUSE: He suffered a slipped disc while making *Merrill's Marauders* (1962). On May 13, 1961, he underwent what should have been straightforward surgery at Culver City Hospital, but blood poisoning set in. Another operation ensued, during which he was given 55 pints of blood. He survived that and yet more surgery but his condition steadily declined. The blood poisoning was complicated by pneumonia; he died, aged just 42. Tony Curtis was one of the pallbearers. Chandler is buried in the Hillside Mausoleum of Hillside Memorial Park, 6001 West Centinela Avenue, Los Angeles 90045.

Lane Chandler

(ROBERT LANE OAKES)
Born June 4, 1899
Died September 14, 1972
Prolific cowboy. Born in South Dakota (although some sources list Culbertson, Montana as place of birth, while his death certificate states he was born in South Dakota), 6'4" Chandler was the son of a horse rancher and was educated at Montana Wesleyan College before leaving to work as a tour bus driver at Yellowstone National Park. He eventually moved to Los Angeles to seek fame and fortune. While waiting for his big break he worked as a car mechanic. Chandler was signed by Paramount in 1927 as a possible Western star. He went on to make more than 330 films, playing villains and good guys alike, although his

demeanour seemed to favour the baddies. His only lead role was in the silent Western *The Open Range* (1927) as Tex Smith, although for a time he and Gary Cooper vied for the best cowboy roles. Paramount realised that with Cooper, Richard Arlen, Frederic March, and Neil Hamilton, it had too many leading men on the roster and Chandler was dropped as an economy move. Chandler did not just feature in Westerns – he appeared in *Flash Gordon* (1936), *The Secret Of Treasure Island* (1938), *Marie Antoinette* (1938), *I Am The Law* (1938), *Angels With Dirty Faces* (1938), *Buck Rogers* (1939), *The Green Hornet* (1940) and *Charlie Chan In Panama* (1940). His best-known Westerns were *Firebrand Jordan* (released January 28, 1930), *The Lightning Express* (April 30, 1930), *Riders Of The Rio* (December 1, 1930), *Hurricane Horseman* (October 31, 1931), *Cheyenne Cyclone* (December 15, 1931), *Battling Buckaroo* (February 11, 1932), *Texas Tornado* (April 1, 1932), *The Reckless Divider* (July 1, 1932), *Guns For Hire* (September 1, 1932), *The Wyoming Whirlwind* (December 30, 1932), *The Lone Bandit* (February 1, 1935), *The Outlaw Tamer* (March 15, 1935) and *Heroes Of The Alamo* (August 6, 1937). He also appeared in *Zorro Rides Again* (1937) and in the 1959 remake. He spent much of the Forties working as a utility actor for director Cecil B. DeMille, before moving to television in the Fifties and Sixties.
CAUSE: He died in Los Angeles, California of cardio-vascular disease. He was 73.

Lon Chaney

Born April 1, 1883
Died August 26, 1930
'The Man of a Thousand Faces'. Alonso Chaney was born in Colorado Springs. Both his parents were deaf mutes and he used mime to 'talk' to them. After working as a stagehand and vaudeville comedian he became the best-known star of horror films in the Twenties because of his ability to assume numerous personas through his talent and clever make-up (he wrote the entry on cosmetics for one edition of *Encyclopædia Britannica*). Between 1913 (when he appeared in *Poor Jake's Demise*) and 1930 he appeared in over 150 films, many in collaboration with director Todd Browning (b. July 12, 1882, d. October 6, 1962). More often than not his roles included physical discomfort for the 5'9" Chaney. In *The Penalty* (1920) he played a criminal who had lost his legs. Chaney had his calves tied to his thighs and perambulated on his knees for the part. In *The Hunchback Of Notre Dame* (1923) he played Quasimodo with 70lb of padding. He was also Erik, the lead in *The Phantom Of The Opera* (1925). His other film credits include *The Sea Urchin* (1913) as Barnacle Bill, the first of his films in which he donned elaborate make-up, *An Elephant on His Hands* (1913) as Eddie, *Red Margaret, Moonshiner* (1913) as Lon, *Bloodhounds Of The North* (1913) as Mountie, *Remember Mary Magdalen* (1914), *The Menace To Carlotta* (1914) as Giovanni Bartholdi, *The Old Cobbler* (1914) as Wild Bill, *Her Grave Mistake* (1914) as Nunez, *The Oubliette* (1914) as Chevalier Bertrand de la Payne, *Her Bounty* (1914) as Fred Howard, *Virtue Is Its Own Reward* (1914) as Duncan Bronson, *Lights And Shadows* (1914) as Bentley, *The Lion, The Lamb, The Man* (1914) as Fred, *When The Gods Played A Badger Game* (1915), *Where The Forest Ends* (1915) as Paul Rouchelle, *Maid Of The Mist* (1915), *Quits* (1915) as Frenchy, *The Grip Of Jealousy* (1916) as Silas Lacey, *The Girl In The Checkered Coat* (1917) as Hector Maitland, *The Talk Of The Town* (1918) as Jack Lanchome, *The Kaiser, The Beast Of Berlin* (1918) as Theobald von Bethmann-Hollweg, *That Devil, Bateese* (1918) as Louis Courteau, *When Bearcat Went Dry* (1919) as Kindard Powers, *Treasure Island* (1920)

as Blind Pew, *Oliver Twist* (1922) as Fagin, *Quincy Adams Sawyer* (1922) as Obadiah Strout, *All The Brothers Were Valiant* (1923) as Mark Shore and *Laugh, Clown, Laugh* (1928) as Tito Beppi. In 1928 and 1929 he was the top male box-office star – his female peer in both years was Clara Bow. In 1914, nine years after their marriage, he divorced his first wife Cleva Creighton and married Hazel Bennett. His son Creighton (b. Oklahoma City, February 10, 1906, d. July 12, 1973) changed his name to Lon Chaney, Jr to get more work and also appeared in around 150 films, many of them horror features.

CAUSE: He died of throat cancer aged 47 a month before his first talkie, *The Unholy Three* (1930) was released.

He was buried in Forest Lawn Memorial-Parks, 1712 South Glendale Avenue, Glendale, California 91209.

Sir Charlie Chaplin

Born April 16, 1889
Died December 25, 1977

The little tramp with a penchant for little tramps. Born at 8pm in East Street (four days before Adolf Hitler), Walworth, London, the son of music hall performers Charles Chaplin (b. 22 Orcus Street, Marylebone, London, March 18, 1863) and Hannah Harriett Pedlingham Hill (b. 11 Camden Street, Walworth, London, August 6, 1865). About a year after his birth, Chaplin's parents separated. Chaplin's maternal grandmother was committed to an asylum on February 23, 1893. For a time his mother's career was successful enough for her to feed her family. Charles Chaplin Sr's life was blighted by alcoholism, which generally meant that he did not face up to his responsibilities. This often led the family to the workhouse. On May 30, 1896, Charlie and his elder brother Sydney (b. March 16, 1885, three months before his parents' marriage, d. Nice, France, April 16, 1965) were sent to Newington Workhouse. The following year Sydney began training for a life at sea, leaving Charlie to sleep rough in Covent Garden and support himself in a variety of lowly paid jobs. On January 18, 1898, a warrant was issued for the arrest of Charles Chaplin for non-payment of child support. That same day, Charlie left school and two days after that, Sydney left his navy training ship. During that year Charlie and Sydney were admitted to the Lambeth Workhouse on four occasions. Their mother, suffering from the mental problems that had also beset her mother, was committed to Cane Hill Asylum, where she stayed for two months from September 15, 1898. On Boxing Day Charlie got his first real taste of showbiz, appearing as one of Eight Lancashire Lads at the Theatre Royal, Manchester. The year 1901 saw part of the family going their separate ways. Charles was admitted to St Thomas' Hospital, London where he died on May 9, 1901, aged 37 from dropsy, while Sydney sailed around the world as a steward. Two years to the day after her husband's death, Hannah Chaplin was committed to an asylum as a lunatic. Charlie was listed as her next of kin. By this time Charlie had begun to find reasonably regular work in the theatre, playing Sam in *Jim, A Romance Of Cockayne* and then Billy in *Sherlock Holmes*. On his mother's release from the asylum and Sydney's return from sea, Charlie was joined by them both on tour. It was to be a short respite, however. Hannah was recommitted as a lunatic on March 16, 1905. The following year Sydney signed a contract with the theatrical impresario Fred Karno, who also gave Charlie a successful audition in February 1908. In 1910 the Karno troupe sailed for America, where they toured for two years. (Another member of the touring party was a promising comedian called Stan Laurel.) On December 16, 1913, Charlie Chaplin began a $150-a-week contract with the Keystone Film Company. He began turning out films quickly: *Making A Living* (released February 2, 1914) as a swindler, *Kid Auto Races At Venice* (released February 7, 1914) as a tramp, *Mabel's Strange Predicament* (released February 9, 1914) as a tramp (the first outing of his famous attire although this film was released two days after the previous one when he again donned the tramp's garb), *Between Showers* (released February 28, 1914) as a masher, *A Film Johnnie* (released March 2, 1914) as The Film Johnnie, *Tango Tangles* (released March 9, 1914) as a half-cut dancer, *His Favorite Pastime* (released March 16, 1914) as a boozer, *Cruel, Cruel Love* (released March 26, 1914) as Lord Helpus, the title role in *The Star Boarder* (released April 4, 1914), *Mabel At The Wheel* (released April 18, 1914) as a rascal, *Twenty Minutes Of Love* (released April 20, 1914) as a pickpocket, *Mabel's Busy Day* (released June 13, 1914) as a drunken boor, *Mabel's Married Life* (released June 20, 1914) as Mabel's husband and many more. That same year he turned to directing and writing, later turning his hand to editing, producing, composing and choreographing. There is a story that an exec at Charlie Chaplin's studio sent a memo saying that Chaplin would never become a star unless he junked the moustache, cane, bowler, funny walk and ill-fitting suit. Not true – it was a studio joke. At the start of 1915 Chaplin moved to Essanay Studios (formed by Broncho Billy Anderson). The following year, with Sydney and Herbert Clark, Charlie founded Charles Chaplin Music Corporation at 233 South Broadway, Los Angeles. On February 26 of that year he again changed studios, moving to Mutual Film Corporation at a salary of $10,000 per week, with a $150,000 bonus thrown in for good measure. Also in 1916, he became the subject of a cartoon strip, *Pa's Imported Son-in-Law*. On March 22 he was subjected to an attack by the *Daily*

Mail because of a clause in his contract forbidding him to return to England to fight for King and Country. Still he churned out films: *His New Job* (released February 1, 1915) as a film extra, *A Jitney Elopement* (released April 1, 1915), the lead in *The Tramp* (released April 11, 1915), *Work* (released June 21, 1915) as Izzy A. Wake's aide, *The Bank* (released August 9, 1915) as a caretaker, *Shanghaied* (released October 4, 1915) as another tramp, *Carmen* (released December 18, 1915), *Police* (released March 27, 1916) as a tramp, *Charlie Chaplin's Burlesque On Carmen* (released April 1916) as Don Jose, *The Floorwalker* (released May 15, 1916) as a tramp, *The Vagabond* (released June 10, 1916) as a busker, *Chase Me Charlie* (1917) as Charlie, *Easy Street* (released January 22, 1917) as a streetwise police recruit and *A Dog's Life* (released April 14, 1918) as a tramp. In the summer of 1917 Chaplin signed a million dollar-a-year contract with First National and on August 4 he announced "I am ready and willing to answer the call of my country." On October 23, 1918, in Los Angeles, California, he married 16-year-old child actress Mildred Harris (b. Cheyenne, Wyoming, November 29, 1901, d. Los Angeles, California July 20, 1944, from pneumonia following an operation). Harris would be the first in a long line of nubile young girls with whom Chaplin would be publicly associated. The marital home was 2000 DeMille Drive, but not for long. The couple divorced on November 13, 1920, on grounds of Chaplin's mental cruelty. They had one son, Norman Spencer Chaplin (b. Los Angeles, California, July 7, 1919, d. Los Angeles, California July 10, 1919, at 4pm, aged three days) who was born severely handicapped. On February 5, 1919, Chaplin, D.W. Griffith, Mary Pickford and Douglas Fairbanks formed United Artists to produce and sell their own films and those of other independents. That year and 1920 also saw Chaplin working on *The Kid* (released February 6, 1921), which featured Jackie Coogan in the title role. Chaplin hired Edna Purviance to play the part of Coogan's mother and also found a part for Lilita McMurray who, he commented, had "so much innocence mixed with such big breasts". In the summer of 1922 he had a fortnight-long fling with 5'3½" socialite Peggy Hopkins Joyce (b. Berkley, Virginia, May 26, 1893 as Marguerite Upton, d. New York, June 12, 1957) who had been married five times, and every husband a millionaire. In the autumn of 1922 Chaplin supposedly became involved with Pola Negri, although how much of the 'relationship' was genuine and how much a publicity stunt puzzled many. Their engagement was announced on January 28, 1923, but on March 1 it was all off. A day later, they were back together again but on June 28 they split for good. On October 1, 1923, the première of *A Woman Of Paris* was held, a romantic melodrama starring Chaplin's old flame Edna Purviance. However, crowds expecting to see Chaplin slapstick were disappointed and the film flopped. Realising that comedy was what people wanted, Chaplin began preparing the first draft of *The Gold Rush* (1925) in December 1923. Three months later, on March 2, 1924, Lilita McMurray (now calling herself Lita Grey) was signed as leading lady. On November 19, director Thomas Ince died under mysterious circumstances and Chaplin's part, if any, in the death has remained the subject of rumour and speculation from that day on. (See Ince entry for full details.) However, the Little Tramp had other things on his mind. A week after Ince's death he married Lita Grey at Guayamas, Mexico. Like his first wife she was 16 years old, but the second Mrs Chaplin was also pregnant. The union was to produce two sons: Charles Spencer, Jr (b. Los Angeles,

California, May 5, 1925, d. California, March 20, 1968) and Sydney Earle (b. Los Angeles, California, March 30, 1926). Chaplin bribed an official to register his second son's birth as June 28, 1925, to cover up his premarital sex. *The Gold Rush* was premièred at Grauman's Egyptian Theatre on June 26, supposedly two days before the birth of Charles Jr. The film contains two of the most famous scenes in all of Chaplin's films: the dance of the bread rolls and Chaplin eating his boots. (Actually, they were made of liquorice.) The film was officially shot over 405 days although only 170 of those actually saw a camera rolling. In the spirit of realism Chaplin hired 2,500 hobos for a day, although they had to provide their own clothes. On July 6, 1925, Chaplin became the first actor to be featured on the cover of *Time* magazine. His next film was *The Circus* (premièred January 6, 1928), which he wrote, directed, produced, edited and starred in as well as composing the music for the reissued version in 1970. On January 10, 1927, Lita Grey filed for divorce, which was granted on August 22, 1927, and became final a year later on August 25, 1928. On May 5 of that year Chaplin began working on *City Lights*, which would not see the light of day until January 19, 1931. Chaplin plays a tramp whom a blind girl (Virginia Cherrill) believes is a millionaire. Chaplin reshot one scene 342 times until he was satisfied with the shot of the blind girl selling the tramp a flower. Indeed, he shot 125 times more film than he actually used. In the early Thirties Chaplin travelled constantly. On March 25, 1933, he began work on *Modern Times* (released February 5, 1936), yet another Chaplin work with a long gestation. In July of the same year he met the woman who was to become the third Mrs Chaplin. *Modern Times* was seen as a strongly pro-union film. Chaplin had already spoken in favour of the Soviet Union, opinions that were making him decidedly unpopular in America. The film was banned in Nazi Germany and Mussolini's Italy and marked the last appearance of Chaplin's little tramp. The producers of René Clair's *A Nous La Liberté* (1931) considered suing Chaplin for plagiarism but the suit was dropped when Clair professed himself flattered by the film. The female lead was played by Paulette Goddard, whom Chaplin treated abysmally on set. Despite this, they married in Canton, China, sometime in June 1936. Goddard, at 31, was virtually old enough to be the mother of Chaplin's first two wives. The reason for the sudden leap in bridal ages was probably less to do with Chaplin's desire for maturity in women and more to do with the fact that Goddard lied about her age. In October 1938 Chaplin began working on *The Great Dictator* (released October 15, 1940), his lampoon of Adolf Hitler, renamed Adenoid Hynkel. Although regarded as a classic by film students, the US public did not take to the movie and were unimpressed by the fact that Chaplin, who made his money in America, had never renounced his British citizenship (as Stan Laurel, Cary Grant and Bob Hope all did). On April 15, Konrad Bercovici sued Chaplin for plagiarism over *The Great Dictator*. Chaplin later remarked: "Had I known of the actual horrors of the German concentration camps, I could never have made *The Great Dictator*. I could not have made fun of the homicidal insanity of the Nazis." In June 1941 he put a mentally unstable, voluptuous, red-headed 22-year-old starlet by the name of Joan Barry under contract. It would be another instance of Chaplin allowing his libido to rule his head. *The Great Dictator* would be Chaplin's last film for seven years. He had other problems. On June 4, 1942, he and Paulette Goddard were divorced. In late October that year he met 16-year-old Oona O'Neill (b. Spithead,

Bermuda, May 13, 1926, d. Manoir de Ban, Vevey sur Corsier, Vaud, Switzerland, September 27, 1991), daughter of playwright Eugene O'Neill by his second wife Agnes Boulton. A few weeks later, on December 23, the mad Joan Barry broke into his home armed with a gun. She threatened to kill herself and later claimed she and Chaplin had had sex that night. Chaplin denied it. In the morning he gave her some money and she left. Seven days passed, then she repeated her performance and this time Chaplin called the police. In court the judge sentenced Barry to 60 days, suspended, and ordered her to leave Los Angeles. In May 1943 she returned pregnant and later (June 4) claimed Chaplin was the father of her baby. Another appearance resulted in her being jailed for a month and then quickly released to the hospital when it was discovered she was with child. At Carpenteria, Santa Barbara, California, on June 16, 1943, Chaplin married Oona O'Neill. He was 55, she was yet to attain her 17th birthday. However, it would prove to be a genuine love match, producing eight children: actress Geraldine Leigh (b. Santa Monica Hospital, California, August 1, July 31, 1944); RADA-educated Michael John (b. Santa Monica Hospital, Beverly Hills, California, March 6, 1946); Josephine Hannah (b. St John's Hospital, Santa Monica, March 28, 1949); Victoria (b. St John's Hospital, Santa Monica, May 19, 1951); Eugene Anthony (b. August 23, 1953), Jane Cecil (b. May 23, 1957); Annette Emily (b. December 3, 1959) and Christopher James (b. July 8, 1962). The last two were fathered when Chaplin was in his seventies; he called his penis 'The Eighth Wonder of the World'. More pressing engagements took priority in 1943. The daughter that Chaplin hadn't fathered was born on October 2, 1943. In 1942, 55-year-old Chaplin began an affair with Barry, paying for plastic surgery to improve her chances of becoming a star. However, by Christmas of the same year Chaplin had decided that perhaps Barry didn't have what it took after all and reduced the salary his company was paying her. She turned up at his house, threatened him and then took an overdose. In June 1943 Barry filed a paternity suit, naming Chaplin as the father of her unborn offspring. The FBI then charged Chaplin with violating the Mann Act – transporting Barry across state lines for immoral purposes. He was further charged with conspiracy in having Barry thrown in jail for vagrancy, thus depriving her of her constitutional rights. On February 21, 1944, he was arraigned. Five days later, he pleaded not guilty to violating the Mann Act and 17 days later he entered a similar plea to the conspiracy charge. The Mann Act trial lasted from March 21 until April 4, 1944, and defended by Jerry Giesler, Chaplin was acquitted. On May 15 the charges for violation of Barry's civil rights were dropped. The Barry paternity suit opened on December 13 but on January 2, 1945, a retrial was ordered when the jury locked 7–5 in favour of Chaplin. The new case opened on April 4, 1945, and 13 days later was settled in Barry's favour by 11 votes to one. However, blood tests proved beyond all shadow of doubt that he could not be the father of Barry's daughter Carol Ann. Moreover, Chaplin's lawyers proved that some of Barry's bills were being paid by billionaire Paul Getty. On April 11, 1947, the world première of *Monsieur Verdoux*, Chaplin's first film in almost a decade, was held at the Broadway Theater, New York. By now the public was inexorably turning against Chaplin and the film flopped. In the late Forties and early Fifties Chaplin began working on *Limelight* (premièred October 16, 1952). When he sailed to London on September 17, 1952, for the English première his re-entry was barred because of his left-wing views. On January 5, 1953,

the Chaplins moved to Manoir de Ban, Vevey sur Corsier, Vaud, Switzerland. On April 17, 1953, Chaplin declared he would not return to the USA after being described as a 'dangerous alien' in the communist witch hunts. In protest at the treatment of her husband, Oona O'Neill Chaplin renounced her American citizenship. His last two films, *A King In New York* (released September 12, 1957) and *A Countess From Hong Kong* (released January 5, 1967), the latter of which he wrote and directed and in which he played the part of a seasick waiter, were shot in Britain. In September 1964 his autobiography was published, a 500-page book that showed off Chaplin's remarkable memory to the greatest extent. Eight long years later, he was welcomed back to America, where he received an honorary Oscar on April 16, 1972. Three years later, on March 4, 1975, he became Sir Charles. Not everyone liked Chaplin. The 5'6½" Chaplin wasn't the most modest man in the world. "If people don't sit at Chaplin's feet, he goes out and stands where they are sitting," commented Herman Mankiewicz. Comedian W.C. Fields commented, albeit somewhat wryly: "The son of a bitch is a ballet dancer! He's the best ballet dancer that ever lived, and if I get a good chance I'll strangle him with my bare hands."

CAUSE: Chaplin suffered from gout in his last years. When his children were growing up, he banned television from the house though he enjoyed watching it at the end of his life. He died peacefully in his sleep at his Swiss home, Manoir de Ban, Vevey sur Corsier, Vaud. When he died he made his wife, Oona, the richest widow in the world. His funeral was held in the Anglican Church at Vevey on December 27, 1977, but that wasn't the end of Chaplin's story. On March 1, 1978 a 24-year-old Pole and a 38-year-old Bulgarian, both car mechanics, stole his body from its

grave in Vevey Cemetery, Etienne Buenzod. A ransom note for SF600,000 was delivered. For 16 days, the world waited and then on March 17, the body was recovered from a cornfield near Noville and reburied in a vault of concrete. A simple cross marks the spot in the field where the coffin was found.
FURTHER READING: *My Autobiography* – Charlie Chaplin (London: The Bodley Head, 1964); *I Couldn't Smoke The Grass On My Father's Lawn* – Michael Chaplin (London: Leslie Frewin, 1966); *Chaplin: His Life & Art* – David Robinson (London: William Collins, 1985); *The Chaplin Encylopaedia* – Glenn Mitchell (London: B.T. Batsford, 1997); *Chaplin The Tramp's Odyssey* – Simon Louvish (London: Faber & Faber, 2009).

Sydney Chaplin

Born March 30, 1926
Died March 3, 2009
Difficult son. Born in Los Angeles, Sydney Earle Chaplin (named for his father's half-brother) was the younger of the two sons of Sir Charlie Chaplin and his second wife, Lita Grey. The couple divorced in 1927 whereupon his maternal grandmother brought up young Chaplin who by his own admission was a difficult child. He dropped out of several schools and tried to join the army when he was 17 but was turned down. A year later, he was conscripted and served as a bazooka man in Europe with the Third Army under George Patton. Chaplin did not have much contact with his father until he was grown up. He recalled, "He was a strange man. He had great difficulty expressing his feelings to me, which was odd because he expressed emotion on screen so marvellously." Charlie Chaplin cast his son in *Limelight* (premièred October 16, 1952) as Neville and he also appeared in his father's last film *A Countess From Hong Kong* (released January 5, 1967) but it was on the stage as opposed to the screen that Sydney Chaplin flourished. In 1957 he won a Best Featured Actor Tony for *Bells Are Ringing* as Jeff Moss opposite Judy Holliday. Seven years later, he received a Tony nomination for his role opposite Barbra Streisand in *Funny Girl* as Nicky Arnstein. When the film came to be made the role was played by Omar Sharif although Chaplin professed not to be disappointed. "I never had the burning desire for recognition and respect that had driven my father. But then I never had to dance on the streets of London for pennies to stay alive." Chaplin's films included *Land Of The Pharaohs* (1955) as Treneh, *Abdulla The Great* (1955) as Ahmed, *Pillars Of The Sky* (1956) as Timothy, *Four Girls In Town* (1957) as Johnny Pryor and *Follow That Man* (1961) as Eddie Miller. "I wasn't a leading man," he said. "So they slapped a coat of dark greasepaint on me and cast me as an Indian or an Egyptian." From the late Eighties to the early Nineties, he was the owner of a restaurant, Chaplin's, in Palm Springs, California which was financed by a $500,000 present from his stepmother Oona O'Neill Chaplin. His first two marriages ended in divorce. He had one son, Stephan, by his first wife Noelle Adam, a French-born dancer. In 1998 he married Margaret Beebe who survived him. He once said, "I'm no genius. I don't have Dad's capacity for work. I just want to be a good actor."
CAUSE: Chaplin died aged 82 at his home in Rancho Mirage, California of complications following a stroke.

Cyd Charisse

(TULA ELLICE FINKLEA)
Born March 8, 1921
Died June 17, 2008
"Beautiful dynamite". The lady given that nickname by Fred Astaire was born in Amarillo, Texas, the daughter of a jeweller. She took her first steps in showbusiness aged six when she began

ballet lessons after being advised by the family doctor that it would strengthen her muscles and seven years later joined the Ballet Russe under Colonel De Basil. Her little brother was unable to say the word "Sis" and called her "Sid", a name she adopted professionally calling herself Felia Sidorova. On August 12, 1939 she married her ballet teacher Nico Charisse, but their honeymoon was cut short by the outbreak of the Second World War. They had one son, Nicky, in 1942. They appeared together in the short film *Rhumba Serenade* (1941) and she made five more shorts before her feature film debut in 1943 in *Mission To Moscow*. Her next film was the Don Ameche-Janet Blair musical *Something To Shout About* (1943) in which she was billed as Lily Norwood (her mother's maiden name). Choreographer Robert Alton recommended her to MGM and the studio put her under a seven-year contract and changed her name to Cyd Charisse. Alton became her champion and suggested her to producer Arthur Freed who cast her in the opening sequence of *Ziegfeld Follies* (1946). Her first meaty role was in Freed's *The Harvey Girls* (1946) as Deborah in which she sang *It's A Great Big World* with Judy Garland and Virginia O'Brien. In fact, she didn't sing it or any other number in her career – she was tone deaf and her efforts were dubbed. (However, Charisse wasn't dubbed in one film, *It's Always Fair Weather* (1955), and when you hear her tuneless singing, it's easy to see why she generally didn't sing her own songs.) She danced with Gower Champion in the Jerome Kern biopic *Till The Clouds Roll By* (1947) and her ballet skills were much in evidence in *The Unfinished Dance* (1947) as Ariane Bouchet. In 1947 she was divorced. She lost out (to Ann Miller) the role of Nadine Hale in *Easter Parade* (1948) after breaking her leg. That year she married singer Tony Martin and their son Tony Jr was born in 1950. MGM

cast her in *Tension* (1949) as Mary Chandler and *East Side West Side* (1949) as Rosa Senta, two films in which she was not required to dance with the result that she did not shine. She performed with Ann Miller and Ricardo Montalban in *The Kissing Bandit* (1949) in a sequence choreographed by Stanley Donen. She really came to the public's attention in her non-speaking role in *Singin' In The Rain* (1952), directed by Gene Kelly and Donen. There is one particularly memorable scene when 5'7½" Charisse wraps her legs around Gene Kelly. She recalled, "As the camera panned up my legs and my body, I was supposed to exhale a drifting plume of smoke. I had never smoked and it took me a long time, plus a lot of coughing, before I got it right." She worked with Hollywood's two leading terpsichoreans – Kelly and Fred Astaire – but refused to name her favourite, "It's like comparing apples and oranges – they're both delicious." Astaire said of her, "She wasn't a tap dancer, she's just beautiful, trained, very strong in whatever we did. When we were dancing, we didn't know what time it was." She appeared opposite Astaire in Vincente Minnelli's *The Band Wagon* (1953) in which she played Gabrielle Gerard. However, the film while enhancing her dancing reputation did nothing to add to her stock as a leading actress. Her next film *Brigadoon* (1954) in which she played Fiona Campbell was a sleeper, not becoming a hit until many years after its release. Her subsequent films included *Deep In My Heart* (1954), *It's Always Fair Weather* (1955) as Jackie Leighton (although several of her scenes ended on the cutting room floor), and *Meet Me In Las Vegas* (1956) as Maria Corvier opposite Dan Dailey. Her last major film came the following year. In Rouben Mamoulian's *Silk Stockings*, a musical version of the Garbo comedy classic *Ninotchka*, Charisse played Ninotchka Yoschenko. Unsurprisingly, the critics compared Charisse to Garbo and the comparisons were not favourable to the former. The end of the Fifties and the start of the Sixties heralded the beginning of the end of the big studio musicals and their stars had to find work in dramatic films or the theatre. Charisse played Charlotte King, a killer, in *Twilight For The Gods* (1958), showgirl and gangster's moll Vicki Gaye in Nicholas Ray's *Party Girl* (1958), and an emasculating actress in Minnelli's *Two Weeks In Another Town* (1962). That year she also co-starred in the unfinished *Something's Got To Give* (1962) in which her performance can mostly be described as inept. Her co-stars were the comedic talents Marilyn Monroe and Dean Martin so perhaps it is not surprising. She said of herself, "Honestly, the idea of working in movies had never once entered my head. I was a dancer, not an actress. I had no delusions about myself. I couldn't act – I had never acted. So how could I be a movie star?" The following year she and husband Tony Martin formed a nightclub act and spent much of the next twenty years appearing on the stage with occasional guest appearances in television shows like *Hawaii Five-O*, *The Love Boat* and *The Fall Guy*.

CAUSE: On June 16, 2008 she was admitted to Cedars-Sinai Medical Centre after suffering a heart attack. She died the next day.

Maurice Chevalier

Born September 12, 1888
Died January 1, 1972
Ze great lovair. Born in a Paris slum on the right bank of the Seine (29 rue de Retrait, off the rue de Ménilmontant, to be exact), Chevalier was one of nine children, only three of whom survived to maturity. He regarded his Flemish mother as a saint and called her La Louque. His father, an alcoholic painter and decorator, deserted the family leaving La Louque to cope as best she could. The family survived by boiling bones for soup and buying day-old bread because it was cheap. In what little spare time she had, La Louque made lace and sold it for a few francs, working long after dark. When Chevalier's brother, Paul (b. 1886, d. August 1969), landed a job, things improved slightly for the family. Occasionally, they would venture out to one of the cafés that was holding a concert. Maurice was fascinated by the cheap acts and tawdry tat he saw around him and determined that one day he would work there. His persistence paid off in remarkably quick time. He landed a job aged 12 in one of the cafés. 'Le Petit Chevalier', as he was called, entertained the crowds with songs that would have made his mother blush. The audience was made up mostly of whores and pimps. He was paid FF12 a week. While working he met a plump, plain, miserable girl called Georgette in April 1900. She told him that she had often spied on her parents having sex, and it seems that she and the young Maurice indulged in some kind of sexual activity. Georgette often invited Chevalier to join her under a park bench outside a church in Ménilmontant's main square after dark. According to his memoirs Chevalier claimed to have lost his virginity when he was 14 to a blonde girl, named Marguerite, whom he described as "a robust, chesty girl singer". Whether true or an example of man's vanity, Chevalier boasted he made love to her seven times consecutively. They met when she appeared on the bill with him at La Parisiana, a fashionable Paris music hall of the time. By the time he turned 14, Chevalier was solely supporting his mother, his two brothers having married. One night in 1903 in La Parisiana the crowds fell silent as a woman swathed in furs walked to a seat near the stage. It was Mistinguett, whom Maurice had often seen perform in revues. She asked him his age. He

told her he was 15 and she told him that he was pretty enough to reach the top. Not long after, Chevalier began to hone his act, making it appeal to a more sophisticated clientele. It also did wonders for his sex life. In 1908 he made his film début in *Trop Crédule* but didn't appear before the cameras again for three years. He appeared in *Une Mariée Qui Se Fait Attendre* (1911), *Par Habitude* (1911), *Une Soirée Mondaine* (1917) and *Par Habitude* (1923). In 1909, he was booked at the Folies Bergère, as was the 40-year-old Mistinguett. The two of them performed a sketch in which they played lovers who argued, then made up and danced before rolling themselves up in a rug. One night in the confines of the rug Chevalier kissed Mistinguett and before dawn the next day they were in bed together. She already had a beau, so their affair was carried out clandestinely at lunchtime. Several times he proposed and each time she turned him down, but she taught him how to behave in society and how to behave in bed. However, she began to feel the first tinges of jealousy as his star threatened to outshine hers. Then in 1914 he joined the 31st Infantry Regiment to fight the Kaiser. On August 22, 1914, he was hit in the chest by shrapnel and captured by the Hun when they overran the hospital he was placed in. He learned to speak English in the Alten Grabow POW camp from a captured British sergeant. In October 1916 he was released and awarded the Croix de Guerre for bravery. By 1917 he was second on the bill at the Casino de Montparnasse. Top of the bill was his lover Mistinguett, but by now a resentment was brewing in him. Chevalier felt that he should have equal billing; Mistinguett would have none of it. They moved in together in central Paris but one day she caught him with another, younger, woman. To give himself some space Chevalier took a job in London, but the icy atmosphere between the two of them remained when he returned to the French capital. Again he asked Mistinguett for equal billing and again she refused. He walked out. Around this time Chevalier developed the image that would make him world famous – the tuxedo topped off with a straw boater. In 1925 he went to America but flopped when stage fright got the better of him and he returned to France. On October 10, 1927, he married his co-star Yvonne Vallée at Vaucresson. She miscarried but despite this trauma the 5'11½" Chevalier carried on with his philandering ways. On June 28, 1928, having signed a contract with Paramount (he failed a screen test at MGM), the Chevaliers sailed for America on the *Ile de France*. Once he had conquered his nerves, Chevalier became a mammoth hit Stateside. He befriended many glamorous film stars. He became especially close to Marlene Dietrich although, despite what Mme Chevalier feared and probably believed, they never were anything other than very good friends. He appeared in *Innocents Of Paris* (1929) as Maurice Marney (in which he popularised the song 'Louise'), *The Playboy Of Paris* (1930) as Albert, *Paramount On Parade* (1930) and *The Smiling Lieutenant* (1931) as Lieutenant Niki. As his star rose on both sides of the Atlantic, his marriage began to crumble and finally his wife asked for a divorce, which was granted in 1932. Chevalier's next romantic conquests were Kay Francis and Josephine Baker, though the latter remained secret due to the widespread social disapproval of miscegenation at the time. Then Chevalier, 46, met a 19-year-old Rumanian Jewess called Nita Raya. For her he changed his diet, gave up smoking and cut down on his boozing. He was worried by the age gap and even sought the advice of his priest. In 1939 when war broke out he and Nita and her parents went to La Bocca near Cannes then, incredibly, Chevalier returned to German-occupied Paris. He was advised by many, including Charles Boyer, to flee to London but Chevalier would have nothing of it. To the immense fury of the French Resistance he performed for the Nazis at Alten Grabow, the POW camp of which he had once been an inmate (his 'fee' was the release of 10 French prisoners of war) although he pointed out that his girlfriend was a Jew. He also said that the Germans had hinted that if he failed to perform they could make things very difficult for her family. Chevalier was accused of collaborating before his appearance before a 'Purge Committee' exonerated him in 1944. (On August 27, 1944, German radio announced Chevalier had been shot by the French Resistance for collaboration.) Feeling that his actions had been misunderstood, Chevalier became depressed; he believed he would and could never entertain again. Then his great friend Marlene Dietrich rescued him by inviting Chevalier to appear with herself and Noël Coward. Some members of the French contingent on the bill threatened to boycott the show because of the presence of a collaborator but then Dietrich said she would not appear unless Chevalier did. The show revitalised Chevalier and his career although not long after, he and Nita split up. In 1954 he was refused a visit to an America at the height of the McCarthyite witch hunts because of his supposed communist sympathies. Three years later, he was finally allowed in and appeared in *Love In The Afternoon* (1957) as Claude Chavasse and was offered the role of Honore Lachaille in Vincente Minnelli's *Gigi* (1958). His rendition of 'Thank Heaven For Little Girls' and 'I Remember It Well' (with Hermione Gingold) became much-loved classics. On October 21, 1968, he retired from show business, losing a lot of the old Gallic spark in the process. He found retirement difficult.

CAUSE: In March 1971 the Great Lover discovered he was impotent and attempted to kill himself by taking an overdose of pills and slashing his wrists. He recovered but on December 12, 1971, he was placed on a kidney dialysis machine after collapsing at a cinema in the Champs Elysées. He died of a heart attack at 7.30pm following surgery for a kidney problem in Paris, aged 83. His last words were "Y'a de la joie" ("There's fun in the air"). He left around $20 million in his will. About a thousand people attended his funeral in Marnes-la-Coquette. Chevalier was laid to rest in his stage costume, his straw boater placed across his chest. At the cemetery a fight broke out between the press photographers and one of them ended up being pushed into the grave on top of the coffin.

FURTHER READING: *Maurice Chevalier: His Life 1888–1972* – James Harding (London: Secker & Warburg, 1982); *Maurice Chevalier: Up On Top Of A Rainbow* – David Bret (London: Robson Books, 1992); *Thank Heaven For Little Girls: The True Story Of Maurice Chevalier's Life And Times* – Edward Behr (London: Hutchinson, 1993).

Erik Chitty
Born July 8, 1907
Died July 22, 1977
Familiar face. Born in Dover, Kent, the son of a flour miller, Erik Chitty was educated at Dover College and then went up to Jesus College, Cambridge, where he read law and helped to form the Cambridge University Mummers for whom he served as treasurer. Then he studied at RADA and went on to appear in over 350 television programmes but is best known as the decrepit sports teacher "Whiffy" Smithy in the film and television show *Please, Sir!* (TV November 8, 1968–February 13, 1972; film 1971). His acting career was interrupted by the Second World War where he saw

service as a sergeant with the Eighth Army in Egypt and Italy. His other films included *Forbidden* (1948), a judge's clerk in *Your Witness* (1950), *Chance Of A Lifetime* (1950) as Silas Pike, *John Wesley* (1954) as a trustee of Georgia, a ballistics expert in *Time Is My Enemy* (1954), *Windfall* (1955), *Left Right And Centre* (1959) as the deputy returning officer, *The Devil's Disciple* (1959) as Titus, *The Day They Robbed The Bank Of England* (1960) as Gudgeon, *First Men In The Moon* (1964) as Gibbs, an old soldier in *Doctor Zhivago* (1965), *Bedazzled* (1967) as Seed, a clergyman in *A Nice Girl Like Me* (1969), a photographer in *The Railway Children* (1970), *Song Of Norway* (1970) as Helsted, *The Statue* (1971) as Mouser, *Lust For A Vampire* (1971) as Professor Herz, *The Amazing Mr Blunden* (1972) as Mr Claverton, an old waiter in *The Vault Of Horror* (1973), *The Flying Sorcerer* (1973) as Sir Roger, the museum guard in *One Of Our Dinosaurs Is Missing* (1975), *The Seven-Per-Cent Solution* (1976) as James the butler and an organist in *A Bridge Too Far* (1977). He was married to the former actress Hester Bevan and had one son and two daughters.
CAUSE: He died aged 70 of natural causes.

Belle Chrystall

Born April 25, 1910
Died June 7, 2003
Early Brit star. Born in Fullwood, near Preston in Lancashire, Belle Chrystall (no one ever knew her real name as she destroyed her birth certificate) was educated at Preston School for Girls, Westbourne High School and Cheltenham Ladies' College, before studying Law at King's College, London. She decided a career at the bar was not for her. "I never intended to be a lawyer," she said. "In my heart I always knew it was an acting life for me." Her parents felt a career on the boards was not suitable for a young lady but she managed to persuade

them and in 1927 went to RADA, where among her classmates was Charles Laughton. She made her stage début in *Crime* in 1928, and after some two dozen further plays decided that a film career was where she wanted to aim. She landed a small part as Peggy in the movie *A Warm Corner* (1930), for the Gainsborough Studios at Shepherd's Bush, and in 1931 she struck lucky after writing a begging letter to the director Victor Saville. After a successful screen test opposite John Stuart, she was signed up for *Hindle Wakes* (1931) playing Jenny Hawthorne. Her portrayal of the Lancashire mill girl who is discovered spending the weekend with the mill owner's son seemed to augur well for a splendid career. "I was a sensation," was her own less than modest estimation of her performance. "Great things were prophesied for me." 5'2" Belle Chrystall went on to play Vicky Hobson in *Hobson's Choice* (1931) opposite Charles Laughton, Aisla Crane in *The Frightened Lady* (1933), and appeared as Mary Stanton opposite George Curzon and Della Lind in *The Scotland Yard Mystery* (1933), a thriller described by *Picturegoer* magazine as having "more twists and turns than a rollercoaster". This was followed by a showy role as Mary Summers in *Friday The Thirteenth* (1934), opposite Jessie Matthews and Sonnie Hale, and Mavis Tremayne in *The Girl In The Flat* (1934). Her most notable film during the mid-Thirties was Michael Powell's *Edge Of The World* (1937) which was filmed on Foula in Shetland and in which she played Ruth Manson. *Film Pictorial* called her performance "breathtaking" and it seemed that at last Chrystall had been given her big break. More than 60 years after its release, *Edge Of The World* opened the 2000 New York film festival to general acclaim. The actor John Travolta described the film as "beautiful, thrilling and profoundly moving". Towards the end of 1937

Chrystall appeared in the religious short *Follow Your Star,* alongside Arthur Tracy. But she failed to achieve longevity as a major star, with many producers preferring American actors. However, that was not always the case. When the leading lady, Diana Churchill, pulled out of *Yellow Sands* (1938), due to exhaustion (she was honeymooning in the South of France with Barry K. Barnes), Walter Mycroft called for Belle Chrystall. She followed it with the lead, Nora Grayson, in *Anything To Declare?* (1938), *Breakers Ahead* (1938) as Mary, and Sucal Hurrin in *Poison Pen* (1939), with Flora Robson and Robert Newton. Following a number of supporting roles in plays for BBC Radio, in 1940 Belle Chrystall made her final appearance on screen as Ann Upcott in *Castle Of Crime,* directed by Harold French. She then took to modelling, and for a brief spell was the face of Lux soap. In 1946, after her marriage to Roy Proctor (d. 1990), she announced her retirement; the following year she gave birth to a daughter, Chrystal (d. 1999). "I was never as hungry as many contemporaries," Belle Chrystall once opined. "I adored my career on screen and the adulation it brought me, but it was no substitute for marriage and a family."
CAUSE: Belle Chrystall died aged 93 of natural causes.

René Clair

(RENÉ-LUCIEN CHOMETTE)
Born November 11, 1898
Died March 15, 1981
Leading French *cinéaste.* Born in Paris, the son of a soap seller, Clair grew up to be one of France's leading film directors. He wrote and directed his own plays from the age of seven. Like many students, he could produce the work in class but not when it came to examinations and he left school having failed. In World War I he drove ambulances until a spinal injury forced him home. He spent time in a Dominican monastery in 1918. He began acting in films such as *Le Lys De La Vie* (1920), *Parisette* (1921), *L'Orpheline* (1921) and *Le Sens De La Mort* (1922) before deciding acting wasn't for him and moving behind the camera. Among his films were: *Entr'acte* (1924), *Le Fantôme Du Moulin-Rouge* (1925), *Un Chapeau De Paille D'Italie* (1927), one of the best-known satires on French middle-class life, *Les Deux Timides* (1928), *Le Million* (1931), *The Ghost Goes West* (1935), *Quatorze Juillet* (1933), *I Married A Witch* (1942), *Les Belles De Nuit* (1952) and *Tout L'Or Du Monde* (1961). When France was occupied by Germany Clair fled to America. His brother, Henri Chomette (1896–1941), was also a director.
CAUSE: He died in Paris aged 82 of natural causes.

Nicholas Clay

Born September 18, 1946
Died May 25, 2000
Unfulfilled heartthrob. Born in London, Nicholas Anthony Phillip Clay trained at RADA and made his film début in *The Night Digger* (1971) as Billy. It seemed at the beginning of the Eighties that he was destined to become a cinematic heartthrob with his sexy roles in *Excalibur* and *Lady Chatterley's Lover* opposite, respectively, a topless Cherie Lunghi and a naked Sylvia Kristel. But for some reason he did not seem to be able to maintain the momentum and the rest of his career was something of a disappointment. His films included *The Darwin Adventure* (1972) as Charles Darwin, *Victor Frankenstein* (1977) as Henry Clerval, *Lovespell* (1979) as Tristan, *Zulu Dawn* (1979) as Lieutenant Raw, *Excalibur* (1981) as Lancelot, *Lady Chatterley's Lover* (1981) as Oliver Mellors, *Evil Under The Sun* (1982) as Patrick Redfern, *Lionheart* (1987) as Charles De Montfort, *Cannon Movie Tales: Sleeping Beauty* (1987) as Prince and *And Beyond* (2000) as Jackie. In

1980 he married Lorna Heilbron by whom he had two daughters, Ella and Madge.

CAUSE: He died in London aged 53 of cancer.

Jack Clayton

Born March 1, 1921
Died February 26, 1995
Kitchen sink director. Jack Isaac Clayton was born at 95 King's Road, Brighton, the illegitimate son of Beatrice Clayton. He had a sister Jill (1917–1993). After one term at the Arnold House School in London he entered the film industry in 1935 as a runner for Alexander Korda, although Clayton described it in less romantic terms: "[I was the] one who runs messages for everybody, calls the actors and acts as general dogsbody." An industrious worker, he rose to become production manager on Korda's *An Ideal Husband* (1947) via such films as *Wings Of The Morning* (1937) and *Q Planes* (1939). During the Second World War, he served with the RAF film unit. In the early Fifties Clayton became associate producer at Romulus Films. His work included *Moulin Rouge* (1952), *Beat The Devil* (1953), *I Am A Camera* (1955), *Sailor Beware* (1956), *Dry Rot* (1956), *Three Men In A Boat* (1956), and the melodrama *The Story Of Esther Costello* (1957), which starred Joan Crawford. In 1956 he directed Wolf Mankowitz's updated version of Gogol's *The Bespoke Overcoat* and won a prize at Venice and an Oscar for the best short subject. This led to him directing *Room At The Top*, John Braine's 1957 best-seller, although he was loath to hire Laurence Harvey as Joe Lampton. He relented and cast Simone Signoret as Alice Aisgill opposite Harvey. The film, when it was released in 1959, was the first to receive an X certificate and was the first of the genre labelled "kitchen-sink dramas", a tag that Clayton disliked. Signoret won the Best Actress Oscar for her performance, and Clayton was nominated as Best Director, but lost out to William Wyler for *Ben Hur*. His next film was *The Innocents* (1961), adapted from Henry James' novella *The Turn Of The Screw*. It starred Deborah Kerr. This was followed by *The Pumpkin Eater* (1964), based on Penelope Mortimer's book about motherhood, adapted by Harold Pinter, which starred Anne Bancroft and featured Maggie Smith in a small role as the local gossip. His other films included *Our Mother's House* (1967) and *The Great Gatsby* (1974) but neither set the box office alight. Then Clayton suffered a stroke and it was almost ten years before he was ready to work again. Disney hired him to direct Ray Bradbury's *Something Wicked This Way Comes* (1983). It was not a success but has since become something of a cult movie. His penultimate film was based on Brian Moore's book *The Lonely Passion Of Judith Hearne* (1987) and Maggie Smith played the title role. Smith also appeared in his last film, Muriel Spark's *Memento Mori* (1992). Michael Winner said of him, "Jack was a very close friend of mine. He was outside the normal director both as a talent and as a human being. He was an exception. Jack was the most gentle, quiet, wonderful man. He was a meticulous craftsman with enormous heart and sensitivity." On December 13, 1947, he married Mary Lydia Cole, the actor Christine Norden (1924–1988). They divorced in 1953 and the following year he married Katherine Kath, another actor. At an Oscar party after the April 4, 1960 ceremony he met and fell in love with the Israeli actress Haya Harareet (b. Haifa, September 20, 1931 as Haya Neuberg) who had played Esther in *Ben Hur*. They married on August 29, 1984, after Clayton's divorce from Katherine Kath.

CAUSE: Jack Clayton died in Wrexham Park Hospital, Slough, Berkshire, from heart and liver problems. He was 73.

Montgomery Clift

Born October 17, 1920
Died July 23, 1966

Flawed idol. Born at 2101 South 33rd Street, Omaha, Nebraska (his death certificate lists his year of birth as 1921), a twin, Edward Montgomery Clift, the son of a banker, had been a brilliant child actor, amazing Broadway critics when he was 15 in *Fly Away Home* at the 48th Street Theater. Moving to Hollywood he was nominated for an Oscar for his first film *The Search* (1948) and became a much sought after star, appearing in such films as *Red River* (1948), *A Place In The Sun* (1951) (which caused writer Raymond Chandler to comment "Mr Montgomery Clift gives the performance of his career which is not saying a great deal since he had already demonstrated in *The Heiress* that he didn't belong on the same screen with first-class actors"), *I Confess* (1953), *From Here To Eternity* (1953) as Robert E. Lee Prewitt, *Raintree County* (1957) as John Shawnessy, *Suddenly Last Summer* (1959) as Dr Cukrowitz, *The Misfits* (1961) as Perce Howland, *Judgment At Nuremberg* (1961) as Rudolph Peterson and the title role in *Freud* (1962). There was a black side to Clift. He hated his homosexuality and resorted to narcotics to attempt to block it out. His friend Marilyn Monroe described him as "The only person I know who is in worse shape than me." Black moods ran in the family. On October 1, 1962, his pregnant 21-year-old niece, Suzanne, murdered her 27-year-old boyfriend, Pierro Brentani, because he refused to marry her. She was sent to a mental hospital. Six years earlier, on May 12, 1956, Clift was leaving a dinner party at Elizabeth Taylor's Coldwater Canyon home when he was involved in a car crash. His stunning good looks were ruined and his friends believed he was never the same afterwards.
CAUSE: On July 22, 1966, Clift spent the day in seclusion in his bedroom at 217 East 61st Street, a four-storey building in Manhattan with seven rooms, six fireplaces, six baths and a huge garden. He lived with Lorenzo James, his black personal secretary. The two men passed the day without talking to each other. Said James: "This wasn't unusual. There were often days when he wanted to be all alone with his head." For a late lunch Clift ate a goose liver sandwich in the afternoon. At 1am the following morning James bade his boss goodnight and mentioned *The Misfits* was on television that night and did he want to watch it. Clift's answer was emphatic: "Absolutely not!" At 6am James went to wake Clift but received no answer and noted that the bedroom door was locked, which was unusual. Unable to break it down he went into the garden and put a ladder to the bedroom window. When he reached it, he saw Clift lying prone on his bed. He called Clift's doctor and lawyer. However, because Clift's personal physician was away a locum came in his stead and pronounced the actor dead at 45. He found Clift "lying face up in bed, glasses on, no clothes on. Right arm flexed. Both fists clenched. No evidence of trauma. Rigor present. Underclothes and pants scattered about on floor of bedroom. Liquor cabinet in bedroom. No empty bottles lying about. No notes, weapons, etc . . ." Death was due to "Occlusive coronary arteriosclerosis with pulmonary edema". Clift had also been suffering from a calcium deficiency for four years. One hundred and fifty people attended his funeral at St James Episcopal Church and then he was interred at Friends Cemetery, Prospect Park, Brooklyn. His gravestone was designed by John Benson, who also designed President John F. Kennedy's memorial at Arlington, Virginia. Shortly afterwards, Clift's mother sold his New York home to a couple with three children. The sale had one stipulation –

they must agree to a plaque being placed in the front stating "Montgomery Clift lived here in 1960–1966". They agreed but for some time were pestered by fans, sightseers and weirdos who would ring the bell at all hours of the day and night. The problem was solved by planting a bush in front of the memorial. It stands there to this day but is completely covered. No one calls now.

FURTHER READING: *Monty: A Biography Of Montgomery Clift* – Robert LaGuardia (New York: Donald I. Fine, 1977); *Montgomery Clift: A Biography* – Patricia Bosworth (New York: Bantam, 1978).

Jimmy Clitheroe
Born December 24, 1921
Died June 6, 1973

'The Clitheroe Kid'. James Robinson Clitheroe was born at 58 Wilkin Street, Clitheroe, Lancashire, the son of James Robert Clitheroe, a cotton weaver, and Emma Pye (d. 1973). He was raised and educated in the nearby village of Blacko, near Nelson. He joined a juvenile touring troupe called the Winstanley Babes, where, among other talents, he became a female impersonator. In 1933 he was stricken with a glandular problem and his growth was stunted. He never reached puberty and was forever stuck as a "boy". He stood just 4′2″ and weighed only five stone. He refused to discuss his stature with anyone. He made his film début in *Old Mother Riley In Society* (1940) playing Boots. He followed that with a performance as Jimmy in *Much Too Shy* (1942) and Joey in *Rhythm Serenade* (1943). In 1945 he teamed up with Albert Burdon, and they appeared together in revue and pantomime. He appeared as Sonny in *Somewhere In Politics* (1949) and Jimmy in *School For Randle* (1949). From May 5, 1958 until August 18, 1972, he starred as *The Clitheroe Kid*, the longest-running radio comedy programme in history and one that attracted 10 million listeners at its peak. In 1959 Clitheroe took part in the Royal Command Variety Show and he starred in the television series *Holiday Hotel*. His catchphrase – "Some mothers do 'ave 'em" – caught the public's imagination. His last film was *Rocket To The Moon* (1967) in which he played Tom Thumb. Clitheroe was not a homosexual or asexual but believed that his medical condition made marriage an unlikely prospect. He spent much of his private life living reclusively with his mother behind the high walls of his home in Bispham Road, Blackpool.

CAUSE: Jimmy Clitheroe was never the most vigorous of men and his health began to fail in the early Seventies. In April 1973 he was found unconscious in the bedroom of a Plymouth hotel, but recovered in Freedom Fields Hospital, Plymouth. Two months later, on June 6, 1973, the day of his mother's cremation, Clitheroe was found unconscious in bed by relatives arriving for the funeral. He died the same day in Victoria Hospital, Blackpool. He was 51. The inquest was told that he had swallowed at least four barbiturate sleeping pills and seven brandies. A verdict of "accidental death due to the combined toxic effects of barbiturates and alcohol" was recorded. His £102,306 fortune, intended for his mother, went, after a number of small bequests, to the Cancer Research Campaign.

Colin Clive
(COLIN GLENN CLIVE-GREIG)
Born January 20, 1898
Died June 25, 1937

The mad scientist. Born in Saint-Malo, France, the son of a British colonel, the 6′ bisexual Clive intended to have a military career until his hopes were wrecked by a knee injury. He turned to the stage and first came to attention as Captain Denis Stanhope in James Whale's production of *Journey's End* at London's Savoy Theatre on January 21,

1929. The play had opened the previous month starring Laurence Olivier as Stanhope but he was unavailable for the West End run. Whale and author R.C. Sheriff searched through *The Spotlight* but were unable to find someone suitable. The 5'4" lesbian actor and playwright Jeanne de Casalis (b. Basutoland, South Africa, May 22, 1897, as De Casalis de Pury, d. London, August 19, 1966) recommended her boyfriend Colin Clive (whom she would marry in June 1929). Whale and Sheriff were unsure but agreed to meet Clive. When he read for them they knew that they had their man. However, Clive was nervous and hesitant and during rehearsals offered to resign but Whale refused to let him. At one run-through Sheriff suggested that Clive have a tot of whisky to calm his nerves. Several shots later, Clive's rendition was perfect. Some authorities have suggested that this is where Clive's alcoholism had its roots. Others have suggested it was his inability to come to terms with his bisexuality. David Manners, who appeared in *Journey's End* with Clive, said, "There seemed to be a split in his personality: one side that was soft and gentle; the other, a man who took to alcohol to hide from the world his true nature . . . Today he would find help. Everyone of us wanted to help then, but when he was on the bottle, which was most of the time, he put on the mask of a person who repelled help and jeered at his own softness. He was a fantastically sensitive actor – and, as with many great actors, this sensitivity bred addiction to drugs or alcohol in order to cope with the very insensitive world around them." On the day the play opened Clive was knocked down by a bus in the Strand but did not let this minor mishap stop the show going on. When the chance came to make the film version for Whale only one man could play Captain Denis Stanhope but Clive's first screen test was described as "an inarticulate mumble". Nevertheless, Clive was cast and *Journey's End* was shot between November and December 29, 1929, being premièred in Glendale, California on March 13, 1930. Clive's next film was *The Stronger Sex* (1931) in which he appeared as Warren Barrington. Then came the role that made his career and set the standard thereafter for portrayals of mad scientists – Dr Henry Frankenstein in James Whale's *Frankenstein* (released December 1931). Although Carl Laemmle wanted Leslie Howard for the part, Whale was insistent that Colin Clive was the perfect choice. Boris Karloff's casting was suggested by Whale's boyfriend, David Lewis. Years before method acting, the fight scene was so realistic that Clive dislocated his arm. His co-star Mae Clarke said of Clive, "Colin Clive was the dearest, kindest man who gave you importance. He was wonderful, so clever. When he started acting in a scene, I wanted to stop and just watch . . . Colin was electric. I was mesmerised by him . . . When he looked at me, I'd flush . . . He was the handsomest man I ever saw – and also the saddest. Colin's sadness was elusive; the sadness you'd see if you contemplate many of the master painters and sculptors of the face of Christ." Clive's next role was as Rupert Harvey in *Lily Christine* (1932). Then he starred as Sir Christopher Strong opposite Katharine Hepburn in her first starring role in *Christopher Strong* (1933), followed by *Looking Forward* (1933) as Geoffrey Fielding and *The Key* (1934) as Captain Andrew Kerr before being reunited with James Whale for *One More River* (1934) as Sir Gerald Corven. Whale asked Clive to stay in Hollywood to appear in another of his films. During the interim Clive busied himself by appearing in *Jane Eyre* (1934) as Edward Rochester, *Clive Of India* (1935) as Captain Johnstone and *The Right To Live* (1935) as Maurice Trent, a remake of Somerset

Maugham's *The Sacred Flame* (1929). The new Whale film was *Bride Of Frankenstein* (1935) and Clive reprised his part as Dr Henry Frankenstein. Clive made just six more films: *The Girl From 10th Avenue* (1935) as John Marland, *Mad Love* (1935) as Stephen Orlac, *The Man Who Broke The Bank At Monte Carlo* (1935) as Bertrand Berkeley, *The Widow From Monte Carlo* (1935) as Lord Eric Reynolds, and *History Is Made At Night* (1937) as Bruce Vail, during the filming of which he broke down and wept hysterically on the sound stage, his appearance wrecked by his alcoholism. His last film was *The Woman I Love* (1937) in which he played Captain Thelius.

CAUSE: Colin Clive died at the Cedars of Lebanon Hospital, Los Angeles, of pulmonary tuberculosis caused by alcoholism.

Rosemary Clooney
Born May 23, 1928
Died June 29, 2002

Georgie's aunt. The singer who had a successful movie career was born in Maysville, Kentucky, but her parents separated not long after her birth and she was raised by her paternal grandparents. Her grandfather was a political animal and when he ran for the mayoralty Clooney and Betty, her younger sister (b. Maysville, Kentucky, 1931, d. 1976 of a brain aneurysm), sang at the campaign meetings and no doubt their mellifluence helped in his subsequent re-election to three successive terms. In 1941 the Clooney sisters moved to Cincinatti, Ohio, to live with their mother's parents. They spent their days in school and their nights appearing on local radio station WLW for $20 a night. Their uncle acted as a chaperone and they toured the locale before being signed up by the Tony Pastor Orchestra in 1945. They toured with this band for three years. The sisters were still chaperoned by their uncle but that did not stop Rosemary falling for a bandmember.

The mystery man proposed marriage and Rosemary agreed but changed her mind because of her single-minded resolve to get on with her career before getting off with a man. (The man was identified only as "Dave" in her 1977 autobiography *This For Remembrance*.) With the end of the Second World War came the beginning of the end of the big band era and Rosemary Clooney decided to go solo. In 1946 she recorded 'I'm Sorry I Didn't Say I'm Sorry When I Made You Cry Last Night'. She was to say of the session that she "was not able to sing above a whisper. Fear. Fear and this thing I was feeling inside about Dave." Nonetheless, critics hailed her "new" style. Clooney moved to New York and signed a contract with Columbia Records and recorded some songs with Frank Sinatra before the Chairman of the Board left for Capitol. A meeting with Mitch Miller, the producer, proved fruitful and in 1951 he got her to record 'Come On-A My House'. The previous year she had appeared on the television show *Songs For Sale* and then recorded 'Big Brown Eyes', which sold more than half a million copies. Despite hating her new song, it went on to sell more than a million copies and hit the number one spot. The hits continued including: 'Tenderly', 'Suzy Flowflake', 'Botcha Me', 'Hey There' (UK number four), 'This Ole House' (UK number one), 'Christmas', and 'Mambo Italiano' (UK number one). On July 13, 1953 she married the actor Jose Ferrer in Durant, Oklahoma. They moved into the house in Beverly Hills where the singer Russ Columbo had shot himself on September 2, 1934, and where George and Ira Gershwin had written 'Foggy Day'. Clooney was signed to Paramount and made her screen début in 1953 in *The Stars Are Singing* playing Terry Brennan. This was followed by *Here Come The Girls* (1953) in which she played Daisy Crockett, *Red Garters* (1954) as Calaveras Kate, and *Deep In My Heart*

(1954). She appeared in *White Christmas* (1954) playing Betty Haynes opposite Bing Crosby and not long after fell pregnant. Her son Miguel José was born in Santa Monica, California on February 7, 1955. He became an actor in *Twin Peaks* and *Robocop* and in 1991 married Leilaui Sarelle (b. September 28, 1959) who played Roxy, Sharon Stone's lesbian lover in *Basic Instinct* (1992). The Jose Ferrers were to have four more children (Maria Providencia in August 1956, Gabriel Vincente in 1957, Monsita in 1958 and Rafael on March 23, 1960) but he found it impossible to stay faithful and she found herself unable to sing. They filed for divorce in 1961 and although the decree nisi was issued the decree absolute was never finalised. To compensate she became a vocal supporter of presidential candidate John F. Kennedy and was horrified at his assassination on November 22, 1963. She was angry and disgusted that her husband didn't share her sorrow. It was the catalyst for their divorce which came in late 1967. In the middle of the flower power era she began a two-year affair with a drummer a decade and a half younger than her. She was later to describe it as "the happiest times I could ever remember having with a man". On June 5, 1968 she was standing a few feet from Senator Bobby Kennedy when he was assassinated. The awful event caused the end of her relationship and also caused her to have a nervous breakdown. She was sent to a mental hospital. Slowly, she regained her sanity and in 1975 Bing Crosby invited her to go on tour with him. Two years later she formed Four Girls Four with Margaret Whiting, Helen O'Connell and Rose Marie. They toured for the next six years. She appeared in the television hospital drama *ER* opposite her nephew, George Clooney. She was nominated for an Emmy for her role as an Alzheimer's sufferer who could only communicate through song. In 1997 she married Dante Di Paulo, whom she had met again in 1973 when he pulled up alongside her at a traffic light. CAUSE: Rosemary Clooney underwent surgery for lung cancer on January 11, 2002 at the Mayo Clinic in Minnesota and the upper left lobe of her lung was removed. In early June 2002 the cancer returned with a vengeance. She died aged 74 of lung cancer in Beverly Hills, California. She was surrounded by her husband, her five children and nephew George Clooney.

Andy Clyde
Born March 25, 1892
Died May 18, 1967
The best friend. Born in Blairgowrie, Scotland, Clyde began his show business career in Twenties vaudeville before becoming an extra at Mack Sennett Studios. He became known for playing the hero's sidekick, such as Hopalong Cassidy's grizzled mate California Carlson. He made his début in the silent film *A Small Town Idol* (1921) and went on to appear in *Million Dollar Legs* (1932), *Annie Oakley* (1935) as MacIvor, *Three Men From Texas* (1940) as California Carlson, *Abe Lincoln In Illinois* (1940), *The Green Years* (1946) as Saddler Boag, *Abilene Trail* (1951) as Sagebrush and his last film *Pardon My Nightshirt* (1956). He also appeared on television in *The Real McCoys* (1957–63) as George MacMichael, *Lassie* (1958–64) as Cully Wilson and *No Time For Sergeants* (1964–65) as Grandpa Jim Anderson. Married to actress Elsie Maud Tarron, a Mack Sennett bathing beauty, his brother David (b. 1887, d. San Fernando Valley, California, May 17, 1945) and sister Jean (d. 1962) were also actors. CAUSE: He died aged 75 of natural causes in Los Angeles, California. He was interred in Forest Lawn Memorial-Parks, 1712 South Glendale Avenue, Glendale, California 91209.

Lee J. Cobb

(LEO JACOB)
Born December 8, 1911
Died February 11, 1976
Mr Menace. Born in New York, Cobb
was a child prodigy on the violin until
he broke his wrist. His ambition to be
an actor was stifled by his parents, so
he ran away from home. He appeared
in various bit parts in films such as *The
Vanishing Shadow* (1934), *North Of The
Rio Grande* (1937) as Wooden, *Ali
Baba Goes To Town* (1937), *Danger
On The Air* (1938) as Tony while
simultaneously working with the
influential Group Theater in New
York. His apogee on stage came in
1949 with the first production of
Arthur Miller's *Death Of A Salesman* in
which Cobb played the leading role of
Willy Loman. His performance became
the standard by which all subsequent
productions were based. (He recreated
the part for a TV movie in 1966.) His
film work continued apace; his parts
were usually those of big-mouthed yobs
or other unpleasant or intimidating
characters. Cobb said he was cast in
less sympathetic roles because he lost
his hair when he was just 20. (He wore
a wig on stage, TV and film.) A perfect
example of this came in *12 Angry Men*
(1957) when he played the juror
holding out for conviction while Henry
Fonda's character strove to persuade
the other jury members that there
was an element of doubt in the
prosecution's case. He was twice
nominated for Academy Awards.
Firstly, for the inappropriately named
union racketeer Johnny Friendly in *On
The Waterfront* (1954) and then as the
overbearing patriarch Fyodr in *The
Brothers Karamazov* (1958). From
September 19, 1962, until 1966 he was
a regular on the television series *The
Virginian*, playing Judge Henry Garth.
One of his last memorable roles was
that of Lieutenant William F.
Kinderman in William Friedkin's *The
Exorcist* (1973). Other films included:
Golden Boy (1939) as Mr Bonaparte,
Tonight We Raid Calais (1943) as
Bonnard, *Buckskin Frontier* (1943) as
Jeptha Marr, *The Song Of Bernadette*
(1943) as Dr Dozous, *Anna And The
King Of Siam* (1946) as Kralahome
(The Siamese Prime Minister),
Boomerang! (1947) as Chief Robinson,
Call Northside 777 (1948) as Brian
Kelly, *Sirocco* (1951) as Colonel
Feroud, *Green Mansions* (1959) as
Nuflo, *Exodus* (1960) as Barak Ben
Canaan, *Four Horsemen Of The
Apocalypse* (1961) as Julio Madariaga,
How The West Was Won (1962) as
Marshal Lou Ramsey, *Come Blow Your
Horn* (1963) as Mr Baker, *Our Man
Flint* (1965) as Lloyd C. Cramden, *In
Like Flint* (1967) as Lloyd C.
Cramden, *Coogan's Bluff* (1968) as
Lieutenant McElroy, *The Man Who
Loved Cat Dancing* (1973) as
Lapchance and *That Lucky Touch*
(1975) as Lieutenant General Henry
Steedman.
CAUSE: Cobb died of a heart attack
aged 64 in Los Angeles, California.

Charles Coburn

Born June 17, 1877
Died August 30, 1961
Monocled cinematic grandfather. Born
Charles Douville Coburn in Savannah,
Georgia, he began his theatrical career
selling programmes, gradually working
his way up the ladder to become
theatre manager. He then turned to
acting, making his Broadway début in
1901. Among his film credits are: *Boss
Tweed* (1933) his first film, *Of Human
Hearts* (1938) as Dr Charles Shingle,
Idiot's Delight (1939) as Dr Hugo
Waldersee, *Stanley And Livingstone*
(1939) as Lord Tyce, *The Story Of
Alexander Graham Bell* (1939) as
Gardner Hubbard, *The Road To
Singapore* (1940) as Joshua Mallon IV,
Edison The Man (1940) as General
Powell, *The Devil And Miss Jones*
(1941) as Merrick, for which he was
nominated for a Best Supporting Actor
Oscar, *Kings Row* (1942) as Dr Henry
Gordon, *Heaven Can Wait* (1943) as

Hugo Van Cleve, *The More The Merrier* (1943) as Benjamin Dingle, for which he won an Oscar as Best Supporting Actor, *Wilson* (1944) as Professor Henry Holmes, *The Green Years* (1946) as Alexander Gow, for which he was nominated for a Best Supporting Actor Oscar, *Yes Sir That's My Baby* (1949) as Professor Jason Hartley, *Monkey Business* (1952) as Mr Oliver Oxley, *Has Anybody Seen My Gal?* (1953) as Samuel Fulton, *Gentlemen Prefer Blondes* (1953) as Sir Francis Beekman, *The Remarkable Mr Pennypacker* (1959) as Grampa and *Pepe* (1960), his final film. He was a keen race-goer and had his own stable of horses. He wore the monocle not for effect but because of an eye complaint.

CAUSE: He died of a heart attack, aged 84, in New York.

James Coburn

Born August 31, 1928
Died November 18, 2002
Rangy leading man. Born in Laurel, Nebraska, James Harrison Coburn III took an early interest in acting, playing Herod in a school play at the age of four. Coburn always said that he had been fascinated by the cinema from the beginning. His father's garage business, in Laurel, went bust during the Depression and the family moved to Compton, California, where his father worked as a mechanic. When the Second World War broke out in America in 1941 Coburn was a jack of all trades in a cinema: the cleaner, the janitor and the ticket collector. Then he went to Los Angeles City College where he studied acting, though with directing as much as acting in mind. In 1955 Coburn moved to Manhattan, where he found work in a Remington shaving advertisement. He studied under Stella Adler and this led to breaks off-Broadway and on television, including the live Studio One television shows. He made his film début in *Ride Lonesome* (1959) as Whit and then played Purdy in *Face Of A Fugitive*

(1959) before being cast as Britt in *The Magnificent Seven* (1960). It made a star of him and he went on to appear in *The Murder Men* (1961) as Arthur Troy, *Hell Is For Heroes* (1962) as Corporal Frank Henshaw, *The Great Escape* (1963) as Flying Officer Louis Sedgwick, *Charade* (1963) as ruthless killer Tex Panthollow, *The Man From Galveston* (1963) as Boyd Palmer, *The Americanization Of Emily* (1964) as Lieutenant Commander 'Bus' Cummings, *Major Dundee* (1965) as Samuel Potts, *A High Wind In Jamaica* (1965) as Zac, *Our Man Flint* (1966) as Derek Flint, *What Did You Do In The War, Daddy?* (1966) as Lieutenant Christian, *Dead Heat On A Merry-Go-Round* (1966) as Eli Kotch, *Duffy* (1968) as Duffy (critic Pauline Kael opined of his performance, "James Coburn the actor has disappeared, and his body is now inhabited by a dimpled, grinning star – a spastic zombie"), *Candy* (1968) as Dr Krankheit, *Hard Contract* (1969) as John Cunningham, *Last Of The Mobile Hot Shots* (1969) as Jeb, *Una Ragione Per Vivere E Una Per Morire* (1972) as Colonel Pembroke, *Pat Garrett And Billy The Kid* (1973) as Sheriff Patrick J. Garrett, *Harry In Your Pocket* (1973) as Harry, *Bite The Bullet* (1975) as Luke Matthews, *Hard Times* (1975) as Spencer 'Speed' Weed, *Sky Riders* (1976) as Jim McCabe, *Midway* (1976) as Captain Vinton Maddox, *Cross Of Iron* (1977) as Sergeant Rolf Steiner, *Goldengirl* (1979) as Jack Dryden, *Loving Couples* (1980) as Walter, *High Risk* (1981) as Serrano, *Young Guns II: Blaze Of Glory* (1990) as John Chishum, *Hudson Hawk* (1991) as George Kaplan, *Eraser* (1996) as Chief Beller, *Skeletons* (1996) as Frank Jove, *Affliction* (1997) as Glen Whitehouse (for which he won an Oscar, saying at the ceremony "I've been working and doing this work for over half my life and I finally got one right, I guess"), *Intrepid* (2000) as Captain Hal Josephson, *Proximity* (2001) as Jim

Corcoran, *Yellow Bird* (2001) as Reverend Increase Tutwiler, *Snow Dogs* (2002) as Thunder Jack Johnson and *American Gun* (2002) as Martin. In July 1973 Coburn was a pallbearer at the funeral of the actor (and his martial arts instructor) Bruce Lee. Six years later, in 1979, 6'3" Coburn began suffering from arthritis that left one hand crippled. In an interview, he said: "I couldn't stand up. It caused me such difficulty, I never wanted to get up. I'd break out in a sweat every time I tried. An actor's got to be able to move, and I couldn't. I was in agony every time I moved. Having rheumatoid arthritis practically stopped my career. Arthritis didn't affect my voice, so I did narrations, commercials, stuff like that. But I was sick most of that time." By 1999 he was telling friends that he had "healed himself" by taking sulphur-based pills. Although his knuckles remained gnarled, the pills cured him of the excruciating pain. He once said, "Actors are boring when they are not working. It's a natural condition, because they don't have anything to do. They just lay around, and that's why so many of them get drunk. They really get to be boring people. My wife will attest to that." Coburn had a long relationship with the singer Lynsey de Paul (b. Cricklewood, June 11, 1948 as Lynsey Reuben). He was married twice. In 1959 he married Beverly Kelly and helped raise her daughter, Lisa (b. 1957), a website designer. Their son, James IV (b. 1961), works as a sound mixer. The couple was divorced in 1979. On November 22, 1993, Coburn married Paula Murad. CAUSE: On the afternoon of November 18, 2002, Coburn was listening to music at his home in Beverly Hills when he suffered a heart attack. His wife, Paula, was with him. He was pronounced dead at Cedars-Sinai Medical Center in Los Angeles. Coburn and his wife had placed their five-storey home on the market the previous month for £3 million in order, they said, to spend their remaining years travelling the world.

Steve Cochran

(ROBERT ALEXANDER COCHRAN)
Born May 25, 1917
Died June 15, 1965
He-man. Born in Eureka, California, Steve Cochran, the son of a Californian lumberman, was raised in Wyoming and attended university there. A handsome, dark actor with a menacing air that he used to good effect in films, he never quite became an A-list star but his active and turbulent love life kept him busy away from the cameras. He once planned to hire six late-teen foreign domestics so "they couldn't leave me for two years and I'd always have six girls about the house." He began his career in the theatre where he worked (in the dressing room and on the stage) with Mae West before he was given a contract with Samuel Goldwyn in 1945 and made his début in *Wonder Man* (1945) as Ten-Grand Jackson (he first appeared on screen in *Hollywood Canteen* in 1943). In 1949 he signed a contract with Warner Bros that was to last until 1952. His films included *Boston Blackie's Rendezvous* (1945) as James Cook, *Boston Blackie Booked On Suspicion* (1945) as Jack Higgins, *The Kid From Brooklyn* (1946) as Speed McFarlane, *The Chase* (1946) as Eddie Roman, *The Best Years Of Our Lives* (1946) as Cliff Scully, *Copacabana* (1947) as Steve Hunt, *A Song Is Born* (1948) as Tony Crow, *White Heat* (1949) as Big Ed Somers, *The Damned Don't Cry* (1950) as Nick Prenta, *Highway 301* (1950) as George Legenza, *Dallas* (1950) as Brant Marlow, *Tomorrow Is Another Day* (1951) as Bill Clark/Mike Lewis, *Storm Warning* (1951) as Hank Rice, *Inside The Walls Of Folsom Prison* (1951) as Chuck Daniels, *Jim Thorpe – All-American* (1951) as Peter Allendine, *Raton Pass* (1951) as Cy Van Cleave, *The Tanks Are Coming* (1951) as

Francis Aloysius 'Sully' Sullivan, *Operation Secret* (1952) as Marcel Brevoort and *The Lion And The Horse* (1952) as Ben Kirby. After his contract was dropped Cochran's career seemed to falter even though he set up his own production company. In May 1953, Cochran was sued for $405,000 after he hit boxer Lenwood 'Buddy' Wright over the head with a baseball bat at a New Year's Eve party. The judge awarded Wright $16,500. That same year he refused to pull over his red Porsche in Culver City after police indicated that he should. A five-mile chase ensued and Cochran only stopped when the police fired warning shots into the air. In 1955 Cochran was arrested in Durban, South Africa. He was accused of adultery with the wife of Arthur Cecil Miller, the jockey. The charges were eventually dropped. His mid- to late-Fifties films included *She's Back On Broadway* (1953) as Rick Sommers, *Shark River* (1953) as Dan Webley, *The Desert Song* (1953) as Captain Fontaine, *Back To God's Country* (1953) as Paul Blake, *Private Hell 36* (1954) as Cal Bruner, *Carnival Story* (1954) as Joe Hammond, *Come Next Spring* (1956) as Matt Ballot, *Slander* (1956) as H.R. Manley, *The Weapon* (1957) as Mark Andrews, *Il Grido* (1957) as Aldo, *I Mobster . . . The Life Of A Gangster* (1958) as Joe Sante, *Quantrill's Raiders* (1958) as Wes, *The Big Operator* (1959) as Bill Gibson and *The Beat Generation* (1959) as Detective Sergeant Dave Culloran. In August of 1960 Cochran's boat, a 40-ft schooner, sank in Los Angeles harbour. Aboard were Cochran, two 19-year-old women, Hedy Graaberg and Nicole Mackay, two dogs and a miniature chimpanzee. All scrambled to safety. The following year he made *The Deadly Companions* (1961) playing Billy. Over the next two years he made just one film, *Of Love And Desire* (1963) in which he played Steve Corey opposite Merle Oberon. Cochran married three times: to artist Florence Lockwood

from whom he was divorced in 1946; singer Fay McKenzie (married from 1946 to 1948) and Jonna Jensen, a 23-year-old Danish-born Beverly Hills secretary, whom he married in 1961 but from whom he was estranged at the time of his death.
CAUSE: In the winter of 1964 Cochran and an all-female crew set sail in his 40-ft schooner, *The Rogue*, from San Pedro. The plan was to scout for locations for future films but the press believed that it was just a publicity stunt. The female crew disembarked in Ensenada and Cochran sailed alone to Acapulco. There he advertised for another all-female crew and hired three friends – Eugenia Bautista, 25, Eva Montero Catsellanos, 19, and Lorenza Infante de la Rose who was just 14. *The Rogue* was intercepted by the Coast Guard off Port Champerico in Guatemala on June 27, 1965 where Cochran's body was discovered apparently dead from acute infectious oedema. The three crew members, demented with thirst and heatstroke, were interviewed by the authorities and they said that Cochran had died shortly after 5am on June 15, leaving them helpless on the Pacific Ocean until the Coast Guard came upon them. In an interview given to UPI, the news agency, the women said that the boat had become caught up in a hurricane and Cochran battled for two days and two nights before he died. Cochran's body was badly decomposed when it was brought ashore. Rumours persist to this day that Cochran was murdered. He suffered from blinding headaches and fainting spells and one day awoke paralysed, unable to move anything but his head. The symptoms resembled a poisoning and when the police boarded the vessel, they suspected foul play. The coroner's verdict of a lung infection did nothing to allay the suspicions. His former co-star Merle Oberon tried to use her influence to push for further police investigations but without success. Then Cochran's estranged

third wife came forward to claim her share of what was thought to be an estate valued at $160,000. There was a shock for her when the estate totalled just $60,000, Cochran having given his 85-year-old mother $100,000 a few months before his death. Cochran's daughter by his first marriage, Xandria, from whom he was also estranged, also wanted her share of the money. In the end because a will could not be found, the estranged wife and the estranged daughter shared $25,000. Cochran is buried in Lot 4, Block 238 of Monterey Cemetery in California.

Iron Eyes Cody
(OSKIE CODY)
Born April 3, 1906
Died January 4, 1999
'The Crying Indian'. Cherokee Iron Eyes Cody was born in the Oklahoma Territory and began in movies when his father's ranch was used as a location for a Paramount movie and he ended up being hired as a technical adviser. In all he appeared in over 200 films, becoming the most famous Native American Indian actor in the world. In the Seventies his face, with a tear rolling down it, became famous as part of an ecology campaign. In the usually reliable Katz his death is reported as having occurred in 1991. His films included *Back To God's Country* (1919), *Fighting Caravans* (1931), *Oklahoma Jim* (1931), *Texas Pioneers* (1932), *Rustlers Of Red Dog* (1935), *Toll Of The Desert* (1936), *Ride, Ranger, Ride* (1936), *Custer's Last Stand* (1936) as Brown Fox, *The Riders Of The Whistling Skull* (1937), *Wild Bill Hickok* (1938), *Union Pacific* (1939), *Young Buffalo Bill* (1940), *Young Bill Hickok* (1940), *Saddlemates* (1941) as Black Eagle, *Springtime In The Rockies* (1942) as White Cloud, *Perils Of Nyoka* (1942), *King Of The Stallions* (1942), *Bowery Buckaroos* (1947) as Indian Joe, *Train To Alcatraz* (1948) as Geronimo, *Massacre River* (1949) as Chief Yellowstone, *Cherokee Uprising* (1950)

as Longknife, *Son Of Paleface* (1952) as Chief Yellow Cloud, *Heller In Pink Tights* (1960) and *Ernest Goes To Camp* (1987). He married Bertha Darkcloud known to all as Birdie (b. 1906, d. 1977) in 1924 and they had two sons: Arthur and Robert. He attempted suicide after the death of his wife. He then began a relationship with his wife's former secretary, Sandy Redhawk, at the suggestion of Birdie as she lay on her deathbed.
CAUSE: Iron Eyes Cody died of natural causes in Los Angeles, California, aged 92.
FURTHER READING: *Iron Eyes: My Life As A Hollywood Indian* – Iron Eyes Cody as told to Collin Perry (London: Frederick Muller, 1982).

Frank Coghlan, Jr
Born March 15, 1916
Died September 7, 2009
"The perfect example of a homeless waif". Born in New Haven, Connecticut, his parents moved to Los Angeles when their son was a baby and he began working in films as an extra when he was three. Using the name Junior Coghlan, he had bit parts in *The Spanish Dancer* (1923) and Charlie Chaplin's *A Woman Of Paris: A Drama Of Fate* (released October 1, 1923). Cecil B. DeMille then signed Coghlan to a five-year contract and described him as "the perfect example of a homeless waif". In the Twenties and Thirties Coghlan's all-American appeal meant he was one of the busiest of child actors. He appeared in *The Yankee Clipper* (1927), *Slide, Kelly, Slide* (1927), *The Public Enemy* (1931) and *The Last Of The Mohicans* (1932). As he got older, Coghlan was reduced to playing smaller parts before becoming Billy Batson in the 12-part *Captain Marvel* series in 1941. "I had no idea who Captain Marvel or Billy Batson were," Coghlan said, "[then] I said to myself, 'Hey, I do kind of look like that kid'." Batson became the superhero by uttering the word

"Shazam!" and a giant flash and a cloud of white smoke appeared. "Every time we did that, they ignited flash powder, which was in a trough in front of me," said Coghlan. "And if the wind was unkind, I'd get the powder flash in my face and lose some eyebrows." When the smoke cleared Batson had become the mighty Captain Marvel (played by Tom Tyler). The show was the first to bring a comic book superhero to the silver screen. Coghlan became a naval flier in the Second World War. After the conflict he remained in the navy until his retirement as a lieutenant commander in 1965. Coghlan was married three times. His first two wives predeceased him.

CAUSE: Coghlan died in his sleep in an old people's home at Saugus, California. He was 93.

Herman Cohen

Born August 27, 1925
Died June 2, 2002

Schlockmeister. Born in Detroit, Michigan, he attended Central High School. Cohen's film career began when he was 12 and he got a job as the assistant to a janitor in a local cinema. He was paid in free tickets. After serving in the military, he joined the publicity department of Columbia Pictures. His first on-screen credit came with *Bride Of The Gorilla* (1951) where he was assistant producer. He was associate producer of *Bela Lugosi Meets A Brooklyn Gorilla* (1952), in which Bela Lugosi meets a gorilla from Brooklyn. His big break came in 1957 with *I Was A Teenage Werewolf*, a drive-in film that cost less than $100,000 and was savaged by the critics for its tacky props, ham acting and corny lines. But it became a surprise hit, taking more than $2 million at the box office. It starred Michael Landon as a troubled teen, Tony Rivers, who turns to a hypnotherapist (Whit Bissell) to cure his aggression. Instead, the evil doctor gives him an experimental potion that

turns him into a werewolf. The appearance of the werewolf – a furry beast with claws and fangs, dressed in jacket and jeans, became an icon of the teen horror genre. Cohen was warned that the movie would destroy his reputation but he ignored the naysayers and even made an uncredited cameo appearance in the manner of Alfred Hitchcock. The film was later re-released as "starring Michael Landon, star of *Bonanza*". Cohen went on to make a series of similar pictures, most of which featured teenagers being turned into monsters by adults. They included the double billed *I Was A Teenage Frankenstein* (1957) and *Blood Of Dracula* (1957) (which offered free smelling salts to patrons and advised not to eat before seeing the film). In 1959 Cohen moved to England where he made a series of grisly films about the sadistic excesses of serial killers. In one of the genre, *Horrors Of The Black Museum* (1959), a crime writer orchestrates a series of gruesome murders using devices such as a pair of binoculars which jab spikes into the user's eyes. Cohen began to work with the ageing and temperamental Joan Crawford to make *Berserk!* (1968), in which she plays a ringmaster in a circus where the performers are murdered one by one, and *Trog* (1970), Crawford's 81st and last movie, in which she is a female scientist who tries to train a man-ape discovered down a pothole. In both films Cohen begged Crawford not to drink in the mornings before shooting, ignoring her protestations that she was just "a little sipper". Crawford insisted on providing her own unsuitably abbreviated wardrobe. "Save your money, Herm," she told him. "I've been hustling clothes all my life." After *Craze* (1973), a comic horror starring Jack Palance, Trevor Howard and Diana Dors, Cohen retired from producing and formed a film distribution company. He never married.

CAUSE: Cohen died aged 76 of throat

cancer at Cedars-Sinai Medical Center in Los Angeles, California. He was buried in Clover Hill Park Cemetery, 3607 West 14 Mile, Royal Oak, Detroit.

Harry Cohn

Born July 23, 1891
Died February 27, 1958
Hollywood's most loathed mogul. The second son of a German immigrant tailor, 5'10" Harry Cohn was born in New York, New York. He became a pool hustler, a fur salesman and then a record plugger before landing a job as Carl Laemmle's secretary in 1918. With brother Jacob, known as Jack (b. New York, New York, October 27, 1889, d. 1956 of an embolism) and Joseph Brandt he went on to found CBC Film Sales Company (nicknamed 'Corned Beef and Cabbage') which, on January 10, 1924, became Columbia Pictures Corporation, where he created a régime of despotic autocracy. He would brandish a riding crop and bang it down on his desk to intimidate underlings. The company offices were on Sunset Boulevard, an area known as 'Poverty Row'. However, Cohn steered Columbia through the advent of talkies, the Great Depression and the coming of television. Cohn was generally despised by the Hollywood community. Gossip columnist Hedda Hopper stated: "You had to stand in line to hate him." Screenwriter Ben Hecht nicknamed him 'White Fang'. He modelled his office on that of Mussolini, whom he admired for making the trains run on time; a framed photograph of *Il Duce* sat on his desk. Cohn could rarely speak a sentence without a cuss-word and spied on his employees using informers and hidden microphones. However, he spared no expense to cultivate and promote the careers of his favourites, including Rita Hayworth (who annoyed him by constantly getting married, which eroded her box-office appeal) and Kim Novak. He revelled in his notoriety ("I don't get ulcers, I give

them") and his charitable acts were kept a closely guarded secret. He liked to sack people – usually on Christmas Eve. For some time there developed a power struggle to be the head of the company between Cohn and his brother which came to a head in 1932 when Jack successfully foiled his brother's attempt to topple him and consolidated his power base. The megalomaniac studio boss in the Robert Aldrich film *The Big Knife* (1955) was supposedly based on Cohn. He had a unique way of judging films: "By the itch of my ass." Cohn would watch a film until he started to squirm in his seat and that was when he knew it was going wrong. No squirming, it was a hit. And it seemed to work for him. Among the films he produced were *Only A Shop Girl* (1922), *Yesterday's Wife* (1923), *Innocence* (1923), *Discontented Husbands* (1924), *When Husbands Flirt* (1925), *Birds Of Prey* (1927), *Sally In Our Alley* (1927), *Stage Kisses* (1927), *Lady Raffles* (1928), *Broadway Daddies* (1928), *Ransom* (1928), *Beware Of Blondes* (1928), *Virgin Lips* (1928), *Sinner's Parade* (1928), *Trial Marriage* (1929), *Broadway Scandals* (1929), *Acquitted* (1929), *Wall Street* (1929), *Murder On The Roof* (1930), *Personality* (1930), *Vengeance* (1930), *Guilty?* (1930), *Sisters* (1930), *Ladies Must Play* (1930), *Madonna Of The Streets* (1930), *Platinum Blonde* (1931), *Forbidden* (1932) and *It Happened One Night* (1934). He married twice. His first wife was actress Rose Barker, whom he married on September 18, 1923, and then divorced on July 28, 1941. His second wife was former actress Joan Perry (b. Pensacola, Florida July 7, 1911, as Elizabeth Miller, d. Montecito, California, September 16, 1996, from emphysema) whom he wedded in a room of the St Regis Hotel in New York City on July 31, 1941. Their daughter, Jobella, died 30 minutes after her birth in 1943. Cohn was not charged by the doctor, who said it was not his custom to issue an invoice in circumstances where he was powerless to save a baby. Cohn asked him why his daughter had died and was told that not enough research had been done into infant mortality for an accurate answer. The very next day Cohn sent the doctor a cheque for $100,000 to fund research. Cohn went on to have two sons: John Perry, b. April 18, 1945, at 5.45am (at the studio Cohn opened a bottle of 100-year-old brandy and offered a small glass to a dozen of his top executives. One proposed a toast to the new baby "May he be just like his father" at which Cohn knocked the glass out of the man's hand. "Don't ever say that!" he raged, "I want my son to have friends") and Harrison Perry b. 1946 (who later changed his name to Harry Cohn, Jr); and an adopted daughter, Catherine Perry. Joan Perry Cohn went on to marry actor Laurence Harvey on October 17, 1968, and divorced him in 1972. CAUSE: He died in Phoenix, Arizona, of a heart attack, aged 66. As was his custom he was staying at the Biltmore Hotel when he fell ill. He was placed in an ambulance and driven to St Joseph's Hospital but died a block away. Mrs Cohn told a priest that in his dying moments Cohn had called out the name of Jesus Christ. The priest told Mrs Cohn that, for this reason, her husband should be baptised a Christian and this was duly done. His funeral, on March 2, 1958, was non-denominational and no reference was made to the fact that Cohn was Jewish. It was held on a Sunday (to allow attendance and so as not to disrupt studio filming) and was one of the most well-attended funerals in Hollywood history prompting Red Skelton to comment, "Well, it proves what they always say: give the people what they want to see and they'll come out for it." In his will, written on St Valentine's Day 1957, Cohn had ordered that no funeral service take place. Columbia executives persuaded Mrs Cohn to ignore her husband's wish. He was buried in Hollywood Memorial Park, 6000 Santa Monica Boulevard, Hollywood, California 90038 because, "It's right by the water and I can see the studio from it." FURTHER READING: *King Cohn* – Bob Thomas (London: Barrie & Rockliffe, 1967).

Claudette Colbert

(LILY CLAUDETTE CHAUCHOIN)
Born September 13, 1903
Died July 30, 1996
'The Fretting Frog'. Arriving in New York from her native Paris when still a child, the 5'4½" Colbert had dreams of becoming a fashion designer and then a successful Broadway actress. Leaving school she enrolled in The Art Students' League and worked in a dress shop to pay her fees and living expenses. She finally got to Broadway in 1923, appearing in *The Wild Westcotts* and adopting the stage name Claudette Colbert. She played leading roles on the Great White Way for two years from 1925 until deciding she wanted to give films a try. Her first feature, Frank Capra's *For The Love Of Mike* (1927), was a disaster. When the Great Depression forced the closure of many theatres, she became stuck with working in films, much to her initial dismay. *The Lady Lies* (1929) and *The Hole In The Wall* (1929) were more successful. Her appearance with Frederic March in *Manslaughter* (1930) was the first in which her star was obviously beginning to rise. However, it was when Colbert began appearing in talkies, such as Cecil B. DeMille's *The Sign Of The Cross* (1932) as Poppaea, and appeared taking a bath in asses' milk in *Cleopatra* (1934) that she really shone. She won her only Oscar for the part of Ellie Andrews in Frank Capra's *It Happened One Night* (1934). Legend has it that Colbert was convinced she wouldn't win and she decided to get away from Hollywood on the night of

the ceremony, only to be rushed back on the pillion of a motorbike to accept the prize wearing a brown felt hat and her travelling clothes. The following year she was again nominated, for *Private Worlds* (1935) as psychiatrist Dr Jane Everest. She also appeared in *I Cover The Waterfront* (1933) as Julie Kirk, *Four Frightened People* (1934) as Judy Cavendish, *She Married Her Boss* (1935) as Julia Scott, *I Met Him In Paris* (1937) as Kay Denham, *Maid Of Salem* (1937) as Barbara Clarke, *Midnight* (1939) as Eve Peabody, *Skylark* (1941) as Lydia Kenyon, *No Time For Love* (1943) as Katherine Grant and *Since You Went Away* (1944) as Anne Hilton, for which she was nominated for her third Academy Award. Although she didn't retire until 1992 Colbert's last major movie hit came with *The Egg And I* (1947) in which she played Betty MacDonald, a sophisticated New Yorker who married a chicken farmer. "Part of ageing gracefully is acceptance of the prominence of youth in our profession. In my final picture *Parrish*, I shared the screen with Troy Donahue and Connie Stevens and so on . . . I've never objected to youth, but I'm less happy about untalented actors and salacious story-lines." Convinced the right side of her face left a lot to be desired, she insisted she was only ever photographed from the left side, going so far as, so legend has it, putting green paint on the right side so the cameraman couldn't film it. She was aware of what was required to be a star in Hollywood, once commenting: "The casting couch? There was only one of us ever made it to stardom without it – that was Bette Davis." Twice married, she first walked up the aisle with actor-director Norman Foster (b. Richmond, Indiana, December 13, 1900, as Norman Hoeffer, d. 1976) in 1928, divorcing him on August 30, 1935. (He went on to marry Sally Blane.) Bizarrely, they never lived together. Four months later, on Christmas Eve, she married Dr Joel Pressman in Yuma, Arizona. They were together until his death from cancer in Los Angeles on February 26, 1968. In fact, 'together' is something of an exaggeration. Colbert claimed they stayed married because each maintained a separate residence. This gave her free rein to live a bisexual lifestyle which she did, having affairs with, among others, Marlene Dietrich. *The New York Times* in its obituary stated: "She could appear worldly and sophisticated yet down to earth, and this quality, combined with acute attention to camera angles, lighting and other professional details, helped her to sustain a remarkably durable career that encompassed more than 60 films and many stage appearances."
CAUSE: She died in Cobblers Cove, Barbados, aged 92, of natural causes.

Barbara Colby
Born July 2, 1940
Died July 24, 1975
A riddle. Colby was the ex-daughter-in-law of Ethel Merman and had only bit parts in films such as *California Split* (1974) but appeared on television including: *Columbo: Murder By The Book* (1971) as Lily LaSanka, *The Mary Tyler Moore Show* (1970) and an early appearance in *Gunsmoke*. She also appeared on stage.
CAUSE: She was leaving her yoga class in Los Angeles when she was shot by two men. At the time she was appearing in the play *Murderous Angels*, the plot of which concerns someone who is murdered for revenge.

Jack Cole
(JOHN EWING RICHTER)
Born April 27, 1911
Died February 17, 1974
Choreographer *par excellence*. Born New Brunswick, New Jersey, Cole's professional career began with Ted Shawn and Ruth St Denis's Denishawn modern dance ensemble but he disagreed with their pseudo-Orientalism

and studied India's bharata natyam instead. He developed a nightclub act, which fused Indian dance and jazz. Cole was a weird looking man with high cheekbones and one lopsided eye and he dressed like an Indian swami. He moaned at customers who chatted while he was on stage and once wearing just harem pants, chased an unfortunate patron down the street, a knife in his hand. It was only a matter of time before Hollywood came calling and Cole and his dancers first appeared in *Moon Over Miami* (1941). Rita Hayworth at Columbia Pictures championed his work as did Betty Grable at Fox. Cole worked with most of the sex symbols of the Fifties: Hayworth, Grable, Lauren Bacall, Mitzi Gaynor, Ann Miller, Jane Russell, Lana Turner, and the biggest of them all, Marilyn Monroe. He first worked with Monroe on *Gentlemen Prefer Blondes* (released July 15, 1953). She wore a form-fitting fuchsia evening gown for one number which designer Travilla lined with felt to ensure Marilyn's body had a fluidity to its movement. Under the felt, Monroe went commando as she so often did. Remembered co-star Jane Russell, "Marilyn and I had never danced before; we were a pair of klutzes. Jack was horrible to his own dancers, but with us, the two broads, he had the patience of Job. He would show us and show us and then turn us over to Gwen [Verdon, Cole's protégée who became a star in her own right]." Cole and Monroe worked together on *River Of No Return* (released April 30, 1954), *There's No Business Like Show Business* (released December 16, 1954), *Bus Stop* (released August 31, 1956), *Some Like It Hot* (released March 29, 1959) and *Let's Make Love* (released September 8, 1960). His other films included: *Kismet* (1944), *Tonight And Every Night* (1945), *Gilda* (1946), *The Jolson Story* (1946), *Down To Earth* (1947), *On The Riviera* (1951), *David And Bathsheba* (1951), *Meet Me After*

The Show (1951) *The Farmer Takes A Wife* (1953), *Kismet* (1955), *Gentlemen Marry Brunettes* (1955) and *Les Girls* (1957). Cole did not suffer fools gladly in the studio; he swore at dancers, dragged one girl across the floor by her hair and threatened to throw another out a second-story window. When one dancer fainted during a particularly brutal rehearsal the others stepped over her body, so afraid were they to stop. CAUSE: Cole died from cancer at Hollywood, California aged 62.

Charlotte Coleman
Born April 3, 1968
Died November 14, 2001
Eccentric talent. Charlotte Ninon Coleman was born in London, the elder daughter of the producer-director Francis Coleman and the actress Ann Beach (b. Wolverhampton, Staffordshire, June 7, 1938). Sister Lisa Coleman (b. Charing Cross, London, 10 July, 1970) is also an actress and former nude model. Charlotte was educated at St Michael's Primary School, Highgate, and Camden School for Girls – from where she was expelled – and also attended the Anna Scher Children's Theatre in Islington. Something of a wild child, she told one interviewer, "I graffitied the house, I was smoking at 12, had boyfriends at 13, lost my virginity early, had my nose pierced at 14, shaved my head completely and then had a bluebird tattooed on my bottom when I was 15." She left her family's home in Muswell Hill, north London, at 14 to live with a friend. Charlotte Coleman's break came playing Sue Peters in the children's television series *Worzel Gummidge* (1979) and then played the lead role, Marmalade Atkins, in *Educating Marmalade* (1981). Coleman paid for her own education at the extremely liberal school, Dartington Hall in Devon, from the money she earned from Marmalade Atkins. She made her film début in *Bearskin: An Urban Fairytale* (1989) and played Ros

in *Sweet Nothing* (1990). Her next television role was the controversial lesbian drama *Oranges Are Not The Only Fruit* (1990) in which she played Jess and romped naked with Cathryn Bradshaw. She found her lesbian scenes too embarrassing to watch at screenings, but she won the Royal Television Society's 1991 Best Performance Award for a Scripted Fictional Performance and was nominated for a BAFTA Best Actress award. Another television series, *Freddie And Max* (1990), followed in which Coleman starred with Anne Bancroft. She was in *Map Of The Human Heart* (1992) as Julie and then co-starred in the film that was to rejuvenate the British cinema and make Hugh Grant a star. Richard Curtis' *Four Weddings And A Funeral* (1994) was the most successful British film in many a long year. Coleman won a BAFTA nomination for Best Supporting Actress for her role as Scarlet, Hugh Grant's chaotic and eccentric flatmate. She returned to a lesbian role in the television drama *Giving Tongue* (1996), as the former teenage girlfriend of a campaigning anti-blood sports Labour MP (played by Clare Holman). "I've kissed more women than men on set," she said, "and I'm heterosexual." She also appeared in *The Young Poisoner's Handbook* (1995), as the sister of the real-life mass poisoner Graham Young, *Different For Girls* (1996) as an editorial assistant trying to get her transsexual boss sacked, *The Revengers' Comedies* (1998) as Norma, *The Man With Rain In His Shoes* (1998) as Alison Hayes, *Shark Hunt* (1998), *Beautiful People* (1999) as Portia Thornton, *Bodywork* (1999) as Tiffany Shades and *A Loving Act* (2001) as Police Detective Jane Thompson. She relaxed by driving, riding, knitting and playing snooker. Charlotte Coleman was unmarried. CAUSE: She died aged 33 after an asthma attack in Holloway, north London.

Ronald Colman

Born February 9, 1891
Died May 19, 1958

The personification of the English gentleman. Ronald Charles Colman was born in Richmond, Surrey, the second son of a silk importer. A bright child, his parents intended him to go to Oxford University, although at school he took part in amateur theatre. His world collapsed in 1907 with the death of his father from pneumonia. Shortly thereafter he became an office boy in a shipping company. In his spare time he appeared in amateur dramatics with the Bancroft Amateur Dramatic Society. In 1909 he joined the territorial army and served in the London Scottish Regional Guards. At the outbreak of hostilities in 1914 his regiment was sent to the front and Colman took part in action in Ypres and was wounded in Messines. His bravery was rewarded with a medal but he was sufficiently sick to be sent home in May 1915. His service left him with a limp and he spent much time and considerable effort hiding his infirmity from everyone. At home he discussed his future with various relatives and considered a career in the diplomatic corps but while he was making his mind up he was given a part in a play. For a role in Sir Rabindranath Tagore's 1916 work *The Maharani Of Arakam* he had no lines and was blacked up. Still, it was a start. On March 17, 1917, he opened in *Damaged Goods* at the St James's Theatre. He played a husband infected with syphilis. Despite its daring subject matter, the play was a hit and only closed when the Germans repeatedly bombed the area. In 1919 he made his first film, *The Toilers* (1919) playing Bob. However, it wasn't a success (a casting card said he did not screen well) nor were his subsequent films: *Snow In The Desert* (1919) as Rupert Sylvester, *Sheba* (1919), *A Daughter Of Eve* (1919), *A Son Of David* (1920) as Maurice Phillips, *Anna The Adventuress* (1920) as Brendan and *Handcuffs Or*

Kisses (1921) as Lodyard. Meanwhile, on September 18, 1920, in London's Hanover Square Registry Office, he married his live-in actress girlfriend Thelma Victoria Raye. Deciding to give America a try, he sailed for Broadway and arrived with "$37, three clean collars and two letters of introduction" but found work hard to come by, living on "dish-washing jobs and a diet of soup and rice pudding". His big break came not on stage but in the cinema when he was offered the role of Captain Giovanni Severini, Lillian Gish's lover, in *The White Sister* (1923). The movie, shot on location in Italy, was not a happy experience for Thelma Colman. She had difficulty in coping with a husband who was public property and they separated. (They were divorced in 1935.) *The White Sister* was a massive hit and its success prompted Samuel Goldwyn to offer 5'11" Colman a contract. His first starring feature was *The Dark Angel* (1925) as a blinded soldier, Captain Alan Trent, opposite Vilma Bánky and he also appeared in *Stella Dallas* (1925) as Stephen Dallas, a silent (!) version of Oscar Wilde's *Lady Windermere's Fan* (1925) as Lord Darlington and the Foreign Legion adventure *Beau Geste* (1926) as Michael 'Beau' Geste. Colman made the transition to sound movies easily. His first was *Bulldog Drummond* (1929) as Hugh 'Bulldog' Drummond, which won him an Oscar nomination for Best Actor. His other films included: *Condemned* (1929) as Michel (another Oscar nod), *The Devil To Pay!* (1930) as Willie Leyland, *Raffles* (1930) as A.J. Raffles, *Arrowsmith* (1931) as Doctor Martin Arrowsmith, *Bulldog Drummond Strikes Back* (1934) as Captain Hugh 'Bulldog' Drummond, *The Man Who Broke The Bank At Monte Carlo* (1935) as Paul Gaillard, *Clive Of India* (1935) as Robert Clive, *A Tale Of Two Cities* (1935) as Sydney Carton, *Lost Horizon* (1937) as Robert Conway, *The Prisoner Of Zenda* (1937) as Rudolph

Rassendyll/King Rudolf V, *If I Were King* (1938) as François Villon, *Random Harvest* (1942) as Charles Rainer/John 'Smithy' Smith (and his third Best Actor Oscar nomination), *Kismet* (1944) as Hafiz and a cameo role in *Around The World In 80 Days* (1956). He won a Best Actor Oscar for playing Anthony John in *A Double Life* (1947). Nine years earlier, on September 30, 1938, at his San Ysidro Ranch home, he had married Benita Hume. They had one daughter, Juliet Benita (b. July 1944), who wrote her father's biography.
CAUSE: He died in Santa Barbara, California, aged 67 from a lung infection. He left £10,436 1s 7d.

Kenneth Connor, MBE
Born June 6, 1916
Died November 28, 1993
Carry On stalwart. Born in London. Connor made his stage début aged two in a charity show put on by his sailor father. He took drama lessons and in 1933 was accepted at the Central School Of Speech & Drama. His film début came in 1939 but it is for the 17 *Carry On*s he made between 1958 and 1978 that he is best remembered by cinema audiences. He began as national serviceman Horace Strong in *Carry On Sergeant* (1958) and continued through PC Constable in *Carry On Constable* (1960), Sam Twist in *Carry On Regardless* (1960), the cowardly Hengist Pod in *Carry On Cleo* (1964), Lord Hampton of Wick in *Carry On Henry* (1971), Mayor Frederick Bumble in *Carry On Girls* (1973), Major Leep in *Carry On Behind* (1975), the officious Captain S. Melly in *Carry On England* (1976) and the final *Carry On Emmannuelle* (1978) in which he played the chauffeur Leyland. In his later years he appeared as Monsieur Alphonse, the undertaker with 'the dicky ticker', in the BBC sitcom *Allo Allo*.
CAUSE: He died aged 77 of cancer at his home in Harrow-on-the-Hill, Middlesex.

Mabel Constanduros
(MABEL TILLING)
Born March 29, 1880
Died February 8, 1957
Cockney comedienne. Mabel
Constanduros was born in Devonshire
House, Peckham Road, Camberwell,
south London, one of seven children of
Richard Stephen Tilling, managing
director of Thomas Tilling & Son, a
bus company, and Sophie Thorn. After
school Mabel became her father's
private secretary. In 1910 she became
involved in the local amdram society
and then studied at the Central School
of Speech Training. On March 23,
1925 she made her first broadcast on
BBC wireless. On September 1, 1925
the Buggins family, which she created,
made their initial appearance on the
radio in *The Buggins Family Out For A
Day*. She appeared in more than 250
Buggins shows in which she played all
six speaking parts: Grandma Buggins,
Mrs Buggins, her three children
(Emma, Alfie, and Baby Buggins), and
Aunt Maria. The show was so popular
that the Ministry of Food even used
Mrs Buggins to broadcast recipes
during the Second World War. The last
episode aired in 1948. Despite the
show's undoubted success she always
believed that she was underpaid. She
made her film début in *Ag And Bert*
(1929) playing Aggie Buggins and went
on to appear in *Radio Parade* (1933),
Hope Of His Side (1935) as Mrs
Scodger, *Salute John Citizen* (1942) as
Mrs Bunting, *Rose Of Tralee* (1942) as
Mrs Thompson, *Medal For The General*
(1944) as Mrs Bates, *My Ain Folk*
(1945) as Mrs Mackenzie and *Easy
Money* (1948) as Grandma Stafford.
She also wrote more than 100 plays on
her own and many more in
collaboration with others. In the early
years of the twentieth century she
married Athanasius Constanduros
(d. 1937), an insurance broker. They
had three children, of whom only a
son, Michael, survived into adulthood.
It was not a happy marriage and in her
autobiography, *Shreds And Patches*, she
rarely mentions her husband and never
favourably.
CAUSE: Mabel Constanduros died of a
heart attack in the Royal West Sussex
Hospital, Chichester. She was 76. She
left £12,168.

Richard Conte
Born March 24, 1910
Died April 15, 1975
The cynical type. Born in Jersey City,
New Jersey, the son of a barber,
Richard Nicholas Peter Conte did the
usual rounds of tedious jobs before
heading for show business, landing a
job as a performing waiter. He was
spotted by Elia Kazan who sent him to
the Neighborhood Playhouse in New
York. Conte never looked back and
appeared in *Heaven With A Barbed
Wire Fence* (1939) as Tony,
Guadalcanal Diary (1943) as Captain
Davis, *Captain Eddie* (1945) as Private
Bartek, *13 Rue Madeleine* (1946) as Bill
H. O'Connell, *Call Northside 777*
(1948) as convicted murderer Frank
Wiecek, *Cry Of The City* (1948) as
wounded hoodlum Martin Rome,
House Of Strangers (1949) as Max
Monetti, *Under The Gun* (1950) as Bert
Galvin, *Hollywood Story* (1951) as
Larry O'Brien, *New York Confidential*
(1955) as Nick Magellan, *Little Red
Monkey* (1955) as Bill Locklin, *Full Of
Life* (1956) as Nick Rocco, *Ocean's
Eleven* (1960) as Anthony Bergdorf,
The Greatest Story Ever Told (1965) as
Barabbas, *Operation Cross Eagles* (1969)
as Lieutenant Bradford, *The Godfather*
(1972) as Emilio Barzini, *Anastasia Mio
Fratello* (1973) as the head of Murder,
Inc. Alberto Anastasia, *Eroticofollia*
(1974) and *Roma Violenta* (1975).
CAUSE: He died of a heart attack in Los
Angeles, California, aged 65. He was
buried in Westwood Memorial
Cemetery under a stone bearing
his name, dates and the legend
"Actor–Writer–Painter–Composer–
Poet".

Jackie Coogan

Born October 26, 1914
Died March 1, 1984

'The Kid'. John Leslie Coogan was born in Los Angeles, California. Both parents worked in vaudeville and it seemed only logical that Jackie should step into their shoes. They could not have realised what a massive impact he would make in the Charlie Chaplin movie *The Kid* (1921) in which Jackie played the title role. He became an immense world-wide celebrity and had his every cough and spit reported in the press. However, his parents kept a tight grip on the young star's money, placing it in trust for him. He was offered $1 million plus a percentage of profits for two years and given a $500,000 signing-on fee when he joined Metro from First National. By contrast, his parents allowed him $6.25 pocket money each week. Coogan appeared in *Trouble* (1922) as Danny, the lead in *Oliver Twist* (1922), *Circus Days* (1923) as Toby Tyler, *Long Live The King* (1923) as Crown Prince Otto, *Little Robinson Crusoe* (1924) as Mickey Hogan, *Johnny Get Your Hair Cut* (1927) as Johnny O'Day (unbelievably, a film that featured his hair before and after his famous bob was cut) and his last film as a child star *Buttons* (1927) as Buttons. As many child actors have found to their cost, when age and puberty kick in the audience loses interest, and such was the case with Coogan. He attempted a comeback playing Mark Twain's ragamuffin hero Tom Sawyer in two films, *Tom Sawyer* (1930) and *Huckleberry Finn* (1931), but his ship had, it seemed, sailed. However, Coogan still had his inheritance to look forward to, which was due in 1935. That year his father and another child star, Junior Durkin, were killed in a car crash. Coogan's mother and her new husband seemed reluctant to hand over the money and so, on April 11, 1938, Coogan sued them. He had married Betty Grable at St Brendan's Catholic Church, Los Angeles, on November 20, 1937 and was unable to provide for the new Mrs C. However, by the time the case was eventually settled, out of the $4 million that he was expecting only $252,000 remained, of which Coogan received approximately half. One good thing to come out of the fiasco was the passing of the Coogan Act to prevent parents or anyone else ripping off prodigious children. The case had put a strain on Coogan's marriage to Grable and on October 11, 1939, they were divorced. Money was one of the major factors in the split. During World War II Coogan served in the air force and was the first glider pilot to fly behind enemy lines and land allowing soldiers to fight. After the war he began making films once more but was confined to playing unpleasant characters. His work, some of it dross, includes: *Kilroy Was Here* (1947) as Pappy Collins, *French Leave* (1948) as Pappy, *Skipalong Rosenbloom* (1951) as Buck James, *Outlaw Women* (1952) as Piute Bill, *The Joker Is Wild* (1957) as Swifty Morgan, *The Buster Keaton Story* (1957) as Elmer Case, *High School Confidential!* (1958) as Mr A, *Night Of The Quarter Moon* (1959), *Lonelyhearts* (1959) as Ned Gates, *Sex Kittens Go To College* (1960) as Wildcat MacPherson, *When The Girls Take Over* (1962) as Captain Toussaint, *Girl Happy* (1965) as Sergeant Benson, *Manchu Eagle Murder Caper Mystery* (1973) as Detective Anderson and *Won Ton Ton, The Dog Who Saved Hollywood* (1976). In 1964 he landed the role of Uncle Fester on the TV show *The Addams Family* and later said that it was his favourite part. Following his divorce from Betty Grable, he married three more times. He wedded actress Flower Parry in Gardnerville, Nevada, on August 10, 1941 (divorced June 29, 1943), and had one son, Anthony (b. Los Angeles, March 4, 1942). Actress Ann McCormick became his third wife in Los Angeles on December 26, 1946 (divorced September 20, 1951) and the couple had one daughter, Joan (b. Los Angeles, April 2, 1948). His final marriage was to dancer Dorothea Lamphere in April 1952. The Coogans kept the marriage secret until July 1953. They had a daughter, Leslie (b. 1953), and a son, Christopher (b. July 9, 1967).

CAUSE: In February 1984 Coogan travelled to Malibu to stay with his daughter, Leslie. At the beginning of March he suffered a heart attack around 10am and was rushed to Santa Monica Medical Center, 1225 15th Street, Santa Monica, where he succumbed at 1.37pm. He was 69 and had been suffering from arteriosclerotic heart disease for 20 years and hypertensive cardiovascular disease for 25 years. He was buried in Grave 47, Tier 56 of Section F of Holy Cross Cemetery & Mausoleum, 5835 West Slauson Avenue, Culver City, California 90230.

Pat Coombs

Born August 27, 1926
Died May 25, 2002

Bird-like spinster. Patricia Doreen 'Pattie' Coombs was born in Camberwell, London ("I'm a real Cockney," she said, "born within the sound of Bow Bells"); her father worked for Employers' Liability, the forerunner of Commercial Union and Pattie was educated at the County School for Girls in Beckenham, Kent, from where she became a kindergarten teacher for three years, lacking the confidence to do anything positive about her acting ambitions.
Encouraged by Harold Pinter's first wife, the actress Vivien Merchant, Coombs eventually went to the London Academy of Music and Dramatic Arts. She was best known as a foil to innumerable comedians such as Dick Emery, Bob Monkhouse, Eric Barker, Eric Sykes, Tony Hancock, Terry Scott, Marty Feldman, Roy Hudd, Irene Handl, Reg Varney, Stephen Lewis, Charlie Chester,

Arthur Askey and many more. Beginning her career on radio Coombs first came to public notice as Nola Pervis, the dim-witted daughter of Irene Handl in Arthur Askey's *Hello, Playmates* (1954–55). Her first film role was as a simpering girl with Norman Wisdom, Hattie Jacques and John Le Mesurier in *Follow A Star* (1959). She also played Henrietta Salt in the film version of Roald Dahl's *Willy Wonka And The Chocolate Factory* (1971). Pat Coombs also appeared in *Carry On Doctor* (1968), *Carry On Again, Doctor* (1969), *On The Buses* (1971), and Spike Milligan's *Adolf Hitler: My Part In His Downfall* (1972) playing his mother. She appeared with Dick Emery in the 1972 film *Ooh! . . . You Are Awful* and with her old friend Peggy Mount in the television show *Lollipop Loves Mr Mole* (October 25–November 29, 1971), later known as *Lollipop* and created by Jimmy Perry. The two of them also appeared together in the sitcom *You're Only Young Twice* (September 6, 1977–August 11, 1981) which was set in an old people's home, Paradise Lodge. "I never wanted to play St Joan or any of those serious parts," she once said. "I was never a leading lady; the only talent I had was for mimicry and doing funny voices." Pat Coombs never married, living with her parents until her late forties. "I've never been wildly ambitious; I think if I'd been married, my career would have gone out of the window. I've had affairs," she once confessed, "but not with actors – with sailors."

CAUSE: A heavy smoker throughout her life, Coombs had osteoporosis diagnosed in 1995. Pat Coombs died after complications from emphysema in Denville Hall in Northwood, west London, aged 75.

Gary Cooper

(FRANK JAMES COOPER)
Born May 7, 1901
Died May 14, 1961
Cooper the All-American Man.

Slow-talking, shy, awkward and seemingly gauche. Despite these setbacks Gary Cooper became one of Hollywood's best-loved actors and most successful ladies' men. Cooper was born in Helena, Montana. His parents were English. His father Charles H. (b. Bedfordshire, 1866, d. 1946) was a lawyer who went on to become a Montana State Supreme Court judge; Cooper's mother was Alice Brazier (b. Gillingham 1873, d. California Convalescent Hospital, 1966). The Coopers sent their son to Dunstable, an English public school, where he was teased. Many believe this is where his shyness originated. In 1920 he went up to Wesleyan College, Bozeman, Montana and, following a car crash that resulted in a broken hip and his famous walk, he transferred to Grinnell College in Iowa where he studied agriculture. Among his early jobs were photographing babies, serving as a guide in Yellowstone Park and selling adverts on theatre curtains. Cooper showed a flair for art but when he found himself unable to make a living from it, he began working as an extra in films. When he learned the rates of pay for the lead stars he decided to become an actor, eventually appearing in over 100 films. He changed his name to Gary at the suggestion of his agent, Nan Collins. It came from the Indiana town that was her home town, and later home to the Jackson Five. Cooper's first major part came as Abe Lee in *The Winning Of Barbara Worth* (1926). The film was poorly received but Cooper impressed enough for Paramount Pictures to offer him a contract. He appeared in *It* (1927) which starred his lover Clara Bow, but it was his brief appearance (127 seconds) in *Wings* (1927) as Cadet White, a pilot who realised he was going to die, that made him a star. He began playing bigger and bigger roles in films such as *Beau Sabreur* (1928) as Major Henri De Beaujolais (a sequel to *Beau Geste*. In 1939 he starred as Beau Geste, making him perhaps the only actor to have starred in a sequel and then a remake), *The First Kiss* (1928) as Mulligan Talbot, *Lilac Time* (1928) as Captain Philip Blythe and *The Virginian* (1929), which consolidated the image of Cooper as a cowboy even though less than one-quarter of his films were Westerns. Cooper's performance as Lieutenant Frederick Henry in Ernest Hemingway's *A Farewell To Arms* (1932) impressed so much that the author personally insisted on Cooper for the part of Robert Jordan in his *For Whom The Bell Tolls* (1943). On December 15, 1933, Cooper married Veronica Balfe, known to all as 'Rocky', at her mother's home in Park Avenue, New York. They had one daughter, Maria (b. Los Angeles, September 15, 1937). In the mid- to late Thirties Cooper began showing he could play subtle comedy and light roles as well as the rough and tumble cowboy stuff. He impressed in *Mr Deeds Goes To Town* (1936) as Longfellow Deeds and *Meet John Doe* (1941) in the title part. However, he didn't always show sound judgment. "*Gone With The Wind* is going to be the biggest flop in Hollywood history. I'm just glad it'll be Clark Gable who's falling flat on his face and not me," he once commented. However, he could still cut the mustard with adventure films such as *Beau Geste* (1939) as Michael 'Beau' Geste, *North West Mounted Police* (1940) as Dusty Rivers, *Sergeant York* (1941) as Alvin C. York (which won him an Oscar as Best Actor), *The Pride Of The Yankees* (1942) as tragic baseball legend Lou Gehrig, *Saratoga Trunk* (1945) as Colonel Clint Maroon and *Distant Drums* (1951) as Captain Quincy Wyatt. In the Forties 6'2" Cooper was used as a political tool to oppose anything and everything left-wing. He was politically naïve. In 1944 he was persuaded by Cecil B. DeMille and Hedda Hopper to oppose the re-election of President Franklin D. Roosevelt (1882–1945). Cooper commented publically that he didn't "like the company he's keeping", presumably a reference to FDR's Jewish advisers. At a congressional hearing on October 23, 1947 (shortly after being named Least Co-operative Star by the Hollywood Women's Press Association), he showed his ignorance of Karl Marx by stating: "From what I hear about communism, I er, don't like it because, er, it isn't, er, on the level." Of Arthur Miller's *Death Of A Salesman* he said, "Sure there are fellows like that, but you don't have to write plays about them." Cooper was once described by Carl Sandburg as "one of the most beloved illiterates America has ever known". In the Fifties he was troubled with back pain, excessive weight and his wife left him during 1951 and 1952. He also had a facelift in 1958 after critics savaged him for playing an 18-year-old's lover and wore a wig to hide his baldness. (Following his death, his widow married the plastic surgeon.) It was ironic in the extreme that Cooper's career was rescued by a writer with Communist sympathies. Carl Foreman had written a script about Will Kane, a Western marshal in a town called Hadleyville. Kane has to defend himself on his wedding day from an old enemy who has sworn to kill him. Everyone, including his bride, deserts him. Gregory Peck turned down the chance to star in *High Noon* (1952) because he thought he could not do the part justice. Cooper had no such qualms and went on to pick up a Best Actor Academy Award. He agreed to star in the film for $60,000, one-fifth of his usual take-home pay, plus a share of the profits. Coop was in agony for much of the filming (September through October 1951) as he had recently undergone an operation for a hernia and then found out he had a bleeding duodenal ulcer. (John Wayne hated the film so much he made *Rio Bravo* [1959] to counter it.) However,

the rest of Cooper's career was awash with mediocre films. Said Fred Zinneman, "He had magic. The only time he was in trouble was when he tried to act." Cooper was equally well-known for his riotous love life. Despite being married, he had affairs with beautiful and famous stars such as Clara Bow ("He's hung like a horse and can go all night," she once generously confided), Ingrid Bergman ("Ingrid loved me more than any woman in my life loved me. The day after the picture [*Saratoga Trunk*] ended, I couldn't get her on the phone"), Lupe Velez (they often indulged in phone sex but it was a stormy relationship and at one time she tried to shoot him), Marlene Dietrich, Patricia Neal (they had a fling in 1950 but Cooper's Catholic wife wouldn't give him a divorce), Tallulah Bankhead (when asked why she was going to Hollywood she said "for the money and to fuck that divine Gary Cooper") and Cecil Beaton (or so Beaton claimed). He became a Roman Catholic on April 9, 1959, two years before his death.

CAUSE: In April 1960 he had an operation in Boston for cancer and later had part of his bowel removed. On December 27, 1960, Rocky Cooper was told her husband had inoperable lung cancer. Twelve days later, on January 8, 1961, the Friars Club of Hollywood gave a testimonial dinner for Cooper. On February 27 he was told the truth about his illness by his wife. HH Pope John XXIII sent a message of goodwill to the dying actor. On April 17, 1961, Cooper was too ill to personally receive his special Oscar "for his many memorable screen performances and for the international recognition he, as an individual, has gained for the film industry." It was accepted on his behalf by a tearful Jimmy Stewart. Cooper watched the telecast from his home 200 North Baroda Drive in the Holmby Hills. He died there 27 days later at 12.47pm.

He was buried in the Grotto of Our Lady of Lourdes in the Holy Cross Cemetery & Mausoleum, 5835 West Slauson Avenue, Culver City, California 90230. In May 1974 his remains were moved to the Sacred Cross Cemetery in Southampton, Long Island.
FURTHER READING: *The Gary Cooper Story* – George Carpozi (London: Star Books, 1975); *The Last Hero: A Biography Of Gary Cooper* – Larry Swindell (London: Robson Books, 1987); *Cooper's Women* – Jane Ellen Wayne (London: Robert Hale, 1989).

Maxine Cooper
Born May 12, 1924
Died April 4, 2009
Activist actress. Born in Chicago, Illinois, Cooper became interested in acting while at Bennington College in Vermont amd then moved to the Pasadena Playhouse in Pasadena, California. In 1946 she entertained American troops serving overseas. In 1947 she lived in London where she appeared in several BBC television plays including *You Can't Take it With You* (1947) and *I Killed The Count* (1948). Back in Tinseltown, she appeared in several television shows and made her film debut as Velda, Mike Hammer's secretary in the Mickey Spillane classic *Kiss Me Deadly* (1955). The film later inspired Quentin Tarantino to make *Pulp Fiction* (1994) although Cooper refused to make a cameo appearance. Cooper's other films included *Autumn Leaves* (1956), *Zero Hour!* (1957) and the psychological horror movie *Whatever Happened To Baby Jane?* (premièred October 26, 1962). On her retirement she became a political activist organising a march in support of Martin Luther King, Jr and several protests during the Vietnam War. She was a vocal opponent of George W. Bush. On July 17, 1957 she married the Oscar-nominated screenwriter and producer Sy Gomberg (b. New York,

August 19, 1918, d. Brentwood, California, February 11, 2001). They had three children: a son, Chris, and two daughters, Katherine and Marsha. CAUSE: Maxine Cooper died aged 84 of natural causes at her home in Los Angeles.

Harry H. Corbett, OBE
Born February 28, 1925
Died March 21, 1982
Comedy totter. Born in Rangoon, Burma, the son of an Army officer, Harry Corbett was raised in Manchester by an aunt after his mother died in 1928. After Second World War service in the Royal Marines he began his acting career in repertory in Chorlton and then spent ten years with the Theatre Workshop company. He went on to appear in numerous stage productions but it is as Harold Steptoe that he will be remembered. Scriptwriting geniuses Ray Galton and Alan Simpson created the tale of the two totters during time they had allocated to Tony Hancock but he decided to dispense with their services. Thus *Steptoe And Son* was born. Originally part of Comedy Playhouse, it soon had a life of its own and ran from June 14, 1962 until December 26, 1974. There were also a couple of film versions, *Steptoe And Son* (1972) and *Steptoe And Son Ride Again* (1974). Corbett's other films included *The Passing Stranger* (1954), *Nowhere To Go* (1958), *In The Wake Of A Stranger* (1959), *Shake Hands With The Devil* (1959), *Shakedown* (1960), *Cover Girl Killer* (1960), *The Big Day* (1960), *The Unstoppable Man* (1960), *Marriage Of Convenience* (1960), *Time To Remember* (1962), *Sparrows Can't Sing* (1963), *Ladies Who Do* (1963), *What A Crazy World* (1963), *Rattle Of A Simple Man* (1964), *Joey Boy* (1965), *Carry On Screaming* (1966) as Detective Inspector Bung (a snatch of the Steptoe theme tune is played in one scene in homage to his television character), *The Sandwich Man* (1966), *The Magnificent*

Seven Deadly Sins (1971), *Percy's Progress* (1974), *Hardcore* (1976) and *Adventures Of A Private Eye* (1977). He also starred in the television sitcoms *Mr Aitch* (January 6–April 21, 1967) as Harry Aitch, *The Best Things In Life* (August 12, 1969–July 13, 1970) as Alfred Wilcox and *Grundy* (July 14–August 18, 1980) but it was for the ever-aspiring, ever-failing 'Arold that he is justly famous. He was married twice. Firstly to the actress Sheila Steafel and then in September 1969 to RADA-trained actress Maureen Blott (b. 1944 as Maureen Crombie, d. November 1999 of cancer) with whom he had two children Jonathan (b. 1966) and Susannah (b. March 1968), now a successful actress herself. Maureen, 5', was already married to a Catholic who would not give her a divorce when she met Corbett. She changed her name by deed poll to Corbett when she moved in with him. They had their children before they were able to marry. The "H" in his name stood for "Hanything" – it was just a device to differentiate himself from the puppeteer who created Sooty.
CAUSE: Corbett suffered a heart attack in 1979 while filming *Grundy*. He cut down on his smoking, changing from 60 unfiltered fags a day to 20 filtered. Three years later, he died from a second attack aged 57.

Ellen Corby
(ELLEN HANSEN)
Born June 3, 1911
Died April 14, 1999
Grandma Walton. Born in Racine, Wisconsin, Ellen Corby spent a dozen years working behind the scenes before deciding her future lay in acting. She was nominated for an Oscar for her role as Aunt Trina in *I Remember Mama* (1948) and her other movies included *Little Women* (1949), *Madame Bovary* (1949), *Shane* (1953), *Vertigo* (1958), *Hush . . . Hush, Sweet Charlotte* (1965), *The Night Of The Grizzly*

(1966) and *Support Your Local Gunfighter* (1971). To viewers of the small screen she was best known as Esther Walton in the long-running CBS series *The Waltons*, a role that won her three Emmys (1973, 1975 and 1976). She also played Mother Lurch in *The Addams Family*. She married cameraman Francis Corby.
CAUSE: She suffered a stroke in 1976 that necessitated her leaving Walton mountain for 18 months to recuperate. She died of natural causes aged 87.

Jeff Corey
Born August 10, 1914
Died August 16, 2002
Blacklistee. Born in Brooklyn, New York, Corey had political leanings in high school. Unfortunately for him, they happened to be leanings towards the Left. Corey attended several meetings of the Communist Party but never joined. In the Thirties he worked as a salesman selling sewing machines before landing a small part as a spear carrier in a Broadway production of *Hamlet* starring Leslie Howard. Howard was so impressed that Corey was given the role of Rosencrantz on tour. In 1939 he made his film début in *One Third Of A Nation* as an extra at the scene of a fire. He then went on to appear in *Third Finger, Left Hand* (1940) as Johann, *Bitter Sweet* (1940), *You'll Find Out* (1940) as Mr Corey, *Small Town Deb* (1941) as Hector, *The Devil And Daniel Webster* (1941) as Tom Sharp, *Petticoat Politics* (1941) as Henry Trotter, a reporter in *The Lady From Cheyenne* (1941), the cook in *Mutiny In The Arctic* (1941), *The Reluctant Dragon* (1941), *North To The Klondike* (1942) as Lafe Jordon, an orderly in *Roxie Hart* (1942), the medical examiner in *Who Is Hope Schuyler?* (1942), *The Man Who Wouldn't Die* (1942) as Coroner Larson, *The Postman Didn't Ring* (1942) as Harwood Green, *Girl Trouble* (1942) as Mr Mooney, *My Friend Flicka* (1943) as Tim Murphy, the

crypt keeper in *Frankenstein Meets The Wolf Man* (1943) and *The Moon Is Down* (1943) as Albert before joining USS *Yorktown* in 1943 as a combat photographer. In October 1945 his photography of a kamikaze attack was recorded in dispatches. Demobbed, he returned to Hollywood and minor and non-speaking parts. He appeared in *It Shouldn't Happen To A Dog* (1946) as Sam Black, *California* (1946) as Clem, a bank clerk in *Somewhere In The Night* (1946), *The Killers* (1946) as Blinky Franklin, a reporter in *Miracle On 34th Street* (1947), *Ramrod* (1947) as Bice, *Brute Force* (1947) as Freshman, *Hoppy's Holiday* (1947) as Jed, *Canon City* (1948) as Carl Schwartzmiller, *Alias A Gentleman* (1948) as Zu, an immigration officer in *I, Jane Doe* (1948), *Joan Of Arc* (1948) as her prison guard, *Kidnapped* (1948) as Shuan, *The Wreck Of The Hesperus* (1948) as Joshua Hill, *Wake Of The Red Witch* (1948) as Mr Loring, a doctor in *Home Of The Brave* (1949), *City Across The River* (1949) as Lieutenant Macon, *Hideout* (1949) as Beecham, *Roughshod* (1949) as Jed Graham, *Follow Me Quietly* (1949) as Police Sergeant Art Collins, *Bagdad* (1949) as Mohammed Jao, *The Outriders* (1950) as Keeley, *The Next Voice You Hear . . .* (1950) as Freddie Dibson, *The Nevadan* (1950) as Bart, *Singing Guns* (1950) as Richards, *Rock Island Trail* (1950) as Abe Lincoln, *Bright Leaf* (1950) as John Barton, *Red Mountain* (1951) as Sergeant Skee, *The Prince Who Was A Thief* (1951) as Emir Mokar, *New Mexico* (1951) as Coyote, *Never Trust A Gambler* (1951) as Lou Brecker, *Fourteen Hours* (1951) as Sergeant Farley, *Rawhide* (1951) as Luke Davis, *Only The Valiant* (1951) as Joe Harmony and *Superman And The Mole Men* (1951) as Luke Benson. Corey may have become a star and then again he may not. His world came crashing down in September 1951 when he was interrogated before the House Un-American Activities Committee and pleading the 5th Amendment refused to name names. With a wife, Hope, and three daughters, Jane, Eve and Emily, to support Corey began working as a labourer earning $14-a-day. Using the same government grant to help ex-servicemen that Rod Steiger used, Corey took a degree in speech therapy at the University of California at Los Angeles. He then converted his garage into an acting studio and began to teach. He quickly became the most in-demand teacher in Hollywood and his students numbered Robert Blake, Richard Chamberlain, James Coburn, James Dean, Jane Fonda, Jack Nicholson, Leonard Nimoy, Anthony Perkins, Barbra Streisand and Robin Williams. It would be 12 years, however, before Corey stepped in front of the cameras again. He appeared in *The Yellow Canary* (1963) as Joe, *Lady In A Cage* (1964) as George L. Brady, Jr, *Once A Thief* (1965) as Lieutenant Kebner, *Mickey One* (1965) as Fryer, *The Cincinnati Kid* (1965) as Hoban, *Seconds* (1966) as Mr Ruby, *In Cold Blood* (1967) as Mr Hickock, *The Boston Strangler* (1968) as John Asgeirsson, *True Grit* (1969) as Tom Chaney/Tom Chambers/Therin Chilnsford, *Butch Cassidy And The Sundance Kid* (1969) as Sheriff Steve Bledsoe, *Impasse* (1970) as Wombat, *Cover Me Babe* (1970) as Paul, *Beneath The Planet Of The Apes* (1970) as Caspay, *Getting Straight* (1970) as Dr Willhunt, *They Call Me Mister Tibbs!* (1970) as Captain Hank Marden, *Little Big Man* (1970) as Wild Bill Hickok, *Catlow* (1971) as Merridew, *Paper Tiger* (1975) as Mr King, *The Premonition* (1976) as Detective Lieutenant Mark Denver, a doctor in *The Last Tycoon* (1976), *Moonshine County Express* (1977) as Hagen, *Oh, God!* (1977) as Rabbi Silverstone, *Jennifer* (1978) as Luke Baylor, *The Wild Geese* (1978) as Mr Martin, *Up River* (1979) as Bagshaw, *Battle Beyond The Stars* (1980) as Zed, *The Sword And The*

Sorcerer (1982) as Craccus, *Rooster: Spurs Of Death!* (1983) as Kink, *Conan The Destroyer* (1984) as Grand Vizier, *Creator* (1985) as Dean Harrington, *Messenger Of Death* (1988) as Willis Beecham, *Bird On A Wire* (1990) as Lou Baird, *Ruby Cairo* (1993) as Joe Dick, *Surviving The Game* (1994) as Hank, *Color Of Night* (1994) as Ashland and a professor in *Ted* (1998). He also became a regular on the small screen appearing both in front and behind the cameras. He directed episodes of *Night Gallery*, *Alias Smith & Jones*, *The Bob Newhart Show*, and *Anna And The King* among others. CAUSE: He died in Santa Monica, California, of complications from a fall. He was 88.

Dolores Costello

Born September 17, 1905
Died March 1, 1979
Blonde beauty. The 5'4" daughter of actor Maurice Costello (b. Pittsburgh, Pennsylvania, February 22, 1877, d. Hollywood, California, October 28, 1950, from a heart ailment) and sister of five-times married 5'2" actress Helene Costello (b. New York, June 21, 1903, d. Los Angeles, California, January 26, 1957, from pneumonia, tuberculosis and drugs), she was born in Pittsburgh, Pennsylvania. She appeared regularly as a child with her sister in their father's films. Her first major adult role was in *The Little Irish Girl* (1926), a film written by Darryl F. Zanuck, with whom she began a brief affair. It ended when her father told Zanuck's wife and she threatened to leave him. On November 24, 1928, in Beverly Hills, Costello became the third wife of John Barrymore, by whom she had two children, Dolores Ethel Blyth Barrymore (b. August 8, 1930) and actor and father of Drew, John Blyth Barrymore (who is noticed elsewhere in this book). They were divorced on October 9, 1935. On November 29, 1939, she married Dr

John Vruwink in Prescott, Arizona. They divorced on July 12, 1951, at which time she claimed: "He seldom talked to me, and when he did, he only criticised." She also had an affair with Conrad Nagel. She spoke with a lisp, which made her transition to talkies rather difficult until she had speech therapy. Her films included: *Glorious Betsy* (1928), *Noah's Ark* (1929), *Expensive Women* (1931), *Little Lord Fauntleroy* (1936), *King Of The Turf* (1939), *The Magnificent Ambersons* (1942) as Isabel Amberson Minafer and many more. She retired after *This Is The Army* (1943). CAUSE: She died in Fallbrook, California, aged 73 from emphysema. She was buried at the Catholic Calvary Cemetery, 4201 Whittier Boulevard in Los Angeles, California.

John Costelloe

Born November 8, 1961
Died December 16, 2008
Tragic macho man. A former fireman, he worked eleven years at Ladder Companies 109 and 110 in Brooklyn before retiring in 1998. While still a fireman Costelloe made his film debut in *Black Rain* (1989). His other films included *Last Exit To Brooklyn* (1989) as Tommy, *Die Hard 2* (1990) as Sergeant Oswald Cochrane, *Billy Bathgate* (1991) as Lulu, a cop in *Manhattan Murder Mystery* (1993), *Who Do I Gotta Kill?* (1994) as Billy 'Bink-Bink' Borelli, *Kiss Of Death* (1995) as Cleary, *Crooked Lines* (2003) as Manny, *The Kings Of Brooklyn* (2004) as Miller and *Doubt* (2008) as Warren Hurley. He was best known for his role on television as short-order cook Jim "Johnny Cakes" Witowski who had an affair with closeted gay mobster Vito Spatafore on *The Sopranos*. CAUSE: He died in the basement bedroom of his Sunset Park, Brooklyn home from a self-inflicted gunshot wound. He was 47.

Joseph Cotten
Born May 15, 1905
Died February 6, 1994
Mr Nearly. Sturdy leading man who never quite achieved stardom. Born in Petersburg, Virginia, Joseph Cheshire Cotten's voice was perfect for radio and he appeared in many of Orson Welles' wireless plays before making his screen début in *Too Much Johnson* (1938) as Augustus Billings and appearing in *Lydia* (1941) as Michael Fitzpatrick before making his mentor's *Citizen Kane* (1941) and following that with the Welles films *The Magnificent Ambersons* (1942) as Eugene Morgan, *Journey Into Fear* (1942) as Howard Graham, *Othello* (1952), *Touch Of Evil* (1958) and *F For Fake* (1974). In the Fifties he worked in many foreign films, horror stories and TV movies. When he was about eight years old a black family servant named Thelma took him into a tent in his backyard and sexually molested the young Cotten. It didn't seem to bother him too much. Frequently thereafter, Cotten has said, he'd ask Thelma when they were going to go to the tent again. Cotten played cuckolded husband George Loomis in *Niagara* (1953), the film that made Marilyn Monroe a star. His other films included *Gaslight* (1944) as Brian Cameron, *The Third Man* (1949) as Holly Martins, *The Oscar* (1966) as Kenneth Regan, *Tora! Tora! Tora!* (1970) as Secretary Of War Henry L. Stimson, *The Abominable Dr Phibes* (1971) as Dr Vesalius, *Airport '77* (1977) as Nicholas St Downs III and *Heaven's Gate* (1980) as Reverend Doctor. He was married twice. His first wife was magazine editor Lenore La Mont, whom he married in October 1931. She died of cancer aged 55 in Rome on January 7, 1960. Nine months later, on October 20, 1960, he married Patricia Medina, ex-wife of Richard Greene.
CAUSE: He died in Westwood, California, of pneumonia. He was 88.
FURTHER READING: *Vanity Will Get You Somewhere: An Autobiography* – Joseph Cotten (New York: Avon Books, 1988).

Alexander Courage
Born December 10, 1919
Died May 15, 2008
Mr Music. Alexander Mair Courage, Jr, known to all as Sandy, was born in Philadelphia, Pennsylvania and raised in New Jersey. He first learned to play the piano and then studied the horn and cornet at the Eastman School of Music in Rochester, New York, graduating in 1941. He joined the Army Air Corps on January 6, 1942 and became a bandleader. He joined CBS Radio as a composer at the end of hostilities and in 1948 became an orchestrator at MGM. He worked on big budget musicals including *Showboat* (1951), *The Band Wagon* (1953), *Seven Brides For Seven Brothers* (1954), *Kismet* (1955), *Guys And Dolls* (1955), *Oklahoma!* (1955), *It's Always Fair Weather* (1955), *Funny Face* (1957), *Les Girls* (1957), *Gigi* (1958), *My Fair Lady* (1964), *Doctor Dolittle* (1967) for which he was nominated for an Oscar and *Hello, Dolly!* (1969). He received an Oscar nod for *The Pleasure Seekers* (1963). Composer John Williams said of Courage, "He was one of the architects of the MGM sound, a particular style of orchestration, which was an extension and development of what was done in the theatre in the 1920s." He also worked on various television shows and is probably best known for writing the theme tune to *Star Trek* (1966–1969). He also was responsible for the whooshing sound of the Enterprise doors opening and closing – made by breathing into a microphone. His later work included *Fiddler On The Roof* (1971), *The Poseidon Adventure* (1972), *Superman IV: The Quest For Peace* (1987), *Basic Instinct* (1992), *Jurassic Park* (1993) and *The Mummy* (1999). He also worked on more than 100 episodes of *The Waltons*. He won a 1988 Emmy

as principal arranger for the ABC television special *Julie Andrews: The Sound of Christmas*. He was married three times.

CAUSE: Courage died in Pacific Palisades, California after suffering a number of strokes. He was 88 and had been ill for three years.

Sir Noël Coward

Born December 16, 1899
Died March 26, 1973

Gay icon. Born in Waldegrave Road, Teddington, Middlesex, 5'11" Noël Peirce Coward was responsible for some of the best light comedies ever written in the English language, such as *Private Lives*, *Hay Fever* and *Tonight At 8.30*, as well as being a pungent wit and keen aphorist. Nicknamed 'The Master', he was asked why. In a rare fit of modesty he replied, "Oh, you know, jack of all trades, master of none." He wrote, produced, co-directed and starred in the war epic *In Which We Serve* (1942), based on the life of his friend Lord Mountbatten, for which he was nominated for the Best Writer Oscar. He was also fêted for his humorous songs such as 'Mad Dogs & Englishmen', 'There's Always Something Fishy About The French' and 'Don't Put Your Daughter On The Stage, Mrs Worthington' (written about the grandmother of actors Edward and James Fox). As a boy he showed a remarkable precocity. On September 7, 1910, his mother, Violet, saw an advert placed by Lila Field in the *Daily Mirror* for boys to appear in a play called *The Goldfish*. On September 13 Violet took Noël along and he sang 'Liza Ann' from *The Orchid* and, because there was no piano, she la-la'd as he danced. Miss Field was suitably impressed and told Mrs Coward the fee would be a guinea and a half per week. Mrs Coward was embarrassed and blushed, saying she could not afford that kind of money. No, no, no, Miss Field replied, that was Noël's fee. Coward left school without

much of a formal education. Patrick Garland interviewed him for an *Arena* profile on BBC TV in 1969. He asked Coward how he educated himself and received the following reply from the homosexually inclined Master: "Reading. I belonged to the Battersea Park Public Lavatory. Erm, library, a Freudian slip." Claudette Colbert, appearing in a performance of Coward's *Blithe Spirit* in New York, was experiencing difficulty remembering her lines. She apologised to Coward: "I'm so sorry, Noël, this morning I knew the lines backwards." "That's how you're saying them now, dear," came the waspish retort. (This story is also told about Coward and Dame Edith Evans.) Towards the end of her long life, Lady Diana Cooper was best remembered as a society beauty and engaging eccentric. She had spent a good deal of her early career on the stage but came off second-best in a battle of wits with Noël Coward. She had starred as a non-speaking statue in the religious play *The Miracle* when she bumped into the Master. "Didn't you write *Private Lives*?" Lady Cooper asked Coward. "I saw it and didn't think it was very funny." Coward retorted, "Didn't you appear in *The Miracle*? I saw it and absolutely screamed." Once, on leaving a hotel in New York, Coward was accosted by a woman who gushed, "You remember me? I met you with Douglas Fairbanks." "Madam," replied Coward, "I don't even remember Douglas Fairbanks." Occasionally, he was bested. One day he bumped into the American playwright Edna Ferber who was fetchingly clad in masculine attire. "Why Edna," said the Master, "you almost look like a man." To which she responded, "So do you." Coward and Bea Lillie were staying in Paris one night in separate rooms when she felt the inclination to be naughty. She assumed a deep voice, knocked on Coward's hotel room door and asked, "Have you got a gentleman in there, sir?" Without missing a beat, Coward replied, "Just a minute, I'll ask him." Every great performer and writer sometimes has a failure. Noël Coward's was *Sirocco,* which was booed by the audience. Coward's mother, who was slightly deaf, mistook the jeers for cheers. The producer of the play, Basil Dean, made the same mistake and kept raising and lowering the curtain. Coward was linked romantically with Gertrude Lawrence but he told interviewer Gore Vidal that he had never had sex with a woman. "Not even with Gertie Lawrence?" persisted Vidal. "Particularly not with Miss Lawrence," came the reply. Coward's godson, Sheridan Morley, wrote one of the first biographies of him although Morley was forbidden from mentioning his subject's homosexuality. Morley pleaded with Coward, arguing that it would make no difference to the public's perception of him. He cited the case of the critic T.C. Worsley, who had recently (1966) come out. Coward was adamant. "There is one essential difference between me and Cuthbert Worsley. The British public at large would not care if Cuthbert Worsley had slept with mice." Anyway, despite the lack of indiscretion in his posthumously published diaries, we know of some of Coward's conquests. One was Prince George, the Duke of Kent, the father of the present Duke. Another was the actor Tom Tryon and a third was the writer Michael Thornton. Among his films were *Brief Encounter* (1945) which he wrote, *Around The World In 80 Days* (1956), *Our Man In Havana* (1959), *Boom* (1966) and *The Italian Job* (1969). CAUSE: In the early hours of March 26, 1973, Coward suffered a heart attack in the bathroom of his home Firefly in Kingston, Jamaica. His servants helped him into bed but he refused to let them call his close friends and sometime lovers Cole Lesley (b. Farningham, Kent, 1909, as Leonard Cole, d. January 3, 1980, of a heart attack) and

Graham Payn (b. Pietermaritzburg, South Africa, April 25, 1918), nicknamed 'Little Lad'. He fell asleep on the bed and died. On May 24, 1973, a service of thanksgiving for the life of Coward was held in St Martin-in-the-Fields in London. FURTHER READING: *Present Indicative – Noël Coward* (London: William Heinemann, 1937); *The Life Of Noël Coward* – Cole Lesley (London: Penguin, 1979); *Noël* – Charles Castle (London: Abacus, 1974); *Noël Coward* – Clive Fisher (London: Weidenfeld & Nicolson, 1992); *My Life With Noël Coward* – Graham Payn with Barry Day (London & New York: Applause, 1994); *Noël Coward: A Biography* – Philip Hoare (London: Sinclair Stevenson, 1995); *Genius And Lust: The Creativity And Sexuality Of Cole Porter And Noël Coward* – Joseph Morella & George Mazzei (London: Robson Books, 1996).

Wally Cox
Born December 6, 1924
Died February 15, 1973
Marlon's best pal. Wallace Maynard Cox was born in Detroit, Michigan, but his family moved to Evanston, Illinois, where he was befriended by the young Marlon Brando. The 5′6″ Cox was a weedy bespectacled specimen, very much the opposite of the brawny Brando but nonetheless the two became virtual lifelong friends. After the Second World War Brando piqued Cox's interest in becoming an actor and he began appearing on television in the late Forties and early Fifties. His role as science teacher Robinson Peepers in the sitcom *Mr Peepers* (July 3, 1952–June 12, 1955) brought him fame but not happiness. Despite two Emmys Cox hated the character and insisted that he was nothing like the man he called 'Mr Goodboy'. He was the voice of the cartoon superhero Shoeshine Boy a.k.a. Underdog in *The Underdog Show* (October 3, 1964– September 1, 1973). On June 7, 1954,

he married Marilyn Gennaro. He
played a shoe salesman in Marilyn
Monroe's unfinished last film
Something's Got To Give (1962).
CAUSE: Cox was found dead at his
home on Roscomare Road in Bel Air.
The Bel Air Patrol was called at
7.30am by his wife, Pat. The
authorities found an almost empty
bottle of the sleeping pill Placidyl on
the nightstand and also a partially
finished note in the typewriter. Despite
the likelihood of suicide, coroner to the
stars Thomas Noguchi listed death as
being due to "severe coronary disease
due to arteriosclerosis". Cox was 48.
He was cremated but his ashes
remained at his lover Marlon Brando's
home until Brando's own death in
2004 when their ashes were scattered
together at Death Valley.

Buster Crabbe

(CLARENCE LINDEN CRABBE)
Born February 17, 1907
Died April 23, 1983
Born in Oakland, California, Crabbe
was raised in Hawaii, where he became
an expert swimmer. He represented his
country in the 1928 Amsterdam
Olympic Games, coming fourth, but
four years later in Los Angeles he won
the 400m freestyle gold. After retiring
from competitive swimming he became
an actor. Best known for his portrayal
of sci-fi hero Flash Gordon beginning
in 1935 (*Mars Attacks The World*
[1938], *Flash Gordon's Trip To Mars*
[1938], *Flash Gordon Conquers The
Universe* [1940], etc.) he appeared in
over 100 films including *King Of The
Jungle* (1933) as Kaspa The Lion Man,
Tarzan The Fearless (1933) as Tarzan,
King Of Gamblers (1937) as Eddie,
Murder Goes To College (1937) as Strike
Belno, *Billy The Kid Wanted* (1941),
Billy The Kid's Roundup (1941), *Sheriff
Of Sage Valley* (1942), *The Mysterious
Rider* (1942), *Law And Order* (1942),
Billy The Kid Trapped (1942), *Billy The
Kid's Smoking Guns* (1942), *The Kid
Rides Again* (1943), *Fugitive Of The*

Plains (1943), *Cattle Stampede* (1943),
The Renegade (1943), *Blazing Frontier*
(1943) all as William H. 'Billy The
Kid' Bonney. He also appeared in
another long series as Billy Carson.
When he left full-time acting, he
became a swimming pool salesman.
CAUSE: He died of a heart attack in
Scottsdale, Arizona, aged 75.

Joan Crawford

(LUCILLE FAY LeSUEUR)
Born March 23, 1905
Died May 10, 1977
The ultimate Hollywood star. "I love to
play bitches," Joan Crawford once said.
From what her daughter has told the
world it seems as if she behaved in a
similar way off-screen as well. In the
Forties Hedda Hopper stated: "Joan
Crawford is the only Hollywood star I
know who manufactured herself." That
process began in San Antonio, Texas
where Crawford was born the second
daughter and youngest child of a
French-Canadian labourer who
deserted the family before she was
born. Nicknamed 'Billie' by her elder
brother, Hal, the family took the
surname Cassin when Joan's mother
began a relationship with impresario
Henry Cassin who also ran a bail bond
company. In 1911 the Cassins moved
to Lawton, Oklahoma, where Henry
owned a theatre. Young Billie was
something of a tomboy, preferring the
company of boys to playing with girls.
Cassin allowed his stepdaughter Billie
to spend time around his theatre and
she was taught dance and make-up by
the dancers. Billie received little or no
affection from her mother who much
preferred Hal and made no secret of it.
Aged eight Billie cut an artery in her
foot and was told she would walk with
a limp for the rest of her life. Showing a
steely determination beyond her years,
she underwent two operations and
still kept her ambition of being a
professional dancer. When Billie
discovered some money hidden by
Henry Cassin she and Hal were sent off

to Phoenix, Arizona, while the matter was sorted out. It seemed that a criminal had put his surety in gold coins and Cassin decided to keep them thinking no one would doubt his word against that of a criminal. He probably returned the money since the charges were dropped. Reunited, the family moved to Kansas City, Missouri. Billie was sent to the local Catholic school. Joan Crawford always claimed she was a Papist until around the middle of her life when she announced via countless interviews that she was a Christian Scientist. In 1919 Henry Cassin died and Billie began work in a local laundry run by her mother. In 1923 she entered the prestigious Stephens College in Columbia, Missouri, but stayed only four months, feeling out of her depth. Back home she entered dancing competitions and won many trophies for the Charleston, eventually getting a job dancing at the Oriole Terrace nightclub in Detroit, although at 5'1" (she claimed 5'4") she was considerably shorter than the other chorines. The girls who didn't have regular boyfriends would often accept dinner from one or other of the "stagedoor johnnies" who hung around after the show. After dinner the men would propose a nightcap in their motel room. At first Lucille (she had dropped Billie thinking Lucille would look better on marquees) refused but soon saw no harm in it. After one show she had been in the man's room no longer than half an hour when the police raided the motel and she was arrested for prostitution. The incident shocked Lucille, although later her police record was destroyed on the personal orders of her friend, the FBI chief J. Edgar Hoover. Lucille may also have got married. According to Patricia Fox-Sheinwold in her 1981 book *Gone But Not Forgotten*, Lucille secretly married saxophonist James Welton. The story also appeared in *The New York Post* of January 29, 1982. They were supposedly divorced in the late

Twenties in Los Angeles. There is also a rumour that she appeared in a pornographic film, although no copy has ever surfaced. There was a film called *The Casting Couch* but it was made in 1918, seven years before Lucille arrived in Hollywood and when she would have been just 13. Stories vary depending on who is telling them, but somehow Lucille wangled a screen test for Metro-Goldwyn-Mayer along with a dozen other girls. On Christmas Day 1924 a telegram arrived offering her a $75-a-week five year contract with MGM. The contract was certainly strict – it even stipulated what time she had to be in bed. She made her film début in a bit part in *Pretty Ladies* (released July 14, 1925) and in the middle of that year publicity man Pete Smith decided his newest starlet needed a name change. A competition to "Name A Star" was held in *Movie Weekly* magazine and the winning entry was Joan Arden. However, an actress already existed with that name and, unsurprisingly, she complained. The second choice was Joan Crawford. Lucille hated her new name with a passion. MGM began to groom Joan Crawford for stardom and placed her in a number of silent films including *The Boob* (1926), *The Taxi Driver* (released March 8, 1927), *The Unknown* (June 13, 1927), *Spring Fever* (released October 18, 1927) and *West Point* (released January 2, 1928). She was loaned out to First National to make *Tramp, Tramp, Tramp* (May 24, 1926) with Harry Langdon. No one really picked up on Joan Crawford until she showed her terpsichorean talent in *Our Dancing Daughters*. The day of its release (October 8, 1928), a month before she began shooting a sequel, *Our Modern Maidens* (released September 7, 1929), she got engaged to the actor Douglas Fairbanks, Jr. They married at St Malachy's Roman Catholic Church, New York, on June 3, 1929. Both said that they were 21 years old (she was, in fact, 24). That same year Joan appeared in her first talkie, Jack Conway's *Untamed* (released November 30, 1929), and a further sequel, *Our Blushing Brides* (August 2, 1930). She appeared with her lover Clark Gable for the first time in Harry Beaumont's *Dance, Fools, Dance* (March 21, 1931) and went on to star with him in *Laughing Sinners* (July 4, 1931, also directed by Harry Beaumont) and Clarence Brown's *Possessed* (November 28, 1931) before appearing as Flaemmchen in *Grand Hotel* (April 12, 1932), the first film with an all-star cast. Directed by Edmund Golding, it featured Greta Garbo, John Barrymore, Wallace Beery, Lionel Barrymore, Lewis Stone and Jean Hersholt and won the Best Picture Oscar. She followed that up by playing Sadie Thompson in Lewis Milestone's *Rain* (October 13, 1932), an adaptation of a Somerset Maugham story. The following year she and Fairbanks were divorced. She appeared opposite Franchot Tone (whom she would marry on October 11, 1935 and divorce less than four years later on April 11, 1939) in *Today We Live* (April 15, 1933) and Fred Astaire in his film début *Dancing Lady* (December 1, 1933). Joan Crawford became a reliable but not spectacular actress appearing in, among others, *Sadie McKee* (May 19, 1934), *Chained* (September 1, 1934), *Forsaking All Others* (December 21, 1934), *The Gorgeous Hussy* (September 5, 1936), *Love On The Run* (November 28, 1936), *The Bride Wore Red* (October 15, 1937), *Mannequin* (January 21, 1938), *The Women* (September 22, 1939), *Strange Cargo* (April 26, 1940), *A Woman's Face* (May 16, 1941) and *Above Suspicion* (August 6, 1943). Her career waned and on May 3, 1938, she was labelled "box office poison" by *The Independent Film Journal* in an advertisement created by Harry Brandt, the president of the Independent Theater Owners Association. "Among those players whose dramatic ability is

unquestioned, but whose box office draw is nil, can be numbered Mae West, Edward Arnold, Greta Garbo, Joan Crawford, Katharine Hepburn, Marlene Dietrich and Fred Astaire." Joan, who kept a very careful eye on her press coverage, was devastated by the attack. In 1939 she adopted a baby girl who became Christina Crawford and two years later adopted a baby boy named Christopher. In Hidden Valley, Ventura, California, on July 21, 1942, she married Frederik Kormann, better known as the actor Phillip Terry, six weeks after meeting him. Her home life may have been happy but her professional one was assuredly not. In 1943, MGM chief Louis B. Mayer released her from her contract. "The consensus of opinions among the top brass," she said, "was that I was washed up again." Apart from a cameo appearance as herself in *Hollywood Canteen* (released December 16, 1944) Joan Crawford was absent from the screen for two years. When she learned that Barbara Stanwyck had turned down the part of Mildred Pierce, she persuaded Warner Brothers to cast her in the maternal role. It was said that Bette Davis also declined the part, although Davis denied that. Normally, Crawford shunned motherly parts because she did not want to be typecast in them. Director Michael Curtiz wasn't so sure. "She comes over [to Warners] with her high-hat airs and her goddamn shoulder pads. Why should I waste my time directing a has-been?" Crawford dumped the shoulder pads and even made a screen test for Curtiz. *The New York Daily News* enthused, "She gives the best performance of her career." *Mildred Pierce* (released September 29, 1945), the story of a woman who sacrificed everything, even committing murder for her daughter (Ann Blyth), won Joan Crawford her only Oscar. However, Crawford deemed herself too ill to attend the ceremony at Grauman's Chinese Theater on March 7, 1946, telling her publicist Henry Rogers, "Henry, I can't do it, I'm so frightened. I know I'm going to lose." However, she had her make-up artist and hairdresser on stand-by at her Bristol Avenue home. Cameras were also stationed outside thanks to Rogers. When Charles Boyer announced the winner, Michael Curtiz stepped up to receive the statuette. Joan made a remarkable recovery and was able to receive the Oscar later that night from Curtiz. Pictures of her in bed clutching the gold trophy pushed every other winner off the front page the next day. *Mildred Pierce* also received nominations for Best Film, Best Supporting Actress (Eve Arden and Ann Blyth), Best Screenplay and Best Black & White Cinematography. The only blot on the landscape was her divorce from Phillip Terry, who was playing the part of Ray Milland's brother in *The Lost Weekend* (1945). (Milland picked up Best Actor and the film won Best Picture.) Joan Crawford was a star once again, signing a seven-year deal paying $200,000 per film. In 1947 she was nominated for another Oscar for *Possessed* (released Christmas Day, 1947) although Loretta Young won for *The Farmer's Daughter*. A third nomination came five years later for *Sudden Fear* (released August 8, 1952) but Shirley Booth triumphed for *Come Back, Little Sheba* (1952). Crawford made her first film in colour in 1953 for MGM, *Torch Song* (October 13, 1953), co-starring Michael Wilding and Gig Young. India Adams dubbed Crawford's singing voice. On May 10, 1955, Crawford married for the fourth (or was it the fifth?) time to Pepsi chairman Alfred Steele. He died on April 19, 1959, but she remained on the company's board of directors. By this time Crawford was 54 years old and her career seemed to be over. Despite the opinions of her detractors she was far from finished. In August 1962 she began to film *Whatever Happened To Baby Jane?* . (released November 7, 1962)

co-starring with her great rival Bette Davis. It was the story of two ageing sisters – Baby Jane Hudson (Davis) and the crippled Blanch Hudson (Crawford) – and their animosity for each other, something that was carried over into real life. Davis was to say, "The best time I ever had with Joan Crawford is when I pushed her down the stairs." Crawford got her revenge. One scene called for Davis to lift her crippled sister and Crawford placed weights under her clothing which put Davis' back out. "Christ, you never know what size boobs that broad has strapped on! She must have a different set for each day of the week! She's supposed to be shrivelling away, but her tits keep growing. I keep running into them like Hollywood Hills." (In 1985, Davis donated her scrapbooks to Columbia University and in every picture Joan Crawford's teeth were blacked out.) Crawford was paid $30,000, $1,500-a-week expenses plus 15 per cent of the worldwide gross profits. The movie was completed in just 21 days, was a box office smash and a critical hit and a sequel was lined up, *Hush . . . Hush, Sweet Charlotte* (1965), but Crawford dropped out and Davis starred opposite Olivia De Havilland. Davis was nominated for an Oscar, much to Crawford's disgust, and she actively campaigned against her co-star, even offering to collect the other nominee's award if they were unable to attend. On the big night the Oscar went to Anne Bancroft and Joan stepped up to receive it. Davis was later to remark, "Why am I so good at playing bitches? I think perhaps it's because I'm not a bitch. Maybe that's why Miss Crawford always plays ladies." Joan Crawford was to make only five more films and she began to drink heavily. The Pepsi bottle that she always carried with her was full of vodka. Her last films were *Strait Jacket* (released January 23, 1964), *I Saw What You Did* (released July 22, 1965), *Berserk* (released January 11, 1968) and *Trog* (1970).

CAUSE: Joan believed her Christian Science faith would cure her of the cancer that spread through her body. Her weight dropped alarmingly (shortly before her death from pancreatic cancer and acute coronary occlusion she weighed just five stone) but still she kept the faith. On the morning of her death she insisted on making breakfast for her housekeeper and a fan who had stayed over at her New York home. (Joan was an inveterate letter writer sending out between 5,000 and 10,000 items each month and 6,000 at Christmas.) The meal prepared, she returned to her bed and died. Rumours persist that Joan Crawford committed suicide. Debbie Reynolds was certainly convinced that she did. "There were too many coincidental events leading up to [her death]. I just feel Joan found some way to end this life before she looked too bad, before she had to suffer the ravages of decay any more." Joan Crawford's reputation was ruined posthumously in November 1978 when her adopted daughter, Christina, penned a vitriolic memoir entitled *Mommie Dearest* in which she portrayed Crawford as a vicious woman who regularly beat her children with wire coat-hangers. Both Christina and Christopher were excluded from Joan's will "for reasons which are well known to them". The book was made into a film in 1981 starring Faye Dunaway in the title role. However, that film has become an unintended camp classic.
FURTHER READING: *Joan Crawford: A Biography* – Bob Thomas (London: Weidenfeld & Nicolson, 1979); *Bette & Joan: The Divine Feud* – Shaun Considine (London: Sphere, 1990); *Joan Crawford: The Last Word* – Fred Lawrence Guiles (London: Pavilion, 1995).

Laird Cregar
Born July 28, 1916
Died December 9, 1944
Screen heavy. Born in Philadelphia, Pennsylvania, the youngest of six sons, Samuel Laird Cregar was a strapping 6'3" hulk of a man who used his bulk to good effect as a nightclub bouncer. In 1940 he turned to acting and appeared in *Granny Get Your Gun* (1940) and then as a fur trapper in Paul Muni's *Hudson's Bay* (1940) as Gooseberry. Over the next four years he made some memorable appearances as unpleasant characters, in *Oh Johnny, How You Can Love* (1940), *I Wake Up Screaming* (1941) as Ed Cornell, *Charley's Aunt* (1941) as Sir Francis Chesney, *Ten Gentlemen From West Point* (1942) as Major Sam Carter, *This Gun For Hire* (1942) as nightclub owner Willard Gates, *The Lodger* (1944) as Slade and *Hangover Square* (1945) as George Harvey Bone. He was unmarried.
CAUSE: He died in Los Angeles, California, of a heart attack brought on by a crash diet. He weighed over 21st but wanted to be a leading man and thought he could achieve that ambition if he was slim. He lost 7st but the sudden weight loss proved too much for his system to cope with. He was just 28. He was buried in the Court of Freedom at Forest Lawn Memorial-Parks, 1712 South Glendale Avenue, Glendale, California 91209.

Hume Cronyn
Born July 18, 1911
Died June 15, 2003
Versatile old-timer. Hume Cronyn, once rather unkindly described by a critic as "jaunty and jug-eared", was probably best known for his long-running on-screen and off-screen partnership with Jessica Tandy. Hume Blake Cronyn was born in London, Ontario, Canada, the youngest child of Sir Hume Blake Cronyn, a financier and Unionist MP, and his wife Frances Amelia Labatt, heiress to the brewing empire. His great-grandfather was the first Bishop of Huron, and his grandfather the first white child born in what is now London, Ontario. A trip to

the West End during a holiday in England led to the seven-year-old Cronyn wanting to become an actor. Hume was educated at Ridley College, Ontario, where he was bullied because he was short (he grew to be just 5'6"), so he took up boxing in self-defence and became one of the school's most successful featherweights. Something of a rebel, he did not take kindly to the rigid discipline at school or home, later remembering that "everything seemed to be frowned on by my family as being socially unacceptable". This applied especially to acting. Cronyn was "encouraged" to study law at McGill University, where he became involved in amateur dramatics and won a place on the Canadian Olympic boxing team. Just a year into his law degree he decided to become an actor and made his professional début in 1931 on a visit to Washington, DC with the National Stock Company, where he played the paper boy in *Up Pops The Devil*. He then became a student of Max Reinhardt at Salzburg, before going to New York where he attended a course at the American Academy of Dramatic Art, where he impressed classmates by arriving in an air-cooled Buick roadster. In reaction to his early life he soon became "the dandy of the speakeasies", and was regularly "flat broke" despite his then enormous allowance of $173 a week. Cronyn first appeared on Broadway in 1934, playing the janitor in *Hipper's Holiday* at the Maxine Elliott Theater, and then taught at the academy until 1938. He also directed numerous productions at the Barter Theater in Virginia and added to his growing reputation for comedy in *Three Men On A Horse* (1935) playing Erwin Trowbridge. After appearing on stage as Leo Davis in *Room Service* (1937), Cronyn was exasperated when he met the film mogul Harry Cohn, who suggested that he might do a screen test for "some part" in the film version. An angry Cronyn replied that it should not be

necessary to test someone who had been playing the part for months, and walked out. Later when interviewed by Paramount, he would agree to a test only if they gave him no fewer than four scenes. For good measure, he recalled, "I also pointed out that because I was principally a stage actor I would only be available for film-making at certain times." Surprisingly, Paramount accepted the terms and offered him a contract for seven years; but Cronyn turned down the offer feeling the salary of $250 was not enough. Two years later when Alfred Hitchcock saw Cronyn's Paramount test, he immediately offered him the part of Herbie Hawkins in *Shadow Of A Doubt* (1943). When the film, which dealt with teenager Charlie's realisation that her beloved uncle may be a serial killer, came out, Cronyn stole the show from Joseph Cotten with his portrayal of a nosy neighbour who is obsessed with pulp murder stories. He was also a notable Arthur Keats, the lawyer in the original version of *The Postman Always Rings Twice* with Lana Turner (1946). Cronyn played Gerard, a policeman, in *The Phantom Of The Opera* (1943) and the traitor Andre Duval in *The Cross Of Lorraine* (1943), then worked with Hitchcock again in *Lifeboat* (1944). He was Stanley 'Sparks' Garrett, the shy radio operator alongside Tallulah Bankhead in a boat floating in the Atlantic, as a *Daily Express* with a headline declaring that there would be no Second World War drifted past. (Based on a John Steinbeck novelette, the character of the radio operator was the only one who did not feature in the original work.) Such was the hardship in filming that Cronyn cracked two ribs. Cronyn's reputation was firmly established when he signed a contract with MGM and appeared as Paul Roeder opposite Spencer Tracy in *The Seventh Cross* (1944). This was the first time on screen that he played opposite Jessica Tandy, whom he had married on September 27, 1942 after a brief marriage to Emily Woodruff, a drama student. His performance in the picture won him an Oscar nomination for what was only his third major role; and for the next 13 months he turned down every script he was offered. Cronyn appeared as Papa Lecklie with Jessica Tandy again in MGM's *The Green Years*, in which she played his daughter. She was largely shown standing behind chairs or carrying trays to conceal the fact that she was heavily pregnant. Among Cronyn's immediate postwar films were *Brute Force* (1947) in which he played Captain Munsey, *The Bridge Goes Wild* (1948) as John McGrath and *Top O' The Morning* (1949) as Hughie Devine. While filling in his time between roles he was also busy writing screenplays, directing his wife in such productions as *Portrait Of A Madonna*, and producing television shows. In 1948 he collaborated with Hitchcock again on *Rope*, which Cronyn had adapted for screen from the stage play. The film was notable for Hitchcock's 10-minute-long single takes, a technique he also employed in *Under Capricorn*, which starred Ingrid Bergman as the wife of a hardened Australian farmer; but neither film proved successful at the box office, and Hitchcock then abandoned the idea. Cronyn remained one of Hitchcock's closest friends. When an unflattering biography written by Donald Spoto (*Alfred Hitchcock The Dark Side Of Genius*) appeared after the director's death in April 1980, Cronyn wrote to the *New York Times* to complain about some of the claims in the book, such as the suggestion that Hitchcock had filmed *The Birds* as a symbolic rape of Tippi Hedren. Cronyn accepted the part of Professor Rodney Elwell in the Cary Grant film *People Will Talk* (1951) in order to work with another friend, the director Joseph L. Mankiewicz. Cronyn returned to the theatre after this film and starred for two years opposite Jessica Tandy in the

Broadway hit *The Fourposter*. The couple toured with the production until 1953, and Cronyn remained in the theatre for the rest of the decade. In 1963 he worked again with Mankiewicz in the epic flop *Cleopatra*. Cronyn was the Egyptian queen's adviser, Sosigenes. The following year he was Polonius opposite Richard Burton in John Gielgud's production of *Hamlet*. In 1969 Cronyn was diagnosed as suffering from optic cancer and had his left eye removed. He continued working, appearing in Mankiewicz's *There Was A Crooked Man* in which he played Dudley Whinner, *The Arrangement* as Arthur, and *Gaily Gaily* as 'Honest' Tim Grogan. Cronyn surprised his theatrical fans by appearing in the disastrous comedy *Honky Tonk Freeway* (1981) playing Sherm. Afterwards, he explained that he took the part "to work with John Schlesinger, and for no other reason". In 1978 Cronyn appeared again with Jessica Tandy in one of his most successful stage roles, Weller Martin in *The Gin Game*. The show was extremely well received on Broadway and toured Britain, Canada and the Soviet Union. He then returned to writing, collaborating with the English writer Susan Cooper (b. Burnham, Buckinghamshire, May 1935) on a play called *Foxfire*. This was based on a series of recollections of country life, and starred Cronyn and Jessica Tandy as an old hillbilly couple. He collaborated again with Susan Cooper in 1985 on the television film *The Dollmaker*, which starred Jane Fonda and won him a Best Screenplay award. Cronyn and Jessica Tandy starred together as an elderly couple rejuvenated by aliens in *Cocoon* (1985) and as the owners of a decrepit diner in *Batteries Not Included* (1987). In 1988 they again worked together, in the sequel *Cocoon: The Return*, in which they decided to emigrate to outer space for their retirement. Cronyn was the business brains of the partnership, finding the scripts, drawing up the contracts and scheduling their engagements. When not acting he enjoyed fishing and hiking. He and Jessica Tandy had a house in Connecticut and a large apartment in Manhattan, which housed their collection of modern painting and pre-Columbian art. They rarely watched television. Jessica Tandy died in 1994. The Cronyns had two children, a son (Christopher, b. Los Angeles, California, July 22, 1943) and daughter (Tandy, b. Los Angeles, California, November 26, 1945). Two years later in July 1996 Cronyn married Susan Cooper, who survived him.

CAUSE: He died of prostate cancer in Fairfield, Connecticut. He was 91.

Bing Crosby

(HARRY LILLIS CROSBY)
Born May 2, 1903
Died October 14, 1977
The heartless groaner. Crosby's great-grandfather was one of the founders of Portland, Oregon, and Olympia, Washington. Crosby was born at 1112 North J Street, Tacoma, Washington, one of six children, and was baptised on May 31 in St Patrick's Church, 1122 North J Street, Tacoma, just along from his birthplace. His nickname, originally Bingo, came from a cartoon strip *The Bingsville Bugle*. By the age of 12 he had won seven medals for swimming. At school he played football, basketball and baseball. He suffered from colour blindness. He began singing professionally with the Paul Whiteman Band in 1926 and, four years later, he made his film début with them. In 1931 he left Whiteman to go solo and quickly signed a recording contract, landing himself a regular spot in a nightclub. Soon his records would sell in their millions. Following the tragic death of Russ Columbo, his only real rival, on September 2, 1934, Crosby became the most popular singer of the Thirties. In the Thirties he appeared in films in which he could croon his romantic songs while in the Forties he began appearing in the celebrated *Road* pictures with Bob Hope and Dorothy Lamour. The first was *Road To Singapore* (1940). Four years later, he won his first Oscar for playing Father O'Malley in *Going My Way* (1944). The following year he was nominated for *The Bells Of St Mary's* (1945) reprising his role as Father O'Malley. His third and final Oscar nod came with *The Country Girl* (1954) in which he played Frank Elgin, an alcoholic actor. His large ears were often taped back for films. It was in the film *Holiday Inn* (1942) that he introduced the song that until relatively recently was the best-selling single of all time. Songwriter Irving Berlin was insecure about many of his songs. When he heard 'White Christmas' Crosby said, "I think you'll be okay with this one, Irving." Over the course of his career Crosby appeared in countless television and radio programmes, 70 films and sold over 500 million records. He became an immensely wealthy man – second only to his chum Bob Hope – and his fortune was estimated at between $200 million and $400 million. However, money didn't seem to make Crosby happy. He married singer Dixie Lee (b. Harriman, Tennessee, November 4, 1911, as Wilma Winifred Wyatt, d. November 1, 1952) on September 29, 1930, at the Church of the Blessed Sacrament on Sunset Boulevard. At the end of her life, as she lay dying of cancer, Crosby went off to Europe to play golf. He was also on the golf course when his twin sons were born – ironically, he was himself to die after suffering a heart attack on a golf course. They had four sons: Gary Evan (b. Los Angeles, California, June 27, 1933 – he was named for Gary Cooper; Crosby was playing golf as Dixie went into labour), who later became an alcoholic and drug addict; Philip Lang (b. California, July 13, 1934); Dennis

Michael (b. California, July 13, 1934, d. May 7, 1991, by his own hand, using a 12 bore shotgun) and Lindsay Harry (b. California, January 5, 1938, d. Las Vegas, Nevada, December 11, 1989, by his own hand, using a rifle). Crosby became an alcoholic and when he died his family asked for donations to be sent to an organisation for abused children. He eloped to Las Vegas with Olive Kathryn Grandstaff (b. West Columbia, Texas, November 25, 1933) on October 24, 1957. They had three children: Harry Lillis, Jr (b. Queen of Angels Hospital, Hollywood, August 8, 1958, at 11.32am), Mary Frances (b. Queen of Angels Hospital, Hollywood, September 14, 1959) and Nathaniel (b. Queen of Angels Hospital, Hollywood, October 29, 1961, at 11.20pm). Mary was to gain notoriety as the woman who shot J.R. in the TV soap *Dallas*. Of all the Crosby children, she has achieved the most in show business. Nathaniel won the US Amateur Golf Championship in 1981. Crosby was estranged from most of his family. Despite his image as a good guy, it seems he would do almost anything to fulfil his ambitions – but at what cost to his personal happiness?

CAUSE: Crosby was playing golf at La Moralejo Golf Club in Spain when, having just completed the 17th hole, he suffered a massive heart attack. He was dead before the ambulance could get to Madrid's Red Cross Hospital. He was 74. He said he wanted his epitaph to read "He was an average guy who could carry a tune." In his will, Crosby stated that none of his sons could use a trust fund he had set up for them until they reached 65. After his death, Crosby's son Gary wrote a book saying his father tortured him. Said his old friend Bob Hope, "Bing used to sing to me too but I didn't feel I had to write a book about it."

FURTHER READING: *Bing Crosby: The Hollow Man* – Don Shepherd & Robert F. Slatzer (London: W.H. Allen, 1981).

Alan Crosland
Born August 10, 1894
Died July 16, 1936
Sound pioneer. The name of Alan Crosland has been virtually forgotten in the pantheon of Hollywood pioneers but he was the director of the first talkie, *The Jazz Singer* (1927). He almost never lived to become a part of history, as he was involved in a car crash in 1925 that almost killed him. Born in New York into an upper middle class family, he was raised at East Orange, New Jersey and educated at Dartmouth College but left before graduation. A trip to England left him with a hybrid Anglo-Yankee accent that raised eyebrows. He began professional life working as a writer with the *New York Globe*, writing articles and short stories on the side for movie magazines. In 1912 he moved into the film industry at Edison Studios in The Bronx where he did various jobs to build up experience. In 1916 he began directing films beginning with *The Fear Market*. His films included: *Kidnapped* (1917), *The Light In Darkness* (1917), *Chris And His Wonderful Lamp* (1917), *Knights Of The Square Table* (1917), *The Little Chevalier* (1917), *The Story That The Keg Told Me* (1917), *The Apple-Tree Girl* (1917), *Friends, Romans And Leo* (1917), *The Unbeliever* (1918), the studio's last feature film, and *The Whirlpool* (1918). Crosland joined the army and served in the Army Photo Service. In 1919 he was signed by William Randolph Hearst to direct epic costume dramas. In 1920 he helmed *The Flapper (1920)*, one of the last films made by Olive Thomas before her death in September of that year. In 1923 he joined Goldwyn-Cosmopolitan where he made his name with *Under The Red Robe* (1923). He was also the first director that studio bosses turned to when dealing with a temperamental star. By 1925 Crosland was working for Jesse L. Lasky's Famous Players-Lasky Company when Warner Bros approached him to work in Hollywood.

He made *Don Juan* (released August 6, 1926), the first film to contain synchronised music and sound effects, and *The Beloved Rogue* (released March 12, 1927) both with his friend and role model John Barrymore. Paul Bern, Jean Harlow's future husband, wrote the screenplay for *The Beloved Rogue*. Crosland was then chosen to direct *The Jazz Singer*, the film for which he should be famous. Crosland would, it was hoped, be able to cope with the egotistic Al Jolson after George Jessel (who had starred in the Broadway production) walked out over pay in June 1927. The film cost $500,000 and had just 281 spoken words (mostly incidental to the songs and ad-libbed by Jolson). It made $3,000,000. Crosland directed another part-talkie smash hit, *Glorious Betsy* (1928), a costume epic starring Dolores Costello. Crosland tried to make an early colour film, *On With The Show!* (1929) – a musical with Betty Compson and Arthur Lake. It was a flop as was his next film *Captain Thunder* (1930). His career ended as he began directing B-movies rather than A-list hits. Crosland married three times. In 1917 he wed the actress Juanita Fletcher by whom he had one son, Alan Crosland, Jr (1918–2001), a television director. The couple divorced in 1921. In 1925 he married the actress Elaine Hammerstein (b. Philadelphia, Pennsylvania June 16, 1897, the granddaughter of Oscar Hammerstein I, d. Mexico August 13, 1948 in a car crash), and they divorced after five years. On December 21, 1930 he married the 5'2" actress Natalie Moorhead (b. Pittsburgh, Pennsylvania July 27, 1898 d. Montecito, California October 6, 1992). They divorced on July 15, 1935.
CAUSE: Crosland, 41, was driving his car on Sunset Boulevard in Los Angeles, California on the morning of July 10, 1936 when he hit some roadworks and his car turned over twice. He had multiple broken bones and a suspected skull fracture. Fewer than four days later, he contracted pneumonia and died on July 16, 1936. His last film, *The Case Of The Black Cat* (1936), was completed by William C. McGann. He was buried in Grave 727S, Row 7, Garden of the Exodus, Hollywood Forever Cemetery, 6000 Santa Monica Boulevard, Hollywood, California.

George Cukor
Born July 7, 1899
Died January 23, 1983
'The women's director'. George Dewey Cukor (he was named after the US naval hero Admiral George Dewey) was born in New York, New York, and began directing on Broadway in the Twenties before moving west in February 1929 to work as a dialogue director on *River Of Romance* (1929) and *All Quiet On The Western Front* (1930). His first directing role proper came in 1930 with *The Royal Family Of Broadway*. A meeting with David O. Selznick led to Cukor directing Katharine Hepburn in her first film, *A Bill Of Divorcement* (1932). They would work together ten times. He began directing some memorable films, including *Dinner At Eight* (1933), *Little Women* (1933), *David Copperfield* (1935), *Sylvia Scarlett* (1936), *Romeo And Juliet* (1936), *Camille* (1937), *The Prisoner Of Zenda* (1937) and began work on *Gone With The Wind* (1939) on January 26, 1939. He was sacked on February 12. There have been any number of theories to explain the firing. The 5'9" Cukor was a middle-class, Jewish and a (very closeted) homosexual (John Carradine recalled, "He was the type of gay Jew who would never dream of admitting to anyone that, yes, he was gay and he was Jewish. Above all he wished to be thought very rich yet very common . . .". In his younger days Clark Gable had serviced Billy Haines, a friend of Cukor. Haines would have told Cukor and this made Gable

unhappy at the knowledge the director knew of his gay past. Cukor constantly called Gable "Dear" or "Darling" on set, but then he did the same to everyone, both male and female. Did Gable see this as an unsubtle dig at his masculinity? Gable claimed, "Fuck this! I won't be directed by a fairy – I have to work with a real man." Gable believed that Cukor would favour Vivien Leigh. Producer David O. Selznick didn't believe Cukor good enough. You pays your money . . . His dismissal rankled with Cukor for the rest of his long life, although he churned out notable fare such as *The Philadelphia Story* (1940), *Gaslight* (1944), *Adam's Rib* (1949), *A Star Is Born* (1954), *Lust For Life* (1956), *Bhowani Junction* (1956), *Let's Make Love* (1960) starring Marilyn Monroe and Yves Montand ("You never really know about chemistry. I directed Monroe and Montand in *Let's Make Love*, which they proceeded to do. Miss Signoret was accompanying her husband, but right under her nose he had an affair with Marilyn. They were intoxicated with each other. But on the screen? Marilyn. Yves. Nothing!"), MM's last, unfinished, film *Something's Got To Give* (1962) and *My Fair Lady* (1964), which won him his only Oscar. Cukor was a committed Anglophile and his home was a retreat for many ex-pat Brits including David Niven, J.B. Priestley, Christopher Isherwood and Ronald Colman. His last film, made at the age of 82, was the disappointing *Rich And Famous* (1981), his first film for MGM for 25 years. Cukor's sex life mainly consisted of one-night stands. He was terrified of his homosexuality becoming public knowledge and went to great trouble to cover his tracks.
CAUSE: He died in Cedars-Sinai Hospital Medical Center, 8700 Beverly Boulevard, Los Angeles, California, aged 83, from heart failure at 10.58pm. He was buried in Forest Lawn Memorial-Parks, 1712 South Glendale Avenue, Glendale, California 91209.
FURTHER READING: *George Cukor: A Double Life* – Patrick McGilligan (London: Faber, 1992); *George Cukor, Master Of Elegance: Hollywood's Legendary Director And His Stars* – Emanuel Levy (New York: William Morrow, 1994).

Finlay Currie
Born January 20, 1878
Died May 9, 1968
Authoritarian old man. Formerly a choirmaster and organist, William Finlay Currie was born at 35 Cumberland Street, Edinburgh, the illegitimate son of Annie Currie, a Post Office clerk (his birth certificate names no father). He was educated at George Watson's College in Edinburgh and turned to acting, first appearing on stage on May 3, 1898 as a courtier in W.H. Murray's *Cramond Brig* at The Pavilion, Edinburgh. Currie made his London début in June 1902 at the South London Music Hall, billed as "Harry Colvo, the double-voiced vocalist". In 1906 he toured America, including a stint in New York at Tony Pastor's renowned Vaudeville Theater on 14th Street. He then went to Australia for more than ten years where he worked in the company managed by Sir Benjamin Fuller. Back in England, he appeared in more than 20 West End plays between 1930 and 1950. He made his film début in *The Frightened Lady* (1932) as Brooks. His best role was probably as the criminal Magwitch in David Lean's *Great Expectations* (1946). His other films included *Rome Express* (1932), *Excessive Baggage* (1933) as Inspector Toucan, *Little Friend* (1934) as Grove, *Edge Of The World* (1937) as James Gray, *49th Parallel* (1941) as Albert, *I Know Where I'm Going!* (1945) as Ruairidh Mor, *Bonnie Prince Charlie* (1948) as the Marquis of Tullabardine, *Whisky Galore!* (1949), *The Black Rose* (1950) as Alfgar, *The Mudlark* (1950) as Queen Victoria's 'friend' John Brown,

Quo Vadis as Peter the Apostle, *People Will Talk* (1951) where he played Sunderson, *Ivanhoe* (1952) as Cedric, *Zarak* (1956) as the Mullah, *Ben-Hur* (1959) as Balthazar, *Solomon And Sheba* (1959) as David, *Kidnapped* (1960) as Cluny MacPherson, *Francis Of Assisi* (1961) as the Pope, *Murder At The Gallop* (1963) as Old Enderby, *Billy Liar* (1963) as Duxbury, *The Fall Of The Roman Empire* (1964) as a senator and *Bunny Lake Is Missing* (1965) his final film. He was married to the American variety actress Maud Courtney (1884–1959), who first appeared on the London stage in 1901. She was the original performer of the song 'The Honeysuckle And The Bee'. They had two children, George and Marion. Currie's hobby was collecting books on Rabbie Burns.

CAUSE: He died at the age of 90 in the Chalfont and Gerrards Cross Hospital, Gerrards Cross, Buckinghamshire, of kidney and heart failure. He was worth £1,588 at the time of his death.

Michael Curtiz

(MIHÁLI KERTÉSZ)
Born December 24, 1886
Died April 10, 1962
Mixed-up director. Curtiz was born in Budapest, Hungary, the son of a Jewish architect and an opera singer. Despite working in Hollywood from 1926, he never quite mastered the English language. Among his verbal lapses were "Don't talk to me while I'm interrupting" and "Keep quiet. You are always interrupting me in the middle of my mistakes." He once told Gary Cooper, "Now ride off in all directions." Approached by a man he didn't know, Curtiz was greeted with, "Hello, stranger." Replied the director, "What do you mean, stranger? I don't even know you." According to David Niven, while directing the 1936 classic *The Charge Of The Light Brigade* Curtiz shouted a request for some riderless chargers to be brought onto the set: "Okay, bring on the empty horses!"

Niven and his co-star Errol Flynn fell about laughing. Curtiz was furious. "You lousy bums. You and your stinking language . . . you think I know fuck nothing . . . well, let me tell you – I know FUCK ALL!" *Casablanca* (1942) won three Oscars and director Curtiz accepted his with the words "So many times I have a speech ready but no dice. Always a bridesmaid, never a mother." Among his 170-plus films were: *Az Utolsó Bohém* (1912), *Rablélek* (1913), *Házasodik Az Uram* (1913), *Bánk Bán* (1914), *A Kölcsönkért Csecsemök* (1914), *Makkhetes* (1916), *Karthausi* (1916), *Farkas* (1916), *Árendás Zsidó* (1917), *Tatárjárás* (1917), *Halálcsengö* (1917), *Varázskeringö* (1918), *99* (1918), *Die Dame Mit Dem Schwarzen Handschuh* (1919), *Miss Tutti Frutti* (1920), *Boccaccio* (1920), *Namenlos* (1923), *General Babka* (1924), *The Third Degree* (1926), *Madonna Of Avenue A* (1929), *Bright Lights* (1930), *God's Gift To Women* (1931), *20,000 Years In Sing Sing* (1932), *Private Detective 62* (1933), *Captain Blood* (1935), *Anthony Adverse* (1936), *Kid Galahad* (1937), *The Adventures Of Robin Hood* (1938), *Angels With Dirty Faces* (1938), *The Private Lives Of Elizabeth And Essex* (1939), *The Sea Hawk* (1940), *Yankee Doodle Dandy* (1942), *Mildred Pierce* (1945), *Night And Day* (1946), *Life With Father* (1947), *Flamingo Road* (1949), *Young Man With A Horn* (1950), *Jim Thorpe – All American* (1951), *The Story Of Will Rogers* (1952), *King Creole* (1958), *The Adventures Of Huckleberry Finn* (1960), *Francis Of Assisi* (1961) and *The Comancheros* (1961).

CAUSE: Curtiz died of cancer aged 75 in Hollywood, California. He was buried in Forest Lawn Memorial-Parks, 1712 South Glendale Avenue, Glendale, California 91209.

Peter Cushing, OBE

Born May 26, 1913
Died August 11, 1994
Horror star. One of the truly nice men in the film world, it was ironic that Peter

Cushing made his name in so many fright-inducing films. He was born in Kenley, Surrey, weighing a whopping 10lb but grew into a man with a thin, hawk-like appearance. On leaving school he became a surveyor's clerk and studied at the Guildhall School of Music and Drama. In 1935 he made his stage début as Captain Randall in *The Middle Watch* at the Connaught Theatre, Worthing. His *Broadway* début was to come two years before his first West End appearance. The débuts were, respectively, November 21, 1941, Mansfield Theater, playing Percival in *The Seventh Trumpet*; August 6, 1943, Phoenix Theatre, playing Alexander I and Captain Rambalel in *War And Peace*. The reason for this was because he had gone to Hollywood to appear in a number of films including: *The Man In The Iron Mask* (1939), *Women In War* (1940) as Captain Evans, *A Chump At Oxford* (1940) as Jones, *The Hidden Master* (1940) as Robert Clive Of India and *They Dare Not Love* (1941) as Sub-Lieutenant Blacker. He returned to England to make his first film, *Hamlet* (1948), in which he played Osric. Starting in the mid-Fifties he began to appear in Hammer Films productions. They were almost exclusively horror films and he excelled in many of them but also found time to play the world's greatest detective and one of sci-fi's greatest heroes. His films included: *Alexander The Great* (1956) as Memnon, *The Curse Of Frankenstein* (1957) as Baron Victor Frankenstein, *The Abominable Snowman* (1957) as Dr John Rollason, *Dracula* (1958) as Dr Van Helsing, *The Revenge Of Frankenstein* (1958) as Dr Victor Stein, *The Hound Of The Baskervilles* (1959) as Sherlock Holmes, *The Mummy* (1959) as John Banning, *The Hellfire Club* (1960) as Merryweather, *The Brides Of Dracula* (1960) as Dr Van Helsing, *Sword Of Sherwood Forest* (1960) as Sheriff Of Nottingham, *The Evil Of Frankenstein* (1964) as Baron Frankenstein, *The Gorgon* (1964) as Dr Namaroff, *Dr Who And The Daleks* (1965) as Dr Who, *She* (1965) as Major Horace Holly, *Dr Terror's House Of Horrors* (1965) as Dr Sandor Schreck, *Island Of Terror* (1966) as Dr Brian Stanley, *Daleks: Invasion Earth 2150 AD* (1966) as Dr Who, *Night Of The Big Heat* (1967) as Dr Vernon Stone, *Frankenstein Created Woman* (1967) as Baron Victor Frankenstein, *The Blood Beast Terror* (1967) as Inspector Quennell, *Scream And Scream Again* (1969) as Major Benedek, *Frankenstein Must Be Destroyed* (1969) as Baron Victor Frankenstein, *The Vampire Lovers* (1970) as General von Spielsdorf, *I, Monster* (1971) as Frederick Utterson, *Twins Of Evil* (1971) as Gustav Weil, *Horror Express* (1972) as Dr Wells, *Dr Phibes Rises Again* (1972), *Dracula AD 1972* (1972) as Lawrence Van Helsing/Professor Larimer Van Helsing, *The Creeping Flesh* (1973) as Emmanuel Hildern, *And Now The Screaming Starts!* (1973) as Dr Pope, *The Satanic Rites Of Dracula* (1974) as Professor Larimer Van Helsing, *The Legend Of The 7 Golden Vampires* (1974) as Professor Larimer Van Helsing, *Frankenstein And The Monster From Hell* (1974) as Baron Frankenstein, *The Beast Must Die* (1974) as Dr Christopher Lundgren, *Tender Dracula* (1975) as MacGregor, *Legend Of The Werewolf* (1975) as Paul Cataflanque, *Land Of The Minotaur* (1976) as Baron Corofax, *Star Wars* (1977) as Grand Moff Wilhuff Tarkin, *Hitler's Son* (1978) as Heinrich Hussner, *Black Jack* (1980) as Sir Thomas Bedford and *Biggles* (1986) as Colonel Raymond. He became somewhat weary of his horror film tag: "If I played Hamlet, they'd call it a horror film." On April 10, 1943, at Kensington Register Office he married Helen Beck (b. St Petersburg, Russia February 8, 1905, d. Kent January 14, 1971). There were no children.

CAUSE: He died of cancer aged 81 in Canterbury, Kent. He left £282,163. FURTHER READING: *An Autobiography* – Peter Cushing (London: Weidenfeld & Nicolson, 1986).

D

Robert Dalban

(GASTON BARRÉ)
Born July 19, 1903
Died April 3, 1987
L'acteur du police. Born in
Celles-sur-Belle, Deux-Sèvres, France,
Dalban was a talented and
wide-ranging actor but usually found
himself cast as a policeman. His films
included: *Passeurs D'Hommes* (1937),
L'Alibi (1937), *Promesse A L'Inconnue*
(1942), *Peloton D'Exécution* (1945), *Le
Jugement Dernier* (1945), *Quai Des
Orfèvres* (1947) as Paulo, *Fandango*
(1948), *Au-Delà Des Grilles* (1948) as
Bosco, *Berlin Express* (1948), *Le Secret
De Monte-Cristo* (1948) as Mathieu
Loupian, *Un Homme Marche Dans La
Ville* (1949), *Quai De Grenelle* (1950) as
Café Owner, *Ouvert Contre X* (1952) as
Inspector Sylvestre, *Destinées* (1953),
Mandat D'Amener (1953) as Alexandre
Brion, *Minuit, Champs-Élysées* (1954)
as Inspector Bougeaud, *Obsession*
(1954) as Inspector Chardin, *M'sieur
La Caille* (1955) as Dominique le
Corse, *Les Diaboliques* (1955) as the
petrol pump attendant, *Paris Canaille*
(1956), *A La Manière De Sherlock
Holmes* (1956) as Commissioner
Sanois, *Zaza* (1956) as Gascard, *La
Tour, Prends Garde!* (1957) as Barberin,
Je Reviendrai A Kandara (1957) as
Cardelec, *Marie-Octobre* (1959) as
Léon Blanchet, *La Menace* (1960),
Quai Du Point-Du-Jour (1960) as
Dominique, *La Prostitution* (1962) as
Robert, *L'Oeil Du Monocle* (1962), *Le
Repos Du Guerrier* (1962) as the police
sergeant, *Chair De Poule* (1963) as
the brigadier, *Les Tontons Flingueurs*
(1963) as Jean, *Les Gorilles* (1964) as
Montecourt, *Le Gentleman De Cocody*
(1964) as Pepe, *Fantômas* (1964) as the
magazine editor, *Trois Enfants Dans Le
Désordre* (1966) as Gaubert, *Fantômas
Contre Scotland Yard* (1966), *Un Idiot A
Paris* (1967) as Patouilloux, *Le Pacha*
(1967) as Inspector Gouvion, *Faut Pas
Prendre Les Enfants Du Bon Dieu Pour
Des Canards Sauvages* (1968) as
Casimi, *Las Bellas* (1969), *Le Cerveau*
(1969), *Mon Oncle Benjamin* (1969) as
Jean-François, *Elle Boit Pas, Elle Fume
Pas, Elle Drague Pas, Mais . . . Elle
Cause!* (1970) as Belpech, *Point De
Chute* (1970) as the inspector, *Il
Etait Une Fois Un Flic* (1971) as the
superintendent in Nice, *Quelques
Messieurs Trop Tranquilles* (1972) as the
inspector, *L'Insolent* (1972) as Roger,
La Valise (1973) as Mercier, *Comment
Réussir Dans La Vie Quand On Est Con
Et Pleurnichard* (1974), *La Gifle* (1974),
Le Téléphone Rose (1975), *L'Incorrigible*
(1975) as Freddy, *Le Maestro* (1977),
Dracula Père Et Fils (1977), *Coup De
Tête* (1979), *La Boum* (1980) as Serge,
Les Compères (1983) as the hotel
receptionist and *P'tit Con* (1984) as
the concierge. To English television
viewers, Dalban is best known as the
captain in the classic serial *The
Adventures Of Robinson Crusoe*,
broadcast on the BBC between
October 12 and December 30, 1965.
CAUSE: Dalban died in Paris, France,
aged 83.

Suzanne Dalbert

Born May 12, 1927
Died December 31, 1970
French sex kitten. Born in Paris, she
was discovered by Hal Wallis who
brought her to America. She made her
début playing a sexy student, Susan
Duval, in *The Accused* (1948).
Although attractive she adorned a
number of films but didn't quite have
that spark needed to illuminate
Tinseltown. She returned to France
desperately unhappy. Her movies
included: *Trail Of The Yukon* (1949) as
Marie Duval, *Breakthrough* (1950) as
Collette, *Mark Of The Gorilla* (1950)
as Nyobi, *Target Unknown* (1951) as
Theresa, *My Favorite Spy* (1951) and

Thunderbirds (1952) as Marie Etienne.
CAUSE: Suzanne died aged 43 by her
own hand. She overdosed on sleeping
pills.

James Daly

Born October 23, 1918
Died July 3, 1978
Patriarch. Originally a Broadway actor,
Wisconsin Rapids-born Daly began
appearing on television in 1945 and
was a regular face on the screen
throughout the Fifties and Sixties.
He guested on *Dr Kildare* and *Mission:
Impossible* and his final TV role was in
Roots: The Next Generation. He made
his film début in *The Court Martial Of
Billy Mitchell* (1955) and also appeared
in *The Young Stranger* (1957), *I Aim
At The Stars* (1960) and *Planet Of The
Apes* (1968) as Honorius. His daughter
is the *Cagney & Lacey* actress Tyne
Daly (b. Madison, Wisconsin,
February 21, 1946) and his son is
the actor Timothy Daly (b. New York,
March 1, 1956).
CAUSE: Daly died aged 59 of a heart
attack in Nyack, New York, where he
was rehearsing a play. After his death,
a gay lover sued his estate.

Dorothy Dandridge

Born November 9, 1922
Died September 8, 1965
'The black Marilyn Monroe'. Born in
Cleveland, Ohio, Dorothy Jean
Dandridge was the daughter of
clergyman Cyril Dandridge (b.
Cleveland, Ohio, October 25, 1895,
d. Cleveland, Ohio 1989) and actress
Ruby Jean Butler (b. Witchita, Kansas
March 1, 1899, d. Los Angeles,
California, October 17, 1987). Her
parents did not have a happy marriage.
Ruby had walked out (not for the first
time) when she was five months
pregnant with Dorothy. When she was
just four-years-old Dorothy and sister
Vivian Alferetta (b. Cleveland, Ohio,
April 22, 1921, d. Seattle, Washington
October 21, 1991) were put on stage.
They sang and danced and were billed

as "The Wonder Children". In 1937
she made her first film appearance, in
The Marx Brothers' *A Day At The
Race,* but it didn't lead to the breaks
she hoped for. When she was 16 she
was thrown onto a bed and assaulted
by a female friend of her mother's,
Eloise Matthews. The woman, a
lesbian, excused her action by saying
that she was checking to see if
Dandridge was still a virgin, but was
probably really just satisfying her own
sexual urges. The incident scarred
Dandridge so badly that she acquired a
frigid attitude toward sex and abstained
until she married. Her first sexual
encounter with a man finally came on
her September 1942 wedding night
with her first husband, Harold
Nicholas of the tap dancing duo the
Nicholas Brothers. Their daughter,
Harolyn Suzanne known to the family
as Lynn, was born on September 2,
1943 at Rose Maternity Hospital in
Los Angeles. She was severely brain
damaged. An interlocutory divorce was
granted on September 29, 1950 and
the decree absolute in October 1951.
She cited his extreme cruelty, mainly
his constant womanising. Dorothy
made a number of films in the Forties
but almost always in small bit parts.
Away from the screen she began a
successful nightclub act but racism
meant she was never entirely
comfortable about how she would be
received. Although hotel and casino
owners were more than happy for her
to sing for her supper, they did not
allow her to use the facilities enjoyed by
other patrons. It was even reported that
one hotel emptied its swimming pool
lest Dorothy pollute the water. In 1953
she had an affair with Peter Lawford,
but knew it could never go anywhere
because the scandal would kill both
their careers. One friend commented:
"Peter didn't have the courage to take
Dorothy Dandridge to parties. He'd
have me pick her up and I'd walk into
the party with her; then she'd hook up
with Peter. I once took her to a party at

[agent] Charlie Feldman's house . . . When we walked in every man in the room started paying attention to her – Richard Burton, William Holden, David Niven, all of them. She was a gorgeous woman and a very nice person." In 1954 she made an all-black version of *Carmen* entitled *Carmen Jones*. She became the first black woman to receive an Academy Award nomination for Best Actress but lost out to ice maiden Grace Kelly. She had an affair with director Otto Preminger while making *Carmen Jones* for which she was paid $18,000. (Strangely, considering she worked in a nightclub, her singing was dubbed in the film.) In 1959 she starred opposite Sydney Poitier in *Porgy And Bess*, for which she won a Golden Globe. That same year on June 22 she married restaurateur Jack Denison in the Greek Orthodox Cathedral of St Sophia in Beverly Hills. It was not a happy match: he beat her up and spent her money on a failed nightclub venture. They divorced after three years and she declared herself bankrupt. She died shortly before she was due to perform at a New York gig. CAUSE: On the morning of September 8, 1965, Dandridge's manager Earl Mills arrived at her apartment, D2/El Palacio Apartments, 8495 Fountain Avenue, West Hollywood, California, to help with preparations for the New York gig. He had a key but when he tried to let himself in he found the chain was on the door. Thinking Dandridge was asleep, Mills went away for around two hours. He again used his key when he returned but still the door was chained. By now he was worried so he got the tyre jack from his car and broke the door down. Mills discovered Dandridge on the bathroom floor. She was dead. Psychologists tell us women rarely commit suicide in the nude. Dandridge had a blue scarf on her head and some make-up on her face, but otherwise she proved the exception to that rule. Mills called an ambulance and Dandridge's doctor. In

one of Hollywood's many strange tales Dandridge had given a letter to her manager in an envelope addressed to: "To Whomsoever Discovers Me After Death – Important". Inside was the hand-written message:
In case of my death – to whomever discovers it – Don't remove anything I have on – scarf, gown or underwear – Cremate me right away – If I have anything, money, furniture, give to my mother Ruby Dandridge – She will know what to do.
Dorothy Dandridge"
Following an autopsy, Dandridge was embalmed and then cremated and interred in the Columbarium Of Victory, Freedom Mausoleum at Forest Lawn Memorial-Parks, 1712 South Glendale Avenue, Glendale, California 91209. A memorial service was attended by Sidney Poitier, Sammy Davis, Jr, James Mason, Pearl Bailey and her former lover Peter Lawford. Two days after her death reports began to circulate that she had died from a blood clot caused by a fractured toe. In November 1965 the Los Angeles County Medical Examiner announced "Dorothy Dandridge died as a result of an overdose of drugs [Tofranil, an anti-depressant] used to treat psychiatric depression." In her bank account was the sum total of $2.14. FURTHER READING: *Dorothy Dandridge A Biography* – Donald Bogle (New York: Amistad, 1997).

Bebe Daniels
(PHYLLIS DANIELS)
Born January 14, 1901
Died March 16, 1971
Radio star. Born in Dallas, Texas, she was raised in Los Angeles and began making films aged nine. Five years later, 5′3″ Bebe graduated to adult films. She made over 200 shorts. In April 1921 she was jailed for ten days for speeding in Santa Ana, California. Remarkably, her cell was furnished by a large department store and restaurants competed with each other to feed her.

Nearly 800 Hollywood dignitaries visited her. She rarely spent time in her cell except when posing for photographs. She was hounded by the press for interviews finally becoming exhausted and refusing one request with the words, "No, tell him I'm out." She was let out of prison after nine days for good behaviour and Paramount immediately capitalised on the free publicity by starring her in a film called *Speed Girl* (1921). In 1936 she moved to England with husband Ben Lyon (they married in June 1930) where they stayed for ten years. They returned to the States in 1946 but by 1949 were back in England where they starred in the successful radio show *Life With The Lyons* and appeared in films such as *Life With The Lyons* (1954) and *The Lyons In Paris* (1956).

CAUSE: In 1963 she suffered the first of a series of strokes that partially disabled her. She died in London of a cerebral haemorrhage aged 70.

Linda Darnell

(MONETTA ELOYSE DARNELL)
Born October 16, 1923
Died April 10, 1965
'The Girl With The Perfect Face'. Born Dallas, Texas, at 4.40am, the daughter of a post office worker, Darnell was biologically precocious. She began modelling aged eleven and later won a beauty contest that had a screen test with RKO as its prize. In 1939 she was contracted to 20th Century Fox on a seven-year term. In many of her films her exotic looks were capitalised on and she was cast as the innocent *ingénue*. She rose to become a very popular star in the Forties but found work hard to come by when her Fox contract ended. She moved to television and the stage. She gained weight and found summer stock to be the only way of supporting herself. Her films included: *The Mark Of Zorro* (1940) as Lolita Quintero, *Brigham Young – Frontiersman* (1940) as Zina Webb, *Blood And Sand* (1941)

as Carmen Espinosa, *The Loves Of Edgar Allan Poe* (1942) as Virginia Clemm, *Buffalo Bill* (1944) as Dawn Starlight, *Hangover Square* (1945) as Netta Longdon, *My Darling Clementine* (1946) as Chihuahua, *Unfaithfully Yours* (1948) as Daphne De Carter, *Slattery's Hurricane* (1949) as Aggie Hobson, *No Way Out* (1950) as Edie Johnson, *Night Without Sleep* (1952) as Julie Bannon, *Blackbeard The Pirate* (1952) as Edwina Mansfield, *Second Chance* (1953) as Clare Shepherd, *Dakota Incident* (1956) as Amy Clarke, *Zero Hour* (1957) as Ellen Stryker and *Black Spurs* (1965) as Sadie. She married three times. Her first husband was cameraman J. Peverell Marley (b. San Jose, California, August 14, 1901, d. 1964) with whom she eloped to Las Vegas on April 18, 1943. Five years later they adopted a daughter, Charlotte Mildred, whom they nicknamed Lola. They divorced in 1951. Husband number two was brewer Philip Liebmann and they married in Bernalillo, Mexico, on February 25, 1954. Less than two years later, in December 1955, they divorced. Her final husband was airline pilot Merle Roy Robertson. They married on March 3, 1957, and divorced on November 23, 1963, the day after President Kennedy was assassinated.

CAUSE: Darnell was terrified of fire. She almost had to be forced onto the set of *Forever Amber* (1947) for the scene featuring the Great Fire of London and the previous year in *Anna And The King Of Siam* (1946) she played Tuptim, who was burned at the stake, and was herself slightly hurt. In 1965 she fell ill during a tour and stayed with her former secretary in Chicago. On April 8, 1965, she noticed one of her old films, *Star Dust* (1940), was playing on the late show and suggested watching it. When the film finished the secretary went to bed but Darnell remained on the settee, smoking a cigarette. She obviously did not realise just how tired she was because Darnell soon fell into a deep sleep, the cigarette still alight. The secretary escaped the blaze but Darnell was trapped. She was eventually rescued by firemen but died two days later in Cook County Hospital at 3.25pm. She was 41. Her remains were cremated but were not buried until September 1975, a full ten years after her death.

Frankie Darro
(FRANK JOHNSON)
Born December 22, 1917
Died Christmas Day, 1976
Youthful-looking star. Born in Chicago, Illinois, his parents were both circus acrobats. Darro, who made his first film when he was six, was of small stature and continued to play teenagers well into his twenties. As he matured he played jockeys or other horse-bound characters. By the mid-Fifties he was doing stunt work and all but disappeared from public view.
CAUSE: He died in Huntington Beach, California, of a heart attack three days after his 59th birthday.

Bella Darvi
(BELLA WEGIER)
Born October 23, 1928
Died September 11, 1971
Polish plaything. Born in Sosnowiec, Darvi emigrated to Paris with her parents. She was interned in Osnabrück and Auschwitz concentration camps during World War II. In 1950 she married wealthy businessman Alban Cavalade but they were divorced after two and a half years. She was a regular at the Cannes film festival and apparently slept with any journalist who showed an interest in her, although many recounted she never seemed to be particularly enthusiastic or to enjoy herself in bed. She spoke French, German, Italian and Polish. She met Darryl F. Zanuck in the French capital in June 1951 and quickly began an affair with him.

Although a talented man, Zanuck often thought with his genitals and not his brain and employed dozens of women because he wanted to bed them. If they became a success it was all well and good, but if not there was always someone else. Bella was one of the unfortunate ones. In November 1952 she went to America and stayed at the Zanucks' beach house; Zanuck arranged for her to have a screen test. Her name was changed to Darvi for DARryl and VIctoria, Zanuck's wife. The now defunct *New York Journal-American* reported on July 11, 1953: "A newly arrived French doll by the name of Bella Darvi, who has a voice like Marlene Dietrich, eyes like Simone Simon and the allure of Corinne Calvet, is hitting Hollywood with the impact of TNT. She's got zip, zoom and zowie and in *parlez-vous*, she's *ravisante, chi chi* and *très élègante*. In any language that's hot stuff." Readers who may think this kind of guff is a relatively modern phenomena should note that it's been around as long as Hollywood. Darvi appeared in two American films – *Hell And High Water* (1954) and *The Racers* (1954) and both flopped. Zanuck, who was still bedding her, put her in *The Egyptian* (1954) – but the public still didn't take to her. Even *Variety* commented: "A weak spot in the talent line-up is Bella Darvi who contributes little more than an attractive figure. Her thesping . . . is something less than believable or skilled." Finally, Mrs Zanuck threw her out of the house and Bella was dispatched to Monte Carlo, where Darryl F. followed. The move resulted in the break-up of his marriage. Zanuck and Darvi split when he discovered Bella preferred the company of women to men – both in and out of bed. She also gambled away hundreds of thousands of francs. When her looks began to fade she sought solace in drink and drugs.
CAUSE: In the spring of 1968 Darvi tried to kill herself with an overdose of

barbiturates. It was just one of many attempts at suicide. She finally succeeded when she gassed herself aged 42 in Monte Carlo.

Jules Dassin

Born December 18, 1911
Died March 31, 2008
Leftie filmmaker. Julius Samuel Dassin was born in Middletown, Connecticut, one of the eight offspring of Jewish-Russian immigrant parents. The family moved to Harlem when he was still young and Dassin developed an interest in drama when he was still in school. After the Grand Tour he returned to New York in 1936 and learned Yiddish so he could join Jewish theatre companies. He joined the Jewish Socialist collective the Artef Players and appeared in a number of Marxist plays. He went to Hollywood for six months as an apprentice director at the instigation of RKO. He did very little – the most interesting task was watching Alfred Hitchcock make *Mr And Mrs Smith*: "He would never print a take without shouting in my direction 'Is that all right for you?'" – and after the allotted time RKO did not renew Dassin's contract. He found a job at MGM and somehow a rumour started that he was the nephew of the studio boss Louis B Mayer, a rumour that Dassin did nothing to disavow anyone of. On October 25, 1941 his film of the Edgar Allen Poe story *The Tell-Tale Heart* was released. It won awards and Dassin a seven-year contract. Three years later, he went on strike for fourteen months after MGM refused to let him change the script of *The Canterville Ghost*. He lost and left the studio and joined Universal where with producer-scriptwriter Mark Hellinger and writer Richard Brooks he made the prison drama *Brute Force* (released June 30, 1947) starring Burt Lancaster as prisoner Joe Collins and Hume Cronyn as Captain Munsey, a sadistic prison warder who hit convicts as he listened to Wagner. The film was so violent that it had to be toned down before its release. Next was the double Oscar-winning *The Naked City* (released March 4, 1948), which was Hellinger's final film. It was the story of a manhunt through the seamier side of New York and written by Marvin Wald. Dassin joined 20th Century Fox where he made *Night And The City* (released April 1950), made in London with Richard Widmark. Shortly after filming wrapped, Frank Tuttle and Edward Dmytryk named Dassin as a communist in testimony before the House Committee on UnAmerican Activities. Dassin was blackballed at every studio and moved to France in 1953. For two years he struggled to earn a living until he made *Rififi* (1955), which won him the Best Director prize at the Cannes Film Festival. At the festival he met and subsequently married Melina Mercouri. Their first film together was *He Who Must Die* (1957), the story of a passion play. Their best-known collaboration was *Pote Tin Kyriaki* (*Never On Sunday*) (released October 1, 1960), the story of a kind-hearted prostitute who charges her punters what they could afford and never worked on Sundays. The film cost just $150,000 to make and its theme tune, by Manos Hadjidakis, became an international hit. His version of *Phaedra* (released September 1962) with Mercouri, Raf Vallone and Anthony Perkins flopped but *Topkapi* (released September 17, 1964) was a success and won a Best Supporting Actor Oscar for Peter Ustinov. 1967 was a memorable year for Dassin – he returned to America to work, staged a successful Broadway musical of *Never On Sunday* under the title *Ilya Darling* and when the colonels seized power in Greece he and Mercouri helped in the fight against them. When the junta was overthrown Dassin and Mercouri returned to Greece where they worked in the theatre and films. His last film was *Circle Of Two* (released May 7,

1981), notable only for a topless scene from Tatum O'Neal playing a schoolgirl who has an affair with 60-year-old artist Ashley St Clair (Richard Burton). In 1932 he married Béatrice Launer, with whom he had two daughters, songwriter Richelle (b. 1940) and actress Julie (b. Los Angeles July 19, 1945) and a son. Joe Dassin (b. New York November 7, 1938) was a popular singer in France until his death from a coronary aged 42 on 21 August 1980. The marriage ended in divorce in 1962 and on May 18, 1966 he married Melina Mercouri. He founded the Melina Mercouri Foundation after her death in 1994. CAUSE: Jules Dassin died aged 96 of complications from flu at Hygeia Hospital, Athens, Greece.

Marion Davies

(MARION CECILIA DOURAS)
Born January 3, 1897
Died September 22, 1961
Misunderstood mistress. Born in Brooklyn at 6am, lawyer's daughter Marion Davies would probably rate no more than a footnote in most movie books were it not for her long-lasting relationship with newspaper magnate William Randolph Hearst. He ordered his newspapers to overhype her as an actress but as Dorothy Parker said of her, "She has two expressions: joy and indigestion." She had three older sisters and all four eventually went onto the stage. The 5′4½″ Marion was blonde, beautiful, graceful and stuttered in a most delightful way. She was in the chorus of the revue *Stop! Look! Listen!* when she met Hearst, who was immediately taken with her. (However, a story that he attended her 1916 show *Ziegfeld Follies* every night for eight weeks just so he could see her seems to be without provenance.) He was 34 years older than her and married. Mrs Hearst wouldn't give him a divorce and Marion showed a modernity ahead of her time by agreeing to a relationship without the benefit of clergy. Hearst

began his master plan to make Marion a superstar and help her family into the bargain. Her father, Bernard J. Douras, became a magistrate, thanks to Hearst's influence. As for Marion, Hearst hired the best vocal, posture and acting coaches for his young protégé and placed her in films shot in his New York studio. Her first feature film, *Cecilia Of The Pink Roses* (1918), in which she played the poor little rich girl lead, was treated by Hearst's film critics with a reverence worthy of the Second Coming. Other, more discerning, journalists wrote it off as nothing very special. Her films, *When Knighthood Was In Flower* (1922) in which she played Henry VIII's sister Mary Tudor, *Little Old New York* (1923) in which she was resilient Irish girl Patricia O'Day and *Janice Meredith* (1924) in which she took the lead part of a wealthy New Jersey landowner's daughter were more successful. Again the Hearst press was undiluted in its praise, the chief cheerleader being Louella O. Parsons. Hearst hired writer Frances Marion at $2,000 a week to create roles for Marion. However, when it was suggested that Marion had a gift for light comedy that could be exploited Hearst wouldn't listen. He felt that Marion was going to be the next Mary Pickford. When he moved his studio to Culver City, California, in 1924, Marion became the mistress of his massive monstrosity, San Simeon. Hearst allowed no alcohol to be served at his parties but his wily mistress would sneak off to the ladies and the bottle of gin she kept there. Davies was paid $10,000 a week to appear in films and was kept in splendour on the set, where she enjoyed the use of a 14-room 'dressing room'. As if that was not enough, Hearst also had an 118-room, 55-bathroom mansion built for her at 415 Palisades Beach Road, Santa Monica. The walls were decorated with a dozen portraits of Marion in her most famous roles, all commissioned by Hearst. The tycoon used his newspaper empire whenever he could to further Marion's career and, if necessary, blocked others who got in her way. When Norma Shearer beat off Marion for the lead in *The Barretts Of Wimpole Street* (1934) Hearst forbade any of his papers from mentioning Shearer's name. It wasn't a completely one-way street, however. Davies didn't waste her money. She invested in property and was wealthy enough to help Hearst out in the late Thirties, when he was bankrupt, by lending him $1 million. In 1941 both were deeply hurt by Orson Welles' film *Citizen Kane* and its supposed portrayal of their relationship. Marion wasn't the vacuous plaything that Susan Alexander was in the film. The last word in the film, "Rosebud", was supposedly Hearst's nickname for Marion's pudenda. When Hearst began to ail, Marion stood by him, but when he died aged 88 on August 14, 1951, in 1011 North Beverly Drive, Beverly Hills she was asleep and his body was removed before she was informed of his demise. Mrs Hearst banned her from his funeral. Three months later, on October 31, 1951, she married Captain Horace G. Brown, Jr in Las Vegas, Nevada. In 1957 she gave $1.5 million to a children's hospital in Los Angeles. Her other films included: *Beverly Of Graustark* (1926) as student Beverly Calhoun, *Tillie The Toiler* (1927) as stenographer Tillie Jones, *Quality Street* (1927) as schoolteacher Phoebe Throssel, *Show People* (1928) as wannabe actress Peggy Pepper, *Not So Dumb* (1930) as bimbo Dulcinea Parker, *The Floradora Girl* (1930) as Daisy, *It's A Wise Child* (1931) as benevolent meddler Joyce, *Five And Ten* (1931) as heiress Jennifer Rarick, *Polly Of The Circus* (1932) as acrobat Polly Fisher, *Blondie Of The Follies* (1932) as Blondie McClune, *Going Hollywood* (1933) as Sylvia Bruce, *Page Miss Glory* (1935) as hotel chambermaid Loretta, *Cain And Mabel* (1936) as former waitress-turned-actress Mabel O'Dare and *Ever Since Eve* (1937) as stenographer Marge Winton.

CAUSE: She died in Hollywood aged 64 of cancer. She was buried a few feet from Tyrone Power in Hollywood Memorial Park, 6000 Santa Monica Boulevard, Hollywood, Los Angeles 90038.

FURTHER READING: *The Intimate Biography Of Marion Davies* – Fred Lawrence Guiles (New York: Bantam, 1973).

Bette Davis

(RUTH ELIZABETH DAVIS)
Born April 5, 1908
Died October 6, 1989
Mother Goddam. Ruth Elizabeth Bette Davis was born in Lowell, Massachusetts, home of the witchcraft trials; her ancestors were accused of sorcery. She had one sister, Barbara, known as Bobby (b. Winchester, Massachusetts, October 25, 1909, d. July 1979 of a heart attack). The 5'3" Bette made her first professional appearance playing a dancing fairy in *A Midsummer Night's Dream* for the Mariarden School of Dance on July 23, 1925. Her early professional life was full of setbacks. In September 1927 she auditioned for Eva Le Gallienne in New York and was turned down with the cutting comment, "You are a frivolous little girl." Her first screen test in 1929 was not a roaring success either. "Her features are too irregular. She isn't glamorous or beautiful enough. She is a problem to light and she doesn't have enough s[ex] a[ppeal]." When studio boss Sam Goldwyn saw the test he yelled, "Who in hell did this to me? She's a dog!" When Bette saw the test herself she "ran from the projection room screaming". She took another screen test on October 14, 1930, this time for Universal and was offered a contract. On December 8, 1930, she set out for Hollywood by train with her indomitable mother, Ruthie (b. Lowell,

Massachusetts, September 16, 1885, d. 655 Ramona Street, Laguna Beach, California, July 1, 1961, at 8am of coronary thrombosis). A young studio worker was sent to meet Davis at the station when she arrived on December 13, 1930. He returned empty-handed with the words: "No one faintly like an actress got off the train." Her first films – *Bad Sister* (released March 29, 1931) as Laura Madison, *Seed* (released May 14, 1931) as Margaret Carter and *Way Back Home* (released November 13, 1931) as Mary Lucy – were not roaring successes, although after seeing *Seed*, Louella O. Parsons noted: "Keep an eye on Bette Davis; that girl has something worth developing." In September 1931 she was sacked by Universal. On November 18, 1931, she signed her first contract with Warner Bros at $300 a week. The contract was just for one film, *The Man Who Played God* (released February 10, 1932) in which she played Grace Blair, but Bette impressed enough for the studio to offer her a 26-week extension and raise her wages to $400 a week. However, over the first three years of the contract it became obvious that Warners had no real idea of where to place Bette. After directing a trio of unknown starlets in *Three On A Match* (released October 28, 1932) Mervyn Le Roy commented, "I think Joan Blondell will be a big star, Ann Dvorak has definite possibilities, but I don't think Bette Davis will make it." On August 18, 1932, in Yuma, Arizona, she lost her virginity aged 24 when she married her first husband, musician Harmon 'Ham' Oscar Nelson, Jr (b. Massachusetts July 5, 1907, d. Los Angeles, California September 28, 1975). Davis claimed that she had suggested the name Oscar for the Academy Award (known previously as 'the Statuette') after her first husband. Her friend Roy Moseley believed this was how the Oscar came to be known. The marriage would not be an especially happy one. Ham was a pleasant enough fellow but Bette

believed he lacked ambition. He was also unhappy at her being the breadwinner. Added to this he was a chronic masturbator, a premature ejaculator and, Bette believed, possessed of homosexual tendencies. She had a number of affairs while they were married, notably with Howard Hughes and William Wyler. Nelson was not naïve and when he discovered his wife was sleeping with Hughes he cunningly placed a tape recorder under the bed to capture the sounds of their lovemaking. He later blackmailed Hughes for a not inconsiderable sum of money. The affair with Wyler was more serious; she would later describe him as the love of her life. It began during the filming of *Jezebel* (premièred March 10, 1938) and ended in October 1938 when Wyler sent Davis an ultimatum in a letter – divorce her husband, Ham Nelson, and marry him or he would marry someone else. The following week he married actress Margaret Tallichet. (The next film Wyler and Davis made together was, ironically, entitled *The Letter* [released November 22, 1940].) Bette began working on *Of Human Bondage* (1934) playing the cockney Mildred Rogers on February 12, 1934, and when the film was released on June 8 she received rave reviews. *Life* called it "perhaps the finest performance ever given on screen." *Variety* was equally effusive about *Dangerous* (released December 25, 1935), in which Davis played Joyce Heath, saying, "This is perhaps her best achievement." It was certainly considered so at the time because, on March 5, 1936, Davis won an Oscar for her performance. However, all was not yet roses in Davis' professional career. On June 20, 1936, a day after her lawyer sent the studio a letter asking for her contract to be reviewed, she was suspended by Warner Bros. Jack Warner offered to raise her salary from $1,600 to $2,000 but Bette held out for $3,500. Her co-star Barbara Stanwyck called Davis "an egotistical little bitch". She had a point: Davis also added that she would return to the studio if the films she was offered were suitable to her talents. Warners refused to budge. On August 3, 1936, Bette left the country to make films in Europe. But Jack Warner wasn't giving up that easily. "It is high time something were done to make people under contract to the studios realise that a contract is not a mere scrap of paper to be thrown aside because they happen to make a good picture or two," he grouched. On September 9, 1936, Warner Bros issued an injunction in England against Bette making films outside the studio. On October the case came to trial. Bette was represented by Sir William Jowitt (1885–1957) and Warners by the equally distinguished Sir Patrick Hastings (1880–1952). In court one day he became so frustrated by Bette that he pulled his wig off and threw it onto the floor. Despite this petulance he won the case for the studio after five days and Bette was ordered to pay costs. She wrote an apologetic note to Warner and found that he agreed to waive part of the costs and began to put her in more suitable pictures. One such was *Jezebel*, regarded by many as the best film ever produced by Warners. On November 22, 1938, Ham Nelson filed for divorce, which was granted on December 6, of the same year. Three months later, on February 23, 1939, *Jezebel* won Bette her second Oscar. She also appeared in *Kid Galahad* (premièred May 26, 1937) as Louise 'Fluff' Phillips, *That Certain Woman* (released September 15, 1937) as Mary Donnell, *It's Love I'm After* (released November 20, 1937) as Joyce Arden, *The Sisters* (released October 14, 1938) as Louise Elliott Medlin starring opposite Errol Flynn, *Dark Victory* (released April 20, 1939) as Judith Traherne, *Juarez* (released April 24, 1939) as Empress Carlotta von Habsburg and *The Old Maid* (released August 16, 1939) as Charlotte Lovell, which also won rave reviews. In 1939 she made *The Private Lives Of Elizabeth And Essex* (premièred September 27, 1939) in which she played Elizabeth I who, despite the claims of her supporters, was decidedly not a virgin. Playing Essex was Errol Flynn, with whom Bette had worked a year earlier. They did not get on. She believed he was overrated, while he believed her dislike of him stemmed from a refused invitation from her to him for drinks. Whatever the truth there was no love lost, as was evident in one scene in the film, where Elizabeth had to slap Essex. Bette did not pull her punch and whacked Flynn with all the might she could muster. She almost knocked him out. Bette later rejected the part of Scarlett O'Hara in *Gone With The Wind* (1939) because she thought she'd have to work with Flynn again. At 8pm on December 31, 1940, in Arizona, Bette married for the second time. Her new husband was 6' Arthur Farnsworth, Jr (b. Rutland, Vermont, December 15, 1908). Because of her commitments to *The Bride Came C.O.D.* (1941) as Joan Winfield and the film she badly wanted, *The Little Foxes* (1941) in which she played Regina Hubbard Giddens, there wasn't much of a honeymoon. In October 1941 Farnsworth fell seriously ill with lobar pneumonia and Bette flew (which she hated) to his side, interrupting work on *In This Our Life* (1942). Much to the studio's disquiet, she stayed by his side until his condition improved and then went back to work by train. Her film *Now, Voyager* (released October 22, 1942) contains one of the most famous of all movie scenes: in a romantic gesture that had women all over the world swooning Jerry Durrance (Paul Henreid) lights two cigarettes before handing one to Charlotte Vale (Bette). In spring 1943 Bette finished *Old Acquaintance* (1943) and went on holiday to Mexico while husband Farney went to Franconia. The separate vacations prompted rumours of marital discord and certainly Bette had an affair with *Old Acquaintance* director Vincent Sherman. But in the summer husband and wife were together again and seemingly happy to be so. On August 23, Farney had lunch with their lawyer. As he walked back to his car he cried out, fell backwards and landed on the pavement outside a cigar shop at 6249 Hollywood Boulevard. Blood poured from his nose and ears. He never regained consciousness and died on August 25 at Hollywood Presbyterian Hospital. Rumours immediately started as to what had happened. An inquest stated it was an accident but murder was discussed and a number of men, including Vincent Sherman and her third husband, claimed Bette admitting pushing her husband over. The mystery remains. Her career faltered somewhat in the mid- to late Forties but her private life was boosted. She refused the lead role in *Mildred Pierce* (1945), a part that won an Oscar for Joan Crawford. On November 29, 1945, in the Mission Inn, Riverside, California, she married sailor William Grant Sherry (b. Amagansett, New York, April 13, 1914) and, on May 1, 1947, she gave birth to daughter Barbara Davis, known as B.D. As Bette attempted to find a successful film she and Sherry split and then reconciled. It would have been a foolish person to write off Bette Davis professionally and on April 11, 1950, she began work on a film that would see her back with a bang. She was signed to play Margo Channing in Joseph L. Mankiewicz's *All About Eve* (premièred October 13, 1950). Bette wasn't the first choice for Margo, although in retrospect *only* Bette could have played her. Bette *was* Margo. The first choice was Marlene Dietrich and then Claudette Colbert, who actually signed for the part. However, she was injured in another film and withdrew, much to her disappointment even 40 years later. Jeanne Crain was considered, then Gertrude Lawrence

and finally Ingrid Bergman before the call came for Bette. On the set she met an actor called Gary Franklin Merrill (b. Hartford, Connecticut, August 2, 1915, d. Falmouth, Maine, March 5, 1990), who was playing Bill Sampson and she fell in love with him almost immediately. It was in *All About Eve* that she delivered her most famous movie line: "Fasten your seat belts; it's going to be a bumpy night." It was believed that Bette based the character of Margo on Tallulah Bankhead, who wasn't best pleased. Bette was nominated for an Oscar for her performance but lost out on March 29, 1951, to Judy Holliday for *Born Yesterday* (1950). Following the film's success Bette sent a telegram to Mankiewicz. "Thanks, Joe, for raising me from the dead." Meantime, her marriage to William Grant Sherry was breaking up and she filed for divorce. During filming he sent her a telegram asking her to reconsider. She cruelly and sarcastically read the telegram aloud to the whole company. Bette had an unpleasant side to her character. Every so often she would sort through her Rollerdex and tear out the details of those who had upset her. They would never be restored. On July 28, 1950, she and Sherry were divorced. That same day she married Gary Merrill. Just over three months later, on November 6, 1950, Bette was invited to make her hand- and footprints in the wet cement outside Grauman's Chinese Theater. The Gary Merrills adopted two children: Margot Mosher (b. January 6, 1951) who was mentally retarded and Michael Woodman (b. January 5, 1952). Bette turned down the part of Lola in *Come Back, Little Sheba* (1952) that won Shirley Booth an Oscar (during her acceptance speech Booth thanked Davis). On March 16, 1953, Bette underwent an operation to correct osteomyelitis of the jaw. In 1955 she again played Elizabeth I, in her first film for three years, called *The Virgin Queen* (released

July 22, 1955). She was to make only four films over the next six years and in that time, on July 7, 1960, she divorced Gary Merrill. Once again her career seemed to be in the doldrums. Then it was revived again on May 9, 1962, when she signed to appear opposite her great rival Joan Crawford in Robert Aldrich's *Whatever Happened To Baby Jane?* (premièred October 26, 1962). Bette was paid $60,000, $600 a week expenses plus 10% of the gross profits. During filming Joan sent Bette little presents and notes. Bette sent them back, saying that while she appreciated the gesture she did not have the time to reciprocate. After a little while the presents began arriving at the Davis home once again. Bette was furious. "What is this crap? Christ, I'm 54 years old and my figure is shot to hell. She's 58 if she's a day and she's still coming on like a dykey schoolgirl with a crush on the boobs and twat at the next schoolroom desk!" The presents stopped. The exterior shots of the Hudson house were shot at 172 South McCadden Place, Los Angeles. Davis was not happy with Aldrich's hiring of 24-year-old Victor Buono as Edwin Flagg for the film and tried to get the director to fire him but Aldrich stood resolute. After the first scenes were in the can Davis strode up to Buono and said, "I confess that before we began, I did not care for Bob's choice of you, and I tried to persuade him not to use you. He was right and I was wrong. I hope you will accept my apology, because you are absolutely marvellous." Despite her infamous feud with Joan, Bette kept a picture of Crawford in her home. Nine days after shooting wrapped on *Whatever Happened To Baby Jane?* Bette placed an advertisement in *Variety*. It read:
"*Situation Wanted, Women Artists Mother of three – 10, 11, 15 – divorcee, American. Thirty years experience as an actress in motion pictures. Mobile still and more affable than rumor would have it. Wants steady employment in Hollywood.*

(Has had Broadway.) Bette Davis, c.o. Martin Baum, G.A.C., References Upon Request." It would be fair to say the advert shocked Hollywood. It was placed before *Whatever Happened To Baby Jane?* was released and, obviously, before it was a hit. In later years, Bette claimed the ad was a joke. Nothing could have been further from the truth. She was desperate for work. On February 25, 1963, Bette was nominated for an Oscar for *Whatever Happened To Baby Jane?* but lost out. She signed to do another film with Joan Crawford, *Hush . . . Hush, Sweet Charlotte* (released December 15, 1964), playing Charlotte Hollis, but Joan backed out, feigning illness and Olivia De Havilland filled the gap. Bette made few films in the late Sixties and Seventies moving to television movies such as *Madame Sin* (1972), *Scream, Pretty Peggy* (1973), *Dark Secret Of Harvest Home* (1978), *Strangers: The Story Of A Mother And Daughter* (1979), *White Mama* (1980) and *Little Gloria . . . Happy At Last* (1982). In May 1977 her rival Joan Crawford died and her adopted daughter Christina penned the vicious *Mommie Dearest* the following year. Bette, whose relationship with B.D. was fraught, must have wondered if her daughter would do the same when she was dead. She didn't have to wait that long. On Mother's Day 1985 B.D. published a searing account of Bette entitled *My Mother's Keeper*. It became a number one bestseller with its tales of alcoholism, abuse and downright nasty behaviour. It caused a rift between mother and daughter that was never healed. Bette made her penultimate film, *The Whales Of August* (premièred October 16, 1987) as Libby Strong, with another Hollywood survivor, Lillian Gish. They didn't always get on. Directing was Lindsay Anderson and when, one day, he said to Lillian, "Miss Gish, you just gave us a marvellous close-up!" Bette rejoined, "She ought to know about close-ups. Jesus, she was

around when they invented them! The bitch has been around forever, you know!" Lillian Gish got her own back: "That face! Have you ever seen such a tragic face? Poor woman. How she must be suffering! I don't think it's right to judge a person like that. We must bear and forbear."

CAUSE: On June 9, 1983, Bette underwent a mastectomy at the New York Hospital and then on the 18th she suffered a stroke. (She later claimed that B.D.'s book did her more harm than the stroke.) Later that year her third misfortune occurred when she broke her hip. On September 22, 1989, she received the Donostia Award for Lifetime Achievement in Spain at the San Sebastian Film Festival. Bette commented drily: "If they'd waited any longer to give me this award, I wouldn't be here to receive it." She stayed in Spain for more events but on October 3 fell ill with what was assumed to be influenza. She was taken to The American Hospital, 63 boulevard Victor Hugo, Paris, where she was informed her cancer had returned. She died from breast cancer at 11.20pm, three days after admittance. She had told her friend Roy Moseley that when she died she would be ignored, forgotten by the world's press. He told her she was wrong and, indeed, her death did make world headlines. She was buried at 11am on October 12, in Forest Lawn-Hollywood Hills, 6300 Forest Lawn Drive, Los Angeles, California 90068. B.D. did not attend. Interviewed in June 1987 about her own mortality, Bette said: "I would hate to pass on after a long lingering illness. It should be something sudden. And I don't want anyone sending money to any little charity instead of flowers. I want millions of flowers. I want it to be ludicrous with flowers . . . I want everyone to weep. Copiously."

FURTHER READING: *Mother Goddam: The Story Of The Career Of Bette Davis*

– Whitney Stine With A Running Commentary By Bette Davis (London: W.H. Allen, 1975); *Bette: A Biography Of Bette Davis* – Charles Higham (London: NEL, 1981); *This 'N That* – Bette Davis with Michael Herskowitz (New York: Berkeley, 1988); *Bette Davis: An Intimate Memoir* – Roy Moseley (London: Sidgwick & Jackson, 1989); *No Guts, No Glory: Conversations With Bette Davis* – Whitney Stine (London: Virgin, 1990); *Bette & Joan: The Divine Feud* – Shaun Considine (London: Sphere, 1990); *The Passionate Life Of Bette Davis* – Lawrence J. Quirk (London: Robson Books, 1990); *All About Bette: Her Life From A–Z* – Randall Riese (Chicago: Contemporary Books, 1993); *More Than A Woman: An Intimate Biography Of Bette Davis* – James Spada (London: Little, Brown, 1993); *Bette Davis Is The Girl Who Walked Home Alone* – Charlotte Chandler (London: Simon & Schuster, 2006); *Dark Victory: The Life Of Bette Davis* – Ed Sikov (London: Aurum, 2007).

Brad Davis
(ROBERT DAVIS)
Born November 6, 1949
Died September 8, 1991
Thesp with a tragic secret. Born in Tallahassee, Florida, the son of dentist Eugene Davis and Anne Creel, Davis was an intense but unknown actor to most when he was cast as drug smuggler Billy Hayes in Alan Parker's harrowing *Midnight Express* (1978). The story of an American student caught attempting to smuggle heroin out of the country made international headlines. For a brief period Davis' star shone, but was quickly extinguished. As stardom faded, other things came along to take its place. Those other things were drink and drugs. In 1981 Davis joined Alcoholics Anonymous and in 1983 confessed he had taken "every known drug under the sun, singly and in combinations." His films included: *Eat My Dust!* (1976), *A Small*

Circle Of Friends (1980) as Leonardo DaVinci Rizzo, *Chariots Of Fire* (1981) as Jackson Scholz, *Querelle* (1982) as Querelle, *Il Cugino Americano* (1986) as Julian Salina, *Heart* (1987) as Eddie, *Cold Steel* (1987) as Johnny Modine and *Hangfire* (1991) as Sheriff Ike Slayton. He married his agent Susan Bluestein in 1976 and they had a daughter, Alexandra, born in 1983. Prior to Hollywood, he was known to be homosexual. Among his lovers was Timothy Patrick Murphy (who is noticed elsewhere in this book). The late author and gay rights activist Vito Russo revealed: "Brad was nonchalant about his gayness before he headed out west. He was always horny, and the first to say so . . . I had no idea he had a bisexual side. He either hid it well or going to Hollywood just coaxed it out of him – if out is the right word and in this context it ain't."

CAUSE: In 1985 Davis was diagnosed HIV positive, but kept his condition secret, fearing that if it became known he was infected he would be virtually unemployable. He was probably right. He didn't go for early treatment in case gossip leaked out. Despite the biography on imdb.com, Davis contracted AIDS through gay sex not "heterosexual contact". He finally succumbed to AIDS aged 41 in Studio City, Los Angeles, California. Gay author Armistead Maupin stated, "I'm tired of people being congratulated posthumously on their brave battle. It wasn't that brave if we didn't know about it while it was going on."

Sammy Davis, Jr
Born December 8, 1925
Died May 16, 1990
Hollywood's only one-eyed Jewish negro. Born in Harlem, New York, Davis was a child entertainer, who was treading the boards before his third birthday. The early work made Sammy miss school, with the result that he had difficulty writing, although he was a voracious reader. He never personalised autographs because he couldn't spell names correctly. He made his movie début in *Rufus Jones For President* (1933) playing Rufus Jones, but apart from one more film (*Sweet And Low* [1947]), didn't make any more films until the late Fifties. He was part of the Wil Mastin (his 'uncle') group entertaining nationwide. In 1945, following two years in the army – where he was subjected to horrific racism, including having his nose broken several times and offered a beer laced with urine – things began taking off for Sammy and the group was renamed the Wil Mastin Trio Starring Sammy Davis, Jr. He began appearing regularly on television and in nightclubs in the Fifties earning $25,000 a week at the Sands in Las Vegas. In November 1954 he was involved in a car crash that resulted in him losing his left eye. He became associated with the hard-living, hard-drinking Rat Pack (other members included Frank Sinatra, Dean Martin, Peter Lawford and Joey Bishop). His films included: *Anna Lucasta* (1958) as Danny Johnson, *Porgy And Bess* (1959) as Sportin' Life, *Ocean's 11* (1960) as singing dustman Josh Howard for which he was paid $100,000, *Sergeants 3* (1962) as Jonah Williams, *Robin And The 7 Hoods* (1964) as Will, *Salt And Pepper* (1968) as Charles Salt, *Sweet Charity* (1969) as Big Daddy, *Elvis – That's The Way It Is* (1970) playing himself, *James Dean, The First American Teenager* (1975) again playing himself, *The Cannonball Run* (1981) as Fenderbaum, *Cracking Up* (1983) as Mr Billings and *Cannonball Run II* (1984) reprising his role as Fenderbaum. In 1985 he had a hip replaced that enabled him to dance again and four years later, having beaten drink and cocaine problems, he went on a world tour with Frank Sinatra and Liza Minnelli. He caused a sensation in the autumn of 1957 when he began dating blonde star Kim Novak who had just finished filming

Alfred Hitchcock's *Vertigo*. Novak was being groomed for stardom by Harry Cohn and the Columbia chief didn't want the beautiful blonde dating a black man. Cohn arranged for his friend the gangster Mickey Cohen to have Davis taken out into the desert and poke a sharp stick into his other eye and, for good measure, break both his legs. Davis had one chance – marry a black girl and quickly. On January 10, 1958, after a sum of money had changed hands, Davis married twice-divorced 23-year-old black singer Loray White, who already had a six-year-old daughter. The ceremony took place in the Emerald Room of the Sands Hotel and Harry Belafonte was best man. On April 23, 1959, they were divorced, amid rumours the marriage had never been consummated. Davis paid Loray $25,000 for the divorce. On November 13, 1960, he married Swedish-born actress May Britt, with Frank Sinatra as best man. A daughter, Tracey, was born on July 5, 1961, and two adopted sons, Mark and Jeff, came along later. The marriage wrecked Britt's career and when Sammy arrived in Washington, DC in 1960 he was greeted by signs reading "Go Back To The Congo You Kosher Coon". Even when he appeared at the 1960 Democratic Convention in support of John F. Kennedy he was jeered by the Mississippi delegation. On January 17, 1961, Sammy was 'disinvited' to the inauguration of the 35th President because Kennedy feared Sammy would upset Southern Congressmen. On November 1, 1967, Sammy and May went their separate ways and were divorced on December 19, 1968. On May 11, 1970, he married black dancer Altovise Gore (who appeared in *Can't Stop The Music* [1980]) and in 1990 they adopted a son, Manny (b. 1976). Sammy also had one of the world's largest collections of hardcore pornography and presented the première of the notorious *Deep Throat*, starring Linda Lovelace, in several countries.

CAUSE: In 1988 Sammy began to suffer from a bad throat. Years of smoking had done him harm. He would smoke as he sang and exhale with a note, despite being warned not to do so by Nat 'King' Cole. In September 1989 he contracted throat cancer. In February 1990 he was admitted to Cedars-Sinai Hospital Medical Center, 8700 Beverly Boulevard, Los Angeles, California. Doctors told him he needed an operation but he realised that if he went through with it, he would never sing again. He refused the treatment. On March 13, 1990, he was discharged from the hospital with a large tumour sticking out of his neck. He died of a heart attack, pneumonia and laryngeal carcinoma aged 64 at 5.59am at his home, 1151 Summit Drive, Beverly Hills. On May 18 he was buried, between his father and Wil Mastin, in Forest Lawn Memorial-Parks, 1712 South Glendale Avenue, Glendale, California 91209. Among the 1,200 or so mourners were Bill Cosby, Billy Crystal, Tony Danza, Angie Dickinson, Robert Guillaume, Gregory Hines, Michael Jackson, Shirley Maclaine, Dean Martin, Liza Minnelli, Ricardo Montalban, Carroll O'Connor, Burt Reynolds, Jill St. John, Frank Sinatra, Ben Vereen, Robert Wagner and Stevie Wonder. Altovise Davis was later served with a $7.5-million tax bill. FURTHER READING: *Hollywood In A Suitcase* – Sammy Davis, Jr. (London: Star Books, 1981).

Lisa De Leeuw

Born July 3, 1958
Died November 11, 1993
Porn starlet. Born in Moline, Illinois, De Leeuw came to Hollywood looking for fame and fortune and ended up in hardcore porn movies. One critic described her, somewhat uncharitably, as an "incredibly ugly, big-titted female with the personality of Andrea Dworkin"! Among her 180 or so films were *800 Fantasy Lane* (1979), *1001 Erotic Nights* (1982), *The Blonde*

Next Door (1982), *Aunt Peg Goes To Hollywood* (1982), *Behind The Scenes Of An Adult Movie* (1983), *Foxholes* (1983), *Chocolate Cream* (1984), *With Love, Lisa* (1985) and *Beverly Hills Cox* (1986).

CAUSE: She died aged 35 of AIDS contracted through heavy drug use.

James Dean

Born February 8, 1931
Died September 30, 1955

Teen icon. The 5'8" James Byron Dean made just three films (*East Of Eden* [1955], *Rebel Without A Cause* [1955] and *Giant* [1956]) but is still one of the most recognisable of all showbiz icons more than 40 years after his death. Born at 2am in Byron, Indiana, an only child, his beloved mother, Mildred (b. Grant County, Indiana, September 15, 1911), died in Santa Monica of a uterine carcinoma when he was nine on July 14, 1940, at 2.40pm. On April 9, 1949, he won first prize in the Indiana State Speech Tournament and two months later moved to Los Angeles in preparation for attending Santa Monica City College and then the University of California at Los Angeles, where he appeared in *Macbeth*. In December 1950 he was taken on by his first agent, Isabelle Draesemer, and appeared in a Pepsi advert on the 13th of that month. In October 1951 he moved to New York City and appeared in a number of plays. Dean's Hollywood career was short. He was cast in *East Of Eden* on March 5, 1954, and 18 months later he was dead; his legend was about to begin. His *Giant* co-star Rock Hudson wasn't impressed: "I don't mean to speak ill of the dead, but he was a prick . . . he was selfish and petulant, and believed his own press releases." One of the biggest mysteries of Dean's life was his sexuality. Was he straight? Gay? Bisexual? A masochist? Most authors think that Dean was sexual. He would have sex with whomsoever he fancied – male or female. "I'm certainly not going through life with one hand

tied behind my back," was his own stance. The following have asserted (or had asserted on their behalf) a sexual relationship with Dean: beautiful Swiss blonde Ursula Andress, Pier Angeli, Rogers Brackett (b. 1916, his mentor), Betsy Palmer (best known for TV soap *Knots Landing* and being the original killer in *Friday The 13th* [1980]) and actress Beverly Wills.

CAUSE: Dean was a speed freak who loved racing his cars and motorbikes at reckless and dangerous speeds. In May 1954 Dean bought a red 1953 MG. Ten months later, he splashed out on a white, 1500cc Porsche 356 Super Speedster. On September 21, 1955, Dean purchased for $3,700 a silver Porsche 550 Spyder that he nicknamed 'The Little Bastard'. It was travelling in this last car at 5.45pm on Friday September 30, 1955, that Dean met his death, approximately 28 miles northeast of Paso Robles, California. Dean was driving with his 28-year-old mechanic Rolf Wütherich (himself to die in a car crash on July 28, 1981) when they saw another car in the distance. "That guy's gotta see us. He's gotta stop," said Dean and did not attempt to slow down. The driver of the other car, a 1950 Ford Sedan, 23-year-old college student Donald Gene Turnupseed, did see Dean's car but only at the last second, when collision at the junction of US 466 and Highway 41 was inevitable. Dean's neck was broken and he suffered numerous internal injuries. Wütherich also suffered serious wounds but Turnupseed was only dazed and superficially cut. Dean was pronounced dead on arrival at Paso Robles War Memorial Hospital. Turnupseed has never spoken publicly about the accident. Ironically, shortly before his death, Dean took part in an advertisement campaign for road safety. He told teenagers to slow down "because the life you save could be mine."

FURTHER READING: *James Dean: A*

Short Life – Venable Herndon (London: Futura, 1974); *James Dean: The Mutant King* – David Dalton (London: Plexus, 1983); *The Death Of James Dean* – Warren Newton Beath (New York: Grove Press, 1986); *The Unabridged James Dean: His Life And Legacy From A–Z* – Randall Riese (Chicago: Contemporary Books, 1991); *James Dean Little Boy Lost: An Intimate Biography* – Joe Hyams with Jay Hyams (London: Hutchinson, 1992), *The James Dean Story: A Myth-Shattering Biography Of An Icon* – Ronald Martinetti (New York: Birch Lane Press, 1995); *Rebel: The Life And Legend Of James Dean* – Donald Spoto (New York: HarperCollins, 1996).

Sandra Dee

(ALEXANDRA ZUCK)
Born April 23, 1944?
Died February 20, 2005
Girl next door. "Look at me, I'm Sandra Dee, lousy with virginity" so sang Rizzo in the hit musical *Grease* but the song got it wrong, terribly wrong. Sandra Dee was born in Bayonne, New Jersey to an enthusiastic and overly ambitious stage mother and an alcoholic bus driver father. Her mother added two years to her daughter's age so that she could begin work earlier. John Zuck was deserted by his wife for Eugene Douvan, a wealthy businessman 40 years her senior. Douvan was also a predatory paedophile who insisted that six-year-old Alexandra sleep between him and her mother on their wedding night. Two years later, he began to have sex with the eight-year-old, an abuse that continued until she was 12 and he died of a heart attack. "Daddy started having sexual intercourse with me. It was scary. He molested me whenever he wanted to and there was opportunity. He'd say, 'Let's snuggle,' and I never fought back." Alexandra began refusing to eat so her mother began to force-feed her but by the age of nine she was anorexic. Her mother pushed her daughter into

modelling and when she was 10, Alexandra was earning $70,000 a year. She made her film début as Evelyn Leslie, the youngest of four sisters in the film *Until They Sail* (1957). The lead role in *Gidget* (1959) made her a star but aged 15 she was 5'5" and weighed just 6st 6lbs. To control her weight, she ate 2oz of Epsom salts as an emetic after every meal. But her body developed a tolerance and she increased the dosage until one day she swallowed 8oz and collapsed with a heart attack. She was rushed to hospital but survived to continue making films such as *Imitation Of Life* (1959) as Susie and *A Summer Place* (1959) as Molly Jorgenson. She travelled to Portofino, Italy to film *Come September* (1961) in which she played Sandy Stevens and was swept off her feet by her leading man Bobby Darin, the singer. However, she did not like him at their first meeting. By the end of filming he had proposed and eight weeks later, on December 1, 1960, they were married in a hurried ceremony in Elizabeth, New Jersey. Their wedding night was not a success – understandably terrified of sex, Sandra slept on the settee. Eventually, the marriage was consummated but because of the anorexia she suffered six miscarriages. Jealous of her husband's fans, she took to drink and later amphetamines. Gambling became another addiction and one night she lost $25,000 at blackjack. The marriage was in trouble and on March 7, 1967 they divorced. They had one son, Dodd Mitchell. But she still carried a torch for Darin and was devastated by his premature death in December 1973 from a congenital heart defect. Her later films included *If A Man Answers* (1962) and *That Funny Feeling* (1965) but the effects of the drugs, booze, gambling and after-effects of the anorexia played havoc with her looks and ability to work. Her last film was *Ad Est Di Marsa Matruh* (1971). She made occasional television appearances but never lived up to her early promise.

CAUSE: In 2000 she was diagnosed with throat cancer and kidney failure. She died in Los Angeles from kidney disease and pneumonia. She was 60.

Nicole DeHuff

Born January 6, 1974
Died February 16, 2005
Tragic entrant. Dark-haired Nicole Renee DeHuff was born in the unusually named Oklahoma town of Antlers and studied at the Carnegie Mellon Acting Conservatory. She made her film début in the comedy *Meet The Parents* (2000) playing Deborah Byrnes opposite Robert DeNiro and Ben Stiller. She went on to appear in *Suspect Zero* (2004) as Katie Potter. She featured in the TV shows *CSI: Miami, Monk* and *The Practice*. Nicole was married on November 11, 2000 to the producer Ari Palitz, but had no children.

CAUSE: Feeling ill, she attended hospital in Los Angeles but was twice sent home and told not to worry, that there was nothing serious amiss. Tragically, the doctors misdiagnosed her and she died of pneumonia, aged only 31.

Albert Dekker

Born December 20, 1905
Died May 3, 1968
Suave with a secret. Born in Brooklyn, New York, Dekker attended Bowdoin College, Maine, with an ambition to become either a psychiatrist or a psychologist. However, he proved so impressive in college plays that a former pupil badgered Dekker into giving acting a shot and even wrote a letter of introduction for him to Alfred Lunt. Dekker finally agreed and Lunt was to say later of him, "Al has a fine mind and a soul in which unkindness is wholly absent." It was in 1927 that Dekker made his stage début playing a beggar in *Kismet*. His first Broadway appearance came with a variety of plays the same year. Dekker was a natural on both stage and in films, which he entered in 1937. He was handsome, tall (6'3"), sandy haired and blue eyed. In 1929 he married actress Esther Guernini and fathered two sons and a daughter. His first film was *The Great Garrick* (1937) as LeBrun and he went on to appear in over 70 more, including *She Married An Artist* (1938) as Whitney Holton, *Extortion* (1938) as Jeffrey Thompson, *Marie Antoinette* (1938) as Comte de Provence, *Never Say Die* (1939), *Hotel Imperial* (1939), *The Man In The Iron Mask* (1939) as Louis XIII, *Beau Geste* (1939) as Schwartz, *Rangers Of Fortune* (1940) as George Bird, *Strange Cargo* (1940) as Moll, *Dr Cyclops* (1940) as mad scientist Dr Thorkel, *You're The One* (1941) as Luke Laramie, *Reaching For The Sun* (1941) as Herman, *Honky Tonk* (1941) as Brazos Hearn, *Blonde Inspiration* (1941) as Phil Hendricks, *Night In New Orleans* (1942) as Police Lieutenant William Richards, *In Old California* (1942) as Britt Dawson, *Wake Island* (1942) as Shad McClosky, *The Forest Rangers* (1942) as Twig Dawson, *Buckskin Frontier* (1943) as Gideon Skene, *Incendiary Blonde* (1945) as Cadden, *California* (1946) as Mr Pike, *Two Years Before The Mast* (1946) as Brown, *Wyoming* (1947) as Lassiter, *Slave Girl* (1947) as Pasha, *Tarzan's Magic Fountain* (1949) as Mr Trask, *Destination Murder* (1950) as Armitage, *As Young As You Feel* (1951) as Louis McKinley, *Illegal* (1955) as Frank Garland, *She Devil* (1957) as Dr Richard Bach, *Machete* (1958) as Don Luis Montoya, *Suddenly, Last Summer* (1959) as Dr Hockstader and Sam Peckinpah's *The Wild Bunch* (1969) as Pat Harrigan. In 1944 he was elected as a Democrat to the 57th District in the California State Assembly, where he served a two-year term. Back on stage he wowed audiences as Willy Loman in Arthur Miller's *Death Of A Salesman* and won a Tony for his part as the Duke of Norfolk in Robert Bolt's *A Man For All Seasons*. Then in

the mid-Fifties Dekker's seemingly charmed existence came to an end. He was furious at the McCarthy witch hunts and was one of the few brave enough to speak out, calling the junior senator from Wisconsin "insane". Despite his political record Dekker was damned, received death threats and found himself blacklisted. It was almost 20 years before Dekker was able to work regularly again. His 16-year-old son, Jan, shot and accidentally killed himself in 1967. That tragic demise would be as nothing compared to his father's the following year.

CAUSE: Albert Dekker's death at 62 is one of the most puzzling in Hollywood history. He was discovered dead in his Hollywood home, 1731 North Normandie, kneeling in the bath. In each arm was a dirty hypodermic needle, a noose was around his neck, a scarf covered his eyes, a horse's bit was in his mouth with the reins tied tightly behind his head, a leather belt was around his neck, another around his chest and leather ropes connected the two. A third leather belt around his waist was tied with a rope to his ankles, which were tightly bound. The rope then went back up his body around his wrists and was held in his hands, which were manacled with handcuffs. The word "Whip" was written in red lipstick on his right buttock above two needle marks. Around his nipples were sun rays, also in lipstick. On his thorax was the words "Make me suck" with "Slave" and "Cocksucker" on his chest. A vagina was drawn on his lower belly. To add to the disturbing sight, lividity had sent the lower half of his body purple. The coroner stated it was an "accidental death, not suicide" but many of his friends believed he had been murdered. They pointed to the fact that $70,000 in cash was missing along with a tape recorder and expensive photographic equipment. Coroner Dr Thomas T. Noguchi (on whom TV pathologist *Quincy, M.E.* was based) believes Dekker died of auto-asphyxiation during a sex game that went horribly wrong. The case is closed.

Dolores Del Rio
(LOLITA DOLORES MARTÍNEZ ASÚNSOLO Y LÓPEZ NEGRETE)
Born August 3, 1905
Died April 11, 1983
Beautiful brunette bombshell. Born in Durango, Mexico, Dolores Del Rio was the St Joseph's Convent-educated daughter of the president of a bank and the cousin of Ramon Novarro. The family fled their massive ranch in 1909 to escape Pancho Villa. The 5'3½" Dolores Del Rio was never really taken seriously in Hollywood, probably because of her accent, even though she could speak English, French, German and Spanish. Producers tended to regard her more as window dressing. Back home in Mexico, she was respected and won four Arieles, the Mexican Oscar, and one Quixote, the Spanish Oscar. Aged 16 she married Jaime Martinez Del Rio, a wealthy aristocrat lawyer 18 years her senior and homosexual, and met film director Edwin Carewe in Mexico City. He took her back to Tinseltown and told her he would marry her, even though he was also a newlywed. She appeared in *Joanna* (1925) as Carlotta de Silva, *The Whole Town's Talking* (1926) as Rita Renault, *High Steppers* (1926) as Evelyn Iffield, *Pals First* (1926) as Jeanne Lamont, *What Price Glory* (1926) as Charmaine de la Cognac, *Resurrection* (1927) as Katyusha Maslova, *Revenge* (1928) as Rascha, *Ramona* (1928) as Ramona, *No Other Woman* (1928) as Carmelita de Granados, *The Trail Of '98* (1929) as Berna, *Evangeline* (1929) as Evangeline, *Girl Of The Rio* (1932) as Dolores, *Bird Of Paradise* (1932) as Luana, *Flying Down To Rio* (1933) as Belinha de Rezende, *Madame DuBarry* (1934) as Madame DuBarry, *I Live For Love* (1935) as Donna Alvarez, *Accused* (1936) as Gaby Seymour, *Lancer Spy*

(1937) as Dolores Daria Sunnell, *Ali Baba Goes To Town* (1937), *International Settlement* (1938) as Leonore Dixon and her final major American film *Journey Into Fear* (1942) as Josette Martel. By 1928 she had separated from her husband. Jaime Del Rio died in a German hospital of blood poisoning, but no marriage to Edwin Carewe materialised. Instead, on August 6, 1930, in Santa Barbara, California, Dolores wed MGM art director Cedric Gibbons (b. Dublin, March 23, 1893, d. 1960). They were together until January 17, 1941. Before the divorce she romanced Orson Welles. The latter met Dolores in a nightclub and told her he had been in love with her from the age of 11. When she left the club that night Welles ran down the street after her. Even though she was ten years older, she was intrigued by his genius and he by her . . . well, by her. Dolores went on to marry Lewis Riley, a millionaire, on November 24, 1959. She had moved back to Mexico City by this time and appeared in several more films, including *Flor Silvestre* (1943) as Esperanza, *María Candelaria* (1944) as María Candelaria, *Bugambilia* (1945) as Amalita de los Robles, *La Casa Chica* (1949) as Amalia Estrada, *Deseada* (1951) as Deseada, *Reportaje* (1953) as María Enriqueta, *Señora Ama* (1954) as Dominica, *El Pecado De Una Madre* (1960) as La Madre, *Rio Blanco* (1967) and *C'Era Una Volta* (1967). Dolores maintained that the secret of beauty was to "Take care of your inner, spiritual beauty – that will reflect in your face." She also didn't drink, didn't smoke and slept a remarkable 16 hours a day.
CAUSE: She died aged 77 in Newport Beach, California, of liver failure.

Dom DeLuise

Born August 1, 1933
Died May 4, 2009
Podgy second banana. Born in Brooklyn, the youngest of three children of a dustman and a housewife, Dominick DeLuise attended the High School for Performing Arts in Manhattan. Of his father, an Italian immigrant, DeLuise said, "I was really in this acting thing alone. My father was a peasant, a blue-collar worker, who was amazed that I got paid for what I do. He used to say, 'If you can make money with your mouth, God bless you!'" DeLuise began appearing on television in the late Fifties in *Tinker's Workshop* but it was the Sixties before he was a regular guest star in programmes such as *The Shari Lewis Show*, *The Munsters*, *Please Don't Eat The Daisies*, *The Girl from U.N.C.L.E.* and *The Ghost And Mrs Muir*. He made his Broadway debut in 1963 as Muffin T. Ragamuffin in *The Student Gypsy* and his film debut the following year in *Diary Of A Bachelor* (1964) as Marvin Rollins. His dimwitted spy Julius Pritter stole the show in the Doris Day film *The Glass Bottom Boat* (1966) and it became a virtual given that DeLuise would do his best to steal any scene he played. "I became a comedian when they laughed at my serious acting." he revealed. He often worked with Mel Brooks and Burt Reynolds. His films included: *What's So Bad About Feeling Good?* (1968) as J. Gardner Monroe, *The Twelve Chairs* (1970) as Father Fyodor, *The Adventure Of Sherlock Holmes' Smarter Brother* (1975), *Silent Movie* (1976), the deranged studio boss Adolf Zitz in *The World's Greatest Lover* (1977), *The Muppet Movie* (1979), *Hot Stuff* (1979), which was the first film he directed, a compulsive eater in *Fatso* (1980), *Smokey And The Bandit II* (1980), *History Of The World – Part I* (1981) as Nero, *Cannonball Run* (1981), *The Best Little Whorehouse In Texas* (1982), *Cannonball Run II* (1984), *Spaceballs* (1987) as the voice of Pizza the Hutt, *Loose Cannons* (1990) as fat pornographer Harry "the Hippo" Gutterman, *Robin Hood: Men In Tights* (1993) as Don Giovanni and the horror spoof *The Silence Of The*

Hams (1994) as Dr Animal Cannibal Pizza. His later television career was not as successful. His sitcom *Lotsa Luck* ran from 1973 until 1974 and the syndicated *Dom DeLuise Show* also only ran for two years. His hosting of *Candid Camera* in 1991 was also a flop. As DeLuise's film work began to dry up, he found an outlet in food and wrote a number of recipe books including *Eat This . . . It'll Make You Feel Better!* (1988) and *Eat This Too!: It'll Also Make You Feel Better* (1997). He also wrote a number of books for children. On November 23, 1965 he married the actress Carol Arthur (b. Hackensack, New Jersey August 4, 1935). They had three sons all of whom became actors: Peter (b. New York November 6, 1966), Michael (b. Los Angeles, California August 4, 1969) and David (b. Burbank, California November 11, 1971).

CAUSE: 5'10" DeLuise was fat for most of his life, at one stage reaching 24 stone. In 1993 doctors refused to perform hip replacement surgery until DeLuise lost seven stone. He did but regained some weight after the operation. DeLuise died aged 75 at St John's Health Center in Santa Monica from kidney failure and respiratory complications from cancer. He was cremated and his ashes buried with his parents in New York.

Roger Delgado

(ROGER CAESAR MARIUS BERNARD DE DELGADO TORRES CASTILLO ROBERTO)
Born March 1, 1918
Died June 18, 1973
The Master. Delgado, the son of a Spanish banker father and a French mother, was born in London during the last air raid of the First World War. He longed to be in drama but followed his father's footsteps and began working in a bank. Then, one Friday in 1938, after 18 months in the job he walked out of his City bank and on the following Tuesday began rehearsals with the Nelson Repertory Company at the Theatre Royal, Leicester, for a production of *You Can't Take It With You*. He then found a niche playing villains and appeared in all forms of show business except cabaret and ice shows. His best-known villain was on television playing Dr Who's nemesis, the renegade Time Lord known as The Master, a mantle he took up in an episode called *Terror Of The Autons* on January 2, 1971. His films included: *The Broken Horseshoe* (1953), *Blood Orange* (1953) as Marlowe, *Storm Over The Nile* (1955), *Mark Of The Phoenix* (1958), *The Stranglers Of Bombay* (1960), *The Terror Of The Tongs* (1961) as Tang Hao, *The Road To Hong Kong* (1962) as Jhinnah, *Masquerade* (1965) as Ahmed Ben Faïd, *The Mummy's Shroud* (1967) as Hasmid and *The Assassination Bureau* (1969).
CAUSE: He was killed aged 55 in a car crash while working in Turkey. Ironically, one of his hobbies was driving fast sports cars. Delgado was working on a film called *Bell Of Tibet* when the hired car he was in plunged into a ravine near Neveshir. Police said the crash was caused by the chauffeur taking a bend too quickly.

Dorothy Dell

(DOROTHY DELL GOFF)
Born January 30, 1915
Died June 8, 1934
Tragic starlet. Born Hattiesburg, Mississippi, Dorothy was an absolute stunner, becoming Miss New Orleans and then winning both the Miss America and Miss Universe titles in 1930. She landed a job with the Ziegfeld Follies in 1931 and then signed a contract with Paramount. She appeared in *Wharf Angel* (1934) as Toy with Victor McLaglen. She then played nightclub singer Bangles Carson in the Shirley Temple flick *Little Miss Marker* (1934). The childhood best friend of Dorothy Lamour, she was promoted as Paramount's answer to Alice Faye. It was not to be.
CAUSE: In June 1934, blonde Dorothy

and her boyfriend, a Beverly Hills doctor, attended a party in the Altadena Hills. On the way home their car went over an embankment, smashed into a telephone pole and hit a boulder. Dorothy died immediately, her lover a few hours later. Her final movie, *Shoot The Works* (1934), in which she played Lily Raquel, was released posthumously.

Cecil B. DeMille

Born August 12, 1881
Died January 21, 1959
Epic director. Born in Ashfield, Massachusetts, the man who made biblical cinematic epics was the younger son of an Episcopal lay preacher, Henry Churchill De Mille (b. Washington, North Carolina September 4, 1853 d. Pompton Lakes, New Jersey, February 10, 1893 from typhoid fever) and (Matilde) Beatrice Samuel (b. Liverpool, January 30, 1853 d. Hollywood, California, October 8, 1923), a teacher. A sister Agnes Beatrice (b. May 23, 1891, d. February 12, 1895) did not survive childhood. The spelling of the surname remains difficult for authors. It was Henry De Mille but Cecil B. began as de Mille, then became De Mille before finally settling on DeMille. 5'11" Cecil Blount DeMille enrolled at Pennsylvania Military College in 1898. He then followed in the footsteps of his brother, William Churchill (b. North Carolina July 25, 1878, d. Playa del Rey, March 4, 1955) by joining the American Academy Of Dramatic Arts whence he graduated in 1900. He worked as an actor, stage manager and playwright (albeit unsuccessfully – alone and collaborating with his brother William, he wrote several plays, all of which failed) before co-founding The Jesse L. Lasky Feature Play Company (later Paramount) in November 1913 with Lasky and his brother-in-law Samuel Goldfish (later Goldwyn). DeMille was appointed director-general of the company,

despite the fact that he had little or no experience with a camera. His first film (which he co-directed, wrote, produced and appeared in) was *The Squaw Man* (released February 15, 1914), which began shooting on December 29, 1913 on a budget of $20,000. DeMille said, "When I came to Los Angeles I knew nothing of the making of films, but I had the big idea. I had seen picture plays that were almost dramas. When anyone told me that such and such a thing could not be done, I got someone who could do it." DeMille became an expert at the art of self-publicity, often appearing in prologues to his films. He became known for his image of bald head, boots and megaphone. He wore boots on set in the early days to protect him from snake bites and kept them as an affectation ever after. "He wore baldness like an expensive hat, as though it were out of the question for him to have hair like other men," said Gloria Swanson. *The Squaw Man* made $250.000 and DeMille never looked back. He introduced a number of innovations that later became standard in films: the listing of actors' names in on-screen credits, the use of proper sets rather than painted scenery for indoor scenes, and the use of extra lighting apart from the sun to emphasise certain aspects of the screen image (he called this "Rembrandt" lighting). He would also go on to invent the boom mike. Seemingly tireless, he once directed two films at the same time, one by day and one by night. He also began to live the life of a very rich man with a chauffeured limousine, a mansion, a ranch, and a yacht. He also had interests in land, oil, banking, and racetracks and an early airline. He made *Brewster's Millions* (released April 15, 1914), *The Master Mind* (released May 11, 1914), *The Virginian* (released September 7, 1914), *Rose Of The Rancho* (released November 15, 1914), *After Five* (released January 28, 1915), *The Warrens Of Virginia* (released February 15, 1915), *The Wild*

Goose Chase (released May 27, 1915),
Carmen (released October 31, 1915),
Maria Rosa (released May 7, 1916),
The Trail Of The Lonesome Pine
(released February 13, 1916), *Sweet
Kitty Bellairs* (1916), *A Romance Of The
Redwoods* (released May 14, 1917), *Old
Wives For New* (released May 19,
1918), *You Can't Have Everything*
(released July 7, 1918), *Don't Change
Your Husband* (released January 26,
1919), *For Better, For Worse* (released
April 27, 1919), *Male And Female*
(released November 23, 1919) which
contained a scene of Gloria Swanson
preparing for a bath, *Why Change Your
Wife?* (premièred May 21, 1920)
described by one critic as "the most
gorgeously sensual film of the month;
in decoration the most costly; in
physical allure the most fascinating; in
effect the most immoral", *Saturday
Night* (released January 29, 1922) and
Adam's Rib (released September 24,
1923). Following a series of scandals a
new morality invaded Hollywood and
DeMille, ever quick to jump on a
bandwagon, began making biblical
films or movies with a message such as
Manslaughter (released September 24,
1922). A move to MGM saw DeMille
remake *The Squaw Man* (released
September 5, 1931) but it was terrible.
At the age of 50 DeMille was jobless
and in trouble with the IRS. With no
other choice, he returned to Paramount
where he spent the rest of his career.
He was convinced that he could revive
his career with another historical
drama. He was given a one-picture deal
on a greatly reduced salary and strict
instructions to remain within budget.
The Sign Of The Cross (1932) about
oppressed Christians in pagan Rome
was a gamble that paid off. DeMille's
next two films, both modern-day
stories, lost money, and thereafter he
played it safe with heroic tales of the
past. He made two versions of *The Ten
Commandments* 33 years apart (released
November 23, 1923 and released
October 5, 1956) and when asked why

he made so many biblical-themed
films, he replied, "Why let 2,000 years
of publicity go to waste?" DeMille was
not one to suffer inaccuracies in his
films. He spent $100,000 researching
for his epic *Cleopatra* (released October
5, 1934). This even stretched to
sending researchers to Egypt to check
what colour the pyramids are. (They
returned with the news that they are
the same colour the man in the street
thought they were – sandy brown.)
That said, at one point in DeMille's
The Crusades (released October 25,
1935), the actor playing the king looks
at his wristwatch. In 1937 DeMille was
nominated for senator by the
Republicans but declined the
nomination. For a time he was
Anthony Quinn's father-in-law
(the actor was married to Katherine
DeMille from October 5, 1937 until
1941). When DeMille was given the
honour of preserving his handprints in
cement at Grauman's Chinese Theater,
he was too busy on set to leave, so the
cement was brought to the shoot.
DeMille had some peculiar habits. He
had a collection of over 200 shrunken
heads and he was a foot fetishist.
Actress Paulette Goddard revealed, "I
actually used my bare feet to get better
roles out of him." His later films
included: *North West Mounted Police*
(released October 22, 1940), *Reap The
Wild Wind* (premièred March 18,
1942), *Unconquered* (premièred
September 24, 1947), *California's
Golden Beginning* (1948), *Samson And
Delilah* (released December 21, 1949)
and *The Greatest Show On Earth*
(premièred January 10, 1952) all of
which he also produced except for the
fourth in this list. *The Greatest Show On
Earth* won DeMille a Best Picture
Oscar. He also had a small career as an
actor – usually, though not always,
playing himself. He was the narrator
on *Reap The Wild Wind* (1942) and
Unconquered (1947), the voice of God
on *The Ten Commandments* (1956) and
played himself in *Sunset Blvd.* (1950).

In 1949 he received the Irving G. Thalberg Award, his first Oscar in 36 years of work. He married Constance Adams (b. Orange, New Jersey, April 27, 1874, d. Los Angeles, California, July 17, 1960 from pneumonia), nine years his senior, on August 16, 1902, in Orange, New Jersey, and had a daughter Cecilia (b. Orange, New Jersey, October 5, 1908, d. Los Angeles, California, June 23, 1984). They also adopted two sons, John (b. 1909 as John Gonzales) in 1914 and Richard (b. February 12, 1922) in 1940 (although he was with the family from babyhood) and a daughter 5'3¾" Katherine (b. Vancouver, British Columbia, Canada, June 29, 1911 as Katherine Lester d. Tucson, Arizona, April 27, 1995 from Alzheimer's disease) in 1920. Like many powerful men DeMille took several mistresses after his wife lost interest in sex but remained devoted to her. The most famous anecdote regarding DeMille is one oft told but worth repeating. It relates to one of his Biblical epics, when he had five cameras ready to capture the action from various angles. It would be a tremendous scene and all had to be done in one take. DeMille called action and the scene began. When he called "Cut" he contacted all the cameramen on radio microphones. "Number 1, did you get the shot?" "Yes, Mr DeMille." "Number 2?" "Yes, Mr DeMille", and so on. Then it was number five's turn. "Well?" asked DeMille. "Ready when you are, Mr DeMille."
CAUSE: He died of a heart seizure at 5am in Hollywood, California, aged 77. He was buried on January 23, 1959, with the funeral taking place at St Stephen's Episcopal Church, 6126 Yucca Street. He was laid to rest beside his brother (who once commented, "The trouble with Cecil is that he bites off more than he can chew – and then chews it") in the Hollywood Memorial Park, 6000 Santa Monica Boulevard, Hollywood, California 90038.

FURTHER READING: *Cecil B. DeMille –* Charles Higham (New York: Da Capo Press, 1973); *Cecil B. DeMille And The Golden Calf –* Simon Louvish (London: Faber & Faber, 2007).

Ted Demme

Born October 26, 1963
Died January 13, 2002
Jonathan's nephew. Ted Demme was born in New York and began working as a production assistant at MTV. He co-directed the video for Bruce Springsteen's 'Streets Of Philadelphia' but his first motion picture was *Who's The Man?* (1993). He was best known for directing *Blow* (2001) which starred Johnny Depp and Penelope Cruz and was the story of the real-life drug kingpin George Jung, who established the US cocaine market in the Seventies. Demme was married to Amanda Scheer and they had two children, a five-year-old daughter and a two-month-old son.
CAUSE: Demme suffered a heart attack while playing in a celebrity basketball game at the private Crossroads School in Santa Monica. He was rushed by paramedics to the Santa Monica UCLA Medical Center in full cardiac arrest shortly after 5pm. Efforts to revive Demme failed and he was pronounced dead about 20 minutes later. He was 38.

Michael Denison, CBE

Born November 1, 1915
Died July 22, 1998
True Brit. Born in Doncaster, Yorkshire, John Michael Terence Wellesley Denison attended Harrow and Magdalen College, Oxford (BA in modern languages), before studying at the Webber-Douglas School. In August 1938 he made his first appearance on stage at Frinton-on-Sea playing Lord Fancourt Babberley in *Charley's Aunt*. It was to be the start of a long and distinguished stage career. He made his first film *Inspector Hornleigh On Holiday* in 1939 and his second a year later,

Tilly Of Bloomsbury, playing Dick Mainwaring. From 1939 until 1946 he served with the Royal Signals and Intelligence Corps. He resumed his career after the cessation of hostilities and went on to appear in *Hungry Hill* (1947) as Henry Broderick, *My Brother Jonathan* (1948) as Jonathan Dakers, *The Glass Mountain* (1949) as Richard Wilder, *The Importance Of Being Earnest* (1952) as Algernon Moncrieff, *There Was A Young Lady* (1953) as David Walsh and *Shadowlands* (1993) as 'Harry' Harrington, his last film and his first for over 30 years. On television he took the lead role in the drama *Boyd, QC* from 1956 for eight years. In 1939 he married the actress and authoress Dulcie Gray. He contributed a number of articles (most notably the one on Noël Coward) to *The Dictionary Of National Biography*.
CAUSE: He died of cancer aged 82 at his home, Shardeloes, in Amersham, Buckinghamshire.

Peter Denyer
Born August 20, 1947
Died September 18, 2009
Comedic character. Born illegitimately at Dartford, Kent, Peter John Denyer was raised by adoptive parents and attended Erith Grammar School. He trained at the Bristol Old Vic and began his career aged 19 at The Playhouse in Sheffield in Alan Cullen's musical *The Stirrings In Sheffield On Saturday Night*. In 1967 he appeared in the National Youth Theatre's hit musical *Zigger Zagger* at the Strand Theatre in the West End. The following year, he was cast as dopey Dennis Dunstable in the sitcom *Please Sir!* (November 8, 1968–February 13, 1972) – he said, "I auditioned for the role in 1967 and got the part because, I suspect, I looked stupider than anyone else at the auditions" – and reprised the role in the 1971 film version. He appeared in only the first series of *The Fenn Street Gang*. To capitalise on his success in *Please Sir!* Denyer recorded a

sentimental ballad in 1972 called 'Beggar Boy' and appeared in a mediocre film about banning pop music called *Never Too Young To Rock* (1975). He found work hard to come by, such was his association with Dennis Dunstable. It was not until he appeared as the homosexual Michael Simpson in the sitcom *Agony* (March 11, 1979–March 1, 1981) that Denyer returned to the public's attention. Seven years later, he was cast as Ralph Dring in the BBC sitcom *Dear John* (February 17, 1986–October 12, 1987, plus 1987 Christmas special) and he had another crack at fame. But then the series was cancelled, as it was cheaper for the BBC to buy in the American version with Judd Hirsch than to make original episodes. As acting work dried up, he moved behind the cameras in 1990 and began writing, directing and producing pantomimes. He also played the dame in pantomimes. Denyer was unmarried.
CAUSE: Denyer died aged 62 at Cheltenham, Gloucestershire.

Guillaume Depardieu
Born April 7, 1971
Died October 13, 2008
Difficult son. Guillaume Jean Maxime Antoine Depardieu was born in Paris, the son of Gerard Depardieu. They endured a tempestuous relationship and had a very public falling-out in 2003. Although he appeared in several films it was more for his private life that Depardieu made headlines. On September 16, 2003 he was sentenced to prison for nine months, eventually suspended and fined, for threatening a man with a gun in Trouville, France. He married Elise Ventre on December 30, 1999 and had a daughter Louise by her in January 2001. They separated the year their daughter was born. Among Depardieu's films were *Pas Si Méchant Que Ca* (1974) as Guillaume, *Tous Les Matins Du Monde* (1991) as Young Marin Marais, *Les Paroles Invisibles* (1992), *Cible Emouvante*

(1993) as Antoine, *Marthe* (1997) as
Simon, . . . *Comme Elle Respire* (1998)
as Antoine, *Process* (2004) as the
husband, *Célibataires* (2006) as Ben,
Versailles (2008) as Damien, *Stella*
(2008) as Alain Bernard and *Les
Inséparables* (2008) as Boris.
CAUSE: In 1995 Depardieu was
involved in a motorcycle accident and
while in hospital his leg became
infected. Despite two years of
treatment the infection refused to be
cleared up and in constant pain
Depardieu agreed to have his leg
amputated. His resistance was low
afterwards and while filming *L'Enfance
D'Icare* on location in Romania he
contracted pneumonia. He died at the
Garches Hospital, France aged 37.

John Derek
(DEREK DULLIVAN HARRIS)
Born August 12, 1926
Died May 22, 1998
Lucky blighter. To a whole generation
of film-goers John Derek is known only
as the man who married Bo Derek (b.
Torrance, California, November 21,
1956, as Mary Catherine Collins), the
beautiful, corn-braided, 5'4" blonde
who first came to the public's attention
in *10* (1979) starring opposite Dudley
Moore. However, there was much
more to John Derek than his wife Bo.
He was also the man who married
beautiful blondes Ursula Andress and
Linda Evans. Oh, and he also had
something of an acting career. Born in
Hollywood, California, the son of an
actor-turned-architect, 5'10½" Derek
began his movie career by being offered
a contract by David O. Selznick as a
teenager. His first job was acting in
the film *I'll Be Seeing You* (1944) as
Lieutenant Bruce; bizarrely, he was
listed as Dare Harris on the credits. A
steady rather than an overly charismatic
actor, he went on to appear in *Knock
On Any Door* (1949) as street punk
Nick Romano, *All The King's Men*
(1949) as Tom Stark, *Rogues Of
Sherwood Forest* (1950) as Robin, Earl

of Huntington, *Mask Of The Avenger*
(1951) as Captain Renato Dimorna,
Saturday's Hero (1951) as Steve Novak,
Thunderbirds (1952) as Gil Hackett,
Scandal Sheet (1952) as Steve
McCleary, *Sea Of Lost Ships* (1953)
as Grad Matthews, *Prince Of Pirates*
(1953) as Prince Roland, the title role
in *The Adventures Of Hajji Baba*
(1954), Cecil B. DeMille's *The Ten
Commandments* (1956) in which he
played Joshua, *Fury At Showdown*
(1957) as Brock Mitchell, *Omar
Khayyam* (1957) as Young Prince
Malik, *Exodus* (1960) as Taha, *Once
Before I Die* (1965) as Bailey and his
last film *Nightmare In The Sun* (1965).
Derek had many opportunities to
appear in better films, but felt he
was hamstrung by his studio.
Consequently, he never let any of his
wives become bound by studio
contracts. He was also picked on by the
press because of his pretty boy looks.
One critic carped that if John Derek
wore a wig he would look like Rita
Hayworth. Derek saved his charisma
for off-screen, capturing the hearts of
some of the world's most beautiful
women. Following the divorce from his
little-known first wife, Princess Pati
Behrs Eristoff (they had a quadriplegic
son, Russell, b. 1950, and a daughter
Sean Catherine, b. October 16, 1953),
he married Ursula Andress (b. Berne,
Switzerland, March 19, 1936) in Las
Vegas on February 2, 1957, and
divorced her ten years later, following
his affair with Linda Evans and
Andress' fling with Jean-Paul
Belmondo. The 5'7" Evans (b.
Hartford, Connecticut, November 18,
1942, as Linda Evanstad) became Mrs
Derek only to be dumped for Bo,
whom he married in 1974. He guided
her career in a Svengali-like manner to
see her become, for a time, the world's
number one sex symbol. He wrote,
photographed, directed and she starred
in (usually without her clothes on) the
following films: *Fantasies* (1981),
Tarzan, The Ape Man (1981) (he didn't

write this one), *Bolero* (1984) and *Ghosts Can't Do It* (1991). In 1979 he directed and she produced a hardcore porn film.

CAUSE: After suffering from heart trouble for many years, he finally succumbed in Santa Maria, California, aged 71.

FURTHER READING: *Cast Of Characters* – Sean Catherine Derek (New York: Leisure Books, 1982).

Jerry Desmonde
(JAMES ROBERT SADLER)
Born July 20, 1908
Died February 11, 1967
Gentlemanly foil. Born in of all places, although you would never know it from his accent, Middlesbrough, he began his professional career on July 20, 1922, teaming up with the rest of his family to become one of The Four Sadlers. He didn't intend to join the family act but his sister Elsie left the troupe when she eloped and Jerry put on a wig and her clothes and for two years was 'Elsie'. In 1927 he toured America in a show called *This Year Of Grace*. He later became a stooge to Scottish comedian Dave Willis and worked with his wife, Peg, as Peg & Jerry for seven years before becoming straight man to Sid Field on stage and in two films – *London Town* (1946) and *Cardboard Cavalier* (1949) playing Lovelace. However, shortly after opening with Field in a 1949 production of *Harvey*, Desmonde was sacked. Field had dropped out of the show through ill-health and newspapers began asking if he would be as funny without Desmonde. Field refused to return to the show until his former stooge had been replaced. He also worked with Arthur Askey, Bob Hope and Nat Jackley. On television he was a regular panelist on *What's My Line?* and also presented *The 64,000 Question* from 1956 until 1958. Yet he was probably best known for his work with Norman Wisdom in films such as *Trouble In Store* (1953) in which he

played store boss Augustus Freeman, *Man Of The Moment* (1955) as Jackson, *Up In The World* (1956) as Major Willoughby, *Just My Luck* (1957), *A Stitch In Time* (1963) as Sir Hector and *The Early Bird* (1965) as Mr Hunter. His other films included: *The Perfect Woman* (1949), *The Malta Story* (1953), *Alf's Baby* (1953) as Alf Donkin, *The Angel Who Pawned Her Harp* (1954) as Parker, *Ramsbottom Rides Again* (1956) as Blue Eagle, *A King In New York* (1957) as Prime Minister Voudel, *Follow A Star* (1959) as Vernon Carew, *Carry On Regardless* (1961) as Martin Paul, *A Kind Of Loving* (1962), *Stolen Hours* (1963), *The Beauty Jungle* (1964) and *Gonks Go Beat* (1965) as the Great Galaxian. He was as fastidious off-screen as on-, rarely being seen without highly polished shoes and a smartly pressed suit.

CAUSE: He died by his own hand aged 59 in London.

Brandon De Wilde
Born April 9, 1942
Died July 6, 1972
Young talent. Born into a theatrical family at Brooklyn, Andre Brandon De Wilde was raised in Baldwin, Long Island. At seven he made his Broadway debut in *The Member Of The Wedding*, becoming the first child actor to win the Donaldson Award. He also starred in Fred Zinnemann's 1952 movie version. 1952 was the pinnacle of his career – he played Joey Starrett who worships the loner gunman (Alan Ladd) in *Shane* (premièred April 23, 1953), which resulted in his nomination for a Best Supporting Actor Oscar. From 1953 until 1954 he had his own series on television, *Jamie* in which he played Jamison Francis McHummber, but it was cancelled in a contractual dispute. In 1956 he was Skeeter opposite Walter Brennan, Phil Harris, and Sidney Poitier in *Good-bye, My Lady*. The following year he was Joey Adams in *Night Passage* (1957),

and then Brian Turner in *The Missouri Traveler* (1958), Arthur Bartley in *Blue Denim* (1959) co-starring Carol Lynley before appearing as Clinton Willart with Warren Beatty and Eva Marie Saint in *All Fall Down* (1962). After *Shane*, his second biggest role is probably in *Hud* (1963) opposite Paul Newman. De Wilde was the only lead actor in the film not to receive a nod from the Academy. He was Bucky Calloway in *Those Calloways* (1965) before he played John Wayne's son, Ensign Jeremiah Torrey in *In Harm's Way* (1965) but made only two more films one as an extra (*The Trip* in 1967) before his untimely death. His last cinematic role was playing Josh in *Wild In The Sky* (1972). As his cinematic career waned he tried his hand at music but with little success. In 1963 he married Susan M. Maw by whom he had a son, Jesse, but the marriage ended in divorce in 1969. In 1972 he married Janice Gero.

CAUSE: De Wilde was appearing in the play *Butterflies Are Free* in Lakewood, Colorado when his motorcycle swerved to avoid a car and hit a building site trailer. De Wilde was trapped under his bike for some time before he was freed and taken to Denver General Hospital. He died four hours later. He was interred at Hollywood, California but his remains were later dug up and reburied at Pinelawn Memorial Park, Pinelawn Road and Wellwood Avenue, Farmingdale, New York NY11735. His father, Frederic (b. February 7, 1914), died in April 1980 and mother, Eugenia (b. January 3, 1916), in May 1987. The song 'In My Hour Of Darkness' was written by Emmylou Harris and Gram Parsons about De Wilde.

Brad Dexter

(BORIS MILANOVICH)
Born April 9, 1917
Died December 12, 2002
Frank's pal. Born in Goldfield, Nevada, the son of Serbian emigres,

Dexter grew up speaking Serbo-Croat. He became a lifelong friend of Karl Malden, another Serb, after they met in the air force during the Second World War. They also appeared in stage and film versions of *Winged Victory* (1944), a drama about airmen designed to bolster wartime morale in which Dexter played the role of Jack Browning. After the war, Dexter, who had been a talented amateur boxer, studied acting at the Pasadena Playhouse and changed his name to Barry Mitchell. His earliest films included *Heldorado* (1946) as Alex Baxter and *Sinbad The Sailor* (1947) as Muallin with Douglas Fairbanks, Jr, but his big break came with *The Asphalt Jungle* in 1950. He played Bob Brannom and it was the start of a career that often saw him portraying thugs and villains. He played jewel thief and murderer Victor Rawlins in *99 River Street* (1953) and gangster Gil Clayton in *Violent Saturday* (1955). He was the flamboyant real-life hoodlum Bugsy Siegel in *The George Raft Story* (1961). "I love playing heavies," he said. "It's the best-written character." In January 1953, he married singer Peggy Lee in the garden of her hilltop home in Los Angeles but by September they were divorced. Dexter said afterwards, "I doubt if I'll ever get married again. I can't put up with 'What are you doing?' and 'Where have you been?'" He was comforted by Marilyn Monroe, whom he had met on the set of *The Asphalt Jungle*. Dexter insisted that he and the 20th century's leading sex symbol were just friends, though it was not only showbiz reporters who speculated on the relationship: her husband Joe DiMaggio threw a fit when he first found Dexter in his home. Dexter often worked on television westerns and played Beero, the Belden foreman in *Last Train From Gun Hill* (1959). It was following this that John Sturges signed him to play the most famous unknown in Hollywood. Yul Brynner was the only star name in *The Magnificent Seven* although Steve McQueen, James Coburn, Robert Vaughn and Charles Bronson would all become household names. That fate was not for Brad Dexter who played Harry Luck in the movie. Years later James Coburn struggled to complete the line-up, stumbling over "what's-his-name . . . the guy that nobody can remember". Dexter and Charles Bronson were reunited on the flying drama *X-15* (1961), in which Dexter played Major Anthony Rinaldi and Frank Sinatra produced. It was the beginning of a long working relationship. Dexter and Sinatra appeared together in the war films *None But The Brave* (1965), which Sinatra directed, and *Von Ryan's Express* (1965), and Ol' Blue Eyes appointed Dexter as vice-president of Sinatra Enterprises. On May 10, 1964, during the filming of *None But The Brave* on the island of Kauai in Hawaii, Sinatra went swimming during a break in filming. With him was Ruth Koch, the wife of the film's executive producer Howard Koch. Suddenly those on the beach realised that an undertow had pulled the couple away from the shore and they were drowning in the rough water. Dexter raced into the ocean and kept the heads of the nearly unconscious pair above water until lifeguards arrived. The incident became worldwide news. Afterwards, Dexter refused to talk to the press about the incident, describing Sinatra as "one of my closest friends". Years later, when interviewed by Kitty Kelley for her biography of Sinatra, *His Way* (1986), Dexter revealed that he had not spoken to Sinatra for years. "I realise now that my rescue efforts probably severed the friendship there and then," he said. "He never thanked me, then or later. I didn't see the love–hate relationship all that clearly at the time, but it certainly became obvious later on." Dexter produced *The Naked Runner* (1967), a secret agent melodrama with Sinatra as star, but the two men fell out over Sinatra's

relationship with the 30 years younger Mia Farrow. Dexter's other films included *Macao* (1952) as Vincent Halloran, *Between Heaven And Hell* (1956) as Lieutenant Joe Johnson, *Run Silent Run Deep* (1958) as Lieutenant Gerald Cartwright, *Vice Raid* (1959) as Vince Malone, *Twenty Plus Two* (1961) as Leroy Dane, *Taras Bulba* (1962) as Shilo, *Kings Of The Sun* (1963) as Ah Haleb, *Johnny Cool* (1963) as Lennart Crandall, *Invitation To A Gunfighter* (1964) as Kenarsie, *Blindfold* (1965) as Detective Harrigan, *Bus Riley's Back In Town* (1965) as Slocum, *Jory* (1972) as Jack, *Shampoo* (1975) as Senator East, *The Private Files Of J. Edgar Hoover* (1977) as Alvin 'Creepy' Karpis, *House Calls* (1978) as Quinn, *Winter Kills* (1979) as Captain Heller One and *Tajna Manastirske Rakije* (1989) as Veljko Pantovich. Dexter married secondly the Star-Kist tuna heiress Mary Bogdonovich and they were together until her death in 1992. In 1994 he married June Deyer.
CAUSE: Dexter died aged 85 in Rancho Mirage, California, from emphysema.

Khigh Dhiegh
(KENNETH DICKERSON)
Born 1910
Died October 25, 1991
Actor-philosopher. Born in Spring Lake, New Jersey, Khigh Dhiegh (pronounced Ki Dee) was of Anglo-Egyptian-Sudanese extraction. His best known role was as the villainous Wo-Fat in *Hawaii Five-O*. The original plan was for Wo-Fat, Steve McGarret's nemesis, to be killed at the end of the pilot *Cocoon* but Jack Lord was so taken with the character that he was reprieved and lived to annoy and irritate McGarret for a further 12 years. Dhiegh was a leading proponent of the ancient Chinese philosophy I Ching. He owned a Taoist shrine in Tempe, Arizona. Prior to becoming an actor he owned a bookshop in New York or possibly he worked in his mother's bookshop

(sources vary). He then studied theatre under David Belasco. He wrote eleven books, crafted jewellery and taught philosophy at the University of California in Los Angeles. His films included *Time Limit* (1957) as Colonel Kim, *The Manchurian Candidate* (1962) as Dr Yen Lo, *13 Frightened Girls* (1963) as Kang, *Seconds* (1966) as Davalo, *The Destructors* (1968) as King Chou Lai, *The Hawaiians* (1970) as Kai Chung, *The Mephisto Waltz* (1971) as Zanc Theun and *Goin' Coconuts* (1978) as Wong. Khigh Dhiegh had his own series called *Khan* in which he played a private detective in San Francisco's Chinatown who solved crimes with the help of his two children, Anna and Kim. Khan's daughter Anna was played by Irene Yah-Ling Sun who appeared in many *Hawaii Five-O* episodes. However, the show was not well received by the public and was cancelled after just four episodes, running from February 7 until February 28, 1975. He was married to Mary and had two children: Kenneth Dickerson, Jr, and Kathleen Dickerson.
CAUSE: He died in Mesa, Arizona, of kidney and heart failure. He was 81.

Gloria Dickson
(THAIS DICKERSON)
Born August 13, 1916
Died April 10, 1945
Party girl. Born in Pocatello, Idaho, the daughter of a banker who died when she was 12, she began acting in local repertory companies before making her movie début in Mervyn LeRoy's *They Won't Forget* (1937) as Sybil Hale. (Another beauty, Lana Turner, also appeared in the film in a minor role.) She worked steadily, if not spectacularly, in films such as *Racket Busters* (1938) as Nora Jordan, *Heart Of The North* (1938) as Joyce MacMillan, *Gold Diggers In Paris* (1938) as Mona, *Private Detective* (1939) as Mona Lannon, *Cowboy Quarterback* (1939) as Evelyn Corey,

They Made Me A Criminal (1939) as Peggy, *No Place To Go* (1939) as Gertrude Plummer, *On Your Toes* (1939) as Peggy Porterfield, *This Thing Called Love* (1940) as Florence Bertrand, *I Want A Divorce* (1940) as Wanda Holland, *The Affairs Of Jimmy Valentine* (1942), *Lady Of Burlesque* (1943) as Dolly Baxter and *Rationing* (1944) as Miss McCue.
CAUSE: Like many in Hollywood Gloria enjoyed the socialising almost as much as, if not more than, acting and began to overindulge in drink and drugs. She burned to death in the bathroom of her Hollywood home in a fire probably caused by a carelessly dropped cigarette. She was 28.

Marlene Dietrich
(MARIE MAGDALENE DIETRICH)
Born December 27, 1901
Died May 6, 1992
"The world's most glamorous grandmother". Born at 9.15pm in Sedanstrasse, Schöneberg, Germany, at 53 Sedanstrasse, the daughter of Lieutenant Louis Erich Otto Dietrich (b. 1868, d. Nussbaumallee, Germany August 5, 1908 from syphillis), who despite the assurances of previous biographers did not win the Iron Cross during the Franco-Prussian War, and (Wilhelmine Elisabeth) Josephine Felsing (b. November 1876, d. Berlin, Germany, November 6, 1945 of a heart attack). The couple married in 1898 not in 1883 as Dietrich claimed. The early life of 5'5" Marlene (the name came from combining her first two Christian names) is shrouded in mystery due to her own obfuscation and that of press agents when she first arrived in America in 1930. Dietrich lost her virginity aged 15 to her violin teacher, Professor Robert Reitz, a violinist in Weimar. Being married with children, a music teacher and the man who took her virginity, Reitz might have had a profound influence on Dietrich's later life, because she was adept at sticking a musical saw between

her legs and playing it. Dietrich's sister, (Ottilie Josephine) Elisabeth, was born on February 5, 1900. Lieutenant and Frau Dietrich soon fell out of love and in 1910 had separate telephone numbers installed albeit under the same roof. By the time Dietrich was six she had lived in four different homes and would soon be in a fifth with her widowed mother. Marlene Dietrich began acting on the stage and made her first film in 1919, *Im Schatten Des Glücks*. As she appeared in more films including *So Sind Die Männer* (1922) as Kathrin, *Der Mensch Am Wege* (premièred June 6, 1923) as Krämerstochter, *Tragödie der Liebe* (premièred October 8, 1923) as Lucy, *Der Sprung Ins Leben* (premièred February 4, 1924) as Mädchen am Strand, *Manon Lescaut* (premièred February 15, 1926) as Micheline, Sein größter Bluff (premièred May 12, 1927) as Yvette and *Cafe Elektrik* (premièred November 25, 1927) as Erni Göttlinger and plays, her reputation began to grow. On May 17, 1923 she married Rudolf Sieber (b. Aussig, near Prague, February 20, 1897) and on December 13, 1924 their daughter, Maria Elisabeth, was born. Although they lived separate lives Herr und Fräu Sieber remained good friends until his death in San Fernando on June 24, 1975. In 1930 she was "discovered" by Josef Von Sternberg when he directed her in *Der Blaue Engel* (premièred April 4, 1930) in which she played the sensuous Lola Lola. On the strength of that film she was offered a contract by Paramount where she shone brightly from 1931 until 1937. She was promoted as the studio's answer to MGM's Greta Garbo. Six of her first seven Stateside films – *Morocco* (premièred November 14, 1930) as Amy Jolly, *Dishonored* (premièred March 5, 1931) as Marie Kolverer/X27, *Shanghai Express* (premièred February 5, 1932) as Shanghai Lily, *Blonde Venus* (premièred September 22, 1932) as Helen Faraday, *The Scarlet Empress*

(premièred May 19, 1934) as Catherine II/ Sophia Frederica and *The Devil Is A Woman* (premièred May 3, 1935) as Concha Perez – were directed by von Sternberg who worked hard on her image transforming her into the sex symbol she became. For a time she was Hollywood's highest paid actress. Bisexual, she shared a lesbian lover with Greta Garbo (Mercedes De Acosta, whom Marlene first bedded on September 16, 1932). Mae West revealed: "She wanted to wash my hair. She came into my dressing room – we were both at Paramount – and made the offer. I had to turn her down – I was afraid she didn't mean the hair on my head . . ." Among her other lovers were Yul Brynner, Maurice Chevalier, Douglas Fairbanks, Jr, Jean Gabin, John Wayne, Orson Welles, Brian Aherne and General George S. Patton. She denied sleeping with Ernest Hemingway, whom she nicknamed 'Papa', saying, "It was too special for that . . ." When she met a man she admired Dietrich would drop to her knees and undo his flies because it gave her power over him. For bed, she preferred women. She used ice water and vinegar douches to avoid pregnancy. It seemed to work. Despite numerous lovers she only had one child. However, she would insist that her lovers were out of the house before her daughter awoke and then return after breakfast as if nothing had happened. Dietrich once said the diaphragm was the greatest invention since pancake make-up. Richard Burton said of her, "She's like a skeleton risen from the grave. Beautiful and extraordinary." Like many Hollywood stars she had a facelift and like many women she was a firm believer in astrology (as was Hitler). In 1937 she made a film in England and was approached by Nazi agents. Hitler wanted to have an affair with her, but she turned the Führer down. (Later, she worried that had she agreed, she might have been able to stop him persecuting Jews.) As a consequence her films were banned in Germany. She became an American citizen in 1938 and was awarded medals by the French, Russians and Americans for her morale-boosting work in World War II. Her movie career waned and she was labelled "box office poison" by *The Independent Film Journal* in 1938, along with other established Hollywood greats including Greta Garbo, Joan Crawford and Fred Astaire. In the Fifties she reinvented herself as a nightclub entertainer with smoky renditions of songs such as 'Falling In Love Again' and 'Lili Marlene'. As she grew older, Dietrich became more reclusive. In 1978 she moved into a two-room flat at 12 avenue Montaigne in Paris. She left only on very rare occasions, preferring to contact the outside world by telephone – her phone bills could be as much as $7,500 a month. In 1987 she auctioned some knick-knacks and raised $81,500. Her other films included: *I Loved A Soldier* (1936) as Anna Sedlak although the movie was never complated, *Desire* (premièred April 11, 1936) as Madeleine de Beaupre, *Angel* (premièred November 3, 1937) as Maria Barker, *Destry Rides Again* (premièred November 29, 1939) as Frenchy, *Seven Sinners* (released November 1940) as Bijou Blanche, *Manpower* (premièred July 1941) as Fay Duval, *Pittsburgh* (premièred November 11, 1942) as Josie Winters, *Golden Earrings* (premièred August 27, 1947) as Lydia, *Stage Fright* (premièred February 23, 1950) as Charlotte Inwood, *Rancho Notorious* (premièred May 15, 1952) as Altar Keane, *Around The World In 80 Days* (premièred October 17, 1956), *Touch Of Evil* (premièred February 1958) as Tanya and *Judgment At Nuremberg* (released December 19, 1961) as Madame Bertholt.

CAUSE: Marlene was bedridden for the last five years of her life. She died aged 90 of natural causes at her Parisian flat. A funeral service attended by over 1,500 people was held at the Madeleine Church in Paris. Her daughter put a St Christopher's medal, a wooden crucifix and a locket containing photos of Dietrich's grandsons in the coffin. On May 16 her body was flown to Berlin where she was buried in the city's Friedenau Cemetery. Her funeral service was disrupted by neo-Nazis handing out anti-Dietrich pamphlets. She suffered the same fate as Joan Crawford and Bette Davis in having her daughter write a less than complimentary biography of her.

FURTHER READING: *Dietrich: The Story Of A Star* – Leslie Frewin (London: Coronet, 1974); *Marlene: The Life Of Marlene Dietrich* – Charles Higham (New York: W.W. Norton, 1977); *Dietrich* – Donald Spoto (London: Bantam Press, 1992); *Marlene Dietrich: Life And Legend* – Steven Bach (London: HarperCollins, 1992); *Dietrich* – Malene Sheppard Skærved (London: Life & Times, 2003).

Walt Disney

Born December 5, 1901
Died December 15, 1966
The man who made magic. Walter Elias Disney was born at 1249 Tripp Avenue, Chicago, and discovered he could make money out of his drawing talent aged 10 when he swapped cartoons for free haircuts. During World War I he worked as an ambulance driver. At his first job interview he was told he had no talent; on the train journey home he created Mickey Mouse. He was supposedly inspired by the mice playing in the waste paper basket in his studio. Originally due to be called Mortimer, until Mrs Disney intervened, the rodent has made more money for Disney and the Disney Organisation from off-screen merchandising than he ever has from film revenues. The first film that the mouse appeared in was *Steamboat Willie* (1928) and since then

he's won an Oscar, been honoured by the League of Nations and has been sent more fan mail than any other film star. On his 50th birthday in 1978 he travelled across America and even performed for President Carter at the White House. Disney produced over 600 films, beginning with *Tommy Tucker's Tooth* (1922), moving on to produce feature-length cartoons. When the first, *Snow White And The Seven Dwarfs* (1937), won an Academy Award, Disney was presented with one full-size Oscar and seven miniature ones. The nephew of the creator of Pinocchio, the star of Disney's 1940 film of the same name, wanted the Italian government to sue Disney for making the wooden boy too American. It took 14 years for *Peter Pan* (1953) to hit the screen from the time Disney bought the rights to make a film of the story. Disney was something of a perfectionist and demanded such high standards that in 1941 his technicians went on strike. In 1950 the company began making live action films, beginning with *Treasure Island* starring Robert Newton as Long John Silver, Bobby Driscoll as Jim Hawkins and *Dad's Army*'s John Laurie as Blind Pew. Disney had an almost anti-Semitic point of view and also had strange beliefs when it came to women. He had virtually no sexual interest in them, seeing them only as friends. He married Lillian Bound only because his brother, with whom he shared a home, had married and Walt was not cut out for bachelor life. They wed on July 13, 1925, and had one daughter, Diane Marie (b. December 18, 1933), and one adopted daughter, Sharon Mae (b. 1931). Said Alfred Hitchcock, "Disney, of course, has the best casting. If he doesn't like an actor, he just tears him up."
CAUSE: On November 7, 1966, in St Joseph's Hospital, Burbank, which was just across the road from the Walt Disney Studios Disney's left lung was removed because it was cancerous (due to his chain smoking). Another operation was performed a fortnight later and then he was released. On December 5, he was readmitted to the hospital and died there ten days after his 65th birthday. He was cremated two days later and his ashes interred in the Court of Freedom at Forest Lawn Memorial-Parks, 1712 South Glendale Avenue, Glendale, California 91209. Despite the rumours, he is not frozen waiting to be thawed out and rejuvenated.
FURTHER READING: *Walt Disney: A Biography* – Bob Thomas (London: Star, 1981); *The Real Walt Disney: A Biography* – Leonard Mosley (London: Grafton, 1986); *The Disney Films* – Leonard Maltin (New York: Hyperion, 1995).

Divine

(HARRIS GLENN MILSTEAD)
Born October 19, 1945
Died March 7, 1988
Disco diva. Larger than life (27st) transvestite who achieved a certain fame in underground films. Born in the Women's Hospital, Baltimore, Maryland, Glenn Milstead (so called to avoid confusion with his father, also called Harris) he weighed only 5lb 4oz at birth. However, he soon began to put on weight at an alarmingly fast rate. At 15 he weighed over 16st. It seemed as if he was destined to be yet another gay hairdresser when he was discovered in 1965 by John Waters who cast him in his first movie, *Roman Candles* (1966). It was at this time that Waters renamed Glenn Milstead. Waters unashamedly set out "to make the trashiest motion pictures in cinema history". Some would say he succeeded. In 1968 he cast Divine as Jackie Kennedy in *Eat Your Make-Up*. The next film was *The Diane Linkletter Story* (1969). The 20-year-old daughter of American TV personality Art Linkletter, she committed suicide on October 5, 1969, by throwing herself out of a sixth-floor window. Waters

made the film with Divine as Diane the day after her death. That same year Waters cast Divine in *Mondo Trasho*, a 90-minute film that cost $2,000 to make. The actor playing a naked hitchhiker; Waters and three others were arrested during filming and charged with public indecency. The next year he appeared as Lady Divine in Waters' paean to gore king Herschell Gordon Lewis, *Multiple Maniacs* (1970), his first talkie. The budget for that was $5,000. Two years later came Waters' most shocking and notorious film. *Pink Flamingoes* (1972) starred Divine as Babs Johnson, 'the filthiest person alive'. At the end of the film Divine ate poodle excrement. In 1974 Divine appeared as Dawn Davenport in *Female Trouble*, a film that cost $25,000. It was the story of a teenage delinquent from her earliest days to her execution in the electric chair as a convicted murderer, and was Divine's favourite film. Divine then appeared in various stage plays and made records before returning to the big screen in the Eighties. A promised cameo role in Village People's *Can't Stop The Music* (1980) never materialised. Divine and gay icon Tab Hunter played lovers, Francine and Elmer Fishpaw, in John Waters' *Polyester* (1981); Elmer was a pornographer by trade. Filming began on September 1, 1980, and when the film was released in May 1981, cinema audiences received a scratch-and-sniff card so they could 'enjoy' the smells of the various scenes. In 1985 Divine was again cast opposite Hunter in Paul Bartel's Western spoof *Lust In The Dust*. The following year he appeared in *Trouble In Mind* (1986), a film described by one critic as "an unusual screen experience that almost defies description". In February 1988, as *Hairspray* (1988) was on general release, in which Divine co-starred with Ricki Lake (he played her mother), Sonny Bono and Debbie Harry, he was offered the role of Uncle Otto on the hit TV sitcom *Married . . . With*

Children. It was a part he was never destined to play. Divine's last film was the posthumously released *Out Of The Dark* (1989) about a killer murdering phone sex girls. John Waters released his tribute to Divine, entitled simply *Divine*, two years after the actor-singer's death.

CAUSE: Divine died aged 42 of hypertrophic cardiomyopathy with cardiomegaly in room 252 of the Regency Plaza Suites Hotel, 7940 Hollywood Boulevard, a day after learning he owed the taxman approximately $100,000. It took six officers of the coroner to lift Divine's body into the paddy wagon for the journey to the morgue. On March 10 he was buried in Prospect Hill Cemetery, Towson, Maryland. For a man used to wearing extravagant clothing, he was soberly dressed in his coffin wearing a black Tommy Nutter suit, black polo neck shirt and Andrew Logan jewellery. Ironically, when he was a teenager Divine would host parties decorated with flowers stolen from that very cemetery.

FURTHER READING: *Not Simply Divine –* Bernard Jay (London: Virgin, 1993).

Troy Donahue
(MERLE JOHNSON, JR.)
Born January 27, 1936
Died September 2, 2001
Fifties teen heartthrob. Born in New York City, Donahue moved at 19 to Hollywood, where he was discovered by Warner Bros. It was the release of *A Summer Place* (1959) in which he played Sandra Dee's young lover that made him for a time the studio's top box office draw. During his heyday, Donahue split his time between the movies and television, appearing as Sandy Winfield II in ABC's detective series *Surfside Six* (October 3, 1960–September 24, 1962). Merle Johnson, Jr. became Troy Donahue thanks to Henry Willson, the same film agent who renamed Roy Scherer, Jr. as Rock Hudson. "It was part of me

10 minutes after I got it. It feels so natural, I jump when people call me by my old name. Even my mother and sister call me Troy now," he said. He went on to star in a series of teen romances including *Parrish* (1961), *Rome Adventure* (1962) and *Palm Springs Weekend* (1963). He took a bit part in 1974's *Godfather Part II*, playing Merle Johnson. But with his career in decline, Donahue became a drug addict and alcoholic, and spent a summer homeless in New York's Central Park. He stopped drinking in the early Eighties. "I realised that I was going to die, and I was dying – or worse than that, I might live the way I was living for the rest of my life," Donahue said at the time. To many, Donahue is known only as part of a lyric in a song from *Grease* – 'Look At Me I'm Sandra Dee'. Donahue was married four times: to the actress Suzanne Pleshette on January 4, 1964 but they divorced on September 8, 1964; another actress Valerie Allen (1966–1968); to secretary Alma Sharp on November 15, 1969; and to Vicky Taylor (1979–1981). At the time of his death he lived in Santa Monica with his fiancée, mezzo soprano Zheng Cao. However, there were rumours that Donahue was a homosexual, perhaps fuelled by the shortness of all his marriages. In 1984 he told *People* magazine, "I am not gay. Once in a while people get me confused with another blond, blue-eyed actor who was around at the same time, but it's no big deal." The actor Donahue was referring to was Tab Hunter.
CAUSE: Donahue died at St John's Hospital and Medical Centre in Santa Monica after suffering a heart attack four days earlier. He was 65.

Robert Donat

Born March 18, 1905
Died June 9, 1958
The man who bested Clark Gable. Born in Withington, Manchester, to a Polish civil engineer father and an English mother, Friederich Robert Donat was sent to elocution lessons to cure a childhood stammer. He was still a teenager (16) when he made his acting début on stage in Birmingham and spent the rest of his career alternating between stage and the big screen. The 6′ Donat made his movie début in *That Night In London* (1932) as Dick Warren and made only 19 more over the next 26 years. But oh, what films they were. Following his appearance as Thomas Culpepper in *The Private Life Of Henry VIII* (1933) he was offered work in America but made only one film there, playing Edmond Dantes in *The Count Of Monte Cristo* (1934). He turned down *Captain Blood* and *The Adventures Of Robin Hood* because his chronic asthma was exacerbated by the warm weather in Los Angeles. He also suffered from severe depression. (Both parts went to helping the career of Errol Flynn.) Back in England he returned to the stage and appeared in *The 39 Steps* (1935) as Richard Hannay, *The Ghost Goes West* (1935) as Murdoch Glourie/Donald Glourie, *The Citadel* (1938) as Dr Andrew Manson (for which he was nominated for Best Actor Oscar), *The Young Mr Pitt* (1942) as The Earl of Chatham, *Captain Boycott* (1947) as Charles Stewart Parnell, *The Winslow Boy* (1948) as Sir Robert Morton and *Cure For Love* (1950) as Sergeant Jack Hardacre, a film he also produced, directed and wrote. It was for his performance as kindly schoolteacher Mr Chipping in *Goodbye, Mr. Chips* (1939), based on James Hilton's novel, that Donat won the Best Actor Oscar, beating out Clark Gable's Rhett Butler in *Gone With The Wind*, Laurence Olivier's Heathcliffe in *Wuthering Heights*, Mickey Rooney's *Babes In Arms* and James Stewart's *Mr Smith Goes To Washington*. Donat, a shy man by nature, didn't attend the ceremony, which was held on February 29, 1940, to collect his award in person. He married twice. His first wife

(in Wilmslow, Cheshire, in 1929) was Ella Annesley Voysey and they had two sons, John (b. September 19, 1933) and Brian (b. August 3, 1936), and a daughter, Joanna (b. May 19, 1931). In London on May 4, 1953, seven years after his divorce, he married actress (Dorothy) Renée Ascherson (b. 1920). They separated in 1956.

CAUSE: For the last five years of his life 6' Donat was a martyr to his asthma. It made him a virtual invalid. He died of a chronic asthma attack in London. His last film, *The Inn Of The Sixth Happiness* (1958), was released posthumously. His last words on screen were to Ingrid Bergman: "Stay here for a time. It will comfort me as I leave to know it. We shall never see each other again, I think. Farewell." Donat left £25,236 11s 5d.

Brian Donlevy

(GROSSON BRIAN BORU DONLEVY)
Born February 9, 1899
Died April 5, 1972
Hollywood realist. Born in Portadown, County Armagh, Ireland, Donlevy went to America with his family aged two and was raised in Wisconsin. Aged 17 he ran away from home to join the army and ended up fighting Mexican bandit Pancho Villa. During World War I he was a pilot with the Lafayette Escadrille. He also spent a couple of years at the US Naval Academy in Annapolis, Maryland. In the Twenties he became New York's best-known male model, the same decade he made his film début. When he played Knuckles Jacoby in *Barbary Coast* (1935) the costume department placed him in the black shirt Clark Gable had worn in *Call Of The Wild* (1935) in the hope it would bring Donlevy luck. It did more than that. It made his name and he wore it for years afterwards, being offered a contract by Fox (although his pompous attitude meant he was disliked as much on set as his character was off). His films included: *36 Hours To Kill* (1936) as Frank Evers,

Strike Me Pink (1936) as Vance, *Human Cargo* (1936) as Packy Campbell, *In Old Chicago* (1937) as Gil Warren, *Sharpshooters* (1938) as Steve Mitchell, *Battle Of Broadway* (1938) as Chesty Webb, *Jesse James* (1939) as Mr Barshee, *Beau Geste* (1939) as Sergeant Markoff, for which he was nominated for an Oscar, *Destry Rides Again* (1939) as Kent, *Brigham Young – Frontiersman* (1940) as Angus Duncan, *Billy The Kid* (1941) as Jim Sherwood, *I Wanted Wings* (1941) as Captain Mercer (it was filmed on a real military camp and Donlevy was saluted by real soldiers so often he took to wearing a sign that said 'Actor'), *Birth Of The Blues* (1941) as Memphis, *Two Yanks In Trinidad* (1942) as Vince Barrows, *Nightmare* (1942) as Daniel Shane, *Stand By For Action* (1943) as Lieutenant Commander Martin J. Robertson, *Our Hearts Were Growing Up* (1946) as Tony Minnetti, *The Virginian* (1946) as Trampas, *Canyon Passage* (1946) as George Camrose, *Song Of Scheherazade* (1947) as Captain Gregorovitch, *Killer McCoy* (1947) as Jim Caighn, *Kiss Of Death* (1947) as Assistant District Attorney Louie DeAngelo, *Command Decision* (1948) as General Clifton Garnet, *Impact* (1949) as Walter Williams, *Shakedown* (1950) as Nick Palmer, *Kansas Raiders* (1950) as William Quantrill, *Hoodlum Empire* (1952) as Senator Bill Stephens, *The Big Combo* (1955) as McClure, *Escape From Red Rock* (1958) as Bronc Grierson, *Juke Box Rhythm* (1959) as George Manton, *How To Stuff A Wild Bikini* (1965) as B. D., *Arizona Bushwhackers* (1968) as Mayor Joe Smith and his last movie *Pit Stop* (1969) as Grant Willard. He readily accepted that Hollywood was all illusion so he made a list of what was needed to be done to prepare himself for a day on set: 1) Insert dentures; 2) Don hairpiece; 3) Strap on corset; 4) Lace up 'elevator' shoes. He married three times, firstly to Ziegfeld Follies girl Yvonne Grey on October 5, 1928

(they divorced in February 1936). In Tijuana, Mexico, on December 22, 1936, he married singer-actress Marjorie Lane and had one daughter, Judith Ann (b. February 20, 1943). They divorced in 1947. On February 25, 1966, he wed Lillian Lugosi, widow of Bela Lugosi. Away from the cameras Donlevy had two completely unrelated interests – writing poems and gold mining. Following his retirement in 1969 he moved to Palm Springs where he began composing short stories.
CAUSE: In 1971 he was admitted to the Motion Picture County Hospital, Woodland Hills, California, for throat surgery. On March 10, 1972, he was readmitted and died there aged 73 of throat cancer, less than four weeks later.

Casey Donovan
(CALVIN CULVER)
Born November 2, 1943
Died August 10, 1987
Gay superstar. Born in East Bloomfield, New York, a former private school teacher, Donovan was the first male porn star to have his name above the title. He was anonymous in his early films until fan letters began arriving in sack loads from men wanting to know his identity, so he assumed the name of a character he played in a film. His movies included: *Ginger* (1971), *Boys In The Sand* (1971), *Fun And Games* (1973), *The Opening Of Misty Beethoven* (1976), *L.A. Tool & Die* (1981), *Sleaze* (1982), *Hotshots* (1983), *Boys In The Sand II* (1984) and *Inevitable Love* (1985).
CAUSE: He died of AIDS aged 43 in Inverness, Florida.

Françoise Dorléac
Born March 21, 1942
Died June 26, 1967
Dedicated actrice. Born in Paris, France, she was one of four daughters of minor French stage actor Maurice Dorléac. Françoise showed a determination to achieve something for

herself. When she took ballet lessons, she practised so long that her toes bled. Her little sister was the actress Catherine Deneuve (b. October 22, 1943) but the two girls could not have been more different. Françoise threw herself into everything with a passion and determination, whereas Catherine was described by their mother as a "tender, fragile little girl". Françoise made her stage début aged 10 and began modelling five years later, which led directly to her first film. She was spotted by a talent scout and landed a small part in *Mensonges* (1957). Back at school she dreamed of being a successful actress. Her first feature film was playing Madeleine in *Les Loups Dans La Bergerie* (1959) about some hoodlums who hide out in a borstal. Her appearance in *Les Portes Claquent* (1960) led to Catherine's film début. The producers were looking for someone to play Françoise's sister in the film and she recommended her real-life sibling. In 1961 she appeared in five films but just one, *Arsène Lupin Contre Arsène Lupin* (1962), over the next three years. It was her performance as mistress Nicole in François Truffaut's *La Peau Douce* (1964) that first brought her international recognition. Françoise began spending hours perfecting her image. "I want to dress so that everybody tries to dress like me, and nobody can. I love it when you are completely dressed and you look naked. I wear chain belts to look fragile, like a slave. Every time I go out, even if it's 6 o'clock in the morning, when nobody can see, it's still important [to] keep a certain class, but look erotic." Her first major American film was the espionage adventure *Where The Spies Are* (1965) in which she played Vikki opposite David Niven. She played Mrs Genghis Khan, Bortei, in *Genghis Khan* (1965) and was the bored, flirtatious Teresa in Roman Polanski's *Cul-De-Sac* (1966). However, success didn't make her happy. "I find that with each picture, I

become more insecure, less confident about my ability to do good work." She lived with her mum and dad until she was 23, when Madame Dorléac insisted she stand on her own two feet. Her mother found her a new home, which was across the street from the family house. She played Catherine's twin, Solange Garnier, in *Les Demoiselles De Rochefort* (1967) before appearing in *Billion Dollar Brain* (1967) as double agent Anya. She never married.
CAUSE: In the summer of 1967 she went on holiday in St Tropez with Catherine. Driving alone to Nice airport she lost control of her car, smacked into a concrete road sign and burned to death when the vehicle caught alight. She was just 25.

Diana Dors

(DIANA MARY FLUCK)
Born October 23, 1931
Died May 4, 1984
Britain's answer to Marilyn Monroe. It is a cliché but none the less true that the life story of Diana Dors reads like a soap opera. Born in the Haven Nursing Home, Kent Road, Swindon, Wiltshire, her mother, Mary, decided that young Diana would have all the opportunities she never had. To get rid of her West Country accent Diana was given elocution lessons. She also attended dancing and piano lessons, although she quickly became bored with the latter and gave up, to the fury of her father. At school she was something of a practical joker and often played truant to go to the cinema. At the age of eight she wrote an essay about what she wanted to do when she grew up and revealed her plans to be a Hollywood star with a swimming pool and a cream-coloured telephone. During World War II she entertained the GIs and at the age of 12½ put peroxide streaks in her naturally brown hair. With her precocious figure she soon found herself leered after by many a Yank who, as many an Englishman complained, were "Over

paid, oversexed and over here". She attended dances with her mother, who had made a friend of the camp cook, with the result that a goodie bag of desirables went home with her after each do. Diana was also not averse to the company of local boys and for a time dated a 17-year-old called Desmond Morris, later to be famous in his own right. Expelled from school and on holiday in Weston-super-Mare Diana entered a beauty contest and came third. A picture of her appeared in the local paper and this got her a job as a model for the art school. It also led to her appearing on radio and in a number of stage productions. In September 1945, 5'5" Diana began attending the London Academy of Music and Dramatic Art (LAMDA). It was at LAMDA that Diana became a fully fledged blonde. To give her some income she also began showing her 36-24-35 figure nude for a camera club in London at a wage of a guinea an hour. At the end of her first year she passed all her exams with distinction and landed her first film role as the flashy Mildred in *The Shop At Sly Corner* (1947), which starred Oscar Homolka and Muriel Pavlow. Diana was paid £8 per day for her work and also changed her name. Imagining her name up in lights she wondered, "What on earth would I do if the letter 'L' went out?" She adopted her grandmother's name, which was Dors, and so Diana Dors was born at Wharton Studios, Isleworth. When she told the director her age he wouldn't believe her and the crew were convinced her magnificent *embonpoint* was the result of gaffer tape rather than nature's gift. She made three films altogether in 1947 earning £10 a day as a jitterbugger in *Holiday Camp* and the same fee as a dance hall hostess in *Dancing With Crime*. When she went home she took her earnings with her (including the guineas she made posing nude for the camera club) and proudly displayed £150 in notes. Her father, never her greatest fan, was initially not impressed that his 15-year-old daughter was making more money than him. In 1948 she landed the role of Charlotte in David Lean's *Oliver Twist* and was also offered a 10-year contract by Rank beginning at £10 a week. At LAMDA she was awarded the Alexander Korda Cup for the most promising student and her acceptance speech was written by her father, who by now was finally beginning to see the talent in his daughter that everyone else did. At the Rank School they put her in a number of films in bit parts including *Good Time Girl* (1949) as delinquent Lyla Lawrence, *It's Not Cricket* (1949) as an aspiring secretary, *The Calendar* (1948) as the maid Hawkins and *My Sister And I* (1948) as a gofer. She appeared as Diana Hopkins in both *Here Come The Huggetts* (1948) and *Vote For Huggett* (1949). For the second film Diana attended her first and only press screening. The media were not enamoured with the film. It was while filming yet another 'bad girl' role, Ada Foster, in *A Boy, A Girl And A Bike* (1949) in Yorkshire that Diana lost her virginity to actor Gil Gynt, brother of the actress Greta Gynt who had presented her with the Alexander Korda Cup in her LAMDA days. (It was for Diana, as for so many, a disappointing experience.) Back in London Diana rented a flat just off the King's Road for the bargain sum of £5 a week. In 1948 she fell pregnant and had an abortion, which cost her £10. When she was 19 she suddenly found herself unemployed when the Rank Charm School closed and all contracts were terminated. Her latest film, *Diamond City* (1949) in which she played Dora, had not been a success. In May 1951, while filming *Lady Godiva Rides Again* (1951), she met a handsome charmer called Dennis Hamilton (b. Brymbro, North Wales, October 23, 1924, as Dennis Hamlington Gittins). On July 2, 1951, having known each other just five weeks, they went to Kensington Registry Office to be married. Diana, 19, claimed to be 22 but had a letter from her parents giving their permission for the marriage to go ahead. The ceremony didn't actually take place that day, though the next day they were married. Hamilton had rung the press and a veritable posse of journalists and paparazzi turned up to see the happy couple. Meanwhile, the registrar had received a phone call telling him the letter from Mr & Mrs Fluck was a forgery but Hamilton was not a man to be turned away lightly. The wedding went ahead after he threatened to knock the registrar's teeth out. They moved into a house in Beauchamp Place, Knightsbridge, and Diana landed a job as Ruby Bruce on *The Last Page* (1952), which paid her £450. When no more work arrived they moved to Dunsfold in Surrey, unable to afford the luxury of SW3. Hamilton then approached the newspapers with a story that Diana had turned down a £400-a-week Hollywood salary to stay in the country she loved. The scam garnered press coverage but no work. Another abortion followed. One day Hamilton bought Diana a Rolls-Royce and she began arriving at jobs in the car, prompting people to speculate that she must be doing well. How little they knew. In 1952 she also appeared in two flop stage plays. She turned to variety and her first appearance at the notorious Glasgow Empire was met by complete silence. Once she was off stage she moaned to the stage manager that she was terrible. "Och no, at least they didn't throw things," were his consoling words. In 1953 she made the prison drama *The Weak And The Wicked* (1953) playing Betty Brown. She also had an affair with comedian Bob Monkhouse and when Dennis Hamilton found out he threatened to slit Monkhouse's eyeballs with a cutthroat razor. Monkhouse only escaped by kneeing Hamilton where it hurts. *The Weak And The Wicked* was a hit but it was Diana's next prison film that would finally transform her from a primarily B-picture actress to a fully fledged star. *Yield To The Night* (1956) starred Diana as Mary Hilton, a woman condemned to death for the murder of her ex-boyfriend's girlfriend. Despite the oft-repeated rumour, the film wasn't based on the story of 28-year-old Ruth Ellis. The latter was executed on July 13, 1955, for the murder of her racing driver boyfriend David Blakely, 25, outside the Magdala Tavern, South Hill Park, Hampstead, on April 10, 1955. The story for the film, written by Joan Henry, was conceived in 1953, two years before the Blakely murder. In 1956 Diana was voted Variety Club Show Business Personality Of The Year and *Yield To The Night* was chosen as the year's Royal Command Film Performance. On June 23, 1956, Diana arrived in New York aboard the *Queen Elizabeth II* to begin her American odyssey. Flying out to Los Angeles she began filming *I Married A Woman* (1956) for RKO, for which she was paid £35,000. Although mega bucks were offered, Diana quickly tired of the superficiality that typified and typifies Tinseltown. On August 19, they threw a party at their new home, Hillside House on Coldwater Canyon, and one photographer, Stewart Sawyer, seeing an eye for a picture pushed Diana into the swimming pool. Dennis Hamilton beat him up but the next day the newspapers were full of Hamilton's bad behaviour, not the snapper's. During the filming of her next movie, *The Unholy Wife* (1957) in which she played Phyllis Hochen, Diana began an affair with her co-star Rod Steiger. The film flopped and Diana returned to England without a husband. However, Hamilton was not one to give up the easy life that easily and he talked Diana into giving him another chance. Diana appeared on *This Is Your Life* on April 1, 1957, and the final guest was Hollywood photographer

Stewart Sawyer. It was all Diana could do at the end of the show to stop Hamilton beating Sawyer up again. The final split with Hamilton came when he pulled a shotgun on her and made her sign everything over to him. On Boxing Day of that year Diana threw a party and met a young comedian called Dickie Dawson (b. Gosport, Hampshire, November 20, 1932). They began dating and in early 1959 Diana flew to America. It was while she was there on January 31, that Dennis Hamilton died in London of tertiary syphilis. On April 12, 1959, Diana and Dickie Dawson were married in New York. At 9.55pm on February 4, 1960, Mark Richard Dawson was born weighing 6lb 15oz in the London Clinic. Another son, Gary, followed on June 27, 1962 at the Cedars of Lebanon Hospital, Los Angeles. He weighed 10lb 2oz. Over this period Diana appeared in *Tread Softly Stranger* (1958) as Calco, *Passport To Shame* (1958) as Vicki, *On The Double* (1961) as Sergeant Bridget Stanhope, *Scent Of Mystery* (1960) as Winifred Jordan (the film was the world's first feature film in 'smell-o-vision'), *King Of The Roaring 20s – The Story Of Arnold Rothstein* (1961) as Madge, *Mrs. Gibbon's Boys* (1962) as Myra and *West 11* (1963) as Georgia. Diana began an affair with Darryl Stewart and when Dawson found out he petitioned for divorce. Darryl dumped her soon afterwards. Back in England Diana was dropped by her agent and found work difficult to come by. She took anything that was offered – gay clubs, working men's venues, anything to pay the bills. In 1967 the Inland Revenue sent Diana a bill for £48,413. Instead of fretting she bought the house that would be hers for the rest of her life, Orchard Manor, Shrubs Hill Lane, Sunningdale, Berkshire. *Hammerhead* (1968) enabled her to furnish the house as she liked. On October 10, 1968, she set out for work on a television series called *The*

Inquisitors. Its two stars were Tony Selby and a RADA-educated actor called Alan Lake (b. Stoke-on-Trent, November 24, 1940). When he heard who his new co-star was to be, Lake complained, "Oh no, not Madame Tits and Lips!" However, within days they were very much in love and he proposed. On November 23, 1968, they were married at Caxton Hall, Westminster. A son, Jason David, was born in London on September 11, 1969, weighing 7lb 14oz. On October 16, 1970, Alan Lake was sentenced to 18 months' imprisonment for his part in a pub brawl on July 13. (Also jailed, for three years, was pop star Leapy Lee.) Just over three weeks later, on November 5, Diana appeared in the first episode of the Yorkshire Television sitcom *Queenie's Castle* as Queenie Shepherd. Lake was released on October 16, 1971, after exactly a year behind bars. Diana's only film that year was *Hannie Caulder* (1971), which was filmed in Spain. On February 20, 1972, Lake broke his back in a riding accident and was thought by some medical staff to be beyond help. Around this time Diana appeared in *Every Afternoon* (1972) as Margaretha, *The Amazing Mr Blunden* (1972) as the Housekeeper Mrs Wickens, *The Amorous Milkman* (1972) as Rita, *Theatre Of Blood* (1973) as Maisie Psaltry and *Steptoe And Son Ride Again* (1973). Out of hospital, Alan Lake began drinking very heavily. The Lakes' housekeeper suggested he visit her local church and soon he was a proselytising Roman Catholic and Diana was one of his first converts. In 1975 Diana fell pregnant and was advised by doctors to have an abortion but knowing the Catholic Church's abhorrence of abortion she decided to go ahead. She miscarried later that year. The sadness sent Alan Lake back onto the booze. Diana subsequently appeared in some dreadful films, many verging on soft porn, to pay the bills, including *Rosie* (1975), *Adventures Of*

A Taxi Driver (1976) as Mrs North, *Adventures Of A Private Eye* (1977) as Mrs Horne and *Confessions From The David Galaxy Affair* (1979) as Jenny Stride. She also appeared as Mrs Bott in the LWT series *Just William*. In 1978 she published her first book, *For Adults Only*, and then worked on its sequel *Behind Closed Dors*. Both became bestsellers. In December 1979 the Inland Revenue again pounced, sending Diana a demand for £12,000. In October 1981 Diana's autobiography, *Dors By Diana*, was published. The following year she became an agony aunt for the *Daily Star*. In October 1982 she featured on *This Is Your Life* for a second time. In May of the following year she went on a television diet on TV-am but in February 1984 she was fired from the breakfast station over irregularities. The next month she began work on her last film, *Steaming* (1985) playing Violet, set in a ladies' steam room. CAUSE: On November 23, 1974, Diana fell ill and the next day collapsed into a coma with meningitis. However, within seven weeks she was well enough to rehearse a new play. In June 1982 she was rushed to hospital with severe stomach pains. An operation revealed that an ovarian cyst had burst and had been malignant. Diana Dors had cancer. On September 3, 1983, she underwent yet another operation for cancer. She was put on a course of tablets. On April 30, 1984, an operation discovered that the cancer had spread throughout her body, even to her bone marrow. She never left the hospital in Windsor, Berkshire and died at 9pm four days later. After the funeral back at Orchard Manor Alan Lake removed the mourning suit he had worn and, going into the garden, burned it. At 1.45pm on October 10, 1984, 16 years to the day of his meeting with Diana, Alan Lake blew his brains out in their son Jason's bedroom. Diana Dors left £208,000. Alan Lake left £132,702.

FURTHER READING: *Swingin' Dors –*
Diana Dors (London: WDL Books,
1960); *Dors & Diana: An Intimate
Biography –* Wolf Rilla (London:
Everest Books, 1977); *Diana Dors:
Only A Whisper Away –* Joan Flory &
Damien Walne (London: Javelin
Books, 1988); *Come By Sunday: The
Fabulous, Ruined Life Of Diana Dors –*
Damon Wise (London: Sidgwick &
Jackson, 1998).

Jack Douglas
(JACK ROBERTON)
Born April 26, 1927
Died December 18, 2008
"Phwaay". Born in Newcastle-upon-
Tyne, the son of an impresario, Jack
Douglas was raised on a farm in
Meriden which made pork pies. At 15,
he left school to work for his father and
became a producer until an actor fell ill
and Douglas stood in. During the
Second World War he toured in a show
called *Hi There* and then after demob,
found work in panto and summer
seasons. He became a straight man to
Joe Baker, Arthur Haines and Benny
Hill before creating his own character
of Alf Ippititimus after going on solo at
Butlin's in Clacton-on-Sea, Essex one
night. He formed a double act with Des
O'Connor that reached its apogee with
the 1966 Royal Variety Show. He never
played a major role but became a
stalwart in the *Carry On . . .* films
appearing in the last seven films of the
original series, *Carry On Matron* (1972)
as the twitching father (with only one
line "Could you get me *The Guinness
Book Of Records* please?" plus a few
twitches), *Carry On Abroad* (1972) as
Harry, *Carry On Girls* (1973) as
William, *Carry On Dick* (1974) as
Sergeant Jock Strapp, *Carry On Behind*
(1975) as Ernie Bragg, *Carry On
England* (1976) as Bombardier Ready
and *Carry On Emmannuelle* (1978) as
Lyons. He also appeared in the
appalling *Carry On Columbus* (1992) as
Marco the Cereal Killer, his last film,
but had severe reservations about it. He

was paid a one-off fee for the six weeks
he worked on each *Carry On*. He also
appeared in the television series *Carry
On Laughing*. He once commented,
"The *Carry On*s never stopped being
popular, they were an institution. It
was amazing that they came out and
people went to see them, because
people could take their families and
there was no question of any filth
whatsoever. They appeal to children
and to their grandparents, there was
something for everyone." He also
appeared in the Cannon and Ball film
Boys In Blue (1982). Douglas who
stood 6′4″ wrote *What A Performance*,
a musical based on the life of Sid
Field.
CAUSE: Douglas died at St Mary's
Hospital, Newport on the Isle of Wight
from pneumonia. He was 81.

Marie Dressler
(LEILA MARIE KOERBER)
Born November 9, 1868
Died July 28, 1934
Hefty star. Born in Coburg, Canada,
she began her career on stage when she
was 14 before moving into opera for a
time. By 1892 she was a vaudeville and
Broadway star and in 1910 played the
comedic character Tillie on stage to
great acclaim. She made her film début
at a salary of $2,500 a week in the title
role in *Tillie's Punctured Romance*
(1914), the first American full-length
comedy. Mack Sennett learned that
his former director D.W. Griffith was
making a feature film (*Birth Of A
Nation*) so he determined to get in first.
The film was shot in 14 weeks from
April to July 1914 and the cast
included Charlie Chaplin, Mabel
Normand, Edgar Kennedy, Chester
Conklin, Minta Durfee (Mrs Fatty
Arbuckle) and Al St John. The film was
released in America on November 14,
1914, to tremendous acclaim and in
Britain in spring 1915. A sequel, *Tillie's
Tomato Surprise* (1915), was made and
that was also successful so a third film
went into production, *Tillie Wakes Up*

(1917). Despite the fact that he was the one who signed her in the first place Dressler sued Sennett claiming that her husband (George Hoppert) had been promised the distribution rights to the film but the suit was dismissed. Her career had its ups and downs but was not affected by the advent of the talkies. She appeared with Greta Garbo in *Anna Christie* (1930) and that same year won the Best Actress Oscar for *Min And Bill* (1930) playing opposite Wallace Beery. She worked with Beery three times and said of him, "He never struck me, except in self-defence." She was nominated again as Best Actress for her role as Emma (Thatcher Smith) in *Emma* (1932). Dressler stood 5'7" tall and "homely" was one of the kinder descriptions about her bulk. One critic said that she had "an ample figure like a rain barrel and a face that fell into folds like those of a St Bernard".

CAUSE: She died in Santa Barbara, California, of cancer. She was 65.

Bobby Driscoll

Born March 3, 1937
Body found March 30, 1968
Tragic child star. Born in Cedar Rapids, Iowa, Robert Cletus Driscoll and his family moved to California in 1943 when he was 6 years old. After being told by a barber that their son ought to be in pictures the Driscolls took young Bobby for an audition at MGM. The studio was suitably impressed and he made his film début in *Lost Angel* (1943) playing a character called Bobby opposite Margaret O'Brien, another child star who was not destined for adult stardom. He was able to learn lines like a pro and Bobby was soon fêted as the leading child star earning $500 a week. He appeared with Anne Baxter in *Sunday Dinner For A Soldier* (1944) as Jeep Osborne; he was in *The Sullivans* (1944) as Al Sullivan, *The Big Bonanza* (1944) as Spud Kilton, the tragically ironically entitled *Identity Unknown* (1945) as Toddy

Loring, a boy with a wounded dog in *Miss Susie Slagle's* (1946) and *From This Day Forward* (1946) as Timmy Beesley. He appeared in the Alan Ladd vehicle *O.S.S.* (1946) as Gerard, and bowled over his co-stars Myrna Loy and Don Ameche in *So Goes My Love* (1946) for Universal in which he played Percy Maxim. Ameche commented, "He's got a great talent. I've worked with a lot of child players in my time but none of them bore the promise that seems inherent in young Driscoll." When he was signed to appear in *Song Of The South* (1946) as Johnny, he became the first "live" star to be given a contract with the Disney studios. Driscoll made five more films for Disney – all successful. His portrayal of Jim Hawkins, the cabin boy, in *Treasure Island* (1950) was masterful. He told reporters that he was going to save his money, go to college and become a G-man. On March 23, 1950, he was presented with a special Oscar by Donald O'Connor for his work in *The Window* (1949) as Tommy Woodry and *So Dear To My Heart* (1949) as Jeremiah 'Jerry' Kincaid. At the ceremony Driscoll who as a teenager was plagued by severe acne thanked "God for giving me such a wonderful mother and father". His was the voice of *Peter Pan* (1953) in the film of the same name. He also appeared in *If You Knew Susie* (1948) as Junior, *When I Grow Up* (1951) as Josh/Danny Reed, *The Happy Time* (1952) as Bibi, *The Scarlet Coat* (1955) as Ben Potter. In 1956 he married Marilyn Brush and they had a son before they separated unamicably. Within a few short years his career would be over. Like many child actors Driscoll found it difficult to obtain work once he reached his late teens. He also found it difficult to mix with his peers and when they ignored or rejected his friendship he "fought back [and] became cocky and belligerent". By the time he was 16 he was a heroin addict. His last film, and also the last for his co-star Frances Farmer, was *The Party Crashers* (1958) in which he played Josh Bickford. The following year he was arrested for possession of heroin and jailed. In 1960 his troubles worsened and he was arrested on a charge of possession of a deadly weapon after he pistol-whipped some youths who were verbally abusing him. In 1961 he was arrested for breaking into a vet's and then for forging a cheque and later on more drugs charges. He was sentenced to six months in the Narcotics Rehabilitation Center of Chino State Penitentiary. On his release he moved to New York and dropped from view. His mother blamed the drugs for destroying her once handsome son. "Drugs changed him. He didn't bathe, his teeth got loose. He had an extremely high IQ but the narcotics affected his brain. We didn't know what it was. He was 19 before we knew."

CAUSE: A body was discovered by two children playing in an abandoned tenement on New York's Avenue A on the Lower East Side in Greenwich Village on March 30, 1968. The cause of death was hardening of the arteries, a heart attack and hepatitis due to drug abuse. The unidentified corpse was fingerprinted and then buried in a pauper's grave on Hart Island off the Bronx. In September 1969, Driscoll's mother contacted the Disney Organisation. Driscoll's father was dying and wanted to find her missing son. She had been to the FBI but J. Edgar Hoover's G-men were unhelpful. The powerful Disney Organisation intervened to put pressure on various authorities. It was then discovered that the corpse found in New York was that of Driscoll, the one-time Oscar winning actor. The find came a fortnight after the death of Driscoll's father. He was less than a month past his 31st birthday. He once complained bitterly, "I was carried on a satin cushion and then dropped in a garbage can."

Joanne Dru
(JOANNE LACOCK)
Born January 31, 1923
Died September 11, 1996
Gutsy heroine. Born in Logan, West Virginia, the sister of American TV personality Peter Marshall, Joanne Dru began her career on stage in New York in 1940. In September 1941 she married singer Dick Haymes (b. Buenos Aires, Argentina, September 13, 1916, d. March 29, 1980) and had three children: Dick, Jr (b. 1942), Helen (b. 1944) and Barbara (b. 1949). They were divorced in 1949 and she married actor John Ireland in the same year. That marriage lasted seven years and produced two sons John and Peter. In 1972 she married C.V. Wood, Jr. He died in 1993. She began in films with *Abie's Irish Rose* (1946) playing Rosemary Murphy but it was appearing in Westerns such as *Red River* (1948) as Tess Millay, *She Wore A Yellow Ribbon* (1949) as Olivia Dandridge and *Wagonmaster* (1950) as Denver that made her name. Oddly, she hated horses. Her other films included: *All The King's Men* (1949) as Anne Stanton, *711 Ocean Drive* (1950) as Gail Mason, *Mr Belvedere Rings The Bell* (1951) as Miss Tripp, *The Pride Of St Louis* (1952) as Patricia Nash Dean and *Sylvia* (1965) as Jane Phillips.
CAUSE: She died aged 76 in Beverly Hills, California, of lymphedema.

Pete Duel
(PETER ELLSTROM DEUEL)
Born February 24, 1940
Died December 31, 1971
The frustrated stage actor. To outsiders it seemed that Pete Duel had everything to live for – a loving girlfriend, a nice home, money and a hit TV series. Yet, it was not enough. He was born in Rochester, New York, the eldest child of Dr Elsworth Shault Deuel and Lillian Marcella Ellstrom, a Swedish-American. Brother Geoffrey, born in 1942, and sister Pamela, born three years later, completed the family.

Peter Deuel grew up wanting to be a pilot but discovered he had 20/30 eyesight and changed his plans to medicine. During two years studying to be a doctor at St Lawrence University, Watertown, New York, the college attended by both his father and grandfather, Deuel appeared in every play staged by the drama department. Deciding a life of medicine was not after all for him, Deuel joined the American Theatre Wing where he spent a further two years studying Shakespeare, restoration comedy, elocution, fencing, dancing and body movement. In 1962 Deuel landed his first paid job as an actor, a small part in an off-Broadway production of *Electra* at the Players' Theater in Greenwich Village where he also served as Assistant Stage Manager. Deuel made his TV début in a one hour production from the Armstrong Theater and then went on tour with Tom Ewell in the Broadway hit *Take Her, She's Mine*. On his return he decided to find his fortune in Hollywood. Arriving in the movie capital Pete Deuel was cast in mainly villainous roles before landing a part, John Cooper, in the TV series *Gidget*, which premièred on September 15, 1965. This led to his casting in one of the lead parts, David Willis, in *Love On A Rooftop* the following year. This vehicle gave him the opportunity to show off his talents in both comic and tragic situations. In 1967 Deuel made his film début as Mike Brewer in *The Hell With Heroes* and impressed so much that he was signed to a seven-year contract by Universal. Appearing as a guest star in a number of shows including *The Fugitive*, *The Virginian*, *A Man Called Ironside*, 6′ Deuel was signed to play the role of Hannibal Heyes (alias Joshua Smith) in a new ABC TV series entitled *Alias Smith & Jones* about two Kansas train robbers who have been promised an amnesty if they can stay out of trouble for one year. The series débuted in Britain in April 1971 on BBC2 and was an instant hit. For the sake of simplicity Pete had by now altered the spelling of his surname to Duel. However, filming a weekly series was a hard slog and Duel did not really relish the demands put upon him. In August 1971 he collapsed on set with the flu and was sent home. A reputation for being difficult followed, although Pete claimed he was not hard to work with, merely a perfectionist. It is thought he was hoping another less strenuous series would rescue him from *Alias Smith & Jones* and then allow him to return to 'proper' acting on Broadway. Of acting in a series Pete had said, "The quantity of work is Herculean and the quality is often non-existent." A salary increase quietened him temporarily. "Contractually, I have to do this series," he told a journalist friend, "or some other trash." Duel was a politically active Democrat and was vocal in his support for Eugene McCarthy. In November 1971 Duel stood for election to an executive post in the Screen Actors' Guild, the union, and was bitterly disappointed when he lost. When the telegram arrived informing him of his defeat he tacked it to a wall and then, taking his revolver, blasted a hole through it. A keen environmentalist and 20 years ahead of his time, Pete loved to picnic far from civilisation, but he always tried to leave the countryside tidier than when he had arrived. Pete refused to buy containers that could not be recycled and campaigned to persuade everyone else to do the same. When he signed an autograph, more often than not he would preface his signature with the words "Peace and Ecology Now". A poet as well as an actor, Pete Duel was a typical man of the Sixties. However, he found his release in alcohol rather than drugs. Thrice arrested for drink-driving, he lost his licence but escaped jail by promising the judge he would give up the bottle. Pete received a $1,000 fine and was sentenced to 180 days jail, suspended for two years. Just a week after his plea to the judge, Pete Duel would die by his own hand. In December he volunteered to spend two weekends working for a charity telethon – Toys for Tots. A picture taken at the time shows Duel holding a toy gun to his head. Often, while in the make-up chair for the show, Duel would place his prop gun to his head. CAUSE: On Thursday December 30, 1971, Pete worked, as usual, on *Alias Smith & Jones*, and was in high spirits according to the crew. At his home at 2552 Glen Green Terrace, a two-bedroomed bungalow in the Hollywood Hills, Pete read through the script for the next day. He had one visitor that night – his girlfriend, 29-year-old Diane Ray, a secretary and aspiring actress. Together they watched the latest episode of *Alias Smith & Jones* (Duel was not happy with the edition) and a Lakers basketball game. Duel drank a lot that evening, leading to an argument with Diane, who went to bed. At 1.25am Pete walked into the bedroom and stared at her for a long moment before going to a dresser where he took out a package that Diane thought was a forgotten Christmas present. Taking the box into the living room, Pete smiled at his girlfriend and said, "I'll see you later." A few moments later, Diane heard a loud sound like a firecracker. Going to find out what had happened, she saw Duel lying nude in front of the Christmas tree, a .38 revolver by his side and blood oozing from his right temple. Gathering her wits about her Diane called the police. At first, the authorities did not want to write the death off as a suicide and cited Pete's open-house policy for aspiring and out-of-work actors as a possible factor. Perhaps, they argued, one of the resting thespians, jealous of Pete's success, had killed him. There was no evidence, however, that anyone apart from Duel and Ray had been in the house. Pete's friends dismissed the suicide theory and claimed it was an accidental death.

However, none of them came up with a satisfactory answer as to why ecologist Pete had bought a gun, if not to kill himself. It may be interesting to note that when he arrived in Hollywood, Pete had given himself five years before returning to Broadway. At the time of his death, Pete had spent six years in Tinseltown and the success of *Alias Smith & Jones* threatened to extend that period by some years. A memorial service was held on January 2, 1972, at the Hindu-Christian Self Realisation temple in Pacific Palisades, California. (Pete was not a member but his manager was.) Pete's funeral took place on January 5, 1972, at the Baptist Church in Penfield, New York. Even now, almost 30 years after his death, Pete Duel and all that he stood for are remembered not just for what might have been but also for what he achieved in his ever-so brief life. He once said, "Fame in show business is not in proportion to actual achievement." His business manager has an enduring memory of Pete Duel. John Napier writes, "I shall never forget early one morning about 4am one summer when Pete stood in front of my home, barefoot in blue jeans, looking out over the vast valley stretching far in the distance and began in a loud, strong, beautiful voice, to recite *Hamlet*. Even in my sleepless stupor I was suddenly caught up in the beauty of the speech as his *Hamlet* reverberated around the hills. When he came near the end of the speech the sun began to peek its brilliant head over a nearby mountain as if to pay tribute to a fine performance. 'I love you sun,' he yelled and we broke into gales of laughter. Neighbours, be damned. It was a happy time. There were many happy times like that."

Howard Duff

Born November 24, 1913
Died July 8, 1990
Mr Grit. Born in Bremerton, Washington, Duff was the original

Sam Spade on the wireless before World War II. He made his film début in *Brute Force* (1947) and went on to appear in over 40 films. Mostly, he was cast as a gritty, dependable character rather than a lead. He appeared on several TV shows such as *Bonanza, The Twilight Zone, The Virginian, Batman, Alias Smith & Jones, Kung Fu, Knots Landing, Flamingo Road* and *Dallas*. His films include: *The Naked City* (1948) as Frank Niles, *Red Canyon* (1949) as Lin Sloane, *Johnny Stool Pigeon* (1949) as George Morton, *Calamity Jane And Sam Bass* (1949) as Sam Bass, *Spy Hunt* (1950) as Roger Quain, *Shakedown* (1950) as Jack Early, *Woman In Hiding* (1950) as Keith Ramsey, *Models, Inc.* (1952), *Tanganyika* (1954) as Dan Harder, *Private Hell 36* (1954) as Jack Farnham, *While The City Sleeps* (1956) as Kaufman, *Kramer vs. Kramer* (1979) as John Shaunessy and *Oh, God! Book II* (1980). In Glenbrook, Nevada, on October 21, 1951, he married actress Ida Lupino. Their daughter, Bridget, was born six months later on April 23, 1952. They separated in 1972 but didn't get divorced until 1984.
CAUSE: He died aged 76 of a heart attack in Santa Barbara, California.

Jim Dukas
Born June 6, 1926
Died December 14, 2008
The pal. Jim Dukas was never a star but he worked with many actors who were including Woody Allen, Jackie Gleason, Steve McQueen, Robert Redford and Frank Sinatra. His voice was well known in radio and television advertisements. He made his debut in *The Great St Louis Bank Robbery* (1959) as Willie the driver and among his films were *The Hustler* (1961) as Kibitzer, *The Detective* (1968), *Coogan's Bluff* (1968) as the prison hospital doctor, *The Private Files Of J. Edgar Hoover* (1977) as Frank, *Brubaker* (1980), *Ironweed* (1987) as Finny and *Astoria* (2000) as Kostas. Oddly, because he didn't have a driver's licence he had to get a provisional one to drive the getaway car in *The Great St Louis Bank Robbery*.
CAUSE: He died aged 82 of cancer in his New York City home at West 34th Street near the Lincoln Tunnel and Madison Square Garden.

Dominique Dunne
Born November 20, 1959
Died November 4, 1982
Promise unfulfilled. Dominique Ellen Dunne was born in Santa Monica, California, the daughter of Roman Catholic journalist Dominic Dunne (b. Hartford, Connecticut, October 29, 1925, d. Manhattan, New York, August 26, 2009) who covered the O.J. Simpson and Menendez brothers trials for *Vanity Fair*, the sister of actor Griffin Dunne (b. New York, June 8, 1955), the niece of novelist John Gregory Dunne (b. Hartford, Connecticut, May 25, 1932, d. Manhattan, New York, December 30, 2003) and his author wife Joan Didion (b. Sacramento, California, December 5, 1934) who co-wrote *A Star Is Born* (1976). Following her parents' divorce Dominique moved to New York and then to Beverly Hills where she attended the high school popularised in *Beverly Hills 90210*. Then it was off to study acting at the University of Colorado. The 5'1" Dunne made her film début as Polly Ames in *The Haunting Of Harrington House* (1981) but it was as the elder sister, Dana Freeling, in *Poltergeist* (1982) that she made her name and showed her real talent. She soon began to be a regular on the Beverly Hills social scene and, by all accounts, was liked by everyone who encountered her. It seemed as if the world was at her feet.
CAUSE: In 1982 Dominique began to see 26-year-old John David Sweeney, a chef at the popular Los Angeles niterie Ma Maison. However, Sweeney was a jealous control freak with a violent temper. When Dominique landed the

part of someone who had been beaten up on *Hill Street Blues*, she didn't need very much make-up, thanks to Sweeney. It became too much for Dominique and on the night before Halloween she ended the relationship. Sweeney turned up at her home, 8723 Rangely Avenue, West Hollywood, to effect a reconciliation but Dominique had had enough. However, Sweeney was not a man to take no for an answer and he dragged her outside and put his hands around Dominique's throat. The police were called but when they arrived, Dominique was already lying unconscious in the front garden. When he saw the police Sweeney mumbled, "I killed my girlfriend." An ambulance rushed the comatose Dominique to Cedars-Sinai Hospital Medical Center, 8700 Beverly Boulevard, Los Angeles. She lay in a coma for five days until her heart simply stopped beating. The hospital remains very keen to state that it did not switch off her life support system. Dominique died at 11am. Cause of death: anoxic encephalopathy due to strangulation. She was just 22. Her funeral was held on November 6 at Westwood Catholic Church. It was widely attended and Dominique was laid to rest in grave number 189, Section D of Westwood Memorial Park, 1218 Glendon Avenue, Los Angeles, California 90024. While in prison awaiting trial Sweeney attempted to kill himself using a throwaway razor. In November 1983 he was convicted of assault and unintentional manslaughter and sentenced to 62 years in prison. However, he was released in June 1986 after having served just over two and a half years. Remarkably, he went back to working as a chef in Los Angeles. Dominique's mother, Ellen Griffin Dunne, set up a support group, Justice for Victims of Homicide, for grieving relatives. When Dominique's family and friends discovered where Sweeney was working they picketed the restaurant handing out flyers that read,

"The hands that will prepare your meal tonight also murdered Dominique Dunne." Sweeney was sacked, changed his name to John Maura, and left the area.

Irene Dunne
Born December 20, 1898
Died September 4, 1990
Adaptable performer. Born in Louisville, Kentucky, 5'5" Irene Marie Dunne was the daughter of Joseph Dunne, a steamship inspector and Adelaide Henry, an accomplished pianist, who encouraged her to follow in her footsteps. In 1911 Joseph Dunne died and the family moved to 917 West Second Street, Madison, Indiana, where they boarded with her mother's family. Irene, a devout Roman Catholic, landed a job as a teacher in East Chicago, Indiana, but decided instead to go to the Chicago Musical College. After graduating she failed an audition for the New York Metropolitan Opera. She got a job with a touring company where she learned her acting trade. On July 16, 1928, she married Francis Dennis Griffin, a New York dentist and they adopted a four-year-old girl, Anna Mary Bush, on March 17, 1936. They were together until Griffin's death on October 15, 1965. Under contract to RKO she made her film début in *Leathernecking* (1930) playing Delphine Witherspoon. She soon earned a reputation as someone who could play across the board, including comedies, melodramas and musicals. Her 42 films included: *The Great Lover* (1931) as Diana Page, *Cimarron* (1931) as Sabra Cravat, a performance that earned her a nomination for Best Actress Oscar, *Bachelor Apartment* (1931) as Helene Andrews, *Thirteen Women* (1932) as Laura Stanhope, *Back Street* (1932) as Ray Schmidt, *No Other Woman* (1933) as Anna Stanley, *If I Were Free* (1933) as Sarah Cazenove, *Magnificent Obsession* (1935) as Helen Hudson, *Theodora Goes Wild* (1936) as Theodora

Lynn, earning her second nomination for Best Actress Oscar, *Show Boat* (1936) as Magnolia Hawks, *High, Wide, And Handsome* (1937) as Sally Watterson, *The Awful Truth* (1937) as Lucy Warriner provided her third Best Actress Oscar nomination, her fourth came with *Love Affair* (1939) in which she played Terry McKay, *My Favorite Wife* (1940) as Ellen Arden, *Anna And The King Of Siam* (1946) as Anna Owens, *Life With Father* (1947) as Vinnie Day, *I Remember Mama* (1948) as Mama Hansen which earned her a fifth and final Best Actress Oscar nomination and *It Grows On Trees* (1952) as Polly Baxter. At her peak she was earning $400,000 a year. Very right wing, she criticised Farrah Fawcett and Vanessa Redgrave for having children out of wedlock. Dunne retired in 1952 to become an advocate of Republican policies. She was appointed the American delegate to the United Nations by President Dwight D. Eisenhower in 1957 and was a staunch supporter of Ronald Reagan's bid for the presidency.

CAUSE: She died in Los Angeles, California, of heart failure. She was 91.

E

Milt Ebbins

Born February 20, 1912
Died March 4, 2008
The manager. Milton Keith Ebbins was born in Springfield, Massachusetts, and started his career in the early 1930s as a trumpeter and bandleader. Realising that being in the public eye was not his forte he became an agent and manager. His clients included Count Basie, Sarah Vaughn, Billy Eckstine, Vic Damone, Elizabeth Montgomery, Patty Duke, Mort Sahl and Peter Lawford. He was also producer of films for his clients and his 35-year long relationship with Lawford gave him an entrée to the Rat Pack and the Kennedy administration. Ebbins helped organise the 1961 Kennedy inauguration and the 1962 Madison Square Garden birthday party. It was to Ebbins that Peter Lawford turned on August 4, 1962 when the actor received a phone call from Marilyn Monroe. He advised Lawford not to visit Fifth Helena Drive and instead rang Marilyn's lawyer Mickey Rudin. He married Lynne Sherman in 1940 and they had one son, Gary, also a personal manager. His brother, Bernie, worked as a road manager for many of his brother's clients and died aged 88 on December 27, 2004 at Cedars-Sinai Medical Center in Los Angeles.
CAUSE: Ebbins died aged 96 from heart failure in Los Angeles, California.

Johnny Eck

(JOHN ECHKARDT)
Born August 27, 1911
Died January 5, 1991
Cinematic oddity. Born in Baltimore, Maryland, 20 minutes after his normal-sized twin brother Robert, Johnny Eck stood just 1'6". Aged 12, he joined a sideshow where he was billed as "Johnny Eck, The Half-boy". He made just four films but one was the notorious Tod Browning movie *Freaks* (opened on July 8, 1932) which was banned for many years in the UK. It was the story of a circus freak show and featured many malformed actors who had worked in sideshows. Of his fellow performers, Eck said, "I met hundreds and thousands of people, and none finer than the midgets and the Siamese twins and the caterpillar man and the bearded woman and the human seal with the little flippers for hands. I never asked them any embarrassing questions and they never asked me, and God, it was a great adventure." The film originally ran to 90 minutes but was cut to 64 and the 26 minutes of footage have been lost. It starred Olga Baclanova as a heartless trapeze artiste. In 1937, with his twin brother, Johnny performed a sawing-in-half illusion. His other films were: *Tarzan The Ape Man* (1932), *Tarzan Escapes* (1936) and *Tarzan's Secret Treasure* (1941).
CAUSE: Eck died in his home city of Baltimore, Maryland aged 79.

Herb Edelman

Born November 5, 1930
Died July 21, 1996
Tall baldie. Herbert Edelman was born in Brooklyn, New York, and educated at Brooklyn College and Cornell University before being called up to the army. On demob, he became a cab driver while waiting for his break as an actor. He made his Broadway debut in 1963 in the play *Lorenzo* and his big break came at the Biltmore Theatre when he played the part of Harry Pepper, the telephone repairman in Neil Simon's *Barefoot In The Park*, a role he reprised in the 1967 film version. He appeared in more than 50 television programmes including *Cagney & Lacey*, *Highway To Heaven*, *Charlie's Angels*, *Chico And The Man*, *Murder, She Wrote*, *The Fall Guy*,

Fantasy Island, Cannon, The Love Boat, MacGyver, Knots Landing but was best known for his starring roles in *Big John, Little John* (1976) as Big John Martin (helped by his 6ft 5in height), *Ladies' Man* (1980–81) as Reggie, Harry Nussbaum in *9 To 5* (1982–83) and Richard Clarendon in *St Elsewhere* (1982–88). In 1985 he began appearing as Stanley Zbornak in *The Golden Girls* (until 1992) forever trying to win back Dorothy (Bea Arthur). His work won him two Emmy nominations (in 1987 and 1988). His film work included *In Like Flint* (1967) as the Russian prime minister, *The Odd Couple* (1967) as Murray, *The War Between Men And Women* (1972) as Howard Mann, *The Way We Were* (1973) as Bill Verso, *The Front Page* (1974) as Schwartz and *California Suite* (1978) as Harry Michaels. He married the actress Louise Sorel (b. New York 6 August 1940 as Louise Cohen) in 1964 and had two daughters by her. They divorced in 1970.
CAUSE: Herb Edelman died in Woodland Hills, California, aged 65 from emphysema.

Nora Eddington

Born February 25, 1924
Died April 10, 2001
Mrs Errol Flynn II. Born in Chicago, Illinois, the daughter of Jack Eddington, who worked for the Los Angeles County Sheriff's Office. When Flynn spotted her in 1943 Nora was working on a tobacco stand in Los Angeles Hall of Justice. He was in the courtroom on trial for rape. He wooed Nora and they had a platonic relationship until one night when he raped her. Despite this assault, Flynn charmed his way back into Nora's life and she married the legendary hellraiser by proxy in Mexico in September 1944 and gave birth to his daughters Deirdre (b. Mexico City, January 10, 1945 at 10.50pm) and Rory (b. Hollywood, California, March 12, 1947). Flynn was his usual self and

the couple were divorced on July 7, 1949 in Nevada. The following year she married the singer Dick Haymes who had been married to Joanne Dru and would later marry Rita Hayworth. Nora divorced Haymes in 1953. Her third husband was Richard Black and by him she had one son, Kevin, who died when he was 10. Nora appeared in three films *Unusual Occupations* (1947), *Adventures Of Don Juan* (1948) and *Cruise Of The Zaca* (1952).
CAUSE: She died aged 77 of kidney failure in Los Angeles, California.

Nelson Eddy

Born June 29, 1901
Died March 6, 1967
'The Singing Capon'. Born in Providence, Rhode Island, a descendant of 8th American President Martin Van Buren, blond baritone Eddy began his career as a boy soprano. In 1915 his parents separated and he went to live with his mother in Philadelphia. Needing to support the family, he left school and took a number of writing jobs before landing his first professional gig in 1922 in *The Marriage Tax* at the Philadelphia Academy of Music. His career blossomed and he took a number of jobs with various Philadelphia ensembles. He began appearing on radio from the late Twenties and in 1933 was offered a contract by RKO but preferred to sign for MGM. He made his film début in *Broadway To Hollywood* (1933) but his star didn't shine brightly until he was teamed with Jeanette MacDonald in *Naughty Marietta* (1935). It was to be the first of eight films they would make together, during the course of which the duo became immensely popular; indeed, they were often referred to as 'America's Sweethearts'. He also sang with Eleanor Powell, Virginia Bruce and Ilona Massey. Following the end of his film career in 1947 Eddy began touring nightclubs. On January 19, 1939, Eddy married Ann Denitz

Franklin (d. August 28, 1987). There were no children from the marriage. CAUSE: On March 5, 1967, he suffered a stroke while appearing in the Blue Sails Room of the Sans Souci Hotel in Miami Beach. Taken to Mount Sinai Hospital, he died the next day aged 65. He was buried in Hollywood Memorial Park, 6000 Santa Monica Boulevard, Hollywood, California 90038.

Jimmy Edwards, DFC
Born March 23, 1920
Died July 7, 1988
Blusterer. Born in Barnes, Surrey, James Keith O'Neill Edwards was the eighth of nine children (last of five sons) of Professor Reginald Walter Kenneth Edwards, lecturer in Maths at King's College, London. He was educated at St Paul's Cathedral School, King's College School and went up to St John's College, Cambridge where he read history. He came to fame on the radio in the show *Take It From Here* in which he created the character of Pa Glum (later transferred to TV). To television viewers he was best known for his portrayal of the headmaster of Chiselbury School in the sitcom *Whack-O!* (from October 4, 1956). He was instantly recognisable by his enormous handlebar moustache (said to be 11″ across and grown to hide facial scars suffered during World War II). He appeared in *Murder At The Windmill* (1948), *Treasure Hunt* (1952), *Three Men In A Boat* (1955), *Bottoms Up!* (1959, a *Whack-O!* spin-off), *Nearly A Nasty Accident* (1961), *The Plank* (1967) and others. He stood as a Member of Parliament for the Conservative Party in the 1964 General Election in the Paddington North constituency. A homosexual, he married air hostess Valerie Seymour in 1958 but they divorced in 1969 when she discovered he was continuing to sleep with men (on honeymoon he had told her he was a reformed homosexual). In 1976 an Australian drag artist Ramon Douglas sold the story of his ten-year 'loving relationship' with Edwards. CAUSE: He died of pneumonia in London's Cromwell Hospital. He was 68 and had been ill for some time. FURTHER READING: *Six Of The Best* – Jimmy Edwards (London: Robson Books, 1984).

Julie Ege
(JULIE DZULI)
Born November 12, 1943
Died April 29, 2008
"New sex symbol of the Seventies". Rarely was a Seventies comedy or sex romp complete without the presence of the beauteous Julie Ege. Born in Sandnes, southwest Norway she began modelling aged 15 and at 18 was crowned Miss Norway. She entered but did not win Miss Universe. Brains as well as beauty saw her get a degree in English and History at the University of Oslo. To improve her English, she moved to London in 1967 to work as an au pair. Within two months her 36-24-36 charms were adorning *Penthouse*, which led to her third film *On Her Majesty's Secret Service* (released December 18, 1969). Next she played lusty Swedish au pair Inga Giltenburg in Marty Feldman's *Every Home Should Have One* (1970). "It was my first real part with dialogue. They wanted me to look and sound like a Scandinavian nanny so I gave them just that. It was really difficult," she joked. "Once the film opened, all the newspapers carried a photo of me with the caption 'Every Home Should Have One'. I was famous overnight and was not prepared for all the decision-making so crucial at that moment," she confessed. Her sex symbol credentials were confirmed as Voluptua in *Up Pompeii* (1971). She was given a role as Nala in the Hammer film *Creatures The World Forgot* (released April 18, 1971) after turning down the opportunity to appear opposite Peter Sellers in *There's A Girl In My Soup* (1970). She did not

enjoy the African location shoot and had recently given birth to her first daughter. "They made me wear this awful wig and my bikini was a far cry from the one Raquel Welch wore," she recalled. "I had dirt smeared all over me. My newborn child was back in England and after a few days I got homesick." She was offered the Martine Beswick role in Hammer's *Dr Jekyll And Sister Hyde* in 1972 but turned it down. "I was by then very reluctant about doing nudity," she said. "Many people think I did so much nudity in my films. I did a short scene in *Every Home Should Have One*, and two bathtub scenes in *Not Now Darling* and *The Mutations*." She appeared in several sex comedies and horror films where a pretty girl was required in the Seventies including *The Magnificent Seven Deadly Sins* (released November 1971) as Ingrid, *Rentadick* (1972) as Utta, *Not Now Darling* (released March 1973) as Janie McMichael, *Percy's Progress* (released August 1974) as Miss Hanson, *The Mutations* (released October 1974) as Hedi, *The Legend Of The Seven Golden Vampires* (released October 6, 1974) and *The Amorous Milkman* (released January 1975) as Diana. The film's poster showed a contented cat licking its lips above the unsubtle legend, "If your pussy could only talk". Her last film was the drama *Fengslende dager* for Christina Berg (1988) in which she was Krags hustru. Ege was under no illusions about the reasons for her fame – "To be honest, I was never really that proud of my performance in films, but I gave it my best and enjoyed the work very much" – and when she retired, she retrained as a nurse. She married and divorced twice. In the Seventies, Ege lived with Tony Bramwell, the Beatles associate, and even recorded a version of the John Lennon song 'Love'.
CAUSE: In 1986, she was diagnosed with breast cancer and underwent a mastectomy. She later had lung cancer and died in Oslo. She was 64.

Sergei Eisenstein
Born January 23, 1898
Died February 11, 1948
Leading Soviet film-maker. Sergei Mikhalovich Eisenstein was born in Riga, Latvia, and could speak English, French, German and Russian by the time he was ten. In 1917 he began studying at the St Petersburg Institute of Civil Engineering but forsook the fascinating world of engineering for the more precarious one of the theatre. At the outbreak of civil war in Russia he joined the Bolsheviks while his father sided with the Mensheviks. In 1920 he began directing an amateur troupe. He joined a theatre as a scenic designer and two years later was appointed artistic head of an offshoot. He greatly admired D.W. Griffith. Eisenstein's first directorial film was *Stachka* (1925) about the conflict following the Great October Socialist Revolution. *Pravda* praised the film; the public didn't. It was his next film that cemented Eisenstein's reputation. *Bronenosets Potemkin* (1925) was undoubtedly one of the greatest, most moving films ever made. The movie premièred at the Bolshoi Theatre in December 1925 but again, public reaction was lukewarm. His film *Oktyabr* (1927) commemorated the tenth anniversary of the Bolshevik rise to power. The Soviet authorities put the entire city of Leningrad at his disposal but not everyone enthused over the director and he was subject to harassment by unfriendly police. The admiration of his peers more than made up for this, however. In 1930 he arrived in America and was greeted as a conquering hero by some and as evil personified by others. The publicity machine went into overdrive and Eisenstein was photographed with Mickey Mouse and Rin Tin Tin, much to his discomfort. He began work on *Que Viva Mexico* (1932) but abandoned the film without completing it when his finance ran out. Disappointment, jealousy from his fellow workers and the failure

to complete *Bezhin Meadow* all contributed to Eisenstein's nervous breakdown in 1937. His next film *Aleksandr Nevsky* (1938) was a success at home and abroad although some of his early fans expressed disappointment with it. His final work, *Ivan Groznyi* (1942–1946), was envisaged as a monumental triptych. However, only two parts were completed and the second of those was banned by Stalin because of its unflattering portrayal of the secret police. The ban wasn't lifted until 1958.

CAUSE: He died of a heart attack aged 50 in Moscow.

Jack Elam

Born November 13, 1918
Died October 20, 2003
Wild-eyed film cowboy. Born in Miami, Arizona, Jack Elam lost his left eye aged 12 when a fellow Boy Scout stabbed a pencil into it. The 6'2" Elam began his professional life as an accountant and hotel manager. He got his start in show business by offering his accounting services free of charge in exchange for a role in a film. He appeared as a baddie in more than 130 films in a career spanning more than 50 years. His films included *Trailin' West* (1944) as the killer, *Mystery Range* (1947) as Burvil Lambert, *One Way Street* (1950) as Artie, *A Ticket To Tomahawk* (1950) as Fargo, *High Lonesome* (1950) as Bob Jessup, the 1951 classic *Rawhide* as Tevis, *Rancho Notorious* (1952) as Mort Geary, *High Noon* (1952) as Charlie, *Ride, Vaquero!* (1953) as Barton, *Cattle Queen Of Montana* (1954) as Yost, *The Man From Laramie* (1954) as Chris Bouldt, *Kismet* (1955) as Hassan-Ben, *Tarzan's Hidden Jungle* (1955) as Burger, *Gunfight At The OK Corral* (1957) as Tom McLowery, *Pat Garrett & Billy The Kid* (1973) as Alamosa Bill, *Cannonball Run II* (1984) as Dr Nikolas von Helsing, and *Shadow Force* (1993) as Tommy. Twice married: to Jean (1937 until her death in 1961)

and to Margaret Jennison (from 1961 until his death). He fathered a son, Scott, and two daughters, Jeri and Jacqueline. He disliked critics ascribing psychological characteristics to his roles. "I robbed the bank because I wanted the money. Nobody cared what my problem was and I didn't either."

CAUSE: Elam died aged 84 in Ashland, Oregon, having been ill for some time.

Denholm Elliott, CBE

Born May 31, 1922
Died October 6, 1992
Smoothy with a secret. Born at 48 Lexham Gardens, Kensington, London (the street where Kenny Everett would die of the same illness that killed Elliott) Denholm Mitchell Elliott was the second son of Myles Layman Farr Elliott (d. 1933), a barrister, and Nina Mitchell (d. 1966). Elliott, who had lost the tip of his right thumb in a lawnmower accident, began his acting career at Ripley Court, his prep school, in Surrey. In 1933 his father was killed by terrorists while he was serving as a crown prosecutor in Palestine, and Elliott was sent off to Malvern College, hating every second of public school life. In an unusual turn, he began to steal anything that was not nailed down and was sent to a psychiatrist who recommended that he be sent to the Royal Academy of Dramatic Art. His studies were interrupted after two terms when he joined the RAF as a gunner in 1940. Two years later, he was shot down off Denmark and sent as a prisoner of war to Stalag 8B at Lansdorf, Silesia. He began acting again while being held prisoner. Released in 1945 he quickly made up for lost time, making his stage début in July of that year at the Amersham Playhouse. He made his first film, *Dear Mr Prohack*, in 1949 and went on to appear in David Lean's *The Sound Barrier* (1952) (impressing Sir Alexander Korda so much that he was offered a five-figure contract and the lead in a mooted Lawrence of Arabia

biopic), *The Cruel Sea* (1953), *The Heart Of The Matter* (1953), *Alfie* (1966), *The Night They Raided Minsky's* (1968), *Percy* (1970), *A Bridge Too Far* (1977), *The Boys From Brazil* (1978), *Raiders Of The Lost Ark* (1981), *Brimstone And Treacle* (1982), *Trading Places* (1983), *Maurice* (1987) (E.M. Forster's posthumously published novel about homosexuality), *Indiana Jones And The Last Crusade* (1989) and the disappointing movie version of hit sitcom *Rising Damp* (1980). On television he appeared in *Clayhanger*, *Blade On The Feather* (1980) for which he won a BAFTA award, *Bleak House*, *Hotel Du Lac* and many others. He won a Best Supporting Actor Oscar nomination for his performance as Mr Emerson in Merchant-Ivory's *A Room With A View* (1985). In 1984 and 1985 he won BAFTA awards for *A Private Function* and *Defence Of The Realm* (1985). Gabriel Byrne, his co-star, said, "Never act with children, animals or Denholm Elliott." Elliott often accepted roles purely for their financial reward. On March 1, 1954, he married the actress Virginia Anne McKenna but they divorced in 1957. On June 15, 1962 he married the American model Susan Robinson (b. 1942). They had two children: Jennifer Sarah Elliott (b. New York, June 8, 1964) and Mark (b. January 23, 1967).

CAUSE: Through two marriages, Elliott carried on gay affairs that were to result in his death at the age of 70 from AIDS-related tuberculosis at his long-time home of Santa Eulalia, Ibiza, Spain. He was already HIV positive when he was appointed CBE in 1988. He left less than £125,000. His ashes were scattered in the garden of Santa Eulalia. His daughter was shocked to learn of her father's bisexuality and it sent her on a downward spiral of heroin addiction and despair. She found out in a most hurtful way. The teenaged Jennifer was confronted by a stranger on the King's Road in London who said, "Your dad is Denholm Elliott. Did you know he is gay? Well, he can kiss my arse any time he wants." Jennifer was regularly smoking cannabis by the age of 13, and by 15 was taking heroin. She managed to conceal her addiction from her parents, but shortly before her 18th birthday confessed that she was an addict. By the time she was 20, Jennifer had left home and was begging on the streets of London. By 24, she had fled to America, where she resorted to prostitution to fund her next heroin fix, selling her body for £30 a time. Her father hired a private detective to track her down and paid for endless stints in expensive rehabilitation clinics, all to no avail. Following her father's death, her mother set up a charitable project to help AIDS patients and Jennifer worked there. She told one newspaper of her battle with heroin, "It's total despair and you begin to think, 'I really can't handle this.' I'll never be clear of drugs. I hate it. I would love more than anything in the world to be free. I get so angry with myself the minute I start to go back. I feel so despairingly low." When the Denholm Elliott Project closed through lack of money, Jennifer divided her time between London and America, drifting between working in a bar and not working at all. In 1999 she moved to the family villa in Ibiza. It seemed her life was on the up. She put on weight as she ate a healthy diet and got a suntan as she motored around the island on her scooter. However, the drug use had left its mark. She suffered insomnia and her short-term memory was affected. She had to write things down on paper to remember them but would forget where she had left the bits of paper. As a result she couldn't keep a job and thus had money worries. Added to this, a close friend on the island died and her mother fell ill. Then her long-term boyfriend ended their relationship. Jennifer had to leave her home in the summer because her mother rented it out to make some money. In June 2003 Jennifer Elliott hanged herself from the branch of a tree in the garden at Santa Eulalia. In the house, she left a heartbreakingly simple handwritten note saying that she couldn't go on. Almost ten years earlier, she had written, "There's a point you reach when you are ready to kill yourself. You can't stand any more pain."

Michael Elphick
Born September 19, 1946
Died September 7, 2002
Rough diamond. Despite his London accent, Michael John Elphick was born in Chichester, West Sussex, the son of a librarian, but left at 15 to work as an electrician for Laurence Olivier's company. It was Olivier who suggested that Elphick go to the Central School of Speech and Drama and soon Elphick was a regular on stage and screen. Despite his later years when he was a familiar face on television, Elphick also made several films. He made his début in Stanley Baker's *Where's Jack?* (1969) about highwayman Jack Sheppard in which Elphick played Hogarth. He went on to appear in *Hamlet* (1969) as Captain, *Fräulein Doktor* (1969) as Tom, *Cry Of The Banshee* (1970) as Burke, *See No Evil* (1971) as Gypsy Tom, *O Lucky Man!* (1973), *Stardust* (1974) and *The Odd Job* (1978) as Raymonde. In the Seventies he began to appear on television on a regular basis. He was the second porter in *Three Men In A Boat* (1975), *The One And Only Phyllis Dixey* (1978) and Dennis Potter's *Blue Remembered Hills* (1979) as Peter, in which a group of adults played children. Back on the big screen he was Jimmy's father in *Quadrophenia* (1979), Burgess in *The First Great Train Robbery* (1979) and the night porter in *The Elephant Man* (1980). Then he took the lead role of Private Gerhard Schultz in the comedy *Private Schultz*. The following year he was the Detective Chief Superintendent in *Smiley's People*. In 1983 he signed to play troublemaking Irish brickie Magowan in *Auf Wiedersehen, Pet.*

His other films included *Privates On Parade* (1982) as Sergeant-Major Red Drummond, *Gorky Park* (1983) as Pasha, *Curse Of The Pink Panther* (1983) as Valencia Police Chief, *Ordeal By Innocence* (1984) as Inspector Huish, *Memed My Hawk* (1984) as Jabbar, *The Supergrass* (1985) as Constable Collins, a sentry in *Pirates* (1986), *Withnail And I* (1987) as Jake, *Little Dorrit* (1988) as Mr Merdle, *I Bought A Vampire Motorcycle* (1990) as Inspector Cleaver, *Buddy's Song* (1990) as Des, *The Krays* (1990), *Let Him Have It* (1991) as Prison Officer Jack and *Dead In The Water* (2001) as Lionel Stubbs. In the mid-Eighties he signed to appear in two long-running series that made him a popular face on television. From April 15, 1985 until June 18, 1989, he played the working-class Sam Tyler in *Three Up, Two Down* opposite Angela Thorne's snobbish Daphne Trenchard. In 1986 he also began appearing as Ken Boon, a biker, a private detective and a loser. In 1993 he played Harry Salter, a former Fleet Street journalist, in *Harry* but the public did not warm to the show. He played another journalist, Peter Campling, in *The Fix* (1997), a story about the bribing of Sheffield Wednesday footballers in 1963. In the spring of 2001 he joined the soap opera *EastEnders* as Harry Slater, a paedophile who had raped his 13-year-old niece and fathered her daughter. Aged 19, Elphick suffered an ulcer due to his heavy drinking and in 1988 was given a year to live. He remained teetotal for four years afterwards but then started drinking again. He drank heavily to cope with the death of his girlfriend of 34 years Julia Alexander (b. 1945, d. London, March 1996 of breast cancer), a teacher of dyslexic children, and the mother of his daughter, Kate (b. March 1975). He contemplated suicide after her death. In 1979 as Julia Alexander was beginning her long and unsuccessful battle with the cancer that was to kill her Elphick began a five-year affair with blonde actress Hetty Baynes (b. 1961). "Michael did tell me there was someone in his life, but because they weren't married, I persuaded myself that it wasn't serious," said Baynes who later went on to marry and divorce the much older film director Ken Russell. "By the time I realised that he might as well have been married, it was too late. I was madly in love with him." Elphick was sacked from *EastEnders* due to his alcoholism. He had turned up drunk to the British Soap Awards, much to the dismay of the show's executives.

CAUSE: On Thursday, September 5, 2002 Elphick collapsed outside his local, Isobar at 61 Walm Lane, Willesden, in north London. The next day he went into the pub to tell regulars that he was OK. Twenty-four hours later, Elphick collapsed at his home, 31 Cranhurst Road, in Willesden, with a heart attack. He died in hospital the same day aged 55. His funeral was held in Chichester, West Sussex, and one of the songs played was 'The Great Pretender'.

Dick Emery

Born February 19, 1915
Died January 2, 1983
Character comedian. Born in University College Hospital, St Pancras, London, Richard Gilbert Emery was not a matinée idol to look at but he seemed to have no trouble attracting gorgeous women. His parents were the music hall act Callan & Emery. During the Second World War he joined the RAF and then Ralph Reader's Gang Show in 1942. After demob he worked with Tony Hancock at the Windmill Theatre in 1948 before finding a measure of fame on the radio show *Educating Archie*. It was his appearances in *The Army Game* (from September 27, 1960) as Private 'Chubby' Catchpole that finally propelled him to stardom. *The Dick Emery Show* began on BBC1 on

July 13, 1963, and ran for eighteen years and 166 episodes. His characters, such as old man Lampwick, the tramp College, camp Clarence ("Hello, honky-tonks"), sex starved Hettie and randy Mandy ("Oooh, you are awful . . . but I like you"), became national institutions. In 1960 he appeared in *Light Up The Sky* and followed that with *A Taste Of Money* (1960), *The Wrong Arm Of The Law* (1963), *Baby Love* (1968), played Bateman in *Loot* (1970) and brought many of his characters to the big screen in 1972 for *Ooh, You Are Awful*. Dick who suffered badly from nerves and was usually physically sick before a performance was married five times. He had a son by his first wife, Zelda, but she left him after five years. He married secondly on August 13, 1946, to Irene Dorothy Ansell but the marriage lasted only a few months. Wife number three was Iris Tully by whom he had a son. She died of a brain tumour. In 1958 he married 18-year-old Victoria Chambers. They had two children. His fifth wife was the singer and actress, Josephine Sheila Blake whom he married on November 1, 1969. There were no children. When Emery died he was living with a dancer, Fay Hillier.

CAUSE: He died aged 67 in the intensive care unit of King's College Hospital, London. He had fallen ill in December 1982 after taking pills for gout. He moved to King's College from a private clinic after contracting a respiratory infection. He seemed to be recovering but died suddenly after a relapse. He left £311,437 in his will. Before his body was taken to a chapel of rest, it was left overnight in a garage in Patcham Terrace, Battersea. He was cremated at Mortlake, London, on January 13, 1983.

Harry Endo

Born July 20, 1922
Died January 9, 2009
Late bloomer. Born in Colorado, Endo

worked for Territorial Savings Bank for whom he made an advertisement and was spotted by the producers of a new police show. Endo was cast as scientist Che Fong in *Hawaii Five-O*. He played in 111 episodes of the series. Doug Mossman, who was Detective Frank Kamana on the show, said Fong was "the all-encompassing forensic genius, who was supposed to know everything about everything". Endo retired from acting in the Eighties. His wife, Myrtle, to whom he was married for more than 60 years, died two months after he did. She was 85.

CAUSE: Endo died aged 86 at Brooklyn Methodist Hospital, New York of a stroke.

René Enriquez

Born November 24, 1933
Died March 23, 1990
Gay caballero. Enriquez, who attended the American Academy of Dramatic Arts, played the perpetually worried Lieutenant Ray Calletano on the hit cop show *Hill Street Blues*. He appeared in a few films including *Bananas* (1971) as Dias, *Serpico* (1973), *Harry And Tonto* (1974), *Under Fire* (1983) as President Anastasio Somoza, *The Evil That Men Do* (1984) as Max Ortiz and *Bullet Proof* (1988) as General Brogado. He also appeared in a number of TV movies on television and in episodes of *Charlie's Angels, Benson, WKRP In Cincinnati* and *Quincy, M.E.*

CAUSE: In biographies and interviews Enriquez told of a wife who had tragically died. It was a lie. He was a homosexual bachelor who contracted AIDS in 1987. As he became more and more ill he told his family, friends and fans he was suffering from cancer. His publicist and long-time friend Henry Bollinger revealed, "René told me he was dying of pancreatic cancer. He never told me anything about a gay lifestyle. He made clear to me before his death that he wanted no autopsy performed on his body and wanted no funeral. He did not want his friends to

come together after he had passed." The true cause of death, AIDS, only became known when his death certificate was published. Cause of death was given as "cytomegalovirus enteritis due to Acquired Immune Deficiency Syndrome (AIDS)". The only people privy to Enriquez's terrible secret were his two sisters and his 25-year-old Hispanic lover.

Peg Entwhistle

(LILLIAN MILLICENT ENTWHISTLE)
Born July 1, 1908
Died September 18, 1932
Tragic Hollywood icon. Like many girls Peg Entwhistle dreamed of acting stardom. Born into a theatrical family in Port Talbot, Wales, she was raised in London but travelled from her home (53 Comeragh Road, Barons Court, London W14) to America with just one aim – to be a successful actress. In 1925 she made her Broadway début in *Hamlet* as part of the prestigious New York Theater Guild. Two years later, aged 19, she became one of the youngest ever actresses to star on the Great White Way. It seemed she could do no wrong. She received excellent notices for her role in *Tommy*, which opened at the Gaiety Theater on January 10, 1927, and ran for 232 performances. Her co-star was Sidney Toler, best known to cinema audiences as the masterful Oriental sleuth Charlie Chan. She married actor Robert Keith in 1927 but they divorced two years later. His son was the actor Brian Keith (b. New Jersey, November 14, 1921, d. 91a Malibu Colony Road, Malibu, Los Angeles 90265, June 24, 1997, from a self-inflicted gunshot wound to the head). Then Peg's luck really began to change, and not for the better. The 1931–2 season was an unmitigated disaster. Eight consecutive failures haunted her. In April 1932 she moved to Hollywood, hoping the West Coast would herald a change of fortune. She appeared with Billie Burke in *The Mad Hopes* but the play closed after just a

fortnight of playing to half-empty theatres. To Peg it was another defeat. After some months of looking for movie work, she was signed to RKO. Her first film was called *Thirteen Women* (1932) and starred Myrna Loy and Irene Dunne; Peg only had a bit part. When filming wrapped in August, the studio declined to pick up her contract. Peg was desolate. She began to think she was jinxed. She tried to raise the money to go back to New York and Broadway, her first love, but was unable to. Distraught, she resorted to what many actresses have done to pay the rent – she posed for pin-ups and nude photographs.

CAUSE: On September 18, 1932, Entwhistle left 2428 Beachwood Canyon Drive, the home she shared with her Uncle Harold, her only living relative, telling him she was going to buy a book and perhaps see a friend. Instead, she walked in the opposite direction to the foot of Mount Lee, where she struggled through the dense terrain up to the famous HOLLYWOODLAND sign, built in 1923 at a cost of $21,000 and illuminated by 4,000 bulbs. She took off her jacket and folded it neatly. She placed her handbag on top of it and, using the electrician's ladder, she climbed to the top of the 50-foot 'H' and looked down at the city that had rejected her. No one knows for how long she stood there before she flung herself off and plunged to her death in the dark void below. She was just 24 years old. Her mangled body lay unidentified for several days. The next morning a woman called the Central Los Angeles Police Department to report, "I was hiking near the Hollywoodland sign today and near the bottom I found a woman's shoe and jacket. A little further on I noticed a purse. In it was a suicide note. I looked down the mountain and saw a body. I don't want any publicity in this matter, so I wrapped up the jacket, shoes and purse in a bundle and laid them on the steps of the Hollywood Police Station." The note read: "I am afraid I am a coward. I am sorry for everything. If I had done this a long time ago, it would have saved a lot of pain. P.E." The note was published in the *Los Angeles Times* and Uncle Harold officially identified Peg's body. Ironically, in the post was a contract from the Beverly Hills Community Players offering her a juicy part in their next production – that of a girl who commits suicide at the end of the third act. Peg had died from multiple fractures of the pelvis and following her funeral at W.M. Strothers Mortuary, 6240 Hollywood Boulevard, was cremated at Hollywood Memorial Park and her ashes interred next to her father at Oak Hill Cemetery, Glendale, Ohio, on January 5, 1933. Although Peg didn't achieve lasting fame as an actress, she does have an epitaph of a kind. It was Entwhistle's performance in Ibsen's *The Wild Duck* in Boston that inspired Bette Davis to become an actress.

Leif Erickson
(WILLIAM WYCLIFFE ANDERSON)
Born October 27, 1911
Died January 29, 1986
Bland blond. Born in Alameda, California, the son of a sea captain and a writer, he began his career in showbusiness as a big band singer and trombonist and indeed his film debut was as the band singer with Ted Fio Rito in *The Sweetheart Of Sigma Chi* (1933) and followed that with *Air Tonic* (1933). He began using the name Glenn Erickson and with that moniker he played Lawrence (a corpse!) in *Wanderer Of The Wasteland* (1935). He adopted the Leif Erickson name for good with *Conquest* (1937) as Paul Lachinski. He worked steadily for most of his career but never attained stardom on the big screen. His best role was probably one he played on stage as well, Bill Reynolds, Deborah Kerr's macho husband, in Vincente Minnelli's *Tea And Sympathy* (released

September 27, 1956). His films included: *College Holiday* (1936) as Dick Winters, *Waikiki Wedding* (1937) as Dr Victor Quimby, *Thrill Of A Lifetime* (1937) as Howdy Nelson, *The Big Broadcast Of 1938* (1938) as Bob Hayes, *Ride A Crooked Mile* (1938) as Johnny Simpkins, . . . *One Third Of A Nation* . . . (1939) as Peter Cortlant, *Sorry, Wrong Number* (1948), *The Snake Pit* (1948), *Fourteen Hours* (1951), *Invaders From Mars* (1953), *On The Waterfront* (1954), *Twilight For The Gods* (1958), *A Gathering Of Eagles* (1963), *Roustabout* (1964) and *The Carpetbaggers* (1964). If not for his role as Big John Cannon in the television Western *The High Chaparral* from 1967 until 1971, Erickson would probably be remembered only as the husband of mentally unstable star Frances Farmer. They eloped to Yuma, Arizona on February 8, 1936. They divorced on June 12, 1942, the same day that Erickson married 5'4" actress Margaret Hayes (b. Baltimore, Maryland December 5, 1916 as Florette Regina Ottenheimer d. Miami Beach, Florida January 26, 1977 of cancer and hepatitis). The marriage lasted just one month. In 1945 Erickson married Ann Diamond by whom he had two children: William Leif (b. California December 17, 1946 d. San Luis Obispo February 11, 1971 in a car crash) and Susan Irene (b. 1950). CAUSE: Erickson died from cancer at Pensacola, Florida. He was 74.

Barry Evans

Born June 18, 1943
Died February 10, 1997
Poor man's Robin Askwith. Barry Joseph Evans was born in Guildford, Surrey, and grew up in an orphanage in Twickenham. Aged 18 he won a John Gielgud scholarship to the Central School of Speech and Drama. Following graduation, he found work with regional repertory companies and some "spear-carrying parts" at the National Theatre before Clive Donner's *Here We Go Round The Mulberry Bush* (1967) launched him as Jamie McGregor, a teenage boy (he was in his mid-twenties at the time) farcically intent on losing his virginity. Critics praised his performance as "a definitive portrait of a boy on the threshold of manhood". He landed a role as the naïve and nervous medical student Michael A. Upton in the popular TV series *Doctor In The House* (July 12, 1969–July 3, 1970) and its successor *Doctor At Large* (February 28–September 12, 1971). His youthful good looks drew an enthusiastic response from female viewers. Ironically, Evans was bisexual with a strong homosexual streak. He left the series and his place was taken by Robin Nedwell who was also to die prematurely and whose death is noticed elsewhere in this book. Evans' films included *Alfred The Great* (1969) as Ingild, *Die Screaming, Marianne* (1971) as Eli Frome and the sex comedy *Adventures Of A Taxi Driver* (1976) as Joe North. Finding work difficult to come by, he returned to television sitcomland and the role of English teacher Jeremy Brown in the comedy series *Mind Your Language* (December 30, 1977–December 15, 1979 and again later January 4–April 12, 1986). As he aged, Evans found work less easy to come by and in 1993 left London and began working as a taxi driver in Melton Mowbray. He never married. CAUSE: Evans was discovered dead with four and a half times the legal drink-drive limit in his blood at his rundown home, in Claybrooke Magna, Leicestershire. On a nearby table was an empty bottle of whisky and a spilled bottle of aspirins priced before decimalisation plus a will he had made out three days earlier. The cause of death was given as "acute alcohol poisoning". His body was discovered by police when they went to his house to tell him that they had recovered his stolen car. The police said there were unusual circumstances surrounding the

death. His telephone lines had been cut, his credit cards were missing and his car had been found driven by other people on the day of his death. James Leadbitter, 18, of Hinckley, Leicestershire, was arrested over the theft and later accused of attempted murder. He told police that he was a friend of Evans and had visited him on the day he died to say he would not be calling round again. Leadbitter said the actor became upset and drank half a bottle of whisky. On January 26, 1998, Leadbitter was found not guilty at Nottingham Crown Court of the attempted murder of Evans. The Crown Prosecution Service admitted it had "no real prospect" of a conviction against Leadbitter, who denied the charge. On October 14, 1998 Martin Symington, the coroner for Leicester and South Leicestershire, recorded an open verdict on Evans' death. Mr Symington said there was insufficient evidence to prove Evans had intended to kill himself. He added, "Was he perhaps contemplating taking the tablets and the alcohol together, but passed out before he could use the tablets?" A friend, Lawrence Brown, told the inquest, "I got the impression he was missing the publicity of being an actor and that he'd like to get back into acting, but never really did anything about it. He used to discuss what he had done and showed me videos of his work."

Dale Evans
(FRANCES OCTAVIA LUCILLE WOOD SMITH)
Born October 31, 1912
Died February 7, 2001
'The Queen of the Cowgirls'. Frances Smith became famous as Dale Evans, the beloved wife of cowboy hero Roy Rogers who took second place to his horse, Trigger. It was even reported that Dale Evans had dyed her hair yellow to match Trigger's tail. Dale Evans added, "You've got to remember that the bit where Roy said 'Goodbye'

to me, reared up on Trigger, and rode off, was the bit where the kids were getting out their bags of popcorn. Even if he kissed me on the nose, we got a ton of letters saying: 'We can't stand the mushy stuff – cut it out next week.'" Between 1951 and 1956 the two of them made 194 half-hour episodes of *The Roy Rogers Show*. When Trigger finally died in 1966, "it was like losing one of the family". Roy Rogers and Dale Evans created a special museum in Victorville, California, where Trigger's stuffed carcass was exhibited. Dale Evans' buckskin mount Buttermilk is also on display there, as is Bullet, the German shepherd dog. In real life the couple were devoted. Rogers revealed their secret was "to give 90 and take 10, both sides, and don't fester. Keep everything you feel right out in front, so's you've only got to look at your wife once to ask, 'Hey, what's wrong?'" Their life was also beset with tragedy. After their first child, a daughter, died in infancy, they adopted nine children. But Debbie, a Korean-born daughter, was killed in a bus crash near San Clemente, California, on August 17, 1964, and a son, Sandy, choked to death in Germany on October 31, 1965 while serving with the army. Born in Uvalde, Texas, Frances Smith was not a popular child. To compensate she eloped in January 1927, aged 14, with an older classmate, Thomas Frederick Fox. A son, Frederick, was born on November 28, 1927 but by October 1929 the relationship was over. Standing on her own two feet, she found work at three separate radio stations in Louisville, Kentucky, where she was renamed Dale Evans, a name she originally disliked. In late 1929 she married August Wayne-Johns but he objected to his wife working in show business, and they divorced in 1935. That year she met pianist Robert Dale Butts in Dallas and married him. In Chicago she sang with Paul Whiteman's Orchestra and with Fats

Waller. Spotted on tour in Hollywood Darryl Zanuck gave her a contract at $400 a week. She was dumped after six months but had the taste for Tinseltown and signed a one-year contract with Republic Studios, appearing in such films as *Swing Your Partner* (1941) and *Casanova In Burlesque* (1943). She met Roy Rogers while touring the country with the Hollywood Victory Committee. She later said, "I was impressed by Roy because he was very clean-cut looking and no Hollywood act, a very real person. A very real person. He reminded me of my brother." Herbert Yates, head of Republic Studios, decided that her riding skill made her the perfect screen partner for Rogers. She recalled: "I was friends with the Pioneers in Chicago, when I was on CBS there, and I made seven pictures at Republic Studios before I worked with Roy. Mr Yates saw the musical *Oklahoma!* in New York and he decided that Roy's pictures should be like *Oklahoma!* with the girl's part built up, and that there would be more music, more horses. The chemistry was right between us, apparently, because after I made one picture, the exhibitors said, 'Don't break the team up.'" *The Cowboy And The Senorita* (1944) was the first of 28 pictures they made together. Her marriage with Robert Butts did not long survive and they divorced in 1946. That year on November 5 Arlene Wilkins Rogers died, a week after childbirth and on December 31, 1947 Rogers and Evans were married at the Flying L Ranch near Davis, Oklahoma. The couple recorded more than 400 songs together, and at the peak of their popularity in the early Fifties they had more than 2,000 fan clubs around the world. Both were Right-wing Christians who saw Reds under the bed and both were staunch supporters of President Ronald Reagan. Dale Evans was named California Mother of the Year in 1967 and Texan of the Year in 1970. She

had three stars on the Hollywood Walk of Fame. She also wrote more than 20 books, including *Angel Unaware* (1991), the story of the couple's daughter Robin, who had had Down's syndrome and heart problems and died from mumps on August 24, 1952, two days before her second birthday. CAUSE: She suffered a stroke in 1996, after which she was confined to a wheelchair. Dale Evans died aged 88 in Los Angeles, California, of congestive heart failure. She was buried in Sunset Hills Memorial Park, Apple Valley, San Bernardino County, California, along with Roy Rogers.

Dame Edith Evans
Born February 8, 1888
Died October 14, 1976
Imperiousness personified. Born in Ebury Square, London, Edith Mary Evans was a milliner before becoming an actress and making her professional stage début on August 1, 1912. It was to be the start of a long (66-year) and distinguished theatrical career, including appearances in *Troilus & Cressida* as Cressida, *Hamlet* as the Queen, *The Merchant Of Venice* as Portia, *The Merry Wives Of Windsor* as Mistress Page, Helena in *A Midsummer Night's Dream*, Cleopatra in *Antony & Cleopatra*, *The Taming Of The Shrew* as Katherine, the nurse in *Romeo & Juliet* and the definitive Lady Bracknell in *The Importance Of Being Earnest*. She made her film début in 1915 in *A Welsh Singer* and went on to appear in *The Last Days Of Dolwyn* (1948) as Merri, *Look Back In Anger* (1959) as Ma Tanner, *The Nun's Story* (1959) as Mother Superior, *Tom Jones* (1962), *Young Cassidy* (1965), *The Whisperers* (1966) as Mrs Ross, *The Mad Woman Of Chaillot* (1968), *Crooks And Coronets* (1969), *Scrooge* (1970) as the Spirit of Christmas Past and *The Slipper And The Rose* (1975) as the Dowager Queen. She also recreated her Lady Bracknell to excellent effect in *The Importance Of Being Earnest* (1951).

Playwright Robert Bolt's *Gentle Jack* opened at the Queen's Theatre in London on November 28, 1963. It starred the venerable Dame Edith and waspish Kenneth Williams in the title role as Jack of the Green. Williams had appeared in a number of *Carry On* films and on Tony Hancock's radio show, whereas Evans' experience was mostly in the theatre. She was not overly ecstatic about the casting and made her feelings known to producer Hugh 'Binkie' Beaumont. "Why on earth have you cast that Kenneth Williams?" "I think he'll be rather good," replied Beaumont. "Why?" "Well," the Dame said slowly. "He's got such a peculiar voice!" Like the old trooper that she was, Dame Edith had no thoughts of retirement. However, as she got older her faculties began to desert her. After one performance the audience turned on her. As she left the stage she turned to Kenneth Williams and said, "I distinctly heard one 'Bravo!'" "No," said Williams, "he shouted 'Go 'ome!'" Towards the end of her life Dame Edith was appearing at the Riverside Studios. When a helpful stage-hand said to her, "This way, dear", she was not impressed: "'Dear!' They'll be calling me 'Edie' next!" A devout Christian Scientist, Dame Edith married George 'Guy' Booth on September 9, 1925, at St Saviour's Church, near Claverton Street, London. He died from a brain tumour ten years later at 9.30am on January 9, 1935. There were no children. Away from work, she relaxed by gardening, reading and watching football on television.
CAUSE: In July 1971 she suffered a massive heart attack, from which she recovered to work again. She died of natural causes five years later at 12.20pm in her bed at home, Gatehouse in Kilndown, Kent, aged 88. She left £130,545.
FURTHER READING: *Dame Edith Evans: Ned's Girl* – Bryan Forbes (Boston: Little, Brown, 1977).

Tom Ewell
(SAMUEL YEWELL TOMPKINS)
Born April 29, 1909
Died September 12, 1994
Mr Average. Born in Owensboro, Kentucky, Ewell began his acting career in rep in 1928. In New York he studied at the Actors Studio along with Montgomery Clift and Karl Malden. He made his Broadway debut in 1934 and his first film six years later in *They Knew What They Wanted* (1940). He was a comfortable support actor until he was noted for his performance as Warren Attinger in George Cukor's romantic comedy *Adam's Rib* (released November 18, 1949). Standing 5'10¾", Ewell appeared opposite two of the twentieth century's greatest sex symbols Marilyn Monroe and Jayne Mansfield. In 1952 he appeared in the stage production of *The Seven Year Itch* as bored Richard Sherman who contemplates an affair with an unnamed sexy girl while his wife is away from their New York home for the summer. Vanessa Brown (1928–1999) played The Girl in the original play, which won Ewell a Tony in 1953, but Marilyn Monroe replaced her in the 1955 film. Ewell won a Golden Globe for his performance. A year later, he played Tom Miller opposite Mansfield in *The Girl Can't Help It* (released December 1, 1956). As his cinematic and theatrical careers wound down, Ewell began appearing on television – he had his own show for a time and his last job was in a 1986 episode of *Murder, She Wrote*. He claimed never to have seen any of his performances except by accident when his wife had the television on. He married Judith Abbott on March 18, 1946 but they divorced the following year. On May 5, 1948 he married advertising copywriter Marjorie Sanborn, by whom he had one son, and they were happily married until his death.
CAUSE: Ewell died in Woodland Hills, California, aged 85, of natural causes.

F

Douglas Fairbanks

(DOUGLAS ELTON ULMAN)
Born May 23, 1883
Died December 12, 1939
Swashbuckler. Born in Denver,
Colorado, Fairbanks' father,
(Hezekiah) Charles Ulman (b.
Berrysburg, Pennsylvania, September
15, 1833), founded and was President
of the US Law Association. (In 1917 a
mountain peak in Yosemite National
Park was named in his honour.)
Fairbanks' parents divorced after his
father's unwise investments in a Denver
silver mine. Douglas was educated at
the Jervis Military Academy, East
Denver High School (he was expelled
in April 1899) and the Colorado
School of Mines. In 1900 Douglas and
his elder brother, Robert Payne (b.
March 13, 1882, d. 1948) legally took
the surname Fairbanks, which was
the surname of their mother's second
husband. In 1901 Douglas began
acting and in 1903 made his Broadway
début, but he then lost interest in the
theatre and went to work for a firm of
New York stockbrokers as a clerk. He
was a keep fit fanatic and had signed
the pledge aged 12 at the insistence
of his mother. He was, however, a
chain-smoker. On July 11, 1907,
Fairbanks married Anna Beth Sully
(b. Providence, Rhode Island, June 20,
1888, at 4pm, d. 1967). Their son,
Douglas Jr, arrived in New York at
4.15am on December 9, 1909. (Some
sources list 1907 as his birthday.)
Douglas Sr, soon returned to the
acting world and, before the outbreak
of World War I, was reasonably
established as a leading man and an
adequate comedian. He began making
films in 1915 with *The Lamb*, *Martyrs
Of The Alamo* and *Double Trouble*. He

was signed by Triangle at a salary of
$2,000 a week and made eleven films
for the company. Triangle was owned
and run by D.W. Griffith, Mack
Sennett and Thomas Ince. Fairbanks
appeared in *His Picture In The Papers*
(1916) as Pete Prindle, *The Habit Of
Happiness* (1916) as Sunny Wiggins,
Reggie Mixes In (1916) as Reggie Van
Deuzen, *The Half-Breed* (1916) as Lo
Dorman, *Flirting With Fate* (1916) as
Augy Holliday, *Intolerance* (1916) and
Manhattan Madness (1916) as Steve
O'Dare among other roles. D.W.
Griffith did not appreciate either
Fairbanks' sense of humour or his
practical joking and there was a
parting of the ways between the two
of them. In 1916, the 5'10" Fairbanks
formed the Douglas Fairbanks Film
Corporation and took control of every
aspect of his films. He performed all
his own stunts, keeping himself fit by
exercising every day. He starred in
American Aristocracy (1916) as Cassius
Lee, *The Matrimaniac* (1916) as Jimmie
Conroy, *The Americano* (1916) as Blaze
Derringer, *Wild And Woolly* (1917) as
Jeff Hillington, *Down To Earth* (1917)
as Billy Gaynor, *Reaching For The
Moon* (1917) as Alexis Caesar
Napoleon Brown, *He Comes Up Smiling*
(1918) as Jerry Martin and *Arizona*
(1918) as Lieutenant Denton. On
February 5, 1919, Fairbanks, Charlie
Chaplin, D.W. Griffith and Mary
Pickford formed United Artists to
produce and sell their own films and
those of other independents. Having
divorced his wife the same year,
Fairbanks married Mary Pickford,
'America's Sweetheart', on March 28,
1920. They lived in Pickfair, their
42-room Hollywood mansion situated
at 1143 Summit Drive, Beverly
Hills. Pickfair became the mecca for
Hollywood social life and everyone
who was anyone was invited there.
Almost. Douglas Jr said he was never
invited to spend a night at the house
during his father's lifetime. Gloria
Swanson was later to claim that parties

there were not exactly the most exciting events in the world. It was during his marriage to Pickford that Fairbanks made some of his best and most memorable films, such as *The Mark Of Zorro* (1920) as Don Diego Vega/Zorro, *The Three Musketeers* (1921) as D'Artagnan, *Robin Hood* (1922) as the Earl Of Huntingdon/ Robin Hood, the title role in *The Thief Of Bagdad* (1924), *Don Q Son Of Zorro* (1925) as Don Cesar de Vega/Zorro, the leads in *The Black Pirate* (1926) and *The Gaucho* (1928) and *The Iron Mask* (1929) reprising his role as D'Artagnan. He wrote the screenplays for many of them under the pseudonym Elton Thomas. In 1922 Fairbanks was promoting his film *Robin Hood*. One stunt called for him to pose on a New York rooftop with a bow and arrow. Unfortunately, Fairbanks carelessly fired the arrow and saw it fly through the air before landing in the backside of a tailor. The man ran into the street shouting something about Red Indians; it cost Fairbanks $5,000 to settle out of court. Following his divorce from Mary Pickford in January 1936 Fairbanks stopped acting. In Paris on March 7, 1936, he married for the third and final time, to Sylvia, Lady Ashley (b. London, 1904, as Edith Louise Sylvia Hawkes, d. Los Angeles, June 30, 1977, of cancer). Fairbanks' feet were among the first to be enshrined in cement at Grauman's Chinese Theatre. He was the first president (1927–1932) of the Academy of Motion Picture Arts and Sciences, the body that hands out the Oscars. He was awarded a posthumous statuette in 1940. In 1930 he set a record for the world's longest ship-to-shore telephone call – 7,400 miles. Fairbanks nicknamed his pets after fictional or historical characters. He had a mastiff called Marco Polo and a terrier called Zorro. Mary Pickford said of him: "In his private life, Douglas always faced a situation in the only way he knew, by running away from it."

CAUSE: He died of a heart attack in his sleep in Santa Monica, California, aged 56.

Douglas Fairbanks, Jr,
Hon KBE, DSC
(DOUGLAS ELTON FAIRBANKS)
Born December 9, 1907
Died May 7, 2000
Anglophile actor. Unlike his father, 6'1" Douglas Jr was never really a swashbuckler, nor did he ever want to be one. "I never tried to emulate my father. Anyone trying to do that would be a second-rate carbon copy," he once said. "I was determined to be my own man, although having the Fairbanks name did make it easier to get into an office to see someone." He arrived in New York at 4.15am on December 9, 1907. As a youngster Fairbanks was rather plump and shy, which didn't really endear him to his father. In 1919 his parents divorced. He made his film début in *The Three Musketeers* (1921), a movie that starred his father. Fairbanks fought his way up the Hollywood tree in bit parts and occasionally by writing scripts. He was cast as Stephen Harlow, Jr in *Stephen Steps Out* (1923), which his father disliked, but which led to a contract with Paramount in 1924. He used whatever money he was paid to support himself and his mother, who had invested her $500,000 divorce settlement unwisely. His films included: *Wild Horse Mesa* (1925) as Chess Weymer, *Stella Dallas* (1925) as Richard Grosvenor, *Padlocked* (1926) as Sonny Galloway, *Man Bait* (1926) as Jeff Sanford, *Broken Hearts Of Hollywood* (1926) as Hal Terwilliger, *Women Love Diamonds* (1927) as Jerry Croker-Kelley, *Is Zat So?* (1927) as G. Clifton Blackburn, *Dead Man's Curve* (1928) as Vernon Keith, *Modern Mothers* (1928) as David Starke, *A Woman Of Affairs* (1928) as Geoffrey Merrick, *The Jazz Age* (1929) as Steve Maxwell and *Our Modern Maidens* (1929) as Gil Jordan. One of his co-stars in that film was Joan Crawford

and, a month before filming began, they became engaged. They were married in St Malachy's Roman Catholic Church in New York on June 3, 1929. Some believed that Joan married Fairbanks more for social cachet than for love. Certainly his mother disapproved, calling Crawford "a strange, moody girl, over-flamboyant in her dress, and alternating between gushing enthusiasm and gauche aloofness." Fairbanks' stepmother Mary Pickford was also not best impressed by her new stepdaughter-in-law. The marriage was brief (they divorced on May 12, 1933) but reasonably happy while it lasted. Fairbanks always spoke favourably of Crawford in later years. It was with his portrayal of gigolo Joe Massara in *Little Caesar* (1930) that he finally began to step out from under his father's enormous shadow. Successful appearances in *Outward Bound* (1930) as Henry and *The Dawn Patrol* (1930) as Douglas Scott led Warner Bros to offer him a starring contract. In the early Thirties Fairbanks travelled to London where he appeared in Alexander Korda's *Catherine The Great* (1934) as Grand Duke Peter. It was to be the start of a virtual lifelong love of Britain. He appeared on stage with Gertrude Lawrence and also in the gossip columns when they had a fling. He even formed a film production company in England but ran into financial difficulties and returned to Hollywood where David O. Selznick cast him as Rupert of Hentzau in *The Prisoner Of Zenda* (1937), generally regarded as his best film. He spent the late Thirties commuting between England and America, becoming acquainted socially with the royal family. On April 22, 1939, he married, as her second husband, Mary Lee Eppling. The union was to produce three daughters and was regarded as a happy marriage. When the dark clouds of war circled over Britain, Fairbanks remained loyal to his friends and

appeared in a number of pro-British films, including *Gunga Din* (1939) as Sergeant Ballantine, *The Sun Never Sets* (1939) as John Randolph and *Rulers Of The Sea* (1939) as David 'Davie' Gillespie. He and Constance Bennett were among the first Hollywoodites to urge America to support Britain. Fairbanks joined the US Navy, reaching the rank of Lieutenant-Commander and in 1944 was awarded the Distinguished Service Cross. He was also the first American officer to command a British flotilla during a commando operation. In 1949, in recognition of "furthering Anglo-American amity", George VI awarded Fairbanks a knighthood but, as he retained his American citizenship, he was unable to style himself Sir Douglas unlike his fellow New Yorker Sir Yehudi Menuhin, later Baron Menuhin. Fairbanks' most financially successful film was *Sinbad The Sailor* (1947) in which he played the lead. He and his wife moved permanently to London in 1950 and bought a house at 28 The Boltons, SW10. In 1952 the Queen and Duke of Edinburgh visited for dinner. In 1963 Fairbanks unwittingly became caught up in the sensational divorce trial of Margaret, Duchess of Argyll, the society beauty who became engaged in a series of scandals. Deb Of The Year 1930, Cole Porter put her in his song *You're The Top*. On March 3, an infamous case involving the Duchess opened in an Edinburgh court room. The evidence presented to the court included pictures of her fellating a man whose head had been chopped off by the camera. The identity of the man was finally confirmed in August 2000 as Fairbanks. The actor's identity was not revealed in court nor in Lord Denning's subsequent report. The judge, Lord Wheatley, delivered his judgment on May 8, and took 40,000 words to attack the morals of the Duchess. It was also alleged that Fairbanks had a threesome with

Profumo scandalites Christine Keeler and Mandy Rice-Davies, although he strongly denied that. In the film *Scandal* (1988) the Fairbanks character, played by Trevor Eve, is credited only as "The Matinee Idol". When his arthritis was affected by the English damp in 1970, Fairbanks reluctantly retired to Florida. Following the death of Mary Lee Fairbanks, he married Vera Shelton on May 30, 1991. Two years earlier, he admitted: "I've led an enormously lucky life." CAUSE: Douglas Fairbanks, Jr died of respiratory problems in Mount Sinai Hospital, New York, aged 92. He was buried next to his father. FURTHER READING: *The Salad Days –* Douglas Fairbanks, Jr (London: Collins, 1988); *A Hell Of A War –* Douglas Fairbanks, Jr (New York: St Martin's Press, 1993).

Chris Farley

Born February 15, 1964
Died December 18, 1997
John Belushi for the Nineties. Born in Madison, Wisconsin, supersized (21-stone) Christopher Crosby Farley attended Marquette University where he studied theatre and communications. He made just ten films after achieving fame Stateside on *Saturday Night Live*. Farley confessed his hero was former *Saturday Night Live* star John Belushi: "[I] dreamed of being John Belushi. That's why I went the [comedy troupe] *Second City, Saturday Night Live* route. I wanted to follow him." Sadly, he did – all the way. Farley, who had been to rehab at least a dozen times, was a glutton with both food and drugs. "I have a tendency toward the pleasures of the flesh. It's a battle for me, as far as weight and things like that." His films included *Wayne's World* (1992), *Coneheads* (1993) as Ronnie, *Wayne's World 2* (1993) as Milton, *Airheads* (1994) as Wilson, *Black Sheep* (1996) as Mike Donnelly and *Beverly Hills Ninja* (1997) as Haru.

CAUSE: Farley, who lived on the 60th floor of the John Hancock Building, Michigan Avenue, Chicago, liked to party with prostitutes, believing his gross size put off ordinary women. On December 17, 1997, a friend hired a hooker called Heidi for him at a cost of $2,000. She escorted the corpulent star to a party at 11am where people were doing drugs. After leaving the party Heidi took Farley to her home where they smoked crack and snorted heroin. Farley told her he was unable to sleep and had been up for four days solid. They moved to the bedroom but Farley discovered he was impotent. They left and went to his home where at 11pm she demanded payment. Farley claimed his friend was to pay her and then tried to have sex with her but again was impotent. Heidi hung around for four hours waiting for the stoned and by now drunk Farley to get an erection but without success. She decided to leave but as she did Farley collapsed in front of her breathing heavily. He wheezed, "Don't leave me." So, as any good citizen would, she left . . . but not before taking a picture of him! Around two the next afternoon Farley's brother, John, discovered him lying where he had fallen. He called the emergency services but Farley was pronounced dead at the scene. He was 33, as was John Belushi when he died. The coroner declared, "Chris Farley died of opiate (morphine) and cocaine intoxication and his death was determined to be accidental." Prozac, morphine, marijuana and the antihistamine fexofenadine were also found in his system although the coroner ruled they did not contribute to his death. His mammoth weight, which caused a narrowing of three coronary arteries, did. On December 19, his corpse was taken to the McKeon Funeral Home, 634 West 37th Street, Chicago, before being shipped to Madison, Wisconsin, where a private funeral took place on December 23, at Our Lady Queen of

Peace Roman Catholic Church. Over
500 people attended, including Tom
Arnold (who was Farley's sponsor at
Alcoholics Anonymous), Dan Aykroyd
(who sported a leather jacket over his
suit, as he had done at John Belushi's
funeral), John Goodman, Chris Rock,
Adam Sandler and George Wendt. He
was interred in Resurrection Cemetery,
Madison.

Frances Farmer

Born September 19, 1913
Died August 1, 1970
Rebel with a cause. Born in Seattle,
Washington, the daughter of a lawyer,
Frances Elena Farmer is remembered
now as the mentally disturbed star
who was locked up by her mother. Her
story is much sadder than that brief
outline indicates. After graduating
from Washington State University, the
beautiful blonde signed a seven-year
contract with Paramount in 1936. On
February 8 of that year she eloped to
Yuma, Arizona, with *The High
Chaparral* star Leif Erickson. That year
she also made what was probably her
best film, *Come And Get It*, but soon
tired of what she saw as the phoniness
of Hollywood and went east to
Broadway where she was a hit in the
play *Golden Boy*. She had an affair with
playwright Clifford Odets who wrote
Golden Boy but it was not to last and
she went back to her husband. They
fought constantly. In 1942 she
appeared opposite Tyrone Power in
Son Of Fury. But it was to be a year of
highs and lows – tremendous lows.
She and Erickson were divorced on
June 12. On October 19 she was
arrested after she smacked a
policeman who stopped her for driving
through a blackout area with her lights
on. Three months later, on January
14, 1943, she was again arrested after
hitting a hairdresser on the set. She
was put under psychiatric care. Six
days later, a judge ordered that she
should receive electroshock treatment
as a 'cure' for her eccentric behaviour.

At 3.25pm on May 22, 1945, Farmer
was sent to Washington State Asylum
35 miles south of Seattle, where she
would stay until March 25, 1950.
During her 3,040-day incarceration
she was raped on numerous occasions
by warders, given ice water baths,
strapped into a straitjacket and nibbled
at by rats. Exactly a year after she was
let out of the asylum, she was released
from the jurisdiction of the hospital
but the information was kept from her
by her neurotic mother until 1953. In
July 1953 her mother was discharged
as her legal guardian and Frances
landed a job as a dogsbody in a hotel.
Her Paramount contract had been
worth $200,000 a year. This job paid
75¢ an hour. She married again, this
time to Seattle engineer Alfred Lobley
on July 27, 1953, even though she
confessed she didn't really love him.
Frances had by now become an
alcoholic. She found a job as a typist
in Eureka, California. She divorced
her husband on March 7, 1958.
Thirteen days later, she married
Leland Mikesell in Las Vegas; they
were divorced in 1963. Frances
made another film and reinvented
herself as a folk singer, appearing on
The Ed Sullivan Show. It was later
revealed that her 'mental illness'
was actually caused by a case of
hypoglycemia and could have been
treated with proper diagnosis and
diet. She became a forgotten figure
until her posthumously published
autobiography, *Will There Really Be A
Morning?*, was made into the movie
Frances (1982) starring Jessica Lange.
CAUSE: She died of cancer of the
aesophagus in Indianapolis, Indiana,
aged 56. She was alone at the time.
FURTHER READING: *Will There Really
Be A Morning?* – Frances Farmer
(London: Fontana, 1984).

Charles Farrell

Born August 6, 1900
Died August 27, 1988
The first. Born in Dublin, Ireland,

Charles Farrell was a dependable supporting actor. He appeared in more than 50 films including: *The Man At Six* (1931) as George Wollmer, *Money For Nothing* (1932) as Digger, *Boys Will Be Boys* (1935) as Louis Brown, *The Rebel Son* (1938) as Tovkatch, *Jailbirds* (1940) as Spike Nelson, *I Became A Criminal* (1947) as Curley, a barman in *The Sheriff Of Fractured Jaw* (1958), a policeman in *Oh! What A Lovely War* (1969), the landlord in *The Vampire Lovers* (1970), the slave seller in *Countess Dracula* (1971) and the chauffeur in *The Abominable Dr Phibes* (1971). A homosexual, he was one of "The Five Queens" as called by Beryl Formby in the film *Bell-Bottom George* (1943) in which he played Jim. The other "Queens" were Charles Hawtrey, Peter Murray Hill, Reginald Purdell and Manning Whiley.
CAUSE: He died in London aged 88 of natural causes.

Charles Farrell
Born August 9, 1901
Died May 6, 1990
The second. Born in Onset Bay on Cape Cod, Massachusetts, 6'2" Charles David Farrell was educated at Boston University and went onto the stage. He made his film début as an extra in *The Cheat* (1923) and was a regular if unspectacular support until 1927 when he appeared in the Oscar-nominated *Seventh Heaven* with Janet Gaynor. For seven years the pair were *the* Hollywood romantic pair of screen lovers. They appeared in *Street Angel* (1928), *Lucky Star* (1928) and *Sunny Side Up* (1929). His stardom faded as quickly as it came and his career was all but over by the mid-Thirties. He retired from the big screen in 1941. He founded the Palm Springs Racquet Club and made a fortune. On January 7, 1959, Farrell sold the Racquet Club to businessmen William W. Beacom and Robert S. Morton for $1.2 million but stayed on

as chairman and managing director. It was sold again in 1964. Film historian Carlos Clarens said of him, "Charles Farrell was a closeted movie star, married to a closeted movie star. He was anti-Semitic, and didn't like that more clubs in Hollywood were letting Jews in, so he and his pal Ralph Bellamy went to Palm Springs and started the Racquet Club – which was restricted . . . No, he never came out." William Gargan once called Farrell a fairy in the Club bar and Farrell knocked him out with one punch. (It was at the Racquet Club that Marilyn Monroe's patron and mentor Johnny Hyde died of a heart attack on December 17, 1950.) In the Fifties Farrell spent seven years as mayor of Palm Springs and simultaneously appeared in the television sitcom *My Little Margie* (June 16, 1952–August 24, 1955) as Vernon Albright. He intensely disliked his co-star Gale Storm and the feeling was mutual. On St Valentine's Day 1931 he married the 5'4" actor Virginia Valli (b. Chicago, Illinois, June 10, 1895 as Virginia McSweeney, d. Palm Springs, California, September 24, 1968, aged 73 following a stroke two years earlier). Of them, Bette Davis commented, "It was very different then. One wasn't always sure what to judge on. But if a woman wore pants a lot, we suspected . . . I worked with Charlie Farrell, and I never guessed he was reputed to be . . . gay. Of course he would flirt with any ladies on the set, it was expected and normal . . . The one we suspected was his wife. And it was because she wore pants quite often and she just adored golf!"
CAUSE: He died in Palm Springs, California, aged 88 of a heart attack. He had been increasingly reclusive in his last years, spending his days in a dressing gown watching television. He was buried alongside his wife in Section 10-3, Lot F of Welwood Murray Cemetery, Palm Springs, Riverside County, California.

Glenda Farrell

Born June 30, 1904
Died May 1, 1971
Perky blonde. Born in Enid,
Oklahoma, Farrell learned her trade in
rep before graduating to Broadway in
1928. She was spotted by Warner Bros
in *Lucky Boy* (1929) and signed to a
contract. She specialised in playing
good-time girls such as Olga Strassoff,
a gangster's moll, in *Little Caesar*
(1930) and the prostitute Marie Woods
in *I Am A Fugitive From A Chain Gang*
(1932) and her tough looks meant she
could not play romantic leads. She was
teamed with Joan Blondell in *Havana
Widows* (1933) and played hard-bitten
journalist Florence Dempsey in *The
Mystery Of The Wax Museum* (1933).
Farrell played supporting roles in A
films and leads in Bs. In 1936 she
began starring in the Torchy Blane
reporter series commencing with *Smart
Blonde*. The original character (created
by Frederick Nebel) was a man but it
had a sex change to accommodate
Farrell. She played in seven of the nine
films. A fast-talker Farrell was once
said to have delivered a 400-word
speech in just 40 seconds. Her career
stalled at the end of the Thirties as the
brassy blonde fell from favour. She
moved back to the theatre and
television where she won a Best
Supporting Emmy for the *Ben Casey*
episode *A Cardinal Act Of Mercy*. She
was married twice. Her first husband
(in 1921) was Thomas A. Richards (b.
January 8, 1899, d. Los Angeles,
California, January 4, 1946) and they
had a son, Thomas, Jr (b. Hollywood,
California, October 7, 1921, d.
Woodland Hills, California, May 9,
2004). An attempt to forge a vaudeville
act was unsuccessful and the couple
was divorced in 1929. Their son
changed his surname to Farrell
following his parents' divorce. On
January 19, 1941, she married Dr
Henry Ross in Passaic, New Jersey.
They remained married until her death.
CAUSE: She was appearing on

Broadway in 1969 in *40 Carats* when
she was diagnosed with inoperable lung
cancer. She died in her New York
home. She was 66. She was buried in
Section 7, Row D, Grave 211 at the
US Military Academy Post Cemetery,
West Point, Orange County, New
York. Her first husband's service in the
First World War allowed Farrell to be
buried in a military cemetery.

Rainer Werner Fassbinder

Born May 31, 1945
Died June 10, 1982
Deutsche wunderkind. Born in Bad
Wörishofen, Bavaria, the son of a
doctor-cum-slum landlord who
became wealthy on the rents of others,
Fassbinder was sent to collect the rent
from the mostly immigrant tenants. As
a boy Fassbinder spent much of his
time watching movies. Deciding to
make them his career, he was turned
down by the prestigious Berlin Film
Institute. Barely out of his teens he
began making amateur films. He
became an actor in 1967, joining the
Munich Action Theatre and two years
later made his first feature. Between
1969 and 1982 he directed over 30
films, usually using the same cast
and crew, who flourished under
his autocratic control. His corpus
included: *Der Stadtsreicher* (1965),
Das Kleine Chaos (1966), *Katzelmacher*
(1969), *Warum Laüft Herr R Amok?*
(1970), *Wildwechsel* (1972), *Die Bitteren
Tränen Der Petra Von Kant* (1972),
Angst Vor Der Angst (1976) and *Querelle*
(1982). Fassbinder never achieved
worldwide fame and in later years
became paranoid due to his
overindulgence in drugs and alcohol.
A homosexual, he nonetheless married
Ingrid Caven who had appeared in
many of his films.
CAUSE: He died by his own hand of a
drug overdose aged 37, four years to
the day after his boyfriend hanged
himself in the Munich home he and
Fassbinder shared.

Farrah Fawcett

(MARY FERRAH LENI FAWCETT)
Born February 2, 1947
Died June 25, 2009
Charlie's most successful and sexiest
angel. Born at 3.10pm at Memorial
Hospital, Corpus Christi a small oil
town in Texas, the daughter of James
William Fawcett (b. 1918), a pipe fitter
in the oil industry, and housewife
Pauline Alice Evans (b. January 30,
1914, d. March 4, 2005). She was born
with a tumour obstructing her digestive
tract and had to undergo an operation
when she was only 28-days-old. Her
older sister, Diane (b. Montgomery,
Texas October 27, 1938), died of lung
cancer on October 16, 2001, aged 63.
She was educated at WB Ray High
School before enrolling at the
University of Texas in 1965 to read
microbiology, later changed to
sculpture. She was voted one of the 10
most beautiful women on campus. She
began a relationship with jock Gregg
Lott who said that she was "gorgeous –
like a frisky palomino, all legs, teeth
and spirit". She dropped out of
university after a year when modelling
and casting agencies began to call.
She moved to Hollywood where she
changed her first name to Farrah.
"I never had a burning desire to
be an actress," she said. "I came to
Hollywood as a lark." She appeared as
window dressing in shows like *The
Flying Nun* and *The Partridge Family*
and appeared in advertisements for a
range of products including Wella
shampoo, Noxema shaving cream (her
advert showed during the 1973
Superbowl) and Ultra Brite "the
toothpaste with sex appeal". In 1969
she made her film début appearing in
the French movie *Un Homme Qui Me
Plaît* (released in America as *Love Is A
Funny Thing* on March 26, 1970). She
made her American film début playing
Raquel Welch's lesbian lover in *Myra
Breckinridge* (released June 24, 1970).
On August 24 and November 24,
1970, she was arrested for shoplifting
after she took clothes from boutiques,
and was convicted both times on the
lesser charge of trespassing and fined
$125 and $265, respectively. In her
defence, Fawcett claimed to be
returning clothes at both stores,
substituting new ones of equivalent
value, because they refused to exchange
the merchandise. "I was just taking
justice into my own hands," she
explained. "I don't think I was wrong,
but I'd never do it again. I realise now
there are certain things you can't do
anything about, and you just don't let
them bother you." Casting directors
weren't knocking down her door so she
returned to the small screen. She
appeared in the television movies
The Feminist And The Fuzz (aired
January 26, 1971), *The Great American
Beauty Contest* (aired February 13,
1973), *The Girl Who Came Gift-Wrapped*
(aired January 26, 1974) and as an air
hostess in *Murder On Flight 502* (aired
November 21, 1975). She appeared in
the sci-fi film *Logan's Run* (released
June 23, 1976) but stardom eluded her.
In 1968 she had met actor Lee Majors
(b. Wyandotte, Michigan April 23,
1939 as Harvey Lee Yeary). They
married on July 28, 1973 on the Swan
Lake Terrace of the Bel Air Hotel in
West Los Angeles and she became
Farrah Fawcett-Majors. He then
landed the role of Colonel Steve
Austin, the astronaut who is almost
killed in a crash and rebuilt at a cost of
six million dollars. She landed a regular
bitpart as Sue Ingham in the detective
series *Harry O*. She came to the
attention of Aaron Spelling and
Leonard Goldberg who were looking to
cast three women as private detectives
in a new series, to be called *Charlie's
Angels*. The show premièred on
September 22, 1976 and soon became
a hit with much of the attention
focused on Fawcett-Majors's Jill
Munroe, the blonde, athletic angel.
Women the world over adopted her
hairstyle which was described as "a
work of art that looked as if it had just

come out of the sea and been tossed by the wind into a state of careless perfection". A swimsuit poster that showcased her prominent nipples reputedly sold eight million copies (sales vary according to the source from six, seven, eight, 12 and even 30 million) worldwide. She wore a swimsuit rather than a bikini because of a scar from childhood on her stomach. At the end of the first series the programme was rated the number five network show, the highest-rated television début in history at that time. Fawcett-Majors remarked, "When the show got to be number three, I figured it was our acting. When it got to be number one, I decided it could only be because none of us wears a bra." Majors found it difficult to deal with his wife's new found fame which eclipsed his own. A traditionalist, he had it written into her contract that she would be home at 6.30pm to cook his dinner. Fawcett-Majors was also unhappy with her pay packet – said to be $10,000 an episode – and when a rise was refused, she walked out. One unnamed executive appeared to be unworried by the departure of the show's biggest star. Her replacement would be "another well-stacked blonde with good bod and great-looking legs who can wear a T-shirt well and read four lines of dialogue off an idiot card." Nonetheless, Spelling and Goldberg sued her for breach of contract and won. Replaced by Cheryl Ladd, playing her sister Kris Munroe, Fawcett-Majors was forced to appear in six episodes over the next two series. She signed a £3 million contract with cosmetics giant Fabergé but was gaining a reputation for being difficult. She appeared topless in the film *Saturn 3* (released February 15, 1980), playing the lover of Kirk Douglas. She was in *Somebody Killed Her Husband* (1978) and *Sunburn* (released August 10, 1979). She also was Burt Reynolds's love interest in the comedy *The Cannonball Run* (released June 19,

1981). Deciding to take roles both on the big and small screens that played against her looks, Fawcett played a battered wife in *The Burning Bed* (aired October 8, 1984), an intelligent schoolteacher persecuted by her mother-in-law in *Between Two Women* (aired March 10, 1986), a vengeful rape victim in *Extremities* (released August 22, 1986; she also appeared off-Broadway in the play of the film in 1983 replacing Karen Allen), *Nazi Hunter: The Beate Klarsfeld Story* (aired November 23, 1986), Alan Pakula's *See You In The Morning* (released April 14, 1989), *Double Exposure* (aired April 24, 1989) as the *Life* photographer Margaret Bourke-White, and a white-trash mother accused of killing her children in *Small Sacrifices* (aired November 12, 1989). By this time she was ensconced with 6′1″ (Charles Patrick) Ryan O'Neal (b. Los Angeles, California April 20, 1941), the best friend of Lee Majors, who had been tasked to look after her while Majors was away filming. O'Neal took the request seriously and Majors and Fawcett-Majors separated on their sixth wedding anniversary. They divorced on February 16, 1982. It would be a tempestuous relationship, peppered with violence according to O'Neal's daughter, Tatum. "Farrah was innocent," she said. "Dad was a Svengali for her. He took over her life, but there was a price. He had a terrible temper and was very violent." For her part, 5′6″ Fawcett said, "Ryan was a physical person. He was a bully, but I was never afraid of him." At Los Angeles on January 30, 1985 she gave birth to his son, Redmond James, who was expelled aged 13 from school for smoking marijuana. He later became a heroin addict. In 1994 she posed nude for *Playboy* and the issue sold four million copies. She made a video for the magazine in July 1997 to celebrate her fiftieth birthday. *All Of Me* featured her sculpting in the nude, covered only in body paint. That year also marked a split from O'Neal. Despite her claims to the contrary, she began drowning her sorrows with tequila and cannabis. In 1991 she appeared with O'Neal in *Good Sports*, a short-lived sitcom. On June 6, 1997 she appeared on *The Late Show With David Letterman* and rambled incoherently for almost 20 minutes. Later she denied that she had been drunk or stoned. On the show she admitted that she did not like the way she looked. She began to have plastic surgery with, frankly, disastrous results. She had cheek implants and a nose job, then more than one full facelift, as well as eyebrow and eyelifts, and the tip of her nose raised. On January 28, 1998 her next boyfriend James Orr (b. Canada 1953) reportedly proposed to her in a restaurant and she refused. An argument ensued. They left the eaterie but Fawcett refused to let the matter drop. She confronted Orr at his home brandishing a baseball bat. His response was to crack her head on his driveway and kick her in the stomach. On October 29, 1998 he was convicted and sentenced to three years' probation. But the judge ruled that by turning up with the baseball bat she had incited his violence. She starred in Robert Altman's *Dr T And The Women* (2001), as Richard Gere's wife, a woman in mid-breakdown who is reduced to a childlike state. The part required her to appear nude. During her career, Fawcett was nominated for three Emmys and six Golden Globes but never won. In 2003 her son appeared in court charged with forging a cheque. The prosecution agreed to drop the charge if he went into rehab. He failed to complete the course and in a Texas court in 2004 Fawcett admitted that her son was "still addicted to heroin". She made an embarrassing six-part reality show, *Chasing Farrah*, for an obscure cable channel, TVLand, in 2005. Her final years were characterised by dreadful plastic surgery and her son's drug addiction. "I became famous," she once said, "almost before I had a craft."

In her will Fawcett left $4.5 million to her drug addict son, Redmond. She bequeathed $100,000 to ex-boyfriend Greg Lott, $500,000 to her nephew Greg Walls and the same amount to her father James. Ryan O'Neal and "best friend" Alana Hamilton received nothing.

CAUSE: In September 2006 Fawcett was diagnosed with anal cancer. Abstinence and the HPV vaccine are the most reliable forms of prevention against this type of cancer, which, in most cases, is sexually acquired. On February 2, 2007 the disease went into remission, only to return three months later in May 2007. She travelled to Germany in early 2009 for embryonic stem-cell cancer treatment that was not available in America in the hope of a cure but the cancer had returned with a vengeance. It moved on to her liver by April 2009. The treatment caused her hair to fall out. Ryan O'Neal commented, "The hair is gone. Her famous hair. I have it at home. She didn't care. I rub her head. It's kind of fun, actually, this great, tiny little head. How she carried all that hair I'll never know. She doesn't have a vanity about it." On April 5, 2009 as his mother was fighting for her life Redmond O'Neal was jailed on drug charges. He had been arrested on charges of trying to smuggle drugs into a jail facility in Castaic. In the week of her death O'Neal told television interviewer Barbara Walters that he and Fawcett would be married. It was not to be. She died at 9.28am in the intensive care unit at St John's Health Center in Santa Monica, California after receiving the Last Rites. She was 62. Her funeral took place on June 30, 2009 at the Roman Catholic Cathedral of Our Lady of the Angels. Attendees included Lee Majors, Cheryl Tiegs and Jackie and Joan Collins. She is buried at the Westwood Village Memorial Park in Los Angeles, California.
FURTHER READING: *Farrah An Unauthorised Biography* – Patricia

Burstein (New York: Signet, 1977); *Farrah & Lee* – Connie Berman (New York: Grosset & Dunlap, 1977).

Alice Faye
(ALICE JEANNE LEPPERT)
Born May 5, 1912
Died May 9, 1998
Thirties sweetheart. Born in New York City's notorious Hell's Kitchen, the daughter of a policeman, she began her showbiz career as a 13-year-old dancer. She took her name from a star of the time, Frank Fay. In 1934 Rudy Vallee gave her a job as a singer on his radio show and persuaded his film studio to cast her in his latest venture, *Scandals* (1934). Judging by her appearance in her first nine films, the 5'5" Faye seemed destined to be the new singing Jean Harlow. However, in 1936 her parts changed and she appeared in a more gentle, subtle light in *Poor Little Rich Girl* and *Sing, Baby Sing*. Henry King, who directed her in *In Old Chicago* (1937), attributed her success to "a deep-seated human warmth, so genuine, so real that everyone felt it. It's truly a gift." On September 4, 1937, she eloped to Yuma, Arizona, with tenor Tony Martin. (On March 22, 1940, they were divorced on the grounds of his mental cruelty.) On May 12, 1941, she eloped again. This time her beau was bandleader Phil Harris and they were to remain married for over 50 years. They had two daughters: Alice (b. May 19, 1942) and Phyllis (b. April 26, 1944). Alice Faye's star shone brightly for eleven years in over thirty films. She retired from movie making after *Fallen Angel* (1945), following the rise of Betty Grable. Her comeback in 1962, to make *State Fair*, was a disappointment to her. She commented, "I don't know what happened to the picture business. I'm sorry I went back to find out. Such a shame." Her last film was *The Magic Of Lassie* (1978).
CAUSE: She died of stomach cancer in Rancho Mirage, California, five days

after her 86th birthday. She was buried in Palm Springs Mausoleum, Palm Springs, California.

Marty Feldman
Born July 8, 1934
Died December 3, 1982
Bug-eyed comedy genius. Born in Canning Town, east London, the son of a Jewish dressmaker, Feldman left grammar school aged 15 determined to be a jazz trumpeter. (He and actress Fenella Fielding were not siblings, although a number of reference books state that they are.) Feldman became part of a comedy trio called Morris, Marty & Mitch, but they were not especially good. In 1955 he met comedian Barry Took at the Empire Theatre, York. The two men quickly became close friends, finding they had much in common. In 1959 they began writing comedy to amuse themselves, but soon found themselves much in demand writing for *The Army Game* and *Bootsie & Snudge*; Feldman also compiled scripts for *Educating Archie*. In 1961 he became ill with a hyperthyroid condition, an ailment that brought about his famous 'bug-eyed' appearance. His behaviour also became erratic. He told Took he could only write during the hours of darkness and to the strains of jazz music. Of course, in effect that meant he didn't write at all. However, following an operation, he returned to normal. In late 1964 the pair were approached by the BBC to write what was to become one of the funniest radio shows of all time – *Round The Horne*. At first they demurred but had second thoughts and produced a hilarious script, featuring characters such as Rambling Syd Rumpo, J. Peasmold Gruntfuttock, Julian and Sandy, Dame Celia Molestrangler and ageing juvenile Binkie Huckaback, Chou En Ginsberg, M.A. (Failed) and Charles and Fiona. In 1967 Feldman left *Round The Horne* and began appearing on television in *At Last The 1948 Show*

(from February 15 until November 7, 1967) and his own show, *It's Marty* (from April 29, 1968, until January 13, 1969). He moved to Hollywood and began appearing in movies such as Mel Brooks' *Young Frankenstein* (1974) as Igor and *Silent Movie* (1976) as Marty Eggs, *The Adventure Of Sherlock Holmes' Smarter Brother* (1975) as Orville Sacker, *To See Such Fun* (1977), *The Last Remake Of Beau Geste* (1977) as Digby Geste, *In God We Tru$t* (1980) as Brother Ambrose, *Slapstick (Of Another Kind)* (1982) as Sylvester and *Group Madness* (1983) as himself. He was chosen to present the Oscar for Best Short Film on March 29, 1977, at the Dorothy Chandler Pavilion, Los Angeles. Feldman decided he would play a joke on the night. He had a plaster replica of the statuette made so that he could pretend to drop it as he presented it to the winner. Then, in a moment of triumph, he could produce the real prize. Not a great gag, one must admit, but vaguely amusing. However, things didn't go according to plan. The fake Oscar refused to break and so Feldman threw it on the floor and jumped up and down on it. The watching audience, not in on the joke, was horrified at this strange-looking Englishman sacrilegiously vandalising this symbol of American cinema. Feldman lost many friends that night. The only saving grace was that the show was watched by the smallest TV audience ever. He married Lauretta Sullivan. There were no children.
CAUSE: He died of a heart attack aged 48 in Mexico City during the filming of *Yellowbeard* (1983) in which he played Gilbert.
FURTHER READING: *Round The Horne: The Complete And Utter History* – Barry Took (London: Boxtree, 1998).

Federico Fellini
Born January 20, 1920
Died October 31, 1993
Mendacious film *auteur*. Born in Rimini,

Italy, it is difficult to ascertain the truth about Fellini's childhood since many of the tales he told were riddled with discrepancies. He was a self-confessed liar. He left home in 1938 to become a cartoonist and proofreader in Florence. He then became a journalist specialising in crime before becoming a joke writer for films. A meeting with Roberto Rossellini opened the way for mainstream movie work. His best, most famous and first internationally recognised work was *La Dolce Vita* (1959), a critical look at modern Rome. It introduced the word *paparazzi* to the English language. Fellini originally wanted Marilyn Monroe to play the part of Sylvia Rank in the film, but was turned down. Anita Ekberg played the role. His wife Giulietta Massina appeared in many of his films, which included *Luci Del Varietà* (1950), *Lo Sceicco Bianco* (1950), *La Strada* (1954) which won a Best Foreign Film Oscar, *Le Notti Di Cabiria* (1957) which won his second Best Foreign Film Oscar, *8½* (1963) which won his third Best Foreign Film Oscar, *Giulietta Degli Spiriti* (1965), *Satyricon* (1969), *Roma* (1972), *Amarcord* (1974) which won his fourth Best Foreign Film Oscar, *Casanova* (1976), *La Città Delle Donne* (1980), *Ginger E Fred* (1985), *Intervista* (1987) and *La Voce Della Luna* (1989).
CAUSE: He died in Rome of a heart attack aged 73.

Fernandel
(FERNAND JOSEPH DÉSIRÉ CONTANDIN)
Born May 8, 1903
Died February 26, 1971
Rubber-faced clown. Fernandel had no illusions about his looks. In fact, when he first saw himself on screen it virtually put him off acting. Thankfully, he reconsidered. One French film critic noted: "When Fernandel is on a film set there's a whiff of garlic in the air, the sun shines, and those who don't talk like Provençals begin to sound like they

were speaking with an accent." Born in Marseilles, the son of an office worker who spent his weekends in amdram, Fernandel made his stage début aged five, singing military songs with his older brother and later won trophies at amateur concerts. Leaving school, he began work in a bank but was sacked from three consecutive positions for, respectively, smoking outside the manager's office, singing during office hours and telling so many jokes that no one got any work done. His stage name came about from his future mother-in-law. When he went to pick up his girlfriend, Henriette Manse, her mother would cry out "Ah, voilà, le Fernand d'elle!" ("Here's her Fernand.") Married life (he took the plunge in 1925 and had three children) taught him responsibility and he landed a job in the accounts department of a soap factory. One day the manager of the local Odeon in Marseilles asked Fernandel to fill in for an errant singer. Nervously he agreed. That night he launched into one song after the other, not allowing the audience to interrupt. To his amazement when he did finally pause for breath he found them cheering, not jeering. The result was a national tour. Film director Marc Allégret was in the audience one night and was impressed by what he saw. Fernandel was given a part in Sacha Guitry's *Le Blanc Et Le Noir* (1930). It was the first of 150-plus films that saw him become one of France's highest paid actors and develop a friendship with writer-director Marcel Pagnol. They began to collaborate on films including *Regain* (1937) (banned in Britain until 1956 because of an implied gang rape), a satire of the French film world *Le Schpountz* (1938), *La Fille Du Puisatier* (1940) and *Nais* (1945) based on a story by Emile Zola in which Fernandel plays a hunchbacked labourer. On their first film, *Angèle* (1934), Pagnol cast Fernandel as a village idiot. During filming Pagnol decided to rewrite one

scene on the spot. Fernandel protested that he couldn't learn six new sides (script pages) so Pagnol suggested he hide them in his hat. The scene was shot without rehearsing, and critics applauded Fernandel's sensitive characterisation, especially the way he lowered his eyes every so often! In 1936 Fernandel was the third most popular box-office star in France; the following year he took over top place from Charles Boyer. By the time of his 35th birthday Fernandel was making around one film every two months. He would rise between 5am and 6am, having slept just four hours. Over strong coffee, he would personally answer his hundreds of fan letters before going to the studio or location. During World War II he appeared in films in Vichy France along with a host of other notables. He was arrested on August 28, 1944, for collaboration, but later exonerated. After the war he continued making films. Probably his best-known role outside France was that of the Roman Catholic priest Don Camillo in Julien Duvivier's film *Le Petit Monde De Don Camillo* (1952). Although he was initially reluctant to take part, the film was a massive international success and Fernandel was personally invited to the Vatican by Pope Pius XII who labelled him "the second best-known priest in Christendom". The film was based on Giovanni Guareschi's tales of two bigots in an Italian town – the communist mayor and the curate. One thing did upset Fernandel. He took a salary rather than a cut of the profits, little knowing the success the film would have; it made director Duvivier rather wealthy. Duvivier also directed the equally successful sequel, *Le Retour De Don Camillo* (1953) but the next in the series (without Duvivier) *Don Camillo Monseigneur* (1961) suffered from poor direction. Mike Todd wanted Fernandel to play Passepartout to David Niven's Phileas Fogg in *Around The World In 80 Days* (1956) but the Frenchman demurred, claiming his English was not sufficiently good. The part went to the Mexican Cantinflas, although Fernandel did play a cameo role. His choice of films in his latter years was mostly poor, teaming him with comedians from other countries, usually to no good effect. In 1965 he appeared with his son in *L'Age Ingrat* and returned as Don Camillo in *Don Camillo A Moscou* (1965).

CAUSE: Fernandel fell when he was on his boat and bruised his chest. Some time later he began to suffer pains that he believed were a direct result of the fall. In the summer of 1970 he was filming *Don Camillo Et Les Contestataires* in Italy when he collapsed with pleurisy. He was returned to his Paris flat where he was told to get plenty of rest. However, his condition worsened and he died of lung cancer aged 67.

Lolo Ferrari

(EVE VALOIS)
Born February 9, 1963
Died March 6, 2000
Huge-busted model. Born to a middle-class family in Clermont-Ferrand, France, Lolo Ferrari became infamous for her huge silicone-inflated breasts. She had more than 30 operations on various parts of her body. Her breasts were inflated with three litres of surgical serum and were designed by an aircraft engineer. She could not sleep on her back or stomach, had difficulty breathing and was scared to fly lest her breasts explode. She appeared as a regular on the television show *Eurotrash* from September 1996 until 1999. In February 1996, she released a single called 'Airbag Generation'. A second was entitled 'Set Me Free'. As well as appearing in porn films, she also appeared in the movies *Camping Cosmos* (1995) as Mme Vandeputte and *Quasimodo D'El Paris* (1999) as La fée. In 1988 she married Eric Vigne

(b. 1948). At one stage it was stated that 5'7" Lolo's breasts measured 71" or 54G bra size. Lolo, by the way, is French slang for "tits".

CAUSE: She died aged 37 in Grasse, France, of what was originally thought to be an overdose of prescription drugs. On June 8, 2000, Eric Vigne was arrested on suspicion of failing to prevent her death. In February 2002, a report was issued stating that Lolo had died of suffocation. On February 27, 2002, Vigne was placed under formal investigation – one step short of being charged with murder. In November 2002, a court in Aix-en-Province decided that there was sufficient evidence to proceed with the murder trial of Eric Vigne.

Jose Ferrer

(JOSÉ VICENTE FERRER DE OTERO Y CINTRÓN)
Born January 8, 1909
Died January 26, 1992
Latin lover. Born in Santurce, Puerto Rico, Ferrer was educated at Princeton University, where he studied architecture. Changing direction, he made his acting début on a Long Island showboat in 1934. The following year he appeared in summer theatre in Suffern, New York. He then joined Joshua Logan's company and toured doubling up as assistant stage manager. His Broadway début came at the 48th Street Theater on September 11, 1935, playing a policeman in *A Slight Case Of Murder*. He spent much of the next 50 years touring America in various plays. He also appeared in over 50 films and innumerable television productions, including *Joan Of Arc* (1948) as The Dauphin, for which he was nominated for a Best Supporting Actor Oscar, losing out to Walter Huston for *Treasure Of The Sierra Madre* (1948), the lead in *Cyrano De Bergerac* (1950), which won him the Best Actor Academy Award, *Crisis* (1950) as Raoul Farrago, *Moulin Rouge* (1952) as Henri de Toulouse-Lautrec and

The Comte de Toulouse-Lautrec, which earned him a Best Actor Oscar nomination, *Anything Can Happen* (1952) as Giorgi, *Miss Sadie Thompson* (1953) as Alfred Davidson, *The Caine Mutiny* (1954) as Lieutenant Barney Greenwald, *Deep In My Heart* (1954) as Sigmund Romberg, *The Cockleshell Heroes* (1955) as Major Stringer, *I Accuse!* (1958) as Captain Alfred Dreyfus, which he also directed, *The High Cost Of Loving* (1958) as Jim Fry, *Lawrence Of Arabia* (1962) as Bey Of Deraa, *Cyrano Et D'Artagnan* (1963) as Cyrano de Bergerac, *The Greatest Story Ever Told* (1965) as Herod Antipas, *Ship Of Fools* (1965) as Rieber, *Cervantes* (1966) as Hassan Bey, *The Swarm* (1978) as Dr Andrews, *The Amazing Captain Nemo* (1978) as Captain Nemo, *The Fifth Musketeer* (1979) as Athos, *To Be Or Not To Be* (1983) as Professor Siletski, *Dune* (1984) as Padishah Emperor Shaddam IV and *Hired To Kill* (1991) as the leader of the rebels. Of his career he had few illusions: "The truth is I made a few good movies in the Fifties then went into freefall." He was possessed of a sense of humour that didn't always place him in favourable positions. Interrogated during the McCarthy witch hunts on May 22, 1951, he was asked about an alleged communist past and his attendance of communist fund-raising events during the war. Ferrer admitted attending the events but said that when he played Iago to Paul Robeson's Othello, he didn't notice that the actor was either a communist or black! Ferrer was married four times. His first wife was Uta Hagen, whom he married on December 8, 1938. They divorced in 1948, eight years after the birth of their daughter, Leticia Thyra. On June 19, 1948, Ferrer married actress Phyllis Hill in Greenwich, Connecticut. The couple was divorced on July 7, 1953. Six days later, Ferrer married singer Rosemary Clooney in Durant, Oklahoma. They had five children:

actor Miguel (b. February 7, 1955) who is married to actress Leilani Sarelle, Roxy in *Basic Instinct* (1992); Maria (b. August 1956); Gabriel (b. 1957) who married singer Debby Boone in 1979; Monsita (b. 1958) and Rafael (b. March 23, 1960). Ferrer and Clooney were divorced in 1967. Sometime in the late Sixties, amid great secrecy, Ferrer married Stella Daphne Magee. "The date of our marriage is known to only three people: my wife, myself and the man who married us. Even my children don't know."

CAUSE: He died in Coral Gables, Florida, aged 83, after a short illness.

Mel Ferrer

Born August 25, 1917
Died June 2, 2008
Hepburn's handsome husband. Melchor Gaston Ferrer was born in Elberon, New Jersey, the son of a Cuban-born surgeon and a Manhattan socialite who was an ardent anti-Prohibitionist. Ferrer was educated privately before going to Princeton where he won the Playwright's Award before dropping out to try his hand as an actor. Success was not immediate and to pay for his keep while he worked in rep at the Cape Cod Playhouse in Massachusetts, he edited a newspaper in Vermont, wrote a children's book, *Tito's Hat*, which was published by Doubleday in 1940 and worked as a DJ. Two years earlier, he had made his debut on Broadway as a dancer in two unsuccessful musicals, Cole Porter's *You Never Know* and *Everywhere I Roam*, a historical romp. He appeared in two straight roles before he was stricken with polio, which left him with a shrivelled arm, after which he moved into producing and directing for NBC Radio. He was determined to overcome the disability and exercised until his arm was back to normal. That led to Columbia Pictures giving 6ft 3in Ferrer a job as a dialogue coach and then

director of the B movie, *The Girl Of The Limberlost* (released October 11, 1945). He returned to the Great White Way where he worked with José Ferrer (no kin) on two plays. He had a minor role as Father Serra in John Ford's *The Fugitive* (released November 3, 1947) before he co-founded the La Jolla Playhouse with Gregory Peck, Dorothy McGuire, Jennifer Jones and Joseph Cotton. Ferrer's only truly successful film as a director was *The Secret Fury* (released February 21, 1950), a thriller starring Claudette Colbert and Robert Ryan. The year before he had made his debut as an actor in the film *Lost Boundaries* (released July 2, 1949) as Scott Mason Carter, a fair-skinned black who finds it difficult to get work because of his colour and has to pretend he is white. His subsequent films included Nicholas Ray's *Born To Be Bad* (released August 27, 1950) as Gabriel "Gobby" Broome, Robert Rossen's *The Brave Bulls* (released April 18, 1951) as matador Luis Bello, and Fritz Lang's *Rancho Notorious* (released March 1, 1952) as Marlene Dietrich's outlaw boyfriend Frenchy Fairmont before stardom, or at least celebrity, beckoned in George Sidney's dazzling *Scaramouche* (released June 27, 1952) in which Ferrer was Noel, Marquis de Maynes. One critic said that Ferrer was "a hissable villain and a convincing lover of Marie Antoinette, his coldly aristocratic mien perfect for the role". Ferrer played a seven-minute fencing scene with Stewart Granger but said, "I avoided fencing with Mel as much as possible as he never could concentrate if there was a pretty girl around." Ferrer consolidated his fame as the bitter, crippled puppeteer Paul Berthalet in Charles Walters's *Lili* (released September 21, 1953). He was signed to play King Arthur in Richard Thorpe's *Knights Of The Round Table* (released January 15, 1954), which was filmed in London when he met Audrey Hepburn at a party given by Gregory Peck.

Ferrer said, "She knew all about the La Jolla Playhouse, and said she'd seen *Lili* three times. Finally, she said she'd like to do a play with me." In February 1954 they opened on Broadway in Jean Giraudoux's *Ondine* but he received public opprobrium because he insisted on sharing her curtain calls. The actor Robert Flemyng, a friend of them both, said, "Mel's success in *Lili* did not bear the fruits that he might have hoped for and, in the course of time, he was not pleased to be Mr Hepburn." On 25 September 1954 he married Hepburn. Their son, Sean (who stands 6'3", like his father), was born in Lucerne, Switzerland, on July 17, 1960, after Hepburn had suffered two miscarriages. Some saw him as Svengali to her Trilby. "Ferrer used Audrey's crush on him to rule her with an iron fist," said director Alfred Lunt, though the actor William Holden felt that the relationship was evenly balanced: "Audrey allows Mel to think he influences her." Ferrer played Prince Andrei Bolkonsky in Raoul Walsh's *War And Peace* (released August 21, 1956) opposite Hepburn and Henry Fonda. He appeared in Henry King's *The Sun Also Rises* (released December 29, 1957) as Robert Cohn and *The World The Flesh And The Devil* (released May 20, 1959) as Benson Thacker before directing Hepburn in *Green Mansions* (released September 3, 1959), the biggest flop of her career. Directing was his first love; he suffered from stage fright and said, "I curl up inside and freeze when I have to act. I much prefer sitting on the sidelines and trying to get the best out of other people." However, after the flop he returned to acting, appearing in bit parts in *The Fall Of The Roman Empire* (released March 24, 1964), Hepburn's *Paris When It Sizzles* (released April 8, 1964) and *Sex And The Single Girl* (released December 25, 1964). He produced Hepburn's last cinematic hit, a screen version of the play *Wait Until Dark* (released

October 26, 1967) in which she played a blind girl who beat smugglers. It was to be their last collaboration and they divorced on December 5, 1968. The rest of Ferrer's career was made up of appearances on television shows like *Hawaii Five-O, Ellery Queen, Fantasy Island, Murder, She Wrote* and more than 50 appearances as Philip Erikson in the soap *Falcon Crest* and small budget European films. His marital life was complicated. Apart from Hepburn, Ferrer married actress Frances Pilchard on October 23, 1937. They divorced in 1939. In 1940 he married Barbara C. Tripp by whom he had a son, Christopher (b. February 4, 1944) and a daughter, Mela (b. January 22, 1943). After their divorce, he remarried Frances Pilchard in 1944 and had a son Mark Young (b. June 19, 1944) and a daughter, Pepa Phillippa (b. August 19, 1941). A second divorce followed and after he and Hepburn were divorced he married Belgian Elizabeth Soukhotine on February 19, 1971. She survived him.
CAUSE: Ferrer died aged 90 at his ranch near Santa Barbara, California, from heart failure. He was cremated and his ashes buried at Carpenteria, California.

Sid Field

Born April 1, 1904
Died February 3, 1950
Tragic comedian. Sidney Arthur Field was born in Birmingham, an only child. A tall gangling man, he spent 20 years in show business before becoming an overnight sensation on March 18, 1943, with the revue *Strike A New Note*. He made just three films: *That's The Ticket* (1940) as Ben, *London Town* (1946) as comedian Jerry Sanford, for which he was paid £30,000, and *Cardboard Cavalier* (1949) as barrow boy Sidcup Buttermeadow, for which he earned £18,600. Moreover, he appeared in only four London shows, yet many who saw Field regard him as the

funniest man they ever had the pleasure to watch.
CAUSE: Playing golf one Sunday in July 1949 he suffered a series of minor heart attacks but finished his game. Three weeks later, a more serious coronary stopped him playing golf. A specialist diagnosed serious heart trouble in August. He went into a nursing home (actually a maternity home) in Wimbledon and suffered another heart attack the day after he was admitted. He was released after six weeks and went on a convalescing cruise to South Africa. On holiday, he suffered yet another mild attack. Once again in England, he went back to work and one day after returning from the theatre he suffered a more serious attack. The following morning he died aged 44 of a heart attack at his home, Arran Cottage, on Wimbledon Common. He left £31,735 18s 8d.
FURTHER READING: *What A Performance: A Life Of Sid Field* – John Fisher (London: Seeley Service, 1975).

Dame Gracie Fields

(GRACE STANSFIELD)
Born January 9, 1898
Died September 27, 1979
'Our Gracie'. Gracie Fields was born over her paternal grandmother's fish and chip shop at 9 Molesworth Street, Rochdale, Lancashire the eldest daughter (of three) of engineer Fred Stansfield (1874–1956). There was also a son. Her mother, Sarah Jane 'Jenny' Bamford (1879–1953), was the archetypal stage mother and wanted her daughter to be a star. Gracie left school on February 11, 1910 aged 12 to enter show business and changed her name to Gracie Fields when she was told her real name was too long. In 1913 she branched out into the field of comedy to add another string to her singing bow. In 1916 she became the leading lady in a troupe formed by bald, bespectacled, womaniser Archie Pitt (b. 1895 as Archibald Sellinger) whom she married on April 21, 1923.

(Gracie's sister, Betty, likened Pitt to Svengali and Grace to Trilby in George Du Maurier's novel. Incidentally, the hat was named after the character, not the other way round.) The marriage wasn't a happy one. "It was like being married to a balance sheet," said Gracie years later. Nonetheless, when Pitt's revue *Mr Tower Of London* opened in the capital at the Alhambra Theatre, Leicester Square, on February 25, 1924, Gracie became an overnight sensation. During the day she made records, in the evening she appeared at the theatre and when the curtain came down she went into cabaret. The money was rolling in (£700 a week) and Pitt was enjoying the trappings of celebrity. Gracie wasn't. They lived in a house called Tower on The Bishop's Avenue, Hampstead, London N2. "They" happened to be Gracie, Archie and his mistress. In 1931 when they were on the verge of separation he made her into a film star. Her début was *Sally In Our Alley* (1931) playing Sally Winch and singing the famous title song which Gracie was later to call "that wretched song". The early films, such as *Looking On The Bright Side* (1932) as Gracie, for which she was paid £20,000, *This Week Of Grace* (1933) as Grace Milroy, *Sing As We Go* (1934) as Gracie Platt, *Love, Life And Laughter* (1934) as Nellie Gwynn, and *Look Up And Laugh* (1935) playing Gracie Pearson, were poor but in spite of this they were enormously popular with the public. In 1935 short (5'5") Italian director and film comedian Monty Banks was hired and the quality improved. The films included *Queen Of Hearts* (1936) as Grace Perkins, *Keep Smiling* (1938), *We're Going To Be Rich* (1938) and *Shipyard Sally* (1939). In 1938 she made the first of her three films in America but she never became a huge star Stateside. In June 1939 she fell victim to cervical cancer (although she didn't admit to the illness until 1964) and was admitted to Chelsea Hospital for Women. Bulletins of her health appeared regularly in newspapers and on the radio and prayers were said in churches to aid her recovery. Some even knelt in prayer outside the Chelsea hospital where she was recuperating. She had separated privately from Archie Pitt in 1932 and was now involved with Monty Banks. In January 1940 Gracie was divorced and Pitt married his long-term mistress. Two months later, on March 19, Gracie and Banks were married in Santa Monica. On November 12, 1940 Archie Pitt died of cancer in London aged 45. A more pressing problem presented itself for Gracie. Monty Banks was still an Italian citizen and, as such, could be interned as an enemy alien. He and Gracie went to live in America, taking £34,000 with them. From being the people's sweetheart she was vilified as a deserter by the press and her popularity hit rock bottom. Even her work for ENSA (nicknamed by a wag Every Night Something Awful) did not endear her to the public. After the war she moved to Capri and slowly began to regain acceptance. On February 18, 1952 she married Boris Alperovici (b. Bessarabia 1904, d. 1983). She became a CBE in February 1938 and a DBE in the 1979 New Year's Honours List. CAUSE: She died in La Canzone-del-Mare, Capri aged 81 from pneumonia. She was buried in the non-Catholic cemetery on the island two days later. She was worth £4 million at the time of her death with just £270,153 held in England. FURTHER READING: *Gracie Fields* – Muriel Burgess with Tommy Keen (London: Star, 1981).

W.C. Fields

(WILLIAM CLAUDE DUKENFIELD)
Born January 29, 1880
Died December 25, 1946
Misanthropic alcoholic. Born in Philadelphia, Pennsylvania, the son of a cockney immigrant Civil War vet who sold fruit and veg. When he was nine,

Fields became a juggler, believing himself to become the world's greatest. Two years later, aged 11, he ran away from home and stole food to sustain himself. He got into several fights and claimed that his trademark nose was the result of a particularly nasty beating. He became 'Fields' when he lost the 'Duken' and theatre owners always called him 'Fields' rather than 'Field'; he became fed up with correcting them and so became W.C. Fields. In 1913 he appeared on a bill with Sarah Bernhardt, breaking a rule she had made never to work with jugglers. He made his film début in 1915 in a film called *Pool Sharks*. He signed with Paramount but was dropped because of his poor attitude. In 1932 he signed a contract with Mack Sennett and made four classic short films: *The Dentist* (1932), *The Fatal Glass Of Beer* (1933) as Mr Snavely, *The Pharmacist* (1933) and *The Barber Shop* (1933) as Cornelius Hare. Under the terms of his contract he was paid his weekly wages in two equal instalments – every Monday and Wednesday. He also wrote many of his films under pseudonyms including Mahatma Kane Jeeves, Charles Bogle and Otis J. Criblecoblis. After the success of *International House* (1933), in which he played Professor Henry R. Quail, Fields moved back to Paramount and was put under a long-term contract. Unfortunately, the studio didn't know what to do with him and at first placed him in other people's films. He was a success in *The Old-Fashioned Way* (1934) as The Great McGonigle and *It's A Gift* (1934) as Harold Bissonette, but was so irritated by his co-star Baby Leroy (b. Los Angeles May 12, 1932, as Leroy Winebrenner) that he spiked the one-year-old's orange juice with gin. Fields' own drinking soon got out of hand and he was missing from the screen for two years following his Mr Micawber in *David Copperfield* (1935) and Professor Eustace McGargle in

Poppy (1936). At one stage he was drinking several bottles of martini a day and when he ran out he would summon more by blowing on a hunting horn! It was said that when he went away he took three cases – one for clothes and two for his booze. He gave up drinking for most of 1937 and returned to film-making with *The Big Broadcast Of 1938* (1938) as T. Frothingill Bellows/S.B. Bellows. Then he signed a contract with Universal under which he was paid $125,000 for each film plus $25,000 for writing the story. This usually consisted of jottings on scraps of paper (much the same way Benny Hill wrote his TV shows). He also included rude jokes. He turned down the part of the wizard in *The Wizard Of Oz* to write a book. He was drunk during the entire filming of *My Little Chickadee* (1940), annoying co-star Mae West by pinching her *derrière* and calling her "My little brood mare". "There's no one quite like Bill . . . thank God," said *la* West. Writer Leo Rosten said of him: "Any man who hates small dogs and children can't be all bad." Fields himself said: "I'm free of all prejudice. I hate everyone equally." He distrusted banks and kept small amounts under fictitious names in banks all over the world, including Nazi Germany "in case the little bastard wins". His last years were plagued with alcoholism and polyneuritis. He married Harriet Hughes on August 8, 1900, in San Francisco. They had one son, William Claude, Jr, who was born on July 28, 1904. The couple separated quite early on and W.C. was henceforth accompanied by actress Carlotta Monti (b. 1907, d. December 8, 1993). CAUSE: He died on Christmas Day, a festival he professed to hate, aged 66, from a massive stomach haemorrhage in Las Encinas Sanatorium, Pasadena, California. Despite claiming to dislike children, Fields left a large share of his $1.3-million fortune to an orphanage. He was buried in Forest Lawn

Memorial-Parks, 1712 South Glendale Avenue, Glendale, California 91209. FURTHER READING: *W.C. Fields By Himself: His Intended Autobiography With Hitherto Unpublished Letters, Notes, Scripts And Articles* – Commentary by Ronald J. Fields (London: W.H. Allen, 1974).

Peter Finch

Born September 28, 1916
Died January 14, 1977
Womanising, hard-drinking he-man. Peter George Frederick Ingle Finch was born illegitimately in a nursing home in Courtfield Gardens, South Kensington, London SW5, the son of Lieutenant-Colonel Wentworth Edward Dallas 'Jock' Campbell (b. Gloucestershire, 1887, d. 1974) and Alicia Gladys 'Betty' Finch. He was raised as the son of Betty's husband, George Ingle Finch (b. Orange, New South Wales, August 4, 1888, d. The Grange, East Hanny, Berkshire, November 22, 1970) and Peter didn't meet his biological father until he was 45. Raised in France, India and Australia, Finch (who was convinced his surname was pronounced Fink) found employment in a variety of jobs including working on *The Sun* in Sydney before becoming a comedian's straight man. He turned to acting in 1935, making his first film, *The Magic Shoes* (1935), the same year although the film never saw the light of day. He was blessed with a resonant voice and Finch soon found himself in great demand on the radio. On April 21, 1943 he married Tamara Tchinarova (b. Bessarabia, 1919) in St Stephen's, Bellevue Hill, Sydney. Their daughter, Anita, arrived on October 27, 1950. He made a few films including *Mr Chedworth Steps Out* (1939) as Arthur Jacobs, *The Rats Of Tobruk* (1944) as Peter Linton and *A Son Is Born* (1946) before arriving in Britain in 1949 with his mentor Laurence Olivier. He repaid Olivier's kindness by having an affair with Lady Olivier, Vivien Leigh.

It was in the Fifties that Finch came into his own as a leading man, blossoming in the Sixties and appearing on the stage and in films such as *The Wooden Horse* (1950), *The Story Of Robin Hood And His Merrie Men* (1952) as the Sheriff of Nottingham, *The Story Of Gilbert And Sullivan* (1953) as Rupert D'Oyly Carte, *The Heart Of The Matter* (1953) as Father Rank, *Elephant Walk* (1954) as John Wiley, *Father Brown* (1954) as Flambeau, *A Town Like Alice* (1956) as Joe Harman which won him his first Best Actor BAFTA, *The Battle Of The River Plate* (1956) as Captain Langsdorff, *The Nun's Story* (1959) as Dr Fortunati, *Kidnapped* (1960) as Alan Breck Stewart, *The Sins Of Rachel Cade* (1960) as Colonel Henry Derode, the lead in *The Trials Of Oscar Wilde* (1960) which won him a second Best Actor BAFTA, *No Love For Johnnie* (1961) as Johnnie Byrne which won him a third Best Actor BAFTA, *Girl With Green Eyes* (1964) as Eugene Gaillard, *The Flight Of The Phoenix* (1965) as Captain Harris, *Far From The Madding Crowd* (1967) as William Boldwood which won him another Best Actor BAFTA, *Sunday, Bloody Sunday* (1971) as Dr Daniel Hirsh which saw him nominated for an Oscar, *Lost Horizon* (1972) as Richard Conway, *A Bequest To The Nation* (1973) as Admiral Lord Nelson, *Network* (1976) as Howard Beale which won him a Best Actor BAFTA and Oscar and *Raid On Entebbe* (1976) as Yitzhak Rabin. He divorced his first wife on June 17, 1959 and on July 4 of that year married the actor Yolande Turner (b. South Africa, December 12, 1935, d. London, November 6, 2003) in Chelsea register office. They had two children: Samantha (b. April 27, 1960) and Charles (b. August 1, 1962) before their divorce on November 11, 1965. On November 9, 1973 he married Jamaican-born Eletha Barrett in Rome. Their daughter, Diana, arrived in December 1969.

Finch also had affairs with Kay Kendall and Mai Zetterling among many others.

CAUSE: He died in Beverly Hills, California, aged 60, from a heart attack while promoting *Network*. A lifelong Buddhist, he was given a Roman Catholic funeral service at the Church of the Good Shepherd in Los Angeles and was buried in Hollywood Memorial Park, 6000 Santa Monica Boulevard, Hollywood, California 90038.

FURTHER READING: *Peter Finch A Biography* – Trader Faulkner (London: Angus & Robertson, 1979); *Finch, Bloody Finch* – Elaine Dundy (London: Magnum, 1981).

Bud Flanagan, OBE
(CHAIM REEVEN WEINTROP)
Born October 14, 1896
Died October 20, 1968
Crazy Gangster. Born in Hanbury Street, Whitechapel (the site of a Jack the Ripper murder) in the East End of London, the fifth son and youngest of ten children of Polish Jewish refugees, his name was changed to Robert Winthrop by the registrar who registered his birth. Aged 13 he developed a magic act – Fargo, the Boy Wizard. In 1910 he walked to Southampton and set off for fame and fortune in America. Stateside, he worked as a paper-boy, a messenger and, for one night only, a boxer. Returning to England in 1915 to sign up for World War I, he met Chesney Allen in Flanders. They were not to meet again until after the war. One Sergeant-Major Flanagan, an anti-Semite, made the Jewish recruit's life a misery, so Winthrop became determined to get his revenge and make the name of Flanagan laughed at the length and breadth of Britain. Back in civvy street, he formed a number of partnerships adopting the name Flanagan. In 1925 he married Anne 'Curly' Quinn in Chester-le-Street. They had one son, Buddy (b. 1926), a difficult person who died of leukaemia

in Los Angeles in 1955. In 1926 Flanagan again bumped into Chesney Allen and they formed a duo. At first it was less than successful and they considered becoming bookmakers. In 1929 they made their London début at the Holborn Empire. With Allen, Flanagan was famous for singing 'Underneath The Arches', a song he had written. (His last job was singing the theme tune to *Dad's Army*.) Among his films were *The Bailiffs* (1932), *Wild Boy* (1934), *Underneath The Arches* (1937), *Okay For Sound* (1937), *Alf's Button Afloat* (1938), *The Frozen Limits* (1939), *Gasbags* (1940), *We'll Smile Again* (1942), *Here Comes The Sun* (1944), *Dunkirk* (1958) and *Life Is A Circus* (1958).

CAUSE: He died in hospital, in London, aged 72 from a heart attack. He left £29,134 in his will.

Ian Fleming
Born May 28, 1908
Died August 12, 1964
James Bond's dad. Ian Lancaster Fleming, the man who created the world's greatest fictional spy, was born at 27 Green Street, in London's Mayfair, the second of four sons of Valentine Fleming (b. Newport, Fife, New Brunswick, 1882, k. in action Gillemont Farm, France, May 20, 1917 at 3.30am), a wealthy Eton- and Oxford-educated banker who in 1910 became Conservative MP for South Oxfordshire, and Evelyn Beatrice Ste Croix, née Rose (b. 1885, d. Brighton, July 20, 24 or 27, 1964 of a stroke), the beautiful, flamboyant daughter of a Berkshire solicitor. Fleming's elder brother Peter, OBE, married the actor Celia Johnson (who is noticed elsewhere in this book) on December 10, 1935 and Ian often felt in the shadow of Peter. Fleming was educated at Durnford preparatory school and at Eton College. At Eton Fleming edited a school magazine called *The Wyvern*. Rather than following Peter to Oxford, Fleming went to the Royal Military

College, Sandhurst in the autumn of 1926. But military life was not to his taste and he left in disgrace on September 1, 1927, after an incident with a woman in which he contracted gonorrhoea. In a bid to salvage his life and reputation he was sent to a finishing school for men in Kitzbühel, Austria. There he met a former spy called Ernan Forbes Dennis who, with his wife the novelist Phyllis Bottome, encouraged Fleming to learn languages and write stories. It seemed as if Fleming was destined for a career as a diplomat, only for him to fail the Foreign Office entrance exam. His mother got him a job with Reuters News Agency but then under family pressure he went to work in the City. From 1933 to 1935 he worked for a small bank, Cull & Co. He then joined Rowe and Pitman, a leading firm of stockbrokers, where he was bored rigid. On July 26, 1939 he became personal assistant to Admiral John Godfrey, the director of naval intelligence. In this secret world Fleming flourished and quickly became a commander, working on anti-German black propaganda. In May 1941 he travelled to America with Admiral Godfrey and wrote a plan for the creation of an Office of Co-ordinator of Information (the forerunner of the Office of Strategic Services, which evolved into the Central Intelligence Agency). From 1941 until 1942 Fleming was in charge of Operation Goldeneye, a plan to maintain vital intelligence should the Germans take over Spain and Gibraltar. It was at this time that Fleming's interest in writing spy fiction was born. However, after being demobbed on November 10, 1945, he joined the Kemsley newspaper group at 200 Gray's Inn Road, which owned *The Sunday Times*, as foreign manager. He later laboured under the name Atticus before his retirement. Fleming used the charm and wit that had made him a successful spy to negotiate a contract that allowed him to take three

months' holiday every winter in Jamaica. In 1945 he had spent £2,000 buying, sight unseen, some land at Oracabessa, on Jamaica's North Shore where he built a house he called Goldeneye. There he entertained his long-term girlfriend Ann Rothermere (b. Stanway, Gloucestershire, June 19, 1913 as Ann Geraldine Mary Charteris, d. Sevenhampton Place, Highworth, Sevenhampton, July 12, 1981 of cancer), the wife of the owner of the *Daily Mail*, the 2nd Viscount Rothermere. When her first husband, the wealthy banker Shane Edward Robert O'Neill, the 3rd Baron O'Neill (b. February 6, 1907), whom she had married on October 6, 1932, was killed in action in Italy on October 24, 1944, it was expected that she would marry Fleming but he demurred and instead she married Esmond Cecil Harmsworth (b. May 29, 1898, d. July 12, 1978) on June 28, 1945. Nevertheless, she continued her affair with Fleming and at 11 Randolph Crescent, Edinburgh in August 1948 gave birth to his daughter, Mary, who lived only eight hours. In October 1951 she finally divorced Rothermere and married Fleming in Port Maria town hall, Jamaica, five months later on March 24, 1952. Noël Coward and Cole Lesley were the only witnesses. The Flemings' only child, a son named Caspar Robert, was born in London on August 12 that year. Noël Coward and Clarissa Eden, wife of the future prime minister Sir Anthony, were among the godparents. James Bond was born on January 15, 1952 shortly after breakfast when Fleming wrote the first words, on a 20-year-old Imperial portable typewriter, that were to become his first book, *Casino Royale*. The name came from James Bond's *Field Guide To Birds Of The West Indies*, a book that Fleming kept on his breakfast table. Recalled Fleming, "I wanted the simplest, dullest, plainest-sounding name I could find. James Bond seemed perfect." He said that the creation was "a counter-irritant or antibody to my hysterical alarm at getting married". Fleming wrote for three hours every morning – between 9am and midday – for seven weeks. The casino of the title, Royale-les-Eaux, is where Bond challenges the Soviet agent Le Chiffre, a.k.a. Herr Ziffer, over the roulette table. The 62,000-word book was published to critical acclaim on April 13, 1953. Thereafter Fleming used his Caribbean holidays to write a James Bond story every year until his death in 1964. Not everyone was enamoured of Fleming's writing, which he described as being for "warm-blooded heterosexuals in railway trains, aeroplanes and bed". In 1958 the journalist Paul Johnson criticised the books in *The New Statesman* for their "sex, snobbery and sadism". Harold Nicolson wrote in his 1959 diary that *Goldfinger* had an "underlying atmosphere of violence, luxury and lust . . . [It is] an obscene book, liable to corrupt". Labour Party leader Hugh Gaitskell told the author, "I am a confirmed Fleming fan – or should it be addict? The combination of sex, violence, alcohol and – at intervals – good food and nice clothes is, to one who lives such a circumscribed life as I do, irresistible." Fleming's next books were *For Your Eyes Only* (1960), a collection of short stories, *Thunderball* (1961), a novel based on a treatment by Kevin McClory and Jack Whittingham and *The Spy Who Loved Me* (1962). On March 25, 1961 his co-writers on *Thunderball* sued him for stealing their plot. The case would not be settled for two years. It finished in November 1963 with Fleming acknowledging that McClory and Whittingham had written the book with him. McClory received the film rights and disclaimed interest in the novel and went on to co-produce the 1965 box-office smash. (McClory also agreed not to use his *Thunderball* material for ten years. He was later to remake the film as *Never Say Never*

Again [released on October 7, 1983] and once again starring Sean Connery as 007.) On April 12, 1961 Fleming suffered a heart attack. Then, just as things began to look incredibly bleak (he was suffering marital difficulties as well as health worries), his career took off and his books became best sellers in America, helped by an endorsement from President Kennedy in *Life* magazine on March 17, 1961. Fleming wrote 12 Bond novels and two collections of short stories. In June 1961 Fleming signed a $50,000 deal with the producers Cubby Broccoli and Harry Saltzman for film options on all the Bond books apart from *Casino Royale*. This was the first book to be dramatised when on October 21, 1954 it was aired live on American television. Barry Nelson became the first (and to date only) American Bond. Peter Lorre played his nemesis Le Chiffre in this studio-bound version which cost CBS $1,000. When the film version of *Casino Royale* was made, it was a spoof and a terrible one at that. Released on April 19, 1967 one critic said it was "filled with plot holes you could drive Aston Martins through". It starred Peter Sellers, Ursula Andress, David Niven, Orson Welles and Woody Allen. The first official Bond film *Dr No* starred Sean Connery and Ursula Andress and opened on October 6, 1962. However, Fleming was not impressed by Connery. His choices were James Stewart, Richard Burton or James Mason but he did not have a say in the casting. Away from Bond, Fleming also wrote the children's story *Chitty Chitty Bang Bang* which became a successful film in 1968.
CAUSE: Following the box-office success of *Dr No*, Fleming wrote *On Her Majesty's Secret Service* (1963) which was released as a film (the sixth Bond film) on December 18, 1969. His success (Fleming sold 30 million books during his lifetime – a figure that doubled in the two years after his death) bought homes including

a Regency house at 16 Victoria Square, London and residences in Bekesbourne, near Sandwich in Kent and later Sevenhampton Place, Highworth, Sevenhampton, near Swindon in Wiltshire, as well as Goldeneye in Jamaica. But his health had been permanently damaged, not helped by his excessive drinking and smoking (70 a day). He died aged 56 from heart complications in the Kent and Canterbury Hospital at 1am on August 12, 1964. He was buried at Sevenhampton, Wiltshire. Fleming left £302,147 (gross) and £289,170 (net). On October 2, 1975 Caspar, his depressive son who became a drug addict and had attempted suicide several times, killed himself aged 23 with a drugs overdose. He left a note saying, "If not this time, it will be the next." When Ann Fleming died six years later she left £926,456.

FURTHER READING: *The Life Of Ian Fleming* – John Pearson (London: Jonathan Cape, 1966); *Peter Fleming A Biography* – Duff Hart Davis (London: Jonathan Cape, 1974); *The Complete James Bond Movie Encyclopaedia* – Steven Jay Rubin (Chicago: Contemporary Books, 1990); *Ian Fleming* – Andrew Lycett (London: Weidenfeld & Nicolson, 1995).

Victor Fleming
Born February 23, 1883
Died January 6, 1949
Director extraordinaire. Born in Pasadena, California, 6'1" Fleming was responsible for some of the most memorable Hollywood films of all time. He began his working life as a mechanic before becoming a photographer. Fleming became involved in film-making aged 27. During World War I he worked in intelligence and was President Woodrow Wilson's chief cameraman when he went to Europe. Among Fleming's films were *Woman's Place* (1921), *Red Hot Romance* (1922), *Dark Secrets* (1923), *Law Of The Lawless*

(1923), *To The Last Man* (1923), *Code Of The Sea* (1924), *Adventure* (1925), *Lord Jim* (1925), *The Way Of All Flesh* (1927), *The Virginian* (1929), *Renegades* (1930), *Around The World In 80 Minutes With Douglas Fairbanks* (1931), *Red Dust* (1932), *Bombshell* (1933), *Treasure Island* (1934), *Reckless* (1935), *Captains Courageous* (1937), *Test Pilot* (1938), *The Wizard Of Oz* (1939), *Gone With The Wind* (1939), for which he won an Oscar, *Dr Jekyll And Mr Hyde* (1941) and *Joan Of Arc* (1948). He married Joan Blair in 1931. CAUSE: He died aged 65 in Arizona from a heart attack. He was buried in Hollywood Memorial Park, 6000 Santa Monica Boulevard, Hollywood, California 90038.

Errol Flynn
Born June 20, 1909
Died October 14, 1959
Hell-raiser. Born in Hobart, Tasmania, Australia, the name of 6'2" Errol Leslie Thompson Flynn has become a synonym for a hard-living, heavy drinking, womanising roustabout. His biologist father bought the first live duck-billed platypuses to Europe, though Errol managed to kill two on the journey by feeding them tadpoles. Much of what we know about Flynn is in dispute because he was such a masterful storyteller. "The only thing you could be certain of about Errol," recalled his good friend David Niven, "is that whatever it was, he would let you down." Producer Jack L. Warner commented, "You know Flynn, he's either got to be fighting or fucking." The notoriously priapic actor claimed he lost his virginity to the family maid in Tasmania when he was 12 years old. He was expelled from Sydney Church of England Grammar School for stealing (or was he caught having sex with a female pupil on a pile of coal in the basement?). He travelled to New Guinea, where he worked as a slave trader. That 'career' ended when he was accused of murder but was

acquitted when his plea of self-defence was accepted (or was it because the authorities couldn't find the body?). Flynn began his acting career not in films but on stage in the uninspiring town of Northampton. He was eventually sacked from the company for throwing a director's wife down a flight of stairs. On June 19, 1935, he married Lili Damita in Yuma, Arizona, and fathered a son, Sean (b. Los Angeles, May 31, 1941, disappeared in Vietnam, 1970). The couple was divorced on March 31, 1942, in Los Angeles. He became a Hollywood star after Jack Warner took a chance and cast him as Dr Peter Blood in the epic *Captain Blood* (1935). Flynn wanted to be a writer and had two novels *Beam Ends* and *Showdown* and several articles published. However, he failed to make headway in that direction, probably because he lacked the necessary dedication to apply himself to the writer's craft, so he returned his efforts to the big screen. During the Spanish Civil War Flynn journeyed to Spain with a shadowy figure, Dr Herman Erben. It is Flynn's friendship with Erben, a card-carrying Nazi who was thrown out of Austria for dressing like his hero Adolf Hitler, that is one of the most controversial episodes of his life. According to a biography of Flynn by respected author Charles Higham, the actor was himself a Nazi spy during WWII. Another writer, William Donati, has examined all the thousands of documents on Flynn but has found nothing to substantiate Higham's accusations. Still, the rumours refuse to die. The FBI kept Flynn under surveillance but were unable to prove he was a Nazi, or that he had any political affiliations or interest at all. Flynn did not fight for the Allies in World War II – not because of any misguided sense of loyalty to the Führer, but because, despite his seemingly indestructible physique, he was a very sick man. By the age of 28, the year his

swashbuckling reputation was made with *The Adventures Of Robin Hood* (1938), Flynn was suffering from an enlarged heart, malaria, spots on the lungs and tuberculosis, all exacerbated by his drinking. He regularly collapsed on set. When he tried to enlist in the army he was registered 4F. Flynn kept himself amused with other pursuits instead of fighting, not all of them legal. In October 1942, the actor was charged and acquitted of raping two young girls, Peggy Satterlee and Betty Hansen at 345 St Pierre Road, Bel Air. They claimed Flynn kept his socks on during intercourse. At his trial, for which he could have been sentenced to up to 150 years in prison, Flynn hired Hollywood's best-known troubleshooter, Jerry Giesler, to defend him. The legal eagle tore into the two girls, destroying their reputations in the process. In 1996 Betty Hansen spoke publicly for the first time about the case. "He was the first love in my life," she commented. "He is the first and maybe the last." Flynn had made preparations to fly abroad if the verdict had gone against him. He also lied on oath and was almost certainly guilty of the offence. The narrow escape at the trial did nothing to diminish Flynn's appetite for very young girls. He spent his final years with teenager Beverly Aadland (b. September 17, 1942). Again according to Higham, Flynn was an active bisexual who had an affair with fellow actor Tyrone Power and, possibly, with billionaire Howard Hughes. One of the most enduring rumours about Flynn is that he was the very proud possessor of an enormous penis. This is another story that just doesn't stand up when scrutinised. His close friend and biographer Earl Conrad and second wife Nora Eddington both confirm that he was of normal dimensions in the trouser department. Thrice-married, Flynn took refuge in drink and drugs. He even called his house Cirrhosis By the Sea. His marriage to cigar seller Nora

Eddington (married by proxy in September 1944, divorced on July 7, 1949, following the birth of two daughters – Deirdre [b. Mexico City, January 10, 1945] and Rory [b. Los Angeles, March 12, 1947]) was wrecked because of his morphine addiction. He married actress Patrice Wymore on October 23, 1950, in the Lutheran Chapel in Nice. Their daughter, Arnella Roma, was born in the Italian capital on Christmas Day 1950. Flynn's films included *In The Wake Of The Bounty* (1933) as Fletcher Christian, *Murder At Monte Carlo* (1934) as Dyter, *Don't Bet On Blondes* (1935) as David Van Dusen, *The Charge Of The Light Brigade* (1936) as Major Geoffrey Vickers, *The Perfect Specimen* (1937) as Gerald Beresford Wicks, *Another Dawn* (1937) as Captain Denny Roark, *The Prince And The Pauper* (1937) as Miles Hendon, *The Dawn Patrol* (1938) as Captain Courtney, *Dodge City* (1939) as Wade Hatton, *The Private Lives Of Elizabeth And Essex* (1939) as the Earl of Essex (during which he feuded constantly with co-star Bette Davis), *The Sea Hawk* (1940) as Geoffrey Thorpe, *Santa Fe Trail* (1940) as Jeb Stuart, *Virginia City* (1940) as Kerry Bradford, *Dive Bomber* (1941) as Lieutenant Doug Lee, *They Died With Their Boots On* (1941) as George Armstrong Custer, *Edge Of Darkness* (1942) as Gunnar Brogge, *Gentleman Jim* (1942) as champion boxer James J. Corbett, *Objective, Burma!* (1945) as Captain Nelson, *Never Say Goodbye* (1946) as Phil Gayley, *Cry Wolf* (1947) as Mark Caldwell, the lead in *Adventures Of Don Juan* (1948), *That Forsyte Woman* (1949) as Soames Forsyte, *Rocky Mountain* (1950) as Lafe Barstow, *Montana* (1950) as Morgan Lane, *Kim* (1950) as Mahbub Ali, *Mara Maru* (1952) as Gregory Mason, *The Master Of Ballantrae* (1953) as Jamie Durrisdeer, *Istanbul* (1957) as James Brennan and *The Sun Also Rises* (1957) as Mike Campbell. In the end what did

for Errol Flynn was Errol Flynn, who lived every day as if it was his last. CAUSE: Flynn died in Vancouver, Canada, aged 50, from a heart attack. Other contributory factors included myocardial infarction, coronary thrombosis, coronary arteriosclerosis, fatty degeneration of the liver, portal cirrhosis of the liver and diverticulosis of the colon. He was buried in Forest Lawn Memorial-Parks, 1712 South Glendale Avenue, Glendale, California 91209. A rumour persists that he was interred with half a dozen bottles of whisky. His final resting place remained unmarked until 1979. FURTHER READING: *Errol Flynn: The Untold Story* – Charles Higham (New York: Doubleday, 1980); *Errol Flynn: The Spy Who Never Was* – Tony Thomas (New York: Citadel Press, 1990).

Henry Fonda
Born May 16, 1905
Died August 12, 1982
Founder of a dynasty. Born in Grand Island, Nebraska, Henry Jaynes Fonda was encouraged to act by Do Brando, mother of Marlon, and one of the founders of the Omaha Community Playhouse. She cast him in a 1925 production of *You And I*. Shy at first, Fonda soon took to acting: "I discovered the magic of the theatre that I had never known anything about before. I liked the feeling of being up there . . . I lost most of my shyness and began to relax." As well as acting, Fonda designed and painted sets to survive until he became a star on Broadway as Dan Harrow in *The Farmer Takes A Wife* in 1935. He was spotted by a film producer and reprised his role in the movie version. On Christmas Day 1931 he married actress Margaret Sullavan in Baltimore's Kernan Hotel. In less than five months they separated and Fonda went back to sharing a New York flat with James Stewart. Said Fonda, "Christ, I suppose they'll call

Jimmy and me fags after we're gone just because we lived together. Hell, if we hadn't shared the food and rent, we would never have made it." The one taboo subject between the two of them was politics. Fonda was a Democrat while Stewart was a fervent Republican. Fonda said Ronald Reagan (Stewart's close friend) made him "physically ill" and that he "couldn't stomach any of the Republicans, most of all Richard Nixon." On September 16, 1936, with director Josh Logan as best man, Fonda married socialite divorcée Frances Seymour Brokaw (b. 1908) in New York's Christ Church. Their daughter Jane was born on December 21, 1937, in New York City, while son Peter Henry arrived on February 23, 1940, also in the Big Apple. In December 1949, Fonda announced a separation; five months later, on April 14, 1950, his wife, committed to a sanatorium with a mental illness, killed herself. She was 42. Neither Jane nor Peter were told the truth about their mother's death for many years. On December 28, 1950, Fonda married Susan Blanchard (b. 1928), stepdaughter of Oscar Hammerstein, II, and 23 years younger than him. The ceremony took place in Hammerstein's New York home. In November 1953 the couple adopted Amy, an eight-month-old girl from Connecticut. In May 1956 the Fondas divorced. Marriage number four was on March 10, 1957, to Afdera Franchetti. They met in 1955 at a party for Dino De Laurentiis-Carlo Ponti's film War And Peace. Afdera was the daughter of a 6'6" Venetian nobleman who named his children after the exotic places he had visited. His eldest daughter was named Simba ('lion' in Swahili), next was Lorian (named after the place elephants go to die) and the brother was named Nanook or Nanucki after a conquest of the North Pole. Afdera was a volcano. Their courtship was conducted primarily in secret because Fonda was not yet

divorced and Afdera was engaged to someone else. They did go to Roman nightclubs, but mostly they spoke on a transatlantic phone. He proposed in late summer 1956 and they became engaged at Christmas of the same year. They married in the drawing room of Fonda's East 74th Street townhouse in Manhattan. The ceremony was performed by a New York State Supreme Court judge, and a sulky 16-year-old Peter Fonda was his father's best man. When the wedding pictures were developed, Afdera was revealed to have big black marks under her eyes from crying and her brother's fists. (He disapproved of the match because Fonda was non-Catholic and thrice-married, so he took it out on his sister.) She took a pair of scissors and cut out all the eyes in the photos. The honeymoon was delayed because Fonda had to finish 12 Angry Men (1957). The couple eventually went on their honeymoon in July and took Jane Fonda with them. Afdera was only five years older than Jane and although Afdera liked her new stepdaughter the feeling was not reciprocated. (Peter and Afdera were cold towards each other.) They flew to a draughty chalet in Canada. Fonda had a cold and Mrs F. was still feeling the effects of her brother's beating. They visited Pamplona, Venice and Cap Ferrat. Problems quickly appeared as Fonda realised he did not fit into his wife's social milieu. Eventually, Afdera left him for another man. She attended John F. Kennedy's inaugural ball alone and never went back to her husband. They were divorced in 1961. Mrs F. claimed that in the years they were married she never went into the kitchen and never wrote a cheque. On December 3, 1965, Fonda married for the fifth and final time. His new wife was Shirlee Mae Adams and the ceremony took place on Mineola, Long Island. Throughout his life, Fonda found it difficult to show his feelings and admitted, "I was ashamed that a guy with a solid background like mine kept screwing up his personal life." His private life may have been a mess but his professional one was a soaraway success. His films include *Spendthrift* (1936) as Townsend Middleton, *The Trail Of The Lonesome Pine* (1936) as Dave Tolliver (cartoonist Al Capp based Li'l Abner on Fonda's Tolliver), the lead in *Slim* (1937), *You Only Live Once* (1937) as Eddie Taylor, *That Certain Woman* (1937) as Jack Merrick, *I Met My Love Again* (1938) as Ives Towner, *Jezebel* (1938) as Preston Dillard, *Blockade* (1938) as Marco, *Drums Along The Mohawk* (1939) as Gilbert Martin, *Jesse James* (1939) as Frank James, the lead in *Young Mr Lincoln* (1939), *The Story Of Alexander Graham Bell* (1939) as Bell's assistant Thomas Watson, *The Grapes Of Wrath* (1940) as Tom Joad, *Lillian Russell* (1940) as Alexander Moore, *The Return Of Frank James* (1940) as Frank James, the lead in *Chad Hanna* (1940), *Wild Geese Calling* (1941) as John Murdock, *Rings On Her Fingers* (1942) as John Wheeler, *The Magnificent Dope* (1942) as Tad Page, *Tales Of Manhattan* (1942) as George, *The Ox-Bow Incident* (1943) as Gil Carter, *My Darling Clementine* (1946) as Wyatt Earp, *Daisy Kenyon* (1947) as Peter Lapham, *Fort Apache* (1948) as Lieutenant-Colonel Owen Thursday, *Mister Roberts* (1955) as Doug Roberts, *War And Peace* (1956) as Pierre Bezukhov, *Stage Struck* (1958) as Lewis Easton, *The Longest Day* (1962) as Brigadier General Theodore Roosevelt, Jr, *How The West Was Won* (1962) as Jethro Stuart, *Sex And The Single Girl* (1964) as Frank Broderick, *Battle Of The Bulge* (1965) as Lieutenant Colonel Kiley, *A Big Hand For A Little Lady* (1966) as Meredith, *The Boston Strangler* (1968) as John S. Bottomley, *Once Upon A Time In The West* (1968), and *The Swarm* (1978) as Dr Krim, but towards the end of his life he became better known as the father of Jane, rather than as a star in his own right. However, it is wise never to write off the elderly: Fonda won a Best Actor Oscar for *On Golden Pond* (1981) with his portrayal of Norman Thayer, Jr.

CAUSE: In his declining years Fonda suffered heart problems. On May 15, 1981, during an operation at Cedars-Sinai Hospital Medical Center, 8700 Beverly Boulevard, Los Angeles, California, doctors discovered Fonda not only had prostate cancer but that the disease had spread throughout his body. A pacemaker was fitted to ease his heart problems. On August 7, 1982, he was readmitted to Cedars-Sinai Hospital Medical Center. Five days later at 8.15am Fonda died, aged 77, following cardio-respiratory arrest. Later that day his widow and children held a press conference in the driveway of the family home – 10744 Chalon Road, Bel Air. Shirlee Fonda said, "He had a very good night the night before. He talked to all of us. He was never unconscious at any time. He woke up this morning, sat up in bed, and quietly stopped breathing." On August 13, 1982, Fonda was cremated at Grandview Cemetery, Glendale, California.

FURTHER READING: *The Fabulous Fondas* – James Brough (New York: David McKay, 1973); *Fonda: My Life* – Henry Fonda As Told To Howard Teichmann (London: W.H. Allen, 1982); *The Fondas: A Hollywood Dynasty* – Peter Collier (London: HarperCollins, 1991).

Kam Fong

(KAM TONG CHUN)
Born May 27, 1918
Died October 18, 2002
Forever Chin Ho. Born in Honolulu, one of seven children, the family ran a sweet factory but when his father had an affair the family found themselves in reduced circumstances. His name means "golden temple" but when he went to school his teacher misunderstood and called him Kam Fong, a name he later adopted legally.

After he finished his education he became a welder at Pearl Harbor and was there when the Japanese attacked on December 7, 1941. He recalled: "I looked across the bay and I saw the USS *Arizona* burning and I cried." In 1944 further tragedy was to haunt him when his wife Esther, son Donald and daughter Marilyn were killed when an American B-24 bomber crashed after colliding with another B-24 above his house. Fong tried to shoot himself but his mother stepped in to stop him. He took a job in which he often put his life on the line with the Honolulu police force. He earned the nickname 'A&B' Chun because of his handling of cases involving assault and battery. He married Gladys Lindo and fathered four more children, finally giving up his police work in 1961 after 17 years to become an estate agent and a DJ. He also dabbled in acting and had his own television series for children *Kam Fong's Comedies*. He also appeared in the films *Ghost Of The China Sea* (1958), *Gidget Goes Hawaiian* (1961), *Seven Women From Hell* (1961) and *Diamond Head* (1963). Five years later, he signed to play the Irish-Hawaiian detective Chin Ho Kelly in the hit series *Hawaii Five-O*. He stayed with the series for ten years before finally being killed off while working undercover. The character was named after Chin Ho, a Hawaiian benefactor, and Roy Kelley, a Waikiki hotel developer. He went back to DJing and in 1988 he ran for governor of Hawaii under the slogan "Give a damn – vote for Kam".

CAUSE: He died in Honolulu aged 84 from lung cancer.

Horton Foote

Born March 14, 1916
Died March 4, 2009
America's biographer. The man who won a Pulitzer Prize and two Academy Awards was born Albert Horton Foote, Jr at Wharton, Texas, one of three sons of Albert Horton Foote, a haberdasher, and Hallie Brooks who taught piano. In 1932 he left for Dallas to become an actor and later spent two years studying theatre at the Pasadena Playhouse in California, then in 1935 went to New York to become a Broadway star. One day he met choreographer Agnes De Mille who wondered if he had considered writing. "No," he said. "What on earth would I write about?" De Mille, said, "Write what you know about." His first effort was a one-act play called *Wharton Dance*, about Friday night dances in his hometown and Foote wrote himself the lead role. In 1941 the American Actors Company put on his three-act drama *Texas Town*, with Foote in the lead. When not acting and waiting for his big break Foote worked as a lift attendant and in a bookshop. One day Lillian Vallish (b. Mount Carmel, Pennsylvania July 18, 1923), a Vassar student, came into the shop and Foote asked her out. They married on June 4, 1945 and had four children – Hallie (b. 1953), Horton (b. 1954), Walter and Daisy (b. 1963) – before her death on August 5, 1992. In 1950 Foote began writing for *The Gabby Hayes Show* but it was with *The Trip To Bountiful* (broadcast March 1, 1953) starring Lillian Gish as the homesick widow Carrie Watts that made his name. When it was made as a film in 1985 Geraldine Page won a Best Actress Oscar and Foote was nominated for the screenplay. One of Foote's earliest film jobs was to adapt Harper Lee's *To Kill A Mockingbird* for the big screen. Released on Christmas Day 1962, the film won Gregory Peck a Best Actor Oscar as lawyer Atticus Finch defending a black man on rape charges in racially divided Alabama in 1932. Foote won an Oscar for his screenplay and the film marked an early screen appearance if not the first for Robert Duvall as Arthur "Boo" Radley. Harper Lee said that Foote "looked like God, only clean shaven." His next film was *Baby, The Rain Must Fall* (1965), which starred Steve

McQueen. Then it all went wrong. Hollywood bosses hated his adaptation of his own play *The Chase* and hired Lillian Hellman to rewrite it. Otto Preminger gave Foote a job to write *Hurry Sundown* (1967), but the producer never used a word of Foote's work. Depressed, Foote moved to a New Hampshire farm and contemplated giving up writing. The death of his parents inspired Foote to write the nine-play cycle *The Orphans' Home*, which marked his comeback. As he wrote the cycle, he also worked on *Tender Mercies* (1983), written specifically with Robert Duvall in mind for the role of Mac Sledge, a finished, alcoholic singer who is saved by the love of a young Vietnam War widow and her small son. Duvall won the Best Actor Academy Award and Foote received his second Oscar for the screenplay. In 1995 he won the Pulitzer Prize for *The Young Man From Atlanta*, about a couple nearing retirement in Fifties Houston whose son killed himself because he may have been gay. Of his work, Foote said, "I believe very deeply in the human spirit and I have a sense of awe about it because I don't know how people carry on. I've known people that the world has thrown everything at to discourage them, to kill them, to break their spirit. And yet something about them retains a dignity. They face life and they don't ask quarters. I don't think I'll ever stop writing. I write almost every day. I'd write plays even if they were never done again. You're at the mercy of whatever talent you have."

CAUSE: Horton Foote died in his sleep at his apartment in Hartford, Connecticut, aged 92 after a brief illness.

John Ford
(SEAN O'FEENEY)
Born February 1, 1895
Died August 31, 1973
The Western director. One-eyed Ford was born in Cape Elizabeth, Maine, the youngest of 13 children. His father was a publican and young John joined his elder brother in show business before making his name (adopted in 1923) as the foremost director of westerns. He helped the careers of numerous actors, including John Wayne and Henry Fonda, despite his low opinion of the profession: "Actors are crap," he once said. His films included *Red Saunders Plays Cupid* (1917), *Trail Of Hate* (1917), *Cheyenne's Pal* (1917), *Straight Shooting* (1917), *Bucking Broadway* (1917), *Delirium* (1918), *Wild Women* (1918), *Thieves' Gold* (1918), *Hell Bent* (1918), *Three Mounted Men* (1918), *Rustlers* (1919), *By Indian Post* (1919), *Gun Law* (1919), *Bare Fists* (1919), *Ace Of The Saddle* (1919), *Rider Of The Law* (1919), *Marked Men* (1919), *Just Pals* (1920), *Desperate Trails* (1921), *Action* (1921), *Little Miss Smiles* (1922), *Hoodman Blind* (1923), *Cameo Kirby* (1923), *North Of Hudson Bay* (1923), *Hearts Of Oak* (1924), *Kentucky Pride* (1925), *Thank You* (1925), *3 Bad Men* (1926), *Upstream* (1927), *Four Sons* (1928), *Hangman's House* (1928), *Riley The Cop* (1928), *Salute* (1929), *Men Without Women* (1930), *Born Reckless* (1930), *Arrowsmith* (1931), *Flesh* (1932), *Pilgrimage* (1933), *Doctor Bull* (1933), *Steamboat 'Round The Bend* (1935), *The Informer* (1935), for which he won his first Oscar, *Mary Of Scotland* (1936), *Wee Willie Winkie* (1937), *Submarine Patrol* (1938), *Stagecoach* (1939) starring John Wayne, for which Ford was nominated for an Oscar, *Drums Along The Mohawk* (1939) starring Henry Fonda, *Young Mr Lincoln* (1939) starring Fonda, *The Grapes Of Wrath* (1940), for which he won his second Oscar, *Tobacco Road* (1941), *How Green Was My Valley* (1941), for which he won his third Oscar, *Torpedo Squadron* (1942), *Sex Hygiene* (1942), *The Battle Of Midway* (1942), *They Were Expendable* (1945), *My Darling Clementine* (1946), *Fort Apache* (1948), *3 Godfathers* (1948), *She Wore A Yellow Ribbon* (1949),

Wagonmaster (1950), *Rio Grande*
(1950) starring Wayne, *What Price
Glory* (1952), *The Quiet Man* (1952)
starring John Wayne, for which Ford
won his fourth and final Oscar,
Mogambo (1953) starring Ava Gardner,
Mister Roberts (1955), *The Searchers*
(1956) starring John Wayne, *The Man
Who Shot Liberty Valance* (1962),
Cheyenne Autumn (1964) and *Chesty: A
Tribute To A Legend* (1970). Ford once
observed of his craft: "Anybody can
direct a picture once they know the
fundamentals. Directing is not a
mystery, it's not an art. The main thing
about directing is: photograph the
people's eyes."
CAUSE: Ford died of cancer in Palm
Desert, California. He was 78.

George Formby, OBE

(GEORGE HOY BOOTH)
Born May 26, 1904
Died March 6, 1961
Silly songstrel. Born at 3 Westminster
Street, Wigan, Lancashire, George was
the eldest of seven surviving children
(four girls and three boys) of James
Lawler Booth (b. Ashton-under-Lyne,
Lancashire, October 4, 1875, the
illegitimate son of a 4' tall prostitute
with a fierce temper, d. Newcastle
Empire, February 8, 1921 of a
haemorrhage), a reasonably successful
music hall comedian who was billed as
"The Wigan Nightingale" and Eliza
Hoy (b. 1879, d. August 1981), a
devout Roman Catholic. The couple
was married at Wigan Register Office
on August 11, 1899. Their first six
children died in infancy although James
Booth was reputed to have fathered
several children out of wedlock. George
was born blind until a sneezing fit
miraculously caused his eyesight to
return when he was a few months old.
His siblings were Louisa (b. Wigan,
Lancashire, 1900, d. Wigan,
Lancashire, 1900), Beatrice (b. Wigan,
Lancashire, 1901, d. Wigan,
Lancashire, 1902), Edith Lillian (b.
Wigan, Lancashire, 1903, d. Wigan,

Lancashire, 1903), a child (b. Wigan,
Lancashire, 1905, d. Wigan,
Lancashire, 1905), Louisa (b. Wigan,
Lancashire, 1906), a child (b. Wigan,
Lancashire, 1907, d. Wigan,
Lancashire, 1907), Frances (b. Wigan,
Lancashire, 1908, d. Wigan,
Lancashire, 1909), Ella (b. Wigan,
Lancashire, 1910, d. Wigan,
Lancashire, 1998), Mary (b. Wigan,
Lancashire, 1912, d. Wigan,
Lancashire, 1987), Frank Allen (b.
Wigan, Lancashire, 1913, d. Wigan,
Lancashire, 1983), Ethel (b. Wigan,
Lancashire, 1915, d. Wigan,
Lancashire, 1998) and Edward (b.
Wigan, Lancashire, 1918). George left
school aged seven and became a stable
boy with his eye on becoming a jockey.
His father hired a schoolteacher to
educate the boy but he was more
concerned with the form of the
racehorses with the result that George
was almost illiterate. In 1921, George
was 16 and by this time was too tall for
a career in the saddle. That year, on
February 8, his father died and George
saw a show at London's Victoria Palace
Theatre in which a comedian called
Tommy Dixon did an impression of
him and used his act. Young George
was annoyed by the plagiarism and
decided he would use his father's act.
This happened in April 1921 at the
Hippodrome, Earlestown. In deference
to the old man he used his mother's
maiden name and announced he would
not be known as George Formby until
he topped the bill in his own right.
Three years later, in August 1924, he
achieved his ambition, at least of
appearing in London (he was a support
act) and was billed as George Formby,
Jr. It was in 1925 that he began playing
the instrument that was to make
him famous – the ukulele. When he
stopped impersonating his father his
career began to soar and in 1929 he
began singing and recording his "silly
little songs". On September 13,
1924, at Wigan Register Office, he
married Beryl Ingham (b. Accrington,

September 9, 1900), a clog dancer, and in 1928, she took over the management of his career. Under her guidance George became a millionaire but at a price. Her control was rigid. He was not allowed to kiss his leading ladies and she placed him on an allowance of just five shillings a day. She also nagged him incessantly but claimed that George wanted her with him and was miserable when she was not in his presence. He made his film début while still a stable boy in *By The Shortest Of Heads* (1915) but his first feature film was Bert Tracey's *Boots! Boots!* (1934) in which he played John Willie. He was paid £200 plus 10 per cent of the profits for a 15-day shooting schedule. During filming, as with his stage work, Beryl made sure that George did not associate too closely with any of his co-stars. She even went so far as to ensure that the scenes featuring a 12-year-old Betty Driver (later Betty Turpin Williams in *Coronation Street*) ended up on the cutting room floor because George was friendly towards her. He followed *Boots! Boots!* with Arthur Mertz's *Off The Dole* (1935) again as John Willie, *No Limit* (1935) as George Shuttleworth (with a budget of £30,000), *Keep Your Seats, Please* (1936) as George (both helmed by Monty Banks who later declared, "The only time you'll ever get me directing anything where that fucking Formby woman is concerned will be when she's playing the murder victim, and the scene's for real"), *Feather Your Nest* (1937) as Willie, *Keep Fit* (1937) as George Green for which he was paid £25,000, *I See Ice* (1937) as George Bright, *It's In The Air* (1938) as George Brown, *Trouble Brewing* (1939) as George Gullip, *Come On George* (1939) as George, *Let George Do It* (1940) as George Hepplewhite, *Spare A Copper* (1940) as George Carter, *Turned Out Nice Again* (1941) as George Pearson, *South American George* (1941) as George Butters/Gilli Vanetti, *Much Too Shy* (1942) as George Andy, *Get*

Cracking (1943) as George Singleton, *Bell-Bottom George* (1943) as George Blake, *He Snoops To Conquer* (1945) as George Gribble, *I Didn't Do It* (released in July 1945) as George Trotter and *George In Civvy Street* (1946) as George Harper. On September 27, 1936 at Blackpool's Feldman Theatre, he recorded the first version of 'When I'm Cleaning Windows', his saucy song about what a vision technician sees on the job. The BBC's Director-General Lord Reith banned the song. "If the public wants to listen to Formby singing his disgusting little ditty, they'll have to be content to hear it at cinemas, not over the nation's airwaves." The song shifted 150,000 copies within a month of its release but the follow-up 'Window Cleaner No. 2' was even saucier and upset the normally unflappable Beryl. In *Feather Your Nest* George sang what was to become virtually his signature song 'Leaning On A Lamppost'. As often happens when stars popularise a song, Beryl asked the composer Noel Gay to add George's name to his in the songwriting credits. Gay refused. On June 18, 1937 Beryl underwent a hysterectomy in a private nursing home in London. Beryl was determined not to become a mother – a decision she later came to regret – and the operation was her way of ensuring this never happened. It was an unusual decision because Beryl rarely slept with her husband anyway and told him that since she didn't want sex with him, no other woman would either. It was a rather foolish assumption on her part. It is believed that while Beryl was away from the set recovering, George had a fling with his *Keep Fit* co-star Kay Walsh. It was not to be his last fixture playing away from home. On November 15, 1937, George appeared in his first Royal Variety Show at the London Palladium alongside fellow Lancastrian Gracie Fields. He was a massive star in the Soviet Union and in

1943 he was awarded the Order of Lenin. Following his last film, the Formbys travelled the world and George appeared in various stage shows including pantomime. Both suffered from ill health and George left the play *Zip Goes A Million* not as was assumed at the time because of an argument over pay but because he suffered an undiagnosed heart attack. He announced his retirement (again) after spending nine weeks recuperating. In September 1952 he was stricken with gastroenteritis and a suspected blood clot on the lung. In October 1953 he was back at work. In the summer of 1960 he began an affair with the gold-digging lesbian singer Yana. His last public performance was in November 1960 at London's Dorchester Hotel. On Christmas Day 1960 Beryl Formby died aged 60 of uterine cancer. On St Valentine's Day 1961 George became engaged to teacher Pat Howson (b. February 14, 1925), the daughter of family friends. CAUSE: On February 22, 1961, George suffered a heart attack while having dinner with his future in-laws. Prompt action from a doctor who lived three doors away saved his life and he was taken to St Joseph's Roman Catholic Hospital in Preston. On the morning of March 6, Pat Howson went out to buy her wedding ring, announcing that the ceremony had been brought forward to March 8. George Formby died that afternoon. He was 56. More than 150,000 people attended his funeral on March 10 at St Charles' Roman Catholic Church, Warrington. He was buried next to his father in Manchester Road Catholic cemetery, Warrington. Most of his £135,142 5s. 9d fortune went to his fiancée, much to the outrage of his family, none of whom had been close to him. On May 13, 1963, Eliza Booth and her daughters sued to overturn George's final will. In a fit of generosity Pat Howson offered Eliza Booth a one-off payment of £5,000 and the sisters £2,000 each,

even though George had not wanted them to have anything. She also agreed to meet the costs of both parties. The deal was grudgingly accepted but then the Booth women sought to have the ruling overturned. The matter was finally settled in Pat Howson's favour in September 1965 only after invention by the Solicitor-General Sir Dingle Foot. She died of cancer in a Lytham nursing home, aged 46, on November 22, 1971. Shortly before her death, Pat had announced that she intended to become a nun. FURTHER READING: *George Formby* – John Fisher (London: Woburn-Futura, 1975); *George Formby: A Troubled Genius* – David Bret (London: Robson Books, 2001).

Mimi Forsythe
(MARIE G. ARMSTRONG)
Born 1922
Died August 17, 1952
Tragic starlet. Mimi Forsythe made only two films before retiring. She landed one of those by accident. The role of Tamara in *Three Russian Girls* (1944) was slated for Oona O'Neill, but she withdrew when she married Charlie Chaplin. Mimi was cast and was a moderate success. Later she appeared as Julia Westcott in *Sensations Of 1945* (1944). She retired after marrying producer Benedict Bogeaus, but had a breakdown when he left her. CAUSE: She died by her own hand during a fit of depression in Hollywood, aged 30.

Barry Foster
Born August 21, 1927
Died February 11, 2002
Everyman. Barry Foster was born in Beeston, Nottinghamshire, the only child of toolsetter Charles Waterton Foster and Dora Dewey. After the family relocated to Hayes, Middlesex, during the depression, he was educated at Southall County Grammar School. In 1945, he joined the Fleet Air Arm as an air mechanic. From 1946 to 1947

he served on an FAA station on the Cromarty Firth, keeping grounded Barracudas ticking over. Before he was demobbed he took a course in photography and then having worked in a research laboratory for EMI, he considered becoming an industrial chemist. Deciding he would like a career on the stage, he then studied on a scholarship at the Central School of Speech and Drama. He made his first appearance on stage in August 1952 playing Lorenzo in *The Merchant Of Venice* in Cork in the Republic of Ireland. His first London part came nearly three years later in January 1955 as the electrician in Joseph Losey's production of Michael Burn's play, *The Night Of The Ball* at the New Theatre. He made his film début in *High Flight* (1956) as Wilcox and also appeared in *The Battle Of The River Plate* (1956) as Captain Bell's messenger, *Yangtse Incident* (1957) as PO McCarthy RN, *Sea Of Sand* (1958) as Corporal Matheson, *Sea Fury* (1958) as Vincent, *Dunkirk* (1958) as Don R, *Yesterday's Enemy* (1959), *Surprise Package* (1960) as US Marshal, *Playback* (1963) as Dave Hollis, *King And Country* (1964) as Lieutenant Webb, *The Family Way* (1966) as Joe Thompson, *Robbery* (1967) as Frank, *Twisted Nerve* (1968) as Gerry Henderson, *Inspector Clouseau* (1968) as Addison Steele, *The Guru* (1969) as Chris, *Battle Of Britain* (1969) as Squadron Leader Edwards, *Ryan's Daughter* (1970) as the republican commandant Tim O'Leary, *Frenzy* (1972) as the murderous grocer Robert Rusk, *Der Letzte Schrei* (1974) as Edward, *A Quiet Day In Belfast* (1974) as John Slattery, *The Wild Geese* (1978) as Thomas Balfour, *Danger On Dartmoor* (1980) as Green, *Heat And Dust* (1982) as Major Minnies, *The Whistle Blower* (1986) as Charles Greig, *Three Kinds Of Heat* (1987) as Norris, *Beyond The Next Mountain* (1987), *Maurice* (1987) as Dean Cornwallis, *The Killing Game* (1988) as Jack, *King Of The Wind* (1989) as Mr Williams,

The Free Frenchman (1989) as Major Trent and a doctor in *Rancid Aluminium* (2000). His first television big break came in 1965 when he played a young oil executive in *Mogul*, but he disliked the "factory-like atmosphere involved in doing a long series" and it would be five years before he returned to the small screen. It was as the Commisaris Piet Van Der Valk in the television series *Van Der Valk* (September 13–October 10, 1973, September 5–November 21, 1977, January 16, 1991–March 1992) that he became famous. Created by Nicolas Freeling, the show only ran for 13 episodes but acquired a hardcore following and when fans addressed letters to "Van Der Valk, London" or "Herr Foster, England", they usually reached their destination. The theme tune 'Eye Level', written by the Dutch composer Jan Stoeckhart under the *nom de plume* of Jack Trombey and performed by the Simon Park Orchestra, even reached number one in the charts for four weeks. Some claimed that *Van Der Valk* did not fare well because it clashed in the schedules with *Till Death Us Do Part*. An attempt to revive the show in 1976 failed because of union intervention so it took another year before the commisaris was back pounding the water-filled streets of Amsterdam. The show was back again in 1991 at a cost of £6 million and 13 million people tuned in. Foster said that he was "the wrong shape, the wrong size, the wrong colour to be a British police hero". He once opined of Van Der Valk, "He can be just like the kids. It is the style of the place. The police over here cannot be astonished, and this is one thing about the character Van Der Valk. He is understanding and does not disapprove. That isn't his job, anyway. He's a lovely guy to play, a thoughtful, unorthodox cop with a touch of the private eye." Some critics compared Foster's character to Inspector Morse which was ironic because Foster was forever being recognised in the streets as John Thaw. In 1955 Barry Foster married Judith Shergold, a former singer in West End musicals. They had two daughters, Joanna and Miranda, who are actresses, and a son, Jason. Barry Foster attributed his versatility partly to a lack of distinguishing features, once remarking: "I'm neither very tall nor very short. You can't look at my face and say, "He's the killer', or 'the guy next door', or 'the mad scientist'. All I've got is my curly hair – which everyone thinks is a wig anyway." CAUSE: Barry Foster died aged 74 of a heart attack in Guildford, Surrey.

John Frankenheimer

Born February 19, 1930
Died July 6, 2002
Televisual graduate. John Michael Frankenheimer was born in an affluent section of Queens in New York, the son of a stockbroker and an Irish Catholic mother. He attended the Roman Catholic LaSalle Military Academy in Long Island, but by the time he graduated in 1947 he had lost his faith. Then he matriculated at Williams College in Massachusetts where he studied English. He also showed promise as a tennis player and for a time considered that as a profession. He also contemplated becoming an actor but was too shy to tread the boards. He joined the US air force and worked in the post room of the Pentagon. He was then transferred to the new movie squadron based at Burbank in California. Frankenheimer was allowed a certain latitude provided his men kept out of trouble. Determined to keep their noses clean, he sent them to lunch at 9.30am and performed every task – lighting, photography and editing – himself. Frankenheimer was demobbed in 1953 and moved to New York where he landed a job as an assistant director at CBS. In 1954 he directed *The Plot Against King Solomon*. During the course of the next five years

Frankenheimer directed 152 live shows, which included versions of *The Last Tycoon*, *For Whom The Bell Tolls* and *The Turn Of The Screw*, and winning 14 Emmys. He made his feature film début with *The Young Stranger* (1956). However, the film was not critically well received and Frankenheimer returned to television. His next movie was *The Young Savages* (1961), a tale of gang warfare between Puerto Ricans and Italians. His next two films, *Birdman Of Alcatraz* (1962) about the murderer Robert Stroud (who despite the film never actually kept birds in Alcatraz) and *All Fall Down* (1962) about sibling rivalry, established his reputation. Frankenheimer only took over *Birdman Of Alcatraz* when Charles Crichton, the original director, dropped out. Two of his most popular films, *The Manchurian Candidate* (1962) ("a brilliant spy thriller" – Halliwell), about a politician based obviously on the deranged Senator Joe McCarthy, which gave Angela Lansbury an Oscar nomination and *Seven Days In May* (1964) about a *coup d'état*, borrowed from his TV days and saw the screen replete with television monitors. Frankenheimer was no slouch when it came to utilising others' ideas. He borrowed Gregg Toland's (director of photography on *Citizen Kane*) trick of using deep focus lenses so that foreground and background were in equally sharp relief. He also borrowed heavily from Soviet director Sergei Eisenstein and used his editing ideas in an early Frankenheimer flick *The Young Savages* (1961). For *The Train* (1964) Frankenheimer threw out the original script and had a new one written at great cost. As the years went by Frankenheimer fell from favour not just because it seemed the public wanted less intelligent films but also because Frankenheimer ran out of steam and ideas. The film that really wrecked his reputation was *Seconds* (1966), a sci-fi film that saw John Randolph, a Wall

Street worker, transformed into Rock Hudson by plastic surgery. The cinematographer James Wong Howe argued against Frankenheimer's desire to use a fish-eye lens but still went on to win an Academy Award nomination. However, the public did not warm to the film. The rest of Frankenheimer's canon barely rose above the adequate. They included *99 And 44/100 Per Cent Dead* (1974), *French Connection II* (1975), *Black Sunday* (1976), *Prophecy* (1979), *The Challenge* (1982), *52 Pick Up* (1986), *Year Of The Gun* (1991), *The Island Of Dr Moreau* (1996) and *Ronin* (1998). In the Seventies he developed a drink problem which he said came as a result of the assassination of his close friend Robert F. Kennedy. Kennedy was staying at Frankenheimer's house, and Frankenheimer drove him to the Ambassador Hotel the night he was killed in June 1968. 6'3" Frankenheimer was an ardent Francophile speaking fluent French and cooking French food. He was married three times. His first wife (in 1951) was Joanne Evans. It was a marriage of convenience. He was due to be called up and he forced the air force to pay for her to live with him. They had an agreement to divorce when he was demobbed and they did. In 1954 he married Carolyn Miller, and he had two daughters, Elise and Kristi, before their divorce. In 1964 he married Evan Evans.

CAUSE: He died aged 72 at Cedars-Sinai Medical Center, Los Angeles, of a stroke due to complications following spinal surgery.

Mark Frechette

Born December 4, 1947
Died September 27, 1975
Jailbird. In 1970 Frechette was signed to star in Michelangelo Antonioni's movie *Zabriskie Point*. The film was about a disaffected youth who fell into a life of crime and eventually died in a police cell.

CAUSE: Four years later, in April 1974, the by now disaffected Frechette, then aged 26, was jailed for 15 years in Boston, Massachusetts, for attempted bank robbery. While still in custody in Walpole State Prison, Norfolk, Massachusetts, he was found dead in the prison gym, a 150lb weightlifting bar having fallen on his throat.

Lynne Frederick

Born July 25, 1954
Died April 27, 1994
Impossible gold digger. Born in Hillingdon, Middlesex, the daughter of a Thames TV casting director, Lynne Frederick was one of a gaggle of attractive brunettes in and around the film world in the Seventies. She was always there or thereabouts, never quite making the final cut. She appeared as Mary Custance in *No Blade Of Grass* (1970) and followed that with *Nicholas And Alexandra* (1971) as Grand Duchess Tatiana, *Vampire Circus* (1972) as Dora Mueller, *The Amazing Mr Blunden (1972) as Lucy Alen, Henry VIII And His Six Wives* (1973) as Catherine Howard, *Giubbe Rosse* (1974), *Largo Retorno* (1975), *Voyage Of The Damned* (1976) as Anna Rosen, *Schizo* (1977) as Samantha and *The Prisoner Of Zenda* (1979) as Princess Flavia. Like many actresses she posed for topless pictures, and appeared nude in *Schizo*. She had been romantically involved with (Sir) David Frost before hooking up with Peter Sellers. They married in Paris on February 18, 1977, and appeared together in *The Prisoner Of Zenda* but separated not long afterwards. In October 1979 they reconciled, but Sellers became increasingly jealous of his young wife. They separated again but before the divorce could be finalised, Sellers died of a heart attack. Frederick flew to London, where she played the part of the grieving widow to perfection and much to the annoyance of Sellers' children. Following his death from a heart attack (he left her $9.6 million in his will), she resumed

her affair with David Frost and they married on January 24, 1981. They were together for 18 months and one miscarriage before the divorce. Before she hit 30, Frederick married (in December 1982) her third wealthy husband, Californian heart specialist Barry Unger. They had a daughter, Cassie, before their 1991 divorce. Strangely, Frederick remained Mrs Peter Sellers on her credit cards even after two more failed marriages.

CAUSE: Following her third divorce she began drinking heavily (mostly vodka) and dabbling in drugs. She spent £2,500 a week on cocaine and was banned from several restaurants because of her drunken behaviour. Frederick rose late and drank by herself; she even stopped opening her post after a while. She binged on food, reaching 14st shortly before her death. She died aged 39 in Los Angeles, California, after choking on spaghetti and meatballs. Her funeral took place at the Little Chapel of the Dawn in Santa Monica.

Billy Fury
(RONALD WYCHERLEY)
Born April 17, 1940
Died January 28, 1983
Britain's Elvis. Born at 126 Smithdown Road, Garston, Liverpool, the elder son of Albert Edward Wycherley, a cobbler, and Sarah Jane (known as Jean) Homer, the young Ron Wycherley went to school with Ringo Starr (St Silas' Primary School) and then went to Wellington Road Secondary Modern but was a sickly child (he had rheumatic fever at the age of six which damaged his heart valves). Despite poor health Ron became a rivet thrower in an engineering factory and then landed a job as a deckhand on a tugboat in the Mersey estuary. A self-taught guitarist, he occasionally played as part of the Formby Skiffle Group under the name Stean Wade. In 1958 he sent a tape of six of his own songs to the impresario Larry Parnes,

who invited him to perform backstage to Marty Wilde at the Birkenhead Essoldo. The impromptu audition was successful and he was given a spot in that night's show. Billy was signed to a management contract by Parnes and given the name Billy Fury. On November 26, 1958, he signed with Decca Records, having been turned down by Philips. Unlike today's instant pop stars who tour after one single, Billy Fury was sent on a tour of Britain to learn his trade and get his name known. His blond hair and skin-tight, lamé suits wowed teenagers wherever he went. On February 27, 1959, he had a hit with his own song, 'Maybe Tomorrow', reaching number 18 and staying in the hit parade for nine weeks. He followed that with the self-penned 'Margo' (number 28, June 1959), 'Colette' (number 9, March 1960) and 'That's Love' (number 19, May 1960). In October 1959 his act was terminated at the Theatre Royal, Dublin, after it was deemed "offensive" by the management. He toned down his stage act and began appearing on the Jack Good television shows *Oh Boy!*, *Boy Meets Girl*, and *Wham!*. Before one tour, in Liverpool, Parnes and Fury auditioned (but turned down) the nascent Beatles as Fury's potential backing group. Instead, Parnes assembled the Blue Flames, led by pianist Georgie Fame. After releasing *The Sound Of Fury* in June 1960, Fury was deserted by the Blue Flames. Disappointed by what he saw as their lack of loyalty Fury began to cover American hits such as 'Halfway To Paradise' (number 3, May 1961), 'Jealousy' (number 2, September 1961) and 'I'd Never Find Another You' (number 5, December 1961). 'Halfway To Paradise' and 'Jealousy' earned silver discs for sales of 250,000. Fury became very wealthy, owning homes in St John's Wood, London and Dorking, Surrey, where his house was set in 12 acres. In 1959 he made his acting début as a Teddy boy in *Strictly For*

Sparrows, a television play by Ted Willis. He made his film début in 1962 playing Billy Universe in Michael Winner's *Play It Cool*. The film was a popular success although Fury was, to all intents and purposes, playing himself. He was also in *I've Gotta Horse* (1965) as Billy and played Stormy Tempest in the David Essex vehicle *That'll Be The Day* (1973). In 1965 he made his only appearance on American television and also appeared for the only time in panto with *Aladdin* at the New Theatre, Oxford. He signed a new recording contract with EMI's Parlophone label and released 11 singles between 1966 and 1968 but they nearly all flopped. In 1971 he founded his own record company, Fury, to release his own work and that of other singers including Shane Fenton (later Alvin Stardust). In 1974 he took part in a rock'n'roll revival tour with Marty Wilde and four years later he re-recorded his early hits for the K-Tel company after being declared bankrupt, thanks to unscrupulous management. In the Seventies he bought a 100-acre farm near Llandovery in north Wales, where he bred sheep and horses and became a keen ornithologist. He began recording again in 1981 and his final album, *The One And Only*, was released posthumously in March 1983. Three singles released between September 1982 and June 1983 only dented the lower reaches of the charts. For eight years from 1959 he lived with the spiritualist Audrey Valentine (Lee) Middleton (b. Sheffield, February 14, 1935). She later married the homosexual DJ Kenny Everett (b. 14 Hereford Road, Seaforth, Liverpool, December 25, 1944 at 3am as Maurice Cole, d. Lexham Gardens, Kensington, London, April 4, 1995 at 10.43am aged 50 of AIDS). On May 31, 1969, Fury was married to the ex-model Judith Hall, a friend of Lee Middleton, but they divorced with Fury commenting, "We were two people who never should have got married." From 1971 until his death, he lived with Lisa Fiona Rosen (b. June 18, 1953), now Lisa Voice, who became a property magnate and, according to *The Sunday Times* (April 2005), is worth £30 million.

CAUSE: Billy Fury suffered from poor health for many years which blighted his career. In 1971 he developed a serious heart condition. He underwent an operation to repair two valves in his heart. He said, "Before the operation I couldn't even walk around the block without getting weak . . . I really came to accept that I would go out under the anaesthetic and never wake up. When I saw the nursing sister looking down at me after the operation it was the most beautiful sight I had ever seen." He hoped one day to open a bird sanctuary on his farm on the Surrey–Sussex border but it was not to be. Later in the decade Fury again underwent major heart surgery. In March 1982 he collapsed, suffering from paralysis and temporary blindness. He recovered but it was to be a temporary respite. Fury died aged 42 of heart disease in St Mary's Hospital, Harrow Road, Westminster, London. He was buried on February 4, 1983 at Paddington New Cemetery, Mill Hill, London. A lectern was inscribed in his honour in Liverpool Cathedral. He was worth less than £40,000 at the time of his death.

G

Clark Gable

Born February 1, 1901
Died November 16, 1960

The King of Hollywood. Clark Gable was born in Cadiz, Ohio, at 4.30am, the son of thrice-married William Henry Gable (b. 1870 d. August 4, 1948 of a heart attack), an oil driller, and Adeline Hershelman (b. 1870 d. Meadville, Pennsylvania November 14, 1901 of an epileptic fit). Some sources report that Gable was mistakenly listed on his birth certificate as a female. It was an inauspicious start to a life that had 6′1″ Gable labelled "The King Of Hollywood" in 1937 and hit its apotheosis two years later with *Gone With The Wind* (1939) even though he did not want to be in the film. It was an odd monicker, because Gable, a freemason, was, by his own admission, a poor lover, underendowed, had false teeth and bad breath. He and Cary Grant would exchange unwanted monogrammed Christmas gifts. *Mogambo* (1953) co-star Ava Gardner said, "He's the kind of guy who, if you say, 'Hiya Clark, how are you' is stuck for an answer." Even fourth wife, Carole Lombard, opined, "Listen, he's no Clark Gable at home." Despite all this, Gable was still one of the most popular figures in Hollywood. He finished full-time education when he was 14 and worked in a tyre factory in Akron, Ohio. There he became interested in the theatre and worked his evenings free of charge as a call boy. Just as it seemed he was about to achieve his break, his father took him to drill for oil in Oklahoma. However, in 1922 he abandoned his father and joined a repertory company headed by Josephine Dillon (b. Denver, Colorado January 26, 1884, d. Verdugo City,

California, November 10, 1971). On December 13, 1924, Gable married her (some sources list December 18 and say that the marriage was never consummated) and moved to Hollywood, where he began appearing in bit parts. She arranged for him to have a makeover – he had a new hairstyle and his rotten teeth were repaired. He appeared in *White Man* (1924), *Forbidden Paradise* (1924), *Declassée* (1925), *The Merry Widow* (1925) and *North Star* (1926) as Archie West but stardom eluded him. He left his wife (they divorced on April Fool's Day 1930) and began touring, ending up on Broadway where Lionel Barrymore arranged a screen test for him. Preparing for his film *Little Caesar* in 1930, director Mervyn LeRoy made what he thought was an excellent test of Gable. When he screened it for executives Darryl F. Zanuck and Jack L. Warner, he was told, "Why do you throw away $500 of our money on a test of that big ape? Didn't you see those ears when you talked to him? And those big feet and hands, not to mention that ugly face of his?" In December 1930 Gable signed a contract with MGM at $350 a week, reporting to Irving Thalberg. Around May 1931 he began an affair with Joan Crawford that was to last on and off for the rest of his life. On June 19, 1931 at the Santa Ana Courthouse, Gable married, as her fourth husband, the wealthy socialite Ria Franklin Prentiss Lucas Langham (b. January 17, 1884 as Maria Franklin d. Houston, Texas, September 24, 1966). Between 1931 and 1933 he appeared in *Night Nurse* (1931) as Nick, *Dance, Fools, Dance* (1931) as Jake Luva, *The Painted Desert* (1931) as Rance Brett, *Laughing Sinners* (1931) as Carl Loomis, *Sporting Blood* (1931) as Rid Riddell, *Possessed* (1931) as Mark Whitney, *Strange Interlude* (1932) as Ned Darrell, *No Man Of Her Own* (1932) as Babe Stewart, *Polly Of The Circus* (1932) as Reverend John Hartley, *Hold Your Man*

(1933) as Eddie and *Dancing Lady* (1933) as Patch Gallagher. However, it was his performance in Clarence Brown's *A Free Soul* (released June 20, 1931) that made his name. Gable played Ace Wilfong, a gangster, who roughed up Jan Ashe (Norma Shearer). Shearer's husband, Irving Thalberg, suggested the scene thinking that it would turn the audience against the character. In fact, it had the opposite effect. "It was Clark who made villains popular," said Shearer later. "Instead of the audience wanting the good guy to get the girl, they wanted the heavy to win her." The following year he was in *Red Dust* (1932) as Dennis Carson opposite the gorgeous Jean Harlow and became MGM's leading man. Gable was not happy though. In 1933 Gable was fretful over his private life and began to drink heavily. One night he was driving to Sunset Boulevard from the Hollywood Hills when he took a corner too sharply and hit and killed a pedestrian. Determined to save Gable and MGM from any harmful publicity studio mogul Louis B. Mayer bribed one of his junior executives to take the rap for Gable. The man served a year on a manslaughter charge having obtained a promise from Mayer of a guaranteed lifetime's employment at the studio. It was in June of that year that all of Gable's remaining teeth were removed after an infection. Gable began moaning about the type of role he was required to play – usually a brute – and complained to Mayer. The mogul decided to punish the star by lending him to Columbia to play Peter Warne in what was thought to be a minor film originally called *Night Bus* and directed by Frank Capra. The film became *It Happened One Night* (1934) and won Gable an Oscar, which he later gave to the son of a friend. It was said that when Clark Gable removed his shirt in the film and revealed a bare chest, the sales of vests plummeted. The film is also responsible for magic time. Gable left his motel room at 2am,

drove around New York, wrote a story for his newspaper and returned to his room, where the clock still said 2am! From 1934 Gable could do virtually no wrong (apart from 1937 when he starred as Charles Stewart Parnell in the flop *Parnell* and was sued for $150,000 by an Englishwoman, Violet Norton, a 47-year-old woman from Essex over the paternity of her daughter, Gwendoline, born in June 1923!). She claimed that Gable had seduced her when he visited England in September 1922 but Gable had not been issued a passport until 1930. It was an elaborate publicity stunt) and he appeared in *Chained* (1934) as Michael Bradley, *Forsaking All Others* (1934) as Jeff Williams, *The Call Of The Wild* (1935) as Jack Thornton, *China Seas* (1935) as Captain Alan Gaskell, *Mutiny On The Bounty* (1935) as Fletcher Christian, *Cain And Mabel* (1936) as Larry Cain, *San Francisco* (1936) as Blackie Norton, *Saratoga* (1937) as Duke Bradley, *Too Hot To Handle* (1938) as Chris Hunter and *Test Pilot* (1938) as Jim Lane. In *Mutiny On The Bounty* (1935) he played Fletcher Christian opposite Charles Laughton as Captain Bligh and was nominated for an Oscar. On tour to promote the film, Gable was mobbed wherever he went. "This power over women that I'm supposed to have was never noticed when I was on Broadway," he said. "I don't know when I got it. And by God, I can't explain it." In November 1935 he and the second Mrs Gable separated. He had impregnated Loretta Young and their daughter, Judy Lewis, was born on November 6, 1935, but didn't find out the truth of her parentage until 1957. The world was told that Young had adopted a daughter. At a party on January 25, 1936, Gable bumped into the foul-mouthed blonde actress Carole Lombard and they began a relationship. On December 9, 1937, he was "crowned" King Of Hollywood by columnist Ed Sullivan in a ceremony at the El Capitan Theatre in Hollywood. Standing nearby was Carole Lombard who whispered *sotto voce*, "If Clark had an inch less, he'd be Queen of the Movies." Oddly, what was unknown to the public was that Lombard was making more money than her boyfriend. Gable was cast as Chris Hunter in *Too Hot To Handle* (1938) opposite Myrna Loy who had been named Queen of Hollywood in the poll. During the filming, with Lombard on set, he rescued Loy from a burning plane. Loy was never sure if she had been in real danger or if it had been a publicity stunt. Lombard was not impressed when Gable continued holding Loy after the cameras had stopped rolling. On December 14, 1938 Gable announced that he and the second Mrs Gable were seeking a divorce. On January 13, 1939 David O. Selznick announced that the long search to find Scarlett O'Hara in *Gone With The Wind* had been completed and that Vivien Leigh had been chosen over dozens of American hopefuls. Gable was the second choice for Rhett Butler and did not want to play the role anyway. Gary Cooper opined, "*Gone With The Wind* is going to be the biggest flop in Hollywood history. I'm just glad it'll be Clark Gable who's falling flat on his face and not me." The film began shooting on January 26, 1939 and Gable shot his first scenes with Leigh five days later. She complained about his bad breath and he complained about virtually everything from his costumes to the script or lack of one to Selznick's insistence that he speak his lines in a southern accent – Gable refused, hoping that he would be sacked. In his younger days Gable had not been averse to doling out sexual favours to gay men in return for work or a meal. One of these encounters had been with William Haines, an actor whose career was ruined when he was caught in bed with another man at the YMCA. Haines was a popular man and his

Hollywood friends gathered round and offered him jobs to decorate their mansions. One of his clients was George Cukor, the director of *Gone With The Wind*. When Gable saw Haines and Cukor laughing and joking he was convinced that Haines was telling the closeted gay Cukor that he and Gable had been lovers. Gable went to see Selznick and demanded that Cukor be sacked. On February 12, Cukor was removed and replaced by Victor Fleming, who had spats with Leigh and at one stage left the production for a fortnight after suffering a breakdown. Sam Wood took over until Fleming was fit enough to return. *Gone With The Wind* ended on June 27, 1939, with post-production work (including a fifth version of the opening scene) going to November 11, 1939. Gable was bitterly disappointed not to win another Oscar for his portrayal of Rhett Butler. Eight months earlier, on March 29, 1939, exactly three weeks after his divorce from Ria, Gable and Lombard were married at the First Methodist Episcopal Church, Kingman, Arizona by the Reverend Kenneth Engle. At 3am on April 2, the happy couple went to her home where her mother and brothers were waiting whereupon Gable went straight to bed. To her puzzled mother, Lombard said, "Clark's tired and he has enough trouble performing under the best of circumstances." On January 25, 1940, MGM gave Gable a new seven-year contract at $7,500-a-week. Gable's next film was *Strange Cargo* (1940) as convict André Verne in his last film with Joan Crawford followed by *Boom Town* (1940) as Big John McMasters – Gable's last film with Spencer Tracy, *Comrade X* (1940) as McKinley B. Thompson, *They Met In Bombay* (1941) as Gerald Meldrick opposite Rosalind Russell, *Honky Tonk* (1941) as Candy Johnson with Lana Turner and *Somewhere I'll Find You* (released August 1942) as Jonathon Davis also with Lana Turner, then tragedy struck.

In December 1940, Gable and Lombard had an audience with President Franklin D. Roosevelt who told them that America must help Britain in her war effort. For days after, Lombard spoke of nothing else. When America was attacked on December 7, 1941 the couple determined to help even more. The Secretary of the Treasury Henry Morgenthau, Jr asked MGM if it would allow any of its stars to travel the country selling war bonds. Lombard was asked to go to Indiana, her home state and she agreed but the studio refused to let Gable go with her because he was filming *Somewhere I'll Find You* so she went with her mother and Otto Winkler, Gable's PR. She left California on January 12, 1942. Three days later, she was in Indianapolis where she sold more than $2,017,513 of war bonds. Each one came with a personally signed photograph of Lombard. It took her more than six hours to sign all the pictures and never once did she complain. Missing Gable, she decided to fly back and despite the reservations of her mother and Mr Winkler, they set off at 4am the next day. Some time after 7.07pm, the plane crashed into Table Rock Mountain near Las Vegas killing all on board. Lombard, 33, was decapitated on impact. Gable flew out to Nevada but there was nothing that he could do. The remains were gathered up and put into wooden crates. Gable accompanied the crates marked Lombard, her mother and Mr Winkler but in truth no one knew who was in them and for all he knew Gable may have accompanied the remains of some of the military personnel who also died. Gable turned to drink to numb his pain. Lombard left her entire estate to her husband, much to the annoyance of her brothers who never spoke to him again. After *Somewhere I'll Find You* Gable was not to make another film for three years. Gable's friend and sometime lover Joan Crawford took Lombard's role in *They All Kissed The*

Bride (1942) and donated her $125,000 fee to the Red Cross. "My agent made the deal," she said. "When he took 10 per cent, I fired the bastard." On August 12, 1942, Clark Gable enlisted in the air force as 191-257-41 Gable. He was photographed shaving off his moustache but no pictures were taken of him after his haircut so as not to showcase his enormous ears. On October 28, he became 056-5390 2nd Lieutenant Gable and on January 7, 1943, he got his officer's wings. On January 28 he was assigned to 508th Squadron of the 351st Heavy Bombardment Group. For a time he was stationed at RAF Polebrook whence he flew five combat missions, including one to Germany, as an observer-gunner in B-17 Flying Fortresses between May 4 and September 23, 1943. Despite reports Gable was not awarded the Distinguished Flying Cross. Hitler supposedly put a bounty on Gable's head. The actor rose to the rank of major before he was discharged. Captain Ronald Reagan signed Gable's discharge papers. Back in Hollywood, Gable chased women most of whom were more than happy to be caught. His films *Homecoming* and *Command Decision* (both 1948) were forgettable flops. In Santa Barbara on December 20, 1949 he married, as her fourth husband, Sylvia, Lady Ashley (b. Paddington, London, April 1, 1904 as Edith Louisa Hawkes, d. Los Angeles, California, June 30, 1977, of cancer) who had been the second wife of Douglas Fairbanks. Gable divorced her on May 31, 1951. To avoid a hefty tax bill, Gable travelled to Europe and made *Never Let Me Go* (1953), *Mogambo* (1953) and *Betrayed* (1954). In 1954 his contract with MGM ended after arguments with new boss Dore Schary. He filmed *Soldier Of Fortune* and *The Tall Men* (both 1955). On July 11, 1955 he married for the fifth and final time to Kay Williams Capps de Alzaga Ungue Spreckels (b. August 7, 1916, d. Houston, Texas, May 25, 1983, of heart failure). Gable's finest performance came, perhaps, in *The Misfits* (1961). Filming was due to begin in the autumn of 1959 but Marilyn Monroe's commitment to *Let's Make Love* (1960) and Gable's to *It Happened In Naples* (1960) delayed shooting. The new start date was March 30, 1960, but an actors' strike delayed the filming of *Let's Make Love* by five weeks which, in turn, delayed *The Misfits*. Almost immediately after the completion of *Let's Make Love*, Marilyn flew to New York for costume fittings. Finally, shooting began at 9am on July 18, 1960, only to shut down a week later because director John Huston's gambling caused a cash flow problem, a situation that was to cause further stoppages later in the shoot. Marilyn's first scene was filmed on July 21. Shooting was postponed on July 30, and again on August 1, because Marilyn was 'indisposed'. After numerous problems the film wrapped on November 4, 1960. It had run 40 days over schedule and cost $3,955,000, making it the most expensive black-and-white film then made. Coincidentally, Gable also appeared opposite Jean Harlow, the century's other most potent sex symbol, in her last film (*Saratoga*, [1937]). Gable, who had dieted from 16st to 14st for the film, was worn out by Marilyn's continual lateness on the set and failure to learn her lines. However, he never publicly criticised her. To alleviate his boredom, the 59-year-old star often performed his own stunts, against all advice. One involved him being dragged behind a truck travelling at 30mph. When Gable's scenes were finished on November 4, he remarked, "Christ, I'm glad this picture's finished. She near gave me a damn heart attack. I've never been happier when a film ended." The following day he suffered a heart attack.

CAUSE: Gable died eleven days after the heart attack. The usual line was to blame Marilyn Monroe for Gable's demise but it must be remembered that Gable had volunteered to do his own stunts (at age 59) and had smoked 60 cigarettes a day for 30 years. Gable was cremated and his ashes interred at Forest Lawn Memorial-Parks, 1712 South Glendale Avenue, Glendale, California 91209. Gable once told a reporter his epitaph would read "He was lucky and he knew it." However, his final resting place, next to Carole Lombard, bears no such legend. His much-longed-for son, John Clark, was born on March 20, 1961, after his father's death. (Gable also fathered Loretta Young's daughter but the paternity was not admitted until long after his death.)

FURTHER READING: *Clark Gable –* George Carpozi, Jr. (New York: Pyramid Books, 1961); *Dear Mr. G – The Biography Of Clark Gable –* Jean Garceau with Inez Cocke (London: Four Square, 1961); *Long Live The King: A Biography Of Clark Gable –* Lyn Tornabene (New York: Pocket Books, 1976); *Gable & Lombard –* Warren G. Harris (London: Corgi, 1977); *Gable's Women –* Jane Ellen Wayne (New York: Prentice Hall Press, 1987); *Clark Gable: Portrait Of A Misfit –* Jane Ellen Wayne (London: Robson Books, 1993); *Clark Gable: Tormented Star –* David Bret (London: JR Books, 2007).

Eva Gabor

Born February 11, 1919
Died July 4, 1995

Glamorous sister. Born in Budapest, Hungary, Eva Gabor was the first of the legendary sisters to migrate to America. The Gabor sisters' habit of rewriting history is legendary, so much of what they 'reveal' must be treated with caution. Eva married Eric Drimmer in 1939 and divorced him less than three years later, on February 24, 1942. She began appearing in films in 1941 and featured in, among others, *Forced*

Landing (1941) as Johanna Van Deuren (shot in just ten days), *Pacific Blackout* (1941) as Marie Duval, *Star Spangled Rhythm* (1942), *The Wife Of Monte Cristo* (1946) as Madame Maillard, *Song Of Surrender* (1949) as Countess Marina, *Tarzan And The Slave Girl* (1950), *Love Island* (1952) as Sarna, *Captain Kidd And The Slave Girl* (1954), *Artists And Models* (1955) as Sonia, *Don't Go Near The Water* (1957) as Deborah Aldrich, *Gigi* (1958) as Liane d'Exelmans, *It Started With A Kiss* (1959) as Marquesa de la Rey, *Youngblood Hawke* (1964) as Fannie Prince and *The Princess Academy* (1987) as Countess Von Pupsin. She was probably best known for her role as Lisa Douglas on the TV series *Green Acres*. Like all the Gabors, she made several trips up the aisle. In September 1943, she married millionaire estate agent Charles Isaacs (divorced April 5, 1949, four days after Zsa Zsa married George Sanders). On April 6, 1956, Dr John Williams became the third Mr Gabor – the couple separated on November 28 of the same year. On October 6, 1959, she wed Richard Brown, a match that proved to be her longest marriage (13 years) and on September 27, 1973, she married tycoon Frank Gard Jameson (divorced 1983). Away from the screen she was chairman of the world's largest wig-making company. Eva (pronounced A-va) bore a striking resemblance to her elder sister, something which, on occasion, she used to her advantage. Swimming nude one day she was greeted by someone calling "Hello, Eva." "No, darlink, Zsa Zsa," came the reply.
CAUSE: In June 1995 Eva was holidaying with friends at her home in Baja, Mexico. On the 20th of that month she supposedly "ate a bad piece of fruit", which led to viral pneumonia. This made her giddy and she fell down her stairs, breaking her hip. She was flown back to America, thanks to the generosity of her 'boyfriend' TV personality Merv Griffin, and admitted to Cedars-Sinai Hospital Medical Center, 8700 Beverly Boulevard, Los Angeles, California, on June 21. Her condition deteriorated and she died aged 76 of respiratory failure due to adult respiratory distress syndrome and bilateral pneumoccal pneumonia at 10.05am. She was buried in Westwood Village Memorial Park, 1218 Glendon Avenue, Los Angeles, California 90024.
FURTHER READING: *Such Devoted Sisters: Those Fabulous Gabors* – Peter H. Brown (London: Robson Books, 1986).

Don Galloway
Born July 27, 1937
Died January 8, 2009
Ironside's friend. Born in Brooksville, Kentucky, the son of Paul Galloway and Malee Poe, Donald Poe Galloway began his acting in the Fifties in the soap opera *The Secret Storm*. He signed with Universal Studios in 1963 and guest starred in a number of shows before landing the role of Sergeant Ed Brown in the cop show *A Man Called Ironside* (1967–1975). Eighteen years later, he reprised the role in a television film, *The Return Of Ironside*. His other films included: *The Rare Breed* (1966) as Jamie Bowen, *Gunfight In Abilene* (1967) as Ward Kent, *Ride To Hangman's Tree* (1967) as Nevada Jones, *Rough Night In Jericho* (1967) as Jace, *Satan's Mistress* (1982) as Carl, *The Big Chill* (1983), *Two Moon Junction* (1988) as Senator Delongpre, *Listen To Me* (1989) as a coach at Harvard and *The Doom Generation* (1995). 6'2" Galloway became a reserve deputy sheriff for the San Bernardino County Sheriff's Department in 1993. On September 27, 1963 he married first wife, Linda Dale Robinson, by whom he had two daughters, Tracy and Jennifer. In 1989 he married Linda Marie. He retired from acting in the Nineties.
CAUSE: Galloway suffered a stroke on

Christmas 2008 and was taken into hospital where he stayed until his death at the Renown Regional Medical Center, Reno, Nevada. He was 71. By coincidence his mother died in Christmas 1989 and his mother-in-law at Christmas 2007.

Matthew Garber

Born March 25, 1956
Died June 13, 1977

Child star. Matthew Garber was born in London and made his film début in *The Three Lives Of Thomasina* (1963) playing Geordie but he shot to fame as Michael Banks in *Mary Poppins* (1964). Garber was an unenthusiastic star and made just one more film, Disney's *The Gnome-Mobile* (1967) in which he portrayed Rodney Winthrop. By coincidence the actress who played his sister, Elizabeth, in the film was Karen Dotrice who had also been his screen sister in *Mary Poppins*.
CAUSE: Garber died aged 21 in Hampstead of pancreatitis.

Greta Garbo

(GRETA LOVISA GUSTAFSSON)
Born September 18, 1905
Died April 15, 1990

Solitary Swede. 5′6″ Greta Garbo was the most enigmatic of all film stars. Frederic March revealed, "Co-starring with Garbo hardly constituted an introduction." Friends called her "GG" or if they were less well acquainted "Miss G". No one called her "Greta". She retired nearly 50 years before her death yet her legend lived on. Greta Garbo was born in Södra Maternity Hospital, Stockholm, Sweden, at 7.30pm weighing 7lb 7oz, the second and younger daughter of Karl Alfred 'Kalle' Gustafsson (b. Frinnaryd, Sweden, May 11, 1871 as Karl Alfrid Johansson, d. June 1, 1920 of inflammation of the kidneys) and Anna Lovisa Karlsdotter (b. Högsby, September 10, 1872, d. Scarsdale, New York, October 18, 1944 of a coronary thrombosis). Their son Sven Alfred was

born in Södra Maternity Hospital, Stockholm, Sweden on July 26, 1898 – 10 weeks after his parents were married. Between 1929 and 1930 he would make three films, two as Sven Garbo and one as Sven Gustafsson. He died of an acute heart attack at the Desert Hospital, Palm Springs, on January 27, 1967. On June 14, 1919, Garbo graduated from school and was confirmed on April 18, 1920. Garbo lost her virginity one summer in her early teens, when she and her prettier elder sister, Alva Maria (b. Stockholm, Sweden, September 20, 1903, d. Stockholm, Sweden, April 21, 1926 of lymphatic cancer), had sex together outdoors in a tent. Soon thereafter, a local boy also made use of the same tent to have sex with Greta. When she was 14 she worked in a barber's shop preparing customers for a shave. She then modelled hats in a shop, which led to a newspaper advert that went on to an advertising film which was spotted by Eric Petchser, a director of Swedish comedies. He cast her in *Luffar-Petter* (premièred Boxing Day, 1922 at the Odeon Theatre, Stockholm) in which she played a character called Greta. Mauritz Stiller (b. Helsinki, July 17, 1883 as Movscha Stiller) saw this and starred her in the four-hour long *Gösta Berlings Saga* (premièred March 10 – Part 1 – and March 17 – Part 2 – 1924 at the Röda Kvarn, Stockholm) as Countess Elisabeth Dohna and renamed her Greta Garbo on December 4, 1923. (He had already chosen the name – he was looking for someone to inherit it.) Stiller was offered a contract by MGM but he refused to sign it unless his lover and protégée Garbo was offered a deal as well. "Tell her in America men don't like fat women," boss Louis B. Mayer said to Stiller, but common sense prevailed. It took some time for MGM to appreciate the treasure they had unwittingly uncovered. The press office labelled her, "The Mysterious Stranger" because of her lack of desire to do publicity. Her first American film was *The Torrent* (1926) as Leonora Moreno. It was lucky that sound films had yet to make their appearance because Garbo couldn't speak a word of English at the time. *The Torrent* made Garbo a star and Mayer offered her a higher salary even before the film's February 21, 1926 première at the Capitol Theater, New York and Loew's State Theater, Los Angeles. Stiller was replaced for Garbo's next film, *The Temptress* (premièred October 10, 1926 at the Capitol Theater, New York) and as her career soared, his died. In 1927 he went back to Sweden after she ignored his entreaties to join her. (He died of infective pleurisy on November 7, 1928.) Garbo's beauty astounded moviegoers in America. Her films included *Flesh And The Devil* (premièred January 9, 1927 at the Capitol Theater, New York) in which she played Felicitas Von Kletzingk. Her co-star was John Gilbert and, by all accounts, the romance carried on off screen as well. In *Love* (premièred November 29, 1927 at the Embassy Theater, New York) Garbo played Anna Karenina and was again teamed with Gilbert, possibly so the promoters could write the line "Garbo and Gilbert in *Love*". In *Wild Orchids* (premièred February 16, 1929) she was Lillie Sterling. This film was originally entitled *Heat* until wiser heads prevailed and it was realised that marquees carrying the legend "Greta Garbo in *Heat*" would be unacceptable. Garbo ended the affair with Gilbert in 1929. It was her first talkie, *Anna Christie* (premièred January 22, 1930 at the Criterion Theater, Los Angeles), in which she played the lead role of a waterfront prostitute, that won her an Oscar nomination and worldwide interest – "Garbo Talks!" – an interest that she shunned with a passion. Her next film, *Romance* (premièred July 18, 1930 at Loew's State Theater, Los Angeles), in which she was cast as Rita Cavallini, won her another Oscar

nomination but no trophy. When she made her first comedy *Ninotchka* (premièred November 10, 1939 at the Radio City Music Hall, New York) playing Ninotchka, the tag ran "Garbo Laughs!" For *Camille* (premièred December 12, 1936 at the Plaza Theater, Palm Springs), in which she appeared as the consumptive heroine Marguerite Gautier, one wag suggested the line should read "Garbo Coughs!" Nonetheless, both films won her Oscar nominations. Garbo was the favourite actress of Adolf Hitler. On May 3, 1938 she was labelled "box office poison" by *The Independent Film Journal* in an advertisement paid for by Harry Brandt, the president of the Independent Theatre Owners Association. "Among those players whose dramatic ability is unquestioned, but whose box office draw is nil, can be numbered Mae West, Edward Arnold, Greta Garbo, Joan Crawford, Katharine Hepburn, Marlene Dietrich and Fred Astaire." It did not seem to harm her legend. Her other films included *Mata Hari* (premièred New Year's Eve, 1931 at the Capitol Theater, New York) in the title role, *Grand Hotel* (premièred April 12, 1932 at the Astor Theater, New York) as Grusinskaya, *As You Desire Me* (premièred June 3, 1932 at the Capitol Theater, New York) as Zara/Countess Maria Varelli, *Queen Christina* (premièred Boxing Day, 1933 at the Astor Theater, New York) as Queen Christina. (In the closing scene Garbo's character sails off into exile but the wind in her hair is blowing in a different direction from that through the sails directly behind her), *Anna Karenina* (released August 20, 1935) as Anna Karenina, *Conquest* (premièred November 5, 1937 at the Capitol Theater, New York) as Marie Walewska and *Two-Faced Woman* (released December 4, 1941) as Karin Borg Blake/Katherine Borg. Then it all ended. Garbo announced her retirement. She never explained why except to say, "I have made enough faces." Director Clarence Brown stated: "She has this great appeal to the world because she expresses her emotions by thinking them. Garbo does not need gestures and movements to convey happiness, despair, hope and disappointment, joy or tragedy. She registers her feelings literally by radiating her thoughts to you." The diarist Alistair Cooke remarked that Garbo was "every man's harmless fantasy mistress. She gave you the impression that if your imagination had to sin, it could at least congratulate itself on its impeccable taste." Her retirement was long. Despite rumours of comebacks none ever materialised. She refused to appear on the radio, once turning down $25,000 for a single show. She was awarded an honorary Oscar in 1954 but didn't bother to show up to collect it. She spent her reclusive years travelling around Europe and living in Manhattan. Every day she would take the same route from her home, The Campanile, 450 East 52nd Street, for her morning constitutional and every day fans would approach her and ask her the time. She always told them. Although predominantly lesbian, she had probable affairs with designer Cecil Beaton (who was himself predominantly homosexual) and actors John Gilbert, George Brent and conductor Leopold Stokowski. She continued her sex life in other ways, too. Garbo liked to masturbate frequently while looking at photos of her favourite film actors. For many years historians speculated over a possible affair with socialite Mercedes de Acosta who also claimed to have slept with Marlene Dietrich. On April 15, 2000, at the Rosenbach Museum and Library in Philadelphia, 25 secret letters from Garbo to de Acosta were unsealed along with 88 other items including notes that accompanied flowers, photographs, telegrams, and poems. However, although the

documents verified the two women's 28-year friendship they neither confirmed nor refuted the existence of a sexual relationship between them. The Garbo enigma remained intact. Speaking in 1963 Clarence Brown said: "Today she is still the greatest. She is the prototype of all stars."
CAUSE: In March 1987, Garbo, then 81, tripped over her vacuum cleaner and sprained her right ankle. She was taken to hospital but fearful of having her privacy invaded, she checked herself out. She holidayed alone in Klosters in July 1988. The following month she suffered a minor heart attack. On January 5, 1989, she was rushed by ambulance to New York Hospital but she was allowed home two days later. Her kidneys had begun to fail and after much argument Garbo began dialysis in June 1989 three times a week. On April 11, 1990, Garbo again went to New York Hospital where she died of pneumonia four days later at 11.30am on Easter Sunday, aged 84. She was cremated at the Garden State Crematory in New Jersey on Easter Monday. Her estate was worth almost $55 million. Her ashes were buried in Skogskyrkogården, Stockholm.
FURTHER READING: *Garbo: The Authentic Life Story* – John Bainbridge (London: Frederick Muller, 1955); *Garbo: Her Story* – Antoni Gronowicz (New York: Simon & Schuster, 1990); *Loving Garbo* – Hugo Vickers (London: Jonathan Cape, 1994); *Greta Garbo: A Life Apart* – Karen Swenson (New York: Scribner, 1997).

Ava Gardner

Born December 24, 1922
Died January 25, 1990
Glamorous brunette. Known for her foul mouth and fiery relationship with Frank Sinatra, Ava Lavinia Gardner was born, one of six children, in Brogden, North Carolina. Her film career began when her picture was spotted in a shop window by an MGM

talent scout. After a screen test in 1940 she was put under a $50-a-week contract and appeared in bit parts in several films including *H.M. Pulham, Esq.* (1941), *Fancy Answers* (1941), *We Were Dancing* (1942), *This Time For Keeps* (1942), *Sunday Punch* (1942), *Reunion In France* (1942), *Kid Glove Killer* (1942), *We Do It Because . . .* (1942) and *Calling Dr Gillespie* (1942) before making her first major appearance in *Three Men In White* (1944) in which she played Jean Brown. On January 10, 1942, in a small Presbyterian church in the foothills of the Santa Ynez Mountains, 21-year-old Mickey Rooney, the 5′3″ cinematic Andy Hardy, was an ecstatically happy young man. He had just married the lush, 5′7″, 19-year-old, 36-23-37 actress. That night Ava lost her virginity to him. Despite the fact that he was something of a playboy, Rooney was nervous as he undressed for bed – indeed, he put his legs into the arms of his pyjamas! His bride was terrified – her mother had warned her that sex was terrible and had to be endured and not enjoyed. However, once Ava got over her initial shyness she found she actually enjoyed the event and looked forward to a repeat performance. It was not to be – Rooney was a golf fanatic and made for the green after breakfast. Not surprisingly, Ava, who was a bit of a hick at the time of her marriage, wised up to Mickey the Mite within a short time and ditched him. They were divorced on May 21, 1943. While her private life may have been troubled, her professional one certainly wasn't. She featured in *Maisie Goes To Reno* (1944) as millionaire's wife Gloria Fullerton, *She Went To The Races* (1945) as Hilda Spotts, *Whistle Stop* (1946) as love-torn small-town girl Mary, *The Killers* (1946) as gangster's moll Kitty Collins, *The Hucksters* (1947) as good-time girl Jean Ogilvie, *Singapore* (1947) as amnesiac war victim Linda Gordon Van Leyden, *One Touch Of Venus*

(1948) as statue Venus, *East Side, West Side* (1949) as the other woman Isabel Lorrison and *The Bribe* (1949) as Elizabeth Hintten. On October 17, 1945, she married bandleader Artie Shaw at 1112 South Peck Drive, Beverly Hills. She wore the same blue outfit she had worn when she married Mickey Rooney. They divorced after two years. In Philadelphia on November 7, 1951, she married Frank Sinatra. It had been a stormy courtship and continued into a volatile marriage. She had an abortion, something which upset him deeply. Director John Ford tried to embarrass Gardner at a dinner for the British Governor of Uganda during the filming of *Mogambo* (1953) (for which Gardner would be Oscar-nominated for her portrayal of Eloise Y. 'Honey Bear' Kelly). Ford asked Gardner what she saw "in that 120-pound runt you're married to" – i.e. Sinatra. "Well," replied Ava, "there's 10lbs of Frank and 110lbs of cock." The Governor was amused but the response caused Ford to choke. She and Ol' Blue Eyes separated in 1954 and were divorced three years later on July 5, 1957. After a subsequent so-so career, which included films such as *Show Boat* (1951) as Julie LaVerne, *The Snows Of Kilimanjaro* (1952) as Cynthia Street, *The Barefoot Contessa* (1954) as Maria Vargas, *Around The World In 80 Days* (1956), *Bhowani Junction* (1956) as Victoria Jones, *55 Days At Peking* (1963) as Baroness Natalie Ivanoff, *Mayerling* (1968) as Empress Elizabeth, *The Life And Times Of Judge Roy Bean* (1972) as Lily Langtry and *Earthquake* (1974), Ava moved to Spain, where she became more famous for her affairs with a series of Spanish bullfighters, among others, than for her films. She lived her final years in reclusive luxury in London, making occasional forays to appear in such television series as *Knots Landing* and *AD*.

CAUSE: In her final years Gardner suffered from consistently bad

health. She endured two strokes and pneumonia. She died aged 67 in her London home, 34 Ennismore Gardens, Westminster, London SW7, of bronchopneumonia, fibrosing alvealitis and systemic lupus erythematosis.
FURTHER READING: *Ava's Men: The Private Life Of Ava Gardner* – Jane Ellen Wayne (London: Robson Books, 1990).

John Garfield
(JACOB JULIUS GARFINKLE)
Born March 4, 1913
Died May 21, 1952
Jewish gangster. Born in the Bronx, New York, the son of Russian-Jewish immigrants, Garfield fell into trouble early on in his life following the death (when he was seven) of his mother, who nicknamed him 'Juli'. He joined several gangs and played truant from school. Although he was steered into the theatre, Garfield never lost the chip on his shoulder. He began making films in the late Thirties (an appearance in *Footlight Parade* [1933] is disputed) and soon became one of Hollywood's best-known tough guys. He appeared in *They Made Me A Criminal* (1939), *Juarez* (1939) as Porfirio Diaz, *Daughters Courageous* (1939) as Gabriel Lopez, *Castle On The Hudson* (1940) as Tommy Gordon, *The Sea Wolf* (1941) as George Leach, *Out Of The Fog* (1941) as Harold Goff, *Dangerously They Live* (1942) as Dr Michael Lewis, *Tortilla Flat* (1942) as Danny, *Air Force* (1943) as Sergeant Joe Winocki, *Destination Tokyo* (1943) as Wolf, *Between Two Worlds* (1944) as Tom Prior, *Pride Of The Marines* (1945) as Al Schmid, *The Postman Always Rings Twice* (1946) as Frank Chambers (Garfield was released from the army to appear), *Nobody Lives Forever* (1946) as Nick Blake, *Humoresque* (1946) as Paul Boray, *Body And Soul* (1947) as Charlie Davis, *Force Of Evil* (1948) as Joe Morse, *We Were Strangers* (1949) as Tony Fenner, *The Breaking Point* (1950) as Harry Morgan and *He Ran*

All The Way (1951) as Nick Robey. Garfield was called to testify before the House Un-American Activities Committee to explain his alleged involvement with left-wing groups. He was terrified of losing his fame and fortune and, denying he was or had ever been a Communist, he thanked the Committee for its protection of America "from the Red menace". One Committee member stated Garfield was "an intensely loyal American", but another was "not entirely convinced of the entire accuracy and cooperation" of the actor's testimony. Dissatisfied, he still found himself blacklisted by producers and found work at $100 a time on Broadway. In the weeks leading up to Garfield's unexpected death, rumours flew in Washington that a big Hollywood star was to be indicted for lying to the House Committee. No one doubted the star was Garfield. There was even a rumour that Garfield was ready to talk and "make a clean breast of his Un-American activities" when called to testify before the House committee. It was said he had been promised immunity if he named names of Hollywood Reds. He was summoned to testify a second time but was noncommittal. He collaborated with a journalist to write an article for *Look* magazine entitled "I Was A Sucker For A Left Hook". He died before the article was published. Like many actors Garfield was superstitious and carried an old pair of shoes with him that featured in every film he made. He married Roberta Seidman in 1932. He had three children: Katherine (b. 1939, d. 1945 of a throat infection), actor David Patton (b. 1942) and actress Julie Patton (b. January 10, 1946).
CAUSE: Garfield died aged 39 from a coronary thrombosis in the second-floor apartment of his mistress, Iris Whitney, a 36-year-old Broadway actress, at 3 Gramercy Park, New York. Just seven days prior to this, showbiz columnist Earl Wilson had

reported the actor and his wife had separated and that Garfield had left their apartment at 88 Central Park West, and was staying at the Hotel Warwick on 54th Street. The first report of Garfield's sudden death came from Dr Charles Nammack, Iris Whitney's GP, who made a 'routine report' to the Medical Examiner's office about the death, which the doctor ascribed to a cardiac condition. Assistant Medical Examiner Dr Eugene Clark, examining the body, confirmed Dr Nammack's diagnosis and left saying that no autopsy was necessary. The police arrived to prepare a report on the death, but were refused admittance to the flat by Whitney. For an hour there was a stand-off until the police broke the door down. Whitney claimed she believed the police were the press. Two days earlier, she told the police, Garfield had spent the night playing poker, then had a normal day. That evening the couple dined at Luchow's Restaurant on 14th Street and then walked the few blocks to her apartment. Drinking coffee around 9pm, Garfield complained of tiredness. In the back of her mind, Whitney said, was the actor's history of heart trouble. He had had a mild heart ailment for several years. In 1949, he collapsed after a tennis match and was ordered to take a complete rest. Then he suffered a heart attack in 1951. His interrogation by the House Un-American Activities Committee hadn't helped matters. She offered to call a doctor but he refused to let her. Garfield then went to the bedroom while she slept on the living room settee. The next morning at 9am she took him some orange juice. "He couldn't seem to open his eyes," she told police. "He wouldn't reach for the juice. He just didn't respond. I shook him and there wasn't any response. I called my physician, Dr Nammack. He said he'd be right over. When he got here, he told me Mr Garfield was dead . . ." Whitney had been sleeping

with the actor for around two months, but apparently that was long enough for her to opine: "He was a very sweet dear boy. He has a nice family. But he was troubled and he came to me for help. He needed help. He wanted someone who was sympathetic to him. I don't think I could say more. I don't want to talk about it . . ." Within hours of his death, fans had gathered in a silent vigil outside the Gramercy Park apartment. In a bid to hush the scandal of a star being found dead in another woman's bed the spin doctors went to work. Famed lawyer Louis Nizer, saying he represented both Garfield and his wife, expostulated: "Neither of them had taken any action for a separation or divorce, or even contemplated doing so. They have had quarrels like any husband or wife. But they were together at my house only two nights ago . . ." He didn't add they weren't two nights later. Barry Hyams, a press agent for the American National Theater and Academy, which produced the Clifford Odets play *Golden Boy* that Garfield had starred in until only a few weeks before his death, offered yet another explanation of why John was found dead in Iris Whitney's bed. Hyams said Garfield was seeing Miss Whitney to discuss his plans to produce a play called *The Fragile Fox* in the autumn. Laughably he added, "That is the only reason I can think of for his visiting Miss Whitney. She is interested in the financing of plays." Garfield was buried in Westchester Hills Cemetery, 400 Saw Mill River Road, Hastings-on-Hudson, New York 10706.

Judy Garland
(FRANCES ETHEL GUMM)
Born June 10, 1922
Died June 22, 1969
Tragic talent. Where to start with the life of Judy Garland? Singer. Actress. Oft-married. Bisexual. Drug addict. Mother of Liza Minnelli. She was all this and much, much more. Born at

5.30am in the local hospital of Grand Rapids, Minnesota, the daughter of 5'11" homosexual Frank Avent Gumm (b. Murfreesboro, Tennessee, March 20, 1886, d. Cedars of Lebanon Hospital, Los Angeles, California November 17, 1935, of spinal meningitis), and a stage mother, Ethel Marion Milne (b. Marquette, Michigan, November 17, 1893, d. Los Angeles, California, January 5, 1953, of a heart seizure). The Gumms badly wanted a boy and a newspaper advertisement announced the birth of Francis Gumm, Jr. Judy's career began when she was under three-years-old. She took part in an act with her two elder sisters on a cold Boxing Day 1924. In August 1934 the three sisters arrived at a theatre to perform and as they stood outside looking at their names up in lights their pride turned to anger when they saw themselves listed as "The Glum Sisters". At various times they had been billed as "The Crum Sisters", "The Dumb Sisters" and even "The Rum Sisters". Entertainer George Jessel suggested they adopt the name of the New York World-Telegram theatre critic Robert Garland and young Frances went one further by taking as her Christian name the title of her favourite song of the time 'Judy' by Hoagy Carmichael. That night Jessel introduced "The Garland Sisters – featuring Little Miss Judy Garland with the big voice". The stories of how Judy Garland came to the attention of MGM are varied but she signed a contract with the studio. Another story has it that Judy Garland became a star by complete accident. She appeared with 15-year-old Deanna Durbin in a short film called Every Sunday (1936) described by Garland as "sort of jazz versus opera" and on the credits as "A Tabloid Musical". Garland played an American with "an apple in my hand and a dirty face" while Durbin played a European princess. Louis B. Mayer was impressed and told an aide to sign up

"the flat one" meaning Durbin who didn't always hit the right note. The flack misheard thinking the movie mogul had said "the fat one" and offered a contract to chubby Judy Garland. Her MGM contract was signed (by Ethel, for Judy was a minor) on September 27, 1935 and officially started four days later. Her starting salary was $100 per week with options for seven years. The seven years worked out as follows: Year One: 6 months at $100 per week with a 20 week guarantee of work; 6 months at $200 per week with a 20 week guarantee; Year Two: $300 per week with a 40 week guarantee; Year Three: $400 per week with a 40 week guarantee; Year Four: $500 per week with a 40 week guarantee; Year Five: $600 per week with a 40 week guarantee; Year Six: $750 per week with a 40 week guarantee and finally, in year seven she would earn $1,000 per week, again with 40 weeks of work guaranteed. Mayer was to take more than a passing interest in Garland and would often summon her to his office where he would fondle her breasts. He ignored her complaints and invited other MGM execs to follow his lead. Garland was to say later, "When Dad died MGM took over as my father. In our house the word of Louis B. Mayer became the law. When Mother wanted to discipline me, all she had to say was 'I'll tell Mr Mayer.'" Less than a year after her contract with MGM was issued, Judy signed a recording contract with Decca Records. On 12 June 1936, just two days after her 14th birthday, she recorded 'Stompin' At The Savoy'/ 'Swing Mr Charlie' with Bob Crosby and His Orchestra for Decca in New York. They were the first Judy Garland songs ever to be released. It was Garland's scene stealing performance in Broadway Melody Of 1938 (released August 20, 1937) as Betty Clayton during which she sang 'You Made Me Love You' to a picture of Clark Gable that captured hearts the world over. Bosley Crowther wrote in *The New York Times*, "There are individual successes in the film . . . the amazing precocity of Judy Garland, Metro's answer to Deanna Durbin . . . Miss Garland particularly has a long tour de force in which she addresses lyrical apostrophes to a picture of Clark Gable. The idea and words are almost painfully silly – yet Judy . . . puts it over – in fact with a bang." It was *The Wizard Of Oz* (premièred August 12, 1939) and her portrayal of Dorothy Gale that made her an international star. (Incidentally, she became such a huge favourite of gays that they nicknamed themselves "Friends of Dorothy".) Garland almost never played the role. Mayer told ambitious songwriter Arthur Freed to find a project and then, maybe, he would consider allowing him behind a camera. Freed searched in MGM's archive but nothing was suitable but then someone mentioned a property written by L Frank Baum and then owned by Samuel Goldwyn. Freed saw potential in *The Wizard Of Oz*, which was more than Goldwyn did and, more presciently, he saw Judy in the role of Dorothy Gale. Freed began secret negotiations with Goldwyn and bought the rights. Mayer agreed with Freed that it was a good property but refused to countenance letting Judy play Dorothy. The film, Mayer decided, would star Shirley Temple, then under contract to Fox. He summoned Freed to his office and told him the news. Freed was to be associate producer. The plans hit problems when Fox refused to loan Temple. Back to Plan A and Judy was told the role was hers. She was also told to lose weight and put on a special diet. Richard Thorpe was hired to direct and Harold Arlen and Edgar Yipsel "Yip" Harburg to write the score. MGM threw all their resources into *The Wizard of Oz*. Judy was more concerned with her education. When the film wrapped on March 16, 1939 she would graduate

from Hollywood High School. At least that was the plan. It was customary then that when child actors came to school leaving age they would enrol in a local school for a few days before the end of term and then graduate with the class. Judy could not attend the day school at the studio and was assigned a tutor, Rose Carter, who was with her for eight hours a day. Whenever Judy was not in front of the cameras she was being tutored. Filming began on October 13, 1938 but according to Margaret Hamilton who played Miss Almira Gulch/the Wicked Witch of the West, it was not a happy set. The four male principals – Bert Lahr (Zeke/Cowardly Lion), Ray Bolger (Hunk/Scarecrow), Jack Haley (Hickory/Tin Man) and Frank Morgan (Professor Marvel/Emerald City doorman/taxi driver/Wizard's minder/Wizard of Oz) – were worried that Judy would upstage them and played not with her, but against her. Hamilton was horrified to learn that Judy was on drugs to cope with her hectic schedule. The main thing that excited Judy during filming was the thought of graduating and she proudly showed Margaret Hamilton the dress she intended to wear. However, when filming was over Judy was sent on a tour with Mickey Rooney and never got to graduate in the dress. Margaret Hamilton telephoned the publicity department to protest only to be told that Louis B Mayer had expressly ordered the tour. *The Wizard Of Oz* premièred at Oconomowoc, Wisconsin on 12 August 1939 followed by premières in Hollywood three days later and in New York at the Capitol Theatre at 51st Street on 17 August 1939. The original plan was for W C Fields to play the title role but he wanted $100,000 and the studio was prepared to offer only $75,000. Ray Bolger was the original Tin Man and Buddy Ebsen the Scarecrow but Bolger insisted on swapping parts because his childhood hero Fred Stone had played the Scarecrow on stage in 1902. Ebsen then had to drop out when he had a severe allergic reaction to the make-up used for the Tin Man. Le Roy then sacked the director Richard Thorpe and scrapped the first week's footage. George Cukor stood in as director until Victor Fleming took over. On November 4, Jack Haley was hired to replace Ebsen as the Tin Man although it is Ebsen's voice that you can hear on the soundtrack. Yip Harburg remembered, "Here was Dorothy a little girl from Kansas, a bleak place where where were no flowers, where there was no colour of any kind. What does a child like this want? The only colourful thing in her life was a rainbow." In fact, the song nearly did not make it into the final film. It was thought 'Over The Rainbow' was too cloying and sentimental and was dropped from the final edit. It was put back into the film after a sneak preview revealed that the film was rather slow and needed to quicken the pace and also because it was too late to compose another number. The film was a spectacular in more ways than one. Seven assistant directors worked on the picture and 15 people contributed to the final script. All of MGM's 29 sound stages were used for the 65 sets and the cast finally numbered 600. The budget ran to $2.78 million, an unheard of figure for that time but the first weekend's takings were $5.35 million. After the previews MGM began to realise that they had potentially a massive hit on their hands and in Judy, a huge star. However, for some reason the studio did not treat Judy with the respect that was her due. They insisted that she was only a success because of them and sent her on a cross-country tour (the one Margaret Hamilton tried to block). The film contains a few errors. At the start of the film Auntie Em (Clara Blandick) is counting chickens. She announces: "Sixty-seven, sixty-eight, sixty-nine", then puts a further three in

her apron and takes one from Dorothy, saying "Seventy." It should have been "Seventy-three." On the table by the window is an oil lamp, but it disappears before the window is blown open in the storm. And have a close look at the set when the bed is moving around the room during the tornado. Although the pictures on the wall move, the bottles on the table stay where they are. Dorothy's hair changes length at least three times during the movie. When she is taken to the Wicked Witch's castle, her hair is mid-length. When Toto runs away her barnet hangs down to her waist, but when the Witch is turned into an hourglass, the hair is shoulder length. When the Scarecrow (Ray Bolger) receives a brain, he states: "The sum of the square roots of any two sides of an isosceles triangle is equal to the square root of the remaining side." Actually, it's not. In Pythagorean theory the square of the length of the hypotenuse of a right-angled triangle is equal to the sum of the squares of the lengths of the other two sides. Nonetheless, Judy Garland's performance endeared her to the cinema-going public, and even earned her a special Oscar as the "best juvenile performer of the year". Judy also appeared regularly opposite the young Mickey Rooney in films such as *Thoroughbreds Don't Cry* (released November 25, 1937) as Cricket West, *Babes In Arms* (premièred October 10, 1939) as Patsy Barton, *Strike Up The Band* (released September 27, 1940) as Mary Holden, *Babes On Broadway* (released December 31, 1941) as Penny Morris and *Girl Crazy* (released November 26, 1943) as Ginger Gray as well as *Love Finds Andy Hardy* (released July 22, 1938) and *Andy Hardy Meets Debutante* (released July 5, 1940) all as Betsy Booth. On July 28, 1941 Garland eloped to Las Vegas with composer David Rose (b. London June 15, 1910, d. Burbank, California, August 23, 1990). The marriage was fated not to last and they divorced in

February 1943, following an abortion. Judy also became estranged from her mother and began popping pills in a bid to keep her weight down and to sleep. It led to a lifelong addiction. On June 15, 1945, she married homosexual film director Vincente Minnelli. Their daughter, Liza May, was born on March 12, 1946, in Los Angeles. One day Judy caught Minnelli in bed with the male hired help. (Continuing the family tradition of unconventional sexual partnerships, Liza married gay entertainer Peter Woolnough Allen [b. Tenterfield, Australia, February 10, 1944] on March 3, 1967, in New York City. He died of AIDS on June 18, 1992.) Judy Garland's marital life was traumatic – she suffered breakdowns and even considered suicide at one point. However, on screen she was still a dream in films such as *For Me And My Gal* (released October 21, 1942) as Jo Hayden and *Meet Me In St. Louis* (released November 22, 1944) as Esther Smith. The latter provided more cinematic bloopers. During the 'Trolley' song one of the extras shouts, "Hi, Judy." When Esther dances with her little sister Tootie (Margaret O'Brien), the younger girl is wearing pink slippers, but later they are blue. She also starred in *The Clock* (released March 22, 1945) as Alice Mayberry, *Ziegfeld Follies* (released March 22, 1946), *Easter Parade* (released June 30, 1948) as Hannah Brown and *Summer Stock* (released August 31, 1950) as Jane Falbury. It was around the late Fifties that Judy's private battles began to overtake her professional life. Joan Crawford commented, "I didn't know her well, but after watching her in action I didn't want to know her well." She divorced Minnelli on March 23, 1951. On June 8, 1952, at 6pm at the Hollister, California, ranch of Robert Law, a friend of the couple, she married former test pilot Sid Luft. The ceremony lasted just five minutes. Judy spent her wedding night at the theatre performing in her show at the Curran

Theater in San Francisco. The two had met at a cocktail party hosted by Jackie Gleason. Garland was already a double divorcée, while Luft had been married to the lesbian actress Lynn Bari, known as the 'Queen of the GIs'. He ignored Garland at first. They began dating when Judy found she could talk easily to Luft, who arranged for her 1951 season at the London Palladium. She later claimed it was love at first sight. Their daughter, Lorna, was born on November 21, 1952, but the couple spent much time apart – she working, him arranging her gigs. When they were together, arguments escalated into violence and Judy would find herself on the wrong end of Luft's fists. In 1953 the couple decided to combine their efforts in a production company, Transcona Enterprises, and make a film for Judy to star in. The film was *A Star Is Born* (premièred September 29, 1954) and it garnered Judy an Academy Award nomination for her role as Esther Blodgett/Vicki Lester. The marital problems continued and in 1958 Judy even filed for divorce, though she later withdrew the petition. After the couple was reconciled, Judy gave birth on March 29, 1959, to her third child, a son called Joseph Wiley. They again separated in January 1961 after a sabbatical in London. On April 29, 1962, Garland filed for divorce; Luft retaliated by threatening to have her declared an unfit mother. A bitter custody battle ensued, resulting in joint custody of the children. Meanwhile, Judy had met Mark Herron, who was to become her fourth husband. Bizarrely, at the time – and during the marriage – he was having an affair with Peter Allen, Judy's son-in-law. The Lufts were finally divorced in Santa Monica on May 19, 1965. Absent from major films for the seven years following *A Star Is Born*, Judy was again Oscar-nominated for *Judgment At Nuremberg* (released December 19, 1961) as Irene Hoffman. On November 14, 1965, she married

Mark Herron at the Little Chapel of the West in Las Vegas. They were together less than six months after the ceremony and divorced on April 11, 1967. Judy claimed that Herron drank and hit and kicked her. Her final years were a series of setbacks and disappointments. On March 15, 1969, at Chelsea Registry Office she married for the fifth time to gay club manager Mickey Deans (né Devinko). Three months later, she was dead.

CAUSE: On June 21, 1969, Judy and Deans were at home – 4 Cadogan Lane, Chelsea – with Deans' close friend Philip Roberge, watching the documentary about the House of Windsor, *The Royal Family*, when Judy and her husband had a row. She ran into the street shouting and after a time he went after her. Unable to find her he returned to the house and went to bed. At approximately 10.40am the next morning the telephone rang for Judy. Deans scoured the house and discovered the bathroom door was locked. He banged on it but received no reply. He climbed in through the bathroom window and found Judy dead, sitting on the toilet. Rigor mortis had already set in. She was only 47. The official cause of death was given as "Barbiturate Poisoning (quinalbarbitone), incautious self-overdosage, accidental." Following Judy's autopsy performed by Dr Gavin Thurston at Westminster Hospital, her corpse was taken back to America three days later. On June 27, her body lay in state at Campbell's Funeral Home, Madison Avenue, New York and almost 22,000 fans paid homage to her. She was buried in Mausoleum Unit 9, Section HH, Crypt 31 of Ferncliff Cemetery and Mausoleum, Secor Road, Hartsdale, New York 10530. Marcella Rabwin originally discovered Judy and was later asked if she had any regrets about putting her on the road to stardom. Her answer was definite: "For having given the world that great talent? No."

FURTHER READING: *Weep No More My Lady: An Intimate Biography Of Judy Garland* – Mickey Deans & Ann Pinchot (London: Mayflower, 1973); *Little Girl Lost: The Life & Hard Times Of Judy Garland* – Al DiOrio, Jr. (London: Robson Books, 1975); *Judy Garland* – Anne Edwards (London: Corgi Books, 1976); *Heartbreaker* – John Meyer (London: Star Books, 1987); *Judy Garland* – David Shipman (London: Fourth Estate, 1992); *Judy Garland* – Paul Donnelley (London: Haus, 2007).

Peggy Ann Garner
Born February 3, 1932
Died October 16, 1984
Child star. Born in Canton, Ohio, her parents, Virginia and William H. Garner separated when she was four and her pushy mother took young Peggy Ann to New York where she modelled children's clothes. Two years on they decamped to Hollywood where Peggy Ann began her acting career. She made her first film when she was just six – *Little Miss Thoroughbred* (1938) and then played Carole Lombard's daughter, Ellen Eden, in *In Name Only* (1939). She played smaller roles in *Blondie Brings Up Baby* (1939) as Melinda Mason, *Abe Lincoln In Illinois* (1940), *Eagle Squadron* (1942), *The Pied Piper* (1942) as Sheila Cavanaugh, *Jane Eyre* (1944) as the young Jane Eyre and *The Keys Of The Kingdom* (1944) as Nora. In 1943 Garner had been contracted to Twentieth Century Fox but after Jane Eyre MGM wanted to buy half her Fox contract and star in a film about horses called *National Velvet* (1945) but Darryl F. Zanuck refused to countenance the idea. The role went to one of her co-stars in *Jane Eyre*, a young English girl by the name of Elizabeth Taylor. Zanuck promised Virginia Garner that he had a better role for her daughter. The part was Francie Nolan and the film was *A Tree Grows In Brooklyn* (1945). She was paid $1,250 weekly for the duration of the

film. It was a sensation, it made Fox a fortune and on March 7, 1946 Garner was presented with a miniature Oscar as Outstanding Child Actress Of 1945. As with so many who achieved stardom early, it was all downhill from there and 5′4″ Garner was never to match that success. Her parents' divorce was finalised in 1947 and Garner asked a judge to place her with her father not her stage door mother. In the Fifties she spent time in New York studying with the Actors Studio and appearing on television. In the Sixties she worked as an estate agent and then sales manager for a Pontiac dealership in Santa Monica. The second big break never came. Peggy Ann Garner was married three times. On February 22, 1951 she married Richard Hayes (b. Brooklyn, New York January 5, 1930) and TV legend Ed Sullivan gave her away. They divorced on October 13, 1953. On May 16, 1956 she married the actor Albert Salmi who is noticed elsewhere in this book and on March 30, 1957 gave birth to her only child, a daughter Catherine Ann. On May 17, 1995 she died of premature heart disease at the age of 38. Garner and Salmi were divorced on March 13, 1963. On August 7, 1964 she married Kenyon Foster Brown and divorced him four years later.

CAUSE: Garner died of pancreatic cancer at Woodland Hills, Los Angeles, California. She was 52. Her pushy mother who was born on March 24, 1911 outlived both her daughter and granddaughter and died on November 5, 1995.

Greer Garson

Born September 29, 1904
Died April 6, 1996
Statuesque performer. Born in London, Eileen Evelyn Greer Garson was educated at the University of London and set her heart on becoming a teacher. However, fate intervened and she went to work for an advertising agency performing in amdram on the

side. In 1932 she decided to give full-time acting a shot and made her professional début in Birmingham followed two years later by her first appearance on the West End stage. Fortuitously, she was spotted by Louis B. Mayer, who offered her a contract with MGM. The studio was in dire need of someone to replace Norma Shearer and Greta Garbo and Greer Garson was it. On September 28, 1933, she married civil servant Edward Alec Abbot Snelson but they divorced on May 12, 1941. Two years earlier she had made her film début and won an Academy Award nomination in *Goodbye, Mr Chips* (1939) as Katherine Chipping. She became an overnight star. She followed that with *Remember?* (1939) as Linda Bronson, *Pride And Prejudice* (1940) as Elizabeth Bennet, *When Ladies Meet* (1941) as Claire Woodruff and *Blossoms In The Dust* (1941) as Edna Gladney, for which she received another Oscar nomination. It was her next film that is regarded as her finest work. In *Mrs Miniver* (1942) she played the indomitable Kay Miniver. Norma Shearer turned down the title role because she didn't want to play a middle-aged woman with a 20-year-old son on screen. As history reveals, the part went to Greer Garson who was 15 months younger than Shearer. It won her an Oscar – and a husband, Richard Ney, who played her son in the film. The next year on July 24, 1943, they married. However, the marriage was not to last and on September 25, 1947, they divorced. On July 15, 1949, Garson married millionaire rancher Edward E. 'Buddy' Fogelson. They were together until his death in December 1987. Despite the oft-repeated rumours, Greer Garson did not ramble on for over an hour when accepting her Oscar. It *was* the longest speech in Oscar history, *but* lasted only five minutes. Her subsequent films included: *Random Harvest* (1942) as Paula, *Madame Curie* (1943) as Marie Curie, for which she

received another Oscar nomination, *Mrs Parkington* (1944) as Susie Parkington, for which she received another Oscar nomination, *The Valley Of Decision* (1945) as Mary Rafferty, for which she received another Oscar nomination, *Adventure* (1945) as Emily Sears, *Desire Me* (1947) as Marise Aubert, *Julia Misbehaves* (1948) as Julia Packett, *That Forsyte Woman* (1949) as Irene Forsyte, *The Miniver Story* (1950), in which she – not terribly successfully – reprised her role as Kay Miniver, *Scandal At Scourie* (1953) as Mrs Patrick J. McChesney, *Julius Caesar* (1953) as Calpurnia, *Her Twelve Men* (1954) as teacher Jan Stewart (who attempts to educate 13 boys), *Strange Lady In Town* (1955) as Dr Julia Winslow Garth, *Sunrise At Campobello* (1960) as Eleanor Roosevelt and yet another Oscar nod and *The Singing Nun* (1965) as Mother Prioress. Greer Garson gave millions of dollars to the Southern Methodist University in Dallas, who built the Greer Garson Theater. There were three conditions attached to her generosity. The theatre had to be a working circular stage; the first production had to be *A Midsummer Night's Dream* and, finally, it had to have an extra Ladies room. Not everyone was a fan however. "I gave up being serious about making pictures years ago, around the time I made a film with Greer Garson and she took 125 takes to say 'No'," quipped Robert Mitchum.
CAUSE: Greer Garson died aged 91 in Dallas, Texas, from heart failure.

Janet Gaynor
(LAURA GAINOR)
Born October 6, 1906
Died September 14, 1984
Mary Martin's husband. Born in Philadelphia, Pennsylvania, she was raised in Chicago from the age of eight and, after working in a shoe shop for $18 a week, joined Fox when she was 19. She appeared, usually uncredited, in numerous films, until she was

noticed in F.W. Murnau's *Sunrise* (1927). It was her performance in that film and in Frank Borzage's *Seventh Heaven* (1927) as Diane and *Street Angel* (1928) as Angela that won her the very first Best Actress Academy Award. It was also the first and only time a statuette was awarded for multiple films. *Seventh Heaven* was her first teaming with screen lover Charles Farrell. For twelve films and seven years they were Fox's leading screen lovers. Away from the screen was a different matter. Of the two Gaynor was, by far, the more masculine. In 1930 she ran away to Honolulu, fed up with the roles she was allocated. She went on strike for seven months before agreeing to return, by which time Fox had merged with 20th Century and her services were less in demand. She retired from the screen in 1939. To disguise Tyrone Power's homosexuality, Fox arranged 'dates' with, among others, the 5′ Gaynor. A lesbian, she nonetheless wed three times. She married San Francisco lawyer Lydell Peck on September 11, 1929, and was divorced on April 11, 1934. She eloped to Yuma, Arizona, with designer Gilbert Adrian (b. Naugatuck, Connecticut, March 3, 1983, as Adrian Adolph Greenberg, d. September 1959, of a stroke) on August 14, 1939, to shake off her "particular corridor and know the other side of life". Their son, Robin Gaynor Adrian, was born on July 6, 1940. On Christmas Eve, 1964, she married Paul Gregory, a friend of Charles Laughton and 15 years her junior. Her films included: *Two Girls Wanted* (1927) as Marianna Wright, *Four Devils* (1928) as Marion, *Sunny Side Up* (1929) as Molly Carr, *Lucky Star* (1929) as Mary Tucker, *High Society Blues* (1930) as Eleanor Divine, *Delicious* (1931) as Heather Gordon, *Daddy Long Legs* (1931) as Judy Abbott, *State Fair* (1933) as Margy Frake, *Carolina* (1934) as Joanna Tate, *The Farmer Takes A Wife* (1935) as Molly Larkins,

Ladies In Love (1936) as Martha Kerenye, *Small Town Girl* (1936) as Katherine Brannan, *A Star Is Born* (1937) as Esther Blodgett/Vicki Lester for which she was nominated for an Oscar, *Three Loves Has Nancy* (1938) as Nancy Briggs and *Bernardine* (1957) as Mrs Wilson.

CAUSE: She was badly hurt in a San Francisco car crash with her husband and lover Mary Martin on September 5, 1982. She suffered eleven broken ribs, a broken pelvis and collarbone and assorted internal injuries. Following two major operations at San Francisco General Hospital, she was released in January 1983. However, she never fully recovered from the accident and died in Desert Hospital, Palm Springs, California, from pneumonia aged 77. She was buried in Section 8, Lot 193 of Hollywood Memorial Park, 6000 Santa Monica Boulevard, Hollywood, California 90038.

Liz Gebhardt

Born April 12, 1945
Died August 10, 1996

Sitcom regular. Born at Liverpool Elisabeth Ann Gebhardt began her career on television in 1966 and two years later she achieved national fame playing the mousy devout Catholic Maureen Bullock who had a less than secret crush on her form teacher, Mr Hedges in the sitcom *Please Sir!* (November 8, 1968–February 13, 1972). She reprised her role in the 1971 movie version but only played the character for two series of the follow up *The Fenn Street Gang*. She had made her film debut as Calpurnia's maid in *Julius Caesar* (1970). She appeared in the television film *The Naked Civil Servant* (1975) but as with so many actors who are associated with one part found work difficult to come by. She made a few guest appearances in shows like *Dear Mother... Love Albert, Z Cars, Doctor On The Go, Don't Wait Up, Grange Hill, The Bill* and *Keeping Up Appearances*. She was married to Ian Talbot.

CAUSE: Gebhardt died at London of cancer. She was 51.

Kurt Gerron

(KURT GERSO)
Born May 11, 1897
Died October 28, 1944

Rotund German star. Born in Berlin to Jewish parents Kurt Gerron studied to become a doctor before switching to the stage in 1920. That year he also began to make movies. His films included: *Spuk Auf Schloß Kitay* (1920), *Die Apotheke Des Teufels* (1921), *Vorderhaus Und Hinterhaus* (1925), *Im Weißen Rößl* (1926), *Die Goldene Schmetterling* (1926), *Die Tragödie Eines Verlorenen* (1926), *Feme* (1927), *Glanz Und Elend Der Kurtisanen* (1927), *Einbruch* (1927), *Casanovas Erbe* (1927), *Die Marquise Von Pompadour* (1930) as Ludwig XV and *Trapeze* (1931) as Grimby. In Berlin on August 28, 1928 he starred in the original version of Kurt Weill's and Bertolt Brecht's *Die Dreigroschenoper* playing Tiger Brown. In 1930 he became the director of a Berlin theatre and directed *Der Rote Faden* which starred Marlene Dietrich. He also appeared with Dietrich in *Der Blaue Engel* (1930) as Kiepert, the magician. He directed a few shorts and five features for the German film company UFA. He was working on the film *Kind, Ich Freu Mich Auf Dein Kommen* (1933) when the Nazis came to power. He left Germany and travelled around Europe before settling in Holland where he worked as a director. In 1940 the Germans invaded and Gerron was forced to appear in the propaganda film *Der Ewige Jude* (1940). In 1943 he was sent to a concentration camp where he organised a theatre group. In 1944 he was moved to Theresienstadt concentration camp where he directed the propaganda documentary *Der Fuhrer Schenkt Den Juden Eine Stadt* (1944). He was soon deported to another camp.

CAUSE: He and his wife died in the gas

chambers at Auschwitz three months before its liberation. In 2003 a documentary about Gerron entitled *Prisoner Of Paradise* was nominated for an Oscar.

Irving Gertz
Born May 19, 1915
Died November 14, 2008
The music man. Irving Gertz was born in Providence, Rhode Island, the youngest of eight children. Always musical, he began playing when he was young and showed proficiency at a number of different instruments including the clarinet, piano, string bass and tuba. He was educated at the Providence College of Music. He composed music for the Providence Symphony Orchestra but his interest in films influenced his career decisions and he joined Columbia Pictures' music department in Hollywood in 1938. The Second World War interrupted his life and he became an artillery gunner and then as an officer in the Army Signal Corps. After being demobbed he rejoined Columbia and started writing film music. He left Columbia to write music for plays based on films for NBC Radio before making a move to Universal-International in the early 1950s. He joined 20th Century Fox in 1960 and worked there until his retirement in 1968, composing and music directing. A prolific writer, Gertz wrote for more than 200 films and television programmes including *Dragnet* (released August 16, 1947), *Bulldog Drummond Strikes Back* (released September 4, 1947), *It Came From Outer Space* (released May 26, 1953), *Francis Joins The WACS* (released October 24, 1954), *Abbott And Costello Meet The Mummy* (released June 1955), *The Creature Walks Among Us* (released April 26, 1956), *The Incredible Shrinking Man* (released April 1957), *The Alligator People* (released July 1959) and *Hell Bent For Leather* (released February 1, 1960). He worked on

several television shows including *Daniel Boone, The Invaders, Land Of The Giants, Peyton Place* and *Voyage To The Bottom of the Sea.* In 1944 he married Dorothy Stadler and they had two daughters, Susie Anson and Madeleine Herron.
CAUSE: Gertz died aged 93 at his West Hollywood home, from natural causes.

Brian Gibson
Born September 22, 1944
Died January 4, 2004
Distinguished director. Brian Gibson was born the son of a carpenter and a shop assistant. He was educated at Southend High School before winning a state scholarship to St Catherine's College, Cambridge, where he studied medicine. He then took a second degree studying History of Science at Darwin College. His first professional gig was working on BBC's *Horizon* before changing tack to produce drama documentaries. With Dennis Potter, Gibson collaborated on *Where Adam Stood* (based on *Father And Son*, the 1907 memoir by Edmund Gosse). This was followed by Potter's *Blue Remembered Hills* (1979) starring Helen Mirren and Colin Welland in an award-winning film about primitive childhood behaviour which required actors to play children pretending to be adults. Gibson received a BAFTA award for *Joey*, the story of Joey Deacon, a brain-damaged child who, later in life, found a handicapped friend to unlock his latent intellect. Joey was the subject of a *Blue Peter* appeal. His film *The Billion Dollar Bubble* (1976) gave James Woods an early success in his career. The low-budget films led to Gibson's first feature film, *Breaking Glass* (1980), which he wrote himself in four days. He discovered the punk singer Hazel O'Connor while researching the film. The success of *Breaking Glass* took him to Hollywood but he was often very choosy over his material. During his 12 years in Hollywood, he gave one tenth of his

income each year to charity, for the education of disadvantaged children. This continued on his return to Britain. He produced many films for HBO, including *The Josephine Baker Story* (1991), which starred his first wife Lynn Whitfield, and won an Emmy for Best Director. *Murderers Among Us* (1989) – the tale of Nazi hunter Simon Wiesenthal – was nominated for several Golden Globe and Emmy awards. His mainstream work included *Poltergeist II* (1986) and *What's Love Got To Do With It?* (1993), the story of Ike and Tina Turner, which won Oscar nominations for its stars Angela Bassett and Laurence Fishburne. Gibson's last Hollywood film was *The Juror* (1996) with Demi Moore and Alec Baldwin and a $44 million budget. Back in Britain he directed the cult film *Still Crazy* (1998) starring Billy Connolly, Stephen Rea and Jimmy Nail. In 1990 he married Lynn Whitfield (b. Baton Rouge, Louisiana, May 6, 1953 as Lynn Butler-Smith), by whom he had a daughter, Grace. After their 1992 divorce he married the artist Paula Guarderas, with whom he had another daughter, Raphaela.

CAUSE: Brian Gibson died from Ewing's sarcoma (bone cancer). He was 59.

Sir John Gielgud

Born April 14, 1904
Died May 21, 2000
Silken-voiced patrician actor. Arthur John Gielgud was born in 7 Gledhow Gardens, South Kensington, London, the third child and second son (of two) of four children to stockbroker Frank Gielgud and great-nephew of the actress Ellen Terry. He was educated at Westminster School (spending his free afternoons watching ballet) and then went to Lady Benson's School and RADA, winning scholarships to both. His first stage appearance came when he was 17 on November 7, 1921, at the Old Vic playing the Herald in *Henry V*. Shakespeare soon became Gielgud's

forte and his *Hamlet* was regarded as the finest of the twentieth century. However, Gielgud was nothing if not versatile and his first job after leaving RADA in December 1923 was playing Charles Wykeham in the farce *Charley's Aunt*. In May 1924 he played Romeo for the first time. He made his film début that year in *Who Is The Man?* (1924) as Daniel but it wasn't until late in life that he began appearing regularly on screen. Gielgud was never out of work, moving with ease between productions. In January 1928 he made his Broadway début at the Majestic Theater playing Grand Duke Alexander in Alfred Neumann's *The Patriot*. The show closed after only a dozen performances. A number of London assignments were equally unsuccessful but he at least had the consolation of seeing his name in lights in June 1928 at the Globe Theatre for the farce *Holding Out The Apple*. In September 1929 he joined the Old Vic company. His second film, *The Clue Of The New Pin* (1929) in which he played Rex Trasmere, was also released that year. On July 7, 1930, at the Lyric Theatre, Hammersmith, he played John Worthing in *The Importance Of Being Earnest* for the first time before rejoining the Old Vic company. Gielgud became a star on February 2, 1933, following his performance in the lead role of *Richard Of Bordeaux* at the New Theatre. The play ran for a year. In November 1934 he began the first of 155 performances in *Hamlet*. Gielgud's 1935 production of *Romeo & Juliet* for the Oxford University Drama Society is rightly acclaimed. Among the cast were Dame Peggy Ashcroft, Dame Edith Evans, Christopher Hassall as Romeo and Sir Terence Rattigan. After a triumphant first night Gielgud stood on the stage taking the plaudits. When the cheering had died down, he said that Ashcroft and Evans were "the like of whom I shall never meet again!" He had appeared in *Insult* (1932) as Henri Dubois, *The Good Companions* (1933) as Inigo Jollifant and *Secret Agent* (1936) as Edgar Brodie/Richard Ashenden. During the Second World War Gielgud toured extensively entertaining troops abroad while managing to maintain a presence on the West End stage. He played Benjamin Disraeli in *The Prime Minister* (1941), narrated *An Airman's Letter To His Mother* (1941) and was the voice of the ghost in *Hamlet* (1948). It would be his last film for five years. From the mid-Fifties he began to appear with regularity on television and in films. As well as being celebrated for being one of the best actors of the twentieth century Gielgud was also famous for his verbal blunders, lovingly known as Gielgudies. He saw an under par performance from an ill Richard Burton in *Hamlet* and told him "I'll come back when you're better . . . in health, of course." Early in his career Gielgud was the guest of an old and distinguished but very boring playwright when a man passed their table without stopping. "Thank goodness, he didn't stop. He's more boring than Eddie Knoblock," Gielgud commented. His dining companion at the time was Eddie Knoblock. Having graduated from RADA Peter Sallis was cast by Gielgud as the gardener in *Richard II*. Gielgud then turned to cast two other roles before turning back to Sallis saying, "We've got two men playing Bushy and Bagot, very beautiful. You'll make a good contrast." One day after a performance Gielgud approached a man to whom he said, "How pleased I am to meet you. I was at school with your son." The man was puzzled. "I have no son. We were at school together." Casting *The Laughing Woman*, a play about a sculptor and his mistress, Gielgud was chatting to Emlyn Williams: "Bronnie is insisting on Stephen Haggard for the part. He's splendid but much too well bred. It calls for an actor who would convey someone savage, uncouth – Emlyn, you should be playing it." Dudley Moore's

first appearance on Broadway was in *Beyond The Fringe*. Gielgud gave him a letter of recommendation for Lilli Palmer. It read, "Darling Lilli, This will introduce to you the brilliant young pianist from *Beyond The Fringe* Stanley Moon . . ." When Clement Attlee was Prime Minister Sir John Gielgud had dinner with him in a hotel at Stratford-upon-Avon. Sir John sat next to Attlee's daughter. Discussing houses, Gielgud remarked, "I have a very convenient home in Westminster (it was at 16 Cowley Street, SW1) and where do you live?" A startled Miss Attlee replied, "Number ten Downing Street." The two knighted Johns of the theatre, Gielgud and Mills, starred in a provincial tour of Charles Wood's play *Veterans*. Booked to appear in Brighton the audience was shocked by the many four-letter words in the script. It was too much for one man. He shouted out that the two respected actors ought to be ashamed of themselves for appearing in such a dreadful play. He took his wife's hand and led her from their seats. One woman was not quick enough. "Get out of my fucking way!" he shouted at Mary Haley Bell, a.k.a. Lady Mills. Gielgud was once instructing members of the cast to wear jockstraps under their leotards. One of the bit part actors piped up. "Does that apply to those of us who only have small parts, Sir John?" Gielgud was knighted in the June 2, 1953, Coronation Honours List, six years after his rival Laurence Olivier. Later that year, on October 21, Gielgud was arrested in a Chelsea public lavatory and charged with importuning. At home in Cowley Street that night Gielgud contemplated suicide. He turned up at the magistrate's court the next morning and pleaded guilty but lied to the court, telling the bench he was a self-employed clerk who earned £1,000 a year. The magistrate, E.R. Guest, fined him £10 and told him to visit a doctor. Gielgud appeared in, among other films, *Julius Caesar* (1953) as Cassius, *Richard III* (1954) as George, Duke of Clarence, *Around The World In 80 Days* (1956) as Foster, *The Barretts Of Wimpole Street* (1957) as Edward Moulton-Barrett, *Saint Joan* (1957) as Warwick, *North West Frontier* (1959), *Becket* (1964) as King Louis VII, for which he was nominated a Best Supporting Actor Oscar, *The Charge Of The Light Brigade* (1968) as Lord Raglan (Gielgud was required to deliver his lines while sitting on a horse. The idea was the horse would move and then Gielgud would deliver his words. On ten occasions, he spoke his lines perfectly but the trusty steed failed to budge even an inch. Said the director, Tony Richardson, "No, John. I want you to advance the horse five paces and then say your lines." Gielgud replied, "I know that but does the horse?"), *The Shoes Of The Fisherman* (1968) as the Elder Pope, *Oh! What A Lovely War* (1969) as Count Leopold Von Berchtold, *Julius Caesar* (1970) as Julius Caesar, *Lost Horizon* (1973) as Chang, *Gold* (1974) as Farrell, *Murder On The Orient Express* (1974) as Beddoes, *Galileo* (1975) as the old Cardinal, a doctor in *Joseph Andrews* (1977), *Murder By Decree* (1979) as Lord Salisbury, the Prime Minister who covers up the royal family's involvement in the Jack the Ripper outrages, *The Elephant Man* (1980) as Carr Gomm, *Caligula* (1980) as Nerva, *Chariots Of Fire* (1981) as the Master of Trinity College, *Sphinx* (1981) as Abdu Hamdi, *Arthur* (1981) as Hobson for which he won a Best Supporting Actor Oscar, delivering such memorable lines as "I'll alert the media" when Arthur Bach (Dudley Moore) announces he is going to have a bath and "One normally has to go to a bowling alley to meet a woman of your stature," to prostitute Linda Marolla (Liza Minnelli)), *Gandhi* (1982) as Lord Irwin, *The Wicked Lady* (1983) as Hogarth, *Arthur 2: On The Rocks* (1988) as Hobson, *Prospero's Books* (1991) as Prospero, *Haunted* (1995) as Doctor Doyle, *Shine* (1996)

as Cecil Parkes, *The Tichborne Claimant* (1998) as Cockburn and *Elizabeth* (1998) as Pope Paul IV. Gielgud was unmarried but lived with his long-term boyfriend, Martin Hensler (d. February, 1999 of cancer), for 40 years.

CAUSE: Gielgud died aged 96 of natural causes in his sleep at his home, South Pavillion, Wotton Underwood, Aylesbury, Buckinghamshire. He left £1,477,626.

Jerry Giesler

(HAROLD LEE GIESLER)
Born November 2, 1886
Died January 1, 1962
'The magnificent mouthpiece'. When stars were in trouble, the call went out "Send for Giesler". Born in Wilton Junction, Iowa, super-lawyer Giesler had poor eyesight, a huge belly, a Bobby Charlton hairstyle and a high-pitched voice. Nonetheless, he was a tiger in the courtroom. His first case was defending fellow legal eagle Clarence Darrow for allegedly bribing a lawyer. Giesler specialised in murder cases and divorce battles. He patented the much-maligned method of attacking alleged rape victims over their past history in a bid to free his client. It usually worked. He defended Errol Flynn when he was charged with rape in January 1943. On April 4, 1944, he saw Charlie Chaplin acquitted on a charge of violating the Mann Act, taking a female across state lines for immoral purposes. He was in Robert Mitchum's corner when the legendary hell-raiser was busted for possession of pot on August 31, 1948. In 1951 he defended stripper Lili St. Cyr after she was arrested at Ciro's nightclub in Los Angeles for "lewd and lascivious behaviour". She was acquitted after an hour's deliberation. He was Lizabeth Scott's lawyer when she sued scandal magazine *Confidential* over a story hinting she was a lesbian and hired gay call-girls. For once Giesler was on the losing side. In 1958 he represented

Lana Turner and her daughter following the death of Lana's gangster boyfriend Johnny Stompanato. Giesler was by Marilyn Monroe's side when she decided to divorce second husband Joe DiMaggio in 1954, by Barbara Hutton's side when she divorced Cary Grant and brokered Lady Sylvia Ashley's separation from Clark Gable. He successfully defended the boxer Kid McCoy on a charge of murder (even though the pugilist admitted killing his mistress) and was in Bugsy Siegel's corner over the only crime he was ever prosecuted for, the shooting of squealer Harry 'Big Greenie' Greenbaum in Los Angeles on November 22, 1939. One of his last high-profile cases was investigating the death of TV's Superman, George Reeves. He dropped the case, possibly after being warned off. In the wake of the investigation, Giesler began carrying a gun.

CAUSE: He died in his Beverly Hills office from a heart attack aged 76. Private detective Milo Speriglio, who investigated the death of Marilyn Monroe, believes that Giesler was murdered by one of his mob clients, from whom he charged $100,000 for his services.

FURTHER READING: *The Jerry Giesler Story* – Jerry Giesler as told to Pete Martin (New York: Simon & Schuster, 1960).

John Gilbert

(JOHN CECIL PRINGLE)
Born July 10, 1899
Died January 9, 1936
Romantic idol. Born in Logan, Utah, 70 miles north of Salt Lake City, he was delivered without the presence of a doctor or midwife during the worst storm of the decade. John Gilbert signed for Ince-Triangle Films in 1915 and made his début in *Matrimony* (1915) as an uncredited extra. He appeared in several films, producing a workmanlike performance but not showing any real star quality. However,

he quickly moved up the ranks, signed a contract with Fox and made *Shame* (1921) as William Fielding/David Field, *Ladies Must Live* (1921) as the gardener, the title role in *Gleam O'Dawn* (1922), *Arabian Love* (1922) as Norman Stone, *The Yellow Stain* (1922) as Donald Keith, *Honor First* (1922) as Jacques Dubois/Honoré Dubois, *Monte Cristo* (1922) as Edmond Dantes, Count of Monte Cristo, *Calvert's Valley* (1922) as Page Emlyn, *The Love Gambler* (1922) as Dick Manners, *A California Romance* (1922) as Don Patricio Fernando, *Truxton King* (1923) as Truxton King, *The Madness Of Youth* (1923) as Jaca Javalie, *St Elmo* (1923) as St Elmo Thornton, *The Exiles* (1923) as Henry Holcombe, the title role in *Cameo Kirby* (1923), *Just Off Broadway* (1924) as Stephen Moore, *The Wolf Man* (1924) as Gerald Stanley and *The Lone Chance* (1924) as Jack Saunders for the studio before signing for MGM in 1924. It was, in hindsight, to be a disastrous choice. Gilbert became a massive star at MGM, appearing in films such as *He Who Gets Slapped* (1924) as Bezano, *The Merry Widow* (1925) as Prince Danilo Petrovich and *The Big Parade* (1925) as young soldier James Apperson. It was probably Gilbert's best work. His popularity continued through *La Bohème* (1926) as Rodolphe in which he played opposite Lillian Gish and three films opposite his real-life lover Greta Garbo: *Flesh And The Devil* (1926) as Leo von Sellenthin, *Love* (1927) as Captain Count Alexei Vronsky and *A Woman Of Affairs* (1928) as Neville Holderness. They were due to marry on September 8, 1926, but Garbo jilted Gilbert by standing him up on what was supposed to be their wedding day. MGM boss Louis B. Mayer was less than sympathetic: "Why do you have to wait to marry her? Why don't you just go on fucking her and forget about the wedding?" he asked Gilbert, somewhat unfeelingly. Gilbert lost his temper,

grabbed hold of Mayer and tried to strangle him before pushing him into a fireplace, where he broke his glasses. Not an especially wise thing to do. In front of the assembled guests, Mayer screamed, "You're through! I'll destroy you if it costs me one million dollars!" Gilbert was unperturbed, having signed a contract for that very amount with Mayer's hated opponent, Nicholas Schenck, a top execuive with MGM's parent company. A few months later, Gilbert and Garbo were back in bed together – much to the disgust of Mayer, who hated them both. Mayer was as good as his word, ruining Gilbert's career by casting him in third-rate films and by spreading rumours about his unreliability. Gilbert lapsed into alcoholism. His later films included *Redemption* (1930) as Fedya, *Way For A Sailor* (1930) as Jack, *Wir Schalten Um Auf Hollywood* (1931), *Gentleman's Fate* (1931) as Jack Thomas, *Downstairs* (1932) as Karl, *Queen Christina* (1933) as Don Antonio de la Prada, his last film with Greta Garbo, and *The Captain Hates The Sea* (1934) as Steve Bramley. Gilbert was married four times. On August 26, 1918, he married Olivia Burwell in Hollywood. They divorced in 1921, when he married Leatrice Joy. Their daughter, also named Leatrice Joy, was born on September 6, 1924. The couple was divorced in June 1926. On May 9, 1929, he eloped to Las Vegas with actress Ina Claire. They divorced in Los Angeles on August 4, 1931. On August 10, 1932, he married actress Virginia Bruce and their daughter, Susan Ann, was born on August 2, 1933. They divorced on May 25, 1934, due to his drinking. For years the story has done the rounds that Gilbert's voice was the reason his career faltered. This is simply not true. His demise can be laid squarely at the door of Louis B. Mayer.
CAUSE: Gilbert's death at the age of 36 at 9.05am on January 9, 1936, was officially put down to heart failure. In

fact, he choked to death on his tongue after being given something to help him sleep. He passed away in Los Angeles, California. He was cremated and his ashes buried in Whispering Pines at Forest Lawn Memorial-Parks, 1712 South Glendale Avenue, Glendale, California 91209. Among those in attendance were John Barrymore, Gary Cooper, Marlene Dietrich, Cedric Gibbons, Samuel Goldwyn, Myrna Loy, David O. Selznick, Irene Mayer Selznick, Irving Thalberg and King Vidor. Dietrich caused a spectacle by fainting as she approached the open coffin. She later bought at auction the sheets on which she and Gilbert had had sex.
FURTHER READING: *Dark Star: The Meteoric Rise And Eclipse Of John Gilbert* – Leatrice Gilbert Fountain with John R. Maxim (London: Sidgwick & Jackson, 1985).

Dorothy Gish
(DOROTHY ELIZABETH DE GUICHE)
Born March 11, 1898
Died June 4, 1968
The lesser-known sister. Born in Dayton, Ohio, 5′ Dorothy Gish was part of an acting family that included her mother Mary Gish (d. New York, September 16, 1948) and sister Lillian Gish. When legendary director D.W. Griffith showed an interest in the sisters for one of his films Dorothy imperiously replied, "Sir, we are of the *legitimate* theatre." It was Dorothy who was probably the more talented, but Lillian allowed herself to be moulded by Griffith and she became the more famous and infinitely more durable star. Dorothy made over 100 films, including *An Unseen Enemy* (1912) as the younger sister (her and Lillian's début), *Gold And Glitter* (1912), *My Baby* (1912), *Brutality* (1912), *My Hero* (1912), *Pa Says* (1913), *Almost A Wild Man* (1913), *Oil And Water* (1913), *Just Gold* (1913), *Her Mother's Oath* (1913), *Their First Acquaintance* (1914), *Silent Sandy* (1914), *Sands Of Fate*

(1914), *Liberty Belles* (1914), *Her Mother's Necklace* (1914), *Her Father's Silent Partner* (1914), *Granny* (1914), *A Duel For Love* (1914), *Down The Road To Creditville* (1914), *Arms And The Gringo* (1914), *The Avenging Conscience: Thou Shalt Not Kill* (1914), *Victorine* (1915), *Out Of Bondage* (1915), *Minerva's Mission* (1915), *Her Mother's Daughter* (1915), *Her Grandparents* (1915), *How Hazel Got Even* (1915), *Bred In The Bone* (1915) as Mercy, *Jordan Is A Hard Road* (1915) as Cora Findley, *Betty Of Greystone* (1916) as Betty Lockwood, *Little Meena's Romance* (1916) as Meena, *Susan Rocks The Boat* (1916) as Susan Johnstone, *Atta Boy's Last Race* (1916) as Lois Brandon, *Children Of The Feud* (1916) as Sairy Ann, *Her Official Fathers* (1917) as Janice, *The Hun Within* (1918) as Beth, the lead roles in *Battling Jane* (1918), *Boots* (1919), *Peppy Polly* (1919) and *Nugget Nell* (1919), *Turning The Tables* (1919) as Doris Pennington, *Remodeling Her Husband* (1920) as Janie Wakefield, *Mary Ellen Comes To Town* (1920) as Mary Ellen, *Little Miss Rebellion* (1920) as Grand Duchess Marie Louise, *Orphans Of The Storm* (1921) as Louise Girard, *Fury* (1923) as Minnie, *Romola* (1924) as Tessa, *Nell Gwyn* (1926) as Nell Gwyn, *Tiptoes* (1927), *Madame Pompadour* (1927) as Madame Pompadour, *Our Hearts Were Young And Gay* (1944) as Mrs Skinner and *The Cardinal* (1963) as Celia. In 1920 she married actor James Rennie. They divorced 15 years later.
CAUSE: She died aged 70 in Rapallo, Italy, of bronchial pneumonia.

Lillian Gish

(LILLIAN DE GUICHE)
Born October 14, 1893
Died February 27, 1993
'The First Lady of the Silent Screen'. Born in Springfield, Ohio, 5′4″ Lillian Gish was not only one of the leading actresses of the silent era, she also had one of the longest careers in cinematic history – 75 years. Appearing with her sister in many films, Lillian Gish became a star through her performance in D.W. Griffith's *The Birth Of A Nation* (1915) as Elsie Stoneman, though she had made over 35 films prior to that. Griffith fell in love with her and before their falling out (over money) she appeared in his *Intolerance* (1916), *Hearts Of The World* (1918) as Marie Stephenson, *Broken Blossoms* (1919) as Lucy Burrows, *Way Down East* (1920) as Anna Moore and *Orphans Of The Storm* (1921) as Henriette Girard. She excelled in the silent flicks *The Scarlet Letter* (1926) as Hester Prynne and *The Wind* (1928) as Letty Mason. Her career did not end with the advent of the talkies, unlike many of her contemporaries. She was masterful in *Duel In The Sun* (1946) as Laura Belle McCanles, for which she was nominated for a Best Supporting Actress Academy Award, and *The Night Of The Hunter* (1955) as Rachel Cooper, and was still wowing audiences almost 40 years later in *The Whales Of August* (1987) as Sarah Webber. In the latter, she played opposite Bette Davis; the two had a somewhat spiky relationship. Director Lindsay Anderson remembered, "Lillian Gish did confide that one of the advantages of being old was not having to do love scenes any more . . . At one point, Bette Davis asked me if I'd found out anything about the rumours about Lillian [being a lesbian]. 'Is she or isn't she?' she hissed. I whispered to her, 'Don't ask me, Bette. Ask her long-time girlfriend.' "
CAUSE: She died in New York of heart failure. She was 99 years old.

Brian Glover

Born April 2, 1934
Died July 24, 1997
Bluff Yorkshireman. Born in Sheffield, South Yorkshire, the bald Glover worked as a teacher and part-time wrestler (under the name Leon Arras –

from Paris, France) before finding fame as a teacher in *Kes* (1968), the story of a boy and his kestrel. He went on to appear in *O! Lucky Man* (1972), *Mister Quilp* (1975), *Sweeney!* (1976), *Joseph Andrews* (1977), *The First Great Train Robbery* (1978), *An American Werewolf In London* (1981), *The Company Of Wolves* (1984) as the amorous boy's dad, *Ordeal By Innocence* (1984), *Alien 3* (1992) as Andrews and *Leon The Pig Farmer* (1993) as Brian Chadwick. On television he was known as the distinctive voice of advertisements for tea and bread. He had two children: a daughter, Maxine, by his ex-wife, Elaine Foster, whom he married on July 10, 1954, and a son, Gus (b. 1982), by his second wife Tara Angleen Kamla Prem, a film producer to whom he was married on October 2, 1996. CAUSE: Glover died aged 63 from a brain tumour at Trinity Hospice, Clapham, south London. An operation to remove the growth in 1996 had been only partially successful. His funeral was held at Brompton cemetery on July 30. He left £650,816.

Paulette Goddard
(PAULINE MARION LEVY)
Born June 3, 1905
Died April 23, 1990
Chaplin's cast-off. Born in Great Neck, New York, probably the only reason the name of Paulette Goddard is known today is because she was the third wife of comedian Sir Charlie Chaplin. On October 1, 1937, she screen-tested unsuccessfully for the part of Scarlett O'Hara in *Gone With The Wind* (1939). Paulette was somewhat famed for her collection of jewels, all of which she had managed to cadge from a bevy of husbands and assorted lovers. Goddard once told Marlene Dietrich, "Never, ever sleep with a man until he gives you a pure white stone (diamond) of at least ten carats." Her third husband was actor Burgess Meredith, and her fourth the novelist Erich Maria Remarque, who

wrote *All Quiet On The Western Front*. Paulette's first husband was one Edgar James, whose true occupation was uncertain. Rumour had it that Mr James was a professional gambler who used Paulette as a 'shill' in some of his games to extract takings from suckers. They met when she was appearing in the Ziegfeld Follies in Palm Beach. He followed her back to New York, where they were married in November 1927. Her films included *Berth Marks* (1929), *Young Ironsides* (1932), *Pack Up Your Troubles* (1932), *Modern Times* (1936), *Dramatic School* (1938) as Nana, *The Women* (1939) as Miriam Aarons, *The Cat And The Canary* (1939) as Joyce Norman, *The Ghost Breakers* (1940) as Mary Carter, *The Great Dictator* (1940) as Hannah, *North West Mounted Police* (1940) as Louvette Corbeau, *Second Chorus* (1940) as Ellen Miller, *Nothing But The Truth* (1941) as Gwen Saunders, *Hold Back The Dawn* (1941) as Anita Dixon, *Reap The Wild Wind* (1942) as Loxi Claiborne, *The Forest Rangers* (1942) as Celia Huston, *So Proudly We Hail!* (1943) as Lieutenant Joan O'Doul, *I Love A Soldier* (1944) as Eve Morgan, *The Diary Of A Chambermaid* (1946) as Célestine, the lead in *Kitty* (1946), *Suddenly, It's Spring* (1947) as Mary Morely, *Unconquered* (1947) as Abby Hale, *On Our Merry Way* (1948) as Martha Pease, the title role in *Anna Lucasta* (1949), *Bride Of Vengeance* (1949) as Lucretia Borgia, *Babes In Bagdad* (1952) as Kyra, *Sins Of Jezebel* (1953) as Jezebel, *Paris Model* (1953) as Betty Barnes, *Vice Squad* (1953) as Mona and *Charge Of The Lancers* (1954) as Tanya. CAUSE: She died in Ronco, Switzerland, of heart failure aged 84.

Alexander Godunov
Born November 28, 1949
Died May 18, 1995
Blonde balletomane. Born in Sakhalin and raised in Riga, Latvia, 6′2″ Boris Alexander Godunov was the first

Bolshoi Ballet dancer to defect to the West (on August 21, 1979) although his wife and co-star Ludmila Vlasova refused to join him. He joined the American Ballet Theater but was fired in 1982. He became an actor linking up (in 1982 following his divorce) with beautiful British actress Jacqueline Bisset (in 1985 *People* called them "the most torrid twosome in showbiz") and appeared in *Witness* (1985) as Daniel Hochleitner, *The Money Pit* (1986) as Max Beissart, *Die Hard* (1988) as terrorist Karl, *Waxwork II: Lost In Time* (1992) as Scarabis and *The Zone* (1995) as Lothar Krasna.

CAUSE: He died of heart failure coupled with acute alcoholism aged 45, in Shoreham Towers, 8787 Shoreham Drive West Hollywood, California. He lay dead for two days before his corpse was discovered.

Samuel Goldwyn
(SCHMUEL GELBFISZ)
Born July 1879
Died January 31, 1974
Film producer and malapropist. Goldwyn was born in Warsaw, Poland, the eldest child of Hasidic Jews. He migrated, alone, to Birmingham, England, when he was 14. Two years later, he travelled again alone to Castle Garden, New York, where he eventually became an expert glove cutter and then glove salesman. On May 8, 1910, he married Blanche Lasky and in December 1913, calling himself Samuel Goldfish, he formed, along with brother-in-law Jesse Lasky and Cecil B. DeMille, the Jesse L. Lasky Feature Play Company. Their first film, *The Squaw Man* (1913), was such a success it allowed the company to make over 20 films in their first 12 months of business. On March 14, 1916, Goldwyn was divorced. Three months later, on June 28, 1916, the company merged with Adolph Zukor's Famous Players. The same year, after some in-fighting, Goldfish (given a

$900,000 golden handshake) formed a new partnership with Edgar Selwyn and others calling their company Goldwyn. On December 16, 1918, he legally adopted the name Goldwyn. Despite high ideals, the company suffered financially in its formative years. In April 1924 the Goldwyn company merged with Metro Pictures and Louis B. Mayer Productions to form Metro-Goldwyn-Mayer, although Goldwyn had nothing to do with the new company; he had been bought out with a million dollars. The same year he formed his own company and quickly the legend "Samuel Goldwyn Presents" came to represent great entertainment. On April 23, 1925, he married the Broadway actress Frances Howard (b. Nebraska, 1903, d. 1976). However, Goldwyn is probably equally well known for the malapropisms he made throughout his life. Most of them are almost certainly apocryphal. Goldwyn complained in his high-pitched, Polish-accented voice, "None of them are true. They're all made up by a bunch of comedians and pinned on me." Here are some of the best known:
"And don't try coming back to me on bended elbows."
"Any man who goes to a psychiatrist ought to have his head examined."
"Anything that man says, you've got to take with a dose of salts."
"Even if they had it in the streets, I wouldn't go" – on Mardi Gras.
"Frances (Howard, his second wife) *has the most beautiful hands in the world and someday I'm going to make a bust of them."*
"Gentlemen, for your information, I'd like to ask a question . . ."
"Gentlemen, include me out."
"Give me a smart idiot over a stupid genius any day."
"Go ahead but make some copies first" – to his secretary when asked if she could destroy some old files.
"He's living beyond his means, but he can afford it."

"I am going out for some tea and trumpets."

"I am very sorry that you felt it was too blood and thirsty" – telegram to James Thurber, who supposedly replied, *"Not only did I think so, but I was horror and struck."*

"I can get [Red] Indians – all I want. All I've got to do is ring up the reservoir" – after being told that the Western he was working on needed some extra Native Americans.

"I feel the same sort of victim as Frankenstein."

"I had a great idea this morning, but I didn't like it."

"I love the ground I walk on. Just look at what it has done for me."

"I never put on a pair of shoes until I've worn them for five years."

"I ran into George Kaufman last night. He was at my house for dinner."

"I read part of it all the way through."

"I want you to cohabit with me" – to a female writer with whom he wanted to collaborate on a story.

"I was always an independent, even when I had partners."

"I will not stand to have you treat me like the dirt under my feet."

"If you can't give me your word of honour, will you give me a promise?"

"I've been laid up with intentional flu."

"I've gone where the hand of man has never set foot."

"I've just returned from 10 Drowning Street, so I know what I'm talking about."

"If I entered into an agreement with that man, I should be sticking my head in a moose."

"It rolls off my back like a duck" – on criticism.

"It will create an excitement that will sweep the country like wild flowers."

"It's more than magnificent. It's mediocre!"

"It's not worth the paper it's written on" – on a verbal contract. Although this is usually reported as *the* Goldwynism, a slightly different version is also said to have been: *"That fellow is a crook. His word isn't worth the paper it's written on."*

"Let's bring it up to date with some snappy nineteenth-century dialogue."

"Modern dancing is so old-fashioned."

"My! What will they think of next?" – on seeing a sundial at Jack Warner's house (or possibly at Sam Harris' home).

"My autobiography should only be written after I'm dead."

"Our comedies are not to be laughed at."

"Sex will outlive us all."

"(These people) are always biting the hand that laid the golden egg."

"To hell with the cost – we'll make it anyway" – when told a story was too caustic.

"Tomorrow we shoot, whether it rains, whether it snows, whether it stinks."

"What we want is a story that starts with an earthquake and works its way up to a climax."

"When I want your opinion, I'll give it to you" – to a young writer.

"When it comes to ruining a painting, he's an artist" – on an abstract artist.

"Why call him Joe? Every Tom, Dick and Harry is called Joe."

"Why should people go out and pay money to see bad films when they can stay at home and watch bad television for nothing?"

"You are partly one hundred per cent right."

"You just don't realise what life is all about until you have found yourself lying on the brink of a great abscess."

"You write with great warmth and charmth." (Very apocryphal.)

"You've got to take the bull by the teeth." Of his rival Louis B. Mayer, Goldwyn supposedly commented, "We're like friends. We're like brothers. We love each other. We'd do anything for each other. We'd even cut each other's throats for each other." He detested being taken for an ill-educated buffoon, but sometimes he was his own worst enemy. One day Goldwyn approached newspaper columnist and *What's My Line?*'s resident panellist Dorothy Kilgallen and told her he was to be the mystery guest on her show. Kilgallen could do nothing except disqualify herself from the broadcast. Later Goldwyn confessed his folly to Bennett

Cerf. "I told Dorothy Kilgallen I was going to be a guest on her show." That week Dorothy Kilgallen and Bennett Cerf both disqualified themselves from *What's My Line?*

CAUSE: In 1969 Goldwyn suffered a severe stroke that left him mute and partially paralysed. He was bedridden or confined to a wheelchair for the rest of his life. In January 1974 he was admitted to St John's Hospital, Santa Monica, "for treatment of a kidney ailment". Goldwyn died at 2am of heart failure in his home in Laurel Lane, Los Angeles. He was just six months short of his 95th birthday. He was buried in a short, private ceremony in Crypt B of Forest Lawn Memorial-Parks, 1712 Glendale Avenue, Glendale, California 91209. His estate was worth $16,165,490.24.

FURTHER READING: *Goldwyn: A Biography Of The Man Behind The Myth* – Samuel Marx (New York: W.W. Norton, 1976); *The Goldwyn Touch: A Biography Of Sam Goldwyn* – Michael Freedland (London: Harrap, 1986); *Goldwyn: A Biography* – A. Scott Berg (London: Hamish Hamilton, 1989).

Lucy Gordon
Born May 22, 1980
Died May 20, 2009
Wasted life. Born in Oxford, she was educated at £10,000-a-year Oxford High School where she passed nine GCSEs. She began modelling while in the fourth year at secondary school and was later signed to the Select modelling agency. She made her film debut in *Perfume* (2001) in the bit part of Sarah. She had another bit part in *Serendipity* (released October 2001). The following year she appeared in the larger role (of Isabelle) in the military drama *The Four Feathers* (premièred September 17, 2002). She made no films for three years before returning with *Les Poupées Russes* (2005) in which she was Celia Shelburn. She played television reporter Jennifer Dugan in

Spider-Man 3 (2007). She was Kate Hardwick in *Frost* (released June 12, 2009). She played a hitchhiker in *Brief Interviews With Hideous Men* (released September 25, 2009) before her biggest role, that of actress Jane Birkin in a biopic of singer-songwriter Serge Gainsbourg, Joann Sfar's *Serge Gainsbourg, Vie Héroïque* (released January 20, 2010).

CAUSE: Two days before her 29th birthday, Gordon hanged herself in the two-bedroom £2,000-a-month rented flat in La Rue des Petites Ecuries, Paris, France that she shared with her much older cinematographer boyfriend, Jérome Alméras. Gordon left two suicide notes; one detailing her last wishes regarding her estate, the other a letter for her parents.

Cliff Gorman
Born October 13, 1936
Died September 5, 2002
Powerful stage presence. Born in Queens, New York, Gorman was educated at the Manhattan High School of Music and Art and later got a B.Ed. from New York University. Before turning to acting he worked as a trucker, an ambulance driver and a probation officer working with juvenile delinquents. He then landed a job with Jerome Robbins' American Theater Lab. This led to the role of Emory in Mart Crowley's gay play *The Boys In The Band* at the Theater Four from April 15, 1968. Written in five weeks, the play was said to have earned Crowley more than $1 million. The play ran for 1,002 performances, finally closing on September 6, 1970. A film version opened on March 17, 1970 with Gorman reprising his role. Gorman had made his film début playing a gay character in George Cukor's *Justine* (1969). Gorman's next big role was playing the comedian Lenny Bruce in the Julian Barry play *Lenny*. However, when Bob Fosse came to make the film version in 1974 he overlooked Gorman in favour of

Dustin Hoffman. However, Hoffman had seen Gorman on stage and told Fosse that Gorman was the only man for the part. It was only when Fosse said that Gorman was not a big enough "name" that Hoffman finally relented and agreed to make the film. In 1980 Fosse attempted to make up for his decision by casting Gorman as a Lenny Bruce-type comedian in *All That Jazz* (1980). In 1977 Gorman was nominated for a Tony for his portrayal of Leo Schneider in Neil Simon's play *Chapter Two*. Gorman's other films included *Cops And Robbers* (1973), *An Unmarried Woman* (1978), *Hoffa* (1992), *Ghost Dog: The Way Of The Samurai* (1999) and *King Of The Jungle* (2001). He was married to Gayle. CAUSE: Gorman died aged 65 of acute leukaemia.

Betty Grable

(RUTH ELIZABETH GRABLE)
Born December 18, 1916
Died July 2, 1973
'Million Dollar Legs'. Betty Grable was born at 3858 Lafayette St, St Louis, Missouri. A sister, Marjorie, was born on April 17, 1909 (d. 1980 from a stroke), and a brother, John Karl, was born in 1914, but died in 1916 of bronchial pneumonia. Betty began her Hollywood career before she was 14, thanks to a pushy mother who was adept at falsifying documents, including legal ones when it suited. Lillian Grable, known as Billie, listed her 13-year-old daughter as 16. Billie appeared in black face in the chorus of *Let's Go Places* (1930) at Fox, but when the executives discovered her true age *after* the film, she was sacked. Undeterred, Lillian took her along to the Goldwyn Studios, where Betty was one of 20 (along with Lucille Ball, Ann Dvorak, Virginia Bruce and Paulette Goddard) chosen to be the original Goldwyn Girls. She appeared in bit parts in films such as *Palmy Days* (1931) and *The Kid From Spain* (1932). She was in a crowd scene in *Kiki*

(1931) and played a model in *The Greeks Had A Word For It* (1932). It was while filming *Palmy Days* when she was only 15 that she started dating actor George Raft, who was some 21 years older than her. However, she was closely chaperoned by her mother and Raft finally gave up, saying, "I'm giving her back till she grows up." Her next boyfriend was 19-year-old Kansas-born drummer Charlie Price, to whom she lost her virginity, aged 16. Arranging a date in San Francisco's foggy beaches, Price took Grable, her chaperoning mother and another couple out in his 1933 Oldsmobile convertible and gave Mrs Grable rather a large amount of wine to drink. So much, in fact, that she passed out and that's when Price made his move on Betty; her mother lay nearby in a drunken slumber as the two couples made out in the sand dunes. Betty originally appeared in films under the name Frances Dean before reverting to her real name for *Hold 'Em Jail* (1932). In the latter part of 1932 Betty joined the Frank Fay musical *Tattle Tales*. Fay was an alcoholic and this caused the play to close not long after it opened. Betty subsequently landed a job as a singer with the Ted Fio Rito Orchestra. In the summer of 1933 they let her go, claiming her voice wasn't suitable for recording, though she did appear in the film *The Sweetheart Of Sigma Chi* (1933) as part of the orchestra. She relocated to San Francisco and joined the Jay Whidden Orchestra who were resident at the city's Mark Hopkins Hotel. Over the next five years Betty featured in 16 films including two – *The Gay Divorcee* (1934) and *Follow The Fleet* (1936) – that starred Fred Astaire and Ginger Rogers. RKO was so impressed by her performance in *The Gay Divorcee* they signed her to a contract, plucked her eyebrows, dyed her hair platinum and put her in *The Nitwits* (1935) as Mary Roberts, *Old Man Rhythm* (1935) as Sylvia and *Don't Turn 'Em Loose* (1936) as Mildred. In the late summer of 1935 Betty met and fell in love with 20-year-old Jackie Coogan. (Lillian was not slow to grasp that Jackie would inherit a $4-million fortune when he turned 21 later that year.) The publicity generated by the affair made Betty a household name. It resulted in a national tour with Coogan, but still the studios didn't seem to know what to do with her. RKO lent her to 20th Century Fox for *Pigskin Parade* (1936). On November 20, 1937, she married Jackie Coogan at St Brendan's Catholic Church, Los Angeles. Finally, Paramount offered her a two-year contract and she appeared in *This Way Please* (1937) as Jane Morrow, *Thrill Of A Lifetime* (1937) as Gwen, *College Swing* (1938) as Betty, *Give Me A Sailor* (1938) as Nancy Larkin, *Campus Confessions* (1938) as Joyce Gilmore (the first film that gave her top billing), *Million Dollar Legs* (1939) as Carol Parker and *Man About Town* (1939) as Susan Hayes. While filming the latter, Betty collapsed on set and was rushed to hospital with acute appendicitis. Production resumed a month later, with Dorothy Lamour playing Betty's part, though Betty was well enough to appear in a speciality number. On October 11, 1939, Betty and Coogan were divorced, due to financial worries. When she completed *Million Dollar Legs* (the legs in question belonged to a racehorse) Paramount dropped her contract. However, Darryl F. Zanuck was always looking for new talent for 20th Century Fox and he offered Betty a contract. Zanuck did not have a specific project in mind for Betty when he signed her, so she was immediately loaned to Broadway for the show *Dubarry Was A Lady*. It was a smash, one of the highlights being Betty's duet with Charles Walters on 'Well Did You Evah'. Although the musical ran for a year Betty left the cast in June 1940 to appear in the film that made her a fully fledged film star, *Down Argentine Way* (1940) starring as Glenda Crawford opposite Don Ameche. Making her

Hollywood début in the film was Carmen Miranda. She only landed the part because the original choice, Alice Faye, fell ill. As soon as filming was completed, Betty went on to play Alice Faye's sister in *Tin Pan Alley* (1940). Many thought there would be fireworks between the two leading ladies, but they got on splendidly, becoming lifelong friends. Betty then went on a working holiday to Chicago with boyfriend Victor Mature and met bandleader Harry Haag James (b. Albany, Georgia, March 15, 1916, d. July 5, 1983, of cancer). Betty was voted Best Figure of 1941 and back in Hollywood she made *Moon Over Miami* (1941), playing the part of Kay Latimer. The film was a hit but then Betty appeared in three turkeys – *A Yank In The RAF* (1941) as Carol Brown, *I Wake Up Screaming* (1941) as Jill Lynn and *Footlight Serenade* (1942) as Pat Lambert. She hit the big time again with *Song Of The Islands* (1942) as Eileen O'Brien, in which she co-starred with Victor Mature. In *Springtime In The Rockies* (1942), in which she played Vicky Lane, her co-stars were Cesar Romero, Carmen Miranda and Harry James, whom she by now fancied something rotten. In 1943 she made *Sweet Rosie O'Grady* (1943) as Madeleine Marlowe/Rosie O'Grady, and became the top box-office draw. Her footprints were enshrined at Grauman's Chinese Theater on Hollywood Boulevard, she married Harry James on July 5 at the Frontier Hotel in Las Vegas and her legs were supposedly insured for $1 million by Lloyds of London. One of the most famous images of World War II was a portrait of Betty taken from behind, which subsequently adorned many a fighter plane. Photographed by Frank Powolney (b. 1899, d. January 1984 of a heart attack), the publicity department at Fox labelled it "the picture that launched a million dreams." The stories about how the pic came to be taken are legion. One has it that Betty was pregnant or had a flabby tummy and didn't want to be photographed from the front. Another reports Fox chief Darryl Zanuck entering the studio and Betty turning round to say hello as the picture was being taken. Photographer Powolney insists that Betty was trying on different swimsuits and as she was walking away to change she looked over her shoulder. Powolney thought it would make a good shot and that was that. Not long after the shoot Betty underwent an abortion (her second). At 4.45am on March 3, 1944, at the Cedars of Lebanon Hospital, Betty gave birth to Victoria Elizabeth James. Five months later she began work on *Billy Rose's Diamond Horseshoe* (1945). Next up was her least favourite of her own films, *Pin-Up Girl* (1944) in which she played Lorry Jones. Critics gave it mixed reviews but it was a box-office hit. Zanuck cast Betty and June Haver in *The Dolly Sisters* (1945) and, for once, Betty did not gel with a co-star. Nevertheless, Fox and Betty had another hit on their hands. Zanuck decided he wanted to enlarge Betty's appeal and suggested the lead in *The Razor's Edge*. Betty demurred, saying: "I'm a song and dance girl. I can act enough to get by. But that's the limit of my talents." No one said no to Darryl F. Zanuck, and he suspended Betty until virtually the end of 1946 when she began to film *The Shocking Miss Pilgrim* (1947) as Cynthia Pilgrim. The film had a Victorian setting, which meant Betty didn't show her legs, and Fox was inundated with thousands of letters of complaint. In *Mother Wore Tights* (1947) Betty played Myrtle McKinley Burt opposite Dan Dailey, who became her close friend. On May 20, 1947, after a difficult labour, Betty bore her second daughter, Jessica, at Cedars of Lebanon Hospital. Harry James could not be reached in Atlantic City to be told about his daughter's arrival and Betty took out her fury on the medical staff. Sensing

an apparent indifference in James, she began smoking heavily and drinking too much. Her next film, *That Lady In Ermine* (1948), was not a success ("Audiences stayed away from *The Lady In Ermine* like it was 'The Lady With Leprosy'. I thought, well there's one consolation, it can't get any worse than this. Then along came *The Beautiful Blonde From Bashful Bend*") and probably heralded the beginning of the end of her career. She also did not like her co-star Douglas Fairbanks, Jr. *When My Baby Smiles At Me* (1948) in which Betty played Bonny was a mild hit but the next film, *The Beautiful Blonde From Bashful Bend* (1949), flopped. The following year she remade one of her earlier pictures, *Coney Island* (1943), as *Wabash Avenue*. Zanuck, ever fearful of diminishing box-office returns, introduced a newcomer, Mitzi Gaynor, in Betty's next movie, *My Blue Heaven* (1950). *Call Me Mister* (1951) saw her fourth and final pairing with her pal Dan Dailey. Zanuck put Betty in the strenuous *Meet Me After The Show* (1951) and then ordered her to work on a similarly energetic film immediately afterwards. When Betty refused, he suspended her again. Returning, she appeared in *The Farmer Takes A Wife* (1953) as Molly Larkin and *How To Marry A Millionaire* (1953) as Loco Dempsey, starring opposite Marilyn Monroe and Lauren Bacall. As with Alice Faye, studio gossips believed Grable and Monroe would hate each other but as with Faye, Marilyn and Betty became firm friends. In July 1953 Betty walked out of her Fox contract, having been suspended for a third time when Zanuck wanted to lend her to Columbia. Two years later, Zanuck asked her to appear in *How To Be Very, Very Popular* (1955) as Stormy Tornado after Marilyn Monroe had nixed the part. When it was released in July 1955 the critics were unimpressed. It was over. She turned to theatre and began appearing in shows such as *Guys And Dolls* with Dan Dailey and

Hello Dolly. In October 1965 she and Harry James were divorced. Some shows were more successful than others.

CAUSE: On April 10, 1972, Betty and Dick Haymes presented the Oscar for Best Scoring. During the ceremony Betty felt a pressing in her chest, but continued anyway. After the show she was due to fly out of Los Angeles but had difficulty breathing and was taken to St John's Hospital, Santa Monica, where she was diagnosed with lung cancer. On May 6, 1972, she underwent an operation to see if the cancer had spread to her lymph glands. It had. She underwent chemotherapy and convalesced at home, 164 Tropicana Road, Las Vegas. Bills needed to be paid and so she returned to work. The cancer returned with a vengeance and she was readmitted to St John's in September 1972, where she underwent yet more surgery. The cancer's advance in her lungs had been halted but it had spread to her intestines. Once again she returned to work. On April 24, 1973, a spokesman at St John's announced Betty was ill with a duodenal ulcer. Not long after, she underwent a hysterectomy. Betty was sent home but later readmitted to St John's where she died, around 5pm, aged 56. Her funeral was held at All Saints Episcopal Church, Beverly Hills. Betty was cremated and her ashes interred in the Sanctuary of Dawn at Inglewood Memorial Park, 720 East Florence Avenue, Inglewood, California 90301. After Betty's death her daughter Jessie visited her mother's safe deposit box. At the very bottom, underneath a few documents, lay an envelope containing a note. Betty had written: "Sorry, there's nothing more."

FURTHER READING: *Betty Grable: The Reluctant Movie Queen* – Doug Warren (London: Robson Books, 1982); *Pin-Up: The Tragedy Of Betty Grable* – Spero Pastos (New York: Berkeley, 1987).

Lew Grade, Baron Grade of Elstree

(LOUIS WINOGRADSKY)
Born December 25, 1906
Died December 13, 1998

The ultimate showman. Lord Grade was born in Tokmak, near Odessa, Ukraine, the eldest of four children, three boys and a girl, of Isaac Winogradsky (b. Odessa, Russia, 1879, d. Hammersmith Hospital, London, October, 1935 of Hodgkin's disease), and his wife, Golda (later Olga) Mary Eisenstadt (b. Alexandrovsk, Russia, 1886, d. Grosvenor House Hotel, Park Lane, Mayfair, London, January 16, 1981) who married exactly nine months before his birth. The other children were Boris (later Barnet, then (Sir) Bernard Delfont, then Baron Delfont of Stepney; b. Tokmak, September 5, 1909, d. July 28, 1994), Lazarus (later Leslie) (b. London, June 3, 1916, d. France, October 15, 1979 from the effects of a stroke) and Rita (b. London, January 23, 1925). Isaac Winogradsky was an enthusiastic businessman but all his endeavours ended in failure; it was his wife who was the powerhouse in the family. In 1912 Isaac Winogradsky moved his family from Russia to London's East End. Young Louis was sent to Rochelle Street School in Shoreditch, but because he could not speak English was put in a class with younger children. A keen intelligence, a photographic memory and the ability to learn quickly resulted in him being more fluent than his parents. He won a scholarship to college but decided to work instead and, aged 15, took a job in a clothing company. Two years later, with his father, he set up an embroidery factory. Adopting the name Louis Grad, he became a dancer and called himself the world champion Charleston dancer after winning a contest at the Albert Hall that was judged by the impresario C.B. Cochran and Fred Astaire. In 1926 he became a professional hoofer and toured Britain and Europe (appearing at the Moulin Rouge, a Parisian newspaper misspelled his name as Grade and he accepted the mistake) as "Lew Grade, the Dancer with the Humorous Feet". In the following decade he retired from dancing and began a new career as a show business agent. With Joe Collins, the father of actor Joan (b. Bayswater, London, May 23, 1933) and novelist Jackie (b. Fordwych Road, Hampstead, north London, October 4, 1937), Grade formed the Collins and Grade Agency and booked acts that he had seen when he was touring as a dancer. During the Second World War he served briefly as an entertainment officer in the army but left because he was unfit for duty – the Charleston had wrecked his knees. On June 23, 1942, at Caxton Hall register office in London, he married Kathleen Sheila Moody (b. June 23, 1921), a singer and dancer and formerly one of Beams' Breezy Babes. Kathy Grade was a Roman Catholic and, as a result, Olga Winogradsky refused to attend the ceremony, although the two women later became good friends. In 1952 they adopted a son, Paul (b. August 1952), after Kathy had several miscarriages. Grade claimed that his marriage was the "best deal I ever made". In January 1943 he and Collins split and Grade took over his brother's business while Leslie was serving his country. On demob the brothers formed Lew and Leslie Grade Ltd. Despite his blustery exterior, Grade was nervous and to hide his fear he took to smoking huge cigars. In time Lew and Leslie Grade Ltd became the second largest theatrical agency in Europe after William Morris. In America they represented, among others, Jack Benny, Bob Hope, Lena Horne, Danny Kaye, Dorothy Lamour and Louis Armstrong. The advent of independent television in Britain in the Fifties allowed them to expand their portfolio. With theatre impresarios Prince Littler and Val Parnell, who ran the Stoll Moss group, and Binkie Beaumont, Grade formed the Independent Television Corporation (ITC). The company took a stake in ATV which had the franchise for weekday television in London and weekend TV in the Midlands. ATV moved into America, purchased Elstree film studios and, in 1965, took over Stoll Moss, Britain's biggest theatre chain and then bought Northern Songs, which had the rights to The Beatles' song publishing, and Pye Records. Among the ATV fare was *Emergency Ward Ten, The Saint, The Power Game, Danger Man, The Prisoner, The Persuaders, Stingray, Thunderbirds, Captain Scarlet* and *Space 1999*. In 1976, in a joint project with Italian television, he produced the biblical epic, *Moses The Lawgiver*, starring Burt Lancaster. He followed it with the even more ambitious *Jesus Of Nazareth* (1977), and claimed that Pope Paul VI had suggested the film during an audience at the Vatican. Pope John Paul II was a fan and Grade became one of the few Jews to be a papal knight. Grade's next success was *The Muppet Show*, an offshoot of the multi-Emmy award-winning *The Julie Andrews Hour*. The puppet show ran for 120 episodes over five years and spawned five films and numerous videos. Grade also produced *The Tamarind Seed* (1974), *The Return Of The Pink Panther* (1974), *Farewell My Lovely* (1975), *The Eagle Has Landed* (1976), *The Cassandra Crossing* (1976), *The Boys From Brazil* (1978) and *The Big Sleep* (1978). His *Raise The Titanic* (1980) was a costly flop prompting Grade to quip, "It would have been cheaper to lower the Atlantic." Two films were more successful – *On Golden Pond* (1981) and *Sophie's Choice* (1982), although the euphoria was tempered by a court battle with the Australian entrepreneur Robert Holmes à Court that resulted in Grade leaving the company amid much rancour. In June 1982 Grade became chairman and chief executive of the London-based Embassy Communications International but the only noteworthy film was *Champions* (1984), the tale of jockey Bob Champion who beat cancer to win the Grand National. His last film was *Something To Believe In* (1998) but it was not a notable success. Lew Grade was knighted in 1969 and made a peer in 1976. His only hobby was work and he was usually at his desk by 7am. He rarely took holidays and loved making and executing deals. He relied on handshakes rather than written contracts and expected others to honour the same. Lew Grade, like Samuel Goldwyn, often found quotes and anecdotes attributed to him. Many he denied but some he confessed to. Among his pearls: "All my shows are great. Some of them are bad, but they are all great." One day he and Leslie were in a restaurant when Leslie suddenly jumped up, "I've forgotten to lock the office safe." "Don't worry," said Lew, "we are both here." When car phones started to become fashionable Bernie Delfont had one fitted in his Rolls-Royce so Lew had to get one to keep up with his brother. One day on the five minute drive from his flat to his office, he rang Delfont. "Hang on," said Bernie, "I'm on the other line." During pre-production on *Jesus Of Nazareth*, Grade was asked the names of the disciples. "Well, there's Luke and Matthew and John . . . I'll let you know the others when I've finished reading the script." He denied all of these had ever occurred. Ones he did admit to include: "My English isn't so good. I leave you to put in any grammar"; "The trouble with this business is that the stars keep 90 per cent of my earnings"; "When I get home, I have my food in front of the TV, then I start phoning. You get much better results phoning people when they're quiet and happy. I love the phone. I don't believe in writing letters"; "When I whisper I'm still shouting" and

"I have one week's holiday a year. I don't really need any more. When I've made a sale, that's a holiday."
CAUSE: Still working, he died of heart failure in the London Clinic, 20 Devonshire Place. He was 91. Three days later he was buried in the Liberal Jewish cemetery in Willesden, north London. He left £8,423,342.
FURTHER READING: *The Grades* – Hunter Davies (London, Weidenfeld & Nicolson, 1981); *Still Dancing My Story* – Lew Grade (London: Collins, 1987).

Sheilah Graham
(LILY SHEIL)
Born September 15, 1904
Died November 17, 1988
Gossip columnist. Born in London, the youngest of six Jewish children, Sheilah Graham became one of Hollywood's best-known gossip columnists and was equally infamous for her affair with married writer F. Scott Fitzgerald. The affair began when they met in the legendary Garden of Allah (a notorious hotel complex owned by Alla Nazimova), at 8150 Sunset Boulevard, on July 14, 1937, and lasted until his death from a heart attack on December 21, 1940, aged 44, in Hayworth Avenue, Hollywood, California. Rumours persist that they were having sex when he expired, although she claims he was sitting in an armchair reading *The Princeton Alumni Weekly* when he suffered a coronary, stood up and fell to the floor, where he expired. When the affair began he was shocked by her admission to having taken eight lovers before him. Incredibly, during all their time together, she never saw him naked. Like many Hollywood writers, Graham appeared in a few films, usually playing herself. They included *That's Right You're Wrong* (1939), *Jiggs And Maggie In Society* (1947), *Impact* (1949), *Challenge The Wild* (1954) and *College Confidential* (1960).
CAUSE: She died aged 84 in West Palm Beach, Florida, of natural causes.
FURTHER READING: *A State Of Heat* –

Sheilah Graham (London: W.H. Allen, 1973); *My Hollywood: A Celebration And A Lament* – Sheilah Graham (London: Michael Joseph, 1984); *Intimate Lies* – Robert Weston (New York: HarperCollins, 1995).

Stewart Granger
(JAMES LABLACHE STEWART)
Born May 6, 1913
Died August 16, 1993
English swashbuckler. Granger was a handsome, smooth actor who changed his name to avoid confusion with the American actor of the same name. Born at 2am on the Old Brompton Road, London, the second of the two children of Major James Stewart, MBE (1861–1938), of the Royal Engineers, and Frederica Lablache, he became a film extra in *A Southern Maid* at the behest of his friend Michael Wilding in 1933. He studied at the Webber-Douglas Theatre School and made his stage début in Hull in *The Cardinal* (1935). He made his film *début* in 1938 in a movie called *So This Is London*. In 1940 Granger enlisted in the Gordon Highlanders as a private but disliked having to spend his time in the company of so many men but felt that he had to do his bit. On September 10, 1938 he had married the actress Elspeth March and she was pregnant when he joined up. The baby died shortly after birth and she suffered further miscarriages before their son, Jamie, was born in 1944. A daughter, Lindsay, followed two years later. Granger later transferred to the 6th battalion of the Black Watch after securing a commission as a second lieutenant. In 1942 he was invalided out with a stomach ulcer, a fortuitous accident because shortly after, most of his unit was wiped out in north Africa. The following year Granger was back in front of the cameras, cast as the Marquis of Rohan in Gainsborough Pictures' *The Man In Grey* (1943); however, he swapped roles with his close friend James Mason and achieved stardom as Peter Rokeby. He played a spiv in *Waterloo Road* (1945) but the public preferred Granger in costume dramas such as Apollodorus in *Caesar And Cleopatra* (1945). However, not everyone liked them. Of his playing the violinist Paganini in *The Magic Bow* (1946), the *Daily Graphic* said that "he appears to be sawing wood with one hand and milking a cow with the other". On April 13, 1948 he and March were divorced. He had been romancing Jean Simmons (who is noticed elsewhere in this book), his co-star in the comedy *Adam And Evelyne* (1949). Granger appeared in *King Solomon's Mines* (released November 9, 1950) with Deborah Kerr, with whom he had had an affair while married to Elspeth March. Granger signed a seven-year deal with MGM and prepared to marry Simmons. Then it began to unravel. Granger's friend Cary Grant suggested that his close pal Howard Hughes, then owner of RKO, arrange the wedding to save the happy couple the fuss and help them to avoid the press. For some reason Granger agreed. He and Simmons flew to Tucson, Arizona where they married on December 21, 1950 in the home of one of Hughes's lawyers. Granger's very close friend Michael Wilding was best man. They also enjoyed a honeymoon at Hughes' expense. Then Hughes began to show his obsession with Simmons. He bought her contract from J. Arthur Rank without consulting her or her husband. He interfered in her career refusing to let her play in William Wyler's *Roman Holiday* so the part went to Audrey Hepburn. Her contract with Rank had committed her to three more films but Hughes wanted her to sign a seven-year contract with him or he threatened to put her "in three of the lousiest movies you've ever seen". At one stage Granger even contemplated killing Hughes. He would leave him and Simmons alone at their cliff front home, then Simmons would scream

and Granger would rush in to protect her honour and push Hughes to his death on the rocks below. He abandoned the plan and instead resorted to a legal solution. They won an out-of-court settlement of $250,000, plus $35,000 costs. He turned down the male leads in *Quo Vadis?* (1951), *From Here To Eternity* (1953), and *Ben-Hur* (1959). Instead he appeared in *Fanny By Gaslight* (1943), *Captain Boycott* (1947), *Blanche Fury* (1948) as Philip Thorn although his co-star Valerie Hobson recalled Granger as "not an easy actor to work with because he was a worrier and rather moody", *King Solomon's Mines* (1950), *Scaramouche* (1952), *The Prisoner Of Zenda* (1952), *Young Bess* (1953), opposite Simmons, *Beau Brummell* (1954), *Bhowani Junction* (1956) and many, many more. He didn't much like any of his movies – "I've seldom, if ever, made a film I have really liked or been proud of . . . To spend a life making even reasonable films is bad enough, but to spend one, as I have, making terrible ones tends to be a little dispiriting" – or the film business. "The cinema world is not easy. It's full of envy from little people – heads of studios, for example, who hate people for their attractiveness". He was in *Moonfleet* (1955), *The Last Hunt* (1956), *Bhowani Junction* (1956), and *North To Alaska* (1960) and then his star began to wane. On August 12, 1960 he and Simmons were divorced. Their daughter, Tracy, had been born on September 10, 1956 and named after her godfather Spencer Tracy. On June 12, 1964 at Geneva City Hall Granger married the former Miss Belgium, Caroline Lecerf (b. 1942), but they divorced in 1969, a year after the birth of their daughter, Samantha (b. 1968). In 1967 he had renounced the American citizenship he had taken up in 1956. He is best known for his action costume films such as *Scaramouche*, a dramatic swashbuckling film starring Granger in the title role

plus Mel Ferrer, Eleanor Parker and Janet Leigh. The producer hired Jean Heremans, a European fencing champion, to teach the cast how to buckle their swashes. His teaching was not altogether successful. In one scene Heremans stood in for Mel Ferrer to 'fight' Granger. They began to fight but Granger's sword broke and a piece of metal flew off into Heremans' eye cutting his eyelid but, fortunately, not his eyeball. Later during filming another sword fight resulted in Granger being stabbed in the face when he didn't parry an attack with sufficient might. Unsurprisingly, Granger was getting rather worried and asked about insurance. He was told there wasn't any because none of the other stars had ever asked for it. He sought out MGM's Mr Fix-it Eddie Mannix (whose wife had an affair with Superman George Reeve). Eventually, Mannix agreed to Granger's demands. In another scene a chandelier was to fall towards Granger and he was to roll out of the way and continue fighting. An elaborate mechanism was constructed to stop the iron chandelier a foot above Granger so the camera would be able to get the most dramatic of shots. Granger was no fool and asked to see the device in action before he lay beneath it. The director was unhappy. The setting up had taken an hour and would take a further sixty minutes to reset it. Anyway, the man who had arranged it was the best in the business. Nonetheless, 6'3" Granger was adamant. The order was given and the chandelier began its descent and didn't stop until it embedded itself two inches into the ground. The director threw up and, to add insult to injury, Granger found out that the insurance policy he had fought so hard for hadn't become operative! The slip-ups continued on the film. In another scene he was due to fight on the ledge of a theatre box 20 feet above the ground. A special corset had been designed with a wire attached to the ceiling in case he fell. During rehearsals the corset prevented Granger from moving freely so he took it off. Back on the ledge he fell and landed, hurting his shoulder, an injury that would trouble him for the rest of his life. Finally, Granger was scheduled to 'fight' Mel Ferrer across the theatre seats. The seating had been bought from a cinema and were the usual tip-up variety. Both actors were warned not to let their legs slip down the gap. As the 'fight' progressed, vainglory got the better of Granger and, as he performed a dramatic slash with his sword, his leg fell down the gap and he collapsed. Luckily, he twisted himself as he fell but the seat was ripped from its mooring with a tremendous bang. Granger lay stunned on the floor as the assistant director rushed up to him. "Oh, Jesus Christ, he's killed himself." Granger's sense of mischievousness took over and he lay still, trying not to breathe. "It's bad George, he's not breathing. I think the poor bastard's dead." Then came the words that sum up Hollywood from director George Sidney. "What the hell are we going to do? The film's only half-finished." Granger let out a choke, "Call a doctor, you mercenary prick." To top all that, Granger was approached by a fan at the première who marvelled at the work by the 'stuntman'. When Granger said he had done all his own stunts, he was met with derision. "Oh, come on, Mr Granger. We know actors like you never take risks. We know it's someone else." CAUSE: Granger died of cancer at St John's Hospital & Health Center, Santa Monica, California, aged 80. FURTHER READING: *Sparks Fly Upward* – Stewart Granger (London: Granada, 1982); *Stewart Granger: The Last Of The Swashbucklers* – Don Shiach (London: Aurum, 2005).

Bob Grant

Born April 14, 1932
Found dead November 8, 2003
Toothsome funster. Some actors are destined to be linked with just one role in the public consciousness – Bob Grant was one such actor. No matter how he tried to break away from the role of the lecherous bus conductor Jack Harper in the television and film versions of *On The Buses*, the public would not let him. Grant was born in Hammersmith, west London and studied at the Royal Academy of Dramatic Art, working in his spare time as both (ironically) a bus conductor and a frozen food salesman. During his National Service he was commissioned in the Royal Artillery and later worked in rep before arriving in London. In 1961 he was in *Big Soft Nellie* at Joan Littlewood's Theatre Royal, Stratford East. On May 8, 1962 he got the lead in Lionel Bart's *Blitz!* at the Adelphi, a job that lasted for two years. Returning to east London he appeared in *Sparrers Can't Sing* and *Instant Marriage*, for which he wrote both the dialogue and lyrics. Grant then appeared as the bibulous foreign secretary George Brown in the dramatisation of *Mrs Wilson's Diary*, written by Richard Ingrams and John Wells. When Brown resigned from office on March 16, 1968 over the conduct of government business, Grant offered to withdraw from the part. On February 28, 1969 the first edition of *On The Buses* left London Weekend Television's garage. Written by the Ronnies Wolfe and Chesney, the sitcom had originally been offered to the BBC who declined to buy a ticket. The show gave LWT one of its biggest comedy hits, running for 74 episodes over seven series and spawning three films made by Hammer – *On The Buses* (1971), *Mutiny On The Buses* (1972) and *Holiday On The Buses* (1973). The first film was the top British box office movie of 1971, beating off all comers including *Diamonds Are Forever*, the James Bond film. The series (and films) revolved around the bachelor bus driver Stan Butler (Reg Varney) who lived at home with his doting mum (Cicely Courtneidge, then Doris Hare),

slatternly sister Olive (Anna Karen) and her work-shy husband Arthur (Michael Robbins). Butler worked with Harper (who lived a few doors away) for the Home Counties-based Luxton and District Traction Company where they operated the No 11 green double-decker bus between the Cemetery Gates and the depot. When not on board they spent their time eyeing up the mini-skirted clippies and baiting their boss, Inspector Cyril Blake (Stephen Lewis). Towards the end of the run (it finished on May 6, 1973) Grant and Lewis began writing scripts for the show. *On The Buses* was transferred to America and emerged as the sitcom *Lotsa Luck* but it was not very successful, running from September 10, 1973 until May 24, 1974. Dom DeLuise played Stan Belmont while Jack was transformed into a character called Bummy. When the show ended Grant carried on writing, producing several more comedies, including *Home Is Where Your Clothes Are* and *No Room For Love*. He toured Australia in the comedy *No Sex Please, We're British*, and appeared in musicals and pantomimes in the provinces. He could never regain the success of *On The Buses* and this troubled him deeply. Twice wed, when he married Kim Benwell in 1971 hundreds of fans forced the newlyweds to leave their hired Rolls-Royce, and the guests the double-decker, to walk to the reception. CAUSE: Bob Grant suffered from depression and in 1987 he disappeared for five days before responding to a public appeal by his wife. He disappeared again in 2003 and was found dead in Gloucestershire on November 8. He was 71.

Cary Grant
(ARCHIBALD ALEC LEACH)
Born January 18, 1904
Died November 29, 1986
Mr Smoothie. Handsome 6'1" debonair Cary Grant was the epitome of the well-groomed gentleman. Born in the Horfield district of Bristol, Archie Leach had an inauspicious start to life. Two of his biographers explain his circumcision by stating that he was the illegitimate son of a Jewish woman who either ran away or died in childbirth. There is no documentary evidence to support this assertion, however. In 1948 he gave $25,000 to the new state of Israel "in memory of my dead Jewish mother", yet at the age of 79 he denied his mother was Jewish. The same authors claim that in 1910 Archie, then six years old, joined the music hall act the Bob Pender Troupe, with his father's blessing. They go on to state that when the Bristol run ended Archie went with the troupe to Germany, Paris and London. On March 15, 1911, he sailed for New York aboard the ill-fated *Lusitania* (it was sunk four years later during World War I). The Broadway show was popular but failed because the $2.50 ticket prices were too high for most New Yorkers. So, according to the aforementioned sources, they returned to Bristol and Archie went to the Bristol Road Infant School. Again, there is no firm evidence to support this. Sometime in either 1913 or 1914 Archie came home from school and was told his mother "had died suddenly of a heart attack and had to be buried immediately". In fact, she had suffered a nervous breakdown and had been admitted to the Country Home for Mental Defectives in Fishponds, Bristol, by her husband. Mother and son were not to meet again until he was 32. In 1915 he won a scholarship to Fairfield Grade & Secondary School, enrolling on September 2. On March 13, 1918, he was expelled from school for stealing "a valise containing paints". Three days later, he rejoined Pender's touring troupe. They travelled to America again on July 21, 1920. In 1921 Archie, then 17, moved in with gay designer (and future Oscar winner) Orry-Kelly in Greenwich Village.

Archie toured America and Canada in the revue *Good Times*. In 1923 and for two years afterwards he toured with the renamed Lomas Troupe (run by Pender's daughter). Encouraged by his friends Archie began to try straight theatre and again went on tour in 1926. Back in New York he befriended up-and-coming comedians George Burns and Gracie Allen. He was also on good terms with the sexually ambiguous Moss Hart, who took parts of Archie's character and weaved them into his first successful stage play, *Once In A Lifetime*. In 1928 Archie joined the prestigious William Morris Agency. In 1929 both he and Jeanette MacDonald had screen tests for Paramount Publix Pictures at the company's Astoria studios in Long Island City. MacDonald's was sent to Hollywood but Leach's was rejected immediately. An executive told him, "You're bow-legged and your neck is too thick." Young Archie didn't seemed destined for stardom, but he refused to give up. Cary Grant was to tell later interviewers that he returned to England following this disappointment, where he made a success of himself as a theatre actor. That was not true. From May 8–13, 1931, he made his film début in a ten-minute movie entitled *Singapore Sue*. He was paid $150. In November he was spotted by Paramount chief B.P. Schulberg in a screen test for an actress and offered a long-term contract, which he signed on December 7, 1931, the day it could be said that Cary Grant was born. Fay Wray called him 'Cary' and a studio flack came up with 'Grant'. His first feature film (out of 72) was *This Is The Night* (1932), a light comedy of the type that was to make him a star. His co-stars were Lili Damita, who would marry Errol Flynn, and Thelma Todd, who would die under mysterious circumstances. Around this time Cary met a man who was to play a very important part in his life – Randolph

Scott. The two men decided to move in together. To protect their stars from the rumour mill, the studio announced the two men were sharing to save money on bills. Most of the public swallowed this hogwash. Each man was earning $450 a week and could easily afford a rent of $75 per month. When the two men turned up to Hollywood events together the studio quickly assigned them dates. Paramount placed Grant in a series of films including *Sinners In The Sun* (1932), *Blonde Venus* (1932) (opposite Marlene Dietrich), *The Devil & The Deep* (1932) and *She Done Him Wrong* (1933) as Captain Cummings, in which he co-starred with Mae West. The last of these, shot in 18 days without retakes, was the film in which Mae uttered the immortal but oft-misquoted line, "Why don't you come up sometime . . . See me?" and described him as "warm, dark and handsome". On February 9, 1934, at Westminster registry office, Cary married Virginia Cherrill, a protégée of Charlie Chaplin. Just over a year later, on March 26, 1935, the marriage was over. By 1935 he had made over 20 films and was described as a star, but in a poll held by *Motion Picture Herald* to find the top stars, Cary received less than 1% of the votes cast. In the summer of 1936 he resumed living with Randolph Scott. His professional reputation continued to climb over the next decade in movies such as *I'm No Angel* (1933) as Jack Clayton, *Alice In Wonderland* (1933), *Sylvia Scarlett* (1935) (with Katharine Hepburn; the film, directed by the homosexual George Cukor, was full of sly digs at Cary's bisexuality), *Suzy* (1936) with Jean Harlow and *The Toast Of New York* (1937). It was following his performance in *Topper* (1937) as George Kerby that he entered the strata of superstardom and became a popular box-office draw. Classic comedies followed, including *Bringing Up Baby* (1938) as David Huxley (again with Katharine Hepburn, in which he became the first man to use the word 'gay', in the sense of 'homosexual', in movies), *The Philadelphia Story* (1940) as C.K. Dexter Haven (he donated his $125,000 fee to the British War Relief Fund) and *My Favorite Wife* (1940) as Nick Arden. Cary's portrayal of newspaperman Roger Adams in *Penny Serenade* (1941) earned him his first Best Actor Oscar nomination. He lost out to Gary Cooper for *Sergeant York* (1941). Katharine Hepburn described him as "a personality functioning. A delicious personality who has learnt to do certain things marvellously well. He can't play a serious part or, let me say, the public isn't interested in him in that way, not interested in him at all, which I'm sure has been a big bugaboo to him. But he has a lovely sense of timing, an amusing face and a lovely voice." Romance once again beckoned and when Cary married Woolworth's heiress Barbara Hutton on July 8, 1942, at Lake Arrowhead, California, they were nicknamed 'Cash and Cary'. Cooed Barbara, "It's sheer heaven." Three years later, on August 30, 1945, they divorced. Throughout the Forties Grant managed to combine his light comedies (*The Talk Of The Town* [1942] as Leopold Dilg, *Arsenic & Old Lace* [1944] as Mortimer Brewster) with dramas (Alfred Hitchcock's *Suspicion* [1941] as Johnnie Aysgarth and the Oscar-nominated *None But The Lonely Heart* [1944]) and adventure films (*Destination Tokyo* [1944]). He also may have worked for British Intelligence before and during the war. In 1946 he played gay composer Cole Porter in the biopic *Night And Day* (1946). It could have been the Cary Grant Story – the tale of an unemotional workaholic who ignores his wife to spend time pursuing his career. Later that year he again teamed with Hitchcock to co-star in *Notorious* with Ingrid Bergman. On Christmas Day 1949 he married for the third time. This time his bride was the

actress Betsy Drake, 19 years his junior, and the ceremony took place in Phoenix, Arizona. In the next two decades Grant appeared in much the same fare, offering the public what they wanted. He starred in two more Hitchcock thrillers – *To Catch A Thief* (1955) and *North By Northwest* (1959). Alfred Hitchcock had a sadistic sense of humour and it is just possible that the title of *To Catch A Thief* was a sly dig at Grant's own brush with thievery. Cary played John Robie, a retired jewel thief living in the French Riviera. When a series of thefts occur with Robie's modus operandi he sets out to uncover the thief and prove his innocence. One scene called for Cary to run across rooftops without a safety net, despite his fear of heights. "I've always felt queasily uncertain whether or not Hitchcock was pleased to see me survive each day's work. I can only hope it was as great a relief to him as disappointment." In *North By Northwest* Cary played advertising executive Roger Thornhill who is kidnapped by a Soviet spy ring after they mistake him for someone else. Cary's co-star was supposed to be Sophia Loren but she was replaced after contractual difficulties by Eva Marie Saint. One memorable scene shot in the first week of October 1958 featured a plane crop-dusting a field that turns out to be an assassin intent on murdering Thornhill. Hitchcock liked to see well-turned-out actors looking messy, so he was pleased when Cary ruined his suit crawling through the dust and dirt. However, Hitch wasn't pleased with the look of fear on Cary's face until fate intervened. Cary saw a tarantula crawl over his hand; he screamed and Hitchcock filmed the expression, although he edited the scream out of the final cut. Despite his handsome appearance, not all leading ladies took to Cary Grant. Joan Fontaine called him "an incredible boor" and his *Indiscreet* (1958) co-star Ingrid Bergman opined: "He was not only stingy, he worried about everything . . . the vainest man I ever met. I never had an affair with Cary – but, then who among his leading ladies did?" Grant's meanness was legendary. At Christmas he would swap unwanted monogrammed gifts with Clark Gable. He would also check restaurant bills. "That doesn't make me a cheapskate," he insisted. "I've saved hundreds of dollars by finding mistakes in the totals of restaurant checks. I don't mind paying what I owe, but I certainly object to being charged for something I didn't receive." In 1958 he began taking LSD, a drug at the time used to remove inhibitions and combat impotence. On October 19 of that year he and Betsy Drake separated, although the actual divorce didn't occur until August 1962. On July 22, 1965, at the Desert Inn in Las Vegas, Nevada he married Dyan Cannon, another actress, and she gave birth to his only child, Jennifer, seven months later on February 26, 1966. He continued to take LSD and encouraged his wife to do the same. Later she told a reporter: "I'm telling you, if I'd stayed in that marriage I'd be dead today. Dead. Dead. Dead. Dead. Really dead! In a grave! Dead! I don't want to talk about him. He's a real pain." She sued for divorce on August 22, 1967. Following the film *Walk, Don't Run* (1966) Grant announced his retirement from the screen in 1969 and became an executive for Fabergé, the make-up company. (Odd because he never used make-up on screen.) In July 1969 he was questioned by police after a woman claimed Cary had picked up her young son at a motorway junction in Los Angeles. On April 7, 1970, he was presented with an honorary Oscar by Frank Sinatra, the same year he made an uncredited appearance in *Elvis – That's The Way It Is*. He reacted with fury in November 1980 when comedian Chevy Chase publicly called him "a great physical comic, and I understand he was a homo – What a

gal!" on the *Tomorrow Show*. He filed a $10-million lawsuit against Chase though, understandably, he did not follow through with the writ. On April 15, 1981, he married for the fifth and final time. His bride was Barbara Harris, a British PR. Grant was sensitive about his age. An old story has it that an inquisitive magazine once sent him a telegram enquiring about his age: "How old Cary Grant?" to which he replied, "Old Cary Grant fine. How you?" Sadly, it never happened. CAUSE: In October 1984 he suffered a minor stroke and was warned to take things easy. Grant was a relatively private man, rarely gave interviews and never wrote an autobiography. It therefore came as a surprise to his fans when he agreed to tour America giving talks about himself. He called the 90-minute session "A Conversation with Cary Grant". With wife Barbara, Grant arrived in Davenport, Iowa, on November 28, 1986, and booked into the Blackhawk Hotel. The following day they went sightseeing before arriving at the Adler Theater on 3rd Street. Not long after arriving, Grant felt sick and threw up. A wheelchair took him to his dressing room and then back to his hotel. He ignored calls to summon a doctor. The night's show was cancelled and finally doctors were called. He was rushed to St Luke's Hospital, becoming comatose on the way. Grant was pronounced dead at 11.22pm from a massive intracerebral haemorrhage – a major stroke. On December 1, 1986, he was cremated as per his wishes.
FURTHER READING: *Cary Grant: Haunted Idol* – Geoffrey Wansell (London: Fontana, 1984); *Cary Grant* – Chuck Ashman & Pamela Trescott (London: Star, 1988); *Cary Grant: A Touch Of Elegance* – Warren G. Harris (London: Sphere, 1988); *Cary Grant: The Lonely Heart* – Charles Higham & Roy Moseley (London: NEL, 1989); *An Affair To Remember: My Life With Cary Grant* – Maureen Donaldson and

William Royce (London: Macdonald, 1989); *Cary Grant: A Class Apart* – Graham McCann (London: Fourth Estate, 1996).

Johnny Grant
Born May 9, 1923
Died January 9, 2008
The Mayor of Hollywood. Johnny Grant was emcee at more than 500 ceremonies inducting celebrities into the Hollywood Walk of Fame. He also produced Hollywood's annual Christmas Parade. Born in Goldsboro, North Carolina, John Grant, Jr was a cub reporter for radio station WGBR who hitchhiked to Washington to cover President Franklin D. Roosevelt's third inauguration. Small in stature, Grant had to sit in a tree to get a view and write his report. In 1943, he joined the army and following demob he arrived in Hollywood where he landed the part of a reporter in *The Babe Ruth Story* (released September 6, 1948). Six years later, he played Ed Harrison in *Irving Berlin's White Christmas* (released October 14, 1954), and was himself in *The Oscar* (released July 8, 1966). He made fifteen trips to Korea (beginning in 1951) and fourteen to Vietnam to entertain the troops and was a popular radio presenter but it was as the honorary mayor of Hollywood, a title bestowed upon him in 1980 by the Hollywood Chamber of Commerce, that he was best known. He never married.
CAUSE: Grant died in his 14th-floor suite of the Hollywood Roosevelt Hotel, apparently of natural causes. He was 84.

Sid Grauman
Born March 17, 1879
Died March 5, 1950
The most trodden-on man in Hollywood. Indianapolis, Indiana-born Grauman began in the movie business with a cinema in the Yukon shortly before the start of the twentieth century. He moved to San Francisco,

where he opened several cinemas. On October 18, 1922, he opened the Egyptian Theater on Hollywood Boulevard. His more famous venue, Grauman's Chinese Theater at 6925 Hollywood Boulevard, Central Hollywood, opened on May 19, 1927. Most visitors to Hollywood travel to this location of hundreds of celebrity footprints (and handprints). One of Tinseltown's greatest tourist attractions (2 million trippers a year) may have been started with a blunder. Theories abound as to how the tradition started. It is said that Norma Talmadge visited the construction site of the theatre and accidentally stood in some wet cement. According to this version of the story, the owner, Sid Grauman, witnessed the event and was inspired with the idea of a permanent record of celebrities. Another version has it that Talmadge, Douglas Fairbanks and Mary Pickford arrived for a visit and that it was Pickford who stepped in the cement. A third account is based around an incident at Pickfair, the home of Pickford and Fairbanks. Mary Pickford's dog, Zorro, allegedly ran in some wet cement at the house. Inspired by the accident, Pickford rang Sid Grauman with the idea that she and Fairbanks put their footprints in cement outside the theatre and start a tradition. Pickford said that she generously let Grauman take the credit because he was a good friend and did own the theatre after all. Grauman himself provided fourth and fifth versions. According to one, he accidentally trod in some wet cement and was shouted at by one of his employees (is this likely?) when the idea struck him. He immediately called Pickford, Fairbanks and Talmadge and asked them to the site, whereupon he immediately told them of his concept. Alternatively, Grauman was told off as a child for ruining some wet cement and this was his adult revenge. Other stories abound, but since all the participants in the history are dead

we'll probably never know for sure. The 100th ceremony featured the impressions of Jackie Cooper. There is another showbiz blunder with regard to Grauman's. Burt Reynolds was so nervous when leaving his footprints that he mis-spelt his name!
CAUSE: He died in Hollywood aged 70 of natural causes.

Leslie Graves
Born September 29, 1959
Died August 23, 1995
Tragic beauty. Born in Silver City, New Mexico, Leslie Graves became an actress at an early age, appearing on *Sesame Street* when she was nine years old and then starring in the short-lived television series *Here We Go Again* in 1972 where she played Cindy Standish, Larry Hagman's stepdaughter. In 1975 she retired from acting. In 1980 she posed nude for some raunchy pictures, telling the world, "It's a sort of coming into adulthood present for myself. It's like saying, 'Hey world – look! I'm a woman and proud of it.'" In 1981 she played Alison Dumont in *Piranha II: The Spawning*. The fish must have had an effect on her because she retired from acting to work on a shrimp boat in Texas. However, her retirement was brief and she returned to play the spoiled 15-year-old debutante Brenda Clegg in the soap opera *Capitol* from March 26, 1982, a part she held for two years. That same year she appeared in *Death Wish II*. She once opined, "I'm easily waylaid. I love men who are tender, men who know how to touch me softly. Lord knows I've been pawed by enough creeps in my life." They were attracted to her tiny but voluptuous shape. She stood just 4'11" but measured 36D-22-31. She was married to Jerry Schoenkopf by whom she had two children, Amanda and Jimmy, born a year before his mother's death.
CAUSE: When not acting Leslie Graves liked to keep herself to herself. She died, aged 35, of an AIDS-related illness in Los Angeles, California. It seems likely that she contracted the disease from her heroin addiction.

Charles Gray
(DONALD MARSHALL GRAY)
Born August 29, 1928
Died March 7, 2000
Supercilious villain. Born in Bournemouth, Dorset, the son of a surveyor, Donald Gray began his working life as an estate agent before becoming a thespian with the Regents Park Open Air Players in 1952. His first paid job was as the wrestler Charles in *As You Like It*, a role that inspired him to change his own Christian name. He appeared on the stage regularly on both sides of the Atlantic before making the transition to movies in 1958. He usually played villains and his most memorable portrayal was probably Ernst Blofeld (the third actor in the role after Donald Pleasence and Telly Savalas), the villain with the white cat in his arms, in *Diamonds Are Forever* (1971) closely followed by the narrator in *The Rocky Horror Picture Show* (1975). He dubbed the voice of Jack Hawkins in many films when the latter suffered from cancer. Gray's films included: *The Unknown Terror* (1957) as Jim Wheatley, *Ride A Violent Mile* (1957), *I Accuse!* (1958) as Captain Brossard, *Tommy The Toreador* (1959) as Gomez, *The Entertainer* (1960), *Masquerade* (1965) as Benson, *The Night Of The Generals* (1967) as General von Seidlitz-Gabler, *You Only Live Twice* (1967) as Henderson, *The Devil Rides Out* (1968) as Mocata, *Mosquito Squadron* (1969) as Hufford, *Cromwell* (1970) as The Earl of Essex and *The Tichborne Claimant* (1998) as Arundell. A homosexual bachelor, 6'2" Gray was a close friend of Ava Gardner when she lived in London during her final years.
CAUSE: He died in Brompton Hospital, London, having smoked heavily and drunk a bottle and a half of pink gin a day for more years than he could

probably remember. His funeral took place on March 17, 2000.

Spalding Gray

Born June 5, 1941
Found dead March 8, 2004
Monologist. Spalding Gray was born at Barrington, Rhode Island, and he and his two brothers were raised as Christian Scientists. An unruly schoolboy, he set off cherry bombs in the school lavatory and threw rotten eggs in the halls. Worried about his poor academic performance – he was dyslexic – his parents enrolled him at Fryeburg Academy, Maine, where his grades improved. His interest in acting was born at Emerson College, Boston and he landed work in rep on Cape Cod after graduating in 1965. He then worked at a small theatre in Saratoga, New York, before moving to New York City in 1967 to live with his girlfriend, Elizabeth LeCompte. The suicide of his mother the same year led him into a depression that lasted for nine years and ended in his own nervous breakdown. In 1979 Gray and LeCompte formed the Wooster Group and put on the autobiographical *Sakonnet Point*, named after the Rhode Island resort where Gray had enjoyed school summer holidays. Gray wrote his first monologue, *Sex And Death To The Age 14*, using his childhood experiences against the major events of the day, including the polio epidemic, which Gray survived by "washing my hands with rubbing alcohol and staying out of crowded movie theatres". Gray's monologues were always performed at a bare desk with a glass of water his only prop. Gray's most famous monologue was *Swimming To Cambodia*, loosely based on his experiences while acting in *The Killing Fields*, filmed on location in Thailand in 1983. Three years later, *Swimming To Cambodia* was turned into a film, directed by Jonathan Demme. His next monologue was the 1986 *Terrors Of Pleasure*. Although the talks became

successful Gray found it difficult to handle the fame and in 1992 suffered a midlife crisis as he approached the age at which his mother took her own life. His films included: *Cowards* (1970), *The Farmer's Daughter* (1973) as George, the United States consul in *The Killing Fields* (1984), a travel agent in *Almost You* (1985), *Seven Minutes In Heaven* (1985) as Dr Rodney, *Hard Choices* (1985) as Terry Norfolk, *Stars And Bars* (1988) as Reverend Cardew, *Clara's Heart* (1988) as Dr Peter Epstein, *Beaches* (1988) as Dr Richard Milstein, *Straight Talk* (1992) as Dr Erdman, *Bliss* (1997) as Alfred, *How High* (2001) as Professor Jackson, *Kate & Leopold* (2001) as Dr Geisler and *The Paper Mâché Chase* (2003) as Dr Calhoun. He married twice: firstly to Renée Shafransky from whom he was divorced, and secondly to Kathleen Russo by whom he had two sons and a stepdaughter.
CAUSE: In 2001 Gray suffered a broken hip, fractured skull and sciatic nerve damage in his foot after a van crashed into his hire car in Ireland. Unimpressed by Irish hospitals, he wrote and performed a monologue about his experiences, then began a book, *Black Spot*. He became more angry and depressed about his injuries as time went on. "I can't take long walks," he complained. "I don't feel whole any more. I've been maimed and there's been no acknowledgement of it." In October 2002 he tried to jump from a bridge near his Long Island home, but was talked down by a passer-by. On Sunday, January 10, 2004 he went missing and was later seen on the Staten Island ferry. His body was recovered from the East River two months later.

Hughie Green

Born February 2, 1920
Died May 3, 1997
Sincere showman. Readers may be surprised by the inclusion of Hughie Green in a book of film actors,

nevertheless he did appear in ten films between 1935 and 1978, with a television movie in 1993. He was also for a time the biggest child star in Britain. Hugh Hughes Green was born at his parents' central London flat, 8 Weymouth Court, 1 Weymouth Street, in Marylebone. His father was 6'3" Major Hugh Aitchison Green (b. Hanging Shaw, Glasgow, July 30, 1886, d. Mezzanine Floor, Chiltern Court, Baker Street, London, October 23, 1959 of a myocardial fibrosis and coronary thrombosis) and his mother Violet Eleanor Price (b. 1894, d. Wellington Hospital, London, February 13, 1975 of stomach and liver cancer). His parents were not a loving couple. While some described them as unconventional, their grandson was blunter calling them "satanic". Violet Green didn't want her son at all. As a result, they travelled frequently without him. His education was peripatetic. While his parents lived beyond their means, he was shunted from school to school. He went to Francis Holland School, Clarence Gate, Regent's Park, London; Egerton House School, Dorset Square, Marylebone; St Margaret's, Bromley, Kent; and Arnold House School, Loudoun Road, St John's Wood, London. He finished his full-time education in December 1933, two months before the then school leaving age of 14. Within a year Hughie Green was the highest-paid child entertainer in Britain and a film star. In September 1932 his father had arranged for Hughie to sign a deal with the Fox Film Corporation worth £10,000 a year. But the 1913 Children (Employment Abroad) Act expressly forbade any child under 14 to leave the UK for the purposes of entertaining. The penalty for the parents was two years' hard labour. Hughie produced a revue starring children that led to an audition at the BBC. He passed and was cast as Emil in a wireless production of *Emil And The Detectives* in 1934. He became in great demand

for his revue *Hughie Green's Gang Show*. For the next five years he toured with the show constantly. One of the other boys in the *Gang Show* was named Toney Entwhistle. He stayed in touch with Hughie and later changed his name to Antony Beauchamp. He became a society photographer and war artist. On October 18, 1949 in America he married Sarah, the actress daughter of Sir Winston Churchill. They separated in 1955 and on August 18, 1957 he committed suicide with an overdose of barbiturates. Beauchamp was not really a friend of Hughie – he was so imperious, so convinced that he was always right that Hughie had virtually no friends as a child. By the time he was 14 Hughie was drinking alcohol and taking Benzedrine, or speed. He began to appear in films, including Carol Reed's *Midshipman Easy* (1935) in the title role alongside Margaret Lockwood and Harry Tate. The film was a critical and financial success but never became a classic. He failed the audition for MGM's *David Copperfield*, a part that went to Freddie Bartholomew. In 1937 he got Vera May Hands, a 17-year-old theatre usherette, pregnant and she gave birth to his first illegitimate child, Barry, on March 17, 1938 at Dudley Road Hospital, Birmingham. (He would go on to have four illegitimate daughters, all but one will not be identified in this book.) That same year he made *Melody And Romance* (1937) playing Hughie Hawkins. His later films included: *Music Hall Parade* (1939) as Eve Becke, *Down Our Alley* (1939) as Hughie Dunstable and *Tom Brown's School Days* (1940) as Walker. In October 1939 the Gang Show came to an end because many of the personnel had signed up for the forces. On February 2, 1941 Green volunteered for the Royal Canadian Air Force. On May 24, 1941 he enrolled in Regina, Saskatchewan. However his parents were not happy about this interruption of his showbiz career and desperately tried to pull strings to stop him serving. Major Green even managed to land Hughie a part in a show called *Golden Wings* in America, so Hughie had to swap his uniform for a costume. In 1935 he had met (Audrey) Claire Wilson (b. February 20, 1922, d. St George's Nursing Home, St George's Square, Westminster, London, March 9, 1995 of brain cancer), the woman who was in September 1942 to become his wife and the mother of his legitimate children. The Greens' daughter Linda was born in the Royal Victoria Hospital in Montreal on April 20, 1944, and their son Christopher Hugh Whitney was born in Montreal on July 24, 1947. His parents were horrified at the marriage and became the in-laws from hell, sending anonymous hate mail to their daughter-in-law. Hughie called in the police who identified the sender as Hughie's father. Hughie hired the 6′2″ flamboyantly homosexual lawyer David Jacobs (b. 1922, committed suicide 2 Princes Crescent, Hove, Sussex, December 15, 1968), who also represented The Beatles, Judy Garland, Diana Dors and Laurence Harvey to "scare the living shit out of my father and secure . . . a pledge that . . . he . . . will . . . cease and desist from ever doing anything of this nature again". At 10.30am on October 23, 1959 Jacobs arrived at the mezzanine floor, five floors below where Hughie and his family lived at Chiltern Court, Baker Street, London with the appropriate legal paperwork and the hate mail. Major Green aimed a kick at the made-up solicitor, breaking his wrist before falling back onto the marble floor dead from a myocardial fibrosis and coronary thrombosis. In July 1945 Hughie appeared in *The Hughie Green Comedy Show* for the Canadian Broadcasting Corporation, produced by Jackie Rae (who would become the first host of *The Golden Shot*). The show flopped and it seemed as if Green's career could be over. Ben

Lyon came to the rescue and helped Hughie get the role of Freddie Perch in *If Winter Comes* (1947) which starred Walter Pidgeon and Deborah Kerr. His last New York stage appearance came in December 1948 in Shaw's *Captain Brassbound's Conversion*. He also appeared in *Hills Of Home* (1948) as Geordie Howe, *Paper Orchid* (1949) as Harold Croup and *Men Of The Sea* (1951) as Jack Easy. In 1949 the call came from the BBC to sit in for the radio presenter Carroll Levis who had suffered a nervous breakdown. The talent show *Opportunity Knocks* was the programme that Green devised to replace Levis and it ran from February until the autumn of 1949. After that one series Green was informed that the BBC did not intend to renew his contract despite the show attracting more than 13 million listeners. A new show produced by the Carroll Levis Organisation took to the air instead. Two of Levis' staff rang Green and told him that BBC officials had been bribed to let the Levis show back on air. In 1950 Green called in Scotland Yard and sued the BBC claiming they were "conspiring to prevent [*Opportunity Knocks*] being screened". The case rumbled on for five years and the strain turned Hughie's hair white. On May 27, 1955 he lost and went bankrupt owing £30,000. Billy Butlin offered him work at his holiday camp in Skegness. Although the BBC did not want the show others did. *Opportunity Knocks* appeared in a 95-week run on Radio Luxembourg and one of the early discoveries was the singer David Whitfield. In 1957 thanks to a loan from his wife's grandmother Hughie was discharged from bankruptcy. On September 22, 1955 Associated Rediffusion launched Channel Nine, the first independent television channel in Britain, and Hughie was to find his fame restored there in various game shows. His show *Double Your Money* ran on Monday nights from September 26, 1955 until 1968. 6′2″

Green realised that the people were the stars and he made sure never to outshine them. Among the hostesses were Monica Rose and Amanda Barrie (although she only lasted a few months in 1959). In 1956 *Opportunity Knocks* arrived on television and ran until 1978. Among its discoveries were Pam Ayres, Bobby Crush, Frank Carson, Freddie 'Parrot Face' Davies, Les Dawson, Mary Hopkin, Bonnie Langford, Little & Large, Tom O'Connor, Peters & Lee, Freddie Starr and Lena Zavaroni. Before his divorce from Claire, Green was an unfaithful husband who often bedded the wives of men that he worked with or knew. He had affairs with two sisters Pat Hughes and her sister Gwendoline Helen Claremont (b. Acton, west London, April 8, 1916). Claire, too, was unfaithful taking a couple of lovers. They separated in 1960. On April 3, 1965 a drunk and drugged Hughie crashed his car into a 17-ton lorry while driving to Reading. It took 40 minutes for fire crews to cut him out of the wreckage, which gave him some time to sober up before he got to the hospital. He had concussion, six broken ribs, leg and spinal injuries and a blood clot between the liver and lungs. In 1971 he began to present *The Sky's The Limit* for Yorkshire TV. In 1974 the show had a new producer Jess Yates, the host of the religious show *Stars On Sunday*. Yates dispensed with the homely hostesses and introduced dolly birds and jazzed up the set, much to Hughie's annoyance. Ratings fell. Yates did not know that his wife had been sleeping with Green for two decades. Green also bedded and photographed Yates' girlfriend, Anita Kay, a busty brunette who had appeared nude in the revue *Pyjama Tops*. On July 7, 1974 the *News Of The World* ran the story of Yates and Anita Kay which wrecked his career. Both men suffered although Yates more so. The show was dropped after that series. That year Hughie and Claire had a brief reconciliation. It

was not to last and on May 3, 1975 at Caxton Hall, Westminster, she married the actor David Langton (b. Motherwell, Scotland, April 16, 1912 as Basil Langton-Dodds, d. 17 Avonbank Paddocks, Stratford-upon-Avon, Warwickshire, April 25, 1994 of a heart attack) who played Lord Bellamy in *Upstairs Downstairs*. Three years later, he made his last film, *What's Up Superdoc!* (1978) as Bob Scratchitt. That year *Opportunity Knocks* was dropped by ITV. Hughie offered it to the BBC who accepted it but not him. On June 17, 1981 65-year-old Gwen Claremont, Hughie's former girlfriend, committed suicide in Holland Park by dousing herself in petrol and setting it alight. She died of 100 per cent burns in Queen Mary's Hospital, Roehampton. She left a note claiming that she had cancer but when an autopsy was performed no sign of the disease could be found. In 1989 he unsuccessfully sued the New Zealand Broadcasting Company for running what he saw as a plagiarised *Opportunity Knocks*. In 1996 he took the BBC to task for a line in the sitcom *The Vicar Of Dibley*: "There hasn't been a bus through the village since Hughie Green died." His unctuous catchphrase "I mean that most sincerely, folks" was a gift for impressionists of the day. He held very right-wing views, was homophobic, wanted to hang drug dealers (even though he was a lifelong drug abuser), a snob and did not suffer fools at all, never mind gladly. He also did not like children, including his own, and the feelings were reciprocated. His daughter publicly called him "a monster" while his son in perhaps a touch of understatement said that "he wasn't a very nice man".

CAUSE: In August 1996 Hughie Green was diagnosed with cancer of the oesophagus. He died aged 77 of internal bleeding caused by the cancer at the Royal Marsden Hospital in London. Half of his ashes were scattered at Wemyss Bay on the Clyde in Scotland on August 6. Five days later, on August 11, the other half were scattered over Mount Royal, overlooking Montreal. He left £276,182, most of which came from the sale of his flat. At his funeral at Golders Green Crematorium, Hoop Lane, London on May 9, 1997 his drinking friend Noel Botham, a journalist, revealed that Green was the real father of a celebrated television personality. He did not identify the celebrity who, on December 11, 1997, turned out to be Paula Yates (b. Deganwy Castle, Colwyn Bay, Clwyd, Wales, April 24, 1959, d. St Luke's Mews, Notting Hill, west London, September 17, 2000 from an overdose of heroin). Paula Yates' funeral was held at the church of St Mary Magdalene in Faversham, Kent – the church where she had married the singer Bob Geldof (b. Dublin, Ireland, October 5, 1951) on August 24, 1986 and where their three children had been baptised. She was cremated at Charing Crematorium in Ashford, Kent.

FURTHER READING: *Opportunity Knocked* – Hughie Green (London: Frederick Muller, 1965); *Hughie And Paula The Tangled Lives Of Hughie Green And Paula Yates* – Christopher Green with Carol Clerk (London: Robson Books, 2003).

Nigel Green

Born October 15, 1924
Died May 15, 1972
Imposing presence. Born in Pretoria, South Africa, Green was a regular face in the movies in the Fifties and Sixties although he never achieved stardom. His films include *Stranger From Venus* (1954), *The Sea Shall Not Have Them* (1954), *As Long As They're Happy* (1955) as Peter, *Reach For The Sky* (1956) as Streatfield, *Sword Of Sherwood Forest* (1960) as Little John, *Beat Girl* (1960) as Simon, *Pit Of Darkness* (1961) as Jonathan, *The Man*

At The Carlton Tower (1961) as Lew Daney, *Mysterious Island* (1961) as Tom, *The Prince And The Pauper* (1962), *Doctor From Seven Dials* (1962) as Inspector Donovan, *Saturday Night Out* (1963) as Paddy, *Jason And The Argonauts* (1963) as Hercules, *The Masque Of The Red Death* (1964) as Ludovico, *Zulu* (1964) as Colour Sergeant Bourne, *The Ipcress File* (1965) as Dalby, *The Face Of Fu Manchu* (1965) as Denis Nayland Smith, *The Skull* (1965) as Inspector Wilson, *Let's Kill Uncle* (1966), *Deadlier Than The Male* (1966) as Carl Petersen, *Khartoum* (1966) as General Wolseley, *Tobruk* (1967) as Colonel Warren, *Countess Dracula* (1971) as Captain Dobi and *Gawain And The Green Knight* (1973) as the Green Knight.
CAUSE: He died aged 47 in Brighton from an accidental overdose of sleeping pills.

Sydney Greenstreet

Born December 27, 1879
Died January 18, 1954
Villainous heavyweight. The movie career of 21-stone Sydney Hughes Greenstreet lasted just eight years, but featured some very memorable performances. Born in Sandwich, Kent, one of eight children, he tried a variety of jobs before opting for acting in 1902. He made the theatre his life until his film début aged 61 in *The Maltese Falcon* (1941) playing Kasper Gutman, for which he was nominated for an Oscar. Nicknamed Tiny, his other films included *They Died With Their Boots On* (1941) as Lieutenant General Winfield Scott, *Casablanca* (1942) as Senor Ferrari, *Background To Danger* (1943) as Colonel Robinson, *Between Two Worlds* (1944) as Thompson, *The Mask Of Dimitrios* (1944) as Mr Peters, *Pillow To Post* (1945) as Colonel Michael Otley, *Three Strangers* (1946) as Jerome K. Arbutny, *Devotion* (1946) as Thackeray, *The Woman In White*

(1948) as Count Alessandro Fosco, *Ruthless* (1948) as Buck Mansfield and *Flamingo Road* (1949) as Sheriff Titus Semple, after which he retired from the cinema.

CAUSE: He died in Hollywood, California, aged 74 from the effects of diabetes and Bright's Disease. He was buried in Forest Lawn Memorial-Parks, 1712 South Glendale Avenue, Glendale, California 91209.

Jane Greer

Born September 9, 1924
Died August 24, 2001

Film noir's seductive bad girl. Bettejane Greer was born along with her twin brother, Donne, in Washington, DC. At the age of 5 she went on the stage thanks to a starstruck mother. By the age of 12 she was a professional model although disaster struck three years later when she was afflicted with Bell's Palsy which paralysed one side of her face and required intensive physiotherapy. By the time she was 17 5'5" Greer was being paid $100 a week singing with Ralph Hawkins' band and performing rumbas and other Latin American songs with Enrico Madriguero's Orchestra at the Del Rio nightclub in Washington. She couldn't speak Spanish and learned the words phonetically: "Later I found out I was singing dirty lyrics." In 1942, thanks to her mother who was working in the War Department, she modelled for an army recruiting poster, wearing a light khaki cotton twill uniform. When the picture was published in *Life* on June 8, 1942, she was soon approached by a number of Hollywood studios, and eventually summoned to California by Howard Hughes, who gave her money, ordered her not to go out with anyone, and then left her alone for six months. She later said, "Howard Hughes was obsessed with me. But at first it seemed as if he were offering me a superb career opportunity." However, she found Hughes' regime stifling and

to escape began to sing on the crooner Rudy Vallee's radio show. Hughes was not amused and absolutely furious when she married Rudy Vallee on December 2, 1943 in the Westwood Village Community Chapel, Los Angeles. However, Vallee was a serial adulterer and she soon issued divorce proceedings. The divorce came through in Los Angeles on July 27, 1944. They remained friendly, with Vallee commenting, "A more charming, talented and gracious person I shall never know." Kirk Douglas later recalled, "Beautiful Jane could also be very funny. I loved hearing her stories of her brief marriage to Rudy Vallee at the age of 17 [sic], and how he would insist that she wear black panties, black net stockings and black shoes with heels so high she teetered." The following year she made her film début in *Pan-Americana* (1945) as Miss Downing and then appeared in *Dick Tracy* (1945) as Judith Owens (the first time she was billed as Jane Greer). It was her role as Kathie Moffat in *Out Of The Past* (1947) that made her a poster girl for the film noir crowd. "I was believable," she later recalled, "because although my character Kathie was a bitch, a liar and a killer, she looked soft and innocent." The critic James Agee wrote, "Jane Greer can best be described, in an ancient idiom, as a hot number." On August 21, 1947, she married lawyer-producer Edward Lasker, the son of a millionaire, and by him had three sons, Albert on June 23, 1948, Lawrence on October 7, 1949 and Steven on May 9, 1954, before their divorce in Juarez, Mexico, on November 6, 1963. She began making fewer and fewer films – 13 in 17 years because, "I didn't want the children to grow up, and when asked what their mother did, say, 'Oh, Mum's a gun moll in the movies.'" The films included *You're In The Navy Now* (1951), a comedy with

Gary Cooper, *The Company She Keeps* (1951), *You For Me* (1952), *The Prisoner Of Zenda* (1952) and *Desperate Search* (1952). In *Run For The Sun* (1956) she caught a virus on location in the Mexican jungle and her marriage was beginning to fall apart. Jane Greer's last lead role in a major film was her outstanding performance as the virtuous second wife of Lon Chaney (James Cagney) in *Man Of A Thousand Faces* (1958). Over the next two decades she took on smaller roles in films such as *Where Love Has Gone* (1964) which starred Susan Hayward and Bette Davis and was based on Lana Turner's tempestuous romance with Johnny Stompanato. In 1983 she played the mother of Kathie Moffat (Rachel Ward) in *Against All Odds*, a disappointing remake of *Out Of The Past*. The only effect, wrote one critic, was to sully the image she had created in 1947. From 1963 until his death from lymphoma on January 31, 2001, she lived with the actor Frank London (b. Philadelphia, Pennsylvania, November 21, 1924). Her nieces, 5′8″, 34D-27-34 Liza Jamie (b. El Paso, Colorado Springs, Colorado, August 31, 1963) and 5′8″ Robin (b. Hollywood, California, May 27, 1960), brought shame to the family name when they wrote a best-selling book *You'll Never Make Love In This Town Again* in which they regaled readers with their sexual exploits with some of Hollywood's biggest names. Liza became a prostitute although Robin was a successful actress and from 1983 until 1985 she played Sydney Price on the ABC soap *Ryan's Hope*. One of Robin's closest friends was Nicole Brown Simpson (b. Frankfurt, West Germany, May 19, 1959, m. 875 South Bundy Drive, Beverly Hills, California, June 12, 1994, aged 35). Nicole's daughter, Sydney (b. October 17, 1987) was named after her friend's character.

CAUSE: She died in Los Angeles, California, aged 76 of cancer.

James Gregory
Born December 23, 1911
Died September 16, 2002
The famous unknown actor. Born in the Bronx, he grew up in the New York suburb of La Rochelle. As a youngster, he demonstrated a talent for both acting and golf, being elected president of the school drama club, and he might have chosen a career in either. But his first proper employment, after a series of jobs as golf caddy, waiter and clerk, was on Wall Street. He had been offered a job after caddying for a stockbroker called John R. Dillon. He worked as a runner after the crash of October 1929 and within five years he had been promoted to the post of private secretary to a stockbroker. In his spare time Gregory simultaneously acted with local drama groups, and in 1935 he was acting professionally, performing with a travelling company in plays up and down the east coast of America. Then, in 1939, he made his Broadway début in a production of *Key Largo*. During the Second World War Gregory served in the US Navy and Marine Corps in the Pacific, spending 83 days on Okinawa. On his return to the stage, he appeared in a further 25 Broadway productions, including in 1948 Arthur Miller's *Death Of A Salesman*, in which he played Biff. That same year he made his film début as Albert Hicks, a police patrolman in *The Naked City*. In the early Fifties Gregory moved into live television: "I once played five live shows on television within a period of 10 days. I set a record that's never been beat. Can you imagine the running around I had to do in New York to make all the rehearsals and not get mixed up in the characterisations? I was lucky. Well, not only lucky, I was a good actor." In 1954 he appeared in *Danger*, the first television show directed by John Frankenheimer. He then split his time between the stage and the big and small screens. He appeared in television dramas such as *Gunsmoke*,

Bonanza, Wagon Train, and *Rawhide.* If an American cop was required on the television screen, the chances were that he would be embodied by James Gregory. He had roles in the very first episode of *The Twilight Zone* (October 2, 1959), *Columbo, McCloud, Alfred Hitchcock Presents,* and Pentagon spy Jonathan Kaye in *Cocoon,* the September 20, 1968 pilot of the longest continuously running cop show on American television *Hawaii Five-O.* From April 16, 1959 to September 22, 1961, he was Barney Ruditsky in *The Lawless Years,* a series based on the exploits of a real detective in New York City in the 1920s. He also played Inspector Frank Luger from January 23, 1975 to September 9, 1982 in *Barney Miller,* about a Jewish policeman portrayed by Hal Linden. On the big screen his best-known role was probably as the right wing Senator Iselin in John Frankenheimer's *The Manchurian Candidate* (1962), about a brainwashed Korean War hero. His other films included *The Young Stranger* (1957) as Sergeant Shipley, *Al Capone* (1959) as Schaefler, *PT-109* (1963) as Commander C.R. Ritchie (the future President John F. Kennedy's commanding officer), *The Sons Of Katie Elder* (1965) in which Gregory played Morgan Hastings, a murderer who kills the witnesses to his crimes, *Beneath The Planet Of The Apes* (1969) as Ursus, the gorilla commander who believes the only good human is a dead human and *Shootout* (1971) as Sam Foley. In 1944 he married Anne Miltner.

CAUSE: Gregory retired to Arizona in 1986 after suffering two strokes. He died in Sedona aged 90.

John Gregson
Born March 15, 1919
Died January 8, 1975
Handsome British hero. Born in Liverpool, Gregson worked in amdram before appearing at the Liverpool Old Vic and moved into the cinema with

Saraband For Dead Lovers (1948) and went on to appear in almost 40 films, including *Scott Of The Antarctic* (1948) as P.O. Green, *London Belongs To Me* (1948), *Whisky Galore!* (1949) as Sammy MacCodrun, *Cairo Road* (1950), *Treasure Island* (1950) as Redruth, *The Lavender Hill Mob* (1951) as Farrow, *Venetian Bird* (1952) as Renzo Uccello, *The Titfield Thunderbolt* (1953) as Gordon, *Angels One Five* (1953) as Pilot Officer 'Septic' Baird, *To Dorothy A Son* (1954) as Tony Rapallo, *Above Us The Waves* (1955) as Lieutenant Alec Duffy, *The Battle Of The River Plate* (1956) as Captain Bell, *Rooney* (1958) as James Ignatius Rooney, *Hand In Hand* (1960) as Father Timothy, *The Treasure Of Monte Cristo* (1961) as Renato, *The Longest Day* (1962) as the British vicar and *Fright* (1971) as Dr Cordell. Probably his best-loved film was the gentle British comedy *Genevieve* (1953), in which he portrayed veteran car racer Alan McKim. On the small screen he was known for the detective drama *Gideon's Way* (1965) as Commander George Gideon. He was married to actress Thea Gregory and fathered six children.

CAUSE: He died of a heart attack on holiday in Porlock Weir, Somerset, aged 55.

Joyce Grenfell, OBE
(JOYCE IRENE PHIPPS)
Born February 10, 1910
Died November 30, 1979
Horsey comedienne. Born in London, the daughter of an American architect and the niece of Lady Nancy Astor, Grenfell was educated at Francis Holland School and then a Christian Science establishment before attending a finishing school in Paris. She began attending RADA but dropped out in 1929 to marry Reginald Grenfell. For three years from 1936 she was radio critic of the *Observer.* In 1939 she began her stage career with witty talks, entertaining monologues and silly

songs. In 1946 she was made an OBE. She appeared in over 20 films, including *A Letter From Home* (1941), *While The Sun Shines* (1947) as Daphne, *Stage Fright* (1950), *Laughter In Paradise* (1951) as Elizabeth Robson, *The Pickwick Papers* (1952) as Mrs Leo Hunter, *The Million Pound Note* (1953) as the Duchess of Cromarty, *Genevieve* (1953) as the owner of a hotel, *Forbidden Cargo* (1954) as Lady Flavin Queensway, *The Belles Of St Trinian's* (1954) as WPC Ruby Gates, *Blue Murder At St Trinian's* (1957) as Sergeant Gates, *The Good Companions* (1957) as Lady Parlitt, *The Pure Hell Of St Trinian's* (1961) as Sergeant Ruby Gates and *The Yellow Rolls-Royce* (1965) as Hortense Astor. In 1954 she toured the world with her show *Joyce Grenfell Requests The Pleasure*.

CAUSE: She died of cancer at her London home, 34 Elm Park Gardens, Chelsea, aged 69, a month before she was due to become Dame Joyce Grenfell. She left £196,358.

Lita Grey

(LILLITA LOUISE MACMURRAY)
Born April 15, 1908
Died December 29, 1995
Charlie's darling. Born in Hollywood, California, the name of Lita Grey would be virtually forgotten – she made less than half a dozen films – if it was not for the fact that she married Charlie Chaplin. She first appeared in a Chaplin film when she was 12, playing in *The Kid* (1921). She played a maid in *The Idle Class* (1921). On March 2, 1924, now calling herself Lita Grey, she was signed as leading lady for Chaplin's *The Gold Rush* (1925). On November 26, 1924, he married her at Guayamas, Mexico. Like his first wife she was 16 years old, but the second Mrs Chaplin was also pregnant by the time of the wedding. The union was to produce two sons: Charles Spencer, Jr (b. Los Angeles, California, May 5, 1925, d. California, March 20, 1968) and Sydney Earle (b. Los Angeles,

California, March 30, 1926). Chaplin bribed an official to register his second son's birth as June 28, 1925, to cover up his premarital sex. *The Gold Rush* was premièred at Grauman's Egyptian Theatre on June 26, supposedly two days before the birth of Charles, Jr. The scenes featuring Grey were cut from the final edit. On January 10, 1927, Grey filed for divorce, which was granted on August 22, 1927, and became final a year later on August 25, 1928. She appeared in just two more films: *Mr Broadway* (1933) as herself and *The Devil's Sleep* (1951) as Judge Rosalind Ballentine.

CAUSE: She died aged 87 of cancer in Los Angeles, California.

D.W. Griffith

(DAVID LEWELYN WARK GRIFFITH)
Born January 22, 1875
Died July 24, 1948
Cinematic legend. Born on a farm near Crestwood, Oldham County, Kentucky, the son of a doctor who fought in the Mexican War and served in the Kentucky legislature, Griffith was one of the earliest pioneers of movies, but he didn't have the gift of foresight. He once commented: "It'll never be possible to synchronise the voice with the pictures." Nonetheless, he was a prolific writer, director and producer. He directed over 500 films, wrote over 200, produced over 40 and found time to act in over 30! Acting was his passion and it was only when he found himself short of money that he began to take a number of menial jobs before joining Biograph. From 1908 he wrote and directed films for them, forming a partnership with cameraman Billy Bitzer before leaving in September 1913 for Reliance-Majestic. It was his American Civil War film epic *The Birth Of A Nation* (1915) (which he wrote, directed, produced, edited and composed the music for) that made his name. It cost $91,000 to make and recouped $5 million. It was the first film shown in the White House and President Woodrow Wilson loved it. It

also brought criticism and controversy over charges of racism for its sympathetic portrayal of the Ku Klux Klan (membership trebled) and less sympathetic showing of blacks. Only one black actor was hired. All the rest of the 'black' faces are made-up white ones. On the other hand, many historians regard the movie as the most important development in the art film genre. The film lasted for almost three hours and tickets cost a remarkable $2 each. His next major film, which took two years and $2.5 million (much of it Griffith's own money) to make was the epic *Intolerance* (1916). (On July 20, 1915, while making *Intolerance*, Griffith had teamed up with Thomas Ince and Mack Sennett to form the Triangle Motion Picture Company. They built a studio for Mabel Normand to make *Mickey* [1918] but their hopes of making her a big star were dashed when she signed for Samuel Goldwyn.) *Intolerance* was a commercial disaster and Griffith found himself in financial trouble. To get out of dire straits he worked tirelessly and on February 5, 1919, Griffith, Charlie Chaplin, Mary Pickford and Douglas Fairbanks formed United Artists to produce and sell their own films and those of other independents. His first film for the new venture was *Broken Blossoms* (1919). During the filming of *Way Down East* (1920) his star Lillian Gish was made to suffer for her art. She endured permanent damage to her hand by having to trail it in icy water. The film turned out to be Griffith's second most commercially successful. He worked steadily without ever quite finding success again and his last film, the appropriately named *The Struggle* (1931), was a disaster. A womaniser, he married twice. His first wife (on May 14, 1906, at the Old North Church, Boston) was Linda Arvidson. Separated since 1911, they divorced on March 2, 1936. Number two (also on March 2, 1936) was Evelyn Baldwin, 35 years his junior.
CAUSE: On July 23, 1948, he suffered a cerebral haemorrhage in his rooms at the Knickerbocker Hotel, 1714 North Ivar Avenue, Hollywood, California, and died, without regaining consciousness, at 8.24am the next day at the Temple Hospital, aged 73. He was buried in Mount Tabor Methodist Church's graveyard.
FURTHER READING: *D.W. Griffith: An American Life* – Richard Schickel (New York: Simon & Schuster, 1984).

Sir Alec Guinness, CH
(ALEC GUINNESS DE CUFFE)
Born April 2, 1914
Died August 5, 2000
The invisible man. Like his contemporary, Olivier, Guinness was one of the most famous actors in the world and yet could walk down a crowded Oxford Street totally unrecognised. Born in Marylebone, London, the illegitimate son of a prostitute, Guinness' father was 64-year-old banker Andrew Geddes. When he was five, his name was changed to Alec Stiven when his mother married a Scottish army captain. Stepfather and stepson did not see eye to eye although the boy liked the sound of his new name. By the age of 14 he had been known by three different surnames and had lived in thirty different residences. His interest in the theatre was cultivated in school until his headmaster told him he would never succeed as an actor and so Guinness began to work at an advertising agency. While at the agency he spent every spare moment at the theatre and eventually applied to RADA for an audition. Guinness rang up John Gielgud in the naïve hope that Gielgud would take him under his wing and teach him how to be an actor. It very nearly worked and Gielgud recommended Martita Hunt as a drama teacher. The two men were later to become firm friends. Guinness made his film début in *Great Expectations* (1946) but it was his performance as eight members of the

D'Ascoyne family in *Kind Hearts And Coronets* (1949) that brought him to public notice. *The Lavender Hill Mob* (1951) and *The Man In The White Suit* (1956) helped to cement his reputation as a fine actor. His portrayal of the Catholic detective Father Brown in the 1954 film of that name was not only eminently watchable but also led him inexorably to Rome as well. In order to rehearse for each part, Guinness imbued each of his characters with a particular walk. One of the most memorable came as Colonel Nicholson in his Oscar-winning film *The Bridge Over The River Kwai* (1957). The walk when the stubborn soldier is released from a sweat box came from Guinness' son when the boy was recovering from polio. Guinness also excelled in *Lawrence Of Arabia* (1962) but was curiously underused in *Dr Zhivago* (1965). In 1977 he played Obi-Wan Kenobi in the mega hit *Star Wars* (1977), never his favourite film although a clever contractual agreement assured him of 2% of the profits. Guinness made £6 million from merchandising of his image. On television he was a sensation as the spymaster George Smiley in a number of adaptations of John Le Carré's books. In 1955 he was appointed CBE with his knighthood arriving four years later. He became a Companion of Honour in 1994. A very private man, in June 1938 he married Merula Salaman. They had one son, Matthew, who acted for a time.

CAUSE: Guinness died aged 86 of cancer at King Edward VII Hospital, Midhurst, Hampshire.

FURTHER READING: *My Name Escapes Me The Diary Of A Retiring Actor* – Alec Guinness (London: Hamish Hamilton, 1996).

Deryck Guyler

Born April 29, 1914
Died October 8, 1999

Old faithful. Born in Wallasey, Merseyside, Deryck Guyler spent much of his career on the small screen making the occasional foray on to the big one. He became well known on the radio show *ITMA*, and his appearance on the show marked the first time a Scouse accent had been broadcast to the nation. When gay actor Richard Wattis left the cast of *Sykes*, Guyler joined as friendly bobby 'Corky' Turnbull. He was also well known as the pompous ex-Desert Rat school janitor Norman Hesquith Potter on the LWT sitcom *Please Sir!* An expert player of the washboard, Deryck Guyler appeared in *Mad About Men* (1954), *Nurse On Wheels* (1963), *A Hard Day's Night* (1964), *Ferry Cross The Mersey* (1965) as Trasler, *Carry On Doctor* (1968) as Mr Hardcastle, *Please Sir!* (1971) as Norman Potter, *Barry Mackenzie Holds His Own* (1974) and *One Of Our Dinosaurs Is Missing* (1976) as Harris.

CAUSE: He died in Brisbane, Australia, of natural causes, aged 85.

Fred Gwynne

Born July 10, 1926
Died July 2, 1993

Lugubrious star. Born in New York, New York, 6'5" Frederick Hubbard Gwynne grew up in South Carolina, Florida and Colorado. He was primarily known for his performances in the sitcoms *Car 54, Where Are You?* (from September 17, 1961, until September 8, 1963) as Officer Francis Muldoon and *The Munsters* (from September 24, 1964, until September 1, 1966) as Herman Munster and other television work. He also appeared in several films, including *On The Waterfront* (1954) as Slim, *Munster, Go Home* (1966) reprising his role as Herman Munster, *Simon* (1980) as Korey, *The Cotton Club* (1984) as Frenchy Demange, *Ironweed* (1987) as Oscar Reo, *Fatal Attraction* (1987) as Arthur, *Disorganized Crime* (1989) as Max Green, *Pet Sematary* (1989) as Jud Crandall and *My Cousin Vinny* (1992) as Judge Chamberlain Haller.

He also wrote around a dozen popular children's books, including *The Battle Of The Frogs And Mice*, *A Chocolate Moose For Dinner*, *The King Who Rained*, *A Little Pigeon Toad* and *Pondlarker*. He was married with two sons and two daughters.

CAUSE: In January 1993 Gwynne fell ill with what was diagnosed (on February 3) as pancreatic cancer. An operation at John Hopkins Medical Center in Baltimore, Maryland, revealed that the disease had spread incurably. He died aged 66 at 8am at his farm home on Stone Road, Taneytown, Maryland. On July 3, his funeral service took place at Sandymount Methodist Church. He was interred in an unmarked grave.

H

Joan Hackett

Born May 1, 1933
Died October 8, 1983
Plain talent. Born in New York, Hackett, like many modern actors, appeared as often on television as she did on the big screen. After leaving New York University she became a fashion model before changing direction and studying under Lee Strasberg. She first began to make her mark in the cinema with *The Group* (1966) and followed that with *Support Your Local Sheriff* (1969), *Rivals* (1972), *The Terminal Man* (1974), *Treasure Of Matacumbe* (1976), *One Trick Pony* (1980), *Only When I Laugh* (1981) as Toby Landau for which she was nominated for an Oscar and *The Escape Artist* (1982).
CAUSE: Hackett, a lesbian who liked to smoke cigars, died of cancer aged 50 in Encino, California. She was buried in Crypt 2314 in the Abbey of the Psalms in Hollywood Memorial Park, 6000 Santa Monica Boulevard, Hollywood, California 90038.

William Haines

Born New Year's Day, 1900
Died Boxing Day, 1973
The first gay martyr. In Hollywood, and in London for that matter, a large number of actors are homosexual or bisexual. Many of the biggest stars now working in films are gay but not one of them has the courage to come out and reveal their sexuality. They will not come out because they fear that their careers will be wrecked – that the so-called sophisticated public will not accept a known homosexual as a leading man – and they are absolutely right. Most actors stay silent for the sake of their careers and many like

Charles Laughton and Rock Hudson get married, often to lesbians. These so-called lavender marriages are very popular in show business – two careers are potentially saved and as long as both parties are careful no one – i.e. the paying public – is any the wiser. William Haines was different. He was a top box office draw but he was also openly homosexual. Haines was born in Staunton, Virginia and educated at a military school. Aged 14, he ran away from home. He worked at various menial jobs until he was spotted by a Samuel Goldwyn talent scout and put in a new faces competition. Haines was the male new face and Eleanor Boardman the female. Both were given contracts and he made his début in *Brothers Under The Skin* (1922). He became one of the leading actors in the Twenties. Haines befriended Joan Crawford who proposed to him but he turned her down. He already had a "wife". In 1930 Haines and his boyfriend Jimmy Shields bought an antique shop and he gave decorating advice gratis to friends. In 1933 he was discovered in bed with another man at the YMCA and arrested. His last film was *The Marines Are Coming* (1934). MGM's Louis B. Mayer gave Haines the choice – career and marriage or boyfriend. Haines picked Shields and it was a decision that he never regretted. He and Shields were together for 50 years. Joan Crawford said that "the happiest marriage I've seen in Hollywood is Billy Haines and Jimmy Shields". The two men became professional interior designers and prospered thanks to the good offices of friends like Crawford, Marian Davies and Carole Lombard who hired them and then recommended their services to friends. On June 3, 1936 while at their beach house in El Porto, California, they gave Jimmy Walker, a small boy, six cents. The boy's father asked him where he had got the money and when he learned it was from two "interior designers" he and some friends beat up Haines and Shields. The two men never returned to the area but refused to press charges against the thugs.

CAUSE: Billy Haines died of cancer, aged 73. Miserable without his boyfriend, Jimmy Shields died by his own hand, six months later. His suicide note read, "It's no good without Billy."

Alan Hale, Jr

Born March 8, 1918
Died January 2, 1990
Bluff character. Born in Los Angeles, California, the son of character actor Alan Hale (b. Washington, DC, February 10, 1892, d. Hollywood, California, January 22, 1950) whom he closely resembled, Alan began playing much the same type of role as his father. He began appearing in films in the Thirties and went on to feature in, among others, *Wild Boys Of The Road* (1933), *I Wanted Wings* (1941), *Top Sergeant* (1942) as Cruston, *To The Shores Of Tripoli* (1942) as Tom Hall, *Rubber Racketeers* (1942) as Red, *Eagle Squadron* (1942) as Olsen, *Wake Island* (1942), *Sweetheart Of Sigma Chi* (1946) as Mike Mitchell, *Sarge Goes To College* (1947) as Sarge, *It Happened On 5th Avenue* (1947) as Whitey, *Riders In The Sky* (1949) as Marshal Riggs, *Sierra Passage* (1950), *The West Point Story* (1950) as Bull Gilbert, *Honeychile* (1951) as Joe Boyd, *Hometown Story* (1951) as Slim Haskins, *Lady In The Iron Mask* (1952) as Porthos, *At Sword's Point* (1952) reprising his portrayal of Porthos, *Young At Heart* (1954) as Robert Neary, *Captain Kidd And The Slave Girl* (1954), *Many Rivers To Cross* (1955) as Luke Radford, *The True Story Of Jesse James* (1957) as Cole Younger, *Up Periscope* (1959) as Malone, *Bullet For A Badman* (1964) as Leach, *The Fifth Musketeer* (1979) once again as Porthos, *Hambone And Hillie* (1984) as McVickers and *Back To The Beach* (1987). He also appeared as the lead in a number of television series such as *Biff Baker, U.S.A.* (November 13,

1952–March 26, 1953), *Casey Jones* (1957) and his most enduring role as the skipper Jonas Grumby on *Gilligan's Island* (September 26, 1964–September 4, 1967), *The New Adventures Of Gilligan* (September 7, 1974–September 4, 1977), a cartoon series, *Rescue From Gilligan's Island* (October 14–21, 1978), *The Castaways On Gilligan's Island* (May 3, 1979), *The Harlem Globetrotters On Gilligan's Island* (May 15, 1981) and *Gilligan's Planet* (September 18, 1982–September 10, 1983), another cartoon series. He was not happy with *Casey Jones*: "We were betwixt and between whether we should make *Casey* for adults or for kids. Apparently, it showed." Hale even confessed never having seen an episode of the show. Away from the world of show business Hale owned a seafood restaurant on La Cienega Boulevard in Los Angeles called the Skipper's Lobster Barrel.

CAUSE: In 1989 Hale was diagnosed with cancer of the thymus. However, even though he underwent an operation to remove the malignancy, the cancer had spread to his lungs and stomach. He died of acute respiratory failure in St Vincent's Medical Center, 2131 West 3rd Street, Los Angeles at 5.45pm. On January 6, 1990, Hale was cremated and his ashes were scattered at sea off Port Fermin, Los Angeles.

FURTHER READING: *The Unofficial Gilligan's Island Handbook* – Joey Green (New York: Warner Books, 1988).

Monte Hale

(SAMUEL BUREN ELY)
Born June 8, 1919
Died March 29, 2009
Singing cowboy. Born in Ada, Oklahoma and raised at San Angelo, Texas, Hale began singing in local clubs when he was 13, having saved $8.50 to buy a guitar by picking cotton and pecans. He appeared on the wireless before joining the Stars Over Texas Bond Drive as a singer during the Second World War. Its chairman

Phil Isley, the father of Jennifer Jones, recommended Hale to Herb Yates, the head of Republic Pictures, who offered the singer a seven-year contract after Hale had hitchhiked to California where he took a screen test and appeared in *The Big Bonanza* (1944) as a singer. Two years later, Hale appeared in *Home On The Range*, the first of 19 films in which he took the lead role. Along with Gene Autry, Eddie Dean and Roy Rogers, 6'5" Hale was one of the top B-movie cowboy stars of the Forties. Hale's Westerns featured more action and fewer musical production numbers than those of Autry or Rogers, meaning he usually sang fewer songs per movie. His films included: *The Topeka Terror* (1945), *Steppin' In Society* (1945), *Oregon Trail* (1945), *Bandits Of The Badlands* (1945) as Dr Steve Carson, *Rough Riders Of Cheyenne* (1945) as Ward Tuttle, *Colorado Pioneers* (1945), *The Phantom Rider* (1946), *California Gold Rush* (1946) as Pete, *Sun Valley Cyclone* (1946) as Jeff, *Along The Oregon Trail* (1947) as Monte Hale, *California Firebrand* (1948) as Monte Hale, *Son Of God's Country* (1948) as US Marshal Monte Hale, *Prince Of The Plains* (1949) as Bat Masterson, *Law Of The Golden West* (1949) as Buffalo Bill Cody, *Outcasts Of The Trail* (1949) as Pat Garrett, *South Of Rio* (1949) as Jeff Lanning, *San Antone Ambush* (1949) as Lieutenant Ross Kincaid, *Ranger Of Cherokee Strip* (1949) as Steve Howard, *Pioneer Marshal* (1949) as Marshal Ed Sherwood/Ted Post, *The Vanishing Westerner* (1950) as Chris Adams, *The Old Frontier* (1950) as Barney Regan and *The Missourians* (1950) as Bill Blades. Around this time his career ground to a halt and he returned to singing in clubs around America and the occasional TV appearance. He shone in the small role of Bale Clinch, Rock Hudson's lawyer, in *Giant* (1956). Hale's last film was *Guns Of A Stranger* (1973), with Marty Robbins as a singing cowboy. Hale also appeared as a comic book hero from 1948 until 1956, published in 27 languages. He helped to found a Western museum with Gene Autry. Hale donated his own white hat, guns, gun belt and other prized treasures. Hale was married twice but died childless. CAUSE: Hale, 89, died of age-related causes at his Studio City home following a lengthy illness.

Jack Haley
Born August 10, 1899
Died June 6, 1979
The tin man. Born in Boston, Massachusetts, John Joseph Haley's most famous role came about by accident. The part of the Tin Man in *The Wizard Of Oz* (1939) was originally due to be played by Buddy Ebsen. Unfortunately, he suffered a bad skin reaction to the silver make-up and had to be hospitalised. The part eventually went to Haley, who began his career in vaudeville working as a singer and dancer before making the transition to Broadway and then to films. His movies included *Broadway Madness* (1927), *Salt Water Daffy* (1933) as Elmer, *Here Comes The Groom* (1934) as Mike Scanlon, *Redheads On Parade* (1935) as Peter Mathews, *Coronado* (1935) as Chuck Hornbostel, *Poor Little Rich Girl* (1936) as Jimmy Dolan, *Mister Cinderella* (1936) as Joe Jenkins, *She Had To Eat* (1937) as Danny Decker, *Danger – Love At Work* (1937) as Henry MacMorrow, *Rebecca Of Sunnybrook Farm* (1938) as Orville Smithers, *Alexander's Ragtime Band* (1938) as Davey Lane, *Moon Over Miami* (1941) as Jack O'Hara, *Beyond The Blue Horizon* (1942) as Squidge, *Higher And Higher* (1944) as Mike O'Brien, *People Are Funny* (1946) as Pinky Wilson and *Make Mine Laughs* (1949). A devout Catholic, Haley was made a Knight of Malta by the Pope. On February 25, 1921, he married Ziegfeld Follies dancer Florence McFadden. They had two children: son Jack Jr (b. Los

Angeles, California, October 25, 1933) who married Liza Minnelli and daughter Gloria (b. 1928).

CAUSE: Haley died of a heart attack in Los Angeles, California, aged 79. He was buried in Grave 2 of the Grotto in the Holy Cross Cemetery, 5835 West Slauson Avenue, Culver City, California 90230.

Kevin Peter Hall

Born May 9, 1955
Died April 10, 1991

Tall guy. Born in Pittsburgh, Pennsylvania, Hall was educated at Penn Hills High School in Pittsburgh before attending George Washington University in the American capital and got a degree in acting while playing scholarship basketball. He represented the University of Southern California at the Edinburgh Festival. His best-known film roles were as the lead in *Harry And The Hendersons* (1987) and *Predator* (1990). He stood 7'2" and was married to Alaina Reed (b. Springfield, Ohio, November 10, 1946) and had two children.

CAUSE: Hall died of AIDS in Hollywood, California. He was 35.

Leslie Halliwell

Born February 23, 1929
Died January 21, 1989

Cinematic encyclopædist. Born in Bolton, Lancashire, the youngest (by 13 years) of three children, bearded Robert James Leslie Halliwell was educated at St Catherine's College, Cambridge, and began his career as a journalist on *Picturegoer*. He became a cinema manager and then a publicist for Rank before moving to the now defunct Southern TV as a film buyer in 1958. The following year he moved to Granada TV and eventually became their film buyer taking over that responsibility for the whole ITV network in 1968. He added Channel 4 to his remit when that station began broadcasting on November 2, 1982. But it is for two remarkable reference

works that Halliwell earned his place in the movie pantheon. *Halliwell's Filmgoer's Companion* was first published in 1965 (with a foreword by Alfred Hitchcock) and 12 years later saw the advent of *Halliwell's Film Guide*. Both books deserve their place on the bookshelf of the serious movie lover. It should be pointed out, however, that Halliwell disliked almost every film made after 1950, regarding the Thirties and Forties as the golden era of Hollywood.

CAUSE: Halliwell died of abdominal cancer aged 59 at the Princess Alice Hospital, Esher, Surrey.

Bernie Hamilton

Born June 12, 1928
Died December 30, 2008

Irascible second banana. Born in East Los Angeles, Hamilton ran away from home as a teenager and lived in a garage. He became interested in acting while at school and made his film debut in 1950 as Ernie, a baseball player in *The Jackie Robinson Story*. He was a little-noticed bitpart player until 1964 when he appeared in the film *One Potato, Two Potato* as Frank Richards, the black husband of a white woman (Barbara Barrie). He became famous if not a star as Starsky and Hutch's short-tempered boss Captain Harold Dobey in the popular 1970s cop show. He appeared in more than twenty films and became a record producer releasing R'n'B and gospel records on the Chocolate Snowman label. He even released a record of his own, *Captain Dobey Sings The Blues*. His brother was the jazz drummer Chico Hamilton. Bernie Hamilton was divorced with two children.

CAUSE: Hamilton died of a heart attack at Cedars-Sinai Medical Centre in Los Angeles. He was 80.

Margaret Hamilton

Born December 9, 1902
Died May 16, 1985

'A woman with a heart of gold and a

corset of steel.' Born in Cleveland, Ohio, Hamilton began acting after a career as a nursery school teacher. Her early stage work was unsatisfactory (to her) and it was only after her arrival in Hollywood in 1933 that she began to flourish. She appeared in over 70 films but it was her performance as Miss Almira Gulch/The Wicked Witch Of The West in *The Wizard Of Oz* (1939) that she is most fondly remembered. Her other films included *Another Language* (1933) as Helen Hallam, *Hat, Coat, And Glove* (1934) as Madame DuBarry, *There's Always Tomorrow* (1934) as Ella, *Way Down East* (1935) as Martha Perkins, *These Three* (1936) as Agatha, *Chatterbox* (1936) as Emily Tipton, *The Trail Of The Lonesome Pine* (1936), *Mountain Justice* (1937) as Phoebe Lamb, *Laughing At Trouble* (1937) as Lizzie Beadle, *I'll Take Romance* (1937) as Margot, *You Only Live Once* (1937) as Hester, *Mother Carey's Chickens* (1938) as Mrs Fuller, *Main Street Lawyer* (1939) as Lucy, *Babes In Arms* (1939) as Martha Steele, *I'm Nobody's Sweetheart Now* (1940) as Mrs Thriffie, *My Little Chickadee* (1940) as Mrs Gideon, *Play Girl* (1941) as Josie, *Meet The Stewarts* (1942) as Willametta, *Johnny Come Lately* (1943) as Myrtle Ferguson, *The Ox-Bow Incident* (1943) as Mrs Larch, *George White's Scandals* (1945) as Clarabell, *Janie Gets Married* (1946) as Mrs Angles, *Driftwood* (1947) as Essie Keenan, *Texas, Brooklyn And Heaven* (1948) as Ruby Cheever, *Wabash Avenue* (1950) as Tillie Hutch, *People Will Talk* (1951) as Miss Sarah Pickett, *Angel In My Pocket* (1969) as Rhoda, *Brewster McCloud* (1970) as Daphne Heap and *The Anderson Tapes* (1971) as Miss Kaler.
CAUSE: She died in New Brunswick, Canada, of a heart attack, aged 82.

Tony Hancock
Born May 12, 1924
Died June 25, 1968
The Lad Himself. Born in Birmingham, one of three sons (the elder was killed in the Second World War, the younger became a showbiz agent and keeper of his brother's reputation), Anthony John Hancock was undoubtedly one of the most successful post-war comedians Britain has produced. Like many comedians, he was also a manic depressive (Harry Secombe substituted for Hancock in three episodes of the radio show because the star was in a mental hospital) and abhorred the physical act of parting with money. He rarely carried cash. Once, after writing a cheque for £5,000, Hancock had to drink whisky to recover. Starting on the radio on November 2, 1954, with his 'repertory' company of Hattie Jacques, Sid James, Bill Kerr and Kenneth Williams, *Hancock's Half Hour*, after a slow start, became required listening for virtually the whole country. The scripts were written by Ray Galton and Alan Simpson (who met when both were patients in a TB clinic). Williams used many funny voices on the show and pioneered the catch-phrase "Stop messin' about!" which Hancock was later to dismiss as "a cardboardian stereotype". On July 6, 1956, the show moved to television. Only Sid James made the transition as a regular from the wireless to the small screen. Kerr disappeared completely, Williams vanished after six weeks and Jacques made only rare appearances. It seemed Hancock could do no wrong, although he disliked the shows, calling the set "a bloody death cell . . . with an execution once a week." His programmes contained classic one-liners, viz:. "A pint?! Have you gone mad – that's very nearly an armful!" (*The Blood Donor*) and "Does Magna Carta mean nothing to you? Did she die in vain?" (*Twelve Angry Men*). However, his national popularity was not enough for the Lad Himself. He yearned for international success and made a number of unsuccessful films such as *The Rebel* (1961), which he hated, and *The Punch & Judy Man* (1962), playing Wally

Pinner, as an attempt to cross over to a wider audience. Hancock abandoned Sid James but, more importantly, he jettisoned his writers Galton and Simpson (who went on to create *Steptoe & Son* in the time they had allocated for writing more *Hancock*s). Without financial remuneration, Galton & Simpson had worked on three scripts tailor-made for Hancock. He rejected them all. It was the biggest blunder of his career. If ever there was a comedian who could not function without writers, that comedian was Tony Hancock. He made a series for independent television that began on January 3, 1963, and ran for 13 weeks. It went down like the proverbial lead balloon. Another ITV series, called simply *Hancock's* (in 1967), saw Hancock as the wholly unbelievable owner of a nightclub. It was a disaster. Hancock began drinking even more heavily and had difficulty remembering his lines. Gerald Thomas, director of the highly successful *Carry On* films, proposed a film that would reunite Hancock with Sid James. James was enthusiastic but Hancock nixed the idea. Hancock was a strange mixture. He hated to be touched. He was a violent husband to his two wives. He also had a secret gay side that led him to patronise certain bars in Soho. Indeed, he had attempted to seduce singer Matt Monro in October 1962 and received a smack in the face for his troubles. CAUSE: In March 1968 Hancock went to Australia in an attempt to revive his flagging career. He was to film 13 shows returning to his old character. With three episodes in the can and after rehearsals for the fourth finished, Hancock returned to his Sydney hotel room. The next day, June 25, 1968, four days after his second divorce, Tony Hancock committed suicide, overdosing on barbiturates washed down with vodka. He was 44 years old. He left two suicide notes one of which contained the poignant phrase, "Things seemed to go wrong too many times." Comedian Willie Rushton was given the task of escorting Hancock's ashes back to England. However, the plane was filling up and the seat next to Rushton was required. He explained his dilemma to a stewardess who took the urn to the first-class cabin. As Rushton went to collect it there was a single red rose and a note by it. The note read, "Thank you for making us laugh." He left £32,559.

FURTHER READING: *Tony Hancock –* Philip Oakes (London: Woburn-Futura, 1975); *Tony Hancock: 'Artiste' –* Roger Wilmut (London: Methuen, 1986); *When The Wind Changed: The Life And Death Of Tony Hancock –* Cliff Goodwin (London: Century, 1999).

Irene Handl

Born December 28, 1901
Died November 29, 1987
Reliable straight woman. Irene Handl who was born at 13 Leith Mansions, Paddington, London, the second daughter of a Viennese banker, was one of the mainstays of British comedy for many, many years. She worked with almost every comedian going. She began acting in the Thirties on the stage, making her first film playing a chambermaid in *Missing, Believed Married* (1937). She was a stalwart, never quite making the big time until the television show *For The Love Of Ada* (1970) playing Ada Cresswell opposite Wilfred Pickles. The film version was not a success. Many of her other films were, including *Spellbound* (1940) as Mrs Nugent, *Give Us The Moon* (1943) as Miss Haddock, *Brief Encounter* (1946), *The History Of Mr Polly* (1949), *Cardboard Cavalier* (1949) as Lady Agnes, *The Belles Of St Trinian's* (1954) as Miss Gale, *A Kid For Two Farthings* (1955) as Mrs Abramowitz, *Carry On Nurse* (1958) as Madge Hickson, *I'm All Right Jack* (1959) as Mrs Kite, *Carlton-Browne Of The F.O.* (1959) as Mrs Carter, *School For Scoundrels* (1960) as Mrs Stringer,

Carry On Constable (1960), *Doctor In Love* (1960) as Professor MacRitchie, *The Rebel* (1961) as Mrs Crevatte, *The Pure Hell Of St Trinian's* (1961) as Miss Harker-Parker, *The Italian Job* (1969) as Miss Peach, *Doctor In Trouble* (1970) as Mrs Dailey, *The Private Life Of Sherlock Holmes* (1970) as Mrs Hudson, *Confessions Of A Driving Instructor* (1976) as Miss Slenderparts, *Stand Up, Virgin Soldiers* (1977) as Mrs Phillimore, *Adventures Of A Private Eye* (1977) as Miss Friggin, *Come Play With Me* (1977) as Lady Bovington, *The Last Remake Of Beau Geste* (1977) as Miss Wormwood, *The Hound Of The Baskervilles* (1978) as Mrs Barrymore and *Absolute Beginners* (1986) as Mrs Larkin. She never married.
CAUSE: She died in her sleep at 31 Viscount Court, 1 Pembridge Villas, Kensington, west London, aged 85. She left £376,134.

Tommy Handley
Born January 17, 1892
Died January 9, 1949
It's that man again! Born at 13 Threlfall Street, Toxteth Park, Liverpool, the son of a dairy farmer, he began his professional showbiz career in 1917, first broadcasting seven years later. It was the wireless that made Tommy Handley a star – his show *ITMA* becoming required listening for millions of Britons for ten years from July 12, 1939 until the last show on January 5, 1949. Handley made few feaure films but they included *Elstree Calling* (1930), *Tommy Handley In Making A Christmas Pudding* (1933) playing himself, *Two Men In A Box* (1938), *It's That Man Again* (1942) as Mayor Handley and *Time Flies* (1943) as Tommy. It is a common misconception to presume the "man" in *ITMA* was Handley himself. It wasn't. As his biographer and *ITMA* scriptwriter, Ted Kavanagh, reveals, the "man" was actually Adolf Hitler. Handley's hobbies included cycling, golf, reading and attending criminal

trials at the Old Bailey. On February 19, 1929 he married (Rosalind) Jean Allistone (d. 1958) in London. There were no children.
CAUSE: Tommy Handley died of a cerebral haemorrhage in a London nursing home at 29 Cleveland Gardens, Paddington, eight days before his 57th birthday. He left £63,181 11s 6d.
FURTHER READING: *Tommy Handley* – Ted Kavanagh (London: Hodder & Stoughton, 1949).

William Hanna
Born July 14, 1910
Died March 21, 2001
Animator extraordinaire. With his partner Joseph R. Barbera, William Denby Hanna was responsible for some of the most popular cartoons of the twentieth century. The names of Hanna-Barbera have become renowned as probably the most successful television animators in the world. Among their creations were *Top Cat* (based on Bilko), *The Flintstones* (based on *The Honeymooners*), *Huckleberry Hound, Yogi Bear, Quick-Draw McGraw, The Jetsons, Touché Turtle, Atom Ant, Secret Squirrel, Wait Till Your Father Gets Home, Wacky Races, The Perils Of Penelope Pitstop, Dastardly And Muttley In Their Flying Machines* and, possibly the most popular, *Scooby Doo, Where Are You?* Hanna-Barbera began their working partnership in 1939 while working at MGM where they created a series of Oscar-winning *Tom and Jerry* cartoons. They formed their own independent production company in 1957 and have since created more than 150 cartoon series. Bill Hanna was born in Melrose, New Mexico, the son of William John Hanna and Avice Joyce Denby. After school he studied journalism and engineering at college and worked as a structural engineer for a building firm. One of his first jobs was to oversee the building of the Pantages Theater in Hollywood. The Depression cost him his job but he found work as a general dogsbody at a

cartoon company, and in 1930 joined the company that made *Looney Tunes* and *Merrie Melodies*. On June 7, 1937, he joined MGM in Culver City and the following month Joe Barbera joined the staff. The two became firm friends and began working together unofficially. In 1939 they created *Tom And Jerry*. The two almost decided on a dog and a fox before plumping for the cat and the mouse. Tom and Jerry first appeared in *Puss Gets The Boot* which won an Academy Award for Best Cartoon Short in 1940. Over the next fifteen years, under the supervision of producer Fred Quimby, they created 113 cartoons featuring the cat and the mouse. Between 1940 and 1952 they won seven Oscars and 12 nominations. Barbera was responsible for drawing the story board while Hanna spent his time on the technical side of productions. In 1955 and 1957 they won two more Academy Award nominations. It was in July 1957 when MGM began cutting back their cartoon output that the two men formed their own company. December 14, 1957 saw the début of their first television show, *Ruff And Reddy*. As well as their original programming Hanna-Barbera produced animated versions of popular live-action shows or popular personalities such as Fonz and the *Happy Days* Gang, The Harlem Globetrotters and many more. Hanna married Violet B. Wogatzke on August 7, 1936 and had two children, David William and Bonnie Jeane. CAUSE: Hanna died aged 90 at his home in North Hollywood, California, from natural causes. He is buried in Ascension Cemetery, Lake Forest, Orange County, California.

Sir Cedric Hardwicke

Born February 19, 1893
Died August 6, 1964
Fruity-voiced thesp. Born in Stourbridge in the West Midlands, the only son of a doctor (there were two younger daughters), Cedric Webster Hardwicke intended to follow in his father's footsteps but didn't pass the requisite exams and instead enrolled in RADA. In 1913 he joined Frank Benson's Shakespeare Company and the following year moved to the Old Vic. In 1913 he had also made his first film, *Riches And Rogues* (1913), but didn't appear before the cameras again for 13 years. Meanwhile, his theatre career flourished playing Magnus in *The Apple Cart*, Captain Andy in *Show Boat* and Edward Barrett in *The Barretts Of Wimpole Street*. In 1914 he joined the army, where he stayed for seven years. He was the last British officer to leave the war zone. In 1927 he married actress Helena Pickard (d. 1959) and had one son, Edward, who became an actor and was well known to television audiences as Dr Watson to Jeremy Brett's Sherlock Holmes. Following his divorce, Cedric Hardwicke married actress Mary Scott in 1959 and had another son before another divorce. His films included *Nelson* (1926) as Horatio Nelson, *The Dreyfus Case* (1931) as Captain Alfred Dreyfus, *Nell Gwyn* (1934) as Charles II, *Jew Suess* (1934) as Rabbi Gabriel, *Bella Donna* (1934) as Dr Isaacson, *Peg Of Old Drury* (1935) as David Garrick, *Becky Sharp* (1935) as the Marquis of Steyne, *Tudor Rose* (1936) as the Earl of Warwick, *Things To Come* (1936) as Theotocopulos, *King Solomon's Mines* (1937) as Allan Quartermain, *Stanley And Livingstone* (1939) as Dr David Livingstone, *The Hunchback Of Notre Dame* (1939) as Jean Frollo, *Tom Brown's School Days* (1940) as Doctor Arnold, *The Ghost Of Frankenstein* (1942) as Dr Ludwig Frankenstein, *The Lodger* (1944) as Robert Burton, *Wilson* (1944) as Senator Henry Cabot Lodge, *The Picture Of Dorian Gray* (1945), *Nicholas Nickleby* (1947) as Ralph Nickleby, *Tycoon* (1947) as Frederick Alexander, *I Remember Mama* (1948) as Mr Hyde, *The Winslow Boy* (1948) as Arthur Winslow, *A Connecticut Yankee In King Arthur's*

Court (1949) as King Arthur, *The Desert Fox: The Story Of Rommel* (1951) as Dr Karl Strolin, *Salome* (1953) as Caesar Tiberius, *Richard III* (1954) as Edward Plantagenet, *Around The World In 80 Days* (1956) as Sir Francis Gromarty and *The Pumpkin Eater* (1964). He was knighted in 1934. Towards the end of his life, he suffered from impotence and nicknamed himself "Sir Seldom Hardprick". CAUSE: He died in New York aged 71 from a lung ailment.

Jean Harlow

(HARLEAN HARLOW CARPENTER)
Born March 3, 1911
Died June 7, 1937
Platinum blonde. After Marilyn Monroe, Jean Harlow is probably the most potent female sex symbol of the twentieth century. Born at 7.40pm weighing 9lb at 3344 Olive Street, Kansas City, Missouri, 34-24-36 Harlow began making films in 1928, appearing in *Honor Bound*, but went unnoticed until *Double Whoopee* (1929) where she played opposite Laurel & Hardy. In *The Saturday Night Kid* (1929) she was cast as Hazel. The star of the film was Clara Bow, whose mantle as the cinema's leading sex symbol Jean Harlow would soon inherit. When she was 18 and still known by her real name she had a screen test for *Hell's Angels* (1930). It didn't go well. Screenwriter Joseph Moncure March observed, "My God, she's got a shape like a dustpan." Director Howard Hughes concurred: "In my opinion, she's nix." She still got the part and became notorious for asking Ben Lyon on screen, "Would you be shocked if I changed into something more comfortable?" The 5′2½″ Jean's first marriage ended in a steamy divorce in January 1931 after Charles Fremont McGrew II (whom she married in Waukegan, Illinois, on September 20, 1927) accused Jean of posing for indecent pictures. While still married, Jean was constantly seen with

a parade of handsome leading men, at parties, at dinners, horseback riding and at the beach. She was the toast of Hollywood, the most desired girl in town, indeed the world. Jean was given the house, money McGrew owed her, and $375-a-month alimony – plus the assurance that she could have the use of a car for as long as she lived. But Jean gave back everything. She only wanted a moral victory – and the judge gave it to her. That year she appeared in *City Lights* (1931), *Iron Man* (1931) as Rose, *The Public Enemy* (1931) as Gwen Allen, *Goldie* (1931) as Goldie, *Platinum Blonde* (1931) as Ann Schuyler and *The Secret Six* (1931) as Anne Courtland. She was no stranger to death. Canine superstar Rin Tin Tin died in her arms on August 8, 1932, and her second husband, MGM producer Paul Bern, died at their home, 9820 Easton Drive, Beverly Hills, of a gunshot wound just two months after their wedding, under bizarre circumstances. Still only 22, she married for the third time (to Harold G. 'Hal' Rosson in Yuma, Arizona, on September 18, 1933) but that match was destined not to last either. A divorce was granted on the grounds of her husband's cruelty. Meanwhile, she appeared in *Talking Screen Snapshots* (1932), *Three Wise Girls* (1932) as Cassie Barnes, *The Beast Of The City* (1932) as Daisy Stevens, *Red-Headed Woman* (1932) as Lillian 'Red' Andrews Legendre, *Red Dust* (1932) as Vantine, *Dinner At Eight* (1933) as Kitty Packard, *Hold Your Man* (1933) as Ruby Adams and *Bombshell* (1933) as Lola Burns. Novelist Graham Greene noted, "There is no sign her acting would ever have progressed beyond the scope of the restless shoulders and the protuberant breasts; her body technique was the gangster's technique – she toted a breast like a man totes a gun." To make her nipples stick out, she rubbed them with ice before a scene and rarely wore a bra. CAUSE: In 1936, while working on the movie *Saratoga*, Harlow fell ill. She suffered from colds and had three impacted wisdom teeth removed. She was hospitalised for several weeks. Harlow's mother, known as Mother Jean Bello, took control of her daughter's convalescence. She made sure Jean slept at night, even if that meant the use of drink and drugs. In the morning she would shake her daughter awake and make her drink coffee. At the end of each day, Harlow would drowsily attempt to learn her lines for the next day, before falling into bed dog tired. Her nights were not helped by her mother, a devout Christian Scientist, praying aloud in her room. Harlow told her boyfriend, William Powell, and her agent how ill she felt but Mother Jean's religious beliefs would not allow her daughter to seek conventional medical advice. With the film just six days from wrapping, Harlow collapsed on the set. She would never return. Her mother took her home and refused admittance to all visitors, telling callers that her daughter was resting peacefully with no signs of illness. Jean complained of feeling hot but her mother told her to concentrate on feeling cold as she was and all would be well. When Harlow did not return to the set emissaries from the studio were sent to her house at 512 North Palm Drive, Beverly Hills, but again Mother Jean refused to admit anyone. Even Clark Gable was turned away. He later returned with Harlow's agent and two men from the studio. Finally, they saw Harlow and were horrified by her poorly condition. They insisted Mother Jean call a doctor. She laughed at them, saying she had told the sickness to leave her daughter's body and soon Jean would be well again. In the end a doctor was called and diagnosed inflammation of the gall bladder, demanding that surgery be performed immediately. Mother Jean refused to consider the idea. Didn't these fools know that she, Mother Jean, would cure her daughter? Eventually,

she agreed that the physician could administer painkillers but only on condition that she would continue her form of healing. Nurses did what they could for Jean but her damaged kidneys were making their work all but superfluous. They insisted Jean be taken at once to the hospital for surgery but Mother Jean still refused. "There is no death," she insisted. Eventually, William Powell rang studio head Louis B. Mayer to inform him of his star's condition. Within minutes of Mayer's edict coming through Harlow was in an ambulance being rushed to hospital. When she was examined it was decided she was too weak to be operated on. She was given blood transfusions but it was too late, much too late. She died, because of Mother Jean's blundering stubbornness, at 11.37am. Just 26 years old, Harlow was buried in the Jean Harlow room of The Great Mausoleum at Forest Lawn Cemetery. The room cost her boyfriend, William Powell, a reputed $25,000.

FURTHER READING: *Deadly Illusions: Who Killed Jean Harlow's Husband?* – Samuel Marx & Joyce Vanderveen (London: Century, 1991); *Platinum Girl: The Life And Legends Of Jean Harlow* – Eve Golden (New York: Abbeville Press, 1991); *Bombshell: The Life And Death Of Jean Harlow* – David Stenn (New York: Doubleday, 1993).

Radie Harris
Born October 24, 1904
Died February 22, 2001
Monoped gossip columnist. Born one of five children and a twin (she had a brother, Lawrence) in New York City, New York, Radie Harris was 14 years old when she was thrown from her horse in Maine and as a result of the injury had to have her left leg amputated below the knee. She became a journalist with the *New York Morning Telegraph*, later presented a radio show on CBS and wrote a column for the *Hollywood Reporter* called Broadway Ballyhoo.

Unlike her rivals Hedda Hopper and Louella Parsons, Harris' columns were much gentler as she enjoyed the confidence of those she wrote about. She appeared in the film *Stage Door Canteen* (1943). She never married. CAUSE: Radie Harris died aged 96 in Englewood, New Jersey, from natural causes.
FURTHER READING: *Radie's World –* Radie Harris (London: W.H. Allen, 1975)

Richard Harris
Born October 1, 1930
Died October 25, 2002
Irish troublemaker. Born in Limerick in the Republic of Ireland, the fifth of eight children of a flour mill owner, Ivan Harris and his wife Mildred Harty (d. December 1959 of cancer), a staunchly Roman Catholic family, Richard St John Harris was educated by the Jesuits at Crescent School. He wanted to become a rugby international and played for Munster before a bout of tuberculosis when he was 19 wrecked his dreams. He was bedridden for two years during which time he read prodigiously and decided to become an actor. He travelled to London in 1953 to fulfil his ambition. He had just £21 in his pocket. He was accepted by LAMDA after RADA turned him down and then studied at Joan Littlewood's Theatre Workshop before making his London stage début in 1956. On February 9, 1957, at the Church of Notre Dame de Paris, Leicester Place, London he married the Honourable (Joan) Elizabeth Rees-Williams (b. 1 May, 1936, daughter of David, 1st Baron Ogmore). Their reception was held at the House of Lords. By Harris, she had three sons: the film director Damian (b. Queen Charlotte's Hospital, London, August 2, 1958) and the actors Jared (b. London, August 24, 1961) and Jamie (b. London, May 15, 1963). Harris was present at the birth of Damian and fainted during the

proceedings. They divorced on July 25, 1969 and she went on to marry (Sir) Rex Harrison on August 26, 1971 in Oyster Bay, Long Island, New York. They divorced on December 16, 1975. Harris quickly acquired a reputation for heavy drinking and fighting, so perhaps it is fitting that his first film was called *Alive And Kicking* (1958) which starred Sybil Thorndike and Stanley Holloway. In 1963 he played a miner in Lindsay Anderson's *This Sporting Life* and was nominated for an Oscar for his performance. Harris used the money he made from the film to prevent the closure of his father's mill. In 1967 he played King Arthur in *Camelot* despite the fact that the producers wanted Richard Burton who had created the role on stage. In the Eighties Harris bought the rights to the stage version for £1 million and toured the world for five years with the show, becoming a multi-millionaire in the process. In 1968 he had a smash hit with his version of the maudlin song 'Macarthur Park'. He was nominated for another Oscar in 1990 for *The Field* for his performance as 'Bull' McCabe who is fighting to save his land. Harris created as many headlines off the screen as he did on. He and Marlon Brando had a well-publicised feud during the making of *The Mutiny On The Bounty*. "I called him a gross, misconceived, bloody animal. It was a legendary punch-up and it stuck with me." Harris also had fights with Kirk Douglas and Charlton Heston during the filming of Sam Peckinpah's *Major Dundee* (1964) – Heston called him "very much the professional Irishman and an occasional pain in the posterior". On December 17, 1983, the IRA exploded a bomb outside Harrods which killed six people and injured 90. Harris praised the bombers and it was only when public revulsion reached a peak that he then came out with a pious piece of hypocrisy. He claimed that *Daily Express* gossip journalist Philip Geddes, a 24-year-old victim, "was a friend of mine". Hardly. The previous time that the two men had met was in Langan's Brasserie and Harris punched Geddes in the face. Two years previously, Harris had been told that he had hypoglycaemia and warned that unless he moderated his prodigious drinking, he would be dead within 18 months. On August 11, 1981, he went into the Jockey Club in Washington and ordered two bottles of Chateau Margaux 1947 at a cost of £325 each. He had decided to say goodbye to alcohol in style. In the Nineties he lived at the Savoy hotel and claimed that his friends were the winos who populated the Strand. In December 2001 a young woman in a mini-skirted Santa Claus outfit collecting for charity walked into Harris' local, the Coal Hole on the Strand. He rushed over and she good-naturedly ruffled his hair and rubbed his stubble, "Hello, grandad, have you been a good boy this year?" They chatted for ten minutes and then she left saying, "I don't know who that tramp was but he has just given me a donation of a thousand pounds." The dyslexic Harris once said, "My life has been a rollercoaster of money, booze and high adventure. I drank, I screwed and I put the 'Great' into British films." His films included *Shake Hands With The Devil* (1959) as Terence O'Brien, *The Wreck Of The Mary Deare* (1959) as Higgins, *The Long And The Short And The Tall* (1960) as Corporal Johnstone, *A Terrible Beauty* (1960) as Sean Reilly, *The Guns Of Navarone* (1961) as Squadron Leader Howard Barnsby RAAF, *Mutiny On The Bounty* (1962) as Seaman John Mills, *Il Deserto Rosso* (1964) as Corrado Zeller, *The Heroes Of Telemark* (1965) as Knut Straud, *La Bibbia* (1966) as Cain, *Hawaii* (1966) as Rafer Hoxworth, *The Circle* (1967), *Caprice* (1967) as Christopher White, *Camelot* (1967) as King Arthur, *A Man Called Horse* (1970) as John Morgan, *Cromwell* (1970) as Oliver Cromwell, *The Molly Maguires* (1970) as James McParlan/

McKenna, *Bloomfield* (1971) as Eitan which he also directed, *Man In The Wilderness* (1971) as Zachary Bass, *The Deadly Trackers* (1973) as Sheriff Sean Kilpatrick, *99 And 44/100 Per Cent Dead* (1974) as Harry Crown, *Juggernaut* (1974) as Fallon, *Ransom* (1975) as Gerald Palmer, *Robin And Marian* (1976) as King Richard, *Echoes Of A Summer* (1976) as Eugene Striden, *The Return Of A Man Called Horse* (1976) as Lord John Morgan a.k.a. Shunkawakan which he also produced, *The Cassandra Crossing* (1976) as Dr Jonathan Chamberlain, *Gulliver's Travels* (1977) as Gulliver, *Orca* (1977) as Captain Nolan, *Golden Rendezvous* (1977) as John Carter, *The Wild Geese* (1978) as Captain Rafer Janders, *Ravagers* (1979) as Falk, *The Last Word* (1979) as Danny Travis, *A Game For Vultures* (1979) as David Swansey, *Tarzan, The Ape Man* (1981) as Parker, *Your Ticket Is No Longer Valid* (1981) as Jason, *Triumphs Of A Man Called Horse* (1982) as John Morgan, *Martin's Day* (1984) as Martin Steckert, *Highpoint* (1984) as Lewis Kinney, *Strike Commando 2* (1989), *King Of The Wind* (1989) as King George II, *Mack The Knife* (1990) as Peachum, *Patriot Games* (1992) as Paddy O'Neil, *Unforgiven* (1992) as English Bob, *Silent Tongue* (1993) as Prescott Roe, *Wrestling Ernest Hemingway* (1993) as Frank, *Savage Hearts* (1995) as Sir Roger Foxley, *Cry, The Beloved Country* (1995) as James Jarvis, *Trojan Eddie* (1996) as John Power, *Smilla's Sense Of Snow* (1997) as Andreas Tork, *This Is The Sea* (1998) as Old Man Jacobs, *Sibirskij Tsiryulnik* (1998) as Douglas McCraken, *To Walk With Lions* (1999) as George Adamson, *Grizzly Falls* (1999) as Old Harry, *The Royal Way* (2000), *Gladiator* (2000) as Marcus Aurelius, *The Pearl* (2001), *My Kingdom* (2001) as Sandeman, *Harry Potter And The Philosopher's Stone* (2001) as Professor Albus Dumbledore for which he received another Oscar

nomination, *The Count Of Monte Cristo*
(2002) as Abbé Faria, *Harry Potter
And The Chamber Of Secrets* (2002) as
Albus Dumbledore, *San Giovanni –
L'Apocalisse* (2002) as St John/
Teophilus and *Kaena: The Prophecy*
(2003) as Opaz. He was also Maigret in
the television series of 1988. Following
his divorce from his first wife Harris
was married to the tall, glamorous,
Jewish model-actress Ann Turkel (b.
Scarsdale, New York 1947) from June
1974 (in Beverly Hills) until 1981.
CAUSE: Harris died in London's
University College Hospital of
Hodgkin's disease. As he lay dying his
ex-wife Ann Turkel waved her hands
over his body and prayed for him to be
healed.
FURTHER READING: *Richard Harris A
Sporting Life* – Michael Feeney Callan
(London: Sidgwick & Jackson, 1990);
Richard Harris Actor By Accident – Gus
Smith (London: Robert Hale, 1990).

Sir Rex Harrison

*Born March 5, 1908
Died June 2, 1990*
Urbanity personified. Born in Derry
House, Tarbock Road, Huyton,
Merseyside, the son of a stockbroker,
Reginald Carey Harrison became 'Rex'
when he was ten years old. A weedy
child, he joined the Liverpool
Repertory Theatre when he was just 16
and began touring with *Charley's Aunt*
in 1927. He made his film début
three years later in *School For Scandal*
(1930). He signed a contract with Sir
Alexander Korda at London Films but
continued to appear on the stage. In
January 1934 he married fashion model
Noel Marjorie Collette Thomas (d.
1991) who preferred to be known by
her third given name and they had one
son Noel (b. London, January 29,
1935) who became an actor, pop star
and Olympic skier. The couple was
divorced in 1942. Prior to a two-year
stint in the Royal Air Force Volunteer
Reserve, he appeared in *School
For Husbands* (1937) as Leonard

Drummond, *Over The Moon* (1937) as
Dr Freddie Jarvis, *Storm In A Teacup*
(1937) as journalist Frank Burdon,
Sidewalks Of London (1938) as Harley
Prentiss, *Night Train To Munich* (1940)
as Gus Bennett and *Major Barbara*
(1941) as Adolphus Cusins. He
married for the second time at Caxton
Hall Register Office on January 25,
1943; his wife this time was the actress
Lilli Palmer and they had a son Carey
(b. London, February 19, 1944). After
demob Harrison appeared in *The
Rake's Progress* (1945) as playboy
Vivian Kenway and *Blithe Spirit* (1945)
as Charles Condomine before signing a
seven-year contract in Hollywood at
20th Century Fox. He appeared in
Anna And The King Of Siam (1946)
playing King Mongkut to Irene
Dunne's Mrs Anna, *The Ghost And Mrs
Muir* (1947) playing the spirit of sea
salt Captain Daniel Gregg and
Unfaithfully Yours (1948) as the
egomaniacal conductor Sir Alfred De
Carter. His contract with Fox was
ended by mutual consent following his
involvement in a scandal over the
suicide of actress Carole Landis, with
whom he was having an affair. For
some time Harrison preferred the
theatre, occasionally appearing before
the cameras in films such as *The Long
Dark Hall* (1951) as Arthur Groome,
King Richard And The Crusaders (1954)
as Saladin, *The Constant Husband*
(1955) as Charles Hathaway, *The
Reluctant Debutante* (1958) as Jimmy
Broadbent and *Midnight Lace* (1960) as
Anthony Preston. He met actress Kay
Kendall and began an affair with her
only to discover she was dying of
leukaemia. He divorced Lilli Palmer in
February 1957 so he could marry his
new lover with the understanding they
would remarry after Kendall's death.
He and Kendall were married at
Universalist Church of the Divine
Paternity, Central Park West & 76th
Street, New York on June 23, 1957.
They were together when she died at
the London Clinic on September 6,

1959, aged 32. Harrison and Palmer never remarried and on March 21, 1962, he married actress Rachel Roberts (b. Llanelli, Wales, September 20, 1927, d. Los Angeles, California, November 26, 1980) at Genoa Town Hall. He appeared in the epic that bankrupted 20th Century Fox, *Cleopatra* (1963), playing Julius Caesar (and winning an Oscar nomination) but it was the following year that he created his most famous cinematic role, that of Professor Henry Higgins in *My Fair Lady* (1964). He had first played the part on stage in 1956, but his cinematic turn made him an international star. He won his only Oscar for the part. Actress Cathleen Nesbitt, still working as a nonagenarian, played the role of Rex Harrison's mother in the American touring production of *My Fair Lady*. Her legs would no longer carry her to and from her dressing room, so thoughtful stage-hands placed a chair at the side of the stage for her to sit on between her entrances. This resulted in her seeing parts of the show that she had previously missed, as she had been in her dressing room when they were being performed. She was not impressed. She complained to the producer about the 'new' songs he had put into the play: "Something about the rain in Spain . . ." When the show reached San Francisco the audience gave her a standing ovation on her first entrance. The old dear became confused and, thinking the show was over, took a bow and left the stage. In the late Sixties and Seventies Harrison appeared in *The Agony And The Ecstasy* (1965) as Pope Julius II, *Doctor Dolittle* (1967) as Dr John Dolittle, *Staircase* (1969) as Charles Dyer, *Shalimar* (1978) as Shalimar, *The Fifth Musketeer* (1979) as Colbert and *Ashanti* (1979) as Brian Walker. Harrison would have played Ebeneezer Scrooge in *Scrooge* (1970) but a last minute contractual problem meant the role went to Albert Finney. On

February 20, 1971, he was divorced for the fourth time. Not single for long, on August 26 of the same year he married the Honourable Elizabeth Harris (b. May 1, 1936, the daughter of 1st Baron Ogmore of Bridgend and former wife of Richard Harris) at Oyster Bay, Long Island, New York. They were divorced on December 16, 1975. He married for the sixth and final time in New York on December 17, 1978, to Mercia Tinker (b. 1938). His last film was *A Time To Die* (1983) in which he played Van Osten. Generally regarded as a deeply unpleasant man with a fearsome temper (he also had only one eye [the right] and wore a wig), when he was awarded a knighthood in the summer of 1989 one of his friends commented, "What has Rex ever done for England, except live abroad on his illegal income tax and call everybody a cunt?" Even the ceremony didn't please him. "The Queen wasn't properly briefed. She didn't seem to know who I was. Mind you, you'd have to be a complete cunt not to get it right." Noël Coward once said to him, "If you weren't the best light comedian in the country, all you'd be fit for is selling cars in Great Portland Street."

CAUSE: He died in New York of pancreatic cancer aged 82. On his death bed he told younger son, Carey, to drop dead and informed his elder son, Noel, "There was something I always wanted to tell you. I could never stand the sound of your fucking guitar."

FURTHER READING: *Love Honour & Dismay* – Elizabeth Harrison (London: Star Books, 1978); *Rex Harrison* – Allen Eyles (London: W.H. Allen, 1985); *Rex Harrison: The First Biography* – Roy Moseley with Philip & Martin Masheter (London: New English Library, 1987); *Rex Harrison: A Biography* – Nicholas Wapshott (London: Chatto & Windus, 1991); *The Last Of The High Comedians – The Incomparable Rex: A Memoir Of Rex Harrison In The 1980s* – Patrick Garland (London: Macmillan, 1998).

John Hart

Born December 13, 1917
Died September 20, 2009

The other Lone Ranger. Born in Los Angeles, Hart was raised at San Marino, where his mother was a drama critic for the *Pasadena Star-News*. Hart was educated at South Pasadena High School and while there he appeared at the Pasadena Playhouse before landing a Hollywood agent. After featuring in Cecil B. DeMille's 1938 film *The Buccaneer*, he was signed to a contract at Paramount. In 1941 he was drafted into the army. Demobbed, he appeared in the movie serial *Jack Armstrong: The All-American Boy* (1947). In 1952 Hart replaced Clayton Moore as The Lone Ranger after Moore left in a pay dispute. "I don't know how many other actors they looked at, but I got the part," Hart said. "They didn't pay me much, either. It was unbelievable. But being an out-of-work actor, to have a steady job for a while is great." Hart played the masked avenger for 52 episodes before Moore returned to the role. "I got a lot of bad advice about playing the part. I tried the bad advice for about one or two shows and then I said, 'The hell with that, I'll do it my own way.' They wanted me to be like a stiff army major, and it was all wrong. So I just forgot that and slipped into the part, and everybody loved it," he said. After *The Lone Ranger*, Hart went on to star in the 1955 Columbia serial *The Adventures Of Captain Africa*. Two years later, he starred in *Hawkeye And The Last of the Mohicans*, a 1957 syndicated TV series shot in Canada with Lon Chaney, Jr as Chingachgook. While filming he met his Canadian-born actress Beryl Braithwaite, 20. Ten days later, they were married and had one daughter, Robyn. Hart played a newspaper editor in the 1981 movie *The Legend Of The Lone Ranger* which starred Klinton Spilsbury in the title role.

CAUSE: Hart died aged 91 at his home in Rosarito Beach, Mexico. He had been suffering from dementia in his later years.

Phil Hartman

Born September 24, 1948
Died May 28, 1998

'The Sultan Of Smarm'. Born in Brantford, Ontario, Canada, Philip Edward Hartman was little known in Britain but well known in America for his appearances on numerous television shows such as *Saturday Night Live* often impersonating President Bill Clinton. He also appeared in several films including *The Gong Show Movie* (1980), *Weekend Pass* (1984) as Joe Chicago, *Pee-Wee's Big Adventure* (1985) playing a reporter, *Three Amigos!* (1986) as Sam, *Jumpin' Jack Flash* (1986) as Fred, *Blind Date* (1987) as Ted Davis, *Fletch Lives* (1989), *So I Married An Axe Murderer* (1993) as John Johnson, *Loaded Weapon 1* (1993), *Coneheads* (1993) as Marlax, *Sgt. Bilko* (1996) as Major Thorn and *Small Soldiers* (1998) as Phil Fimple. He was wed five times. He married Lisa Jarvis, Carlyle Blackwell, Gretchen Lewis, Lisa Strain (in 1982) and finally Brynn in 1987. He once commented, "I'm 49 years old and I'm cautious of the fact that very few people in comedy have careers after age 50. I think there's a notion in our society, and it may be valid, that people aren't as funny when they get older. It's a stigma still attached to the rebelliousness of youth. I do believe that sooner or later I'll get those great roles like Gary Sinise's part in *Forrest Gump* or Tommy Lee Jones as Two Face in *Batman Forever*."

CAUSE: He was murdered, aged 49, by his wife who shot him as he lay sleeping in bed at home in Encino. His widow then committed suicide.

William Hartnell

Born January 8, 1908
Died April 23, 1975

Forever Dr Who. Born illegitimately in South Pancras, London, Billy Hartnell never knew his father and his mother, Lucy (b. January 1884) was never to marry. He appeared in over 75 films including *The Unwritten Law* (1929), *School For Scandal* (1930), *Too Dangerous To Live* (1939), *Flying Fortress* (1942) as a taxi driver, *The Goose Steps Out* (1942) as a German officer, *Brighton Rock* (1947) as Dallow, *The Pickwick Papers* (1952), *Private's Progress* (1956) as Sergeant Sutton, *Yangtse Incident* (1957) as Leading Seaman Frank, *Carry On Sergeant* (1958) as Sergeant Grimshaw and *This Sporting Life* (1963) as Johnson. He also appeared regularly on television, including *The Army Game*, and was the first Dr Who. He left the show in 1966 after three years because he believed it unsuitable for children and because he was suffering from multiple sclerosis. On May 9, 1929, at Chelsea Register Office, he married Amy Heather Miriam Armstrong McIntyre (b. April 27, 1907, d. December 1984).

CAUSE: Towards the end of his life, he became very vague and absent-minded. He died aged 67 in his sleep, having been hospitalised four months earlier after a series of strokes.

FURTHER READING: *Who's There? The Life And Career Of William Hartnell* – Jessica Carney (London: Virgin, 1996).

Laurence Harvey

(LARUSHKA MISCHA SKIKNE)
Born October 1, 1928
Died November 25, 1973
Mixed-up leading man. Born in Joniskis, Lithuania, Jewish Harvey was raised in South Africa and joined the republic's navy and then army before enrolling in RADA in 1945. He was named Harvey after the London store Harvey Nichols. He made his first film in 1948 playing Francis Merryman in *House Of Darkness*. He followed that with *Man On The Run* (1948) as Detective Sergeant Lawson. He also appeared in *Cairo Road* (1950) as Lieutenant Mourad, *There Is Another Sun* (1951) as Mag Maguire, *I Believe In You* (1952) as Jordie, *King Richard And The Crusaders* (1954) as Sir Kenneth, *I Am A Camera* (1955) as Christopher Isherwood, *Storm Over The Nile* (1955) as John Durrance, *Three Men In A Boat* (1956) as George and *Room At The Top* (1959) as Joe Lampton, the film that made him a star. Hollywood beckoned and he appeared in *Expresso Bongo* (1960) as Johnny Jackson, *The Alamo* (1960) as Colonel William Travis, *Butterfield 8* (1960) as Weston Liggett, *The Wonderful World Of The Brothers Grimm* (1962) as Wilhelm Grimm and his best performance as the brainwashed assassin Raymond Shaw in *The Manchurian Candidate* (1962). (Angela Lansbury played his mother. She was just three years his elder.) He also made *The Running Man* (1963) as Rex Black, *Of Human Bondage* (1964) as Philip Carey, *Life At The Top* (1965) as Joe Lampton, *Darling* (1965) as Miles Brand, *The Spy With A Cold Nose* (1966) as Dr Francis Trevelyan and *A Dandy In Aspic* (1968) as Alexander Eberlin. He married three times. His first wife was the actress Margaret Leighton, whom he married in August 1957. They were divorced in 1960. Wife number two (on October 17, 1968 at the Lyford Cay Club, Nassau) was Joan Cohn, widow of mogul Harry Cohn. They divorced in 1972. On New Year's Eve that year he married model Paulene Stone. Their daughter, Domino, had been born in 1969. During his time with Paulene Stone, Harvey was said to be conducting a homosexual affair with one of his producers. When Harvey died Paulene married American businessman Peter Morton, leaving her daughter in England. She was expelled from four schools and in 1989 5'9" Domino became a ranch hand in the San Diego mountains. Later she joined the San Diego Fire Brigade. In 1994 she began working as a bounty hunter for the

Celes King Bail Bond Agency in South Central Los Angeles. She sold the rights to her life story for £26,000 and then disappeared. She fell prey to heroin addiction and in April 1997 checked herself into the Habilitat rehab clinic on Oahu, Hawaii where she stayed for two years. In March 2005 the film of her story *Domino* was released starring Keira Knightley in the title role. However, all examples of the real Domino's bisexuality were erased from the movie. Harvey also had a long affair with Hermione Baddeley. Sir Robert Stephens said of him: "An appalling man and, even more unforgivably, an appalling actor." CAUSE: He died of stomach cancer at his home in Kidderpore Avenue, Hampstead, north London, aged 45. He was cremated at Golders Green Crematorium. He left £34,349. FURTHER READING: *The Prince Laurence Harvey His Public And Private Life* – Des Hickey & Gus Smith (London: Star Books, 1976).

Imogen Hassall

Born August 25, 1942
Died November 16, 1980
Countess of Cleavage. Busty, brunette and beautiful Imogen Hassall was born in Woking, Surrey, the daughter of the poet Christopher Vernon Hassall (b. London, March 24, 1912, d. of a heart attack on a train in Chatham, Kent, April 25, 1963) and the actor Evelyn Lynett Chapman who were married in 1938. Christopher Hassall was reported to be the gay lover of Ivor Novello and in 1973 Imogen spoke about the difficulty of being thought of as the offspring of a homosexual or bisexual. Some believe that Imogen's difficulties in life sprang from her relationship with her father – comparable to Vanessa and Corin Redgrave discovering that their father was bisexual. Imogen's godfather was the composer Sir William Walton. Her brother Nicholas Edward was born in Chelsea Hospital in April 1941. Their parents split in 1961 and

Christopher Hassall moved to Tonford Manor in Canterbury, Kent. Imogen, who was called 'Jenny' by her family and 'Imo' by her friends, was educated at Dorlands School, Hook Heath, near Woking, Channing School in Highgate, north London (June 1949–May 1951), Elmhurst Ballet School and the Royal Ballet School (from January 10, 1955). In 1959 Princess Margaret visited the school and Imogen managed to spill tea over the royal guest. In the academic year 1959–1960 – her final one – Imogen was head girl. From December 23, 1958 Imogen appeared as Victoria Bowman in a six-week run of *The Amazing Adventures Of Miss Brown* put on by the Rapier Players. Imogen's sweet nature made her a hit with the cast who were surprised to learn that at 16 she was already ordering custom-made bras. One of her castmates said that Imogen had "the most amazing figure and the smallest waist I have ever seen". Imogen made a career out of playing dolly birds although she was talented enough to work with The Royal Shakespeare Company. On October 5, 1960, Imogen enrolled at LAMDA (unlike many of her impoverished contemporaries Imogen had her own car and a flat above her aunt at 88 Kensington Park Road) and on graduation in 1962 spent five months with the RSC. She left to appear in the West End play *The Reluctant Peer* in 1964. Imogen became an adult in the Swinging Sixties, a time when everyone was supposedly at it (apart from the poet Philip Larkin) and Imogen had more than her fair share of lovers. She could not be without a man but she confessed to a friend, "I don't really like sex much, but I feel I ought to because what else have I to offer?" Two years before her death Imogen gave an interview in which she fully expounded her views on sex. She said, "I didn't want the reputation of sleeping around but on the other hand one was, I suppose, doing it . . . I was known as a jet-set girl and with this jet-set girl you slept around. It was a time when men used to phone me in the middle of the night and say come over [and] I used to go. It was something in me that liked to be wanted. I think I knew I was a good lover . . . I could move my body into different positions – and I knew what a man wanted instinctively . . . I loved the fact that people thought my body was super . . . I enjoyed people looking at my body and showing it off. I started having sex when I was 18 and I first had an orgasm when I was 30. Twelve years of complete frustration – but I was a wonderful faker. I don't do that any more – I think I've actually learned to enjoy sex myself – which I didn't before. I think I enjoy making love now and that makes me a good lover. Now I want to enjoy my body in bed – that has taken me a long time. I realise that I used to play a ridiculous game because even though I was happy, I cried a lot." She also had at least one abortion in the early Sixties, an operation that severely restricted her ability to have children. 1963 was a busy year for Imogen on television. On May 5 she appeared in the 'A Sunday Morning' episode of the series *Moonstrike*, in September in the crime drama *Scales Of Justice* and on December 14 she played Nikki in the 'Not Quite Fully Covered' episode of *The Sentimental Agent*. She also appeared in the film *Position Of Trust*. 1964 began well as Imogen opened at the Duchess Theatre on January 15 playing Lady Rosalind, the daughter of the title character, in *The Reluctant Peer*, a play by William Douglas Home, the brother of the prime minister. She made several appearances in *The Saint*: the title role of Sophia, the daughter of Stavros, a Greek innkeeper, in an episode on February 27, 1964 that was based on the 1948 short story *Lucia*; on December 23, 1966 ('Flight Plan') playing Nadya and Malia Gupta on December 22, 1968 ('The People Importers'). In August 1965 Imogen

opened as the Honourable Muriel Pym in *Milestones* for a fortnight at the Yvonne Arnaud Theatre in Guildford, Surrey. Three months later, she was back at the same theatre appearing in a production of Noël Coward's play about drugs, *The Vortex*. In 1965 she also made a brief appearance as Sir Roger's secretary Miss Cartwright in the Norman Wisdom vehicle *The Early Bird*. Halliwell describes the film as "overlong and mainly uninventive". On December 28, 1967 Imogen was Anjali in the 'Escape In Time' episode of *The Avengers*. She was also to appear in *The Champions* (October 9, 1968), *Softly Softly* (February 26, 1970), *The Persuaders* (September 17, 1971), and *Jason King* (March 17, 1972). In late 1966 she filmed *The Long Duel* (1967) in Spain, playing Tara who escapes from the British fort in India but then dies in childbirth. On set Imogen befriended her co-star Charlotte Rampling. However, Rampling pulled away from Imogen, put off by the older woman's obvious instability and she remembers that Imogen also attempted suicide at least once during their brief friendship. The film's stars were Yul Brynner, Trevor Howard and Harry Andrews. She was also in the film *Bedtime* (1967). From February 1, 1968, she played Elsa Levkin in *The Italian Girl* at Wyndham's Theatre. Imogen's portrayal of a doomed girl was described as "quite haunting". Imogen left the play ostensibly to holiday in Italy but in reality because she was unable to cope, much to the disappointment of her co-stars. The following year she played a fur bikini-clad cavegirl Ayak in the Hammer film *When Dinosaurs Ruled The Earth* (1969). In a film full of scantily clad starlets, Imogen stands out with her long lustrous hair and fine supple body. Publicity stills from the film are sought after by collectors of cult memorabilia to this day. In *Mumsy, Nanny, Sonny And Girly* (1969), a whimsically ghoulish horror melodrama, she played Michael Bryant's girlfriend. The next year Imogen made five films. She was in *El Condor* (1970) as Dolores with a nude scene; Franco Nero's evil wife in *The Virgin And The Gypsy* (1970) with a breast-feeding scene; *Toomorrow* (1970), a bizarre science fiction fantasy that starred Olivia Newton-John and in which Imogen played Amy; *Take A Girl Like You* (1970) as Samantha and wallflower-turned-model Jenny Grubb in *Carry On Loving* (filmed April 6– May 15 and released September 1970), a film that made the most of her 35-21-34 assets. In *Bloodsuckers*, also known as *Incense For The Damned* (1972), she is Chriseis, a vampire, and appears topless at the start of the film. In 1970, with enough money from her film work, Imogen bought a house in Betteridge Road, Fulham, which she proudly decorated herself. Around this time she became a regular at film premières, usually turning up in skimpy outfits and to at least one with her breasts barely encased in a fishnet top. Nowadays the tabloid press builds people up and then tears them down – it was no different 30 years ago. Although the press filled pages with photographs of Imogen at various events, they thought nothing of labelling her one of the "Top 10 Bores of the Year". To celebrate Neil Armstrong becoming the first man to walk on the moon, on July 20, 1969, the *Sunday Mirror* published pictures of their "own heavenly body" Imogen in the waves in the Bahamas. In July 1970, Imogen prepared to marry Christopher Long but nothing came of it. On September 20 she was taken to St Stephen's Hospital, Fulham Road, after taking a drugs overdose. Her friends believed it was a cry for help and not a serious attempt to end her life. However, at the end of October she told William Hall of the *Evening News*, "The overdose was an accident. It was certainly not a suicide attempt . . . I'm not the type. I had

been in great pain after paying £300 for an abortion at a Harley Street nursing home. I finally got some painkillers and when I got home I took two pills and lay down to sleep. I woke up in a daze and took two more, then two more, then two more." By the end of that year Imogen was worried that she was not being taken seriously and she had become nothing more than a sexy joke. In 1971 Imogen played Lady Ursula Itchin in *The Jockey Club Stakes*, another play by William Douglas Home, at the Duke of York Theatre. The play closed in November and, before its end, pleased with the response, Imogen decided to hire a PR to give herself some much needed positive press coverage. She arranged a Hallowe'en party for the press on a boat in the Thames and the PR told her how to dress and what to say. Satisfied that his job was done, he left Imogen alone. The next day there was his client resplendent in a witch's hat, topless, holding candles in front of her breasts. In the autumn of that year she met the man who would become her first husband when Kenneth Ives (b. 1933) joined the cast of the play. He was best known as Hawkeye in TV's *The Last Of The Mohicans* and later married comedienne Marti Caine. Early the next year Imogen became pregnant but their daughter, Melanie Ives Hassall, died on November 5, 1972 aged just four days. In June and July 1973 she appeared in Neil Simon's comedy *Barefoot In The Park* and then in October and November she toured in the play *The Mating Game*, playing Julia Carrington "the short-sighted and censorious secretary". In 1973 she starred alongside David Jason (playing Albert Toddey) in Ray Selfe's black comedy *White Cargo* (originally entitled *Albert's Follies*), in which she played Stella, a policewoman working undercover as a stripper to trap white slave traders. The film was made on a budget of £80,000. She married Ives at Bromley Register Office on May 25,

1974. At Christmas 1974 she appeared in the pantomime *Puss In Boots* at Whitehaven. During the run she had a brief fling with co-star Bill Homewood. On June 22, 1975, at 1.10am while living in Hurlingham Road, Fulham, she was stopped by police in Daisy Lane, Putney, and arrested for being drunk in charge of a bicycle. The next day at West London Magistrates Court she was fined £10 with £11 doctors' fees. The same day Imogen tried unsuccessfully to get a quickie divorce. Christmas 1975 and she was in panto in Bournemouth as Maid Marian in *Babes In The Wood*. From 1975 until 1976 she had an affair with Alan Whitehead (b. Oswestry, July 24, 1947), the drummer with the pop group Marmalade. Their first date was at Trader Vic's and Whitehead remembers that half way through the meal she laid down her fork and said, "All right, you've seduced me with your eyes. Let's go," and took him back to her Fulham home. In 1976 she took to the road appearing in the mystery play *Killer* opposite Wilfrid Brambell, and Geoffrey Davies from the medical sitcom *Doctor On The Go*. Imogen spent 1977 out of work. On February 3, 1978 she and Kenneth Ives were divorced. "I always refused what I didn't want in bed. I only forced myself to do something I didn't want sexually in my marriage. It became a nightmare. My husband was physically very handsome – I got married because I thought I ought to – but it was hell – I was on pills – awful." In September 1978 she landed the role of Valerie in the play *Say Who You Are*. One of her co-stars was the Cambridge-educated actor Andrew Knox (b. Hollywood, California, 1944), the son of the Oscar nominated actor Alexander Knox (b. Canada Strathroy, Ontario, Canada, January 16, 1907, d. Berwick-on-Tweed, Northumberland, April 25, 1995 aged 88 of bone cancer). He appeared as the snooty James Gascoigne in the sitcom *Doctor*

On The Go alongside her *Killer* co-star Geoffrey Davies. Imogen became depressed over her relationship failures and inability to have a child: "Desperately I want to be loved. Desperately I don't want to be used any more." On January 15, 1979, she married Knox at the Register Office in Berwick-on-Tweed, Northumberland. According to Imogen it was all over in a fortnight and Knox moved his belongings out of Imogen's home in Schubert Road, Putney. Imogen confessed, "We'd only spent about six nights together. The wedding was all a big joke that I didn't quite see. Andrew and I didn't have a very exciting sex life. Right from the start he had his own separate bedroom. We'd never lived together as man and wife in the normal sense." Knox had a different view. "Our sex life was splendid. It was rip-roaring. We were fornicating all the time we were together, which wasn't just two weeks. It was two months." Imogen told Geoffrey Davies that the marriage was never consummated. That year Imogen made her last film, a minor role in *Licence To Love And Kill* known in the States as *The Man From S.E.X.* From February until August 1980 Imogen toured as Ginnie in the cricket play *Outside Edge*.

CAUSE: Imogen began talking of suicide when she was just 18. She was given Tuinal, a drug that is now banned, at her mother's suggestion and thus began a reliance on pills that would last her entire adult life. Touring in 1980 she took pills to sleep and pills to wake up. Her friends would often receive phone calls in the middle of the night because Imogen was lonely and unable to sleep. Friends would patiently babysit her through the long, lonely, night-time hours as Imogen moaned that people, *i.e.* men, only looked at the surface and only wanted her for one thing. Imogen had attempted to kill herself three times. In June 1980 during the run of *Outside Edge* Imogen suffered an ectopic pregnancy and was rushed to hospital, according to the doctor who treated her she was "minutes from death". (According to her actor friend, Suzanna Leigh, Imogen lost eight babies. In August 1977 Imogen told the *Sunday People* that she had lost a baby the previous month and then split from her restaurateur boyfriend John Granville-Barker.) She left Putney and moved to a semi-detached cottage, 17 Crooked Billet, Wimbledon Village, London, next to The Crooked Billet pub. She began to date a toolmaker called Mick Hayward (b. 1947) but he broke off the relationship a few days before her death. On November 13, Imogen presented her local chemist with a prescription for 20 Dalmane sleeping pills, 20 Daraprim anti-malaria tablets, 50 Tuinal barbiturates and 25 Valium. The pharmacist questioned the large amount but was satisfied by Imogen's explanation that she was about to go on a month-long holiday to Mombasa, Kenya. She was due to leave with Suzanna Leigh on November 16. She died in the early hours of that Sunday morning. She was just 38. At 2pm Imogen's naked body was discovered in her four-poster bed by her housesitter. Her right hand was on the telephone dial and an empty bottle of Tuinal barbiturates beside her. Imogen had often taken drugs and then rang her friends to come and save her. On this Saturday night was she dialling her friends but none of them received the message or did she really intend finally to kill herself? Suzanna Leigh went ahead with the planned holiday. Later, Suzanna Leigh was to tell the story that on Friday, November 14 Imogen was beaten and raped by the friend of a man known to her. Leigh claimed that Imogen's head was badly cut and some hair had been pulled out. However, on November 17, when Imogen was autopsied no sign of sexual assault was discovered. Imogen was buried in the cemetery in Gap Road, Wimbledon, in a ceremony attended by more than 50 mourners. An obituary in

The Stage And Television Today published on November 27 said, "Imogen Hassall was better known for attending premières than for her abilities as an actress." At the inquest held on December 18, the coroner returned a verdict of suicide by barbiturate poisoning. Her will was published on May 11, 1981 and Imogen left £36,145 net (£42,767 gross). In 1987 Andrew Knox took his own life, throwing himself off the Jersey ferry. His body was never found.
FURTHER READING: *Tuesday's Child – The Life And Death Of Imogen Hassall –* Dane Leissner (Baltimore: Luminary Press, 2002).

Signe Hasso

(SIGNE LARSSON)
Born August 15, 1910
Died June 7, 2002
Garbo's 'replacement'. Signe Hasso was born in Stockholm and lived with her mother, grandmother and two siblings in a one-room apartment. Her father and grandfather had died by the time she was four. By the age of 12 she was studying at the Royal Dramatic Theatre. Her wholesome good looks soon attracted the attention of film-makers and in 1938 she received an award for her part in the film *Karriär*. One of her early champions was Harry Hasso, whom she married. Encouraged by the enthusiasm she moved to New York to learn English. By 1941 she was ready to appear on Broadway. Fate – in the form of the Japanese attack on Pearl Harbour on December 7, 1941 – intervened and she moved to the West Coast. She was given a part in a wartime propaganda film called *Journey For Margaret* (1942). She supplemented her income by becoming Hollywood correspondent for a Stockholm newspaper. Her marriage fell victim to the war and she was divorced in 1942. Her films included *Assignment In Brittany* (1943), *Heaven Can Wait* (1943), *The Story Of Dr Wassell* (1943), *The Seventh Cross*

(1944) as Toni, *Johnny Angel* (1945) as
Paulette Girard, *The House On 92nd
Street* (1945) as Elsa Gebhardt, *A
Scandal In Paris* (1946) as Therese de
Pierremont, *Where There's Life* (1947)
as General Katarina Grimovich, *A
Double Life* (1947), *To The Ends Of
The Earth* (1948) as Ann Grant. After
her performance in *Crisis* (1950),
starring Cary Grant, Signe Hasso
arrived in London to play Rebecca
West in Ibsen's *Rosmersholm* at the St
Martin's Theatre. "She decorated the
stage admirably," noted the *Daily
Telegraph*'s Patrick Gibbs, who noticed
"a certain artificiality in her acting".
In 1956 she appeared in the lead in
Schiller's *Mary Stuart* opposite Eva Le
Gallienne's Elizabeth at the Colonial
Theater in Boston. In 1958 she
appeared in Philip Mackie's thriller
The Key Of The Door at the Lyric,
Hammersmith alongside Michael
MacLiammoir. The critic W.A.
Darlington found that she
acted "decoratively if rather too
melodramatically". She continued to
work regularly in the theatre and
cinema and on television in America
and Europe until the mid-Eighties. She
also wrote articles and short stories, as
well as songs in English, German and
Swedish. In 1972 the King of Sweden
appointed her a Knight First Class of
The Royal Order of Vasa. She was
married three times and had a son, who
was killed in a car crash in 1957. She
was on Broadway when she heard the
news, playing Orinthia in Bernard
Shaw's *The Apple Cart*. She forced
herself to carry on with the part.
CAUSE: Signe Hasso died aged 91 in
Los Angeles, California, of pneumonia
resulting from her treatment for lung
cancer.

Henry Hathaway

Born March 13, 1898
Died February 11, 1985
Western cultist. Born in Sacramento,
California, Henry Hathaway began his
career as a child actor working for

director Allan Dwan before moving
behind the cameras and up the pecking
order. He began directing B Westerns
with *Wild Horse Mesa* (1932) and
followed up with *Heritage Of The Desert*
(1932), *The Thundering Herd* (1933),
Under The Tonto Rim (1933), *Sunset
Pass* (1933), *Man Of The Forest* (1933),
Come On Marines (1934), *The Lives Of
A Bengal Lancer* (1935), which won
him his only Oscar nomination, *Peter
Ibbetson* (1935), *I Loved A Soldier*
(1936), *The Trail Of The Lonesome Pine*
(1936), *Go West Young Man* (1936),
Brigham Young – Frontiersman (1940),
Ten Gentlemen From West Point (1942),
China Girl (1942), *Nob Hill* (1945), *13
Rue Madeleine* (1946), *Call Northside
777* (1948), *Rawhide* (1951), *The Desert
Fox: The Story Of Rommel* (1951),
You're In The Navy Now (1951), *O.
Henry's Full House* (1952) and *Niagara*
(1953), the film that made Marilyn
Monroe a star. Hathaway told Marilyn
he wanted her to wear her own clothes
for the film and was amazed and
disbelieving when she told him she
didn't own any. It was only when he
visited her apartment and saw her
"closet . . . and in the back was one
black suit [which she wears in the
famous bell pealing scene when she is
murdered] . . . She said she's bought it
for Johnny Hyde's funeral. 'That's why
I have to borrow clothes from the
studio when I have to go out. I don't
have any of my own,' she told me."
Hathaway was not looking forward to
the assignment. He had heard Marilyn
could be 'difficult', but was delighted
to discover that she was a joy to work
with. "Joe [DiMaggio] was there to
keep her happy," he recalled. He also
made *23 Paces To Baker Street* (1956)
(London, Hollywood, is never the same
as London, England – Van Johnson's
flat in Portman Square has a view that
overlooks the Savoy Hotel, in reality
two miles away), *North To Alaska*
(1960), *Of Human Bondage* (1964), *The
Sons Of Katie Elder* (1965), *True Grit*
(1969), *Raid On Rommel* (1971) and

Hangup (1974). Hathaway was known to be exceptionally rude to his fellow workers.

CAUSE: He died from a heart attack in Hollywood, California, aged 86.

Rondo Hatton

Born April 22, 1894
Died February 2, 1946
Pug ugly. Although by no means the most handsome actor in the world, Charles Laughton still needed make-up to portray ugly characters such as Quasimodo. Sadly, Rondo Hatton had no need for cosmetics. He was born in Hagerstown, Maryland, and grew up a handsome young man. Then he was struck down with acromegaly, a disease that affects the pituitary gland and results in distorted bones. Nevertheless, his illness meant that he became a star of sorts. He made his film début in *Hell Harbor* (1930) and went on to appear in *In Old Chicago* (1937) as Rondo, *The Hunchback Of Notre Dame* (1939) as first 'Ugly Man' contestant, *Chad Hanna* (1940), *Sleepy Lagoon* (1943) as a hunchback, *The Ox-Bow Incident* (1943) as Gabe Hart, *The Pearl Of Death* (1944) as The Creeper, *The Princess And The Pirate* (1944), *The Spider Woman Strikes Back* (1946) as Mario. Unbelievably, Hollywood decided to make a film about Hatton's deformity. Perhaps mercifully, he died before *The Brute Man* (1946) could be released.

CAUSE: He died of a heart attack in Beverly Hills, California, aged 51.

Jeremy Hawk

(CEDRIC JOSEPH LANGE)
Born May 20, 1918
Died January 15, 2002
Reliable straight man. Born in Johannesburg, South Africa, the son of Douglas Lange, a South African film star who performed under the name Douglas Drew, and June Langley. When the boy was two, his parents divorced, and he returned to Britain with his mother, June, who married a Yorkshire wool merchant, John Moore. At Harrow School, he developed an interest in the theatre because of his friendship with Terence Rattigan, the cricket team captain. Although he worked in his stepfather's wool business for a short time on leaving school, Lange was determined to become an actor and trained at RADA. He liked the name Jeremy and added it to his nickname, 'Hawk' because of his noticeable nose, Jeremy Hawk. After the Second World War broke out, Hawk became a regular in the *New Faces* revue at London's Comedy Theatre (1940), which established him as a comedy performer. He then appeared as Albert in *Ladies In Retirement* (St Martin's Theatre, 1941) and, after serving with the Army in North Africa and Italy, and entertaining the troops with ENSA, continued to appear in West End comedies for almost 50 years. He played Dr Sanderson, the comedian Sid Field's foil, in the long-running *Harvey* (Prince of Wales Theatre, January 1949). Hawk was chosen by Granada Television to host *Criss Cross Quiz* (1957–62), which became the third most popular programme nationwide in the year in which it began. Hawk's appearances in *The Benny Hill Show* had led to his acting in Hill's first film, the Ealing Studios comedy *Who Done It?* (1955), in which the star played an ice-rink sweeper who sets himself up as a private eye. Previously, Hawk had taken small roles on screen and subsequently played an instructor in *Dentist In The Chair* (1960), a professor in *Dentist On The Job* (1961), Admiral Saintsbury in *Mystery Submarine* (1963), a bank manager in the crime drama *The Trygon Factor* (1963) and an elderly priest in *Stealing Heaven* (1988). Hawk also appeared in the 1957 Boulting Brothers comedy *Lucky Jim* as Bill Atkinson. His last role was as the queen's second bishop in the acclaimed film *Elizabeth* (1998). His

television roles were character parts in series such as *The New Avengers* (1976), *The Professionals* (1978), the sitcom *Sorry!* (1987) and Agatha Christie's *Poirot* (1992), but he became a celebrity again after appearing in a Seventies commercial for Cadbury's Whole Nut chocolate, which featured a catchy tune about "Nuts, whole hazelnuts". He also guest-starred in *2point4 Children* (1996), the BBC sitcom that featured Belinda Lang – his daughter from his second marriage, to the actress Joan Heal. Hawk was married three times.

CAUSE: He died in Reading, Berkshire, of natural causes, aged 83.

Jack Hawkins

Born September 14, 1910
Died July 18, 1973
Stolid Englishman. Born in Lyndhurst Road, Wood Green, London, John Edward Hawkins began acting as soon as he became a teenager and his first film was *Birds Of Prey* (1930) as Alfred. He quickly achieved a reputation as a first-class actor in films such as *The Lodger* (1932) as Jack Martin, *Death At Broadcasting House* (1934) as Herbert Evans, *Murder Will Out* (1939) as Stamp, *The Fallen Idol* (1948) as Detective Ames, *Bonnie Prince Charlie* (1948) as Lord George Murray, *The Elusive Pimpernel* (1951) as the Prince Of Wales, *No Highway* (1951) as Dennis Scott, *Mandy* (1952) as Searle, *The Cruel Sea* (1953) as Captain Ericson, *Front Page Story* (1954) as Grant, and *Land Of The Pharaohs* (1955) as Pharaoh Khefu. In 1954 21-year-old Ivy Nicholson had the chance to become a big star. She was tested by Howard Hawks for a role in his million-dollar epic *Land Of The Pharaohs*. Her instructions read: "You're quarrelling, and he slaps you. Just react naturally, as you would if you'd really been slapped." Jack Hawkins appeared with her and when he faked the slap, Ivy let out a bloodcurdling scream and sank her

teeth deep into his arm. The test was suspended and poor old Ivy was sent home with the words, "We don't think you're up to the part." She was never heard of again. Her replacement fared rather better. Her name was Joan Collins. Hawkins starred in *The Bridge On The River Kwai* (1957) as Major Warden, *Ben-Hur* (1959) as Quintus Arrius, *Lawrence Of Arabia* (1962) as General Allenby, for which he was criticised by the real-life Allenby family, *Zulu* (1964) as Swedish missionary Reverend Otto Witt, *Lord Jim* (1965) as Captain Marlowe and *Masquerade* (1965) as Colonel Drexel. In 1966 he lost his voice following surgery for cancer of the larynx. However, he continued acting and his voice was dubbed by, among others, Charles Gray. Hawkins appeared in *Poppies Are Also Flowers* (1966) as General Bahar, *Shalako* (1968) as Sir Charles Baggett, *Monte Carlo Or Bust* (1969) as Count Levinovitch, *Oh! What A Lovely War* (1969) as Emperor Franz Josef, *Kidnapped* (1971) as Captain Hoseason, *Nicholas And Alexandra* (1971) as Count Fredericks, *Young Winston* (1972) as Mr Welldon and *Theatre Of Blood* (1973) as Solomon Psaltery. In 1932 he married actress Jessica Tandy in Winchmore Hill, London. Their daughter, Susan, was born in 1934 and they were divorced in 1940. On October 31, 1947, Hawkins married actress Doreen Lawrence. They had three children: Nicholas (b. St George's Hospital, London, 1948), Andrew (b. St George's Hospital, London, June 10, 1950) and Caroline (b. 1954).

CAUSE: Hawkins died of cancer at 12.10am in St Stephen's Hospital, Fulham Road, London, aged 62. He left £13,019.

Howard Hawks

Born May 30, 1896
Died December 26, 1977
Master film-maker. Born in Goshen, Indiana, the son of wealthy lumberman

Frank Winchester Hawks (b. Goshen, Indiana, October 16, 1864), Howard Winchester Hawks was the eldest in a family of five children. He studied mechanical engineering at Cornell University, developing an enthusiasm for racing, a passion that continued into his seventies. After seeing service in World War I he moved to Hollywood where he took a variety of jobs before selling a tale to Fox with the condition that he be allowed to direct. *The Road To Glory* (1926) was an aptly named film since it set him on the road to fame, money and success. On March 30, 1928, he married the perpetually sick Athole Shearer (b. November 20, 1900, d. March 17, 1984), Norma's big sister. They had two children: David (b. 1929) and Barbara (b. May 20, 1936). Hawks turned down a key role at MGM because of Louis B. Mayer's often malign influence and remained for the most part a freelance director. His films included: *Fig Leaves* (1926), *Paid To Love* (1927), *Trent's Last Case* (1929), *The Dawn Patrol* (1930), *Scarface* (1932), *Viva Villa!* (1934), *Barbary Coast* (1935), *Bringing Up Baby* (1938), *Only Angels Have Wings* (1939), *His Girl Friday* (1940), *Sergeant York* (1941), *The Outlaw* (1943), *To Have And Have Not* (1944), *The Big Sleep* (1946), *Red River* (1948), *I Was A Male War Bride* (1949), *O. Henry's Full House* (1952), *Monkey Business* (1952), *The Big Sky* (1952), *Gentlemen Prefer Blondes* (1953), *Land Of The Pharaohs* (1955), *Rio Bravo* (1959), *El Dorado* (1967) and *Rio Lobo* (1970). Following his divorce, he married screenwriter Nancy 'Slim' Gross (b. 1917). Gary Cooper gave the bride away. Their daughter Kitty was born on February 11, 1946, but the Hawkses divorced in 1948. Following the split with his fiancée Marian Marshall (who later married Robert Wagner), Hawks married New York model Dee Hartford (b. 1927) on February 20, 1953. Their son Gregg was born in 1953 but Hawks underwent his third divorce in 1960. (His ex-wife married Stuart Cramer, who was married to Jean Peters, who had been married to Howard Hughes.) He was awarded an honorary Oscar in 1974.

CAUSE: Aged 81, he died in Palm Springs, California, following a fall.

Sir Nigel Hawthorne, CBE

Born April 5, 1929
Died Boxing Day, 2001

Erudite actor. Film success for Nigel Hawthorne came late in life. He personified the civil service for many (including Margaret Thatcher) in the television sitcoms *Yes, Minister* (February 25, 1980–December 17, 1984) and *Yes, Prime Minister* (January 9, 1986–January 28, 1988) in which he excelled as the officious Sir Humphrey Appleby. Co-star Derek Fowlds remembers, "Together with Paul Eddington, the three of us were together for seven, eight years. We were really good mates. We had many happy hours doing those shows . . . they were very special times." Yet in his posthumously published autobiography Hawthorne claims that he and Eddington were not very close at all. "I wouldn't have said we were great friends. I used to get the feeling that he never thought either Derek or I were quite up to it." Born in Coventry, Nigel Barnard Hawthorne was the elder of two sons and four children of Dr Charles Barnard Hawthorne and (Agnes) Rosemary Rice. In August 1932 the family sailed for South Africa. It was in Cape Town that Hawthorne first became interested in acting and appeared in a school production of *The Pirates Of Penzance*. However, his first job on leaving school was as a clerk in the motor department of an insurance company. He then enrolled at the University of Cape Town where he again became involved with acting and also radio presenting in the campus' small broadcasting studio. His first professional gig came in the second year at university in a production of *Home Of The Brave*. His studies had begun to suffer as he spent more time concerned with the theatre and eventually left without completing his degree. On his 21st birthday he joined the Hofmeyr Theatre as assistant stage manager at a salary of £3 per week. Fearing that he would not learn very much in the confines of South Africa, Hawthorne decided that he needed to return to Britain. He arrived on April 6, 1951 and landed a job almost immediately, earning £7 a week. He spent the next twenty or so years appearing in various plays on tour and in the West End before learning that Richard Attenborough was casting for a film about the early life of Winston Churchill. The producer/writer was Carl Foreman and he was singularly unimpressed by Hawthorne when he presented himself at audition. The next day Hawthorne returned sporting an obviously fake beard and was delighted and not a little amazed when he was given the role of a Boer sentry in *Young Winston* (1972). His other films included *S*P*Y*S* (1974) as Croft, *The Hiding Place* (1975) as Pastor De Ruiter, *Sweeney 2* (1978) as Dilke, *The Sailor's Return* (1978) as Mr Fosse, *Watership Down* (1978) as Campion, *The Knowledge* (1981) as Mr Burgess, *History Of The World: Part I* (1981) as Citizen Official, *The World Cup: A Captain's Tale* (1982), *The Plague Dogs* (1982) (voice) as Dr Robert Boycott, *Gandhi* (1982) as Kinnoch, *Firefox* (1982) as Pyotr Baranovich, *King Of The Wind* (1989) as Achmet, *En Håndfull Tid* (1989) as Ted Walker, *Relatively Speaking* (1990) as Philip Carter, *Freddie As F.R.O.7* (1992) as Brigadier G, *Demolition Man* (1993) as Dr Raymond Cocteau, *Richard III* (1995) as George, Duke of Clarence, *Twelfth Night: Or What You Will* (1996) as Malvolio, *Murder In Mind* (1997) as Dr Ellis, *Amistad* (1997) as Martin Van Buren, *The Object Of My Affection* (1998) as Rodney Fraser, *At Sachem Farm* (1998) as Uncle Cullen (which he also executive produced), *Atatürk: Founder Of Modern Turkey* (1999) as Sir Percy Loraine, *The Winslow Boy* (1999) as Arthur Winslow, *The Big Brass Ring* (1999) as Kim Mennaker, *A Reasonable Man* (1999) as Judge Wendon and *The Clandestine Marriage* (1999) as Lord Ogleby, a film on which he was also associate producer. Hawthorne caused a storm at the National Theatre in 1992 for his portrayal of "mad" King George III in Alan Bennett's excellent *The Madness Of George III*. Yet when the film came to be made in 1994 its title was changed to *The Madness Of King George* lest unintelligent Americans think it was the third film in a series. Hawthorne had two long-standing relationships – one of 27 years with Bruce Palmer (d. 1992 of AIDS) and one of 22 years with Trevor Bentham, a screenwriter 14 years his junior. Although Hawthorne was, like many actors, "out" in the profession the public were unaware of his homosexuality. In 1994 he was outed by the gay magazine *The Advocate*, less than a week before he was due to fly to Los Angeles for the Oscar ceremony where he had been nominated for his performance in *The Madness Of King George*.

CAUSE: Nigel Hawthorne died at his home, Fabdens, in Thundridge, Hertfordshire, at 9.30am on Boxing Day. He was 72 and had been suffering from cancer of the pancreas for two years. He left £346,663 in his will.

FURTHER READING: *Straight Face – Nigel Hawthorne* (London: Hodder & Stoughton, 2002).

Charles Hawtrey

(GEORGE FREDERICK JOFFRE HARTREE)
Born November 30, 1914
Died October 27, 1988

The weedy bespectacled one. Born in Hounslow, Middlesex, he was a child actor who cheekily acquired the name of venerated stage manager and actor Sir Charles Hawtrey. After studying at

Italia Conti, Hawtrey began his career in 1921 as a boy soprano and moved to the stage in 1925 in *The Windmill Man*, playing an Arab. His London début came on December 26, 1927, and two years later he began his radio career, appearing with Will Hay among many others. He was also the snobby Hubert Lane in a dramatisation of *Just William*. He made his first film appearance in *Marry Me* (1932) as Billy Hart and was a regular over the years, often appearing alongside his friend Will Hay. His work included *Well Done, Henry* (1936) as Rupert McNab, *Sabotage* (1936), *Good Morning, Boys* (1937) as Septimus, *Where's That Fire?* (1939) as Woodley, *The Ghost Of St Michael's* (1941) as Percy Thorne, *Let The People Sing* (1942) as Orton, *The Goose Steps Out* (1942) as Max, *A Canterbury Tale* (1944) as Thomas Duckett, *Passport To Pimlico* (1949) as Bert Fitch, *The Galloping Major* (1951) as Lew Rimmel, *Brandy For The Parson* (1952) as George Crumb, *You're Only Young Twice* (1952) as Adolphus Hayman, *Paid To Kill* (1954) as Bill, *Man Of The Moment* (1955) and *Timeslip* (1956). In 1957 he was cast in the Granada TV sitcom *The Army Game* as Private 'Professor' Hatchett and featured in its movie spin-off, *I Only Arsked!* (1958). That same year Hawtrey was cast in a comedy film that was undoubtedly inspired by *The Army Game*. None of the cast could know what a success *Carry On Sergeant* (1958) would be or what it would lead to. It made Hawtrey, playing Private Peter Golightly, a household name. He would go on to appear in 23 *Carry On*s. They were: *Carry On Nurse* (1958) as Humphrey Hinton, *Carry On Teacher* (1959) as music master Michael Bean, *Carry On Constable* (1960) as PC Timothy Gorse, *Carry On Regardless* (1961) as Gabriel Dimple, *Carry On Cabby* (1963) as taxi driver Terry 'Pintpot' Tankard, *Carry On Jack* (1964) as Walter Sweetley, *Carry On Spying* (1964) as agent Charlie Bind: number 000, *Carry On Cleo* (1964) as 'dirty old sage' Seneca, *Carry On Cowboy* (1965) as Red Indian Chief Big Heap, *Carry On Screaming!* (1966) as Dan Dann the lavatory man, *Carry On . . . Don't Lose Your Head* (1967) as French aristocrat Duc De Pommfrit, *Carry On . . . Follow That Camel* (1967) as Foreign Legionnaire Captain Le Pice, *Carry On Camping* (1969) as Charlie Muggins (trivia note: Charlie beds down with the Potters [Terry Scott and Betty Marsden] in their tent in a blue sleeping bag but, in the morning, when they do a bunk, it has miraculously changed to a green and yellow patterned one), *Carry On Again Doctor* (1969) as Dr Ernest Stoppidge, *Carry On Up the Jungle* (1970) as King Tonka/Walter Bagley, *Carry On Loving* (1970) as private dick James Bedsop, *Carry On Henry* (1971) as Sir Roger de Lodgerley, *Carry On At Your Convenience* (1971) as Charles Coote, *Carry On Matron* (1972) as Dr Francis A. Goode and *Carry On Abroad* (1972) as alcoholic mummy's boy Eustace Tuttle. In real life, Hawtrey's drinking worsened to the extent that he was sacked from the series and played a parody of himself in his last *Carry On*. The story is told of Lord Olivier being chauffeured to Pinewood to work on *Lady Caroline Lamb* (1972) when he saw a familiar figure shuffling along the road carrying two old brown paper carrier bags. Drawing closer he saw it was Hawtrey and he gave him a lift to the studio. Later, in the studio's restaurant, he expressed amazement that the producers didn't pay for drivers. "No, we get no transport whatsoever," Joan Sims responded. "They won't pay a halfpenny for any extra comforts." Olivier left saying he felt they deserved better. Said Kenneth Williams, "He'd never put up with *Carry On* conditions." "Oh. I wondered why they'd never cast him," Sims responded. Hawtrey was eccentric, preferring to communicate in a telegraphese nonsense language that baffled many of his *Carry On* co-stars, although Joan Sims could translate perfectly. A homosexual, Hawtrey lived alone, entertaining a succession of young men in a former smuggler's cottage in Middle Street, Deal, Kent. On August 5, 1984, his home caught fire and he had to be rescued, naked and *sans toupée*, accompanied by a young man in his twenties who was clad only in a pair of trousers. *Carry On* co-star Kenneth Williams was jealous of Hawtrey's comfortable acceptance of his sexuality: "He can sit in a bar and pick up sailors and have a wonderful time. I couldn't do it." Hawtrey was banned from a number of pubs around his home because of his drunkenness. Instead, he sent a taxi to collect his supplies from an off-licence and often failed to pay the taxis.

CAUSE: In May 1984 he suffered a heart attack and on September 22, 1988, his heart stopped beating because of a serious artery condition. Doctors informed the actor, who had no visitors, that he must face double amputation of the legs or die. Hawtrey refused and he died in a Deal nursing home aged 73. His death certificate is a measure of how much he had alienated his friends. No one was close enough to even know his birthday. It merely reads "Born *circa* 1915".

Will Hay

Born December 6, 1888
Died Easter Monday (April 18), 1949
Brit comic. Born in Stockton-on-Tees, William Thomson Hay was the second of three sons of a Scottish engineer. On leaving full-time education he became a reporter and married Gladys Perkins on October 7, 1907. They had three children, William, Gladys and Joan, before their 1934 separation. (They never got around to formalising a divorce.) Not long after getting married Hay began a musical hall career that led inexorably to radio and then films. He made 18 well-received films that are often still shown on daytime

television. They were: *Those Were The Days* (1933) as Magistrate Brutus Poskett, *Radio Parade Of 1935* (1934) as William Garland, *Dandy Dick* (1935) as the Reverend Richard Jedd, which he also wrote, *Boys Will Be Boys* (1935) as Dr Alec Smart, which he also wrote, *Windbag The Sailor* (1936) as Captain Ben Cutlet, which he also wrote, *Where There's A Will* (1936) as Benjamin Stubbins, which he also wrote, *Oh, Mr Porter!* (1937) as William Porter, *Good Morning, Boys* (1937) as Dr Benjamin Twist, *Old Bones Of The River* (1938) as Professor Benjamin Tibbetts, *Hey! Hey! USA* (1938) as Dr Benjamin Twist, *Where's That Fire?* (1939) as Captain Viking, *Convict 99* (1939) as Dr Benjamin Twist, *Ask A Policeman* (1939) as Sergeant Dudfoot, *The Ghost Of St Michael's* (1941) as William Lamb, *The Goose Steps Out* (1942) as William Potts/Muller, which he also directed, *The Black Sheep Of Whitehall* (1942) as Davis, which he also directed, *The Big Blockade* (1942) as Skipper and *My Learned Friend* (1943) as William Fitch, which he also directed. Away from entertainment, he was a keen amateur astrologer, who discovered a white spot on Saturn and was made a fellow of the Royal Astronomical Society.

CAUSE: Will Hay suffered a stroke in 1946 from which he only partially recovered. A further embolism caused his death aged 60 in the early hours of Easter Monday, April 18, 1949, at his London flat, 16 Chelsea Embankment. He was buried in the garden of remembrance, Streatham. He left £27,155 9s 8d.

Sessue Hayakawa

Born June 10, 1889
Died November 23, 1973
Oriental lead. Born in Nanaura, Chiba, Japan, Hayakawa began acting after being rejected by the Imperial Navy due to a hearing loss. He joined an acting troupe directed by his uncle and later formed his own Japanese Imperial

Company which toured the world. After emigrating to Chicago he was discovered by director Thomas Ince and began his career in movies in *The Hateful God* (1913). He also appeared in *The Wrath Of The Gods* (1914) as Lord Yamaki, *After Five* (1915) as Oki, *The Secret Sin* (1915) as Lin Foo, *Alien Souls* (1916) as Sakata, *The Soul Of Kura San* (1916) as Toyo, *Each To His Kind* (1917) as Rhandah, *Forbidden Paths* (1917) as Sato, *Hashimura Togo* (1917) as Hashimura Togo, *His Birthright* (1918) as Yukio, *The Courageous Coward* (1919) as Suki Iota, *His Debt* (1919) as Goto Mariyama, *Li Ting Lang* (1920) as Li Ting Lang, *An Arabian Knight* (1920) as Ahmed, *Black Roses* (1921) as Yoda, *Five Days To Live* (1922) as Tai Leung, *Sen Yan's Devotion* (1924), *Daughter Of The Dragon* (1931) as Ah Kee, *Atarashiki Tsuchi* (1937) as Iwao Yamato, *Yoshiwara* (1937) as Isamo, *Tempête Sur L'Asie* (1938) as Le Prince Ling, *Malaria* (1942), *Tokyo Joe* (1949) as Baron Kimura, *Mask Of Korea* (1950) as Ying Tchai, *Three Came Home* (1950) as Colonel Suga, *House Of Bamboo* (1955) as Inspector Kito, *The Geisha Boy* (1958) as Mr Sikita, *Green Mansions* (1959) as Runi, *Hell To Eternity* (1960) as General Matsui, *The Swiss Family Robinson* (1960) as a pirate chief and his final film *The Daydreamer* (1966) as the voice of the Mole. He was a major silent star but faded with the advent of sound. It was said he earned $7,500 a week, gambled regularly in Monte Carlo, and once lost $965,000 in one night. The apotheosis of his career was reached in October 1956 when he was given the dream role of Colonel Saito in David Lean's *The Bridge On The River Kwai* (1957). He was nominated for a Best Supporting Actor Academy Award. His hobby was boxing and he would often spar in the ring after a day of filming.
CAUSE: He died in Tokyo, Japan, of a cerebral thrombosis, aged 83.

Sterling Hayden
(STERLING RELYEA WALTER)
Born March 26, 1916
Died May 23, 1986
'The Most Beautiful Man In The Movies'. Born in Upper Montclair, New Jersey, his father died when the boy was nine so James Hayden adopted him and renamed him Sterling Walter Hayden. 6'5" Hayden worked as a sailor and decided he wanted to buy his own vessel. To raise the money he turned to modelling. He was 25 before he made a film, appearing in *Virginia* (1941) as Norman Williams. After *Bahama Passage* (1941) in which he played Adrian, Hayden joined the US Marines in 1942 using the name John Hamilton to disguise his Hollywood background and was then seconded to the Office of Strategic Services – the predecessor of the CIA – to support the partisans in Yugoslavia. He became a first lieutenant on September 13, 1944, a captain on February 14, 1945 and won the Silver Star for gallantry. He was demobbed on Christmas Eve, 1945. It would be 1947 before he began acting again in *Blaze Of Noon* (1947) as Tad McDonald. A brief flirtation with the Communist Party followed and he appeared in *Manhandled* (1949) as Joe Cooper, *El Paso* (1949) as Bert Donner, *The Asphalt Jungle* (1950) as Dix Handley, during the filming of which he suffered acute alcohol and mental problems, *Journey Into Light* (1951) as John Burrows, *Flaming Feather* (1951) as Tex McCloud, *Flat Top* (1952) as Dan Collier, *Denver And Rio Grande* (1952) as McCabe, *Take Me To Town* (1953) as Will Hall, *Fighter Attack* (1953) as Steve, *Naked Alibi* (1954) as Chief Joe Conroy, *Arrow In The Dust* (1954) as Bart Laish, *Crime Wave* (1954) as Detective Lieutenant Sims, *Prince Valiant* (1954) as Sir Gawain, *Johnny Guitar* (1954) as Johnny Guitar, *Battle Taxi* (1955) as Captain Russ Edwards, *Crime Of Passion* (1957) as Bill Doyle, *Valerie* (1957) as John Garth, *Zero Hour*

(1957) as Treleaven, *Terror In A Texas Town* (1958) as George Hansen, *Dr Strangelove Or: How I Learned To Stop Worrying And Love The Bomb* (1964) as General Jack D. Ripper, *Deadly Strangers* (1974) as Malcolm Robarts, *1900* (1976) as Leo Dalco, *Nine To Five* (1980) as Russell Tinsworthy and *Venom* (1982) as Howard Anderson. When the McCarthy witch hunts came along Hayden avoided being blacklisted by betraying his former friends and colleagues, along with Lloyd Bridges, Lee J. Cobb, Elia Kazan, Marc Lawrence, Isobel Lennart, Clifford Odets, Larry Parks, Budd Schulberg, Jerome Robbins and Frank Tuttle. Hayden played the part of Police Chief McCluskey in *The Godfather* (1972). In one scene he is shot in the neck by Michael Corleone (Al Pacino) and grabs his neck, but in the next shot he is bleeding from the forehead. In another gaff, one scene in *The Godfather* is set in 1945, yet you can see a US flag with 50 stars; in 1945 there were only 48 States of the Union. Hayden retired in 1958, only returning to acting when the pay cheque demanded it. He was married three times: to Madeleine Carroll (February 14, 1942–May 8, 1946); Betty Ann Noon (April 25, 1947–April 23, 1953) by whom he had three sons and a daughter and Catherine Devine McConell (March 1960 until his death) by whom he had two more sons.
CAUSE: He died in Sausalito, California, aged 70, of cancer.

Allison Hayes

(MARY JANE HAYNES)
Born March 6, 1930
Died February 27, 1977
B-movie goddess. Born in Charleston, West Virginia, 37-23-36 Hayes was Miss Washington, DC, in the 1949 Miss America beauty contest. She began appearing regularly on television and this lead to her film début in *So This Is Paris* (1954) as Carmen. She

worked regularly but never really made the transition to A pictures. Her movies included *Francis Joins The WACS* (1954) as Lieutenant Dickson, *Count Three And Pray* (1955) as Georgina Decrais, *Sign Of The Pagan* (1955) as Iloico, *Mohawk* (1956), *Zombies Of Mora Tau* (1957) as Mona Harrison, *The Unearthly* (1957) as Grace Thomas, *The Undead* (1957) as Livia, *The Disembodied* (1957) as Tonda Metz, *Hong Kong Confidential* (1958) as Elene Martine, *Attack Of The 50 Foot Woman* (1958) as Nancy Fowler Archer, *Wolf Dog* (1958) as Ellen Hughes, *Pier 5 Havana* (1959) as Monica Gray, *A Lust To Kill* (1959) as Sherry, *Who's Been Sleeping In My Bed?* (1963) and *Tickle Me* (1965) as Mabel.
CAUSE: She died of blood poisoning in La Jolla, California, aged 46.

Gabby Hayes

Born May 7, 1885
Died February 9, 1969
Perennial sidekick. Born in Wellsville, New York, thousands of miles from the Wild West, George Francis Hayes nonetheless carved out a career as arguably the most popular and recognisable 'pardner' of all time. He was known for his whiskers, his toothless smile and his phrases, such as "Yer durn tootin' buckaroo". In around 200 films he worked alongside Roy Rogers, Gene Autry, Hopalong Cassidy and many, many more. His films included his début *Smiling Irish Eyes* (1922) as a taxi driver, *Freighters Of Destiny* (1931) as Jim, *Klondike* (1932) as Tom Ross, *Dragnet Patrol* (1932), *Without Honor* (1932), *Love Me Tonight* (1932), *Texas Buddies* (1932) as Cy, *Trailing North* (1933) as Flash Ryan, *Riders Of Destiny* (1933) as Denton, *In Old Santa Fe* (1934) as Cactus, *The Return Of Casey Jones* (1934), *West Of The Divide* (1934) as Dusty Rhodes, *Randy Rides Alone* (1934) as Marvin Black aka Mat the Mute, *Tombstone Terror* (1935) as Soupy Baxter, *The Lost City* (1935) as

Butterfield, Cecil B. DeMille's *The Plainsman* (1936), as Breezy, *Mr Deeds Goes To Town* (1936), *I Married A Doctor* (1936) as Windy Halliday, *Hearts In Bondage* (1936) as Ezra, *Valiant Is The Word For Carrie* (1936), *The Bells Of Rosarita* (1945) as Gabby Whittaker, *Albuquerque* (1948) as Juke and, his last film, *The Cariboo Trail* (1950) as Grizzly.

CAUSE: He died from heart problems aged 83 in Burbank, California.

Helen Hayes
(HELEN BROWN)
Born October 10, 1900
Died March 17, 1993
'The First Lady of the American Theatre'. Born in Washington, DC, Helen Hayes' heart belonged to the stage and that was where she did her best work. She made a few films and television appearances, including *The Weavers Of Life* (1917) as Peggy, *Arrowsmith* (1931) as Leora Tozer Arrowsmith, *What Every Woman Knows* (1934) as Maggie Wylie, *My Son John* (1952) as Lucille Jefferson, *Anastasia* (1956) as the Dowager Empress, *Airport* (1970) as Ada Quonsett, *Herbie Rides Again* (1974) as Mrs Steinmetz, *One Of Our Dinosaurs Is Missing* (1976) as Hettie and *Candleshoe* (1977) as Lady St. Edmund. She also played Miss (Jane) Marple in the television movies *A Caribbean Mystery* (1983) and *Murder With Mirrors* (1985) and was Ernesta Snoop in *The Snoop Sisters*. Comedian Beatrice Lillie one day visited Blackwell's Island on New York's East River with Helen Hayes and her husband the playwright Charles MacArthur (the adoptive parents of *Hawaii Five-O* actor James 'Danno' MacArthur). One thing had escaped the minds of the theatrical threesome. Blackwell's Island was home to high-security mental institutions. A guard refused them admission to the East 79th Street Pier Ferry without documentation. Lillie decided to announce herself. "I am

Beatrice Lillie and this lady is Helen Hayes and we both have performances to give tonight." Unfortunately, the guard was obviously not a theatre-goer, and this made little impression. Lillie tried again. "I am Lady Peel. Miss Hayes is the First Lady of the American Theatre and this gentleman is the distinguished playwright Mr Charles MacArthur." The guard replied, "Look, lady. We already have more than our fair share of Lillies and First Ladies. Probably some MacArthurs too. Either you show me a pass or you get back to tea with Greta Garbo and Lady Astor!"

CAUSE: She died in Nyack, New York, from congestive heart failure, aged 92.

John Michael Hayes
Born May 11, 1919
Died November 19, 2008
Hitch's collaborator. Born in Worcester, Massachusetts, the son of a song and dance man Hayes began writing while still young – he was editor of the *Boy Scout Journal* and a cub reporter for the *Worcester Telegram*. During the Second World War he served in the army but never left the continent and performed in troop shows. He began writing for radio before moving to the big screen. It was for his collaboration on four films with Sir Alfred Hitchcock – *Rear Window* (released August 1, 1954), *To Catch A Thief* (released August 5, 1955), *The Trouble With Harry* (released October 3, 1955) and *The Man Who Knew Too Much* (released June 1, 1956). In *Rear Window*, photographer L.B. Jefferies (James Stewart) is confined to a wheelchair after breaking his leg and spies on his Greenwich Village neighbour who he thinks is a murderer. Hayes is said to have based the character of fashion model Lisa Carol Fremont (Grace Kelly) on his own model wife, Mildred. "The thing was, in the story of *Rear Window*, there was no woman, and Hitch wanted a woman," Hayes said. "He had done

Dial M For Murder with Grace Kelly and said, 'We have to have a girl, and I want to use Grace Kelly.' He told me to spend a week or two with her to get to know her, which I did. My wife was a very beautiful girl, a high-style fashion model, so I used the world I knew and I made Grace Kelly a model. It still has a life of its own. I brought dialogue, character and humour to Hitch. He had the suspense, and we melded very well. He liked my sometimes flippant dialogue, and so did the audience." The Mystery Writers of America gave 5'10" Hayes an Edgar Award for the film, which also received an Oscar nomination. When he showed Hitchcock the small ceramic statuette, the director examined it and then said, "You know, they make toilet bowls out of the same material." After he had finished work on *The Man Who Knew Too Much* Hitchcock hired Angus MacPhail to polish the screenplay and demanded that Hayes share the byline. Hayes refused and took the matter to the Writers' Guild for arbitration. They decided in his favour but it wrecked his relationship with Hitchcock. "I enjoyed working with him professionally, but off the screen he wasn't so likable. He was egotistical to the point of madness." After Hitchcock, Hayes wrote the screenplay for *Peyton Place* (premièred December 11, 1957) and was nominated for a second Oscar. He wrote *Butterfield 8* (released November 4, 1960) which won an Academy Award for Elizabeth Taylor. He also wrote *The Carpetbaggers* (released April 9, 1964) and *Harlow* (released June 23, 1965). His wife Mildred Louise "Mel" Hicks, whom he married on August 29, 1950, died in June 1989. They had four children: two sons, Garrett Michael and Corey, and two daughters, Meredyth and Rochelle. CAUSE: Hayes died in his sleep of age-related causes at a retirement community in Hanover, New Hampshire. He was 89.

Will Hays
Born November 5, 1879
Died March 7, 1954

Puritanical censor. Following the arrest of Fatty Arbuckle for a rape and manslaughter he didn't commit, 12 Hollywood moguls got together and decided they would appoint a censor themselves rather than waiting for the government to foist one on them. On December 8, 1921, they wrote to Postmaster General Will Hays, offering him the job. He was offered a renewable three-year contract with a salary of $115,000 a year, a $2-million life insurance policy and unlimited expenses. He accepted the position on January 14, 1922, taking office exactly two months later. In 1930 he created the Motion Picture Production Code, the aim of which was to "govern the Making of Talking, Synchronised and Silent Motion Pictures". Many in the industry were outraged by the appointment of the Republican Hays. Born in Sullivan, Indiana (population 2,166), William Harrison Hays (he never used his full name) was proud to declare himself "100% American", conveniently forgetting about his English and Dutch heritage. John T. Hays, Hays' father, himself a Republican lawyer, instilled strict puritanical views into his sons including not borrowing and abstaining from alcohol. On leaving university, he joined his father in the law firm Hays & Hays. Will Hays, a devout Presbyterian, became a mason and quickly moved up the Republican ladder until President Warren G. Harding appointed him Postmaster General on March 5, 1921. Despite two decades in Republican politics, Hays actually only held elective office once – he was Sullivan's lawyer. Hays resigned as head of the Motion Picture Producers and Distributors of America, Inc. (MPPDA) in September 1945. He was twice married. His first trip up the aisle, with Helen Louise Thomas, (in 1902) ended in divorce and in 1930 he

married Jessie Heron Stutsman.
CAUSE: Hays died in Sullivan, Indiana, aged 74, of natural causes.

Louis Hayward
Born March 19, 1909
Died February 21, 1985
The first Saint. Born in Johannesburg, South Africa Louis Charles Hayward was educated in England and managed a London club before becoming an actor. In 1931 Noël Coward took the handsome 5'10½" Hayward under his wing and the two men began an affair. The relationship ended bitterly – Hayward liked to make the Master jealous and took it a step too far when he had an affair with heiress Natasha Paley who would marry Jack Wilson, another of Coward's boyfriends. Hayward made his film debut in *Self Made Lady* (1932). He made his only Broadway appearance on January 16, 1935 when he opened in Coward's *Point Verlaine*, which led him to being awarded a contract on the west coast. His big break came in the extended romantic prologue of *Anthony Adverse* (1936). He spent the rest of the decade in mainly B pictures. He was the first cinematic Simon Templar in *The Saint In New York* (1938). He played good and evil twins in *The Man In The Iron Mask* (1939), but he flopped in *The Son Of Monte Cristo* (1940). He was given a plum part in Orson Welles's *The Magnificent Ambersons* (1941) but it was edited down to nothing. Hayward won a Bronze Star for his courage under fire during the Battle of Tarawa in the Second World War. He played twins in *And Then There Were None* (1945) and appeared in *Monte Cristo* (1946), *The Black Arrow* (1948), *Fortunes Of Captain Blood* (1950) as Captain Peter Blood, *The Lady And The Bandit* (1951) as Dick Turpin, *Captain Pirate* (1952) as Captain Peter Blood, *The Royal African Rifles* (1953) as Denham and *The Saint's Return* (1953) as Simon Templar. He was also a regular on television. He retired in

the mid-Seventies. He was married three times. His first wife from November 16, 1938 until May 11, 1945 was the actress Ida Lupino. In 1945 he entered a five-year marriage with Peggy Morrow Field and in 1953 he married June Hanson by whom he had one son, Dana (d. January 2007). CAUSE: Hayward died of lung cancer and renal failure at Palm Springs, California. He said on the diagnosis of the lung cancer, "I got precisely what I deserved after a four-pack-a-day habit for 50 years." He was 75.

Susan Hayward
(EDYTHE MARRENER)
Born June 30, 1917
Died March 14, 1975
Fiery redhead. Born at 3507 Church Avenue, Brooklyn, New York, she studied to be a dress designer before changing her mind and becoming a model. Like many a hopeful, the 5'1" Marrener travelled to Hollywood when she learned of the hunt for an actress to play Southern belle Scarlett O'Hara in *Gone With The Wind* (1939). Although she was unsuccessful in auditions for the role, she stayed in Tinseltown and her name was changed to Susan Hayward (after agent Leland Hayward). She began appearing in a number of films in bit parts, including *Hollywood Hotel* (1938), *The Amazing Dr Clitterhouse* (1938), *The Sisters* (1938), *Comet Over Broadway* (1938), *Campus Cinderella* (1938) and her first billed film *Girls On Probation* (1938) as Gloria Adams. In 1939 she signed a contract with Paramount. Gradually the roles she was assigned became larger and the films more expensive. She was Isobel Rivers in *Beau Geste* (1939), Estelle Masterson in *I Married A Witch* (1942), Drusilla Alston in *Reap The Wild Wind* (1942), Charmian Kittredge in *Jack London* (1943), Kate Benson in *Young And Willing* (1943) and Mildred Douglas in *The Hairy Ape* (1944). On July 23, 1944, at St Thomas' Episcopal Church, Los

Angeles, she married actor Jess Barker. On February 17, 1945, at St John's Hospital, Santa Monica, she gave birth to non-identical twins Gregory and Timothy. In 1946 Walter Wanger put her under personal contract and her star began to soar. In 1947 she played alcoholic Angelica Evans in *Smash-Up – The Story Of A Woman* and earned herself the first of her five Academy Award nominations. *My Foolish Heart* (1949), in which she played unmarried mother Eloise Winters, was her second Oscar nod. In 1951 Darryl F. Zanuck bought out her contract for $200,000 and called her "my $12-million baby", that being the amount he had expended on three of her films. Over the next five years her films raked in enormous amounts for the company, but Zanuck began to dislike her, supposedly because she had spurned his sexual advances. It was third time unlucky for Hayward in *With A Song In My Heart* (1952) as disabled chanteuse Jane Froman – she was again beaten to an Oscar. Her other films of the time included *Rawhide* (1951) as Vinnie Holt, *I'd Climb The Highest Mountain* (1951) as Mary Elizabeth Eden Thompson, *David And Bathsheba* (1951) as Bathsheba, *The Snows Of Kilimanjaro* (1952) as Helen, *White Witch Doctor* (1953) as Ellen Burton, *Demetrius And The Gladiators* (1954) as Messalina, *Untamed* (1955) as Katie O'Neill, *Soldier Of Fortune* (1955) as Jane Hoyt and *Top Secret Affair* (1957) as Dorothy 'Dottie' Peale. Her marriage to Barker broke down and they divorced in 1955. A bitter custody battle ensued during which Hayward attempted suicide on April 25. On February 9, 1957, she married lawyer Eaton Floyd Chalkley, Jr (b. 1908, d. Fort Lauderdale, Florida, January 9, 1966, of hepatitis) in Phoenix, Arizona. He was by her side when she finally won a Best Actress Oscar for her portrayal of killer Barbara Graham in *I Want To Live!* (1958). The Sixties were not a good decade professionally for

Hayward and she retired in 1964, but made the occasional foray into film-making. On June 30, 1966, she was baptised a Roman Catholic. Her final public appearance came on April 2, 1974, at the Oscars when, with Charlton Heston, she presented the Best Actress award. She asked expert Frank Westmore to do her make-up. He was shocked by her appearance. The cobalt treatments that she had been undergoing to combat a brain tumour had wrecked her hair, eyelashes and eyebrows. Her body was thin and she suffered seizures. He was to say later, "I was never more proud of my craftsmanship than when I saw Susan walk out on that stage . . . She looked not much different from the Susan Hayward of 1945, and that's how the world will remember her."
CAUSE: In 1956 she played Bortai in Howard Hughes' execrable *The Conqueror*. It was a part that almost certainly led to her early death. Around half the cast and crew became stricken with cancer after working on the film, which had been shot in St George, Utah, near the site of atom bomb tests. Susan was diagnosed with tumours on her vocal chords in 1968. In March 1972 a tumour was discovered on one of her lungs during a regular medical. Then she began suffering from blinding headaches. She put them down to hangovers, but a scan revealed tumours on her brain as well. In April 1972 she suffered her first seizure and a trip to the hospital revealed 20 tumours growing rapidly in her brain. She underwent immediate chemotherapy. On March 30, 1973, her son, Timmy, applied to be made conservator, but she fought the application and he withdrew it. On July 17, 1973, the *National Enquirer* published an interview with him and a picture of Susan having a seizure. Her condition gradually worsened and on October 17, 1974, she went into a coma that lasted four days. Doctors feared the worst and had informed her family. She recovered

and went home to die. By February 1975 no one other than close family was allowed to visit. There were three exceptions – close friend Ron Nelson, Katharine Hepburn and Greta Garbo. Hayward's bedroom stank from the oozings from her body and because she could no longer control her bowels. On March 6, 1975, she went into another four-day coma. At 2.24pm Susan Hayward died of a massive seizure, during which she bit off her tongue, in Laurel Way, Hollywood, California. Ron Nelson performed extreme unction on the body. She was buried in the cemetery of Our Lady of Perpetual Help, Center Point Road, Carrollton, Georgia 30117.

FURTHER READING: *A Star Is A Star Is A Star! The Lives And Loves Of Susan Hayward* – Christopher P. Andersen (London: Robson Books, 1981); *Red: The Tempestuous Life Of Susan Hayward* – Robert LaGuardia & Gene Arceri (London: Robson Books, 1990).

Rita Hayworth

(MARGARITA CARMEN CANSINO)
Born October 17, 1918
Died May 14, 1987

'Love goddess'. Born in Brooklyn, New York, Margarita Carmen Cansino was the gorgeous flame-haired 36C-24-36 daughter of 5′6″ Eduardo Cansino (b. 1896, d. December 24, 1968), a sleazy professional dancer, who seduced her. The teenage Margarita was also his dancing partner and this seemed to fuel Cansino's lust. It is often thought that, in many cases, family members are aware of incest but give it tacit approval by keeping quiet; the daughter believes she is keeping the family together and thus remains silent. Certainly, Margarita's two brothers, Sonny (b. October 13, 1919, d. March 1974, of cancer) and Vernon (b. May 21, 1922, d. April 1974), were aware of their father's reputation. The family lived in a three-bedroom house in a strange arrangement – one bedroom was for the boys, one for Eduardo and

the other was shared by mother and daughter. The mother, Volga Haworth (b. August 25, 1897, d. January 25, 1945, at 9.30pm of generalised peritonitis due to a ruptured appendix), also took to travelling with her husband and daughter leaving the young boys home alone. It seemed, to her, better to protect her daughter and risk charges of abuse for her sons. In 1926 Margarita made her film début in *La Fiesta* and went on to appear in *Cruz Diablo* (1934) and *Paddy O'Day* (1935) as Tamara Petrovitch. She appeared in *Under The Pampas Moon* (1935), billed as Rita Cansino. She became Rita Hayworth (abbreviating 'Margarita' and slightly changing her mother's maiden name) in *The Shadow* (1937) and learned her trade in B movies. Determined to succeed she took elocution lessons, lost weight and raised her hairline with electrolysis. Although at one time she was a singer with Xavier Cugat's orchestra, movie bosses obviously didn't think this qualified her to sing on film. Thus, her voice was dubbed by Ann Greer in *Gilda* (1946) and *Pal Joey* (1957). She began to appear in bigger budget films such as Howard Hawks' *Only Angels Have Wings* (1939) as Judy McPherson. However, it was her performance in *Blood And Sand* (1941) as Dona Sol Des Muire that made her a star. She appeared opposite Fred Astaire in *You'll Never Get Rich* (1941); at first he was wary of her, but soon came to appreciate her dancing skills. In September 1943 she filed for divorce from her first husband, Edward Judson (whom she had married on May 29, 1937), having begun an affair with Victor Mature, but the couple never made it up the aisle and she married Orson Welles on September 7, 1943, instead (the day her divorce came through). Their daughter, Rebecca, was born on December 17, 1944. A cousin of Ginger Rogers, Rita's portrait was stuck to the side of the first atom bomb exploded at Bikini Atoll. During her marriage to Welles she made probably her best musical, *Cover Girl* (1944). Two years later came the high point of her cinematic career in *Gilda* (1946), which raked in $4 million domestically alone. Rita appeared opposite Glenn Ford who later commented of the project: "I've never played anyone but myself on screen. No, I take that back. Once I tried to throw myself into the role of a Spanish gypsy. The picture was *The Loves Of Carmen* with Rita Hayworth and it was the biggest bomb in history." By this time the marriage was suffering and Columbia chief Harry Cohn ordered husband and wife to appear together in *The Lady From Shanghai* (1948), believing the close proximity of working together would bring about a reconciliation. In the event it served only to force them further apart and in 1948 they divorced. Suspended by Cohn, Rita lost $248,000 a year. Husband number three, on May 27, 1949, was playboy Prince Aly Khan and during this marriage Rita had a daughter, Yasmin (b. Lausanne, Switzerland, December 28, 1949), but rarely appeared on screen. Divorced on September 23, 1953, and broke, she returned to Hollywood but met with mixed fortunes. On September 24, 1953, she married bandleader Dick Haymes but that, too, ended in divorce after two years. Her fifth marriage (to James Hill on February 2, 1958) was no happier. On May 12, 1960, Rita collapsed when she heard Khan had been killed in a car crash in France. During the Fifties she appeared in only one really successful film, *Pal Joey* (1957), as Vera Simpson. Her last film was *The Wrath Of God* (1972) as Senora De La Plata. After this she was hired for the British film *Tales That Witness Murder*, but was sacked, whereupon she retired. On March 9, 1977, it was revealed that she was "gravely disabled as a result of mental disorder or impairment by chronic alcoholism" and was "unable or

unwilling to accept responsibility for her treatment." Four years later in June 1981, it was revealed that she was actually suffering from Alzheimer's disease. Speaking of her poor romantic track record, Hayworth once commented, "Every man I've ever known has fallen in love with Gilda and wakened with me."
CAUSE: She died at the San Remo Apartments, 145–146 Central Park West, New York, aged 68, from Alzheimer's disease.
FURTHER READING: *Rita: The Life Of Rita Hayworth* – Edward Z. Epstein & Joseph Morella (London: W.H. Allen, 1983); *If This Was Happiness: A Biography Of Rita Hayworth* – Barbara Leaming (London: Weidenfeld & Nicolson, 1989).

Edith Head
(EDITH CLAIRE POSENER)
Born October 28, 1897
Died October 24, 1981
Hollywood's most decorated. Born in San Bernardino, California, an only child, lesbian prude Edith Head began working as a language teacher (French and Spanish) in La Jolla before moving to a girls' school in Hollywood. She lied her way into a job at Paramount and managed to stay there for almost 50 years, designing for almost every star that ever graced the big screen. She created outfits for Jean Harlow, Dorothy Lamour, Elizabeth Taylor, Grace Kelly, Hedy Lamarr, Marlene Dietrich, Barbara Stanwyck and Bette Davis to name but eight. Her work was rewarded with eight Oscars and 35 nominations. Her films included *She Done Him Wrong* (1933), *Death Takes A Holiday* (1934), *Wells Fargo* (1937), *The Big Broadcast Of 1938* (1938), *The Cat And The Canary* (1939), *Road To Singapore* (1940), *The Texas Rangers Ride Again* (1940), *Road To Zanzibar* (1941), *My Favorite Blonde* (1942), *I Married A Witch* (1942), *Holiday Inn* (1942), *Road To Morocco* (1942), *Star Spangled Rhythm* (1942), *Double*

Indemnity (1944), *The Lost Weekend*
(1945), *Notorious* (1946), *The Virginian*
(1946), *My Favorite Brunette* (1947),
Road To Rio (1947), *My Friend Irma*
(1949), *The Great Gatsby* (1949),
*A Connecticut Yankee In King Arthur's
Court* (1949), *The Heiress* (1949), for
which she won her first Oscar, *Samson
And Delilah* (1949), for which she won
her second, *Sunset Blvd.* (1950), *All
About Eve* (1950), for which she won
her third Academy Award, *A Place In
The Sun* (1951) for which she won her
fourth, *My Favorite Spy* (1951), *Road
To Bali* (1951), *The Greatest Show On
Earth* (1952), *Roman Holiday* (1953)
and her fifth Oscar, *Houdini* (1953),
Shane (1953), *Rear Window* (1954),
The Country Girl (1954), *The Bridges At
Toko-Ri* (1954), *White Christmas*
(1954), *Sabrina* (1954), which won her
a sixth Oscar, *To Catch A Thief* (1955),
The Ten Commandments (1956),
Gunfight At The O.K. Corral (1957),
Vertigo (1958), *King Creole* (1958),
Alias Jesse James (1959), *The Facts Of
Life* (1960) and her seventh Oscar, *G.I.
Blues* (1960), *Breakfast At Tiffany's*
(1961), *Blue Hawaii* (1961), *The Man
Who Shot Liberty Valance* (1962), *The
Birds* (1963), *Hud* (1963), *The Nutty
Professor* (1963), *Marnie* (1964), *The
Sons Of Katie Elder* (1965), *The Great
Race* (1965), *Barefoot In The Park*
(1967), *Sweet Charity* (1969), *Butch
Cassidy And The Sundance Kid* (1969),
Airport (1970), *Myra Breckinridge*
(1970), *The Life And Times Of Judge
Roy Bean* (1972), *The Sting* (1973),
which won her an eighth and final
Academy Award, *Airport 1975* (1974),
Rooster Cogburn (1975), *The Man Who
Would Be King* (1975), *The Great
Waldo Pepper* (1975), *Gable And
Lombard* (1976) and *Airport '77* (1977).
"Edith Head gives good wardrobe" was
a famous piece of graffiti, but the lady
herself was unamused by it. Indeed,
she had little in the way of a sense of
humour. She married twice. Her first
marriage to Charles Head, which
ended in 1938, was rarely discussed.

Her second was to Wiard Boppo Ihnen
and they were together for 39 years
until his 1979 death, aged 91.
CAUSE: She died in Los Angeles,
California, of bone marrow disease,
four days before her 84th birthday.

Sophie Heathcote
Born December 25, 1972
Died January 4, 2006
Taken too soon. Born in Melbourne,
Heathcote began her professional
career playing Stephanie Brennan in
the medical drama *A Country Practice*
(1990–91). Her first film was *Reckless
Kelly* (1993), a year before she
graduated from Australia's National
Institute of Dramatic Art. Working all
over the world, she appeared in *Soldier
Soldier* in England and played Sam, a
sexy lesbian dancer, in *Raw FM* (1997)
in her homeland. In 2000 she won an
Australian Film Institute award for
Grass Roots. She retired from acting in
2001 to concentrate on her all-natural
skin care range, Ki, which she founded
in 1998. In 2005 Heathcote, her
husband Chris Clarke and two young
children moved to New York.
CAUSE: Suffering from skin and
pancreatic cancer Heathcote died
from an aneurysm at Connecticut. She
was 33.

Eileen Heckart
Born March 29, 1919
Died December 31, 2001
Gravel-voiced actress. Born in
Columbus, Ohio, Anna Eileen Heckart
first received plaudits from the
critics on Broadway in 1953 as the
love-starved Rosemary Sidney in *Picnic*.
The following year she created the role
of Mrs Daigle in *The Bad Seed*, a part
she reprised in the 1956 film version,
gaining an Oscar nomination as
supporting actress. Earlier in 1956 she
made her film début in *Miracle In The
Rain*, which starred Jane Wyman and
Van Johnson. That year, she also
appeared in *Somebody Up There Likes
Me* and *Bus Stop*. In 1969, she created

the stage role of the domineering mother of a blind young man in *Butterflies Are Free* and repeated it in the 1972 movie, which won her an Oscar. A week after collecting the Oscar she went to sign on and the whole benefits office burst into applause. She was awarded Emmys in 1967, for a production called *Save A Place For Me* at Forest Lawn and in 1994, for an episode of *Love & War*. In 2000, she won a special Tony award for her lifetime of theatre work. She married John Harrison Yankee, Jr. in 1944 and by him had three sons, Mark, Philip, and Luke. He died in 1997. CAUSE: She died of cancer at her home in Norwalk, Connecticut. She was 82.

Neal Hefti

Born October 29 1922
Died October 11, 2008
Maestro. Neal Paul Hefti was born into a musical family in Hastings, Nebraska. For Christmas 1933 he was given a trumpet and quickly began winning prizes. In 1941 Hefti moved to New York, where he played trumpet in the bands of Charlie Barnet and Charlie Spivak. Two years later, he moved with Spivak's band to Hollywood in 1943 to appear in the film *Pin Up Girl*, starring Betty Grable and stayed on when the band returned to the east coast. In October 1945 Hefti married vocalist, Frances Wayne (b. Boston, Massachusetts August 26, 1919 d. Boston, Massachusetts February 6, 1978), and began a career as a studio arranger and conductor. "Whatever the studio wanted me to do, I learned how," he said, "I did big bands, vocal doo-wahs, pop artists, catalogue music. I loved it all." In 1961 he became Frank Sinatra's producer at Reprise Records. Hefti wrote the theme tune to *Batman* as well as *How To Murder Your Wife* (1964) and *Sex And The Single Girl* (1964), *Barefoot In The Park* (1967) and *The Odd Couple* (1968). CAUSE: Hefti died of a heart attack at Toluca Lake, California. He was 76.

Margaux Hemingway

(MARGOT HEMINGWAY)
Born February 19, 1955
Died June 30, 1996
Flawed beauty. Born in Portland, Oregon, the granddaughter of novelist Ernest Hemingway, 6' Margot (she changed her name to match the Château Margaux her parents were supposedly drinking when she was conceived) was raised on a farm in Ketchum, Idaho. She made her film début in *Lipstick* (1976) as rape victim Chris McCormick (in which little sister Mariel played her screen sister) and in which she appeared topless. She landed a $1-million contract – the largest then signed – with cosmetic firm Fabergé on May 20, 1975, making her one of the first supermodels and earning her a place in *The Guinness Book Of Records*. Her face regularly adorned magazine covers. She appeared in *Killer Fish* (1978) as Gabrielle, *They Call Me Bruce?* (1982) as Karmen, *Over The Brooklyn Bridge* (1984) as Elizabeth, *La Messe En C Mineur* (1990) as Sophie, *Inner Sanctum* (1991) as Anna Rawlins, in which she is briefly topless, *Love Is Like That* (1992) as Jackie, *Deadly Rivals* (1992) as Agent Linda Howerton, *Frame-Up II: The Cover-Up* (1993) as Jean Searage, *Inner Sanctum II* (1994) as Anna Rollins, *Double Obsession* (1994) as Heather Dwyer, in which she bares her right breast, and *Vicious Kiss* (1995). Away from the screen she was desperately unhappy. In Paris on June 21, 1975, she married hamburger baron Erroll Wetson but they were divorced after less than three years. She wed Bernard Foucher in 1980 and that too ended in divorce after five years. She began to drink heavily and put on weight. On December 4, 1987, she entered the Betty Ford Center in a bid to conquer her alcoholism. She left believing she had beaten her demons and 30lb lighter. To show off her new figure she posed nude for *Playboy* in May 1990, but ultimately her period of rehab

wasn't sufficient to pull her around. In the end she lived alone and had few friends.

CAUSE: On July 2, 1996 (the 35th anniversary of her grandfather's death), Margaux's neighbours alerted police to the fact that they hadn't seen the actress since June 29. On breaking into her Santa Monica, California, studio flat via a second-floor window, police discovered Margaux's body; it was in an advanced state of decomposition and dental records had to be utilised for identification. The Los Angeles Coroner's Office announced that Margaux Hemingway had committed suicide by taking an overdose of Phenobarbital. She was the fifth member of her family to commit suicide. She was buried in Ketchum Cemetery, Ketchum, Idaho. "In my case drink became such a problem, I thought about suicide," she had once said, ominously. "It's like I'm genetically programmed for disaster."

David Hemmings

Born November 18, 1941
Died December 3, 2004

Sixties heart-throb. Born in Guildford, Surrey, the son of a dance band pianist who gave it up for an office job to support his family, Hemmings began his film career aged 12 appearing in *The Rainbow Jacket* (1954). He was also a boy soprano for whom Benjamin Britten wrote some of his important child roles. His first success, and of enduring significance, came on September 14, 1954 when, aged 12, he sang the treble role of Miles, the sinister child, opposite Joan Cross and Peter Pears in the world première of Britten's *The Turn Of The Screw*. When Hemmings' voice broke he studied painting at the Epsom School of Art, where he staged his first exhibition at 15. In his early British films he was often cast as a misunderstood and belligerent youth, leading to his role in Michelangelo Antonioni's *Blowup*, which won the Palm d'Or at Cannes in 1967. "I desperately wanted to work for him," Hemmings later said of Antonioni. "This was a job you seek." He played Thomas, a fashion photographer, reportedly based on David Bailey, who believes he may have unwittingly photographed a dead man. The sequence was shot in Maryon Park in East Greenwich. Scenes in which he photographed a model, played by Verushka, have often been ranked among the sexiest moments captured on screen. He was also in the science-fiction romp *Barbarella* (1968) opposite Jane Fonda and the film version of the stage musical *Camelot* (1967). He rode with Lord Cardigan as a dashing, insubordinate cavalry officer in Tony Richardson's revisionist *The Charge Of The Light Brigade* (1968). On April 22, 1975, 5'10" Hemmings played the title role in *Jeeves*, a short-running collaboration between Alan Ayckbourn and Andrew Lloyd Webber at Her Majesty's Theatre. The show closed five weeks later. With *Running Scared* (1972) he began a career as a director of several movie and television productions in Britain, Australia and Canada. His directing credits included the movie *Just A Gigolo* (1979) and the television shows *Magnum, P.I.* (1980), *The A-Team* (1983), *Airwolf* (1984) and *Quantum Leap* (1989). Of his apparent long absence, he famously remarked: "People thought I was dead – I was just directing *The A-Team*." He returned to acting with the role of Cassius, the master of ceremonies, in *Gladiator* (2000). Other recent roles included parts in *Spy Game* (2001) as Harry Duncan, *Last Orders* (2001) as Lenny, *Mean Machine* (2001) as the governor, *Gangs Of New York* (2002) as Mr Schermerhorn and *The League Of Extraordinary Gentlemen* (2003) as Nigel. Hemmings married four times. His first wife was Genista Ouvry whom he married on March 25, 1961 at St John's Church, Hurst Green, Surrey and by whom he had two children. Their daughter Deborah was born on April 13, 1962. They divorced in 1967. On November 16, 1968 he married Gayle Hunnicutt by whom he had a son, Nolan (b. September 23, 1970), named after Hemmings' character in *The Charge Of The Light Brigade*. On July 23, 1974 Hunnicutt filed for divorce and received her decree nisi on December 19, 1974. The following year on March 19, 1976 at Chelsea Register Office he married his secretary, Baroness Prudence de Casembroot, by whom he had three children. Son George was born six weeks after the wedding. Charlotte was born on February 16, 1983 and William arrived on July 25, 1984. He had a couple of significant affairs – with a British journalist based in California, and with Tessa Dahl, daughter of the writer Roald Dahl. Hemmings became an alcoholic with the strain of juggling two women – his wife and Dahl. Eventually, he and Dahl booked themselves into a drying out clinic in Minnesota. He and his wife were divorced in 1997. On October 18, 2002 he married Lucy Williams, a former assistant to the milliner David Schilling. Away from show business, Hemmings was a talented artist, poet, amateur magician, brilliant mimic and raconteur. He loved the Sixties, he loved being recognised and he loved living life to the full. "I had as much debauchery as anyone else," he once said.

CAUSE: Hemmings died of a heart attack while filming *Samantha's Child* in Bucharest, Rumania. Paramedics on the film set were unable to revive him. He was 62.

Paul Henreid

(PAUL GEORGE JULIUS HERNREID RITTER VON WASEL-WALDINGAU)
Born January 10, 1908
Died March 29, 1992
Cigarette lighter extraordinaire. Born in Trieste, Austria, he was discovered

by Otto Preminger in 1933. Henreid became a leading light in Max Reinhardt's Viennese theatre. He emigrated first to England in 1935 and then to America in 1940, where he became a US citizen and film star. He participated in one of the most memorable cinematic scenes of all time. In *Now Voyager* (1942) as Jerry Durrance in Rio he lights two cigarettes and passes one to Bette Davis. This scene was Henreid's own idea. It was a habit for him and his wife Lisl (whom he married in 1936). "Back when cars didn't have lighters, and I was driving and wanted to smoke, she would light our cigarettes that way." He played Victor Laszlo opposite Ingrid Bergman in *Casablanca* (1942) and later moved behind the cameras to direct for film and TV. His films included *Goodbye, Mr Chips* (1939) as Staefel, *Of Human Bondage* (1946) as Philip Carey about which Richard Winnington commented, "He looks as though his idea of fun would be to find a nice cold damp grave and sit in it", *Song Of Love* (1947) as Robert Schumann, *Siren Of Bagdad* (1953) as Kazah, *Deep In My Heart* (1954) as Florenz Ziegfeld, *Meet Me In Las Vegas* (1956) as Pierre, *Four Horsemen Of The Apocalypse* (1961) as Etienne Laurier, *Operation Crossbow* (1965) as General Ziemann and his last film *Exorcist II: The Heretic* (1977) as the Cardinal. Henreid was interested in almost everyone. "Only on rare occasions have I met someone who didn't interest me in some manner. Each person has a story to tell."

CAUSE: He died in California of pneumonia aged 84.

Jim Henson

Born September 24, 1936
Died May 16, 1990
Muppeteer. James Maury Henson, the man who created the Muppets, was born in Greenville, Mississippi. He became a professional puppeteer in the Forties creating characters that would feature on the television series *Sesame*

Street. In 1965 he won an Oscar for the short film *Time Piece.* Four years later, he had a world-wide hit with the Muppets as creator, producer, writer and vocal artiste. His films included *Frog Prince* (1972), *The Great Muppet Caper* (1981), *The Dark Crystal* (1982), *The Muppets Take Manhattan* (1984), *Labyrinth* (1986) and *Muppet*vision 3-D* (1991).

CAUSE: He died of a bacteriological condition in New York aged 53.

Audrey Hepburn

(EDDA KATHLEEN VAN HEEMSTRA HEPBURN-RUSTON)
Born May 4, 1929
Died January 20, 1993
Will-o'-the-wisp. Born at 48 rue Keyenveld, Brussels, Belgium, she was the gamine 5'7½" daughter of Anglo-Irish Joseph Victor Anthony Hepburn-Ruston (b. Ouzice, Austria, 1889, d. Ireland, 1980), an extreme right winger and director of the Brussels branch of the Bank of England and Baroness Ella van Heemstra (b. 1900), a Dutch aristocrat. Following her parents' divorce in 1935 she was sent to school in London but was on holiday with her mother on September 1, 1939, when war broke out. She stayed in Holland for the duration and studied ballet. She also worked for the resistance for a while, entertaining the troops. At the cessation of hostilities she joined the Ballet Rambert in London. Audrey became a model and chorus girl before landing small parts in films such as *The Lavender Hill Mob* (1951) as Chiquita. It was in 1951, when she was cast as Gigi on Broadway at the behest of Colette, that she became a star. She won an Oscar for Princess Ann in *Roman Holiday* (1953) opposite Gregory Peck and appeared in *Sabrina* (1954) as Sabrina Fairchild, for which she was nominated for another Oscar, King Vidor's *War And Peace* (1956) as Natasha Rostov, *Love In The Afternoon* (1957) as Ariane Chavasse, *Funny Face* (1957) opposite Fred

Astaire and *The Nun's Story* (1959) as Sister Luke, which earned her another Oscar nod. In Burgenstock, Switzerland, on September 25, 1954, she married Mel Ferrer and their son, Sean, was born in Lucerne on January 17, 1960. The following year she appeared in *Breakfast At Tiffany's* (1961) as Holly Golightly and received her third (unsuccessful) Oscar nomination. She played Eliza Doolittle in the film version of *My Fair Lady* (1964), as Nicole Bonnet in *How To Steal A Million* (1966), as Joanna Wallace in *Two For The Road* (1967) and appeared as a blind woman terrorised by unknown forces in *Wait Until Dark* (1967), which earned her fifth and final Oscar nomination. Thereafter she announced her retirement. On November 20, 1968, she and Ferrer were divorced. She met her second husband, Dr Andrea Dotti (b. March 18, 1938), in the early Sixties at a party. However, it wasn't until June 1968 on a cruise of the Greek islands that they got talking and Audrey told him she did not remember meeting him before. Audrey had by then split from her first husband, and had been invited by two friends to join them on their luxury yacht. The vessel was full of immensely rich people but the one who caught her eye was 30-year-old psychiatrist Dr Dotti. As a 14-year-old boy he had seen Audrey in *Roman Holiday* (1953) and had rushed home to tell his mother that he had fallen in love with the star and would, one day, marry her. Dotti proposed to Audrey at Christmas 1968 in Rome. They married on January 18, 1969, in the town hall of Morges in Switzerland. The ceremony was conducted by the registrar Madame Denise Rattaz, who at one point had to stop the ceremony because she herself was crying. Audrey wore a pink suit, a gift designed by Givenchy, and her bridesmaids included Yul Brynner's wife Doris and the lesbian actress Capucine. There were three dozen guests. Audrey fell pregnant in April 1969 and gave birth to son, Luca, by Caesarean section on February 8, 1970, in the Cantonial Hospital, Lausanne, Switzerland. The joy was tempered by Dotti's philandering. In August 1970 the couple healed their rifts. Not for long. Dotti was soon back on the town with various women and things were not helped when Audrey had a miscarriage. In an attempt to patch things up the couple had a 'honeymoon' in Hawaii. It didn't work and Audrey began an affair with actor Ben Gazzara but it was not to last and she became romantically entangled with Robert Wolders, the widower of actress Merle Oberon, and "the only Dutchman to be cast as a Texas lawman" in the hit TV series *Laredo*. Audrey and Dotti were divorced in 1982, a year after she began living with Wolders. She had made a brief comeback in *Robin And Marian* (1976) as Lady Marian and also appeared in *Bloodline* (1979) as Elizabeth Roffe, *They All Laughed* (1981) as Angela Niotes and her last film *Always* (1989) as Hap. She spent her final years as a goodwill ambassador for UNICEF.

CAUSE: She died in Tolochenaz, Switzerland of colon cancer aged 63. Robert Wolders and her two sons were by her side. She was buried four days later.

FURTHER READING: *Audrey: A Biography Of Audrey Hepburn* – Charles Higham (London: New English Library, 1986); *Audrey: An Intimate Portrait* – Diana Maychick (London: Pan Books, 1994); *Audrey: Her Real Story* – Alexander Walker (London: Orion, 1995).

Katharine Hepburn

Born May 12, 1907
Died June 29, 2003

'Katharine of Arrogance'. Though Katharine Hepburn made only some 40 films in a career that spanned more than half a century, she won four Oscars and was nominated eight more

times, more than any other star (her record stood until Meryl Streep overtook her in 2003). Her poise, her voice, her lack of pretension, her style made her unique in Hollywood. Tallulah Bankhead once described her voice as "nickels dropping in a slot machine" although the lady herself said it was a cross "between Donald Duck and a Stradivarius" but was actually caused by nodules on her vocal cords when she was young. Katharine Houghton Hepburn was born at 3.47pm at 22 Hudson Street, Hartford, Connecticut, the second of six children born to Dr Thomas Norval Hepburn (b. Hanover County, Virginia, December 18, 1879, Hartford, Connecticut as Norval Thomas Hepburn, d. November 20, 1962 of complications following a burst gall bladder), a noted urologist, and Katharine Martha Houghton (b. Connecticut, February 2, 1878, d. 201 Bloomfield Avenue, Hartford, Connecticut, March 17, 1951). Both were tall for their time, he stood 5'11" while his wife was 5'8". Kate stood 5'7". The other children were: Thomas Houghton (b. 22 Hudson Street, Hartford, Connecticut, November 8, 1905), Richard Houghton (b. 133 Hawthorn Street, Hartford, Connecticut, September 8, 1911, who was educated at Harvard and became a playwright; he married twice, firstly to Elizabeth Ballard and then to Estelle Morrison. Both marriages ended in divorce and he died in October 2000), Robert Houghton (b. 133 Hawthorn Street, Hartford, Connecticut, April 4, 1913, who was educated at Harvard and became a doctor; he married Susanna Floyd), Marion Houghton (b. 352 Laurel Street, Hartford, Connecticut, April 24, 1918, m. June 12, 1938 Ellsworth Grant, d. 1986 of a heart attack) and Margaret Houghton known as Peg (b. 352 Laurel Street, Hartford, Connecticut, May 17, 1920, who married and divorced the engineer Thomas Perry and became a farmer in

Canton, New Jersey. She gave birth to twins in Washington, DC in 1942 and needed a blood transfusion. The blood was provided by Kate's ex-husband). The Hepburns did not court polite society. In fact, Dr Hepburn angered people by publicising the dangers of venereal disease while Mrs Hepburn was a suffragette who campaigned vigorously for women's rights, at one point picketing the White House. "We were snubbed by everyone," Katharine Hepburn recalled, "but we grew quite to enjoy that." Within the family, though, the atmosphere was intensely competitive. Her father insisted that all the children become athletes, and her childhood was dedicated to swimming, riding, golf and tennis – a regime that left her, in her own words, "very strong and utterly fearless". She wore trousers long before it was socially acceptable for young girls to do so and shaved her hair so local boys couldn't grab it. Of her siblings she was closest to Tom, a sensitive boy. Kate adored him and he her. They spent much of their time together and the spring of 1921 was no exception. Two days after Easter, Tom, Kate and their mother travelled to Mary Towle's house at 26 Charlton Street in New York's Greenwich Village. She had been at college with Mrs Hepburn and was Tom's godmother. On Saturday, April 2, Mary Towle invited eight neighbourhood teens over to play with Tom and Kate. The children had lots of fun and games. Tom was a success although Kate was shy and reserved. At 10.15pm, the other children long gone, the Hepburns went to bed. However, at 8am the next morning, when Tom had not come down for breakfast, Kate went to his attic bedroom to wake him. She found him next to the bed, knees bent, hanging from a rafter by a torn sheet. She managed to cut him down but was unable to revive him. The next-door neighbour, Judge Bertha Rembaugh, took charge and a doctor pronounced death had occurred at

3am. No one knows for sure why Tom died. Local newspapers announced the death as a suicide. Kate felt it must have been an accident. Two days before his death they had seen the film *A Connecticut Yankee In King Arthur's Court* in which a man was hanged from a tree. Kate assumed her brother had tried to imitate the actor with tragic consequences. Their father believed that it had been an accident. Dr Hepburn had told his children of a trick whereby one pretended to hang and held the neck in a certain position so that the airway was not cut off. Did Tom try this but with a sheet instead of a rope and been unable to stop the sheet slipping? Another theory was that Tom killed himself in despair at having been rejected by a local girl. Yet another was that Tom had fallen in love with an older boy called Tracy Walker whose mother was a prostitute. Tracy lured Tom into the Hartford woods in order, Tom believed, to consummate their passion only for Tom to be cruelly disabused. Three other boys from their school jumped out and called Tom "a faggot". A fortnight later, Tom and Kate travelled to Mary Towle's in New York. Whatever the reason, Tom wanted to die. He tore a sheet and braided it into a rope. Tying one end to a large metal bedspring on the floor, he fashioned a noose, tossed the sheet rope over a rafter and put his head in the noose. Climbing onto a packing case, he jumped but the sheet rope was too long and he landed on his feet. Tom then bent his knees and pushed forward with all his strength. He died of slow strangulation. According to the police, Tom Hepburn, 15, had done "hard work to die". In memory of her brother Kate adopted his birthday and did not admit her real natal day until the publication of her autobiography, *Me*, when she was in her eighties. It was not the first suicide in the family. Alfred Houghton, Kate's 41-year-old grandfather, shot himself in the head on October 29, 1892, while suffering from melancholia. Two of Kate's uncles on her father's side also died by their own hands. On April 16, 1915, Charlie Hepburn flung himself out of the fourth storey of his home and impaled himself on the railings below. He died at 4.55pm, never regaining consciousness. On April 5, 1921, Sewell Hepburn killed himself at his home, 54 State Circle, in Annapolis, Maryland, with carbon monoxide poisoning, locking his garage doors and turning on his car's ignition. Kate was educated by private tutors and then at the Hartford School for Girls but she did not excel academically. She was later sent to Bryn Mawr College (her mother's alma mater) to study drama but again she did not put too much effort into her studies. On October 20, 1927, she was suspended for five days after being caught smoking in the dorm. She graduated on June 7, 1928 and later that year lost her virginity to the bisexual stage manager Kenneth MacKenna. 1928 was a busy year sexually for Katharine Hepburn. It was the year she began an affair with Laura Barney Harding, the American Express heiress. Even after the flames of passion had died, they remained very close friends until Harding's death in 1994. On December 12, 1928, at 201 Bloomfield Avenue, Hartford, amid some unexplained secrecy, Kate married the wealthy socialite Ludlow 'Luddy' Ogden Smith (b. 1897; m. (secondly) September 26, 1942 Elizabeth Albers (b. 1918), d. 1979 of prostate cancer) in a ceremony conducted by the Reverend Sewell Stavely Hepburn, her paternal grandfather, and, at 83, the oldest Episcopalian minister in Virginia. Cocking another snook at conventionality, Kate posed nude for sculptures by Robert J. McKnight. During her courtship with Luddy she had posed for several hundred nude photographs taken by her boyfriend and his best friend (and some say

lover), John G. 'Jack' Clarke. Kate and Luddy honeymooned in Bermuda – with Jack Clarke and Laura Harding for company. The marriage was a disaster. "I was a terrible pig. In those days it was all me, me, me," she recalled. "All I thought about was what Luddy could do to make me happy." One thing to make her happy was a name change. Kate persuaded her new groom to change it to S. Ogden Ludlow so that she would not be called Kate Smith. However, she had no desire to settle down to domesticity. She had a career to think about. After three weeks they separated, although the marriage was not dissolved until Kate travelled to Mérida, Mexico, on April 22, 1934. Eight days later, she filed for divorce and it became final on May 30, 1934. However, on September 19, 1942, Luddy filed a divorce suit against Kate in Hartford charging desertion and claiming that he doubted the validity of the 1934 Mexican divorce. After graduating she found work with a Baltimore repertory company and then through some string pulling, landed her first role on Broadway, suitably enough as a rich schoolgirl in *These Days*. The play opened at the Cort Theater on November 12, 1928 and closed after just eight performances. Kate didn't suffer fools gladly and she was fired from several shows for arguing with the director. Her breakthrough came on March 11, 1932, when she played Antiope, an Amazon queen, in *The Warrior's Husband*, an updated version of *Lysistrata* in Broadway's Morosco Theater. However, even from this play she was sacked and reinstated twice before the opening night. Kate was a bag of nerves before the curtain went up and was sick twice. The part required her to enter by leaping down a flight of 40 steep steps three at a time while carrying a large stag (actually a stuffed deer) on her shoulders. The show ran for 83 performances and Kate was paid $150 a week (later reduced to

$75 when box office takings dwindled). The play received mixed notices but Kate's were universally good. An RKO talent scout in the audience was so impressed by this feat – or was it the short skirt she wore – that he offered her a film test. The test was directed by Lillie Messenger and shot at a studio hired by RKO at West 59th Street and Tenth Avenue in New York. She acted a scene from *Holiday*. David O. Selznick needed someone to play opposite John Barrymore in *A Bill Of Divorcement* (1932). Selznick was at first unsure of Kate's ability but he was persuaded by his wife, Irene Mayer Selznick, and the director George Cukor. Kate was then earning $75 a week but demanded – and got – $1,500 a week, with three weeks guaranteed work plus a week of rehearsal. With the faithful Laura Harding in tow, Kate set off for Hollywood on July 1, 1932. During the long train journey, Kate had stood on the observation platform but as the train left Albuquerque a piece of steel rail had hit her in the eye. When the train pulled into Pasadena three days later both her eyes were horribly swollen. Leland Hayward and Myron Selznick met her at the station and the men were horrified to see her appearance. "*This* is what David's paying $1,500 a week for?" reputedly said Myron Selznick. (He later denied making any such comment "although it makes a good line.") They took her to the studios where she was introduced to David O. Selznick but the meeting was awkward. Next they met the homosexual director George Cukor who criticised her hair and clothes. They began arguing when John Barrymore wandered by. Seeing Kate's red eyes he assumed that she had been drinking and offered her his own curative. "I also hit the bottle occasionally, my dear. But I have a perfect disguise. You see this little phial of eyedrops? When I use it, it clears up the inflammation right away. People think I've been cold sober." Kate

protested, "Mr Barrymore, I have something in my eye." Barrymore looked at her and wandered off, saying, "That's what they all say, my dear." Cukor arranged for Kate to visit an optometrist who removed the pieces of grit but Kate had to wear an eye patch for several days afterwards. During filming with Barrymore the Great Profile invited Kate to his dressing room whereupon he stripped off. Kate was terrified. "My dear, any young girl would be thrilled to make love to the great John Barrymore," he said. "Not me," said Kate. "My father doesn't want me to make babies." On set he pinched her behind. She turned on him, "If you do that again, I'm going to stop acting." "I wasn't aware you'd started, my dear," said Barrymore. Both were later to deny the exchange occurred. "I would never have been so gratuitously cruel to a young newcomer like that. Coming from me, it might have seriously inhibited her acting," he said. Barrymore was later to claim that he did seduce Kate. In Hollywood Kate discovered that her outspoken ways with directors and crew meant that she was no more popular there than she had been on Broadway. She refused to do promotional interviews or pose for publicity stills or go on "dates" with male stars. She read her fan mail sitting on the pavement outside RKO. She played practical jokes on her co-workers and took to walking around with a pet monkey on her shoulder. George Cukor described her behaviour as "idiotic". Nevertheless, Cukor became a close friend, and showed her the difference between stage and film acting. "George taught me how to be funny," Hepburn later recalled. Her second film for RKO was supposed to be *Three Came Unarmed* in which she was set to appear opposite the bisexual Joel McCrea. The film never came to fruition because of script problems. Her next film saw her working with another homosexual director. However, unlike George Cukor, Dorothy Arzner insisted on absolute silence on her set for *Christopher Strong* (opened on March 10, 1933) in which Kate played Lady Cynthia Darrington, an aviatrix (based on the English flier Amy Johnson). Arzner referred to Kate as "Miss Hepburn" for the entirety of the shoot. It was not a happy experience. The weather was poor and Kate fell ill with a mix of the flu and gynaecological problems. The two women argued frequently and the film was not even redeemed by being a box office success. Arzner was due to direct the next Hepburn vehicle but the mauling she received over *Christopher Strong* meant she pulled out of the project. Lowell Sherman stepped into the breach. While the script was being worked on, Kate began an affair with her theatrical agent Leland Hayward, who was charming, groomed, intelligent, loquacious, and even owned a gold mine but was incapable of fidelity. The film, *Morning Glory* (1933), which was shot in just 17 days, won Kate her first Oscar. She played Eva Lovelace, a tomboy who longed to be a star and received top billing (above Douglas Fairbanks, Jr with whom she had a brief fling) in the movie posters. It was a perfect role for her. Oddly, she was not the first choice. The studio wanted Constance Bennett. The writer Zoë Akins had based the character on Tallulah Bankhead. For her next film she appeared as Jo March in Cukor's version of Louisa May Alcott's *Little Women* (opened November 1933) for which she won the Venice Film Award. The film, which was the last that David O. Selznick supervised at RKO, was also a hit at the box office. *Spitfire* (1934), in which Kate played Trigger Hicks, a wild girl of the mountains, proved that her talent did not extend to playing primitive or uncouth. On Boxing Day, 1933 she opened in New York in the Dorothy Massingham play *The Lake*. It was a mistake. The next day Dorothy Parker wrote a famous review, "Go to the Martin Beck

[theatre] and watch Katharine Hepburn run the gamut of emotion from A to B". Kate was later to describe the quote as "extremely funny and accurate". Kate's voice had run up and down the scale and she employed a vocal coach called Suzanne Steele to help her. She also ended up in bed with Steele which brought her affair with Laura Harding to a temporary end. It took her $13,675.75 – all her savings – to buy the play out from the producer and her former lover Jed Harris (b. Vienna, Austria, February 25, 1900 as Jacob Horowitz, d. New York, November 14, 1979) and stop it going to Chicago where she would have faced further humiliation. The play closed on February 10, 1934 after 55 performances. Two days later, she sailed for France aboard the SS *Paris* for a holiday with Suzanne Steele. Kate did not attend the Academy Awards at which she won her first Oscar, which were held on March 16, 1934 at the Ambassador Hotel, Los Angeles, setting a precedent that would last for 40 years. Aboard the *Paris* with her girlfriend she wired Leland Hayward asking him to forward it to the Academy. It read: "I do not believe in acting contests, finding them silly, and therefore must refuse your offer of an award." Hayward did not do as he was asked and instead sent a gracious thank you in Kate's name to the Academy. By the time the ship arrived in France Kate and Suzanne Steele had fallen out and Kate wired Laura Harding asking her to take her back. She was also bored by France and spent just four days in the country before returning to America. Aboard the ship on the return voyage were Ernest Hemingway and Marlene Dietrich. Kate began a brief but passionate affair with Papa Hemingway. Her next film was J.M. Barrie's *The Little Minister* (1934) in which she played Lady Babbie. Kate later confessed that jealousy had spurred her to take away the part from her love rival Margaret Sullavan, not

that she gained much by the theft. The film opened at Radio City Music Hall in late 1934 to the largest crowd in the cinema's history but flopped everywhere else. Meanwhile, her next film, Philip Moeller's *Break Of Heart* (1935) was another flop. Kate next played Constance Dane Roberti, a composer who falls in love with Charles Boyer's alcoholic conductor, Franz Roberti. The film, called *The Music Man*, had been intended as a vehicle for Kate and John Barrymore but Francis Lederer replaced him after he and Kate fell out spectacularly. Although Boyer had only recently married, he and Kate began an affair that lasted as many cinematic flings do – only for the length of filming. Then came the title role in George Stevens' *Alice Adams* (1935). Critics applauded Kate's performance as Alice, a social-climbing, small-town girl and she was nominated for a Best Actress Academy Award. Kate had a 10-day affair with her co-star Fred MacMurray during filming. Frank Albertson was cast as Alice's brother although Kate thought him too common for the role. She later admitted that he was terrific. Hattie McDaniel played the slatternly maid, Malena. The film was also nominated for a Best Picture Oscar. At the ceremony, held at the Biltmore Hotel on March 5, 1936, it lost out to *Mutiny On The Bounty* and Kate lost to Bette Davis for *Dangerous*. It was around this time that her affairs with Laura Harding and Leland Hayward ended. Hayward married Margaret Sullavan on November 15, 1936 and Kate went back east to live her own life. In Kate's next film, *Sylvia Scarlett*, (released on January 3, 1936) she played the title role who masquerades as a boy, Sylvester Scarlett, to escape from France. She also had her head shaved. The film was based on the Compton Mackenzie book *Early Life And Adventures Of Sylvia Scarlett*. The talented cast included Cary Grant as the crook Jimmy Monkley, Brian

Aherne as Sylvia's love interest Michael Fane and Edmund Gwenn as her father. Grant was paid $15,000 for his part while Kate received $50,000. Cast and crew believed that they had a hit on their hands and Kate even attended the preview in Huntingdon Park, breaking her usual rule. The film was way ahead of its time and three-quarters of the audience walked out while the rest stayed to boo and jeer. They did not like or understand the bisexual overtones and in a bid to soften the story Cukor changed the beginning and the ending which he later admitted was a mistake. Kate and the director George Cukor told the producer Pandro Berman that they would make the next film for nothing to make up for the disappointment. He was not impressed, and said, "Don't bother." Following a series of flops Kate was disheartened and began to doubt her ability, even believing her career might be about to peter out. Her next film, *Mary Of Scotland* (released on July 30, 1936), though directed by John Ford, in which Kate played Mary, Queen of Scots, was laughable. Ford, who disapproved of her fondness for trousers, challenged Kate to a game of golf at $100 a hole. He added the side bet, "If you lose you'll agree to come to the studio at least one day dressed like a woman." Hepburn replied, "And if I win will you come dressed as a gentleman?" Kate believed that Mary was "a bit of an ass" and that her cousin Elizabeth I would have made a better subject. During filming Kate believed that John Ford saved her life. "I was riding at full gallop and suddenly he yelled, 'Duck!' I did and if I hadn't I'd have been killed instantly. There was a branch I hadn't seen." Her next film, *A Woman Rebels* (1936), in which Kate played Pamela Thistlewaite, also flopped. Next was a film version of J.M. Barrie's *Quality Street* (1937) – another failure to add to a worryingly long list. Kate decided to take a break from film-making and return to the theatre. In November 1936 she began dating the eccentric billionaire Howard Hughes. Back in Hollywood, in the winter of 1937, Kate was depressed. She was then sent a script for a story about life in a New York theatrical boarding house. *Stage Door* (which opened on November 12, 1937), directed by Gregory La Cava in which she starred with Ginger Rogers and Constance Collier, gave her back some much-needed confidence. Kate seemed more comfortable in comedies and reached her comic peak playing Susan Vance, a scatterbrained Connecticut heiress in Howard Hawks' screwball comedy *Bringing Up Baby* (released February 18, 1938), with Cary Grant (the baby of the title was a leopard). During filming Kate was in high spirits and became rather talkative. Hawks called for silence on the set but Kate carried on with her conversation. Eventually, she realised everyone was looking at her and asked Hawks what was going on. "I was waiting for the parrot to stop talking," he said. Kate beckoned him to one side. "Howard, these people are friends of mine. If you say things like that to me, you're liable to get into trouble." Hawks recalled, "I glanced up and there was an electrician in the flies above us with a big lamp. I called up to him, 'Eddie, if you had a choice of dropping that lamp on me or Miss Hepburn, which would you choose?' And he called back, 'Step aside, Mr Hawks.'" Kate was also quick to improvise. During one scene her shoe broke and as she limped around the set, she said to Cary Grant, "I was born on the side of a hill." The picture is still routinely cited as one of the best examples of its kind although at the time it proved too sophisticated for the mass audiences. It was also her last film for RKO and it lost the studio $365,000. On May 3, 1938, Kate was included in a list of "box office poison" created by Harry Brandt, the president of the Independent Theatre

Owners Association along with Marlene Dietrich, Greta Garbo, Kay Francis, Joan Crawford and others. "They say I'm a has-been," said Kate. "If I weren't laughing so much, I'd cry." However, that may not have been the complete truth. Stories have emerged that the next day Kate threatened to commit suicide by jumping from a studio window. It took 90 minutes of persuasion from Cary Grant to talk her back into the room and safety. Kate next made *Holiday* (released on June 15, 1938) on a loan-out to Columbia from RKO who wanted to get rid of her. It cost Kate $75,000 to make *Holiday* but she more than recouped that as her fee from Columbia was $150,000. In the late Thirties Hollywood was awash with the excitement of filming *Gone With The Wind*, Margaret Mitchell's epic novel. Kate wanted to play Scarlett O'Hara, as did almost every other actress of the period. Her contract was up for renewal and Kate said that she would not return to the studio unless she was allowed to play Scarlett. A stumbling block was David O. Selznick who did not want her to play the role despite the pleas from Kate's friend George Cukor who was hired to direct the picture. "She has no sex appeal," said Selznick. When Kate approached him and demanded to know why he would not cast her, he was blunt: "Because, my dear, I can't see Rhett Butler chasing you for twelve years." Kate spent the summer of 1938 at her home, Fenwick, in Connecticut. However, the house was all but destroyed by a hurricane in September of that year and had to be rebuilt. Kate was offered two story ideas by Philip Barry, the author of *Holiday*, one about a father and daughter which was of no interest and the other about an heiress called Tracy Lord. Kate was interested in the Tracy Lord story "provided I don't play Scarlett O'Hara first". On January 17, 1939, the chimney in her New York home at 244 East 49th

Street caught fire and she had to evacuate while firemen put out the blaze. On March 28, 1939, Kate opened in the Tracy Lord tale, now entitled *The Philadelphia Story* at the Shubert Theatre on Broadway. Despite a talented cast including Joseph Cotten and Dan Tobin, Kate was convinced that the play in New York was going to be yet another disaster to add to her catalogue of woes. She could not have been more wrong. The play ran for 415 performances, grossing $961,310.37 and then 254 more shows on tour, grossing a further $753,538.50. Kate took 10 per cent as salary and owned a further quarter share in the production. *The Philadelphia Story* made her a very rich woman. Kate decided to make a film version and Howard Hughes bought the rights for her. However, Kate's temperament, not to mention her "box office poison" label, made it all but impossible to sell. Louis B. Mayer at MGM was a friend and admirer of Kate's and he agreed to make *The Philadelphia Story* with her and Spencer Tracy and Clark Gable. When approached they refused to work with Kate and she was forced to accept two lesser stars – Cary Grant and James Stewart. George Cukor was at the helm for the filming in July and August of 1940. Grant insisted on top billing and a salary of $137,500 which he donated to the British War Relief Fund. Stewart's performance won him a Best Actor Oscar and the film revitalised Hepburn's career winning her another Academy Award nomination (although she lost to Ginger Rogers for *Kitty Foyle*). Finished five days under schedule, it proved to be one of the great Hollywood comedies. *The Philadelphia Story* was released on December 25, 1940 and took $594,000 during its first six weeks at Radio City Music Hall. The film was later remade as a musical, *High Society*. Despite a cast of Frank Sinatra, Bing Crosby, Grace Kelly and Louis Armstrong and a music score by Cole Porter, audiences have tended to prefer the original. As the film was going into production Kate began an affair with Claudette Colbert that was to last eight years. She was also the bridesmaid when Laurence Olivier married Vivien Leigh in August 1940. Her next picture, *Woman Of The Year* (shooting began August 29, 1941; released February 1942, the film was originally entitled *The Thing About Women*) was the first of nine movies she made with Spencer Tracy. At first it seemed they were destined not to get along. When Joseph L. Mankiewicz introduced Kate to Tracy, she commented on their height disparity, "I'm afraid I'm a little tall for you, Mr Tracy." "Don't worry, Kate," Mankiewicz said, "he'll soon cut you down to size." And so he did. (Although this has become the accepted Hollywood story, one biographer claims that the words were uttered to Leslie Howard by Kate in November 1931.) By the end of the Thirties audiences were growing tired of her superior ways; Tracy's gruff put-downs helped to make her more acceptable. Off screen, their relationship was perhaps more complicated than Hepburn chose to declare. "I don't believe in marriage," she proclaimed. "It's bloody impractical to love, honour and obey. If it weren't, you wouldn't have to sign a contract." Like many of Hepburn's claims, this was disingenuous. In her autobiography, she barely touched on Tracy's alcoholism, nor explained why Tracy, though he lived with her for 25 years, never divorced his wife. Interestingly, Kate's parents disapproved of Spencer Tracy. Their disapproval was not his unwillingness to marry their daughter, nor his abusive alcoholism, nor his penchant for prostitutes and the resulting social diseases that brought, nor his bisexuality (he had affairs with Lew Ayres, Johnny Mack Brown and "half the women in Hollywood"). They disapproved because he bored them and in the Hepburn household that was a terrible sin. On the silver screen, though, there was no ambiguity. "On screen Spencer and I are the perfect American couple," she once opined. "I needle him. If he put a big paw out and put it on my head, he could squash me. I think that is the romantic, ideal picture of the male and female in this country." In *Woman Of The Year*, which was filmed in MGM's studios at Culver City between August and October 1941, Hepburn was Tess Harding, an ambitious politician, Tracy – Sam Craig a sports journalist; inevitably there were spats; no less inevitably, love emerged triumphant. The film won an Oscar for Best Screenplay and Kate received a Best Actress nomination (losing out to Greer Garson for *Mrs Miniver*). In George Cukor's *Keeper Of The Flame* (released in December 1942) Tracy again appeared as a journalist, but this was a melodrama, with Hepburn as a widow who is made to admit that her husband was a fascist. Cukor recalled, "It was Kate's last romantic glamour girl part, and she acted with some of that artificiality she's supposedly left behind at RKO . . . I don't think I really believed in the story, it was pure hokey-pokey, and her part was phony." *Without Love* (1945) concerned another widow, who lets a scientist move in with her. Next came an "epically dreary" Western, *The Sea Of Grass* (released April 25, 1947), directed by Elia Kazan, which starred Tracy as Colonel James Brewton, a cattle tycoon so obsessed by his work that he alienates his family. The two of them were back on form in Frank Capra's *State Of The Union* (premièred in Washington, DC, April 7, 1948 and released nationwide 23 days later), which presented Tracy as a candidate for the presidency, and Hepburn as the estranged wife who returns to his side. The film contained many cruel barbs at President Harry S Truman but by all accounts he liked the film. The delightful *Adam's Rib* (released November 18, 1949), shot in New York by George Cukor, saw Kate as militant feminist lawyer Amanda Bonner defending a dumb blonde (Judy Holliday) for shooting her unfaithful husband. Tracy was the prosecutor Adam Bonner. When the studio began to create the publicity materials Spencer Tracy insisted on top billing. Garson Kanin, the writer, remonstrated with him, "Spencer, didn't you ever hear of ladies first?" Tracy replied, "This is a movie, chowderhead, not a lifeboat." *Pat And Mike* (released June 13, 1952), with Tracy as a sports promoter who takes on Hepburn as Pat Pemberton, the all-round champion, was enjoyable enough. *The Desk Set* (released May 1957), although an enjoyable movie to make, proved a disappointment. In January 1962 an article appeared in *Look* that revealed their relationship for the first time as well as Tracy's alcoholism and his fiery temper. Both Tracy and Hepburn were angry and disappointed by the feature. In their swansong, *Guess Who's Coming To Dinner?* (released December 12, 1967), which finished shooting ten days before Tracy's death, they were a liberal couple, Christine and Matt Drayton, whose principles begin to slip when their daughter Joey (played by Kate's niece, Katharine Houghton) announces her engagement to John Prentice, a black man (Sidney Poitier). It was said that Kate had only taken her rather underwritten part in *Guess Who's Coming To Dinner?* to be near Tracy at the end. Even if this were so, she was rewarded with yet another Oscar. But she rejected any suggestion of altruism in the devotion she showed in his final illness. "Self-sacrificing women give me melancholia," she observed. "My mother, who was an angel, said, 'Please yourself, then at least you're sure somebody is pleased.'" For some years after meeting Tracy, the films that

Hepburn made without him such as *Stage Door Canteen* (1943) playing herself; *Dragon Seed* (1944) as Jade opposite Turhan Bey; *Undercurrent* (November 28, 1946) as Ann Hamilton and *Song Of Love* (1947), in which she played Clara Schumann were wholly forgettable. The notable exception was *The African Queen* (released in December 1951), in which she won her second Oscar as Rose Sayer, a prissy spinster, whose missionary brother (played by Robert Morley) has died, and who conceives an affection for Charlie Allnutt, Humphrey Bogart's gin-soaked river trader. The film has become a classic. Director John Huston told Kate to base her portrayal of Rosie on Eleanor Roosevelt. Filmed on location on the Ruiki River and Butiaba in the Belgian Congo and the Murchison Falls and Lake Albert in Uganda between May and July 17, 1951, every member of the cast and crew suffered from malaria and diarrhoea. Well, not quite everyone. Huston and Bogart escaped the torment because neither of them ever drank any water. Hepburn took a dim view of their nightly binges and, like her character in the film, found consolation in the Bible. Owing to the illnesses much of the film was eventually shot at Isleworth and Shepperton Studios. Staying in London, Kate lived at Claridge's but upset the hotel management by wearing trousers in the lobby. When it was pointed out that this behaviour was not allowed she used the servants' entrance for the rest of her stay. Based on C.S. Forester's novel, Columbia had originally intended *The African Queen* for Charles Laughton and Elsa Lanchester and then, when they sold it to Warner Bros in 1939, for David Niven and Bette Davis. The irascible Davis (of whom Kate once said, "There's not a camera lens in Hollywood which could make her look 25") argued with the chosen producer and the project fell into abeyance.

Bogart initially hated making the film but gradually threw himself into his character and won his only Oscar. Kate was nominated for a Best Actress Academy Award but lost out to Vivien Leigh for *A Streetcar Named Desire*. Hepburn returned to the theatre, playing Rosalind in *As You Like It* on Broadway and on tour. On June 27, 1952 she scored a success in London for 12 weeks as Epifania in George Bernard Shaw's *The Millionairess*, directed by Michael Benthall. The casting was apt, for Shaw himself had described her as "the born decider, dominator, organiser, tactician, mesmeriser". Kate travelled over with Constance Collier but producer Binky Beaumont refused to pay for the flight of Collier's (and later Hepburn's) secretary Phyllis Wilbourn. Kate cashed in the two aeroplane tickets and bought three for a sea voyage instead. All three women were hopelessly seasick during the entire journey which ended in Southampton on March 19, 1952. When the play opened in New York at the Shubert Theatre on October 17, 1952 it was a flop, partly because of bad reviews and partly because Kate lost her voice on the opening night. Hepburn wanted to make a film of *The Millionairess*, but the funds were never forthcoming. On August 6, 1953, in Hartford Hospital, Kate underwent surgery for the removal of a number of skin cancers, thought to be the result of too much sun while filming *The African Queen*. She recuperated at Fenwick. Next, she gave one of her finest performances in David Lean's *Summer Madness* (1955), about Jane Hudson, a lonely American spinster secretary, who finds romance with Renato di Rossi (Rossano Brazzi) in Venice. The film resulted in yet another nomination for an Academy Award. From May 2 until November 2, 1955, she toured Australia with the Old Vic company (including the homosexual Bobby Helpmann), playing Portia in *The Merchant Of*

Venice, Beatrice in *Much Ado About Nothing*, Katherine in *The Taming Of The Shrew* and Isabella in *Measure For Measure*. In both Sydney and Melbourne the mayors announced, "I am delighted to welcome Mr Hepburn and Miss Helpmann to our fair city." Two years later, on July 10, 1957, she returned to Shakespeare, again appearing as Portia and Beatrice, this time at Stratford, Connecticut, where she also performed on June 3, 1960 as Viola in *Twelfth Night*, and then on July 22 as Cleopatra. On the screen, meanwhile, Hepburn had made an appalling comedy, *The Iron Petticoat* (released in July 1956), with Bob Hope, written by Ben Hecht (although he asked for his name to be removed from the final credits) and directed by Ralph Thomas. It was filmed at Pinewood Studios and Kate played Captain Vinka Kovelenko, a Russian air force officer assigned to an American base in Germany. Nor was *The Rainmaker* (1956), in which she was Lizzie Curry, a confirmed spinster, who discovers love at the last gasp through the good offices of Starbuck (Burt Lancaster), very good yet she was nominated for an Academy Award. Although she eschewed motherhood in real life, Kate began to play mothers in reel life. She was Violet Venable in a version of Tennessee Williams' *Suddenly Last Summer* (opened December 22, 1959) for which she was nominated for an Academy Award. It was not a happy experience. She fell out badly with director Joseph L. Mankiewicz and at the end of filming spat in his face in front of an astonished cast and crew. She repeated the action in the face of producer Sam Spiegel. In Sidney Lumet's version of Eugene O'Neill's *Long Day's Journey Into Night* (1962) in which she starred as Mary Tyrone alongside Ralph Richardson (Jason Robards and Dean Stockwell played her sons) she received yet another Oscar nomination. In *The Lion In Winter* (1968) she played Eleanor of

Aquitaine and co-starred with Peter O'Toole (King Henry II), Anthony Hopkins (as King Richard the Lionheart) and Timothy Dalton (King Philip). O'Toole remembered, "Meeting Kate was the greatest experience of my life. I had first met her in London when I was in *The Long And The Short And The Tall*, and I was pissing in the sink, because someone was using the toilet, when she walked into my dressing room. I heard her say, 'I'm Kate Hepburn.' I pretended I was washing my hands and arranged my clothes hastily." All these performances received critical accolades; for the last of them Hepburn won her third Oscar. She showed no inclination to rest on her laurels. Bryan Forbes' *The Madwoman Of Chaillot* (1969) which was filmed in the South of France and *The Trojan Women* (in which she played Hecuba) (1971) proved unsuitable for the screen. The musical *Coco*, in which she starred from December 18, 1969, proved unsuitable for Broadway. Kate's final performance was on August 1, 1970. The film of Edward Albee's *Delicate Balance* (1975), with Paul Scofield, Joseph Cotten and Lee Remick, though well intentioned and well acted, was not for a mass market. *Rooster Cogburn* (1975) was a sequel to *True Grit*, the Western which had won its star John Wayne his only Oscar. Filmed in Oregon in the autumn of 1974, Kate played a Bible-thumping spinster who learns to use a rifle against outlaws. On April 2, 1974, Kate made her first appearance at the Oscars to present the Irving Thalberg Award to her friend the producer Lawrence Weingarten. Wearing a black Mao suit, Kate received a standing ovation at the Dorothy Chandler Pavilion. Kate appeared as Miss Pudd in the awful *Olly Olly Oxen Free* (1978). *On Golden Pond* (1981), a study of old age and family relationships, gave Hepburn as Ethel Thayer her first success in films for 13 years. She bestowed warmth and humanity as the wife of a grouchy

Henry Fonda, who also won an Oscar. "You don't have to act old when you're our age," she reflected. As a gift she gave Fonda one of Spencer Tracy's hats and he painted a picture of it which he gave to Kate. The film would have made a fitting end to Kate's career but she insisted on making the disastrous *Grace Quigley* (1984), with Nick Nolte, about an old woman so sold on euthanasia that she hires a hit man to murder her. And she continued to appear on television, in *Mrs Delafield Wants To Marry* (1986) and *Penthouse Paradise* (1989). Her final screen appearance was a cameo part as Warren Beatty's aunt in *Love Affair* (1994). Katharine Hepburn mostly lived in a magnificent four-storey New York brownstone house at 244 East 49th Street that she had bought in 1937 for $33,000. In the winter of 1974–75 she fell out with her neighbour, the homosexual composer Stephen Sondheim, whose late-night piano playing annoyed her. After he had written one song late at night for the musical *Company* (it was usually said to be 'The Ladies Who Lunch', but according to one probably apocryphal version of the story, it was 'You Could Drive A Person Crazy'), Sondheim and his young male guest looked out of a window to see Kate glaring malevolently back at them. The composer went out the next day and bought an electric piano and headphones. In 1996 she moved permanently to Connecticut. "Life's what's important," she was wont to say. "Walking, houses, family. Birth, pain and joy – and then death. Acting's just waiting for the custard pie." Her New England upbringing left her dissatisfied with her lot. "I could have accomplished three times what I've accomplished. I haven't realised my full potential. It's disgusting."
CAUSE: Katharine Hepburn, who had been in ill-health for some years, died at her home in Fenwick, an upper-class borough of Old Saybrook,

Connecticut. She had suffered from Parkinson's disease and a large malignant tumour had grown on her neck. A friend of the actor, Cynthia McFadden, said that she died surrounded by family. On June 10–11, 2004, Sotheby's in New York auctioned 684 lots of Hepburn's belongings, including items of clothing and paintings she had created.
FURTHER READING: *Tracy And Hepburn* – Garson Kanin (New York: Bantam, 1972); *Kate: The Life Of Katharine Hepburn* – Charles Higham (New York: W.W. Norton, 1975); *Katharine Hepburn: A Biography* – Gary Carey (London: New English Library, 1985); *Katharine Hepburn: A Biography* – Anne Edwards (London: Coronet, 1987); *Young Kate* – Christopher Andersen (New York: Delta, 1988); *Me: Stories Of My Life* – Katharine Hepburn (New York: Ballantine Books, 1992); *Katharine Hepburn* – Barbara Leaming (London: Weidenfeld & Nicolson, 1995); *An Affair To Remember: The Remarkable Love Story Of Katharine Hepburn And Spencer Tracy* – Christopher Andersen (New York: William Morrow & Co., 1997); *Kate Remembered* – A. Scott Berg (London: Simon & Schuster, 2003); *Katharine The Great (1907–1950) Secrets Of A Lifetime . . . Revealed* – Darwin Porter (New York: Blood Moon Productions, 2004).

Charlton Heston

(JOHN CHARLES CARTER)
Born October 4, 1923
Died April 5, 2008
Epic star. Charlton Heston played more "great man" roles than almost anyone in cinematic history. He was Moses in Cecil B DeMille's 1956 remake of *The Ten Commandments*, the title roles in *Ben-Hur* (1959) and *El Cid* (1961), Michelangelo in *The Agony And The Ecstasy* (1965), John the Baptist in *The Greatest Story Ever Told* (1965), General Gordon in *Khartoum* (1966) and Mark Antony in *Julius*

Caesar (1970). He said, "I have played three presidents, three saints and two geniuses. If that doesn't create an ego problem, nothing does." He was an actor of limited range, renowned in real life for lacking a sense of humour. However, towards the end of his life he was best known for his right-wing political views and presidency of the National Rifle Association. At the 2001 NRA conference, he held a 230-year-old musket above his head and declaimed, "I have only five words for you: From my cold, dead hands." Heston was born in Evanston, Illinois, and grew up at St Helen, Michigan, where his father, Russell Carter, owned a lumber mill. His parents were divorced in the mid-1930s and his mother, Lilla Charlton, married Chester Heston, a heating appliance superintendent. When he became an actor he adopted his mother's maiden name but preferred to be called Chuck by friends, family and indeed strangers. Heston began acting at Northwestern University, appearing in the title role of a 16mm silent production of Ibsen's *Peer Gynt* (1942), directed by the independent filmmaker David Bradley. Seven years later, Bradley made another 16mm film, a version of Shakespeare's *Julius Caesar* where Heston was cast as Mark Antony. Heston began appearing regularly in theatre and on television before being signed by Paramount producer Hal B. Wallis. Heston made his Hollywood film debut in *Dark City* (released October 17, 1950), a film noir. Two years later, Cecil B. DeMille cast him in his first major role as Brad Braden, the manager of a failing circus who makes it into a success once again in the double Oscar-winning *The Greatest Show On Earth* (premièred January 10, 1952). Heston later commented, "A lady wrote a letter to DeMille which said, 'I thought the circus master fitted in very well with the real actors.' I've always said that was the best review I ever had." Heston was not able to

capitalise on the film's success and for four years was only cast on television, in Westerns and action films including *The Savage* (released September 1952) as Jim Aherne Jr, *The President's Lady* (released May 21, 1953) as President Andrew Jackson, *Pony Express* (released June 5, 1953) as Buffalo Bill, *Arrowhead* (released August 3, 1953) as Ed Bannon, *The Naked Jungle* (released March 3, 1954) as Christopher Leiningen, *The Far Horizons* (released May 20, 1955) and *The Private War Of Major Benson* (released August 2, 1955) as Major Bernard R. "Barney" Benson. It was Cecil B. DeMille who saved Heston from a career of B movies when he hired him to play Moses in a remake of his own *The Ten Commandments* (released October 5, 1956; premièred November 14, 1956). DeMille thought Heston looked like Michelangelo's statue of Moses complete with the broken nose 6′3″ Heston got playing football in college. Heston commented, "If you can't make a career out of two DeMilles, you'll never make it." Heston did make a career and after playing another president (Andrew Jackson) in *The Buccaneer* (released December 1, 1958), and appearing in *Touch of Evil* (released April 23, 1958), the last film made in Hollywood by Orson Welles, he moved onto another big role as Judah Ben-Hur, a First Century Jewish prince sold into slavery, in William Wyler's *Ben-Hur* (premièred November 18, 1959). The film was a smash at the box office and won eleven of the twelve Oscars it was nominated for including Best Film, Best Director and Best Actor for Heston. Heston spent weeks learning how to drive a chariot for the famous race scene. Not everyone was enamoured of the film; one critic wrote, "Loved Ben, hated Hur." Heston followed that up by playing the lead in *El Cid* (released December 14, 1961), in which, at the end, his corpse is strapped to his horse so that he could be seen to be leading his men into battle. He appeared in

Sam Peckinpah's Western *Major Dundee* (released April 7, 1965) and fell out with the director. He said, "Sam is the only person I've ever physically threatened on a set." Heston continued his great man role-playing in the Oscar-nominated *The Agony And The Ecstasy* (released October 7, 1965) when he took the role of Michelangelo opposite Rex Harrison's Pope Julius II. The following year he played General Gordon in the Oscar-nominated *Khartoum* (released June 15, 1966) opposite Laurence Olivier as the Mahdi. Heston was the astronaut George Taylor who landed on a future earth run by apes in the Oscar-nominated sci-fi classic *Planet Of The Apes* (released February 8, 1968). He refused any more than a cameo role in the sequel *Beneath The Planet Of The Apes* (1970). He said, "I told Dick Zanuck, 'I know you can't make this movie if I'm not in it, but I really don't want to do it. We've already told the story in the first one. The rest of them are just going to be 'Adventures Among The Monkeys'. I'll do it but in this one kill me off. And give whatever money you want to pay me to a charity.'" (In 2001 Charlton took a cameo role as an ageing ape in Tim Burton's remake). In 1970, he was Mark Antony for the second time in his film career followed in 1972 by another portrayal in *Antony And Cleopatra* (released in London March 2, 1972; Washington DC première September 26, 1973), which he also directed and co-wrote. He was Cardinal Richelieu in *The Three Musketeers* (released March 28, 1974), reprised the role in *The Four Musketeers* (released February 26, 1975), was Henry VIII in *The Prince And The Pauper* (released in London June 3, 1977) and in the meantime was respectively Alan Murdock and Stewart Graff in the disaster movies *Airport 1975* (released October 18, 1974) and *Earthquake* (released November 15, 1974). Of the latter film, Pauline Kael said, "He's not a bad actor, but he's

humourlessly unresilient. He underacts grimly and he turns into a stereotype of himself." From 1966 to 1971, Heston was president of the Screen Actors' Guild, following in the footsteps of Ronald Reagan. He made fewer films after that and turned down the Roy Scheider role in *Jaws* (1975) and the ambassador in *The Omen* (1976) but played Jason Colby initially in *Dynasty* and then in the spin-off series *The Colbys*. He appeared on the London stage in *The Caine Mutiny Court Martial* (1985) and in a two-hander, *Love Letters*, in which he toured America with his wife in 1997. Much of his later work was parodying his earlier roles and his real-life lack of a sense of humour was used for comedic effect in *Wayne's World 2* (released December 10, 1993). His final film appearance was playing Joseph Mengele in *My Father, Rua Alguem 5555* (2003). The year before, the left-wing filmmaker Michael Moore had interviewed Heston in his position as NRA president for the documentary *Bowling For Columbine* (2002). Heston walked out mid-interview and later claimed that Moore had set him up. Ironically, on June 16, 1968 Heston and Gregory Peck, James Stewart and Kirk Douglas appeared on television calling for gun control after the assassination of presidential hopeful Senator Robert F. Kennedy. Heston resigned as president of the NRA and on August 9, 2002 made public the news that he was suffering symptoms consistent with the onset of Alzheimer's disease. Announcing his dementia, Heston said, "My Dear Friends, Colleagues and Fans: My physicians have recently told me I may have a neurological disorder whose symptoms are consistent with Alzheimer's disease. So . . . I wanted to prepare a few words for you now, because when the time comes, I may not be able to. I've lived my whole life on the stage and screen before you. I've found purpose and meaning in your response. For an actor there's no greater loss than the loss of his audience. I can part the Red Sea, but I can't part with you, which is why I won't exclude you from this stage in my life. For now, I'm not changing anything. I'll insist on work when I can; the doctors will insist on rest when I must. If you see a little less spring in my step, if your name fails to leap to my lips, you'll know why. And if I tell you a funny story for the second time, please laugh anyway. I'm neither giving up nor giving in. I believe I'm still the fighter that Dr Martin Luther King and John F. Kennedy and Ronald Reagan knew, but it's a fight I must someday call a draw. I must reconcile courage and surrender in equal measure. Please feel no sympathy for me. I don't. I just may be a little less accessible to you, despite my wishes. I also want you to know that I'm grateful beyond measure. My life has been blessed with good fortune. I'm grateful that I was born in America, that cradle of freedom and opportunity, where a kid from the Michigan Northwoods can work hard and make something of his life. I'm grateful for the gift of the greatest words ever written, that let me share with you the infinite scope of the human experience. As an actor, I'm thankful that I've lived not one life, but many. Above all, I'm proud of my family . . . my wife Lydia, the queen of my heart, my children, Fraser and Holly, and my beloved grandchildren, Jack, Ridley and Charlie. They're my biggest fans, my toughest critics and my proudest achievement. Through them, I can touch immortality. Finally, I'm confident about the future of America. I believe in you. I know that the future of our country, our culture and our children is in good hands. I know you will continue to meet adversity with strength and resilience, as our ancestors did, and come through with flying colours – the ones on Old Glory. William Shakespeare, at the end of his career, wrote his farewell through the words of Prospero, in *The Tempest*.

It ends like this, 'Be cheerful, sir. Our revels now are ended. These our actors, as I foretold you, were all spirits and are melted into air, into thin air: And, like the baseless fabric of this vision, the cloud-cap'd towers, the gorgeous palaces, the solemn temples, the great globe itself, yea all which it inherit, shall dissolve and, like this insubstantial pageant faded, leave not a rack behind. We are such stuff as dreams are made on, and our little life is rounded with a sleep'. Thank you, and God bless you, everyone." When George Clooney made some unflattering remarks about Heston's illness, he responded, "It's funny how class can skip a generation, isn't it? I don't know the man – never met him, never even spoken to him. But I feel sorry for George Clooney – one day he may get Alzheimer's disease. I served my country in World War II. I survived that – I guess I can survive some bad words from this fellow." On March 17, 1944 Heston married Lydia Clark (b. Two Rivers, Wisconsin April 14, 1923) and they had two children, Fraser Clarke (b. Los Angeles February 12, 1955 weighing 7lb 14½oz; he played the infant Moses in *The Ten Commandments* and is now a director) and adopted daughter Holly Ann (b. 1963).

CAUSE: Heston was in poor health for some years before his death. In 1996, he had a hip replacement. He was diagnosed with prostate cancer in 1998. He died on April 5, 2008 from complications arising from Alzheimer's disease at his home in Beverly Hills with his wife Lydia at his side. He was 84. His funeral occurred a week later and was attended by 250 people including former First Lady Nancy Reagan, Governor Arnold Schwarzenegger of California, Olivia de Havilland, Keith Carradine, Pat Boone, Tom Selleck, Oliver Stone and Rob Reiner.

FURTHER READING: *The Actor's Life: Journals 1956–1976* – Charlton Heston (London: Penguin Books, 1980), *In the*

Arena: The Autobiography – Charlton Heston (London: HarperCollins, 1995).

Jon-Erik Hexum
Born January 5, 1957
Died October 18, 1984
Tragic hunk. Born in New Jersey, it was said that handsome 6'1" Hexum had a guaranteed golden future ahead of him in Hollywood. He starred as macho time-traveller Phineas Bogg in the sci-fi show *Voyagers* and then he appeared with Joan Collins in the TV movie *The Making Of A Male Model* (1983). The pair reputedly became a couple off screen. Collins tried and failed to use her influence to get Hexum cast as her lover, Dex, on *Dynasty*. (The part went to Michael Nader.) Instead, Hexum was cast as Mac Harper, the lead in the series *Cover Up* at Fox in Century City. Mac Harper was a fashion photographer, a former Green Beret and, ironically, a weapons expert, who doubled as a secret agent.
CAUSE: Off screen Hexum was a practical joker, forever fooling around. It was his sense of fun and jolly japes that cost him his life. On Friday October 12, 1984, Hexum left his home, 2108 Kenwood Avenue, Burbank, and travelled to the studio. At about 5.15pm 26-year-old Hexum jokingly placed a .44 Magnum against his temple, smiled and said, "Let's see if I've got one for me" and pulled the trigger. Although the weapon was loaded with three empty cartridges and two blanks (a wad of cotton and a small charge) it was still enough to shatter his skull. He immediately collapsed into a coma. A witness at the studio commented: "Jon smiled and pulled the trigger. There was a loud bang and a bright flash, then black smoke. Jon screamed in agony, then looked kind of amazed as he slumped back onto the bed with blood streaming from a severe head wound. It was horrible." A crew member rushed over and tried to stem the bleeding. Hexum was rushed to Beverly Hills Medical Center, 1177 South Beverly Drive, Los Angeles, where his condition was declared to be extremely critical. Six days later, he was pronounced brain dead. His organs were transplanted and his death was ruled as 'accidental'. He was cremated at a private funeral in Grandview Crematory, Glendale, California. His ashes were scattered in Malibu.

Benny Hill
(ALFRED HAWTHORNE HILL)
Born January 21, 1924
Found dead Easter Monday (April 20), 1992
Sad comic. Best known for his television shows Benny Hill made only the occasional foray into films, including *Those Magnificent Men In Their Flying Machines* (1965), *Chitty Chitty Bang Bang* (1966) as the toy maker and *The Italian Job* (1969) as the computer expert. In *Star Turns*, his dual biography of Benny Hill and Frankie Howerd, the scriptwriter Barry Took investigates the sex lives of both comedians. One was a closet homosexual although very open about it in showbiz circles while the other was suspected of similar tendencies. Benny Hill's friends jumped to his defence insisting any accusation of homosexuality was simply wrong and ill-informed. And they were right. Benny Hill was born above a lamp shop in Bernard Street, Southampton (although he knocked a year off his age in later life insisting he was born in 1925), the middle of three children: Leonard Ernest (b. Southampton, January 30, 1922, d. June, 1990 of a heart attack) and Diana Helen (b. Southampton, January, 1933, d. Australia, 1987, of leukaemia). Hill was exceptionally close to his mother, Helen Cave (b. June 21, 1894, d. Southampton General Hospital, February, 1976), but kept his distance from his father Alfred Hawthorn (b.

Leytonstone, December 12, 1893, d. May, 1972) who by all accounts was a stern man known as 'The Captain'. In 1941, aged 17, young Alfred left Southampton and travelled to London to seek fame and fortune in the precarious world of show business. Not long after his arrival in the capital city Hill was propositioned by a gay comedian looking for a new partner (for his act). He plied the youngster with booze and edged closer on the settee. An arm around the shoulder, a hand on the knee. It was only when he leaned forward to kiss him that Hill jumped up and ran away. Later, when asked by a group of gay dancers if he was queer, Hill is said to have replied that he felt very well. When the matter was pressed he said, "Not really but I have my funny little ways." Hill was said to have had two great loves in his life which left him unable to give himself completely to any other woman. The second of these was actress Annette André, star of *Randall & Hopkirk (Deceased)*. It was claimed that whenever she came on screen he had to leave the room. However Hill would have wanted it otherwise, the relationship was always a friendship and never a romance. "We used to laugh together and were good friends, but that was it," she said many years later. "I never had an affair with him, I didn't want to." It came as a shock to her when Hill proposed one day in 1963. She declined and never spoke to him again until just two months before his death in 1992. It was on *The Benny Hill Show*, broadcast on Thames TV from 1969 until 1989, that Hill began to attract massive audiences and three BAFTA (British Oscar) awards (for Best Light Entertainment Programme (1971), Best Light Entertainment Production and Direction, and Best Script (both 1972)). However, the show also brought a great deal of criticism from feminists, much of it ignorant. The readers of a women's magazine voted *The Benny Hill Show*

their least favourite programme. In 1987 Colin Shaw, the director of regulatory body the Broadcasting Standards Council, declared, "It's not as funny as it was to have half-naked girls chased across the screen by a dirty old man. Attitudes have changed. The kind of behaviour that gets a stream of men sent to magistrates' courts each year isn't at all amusing." Alternative comedian Ben Elton wondered aloud if in the days when it was unsafe for women to walk in parks, was it a good idea for a show to be broadcast showing Benny Hill chasing women in their underwear? Hill was outraged at Elton breaking the unwritten rule that one comic does not publicly criticise another. Without specifically naming anyone he hit back. "They criticise me for chasing girls through a park, when in real life it's not safe for a girl to walk through parks alone. If they watched the show properly, they would see it's always girls chasing me." The girls were nicknamed in the press 'Hill's Angels' after the gorgeous trio in the cop show *Charlie's Angels*. Sue Upton, one of the original Angels and a close friend of Hill, came to his defence. She stated somewhat naïvely, "Benny isn't the dirty old man people think . . . He is the perfect gentleman when he dates his glamour girls. They all say so. He always walks on the road side of the pavement. That's the height of good manners." Yet others told a different tale. One young and very attractive brunette actress tells of being invited for a Chinese meal by Hill and then back to his flat at 2 Queensgate, London SW7, where Hill expected sexual favours. When she declined to service the fat comic he asked her to leave and she never got to appear on his show. Beautiful model and actress Stefanie Marrian (b. October 9, 1949) was just 16 when she went to see Hill about work on his TV show in 1966. In October 1985 Marrian told newspapers that Hill had invited her to his flat for an "audition" whereupon he produced a bottle of champagne to help her relax. As he poured the drink, Hill told her there were three ways to become a success. "Either you need talent which you don't have, or outstanding beauty which you don't have either. Or you scratch my back and I'll scratch yours." Stefanie Marrian then related how Hill showed her how to pleasure him. He took her into his bedroom where he stripped her before taking off his own clothes except his shorts. Stefanie grabbed her clothes and bolted for the door. A few days later, she went back. "I'd never seen a man naked before and the sight of Benny was no laughing matter," she said. "He didn't want to make love, but enjoyed me masturbating him on his purple bed. I hated the sight of his naked body, but he loved me wanking him. It was like a holy ritual and I was his virginal creature." 33½-22-34 Stefanie who went on to become *The Sun* Page 3 Girl of the Year in 1976 related how Hill would strip off and lay on his bed with her between his legs stroking him. "I always kept my knickers on and he would never touch me. He would constantly put me down and make me feel dirty. Each time we met I would masturbate him, no matter where we were." According to the model she pleaded with the corpulent comic to make love to her not long after she had lost her virginity aged 17. She tried everything in her repertoire of tricks to turn Hill on including wearing stockings and garters and bending over in front of him while wearing no knickers but nothing seemed to work. "He kept saying he was afraid of making me pregnant. But once when he did try to touch me up, he did it wearing rubber gloves. He would also invite his friends round and expect me to sleep with them, but I would always refuse." Blonde model Nikki Critcher claimed that one day in the studio Hill had squeezed her bosom so hard she had to slap his face to make him let go. "I'd been warned by other girls that

Benny was always trying it on, but I'd never seen that side of him until one day he suddenly grabbed my breasts. I feel sorry for Benny. I think he was very lonely." His former producer Dennis Kirkland completely refutes both stories. Former model Cherie Gilham has revealed how she would give the corpulent comic "a sympathy blowjob". In *Star Turns* Barry Took opines that 5'10" Benny Hill's sex life was carried out with prostitutes in faraway places like Marseilles, Hamburg, Tokyo and Bangkok. It seems that Benny Hill didn't have to go far to get his kicks after all. However, perhaps the most poignant statement is made by Hill himself. "In relations between the sexes the male is always disappointed."

CAUSE: In February 1992 Benny was admitted to the Cromwell Hospital after suffering a minor heart attack. The situation was exacerbated because in 1976 he had had a kidney removed and the remaining one began to create water which settled on his chest making breathing difficult. On March 8 he was readmitted after suffering a panic attack. He was released five days later and went home to 7 Fairwater House, Twickenham Road, Teddington, Middlesex. (Benny Hill moved from his long-term residence, 2 Queensgate, when the rent went up.) It was there that he was discovered sitting on the settee in front of his two televisions and two videos. He had died of a heart attack probably on April 18. He was 68. He was buried in Southampton next to his parents. He left £7,548,192, and no will.

FURTHER READING: *The Benny Hill Story* – John Smith (London: W.H. Allen, 1988); *Saucy Boy: The Revealing Life Story Of Benny Hill* – Leonard Hill (London: Grafton, 1992); *Benny: The True Story By His Best Friend* – Dennis Kirkland with Hilary Bonner (London: Smith Gryphon, 1992); *The Benny Hill Story* – Margaret Forwood (London: Robson Books, 1992); *Star Turns: The*

Life And Times Of Benny Hill & Frankie Howerd – Barry Took (London: Weidenfeld & Nicolson, 1992); *Funny Peculiar: The True Story Of Benny Hill* – Mark Lewisohn (London: Pan, 2003).

Dame Wendy Hiller
Born August 15, 1912
Died May 14, 2003
Theatrical dame. Wendy Margaret Hiller was born in Bramhall, Cheshire, the daughter of Frank Watkin Hiller, a Manchester cotton manufacturer, and Marie Elizabeth Stone. She was sent to Winceby House School in Bexhill, Sussex, to rid her of her Mancunian accent. The reason for the elocution was not to aid a stage career but because it was thought that a regional accent would count against her chances of marrying. In fact she married a northern research chemist and schoolmaster, Ronald Gow (b. Heaton Moor, November 1, 1897, d. April 27, 1993) by whom she had a son and a daughter, who had written *Love On The Dole*, the 1934 play about the Depression which brought her sudden fame as Sarah Hardcastle. Her work was seen by George Bernard Shaw who, in July 1936, invited her to perform in two of his plays at the Malvern Festival, *Pygmalion* (as Eliza Doolittle) and *Saint Joan* (in the title role). She gained a reputation by appearing in Shavian plays and films, in Ibsen, and in modern adaptations (some by her husband) of novels by Walter Greenwood, Thomas Hardy, Henry James, and others. She made her movie début in *Lancashire Luck* (1937) playing Betty Lovejoy. Her second film was *Pygmalion* (1938) for which she was nominated for a Best Actress Oscar (losing out to Bette Davis in *Jezebel*). Her other films included: *Sons And Lovers* (1960), Alice More in *A Man For All Seasons* (1966) for which she was nominated for a Best Supporting Actress Oscar (she was beaten by Sandy Dennis for

Who's Afraid Of Virginia Woolf? but collected Paul Scofield's Best Actor Oscar for him), *Murder On The Orient Express* (1974) as the Countess, David Lynch's *The Elephant Man* (1980), with John Hurt, and *The Lonely Passion Of Judith Hearne* (1987). She won a Best Supporting Actress Oscar for her performance in Terence Rattigan's *Separate Tables* (1958) although she was not present at the ceremony on April 6, 1959 and the producer Harold Hecht collected the gong. She later said, "All you could see of me in the picture was the back of my head. Unless they give some award for acting with one's back to the camera, I don't see how I could have won. They cut my two best scenes and they gave one to Rita Hayworth . . . I am sure the honour is very nice. I hope this award means cash – hard cash. I want lots of lovely offers to go filming in Hollywood, preferably so I can avoid all the horrid cold [in England]." She was appointed OBE in 1971 and DBE in 1975. Asked by Sheridan Morley how she wanted to be remembered, if at all, she said, "Oh, I think a little posterity must always be nice. After I'm dead I'll probably be a cult and they'll have entire seasons of me at the National Film Theatre. Thank God I won't have to watch them all."
CAUSE: She spent much of the last decade of her life as an invalid cared for by her children. She died in Beaconsfeld, Buckinghamshire.

Pat Hingle
(MARTIN PATTERSON HINGLE)
Born July 19, 1924
Died January 3, 2009
Everyman. Born in Miami, Florida, the son of a building contractor who died when his son was young, Hingle, his mother and two siblings travelled across the States as she looked for work. He enrolled in the University of Texas but dropped out to enlist in the

navy during the Second World War. Demobbed in 1946, he went back to university and joined a drama club. However, he was recalled to service during the Korean War. In the early Fifties he moved to New York and joined the Actors Studio where he landed roles on stage and in film and television. While waiting for his big break he worked as a Bible salesman, playground attendant, farmhand, usher, waiter and a clerk at Bloomingdale's. Early films included *On The Waterfront* (1954) as the barman Jocko who winds up Marlon Brando and *No Down Payment* (1957) as Herman Kreitzer. In 1954–55 he played Gooper in Tennessee Williams's *Cat On A Hot Tin Roof* on Broadway. In 1957 he appeared in *The Strange One* reprising a 1953 theatre role, winning acclaim for both performances. In 1959 while appearing in the Archibald MacLeish play *J.B.* he fell down a lift shaft and had to have the little finger on his left hand amputated. He played a variety of parts including a gay J. Edgar Hoover in the HBO movie *Citizen Cohn* (1992) and Warren Beatty's father in the 1961 film *Splendor In The Grass*. "I can be a truck driver, a doctor, a lawyer, a hanging judge, whatever," he said. "And looking like I do has allowed me to make a good living in all kinds of media. It's a blessing and I'm aware of it." He was Police Commissioner Gordon in the *Batman* films, beginning in 1989 and played Bobo Justus the sadistic gangster who stubbed out a cigar on Anjelica Huston's hand in *The Grifters* (1990). On June 3, 1947 he married Alyce F. Dorsey and they had three children, Bill Hingle, Jody Smith and Molly Mantione. The marriage ended in divorce and on 25 October 1979 he married Julia Wright.
CAUSE: Hingle died at his home in Carolina Beach, North Carolina aged 84. The cause was myelodysplasia, a blood disorder, with which he was diagnosed in November 2006.

Dame Thora Hird
Born May 28, 1911
Died March 15, 2003
Grande dame. Born in Morecambe, Lancashire, the daughter of James Henry Hird the manager of the Royalty Theatre, Morecambe, where she began her career in 1931, and Mary Jane Mayor. She appeared in rep until making her London début in 1944. Best known in her later years for her work on religious programmes, sitcoms (*Last Of The Summer Wine*, etc) and with Alan Bennett, she appeared in several films. She made her début in *The Big Blockade* (1940) playing a German barmaid and went on to appear in *48 Hours* (1942) as Ivy Dawking, *The Weaker Sex* (1948) as Mrs Gaye, *The Entertainer* (1960) as Ada Lapford, *A Kind Of Loving* (1962) as Mrs Rothwell, *Term Of Trial* (1962) as Mrs Taylor, *Rattle Of A Simple Man* (1964) as Mrs Winthram and *The Nightcomers* (1972) as Mrs Grose. In 1988 she won a Best TV Actress BAFTA as Doris for Alan Bennett's monologue in *A Cream Cracker Under The Settee* (1987). On May 3, 1937, she married the musician James 'Scottie' Scott (d. 1994) by whom she had one daughter Janette (who was engaged to Sir David Frost and married Mel Tormé). She was made OBE in 1983 and created DBE ten years later.
CAUSE: She died aged 91 in Brinsworth House, Twickenham, Middlesex, following a stroke.

Alfred Hitchcock
Born August 13, 1899
Died April 29, 1980
Nightmare creator. Born at 517 Leytonstone High Road, east London, the second son and youngest of three children, Alfred Joseph Hitchcock was educated at St Ignatius College, Stamford Hill, London, (from October 5, 1910, until July 25, 1913) and this Jesuitical upbringing undoubtedly influenced much of his outlook on life. When

Hitchcock was five his father (who died on December 12, 1914) arranged to have him locked up in a police station for ten minutes as a punishment for being naughty. Hitch joined the Islington Film Studios in November 1920 and five years later directed his first film, *The Pleasure Garden* (1925). His interest in matters criminal developed as a boy, when he was in the habit of attending trials at the Old Bailey. He used this background and his knowledge of Jack the Ripper to make his first thriller, *The Lodger* (1926). It was also the first time he took a cameo part in a movie, a quirk that he was to maintain throughout his film-making career. Three years later, he showed the first signs of the talent and promise that would arrive in later years when he made *Blackmail* (1929). In the Thirties Hitchcock became the master of the suspense thriller. He found great satisfaction in carefully crafting each film and really thought the actual execution to be a bore. His famous comment "Actors should be treated like cattle" only meant that they were there to bring to life his vision and for no other reason. His success in films such as *The 39 Steps* (1935) and *Sabotage* (1936) inevitably meant that Hollywood came a-calling and in 1939 he set off for Tinseltown, where he directed *Rebecca* (1940). It won a Best Film Oscar. Hitchcock made his life in Hollywood although he didn't renounce British citizenship until April 20, 1955. From the mid-Forties Hitchcock's name became a by-word for well-crafted suspense-laden movies. He made a string of memorable thrillers, including *Spellbound* (1945), *Dial M For Murder* (1954), *Rear Window* (1954), *To Catch A Thief* (1955) *North By Northwest* (1959) and *The Birds* (1963). In the latter, the creatures that follow the children have no shadows. This was because they were painted on to the celluloid after the scene was shot. One scene in the film nearly resulted in female lead

Tippi Hedren losing an eye. She was placed in a small room (her attic on film) and numerous birds were tied to her so they could not fly away. They then began to peck as she flapped her arms to shush them away though, of course, the cords prevented them from escaping. "Finally, one gull decided to perch on my eyelid," Hedren recalled, "producing a deep gash and just missing my eyeball. I became hysterical." As a result of the incident, Hedren collapsed and shooting was abandoned for a week to allow her to recover. This period also saw the production of *Marnie* (1964), *Torn Curtain* (1966) and *Frenzy* (1971). His most famous feature is probably *Psycho* (1960), the story of the mother-fixated Norman Bates, proprietor of the Bates Motel. It is claimed by amateur film psychologists that Hitchcock had a fascination for glacial blondes such as Grace Kelly and Tippi Hedren but because he believed they would never be physically interested in him, he sought to 'punish' them, exacting his revenge by having dastardly things happen to them in his films. A notorious practical joker, some of his japes definitely went a little too far. One revolved around a rather brash cameraman who boasted he could stay alone in the studio all night and not be afraid. Hitchcock heard about it and bet the man he would not stay. The wager was made and Hitchcock arranged for the man to be handcuffed to a camera just before the studio was locked for the night. As he was leaving, Hitchcock handed the man a bottle of brandy to keep his spirits up. Unbeknownst to this latest victim of a Hitchcockian jape, the bottle was laced with a very strong laxative. When the unfortunate man was discovered in the morning he was in tears, as he had badly despoiled himself. On December 2, 1926, Hitchcock married Alma Reville (b. 69 Caroline Street, Nottingham, August 14, 1899, d. 1982) and they had one daughter, actress Patricia (b. 153 Cromwell Road, London, July 7, 1928). By the time he was 40 years old Hitchcock had decided to become celibate, although that decision may have been caused by his diabetes. He was created an honorary KBE in the 1980 New Year's Honours List. The devoutly Catholic Hitchcock donated £20,000 for a chapel to be built at the Jesuit school of the present author. The gift was kept a secret until after his death. CAUSE: He died at 9.17am in Beverly Hills, California, of an enlarged heart and liver and kidney failure.

FURTHER READING: *Hitch: The Life And Work Of Alfred Hitchcock* – John Russell Taylor (London: Faber & Faber, 1978); *The Art Of Alfred Hitchcock* – Donald Spoto (New York: Dolphin, 1979); *The Dark Side Of Genius: The Life Of Alfred Hitchcock* – Donald Spoto (New York: Ballantine, 1983).

Valerie Hobson

Born April 14, 1917
Died November 13, 1998
Faithful wife. Born in Larne, County Antrim, Ireland, the daughter of a Royal Navy captain, Valerie Babette Louise Hobson seemed destined for the stage from the age of two when she would wrap herself in a towel and pretend to be the Queen of Sheba. She began to learn ballet aged five but fell victim to scarlet fever, necessitating a lengthy spell of convalescence. When she got out of bed again she was too tall for ballet. She was educated at RADA and became a stalwart of the British and Hollywood cinema, appearing in *Two Hearts In Waltz Time* (1934) as Susie, *Oh, What A Night* (1935) as Susan, *Chinatown Squad* (1935) as Janet Baker, *The Mystery Of Edwin Drood* (1935) as Helena Landless, *Bride Of Frankenstein* (1935) as Elizabeth Frankenstein, *Werewolf Of London* (1935) as Lisa Glendon, *No Escape* (1936) as Laura Anstey, *When Thief Meets Thief* (1937) as Glory Fane,

The Drum (1938) as Mrs Carruthers, *Q Planes* (1939) as Kay Lawrence, *Sabotage Agent* (1943) as Maruschka Brunn, *Great Expectations* (1946), *Blanche Fury* (1947) as Blanche Fury, *Kind Hearts And Coronets* (1949) as Edith, *Meet Me Tonight* (1952) as Stella Cartwright, *The Card* (1952) as Countess of Chell, *Background* (1953) as Barbie Lomax and *Monsieur Ripois* (1954) as Catherine. "I've thought this out carefully, why I went on the stage. Why I needed an audience. I was a very plain, wishy-washy child. Large, wistful eyes. A real gumdrop. Awful. My sister was exquisite. She could never believe this pasty-faced mouse was her sister. Everybody called me Monkey." In 1954 she appeared in *The King & I* at Drury Lane. That year she retired from acting to marry (on December 31) rising Conservative politician John Profumo. (She had previously been married to Anthony Havelock-Allan by whom she had two sons, Simon and Mark. Simon had been born severely mentally disabled and was put in a home, where he died.) It seemed as if Profumo might be destined for Number 10 . . . then it all came crashing down. On July 8, 1961, Profumo, by then War Minister, met good-time girl Christine Keeler at the swimming pool at Cliveden, home of Lord Astor. (She was naked at the time and Valerie Hobson handed her a towel to cover her modesty.) After that initial meeting, 'Jack' Profumo regularly enjoyed Keeler's favours, a generosity she also shared with Soviet naval attaché Evgeny Ivanov, with obvious implications for national security. The rumours of Profumo's affair with Keeler came to the ears of Labour MP Colonel George Wigg, who raised the matter under parliamentary privilege during a debate on the Vassall enquiry in which two journalists had been imprisoned for refusing to reveal their sources. The Home Secretary Henry Brooke refused to comment and criticised Labour for even raising the matter. Nonetheless, Profumo was roused from his Regents Park bed – the one he had once shared with Christine Keeler – and questioned by senior Tories over the allegations. Told that nothing less than a personal statement would satisfy his critics, Profumo stood at the Dispatch Box shortly after 11am on March 22, 1963, and, flanked by Harold Macmillan, Iain Macleod, R.A. Butler and the Attorney-General, blatantly lied to the House of Commons. Before a hushed House (it is Commons procedure that a member is not questioned or interrupted during a personal statement) Profumo denied any "impropriety whatsoever in my acquaintance with Miss Keeler". The lie was to destroy not only Profumo's political career and reputation but also help bring about the fall of the Tory government in the 1964 General Election. On June 4, 1963, Profumo resigned from the government and entered a life of charity working for the dregs of society in Toynbee Hall. Valerie Hobson publicly stood by her husband to the end.

CAUSE: She died in London of a heart attack, aged 81.

William Holden

(WILLIAM FRANKLIN BEEDLE, JR)
Born April 17, 1918
Found dead November 16, 1981
Golden boy. Born in O'Fallon, Illinois, the son of a wealthy family, Holden was noticed in an amateur college production and signed to Paramount. His first movie was *Prison Farm* (1938) but it was *Golden Boy* (1939) that first attracted critical acclaim, though the war abruptly interrupted the momentum of his career. After serving as an Army lieutenant, he appeared in *Dear Ruth* (1947) as Lieutenant William Seacroft. Director Billy Wilder saw something more than a pretty boy in Holden and cast him as the writer-chancer Joe Gillis in *Sunset Blvd.* (1950) after Montgomery Clift turned down the part. The film earned Holden

a Best Actor Oscar nomination. (When Ronald Reagan married Nancy Davis on March 4, 1952, Holden was best man.) Wilder also placed Holden in *Stalag 17* (1953) as Sefton, a cynical prisoner of war, a role that won the actor an Oscar. Within three years he was the highest paid performer in Hollywood and the number one box-office draw. He appeared in *The Country Girl* (1954) as Bernie Dodd, *The Bridges At Toko-Ri* (1954) as Lieutenant Harry Brubaker (USNR), *Executive Suite* (1954) as McDonald Walling, *Sabrina* (1954) as David Larrabee, *Love Is A Many-Splendored Thing* (1955) as Mark Elliott, *The Bridge On The River Kwai* (1957) as Shears (for which he was paid $300,000 plus 10% of the gross profits) and *The World Of Suzie Wong* (1960) as Robert Lomax. The Sixties saw Holden's popularity decrease and his drinking increase. The last 20 years of his life failed to produce anything like the performances of the Fifties. He occasionally showed flashes of brilliance, but for the most part concentrated on drinking and his on-off actress girlfriend Stefanie Powers. His final films included *The Wild Bunch* (1969) as Pike Bishop, *The Towering Inferno* (1974) as James Duncan, *Network* (1976) as Max Schumacher, for which he was nominated for an Oscar, *Damien: Omen II* (1978) as Richard Thorn, *Ashanti* (1979) as Jim Sandell, *When Time Ran Out . . .* (1980) as Shelby Gilmore, *The Earthling* (1980) as Patrick Foley and *S.O.B.* (1981) as Tim Culley. Holden was at times ridiculously tight with money and at other times foolishly generous. He had a passion for secrecy that bordered on paranoia and would nearly always settle lawsuits so that he wouldn't have to testify in court. On July 26, 1966, Holden was involved in a car accident in Prato, Italy, that resulted in the death of 42-year-old Valerio Giorgio Novelli. Holden had been driving at over 100mph at the time and on July 26, 1966, he was charged with manslaughter. On October 26, 1967, he was found guilty of manslaughter and sentenced *in absentia* to eight months in jail suspended. He also paid Novelli's widow $80,000. Holden married just once. His wife was actress Brenda Marshall (b. Negros, The Philippines, 1917, as Ardis Ankerson) and they tied the knot on July 13, 1941. They had two sons and divorced in 1973. CAUSE: "If somebody had said to me 'Holden's dead' I would have assumed that he had been gored by a water buffalo in Kenya, that he'd died in a plane crash approaching Hong Kong, that a crazed, jealous woman had shot him and he'd drowned in a swimming pool. But to be killed by a bottle of vodka and a night table – what a lousy fade-out for a great guy." Thus spake Billy Wilder when he heard of Holden's demise. William Holden lived on the fourth floor, number 43, of the 13-storey Shorecliff Towers, located at 535 Ocean Avenue, Santa Monica, California. He valued his privacy, barely acknowledging his neighbours, and that is perhaps why he died. Holden had not been seen by anyone for some time and so the building manager, Bill Martin, decided to investigate on Monday November 16, 1981. He discovered Holden in his bedroom. He was wearing only his pyjama jacket and had a 2½-inch gash on his forehead. He was also very dead and had been for some time, possibly at least four days. Two days later, Holden was autopsied by Dr Thomas T. Noguchi (the role model for TV's *Quincy, M.E.*) and assigned the case number 81-14582. Noguchi determined that Holden's blood alcohol level was .22. In California to be .10 was enough to be arrested for drink-driving (assuming you were in a car, of course . . .). Around Holden's body were several blood-soaked tissues and empty booze bottles. Noguchi deduced that in a drunken state

Holden had slipped, hit his head on the bedside table and attempted to mop up the blood. However, the alcohol prevented him from thinking straight and he passed out within ten minutes, dying within the half-hour. He had made no attempt to telephone for help. In accordance with his wishes, no funeral service was held and Holden's body was cremated and his ashes scattered on the ocean. He left Stefanie Powers $250,000 in his will. FURTHER READING: *Golden Boy: The Untold Story Of William Holden* – Bob Thomas (London: Weidenfeld & Nicolson, 1983).

Judy Holliday
(JUDITH TUVIM)
Born June 21, 1921
Died June 7, 1965
Blonde comedienne. Born in Lying In Hospital, 23rd Street & Second Avenue, New York, New York, shortly before midnight Holliday won a Best Actress Oscar for *Born Yesterday* (1950) and a Tony for *The Bells Are Ringing*, but never was a luvvie. "Acting is a very limited form of expression and those who take it seriously are very limited people," she once commented. Her films included *Winged Victory* (1944) as Ruth Miller, *Adam's Rib* (1949) as Doris Attinger, *The Marrying Kind* (1952) as Florence Keefer, *It Should Happen To You* (1954) as Gladys Glover, *The Solid Gold Cadillac* (1956) as Laura Partridge and *Bells Are Ringing* (1960) as Ella Peterson. When Judy was 20 years old she lost her virginity to Yetta Cohn, a female employee of the New York Police Department. A year or so later, Holliday had her first sexual experience with a man when schizophrenic English actor John Buckmaster (brother-in-law of Robert Morley and son of Gladys Cooper) raped her, or so Holliday claimed. Just how emotionally wrenching was Judy's rape? Well, she said she wanted to have sex with Buckmaster again, but that he ignored

her thereafter. She married Columbia Records executive David Oppenheim on January 4, 1948, and had one son, Jonathan Lewis (b. Doctors Hospital, New York, November 11, 1952). She was divorced by her husband in March 1957.

CAUSE: Judy underwent a mastectomy on October 12, 1960. In 1963 she was diagnosed with throat cancer, although her doctor didn't tell her the truth about her condition. Instead, she was told she had a curable disease similar to cancer for which the treatment was also similar to that for cancer. The disease became progressively worse and Judy was given heroin to ease her pain. On May 26, she was admitted to Mount Sinai Hospital, New York, where she died 12 days later at 5am, aged 43.

FURTHER READING: *Judy Holliday: An Intimate Life Story* – Gary Carey (London: Robson Books, 1983).

The Hollywood Kids

(LANCE HOWARD BROWNE)
Born September 18, 1955
Died May 9, 1994
(JOHN ALTON NICHOLS)
Born July 13, 1953
Died April 7, 1995
(JAMES ROBERT ROSE)
Born June 19, 1959
Died July 11, 1992

Premier modern day gossipists. Three young wannabes who lusted after Hollywood stardom but found they didn't have the requisite ability or luck to make it. What they did have was access to the hottest gossip in Tinseltown and began giving their own gossip sheet away on the streets around Melrose Avenue. Each issue contained a celebrity interview, a guide to who was hot and a number of 'blind items' in which the identity of the star was hidden by a pseudonym such as 'Missy Hot TV Star' or 'Mr Old Movie Hunk'. Their fame spread and they hosted their own radio show and wrote their own column in *Movieline* magazine for which they were paid

$1,000 per month. *Gilligan's Island* star Jim Backus commented: "Hedda and Louella would have been jokes except for their power. Thank God no one in Hollywood has that power. Now you have the Hollywood Kids as gossips. They're rather ridiculous, like those old bags were, but at least they have no power. Claws but no power!" The Hollywood Kids made no secret of their homosexuality. Jimmy was the first to succumb to the disease that was ravaging much of Hollywood. John and Lance were lovers and both were stricken with the deadly virus.

CAUSE: All three succumbed to AIDS in California. Jimmy, 33, died in Sacramento, Lance, 38, in Los Angeles and John, 41, in Alameda.

John Holmes

(JOHN CURTIS ESTES)
Born August 8, 1944
Died March 12, 1988

Huge porn star. Born in Ashville, Ohio, at the age of two his name was changed to John Curtis Holmes. Like many actors Holmes liked to spin a web of deceit to glamorise his background. In fact, he was something of a nerd at school, regularly studying the Bible and not, as he was to claim, sleeping with all the girls in his class bar three. It seems unlikely that Holmes lost his virginity before leaving home. Aged 16 he joined the army and spent two years serving Uncle Sam. Back in Los Angeles he fell into making porn films and soon became famous for the size of his penis – reportedly 14″, more likely 12″ or 10″. On his first shoot Holmes was paid $100 by cheque but it bounced and so in future he always demanded payment in cash. It is estimated he appeared in over 400 porn films becoming internationally famous for the Johnny Wadd detective series he made in the mid-Seventies. His films included *Sex Psycho* (1970), *Sex And The Single Vampire* (1970), *Doctor I'm Coming* (1970), *My Tongue Is Quick* (1971), *Blonde In Black Lace* (1971),

Double Exposure (1972), *Ride A Cocked Horse* (1973), *Johnny Wadd* (1973) as Johnny Wadd, *Suburban Satanist* (1974) as Barney, *Confessions Of A Teenage Peanut Butter Freak* (1974), *Tell Them Johnny Wadd Is Here* (1975) as Johnny Wadd, *Personal Services* (1975) as B.C. Buzzard, *In Memory Of Connie* (1975), *Fantasm* (1975) as Neptune, *Around The World With Johnny Wadd* (1975), *Tapestry Of Passion* (1976), *Little Orphan Dusty* (1976), *Cheri* (1976), *Young, Hot'N'Lusty Teenage Cruisers* (1977), *Hard Soap, Hard Soap* (1977), *Flesh Of The Lotus* (1977), *Female Athletes* (1977), *Fantastic Orgy* (1977), *I Am Always Ready* (1978), *Blonde Fire* (1978) as Johnny Wadd, *Superstar John Holmes* (1979), *Dracula Sucks* (1979), *Anal Ultra Vixens* (1979), *Inside Desiree Cousteau* (1979), *Lust Vegas Joyride* (1980), *Let Me Count The Lays* (1980), *Swedish Erotica 6* (1981), *Homecoming* (1981), *Sweet Alice* (1983), *The Private Pleasures Of John C. Holmes* (1983), his only gay feature film, *Nasty Nurses* (1983), *Passion Pit* (1985), *The Good, The Bad And The Horny* (1985), *Erotic Gold* (1985), *Saturday Night Beaver* (1986), *Return Of Johnny Wadd* (1987) and *Ginger Lynn The Movie* (1988). Away from the camera Holmes became a cocaine addict (taking so much it made his nose bleed) and this caused his world to come tumbling down on July 1, 1981. At 8763 Wonderland Drive, Laurel Canyon, four people were discovered brutally murdered and a fifth maimed beyond recognition. On November 30, 1981, Holmes was arrested and charged with murder when his palm print was discovered at the house above one of the victims. The prosecution contended the killings had been revenge for an armed robbery at the house of Holmes' club-owning drug dealer Adel Nasrallah, a.k.a. Eddie Nash, and his large black bodyguard Gregory Diles. Holmes had double-crossed his dealer, agreeing to split any profits with the robbers.

Holmes refused to identify the killers and spent 110 days in prison on contempt charges. In prison he made pots of money from either drug dealing or homosexual acts. Some believe he contracted the HIV virus in jail. However, he was also addicted to drugs, coprophilia and other forms of deviant sex with transsexuals, low-rent prostitutes and very young girls, so who really knows. He also had anal sex with porn star Joseph Yale who died of AIDS, and away from the camera preferred men sexually. Holmes was certainly HIV+ by April 1986 and probably earlier, during which time he carried on working in porn films. One unidentified Italian actress (Moana Pozzi?) reputedly died of AIDS after working with Holmes. In October 1986 Holmes underwent an operation for piles. He was twice married. In 1968 he married nurse Sharon Gebenini. They were divorced in 1984. In Las Vegas on January 23, 1987, he wed brunette ex-porn star Laurie Rose (b. 1963) who worked under the name Misty Dawn and had a penchant for anal sex. Her first words on seeing Holmes were "I can't wait to get that man up my ass." The central character in the film *Boogie Nights* (1997) was supposedly based on Holmes.

CAUSE: Holmes died aged 43 of pneumonia and encephalitis caused by AIDS in room 101a of the Veterans' Administration Hospital, Plummer Street, Sepulveda, California. He was cremated at Forest Lawn Memorial-Parks, 1712 South Glendale Avenue, Glendale, California 91209.

Oscar Homolka
Born August 12, 1898
Died January 27, 1978
Character villain. Born in Vienna, the stocky, bushy-eyebrowed Homolka began his career, as so many film actors did, on stage. He trod the boards in Germany and Austria before making his move into movies. He fled Europe when Hitler rose to power and settled

in America, where he carved a niche for himself playing villains. His films include *Dreyfus* (1930) as Major Ferdinand Walsin-Esterhazy, *Sabotage* (1936) as Carl Verloct, *Ebb Tide* (1937) as Captain Therbecke, *The Dreyfus Case* (1940) again as Major Ferdinand Walsin-Esterhazy, *Seven Sinners* (1940) as Mr Antro, *The Invisible Woman* (1940) as Blackie Cole, *I Remember Mama* (1948) as Uncle Chris, for which he was nominated for a Best Supporting Actor Oscar, *Anna Lucasta* (1949) as Joe Lucasta, *Top Secret* (1952) as Zekov, *The Seven Year Itch* (1955) as Dr Brubaker, *War And Peace* (1956) as General Kutuzov, *A Farewell To Arms* (1957) as Dr Emerich, *The Key* (1958) as Van Dam, *Mr Sardonicus* (1961) as Krull, *The Long Ships* (1963) as Krok, *Funeral In Berlin* (1966) as Colonel Stok, *The Happening* (1967) as Sam, *The Madwoman Of Chaillot* (1969) as the Commissar, *Song Of Norway* (1970) as Engstrand, *The Executioner* (1970) as Racovsky and his final film *The Tamarind Seed* (1974) as General Golitsyn. A regular on television, he was married four times: to Grete Mosheim, Florence Meyer by whom he had two sons, Baroness Vally Hatvany and actress Joan Tetzel (b. June 21, 1923) from 1949 until her death on October 31, 1977.
CAUSE: He died in Sussex aged 79 from pneumonia.

Morag Hood

Born December 12, 1942
Died October 5, 2002
TV heroine. Born in Glasgow, the daughter of a carpenter who worked in local theatres and cinemas, Morag Hood was educated at Bellahouston Academy, Glasgow. At Glasgow University she read English, French and Economics, and set up *Roundup*, a current affairs programme for teenagers shown on Scottish Television. It was her portrayal of Natasha Rostova in the television adaptation of Tolstoy's epic novel *War And Peace* in 1972 that imprinted her face on the public consciousness. *War And Peace*, which co-starred Alan Dobie and Anthony Hopkins, took three years to produce, with location filming in Yugoslavia and extensive special effects work. In total the series lasted 15 hours, eight hours longer than the longest film version ever made – too long in the opinion of most viewers. Morag Hood was in her late twenties and largely unknown when she was cast from 1,000 actresses who applied. Her success was reflected in a boom in the number of babies christened Natasha. As well as Natasha, Morag Hood took minor roles in a number of television serials, including *Dr Finlay's Casebook*, *Z-Cars* and *Coronation Street*. In 1979, she played the forthright Maggie Drum in *The Camerons*, a television serial about 20 years in the life of a Scottish family in late Victorian times. She also appeared on television in *Square Mile Of Murder*, *Breeze Anstey*, *Keep Smiling*, *The Personal Touch* and *Persuasion*. Her films were few and far between. She appeared in *Wuthering Heights* (1970) as Frances, *Diversions* (1980) and *Ill Fares The Land* (1981) as Barclay. She was unmarried.
CAUSE: She died aged 59 from cancer in a London hospice.

Bob Hope

Born May 29, 1903
Died July 27, 2003
Cinematic comedian. Leslie Townes (birth register spells name Towns) Hope was born the fifth of seven sons to the alcoholic William Henry Hope (b. London, 1870, d. 1937) and Avis Townes (b. Cardiff, Wales, 1875, d. Cleveland, Ohio, January 22, 1934 of cancer) in the south London suburb of Eltham but went on to become an American icon and one of its richest men with a fortune guestimated to be $400,000,000. His siblings were: Ivor (b. Monmouthshire, Wales, 1892, d. Gates Mill, Ohio, 1969, of a heart attack), James Francis (b.

Monmouthshire, Wales, 1893), Emily (b. Monmouthshire, Wales, July 1895, d. 1899 of diphtheria), Frederick Charles (b. Barry, 1897), William John 'Jack' (b. 1899, d. Boston, Massachusetts, August 6, 1962 of cancer), Sidney (b. 1905, d. Ridgefield Corners, Ohio, 1946 of cancer) and George Percy (b. Cleveland, Ohio, 1909, d. 1969 of cancer). Bob Hope was almost as famous for his uniquely shaped nose which became the butt of many a joke in his films. He once said, "It was my mother who discovered my nose. 'Call back the doctor,' she cried. 'He's taken the baby and left the stork.'" In March 1908 Hope left England aged four bound for Cleveland, Ohio. At school kids called him 'Hopelessly' and then 'Hopeless' after he announced his name as "Hope, Leslie". On December 20, 1920, he became an American citizen. While singing at a family gathering his voice cracked causing everyone to laugh. From that moment, Hope resolved to be a funny man. After high school he had a short stint as an amateur boxer using the nom de punch Packie East. He also briefly ran a dance school. 5'10" Hope and partner George Byrne joined Fatty Arbuckle's touring company. They worked in black face for a time. He made his Broadway début in 1927 in *Sidewalks Of New York*. Splitting from Byrne in 1928, he became a stand-up comedian changing his name to Lester T. Hope but success eluded him and soon he was $4,000 in debt. Eventually, he became emcee at a small nightclub. That led to a six-month contract at Stratford Theater. He adopted the name Bob after the agent Bob O'Donnell. He made his feature film début in 1938, the same year he got his own radio series which lasted for 1,145 programmes. He had appeared in some shorts from *Going Spanish* in 1934. His best-known films are the *Road To . . .* series. Co-starring with Dorothy Lamour and his friend Bing Crosby,

the first was *Road To Singapore* (1940) which began filming in November 1939 and premièred on April 13, 1940 at the Paramount Theater in New York. The trio made seven films in the series: *Zanzibar* (1941), *Morocco* (1942), *Utopia* (1945), *Rio* (1948), *Bali* (1952) and *Hong Kong* (1962). Hope and Crosby had met in 1932 and became firm friends – unusually, on stage as well as off. Of Gary Crosby's book claiming that his father tortured him, Hope commented, "Bing used to sing to me too, but I didn't feel I had to write a book about it!" Hope tried to enlist in the army during the war but was told that he would be more useful entertaining the troops. Hope's troupe became a staple diet of army life. He made six overseas tours during the Second World War and in December 1990 travelled to Saudi Arabia to entertain troops fighting in Operation Desert Storm. His conservative stand on Vietnam did not win him many friends. In the Seventies Chevy Chase commented, "Bob Hope is still about as funny as he ever was. I just never thought Bob Hope was that funny in the first place." Hope employed an army of writers – the first one, Al Boasberg, in October 1929. Groucho Marx once commented that Hope wasn't at all funny. He was just a translator of funny lines written for him. Hope was friendly with every American president – Democrat and Republican – from Eisenhower to Reagan. He was also equally famous for his love of golf, hosting the annual Bob Hope Desert Classic in Palm Springs. The tournament raised more than $10,000,000 for charities. Combining his two loves, he once said of playing golf with President Jerry Ford: "He draws a big crowd – you know how people gather at the scene of an accident." Hope's wisecracking extended to his private life. "I hate to see my name in print and I do everything I can to avoid interviews. If there's any publicity about me, I want

it to come naturally. At least that's what I tell my eight press agents."
In 1990 Hope surprised many, particularly his liberal antagonists, by coming out in favour of gun control. "I am not going to stop until Congress does something about this . . . Mandatory gun registration is a step in the right direction." Hope received more than 1,000 awards and citations for his humanitarian and professional efforts. His signature tune was 'Thanks For The Memory' which was the way he signed autographs. In retirement he spent most of his time at a 25,000 square foot home in Palm Springs. "George Burns and I, for excitement on a Saturday night, sit around and see whose leg falls asleep first." In 1998 Hope was awarded an honorary knighthood. His films included: *The Big Broadcast Of 1938* (1938), *College Swing* (1938), *Give Me A Sailor* (1938), *Thanks For The Memory* (1938), *Never Say Die* (1939), *Some Like It Hot* (1939), *The Cat And The Canary* (1939), *The Ghost Breakers* (1940), *Caught In The Draft* (1941), *Nothing But The Truth* (1941), *Louisiana Purchase* (1941), *My Favorite Blonde* (1942), *Star Spangled Rhythm* (1942), *They Got Me Covered* (1942), *Let's Face It* (1943), *The Princess And The Pirate* (1944), *Monsieur Beaucaire* (1946), *My Favorite Brunette* (1947), *Where There's Life* (1947), *Variety Girl* (1947), *The Paleface* (1948), *Sorrowful Jones* (1948), *The Great Lover* (1949), *Fancy Pants* (1950), *The Lemon Drop Kid* (1951), *My Favorite Spy* (1951), *Son Of Paleface* (1952), *Off Limits* (1953), *Here Come The Girls* (1953), *Casanova's Big Night* (1954), *The Seven Little Foys* (1954), *That Certain Feeling* (1956), *The Iron Petticoat* (1956), *Beau James* (1957), *Paris Holiday* (1958), *Alias Jesse James* (1959), *The Facts Of Life* (1960), *Bachelor In Paradise* (1961), *Critic's Choice* (1963), *Call Me Bwana* (1963), *A Global Affair* (1964), *I'll Take Sweden* (1965), *Boy, Did I Get A Wrong Number!* (1966), *The Oscar*

(1966), *Eight On The Lam* (1967), *The Private Navy Of Sergeant O'Farrell* (1968), *How To Commit Marriage* (1969), *Cancel My Reservation* (1972), *The Muppet Movie* (1979), *Masterpiece Of Murder* (1985), *The Best Show In Town* (1989) and *Entertaining The Troops* (1989). A mystery surrounds Bob Hope's marital status. According to all the authorised biographies, on February 19, 1934, Bob Hope married Dolores Reade (b. New York, May 27, 1909) in the Catholic church in Erie, Pennsylvania, after a whirlwind two-month romance. However, there is no record of Bob Hope marrying Dolores Reade in Erie on that date or any other for that matter. There *is* a record of Leslie T. Hope, a salesman of 3323 Yorkshire Road, Cleveland, Ohio, marrying Grace Louise Troxell, a secretary of 642 West 64th Street, Chicago, Illinois, in Erie on January 25, 1933. Grace Louise Troxell was Hope's Vaudeville partner and was still appearing with him in his act in July 1934 according to the *New York Herald Tribune*, five months after he supposedly married Dolores Reade. Following her divorce from Hope (although when this happened, no one knows) Troxell married David Halper, a Chicago bookmaker. Here the story takes another twist. After she married Halper, Troxell gave birth to a daughter. For years that daughter received a monthly cheque from Bob Hope. In the Eighties Hope's former publicist wrote a biography of him that omitted the first marriage and child support though he admitted that he was aware of both. On August 4, 1934 the *New York Herald Tribune* ran a story announcing Bob Hope's engagement to Dolores Reade. Milton Berle, the comedian, attended the nuptials which he said occurred in a Catholic church in Manhattan sometime in autumn 1934 or spring 1935. Berle quipped that he would not go to a wedding in Erie, Pennsylvania even if the Pope was getting married. Whenever they wed the Hopes had a happy marriage. They adopted four children Linda Theresa (b. July 1939), Tony Reade (b. 1940), and brother and sister Honora Avis Mary and (William) Kelly Francis.

CAUSE: Bob Hope died aged 100 at his home in Toluca Lake, California, of pneumonia.

FURTHER READING: *I Never Left Home* – Bob Hope with Carroll Carroll (New York: Simon & Schuster, 1944); *Have Tux, Will Travel* – Bob Hope as told to Pete Martin (New York: Simon & Schuster, 1953); *Bob Hope* – Joe Morella, Edward Z. Epstein & Eleanor Clark (New York: Arlington House, 1973); *Bob Hope: Portrait Of A Superstar* – Charles Thompson (London: Fontana, 1981); *Bob Hope A Life In Comedy* – William Faith (New York: G.P. Putnam, 1982); *Bob Hope: A Comic Life* – Pamela Trescott (New York: Acropolis, 1985); *Don't Shoot, It's Only Me* – Bob Hope with Melville Shavelson (New York: G.P. Putnam, 1990); *The Secret Life Of Bob Hope* – Arthur Marx (1993).

Miriam Hopkins

Born October 18, 1902
Died October 9, 1972
Diminutive beauty. Born in Bainbridge, Georgia, 5'2" Ellen Miriam Hopkins was educated at Syracuse University and wanted to become a ballerina, but a broken ankle forced her to reconsider and she joined a revue as a chorine in 1921. Two years later, she became a successful Broadway actress and signed a contract with Paramount on June 25, 1930, making her film début in *Fast And Loose* (1930) as Marion Lenox. In 1935 she signed for Goldwyn and, four years later to Warner, where she feuded with Bette Davis who said, "Miriam is a perfectly charming woman socially. Working with her is another story." Her star fell in the Forties and she returned to Broadway, making the occasional film. Her movies included *Dr Jekyll And Mr Hyde* (1931) as Ivy

Pearson, *24 Hours* (1931) as Rosie Duggan, *World And The Flesh* (1932) as Maria Yaskaya, *Trouble In Paradise* (1932) as Lily Vautier, *Design For Living* (1933) as Gilda Farrell, *She Loves Me Not* (1934) as Curly Flagg, *The Richest Girl In The World* (1934) as Dorothy Hunter, *Splendor* (1935) as Phyllis Manning Lorrimore, *Barbary Coast* (1935) as Mary 'Swan' Rutledge, the lead in *Becky Sharp* (1935) for which she was nominated for an Oscar, *These Three* (1936) as Martha Dobie, *Men Are Not Gods* (1936) as Ann Williams, *The Old Maid* (1939) as Delia Lovell Ralston, *Old Acquaintance* (1943) as Mildred Drake, *The Mating Season* (1951) as Fran Carleton, *Carrie* (1952) as Julie Hurstwood, *Fanny Hill* (1964) as Mrs Maude Brown and *Savage Intruder* (1968). She married four times. On May 11, 1926, she married actor Brandon Peters. On June 2, 1928, she married Austin 'Billy' Parker before her divorce from Peters had come through. They divorced in 1931. On September 4, 1937, she eloped to Yuma, Arizona, with Anatole Litvak. They divorced on October 11, 1939. In 1945 she married journalist Ray Brock but that marriage only lasted six years. Her lovers included Maurice Chevalier, Bing Crosby, John Gilbert, William Randolph Hearst, Frederic March, Robert Montgomery, Franchot Tone and King Vidor. She once said, "When I can't sleep, I don't count sheep. I count lovers and by the time I reach 38 or 39 I'm asleep."

CAUSE: She died aged 69 in New York of a heart attack. She was buried in Bainbridge, Georgia.

Hedda Hopper

(ELDA FURRY)
Born May 2, 1885
Died February 1, 1966
Bitchy old-time gossip. With her rival Louella O. Parsons, gossip columnist Hedda Hopper was one of the most hated and feared people in Hollywood. If the pen is indeed mightier than the

sword, then Hedda wielded hers with great ferocity. It was believed by many the reason for her vitriol was to 'punish' successful actors, Hedda having failed to make the grade herself as a star, although she appeared in nearly 150 films. Born in Hollidaysburg, Pennsylvania, the daughter of a butcher, 5'7" Hedda Hopper used a number of names, calling herself Elda Curry, Ella Furry and Elda Millar before marrying DeWolf Hopper on May 8, 1913, in New York. Her ambition was to be a theatre actress and she travelled to New York to further her dreams. She appeared in a number of plays, but usually before they hit Broadway or she joined the cast for the touring production. Her acting career was temporarily halted by the birth of her son, Bill, on January 26, 1915. (He went on to play Detective Paul Drake in the TV series *Perry Mason*.) That year DeWolf tried his hand at films for the newly formed Triangle Company but his stage technique let him down somewhat. It was his wife's turn and Hedda made her début in *The Battle Of Hearts* (1916) earning a $100 a week contract in the process. She appeared in many 'vampy' roles in films including *Nearly Married* (1917), *The Beloved Traitor* (1918), *Isle Of Conquest* (1919) and *Women Men Marry* (1922) before being downgraded to supporting parts. In 1922 she and her husband divorced and Hedda became a regular on the Hollywood social scene. Her brief appearances in innumerable films earned her the nickname 'The Queen of Quickies'. In 1936 she began a radio show detailing snippets of Hollywood gossip. A recent trip to England had left her speaking with a pronounced English accent. The station was not impressed and she was fired. Tenacious to the end, Hedda persevered and landed another show. She remarked: "I wasn't allowed to speak while my husband was alive, and since he's gone, no one's been able to shut me up." In

1937 Esquire Feature Syndicate signed her up to write a newspaper gossip column. Her first attempts appeared in 13 newspapers. One of the first newspapers to carry her work, from February 14, 1938, was the *Los Angeles Times* owned by the powerful press baron William Randolph Hearst. For almost the next 30 years she wrote for dozens of newspapers, detailing the lives, affairs and careers of Hollywood stars. Her columns were so successful she was able to afford a splendid home, which she called "The House That Fear Built". She became notorious for her rivalry with Louella O. Parsons, her feuds with, among others, the actress Constance Bennett and society queen Elsa Maxwell, and her enormous collection of hats. Hopper took a dislike to people for the pettiest reasons, but for the most part Hollywood was too scared to protest too vociferously. Occasionally, one star hit back. Hedda disliked Elizabeth Taylor for falling in love with Eddie Fisher and thus bringing about his divorce from Debbie Reynolds. When Michael Wilding married Taylor he came into the firing line as well. Hedda ordered Taylor and Wilding to visit her at home and tried to stop their wedding by saying he was too old for her (he was almost 20 years her senior) and that he was a homosexual. Taylor and Wilding repaired to the home of Wilding's friend Stewart Granger and related what had happened. Granger was furious, rang Hopper and let her have it with both barrels. "I think you're a monumental bitch. How bloody dare you accuse a friend of mine of being a queer? You raddled, dried up, frustrated old cunt." Although Hedda became friends again with Taylor and Wilding, she used every opportunity to castigate Granger. Fellow British actor Ray Milland was also not a fan. He opined: "She was a venomous, vicious and pathological liar and quite stupid." After the Forties she rarely appeared on screen and when

she did she usually played herself, as she did in *Breakfast In Hollywood* (1946), *Sunset Blvd.* (1950), *The Patsy* (1964) and *The Oscar* (1966).
CAUSE: Aged 80, she died of double pneumonia in Cedars of Lebanon Hospital, Los Angeles, California.
FURTHER READING: *Hedda And Louella* – George Eells (London: W.H. Allen, 1972).

Leslie Howard

(LESLIE HOWARD STAINER)
Born April 3, 1893
Died June 1, 1943
Quintessentially English. Born in London, the son of Hungarian immigrants, he was educated at Dulwich College. He became a bank clerk until the outbreak of war. Serving in World War I he suffered from shell shock and was invalided home. He began acting as a form of therapy and made his film début in *The Heroine Of Mons* (1914). He moved to America and there his career really took off, reaching its apogee playing Ashley Wilkes in *Gone With The Wind* (1939) alongside Clark Gable and Vivien Leigh. Actually, Howard rarely met Gable since their scenes did not coincide and each man was on set at different times. The 6' Howard's other films included *Secrets* (1933) as John Carlton, *Captured* (1933) as Captain Fred Allison, *Of Human Bondage* (1934) as Philip Carey, *British Agent* (1934) as Stephen Locke, Sir Alexander Korda's *The Scarlet Pimpernel* (1935) as Sir Percy Blakeney, Romeo in *Romeo & Juliet* (1936), Professor Henry Higgins in *Pygmalion* (1938), *Pimpernel Smith* (1941) as Professor Horatio Smith and Spitfire inventor R.J. Mitchell in *The First Of The Few* (1942). Pipe-smoking Howard, a hypochondriac who could be surly and self-obsessed, married Ruth Evelyn Martin in 1916. They had one son, actor Ronald (b. London, April 7, 1918, d. February 16, 1997) and one daughter, Leslie Ruth (b.

October 1924). Both have written books about their father. Howard had a five-year long affair with Violette Cunnington (b. 1913, d. May 1943 of blood poisoning) whom he met on the set of *Pygmalion*.
CAUSE: At the outbreak of World War II he returned to the UK to do his bit. In May 1943 he set out on a propaganda mission to Spain and Portugal. He never made it back. His unarmed plane, a DC-3 Dakota on commercial flight 777A, was shot down by eight German Junkers. Mystery surrounds the trip. It was delayed supposedly because Howard had forgotten some silk stockings for one of his lady friends and finally took off at 7.35am. The flight should have taken seven hours and landed at Whitchurch, near Bristol, but disappeared at 10.54am when the Dutch pilot radioed that he was being attacked. No one on board stood a chance. The 13 passengers included a Winston Churchill lookalike, Alfred Chenhalls, who was Howard's accountant, plus three men the Nazis knew were helping the British war effort. Over 50 years after the crash, a young RAF squadron leader tracked down the Luftwaffe pilots and their leader, Oberleutnant Herbert Hintze, claimed the plane was shot down by accident. Another theory holds that Howard was on a secret mission and that was why the plane was downed. The greatest, and saddest, irony of it was that the British knew that the Germans were aware of the mission. They could not intervene because that would have alerted the Nazis to the fact their code had been deciphered.
FURTHER READING: *In Search Of My Father* – Ronald Howard (London: William Kimber, 1981).

Trevor Howard

(TREVOR WALLACE HOWARD-SMITH)
Born September 29, 1913
Died January 7, 1988
Authoritarian figure. Born in Cliftonville

and trained at RADA, Howard appeared on stage for a decade before making his film début. He went on to appear in over 70 films including romances, war films and spy movies. Robert Mitchum once opined, "You'll never catch Trevor Howard acting", but it wasn't an insult. Howard was not a luvvie in any sense of the word. In fact, he regarded acting as a game, but one that he was rather good at. He first made his name in David Lean's romantic weepie *Brief Encounter* (1945) as Alec Harvey, for which he was paid just £500. To add insult to injury, Howard was not invited to the press screening and the film's writer, Noël Coward, ignored him at the première because he didn't recognise him. Nonetheless, other members of the industry did recognise Howard and he starred in some riveting films. He was in *The Passionate Friends* (1949), *The Third Man* (1949) as Major Calloway, *The Heart Of The Matter* (1953), *Sons And Lovers* (1960) which earned him an Oscar nomination and was Captain Bligh to Marlon Brando's bizarre Fletcher Christian in *Mutiny On The Bounty* (1962). A heavy drinker, he preferred the description 'eccentric' to 'hell-raiser'. He was once arrested in Vienna for conducting the band in a restaurant while dressed in his army uniform from *The Third Man*. He married Helen Cherry in 1944. There were no children.
CAUSE: Howard died aged 74 in Bushey, Hertfordshire, after a short illness. He left £3,024,130.
FURTHER READING: *Trevor Howard: A Gentleman And A Player* – Vivienne Knight (London: Muller, Blond & White, 1986).

Frankie Howerd, OBE

(FRANCIS ALICK HOWARD)
Born March 6, 1917
Died Easter Sunday (April 19), 1992
Camp comic. Born in York's City Hospital, the elder son of three children of Frank Alfred William

Howard (b. 1886, d. May 12, 1935) and Edith Florence Morrison (b. 1888, d. June 7, 1962), Frankie Howerd won a scholarship to Shooters Hill Grammar School in Woolwich, London and went there with an ambition to become a saint. He turned to acting in a bid to cure a stammer but at 17 his nervousness led him to fail an audition for RADA. He became a clerk by day and attempted a stand-up routine as Ronnie Ordex at night. It was a failure: as the spotlight came on, Howerd went off. He failed to join ENSA and joined the regular army where he became a sergeant in the Royal Artillery. On July 31, 1946 he made his professional début at the Sheffield Empire. His bill matter listed him as "Frankie Howerd: The Borderline Case" and his act lasted eight minutes. By 1948 he was top of the bill at the London Palladium with a script written by Eric Sykes. He made his first film in 1953 *The Runaway Bus* in which he played Percy Lamb, a relief bus driver. Howerd also consolidated his radio and stand-up work. He developed a number of catchphrases including "And the best of luck", "I was *a*-mazed", "Just make meself comfy", "Ladies and gentle-*men*!", "Oooh, no missus", "Nay, nay and thrice nay", "No, don't mock", "Please yourselves", "Poor old girl, she's past it", "Shut your face" and, most famously, "Titter ye not". Having seen the success of (Sir) Norman Wisdom, studios began to hire Howerd to appear in their vehicles. In 1955 he appeared as an emcee in *An Alligator Named Daisy*, had a bit part as a barrow boy in the Ealing comedy *The Ladykillers* and as greyhound owner Willy Joy in *Jumping For Joy*. In July and August 1956 he filmed *A Touch Of The Sun*, in which he used George Formby's catchphrase "Turned out nice again". On May 19, 1958 *Further Up The Creek* began shooting and was released on October 20 of the same year. It was a follow-up to *Up The Creek* which had starred Peter Sellers. *Further Up The Creek* was a flop. Howerd played a Bilko-esque bosun called Dibble who always had an eye open for a moneymaking scheme. The late Fifties and early Sixties were a bad time for him professionally and he began to suffer from depression. In 1961 he guest starred as a church organist in *Watch It, Sailor!* and the following year was a road workman in *The Fast Lady*. In July 1962 he filmed Michael Winner's *The Cool Mikado* (released on May 19, 1963) playing Ko-Ko Flintridge and later said, "I can say without equivocation that not only was it the worst film ever made but the only production in show business that I'm positively ashamed of having appeared in." Then on April 6, 1963 his star rose again with an appearance on the television show *That Was The Week That Was*. That led to the lead role as Pseudolus in *A Funny Thing Happened On The Way To The Forum* which opened on October 3, 1963 at the Strand Theatre. He stayed with the show until July 3, 1965 and left "before I get stale". His subsequent films, *The Great St Trinian's Train Robbery* (1966) as Alphonse of Monte Carlo/Alfred Askett, *Carry On Doctor* (1967) as Francis Kitchener Bigger (he was paid £7,500 for the five week shoot between September 18 and October 20, 1967), *Carry On Up The Jungle* (1970) as Professor Inigo Tinkle (filmed from October 15, 1969, he was paid £9,000 for six weeks' work although the role was initially intended for Kenneth Williams), *Up Pompeii!* (1971) as Lurcio, fared rather better. He resurrected the Lurcio character twice in slightly different guises as Lurkalot and Richard the Lion-Heart in *Up The Chastity Belt* (filmed between April 20 and May 25, 1971) and as Lurk in *Up The Front* (1972). "The film I enjoyed making the most" was how he described *The House In Nightmare Park* (filmed between November 6 and December 16, 1972 at Pinewood

Studios) in which he played Foster Twelvetrees. His last film was *Sgt. Pepper's Lonely Hearts Club Band* (1977) and he said, "They only got me because they couldn't get Ronald Colman." The film flopped and his career again took a downturn in the late Seventies. He was in the doldrums for five years until 1981 when he appeared in *Die Fledermaus*, and his TV career again took off. From the Fifties he appeared in several television series including *The Howerd Crowd* (BBC, January 12, 1952–August 27, 1955 and then ATV, August 17, 1958), *Frankly Howerd* (BBC, May 1–June 5, 1959), *Frankie Howerd* (BBC, December 11, 1964–March 29, 1966), *The Frankie Howerd Show* (ATV, August 9–September 13, 1969), *Up Pompeii!* (BBC1, March 30–October 26, 1970), *Whoops Baghdad* (BBC1, January 25–March 1, 1973), *An Evening With Francis Howerd* (BBC2, April 30–May 14, 1973), *The Howerd Confessions* (Thames TV, September 2–October 7, 1976), *Frankie Howerd Strikes Again* (Yorkshire TV, September 1–October 6, 1981), *Then Churchill Said To Me* (BBC2, made in 1982 but unseen because of the Falklands war, finally broadcast April 8–September 10, 2000), *All Change* (Yorkshire TV, November 15,1989–March 12, 1991) and *Frankie's On . . .* (Central TV, June 21–July 12, 1992). A promiscuous homosexual, Frankie Howerd would never be seen in public without his wig. He suffered from alopecia which left a saucer-sized bald spot on his forehead from his early twenties. He was extremely sensitive about his rug and once had a second assistant at Pinewood fired when he walked into the dressing room and saw Frankie minus toupe. He never married. A story is told of a showbiz dinner in 1966 at which the room was packed with people keen to see Frankie. One of those on the top table turned to Tommy Cooper and said, "Well, there's one thing you can say for

Frankie. He certainly puts bums on seats." "Yes," said Tommy, "safest place for them."

CAUSE: On April 3, 1992 he was admitted to the intensive care unit of the Harley Street Clinic, Weymouth Street, London, suffering from respiratory problems. Four days later, he was moved from the ICU and was discharged on April 14. On Good Friday he had lunch at this favourite restaurant Al Gallo d'Oro with his loyal sister Betty (b. October 1921) who had moved into his home at 27 Edwardes Square, Kensington, London to look after him. It seemed that he was rallying and his specialist said that he could finish his recuperation at his Somerset bolthole. Frankie lay on the settee for a nap and his long-term boyfriend Dennis Heymer (they moved in together in 1956) checked on him every 15 minutes. On the fourth attempt Heymer noticed that his lover was not breathing and Betty rang 999. An ambulance rushed him to Charing Cross Hospital but on the way he suffered a heart attack and died. He was 75. On April 29, 1992 Frankie Howerd was buried at St Gregory's, Weare in Somerset. A memorial service was held at St Martin-in-the-Fields on July 8, 1992. He left £1,327,198.

FURTHER READING: *Titter Ye Not The Life Of Frankie Howerd* – William Hall (London: Grafton, 1992); *Star Turns The Life And Times Of Benny Hill & Frankie Howerd* – Barry Took (London: Weidenfeld & Nicolson, 1992); *The Complete Frankie Howerd* – Robert Ross (London: Reynolds & Hearn, 2001); *Frankie Howerd Stand Up Comic* – Graham McCann (London: Fourth Estate, 2004).

Newton House
Born November 1, 1911
Died July 23, 1987
Make-up and Stetsons. Born in Holly, Colorado the son of actor and Rudolph Valentino's stunt double-in Jack House, Newton House began his film

career early, due in no small part to his expertise around horses. By the time he was 15 he had won a dozen trophies for trick riding. He made his film debut at 12 in *Which Shall It Be?* (1924). He followed that up with *The Spirit Of The USA* (1924) as Little Silas Gains, *The Ridin' Kid From Powder River* (1924) as Bud, *Shattered Lives* (1925) as Chick Connors, *Little Annie Rooney* (1925) and *The Buckaroo Kid* (1926). In 1927 and 1928 Universal cast him in a 13-part serial with the title *The Champion Boy Rider*. The series encompassed *The Riding Whirlwind* (1927), *Red Warning* (1927), *Clearing The Trail* (1927), *The Racing Wizard* (1927), *Riding Gold* (1928), *Buckskin Days* (1928), *Winged Hoofs* (1928), *A Son Of The Frontier* (1928), *The Untamed* (1928), *The Fighting Kid* (1928), *The Ride For Help* (1928), *Ropin' Romance* (1928) and *The Danger Trail* (1928). His other films included: *A Final Reckoning* (1928) as Ruben Whitney, *The Girl Of The Golden West* (1930) as a Pony Express rider, *We Live Again* (1934), *Devil Dogs Of The Air* (1935) and *Shipmates Forever* (1935). In an unusual move for a macho cowboy House moved behind the camera but not as a cameraman but as a make-up artist. He did the cosmetics on *Stanley And Livingstone* (1939) and *Drums Along The Mohawk* (1939). He made one more appearance in front of the camera, *Son Of Zorro* (1947) as Haynes before his retirement. CAUSE: He died of natural causes in Colton, California at the age of 75.

Gusti Huber
Born July 27, 1914
Died July 12, 1993
Matriarch. Auguste Huber was born in Wiener Neustadt, Austria-Hungary, and was a mainstay in the German cinema before the Second World War. She began working in the theatre in Zurich before moving into films. Between 1940 and 1944 she worked in the Viennese Castle Theatre. Her

films included *Ein Walzer Um Den Stephansturm* (1935), *Buchhalter Schnabel* (1935), *Tanzmusik* (1935) as Hedi Baumann, *Fiakerlied* (1936), *Savoy-Hotel 217* (1936) as Daria Plagina, *Die Unentschuldigte Stunde* (1937) as Käte Riedel, *Land Der Liebe* (1937) as Prinzessin Julia, *Der Mann, Von Dem Man Spricht* (1937) as Bianca Zaratti, *Der Optimist* (1938), *Kleiner Mann – Ganz Groß!* (1938), *Das Mädchen Gon Gestern Nacht* (1938) as Jean Miller, *Eine Frau Für Drei* (1939) as Marguerite Kranz, *Wie Konntest Du, Veronika!* (1940), *Herz – Modern Möbliert* (1940), *Jenny Und Der Herr Im Frack* (1941) as Jenny, *Gabriele Dambrone* (1943), *Am Abend Nach Der Oper* (1944), *Wie Ein Dieb In Der Nacht* (1945) and *The Diary Of Anne Frank* (1959) as Mrs Edith Frank. Her second marriage was to an American soldier and she moved to the States permanently. From 1952 she appeared on the American stage including *Dial M For Murder* in 1953 on Broadway but rarely stepped before the cameras. In 1961 she retired from acting and lectured regularly in New York on the legacy of Anne Frank. Her daughter was Bibi Besch and her granddaughter is Samantha Mathis.

CAUSE: She died of heart failure in Mount Kisco, New York, aged 79.

Rock Hudson

(ROY HAROLD SCHERER, JR)
Born November 17, 1925
Died October 2, 1985
Secret gay. Born in Winnetka, Illinois, Hudson was never cast in school plays because he simply couldn't remember lines. He began his working life as a postman before becoming a truck driver, doing which job he was discovered by the gay agent Henry Willson, who was also responsible for launching the careers of Tab Hunter and Rory Calhoun. He renamed his discovery after the Rock of Gibraltar and the Hudson River. As the world now knows Hudson's career was based

on a sham. Rather than the lady-killer of celluloid fame, he was, in fact, a promiscuous homosexual who regularly trawled gay bars looking for pick-ups. "Rock Hudson was emotionally constipated. He hated having to play hetero on screen, he hated having to pretend off screen, and he hated anyone saying he was gay," revealed openly gay actor Paul Lynde. "We acted together, but we could never have socialised. I let it all hang out; he left it all hanging in. And now that he's not a big star any more, he's still just as uptight." It was Rock Hudson's looks rather than his talent that made him a movie star. He made his first film appearance in *Fighter Squadron* (1948) and went on to appear in *Winchester '73* (1950) as Young Bull, *I Was A Shoplifter* (1950), *Tomahawk* (1951) as Corporal Burt Hanna, *Bright Victory* (1951) as Dudek, *Horizons West* (1952) as Neil Hammond, *Has Anybody Seen My Gal?* (1952) as Dan, *Sea Devils* (1953) as Gilliatt, *The Lawless Breed* (1953) as John Wesley Hardin, *Seminole* (1953) as Lance Caldwell, *Taza, Son Of Cochise* (1954) as Taza, *Bengal Brigade* (1954) as Captain Jeffrey Claybourne, *Magnificent Obsession* (1954) as Bob Merrick, *All That Heaven Allows* (1955) as Ron Kirby, *Captain Lightfoot* (1955) as Michael Martin, *Written On The Wind* (1956) as Mitch Wayne, *Never Say Goodbye* (1956) as Dr Michael Parker, *Giant* (1956) as Jordan 'Bick' Benedict, *A Farewell To Arms* (1957) as Lieutenant Frederick Henry, *Battle Hymn* (1957) as Colonel Dean Hess, *Twilight For The Gods* (1958) as Captain David Bell, *Come September* (1961) as Robert Talbot, *Tobruk* (1967) as Major Donald Craig, *Ice Station Zebra* (1968) as Commander James Ferraday, *Hornet's Nest* (1970) as Captain Turner, *Darling Lili* (1970) as Major William Larrabee ("I heard that my *Darling Lili* taskmasters, Blake Edwards and Julie Andrews, were implying to the press that I'm gay. I could hardly believe it! Talk about the kettle calling the pot black!"), *Pretty Maids All In A Row* (1971) as Michael 'Tiger' McDrew and *Avalanche* (1978) as David Shelby. At one point in the Fifties it seemed as if Hudson's secret was going to be revealed by *Confidential* magazine, so Henry Willson arranged for Hudson to marry 5'9½" Phyllis Lucille Gates (b. Dawson, Minnesota December 7, 1925 d. Marina del Ray, California January 4, 2006 from lung cancer), a secretary in his office. Hudson and Gates eloped to Santa Barbara on November 9, 1955. Gates claimed that she had no idea of her husband's true sexuality and that she had only met him when Willson arranged the match. They divorced on August 13, 1958 and neither ever remarried. After her death many came forward to claim that Gates was a lesbian. According to actor John Carlyle, a Willson client, he and his boyfriend used to double date with Hudson and Gates on weekend trips to Palm Springs, California, before their marriage. In 1953 Hudson's close friend Mark Miller and his lover, matinee idol George Nader, shared a house in Studio City, and it was there that Hudson met Gates at a small party. She arrived with Hudson's then live-in boyfriend, Jack Navaar, with whom she had just been to the pictures. It was also alleged that she tried to blackmail Hudson after they separated. She also apparently tried to extort money from a woman she had had an affair with but the money didn't care – her husband was gay too. Shortly before her death she was named as correspondent with another woman in a divorce suit filed by the husband. Hudson appeared in a number of romantic comedies such as *Pillow Talk* (1959) as Brad Allen and *Lover Come Back* (1961) as Jerry Webster playing opposite Doris Day and in the Seventies was known to television audiences for his portrayal of San Francisco police chief Stewart

Macmillan in *Macmillan And Wife*. He deeply disliked his co-star Susan Saint James. "I tell you the truth. I wouldn't even stand next to her at a cocktail party!" On his 50th birthday he walked down the staircase at home wearing only a nappy while a band played 'You Must Have Been A Beautiful Baby'. For some time in the late Seventies and early Eighties Hudson was absent from public view. In 1984 he was signed to appear on the glossy soap *Dynasty*. The show was created for ABC and Aaron Spelling by Esther Shapiro and her husband Richard as a rival to CBS's *Dallas*. In America the series gradually gained momentum and overtook *Dallas* in the ratings, something it never achieved in Britain. *Dynasty* relied as much on its big name guest stars as well as its outlandish plots to win over audiences. On October 9, 1984, it was announced that Rock Hudson had signed to play handsome horse breeder Daniel Reece for six episodes with an option for four more and a spin-off series the next year. When Hudson arrived on set at the end of October he looked ill, seriously ill. His previously muscular 6'6" frame was nearly skeletal and his clothes hung from the bones. All sorts of rumours about the nature of Hudson's condition were doing the rounds; AIDS was still virtually unknown to the public at large at the time. In an interview with *U.S.A. Today* Hudson claimed his weight loss was due to a stringent diet and that he was more than happy with his appearance. It was not a convincing explanation. One scene was to cause controversy not just on the *Dynasty* set but around the world. Millionaire Daniel Reece, who owned the Delta Rho Stables, was an old flame of Krystle Carrington, played by Linda Evans, and the script called for the two to kiss. According to his authorised biography, Hudson returned to his home, known as 'The Castle', at 9402 Beverly Crest Drive, Beverly Hills, California, and flung the script across the room. He discussed his dilemma with his close friend Mark Miller – should he admit he had AIDS and finish his career, or kiss Linda Evans? At that time no one knew for certain how the HIV virus was passed on and it was believed that casual contact – even touching – was enough to transmit the virus. Hudson made a decision. Throughout his career he had always put his career first. Career. Sex. People. They were the three driving forces in his life. Dying from AIDS, there would be no exception to his rule. Prior to the scene Hudson was sitting next to Joan Collins in the make-up room. He chain-smoked and small-talked as the technicians performed their wizardry – trying to make Hudson look human. After he left for the set Joan Collins' openly gay hairdresser speculated that Hudson had the deadly AIDS virus. Immediately prior to the kiss Hudson utilised every mouthwash and gargle he could find and then kissed Linda Evans. As soon as the director shouted, "Cut!" Evans rushed to her dressing room, where she spent 15 minutes cleaning her teeth, using antiseptic mouthwashes and harshly washing her face. The next day Evans told Joan Collins she had gone through with the kiss because she did not want to hurt Hudson's feelings! Back home Hudson said to Mark Miller, "The fucking kiss is over with. Thank God!" Miller said Hudson thought it one of the worst days of his life. The episode aired on February 6, 1985. Former actor George Nader is Mark Miller's boyfriend and the two men were with Tom Clark, Hudson's former lover, the closest friends Hudson had in the world, when the episode screened – Nader taped the programme as he watched it. He commented afterwards, "I could see where Rock kept his lips closed and hit Linda on the side of the cheek for a brief, chaste kiss. He did not open his mouth, no saliva was exchanged." Hudson completed his contract with

Dynasty, smoking 40 cigarettes a day on the set and drinking vodka as if it was water. When it was announced that Hudson was suffering from AIDS the cast and crew of *Dynasty* were united in their sympathy for him. No one seemed bothered that Hudson may have exposed Linda Evans to a deadly disease. (Remember, at that time no one knew for certain just how contagious the disease was or exactly how it was passed on.) The reaction from the public was different and Hudson was widely criticised for his thoughtless actions. Even Mark Miller admitted he was worried about touching Hudson, despite knowing he could not get the disease through touch alone. His official biographer Sara Davidson wrote, "Rock did not give the matter [of kissing Linda Evans] a second thought, once it was over. It was a lifelong pattern: he didn't seem vulnerable to guilt."

CAUSE: Rock's condition became apparent when he appeared alongside Doris Day at a press conference on July 15, 1985, in Carmel, California, the town that elected Clint Eastwood mayor. Hudson's weight had dropped from just under 14st to a worrying 9st and his waist had shrunk from 38″ to 33″. It was patently clear that something was terribly wrong with him although his publicist, Dale Olson, maintained that Hudson was happy with the weight loss and intended to buy a whole new wardrobe. Ten days later in Paris, Hudson's publicist, Yannou Collart, announced he was suffering from AIDS. He had been diagnosed as HIV+ on June 5, 1984. However, Hudson continued to have sex with his boyfriend Marc Christian until February 1985. In September 1984 Hudson told his secret to a friend and asked how to put condoms on. "I've never worn [one] in my life. Won't I give the show away if I suddenly have to put one on?" Hudson's doctor later revealed that if the actor had stayed in Paris, his condition might have stabilised and he may have survived longer. However, that was never Hudson's style and he travelled around Europe with a young friend until he returned to the States to work on *Dynasty*. On October 7, 1984, Hudson told Mark Miller that his blood was clear of the virus and he was safe. What he didn't tell him was that he had to stay on the treatment for his blood to remain clear. A week later, he continued to lose weight. In November he began to lose interest in sex. He developed impetigo, causing itching sores over his body, his teeth began to fall out and his body was covered in rashes that could not be alleviated by cortisone because that affected his immune system. He returned to America on July 30, 1985, and was admitted to UCLA Medical Center. On August 24, Marc Christian went to visit palimony lawyer Marvin Mitchelson. Later that month, Hudson went to his beloved home, 'The Castle', for the last time. His death was announced at 9.15am on October 2, 1985. A mortuary van arrived at 10.45am and, after its windows were blacked out with Hudson's butler James Wright's towels, his corpse was taken to the crematorium. The back of the van had no lock, so Tom Clark had to hold the doors shut while straddling Rock's body. At the crematorium the corpse was placed in a cardboard box and burned.

FURTHER READING: *Rock Hudson: Public And Private* – Mark Bego (New York: Signet, 1986); *Idol Rock Hudson: The True Story Of An American Film Hero* – Jerry Oppenheimer & Jack Vitek (New York: Villard Books, 1986); *Rock Hudson: His Story* – Rock Hudson and Sara Davidson (London: Bantam, 1987); *My Husband Rock Hudson: The Real Story Of Rock Hudson's Marriage To Phyllis Gates* – Phyllis Gates And Bob Thomas (London: Angus & Robertson, 1987); *The Trial Of Rock Hudson* – John Parker (London: Sidgwick & Jackson, 1990).

Glenn Hughes
Born July 18, 1950
Died March 4, 2002

The Leatherman. Glenn Michael Hughes was born in the Bronx. In 1977, while working as a tollbooth collector at the Holland Tunnel in New Jersey, he answered for a dare an advertisement for "gay singers and dancers, very good-looking and with mustaches [*sic*]". The advert was placed by a Moroccan-born music producer called Jacques Morali. From the response he put together Village People. To Morali's amazement the group appealed to straight people and teenage girls as well as his targeted audience. Soon Village People were a world-wide phenomenon scoring massive international hits such as 'Y.M.C.A.' (number one in the UK, number two in the US), 'In The Navy', 'Go West' and 'Can't Stop The Music'. It was in the film of the same name that Hughes played himself in the fictionalised version of how the group came to be formed. The band split in 1985 but were reformed a few years later by Randy Jones, the cowboy, with most of the original line-up. Hughes left the band through ill-health in 1996 but continued to work with the group's administration until the time of his death. He also sang on the band's most recent two house music singles 'Loveship 2001' and 'Gunbalanya' under the name Village People alias The Amazing Veepers. The latter tune, which means "in the tribe", was written in Australia with a group of Aborigines during a documentary filmed by the country's public television network. Both singles were released on the group's own label, Plenty Big Music. Hughes also kept in touch with fans answering emails. He never married. CAUSE: Hughes, who had been ill for several years, died of lung cancer in his Manhattan apartment. He was 51. Village People's manager, Mitch Weiss, said that the cancer was in the final stages when it was detected in Hughes, and there was nothing medical experts could do. "It came as a surprise to everyone," he said. In accordance with his wishes Hughes was buried in his leather stage outfit. The other Village People acted as pallbearers at Hughes' funeral. Alexander Briley, the original and current GI, sang 'Where Do I Go?' from *Hair* during the ceremony, which Hughes had also requested. "Glenn had a talent for keeping things light and could make you laugh even on your worst day," Hughes' sister, Cindy, said at his funeral. "His quick wit, terrific dancing and fabulous voice were his trademarks."

Howard Hughes

Born September 24, 1905
Died April 5, 1976
Extremely eccentric. Born in Humble, Texas, Howard Robard Hughes, Jr was an aviator, founder of Trans World Airlines, billionaire, film producer, owner of RKO Pictures, bra inventor, lover of beautiful women (and handsome men) and much more, but it is for his numerous eccentricities that he is best known. The son of a man who invented a tool for drilling, Hughes was left a tremendous fortune on his father's death on January 14, 1924. In an attempt to become his own man and escape from his father's shadow, Hughes became a Hollywood producer. His first work of note was *Hell's Angels* (1930), the film that propelled Jean Harlow to stardom. Other Hughes films included *The Front Page* (1931), *Scarface* (1932), *The Outlaw* (1943), *The Big Steal* (1949), *Flying Leathernecks* (1951), *Underwater* (1955) and *The Conqueror* (1956). Hughes was obsessed with women's breasts, to the point of mania. He designed a special bra for Jane Russell to wear in *The Outlaw*. However, unbeknown to him, she found it uncomfortable and never wore it. He instructed chauffeurs who drove his starlets to the studios to go via a route that ensured there were few if any bumps on the road so their breasts wouldn't bounce. He also took an obsessional interest in their private lives, insisting they did not date anyone and had them tailed to make sure they followed his orders. His name was romantically linked to actresses Carole Lombard, Bette Davis, Terry Moore (who claimed to have married him), Ginger Rogers, Ida Lupino, Marian Marsh and Jean Harlow. According to one biographer (Charles Higham), Hughes also had affairs with Cary Grant, Randolph Scott, Tyrone Power and Richard Cromwell, the gay first husband of Angela Lansbury, among others. Yet other biographers (notably Peter Harry Brown and Pat H. Broeske) disdain the rumours. Since all four men are dead, we will never know for sure. In December 1970 novelist and biographer Clifford Irving decided to write the authorised biography of reclusive billionaire Howard Hughes. Irving forged a correspondence between himself and Hughes and presented it to the publishing execs, demanding $750,000. On December 7, 1971, publishing house McGraw-Hill announced the book in a 550-word press release, saying it would be published on March 27, 1972. Rosemont Enterprises Inc., Hughes' main company, denied the book was genuine. To cover himself, Irving explained that Hughes was so paranoid he had not even told his own men, an explanation that sated McGraw-Hill. Cheques were issued to an H.R. Hughes and deposited in an account at Credit Suisse, opened by Irving's wife, Edith. At 6.45pm on January 7, 1972, from the ninth-floor suite of the Britannia Beach Hotel in Nassau, Hughes made his first public utterance in 15 years when he denounced the book as a fake in a phone link to journalists at the Sheraton Hotel in Los Angeles. Hughes also lied about himself to them, saying he regularly cut his nails and that he wasn't terrified of catching germs. It was when the Swiss

banks broke their traditional vow of secrecy to reveal that H.R. Hughes was a woman (Helga Rosencrantz Hughes) that the plot quickly began to unravel. Hughes informed the I.R.S. that he had not received a penny of the $750,000 advance and, as such, had no intention of paying tax on it. This caused the tax men to begin an investigation. Signatures on the back of cashed cheques were examined and re-examined. On January 28, 1972, Irving admitted that his wife was the mysterious H.R. Hughes and his lawyer, Martin Ackerman, promptly resigned. On February 7, Irving and his wife appeared before a grand jury in New York and took the Fifth Amendment. Then the I.R.S. demanded $500,000. During the hearings singer Baroness Nina van Pallandt revealed that she had travelled to Mexico with Irving during the time Irving had said he was interviewing Hughes; the writer had not left her side long enough to meet Hughes. Four days after the indictments, both Irvings pleaded guilty to all charges. On June 16, 1972, in the Southern District of New York, Judge John M. Cannella sentenced Edith Irving to two years in prison, all but two months of which were suspended. She was then tried in Zurich on March 8, 1973, and sentenced to a further two years' imprisonment. She was released on parole on May 5, 1974. Irving was fined $10,000 and spent 17 months of a 30-month sentence in three Federal prisons, including two stays in solitary confinement. Upon his release on parole in early 1974, he was divorced and wrote the story of the hoax. In June 1975 Irving was declared bankrupt with assets of $410 and debts of $55 million. In his later years Hughes became extremely eccentric – keeping his own faeces and urine in jars, walking around with tissue boxes on his feet, letting his toenails grow to extreme length, hiding in seclusion in darkened rooms, surrounding himself with teetotal Mormons and sending men to catch flies by hand.

CAUSE: Hughes died aged 70 on board an aeroplane bound for Texas. Higham also alleges that the cause of Hughes' death may well have been AIDS, while Brown and Broeske examine the theory that he was murdered.

FURTHER READING: *Howard Hughes: Bashful Billionaire* – Albert B. Gerber (London: New English Library, 1972); *Hoax: The Inside Story Of The Howard Hughes–Clifford Irving Affair* (London: Andre Deutsch, 1972); *The Real Howard Hughes Story* – Nelson C. Madden (New York: Manor Books, 1976); *The Hughes Papers* – Elaine Davenport & Paul Eddy with Mark Hurwitz (London: Sphere, 1977); *'Project Octavio'* – Clifford Irving & Richard Suskind (London: Allison & Busby, 1977); *Citizen Hughes* – Michael Drosnin (London: Hutchinson, 1985); *Howard Hughes: The Secret Life* – Charles Higham (London: Sidgwick & Jackson, 1993); *Howard Hughes: The Untold Story* – Peter Harry Brown and Pat H. Broeske (London: Little, Brown, 1996).

John Hughes
Born February 18, 1950
Died August 6, 2009
The J.D. Salinger of the movie world. John Wilden Hughes Jr was born in Lansing, Michigan, the son of a salesman and a volunteer charity worker. In 1963 the family relocated to Chicago. "I didn't have this tortured childhood," he said, "I liked it." Hughes went through a hippy period and claimed that Bob Dylan's *Bringing It All Back Home* and The Beatles' 'White Album' changed his life. In 1970 he married Nancy Ludwig and then dropped out of the University of Arizona. He made ends meet by writing 100 jokes a day which he sold to comedians for $5 each, except for Joan Rivers who paid him $7. In 1977 his son John III was born and two years later he left his job as an advertising

copywriter to become editor of *National Lampoon*. A second son, Jamie, arrived in 1980. Hughes began working as a script doctor but his own work failed to find favour. His *National Lampoon's Class Reunion* (1982) was a massive flop and the nautical yarn *Nate And Hayes* (released November 18, 1983) sank without trace. Then he hit pay dirt with *National Lampoon's Vacation* (1983) and *Mr Mom* (1983). His own directorial debut came with *Sixteen Candles* (1984), about a girl (Molly Ringwald) whose family forgets her birthday. His next film was the one that made his reputation. Five schoolchildren with very different characters – "a brain, an athlete, a basket case, a princess and a criminal" – are all given detention. *The Breakfast Club* (1985) was a massive hit. At the time Hughes claimed that one of the characters was based on him but later said that he had been joking: "People ask me, 'Were you the geek?' No, I wasn't. 'So which one were you?' I don't get it. Who was Alfred Hitchcock in his movies? Janet Leigh? Did anyone even ask him? But I get asked, so I make up an answer." Hughes looked for very high standards in his crews. "In a town full of people who are impossible to work for," editorialised *Premiere* in 1992, "he's impossible to work for." In 2005, Peter Bart wrote in *Variety* that "working with Hughes during his peak years was akin to a tour of duty at Abu Ghraib. He randomly fired aides and [assistant directors] and daily reminded everyone around him that he was the resident genius." Hughes had firm views on his target audience: "Many filmmakers portray teenagers as immoral and ignorant with pursuits that are pretty base . . . But I haven't found that to be the case. I listen to kids. I respect them . . . Some of them are as bright as any of the adults I've met. My generation had to be taken seriously because we were stopping things and burning things. We were able to initiate change, because

we had such vast numbers. We were part of the baby boom, and when we moved, everything moved with us. But now, there are fewer teens, and they aren't taken as seriously as we were. You make a teenage movie, and critics say, 'How dare you?' There's just a general lack of respect for young people now." Molly Ringwald, the star of three films written by Hughes, said, "I think the reason why I like working with John is that he really understands kids because he genuinely likes young people. He doesn't condescend to them. He treats us not like adults or kids, just as a person. He writes about kids in a really intelligent way. And he's a good person." Ally Sheedy, who starred with Ringwald in *The Breakfast Club*, added, "He's very vulnerable. And I think he likes to write about young people because that's a real part of him. There's something open about him. There's something childlike about him. He likes to play. He likes to laugh." After the "Brat Pack" movies *Weird Science* (1985), *Pretty In Pink* (1986), *Ferris Bueller's Day Off* (1986) and *Some Kind Of Wonderful* (1987) Hughes broadened his writing with *Planes, Trains And Automobiles* (1987), then the romantic comedy *She's Having A Baby* (1988). He increased his scriptwriting output: *The Great Outdoors* (1988), *National Lampoon's Christmas Vacation* (1989), *Home Alone* (1990), which took more than $285 million at the American box office, *Career Opportunities* (1991), *Home Alone 2: Lost In New York* (1992), *Dutch*, aka *Driving Me Crazy* (1992) *Beethoven* (1992); *Dennis* (1993), *Baby's Day Out* (1994), *Miracle On 34th Street* (1994); *101 Dalmatians* (1996), *Flubber* (1997) and *Home Alone 3* (1997) but lost quality control. On occasion he used the nom de plume Edmond Dantès, the real name of the Count of Monte Cristo. His other directorial films included *Uncle Buck* (1989) and his last *Curly Sue* (1991). Perhaps Hughes who virtually retired to a farm in northern Illinois and rarely gave interviews was aware that his work was not as good as it had been or indeed could have been. "I don't think I'm making any great statements," he said in 1998, "and I certainly don't think I'm making art."

CAUSE: Hughes died aged 59, of a heart attack on a morning walk while visiting family in Manhattan.

Jeffrey Hunter

(HENRY HERMAN McKINNIES, JR)
Born November 23, 1925
Died May 27, 1969
Pretty boy. Born in New Orleans, Louisiana, Hunter served in the US Navy and on demob signed a contract with 20th Century Fox in 1950 and was cast in a variety of roles. He was often compared with and cast alongside Robert Wagner. Probably his most memorable appearance was as Jesus in MGM's *King Of Kings* (1961). He was the original captain (Christopher Pike) in the pilot of the sci-fi TV series *Star Trek*. However, he was unavailable when shooting began on the series' second pilot, *Where No Man Has Gone Before*, on July 19, 1965. He married three times: in 1950 to actress Barbara Rush by whom he had a son, Christopher (b. 1952) and from whom he was divorced on March 29, 1955, in Los Angeles; to actress Dusty Bartlett in 1957 by whom he had another son, Todd (b. 1959) and from whom he was divorced in 1967; and actress Emily McLaughlin whom he married on February 4, 1969, four months before his death.

CAUSE: Hunter died aged 43 in Van Nuys, California, as a result of brain surgery following a fall.

Kim Hunter

(JANET COLE)
Born November 12, 1922
Died September 11, 2002
Expressive actress. Born in Detroit, Michigan, she was the only daughter (there was a son, born in 1913) of Donald Cole, who died when she was

three, and Grace Mabel Lind, who remarried Bliss Stebbins, a retired Miami businessman. A lonely child, she was educated at Miami Beach High School and developed a strong fantasy life acting in front of mirrors. She made her first stage appearance in Miami in November 1939 playing Penny in *Penny Wise* with a small theatre group. She moved to New York to study at the Actors' Studio. Performances at the Pasadena Playhouse, near Hollywood, brought her to the attention of David O. Selznick and he signed her to a seven-year contract. Selznick suggested she change her name to Kim and an RKO secretary suggested the last name of Hunter. She appeared in *The Seventh Victim* (1943) as Mary Gibson, a young woman who goes to New York to rescue her sister from a group of devil-worshippers. She was also in *Tender Comrade* (1943) as Doris Dumbrowski, *When Strangers Marry* (1944) as Millie Baxter, *A Canterbury Tale* (1944) as Johnson's girl and *You Came Along* (1945) as Frances Hotchkiss. She was cast as June opposite David Niven in Michael Powell and Emeric Pressburger's fantasy war tale *A Matter Of Life And Death* (1946), after being recommended by Alfred Hitchcock who was influenced by his 14-year-old daughter, Patricia. June was the WAC who talked to an English pilot trapped in a burning aeroplane as it hurtles towards the ground. The pilot is then tried, apparently for the crime of being English, but is later acquitted because of June's love for him. Film critic Leslie Halliwell described the film as deserving "full marks for its sheer arrogance, wit, style and film flair". She appeared as Stella Kowalski, the abused wife of a brutish husband, in *A Streetcar Named Desire* at the Ethel Barrymore Theater, New York, from December 3, 1947. Four years later, she won a Best Supporting Actress Oscar for reprising the role on film. The movie brought Method acting to a wide audience for the first time. Director Elia Kazan kept the Broadway cast except for Blanche Du Bois who was played on screen by Vivien Leigh. Because of the era it was difficult to bring Tennessee Williams' play to the screen with its homosexuality, rape and nymphomania. Homosexuality was absent from the film version and Blanche's nymphomania was toned down but the rape scene was included although it was more suggestive than graphic. The film also won Oscars for Best Actress (Leigh), Best Supporting Actor (Karl Malden) and Best B&W Art Direction/Set Decoration (Richard Day and George James Hopkins). Marlon Brando lost out on the Best Actor statuette to Humphrey Bogart for *The African Queen*. During filming when 5'3" Kim Hunter went for a sleep in her trailer, Brando would shake it violently yelling, "Earthquake! Earthquake!" Although it looked as if Hunter would have her pick of parts, it was not to be. In 1949 she had been a sponsor of a World Peace Conference in New York and the Red-hunting followers of Joseph McCarthy picked up on this and blacklisted her after she was named as a fellow traveller in a rabidly anti-communist magazine called *Red Channels*. During that decade Hunter was offered very few roles. Her films during that period were: *Deadline – U.S.A.* (1952) as Nora Hutcheson, *Storm Center* (1956) as Martha Lockridge, *The Young Stranger* (1957) as Helen Ditmar, *Bermuda Affair* (1958) as Fran West and *Money, Women And Guns* (1959) as Mary Kingman. She said, "For a long while, I wouldn't talk about it at all. I do now, because there's a whole new generation that doesn't remember. And the more one knows, the more one can see, and not allow history to repeat itself." It wasn't until the late Sixties that Kim Hunter's career was completely back on track. Her portrayal of the kindly Dr Zira in *Planet Of The Apes* (1968) won her many plaudits despite her face

and entire body being covered in the chimpanzee suit. Her expressive eyes and movements connected with the audience. She reprised her role in *Beneath The Planet Of The Apes* (1970) and *Escape From The Planet Of The Apes* (1971) although she confessed to being pleased when Zira was killed off in the third in the series. She also appeared in *The Swimmer* (1968) as Betty Graham opposite Burt Lancaster as Ned Merrill, a man who decided to swim home via the pools of his friends (even though Lancaster suffered from mild hydrophobia), *Dark August* (1976) as Adrianna Putnam, *The Kindred* (1986) as Amanda Hollins opposite a deranged Rod Steiger, *Midnight In The Garden Of Good And Evil* (1997) as Betty Harty, *Abilene* (1999) as Emmeline, *Out Of The Cold* (1999) as Elsa Lindepu and *Here's To Life!* (2000) as Nelly Ormond. She was also regularly featured in television movies including: *Dial Hot Line* (premièred March 8, 1970) as Mrs Edith Carruthers, *In Search Of America* (premièred March 23, 1971) as Cora Chandler, *Columbo: Suitable For Framing* (premièred November 17, 1971) as Edna Matthews, *The Magician* (premièred March 17, 1973) as Nora Cougan, *Unwed Father* (premièred February 27, 1974) as Judy Simmons, *Born Innocent* (premièred September 10, 1974) as Mrs Parker (a film that caused a sensation because of the scene – later cut – when Linda Blair, playing a juvenile delinquent, was raped with a broom handle), *Bad Ronald* (premièred October 23, 1974) as Elaine Wilby, *Ellery Queen: Too Many Suspects* (premièred March 23, 1975) as Marion McKell, *The Dark Side Of Innocence* (premièred May 20, 1976) as Kathleen Hancock, *The Golden Gate Murders* (premièred October 3, 1979) as Sister Superior, *F.D.R.: The Last Year* (premièred May 15, 1980) as Lucy Rutherford, *Skokie* (premièred November 17, 1981) as Bertha Feldman, *Drop-Out Mother* (1988) as

Leona, *Bloodlines: Murder In The Family* (1993) as Vera Woodman, *Triumph Over Disaster: The Hurricane Andrew Story* (1993) as Elsa Rael and *Blue Moon* (1999) as Sheila Keating. Kim Hunter was married twice. Her first husband was Marine Captain William A. Baldwin from February 11, 1944 until 1946 and by whom she had a daughter, Kathryn, who became a judge in Connecticut. She was married to the actor Robert Emmett from December 20, 1951 until his death in 2000. They had one son, Sean. CAUSE: Kim Hunter died aged 79 in New York from a heart attack.

John Huston
(JOHN MARCELLUS HUSTON)
Born August 5, 1906
Died August 28, 1987
Hell-raising director and actor. Born in Nevada, Missouri, Huston worked as a boxer, an officer in the Mexican cavalry and a magazine editor before turning his hand to script writing. He was the Oscar-winning son and father of Oscar winners. He was the son of Walter Huston who won an Academy Award for *The Treasure Of The Sierra Madre* (1948) (which John directed) and father of Anjelica Huston who won her Oscar for *Prizzi's Honor* (1985) (which, needless to say, John also directed). John's own trophy came for *The Treasure Of The Sierra Madre*. His first time as director was *The Maltese Falcon* (1941) and it brought instant fame. Huston was also a celebrated actor but was as well known for his womanising (five marriages) and hard drinking. In 1960 he was hired at a salary of $300,000 to direct what turned out to be the last film of Marilyn Monroe and Clark Gable. Filming of *The Misfits* (1961) was due to begin in the autumn of 1959 but Marilyn's commitment to *Let's Make Love* and Clark Gable's to *It Happened In Naples* delayed shooting. The new start date was March 3, 1960, but an actors' strike delayed by five weeks the filming of *Let's Make Love*

which, in turn, delayed *The Misfits*. Finally, shooting began at 9am on July 18, 1960, and shut down a week later because John Huston's gambling caused a cash flow problem. On August 25, filming shut down because Huston had bled the company financially dry. Three days later, Marilyn entered Westside Hospital in Los Angeles. Frank Taylor announced filming would be suspended for a week. It gave Huston time to find new finance. One scene half an hour or so into the film called for Rosalyn (Monroe) to eat eggs that Gay (Gable) had prepared for her. Before Huston had the shot he wanted, Marilyn had chomped her way through two dozen eggs. In one scene 32 minutes into the film, Rosalyn is lying naked in bed when Gay comes into the room and kisses her. As she sits up, her bare breast is revealed. Director Huston cut the scene in the final edit. After numerous problems the film wrapped on November 4, 1960. It had cost $3,955,000 – the most expensive black-and-white film then made – and gone 40 days over schedule. Not everything Huston turned his hand to was for adults, or a success. Columbia Studios paid $9 million for the rights to the musical *Annie* (1982) to be directed by Huston. But the film, set in 1933, features a visit by the characters to Radio City Music Hall to see *Camille*, which wasn't made until 1936. Also, *Camille* would not have been shown at the Radio City Music Hall, but at the Capitol Theater on Broadway. Huston's other directorial films included *Key Largo* (1948), *The Asphalt Jungle* (1950) the first time he worked with Marilyn Monroe and for which he was nominated for an Oscar, *The Red Badge Of Courage* (1951), *The African Queen* (1951) which was only the third American film to be made on location in Africa and for which he was nominated for an Oscar, *Moulin Rouge* (1952) which he also wrote and produced and for which he was nominated for an Oscar, *Beat The Devil*

(1954) which he also wrote and produced, *Moby Dick* (1956) which he also wrote and produced, *Heaven Knows, Mr Allison* (1957) which he also wrote and for which he was nominated for an Oscar, *Freud* (1962) in which he also acted, *The List Of Adrian Messenger* (1963), *The Night Of The Iguana* (1964) which he also wrote, *Casino Royale* (1967) in which he also acted, *Reflections In A Golden Eye* (1967) which he also produced, *The Life And Times Of Judge Roy Bean* (1972), *The Man Who Would Be King* (1975) which he also wrote and for which he was nominated for an Oscar and *Under The Volcano* (1984). On September 25, 1933, Huston ran over and killed a pedestrian on Sunset Boulevard. MGM chief Louis B. Mayer paid out $400,000 to hush up the incident and Huston left for England for an indefinite period.
CAUSE: Huston died in Middletown, Rhode Island, aged 81 of emphysema.
FURTHER READING: *An Open Book –* John Huston (London: Columbus Books, 1988); *The Hustons –* Lawrence Grobel (London: Bloomsbury, 1990).

Walter Huston
(WALTER HOUGHSTON)
Born April 6, 1884
Died April 7, 1950
Solid patriarch. Born in Toronto, Ontario, Canada, he studied drama and became a theatre actor before making the transition to films. He played Trampas in *The Virginian* (1929) but came to notice playing the president in *Abraham Lincoln* (1930). He developed into a stolid, reliable performer and was in, among others, the following films: *The Bad Man* (1930) as Pancho Lopez, *Night Court* (1932) as Judge Moffett, *Law And Order* (1932) as Frame Johnson, *Rain* (1932) as Reverend Alfred Davidson, *Rhodes Of Africa* (1936) as Rhodes, *Dodsworth* (1936) as Sam Dodsworth, *Swamp Water* (1941) as Thursday

Ragan, *The Maltese Falcon* (1941) as Captain Jacobi, *Edge Of Darkness* (1942) as Dr Martin Stensgard, *Yankee Doodle Dandy* (1942) as Jerry Cohan, *The Outlaw* (1943) as Doc Holliday, *Dragonwyck* (1946) as Ephraim Wells and *The Treasure Of The Sierra Madre* (1948) as Howard, a part that won him a Best Supporting Actor Academy Award.
CAUSE: He died in Hollywood, California, the day after his 66th birthday, after suffering an aneurysm.
FURTHER READING: *The Hustons –* Lawrence Grobel (London: Bloomsbury, 1990).

Jim Hutton
(DANA JAMES HUTTON)
Born May 31, 1934
Died June 2, 1979
Talent unfulfilled. Born in Binghamton, New York, Jim Hutton looked as though he would become a modern James Stewart before ill-health tragically cut short his career. He made his film début in *A Time To Love And A Time To Die* (1958) as Hirschland and went on to appear in *Where The Boys Are* (1960) as TV Thompson, *Bachelor In Paradise* (1961) as Larry Delavane, *Period Of Adjustment* (1962) as George Haverstick, *Looking For Love* (1964) as Paul Davis, *Major Dundee* (1965) as Lieutenant Graham, *The Trouble With Angels* (1966) as Mr Petrie, *The Green Berets* (1968) as Sergeant Petersen and *Psychic Killer* (1975) as Arnold Masters. He was also probably the best Ellery Queen in either television or movies. His son is the actor Timothy Hutton.
CAUSE: He died of liver cancer aged 45 in Los Angeles, California.

Joe Hyams
Born June 6, 1923
Died November 8, 2008
Hollywood hack. Joseph Irving Hyams was born in Cambridge, Massachusetts and was at Harvard when the United States entered the Second World War

in December 1941. In 1942 Hyams joined up and was wounded in the South Pacific. He worked as a reporter on the *New York Herald Tribune* from 1951 to 1964 before joining the *Saturday Evening Post*. It was while lounging by the Beverly Hills Hotel pool that Hyams met Humphrey Bogart's press agent who arranged for the hack to interview Bogie the next day. When Hyams arrived, Bogart offered him a drink, which the teetotal reporter refused. Bogart was not impressed. "I don't trust any bastard who doesn't drink, especially a pipe-smoking newspaperman . . . or a man who has more hair than I have." Hyams walked out saying, "I don't drink and I certainly have more hair on my head than you do." Bogart liked his cheek and the two men became friends. Hyams was the first reporter to learn of Bogart's death from cancer on January 14, 1957. Bogart's widow Lauren Bacall told him. "It was the last story he could give you," she said, "and he wanted you to have it first." He wrote a biography of Bogart *Bogie* (1966) – for which Bacall wrote the foreword – and then wrote *Bogart & Bacall: A Love Story* (1975), for which she shunned him. In 1955 he wrote of the formation of the Rat Pack (so named by Bacall but initially labelled the Clan), from information given him by Bogart, who acted as the group's publicist. Hyams was also a friend of James Dean and wrote (with one of his own sons) *James Dean: Little Boy Lost* (1992). He also collaborated with President Reagan's son Michael on *Michael Reagan: On The Outside Looking In* (1989). As well as his biographies, Hyams wrote two novels *The Pool* (1978) and *Murder At The Academy Awards* (1983). A womaniser, Hyams was married four times. His third wife was the German actress Elke Sommer – they divorced in 1981. He became interested in martial arts during the war after being beaten up because he was Jewish.

CAUSE: Hyams died aged 85 at Denver, Colorado of coronary artery disease.

Wilfred Hyde-White

Born May 12, 1903
Died May 6, 1991
The Englishman abroad. Born in Bourton-on-the-Water, Gloucestershire, Hyde-White was educated at Marlborough and RADA, making his film début in 1934. In a career spanning almost 70 years he appeared in innumerable plays and television shows and over 150 films including *The Winslow Boy* (1948), *The Third Man* (1949), *The Browning Version* (1950), *Let's Make Love* (1960), *My Fair Lady* (1964) as Colonel Pickering and *Carry On Nurse* (1959) in which a daffodil is utilised as a thermometer. His son, Alex, is also an actor.

CAUSE: He died of congestive heart failure in Palm Springs aged 87.

I

Thomas Ince

Born November 6, 1882
Died November 19, 1924
Hollywood riddle. Born in Newport, Rhode Island, Thomas Harper Ince was born into a theatrical family and made his stage début aged six and his first appearance on Broadway nine years later. However, acting wasn't his strong suit and he worked as a lifeguard and a promoter. In 1907 he married Eleanor Kershaw and fathered three sons, William, Thomas, Jr and Dick. In 1910 he landed a job with Biograph and found his forte as a director and producer moving to Carl Laemmle's Independent Motion Pictures Company. Then, in 1911, he joined the New York Motion Picture Company and moved west to make Westerns. In October 1911 he created a series of sets nicknamed 'Inceville', where he shot whatever outdoor scenes were necessary. In 1912 he hired William Desmond Taylor to act in his film *The Counterfeiter* (1913). On July 20, 1915, he teamed up with D.W. Griffith and Mack Sennett to form the Triangle Motion Picture Company. They built a studio for Mabel Normand to make *Mickey* (1918) but their hopes of making her a big star were dashed when she signed for Samuel Goldwyn. Always looking for new talent, Ince signed Olive Thomas to star in his films. In June 1917 Ince broke with Triangle and joined Adolph Zukor but the partnership ended quickly. On November 8, 1919, Ince, Allan Dwan, Marshall Neilan, Mack Sennett, Maurice Tourneur and George Loane Tucker formed Associated Producers, an independent film company. Among Ince's films were *Sweet Memories* (1911), *Over The Hills*

(1911), *Little Nell's Tobacco* (1911), *In Old Madrid* (1911), *His Nemesis* (1911), *Her Darkest Hour* (1911), *Their First Misunderstanding* (1911), *The Law Of The West* (1912), *For Freedom Of Cuba* (1912), *Custer's Last Raid* (1912), *The Altar Of Death* (1912), *The Favorite Son* (1913), *The Battle Of Gettysburg* (1913), *In Love And War* (1913), *Jim Cameron's Wife* (1914), *Out Of The Night* (1914), *His Hour Of Manhood* (1914), *Rumpelstiltskin* (1915), *Matrimony* (1915), *Madcap Ambrose* (1916), *Civilization* (1916), *Shell 43* (1916), *The Return Of Draw Egan* (1916), *Somewhere In France* (1916), *Truthful Tulliver* (1916), *Sawdust Ring* (1917), *Shark Monroe* (1918), *23 Hours' Leave* (1919), *Silk Hosiery* (1920), *Let's Be Fashionable* (1920), *Lying Lips* (1921), *Hail The Woman* (1921) and *Free And Equal* (1925).
CAUSE: Ince's death has been shrouded in mystery for years. What is certain is that he was a weekend guest aboard *Oneida*, the luxury 280-foot yacht of billionaire press baron William Randolph Hearst. Other guests included Hearst's mistress Marion Davies, Charlie Chaplin, Louella Parsons, novelist Elinor Glyn and actresses Aileen Pringle and Seena Owen. On November 19, 1924, the Associated Press issued the following bulletin: "Thomas H. Ince, nationally known motion picture producer, died at 5.30 o'clock this morning at his home in the Hollywood foothills, it was announced at his Culver City studio. "Death was due to angina pectoris. He became ill on a trip to San Diego, was taken from a train at Del Mar Monday night and brought to his home here last night. The attack was sudden. He had been active in his motion picture work up to the time he was stricken . . ." A later wire service story added some more details that really didn't add up. After repeating AP's story that the death was due to "angina pectoris", which in itself isn't fatal – the condition is a syndrome of insufficient coronary

circulation – it added, "His death ended an illness which began Monday night while he was en route to San Diego. The suddenness of the attack prompted his friends to take him from a train at Del Mar, then to hurry him to Los Angeles in a special car, during which journey he was attended by two specialists and three nurses. From Los Angeles he was taken to his Canyon home, where his wife, his two sons, and two brothers rushed to his bedside before the end came." The bulletin posed more questions than it answered. What was Ince doing in San Diego, one hundred miles south of Hollywood, and a place that didn't then figure prominently in film-making? If a location scene was being shot, why did it require someone as important as Ince to oversee it? Who were the mysterious "friends" Ince was travelling with? How many of them were present? Where did the "two specialists and three nurses" come from? Who were they? If Ince's condition was serious enough to cancel the trip, why wasn't he taken to the nearest hospital rather than endure an eighty-mile train and ten-mile car journey back to his home? On November 21, Ince was buried. *The Los Angeles Times* announced "MOVIE PRODUCER SHOT ON HEARST YACHT" in its first edition and then yanked the story from all subsequent editions. Then the publicists announced that Ince had already been to San Diego over the previous weekend, and had travelled not by train but aboard the yacht *Oneida*. The yacht dropped anchor early Saturday and left San Pedro Harbor. It arrived in San Diego early Sunday and by that time Ince was desperately ill. Despite this, no doctor was called to the vessel. The only doctor aboard was Dr Daniel Carson Goodman, a doctor of letters not medicine. Early Monday, after no improvement in his condition, Ince was brought to shore. Officially, no one explained how. From reports that

circulated later, Ince was said to have been carried off the *Oneida* to a dinghy, then brought to shore and carried aboard the Los Angeles-bound AT&SF morning train. Still the puzzles continued. At Del Mar, 20 miles out of San Diego, Ince was in such discomfort that Dr Goodman took him off the train, flagged down a passing car and again, instead of taking him to a hospital, brought him to a hotel! Goodman then telephoned a Dr T.A. Parker, of nearby La Jolla, who rushed to the hotel. Arriving, he found a shirtsleeved Ince lying in bed in the suite Goodman had thoughtfully taken for the ailing producer. Undressing Ince, Parker diagnosed heart trouble and wrote a prescription. Parker questioned Ince and later said he learned that the movie maker's distress had been brought on by a great deal of smoking, too much eating and heavy drinking over the previous 24 hours. Still, Ince was not sent to a hospital but Parker did call a nurse, Jessie Howard, to be in attendance. According to a later statement from Parker, "I left him with instructions to Dr Goodman to let Mr Ince rest and to be given medication I prescribed. I called later that night and was told Mr Ince appeared much improved. I said I would see the patient again in the morning. But when I arrived at the hotel on Tuesday, I found a note left with the hotel clerk informing me that Mr Ince had left for home." Ince's inexplicable departure mystified Dr Parker. (Even more strangely, no one has been able to trace a Dr T.A. Parker of La Jolla. Did he exist? Was he an actor hired to give credibility to the coronary story?) Nurse Howard was no less bemused. She also wondered out loud what had gone on aboard the *Oneida*. From the sketchy description offered by the desperately ill Ince, she had every good reason to wonder. "He told me that he had drunk considerable liquor aboard the yacht. He attributed his illness to the amount of liquor he consumed. I saw myself in the hotel room how bad off he was. He was seized by a coughing spell that brought up traces of blood." So what did happen aboard the *Oneida*? One report had Charlie Chaplin firing a gun. Another had Ince being "carried off the yacht in San Diego with a gaping hole in the back of his head . . ." If Ince was wounded, how did the assault occur and by whom? Perhaps a clue can be found in Marion Davies' posthumously published autobiography, *The Times We Had: Life With William Randolph Hearst.* "There were some men who were a bit strenuous in their pursuit of me. That happened occasionally, but the moment W.R. (Davies' nickname for Hearst) would arrive, they'd all run for shelter. Nobody ever dared to stand up to him, and I didn't ever give anybody encouragement. I was a jolly, happy, free catch with everybody. I'd say hello, and that was as far as it ever went." Hearst's friends, colleagues and enemies were aware of the high degree of possessiveness with which he held onto Marion Davies. From his wife and mistress he demanded total and absolute loyalty, love, and devotion. He also had a fierce temper. He would lose his rag under the slightest provocation. In later years Davies spoke in support of Ingrid Bergman during her scandal-plagued romance with Roberto Rossellini. The editor of Hearst's *Los Angeles Herald-Examiner* cut Davies' quotes, but they appeared in the arch-rival *Los Angeles Times*. It was only Davies' intervention that saved the editor's job. Everyone aboard the *Oneida* subsequently remained silent about that fateful weekend. Did Charlie Chaplin fire a shot onboard the yacht? What role, if any, did Hearst play in Ince's demise? The public and certain sections of the press demanded an inquiry into Ince's death. The silence from the Hearst organisation was deafening. San Diego County District Attorney Chester C. Kemply interviewed Dr Parker and nurse Howard but didn't attempt to speak to anyone aboard the *Oneida* before announcing his verdict: "I am satisfied that the death of Thomas H. Ince was caused by heart failure as the result of an attack of acute indigestion. There will be no investigation into the death of Ince, at least so far as San Diego County is concerned. As there is every reason to believe that the death of Ince was due to natural causes, there is no reason why an investigation should be made." One would have imagined that Kemply would have at least wondered why alcohol was being served aboard the *Oneida*, but he neatly passed the buck, stating that as the ship sailed from San Pedro the booze had been bought there as well. As for who might have fired a shot and why, there are a number of theories. One postulates that Charlie Chaplin was having a secret affair with Marion Davies and that Hearst found out. According to this version of events, on the night in question Hearst saw Marion Davies with a man and, assuming him to be Chaplin, shot him. It was only when Davies screamed that Hearst realised he had shot Ince in error. Or, Charlie Chaplin was having a secret affair with Marion Davies and when he saw Ince innocently chatting to Davies, Chaplin shot him. A third version involves a complete newcomer to the story. Marion Davies' secretary, Abigail Kinsolving, claimed she was raped by Ince that weekend. Not long after giving birth to a child, Louise, she was killed in a mysterious car crash near Hearst's San Simeon estate. Her body was discovered by two of Hearst's bodyguards and a suicide note was supposedly found in the wreckage, although it was dissimilar to other samples of her writing. Did Abigail Kinsolving shoot Ince in revenge for raping her? Marion Davies discreetly paid for the child's education and Hearst set up a trust fund for Mrs Ince.

Jill Ireland
Born April 24, 1936
Died May 18, 1990
Gutsy dame. Born in London, beautiful blonde Jill Dorothy Ireland began her showbiz career aged 15 as a Tiller Girl at the London Palladium. She was cast in two other shows when she turned 16 and at 17 she went off to Paris. Following her appearance in *Oh . . . Rosalinda!!* (1956) she was signed to a contract by Rank and met actor David McCallum. They married and their son Paul was born 13 months later. Jill appeared in *There's Always A Thursday* (1957) as Jennifer Potter, *Robbery Under Arms* (1957) as Jean Morrison, *Carry On Nurse* (1958) as Jill Thompson, *Girls Of The Latin Quarter* (1959) as Jill, *So Evil, So Young* (1961), *Raising The Wind* (1961) as Janet, *Jungle Street* (1961) as Sue, *Twice Round The Daffodils* (1962) as Janet and *The Battleaxe* (1962) as Audrey Page. Two more sons Jason and Valentine arrived before she and McCallum were divorced in 1967. The following year, on October 5, she married Charles Bronson. Their daughter Zuleika (named after Max Beerbohm's heroine) was born on August 4, 1971, in Los Angeles. She and Bronson worked in many films together – "I think I'm in so many of his pictures because no other actress would work with him," she once joked. Her films, with and without Bronson, included: *The Karate Killers* (1967) as Imogen, *Villa Rides* (1968), *Città Violenta* (1970) as Vanessa, *Someone Behind The Door* (1971) as Frances, *The Valachi Papers* (1972) as Maria, *The Mechanic* (1972), *Breakout* (1975) as Ann Wagner, *Hard Times* (1975) as Lucy Simpson, *Breakheart Pass* (1975) as Marcia Scoville, *From Noon Till Three* (1976) as Amanda Starbuck, *Love And Bullets* (1979) as Jackie Pruit, *Death Wish II* (1982) as Geri Nichols, *Assassination* (1987) as Lara Royce Craig and *Caught* (1987) as Janet Devon.

CAUSE: In May 1984 she was diagnosed as having breast cancer and underwent a mastectomy. She died in Malibu, California, aged 54, from cancer.
FURTHER READING: *Life Wish* – Jill Ireland (London: Arrow, 1988).

John Ireland
Born January 30, 1914
Died March 21, 1992
The King's Man. Born in Vancouver, British Columbia, Canada, John Benjamin Ireland was raised in New York. He began his professional career as part of a water carnival before moving into legitimate theatre. He made his film début in the classic war epic *A Walk In The Sun* (1945) as Private Windy Craven. Due to his height (he was 6'1"), Ireland usually found himself cast as a heavy but in 1949 he was nominated for a Best Supporting Actor Oscar for his role as the journalist Jack Burden in *All The King's Men*. He lost to Dean Jagger for *12 O'Clock High* and the following decade was not kind to Ireland. He found himself in starring roles, albeit almost exclusively in B-movies. He decided to seek his fame abroad and appeared in many Italian films with the occasional return to Tinseltown for films like *Spartacus* (1960) where he played Crixus. His films included: *It Shouldn't Happen To A Dog* (1946) as Benny Smith, *Wake Up And Dream* (1946) as Howard Williams, *Railroaded!* (1947) as Duke Martin, *I Love Trouble* (1948) as Reno, *Red River* (1948) as Cherry Valance, *I Shot Jesse James* (1949) as Bob Ford, *Anna Lucasta* (1949) as Danny Johnson, *Cargo To Capetown* (1950) as Steve Conway, *Little Big Horn* (1951) as Lieutenant John Haywood Scarf, *Red Mountain* (1952) as General John Quantrell, *Hurricane Smith* (1952) as Hurricane Smith, *The Return Of Jesse James* (1950) as Johnny Callum, *Vengeance Valley* (1951) as Hub Fasken, *The Bushwhackers* (1952) as Jefferson Waring, *Combat Squad* (1953)

as Sergeant Fletcher, *The Fast And The Furious* (1954) as Frank Webster, *Stormy Crossing* (1957) as Griff Parker, *Gunfight At The O.K. Corral* (1957) as Johnny Ringo, *Med Mord I Bagaget* (1959) as Johnny Greco, *55 Days At Peking* (1963) as Sergeant Harry, *I Saw What You Did* (1965) as Steve Marak, *Odio Per Odio* (1967) as Cooper, *Fort Utah* (1967) as Tom Horn, *Dalle Ardenne All'Inferno* (1967) as Captain O'Conner, *Corri, Uomo, Corri* (1968) as Santillana, *Arizona Bushwhackers* (1968) as Dan Shelby, *Villa Rides* (1968), *Femmine Insaziabili* (1969), *Quel Caldo Maledetto Giorno Di Fuoco* (1969), *Lo Strangolatore Di Vienna* (1971), *Northeast Of Seoul* (1972) as Flanaghan, *The House Of Seven Corpses* (1974) as Eric Hartman, *Farewell, My Lovely* (1975) as Lieutenant Nulty, *Marilyn: The Untold Story* (1980) as John Huston, *Graveyard Story* (1990) as Dr McGregor, *Big Bad John* (1990), *Sundown: The Vampire In Retreat* (1991) as Ethan Jefferson and *Waxwork II: Lost In Time* (1992) as King Arthur. Ireland married three times. His first wife was Elaine Sheldon Rosen (1940–1948). Then came Joanne Dru (1949–1956) by whom he had two sons, John and Peter. In 1962 he married Daphne Myrick Cameron and they were together until his death. CAUSE: John Ireland died in Santa Barbara, California of leukaemia.

J

Gordon Jackson, OBE

Born December 19, 1923
Died January 15, 1990
Dour Scot. Depending on how old
you are, Gordon Cameron Jackson
is probably best known to television
viewers of the Sixties as Angus
Hudson, the butler in *Upstairs,
Downstairs* and to Seventies viewers
as the tough-talking George Cowley in
The Professionals. He was also a prolific
actor on stage and in films. Born in
Glasgow he appeared in *One Of Our
Aircraft Is Missing* (1942), *The Captive
Heart* (1946) as Lieutenant Lennox,
Whisky Galore! (1949) as George
Campbell, *Eureka Stockade* (1949)
as Torn Kennedy, *Happy Go Lovely*
(1951) as Paul Tracy, *Castle In The
Air* (1952), *Meet Mr Lucifer* (1953)
as Hector McPhee, *The Quatermass
Xperiment* (1955), *Women Without
Men* (1956) as Percy, *Blonde Bait*
(1956) as Percy, *The Navy Lark*
(1959) as Leading Seaman Johnson,
Greyfriars Bobby (1961), *Mutiny On
The Bounty* (1962) as Edward
Birkett, *The Great Escape* (1963) as
MacDonald, *Those Magnificent Men In
Their Flying Machines, Or How I Flew
From London To Paris In 25 Hours 11
Minutes* (1965) as McDougal, *The
Ipcress File* (1965) as Carswell, *The
Night Of The Generals* (1967) as
Captain Engel, *Hamlet* (1969) as
Horatio, *The Prime Of Miss Jean Brodie*
(1969) as Gordon Lowther, *Scrooge*
(1970), *Kidnapped* (1971) as Charles
Stewart and *Gunpowder* (1987) as
Sir Anthony Phelps.
CAUSE: He died of bone cancer in the
Cromwell Hospital. He was 66 and left
£742,068.

Hattie Jacques

(JOSEPHINA EDWINA JACQUES)
Born February 7, 1922
Died October 6, 1980
'Oooh, matron!' Hattie Jacques was
born at 125 High Street, Sandgate,
Kent, the daughter of Lieutenant
Robin Jacques (d. 1922), a former test
pilot in the Royal Flying Corps, and
Mary Adelaide Thorn. Her father was
killed in a flying accident the year she
was born and Hattie and her brother,
the three-times married book illustrator
Robin Jacques (b. March 27, 1920, d.
March 18, 1995), were raised by their
grandparents. She was educated at
Godolphin and Latymer Upper School
in Hammersmith, west London, and
trained briefly as a hairdresser. Hattie
became a national institution for her
work on the *Carry On . . .* series. She
was also one of the most popular
actresses in Britain, known for her
warmth and generosity. Kenneth
Williams described her as being like
"a kiss on a winter's day". Her agent
recalled, "If she had one fault, it was
that she could be easily put upon. She
was getting constant requests to do
charity work and she'd try to attend
every one." Producer Peter Rogers
described her as "the Mother Superior
of the *Carry On . . .* family . . . That
is the sort of person she was – a
tower of strength, kind, generous,
understanding, with a wonderful sense
of humour." She spent two years
during the Second World War as a Red
Cross nurse (possibly handy training
for playing a matron five times in the
*Carry On*s), and then as a welder in
a north London factory where she
discovered she could make people
laugh, possibly as a defence mechanism
because of her size. She made her stage
début in 1944 at the Players Theatre in
London, singing Victorian songs. At
Christmas she became a large, bossy,
but vulnerable pantomime fairy queen,
which she later confessed was her
favourite part. She toured with the
Young Vic company in *The King Stag*

as Smeraldina (1947–1948). She also appeared on radio in *ITMA* as Sophie Tuckshop (1948–1949), *Educating Archie* as Agatha Dangelbody (1950–1954) and *Hancock's Half Hour*. Her films included *Oliver Twist* (1948) as a singer at the Three Cripples pub, *Trottie True* (1949) as Daisy Delaware, *Scrooge* (1951) as Mrs Fezziwig, *The Pickwick Papers* (1952) as Mrs Nupkins, *Mother Riley Meets The Vampire* (1952) as Mrs Jenks, *All Hallowe'en* (1952) as Miss Quibble, *Our Girl Friday* (1954) as Mrs Patch, *The Square Peg* (1958) as Gretchen, *The Night We Dropped A Clanger* (1959) as Ada, *The Navy Lark* (1959), *School For Scoundrels* (1960), *She'll Have To Go* (1962) as Miss Richards, *The Punch And Judy Man* (1963) as Dolly Zarathusa and *Monte Carlo Or Bust* (1969). She appeared in the following *Carry On*s: *Sergeant* (1958) as Captain Clark, a no-nonsense army doctor, *Nurse* (1958) as Matron, *Teacher* (1959) as maths mistress Grace Short at Maudlin Street School, *Constable* (1960) as Woman Police Sergeant Laura Moon, *Regardless* (1961) as a hospital sister, *Cabby* (1963) as Peggy Hawkins, the neglected wife of a cab firm owner who sets up her own rival organisation, *Doctor* (1968) as Matron, *Camping* (1969) as Miss Haggerd, *Again, Doctor* (1969) as Matron, *Loving* (1970) as Sophie Bliss (née Plummit), who runs a dating agency with her boyfriend, *At Your Convenience* (1971) as Beattie Plummer, *Matron* (1972) as Matron, *Abroad* (1972) as Floella the fiery-tempered hotelier and *Dick* (1974) as Martha Hoggett. From January 29, 1960 until November 16, 1965 she played Eric Sykes' twin sister in the highly successful BBC sitcom *Sykes* which was set at 24 Sebastopol Terrace, Acton, west London. Seven years later on September 14, 1972 the series was revived although the action had now moved to 28 Sebastopol Terrace. The show ended at her early

death. She was married to actor John Le Mesurier from November 10, 1949 until May 28, 1965 and they had two sons, Robin Mark (b. March 22, 1953) and Kim Charles "Jake" (b. October 12, 1956, d. Barcelona, Spain October 6, 1991 of a heroin overdose). In 1962 she began an affair with her new driver John Schofield that lasted until 1966 when he ran off with an Italian heiress. While Schofield lived in the main bedroom, Le Mesurier moved into the attic.

CAUSE: Hattie Jacques's health began to fail in 1980 after the death of her mother. Her weight increased but she continued to smoke. She was admitted to Charing Cross Hospital in early October 1980 but persuaded staff to let her go home at 67 Eardley Crescent, Earl's Court, London, without telling them she had agreed to do a charity gig on the Sunday night. However, chest pains prevented her from going. Taking a hot water bottle, she went to bed early. The next day she had not come down and was found dead in bed by her son Jake. She was 58 and had succumbed to a heart attack. A memorial service was held at St Paul's, Covent Garden. She left £151,503.

FURTHER READING: *Hattie: The Authorised Biography Of Hattie Jacques* – Andy Merriman (London: Aurum, 2007).

Sam Jaffe

Born March 10, 1891
Died March 24, 1984
Small fry. Born in New York, Shalom Jaffe gave up a relatively successful stage career to become a maths teacher. He returned to acting in 1915 and made his film début 19 years later. He appeared in *The Scarlet Empress* (1934) as Grand Duke Peter, *Lost Horizon* (1937) as High Lama, *Gunga Din* (1939) as Gunga Din, *13 Rue Madeleine* (1946) as Mayor Galimard, *The Accused* (1948) as Dr Romley, *The Asphalt Jungle* (1950) as Doc Riedenschneider, for which he was

nominated for a Best Supporting Actor Oscar and won Best Actor at the Venice Film Festival, *The Day The Earth Stood Still* (1951) as Professor Jacob Barnhardt, *The Barbarian And The Geisha* (1958) as Henry Heusken, *Ben-Hur* (1959) as Simonides, *Tarzan's Jungle Rebellion* (1965) as Singleton, *The Great Bank Robbery* (1969) as Brother Lilac, *Battle Beyond The Stars* (1980) as Dr Hephaestus, *Nothing Lasts Forever* (1984) as Father Knickerbocker and *Río Abajo* (1984) as El Gabacho. He married twice. His first wife was actress Lillian Taiz Jaffe (d. 1941) and his second (from 1955) was actress Bettye Ackerman (b. Cottageville, South Carolina, February 28, 1928) with whom he appeared in the television series *Ben Casey*.
CAUSE: He died in Beverly Hills, California, from cancer, at the age of 93.

Dean Jagger

Born November 7, 1903
Died February 5, 1991
Old before his time. Ira Dean Jagger was born in Lima, Ohio, and, like Sam Jaffe, was a teacher before he turned to acting. He appeared on radio, vaudeville, and in films and later television. His movies included: *The Woman From Hell* (1929) as Jim, *Men Without Names* (1935) as Jones, *Wings In The Dark* (1935) as Tops Harmon, *Home On The Range* (1935) as Thurman, *People Will Talk* (1935) as Bill Trask, *Car 99* (1935) as Officer Jim Burton, *Star For A Night* (1936) as Fritz Lind, *Revolt Of The Zombies* (1936) as Armand Louque, *It's A Great Life* (1936) as Arnold, *Thirteen Hours By Air* (1936) as Hap Waller, *Pepper* (1936) as Bob O'Ryan, *Woman In Distress* (1937) as Fred Stevens, *Exiled To Shanghai* (1937) as Fred Sears, *Escape By Night* (1937) as Capper Regan, *Dangerous Number* (1937) as Dillman, *Brigham Young – Frontiersman* (1940) as Brigham Young, *Western Union* (1941) as Edward Creighton,

The Omaha Trail (1942) as 'Pipestone' Ross, *Valley Of The Sun* (1942) as Jim Sawyer, *The North Star* (1943) as Rodion, *I Escaped From The Gestapo* (1943) as Lane, *I Live In Grosvenor Square* (1945) as Sergeant John Patterson, *Sister Kenny* (1946) as Kevin Connors, *Driftwood* (1947) as Dr Steve Webster, *Twelve O'Clock High* (1949) as Major Harvey Stovall for which he was nominated for a Best Supporting Actor Oscar, *Dark City* (1950) as Captain Garvey, *Warpath* (1951) as Sam Quade, *Rawhide* (1951) as Yancy, *It Grows On Trees* (1952) as Phil Baxter, *The Robe* (1953) as Justus, *Private Hell 36* (1954) as Captain Michaels, *White Christmas* (1954) as General Waverly, *Executive Suite* (1954) as Jesse Grimm, *Bad Day At Black Rock* (1955) as Tim Horn, *On The Threshold Of Space* (1956) as Dr Hugh Thornton, *Bombers B-52* (1957), *King Creole* (1958) as Mr Fisher, *The Proud Rebel* (1958) as Harry Burleigh, *The Nun's Story* (1959) as Dr Van Der Mal, *Elmer Gantry* (1960) as William L. Morgan, *Day Of The Evil Gun* (1968) as Jimmy Noble, *The Kremlin Letter* (1970), *So Sad About Gloria* (1973), *The Great Lester Boggs* (1975) and *Alligator* (1980) as Slade. He won an Emmy in 1980.
CAUSE: He died aged 87 in Santa Monica, California, from heart disease.

Sid James

(SIDNEY JOEL COHEN)
Born May 8, 1913
Died April 26, 1976
South African cockney. Many people would have placed wagers on Sid James' birthplace, and would confidently assert that he was born well within the sound of the bells of St Mary-le-Bow making him a fully fledged cockney. Those people would have lost their money, because Sid James began life several thousand miles from east London in Hancock Street, Newcastle, Natal, South Africa. Within a week of his birth (reported on his

death certificate as May 6, 1913) his forenames were replaced by the more Judaic Sollie. He became Sidney again aged eight, to avoid confusion at school with his cousin, who became a surgeon. He also changed his surname to the one that subsequently became known by millions of film fans. Despite the tales of derring-do later recounted by the adult Sid James he began his real working life in 1930 as a hairdresser at the Marie Tudor salon. It was there he met his first wife, Berthe Sadie Delmont (b. 1912, d. 1966), nicknamed 'Toots'. In 1932, determined to escape from his mother's apron strings, he moved to Kroonstad where he became a favourite of the ladies who have their hair cut. He also began to teach ballroom dancing and attempted to seduce as many women as possible. He hated cutting hair and yearned for a career on the stage and to make lots of money. He returned to Johannesburg, where he married Toots on August 12, 1936, in the Central Register Office. As a 'wedding present', Sid's father-in-law bought him his own hairdressing establishment, Maison Renée. In reality, the gift was an attempt to prevent Sid following his acting dreams and taking Toots away. Just 80 days into the marriage, Toots discovered Sid was seeing someone else. The someone else was pregnant and Toots' father paid the other woman hush money to leave the country and never mention who the father of her daughter was. The situation repeated itself again in February 1937 when a son arrived. More affairs followed before James' first legitimate child, Elizabeth, was born in December 1937. Six months earlier, he had joined the Johannesburg Repertory Players. In 1939 he made his professional acting début – on the wireless. That year he also met Meg Sergei (b. August 1913) and began an affair that resulted in Toots filing for a divorce. He also began getting involved in bar room brawls, which later in the

Sid James mythology evolved into professional boxing (he was never actually a boxer). James compared his face to "a bed that has been slept in with the sheets left rumpled". His pockmarked skin was the result of acne and the wrinkles were suffered by all the male Cohens. However, his nose did get broken during a fight. A large man had made anti-Semitic remarks and Sid waded into him, little knowing he had several equally well-built friends with him. They stamped on Sid's hands and one of his little fingers was so badly hurt that it was to remain paralysed until his death. In February 1941 a 17-year-old trainee at Maison Renée gave birth to Sid's illegitimate son. His father-in-law then took a contract out on Sid, who joined the decidedly less dangerous ranks of the army to escape. He soon joined an entertainment unit and underwent an unsuccessful operation (performed by his cousin) to treat his haemorrhoids. In 1943 he and Meg Sergei were married. In January 1945 a new recruit joined the concert party and, after a shaky start, Sid and Larushka Skikne became lifelong friends. He, too, became an actor, under the name Laurence Harvey. James arrived in London, virtually penniless, on December 25, 1946. However, his determination saw him cast in a film within days of his arrival. After that he never looked back. He appeared in *Black Memory* (1947) as Eddie Clinton, *The October Man* (1947), *It Always Rains On Sunday* (1948) as a bandleader, *No Orchids For Miss Blandish* (1948), *Night Beat* (1948) as Nixon, *Once A Jolly Swagman* (1948) as Rowton and many others. His daughter Reine Christina arrived on April 26, 1947, at the Royal Northern Hospital, Islington. He was quickly on his way to becoming a stalwart of British films in the Fifties, taking any part rather than face unemployment and uncertainty. His films included *The Small Back Room* (1949) as Knucksie the barman, *Paper Orchid* (1949) as crime reporter Freddie Evans, *The Man In Black* (1949) as Henry Clavering, *Give Us This Day* (1949) as Murdin, *The Lady Craved Excitement* (1950) as Carlo, *Lady Godiva Rides Again* (1951) as Lew Beeson, *The Lavender Hill Mob* (1951) as safecracker Lackery, *The Magic Box* (1951), *Miss Robin Hood* (1952) as Sidney, *Time Gentlemen Please!* (1952) as Eric Hace, *The Venetian Bird* (1952) as Bernardo, *The Titfield Thunderbolt* (1953) as train driver Hawkins, *Escape By Night* (1953) as Gino Rossi, *Father Brown* (1954) as Parkinson, *Aunt Clara* (1954) as Honest Sid, *For Better, For Worse* (1954), *The Belles Of St Trinian's* (1954) as Benny, *A Kid For Two Farthings* (1955) as Iceberg, *The Glass Cage* (1955) as Tony Lewis, *Quatermass II* (1957) as Jimmy Hall, *The Story Of Esther Costello* (1957) as Ryan, *I Was Monty's Double* (1958), *The Sheriff Of Fractured Jaw* (1958) as a drunk, *The 39 Steps* (1959) as Perce and many, many more. Meanwhile, in 1948, with a wife and an 18-month-old daughter, Sid began an affair with a teenage actress called Valerie Ashton (b. Hartlepool December 13, 1928, as Valerie Elizabeth Patsy Assan). He separated from his wife in 1950 and moved in with Valerie. He was divorced on August 17, 1952, and, four days later, he and Valerie were married. On February 19, 1954, their son Stephen was born in the London Clinic. On November 2 of that year Sid began appearing on the radio show *Hancock's Half Hour*, which transferred to television on July 6, 1956. Sid was one of the few cast members to make the transition from the wireless to the small screen. During his third marriage Sid's gambling began to spiral out of control and he often borrowed money from friends to pay his debts, with little likelihood of repayment. On October 7, 1957, Susan Valerie James was born at Queen Charlotte's Hospital, Hammersmith. In January 1958 Sid

signed to make the (unsuccessful) Associated-Rediffusion sitcom *East End, West End*, playing a wide-boy. In 1959 Sid was approached to appear in the fourth of what had the makings of a successful series of films. It was called *Carry On Constable* (1960) and he took over the role assigned to Ted Ray who was dropped from the series for legal reasons. Sid played Sergeant Frank Wilkins, who has to lick three newcomers – played by Kenneth Connor, Leslie Phillips and Kenneth Williams – into shape. Also in the Sixties Sid renounced his South African citizenship and became a British subject, although at heart he still felt himself to be a Springbok and cheered for that national team rather than that of his adopted home. Apart from the *Carry On*s Sid also appeared in *Raising The Wind* (1961) as Sid, *The Pure Hell Of St Trinian's* (1961) as Alphonse O'Reilly, *The Green Helmet* (1961) as Richie Launder and *The Big Job* (1965) as George Brain. *Carry On Constable* (1960) was the first of 19 *Carry On*s that Sid was to appear in, often playing a character called Sid. The others were: *Carry On Regardless* (1961) as Bert Handy, *Carry On Cruising* (1962) as Captain Wellington Crowther, *Carry On Cabby* (1963) as taxi boss Charlie Hawkins, *Carry On Cleo* (1964) as Mark Antony, *Carry On Cowboy* (1965) as Johnny Finger/The Rumpo Kid, which was his favourite of the series, *Carry On . . . Don't Lose Your Head* (1967) as the saviour of 'French aristos' Sir Rodney Ffing a.k.a. The Black Fingernail, *Carry On Up The Khyber* (1968) as Sir Sidney Ruff-Diamond (an in-joke, since he really was a rough diamond), *Carry On Doctor* (1968) as Charlie Roper, *Carry On Camping* (1969) as Sid Boggle, *Carry On Again, Doctor* (1969) as Gladstone Screwer, *Carry On Up The Jungle* (1970) as Bill Boosey, *Carry On Loving* (1970) as Sidney Bliss, *Carry On Henry* (1971) as King Henry VIII, *Carry On At Your Convenience* (1971) as factory owner Sid Plummer, *Carry On Matron* (1972) as Sid Carter, *Carry On Abroad* (1972) as Vic Flange, *Carry On Girls* (1973) as Sidney Fiddler and *Carry On Dick* (1974) as Dick Turpin/Reverend Flasher. He also appeared in the television series *Citizen James* (BBC, November 24, 1960–November 23, 1962) as Sidney Balmoral James, *Taxi!* (BBC, July 1963–August 1963), *George And The Dragon* (ATV, November 19, 1966–October 31, 1968) as chauffeur/handyman George Russell, *Two In Clover* (Thames TV, February 18, 1969–March 19, 1970) as Sid Turner and *Bless This House* (Thames TV, February 2, 1971–April 22, 1976) as Sid Abbott, the put-upon father of two teenagers. (When a film version was made Sid insisted that Robin Stewart, who played his son in the TV series, was dropped from the cast.) In 1974 Sid was voted Funniest Man On Television by readers of *TV Times*. CAUSE: On May 13, 1967, while filming *George And The Dragon* Sid suffered a massive heart attack. His health was so poor during the making of *Carry On Doctor* (1968) that it was fortunate that all his scenes required him to be in bed. As well as his gambling Sid James was a dedicated philanderer, attempting to seduce as many women as possible, and usually successfully. One of his conquests was his *Carry On . . .* co-star Barbara Windsor. It was when the affair with Windsor petered out that Sid began to lose the will to live. He told friends that if the affair ended he would be dead within a year. He drank a bottle of whisky a day and preferred to work rather than spend time at home with his wife. In 1976 he began a tour of the play *The Mating Game*. It was on stage at the Empire Theatre, Sunderland, that he suffered a fatal heart attack and died on the way to hospital. He was 63 years old. He left £68,012. FURTHER READING: *Sid James* – Cliff Goodwin (London: Century, 1995).

Emil Jannings
(THEODOR FRIEDRICH EMIL JANENZ)
Born July 23, 1884
Died January 3, 1950
Oscar's first. Born in Rorschach, Switzerland, 6′ Jannings began acting in Berlin with Max Reinhardt's Deutsches Theatre Company before moving to films at the suggestion of Ernst Lubitsch. He appeared in over 70 films including *Passionels Tagebuch* (1914), *Im Schützengraben* (1914), *Arme Eva* (1914), *Unheilbar* (1916), *Stein Unter Steinen* (1916), *Nächte Des Grauens* (1916), *Frau Eva* (1916), *Die Ehe Der Luise Rohrbach* (1916), *Die Bettlerin Von St Marien* (1916), *Aus Mangel An Beweisen* (1916), *Lulu* (1917), *Der Ring Der Giuditta Foscari* (1917), *Fuhrmann Henschel* (1918), *Ein Fideles Gefängnis* (1918), *Die Brüder Karamasoff* (1918), *Die Augen Der Mumie Ma* (1918) as Radu, *Die Tochter Des Mehemed* (1919), *Madame DuBarry* (1919) as Louis XV, *Der Schädel der Pharaonentochter* (1920), *Das Große Licht* (1920), *Colombine* (1920), *Algol* (1920) as Robert Herne, *Vendetta* (1921), *Der Schwur Des Peter Hergatz* (1921), *Othello* (1922) as Othello, *Das Weib Des Pharao* (1922) as Pharaoh Amenes, *Das Wachsfigurenkabinett* (1923) as Harun al Raschid, *Quo Vadis?* (1924), *Peter The Great* (1924), *Variete* (1925) as jealous trapeze artist Boss Huller, *Faust* (1926) as Mephisto, *The Way Of All Flesh* (1927) as August Schilling, *The Last Command* (1928) as General Dolgorucki/Grand Duke Sergius Alexander, *The Patriot* (1928) as Czar Paul I, *Liebling Der Götter* (1930) as Albert Winkelmann, *Der Blaue Engel* (1930) as Professor Immanuel Rath, *Stürme Der Leidenschaft* (1932) as Gustav Bumke, *Die Abenteuer Des Königs Pausole* (1933), *Traumulus* (1936) as Professor Niemeyer, *Die Entlassung* (1942) as Bismarck, *Wo Ist Herr Belling?* (1945), *Das Kommt Nicht Wieder* (1958) and *Das Gab's Nur Einmal* (1958). It was the success of *Variete* that led him

to sign a three-year contract with Paramount and he subsequently won the first Best Actor Oscar for *The Way Of All Flesh* and *The Last Command*. He was acclaimed for his portrayal of the university professor opposite Marlene Dietrich in *Der Blaue Engel/The Blue Angel* but while she went on to become a huge star Jannings was let down by his poor English and returned to Germany where he appeared in propaganda films for the Nazis. Following the war he was blacklisted by the victorious Allies and retired to Austria, a broken man.
CAUSE: He died aged 65 in Strobl, Austria, of cancer.

David Janssen

(DAVID HAROLD MEYER)
Born March 27, 1931
Died February 13, 1980
The original fugitive. David Janssen was born in Naponee, Nebraska, the son of Harold Edward Meyer, but his parents separated while he was still in nappies. His mother, Berniece, a former Ziegfeld girl, married Eugene Janssen and the family settled in Los Angeles. Young David was educated at Fairfax High School in Hollywood and made his film début aged 14 in *It's A Pleasure* (1945). Aged 18 he signed a contract with 20th Century Fox but they dropped him, supposedly because of his big ears and receding hairline. (His appearance gave rise to the rumour that he was, in fact, the illegitimate son of Clark Gable.) He then made 32 films for Universal but never became a really big star on the big screen. On July 1, 1957, his first major television series *Richard Diamond, Private Eye* aired on CBS. Diamond was an ex-NYPD cop who became a private detective. The show moved to NBC for its final year, ending on September 6, 1960. Three years and eleven days later, the show that would make Janssen a star premièred on ABC. He played Dr Richard Kimble, a man wrongly accused of uxoricide in

The Fugitive. The show was based on the real life murder in Cleveland, Ohio, on July 3, 1954 of Marian Sheppard whose husband Dr Sam was convicted on December 21, 1954 and sentenced to life imprisonment for her murder. After 12 years of incarceration Sheppard was cleared on November 16, 1966. He died on April 6, 1970. The show ended on August 29, 1967 when the one-armed man confessed before being shot by Kimble's nemesis, Lieutenant Philip Gerard. The finale received a 72 per cent share of American television viewers; a record that stood until the episode of *Dallas* when it was revealed who had shot J.R. Ewing (the first time). Janssen then appeared as Jim O'Hara in the short-lived series *O'Hara, US Treasury* (September 17, 1971–September 8, 1972) before scoring his final TV hit as San Diego private detective Harry Orwell in *Harry-O* (September 12, 1974–August 12, 1976). The show co-starred *High Chaparral* star Henry Darrow and featured Keye Luke (Charlie Chan's Number One Son) and early appearances from the beautiful Farrah Fawcett-Majors. His other films included *Francis Goes To West Point* (1952) as Corporal Thomas, *Francis In The Navy* (1955) as Lieutenant Anders, *To Hell And Back* (1955) as Lieutenant Lee, *The Green Berets* (1968) as George Beckworth, *The Shoes Of The Fisherman* (1968) as George Faber, *Macho Callahan* (1970) as Diego Callahan and *Covert Action* (1978) as Lester Horton. 6' David Janssen was married twice. His first wife in 1958 was Ellie Graham. They divorced in 1973. She claimed that Janssen was a womaniser who slept with 31 women during the last 18 months of their marriage. Two years later he married Dani Saval Crayne Greco.
CAUSE: David Janssen awoke suffering from chest pains on February 13, 1980. He went to the bathroom and collapsed. At 5.55am his wife Dani

rang for an ambulance but he was pronounced dead at Santa Monica Hospital, 1225 15th Street, Santa Monica, California, aged 48 of heart failure. He was buried on February 17, 1980 at Hillside Memorial Park in Culver City. Pallbearers included Milton Berle, Rod Stewart, Gene Kelly, Richard Harris and Gregory Peck.

Maurice Jarre
Born September 13, 1924
Died March 29, 2009
Monsieur Musique. Born in Lyon, France Maurice-Alexis Jarre studied music at the Conservatoire de Paris, training initially as a kettledrum player. At the school, he studied under the Swiss composer Arthur Honegger, the timpanist Félix Passerone and Joseph Martenot, inventor of the Martenot Waves, an electronic keyboard that virtually evolved into the modern synthesiser. He spent a dozen years as permanent composer at the Theatre National Populaire. Jarre began composing film soundtracks – more than 150 in total – in 1950 and won three Oscars, all from films directed by Sir David Lean – *Lawrence Of Arabia* (1961), *Doctor Zhivago* (1965) and *A Passage To India* (1984). Interestingly, Jarre was the third choice for *Lawrence Of Arabia*; producer Sam Spiegel wanted Sir William Walton while Lean asked Malcolm Arnold. Both men turned down the invitation. Jarre composed and recorded all the music for the 3½ hour film in just six weeks. He also conducted the music despite the onscreen credit for Sir Adrian Boult. Jarre earned a further six Oscar nominations for films: *Les Dimanches De Ville D'Avray* (1962), *The Life And Times Of Judge Roy Bean* (1972), Moustapha Akkad's *The Message* (1976); Peter Weir's *Witness* (1985), for which he won a BAFTA; Michael Apted's *Gorillas In The Mist* (1988); and Jerry Zucker's *Ghost* (1990). Jarre's other films included: *Is Paris Burning?* (1966), *The Damned* (1969), *Ryan's*

Daughter (1970), *The Man Who Would Be King* (1975), *The Tin Drum* (1979), *Circle Of Deceit* (1981), *The Year Of Living Dangerously* (1982), *Fatal Attraction* (1987), *No Way Out* (1987) and *Dead Poet's Society* (1989), for which he won a further BAFTA. He also composed the music for the epic television series *Jesus Of Nazareth* in 1977. His last score was for *Uprising* (2001), a television film about the Holocaust. Diminutive French president Nicolas Sarkozy said, "He showed everyone that music is just as important as images for the beauty and success of a film." Jarre was married four times.
CAUSE: Jarre of cancer died at his home in Malibu, California, aged 84.

Jean Louis
Born October 5, 1907
Died April 20, 1997
Le designer. Jean Louis Berthault achieved fame with the dress he created for Rita Hayworth in *Gilda* (1946). "That dress seemed marvellous from the first moment I thought of it," he told one interviewer. "Rita made it sexy because of the casualness with which she wore it. There was something voluptuous about her ease." Jean Louis was born in Paris, France and travelled to New York in 1935 on a speculative trip. He stayed and was soon designing for the Duchess of Windsor and Mrs Harry Cohn who recommended him to her husband. From 1944 until 1958 Columbia films bore the line "Gowns by Jean Louis" in the credits. When he was hired to work on *Gilda* Rita Hayworth had not long had a baby and, unlike today's female celebrities, she still had her baby belly. Jean Louis' solution was to flatten her stomach with a tight tie that flowed into a bow. Flame-moulded plastic bars held up the strapless frock. When later he worked with Kim Novak she did not want her gowns to have any support up top, so she glued herself into her outfits tearing skin and material at the end of

each day's shooting. Stars trusted Jean Louis because he made them feel glamorous and womanly, not slutty or slatternly. He designed for Judy Holliday in *Born Yesterday* (1950) for which he was nominated for his first Oscar, *It Should Happen To You* (1954) for which he was nominated for his fifth Oscar and *The Solid Gold Cadillac* (1956) for which he finally won an Academy Award; Rita Hayworth again in *Affair In Trinidad* (1952) for which he was nominated for his second Oscar; and *Pal Joey* (1957) and his eighth nomination; Deborah Kerr in *From Here To Eternity* (1953) for which he was nominated for his third Oscar; Marlene Dietrich's 1953 cabaret tours; Judy Garland in *A Star Is Born* (1954) for which he was nominated for his fourth Oscar and *Judgment At Nuremberg* (1961) and his 10th nomination; Joan Crawford in *Queen Bee* (1955) for which he was nominated for his sixth Oscar; Kim Novak in *Bell, Book And Candle* (1958) for which he was nominated for his ninth Oscar; Susan Hayward in *Back Street* (1961) for which he was nominated for his 11th Oscar; Vivien Leigh in *Ship Of Fools* (1965) and his 12th Academy Award nomination; Shirley MacLaine in *Gambit* (1965) for which he was nominated for his 13th Oscar; Julie Andrews in *Thoroughly Modern Millie* (1967) for which he was nominated for his 14th Oscar and Nancy Reagan on the night her husband was elected president (1980). On May 19, 1962, the infamous night that Marilyn Monroe sang a breathy 'Happy Birthday' to President Kennedy, Jean Louis designed the outfit that she was almost wearing. Marilyn had to be sewn into the gown and Jean Louis recalled, "It was nude, very thin material, embroidered with rhinestones, so she would shine in the spotlight. She wore nothing, absolutely nothing underneath. It cost about $5,000. It didn't look very pretty from the back, but ..." He was married

twice. His first wife was Maggy and on September 10, 1993, six years after her death he married her best friend, the actor Loretta Young.
CAUSE: He died, aged 89, of natural causes at his home in Palm Springs, California.

Peter Jeffrey
Born April 18, 1929
Died Christmas Day, 1999
Moustachioed character actor. Born in Bristol and educated at Harrow and Pembroke College, Cambridge, he had no formal training but nonetheless appeared with the Royal Shakespeare Company and at the National Theatre. Mainly known for his television work, he also made several films including: *Becket* (1964), *If . . .* (1967) as the headmaster, *Ring Of Bright Water* (1969), *Anne Of The Thousand Days* (1970), *The Odessa File* (1974), *The Return Of The Pink Panther* (1975), *Midnight Express* (1978) and *The Adventures Of Baron Munchausen* (1989).
CAUSE: He died from cancer in Stratford-upon-Avon, Warwickshire, aged 70. His second wife, five children from his first marriage and two step-daughters were with him when he died.

Butch Jenkins
Born August 29, 1937
Died August 14, 2001
Child star. Born in Los Angeles, California, the son of Captain Jack Jenkins of the US Ferry Command and the actress Doris Dudley, Jackie Jenkins was raised in Santa Monica where by the age of six he already had a reputation as a tearaway. He even set fire to his own home but rather than punish him, his mother decided to channel his energy into showbusiness. He was spotted being a brat on the beach by an MGM scout at the time the studio was looking for a child to play Ulysses Macauley in the film of William Saroyan's novel *The Human*

Comedy (1943). The buck-toothed six-year-old was chosen to appear in the film, alongside Mickey Rooney. He made a dozen films in just five years before he retired aged 11 when he developed an unfortunate stutter that he never recovered from. His filmography runs: *Reward Unlimited* (1944), *An American Romance* (1944) as Thomas Jefferson Dangos, *National Velvet* (1944) as Donald Brown, *Our Vines Have Tender Grapes* (1945) as Arnold Hanson, *Little Mister Jim* (1946) as Little Jim Tukker, *Boys' Ranch* (1946) as Butch, *My Brother Talks To Horses* (1947) as Lewie Penrose, *My Old Town* (1948), *Summer Holiday* (1948) as Tommy, *The Bride Goes Wild* (1948) as Danny and *Big City* (1948) as Louis Keller. Fortunately, unlike so many stage parents, Jenkins's mother and father wisely invested his earnings leaving Butch financially settled. The family moved to Dallas and he later attended the State University of Iowa. In 1957 he married and fathered three daughters but the marriage ended in divorce in 1964. In 1966 he remarried. Standing 6'4", he owned a car wash franchise. Of his time in showbusiness, he said, "I have never regretted leaving the picture business and am very grateful to my mother for taking me away from it. I enjoyed the first few years of acting in movies but I certainly don't miss it. In fact, when I've had offers to return a few times, I wasn't even tempted. There may be a better way to live than on a lake with a couple of cows, a wife, and children but being a movie star is not one."
CAUSE: Jenkins died aged 63 in his sleep at his home in Asheville, North Carolina.

Claudia Jennings

(MARY EILEEN CHESTERTON)
Born December 20, 1949
Died October 3, 1979
Playboy superstar. Born in Minnesota but raised in Milwaukee, Wisconsin,

5'6" Mary, known to her friends as 'Mimi', moved again in 1966 to Evanston, Illinois, where she graduated from high school. She showed an early interest in drama and joined the Hull House theatre company in Chicago. In September 1968, 35-23-36 Claudia began working as a receptionist at the offices of *Playboy* magazine, where she was spotted by photographer Pompeo Posar who eventually persuaded her to do a test shoot for him. She kept refusing, saying, "Oh no, I got no boobs." It was the lure of a $5,000 cheque that finally persuaded her and she became *Playboy*'s Playmate of the Month for November 1969, going on to reach the dizzy heights of becoming 1970's Playmate of the Year. She used *Playboy* as a springboard to films and appeared in *The Stepmother* (1971), *Jud* (1971) as Sunny, in which she appeared topless, *The Love Machine* (1971) as Darlene, *Unholy Rollers* (1972) as Karen Walker, in which she appeared topless, *Group Marriage* (1972) as Elaine, *The Single Girls* (1973) as Allison, in which she appeared topless, *40 Carats* (1973) as Gabriella, *Truck Stop Women* (1974) as Rose, in which she appeared topless, *Grotesque* (1975), *'Gator Bait* (1976) as Desiree Thibodeau, in which she appeared topless, *The Man Who Fell To Earth* (1976), in which she appeared topless, *Sisters Of Death* (1976), *The Great Texas Dynamite Chase* (1977) as Candy Morgan, *Moonshine County Express* (1977) as Betty Hammer, *Impulsion* (1978), in which she appeared topless, *Deathsport* (1978) as Deneer, in which she appeared topless and *Fast Company* (1979) as Sammy. For five years from 1970 she lived with songwriter/producer Bobby Hart. Their split sent her on a downward spiral. She was short-listed to take over from Kate Jackson on *Charlie's Angels*, but lost out to Shelley Hack in May 1979.
CAUSE: Claudia began seeing Stan Herman, a Beverly Hills estate agent, in 1979 but the relationship wasn't a

healthy one and they spilt. She was on the way to collect her belongings from his Malibu home when she fell asleep at the wheel of her Volkswagen convertible and was involved in a head-on collision. She died as rescuers tried to cut her from the wreckage. She was 29.

Humphrey Jennings, OBE

Born August 19, 1907
Died September 24, 1950
Documentarian. Frank Humphrey Sinkler Jennings was born at The Gazebo, Walberswick, Suffolk, the only child of the architect Frank Jennings and Mildred Jessie Hall. After earning a First from Pembroke College, Cambridge, he received a scholarship to complete an unfinished doctorate. In 1934 he joined the GPO Film Unit but his interests were diverted by organising surrealist exhibitions. In 1939 he made a documentary, *Spare Time*, about what the working class got up to in their leisure periods. Although he never lost his interest in painting, he turned full time to documentary making and directed 20 films over the next 11 years. Mostly, he worked for the GPO Film Unit (later the Crown Film Unit) and his best work was produced during the Second World War – *Listen To Britain* (1942), *Fires Were Started* (1943), *V-1* (1944) and *Diary For Timothy* (1945). In October 19, 1929, Jennings married Cicely Mary Wilhelmina Raimonde Cooper (b. 1908) and by her had two daughters: Mary-Lou (b. September 1933) and Charlotte (b. August 1935). CAUSE: Jennings died aged 43 as a result of a fall on the Greek island of Poros while scouting for locations for the European Economic Commission.

Stratford Johns

Born February 22, 1925
Died January 29, 2002
Bluff blusterer. Born in Pietermaritzburg, South Africa, Alan Stratford Johns, the son of a train driver, served in the South African navy before moving to England in 1948. After a brief career in accountancy, he became an actor and appeared in 30 films and more than 200 television programmes. It was his role as the tough-talking Charlie Barlow in *Z-Cars* (1962–1965) and then its spin-offs *Softly Softly* (1966–1972) and *Barlow At Large* (1971) that Johns became well known. His films included *The Ship That Died Of Shame* (1955) as a garage worker, *The Night My Number Came Up* (1955) as Sergeant, a security guard in *The Ladykillers* (1955), a policeman in *Who Done It?* (1956), *Tiger In The Smoke* (1956) and *The Long Arm* (1956), a man on an upturned life boat in *A Night To Remember* (1958), *Two Letter Alibi* (1962) as Bates, *The Great St Trinian's Train Robbery* (1966) as The Voice, *Rocket To The Moon* (1967) as Warrant Officer, *Cromwell* (1970) as President Bradshaw, *The Strange Case Of The End Of Civilisation As We Know It* (1977) as Chief Commissioner, *George And Mildred* (1980) as Harry Pinto, *The Fiendish Plot Of Dr Fu Manchu* (1980) as Ismail, *Dance With A Stranger* (1985) as Moorie Conley, *Car Trouble* (1985) as Reg Sampson, *Wild Geese II* (1985) as Mustapha El Ali, *Foreign Body* (1986) as Mr Plumb, *Salome's Last Dance* (1988) as Herod/Alfred Taylor, *The Lair Of The White Worm* (1988) as Peters and *Splitting Heirs* (1993) as Butler. Johns' home life left a lot to be desired. In 1976 he and wife Nanette split after she confessed to ten lovers but were reconciled in 1983. In June 1988, the 18-stone Johns was arrested after he was accused of hitting Nanette at their home at 29 Mostyn Road, Wimbledon, south-west London. His eldest daughter, Frith (b. 1956), was sent to jail for possession of drugs. On April 4, 1989, his younger son, Alan (b. 1963), was jailed for two and a half years for selling cannabis worth £30,000. The court was told that Alan Stratford-Johns began taking heroin when he was 13.

He was later disowned by his father when he sold a story to newspapers about him for £4,000. His younger daughter, Lissa (b. 1968) was hooked on amphetamines by the time she was 15 and at 17 was in hospital suffering from bleeding ulcers. Only daughter Peta seemed immune.

CAUSE: He suffered two strokes and had been in poor health for six years leading up to his death. He died of a heart attack at his home in Heveningham, Suffolk, aged 77.

Dame Celia Johnson
Born December 18, 1908
Died April 24, 1982
Theatrical dame. Born in Ellerker Gate, Richmond, Surrey, Celia Elizabeth Johnson was the daughter of a doctor and was educated at RADA. She made her professional début on the stage at the Theatre Royal, Huddersfield, on July 23, 1928 as Sarah in *Major Barbara*. The stage was to dominate her professional life for more than fifty years. She made her film début in *A Letter From Home* (1941) and next appeared in *In Which We Serve* (1942) playing Noël Coward's wife Alix Kinross, *Dear Octopus* (1943) as Cynthia and *This Happy Breed* (1944) as Ethel Gibbons. It was her performance as Laura Jesson in David Lean's *Brief Encounter* (1945) for which she is best remembered. One review said that "what is most exceptional about it is that it dares to allow its average characters to remain average" adding that Johnson's face "is touched by life rather than retouched by an ever-hovering make-up man". Her performance was nominated for an Oscar but she lost out to Olivia de Havilland in *To Each His Own*. Subsequently, her films were few and far between. She was in *The Astonished Heart* (1949) as Barbara Faber, *The Holly And The Ivy* (1952) as Jenny Gregory, *A Kid For Two Farthings* (1955) as Joanna, *The Good Companions* (1957) as Miss Trant, and *The Prime Of Miss Jean Brodie* (1969) as Miss MacKay. On December 8, 1935 she married the travel writer Peter Fleming, OBE (b. 27 Green Street, Park Lane, London W1, May 31, 1907, d. Black Mount, Argyllshire, August 18, 1971 of a heart attack), the elder brother of the writer Ian Fleming. They had one son, Nicholas Peter Val (b. More's Gardens, Chelsea, London, January 3, 1939), and two daughters, Kate (b. May 24, 1946) and Lucy (b. Merrimoles House, Nettlebed, Oxfordshire, May 15, 1947). She was appointed CBE in June 1958 and awarded a damehood in the Birthday Honours List of 1981.

CAUSE: She died at home, Merrimoles House, Nettlebed, Oxfordshire, of a stroke suffered while playing bridge. She was 73 and left £150,557.

FURTHER READING: *Celia Johnson A Biography* – Kate Fleming (London: Weidenfeld & Nicolson, 1991).

Sunny Johnson
(SUNNY SUZANNE JOHNSON)
Born September 21, 1953
Died June 19, 1984
Unfulfilled potential. Born in San Bernardino County, California, she made her first film appearance playing a student in *Animal House* (1978). That was followed by *Almost Summer* (1978), *Why Would I Lie?* (1980), *Dr Heckyl And Mr Hype* (1980) as Coral Careen, *Where The Buffalo Roam* (1980), *The Night The Lights Went Out In Georgia* (1981) as Melody Bartlett and her most famous film *Flashdance* (1983) as Jeanie Szabo.

CAUSE: She died of a ruptured aneurysm aged 30 in Los Angeles. She was discovered unconscious in her bathroom and passed away a few days later.

Van Johnson
Born August 25, 1916
Died December 12, 2008
Boy-next-door. Charles Van Dell Johnson was born in Newport, Rhode

Island, the son of estate agent Charles Johnson and alcoholic Loretta Snyder who walked out when her son was three. Early visits to local theatres sparked his interest in acting and in 1934 he went to New York to seek fame and fortune with $5 and all his worldly goods in a straw suitcase. In May 1936 he appeared in the chorus line of the Broadway musical-revue *New Faces Of 1936*. Three years later, he was in the chorus line of the Rodgers and Hart musical, *Too Many Girls*. He later progressed to understudy for the three male leads Eddie Bracken, Richard Kollmar and Desi Arnaz. Johnson went west where he appeared in bits part in the film version of *Too Many Girls* (released October 8, 1940) and *Personalities* (1942) before Warner Bros offered him a six-month contract at $300 a week. He made one film at the studio. "First the zenith, then the nadir. Warner Bros. dropped me after *Murder In The Big House*," he said. Disillusioned, Johnson was planning his return east when he had dinner with Desi Arnaz and Lucille Ball at Chasen's restaurant. He later recalled, "Lucille tried to cheer me up, but I just couldn't seem to laugh. Suddenly she said to me, 'There's Billy Grady over there; he's MGM's casting director. I'm going to introduce you, and at least you're going to act like you're the star I think you will be.'" MGM signed Johnson to a $350-a-week contract and his first film for them was *For The Common Defense!* (released June 20, 1942). Around this time, Johnson began wearing the item of clothing for which he would become known offstage – red socks. Johnson joined the Lionel Barrymore *Dr Gillespie* series (which replaced *Dr Kildare*) as Dr Randall "Red" Adams (later Ames) beginning with *Dr Gillespie's New Assistant* (1942) and appeared in four films over the course of three years. It was during the Second World War that Johnson became MGM's boy-next-door in films including the fantasy romantic-drama *A Guy Named Joe* (released December 24, 1943) as Ted Randall and *Thirty Seconds Over Tokyo* (released November 15, 1944) as Ted Lawson and became one of the era's top box-office draws. However, it was lucky that Johnson ever became a star in the first place. On April 1, 1943 he was involved in a car crash near MGM when another driver jumped a red light in Culver City and hit Johnson's DeSoto convertible, causing it to roll on its side. The actor suffered severe facial injuries, a fractured skull, a severed artery in his neck and bone fragments piercing his brain. He spent a long time in hospital during which time he had several operations and a metal plate inserted on the left side of his head, which left him rated 4-F and thus ineligible for military service. He was also left with a badly scarred forehead. "They tell me I was almost decapitated, but I never lost consciousness," he remembered. "I spent four months in the hospital after they sewed the top of my head back on. I still have a disc of bone in my forehead five inches long." *Two Girls And A Sailor* (premièred April 27, 1944) in which he played John Dyckman Brown III was the first film in which he received top billing. Despite his never actually being in the military, he joked in 1945, "I'd been in every branch of the service, all at MGM." That year he was second in the annual Top 10 Box Office list (behind Bing Crosby). Tinseltown's tittle-tattlers nicknamed him "The Voiceless Sinatra". Esther Williams tried to explain his appeal, "He was probably one of the most charming, gregarious of the stars I worked with. If you look at any of his pictures, look at *Thirty Seconds Over Tokyo*. You'll see why he was a big star, because he had this wonderful, boyish quality with those freckles and that smile. He was so natural. He was a wonderful companion and I liked working with him a lot. I once wondered why he was so moody and I talked to Keenan [Wynn] because he was Van's very good friend. He said, 'He's not angry or upset with you. He's Swedish.' I think Van had some unhappy stuff in his life, but we didn't get into it. We were just kind of like buddies." June Allyson added, "He was very, very down-to-earth. I think he was the man every girl would like to marry. I just loved working with him. He was delightful, he was funny, and he was always prepared." Then it all began to crumble. In 1946 he was rated third in the box office top ten – it would be his last appearance in the list. On January 25, 1947 actor Keenan Wynn divorced his wife Eve Abbott Wynn (b. Buffalo, New York May 8, 1914; Fort Lauderdale, Florida, d. July 19, 2004), the mother of his two young sons, Ned and Tracy Wynn. Four hours later, she married Van Johnson at Juarez, Mexico. When Johnson married it was said that his teenage girl fans were so distraught, they wore their bobby socks at half-mast. The press turned on him because of the marriage but he continued working at MGM until 1954 when he went freelance after they cut him loose. Johnson was never known to have asked for a raise or turned down a part he was told to play. In 1985, he said of his years at MGM, "It was one big happy family and a little kingdom. Everything was provided for us, from singing lessons to barbells. All we had to do was inhale, exhale and be charming. I used to dread leaving the studio to go out into the real world, because to me the studio was the real world." Between 1947 and 1954 his films included *The Bride Goes Wild* (released March 3, 1948) as Greg Rawlings, *State Of The Union* (released April 30, 1948) as "Spike" McManus, *Command Decision* (premièred December 23, 1948), *In The Good Old Summertime* (released July 29, 1949) as Andrew Delby Larkin, *Battleground* (released November 9, 1949) as Holley, *Three Guys Named Mike* (released

March 1, 1951) as Mike Lawrence, *The Caine Mutiny* (premièred June 24, 1954) as Lieutenant Steve Maryk, *Brigadoon* (released September 8, 1954) as Jeff Douglas and *The Last Time I Saw Paris* (released November 18, 1954). After MGM his career began to wane. Among his later films were *Kelly And Me* (released April 10, 1957) as Len Carmody, *Wives And Lovers* (released August 28, 1963) as Bill Austin, *Divorce American Style* (London première August 17, 1967) as Al Yearling, *Yours, Mine And Ours* (released April 24, 1968) as Warrant Officer Darrel Harrison and *The Purple Rose Of Cairo* (released March 1, 1985) as Larry. Johnson turned down the role of Eliot Ness in the television crime series *The Untouchables* in 1959. He turned to episodic television and appeared on many shows including *Alfred Hitchcock Presents, Batman, Black Beauty, Fantasy Island, Glitter, Love, American Style, The Love Boat, Maude, McCloud, McMillan & Wife, Murder, She Wrote, Nanny And The Professor, Quincy M.E., Tales Of The Unexpected, The Virginian* and *Rich Man, Poor Man* which earned him an Emmy nomination. Away from the camera, 6′1″ Johnson painted, his art selling for up to $10,000 a piece. He recalled, "I was on the Onassis yacht with Winston Churchill. He got his canvas out and so did I. He was working away, and he growled at me, 'Don't just sit there and stare! Get some paint and splash it on!'" His other hobby, like Rock Hudson, was embroidery. Johnson had one daughter, Schuyler Van (b. January 6, 1948), but his marriage did not end amicably. They separated in 1962 and were divorced on May 3, 1968. "She wiped me out in the ugliest divorce in Hollywood history," he said. She said, "[MGM] needed their 'big star' to be married to quell rumours about his sexual preferences and unfortunately, I was 'It' – the only woman he would marry." The openly gay writer Arthur Laurents wrote in his memoirs, "A sunny male star caught performing in public urinals once too often was ordered by his studio to get married. His best friends, a young comedian and his wife, divorced so that he could marry the wife." Johnson's stepson Ned Wynn said that his mother told him that Johnson had left her 'for a man – a boy, really. He's the lead boy dancer [in London West End show *The Music Man*]."

CAUSE: Johnson had skin cancer surgery in 1963. He moved into Tappan Zee Manor, an old people's home, at Nyack, New York in 2001. He died there of natural causes. He was 92. Prior to that, he lived in a penthouse at 405 East 54th Street in Manhattan with two cats. He had been estranged from his daughter for many years. In his late seventies, he opined, "Maybe Garbo and Crawford and Marlene had the right idea. Get out of the damned spotlight while you can still be remembered for your earlier glories, not as some old relic." A biography appeared about Johnson in 2001, which mentioned that he was homosexual. An anonymous friend reviewed the book saying, "First of all, rumours of homosexuality are false . . . Van is a warm, non-judgmental, kind and humorous human being. All this and more besides being an outstanding actor." Another review was written by Johnson's daughter who said, "I can tell you that is an excellent work and came out extremely well. Some of it was hard to get through, being an interested party, but also somewhat cathartic and nice to put away on a shelf as part of my distant past, best left on the shelf, once read . . . Would that the living of some of it had been that easy!"

Al Jolson

(ASA YOELSON)
Born circa *1885*
Died October 23, 1950
'You ain't heard nothin' yet!' Like many Jewish immigrants to the United States from eastern Europe, the exact date of Al Jolson's birth is unknown and he chose the day he wished to celebrate as his birthday (May 26, 1886). He was born in Srednicke, Riga, Latvia, the son of a cantor, and first sang in public in his father's synagogue. He emigrated to America and joined vaudeville where he was celebrated for singing in blackface. He was sued by his brother for $25,000; Harry Jolson claimed Al agreed to pay him $150 per week not to go into showbiz. It was in 1923 that he made his movie début in *Mammy's Boy* (1923) as Al. He made cinematic history in the first talkie *The Jazz Singer* (1927) as Jakie Rabinowitz (Jack Robin) when he uttered the immortal line "You ain't heard nothin' yet!" In fact, the film was not supposed to be a talkie. It was a musical and Jolson ad-libbed his famous line. For his part in the film Warner Bros offered Jolson shares in their company in lieu of a salary. He turned down their offer preferring to take the cash ($75,000) and in doing so passed on a fortune. He appeared in *The Singing Fool* (1928) as Al Stone, *Sonny Boy* (1929) as Al, *Mammy* (1930) as Al Fuller, *Hallelujah, I'm A Bum* (1933) as Bumper, *Swanee River* (1939) as E.P. Christy and *Rose Of Washington Square* (1939) as Ted Cotter. His popularity began to wane as fashions changed but it picked up when he entertained troops in the Forties. Two biopics were made. He screen-tested to play himself in *The Jolson Story* (1946) and failed. However, he can be seen in some long shots and it is his voice you hear singing. Jolson never made any secret of his enormous ego. In fact, he played up to it on his radio shows, once joking he had carved his initials on a tree "AJWGE" – Al Jolson World's Greatest Entertainer. George Burns quipped, "It was easy enough to make Jolson happy. You just had to cheer him for breakfast, applaud wildly for lunch and give him a standing ovation for dinner."

CAUSE: He died in San Francisco,

California, aged about 65, of a heart attack. He was buried in the Al Jolson Memorial in Hillside Memorial Park, 6001 West Centinela Avenue, Los Angeles, California 90045.
FURTHER READING: *Al Jolson: You Ain't Heard Nothin' Yet!* – Robert Oberfirst (San Diego: A.S. Barnes, 1980); *Jolson: The Story Of Al Jolson* – Michael Freedland (London: Virgin, 1995).

Carolyn Jones
Born April 28, 1929
Died August 3, 1983
Forever Morticia. Born in Amarillo, Texas, of Comanche Indian ancestry, 5'5" Carolyn Sue Jones appeared in almost 40 films, but despite an Oscar nomination (for *The Bachelor Party* [1957]) it was for her continuing role as Morticia Addams on *The Addams Family* that she is best known. She began acting with the Pasadena Playhouse, progressing to films in the early Fifties. She appeared in *Road To Bali* (1952) as Eunice, *The Turning Point* (1952), *House Of Wax* (1953) as Cathy Gray, *The Big Heat* (1953) as Doris, *Geraldine* (1954) as Kitty, *The Tender Trap* (1955) as Helen, *East Of Eden* (1955), *The Seven Year Itch* (1955) as Miss Finch, *The Opposite Sex* (1956) as Pat, *Invasion Of The Body Snatchers* (1956) as Theodora 'Teddy' Belicec, *The Man Who Knew Too Much* (1956) as Cindy Fontaine, *Baby Face Nelson* (1957) as Sue, *Marjorie Morningstar* (1958) as Marsha Zelenko, *King Creole* (1958) as Ronnie, *A Hole In The Head* (1959) as Shirl, *How The West Was Won* (1962) as Julie Rawlings, *A Ticklish Affair* (1963) as Tandy Martin, *Color Me Dead* (1969) as Paula Gibson and *Good Luck, Miss Wyckoff* (1979) as Beth. She was also Marsha, Queen of Diamonds in *Batman* and appeared as Myrna Clegg in the soap *Capitol* but had to leave through ill-health. On April 10, 1953, she married actor-turned-writer and producer Aaron Spelling. They were divorced during the first series of *The Addams Family*. In 1968 she married conductor Herbert Greene but that, too, ended in divorce.
CAUSE: In March 1981 she was diagnosed with colon cancer. When an exploratory operation was performed it was discovered the cancer had also spread to her liver. Surgeons removed two-thirds of her colon but Carolyn kept her illness secret, telling friends she was suffering from ulcers. She continued to work and for a time it looked as if the disease was in remission, but then in 1982 it returned with a vengeance. In July 1983 she married her actor lover Peter Bailey-Britton (b. 1950). She died the next month, weighing just over 3st, at her home, 8967 Norma Place, West Hollywood, California 90069. She was 54. Cause of death was given as "metastic carcinoma". She was cremated on August 4, 1983.

Peter Jones
Born June 12, 1920
Died April 10, 2000
Comedy all-rounder. Born in Wem, Shropshire, Peter Jones excelled in all forms of showbiz – he was a talented theatre actor and director, a whiz on the radio show *Just A Minute*, a success on TV sitcoms such as *The Rag Trade* and a much-in-demand film performer. His father was a cabinet maker and he wanted his son to have a solid career and sent him to boarding school to prepare him for this. However, at the age of 14, Peter contracted tuberculosis and was sent to a sanatorium to recuperate. There he began writing and performing sketches for the other patients. He made his professional début in 1936 in Wolverhampton playing a reporter from *The Times* in *The Composite Man*. The management decided he was not up to scratch and sacked him. Undeterred, he carried on acting and made his West End début at the Haymarket Theatre on April 6, 1942, in *The Doctor's Dilemma* where he again

played a gentleman of the fourth estate. It was to be the start of 60 years' almost continuous employment. In 1951 he became a star on the wireless, appearing alongside his friend Peter Ustinov in the comedy show *In All Directions*. Much of the dialogue was improvised, a skill he showed to a greater extent in *Just A Minute*. His next big hit was starring in *We're In Business*, which he co-wrote with Barry Took and Marty Feldman. In the Seventies he was the narrator of the radio programme *The Hitch Hiker's Guide To The Galaxy* and reprised that role when the series hit the small screen in 1981. He featured in many television programmes. From March 13, 1967, until March 26, 1968, he played Gerald Garvey in the BBC sitcom *Beggar My Neighbour*. He appeared as Sidney Rochester in the LWT comedy *Kindly Leave The Kerb* in May 1971. He created, wrote and starred in the BBC show *Mr Big* (1977) about a small-time crook and his nefarious family. He co-wrote and starred in the Central show *I Thought You'd Gone* in 1984. However, it was for his portrayal of the harassed factory owner Harold Fenner in BBC's *The Rag Trade* that he was best loved. The show began on October 6, 1961, and also starred Miriam Karlin as shop steward Paddy, Reg Varney, Esma Cannon, Sheila Hancock, Barbara Windsor and Irene Handl. It ran until March 30, 1963. The show was revamped by LWT on September 11, 1977, and once again starred Jones and Karlin but Christopher Benny stood in for Varney, Diane Langton replaced Barbara Windsor, future *EastEnder* Gillian Taylforth played Lyn and Anna Karen played Olive, not a million miles from the character of the same name she played in *On The Buses*, which was written by the same team of Ronald Wolfe and Ronald Chesney. Peter Jones made his film début in *Fanny By Gaslight* (1944) and went on to appear in *The Browning Version*

(1950), *The Yellow Balloon* (1953), *Albert R.N.* (1953), *Blue Murder At St Trinian's* (1957), *Danger Within* (1958), *The Bulldog Breed* (1961), *Romanoff & Juliet* (1961), *A Stitch In Time* (1963), *Press For Time* (1966), *Carry On Doctor* (1968), *The Return Of The Pink Panther* (1975), *Carry On England* (1975) and *Chariots Of Fire* (1981) among many others. Jones, a kindly man who helped the present author with a previous book, was married to the American actress-writer Jeri Sauvinet who passed away in 1999. They had three children: actress Selena Carey-Jones, producer Bill Dare who created the hit radio show *Dead Ringers* and Charles Jones, who was not involved with entertainment.
CAUSE: He died after a long illness, aged 79.

Alex Jordan
(KAREN ELIZABETH HUGHES)
Born September 20, 1963
Died July 2, 1995
Brit tragedy. Born in Liverpool blonde Karen Hughes emigrated to Australia before ending up in America where she made a name for herself in hardcore pornographic films. During her career she appeared in 207 skin flicks including *Wicked Thoughts* (1992), *Talk Dirty To Me 9* (1992), *Tailiens 2* (1992), *Tailiens 3* (1992), *Single White Woman* (1992), *Seymore Butts: In The Love Shack* (1992), *Sex Stories* (1992), *Maneater* (1992), *Bonnie & Clyde – Outlaws Of Love* (1992), *Beverly Hills 90269* (1992), *Vampire's Kiss* (1993), *Spermacus* (1993), *One Of Our Porn Stars Is Missing* (1993), *Lethal Lolita* (1993), *The Joi Fuck Club* (1993), *Cheerleader Nurses* (1993), *Cheerleader Nurses 2* (1993), *Bonnie And Clyde: Desperado* (1993), *Titty Slickers 2* (1994), *Interview With A Vamp* (1994) and *Buttman's Butt Freak 2* (1996).
CAUSE: Alex hanged herself aged 31 in her bedroom closet in Marina Del Rey, California. Supposedly, she was depressed over the death of her pet

parrot. Her friend and neighbour Summer Knight discovered the body.

Brenda Joyce

(BETTY GRAFFINA LEABO)
Born February 25, 1917
Died July 4, 2009
Blonde Jane. Born in Excelsior Springs, Missouri (some sources say 1912), she moved to Los Angeles where she became a model to pay for her university fees. She was signed by 20th Century Fox after talent scouts saw a magazine layout of her and her name was changed to Brenda Joyce after silent star Alice Joyce. She was named Fox's Discovery of the Year for 1939 and her film debut came as Fern Simon in *The Rains Came* (released September 15, 1939), an adaptation of the Louis Bromfield novel that starred Myrna Loy, Tyrone Power and George Brent. She was relegated to B movies supposedly because the studio disapproved of her 1941 marriage to Owen Ward, having groomed her as a sexy spinster. The marriage produced three children – Pamela Ann, Timothy Owen and Beth Victoria – before it ended in divorce in 1949. Joyce seemed to lose interest in her career when her children were born but she was persuaded to return to play Jane opposite Johnny Weissmuller in *Tarzan And The Amazons* (released April 29, 1945) after Maureen O'Sullivan decided she no longer wanted to play the ape man's mate. 5′4″ Joyce played the part four times and was the only Jane to play opposite two Tarzans in talkies. Karla Schramm was the only actress of the silent era to play Jane opposite two different Tarzans. Joyce's other Tarzan films were *Tarzan And The Leopard Woman* (released January 1946), *Tarzan And The Huntress* (released April 5, 1947), *Tarzan And The Mermaids* (released May 15, 1948) and finally *Tarzan's Magic Fountain* (released February 5, 1949), opposite Lex Barker, which turned out to be her last film. She married a second time

but that match also ended in divorce. She worked for ten years in the Department of Immigration at Washington, DC helping new immigrants find housing and work. CAUSE: She died aged 92 of pneumonia in a nursing home in Santa Monica. She had been diagnosed with dementia ten year earlier.

Yootha Joyce

(YOOTHA JOYCE NEEDHAM)
Born August 20, 1927
Died August 24, 1980
Toothsome comedy battleaxe. Yootha Joyce was born at 19 Bolingbroke Grove, Battersea, south London, the only child of the singer Percival Henry John (Hurst) Needham, and Jessie Maud née Revitt. Her father had been a promising singer but his voice was ruined when he contracted emphysema during the First World War. Her mother gave up her singing career when she gave birth although, to be fair, her mother was only rarely employed professionally. Joyce was educated in Battersea, Petersfield, and Croydon before enrolling at RADA. In 1944 she became an assistant stage manager at the Grand Theatre, Croydon, and then toured with ENSA. She left RADA a year early and began working in rep, dropping her surname and adopting her middle name as her last name. Her husband, the actor (John) Glynn Edwards (they married on December 8, 1956 and divorced in 1968), recommended her to Joan Littlewood who offered her a permanent place in her company. On February 17, 1959 she appeared in the original version of Frank Norman's and Lionel Bart's East End gangster play *Fings Ain't Wot They Used T'Be* at the Theatre Royal, Stratford East. The supporting cast included Miriam Karlin, Brian Murphy, George Sewell, and a young Barbara Windsor. On February 11, 1960 the play opened at the Garrick Theatre in the West End where it was watched by the

scriptwriters Frank Muir and Denis Norden who cast her in their sitcom *Brothers In Law* (April 17–July 10, 1962). She landed roles in other comedies and dramas such as *Z Cars*, *Dixon Of Dock Green* and *The Saint*. She made her film début in *Sparrows Can't Sing* (1963) playing a barmaid. She also appeared in *The Pumpkin Eater* (1964), *Fanatic* (1965) as Anna, *Catch Us If You Can* (1965) as Nan, *Kaleidoscope* (1966) as the museum receptionist, *A Man For All Seasons* (1966) as Averil Machin, *Charlie Bubbles* (1967), *Stranger In The House* (1967), *Our Mother's House* (1967) as Mrs Quayle, *All The Right Noises* (1969) as Mrs Byrd, *Fragment Of Fear* (1970) as Miss Ward-Cadbury, *The Night Digger* (1971) as Mrs Palafox, *Burke And Hare* (1971) as Mrs Hare, *Nearest And Dearest* (1972) as Mrs Rowbottom and *Steptoe And Son Ride Again* (1973) as Lennie's wife. Joyce's voice could be harsh and she used it to full effect in the television series that made her a star. In *Man About The House* (August 15, 1973–April 7, 1976) she played the sexually frustrated Mildred Roper to Brian Murphy's timorous and lazy George. The show was so successful and the characters so popular that the creators, Johnnie Mortimer and Brian Cooke (who were former Fleet Street cartoonists), gave them their own spin-off series, *George And Mildred* (September 6, 1976–December 25, 1979). A film version was made in 1980.
CAUSE: Yootha Joyce died in a London clinic four days after her 53rd birthday from cirrhosis of the liver. From 1970 until her death, unknown to the public, she had been a prodigious drinker due to depression. She left £101,536.

Raul Julia

(RAUL RAFAEL CARLOS JULIA Y ARCELAY)
Born March 9, 1940
Died October 24, 1994
Hispanic hero. Born in San Juan,

Puerto Rico, he made his New York début in 1964, moving to films five years later. His work included *Stiletto* (1969), *The Organization* (1971) as Juan Mendoza, *The Panic In Needle Park* (1971) as Marco, *Eyes Of Laura Mars* (1978) as Michael Reisler, *Tempest* (1982) as Kalibanos, *The Escape Artist* (1982) as Stu Quinones, *Compromising Positions* (1985) as David Suarez, *Kiss Of The Spider Woman* (1985) as Valentin Arregui, *The Morning After* (1986) as Joaquin Manero, *Tequila Sunrise* (1988) as Carlos/Escalante, *Romero* (1989) as Archbishop Oscar Romero, *Presumed Innocent* (1990) as Sandy Stern, *The Rookie* (1990) as Strom, *The Addams Family* (1991) as Gomez Addams, *Addams Family Values* (1993) as Gomez Addams and *Street Fighter* (1994) as General M. Bison.
CAUSE: Julia died in Manhasset, New York, of complications following a stroke. He was 54.

Katy Jurado

(MARIA CRISTINA JURADO GARCIA)
Born January 16, 1924
Died July 5, 2002
Fiery-eyed Mexican. Katy Jurado was born in Guadalajara, near Mexico City, the daughter of a former landowner who was relieved of his property during the revolution. Films attracted her from an early age and she made her first film at 16, after marrying the author Victor Velazquez, which allowed her to act in films without parental consent. The couple had two sons, but divorced in 1950. In the Forties, she made more than a dozen films, most notably *Nosotros Los Pobres* (1947), directed by Ismael Rodriguez and starring Pedro Infante. When Jurado wasn't acting she supplemented her income by working as a journalist and covering bullfights. In 1951 she was spotted by Budd Boetticher who had gone to Mexico to shoot *The Bullfighter And The Lady*. He spotted Jurado in the audience at a bullfight. She was wearing a white dress

and, Boetticher said, "She looked like a Goddess." He cast her as the wife of a bullfighter even though she couldn't read a word of the English script. The following year Fred Zinnemann cast her as Helen Ramirez, the passionate ex-girlfriend of Will Kane (Gary Cooper), the honourable sheriff. The casting was in complete contrast to the virginal (on screen at least) Amy Kane (Grace Kelly), the marshal's new bride. Kane was originally called Doane but Jurado was unable to pronounce that name. Her performance won her a Golden Globe Award for Best Supporting Actress. It was said that Jurado was furious at the number of close-ups allocated Kelly. "Grace and I got along just fine, despite rumours of battles on set," she later said. *High Noon* was the first of a series of Westerns for her, many of them unworthy of her abilities. "I was always asked to play roles where I was the contrasting or multicultural character," she said. "Sometimes that worked for me – often it didn't." In 1954 she was nominated for an Oscar after her performance in *Broken Lance* (1954) as Senora Devereaux, the wife of a cattle baron played by Spencer Tracy. In Mexico, she won the Ariel, the country's highest acting accolade, three times. In 1956 she was cast as a bare-back rider and snake-charmer in *Trapeze* with Burt Lancaster, Tony Curtis and Gina Lollobrigida. Jurado and Lollobrigida did not see eye to eye,

prompting director Carol Reed to observe that "the actors were more trouble than the animals". In *The Badlanders* (1958) she took the part of Anita, a prostitute who fell for a cowboy played by Ernest Borgnine. She and Borgnine became close off screen too and on December 31, 1959 they married. It was a tempestuous marriage. They divorced on June 3, 1963 with Borgnine declaring, "Katy was beautiful. But a tiger." Her other films included *The Man From Del Rio* (1956), *One Eyed Jacks* (1961), *I Briganti Italiani* (1961) and *Barabbas* (1962). She also appeared on the television shows *The Westerner*, *The Virginian* and *Alias Smith & Jones*. Following her divorce from Borgnine she retired from films and returned to Mexico. In 1966 she was back working as a character actress. She appeared alongside Elvis Presley as Annie Lightcloud in *Stay Away Joe* (1968) and for the part, she gained 22 pounds in 22 days, and days before filming she broke her foot – which explains her limp throughout the film. In 1973, she starred as Ma Baker in *Pat Garrett And Billy The Kid*, directed by Sam Peckinpah. She also appeared in *Under The Volcano* (1984) and *Divine* (1998), which brought her an Ariel nomination. She had previously won Ariels for *El Bruto* (1952) and *Caridad* (1972).
CAUSE: Katy Jurado died aged 78 of a heart attack in Cuernavaca, Morelos, Mexico.

K

Pauline Kael

Born June 19, 1919
Died September 3, 2001
Rude critic. Born in Sonoma County, California, Pauline Kael studied philosophy at the University of California at Berkeley but left without taking a degree. She came late to journalism; she was 35 before she penned her first review (of *Limelight* which she slated as "Slimelight"). Her critical career lasted 38 years, mostly with the *New Yorker*, during which time she delighted readers and annoyed film-makers in equal measure. She was called "the most brilliantly ad hoc critic of her time" by one fellow critic. Kael enjoyed championing movies that she believed in even if the public consensus was against her. She called *Rain Man* "a wet piece of kitsch". Of a famous albeit unnamed actress she commented, "She makes a career of seeming to overcome being miscast." For ten years from 1955 she was a cinema manager in Berkeley. Then she and daughter, Gina, moved to the East Coast of America where she began reviewing for several magazines although she lost her job with *McCall's* when she criticised *The Sound Of Music*. In 1979 and 1980 she took a break from reviewing and worked for Warren Beatty as a production executive and also as a scout for Paramount. She retired in March 1991. She published several books of movie criticism.
CAUSE: Kael died aged 82 at her home in Great Barrington, Massachusetts, from Parkinson's disease.

Madeleine Kahn

Born September 29, 1942
Died December 3, 1999
Quirkily original. Born in Boston, Massachusetts, and raised there and in New York, Madeleine Kahn is probably best known for her work with Mel Brooks. She studied speech therapy at Hofstra University on Long Island and also appeared in drama there. She was warned by a teacher that her baby way of talking would hinder her career but instead Kahn used it to her advantage. She became a regular at New York's Upstairs at the Downstairs Club and on television's *Tonight Show With Johnny Carson*. It was Peter Bogdanovich who spotted her potential and cast her in her first two films. Her movies included *The Dove* (1968) as Sigfrid, *What's Up, Doc?* (1972) as Eunice Burns, a teacher in *From The Mixed-Up Files Of Mrs Basil E. Frankweiler* (1973), *Paper Moon* (1973) as the floozy Trixie Delight for which she was nominated for a Best Supporting Actress Oscar, *Young Frankenstein* (1974) as Elizabeth, *Blazing Saddles* (1974) as Lili Von Shtupp (shtupp is Yiddish for fuck) for which she was nominated for her second Best Supporting Actress Oscar, *The Adventure Of Sherlock Holmes' Smarter Brother* (1975) as Jenny Hill, *At Long Last Love* (1975) as Kitty O'Kelly, *Won Ton Ton, The Dog Who Saved Hollywood* (1976) as Estie Del Ruth, *High Anxiety* (1977) as Victoria Brisbane, *The Cheap Detective* (1978) as Mrs Montenegro, *Happy Birthday, Gemini* (1980) as Bunny Weinberger, *Wholly Moses* (1980) as the witch, *History Of The World: Part I* (1981) as Empress Nympho, *Yellowbeard* (1983) as Betty, *Clue* (1985) as Mrs White, *An American Tail* (1986) as Gussie Mausheimer, *Betsy's Wedding* (1990) as Lola Hopper, *Nixon* (1995) as Martha Mitchell, *A Bug's Life* (1998) as Gypsy and *Judy Berlin* (1999) as Alice Gold. She was the only cast member who could actually sing and dance in Bogdanovich's execrable musical *At Long Last Love* but she did seem to pick an unusually large number of bad films. On stage she fared rather better, picking up a Tony award in 1993 for

The Sisters Rosensweig. In October 1998 she married lawyer John Hansbury. CAUSE: She died of ovarian cancer aged 57 in New York.

Boris Karloff

(WILLIAM HENRY PRATT)
Born November 23, 1887
Died February 2, 1969
The horror star. Born in Camberwell, London, the unfortunately named Bill Pratt was the youngest of nine children (eight boys) of Edward John Pratt, a civil servant with the Indian Salt Revenue Service. He intended to follow his father into diplomacy but instead emigrated to Montreal, Canada, in 1909 where he worked on a farm being paid $10 a month. He became interested in drama and joined various repertory companies touring Canada and America. He took his name in 1911 from a seventh-century ancestor, adding Boris because he liked the sound of it. During one foray to the States he made his first film, *The Dumb Girl Of Portici* (1916), which starred Anna Pavlova. He thought no more of filmdom until he found himself unemployed three years later and decided to have a crack at acting in movies. However, like many, he was not an overnight success and worked as a lorry driver and dug ditches to support himself while waiting for the big break. His early films included *The Prince And Betty* (1919), *The Masked Raider* (1919), *The Lightning Raider* (1919), *His Majesty, The American* (1919), *The Last Of The Mohicans* (1920) as a Native American, *The Deadlier Sex* (1920) as Jules Borney, *The Hope Diamond Mystery* (1921), *Without Benefit Of Clergy* (1921) as Ahmed Khan, *Omar The Tentmaker* (1922) as Imam Mowaffak, *The Infidel* (1922) as the Nabob, *The Prisoner* (1923) as Prince Kapolski, *Dynamite Dan* (1924) as Tony, *Forbidden Cargo* (1925) as Pietro Castillano, *The Prairie Wife* (1925) as Diego, *Her Honor, The Governor* (1926) as Snipe Collins,

The Golden Web (1926) as Dave Sinclair, *Flaming Fury* (1926) as Gaspard, *The Princess From Hoboken* (1927) as Pavel, *The Devil's Chaplain* (1929) as Boris, *Anne Against The World* (1929), *The Unholy Night* (1929) as Abdoul, *The Bad One* (1930) as Monsieur Gaston, *The Utah Kid* (1930) as Baxter, *The Mad Genius* (1931) as Fedor's father, *The Guilty Generation* (1931) as Tony Ricca and *Young Donovan's Kid* (1931) as Cokey Joe. He first came to notice in *The Criminal Code* (1931) as Ned Galloway, a role he had played on stage. It was later the same year that his star really shone, when James Whale cast him as the monster in *Frankenstein.* To add mystery, in the opening credits, Karloff was billed as '?'. The part had been turned down by Bela Lugosi but 6' Karloff was a natural and forever after would be associated with horror films. The costume he wore to transform himself into the monster weighed a staggering 67lb. Off screen Karloff was a kind, gentle man with a passion for cricket. His later films included *Scarface* (1932) as Gaffney, *The Mummy* (1932) as Imhotep/Ardath Bey, *The Mask Of Fu Manchu* (1932) as Dr Fu Manchu, *The House Of Rothschild* (1934) as Count Ledrantz, *The Ghoul* (1934) as Professor Morlant, *The Black Cat* (1934) as Hjalmar Poelzig, *Bride Of Frankenstein* (1935) as the monster, *The Raven* (1935) as Edmond Bateman, *The Walking Dead* (1936) as John Ellman, *Charlie Chan At The Opera* (1937) as Gravelle, *West Of Shanghai* (1937) as Wu Yen Fang, James Lee Wong in *Mr Wong, Detective* (1938), *The Mystery Of Mr Wong* (1939), *Mr Wong In Chinatown* (1939), *The Fatal Hour* (1940) and *Doomed To Die* (1940), *The Man They Could Not Hang* (1939) as Dr Henryk Savaard, *Devil's Island* (1939) as Dr Charles Gaudet, *Son Of Frankenstein* (1939) as the monster, *Before I Hang* (1940) as Dr John Garth, *Black Friday* (1940) as Dr Ernest Sovac, *The Man With Nine*

Lives (1940) as Dr Leon Kravaal, *The Boogie Man Will Get You* (1942) as Professor Nathaniel Billings, *House Of Frankenstein* (1944) as Dr Gustav Niemann, *The Body Snatcher* (1945) as John Gray, *Isle Of The Dead* (1945) as General Nikolas Pherides, *Dick Tracy Meets Gruesome* (1947) as Gruesome, *The Secret Life Of Walter Mitty* (1947) as Dr Hugo Hollingshead, *Unconquered* (1947) as Chief Guyasuta, *Abbott & Costello Meet The Killer, Boris Karloff* (1949) in which Karloff doesn't actually play the killer (he is Swami Talpur), *Colonel March Investigates* (1952) as Colonel March, *Abbott & Costello Meet Dr Jekyll & Mr Hyde* (1953) as Dr Henry Jekyll/Mr Hyde, *Voodoo Island* (1957) as Phillip Knight, *Grip Of The Strangler* (1958) as James Rankin (Dr Richard Tennant), *Frankenstein – 1970* (1958) as Baron Frankenstein, *The Raven* (1963) as Dr Scarabus, *El Coleccionista De Cadáveres* (1967) as Charles Badulescu, *Targets* (1968) as Byron Orlok, *Isle Of The Snake People* (1968) as Carl van Molder, *House Of Evil* (1968) as Matthias Morteval and *Curse Of The Crimson Altar* (1968) as Professor John Marshe. In 1923 he married dancer Helen Vivien Soule but that ended in divorce five years later. In 1930 he married librarian Dot Stine but they divorced after one daughter (Sara Jane who was born in 1938) 16 years later on April 9, 1946. Two days later, he married Evelyn Hope Helmore in Boulder City, Nevada.
CAUSE: Aged 81, 6' Karloff died in Midhurst, Sussex, from a respiratory disease. He had spent his final years in a wheelchair due to crippling arthritis. He left £2,480. On February 3, 2000 Karloff's daughter sued Universal City Studios for $10 million. She alleged that Universal had cheated her out of her share of the royalties from the merchandising of her father's image and likeness. On December 15 a confidential settlement was reached between the two parties and all records sealed.

Frances Kavanaugh
Born February 5, 1915
Died January 23, 2009
"The Cowgirl of the Typewriter". Frances Kavanaugh was unusual in Hollywood – she wrote Westerns. Born in Dallas and raised in Houston, Texas, she grew up in a horsey atmosphere that, she said, "gave me the feeling of Westerns". She took a degree in accountancy at the University of Texas and moved west with her parents in 1940. She enrolled in Max Reinhardt's drama workshop and began writing two-handers for her fellow students. A visitor to the class one day was the independent B-western producer-director-writer Robert Emmett Tansey and he offered Kavanaugh a job with his production company on the Monogram lot. Her job was to rewrite dialogue but one day the script was so bad that no amount of rewriting could save it, so Tansey told her to go home and see if she could do better. She could and he hired her as his chief scriptwriter. Her first screenplay was for the Keene western *Dynamite Canyon* (released August 8, 1941) and over the next ten years she wrote more than 30 film scripts for cowboy stars such as Tom Keene, Bob Steele, Eddie Dean, Jimmy Wakely, Ken Maynard and Duncan Renaldo. In 1951 she married Robert L. Hecker and after some television writing, she retired to raise a family – she had two children, Robbie-Jane Wedeen and Robert K. Persson-Hecker. In 1945 she wrote *Song Of Old Wyoming* (released October 12, 1945) and Tansey suggested she write a whip into the script for Cheyenne Kid, played by Al La Rue. The gimmick was a success and soon the then unknown actor was given his own series as the whip-wielding, black-outfitted Lash LaRue.
CAUSE: Frances Kavanaugh died at her home in Encino after a long battle with lymphoma. She was 93.

Danny Kaye

(DAVID DANIEL KAMINSKI)
Born January 18, 1913
Died March 3, 1987
All-rounder. Born in Brooklyn, New York, 5'11" Kaye grew up in a household in which the first language was Yiddish. While still in his early teens he became a stand-up comedian in hotels in the Catskills resort. He spent much time in the Thirties appearing in cabaret and later on Broadway, where he was spotted by Samuel Goldwyn. He was a hit in the Forties but by the Fifties his film career was almost over and so he turned to television. His films included *Up In Arms* (1944) as Danny Weems, *Wonder Man* (1945) as Buzzy Belew/Edwin Dingle, *The Kid From Brooklyn* (1946) as Burleigh 'Tiger' Sullivan, *The Secret Life Of Walter Mitty* (1947) as Walter Mitty, *A Song Is Born* (1948) as Professor Hobart Frisbee, *The Inspector General* (1949) as Georgi, *On The Riviera* (1951) as Jack Martin/Henri Duran, *Hans Christian Andersen* (1952) as Hans Christian Andersen, *White Christmas* (1954) as Phil Davis, *Knock On Wood* (1954) as Jerry Morgan/Papa Morgan, *The Court Jester* (1956) as Hawkins, *Me And The Colonel* (1958) as S.L. Jacobowsky, *The Five Pennies* (1959) as Loring 'Red' Nichols, *The Man From The Diner's Club* (1963) as Ernest Klenk and *The Madwoman Of Chaillot* (1969). Kaye had an aversion to autograph hunters, often telling them that he only looked like Danny Kaye. On January 3, 1940, he married Sylvia Fine (b. New York, August 29, 1893 or 1913, d. October 28, 1991, of emphysema) and she quickly took over the running of her husband's life. Far from being the ideal couple as portrayed in the press it was a marriage of convenience and domination, both Sylvia's. Their only daughter, Dena, was born in New York on December 17, 1946. In December 1983 he and Sylvia legally warned their daughter that if she were to write a book about "the family's dirty laundry" she would be disinherited. Was the only "dirty laundry" the dysfunctional state of her parents' marriage or was there more to it? For years rumours have circulated that Kaye was homosexual. In particular, it is said he had an affair with Laurence Olivier. Dame Peggy Ashcroft commented, "Of course I knew Laurence Olivier and Danny Kaye were having a long-term affair. So did all of London. So did their wives. Why is America always the last to know?" Elsa Lanchester added, "Danny Kaye is an acquired taste. On the screen, he wasn't the least bit funny. Rather, he was egotistical and one of those comedians who secretly envy dramatic actors. Add to that his ever-present and unpleasant wife, and his being as they say in the closet, and he was no picnic to work with." Kaye's biographer argues that there is no substantive evidence to support allegations of an affair, merely supposition. Two of Olivier's biographers report on the affair and Olivier told his own editor that he had dropped tales of homosexuality from his own autobiography because he didn't want to upset his wife, Joan Plowright. Gay actor-turned-designer Billy Haines said of Kaye: "I think that he's the most repressed innate homosexual I ever met. Do not ask me if he's been with this one or that one, I have no idea if he's ever done it. But it's *there*, in him."
CAUSE: In November 1962 Kaye underwent an emergency appendectomy. In 1982 he was operated on for a hernia and the following year for a "leg condition". This led to pains in his chest and he underwent a heart bypass procedure. During the operation Kaye contracted Hepatitis C, for which he was hospitalised several times. The chief surgeon was Dr Hyman Engelberg who had been Marilyn Monroe's doctor. Rumours surfaced that Kaye had, in fact, contracted AIDS from the

infected blood, because there was no screening in those days. However, his doctor insisted it was hepatitis. Kaye became weaker and died in Cedars-Sinai Hospital Medical Center, 8700 Beverly Boulevard, Los Angeles, California, from "a heart attack brought on by internal bleeding and post-transfusion hepatitis". He was 74. His body was taken to Hillside Memorial Park, 6001 West Centinela Avenue, Los Angeles, California 90045 but then was moved to a crematorium and then his ashes were taken to New York. His widow, Sylvia, as manipulating in death as she was in life, left strict instructions that the exact location of his final resting place was never to be revealed.
FURTHER READING: *Nobody's Fool: The Lives Of Danny Kaye* – Martin Gottfried (New York: Simon & Schuster, 1994).

Elia Kazan

(ELIA KAZANJIOGLOU)
Born September 7, 1909
Died September 28, 2003
Gadge. The method director who was regarded by some as the greatest single influence on post-war American theatre and cinema. Kazan was born in Constantinople, Turkey, the son of George Kazanjioglou and Athena Shishmanoglou (b. Makrikeu, Constantinople, Turkey, d. 1976 of cancer) into an Armenian family. When he was four, his parents moved to America and settled in New York where his father became a carpet dealer. Kazan was educated at Williams College, New York (enrolling in the autumn of 1926 and graduating in 1930), and Yale, and studied for the stage at Yale Dramatic School. In 1932, he joined the Group Theater as an actor and assistant stage manager. He was with the company on its successful visit to London with *Golden Boy* in 1938. Kazan directed his first stage play in 1935, and though he went on acting regularly for a decade, and occasionally in films, it was as a

Broadway director that he made his name. His work included *Thunder Rock* (opening at the Mansfield Theater on November 14, 1939; running for 23 performances); *The Skin Of Our Teeth* (opening at the Plymouth Theater, November 18, 1944; running for 355 performances); *Jacobowsky And The Colonel* (opening at the Martin Beck Theater, March 14, 1939; running for 415 performances); *Deep Are The Roots* (opening at the Fulton Theater, September 26, 1945; running for 477 performances); *Camino Real* (opening at the National Theater, March 19, 1953; running for 60 performances); *Tea And Sympathy* (opening at the Barrymore Theater, September 30, 1953; running for 712 performances); William Inge's *The Dark At The Top Of The Stairs* (opening at the Music Box Theater, December 5, 1957; running for 468 performances) and Archibald MacLeish's *J.B.* (opening at the Anta Theater, December 11, 1958; running for 364 performances). In 1963 he became co-director of the Repertory Theater of the Lincoln Center for the Performing Arts, staging Arthur Miller's *After The Fall* (January 23, 1964) and *Incident At Vichy*, as well as *The Changeling*. Kazan forsook the theatre because, "There is no damned theatre any more. It's boring and archaic and I never go to the theatre. I hate the theatre. Movies is where all the action is." Kazan had made his film début in 1934 in Ralph Steiner's short *Pie In The Sky*. Three years later, he directed a documentary about Tennessee miners, *The People Of The Cumberland*. He was also responsible for a full-length documentary for the US Department of Agriculture, *It's Up To You* (1941), about food rationing. His feature film directing career began in 1945 when he made the big screen version of the Broadway play *A Tree Grows In Brooklyn* for Fox. When he landed in Tinseltown, he was advised to change his name to Cezanne. Kazan protested that there was already a celebrated painter of that name. A Fox executive responded, "You make just one good picture, and nobody will ever remember the other guy." He directed an "epically dreary" Western *The Sea Of Grass* (released April 25, 1947) which starred Spencer Tracy as Colonel James Brewton, a cattle tycoon so obsessed by his work that he alienates his family. Kazan's next film, the thriller *Boomerang!* (1947) starring Dana Andrews, Jane Wyatt, Lee J. Cobb, Sam Levene, Ed Begley, Sr and Karl Malden was shot entirely on location. In the summer of 1947 he filmed Laura Z. Hobson's novel *Gentlemen's Agreement* for 20th Century Fox and hired Gregory Peck, Dorothy McGuire, John Garfield and Celeste Holm. It was a film about a Gentile writer who poses as a Jew to expose anti-Semitism but Jews Louis B. Mayer and Samuel Goldwyn could not understand why the Gentile Darryl F. Zanuck wanted to make it. Peck was a Catholic and Garfield was the only principal cast member who was Jewish. Fox's tag line for the film was "The Picture That Calls A Spade, A Spade". On March 20, 1948, at the Oscars held at the Shrine Auditorium, Los Angeles, the film, which had opened in New York in November 1947 and Hollywood just before Christmas 1947, won Best Picture, Best Director (for Kazan) and Best Supporting Actress (for Holm). Holm obviously did not expect to win. As Donald Crisp announced her name she was sitting knitting and dropped the ball of yarn under her seat. Crisp stayed on stage to present Kazan with his gong. Gregory Peck was nominated as Best Actor but lost out to Ronald Colman in *A Double Life* (1947). Dorothy McGuire lost to Loretta Young in *The Farmer's Daughter* (1947) for the Best Actress Oscar. Moss Hart was also nominated for Best Screenplay and Harmon Jones for Best Film Editing. Zanuck had been wary of hiring Kazan because "I am naturally suspicious of deep

thinkers in relation to motion pictures. They sometimes think so deep that they miss the point." Kazan's next film was also a thinker. *Pinky* (1949) was a racial drama about a light-skinned black girl (Jeanne Crain) who passed for white until she went home to Mississippi. Another thriller followed. *Panic In The Streets* (1950) saw the nascence of the punchy realism that was to infect Kazan's future work. Richard Widmark played Dr Clinton Reed, a New Orleans public health official, who has 48 hours to find Blackie (Jack Palance), a criminal who unknowingly carries a deadly virus. Edna and Edward Anhalt won the Best Motion Picture Story Oscar for *Panic In The Streets*. For his next film Kazan turned to Tennessee Williams' *A Streetcar Named Desire*. Kazan had already directed Marlon Brando in the 1947 Broadway production and contrasted Brando's brooding, instinctive Stanley Kowalski against the conventional histrionics of Vivien Leigh (who replaced the original Jessica Tandy) as Blanche Dubois. *A Streetcar Named Desire* was filmed on location in New Orleans, Louisiana and the Warner Bros studios between August 14 and mid-October 1950 and released on March 22, 1951. The film required 68 rewrites from the stage version to appease the various censorious bodies. Blanche's nymphomania was toned down and mentions of her first husband's homosexuality excised. Kazan wrote of Brando's portrayal of the animally magnetic, uncouth, slobbish Kowalski, "If there is a better performance by a man in the history of film in America, I don't know what it is." The film received Best Picture, Best Actor, Best Actress, Best Supporting Actor, Best Supporting Actress, Best Director, Best Screenplay, Best Cinematography, Best Black & White Art Direction, Best Sound Recording, Best Scoring Of A Dramatic Picture and Best Black & White Costume Design nominations.

On March 20, 1952, only Leigh (Best Actress), Karl Malden (Best Supporting Actor as Mitch) and Kim Hunter (Best Supporting Actress as Stella Kowalski) went home from the RKO Pantages Theater in Hollywood clutching Oscars. Kazan worked again with Brando in *Viva Zapata!* (1952) even though studio honcho Darryl Zanuck did not want Brando. Kazan stood firm and Brando repaid his belief, receiving his second Oscar nod and his second defeat, losing to Gary Cooper in *High Noon*. Kazan's next film was *Man On A Tightrope* (1953) starring Frederic March, Terry Moore, Cameron Mitchell, Gloria Grahame and Adolph Menjou. Then he was back working with Brando in *On The Waterfront* (filmed in Hoboken, New Jersey between November 17, 1953 and January 1954 and released on July 14, 1954). The powerful film about whistle blowing had parallels in real life. On April 13, 1952, Kazan named names before the House of Un-American Activities Committee about former Communist comrades in the theatre. Having admitted his membership of the Communist Party during his days with the Group Theater, he declined at first to name fellow artists but he later changed his mind. The next day he placed an advertisement in *Daily Variety* and *The New York Times* praising his own behaviour. Kazan did not need to testify. His Broadway career would have been safe as the black list only affected the West Coast. Rumours circulated that Fox had paid Kazan a large sum of money for testifying. His actions had cost him friends and would haunt him for the rest of his life. Brando was furious with Kazan for informing but full of admiration for his talent as a director. Arthur Miller refused to write the screenplay because of his disgust at Kazan's actions. It was written by another informer Budd Schulberg and it co-starred Lee J. Cobb who had also blabbed about who was a

communist or had sympathies. Many of the film's leading characters were based on real people. Terry Malloy (Brando) was based on Anthony De Vincenzo, a whistle-blowing docker; Roman Catholic priest John M. Corridan was the basis for Father Barry (Karl Malden) and Johnny Friendly (Lee J. Cobb) was the gangster Anthony Anastasio (b. Italy 1906, d. 1963 of natural causes), the brother of Albert Anastasia who was known as the Lord High Executioner of Murder Inc. On March 30, 1955, *On The Waterfront* won Oscars for Brando, Best Film, Best Director (Kazan), Best Supporting Actress (Eva Marie Saint), Best Screenplay, Best Black & White Cinematography, Best Black & White Art Direction and Best Editing. Other nominations were two Best Supporting Actors (Malden and Cobb) and Best Dramatic Score. The film was Kazan's way of rationalising his behaviour in naming names. In *East Of Eden* (filmed between May 27 and August 9, 1954 and premièred in New York on March 9, 1955), his first colour and widescreen film, Kazan introduced another superb method actor in James Dean whose casting had been announced by Warner Bros on March 6, 1954. It was Kazan's last major hit apart from *Splendour In The Grass*. Written by Paul Osborn from John Steinbeck's novel, *East Of Eden* was lauded as Kazan's best work so far. More Oscar nominations followed. Best Actor (James Dean), Best Supporting Actress (Jo Van Fleet), Best Director and Best Screenplay but only Van Fleet won on March 21, 1956. *Baby Doll* (1956) starred Carroll Baker, Eli Wallach and Karl Malden and revealed Kazan's fondness for long scenes. After filming *East Of Eden* in colour Kazan reverts to monochrome for this film and his next. *A Face In The Crowd* (1957) shows the abuse of television's power over the masses. Written by Budd Schulberg, a TV executive creates a star out of a tramp.

Kazan's next film was *Wild River* (1960) about schemes to flood the Tennessee Valley and build dams at the end of the Depression. It was a flop. *Splendour In The Grass* (1961) introduced Warren Beatty to the screen as Natalie Wood's love interest. It turned out to be a real affair as well as a reel one. Beatty was called "the most exciting American male in movies" by *Life* magazine. On April 9, 1962, at the Santa Monica Civic Auditorium, William Inge won the Best Writing Oscar while Natalie Wood lost out to Sophia Loren for *Two Women* (1961) in the Best Actress category. Resorting at length to his own youthful memories in *America, America* (1963), known in Britain as *The Anatolian Smile*, Kazan seemed defeated by the mass of material he had taken from his own book. In *The Arrangement* (1969), another semi-autobiographical film from his shrill novel, the issue of selling out again cropped up. Kazan's final film was *The Last Tycoon* (1976), based on F. Scott Fitzgerald's last and unfinished novel, with a script by Harold Pinter. The movie flopped. In 1987 the Directors' Guild of America awarded Kazan the D.W. Griffith Award. In 1999, as a result of his stance during the HUAC hearings, there was controversy when he won a lifetime achievement Oscar. John Sanford whose late wife Marguerite Roberts had been a victim of the black list spoke for many when he said, "Kazan is a fink bastard. The son of a bitch deserves nothing more than a kick in the ass." The *Village Voice* put a caricature of Kazan on its cover holding a golden rodent instead of an Oscar with the headline "Hollywood's #1 Rat". Film historian Patrick McGilligan said, "He didn't name anyone in the cell. He named the people he didn't like. He named the people who he felt condescended to him . . . He was a cut-throat guy." Hollywood was divided. Charlton Heston, not surprisingly, was in favour

of presenting Kazan with the award, as was director Mark Rydell, actors Warren Beatty, Kim Hunter, Karl Malden, and Tom Arnold who said, "If we didn't honour backstabbers in this town, there would be no awards ceremony." Martin Landau, a friend of Kazan, admitted, "As an artist he deserves to be honoured, as a man he doesn't." Rod Steiger, who had appeared in *On The Waterfront*, also thought Kazan should not be honoured. On March 21, 1999, at the Dorothy Chandler Pavilion, 500 people gathered outside, many with banners declaring "Honor Courage, Not Kazan", "Best Supporting Snitch", "Blacklisted Directors Coulda Been Contenders" and "Kazan – the Linda Tripp of the 50s". At the Academy Awards, whenever a celebrity leaves their seat someone – a filler – sits in so that the auditorium never looks less than full. The presentation to Kazan was to be made after a commercial break. During the break so many of the audience left their seats so as not to be present when Kazan received his trophy that producers worried that they did not have enough fillers. Robert De Niro and Martin Scorsese presented the Oscar to Kazan. Karl Malden, Warren Beatty, Kathy Bates, Lynn Redgrave, Kurt Russell, Meryl Streep, Billy Bob Thornton, Laura Dern, Linda Hunt and Debbie Allen stood to applaud. Steven Spielberg, Jim Carrey and Patrick Stewart clapped but remained seated. Ed Harris, Amy Madigan, Nick Nolte, Ian McKellen, Brendan Fraser, Holly Hunter, David Geffen and Sherry Lansing remained seated and passive. Elia Kazan was married three times. By his first wife, Molly Day Thatcher (d. December 1963), whom he married on December 2, 1932, he had two sons, Chris (b. 1938) and Nick (b. 1946), and two daughters, Judy (b. 1936) and Katharine (b. 1947); by his second wife, the actor and director Barbara Loden (b. Marion, North

Carolina, July 8, 1932, d. New York, September 5, 1980 of liver and breast cancer), whom he married on June 5, 1967, he had one son, Leo (b. New York, January 2, 1962). He married Frances Rudge on June 28, 1982 and became stepfather to her two children. CAUSE: Kazan died in Manhattan, three weeks after his 94th birthday, of natural causes.

FURTHER READING: *A Life* – Elia Kazan (London: Andre Deutsch, 1988).

Moe Keale
Born December 13, 1939
Died April 15, 2002
'Truck'. Wilfred Nalani Keale was born in Niihau, a seventh child, but grew up on Oahu, Hawaii. His father came from Niihau, his mother from Kauai. Keale learned to play the ukulele when he was 4. He played the instrument as a boy growing up in Palolo Valley, taking it to Palolo Elementary School and Kaimuki High School and, later, as a beach boy, to Waikiki. As a beach boy, his long hair earned him a nickname that stuck for years 'Animal'. He was a professional high-diver, a part-time electrician and a radio DJ. A frequent nightclub performer, Keale was the lead singer in Eddie Kamae's Sons Of Hawaii in the late Sixties. He also had his own group, Moe Keale & Anuenue. In 1978, he recorded a solo album, *South Sea Island Magic*. He began acting in 1959 with a role in the Spencer Tracy feature film *The Devil At Four O'Clock*, which was followed by a long run in New York of the stage production of *Paradise Island*. He became a regular in the cast of the hit cop show *Hawaii Five-O* playing Truck Kealoha just as the show was ending. He had also worked on the set as an electrician. He was married to Carol and had a son Scott Nalani.
CAUSE: Keale nearly died in 2001 when he suffered a heart attack while working out at 24 Hour Fitness in the Windward City Shopping Center. Police officers saved his life. He died after a heart attack at Castle Medical Center in Honolulu, Hawaii. On May 4 a musical celebration in remembrance of Keale took place at the Kuhio Beach Hula Mound. A ceremony was held at sunset and his ashes were scattered at sea.

Buster Keaton
Born October 4, 1895
Died February 1, 1966
'The Great Stone Face'. Born in Piqua, Kansas, despite the legend, little Joseph Frank (later Francis) Keaton was *not* nicknamed 'Buster' by family friend Harry Houdini after the six-month-old fell down the stairs and the great escapologist allegedly said to Mr Keaton: "That was some buster he took falling down the stairs." Keaton took part in his parents' act – he would be thrown around the stage by his father and to make it easier to pick up the small boy his mother sewed a suitcase handle onto the back of his jacket. The young Buster had a tough upbringing: on one occasion Mr Keaton beat up a heckler using his son as a weapon and Sarah Bernhardt once threatened to have Mr Keaton arrested for child abuse. Buster taught himself to read and write, having only had one half day of formal schooling in his life. Working in vaudeville, he was invited to join Fatty Arbuckle and the two men became firm friends. Keaton was a notorious practical joker, as was Arbuckle. One day they turned up at the Beverly Hills mansion of a friend pretending to be from the gas board investigating a leak and proceeded to dig up the finely manicured lawn. A chronic ear infection during World War I left Keaton virtually deaf. His films included *The Butcher Boy* (1917) as a customer, *His Wedding Night* (1917), *Coney Island* (1917), *A Country Hero* (1917), *Moonshine* (1918) as an assistant revenue officer, *Good Night, Nurse!* (1918) as a doctor and a visitor, *The Garage* (1919) as an assistant to the garage owner, *The Saphead* (1920), Keaton's first feature

in which he played Bertie Van Alstyne, *Neighbors* (1921) as the boy, *The High Sign* (1921), *The Goat* (1921), *The Boat* (1921) as a husband, *The Paleface* (1922) in the title role, *The Blacksmith* (1922), *The Frozen North* (1922), *Daydreams* (1922), *Cops* (1922), *Go West* (1923) as Buster, *The Balloonatic* (1923), *Sherlock, Jr* (1924) as the projectionist, *The Iron Mule* (1925), *Go West* (1925) as Friendless/Homer Holiday, *The General* (1927) as Johnnie Gray, *Spite Marriage* (1929) as Elmer, *Doughboys* (1930) as Elmer, *Sidewalks Of New York* (1931) as Homer Van Dine Harmon, *Casanova Wider Willen* (1931) as Reginald Irving, *The Passionate Plumber* (1932) as Elmer Tuttle, *The Gold Ghost* (1934), *Palooka From Paducah* (1935), *Three On A Limb* (1936), *Grand Slam Opera* (1936) as Elmer Butts, *Blue Blazes* (1936) as Elmer, *Jail Bait* (1937), *The Villain Still Pursued Her* (1940) as William, *The Spook Speaks* (1940), *Li'l Abner* (1940) as Lonsome Polecat, *She's Oil Mine* (1941), *That's The Spirit* (1945), *You're My Everything* (1949), *The Lovable Cheat* (1949) as Goulard, *Sunset Blvd.* (1950) as himself, *Limelight* (1952) as Calvero's partner, *Around The World In 80 Days* (1956) as a train conductor, *The Adventures Of Huckleberry Finn* (1960) as a lion tamer, *The Triumph Of Lester Snapwell* (1963) as Lester Snapwell, *It's A Mad Mad Mad Mad World* (1963) as Jimmy The Crook, *Beach Blanket Bingo* (1965), *How To Stuff A Wild Bikini* (1965) as Bwana the witch doctor, *Sergeant Deadhead* (1965) as Private Blinken and *A Funny Thing Happened On The Way To The Forum* (1966) as Erronius. Keaton was initially careful to ensure his films were produced and crafted the way he wanted. A move to MGM robbed him of this input and his work began to suffer accordingly. A gourmet cook, he became a virtual alcoholic towards the end of his life. It was only in the Fifties that a new audience began to appreciate his work and he appeared in Chaplin's *Limelight*, despite being one of the Little Tramp's greatest comedy rivals. Keaton was awarded a special Oscar in 1962. On May 31, 1921, he married Natalie Talmadge, sister of Norma. They had two sons: Joseph (born June 2, 1922) and Robert (b. February 3, 1924). The Keatons divorced in 1933. Before his divorce was finalised Keaton married Mae Scribbins on January 8, 1933. They remarried on October 17, 1933. The couple was divorced on October 14, 1936. Keaton's third and final wife was dancer Eleanor Norris; they wed on May 29, 1940.

CAUSE: He died at 6.15am aged 70 in Los Angeles, California, from lung cancer. He was buried in Forest Lawn-Hollywood Hills, 6300 Forest Lawn Drive, Los Angeles 90068. His widow placed a rosary in one pocket and a pack of playing cards in the other.

FURTHER READING: *Buster Keaton: Cut To The Chase* – Marion Meade (HarperCollins, 1995).

Howard Keel

(HAROLD CLIFFORD LEEK)
Born April 13, 1917
Died November 7, 2004
Broad-shouldered baritone. A star of Fifties musicals, Howard Keel later found his career revived as Clayton Farlow in *Dallas*. Born in Gillespie, Illinois, the son of a naval captain turned coalminer, who beat his children when he was drunk. Keel's mother, a strict Methodist, forbade her two sons from having any entertainment. "I had a terrible, rotten childhood," Keel remembered. "My father made away with himself when I was 11. I had no guidance, and Mum was six feet tall, bucktoothed and very tough. I was mean and rebellious and had a terrible, bitter temper. I got a job as an auto mechanic, and I would have stayed in that narrow kind of life if I hadn't discovered art. Music changed

me completely." In the late Thirties Keel moved to Los Angeles, California and aged 20 was befriended by a woman who took him to a concert at the Hollywood Bowl featuring the baritone Lawrence Tibbett. Keel was inspired, and he started taking vocal lessons at 25 cents an hour. His first semi-professional opportunity came as a singing waiter at the Paris Inn Restaurant in downtown Los Angeles at $15 a week and two meals a day. Keel worked for five years at Douglas Aircraft in Santa Monica during the Second World War. He auditioned for Oscar Hammerstein II who was looking for young singers to play Curly in the growing number of touring *Oklahoma!* companies. Hammerstein approved, and soon, under a new name, Howard Keel, he was singing 'Oh, What A Beautiful Morning' in New York eight times a week. He sometimes replaced John Raitt in Rodgers & Hammerstein's other hit, *Carousel*. On occasion he would appear in a matinee of *Oklahoma!* and an evening performance of *Carousel*. He appeared in *Carousel* for eighteen months in London. However, Rodgers & Hammerstein were notorious for underpaying their actors and denying them billing. Keel did not like receiving just $250 a week for the unbilled starring role in a sell-out musical. As soon as his contract expired, he returned to Los Angeles where he was signed to MGM at $850 a week. Keel became an overnight star in his first MGM film playing Frank Butler to Betty Hutton's Annie Oakley in *Annie Get Your Gun* (released on April 12, 1950). He became a staple of the musical genre appearing opposite Esther Williams (*Pagan Love Song* (1950), *Texas Carnival* (1951), *Jupiter's Darling* (1955)), Ann Blyth (*Rose Marie* (1954), *Kismet* (1955)), Kathryn Grayson (*Show Boat* (1951), *Lovely To Look At* (1952), *Kiss Me Kate* (1952)) and Doris Day (*Calamity Jane* (1953)). His own favourite film was the

exuberant *Seven Brides For Seven Brothers* (1954). "It was a fine cast and lots of fun to make," Keel later remarked, "but they did the damn thing on the cheap. The backdrops had holes in them, and it was shot on the worst film stock. As it turned out, the miracle worker was George Foley, the cinematographer. He took that junk and made it look like a Grandma Moses painting." When the era of the big musical ended Keel took to the road with touring versions of his big hits. At the age of 64, when most are contemplating retirement he became a television star in the then biggest show on the box, *Dallas*. He stayed with the show as good guy Clayton until *Dallas* ended on May 3, 1991. "The show was enormous," Keel recalled. "I couldn't believe it. My life changed again. From being out of it, I was suddenly a star, known to more people than ever before. Wherever I went, crowds appeared again, and I started making solo albums for the first time in my career." During his musical career, he had sung on cast albums only. He had one Top 10 (*And I Love You So* in 1984) and one Top 20 album (*Reminiscing – The Howard Keel Collection* in 1985) in the UK. He also sang on *Dallas The Album* soloing with a song called 'JR, Who Do You Think You Are?' When he left MGM his career floundered somewhat. He was St Peter in the unsuccessful *The Big Fisherman* (1959). Most of his other films were westerns: *Waco* (1966), *Red Tomahawk* (1967), *The War Wagon* (1967) (with John Wayne and Kirk Douglas) and *Arizona Bushwhackers* (1968). He also worked in England in *The Day Of The Triffids* (1962). Keel was married three times and divorced twice: first to actress Rosemary Cooper (1943–October 1948), then to dancer Helen Anderson (January 3, 1949– 1970). They had three children: Kaija Liane (born January 14, 1950), Kristine (born June 21, 1952), and Gunnar Lewis (born June 3, 1955). On

December 21, 1970 he married former airline stewardess Judy Magamoll.
They had one daughter, Leslie (born September 1, 1974). He also had 10 grandchildren and one great-granddaughter.
CAUSE: Keel died at 12.42am of colon cancer at his home in Palm Desert. He was 87.

Keiko
Born 1976
Died December 12, 2003
The biggest movie star of all time. Born and captured near Iceland in 1979, Keiko, an Orca whale, was sold to a marine adventure park where the 34'9" mammal lived a private life. In 1993 this was changed when he was cast as the eponymous hero in *Free Willy* (1993), the tale of a boy (James Richter) who befriends a captive whale and encourages him to jump over a sea park wall for freedom. The movie was such a success taking $77.7 million at the American box office that two sequels were made *Free Willy 2: The Adventure Home* (1995) and *Free Willy 3: The Rescue* (1997). The law of diminishing returns kicked in and the sequels took $30.1 million and $3.52 million. No more *Free Willy* films. A naturally shy and retiring performer, Keiko did not receive top billing in the films that made him a star. His modesty led to problems because after the third film he, like many stars before him, was all but forgotten. The biggest movie star of all time was discovered to be down on his uppers and a fund was started to send him back to Iceland. In July 2002 he was released into the wilds but, and it has to be said, Keiko was a rather ungrateful mammal. Despite the large sums of money involved (said to be £14 million), he decided he did not want to be free and anyway he missed his human friends. He swam 870 miles to Helsa, Norway, in September 2002 where locals delighted in playing with him. As usual, the authorities thought that they knew best and they banned anyone from approaching the friendly mammal.
CAUSE: Keiko died aged 27 of pneumonia in the Taknes fjord in Norway.

DeForest Kelley
Born January 20, 1920
Died June 11, 1999
Forever Dr McCoy. Born in Atlanta, Georgia, Jackson DeForest Kelley's first public performances came singing in the church choir. His talent was recognised and he landed a job on WSB-Atlanta radio. Travelling to California to visit a relative, he fell in love with the West Coast and moved there. He joined the Long Beach Theater Group and met another budding thespian Carolyn Dowling. They were married in September 1945. Spotted in a US Navy training film, Kelley was screen-tested by Paramount and offered a contract. He was to spend two and a half years at the studio.
He made his motion picture début in *Fear In The Night* (1947) and appeared in several other films including *Gunfight At The O.K. Corral* (1957) as Morgan Earp, *Raintree County* (1957), *Warlock* (1959) and *Gunfight At Comanche Creek* (1963) usually playing the baddie. However, cinematic fame eluded him. That all changed in 1966 when he was chosen to star in a new TV series called *Star Trek*. He made the character of the irascible Dr Leonard 'Bones' McCoy his own, with his catch-phrase "He's dead, Jim" and his rows with the highly logical (and, to Bones, highly infuriating) Mr Spock, the ship's second-in-command. *Star Trek* was cancelled in 1969 and no doubt Kelley would have been another movie footnote had not the series been revived on the big screen in 1979. He continued to play Dr McCoy in *Star Trek II: The Wrath Of Khan* (1982), *Star Trek III: The Search For Spock* (1984), *Star Trek IV: The Voyage Home* (1986), *Star Trek V: The Final Frontier* (1989) and *Star*

Trek VI: The Undiscovered Country (1991).

CAUSE: In August 1997 he was diagnosed with stomach cancer. Eighteen months later, he left the home he shared with Carolyn, his wife of 54 years, at 15463 Greenleaf Street, Sherman Oaks, California 91403 and moved into the Motion Picture & TV Hospital Country Home, 23388 Mulholland Drive, Woodland Hills, California. Coincidentally, Carolyn Kelly had also been admitted there, having broken her leg. He died at 12:15pm aged 79 from respiratory failure and a carcinoid tumour with metastasis. He was cremated on June 15, and his ashes were scattered at sea off the coast of Los Angeles County.

Gene Kelly

Born August 23, 1912
Died February 2, 1996
Hoofer. The temperamental and difficult bisexual Eugene Curran Kelly was born in Pittsburgh, Pennsylvania, and studied economics at university before deciding to concentrate full-time on showbiz. He became a star on Broadway in *Pal Joey* and then made his Hollywood début for MGM in *For Me And My Gal* (1942) as Harry Palmer. Judy Garland supposedly had a hand in landing him the part. He quickly established himself as a popular song-and-dance man, although he was not quite as successful in non-musicals. His canon included: *Du Barry Was A Lady* (1943) as Alec Howe/Black Arrow, *The Cross Of Lorraine* (1943) as Victor La Biche, *Thousands Cheer* (1943) as Eddie Marsh, *Christmas Holiday* (1944) as Robert Monette, *Anchors Aweigh* (1945) as Joseph Brady, for which he was nominated for an Oscar, *Ziegfeld Follies* (1946), *The Pirate* (1948) as Serafin, *The Three Musketeers* (1948) as D'Artagnan, *Black Hand* (1949) as Johnny Columbo, *Take Me Out To The Ball Game* (1949) as Eddie O'Brien, which he also choreographed, *On The Town* (1949) as

Gabey, which he also directed, *Summer Stock* (1950) as Joe D. Ross, *An American In Paris* (1951) as Jerry Mulligan, *It's A Big Country* (1951) as Icarus Xenophon, *The Devil Makes Three* (1952) as Captain Jeff Eliot, *Singin' In The Rain* (1952) as Don Lockwood, which he also directed, *Brigadoon* (1954) as Tommy Albright, which he also choreographed, *The Happy Road* (1957) as Mike Andrews, which he also directed, *Les Girls* (1957) as Barry Nichols, *Marjorie Morningstar* (1958) as Noel Airman, *Let's Make Love* (1960) as himself, *Inherit The Wind* (1960) as E. K. Hornbeck, *Viva Knievel!* (1977) as Will Atkins and *Xanadu* (1980) as Danny McGuire. He also directed *Hello, Dolly!* (1969). Kelly was awarded a special Oscar in 1951 "in appreciation of his versatility as actor, singer, director and dancer, and especially for his brilliant achievements in the art of choreography". In 1984 his home, 725 North Rodeo Drive, Beverly Hills, California 90210, was razed to the ground by a fire. He lost everything, including his prized Oscar, but rebuilt the house down to the last detail, on the same spot. He married actress Betsy Blair on September 22, 1941. Their daughter, Kerry, was born on October 16, 1942. The couple was divorced in Las Vegas on April 3, 1957. On August 6, 1960, he married dancer Jeanne Coyne. They had a son, Timothy (b. March 3, 1962) and a daughter, Bridget (b. June 10, 1964). The second Mrs Kelly died of leukaemia in Los Angeles on May 10, 1973. On July 24, 1990, the 77-year-old Kelly married 36-year-old Patricia Ward in Santa Barbara.

CAUSE: In 1994 he was admitted to a San Francisco hospital suffering from a severe headache. In July of the same year he suffered a massive stroke followed by another one in February 1995. He spent the remainder of his life in bed, watching his old films on video. He died at home of sepsis, acute renal failure, cerebrovascular accident, diabetes mellitus, coronary disease and prostate cancer. He was cremated at Westwood Memorial Park.

Grace Kelly

Born November 12, 1929
Died September 14, 1982
Ice maiden. For many years the image of Grace Kelly, who became HSH Princess Grace of Monaco, was one of a virginal, almost glacial, blonde beauty. Gradually, after her death the edifice began to crumble and the real woman was revealed. Grace Patricia Kelly was born at 3901 Henry Avenue, Germantown, Philadelphia, Pennsylvania, the daughter of 6'2" John Brendan Kelly (b. October 4, 1889, d. Philadelphia, June 20, 1960, of stomach cancer), a devout Catholic, double Olympic Gold Medal-winning sculler and prominent citizen of Philadelphia. Grace became a model in New York and began to think in terms of a film career. She also began to think in terms of men. She lost her virginity to a much older, married man, the husband of a close girlfriend, one afternoon in 1948 at his house when his wife was away. As Grace later told a friend, "It all happened so quickly. I remember it was raining very hard and her husband told me she would be gone for the rest of the afternoon. I stayed, talking to him, and before I knew it we were in bed together, without understanding quite why." Although Grace remained friendly with the couple, she and the husband never repeated the experience. Grace's husband-borrowing shenanigans didn't stop with that first encounter. As her career progressed she acquired an unsavoury reputation: as that of an actress who slept with most of her leading men, particularly enjoying the ones that were married. They included Ray Milland, William Holden, Oleg Cassini, Gary Cooper and Bing Crosby. Grace's April 18, 1956, marriage into the Monégasque royal house of Grimaldi, and the title of

Princess that went with it, plus the raising of a family, rehabilitated her tarty reputation somewhat. Even then, awkward moments still arose from her husband-borrowing past. Rainier III, Grace's princely husband, once asked actor David Niven who, of all the actresses in Hollywood, he had best enjoyed in bed. Without thinking to whom he was speaking, the dashing actor, whose bed had been Graced years earlier, replied, "Grace." Realising what he had said, Niven quickly mumbled, "Gracie, er Gracie Fields." Grace had received little parental support or encouragement for her ambitions. When she won an Oscar for *The Country Girl* (1954), her father retorted, "I can't believe it! I simply cannot believe Grace won. Of the four children, she's the last one I expected to support me in my old age." Grace made her movie début in *Fourteen Hours* (1951) as Mrs Fuller and went on to appear in *High Noon* (1952) as Amy Kane (signed for the film because she was unknown and, therefore, cheap), *Mogambo* (1953) as Linda Nordley, for which she was nominated for an Oscar, *Rear Window* (1954) as Lisa Carol Fremont, the first of three films for Alfred Hitchcock, *Green Fire* (1954) as Catherine Knowland, *Dial M For Murder* (1954) as Margot Wendice, *The Bridges At Toko-Ri* (1954) as Nancy Brubaker, *To Catch A Thief* (1955) as Frances Stevens, *The Swan* (1956) as Princess Alexandra and the appropriately named *High Society* (1956) as Tracy Samantha Lord. Following that film she retired to marry Prince Rainier and raise a family: Caroline Louise Marguerite (b. Royal Palace Library, Monaco, January 23, 1957, at 9.27am, weighing 8lb 3oz), Albert Alexandre Louis Pierre (b. Royal Palace, Monaco, March 14, 1958, weighing 8lb 11oz) and Stéphanie Marie Elisabeth (b. Royal Palace, Monaco, February 1, 1965, weighing 6lb 10oz). Despite the occasional yearning, she never returned to acting. Towards the end of her life, she suffered the onslaught of the menopause and put on weight, an increase put down to excessive drinking by some. In 1976 she also began an affair with Robert Dornheim, a film producer 16 years her junior. She also had a number of flings with other young men, whom she called her 'Toy Boys'. CAUSE: On September 13, 1982, Grace drove her 1972 Rover 3500 (registration plate 6359MC) from the weekend retreat at Roc Agel towards the royal palace through the village of La Turbie on CD37. As she approached a hairpin bend at 9.54am the car shot over the edge of the road and after turning over a few times landed upside down on its roof 120ft from the road. The passenger, Princess Stéphanie, crawled out through the driver's door and begged the passers-by to "Sauvez, Maman!" At around 11am Grace was taken to the Princess Grace Hospital in Monte Carlo where she was placed on a life support system. When it became obvious that she would not recover, the machine was switched off and she died sometime after 10pm. Her funeral was held on September 18, 1982, at the Byzantine Cathedral where she had married 26 years earlier. Attending the ceremony were Cary Grant, Diana, Princess of Wales – herself to die in a car crash almost 15 years later – the King and Queen of Belgium, the Queen of Sweden, Mme Mitterand and Nancy Reagan, who brought with her an enormous retinue of armed bodyguards. Grace was finally laid to rest three days later in the Grimaldi family vault. What had caused the crash remains something of a mystery. According to some, Grace had been distracted by an argument with the rebellious Stéphanie. Others claim sabotage but the most likely theory is that Grace suffered a minor stroke. If it had occurred at home, she would have survived but driving a car left her unable to control the vehicle or prevent the crash.

FURTHER READING: *Grace: The Secret Lives Of A Princess – An Intimate Biography Of Grace Kelly* – James Spada (London: Sidgwick & Jackson, 1987); *Rainier & Grace* – Jeffrey Robinson (London: Simon & Schuster, 1989); *The Life And Loves Of Grace Kelly* – Jane Ellen Wayne (London: Robson Books, 1991); *The Grimaldis Of Monaco: Centuries Of Scandal, Years Of Grace* – Anne Edwards (London: HarperCollins, 1993); *Grace* – Robert Lacey (London: Sidgwick & Jackson, 1994); *The Ruling House Of Monaco: The Story Of A Tragic Dynasty* – John Glatt (London: Piatkus, 1998).

Rachel Kempson

Born May 28, 1910
Died May 24, 2003
Lady Redgrave. The wife of Sir Michael and mother of Vanessa, Corin and Lynn, and grandmother to Jemma, Joely and Natasha was happier on stage than in films. Rachel Kempson was born at Dartmouth, where her father was headmaster of the Royal Naval College, and later studied at RADA. She began her career in the Thirties as one of the most beautiful and promising Shakespearean actresses on the British stage. On July 18, 1935, she married Michael Redgrave after she refused his entreaties merely to live in sin and they often appeared on stage together. However, most commentators felt that she subsumed her acting ambition into raising her family. It may also have been an escape from her husband's homosexual affairs and other infidelities. She had an affair with the bisexual actor-director Glencairn Alexander Byam Shaw, CBE (b. December 13, 1904, d. Goring-on-Thames, April 29, 1986) who numbered Siegfried Sassoon among his lovers. She excelled as Lady Manners in the television drama *The Jewel In The Crown* (1984) and also appeared in *Elizabeth R* (1971) and *Jennie: Lady Randolph Churchill* (1974). Her films included: *The Captive Heart*

(1946) as Celia Mitchell, *Georgy Girl* (1966) as Ellen Leamington with her daughter Lynn in the lead, *The Charge Of The Light Brigade* (1968) as Mrs Codrington, *The Virgin Soldiers* (1969) as Mrs Raskin (again with Lynn in the starring role) and *Out Of Africa* (1985) as Lady Belfield.

CAUSE: Rachel Kempson died four days before her 93rd birthday of a stroke at granddaughter Natasha's home in Millbrook, New York.

Kay Kendall

(KAY JUSTINE KENDALL MCCARTHY)
Born May 21, 1927
Died September 6, 1959
Comedienne cut down in her prime. Born at Stanley House, Hull Road, Withernsea, near Hull, Yorkshire, the daughter of Justin McCarthy – professionally known as Terry Kendall – and Gladys Drewery, and the granddaughter of music hall artiste Marie Kendall (1873–1964), it seemed only logical that Kay should go on the stage. She was a sickly child who easily tired. She appeared in bit parts in a number of films including *Fiddlers Three* (1944), *Dreaming* (1944), *Champagne Charlie* (1944) and *Waltz Time* (1945) before being chosen by Sid Field to appear in his forthcoming début *London Town* (1946). The film was a disaster and Kay was slated by the critics. Her next films – *Caesar And Cleopatra* (1946), *Dance Hall* (1950) as Doreen, *Happy Go Lovely* (1951) playing a secretary, *Lady Godiva Rides Again* (1951) as Sylvia, *Wings Of Danger* (1952) as Alexia LaRoche, *It Started In Paradise* (1952) as Lady Caroline, *Street Of Shadows* (1953) as Barbara Gale, *The Square Ring* (1953) as Eve Lewis and others were equally unsatisfactory. Kay began to get depressed over what she saw as her failure to achieve a real measure of success and regularly told her family she would throw herself out of a window to her death. Her sister, Kim, recalls: "She was always depressed [but]

by the thirteenth time we used to open [the window] and say 'Help yourself'." Her big break finally came as Rosalind Peters in the light comedy *Genevieve* (1953). She appeared opposite Dirk Bogarde in *Doctor In The House* (1954) as Isobel but there was obviously no romance in any house. On the romantic front she had been wooed and won by Sydney Chaplin, Lord Hanson's brother Bill who was to die of cancer aged 32, Prince Carl Johan of Sweden and grocery tycoon James Sainsbury. It was during the filming of *The Constant Husband* (1955), in which Kay played Monica Hathaway, that she began an affair with an inconstant husband, Rex Harrison. As filming ended they went their separate ways but neither could get the other out of their mind. Throwing caution to the wind, they began a full-blown affair. However, it wasn't without its unfortunate moments. During a lunch with Diana Dors and Dennis Hamilton, Kay kept clinging to Rex and begging him to tell her he loved her and would marry her. Harrison's response was to tell her to shut up, then he "clouted her in the ear." After the hotel lunch they went for a boat trip and Kay again needled Rex into talking about marriage. To gain his attention she threw herself overboard, knowing he would have to rescue her because she couldn't swim. She eventually won him round and they moved in together. Kay had suffered from anaemia for most of her life but her *joie de vivre* made many of her friends forget how weak she really was. Kay's first Hollywood film was *Les Girls* (1957) in which she played Lady Sybil Wren and starred opposite Gene Kelly and Mitzi Gaynor. During filming in New York, Rex went to see her doctor and told him he loved Kay and wanted to marry her. He was then horrified to be told she was suffering from myeloid leukaemia and would be dead within three years. He determined to keep the true prognosis from her, but told his

wife Lilli Palmer. They decided to divorce so Rex could marry and look after Kay, and planned to remarry after her death. As soon as Lilli filed for divorce, Rex and Kay became engaged. Ten days after the engagement, they were at a party and Kay disappeared outside with Frank Sinatra who was looking for a breath of fresh air. Harrison believed that Sinatra was making a play for Kay (he wasn't) and he smacked him twice. The normally fiery-tempered Sinatra turned the other cheek and went back inside. Rex and Kay were married at the Universalist Church of the Divine Paternity, Central Park West & 76th Street, New York on June 23, 1957.
CAUSE: Shortly before she was due to begin work on what would be her penultimate film, *The Reluctant Debutante* (1958) in which she played Sheila Broadbent, the Harrisons flew to Switzerland on holiday, their first together as man and wife, but Kay fell ill. After the film they moved to a rented home in Cheyne Walk, London. While he worked she became more ill. She was approached to appear in *Once More With Feeling* (1960) as Dolly Fabian and her doctors agreed it would be better for her to work. Filming began in Paris in April 1959 but Rex had refused to allow the Columbia Studio doctors to examine Kay lest they discover the seriousness of her condition. It was a risky business and he laid himself open to all sorts of financial penalties if Kay became too ill to work. That did happen and Rex claimed he had passed on a cold to his wife which had turned into bronchial pneumonia. She was taken to London by train and booked into the London Clinic but rallied enough to be discharged after four days and returned to the French capital. When the film was completed the Harrisons went on holiday to Portofino and then on to Switzerland. In August 1959 they returned to Portofino but her condition

deteriorated and she was taken again by train to the London Clinic. She lapsed into a coma on September 6, 1959 as the hospital was issuing a bulletin saying she was "gravely ill". She died without regaining consciousness at 12.30pm. Her last words were to her husband: "I love you with all my heart." She left £2,313 16s 7d.

Joseph P. Kennedy
Born September 6, 1888
Died November 18, 1969
The Ambassador. Although best-known now for being the progenitor of the Kennedy political dynasty, Joseph Patrick Kennedy was one of the first to become involved in the movie industry and had a long-running affair with Gloria Swanson. Born at 151 Meridian Street, East Boston, Massachusetts, Kennedy's father, Patrick John, known as PJ, served in the Massachusetts House of Representatives. Joe was educated at Harvard, graduating in 1912. One story from Harvard shows the man that Joe Kennedy would become. His father's people bribed one of Joe's college mates to allow Joe to win a coveted baseball blue. By the age of 25 Kennedy was Boston's youngest bank president. On October 7, 1914 at Boston, he married Rose Elizabeth Fitzgerald (b. 4 Garden Court Street, North End, Boston, July 21, 1890, d. Hyannis Port, January 20, 1995) and they started a family almost immediately. Eldest son Joseph Patrick, Jr was born on July 25, 1915 in Villa Napoli, 201 Atlantic Avenue, Hull, Massachusetts. Handsome, personable, intelligent, argumentative and with a hair-trigger temper, Joe who was educated at the London School of Economics and Harvard was destined by Joe, Sr to become the first Catholic American president. Those hopes and dreams died on August 12, 1944 when he was killed in action over Suffolk. The dream was transferred to the next

son, John Fitzgerald (b. 83 Beals Street, Brookline, Massachusetts, May 29, 1917, k. Deeley Plaza, Dallas, Texas, 22 November 1963 at 12.30pm), who did become the American President on November 8, 1960 beating off Richard Nixon. Reports have long persisted that Joe Kennedy bought the presidency for his son. However, that story is outside the scope of this book. Joe's other children were Rosemary (b. Brookline September 13, 1918, d. Fort Atkinson Memorial Health Hospital, Wisconsin, January 7, 2005) who was mentally deficient; Kathleen known as 'Kick' (b. Brookline February 20, 1920, k. Crevenne Mountains, Ardeche, France May 13, 1948, in an aeroplane crash); Eunice Mary (b. Brookline, July 10, 1921); Patricia (b. Brookline, May 6, 1924) who married the actor Peter Lawford; Robert Francis (b. Brookline, Massachusetts, November 20, 1925, k. Ambassador's Hotel, Los Angeles, California, June 6, 1968, by assassination) who became Attorney-General under his brother and was, like his brother, Marilyn Monroe's lover; Jean Ann (b. Boston, February 20, 1928) and Edward Moore (b. St Margaret's Hospital, Dorchester, Brookline, Massachusetts, February 22, 1932). Joe made his not inconsiderable wealth from insider dealing and bootlegging when Prohibition was introduced in America. By the mid-Twenties his fortune was estimated at $2 million. On February 7, 1926, he bought the Film Booking Offices of America sight unseen from its English owners for $1 million. The company specialised in low-budget Westerns and melodramas. On November 11, 1927, he met Gloria Swanson for the first time in the Renaissance Room of the Savoy Plaza Hotel on 5th Avenue and 59th Street. They began an affair that was to wreck her third marriage, to Henri, Marquis de la Falaise. Swanson had joined United Artists in a bid to

manage her own affairs. However, the deal had been disastrous and she was virtually broke when she met Kennedy. In early January 1928 their affair was consummated at the Royal Poinciana Hotel. Swanson remembered, "He was like a roped horse, rough, arduous, racing to be free. After a hasty climax, he lay beside me stroking my hair. Apart from his guilty, passionate moanings, he had said nothing cogent." In March 1928, Kennedy and Swanson met with the egotistical Erich von Stroheim and, two months later, contracts were signed to make *Queen Kelly*, an expensive epic that would showcase Swanson. Filming began at the FBO studios in Hollywood in November 1928. In 1929 Joe bought the 15-room, nine-bathroom house at Hyannis Port that would become the Kennedy compound. In spring of that year production on *Queen Kelly* shut down and Kennedy sacked von Stroheim. Kennedy had lost interest in the film but his passion for Swanson was as strong as ever. He hired Edmund Goulding to direct *The Trespasser*, Swanson's first talkie. Their affair fizzled out in 1929 and Swanson was shocked to discover that a fur coat he had given her had actually been paid for out of her money. Kennedy was not finished with Hollywood stars. He had affairs with actresses Betty Compson, Nancy Carroll, Constance Bennett and Marlene Dietrich who supposedly also bedded Joe, Jr and Jack. On August 9, 1929, a teenager called Eunice Pringle alleged that she had been raped in a broom cupboard by Alexander Pantages, who owned the Hollywood Pantages cinema on Hollywood and Vine and sixty other picture palaces. His only rival was the Orpheum Circuit, later owned by RKO, an offspring of Joe Kennedy's FBO. At his trial Pantages was defended by Jerry Giesler but despite his eloquence the jury found Pantages guilty and he was sentenced to fifty years in jail. In 1931

Giesler managed to get the appeal heard and the charges against Pantages were dismissed. On her deathbed Eunice Pringle confessed that the whole thing had been a set-up engineered by Joe Kennedy who wanted to own Pantages' cinema circuit. On December 9, 1937 Kennedy was appointed as American Ambassador to the Court of St James's. On February 23, 1938 he sailed for England. In March 1938, Kennedy arrived in London to take up the seals of office, a post he would hold until November 1940 when he resigned after giving an interview critical of President Franklin D. Roosevelt. The rest of Kennedy's life was devoted to ensuring that the name of Kennedy was a formidable one in American political life.

CAUSE: On a Palm Beach golf course on December 19, 1961, Joe Kennedy collapsed and was taken home by his niece, Ann Gargan. Rose Kennedy insisted that her husband was fine and she went out to play her own game of golf. A few hours later, Joe Kennedy's condition had worsened and he was taken to hospital where doctors found that he had suffered a massive stroke. He had a blood clot in a brain artery, was paralysed down his right side and unable to speak. Despite being incapacitated he lived for eight more years, outliving President John F. Kennedy and Senator Bobby Kennedy and through Senator Teddy Kennedy's scandal at Chappaquiddick. Ambassador Joseph P. Kennedy died at Hyannis Port, Massachusetts, at 11.05am, aged 81. He was buried in the Kennedy family plot in Brookline.

FURTHER READING: *Gloria And Joe* – Axel Madsen (New York: Berkley Books, 1989).

Troy Kennedy Martin

Born February 15 1932
Died September 15, 2009

Passionate writer. Francis Troy Kennedy Martin was born in Rothesay on the Isle of Bute, and named for a Roman Catholic priest who had helped his father. After a short-term commission in the Gordon Highlanders, Kennedy Martin wrote his first play for the BBC *Incident At Echo Six* (1958) about National Servicemen in Cyprus. He joined the BBC full time and his first series was *Storyboard* in 1961. It was on January 2, 1962 that the first episode of the show that was to make his name was broadcast. *Z-Cars* was lauded by the critics and lambasted by the Police Federation. Kennedy Martin had conceived the idea of the gritty police show while recuperating from a bout of mumps in bed and listening to police frequencies on his VHF wireless. The show was set in the fictional Newtown – in reality Kirkby, a town north of Liverpool. The show's title came about because the policemen were taken off the beat (as part of an improvement scheme) and put in Ford Zephyrs. After a series of disagreements with launch producer Elwyn Jones, Kennedy Martin left *Z-Cars* in 1964. Kennedy Martin moved to the big screen and for $100,000 scripted *The Italian Job* (released June 2, 1969), starring Michael Caine. "My brother came up with the idea, but his idea was to set it in London, around Regent Street," Kennedy Martin said. "We decided a financial agreement and I took it on. I decided to change it to Turin because it has a computer operated traffic light system." Kennedy Martin had Robert Redford in mind for the Charlie Croker role and saw the film as a rather dark story. However, when the producers at Paramount cast Noël Coward and Benny Hill opposite Caine, he realised that he was outflanked and "I just let them get on with it". As for the film's climax (a coach loaded with stolen gold bullion worth $4 million teetering on the edge of a ravine in the Alps), Kennedy Martin had devised a completely different denouement, involving a deadly encounter between the British robbers and the Mafia. He commented, "None of us liked the ending at the time. I didn't even write the final scene in the film. [Producer] Michael Deeley added it after they'd run out of money. [Director] Peter Collinson hated it so much he wouldn't film it and made the assistant director do it instead." Kennedy Martin's next film was *Kelly's Heroes* (released June 23, 1970), a black comedy set in the Second World War and starring Clint Eastwood, with Telly Savalas and Donald Sutherland, as three GIs trying to steal gold bullion from behind enemy lines. *The Jerusalem File* (1972) came next but Kennedy Martin did not make another film until 1978 when he wrote *Sweeney 2* (released April 1978), which was based on the television series, *The Sweeney*, created by his younger brother, Ian Kennedy Martin. Other films scripted by Kennedy Martin were Walter Hill's *Red Heat* (premièred June 14, 1988) and the Tom Hooper-helmed *Red Dust* (2004). Ian Kennedy Martin said of his brother's Hollywood sojourns, "He loves meeting film producers who are actually involved with the Mafia, he likes pretty girls." Back on the small screen he wrote the espionage drama *Reilly, Ace Of Spies* (1983) for Thames TV and the 1985 thriller *Edge Of Darkness* for the BBC, which won three Baftas. In 2001 Kennedy Martin said he preferred TV to film. "A television series fits my form better because of its long form. It's like writing a novel, and movies are really just a short story," he said. Troy Kennedy Martin married, in 1967, Diana Aubrey, an actress, with whom he had a son and a daughter. CAUSE: He died in Ditchling, East Sussex, of liver cancer. He was 72.

Evelyn Keyes

Born November 20, 1916
Died July 4, 2008
Scarlett O'Hara's little sister. Born in Port Arthur, Texas, the daughter of an oilman who died before she was a year old, 5'4" Evelyn Louise Keyes moved with her mother to Atlanta, Georgia. At school there she had her first experience of theatre and was also a cheerleader. In 1935 a talent scout from Universal visited Atlanta to find a "New Screen Beauty for 1936" and Keyes's sister sent in her picture which was selected from hundreds of hopefuls. Keyes was given a screen test, which was not a success, but the ambitious youngster persuaded one of the judges to write her a recommendation letter to an agent. With the letter in her luggage, she set off for Hollywood where she met Cecil B DeMille who cast her as Madeleine in *The Buccaneer* (premièred January 7, 1938). She recounted, "Years later I heard DeMille detested women with painted nails. I hadn't had the chance to make myself up since a car was sent early to take me to his office. He signed me to a long-term contract on the spot!" She appeared in seven more films, some in bit parts, some in slightly larger roles before she was signed to play Suellen O'Hara in *Gone With The Wind* (premièred December 15, 1939). Her previous films were *Dangerous To Know* (released March 11, 1938), a nurse in *Men With Wings* (released July 16, 1938), *Sons Of The Legion* (released September 18, 1938) as Linda Lee opposite Tim Holt, *Artists And Models Abroad* (released December 20, 1938), *Paris Honeymoon* (released January 25, 1939), *Sudden Money* (released March 31, 1939) as Mary Patterson and *Union Pacific* (premièred April 27, 1939) as Mrs Calvin. For *Paris Honeymoon*, with Bing Crosby, she asked the director what she should do. "Just swoon, darling, every time you hear Bing croon," was his response. *Gone With The Wind* made her name and for years after fan letters arrived at her home in Montecito, near Santa Barbara, California, which was a replica of Tara, the O'Hara family residence in the film. Although she made 40 or so more films, none reached the heights of *Gone*

With The Wind. She played the prissy Miss Vlissingen in *Slightly Honorable* (released January 20, 1940) and then signed a contract with Columbia where she was teamed with Glenn Ford in six films. She starred opposite Boris Karloff in *Before I Hang* (released September 17, 1940) and Peter Lorre in *The Face Behind The Mask* (released January 16, 1941). Her other films included: *Beyond The Sacramento* (released November 11, 1940) as Lynn Perry, *Here Comes Mr Jordan* (premièred July 23, 1941) as Bette Logan, *Ladies In Retirement* (released September 9, 1941) as Lucy (during filming she became involved with director Charles Vidor although he was married to the actress Karen Morley at the time; at the same time fan magazines voted Keyes "the girl with the perfect leg measurements"), *The Desperadoes* (released May 25, 1943) as Allison McLeod, *Dangerous Blondes* (released September 23, 1943), *There's Something About A Soldier* (released November 30, 1943), *Nine Girls* (released February 17, 1944) as Mary O'Ryan, *A Thousand And One Nights* (released July 20, 1945) as the genie, *Renegades* (released July 13, 1946) as Hannah Brockway, *The Jolson Story* (released October 10, 1946) as Julie Benson, *Johnny O'Clock* (released January 23, 1947) as Nancy Hobson, *Mrs Mike* (released December 23, 1949) as Kathy Flannigan and *The Iron Man* (released August 18, 1951) as Rose Warren after which she left Hollywood and went to Mexico and then Europe. She returned to Tinseltown as Helen Sherman, the holidaying wife of Richard Sherman (Tom Ewell) in the Marilyn Monroe comedy *The Seven Year Itch* (released June 3, 1955). Her boyfriend Mike Todd cast her in *Around The World In Eighty Days* (premièred October 17, 1956), and although the role was small she made money because she had invested in the film. After her marriage to Artie Shaw, she moved to a castle near Barcelona and did not return to America until she wrote a novel, *I Am A Billboard* in 1971. She was in the news again in 1977 with her autobiography *Scarlet O'Hara's Younger Sister: My Lively Life In And Out Of Hollywood.* Showing a proficiency with words, she became a showbusiness columnist for *The Los Angeles Times* in the early Eighties. "I was supposed to be secretly ashamed of acting in movies instead of raising a family," she wrote of her Hollywood days. "There was that constant pull between what felt natural to me and what was expected. I hated Hollywood and . . . only went back because what else could I do? To become a big movie star like Joan Crawford, you need to wear blinkers and pay single-minded attention to your career. Nobody paid attention to me, including me. I was the original Cinderella girl, looking for the happy ending in the fairy story. But my fantasy prince never came." She returned to acting in the mid-1980s, appearing in *A Return To Salem's Lot* (released May 1987) as Mrs Axel and *Wicked Stepmother* (released February 3, 1989). She eloped with businessman Barton Leon Bainbridge in 1938. He shot himself in his car on July 19, 1940 after she left him for director Charles Vidor. They married on March 13, 1943 but they separated in November 1944 and divorced on May 18, 1945. She was linked in the gossip press with Howard Hughes and Glenn Ford. On July 23, 1946 she married the director John Huston. The marriage upset Columbia studio boss Harry Cohn who had designs on her himself and he had his revenge by saying that she would not be any more successful. She responded by suing the studio – always a foolish move – for breach of contract. She lost and was forced to freelance. "It wasn't the right move," she said later. "I was advised badly by agents because when all the other studios heard of my actions they became too scared to hire me in case I tried the same on them." She and Huston divorced on February 10, 1950. In September 1957 she married the bandleader Artie Shaw. They divorced in 1985. "I was always interested in the man of the moment," said 35½-25½-35 Keyes, "and there were many such moments."

CAUSE: In December 2004 Keyes sued the estate of Artie Shaw over what she believed was her entitlement. In July 2006, at Ventura, California a jury unanimously decided that Keyes was entitled to $1,420,000. She suffered from Alzheimer's disease in her latter years. She died aged 91 at an old people's home Montecito, California, from uterine cancer and Alzheimer's.

Richard Kiley

Born March 31, 1922
Died March 5, 1999
Ubiquitous performer. Born in Chicago, Illinois, Richard Paul Kiley found success in films, television and on stage. Like many he began his career on radio making his film début in *The Mob* (1951). Among his films are *The Blackboard Jungle* (1955), *Looking For Mr Goodbar* (1977) as Theresa's policeman father, *Endless Love* (1981), *Howard The Duck* (1986) and the voice of the tour guide in *Jurassic Park* (1993). In 1966 he won a Tony Award as Don Quixote in *Man Of La Mancha*. He also won three Emmys for his work on *The Thorn Birds* (1983), *A Year In The Life* (1988) and *Picket Fences* (1994).

CAUSE: He died of bone marrow disease in Warwick, New York, at the age of 76.

Ward Kimball

Born March 4, 1914
Died July 8, 2002
Disney's right-hand man. Ward Walrath Kimball was born in Minneapolis, Minnesota, the son of a travelling salesman. After studying art at Santa Barbara, California, Kimball joined the Walt Disney Studio in 1934 aged 20. It was while working there that he met his wife Betty Lawyer, by whom he had a son (animator John) and two daughters. Kimball began as an apprentice animator and worked his way up the company becoming a director and producer on many Disney feature films and television shows. Disney referred to him as one of the 'Nine Old Men', meaning an experienced animator who stayed with the studio and whose opinions were respected. He worked on the *Silly Symphonies* series, *Mickey Mouse* shorts and many of the sequences in *Snow White And The Seven Dwarfs* (1937), Disney's first full-length feature film. His crowning achievement came in 1940 when Disney called upon Kimball to help with a character in *Pinocchio*. Kimball created Jiminy Cricket and Disney was so impressed the film was rewritten to accommodate Jiminy Cricket as the film's co-star. Kimball also worked on the five crows for *Dumbo* (1941), Panchito in *The Three Caballeros* (1945), the Peter and the Wolf segment of *Make Mine Music* (1946), the two mice and their arch-foe Lucifer the Cat, for *Cinderella* (1950), the Mad Hatter's Tea Party and the Cheshire Cat for *Alice In Wonderland* (1951). However, he was not responsible for the appearance of Captain Hook in *Peter Pan* (1953) despite the usual credits. In 1953 he made *Toot, Whistle, Plunk And Boom*, the first Cinemascope cartoon, for which Kimball received an Oscar. He moved away from animation to television in the Fifties and worked with the rocket scientist Wernher von Braun on *Man In Space* (1955), *Man On The Moon* (1955) and *Mars And Beyond* (1957). He and von Braun also worked on the Tomorrowland exhibition at California's newly opened Disneyland. Kimball also conducted a Dixieland band at the park. In 1969 he created a 30-minute feature called *It's Tough To Be A Bird*, which won him a second Academy Award. He retired

from Disney on August 31, 1973, his contributions unrecognised by the public at large. Disney aggressively refused to allow his animators to take credit for their own work.

CAUSE: Kimball died in Arcadia, California, aged 88 of natural causes.

Klaus Kinski

(NIKOLAUS GÜNTHER NAKSZYNSKI)
Born October 8, 1926
Died November 23, 1991
Eccentric thespian. Born in Sopot, in the free state of Danzig (now Gdansk, Poland), Kinski's behaviour off screen was often as outrageous as that on. He worked as an undertaker's assistant and delivered milk and newspapers to earn some money as a child. He also had an early interest in sex and the reciprocal object of his interest was his sister Inge. He was expelled from school aged 15 for playing truant and decorating his textbooks with drawings of genitalia. At 16 he was conscripted but soon deserted. Kinski ended up being shot four times by the Allies and was sent to a prisoner of war camp in Colchester. After the war he took an interest in acting and auditioned for the Berlin Schlosspark Theatre. It was then he carried on with his interest in very young girls, subsequently admitting to sex with numerous teenagers, some as young as 13. However, Kinski didn't limit himself to young girls, and confessed to sex with fiftysomething virgin lesbians as well. Kinski became famous with the German New Wave. He worked often with Werner Herzog, even though he professed to hate him: "I absolutely despise this murderer Herzog . . . Big red ants should piss in his eyes, eat his balls, penetrate his arsehole, and eat his guts," he once stated. Kinski appeared in around 150 films including *Morituri* (1948), *Das Kalte Herz* (1950), *Decision Before Dawn* (1951), *Um Thron Und Liebe* (1955), *Kinder, Mütter Und Ein General* (1955), *Hanussen* (1955), *Geliebte Corinna* (1956), *A Time To Love And*

A Time To Die (1958) as a Gestapo lieutenant, *Die Seltsame Gräfin* (1961) as Stuart Bresset, *Der Rote Rausch* (1962), *Die Tür Mit Den Sieben Schlössern* (1962) as Pheeny, *The Counterfeit Traitor* (1962) as Kindler, *Piccadilly Null Uhr Zwölf* (1963) as Whitey, *Der Zinker* (1963) as Krishna, *Der Schwarze Abt* (1963) as Thomas, *Scotland Yard Jagt Dr Mabuse* (1963) as Joe Rank, *Die Gruft Mit Dem Rätselschloß* (1964) as George, *Neues Vom Hexer* (1965) as Edwards, *Doctor Zhivago* (1965) as Kostoyed, *Das Geheimnis Der Gelben Mönche* (1966) as Caporetti, *Le Carnaval Des Barbouzes* (1966) as Gomez, *Psycho-Circus* (1966) as Manfred, *Our Man In Marrakesh* (1966) as Jonquil, *¿Quien Sabe?* (1967) as El Santo, *Se Incontri Sartana Prega Per La Tua Morte* (1968) as Morgan, *Deadly Sanctuary* (1968) as the Marquis De Sade, *Il Dito Nella Piaga* (1969) as Haskins, *Nella Stretta Morsa Del Ragno* (1970) as Edgar Allan Poe, *El Conde Drácula* (1970) as Renfield, *Il Venditore Di Morte* (1971) as Chester Conway, *Lo Chiamavano King* (1971) as Brian Foster, *La Bestia Uccide A Sangue Freddo* (1971) as Dr Bernhard Keller, *Aguirre, Der Zorn Gottes* (1972) as Don Lope de Aguirre, *Il Ritorno Di Shanghai Joe* (1974), *Mivtza Yonatan* (1977) as Boese, *Nosferatu: Phantom Der Nacht* (1979) as Count Dracula, *Buddy Buddy* (1981) as Dr Hugo Zuckerbrot, *Android* (1982) as Dr Daniel, *Venom* (1982) as Jaemel, *The Secret Diary Of Sigmund Freud* (1984) as Dr Max Bauer, *The Little Drummer Girl* (1984) as Kurtz, *Code Name: Wild Geese* (1984) as Charleton, *Nosferatu A Venezia* (1986) as Nosferatu, *Cobra Verde* (1988) as Francisco Manoel da Silva and *Paganini* (1989) as Niccolo Paganini. Kinski was once committed to a lunatic asylum for 90 days. His daughters, Nastassja and Pola, are both actresses.

CAUSE: He was discovered dead aged 65 in Lagunitas, California, apparently from natural causes.

FURTHER READING: *All I Need Is Love: A Memoir* – Klaus Kinski (New York: Random House, 1988).

Hildegard Knef

Born December 28, 1925
Died February 1, 2002

Teutonic scandalite. Born in Ulm, Germany, Hildegard Frieda Albertine Knef grew up in Berlin and trained as a draughtswoman for trick photography at the UFA film studios, and at the film academy at Babelsberg. Following her father's premature death, she was raised by her grandfather and mother. At the end of the Second World War her grandfather, who had lost everything in a bombing raid, committed suicide and Knef, who had briefly been in love with a fanatical Nazi officer, was imprisoned by the Russians as a spy. To break her spirit, she was kept in solitary confinement and woken up at odd hours. Once a corpse was put in her cell for "company". She appeared in Wolfgang Staudte's *Die Mörder Sind Unter Uns* (1946), the first German film to deal with the horrors of the war. Five years later, in 1951, she appeared naked on screen for a few seconds in *Die Sünderin*, in which she played a prostitute. The film was banned in some towns and in restaurants people would get up in order not to sit next to her. Her career was unharmed by the scandal. Following the success of *Entscheidung Im Morgengrauen* (1951), she went to seek her fortune Stateside with her American husband Kurt. Marlene Dietrich became a mentor and her name was changed to Hildegard Neff. She starred with Tyrone Power, Gregory Peck and Ava Gardner in *The Snows Of Kilimanjaro* (1952). Legend has it that she refused to accept a studio contract because Hollywood insisted she change her name legally and pretend that she was Austrian. 5′6″ Knef appeared on Broadway in 1954 playing the lead in Cole Porter's *Silk Stockings*, a musical version of Ernst Lubitsch's *Ninotchka*. Ella Fitzgerald called her "the world's greatest singer without a voice". The musical ran for 675 performances. Then she returned to Germany where some of the media accused her of selling out. A botched plastic surgery kept her in the news but her greatest days were behind her. She was married three times. Firstly to Kurt Hirsch in 1950. They divorced after four years. In 1961 she married the British actor and director David Cameron and had one daughter, Christina, the subject of a bitter custody battle. They divorced in 1975. Husband number three was Paul von Schell. "Success and failure are both greatly overrated," she once observed, "but failure gives you a whole lot more to talk about."

CAUSE: The last years of her life were spent in a wheelchair thanks to emphysema. She lapsed into a coma for three weeks in 2001 after a flight not equipped with oxygen. She died a few months later in Berlin from a lung infection. She was 75.

John Kobal

(IVAN KOBALY)
Born May 30, 1940
Died October 28, 1991

Film archivist. Born in Linz, Austria to a Ruthenian father and an Austrian mother, he claimed that one of his earliest memories was creeping into a Rita Hayworth film being shown to the occupation forces in a hall next to his grandmother's house in Salzburg. The family emigrated to Ottawa, Canada when he was ten. In Canada he became an inveterate cinemagoer and began to collect old film stills. He often skipped school to attend the cinema. His favourites were films pertaining to Marie Antoinette, Napoleon and his mistress Marie Walewska. On one rare visit to the classroom he embarrassed himself by insisting that Napoleon had an affair with Greta Garbo. Aged 18, he travelled to New York to become an actor but in 1960 moved to London where he lived for the rest of his life.

Failing to land a place in a drama school, he instead trod the boards in provincial theatres for four years. As he travelled he scoured secondhand bookshops for pictures and cinema magazines. Wherever he lived, he carried the picture collection with him, always adding to it whenever the opportunity arose. Often that opportunity arose in the dustbins of film studios and 6'4" Kobal, an insomniac, spent many hours searching for hidden treasures. As news of his collection grew, many people began to borrow stills. Finally, he started to ask for a deposit just to make sure of their return. Gradually the Kobal Collection evolved as a commercial archive. The collection began in a room in his flat, then three rooms, then an office with a staff of 12 with five phones in Covent Garden. He also began writing books utilising his library but his work needed heavy editing. He wrote a biography of Rita Hayworth, *Film-Star Portraits Of The Fifties: 163 Glamour Photos*, *Great Film Stills Of The German Silent Era* and a collection of conversations with old movie stars, *People Will Talk*. At the time of his death he had written the first volume of a gigantic two-volume biography of Cecil B. DeMille, appropriately entitled *Mammoth*. CAUSE: John Kobal died of pneumonia caused by AIDS, aged 51, in London.

Sir Alexander Korda

(SÁNDOR LASZLO KELLNER)
Born September 16, 1893
Died January 23, 1956
Cinematic knight. Born in Pusztatúrpásztó, Hungary, the son of a land agent, Korda worked as a proofreader and then journalist before publishing a novel using the name Alexander Korda. In 1911 he travelled to Paris but, unable to find work, returned to Budapest. He landed a job translating French films into Hungarian for subtitling. In 1912 he founded a film magazine and the following year began to write and direct

short comedy films with a group of friends. When war broke out in 1914 Korda was excused duties because of poor eyesight and continued to work as a film producer and director. He travelled to Transylvania to create movies with a theatre company there but the war forced his return to Budapest once more. Home again he built a studio called the Corvin. Their first film was a huge success. However, storm clouds were gathering over Hungary after the war and Korda, along with many others, was arrested. On his release he went home, bathed, changed his clothes and left Hungary forever. He migrated to Vienna where he was employed at Sascha Studios. He made, among others, *Prinz Und Bettelknabe* (1920), *Die Tragödie Eines Verschollenen Fürstensohnes* (1922) and *Samson Und Delila* (1922). In 1923 he moved again arriving in Berlin (where he made *Das Unbekannte Morgen* [1923], *Jedermanns Frau* [1924], *Tragödie Im Hause Habsburg* [1924], *Der Tänzer Meiner Frau* [1925], *Madame Wünscht Keine Kinder* [1926] and *Eine Dubarry Von Heute* [1927]) and then three years later arriving in Hollywood. He cast his wife, Maria Corda, in the leading role of his production of *The Private Life Of Helen Of Troy* (1927). He also made *The Stolen Bride* (1927), *Yellow Lily* (1928), *Night Watch* (1928), *Love And The Devil* (1929), *Her Private Life* (1929), *The Squall* (1929), *Lilies Of The Field* (1930) and *Princess And The Plumber* (1930). In 1930 he moved to Europe and joined the Paramount Film Company, making *Marius* (1931). In 1931 he settled in London after making *Service For Ladies* (1932). In February 1932 he founded his own company, London Film Productions, utilising a picture of Big Ben as the company trademark. His studios at Denham, finished in 1937, were the most sophisticated in Europe. An economic downturn forced the closure of the studios in 1939 but the bespectacled

Korda continued to make films. He once quipped, only half in jest, "The art of film-making is to come to the brink of bankruptcy and stare it in the face." During World War II Korda worked for British intelligence gathering information. Alexander Korda was pale, overweight, loathed any form of exercise, suffered chronic insomnia, chain-smoked smelly cigars and drank to excess. He was also probably the most successful British (he became a subject in 1936) film director and producer. He was responsible for *The Private Life Of Henry VIII* (1933), *The Girl From Maxim's* (1933), *Catherine The Great* (1934), *The Private Life Of Don Juan* (1934), *The Scarlet Pimpernel* (1934), *Sanders Of The River* (1935), *The Ghost Goes West* (1935), *Things To Come* (1936), *Rembrandt* (1936), *I, Claudius* (1937), *Elephant Boy* (1937), *Return Of The Scarlet Pimpernel* (1938), *The Drum* (1938), *The Divorce Of Lady X* (1938), *The Four Feathers* (1939), *21 Days* (1940), *The Thief Of Bagdad* (1940), *That Hamilton Woman* (1941), *To Be Or Not To Be* (1942), *Jungle Book* (1942), *Perfect Strangers* (1945), *An Ideal Husband* (1947), *Anna Karenina* (1948) and *The Third Man* (1949). He was married three times. His first wife was actress Maria Farkas (she subsequently went under the name Maria Corda) whom he married in 1921 and divorced ten years later. In Antibes on June 3, 1939, he married actress Merle Oberon. They divorced in Juarez, Mexico, on June 4, 1945. His final marriage (1953) was to Alexandra Irene Boycun (d. 1966).
CAUSE: In 1945 he suffered a heart attack while dining at Romanoff's restaurant in Los Angeles with Merle Oberon, Gracie Fields and Monty Banks. His life was saved by a doctor who also happened to be dining. He died at 20 Kensington Palace Gardens, London, aged 62, of a heart attack and was cremated at Golders Green. He left £385,684 11s 9d.

Harvey Korman
Born February 15, 1927
Died May 29, 2008
Second banana. Harvey Herschel Korman was born in Chicago, the son of a salesman. Describing himself as an "insecure loner", he studied drama at school but resorted to selling aluminium cladding door-to-door, waiting tables, selling cars and being a doorman while he waited for his break. To keep his hand in, he did voiceovers for cartoons and adverts. "For 13 years," he said, "I tried to get on Broadway, on off-Broadway, under or beside Broadway." He worked on television with Red Skelton and Danny Kaye before spending ten years on *The Carol Burnett Show* where he won a Golden Globe Award in 1975, plus four Emmys. He left for his own show but it flopped, as did other projects he worked on. "On one show, I got cancelled in the middle of making the pilot." He admitted, "I didn't have whatever it takes to be a star. I come across as kind of snobbish and maybe a little too bright. Give me something bizarre to play, or put me in a dress and I'm fine." He made his first film in 1961, the Herschel Gordon Lewis exploitation movie *Living Venus*. The following year he won good reviews as Gypsy Rose Lee's press agent in *Gypsy*, the story of the stripper's life. It was his role as the bombastic, vain Hedley Lamarr in Mel Brooks's classic comedy *Blazing Saddles* (released February 7, 1974) that gave him his greatest success. His most memorable scene came as he ordered his men to arrest all types of criminal. "I want you to round up every vicious criminal and gun slinger in the West . . . I want rustlers, cut-throats, murderers, bounty hunters, desperados, mugs, pugs, thugs, nitwits, halfwits, dimwits, vipers, snipers, con men, Indian agents, Mexican bandits, muggers, buggerers, bushwhackers, hornswogglers, horse thieves, bull dykes, train robbers, bank robbers, ass-kickers, shit-kickers and

Methodists," he yelled. Brooks also cast him in *High Anxiety* (released December 25, 1977), *History Of The World, Part 1* (released June 12, 1981) and *Dracula: Dead And Loving It* (released December 22, 1995) as Dr Jack Seward. "You could get rock-solid comedy out of him," said Brooks. "He could lift the material. He always made it real, always made it work." 6'3½" Korman was married twice. On August 27, 1960 he married Donna Ehlert, by whom he had a son, Christopher, and a daughter, Laura. They divorced in 1977. Five years later, on September 8, 1982, he married Deborah Fritz and had two daughters, Katherine and Laura, with her.

CAUSE: In January 2008 Korman underwent an operation on a non-cancerous brain tumour. A day after he was discharged, he was re-admitted to hospital because of a ruptured abdominal aortic aneurysm. It killed him four months later at UCLA Medical Center, Los Angeles, California. He was 81.

Stanley Kubrick

Born July 26, 1928
Died March 7, 1999

Reclusive loon. Born in The Bronx, New York, Kubrick began his career as an apprentice photographer with *Look* magazine. In the Fifties he made some short films for RKO and was spotted by producer James B. Harris. Their reputation was made with *The Killing* (1956) and enhanced by the anti-war film *Paths Of Glory* (1957). Kubrick went on to make some remarkable films, such as *Spartacus* (1960), *Lolita* (1962), *Dr Strangelove Or: How I Learned To Stop Worrying And Love The Bomb* (1964), *2001: A Space Odyssey* (1968), *A Clockwork Orange* (1971) (which was banned by Kubrick in Britain because of fears of imitative violence and after he received death threats), *Barry Lyndon* (1975), *The Shining* (1980) and *Full Metal Jacket* (1987). Kubrick

developed a reputation as an eccentric when it came to both his films and his life. He lived in Harpenden, Hertfordshire as a recluse and demanded total secrecy for his films. He was pedantic to the point of irritation and had an intercom installed in his house so that he wouldn't have to speak to visitors directly. Kubrick's last months were spent in an ultimately futile legal battle with the brilliant investigative magazine *Punch* after it ran a light-hearted gossip piece about the director's well-known eccentricities. His last film, *Eyes Wide Shut* (1999) which co-starred real life husband and wife Tom Cruise and Nicole Kidman, was neither a critical nor a commercial success. George C. Scott said Kubrick was "very meticulous and hates everything that he writes or has anything to do with. He's an incredibly, depressingly serious man . . . paranoid . . . He's a perfectionist and he's always unhappy with anything that's set."

CAUSE: He died of a heart attack in Harpenden aged 70.

Akira Kurosawa

Born March 23, 1910
Died September 6, 1998

Japanese auteur. Born in Omori, Tokyo, the youngest of a soldier's eight children, Kurosawa, who stood over 6' tall, originally wanted to become a painter but found he could not eke out an existence doing that and so applied for a job as an assistant director at a film studio in 1936. His first solo directorial effort was *Sugata Sanshiro* (1943) but he always referred to *Drunken Angel* (1948) as his first 'real' film. In 1950 he made *Rashomon*, which was remade as *The Outrage* (1964). Probably his best-known film is *The Seven Samurai* (1954), which was reworked as the Western *The Magnificent Seven* (1960). *The Idiot* (1951), based on Dostoevsky's novel, was also well received, as was *The*

Lower Depths (1957), based on the work of the same name by Gorky. He was meticulous when it came to detail, with the result that his films became too expensive to finance from the mid-Sixties. When *Dodeska-Den* (1971) flopped, he attempted suicide by cutting his wrists with a razor. Four years later, *Dersu Uzala* (1975) won an Oscar for Best Foreign Film. He made only six films in the last 25 years of his life including his only Oscar nomination, *Ran* (1985), which means 'wretchedness' in Japanese and was his version of *King Lear*. He was awarded an honorary Oscar in 1990.

CAUSE: Kurosawa died of a stroke in Setagaya, Tokyo, aged 88.

L

Barbara La Marr

(REATHA WATSON)
Born July 28, 1896
Died January 30, 1926
'The girl who was too beautiful'. Born in Yakima, Washington State, 5'4" Barbara La Marr has achieved a measure of fame for being one of Hollywood's earliest drug-related deaths. She was raised in California's Imperial Valley and was soon well known around Los Angeles. She was arrested aged 14; in court, the judge decreed she was "too beautiful to be alone in a big city". The incident prompted her to make a break with her past; to mark her decision, she took the stage name Barbara La Marr. After several failed marriages she worked as a dancer in burlesque and then married vaudeville actor Ben Deely. A move to New York saw her change tack and become a writer. Using the exotic *nom de plume* Folly Lytell she wrote six scenarios for Fox. She first came to notice as an actress in Douglas Fairbanks' *The Nut* (1921) as Claudine Dupree. La Marr lived like a movie star, and that meant extravagantly. She was paid $250,000 a film and kept her supply of cocaine on a silver salver on her grand piano. She married five times and when her fifth husband couldn't afford a wedding ring, MGM's Paul Bern, who had a crush on her, paid for it. He also supplied the illegal booze for their honeymoon. He was also in love with her and when one night she stood him up at a party he was discovered with his head down a flushing toilet trying to drown himself. All he succeeded in doing was getting the seat jammed on his head. She married for the first time when she was 17. Her husband was Jack Lytell (1914) but he died from pneumonia not long after the wedding. On June 2, 1914, she wed lawyer Lawrence Converse. Since he already had a wife and three children, he was arrested on June 3 and jailed. He banged his head against the cell bars while calling for La Marr, knocking himself unconscious in the process. He died on June 5, following a blood clot on the brain. From October 13, 1916 until 1917 she was married to dancer Phil Ainsworth who was sent to San Quentin for passing rubber cheques. In 1918 she married Ben Deely but separated from him in April 1921. Before her divorce came through she married Western actor Jack Dougherty in May 1923. By 1924 she had become addicted to drink and drugs. She was also very free with her sexual favours. She had an affair with John Gilbert but that ended about the same time that her career went into decline. Barbara was dropped by Louis B. Mayer and moved to First National for her last three films. She then moved back east. She rarely slept more than two hours a day because she believed life was for living. Her films included *Harriet And The Piper* (1920), *Flame Of Youth* (1920), *Desperate Trails* (1921) as Lady Lou, *The Three Musketeers* (1921) as Milady de Winter, *Trifling Women* (1922) as Jacqueline de Séverac/Zareda, *The Prisoner Of Zenda* (1922) as Antoinette de Mauban, *Quincy Adams Sawyer* (1922) as Lindy Putnam, *Saint Elmo* (1923) as Agnes Hunt, *Souls For Sale* (1923) as Leva Lemaire, during which she was given morphine for a sprained ankle, *Strangers Of The Night* (1923) as Anna Valeska, *The Eternal Struggle* (1923) as Camille Lenoir, *The Eternal City* (1923) as Donna Roma, *Sandra* (1924) as Sandra Waring, *Thy Name Is Woman* (1924) as Guerita, *The Shooting Of Dan McGrew* (1924), *The White Moth* (1924) as the White Moth, *The Heart Of A Siren* (1925) as Isabella Echevaria, *The White Monkey* (1925) as Fleur Forsyte and *The Girl From*

Montmartre (1926) as Emilia. On February 16, 1923, she adopted a son, Marvin Carville La Marr. On her death her son was adopted by actress ZaSu Pitts and his name was changed. CAUSE: She died at her parents' home in Altadena, California. Officially her death was due to anorexia but she also suffered from tuberculosis and nephritis and her consumption of booze and drugs further hastened her end. She was just 29 years old. She was buried in the Cathedral Mausoleum of Hollywood Memorial Park, 6000 Santa Monica Boulevard, Hollywood, California 90038.

Alfred 'Lash' La Rue
Born June 15, 1917
Died May 21, 1996
Bullwhip Kid. Lash La Rue, one of those cinematic cowboys popular in the Forties, grew up in Gretna, Louisiana, and following his father's early death, mother and son relocated to California. After dropping out of education, he became a barber. He was screen-tested but turned down because, he believed, he resembled Humphrey Bogart. A couple of bit parts lead to his first cowboy picture, *Song Of Old Wyoming* (1945), as the Cheyenne Kid and he went on to appear in innumerable films, made cheaply (average budget $20,000) and quickly. In that first film he brandished a 20-foot bullwhip and it became his trademark. He followed that up with *Law Of The Lash* (1947) as Cheyenne, *Ghost Town Renegades* (1947) as Cheyenne Davis, *Return Of The Lash* (1947) as Cheyenne Davis, *Cheyenne Takes Over* (1947) as Cheyenne Davis, *The Enchanted Valley* (1948) as Pretty Boy, *Son Of Billy The Kid* (1949) as Jack Garrett, *Mark Of The Lash* (1949) as himself, *Outlaw County* (1950), *King Of The Bullwhip* (1951) as himself and the last 'Lash' film, *Vanishing Outpost* (1951). Spurned by cinema thereafter, La Rue turned to the small screen for *Lash Of The West* (1952–1953). When that ended, he was caught stealing candy

from a baby in Florida, was accused of vagrancy, drunk and disorderly behaviour and possession of marijuana. In his spare time he wrote scripts for porn films. He subsequently found the Lord and became an evangelist. In 1984 a magazine ad for work brought him parts on two films but they were not successful. He was married and divorced ten times, making him (probably) Hollywood's most married star. CAUSE: He died in Burbank, California, aged 78, from emphysema.

Alan Ladd
Born September 3, 1913
Died January 29, 1964
Frightened and insecure tough guy. Born an only child in Hot Springs, Arkansas, Alan Walbridge Ladd was, in 1932, an American diving champion and also held the 50-yards freestyle record. That same year he became an actor at Universal but was dropped after four months. He then became a grip at Warner Bros earning $4.50 a week. In October 1936 he married Marjorie Jane 'Midge' Harrold (b. October 25, 1915, d. May 1, 1957) and their son, Alan, Jr, was born on October 5, 1937. In 1938 former actress Sue Carol (b. Chicago, Illinois, October 30, 1906, as Evelyn Jean Lederer, d. February 4, 1982, after a stroke) became his agent and promoted him with a fierce enthusiasm. On March 13, 1942, following his July 1941 divorce, Sue Carol became his second wife and he her fourth and final husband. Their son, David, was born on February 5, 1947, and went on to marry (in May 1974) Charlie's Angel Cheryl Ladd (née Stopplemoor). His third wife was Dey Young whose sister, actress Leigh Taylor Young, was the second wife of Ryan O'Neal whose long-term live-in girlfriend was Farrah Fawcett whom Cheryl Ladd replaced on *Charlie's Angels*. Their daughter, Alana, was born on April 21, 1943, and Ladd adopted Sue Carol's daughter,

Carol Lee who was born on July 18, 1932. Alan Ladd's early films included *Tom Brown Of Culver* (1932), *Island Of Lost Souls* (1933), *Pigskin Parade* (1936), *Souls At Sea* (1937), *Hold 'Em Navy* (1937) as Chief Quartermaster, *Born To The West* (1937), *Come On, Leathernecks!* (1938), *The Green Hornet* (1939) as Gilpin, *Rulers Of The Sea* (1939) as Colin Farrell, *Captain Caution* (1940) as Newton, *Brother Rat And A Baby* (1940), *Those Were The Days* (1940) as Keg Rearick, *Her First Romance* (1940), *Petticoat Politics* (1941), *The Black Cat* (1941) as Richard Hartley, *Citizen Kane* (1941) and many more. It was only when the more established actors began to be called up for military duties that Ladd began to establish himself as a lead player. His first major successes came in *This Gun For Hire* (1942) as the vengeful killer Philip Raven and *The Glass Key* (1942) as loner Ed Beaumont. He teamed up with Veronica Lake in these and three other films, a partnership that found favour with the public. Ladd developed a niche as a movie tough guy despite only being 5'5". His career dwindled in the Fifties until he took the title role in *Shane* (1953). Ladd, a morose individual, suffered from insecurity and had a tremendous inferiority complex about his acting. With *Shane* it all came together although even then, Ladd regarded the film as a fluke and was bitterly disappointed not even to be nominated for an Oscar. His career continued to downturn and he attempted suicide in 1963 by shooting himself in the chest. His other films included *Salty O'Rourke* (1945) as Salty O'Rourke, *The Blue Dahlia* (1946) as Johnny Morrison, *Two Years Before The Mast* (1946) as Charles Stewart, *My Favorite Brunette* (1947) as Sam McCloud, *Calcutta* (1947) as Neale Gordon, *Whispering Smith* (1948) as Luke 'Whispering' Smith, *Saigon* (1948) as Major Larry Briggs, *The Great Gatsby* (1949) as Jay Gatsby,

Eyes Of Hollywood (1949), *Branded* (1950) as Choya, *Appointment With Danger* (1951) as Al Goddard, *The Iron Mistress* (1952) as Jim Bowie, *The Red Beret* (1953) as Canada, *Thunder In The East* (1953) as Steve Gibbs, *Desert Legion* (1953) as Paul Lartal, *The Black Knight* (1954) as John, *Hell Below Zero* (1954) as Duncan Craig, *Saskatchewan* (1954) as O'Rourke, *Santiago* (1956) as Cash Adams, *Boy On A Dolphin* (1957) as Dr James Calder, *The Proud Rebel* (1958) as John Chandler, *The Man In The Net* (1959) as John Hamilton, *Guns Of The Timberland* (1960) as Jim Hadley, *All The Young Men* (1960) as Kincaid, *13 West Street* (1962) as Walt Sherill and *The Carpetbaggers* (1964) as Nevada Smith. CAUSE: Ladd committed suicide with a drink and drugs overdose in Palm Springs, California, aged 50. His mother, Ina Raleigh Ladd Beavers (b. West Chester, Pennsylvania, November 25, 1888), had died by her own hand on November 29, 1937, by drinking ant poison. FURTHER READING: *Ladd: A Hollywood Tragedy* – Beverly Linet (New York: Berkley, 1980).

Carl Laemmle

Born January 17, 1867
Died September 24, 1939

Pioneer. Carl Laemmle was born, the 10th of 13 children (eight died during his childhood) of Julius Baruch Laemmle and Rebekka Laemmle, in Laupheim, Württemberg, Germany. At the age of 13 Laemmle became an apprentice stationer and in 1884, following the death of his mother, he emigrated to America to try his luck, landing in Chicago where his older brother, Joseph, was living. In 1889 he became an American citizen. In 1894 he moved to Oshkosh, Wisconsin where he became an accountant for a clothing firm. In 1906 he opened his first cinema and named it the White Front. He quickly bought other premises and set up Laemmle Film Service to buy and

distribute films. He later went into production and in 1909 made 11 short films in New York. In 1910 his company, Imperial Motion Pictures Company of America (IMP) signed Mary Pickford from Biograph and paid her $175 a week, $75 more than she was getting. He also created the world's first film star. Before Pickford, actors had been all but anonymous. In 1912 he co-founded Universal Pictures Corporation, the year after he had bought his first Hollywood studio. In 1915 he began building a studio complex called Universal City. As well as creating the first film star, Laemmle, who stood less than 5' tall, also became notorious for nepotism. Laemmle promoted Lon Chaney in *The Hunchback Of Notre Dame* (1923) and also sponsored Erich von Stroheim's directing career. He also mentored Irving Thalberg. In 1930 Laemmle's studio made the anti-war epic *All Quiet On The Western Front* starring Lew Ayres. After the First World War, Laemmle had been in the vanguard of supporters for rebuilding Germany. In 1936, he sold Universal to a syndicate for a reported $5,500,000. He married Recha Stern on August 28, 1898 by whom he had a son, Julius (later Carl Jr) and a daughter, Rosabelle.
CAUSE: Carl Laemmle died at his home, Dios Dorados in Beverly Hills, California aged 72 from a heart attack. He was buried in Home of Peace Memorial Park, Los Angeles, California. He left an estate worth $4 million.

Veronica Lake

(CONSTANCE FRANCES MARIE OCKLEMAN)
Born November 14, 1919
Died July 7, 1973
'The Girl With The Peek-a-Boo Bangs'. Veronica Lake was born in Brooklyn, New York, the daughter of a sailor. Following her father's death and mother's remarriage the family moved to Montreal, where Lake attended a convent school. Another move

transferred the family to Miami, where she won a beauty contest but was later disqualified because of her age. Following yet another move (this time to the west coast on June 27, 1938) Lake was given elocution lessons at the behest of her mother. One day a friend had an audition at RKO and Lake went along to keep her company. As often happens on these occasions, Lake was the chosen one and given a bit part in *Sorority House* (1939). The following year she began wearing her famous style after her hair accidentally fell over one eye. On September 27, 1941, in Santa Ana, California, she married MGM art director John Detlie, the year of her first big success, *I Wanted Wings* (1941). A temperamental actress, actor Eddie Bracken said, "She was known as 'the bitch' and deserved the title." Lake gave birth to daughter Elaine on August 21, 1942, in Los Angeles. The following year after the success of her portrayal of a failed starlet in *Sullivan's Travels* (1941) she was placed in the Alan Ladd picture *This Gun For Hire* (1942), one of the reasons being she was one of the few Hollywood stars shorter (at 5'2") than 5'5" Ladd. It was a success, as was *The Glass Key* (1942) with Ladd and *I Married A Witch* (1942) where she played opposite Frederic March. In July 1943 she gave birth to son William Anthony but he died of uraemic poisoning aged just one week. By the end of the year she was divorced. In 1944 she made just one film, at $350 a week, *The Hour Before Dawn* (1944), though she was rather busier on the romantic front. She married director André DeToth eight days before Christmas 1944 in Los Angeles. Their son, Michael, was born on October 25, 1945, in Los Angeles; a daughter, Diana, was born on October 16, 1948, also in Los Angeles. During World War II she had to change her hairstyle because the government complained about it! Apparently, women working in munitions factories had copied Lake's style with the result that their hair could and did become entangled in machinery. In the year the war ended she made *Hold That Blonde* (1945) and then *The Blue Dahlia* (1946) again with Ladd. Although Lake's salary had by now been increased to $4,000 a week, neither she nor DeToth were very good at living within their means. In 1948 she was sued by her mother, who argued that Lake had promised her $200-a-week support, rising to $500. The case was settled out of court. That was the year Paramount sacked her and her career began to dry up. In April 1951 she filed for bankruptcy. In June of that year she and DeToth separated, divorcing on June 2, 1952, in Los Angeles. She left Tinseltown for the Big Apple thinking, "The hell with you Hollywood. And fuck you too!" She lived in Greenwich Village and married Joseph McCarthy, a songwriter, on August 28, 1955, in the First Congregational Church, Traverse City, Michigan. They divorced in 1959. On March 22, 1962, the *New York Post* revealed Lake was working as a waitress in the cocktail lounge of the Martha Washington Hotel in New York. In Galveston, Texas, in April 1965, she was arrested for drunk and disorderly behaviour. She appeared on local television and made a horror film, *Flesh Feast* (1970). In the early Seventies she went to Hollywood to promote her autobiography and in June 1972 she married Captain Carlton-Munro. This latest was no more successful than her other attempts at wedlock. As a child she was diagnosed as a schizophrenic but her mother chose to do nothing to help. Later, Lake exhibited many of the classic signs of schizophrenia – heavy drinking, child abuse and promiscuity. Among her lovers were comedian Milton Berle, producer William Dozier, playboy Porfirio Rubirosa, actor Victor Mature, millionaire Aristotle Onassis and many studio hands whom she invited to orgies at her home. She had no illusions about her abilities – "You could put all the talent I had into

your left eye and still not suffer from impaired vision" – nor her sex appeal – "I wasn't a sex symbol, I was a sex zombie."
CAUSE: She died in Burlington, Vermont, of acute hepatitis, aged 53. She was cremated and her ashes were scattered in the Virgin Islands. Only one of her children (son Michael) and none of her husbands attended her memorial service at the Universal Chapel, East 52nd Street, New York.

Hedy Lamarr

(HEDWIG EVA MARIA KIESLER)
Born November 9, 1913
Found dead January 19, 2000
'The Most Beautiful Woman of the Century'. She was born in Vienna, Austria, the only child of a director of the Bank of Vienna and a concert pianist who gave up her career to care for her newborn child. Hedy claimed that she was aware of sex at an early age. Her sexual initiation happened aged nine, when a wealthy woman in her thirties climbed into Hedy's bed. Five years later, she was raped at home by a laundryman, whom she had already fought off once before. He succeeded in his quest on the second attempt. Entranced by films, she hung around Sascha Film Studios and wangled herself bit parts in *Sturm Im Wasserglass* (1929) and *Geld Auf Der Straße* (1930). Her next role was rather more substantial. Billed as Hedy Kiesler she played Käthe Brandt in *Man Braucht Kein Geld* (1931). Her first comedy film was *Die Koffer Des Herr O.F. Herne* (1931) in which she played Helene. It was her next film, usually wrongly identified as her first, that made her a star. Still billed as Hedy Kiesler, her first starring role saw her play Eva in what turned out to be the controversial *Extase/Ecstasy* (1932). The film was banned in America until 1940 – not because of the ten-minute nude swimming scene, nor the sight of her bare buttocks, but because of her face during a sex scene, i.e. simulating

an orgasm. Hedy claimed the director achieved the necessary facial expressions by sticking a pin into her bare *derrière*. The following year, on August 10, 1933, at the Church of St Karls in Vienna, she married for the first time. Her husband was the handsome and fabulously wealthy munitions manufacturer Fritz Mandl, who owned Hirstenberger Patronen-Fabrik Industries and admired Hitler. He was also insanely jealous, trailing his young bride when she went out shopping and bugging her rooms. He also attempted to buy up every copy of *Extase/Ecstasy*, though without success. By 1937 it all became too much for Hedy and she made her escape and fled to Paris, where the marriage was annulled. There she met MGM chief Louis B. Mayer who was touring Europe looking for new talent. He offered her a contract at $125 a week, which she at first turned down. Although she later accepted the offer, she still had to travel to the States at her own expense. At their first meeting Mayer continually patted her behind and told her, "You have spirit. I like that and you have a bigger chest than I thought. You'd be surprised how tits figure in a girl's career." In the States Mayer changed her name to Hedy Lamarr in honour of Barbara La Marr, 'the girl who was too beautiful'. Hedy's first film saw her star opposite Charles Boyer in *Algiers* (1938) as Gaby, a girl who falls in love with a jewel thief. The white turban she wore in the film, and which she designed herself, became a must-wear for millions of women the world over. Boyer wasn't that impressed with his co-star – he was probably one of the few men she encountered who wasn't. In 1939 Hedy made two films – *Lady Of The Tropics* as Manon de Vargnes with the sexually ambiguous Robert Taylor, whom she had to teach how to kiss, and *I Take This Woman* as Georgi Gragore, in which she co-starred with Spencer Tracy. She was later to describe Tracy

as, "A great actor but there were times when he made me cry. He was not precisely my favourite person." Neither film capitalised on the success of *Algiers*, much to the dismay of Louis B. Mayer. To add to his disenchantment with his Viennese whirl, she eloped to get married in Mexicali, Mexico, on March 4, 1939. Her second husband was screenwriter Gene Markey (b. Jacksonville, Michigan, December 11, 1895, d. Miami, Florida, May 1, 1978; he was the second Mr Joan Bennett and would become the third Mr Myrna Loy). Mayer liked big weddings because it created welcome publicity. Elopements were not his way of seeing his stars hitched. The Markeys divorced on September 27, 1940, but a son, James Lamarr Markey, was adopted in November 1941. In the meantime Hedy appeared playing Karen Vanmeer opposite Clark Gable in *Boom Town* (1940). After two failures Hedy needed a hit to silence her critics and *Boom Town* was the answer to her prayers. Her next film, *Comrade X* (1940) as Theodora, was also a success as was *H.M. Pulham, Esq.* (1941) in which she played Marvin Myles. It was at the Hollywood Canteen in 1942 that Hedy met actor John Loder, the man who would become husband number three. That year she made three films: *Crossroads* (1942) as Lucienne Talbot, *White Cargo* (1942) as Tondelayo "a half-caste jungle temptress" and *Tortilla Flat* (1942) as part-Mexican Dolores 'Sweets' Ramirez. According to most accounts Hedy was the first choice to play Ilsa in *Casablanca* (1942) but the part went to her rival Ingrid Bergman. Hedy and Loder were married on May 27, 1943, but the marriage was based more on sex than any real love or understanding of each other's needs. Nonetheless, they stayed together for four years and had two children: Denise (b. Los Angeles, May 29, 1945) and Anthony John (b. Los Angeles, March 1, 1947). (Hedy had a secret gift. During World War II, with composer George Antheil, she invented a radio signalling device that reduced the danger of detection or jamming.) On July 17, 1947, she and Loder were divorced. While still married she appeared in *The Heavenly Body* (1943) as Vicky Whitley, *The Conspirators* (1944) as Irene, *Experiment Perilous* (1944) as Alida Bederaux, *Her Highness And The Bellboy* (1945) as Princess Veronica, *Strange Woman* (1946) as Jenny Hager and *Dishonored Lady* (1947) as the nymphomaniac magazine editor Madeleine Damien. Her last major film was on loan-out to Paramount for Cecil B. DeMille's *Samson And Delilah* (1949) in which she played Delilah opposite Victor Mature's Samson. For her next film back at MGM, *A Lady Without Passport* (1950), she was paid $90,000. It was the story of a Viennese woman, Marianne Lorress, who tries to enter America after becoming stranded in Cuba. After making *My Favorite Spy* (1951) as Lily Dalbray, she went on holiday to Acapulco, met a restaurateur called Ted Stauffer and married him on June 12, 1951. After nine months the marriage was over and they divorced on March 17, 1952, but by this time Hedy's career was also on the wane. She appeared in *L'Amante Di Paride* (1953) as Hedy Windsor, *I Cavalieri Dell'Illusione* (1954), *The Story Of Mankind* (1957) as Joan Of Arc and *The Female Animal* (1957) as Vanessa Windsor. On December 22, 1953, at the Queens County Courthouse, New York, she married oil multi-millionaire W. Howard Lee. Not long after the marriage, she became an American citizen. The marriage ended in divorce in April 1960. On March 4, 1963, in Fresno she married Beverly Hills lawyer Lewis J. Boies, Jr, but they divorced after two years on June 21, 1965. As her career began to fade she entered the newspapers for other, less savoury reasons. On January 27, 1966, then living at 9550 Hidden Valley

Road, Beverly Hills, she was arrested at 9.15pm for shoplifting at 6067 Wilshire Boulevard, Los Angeles. A store detective claimed that the actress, who was under psychiatric care at the time, had stolen $86-worth of goods including a $40 knit suit, a $10 pair of knickers, a dollar's worth of greeting cards and other items. Although Hedy was acquitted on April 26 after five hours of jury deliberation, it did not bode well for her. Later that same year, on February 3, she was sacked from the film *Picture Mommy Dead* for not turning up on the first day of shooting. In November 1971 in Los Angeles she was ordered to pay $15,000 to a man she falsely accused of raping her four years earlier. On August 1, 1991, Hedy was arrested for shoplifting in Florida. The charges were dropped when she signed a document promising not to do it again. She decried her image: "Any girl can be glamorous," she once said. "All you have to do is stand still and look stupid."

CAUSE: Aged 86, Hedy Lamarr was found dead in bed in her four-bedroomed house in Orlando, Florida, by Altamonte Springs Police Lieutenant Chuck Stansel who had befriended her and had run a few errands for her. Her death was investigated because she had died alone. She had spent her last years as a drugged-up recluse playing cards and watching television. She was only spotted by neighbours when she collected her post – at night, a torch in one hand and a walking stick in the other. Despite being fabulously wealthy she was careful with her money. In her will she left her stamp collection to her 11-year-old grandson, the bulk of her estate went to her children, who rarely saw her, but she left money to her secretary, a California engineer she had never met, and $83,000 to Lieutenant Stansel.

FURTHER READING: *Ecstasy & Me: My Life As A Woman* – Hedy Lamarr (London: Mayflower, 1967).

Fernando Lamas

Born January 9, 1915
Died October 8, 1982

Latin lover. Born in Buenos Aires, Argentina, he began acting in his homeland in films such as *En El Ultimo Piso* (1942), *Villa Rica Del Espíritu Santo* (1945), *Historia De Una Mala Mujer* (1948) and *La Historia Del Tango* (1949) before he got the call from MGM to come to Hollywood. His first American film was *The Avengers* (1950) as Andre LeBlanc. He later noted: "It took me several years to realise I didn't have too much talent for acting, not true acting. But by then I couldn't give it up, because I had become too famous." He appeared in *The Law And The Lady* (1951) as Juan Dinas, *Rich, Young And Pretty* (1951) as Paul Sarnac, *The Merry Widow* (1952) as Count Danilo, *The Girl Who Had Everything* (1953) as Victor Y. Raimondi, *Dangerous When Wet* (1953) as André Lanet, *Jivaro* (1954) as Rio Galdez, *Rose Marie* (1954) as James Severn Duval, *The Lost World* (1960) as Manuel Gomez, *D'Artagnan Contro I Tre Moschettieri* (1963), *Kill A Dragon* (1967) as Patrai, *100 Rifles* (1969) as Verdugo and *Won Ton Ton, The Dog Who Saved Hollywood* (1976). He was equally well known for his marriages to beautiful women. In 1940 he married Argentine actress Pearla Mux but the couple was soon divorced. In 1946 he married Uruguayan heiress Lydia Babachi. A daughter, Alexandra, was born the following year. They divorced in 1952. On June 25, 1954, he was wed to actress Arlene Dahl about whom he said: "Being married to Arlene Dahl was very nice, at night-time. But in the daytime, it was like being married to Elizabeth Arden. That is where she spent most of her time. If you asked her which is more important to her, her home life or her career, she would have to tell you the truth: her face." Their actor son, Lorenzo, was born on January 20, 1958. They divorced in August 1960. In 1967 he married actress Esther Williams and on New Year's Eve 1969 they renewed their vows: "Some famous wit said that my wife, Esther Williams, is a star only when she is wet. *He* is all wet! Another rumour is that I made Esther give up her career when we got married. That is a lie! She was already washed up when we got married." They were together when he died.

CAUSE: He died of cancer aged 67 in Los Angeles.

Dorothy Lamour

(MARY LETA DOROTHY SLATON)
Born December 10, 1914
Died September 21, 1996

'The Sarong Girl'. Long before cerebrally challenged footballer David Beckham wore a sarong, film star Dorothy Lamour popularised them. Born in Hotel Dieu Hospital, New Orleans, Louisiana, the young Mary Leta Dorothy Slaton entered a beauty contest with her friend Dorothy Dell, who won. Dell landed a part in a play and insisted the producers hire her friend too. The job lasted a year and Lamour came home and became a secretary, winning the Miss New Orleans beauty title when she was 17. She became a lift operator in Chicago and landed an audition with a theatrical company. It did not bode well. She was described as "Brunette, slender, fairly good-looking" and "Not recommended. Bad style as a singer. Didn't even try as an actress. Doubtful prospect." On May 10, 1935, she married bandleader Herbie Kay in Waukegan, Illinois. She made her first film playing Ulah in *The Jungle Princess* (1936). During that film she was taught how to smoke by Ray Milland, developed skin poisoning from the make-up and became so obsessed with her 'ugly' feet that a plastic pair were made for her by the make-up department. Moreover, an extra was killed when he was attacked by the other 'co-star', Gogo the chimp. She appeared with her idol Carole

Lombard in *Swing High, Swing Low* (1937) as Anita Alvarez and with Randolph Scott in *High, Wide, And Handsome* (1937) as Molly Fuller. She often accompanied Scott to various functions, with the obvious approval of her husband, who knew his wife would be safe with Scott. They divorced on May 1, 1939, and on April 7, 1943, she married 6'3" Captain William Ross Howard III (b. 1907, d. February 15, 1978). Her next films were *The Last Train From Madrid* (1937) as Carmelita Castillo, *The Hurricane* (1937) as Marama, *The Big Broadcast Of 1938* (1938) as Dorothy Wyndham, *Her Jungle Love* (1938) as Tura, *Tropic Holiday* (1938) as Manuela, *Spawn Of The North* (1938) as Nicky Duval, *St Louis Blues* (1939) as Norma Malone, *Man About Town* (1939) as Diana Wilson, *Disputed Passage* (1939) as Audrey, *Typhoon* (1939) as Dea and *Moon Over Burma* (1940) as Arla Dean. It was the first *Road* film that made Lamour beloved the world over. Co-starring Bob Hope and Bing Crosby, *Road To Singapore* (1939), was much improvised. Lamour played Mima and the film was to be the first of a hugely successful series. Hope and Crosby called her 'Mommie', but she admitted, "I was closer to Bob than to Bing, whose moods were changeable – he'd be funny one day and quite remote the next." The sarong worn by Lamour is now in the Smithsonian Institute. To prove "I wasn't limited to leaning against a palm tree or playing straight woman to Hope and Crosby" she played gangster's moll Mabel 'Lucky' DuBarry in *Johnny Apollo* (1940). However, it was the *Road* series that people wanted and she appeared in *Road To Zanzibar* (1941) as Donna Latour, *Road To Morocco* (1942) as Princess Shalmar, *Road To Utopia* (1946) as Sal Van Hoyden, *Road To Rio* (1947) as Lucia Maria de Andrade, *Road To Bali* (1952) as Princess Lala and, under sufferance, in *Road To Hong Kong* (1962) playing herself. She

virtually retired after that, appearing only in *Donovan's Reef* (1963) as Miss Lafleur, *Pajama Party* (1964), *The Phynx* (1970), *Won Ton Ton, The Dog Who Saved Hollywood* (1976) and *Creepshow 2* (1987) as Martha Spruce. CAUSE: She died in North Hollywood aged 81 of natural causes. FURTHER READING: *My Side Of The Road* – Dorothy Lamour as told to Dick McInnes (London: Robson Books, 1981).

Burt Lancaster

Born November 2, 1913
Died October 20, 1994
Prima donna. 6'2" Burton Stephen Lancaster was one of five children born (at 209 East 106th Street) to a New York City post office worker. A tough street kid, he won a basketball scholarship to New York University but dropped out when he was 18 and joined a circus as an acrobat. There, in the early part of 1935, he married June Ernst (b. Australia, 1916), a lady trapeze artist. They were married for three years. He worked under the big top until he was injured. During World War II he joined the army and discovered acting. He got a job on Broadway after being spotted in a lift by a theatrical agent. The 6'2" Lancaster became a star with his first film *The Killers* (1946) playing Ole 'Swede' Anderson. In fact, it was his second film. His first was *Desert Fury* (1947) as Tom Hanson but that was held back from release. He only got the role in *The Killers* because the first choice, Wayne Morris, was too expensive. When he couldn't get acting work, Lancaster supported himself by selling ladies' undies in a shop or as a singing waiter. Two years later, he took control of his career by setting up his own production company, Hecht-Hill-Lancaster. Burt, who was arrogant, argumentative and had a ferocious temper, spent $10,000 to have his teeth straightened. On December 28, 1946, in Yuma,

Arizona, he married former secretary Norma Mari Anderson (b. Webster, Wisconsin, June 30, 1917, d. July 21, 1988, from cirrhosis of the liver, pneumonia and a stroke). His early films included *Sorry, Wrong Number* (1948) as Henry Stevenson, *Kiss the Blood Off My Hands* (1948) as Bill Saunders, *All My Sons* (1948) as Chris Keller, *I Walk Alone* (1948) as Frankie Madison, *Mister 880* (1950) as Steve Buchanan, *Jim Thorpe – All American* (1951) as Jim Thorpe, *Ten Tall Men* (1951) as Sergeant Mike Kincaid, *Come Back, Little Sheba* (1952) as Doc Delaney and *The Crimson Pirate* (1952) as Captain Vallo. It was his performance as Sergeant Milton Warden in *From Here To Eternity* (1953) that won him his first Oscar nomination. Lancaster once admitted: "Most people seem to think I'm the kind of guy who shaves with a blowtorch. Actually I'm exactly the opposite. I'm bookish and worrisome." Lancaster was also extremely insecure and looked for love and sex wherever he could find it, with both men and women. On June 27, 1969, he and Norma were divorced. On September 10, 1990, he wed Susan Scherer (b. California, May 3, 1942, as Susan June Martin) in Los Angeles. He followed *From Here To Eternity* by playing another soldier, Sergeant James O'Hearn, in *South Sea Woman* (1953). Then came *Apache* (1954) as Massai, *Vera Cruz* (1954) as Joe Erin, *The Kentuckian* (1955) as Big Eli, *The Rainmaker* (1956) as Bill Starbuck, *Trapeze* (1956) as Mike Ribble, *Sweet Smell Of Success* (1957) as columnist J.J. Hunsecker, *Gunfight At The O.K. Corral* (1957) as Wyatt Earp, *Separate Tables* (1958) as John Malcolm, *Run Silent Run Deep* (1958) as Lieutenant Jim Bledsoe and the Oscar-winning title role in *Elmer Gantry* (1960) playing a gin-sodden evangelist. It was a just reward considering he had turned down the lead role in *Ben-Hur*, the part that won Charlton Heston an Oscar.

Two years later, he was again nominated for a Best Actor Oscar playing Robert Franklin Stroud in *Birdman Of Alcatraz* (1962). As Lancaster's career developed, his characterisations became less rambunctious and more mellow. He worked on *The List Of Adrian Messenger* (1963), *Seven Days In May* (1964) as General James Mattoon Scott, *The Train* (1964) as Labiche, *The Swimmer* (1968) as Neddy Merrill, *The Scalphunters* (1968) as Joe Bass, *Airport* (1970) as Mel Bakersfeld which he described as "The biggest piece of junk ever", *Lawman* (1971) as Jered Maddox, *Valdez Is Coming* (1971) as Bob Valdez, *Ulzana's Raid* (1972) as McIntosh, *Executive Action* (1973) as Farrington, *The Midnight Man* (1974) as Jim Slade, *Buffalo Bill And The Indians, Or Sitting Bull's History Lesson* (1976) as Ned Buntline, *1900* (1976) as Berlinghieri, *The Cassandra Crossing* (1976) as Mackenzie, *The Island Of Dr Moreau*, (1977) as Dr Paul Moreau, *Zulu Dawn* (1979) as Colonel Durnford, *Atlantic City* (1980) as the small-time crook Lou, for which he was nominated for an Oscar, *Local Hero* (1983) as Felix Happer, *Tough Guys* (1986) as Harry Doyle and *Field Of Dreams* (1989) as Doctor Graham. Lancaster, who invented the idea of 'percentage points' for actors and directors, once said: "I've made up my mind that Hollywood isn't going to get me; I'm going to be one guy who won't let it rot his soul."

CAUSE: Burt Lancaster suffered a stroke on November 20, 1990. From then on although he was aware of what was happening around him, he was unable to respond. His friend Michael Winner remembered, "I saw him on October 10, 1991. It was a sad and tragic sight. We held hands and I cried." Lancaster died aged 80 at his home in Century City, California, from a heart attack.

FURTHER READING: *Burt Lancaster –* Minty Clinch (London: Arthur Barker,

1984); *Burt Lancaster* – Robert Windeler (London: W.H. Allen, 1984); *Against Type: The Biography Of Burt Lancaster* – Gary Fishgall (New York: Scribner, 1995).

Elsa Lanchester
(ELIZABETH LANCHESTER SULLIVAN)
Born October 28, 1902
Died December 26, 1986
Charlie was her darling. Born illegitimately in Lewisham, London, (later Universal wanted to change her birthday to Hallowe'en to cash in on her horror connection) she began her career as a child dancer with Isadora Duncan before becoming a nude model and 'the other woman' in divorce cases, in which she was paid to pretend to be having an affair with a husband. Aged 16 she moved into appearing in dramatic roles in the theatre. She made her first film in 1927 and went on to appear in over 50 movies. She went to Hollywood in 1934 with her husband Charles Laughton, whom she had married on February 9, 1929. After a honeymoon (which was also attended by the groom's mother and brother!) they lived in Karl Marx's old house at 28 Dean Street, London, W1. She claims she did not know her husband was a practising homosexual until, one night, when he confessed to paying young men for sex on their settee. Lanchester claimed she went deaf for a week through shock and when her hearing returned, she decided to stand by her man, provided they sold the settee. Marlene Dietrich commented: "Poor Elsa. She left England because it already had a queen – Victoria. And she wanted to be queen of the Charles Laughton household, once he became a star, but he already had the role." Her films included: *One Of The Best* (1927), *The Constant Nymph* (1928), *Mr Smith Wakes Up* (1929), *The Stronger Sex* (1931) as Thompson, *The Officer's Mess* (1931) as Cora Melville, *The Love Habit* (1931) as Mathilde, *The Private Life Of Henry VIII* (1933)

as Anne Of Cleves, *The Private Life Of Don Juan* (1934), *David Copperfield* (1935) as Clickett, *Naughty Marietta* (1935) as Madame d'Annard, James Whale's *Bride Of Frankenstein* (1935) as Mary Shelley/the monster's bride, *The Ghost Goes West* (1935) as Miss Shepperton, *Rembrandt* (1936) as Hendrickje Stoffels, *Sullivan's Travels* (1942), *Son Of Fury* (1942) as Bristol Isabel, *Passport To Destiny* (1944) as Ella Muggins, *The Spiral Staircase* (1946) as Mrs Oates, *The Big Clock* (1948) as Louise Patterson, *The Inspector General* (1949) as Maria, *Come To The Stable* (1949) as Amelia Potts, for which she was nominated for a Best Supporting Actress Oscar, *Buccaneer's Girl* (1950) as Madame Brizar, *Dreamboat* (1952) as Dr Coffey, *The Girls Of Pleasure Island* (1953) as Thelma, *Androcles And The Lion* (1953) as Megaera, *Three Ring Circus* (1954) as the bearded lady, *Witness For The Prosecution* (1957) as Miss Plimsoll, for which she was nominated for her second Best Supporting Actress Oscar, *Bell, Book And Candle* (1958) as Queenie, *Mary Poppins* (1964) as Katie Nanna, *Pajama Party* (1964) as Aunt Wendy, *That Darn Cat!* (1965) as Mrs MacDougall, *Blackbeard's Ghost* (1968) as Emily Stowcroft, *Willard* (1971) as Henrietta Stiles, *Terror In The Wax Museum* (1973) as Julia Hawthorn, Neil Simon's *Murder By Death* (1976) as Jessica Marbles and *Die Laughing* (1980) as Sophie.
CAUSE: She died of bronchial pneumonia, aged 84, at the Motion Picture & TV Hospital Country Home, 23388 Mulholland Drive, Woodland Hills, California. She was cremated and her ashes scattered at sea.

Carole Landis
(FRANCES LILLIAN MARY RIDSTE)
Born January 1, 1917
Died July 5, 1948
'The Ping Girl'. Born in Fairchild, Wisconsin, the Roman Catholic Carole Landis had a very poor reputation at

Fox, where she was saddled with the nickname 'The studio hooker'. She regularly visited boss Darryl F. Zanuck at 4pm, the time at which he daily had sex with a studio employee. Outspoken, she was the daughter of Alfred Ridste, a Norwegian railroad mechanic, and the Polish Clara Stentek and ran away from home aged 14. She married for the first time (out of five) when she was 17, to 19-year-old Irving Wheeler, on January 14, 1934. The marriage was annulled the following month but the couple remarried on August 25, 1934, and stayed married, if not together, until 1940. They moved to California where Carole worked as a nightclub dancer and singer before landing a contract with Warner Bros that paid her $50 a week. She was given various bit parts in films such as *Varsity Show* (1937), *A Star Is Born* (1937), *A Day At The Races* (1937), *The Emperor's Candlesticks* (1937), *Broadway Melody Of 1938* (1937), *Alcatraz Island* (1937), *The Adventurous Blonde* (1937), *Men Are Such Fools* (1938) as June Cooper, *He Couldn't Say No* (1938), *Girls On Probation* (1938), *Love, Honor And Behave* (1938), *Blondes At Work* (1938) as Carol, *Gold Diggers In Paris* (1938) and *Boy Meets Girl* (1938). Certain of the titles may have been propitious because in 1938 Irving Wheeler launched a $250,000 alienation of affection suit against Busby Berkeley, though it was thrown out by the court. By the time of her divorce from Wheeler she had graduated to speaking parts and was cast as Loana in a Hal Roach production called *One Million B.C.* (1940). For the film she dyed her hair blonde, had a nose job and lost a lot of weight. That year, on July 4, 1940, she married yacht broker Willis Hunt, Jr, but they were divorced just over four months later on November 13, 1940. In 1941 she moved to Fox, where she was known as much for her sexual promiscuity as her B movies. She appeared in *I Wake Up Screaming* (1941)

as Vicky Lynn, *Dance Hall* (1941) as Lily Brown, *Cadet Girl* (1941) as Gene Baxter, *Topper Returns* (1941) as Ann Carrington, *Moon Over Miami* (1941) as Barbara Latimer, *Orchestra Wives* (1942) as Natalie, *A Gentleman At Heart* (1942) as Helen Mason, *My Gal Sal* (1942) as Mae Collins, *It Happened In Flatbush* (1942) as Kathryn Baker and *Wintertime* (1943) as Flossie Fouchere. In the late autumn of 1942 she went on a USO tour to North Africa and met Captain Thomas C. Wallace, whom she married on January 5, 1943, in London. She wrote a story based on the tour and the whirlwind romance, which was made into a film called *Four Jills In A Jeep* (1944). Due to USO tours and illness she only made one film before 1946 and that was *Having Wonderful Crime* (1945), in which she played Helene Justus. She and Wallace were divorced on July 19, 1945, in Reno, Nevada. Rarely without a man, and not often without a husband, she married balding, bespectacled Manhattan millionaire W. Horace Schmidlapp on December 8, 1945, in New York. That year also saw Carole's lesbian affair with future best-selling novelist Jacqueline Susann, who based the character of Jennifer North in *Valley Of The Dolls* on Landis. Her contract with Fox was not renewed in 1946, probably due to her off-screen antics. Her last three films were *Out Of The Blue* (1947) as Mae Earthleigh, *Noose* (1948) as Linda Medbury and *Brass Monkey* (1948) as Kay Sheldon. Despite her marriage to Schmidlapp she seemed incapable of fidelity and had began an affair with the married Rex Harrison in the months leading up to her death. Her official nickname, 'The Ping Girl', which she hated, was a diminution of 'The Purring Girl'. CAUSE: On July 4, 1948, Carole had dinner with Rex Harrison as she had done every night for the previous fortnight according to her maid, Fannie Mae Bolden. When Harrison arrived in the States earlier in the year, reporters asked him about his relationship with Landis. He replied: "I'm a married man and love my wife. Of course I am fond of Miss Landis. We are great friends and that is all. She is also a good friend of my wife." Since Harrison's wife, Lilli Palmer, had left him to go to Switzerland, no one believed that one for a second. At the time, Lilli was still protective of her husband. She denied she left Rex because of his attention to Carole. "We were all good friends and I went to Switzerland because I wanted to ski," she explained. At 3.30pm on July 5, Landis' corpse was discovered by Harrison on the bathroom floor of her 1465 Capri Drive, Pacific Palisades, California, home. She had been dead around 12 hours, according to Coroner Ben H. Brown. An autopsy revealed death was due to a massive overdose of Seconal. A handwritten note addressed to her mother made it clear the overdose was deliberate. It read:

Dearest Mommie,

I'm sorry, really sorry, to put you through this. But there is no way to avoid it. I love you darling. You have been the most wonderful mom ever. And that applies to all our family. I love each and every one of them dearly. Everything goes to you. Look in the files and there is a will which decrees everything.

Goodbye my angel.

Pray for me.

Your baby.

After her demise, Harrison made another announcement: "My wife and I are not estranged and never have been," he stated. "I had planned to join her in New York next Thursday. I do not fear appearing at an inquest into Miss Landis' death, if one is called. She and I were just friends. We dined together Sunday night at her home. She told me that she had general financial problems. My wife and I both plan to attend the funeral. I will talk to members of her family." Harrison told police he had been meeting Carole because of their "common interest in a movie" they were to make together in the autumn. They had spent her last evening "talking about the film," he said. Harrison's claim that Landis had "general financial problems" was dismissed by famed Hollywood lawyer Jerry Giesler. He had brokered a separation from her fourth husband that left Carole comfortable. "I take little stock in that financial distress contributed to Miss Landis' suicide. Money from the sale of her house would have paid all her bills and left a considerable sum besides," said the legal eagle. "She was very honourable about paying her bills. She had written personally to her creditors, assuring them that they would be paid as soon as the sale of the house cleared escrow." At the inquest Harrison declared he knew of no reason why Landis should take her own life. "She appeared to be in good spirits . . . although I don't believe she was entirely happy with her career." Harrison told the court that he had left Landis' home at 9.30pm and visited the home of his friend Roland Culver before returning to find her dead the following afternoon. According to the maid, Harrison came down and told her of Landis' death before they both went back upstairs to the bathroom, where they found the suicide note and Harrison is said to have cried out, "Oh, darling, why did you do it, why did you do it?" On July 8, Coroner Brown closed the case, labelling Carole Landis' death a suicide. She was buried in Lot 814, Section 8 in the Everlasting Love area at Forest Lawn Memorial-Parks, 1712 South Glendale Avenue, Glendale, California 91209. For many years rumours have surfaced that there was a second suicide note, one addressed to Harrison, and that he pocketed it. It is alleged that Landis was pregnant with Harrison's child and he had told her that she would have to raise the baby alone. Illegitimacy would have been one stigma too many for Carole

Landis. Furthermore, outside Roland Culver's house two small suitcases were found with a note asking that they be passed to Rex Harrison. They contained all Harrison's love letters to Landis and mementos of their affair. He burned them.

Michael Landon

(EUGENE MAURICE HOROWITZ)
Born October 31, 1936
Died July 1, 1991
TV hero. Born in Forest Hills, New York, Landon was probably best known for his portrayal of television good guys. He was Little Joe on *Bonanza* for 14 years before moving on to *Little House On The Prairie* as Charles Phillip Ingalls, where he lived for eight years. Finally, he played the earth-bound angel Jonathan Smith in *Highway to Heaven*. He usually had a hand in writing, directing and producing the series in which he starred. He had a brief film career beginning with *These Wilder Years* (1956) and *I Was A Teenage Werewolf* (1957) as Tony Rivers the teenage werewolf. Other films included: *Maracaibo* (1958), *High School Confidential!* (1958) as Steve Bentley, *God's Little Acre* (1958) as Dave Dawson and *The Legend Of Tom Dooley* (1959) as Tom Dooley. Despite his televisual reputation as a God-fearing all-round nice guy, his co-workers didn't rate him especially highly. David Janssen said, "Michael Landon can be a spoiled brat when he wants to be, and he often wants to be", while Nancy Walker opined: "I did a charity function with Landon once. He was smiley and affable when the camera was on him, but, boy, the second it turned off he didn't have time for anyone except the other VIPs in the room."
CAUSE: On April 5, 1991, Landon was admitted to Cedars-Sinai Medical Center suffering from what he believed was an ulcer. Doctors discovered that he had inoperable cancer of the liver and pancreas. On May 8, he appeared on *The Tonight Show With Johnny Carson*. It was to be his last public appearance. Fans began to gather in a vigil outside his $7-million home, 5820 Bonsall Drive, Malibu, California 90265. On July 1, he summoned his nine children to his bedside to say goodbye. He was alone with his 34-year-old wife Cindy Clerico when he passed away at 1.10pm from metatastic pancreatic cancer. He was 54. The following day he was cremated. On July 5, a service of thanksgiving was held for him at Hillside Memorial Park. Among the 500 mourners were Melissa Sue Anderson, Ernest Borgnine, Melissa Gilbert, Brian Keith and President and Mrs Ronald Reagan. At the service, the theme tune to *Little House On The Prairie* was played on loudspeakers!

Fritz Lang

Born December 5, 1890
Died August 2, 1976
Film noir genius. Born in Vienna, Austria-Hungary, the second of two sons of Anton Lang (b. August 1, 1860, d. 1940), an architect and construction company manager, and Pauline "Paula" Schlesinger (b. July 26, 1864, d. 1920 of breast cancer), Friedrich Christian Anton Lang studied art and architecture to please his parents before leaving home at 20 to travel the world, supporting himself by selling his artwork. In 1913 he migrated to Paris and staged an exhibition there the following year. He joined the Austro-Hungarian army during the First World War. Wounded four times and in hospital Lang met film director Joe May in 1916 who encouraged him and hired him to write stories. Once demobbed, he turned to film and had almost immediate success with *Der Herr Der Liebe* (1919). This was followed up with *Harakiri* (1919), *Halbblut* (1919), *Die Spinnen, 1. Teil: Der Goldene See* (1919), *Das Wandernde Bild* (1920), *Die Spinnen, 2. Teil: Das Brillantenschiff* (1920), *Der*

Müde Tod (1921), *Dr Mabuse, Der Spieler* (1922), *Die Nibelungen: Siegfried* (1924), *Die Nibelungen: Kriemhilds Rache* (1924), his masterly *Metropolis* (1927) which had been inspired by the skyline of Manhattan, *Spione* (1928), his study of a child murderer *M* – Peter Lorre in his first starring role and the first German sound film – and *Das Testament Des Dr Mabuse* (1932, *The Last Will Of Dr Mabuse*). Oddly, Lang did not like *Metropolis* calling it "a bit silly and a bit naïve, with all that business about the heart being a link between capital and labour. Well, I know more now." When Hitler came to power in January 1933 Lang fled to Paris although his second wife and collaborator Thea von Harbou (whom he married in 1922), chose to stay behind in Nazi Germany and filed for divorce. He moved to London before settling in America where he became a citizen in February 1935. Although he produced many good films 5'11" Lang faced a constant battle with his masters in Hollywood. For example, *Fury* (1936) was a film about lynching in America. MGM insisted on a white star (Spencer Tracy) and a happy ending. "Lynching in the American Thirties was directed against Negroes, but that was too strong for MGM, so the most I could do was to slip in a few Negroes almost in passing," said Lang. "The ending is terrible but MGM insisted on having that fade-out kiss in the court between Tracy and Sylvia [Sidney]." Lang spent much time on the detail in his film: "An audience learns more about a character from detail in the décor, in the way the light falls in a room, than from pages of dialogue." Some believed that his perfectionism – he washed a studio floor himself to ensure the light fell in the exact way he wanted – earned him a reputation in Hollywood as an "impossible tyrant". His American films included *The Return Of Frank James* (1940), *Western Union* (1941), *Hangmen Also Die* (1943), *The Woman In The Window*

(1944), *Ministry Of Fear* (1944), *Scarlet Street* (1945), *An American Guerrilla In The Philippines* (1950), *Clash By Night* (1952), *Rancho Notorious* (1952), *The Blue Gardenia* (1953), *The Big Heat* (1953), *Moonfleet* (1955) and *Beyond A Reasonable Doubt* (1956). Eventually, Lang became tired of the constant battles and went back to Germany where he returned to his roots by making yet one more film about Dr Mabuse: *Die Tausend Augen Des Dr Mabuse* (1960). Lang was married three times. His first wife from 1919 until her death in 1921 was Lisa Rosenthal. He married Thea von Harbou (b. Tauperlitz, Bavaria, December 27, 1888, d. West Berlin, West Germany, July 1, 1954) on August 26, 1922. It was a second marriage for both of them. They divorced on April 26, 1933. From 1971 until his death he was married to actress Lily Latté (b. Germany 1891, d. Los Angeles, California, November 24, 1984). Of the public perception of his work, he said, "They all say I am dark and pessimistic. Some of my pictures show dark things about men and life, of course. However, I think all my pictures are portraits of the time in which they were made . . . I always made films about characters who struggled and fought against the circumstances and the traps they found themselves in. I don't think that is pessimistic."

CAUSE: Lang died in Beverly Hills, California, aged 85, from natural causes. He was buried in the Enduring Faith Section of Forest Lawn-Hollywood Hills, 6300 Forest Lawn Drive, Los Angeles, California 90068.

Harry Langdon
Born June 15, 1884
Died December 22, 1944
Comedic naïf. Born in Council Bluffs, Iowa, the son of members of the Sally Army, Langdon worked at various jobs before joining the travelling troupe Dr

Belcher's Kickapoo Indian Medicine Show. In 1923 he met Mack Sennett, for whom he made a number of short films. He developed his own persona: face whitened by make-up, mascara, lipstick, a dented hat, wide eyes and not quite all there. His early films included: *Smile Please* (1924), *Shanghaied Lovers* (1924), *Picking Peaches* (1924), *The Luck Of The Foolish* (1924), *All Night Long* (1924), *There He Goes* (1925), *The Sea Squawk* (1925) and *Horace Greeley, Jr* (1925). In 1926 he joined Warner Bros, where he made the best films of his career: *The Strong Man* (1926) as Paul Bergot, *Tramp, Tramp, Tramp* (1926) as Harry, which he also produced, and *Long Pants* (1927) as Harry Shelby. Langdon had worked successfully with Frank Capra and Harry Edwards but when these three films took off, as Tony Hancock would do almost 40 years later, Langdon decided he could do without the services of his collaborators. As with Hancock, it was a fatal mistake. Warner Bros dropped his contract. It could be argued that his success was based not on his talent (either as a comedian or ability to recognise others) but on the lack of productivity of his three main rivals: Charlie Chaplin, Buster Keaton and Harold Lloyd. Although Langdon continued to make films (over 90 in total) he seemed unable or unwilling to adapt to changing fashions and tastes. Sennett later said he thought Langdon was as stupid off screen as he appeared on. He had no head for money and filed for bankruptcy in 1931. Maritally, he fared no better. In 1903 he married actress Rose Frances Mensolf (d. 1962). They divorced in 1929. That same year he married actress Helen Walton, but they divorced after three years. On February 12, 1934, he married for the third time. The woman was Mabel Georgena Sheldon and their son, Harry, Jr, was born on December 16, 1934, followed some time later by a daughter, Virginia. It seems Langdon

and Sheldon couldn't live together but they also couldn't live apart. They divorced, remarried, divorced and remarried for the last time in 1938. CAUSE: He died aged 60 of a cerebral haemorrhage in Los Angeles, California, while dreaming of a comeback.

Joi Lansing
(JOYCE WASSMANDORFF)
Born April 6, 1928
Died August 7, 1972
Blonde bombshell. Born in Salt Lake City, Utah, the daughter of a devoutly Mormon family, she began working as a model when she was 16 and became very successful. The 5'5" Joi was lured into films playing a model in *The Counterfeiters* (1948) and reprised the role in *Julia Misbehaves* (1948), *Easter Parade* (1948) and *The Girl From Jones Beach* (1949). Initially, Joi's acting left rather a lot to be desired, but after all she was picked for her looks and her 39-23-35 figure, not her talent. A year-long break (1950) was spent modelling before Joi returned to the moving cameras in *Two Tickets To Broadway* (1951). Although she made several films, it was on television that she proved she could act and not just look pretty, playing Shirley Swanson on *Love That Bob* and Gladys Flatt on *The Beverly Hillbillies*. Her movies included: *FBI Girl* (1951) as Susan Matthews, *Singin' In The Rain* (1952), *The French Line* (1954), *So You Want To Go To A Nightclub* (1954), *So You're Taking In A Roomer* (1954), *So You Want To Be On A Jury* (1955), *So You Want To Be A V.P.* (1955), *So You Want To Be A Policeman* (1955), *Hot Shots* (1956) as Connie Forbes, *Hot Cars* (1956) as Karen Winter, *So You Think The Grass Is Greener* (1956), *Queen Of Outer Space* (1958), *The Atomic Submarine* (1959) as Julie, *Marriage On The Rocks* (1965) as Lola and *Bigfoot* (1970) as Joi Landis. She was married three times. Her first husband was Jerry Safron. Husband number two was Lance

Fuller (from 1951–1953) and the last was Stan Todd (1960–1972).
CAUSE: She died of breast cancer in Santa Monica, California. She was 44.

Ring Lardner, Jr

Born August 19, 1915
Died October 31, 2000
Oscar-winning blacklistee. Born in Chicago Ringgold Wilmer Lardner was one of four sons of humorist Ring Lardner (b. Niles, Michigan, March 3, 1885 d. East Hampton, New York, September 25, 1933 from alcoholism) – who had wanted to call him Bill but was overruled by readers of his newspaper the *Chicago Tribune* – and Ellis Ashton. Three of the four brothers would die prematurely. He was raised in Long Island where family friends included F. Scott Fitzgerald and Dorothy Parker. After education at Phillips Andover Academy and Princeton he moved to the Soviet Union to study at the Anglo-American Institute in Moscow. He quickly became a communist and his anti-fascist beliefs were strengthened when he stayed in Nazi Germany for a period. In 1935 while working as a journalist on the *New York Daily Mirror* he was approached by David O. Selznick's fledgling company and offered a job as a writer. Selznick had never met Lardner but was persuaded by a secretary who said that she had seen Lardner in New York and thought he might have the potential to be an actor as well. However, when 6′ Lardner arrived at Selznick's California office the secretary was disappointed – it had been Lardner's brother, John (b. 1912, d. March 1960 from a heart attack) who was also a journalist that she had seen. Lardner was given a screentest which he failed and put to work in the publicity department. Nonetheless in 1937 he married the secretary – Silvia Schulman – who had fancied his brother. He was teamed with Budd Schulberg and they worked on *A Star Is Born* (1936). Lardner worked with Ben Hecht on *Nothing Sacred* (1937). He was not covered in glory when he sent a memo to David O. Selznick advising him against buying the rights to *Gone With The Wind* (1939). In Hollywood Lardner's left-wing views were well known – he raised money for the Republicans in the Spanish Civil War and one of his brothers died serving in the Abraham Lincoln Brigade. Lardner joined the Screen Writers' Guild and began discussing Marxist theory. He later said that it was because the prettiest girls attended the meetings. As word got round so work began to dry up but in Hollywood everyone loves a success and in spring 1941 he wrote a script (with Michael Kanin) for Katharine Hepburn. She loved it and showed it to MGM but first she took the precaution of removing the title page bearing the authors' names. Thinking it was by Ben Hecht the studio paid $100,000 for it. *Woman Of The Year* teamed Hepburn with Spencer Tracy for the first time, won Lardner an Oscar and earned him a $2,000-a-week contract. Lardner was turned down for military service on the grounds that he had been "a premature anti-fascist". He made training films for the army during the conflict which in 1945 claimed the life of another of his brothers, David, who was working as a war correspondent for the *New Yorker* and stepped on a landmine. He worked on Otto Preminger's *Laura* (1944), Fritz Lang's *Cloak And Dagger* (1947) and *Forever Amber* (1947). That same year Lardner was one of ten people subpoenaed to appear before the House Committee on Un-American Activities. There were originally 11 summoned but Bertolt Brecht left America. The group believed that they were protected by the First and Fifth Amendments. When he appeared before the committee he was asked by J. Parnell Thomas, the chairman, "Are you or are you not a member of the Communist Party of the

United States?" Lardner began to reply but was interrupted by Thomas. He again began to reply and again Thomas stopped him. "I could answer the way you want," said Lardner, "but I'd hate myself in the morning." Thomas screamed at him to leave the chair. On October 30, 1947, the ten men were cited for contempt of Congress thanks in no small measure to an ambitious young Congressman called Richard Nixon. Lardner was fired by 20th Century Fox and sent to jail for a year. He served nine months and spent his sentence in Darnbury, Connecticut, where a fellow prisoner was J. Parnell Thomas who had been jailed for fiddling his expenses. Released from prison Lardner was unable to find much work and mostly wrote for British television. His return to the cinema under his own name came with *The Cincinnati Kid* (1965) and *M*A*S*H* (1970), the anti-war film about a mobile army surgical hospital. It won Lardner his second Oscar. Lardner, the last surviving member of the Hollywood Ten, spent his final years living in Connecticut. He was married twice. His marriage to Silvia Schulman, which produced a son, Peter, and a daughter, Ann, ended in divorce in 1945. On September 28, 1946 he married his sister-in-law Frances Chaney, the actress widow of his brother David. They had a son, James, but he also raised his niece and nephew.

CAUSE: Lardner died in New York aged 85 from cancer.

Charles Laughton

Born July 1, 1899
Died December 15, 1962
Classically ugly. Born at the Victoria Hotel in Scarborough, Yorkshire, Laughton, the eldest of three sons of a hotelier, was not a well child. He had a glandular complaint that caused him to become fat, and as a result was picked on at home and at school. A Roman Catholic, he was educated at a Jesuit school and wanted to become an actor but instead was sent to train at Claridge's. World War I intervened and he enlisted in the Royal Huntingdonshire Regiment only to be invalided home because of a gas attack in November 1918. Back in Scarborough he returned to learning the hotelier's trade until 1925, when he decided to put his own feelings first and enrolled at RADA. There he won the gold medal in 1927 and the following year made his mark as a "neurotic, greedy, sinister villain" who was "revoltingly brilliant" in *A Man With Red Hair*. That year he also made his first film, *Daydreams* (1928) as Ram Das. On February 9, 1929, he married the actress Elsa Lanchester, but throughout his life was tormented by his homosexuality, of which she professed ignorance until he confessed. He also hated his appearance, described by Josef von Sternberg as "that face that faintly resembled a large wad of cotton wool." Laughton appeared in *Piccadilly* (1929), *Comets* (1930), *The Sign Of The Cross* (1932) as Emperor Nero played as a simpering homosexual, *Payment Deferred* (1932) as William Marble, *Devil And The Deep* (1932) as Commander Charles Storm, *If I Had A Million* (1932) as Phineas V. Lambert and *Island Of Lost Souls* (1933) as Dr Moreau, before achieving acclaim and a Best Actor Academy Award for the lead in Sir Alexander Korda's *The Private Life Of Henry VIII* (1933). He followed this with a series of cinematic biographical portrayals including *The Barretts Of Wimpole Street* (1934) as Edward Moulton-Barrett, *Mutiny On The Bounty* (1935) as Captain William Bligh, for which he was nominated for a Best Actor Oscar, *Rembrandt* (1936) as Rembrandt van Rijn, *I, Claudius* (1937) as Claudius, *The Hunchback Of Notre Dame* (1939) as Quasimodo, *Captain Kidd* (1945) as Captain William Kidd, *Abbott & Costello Meet Captain Kidd* (1952) as Captain William Kidd, *Young Bess*

(1953) as King Henry VIII, *Salome*
(1953) as King Herod and *Spartacus*
(1960) as Sempronius Gracchus.
Laughton became an American citizen
in 1950. His other films included:
Jamaica Inn (1939) as Sir Humphrey
Pengallan, *They Knew What They
Wanted* (1940) as Tony Patucci, *Tales
Of Manhattan* (1942) as Charles Smith,
The Man From Down Under (1943) as
Jocko Wilson, *The Canterville Ghost*
(1944) as Sir Simon de Canterville/The
Ghost, *Because Of Him* (1946) as John
Sheridan, *Arch Of Triumph* (1948) as
Haake, *The Strange Door* (1951) as
Alain de Maletroit, *O. Henry's Full
House* (1952) as Soapy, *Hobson's Choice*
(1954) as Henry Horatio Hobson,
Witness For The Prosecution (1957) as
Sir Wilfrid Robarts, for which he was
nominated for a Best Actor Oscar, and
Advise And Consent (1962) as the
homophobic Senator Seabright Cooley.
He also directed (for the only time in
his career) and wrote the cult classic
The Night Of The Hunter (1955).
Laughton was cast as Mr Micawber in
David Copperfield (1934) but didn't feel
himself up to the task and asked to be
let out of the contract. Reluctantly
director George Cukor agreed. Cukor
later said: "He was the first actor I
encountered who prepared to make a
laughing entrance by going around
doing ha-ha sounds for hours."
Laurence Olivier described Laughton
as "The only actor of genius I've ever
met."
CAUSE: In 1959 he suffered a heart
attack and a nervous breakdown.
Laughton's death three years later at 63
was ascribed to cancer, although the
symptoms he exhibited are what we
would now recognise as AIDS. He died
in the schoolroom of his home in
Hollywood, California.
FURTHER READING: *Charles Laughton:
An Intimate Biography* – Charles
Higham (New York: Doubleday,
1976); *Charles Laughton: A Difficult
Actor* – Simon Callow (London:
Methuen, 1987).

Laurel & Hardy
(ARTHUR STANLEY JEFFERSON)
Born June 16, 1890
Died February 23, 1965
(NORVELL HARDY)
Born January 18, 1892
Died August 7, 1957
The comedy duo. The fat one and the
thin one. To millions of cinemagoers
Laurel & Hardy are the funniest screen
comedians ever. They were born on
separate sides of the Atlantic Ocean –
one in northern England, the other in
southern America. Stan was born in
his grandparents' house in Foundry
Cottages (now 3 Argyle Street),
Ulverston, Lancashire, the second of
four sons and one daughter of the
actors Arthur 'A.J.' Jefferson (b.
Manchester, September 12, 1862, d.
Barkston, January 1949) and Margaret
'Madge' Metcalfe (b. Askrigg, North
Yorkshire, 1860, d. December 1,
1908). (There is now a Laurel & Hardy
museum in Upper Brook Street,
Ulverston.) In 1897 the family moved
to North Shields near Newcastle and
Stan attended King James I Grammar
School in Bishop Auckland and
18 months later moved to Gainford
Academy. In 1905 the Jeffersons
moved to Buchanan Drive in
Rutherglen, Glasgow. He worked as a
box office manager, spending as much
time as he could backstage talking with
the performers, developing a taste for
showbiz. His idols were Laddie Cliff,
Boy Glen, Nipper Lane and Dan Leno.
In 1906, by Stan's own recollection, he
persuaded impresario Albert E. Pickard
to let him perform at the Britannia
Theatre, a.k.a. Pickard's Museum
Music Hall in Glasgow, the oldest
venue in the city. Stan wore a wig and
his father's trousers and "best frock
coat and silk hat", told a few jokes and
sang a song. He performed occasionally
over the next three years before
joining Fred Karno in 1910 where
he performed in various sketches and
understudied Charlie Chaplin. On
October 3 of that year he arrived with

Karno in America but, unhappy with his remuneration, left in 1911. He teamed up with another ex-Karnoite, Arthur Dandoe and, calling themselves The Rum 'Uns From Rome, they developed a successful double act. They were a huge hit in London and it should be remembered that in those days, before television and the establishment of cinema, a single act could keep a performer in work for many years. Many of the jokes in the act were written by 5'9" Stan. The act eventually split and, unable to find a suitable replacement, Stan went solo working for various companies and reuniting with Fred Karno for a September 18, 1912–November 1913 tour of America. The act finished when Charlie Chaplin accepted a $125-a-week offer to star in films in America. Stan, too, decided to stay Stateside and in the summer of 1914 joined a trio, Hurley, Stan and Wren, the highlight of whose act was Stan's impression of Chaplin. That, too, broke up and Stan formed The Stan Jefferson Trio, which metamorphosed into a double act, with Mae Charlotte Dahlberg Cuthbert (b. Australia, May 24, 1888, d. Sayville Nursing Home, Long Island, New York, 1969), known as Mae and Stan Laurel, in April 1917. She became his common-law wife on June 18, 1919, unable to marry him officially because she inconveniently already had a husband back in Australia. Their relationship lasted until 1925 (although she sued him for alimony on December 6, 1937 and the case was settled out of court) and it was Mae who christened him Stan Laurel. Stan, like many superstitious showbiz folk, was worried that his name contained thirteen letters. Mae was looking through a book when she came across a picture of Scipio Africanus Major wearing a laurel wreath on his head. She believed 'Stan Laurel' had a ring to it and the man himself agreed, although he did not legally adopt the name until August

1931. It was in 1917 that Stan made his first film *Nuts In May* (then still billed as Stan Jefferson). His other early films included *Whose Zoo* (1918), *Phoney Photos* (1918), *No Place Like Jail* (1918), *Just Rambling Along* (1918) and *Huns And Hyphens* (1918). In 1918 he signed with Universal to make a few films as the simple Hickory Hiram. Then he moved on to Pathé, Vitagraph and worked for Bronco Billy Anderson. Stan's films included: *Scars And Stripes* (1919), *Mixed Nuts* (1919), *Wild Bill Hiccup* (1920), *Under Two Jags* (1920), *Rupert Of Hee-Haw* (1920), *Oranges And Lemons* (1920), *The Rent Collector* (1921), *Mud And Sand* (1922) as Rhubarb Vaselino (a parody of Valentino's *Blood And Sand*) and *When Knights Were Cold* (1923) (a parody of Douglas Fairbanks' *Robin Hood*). On November 17–29, 1919, Stan had made a short film called *The Lucky Dog* but it was not released until 1922. It was notable only because one of his co-stars was a fat chap called Oliver Hardy, who was playing a thug. On March 2, 1923, Stan was signed by director Hal Roach to appear in a number of one-reel films including *White Wings* (1923), *Save The Ship* (1923), *The Noon Whistle* (1923), *A Man About Town* (1923), *Zeb Vs. Paprika* (1924), *Wide Open Spaces* (1924) and *Short Kilts* (1924). When not appearing on film, Stan polished his art in vaudeville but because he had not developed a persona *à la* Chaplin or Lloyd he was not as popular. In 1926 Roach employed Stan as a director and joke writer because he felt his blue eyes photographed as "dead". However, Stan stood in for an injured actor in *Get 'Em Young* (1926) and was such a hit the studio insisted he remain in front of the cameras. Incidentally, the injured actor was Oliver Hardy. He burned his hand and arm while trying to cook a leg of lamb. Stan and Ollie, known to all and sundry by his nickname 'Babe', first began appearing together in *Duck Soup* (filmed September 1926 and released on March 13, 1927). The pair went on to appear in a whole series of hilarious two-reelers: *Slipping Wives* (filmed October 1926, released April 3, 1927), *Love 'Em And Weep* (filmed January 1927, released June 12, 1927), *Why Girls Love Sailors* (filmed February 1927, released July 17, 1927), *With Love And Hisses* (filmed March 1927, released August 28, 1927), *Sailors, Beware!* (filmed April 1927, released September 25, 1927), *Do Detectives Think?* (filmed May 1927, released November 20, 1927), *Flying Elephants* (filmed May 1927, released February 12, 1928), *Sugar Daddies* (filmed June 1927, released September 10, 1927), *The 2nd Hundred Years* (filmed June 1927, released October 8, 1927), *Call Of The Cuckoos* (filmed June 1927, released October 15, 1927) and *Hats Off* (filmed July–August 1927 and released November 5, 1927). For many years purists have argued what should be the generally accepted "first" Laurel & Hardy film. Many plump for *Putting Pants On Philip*, which was written and filmed in August 1927, directed by Hal Roach and released on December 3, 1927. Others argue that not only had the pair made more than a dozen films prior to *Putting Pants On Philip* but even this is not a typical "Laurel & Hardy" comedy. They didn't use their real names, were not friends, did not wear bowler hats and the film did not feature Stan's odd haircut or Ollie's double take to camera. Whatever the consensus is, all we should be grateful for is that Laurel & Hardy did make comedies and superbly entertaining ones at that. The duo worked with Hal Roach until 1940 when they decided they wanted greater artistic freedom over their work. They formed their own production company but produced no films, instead touring with a stage show. They returned to the cinema, signing a non-exclusive contract with 20th Century Fox on April 23, 1941. However, they were denied any creative

input and the films were poor. Stan recalled, "I can't tell you how much it hurt me to do those pictures and how ashamed I am of them." For that studio and for MGM they produced *Great Guns* (1941), *A-Haunting We Will Go* (1942), *Air Raid Wardens* (1943), *Jitterbugs* (1943), *The Tree In A Test Tube* (1943), *The Dancing Masters* (1943), *The Big Noise* (1944), *Nothing But Trouble* (1944), *The Bullfighters* (1945) and *Atoll K/Robinson Crusoeland* (1950). 6'2" Babe Hardy was born at 125 South Hicks Street (now the site of a laundromat) in Harlem, Georgia, the son of Oliver Hardy (b. Harlem, Georgia, December 5, 1844, d. Harlem, Georgia, November 22, 1892), a lawyer and tax collector, and apparently a descendant of the sailor Nelson wanted to kiss at the Battle of Trafalgar, and Emily Norvell Tant. On the first Saturday in October the town holds its annual Oliver Hardy Festival. After his father's death the family moved to Milledgeville, Georgia, where his mother ran the Baldwin Hotel. Babe, who took the name Oliver in memory of his father, was a boy soprano and occasionally joined tours. He considered following his father into law but when his mother moved to Milledgeville, Georgia, he ran a cinema there. Three years passed before he decided to give acting a try. He played the heavy for Lubin Motion Pictures at $5 a day but when World War I arrived he was rejected as being too fat (he weighed around 20 stone). He moved to Ithaca, New York, where he worked for Pathé Films before going to Jacksonville, Florida (where he got the nickname from an Italian barber who used to pinch his cheeks and cry "Nicea-babee" which was shortened to Babe) and then West to California. He worked for Vitagraph before signing for Hal Roach on February 6, 1926. Throughout his career Babe suffered from an inferiority complex. He thought of himself as Stan's straight man and nothing more. He never watched the rushes at the end of a day's filming because he couldn't bear to see himself on screen. He rarely talked about the films he had made because he felt he didn't know enough to discuss them. The films were mostly masterpieces, namely *The Battle Of The Century* (filmed in October 1927 and released on New Year's Eve, 1927) which was based on the boxing match between Gene Tunney and Jack Dempsey on September 22, 1927 at Soldiers' Field, Chicago; *Leave 'Em Laughing* (filmed October 1927, released January 28, 1928) in which the boys' regular car, the Model T Ford, makes its first appearance; *The Finishing Touch* (filmed between November and December 1927, released February 25, 1928); *From Soup To Nuts* (originally called *Let George Do It* – filmed December 1927–January 5, 1928, released March 24, 1928); *You're Darn Tooting* (filmed January 17–27, 1928, released April 21, 1928); *Their Purple Moment* (filmed February 11–24, 1928 with a new ending shot on March 7, 1928 and released on May 19, 1928) during which their pay was $500 a week for Stan and $400 a week for Babe; *Should Married Men Go Home?* (filmed March 13–21, 1928, released September 8, 1928); *Early To Bed* (filmed May 21–29, 1928, released October 6, 1928); *Two Tars* (filmed June 22–23 and June 26–July 3, 1928, released November 3, 1928); *Habeas Corpus* (filmed July 16– 23 & 29–31 and released December 1, 1928) which was described by the studio as Laurel & Hardy's "first sound picture" but unfortunately the music and effects track (no speech) has been lost; *We Faw Down* (filmed August 23–September 1, 1928, released December 29, 1928); *Liberty* (filmed October 1–17, 1928, released January 26, 1929) which co-starred Jean Harlow; *Wrong Again* (filmed November 21–December 1, 1928, released February 23, 1929); *That's My Wife* (filmed December 11–16, 1928, released March 23, 1929); *Big*

Business (filmed December 19–26, 1928, released April 20, 1929); *Double Whoopee* (filmed February 1929, released May 18, 1929) which also co-starred Jean Harlow, who featured in the publicity pictures; *Bacon Grabbers* (filmed February 16–March 2, 1929, released October 19, 1929), a silent film although released with synchronised music and sound effects; *Angora Love* (filmed March 1929, released December 14, 1929) in which the boys "adopt" a goat – it was their last silent film although released with synchronised music and sound effects; *Unaccustomed As We Are* (filmed March 25–April 1929, released May 4, 1929), their first sound picture co-starred Thelma Todd and was shot mostly at night because the Roach Studios had only the one set of sound equipment and the Our Gang team used it during the day; *Berth Marks* (filmed April 20–27, 1929 and released June 1, 1929) in which all the dialogue was improvised. The version most often shown today is the 1936 reissue which has 'Coo-Coo' as the familiar theme tune over the titles – it wasn't recorded until August 1932 which is why it does not appear in original prints; *Men O'War* (filmed May 11–18, 1929, released June 29, 1929); *The Hollywood Revue Of 1929* (released November 23, 1929); *Perfect Day* (filmed June 8–15, 1929, released August 10, 1929); *They Go Boom* (filmed July 7–13, 1929, released September 21, 1929); *The Hoose-Gow* (filmed August 30– September 14, 1929, released November 16, 1929); *The Rogue Song* (filmed July–September 1929, released January 17, 1930) which was produced by Irving Thalberg, directed by Lionel Barrymore and made in two colour Technicolor; *Night Owls* (filmed October–November 1929, released January 4, 1930); *Blotto* (filmed December 1929, released February 8, 1930); *Brats* (filmed January 1930, released March 22, 1930) in which the boys play themselves and their own sons; *Below Zero* (filmed February–March 1930, released April 26, 1930); *Hog Wild* (filmed April 1930, released May 31, 1930); *The Laurel-Hardy Murder Case* (filmed May 1930, released September 6, 1930); *Pardon Us* (filmed June 24–December 1, 1930, released August 15, 1931); *Another Fine Mess* (filmed September–October 1930, released November 29, 1930); *Be Big!* (filmed November–December 1930, released February 7, 1931); *Chickens Come Home* (filmed January 1931, released February 21, 1931); *The Stolen Jools* (released April 1931); *Laughing Gravy* (filmed February 1931, released April 4, 1931) in which their friendship is tested by Stan's inheritance and their landlord takes a dislike to their dog, Laughing Gravy; *Our Wife* (filmed March 1931, released May 16, 1931), the last Laurel & Hardy film that was also filmed in foreign languages; *Come Clean* (filmed May 1931, released September 19, 1931) in which the opening reads, "Mr Hardy holds that a man should always tell his wife the whole truth. Mr Laurel is crazy too"; *One Good Turn* (filmed June 1931, released on Hallowe'en 1931) during which the Hal Roach Studio reported a loss of $25,005.64 on the 1930–1931 season of Laurel & Hardy films; *Beau Hunks* (filmed September 1931, released December 12, 1931) in which Babe and Stan join the Foreign Legion; *On The Loose* (filmed September 1931, released Boxing Day, 1931); *Helpmates* (filming began October 19, 1931, released January 23, 1932); *Any Old Port* (filmed November 1931, released March 5, 1932); *The Music Box* (filmed December 1931, released April 16, 1932) in which they had to deliver a piano (you can still see the steps at 923-927 Vendome Street, Los Angeles); *The Chimp* (filmed January–February 7, 1932, released May 21, 1932); *County Hospital* (filming began February 20, 1932, released June 25, 1932); *Pack Up Your Troubles* (filmed May–June 1, 1932, released September 23, 1932); *Scram!* (filmed June 18–July 1, 1932, released September 10, 1932); *Their First Mistake* (filmed September 24–October 1, 1932, released November 5, 1932) during which the studio reported a loss of $166,447.88 on the 1931–1932 season of Laurel & Hardy films; *Towed In A Hole* (filmed November 1–10, 1932, released New Year's Eve, 1932); *Twice Two* (filmed November 1932, released February 25, 1933); *The Devil's Brother* (filmed February 4–March 4, 1933, released May 5, 1933); *Me And My Pal* (filmed March 1933, released April 22, 1933); *The Midnight Patrol* (filmed June 24–July 6, 1933, released on August 3, 1933); *Busy Bodies* (filmed July 15–25, 1933, released October 7, 1933); *Wild Poses* (filmed August 1933, released October 28, 1933); *Dirty Work* (filmed August 7–19, 1933, released November 25, 1933); *Sons Of The Desert* (shot between October 2–23, 1933, released December 29, 1933); *Hollywood Party* (filmed March 1933–March 1934, released June 1, 1934); *Oliver The Eighth* (filmed December 15–20, 1933 & January 8–15, 1934, released February 13, 1934); *Going Bye-Bye!* (filmed May 21–26, 1934, released June 23, 1934); *Them Thar Hills* (filmed June 11–20, 1934, released July 21, 1934); *Babes In Toyland* (released November 30, 1934); *The Live Ghost* (filmed November 8–14, 1934, released December 8, 1934); *Tit For Tat* (filmed December 10–20, 1934, released January 5, 1935); *The Fixer-Uppers* (filmed January 11–19, 1935, released February 9, 1935); *Bonnie Scotland* (filmed May 1–June 15, 1935, released August 23, 1935); *Thicker Than Water* (filmed July 1–8, 1935, released August 6, 1935); *The Bohemian Girl* (filmed October 9–November 30, 1935, released February 14, 1936) previewed on December 11, 1935 and five days later, co-star Thelma Todd was discovered dead in a garage. To avoid any bad publicity and ghoul seekers Stan and Hal Roach made the decision to cut most of Todd's scenes from the final print; *Our Relations* (filmed March 16– May 4, 1936, released October 30, 1936); *On The Wrong Trek* (filmed April 1936, released June 1936); *Way Out West* (filmed August 27–November 1936, released April 16, 1937) in which they perform their number one hit, 'The Trail Of The Lonesome Pine' and *Pick A Star* (filmed November 16, 1936–January 1937, released May 21, 1937). In 1937 Hal Roach issued a press release stating that Babe would be making a solo film because Stan had not signed a new contract. In March of that year the *Hollywood Reporter* stated that Stan had formed his own company, Stan Laurel Productions. Stan then dropped his old agents, Claude and Gordon Bostock, and hired Charles Feldman. *Way Out West* did very well at the box office and Roach became desperate to team up Stan and Babe once more. On October 8, 1937, Hal Roach signed a four-picture deal with Stan Laurel Productions. Stan was to be paid $2,500 per week plus $25,000 per film. The first film he made under the new deal was *Swiss Miss* (filmed December 28, 1937–February 26, 1938, released May 20, 1938). The next movie *Block-Heads* (filmed June 1–July 1, 1938, released August 19, 1938) was generally regarded as one of the best Laurel & Hardy feature films. This was followed by *A Chump At Oxford* (filmed June 1939, released February 16, 1940), *The Flying Deuces* (filmed July 22–August 1939, released October 20, 1939), *Saps At Sea* (filmed November–December 1939, released May 3, 1940), *Great Guns* (filmed July 11–August 1941, released October 10, 1941), *A-Haunting We Will Go* (filmed March 15–April 1942, released August 7, 1942), *Air Raid Wardens* (filmed December 1,

1942–January 1943, released April 4, 1943), *Jitterbugs* (filmed February 15– March 1943, released June 11, 1943), *The Tree In A Test Tube* (filmed February–March 1943, released 1943), *The Dancing Masters* (filmed June 1–25, 1943, released November 19, 1943), *The Big Noise* (filmed April 1944, released September 1944) generally regarded as one of the worst films of all time, *Nothing But Trouble* (filmed October 1944, released March 1945), *The Bullfighters* (filmed November– December 16, 1944, released May 18, 1945) and *Atoll K* (filmed August 1950–March 1951, released in 1952). On December 1, 1954, the pair were Guests of Honour on *This Is Your Life*. Both Stan and Babe were exceptionally generous to family and friends (both had to make hefty alimony payments) and often arranged for down on their luck friends to get jobs on their films. Stan was also a practical joker. If Stan was recognised towards the end of his life, the fan would approach and say, "Aren't you . . .?" and Stan would rejoinder, "Oliver Hardy." "What happened to Laurel?" "He went barmy," said Stan with a straight face. Stan spent hours writing to fans, something that Babe didn't feel any obligation to do. He had a rubber stamp made of his signature and would use that to send pictures to fans until he received numerous complaints from admirers wanting a real autograph. Stan's marital track record was, to say the least, convoluted and confusing. As far as can be ascertained, he married the actor Lois Nelson (b. 1896, d. 1990) in Los Angeles on August 23, 1926. He had a daughter by her, also Lois (b. December 10, 1927; m. actor Randy Brooks in 1948 and then Tony Hawes, the man who used to announce the conveyor belt prizes on *The Generation Game*) and a son, Stan, Jr (b. May 7, 1930, d. May 16, 1930). The couple separated in May 1933 and divorced on September 10, 1935. Meanwhile, on April 2, 1934, Stan had married the widower (Virginia) Ruth Rogers (d. 1976) in Agua Caliente, Mexico. When his divorce was finalised they remarried on September 28, 1935 in Los Angeles. They divorced on Christmas Eve, 1936. Ruth Laurel was awarded the family home, two cars, $17,000 and 5 per cent of Stan's gross future earnings until her remarriage or death. On New Year's Day, 1938 Stan married Russian singer-dancer Vera Ivanova Shuvalova, known as Ileana (b. November 6, 1897, d. San Francisco, California, February 7, 1994), in Yuma, Arizona. The second Mrs Laurel picketed their honeymoon claiming the wedding was bigamous. To satisfy himself he was legally wed, Stan remarried Ileana on February 28, 1938. To please his bride they went through yet another ceremony in a Russian Orthodox Church on April 26, 1938. She was a fiery woman who saw nothing wrong in bashing her husband over the head with a frying pan and telling the press all about it afterwards. No matter how many times they said, "I do," it soon became clear that they didn't and they divorced on May 17, 1939. On January 11, 1941, he remarried Virginia Rogers but re-divorced her in Nevada on April 30, 1946. The following month in Yuma, Arizona, he married Russian singer Ida Kitaeva Raphael (b. 1898, d. 1980). Babe's nuptials were slightly simpler. In 1913 he married pianist Madelyn Saloshin (b. 1887) whom he divorced in November 1920 (becoming final on November 17, 1921). On November 24, 1921, he married the alcoholic, mentally disturbed Myrtle Lee Reeves (1897–1983) at the Church of Christ in Hollywood. They separated and reconciled on numerous occasions (for example, she filed for divorce on July 24, 1929 alleging seven years of cruel treatment such as Babe "refusing to explain the evidence of his close proximity to persons using powder and cosmetics"), usually when she was committed to various

sanatoriums, before Babe finally filed for divorce in 1933. Unsurprisingly, he withdrew the suit. On May 18, 1937, Babe finally received his interlocutory divorce. The judge commended Babe for "trying to keep [your] marital difficulties to [your]self". The decree absolute was not issued until February 25, 1940. On March 7, 1940, he married (Virginia) Lucille Jones (b. 1914, d. 1986). The last words should go to the two men themselves. Babe: "Those two fellows we created, they were nice, very nice people. They never get anywhere because they are both so dumb, but they don't know they are dumb." Stan: "We were doing a very simple thing, giving some people some laughs, and that's all we were trying to do."

CAUSE: Television revived the pair's careers in the Fifties and plans were made for them to star in a new series of films. However, before anything could come of this, Babe suffered a stroke at his home at 5429 Woodland Avenue, Van Nuys, early on the morning of September 14, 1956 which left him completely incapacitated. Doctors described his condition as "poor" and, until October 7, Babe was on the critical list. He spent a month at St Joseph's Hospital in Burbank, being released on October 13. He was told by doctors to lose weight and shed around 10 stone. Thousands of fans sent him get well letters and cards. In the last picture taken of the pair (in 1956) Stan looks much the same as he always did. Babe is unrecognisable from his weight loss. In early August 1957, he suffered two strokes that left him comatose. He died at 7.25am on August 7 at 5421 Auckland Avenue, North Hollywood, the home of his mother-in-law, Monnie L. Jones. Cause of death was "acute cerebral vascular accident". He was 65. At 1pm on August 9, 1957, he was given full Masonic rites and then cremated at the Chapel of the Pines and his ashes were buried in the Garden of Hope, the Masonic section of the Valhalla Memorial Park, 10621 Victory Boulevard, North Hollywood, California. He has two memorial plaques – one bears his name, birth and death dates and the legend "Beloved husband". The other, placed by the Sons of the Desert in 1977, reads, "Oliver Hardy 1892–1957. A genius of comedy. His talent brought joy and laughter to all the world." Without a partner and in poor health himself (he was discovered to have diabetes in 1945 and suffered a stroke ten years later in June 1955), Stan retired. He did not attend Babe's funeral. Ida and Lois, Jr did. Stan lived out his retirement comfortably at 1111 Franklin Street, Santa Monica, then 25406½ Malibu Road and finally from 1958 at 849 Ocean Avenue, Santa Monica, where he was listed in the telephone directory. He often received fans to chat about the old days. His wife was fiercely protective of Stan but would quietly leave the room to allow him to entertain his visitors. He watched television but rarely his own films. To the fans who could not visit, he wrote thousands of letters, patiently answering their questions. He turned down an offer of $100,000 to be comedy consultant to Jerry Lewis – Stan did not need the money. In 1961 he was awarded a special Oscar but was too poorly to receive it. He died aged 75 from a heart attack at 1.45pm. He had also been suffering from cancer of the palate. Official cause of death was "myocardial infarction, massive (posterior), arteriosclerosis, atherosclerosis (advanced 12 years); also diabetes mellitus – brittle". He was 74. He, too, was cremated – the ceremony taking place on February 27, 1965 at Forest Lawn Crematory. His ashes were interred in plot 910 of the second terrace in the George Washington Section of Forest Lawn, Los Angeles. His memorial reads, "Stan Laurel 1890–1965. A Master of Comedy. His genius in the art of humor brought gladness to the world

he loved." His two-page will, dated November 3, 1947, leaving everything to Ida Laurel was contested by Virginia Laurel. The suit was dismissed.
FURTHER READING: *Mr Laurel & Mr Hardy* – John McCabe (New York: Signet, 1968); *Stan* – Fred Lawrence Guiles (London: Michael Joseph, 1980); *Laurel And Hardy: The Magic Behind The Movies* – Randy Skretvedt (London: Apollo, 1988); *The Comedy World Of Stan Laurel* – John McCabe (London: Robson Books, 1990).

John Laurie
Born March 25, 1897
Died June 23, 1980
Dour Scot. John Paton Laurie's career spanned almost sixty years yet he is probably best known for the portrayal of the financially astute, i.e. mean, sailor-turned-undertaker James Fraser in *Dad's Army*. Born in Dumfries and educated at Dumfries Academy, he intended to become an architect. From 1916 until 1918 he served with the Honourable Artillery Company. He was invalided out of the service and rarely spoke about his experiences. In 1919 he began training at the Central School of Speech Training at the Royal Albert Hall and made his stage début in March 1921 at the Lyceum Theatre, Dumfries playing John Shand in *What Every Woman Knows*. His London début came as Pistol in *The Merry Wives Of Windsor* on August 16, 1922. He had a highly successful career in the theatre and began appearing in films in 1930 with *Juno And The Paycock* as Johnny Boyle. 5'10" Laurie's other films included: *The 39 Steps* (1935) as John, *As You Like It* (1936) as Oliver, *Jericho* (1937) as Hassan, *Farewell Again* (1937) as Private McAllister, *A Royal Divorce* (1938) as Joseph, *Q Planes* (1939), *The Four Feathers* (1939) as Khalifa, *Convoy* (1940) as Gates, *Old Mother Riley's Ghosts* (1941) as McAdam, *The Life And Death Of Colonel Blimp* (1943) as John Montgomery Murdoch, *Henry V*

(1944) as Captain Jamie, *Fanny By Gaslight* (1944) as William Hopwood, *Caesar And Cleopatra* (1946), *Treasure Island* (1950) as Blind Pew, *Trio* (1950) as Mr Campbell, *Richard III* (1954) as Lord Lovell, *Hobson's Choice* (1954) as Dr MacFarlane, *Campbell's Kingdom* (1957) as Mac, *Kidnapped* (1960) as Ebenezer Balfour, *The Abominable Dr Phibes* (1971) as Darrow, *One Of Our Dinosaurs Is Missing* (1976) as Jock and *The Prisoner Of Zenda* (1979) as the Archbishop. He was married twice, firstly to Florence Saunders who died aged 35 on January 24, 1926 and then in 1928 to Oonah V. Todd-Taylor (b. 1901, d. 1990) by whom he had a daughter, Veronica (b. 1939). A kindly man whose hobby was doing *The Times* crossword he, nevertheless, didn't mince his words. He told *Dad's Army* creators Jimmy Perry and David Croft: "I have played every major Shakespearean role in the theatre and I'm considered the finest speaker of verse in the country, and I end up becoming famous doing this crap!"
CAUSE: He died at his home, Southfield, Chalfont St Peter, Buckinghamshire, from emphysema and a lung ailment. He was 83. He left £44,549.

John Phillip Law

Born September 7, 1937
Died May 13, 2008
Blond beefcake. Born in Los Angeles, the son of John Law, the county's deputy sheriff and actress, Phyllis Sallee, John Phillip Law appeared in films as a child extra. His interest in the art was consolidated at the University of Hawaii, where he studied drama. After a bit part in the play *Come On Strong* (1962), Law moved to Italy where he appeared in a number of films. Director Norman Jewison saw him in one and thought that he would be perfect for the part of Alexei Kolchin, a naïve Soviet sailor, in *The Russians Are Coming, The Russians Are Coming* (released May 25, 1966), a

Cold War comedy which garnered several Oscar nominations and won Law a Golden Globe nomination as most promising newcomer. He returned to Europe to appear in spaghetti western *Da Uomo A Uomo* aka *Death Rides A Horse* (1967) with Lee Van Cleef. Law met Jane Fonda while filming Otto Preminger's awful *Hurry Sundown* (premièred February 6, 1967) in Louisiana. It led to his casting in the part for which he is most remembered – the semi-naked, white panties-clad blind angel Pygar in *Barbarella* (released October 10, 1968). The film followed space traveller Fonda as she hunted for a mad professor called Duran Duran. He was similarly cast as a hunk in Mario Bava's *Danger: Diabolik* (released May 1968). 6ft 5in Law wanted to escape from pretty boy roles and flopped in *Skidoo* (premièred December 2, 1968) as hippie Stash and was not much more successful in the John Flynn film *The Sergeant* (released December 25, 1968) in which Master Sergeant Albert Callan (Rod Steiger) had the hots for Law's character. *New York Times* critic Vincent Canby opined, "As played by John Phillip Law, the private is remarkably dense, and – when not being dense – he is so hostile that it would seem the sergeant would have to be psychotic to run after him with such boozy abandon." Law did not have the talent either to be a ruthlessly ambitious television newsreader Robin Stone in an adaptation of Jacqueline Susann's *The Love Machine* (released August 14, 1971) and his last major hit was the title role in *The Golden Voyage Of Sinbad* (released April 5, 1974). Much of the rest of his oeuvre went straight to video. Law, who spoke Italian, Spanish, French and German, claimed that he had made more than 50 films in two dozen countries. He married and divorced Shawn Ryan by whom he had one daughter, Dawn (b. 1974).
CAUSE: He died in Los Angeles, aged 70, from cancer.

Peter Lawford

(PETER SYDNEY ERNEST AYLEN)
Born September 7, 1923
Died December 24, 1984

The First Brother-in-law. Born at 17 Artillery Mansions, Victoria Street, London, SW1, Lawford has a greater claim to fame than acting as the reputed Hollywood pimp for John F. Kennedy, his presidential brother-in-law. Lawford supposedly set up JFK with numerous starlets during the time he was married to First Sister Patricia Kennedy. Lawford had an unorthodox upbringing. His mother, May Somerville Bunny (b. November 4, 1883, d. January 23, 1972) unkindly described him as "an awful accident". At the time of her son's birth she was married to Major Ernest Vaughan Aylen (b. 1876, d. by his own hand, October 12, 1947) of the Royal Army Medical Corps. However, Lawford's real father was Major Aylen's commanding officer Lieutenant-General Sir Sydney Lawford (b. November 16, 1865, d. February 15, 1953). When Mrs Aylen was handed her newborn son she turned up her nose in disgust. "I can't stand babies," she once commented. "They run at both ends; they smell of sour milk and urine." For over 20 years of marriage Major Aylen had pleaded with his wife to give him an heir. She refused until Sir Sydney began courting her. She believed (rightly as it turned out, the third marriage for both of them) that if she had his baby he would marry her and she would thus become Lady Lawford. Peter described his mother as "an inveterate snob". Lady Lawford continued to meddle in all aspects of her son's life. When he was signed to MGM she went to see studio head honcho Louis B. Mayer and told him she thought her son had homosexual tendencies. Mayer listened patiently and then interviewed Lawford, telling him other young men on the lot had the same 'problem'. Lawford, who was at that time seeing Lana Turner, told Mayer he was not gay and to ask Turner. Mayer did and was apparently satisfied with what he heard. Still the rumours continued, and indeed persist to this day. Lawford was very close to actors Van Johnson and Keenan Wynn and his wife Evie Lynn Abbott. When, on January 25, 1947, Wynn divorced Evie and four hours later married Johnson, wags commented, "Who gets custody of Peter?" Lawford met Patricia Kennedy at a party in London in 1949. He was her cinematic hero, while he was delighted to meet the sister of his friend John F. Kennedy. Their first date was in November 1953, when they went out to dinner in Manhattan. They spent Christmas of that year together with her family in Palm Springs. He proposed on her last night in Los Angeles shortly before she was due to fly to Tokyo to be reunited with a beau, Frank Conniff. However, when Pat suggested a date for a wedding, Lawford hesitated. The next morning he had overcome his doubts, but when he called her she had already left for San Francisco. He rang her in Frisco but was again too late. He had to wait until she arrived in her Tokyo hotel room before he could speak to her and agree the marriage was on. Pat caught the first flight back. The Kennedys insisted the engagement was kept a secret until the official announcement. To reporters Lawford denied the truth almost as the Kennedys were making the announcement, making him look rather silly. Newspaper reports mistakenly published pictures of Jean Kennedy, not Pat, and many of the future bride that did appear were taken when her father was ambassador to the Court of St James's and she was about 14. Ill-informed accusations of cradle snatching were not totally absent. The engagement ring cost Lawford $13,000. They were married on April 24, 1954, at 4pm at St Thomas More Church, East 89th Street, New York. The wedding was not held in St

Patrick's Cathedral because Lawford was not a Catholic. The ceremony lasted just ten minutes and the groom was late. The best man was Lawford's friend Bob Neal, the ushers were John, Bobby and Teddy Kennedy, LeMoyne Billings and Peter Sabiston. Jean Kennedy was the only bridesmaid. Pat's dress was pearl white satin and designed by Hattie Carnegie. Lawford did not invite any of his showbiz friends except Jackie Coogan, who refused to attend because he believed Lawford and Pat were incompatible. As they were pronounced man and wife, the groom did not kiss his bride. A crowd of around 3,000 waited outside the church to see the bride and groom and it took 23 policemen almost half an hour to forge a space for the car to move to the reception, which was held for 300 guests at the Plaza Hotel on Fifth Avenue. There was no prenuptial agreement. However, Lawford was kept in the dark completely about his wife's assets. Each year he was given a blank tax form to sign and send to the Kennedy accountants. He never saw the forms again. One year he was sent by mistake a copy of his wife's tax return and discovered she had paid $286,000 in tax the previous year. Pat was a virgin on the wedding night, which was spent in the bridal suite at the Plaza. Their honeymoon was a fortnight in Hawaii with an overnight stop in Chicago. On the honeymoon Pat showed she was a true Kennedy by insisting on visiting the Hawaiian legislature to see the procedures. Lawford spent the first few days of his honeymoon alone while his wife listened to political speeches and debates. Rose Kennedy was not happy at the fact that Lawford was an Anglican although she relented when the couple promised to raise their children as Catholics. Joe Kennedy had Lawford thoroughly checked out to make sure he wasn't a gold digger. The report also revealed that he was a regular visitor to prostitutes. Kennedy,

Sr was impressed by Lawford's sexual appetites and gave the match his blessing. Lady Lawford announced she wanted her son to marry someone from "court circles" and called the Kennedy family "Irish peasants". When she had dinner with Joe Kennedy she fell into an argument, called him "an old fogey" (he was five years younger than her) and stormed out of the restaurant. She referred to her daughter-in-law as "that bitch". This was a bit strong considering her own interferences and, whether tongue in cheek or not, she entitled her own autobiography *Bitch!* Following his divorce, Lawford went on to marry three more times – to Mary Rowan (b. October 31, 1949), the daughter of TV comedian Dan Rowan on October 30, 1971 (from whom he was divorced on January 2, 1975), to Deborah Gould (b. 1951) on June 25, 1976, from whom he separated after a few short months and, finally, in July 1984 to model Patricia Ann Seaton (b. 1959). He died five months after the nuptials. Following the November 22, 1963, assassination of President Kennedy, Lawford began to indulge in rather more drugs than were good for him. His marriage broke up (he was divorced in 1966) and he was exiled from the court of Camelot. He was estranged from his Rat Pack friend Frank Sinatra and was further ostracised because of his association with Marilyn Monroe. It had been Lawford who had emceed the Birthday Gala at Madison Square Garden for JFK on May 19, 1962, at which Marilyn sang a breathily sexy version of 'Happy Birthday'. According to some reports Lawford was the last person to speak to Marilyn when she telephoned him on the evening of her death. She supposedly told him: "Say goodbye to Pat, say goodbye to Jack [or "the President"] and say goodbye to yourself, because you're a nice guy." His films included: *Poor Old Bill* (1930), *Lord Jeff* (1938) as Benny Potter, *A Yank At Eton* (1942) as

Ronnie Kenvil, *Mrs Miniver* (1942), *Random Harvest* (1942), *Sherlock Holmes Faces Death* (1943), *Corvette K-225* (1943), *The Canterville Ghost* (1944) as Anthony de Canterville, *Son Of Lassie* (1945) as Joe Carraclough, *The Picture Of Dorian Gray* (1945) as David Stone, *It Happened In Brooklyn* (1947) as Jamie Shellgrove, *Easter Parade* (1948) as Jonathan Harrow III, *It Should Happen To You* (1954) as Evan Adams III, *Exodus* (1960) as Major Caldwell, *Ocean's Eleven* (1960) as Jimmy Foster, *The Longest Day* (1962) as Lord Lovat, *Sergeants 3* (1962) as Sergeant Larry Barrett, *Sylvia* (1965) as Frederic Summers, *Harlow* (1965) as Paul Bern, *The Oscar* (1966) as Steve Marks and *Won Ton Ton, The Dog Who Saved Hollywood* (1976). When Lawford went to MGM the company promised to make him the new Ronald Colman and told him that his time would come by the age of 30. Aged 34 he asked a producer, "What happened to the time when I'd be perfect?" and was told, "I guess it just went by."

CAUSE: By the late Seventies Peter Lawford's acting career had virtually ground to a halt. He made the occasional advertisement, appeared on game shows and chat shows and did personal appearances. The occasional acting job surfaced but Peter usually blew it. In December 1977 he flew to Honolulu to appear as Kenneth Kirk in 'Frozen Assets', an episode of the hit CBS cop show *Hawaii Five-O*, which was broadcast on March 30, 1978. The network paid for his room at the Kahala Hilton but any extras were the actor's responsibility. In his nine days he ran up a bill of $1,653, which he failed to pay. For a year the hotel chased its money until it announced CBS would have to pay or they would stop the network's credit facilities. Grudgingly, CBS paid up, but sued Lawford. He never worked for the company again. He borrowed sums of up to $10,000 from friends and made

no effort at repayment. The money was usually spent on drugs. He also tried to raise money with frivolous lawsuits. On September 17, 1983, his daughter by Pat Kennedy, Sydney, married, but Lawford was shunned by his former in-laws. Only Jackie Onassis spent time with him at the reception, where he drank too much. On December 12, 1983, Lawford was admitted to the Betty Ford Center in Rancho Mirage to combat his addictions. On the plane he became drunk on vodka and asked Patricia Seaton where they were heading. She replied, "Betty Ford's" to which Lawford, thinking they were having dinner with her, responded, "Oh good, I've always liked Betty Ford." While there he secretly paid for cocaine to be flown to him via helicopter, which he paid for on his American Express card. In July 1984, 35 per cent of his stomach was removed in an operation at UCLA Medical Center. The day after the operation he married the Roman Catholic Patricia Seaton. Back at home Lawford had become unable to look after himself or control his bodily functions. His wife called his children and suggested he be put in a nursing home. They did not feel that was necessary. In December 1984 he was admitted to Cedars-Sinai Medical Center, Los Angeles, with failing kidneys and liver. As his kidneys stopped working his skin gradually turned yellow. His children stopped off to visit him but then continued on to their Christmas holiday in Jamaica. His wife never left his side. On December 19 he fell into a coma. At 8.50am on Christmas Eve Lawford stirred, his muscles contracted, he sat up and blood poured from his mouth, nose and ears. He fell back, dead. He was cremated on Christmas Day 1984 and his ashes were interred in Westwood Village Mortuary, about 50 yards from Marilyn Monroe's crypt.

FURTHER READING: *The Peter Lawford Story* – Patricia Seaton Lawford with Ted Schwarz (New York: Carroll & Graf, 1988); *Peter Lawford: The Man Who Kept The Secrets* – James Spada (London: Bantam, 1991).

Dorothy Layton

(DOROTHY VIOLET WANNENWETCH)
Born August 13, 1912
Died June 1, 2009
Comedic foil. Born in Cincinnati, Ohio, the daughter of the co-founder of the Western Southern Life Insurance Company, she was educated at a convent school. In 1929 she went on a fortnight visit to a cousin who lived at Santa Barbara, California and never left. She found herself a wealthy lover, Roger Marchetti, a lawyer who represented Howard Hughes, Louis B. Mayer and Bing Crosby. He introduced her to Jean Harlow, Joan Crawford, Greta Garbo and Hughes so she decided that she, too, would like to be an actress. She dumped the surname Wannenwetch for that of her maternal great-grandmother, Layton. Whenever she landed a screen test Marchetti had Max Factor do her make-up and MGM costumier Gilbert Adrian create her frocks. In 1932 Layton was selected as one of the WAMPAS Babies (promising starlets chosen by the Western Association of Motion Picture Advertisers). She then signed for MGM and appeared in a series of comedy shorts for Hal Roach. She made her debut opposite Laurel and Hardy and Thelma Todd in *Chickens Come Home* (released February 21, 1931). Roach cast Layton opposite Laurel and Hardy in *The Chimp* (released May 21, 1932), *County Hospital* (released June 25, 1932) and *Pack Up Your Troubles* (released September 23, 1932). In the same year she was in the Charlie Chase comedy *Young Ironsides* (1932). The following year she appeared in *Pick-Up*, with George Raft but in the spring of that year split from Marchetti and also left

her agent. She made her last film for Roach as Billy Gilbert's secretary in *Fallen Arches* (1933) before appearing in Louis Lewy's *Hollywood On Parade* (1933). In 1934 5'2" Dorothy Layton left Tinseltown and moved to Baltimore, where she married Howard Taylor, who ran a company selling mattresses. They had a son and a daughter.
CAUSE: She died aged 96 in an old people's home at Towson, Maryland from natural causes.

Eva Le Gallienne

Born January 11, 1899
Died June 3, 1991
Stately homo. Born in London and RADA educated, Le Gallienne, "the high priestess of classical drama in America", was one of Hollywood's best-known lesbians. She made her stage début at London's Queen's Theatre on July 21, 1914. The following year she moved to New York where she made her début in *Mrs Botany's Daughters* in October 1915 at the Comedy Theatre. For the next ten years she appeared in London and on Broadway. On October 25, 1926, she opened the Civic Repertory Company on West 14th Street, New York, the company she had founded. She did not always show great judgment and once turned down Bette Davis when the younger woman auditioned for her. She was awarded a special Tony in 1964. In 1978 she won an Emmy for *The Royal Family*. She once told the *Christian Science Monitor*: "I really don't know why I came into the theatre, because I am not a theatrical person at all . . . I do not care for publicity. I appreciate it when people are kind enough to send me telegrams, or come back to say they have enjoyed the performance. I would really, though, much rather slip into the theatre each evening and do my work quietly, because it is the work that I like doing." She made just three films: *Prince Of Players* (1954), *The Devil's Disciple*

(1959) and *Resurrection* (1980), for which she was nominated for an Oscar.

CAUSE: She died of natural causes, aged 92.

John Le Mesurier

(JOHN ELTON HALLILEY)
Born April 5, 1912
Died November 15, 1983

A jobbing actor. Born in Chaucer Road, Bedford, he decided to follow his father and grandfather into the legal profession until the age of 23 when a change of heart led him to acting. From his comfortable middle-class upbringing he began to earn less than £5 a week in repertory after training at the Fay Compton Studio of Dramatic Art. He took his mother's maiden name as his stage name. In 1939 he married blonde impresario June Melville in Highgate. At the outbreak of war he became an air raid warden in Victoria based in Dolphin Square, before he was called up and sent to India. The war wrecked his marriage. In 1947 he met actress Hattie Jacques who was to become his second wife on November 10, 1949 at Kensington Register Office. They had two sons, Robin Mark (b. March 22, 1953) and Kim Charles "Jake" (b. October 12, 1956, d. Barcelona, October 6, 1991 of a heroin overdose). In 1948 he made his film *début* in *Death In The Hand* (1948) as Jack Mottram. It was to be the first of well over 100 films, encompassing everything from comedy to drama to police thrillers to sex films. He appeared in *Old Mother Riley's New Venture* (1949) as Karl, *A Matter Of Murder* (1949) as Ginter, *Mother Riley Meets The Vampire* (1952), *Dangerous Cargo* (1954) as Luigi, *The Baby And The Battleship* (1956), *The Good Companions* (1957) as Monte Mortimer, *Law And Disorder* (1958) as Sir Humphrey Pomfret, *I Was Monty's Double* (1958), *Jack The Ripper* (1959) as Dr Tranter, *I'm All Right Jack* (1959) as Waters, *Carlton-Browne Of*

The F.O. (1959) as Grand Duke Alexis, *The Hound Of The Baskervilles* (1959) as Barrymore, *Ben-Hur* (1959), *School For Scoundrels* (1960), *The Day They Robbed The Bank Of England* (1960) as Green, *The Bulldog Breed* (1960), *Doctor In Love* (1960) as Dr Mincing, *The Rebel* (1961), *The Pure Hell Of St Trinian's* (1961), *The Wrong Arm Of The Law* (1962), *The Punch And Judy Man* (1963), *The Pink Panther* (1963), *The Early Bird* (1965) as Colonel Foster, *Those Magnificent Men In Their Flying Machines, Or How I Flew From London To Paris In 25 Hours 11 Minutes* (1965), *Casino Royale* (1967), *The Italian Job* (1969), *Doctor In Trouble* (1970), *Au Pair Girls* (1972) as Mr Wainwright, *The Alf Garnett Saga* (1972), *Confessions Of A Window Cleaner* (1974) as Inspector Radlett, *Barry Mackenzie Holds His Own* (1974) as Robert Crowther, *The Adventure Of Sherlock Holmes' Smarter Brother* (1975) as Lord Redcliff, *What's Up Nurse!* (1977) as Mr Ogden, *Stand Up, Virgin Soldiers* (1977) as Colonel Bromley-Pickering, *Jabberwocky* (1977) as Chamberlain, *Rosie Dixon – Night Nurse* (1978) as Sir Archibald MacGregor, *Who Is Killing The Great Chefs Of Europe?* (1978) as Dr Deere and *The Fiendish Plot Of Dr Fu Manchu* (1980) as Perkins. His marriage to Hattie failed and they parted on very good terms, divorcing in December 1965. In Fulham Town Hall on March 2, 1966, he married Oldham-born Joan Malin, who had been married to the actor Mark Eden (Alan Bradley in *Coronation Street*) although they went through a separation when she had an affair with his best friend, Tony Hancock. It was his portrayal of the charming Sergeant Arthur Wilson in the BBC sitcom *Dad's Army* that brought Le Mesurier his greatest fame. The casting of Arthur Lowe as the pompous lower-middle-class Captain Mainwaring and Le Mesurier as his long-suffering upper-class NCO was inspirational. It was also a joke that BBC boss Huw Weldon failed to appreciate when he first met the cast. He assumed that Le Mesurier was Mainwaring and Lowe Wilson, and that was the original intention until the writers saw the comic potential in reversing the casting. Kind, caring and considerate, John Le Mesurier had time for everyone as long as they were not boring.

CAUSE: In 1977 he was diagnosed with cirrhosis of the liver. On July 5, 1983, he began haemorrhaging and was taken to Ramsgate Hospital, where the bleeding was halted. A month later he suffered another haemorrhage and was taken to King's College Hospital, London. He was discharged in early September. Back at home in Ramsgate he lived on a salt-free diet and continued work on his autobiography, which he never saw published. In early November he was once more readmitted to Ramsgate Hospital, but by then he was too ill to be moved to a private room. His last words were to his wife: "Darling, I'm fed up of it now and I think I'd like to die. It's all been rather lovely." He subsequently fell into a coma, from which he never woke. At his request his widow put a notice in *The Times* that read "John Le Mesurier wishes it to be known that he 'conked out' on November 15th. He sadly misses family and friends."

FURTHER READING: *A Jobbing Actor* – John Le Mesurier (London: Sphere, 1985); *Lady Don't Fall Backwards* – Joan Le Mesurier (London: Pan, 1989).

Roger Leach

Born April 22, 1948
Died December 1, 2001
TV cop. Born in Sydney, Australia, Leach became best known playing Sergeant Tom Penny for six years from 1984 in *The Bill*. After hanging up his uniform, he became a scriptwriter for the show.

CAUSE: He died aged 53 from cancer in Salisbury, Wiltshire.

Sir David Lean, CBE

Born March 25, 1908
Died April 16, 1991
Epic director. Born in Croydon, Surrey, Lean was the son of devout Quakers who heartily disapproved of his passion for what they regarded as the 'sinful' world of films. While attending a Reading-based Quaker boarding school he sneaked away to go to the cinema without his parents' knowledge. When he left the school he went to work in his father's accountancy office but was gripped by ennui and so left in 1927 to become a lowly tea boy at Gaumont. He steadily worked his way up the promotion ladder and by 1931 was editing feature films such as *These Charming People* (1931), *Insult* (1932), *Song Of The Plough* (1933) and *Matinee Idol* (1933). He also edited *As You Like It* (1936), *Pygmalion* (1938), *French Without Tears* (1939), *Major Barbara* (1941), *One Of Our Aircraft Is Missing* (1942), *In Which We Serve* (1942) and, to prove he had not lost his touch, *A Passage To India* after a 42-year hiatus. His first directorial effort was Noël Coward's war epic *In Which We Serve* (1942) although there is a possibility that he worked uncredited on *Major Barbara* (1941). His next three films were all Coward movies: *This Happy Breed* (1944), *Blithe Spirit* (1945) and *Brief Encounter* (1945), for which he was nominated for an Oscar. Then Lean turned his attention to Dickens and directed *Great Expectations* (1946), for which he was nominated for a second Oscar, and *Oliver Twist* (1948), which starred future BBC executive John Howard Davies in the title role and Alec Guinness as a memorable Fagin with Robert Newton as the villainous Bill Sikes. In 1954 he was nominated for an Oscar for *Summertime* (1955). His production of *The Bridge On The River Kwai* (1957) reunited him with Alec Guinness and brought him international fame, making him a household name and earning seven

Oscars, including Best Film, Best Director and Best Actor (for Guinness). Lean had become the first British director to win an Oscar. It was five years before his next film hit the screen, but *Lawrence Of Arabia* (1962) was certainly worth the wait. It also picked up seven Oscars, including Best Film and Best Director, and made stars of Peter O'Toole and Omar Sharif. Lean worked on his next project for three years and cast Sharif once again, this time in the lead part. *Doctor Zhivago* (1965) picked up five Oscars, mostly technical. Lean was an unsuccessful nominee. He shied away from the potential casting of Sophia Loren as Lara and also nixed Sarah Miles, calling her "a north country slut", just two years before he asked her to marry him (and, anyway, she was born in Ingatestone, Essex). His penultimate film was *Ryan's Daughter* (1970), which won two Oscars, including a Best Supporting Academy Award for John Mills. It took 14 years to write, prepare and finance his last movie, *A Passage To India* (1984), for which Lean received Oscar nominations for writing, directing and editing. Lean married six times but only listed five wives: the mystery wife whose existence was revealed only in 1989 was Isabelle, by whom he had his only child, Peter. His other wives were: actress Kay Walsh (b. London 1914; 1940–1949); actress Ann Todd (b. Hartford, January 24, 1909, d. May 6, 1993; 1949–1957) whom he accused of spreading rumours that he was impotent, homosexual and a child abuser and from whom he fled Britain, returning only in 1984; Mrs Leila Matkar (1960–1978), an Indian woman who left her husband and two children for him and whom he regularly cheated on with his mistresses, including Barbara Cole who worked as continuity assistant on *Lawrence Of Arabia* and *Doctor Zhivago* (the marriage was all but over by 1962); Sandra Hotz (1981–1985) and

Sandra Cooke (1990–1991). He so loved film-making that he once quipped, only half-jokingly, "I hope the money men don't find out that I'd pay them to let me do this."
CAUSE: He died at his London home, Sun Wharf, 30 Narrow Street, Limehouse, E14, aged 83 from natural causes. He had begun work on a film to be called *Nostromo* with Marlon Brando and based on Joseph Conrad's novel when he died. He was buried at Putney Vale Crematorium on April 22.

Heath Ledger
Born April 4, 1979
Died January 22, 2008
Another waste. Heathcliffe Andrew Ledger was born at St John of God Hospital, Subiaco, Perth, Western Australia, the son of Kim Ledger (b. 1950), a racing-car driver and mining engineer and Sally Ramshaw, a French teacher. Ledger and his older sister, Katherine, were named after the protagonists in Emily Brontë's novel *Wuthering Heights*. His parents split when he was ten and divorced a year later. Both found new spouses and both had another daughter – his mother had Ashleigh Bell (b. 1989) and his father Olivia (b. 1997). Katherine persuaded her brother to try acting and he appeared in a school production as *Peter Pan*. This led to his casting in Australian children's television programmes. He was also Western Australia's junior chess champion when he was 10. Six years later, with best friend Tom DiCarlo, he drove to Sydney – about 2,051 miles from home – because he thought he would find more acting opportunities there. He was cast as Snowy Bowles, a gay cyclist, in *Sweat* (1996) and briefly appeared in the soap *Home And Away* (1997). He relocated to Los Angeles after *Roar*, another show he was in, was cancelled. "I went over there with no expectation and all the confidence of youth. I never let anything faze me or anyone look down on me." The first

film Ledger made in America was
10 Things I Hate About You (released
March 31, 1999), a remake of *The
Taming Of The Shrew*. One critic wrote,
"[Ledger is] equally comfortable laying
a dangerous loner or doing a goofy
song and dance to impress [Julia
Stiles's character]." He returned to
Australia to appear in *Two Hands*
(released July 29, 1999) playing a
bouncer in a strip club. Although the
film did not do well outside Australia,
the Australian Film Institute
nominated him for a Best Actor award
and was also nominated in the Film
Critics Circle of Australia Awards.
Ledger waited for a script he liked,
turning down those he felt lacked merit
and was duly forced to borrow money
from his agent to eat. "I'm happy
without money," he said. "I never did
have it, so that was no big deal. And it
was fun saying no – because they really
don't like hearing that word in
Hollywood." He auditioned for the
Mel Gibson film *The Patriot* (2000) but
walked out claiming that he was "giving
a bad reading". His agent wangled a
second invitation and Ledger was cast
as Gabriel Martin. The reviews for the
film were mixed but generally good for
Ledger who "emotes up a storm"
according to one. Some critics began
labelling Ledger "the next Russell
Crowe". Ledger's next film, *A Knight's
Tale* (2001), was also lambasted by the
critics. Ledger did not like the baggage
that came with stardom. "When I saw
the poster," he said of the publicity for
A Knight's Tale, "I was pretty freaked.
The film is an ensemble piece, and
there's just my great, big mug. I'm just
doing what I've always done – being an
actor. Now I'm being made into a
'star', a product, and it's out of my
control." He jumped at his next role in
Monster's Ball (released Boxing Day
2001) after his friend Wes Bentley
dropped out. The film won an Oscar
for the beautiful Halle Berry (b.
Cleveland, Ohio August 14, 1966) but
she was criticised by vocal black

journalists for taking the role. Ledger
then appeared in the fifth version of
E.W. Mason's 1902 novel about
cowardice in the British Army, *The
Four Feathers* (première September 17,
2002). His next two films, *Ned Kelly*
(2003) in which he played the
Australian bushranger and *The Order*
(2003) as Alex Bernier, flopped. He
then made a film about skateboarding
Lords Of Dogtown (2005) playing Skip
Engblom. He played Jacob Grimm in
Terry Gilliam's fictional *The Brothers
Grimm* (2005), in which the brothers
(Matt Damon played Wilhelm) were
portrayed as a pair of conmen. The
film was not a great success but Ledger
and Damon received praise from
critics. *Brokeback Mountain* (released
November 30, 2005) was an unlikely
tale of gay cowboys. Ledger played
ranch hand Ennis del Mar while Jake
Gyllenhaal was rodeo cowboy Jack
Twist and they meet on the fictional
Brokeback Mountain in Wyoming in
1963. They fall in love but when their
job ends they go their separate ways.
But the gay attraction is too much.
Ledger and Gyllenhaal were both
nominated for Best Actor Oscars for
their performances but lost out to
Philip Seymour Hoffman for *Capote*
(2005). After playing gay on screen
Ledger then turned his attentions to a
heterosexual lover (at least in films, if
not in reality) and took the lead role in
Casanova (2005). As with much of his
work, the film was derided but Ledger
was singled out for praise. In 2006
Ledger starred in another Australian
film, *Candy*. He played Robbie in *I'm
Not There* (2007) and then was cast as
The Joker in another Batman film
Christopher Nolan's *The Dark Knight*
(première July 14, 2008). Ledger saw
his character as a "psychopathic, mass
murdering, schizophrenic clown with
zero empathy". To ready himself for
the part, he revealed, "I sat around in a
hotel room in London for about a
month, locked myself away, formed a
little diary and experimented with

voices – it was important to try to find a somewhat iconic voice and laugh. I ended up landing more in the realm of a psychopath – someone with very little to no conscience towards his acts." By the time the film was released, Ledger was dead. 6'1" Ledger never married but he dated the beautiful 5'8" actress Heather Graham (b. Milwaukee, Wisconsin January 29, 1970) from October 2000 until June 2001. She called him the love of her life, adding, "Heath is a great guy . . . I feel really protective of him . . . He's an incredible, amazing person and I'm really lucky to know him." He had a relationship between 2002 and 2004 with Naomi Watts, whom he met on the set of *Ned Kelly*. In the summer of 2004 while filming *Brokeback Mountain* he began seeing Michelle Williams. Their daughter, Matilda Rose, was born in New York on October 28, 2005. The couple split up in 2007. CAUSE: In the late autumn of 2007 Ledger complained to a journalist that he could not sleep and had resorted to taking sleeping pills. In January 2008 he told the actor Christopher Plummer, his co-star in Ledger's last, uncompleted role in the film *The Imaginarium Of Doctor Parnassus* (2009) that he was having difficulty breathing and again mentioned his insomnia. Ex-girlfriend Michelle Williams said, "For as long as I'd known him, he had bouts with insomnia. He had too much energy. His mind was turning, turning, turning – always turning." At 2.45pm on January 22, 2008 Ledger was discovered unconscious in bed at his $24,000-a-month home, 4th Floor, 5A, 421 Broome Street, SoHo, New York, that he had been renting since September 2007, by his Filipina housekeeper, Teresa Carino Solomon (b. 1952), and his masseuse, Diana Lee Wolozin, who had arrived early for a 3pm appointment. At 3.10pm when Ledger had still not stirred, Miss Wolozin rang his mobile but it went through to voicemail. She went into the bedroom where Ledger was naked, laying face down at the foot of the bed. Ledger still did not move so the masseuse shook him. He was cold. Then she rang Ledger's friend, the actress Mary-Kate Olsen who was in Los Angeles. "Heath is unconscious, he's cold to the touch," she told Olsen who responded by saying, "I'm sending my private security there." A few moments later, Miss Wolozin rang Olsen again and said, "I think he may be dead, I'm calling 911." Olsen again insisted, "I already have people coming over." At 3.26pm Miss Wolozin finally rang the emergency services and was advised to try to perform cardiopulmonary resuscitation on the actor. At 3.33pm an ambulance arrived at the same time as the guard summoned by Olsen. The paramedics also performed cardiopulmonary resuscitation and used a defibrillator but it was hopeless and Ledger was pronounced dead at 3.26pm. He was 28-years-old. On February 6, 2008, the Office of the Chief Medical Examiner of New York released its conclusions: "Mr Heath Ledger died as the result of acute intoxication by the combined effects of oxycodone, hydrocodone, diazepam, temazepam, alprazolam and doxylamine. We have concluded that the manner of death is accident, resulting from the abuse of prescription medications. The medications found in the toxicological analysis are commonly prescribed in the United States for insomnia, anxiety, depression, pain, and/or common cold symptoms." A memorial service was held on February 9, 2008 and then Ledger's corpse was cremated at Fremantle Cemetery. His ashes were later interred in a family plot at Karrakatta Cemetery, Perth. On February 22, 2008 at the Kodak Theatre in Hollywood, Ledger posthumously won the Best Supporting Actor Oscar for *The Dark Knight*. Federal investigators interviewed everyone close to Ledger but one person would not speak to them. On August 4, 2008 Murray Weiss of the *New York Post* reported that Mary-Kate Olsen had "refused [through her lawyer, Michael C. Miller] to be interviewed by federal investigators probing the accidental drug death of her close friend Heath Ledger . . . [without] . . . immunity from prosecution." Mr Miller said that Olsen had no idea where the narcotics in Ledger's house had come from: "Despite tabloid speculation, Mary-Kate Olsen had nothing whatsoever to do with the drugs found in Heath Ledger's home or his body, and she does not know where he obtained them." Prosecutors issued a subpoena ordering her to testify before a Grand Jury but on August 6 the U.S. Attorney's Office in Manhattan closed its investigation without filing charges because prosecutors "don't believe there's a viable target". It is still not known where Ledger got the oxycodone and hydrocodone that killed him.

FURTHER READING: *Heath Ledger: His Beautiful Life and Mysterious Death* – John McShane (London: John Blake, 2008); *Heath: A Family's Tale* – Janet Fife-Yeomans (Millers Point: Pier 9, 2008).

Belinda Lee

Born June 15, 1935
Died March 12, 1961
Yet one more tragic beauty. The gorgeous blonde Belinda Lee was born in Budleigh Salterton, Devon, to hotelier Robert Esmond Lee and Stella Mary Graham. She was educated at Rookesbury Park Prep School in Fareham, Hampshire and St Margaret's in Exeter, Devon before attending the Tudor Arts Academy in Surrey and RADA where she was spotted and enrolled at the Rank Film School and groomed for stardom. She made her film début, *Murder By Proxy* (premièred in America on May 15, 1954 and in the UK on March 28, 1955), playing Phyllis Brunner. She also appeared in *Meet Mr Callaghan* (1954) as Jenny Appleby, *Life With The Lyons* (1954) as Violet Hemingway, *The Belles Of St Trinian's* (premièred October 1, 1954) as Amanda, *The Runaway Bus* (1954) as Janie Grey, *No Smoking* (1955) as Miss Tonkins, *Man Of The Moment* (1955) as Sonia, *The Big Money* (1956) as Gloria, *Dangerous Exile* (1957) as Virginia Traill, *The Feminine Touch* (1957) as Susan Richards, *The Secret Place* (premièred on February 6, 1957) as Molly Wilson and *Miracle In Soho* (premièred July 1957) as Julia Gozzi but, soon after, parts began to dry up for her and she was forced to resort to making sex films on continental Europe. Her later work included: *La Venere Di Cheronea* (1958) as Aphrodite, *Le Notti Di Lucrezia Borgia* (premièred March 19, 1959), *Il Mondo Di Notte* (1959), *I Magliari* (premièred September 23, 1959) as Paula Meyer often considered to be her best role, *Ce Corps Tant Désiré* (premièred April 17, 1959 after filming finished on October 23, 1958) as Lina, *Die Wahrheit Über Rosemarie* (premièred October 23, 1959) as Rosemarie, *Brevi Amori A Palma Di Majorca* (premièred December 2, 1959) as Mary Moore, *Marie Des Isles* (filmed between May 29 and September 7, 1959, premièred January 15, 1960) as Marie Bonnard, *Der Satan Lockt Mit Liebe* (premièred March 31, 1960), *Messalina Venere Imperatrice* (1960), *La Lunga Notte Del '43* (premièred September 13, 1960) as Anna Barilari, *Giuseppe Venduto Dai Fratelli* (1960) and the posthumously released *Fantasmi A Roma* (premièred April 1, 1961) as Eileen and *Costantino Il Grande* (1962) as Fausta. On June 5, 1954 she married the photographer Cornel Lucas (b. 1923). They divorced in June 1959 not long after she had an affair with the married society figure Prince Filippo Orsini whom she met while at a party in

Fregene, Italy. On January 25, 1958 she reportedly tried to kill herself with an overdose of barbiturates because the affair with Orsini was nearing its end. Rank claimed that the overdose was accidental. Belinda returned to Britain briefly but in March she rented a small villa in Tor Vaianica. On April 6 Belinda was deported from Italy. The Cannes Film Festival was held on May 2–18, 1958 and paparazzi were surprised to see Belinda and Orsini back together. In December 1958 Belinda left Rank and announced her intention to move to France. In January 1960 Belinda told reporters that she had ended the affair with Orsini. Two months later, they were back together again. In May of that year he sold his story to *France Dimanche* and then on May 26 to the Italian magazine *Oggi*. In October 1960 her new boyfriend, the playboy Gualtiero Jacopetti, was jailed for three months for seducing two underage girls. A German newspaper *Bild Zeitung* also claimed that he had seduced an 11-year-old Gypsy girl and married her to avoid a jail sentence. CAUSE: Belinda was killed aged 25 in a car crash near San Bernadino in California. The driver and two other passengers, her boyfriend Gualtiero Jacopetti and Paolo Cavara, survived. Belinda was sitting in the front passenger seat when a rear tyre burst, causing the car to somersault through the air. Belinda was flung through the windscreen landing face first 63 feet from the car. She died of a fractured skull and a broken neck. She was cremated on March 17 in Los Angeles but since no one wanted to claim her remains she lay uncollected for eight months. In November the *New York Journal-American* reported that Orsini had tried to collect her ashes but permission was refused because he was not a relative. On November 29 Belinda's remains were taken to Rome and buried in the English Cemetery there.

Bernard Lee

Born January 10, 1908
Died January 17, 1981
Forever M. Born in London, the son of an actor, Lee made his first stage appearance in *The Double Event* aged six at the Oxford Music Hall, London, in 1914 and later trained at RADA. Apart from army service from 1940 until 1945, he was a regular on the stage. He appeared in almost 100 films. However, to the public at large, he was probably best known for playing James Bond's no-nonsense boss, M, in 11 films. They were *Dr No* (1962), *From Russia With Love* (1963), *Goldfinger* (1964), *Thunderball* (1965), *You Only Live Twice* (1967), *On Her Majesty's Secret Service* (1969), *Diamonds Are Forever* (1971), *Live And Let Die* (1973), *The Man With The Golden Gun* (1974), *The Spy Who Loved Me* (1977) and *Moonraker* (1979).
CAUSE: He died in London from cancer a week after his 73rd birthday.

Brandon Lee

Born February 1, 1965
Died March 31, 1993
Dashed hopes for the future. The son of Bruce Lee, 5'11" Brandon Bruce Lee was born in Oakland, California, but raised in Hong Kong. Like his father, he was a keen student of martial arts. Brandon was expelled from school for bad behaviour. His first film was *Long Zai Jiang Hu* (1986), by which time he seemed to have put his youthful misdemeanours behind him. He appeared in a couple of *Kung Fu* television movies in 1986 and 1987 but then did not make a film for three years. He appeared as Michael Gold in *Laser Mission* (1990) and then went on to make *Showdown In Little Tokyo* (1991) as Johnny Murata and *Rapid Fire* (1992) as Jake Lo before making the fateful decision to appear as Eric Draven in a film called *The Crow* (1994). Speaking not long before his tragic death, Brandon said, "Because we do not know when we will die, we

come to think of life as an inexhaustible well, everything happens only a certain number of times, and a very small number really. How many times will you remember a certain afternoon of your childhood, an afternoon that is so deeply a part of your being that you can't even conceive of your life without it? Perhaps four, five times more. Perhaps not even that. How many more times will you watch the full moon rise? Perhaps twenty. And yet it all seems limitless."

CAUSE: Brandon Lee allegedly believed that all the males in his family were cursed because his grandfather had annoyed some Chinese merchants. Stories circulated that he was so obsessed with death that he took to driving around Los Angeles in a hearse. He is said to have told friends that he would not live to see his 30th birthday. *The Crow* was shot with a partially non-union crew on Stage 4 of Carolco (now Screen Gems) Studios, 1223 North 23rd Street, Wilmington, North Carolina. The film set had already had its fair share of mishaps. One crew member was badly burned by a live electrical wire; a grip had a blackout while driving and drove a car through the studio's plaster workshop and a carpenter accidentally drove a screwdriver through his hand. On another occasion an actor checked a gun that should have been loaded with blanks and found a live round inside the chamber. On the late evening of March 30, 1993, the 50th day of a 58-day shoot, Lee began to prepare to film a scene in which his character is shot repeatedly. Daniel Kuttner, the prop man, filled the pistol to be used with blanks. His fatal mistake was in not checking the gun barrel for blockages. It was not long past midnight when the director called for action. The film was about a vengeful character and this scene was to show how he and his girlfriend had been killed. The rehearsal went well and the cameras began to roll. Drug dealers, one played by Michael Massee, break into Eric Draven's apartment and discover Draven's girlfriend. Taking a shine to her, he decides to rape her. Draven comes back into the flat carrying a bag of shopping and sees what is going on. At this point, the drug dealer shoots him. The shopping bag contained a small explosive that would simulate gunfire. Massee was standing about a dozen feet from Brandon Lee when he fired the gun containing the blanks and Lee activated the charge in the shopping. Almost immediately, he collapsed to the floor bleeding heavily on his right side. Filming continued as Lee tried to signal he needed help, the crew, all the while, marvelling at Lee's excellent 'performance'. Finally, he managed to call out "Cut, cut, somebody please say cut . . .". The director called "Cut" but Lee lay where he had fallen. Initially, the crew thought Lee was having them on until Michael Massee noticed something was horribly wrong. An ambulance was called while studio hands attempted to comfort him. The distraught actor was taken to New Hanover Regional Medical Center, 2131 South 17th Street where he underwent a six-hour operation led by Warren W. McMurry and was given 60 pints of blood. His heart had twice stopped beating: once in the studio and once in the ambulance on the way to hospital. McMurry revealed that Lee "suffered intestinal injuries and major vascular injuries consistent with a bullet wound". A fragment of bullet was lodged in Lee's spine. Lee's girlfriend, writer Eliza Hutton, whom he was due to marry on April 17 after the film wrapped, arrived at the hospital around noon. One hour and three minutes later, Brandon Lee died of his injuries. He was 28. On April 3 he was buried in Lake View Cemetery, Seattle, Washington, next to his father. *The Crow* was released in the United Kingdom on June 10, 1994. Critic James Cameron-Wilson described it as "a despicable pile of junk, a chaotic, noisy shambles that barely resembles a film."

Bruce Lee

(LEE JUN FAN)
Born November 27, 1940
Died July 20, 1973
Martial artiste. Born in San Francisco's Chinese Hospital, California, the son of actor Lee Hoi Chuen (b. February 1901, d. February 8, 1965) 5'7" Lee was raised in Hong Kong where he was cha cha champion in 1958. Hyperactive as a child, his family nicknamed him "Never sits still". He was born in the Year of the Dragon and began appearing in bit parts in Hong Kong movies from an early age. His movies included: *Fu Gui Fu Yun* (1948), *Xi Lu Xiang* (1950), *Wei Lou Chun Xiao* (1953), *Qian Wan Ren Jia* (1953), *Ku Hai Ming Deng* (1953), *Fu Zhi Guo* (1953), *Zao Zhi Dang Cu Wo Bu Jia* (1956), *Zha Dian Na Fu* (1956) and *Ren Hai Gu Hong* (1960). He travelled to America and was cast as Kato in the television series *The Green Hornet*, which aired from September 9, 1966, until July 14, 1967. Back in Hong Kong he continued to make films such as *Tang Shan Da Xiong* (1971) as Cheng Chao-an, *Jing Wu Men* (1972) as Chen Zhen and *Meng Long Guojiang* (1972) as Tang Lung but it was when he made *Enter The Dragon* (1973) as Lee that he became an international star. He married Linda in August 1964 and they had two children: Brandon and Shannon.
CAUSE: Lee lived in Kowloon, Hong Kong, in an 11-room mansion, with his family. On May 10, 1973, he collapsed while filming in Los Angeles but tests at the hospital showed him to be in fine fettle. On the last day of his life his wife left him in his beloved study at home while she went to lunch with a girlfriend. He later went to a business meeting, where he collapsed. Rushed to hospital, he died officially of a cerebral edema. However,

rumours have long circulated about his death. One theory has it that he was murdered by martial artists furious that he had revealed their secret arts to the West. He was buried in Lake View Cemetery, Seattle, Washington. His gravestone reads: "In memory of a once fluid man crammed and distorted by the classical mess."
FURTHER READING: *The Life And Tragic Death Of Bruce Lee* – Linda Lee (London: Star Books, 1975).

Jack Lee

Born January 27, 1913
Died October 15, 2002
Warring director. The reputation of Jack Lee rests on two excellent Second World War films that he made: *The Wooden Horse* (1950) and *A Town Like Alice* (1956). Wilfred Jack Raymond Lee was born in Slad, Gloucestershire. His father abandoned the family in 1918 leaving Lee's mother to raise him, his three brothers, three half-sisters and half-brother. One of his brothers was the best-selling novelist Laurie Lee, MBE (b. Slad, Gloucestershire June 26, 1914, d. May 14, 1997) and the story of their childhood was told in his book *Cider With Rosie* (1959). Jack Lee was reportedly furious with his brother for revealing their childhood poverty. The two brothers later became totally estranged. Jack (but not Laurie) went to Marling Grammar School in Stroud. After leaving he worked in a plastics factory and rose to the position of junior manager. Unhappy, he left to take a course in photography at the Regent Street Polytechnic. In 1938 he joined John Grierson's GPO Film Unit as an associate producer. He hired Laurie to write scripts. The GPO Film Unit was later merged with the Crown Film Unit and made films for the Ministry of Information during the Second World War. Jack Lee edited the propaganda film *London Can Take It* (1940) which included actual Blitz footage. His favourite film, he later

said, was *Children On Trial* (1945), a study in juvenile delinquency. His first feature-length film was *The Woman In The Hall* (1947), about a female who earned money by writing begging letters to wealthy people. It starred Jean Simmons as Joy Blake and Susan Hampshire as the young Joy. His next film was *Once A Jolly Swagman* (1948) about speedway and starred Dirk Bogarde as Bill Fox. Bogarde was told to take his motorbike home every night, stand it in his bedroom and "love it like a woman" – no easy task for the homosexually inclined actor. In 1948 Lee married Nora Dawson and fathered two sons by her. Two years later, he made *The Wooden Horse* about a group of POWs who escaped from the Germans in Stalag Luft III by digging a tunnel under a vaulting horse. It starred Leo Genn, David Tomlinson and Anthony Steel. However, Lee disagreed with Ian Dalrymple, the producer, on how the film should end and left the production. Dalrymple finished the film himself. Despite the film's success Lee was unemployed for a year afterwards. Six years later, he was back working the Second World War milieu. *A Town Like Alice* was based on Nevil Shute's 1950 book about women and children escaping in Malaysia after their men had been captured by the Japanese. The film won BAFTAs for Virginia McKenna and Peter Finch. Lee's last film was *Circle Of Deception* (1960). In 1963 following the dissolution of his first marriage he married Isabel Kidman (a distant cousin of the actress Nicole Kidman) and settled in Australia. He became chairman of the South Australia Film Commission and helped to launch the careers of, among others, Bruce Beresford and Peter Weir. An attempt to reconcile with brother Laurie was rebuffed and the two men were totally estranged at Laurie's death.
CAUSE: Lee died aged 89 in Sydney, New South Wales, from natural causes.

Alison Leggatt
Born February 7, 1904
Died July 15, 1990
Sturdy stalwart. Born in Kensington, London, 5'5½" Alison Joy Leggatt never really reached stardom but nor did she ever really reach the unemployment queue. In 1924 she was awarded the prestigious Gold Medal at the Central School of Dramatic Art and that year made her stage début. She appeared regularly with Noël Coward and was featured in, among others, the following films: *Nine Till Six* (1932) as Freda, *Waterloo Road* (1944) as Ruby, *This Happy Breed* (1944) as Aunt Sylvia, *Here Come The Huggetts* (1948) as Miss Perks, *Marry Me* (1949) as Miss Beamish, *The Day Of The Triffids* (1962) as Miss Coker, *One Way Pendulum* (1965) as Mrs Groomkirby, *Far From The Madding Crowd* (1967) as Mrs Hurst, *Goodbye, Mr Chips* (1969) as the Headmaster's Wife and *The Seven-Per-Cent Solution* (1976) as Mrs Hudson. She was married to Lieutenant-Commander Shene Clark, R.N. but it ended in divorce.
CAUSE: She died in London of natural causes aged 86.

Janet Leigh
(JEANETTE HELEN MORRISON)
Born July 6, 1927
Died October 3, 2004
Scream queen. Although she made 63 films it was her role as Marion Crane, the office worker who became the murder victim of Norman Bates (Tony Perkins) in Alfred Hitchcock's *Psycho* (released on June 17, 1960) for which she is famous. She earned an Oscar nomination as Best Supporting Actress, a Golden Globe, a Golden Apple award as Hollywood's most co-operative actress and a place in cinematic history. "I thought it was cleverly done," Leigh said. "We weren't allowed to show nudity or a knife entering a body but most people believe they saw it. They did in their imaginations. Having restrictions like

that, I think, was good because it forced film-makers to be more creative." The 45-second killing was voted best screen death by *Total Film* magazine in 2004. Born in Merced, California, the only child of Fred Morrison (b. 1910, d. August 12, 1962), an insurance and real estate agent, and Helen Lita Westergaard, who moved frequently. She was a bright, but troubled teenager, eloping to Reno, Nevada, and marrying when she was just 14 in 1942 to Kenny Carlyle. The marriage was annulled but not before it was consummated. She left high school at 15, and in September 1943 went on to the College of Pacific, where she majored in Music. On October 5, 1945 she married Stanley Reames but the marriage ended in divorce in July 1948. In February 1946 she was discovered by the actress Norma Shearer (who had retired from MGM in 1942), who spotted Leigh's picture at the front desk of a ski lodge near Reno, Nevada where Fred Morrison was reception manager and his wife a maid. Shearer – the widow of boy genius Irving Thalberg – was highly regarded at MGM, and her recommendation opened doors for 5′5″ Leigh and ensured her a seven year contract and careful grooming through a series of inconsequential romantic comedies designed to appeal to impressionable teens. As Leigh herself said of MGM, "They used to keep about 150 people under contract, and if they got one or two out of the 150 that would be great, because they were only paying them $50 a week." The name Janet Leigh was coined by Van Johnson, also an MGM hopeful at that time. Leigh made her first movie, playing Lissy Anne MacBean in the post-Civil War drama *The Romance Of Rosy Ridge*, in 1947 and was soon fêted for her classic beauty and hour-glass figure. She quickly became one of Hollywood's most sought-after actresses averaging around four films a year. Among her

personal favourites was the 1949 classic *That Forsyte Woman* (in which she played June Forsyte and Errol Flynn was Soames), set in the Victorian era, and *Little Women* (premièred on March 10, 1949) in which she played Meg March. "They were such beautiful pictures," Leigh said in a newspaper interview the year she died. "They were just pretty to look at and wonderful escapism. Somehow the studios weren't afraid to make beautiful pictures then." In 1948 she made the Rodgers & Hart biopic *Words And Music* playing Dorothy Feiner Rodgers. Her early Fifties films are forgotten and she did not really come into her own until her marriage to Tony Curtis (b. The Bronx, New York, June 3, 1925 as Bernard Schwartz) on June 4, 1951 in Greenwich, Connecticut. They were the Tom Cruise and Nicole Kidman of their day. They had two daughters: Kelly (b. Santa Monica, June 17, 1956 at 2.14pm) and Jamie Lee (b. Los Angeles, November 22, 1958 at 8.37am). Her movies included *Two Tickets To Broadway* (1951), and the Rafael Sabatini costume epic *Scaramouche* (1952). After her marriage to Curtis, MGM loaned her to Paramount for *Houdini* (1953), their first film together. It was a box office hit, paving the way in 1954 for another costume epic, *The Black Shield Of Falworth*. In 1958, Leigh and Curtis made a third film together, *The Vikings*, which attracted a certain notoriety thanks to the scene in which Curtis removed her Saxon tunic to enable her to row more comfortably. They never made a modern-themed film together. Asked once to describe herself, Leigh said she was "a small-town girl who got lucky and worked hard to learn and improve whatever God had given me". There was a darker side to her, however, and she characterised herself as "mild-mannered until crossed, then ballistic". Josef von Sternberg's *Jet Pilot* (1957) probably marked the breakthrough that might have happened earlier, had it been released when originally made in 1950. One of Howard Hughes' aviation adventures, it was held back for years on his personal whim. In the end, history had overtaken it, and the action scenes that would have looked impressive seven years earlier no longer appeared so. What did work, however, was the humorous badinage between John Wayne and Leigh as Lieutenant Anna Marladovna, a Russian jet ace. It was after seeing her in this film that Orson Welles cast her as Susie Vargas in *Touch Of Evil* (released on April 2, 1958), the last work that Welles was able to finish in America. She played Charlton Heston's wife, kidnapped in a Mexican border town and threatened by Mercedes McCambridge's butch gangster's moll. Despite being set in Mexico it was shot on location in a seedy part of Venice, California. Leigh remembered, "We shot all night long, which I hated. It was a terrible place to work, but also fascinating because we worked in actual derelict hotels." She also worked throughout the film with a broken arm, having suffered an accident shortly before shooting began. "I had my arm set in an unobtrusive way, and I'd have a coat over it and gesture a lot with my other arm." *Psycho* began filming on November 30, 1959 and Leigh was paid $25,000 which worked out at more than $1,000 per minute of screen time that her character was alive. Having stolen $40,000 from her boss, she stays at the Bates Motel but has a change of heart and decides to return her ill-gotten gains. Before she can do so, she is stabbed to death in the shower by the Oedipus complex-suffering Norman Bates. Hitchcock shot the shower sequence in fragments, 71 in all, each lasting between two and three seconds; but such a scene required a huge number of takes – far more than appear in the finished film – to give the editor enough material to work with. In all, it took seven days to shoot, but there is no truth in the rumours that Janet Leigh was naked throughout. In fact, she wore a flesh-coloured moleskin. She later recalled the experience matter-of-factly: "Hitchcock followed the storyboard precisely. We worked on it for about a week, but it went very professionally and quickly. It was, of course, gruelling to stand in a shower getting drenched for a week." It put her off showers for life. There was trouble with censors who claimed they could see 36C-21-36 Leigh's nipple in one shot. Hitchcock took the film back, changed nothing, resubmitted it and the censors were happy. In fact, the hot water did loosen the moleskin and a nipple was exposed. Hitchcock whipped up anticipation by banning press previews and stipulated that no one should be allowed into the cinema after the film had started. He deferred his $250,000 salary and agreed to keep the film within budget, shooting in black and white, which facilitated the use of chocolate sauce in the murder scene. Filming ended on February 1, 1960, and only *Ben-Hur* did better at North American cinemas in that year. Leigh had a cameo role as Eugenie Rose Chaney in the Cold War thriller *The Manchurian Candidate* (opened on October 24, 1962), directed by John Frankenheimer. None of her subsequent films matched the quality of her earlier work. *Night Of The Lepus* (1972), a straight-faced horror-thriller in which America is terrorised by giant rabbits, did little to revive her career. She considered retiring after working with her daughter Jamie Lee in the John Carpenter horror flick *The Fog* (1979). She was reunited with her daughter on screen in 1998 in *Halloween H20*. On September 15, 1962 following her divorce from Tony Curtis on July 11 of that year, she married her fourth husband Robert Brandt, a stockbroker.

CAUSE: Janet Leigh died of vasculitis, inflammation of the blood vessels, an ailment she had battled for a year, surrounded by her family including her husband Robert Brandt and actress-daughters Jamie Lee and Kelly Curtis. She was 77.

FURTHER READING: *There Really Was A Hollywood* – Janet Leigh (New York: Jove, 1985).

Vivien Leigh

(VIVIAN MARY HARTLEY)
Born November 5, 1913
Died July 7, 1967
Limited but beautiful actress. Born in Shannon Lodge, Darjeeling, India, within sight of Mount Everest, one of her fellow boarders at a Catholic school was Maureen O'Sullivan. Both women became successful actresses but Leigh was to have the higher profile. In February 1932 she enrolled at RADA. On a brisk February day in the same year Vivien was waved at by an elegant man on horseback in the Devon village of Holcombe. He was Herbert Leigh Holman, a 31-year-old, Cambridge-educated barrister who bore more than a passing resemblance to Leslie Howard. Vivien decided then and there she would marry him, even though he was engaged at the time to another girl. On December 20, 1932, the determined Vivien got her wish and married Leigh Holman at St James's, Spanish Place, London, and lost her virginity to him that night. Budapest-born film director Sir Alexander Korda was the undisputed king of British film in the Thirties. Among his successes were *The Private Life Of Henry VIII* (1933) with Charles Laughton, Binnie Barnes, Robert Donat, Elsa Lanchester and Merle Oberon and *The Scarlet Pimpernel* (1935) with Leslie Howard, Merle Oberon, Raymond Massey and Nigel Bruce. Korda asked to see Vivien Leigh with a view to offering her a movie contract. The interview at Isleworth Film Studios did not go well. Korda left the actress cooling her heels outside while he dealt with others. It was obvious from the start that Leigh did not particularly impress him. He thought there was nothing to single her out from numerous other beauties he already had in his stable, including his wife Merle Oberon, Wendy Barrie and Diana Napier. Unsurprisingly, Leigh was disappointed but knuckled down to learn her trade. She appeared in two films and a critically acclaimed play before, on May 15, 1935, at the Ambassador's Theatre, Korda watched Leigh in *The Mask Of Virtue* and witnessed an exquisite performance. After the show he went backstage and congratulated the star. "Even a Hungarian can make a mistake," he said. Five years after making her film début in *Things Are Looking Up* (1934), Leigh became world famous in 1939 when she played the role of southern belle Scarlett O'Hara in the movie version of Margaret Mitchell's epic Civil War novel *Gone With The Wind*. Her performance garnered Leigh her first Best Actress Oscar and numerous plaudits from around the globe. Look out for the following bloopers in the famous film. When Scarlett and Melanie (Leigh and Olivia De Havilland) are looking after the wounded, their shadows on the wall behind them do not match their movements. In the scene in Tara's cotton patch, Scarlett slaps her sister, Suellen (Evelyn Keyes), and is then admonished by their father, Gerald O'Hara (Thomas Mitchell), for telling off the servants but no such ticking off is in the film; it was cut before release. After the night of passion with Rhett Butler (Clark Gable) Scarlett lies in bed reliving the fun they had. In comes Mammy (Hattie McDaniel) and takes away a tray containing a silver service – but where did it come from? If they didn't know that the tray had been brought in by Scarlett's daughter (and how could they when that scene had been cut?) audiences were left wondering whether Rhett's seduction techniques included a midnight feast. When Scarlett flees Atlanta she is

bareheaded but as she and Rhett ride through the depot she is wearing a black bonnet. In the next scene on the road to Tara the bonnet disappears. George Reeves (later to become famous as Superman and to die under very mysterious circumstances) played Stuart Tarleton, one of Scarlett's beaux. Curiously, on the credits he is listed as Brent Tarleton. Leigh and her first husband were divorced on August 26, 1940. Five days later, in Santa Barbara, Leigh married acting legend Laurence Olivier. Despite the marriage and a second Academy Award for *A Streetcar Named Desire* (1951) playing Blanche Dubois, Leigh wasn't a particularly well or satisfied woman. She had bouts of tuberculosis and alcoholism and in 1953 showed the first symptoms of what were euphemistically termed 'mental' problems, plus she was a manic depressive. She became a schizophrenic suffering a persecution complex making her 'an instant enemy of everyone'. One of the symptoms of her mental disorder was an irresistible urge to utter obscenities. The tuberculosis heightened Leigh's sex drive dramatically, resulting in her asking friends to arrange anonymous bouts of sex with strangers. Most of her friends demurred. An affair with Peter Finch followed, but the marriage to Olivier was over ("Which one of you is coming to bed with me?" she once asked the two men). In his autobiography Olivier recounted attempts "to try fucking our love back into existence", but without success. They divorced in 1960. She spent her final years with actor John Merrivale. She invented a party game called "Ways to Kill a Baby", whereby players had to invent bizarre methods of slaughtering infants. Her films included: *Look Up And Laugh* (1935) as Marjorie Belfer, *Fire Over England* (1937) as Cynthia, *Storm In A Teacup* (1937) as Victoria Gow, *A Yank At Oxford* (1938) as Elsa Craddock, *Waterloo Bridge* (1940) as Myra,

21 Days (1940) as Wanda, *That Hamilton Woman* (1941) as Emma, Lady Hamilton, *Caesar And Cleopatra* (1946) as Cleopatra, *Anna Karenina* (1948) as Anna Karenina, *The Deep Blue Sea* (1955) as Hester Collyer, *The Roman Spring Of Mrs Stone* (1961) as Karen Stone and *Ship Of Fools* (1965) as Mary Treadwell. Despite being regarded as one of the most beautiful women in the world she did not have a high opinion of herself: "My neck's too long, my hands too big and my voice too small," she once wailed.
CAUSE: She died at 54 Eaton Square, London SW1, of tuberculosis. She was 53. Despite her Catholic upbringing she was cremated and her ashes scattered at her country home Tickerage Mill, Uckfield, Sussex, a five-bedroomed Queen Anne mill house that had once belonged to Lord Snowdon's father. She left £252,681.
FURTHER READING: *Light Of A Star* – Gwen Robyns (London: Leslie Frewin, 1968); *Vivien Leigh: A Biography* – Anne Edwards (London: Coronet, 1982); *Vivien: The Life Of Vivien Leigh* – Alexander Walker (London: Weidenfeld & Nicolson, 1987); *Vivien Leigh* – Hugo Vickers (London: Hamish Hamilton, 1988).

Margaret Leighton, CBE
Born February 26, 1922
Died January 13, 1976
'First Lady of the British Stage'. She began life in Barnt Green, Worcestershire, and throughout her career was best at playing "fragile, sensitive and highly vulnerable women". She made her stage début at Birmingham Repertory Theatre on September 4, 1938, playing Dorothy in *Laugh With Me*. It would be the start of a glittering stage career that saw her win a Tony for her performance in *Night Of The Iguana* (1962). Her first film was Terence Rattigan's *The Winslow Boy* (1948) playing Catherine Winslow. Her subsequent film work included: *Bonnie Prince Charlie* (1948)

as Flora MacDonald, *Under Capricorn* (1949) as Milly, *The Elusive Pimpernel* (1951) as Marguerite Blakeney, *Calling Bulldog Drummond* (1951) as Sergeant Helen Smith, *Carrington, V.C.* (1955) as Valerie Carrington, *The Sound And The Fury* (1959) as Caddy Compson, *Waltz Of The Toreadors* (1962) as Emily Fitzjohn, *7 Women* (1966) as Agatha Andrews, *The Madwoman Of Chaillot* (1969) as Constance, The Madwoman Of Passy, *The Go-Between* (1971) as Mrs Maudsley, for which she was nominated for a Best Supporting Actress Oscar, *Lady Caroline Lamb* (1972) as Lady Melbourne, *A Bequest To The Nation* (1973) as Lady Frances Nelson and *Dirty Knight's Work* (1976) as Ma Gore. She was married three times: her first husband (1947) was publisher Max Reinhardt, but that ended (on January 28, 1955) when he discovered her affair with Laurence Harvey who became her second husband in August 1957. They divorced on November 11, 1960, when he left her for Harry Cohn's widow, Joan. Her final husband (in Los Angeles on July 15, 1964) was the 2nd Mr Elizabeth Taylor, Michael Wilding.
CAUSE: She died aged 53 from multiple sclerosis in Chichester, Sussex.

Christabel Leighton-Porter
Born April 11, 1913
Died December 6, 2000
Wartime heroine. Born in Eastleigh, Hampshire, Christabel Leighton-Porter's fame rests on her portrayal of the *Daily Mirror* cartoon strip heroine Jane in *The Adventures Of Jane* (1949). Artist Norman Petts hired Christabel four times a week to pose for him. "I was starkers so often that Norman said that he would like me there all the time to decorate the place," she laughed. On September 29, 1944, Jane appeared nude for the first time and legend has it the British 36th Division advanced six miles that day. Jane first appeared in the *Daily Mirror*

on December 5, 1932 and the strip ran until October 10, 1959.
CAUSE: She died aged 87 of cancer in London.

Jack Lemmon
Born February 8, 1925
Died June 27, 2001
Mr Nice Guy. Born, monorchid, in a hospital lift in Boston, Massachusetts, because his father (some sources say that it was his mother Mildred) did not want to leave a game of bridge and so was late getting to the hospital, John Ulhler Lemmon III also was born suffering from jaundice. The nurse remarked that he was a yellow Lemmon. The new arrival was the son of the vice-president of the American Doughnut Corporation. Lemmon became the cinematic "everyman" of the twentieth century. Although he is best remembered for his comedic roles, he disliked being thought of as just a comedy actor. He was a total professional and conscientious to the point of obsession. Lemmon had little time for the material trappings of fame, and was always generous to fellow actors. He deflected praise whenever possible, "That thing of Jack Lemmon, Nice Guy, has been passed down over the years," he said. "It makes me wonder. Is everybody else a jerk?" Lemmon had long-running relationships with Walter Matthau, both on and off screen, and Billy Wilder, which lasted for seven films. A man who did not suffer actors' vanities gladly, Wilder once said: "Happiness is working with Jack Lemmon." Lemmon's first experience of acting came when he was nine and the lead in a school play fell ill. Lemmon took over the role and the costume which was far too big for him. He also didn't know the lines so he would walk to the side of the stage for a teacher to whisper the lines to him. Each time he did this the audience laughed. "After that I never wanted to do anything else," he said. At Harvard he just about earned a

degree in war material management.
During the Second World War
Lemmon served in the navy and after
demob became an actor in preference
to joining his father's company. A
self-taught pianist, he played in a New
York beer hall before landing jobs in
radio and television. After appearing in
his first Broadway play, *Room Service*,
in 1953 he was spotted by a Hollywood
talent scout and signed to Columbia
Pictures. Harry Cohn later described
Lemmon as "the nicest actor we've
ever had on the lot" but was at first
unsure of him. He insisted that
Lemmon change his name lest he
provide ammunition for critics.
Lemmon refused, pointing to Walter
Pidgeon and Cohn relented. Lemmon
made his film début opposite the
comedienne Judy Holliday in *It Should
Happen To You* (1954). He won an
Oscar for Best Supporting Actor in the
naval comedy *Mister Roberts* (1955),
which also starred Henry Fonda and
James Cagney. His first venture with
Billy Wilder saw Lemmon "running
around in drag for about 80 per cent of
the film". Lemmon immediately signed
to make *Some Like It Hot* when offered
the role and the film was a smash. The
following year, in *The Apartment*, 5'9"
Lemmon starred opposite Shirley
MacLaine and consolidated his
position as one of America's leading
actors. His choices were not always
spot on, however. Lemmon turned
down the roles that went to Paul
Newman in both *The Hustler* (1961)
and *Butch Cassidy And The Sundance
Kid* (1969). The year before he teamed
up with his friend Walter Matthau to
make *The Odd Couple*, Neil Simon's
comedy about two divorced men trying
to live together. Matthau was the messy
Oscar Madison, Lemmon the fussy
Felix Unger, though Matthau always
felt that the roles should have been
reversed. "I'd be remiss," Lemmon
said, "if I didn't mention my favourite
leading lady. Without a doubt, it's
Walter Matthau. He leads the pack by

a country mile." In 1971 Lemmon
directed his only film *Kotch*, a warm
and sentimental study of a grandfather,
played by Matthau. Two years later,
Lemmon's performance in *Save The
Tiger* won him a second Oscar – this
time for Best Actor. He regarded it
as the most fulfilling performance of
his career although he commented,
"People come up to me and say,
'You're so natural; thank God you
don't act.' I feel like hitting them,
because I knock myself out trying to be
natural." Lemmon called himself the
luckiest man on earth. "The average
actor can't make a living at acting:
he has to take some other job. So
I'm a lucky guy." He renewed his
relationship with Matthau in *Grumpy
Old Men* (1993), the flop *Grumpier Old
Men* (1995) and *The Odd Couple II*
(1998). He also was in Oliver Stone's
JFK (1991), Robert Altman's *The
Player* (1992) and *Short Cuts* (1993).
Lemmon married the actress Cynthia
Boyd Stone in Peoria, Illinois, on
May 7, 1950 and they had one son, the
actor Chris Lemmon (b. Los Angeles,
California, January 22, 1954), before
their divorce in 1956. On August 17,
1962, he married Felicia Farr (b.
Westchester County, New York,
October 4, 1932). They had a daughter,
Courtney (b. January 7, 1966).
CAUSE: He died in Los Angeles,
California, aged 76, from cancer. He is
buried in Westwood Village Memorial
Park, 1218 Glendon Avenue, Los
Angeles 90024.

John Lennon
Born October 9, 1940
Died December 8, 1980
The Head Beatle. Probably more
myths have grown up around John
Lennon than almost any other
musician with the exception of Elvis
Presley. John Winston (later Ono)
Lennon was born at Oxford Street
Maternity Hospital, Liverpool, at
6.30pm on October 9, 1940. He was
raised by his Aunt Mimi when his

mother, Julia (b. March 12, 1914, k. Menlove Avenue, Liverpool, July 15, 1958), found herself not up to the task and his father, Fred (b. 57 Copperfield Street, Toxteth Park, December 14, 1912, d. Brighton General Hospital, April 1, 1976), did a bunk when John was 16 months old. John attended Quarry Bank High School in Liverpool and failed all his O Levels. He met Paul McCartney at Woolton Parish Church Fete on July 6, 1957, and they formed a skiffle group called The Quarry Men. George Harrison was to join the ensemble later and following the death of Stuart Sutcliffe, the sacking of Pete Best and his replacement by Ringo Starr, the luckiest man in pop music, the group settled as The Beatles (named for Lennon's admiration of Buddy Holly, being a pun on The Crickets). The Beatles became the most successful pop group of all time with 17 number one hits in the UK and 20 in the USA. Yet many were initially uncertain about their possible longevity and talent. In 1960, when The Beatles were due to travel to Hamburg, their original booking agent, Allan Williams, received a telegram, from the leader of the group Howie Casey & The Seniors asking for another band: "Don't send them. They're so bad, they'll spoil it for others." In 1961 Williams told John Lennon after they had a disagreement, "You'll never work again." After seeing the future Fab Four perform at the Cavern, Brian Epstein commented, "I want to manage those four boys. It wouldn't take me more than two half-days a week." Having found out that it would take considerably more of his time, Epstein travelled to London to try and obtain a major record deal for his group. On December 18, 1961, EMI Records said, "Whilst we appreciate the talents of this group we feel that we have sufficient groups of this type at the present time under contract and that it would not be advisable for us to sign any further contracts of this nature at present."

Decca Records was equally blunt. After the group auditioned for the company on New Year's Day, 1962, Brian Epstein was later told by Dick Rowe, "Not to mince words, Mr Epstein, we don't like your boys' sound. Groups are out; four-piece groups with guitars particularly are finished." Even Epstein's mother, Queenie, said to Geoffrey Ellis, one of Brian's friends, "You know, Geoffrey, Brian said to me that the Beatles were going to be bigger than Elvis Presley. Isn't it ridiculous? But we've got to let him get it out of his system." On September 15, 1962, the band was interviewed by Peter Jones of the *Daily Mirror* who concluded, "They're a nothing group." On the eve of the group's first tour of the States, Alan Livingstone, head of Capitol Records, said, "We don't think the Beatles will do anything in this market" and went on to reject the group twice more before bowing to the inevitable and releasing 'I Want To Hold Your Hand'. A story has it that Liverpudlian comedian Arthur Askey met the group before they became famous in a recording studio in Liverpool when they were recording a demo and said, "You're not bad, you know. What's your name?" One of them replied, "The Beatles." "My God," said Askey. "You'll never get anywhere with a name like that." Another source reports the incident as happening after a concert which seems more likely as the only time they recorded a demo tape in Liverpool they were calling themselves The Quarry Men. Composer Henry Mancini stated, "The Beatles will never last" and even Prince Philip got in on the act in 1964 when he declared, "The Beatles are on the wane." In February 1964 Brian Epstein was inundated with offers of endorsements and among them were ideas for Beatles wigs, T-shirts, toys, chewing gum, posters and pillowcases. Epstein met with Nicky Byrne of Seltaeb (Beatles spelled backwards), an American firm, and arranged a bizarre contract in which he surrendered nine-tenths of the rights. When the first royalty cheque came in, Byrne gave Epstein a cheque for $9,700. "I suppose I owe you 90% of this," said Epstein before Byrne explained he had already taken his cut – $87,300. It is believed that Epstein's blunder cost the group over £50 million. In an interview with Maureen Cleave published on March 4, 1966, in the *Evening Standard* Lennon declared, "Christianity will go. It will vanish and shrink. I needn't argue with that; I'm right and I will be proved right. We're more popular than Jesus now. I don't know which will go first – rock'n'roll or Christianity. Jesus was all right but his disciples were thick and ordinary. It's them twisting it that ruins it for me." Britain took the remark from the most outspoken of the Fab Four in its stride but when it was reprinted in America in the teenage magazine *Datebook* in July 1966 there was outrage. Radio stations in the Deep South were inundated with complaints from religious zealots and 35 stations banned the group's records. Grand Wizards of the Ku Klux Klan even organised burnings of Beatles records. One angry town put signs reading "Place Beatle Trash Here" on their litter bins. A damage limitation operation was put into action. Despite being ill, Brian Epstein flew from Portmeirion in North Wales, where he was convalescing, to New York on August 6, in the hope of salvaging the forthcoming major tour. Before holding a press conference Epstein rang Lennon at his home in Weybridge, Surrey, to say that the only way to save the tour was for him (Lennon) to apologise. The Beatle's reply was typical. "Tell them to get stuffed. I've got nothing to apologise for. Cancel the tour. I'd rather that than to have to get up and lie. What I said stands." Epstein's press conference went ahead but it did not satisfy either the American media or people. It was left to John to try and salvage the tour. Arriving in the USA on August 11, a

deeply unhappy Lennon, realising the enormity of his remarks, met with the press press that evening in a Chicago hotel room. He declared, "If I had said television is more popular than Jesus I might have got away with it. But I just happened to be talking to a friend and I used the word 'Beatles' as a remote thing, not as what I think – as Beatles, as those other Beatles like other people see us . . . I'm not anti-God, anti-Christ or anti-religion. I was not saying we're greater or better. I believe in God but not as an old man in the sky. I believe what people call God is something in all of us. I wasn't saying the Beatles are better than God or Jesus. I used 'Beatles' because it was easier for me to talk about The Beatles. I wasn't saying whatever they're saying I was saying. I'm sorry I said it really. I never meant it to be a lousy anti-religious thing. I apologise if that will make you happy. I still don't quite know what I've done. I've tried to tell you what I did do but if you want me to apologise, if that will make you happy, then okay, I'm sorry." The tour went off as planned. In Memphis a church held a meeting during the concert at the Mid-South Coliseum to pray for the souls of the audience. The only worrying incident was when a loud firecracker went off during the gig and frightened everyone. The band played on. It was only a matter of time before the Fab Four forged a film career. John was to appear in a number of films including: *A Hard Day's Night* (1964) as himself, *Help!* (1965) as himself, *How I Won The War* (1967) as Private Musketeer Gripweed and *Let It Be* (1970) as himself, among others. On October 26, 1965, The Beatles were awarded the MBE, much to the indignation of various military types who returned their gongs in protest, something Lennon himself was to do on November 26, 1969, in protest at British involvement in Biafra. In 1971 The Beatles were officially wound up and Lennon continued a successful solo career with songs such as 'Give Peace A Chance', 'Instant Karma', 'Power To The People', 'Happy Christmas (War Is Over)', 'Imagine' and 'Whatever Gets You Through The Night'. Then it all went silent for five years as he stayed at home to look after his newborn son, Sean, who had been born on his 35th birthday. He had split from second wife Yoko Ono and had an affair with his secretary May Pang. The reconciliation was blessed with a son, Sean.

CAUSE: In 1980 John Lennon decided to restart his musical career and began recording songs once again for public consumption. He released an album *Double Fantasy*. On November 8, 1980 his song '(Just Like) Starting Over' entered the UK charts. Exactly one month later, as he was returning home to his seventh floor, 34-room complex in Section A of the Dakota Building, 1 West 72nd Street, New York, from a late night recording session with Yoko Ono, Lennon was shot five times in his arm and back with a .38 revolver by deranged 200lb loner Mark David Chapman (b. Fort Worth, Texas, May 10, 1955) who was obsessed with J.D. Salinger's novel *The Catcher In The Rye* and believed that the ex-Beatle had "sold out". Lennon stumbled up the six steps to the building and collapsed in the vestibule. He was taken by police car to Roosevelt Hospital on 9th Avenue and 58th Street. He was pronounced dead at 11.07pm, from major blood loss. He was cremated at Hartsdale Crematorium in New York State. In his British will Lennon left £2,522,317.

FURTHER READING: *John Lennon: Death Of A Dream* – George Carpozi, Jr. (New York: Manor Books, 1980); *Loving John: The Untold Story* – May Pang and Henry Edwards (London: Corgi, 1983); *John Winston Lennon: Volume 1 1940–1966* – Ray Coleman (London: Sidgwick & Jackson, 1984); *John Ono Lennon: Volume 2 1967–1980* – Ray Coleman (London: Sidgwick & Jackson, 1984); *The Lives Of John Lennon* – Albert Goldman (London: Bantam Press, 1988); *The Murder Of John Lennon* – Fenton Bresler (London: Sidgwick & Jackson, 1989); *The Art & Music of John Lennon* – John Robertson (London: Omnibus Press, 1990); *John Lennon: The Life* – Philip Norman (London: HarperCollins, 2008).

Lotte Lenya
(KAROLINE WILHELMINE CHARLOTTE BLAMAUER)
Born October 18, 1898
Died November 27, 1981
Powerful chanteuse. Born in Penzing, Austria-Hungary, Lenya was named after a sister, who died before she was born, and two aunts. Her father was physically abusive, alcoholic and very poor. Before she turned 13 she worked as a prostitute before turning to singing and dancing. She was mainly known for her stage work, usually performing the works of her husband Kurt Weill and Bertolt Brecht. Following Weill's death, she married three homosexual men. Her films included: *The Roman Spring Of Mrs Stone* (1961) as Contessa Magda Terribili-Gonzales, for which she was nominated for a Best Supporting Actress Academy Award, *From Russia With Love* (1963) as Rosa Klebb, *The Appointment* (1969) as Emma Valadier and *Semi-Tough* (1978) as Clara Pelf.

CAUSE: On December 2, 1977, she underwent a hysterectomy at Doctors Hospital in New York. She later contracted cancer of the bladder, for which she was operated on June 6, 1978, at the New York Hospital. In her final years she also began to suffer from osteoporosis. She died of cancer aged 83 in New York at 5.30pm.

FURTHER READING: *Lenya: A Life* – Donald Spoto (London: Viking, 1989).

Sergio Leone
Born January 3, 1929
Died April 30, 1989
Spaghetti Western maker. Born in Rome, Leone began his film career

working with the best. He was second unit director on *Quo Vadis?* (1951) for Mervyn LeRoy and *Ben-Hur* (1959) before progressing to direct his own films such as *Gli Ultimi Giorni Di Pompei/The Last Days Of Pompeii* (1960) and *The Last Days Of Sodom And Gomorrah* (1962). However, it is for his spaghetti Westerns that he is best remembered. He directed *Per Un Pugno Di Dollari/A Fistful Of Dollars* (1964), *Per Qualche Dollaro In Più/For A Few Dollars More* (1965) and *Il Buono, Il Brutto, Il Cattivo/The Good, The Bad And The Ugly* (1966) which rejuvenated the career of Clint Eastwood as The Man With No Name. His next film, the big budget *C'era Una Volta Il West/Once Upon A Time In The West* (1968), flopped and he gave up directing until casting Robert De Niro and James Woods in *Once Upon A Time In America* (1984).

CAUSE: He died of a heart attack in Rome aged 60. Prior to his death he had been working on a film about the siege of Leningrad.

Mervyn LeRoy

Born October 15, 1900
Died September 13, 1987
Diverse director. Born in San Francisco, California, LeRoy originally wanted to be an actor and that, along with joke writing, was how he made his living. He had directed a few films – *No Place To Go* (1927), *Flying Romeos* (1928), *Hot Stuff* (1929) and *Broadway Babies* (1929) – when he joined First National Pictures (a subsidiary of Warner Bros). It was there his name was made with the gangster flick *Little Caesar* (1930) starring Edward G. Robinson who persuaded LeRoy to let him play the lead rather than a supporting part. LeRoy's reputation was confirmed with *I Am A Fugitive From A Chain Gang* (1932). The film was based on the true story of Robert Eliot Burns (who appeared in the film) who was jailed and sentenced to ten years' hard labour for stealing $5.29

worth of food in 1920 in Georgia. He escaped and wrote a book called *I Am A Fugitive From A Georgia Chain Gang*. Although the film was careful not to identify the state, Georgia was furious and tried to sue for libel, issued a warrant for Burns' recapture and threatened LeRoy and anyone else in the film if they ever visited Georgia. Moving away from gangsters, LeRoy also directed the piece of fluff that was *Gold Diggers Of 1933* (1933). On November 11, 1937, he agreed to join MGM as a producer-director, taking with him Lana Turner, whom he had put on a personal contract. There he produced *The Wizard Of Oz* (1939) and directed *Waterloo Bridge* (1940), *Johnny Eager* (1941), *Random Harvest* (1942), *Madame Curie* (1943), *Thirty Seconds Over Tokyo* (1944), *Quo Vadis?* (1951), *Million Dollar Mermaid* (1952), *Latin Lovers* (1953), *Rose Marie* (1954), which he also produced, and many others. In the Fifties he set up his own production company. He replaced John Ford on *Mister Roberts* (1955). His later films included: *The Bad Seed* (1956), *Home Before Dark* (1958), *No Time For Sergeants* (1958), *The FBI Story* (1959), *Gypsy* (1962) and *Moment To Moment* (1965).

CAUSE: He died aged 86 in Beverly Hills, California, from Alzheimer's disease.

Bruce Lester

(BRUCE SOMERSET LISTER)
Born June 6 1912
Died June 13, 2008
Stiff upper lipped serviceman. Born in Johannesburg and educated at Brighton College, Lester gave up a promising tennis career because he could make more money as an actor. After working on the stage, he began appearing in B-movies and made his screen debut in *The Girl In The Flat* (released June 1934), with Belle Crystall. He appeared in *To Be A Lady* (released July 1934) with Chilli Bouchier and was assistant producer Peter Ridgwell in *Death At*

Broadcasting House (released November 1934). He appeared in the reasonably successful *Crime Over London* (released October 22, 1936) with René Ray and Googie Withers and in *Mayfair Melody* (1937) as Dickie, which led to him being signed by Teddington Studios, Warner Bros' British production arm in 1938. He moved to Hollywood where his name was changed to Lester and he bedded Bette Davis. He impressed so much in *Boy Meets Girl* (released August 27, 1938) that Jimmy Cagney suggested that Warner Bros sign him for three years. He excelled as Mr Bingley in MGM's *Pride And Prejudice* (released July 26, 1940), which starred Laurence Olivier and Greer Garson. He later said, "It was the biggest budget of my career and one that brought with it my own dresser, a bungalow on the lot and lunches where one could spot Greta Garbo, Salvador Dalí, Cary Grant and dozens of Munchkins from *The Wizard Of Oz*." During the Second World War, Lester returned to Britain but was told that he would be of more use Stateside and he appeared in morale-boosters such as *A Yank In The RAF* (premièred September 26, 1941) with Tyrone Power, *Eagle Squadron* (released June 16, 1942) with Robert Stack and *Desperate Journey* (released September 26, 1942) with Errol Flynn and Ronald Reagan. After cessation of hostilities Lester began writing screenplays but kept his hand in in front of the cameras. He appeared opposite John Wayne and Claudette Colbert in *Without Reservations* (released May 13, 1946), *Golden Earrings* (released August 27, 1947) and *Celia: The Sinister Affair Of Poor Aunt Nora* (released August 29, 1949). He became a story analyst for Paramount Pictures in the 1950s but enjoyed a full life with wife Jane that enabled him to play tennis and enjoy the Hollywood Cricket Club.

CAUSE: Lester died of natural causes, aged 96 at Los Angeles, California.

Oscar Levant
Born December 27, 1906
Died August 14, 1972
Acerbic wit. Born in Pittsburgh, Pennsylvania, the youngest of four sons in an Orthodox Jewish family from Russia, by the age of eight he was giving piano recitals. As a teenager in 1922 he moved to New York with his mother, Annie Radin, a year after the death of his father, Max Levant, and there he appeared on Broadway. In 1928 he travelled to Hollywood where he made his first film *The Dance Of Life* (1929). He met and befriended George Gershwin in 1925. His hero worship of Gershwin was punctuated with bitchy comments. He once asked him, "George, if you had to do it all over again, would you fall in love with yourself again?" After Gershwin's early death in 1937 Levant became the main interpreter of Gershwin's works for the piano. Although he appeared in 13 films between 1929 and 1955 including *Rhapsody In Blue* (1945), *Humoresque* (1946), *Romance On The High Seas* (1948) which was Doris Day's first film; Levant said of her, "I knew Doris Day before she was a virgin", *The Barkleys Of Broadway* (1949), *An American In Paris* (premièred September 26, 1951), *O. Henry's Full House* (1952) and *The Band Wagon* (1953), Levant's career was beset by mental illness, drug addiciton and stage fright, which led him to cancel concerts at the last moment. His last performance was on August 2, 1958. He said of his professional life, "In some situations I was difficult, in odd moments impossible, in rare moments loathsome, but at my best unapproachably great." He was a regular on the radio show *Information Please*. His wit was often not to everyone's taste. Of Marilyn Monroe's conversion to Judaism, he said, "Now that Marilyn Monroe is kosher, Arthur Miller can eat her." When Frank Sinatra's son was kidnapped, Levant said, "It must have been done by music

critics." His other witty lines included: "What the world needs is more geniuses with humility, there are so few of us left"; "Everyone in Hollywood is gay, except Gabby Hayes – and that's because he is a transvestite"; "Self pity? It's the only pity that counts"; "Zsa Zsa [Gabor] not only worships at the Golden Calf, she barbecues it for lunch"; "Zsa Zsa is the only lady who left the Iron Curtain wearing it"; "Zsa Zsa has discovered the secret of perpetual middle age"; "[I gave up] reading because it took my mind off myself"; "[A good husband] is a man who is unattractive to other women"; "[Egomania is] what goes in one ear – and stays there"; "Imitation is the sincerest form of plagiarism"; "An atheist is a man with no invisible means of support"; "I was thrown out of a mental hospital – I depressed the other patients"; "My favourite exercises are grovelling, brooding and mulling"; "Strip away the false tinsel from Hollywood, and you find the real tinsel inside" and "It's not what you are, it's what you don't become that hurts." Of Levant, Alexander Woollcott said, "There's absolutely nothing wrong with Oscar Levant that a miracle can't fix" while S.N. Behrman opined, "He was a character who, if he did not exist, could not be imagined". Levant was very superstitious. It was forbidden to mention the number 13 in his presence as well as any mentions of death, undertakers, wills, morgues, hearses, graves and their ilk. He thought the names of his siblings, parents and hometown unlucky. He never wore a hat and refused to allow flowers into his home or dressing rooms. Levant drank up to 60 cups of coffee a day and then took sleeping pills to counter the effects of the caffeine. He spent much time with the George S. Kaufmans which prompted Mrs Kaufman to comment, "The servants always expect a little something. I know you haven't any money, so I tipped them $3 each and said it was from you." Levant did not appreciate the kindness. "$3?" he screamed, "Why didn't you give them five? Now they'll think I am stingy." He married and divorced actress Barbara Woodell (b. Lewiston, Illinois May 25, 1910 as Barbara Smith d. Ojai, California January 16, 1997) on January 5, 1932. They divorced a year later. Harpo Marx asked him what had caused the split. "Incompatibility," said Levant, "and, besides, I had the definite feeling that she loathed me." She went on to marry the cinema chain tycoon Arthur Loew. On December 1, 1939 Levant married singer and actress June Gale (b. San Francisco, California July 6, 1911 as June Gilmartin d. Los Angeles, California November 13, 1996): they had three children, Marcia, Lorna, and Amanda. Mrs Levant filed for a legal separation in 1947 and divorce in 1958 but she stayed with him until his death.

CAUSE: In 1952 he suffered a heart attack. Never fully recovered, he began taking drugs. He went into rehab several times with little effect. He had electric shock treatments, which affected his memory. Levant was a virtual recluse from 1961. He died at his home on North Roxbury Drive, Beverly Hills, California aged 65 of a heart attack. He was buried in Westwood Village Memorial Park Cemetery, Los Angeles, California.

Liberace

(WLADZIU VALENTINO LIBERACE)
Born May 14, 1919
Died February 4, 1987
Camp pianist. Born at 635 51st Street, West Allis, Wisconsin, Liberace became loved by millions of women *d'un age certain* the world over for tinkling the ivories. Not everyone was taken with him. "This deadly, winking, sniggering, snuggling, chromium-plated, scent-impregnated, luminous, quivering, giggling, fruit-flavoured, mincing, ice-covered heap of mother love" was how newspaper columnist Cassandra

of the *Daily Mirror* described The Candelabra Kid to his millions of readers on October 22, 1956. Liberace immediately sued for libel, claiming the piece implied he was homosexual and, besides, that it upset his mother. Committing perjury, he denied being gay or indulging in gay practices "because it offends convention and it offends society". A jury found in his favour and awarded him damages of £8,000 and costs of £14,000. Liberace continued his sell-out concerts to ladies who wanted to mother him. He never dared admit he was gay for fear it would offend his blue-rinse matrons although he joked about many other aspects of his life. "I'm enjoying myself so much, I don't want to take your money," (wink) "but I will." He even designed a toilet that disappeared into a hole in the wall. "Why should you have to walk into a bathroom and see a toilet? It's ugly." An attempt to launch himself as a film star never really took off. He usually played himself, whether the part required it or not. He appeared in *South Sea Sinner* (1949) as Maestro, *Footlight Varieties* (1951) as himself, *Sincerely Yours* (1955) as Anthony Warrin, *When The Boys Meet The Girls* (1965) as himself and *The Loved One* (1965) as Mr Starker.

CAUSE: When he contracted AIDS he lost weight, which his publicists put down to an overindulgence in a watermelon diet, thus probably wrecking the sales of that particular fruit. Liberace succumbed to the disease at his home, Casa de las Cloisters, Palm Springs, California. When he died, the *Mirror* ran a light-hearted editorial asking for its money back.

FURTHER READING: *An Autobiography* – Liberace (London: Star Books, 1974); *Liberace* – Bob Thomas (London: Weidenfeld & Nicolson, 1987).

Larry Linville

Born September 29, 1939
Died April 10, 2000
Absolutely Frank. Larry Lavon Linville

was born in Ojai, California, and raised in Sacramento. He studied aeronautical engineering at the University of Colorado before studying at RADA, one of only three Americans to be accepted from 300 applicants. Linville made his film début in *The Stepmother* (1971) as Dick Hill. He followed that with *Kotch* (1971) as Peter. The following year he landed the role of Major Frank Burns in the hit television series *M*A*S*H*, a part he was to play until 1977. The show about the mobile army surgical hospital kept him off the big screen for much of his career. His later films included *School Spirit* (1985) as President Grimshaw, *Blue Movies* (1988) as Dr Gladding, *C.H.U.D. II – Bud The Chud* (1989) as Dr Jewell, *Earth Girls Are Easy* (1989) as Dr Bob, *Rock'n'Roll High School Forever* (1990) as Principal McGree, *Body Waves* (1992) as Himmel, *West From North Goes South* (1993) as Reverend Mr Lowell, *No Dessert Dad, Til You Mow The Lawn* (1994) as J.J., *Fatal Pursuit* (1994) as Shelby, *A Million To Juan* (1994) as Richard Dickerson, *Angel's Tide* (1995) and *Pressure Point* (1997). Away from acting, Linville's life was fraught. He was married four times. He had only one child, Kelly, born in 1970. On December 28, 1989, Linville's fourth wife filed divorce papers in Los Angeles Superior Court accusing him of beating her up. Susan Linville, 13 years the actor's junior, claimed that he became violent and abusive when drunk; physically attacked her more than 20 times during their four year marriage; hit her so severely during one assault in January 1986 that she was bedridden for a week; and on December 18, 1989 threw her to the floor, ripped her clothes off and then walked off with her dog saying she would never see it again. She also claimed support of $12,500 a month. Through his lawyer, Linville denied all the allegations. In the spring of 1993 Linville was accused of groping a very minor Canadian TV personality. At a Winnipeg Press Club party 6'1" Linville posed with a smiling Natalie Pollock, his hand "lightly placed on her breast". She claimed going somewhat over the top, "He clenched my breast. That is the story and that is a crime. I should have decked him. I was traumatised. It was like the shock I felt when my mum got hit by a car and died."

CAUSE: On February 12, 1998, part of his lung was removed during an operation after doctors found a malignant tumour under his sternum. He died aged 60 at Memorial Sloan-Kettering Cancer Center, New York, of pneumonia due to complications from a cancer operation.

Cleavon Little

Born June 1, 1939
Died October 22, 1992
Promising black actor. Born in Chickasha, Oklahoma, one of five children (three sons, two daughters) of Malchi Little, left-handed Cleavon Jake Little was raised in California and educated at San Diego College. He won a scholarship to Juilliard and moved to New York. He was best known for his role in *Blazing Saddles* (1974) although he had several film appearances under his belt and he won a Tony award for his performance in *Purlie*. Little starred in a sitcom called *Temperatures Rising*. It ran for 46 episodes between September 12, 1972 and August 29, 1974. It co-starred Paul Lynde and Joan Van Ark. In 1979 he made a pilot for a show called *Mr Dugan*, about a fictitious politician, but the show was cancelled before it was shown, thanks to pressure from black politicians. Divorced, he had one daughter Adia Millett-Little.

CAUSE: He died from colon cancer at his house in Sherman Oaks, California. He was cremated on October 28 and his ashes scattered in New York Harbour.

Desmond Llewelyn

Born September 12, 1914
Died December 19, 1999
Gadgeteer. Desmond Wilkinson Llewelyn was born in Newport, South Wales, the son of coal mining engineer Ivor Llewelyn (d. 1930 from a heart attack) and Mia Wilkinson (d. 1942). He studied for a career as a chartered accountant but decided to become an actor, attending RADA. At Holy Trinity, Kensington Gore on May 16, 1938 he married Pamela Pantlin (b. 1912) and had two sons: Ivor (b. July 14, 1949) and Justin (b. 1952). During World War II he served as a second lieutenant with the Royal Welch Fusiliers and spent time in a POW camp. He was recaptured trying to escape. He appeared in a number of films, including *The Lavender Hill Mob* (1951), *Further Up The Creek* (1958) as Chief Yeoman, *The Pirates Of Blood River* (1962) as Tom Blackthorne, *Cleopatra* (1963) and *Chitty Chitty Bang Bang* (1968) as Coggins, but it is for his role as James Bond's exasperated quartermaster Q (a.k.a. Major Boothroyd) that he will be remembered. The director originally wanted Q to be Welsh. "My interpretation of the character was that of a toffee-nosed Englishman," Llewelyn once said. "At the risk of losing the part and with silent apologies to my native land, I launched into Q's lines using the worst Welsh accent, followed by the same in English." He appeared in 17 Bond films (on a daily rate), beginning with 1963's *From Russia With Love* and ending with *The World Is Not Enough* (1999). Despite his screen role he revealed, "In real life I'm allergic to gadgets. They just don't work for me, not even those plastic cards for hotel room doors."

CAUSE: He died in a car crash aged 85 near the town of Firle in East Sussex. He was driving home from a book signing when his car was involved in a head-on collision. He was airlifted to a hospital but succumbed to massive internal injuries. His funeral was held at the twelfth-century St Mary The Virgin Church in Sussex. None of the actors who played James Bond attended. Only actress Samantha Bond, the latest Miss Moneypenny, and Colin Salmon, who plays M's chief of staff, were present. Llewelyn's wife, Pamela, who suffers from Alzheimer's disease, did not attend the funeral.

FURTHER READING: *Q: The Biography Of Desmond Llewelyn* – Sandy Hernu (Seaford: S.B. Publications, 1999).

Harold Lloyd
Born April 20, 1893
Died March 8, 1971

'The Man On The Clock'. With Buster Keaton and Charlie Chaplin, Harold Clayton Lloyd made up the triumvirate of silent comedy giants. Born in Burchard, Nebraska, he made his first film in 1912 and five years later adopted an image that would make him world famous. He purchased a pair of horn-rimmed glasses, removed the lenses to avoid reflection from lights and bought a straw boater. He eventually had 20 identical pairs of glasses made. He also, on occasion, took physical risks to raise a laugh. He did, at times, employ a stunt double, but there was usually enough safety equipment around (although not in shot) to prevent Lloyd falling and killing himself. On August 24, 1919, while posing for publicity pictures the fake bomb he was holding turned out not to be fake at all and exploded. Lloyd lost the thumb and forefinger on his right hand and was also temporarily blinded. Eventually, his eyesight returned but for the rest of his career Lloyd wore a special prosthetic under a flesh-coloured glove. Amazingly, he continued to perform the hair-raising stunts for which he had become famous. In 1926 *The New Yorker* described him as "the most affluent and popular of all the stars in the Hollywood heavens". By 1941 he had made $30 million. In 1952 he was awarded a special Oscar. He made over 200 films during the course of his career including: *Algy On The Force* (1913), *Just Nuts* (1915) as Willie Work, *Miss Fatty's Seaside Lovers* (1915), *Soaking The Clothes* (1915), *Once Every Ten Minutes* (1915), *Giving Them Fits* (1915) as Luke de Fluke, *Bughouse Bellhops* (1915) as Luke, *Tinkering With Trouble* (1915), *A Foozle At The Tee Party* (1915) as Luke, *Ruses, Rhymes And Roughnecks* (1915) as Lonesome Luke, *Peculiar Patients' Pranks* (1915) as Lonesome Luke, *Skylight Sleep* (1916), *Ice* (1916), *Braver Than The Bravest* (1916), *Lonesome Luke Leans To The Literary* (1916) as Lonesome Luke, *Luke Lugs Luggage* (1916), *Lonesome Luke Lolls In Luxury* (1916), as Luke, *The Candy Cut-Up* (1916), *Luke Foils The Villain* (1916), *Luke And The Rural Roughnecks* (1916), *Luke Pipes The Pippins* (1916), *Lonesome Luke, Circus King* (1916), *Luke's Double* (1916), *Them Was The Happy Days!* (1916) as Lonesome Luke, *Luke And The Bomb Throwers* (1916), *Luke's Late Lunchers* (1916), *Luke Laughs Last* (1916), *Luke's Fatal Flivver* (1916), *Luke's Society Mixup* (1916), *Luke's Washful Waiting* (1916), *Luke Rides Roughshod* (1916), *Luke, Crystal Gazer* (1916), *Luke's Lost Lamb* (1916), *Luke Does The Midway* (1916), *Luke Joins The Navy* (1916), *Luke And The Mermaids* (1916), *Luke's Speedy Club Life* (1916), *Luke And The Bang-Tails* (1916) and dozens more Lonesome Luke films which were "a tramp imitation of Chaplin", *Somewhere In Turkey* (1918), *Bride And Gloom* (1918) as the groom, *Wanted – $5,000* (1919), *Ask Father* (1919), *A Sammy In Siberia* (1919), *Pistols For Breakfast* (1919), *Count Your Change* (1919), *Captain Kidd's Kids* (1919), *Among Those Present* (1921) as O'Reilly, *Doctor Jack* (1922) as Dr Jackson, *Safety Last* (1923) in which he hangs from a clock high in the air, *Speedy* (1928) as Harold 'Speedy' Swift, *Stout Hearts And Willing Hands* (1932), *The Milky Way* (1936) as Buleigh 'Tiger' Sullivan and *The Sin Of Harold Diddlebock* (1947) as Harold Diddlebock. With the advent of talking pictures, Lloyd quietly retired. Lloyd married his leading lady Mildred Davis on February 10, 1923, at St John's Episcopal Church, Los Angeles. They had one son and two daughters (one adopted) and were together until Davis' death of a heart attack on August 18, 1969.

CAUSE: He died aged 78 of cancer in Beverly Hills, California.

FURTHER READING: *Harold Lloyd's World Of Comedy* – William Cahn (London: George Allen & Unwin, 1966).

Margaret Lockwood, CBE
Born September 15, 1916
Died July 15, 1990
'The Wicked Lady'. Born in Karachi, India, brought to England aged three and trained at Italia Conti and, from 1933, at RADA, Margaret Mary Lockwood began acting as a teenager on stage. Her film début came in *Lorna Doone* (1934) and she was signed by British Lion, the first British actress to be specifically groomed to be a movie star. Over the course of her 45-film career she murdered her best friend, poisoned more than one husband and was a very wicked lady. She spent most of her career working in England with only a brief trip to Hollywood. She starred opposite Maurice Chevalier in *The Beloved Vagabond* (1936) and two years later was cast in Alfred Hitchcock's *The Lady Vanishes* as Iris Henderson. It was her portrayal as Barbara, Lady Skelton in Leslie Arliss' *The Wicked Lady* (1945) that sealed her reputation. It also made her the highest paid actress in Britain, but also one not taken terribly seriously, a fact that sent her career on a downward path. Her contract with Rank, signed in 1943, was terminated in 1951. Following *Cast A Dark Shadow* (1955) she retired from films, concentrating instead on theatre and the new medium of television. She

made a brief comeback as Cinderella's stepmother in *The Slipper And The Rose* (1976). On October 17, 1937, she married Rupert de Leon at Epsom Registry Office. When her marriage ended in 1946 she fought for custody of her daughter, actress (Margaret) Julia Lockwood (b. August 23, 1941), only for her domineering mother to side with her ex-husband. Following the divorce, she never saw her mother again.

CAUSE: In the late-Seventies she began to suffer from vestibulitis, a viral infection of the middle ear. Although it was cured, it left her deaf. She spent her final years living alone in Kingston-upon-Thames, rarely venturing out except to buy cigarettes. Her home contained no memories of her film career. She refused all job offers but was punctilious about replying to all letters, including a request from the present author for help on another project. She died in the Cromwell Hospital, Kensington, London, aged 73 of cirrhosis of the liver. She left £433,705.

FURTHER READING: *Once A Wicked Lady: A Biography Of Margaret Lockwood* – Hilton Tims (London: W.H. Allen, 1989)

Josh Logan
Born October 5, 1908
Died July 12, 1988
Theatre film director. Born in Texarkana, Texas, Joshua Lockwood Logan III didn't make many films, preferring the stage, but the ones he did tended to be notable for some reason. He studied under Stanislavski and his first movie was *I Met My Love Again* (1938) but there then followed a 17-year hiatus during which time he worked in the theatre before he got his second cinematic opportunity. He worked on *Picnic* (1955) and *Mister Roberts* (1955) before being assigned to direct Marilyn Monroe as the fading bar room singer Cherie in *Bus Stop* (1956). He rated Marilyn highly:

"When I tell people Marilyn Monroe may be one of the finest dramatic talents of our time, they laugh in my face. But I believe it. I believe it to such an extent that I would like to direct her in every picture she wants me for, every story she can dig up." Marilyn received the best reviews in her career for the film and Logan is one of the few directors who never criticised the star. "Monroe is as near genius as any actress I ever knew . . . She is the most completely realised actress since Garbo. Watch her work. In any film. How rarely she has to use words. How much she does with her eyes, her lips, with slight, almost accidental gestures . . . Monroe is pure cinema." Next Logan worked on *Sayonara* (1957), for which he was nominated for an Oscar, the Rodgers and Hammerstein musical *South Pacific* (1958), for which Logan had wanted Elizabeth Taylor instead of Mitzi Gaynor but Taylor failed an audition before Rodgers and Hammerstein, *Tall Story* (1960), which he also produced, *Ensign Pulver* (1964), the sequel to *Mister Roberts*, which he also produced, *Camelot* (1967) and Lerner & Loewe's musical *Paint Your Wagon* (1969).
CAUSE: He died aged 79 in New York from Supranuclear Palsy.

Carole Lombard

(JANE ALICE PETERS)
Born October 6, 1908
Died January 16, 1942
'The Profane Angel'. Much loved in Hollywood for her generosity, raucous personality, practical jokes and foul mouth, Carole Lombard's early death shattered all her many friends. Fed up with men making advances, she had her two brothers teach her every swearword they knew. She once said, "I've lived by a man's code designed to fit a man's world, yet at the same time I never forget that a woman's first job is to choose the right shade of lipstick." She once told Harry Cohn that she would do his "shitty little picture but fucking you isn't part of the deal." Born in Fort Wayne, Indiana, her parents divorced when she was eight and her mother took her and her two brothers west to California. Four years later, the tomboy Carole was playing baseball in the street with the neighbourhood boys when she was spotted by film director, Allan Dwan. He cast her in *A Perfect Crime* (1921) and the acting bug caught her, although it would be three more years before she appeared before the cameras again. She went back to school and excelled in track and field athletics. When Carole was 15 she left school and joined a theatre troupe. In October 1924 she was screen-tested by Fox and offered a contract. Her first role was as Sybil Estabrook in *Hearts And Spurs* (1925). In October of the following year she was involved in a car crash that left her face needing 14 stitches and badly scarred. When she recovered she found herself sacked by Fox. Determined to continue as an actress, she was signed by Mack Sennett and then Pathé director Paul Stei in 1929 and stayed for a year. She signed for Paramount in June 1930. She appeared in *High Voltage* (1929) as Billie Davis, *Big News* (1929) as Margaret Banks, *Fast And Loose* (1930) as Alice O'Neil, *The Arizona Kid* (1930) as Virginia Hoyt, *Safety In Numbers* (1930) as Pauline, *Up Pops The Devil* (1931) as Anne Merrick, *It Pays To Advertise* (1931) as Mary Grayson and *I Take This Woman* (1931) as Kay Dowling. She was cast opposite William Powell in *Man Of The World* (1931) as Mary Kendall and, on June 26 of that year, married him. It was a week after Clark Gable had married Rhea Langham. The union didn't work and they divorced in August 1933, but remained on good terms despite him not paying her alimony. She was romanced by Russ Columbo until his early death on September 14, 1934. Privately, Carole told friends that he was the great love of her life. She filmed *No Man Of Her*

Own (1932) with Clark Gable. It would be the only time they appeared on film together. She signed for Paramount Studios, becoming one of their most popular stars. Probably her best performance came in *Twentieth Century* (1934) as Lily Garland (Mildred Plotka) showing her comedic potential opposite John Barrymore. She went on to appear in *Now And Forever* (1934) as Toni Carstairs, *We're Not Dressing* (1934) as Doris Worthington, *Bolero* (1934) as Helen Hathaway, *The Gay Bride* (1934) as Mary Magiz, *Rumba* (1935) as Diana Harrison, *Hands Across The Table* (1935) as Regi Allen, *The Princess Comes Across* (1936) as Princess Olga, *Love Before Breakfast* (1936) as Kay Colby and *My Man Godfrey* (1936) as Irene Bullock, for which she received her only Oscar nomination, *True Confession* (1937) as Helen Bartlett, *Swing High, Swing Low* (1937) as Maggie King, *Nothing Sacred* (1937) as Hazel Flagg, *Fools For Scandal* (1938) as Kay Winters, *In Name Only* (1939) as Julie Eden, *Made For Each Other* (1939) as Jane Mason, *Vigil In The Night* (1940) as Anne Lee, *They Knew What They Wanted* (1940) as Amy Peters, *Mr & Mrs Smith* (1941) as Ann Krausheimer Smith and the posthumously released *To Be Or Not To Be* (1942) as Maria Tura playing opposite Jack Benny. She had legally changed her name to Carole Lombard in 1936, having previously been billed as Carol Lombard until a back room boy misspelled her name. She later said: "I think that 'e' made the whole fucking difference." On March 29, 1939, she married Clark Gable. They nicknamed each other Ma and Pa and lived an idyllic life far away from Hollywood glamour on a 20-acre ranch in the San Fernando Valley. She wore falsies in some films to enhance her figure and was wont to shout at the make-up people, "Okay, bring me my breasts." Her co-star George Raft discovered she wasn't a natural blonde when one day she stripped off in front of him and began applying peroxide to her pubes. "Relax, Georgie," she told him, "I'm just making my collar and cuffs match."

CAUSE: Following America's belated entry into World War II Carole did her bit for the war effort and travelled to Indiana for a war bond rally. On January 16, 1942, having raised over $2 million, she was set to return home, but couldn't decide whether to fly or let the train take the strain. She tossed a coin and decided to fly. Her mother, Elizabeth Knight Peters, had never been on an aeroplane and was frightened of the journey. She had also been warned that 16 was an unlucky number. The plane, TWA Flight #3, took off at 4am with Carole, a nervous Mrs Peters and Carole's publicity man Otto Winkler. The journey was due to take 17 hours. When they stopped off at Albuquerque, New Mexico, to refuel, several passengers were asked to give up their seats so military personnel could be accommodated. Carole used her charms for her, her mother and publicist to be allowed to stay on board. Permission was granted. Following another stop-off in Las Vegas the plane began to climb, but not quickly enough, and 30 miles south-west of Vegas it crashed into Table Rock Mountain, 730ft below the summit. The plane split in two and all 22 people aboard perished. It took two days for rescuers to retrieve the corpses. The front section in which Carole had been sitting was compressed into a block about 10ft long. A few wisps of her blonde hair fluttered in the wreckage. Carole was 33. On January 21, 1942, her remains were buried in the Great Mausoleum, Sanctuary of Trust, at Forest Lawn Memorial-Parks, 1712 South Glendale Avenue, Glendale, California 91209. Eighteen years later, Clark Gable would be laid to rest beside her.

FURTHER READING: *Gable & Lombard* – Warren G. Harris (London: Corgi, 1977).

Jack Lord

(JOHN JOSEPH PATRICK RYAN)
Born December 30, 1920
Died January 21, 1998
Humourless leading man. Born in New
York, unlike many actors 6'2" Jack
Lord did not embrace publicity despite
being the star of a top-rated television
show for 12 years and appearing in
numerous films. Even his birth date is
in doubt. According to his network he
was born on December 30, 1930, yet it
is also claimed he was a war hero (who
spent 16 hours in a lifeboat after his
boat was sunk off East Africa in 1944)
making that date highly improbable
if not downright impossible. The
American Library of Congress lists his
birthday as 1922, yet he supposedly
graduated from John Adams High
School in 1938, making his year of
birth the one given above. However,
when he died some claimed he was in
his early eighties. Lord also supposedly
married Ann Willard in 1942 and
divorced her in 1947, again making
1930 impossible for the year of his
birth. Or he may have married the
daughter of an Argentine diplomat who
left him shortly after the honeymoon
when she discovered she was pregnant.
He supposedly had a son by this
marriage who died aged 13 in 1950 in
an accident. After a career in the
merchant navy, he made his film début
in *Project X* (1949) as John Bates and
went on to appear in *The Tattooed
Stranger* (1950) as Detective Deke Del
Vecchio, *Cry Murder* (1950) as Tommy
Warren, *The Court-Martial Of Billy
Mitchell* (1955) as Commander Zach
Lansdowne, *Williamsburg: The Story Of
A Patriot* (1956) as John Fry, *God's
Little Acre* (1958) as Buck, *The
Hangman* (1959) as Johnny Bishop
and *Dr No* (1962) as Felix Leiter,
Bond's CIA colleague. He was booked
to reprise the role in *Goldfinger* (1964)
until producer Cubby Broccoli
dropped him, fearing he would
overshadow Bond. Jack Lord was
offered the part of Captain Kirk in *Star
Trek* but creator Gene Roddenberry
withdrew the offer when Lord asked to
co-produce the series and own a
percentage of the show. He also turned
down the role of Napoleon Solo in
The Man From U.N.C.L.E. On
September 20, 1968, the pilot of a new
CBS cop show set in the beautiful
surroundings of the Pacific hit the air
under the title *Hawaii Five-O*. Lord
found his niche playing the tough head
of the fictional state police Five-O and
became known for the catch-phrase
"Book 'em, Danno!" As the show grew
in popularity, so did Lord's ego.
Moving to Honolulu permanently he
fancied himself an important local
figure. He was not close to co-star
James MacArthur, who played
McGarrett's sidekick Danno Williams,
and in the last season was positively
furious with newcomer Sharon Farrell
who played Detective Lori Wilson.
Sharon preferred not to wear a bra and
the sight of her bouncing breasts as she
ran was not one that Lord felt was
appropriate for a policewoman. She
left the show after ten episodes. The
show ran for 279 episodes until April 5,
1980. It was claimed that Lord was a
talented painter with several of his
works exhibited world-wide. However,
following his death, a 'friend' alleged
he would send unsolicited work to
museums who, chary of paying for the
costs of returning the paintings, stored
them in their basements unhung.
Supposedly, the porn star Traci Lords
changed her name from Nora Kuzma
in honour of Jack Lord. Jack Lord
solved hundreds of mysteries on
Hawaii Five-O but left innumerable
riddles about his own life. There is only
one thing of which we can be certain:
he brought pleasure to millions.
CAUSE: Jack Lord's final years were
not especially happy ones. Around
1994 he began to suffer from
Alzheimer's disease and was cared for
by his devoted wife, Marie Denarde,
whom he married around 1954. He
died of heart failure at his Honolulu

home at around 8pm with Marie holding his hand.

FURTHER READING: *Booking Hawaii Five-O* – Karen Rhodes (Jefferson: McFarland, 1997).

Peter Lorre

(LÁSZLÓ LÖWENSTEIN)
Born June 26, 1904
Died March 23, 1964

'The Walking Overcoat'. Born in Rozsahegy, Hungary, to the wealthy businessman Alois Löwenstein and his wife Elvira, from the age of four Lorre was raised in Vienna. He left home aged 17 to become an actor and after working in a bank for a while ended up in Berlin playing sexually dysfunctional men. He came to world-wide fame in Fritz Lang's story of child murderer Hans Beckert in *M* (1931). Offers from Hollywood poured in, but 5'5" Lorre spurned them all. He did not want to be typecast as a villain, nor was he overly interested in the financial rewards Hollywood had to offer. As the Nazis consolidated their power the Jewish Lorre moved to Paris and then London where, in the spring of 1934, he married Celia Lovsky (d. 1979) at Westminster Registry Office. Alfred Hitchcock cast him in *The Man Who Knew Too Much* (1934) as Abbott before Lorre finally moved to Hollywood, where he signed for Columbia. At first the studio could not find a workable property for him and he was loaned to MGM, where he excelled as the sexually frustrated plastic surgeon Dr Gogol in *Mad Love* (1935). Lorre shaved his head for the role and, with expert lighting, seemed very frightening. Columbia had him back to star as Raskolnikov in Josef von Sternberg's *Crime And Punishment* (1935). He went back to England to make *Crack-Up* (1936) as Colonel Gimpy for Alfred Hitchcock. Clearly having by now forgotten his early desire not to be typecast, he accepted the role of the Japanese detective Kentaro Moto in a series of B pictures: *Think Fast,*

Mr Moto (1937), *Thank You, Mr Moto* (1937), *Mysterious Mr Moto* (1938), *Mr Moto Takes A Chance* (1938), *Mr Moto's Gamble* (1938), *Mr Moto Takes A Vacation* (1939), *Mr Moto In Danger Island* (1939) and *Mr Moto's Last Warning* (1939). It was in 1941 that he teamed up with Sydney Greenstreet for the first of eight films. Lorre played Joel Cairo to Greenstreet's Kasper Guttman in *The Maltese Falcon* (1941) and the two actors were reunited in *Casablanca* (1942) in which Lorre played Ugarte. During the Second World War Lorre played a variety of characters – heroes, Nazis, Japanese villains and horror characters. He appeared in: *The Cross Of Lorraine* (1943) as Sergeant Berger, *The Constant Nymph* (1943) as Fritz Bercovi, *Background To Danger* (1943) as Nikolai Zaloshoff, *The Mask Of Dimitrios* (1944) as Cornelius Latimer Leyden, *Arsenic And Old Lace* (1944) as Dr Einstein, *Hotel Berlin* (1945) as Johannes Koenig and *Confidential Agent* (1945) as Contreras. On March 13 of that year he was divorced and 73 days later married Karen Verne (b. Berlin, Germany, 1918, as Ingeborg Catharine Marie Rose Klinckerfuss, d. Hollywood, California, December 23, 1967). The marriage was to last almost five years before the couple was divorced. After the war he appeared in *The Beast With Five Fingers* (1946) as Hilary Cummins, *Black Angel* (1946) as Marko, *My Favorite Brunette* (1947) as Kismet, *Quicksand* (1950) as Nick and went back to West Germany to write, directed and star in *Der Verlorene* (1951), then back to the States for *Beat The Devil* (1954) as O'Hara, *20,000 Leagues Under The Sea* (1954) as Conseil, *Around The World In 80 Days* (1956), *The Story Of Mankind* (1957) as Nero, *Hell Ship Mutiny* (1957) as Commissioner Lamoret, *The Buster Keaton Story* (1957) as Kurt Bergner, *Silk Stockings* (1957) as Brankov, *Scent Of Mystery* (1960) as Smiley, *Voyage To The Bottom Of The Sea* (1961) as

Commodore Lucius Emery, *Five Weeks In A Balloon* (1962) as Ahmed, *The Raven* (1963) as Dr Adolphus Bedlo, *The Comedy Of Terrors* (1963) as Felix Gillie, *Muscle Beach Party* (1964) as Mr Strangdour and *The Patsy* (1964) as Morgan Heywood. Following his second divorce he married Annemarie Brenning on July 21, 1950, by whom he had a daughter, Catharine. They separated in October 1962 and were due to have a divorce hearing on the day of his death. Lorre did not take his work too seriously. "Once I had a terrible fight with Jack Warner, who asked me what I thought of a picture I had done with Humphrey Bogart. I told him I didn't go to see it. Mr Warner was furious. I said that I only get paid for making pictures. If he wanted me to see them, he'd have to pay me extra." Lorre attended the funeral of his fellow horror star Bela Lugosi accompanied by Vincent Price. Lugosi was buried in his Dracula cape and Lorre whispered to Price: "Do you think we should drive a stake through his heart just in case?"
CAUSE: Lorre died of a stroke aged 59 in Los Angeles, California. He was buried in Niche 5, T.1, Corridor C of the Cathedral Mausoleum of Hollywood Memorial Park, 6000 Santa Monica Boulevard, Hollywood, California 90038.

Linda Lovelace

(LINDA SUSAN BOREMAN)
Born January 10, 1949
Died April 22, 2002
Deep Throater. Linda Lovelace's is a strange story. In 1972 she became world famous because of a pornographic film about a woman whose clitoris was located at the back of her throat instead of the usual place. The only way she could achieve orgasm was by fellatio or "deep throat". Then she turned her back on the world of porn, claimed that she had been abused by her then husband, Chuck Traynor, and campaigned against pornography.

Then, not long before her death, she posed in a glamour magazine and appeared at several sex festivals where she sold autographed pictures. Linda Boreman was born in the Bronx, New York, the daughter of a retired policeman and a waitress. She was educated at Catholic schools. By her account Boreman's father was henpecked and did nothing to stop his wife's abusive treatment of her children. "He could tiptoe through an earthquake and pretend it wasn't happening," she later said. Mrs Boreman was subject to uncontrollable rages, during which she regularly beat her children. Linda was hit, usually with a belt or whatever her mother had handy, from the time she was four on the slightest pretext. Linda supposedly had sex early and when she was 19 gave birth to a son who was put up for adoption. Then Linda's life changed again when she met an older man named Chuck Traynor in 1970 when she was living with her parents in Florida and recovering from a car accident. He had a drugs charge outstanding against him and had tried to make a living as a pimp. Traynor worked as a production manager on *Deep Throat* and he sensibly married Lovelace to insure himself against her giving testimony against him in court. People queued around the block to see the film and allegedly even Jackie Kennedy Onassis went to see it. *Deep Throat*, which took two weeks to make and cost a few thousand dollars, grossed $600 million at the box office to become the first smash hit of its genre. Linda Lovelace made $1,250, most of which Traynor kept. Her star rose. In 1973 she introduced Elton John on stage in Los Angeles. On May 29, 1974, she arrived in Britain. On June 18 she went to Ascot and wore an entirely diaphanous tiny, teeny minidress. Asked to explain her appeal she said, "From what I've heard, it's the fact that *Deep Throat* was a 'comedy', and because it was on the big screen. Gerard Damiano thought it was the fact that I had that sweet, innocent look. I didn't have bleached blonde hair, I wasn't chewing bubble gum and counting the cracks in the ceiling. As far as what I was doing, I just thought everybody else did that. I didn't know any better. For me, it was cool, because, after being with Mr Traynor and being forced into prostitution, if I did that I felt like I wasn't being abused sexually." A series of books followed purporting to tell Linda Lovelace's story. One of them, *Inside Linda Lovelace*, was prosecuted for obscenity in Britain in 1976 and found not guilty on January 28. In 1980 Linda Lovelace published another autobiography but this one, *Ordeal*, was not a litany of lust like her others but the tale of how she was abused and forced to make *Deep Throat*. "When you see the movie *Deep Throat*," she told an interviewer that year, "you are watching me being raped. It is a crime that movie is still showing; there was a gun to my head the entire time." She claimed that she was forced into sex sessions with a number of men whom Traynor introduced to her. Many of these encounters were filmed. She became a user of painkillers to numb the physical and emotional pain. She had, she alleged, even been forced to have sex with a dog. (A 1969 film supposedly exists called *Dog Fucker* that features Linda having congress with an alsatian.) Men queued up to have sex with her and she slept with a number of Hollywood celebrities including Sammy Davis, Jr. In 1975 she left Traynor for David Winters, who produced her *Linda Lovelace For President* (1976), opposite the former Monkee Mickey Dolenz, an abysmal sex comedy which saw her on the campaign trail following a cross-country bus route mapped out in the shape of a penis. Traynor and Lovelace were divorced. She said, "After I got away from Traynor, it was a lot more fun because I wasn't being

sexually abused. I was walking around with transparent clothes on. I didn't think looking sexy was a terrible thing. I met a lot of people and had a lot of fun at that point." Linda Lovelace appeared on chatshows, filmed a shoe advertisement and the inevitable *Deep Throat II* (1973) and posed for *Playboy* magazine; for a while she even moved into Hugh Hefner's infamous Hollywood mansion. Traynor took up with Marilyn Chambers, another porn star. In 1974 Linda Lovelace married Larry Marchiano, a plumber and TV repairman, by whom she had a son, Dominic, born in 1977, and a daughter, Lindsay, born in 1980. She began a campaign against porn, touring universities and colleges and testified at government and church commissions on the effects of pornography. She was befriended by feminists and the legal scholar Catharine MacKinnon while anti-censorship groups coined the term "Linda Syndrome", referring to porn stars that seek acceptance from society by disavowing their past. In 1996 she and Marchiano were divorced but her health began to suffer and she had huge medical bills. Among other complaints, she had a liver transplant in 1987 after contracting hepatitis C from a blood transfusion. It may well have been the cost of her medical treatment that caused Linda Lovelace's volte face. She posed in lingerie for magazines and appeared at sex festivals, her criticisms of pornography apparently a thing of the past. When *Playboy* compiled its list of the world's 100 sexiest women in 1988, Linda Lovelace was voted number 34, just ahead of Madonna. Interviewed in 1997, Lovelace claimed she had no regrets about her past. "I'm not ashamed or sad about it. I look in the mirror and I look the happiest I've ever looked in my entire life."

CAUSE: On April 3, 2002, Linda Lovelace was involved in a car crash in Denver, Colorado, and suffered massive internal injuries. She was taken off a life-support machine at Denver

Health Medical Center on April 22, dying shortly afterwards. Her former husband, Larry Marchiano, was with their children at the hospital when she died. "Everyone might know her as something else, but we knew her as mum and as Linda," he said. "We divorced five years ago, but she was still my best friend." Ironically, Chuck Traynor died, from a heart attack, exactly three months after Linda Lovelace on July 22, 2002.

FURTHER READING: *Inside Linda Lovelace* – Linda Lovelace (London: Heinrich Hanau, 1974); *The Intimate Diary of Linda Lovelace* – Linda Lovelace as told to Carl Wallin (London: Heinrich Hanau, 1976); *Ordeal An Autobiography* – Linda Lovelace with Mike McGrady (New York: Citadel Press, 1980); *Out Of Bondage* – Linda Lovelace with Mike McGrady (New York: Berkeley, 1986).

Arthur Lowe

Born September 22, 1915
Died April 15, 1982

Pompous character actor. Arthur Lowe was born in his maternal grandfather's home in Spring View Terrace, Hayfield, Derbyshire, the only child of Arthur Lowe (b. Hayfield, Derbyshire, November 1888, d. Hayfield, Derbyshire, August 12, 1971 of a heart attack and chronic bronchitis) and Mary Annie, known as 'Nan', Ford (b. Hayfield, Derbyshire, June 1885, d. Dystleigh Grange, Disley, Derbyshire, December 25, 1981 from a stroke and bronchopneumonia). In 1916 the family moved to Manchester, where Big Arthur became a clerk on the railway at London Road station (now Manchester Piccadilly). Later that year, after the massacre at the Somme, he was called up. He returned to his family in 1918 but was stricken with chronic bronchitis caused by a German mustard gas attack. 'Little Arthur', as he was called to distinguish him from his father, began his education at Chapel Street Elementary Municipal School when he was four. He left in July 1927 and later went to Alma Park Central School in Levenshulme. Little Arthur wanted to join the Merchant Navy but was let down by his poor sight. He worked as a clerk in the cycling department of Brown Brothers at 261-273 Deansgate in Manchester. He was paid £2 10s for a 51-hour week. In February 1939 he joined the Territorial Army, as a cavalry trooper in the Duke of Lancaster's Own Yeomanry. His poor eyesight ensured he was never allowed near the front. In March 1946 he was demobbed and pursued his dream to be an actor. It was a dream that would come true. 'Little Arthur' was known to one generation as Leonard Swindley in *Coronation Street* (the only Weatherfield character ever to get his own spin-off series, *Pardon The Expression*), to another as Captain George Mainwaring in *Dad's Army*, and to a third as the voice of the *Mr Men*. Arthur Lowe was a truly talented actor. He was always in demand for films, television and theatre. The pompous Captain Mainwaring, manager of Martins Bank in Walmington-on-Sea as well as leader of the Home Guard, was not too dissimilar to Arthur Lowe. Both believed things should be done just so and any deviation from this was wrong. They had another disturbing connection. They both had overpowering wives. Elizabeth Mainwaring never appeared on screen. Her footsteps were heard and her backside bearing heavily down on a bunk in the Mainwarings' Anderson shelter was spotted in one episode. Joan Cooper did appear in *Dad's Army*. She played Dolly, the sister of Private Godfrey. It was at Joan Cooper's insistence that she was cast in the role. She was determined that Arthur Lowe should not appear in any performance in which a part wasn't reserved for her. He was a brilliant character actor. She was a mediocre actress who should never have left rep. This was the reason why for the last ten years of his life when Arthur Lowe should have been reaping the benefits of his talent in Hollywood and earning a fortune he was touring crappy theatres starring in crappy plays that were not worthy of his talent. Only in this way could Joan be assured of a part in her husband's personal and professional life. Joan Cooper (b. Birmingham, May 27, 1922) married Arthur Lowe in a register office in Robert Adam Street on January 10, 1948, after her divorce from her first husband, the Canadian actor Richard Gatehouse on December 23, 1947. They had married in Ripon Cathedral, North Yorkshire, in March 1941 and their son, David, was born five months later at her parents' home, Penmore House, Hasland, Chesterfield. It was there in November 1943 that she gave birth to a daughter named Jane. Sadly, four months later, Jane contracted subacute bronchitis and died after choking on her own vomit. In 1946 Joan Gatehouse and Arthur Lowe began an affair – they slept together for the first time on June 13. On August 1, 1946 they moved in together. Nan Lowe did not take to her son's girlfriend – she disapproved of adultery and thought Joan too posh and too much of a luvvie – and the animosity between the two women lasted until death. At the close of 1947 Joan Lowe became pregnant. She was still upset by the death of her daughter and induced a miscarriage by drinking lots of gin (mother's ruin) and lying in a hot bath. The Lowes eventually had a son, Stephen, who was born at Queen Charlotte Hospital, Hammersmith on January 23, 1953 at 6pm, weighing 6lbs 12oz. Stephen later declared that he had been all but ignored by his parents and commented on his mother's voracious sexual appetite. Apparently, Arthur Lowe had little or no desire to make love to his wife every night. It was not that he didn't find her attractive. It was simply that his sex drive was nowhere near as high as hers.

"If you're not fucking me, who are you fucking?" she would shout before indulging in her second vice – booze. She consumed copious amounts of gin which usually set her off on another rant to her husband. The drinking sessions would get heavier and heavier until she passed out and he would wearily put her to bed before sitting on the edge, his head in his hands, wondering what to do next. His films included: *London Belongs To Me* (1948), *Kind Hearts And Coronets* (1949) as a journalist, *The Green Man* (1956), *Stormy Crossing* (1957), *The Boy And The Bridge* (1959), *The Day They Robbed The Bank Of England* (1960), *This Sporting Life* (1963) as Slomer, *If . . .* (1968) as Mr Kemp, *Spring And Port Wine* (1970) as Mr Aspinall, *The Rise And Rise Of Michael Rimmer* (1970) as Ferret, *Adolf Hitler – My Part In His Downfall* (1972) as Major Drysdale, *No Sex, Please – We're British* (1973) as Mr Bromley, *O Lucky Man!* (1973) as Mr Duff/Charlie Johnson/Dr Munda, *Man About The House* (1974) as Spiros, *The Bawdy Adventures Of Tom Jones* (1976) as Dr Thwackum, *The Strange Case Of The End Of Civilisation As We Know It* (1977) as William Watson, *The Lady Vanishes* (1979) as Charters and *Sweet William* (1980) as Captain Walton. CAUSE: In December 1981 and January 1982 he appeared at the Victoria Palace, London, in his first pantomime *Mother Goose* alongside Ian Lavender and John Inman. Naturally, a part was created for Joan – the invented character of the Queen of Gooseland. By this time he was suffering from narcolepsy and two male dancers stood by his side at all times to nudge him in case he fell asleep. In March 1982 Lowe presented an award at the BAFTAs but stumbled over his lines and mispronounced a surname. The audience, thinking it was an act, howled. On April 14 he went to BBC Radio Birmingham to record a morale-boosting broadcast as Captain

Mainwaring for the troops sailing to free the Falkland Islands from the Argentine invaders. That afternoon he took part as usual in the matinee performance of R.C. Sheriff's 1948 play *Home At Seven* at the Alexandra Theatre, Birmingham where he was playing bowler-hatted banker David Preston. At 5.30pm he collected egg and chips from the theatre's canteen and went back to his dressing room to eat. At 6pm he suffered a stroke but Joan insisted that he had just fallen over and banged his head. Worried theatre staff insisted on calling an ambulance. Lowe was taken unconscious to the General Hospital, Birmingham. His wife told the theatre manager to clear Arthur's dressing room and that night she acted opposite Lowe's understudy Vyvian Hall, even though the theatre offered to cancel the performance. Joan Lowe went to the hospital after she had finished the play and was told that her husband had lost the use of one side of his body and would be paralysed if he recovered. At 5am the following morning Arthur Lowe died aged 66 without regaining consciousness. That night she went on with the performance without telling Stephen who heard the news on the wireless. For some reason when she registered his death, Joan Lowe told the registrar that her husband had been born in Cheshire. On April 22 Arthur Lowe was cremated at Sutton Coldfield Crematorium and his ashes scattered in the grounds. Fewer than a dozen people attended the service. His widow was not there because she was touring in Belfast. Why did Arthur Lowe stay with this cold woman? Why didn't he leave her? Because he loved her. Because he loved her he did work that was beneath him. Ultimately, Arthur Lowe did not achieve the acting greatness that could have been his because he loved a drunken nymphomaniac and that is the greatest tragedy of all. He left £205,983. Joan Lowe died on July 1, 1989 from stomach cancer at 3 Chapel Road in Hayfield, Derbyshire, the last home of her in-laws.

FURTHER READING: *Arthur Lowe –* Graham Lord (London: Orion, 2002).

Myrna Loy

(MYRNA ADELE WILLIAMS)
Born August 2, 1905
Died December 14, 1993

'The Queen of Hollywood'. Born in Raidersburg, Montana, Myrna was the redheaded daughter of a cattleman who was the youngest ever person to be elected to the Montana State legislature. She harboured an ambition to be a dancer from an early age and fulfilled that dream when she was 12. After a brief stint as a model, six years later, she was in the chorus of Grauman's Chinese Theater. The 5'6" Myrna began her film career as the silent era was ending. She appeared usually as some kind of vamp or *femme fatale* and her 'Oriental' appearance led her to change her name to the more eastern Loy. Her films included: *Pretty Ladies* (1925), *Sporting Life* (1925), *Ben-Hur* (1925), *The Caveman* (1926), *The Love Toy* (1926), *Exquisite Sinner* (1926), *Don Juan* (1926) as Mai, *When A Man Loves* (1927), *The Climbers* (1927) as Countess Veya, *The Jazz Singer* (1927), *The Girl From Chicago* (1927) as Mary Carlton, *Ham And Eggs At The Front* (1927) as Fifi, *What Price Beauty?* (1928), *A Girl In Every Port* (1928), *Pay As You Enter* (1928) as Yvonne De Russo, *Fancy Baggage* (1929) as Myrna, *The Desert Song* (1929) as Azuri, *The Black Watch* (1929) as Yasmini, *The Great Divide* (1929) as Manuella, *The Devil To Pay!* (1930) as Susan Hale, *Under A Texas Moon* (1930) as Lolita Romero, *Cock O' The Walk* (1930) as Narita, *Bride Of The Regiment* (1930) as Sophie, *The Jazz Cinderella* (1930) as Mildred Vane, *Renegades* (1930) as Eleanore, *Rogue Of The Rio Grande* (1930) as Carmita, *The Truth About Youth* (1930) as Kara, *Transatlantic* (1931) as Kay Graham,

Skyline (1931) as Paula Lambert, *Rebound* (1931) as Evie Lawrence, *The Naughty Flirt* (1931) as Linda Gregory, *A Connecticut Yankee* (1931) as Morgan le Fay, *Body And Soul* (1931) as Alice Lester, *Consolation Marriage* (1931) as Elaine Brandon, *Vanity Fair* (1932) as Becky Sharp, *The Wet Parade* (1932) as Eileen Pinchon, *Thirteen Women* (1932) as Ursula Georgi, *The Mask Of Fu Manchu* (1932) as Fah Lo See, *The Barbarian* (1933) as Diana, *Topaze* (1933) as Coco, *When Ladies Meet* (1933) as Mary Howard and *The Prizefighter And The Lady* (1933) as Belle Mercer Morgan. Just when it seemed as if she had been typecast into playing a certain type of character, W.S. Van Dyke came along and cast her as Nora Charles in *The Thin Man* (1934). She was to appear in the Thin Man sequels as well: *After The Thin Man* (1936), *Another Thin Man* (1939), *Shadow Of The Thin Man* (1941), *The Thin Man Goes Home* (1945) and *Song Of The Thin Man* (1947). Her other films included: *Manhattan Melodrama* (1934) as Eleanor Packer, *Wings In The Dark* (1935) as Sheila Mason, *Petticoat Fever* (1936) as Irene Campton, *The Great Ziegfeld* (1936) as Billie Burke, *Libeled Lady* (1936) as Connie Allenbury, *Parnell* (1937) as Katie O'Shea, *Too Hot To Handle* (1938) as Alma Harding, *Test Pilot* (1938) as Ann Barton, *The Rains Came* (1939) as Lady Edwina Esketh, *Lucky Night* (1939) as Cora Jordan Overton, *I Love You Again* (1940) as Kay Wilson and *Love Crazy* (1941) as Susan Ireland. As she got older her role became more maternal, in movies such as *The Bachelor And The Bobby-Soxer* (1947) as Judge Margaret Turner, *Mr Blandings Builds His Dream House* (1948) as Muriel Blandings, *That Dangerous Age* (1949) as Lady Cathy Brooke, *Midnight Lace* (1960) as Aunt Bea, *The April Fools* (1969) as Grace Greenlaw and *Airport 1975* (1974) as Mrs Devaney. From 1949 until 1954 she was a film adviser to UNESCO.

On screen she often played the part of a perfect wife, something that may have hindered her off screen where she married and divorced four times. Her husbands were: Arthur Hornblow, Jr (June 27, 1936–June 1, 1942), John Hertz, Jr (June 6, 1942–August 21, 1944), Gene Markey (January 1946–August 1950) and Howland H. Sergeant (June 2, 1951–May 31, 1960). In 1991 she was awarded a special Oscar, no doubt to make up for never having been even nominated. CAUSE: On November 1, 1993, she was admitted to Lenox Hill Hospital, New York. She underwent surgery 43 days later but died on the operating table at 6.22pm. She was 88. She was cremated on December 18, 1993 and her ashes were buried at Forestvale Cemetery, Helena, Montana.

Ernst Lubitsch
Born January 28, 1892
Died November 30, 1947
Deft director. After working in films in his native Berlin both as an actor and director, Lubitsch left for Hollywood in 1922 at the invitation of Mary Pickford. Seven years later, he discovered Jeanette MacDonald, who was to say of him: "To me, great people are always simple and Ernst was the simplest man I ever knew. He had no flaw in his greatness, no chi chi, nor false vanity. On the set, he had a greatness of his art, but no 'artiness'." On February 4, 1935, 5'7" Lubitsch became Paramount's production chief, the first time this had happened to a director. His films included: *Fräulein Seifenschaum* (1914), *Der Letzte Anzug* (1915), *Blindekuh* (1915), *Das Schönste Geschenk* (1916), *Der Blusenkönig* (1917), *Das Mädel Vom Ballet* (1918), *Ein Fideles Gefängnis* (1918), *Rausch* (1919), *Die Puppe* (1919), *Meine Frau, Die Filmschauspielerin* (1919), *Ich Möchte Kein Mann Sein* (1919), *Madame DuBarry* (1919), *Anna Boleyn* (1920), *Romeo Und Julia Im Schnee* (1920), *Rosita* (1923) which was his

first American film, *The Marriage Circle* (1924), *Three Women* (1924), *Forbidden Paradise* (1924), *Kiss Me Again* (1925), *Lady Windermere's Fan* (1925), *The Love Parade* (1929) which was his first talkie, *Paramount On Parade* (1930), *Monte Carlo* (1930), *The Smiling Lieutenant* (1931), *Trouble In Paradise* (1932), *If I Had A Million* (1932), *The Merry Widow* (1934), *Bluebeard's Eighth Wife* (1938), *Ninotchka* (1939), *To Be Or Not To Be* (1942) and *Heaven Can Wait* (1943).

CAUSE: Aged 55, he died in Hollywood, California, from a heart attack while filming *That Lady In Ermine* (1948), which was finished by Otto Preminger.

Arthur Lucan

(ARTHUR TOWLE)
Born September 16, 1885
Died May 17, 1954
Old Mother Riley. Born in Boston, Lincolnshire, Towle began in show business in 1900 when he left school. A regular in music halls, in 1913 he married Kathleen 'Kitty' McShane (b. Dublin, May 19, 1898, d. London, March 24, 1964) – she was 15, he 26. They developed the act of Old Mother Riley and her daughter and successfully made it last 40 years, transferring it to 15 cheaply made and highly profitable films (1937–1952). The films were *Old Mother Riley* (1937), *Old Mother Riley In Paris* (1938), *Old Mother Riley, MP* (1939), *Old Mother Riley Joins Up* (1939), *Old Mother Riley In Society* (1940), *Old Mother Riley In Business* (1940), *Old Mother Riley's Ghosts* (1941), *Old Mother Riley's Circus* (1941), *Old Mother Riley Overseas* (1943), *Old Mother Riley Detective* (1943), *Old Mother Riley At Home* (1945), *Old Mother Riley's New Venture* (1949), *Old Mother Riley, Headmistress* (1950), *Old Mother Riley's Jungle Treasure* (1951) and *Mother Riley Meets The Vampire* (1952). Old Mother Riley relied on malapropisms, comical situations and facial expressions for his comedy. By 1951 after a series of fierce

rows, the couple had separated and Kitty did not appear in Arthur's last film, though he supported her financially.

CAUSE: He collapsed from a heart attack just before going on stage in Hull and died. He was 68.

Bela Lugosi

(BÉLA FERENC DEZSÖ BLASKÓ)
Born October 20, 1882
Died August 16, 1956
The horror star for whom it all went horribly wrong. The son of a baker-turned-banker, Lugosi was born in Lugos, Austria-Hungary (now Lugoj, Rumania), hence his name. Following his father's death he left school to work in an ironworks. Deciding to chance his arm at acting he changed his name to Bela Lugossy, which gave him an aristocratic air. In 1911 he altered the spelling to the less pretentious Lugosi, by which name he became world famous. The handsome 6'1″ actor became a favourite and matinee idol but his career was interrupted by World War I. Commissioned as a lieutenant, he was wounded three times and, finally discharged in 1916, went back to his first love. The following year on June 25, he married Ilona Szmik. That same year he began making films including *A Régiséggyüjtö* (1917), *A Leopárd* (1917), *Az Ezredes* (1917), *Álarcosbál* (1918), *Nászdal* (1918) as Bertram, *Küzdelem A Létért* (1918), *Casanova* (1918) and *99* (1918). In March 1919 Hungary was hit by revolution and Lugosi was at the forefront, leading the actors' union and claiming oppression of the profession by producers. That summer the insurrection was suppressed and Lugosi had to flee for his life. His wife refused to follow him into exile and they were divorced. He moved to Vienna and Germany, where he appeared in teutonic films. In December 1921 he moved to New York to appear in a touring play but it was financially unsuccessful and he

resumed his movie career with *The Silent Command* (1923) as Hisston. In 1922 he had married Ilona von Montagh but both soon realised they had made a mistake and they divorced. Lugosi made the occasional film but devoted most of his time to Broadway. In 1927 he opened in an English play about a Transylvanian vampire. *Dracula* played on the Great White Way for over a year and was eventually made into a film (1931), with Lugosi in the title role. He was to the manner born. In the summer of 1929 he had married Beatrice Woodruff and again that ended in a quick divorce. Following the success of *Dracula*, Lugosi was cast as Frankenstein's monster but refused to play the role for fear of getting typecast. (As it turned out, it was already too late for him to avoid that.) The part went to Boris Karloff and made his name. Lugosi played the mad scientist Doctor Mirakle in *Murders In The Rue Morgue* (1932), which flopped. On January 31, 1933, he married his secretary Lillian Arch, by whom he had one son. With a wife to support and by now realising on which side his bread was buttered, Lugosi was cast in a variety of horror and thriller roles including *Chandu The Magician* (1932) as Roxor, *White Zombie* (1932) as Murder Legendre, *The Death Kiss* (1932) as Joseph Steiner, *Night Of Terror* (1933) as Degar, *Island Of Lost Souls* (1933) as Sayer Of The Law, *The Devil's In Love* (1933), *The Black Cat* (1934) as Dr Vitus Verdegast, *The Return Of Chandu* (1934) as Frank Chandler (Chandu The Magician), *Murder By Television* (1935) as Arthur Perry, *Mark Of The Vampire* (1935) as Count Mora, *Chandu On The Magic Island* (1935) as Frank Chandler (Chandu), *The Mysterious Mr Wong* (1935) as Mr Wong, *The Raven* (1935) as the insane Dr Richard Vollin, *The Phantom Creeps* (1939) as Dr Alex Zorka, *Son Of Frankenstein* (1939) as Ygor, *The Wolf Man* (1941) as Bela, *The Ghost Of Frankenstein* (1942) as Ygor, *Frankenstein Meets The Wolf Man* (1943) as Frankenstein's Monster, *The Return Of The Vampire* (1944) as Armand Tesla, *Zombies On Broadway* (1945) as Dr Paul Renault and *The Body Snatcher* (1945) as Joseph. In 1945, when the industry halted production of films about mad scientists, Lugosi found regular work difficult to come by. He also became addicted to drugs, taken at first to ease his sciatica. First, he took morphine, then Demarol and the heroin substitute Methadone. He began to parody his own image in films such as *Scared To Death* (1947) as Professor Leonide, *Abbott & Costello Meet Frankenstein* (1948) as Dracula, *Mother Riley Meets The Vampire* (1952) as Von Housen, for which he was paid $4,000, and *Bela Lugosi Meets A Brooklyn Gorilla* (1952) as Dr Zabor. During the Forties and Fifties he toured America with a horror act and was jeered and laughed at by the audience mainly made up of teenagers. He would even sign autographs while lying in a coffin. In 1953 his marriage collapsed and his wife was granted a divorce on July 17. In April 1955 he was committed as a hopeless drug addict but was only incarcerated for four months in a bid to wean him off narcotics. Released back into the community and buoyed by the fan mail he had received he tried to kick-start his career but could only land the part of Casimir, a deaf mute, in *The Black Sleep* (1956). On August 25, 1955, he married again. The fifth Mrs Lugosi was Hope Lininger. The world's worst film director, Ed Wood, Jr, cast Lugosi in the now notorious *Plan 9 From Outer Space* (1958), generally regarded as the worst film of all time. Horror writer Stephen King wasn't amused by the film. He wrote: "There's nothing funny about watching Bela Lugosi (actually, a stand-in was used for most shots) wracked with pain, a morphine monkey on his back, creeping around a southern California development with his Dracula cape pulled up over his nose." Lugosi himself once said: "I guess I'm pretty much of a lone wolf. I don't say I don't like people at all but, to tell you the truth, I only like [them when] I have a chance to look deep into their hearts and their minds."

CAUSE: Bela Lugosi died aged 73 at his home, 5620 Harold Way, Los Angeles, at 6.45pm of a coronary occlusion with myocardial fibrosis – in other words a heart attack. On August 18, 1956, he was buried in Grave 1, Tier 120 of the 'Grotto' of Holy Cross Cemetery & Mausoleum, 5835 West Slauson Avenue, Culver City, California 90230. At his request he was buried in his Dracula cape.

Keye Luke

Born June 18, 1904
Died January 12, 1991

'Number One Son'. To generations of movie-goers, 5′6″ Keye Luke was the leading Oriental actor working in Hollywood in a career lasting almost 60 years. For someone who spent so much of his life before camera it is strange that the first mystery about Luke concerns his place of birth. For many years it was believed he was born in Canton, China, but now evidence has come to light that seems to suggest he was actually born in New York City. He was raised in Seattle, Washington, where he attended the University of Washington, and joined the film industry as an artist designing movie posters. He also worked as a technical adviser on all things Oriental. Like many behind the scenes he itched to get in front of the camera and his chance came in 1934 when he made his début in *The Painted Veil*. From then on, it seemed that whenever a Chinese character was written into a film or television show the call went out for Keye Luke. His innumerable films included: *Shanghai* (1935), *Oil For The Lamps Of China* (1935), *Mad Love* (1935) as Dr Wong, *King Of Burlesque*

(1935) as Wong and, the first time he portrayed Charlie Chan's number one son, *Charlie Chan In Paris* (1935). It was a role he was to reprise many times in films such as *Charlie Chan In Shanghai* (1935), *Charlie Chan At The Race Track* (1936), *Charlie Chan At The Circus* (1936), *Charlie Chan On Broadway* (1937), *Charlie Chan At Monte Carlo* (1937), *Charlie Chan At The Opera* (1937), *Charlie Chan At The Olympics* (1937), *Mr Moto's Gamble* (1938), *The Feathered Serpent* (1948), *The Sky Dragon* (1949) and, finally, 'winning promotion', *The Amazing Chan And The Chan Clan*, a CBS cartoon series that lasted from September 9, 1972, until September 1, 1974, where he finally voiced Charlie Chan. He also played Kato in *The Green Hornet* (1939) and *The Green Hornet Strikes Again* (1940) and reprised the part on television 50 years later. He was Dr Kildare's rival Dr Lee Wong How in *Dr Gillespie's New Assistant* (1942), *Dr Gillespie's Criminal Case* (1943), *Three Men In White* (1944), *Between Two Women* (1944) and *Dark Delusion* (1947). Other films included: *Disputed Passage* (1939) as Andrew Abbott, *Torchy Blane In Chinatown* (1939), *Barricade* (1939) as Ling, *Sued For Libel* (1940) as Chang, *No, No, Nanette* (1940), *Phantom Of Chinatown* (1940) as James Lee Wong, *They Met In Bombay* (1941) as Chen Ling, *No Hands On The Clock* (1941), *Mr And Mrs North* (1941) as Kumi, *Burma Convoy* (1941) as Lin Taiyen, *Bowery Blitzkrieg* (1941) as Clancy, *Yank On The Burma Road* (1942) as Kim How, *A Tragedy At Midnight* (1942) as Ah Foo, *Spy Ship* (1942) as Hiru, *North To The Klondike* (1942) as Wellington Wong, *The Falcon's Brother* (1942) as Jerry, *Destination Unknown* (1942), *Invisible Agent* (1942), *Somewhere I'll Find You* (1942) as Thomas Chang, *Across The Pacific* (1942), *Let's Go Collegiate* (1942) as Buck Wing, *Mexican Spitfire's Elephant* (1942) as Lao Lee, *Journey*

For Margaret (1942), Salute To The Marines (1943) as 'Flashy' Logaz, Adventures Of Smilin' Jack (1943) as Captain Wing, Dragon Seed (1944), Andy Hardy's Blonde Trouble (1944) as Dr Lee, Secret Agent X-9 (1945) as Ah Fong, First Yank Into Tokyo (1945) as Haan-Soo, Lost City Of The Jungle (1946) as Tal Shan, Tokyo Rose (1946) as Charlie Otani, Waterfront At Midnight (1948) as Loy, Sleep, My Love (1948) as Jimmie, Young Man With A Horn (1950) as Ramundo, Fair Wind To Java (1953) as Pidada, Hell's Half Acre (1954) as Chief Dan, The Bamboo Prison (1954) as Li Ching, World For Ransom (1954) as Wong, Love Is A Many-Splendored Thing (1955), Around The World In 80 Days (1956), Yangtse Incident (1957) as Captain Kuo Tai, Project X (1968) as Sen Chiu, Nobody's Perfect (1968), The Chairman (1969) as Professor Soong Li, The Hawaiians (1970) as Foo Sen, Enter The Dragon (1973), Won Ton Ton, The Dog Who Saved Hollywood (1976), The Amsterdam Kill (1977) as Chung Wei, Just You And Me, Kid (1979) as Doctor Device, Gremlins (1984) as Grandfather, A Fine Mess (1986) as Ishimine, Dead Heat (1988) as Mr Thule, The Mighty Quinn (1989) as Dr Raj, Gremlins 2: The New Batch (1990) as Mr Wing and Alice (1990) as Dr Yang. He appeared on Broadway and was also much in demand on television. He played Thomas Wong on the NBC comedy drama series Kentucky Jones from September 19, 1964, until September 11, 1965. He was amateur crime fighter Dr Fong on the ABC detective show Harry-O in 1976. He portrayed the Kralahome (Prime Minister) frequently arguing with Mrs Anna on the short-lived CBS comedy Anna And The King from September 17, 1972, until New Year's Eve of the same year. However, his best-known television role was as the kindly Shaolin priest Master Po on the ABC western Kung Fu from October 14, 1972, until June 28, 1975. He wore white contact lenses (Po was

blind) and a rather large amount of make-up to hide the fact that he still had a relatively young-looking face. He reprised that part in the television film Kung Fu: The Movie (1986).
CAUSE: He died following a stoke in Whittier, California, aged 86.

Paul Lynde
Born June 13, 1926
Died January 10, 1982
Camp Square. Paul Lynde was celebrated for his vocal talents (his was the voice in many cartoons) and for his outrageous campness on TV shows such as Hollywood Squares where he occupied the middle square. He died before it was in vogue to out gay celebrities. Born in Mount Vernon, Ohio, Paul Edward Lynde was one of six children and the middle of four boys of a butcher. He was taken by his mother to see Ben Hur (1926) and from then on never wanted to be do anything other than be in show business. When he told his father his dream, he recalled, "My dad hit the roof and I hit the road, simultaneously." He graduated from Northwestern University in Evanston, Illinois, and became a stand-up comedian at the Number One Fifth Avenue nightclub in New York. In 1948 he began a two-year residency with The Perry Como Show. He made his film début in New Faces (1954) as himself and went on to appear in Son Of Flubber (1963) as a sports commentator, Bye Bye Birdie (1963) as Harry McAfee, Under The Yum Yum Tree (1963) as Murphy, For Those Who Think Young (1964) as Uncle Sid, Send Me No Flowers (1964) as Mr Akins, Beach Blanket Bingo (1965) as Bullets, The Glass Bottom Boat (1966) as Homer Cripps, How Sweet It Is! (1968) as the Purser, Rabbit Test (1978) as Dr. Roger Vidal and The Villain (1979) as Nervous Elk. On television he was Uncle Arthur in Bewitched (1965–July 1, 1972) and headlined in his own The Paul Lynde Show (1972) and a

sitcom called *Temperatures Rising*. It ran for 46 episodes between September 12, 1972 and August 29, 1974. He was the voice of Mildew Wolf in *The Cattanooga Cats* (September 6, 1969–September 5, 1971) and Sylvester Sneekly, a.k.a. The Hooded Claw in *The Perils of Penelope Pitstop* (September 13, 1969–September 5, 1971).

CAUSE: Paul Lynde's death has never been satisfactorily explained. He was found drowned in his swimming pool in Beverly Hills, California, either as a result of a heart attack or under the influence of alcohol. He had been in ill-health for over a year with an illness thought to be cancer. The coroner who examined his body said that Lynde had the heart of an 88-year old man. He was buried in Amity Cemetery in Amity, Ohio.

M

Bernie Mac

(BERNARD JEFFREY MCCULLOUGH)
Born October 5, 1957
Died August 9, 2008
His own man. Born and raised on the
South Side of Chicago, Illinois, Bernie
Mac began his career as a stand-up
comic in 1977, four years after the
death of his single mother, Mary. He
made his film debut as a doorman in
Mo' Money (1992) and then until 1995
appeared in bit parts in films such as
Who's The Man? (1993), *House Party 3*
(1994) and *The Walking Dead* (1995).
From then on his star began to rise. He
was the star of *The Bernie Mac Show*
(2001–2006), which won him two
Emmy nominations. He appeared in
How To Be A Player (1997), *The Players
Club* (1998), *Life* (1999) starring Eddie
Murphy, *What's The Worst That Could
Happen?* (2001), *Ocean's Eleven* (2001)
and *Charlie's Angels: Full Throttle*
(2001) in which he played a black
Jimmy Bosley as opposed to David
Doyle's staid, middle-aged white John
Bosley. His first starring role came in
Mr 3000 (2004) in which he was a
retired baseball player. He married
Rhonda McCullough in 1977.
CAUSE: Mac had sarcoidosis, an
inflammatory lung disease. He was
admitted to Northwestern Memorial
Hospital, Chicago a week before his
death from pneumonia. He was 50. He
was cremated and his ashes interred at
Washington Memory Gardens
Cemetery, 701 Ridge Road,
Homewood, Illinois.

Jeanette MacDonald

Born June 18, 1903
Died January 14, 1965
'The Iron Butterfly'. Born in
Philadelphia, Pennsylvania, 5'4"
Jeanette Anna MacDonald began

her performing career appearing in
Broadway musicals. Her film début
came in *The Love Parade* (1929) as
Queen Louise appearing opposite
Maurice Chevalier. He commented, "I
never thought she had much of a sense
of humour. When we worked together
she always objected to anyone telling
a risqué story." They reprised their
partnership three more times in *One
Hour With You* (1932), in which
MacDonald played Colette Bertier,
Love Me Tonight (1932) in which she
played Princess Jeanette and *The Merry
Widow* (1934). However, it was her
films made alongside Nelson Eddy
that won hearts the world over. Their
first (of eight films they would make
together) was *Naughty Marietta* (1935)
as Princess Marie de Namours de
la Bonfain. Others were *Rose Marie*
(1936) as Marie de Flor, *Maytime*
(1937) as Marcia Morney/Miss
Morrison, *The Girl Of The Golden West*
(1938) as Mary Robbins, *Sweethearts*
(1939) as Gwen Marlowe, *New Moon*
(1940) as Marianne de Beaumanoir,
Bitter Sweet (1940) as Sarah Millick,
later Sari Linden, and *I Married An
Angel* (1942) as Anna Zador/Briggitta.
Like Eddy she performed with other
partners and her duettists included
Alan Jones (father of singer Jack) and
her husband actor Gene Raymond,
whom she married on June 16, 1937,
at the Wilshire Boulevard Church in
Los Angeles. Following *The Sun Comes
Up* (1949) in which she played Helen
Lorfield Winter, she retired from acting
and concentrated her energies on
singing.
CAUSE: She died of a heart attack in
Houston, Texas, aged 61. She was
interred in the Freedom Mausoleum
on Arlington Road of Forest Lawn
Memorial-Parks.

Fred MacMurray

Born August 30, 1908
Died November 5, 1991
Prodigious performer. Born in
Kankakee, Illinois, 6'3" Frederick

Martin MacMurray, the son of a concert violinist, quickly rose to become one of Hollywood's best-known and favourite comic leading men. He began as a singer and a saxophonist with a big band before making his film début in *Girls Gone Wild* (1929). He signed for Paramount in 1935 and also appeared in *Tiger Rose* (1929), *Car 99* (1935) as Ross Martin, *Hands Across The Table* (1935) as Theodore Drew III, *The Bride Comes Home* (1935) as Cyrus Anderson, *The Trail Of The Lonesome Pine* (1936) as Jack Hale, *Thirteen Hours By Air* (1936) as Jack Gordon, *True Confession* (1937) as Kenneth Bartlett, *Champagne Waltz* (1937) as Buzzy Bellew, *Cocoanut Grove* (1938) as Johnny Prentice, *Remember The Night* (1940) as John Sargent, *Dive Bomber* (1941) as Commander Joe Blake, *Double Indemnity* (1944) as murderer Walter Neff, *The Egg & I* (1947) as Bob MacDonald, *The Caine Mutiny* (1954) as Lieutenant Tom Keefer, *There's Always Tomorrow* (1956) as Clifford Groves, *Face Of A Fugitive* (1959) as Jim Larsen and *The Apartment* (1960) as J.D. Sheldrake. Although undoubtedly leading material he was rarely cast in big budget productions but he didn't seem to mind and turned to television when his career began to falter. The series *My Three Sons* revived his film career and he appeared in *The Absent-Minded Professor* (1961) as Professor Ned Brainard, *Son Of Flubber* (1963) as Professor Ned Brainard, *Follow Me Boys!* (1966) as Lemuel Siddons and *Charley And The Angel* (1973) as Charley Appleby. The horror film about bees *The Swarm* (1978), in which he played the part of Clarence, marked his last cinematic appearance. He was married twice. His first wife was dancer Lillian Lamont (b. 1908) whom he married on June 20, 1936. They adopted two children: Susan (b. 1941) and Robert (b. 1944). Lillian died in Santa Monica on June 22, 1953. A year later, on June 28, 1954, he married June Haver. They adopted twin daughters, Kathryn Marie and Laurie Ann, on December 4, 1956. He was the visual inspiration for the superhero Captain Marvel.

CAUSE: He died of pneumonia aged 83 in Santa Monica, California. He was buried in the Mausoleum, D1, Room 7, of Holy Cross Cemetery, 5835 West Slauson Avenue, Culver City, California 90230.

Gordon MacRae
Born March 12, 1921
Died January 24, 1986
Alcoholic actor. The son of a Scottish toolmaker, Gordon MacRae was a musically gifted child at school, playing the clarinet and piano and singing in the choir. He also excelled at American football and lacrosse. At the 1939–1940 World's Fair he won a singing competition for amateurs. This led to a two-year gig singing with a band. During World War II he served as a navigator. Following the cessation of hostilities he moved to Hollywood and appeared in *The Big Punch* (1948) as Johnny Grant, *The Daughter Of Rosie O'Grady* (1950) as Tony Pastor, *The West Point Story* (1950) as Tom Fletcher, *On Moonlight Bay* (1951) as William Sherman, *By The Light Of The Silvery Moon* (1953) as William Sherman, *The Desert Song* (1953) as Paul Bonnard, *Oklahoma!* (1955) as Curly, *Carousel* (1956) as Billy Bigelow and *The Best Things In Life Are Free* (1956) as B.G. 'Buddy' De Sylva. He married the actress Sheila Stephens on May 21, 1941, and they had four children: actresses Meredith (b. Houston, Texas, 1944) and Heather (b. 1946), Bruce (b. 1948) and Garr (b. 1954). They divorced on April 15, 1967, and on September 25 of that year he married Elizabeth Lambert Schrafft. Their daughter, Amanda, was born on May 2, 1968. MacRae admitted that he had been an alcoholic for much of his life and in 1983

became honorary chairman of the National Council of Alcoholism. CAUSE: He died in Lincoln, Nebraska, of cancer of the jaw and mouth complicated by pneumonia. He was 64 years old.

Guy Madison
(ROBERT OZELL MOSELEY)
Born January 19, 1922
Died February 6, 1996
Uniform dreamboat. Born in Bakersfield, California, Madison had a varied life before joining the navy in 1942. He was a lifeguard, a telephone linesman and a champion swimmer. Once in uniform, he became a marine where he was spotted by a talent scout who recommended him for a small part in *Since You Went Away* (1944). Using a seven-day pass, he played Harold Smith, a sailor who flirts with Jennifer Jones. Even though he was on screen for just three minutes, Madison made a huge impact on the female audience and received 4,000 fan letters. Following demob, he was offered a contract. He said, "I knew stars made lots of money. That meant clothes, cars, maybe a boat. That was for me." However, his performances soon led studio bosses to realise that Madison (the name came from a press agent) was just a pretty face. In 1945 he met actress Gail Russell who was singularly unimpressed by the blond hunk. A few months later they met again at the home of the homosexual agent Henry Willson, the man who named Rock Hudson, Tab Hunter and many more. This time the couple fell in love but it did not stop Gail spending a lot of time with John Farrow, the director and husband of Maureen O'Sullivan. In February 1949, Madison and Gail went on a month-long holiday to get to know each other better and visit her innumerable relatives. On August 31 they married at the Biltmore Hotel in Santa Barbara. The bride wore the outfit designed for her by Edith Head

for the film *Captain China* (1949). Gail's mother, father and brother were notable for their absence from the ceremony. The Guy Madisons honeymooned in Yosemite National Park. Her alcoholism and insecurity caused rows between the couple and they separated. In October 1953 Gail was named as co-respondent by John Wayne's estranged wife, Esperanza 'Chata' Diaz Ceballos. Gail and Madison reconciled but it was never a love match. Gail entered a sanatorium in Seattle, Washington, to try to recover but in November 1953, she was arrested for drink driving. Madison bailed her out but on October 6, 1954 they were divorced. It was in his thirties that Madison began to show some minor acting talent. His pretty boy looks had started to fade and he was able to land parts that allowed him some measure of respectability. However, not all his films were quite so, er, normal. In *The Beast Of Hollow Mountain* (1956) he played Jimmy Ryan, a rancher whose cattle were eaten by a dinosaur that had somehow managed to survive the various travails that had killed off all the other species. In April 1951, Madison turned to television and appeared in the title role in *The Adventures Of Wild Bill Hickok*, a gig that lasted seven years. Six foot Madison would introduce himself on screen as "James Butler Hickok, mister" only for his sidekick Jingles P. Jones (Andy Devine) to pipe up, "That's Wild Bill Hickok, mister. The bravest, strongest, fightingest US marshal in the whole West." Many of the Hickok adventures were made into second-feature films for overseas distribution including *The Yellow Haired Kid* (1952), *Trail Of The Arrow* (1952), *The Ghost Of Crossbones Canyon* (1952), *Behind Southern Lines* (1952), *Two Gun Marshal* (1953), *Six Gun Decision* (1953), *Secret Of Outlaw Flats* (1953), *Border City Rustlers* (1953), *The Two Gun Teacher* (1954), *Trouble On The Trail* (1954), *Outlaw's Son* (1954),

Marshals In Disguise (1954), *The Titled Tenderfoot* (1955), *Timber Country Trouble* (1955), *Phantom Trails* (1955) and *The Matchmaking Marshal* (1955). His other films included: *Till The End Of Time* (1946) as Cliff Harper, *Honeymoon* (1947) as Phil Bowen, *Texas, Brooklyn And Heaven* (1948) as Eddie Taylor, *Massacre River* (1949) as Lieutenant Larry Knight, *Drums In The Deep South* (1951) as Will Denning, *Red Snow* (1952) as Lieutenant Phil Johnson, *The Charge At Feather River* (1953) as Miles Archer, *The Command* (1954) as Captain Robert MacClaw, *5 Against The House* (1955) as Al Mercer, *The Last Frontier* (1955) as Captain Glenn Riordan, *Reprisal!* (1956) as Frank Madden, *On The Threshold Of Space* (1956) as Captain Jim Hollenbeck, *Hilda Crane* (1956) as Russell Burns, *The Hard Man* (1957) as Steve Burden, *Bullwhip* (1958) as Steve, *Jet Over The Atlantic* (1959) as Brett Murphy. In the Sixties he worked mainly in Europe appearing in many spaghetti Westerns and low-budget period pieces such as *La Schiava Di Roma* (1960) as Marco Valerio, *Le Prigioniere Dell'Isola Del Diavolo* (1961) as Henri Valliére, *Rosmunda E Alboino* (1962) as Amalchi, *Il Boia Di Venezia* (1963) as Rodrigo Zeno, *Il Vendicatore Mascherato* (1964) as Massimo, *Sandokan Contro Il Leopardo Di Sarawak* (1964) as Captain Iannis, *Sandokan Alla Riscossa* (1964) as Iannis, *I Misteri Della Giungla Nera* (1964) as Souyadhana, *L'Avventuriero Della Tortuga* (1965) as Alfonso di Montélimar, *I Cinque Della Vendetta* (1966) as Tex, *Testa Di Sbarco Per Otto Implacabili* (1967) as Captain Murphy, *I Lunghi Giorni Dell'Odio* (1967) as Martin Benson, *Il Figlio Di Django* (1967) as Father Fleming, *Un Posto All'Inferno* (1968) as Marc McGreaves, *La Battaglia Dell'Ultimo Panzer* (1968), *Il Re Dei Criminali* (1968) as Professor Wendland, *Sette Winchester Per Un Massacro* (1968) as Colonel Thomas Blake, *Reverendo Colt* (1970) as

Reverend Miller, *Comando Al Infierno* (1970) as Major Carter and a star at the film screening in *Won Ton Ton, The Dog Who Saved Hollywood* (1976). In 1954 he was married a second time. His later wife was Sheilah Connolly and they had three daughters, Bridget (b. 1955), Erin (b. 1956) and Dolly (b. 1957), before their 1963 divorce. Away from the screen he enjoyed hunting and even made his own bows and arrows with which to hunt game.
CAUSE: Madison died aged 74 in Palm Springs, California, of emphysema.

Anna Magnani
Born March 7, 1908
Died September 26, 1973
'Nannarella'. Born in Rome, half-Italian, half-Egyptian and fully illegitimate, Magnani was educated at a convent school but became a singer in a nightclub belting out saucy songs. In 1926 she began appearing in dramas and made her film début in *Scampolo* (1927). It would be seven years before she performed before the cameras again, in *La Cieca Di Sorrento* (1934). In 1935 she married director Goffredo Alessandrini. They were divorced in 1950. By that time she had given birth (in 1942) to a polio-ridden son, Luca, by actor Massimo Serato. She made her name in Roberto Rossellini's *Roma Città Aperta* (1945) and won an Oscar as Serafina Delle Rose in *The Rose Tattoo* (1955) opposite Burt Lancaster and two years later was nominated again for Gloria in *Wild Is The Wind* (1957). Cecil Beaton opined: "She conforms only to the law of nature at its most primitive . . . She is a wild animal with its grace, health and vitality." She found work increasingly difficult to come by after that and returned to Italy where she made films for television.
CAUSE: She died in Rome of a cancerous tumour in the pancreas aged 65. Her funeral was spectacularly well attended.

Jock Mahoney

(Jacques O'Mahoney)
Born February 7, 1919
Died December 14, 1989
Acting jock. Born in Chicago, Illinois, of French, Irish and Cherokee extraction, he was educated at the University of Iowa where he excelled in American football, basketball and swimming. At the outbreak of the Second World War he became a Marine fighter pilot and instructor. Mahoney was a tall (6'4"), handsome, athletic specimen who began making films as a stunt man before playing villains in cheap Westerns. He screen-tested to replace Johnny Weissmuller as Tarzan but lost out to Lex Barker. He appeared in two successful television series before playing the baddie, Coy Banton, in *Tarzan The Magnificent* (1960) and then taking over (as the 13th actor to do so) the part of the Lord of the Jungle from Gordon Scott in *Tarzan Goes To India* (1962) and *Tarzan's Three Challenges* (1963). He did all his own stunts and during the filming of his second Tarzan film he was ill with dysentery, dengue fever and pneumonia. The producer had also decided that he wanted to make a Tarzan television series and Mahoney was too old for this. They parted company reasonably amicably and Mahoney went home to recuperate. He was married three times. His first wife was Lorraine O'Donnell by whom he had two children: Kathleen and James. The second Mrs Mahoney was Margaret Field, whom he married in 1952 and by whom he had a daughter, Princess. He also became stepfather to Margaret Field's children, one of whom is the actress Sally Field. His final marriage in 1967 was to Patricia who was nicknamed Autumn, and she survived him.
CAUSE: In 1973 while filming an episode of *Kung Fu* he suffered a stroke that virtually ended his career. On December 12, 1989, he was involved in a car accident and was admitted to hospital in Bremerton, Washington. Two days after admittance he suffered a second stoke that ended his life at the age of 70.

Karl Malden

(Mladen George Sekulovich)
Born March 22, 1912
Died July 1, 2009
Everyman. Born in Chicago, the son of Petar Sekulovich (b. January 10, 1886 d. October 1975), a Serbian immigrant who worked in a steel mill and later became a milkman and Minnie Sebera (b. March 22, 1893 d. August 15, 1995), a Bohemian immigrant, Malden, the eldest of three brothers, was raised in Gary, Indiana, from the age of five and worked in a steel mill for three years. He twice broke his nose playing football at school, resulting in his bulbous conk. In 1934 he began studying at the Goodman Theatre and paid his fees by building sets. He said, "[The tutors] asked me how much money I had, and I told them I had saved my every dime from working in the mills, which was about $300. Well, they told me the school tuition for a year was $900. But the man in charge of the school made me an offer I'll never forget it. He asked me if I was a gambler. He said if I paid the $300, he would take me on and if I worked hard and proved I had talent, somehow he'd find the rest of the tuition money for me." At the Goodman he met an aspiring actress named Mona Greenberg who was to become his wife on December 18, 1938. They had two daughters: Mila and Carla (b. Los Angeles, California July 5, 1953). After graduation in 1937 he went to Gary, Indiana where he delivered milk but he was invited to New York by playwright Robert Ardrey but the promised role never materialised. Instead he auditioned for the director Harold Clurman and Elia Kazan who were casting *Golden Boy* for the Group Theater. It was to be the start of a long

friendship between Malden and Kazan who persuaded him to change his name – Mladen became Malden and Karl was from a grandfather. "I hadn't met anyone that non-actorish before, non-theater-like," said Kazan of his protégé. "The minute I saw him, I knew he came from something. It turned out to be the steel mills, and it was a thing that was very important for a director, because you feel here is a person who can play difficult parts, rough parts, physical parts, who doesn't get frightened easily, who's all there when I need him." Malden later studied at the Actors Studio. After being demobbed from the army after the Second World War, Malden played a drunken matelot in Clurman and Kazan's production of Maxwell Anderson's 1946 play *Truckline Café*. The play was a disaster but Malden received good notices, as did another young actor by the name of Marlon Brando. Malden had made his film debut in 1940 as Red in *They Knew What They Wanted* (released October 19, 1940) and followed that with *Winged Victory* (released December 20, 1944) as Adams, where he was credited as Corporal Karl Malden, *13 Rue Madeleine* (released January 15, 1947) as Jump Master, Elia Kazan's *Boomerang!* (released March 5, 1947) as Detective Lieutenant White, Henry Hathaway's *Kiss Of Death* (released August 27, 1947) as Segeant William Cullen, *The Gunfighter* (released June 23, 1950) as Mac, *Where The Sidewalk Ends* (premièred June 26, 1950) as Detective Lieutenant Thomas and *Halls Of Montezuma* (released December 1950) as PHM2 C.E. "Doc" Jones. In 1951 Malden reunited with Brando and Kazan to make *A Streetcar Named Desire* (premièred September 18, 1951), the film that won him an Oscar and made him one of Hollywood's leading character actors. On March 20, 1952 Vivien Leigh (Best Actress), Malden (Best Supporting Actor) and Kim Hunter (Best

Supporting Actress) all went home from the RKO Pantages Theatre in Hollywood clutching Oscars. Malden later said that he was probably "the only ex-milkman Vivien ever kissed in a movie." Malden then appeared opposite Jennifer Jones and Charlton Heston in *Ruby Gentry* (1952) and played a policeman in Alfred Hitchcock's *I Confess* (1953) before reuniting with Kazan and Brando to make *On The Waterfront* (premièred July 28, 1954) in which he played Father Barry and won an Oscar nomination. He and Kazan worked together on *Baby Doll* (released December 18, 1956) in which Malden played the devious Southern cotton gin operator Archie Lee Meighan, Carroll Baker's husband. The part won him a BAFTA nomination as Best Foreign Actor and a Golden Glove nomination for Best Motion Picture Actor – Drama. In 1962 he played the doggedly loving boyfriend of Rosalind Russell in Gypsy, and in 1970 he won critical praise for his stalwart General Omar Bradley in *Patton*, starring George C. Scott. His other films included: *Pollyanna* (1960) as Reverend Paul Ford, *The Great Impostor* (1961) as Father Devlin, *Parrish* (1961) as Judd Raike, *One-Eyed Jacks* (1961), the only film directed by Marlon Brando, *Birdman Of Alcatraz* (1962) as brutal prison warder Harvey Shoemaker, *How The West Was Won* (1962) as Zebulon Prescott and *Billion Dollar Brain* (1967) as Leo Newbigen. During filming at Pinewood Studies with Michael Caine, Malden's London hotel room was robbed and his cash stolen, but his travellers' cheques were left untouched. Between 1973 and 1994 he was the public face of American Express travellers' cheques encouraging people, "Don't leave home without them". "After 50 years of doing all those other things in the business, wherever I go, the one thing people will say to me is, 'Don't leave home without it'. What am I going to say? It's kind of

frustrating in a way, but at the same time, American Express has been very good to me, and it's given me independence. I don't have to jump at anything and everything that comes my way," he said. When cinematic work began to dry up in the early 1970s Malden reluctantly moved to the small screen. He recounted, "I felt that I had started at the bottom in the theatre and worked my way up for 20 years, then started at the bottom with bit parts in films and worked my way up for another 20 years. I didn't feel like starting at the bottom again." A cop show called *The Streets Of San Francisco* (1972–1977) gave 6'1½" Malden as Lieutenant Mike Stone another lease of life. Malden garnered four consecutive Emmy nominations as lead actor in a drama series. He won an Emmy for his role in *Fatal Vision* (1984). His last performance came in 2000 playing Father Thomas Cavanaugh who advised President Jed Bartlet in *The West Wing*. In 1989 Malden began a three-year term as president of the Academy of Motion Picture Arts and Sciences and in 1999 used his influence to grant an honorary but controversial Oscar to Elia Kazan. "If anyone deserved this honorary award because of his talent and body of work," Malden said, "it was Kazan." Karl Malden received a Screen Actors Guild award for a lifetime of achievement in 2004.
CAUSE: Malden died of natural causes at his home in Brentwood, California. He was 97.

Louis Malle
Born October 30, 1932
Died November 23, 1995
New Wave auteur. Born in Thumeries, France, Malle began his cinematic career working for Jacques Cousteau and after two years he worked as a cameraman on Jacques Tati's *Mon Oncle* (1958) before making his first solo effort, *Lift To The Scaffold* (1957). His next film *The Lovers* (1958)

aroused condemnation for what was considered at the time to be its explicit sexuality; Malle tended to ignore the criticism. Brigitte Bardot starred in his *Le Privée* (1961) and then he made *Le Feu Follet* (1963) regarded by many as his finest work. In 1978 he once again irked puritans when he made *Pretty Baby*, which featured a 12-year-old Brooke Shields playing a child prostitute. *Atlantic City* (1980) was praised. *Au Revoir Les Enfants* (1987) was an autobiographical film about Jewish children attending a Roman Catholic school during World War II. He married actress Candice Bergen on September 27, 1980.
CAUSE: He died aged 63 of lymphoma complications in his Beverly Hills home.

Joseph L. Mankiewicz
Born February 11, 1909
Died February 5, 1993
Oscar-winning director. Born in Wilkes-Barre, Pennsylvania, Joseph Leo Mankiewicz was the third and youngest of the Mankiewicz family. (Brother Herman wrote most of *Citizen Kane* [1941].) He began as a journalist and then moved into translating German subtitles. He joined Famous Players-Lasky-Paramount where he worked on films including *The Dummy* (1929), *Close Harmony* (1929), *The Man I Love* (1929), *Thunderbolt* (1929), *River Of Romance* (1929), *The Mysterious Dr Fu Manchu* (1929), *Fast Company* (1929), *The Virginian* (1929), *Slightly Scarlet* (1930), *Only Saps Work* (1930), *Finn And Hattie* (1931), *Skippy* (1931), for which he was nominated for an Oscar, *Million Dollar Legs* (1932), *Alice In Wonderland* (1933) and many others before moving to MGM where he became a producer on films such as *Three Godfathers* (1936), *Fury* (1936), *The Gorgeous Hussy* (1936), *Love On The Run* (1936), *The Bride Wore Red* (1937), *Double Wedding* (1937), *The Shopworn Angel* (1938), *A Christmas Carol* (1938), *Huckleberry*

Finn (1939), *Strange Cargo* (1940), *The Philadelphia Story* (1940), *The Feminine Touch* (1941), *Woman Of The Year* (1942) and *Cairo* (1942). Moving to 20th Century Fox he began to direct, "because I couldn't stomach what was being done with what I wrote." His canon included *Dragonwyck* (1946), *The Ghost And Mrs Muir* (1947), *Escape* (1948), *A Letter To Three Wives* (1949), for which he won Oscars as Best Director and Best Screenplay, *House Of Strangers* (1949), *No Way Out* (1950) for which he was nominated for an Oscar, *All About Eve* (1950), probably his best film and certainly the one that showed his talent for bitchy dialogue to greatest effect, and for which he again won Oscars as Best Director and Best Screenplay, *People Will Talk* (1951), *Julius Caesar* (1953), *The Barefoot Contessa* (1954), *Guys And Dolls* (1955), *Suddenly, Last Summer* (1959), *Cleopatra* (1963) and *Sleuth* (1972). He was married three times. On May 20, 1934, he married actress Elizabeth Young. They had a son, Eric, born at Cedars of Lebanon Hospital, Los Angeles, on July 1, 1936. Mr & Mrs Mankiewicz separated on November 24, 1936, reconciled, separated again on April 30, 1937, and finally divorced on May 20, 1937, their third wedding anniversary. He married actress Rosa Stradner (b. Vienna, Austria July 31, 1913) on July 28, 1939 in New York. They had two sons: Christopher (b. October 8, 1940) and Thomas Eddie Mannix (b. June 1942). She was plagued with mental problems and died by her own hand aged 45 via an overdose of sedatives on September 27, 1958. On December 14, 1962, he married production assistant Rosemary Matthews in New York.

CAUSE: Mankiewicz died in Bedford, New York, of heart failure six days before his 84th birthday.

FURTHER READING: *Pictures Will Talk: The Life And Films of Joseph L. Mankiewicz* – Kenneth L. Geist (New York: Charles Scribner's Sons, 1978).

Abby Mann
(ABRAHAM GOODMAN)
Born December 1, 1927
Died March 25, 2008
Serious writer. Born in Philadelphia and raised in the predominantly Roman Catholic East Pittsburgh, he was educated at Temple University and New York University and began his writing career after the Second World War working on early television shows. In 1959 he wrote an episode about a Nazi war crime trial for *Playhouse 90*. Two years later, it became the film *Judgment At Nuremberg* and won Mann an Oscar. On accepting the gong, he said, "A writer worth his salt at all has an obligation not only to entertain but to comment on the world in which he lives." Mann was also nominated for Stanley Kramer's 1965 film *Ship Of Fools*. He won Emmys for the television films *The Marcus-Nelson Murders* (1973), which became the basis for *Kojak*, and *Murderers Among Us: The Simon Wiesenthal Story* (1989) and *Indictment: The McMartin Trial* (1995).

CAUSE: Mann died of heart failure in Beverly Hills. He was 80.

Jayne Mansfield
(VERA JANE PALMER)
Born April 19, 1933
Died June 29, 1967
Pneumatic blonde. Jayne Mansfield was no stranger to notoriety. Her numerous affairs were regularly chronicled in the gossip columns. Promoted as another Marilyn Monroe, 5'5" Jayne simply did not have the talent to compete with the star. Jayne was a publicity stunt maniac and a firm believer in the school of thought that maintained, "Say what you like about me, just spell my name right." She was born by Caesarean section in Bryn Mawr Hospital, Bryn Mawr, Pennsylvania, the only child of successful lawyer Herbert Palmer and his wife Vera. At birth she weighed 9lb 10oz. Her father doted on her and

she on him but when she was three
Herbert Palmer was felled by a massive
heart attack. Her mother remarried
with, according to neighbours,
unseemly haste and the family
relocated to Dallas. When Jayne
was ten she fell in love with Johnny
Weissmuller and plastered her
bedroom walls with his posters.
According to Jayne, never the most
reliable of witnesses, she was upset
when she had to wear a bra and girdle
to hide her fulsome curves. Her claims
for her vital statistics ranged from
around 39-23-36 to 46D-23-37. Her
school friends remember her dressing
to show off her figure; Jayne had the
body of an adult but not the maturity
to match. She eloped to Fort Worth,
Texas, with blond Paul Mansfield (who
was born in 1925 and whom she met
on Christmas Eve 1949) on January 28,
1950 and quickly fell pregnant with her
first child, Jayne-Marie, who was born
at 10.50am on November 8, 1950 in
Austin, Texas. An official wedding took
place on either May 6, 10 or 30, 1950.
After the birth Jayne enrolled in the
University of Texas at Austin and
began to study drama. Paul Mansfield
was not a jealous man but he began to
feel a sense of unease when Jayne
skipped lectures to pose nearly nude
for the art class on the campus. The
money was good, Jayne told him. In
1951 Paul Mansfield was drafted into
the Reserve Officers' Training Corps
(ROTC) and Jayne went to Los
Angeles to enrol in UCLA and also
entered the Miss Southern California
of 1951 contest. Her husband
disapproved, so Jayne pulled out.
The following year Paul was posted to
Camp Gordon in Augusta, Georgia,
where Jayne joined him. She outraged
the other army wives by dying her hair
jet black and doing her aerobics on the
barrack lawn in either a skimpy leotard
or a velvet bikini. After several
complaints she dressed more 'suitably'.
She appeared in an amateur production
of *Anything Goes* on the base. When

Paul was sent to Korea, Jayne took
herself and her dogs and baby off to
Dallas, where she took drama classes
at Southern Methodist University and
earned a living by nude modelling,
both for art classes and, occasionally,
a Dallas photographer. Before he was
shipped off to war Jayne had extracted
a promise from her husband that when
he returned they would all go off to
Hollywood for six months so she could
fulfil her dreams of acting stardom. In
the summer of 1954 Paul returned
from Korea and begrudgingly kept his
promise. Jayne would later claim that
as the car crossed the Californian
border, she insisted her husband stop
the vehicle so she could get out and
kiss the ground, saying, "I am home!"
Never a wallflower, Jayne, now blonde,
rang up Paramount and on April 30,
1954, had a screen test for *Joan Of
Arc*. However, she was told her body
was rather too bountiful to play the
waif-like saint. Much to her husband's
annoyance, Jayne spent what little
money they had buying new outfits
and shoes. *Los Angeles Daily News*
photographers saw her determination
and did test shoots and gave advice for
free. Just as their money finally ran out
Jayne received an inheritance from her
grandmother and used the money to
put down a deposit on a small house
at 9840 Wanda Park Lane. It was the
final straw for Paul Mansfield who
packed his bags and returned to Dallas.
He later launched an ultimately futile
custody suit for Jayne-Marie claiming
that Jayne's nude photos hardly made
her a fit mother. Jayne was helped by
her friend and later lover, he-man actor
Steve Cochran although she later
confessed: "He was not a good lover."
Her first television appearance – all of
30 seconds – came on October 21,
1954, for Lux Video Theater in the live
broadcast of *The Angel Went AWOL*.
Then she was paid $100 for appearing
in *Hangover* (later re-titled *The Female
Jungle*). She told her friend and later
biographer May Mann: "I *loved* me up

there on the screen. I was filled with a chill. I had finally made it and wanted to stay there. 'I love you Jayne Mansfield,' I told my image, 'I'll work hard for you! Nothing or no one could ever make me let you down.' " Then Jayne employed Jim Byron as her press officer. His first stunt was for her to dress up as Father (Mother?) Christmas and visit all the newspaper offices in the area and deliver a bottle of whisky and a kiss to Jim's reporter friends. It got her lots of press coverage. Her next photo opportunity was even bigger. She gatecrashed the party for the Jane Russell film *Underwater* wearing a skin-tight red lamé one-piece swimming costume and proceeded to accidentally fall into the pool, breaking one of the straps on her cozzy as she did so. According to *Variety* of January 12, 1955, the stunt proved Jayne to be "worth her weight in cheesecake". Now that her attempts to break into Hollywood were picking up a little steam, Jayne hired a lawyer, Greg Bautzer (who else?), a manager, Charles Godring, and an agent, Bill Shiffrin. She also began an affair with Jim Byron. A bidding war started for Jayne's services between Warner Bros and Howard Hughes. In bed Byron advised Jayne to go for Hughes while out of bed the astute Shiffrin was advising Warner Bros. Jayne signed for Warners at $250 a week on a six-month renewable contract. It wasn't a good deal and Jayne still found herself caught between her advisers. Byron said she should capitalise on her "tits and ass" while Shiffrin and Bautzer advised a more conservative and ultimately long-term approach. Jayne went for Byron, possibly because he was bedding her but more likely because he was talking to her in terms she could understand – sex sells. Her first three films – *Illegal* (1955) as Angel O'Hara, *Pete Kelly's Blues* (1955) and *Hell On Frisco Bay* (1955) – were disappointing and Warner Bros dropped Jayne's option. She maintained a high

press profile and won several spurious beauty contests during 1955 including Miss Negligee, Miss Nylon Sweater, Miss Freeway, Miss Electric Switch, Miss Geiger Counter, Miss 100% Pure Maple Syrup, Miss 4th of July, Miss Fire Prevention and Miss Tomato! She was also the unnamed and brunette Miss February 1955 in *Playboy*. Columnist Earl Wilson reported: "Jayne surrendered all her privacy and considerable dignity to the daily job of getting her name and picture in the papers. Her home, whether it was a house, apartment, or hotel suite, was always open to reporters, and photographers were constantly running in and out, stumbling over her dogs and cats or her little daughter Jayne-Marie." On October 12, 1955, Jayne opened at the Belasco Theater on Broadway in George Axelrod's play *Will Success Spoil Rock Hunter?* as Rita Marlowe starring opposite Walter Matthau. Of her character, Jayne opined: "She is brassy and extroverted, refreshing and direct and not entirely oblivious of her bombshell of a body. The role gives me a chance to act on stage the way I would like to behave off stage." Jayne did what Jayne knew best. Within days of arriving in New York she was posing in fur bikinis and stilettos. But the publicity was fine – the question was, how would she handle the daily rigours of a play? Like the proverbial duck to water. As Jayne had the traditional first night repast in Sardi's the congratulatory telegrams poured in. Jayne dyed her hair even blonder, dyed one of her dogs pink and killed it in the process, dyed her new Jaguar pink and offered life-size cut-outs of herself to any shop that wanted one. *Will Success Spoil Rock Hunter?* ran for an amazing 452 performances. On May 26, 1956, at a Mae West show, she met bodybuilder and former Mr Universe Mickey Hargitay (b. Hungary, 1930). There were three problems to their relationship: Paul Mansfield, Mrs

Hargitay and their five-year-old daughter. In the meantime 20th Century Fox had bought the film rights to *Will Success Spoil Rock Hunter?* and Jayne was to star in it. The studio was unhappy with the presence of Hargitay, however. In the meantime she played gangster's moll Jerri Jordan in Fox's *The Girl Can't Help It* (1956) and Gladden in the low-budget *The Burglar* (1957) for Columbia. The film of *Will Success Spoil Rock Hunter?* wasn't quite as successful as the stage version, but it made money. Her next films *Kiss Them For Me* (1957) in which she played Alice Kratzner opposite Cary Grant and *The Wayward Bus* (1957) as Camilla were also not well received. Her co-star in *The Wayward Bus* was Joan Collins who went into Mansfield's trailer one day to find Jayne "wearing nothing but a big smile and a small bra, legs akimbo, one foot on a chair. Kneeling before her, razor in hand, was the make-up assistant, liberally applying shaving foam to Jayne's crotch. 'Dick here is getting me ready for a swimming pool shoot tomorrow. Can't have those tell-tale blackies sprouting out from my teeny-weeny bikini, can we? By the way, didja know it's Valentine's Day? Dick's trimming things into a heart shape . . . Mickey can't get enough of it.'" On January 8, 1958, she and Paul Mansfield were divorced and, five days later at 8pm, she and Mickey Hargitay were married at the Wayfarers' Chapel, in Palos Verdes Estates, California. For six weeks they performed a nightclub act at the Las Vegas Tropicana for which their remuneration was $25,000 a week – twenty for her, five for him. They bought what was to become famous as her pink mansion at 10100 Sunset Boulevard. The house had eight bedrooms, 13 baths, a heart-shaped bed and fireplace and a heart-shaped swimming pool that had "I Love You Jaynie" in two foot high gold mosaic

tiles on the bottom. Jayne flew off to England to appear as saloon owner Kate in Fox's *The Sheriff Of Fractured Jaw* (1958) opposite Kenneth More. Just before she departed, she discovered she was pregnant. The film wasn't a success but the shoot was an enjoyable experience for Jayne. However, when she returned to America in the summer of 1958 she found herself more in demand for pictures than movies. At 5am on December 21, 1958, Miklos Jeffery Palmer Hargitay made his début in St John's Hospital, Santa Monica. The following year Jayne disposed of her retinue of Byron, Shiffrin and Bautzer. Looking after her newborn son Jayne was absent from film-making during 1959. In June 1960 she was the guest of honour on *This Is Your Life* and two months later on August 1, 1960, she gave birth to son Zoltan in Santa Monica. In December of that year she and Hargitay were performing their act entitled *The House Of Love* in Las Vegas. Her next films – *Too Hot To Handle* (1960) as stripper Midnight Franklin and *The Challenge* (1960) as bullion thief gang leader Billy in which she went topless for the first time on film – were not especially good. She also made her first European (non-British) film because Mickey Hargitay was offered a part in it – *Gli Amori Di Ercole* (1960), as Queen Dianira. She went on to star in *It Happened In Athens* (1960) as Eleni Costa and *The George Raft Story* (1961) as Lisa Lang, but neither was ever going to set any box-office records and it looked as though her marriage was also failing. A second honeymoon in Nassau in February 1962 almost ended in tragedy when the couple's boat overturned and Jayne was admitted to hospital suffering from shock and exposure, although not the kind she usually coveted. However, the press suspected a hoax, much to Mickey Hargitay's fury. In mid-1963 Jayne was touring the rubber chicken circuit telling a few jokes, singing some songs and then taking her clothes off. It was rather successful. A separation ensued but soon the couple were reunited and daughter Mariska Magdolna was born weighing 8lb 9oz in January 1964 in St John's Hospital, Santa Monica, although rumours have long persisted that her real father was married Brazilian singer Nelson Sardelli. Certainly, Jayne and Mickey were divorced just seven months after the birth on August 26, 1964. Never single for long Jayne married short, hairy, pornographer Matt Climber (b. 1935, as Thomas Vitale Ottaviano) on September 24, 1964, in Baja California, Mexico. None of Jayne's films during this time were remarkable – *Panic Button* (1962) in which she played Angela, *Heimweh Nach St Pauli* (1963), *Dog Eat Dog* (1964) as Darlene, *L'Amore Primitivo* (1964) as Jayne – except one, and that was for all the wrong reasons. *Promises! Promises!* (1963) was a piece of exploitative trash. Film critics Mick Martin and Marsha Porter call it "silly and crude", adding, "The only thing going for this film is the scenes of a next-to-totally naked Jayne Mansfield" and that was about once every nine minutes. Neither respected critics Leonard Maltin nor Leslie Halliwell even bothered to include the film in their directories. *Playboy* magazine asked Jayne to pose for them as part of the publicity machine and since Jayne owned ten per cent of the film she agreed. Seen today the pictures are innocuous, but they were regarded as scandalous at the time and resulted in publisher Hugh Hefner being fined for obscenity. *Promises! Promises!* flopped, and with it Jayne's career. In the summer of 1964 Jayne and a male friend met John Lennon and journalist Chris Hutchins in Los Angeles. The remaining Beatles had gone to the Whiskey-A-Go-Go nightclub on Sunset Boulevard and Jayne suggested joining them. Lennon didn't want to and offered Jayne a

drink. She asked for a cocktail and the ever helpful Chris Hutchins offered to make it and then realised he had no idea what to put in a cocktail. He stood in the kitchen with Lennon examining various bottles until Lennon told him to include "A drop of that, that, that and that, and then you pee in it." Chris made the drink and then handed it to John who added his own special ingredient, which Jayne duly drank pronouncing it "a real humdinger". Flirting with Lennon, she tugged his mop top hair and asked, "Is this real?" Lennon, who loathed being touched, eyed her breasts and inquired, "Are those real?" Jayne smiled and replied, "There's only one way to find out." Just then Jayne's friend announced he would read their fortunes with his tarot cards. The reading proceeded, then suddenly the man stopped, horrified by what the cards revealed: "I see an awful ending to all this." The paranoically superstitious Lennon threw them out. Then he and Chris Hutchins headed for the Whiskey-A-Go-Go to join the others. Jayne turned up and as photographers lined up to take pictures of the Fab Four she eased herself into the frame next to John. George Harrison was not impressed and threw his Scotch and Coke at a photographer, missed, and instead hit Mamie Van Doren square in the face. In the mêlée John told Jayne what had really been in the cocktail and bolted for the door. On October 17, 1965, Jayne gave birth to Antonio Raphael Ottaviano Climber at Cedars of Lebanon Hospital, Los Angeles. Her films, *The Fat Spy* (1965) as Junior and *The Las Vegas Hillbillies* (1966), continued to flop. She was even cut from *The Loved One* (1965). She and Climber split on July 11, 1966, and Jayne's lawyers filed for divorce eight days later. Jayne flew to Caracas, Venezuela, where she had an affair with a student called Douglas Olivares (b. October 1945). She also contracted a venereal disease. By October 1966 Olivares was back in

South America. She took up with short, balding, Jewish lawyer Sam Brody whose wife named Jayne in her divorce petition. Brody had been Jack Ruby's lawyer when the nightclub owner was tried for murdering Lee Harvey Oswald who was alleged to have shot John F. Kennedy . . . who had had an affair with Jayne. The relationship with Brody was violent. He regularly beat her and once smashed her head against a toilet bowl. Still, he wanted to marry her. It was around this time that Jayne supposedly became involved with Anton La Vey's Church of Satan in San Francisco. Jayne, raised a Baptist, had also shown an interest in Catholicism and Judaism. To maintain her extravagant lifestyle Jayne was forced to return to the nightclub circuit. CAUSE: In the spring of 1967 she was sacked from her British tour because of "disfiguring black and blue marks from her knees up". A lack of organisation and Jayne's increasing dependency on alcohol didn't help. On June 28, 1967, Jayne appeared at the Gus Stevens Supper Club in Biloxi, Mississippi. With Sam Brody and her three children, 19-year-old Ronnie Harrison at the wheel of the year-old Buick, Jayne set off for New Orleans, Louisiana, and her next appointment with WESU-TV's *The Midday Show*. At approximately 2.25am the next morning the car was travelling along Route 90. With just 15 miles to go to reach their destination Harrison was temporarily blinded by the reflection of his own headlights in the mist caused by a mosquito-spraying machine at the kerb. When his vision returned it was too late for him to prevent driving at speed into the back of a lorry. He and Brody were flung out of the wreckage, dying instantly. Jayne died of a "crushed skull with avulsion of cranium and brain. Closed fracture of right humerus. Multiple lacerations of hands and lower extremities." Most reports have Jayne being decapitated although Louisiana undertaker Jim Roberts denies this. It was, he says, her blonde wig that was thrown from the wreckage and seen by those at the death site that created the myth. She was 34 years old. She was buried in Fairview Cemetery, Plainfield (Outside of Pen Argyl), Pennsylvania.

FURTHER READING: *Jayne Mansfield: A Biography* – May Mann (London: Abelard-Schuman, 1974); *Jayne Mansfield And The American Fifties* – Martha Saxton (New York: Bantam, 1976); *Pink Goddess: The Jayne Mansfield Story* – Michael Feeney Callan (London: W.H. Allen, 1986); *Here They Are: Jayne Mansfield* – Raymond Strait (New York: SPI, 1992).

Fredric March

(ERNEST FREDERICK MCINTYRE BICKEL)
Born August 31, 1897
Died April 14, 1975
Journeyman with occasional flashes of brilliance. Born in Racine, Wisconsin, 5′10″ March was intended for the world of finance by his family but he had other ideas. He studied economics at the University of Wisconsin and after fighting in World War I he migrated to New York in 1920 and began a career as an actor appearing as a bit part player in various films. He signed to Paramount and began receiving plaudits for his acting although Shelley Winters remembered, "He was able to do a very emotional scene with tears in his eyes and pinch my fanny at the same time." March's stage name came from a diminution of his mother's maiden name, Marcher. His films included *Paris Bound* (1929) as Jim Hutton, *Jealousy* (1929) as Pierre, *Footlights And Fools* (1929) as Gregory Pyne, *The Royal Family Of Broadway* (1930) as Tony Cavendish, *Ladies Love Brutes* (1930) as Dwight Howell, *Manslaughter* (1930) as Dan O'Bannon, *Laughter* (1930) as Paul Lockridge, *My Sin* (1931) as Dick Grady, *Dr Jekyll And Mr Hyde* (1931) as Dr Henry Jekyll/Mr Hyde, for which

he won an Oscar, *Merrily We Go to Hell* (1932) as Jerry Corbett, *Tonight Is Ours* (1933) as Sabien Pastal, *Design For Living* (1933) as Tom Chambers, *The Barretts Of Wimpole Street* (1934) as Robert Browning, *All Of Me* (1934) as Don Ellis, *The Dark Angel* (1935) as Alan Trent, *Anna Karenina* (1935) as Count Alexei Vronsky, *Anthony Adverse* (1936) as Anthony Adverse, *Mary Of Scotland* (1936) as Earl of Bothwell, *A Star Is Born* (1937) as Norman Maine, *Nothing Sacred* (1937) as Wally Cook, *Trade Winds* (1938) as Sam Wye, *There Goes My Heart* (1938) as Bill Spencer, *Victory* (1940) as Hendrik Heyst, *I Married A Witch* (1942) as Wallace Wooley, *The Adventures Of Mark Twain* (1944) as Samuel Langhorne Clemens, *The Best Years Of Our Lives* (1946) as Al Stephenson, for which he won a second Oscar, *Christopher Columbus* (1949) as Christopher Columbus, *Death Of A Salesman* (1951) as Willy Loman, *The Bridges At Toko-Ri* (1954) as Rear Admiral George Tarrant, *Executive Suite* (1954) as Loren Phineas Shaw, *Inherit The Wind* (1960) as Matthew Harrison Brady and *The Iceman Cometh* (1973) as Harry Hope. Married twice, he wed stage actress Ellis Baker in 1923 and Florence Eldridge on May 30, 1927. They adopted two children: Penelope (1932) and Anthony (1935).

CAUSE: Aged 77, he died in Los Angeles, California, of cancer.

Richard Marner

(ALEXANDER MOLCHANOFF-SACHA)
Born March 27, 1921
Died March 18, 2004
Talented character actor. Born in Petrograd (now St Petersburg) in the Soviet Union, he was the eldest son of Colonel Paul Molchanoff, of the Semionovsky regiment, one of the two hereditary Imperial Guards regiments founded by Peter the Great. In 1924 the family fled the Bolsheviks via Finland and Germany, finally ending up in London, where Alexander's grandmother, 'Babushka London', had a home on Harley Street. His great-grandmother – known to the family as 'Babushka Claridges' because of the years spent living in the hotel – was the slavophile Madame Olga Novikoff, who was Tsar Nicholas I's goddaughter. Alexander was educated at Monmouth School, after which he became an assistant to the Russian tenor Vladimir Rosing at Covent Garden. Following a spell in the RAF from which he was invalided out, he decided to become an actor and, changing his name to Richard Marner, he joined a repertory company. Marner appeared in more than two dozen films. His parts ranged from that of an officer in *The African Queen* (1951) to the Russian President Zorkin in *The Sum Of All Fears* (2001), with Ben Affleck, Morgan Freeman and Alan Bates. Marner also played a Vopo captain in *The Spy Who Came In From The Cold* (1965), Colonel Lebotov in *Oh Rosalinda!* (1955), a spacecraft operator in *You Only Live Twice* (1967), and a Greek Bishop in the 65th episode of *Lovejoy* (1994). Having not achieved stardom Marner worked as a salesman for a costume jewellers but his money worries were at an end when he was cast as the benignly idiotic Colonel Kurt von Strohm in the long-running BBC sitcom *'Allo 'Allo* set in the northern French town of Nouvion. Marner appeared in all 85 episodes of the sitcom. It was not the first time Marner had been chosen to play an army officer – he was an SS colonel in *Lili Marlene* (1951), a German NCO in *The Safecracker* (1958), a German colonel in *Circle Of Deception* (1961), and a Russian air force general in *The Mouse On The Moon* (1963). He was an aficionado of the turf and kept a separate bank account for betting. In 1947 he married Pauline and they had one daughter.

CAUSE: Richard Marner died in Perth, Scotland, where he had retired with his wife. He was 82.

Betty Marsden
Born February 24, 1919
Died July 19, 1998
The woman of a thousand voices. Betty Marsden worked in all branches of showbiz. She was a regular on TV comedy shows, began making films in 1938 (*The Sky Raiders* as Miss Quarm) and positively shone on radio. Her other films included *Ships With Wings* (1941) as Jean, *Ramsbottom Rides Again* (1956) as Florrie Ramsbottom, *Carry On Regardless* (1961) as Mata Hari, *The Wild Affair* (1963) as Mavis Cook, *The Leather Boys* (1963) as Dot's Mother, *Carry On Camping* (1969) as Harriet Potter, *Sudden Terror* (1970) as Madame Robiac, *Britannia Hospital* (1982) as Hermione, *The Dresser* (1983) as Violet Manning and *Little Dorrit* (1988) as Mrs Phoebe Barnacle. However, it was on radio that she excelled, especially in the brilliant comedy shows *Beyond Our Ken* and *Round The Horne*, where she played such diverse characters as Daphne Whitethigh, Buttercup Gruntfuttock, Dame Celia Molestrangler, Julie Coolibah, Fanny Haddock, Bea Clissold and Lady Counterblast "many, many times".
CAUSE: She died aged 79 from complications due to heart trouble and pneumonia in Ruislip.

Mae Marsh
Born November 9, 1895
Died February 13, 1968
Silent heroine. Born in Madrid, New Mexico, Mary Wayne Marsh bunked off school to see her big sister, Marguerite Loveridge (d. 1925), act but it was Mae who achieved fame when she was spotted by D.W. Griffith. She appeared in over 150 films but excelled in Griffith's *The Birth Of A Nation* (1915) as Flora Cameron and *Intolerance* (1916) as The Dear One. Sensing her talent Goldwyn poached her, but that studio couldn't find any suitable material for her and the pictures she was given were mediocre.

She returned to her mentor in 1923 for *The White Rose* (1923) giving a superlative performance as Bessie 'Teazie' Williams. She mainly retired in 1925 but made a comeback when talkies were invented and was regularly in demand as a character actress. She appeared in *Rebecca Of Sunnybrook Farm* (1932) as Aunt Jane, *Hollywood Boulevard* (1936) as Carlotta Blakeford, *Drums Along The Mohawk* (1939), *The Grapes Of Wrath* (1940) as Floyd's Wife, *Tobacco Road* (1941), *Tales Of Manhattan* (1942) as Molly, *The Song Of Bernadette* (1943), *Jane Eyre* (1944) as Leah, *Fort Apache* (1948) as Mrs Gates, *My Blue Heaven* (1950), *The Robe* (1953), *A Star Is Born* (1954), *Donovan's Reef* (1963) and *Cheyenne Autumn* (1964). In 1918 she married Louis Lee Adams and had two daughters and a son. All survived her.
CAUSE: Aged 72, she died of a heart attack in Hermosa Beach, California.

Herbert Marshall
Born May 23, 1890
Died January 22, 1966
One-legged wonder. London-born Herbert Brough Falcon Marshall was the epitome of the well-bred Englishman, yet he began his career as an accountant and became business manager to an impresario. That gave him the acting bug and he made his stage début in Brighton in 1911. During World War I he lost his right leg in action but managed to hide his disability well. In 1915 he married actress Mollie Maitland. They divorced in 1928, the year after his first screen appearance with *Mumsie* (1927) as Colonel Armitage. On November 26, 1928, he married his leading lady Edna Best in Jersey City, New Jersey. The following year he made his first major American film, *The Letter* (1929), as Geoffrey Hammond starring opposite Jeanne Eagels. He commuted between London and America appearing on the stage in both countries until 1932 when

he began to work solely in the movies. He appeared in *Trouble In Paradise* (1932) as Gaston Monescu, *Blonde Venus* (1932) as Edward Faraday, *I Was A Spy* (1933) as Stephan, *Four Frightened People* (1934) as Arnold Ainger, *If You Could Only Cook* (1935) as Jim Buchanan, *Girls' Dormitory* (1936) as Dr Stephen Dominick, *Angel* (1937) as Sir Frederick Barker, *Zaza* (1939) as Dufresne, *Foreign Correspondent* (1940) as Stephen Fisher, *The Letter* (1940) as Robert Crosbie, *Andy Hardy's Blonde Trouble* (1944) as Dr M.J. Standish, *Duel In The Sun* (1946) as Scott Chavez, *The Virgin Queen* (1955) as Lord Leicester and *The List Of Adrian Messenger* (1963) as Sir Wilfrid Lucas. Edna Best claimed he had deserted her in 1934 and they finally divorced in Las Vegas on February 7, 1940. Nineteen days later, he married actress Lee Russell. They divorced in 1946. On August 3, 1947, he married Boots Mallory (b. 1913), who would die on December 1, 1958, in Santa Monica. On April 25, 1960, he married for the fifth and final time, to Dee Ann Kahman.
CAUSE: Aged 75, he died of a heart attack at his home in Beverly Hills, California.

Zena Marshall

Born New Year's Day 1926
Died July 10, 2009
The real first Bond girl. Zena Moyra Marshall was born in Nairobi but was raised in Leicestershire after her mother remarried following her husband's early death. Marshall was educated at St Mary's Roman Catholic School, an independent boarding school for girls in Ascot, Berkshire, whose alumni included Princess Caroline of Monaco, the daughter of Grace Kelly, Lady Antonia Fraser, Sarah Hogg, Viscountess Hailsham and Olga Polizzi. Marshall then trained at the Royal Academy of Dramatic Art, before working with ENSA, the Entertainments National Service Association during the Second World War. She made her screen debut as a handmaiden in *Caesar And Cleopatra* (1945) and retired from films after a starring role in the sci-fi film *The Terrornauts* (1967). In 1962 she appeared as Miss Taro, the Chinese double agent in the first Bond film *Dr No*. Although Ursula Andress is assumed to be the first Bond girl, the first female Bond met was Eunice Gayson, who played Sylvia Trench, whom Bond encountered at the casino. The first woman Bond took to bed was Miss Taro before handing her over to a policeman outside her bungalow. In 1964 Somportex published a picture of 5'5" Marshall in the dressing gown she had worn in *Dr No* in a series of bubblegum cards along with other Bond girls also in a state of *deshabille*. The cards caused a scandal with one MP calling them "a disgusting and disgraceful corruption of young children". The semi-naked women were replaced by images of guns and violence and no one complained. Her other films included: *Sleeping Car To Trieste* (1948), *Helter Skelter* (1949), *So Long At The Fair* (1950), *Three Cases Of Murder* (1955) and *Those Magnificent Men In Their Flying Machines* (1965). In 1947 she married the bandleader Paul Adam, though the match was short. There was a second brief marriage, and Marshall married for a third time, to the film producer Ivan Foxwell, who predeceased her on January 16, 2002. They had no children.
CAUSE: Zena Marshall died of cancer in London. She was 83.

Dean Martin

(DINO CROCETTI)
Born June 7, 1917
Died December 25, 1995
Rat Packer. Jokes abounded about 5'11½" Dean Martin's copious consumption of alcohol. "Dean Martin saw a sign that said 'Drink Canada Dry' so he went there and did." "I wouldn't

say Dean has a drinking problem, but his major concern in life is what wine goes with whisky." The humour tends to overlook the role played by Dean Martin in twentieth-century entertainment. Born at 11.55pm, prematurely, at 319 South Sixth Street, Steubenville, Ohio, the son of Gaetano Crocetti (b. Montesilvano, Italy, 1896, d. 1967), an Italian immigrant, and Angela Barra (b. Fernwood, Ohio, December 18, 1897, d. Los Angeles, California, December 25, 1966 at 3.15am), a second-generation Italian immigrant, like many in showbiz he worked at a variety of jobs before breaking into the biz. Among his tasks were petrol pump attendant, steel mill worker, boxer and card dealer for the local mob-run casino. Finally, he turned to singing and rose to the top of the profession, gaining enormous power and vast wealth along the way. As he did so, Martin retreated into himself. People knew of his professional life but only as much of his personal life as he wanted them to know. When he was 27 he had a rhinoplasty. His starting salary as a singer was $50 a week (less than he made working as a croupier) but that soon rose to $750 a week at Atlantic City's 500 Club where, in 1946, he made the acquaintance of a comedian called Jerry Lewis. They formed a partnership that was, initially, unsuccessful. Ditching their scripts they began to ad lib a routine and rapidly became a smash, going on to appear in 16 films together. They were: *My Friend Irma* (1949), *My Friend Irma Goes West* (1950), *At War With The Army* (1951), *That's My Boy* (1951), *Sailor Beware* (1952), *Jumping Jacks* (1952), *The Stooge* (1953), *Scared Stiff* (1953), *The Caddy* (1953), *Money From Home* (1954), *Living It Up* (1954), *Three Ring Circus* (1954), *You're Never Too Young* (1955), *Artists & Models* (1955), *Pardners* (1956) and *Hollywood Or Bust* (1956). They split amid much acrimony – "I still love Dean, but I

don't like him any more," said Lewis – but Dean's solo film début came in the flop *10,000 Bedrooms* (1957). However, critics began to take him seriously when he gave a remarkable performance as the draft dodger in *The Young Lions* (1958). His later films included *Some Came Running* (1959), *Rio Bravo* (1959) as Dude (the film made as an "antidote" to *High Noon* [1953]), *Career* (1959), *Who Was That Lady?* (1956), *Ocean's 11* (1960) the first Rat Pack film, *All In A Night's Work* (1961), *Sergeants 3* (1962), which was produced by Frank Sinatra, *The Road To Hong Kong* (1962), *4 For Texas* (1963) another Rat Pack film, *What A Way To Go!* (1964), *Robin And The 7 Hoods* (1964), another Rat Pack film, *The Sons Of Katie Elder* (1965), *Five Card Stud* (1968), *Airport* (1970) as Vernon Demerest, *Mr Ricco* (1973), *The Cannonball Run* (1981) and *Cannonball Run II* (1984). Dean Martin was cast in the 1962 movie *Something's Got To Give* which starred Marilyn Monroe. When she was fired he gallantly refused to work with another actress; Marilyn died before filming could resume. He first entered the British pop charts on September 18, 1953, with the Top 10 hit 'Kiss' and was still charting over 40 years later. His theme tune was 'Everybody Loves Somebody Sometime', but he topped the charts in 1956 with 'Memories Are Made Of This'. He was married three times. On October 2, 1940, he married Elizabeth Anne MacDonald (b. Chester, Pennsylvania July 14, 1922, d. November 7, 1989) in St Anne's, Cleveland. They had four children: Stephan Craig (b. Evangelical Deaconess Hospital, Cleveland, June 29, 1942); Claudia (b. Ridley Park, Pennsylvania, March 16, 1944); Barbara Gail (b. Ohio Valley Hospital, 1101 Cardinal Avenue, April 11, 1945) and Deana (b. New York, August 19, 1948). The couple was divorced on August 24, 1949. On September 1 of the same year he married model

Dorothy Jean 'Jeanne' Beiggers (b. Florida, March 27, 1927) in Beverly Hills. They had three children: pop singer Dean-Paul (b. St John's Hospital, Santa Monica, November 17, 1951, k. San Bernardino National Forest, March 20, 1987, in a plane crash); Ricci James (b. St John's Hospital, Santa Monica, September 20, 1953) and Gina Carolyn (b. St John's Hospital, Santa Monica, December 20, 1956). They divorced on March 29, 1973. On April 25, 1973, he married beautician Catherine Mae Hawn (b. Ohio, November 5, 1947) in his Bel-Air home, 363 Copa del Oro. They divorced on February 24, 1977. Dean once opined: "I feel sorry for people who don't drink, 'cos when they get up in the morning that's as good as they are going to feel all day."

CAUSE: He died aged 78 of acute respiratory failure caused by emphysema.

FURTHER READING: *Dino: Living High In The Dirty Business Of Dreams* – Nick Tosches (New York: Doubleday, 1992); *Martini Man The Life Of Dean Martin* – William Schoell (New York: Cooper Square, 2003); *Memories Are Made Of This: Dean Martin Through His Daughter's Eyes* – Deana Martin with Wendy Holden (London: Sidgwick & Jackson, 2004); *Dean Martin King Of The Road* – Michael Freedland (London: Robson Books, 2005).

Mary Martin
Born December 1, 1913
Died November 3, 1990
J.R.'s mum. Born in Weatherford, Texas, Mary Martin started her career as a celebrated actress renowned for her Peter Pan (winning a Tony for her performance in 1954) and ended it known as someone's mum. That someone was a pretty big someone, however – her son Larry Hagman, the villainous J.R. Ewing in *Dallas*. Mary, who was a lesbian, also won a Tony for her role in the 1959 production of *The Sound Of Music*. Her films included

The Rage Of Paris (1938), *The Great Victor Herbert* (1939) as Louise Hall, *Kiss The Boys Goodbye* (1941) as Cindy Lou Bethany, *Birth Of The Blues* (1941) as Betty Lou Cobb, *Night And Day* (1946) and *Main Street To Broadway* (1953). Mary Martin married twice. In 1930 she wed lawyer Bernard Hageman. On May 5, 1940, she married literary agent Richard Halliday (b. 1906, d. Brasilia, Brasil, March 3, 1973, following an operation). Their daughter, Mary Heller, was born in 1941. Ethel Merman said of her: "Mary Martin? Oh, she's all right, if you like talent."

CAUSE: She died in Rancho Mirage, California, aged 76, from cancer.

Lee Marvin
Born February 19, 1924
Died August 29, 1987
Gruff-voiced hell-raiser. Of all the people featured in this book, the least likely to have a number one hit record would probably be Lee Marvin. Yet on March 7, 1970, he hit the top slot with 'Wand'rin' Star', a song about a man who can't settle in one place. It stayed at the top for three weeks, as long as the Spice Girls' 'Spice Up Your Life' and 'Viva Forever' combined! Born in New York, he joined the US Marines and was invalided out with a Purple Heart having been wounded in the backside. He joined a theatre company and made his way to Broadway, television and, eventually, his first film, *You're In The Navy Now* (1951), alongside fellow cinema débutant Charles Bronson. He first grabbed attention in the war film *Eight Iron Men* (1952) as Mooney and went on to appear in *The Stranger Wore A Gun* (1953) as Dan Kurth, *Gun Fury* (1953) as Blinky, *The Glory Brigade* (1953) as Corporal Bowman and *Down Among The Sheltering Palms* (1953) as Snively. He carved a niche for himself as a Hollywood hard man throwing boiling coffee in the face of Gloria Grahame in Fritz Lang's *The Big Heat* (1953). He

was in *Seminole* (1953) as Sergeant Magruder, *The Wild One* (1954), *Gorilla At Large* (1954) as Shaughnessy, *The Caine Mutiny* (1954) as Meatball, *I Died A Thousand Times* (1955) as Babe Kossuck, John Sturges' *Bad Day At Black Rock* (1955) as Hector David and *Raintree County* (1957) as Orville 'Flash' Perkins. He appeared in the NBC television series *M Squad* as hard-nosed cop Lieutenant Frank Ballinger from September 20, 1957, unti September 13, 1960. He was often seen on individual television plays before returning to the big screen, doing very little television work afterwards. He began appearing in Westerns such as *The Comancheros* (1961) as Tully Crow, *The Man Who Shot Liberty Valance* (1962) as Liberty Valance and *Cat Ballou* (1965) as Tim Strawn/Kid Shelleen, which won him an Oscar. He led *The Dirty Dozen* (1967) as Major John Reisman, became gangster Walker in John Boorman's violent *Point Blank* (1967) but returned to the West for Josh Logan's *Paint Your Wagon* (1969) as Ben Rumson. Despite being a successful stage show the film was a flop. Nonetheless, it earned Marvin a number one record. Director Logan commented, "Not since Attila the Hun swept across Europe leaving five hundred years of total blackness has there been a man like Lee Marvin." After that Marvin was a steady actor who never found the right project. His later films included *The Iceman Cometh* (1973) as Hickey, *The Klansman* (1974) as Sheriff Bascomb, *Shout At The Devil* (1976) as Flynn O'Flynn, *The Big Red One* (1980) as The Sergeant, *Gorky Park* (1983) as Jack Osborne and *The Delta Force* (1986) as Colonel Nick Alexander. He reprised his portrayal of Major John Reisman in the TV movie *The Dirty Dozen: The Next Mission* (1985). Originally, the role of Reisman was due to be played by John Wayne but he made the ultra-patriotic *The Green Berets* (1968)

instead. On February 5, 1952, Marvin married actress Betty Ebeling in the Wee Kirk O' The Heather, Las Vegas. The ceremony was performed by the Reverend Loveable. They had four children: Christopher (b. 1952); Courtenay (b. 1954), Cynthia (b. 1956) and Claudia (b. 1958). They divorced on January 4, 1967. One of the extras on *Ship Of Fools* (1965) was a 37-24-36, dark-haired, divorced, Roman Catholic singer called Michelle Triola (b. Los Angeles, California, 1933). She and Marvin began an affair. It was to be a fling that made legal history. When they split she sued him in the first 'palimony' suit. "I gave Lee the best years of my life," she claimed while he countered with, "Well, I *also* gave her the best years of *her* life." Explaining the suit, Triola said, "Lee is probably the most pure man I have ever known in my entire life. That's why I have to sue him." Without wishing to ascribe any financial motivation to Triola's action, it should be pointed out that she changed her name legally to Marvin a mere four days before they split. She asked for $3.6 million. On April 18, 1979, the trial ended after 11 weeks and the judge found in favour of Marvin but awarded Triola "an equitable sum of $104,000 to re-educate herself so that she may return from her status as a companion of a motion picture star to a separate, independent, but perhaps more prosaic existence." However, the award was overturned on appeal and Triola was left without a penny. In 1981 she was convicted of "shoplifting two bras and two sweaters from a Beverly Hills department store." In the early Eighties she moved in with married comedian Dick Van Dyke and took to calling herself Michelle Van Dyke. Michelle Triola died in Malibu on October 30, 2009. On October 18, 1970, Marvin had married Pamela Freeley in Las Vegas. They were still together when he died.

CAUSE: Lee Marvin died in Tucson, Arizona, aged 63, from a heart attack. FURTHER READING: *Marvin: The Story Of Lee Marvin* – Donald Zec (London: New English Library, 1979).

The Marx Brothers
Chico
(LEONARD)
Born March 22, 1886
Died October 11, 1961
Groucho
(JULIUS HENRY)
Born October 2, 1890
Died August 19, 1977
Gummo
(MILTON)
Born October 21, 1892
Died April 21, 1977
Harpo
(ADOLPH [ARTHUR])
Born November 23, 1888
Died September 28, 1964
Zeppo
(HERBERT)
Born February 25, 1901
Died November 29, 1979
Comedy family. Born in Yorkville, New York, the sons of Samuel Marx, a Jewish tailor, there were originally six Marx Brothers. Manfred died while still a child. The family resided at 179 East 93rd Street, New York, and soon set off on showbiz careers, joining vaudeville. Groucho was the first to enter the business, followed by Gummo, Harpo, Chico and then Zeppo. By 1914 the four eldest brothers had their own family act. Their names were explained thus by Groucho. "I was the moody one so [I was] called . . . Groucho. The harp player Adolph – who, after Hitler's rise to power changed his name to Arthur – would be known as Harpo. [Milton t]he fellow who wore the gumshoes would be known as Gummo. And the one constantly chasing the pretty chicks would be called Chicko. We didn't think much of the idea at first but it caught on. The 'k' in Leonard's name was accidentally dropped by a typesetter, and it became 'Chico'." Gummo left the act to be replaced by brother Herbert, named Zeppo after a chimpanzee. They made their Broadway début in 1924, a year after a journalist criticised Harpo's voice. He decided to remain mute on stage afterwards. Moving to movies, the Marx Brothers made a number of highly successful film comedies such as *The Cocoanuts* (1929), *Animal Crackers* (1930), *Duck Soup* (1933), *A Night At The Opera* (1935) and *A Day At The Races* (1937). When they released *A Night In Casablanca* (1946), Warner Bros threatened to sue claiming the public would confuse the film with the Bogart epic. Groucho countered by threatening to sue the studio for using the word 'Brothers'. Away from the screen the brothers had other interests. Chico's was womanising. In 1910 he married dancer Betty Karp. Their daughter, Maxine, arrived in 1911. They divorced in 1942. His wife once caught him kissing a chorus girl. He protested his innocence with the explanation: "I wasn't kissing her, I was whispering in her mouth." On August 22, 1958, in Beverly Hills he married actress Mary DeVithas. Zeppo was granted a US patent for a watch that also checked the wearer's heartbeat. He married and divorced Marion Benda and adopted two children. In 1959 he married, as her second husband, Barbara Jane Blakeley (b. Bosworth, Missouri, October 16, 1930) who, after the December 27, 1972 divorce, subsequently married Frank Sinatra. Harpo married actress Susan Fleming on September 12, 1936, but kept the match a secret until November. They adopted four children: Billy Woollcott, Alexander and twins Minnie and Jimmy. Groucho had a successful television career as host of the quiz show *You Bet Your Life*. On one edition of the show a female contestant said she had a dozen children. An amazed Groucho asked why. "Because I love my husband," she

replied. "I love my cigar but I take it out once in a while!" came the rejoinder. Groucho married three times. He wed dancer Ruth Johnson in Chicago on February 4, 1920. They had a son Arthur (b. July 21, 1921), who later wrote books about his father, and a daughter Miriam (b. 1927). Separating in December 1941 the couple was divorced in Los Angeles on July 15, 1942. On July 21, 1945, in Los Angeles, he married Catherine Gorcey, the ex-wife of actor Leo Gorcey. Their daughter, Melinda, was born on August 14, 1946, in Los Angeles. On May 15, 1951, they were divorced. On July 17, 1954, he married for the final time to Eden Marie Hartford. That, too, ended in divorce, this time on December 3, 1969. He once met a priest who said to him, "I want to shake your hand and thank you for all the pleasure you've brought into the world." Groucho grasped the proffered hand with the words, "And I want to thank you for all the pleasure you've taken out of it." Asked by *Playboy* what he would do if he could live his life over again, the immortal Groucho replied, "Try more positions." Widely regarded as one of the funniest on-screen comedians of them all, writer Sir Kingsley Amis dismissed Groucho as, "The most embarrassingly unfunny comedian I have ever encountered." CAUSE: After suffering many years of poor health, Chico died of a heart attack aged 75 in Hollywood. He was buried in Forest Lawn Memorial-Parks, 1712 Glendale Avenue, Glendale, California 91209. Groucho died aged 86 in Los Angeles, of pneumonia. He was buried in Eden Memorial Park, 11500 Sepulveda Boulevard, San Fernando, California 91345. Gummo died aged 84 of lung cancer. He, too, was interred in Forest Lawn Memorial-Parks. Harpo died in Los Angeles during heart surgery aged 75. Zeppo died of cancer aged 78. He was cremated and his ashes scattered at sea.

James Mason
Born May 15, 1909
Died July 27, 1984
The nearly man. Born in Huddersfield, West Yorkshire, James Neville Mason earned a first in architecture from Peterhouse College, Cambridge. He then went on to join the Old Vic and appeared with the Gate Company Players in Dublin before moving into movies although he was sacked from *The Private Life Of Don Juan* (1934) and his official début came as Jim Martin in *Late Extra* (1935). For a time he was a journeyman in films such as *Twice Branded* (1936) as Henry Hamilton, *Troubled Waters* (1936) as John Merriman, *Secret Of Stamboul* (1936) as Larry, *Blind Man's Bluff* (1936) as Stephen Neville, *The Mill On The Floss* (1937) as Tom Tulliver, *The High Command* (1937) as Captain Heverell, *Catch As Catch Can* (1937) as Robert Leyland, *The Return Of The Scarlet Pimpernel* (1938) as Jean Tallien, *I Met A Murderer* (1939) as Mark Warrow, *Alibi* (1942) as Andre Laurent, *Secret Mission* (1942) as Raoul de Carnot, before making his mark in *The Man In Grey* (1943) as the sadist Marquis of Rohan. He also excelled opposite Ann Todd in *The Seventh Veil* (1945) as baddie Nicholas and was splendid as an IRA gunman, Johnny McQueen, in Carol Reed's *Odd Man Out* (1947). In 1947 he moved to America following that film (Mason had been a conscientious objector during the war) and *The Wicked Lady* (1945) in which he played another baddie, Captain Jerry Jackson. Many believe his early work in Hollywood lacked bite. He appeared in *Madame Bovary* (1949) as Gustave Flaubert, *The Reckless Moment* (1949) as Martin Donnelly, *One Way Street* (1950) as Doc Matson, *The Desert Fox: The Story Of Rommel* (1951) as Erwin Rommel, *The Prisoner Of Zenda* (1952) as Rupert of Hentzau, *Five Fingers* (1952) as Albanian valet

Ulysses Diello/'Cicero', *Julius Caesar* (1953) as Brutus, *The Desert Rats* (1953) reprising his role as Erwin Rommel and *20,000 Leagues Under The Sea* (1954) as the submarine *Nautilus*' crazed Captain Nemo. He silenced his critics with his portrayal of Norman Maine in the remake of *A Star Is Born* (1954), played by Frederic March in the 1937 original. He was nominated for a Best Actor Oscar for his work, although he never really liked the film. He also shone in *Journey To The Center Of The Earth* (1959) as Professor Oliver Lindenbrook, Alfred Hitchcock's *North By Northwest* (1959) as Phillip Vandamm menacing Cary Grant, *The Trials Of Oscar Wilde* (1960) as lawyer Sir Edward Carson, *Lolita* (1962) as the middle-aged professor Humbert Humbert obsessed with the young Sue Lyon, *Lord Jim* (1965) as Gentleman Brown, *Genghis Khan* (1965) as Kam Ling, *The Blue Max* (1966) as General Count von Klugermann, *Georgy Girl* (1966) as sugar daddy James Leamington, for which he was nominated for a Best Supporting Actor Oscar, *Mayerling* (1968) as Emperor Franz Joseph, *Age Of Consent* (1969) as Bradley Monahan, in which Helen Mirren appeared nude, *Murder By Decree* (1979) as a bumbling Dr John H. Watson to Christopher Plummer's Holmes, *The Verdict* (1982) as trial lawyer Edward J. Concannon, for which he was nominated for his second Best Supporting Actor Oscar, *The Shooting Party* (1984) and *The Assisi Underground* (1985) as Bishop Nicolini. He also appeared in a number of foreign language films, which neither helped nor harmed his career. Rumours of Mason's supposed homosexuality have long been in circulation, though he married twice. His first wife was Pamela Kellino (b. March 10, 1916, d. June 29, 1996), whom he married at Amersham Registry Office in February 1941. They divorced on August 31, 1964. His second trip up the aisle was with

Clarissa Kaye on August 13, 1971. According to many accounts, Mason was "so opinionated and rude that it was a lesson in self-delusion just to catch a glimpse of him." CAUSE: Mason died of a massive coronary in Lausanne, Switzerland, aged 75. He had suffered heart problems for some time and had a pacemaker fitted. He was buried in Vevey. FURTHER READING: *Before I Forget: An Autobiography & Drawings* – James Mason (London: Sphere, 1982); *Odd Man Out* – Sheridan Morley (London: Weidenfeld & Nicolson, 1989).

Raymond Massey
Born August 30, 1896
Died July 29, 1983
Patriarch. Born in Toronto and educated at Balliol College, Oxford, Massey began his acting career on stage in London in 1922 and progressed to the big screen nine years later. In 1944 he became an American citizen. He was able to play across the spectrum of human endeavour from villains to US President Abraham Lincoln (*Abe Lincoln In Illinois* [1940], for which he was nominated for a Best Actor Oscar and *How The West Was Won* [1962]) to consulting detectives such as Sherlock Holmes in *The Speckled Band* (1932) to abolitionist John Brown in *Santa Fe Trail* (1940) and *Seven Angry Men* (1955). He was also in *The Scarlet Pimpernel* (1935), *Things To Come* (1936), *Fire Over England* (1937), *The Prisoner Of Zenda* (1937), *Arsenic And Old Lace* (1944) as Jonathan Brewster, *A Matter Of Life And Death* (1946) as Abraham Farlan, *East Of Eden* (1955) as James Dean's father Adam Trask and *The Naked And The Dead* (1958). Massey played the wise old Dr Leonard Gillespie on television in *Dr Kildare* from September 28, 1961, until August 30, 1966. He was married three times – in 1921 to Margery Fremantle, actress Adrianne Allan (from November 12, 1929, until July 6, 1939) and (on

July 10, 1939) lawyer Dorothy Ludington Whitney – and two of his three children, Daniel and Anna, followed him onto the boards.
CAUSE: He died of pneumonia aged 86 in Los Angeles. He was buried in Beaverdale Memorial Park, 90 Pine Rock Avenue, Hamden, Connecticut 06515.

Marcello Mastroianni
Born September 28, 1923
Died December 19, 1996
Latin lover. Born in Fontana Liri, Italy, Mastroianni was originally a draughtsman and was sent to a German labour camp in 1942 but escaped and fled to Venice where he hid until the liberation. Joining an amateur theatre group in Rome, he was spotted by Luchino Visconti, who cast him in *White Knights* (1957). He made over 100 films ("but only ten of them are any good"), though his best work was probably as journalist Marcello Rubini in Federico Fellini's *La Dolce Vita* (1959). A lapsed Catholic, he married actress Flora Carabella in 1950 but that didn't stop him fooling around. He had a well-publicised affair with Faye Dunaway, who dumped him in 1971 and fathered a daughter, Chiara-Charlotte, in 1972 by Catherine Deneuve, during a three-year affair. He was nominated for an Oscar on three occasions – for playing Ferdinando in *Divorce, Italian Style* (1962), Gabriele in *A Special Day* (1977) and Romano in *Oci Ciornie* (1987).
CAUSE: He died of pancreatic cancer aged 73 in Paris.

Walter Matthau
(WALTER JOHN MATTHOW)
Born October 1, 1920
Died July 1, 2000
Stolid comedic actor. The actor was born in New York City, the youngest of two sons of Russian-Jewish immigrants, Milton (Melos) Matthow (b. Kiev), an electrician and peddler, and Rose Berolsky (b. Lithuania December 15, 1894, d. New York, January 1979) who worked in a sweatshop. His older brother, Henry, was born July 14, 1918 and died in Long Beach, New York on May 21, 1995. Matthau was raised on the impoverished Lower East Side and sold soft drinks and played bit parts, aged 11, at a Second Avenue Yiddish theatre. His father, who left home when Walter was three, died in 1935 and Matthau was plagued by insecurity. After leaving school he was a boxing instructor, basketball coach and a filing clerk. He was known for his bloodhound face and throaty growl. When filling out an official form in 1937, he declared 'Foghorn' was his middle name. From 1941 to 1945 he served in the United States air force as a radio operator and air gunner. After the war he took advantage of the GI Bill of Rights and returned to New York to study at the New School for Social Research Dramatic Workshop under the renowned German director Erwin Piscator, from whom he acquired "the real feeling for acting". He then joined a summer stock company and began to land parts on Broadway. In 1955 he was in a revival of the musical *Guys And Dolls* playing Nathan Detroit, and the playwright Michael Freeman in *Will Success Spoil Rock Hunter?* opposite Jayne Mansfield. He had made his film début five years earlier in *Atomic Attack* (1950). In his early films he was often cast as the baddie. In *Goodbye Charlie* (1964) he played a film producer, a role based on Alexander Korda. But for a long time it seemed Matthau was destined to remain a supporting player. His big break came in 1965 in Neil Simon's *The Odd Couple*, a comedy of two divorced men trying to live together. Matthau's slob sportswriter, Oscar Madison, won a Tony award (Simon had written the part specifically for him). The two men are quite unable to get on. "Everything you do irritates me," Oscar complains to Felix Unger. "And when you're not

here, the things I know you're going to do irritate me." At 44, Matthau became one of America's leading comic actors. He followed that up with an Oscar as Best Supporting Actor for his performance as Whiplash Willy, a conman lawyer, who forces his only slightly injured client to sue for a million dollars' damages in Billy Wilder's *The Fortune Cookie* (1966). It was the first picture that teamed Matthau with Jack Lemmon, who provided a perfect foil. During shooting Matthau suffered a heart attack, but he was able to resume filming after a seven-week break. Matthau and Lemmon were reunited in 1968 for a film version of *The Odd Couple*. In 1971 Lemmon directed Matthau *in Kotch*, a comedy about a miserable old granddad trying to make it up with his family. Matthau was nominated for another Oscar for his performance. He appeared as Horace Vandergelder opposite Barbra Streisand in the musical *Hello Dolly!* (1969). But they couldn't stand each other. He said of Streisand that she "has as much talent as a butterfly's fart". During the Seventies he starred in more Neil Simon vehicles: *Plaza Suite* (1971), in which he played three parts – an unfaithful husband, a Hollywood producer, and a harassed father-of-the-bride; *The Sunshine Boys* (1975) and *California Suite* (1978). Matthau and Jack Lemmon and Billy Wilder were reunited in 1974 with a Billy Wilder remake of the newspaper comedy *The Front Page*. Matthau, Lemmon and Wilder were together again for *Buddy Buddy* (1981), a remake of the witty French *L'Emmerdeur* which suffered badly by comparison with its original. In the meantime, Glenda Jackson was Matthau's leading lady in *House Calls* (1978), in which he was a recently widowed man seeking a new lover and she was a divorcée. They were together again in the spy film *Hopscotch* (1980). Matthau and Lemmon were together

again in *Grumpy Old Men* in 1993, *Grumpier Old Men* in 1995 and *Out To Sea* in 1997. He and Lemmon rather ill-advisedly made *The Odd Couple II* in 1998, thirty years after the first film. It was not a success. Reports are now circulating that 6'3" Matthau made up as a joke the fact that he was born Walter Matasschanskayasky or Walter Matuschanskayasky and that his real "real" name is Matthow. According to his son, Charlie Matthau, on *Larry King Live*, July 14, 2000, his real name was Walter Matthow, and he changed it to be more exotic. Walter Matthau was married twice. In 1948 he married Grace Johnson. He had a son, David (b. November 2, 1953), and a daughter, Jennie (b. August 2, 1956), by the marriage before the 1958 divorce. On August 21, 1959 he married the actress and writer Carol Marcus (b. New York, September 11, 1925, d. July 20, 2003 of a brain aneurysm; she was previously married to the novelist William Saroyan). They had one son, Charlie (b. December 10, 1962), who directed him in *The Grass Harp* (1995). "I never mind my wife having the last word," he once said. "In fact, I'm delighted when she gets to it."

CAUSE: Matthau suffered a heart attack while making *The Fortune Cookie* (1966) as soon as he became a star. "My doctor gave me six months to live," he quipped, "and then, when I couldn't pay the bill, he gave me six months more." Due to heavy smoking he had heart bypass surgery in 1976. In 1993, he was hospitalised for double pneumonia. In 1995, he had a benign colon tumour removed. In 1999, he was hospitalised again for pneumonia. In the summer of 2000, Matthau was taken to the St John's Health Center after suffering a heart attack but was pronounced dead shortly afterwards at 1.42am. He was 79. He was buried at Westwood Village Memorial Park, 1218 Glendon Avenue, Los Angeles 90024.

Jessie Matthews, OBE
Born March 11, 1907
Died August 19, 1981
Britain's Dancing Divinity. "She was a much greater dancer than Ginger Rogers and I thought a better actress," said Sir Dirk Bogarde. Born at 94 Berwick Street, Soho, London, the seventh of sixteen children of whom eleven reached maturity, Jessie Margaret Matthews was the daughter of a stall holder in Berwick Street market. A brilliant dancer, she was treading the boards before she turned 11 in *Bluebell In Fairyland* in 1919. She was given a job in the chorus line by impresario C.B. Cochran who said she was "an interesting-looking child with enormous eyes and the funniest little nose, wearing clothes which seemed too large for her, and holding with both hands a huge umbrella." She made her film début in *The Beloved Vagabond* (1923) as Pan. At Hammersmith Register Office on February 17, 1926 she married the actor Henry Lytton, Jr (b. 1906, d. Blackpool, September 16, 1965) but they divorced in London on November 21, 1929 because of his adultery. The decree became absolute on June 2, 1930. She was given elocution lessons to rid her of her cockney accent and her star began to ascend in films such as *Out Of The Blue* (1931) as Tommy Tucker, *There Goes The Bride* (1932) as Annette Marquand and *Waltzes From Vienna* (1933) as Rasi. She was signed to a contract by Michael Balcon and appeared in *The Good Companions* (1933) as Susie Dean and *Friday The Thirteenth* (1933) as Millie. Her best musical of the Thirties was probably Victor Saville's *Evergreen* (1934) in which she played Harriet Green/Harriet Hawkes. Due to sign a contract with MGM she suffered a breakdown in 1934 and the American studio pulled out. On January 24, 1931 at Hampstead Register Office she married myopic 5'7" John Robert Hale-Monro, Jr (b. London, May 1, 1902, d. London, June 9, 1959 of

myelofibrosis) known professionally as Sonnie Hale. He had been married to Evelyn Laye and when they divorced on July 11, 1930 Jessie received much unwanted publicity as the "other woman" after being cited as co-respondent. Attending the hearing in the Probate, Divorce and Admiralty Division of the High Court of Justice with Hale, she fainted and was later horrified to hear the judge, Sir Maurice Hill, describe her as "a person of an odious mind". The two women became mortal enemies and on February 28 Jessie was not presented to King George V and Queen Mary when they went to see *The Good Companions* because it was considered "inappropriate". However, the monarch and his consort saw her in the back row of the New Victoria Cinema and smiled and nodded at her. Hale directed her in *Head Over Heels In Love* (1937) in which she was Jeanne, *Gangway* (1937) as Pat Wayne and *Sailing Along* (1938) as Kay Martin. He did not possess Victor Saville's light touch. On December 18, 1934, two months early, she gave birth to John Robert Hale-Monro III, who died aged just four hours. In February 1935 she adopted a daughter, Catherine (b. January 4, 1935). In August 1936 she suffered another serious mental breakdown. Her career was ended in all but name by the Second World War. She suffered yet another breakdown, her marriage ended (in London on July 3, 1944) and she made only the occasional foray into films such as *Tom Thumb* (1958) as Anne and *The Hound Of The Baskervilles* (1978) as Mrs Tinsdale. She had a brief role in the TV series *Edward & Mrs Simpson*. At Chelsea Register Office on August 9, 1945 she married Lieutenant (Richard) Brian Lewis, twelve years younger than her. A son was stillborn on the morning of December 28, 1945. They divorced on October 16, 1958. On March 18, 1963 she took over the part of Mrs (Mary) Dale in the BBC radio series

The Dales. "Sustaining a long personal relationship was just not within her power," said Vincent Shaw. "She wanted to be a star. She was a star and I think she was quite happy with it . . . She was too selfish to want anything else . . . When she ceased to be a big star she was a very lonely lady."
CAUSE: She died of cancer in Eastcote, Middlesex, aged 74. She left £56,503.
FURTHER READING: *Jessie Matthews –* Michael Thornton (London: Hart-Davis, MacGibbon, 1974).

Victor Mature

Born January 29, 1913
Died August 4, 1999
'The Hunk'. Born in Louisville, Kentucky, the second son of immigrants Marcellus G. (1878–1941) and Clara R. (1886–1959), 6′2″ Victor John Mature's career was built more on his physique than his acting ability, as he was the first to admit. He was signed by Hal Roach and made his début in *The Housekeeper's Daughter* (1939) but it was his appearance as a caveman in *One Million BC* that made cinemagoers sit up and take notice. He signed for Fox who placed him opposite his then real-life girlfriend Betty Grable in *I Wake Up Screaming* (1941), *Song Of The Islands* (1942) and *Footlight Serenade* (1942). In 1942 he went into the coast guard, where he stayed for the remainder of the war. In 1946 he portrayed Doc Holliday opposite Henry Fonda's Wyatt Earp in John Ford's historically inaccurate *My Darling Clementine.* Playing a killer in *Kiss Of Death* (1947) he watched as Richard Widmark stole the screen from the supposed star. Mature spent the next decade or so appearing in all sorts of epics including the lead male in Cecil B. DeMille's *Samson & Delilah* (1949) opposite Hedy Lamarr, causing Groucho Marx to comment, "I never go to movies where the hero's tits are bigger than the heroines." The director noticed that Mature, a sensitive, intelligent man, was also, by his own

admission, "a devout coward". He was scared of almost everything – lions, fire, swords, insects, horses, etc. In 1984 he was lured back with a vast salary to play Samson's father, Manoah, in a TV film. Mature stated, "For that money, I'd play his mother." In *The Robe* (1953) he was afraid of a club so the props department fashioned one from a balloon. Mature's fears were not alleviated – he thought the balloon might burst. He had an affair with Rita Hayworth and married five times: Frances Evans (January 30, 1938–1940); Martha Stevenson Kemp (June 18, 1941–February 10, 1943); Dorothy Stanford Berry (February 28, 1948–November 8, 1955), Adrianne Joy Urwich (September 27, 1959–February 6, 1969), Lorey Sabena (1974–until his death) by whom he had his only daughter, Victoria S., born on March 16, 1975. He retired in the Sixties, a very wealthy man, to play golf, but one of his more memorable film appearances that decade was as himself in the frankly bizarre *Head* (1968), starring The Monkees. "I'm no actor," he once said, "and I have 64 pictures to prove it."
CAUSE: Mature died, aged 86, from leukaemia at Rancho Santa Fe, California. He was buried in the family plot at St Michael's Cemetery, Louisville, Jefferson County, Kentucky.

Jenny Maxwell

Born September 3, 1941
Died June 10, 1981
Tragic wannabe. After failing the audition for *Lolita* it looked like New York-born Jennifer Helene Maxwell's career was over before it had started. Then she was cast in *Blue Denim* (1959) as Marion and *Blue Hawaii* (1961) as Ellie Corbett opposite Elvis Presley and it looked as if things could take off. She only made two more films before retiring: *Shotgun Wedding* (1963) and *Take Her, She's Mine* (1963) as Sarah.

CAUSE: Walking with her lawyer husband Tip Roeder both were shot to death outside their Beverly Hills home. The murders remain unsolved.

Louis B. Mayer

(LAZAR MEIR)
Born 1885
Died October 29, 1957
Creator of "more stars than there are in the heavens". Born in Dymer in the Ukraine, the son of 5′4″ Jacob Meir, he moved with his family to England in 1886 but his father was unable to find work and after a year moved to Ireland, while his wife and family sailed for America where he later joined them. Then they moved to St John, New Brunswick, Canada, in 1892. Mayer worked as a scrap metal dealer before moving to Boston on January 3, 1904. At the 15 Emerald Street First Orthodox Synagogue on June 14, 1904, he married Margaret Shenberg (b. 1882, d. Cedars Of Lebanon Hospital, Los Angeles, May 21, 1954, of heart failure). On the wedding documents Mayer lied about his age stating it as "Born July 4, 1882". In fact, like many from Eastern Europe, his date of birth is unsure and he adopted the Fourth of July to show his patriotism. Their daughter Edith was born on August 13, 1905, and then, following a stillbirth, another daughter, Irene, was born at 101 Russell Street, Greenpoint, on April 2, 1907. That same year Mayer bought the Orpheum, an old cinema in Haverhill, Massachusetts, after seeing an advertisement. He spent time and money redecorating the building and then announced a policy of only showing the best films when it opened on November 28 (Thanksgiving), 1907. It worked and he began to purchase other picture palaces until he owned the largest chain in New England. In 1914 he changed tack and began distributing films, starting with D.W. Griffith's *The Birth Of A Nation*

(1915). His next step was to move into production and he joined the Alco company (which later became Metro). On September 15, 1914, he joined a masonic lodge that already numbered Al Jolson, D.W. Griffith and Raymond Hitchcock among its members. On October 14, 1916, he left to become a movie producer and his first film was called *The Great Secret* (1916). He created his own company, Louis B. Mayer Pictures. On April 7, 1920, he had a punch-up with Charlie Chaplin following remarks made by Mayer about the Little Tramp's divorce from Mildred Harris to which Chaplin took exception. The actor took the first swing but the producer won the day. On April 17, 1924, his company merged with Metro and Goldwyn Pictures. For some time films were released as "A Metro-Goldwyn Picture, Produced By Louis B. Mayer" until at Mayer's insistence the name became Metro-Goldwyn-Mayer. Mayer was appointed General Manager and Vice President, a role he would hold until July 25, 1951, when he lost a power struggle to Dore Schary. It was Mayer's vision that made the studio one of the most successful in the Thirties. Mayer spent the most to hire the best and was amply rewarded himself, becoming the highest paid person in America. Mayer ran MGM like a family, rewarding loyalty and punishing those who didn't have the company's best interests at heart. Screenwriter Herman J. Mankiewicz said of him, "He has the memory of an elephant and the hide of an elephant. The only difference is that elephants are vegetarians and Mayer's diet is his fellow man." Mayer went to extreme lengths to protect his 'family', covering up manslaughters by Clark Gable and John Huston. He also maintained a brothel for the exclusive use of visiting VIPs, in which all the prostitutes were film star lookalikes. He had an on-off relationship with his production chief David O. Selznick, who was also his son-in-law. A rabid

Republican, Mayer was instrumental in the foundation of the Academy Of Motion Picture Arts & Sciences. In 1948 his mentally unbalanced wife won a divorce from him. Mayer eloped to Yuma, Arizona, with Lorena Danker on December 3, 1948. When he left MGM, things changed. Ava Gardner reported: "MGM's no great shakes now, but it was a damned sight better when the old man was around. I never liked him much but at least you knew where you stood."

CAUSE: He suffered a kidney infection in October 1957 and on the 28th fell into a coma. He died at 12.35am the next day, aged 72. He was buried in The Chapel Mausoleum's Corridor of Immortality in Home of Peace Memorial Park, 4334 Whittier Boulevard, Los Angeles, California 90023.

FURTHER READING: *Merchant Of Dreams: Louis B. Mayer, MGM And The Secret Hollywood* – Charles Higham (New York: Donald I. Fine, 1993).

Virginia Mayo

(VIRGINIA CLARA JONES)
Born November 30, 1920
Died January 17, 2005
Glamorous second fiddle. Virginia Mayo was born in St Louis, Missouri, the daughter of a newspaper reporter. She became interested in show business at an early age and began her working life in vaudeville. Her movie career almost faltered when David O. Selznick believed that she did not have a future in films. Samuel Goldwyn disagreed and cast her in the 1943 film *Jack London*, which starred her soon-to-be-husband Michael O'Shea (b. Hartford, Connecticut, March 17, 1906, d. Dallas, Texas, December 4, 1973 of a heart attack), whom she married on July 6, 1947 in the Little Church of the Flowers in Glendale, California. They had one daughter, Catherine Mary, who was born in Los Angeles on November 12, 1953. Mayo starred opposite Bob Hope in the 1944

film *The Princess And The Pirate*. Her work was primarily in light comedy and she appeared with Danny Kaye in four films, including *The Secret Life Of Walter Mitty* (1947) in which she played Rosalind van Hoorn. As well as comedy she could play drama and was in 1946's *The Best Years Of Our Lives* as Marie Derry, the unfaithful wife of Fred Derry (Dana Andrews). In the late Forties she made the move from MGM to Warner Bros and was lauded for her role as Verna Jarrett the wife of James Cagney in the crime drama *White Heat* (1949). Her other films included: *The Flame And The Arrow* (1950) as Anne, *Captain Horatio Hornblower* (1950) as Lady Barbara Wellesley, *She's Working Her Way Through College* (1952) as Angela Gardner and *The Silver Chalice* (1954) as Helena, opposite Paul Newman in his film début. She worked less and less from the Sixties onwards, making just ten films between 1965 and her death.

CAUSE: She died aged 84 at a nursing home in Thousand Oaks, California, of pneumonia and heart failure.

Mercedes McCambridge

Born March 16, 1916
Died March 2, 2004
The voice of the devil. Carlotta Mercedes Agnes McCambridge was born at 5am – the daughter of Irish immigrants on the family farm at Blackstone, near Joliet, Illinois. At some point in life, she began giving her birth date as St Patrick's Day 1918. She was educated at a Catholic High School in Chicago, and then studied English and theatre at Mundelein College, Chicago, where she was spotted by a Chicago radio programme director and was given a five-year contract. In 1941, she married her first husband, William Fifield and they migrated to Hollywood, where she continued to work in wireless. She then moved to New York to take the title role in a radio adaptation of the play

Abie's Irish Rose and found steady work in the radio dramas of Orson Welles. In 1945 she made her Broadway début in *A Place Of Our Own* but the play closed after just eight performances. A series of flops followed before McCambridge was chosen to appear in Robert Rossen's *All The King's Men* (released November 8, 1949). The film was based on the career of the corrupt Louisiana governor Huey 'Kingfish' Long and McCambridge played the hard-bitten and aggressive Sadie Burke, a manipulative campaign manager to Governor Willie Stark (Broderick Crawford). On March 23, 1950, the film garnered the Best Picture Oscar, as well as the Best Actor Oscar for Broderick Crawford as Stark. McCambridge also won an Oscar for her performance but if she was hoping that the film would catapult her into megastardom that hope was in vain. She did not fit the Hollywood glamour girl profile and her film work was sporadic. In 1981 she said, "I don't think the Hollywood community is interested in what I can do. That's all right. I've never looked for a job in my life, and I'm not going to start now. I have plenty to keep me busy." Her other credits included *Lightning Strikes Twice* (1951) as Liza McStringer, *Inside Straight* (1951), *The Scarf* (1951), *Giant* (1956) as Luz Benedict, Rock Hudson's haughty older sister, wearing a hat given to her by Gary Cooper, for which she won a second Best Supporting Actress nomination; *A Farewell To Arms* (1957) as Miss Van Campen, *Suddenly Last Summer* (1959) as Mrs Holly, *Cimarron* (1960) as Mrs Sarah Wyatt, *99 Women* (1969), *Thieves* (1977) and *The Concorde – Airport '79* (1979) as Nelli. The on-screen feud with Joan Crawford in *Johnny Guitar* (premièred May 5, 1954) in which she played the homicidal and sexually ambiguous Emma Small was given an added poignancy because the two women could not stand each other off screen –

in her autobiography she called Joan Crawford "a mean, tipsy, powerful, rotten-egg lady". Orson Welles regarded her as "the world's greatest living radio actress" and persuaded her to provide the voice of the demon who possesses Linda Blair in William Friedkin's *The Exorcist* (premièred Boxing Day, 1973). Once she had the role McCambridge was enthusiastic in her preparation. Said Friedkin, "She really went for it. She was chainsmoking, swallowing raw eggs, getting me to tie her to a chair; all these painful things just to produce the sound of a demon in torment. And as she did it, the most peculiar things would happen in her throat. Double and triple sounds would emerge at once, wheezing sounds, very much akin to what you would imagine a demon in torment might sound like." The lady herself said, "I'm a product of 16 years of convent education and I'm still a devout Catholic, so speaking those vile, blaspheming words was an agony for me. Every night when I came home I got down on my knees and gave thanks to God that I had been able to conjure up so much demonic personality. Any child could have wiggled on the bed. If there was any horror in the exorcism, it was me." However, if the audience were shocked by the film's graphic content, McCambridge had a shock as the credits rolled. Her name was omitted. She left the cinema crying and claimed that she would not "at the hands of Mr Friedkin or Warner Bros, sink into senility in shame". The Screen Actors' Guild subsequently forced the inclusion of her name in the credits. She earned a Tony nomination for Best Supporting Actress in *The Love Suicide At Schofield Barracks* (1972). In 1950 she married Fletcher Markle (b. Winnipeg, Manitoba, Canada, March 27, 1921, d. May 23, 1991 of heart failure), a radio and film director. During the course of the 12-year marriage McCambridge became an alcoholic and ended up in hospital after several heavy binges. On March 16, 1963, after her divorce, 5'3" McCambridge was given emergency treatment after swallowing a bottle of sleeping pills. But she eventually recovered, later testifying before a Senate committee on alcoholism and narcotics in July 1969. In 1987, her only child, John Lawrence, the son of her first marriage, committed suicide after murdering his wife and two daughters. Her autobiography *The Quality Of Mercy* punned on her nickname, Mercy.

CAUSE: Mercedes McCambridge died from natural causes at an assisted-living facility in La Jolla, California.

Colonel Tim McCoy

Born April 10, 1891
Died January 29, 1978

Indian expert. Born in Saginaw, Michigan, Timothy John Fitzgerald McCoy was educated at St Ignatius College in Chicago and then moved to Wyoming where he lived on a large ranch. Serving in World War I he reached the rank of Lieutenant-Colonel and was appointed Indian Agent for Wyoming. In 1922 the 5'1" McCoy was hired by a film company as Indian advisor and three years later made the first of his 90-plus films, *The Thundering Herd* (1925), as Burn Hudnall. That year he was signed by MGM where he stayed until the Thirties, leaving as one of the most popular cowboy stars. He worked for Columbia and various independent studios and starred in *The Indians Are Coming* (1935), the first talkie serial at Universal. In 1935 he joined Ringling Brothers Circus and three years later began his own, unsuccessful, Wild West Show. More military service followed before he retired, only to make various comebacks in films and on television. He was married to a Danish journalist called Inga Marie Arvad (b. Copenhagen, October 6, 1913, d. 1973). The latter had an affair with President John F. Kennedy (he nicknamed her Inga-Binga) and was considered a national security risk by the FBI, who put a tap on her phone. McCoy's films included: *War Paint* (1926) as Lieutenant Tim Marshall, *California* (1927) as Captain Archibald Gillespie, *Wyoming* (1928) as Lieutenant Jack Colton, *Beyond The Sierras* (1928) as The Masked Stranger, *Sioux Blood* (1929) as Flood, *Shotgun Pass* (1931) as Tim Walker, *The Fighting Fool* (1932) as Tim Collins, *Two-Fisted Law* (1932) as Tim Clark, *Daring Danger* (1932) as Tim Madigan, *Police Car 17* (1933) as Tim Conlon, *Man Of Action* (1933) as Tim Barlow, *Rusty Rides Alone* (1933) as Tim Burke, *Speed Wings* (1934) as Tim, *Beyond The Law* (1934) as Tim, *Square Shooter* (1935) as Tim Baxter, *Fighting Shadows* (1935) as Tim O'Hara, *Outlaw Deputy* (1935) as Tim Mallory, *Roaring Guns* (1936) as Tim Corwin, *Border Caballero* (1936) as Tim Ross, *Ghost Patrol* (1936) as Tim Caverly, *Two Gun Justice* (1938) as Tim, *Phantom Ranger* (1938) as Tim Hayes, *Lightning Carson Rides Again* (1938) as Bill Carson, *Six Gun Trail* (1938) as Captain William Carson, *Trigger Fingers* (1939) as Bill Carson, *Texas Wildcats* (1939) as Lightning Bill Carson, *Fighting Renegade* (1939) as Lightning Bill Carson/El Puma, *Arizona Gangbusters* (1940) as Tim, *Outlaws Of The Rio Grande* (1941) as Marshall Tim Barton, *Arizona Bound* (1941) as Parson McCall, *The Gunman From Bodie* (1941) as Marshal McCall, *Forbidden Trails* (1941) as Tim McCall, *West Of The Law* (1942) as Marshal Tim McCall, *Below The Border* (1942) as Tim McCall, *Ghost Town Law* (1942) as Marshal Tim McCall, *Down Texas Way* (1942) as Tim, *Around The World In 80 Days* (1956) as Commander and *Requiem For A Gunfighter* (1965) as Judge Irving Short.

CAUSE: He died aged 86 in Nogales, Arizona, from a heart attack.

Jody McCrea

(JOEL DEE MCCREA)
Born September 6, 1934
Died April 4, 2009
Surf 'n' sand star. Born in Los Angeles,
the oldest of three children of Joel
McCrea and Frances Dee, he was
educated at UCLA where he read
theatre studies and threw the javelin for
the track and field team at the 1956
national championship. He began to
appear in Westerns like his father
making his debut in *Lucy Gallant* (1955)
as Tom Dunning and indeed appeared
alongside him in the 1959–1960 TV
Western *Wichita Town*. 6'3" McCrea
featured in film and television Westerns
including: *The First Texan* (1956) as
Lieutenant Baker, *Naked Gun* (1956),
Trooper Hook (1957) as Trooper
Whittaker, *Gunsight Ridge* (1957),
*Sergeant Preston Of The Yukon: The
Criminal Collie* (1958) as Jerry Turner,
Lafayette Escadrille (1958) as Tom
Hitchcock, *Death Valley Days: To Walk
With Greatness* (1962) as Lieutenant
John F. Pershing, *Young Guns Of Texas*
(1962) as Jeff Shelby and *The Broken
Land* (1962) as Deputy Ed Flynn.
However, he found his forte in
surf'n'sand films beginning with *Beach
Party* (1963), which starred Annette
Funicello and Frankie Avalon, and
followed that with *Muscle Beach Party*
(1964) as Deadhead, *Bikini Beach*
(1964) as Deadhead, *Pajama Party*
(1964) as the big lunk, *Beach Blanket
Bingo* (1965) as Bonehead and *How To
Stuff A Wild Bikini* (1965) as Bonehead.
His latter films included: *Young Fury*
(1965) as Stone, *The Girls From Thunder
Strip* (1966) as Pike, *The Glory Stompers*
(1968) as Darryl and *Cry Blood, Apache*
(1970) as Pitcalin. McCrea retired from
acting in 1970 and eventually moved to
New Mexico. In 1966 he had married
actress Dusty Iron Wing. She died in
Hondo, New Mexico on March 31,
1996 of complications from diabetes.
CAUSE: McCrea died of a heart attack at
his ranch in Roswell, New Mexico. He
was 74.

Joel McCrea

Born November 5, 1905
Died October 20, 1990
Mr Nice Guy. The grandson of a man
who drove a stagecoach and another
who was a gold prospector in 1849, it
seemed only right that 6'2" Joel Albert
McCrea should make his name in
Westerns. Raised in South Pasadena,
California, he was one of the few boys at
an all-girls school and later attended
Pomona State College and joined the
Pasadena Playhouse after graduation in
1928. In 1927 he had begun appearing
in films in very small parts, achieving his
first leading role in 1930 in *The Silver
Horde* and going on to appear in over
90 films, making himself a very wealthy
($50 million-plus) man in the process.
He once commented, "The best advice
came from my friend Will Rogers who
told me, 'No matter what you make,
you ought to save half of it,' and I've
always tried to follow that." From the
Thirties onwards he showed a versatility
in his acting, appearing in *Come And Get
It* (1936), *Three Blind Mice* (1938),
Cecil B. DeMille's *Union Pacific* (1939),
Hitchcock's *Foreign Correspondent*
(1940) as Johnny Jones, an
unsophisticated journalist (after Gary
Cooper turned down the part),
Sullivan's Travels (1941), *The Palm
Beach Story* (1942) and Sam
Peckinpah's *Ride The High Country*
(1962). He married Frances Dee
on October 20, 1933, at White
Methodist Church, Rye, New York,
and had three sons: Joel Dee (see above)
(b. September 7, 1934); David
(b. November 15, 1936) and Peter
(b. 1955). For someone in such a
cutthroat profession and despite his
legendary meanness, McCrea was
incredibly popular. Ginger Rogers said,
"Joel truly loves everybody. He expects
to find the best in everyone he meets,
and he does."
CAUSE: He died aged 84 of pulmonary
complications on his 57th wedding
anniversary. McCrea was cremated and
his ashes scattered at sea.

Hattie McDaniel

Born June 10, 1895
Died October 26, 1952
'The coloured Sophie Tucker'. Born in Wichita, Kansas, the 13th child of a Baptist minister, Hattie McDaniel is best known for playing Mammy in *Gone With The Wind* (1939). The role allowed her to make history in three ways: she was the first black person to be nominated for an Oscar, the first to win and the first to sit down at the pre-ceremony dinner. (She also may have been the first black woman to sing on the radio.) She began her career winning a gold medal for acting when she was 16, whereafter she moved into vaudeville and sang with bands. Like many before and since she was occasionally unemployed and, for a time, was a lavatory attendant in Milwaukee. She moved to Hollywood in 1931 and, when she fell on hard times there, took in laundry. She had faith in God (she was a devout member of the Independent Church of Christ) and in herself and finally she got her big break. She appeared in the Western *The Golden West* (1932), which set her on her way. She appeared in over 60 films but it was as Mammy that she is forever remembered. "Everybody loves me," she once said. "When I'm working I mind my own business and do what I'm told." Away from the screen she had definite socialist views. She was married three times. Her first husband's identity is unknown but when he died she married Los Angeles estate agent James Lloyd Crawford in Tucson, Arizona, on March 21, 1941. They divorced and on June 11, 1949, she married painter and decorator Larry C. Williams. They divorced on the grounds of incompatibility on December 5, 1950. She had no children.
CAUSE: She retired because of poor health in 1948. She died aged 57 in the Motion Picture Country House and Hospital, 23450 Calabasas Road, Woodland Hills, San Fernando. She was buried five rows from the kerb near the main entrance of Rosedale Cemetery, 1831 West Washington Boulevard, Los Angeles, California 90007.

Marie McDonald

(CORA MARIE FRYE)
Born July 6, 1923
Died October 21, 1965
'The Body'. As with many actresses, early biographical information on Marie McDonald is sketchy. One source has her born in Vienna and her real name as Cora Froenu, which was changed to Frye when she was eight months old. Another has her born in Burgin, Kentucky. She was raised in Westchester, New York, and then Yonkers, where she wrote for the school newspaper, by-lining her articles "By Ken-Tuck". She won several beauty contests, becoming Miss Yonkers, The Queen Of Coney Island and Miss Loew's Paradise. She left school aged 15 to start modelling and became Miss New York of 1939. On August 28, 1939, she opened in *George White's Scandals Of 1939* at the Alvin Theater. Her co-stars were The Three Stooges, Ann Miller and Ben Blue. Her mother was a typical stage mum until the show went on tour and she lost her hold over Marie. In Hollywood Marie became the model for Dale Arden and Princess Aura in the *Flash Gordon* cartoon strip. In Los Angeles she eloped with Richard Allord but the marriage was annulled a few weeks later. She joined Tommy Dorsey's radio show and in December 1940 auditioned for 20th Century Fox, who turned her down. In 1941 she signed for Universal at $75 a week and dyed her hair blonde. She appeared in minor roles in various films, including *It Started With Eve* (1941), *You're Telling Me* (1942) and *Pardon My Sarong* (1942) as Ferna, a girl who fancied Lou Costello. She had an affair with Bruce Cabot that garnered her acres of newsprint. Universal dropped her

contract, but she then signed for Paramount at $100 a week and was put in *Lucky Jordan* (1942) as Pearl, a sexy secretary. On January 10, 1943, she married, as his third wife, agent Vic Orsatti (b. 1905, d. June 1984). She appeared in *A Scream In The Dark* (1943) as Joan Allen for Republic, but then went back to Paramount for *Riding High* (1943) and *Tornado* (1943) as socialite Diana Linden. She played Gracie, a welder in *I Love A Soldier* (1944), featured in *Our Hearts Were Young And Gay* (1944) and *Standing Room Only* (1944) as Opal, a secretary. *Guest In The House* (1944), in which she played Miriam, earned Marie her first positive reviews. To capitalise on the success, United Artists' press office labelled her 'The Body', a nickname she loathed. For *It's A Pleasure* (1945) as Gale Fletcher her blonde hair was dyed red because the star of the film, Sonja Henie, had a 'no other blondes' clause in her contract. She played the lead in *Getting Gertie's Garter* (1945) for United Artists. In 1947 she signed with MGM and appeared in *Living In A Big Way* (1947) as Margaud Morgan. However, she didn't get on with the star Gene Kelly and the film was not a success. She paid $14,000 to buy herself out of her contract with MGM. In 1947 her marriage broke up. While awaiting a divorce in May 1947 she had an affair with hoodlum Benjamin 'Bugsy' Siegel but he dumped her because of her regular tardiness. Husband number three was multi-millionaire footwear tycoon Harry Karl (b. 1914, d. August 1982 after heart surgery) who would marry Joan Cohn (who married Laurence Harvey) and Debbie Reynolds (on November 25, 1960). She appeared in *Tell It To The Judge* (1949) as Ginger Simmons for Columbia. In November 1950 she began working in the theatre and then made *Once A Thief* (1950) as Flo and *Hit Parade Of 1951* (1950) as Michele. They would be her last films for almost a decade. After several

miscarriages she adopted two children. In 1954 she was charged with driving under the influence. That same year she divorced Karl, claiming that she was allergic to him and that he made her ill. Then they went on holiday and remarried, only to separate again in 1955. On September 12, 1956, their daughter, Tina Marie, was born. In January 1957 she was kidnapped from her Encino home and discovered unharmed 40 miles away. The police found in her home a book about a movie star who is kidnapped. Coincidence or publicity stunt? The ransom note was made up of cuttings from newspapers found in her own fireplace. Marie accused Karl of hiring the kidnappers but he denied it. The case petered out and in March 1958 he sued her for divorce. That year she made her film comeback with Jerry Lewis in *The Geisha Boy* (1958) as Lola Livingston. Her life became a series of ups and downs: a successful play and a conviction for attempting to forge a prescription, a reconciliation with Karl and an accidental overdose of sleeping pills. In 1959 she married agent Louis Bass. In 1960 she divorced him. In 1962 she married lawyer Edward Callaghan. In 1963 she divorced him. An affair with Michael Wilding fizzled out. Her last film was Jayne Mansfield's *Promises! Promises!* (1963), in which she played the wife of Jayne's real-life husband, Mickey Hargitay. Her sixth husband was Donald F. Taylor (b. 1928), who produced *Promises! Promises!*

CAUSE: Donald Taylor found her dead of an overdose at her dressing table at home in Calabasas Hidden Hills, California. She was 42. Unable to bear the grief, he died by his own hand in January 1966.

Roddy McDowall
Born September 17, 1928
Died October 3, 1998
The Queen of the Lavender Mafia. Very few successful child stars grow up

to be successful as adult ones. Even fewer become more successful as adults than they were as children. Usually, they lose their cuteness, their appeal and, consequently, their jobs. Roderick Andrew Anthony Jude McDowall was an exception to the rule. Born in Herne Hill, London, he began making films in England in the Thirties. He appeared in *Yellow Sands* (1938), *Scruffy* (1938), *Sarah Siddons* (1938), *Murder In The Family* (1938) as Peter Osborne, *I See Ice* (1938), *Just William* (1939) as Ginger, *Convict 99* (1939) as Jimmy, *Saloon Bar* (1940) and *This England* (1941) as Hugo among others. In 1941 he travelled the Atlantic to America to appear in John Ford's *How Green Was My Valley* (1941) as Huw and stayed. He starred in *The Pied Piper* (1942) as Ronnie Cavanaugh, *On The Sunny Side* (1942) as Hugh Aylesworth, *Son Of Fury* (1942) as Young Benjamin Blake, *My Friend Flicka* (1943) as Ken McLaughlin, *Lassie Come Home* (1943) as Joe Carraclough, *Thunderhead – Son Of Flicka* (1945) as Ken McLaughlin, *Molly And Me* (1945) as Jimmy Graham, *Rocky* (1948) as Roddy, *Macbeth* (1948) as Malcolm and *Kidnapped* (1948) as David Balfour. In 1948 he began producing as well as starring in films. He made very few films in the Fifties, concentrating instead on television and theatre. His cinematic comeback occurred in the Sixties. He featured in *Midnight Lace* (1960) as Malcolm, *The Longest Day* (1962) as Private Morris, *Cleopatra* (1963) as Caesar Augustus, *The Greatest Story Ever Told* (1965) as Matthew, *That Darn Cat!* (1965) as Gregory Benson, *Planet Of The Apes* (1968) as Dr Cornelius, *Pretty Maids All In A Row* (1971) as Mr Proffer, *Escape From The Planet Of The Apes* (1971) as Cornelius, *Bedknobs And Broomsticks* (1971) as Mr Jelk, *The Life And Times Of Judge Roy Bean* (1972) as Frank Gass, *Conquest Of The Planet Of The Apes* (1972) as Caesar, *The Poseidon Adventure* (1972) as Acres,

Battle For The Planet Of The Apes (1973) as Caesar, *Dirty Mary Crazy Larry* (1974) as George Stanton, *Funny Lady* (1975) as Bobby Moore, *The Cat From Outer Space* (1978) as Mr Stallwood, *Charlie Chan And The Curse Of The Dragon Queen* (1981) as Gillespie, *Fright Night* (1985) as Peter Vincent, *Fright Night Part II* (1989) reprising his role as Peter Vincent, *Angel 4: Undercover* (1993) as Geoffrey Kagen and many, many more. He was the only actor to appear in the *Planet Of The Apes* films and also the television series, where he played Galen. He also had a recurring role as rebel scientist Jonathan Willoway on the television show *The Fantastic Journey*. Away from showbiz (but not too far) McDowall was a successful photographer who published four books of his pictures.
CAUSE: On April 30, 1998, he underwent a left lung and skin biopsy. He died aged 70 at 7.30am of lung cancer at his home, 3110 Brookdale Road, Studio City, Los Angeles, California 91604. The cancer had also penetrated his brain and bones. He was cremated and his ashes scattered in the Pacific.

George "Spanky" McFarland
Born October 2, 1928
Died June 30, 1993
Our Gang's fat boy. Born in Dallas (Fort Worth according to some sources), Texas George Robert Phillips McFarland's parents sent his picture to producer Hal Roach when their son was just two. Roach had always used a fat child in his Our Gang films and he signed McFarland to a contract that lasted until the end of the series in 1944. Stan Laurel taught McFarland how to do a double take on camera. His mother gave him the nickname "Spanky" after she told him off for doing something naughty and promised a punishment. By the time the series ended, he had appeared in more than 150 features and shorts. He is one of

only two Our Gang members to have a star on the Hollywood Walk of Fame (Jackie Cooper is the other). He was also the only cast member to receive onscreen billing. When the series was cancelled he tried his luck as a freelance actor but the jobs did not come in, so identified was he with the Our Gang series. After a stint in the army, he sold insurance, cars and Coca-Cola. He then opened a restaurant but that failed when his landlord ran off with his money. His first marriage ended in divorce and a job in an aeroplane plant did nothing to cheer him up. He moved to Tulsa, Oklahoma where he appeared in adverts before landing a job on KOTV as the host of *The Spanky Show*, a children's television programme in 1955. When the show was cancelled in 1960 he became manager of a wine company. In 1966 McFarland, his wife, 13-year-old son, Emmett Vogan, and eight-year-old daughter moved to Cinnaminson in New Jersey where he became a supervisor for Philco-Ford, instructing salesmen on how to sell televisions. Of his time in showbiz, he said, "I wouldn't take a million dollars for the experience . . . and I wouldn't take a penny to do it again. As a kid I had everything I wanted, we had a good life but when it was over . . . it was over."

CAUSE: McFarland died of a heart attack at Grapevine, Texas. He was 64.

Malcolm McFee
Born August 16, 1949
Died November 18, 2001
Cheeky boy. Born at Forest Gate, London Malcolm Raymond McFee made his acting debut in the *Sisters & Brothers* episode of the television drama *Sanctuary*, playing Terry. Appearances followed in *Ramshackle Road* (1968), *Z Cars* (1969) and *Play For Today: I Can't See My Little Willie* (1970) as Peter Palmer (1970) and he made his film debut in *Oh! What A Lovely War* (1969) as Freddie Smith. It was the first film directed by Richard Attenborough and McFee played one of the three brothers from the same family who went off to fight in World War I. McFee is the last of the three to be killed. It was as the mouthy but charming Peter Craven in *Please Sir!* (November 8, 1968–February 13, 1972) and its sequel *The Fenn Street Gang* (September 24, 1971–July 15, 1973) that McFee became a household face. He reprised the role in the 1971 film version of *Please Sir!* He struggled to find work after the show ended and was reduced to guest appearances in various television shows including *Bless This House*, *The Sweeney*, *Goodnight Sweetheart* and *Birds Of A Feather*. He turned to the theatre to provide his income.

CAUSE: Malcolm McFee died at his home in Braintree, Essex of cancer. He was 52.

Victor McLaglen
Born December 11, 1883
Died November 7, 1959
Brawling giant. One of eight brothers, 6'5" McLaglen was born in Tunbridge Wells, Kent, but raised in South Africa where his clergyman father worked. When he was 14, McLaglen lied about his age and enlisted in the Life Guards, his size fooling the recruiting officer. After three years he left and moved to Canada where, according to McLaglen, before becoming an actor, he worked in 20 jobs including boxer, wrestler, gold miner and policeman. "The only thing which ever thrilled me was boxing," he later reflected. He once fought an exhibition match with heavyweight champion Jack Johnson. He travelled around Australasia, Asia and Africa and was in South Africa in 1914 when World War I started. He joined up and became a lieutenant with the Middlesex Regiment. He was twice wounded in the line of duty. In 1919 he married Enid Mary Lamont (d. Flintridge, California, April 2, 1942) and had one son, film director Andrew

(b. London, July 28, 1920), and a daughter, Sheila (b. London, 1921). Considering his background it was probably not surprising that in his first film, *The Call Of The Road* (1920), McLaglen played a boxer, Alf Truscott. It was the first of over 100 films. He appeared in, among others, *Corinthian Jack* (1921) as Jack Halstead, *Little Brother Of God* (1922) as King Kennidy, *The Glorious Adventure* (1922) as Bulfinch, *The Romany* (1923) as the Chief, *Women And Diamonds* (1924) as Brian Owen, *The Gay Corinthian* (1924) as Squire Hardcastle, *Percy* (1925) as Reedy Jenkins, *Men Of Steel* (1926) as Pete Masarick, *Beau Geste* (1926) as Hank, *What Price Glory* (1926) as Captain Flagg, *The Loves Of Carmen* (1927) as Escamillo, *Mother Machree* (1928) as the Giant of Kilkenny, *Hangman's House* (1928) as Citizen Hogan, *Captain Lash* (1929) as Captain Lash, *Strong Boy* (1929) as Strong Boy, *Hot For Paris* (1929) as John Patrick Duke, *Women Of All Nations* (1931) as Sergeant Flagg, *Wicked* (1931) as Scott Burrows, *Dishonored* (1931) as Colonel Kranau, *Annabelle's Affairs* (1931) as John Rawson, *While Paris Sleeps* (1932) as Jacques Costaud, *Guilty As Hell* (1932) as Detective McKinley, *Hot Pepper* (1933) as Flagg, *Dick Turpin* (1933) as Dick Turpin, *Laughing At Life* (1933) as Captain Easter, *Murder At The Vanities* (1934) as Bill Murdock, *Under Pressure* (1935) as Jumbo, *Professional Soldier* (1936) as Michael Donovan, *Klondike Annie* (1936) as Bull Brackett, *Nancy Steele Is Missing!* (1937) as Dannie O'Neill, *This Is My Affair* (1937) as Jock Ramsay, *Wee Willie Winkie* (1937) as Sergeant MacDuff, *Rio* (1939) as Dirk, *Pacific Liner* (1939) as Crusher McKay, *Full Confession* (1939) as McGinnis, *Ex-Champ* (1939) as Gunner Grey, *Captain Fury* (1939) as Blackie, *Gunga Din* (1939) as Sergeant MacChesney, *China Girl* (1942) as Major Weed, *Tampico* (1944) as Fred Adamson, *Rough, Tough And*

Ready (1945) as Owen McCarey, *Whistle Stop* (1946) as Gillo, *Michigan Kid* (1947) as Curley, *Fort Apache* (1948) as Sergeant Mulcahy, *She Wore A Yellow Ribbon* (1949) as Sergeant Quincannon, *Rio Grande* (1950) as Sergeant Major Timothy Quincannon, *Prince Valiant* (1954) as Boltar, *Bengazi* (1955) as Robert Emmett Donovan, *Around The World In 80 Days* (1956) as a helmsman and *Sea Fury* (1958) as Captain Bellew. McLaglen was one of John Ford's favourite actors and they worked together on several pictures including *The Informer* (1935) which won McLaglen a Best Actor Oscar for playing the traitorous Gypo Nolan, a part McLaglen disliked, calling Nolan "a weak, unintelligent and unresourceful man" which, I suppose, was why he was a traitor. McLaglen became an American citizen in 1933. He had something of a love affair with the military but it was some cause for concern when he founded his own small army in 1936. "In time of war," he said of the Light Horse Troop, "we can be counted upon as a government unit." Many saw the group as proto-fascist. Following the death of his first wife, he married his secretary, Suzanne Bruggemann on November 20, 1943, but they divorced in 1947. On December 19, 1948, he married Margaret Pumphrey. Four years later he was nominated as Best Supporting Actor for his portrayal of Red Will Danaher in *The Quiet Man* (1952). CAUSE: He died aged 75 in Newport Beach, California, from a heart attack.

Maggie McNamara
Born June 18, 1928
Died February 18, 1978
Forgotten talent. Born in New York, one of four children of Irish-American parents, like many actresses she began her career as a teenage model. Discovered by Otto Preminger she worked on various theatrical productions before making her film

début as Patty O'Neill in *The Moon Is Blue* (1953), a part she had played on the stage. Maggie used previously taboo words such as 'mistress', 'seduction' and 'virgin' in the film. The Catholic Legion of Decency condemned the feature as a result, although the Academy Of Motion Picture Arts & Sciences nominated Maggie for a Best Actress Oscar. She didn't win but was signed by Darryl F. Zanuck. She made just two films – *Three Coins In The Fountain* (1954) as Maria Williams and *Prince Of Players* (1955) as Mary Devlin Booth – before leaving showbiz. She made a brief comeback as Florrie Fermoyle in *The Cardinal* (1963) before becoming a secretary for an insurance company. CAUSE: Beset with mental problems for much of her life, she was bereft following the break-up of her marriage to David Swift and killed herself with an overdose of drugs in New York, aged 49.

Steve McQueen

(TERRENCE STEVEN MCQUEEN)
Born March 24, 1930
Died November 7, 1980
Dinky megastar. Born in Beech Grove Hospital, Indianapolis, Indiana, short (5'7"), ultra-macho, dyslexic McQueen was abandoned by his father when still a baby and spent part of his youth in a borstal. He did various jobs before joining the Marines in 1947 and finding himself in jail for going AWOL. He turned to acting in 1952 and made his début in a Yiddish theatre. After various plays he landed a bit part in *Somebody Up There Likes Me* (1956) playing Fidel. He was the lead in the sci-fi film *The Blob* (1958) as Steve Andrews but there was no overnight stardom for McQueen. He competed with the equally egotistical Yul Brynner for screen time as Vin in *The Magnificent Seven* (1960). It wasn't until *The Great Escape* (1963), in which he played Captain Virgil Hilts, that he really became a star. He took the lead in *The Cincinnati Kid* (1965) and was nominated for an Oscar as Jake Holman in *The Sand Pebbles* (1966). Two of his films have been recently remade: *The Thomas Crown Affair* (1968) (remade with Pierce Brosnan and Rene Russo) and *The Getaway* (1972) (with Ali MacGraw; it was remade in the Nineties with Alec Baldwin and Kim Basinger and added nudity). McQueen's other films included: *Bullitt* (1968) as Detective Lieutenant Frank Bullitt, *Papillon* (1973) as Henri 'Papillon' Charriere, *The Towering Inferno* (1974) as Michael O'Hallorhan and *Tom Horn* (1980) in the lead. He married three times. Firstly on November 2, 1956, to actress-singer Neile Adams, a match that produced two children, Terri (b. June 1959, d. 1998 of liver failure) and actor Chad (b. December 28, 1960). They divorced on March 15, 1972. She was to write a memoir that revealed McQueen to be insecure, a bully, self-destructive and possessed of an extremely violent temper. Next, on July 13, 1973, was actress Ali MacGraw (who said, "One thing about Steve, he didn't like the women in his life to have balls") and on January 16, 1980, model Barbara Minty became his third wife. Not everyone liked McQueen. Robert Mitchum said of him: "A Steve McQueen performance just naturally lends itself to monotony. Steve doesn't bring much to the party." CAUSE: McQueen lead a secret bisexual life. Again, Robert Mitchum: "Steve McQueen was notorious for orgies. Honest to God Roman-type sex orgies. The guy always needed an audience. Even sex . . . he had to make it into a party." McQueen died in Clinica de Santa Rosa, Juarez, Mexico, aged 50, from AIDS.
FURTHER READING: *Steve McQueen: The Legend Of A Rebel Superstar* – Malachy McCoy (London: Coronet, 1981); *McQueen: The Untold Story Of A Bad Boy In Hollywood* – Penina Spiegel (New York: Berkley, 1987).

Daniel Melnick

Born April 21, 1932
Died October 13, 2009
Smart producer. Born in New York
City, he was educated at New York's
High School of Performing Arts and
then New York University before
seeing service in the army. In 1954 he
landed a job at CBS before moving to
ABC where he developed programmes
like *The Fugitive, The Untouchables, The
Flintstones* and *77 Sunset Strip*. He
suggested the idea for the spy spoof
series *Get Smart* by telling writers,
"James Bond and Inspector Clouseau –
those are the two biggest hits out there.
Take a hint." Moving to the big screen,
Melnick produced Sam Peckinpah's
Straw Dogs (1971), which led to a job
offer from MGM. Melnick oversaw the
That's Entertainment (1974, 1976)
franchise. He was also responsible
for *The Sunshine Boys* (1975) and
Network (1976), the film that won a
posthumous Oscar for Peter Finch.
Moving to Columbia, he oversaw the
prison drama *Midnight Express* (1978),
Kramer Vs Kramer (1979) and *The
China Syndrome* (1979). From
February until December 1978 he was
president of the studio after the David
Begelman scandal (see Begelman's
entry for full details). In 1979 Melnick
produced Bob Fosse's *All That Jazz*
and then executive produced the sci-fi
horror flick *Altered States* (1980). A
controversial film for the time was
Making Love (1982) about a man
who leaves his wife for another
man. Despite a large proportion of
the denizens of Hollywood being
homosexually inclined, "Everyone was
absolutely terrified it would hurt their
careers," said Melnick. "We finally cast
Harry Hamlin . . . and I had to spend a
lot of time persuading him that it
wouldn't damage his career any more
than Jimmy Cagney playing a damaged
murderer damaged his. We were flying
in the face of one of the last taboos."
Melnick returned to the musical genre
with *Footloose* (1984), starring Kevin
Bacon. In 1987 he made *Roxanne* with
Steve Martin and the experience
prompted Martin to write *L A Story*
(1991). Of his work, Melnick said,
"What I try to do is identify and work
with the most talented people I can
get." In 1955, he married Linda
Rodgers (b. March 5, 1935 which was
her parents' fifth wedding anniversary),
the daughter of the composer Richard
Rodgers, and had a son, Peter, who
became a composer. The couple
divorced in 1971. He never remarried
but had a daughter from another
relationship.
CAUSE: Melnick died at his home in
Los Angeles after suffering from lung
cancer. He was 77.

Adolphe Menjou

Born February 18, 1890
Died October 29, 1963
Hollywood's best-dressed man. Born in
Pittsburgh, Pennsylvania, Adolphe Jean
Menjou worked as an engineer and in a
restaurant before deciding to try
thespianism, more by accident than by
design. His film début came in *The Man
Behind The Door* (1915) as Ringmaster.
He was to make almost 150 films and
the number would have been
considerably higher had he not spent
from 1917 until 1919 serving as a
Captain in the Ambulance Corps. He
resumed acting in 1920 but it was
Charlie Chaplin's *A Woman Of Paris*
(1923), in which he played Pierre Revel,
that brought him fame. The movie
sealed his reputation as a well-dressed
roué about town. He was nominated for
an Oscar for his portrayal of the editor
Walter Burns in *The Front Page* (1931).
Away from the screen, he was as right
wing as they come, belonging to the
John Birch Society and gaily naming
names during the McCarthy witch
hunts. Married three times, his
proudest boast was that he had over
2,000 garments in his wardrobe.
CAUSE: He died of chronic hepatitis in
Beverly Hills, California. He was 73
years old.

Melina Mercouri

Born October 31, 1920
Died March 6, 1994

'The Last Greek Goddess'. Born in Athens, Greece, Maria Amalia Mercouri became better known for her ardent patriotism rather than for acting at the end of her life. The daughter of a politician who became Mayor of Athens, she followed in her father's footsteps by becoming a Greek MP in 1977 and Minister for Culture in 1981, demanding the return of the Elgin Marbles. The high point of her acting career was being nominated for a Best Actress Oscar for playing the prostitute Ilya in *Pote Tin Kyriaki* (1960). In the late Sixties and Seventies she was a thorn in the side of the military junta that ruled Greece and was stripped of her citizenship. She made less than 20 films. She was defeated in her bid to become Mayor of Athens.
CAUSE: She died of lung cancer aged 73 in New York.

Burgess Meredith

Born November 16, 1907
Died September 9, 1997

Raspy-voiced environmentalist. Oliver Burgess Meredith was born in Cleveland, Ohio, and was educated in Amherst College, Massachusetts, and worked as a journalist before travelling to New York in 1933 to join Eva Le Gallienne's company. Two years later, he was a sensation as Mio in Maxwell Anderson's *Winterset* on stage and was equally splendid in the film version in 1936, his movie début. Meredith appeared in dozens of films and TV movies but was probably best known for his portrayal of Mickey in *Rocky* (1976), which saw him nominated for a Best Supporting Actor Oscar. He reprised the role in *Rocky II* (1979), *Rocky III* (1982) and *Rocky V* (1990). He also received an Oscar nod for Harry Greener in *The Day Of The Locust* (1975). On television he played Batman's nemesis The Penguin in several episodes of the camp Sixties TV classic. Blacklisted for a while during the McCarthy era because of his left-wing views, Meredith's other films included: *There Goes The Groom* (1937) as Dick Matthews, *Spring Madness* (1938) as Lippencott, *Tom, Dick And Harry* (1941) as Harry, *San Francisco Docks* (1941) as Johnny Barnes, *The Rear Gunner* (1943) as Private Pee Wee Williams, *The Story Of G.I. Joe* (1945) as Ernie Pyle, *Mine Own Executioner* (1947) as Felix Milne, *The Man On The Eiffel Tower* (1949) as Huertin, *Golden Arrow* (1949) as Dick, *Advise And Consent* (1962) as Herbert Gelman, *A Big Hand For The Little Lady* (1966) as Doc Scully, *Stay Away, Joe* (1968) as Charlie Lightcloud, *Clay Pigeon* (1971) as Freedom Lovelace, *Beware! The Blob* (1972) *as Hobo, The Hindenburg* (1975) as Emilio Pajetta, *The Sentinel* (1977) as Charles Chazen, *The Manitou* (1978) as Doctor Ernest Snow, *Foul Play* (1978) as Mr Hennessey, *The Amazing Captain Nemo* (1978) as Professor Waldo Cunningham, *Clash Of The Titans* (1981) as Ammo, *Santa Claus* (1985) as Ancient Elf, *King Lear* (1987) as Don Learo, *State Of Grace* (1990) as Finn and *Grumpy Old Men* (1993) as Grandpa Gustafson. He married four times. The first Mrs Meredith was Helen Berrian Derby (1932–1935), followed by Margaret Perry (January 10, 1936–July 19, 1938) (who was the daughter of Antoinette Perry after whom the Tonys are named), Paulette Goddard (May 21, 1944–June 6, 1949) and Kaja Sundsten (1950–1979).
CAUSE: He died of Alzheimer's disease in Malibu, California, aged 89.

Una Merkel

Born December 10, 1903
Died January 2, 1986

The best friend. Born in Covington, Kentucky, the daughter of a travelling salesman which meant that she did not start school until she was nine. She studied dance under Tyrone Power's mother and then to support herself, began modelling. She began working as an extra in films and was hired to play Lillian Gish's sister in one because the two women looked alike but a lack of funds meant the project never got off the ground. She was given a screen test alongside two other unknowns Sylvia Sidney and Claudette Colbert. She made a few unremarkable films before a United Artists agent recommended her to D.W. Griffith who was looking for someone to play Ann Rutledge in the film *Abraham Lincoln* (1930). From 1932 until 1938 she was under contract to MGM and often saw herself cast as the heroine's best friend. Her MGM films included *Clear All Wires!* (1933) with Lee Tracy, *Bombshell* (1933) directed by Victor Fleming and starring Jean Harlow, Lee Tracy, Frank Morgan, C. Aubrey Smith, Mary Forbes and Franchot Tone, *Cat's Paw* (1934) opposite Harold Lloyd, *It's In The Air* (1935) with Jack Benny, *Riff-Raff* (1936) again with Harlow, *Saratoga* (1937) with Clark Gable and Harlow in her last film – she collapsed on set on May 29, 1937, and *Test Pilot* (1938) with Gable. She appeared in both the 1934 and the 1952 versions of *The Merry Widow*, but on each occasion she played a different character. One of her best known films is the Western *Destry Rides Again* (released December 29, 1939) for Universal. In it she has a fight with Marlene Dietrich. The following year she played W.C. Fields's daughter in *The Bank Dick*. Merkel's career went into decline in the Forties but strength of personality saw her return and win a Tony in 1956 for the Broadway play *The Ponder Heart*. She played Debbie Reynolds's mother in *The Mating Game* (1959). In 1962, she was nominated for a Best Supporting Actress Oscar for *Summer And Smoke* (1961). Her last film was the Elvis Presley film *Spinout* (1966). 5'4" Merkel was married to Ronald Burla, an aviation designer, from 1932 until 1946. The year before

she came close to death when her mother killed herself by putting her head in the gas oven. Merkel narrowly escaped death again in 1952 when she took an overdose of sleeping pills. CAUSE: She died in Los Angeles, California aged 82 of unknown causes. She was buried at Highland Cemetery, 2167 Dixie Highway, Fort Mitchell, Kentucky.

Ethel Merman

(ETHEL AGNES ZIMMERMAN)
Born January 16, 1909
Died February 15, 1984
'The First Lady Of American Musical Comedy'. A former typist and secretary, she moonlighted in a show at the Brooklyn Paramount in 1928. With her raucous voice, Ethel Merman (born in Astoria, Long Island) often set the Broadway stage alight. It was there she did her best work but, thankfully, there are records of Merman for posterity in the films she made, often playing herself. She made her film début in *Follow The Leader* (1930) as Helen King and followed that up with, among others, *Old Man Blues* (1932) as Helen, *Let Me Call You Sweetheart* (1932), *You Try Somebody Else* (1932), *Time On My Hands* (1932), *Song Shopping* (1933) and *The Big Broadcast Of 1936* (1936) all as herself, *Anything Goes* (1936) as Reno Sweeney, *Alexander's Ragtime Band* (1938) as Jerry Allen, *Stage Door Canteen* (1943) as herself, *Call Me Madam* (1953) as Sally Adams, *There's No Business Like Show Business* (1954) as Molly Donahue, *Won Ton Ton, the Dog Who Saved Hollywood* (1976) as Hedda Parsons and *Airplane!* (1980) as Lieutenant Hurwitz, a hospital patient who thought he was Ethel Merman! Away from the stage Merman was vulgar, bigoted (calling black people "niggers" and referring to "commie Jews") and even demanded a percentage of tickets for every show she was in so she could sell them to touts. Novelist Jacqueline Susann based the character of Helen Lawson in *Valley*

Of The Dolls on Merman. She drank too much, was usually an abusive drunk and married four times. On November 15, 1940, she married agent William R. Smith in Elkington, Maryland. A year later he obtained a divorce on the grounds of desertion. In 1941 she married newspaper executive Robert Daniels Levitt and had two children: Robert Daniels, Jr (b. New York City, August 11, 1945) and Ethel (b. New York City, July 20, 1942, d. 1967, of a drug and drink overdose). They divorced on June 10, 1952. On March 9, 1953, she wed airline boss Robert F. Six and divorced him in December 1960. On June 27, 1964, she married Ernest Borgnine and left him 38 days later. They divorced on November 18, 1964. When she came to write her autobiography one chapter was entitled "Marriage To Ernest Borgnine" followed by a blank page. When asked why, she said: "I only write about things that are important to me." CAUSE: In April 1983 she underwent brain surgery. She died in her sleep ten months later in New York. She was 75.

Russ Meyer
Born March 21, 1922
Died September 18, 2004

The breast man. Russell Albion Meyer was born in Oakland, California, the son of a policeman and a nurse. An autodidact, Meyer began making films in his teens. His first film was *The Immortal Mr Teas* (1959), the first nudie flick to make a profit – $1 million on $24,000 cost. He was off and running and he began to make often bizarre and violent films usually featuring women with huge breasts. His movies included: *Erotica* (made in 1961 on a budget of $4,000), *Heavenly Bodies* (made in 1963 on a budget of $5,000), *Kiss Me Quick!* (1964), *Mudhoney* (made in 1965 on a budget of $60,000), *Motor Psycho* (made in 1965 on a budget of $38,000), *Faster, Pussycat! Kill! Kill!* (made in 1965 on

a budget of $45,000), *Mondo Topless* (made in 1966 on a budget of $12,000), *Finders Keepers Lovers Weepers* (made in 1968 on a budget of $82,000) and *Vixen!* (made in 1968, it grossed more than $6 million profit on an initial outlay of $76,000). Following the success of this last film, Meyer was hired by 20th Century Fox to make proper films. The first of these was *Beyond The Valley Of The Dolls* (1970). It starred Dolly Read (as Kelly MacNamara), Cynthia Myers (Casey Anderson) and Marcia McBroom (Petronella Danforth) as the members of an all-girl rock group who evolve into The Carrie Nations (the name of a nineteenth century temperance campaigner) and it was an enormous hit. Costing $900,000 it grossed $9 million at the American box office. Originally, the film was supposed to be a sequel to the cinematic version of Jacqueline Susann's best-selling novel *Valley Of The Dolls* (1967) but that idea was quickly abandoned. It did not stop Susann from suing for breach of copyright and winning, albeit posthumously, a $2 million settlement. Next Meyer directed a frankly awful version of Irving Wallace's superb novel *The Seven Minutes* (1971), about the world's rudest book. Meyer returned to the sex and schlock formula that had served him so well in films such as *Supervixens* (made in 1975 on a budget of $250,000) and *Beyond The Valley Of The Ultra Vixens* (made in 1979 on a budget of $239,000). He was married three times. His wives were Betty Valvodinos; the 5'7", 38-24-35 *Playboy* Playmate of the Month for June 1955, Evelyn Eugene 'Eve' Turner (b. Griffin, Georgia, December 13, 1928, k. in a plane crash in the Canary Islands, March 27, 1977) from April 2, 1952 until their divorce in 1969; and 37-23-37 Edwina Beth 'Edy' Williams (b. Salt Lake City, Utah, July 9, 1942), a 5'7" actor who made a career of turning up annually to the Academy Awards in the skimpiest outfits she could find, pre-empting the wannabes of today, from June 27, 1970 until November 7, 1975.

CAUSE: Russ Meyer died aged 82 of complications from pneumonia at his home in the Hollywood Hills.

Lewis Milestone

(LEVIS MILSTEIN)
Born September 30, 1895
Died September 25, 1980

The forgotten man. When asked to name a Hollywood director of the past, the name of Lewis Milestone is one that rarely features in anyone but the most keen film student's list. And he died only 30 years ago, after John Wayne and Joan Crawford. He won a Best Film Oscar for *All Quiet On The Western Front* (1930). Milestone showed the horror of wars – the First, Second and Korean conflicts – from the point of view of the ordinary soldier. It was a decision that earned him approbation from many producers. He was born near Odessa in the Ukraine and came to America in 1913, becoming a citizen when he was 18. He worked in various menial jobs such as floor sweeping before he joined the US Signal Corps in 1917 where he worked as an assistant director on army training films. Demobbed in 1919, he headed for Hollywood. He directed his first film, *Seven Sinners*, in 1925, having spent time as a cutter, editor and writer to hone his trade. His fourth film, *Two Arabian Knights* (1927) starring William Boyd and Mary Astor, won a Best Comedy Direction Oscar, the only occasion this award was ever given. His first sound film was *The Betrayal* (1929) an alpine drama starring Gary Cooper and Emil Jannings. His first talkie, *New York Nights* (1929), with Norma Talmadge was not a success and Milestone "refused to put my name on [it], a disappointing backstage melodrama". Milestone did not alter his working techniques for sound when it came to shooting *All Quiet On The Western Front*. "I decreed, 'No two

cameras, nothing different from before. One camera and we shoot the way we've always shot.' And that as far as I was concerned was the big sound revolution. It was that simple. I shot very little footage on the battles because the film was all figured out. Being an editor myself, I pre-edited the whole thing. My idea of drawing each set-up was born on *All Quiet*. The front office was always sitting there waiting for me to say, 'Tomorrow I want 10,000 men.' I made the whole battle scene with 150 fellows." Incidentally, it is Milestone's hand that reaches for the butterfly at the end of the picture. After *All Quiet On The Western Front* for which he was paid $135,000 and which won him his second Academy Award, Milestone worked on films with a non-military theme such as the newspaper story by Charles MacArthur and Ben Hecht *The Front Page* (1931) starring Pat O'Brien and Adolph Menjou, drama such as *Rain* (1932) with Joan Crawford and musicals including *Hallelujah, I'm A Bum* (1933) starring Al Jolson and Harry Langdon with a score from Rodgers & Hart. Milestone made *The Captain Hates The Sea* (1934) for Columbia, which was John Gilbert's last movie. Milestone won praise for *The General Died At Dawn* (1936). Then he got into another dispute, suing Hal Roach who sacked him from *Road Show*. The men settled by Roach agreeing to part finance Milestone's *Of Mice And Men* (1939) starring Lon Chaney, Jr as Lennie and Burgess Meredith as George, a production that the author John Steinbeck liked. It featured Aaron Copeland's first score and was nominated for the Best Picture Oscar. Milestone returned to the military genre with *The Purple Heart* (1944) starring Dana Andrews and Richard Conte, *A Walk In The Sun* (1945) with Dana Andrews and John Ireland, *Halls Of Montezuma* (1951) with Richard Widmark and *Pork Chop Hill* (1959), a film that was beset by arguments with star Gregory Peck. If *All Quiet On The Western Front* was Milestone's definitive take on the First World War then *A Walk In The Sun* represented the second conflict. When Joseph McCarthy was spreading his poison in Washington Milestone was not immune to being smeared but managed to continue working. His last two films were *Ocean's 11* (1960) starring the Rat Pack and as a late replacement for Carol Reed on *Mutiny On The Bounty* (1962) with Marlon Brando and Trevor Howard. *Mutiny* was not the walk in the park that 5'7½" Milestone was expecting. He said, "I thought this was one way of getting rich quick – I get the salary and, at most, it couldn't take two or three months. After I'd signed the contract, I found out that in the previous year all they had on screen was about seven minutes of film. I spent a year on it." In 1936 he married the actor Kendall Lee (b. Washington, DC, September 18, 1903, d. Beverly Hills, California, July 30, 1978). CAUSE: Lewis Milestone died in Los Angeles, California, five days before his 85th birthday, following abdominal surgery. Milestone was buried in the Sanctuary of Tenderness Mausoleum at Westwood Memorial Park, 1218 Glendon Avenue, Los Angeles, California.

Ray Milland

(REGINALD ALFRED JOHN TRUSCOTT-JONES)
Born January 3, 1905
Died March 10, 1986
Heterosexual Cary Grant. Born in Neath, Wales, 6'1" Milland was educated at a military school before opting for acting. His stage name came from the mill lands, a flat area on the banks of the river that Neath stands upon. He appeared in over 100 films and mostly played in comedies until his portrayal of an alcoholic writer in *The Lost Weekend* (1945), which won him a Best Actor Oscar. He had his own show on American television for two years from 1953 and in 1976 was nominated for an Emmy for his role as Duncan Calderwood in *Rich Man, Poor Man Book I*. His character in *Reap The Wild Wind* (1942), Stephen Tolliver, had a curly head of hair while Milland's own locks were straight. To achieve the desired effect the make-up department used hot curling irons on his hair. Milland was convinced this was what caused him to lose his hair (he often wore a wig on screen) and his status as a leading man. His films included: *The Flying Scotsman* (1929) as Jim Edwards, *Just A Gigolo* (1931) as Freddie, *Blonde Crazy* (1931) as Joe Reynolds, *Menace* (1934) as Freddie Bastion, *Charlie Chan In London* (1934) as Neil Howard, *We're Not Dressing* (1934) as Prince Michael Stofani, *Bolero* (1934) as Lord Robert Coray, *Four Hours To Kill!* (1935) as Carl, *Alias Mary Dow* (1935) as Peter Marshall, *Return Of Sophie Lang* (1936) as James Dawson, *Next Time We Love* (1936) as Tommy Abbott, *The Big Broadcast Of 1937* (1936) as Bob Miller, *The Jungle Princess* (1936) as Christopher Powell, *Wings Over Honolulu* (1937) as Lieutenant Samuel Gilchrist, *Ebb Tide* (1937) as Robert Herrick, *Bulldog Drummond Escapes* (1937) as Captain Hugh 'Bulldog' Drummond, *Her Jungle Love* (1938) as Bob Mitchell, *French Without Tears* (1939) as Alan Howard, *Beau Geste* (1939) as John Geste, *Arise, My Love* (1940) as Tom Martin, *Untamed* (1940) as Dr William Crawford, *Are Husbands Necessary?* (1942) as George Cugat, *Forever And A Day* (1943) as Lieutenant William Trimble, *California* (1946) as Jonathan Trumbo, *Kitty* (1946) as Sir Hugh Marcy, *Golden Earrings* (1947) as Colonel Ralph Denistoun, *Sealed Verdict* (1948) as Major Robert Lawson, *Alias Nick Beal* (1949) as Nick Beal, *Rhubarb* (1951) as Eric Yeager, *The Thief* (1952) as Allan Fields, *Something To Live For* (1952) as Alan Miller, *Dial M For Murder* (1954) as Tony Wendice, *The Girl In The Red*

Velvet Swing (1955) as Stanford White, *Three Brave Men* (1957) as Joe DiMarco, *X: The Man With The X-Ray Eyes* (1963) as Dr James Xavier, *Love Story* (1970) as Oliver Barrett III, *Terror In The Wax Museum* (1973) as Harry Flexner, *Escape To Witch Mountain* (1975) as Aristotle Bolt and *Oliver's Story* (1978) as Oliver Barrett III. From September 30, 1932, until his death Milland was married to Muriel 'Mal' Webber. They had one son, Daniel David (b. March 6, 1940), and an adopted daughter, Victoria Francesca. Milland was a keen parachutist and during the filming of *I Wanted Wings* (1941), in which he played Jeff Young, he took off with a pilot to test a plane for filming. In the air he had the urge to jump but the pilot said the plane was low on fuel and that he had to land. Later, retelling the tale, Milland was horrified to learn the 'parachute' that he had intended to use was, in fact, only a prop.
CAUSE: Suffering from lung cancer, he died in Torrance, California, aged 81.

Marjie Millar

Born August 10, 1931
Died April 16, 1966
Blonde ingénue. Born in Tacoma, Washington, attractive Marjie Millar was the protégée of producer Hal Wallis. He took a very deep and personal interest in her career, putting her in *Money From Home* (1953) as Phyllis Leigh and *About Mrs Leslie* (1954) as Nadine Roland. However, in 1958, she was involved in a car crash that left her partially disabled. Giving up all thoughts of acting, she returned to Tacoma where she opened a dance school. On April 23, 1955 she married the television producer John Florea (b. Alliance, Ohio, May 28, 1916, d. Las Vegas, Nevada, August 25, 2000). They divorced in 1957 and she married author John McCallum. That marriage, too, ended in divorce and in 1961 she married sailor Charles Candoo.
CAUSE: She died in Tacoma, from the after-effects of the car crash, following 16 operations on her legs. She was only 34.

Ann Miller

(JOHNNIE LUCILLE ANN COLLIER)
Born April 12, 1923
Died January 22, 2004
'Star lady'. Born in Cherino, Texas, the daughter of John Collier, a prominent criminal lawyer, Miller who was of Irish, French and Cherokee descent (on her grandmother's side) was raised in Houston, where she attended the Albert Sidney Johnson High School. A childhood bout of rickets led to her having dancing lessons and she reportedly had her first tap lesson from Bill 'Bojangles' Robinson. Her parents divorced when she was 10 and she moved to California. Her mother was deaf and received no maintenance from her ex-husband so, to support the family, Miller had to dance at sleazy establishments such as the Black Cat Club. While working at the Bal Tabarin in San Francisco, she was spotted by the RKO talent scout Benny Rubin and at the age of 14 she claimed to be 18 to sign a contract with RKO (hence many reference books list her natal year as 1919). She made her screen début in *New Faces Of 1937*. Her early films included *Stage Door* (1937) as Annie, *Room Service* (1938) as Hilda with the Marx Brothers, and *Radio City Revels* (1938) as Billie Shaw. An early beefier part as Essie Carmichael came in Frank Capra's Oscar-winning comedy *You Can't Take It With You* (1938). Owing to a conflict of interest with her agent Miller asked RKO to be released from her contract. At that time, the dancer Eleanor Powell, who was a big star at MGM, had the same representation. The studio was unhappy to see Ann Miller developing as a rival and Miller believed that if pressure was brought to bear to ensure Powell's continued supremacy her career would suffer. Miller left Hollywood and headed for

Broadway. She appeared in the last (1939) edition of *The George White Scandals*, and, although the show was not successful, everybody admired her big number, 'The Mexiconga'. Her return to Tinseltown came with a series of mostly unsatisfactory short-term contracts. In *Melody Ranch* (1940), she starred as Julie Shelton opposite the singing cowboy Gene Autry ("I was the first girl he ever kissed, apart from his horse") and became known as "the Queen of the Bs" in a run of second features such as *True To The Army* (1942) as Vicki Marlow, *Priorities On Parade* (1942) as Donna D'Arcy and *Reveille With Beverly* (1943) as Beverly Ross, all aimed at encouraging the war effort. In 1948 she was hired by MGM to replace an injured Cyd Charisse in *Easter Parade* playing Nadine Hale. It was not a great part but it placed her opposite Fred Astaire, and Miller made a big enough impression to secure a standard seven-year contract. It led to *On The Town* and steady employment in some of MGM's best-known musicals. Among them were *Lovely To Look At* (1952) as Bubbles Cassidy, a remake of the Fred Astaire/Ginger Rogers film *Roberta*, *Kiss Me Kate* (1953) in which as Lois 'Bianca' Lane she sang 'Too Darn Hot' and 'Always True To You', *Small Town Girl* (1953) as Lisa Bellmount in which she danced a scorching version of 'I've Got To Hear That Beat', *Deep In My Heart* (1954) and *Hit The Deck* (1955) as Ginger. Her last musical was *The Opposite Sex* (1956) as Gloria Dell, an ill-advised remake of *The Women*. In the same year, she played her last film role for two decades – as Doris Patterson, the mother of Dean Jones, in *The Great American Pastime*, a non-musical film about baseball. Realising that the time of the big musical was over, she concentrated on theatre and TV. 5′7″ Miller also featured in a spectacular television advertisement for Heinz Great American Soups, dancing on top of

an eight-foot soup tin, surrounded by 20-foot fountains, a 24-piece orchestra and a long line of high-kicking chorus girls. It ended with her tapping her way into the kitchen, where her husband moaned, "Why must you make such a big production out of everything?" The song she sang was written by comedian Stan Freberg and choreographed by Danny Daniels. Miller had a reputed speed of 500 taps a minute. Her tap shoes were called Moe and Joe and were exhibited in the Smithsonian Institute in Washington. In the theatre she appeared in touring productions of *Can Can*, *Hello, Dolly!*, *Panama Hattie* and *Blithe Spirit*, and made her Broadway comeback (after a 30-year gap) in *Mame*, taking the role originally played by Angela Lansbury. Her most successful stage appearance was in 1979 in *Sugar Babies*, a $1.3 million extravaganza based on the rise of burlesque. Her co-star was her former acting school classmate Mickey Rooney. The show was brought to London in 1988, where she received some of the most favourable notices of her career. In 1998 she appeared in a successful revival of Stephen Sondheim's *Follies* at the Paper Mill Playhouse in New Jersey. She disliked nudity and sex on screen but when she returned to films it was in 2001 when she played Catherine 'Coco' Lenoix, an ageing Hollywood matron, in David Lynch's *Mulholland Drive*, which contained nudity and explicit sex. She was married three times: to Reese Milner on February 16, 1946; to William Moss on August 22, 1958 (they divorced on May 11, 1961) and to Arthur Cameron in 1961. The marriage was annulled the following year. All three were oil millionaires. There were no surviving children. Her daughter died on November 12, 1946, three hours after her birth. Miller had fallen downstairs while nine months pregnant. Miller, who believed in reincarnation, claimed that her difficulty in maintaining relationships with men was due to her being an Egyptian queen in a past life and executing any men who displeased her. Unlike many of her contemporaries at Culver City, she never had a bad word to say about MGM or its studio boss, Louis B. Mayer. "Why, Mr Mayer treated us better than his own horses," she claimed. For his part Mayer was captivated by her and, despite being almost 40 years her senior, regularly took her wining, dining and dancing – always with her mother as chaperone. Not that he misbehaved. "Mr Mayer was the Kissinger of his day," she reported, "very much the gentleman, and he liked me because I was a nice girl." Unfortunately, he was also jealous and possessive. One of the more bizarre stories from that era concerned her nose. After breaking it, she disliked the contour after it mended, so she had an artificial extension made. When she and Mayer argued, he would steal the nose and lock it away in his safe so that she could not go out without him. Then when she fell for an oil millionaire and told Mayer, he cried, he groaned, he hung up the telephone and, within minutes, sent his chauffeur to summon her to his deathbed, where he was dying having swallowed a bottle of sleeping tablets. The ambulance, however, got there first and Mayer recovered. Their relationship was never as cordial thereafter. On her passport, in the space reserved for "occupation", she wrote simply "star lady". She was under no illusions about her talent. "As an actress, I'm terrible," she admitted, "but if Ava Gardner and Lana Turner can act under a good director, I think I still have a chance." Ann Millerisms became almost as legendary as Goldwynisms. Attending a memorial tribute to Oscar Hammerstein, she asked her date, "Why isn't Oscar here tonight?" When she was informed that this was what the concert was about, the lyricist having been dead for 10 years, she replied, "Well, how should I

know? I've been touring in *Mame*." "I do a lot of nutty things, and people think I'm for real," the 35-22-34 star acknowledged. "But all my life I've tried to be an eight-by-10 glossy. I try to give the impression that everything's perfect and that star ladies don't go to the bathroom. It was worse than doing 24 shows a day for those smarty-pants husbands of mine because I was never off stage. I tried to make them believe I was always gorgeous."
CAUSE: She died in Los Angeles, California, from lung cancer. She was 80 years old.

Arthur Miller
Born October 17, 1915
Died February 10, 2005
Mr Marilyn Monroe. In the world of the theatre Arthur Miller is regarded as probably the best American playwright of the twentieth century but outside he is best known as Marilyn Monroe's third husband. Arthur Asher Miller was born in New York City at 5.12am on October 17, 1915 and came of age in the Depression of the thirties. After his father (d. Long Island, New York, 1966) Isidore's women's coats factory collapsed Arthur Miller worked in a variety of jobs before studying journalism at Michigan University in 1934. He began trying his hand at writing plays and discovered a talent. His first Broadway play, *The Man Who Had All The Luck*, opened at the Forrest Theater in New York on November 23, 1944. His first major success came three years later with *All My Sons* (which opened at the Coronet Theater, January 29, 1947), an exposé of war profiteering and individual guilt. His next play, *Death Of A Salesman* (opened on February 10, 1949), a drama about salesman Willy Loman's refusal to face the failure of his career and relationships, won the Pulitzer Prize. It was seen in London in 1949 with Paul Muni in the leading role. In 2003 *Death Of A Salesman* was voted the Play of the Century in a National

Theatre poll. In early Fifties America the mere suspicion of left-wing sympathies could wreck a life, never mind a career. In 1953 Miller produced *The Crucible* about the witch trials of seventeenth-century Salem, Massachusetts. Many saw it as an allegorical attack on the McCarthyite "witch hunts" then prevalent in the USA. Along with many other writers Miller was called to testify before the House Un-American Activities Committee. On June 1, 1957, Miller was convicted of contempt of Congress for his refusal to identify writers believed to hold Communist sympathies. By this time Miller was dating Marilyn Monroe and he later recalled, "The day before I was to appear before the committee the chairman said that if Marilyn Monroe would take a photo with him he would cancel the hearing." Miller refused to use his girlfriend, who had formed Marilyn Monroe Productions in December 1954 in order to make her own films. Miller was not wasteful of his time and wrote two one-act plays, *A View From The Bridge* and *A Memory Of Two Mondays*, in 1955. The following year he rewrote *Death Of A Salesman* as a three-act play. At 7.21pm on June 29, 1956 in a civil ceremony in White Plains Court House, New York, that lasted four minutes Miller married Monroe and had a Jewish celebration on July 1 at the home of Miller's agent in Katonah, New York. Later in the summer of 1956 she and Miller travelled to London to film *The Prince And The Showgirl* which was to be the only film made by the company. The relationship – dubbed The Hourglass and The Egghead – was stormy. Marilyn suffered a miscarriage and Miller found himself unable to cope with his wife's erratic behaviour. He had written a short story for *Esquire* about cowboys which he developed into a film. Made by Seven Artists *The Misfits* was the final nail in his marriage. In November 1960 Marilyn's

co-star Clark Gable died of a heart attack and on January 20, 1961 Miller and Monroe were divorced. In 1963 Miller upset Monroe fans by writing *After The Fall*, a thinly disguised retelling of his marriage woes. It opened on January 22, 1964. Miller disingenuously claimed that Maggie in the story was not Monroe and in a sense he told the truth. Maggie was based on Norma Jeane Mortenson. His next plays included: *Incident At Vichy* (opened December 3, 1964), *The Price* (opened February 7, 1968), *The Archbishop's Ceiling* (opened April 30, 1977), *The American Clock* (opened November 20, 1980), *The Ride Down Mount Morgan* (opened October 11, 1991) and *Mr Peter's Connections* (opened May 17, 1998). Miller married the Roman Catholic Mary Grace Slattery on August 5, 1940, and by her had two children: Jane Ellen (b. Brooklyn, New York, September 7, 1944) and Robert Arthur (b. May 31, 1947). They divorced on June 11, 1956 in Reno, Nevada. On February 17, 1962, four months before the death of Monroe, 6'1" Miller married the Magnum photographer Inge Morath (b. Graz, Austria, May 27, 1923). They had a daughter, Rebecca Augusta (b. Roxbury, Connecticut, August 7, 1963), who became an actor and married Daniel Day-Lewis. They also had a son, Daniel (b. Roxbury, Connecticut, September 15, 1962), who was afflicted by Down's syndrome and put in a home, Southbury Training School in Woodbury, ten miles from the Miller homestead. Miller never acknowledged his son or visited him although Inge Morath was a weekly visitor until her death from cancer in New York on January 30, 2002. In December 2004, Miller announced that he had been living with 34-year-old artist Agnes Barley since 2002. Miller was to declare, "In all my plays and books I try to take settings and dramatic situations from real life, which involve real questions of right and wrong."

CAUSE: Suffering from cancer, heart problems and pneumonia Miller was cared for at his New York home by his sister Joan Copeland. On February 8, 2005, he made the two-hour journey to his home in Roxbury, Connecticut, where he died 48 hours later aged 89 of congenital heart failure. Rebecca Day-Lewis was at his bedside.

FURTHER READING: *Miller The Playwright* (3rd edition) – Dennis Welland (London: Methuen, 1985); *Time Bends A Life* – Arthur Miller (London: Methuen, 1987); *Arthur Miller A Life* – Martin Gottfried (London: Faber & Faber, 2003).

Max Miller

(THOMAS HENRY SARGENT)
Born November 21, 1894
Died May 7, 1963
'The Cheeky Chappie'. Born at 43 Hereford Street, Brighton, East Sussex, the son of a labourer, Max Miller was a music hall comedian who shone with his risqué routines culled from his famous 'Blue Book' and loud attire. Over 6' tall, he kept audiences in stitches by letting them use their imaginations rather than being downright rude. He made 13 feature films: *The Good Companions* (1933) as Millbrau, *Friday The Thirteenth* (1933) as Joe, *Princess Charming* (1934) as Chuff, *Things Are Looking Up* (1935) as Joey, *Get Off My Foot* (1935) as Herbert Cronk, the title role in *Educated Evans* (1936) as Educated Evans, *Don't Get Me Wrong* (1937) as Wellington Lincoln, *Take It From Me* (1937) as Albert Hall, *Thank Evans* (1938) reprising his part as Educated Evans, *Everything Happens To Me* (1938) as Charles Cromwell, *Hoots Mon!* (1939) as Harry Hawkins, *The Good Old Days* (1939) as Alexander the Greatest and *Asking For Trouble* (1942) as Dick Smith. The character of Archie Rice in John Osborne's *The Entertainer* was based on Miller.

CAUSE: On September 14, 1959, he suffered a coronary thrombosis that ultimately forced his retirement. In July 1962 he was felled by a heart attack. He died in Brighton at 11.57pm on May 7, 1963. Considering his deserved reputation as a skinflint, it came as a surprise to many when his estate was valued at just £27,877.

FURTHER READING: *Max Miller: The Cheeky Chappie* – John M. East (London: Robson Books, 1993).

Spike Milligan, KBE (Hon)

Born April 16, 1918
Died February 27, 2002
Sincere Goon. Terence Alan Milligan was born at 3.30pm in Ahmednagar Military Hospital, India. 5'11" Spike Milligan was the son of Leo A. Milligan MSM, RA (d. Newcastle, New South Wales, Australia, January 14, 1969), an Irish Captain in the British Raj in India, and Florence Kettleband (b. 1894). He was educated in a tent in the Hyderabad Sindh desert, and then in a series of Roman Catholic schools in India until the family returned to London in 1931. He left school at 15 to work for Stones Engineering in Deptford, but he was sacked because he repeatedly fused the lights. At the outbreak of the Second World War he joined the Royal Artillery, an experience he would draw on in five volumes of comic memoirs, which began with *Adolf Hitler: My Part In His Downfall* in 1971. In January 1944, he was nearly killed by a mortar bomb near Lauro in the hills to the northeast of Mount Vesuvius. He suffered severe shellshock, started to stammer, and suffered the first of the nervous breakdowns that were to plague him for the rest of his life. Milligan was one of the most original comedians of his age. A prolific output saw him write and star in almost all of the 157 half-hour episodes of *The Goon Show*, write eight series of his own show *Q* and more than 50 assorted books of biography, verse, fiction, letters, games and plays. However, such was the intensity with which he held views that he spent

much time in mental hospitals. "I am condemned never to be taken seriously," he said. Jimmy Grafton, a scriptwriter introduced him to Harry Secombe, who in turn introduced him to Peter Sellers and Michael Bentine. The quartet worked on a radio show that, billed as *Those Crazy People*, later *The Goons*, was first broadcast on May 28, 1951. It ran for 11 series. The weekly programme became a national institution. The Prince of Wales later described it as "one of my favourite programmes", and it lasted for eight years, ending in January 1960. A final performance was given in 1972 to mark the 50th anniversary of the BBC. Characters such as Neddy Seagoon, played by Secombe, Major Bloodnok played by Sellers, and Milligan's own Eccles became the favourites of a generation. Milligan was a comic with a social conscience. He supported CND and the ban on the slaughter of seal pups. He was a member of the World Wide Fund for Nature and Greenpeace. He was fiercely opposed to pornography and smoking (even though as a young man he smoked like a chimney), and he was a compulsive letter-writer. When he wrote to *The Times* in 1990 to ask the paper to make sure his obituary was ready ("as I have not been feeling well lately"), he added that his "most recent exploit was trying to save Rye Hospital" ending with "Yours ailing, Spike". Despite having four children of his own from his three marriages, and two other children, Milligan was obsessed by population growth. When Tony Blair became Prime Minister on May 1, 1997, Milligan wrote to him with a modest proposal to help to remedy the crisis: a ban on births for five years. Spike appeared in the films *Rentadick* (1972) as a customs officer, *Adolf Hitler – My Part In His Downfall* (1972) as Leo Milligan (his father), *The Three Musketeers* (1973) as Monsieur Bonancieux, *Digby, The Biggest Dog In The World* (1973) as Dr Harz, *Man About The House* (1974) as himself, *The Last Remake Of Beau Geste* (1977) as Crumble, *Life Of Brian* (1979) as Spike, *History Of The World: Part I* (1981) as Monsieur Rimbaud and *Yellowbeard* (1983) as a flunkie. He also wrote the segment "Sloth" in *The Magnificent Seven Deadly Sins* (1971). On January 26, 1952, he married June Marlowe and had three children, Laura (b. Royal Northern Hospital, Holloway Road, London, November 2, 1952), Sean (b. September 19, 1954) and Silé (b. December 2, 1956). They divorced in 1960. In the Church of Our Lady of Good Counsel in Rawdon, Yorkshire, on April 28, 1962 he married Patricia 'Paddy' Margaret Ridgeway (d. 1978 of cancer) and they had a daughter (Jane) on May 17, 1966. In July 1983, he married Shelagh Sinclair (b. 1945). Spike had a daughter (Romany) by a Canadian journalist in 1975 and a son (James) after an affair with Margaret Maughan in 1975.

CAUSE: He died in Rye, East Sussex, aged 83, from liver disease. On June 24, 2002, a service of thanksgiving for his life and work was held at St Martin-in-the-Fields, Trafalgar Square, London. The Rev Nicholas Holtam officiated and Stephen Fry read the lesson. Sir Stephen Lamport represented the Prince of Wales. Joanna Lumley read *My Boyhood Dog* by Spike Milligan, Peter O'Toole read *Sonnet XXX* by William Shakespeare and Eddie Izzard read *Have A Nice Day!* by Spike Milligan. Eric Sykes gave an address.

FURTHER READING: *Spike Milligan A Biography* – Pauline Scudamore (London: Grafton, 1987).

Mary Millington

(MARY RUTH QUILTER)
Born November 30, 1945
Died August 19, 1979

Abused and used porn star. To the outside world the tiny, illegitimate, Middlesex-born Mary Millington had much in her favour. A determined and avowed supporter of sexual liberation, she practised what she preached and appeared with gay abandon in several blue films under the name Mary Maxted, including *Eskimo Nell* (1975), *Erotic Inferno* (1975) as Jane, *Keep It Up Downstairs* (1976) as Polly, *Intimate Games* (1976), *I Lust Och Nöd* (1976) and *I'm Not Feeling Myself Tonight* (1976). In 1977, diminutive porn baron David Sullivan moved into film production with *Come Play With Me*. Costing £83,000 to make, the film generated over £3 million in revenue. The star of the film was Mary, playing a character called Sue. When she began working for Sullivan, he paid for her to have plastic surgery and changed her name to Mary Millington. She went on to appear in *What's Up Superdoc!* (1978), *The Playbirds* (1978) as Lucy, *Queen Of The Blues* (1979) as Mary and *Confessions From The David Galaxy Affair* (1979) as Millicent Cumming. Millington became Sullivan's girlfriend but she was emotionally disturbed. She took too many drugs, shoplifted and worked as a prostitute. On a downward spiral, there was just one way out and she took it.

CAUSE: At the age of 33, Mary Millington committed suicide at her Epsom home. Sullivan claimed he cried for a fortnight when told of her death. However, his grief did not stop him from running a lurid story years later in his tacky *Sunday Sport* claiming that Millington was the lesbian lover of film star Diana Dors and that she had tried to seduce Dors' husband, Alan Lake, who (allegedly) hadn't been able to rise to the occasion. Nor did he withdraw her films from circulation. In fact, Sullivan made a sickening 'tribute' film that featured a Millington lookalike lying naked in a coffin. (Later, Sullivan recruited 24-year-old Julie Lee [real name Julie Moxon] to replace Millington in his films and magazines. Lee agreed to marry a wealthy Arab for £1 million but she, too, met with

an untimely death. On May 10, 1983, she was killed in a car crash.)

FURTHER READING: *The Amazing Mary Millington* – Mary Millington and David Weldon (London: Futura, 1979).

Sir John Mills, CBE

(LEWIS ERNEST WATTS MILLS)
Born February 22, 1908
Died April 23, 2005

Consummate pro. John Mills was born at Watts Naval Training College, North Eltham, Suffolk and spent his early years at Belton, near Great Yarmouth, where his father was headmaster (and maths teacher) of the village school. He was educated at Norwich High School For Boys. His sister was the television presenter Annette Mills (b. Chelsea, London, 1890 as Mabel Mills, d. January 10, 1955 of a brain tumour) who created Muffin the Mule. John Mills worked briefly as a clerk before making his theatre début in 1929 in the chorus of a revue. Three years later he made his first film, *The Midshipmaid*, and for a time specialised in juvenile leads. He had a small part in *Goodbye Mr Chips* (1939), in which he played Colley, the old boy who comes back from the First World War to visit the old master. He joined the 346 Company of the Royal Engineers, a searchlight battery based at Royston, Hertfordshire. Commissioned in the autumn of 1940, he was posted to the headquarters of 1st Rifle Battalion, Monmouthshire Regiment, at Trowbridge, Wiltshire. At the end of 1940 he was invalided out with a duodenal ulcer and returned to acting. He appeared in a number of war films to bolster morale including *In Which We Serve* (1942) as Shorty Blake – the film, scripted and produced by Noël Coward, who took the starring role, was based on Lord Mountbatten's destroyer HMS *Kelly*. At one stage during shooting, Mountbatten arranged for 100 sailors to be brought in to replace extras made "seasick" by the hydraulic pumps used to simulate the pitch and roll of the ocean. "There's dysentery in every ripple," observed Coward. Mills claimed to have given Coward the nickname 'The Master'. *We Dive At Dawn* (1943) about a British submarine disabled in the Baltic and *The Way To The Stars* (1945), Anthony Asquith's film about the RAF in the war, followed this. Mills often played clean-cut officer types but showed his versatility in *Cottage To Let* (1941) in which he played a Nazi fifth columnist and *Waterloo Road* (1944) in which he was a cuckolded husband. Stardom came with his portrayal of Pip in David Lean's film *Great Expectations* (1946). He followed this by acting as well as going behind the cameras with *The History Of Mr Polly* (1949) and *The Rocking Horse Winner* (1950), both of which he produced. 5'8" Mills said, "I wasn't a very good producer because I was always dying to get on the floor and didn't really like the office work." He suggested that Mr Polly did not succeed popularly at the time because, "I was a blue-eyed hero up to then and audiences hated seeing me as a little wizened chap with smarmed hair, being a henpecked husband. But I wanted to make those two movies and now I'm rather proud of them." He played the tragic hero Robert Falcon Scott in *Scott Of The Antarctic* (1947) and his subsequent films included: *Morning Departure* (1950) in which he played a submarine skipper resigned to staying down with his ship after it has been hit by a mine, the thriller *The Long Memory* (1952), the guileless Lancashire cobbler Willy Mossop in David Lean's *Hobson's Choice* (1954), *The End Of The Affair* (1955), *The Colditz Story* (1955) as Pat Reid, *War And Peace* (1956) as the cheerful Russian peasant Platon, *Town On Trial* (1957), *I Was Monty's Double* (1958) and *Ice Cold In Alex* (1958) as the alcoholic Captain Anson, in which he was required to drink a pint of cold lager but the director required several takes and by the end of the morning's filming Mills had to be

put to bed, completely drunk. He was also upset that his love scenes were excised, "I was so disappointed in my love scene with Sylvia Syms. Up to then I had made love on the screen to virtually nothing but submarines and tanks, and this was my big chance – and then most of it was cut out." He stayed in the army for *Tunes Of Glory* (1960), in which he played Colonel Barrow opposite his friend of many years, Alec Guinness. "I've been asked a hundred times how I did the quivering eye bit," he said, "but I'm not telling." The performance won him the Best Actor prize at the Venice Film Festival. However, Mills' later claim that he and Guinness had tossed a coin as to which role each should play was one that the director, Ronald Neame, later denied. In 1961 he appeared on Broadway in Terence Rattigan's play about Lawrence of Arabia, *Ross* (a role that coincidentally Guinness had played in the West End). In the Sixties Mills began appearing in international films including *Lady Hamilton* (1967) – he played the cuckolded Sir William Hamilton – and *Lady Caroline Lamb* (1972), with Mills as prime minister George Canning. On occasion he worked with his family. Daughter Juliet first appeared on screen as a three-month-old baby in *In Which We Serve* and sister Hayley made her screen début at age 13 with her father in *Tiger Bay* (1959). They also appeared together in *The Parent Trap* (1961), *The Chalk Garden* (1964) and *The Family Way* (1967). In 1965 he directed the melodrama *Sky West And Crooked*, as a vehicle for Hayley and written by his wife Mary Hayley Bell. The film was a box office flop. "You could have fired a shotgun in any Odeon where it was showing and not hit a soul," he remarked. His other films included Bryan Forbes' *King Rat* (1965) and playing Field Marshal Haig in Richard Attenborough's *Oh! What A Lovely War* (1969). On April 15, 1971, he won a Best Supporting Actor Oscar

for his portrayal of the village idiot in Lean's *Ryan's Daughter* (1970). His later films included *The 39 Steps* (1978), *The Big Sleep* (1978), *Gandhi* (1982), *Who's That Girl?* (1987), Kenneth Branagh's *Hamlet* (1996), *Bean* (1997), and *Bright Young Things* (2003). He was married twice. His first wife was Aileen Raymond, who he married in March 1932 at Marylebone Register Office. After their divorce he married Mary Hayley Bell on January 16, 1941 and by her had a son, Jonathan (b. London Clinic, December 3, 1949), a screenwriter, and two daughters 5'2" Juliet Maryon (b. Royal Northern Hospital, Holloway Road, north London, November 21, 1941) and Hayley Catherine Rose Vivien (b. London, April 18, 1946 at 11.40pm). In May 1976, Mills, who had been appointed CBE in 1960, was knighted in prime minister Harold Wilson's resignation list. The investiture took place at Buckingham Palace on July 28, 1976.
CAUSE: Mills had been in poor health during his last few years, becoming virtually blind in 1992. In August 2002 he was hospitalised with a severe chest infection. It was an affliction that was never to leave him and he died aged 97 at his Denham, Buckinghamshire home. He had nursed his wife through Alzheimer's disease.
FURTHER READING: *Up In The Clouds Gentlemen Please* – John Mills (London: Penguin Books, 1981).

Sal Mineo

Born January 10, 1939
Died February 12, 1976
'The Switchblade Kid'. Born in The Bronx, Salvatore Mineo, Jr was a teen star who progressed to adult success. He was lauded for his Broadway performances in *The Rose Tattoo* in 1951 co-starring Maureen Stapleton and Eli Wallach and *The King & I* a year later with Yul Brynner. After being expelled from school for bad behaviour he was given two choices: borstal or

enrol in an acting school. Acting won but Mineo still took pleasure in beating up anyone who called him a sissy. In 1955 he began making movies. His first filmic forays confirmed his talent and he was Oscar nominated for his portrayal of John, nicknamed Plato, in *Rebel Without A Cause* (1955). His subsequent film career seemed to consist of playing variations of Plato or roles that didn't stretch his acting ability. He appeared in *Somebody Up There Likes Me* (1956) as Romolo, *Rock Pretty Baby* (1956) as Angelo Barrato, *Giant* (1956) as Angel Obregon II and *Dino* (1957) as juvenile delinquent Dino Minetta. Then came *Exodus* (1960), in which he played the part of Holocaust survivor Dov Landau, and another Academy Award nomination. The film caused Mineo problems, however. He was wanted to play the part of an Arab boy in *Lawrence Of Arabia* (1962) but because he had played an Arab-killing Jew in *Exodus* he was banned from entering Jordan, where the movie was filmed. He was absent from the screen for 1961 and was a face in the crowd in *The Longest Day* (1962) as Private Martini and *The Greatest Story Ever Told* (1965) as Uriah. John Ford cast him as Red Shirt in the western *Cheyenne Autumn* (1964) which, apart from playing Milo in *Escape From The Planet Of The Apes* (1971), was his last major film. He was proud of his Italian ancestry: "I'm . . . a wop . . . I was unique. They made all the guys change names, and half of them had to have nosejobs, like Dean Martin, alias Dino Crocetti. And the girls: Anne Bancroft's real name was Italiano – and Paula Prentiss' was Ragusa . . . We ain't all olive-skinned. Look at Connie Stevens or Bernadette Peters." A diminutive bisexual, he was the mentor and gay lover of a very successful Eighties actor who attempts to keep the association quiet today.
CAUSE: With his film career seemingly at an end, Mineo returned to the theatre and began rehearsals at the

Westwood Theater for the play *P.S. Your Cat Is Dead*. The show had played well in San Francisco, prompting wags to comment it should really be called 'P.S. Sal Mineo Is Alive'. At approximately 10pm on February 12, 1976, with opening a week away, Mineo returned to his rented home in West Hollywood just below Sunset Strip, 8563 Holloway Drive, and parked his blue Chevelle in the garage. As he walked to his apartment he was attacked by a man with a knife who stabbed Mineo through the heart. Despite the best efforts of his neighbours Mineo died, aged 37, five minutes later. Witnesses spoke of "A white male with long hair, dressed in dark clothes running away from the scene." It was assumed to be a robbery that went fatally wrong but then police discovered Mineo still was in possession of his wallet. A link to drugs also failed to be substantiated leaving police to believe that Mineo had been murdered during a lovers' tiff. Sal was interred, next to his father, at the Cemetery of the Gate of Heaven, Stevens Avenue, Hawthorne, New York 10532. For two years police hunted Mineo's killer but drew a blank until one day a man in jail confessed to the killing, was charged and, on February 13, 1979, convicted. Lionel Ray Williams, 21, revealed that he had stabbed Mineo just for the hell of it. Police had failed to find a motive for the slaying because there wasn't one. Bizarrely, several leading cast members of *Rebel Without A Cause* all died violent deaths: Nick Adams, James Dean, Mineo and Natalie Wood.

Anthony Minghella, CBE

Born January 6, 1954
Died March 18, 2008
Modern Brit in Hollywood. From working on school series *Grange Hill* to his last project, *No. 1 Ladies Detective Agency* (premièred March 23, 2008), Anthony Minghella was a much-respected voice in the cinematic world. Born on the Isle of Wight, as one of five children, his parents owned a successful ice cream business. He began his career as a lecturer at Hull University before writing scripts for stage, radio and TV. His first major film as a director was *Truly, Madly, Deeply* (premièred November 10, 1990) which he also wrote, that won him a BAFTA for original screenplay. His next film was *Mr Wonderful* (released October 15, 1993) with Matt Dillon and Mary Louise Parker but it was *The English Patient* (premièred November 6, 1996) with which he made his name and reputation. Minghella won Best Director Oscar and was nominated for Best Adapted Screenplay. He received the same nomination four years later for *The Talented Mr Ripley* (premièred December 12, 1999), the second film to be based on the novel by Patricia Highsmith. His other films were: *Play* (2000), *Cold Mountain* (released December 25, 2003) and *Breaking And Entering* (released November 9, 2006). In 2005, 5'8½" Minghella directed Labour's party political broadcast for the General Election. He was chairman of the British Film Institute for four years from 2003. He said, "When I became the chairman of the British Film Institute, I didn't understand how much of my time would be taken up with trying to make a case for the British Film Institute: what it's for, why it exists, why it needs its money." He married producer Carolyn Choa by whom he had two children Max (b. Hampstead, London September 16, 1985) and Hannah.
CAUSE: Minghella suffered a fatal haemorrhage at 5am at Charing Cross Hospital, where he had undergone an operation on a cancerous growth on his tonsils and neck. He was 54. Longtime friend Harvey Weinstein said, "He was my mentor, my partner and, most of all, my brother. The grace, joy and tenderness he brought to his films were symbolic of his life and the many people he touched. There are many

personal and professional moments we have shared together and I will treasure them for the rest of my life." Sydney Pollack added, "Anthony was a realistic romanticist. A kind of poet, disciplined by reality, an academic by training, a musician by nature, a compulsive reader by habit, and to most observers, a sunny soul who exuded a gentleness that should never have been mistaken for lack of tenacity and resolve. The cliché that you don't know anyone well until you've lived through wars with them, is an absolute truth. Sometimes making films is a form of war. Having weathered several with Anthony, I will tell you that his dignity never softened, his artistry never suffered, and his mind remained as sharp and clear in wartime as it was in quietude." Minghella's memorial service was held at the Thomas More Catholic Church, near his home in Hampstead, north London on April 5, 2008. Among the mourners were Tony and Cherie Blair, Gordon and Sarah Brown, the Duchess of York, Jude Law, Renee Zellweger, Helena Bonham-Carter and John Hurt. Jill Scott, who played Precious Ramotswe in Minghella's last film, fainted during the service and had to be carried out by fellow mourners. Minghella left a gross estate of £7,531,190; net £6,581,238.

Vincente Minnelli

(LESTER ANTHONY MINNELLI)
Born February 28, 1903
Died July 25, 1986
Creator of Magic. Born in Chicago, Illinois, the grandson of an Italian revolutionary. Shy, unattractive, effeminate, cosmetic-wearing, inarticulate, beset by a tic and homosexual, Minnelli began his career as a window dresser and then became a photographer's assistant and a costume designer. He had directed a number of stage shows and three films when he was flung into the big time and given the chance to direct Judy Garland in *Meet Me In St Louis* (1944). Production

began on November 10, 1943, although filming didn't start until December 7. Garland was often late or didn't bother to show up at all. She was reliant on drugs and had just finished an affair with Joseph L. Mankiewicz and on the rebound took up with her leading man, Tom Drake. Unfortunately, Drake was gay but Garland took his inability to get an erection as a personal insult. The last day of filming – April 7, 1944 – could not come too soon for her. With all these distractions the film could have been a disaster. It was thanks to Minnelli's skill that it wasn't. The *Los Angeles Times* lauded it as "one of the Great American Family sketches" and the movie became a box-office smash. It was against this background that Garland fell in love with Vincente Minnelli. He had, after all, made her look stunning on film. She and Minnelli began to have dinner together, first with another man present and then alone, and romance blossomed. Not long after the film wrapped they began living together, Judy studiously ignoring the clues to Minnelli's true sexuality. Minnelli worked on *Yolanda And The Thief* (1945) which flopped, *The Clock* (1945) and *Ziegfeld Follies* (1946) the last two which teamed him once again, professionally, with Garland. On January 9, 1945, Minnelli and Garland announced their engagement. Minnelli liked to mould women to his style and tastes and Judy was no exception. Some women may have been horrified by this flagrant interference. Judy loved it. They married on June 15, 1945, in Judy's mother's house and MGM chief Louis B. Mayer gave the bride away. By the end of August, Judy was pregnant and baby Liza arrived in Cedars of Lebanon Hospital, Los Angeles, at 7.58am on March 12, 1946, weighing 6lb 10½oz. He next directed Judy in *The Pirate* (1948), a film about mistaken identities. Judy was out of her head on pills during most of the filming, missing

99 days out of the 135-day schedule. The drugs caused paranoia, the paranoia was addressed to her husband and the film was a financial flop. As they approached their second wedding anniversary, the strains were beginning to tell. Judy had an affair with Yul Brynner and then caught Minnelli in bed with the handyman, the sight of which caused her to attempt suicide. She had him replaced on *Easter Parade* (1948), much to his disappointment and embarrassment. He directed *Madame Bovary* (1949) and *Father Of The Bride* (1950). Then, on December 21, 1950, the couple announced their marriage was at an end. Without the heartache of Judy Garland, Minnelli seemed to thrive and directed highly successful musicals for MGM. His films garnered 20 Oscars and included: *Father's Little Dividend* (1951), *An American In Paris* (1951), which picked up six Academy Awards, *The Band Wagon* (1953), *Brigadoon* (1954), *Kismet* (1955), *Lust For Life* (1956), which won a solitary Oscar, *Designing Woman* (1957) which also won a solitary Oscar, *The Reluctant Debutante* (1958), *Gigi* (1958), which won a staggering nine Oscars including Best Direction for Minnelli, *Four Horsemen Of The Apocalypse* (1961), *The Courtship Of Eddie's Father* (1963), *The Sandpiper* (1965) and *On A Clear Day You Can See Forever* (1970). Following his divorce Minnelli married Georgette Magnani (b. 1931) on February 16, 1954, and fathered a daughter, Tina Nina, in April 1955. On December 31, 1960, he married Denise Gigante. They divorced in August 1971. His final wife was Lee Anderson with whom he began living in 1969.
CAUSE: He died of Alzheimer's disease aged 83 at his home, North Crescent Drive, in Beverly Hills, California. Minnelli was buried in a Catholic funeral at the Wee Kirk O' The Heather, Forest Lawn Memorial-Parks, 1712 Glendale Avenue, Glendale, California 91209.

Carmen Miranda
(MARIA DO CARMO MIRANDA DA CUNHA)
Born February 9, 1904
Died August 5, 1955
'The Brazilian Bombshell'. The enduring image of Carmen Miranda is one of an enthusiastic dancer with the contents of a fruit bowl on her head. She was not born in Brazil but in Marco de Canavezes, near Lisbon, Portugal moving to Rio de Janeiro at an early age. She worked on Brazilian radio and in films such as *A Voz Do Carnaval* (1933) and *Estudantes* (1935) as Mimi, before making her Broadway début in 1939. One critic wrote of that performance: "Her face is too heavy to be beautiful, her figure is nothing to write home about, and she sings in a foreign language. Yet she is the biggest theatrical sensation of the season." Her star shone brightly in Hollywood for a brief period from 1940's *Down Argentine Way* onwards. However, by the end of the decade her welcome had been outstayed. Her films included: *That Night In Rio* (1941) as Carmen, *Weekend In Havana* (1941) as Rosita Rivas, *Springtime In The Rockies* (1942) as Rosita Murphy, *Something For The Boys* (1944) as Chiquita Hart, *Greenwich Village* (1944) as Princess Querida, *Four Jills In A Jeep* (1944) as Carmen Miranda, *If I'm Lucky* (1946) as Michelle O'Toole, *Copacabana* (1947) as Carmen Novarro and *A Date With Judy* (1948) as Rosita Cochellas. It was said she kept her supply of cocaine in a special compartment of her platform shoes. She married producer David Sebastian at the Church of the Good Shepherd, Beverly Hills, on March 17, 1947. He survived her.
CAUSE: She died aged 51 in Beverly Hills, California, of a heart attack, following an appearance on a Jimmy Durante television show. There is a Carmen Miranda Museum in Rio de Janeiro.

Cameron Mitchell

(CAMERON MACDOWELL MITZEL)
Born November 4, 1918
Died July 7, 1994
Rugged star. Born in Dallastown,
Pennsylvania, the son of the Reverend
Charles Mitzel, 5'11" Mitchell began
his career on the Broadway stage and in
1940, appeared in one of the first
television broadcasts in America, *The
Passing Of The Third Floor Back*. Lee
Strasberg regarded Mitchell as one of
the founders of the Actors Studio. After
service as a bombardier in the air force
during the Second World War,
Mitchell made his first film *What Next,
Corporal Hargrove?* (1945). He played
Happy in both stage (he originated the
role of Happy on Broadway) and
cinematic versions (1951) of Arthur
Miller's *Death Of A Salesman*. He
appeared opposite Marilyn Monroe in
How To Marry A Millionaire (1953) and
in the musical *Carousel* (1956). In the
Sixties he appeared in a number of
Italian films but it is for his work on the
television Western *The High Chaparral*
(1967) as Buck Cannon that he will be
most remembered. In 1940, Mitchell
married Johanna Mendel. They had
four children: Robert Cameron (b.
New York July 4, 1941), Charles Emil
"Chip" (b. 1951), Fred and Camille.
The couple divorced in 1960. Two
more marriages ended unsuccessfully.
CAUSE: Mitchell died of lung cancer,
aged 75, at Pacific Palisades,
California. He was buried in lot 83,
section A-23 of Desert Memorial Park,
31705 Da Vall Drive, Cathedral City,
California CA92234.

Carolyn Mitchell

(BARBARA ANN THOMASON)
Born January 25, 1937
Died January 31, 1966
Fit beauty. The blonde 1954 Miss
Muscle Beach of Santa Monica,
Mitchell appeared in *Dragstrip Riot*
(1958) as Betty and Roger Corman's
The Cry Baby Killer (1958) as Carole
opposite Jack Nicholson before giving
up her career to become the fifth
Mrs Mickey Rooney in Mexico in
December 1958. They had four
children: Kelly Ann (b. Santa Monica,
California, September 13, 1959); Kerry
(b. December 30, 1960); Kyle (b.
Santa Monica, California, April 2,
1962) and Kimmy Sue (b. Santa
Monica, California, September 13,
1963). However, she began an affair
with Yugoslavian wannabe actor Milos
Milocevic and on January 21, 1966, she
split from Rooney. On January 24,
Rooney began divorce proceedings.
Six days later, they were reconciled.
CAUSE: Milocevic, who was working as
a chauffeur for Alain Delon, refused to
accept the affair was over and one day
after the reconciliation he murdered
Mitchell in her Brentwood home before
turning the gun on himself.

Robert Mitchum

Born August 6, 1917
Died July 1, 1997
Nonchalant tough guy. An air of
menace seemed to hang over the
slow-talking (but not slow-thinking)
Robert Charles Durman Mitchum, yet
he also could come across as a
pussycat, albeit one with claws. Born
in Bridgeport, Connecticut, his father
was killed in February 1919 and he
wandered through a variety of jobs,
including working with Marilyn
Monroe's husband in a factory. His
long career in movies (130+ films)
supposedly began when Mitchum
wandered by mistake onto the set of
Hopalong Cassidy, where he was spotted
by a producer. Another story is that he
was originally a screenwriter but
realised there was more money to be
made on the other side of the camera.
He played Rigney in *Hoppy Serves
A Writ* (1943) and that year also
appeared in 18 other films. "I played
everything from Chinese laundrymen
to midgets, to Irish washer women to
faggots." He featured in eight *Hopalong
Cassidy* films at $100 a week, "plus all
the horse shit I could take home."

Seven films followed in 1944, before Mitchum made his name with *The Story Of G.I. Joe* (1945) as Lieutenant Bill Walker, for which he was nominated for an Oscar. Almost as soon as that film wrapped he was called up into the army and spent eight months in the military. He was the first male star to refuse to shave his chest. He almost wrecked his career on September 1, 1948, when he was arrested at 8334 Ridpath Drive, Los Angeles, for possession of marijuana and was sentenced to 60 days in Los Angeles County Jail (prisoner #91234) on February 9, 1949. On his release he worked hard to rebuild his reputation in films such as *The Big Steal* (1949) as Lieutenant Duke Halliday, *The Red Pony* (1949) as Billy Buck, *The Racket* (1951) as Captain Thomas McQuigg, *My Forbidden Past* (1951) as Dr Mark Lucas, *One Minute To Zero* (1952) as Colonel Steve Janowski, *Macao* (1952) as Nick Cochran, *The Lusty Men* (1952) as Jeff McCloud, *Angel Face* (1952) as Frank Jessup, *River Of No Return* (1954) as Matt Calder in which he co-starred with Marilyn Monroe, *The Night Of The Hunter* (1955) as the mad Reverend Harry Powell, *Foreign Intrigue* (1956) as Dave Bishop, *The Enemy Below* (1957) as Captain Murrell, *Heaven Knows, Mr Allison* (1957) as Marine Corporal Allison, which was his favourite of his own films, *Thunder Road* (1958) as Lucas Doolin, *The Hunters* (1958) as Major Cleve Saville, *The Sundowners* (1960) as Paddy Carmody, *The Grass Is Greener* (1960) as Charles Delacro, *The Last Time I Saw Archie* (1961) as Archie Hall, *The Longest Day* (1962) as Brigadier General Norman Cota, *Cape Fear* (1962), in which he gave a terrifyingly convincing portrayal of psychopathic rapist Max Cady, *The List Of Adrian Messenger* (1963) as Jim Slattery, *Mister Moses* (1965) as Joe Moses, *El Dorado* (1967) as Sheriff J.B. Harrah, *Villa Rides* (1968) as Lee Arnold, *Ryan's Daughter* (1970) as

Charles Shaughnessy, *The Friends Of Eddie Coyle* (1973) as ex-villain Eddie Coyle, *Farewell, My Lovely* (1975) as private eye Philip Marlowe, *Midway* (1976) as Admiral William F. 'Bull' Halsey, Jr, *The Last Tycoon* (1976) as Pat Brady, *The Big Sleep* (1978) reprising his role as Philip Marlowe, *Cape Fear* (1991) as Lieutenant Elgart, *Woman Of Desire* (1993) as lawyer Walter J. Hill starring opposite Bo Derek and *James Dean: Race With Destiny* (1997) as George Stevens. He married Dorothy Clement Spence (b. 1919) in Dover, Delaware, on March 16, 1940, proposing with the words: "Marry me and you'll be farting through silk." They had two sons: James Robin Spence 'Josh' (b. May 8, 1941) and Christopher (b. October 16, 1943) and one daughter: Petrine Day (b. Good Samaritan Hospital, Los Angeles, California, March 3, 1952, weighing 7lb 10oz). He loved to test the gullibility of the press, often making up stories about himself because he was bored. He told a hack in 1991 that he would like to spend the rest of his life setting up a rehabilitation home for celibate ex-jailbirds. He also told one female reporter who unctuously asked how he maintained his good looks at 60: "It's down to a life of abstention and celibacy." In fact, celibacy was one thing Mitchum didn't practise. In 1962 he had an affair with Shirley MacLaine that almost wrecked his marriage. He also romanced Sarah Miles. In the summer of 1977 while filming *The Big Sleep* he had a fling with blonde 34B-22-33 nude model Lindy Benson (b. Muswell Hill, north London, November 28, 1952). "He was the best lover I've ever had," she later enthused. "He liked to lie with his head on my behind. He said it was the softest pillow ever." Mitchum was also an insomniac. He never took acting seriously: "I got three expressions: looking left, looking right and looking straight ahead," he once commented, adding, "Movies bore me, especially my own." He apparently developed a pot belly so that he wouldn't have to pose with his shirt off. "People think I have an interesting walk. I'm just trying to hold my stomach in." Or was that all a front? Howard Hawks said to him: "You're the biggest fraud I ever met. You pretend you don't care a damn about a scene and you're the hardest working so-and-so I've ever known."

CAUSE: He died aged 79 of lung cancer in Santa Barbara, California. He defied doctors when diagnosed with cancer and emphysema by continuing to smoke a packet of cigarettes every other day and drinking six Martinis for lunch. "Well," he reasoned, "you gotta die of something."

FURTHER READING: *Robert Mitchum –* David Downing (London: Comet, 1985); *Robert Mitchum: A Biography –* George Eells (London: Robson Books, 1988); *Them Ornery Mitchum Boys –* John Mitchum (Pacifica: Creatures At Large Press, 1989).

Tom Mix

Born January 6, 1880
Died October 12, 1940

The silent screen cowboy star. From very early on Hollywood has realised the publicity value of romantic backgrounds for stars. According to the press flacks, 6' Thomas Hezikiah Mix was the son of a cavalry officer, went to military school and fought in the Spanish-American War as one of Teddy Roosevelt's Rough Riders, the Philippines Insurrection, the Boxer Rebellion and the Boer War (on both sides!). He later became a Texas Ranger. He claimed to have been wounded 21 times and even sold maps of his body explaining each scar and mark. After the Texas Rangers, he became a bounty hunter and a US Marshal. When the Mexican Revolution broke out, he went south of the border to fight, was captured and sentenced to death by firing squad, though by some miracle he managed to escape. All fiction. He was born in Mix

Run, Pennsylvania, the son of a lumber worker and although he did join the army he deserted in 1902 after persistent nagging from his wife. He began his professional life in various Western shows, making his film début in *Ranch Life In The Great Southwest* (unreleased until 1910). He appeared in over 300 films, directed over 100, wrote over 70 and produced almost 50. On screen he never drank, smoked or fought without just cause. At one time he was Hollywood's highest-paid star, taking home $17,500 a week at a time when Gary Cooper made just $50 a week. Many stars have their own little luxuries (sometimes not so little) in their dressing rooms and Mix had a boxing ring installed in his to help him keep fit. D.W. Griffith said of him: "He can't act, but he can ride like hell and everybody loves him. I don't know why." Mix spoke slowly, not because he was a slow thinker but because he had trouble with his badly fitting false teeth. Living in a house with nine bathrooms, he dyed his hair black, telling Gene Autry: "The Lord has been good to me. He preserved my hair. I can sure keep it black for Him." He left Hollywood in 1935 to run a circus. He had a less than chivalrous attitude to women, threatening one wife by twirling a loaded gun around his finger but he could also be 'protective'. Out one night with girlfriend Lupe Velez, he tried to strangle another man who began talking to her. Mix married seven times, including the same woman twice. The Mrs Mixes were: Grace I. Allin (1902–1902); Kitty Perine (1905–1906); Olive Stokes (1909–1917) by whom he had a daughter, Ruth (b. 1913, d. 1977); Victoria Forde (1918–December 4, 1930; she was born in New York in 1897 and died in Beverly Hills on July 24, 1964) by whom he had a daughter, Thomasina (b. 1922); Mary Mabel Morgan (1930–1931) by whom he had a daughter, Betty; Mabel Hubbard Ward (February 15, 1932–1934); and Olive

Stokes (1935–1939) again, by whom he had yet another daughter, Bessie Mae. Olive Stokes died in 1972.

CAUSE: He was killed aged 60 in a car crash in Florence, Arizona. A flood had destroyed a bridge and Mix, driving his white convertible at high speed, failed to make a turn and crashed, breaking his neck. A statue of a riderless horse was erected on the spot to honour him.

Bob Monkhouse

Born June 1, 1928
Died December 29, 2003
Mr Comedy. Robert Alan Monkhouse was born at 2am in Beckenham, Kent, the younger son of Wilfred Adrian Monkhouse (d. 1957), a cavalry corporal known as Wammy, and Dorothy Muriel Hansard (d. 1969 of cancer), known as Buddy. Bob's parents found it difficult to show him any affection when he was a child and he was a very fat, unhappy boy with a lifelong stammer he battled to overcome. Monkhouse's grandfather, Frederick John Monkhouse (b. 1861, d. April 1938) was a custard powder tycoon whose death hit the nine-year-old Bob so hard that he was unable to speak for three months. The family firm, Monkhouse Glasscock, held little appeal for the young boy. "I was brought up in an atmosphere of 'Some day son, all this custard will be yours.' But I didn't like the feeling of so much security and the prospect of so much cornflour." He was educated at Dulwich College (the late nostalgia buff Denis Gifford, creator of *Looks Familiar*, was a fellow pupil) where he was known as 'The Oil' because of his fondness for hair tonic. Bob discovered comedy aged six after seeing George Formby in *Boots! Boots!* at the Splendid Cinema, Sydenham, on Easter Monday 1934. As a teenager he began sending jokes to variety hall comedians. He earned his first professional money (five shillings) aged 15, writing for Max Miller. Among the funnies he submitted was "There's going to be no

more clothing coupons for old maids. No, well, they've got enough in their drawers they haven't used yet." His first audition was for the Canadian impresario Carroll Levis at the Golders Green Hippodrome and it was a disaster. "I managed only a couple of jokes before he spoke to me. He said just two words, 'Go home.' I did as he advised and walked off to the sound of my own footsteps. Then I went home and wept. I just couldn't take the rejection." Two years later, he began performing as a stand-up comedian with Denis Goodwin (b. London, July 19, 1929, d. February 26, 1975, aged 45 by his own hand). They styled themselves on Murgatroyd and Winterbottom, a double act formed by Tommy Handley and Ronald Frankau. Goodwin was never a confident stage performer but, out of loyalty, Monkhouse stayed with him when he should have broken up the partnership. He and Goodwin finally split in 1965 when Goodwin went to America. "Muir and Norden were the Fortnum & Mason of scriptwriting. We were the Tesco." Monkhouse also wrote racy pulp novels for the troops under noms de plume including Ramon Le Croix. At 17 Monkhouse trained as a cartoon animator with Gaumont-British under David Low and worked on his act. Before being conscripted into the RAF in June 1946, Bob had made £20,000 from commissioning other writers and artists from his office in Penge and paying them by postal order. In order to entertain the local Young Communists he had to join the party – though he gave his name as Colney Hatch, after the lunatic asylum. Demobbed, he forged a letter from a group captain to the BBC insisting that Corporal R.A. Monkhouse, number 5590996, must have an audition as soon as possible for the sake of his sanity. The BBC replied immediately but the letter found its way to the group captain and it took all of Bob's charm and wit to talk his way out of trouble. He auditioned with a wannabe singer called Gary Miller before Dennis Main Wilson, a young producer not long home from Forces Broadcasting in Hamburg. The usual auditioner awarded low marks – around 20 out of 100. Main Wilson gave Bob 101 and soon the work offers came flooding in. In 1948 Bob made his first appearances on radio and TV in *Works Wonders* and *New To You* respectively. The following year he became the BBC's first contract (12 months) comedian. With Denis Goodwin, he began writing scripts, producing hundreds for radio and TV for performers such as Arthur Askey, Bob Hope, Jack Benny and Jack Buchanan. For a year they wrote up to seven weekly shows simultaneously. He appeared in a few films from 1952 including the first in the *Carry On . . .* series *Carry On Sergeant* in 1958. He once said of himself, "By the age of 28, it was clear to me that I had no talent. What I had was a certain facility, that was all." That facility was to keep him in work for his entire adult life. In 1967, after the BBC had become disillusioned with him, he became host of *Sunday Night At The London Palladium* and then the host of ATV's *The Golden Shot,* taking over from original host Jackie Rae. This was the show that featured the famous Bernie the Bolt, the man who loaded the crossbow fired by a blindfolded contestant at an apple to win the major prize. In 1972, Monkhouse was sacked after too blatantly endorsing a new Wilkinson Sword razor on the programme. Three years earlier, he had almost gone bankrupt when Ronald Markham, the hypnotist and conman, stole the funds of a nightclub called Change Is that he opened in Newcastle on February 9, 1969. Bob claimed that Markham had hypnotised him. By the mid-Seventies Monkhouse had become the king of the TV gameshow hosting such shows as *Family Fortunes, Bob's Full House* and *Celebrity Squares.* In 1977 Monkhouse's name hit the

headlines for all the wrong reasons. An avid movie buff, he had a collection of 1,800 films on 16 mm. On July 11, he was arrested on charges of conspiracy. It was alleged that he had imported films of Columbia Warner and other distributors without the right to do so. He came to trial at the Old Bailey on June 6, 1979. After eleven days of testimony in which Terry Wogan appeared for the prosecution the judge decided there was no case to answer, dismissed it and awarded costs to the defendant. In 1983 he signed a three-year contract worth £200,000 to present a chat show for the BBC. In 1987 and 1992 he was voted After Dinner Speaker Of The Year by the Guild Of Professional Toastmasters, the only two-time recipient. The Nineties saw the return of *Celebrity Squares* and a new show, *Bob's Your Uncle,* that brought back the crossbow, so beloved in *The Golden Shot.* This time it was under the aegis of a lady called Donna Derby (married to the comedian Bradley Walsh) resulting in Bob calling for "Donna – the dart". Bob's sharp wit and determination to always give of his best ensured that he survived the cull of many of his contemporaries and he remained a television favourite up until the time of his death from prostate cancer. A kindly man, Bob was always ready to help. He wrote the foreword to one of this author's previous books and contributed to another. He also gave Jeremy Beadle his first break in television, writing questions for *Celebrity Squares.* In 1995 Monkhouse was devastated when two large books containing years of material were stolen from his dressing room. He was equally dismayed when the press publicised the theft of his "joke books". He offered a £10,000 reward for their safe return and they were back in his possession 18 months later. Monkhouse was a genuine wit and had several thousand one-liners memorised: "I'd never be unfaithful to my wife – I love my house too much." It was not unusual for him to work for two years on a joke to get it right and then repeat it ad infinitum. "If the gag is such a nifty piece of work, you can't wait to do it every night, you know." Interviewers strove to understand what made Monkhouse tick. Professor Anthony Clare in a 1992 episode of his radio programme *In The Psychiatrist's Chair* caused Monkhouse to break down at the suggestion that his mother's possessiveness indicated her love for him. "The fact is that I've made light of serious things because I can't do anything else," explained Monkhouse. In a touch of self-mockery he said, "I'm a hard man to ignore, but well worth the effort." His private life was chequered. He tells of innumerable seductions in his autobiography – some successful and others not so. He slept with Diana Dors whose husband, Dennis Hamilton, threatened to slit Bob's eyeballs with a razor and then put out a contract on his life. Sex with a transsexual chorus girl was not so successful and he rebuffed seduction attempts from Frankie Howerd and Tyrone Power. Twice married, his mother threatened to disinherit him if he married Belfast WAAF Elizabeth. She attended the ceremony at Caxton Hall, Westminster on November 5, 1949 dressed in black. Monkhouse and his mother did not speak again for 20 years, though they were reconciled shortly before her death. Elizabeth suffered four premature births and their first child, a son called Gary Alan, was born three months prematurely on November 24, 1951 severely disabled with cerebral palsy and spent his life in a home. He died in July 1992 of natural causes and was buried on July 14. His second son, Simon (b. July 1954), a teacher, became estranged when he believed Bob was "using" him in interviews. He forbade his father from mentioning him in his autobiography. Then when he was not mentioned by name, Simon Monkhouse again fell out with his father. He died of a heroin overdose in a Thailand boarding house in May 2001. The Monkhouses adopted a daughter, Abigail (b. 1959), who remained close to Bob. The marriage ended in divorce in 1971 and on October 4, 1973 at St Marylebone Register Office he married Jackie Harding (b. August 10, 1936), who had been secretary to Bob and Denis Goodwin. They remained blissfully happy until Bob's death. Monkhouse was a devotee of alternative medicine, taking about 30 vitamin and herbal tablets a day. He topped up his tan with trips to his home in Barbados. He suffered from vitiligo, the skin disease, which left him, beneath his underpants, "a riot of polka dots and moonbeams". He also maintained heroic levels of alcohol consumption, usually two bottles of wine and half a bottle of malt whisky a day. One of his funniest lines came as a result of his family's lack of enthusiasm for his chosen profession, "They laughed when I said I was going to be a comedian . . . they're not laughing now."

CAUSE: He died aged 75 of prostate cancer in Egginton, Bedfordshire.

FURTHER READING: *Crying With Laughter* – Bob Monkhouse (London: Century, 1993; *Over The Limit* – Bob Monkhouse (London: Century, 1998).

Marilyn Monroe

(NORMA JEANE MORTENSON)
Born June 1, 1926
Died August 4, 1962

'The Mmmmmmmm Girl'. For the past ten years or so the name of Marilyn Monroe has been linked more to the various conspiracy theories surrounding her death than to her movie career. More books have been written about her than any other show business celebrity. Despite the preoccupation with her death, Marilyn Monroe remains the most potent sex symbol of the twentieth century. She began life in Los Angeles General Hospital. Her father is listed as Edward

Mortenson, a 29-year-old baker from California, whereabouts unknown. (Some believe that Mortenson was not Norma Jeane's real father and bolted when his wife became pregnant by one of her colleagues, C. Stanley Gifford.) Her Mexican-born mother, Gladys Pearl Monroe (b. Ciudad Porfirio Diaz, May 27, 1900), had recently celebrated her 26th birthday and was working as a film cutter at Consolidated Film Industries at the time of Norma Jeane's birth. Insanity ran in Norma Jeane's family. Her great-grandfather, Tilford Hogan, would hang himself on May 29, 1933, aged 82. In July 1927 her grandmother, Della Mae Monroe Grainger (Tilford Hogan's daughter), attempted to smother the 11-month old Norma Jeane and was committed to Norwalk Metropolitan State Hospital. She died there on August 23, 1927. (Years later Marilyn Monroe would claim she could remember her grandmother trying to smother her. Although many authors have believed this impossible her third husband, Arthur Miller, did believe her.) On November 20, 1929, her uncle Marion Monroe told his wife he was going out to buy newspapers and walked out on his family without explanation, never to return. Gladys Baker (Norma Jeane's mother used the surname of her first husband, Jasper Baker, frequently) decided to use her feminine wiles to ensnare a husband for herself and a father for her latest offspring (she already had a son and a daughter by Jasper Baker). On June 13, 1926, she placed Norma Jeane with Albert Wayne and Ida Bolender, a religious couple who lived in Hawthorne, California, paying them $5 a week to look after her daughter. Meanwhile, Gladys went looking for a man, believing a single woman would be more appealing than a single mother. Gladys visited Norma Jeane every Saturday. The little girl stayed with the Bolenders until 1933 and then moved into another foster home for a brief period. By October 20,

1934, Gladys had saved enough money to put down a $750 deposit on a $6,000 bungalow at 6812 Arbol Drive, Hollywood and mother and daughter finally lived together. To make ends meet Gladys rented out the bungalow except for two rooms for herself and Norma Jeane. Another incident that has puzzled writers is Marilyn's claim that she was molested by a 'Mr Kimmell', one of the lodgers where she lived. When she told her 'foster mother' what the 'star boarder' had done she was admonished for telling tales about such a fine man. It would seem likely that if the incident did happen, it happened at Arbol Drive, for that is really the only place Norma Jeane ever lived that had lodgers. The 'star boarder' was the English actor Murray Kinnell. Marilyn may have slightly changed his name and invented the idea of a 'foster mother' to protect her own mother. The happiness did not last, for in December 1934 Gladys suffered a nervous breakdown and was taken to Los Angeles General Hospital (where Norma Jeane was born) for observation. She was later transferred to Norwalk (where she later died) and was declared a paranoid schizophrenic. On January 15, 1935, Gladys was declared mentally incompetent and her best friend Grace McKee was appointed Norma Jeane's legal guardian. Grace McKee was a kind soul but she was also a practical one. For a while she and Norma Jeane lived with Grace's mother just off Hollywood Boulevard. On August 10, 1935, in Las Vegas Grace married her divorced 6'5" beau Ervin Silliman 'Doc' Goddard, a wannabe inventor and Hollywood stand-in for Joel McCrea. A month later, on September 13, Norma Jeane became the 3,463rd child sent to the Los Angeles Orphans Home. Grace took Norma Jeane on outings, usually to the cinema where she told the little girl that she, too, could become a big star. Grace encouraged Norma Jeane to try out her cosmetics and experiment with various hairstyles and arranged for various foster families to look after Norma Jeane until she was able to provide a home herself. On June 12, 1937, eleven days after her eleventh birthday Norma Jeane left the orphanage for the last time and moved in with Doc and Grace and his three children. Five months later, Norma Jeane was on the move again. Both Doc and Grace were heavy drinkers and one night Doc behaved inappropriately towards Norma Jeane. The girl moved in with her Aunt Olive (wife of the disappeared Marion) until August 1938 when she went to live with one of the most important people in her life, 'Aunt' Ana Lower. Edith Ana Atchison Lower was a 58-year-old Christian Scientist and she was, said Marilyn, "the first person in the world I ever really loved. She was the only one who loved and understood me." In 1941 Norma Jeane moved back in with the Goddards until they announced they were moving to Huntingdon, West Virginia, where Doc had been transferred. They would not be taking Norma Jeane with them. In her usual practical way Grace decided the only thing to do was for Norma Jeane "to get married to the boy next door". Briefly, the girl returned to live with Ana Lower before her wedding to 21-year-old Jim Dougherty on June 19, 1942. Norma Jeane was given away by Ana Lower. At first the marriage was a happy one. Jim Dougherty worked alongside Robert Mitchum and the future actor recalled how lovey-dovey the couple was. Dougherty told the present author that he and Norma Jeane had a very contented marital life. However, cracks gradually began to show. In 1943 the couple relocated to Catalina Island where Dougherty worked as a fitness instructor at the military base. Eventually, much to Norma Jeane's dismay, Dougherty applied for and received duty overseas. He sailed out of Catalina Island and out of the marriage. Meanwhile,

Norma Jeane found work in the Radio Plane factory in Van Nuys, California. It was there she was discovered by army photographer David Conover who had been sent to take pictures of women helping the war effort by his commanding officer, Captain Ronald Reagan. Conover's pictures of the young woman caused a sensation and on August 2, 1945, Norma Jeane, who stood just over 5'5" tall, went to see Emmeline Snively at the Blue Book Model Agency based in the Ambassador's Hotel, Los Angeles. (Bobby Kennedy would be shot dead in the same hotel 23 years later.) Christened Jean Norman, the new model was a success. Emmeline Snively recommended her to Helen Ainsworth, an agent at the National Concert Artists' Corporation. It was Ainsworth who landed Norma Jeane her first interview with Ben Lyon at 20th Century Fox on July 17, 1946. Lyon was impressed by what he saw and two days later arranged a colour screen test for Norma Jeane, without bothering to get the prior approval of his boss Darryl F. Zanuck. The test went well and Norma Jeane was signed to Fox on August 26, 1946, at a fee of $75 per week. Lyon renamed her Marilyn Monroe after Marilyn Miller and Gladys' maiden name. On September 13, she was divorced from Jim Dougherty. (Grace Goddard helped Norma Jeane to get married and she helped Marilyn to get divorced. When Marilyn went to Nevada to establish residency for the divorce she stayed with Grace's Aunt Minnie.) The six-month contract was renewed for a similar period although her salary doubled. Marilyn appeared in *Scudda Hoo! Scudda Hay* (1948) and *Dangerous Years* (1947). However, the option on her contract was dropped on August 25, 1947 after she failed to make much impact in either film. On May 27, 1949, short of money, Marilyn posed nude for photographer Tom Kelley. She was paid a flat fee of $50. The pictures would become among the most celebrated photographs of all time. Between 1947 and 1950 Marilyn made *Ladies Of The Chorus* (1948) for Columbia (she was on contract there from March 9 until September 8, 1948) and returned to Fox to make three films: *A Ticket To Tomahawk* (1950), *The Fireball* (1950) and the feature that garnered her a second chance at Fox, *All About Eve* (1950). Marilyn signed her new contract thanks to her manager and mentor Johnny Hyde on December 10, 1950. Eight days later, Hyde died of a heart attack. On March 29, 1951, Marilyn was a presenter at the Oscars, handing the statuette to Thomas Moulton for Best Sound Recording on *All About Eve*. Finally realising what they had on their hands, Fox signed Marilyn to a seven-year contract on May 11, 1951. It was worth $500 a week with semi-annual increases to a limit of $1,500. The contractual terms were to cause Marilyn an awful lot of resentment in years to come and ended with her going on strike. She then appeared in a succession of mostly unmemorable films but the public noticed her and her fan mail was enormous. In 1952 two momentous incidents occurred. The story of her nude calendar pose became public and she was cast as the unfaithful wife Rose Loomis in *Niagara* (1953), the film that was to make her a star. Marilyn decided to throw herself on the public's mercy and tell the truth about the pictures. It was a successful strategy and the public did not turn against her as the studio feared. *Niagara* was the first film in which Marilyn's name appeared above the title. Behind the scenes Fox was terrified over the sexual content of the story — impotence, adultery, honeymooners — and insisted it be toned down. The right-wing Daughters of the American Revolution campaigned against sex in the movies and were not happy at all with *Niagara*. The *Hollywood Daily Sketch* wrote: "A

film called *Niagara* in which Miss Monroe croons a song called 'Kiss' has proved the last straw for the matrons. And they have made it clear to Miss Monroe's boss, Darryl Zanuck, that Hollywood is in for another purity campaign unless something is done to curb the present spate of suggestiveness in films and publicity. Do their words carry any weight? The film company has postponed the release of a 'Kiss' record by Marilyn Monroe." The film contains what was then the longest walk (Marilyn's) in celluloid history – 116 feet. The camera is trained on 5'5½" Marilyn's backside for the entire stroll. Director Henry Hathaway was not looking forward to the assignment. He had heard Marilyn could be 'difficult'. However, he was delighted to discover that she was a joy to work with. "Joe [DiMaggio] was there to keep her happy," he later recalled. Marilyn's next assignment, in November 1952, was co-starring with Jane Russell in *Gentlemen Prefer Blondes* (1953). Marilyn was a smash as Lorelei Lee, beating out Fox glamour queen Betty Grable for the role. The part allowed Marilyn to show that she could act, sing and dance. Her rendition of 'Diamonds Are A Girl's Best Friend' inspired Madonna and countless other artistes. Marilyn's next smash was the first comedy to be filmed in CinemaScope and teamed her with Grable and Lauren Bacall, in *How To Marry A Millionaire* (1953), the story of how three good-time girls set out to ensnare a rich husband. Most people expected there to be fireworks on set between Monroe and Grable – the upcoming glamour queen and yesterday's version. They were disappointed when the two women became firm friends. The film was released in November 1953 to critical acclaim. Three months later, on January 14, 1954, Marilyn married baseball hero Joe DiMaggio in San Francisco's City Hall. At her new husband's insistence Marilyn dressed conservatively for the ceremony. On their honeymoon they visited Korea, where Marilyn entertained the GIs stationed there. The marriage was not a happy one and was often punctuated by violence. DiMaggio had no patience for what he saw as Hollywood phonies. That patience was stretched to the limit when Marilyn filmed the famous skirt-blowing scene in *The Seven Year Itch* (1955) on September 15, 1954. DiMaggio watched in stony silence as the crowds cheered every time his wife's dress was blown up, before storming off. By October the marriage was over and Marilyn appeared alongside her lawyer Jerry Giesler to announce the separation. She was sporting a nasty bruise on her forehead caused by DiMaggio's fist. That same year Marilyn appeared as saloon singer Kay Weston in *River Of No Return* (1954) opposite her first husband's ex-colleague Robert Mitchum and as singer Vicky in *There's No Business Like Showbusiness* (1954). Neither were great hits. On December 31, 1954, along with bisexual photographer Milton H. Greene, Marilyn formed Marilyn Monroe Productions. The aims of the company were to produce motion pictures worthy of Marilyn's talent and to break the stranglehold, both creative and financial, that Fox held over Marilyn. The studio retaliated by publicly threatening to sue her and privately by spinning against her, playing the 'dumb blonde' card. Marilyn went on strike and a stand-off occurred until the summer of 1955 when *The Seven Year Itch* was released and gave Marilyn her first hit in two years. At the insistence of its shareholders Fox and Marilyn Monroe Productions began to negotiate a new contract. The new document, signed a year to the day after the formation of her company, gave Marilyn director and cinematographer approval, $100,000 per picture, the right to make just four pictures in seven years for the studio, along with $142,500 in

compensation. On May 3, 1956, Marilyn began her first film under the new regime. It was the story of Cherie, a nightclub singer who longed to find a man to accept her for what she was, and a simple-minded cowboy on the look-out for a wife. Co-starring Don Murray, *Bus Stop* (1956) featured what is probably Marilyn's best performance. It was also the first film made under the guidance of Lee Strasberg, the proponent of the 'Method' school of acting that has baffled so many actors and helped so many others. The filming also coincided with her romance with playwright Arthur Miller. The couple was married in a civil ceremony on June 29, 1956, and in a Jewish ceremony two days later. At the time Miller was under investigation by the House Un-American Activities Committee for his supposed left-wing views. Marilyn was wont to combine her honeymoons with work and on this one she and Miller flew to England where she filmed Terence Rattigan's play *The Prince & The Showgirl* (1957) opposite Sir Laurence Olivier. Marilyn was to play Elsie Marina, the showgirl of the title. Ironically, Olivier's wife, Vivien Leigh, had played the role on the London stage but was too old (at 42) for the screen version. Olivier stated that he had expected to fall in love with Marilyn during filming. He was to be disappointed. The leading man and lady did not gel off screen. Olivier was exasperated by Marilyn's behaviour and her reliance on Paula Strasberg. However, despite their differences Olivier was to later state "I was as good as could be; and Marilyn! Marilyn was quite wonderful, the best of all. So. What do you know?" On July 8, 1958, Marilyn announced her next film was to be the Billy Wilder comedy *Some Like It Hot* (1959). The idea originated with *Fanfaren Der Liebe*, a musical in pre-Hitler 1932 Germany. Wilder was working for UFA and had seen the movie in which two musicians disguise themselves to fit into various scenarios: blacking up to play negro music, wearing earrings and bandannas to play gypsy music, wearing drag to play in a girl band, etc. The original had overtones of sadism and lesbianism. Wilder altered the story to make it more palatable for movie audiences in America. It began filming on August 4, 1958 (four years to the day before Marilyn's death) and wrapped on November 6, 1958, 29 days over schedule. It finally cost $2,800,000, having gone $500,000 over budget. Marilyn wanted the film to be shot in colour (as stipulated by her contract) but when the tests were shown, the make-up made the faces of co-stars Tony Curtis and Jack Lemmon look distinctly green, so she agreed to let Billy Wilder shoot in monochrome. Wilder hated colour films. He only shot his previous effort with Marilyn, *The Seven Year Itch*, in colour because of Monroe's contract. Filming was difficult at times because the leading lady was pregnant. Marilyn took 47 takes to deliver the line, "It's me, Sugar". She kept saying, "It's Sugar, me" or, "Sugar, it's me". Following the 30th take, Wilder had the line written on a blackboard. Another line also caused her problems. It was, "Where's the bourbon?" The scene required Marilyn to search through a chest of drawers and deliver the line. Forty times she said either, "Where's the bottle?", "Where's the whisky" or "Where's the bonbon?". Wilder had the line written on a piece of paper and put in the drawer. Then Marilyn became puzzled as to the location of the paper so Wilder placed it in every drawer. Marilyn eventually took 59 takes to film the scene. She was not happy with her opening scene. Remembered Wilder, "She called me after the first daily rushes . . . I hung up and [screenwriter I.A.L.] Diamond and I met and decided it was not good enough. She had just come on originally doing something with that ukulele. And we made up that new

introduction with a new entrance [showing Sugar] coming down to the train through that puff of steam. She was absolutely right about that." Marilyn remembered it slightly differently. "I'm not going back into that fucking film until Wilder re-shoots my opening. When Marilyn Monroe comes into a room, nobody's going to be looking at Tony Curtis playing Joan Crawford. They're going to be looking at Marilyn Monroe." The film was a commercial and critical success, reaching number three at the box office in 1959 earning $7 million and a further $8 million by 1964. Marilyn was paid $100,000 plus a 10 per cent share of the gross profits. It was during this film that co-star Curtis made his notorious remark comparing kissing Marilyn to "kissing Hitler". She could not understand the comment. Her gay publicist, Rupert Allan, remembered Marilyn as saying to him, "That's a terrible thing to say about anybody. I don't understand it either because every morning he would stick in his head and say how beautiful I looked and how wonderful it was and how exciting." Curtis later told *Time Out*, "She was a 600-pound gorilla, y'know. About 680 pounds actually . . . And she was like a mean 6-year-old girl. She would come and tell me that I was funnier than Jack Lemmon, and then she'd tell Jack she wished she were ending up with him at the end of the movie. It got to the point that nobody wanted to talk to her." Not long after filming wrapped Marilyn suffered a miscarriage. On October 1, 1959, she began filming *Let's Make Love* (1960) opposite French actor Yves Montand. It was to be a prescient title. Marilyn and Montand had an affair under the noses of their respective spouses. Marilyn supposedly thought Montand would leave his wife Simone Signoret for her but the Gallic actor evidently saw his dalliance as a mere fling. Perhaps the off-screen events affected Marilyn's performance because *Let's*

Make Love is generally considered to be Marilyn's worst starring film. During the filming of *Some Like It Hot* Arthur Miller had been turning his *Esquire* short story *The Misfits* about a group of disaffected cowboys into a vehicle for his wife. Marilyn's penultimate completed film was to be another fraught with difficulties, despite co-starring with her childhood idol Clark Gable and her friend Montgomery Clift. Filming was delayed by the backlog caused by an actors' strike. Shooting finally began at 9am on July 18, 1960, but it shut down a week later because director John Huston's gambling caused a cash flow problem. Marilyn's first scene was filmed on July 21. Shooting was postponed on July 30, and again on August 1, because Marilyn was 'indisposed'. On August 25, filming shut down because Huston had bled the company financially dry. Marilyn took the opportunity to fly to Los Angeles for a long weekend. Huston had spoken to Marilyn's doctors Hyman Engelberg and Ralph Greenson and told them Marilyn, in his opinion, should be hospitalised for a week to rest. On August 28, Marilyn entered Westside Hospital in Los Angeles. Producer Frank Taylor announced Marilyn had suffered "a breakdown" and that filming would be suspended for a week. It gave Huston time to find new finance. On September 5, Marilyn returned to Reno but was ill again on September 12, 13 and 19. Studio filming began on October 24, with Marilyn and Eli Wallach in a scene involving a truck. The film wrapped on November 4, 1960. It had cost $3,955,000 – the most expensive black-and-white film then made – and gone 40 days over schedule. Marilyn's marriage to Arthur Miller fell apart and the crew of *The Misfits* divided into two camps. Marilyn found Miller's diary where he had written a less than complimentary entry about her. "I'm not just a dumb blonde this time, I'm a crazy dumb blonde. And to think, Arthur did this to me. He was supposed to be writing this for me. He could have written anything and he came up with this." They flew home to New York from Hollywood in separate aeroplanes. On Friday November 11, a week after the film wrapped, the couple announced they would divorce. Five days later, Clark Gable died after suffering a massive heart attack 11 days earlier. The press jumped on Marilyn, claiming her behaviour on the set caused Gable's death. No one mentioned that 59-year-old Gable insisted on doing all his own stunts or the fact that he had smoked 60 cigarettes a day for over 30 years. When the film premièred on January 31, 1961, critics were not kind. Bosley Crowther of *The New York Times* wrote, "Characters and theme do not congeal. There is a lot of absorbing detail in it, but it doesn't add up to a point. Mr Huston's direction is dynamic, inventive and colourful. Mr Gable is ironically vital. (He died just a few weeks after shooting was done.) . . . But the picture just doesn't come off." Marilyn and Arthur Miller were divorced on January 20, 1961, a day chosen to minimise press coverage because it coincided with the inauguration of America's first Roman Catholic President, John F. Kennedy. Marilyn spent much of 1961 hospitalised for various physical and mental ailments. On April 23, 1962, she began filming *Something's Got To Give* opposite Dean Martin. The film was directed by George Cukor who had previously worked with Marilyn on *Let's Make Love*. At the same time that Marilyn was shooting that feature, Elizabeth Taylor was in Rome filming the epic *Cleopatra* (1963), the movie that eventually bankrupted 20th Century Fox. In retrospect, it appears as if the studio wanted Marilyn to leave the film so they could sue her for $1 million for breach of contract and recoup some of the money laid out on

Cleopatra. The script was regularly changed and the new sides were only sent to Marilyn at the last moment. Marilyn was invited to sing 'Happy Birthday' to President Kennedy at his Madison Square Garden birthday party on May 19, 1962, but was forbidden to go by the studio. Feigning a cold, she flew to New York anyway where the MC Peter Lawford introduced her as "the late Marilyn Monroe", a gentle dig at her constant tardiness. Marilyn was escorted by Isadore Miller, her former father-in-law, but rumours have surfaced over the years that she spent the night with the President at the Carlyle Hotel and may even have taken part in an orgy that night. Marilyn's friend Jim Haspiel, who attended the event, disputes this. "I can tell you with *authority*, that I was with Marilyn at her apartment at ten minutes to four in the morning. Categorically, Marilyn was not asleep at the Carlyle Hotel, and I didn't notice the President anywhere nearby us, either!" Nine days after the Madison Square party, Marilyn filmed the famous nude swimming scene for *Something's Got To Give*. The actress was not a good swimmer and utilised an unusual doggy paddle style. She celebrated her 36th birthday with a party on-set. On June 4, she was bedridden with a temperature of over 100 degrees. Four days later, she was fired. An advertisement was placed in *Weekly Variety*, supposedly by the crew 'thanking' Marilyn for losing them their jobs. It was actually placed by Fox, once again spinning against their biggest female draw. Negotiations began in earnest between studio and star; Dean Martin chivalrously refused to appear with anyone else. Marilyn was offered $500,000 for the film plus a bonus if it was completed on time. The film was due to re-shoot from September 16. It was not to be.
CAUSE: Marilyn was buried in Westwood Village Memorial Park, 1218 Glendon Avenue, Los Angeles 90024. Her death has been the subject of enormous speculation for many years and there seems to be no likelihood of it stopping in the near future. Was she murdered? Did she commit suicide? Did she die accidentally? Accounts vary according to who is talking. What is known is that according to the autopsy and death certificate Marilyn died of "acute barbiturate poisoning due to ingestion of overdose". Among the many unanswered questions about her death was the issue of how Marilyn managed to swallow up to 40 Nembutals without having a glass in her room – anyway the water had been turned off at the mains for some decoration. According to biographer Donald Wolfe, Marilyn spent her last afternoon at her home, 12305 Fifth Helena Drive, Brentwood, in the presence of her PR Pat Newcomb and her housekeeper Eunice Murray plus her son-in-law Norman Jefferies. Marilyn and Newcomb had a fight and the PR was asked to leave. That afternoon at around 3.30pm Attorney General Bobby Kennedy arrived at the house with Peter Lawford and the actor told Murray and Jefferies to go to the market. They were gone for about an hour. Later between 9.30 and 10pm Kennedy returned with two men and ordered Murray and Jefferies out of the house. When they came back they found a naked Marilyn lying in a comatose state in the guest cottage, not the master bedroom. An ambulance was called but Marilyn died on the way to the hospital and was returned to her house, placed in bed and the cover-up began. However, that's just one version of events. Another biographer, Donald Spoto, claims that Eunice Murray and Dr Ralph Greenson killed Marilyn by administering a barbiturate enema. Biographer Fred Lawrence Guiles postulates the suicide theory. Probably the most far-fetched theory comes from writer Robert Slatzer (who claims to have married Marilyn in Mexico on October 4, 1952, a day she was shopping in Los Angeles according to

her cheque book) who claimed in 1996
Marilyn was killed because she knew
the truth about the Roswell Incident
and was about to reveal all! Ho-hum.
You pays your money . . .
FURTHER READING: *Marilyn Monroe* –
Maurice Zolotow (London: W.H.
Allen, 1961); *The Agony Of Marilyn
Monroe* – George Carpozi, Jr. (London:
Consul Books, 1962); *The Complete
Films Of Marilyn Monroe* – Mark Ricci
& Michael Conway (Secausus: Citadel
Press, 1964); *Marilyn: The Tragic Venus*
– Edwin P. Hoyt (London: Robert
Hale, 1965); *Norma Jean: The Life Of
Marilyn Monroe* – Fred Lawrence
Guiles (London: W.H. Allen, 1969);
My Story – Marilyn Monroe (New
York: Stein & Day, 1974); *Marilyn* –
Joe Hembus (London: Tandem 1973);
Marilyn Monroe: A Life On Film –
David Robinson & John Kobal
(London: Hamlyn, 1974); *Marilyn
Monroe* – Joan Mellen (London: Star
Books, 1975); *Marilyn Monroe
Confidential* – Lena Pepitone and
William Stadiem (London: Sidgwick &
Jackson, 1979); *Who Killed Marilyn?* –
Tony Sciacca (New York: Manor
Books, 1976); *Finding Marilyn: A
Romance* – David Conover (New York:
Grossett & Dunlap, 1981); *Marilyn
Lives!* – Joel Oppenheimer (London:
Pipeline Books, 1981); *The Last Sitting*
– Bert Stern (London: Black Cat,
1982); *Marilyn Monroe: Murder
Cover-Up* – Milo Speriglio (Van Nuys:
Seville Publishing, 1982); *The Life And
Curious Death Of Marilyn Monroe*
– Robert F. Slatzer (New York:
Pinnacle Books, 1982); *Monroe: Her
Life In Pictures* – James Spada with
George Zeno (London: Sidgwick &
Jackson, 1982); *Marilyn Monroe* –
Janice Anderson (London: W.H.
Smith, 1983); *Marilyn On Marilyn* –
Roger G. Taylor (London: Comet,
1983); *Norma Jeane: The Life And
Death Of Marilyn Monroe* – Fred
Lawrence Guiles (London: Granada,
1985); *Goddess: The Secret Lives Of
Marilyn Monroe* – Anthony B. Summers

(London: Victor Gollancz, 1985);
Marilyn Monroe: A Never-Ending Dream
– Guus Luijters (London: Plexus,
1986); *Marilyn Mon Amour* – André de
Dienes (London: Sidgwick & Jackson,
1986); *Marilyn Monroe: A Life Of The
Actress* – Carl E. Rollyson, Jr. (Ann
Arbor: UMI Research Press, 1986);
The Making Of The Misfits – James
Goode (New York: Limelight Editions,
1986); *The Marilyn Conspiracy* – Milo
Speriglio with Steven Chain (London:
Corgi, 1986); *Requiem For Marilyn* –
Bernard of Hollywood (Bourne End:
The Kensal Press, 1986); *Marilyn
Among Friends* – Sam Shaw & Norman
Rosten (London: Bloomsbury, 1987);
*The Unabridged Marilyn: Her Life From
A–Z* – Randall Riese & Neal Hitchens
(New York: Congdon & Weed, 1987);
Marilyn Monroe: An Appreciation – Eve
Arnold (London: Hamish Hamilton,
1987); *Marilyn At Twentieth
Century-Fox* – Lawrence Crown
(London: Planet Books, 1987); *Marilyn*
– Gloria Steinem & George Barris
(London: Victor Gollancz, 1987);
Conversations With Marilyn – W.J.
Weatherby (London: Sphere, 1987);
*The Marilyn Scandal: Her True Life
Revealed By Those Who Knew Her* –
Sandra Shevey (London: Sidgwick &
Jackson, 1987); *Joe And Marilyn: A
Memory Of Love* – Roger Kahn
(London: Sidgwick & Jackson, 1987);
Marilyn Monroe – Graham McCann
(Cambridge: Polity Press, 1988);
Marilyn: A Biography – Norman Mailer
(London: Spring Books, 1988);
Marilyn – Neil Sinyard (Leicester:
Magna Books, 1989); *Marilyn On
Location* – Bart Mills (London:
Sidgwick & Jackson, 1989); *Marilyn
Monroe And The Camera* – Lothar
Schirmer (London: Bloomsbury,
1989); *Marilyn: A Hollywood Life* – Ann
Lloyd (London: W.H. Smith, 1989);
*Marilyn: The Ultimate Look At The
Legend* – James R. Haspiel (London:
Smith Gryphon, 1991); *Marilyn Monroe
In Her Own Words* – Guus Luijters
(London: Omnibus Press, 1991); *The*

Birth Of Marilyn: The Lost Photographs Of Norma Jean By Joseph Jasgur – Jeannie Sakol (London: Sidgwick & Jackson, 1991); *Marilyn And Me* – Susan Strasberg (London: Doubleday, 1992); *Marilyn: The Last Take* – Peter Harry Brown & Patte B. Barham (London: William Heinemann, 1992); *Marilyn's Men: The Private Life Of Marilyn Monroe* – Jane Ellen Wayne (London: Robson Books, 1992); *Marilyn Monroe: The Biography* – Donald Spoto (London: Chatto & Windus, 1993); *The Marilyn Files* – Robert F. Slatzer (New York: SPI, 1992); *Crypt 33: The Saga Of Marilyn Monroe: The Final Word* – Adela Gregory & Milo Speriglio (New York: Birch Lane Press, 1993); *Young Marilyn: Becoming The Legend* – James R. Haspiel (London: Smith Gryphon, 1994); *My Sister Marilyn: A Memoir Of Marilyn Monroe* – Berniece Baker Miracle & Mona Rae Miracle (London: Weidenfeld & Nicolson, 1994); *Milton's Marilyn* – James Kotsilibas-Davis & Joshua Greene (London: Schirmer Art Books, 1994); *Marilyn: Her Life In Her Own Words* – George Barris (London: Headline, 1995); *The Prince, The Showgirl And Me* – Colin Clark (London: HarperCollins, 1995); *Marilyn's Addresses* – Michelle Finn (London: Smith Gryphon, 1995); *Falling For Marilyn: The Lost Niagara Collection* – Jock Carroll (London: Virgin, 1996); *The Men Who Murdered Marilyn* – Matthew Smith (London: Bloomsbury, 1996); *The Ultimate Marilyn* – Ernest W. Cunningham (Los Angeles: Renaissance Books, 1998); *The Assassination Of Marilyn Monroe* – Donald H. Wolfe (London: Little, Brown, 1998); *Marilyn Monroe* – Barbara Leaming (London: Weidenfeld & Nicolson, 1998); *My Week With Marilyn* – Colin Clark (London: HarperCollins, 2000); *Marilyn Monroe* – Paul Donnelley (Harpenden: Pocket Essentials, 2000); *Cursum Perficio: Marilyn Monroe's Brentwood Hacienda* – Gary Vitacco-Robles (Lincoln: iUniverse, 2000); *To Norma Jeane With Love, Jimmie* – Jim Dougherty as told to LC Van Savage (Chesterfield: BeachHouse Books, 2001); *Victim: The Secret Tapes of Marilyn Monroe* – Matthew Smith (London: Century, 2003); *Marilyn Handbook* – Mike Evans (London: MQ Publications, 2004); *The DD Group: An Online Investigation Into The Death of Marilyn Monroe* – David Marshall (Lincoln: iUniverse, 2005); *Marilyn Monroe: Private and Undisclosed* – Michelle Morgan (London: Constable, 2007); The Genius and the Goddess – Jeffrey Meyer (London: Hutchinson, 2009); *Marilyn Revealed: The Ambitious Life Of An American Icon* – Ted Schwarz (Taylor, 2009); *The Secret Life of Marilyn Monroe* – J. Randy Taraborrelli (London: Sidgwick & Jackson, 2009).

Ricardo Montalbán, KSG

(RICARDO GONZALO PEDRO MONTALBÁN Y MERINO)
Born November 25, 1920
Died January 14, 2009
Latin lover. Born in Mexico City and raised in Torreon, Montalbán was the youngest of four children born to Jenaro Montalbán and Ricarda Merino. In 1940 Montalbán and his brother Carlos moved to New York where Montalbán found work in the play, *Her Cardboard Lover*. The following year he made his film debut in shorts that appeared on Soundies film jukeboxes. Montalbán's first starring film was *He's A Latin From Staten Island* (1941). Towards the end of 1941 Montalbán discovered that his mother was seriously ill so he returned to Mexico for her final days. There he made a dozen films in Spanish and was recognised as a great talent. He went to Hollywood in 1943 and movie bosses wanted to change his name to Ricky Martin but he refused. His first major film was *Border Incident* (1949), opposite George Murphy. On November 21, 1949 Montalbán

became the first Hispanic actor to appear on the front cover of *Life*. Six foot Montalbán found himself cast as Latin lovers, Red Indians or even Asians in films. He was the Blackfoot Indian chief in *Across The Wide Missouri* (1951), a Japanese Kabuki actor in the Oscar-winning *Sayonara* (1957) and a Japanese gangster in *Hawaii Five-O* (1968). In 1967 he played a space villain, Khan Noonien Singh, in *Star Trek*, a role he reprised 25 years later in *Star Trek: The Wrath Of Khan* (1982). To television viewers he was known as the mysterious Mr Roarke on *Fantasy Island* from 1978 with Herve Villechaize intoning "The plane! The plane!" His films included: *Mystery Street* (1950) as Peter Moralas, *Right Cross* (1950) as Johnny Monterez, *Two Weeks With Love* (1950) as Demi Armendez, *Mark Of The Renegade* (1951) as Marcos Zappa, *My Man And I* (1952) as Chu Chu Ramirez, *Sombrero* (1953) as Pepe Gonzales, *Latin Lovers* (1953) as Roberto Santos, *The Saracen Blade* (1954) as Pietro Donati, *Cortigiana Di Babilonia* (1954) as Amal, *La Rivolta Dei Gladiatori* (1958), *The Reluctant Saint* (1962) as Don Raspi, *Love Is A Ball* (1963) as Duke Gaspard Ducluzeau, *Cheyenne Autumn* (1964) as Little Wolf, *Madame X* (1966) as Phil Benton, *The Deserter* (1971) as Natachai, *Escape From The Planet Of The Apes* (1971) as Armando, *Conquest Of The Planet Of The Apes* (1972) as Armando, *Won Ton Ton, The Dog Who Saved Hollywood* (1976), *The Naked Gun: From The Files Of Police Squad!* (1988) as Vincent Ludwig and the grandfather in *Spy Kids 3-D: Game Over* (2003). In 1993 he was awarded a Lifetime Achievement Award by the Screen Actors Guild. On October 26, 1944 he married Georgiana Young (b. Los Angeles, California, September 30, 1923, d. Los Angeles, California, November 13, 2007), the half-sister of Loretta Young and they had four children: Laura (b. August 12, 1945), Mark (b. March 13, 1947), Anita

(b. March 21, 1949) and Victor (b. April 18, 1952). In 1998 HH Pope John Paul II awarded the devoutly Catholic Montalbán a knighthood of the Order of St. Gregory the Great. CAUSE: In 1951 he fell off his horse during the filming of *Across The Wide Missouri* and injured his spine when another horse trampled on him, which left him with a permanent limp. The pain worsened as Montalbán got older and in 1993 he underwent spinal surgery that lasted 9½ hours. The operation left him paralysed from the waist down and confined to a wheelchair. He died at his home in Los Angeles, California from congestive heart failure. He was 88-years-old.

Yves Montand
(IVO LIVI)
Born October 13, 1921
Died November 9, 1991
Gallic charmer. Yves Montand is seen as a great French lover when, in fact, he wasn't French at all. He was born, after a 13-hour labour, in Monsummano Alto, Tuscany, Italy, the son of Jewish peasants. When Mussolini tightened his grip on power the family moved to Marseille. Montand became a music hall star of the Moulin Rouge when he was 19 thanks to the interest shown in his talent by Edith Piaf. Another lucky break came when Marcel Carné cast him in *Les Portes De La Nuit* (1946) as Jean Diego. He then appeared in *L'Idole* (1947) and *Souvenirs Perdus* (1950). On August 14, 1949, he met and, supposedly, fell in love with Simone Signoret and they married on December 22, 1951. She introduced him to extreme left-wing politics (he didn't renounce communism until 1968) and her influential friends such as Jean-Paul Sartre and Françoise Sagan. Meanwhile, Montand's star rose in France and he appeared in films such as *Napoléon* (1955) as Marshal Lefebvre, *Marguerite De La Nuit* (1955) as Monsieur Léon, *Les Sorcières De*

Salem (1957) as John Proctor and *La Legge* (1958) as Matteo Brigante. In 1960 he set off to conquer Hollywood, starring with Marilyn Monroe in *Let's Make Love* (1960) and appearing in a few other films before returning to France where he began to take an active role in politics. His final films were well received and included *Jean De Florette* (1986) as Cesar Soubeyran and *Manon De Sources*, in which he reprised the same part.

CAUSE: Montand died in Senlis, France, from a heart attack. He was 70. FURTHER READING: *You See, I Haven't Forgotten* – Yves Montand with Hervé Hamon and Patrick Rotman (London: Chatto & Windus, 1992).

Maria Montez

(MARIA AFRICA ANTONIA GRACIA VIDAL DA SANTO SILAS)
Born June 6, 1912
Died September 7, 1951

"The Queen of Technicolor". Born in Barahona, Dominican Republic, the second daughter of Isidoro Gracia García, an exporter of guayacan wood and Honorary Vice Consul of Spain and Regla Teresa Maria Vidal, she had ten siblings: Isidoro, Aquilino, Joaquín, David, Ada, Consuelo, Luz, Luis, Jaime and Teresita. She wanted to act from an early age and taught herself English by reading magazines and listening to songs. On November 28, 1932 she married Irish banker William McFeeters, who worked for the First National City Bank of New York in Barahona. They divorced after seven years when the redhead Montez became a model in New York, arriving on July 3, 1939. On her arrival she knocked five years off her age. She was paid $50 for her first magazine cover. After RKO dithered, she signed a contract with Universal for $150-a-week. She changed her name to Maria Montez taking her surname from the dancer and courtesan Lola Montez (who was really called Eliza Rosanna Gilbert and was born in Ireland).

Montez made her film début in *Boss Of Bullion City* (released March 1, 1940) as Linda Calhoun. For someone who couldn't sing, act or dance it is surprising her career lasted as long as it did. She added glamour to eastern adventure tales. Her films, mostly for Universal, included: *The Invisible Woman* (1940) as Marie, *Moonlight In Hawaii* (1941) as Ilani, *That Night In Rio* (1941) as Inez, *South Of Tahiti* (1941) as Melahi, *Bombay Clipper* (1942) as Sonya Dietrich Landers, *Mystery Of Marie Roget* (1942) as Marie Roget, *White Savage* (1943) as Princess Tahia (which earned her the nickname the Queen of Technicolor), *Ali Baba And The Forty Thieves* (1944) as Amara, *Gypsy Wildcat* (1944) as Carla, *Cobra Woman* (1944) as Tollea/Naja, *Sudan* (1945) as Naila, *Tangier* (1946) as Rita and *Pirates Of Monterey* (1947) as Marguerita. Oddly, in 1941, she claimed that her fiancé Lieutenant Commandant Claude Strickland was missing in action. In fact, she had no fiancé and made the announcement to get publicity. If she thought that she did not receive enough attention when she arrived at the Universal commissary, she would leave and return with a noisy entourage. On October 1, 1942 she saw the French actor Jean-Pierre Aumont (1911–2001) at Dearbone train station and said for her it was love at first sight. Montez consulted her astrologer for an auspicious day for the match and they married at her home on July 13, 1943 with Charles Boyer as best man. The guests of honour were her astrologer, Carroll Lighter Norwell, her gardener and two masseurs. The bride and groom kissed 112 times during the ceremony. A few days later, Aumont went off to serve in the war with the Free French Army in North Africa, Italy and France. On February 14, 1946, at 8.14am, Montez gave birth to a baby girl weighing 8lbs 3oz that they named Maria Christina. Under the name Tina Marquand she also became an actress.

In 1946 Montez sued Universal after she barely appeared in *The Exile* (1946). Although she won $250,000 it was not a smart career move. After making *Arabian Nights* (1942) in which she played Sheherazade, she announced, "When I look at myself, I am so beautiful I scream with joy!" The director of *Cobra Woman* (1944) said, "Montez is one of the few actresses whose behaviour is influenced by her work as an actress, if she is a queen, she will demand you to bow before her, even on the breaks, but if she is a slave, you could treat her very bad and she will not complain." In 1946 Montez and Aumont moved to France where they made a number of films in Europe: *Hans Le Marin* (1949), *Portrait D'Un Assassin* (1949), *Il Ladro Di Venezia* (1950), *Amore E Sangue* (1951), *Schatten Uber Neapel* (1951) and *La Vendetta Del Corsaro* (1951). Reports circulated that Hollywood wanted her back but it was not to be. CAUSE: Montez, who had a 36" bust and stood 5'7", liked to take very hot baths perhaps to ease the depression over her weight gains. During one of these she suffered a heart attack and probably drowned at home in Suresnes, near Paris. Her sisters Ada and Teresita found her. Aumont said that she had sunk into the water until just the top of her head from her eyes up was visible. No autopsy was performed. She was 39. Her funeral was in the Saint Pierre of Chaillot Roman Catholic Church, on September 11, 1951. She was buried in section 24E of Cimetière de Montparnasse, Paris. On April 27, 1996 a new airport in Barahona was named the Maria Montez International Airport.

Robert Montgomery
(HENRY MONTGOMERY JR)
Born May 21, 1904
Died September 27, 1981
Dapper star. Born in Fishkill Landing, New York, the elder of two sons of Henry Montgomery, Sr (b. New York,

May 1868, d. June 25, 1922 by jumping off the Brooklyn Bridge) and Mary Weed Barney (b. Bayonne, Hudson County, New Jersey, March 30, 1875). Most biographies report that Montgomery's father was the president of the New York Rubber Company. In fact, the 1920 Federal Census reveals that he was a private secretary. However, he must have had a rapid promotion because the report of his death published in July 1922 reports that he was "the former president of the New York Rubber Company". Montgomery made his Broadway debut in 1924. On April 14, 1928 he married the actress Elizabeth Daniel Allen (b. Louisville, Jefferson County, Kentucky, Boxing Day 1904). A daughter, Martha Bryan, was born on October 13, 1930, but died of spinal meningitis 14 months later. The year before, he had made his film debut in *So This Is College* (1929). That year Montgomery signed a contract with MGM. He became a star after playing opposite Norma Shearer in *Private Lives* (1931). On April 15, 1933 he became a father again when Elizabeth Montgomery was born. She would go on to be an actress and star in the television show *Bewitched*. She died of cancer on 18 May 1995. In 1935, Montgomery was elected President of the Screen Actors Guild, a position he held again in 1946. A son, Robert, was born on April 17, 1936. The next year Montgomery was nominated for a Best Actor Oscar for playing a psychopath who carried around a human head in *Night Must Fall* (1937). He lost out to Spencer Tracy for *Captains Courageous*. He was again nominated for *Here Comes Mr Jordan* (1941) but this time lost to Gary Cooper for *Sergeant York*. He served with the navy during the Second World War, becoming a lieutenant commander. Back in Tinseltown in 1945, he directed some scenes in *They Were Expendable* after John Ford fell ill. Two years later, he made his directorial debut proper with *Lady In The Lake* (1947), in which he also starred. That year, the Republican-supporting Montgomery was a friendly witness before the House Un-American Activities Committee. In 1950 he was divorced. His last film was *The Gallant Hours* (1960), which he narrated and also directed and co-produced with its star, James Cagney. His other films included: *Untamed* (1929), *Their Own Desire* (1929), *The Divorcee* (1930), *The Big House* (1930), *The Sins Of The Children* (1930), *Our Blushing Brides* (1930), *Private Lives* (1931), *The Easiest Way* (1931), *Hell Below* (1933), *When Ladies Meet* (1933), *Forsaking All Others* (1934), *Hide-Out* (1934), *No More Ladies* (1935), *The Last Of Mrs Cheyney* (1937), *Ever Since Eve* (1937), *Live, Love And Learn* (1937), *Yellow Jack* (1938), *Three Loves Has Nancy* (1938), *The Earl Of Chicago* (1940), *Mr And Mrs Smith* (1941), *Rage In Heaven* (1941), *They Were Expendable* (1945), *Ride The Pink Horse* (1947) which he also directed, *June Bride* (1948) and *The Saxon Charm* (1948). From 1950 until 1957 he hosted the Emmy Award-winning television programme *Robert Montgomery Presents*. After the show finished he became convinced that television was censored and controlled by politicians. The only show that would give him airtime was NBC's *Tonight* and some of his more extreme comments were, ironically, censored. He was married to Elizabeth Harkness from December 9, 1950 until his death. He delighted in the success of daughter Elizabeth but was never tempted to return to acting. "If you are lucky enough to be a success," he said, "by all means enjoy the applause and the adulation of the public. But never, never believe it."

CAUSE: 6'1" Montgomery died aged 77 in New York. The cause was cancer, the same disease that killed his daughter Elizabeth and on August 13, 2000, his son Robert.

Clayton Moore
Born September 14, 1908
Died December 28, 1999
The Lone Ranger, always. Born in Chicago, Illinois, Moore was a circus performer and male model who entered movies in 1938 as a stunt man. He appeared in over 70 films most of them B-picture Westerns (two of which co-starred Jay Silverheels, who later played Tonto to Moore's best-known role) but it was for his portrayal of that masked avenger of evil John Reid better known as The Lone Ranger that he became a hero to millions. With the stirring *William Tell Overture* and a hearty "Hi-ho, Silver – Away!" Moore first appeared on television on September 15, 1949 playing the role until 1952 when he was replaced by John Hart. Two years later, he was back for another three-year stint. He also appeared as the Ranger on the big screen twice (*The Lone Ranger* [1956] and *The Lone Ranger And The Lost City Of Gold* [1958]). Most actors don't want to become typecast in one particular part, believing that it limits their working opportunities. Clayton Moore was precisely the opposite – he lived to be The Lone Ranger and would wear his costume at numerous personal appearances, striving to instil the Ranger's code of beliefs in his young fans. However, it all ultimately went wrong for him. In 1980 the four-times married Moore was sued by a studio who wanted to make a new version of the story (*The Legend Of The Lone Ranger* [1981], starring the instantly forgettable Clinton Spillsbury) and didn't want Moore to wear his mask in public. He responded by wearing wraparound sunglasses that looked like a mask and suing. After five years' litigation and much public sympathy, he won the right to don the famous mask in public again. The Lone Ranger Rode Again!

CAUSE: He died of a heart attack aged 91 in West Hills Hospital, 20 miles north-west of Los Angeles. His last request, to be buried in his white hat and black mask, was not honoured.

Cleo Moore

Born October 31, 1928
Died October 25, 1973
Blonde bombshell. Born in Baton Rouge, Louisiana, the blonde 37-22-36 Moore began working life as a model in 1948 and made her film début that year in *Congo Bill* (1948) as Lureen/Ruth Culver. She became known for appearing as the bad girl star of a series of low-budget flicks created by Hugo Haas, including *Strange Fascination* (1952), *One Girl's Confession* (1953) as Mary Adams, *Thy Neighbor's Wife* (1953), *The Other Woman* (1954) as Sherry, *Bait* (1954) as Peggy and *Hit And Run* (1957) as Julie. Her other films included *This Side Of The Law* (1950), *Rio Grande Patrol* (1950) as Peppie, *Dynamite Pass* (1950) as Lulu, *Bright Leaf* (1950) as Cousin Louise, *Hunt The Man Down* (1950) as Pat Sheldon, *Women's Prison* (1955) and *Over-Exposed* (1956) as Lily Krenska alias Lila Crane. She was also rather good at creating publicity, embarking on stunts such as a public seven-minute kiss with a DJ and claiming to be running for Louisiana state Governor. CAUSE: She died in Inglewood, California, of a heart attack, six days before her 45th birthday.

Dudley Moore, CBE

Born Good Friday (April 19), 1935
Died March 27, 2002
'Sex Thimble'. Dudley Stuart John Moore was born in Charing Cross Hospital, London, the son of Jock Moore (b. Glasgow 1898 as John Havlin, d. 1971 of colon cancer), a taciturn, illegitimate Scots railwayman, and his wife, Ada Francis Hughes (b. 1900, d. London, October 16, 1981 of a stroke), a shorthand typist. A sister, Barbara, had been born in 1929. The new arrival was sickly and stunted, his left leg withered below the knee; "It looks like a sweet child's," he was later to say. Both feet were clubbed but the right one corrected itself naturally. Moore's mother shrieked, "This isn't my baby! This isn't my baby!" when she held him for the first time. For much of the first seven years of his life Moore was in hospital, the only child in a ward full of badly wounded soldiers. The nursing staff were not very affectionate towards the small boy. In later years he was to recall that the only kindness shown to him was a goodnight kiss from a nurse. He commented, "In many ways my entire life is based on recapturing that single moment of affection." Like many of small stature or who have physical disabilities 5'2½" Moore was bullied at school. The children at Dagenham County High School, the local grammar school a few hundred yards from where he lived, nicknamed him 'Hopalong'. To escape their attentions he made them laugh. In 1954 he won a music scholarship to Magdalen College, Oxford. However, he hated his time there, feeling insecure socially and sexually. "I felt very ill-equipped. Everybody spoke so factually. I had the feeling I was in the presence of very superior beings. I felt they'd all had a classical education, were older and had done national service, which I hadn't because of my leg. I felt very inferior." At Magdalen he composed and conducted the scores for productions of *Antony and Cleopatra* and Aristophanes' *The Frogs*. Following his graduation, Moore worked as a jobbing jazz pianist. In 1959 he made a record, *Strictly For The Birds*, with the future Beatles producer George Martin. In 1960 he was invited to join the Edinburgh revue show *Beyond The Fringe* alongside Peter Cook, Jonathan Miller and Alan Bennett. Peter Cook wrote the majority of the show (about 67 per cent according to Moore's own estimate) with Alan Bennett and Jonathan Miller contributing the rest. Moore did not write any of it. The show opened on August 22, 1960 at Edinburgh's Lyceum Theatre. Moore's

insecurity came raging to the top: "I felt totally constricted and overpowered. I was completely mute in front of these intellectual giants." The show was a sensation, killing off the traditional theatrical revue and playing in the West End (Fortune Theatre, May 10, 1961) and on Broadway (John Golden Theater, October 1962). Its fans included the Queen, Harold Macmillan and John F. Kennedy. In retrospect *Beyond The Fringe* seems remarkably unbarbed, much more inclined to fantasy and nonsense. In fact, among the sharpest pieces was Moore's parody of Peter Pears and Benjamin Britten in an ornate setting of Little Miss Muffet – one of those parodies which make it difficult to see the original in the same light ever again. Moore didn't lose his virginity until he was 23 and it was during the run of *Beyond The Fringe* that Moore had his first encounter with fellatio. "In terms of oral sex, I never had anybody's mouth around my knob until 1960. I was doing *Beyond The Fringe* in London and there was this girl with huge tits I was just mad for, who one day came to the theatre and said: 'Dudley, I want to suck your cock.' Well, there I was 25 years old and never had it done to me . . . Of course I was never keen on doing it myself but one soon realises there are results from reciprocity." Alan Bennett commented that Moore's stage performance "was often merely a perfunctory interruption of the more prolonged and energetic performance going on in his dressing room". When the show came to the end of its life the BBC hired Moore to star in his own show. During the final months of the run Moore had become close to Peter Cook and he insisted that Cook was hired along with him. Thus *Not Only . . . But Also* was born. The show began on January 9, 1965 and ran until May 13, 1970. The show contained many brilliant comedic moments including the Dud and Pete "Dagenham Dialogues" in which Cook

played the stupid one who thought he knew what he was talking about, who set out to educate Moore, the even stupider one. Sometimes Cook would ad lib causing his partner to corpse. Two additional shows were also recorded in Australia featuring guest star Barry Humphries and broadcast on February 8 and 15, 1971. Cook and Moore were friendly off screen as well with Cook as the natural leader and Moore the natural disciple. "I followed him around like some sort of chihuahua," Moore admitted later. When Cook and his then mistress fled her irate husband and sought refuge at Moore's new home in the middle of the night, they were amazed to discover that it was a replica of Cook's own house – down to the William Morris wallpaper. Cook said of his friend, "Dudley had gone from being a subservient little creep, a genial serf, to become an obstinate bastard who asserted himself." Both men wanted to make the move into films but Cook caused a furious argument by excluding Moore from the writing of *Bedazzled* (1968), their first and best big-screen vehicle. The film was not a success. In 1969 he spoke to the press of his deep depressions and his loss of will to do anything at all for the first time. When Cook's personal life ran into trouble, as it often did, he sought refuge on a five-year tour and in alcohol. Moore followed his partner. When the tour lurched to its end in California in 1975 he broke up the partnership, determined to stay on in Hollywood and have a further crack at the film industry. Moore stayed for 18 months but found no work. Back in England in 1976 Cook released *Derek And Clive* – a three-year-old private tape which gave the old Pete and Dud characters a scatological dimension. Moore was Derek and Cook Clive. Moore returned home and helped Cook to promote the album and make two more. They were poor imitations of the original. Cook became more and more cruel to his friend and the two split. Moore went back to Hollywood for another attempt at stardom. This time it would be third time lucky. He appeared in *The Hound Of The Baskervilles* (1978) as Doctor Watson and *Mr Spiggot And Mrs Ada Holmes And Foul Play* (1978) as Stanley Tibbets. In December 1978 George Segal walked out on the film *10* on its first day of filming. The director Blake Edwards knew Moore from psychoanalysis and immediately cast him in the role of George Webber, a libidinous middle-aged musician, opposite Julie Andrews and the gorgeous Bo Derek. Moore was not going to let this opportunity pass him by. On its release in 1979, the film made 1,000 per cent profit, and its star was voted "Sex Symbol of the Year" by the Hollywood Women's Press Club. The Sex Thimble was born. But then another flop followed. *Wholly Moses* (1980) saw Moore in the dual role of Harvey and Herschel. He later said that it was the only thing in his career he really hated. Moore quickly made another film, *Arthur* (1981), which was a smash. Moore was nominated for a Best Actor Oscar, losing out to Henry Fonda for *On Golden Pond*. John Gielgud won the Best Supporting Actor Academy Award as Hobson, the butler of the spoiled, drunk, rich boy Arthur Bach, and Christopher Cross performed the winning theme song 'Arthur's Theme' ('Best That You Can Do') which he co-wrote with Burt Bacharach, Carole Bayer Sager and Peter Allen. Moore and Gielgud further won the American critics' Golden Globe Award. The film took $30 million at the box office within three months. Moore's star blazed quickly and burned out just as quickly. Although he continued to make films they were mostly eminently forgettable. Who can now remember *Six Weeks* (1982, as Patrick Dalton, a tearful tale of a man and a woman brought together by her dying

daughter), *Romantic Comedy* (1983, as Jason Carmichael, two writers of romantic comedies fall in love), *Lovesick* (1983, as Saul Benjamin, psychoanalyst falls for patient), *Unfaithfully Yours* (1984, as Claude Eastman, a middle-aged musician mistakenly thinks another musician is having an affair with his wife), *Best Defense* (1984, as Wylie Cooper, an American tank goes out of control in Kuwait), *Micki + Maude* (1984, as Rob Salinger, a television personality simultaneously gets his wife and girlfriend pregnant), *Crazy People* (1990, as Emery Leeson, ad-man goes mad, is committed, and enlists asylum inmates in brilliant ad campaign) or *Blame It On The Bellboy* (1992, as Melvyn Orton, an estate agent is mistaken for mafia hit-man)? He resorted to making *Arthur 2: On The Rocks* (1988) reprising his role as Arthur Bach. John Gielgud was recast which was distinctly odd because his character had died at the end of the first film. Towards the end of his life Moore suffered the same depression that had wrecked Peter Cook. His marriage (the fourth) to Nicole Rothschild lay in tatters, destroyed by claims and counter-claims of violence, promiscuity and hard-drug abuse. His fortune, much diminished, had in large part been spent by his wife. On March 21, 1994, they had a violent argument that resulted in Moore being arrested. Nicole was later to admit that she "was drunk as a skunk". Moore was married four times. On June 14, 1968 at Hampstead Register Office, he married the actress Suzy Kendall (b. Belper, Derbyshire, 1944 as Frieda Harriet Harrison). The witnesses were Peter Cook and the novelist Pat Booth. The marriage was dissolved in Kingston, Surrey, on September 15, 1972 on the grounds of "irretrievable breakdown". On September 20, 1975 in Las Vegas he married, as her second husband, the 5′4″ actress Tuesday Weld (b. New York, August 27, 1943 as Susan Ker Weld). Tuesday Weld was actually born on a Friday but changed her name legally when she was 15. They had a son, Patrick Havlin, in February 1976 but separated in 1978 and were divorced in 1980. Between 1980 and 1988 he lived with the actress Susan Anton (b. Oak Glen, California, October 12, 1950) who was 10 inches taller than him but they did not make it legal. At the Little Church of the West in Las Vegas on February 21, 1988 he married 5'8" dyslexic model Brogan Lane (b. 1956 as Denise Lane). They divorced in September 1992. In 1983 or possibly 1984 he had chatted up the woman who was to become his fourth wife, the adopted, silicone-enhanced, 5'5" dyslexic Nicole Rothschild (b. California, February 1964), when she walked in front of his car as he waited at a set of traffic lights. They married on April 16, 1994 and their son, Nicholas Anthony, was born on June 28, 1995. Their relationship was torrid. Nicole who had had lesbian affairs in the past would make love to other women while Moore watched. Her ex-husband and his girlfriend were also in the house. Nicole would also hire $500-a-go prostitutes to dance scantily clad for her husband. He had also been involved with busty actress Anna Leroy in 1960, model Celia Hammond for a year in the early Sixties, actress Shirley Anne Field (b. Bolton, June 27, 1938), 5'8" March 1991 *Penthouse* Pet of the Month Sandi Korn (b. Westchester, New York, December 26, 1966), singer-songwriter Lynsey de Paul (b. Cricklewood, north London, June 11, 1948 as Lynsey Reuben) in 1972, 5'7" actress Candy Clark (b. Norman, Oklahoma, June 20, 1947 as Candace June Clark) plus numerous one-night stands. In June 2001 Moore was awarded the CBE in the Queen's Birthday Honours List. CAUSE: It was in late 1996 that Moore began to have a slight problem with a finger that felt to him slightly out of control. Added to this his balance

was slightly off and his speech slightly slurred. People assumed he was drunk, which made him angry, since he had never had a drinking problem. He underwent some tests in London, but no conclusions were reached. In March 1997 he returned to New Jersey and began preparations for another round of concerts. In the autumn of 1997, when it seemed that the mystery of his failing health would never be resolved, he went to the Mayo Clinic in Minnesota for a comprehensive evaluation. This resulted in open heart surgery and a long rehabilitation stay. However, the rehabilitation programmes did not help and a new search for neurological answers began. By the end of 1997, he had been misdiagnosed with a variety of ailments, ranging from strokes to multiple system atrophy, none of them quite explaining his strange and increasing symptoms. Finally, Dr Martin Gizzi, a neurologist at JFK Medical Center in New Jersey, took a look at his slowed eye movements and recognised the familiar symptom of Progressive Supranuclear Palsy. The reality began to set in that he was truly on a downhill path. He made his illness public in September 1999, explaining that the condition turned his vision hazy, his speech slurred and his walk impaired. In a television interview, he said: "I am trapped in this body and there is nothing I can do about it." During the last few weeks of his life, Moore was barely able to speak and finally was unable to walk. He had used a wheelchair outside of the house but with help he continued to walk inside his home until a few days before his death. Moore died at his home in Plainfield, New Jersey, aged 67 of pneumonia, one of the most common complications of Progressive Supranuclear Palsy. Dudley Moore was buried during a private hour-long ceremony in Watchung, near Plainfield, on April 2, 2002. FURTHER READING: *Dudley Moore –* Douglas Thompson (London: Little,

Brown, 1996); *The Authorised Biography Of Dudley Moore* – Barbara Paskin (London: Sidgwick & Jackson, 1997).

Agnes Moorehead
Born December 6, 1900
Died April 30, 1974
Sterling support star. If you were able to choose in which film to make your début then you could do worse than to choose a controversial and successful film such as *Citizen Kane* (1941). That's what the redheaded Moorehead did. Born in Clinton, Massachusetts, the daughter of a Presbyterian minister (she claimed to believe every word in the Bible) and a mother who outlived her, Agnes Robertson Moorehead was educated at Muskingum College (where she obtained a BA), the University of Wisconsin (where she took an MA in English and public speaking) and the American Academy of Dramatic Art. She later taught speech and drama to schoolchildren, using the long holidays to brush up her own technique, albeit having made her professional début in 1917 with the St Louis, Missouri, Municipal Opera Company. In 1929 she made her first appearance in New York and then began appearing on the radio in various shows. In 1940 she joined Orson Welles' Mercury Theater Company and the following year she was cast in the role of Mrs Mary Kane, the mother of the citizen of the title. It was for her portrayal of Fanny Minafer in Welles' *The Magnificent Ambersons* (1942) that she won the first of her four Academy Award nominations. Her subsequent films included: *The Big Street* (1942) as Violette, *The Youngest Profession* (1943) as Miss Featherstone, *Government Girl* (1943) as Mrs Wright, *Jane Eyre* (1944) as Mrs Reed, *Dragon Seed* (1944), *Since You Went Away* (1944) as Emily Hawkins, *Mrs Parkington* (1944) as Aspasia Conti, for which she won her second Oscar nomination, *Our Vines Have Tender Grapes* (1945) as Bruna Jacobson, *Keep Your Powder*

Dry (1945) as Lieutenant-Colonel Spottiswoode, *Dark Passage* (1947) as Madge Rapf, *The Woman In White* (1948) as Countess Fosco, *Johnny Belinda* (1948) as Aggie McDonald and her third Oscar nod, *Station West* (1948) as Mrs Caslon, *Summer Holiday* (1948) as Cousin Lily, *Caged* (1950) as Ruth Benton, *Black Jack* (1950) as Mrs Birk, *Without Honor* (1950) as Katherine Williams, *Fourteen Hours* (1951) as Christine Hill Cosick, *Show Boat* (1951) as Parthy Hawks, *Main Street To Broadway* (1953) as Mildred Waterbury, *Magnificent Obsession* (1954) as Nancy Ashford, *All That Heaven Allows* (1955) as Sara Warren, *Meet Me In Las Vegas* (1956) as Miss Hattie, *Pardners* (1956) as Matilda Kingsley, *The True Story Of Jesse James* (1957) as Mrs Samuel, *The Story Of Mankind* (1957) as Queen Elizabeth, *Jeanne Eagels* (1957) as Madame Neilson, *Raintree County* (1957) as Ellen Shawnessy, *Pollyanna* (1960) as Mrs Snow, *How The West Was Won* (1962) as Rebecca Prescott and *Hush . . . Hush, Sweet Charlotte* (1964) as the sarcastic housekeeper Velma Cruther, for which she received her fourth and final Oscar nomination. That same year she was cast as the witch Endora in the hit sitcom *Bewitched*. A closeted lesbian (actor Paul Lynde described her as "classy as hell, but one of the all-time Hollywood dykes"), Moorehead was the lover and mentor of a well-known Hollywood actress who went on to marry three times and is forever linked (though not by an affair) with Elizabeth Taylor. Moorehead married twice. When she caught her first husband, John Griffith Lee (June 5, 1930–June 11, 1952), in bed with a woman she shouted at him that if he could have mistresses, so could she. Her second marriage, to Robert Gist, lasted for five years from 1953 until March 12, 1958.
CAUSE: Agnes Moorehead died aged 73 in Rochester, Minnesota, of lung cancer. She was just one of many

including John Wayne, Susan Hayward, Lee Van Cleef and Pedro Armendariz who contracted cancer after working on *The Conqueror* (1956).

Kenneth More

Born September 20, 1914
Died July 12, 1982

The poor man's David Niven. Kenneth Gilbert More was born in Gerrards Cross, Buckinghamshire. After a brief stint working in Sainsbury's, he went to Canada where he worked as a fur trapper before being deported. One of his earliest jobs in the theatre was as a stagehand at the infamous Windmill Theatre, the only London venue to allow nudity on stage, albeit in 'tableaux' (i.e. the performers were not allowed to move). His first task was to rush on stage at the end of each scene during the blackout and hand the girls their dressing gowns, because the Lord Chamberlain's dictum forbade any of them to move if their breasts were bare. On Boat Race nights Hooray Henrys from Oxbridge would invade the theatre determined to make the girls move by putting sneezing powder or chewing gum or pellets in a pea shooter and aiming at the performers. Obviously, when they sneezed their breasts wobbled, to the absolute delight of the audience. When he was promoted to assistant stage manager one of More's more unpleasant tasks was to keep an eye out for men pleasuring themselves. If he saw anything untoward he would alert the commissionaire with the words: "A4 Wanker, *Times*, C17 *Daily Mail*", depending on the seat number and the newspaper that the guilty party was using to cover his furtive activities. The commissionaire would then tell the culprit that the manager wished to see them and they left, no doubt red faced. In 1936 More made his stage début at the Windmill when Eric Woodburn, many years later to make a name for himself as Dr Snoddie in *Dr Finlay's Casebook*, twisted his ankle and was

unable to perform. Unfortunately, Woodburn's was the one part More hadn't learned and he was unable to sing his song either. The audience, not sure if it was a comedy or drama, howled their appreciation and that was the incident that made More decide to become an actor. He appeared in bit parts in a number of films, including *Carry On London* (1937) before the outbreak of war. He failed to get into the RAF because he hadn't passed the School Certificate and failed the medical. Instead he became a lieutenant in the Royal Naval Volunteer Reserve. In 1940 he married Beryl Johnstone (d. 1969) but it wasn't a match made in heaven and they divorced, though not before the birth of a daughter, Susan Jane. Following the end of the war he was cast in *School For Secrets* (1946). Spotted by Noël Coward, the Master cast him as George Bourne in his play *Peace In Our Time* in July 1948. Coward also had desires to cast More elsewhere. However, he was rebuffed. "Oh, Mr Coward, sir! I could *never* have an affair with you, because – because – *you remind me of my father!*" More once told his admirer. Coward approached the object of his lust, ruffled his hair and said, "Hello, son." The two men subsequently became friends and whenever Coward saw him would always call him "Son" as a private joke. More went on to appear in *Scott Of The Antarctic* (1948) as Lieutenant Teddy Evans, *Man On The Run* (1948) as Newman, *Now Barabbas* (1949) as Spencer, *Chance Of A Lifetime* (1950) as Adam, *No Highway* (1951) as Dobson, *Brandy For The Parson* (1952) as Tony Rackham and *The Yellow Balloon* (1953) as Ted Palmer but it was playing Ambrose Claverhouse in *Genevieve* (1953), for which he was paid £2,500, that made him a star. In 1952 he married for the second time. His wife was Mabel Edith Barkby known as 'Bill' and he had a daughter, Sarah Elizabeth (b. King's College

Hospital, London, 1954), by her. He had his biggest cinematic successes in the Fifties with films such as *Doctor In The House* (1954) as Richard Grimsdyke, for which he won a Best Actor BAFTA, *Our Girl Friday* (1954) as Pat Plunkett, *The Deep Blue Sea* (1955) as Freddie Page, *Reach For The Sky* (1956) as legless war hero Douglas Bader, *The Admirable Crichton* (1957) as William Crichton, *The Sheriff Of Fractured Jaw* (1958) as Jonathan Tibbs playing opposite Jayne Mansfield, *A Night To Remember* (1958) as Second Officer Charles Herbert Lightoller in a story about the *Titanic*, *North West Frontier* (1959) as Captain Scott and *The Thirty-Nine Steps* (1959) as Richard Hannay. In the Sixties he was lauded for playing Jolyon Forsyte in a BBC adaption of John Galsworthy's *The Forsyte Saga*. He was paid £15,500 to play the part. More's film work gradually began to dry up, although he played cameo roles in a few biggies and some larger parts, viz. *Sink The Bismarck!* (1960) as Captain Jonathan Shepard, *The Longest Day* (1962) as Captain Colin Maud, *Battle Of Britain* (1969) as Group Captain Baker, *Oh! What A Lovely War* (1969) as Kaiser Wilhelm II and *Scrooge* (1970) playing the Ghost of Christmas Present. From 1974 onwards he played the inquisitive Father Brown in the ATV television series of the same name. It was to be his last major role. On March 17, 1961, he met the beautiful, blonde, Irish, Catholic actress Angela McDonagh Douglas (b. October 29, 1940) while appearing in *The Greengage Summer*. They married in Kensington Congregational Church on St Patrick's Day, 1968 with Roger Moore as the best man.
CAUSE: He died of Parkinson's disease at 27 Rumbold Road, Fulham, London SW7 aged 67. He was worth £186,918 when he died.
FURTHER READING: *More Or Less – Kenneth More* (London: Coronet, 1979).

Morecambe & Wise

(JOHN ERIC BARTHOLOMEW)
Born May 14, 1926
Died May 28, 1984
(ERNEST WISEMAN)
Born November 27, 1925
Died March 21, 1999
Britain's best-loved comedy duo. The two men were not close friends despite their long partnership. (Perhaps because one came from Lancashire and the other Yorkshire?) It was a business relationship, as one critic remarked: "What drove Eric Morecambe? Ernie Wise. What drove Ernie Wise? Money." Eric was an only child but his mother and father had 15 brothers and a sister between them. He wasn't very conscientious at school, coming 45th out of 49 pupils, and didn't bother to turn up for exams. Ernie's career began in a double act with his father known as Carson and Kid, later Bert Carson and the Little Wonder. Eric and Ernie were persuaded by Eric's mum to be a double act. They were sacked from the Windmill because they weren't as funny as another double act, Hancock and Scott – Tony Hancock and Derek Scott. Morecambe & Wise's first BBC show was so awful they urged the corporation to take it off the air. Ernie, like many in showbiz, was very careful with his money in real life and not just on the shows. He bought his house cheaply because it was in the flightpath of Heathrow. Ernie always signed autographs "Ernie Wise, OBE". Their film work was limited to *The Intelligence Men* (1964), *That Riviera Touch* (1966) and *The Magnificent Two* (1967).
CAUSE: Eric died of a heart attack at Cheltenham General Hospital while appearing in a stage show at the Roses Theatre, Tewkesbury alongside his friend Stan Stennett. More than 1,000 people attended his funeral. He left £517,205. In November 1998 Ernie went on a Caribbean cruise but fell ill with two strokes and a heart attack. On January 24, 1999, he was operated on and doctors performed a triple by-pass.

He died of heart failure at 7am at Nuffield Hospital, Wrexham Park, Buckinghamshire. He left £503,299 (gross); £341,484 (net).
FURTHER READING: *Eric & Ernie: The Autobiography Of Morecambe & Wise* – Dennis Holman (London: W.H. Allen, 1973); *Morecambe & Wise* – Graham McCann (London: Fourth Estate, 1999).

Frank Morgan

(FRANCIS PHILLIP WUPPERMANN)
Born June 1, 1890
Died September 18, 1949
The Wizard of Oz. There are some actors who can appear in around 100 films, yet will always be known for just one role. Frank Morgan was just such an actor. Born in New York, one of 11 children, he followed his actor brother into the business, eventually signing for MGM. He appeared in, among many others, *The Daring Of Diana* (1916) as John Briscoe, *Who's Your Neighbor?* (1917) as Dudley Carlton, *At The Mercy Of Men* (1918) as Count Nicho, *The Golden Shower* (1919) as Lester, *Manhandled* (1924) as Arno Riccardi, *Scarlet Saint* (1925) as Baron Badeau, *Love's Greatest Mistake* (1927) as William Ogden, *Dangerous Nan McGrew* (1930) as Muldoon, *Laughter* (1930) as C. Morton Gibson, *Reunion In Vienna* (1933) as Anton, *Hallelujah, I'm A Bum* (1933) as Mayor John Hastings, *Billion Dollar Scandal* (1933) as Masterson, *When Ladies Meet* (1933) as Rogers Woodruf, *Bombshell* (1933) as Pop Burns, *The Affairs Of Cellini* (1934) as the Duke of Florence, for which he was nominated for a Best Actor Oscar, *Escapade* (1935) as Karl, *Dimples* (1936) as Professor Eustace Appleby, *The Great Ziegfeld* (1936) as Jack Billings, *Saratoga* (1937) as Jesse Kiffmeyer, *Mother Carey's Chickens* (1938) as Captain Carey, *Sweethearts* (1938) as Felix Lehman, *Balalaika* (1939) as Ivan Danchenoff, *Broadway Melody Of 1940* (1940) as Bob Casey, *Honky Tonk* (1941) as Judge Cotton,

Tortilla Flat (1942) as the Pirate, for which he was nominated for a Best Supporting Actor Oscar, *Casanova Brown* (1944) as Mr Ferris, *Yolanda And The Thief* (1945) as Victor Budlow Trout, *Courage Of Lassie* (1946) as Harry MacBain, *The Three Musketeers* (1948) as King Louis XIII and *Gold Fever* (1952) as Nugget Jack. However, it is his role in *The Wizard Of Oz* (1939) for which he is best known. Bizarrely, Morgan plays five roles in the film: Professor Marvel, the doorman of the Emerald City, a taxi driver, the Guardian of the Emerald City Gates and the Wizard. What is even stranger is that he wasn't first choice for the part – the producers wanted W.C. Fields.
CAUSE: Morgan had been cast as Buffalo Bill in *Annie Get Your Gun* when he died in his sleep in Beverly Hills, California. He was 59. He was buried in Greenwood Cemetery, 5th Avenue & 25th Street, Brooklyn, New York 11232.

Robert Morley, CBE

Born May 26, 1908
Died June 3, 1992
'The First Gentleman'. Born at Broadoak, Semley, Wiltshire, Robert Adolph Wilton Morley was the future son-in-law of actress Gladys Cooper and Herbert Buckmaster, the man who invented the Buck's Fizz. As a child Morley suffered from chest pains and biliousness, put down to overeating by the family doctor, much to the consternation of his parents who believed he had to be fed to keep his strength up. Originally intended for a career in the diplomatic service, on September 29, 1926, he auditioned for and was accepted at RADA. On May 28, 1928, he made his stage début at the Margate Hippodrome appearing in *Dr Syn*. His first West End appearance came playing a pirate in *Treasure Island* on Boxing Day 1929 at the Strand Theatre. Nine years later, he entered films playing King Louis XVI

in *Marie Antoinette* (1938) and soon gained a reputation as a fine character actor who excelled both in pompous and easygoing parts. He appeared in *Major Barbara* (1941) as Andrew Undershaft, *The Young Mr Pitt* (1942) as Charles James Fox, *I Live In Grosvenor* Square (1945) as the Duke of Exmoor, *The Ghosts Of Berkeley Square* (1947) as General Burlap, *The African Queen* (1951) as Reverend Samuel Sayer, *Melba* (1953) as Oscar Hammerstein, *The Story Of Gilbert And Sullivan* (1953) as W.S. Gilbert, *Beau Brummell* (1954) as King George III, *Beat The Devil* (1954) as Petersen, *The Adventures Of Quentin Durward* (1955) as King Louis XI, *Around The World In 80 Days* (1956) as Ralph, *The Sheriff Of Fractured Jaw* (1958) as Uncle Lucius, *Oscar Wilde* (1959) as Oscar Wilde, *Libel* (1959) as Sir Wilfred, *The Doctor's Dilemma* (1959) as Sir Ralph Bloomfield-Bonington, *The Battle Of The Sexes* (1959) as Robert MacPherson, *The Young Ones* (1961) as Hamilton Black, *The Road To Hong Kong* (1962) as The Leader, *Murder At The Gallop* (1963) as Hector Enderby, *Of Human Bondage* (1964) as Dr Jacobs, *Topkapi* (1964) as Cedric Page, *A Study In Terror* (1965) as Mycroft Holmes, *Genghis Khan* (1965) as the Emperor of China, *Those Magnificent Men In Their Flying Machines, Or How I Flew From London To Paris In 25 Hours 11 Minutes* (1965) as Lord Rawnsley, *Hotel Paradiso* (1966) as Henri Cotte, *Lola* (1969) as Judge Roxborough, *Doctor In Trouble* (1970) as Captain George Spratt, *Who Is Killing The Great Chefs Of Europe?* (1978) as Max and *Little Dorrit* (1988) as Lord Decimus Barnacle. He compiled two collections of unintentional mistakes and was one of the original team captains on *Call My Bluff*. He married Joan Buckmaster (b. July 5, 1910) on February 23, 1940, at Caxton Hall, London. They had two sons, Sheridan (b. December 5, 1941), and Wilton (b. Fairmans Cottage, Wargrave, Berkshire, August 27, 1951,

at 6.30am) and one daughter, Annabel (b. Fairmans Cottage, Wargrave, Berkshire, June 10, 1946). She was born six weeks prematurely and spent the first period of her life living in an airing cupboard. Oddly, both Sheridan Morley and his ex-wife have written biographies of Robert Morley.

CAUSE: For a devoted race-goer such as Morley, it was perhaps appropriate that he died on Derby Day, three days after suffering a stroke from which he never regained consciousness. He was 84.

FURTHER READING: *Robert Morley: Larger Than Life* – Margaret Morley (London: Coronet, 1980); *Robert My Father* – Sheridan Morley (London: Weidenfeld & Nicolson, 1993).

Vic Morrow

Born St Valentine's Day 1929
Died July 23, 1982

Tragedian. Despite a solid body of television movies to his credit, Vic Morrow is known today for two reasons – his daughter is the beautiful and talented actress Jennifer Jason Leigh and he died under tragic circumstances. Vic Morrow was born in the Bronx, New York, one of three children (there was a brother and a sister) of Harry Morrow, an electrical engineer, and Jean Kress, in a typical, middle-class, Jewish family. He left school at 17 to join the US Navy. Using the same government grant to help ex-servicemen that Rod Steiger and Jeff Corey used, Morrow went to Florida State University to study law. Many lawyers need to be good actors and while at university Morrow discovered he preferred acting on stage to acting in a court of law. He said his decision to study "had more to do with the drama of a great courtroom performance than any love of the law". He first studied at Mexico City College (1950) where he "performed in bilingual productions of Shakespeare, Molière and Shaw". He then moved to New York and joined the Actors' Workshop on a two-year course under

Paul Mann. Morrow was asked not to act professionally until his training was over so in order to make ends meet, he drove a cab for a living. He was then cast as Stanley Kowalski in a summer stock production of Tennessee Williams' *A Streetcar Named Desire.* He was signed to MGM and made his film début in Pandro S. Berman's *Blackboard Jungle* (1955) as Artie West, "a tough talking, surly, street punk". He was lauded by the critics but Morrow said, "Sure, the notices were great, but y'da thought they'd picked me up out of an ashcan and made me a star. Hell, I'd already done Shakespeare, Chekhov and all those other cats." Morrow was regularly cast as the bad guy or the heavy in films and he became disillusioned. His films included: *Tribute To A Bad Man* (1956) as Lars Peterson, *Men In War* (1957) as Corporal James Zwickley, *Hell's Five Hours* (1958) as Nash, *King Creole* (1958) as Shark, *God's Little Acre* (1958) as Shaw Walden, *Cimarron* (1960) as Wes Jennings, *Portrait Of A Mobster* (1961) as Dutch Schultz and *Posse From Hell* (1961) as Crip. Morrow moved behind the cameras and began directing after studying at the University of Southern California. He also began directing community theatre. Morrow also began appearing on television and was cast as Sergeant Chip Saunders in the ABC military series *Combat.* The show ran from October 2, 1962 until August 29, 1967 (the day that also saw the very last episode of *The Fugitive* broadcast) and the cast were sent to boot camp for a week to toughen them up. The programme made him a star but also cost him his first marriage. In 1965 he was divorced after seven years from Barbara Turner, an actress and screenwriter, by whom he had two daughters Carrie Ann (b. 1958) and Jennifer Leigh (b. February 5, 1962), and three years later his series for which he had been paid $5,000 a week was cancelled. The divorce (she had

had an affair with Robert Altman), which alienated him from his children, and the end of *Combat* made Morrow depressed and it would be seven years before he was back in front of the cameras in the instantly forgettable *Target: Harry* (1969) in which he played Harry Black. For most of the Seventies 5'9" Morrow appeared in television movies such as *A Step Out Of Line* (premièred February 26, 1971) as Joe Rawlins, *Travis Logan, D.A.* (premièred March 11, 1971) as Travis Logan, *River Of Mystery* (premièred October 1, 1971) as Phil Munger, Truman Capote's *The Glass House* (premièred February 4, 1972) as Hugo Slocum, *The Weekend Nun* (premièred December 20, 1972) as Chuck Jardine, *The Police Story* (premièred March 20, 1973) as Sergeant Joe LaFrita, *Tom Sawyer* (premièred March 23, 1973) as Injun Joe, *Nightmare* (premièred January 8, 1974) as Detective Rausch, *The California Kid* (premièred September 25, 1974) as Sheriff Roy Childress, *Death Stalk* (premièred January 21, 1975) as Leo Brunner, *The Night That Panicked America* (premièred October 31, 1975) as Hank Muldoon, *The Ghost Of Cypress Swamp* (1976) as Toni Stone, *The Man With The Power* (premièred May 24, 1977) as Paul, *The Hostage Heart* (premièred September 9, 1977) as Steve Rockewicz, *Curse Of The Black Widow* (premièred September 16, 1977) as Lieutenant Gully Conti, *Wild And Wooly* (premièred February 20, 1978) as Warden Willis and *Stone* (premièred August 26, 1979) as Morgan Teckington. He also appeared playing Ames in the serial about slavery, *Roots,* and on the big screen in *The Take* (1974) as Manso, *Dirty Mary Crazy Larry* (1974) as Everett Franklin, *The Bad News Bears* (1976) as Coach Roy Turner, *Treasure Of Matecumbe* (1976) as Spangler, *Funeral For An Assassin* (1977) as Michael Cardiff and *The Evictors* (1979) as Jake Rudd. It seemed that he was unable to land strong parts in first-rate films. A second marriage (1975) was doomed to failure and Morrow's mother died in 1978. His younger daughter changed her name to Jennifer Jason Leigh in an effort to escape being labelled "Vic Morrow's kid". Vic saw this as the ultimate act of disloyalty. He began drinking heavily. Then one day in 1982 the call came to appear as Bill Connor in John Landis' film *Twilight Zone: The Movie*.

CAUSE: At 2.30am on July 23, 1982, John Landis was desperately trying to film a scene called Time Out which had Morrow wading knee-deep through the Santa Clara river carrying Renee Chen and My-ca Le, two illegally employed Vietnamese children, one aged 7, the other 6. The children were not professional actors and they weren't on proper work permits. They should also have been in bed but their parents were thrilled to have their family involved in a real Hollywood film so they raised no objection. Landis was keen to get the scene in the bag. The segment was to take place in the jungles of Vietnam, the real location being Indian Dunes Park, a dirt bike park near Six Flags over Magic Mountain theme park. Also in the shot would be a village under military siege, and a helicopter coming towards them. The shot would be littered with gigantic explosions. It didn't go well. Even the special effects people were concerned by the scene. Then the helicopter entered and Landis screamed, "Lower! Lower! Lower!" to direct the chopper downwards. It hovered just 24 feet above the water and cameras filmed the entire event. There was even a cameraman standing on the skid of the helicopter, filming as the explosions went off. Just when the pilot of the helicopter was about to fly away, two more blasts came and he lost control. Extras fled but Morrow lost his grip on Renee and as he struggled to get hold of her, the helicopter landed on top of her and crushed her to death. The 40-ft diameter blades decapitated

Morrow and My-ca Le. The cameras continued to roll. Landis and his assistant director made their way down to the scene, and his assistant found Morrow's torso in the water. The people in the helicopter escaped injury. An announcement was made to the cast and crew: "Leave your equipment where it is. Everyone go home. Please, everyone go home!" Jack Rimmer, one of the fire-safety officers, covered Morrow's torso and placed it on a bank. As he was wading across the river to the village to douse the fires there, Rimmer found My-ca Le's head in the water. A crew member brought over a plastic rubbish bag and placed the little boy's severed head inside. Special effects technician Kevin Quibell located Morrow's head and that was placed in another black plastic bag. On July 25, Landis spoke at Morrow's funeral: "Tragedy can strike in an instant but film is immortal. Vic lives forever. Just before the last take, Vic took me aside to thank me for the opportunity to play this role." Vic Morrow was buried in Block 5 of Mount of Olives at Hillside Memorial Park, 6001 West Centinela Avenue, Los Angeles 90045. The inscription on his gravestone written by Carrie reads 'Victor "Vic" Morrow 1929–1982 I loved him as "Dad" to everyone else he was "Vic"'. In his will, written in purple felt tip pen on yellow paper, just seven months before his death, Morrow left the bulk of his million-dollar estate (house, bank accounts, safety deposit boxes, personal effects and Macho the dog) to Carrie. Jennifer, who had remained estranged from her father, received the token sum of $100. Earlier in his career Morrow had been called upon to fly in a helicopter in the film *Dirty Mary Crazy Larry*. He refused saying, "I'm not getting up in the helicopter. I have a premonition that I'm going to get killed in a helicopter crash." On July 27 both children were buried – Renee is buried in Forest Lawn Glendale and My-ca Le in

Cerritos. Indian Dunes is now owned by the Newhall Ranch Development Company of Newhall, California. They closed the area to movie and film production in the early Nineties for what they termed "agricultural use". Indian Dunes was used for many movies and television programmes, most notably *Black Sheep Squadron* with Robert Conrad and *Some Kind Of Hero* with Richard Pryor. Many silent films and westerns were also filmed there. On January 9, 1984, in a preliminary hearing prior to the court case, Landis openly mocked the prosecutor. On April 23 of the same year, Landis and two co-workers were indicted on three charges of "the involuntary manslaughter of the actors Vic Morrow, Renee Chen and My-ca Le". The trial of Landis and four others eventually opened on September 3, 1986, over four years after the event. On May 29, 1987, all five defendants were acquitted. On June 25, 1988, Landis invited all members of the jury to a private screening of his new film *Coming To America*.

Barry Morse

Born June 10, 1918
Died February 2, 2008
Stalwart. Born in Bethnal Green, east London, 5'10" Morse trained at the Royal Academy of Dramatic Art and made his film debut in the 1942 comedy *The Goose Steps Out* with Will Hay. He worked steadily for the BBC. "I did a great number of television shows for the BBC, not because I was a particularly gifted young actor, but because I was available and willing," he said. "The hardware was so unreliable you'd start a show with two cameras and before you had been on the air for ten minutes they would both be broken down . . . Audiences would be asked to wait for three quarters of an hour for the 'mechanical interruption', while they dragged the camera into a corner and bashed it with spanners to try to make it better." Other early film credits

included *When We Are Married* (1942), *There's A Future In It* (1943), *Daughter Of Darkness* (1948) and *No Trace* (1950). He emigrated to Canada in 1951 where he earned a good living in radio and television. He became a Canadian citizen in 1953. He was best known for playing Lieutenant Philip Gerard in 120 episodes of *The Fugitive* (1963–1967) (for which he said, "I got more hate mail than anyone since Adolf Hitler") and Professor Victor Bergman in *Space: 1999* (1975–76). His last film, a year before his death, was *I Really Hate My Job*, released in 2007. It is likely that Morse played more roles in television, radio, film, and on stage than any other actor; more than 3,000 during his lifetime. On March 26, 1939 he married the actress Sydney Sturgess (b. Ipoh, Malaysia, March 5, 1915, d. Toronto, Ontario, Canada, September 30, 1999 of Parkinson's disease) and they had two children: actress Melanie Virginia Sydney Morse MacQuarrie (b. London, June 13, 1945, d. Montague, Prince Edward Island, Canada February 1, 2005 from a heart attack) and actor Hayward Morse (b. London, September 13, 1947).
CAUSE: Barry Morse died at University College Hospital in London of congestive heart failure. He had been admitted three days earlier after he began experiencing blackouts. He was 89.

Peggy Mount, OBE

Born May 2, 1916
Died November 13, 2001
Battleaxe. Peggy Mount's foghorn voice made her instantly recognisable. Producers used it to good effect - they even starred her in a sitcom called *George And The Dragon*. Margaret Rose Mount was born in Southend-on-Sea, Essex and educated at Leigh North Street School, Southend. Her grandfather had started the first minstrel show on the end of Yarmouth pier. Her father died when she was

nine. Years later she described her mother as "not a nice woman. She never put her arms round me or gave me a kiss. She was always telling me that I was overweight and ugly. If you're told that often enough, you become ugly, and no matter what other people say you believe it." She severed connections with her family and, though she had a sister, they did not speak for more than 50 years. Determined to become an actress, she took lessons under Phyllis Reader at weekends. In the Forties and Fifties she was a stage regular touring the country going wherever there was work. She made her film début in *The Embezzler* (1954) playing Mrs Larkin. *Sailor Beware!* (1956) in which she played Emma Hornett launched Peggy Mount's career as Britain's favourite dragon. She was Ada in the television series *The Larkins* (from September 19, 1958) with David Kossoff portraying her mild husband. The two played a warring couple of country publicans, and a similar theme was developed in a later series, *George And The Dragon* (November 19, 1966–October 31, 1968) which saw her teamed with Sid James. She was in films such as *Ladies Who Do* (1963), *One Way Pendulum* (1964), *Hotel Paradiso* (1966) and was a formidable Mrs Bumble, the beadle's wife, in Lionel Bart's joyous *Oliver!* (1968) opposite Harry Secombe. Rarely off the television screen she worked twice with her friend Pat Coombs, firstly in *Lollipop Loves Mr Mole* (October 25–November 29, 1971) and later in the old people's home comedy *You're Only Young Twice* (September 6, 1977–August 11, 1981). "I've never married," Peggy Mount said, "but I worked with a lot of very eligible men and I've had my chances." In later years, she revealed that in the early Seventies she had unofficially "adopted" a teenage boy, whose own mother had died and whom she regarded as her son. Throughout her life, Peggy Mount suffered from

detached retinas, causing her to have no vision in the centre of her eyes. In 1998, she lost her sight completely while on stage in *Uncle Vanya* at the Chichester Festival Theatre. She said, "The audience had no idea. But soon the word got out and I lost my nerve. Not working is my greatest regret. It was always my wish to die working." CAUSE: Peggy Mount died aged 85 in Northwood, London, following a stroke.

Arthur Mullard
(ARTHUR MULLORD)
Born September 19, 1910
Died December 11, 1995
Cockney heavy. For generations Arthur Mullard was the typical television and movie cockney. His battered face (the result of an early career as a boxer), gruff voice and performances in shows such as *The Arthur Askey Show*, *Romany Jones*, *On The Rocks*, *Hancock's Half Hour*, *Celebrity Squares*, *Bootsie & Snudge*, *Vacant Lot* and *Yus My Dear* endeared him to millions. Born in Peabody Buildings, Essex Road, Islington, London, N1, the son of a labourer, Mullard was a typical Englishman with an attitude that saw him rarely travel further than Southend except when he was working. He lived at 2 Manning House, Fielding Crescent, London, N5, a council maisonette, despite appearing in over 100 films, including *Oliver Twist* (1948), *The Lavender Hill Mob* (1951), *Pickwick Papers* (1952), *The Belles Of St Trinian's* (1954), *The Ladykillers* (1955), *The Loneliness Of The Long Distance Runner* (1962), *The Wrong Arm Of The Law* (1962), *Ladies Who Do* (1963), *Morgan – A Suitable Case For Treatment* (1966), *The Great St Trinian's Train Robbery* (1966), *Casino Royale* (1967), *Chitty Chitty Bang Bang* (1968), *Lock Up Your Daughters!* (1969) and *On The Buses* (1971). Following his retirement he spent most of his time in local pubs boozing, which he said was his main pleasure in life.

Arthur Mullard left school at 14 and despite the recommendation of his teachers ("This boy is a born actor") became a butcher's boy. Joining the army before the legal age of 18 he boxed regularly in the Royal Army Medical Corps, becoming champion and earning a gold medal and a flat nose for his trouble. After three years he left the army and returned to Civvy Street and unemployment. That was when Arthur returned to boxing. For a time he worked as a 'totter' (rag and bone man) with his uncle and also tried his hand and other bits at life modelling for art students. In 1940 he was called up and joined the Royal Artillery Light Anti-Aircraft training camp at Aberystwyth, where he was quickly promoted to sergeant. Following his demobilisation Mullard went back to totting before deciding to take his teachers' advice and have a go at "the acting lark". One of his first jobs was appearing as a heavy in the Mae West play *Diamond Lil* at the Prince of Wales Theatre. It would be the start of a highly successful career in show business. *TV Times* described Arthur as "quite simply the best heavy the British cinema and television have ever produced." However, five months after his death, his daughter Barbara spoke at length about how her father wasn't the lovable cockney with a heart of gold that the public took him for, but a child molester whose behaviour forced his wife to commit suicide. Over the years many offspring of stars have written memoirs that reveal their parents had more in common with Cruella de Ville than the loving family-oriented image they presented to the press. According to Barbara, who admits she has had mental breakdowns and received psychiatric help, "The real [Arthur Mullard] was a domineering pervert" . . . "I loved going on long walks with him across Hampstead Heath. It was only after my 13th birthday that things began to change . . . My mum Flo had gone

into hospital with polio. He needed someone to take her place. First I became his domestic slave, then I became his sex slave. According to him, satisfying his carnal needs was part of my womanly duties." Barbara recalled the first time Mullard allegedly abused her. They were in the kitchen and he reportedly put his penis on the table. In her *naïveté* Barbara thought it was "a long-stemmed mushroom". She reported that her father told her, "You're the fruit that I've grown. I'm entitled to have the first taste. I'm your father. I have to instruct you about life. This is my job." "That's how he rationalised what he was doing," she commented. "He was doing his duty as a good father [. . .] I didn't think, 'I'm being sexually abused, this shouldn't be happening.' I just thought that if your father does something, you accept it and that it is a new experience you are having." Barbara said whenever she washed she would place a lump of wood against the door to wedge it shut. "As I got older he thought having his way with me was part of his conjugal rights. I ceased to be his daughter . . . I was his partner and I had to provide sex for him. Afterwards, he'd wash himself and say, 'Better not let your mother know . . . she'll go potty if she finds out, she'll have a right go at you.'" Again according to their daughter, Mullard beat his wife Flo, regularly punching out her teeth and verbally abusing her. Flo suffered from mental problems brought on, her daughter believes, by Mullard's cruelty and was often institutionalised. Mullard kept Barbara off school to minister to all his needs. When she was 18 Barbara suffered a nervous breakdown. In 1961 Flo Mullard committed suicide aged 49 with a massive drugs overdose. In his autobiography, Mullard recalled his wife's death and said her suicide did not sink in for two days. "Then I went round to the pub, got pissed and cried my eyes out. It was a tragedy that took me a long time to get over because I was shattered. If she had died in hospital, the shock would have not been so great, but a suicide leaves a feeling that something should have been done to prevent it . . . Memories came flooding back of the good times and bad times we shared; things she said and did which made no sense at the time were now crystal clear. She had no fear of death. She was a good mother." Not surprisingly, Barbara blamed her father for the death of her mother. "The quality of my mother's life was zero. On top of everything else she knew that her husband was having sex with her daughter. I knew she knew. One day she did actually come in when something was going on. But she blamed me. She attacked me as if I'd seduced her husband . . . She should have saved me from him but she attacked me. Mum must have known I was being abused, but she was impotent to do anything about it. Suicide was her way of dealing with the problem." Barbara said that Flo had left a note blaming her suicide on what Arthur was doing to her, but claimed he had ripped up the note in front of her. Barbara quickly left home and married but her marriage failed due, she believes, to her father's abuse. She had one son, David. Her second marriage produced three children before her husband died in 1990. Barbara claimed that even when married her father insisted on a "little cuddle" and that the only time that he made no advances was when she was pregnant. Towards the end of her life when Arthur Mullard was ill his daughter nursed her father at her Essex home. When he died he left her just £5,000. The remainder of his estate, estimated at £245,000, went to the National Children's Home. How many of the allegations about Arthur Mullard *et al* are true? The only people who can refute the charges are dead and obviously in no position to answer back. It is interesting that Mullard's younger son, comedian Johnny, said that Arthur had been "a very good father to me and brought me up very well. He taught me about art and poetry and literature. [Arthur admits in his autobiography that he had never read a book from cover to cover.] Arthur was a very clever man. He played the fool, but he went much deeper than the dumb image on television. He was always giving me lots of money. He was very generous to my wife and our children. I certainly was never abused by my father, either mentally or physically." Joan Crawford adopted four children. In her will she wrote, "It is my intention to make no provision herein for my son Christopher or my daughter Christina for reasons that are well known to them." Arthur Mullard did the same to his kids. Could either of them have known how bitter their children's revenge would be?

CAUSE: He died aged 85 in London after a long illness.

FURTHER READING: *Oh, Yus, It's Arthur Mullard* – Arthur Mullard (Everest Books, 1977).

Richard Mulligan

Born November 13, 1932
Died September 26, 2000
Hang-dog actor. Born in New York, New York, Mulligan's face was his fortune and caused perhaps his acting skills to be overlooked. Originally intending to be a playwright, Mulligan found fame on the stage in local theatre rather than behind a typewriter. He was given a big break with his own television show *The Hero* (1966) in which he played Sam Garret, a TV cowboy star. The show flopped. His films included: *Love With The Proper Stranger* (1963) as Louie, a bellboy in *40 Pounds Of Trouble* (1963), *One Potato, Two Potato* (1964) as Joe Cullen, *The Group* (1966) as Dick Brown, *The Undefeated* (1969) as Dan Morse, *Little Big Man* (1970) as General George Armstrong Custer,

Irish Whiskey Rebellion (1972), *From The Mixed-Up Files Of Mrs Basil E. Frankweiler* (1973) as Mr Kincaid, *Visit To A Chief's Son* (1974) as Robert, *The Big Bus* (1976) as Claude Crane, *Scavenger Hunt* (1979) as Marvin Dummitz, *S.O.B.* (1981) as Felix Farmer, *Trail Of The Pink Panther* (1982) as Clouseau, Sr., *Meatballs Part II* (1984) as Coach Giddy, *Teachers* (1984) as Herbert Gower, *Micki + Maude* (1984) as Leo Brody, *The Heavenly Kid* (1985) as Rafferty, *Doin' Time* (1985) as *Mongo Mitchell, A Fine Mess* (1986) as Wayne 'Turnip' Parragella and provided the voice of Einstein in *Oliver & Company* (1988). On the small screen he played Burt Campbell in *Soap* from September 13, 1977 until the show's demise on April 20, 1981. He returned to play Reggie Potter in *Reggie* (August 2–September 1, 1983), the American version of *The Fall And Rise Of Reginald Perrin* but American audiences did not take to the show and it was cancelled after five episodes. More successful was his sitcom *Empty Nest* which ran from October 8, 1988 until July 8, 1995. Mulligan played Dr Harry Weston, a paediatrician whose grown-up daughters returned to the family home. His daughters were played by Dinah Manoff (who was Elaine Lefkowitz on *Soap*) and the lesbian Kristy McNichol who had an affair with Ina Liberace, the pianist's niece.
CAUSE: Mulligan died aged 67 in Los Angeles, California, from cancer.

Paul Muni
(FRIEDRICH MUNI MEYER WEISENFREUND)
Born September 22, 1895
Died August 25, 1967
Perfectionist. Born in Lemberg, Austria-Hungary, the son of an acting family, Muni arrived in the land of opportunity in 1902 and became a staple of Yiddish theatre. In 1926 he made his Broadway début and three years later was nominated for an Oscar for his performance in the film *The Valiant*. It was *Scarface* (1932) that made Muni a star and *I Am A Fugitive From A Chain Gang* (1932) that garnered his second Oscar nomination. His reward for years of sterling cinematic excellence came when he won an Oscar for *The Story Of Louis Pasteur* (1936). In 1955 he won a Tony for his Clarence Darrow-inspired role in the Broadway smash *Inherit The Wind* (Spencer Tracy took the part when the film version was made.) His fifth and final Oscar nomination came in 1959 with *The Last Angry Man*. Bette Davis recalled: "Paul Muni was a fascinating, exciting, attractive man – Jesus, was he attractive! – and it was sad to see him slowly disappear behind his elaborate make-up, his putty noses, his false lips, his beards. One of the few funny things Jack Warner ever said was, 'Why are we paying him so much money when we can't find him?' "
CAUSE: He died in Montecito, California, from heart problems, aged 71.

Janet Munro
Born September 28, 1934
Died December 6, 1972
Born in Blackpool, Lancashire, she looked set for stardom but her career was beset by her tendency to tipple. Her films included *Small Hotel* (1957) as Effie, *The Young And The Guilty* (1958) as Sue, *Tommy The Toreador* (1959) as Amanda, *Third Man On The Mountain* (1959) as Lizbeth Hempel, *Darby O'Gill And The Little People* (1959) as Katie, *Swiss Family Robinson* (1960) as Roberta, *The Day The Earth Caught Fire* (1961) as Jeannie, *Life For Ruth* (1962) as Pat Harris, *Bitter Harvest* (1963) as Jennie Jones and *Sebastian* (1968) as Carol Fancy. She was married to actors Tony Wright (1956–1961) and Ian Hendry (1963–1971).
CAUSE: She choked to death while drinking a cup of tea in London, aged 38.

Ona Munson

(OWENA WOLCOTT)
Born June 16, 1903
Died February 11, 1955
Unfulfilled talent. Born in Portland,
Oregon, 5'2" Munson began her career
in vaudeville before moving to
Broadway where she introduced the
song 'You're the Cream in My Coffee'
in the musical *Hold Everything*. Her
movie career was limited and she
reached her high point playing Rhett
Butler's mistress Belle Watling, the
whorehouse madam, in *Gone With The
Wind* (1939). Thereafter her career
began to go downhill and she became
depressed and began comfort eating. In
the Forties she became the first female
producer at CBS but underwent a
major operation in 1952. She was
married three times: to actor Edward
Buzzell (1926–1930), Stewart
McDonald (1941–1947) and designer
Eugene Berman (1950–1955), who
discovered her corpse. She also took
several lovers including Ernst Lubitsch
and writer Mercedes de Acosta who
also bedded Greta Garbo and Marlene
Dietrich.
CAUSE: She died by her own hand in
New York with an overdose of sleeping
pills. She was 51. Her suicide note
read: "This is the only way I know to
be free again . . . Please don't follow
me." She was buried in Ferncliff
Cemetery & Mausoleum, Secor Road,
Hartsdale, New York 10530.

Audie Murphy

Born June 20, 1924
Died May 28, 1971
Real life hero. Many actors appear
heroic by their cinematic deeds but
Audie Leon Murphy was a true hero.
He was born on Boles Farm, Kingston,
Texas, the seventh of 12 children of
tenant farmer Pat Murphy and Josie
Bell Killian (d. May 23, 1941). His
father deserted the family shortly
before his wife died, leaving the
children to fend for themselves.
Murphy attempted to join the army

after Pearl Harbour but was turned
down for being too young and too
small (5'5½"). He was told to come
back in June 1942 when he turned 18.
He was accepted and in February 1943
was sent to Morocco. His first taste of
battle came on July 10, 1943 when he
took part in the invasion of Sicily.
Exhibiting "coolness and calm fury"
and a very short temper, he went into
battle armed to the teeth. In March
1943, he received the Bronze Star, his
first medal. He won 32 medals before
he turned 21, including five from the
French and one from the Belgians. His
greatest achievement was winning the
Congressional Medal of Honour (for
his actions near Holtzwihr, France on
January 26, 1945). His citation reads,
"2nd Lieutenant Murphy commanded
Company B, which was attacked by six
tanks and waves of infantry. 2nd
Lieutenant Murphy ordered his men to
withdraw to prepare positions in
woods, while he remained forward at
his command post and continued to
give fire directions to the artillery by
telephone. Behind him, to his right,
one of our tank destroyers received a
direct hit and began to burn. Its crew
withdrew to the woods. 2nd Lieutenant
Murphy continued to direct artillery
fire, which killed large numbers of the
advancing enemy infantry. With the
enemy tanks abreast of his position,
2nd Lieutenant Murphy climbed on
the burning tank destroyer, which was
in danger of blowing up at any
moment, and employed its .50 calibre
machine gun against the enemy. He
was alone and exposed to German fire
from three sides, but his deadly fire
killed dozens of Germans and caused
their infantry attack to waver. The
enemy tanks, losing infantry support,
began to fall back. For an hour the
Germans tried every available weapon
to eliminate 2nd Lieutenant Murphy,
but he continued to hold his position
and wiped out a squad, which was
trying to creep up unnoticed on his
right flank. Germans reached as close

as 10 yards, only to be mowed down by his fire. He received a leg wound, but ignored it and continued the single-handed fight until his ammunition was exhausted. He then made his way to his company, refused medical attention, and organised the company in a counterattack, which forced the Germans to withdraw. His directing of artillery fire wiped out many of the enemy; he killed or wounded about 50. 2nd Lieutenant Murphy's indomitable courage and his refusal to give an inch of ground saved his company from possible encirclement and destruction, and enabled it to hold the woods which had been the enemy's objective". His medal was issued on August 9, 1945. He was wounded three times and credited with killing 240 Germans. "I feel no qualms; no pride, no remorse," he said of his death toll. "There is only a weary indifference." Still a young man when the war ended, he turned to Hollywood after an all-expenses paid invitation from James Cagney and became a highly successful cowboy star. He made his film début in *Beyond Glory* (1948) as Thomas and took his first lead the following year in *Bad Boy* (1949) as Danny Lester. After his affair with Jean Peters broke up, on February 8, 1949, he married actress Wanda Hendrix (b. Jacksonville, Florida, November 3, 1928, d. Burbank, California, February 1, 1981 of pneumonia) who divorced him in Los Angeles on April 14, 1950 alleging mental cruelty. As a result of post traumatic stress disorder Murphy suffered nightmares and slept with a loaded gun under his pillow and on one occasion during an argument put the barrel in his wife's mouth. In 1950 he signed to Universal-International Pictures at a salary of $100,000 a year. His films included: *The Kid From Texas* (1950) as Billy the Kid, *Kansas Raiders* (1950) as Jesse James, *The Red Badge Of Courage* (1951) as Henry Fleming, *The Cimarron Kid* (1951) as Bill Doolin, *The Duel At Silver Creek* (1952)

as Luke Cromwell, The Silver Kid, *Tumbleweed* (1953) as Jim Harvey, *Gunsmoke* (1953) as Reb Kittridge, *Column South* (1953) as Lieutenant Jed Sayre, *Ride Clear Of Diablo* (1954) as Clay O'Mara, *Drums Across The River* (1954) as Gary Brannon, *Destry* (1954) as Tom Destry, *To Hell And Back* (1955) his biopic, *Joe Butterfly* (1957) as Private John Woodley, *Ride A Crooked Trail* (1958) as Joe Maybe, *No Name On The Bullet* (1959) as John Gant, *Cast A Long Shadow* (1959) as Matt Brown, *Posse From Hell* (1961) as Banner Cole, *Battle At Bloody Beach* (1961) as Craig Benson, *Six Black Horses* (1962) as Ben Lane, *Apache Rifles* (1964) as Jeff Stanton, *Gunfight At Comanche Creek* (1964) as Bob Gifford, *Bullet For A Badman* (1964) as Logan Keliher and *A Time for Dying* (1971) as Jesse James. On April 23, 1951, in Highland Park Methodist Church, Dallas, Texas, he married Pamela Archer (b. 1922) by whom he had two sons: Terry Michael (b. 1952) and James Shannon (b. 1954). They separated in 1965 but never divorced. As the fashion for cowboy films decreased Murphy found himself looking for work. A television series, *Whispering Smith*, was not a success. He suffered from a drug problem (sleeping pills called Placidyl) and was often violent but the police always dropped the charges. Murphy also had a serious gambling problem and to raise money, took a job as a front man with a company that made prefabs. He owed money to the IRS. He once admitted: "I am working with a handicap. I have no talent."

CAUSE: Just after noon on May 28, 1971, Murphy, 46, and four executives from the prefab company took off from Atlanta, Georgia. A storm blew up and at 11.40am the pilot, Herman Butler, flew the plane into the side of a mountain. All six people aboard were killed but their bodies were not found for three days because of poor weather conditions. On June 7, Murphy was buried in Arlington National Cemetery, Virginia. The government representative at the ceremony was future President George Bush. After that of President John F. Kennedy, it is the second most visited grave at Arlington.

FURTHER READING: *Hero: The Life And Death Of Audie Murphy* – Charles Whiting (New York: Jove, 1991).

Brittany Murphy
Born November 10, 1977
Died December 20, 2009

Life interrupted. Brittany Anne Murphy was born at Atlanta, Georgia, the daughter of Angelo Bertolotti and Sharon Kathleen Murphy who divorced when she was two years old. Living with her mother, they moved to Los Angeles so Murphy could follow a career in the entertainment industry. She said, "When I asked my mum to move to California, she sold everything and moved out here for me. She always believed in me." When she was 14, Murphy was cast in the television series *Drexell's Class* as Brenda Drexell and guest-starred in several other shows. She made her film debut in *Family Prayers* (1993) as Elsie and went on to appear in *Clueless* (1995) as Tai, *Freeway* (1996) as Rhonda, *Bongwater* (1997) as Mary, *Drive* (1998) as Deliverance Bodine, *Falling Sky* (1998) as Emily Nicholson, *The Prophecy II* (1998) as Izzy, *Zack And Reba* (1998) as Reba Simpson, *Drop Dead Gorgeous* (1999) as Lisa Swenson, *Girl, Interrupted* (1999) as Daisy Randone, *Trixie* (2000) as Ruby Pearli, *Angels!* (2000) as Nurse Bellows, *Cherry Falls* (2000) as Jody Marken, *Sidewalks Of New York* (2001) as Ashley, *Summer Catch* (2001) as Dede Mulligan, *Don't Say A Word* (2001) as Elisabeth Burrows, *Riding In Cars With Boys* (2001) as Fay Forrester, *Spun* (2002) as Nikki, *8 Mile* (2002) as Alex Latourno, *Just Married* (2003) as Sarah, *Uptown Girls* (2003) as Molly Gunn, *Little Black Book* (2004) as Stacy Holt, *Sin City* (2005) as Shellie,

The Groomsmen (2006) as Sue, *Love And Other Disasters* (2006) as Emily Jackson, *Happy Feet* (2006) as the voice of Gloria, *The Dead Girl* (2006) as Krista Kutcher, *The Ramen Girl* (2008) as Abby, *Across The Hall* (2009) as June and *Deadline* (2009) as Alice. *Abandoned* (2010) was completed in June 2009 and was in post-production at the time of her death. Five months later, she was sacked from *The Caller* and replaced by Rachelle Lefevre. Stories circulated that she was fired because of her unreliability due to a drugs problem. She had a habit of becoming romantically involved with many of her co-workers. In May 2007 she married the English screenwriter Simon Monjack in a private Jewish ceremony in Los Angeles. In one interview Murphy said, "I don't really take myself very seriously. I've never formally trained in acting, so I'm very instinctual and visceral with decisions. It hasn't really been a plot or scheme in any way, shape or form."

CAUSE: At 8am on December 20, 2009 the Los Angeles Fire Department was called to Murphy's West Hollywood house after she was found on the bathroom floor. The firemen tried to resuscitate Murphy but she was pronounced dead at 10.04am at Cedars-Sinai Medical Center. 32-year-old Murphy was buried in a private funeral at Forest Lawn Hollywood Hills on December 24, 2009. Cause of death ranged from natural causes to an eating disorder to a drugs overdose to a heart attack. An autopsy was inconclusive. In January 2010 Murphy's mother and widower insisted that the death was due to natural causes. Sharon Murphy said, "She had a fear of dying. She would not take too much caffeine. She wouldn't even have a glass of champagne on New Year's. She was just high on life, and people see that as something else I guess." However, various writers speculated that Murphy had a serious drug habit.

Timothy Patrick Murphy

Born November 3, 1959
Died December 6, 1988

Handsome tragedian. Born in Hartford, Connecticut, Timothy Patrick Murphy looked to be destined for a long career. He made his début in the mini-series *Centennial* (1978) playing Christian. His devastating good looks proved attractive to women but off screen Murphy's desires lay with men. A closeted homosexual, he was Spences Langley in the soap opera *Search For Tomorrow* from 1980 until 1981. The following year he signed to play Mickey Trotter, Ray Krebs' cousin, in the glossy soap *Dallas*. A hit with viewers, Mickey wooed and won Lucy Ewing but Murphy decided he wanted to leave. He was written out when his character was involved in a car crash trying to prevent a drunken Sue Ellen from driving off Southfork. He played Chip Craddock in another soap *Glitter*. He played Gene Orowitz in the film *Sam's Son* (1984) and Jeff Richmond in *Doin' Time On Planet Earth* (1988) before illness forced his retirement.

CAUSE: He died aged 29 in Sherman Oaks, California, from AIDS.

N

J. Carrol Naish

Born January 21, 1897
Died January 24, 1973
Versatility personified. Born in New
York, the thin, moustachioed 5′9½″
Joseph Patrick Carrol Naish
(pronounced Nash) was the great-great
grandson of a former Irish Lord
Chancellor but the family had fallen
on hard times by Naish's childhood
and he was raised in a poor area of
Yorkville-Harlem. He joined the navy
aged 16 and then served in the Army
Signal Corps during World War I.
After making a few films he decided
his future belonged on the Great
White Way and headed east. Having
established his reputation on Broadway
he returned to Hollywood as something
of a name. Despite his Gaelic
background he found himself called
upon to play all sorts of ethnic roles,
including that of Chinese detective
Charlie Chan in the TV series *The New
Adventures Of Charlie Chan* (syndicated
from June 1957) and Luigi Basco, an
Italian immigrant, in the CBS sitcom
Life With Luigi (from September 22,
1952, until June 4, 1973). His films
included: *Good Intentions* (1930) as
Charlie Hattrick, *Scotland Yard* (1930)
as Dr Remur, *Homicide Squad* (1931)
as Hugo, *Tiger Shark* (1932) as Tony,
No Living Witness (1932) as Nick,
It's Tough To Be Famous (1932) as
Lieutenant Blake, *The Hatchet Man*
(1932) as Sun Yat Ming, *Two Seconds*
(1932) as Tony, *Crooner* (1932) as
Meyers, *The World Gone Mad* (1933) as
Ramon Salvadore, *Frisco Jenny* (1933)
as Harris, *Elmer The Great* (1933) as
Jerry, *Captured!* (1933) as Guarand,
Blood Money (1933) as Charley, *Ann
Vickers* (1933) as Dr Sorell, *Silent Men*
(1933) as Jack Wilder, *Notorious But*
Nice (1933) as Joe Charney, *What's
Your Racket?* (1934) as Dick Graves,
Return Of The Terror (1934) as Steve
Scola, *One Is Guilty* (1934) as Jack
Allan, *Little Big Shot* (1935) as Bert,
The Lives Of A Bengal Lancer (1935) as
Grand Vizier, *Under The Pampas Moon*
(1935) as Tito, *Front Page Woman*
(1935) as Robert Cardoza, *Captain
Blood* (1935) as Cahusac, *We Who Are
About To Die* (1936) as Nick, *The
Return Of Jimmy Valentine* (1936) as
Tony Scapelli, *The Robin Hood Of El
Dorado* (1936) as Three-Fingered Jack,
Anthony Adverse (1936) as Major
Doumet, *Charlie Chan At The Circus*
(1936) as Tom Holt, *Ramona* (1936)
as Juan Can, *The Charge Of The Light
Brigade* (1936) as Subahdar-Major
Puran Singh, *Crack-Up* (1936) as
Operative #77, *Think Fast, Mr Moto*
(1937) as Adram, *Daughter Of
Shanghai* (1937) as Frank Barden,
Bulldog Drummond Comes Back (1937)
as Mikhail Valdin, *Illegal Traffic* (1938)
as Lewis Zomar, *Her Jungle Love*
(1938) as Kuasa, *Bulldog Drummond In
Africa* (1938) as Richard Lane, *Beau
Geste* (1939) as Rasinoff, *The Corsican
Brothers* (1941) as Lorenzo, *Blood And
Sand* (1941) as Garabato, *That Night
In Rio* (1941) as Machado, *Dr Renault's
Secret* (1942) as Noel, *Gung Ho!* (1943)
as Lieutenant C.J. Cristoforos, *Sahara*
(1943) as war prisoner Giuseppe, for
which he was nominated for a Best
Supporting Actor Oscar, *Waterfront*
(1944) as Dr Carl Decker, *Enter Arsene
Lupin* (1944) as Ganimard, *House Of
Frankenstein* (1944) as Daniel, *A Medal
For Benny* (1945) as Charley Martin,
for which he was again nominated for
an Oscar, *Getting Gertie's Garter* (1945)
as Charles, *The Beast With Five Fingers*
(1946) as Ovidio Castanio, *Humoresque*
(1946) as Rudy Boray, *Joan Of Arc*
(1948) as Count John of Luxembourg,
That Midnight Kiss (1949) as Papa
Donnetti, *Annie Get Your Gun* (1950)
as Chief Sitting Bull, *Rio Grande*
(1950) as General Philip Sheridan,
Denver And Rio Grande (1952) as Gil

Harkness, *Saskatchewan* (1954) as
Batouche, *Sitting Bull* (1954) as Sitting
Bull, *Desert Sands* (1955) as Sergeant
Diepel and *Force Of Impulse* (1961) as
Antonio Marino.
CAUSE: Three days after his 76th
birthday, he died in La Jolla,
California, of emphysema.

Nita Naldi
(ANITA DONNA DOOLEY)
Born April 1, 1897
Died February 17, 1961
Silent vamp. Born in New York she
appeared in the Ziegfeld Follies and
worked in a couple of films before
finding stardom as Miss Gina opposite
John Barrymore in *Dr Jekyll And Mr
Hyde* (1920). Her star was in the
ascendant and was enhanced by
performances in *The Last Door* (1921)
where she played a widow, *A Divorce of
Convenience* (1921) as Tula Moliana
and *Experience* (1921) as Temptation.
She hit the pantheon of stardom with
Blood And Sand (1922) as Doña Sol
opposite Rudolph Valentino. The
public went wild over Valentino, Naldi
and the film which was really the last
silent epic. Unfortunately, as many
discover, when you reach the top there
is only one way to go. Naldi's next
films were disappointing. Then she was
cast as Sally Lung in Cecil B. DeMille's
first version of *The Ten Commandments*
(1923). The advent of sound revealed
her strong New York accent and she
retired from making films after *What
Price Beauty?* (1928) in which she
played Rita Rinaldi. She began
appearing on stage and in television.
CAUSE: She died in New York from
a heart attack in her room at the
Wentworth Hotel and was interred in
Calvary Cemetery, 4902 Laurel Hill
Boulevard, Woodside, New York
11377. She was 64.

Namu
Died July 1966
The first whale star. Namu was the first
killer whale to become a movie star

when he appeared in his own biopic,
Namu The Killer Whale (1966). Namu
was so friendly and intelligent that his
keepers saw fit to finally set him free.
The movie *Free Willy* (1993) was based
on Namu's tale.
CAUSE: He drowned in Seattle,
Washington.

Alan Napier
(ALAN NAPIER-CLAVERING)
Born January 7, 1903
Died August 8, 1988
Holy domestic help! Born in
Birmingham, England, he began his
career in films in 1930 playing
governors, generals and counts before
moving to America in 1939 where he
appeared in over 70 films. Yet it was
his portrayal of Batman's faithful butler
Alfred Pennyworth, in both the classic
camp Sixties TV series and the 1966
spin-off film *Batman*, that made 6'5"
Napier famous. He was the first
member of the cast to be assigned a
role, although prior to casting he had
never heard of Batman because he
never read comics as a child. He was
swayed into being the butler by his
agent's offer of $100,000. Napier's
films included *The Invisible Man
Returns* (1940) as Willie Spears,
A Yank At Eton (1942) as the
Restaurateur, *Cat People* (1942) as
Doc Carver, *Random Harvest* (1942)
as Julian, *Lassie Come Home* (1943) as
Jock, *Madame Curie* (1943) as Doctor
Bladh, *The Song Of Bernadette* (1943)
as Dr DuBeau, *Thirty Seconds
Over Tokyo* (1944) as Mr Parker,
Mademoiselle Fifi (1944) as Count de
Breville, *Hangover Square* (1945) as Sir
Henry Chapman, *Sinbad The Sailor*
(1947) as Aga, *Lured* (1947) as
Inspector Gordon, *Forever Amber*
(1947) as Landale, *High Conquest*
(1947) as Thomas, *Macbeth* (1948),
Johnny Belinda (1948), *Joan Of Arc*
(1948) as Earl of Warwick, *Tarzan's
Magic Fountain* (1949) as Douglas
Jessup, *A Connecticut Yankee In King
Arthur's Court* (1949), *Challenge To*

Lassie (1949) as Lord Provost, *Tarzan's Peril* (1951) as Mr Peters, *Young Bess* (1953) as Robert Tyrwhitt, *Julius Caesar* (1953) as Cicero, *Journey To The Center Of The Earth* (1959) as Dean, *Tender Is The Night* (1962) as Pardo and *Marnie* (1964) as Mr Rutland.

CAUSE: He died of a stroke in Santa Monica, California. He was 85. His wife predeceased him and he was survived by a daughter, a stepdaughter and three grandchildren.

Clarence Nash

Born September 22, 1904
Died February 20, 1985
Absolutely quackers. Oklahoma-born Clarence Nash's talents were used in over 160 films yet he was able to walk down the street totally unrecognised. When his parents moved to California he met Walt Disney and showed the cartoonmeister his repertoire of animal sounds. Disney hired him and from June 9, 1934, Clarence Nash was the voice of Donald Duck. He also provided Donald's voice speaking phonetically in Chinese, French, German, Japanese, Portuguese and Spanish as well as the voices of Huey, Dewey and Louie and Donald's girlfriend Daisy. It could all have been so different for Nash as he once recalled: "I wanted to be a doctor and ended up the biggest quack in the world."
CAUSE: He died of leukaemia aged 80 in Burbank, California. He was survived by his wife and two daughters.

Mildred Natwick

Born June 19, 1905
Died October 25, 1994
Bird-like eccentric. Born in Baltimore, Maryland, she graduated from Bryn Mawr and made her first appearance on stage as an amateur in *The Playboy Of The Western World* in 1929 at the Vagabond Theater in her home city. Her professional début didn't come for another three years, when she appeared as Mrs Noble in *Carry Nation* at the

Biltmore, New York, on October 29, 1932. On May 12, 1933, came her London début as Aunt Mabel in *The Day I Forgot* at the Globe Theatre. She didn't make a film until she was in her mid-thirties and even then seemed to prefer the intimacy of the stage. Her films included: *The Long Voyage Home* (1940) as Freda, *Yolanda And The Thief* (1945) as Aunt Amarilla, *3 Godfathers* (1948), *She Wore A Yellow Ribbon* (1949) as Mrs Allshard, *Cheaper By the Dozen* (1950) as Mrs Mebane, *Against All Flags* (1952) as Molvina MacGregor, *Teenage Rebel* (1956) as Grace Hewitt, *Tammy And The Bachelor* (1957) as Aunt Renie, *Barefoot In The Park* (1967) as Mrs Ethel Banks, reprising a role she had played on Broadway and for which she was nominated for an Oscar, *If It's Tuesday, This Must Be Belgium* (1969) as Jenny Grant, *Daisy Miller* (1974) as Mrs Costello, *At Long Last Love* (1975) as Mabel Pritchard and *Dangerous Liaisons* (1988) as Madame De Rosemonde. Television fame came late to her as one half of a pair of geriatric mystery writers who had a tendency to solve crimes. *The Snoop Sisters* aired on NBC from December 19, 1973, until August 20, 1974, and on ITV from January 24, 1974. Mildred Natwick was Gwendolyn Snoop while Helen Hayes played Ernesta Snoop. Natwick was a lesbian and never married.
CAUSE: She died in New York aged 89 of natural causes.

Alla Nazimova

(ALLA LAVENDERA)
Born May 22, 1879
Died July 13, 1945
'Woman of 1000 Moods'. Despite her talents as a violinist and actress it is as Hollywood's most exotic lesbian that Nazimova is known. Born in Yalta in the Crimea, she was educated at the St Petersburg Conservatory and then studied under Stanislavski before arriving in the early days of Hollywood. She appeared in just over 20 films

including her début *War Brides* (1916) as Joan, *Revelation* (1918) as Joline, *Eye For Eye* (1918) as Hassouna, the title role in *The Brat* (1919), *Billions* (1920) as Princess Triloff, *Camille* (1921) as Marguerite, *A Doll's House* (1922) as Nora Helmer, the title role in *Salome* (1923) in which she hired only homosexual actors in a 'homage' to Oscar Wilde, *The Redeeming Sin* (1925) as Joan and *My Son* (1925) as Ana Silva, after which she retired from the screen to embrace the theatre. She returned to films 15 years later in *Escape* (1940) as Emmy Ritter and followed that up with *Blood And Sand* (1941) as a memorable Senora Augustias, Tyrone Power's mother, *The Song Of Bernadette* (1943), *In Our Time* (1944) as Zofya Orvid, *The Bridge Of San Luis Rey* (1944) as The Marquesa and *Since You Went Away* (1944) as Zosia Koslowska. Nazimova was a very close friend of actress Edith P. Luckett (b. Washington, DC, July 16, 1888, d. Arizona, October 26, 1987, of Alzheimer's disease) and became godmother to her daughter, who grew up to be Nancy Reagan (b. New York, July 6, 1921). She also introduced Rudolph Valentino to his two wives, both members of Nazimova's lesbian coterie. Nazimova founded what was to become a playground of debauchery in Hollywood. The notorious Garden of Allah opened on January 9, 1927, and was located at 8152 Sunset Boulevard and Crescent Heights Boulevard. The hotel collection of 25 bungalows was frequented by Tallulah Bankhead, Bogie and Bacall, Clara Bow, Marlene Dietrich, F. Scott Fitzgerald, Errol Flynn and so many writers it was dubbed the "Algonquin Round Table West". The swimming pool was built in the shape of the Black Sea in homage to Nazimova's origins. The place began to lose some of its magic in the Forties and by the following decade most of the inhabitants were prostitutes and their clientele. It was demolished in 1959 to make way for the Great

Western Bank. Despite her sexual proclivities, Nazimova married twice: in 1904 she wed Russian actor Paul Orleneff. On December 5, 1912, she married actor Charles Bryant in her New York home, only to discover the marriage wasn't legal because Orleneff hadn't granted her a divorce. She lived with Bryant as his common-law wife until 1925.

CAUSE: Nazimova died of a coronary thrombosis in Los Angeles, California, aged 76.

Dame Anna Neagle

(FLORENCE MARJORIE ROBERTSON)
Born October 20, 1904
Died June 3, 1986

'Queen of the British Cinema'. Born in Forest Gate, Essex, the only daughter in a family of three children, she studied to be a dancer and made her first appearance on stage as a dancer in December 1917 at the Ambassadors' Theatre. She worked continuously in the theatre, making her Broadway début at the Selwyn Theater on December 30, 1929, as a dancer in *Wake Up And Dream*. The following year she changed her name to Anna Neagle (her mother's maiden name) and made her first film, *The Chinese Bungalow* (1931) as Charlotte. Two years later, she appeared as Viki in *Goodnight Vienna* (1932), a film directed by the man who would share her personal and professional life for the next 45 years, Herbert Wilcox. Playing the title role in *Nell Gwyn* (1934) made her a star and she became associated with historical biopics such as *Peg Of Old Drury* (1935) in which she played Peg Woffington and *Victoria The Great* (1937), playing Queen Victoria, a role she reprised in *Sixty Glorious Years* (1938). A 1939 foray to America saw her in four pictures for RKO: *Nurse Edith Cavell* (1939) as Edith Cavell, *No, No, Nanette* (1940) as Nanette, *Irene* (1940) as Irene O'Dare and *Sunny* (1941) as Sunny Sullivan. Back in England she returned to the biopic and played aviatrix Amy Johnson in *They Flew Alone* (1941). Following the end of hostilities Neagle's films became less concerned with history and dealt more with light entertainment escapism. She appeared regularly on the London stage. However, in 1950 she returned to real-life roles, taking on the part of World War II heroine Odette Hallowes in the film *Odette*. The following year she played Florence Nightingale in *The Lady With A Lamp* (1951). Her last film, *The Lady Is A Square* (1958) in which she played Frances Baring and which she also produced, was a flop and thereafter she turned her attention to the stage. On August 9, 1943, she married Herbert Sydney Wilcox, CBE (b. Cork, Ireland, April 19, 1892, d. London, May 15, 1977) at Caxton Hall Registry Office, Westminster. There were no children. Noël Coward recalled: "I have just finished reading an autobiography by Herbert Wilcox called *Twenty-Five Thousand Sunsets*. It is curiously endearing. His unquestioning adoration of Anna shines through every page. You would think, from reading it, that dear Anna is the greatest actress, singer and dancer and glamorous star who ever graced the stage and screen. The fact that this is not strictly accurate never for a split second occurs to him." CAUSE: She died of breast cancer in a nursing home, Clare House, in Oakcroft Road, West Byfleet, Woking, Surrey. She was 81. Dame Anna was buried in the City of London Cemetery in Manor Park. She left £151,267.

Robin Nedwell

Born September 27, 1946
Died February 1, 1999
The young doctor. Born in Birmingham, the son of a commercial traveller, Robin Nedwell moved to Cardiff at an early age and was educated at Monkton and Canton High Schools in the city. He joined the Welsh Theatre Company and then trained at the Central School of Speech and Drama. He became famous for playing Dr Duncan Waring in the innumerable *Doctor* programmes although he only took the lead role after Barry Evans (who was also to die young) left the series. Nedwell appeared in *Doctor In The House* (July 12, 1969–July 3, 1970) as Waring and reprised the part in *Doctor In Charge* (April 9, 1972–December 29, 1973), *Doctor At Sea* (April 21–July 14, 1974), *Doctor On The Go* (April 27, 1975–April 10, 1977), *Doctor Down Under* (February 5, 1979–May 10, 1980) and *Doctor At The Top* (February 21–April 4 1991). Nedwell's film work included: *The Vault Of Horror* (1973) as Tom, *Stand Up, Virgin Soldiers* (1977) as Lieutenant Grainger, *The Shillingbury Blowers* (1980) as Peter Higgins and *A Slice Of Life* (1983) as Toby. Other television work included: *The Upchat Connection* (October 24–December 5, 1978) as 'Mike Upchat' taking over when John Alderton refused to make a second series, *West End Tales* (February 16–April 6, 1981) as Fiddler, *Shillingbury Tales* (May 17–June 21, 1981) as Peter Higgins, *The Zany Adventures Of Robin Hood* (1984) as Will Scarlett and *Cluedo* (1990) as Reverend Green. He married Heather Inglis in 1982 and they had one daughter, Amie. His hobbies included collecting swords and Japanese armour. CAUSE: He died aged 52 from a heart attack in Hedge End, Southampton, Hampshire.

Pola Negri

(BARBARA APOLONIA MATHIAS-CHALUPIEC)
Born December 31, 1894
Died August 1, 1987
Silent screen Vamp. Negri is almost totally forgotten (or unheard of) by today's cinema audiences. Yet in her day she was a big star. Born in Janowa, Poland, she wrote and financed her first film, *Niewolnica Zmysłów* (1914). Three years later, she moved to Berlin

to work there before moving to Hollywood in the early Twenties. Her films at Famous Players were for a time very popular. Her love life was tempestuous – she was very publicly engaged to Charlie Chaplin, who dumped her but gallantly allowed the press to report, on March 2, 1924, that it was she who had done the jilting. Her next 'fiancé' was Rudolph Valentino, but they were parted by his sudden death in August 1926. She attended his funeral dressed in black attended by a doctor and nurse who both wore white. Since Valentino was exclusively homosexual and rumours abounded about Negri's sapphic tendencies, it would be a safe bet to assume it was a romance made not in heaven but in a publicist's office. (Gay designer Billy Haines, who was linked publicly with Negri to hide his own homosexuality, confirmed the lesbian rumours. "So very private. In public it was always men. When Valentino died, then she said she was engaged to him. Pola was very willing, she loved the attention. Some of the ladies who liked other ladies wanted as little to do with [fake publicity] as possible.") With typical forthrightness, Tallulah Bankhead called Negri "a lying lesbo, a Polish publicity hound." Nevertheless, lesbian or not, on May 14, 1927, in Seraincourt, near Paris, she married Prince Sergei Mdivani, which made her the sister-in-law of fellow actress Mae Murray. It was supposedly her third trip up the aisle, having previously married Baron Popper and Count Eugene Domski whom she divorced in 1921, or possibly 1923. In August 1928 Negri became one of the first victims to the newly discovered sound films. Her Polish accent made her difficult to understand. Her career troubles were not helped by her histrionics, nor was her marriage. She and her husband were divorced on April 2, 1931, on the grounds of abandonment. She accused him of financial impropriety following the

Wall Street crash. She successfully sued a French magazine for libel after it linked her romantically with Adolf Hitler. Her films included: *Bestia* (1915), *Studenci* (1916), *Arabella* (1916), *Carmen* (1918) as Carmen, *Madame DuBarry* (1919) as Madame DuBarry, *Die Geschlossene Kette* (1920), *Sumurun* (1920) as Taenzerin, *Vendetta* (1921), *Mad Love* (1923), *Bella Donna* (1923) as Bella Donna, *The Cheat* (1923) as Carmelita De Bórdoba, *The Spanish Dancer* (1923) as Maritana, *Shadows Of Paris* (1924) as Claire, Queen of the Apaches, *Men* (1924) as Cleo, *Lily Of The Dust* (1924) as Lily, *East Of Suez* (1925) as Daisy Forbes, *Flower Of Night* (1925) as Carlota y Villalon, *Good And Naughty* (1926) as Germaine Morris, *Hotel Imperial* (1927) as Anna Sedlak, *Barbed Wire* (1927) as Mona Moreau, *The Woman On Trial* (1927) as Julie, *Three Sinners* (1928) as Baroness Gerda Wallentin, *Mazurka* (1935) as Vera, *Madame Bovary* (1937) as Madame Bovary, *Hi Diddle Diddle* (1943) as Genya Smetana and *The Moon-Spinners* (1964) as Madame Habib.

CAUSE: She died aged 92 in San Antonio, Texas, of a brain tumour and pneumonia complications. She was buried in Crypt E-19 of Block 56 in the Main Mausoleum of Calvary Cemetery, 4201 Whittier Boulevard, Los Angeles, California 90023.

Jean Negulesco
Born February 26, 1900
Died July 18, 1993
Arty director. In the Twenties, Negulesco (born in Craiova, Rumania) led a bohemian life as a painter in Paris, becoming a designer of film sets. He worked his way up and sideways until he was handed the assignment of directing *Singapore Woman* (1941). Three years later, he was praised for his work on *The Mask Of Dimitrios* (1944) and *The Conspirators* (1944). His subsequent films included: *Three Strangers* (1946), *Nobody Lives Forever*

(1946), *Humoresque* (1946) (He revealed: "Joan Crawford used continually to knit, whether she was rehearsing, eating, looking at rushes or doing battle with someone. Oscar Levant asked her, 'Do you knit when you fuck?' For days after there were icebergs on the set"), *Johnny Belinda* (1948) for which he was nominated for an Oscar, *Road House* (1948) and *The Forbidden Street* (1949). He spent most of the next decade at 20th Century Fox where he worked on, among other films, *O. Henry's Full House* (1952), *Titanic* (1953), *How To Marry A Millionaire* (1953) with Marilyn Monroe, whom he adored, *Three Coins In The Fountain* (1954), *The Gay Parisian* (1955), *Daddy Long Legs* (1955), *The Rains Of Ranchipur* (1955) and *Boy On A Dolphin* (1957). Following his last film, *Hello-Goodbye* (1970), he spent his time painting and travelling.

CAUSE: Negulesco died aged 93 of heart failure in Marbella, Spain.

Anthony Newley

Born September 24, 1931
Died April 14, 1999
All-rounder. Born illegitimately in Hackney, London, and trained at Italia Conti for all of three weeks, George Anthony Newley made his stage début in April 1946 in Colchester. It took nine more years for his London début, but then things began to happen quickly. His Broadway début came in March 1956 just four months after his West End one. On July 20, 1961, his musical *Stop The World: I Want To Get Off* opened at the Queen's Theatre. Newley also starred as Littlechap and directed. Three years later he wrote *The Roar Of The Grease Paint – The Smell Of The Crowd*. He made his first film in 1948 playing Dick Bultitude in *Vice Versa* (1948). Newley's biggest role that year was as Jack Dawkins a.k.a. The Artful Dodger in David Lean's *Oliver Twist* (1948). He lost his virginity during filming to Diana Dors

who was also in the picture. In 1949 he was called up for National Service but left just as quickly: "I wasn't mature enough to take a man's world, and a psychiatrist gave me a ticket because I simply couldn't adjust." Back in films he made *A Boy, A Girl And A Bike* (1949) as Charlie Ritchie, *Those People Next Door* (1952) as Bob Twigg, *Top Of The Form* (1953) as Percy, *Above Us The Waves* (1955), *The Cockleshell Heroes* (1955) as Clarke, *Port Afrique* (1956) as Pedro, *The Battle Of The River Plate* (1956), *The Good Companions* (1957) as Mulbrau, *Fire Down Below* (1957) as Miguel, *The Lady Is A Square* (1959) as Freddy, a flop film starring and directed by Dame Anna Neagle, and *Killers Of Kilimanjaro* (1959) as Hooky Hook. On May Day 1959 Newley became a pop star when his song 'I've Waited So Long' entered the UK charts, where it would reach number three. It would be the first of a dozen hit singles including 'Personality' (1959/number six), 'Why' (1960/number one), 'Do You Mind' (1960/number one), 'If She Should Come To You' (1960/number four), 'Strawberry Fair' (1960/number three), 'And The Heavens Cried' (1961/number six), 'Pop Goes The Weasel' (1961/number twelve) and 'What Kind Of Fool Am I?' (1961/number 36). In the Sixties Newley and his partner Leslie Bricusse headed for Hollywood where Newley starred in *Doctor Dolittle* (1967), for which Bricusse wrote the Oscar-nominated songs. Four years later, they wrote the songs for *Willy Wonka & The Chocolate Factory* (1971), a cinematic version of his book that author Roald Dahl positively hated. Following the divorce from his first wife, Elizabeth Ann Lynn, whom he married in 1956, Newley married Joan Collins (b. Bayswater, May 23, 1933) in New York on May 27, 1963. Seven months later, on October 12, their daughter, Tara Cynara, was born in Mount Sinai Hospital, New York, to be followed by a son, Alexander Anthony, known as Sacha, on September 8, 1965, also at Mount Sinai Hospital. Newley and Collins filmed the appalling semi-autobiographical *Can Hieronymus Merkin Ever Forget Mercy Humppe And Find True Happiness?* (1969) with Newley as Hieronymus Merkin and Collins as Polyester Poontang. Newley also directed, produced and wrote the music for the film, which was shot in Malta and co-starred George Jessel, Milton Berle, Bruce Forsyth and Patricia Hayes. Not long after the film wrapped Collins and Newley separated and they divorced in August 1970. In the Seventies and Eighties Newley made a few films, appeared on television, wrote *The Good Old Bad Old Days* (1972) and married Dareth Rich, by whom he had a son and a daughter. In 1989 he was inducted into the Songwriters' Hall of Fame. In 1991 Newley returned to live in the UK with his 90-year-old mother and even appeared as Vince Watson in *EastEnders* in 1998.

CAUSE: Aged 67, he died of renal cell cancer in Jensen Beach, Florida.

Paul Newman

Born January 26, 1925
Died September 26, 2008
Salad dresser. Born in Cleveland Heights, an upmarket Jewish suburb of Cleveland, Ohio, Paul Leonard Newman was the second son of Arthur Newman (b. Cleveland, Ohio 1893 d. May 18, 1950) and Theresa Fetsko (b. Hungary July 25, 1897 d. December 1982 of cancer). Not long after their son's birth, the family moved to an eleven-room house in Shaker Heights, Ohio. Newman was educated at Shaker Heights High School, graduating in January 1943, whereupon he earned some money by selling *Colliers Encyclopaedia* door-to-door. He attended Ohio University in Athens, Ohio for four months studying economics. During the Second World War he served in the Pacific with the United States Navy joining in June 1943 – he had hoped to become a pilot until it was discovered that his baby blue eyes which would make him famous the world over were actually colour blind. (He detested people asking to see his eyes and punched one man who asked him to remove his sunglasses. Newman said, "There's nothing that makes you feel more like a piece of meat. It's like saying to a woman, 'Open your blouse, I want to see your tits'.") He saw action aboard the USS Bunker Hill during the Battle of Okinawa in April 1945. On demob in 1946 he went back to university where he graduated from Kenyon College in Gambier, Ohio, in June 1949. That year, on December 6, he married Jacqueline Witt, a tall, brown-eyed blonde. On September 23, 1950 Newman became a father for the first time when Jackie gave birth to a son they named (Alan) Scott. In 1952 Newman campaigned for the Democratic Party's Adlai Stevenson during his unsuccessful presidential campaign. Newman made his Broadway theatre debut on February 19, 1953 as Alan Seymour in the original production of William Inge's *Picnic*, directed by Josh Logan with Ralph Meeker, Eileen Heckart, Arthur O'Connell, Janice Rule, Reta Shaw and Kim Stanley. Inge won the 1953 Pulitzer Prize for Drama for the work, and Logan received a Tony Award for Best Director. Logan did not believe that Newman would be able to play the lead of Hal and gave it to Ralph Meeker despite Newman's interest. An understudy during the run was an ambitious young actress called Joanne Gignilliat Trimmier Woodward (b. Thomasville, Georgia February 27, 1930). One night, after a few drinks, she told Josh Logan, "I've set my hat for that guy . . . I'm gonna get him." A daughter, Susan Kendall, arrived on February 21, 1953. Newman studied Drama at Yale University for a year and also received tuition from Lee

Strasberg at the Actors Studio in New York City. In 1954 Warner Bros offered Newman a seven-year $1,000-a-week contract. After several television appearances Newman made his cinematic début as the toga-clad Basil in the $4.5 million production *The Silver Chalice* (premièred at Saranac Lake, New York December 17, 1954; released nationwide December 20, 1954), it was not an auspicious first film. Newman later described it as "the worst film of the Fifties" and when it was scheduled for a television broadcast in California in 1963 he took out an advertisement in the *Los Angeles Times* apologising and urging people not to watch it. The liberated Greek slave Basil has been asked to design a silver chalice for Jesus to drink from at the Last Supper. The film co-starred Virginia Mayo as Helena, Jack Palance as Simon The Magician and Pier Angeli as Deborra, Basil's love interest. In interviews to promote the film Victor Saville compared Newman to Rudolph Valentino. It did not sway the critics. The *New Yorker* said, "Paul Newman . . . delivers his lines with emotional fervour of a Puttnam Division conductor announcing local stops" while *The New York Times* claimed that his performance was "rarely better than wooden". Things might have been very different – Newman had a screen test with James Dean for *East Of Eden* (1955) but Dean was cast on March 5, 1954. The black and white screen test, directed by Gjon Mili, was shot in New York and still exists. In it, the two actors flirt very openly with each other. An off-screen director calls out, "Hey, you two queens, look over here." "Kiss me," begs Dean clad in jeans and open shirt, and Newman in white shirt and spotted bow tie responds with, "Not here", and then pinches Dean's backside. According to Dean's older boyfriend Rogers Brackett, Dean and Newman became lovers after meeting at the Actors Studio. The affair ended when

Newman's wife, Jackie, discovered it and gave Newman an ultimatum. Writer Lawrence Quirk referred to the incident as Newman's "homosexual panic" in his biography of the actor published in 1997 while Newman was still alive. No writ was ever issued for libel. Despite the appalling debut and a belief that Warner Bros wanted to wreck his career, Newman managed to survive into the Sixties where his magnetic personality charmed a generation. On February 10, 1955 he opened at the Ethel Barrymore Theatre in Broadway in *The Desperate Hours* as Glenn Griffin, a psychotic escaped gangster. During the run a third child, another daughter, Stephanie, was born on February 24. Innumerable fans clamoured after Newman at the stage door after each performance but he disliked signing autographs. His next two films were made on loan to MGM and the second made his name. The first film he made was *The Rack* (released November 2, 1956). Newman played Captain Edward Hall who returned to America after two years in a Korean prisoner-of-war camp where he was brainwashed. The film was released in April 1956 but so few people saw it that it was quietly withdrawn and re-released after the success of Newman's next film. *Somebody Up There Likes Me* (released July 3, 1956) was a biopic of boxer Rocky Graziano. It went into production in January 1956. Directed by Robert Wise, Newman was third choice for the role of Graziano – Montgomery Clift turned it down and James Dean, the second choice, died in a car crash. To get in shape for the role, Newman worked out every day at the Hollywood YMCA. The film reunited Newman with his *Silver Chalice* co-star Pier Angeli who played his wife, Norma. Newman remarked that it was odd that he, a Jew, was playing the Catholic Graziano while Angeli, a Catholic, was playing the Jewish Norma Levine (Unger in real life). In his second film but first with a character name (Fidel) was the young Steve McQueen and the two men became close friends off set during the shoot albeit their relationship was tinged with an undercurrent of rivalry. Also in the film was Sal Mineo as Romolo and Newman befriended him as well. In one scene Newman, McQueen, Mineo and others were all part of a street gang of kids but Newman was 31 and McQueen 25, only Mineo looked authentic. Newman did the round of Tinseltown tattlers to promote the film, including paying homage to ageing gossip queen Hedda Hopper. It paid off. The film won favourable reviews with the the the *Los Angeles Times* declaring, "Newman is excellent" and *Variety* calling him "superb". It almost went wrong when he was arrested for drink driving at Mineola, Long Island. On July 5, 1956 Newman had got drunk at the Jolly Fisherman Restaurant on Main Street, Roslyn, Long Island and got into his car. Losing control of his vehicle, he ploughed the car into bushes and it only stopped when he hit a fire hydrant. With the unimpeachable logic of a drunk, he reversed the car and continued his journey home. He had two strokes of bad luck. Officer Rocky Gaggiano saw Newman and promptly arrested him. When he got to the police station, paparazzi and reporters surrounded him. He believed that the police had tipped them off but in fact they were present for news of a local kidnapping case. One pap recognised Newman and took his photograph, which appeared on the front page of the *Daily News*. Newman spent the night in jail. Recognising that he was developing a drink problem, he went to a psychotherapist recommended by his friend Janice Rule to discover why he needed so much alcohol. He only went three times before asking Rule for help. She later became a psychotherapist after giving up acting. Most of Hollywood expected Newman to get an

Academy Award nod for *Somebody Up There Likes Me* but when the nominations were announced in January 1957 Newman's name was conspicuous by its absence. Wise rang Newman to offer his commiserations and on the night of the Oscar ceremony threw a party for him at his Santa Monica home where he presented the disappointed Newman with a "Noscar" – a spoof award of Uncle Oscar leaning on his sword, resigned to defeat rather than standing erect and proud. Newman returned to television. Three years after *The Silver Chalice* Newman made his second film for Warner Bros – a biopic *The Helen Morgan Story* (released October 5, 1957) with Ann Blyth in the title role. The film had sat gathering dust on the shelves at Warner Bros for years and had been mooted as a vehicle for Jane Wyman or Judy Garland before it was finally made. Gogi Grant dubbed Blyth's singing voice and Michael Curtiz was given the directing job. Most Hollywood biopics are saccharine but *The Helen Morgan Story* concentrated on the dark side of Morgan, her chronic alcoholism and inability to maintain relationships. To add to their woes a television version of the story, also entitled, *The Helen Morgan Story*, aired five months earlier, directed by George Roy Hill, who would later feature in Newman's career. The film would turn out to be Ann Blyth's last. Warner Bros then cast Newman in *Marjorie Morningstar* (1958) but he refused to appear in the film, risking possible suspension. Instead, he returned to MGM, where, reunited with Robert Wise, he made *Until They Sail* (premièred October 8, 1957), a wartime romantic drama, opposite Jean Simmons. Newman played Captain Jack Harding who has an affair with Barbara Leslie Forbes (Simmons) whose husband had just set sail for the front. The film had the tagline, "They Couldn't Have The Love They Wanted, So They Took The Love They Could Get!" By now

Newman and Woodward had gone public with their relationship that would last until his death more than 50 years later and appeared in the television play (and Newman's last live TV drama) *The 80-Yard Run* (broadcast January 16, 1958). Their first feature film together was *The Long, Hot Summer* (released April 3, 1958) which was based on the writings of William Faulkner. Ben Quick (Newman), an arsonist, ingratiates himself with a wealthy family, the Varners. Joanne Woodward was not the first choice for Clara Varner but the original choice Eva Marie Saint fell pregnant and Woodward stepped into her shoes. The film co-starred Anthony Franciosa, Orson Welles, Lee Remick, Angela Lansbury, Mabel Albertson and Richard Anderson. Newman's divorce from his first wife became final on January 28, 1958. Before the divorce, he and Woodward shared Shirley MacLaine's Malibu Beach home with writer Gore Vidal and his boyfriend Howard Austen. Warner Bros then agreed to make *The Left-Handed Gun* (released May 7, 1958) based on Vidal's short television film *The Death Of Billy The Kid*. According to 5'7" Newman, Warner Bros wanted to make the film with a happy ending! The company was not especially interested in the film for which they had budgeted $700,000 and a 23-day shooting schedule. The scenes for the town were filmed on the same set as *High Noon* (1952). Vidal, himself gay, included an in-joke in the title. In some parts of America at the time left-handed was a euphemism for being homosexual – Billy the Kid was actually right-handed. By the time the film was released Joanne Woodward got her man – she and Newman were married at Hotel la Rancho, Las Vegas one day after his divorce from Jackie. They honeymooned in London with Vidal and Austen as their tour guides. Sadly, in February Woodward miscarried while still in London. Newman had to

start work on his next film and had to leave his new wife still hospitalised in London. *Cat On A Hot Tin Roof* (released September 20, 1958) co-starred Elizabeth Taylor and was based on the play by Tennessee Williams, which had won him his second Pulitzer Prize. Taylor was paid $125,000 for her part in the film. As was becoming the norm, Newman was not the first choice to play Brick Pollitt opposite Taylor's Maggie the Cat. The producers wanted Montgomery Clift but he refused the part because of Brick's implied homosexuality. In the Fifties as now, gay actors did not want to play gay on screen lest it harmed their career. Shooting began on March 12, 1958 and thanks to censorship by the Motion Picture Association of America use of the word "homosexual" was forbidden and the third scene had to be rewritten completely. Taylor fell ill during shooting and progress was delayed. It ground to a halt when Taylor's husband, Mike Todd, was killed in an aeroplane crash at 2.40am on March 22, 1958. Four days after that, Woodward won a Best Actress Oscar for *The Three Faces Of Eve*. Taylor returned to the set on April 14, 1958 having lost 12lbs through grief. She was still fragile and went on to have a nervous breakdown. Nevertheless, *Cat On A Hot Tin Roof* was a hit and took more than $10 million at the American box office alone. Tennessee Williams hated the film, which he saw as a bastardisation of his original play. There was a consolation for the playwright – he was paid $450,000 for the film rights. The film was nominated for several Oscars including Best Picture, Best Actor (Newman), Best Actress (Taylor), and Best Director (Richard Brooks), Best Cinematography, Colour (William Daniels), and Best Writing, Screenplay Based on Material from Another Medium. It did not win a single one when the gongs were handed out at the RKO Pantages Theatre in Hollywood on April 6, 1959. Taylor lost to Susan Hayward for playing drug-addicted prostitute and callous killer Barbara Graham in the film *I Want To Live!* On March 9, 1953 Graham and three confederates had broken into the Burbank home of elderly widow Mable Monohan, an action that resulted in the old lady's death and Graham's execution in the gas chamber at San Quentin on June 3, 1955. Newman lost out to David Niven for *Separate Tables* (1958) directed by Delbert Mann and written by Terence Rattigan, John Gay and an unaccredited John Michael Hayes (who is noticed elsewhere in this book). The Newmans bought a former coaching house in Connecticut, dating from 1780. It would become their refuge. Their neighbours and friends were the writer and biographer of Ernest Hemingway, A.E. Hotchner and his wife Ursula who would reoccur in Newman's life much later for a very different reason, far removed from movie making. Newman and Woodward appeared together in his next film, a screwball comedy called *Rally 'Round The Flag, Boys!* (released December 23, 1958). Newman played Harry Bannerman, Woodward his wife Grace Oglethorpe Bannerman and director Leo McCarey wanted Jayne Mansfield for the role of Angela Hoffa but the Newmans used their clout to have their friend Joan Collins cast in the part. To escape from his Warner Bros contract he agreed to make one final film for the studio. He appeared in *The Young Philadelphians* (released May 21, 1959), with Barbara Rush and Robert Vaughn (who won a Best Supporting Actor Oscar nomination). The film, based on the novel by *The Philadelphian* by Richard Powell and directed by Vincent Sherman, was the only Newman-Warner Bros movie to make a profit. Disenchanted with Hollywood he appeared in Elia Kazan's production of *Sweet Bird Of Youth*, a new play by Tennessee Williams that opened at the Martin Beck Theatre in

New York on March 10, 1959. With Newman playing the drifter Chance Wayne were Geraldine Page, Sidney Blackmer, Madeleine Sherwood, Diana Hyland, Logan Ramsey, John Napier, and Rip Torn. The production was nominated for four Tony Awards, including Best Actress for Geraldine Page. The play ran for 375 performances. In the summer of 1959 Newman bought himself out of his Warner Bros contract for $250,000. Two months earlier, on April 8, 1959 Joanne Woodward gave birth to Elinor Teresa known as Nell, his third daughter and fourth child. That year Newman also directed his first film, a short called *On The Harmfulness Of Tobacco*. In January 1960 Newman left the theatre to make the film *From The Terrace* (released July 15, 1960) in which he appeared with Joanne Woodward. It left another dud on his CV although he was paid $200,000, much more than he had ever received at Warner Bros. Newman's next film was Otto Preminger's *Exodus* (released December 15, 1960), about the birth of modern-day Israel and based on the 1958 novel by Leon Uris. The novelist was hired to write the script by Preminger, who threw away his efforts claiming that he had no ear for dialogue and instead gave the job to Dalton Trumbo, one of the blacklisted "Hollywood Ten". Newman was first choice for the role of Ari Ben Canaan, a Palestinian Jewish terrorist. He received another $200,000 cheque for his work, which began on March 27, 1960 in Israel. On the first day Newman arrived with six pages of suggestions of changes to the script but Preminger refused to even look at them. He finally listened to them but would not countenance any of them being used. Newman later described the experience on set as the worst of his career, not helped by hostile Arabs throwing stones at him. The film is now remembered for the superb theme, written by Ernest Gold. It was not a film that Newman would ever be proud of although the *Chicago Tribune* called the 220-minute flick "poignant, suspenseful, harrowing and timely" and it became the most successful Newman movie to date at the box office, taking $21,750,000. Gold's music won an Oscar and Newman's close friend Sal Mineo who played Dov Landau, a survivor of the Warsaw Ghetto, was nominated as Best Actor in a Supporting Role. For Newman, there was again nothing. Next Newman and Woodward appeared together in *Paris Blues* (released September 27, 1961), the fourth of the ten feature films that they would make together. Back in America Newman and Woodard campaigned for John F. Kennedy in his successful presidential campaign against incumbent Vice-President Richard M. Nixon. *Paris Blues* was yet another flop but it didn't matter because two days before, another Newman film opened, one that would really put him on the map. Twentieth Century Fox cast Newman as pool player "Fast Eddie" Felson in *The Hustler* (premièred Washington, DC September 25, 1961). The story had already been made into a television drama starring Cliff Robertson. Director Robert Rossen hired world billiards champion Willie Mosconi to be the film's technical adviser and filled out the rest of the cast with television comedian Jackie Gleason as Minnesota Fats, Piper Laurie as Sarah Packard and in his third film, George C. Scott as Bert Gordon. Mosconi spent a fortnight training Newman but Gleason was already virtually at professional standard. All but one of the shots in the film was actually played by Newman and Gleason. The pool shots were filmed at Ames Pool Hall on the second floor in the Claridge Hotel in Times Square, long since demolished. *The Hustler* made Newman a fully fledged star and Hollywood and beyond fully expected him to be rewarded with his first Academy

Award. When the nominations were announced *The Hustler* was up for nine gongs: Best Picture, Best Director (Robert Rossen), Best Actor in a Leading Role (Newman), Best Actor in a Supporting Role (Gleason), Best Actor in a Supporting Role (Scott but he refused to accept the nomination), Best Actress in a Leading Role (Laurie), Best Writing, Screenplay Based on Material from Another Medium (Sidney Carroll and Robert Rossen) and two more that it actually won – Best Black-and-White Art Direction-Set Decoration (Harry Horner and Gene Callahan) and Best Black-and-White Cinematography (Eugen Schüfftan) on April 9, 1962 at the Santa Monica Civic Auditorium. In the years to come the film's actors became rather unlucky apart from Newman and Scott. Gleason never made another major film, Piper Laurie disappeared from the screen until *Carrie* in 1976 and Robert Rossen fell ill during filming and made just one more film, *Lilith* (1964), before his premature death in 1966, aged just 57. Newman's next film saw him reprise his theatrical role of the drifter Chance Wayne in the cinematic version of *Sweet Bird Of Youth* (premièred March 21, 1962). Newman was paid $350,000 to return to Chance; Geraldine Page also reprised her part as Alexandra Del Lago despite having made only three films before. Madeleine Sherwood and Rip Torn also survived from the theatre to appear in the film. MGM intervened to glam up both Newman and Page much to the annoyance of Tennessee Williams. The result is not satisfactory in cinematic terms although those fans – male and female – that liked seeing Newman shirtless probably did not object. During filming Joanne Woodward gave birth to the couple's second daughter, Melissa Steward known as Lissy, on September 17, 1961. Both Geraldine Page (Best Actress) and Shirley Knight (Best Supporting Actress) who played

Newman's love interest were nominated for Oscars and Ed Begley actually won a Best Supporting Actor for his performance as Boss Finley. Newman, as usual, was ignored by the Academy when the awards were handed out on April 8, 1963 at the Santa Monica Civic Auditorium. Newman made a guest appearance in *Hemingway's Adventures Of A Young Man* (premièred July 18, 1962) written by his friend A.E. Hotchner. During the film Newman had a brief fling with Susan Strasberg who played Rosanna in the movie. She later said, "It was very satisfying, a release of passion and pent-up frustration. I liked Paul but I wasn't going to fall in love with him. He was a married man. I never had any problems sleeping with married men – that hardly makes me a whore. In the theatre, no actor – or actress for that matter – is ever faithful to their lover or spouse." Then Newman made his next major film *Hud* (premièred May 28, 1963), which was directed by Martin Ritt and adapted by Harriet Frank Jr. and Irving Ravetch from the novel *Horseman, Pass By* by Larry McMurtry. Hud Bannon (Newman) was a brash, arrogant, cruel, amoral cowboy with no redeeming features. When his father berates him for breaking the law, Hud responds, "Well, I always say the law was meant to be interpreted in a lenient manner. That's what I always try to do. Sometimes I lean to one side of it and sometimes I lean to the other." Oddly, in the book Hud is a minor character. The co-stars were Patricia Neal as Alma Brown, Melvyn Douglas as Homer Bannon, Hud's father, and Brandon de Wilde as Lonnie Bannon, Hud's nephew. As was often the case with the young men with whom he co-starred, Newman took Brandon de Wilde under his wing. When the Oscar nominations were published Newman was up for Best Actor, one of seven nods for the film. As was happening with disappointing frequency Newman didn't win but his co-stars did –

Melvyn Douglas won the Best Supporting Actor (Brandon de Wilde accepted the award on his behalf) and Patricia Neal won Best Actress (she, too, was not present and Annabella accepted the award on her behalf at the Santa Monica Civic Auditorium on April 13, 1964). James Wong Howe picked up the Academy Award for Best Black-and-White Cinematography. Martin Ritt also lost the Best Director gong and the writers Irving Ravetch and Harriet Frank Jr lost the Oscar for Best Writing, Screenplay Based on Material from Another Medium. *Hud* was also up for Best Black-and-White Art Direction-Set Decoration but lost. On August 28, 1963, Newman, Marlon Brando, Sidney Poitier, Burt Lancaster, Tony Curtis and other actors were among the marchers in the civil rights march on Washington DC, led by Dr Martin Luther King, Jr. Newman's next film was a comedy with wife Woodward, *A New Kind Of Love* (premièred October 30, 1963), followed by *The Prize* (opened Christmas Day 1963), which was loosely based on Irving Wallace's best-selling novel of the same name about the machinations behind the Nobel Prizes. Wallace's book had sold 100,000 copies in the author's homeland but was banned in Sweden because it suggested that the prizes could be fixed. The script written by Ernest Lehman bore little resemblance to the plot of Wallace's novel and the lead female character, Inger Lisa Andersson (played by Elke Sommer), did not even feature in the book. Nonetheless, Newman said, "I had more fun making *The Prize* than any movie I've made so far. I mean just plain fun." Newman finished the year in the top ten box office attractions list, coming in at number nine. He made a guest appearance in the black comedy *What A Way to Go!* (released May 12, 1964) as Larry Flint and then in August Newman appeared at the Democratic National Convention in

Atlantic City to lend his support to President Lyndon B. Johnson. He was also drinking far too much again. His next film *The Outrage* (premièred October 7, 1964), originally entitled *The Rape* and based on the Japanese film *Rashomon* (1951), directed by Akira Kurosawa and starring Toshiro Mifune, told the same story from four very different viewpoints. It didn't do well nor did Newman's next film *Lady L* (released in England December 17, 1965; released in New York May 18, 1966) in which he co-starred with Sophia Loren. Woodward feared that her husband would fall for Loren's undoubted charms and sleep with her. She had nothing to fear – Loren could not stand Newman, finding him uncouth and vulgar. Before flying to Paris for the film Newman and Woodward had appeared in the play *Baby Wants A Kiss*, which opened on April 19, 1964 and was staged by the Actors Studio. Newman played a married homosexual and he and Woodward were paid the Equity minimum of $117.50 each week. The play received poor reviews but was the only Actors Studio production to make a profit. Although his money was poor, he didn't intend to lose out so he began advertising Volkswagens in commercials seen only in West Germany. On April 21, 1965 Woodward gave birth to Newman's sixth child and fifth daughter, Claire Olivia known as Clea. With a mix of hits and misses, Newman's career needed a boost and so he returned to Warner Bros to film *Harper* (released February 23, 1966). Newman played private investigator Lew Harper opposite a strong cast that included Lauren Bacall, Julie Harris, Arthur Hill, Janet Leigh, Robert Wagner and Shelley Winters. It would be the first private eye film on the big screen for some time, the genre having been usurped by the small screen. The lead character was originally called Lew Archer but Newman, like many actors,

was superstitious and realised that his most successful films had all begun with H; therefore Lew Archer became Lew Harper. Newman was paid $750,000 plus 10 per cent of the box office gross for the film. He later claimed that he had based the cynical Lew Harper on Senator Robert F. Kennedy. For the first time, it would be a role that Newman would return to – he again played Lew Harper in *The Drowning Pool* (released July 1975). Newman's career seemed to consist of a flop followed by a hit followed by another flop and so it continued with *Torn Curtain* (released July 14, 1966), which was not one of Alfred Hitchcock's finest films. Newman signed up without seeing the final script and was disappointed when it was shown to him. As with Otto Preminger years before he sent suggestions to the director but like Preminger, Hitchcock ignored them. Returning to the Wild West Newman starred in *Hombre* (released March 21, 1967) where he worked again with Martin Ritt. Reuniting with writers Irving Ravetch and Harriet Frank Jr from *Hud*, cinematographer James Wong Howe also signed on. Newman played John Russell aka Hombre, a white man raised by Apaches, and spent five days on a Red Indian reservation to research the role. The film was an up-to-date version of John Ford's *Stagecoach* (1939) and received excellent reviews but was not a commercial success. Newman and his close friend and rival Steve McQueen were approached to star in the film version of Truman Capote's factual novel *In Cold Blood* (1965) about the Clutter murders even though both men were far too old to play the protagonists. Both declined. Instead Newman made *Cool Hand Luke* (released November 1, 1967) about a convict on a chain gang in the southern states of America. Producer Gordon Carroll did not originally want Newman to play the role of Lucas Jackson; his first choice was Telly

Savalas, then filming *The Dirty Dozen* (1967) in England. The film was an allegory about Jesus – Luke spends much of the film in a white robe and his prison number, 37, is a reference to the *Gospel According To Luke* Chapter 1, Verse 37: "For there is nothing that God cannot do." After eating the 50 hard-boiled eggs, Luke adopts a pose like a crucifixion. *Cool Hand Luke* garnered Newman his fourth Oscar nod and also led to his fourth disappointment. Newman then turned down the lead in *The Swimmer* (1968), a role that went to Burt Lancaster and was a disaster at the box office. Another comedy followed, *The Secret War Of Harry Frigg* (released February 29, 1968), with Newman taking the lead role of conman Private Harry Frigg. By the late Sixties Newman confessed that he was becoming bored with acting. In 1968 he went behind the camera and directed his first feature film. *Rachel, Rachel* (released August 26, 1968) starred Woodward as a frustrated schoolteacher, Rachel Cameron, who at 35, still lives with her mother. In order to get the film made, Newman had to promise Warner Bros that he would make two films for them at half his normal salary. Woodward also had to agree to a film at a smaller than usual salary. The film revived Woodward's career and won four Oscar nominations including Best Actress for Woodward, Best Supporting Actress (Estelle Parsons), Best Writing, Screenplay Based on Material from Another Medium (Stewart Stern) and Best Picture (Newman). It didn't win any. That year Newman spent 25 days campaigning for Senator Eugene McCarthy to win the Democratic nomination for president. Sirhan Sirhan had murdered Senator Robert F. Kennedy in Los Angeles in the first week of June, two months after Martin Luther King had also been cut down by an assassin's bullet. Despite Newman's endorsement, Senator McCarthy lost

the nomination to Vice-President Hubert Humphrey who, in turn, lost to Vice-President Richard Nixon on November 5, 1968. Ever vindictive, Nixon placed Newman at number 19 on his enemies list published on June 27, 1972. Newman appeared again with Woodward in *Winning* (released May 22, 1969), a film about racing cars. Indeed, he began racing professionally in 1972. Woodward feared that he would kill himself but Newman had another problem to deal with. His son, Scott, had grown up to be a handsome but deeply troubled man. In 1905 a film had been made of the exploits of two outlaws called Butch Cassidy and the Sundance Kid. It was said that the real pair had risked their liberty by attending a screening. Almost 65 years later, their story was again brought to the screen directed by George Roy Hill and starring Newman and Robert Redford. *Butch Cassidy And The Sundance Kid* (premièred September 2, 1969), which began shooting on September 16, 1968, would be Newman's last film of the Sixties and arguably his most popular ever. He was paid $750,000 for his work on the film. A regular visitor to the set was Lulu Betanson, the sister of the real Butch Cassidy. Off the set Scott Newman's behaviour was continuing to cause problems for his father. During filming Newman had began an affair with a journalist and occasional actress called Nancy Bacon. The fling ended because of his drinking. Bacon said, "'I finally said to myself, 'I can do better than this.' I told him, 'You're always drunk, and you can't even make love.' I ended it." The affair may have ended but rumours started in July 1969 that all was not well with the Newmans and a separation was inevitable. The gossip writer Joyce Haber wrote about the "fascinating rumours, so far unchecked" that "the Paul Newmans are living apart, according to friends, and will soon get a divorce". The next day the couple spent $2,000 on an advertisement in the *Los Angles Times* that announced, "Recognising the power of the Press and terrified to disappoint Miss Haber and her readers, we will try to accommodate her 'fascinating rumours, so far unchecked' by busting up our marriage, even though we still like each other – Joanne & Paul Newman." The affair continued apace once both had returned to Tinseltown. Bacon recalls, "We were hot and heavy for about a year-and-a-half. He was at my house almost every night for two or three weeks. It was the worst kept secret in Hollywood. People used to joke about it. Referring to his old remark, they'd say, 'Paul may not go out for hamburger, but he sure goes out for Bacon.'" The reviews for *Butch Cassidy And The Sundance Kid* were not totally favourable but the public enjoyed the film and soon it was a box office smash. The decade ended with Newman number two in the box office list (John Wayne was number one). Woodward was not impressed, "Look, he's 44, got six children, and snores in bed. How on earth can he be a sex symbol?" He started the Seventies appearing with his wife in *WUSA* (premièred August 19, 1970), about political corruption in New Orleans. It did not receive a favourable response from the public or critics. His films in the early Seventies were not very good: *Sometimes A Great Notion* (1970), which he also directed, *Pocket Money* (1972), *The Life And Times Of Judge Roy Bean* (released December 18, 1972) and *The MacKintosh Man* (released July 25, 1973) did nothing to solidify Newman's reputation. *The Life And Times Of Judge Roy Bean* would probably be forgotten if not for the fact that it is the only film in which future *Dallas* star Victoria Principal bares her magnificent breasts on screen. Newman directed *The Effect Of Gamma Rays On Man-In-The-Moon Marigolds* (released December 20, 1972), a domestic drama that starred Woodward. In 1973 Newman teamed up again with George Roy Hill and Redford to make *The Sting* (released December 23, 1973). It got his career out of the doldrums. From then on Newman only made films when he wanted to but he starred in the hit *The Towering Inferno* (premièred December 10, 1974) as Doug Roberts, which paired him with Steve McQueen. Both men were paid $1 million for the film, which started filming on May 13 and finished on September 11, 1974. Scott Newman played a bit part as a fireman in the film. In the box office listings for 1974 Newman was ranked third, not bad for someone aged 49. Newman's films in the Seventies were few after the mid-point of the decade. He appeared in *Buffalo Bill And The Indians, Or Sitting Bull's History Lesson* (1976) as Buffalo Bill, *Slap Shot* (1977) as Reggie Dunlop and *Quintet* (1979) as Essex, a film that Newman hates. At Christmas 1977 Newman, with friend and neighbour A.E. Hotchner, brewed up several gallons of their home made salad dressing and gave it to family and friends at Westport. Such was its appeal that the following year the two men sold it in local markets. They then decided to go into business, both investing $20,000. In August 1982 they formed a company to sell and market the dressing, Newman's Own, and in a remarkable act of generosity gave all their profits after tax to charity. The company to date has distributed almost $300 million. The product line has now increased and includes: pasta sauce, iced tea, lemonade, limeade, fruit cocktail juices, popcorn, pretzels, salsa, biscuits, coffee, grape juice, dog and cat food. Newman's Own Lemonade was introduced in 2004. In early 1978 Scott Newman, by now calling himself William Scott, was attempting to forge a music career. On November 19, he was staying at the Ramada Inn in West Los Angeles and was nursing injuries from a motorbike accident, pain that he numbed with copious amounts of drink and drugs. He took eight Valium tablets, snorted cocaine and then took several Quaaludes after which he had difficulty breathing. He was rushed to hospital but was pronounced dead at 1.07am on November 20, 1978. He was 28-years-old. Newman was nominated for an Oscar for the fifth time for *Absence Of Malice* (released December 18, 1981) but lost out at the ceremony on March 29, 1982 to Henry Fonda for *On Golden Pond*. Nomination number six came the following year with *The Verdict* (released December 8, 1982) in which Newman played washed-up, alcoholic lawyer Frank Galvin. This time he lost to Ben Kingsley for *Gandhi*. On March 24, 1986 Newman was presented with an honorary Oscar "in recognition of his many and memorable and compelling screen performances and for his personal integrity and dedication to his craft". He accepted via a satellite link. The following year, Newman finally won an Oscar when he reprised the role of Fast Eddie Felson in the movie *The Color Of Money* (premiered October 8, 1986). Again not present, his award was collected by Robert Wise. Bette Davis who had been celebrating perhaps too enthusiastically that night presented the statuette to Wise. However, when he tried to thank people on Newman's behalf Davis launched into a long tribute to Wise that left no time for Wise to speak. The telecast producer cut his microphone and the orchestra began playing. Newman's other films in the Eighties were: *When Time Ran Out . . .* (1980) as Hank Anderson, *Fort Apache The Bronx* (released 6 February 1981) as Murphy, *Harry & Son* (released March 2, 1984) as Harry Keach, *Shadow Makers* 1989) as General Leslie R. Groves and *Blaze* (1989) as Governor Earl K. Long. In 1987 Newman directed Woodward in a screen version of Tennessee Williams's *The Glass Menagerie* (1987). In 1994

Newman received the Jean Hersholt Humanitarian Award and the following year was nominated for Best Actor for *Nobody's Fool* (1994). Naturally, he didn't win. His final nomination came as Best Supporting Actor in *Road To Perdition* (2002) and again he was a loser in his last film. His final films were *Mr & Mrs Bridge* (1990) as Walter Bridge (with Woodward as Mrs Bridge), *The Hudsucker Proxy* (1994) as Sidney J. Mussburger, *Twilight* (1998) as Harry Ross, *Message In A Bottle* (1999) as Dodge Blake and *Where The Money Is* (2000) as Henry. Newman retired on May 25, 2007. He said, "You start to lose your memory, you start to lose your confidence, you start to lose your invention. So I think that's pretty much a closed book for me." CAUSE: In January 1984 Newman underwent an operation at Sequoia Hospital, Redwood City, California to unclog arteries. Newman, formerly a heavy smoker, was diagnosed with lung cancer in January 2007 but the disease was not made public until June 2008 when Newman underwent treatment at Sloan-Kettering hospital in New York. He died, aged 83, three months later. He was cremated after a private family service.
FURTHER READING: *Paul And Joanne: A Biography Of Paul Newman And Joanne Woodward* – Joe Morella and Edward Z. Epstein (London: W.H. Allen, 1989); *Paul Newman* – Lawrence J. Quirk (Dallas: Taylor Publishing, 1996); *Paul Newman* – Daniel O'Brien (London: Faber & Faber, 2004); *Paul Newman The Man Behind The Baby Blues: His Secret Life Exposed* – Darwin Porter (New York: Blood Moon productions, 2009); *Paul Newman: A Life* – Shawn Levy (London: Aurum, 2009).

Robert Newton

Born June 1, 1905
Died March 25, 1956
Eyeball-rolling baddie. Born in Shaftsbury, Dorset, Newton was a

memorably villainous Bill Sikes in *Oliver Twist* (1948) before Oliver Reed took on that mantle 20 years later. Although he began appearing in films in the early Thirties it was for his no-gooder roles that Newton is best remembered. His films included: *Fire Over England* (1937) as Don Pedro, *Poison Pen* (1939) as Sam Hurrin, *Dead Men Are Dangerous* (1939) as Aylmer Franklyn, *Dangerous Cargo* (1939) as Commander Tomasou, *Jamaica Inn* (1939) as James 'Jem' Trehearne, *Bulldog Sees It Through* (1940) as Watkins, *21 Days* (1940) as Tolly, *Major Barbara* (1941) as Bill Walker, *This Happy Breed* (1944) as Frank Gibbons, *Henry V* (1944) as Ancient Pistol, *Odd Man Out* (1947) as Lukey, *Obsession* (1949) as Dr Clive Riordan, *Waterfront Women* (1950) as Peter McCabe, *Treasure Island* (1950) as Long John Silver (probably his best role), *Tom Brown's Schooldays* (1951) as Dr Arnold, *Blackbeard The Pirate* (1952) as Blackbeard, *Les Miserables* (1952) as Javert, *Androcles And The Lion* (1953) as Ferrovius, *The Desert Rats* (1953) as Bartlett, *Long John Silver* (1954) reprising his portrayal of the one-legged sea cook that he also attempted on television in 1955, before his last film *Around The World In 80 Days* (1956) as Mr Fix, the villain who tries to prevent Phileas Fogg from travelling around the world in the given time. Towards the end of his life, Newton's career suffered because of his alcoholism.
CAUSE: Newton died of a heart attack in Beverly Hills, California. He was 54 years old.

Lionel Ngakane
Born July 17, 1928
Died November 26, 2003
Film pioneer. Lionel Ngakane was born in Pretoria and educated at Fort Hare University College and the University of Witwatersrand. For a brief time he worked as a journalist on the magazines *Zonk* and *Drum* before becoming assistant to Zoltan Korda on his film *Cry The Beloved Country* (1951) in which he also appeared as Absolom Kumalo alongside Sidney Poitier. Korda kept Ngakane on his payroll after the film had wrapped and he moved to England where he met and befriended exiles from South Africa, becoming active in the African National Congress. Ngakane also ran a stall in Portobello Market selling bric-a-brac and later opened an antiques shop in the area. He saved his earnings from the shop to buy a 16-mm cine camera and made his first documentary *Vukani* in 1962, about the evils of apartheid. He also made a short film *Jemima And Johnny* about the racial tensions in Notting Hill in the Sixties. The film won plaudits at the Carthage, Rimini and Venice Film Festivals. In 1967, in Tunis, he was a founder member of the Fédération Panafricaine des Cinéastes, an organisation devoted to promoting independent film-makers in Africa. As an actor Ngakane appeared in *Mark The Hawk* with Eartha Kitt in 1957 and *The Squeeze* in 1977 with Stacey Keach. In 1985 he directed a documentary about Nelson Mandela and, four years later, was a technical consultant on Euzhan Palcy's *A Dry White Season*. In 1994 he returned to South Africa and helped in the creation of the National Film and Video Foundation. He was unmarried.
CAUSE: He died, aged 75, after a long illness. His two brothers and three sisters survived him.

Haing S. Ngor
Born March 22, 1950
Died February 25, 1996
Unlikely star. Born in Samrong Young, Cambodia Ngor was a gynaecologist and obstetrician in his native Phnom Penh until the Khmer Rouge took over and began to torture intellectuals and professionals. Ngor fled to America where he appeared in the film *The Killing Fields* (1984) in which he played

Dith Pran, a translator. Ngor won a Best Supporting Actor Oscar for his portrayal. He continued to appear in films and was in *Dung Fong Tuk Ying* (1986) as Yeung Lung, *The Iron Triangle* (1989) as Tuong, *Vietnam, Texas* (1990), *My Life* (1993) as Mr Ho and *The Dragon Gate* (1999) as Sensei.

CAUSE: In a terrible irony, having escaped the terrors of the Khmer Rouge, Ngor was gunned down outside his home in Los Angeles' Chinatown district.

Wade Nichols

Born October 28, 1946
Died January 28, 1985
Suicide blond. Porn star who made the transition from glamour to mainstream when he landed a job using the name Dennis Parker on the TV soap *Edge Of Night* playing Police Chief Derek Mallory from 1979 until 1984. His films included: *Exploring Young Girls* (1975), *Visions* (1977), *Secret Dreams Of Mona Q* (1977), *Odyssey, The Ultimate Trip* (1977), *Barbara Broadcast* (1977), *Punk Rock* (1979), *Captain Lust And The Pirate Women* (1979) as Handsome Jack, *Love You* (1980) and *Blonde Ambition* (1981). In 1979, he recorded a disco album for Casablanca Records entitled *Like An Eagle*. Jacques Morali, who had created Village People, was the producer.

CAUSE: The bisexual Nichols committed suicide by shooting himself in the head after discovering he had contracted AIDS.

Anna Q. Nilsson

Born March 30, 1888
Died February 11, 1974
"The Most Beautiful Woman in America". Born in Ystad, Skåne län, Sweden Anna Quirentia Nilsson arrived in America in 1905 to seek her fame and fortune. She landed a job as a model where she was nicknamed "The Most Beautiful Woman in America". The modelling led to a film contract with Kalem Company and she made her début as the lead in *Molly Pitcher* (released December 11, 1911). It would be the first of around 200 films. Her movies included: *Seven Keys To Baldpate* (1917), *Heart Of The Sunset* (1918), *Soldiers Of Fortune* (1919), *One Hour Before Dawn* (1920), *The Toll Gate* (1920), *The Luck Of The Irish* (1920), *The Lotus Eater* (1921), *Ponjola* (1923) and *The Midnight Lovers* (1926) as Diana Fothergill. In 1925 she and a friend went riding when a snake scared her horse and threw her against a wall. Taken back to her hotel, a doctor examined her and prescribed rest but after five days the pain in her hip was unabated. The doctor turned out to be a drug addict who had misdiagnosed her and when she returned to Los Angeles she underwent a hip operation. She spent a year in hospital recuperating but was still unable to walk so had another operation. Returning to Sweden, she worked with a therapist who got her walking again. The advent of the talkies ruined her career and she was reduced to bit parts, her last appearance being in *Seven Brides For Seven Brothers* (1954) as Mrs Elcott. 5′7″ Nilsson played herself in *Sunset Boulevard* (1950) and was paid $250. She was married twice: firstly in 1916 to the actor Guy Coombs (b. Washington, DC, June 15, 1882, d. Los Angeles, California, December 29, 1947), they divorced the same year and secondly in 1923 to J. Marshall Gunnerson. They divorced in 1925.

CAUSE: She died in Hemet, California of heart failure. She was 85.

Derek Nimmo

Born September 19, 1930
Died February 24, 1999
Plummy-voiced thespian. Despite his rounded vowels Derek Robert Nimmo was actually born at 26 Springbourne Road in Liverpool, the son of an insurance clerk, Henry Nimmo (d. 1959) and Marjorie Sudbury Hardy. He knocked two years off his age and

reference books give his birthdate as 1932. He was educated at Quarry Bank High School, Harthill Road, Liverpool, the alma mater of politicians Bill Rodgers and Peter Shore and, of course, John Lennon, who took the school's name for his first band. (By coincidence, the first headmaster when the school opened in 1922 was called George Harrison.) Nimmo became interested in acting at school, often playing female roles. He left school at 17, and briefly and reluctantly followed his father into insurance. After national service (he was a corporal in the intelligence corps in Cyprus) he considered becoming a priest but took a job with a paint company paying £12 a week. He organised dances and concerts and met his future wife at one. On April 9, 1955 he married Patricia Sybil Anne Brown: they had two sons, Timothy St John (b. 1956) and Piers James Alexander (b. 1967) and a daughter, Amanda Kate Victoria (b. 1959). In 1952 he became a professional actor and landed his first part at the Hippodrome, Bolton, as Ensign Blades in J.M. Barrie's *Quality Street*. He spent the next four years in rep. Nimmo made his London début in Jean Anouilh's *Waltz Of The Toreadors* at the Criterion Theatre in 1957. He was to become known for playing clergymen and in 1964 he played one for the first time in the farce *See How They Run* at the Vaudeville Theatre. He appeared in the films *The Millionairess* (1960), *Go To Blazes* (1962), *The Amorous Prawn* (1962), *A Hard Day's Night* (1964), *Hot Enough For June* (1964), *Murder Ahoy* (1964), *Joey Boy* (1965), *Casino Royale* (1967) and *One Of Our Dinosaurs Is Missing* (1975) but was best suited to the small screen. From January 31, 1967 to June 17, 1971 he starred in *All Gas And Gaiters* as the self-effacing curate the Reverend Mervyn Noote opposite William Mervyn's bishop and Robertson Hare's archdeacon. The show ran for five series. Running simultaneously, he

played the accident-prone monk Brother Dominic in *Oh Brother!* (September 13, 1968–February 27, 1970). A sequel, *Oh Father!* (September 12–October 24, 1973), followed. Nimmo won the Royal Television Society's silver medal in 1970 and the Variety Club of Great Britain's Show Business Personality of the Year Award in 1971. He again donned clerical garb to play Dean Selwyn Makepiece in *Hell's Bells* (June 9–July 14, 1986). When the television work dried up he took to touring and created his own company Intercontinental Entertainment. He worked in Africa, America, Australia, and the Middle and Far East and was careful about the plays he produced. He abhorred the current trend towards nudity and crudity. In Britain he was best known for his work on the radio programme *Just A Minute*, alongside Kenneth Williams, Peter Jones and Clement Freud. He authored a number of books, including *Derek Nimmo's Drinking Companion* (1979), *Shaken And Stirred* (1984), *Table Talk* (1990) and *Memorable Dinners* (1991) and edited *O Come On All Ye Faithful: A Humorous Church Collection* (1986). CAUSE: On December 3, 1998, Derek Nimmo fell down a flight of stairs at his London home and was taken comatose to Chelsea and Westminster Hospital. He died of pneumonia on February 24, 1999. He left £561,717.

David Niven
Born March 1, 1910
Died July 29, 1983
Tale-teller. "If you want to know about my father's life, you won't find it in his autobiographies. They are all about other people." Thus spoke David Niven's elder son, also called David. And it is certainly true that although his two best-selling volumes of autobiography make for highly entertaining reading, they are by no means an accurate portrayal of Niven's

life or anyone he mentions in their pages for that matter. Like Kenneth Williams, Niven was a brilliant raconteur and believed (possibly rightly) that facts are of secondary importance in a ripping yarn. Niven's tall tales begin even at the moment of his birth. James David Graham Niven was born not in Kirriemuir, Angus, Scotland, as he told everyone, but in Belgrave Mansions, London. On August 21, 1915, his father was killed in action in Gallipoli and his mother married a Tory politician whom David disliked. Niven was expelled from his prep school for stealing a prize marrow and then went to Stowe. In his first autobiography, *The Moon's A Balloon*, Niven recounts the humorous story of how he lost his cherry aged 14 to a Piccadilly prostitute he called Nessie. However, his friend and biographer, Sheridan Morley, believes that 'Nessie' was a composite of many of the hookers that the teenage Niven associated with. Unlike many other public schoolboys Niven's sexual orientation was strictly heterosexual. During a promotional tour for his book, Niven announced that Nessie had written to him when he was around 20 and told him she had married and was now living in Seattle. After that whenever he appeared on TV in America the studio would be flooded by calls from English ladies *d'un age certain* claiming to be his teenage paramour. On July 23, 1926, he was caught cheating in an exam. Stowe didn't expel him, content with merely thrashing him to within an inch of his life. In 1928 he went up to R.M.C. Sandhurst where, in October of that year, he appeared in a play. The following year he joined the Highland Light Infantry. Niven tells the tale of being invited to a swanky fancy dress ball when he was a soldier. Determined to make an impression, he spent hours searching for a costume before finally deciding on a clown's outfit. His make-up was elaborate and for good

measure he brought a few props, such as a string of sausages. As Niven arrived, he thought the butler had a puzzled look on his face but thought no more of it. However, as the door to the drawing room was opened Niven's horror was complete. Everyone in the room was immaculate in evening dress. The young squaddie had the right venue but the wrong night. Again Niven's storytelling comes to the fore. For years Niven told the story of how he sent a telegram to his commanding officer "Request Permission Resign Commission". In fact, the telegram was sent by Niven's older brother, Max. Niven moved to Canada and then on to New York where he became a whisky salesman and racehorse promoter. A trip to Hollywood followed and he got work as an extra in various Westerns. Niven was listed by Central Casting as Anglo-Saxon type #2008 which was odd because his first job was playing a Mexican. His stock rose in Hollywood due in no small part to his friendship with Loretta Young and Sally Blane and his affair with Merle Oberon. His early films included *Cleopatra* (1934), *Without Regret* (1934) as Bill Gage, *Barbary Coast* (1934), *Splendor* (1935) as Clancey Lorrimore, *Mutiny On The Bounty* (1935), *Thank You, Jeeves* (1936) as Bertie Wooster, *Dodsworth* (1936) as Major Clyde Lockert (about which a reviewer wrote "All we can say about this actor is that he is tall, dark and not the slightest bit handsome"), *Rose-Marie* (1936) as Teddy, *The Charge Of The Light Brigade* (1936) as Captain James Randall, *The Prisoner Of Zenda* (1937) as Captain Fritz von Tarlenheim, *The Dawn Patrol* (1938) as Lieutenant Douglas 'Scotty' Scott, *Wuthering Heights* (1939) as Edgar Linton and *Raffles* (1939) as A.J. Raffles. As soon as filming wrapped on *Raffles*, Niven became the first of the British ex-pats in Hollywood to return home to fight in the war. He made just two films during the war, *The First Of The Few*

(1942) as Geoffrey Crisp and *The Way Ahead* (1944) as Lieutenant Jim Perry. His only film of 1945, the year the war ended, was Michael Powell and Emeric Pressburger's fantasy *A Matter Of Life And Death* (1946) as Squadron Leader Peter D. Carter, an RAF pilot taken before his time, and his battle to get back to earth. Unusually, the film was shot in both monochrome and colour. In December 1945 Niven returned to America, where tragedy was waiting. On September 21, 1940, he had married Primula Rollo (b. 1918) in Huish, near Marlborough and they were to have two sons: David, Jr. (b. December 15, 1942, at 9.30am) and James Graham (b. November 6, 1945). On May 21, 1946, Primmie Niven died of a fractured skull and lacerations after falling down a flight of concrete stairs at Tyrone Power's house during a game of sardines. She was 28 although Niven, for some reason, records her age as 25 in his autobiography. For a time after Primmie's death Niven lived with Rita Hayworth (he also had affairs with Ann Todd and Evelyn Keyes). His post-war films were for the most part disappointing and coincided with the end of the British Raj in Hollywood and the death of the studio system. They included *Enchantment* (1948) as General Sir Roland Dane, *Bonnie Prince Charlie* (1948) as Prince Charles, *Soldiers Three* (1951) as Captain Pindenny, *Happy Go Lovely* (1951) as B.G. Bruno, *The Elusive Pimpernel* (1951) as Sir Percy Blakeney, *Appointment With Venus* (1951) as Major Valentine Morland, *Happy Ever After* (1954) as Jasper O'Leary, *The King's Thief* (1955) as Duke of Brampton, *Carrington, V.C.* (1955) as Major Charles 'Copper' Carrington, *Around The World In 80 Days* (1956) as Phileas Fogg, *My Man Godfrey* (1957) as Godfrey Smith, *Bonjour Tristesse* (1958) as Raymond, *Please Don't Eat The Daisies* (1960) as Larry Mackay, *The Guns Of Navarone* (1961) as Corporal Miller, *55 Days At Peking*

(1963) as Sir Arthur Robertson, *The Pink Panther* (1963) as Sir Charles Litton, *Casino Royale* (1967) as Sir James Bond, *Vampira* (1974) as Count Dracula, *Paper Tiger* (1975) as Walter Bradbury, *Candleshoe* (1977) as Colonel Dennis/Mr Gipping/Mr Priory/John, *Death On The Nile* (1978) as Colonel Race, *Escape To Athena* (1979) as Professor Blake, *The Sea Wolves* (1980) as Colonel W.H. Grice, *Trail Of The Pink Panther* (1982) as Sir Charles Litton and *Curse Of The Pink Panther* (1983) again as Sir Charles Litton, although his voice was dubbed by comedian Rich Little because of Niven's final illness. On January 14, 1948 he married Hjördis Paulina Tersmeden at the South Kensington Registry Office. They would adopt two daughters, Kristina and Fiona; although the marriage was happy, it was punctuated by affairs on both sides. In 1951 Niven published his first book, a novel, called *Round The Rugged Rocks*. It was the story of a soldier who through a series of misadventures finds himself a Hollywood star. Niven probably revealed more of himself in this book than he did in his autobiographies, possibly one reason why he would not allow it to be republished in his lifetime after it went out of print. Seven years later, he won an Oscar for *Separate Tables* (1958). In 1971 he published the first volume of his memoirs. After certain publishers professed a lack of faith in the book, *The Moon's A Balloon* (originally entitled *Three Sides Of A Square*) went on to sell 5 million copies world-wide. Four years later *Bring On The Empty Horses* was a thumping success too. He spent much of his time publicising and promoting the book. His final book, a novel called *Go Slowly, Come Back Quickly*, was published in 1981.

CAUSE: In 1981 David Niven was struck down by amyotrophic lateral sclerosis or motor neurone disease. This causes the sufferer to lose both the ability to communicate and use of their limbs. He died from it two years later at Château-d'Oex, Switzerland, accompanied only by his nurse and daughter, Fiona. He left approximately $5 million in his will. His memorial service attracted over five thousand people.

FURTHER READING: *Bring On The Empty Horses* – David Niven (London: Hamish Hamilton, 1975); *The Moon's A Balloon* – David Niven (London: Coronet, 1981); *The Other Side Of The Moon: The Life Of David Niven* – Sheridan Morley (London: Weidenfeld & Nicolson, 1985).

Lloyd Nolan

Born August 11, 1902
Died September 27, 1985
Stalwart detective. Born in San Francisco, California, Lloyd Nolan began his career on the stage in 1927 and six years later made his Broadway début. Nolan began appearing in low-budget fare such as *G-Men* (1935) as Hugh Farrell and *Texas Rangers* (1936) as 'Polkadot Sam' McGee which lead to him being cast in the title role of the series of B-movies that began with *Michael Shayne, Private Detective* (1940). By the middle of that decade he had moved up to A-movies and showed himself to be a versatile performer. He appeared as Officer McShane in *A Tree Grows In Brooklyn* (1945) and FBI agent George A. Briggs in *The House On 92nd Street* (1945). He was also in *The Last Hunt* (1956) as Woodfoot, *A Hatful Of Rain* (1957) as John Pope, Sr and played Dr Swain in *Peyton Place* (1958). He received acclaim for his Broadway portrayal of Captain Queeg in *The Caine Mutiny Court-Martial*. His later films included: *Airport* (1970) as Harry Standish, *Earthquake* (1974) as Dr James Vance, *Prince Jack* (1984) as Joe Kennedy and the posthumously released *Hannah And Her Sisters* (1986) as Evan.

CAUSE: Nolan died of lung cancer in Los Angeles, California. He was 83.

Christine Norden

(MARY LYDIA THORNTON)
Born December 25, 1924
Died September 21, 1988
Britain's first post-war sex symbol. Born in Sunderland, Tyne-and-Wear, buxom Christine Norden became the protégée (and lover) of Sir Alexander Korda who put her in a number of films. She made her début in *Night Beat* (1947) as Jackie and went on to appear in *An Ideal Husband* (1947) as Mrs Marchmont, *Mine Own Executioner* (1947) as Barbara Edge, *The Interrupted Journey* (1949) as Susan Wilding, *Saints And Sinners* (1949) as Blanche, *Reluctant Heroes* (1951) as Gloria Pennie, *A Case For PC 49* (1951) as Della Dainton and *The Black Widow* (1951) as Christine Sherwin before retiring from films for 35 years, making a comeback in *Little Shop Of Horrors* (1986). In the gap she appeared on television in America and in 1967 became the first legitimate actress to bare her breasts on stage. Married five times, including once to cinematographer Jack Cardiff, her last husband named a scientific formula after her.

CAUSE: She died of pneumonia aged 63 in London. She was survived by her fifth husband and son.

Mabel Normand

Born November 16, 1894
Died February 22, 1930
'The Female Chaplin'. Mabel Ethelreid Normand was born in Boston, Massachusetts, the daughter of vaudevillians, and schooled at St Mary's Convent, Westport. Mabel and her parents moved to New York City where the 5'1" Mabel became interested in acting and modelling. She began appearing in films in 1910 for Biograph, then Vitagraph, appearing in more than 200 features. She quickly returned to Biograph, where she worked under Mack Sennett in comedies. On August 28, 1912, when Sennett moved to Keystone Mabel

went with him. They fell in love and even set a wedding date but that came and went and no nuptials followed. Mabel began to appear regularly with Fatty Arbuckle. By May 1, 1916, she was running her own production company. On July 23, 1917, she and Sennett went their separate ways after she was signed by Samuel Goldwyn on a five-year contract at a $3,500-a-week salary. Mabel enjoyed the high life rather too much and began to drink and take drugs. Her favourite read was the *Police Gazette*. She was also in the habit of eating peanuts while riding around Hollywood in her limousine. Sennett persuaded Goldwyn to release Mabel from her contract and she went back to Keystone. Then she met gentlemanly, handsome William Desmond Taylor. Through him, Mabel developed an interest in books; Taylor's ambition and delight was to improve his lady friends' minds through literature. Throughout her career, scandal seemed to dog Mabel. Her co-star Fatty Arbuckle found himself unjustly on the wrong end of the law in September 1921. When William Desmond Taylor was murdered five months later it was another nail in Mabel's professional coffin. Worse was to follow. On New Year's Day 1924 her chauffeur, Horace Greer, shot millionaire clubman Courtland S. Dines while Mabel and Edna Purviance were visiting. The gun was registered to Mabel. According to Greer, Mabel encouraged him to enter Dines' house, and he shot Dines because the bachelor oilman was about to hit him with a bottle during a row. At Greer's trial Mabel behaved in a most peculiar way, joking, waving her hands and holding her feet pigeon-toed. Greer was acquitted. Mabel's star soon flickered out and she developed addictions to booze and cocaine. On September 17, 1926, she married actor Lew Cody (b. Berlin, New Hampshire, February 22, 1884, as Lewis Joseph Coté, d. Beverly

Hills, California, May 31, 1934, of heart disease) when both were drunk.
CAUSE: Mabel died of tuberculosis in a sanatorium in Monrovia, California. Her last words were: "I sigh and surrender." Shortly before that she whispered: "I wonder who killed poor Bill Taylor?"

Ramon Novarro
(JOSÉ RAMÓN GIL SAMANIEGOS)
Born February 6, 1899
Died October 30, 1968
The poor woman's Valentino. Born in Durango, Mexico, the son of a dentist and one of fifteen children, 5'8" Novarro began his career in 1914 as a singing waiter in a Hollywood eatery where he was spotted by dance director Marion Morgan who gave him a job with her vaudeville act. He made his film début in *Joan The Woman* (1916) but it wasn't until he was cast as Rupert of Hentzau in *The Prisoner Of Zenda* (1922) that he became famous. He appeared in *Mr Barnes Of New York* (1922) as Antonio, *Where The Pavement Ends* (1923) as Motauri, *Scaramouche* (1923) as André-Louis Moreau, *The Arab* (1924) as Jamil Abdullah Azam and his most famous film *Ben-Hur* (1925) as Ben-Hur by which time he was earning $10,000 a week. Novarro was MGM's answer to Rudolph Valentino but didn't quite have what it took to inherit Valentino's mantle on his death in 1926. He also shone in Ernst Lubitsch's *The Student Prince In Old Heidelberg* (1927) as Crown Prince Karl Heinrich. In March 1929 he signed a contract with RCA and recorded *The Pagan Love Song* from the film *The Pagan* (1929) in which he played Henry Shoesmith, Jr. It was one of the first hit records originating from a film. By the Forties Novarro's career was over and he had found other ways of amusing himself. On April 29, 1942, he was fined and given a suspended sentence for drunken driving in Los Angeles. On

January 3, 1959, he was again arrested for drunken driving. On February 20, 1962, he was arrested yet again on the same charge and this time sentenced to a fortnight imprisonment. In the last thirty years of his life he made just seven films.

CAUSE: Novarro shared the same sexual preferences as his friend and rival Valentino and when the press inquired about his romantic life, studio publicists put them off with tales of Novarro's deep religious convictions. The only woman he was ever publicly linked with was Greta Garbo when they filmed *Mata Hari* (1931), in which Novarro took the part of Lieutenant Alexis Rosanoff. But since Garbo's biographer describes the film as "the first complete Garbo performance to communicate a coded message to lesbian and gay audiences" it seems the only place romance between the two ever existed was in the febrile imaginations of PRs and the naïve minds of unsophisticated fans. Novarro wasn't quite the devout celibate described in his early press. He had a penchant for rent boys and in the six months leading up to his death he had paid 140 prostitutes for their services. On Hallowe'en 1968 he summoned one more whore to his home, 3110 Laurel Canyon Boulevard, North Hollywood. At 5.30pm 23-year-old Paul Ferguson and his 17-year-old brother, Tom, arrived chez Novarro where he welcomed them with drinks and sent out for cigarettes from the local newsagent. The three carried on boozing, with Novarro recounting anecdotes about his career that went over the heads of the Fergusons, who had never heard of the old actor. All they were interested in was a stash of $5,000 in cash that Novarro supposedly kept in the house. Tom Ferguson, feeling woozy from the booze, went outside to get some fresh air while his brother stayed in the living room where Novarro serenaded him on the piano. After a while Novarro suggested they go somewhere more comfortable and led Ferguson to the bedroom. When Tom Ferguson returned to the house he went looking for his brother and was shocked to find him and the actor naked on the bed indulging in sexual intercourse; clearly Paul hadn't told his brother about the methods he would use to distract Novarro during the caper. Ferguson yelled at his brother to get out and the younger man staggered back to the living room where he rang his girlfriend. After three-quarters of an hour he heard Tom Ferguson calling for him but when he went to the bedroom he was greeted by the sight of a bloodsoaked room and Novarro lying half on the bed. He had three large gashes on the back of his head. The Fergusons half-dragged and half-carried the semi-conscious Novarro to the bathroom where they dunked him under the shower. Novarro mumbled something and Tom Ferguson stooped to listen. "Hail Mary, full of grace . . ." murmured Novarro. They put him back on the bed and Paul Ferguson dressed himself in Novarro's finery, complete with silver-tipped cane. The ailing actor saw a chance to escape and dragged himself to his feet only to be discovered by Paul Ferguson who began to thrash Novarro, splitting his skull and face as he struck. Novarro collapsed to the floor and there drowned in his own blood. Then the regrets came and Paul Ferguson insisted he hadn't meant to kill Novarro. Tom Ferguson came up with the bright idea of making the murder look like a robbery, so the two brothers trashed the old man's home. As a final touch Paul Ferguson placed the silver tip of the cane between Novarro's legs. In the house they found just $45. On November 4, 1968, Novarro was buried in Plot 584, Section C of Calvary Cemetery, 4201 Whittier Boulevard, Los Angeles, California 90023. Thanks to forensic evidence and a 48-minute telephone call made by Tom Ferguson the brothers were arrested two days later. They were tried in July 1969, convicted and sentenced to life imprisonment. They were released in 1976.

Ivor Novello

(DAVID IVOR DAVIES)
Born January 15, 1893
Died March 6, 1951
'The Handsomest Man In England'. One of Britain's greatest songwriters and light actors was born at Llywn yr Eos (Grove of the Nightingales), 95 Cowbridge Road, Cardiff, the only son of David Davies (b. 1852? d. October 1931 of dropsy and a heart attack), a rent collector for Cardiff council, and his wife, Clara Novello Evans (b. 1861, d. March 1, 1943), a singing teacher and choral conductor. After a private education in Cardiff and Gloucester, where he studied harmony and counterpoint with the cathedral organist, Dr (later Sir) Herbert Brewer, the young Ivor gained a scholarship to Magdalen College School, Oxford, where for three of his five years he was a solo treble in Magdalen College choir. His early compositions were inspired by visits to the Gaiety and Daly's theatres in London. His waltz *Spring Of The Year* was featured on a programme given by a choir led by his mother at the Albert Hall. Oddly, his voice didn't break until late 1909 when he was 16 years old. His *The Little Damosel* (1910) attracted much attention. Both compositions were attributed to "Ivor Novello". He changed his name by deed poll in 1927. He moved permanently to London in 1913 and took a flat at 11 Aldwych, which became his London residence for the rest of his life. Aged 22, during the First World War he wrote 'Till The Boys Come Home' ('Keep The Home Fires Burning'), to words by the American poet, Lena Guilbert Ford. Novello was to claim that he earned £15,000 from the song. Money did not inspire generosity, and

like millionaire oil tycoon Paul Getty, Novello installed a payphone in his home. He once gave an actress a diamond brooch. She approached Noël Coward: "Ivor gave me this tiny diamond. Can *you* see it?" Guests always brought their own booze since Novello rationed his measures. In June 1916 he reported to Crystal Palace training depot as a probationary flight sub-lieutenant. Always keen to impress, he had his own tailor make up his uniform. It would not be fair to say that Ivor Novello's forte was flying. He crashed twice and was moved to an Air Ministry office in the Hotel Cecil in London. There he had to learn to use a typewriter but found himself no more adept at that than he had been with an aeroplane's joystick. His first musical success was *Theodore And Co* which featured 13 Novello numbers and opened at the Gaiety Theatre on September 14, 1916. It was produced by George Grossmith and Edward Laurillard with a score written jointly by Novello and Jerome Kern. Novello then contributed four numbers to André Charlot's revue *See-Saw* (opening at the Comedy Theatre on December 14, 1916) and another production by Grossmith and Laurillard, the musical comedy *Arlette* (opening at the Shaftesbury Theatre on September 6, 1917) which featured seven Novello numbers. In 1917 he met the man who would become his long-term (but not only) boyfriend until his death, Robert 'Bobbie' Andrews (1895–1976), coyly described by biographer Peter Noble as "his closest friend". One of his lovers, author J.R. Ackerley, revealed that, "Ivor's equipment did not strike me as very impressive." 5'11" Novello regularly fell in love with women but when the crucial moment came found he was unable to perform. A story has it that Winston Churchill's only homosexual experience was with Novello. When asked what it was like, he replied "musical". Success followed success and he composed *Who's Hooper?* (opened at the Adelphi Theatre on September 13, 1919; a joint score with Howard Talbot), *The Golden Moth* by Thompson and P.G. Wodehouse (opened at the Adelphi Theatre on October 5, 1921), and the revues *Tabs* (opened at the Vaudeville Theatre on May 15, 1918), *A To Z* (opened at the Prince of Wales Theatre October 21, 1921; including Novello's second best known song 'And Her Mother Came Too' first sung by Jack Buchanan, with the lyricist Dion Titheradge), and *Puppets* (opened at the Vaudeville Theatre on January 2, 1924). He made his professional stage début in a straight play at the Ambassadors Theatre on November 23, 1921 playing a young man in *Deburau*, in which the role of Charles Deburau was played by Bobbie Andrews. A year earlier, he had been offered his first film role by the French film director Louis Mercanton in *L'Appel Du Sang* (1920). Novello was cast purely on the strength of a publicity photograph. His next film, *Miarka, Fille De L'Ourse* (1920) was also for Mercanton. Novello made his first English film for Alliance, *Carnival* (1921) as Count Andrea, and went on to appear in *The Bohemian Girl* (1922) as Thaddeus for Alliance, *The Man Without Desire* (1923) for Atlas Biocraft. His first film in America was *The White Rose* (1923) as Joseph Beaugarde, directed by D.W. Griffith for Ideal/United Artists. On June 9, 1924 Novello produced and starred in the successful play *The Rat* about the Parisian thief Pierre 'The Rat' Boucheron at the Prince of Wales Theatre. The play was credited to the pseudonymous David L'Estrange but was written by Novello with his friend, the actor Constance Collier. Filmed for Gainsborough in 1925, it spawned two sequels *The Triumph Of The Rat* (1926) and *The Return Of The Rat* (1928), again for Gainsborough with whom he signed a contract in 1927. Among

Novello's other films were: *Bonnie Prince Charlie* (1923), *The Vortex* (1928) as Nicky Lancaster, *South Sea Bubble* (1928) his last silent film, *Symphony In Two Flats* (1930) as David Kennard and *I Lived With You* (1933) as Prince Felix Lenieff. In 1926 Novello played the title role in Alfred Hitchcock's silent film *The Lodger*, the story of a stranger who is assumed (wrongly) to be Jack the Ripper. The film was the first real Hitchcock thriller. Six years later, the movie was remade as a talkie and was co-written by Novello. The fee from the film *The Constant Nymph* (1928), in which he played Louis Dodd, allowed him to buy Munro Lodge, Littlewick Green, near Maidenhead in Berkshire on November 11, 1927. The price was £4,000 and Novello renamed the five-bedroomed property Redroofs. It was to be his country residence for the rest of his life. Novello returned to the musical stage with the revue *The House That Jack Built* (opened at the Adelphi Theatre on November 8, 1929), to which he contributed eight numbers to a score that also included music by Vivian Ellis, Arthur Schwartz, and Sydney Baynes. In the summer of 1931 Novello moved to Hollywood with a contract from MGM as both a screenwriter and an actor. His talents were scandalously underused: and he made only one minor film as an actor and his biggest contribution was his work on the script for *Tarzan The Ape Man* (1932), for which he reputedly originated the line that gave rise to the now mythical if inaccurate "Me Tarzan. You Jane" (originally – with appropriate pointing – "Tarzan. Jane."). While in Hollywood he had written the play *I Lived With You* and it opened in the West End at the Prince of Wales Theatre on March 2, 1932. It starred Novello, Ursula Jeans and Robert Newton. *Party* opened at the Strand Theatre on May 23, 1932 and starred Benita Hume (the future Mrs Ronald Colman) and Douglas Byng.

Novello returned to London following the death of his father. Exceptionally prolific in the early Thirties Novello had simultaneous London productions of *Fresh Fields* (at the Criterion Theatre from January 5, 1933), *Flies In The Sun* (at the Playhouse Theatre from January 13, 1933), *Proscenium* (at the Globe Theatre from January 14, 1933), and *Sunshine Sisters* (at the Queen's Theatre from November 8, 1933). He met the handsome Christopher Hassall, the father of the beautiful but doomed actress Imogen Hassall, at a midnight supper in Oxford in early 1934 and the two men had an affair that understandably caused much distress to Hassall's wife. They appeared together in Novello's play *Murder In Mayfair* which opened at the Globe Theatre on September 5, 1934. With Hassall, Novello wrote his first musical romance for Drury Lane, *Glamorous Night*, which opened on May 2, 1935. Hassall contributed lyrics to nearly all of Novello's later musical stage shows. On March 23, 1939 at the Theatre Royal, Drury Lane, Novello's most lasting musical stage work *The Dancing Years* opened. The Second World War forced its initial closure and it toured the country before returning to the West End at the Adelphi on March 14, 1942, to run until July 8, 1944.

Novello often filled the cast of his plays with a high percentage of gay men. He only half-jokingly renamed his play *The Dancing Years* "The Prancing Queers". On March 24, 1944, a plain clothes policeman called at 11 Aldwych and charged Novello with unlawful conspiracy to commit offences against the Motor Vehicles (Restriction of Use) Order, 1942. His Rolls-Royce had been used by a supposed fan and assistant, Dora Grace Constable. Novello was none the less deemed liable, and on April 24, 1944 at Bow Street Court he was sentenced to eight weeks in Wormwood Scrubs. Constable was fined £50 with £25 costs. An appeal on May 16, 1944 reduced the sentence

from eight weeks to four, but his brief spell of "porridge" shook him badly both mentally and physically and had lasting effects. On February 16, 1951 his last show, *Gay's The Word*, opened at the Saville Theatre. It starred the comedienne Cicely Courtneidge and for the first time there was no part for Novello. The lyricist was the young and acerbic Alan Melville.

CAUSE: Ivor Novello spent Christmas 1950 at his home Wyndways at Montego Bay in Jamaica but the holiday did not have the restorative powers that he had hoped. He returned to London in February 1951 and unwisely insisted on performing. He died aged 58 at 11 Aldwych, London at 2.15am of a coronary thrombosis. The funeral was held at Golders Green Crematorium at 1pm on March 12, 1951, and his ashes buried under a lilac tree. He left £146,245 2s. 4d, a substantial part going to the faithful Bobbie Andrews. A memorial service at St Martin-in-the-Fields on May 28, 1951 was relayed on loudspeakers to a crowd of several thousand. A scholarship in his memory was established at RADA and his name lives on in the eponymous awards presented annually since 1955.

FURTHER READING: *The Life I Have Loved* – Clara Novello Davies (London: Heinemann, 1940); *Ivor The Story Of An Achievement* – W. Macqueen Pope (London: W.H. Allen, 1952); *Ivor Novello Man Of The Theatre* – Peter Noble (London: The Falcon Press, 1951); *The World Of Ivor Novello* – Richard Rose (London: Leslie Frewin, 1974); *Ivor* – Sandy Wilson (London: Michael Joseph, 1975); *Ivor Novello* – James Harding (London: W.H. Allen, 1987).

Rudolf Nureyev

Born March 17, 1938
Died January 6, 1993
'The Tartar Fury'. Born on a train travelling to Vladivostok, Nureyev became the greatest ballet dancer of the

second half of the twentieth century. Ironically, Nureyev's father was a soldier who hated the ballet. When he joined the Kirov Ballet School, Nureyev shared a room with eight other dancers. On June 16, 1961, the 5′8″ actor defected to the West while in Paris. (Trivia fact: he cut his hair with toenail clippers.) In 1964, with Margot Fonteyn, he received the largest ever number of curtain calls – 64 – for a production of *Swan Lake*. American ballet guru George Balanchine described Nureyev as "the Brigitte Bardot of ballet". Nureyev, who had a record collection numbering several thousand, appeared as the King in an American production of *The King & I*. When the show reached Miami Nureyev only just made his entrance on time and was visibly distracted during the scene. He kept saying "Matt – the phone!" to someone off stage as Mrs Anna (Liz Robertson) tried to explain why the English were not barbarians. Nureyev's calls became ever more frantic and he began to mime the action of a telephone. He dashed through the scene at breakneck speed, surprising not only the audience but his fellow members of the cast into the bargain. After what seemed an interminable age (to Nureyev) the curtain fell and he raced into the wings. It later emerged that Nureyev had made a long-distance call to France before going on stage and had forgotten to replace the receiver. Each minute on stage was costing him a small fortune. An enigmatic figure, Nureyev had a habit of taking midnight walks alone. According to a recent biography, Nureyev, who was not averse to male company, had an affair with Bobby Kennedy. Nureyev made few films. They included *A Leap By The Soul* (pre-1960), *Swan Lake* (1965), *Romeo & Juliet* (1966), *Don Quixote* (1973), *Valentino* (1977), in which he shucked

his clothes to play the great cinematic lover, and *Exposed* (1983).
CAUSE: Nureyev died of AIDS aged 54 in Paris.

Maila Nurmi

(MAILA ELIZABETH SYRJANIEMI)
Born December 21, 1921
Died January 10, 2008
Vampira. Born in Petsamo, Finland (now Pechenga, Russia), she moved to Ohio as a child and when she began modelling she was a natural blonde. She later adopted the persona of Morticia from *The Addams Family* and called herself Vampira. She made her film debut in *If Winter Comes* (1947) and began hosting her own television programme *The Vampira Show* seven years later. Director Ed Wood cast her in *Plan 9 From Outer Space* (1959) as Bela Lugosi's mate. She said of the film, "At the time, I thought it was horrible. I knew immediately I'd be committing professional suicide, but I thought 'What choice do I have?' Somehow, I seemed to be dead already. I love glamour and physical beauty. I've always been fascinated by beautiful men on the screen: Tyrone Power, Robert Walker, with soft-focus filters and velvet voices. That's what Ed Wood was like. Beautiful, dreamy eyes and long, sweeping lashes just beautiful. He didn't make a very pretty lady [in *Glen Or Glenda*], but he made an awfully pretty man." The following year she appeared in *Sex Kittens Go To College* (released August 24, 1960) as Etta Toodie. 5′6½″ Vampira was the inspiration for later horror actresses including Elvira whom she unsuccessfully sued for trademark infringement in March 1989. She was married twice, to Dean Riesner in 1949 and from June 20, 1961 to Fabrizio Mioni.
CAUSE: She died of natural causes in Los Angeles. She was 86.

O

Edmond O'Brien

Born September 10, 1915
Died May 9, 1985
Character ham. Born in New York, O'Brien's career began aged ten when he performed magic tricks for his local neighbourhood and then became interested in amdram. Dropping out of Fordham University, he worked as a bank clerk and appeared in plays, after which he had the luck to be taken on by Orson Welles to join his Mercury Players in 1937. The following year, he made his film début as a prisoner in *Prison Break* (1938). He worked steadily in both leading and supporting roles until his appearance (he was rather heavy) forced him to accept supports only. His films included: *The Hunchback Of Notre Dame* (1939) as Pierre Gringoire, *Obliging Young Lady* (1941) as 'Red' Reddy, *A Girl, A Guy, And A Gob* (1941) as Stephen Herrick, *Winged Victory* (1944) as Irving Miller, *The Killers* (1946) as Jim Reardon, *Fighter Squadron* (1948) as Major Ed Hardin, *Another Part Of The Forest* (1948) as Ben Hubbard, *For The Love Of Mary* (1948) as Lieutenant Tom Farrington, *White Heat* (1949) as Vic Pardo/Hank Fallon, *Between Midnight And Dawn* (1950) as Dan Purvis, *711 Ocean Drive* (1950) as Mal Granger, *Backfire* (1950) as Steve Connolly, *D.O.A.* (1950) as Frank Bigelow, a dying man looking for his murderer, *Warpath* (1951) as John Vickers, *Denver And Rio Grande* (1952) as Jim Vesser, *The Greatest Show On Earth* (1952), *China Venture* (1953) as Captain Matt Reardon, *Julius Caesar* (1953) as Casca, *The Barefoot Contessa* (1954) as press agent Oscar Muldoon, for which he won a Best Supporting Actor Oscar, *Pete Kelly's Blues* (1955) as Fran McCarg, *The Girl Can't Help It* (1956) as Marty Murdock, *1984* (1956) as Winston Smith, *D-Day The Sixth Of June* (1956) as Colonel Alex Timmer, *Stopover Tokyo* (1957) as George Underwood, *Up Periscope* (1959) as Stevenson, *The Longest Day* (1962) as General Raymond D. Barton, *The Man Who Shot Liberty Valance* (1962) as Dutton Peabody, *Birdman Of Alcatraz* (1962) as Tom Gaddis, *Seven Days In May* (1964) as Senator Raymond Clark, for which he was nominated for a second Oscar, *Sylvia* (1965) as Oscar Stewart, *The Wild Bunch* (1969) as Sykes, *Dream No Evil* (1970) as Timothy Macdonald, *99 And 44/100 Per Cent Dead* (1974) as Uncle Frank Kelly and *Lucky Luciano* (1974) as Commissioner Harry J. Anslinger. On February 19, 1941, O'Brien and actress Nancy Kelly (b. Lowell, Massachusetts, March 25, 1921) eloped to Yuma, Arizona. In June 1941 they separated and divorced on February 2, 1942. Six and a half years later, on September 26, 1948, he married actress Olga San Juan (b. Brooklyn, New York, March 16, 1927) in Santa Barbara. They had two daughters: actress Maria (b. 1950) and Bridget (b. 1951) and a son, Brendan (b. May 9, 1962). The couple was divorced in 1976.
CAUSE: Edmond O'Brien died of Alzheimer's disease aged 69 in Inglewood, California. He was buried in Grave 50, Tier 54, Section F of Holy Cross Cemetery & Mausoleum, 5835 West Slauson Avenue, Culver City. California 90230.

Pat O'Brien

(WILLIAM JOSEPH PATRICK O'BRIEN)
Born November 11, 1899
Died October 15, 1983
Responsible character. Born in Milwaukee, Wisconsin, Pat O'Brien began in vaudeville as a dancer and then moved to the legitimate theatre with appearances on Broadway. He made his film début playing a

detective in *Compliments Of The Season* (1930) but it was as the cynical journalist Hildebrand Johnson in *The Front Page* (1931) that he first made his mark. He appeared in several films before joining Warner Bros in 1933, where he stayed for seven years. He was probably best known for playing opposite his real-life close friend James Cagney in films such as *Here Comes The Navy* (1934) as Biff Martin, *Devil Dogs Of The Air* (1935) as Lieutenant William Brannigan, *The Irish In Us* (1935) as Patrick O'Hara, *Ceiling Zero* (1935) as Jake Lee, *Boy Meets Girl* (1938) as J. Carlyle Benson, *Angels With Dirty Faces* (1938) as The Reverend Jerry Connolly, *The Fighting 69th* (1940) as Father Duffy and *Torrid Zone* (1940) as Steve Case. O'Brien, unlike Cagney, enjoyed his time at Warner Bros and, in later years, was called upon to repeat his cry of encouragement in *Knute Rockne, All American* (1940) in which he played Knute Rockne to "win one for the Gipper", Ronald Reagan. After leaving Warner Bros, O'Brien worked for various studios and was working up until two years before his death (he played Delmas in *Ragtime* [1981]). Unusually for Hollywood, and indeed for most of the rest of the world too, O'Brien was married to the same woman for 53 years. He married actress Eloise Taylor on January 23, 1931, and they had one daughter and adopted a son and two more daughters. CAUSE: Pat O'Brien died aged 83 in Santa Monica, California, from a heart attack. He was buried in Grave 62, Tier 56, Section F of Holy Cross Cemetery & Mausoleum, 5835 West Slauson Avenue, Culver City, California 90230.

Donald O'Connor

Born August 28, 1925
Died September 27, 2003
All-rounder. Born into an Irish vaudeville family at St Elizabeth Hospital, Chicago, Illinois Donald David Dixon Ronald O'Connor was one of seven children of John Edward "Chuck" O'Connor, an acrobat with Ringling Brothers-Barnum and Bailey Circus. Three of his siblings did not see adulthood. O'Connor was involved in a car crash when he was a young child that killed his sister, Arlene. Their father died of a heart attack a few weeks later. O'Connor began working in films in 1937 signing a contract with Paramount. His first film was *Melody For Two* (1937) with his two brothers, Jack and Billy. In yet another tragedy Billy later died from scarlet fever. Donald shone in *Sing You Sinners* (released August 17, 1938) opposite Bing Crosby, was Huckleberry Finn in *Tom Sawyer, Detective* (1938) and the 12-year-old Gary Cooper in *Beau Geste* (released September 15, 1939). After a year away when he grew too old for children's roles, he signed for Universal Pictures in 1942 and then appeared in four of the studio's Gloria Jean musicals. In 1944 he joined the army. On demob he was cast opposite Francis the Talking Mule in 1950 and made one film playing Peter Stirling with the animal a year until 1955: *Francis* (1950), *Francis Goes To The Races* (1951), *Francis Goes To West Point* (1952), *Francis Covers The Big Town* (1953), *Francis Joins The WACS* (1954) and *Francis In The Navy* (1955). He left the series and said, "When you've made six pictures and the mule still gets more fan mail than you do . . ." O'Connor had to miss the filming of *White Christmas* (1954) with Crosby after he contracted pneumonia. In between frolicking with Francis O'Connor he appeared in the classic *Singin' In The Rain* (premièred March 27, 1952) as Cosmo Brown. The film won him a Golden Globe for Best Performance by an Actor in a Comedy or Musical. The following year he was Kenneth Gibson in the Irving Berlin musical *Call Me Madam* (1953). It was his favourite performance. "My favourite number is

in there with Vera-Ellen. It's the number I do out in the garden with her to 'It's A Lovely Day Today'. It's a beautiful lyrical number. I think she was the best dancer outside of Peggy Ryan I ever danced with." He appeared in another Berlin musical in 1954 playing Tim Donahue, a member of a performing family, in *There's No Business Like Show Business* (released December 16, 1954) opposite Ethel Merman, Dan Dailey, Johnny Ray and Marilyn Monroe. In 1957 O'Connor played the lead in *The Buster Keaton Story*. His career never really soared again and he spent the rest of it playing guest roles on television programmes and the occasional film such as *Ragtime* (1981) and *Out To Sea* (1997). In the Seventies he had a drink problem. On February 7, 1944 he married Gwen Carter and they had one daughter, Donna Gwen (b. August 10, 1946), before their divorce in 1954. On October 11, 1956 he married Gloria Noble and they had three children: Alicia (b. September 20, 1957), Donald Frederick (b. 1960) and Kevin (b. 1961). Of his career, he said, "I was born and raised to entertain other people. I've heard laughter and applause and known a lot of sorrow. Everything about me is based on showbusiness."
CAUSE: In 1971 O'Connor suffered a heart attack. In January 1999 he was hospitalised with pneumonia. His health was never good afterwards and O'Connor died aged 78 of congestive heart failure at Calabasas, California. He was cremated.

Heather O'Rourke
Born December 27, 1975
Died February 1, 1988
Film moppet. Born in San Diego, California, Heather O'Rourke captured the imagination of the public for her role as Carol Anne Freeling, famous for the cries, "They're heere" and "They're baaack" in the horror trilogy *Poltergeist* (1982), *Poltergeist II: The*

Other Side (1986) and *Poltergeist III* (1988). She also had a recurring role as Heather Pfister on the television sitcom *Happy Days* from 1982 until 1983. Three years earlier, she had been sitting having lunch at MGM with her mother when Steven Spielberg asked if he could talk to her. No, she replied, she didn't talk to strangers. With her mother's permission Spielberg chatted to her and cast her in *Poltergeist*.
CAUSE: On February 1, 1988, she began to suffer stomach ache and was taken to the Children's Hospital of San Diego. She died of pulmonary and cardiac arrest on the operating table, presumably the result of a hereditary weakness of the heart. She was 12 years old. She was buried in Westwood Village Memorial Park, 1218 Glendon Avenue, Los Angeles, California 90024.

Maureen O'Sullivan
Born May 17, 1911
Died June 23, 1998
Tarzan's Jane who became Frank Sinatra's mother-in-law. Born above a draper's shop in Boyle, County Roscommon, Ireland, Maureen Paula O'Sullivan went to the same Catholic school as Vivien Leigh: Convent of the Sacred Heart, Roehampton, and from the age of 9, she wanted to be a pilot. Back in Dublin she met director Frank Borzage at a horse show and he invited her to Hollywood to test for him. She arrived with her mother in 1930. She was Elinor Worthing in *So This Is London* (released June 6, 1930) and then played Eileen O'Brien in Borzage's *Song O' My Heart* (released September 7, 1930). On March 25, 1932 she opened in *Tarzan The Ape Man* (1932) as Jane Parker opposite Johnny Weissmuller. She was to reprise the role of Jane in *Tarzan And His Mate* (released April 20, 1934), *Tarzan Escapes* (released November 6, 1936), *Tarzan Finds A Son!* (released June 16, 1939), *Tarzan's Secret Treasure* (released December 1, 1941) and *Tarzan's New York Adventure* (released

May 1942). Years later, Esther Williams would ask O'Sullivan if she had suffered the same "harassment" from Weissmuller who was determined to show her (Williams) his rather magnificent equipment. O'Sullivan said she did. "What did you do?" asked Williams. "I let him show me." O'Sullivan also faced problems from the simians on set: "Cheetah bit me whenever he could. The apes were all queers, eager to wrap their paws around Johnny Weissmuller's thighs. They were jealous of me, and I loathed them." Before her retirement in 1942 to raise a family and look after her husband who had been discharged from the navy with typhoid, 5'3" O'Sullivan also appeared in, among others, *Fast Companions* (released June 23, 1932) as Sally, *Payment Deferred* (released November 7, 1932) as Winnie Marble, *Strange Interlude* (released December 30, 1932) as Madeline Arnold, *Tugboat Annie* (released August 4, 1933) as Pat Severn, *Stage Mother* (released September 29, 1933) as Shirley Lorraine, *The Thin Man* (released May 25, 1934) as Dorothy Wynant, *The Barretts Of Wimpole Street* (released September 21, 1934) as Henrietta Barrett, George Cukor's *The Personal History, Adventures, Experience, And Observation Of David Copperfield The Younger* (premièred January 8, 1935) as Dora, *Cardinal Richelieu* (released April 28, 1935) as Lenore, *Woman Wanted* (released August 2, 1935) as Ann, *Anna Karenina* (released August 30, 1935) as Kitty, *A Day At The Races* (released June 11, 1937) as Judy Standish, *Between Two Women* (released July 9, 1937) as Claire Donahue, *My Dear Miss Aldrich* (released September 17, 1937) as Martha Aldrich, *A Yank At Oxford* (released February 18, 1938) as Molly Beaumont, *Spring Madness* (released November 11, 1938) as Alexandra Benson, *Let Us Live!* (released March 29, 1939) as Mary Roberts,

Sporting Blood (released July 12, 1940) as Linda Lockwood, *Pride And Prejudice* (released July 26, 1940) as Jane Bennet and *Maisie Was A Lady* (released January 10, 1941) as Abigail Rawlston. On September 12, 1936, she had married John Villiers Farrow (b. Sydney, Australia, February 10, 1904, d. Beverly Hills, California, January 28, 1963, of a heart attack) at St Monica's Church, Santa Monica, and by him had seven children: Michael Damien (b. May 30, 1939, k. October 29, 1958, in a plane crash while taking flying lessons), Patrick Joseph (b. November 27, 1942, committed suicide June 15, 2009 at his art studio in Castleton, Vermont by shooting himself in the head), Maria de Lourdes (b. Beverly Hills, California, February 9, 1945), John Charles (b. Los Angeles, California, September 6, 1946), Prudence Annevilliers (b. Los Angeles, California, January 20, 1948), Stephanie Margarita (b. June 4, 1949) and Theresa Magdalena (b. Los Angeles, California July 22, 1951). Maria de Lourdes became famous as actress Mia Farrow and lost her virginity to Frank Sinatra in the process while Stephanie and Theresa as Tisa also became actresses. Prudence Farrow inspired John Lennon to write the song *Dear Prudence*. Although O'Sullivan adored Farrow he was not faithful to her. When she made her comeback she appeared in, among others, *Bonzo Goes To College* (1952) as Marion Drew, *Duffy Of San Quentin* (released March 16, 1954) and *The Steel Cage* (released December 1954) both as Gladys Duffy, *Wild Heritage* (released August 1958) as Emma Breslin, *Never Too Late* (released November 4, 1965) as Edith Lambert, *Too Scared To Scream* (1985) as Mother, Woody Allen's *Hannah And Her Sisters* (released February 7, 1986) as Norma, *Peggy Sue Got Married* (premièred October 7, 1986) as Elizabeth Alvorg and *Good Ole Boy: A Delta Boyhood* (released November 11,

1988) as Aunt Sue. She also ran Wediquette International, a bridal consulting service. On August 22, 1983 O'Sullivan married James Cushing in Loudonville, New York.

CAUSE: Maureen O'Sullivan died of a heart attack in Scottsdale, Arizona. She was 87-years-old.

Warren Oates

Born July 5, 1928
Died April 3, 1982

Reliable character. Born in Depoy, Kentucky, the son of Bayless E. Oates, who owned a general store, and Sarah Alice Mercer, Warren Mercer Oates enlisted in the US Marines and after service moved to New York in 1954. He worked behind the scenes in television and also took odd jobs to make ends meet. He found a job in front of the cameras but his accent meant that he was more suited to Westerns so he moved to Hollywood. He was cast as a thug most often and appeared in four films by Sam Peckinpah although their collaboration began with the television series *The Rifleman* in 1958. Their first film was *Ride The High Country* (1962). Of his friend he said, "Sam has always believed, and I believe rightly, that he is there to make the film and that anyone who stands in his way is dead. They're in deep, deep trouble. And anyone who doesn't come up to snuff and do their job absolutely perfectly is in deep trouble with Sam." Oates did not see himself in the Western genre: "I feel most uncomfortable in a Western role, because my image of the Western man is John Wayne and I'm just a little shit." He was one of a few character actors almost as well known as the lead. His other films included: *Major Dundee* (1965) as O.W. Hadley, *Return Of The Seven* (1966) as Colbee, *The Wild Bunch* (1969), *Two-Lane Blacktop* (1971), *Dillinger* (1973) as John Dillinger, *Bring Me The Head Of Alfredo Garcia* (1974), *Drum* (1976) as Hammond Maxwell, *1941* (1979) as

Colonel Maddox, *Stripes* (1981) as Sergeant Hulka, *The Border* (1982) as Red, *Tough Enough* (1983) and *Blue Thunder* (1983). Oates was married three times. In 1959 he wed Teddy Farmer by whom he had three children before their 1966 divorce. In 1969 he married Vickery Turner, a match that lasted five years. On August 24, 1977 he married Judy A. Jones.

CAUSE: Oates who stood 5'11" died in Los Angeles, California from a heart attack. He was 53. He was cremated and his ashes scattered in Montana.

Merle Oberon

(ESTELLE MERLE O'BRIEN THOMPSON)
Born February 19, 1911
Died November 23, 1979

'Princess Merle'. Many actors have dark secrets they try to hide. Some of these secrets are due to the stars' sexuality being incompatible with their careers (e.g. Rock Hudson). Some try to hide their criminal past (e.g. Rory Calhoun). Some have a sexual secret of a different nature that they try to keep buried (e.g. the famously handsome, young heartthrob of the Nineties who used to be a male hustler and whose identity, if I revealed it, would give libel lawyers a heart attack). Some keep secret the fact they were 'kept' by an established star – witness the actor who had been a keen sportsman until an injury forced his retirement, around about the time that he met Rock Hudson. The latter took the young man under his wing, arranged for a nose job and acting lessons. In interviews the young man would praise Hudson's altruism and his apartment would be covered with pictures of the two men together. However, when he first hit it big in the Sixties the young man began to distance himself from Hudson and today, with three mega successful TV series and a marriage to an international sex symbol behind him, the all-action hero denies he ever knew anyone called Rock Hudson. It could be argued that there is a good reason for most of the secrecy that permeates Hollywood, but can anyone say there is a good reason for keeping a mother hidden and introducing her to visitors as the maid? That is what 5'4" Merle Oberon did. She further claimed she had been born in Hobart, Tasmania, when she was really born on the border of the Khetwadi and Girgaum suburbs in Bombay, India. Like many hospitals on the subcontinent the maternity unit of St George's was not of a particularly high standard. Baby Estelle was born with a congenital heart defect because of the botched delivery. Merle was baptised on March 16, 1911, and nicknamed 'Queenie' because of the visit of TM King George V and Queen Mary to Delhi and Bombay that year. Her British father died at the Somme in 1916 and her Ceylonese mother took jobs as a nurse in a hospital and then as live-in nurse to various families. In 1919 Merle and her mother moved to Calcutta which was then slightly more Westernised than the rest of the country but which was still subject to violence between Hindus and Muslims. Merle and her mother travelled to Europe in July 1929 and, when Merle arrived in London at the end of the summer, she landed a job as a dance hostess and supplemented her income by appearing in bit parts in films (her first was *The Three Passions* [1929]) not, as rumour has it, by selling her body. Several more minor roles followed before Merle was spotted by Sir Alexander Korda, who realised her potential and began to groom her for stardom. In the meantime, Merle had not been lazy on the romantic front, enjoying affairs with the black pianist Hutch, actor-director Miles Mander and Wadham College, Oxford-educated golfer Charles Sweeney (b. Scranton, Pennsylvania, October 3, 1909, d. Bal Harbor, March 11, 1993) who went on to become the first husband of Margaret, Duchess of Argyll at Brompton Oratory

on February 21, 1933. Merle's big cinematic break came playing Anne Boleyn in Korda's *The Private Life Of Henry VIII* (1933). During the production Merle became unwell. She had been in pain during sex with her numerous lovers and was horrified to see blood in her vagina. She went to a doctor who examined her and told her she had a rare carcinoma in one of her Fallopian tubes. During the operation it was discovered that both tubes were cancerous and had to be removed. Next Merle appeared in Korda's extravagant period dramas such as *The Private Life Of Don Juan* (1934) as Antonita and *The Scarlet Pimpernel* (1934) as Lady Marguerite Blakeney opposite Leslie Howard, with whom she had an affair. Travelling to Hollywood she made *The Dark Angel* (1935) as Kitty Vane for Sam Goldwyn and had a fling with David Niven. To complete her happiness the role resulted in her only nomination for an Oscar. She was cast as Messalina in *I, Claudius* (1937) and shooting began back in England in February 1937. However, the film was beset by difficulties. Co-star Charles Laughton was often unwilling or unable to learn his lines and spent much of the time being shafted (in both the financial and sexual sense) by young hustlers. On March 16, Merle was involved in a car crash and knocked unconscious, bleeding heavily from a cut over her left eye and ear. Due to the combination of Merle's injury and Charles Laughton's masochistic self-loathing, the picture was abandoned. Korda had been wooing Merle with enthusiasm despite her affection for David Niven and he married her in Antibes, France, on June 3, 1939. The year was momentous for Merle and for the world. She co-starred with Laurence Olivier in *Wuthering Heights* (1939) as Cathy Linton to his Heathcliff, even though he was keen for Vivien Leigh to play the part. During the war she helped Korda with his intelligence work and appeared in the following movies: *'Til We Meet Again* (1940) as Joan Ames, *Lydia* (1941) as Lydia MacMillen, *Affectionately Yours* (1941) as Sue Mayberry, *That Uncertain Feeling* (1941) as Jill Baker, *First Comes Courage* (1943) as Nicole Larsen, *Forever And A Day* (1943) as Marjorie, *Dark Waters* (1944) as Leslie Calvin, *The Lodger* (1944) as Kitty Langley and *This Love Of Ours* (1945) as Karin Touzac. She won praise for her portrayal of George Sand in *A Song To Remember* (1945) but by this time had fallen out of love with Korda and in love with cinematographer Lucien Ballard (b. Miami, Oklahoma, May 6, 1908, d. October 1, 1988) whom she married by proxy on June 26, 1945. Like Merle, he, too, was a half-caste and so understood as much of her difficulties as she would reveal to him. (That didn't stop her having an affair with Turhan Bey, her co-star on *A Night In Paradise* [1946].) As Merle grew older her looks began to fade, and with them her career. She was never an especially gifted actress and relied on her exotic looks to get by. In August 1949 she and Ballard were divorced. Her screen appearances became fewer and she instead threw herself in to the social whirl in London, Europe and Hollywood, enjoying more than a few romances including one with a senior member of the royal family. On July 28, 1957, she married Bruno Pagliai in Rome and decided she wanted a family. Unfortunately, due to the operation she had had when she was 20, she was infertile. Instead the couple adopted two children – Bruno, Jr. and Francesca. They lived in Mexico until their 1973 divorce. That year Merle made a half-hearted comeback in a film called *Interval* about a woman desperately searching for her one true love. Merle found love in real life. On January 31, 1975, she married her *Interval* co-star Robert Wolders (b. Rotterdam, Holland, September 28, 1935), an actor who had the distinction of being "the only Dutchman to be cast as a Texas lawman" for his work on the TV Western *Laredo*. Her years with Wolders were brief but happy ones. CAUSE: On November 14, 1978, she underwent a successful heart by-pass operation. However, it left horrible red scars that caused her great pain. Steroids injected into the scar tissue did not help. On Thanksgiving 1979 she suffered a stroke and was taken to Cedars of Lebanon Hospital where she died at 3pm the next day. She was 68. Merle was buried at Forest Lawn Memorial-Parks, 1712 Glendale Avenue, Glendale, California 91209. FURTHER READING: *Merle: A Biography Of Merle Oberon* – Charles Higham & Roy Moseley (London: New English Library, 1983).

Warner Oland

(JOHAN WARNER OLUND)
Born October 3, 1880
Died August 6, 1938
Pseudo-Oriental. It is probably true to say that only in a country like America could a Swede become famous for playing a Chinaman. Yet that is what happened to 5'11" Warner Oland. He brilliantly portrayed the enigmatic and inscrutable Charlie Chan in several movies. 'Jack' Oland didn't wear make-up to play Chan. He simply combed his eyebrows up, his moustache down, grew a goatee and narrowed his eyes. It was not the first time he had played an Oriental. He had also played the villainous Doctor Fu Manchu in *The Mysterious Dr Fu Manchu* (1929), *The Return Of Dr Fu Manchu* (1930) and *Daughter Of The Dragon* (1931), the same year he first played Charlie Chan. He played Chan in *Charlie Chan Carries On* (1931), *The Black Camel* (1931), *Charlie Chan's Chance* (1932), *Charlie Chan's Greatest Case* (1933), *Charlie Chan's Courage* (1934), *Charlie Chan In London* (1934), *Charlie Chan In Paris* (1935), *Charlie Chan In Shanghai* (1935), *Charlie Chan*

In Egypt (1935), *Charlie Chan's Secret* (1936), *Charlie Chan At The Race Track* (1936), *Charlie Chan At The Circus* (1936), *Charlie Chan On Broadway* (1937), *Charlie Chan At Monte Carlo* (1937), *Charlie Chan At The Opera* (1937) and *Charlie Chan At The Olympics* (1937). He even travelled to China to learn more about Orientals and began to learn Chinese so he could accurately enunciate Charlie's Chinese comments. Oland was born in the small village of Nyby, Bjurholm parish of Vasterbotten, Sweden, the son of a Swede, Jonas Olund, and a Russian, Maria Johanna Forsberg. On October 15, 1892, the family moved to Connecticut and he began to take an interest in drama. In the autumn of 1907 he was hired by Alla Nazimova to appear on Broadway. The following year he married Edith Shearn, an actress. His early films included: *Sin* (1915) as Pietro, *Destruction* (1915) as Mr Deleveau, *The Eternal Question* (1916) as Pierre Felix, *Convict 993* (1918) as Dan Mallory, *Mandarin's Gold* (1919) as Li Hsun, *The Yellow Arm* (1921), *East Is West* (1922) as Charley Yong, *His Children's Children* (1923) as Dr Dahl, *One Night In Rome* (1924) as Mario Dorando, *So This Is Marriage?* (1924) as King David, *Curlytop* (1924) as Shanghai Dan, *Riders Of The Purple Sage* (1925) as Lew Walters/Judge Dyer, *Don Q Son Of Zorro* (1925) as Archduke Paul, *Infatuation* (1925) as Osman Pasha, *Don Juan* (1926) as Caesar Borgia, *Twinkletoes* (1926) as Roseleaf, *Tell It To The Marines* (1927) as Chinese bandit leader, *What Happened to Father?* (1927) as W. Bradberry, *The Jazz Singer* (1927) as the Cantor, *Good Time Charley* (1927) as Good Time Charley, *Stand And Deliver* (1928) as Chika, *Chinatown Nights* (1929) as Boston Charley and *The Studio Murder Mystery* (1929) as Rupert Borka.
CAUSE: A consummate pro, Oland had one weakness – he was an alcoholic. It caused his wife to leave him in 1937.

That year he was filming *Charlie Chan At The Ringside* when he upped and left the set never to return. Rumours circulated as to what had happened to him. In fact, in a bid to kick his drinking he had gone to Europe and then to Sweden where he stayed with his mother in Stockholm. There he contracted bronchial pneumonia and died aged 57. He was buried in Southborough Rural Cemetery, Southborough, Massachusetts.

Edna May Oliver
(EDNA MAY NUTTER)
Born November 9, 1883
Died November 9, 1942
Equine-looking character actress. Born in Malden, Massachusetts, she was a staple on the stage and film when it came to playing bossy spinsters. Much of her best work was done before the invention of the Academy Award and she received her only nomination for her portrayal of Sarah McKlennar in *Drums Along The Mohawk* (1939). Among 5'7" Oliver's other films were *Wife In Name Only* (1923) as Mrs Dornham, *Manhattan* (1924) as Mrs Trapes, *Icebound* (1924) as Hannah, *Lovers In Quarantine* (1925) as Amelia Pincent, *Let's Get Married* (1926) as J.W. Smith, *Half Shot At Sunrise* (1930) as Mrs Marshall, *Laugh And Get Rich* (1931) as Sarah Austin, *Fanny Foley Herself* (1931) as Fanny Foley, *Cracked Nuts* (1931) as Aunt Van Varden, *Cimarron* (1931) as Mrs Tracy Wyatt, *Ladies Of The Jury* (1932) as Mrs Livingston Baldwin Crane, *Penguin Pool Murder* (1932) as Hildegarde Withers, *Meet The Baron* (1933) as Dean Primrose, *Ann Vickers* (1933) as Malvina Wormser, *Only Yesterday* (1933) as Leona, *Little Women* (1933) as Aunt March, *Murder On The Blackboard* (1934) reprising her role as Hildegarde Withers, *We're Rich Again* (1934) as Maude, *Murder On A Honeymoon* (1935) once again as Hildegarde Withers, *David Copperfield* (1935) as Betsey Trotwood, *A Tale*

Of Two Cities (1935) as Miss Pross, *Romeo And Juliet* (1936) as Nurse, *My Dear Miss Aldrich* (1937) as Mrs Atherton, *Parnell* (1937) as Aunt Ben Wood, *Paradise For Three* (1938) as Mrs Kunkel, *Nurse Edith Cavell* (1939) as Countess de Mavon, *Pride And Prejudice* (1940) as Lady Catherine de Bourgh and *Lydia* (1941) as Granny. CAUSE: She died in Los Angeles, California, on her 59th birthday, of an intestinal disorder. She was buried at Forest Lawn Memorial-Parks, 1712 Glendale Avenue, Glendale, California 91209.

Laurence Olivier, Baron Olivier of Brighton

Born May 22, 1907
Died July 11, 1989
The greatest actor of all time, probably. Born at 26 Wathen Road, Dorking, Laurence Kerr Olivier was the son of the Reverend Gerald Kerr Olivier (b. April 30, 1869, d. West Sussex, March 30, 1939) and Agnes Louise Crookenden (b. at Kidbrooke, December 1, 1871, d. March 27, 1920). Dame Ellen Terry, one of the greatest Victorian actresses, saw him play Brutus at the age of ten and commented, "The boy is already a great actor." He made his Stratford-upon-Avon Shakespearean début aged 15 in *The Taming Of The Shrew* – he played Katherine. When he made his professional stage début in 1925 at the Brighton Hippodrome in *The Ghost Train*, Olivier was warned by everyone from the box-office manager to the stage manager that there was a tricky doorsill to be overcome on the set. Olivier eventually grew weary of their tiresome warnings and . . . tripped head over heels, landing at the feet of Ruby Miller, the star of the show. In October 1925, the 5'10" Olivier joined a modest repertory company run by Lena Ashwell. The company often played in unusual venues. If they appeared at a school, it was usually on boards over the swimming pool. Most members were asked to perform more than one role in each production. One performance of *Julius Caesar* was performed before a group of schoolboys. It saw Olivier cast as both Antony and Flavius. During one scene a fellow Roman's trousers fell about his ankles from underneath his smart Roman tunic. The audience laughed, as did Olivier, who was summoned to Lena Ashwell's office the next day and summarily sacked. Despite this unpromising start he went on to wow audiences with his stage performances in Shakespearean roles on both sides of the Atlantic. On July 25, 1930, at All Saints Church, Margaret Street, London, Olivier married lesbian actress Jill Esmond (b. London, January 26, 1908, d. Wimbledon, London, July 28, 1990), by whom he had one son, Simon Tarquin (b. London, August 21, 1936). On their wedding night she turned her back on him and it was years before the match was consummated. They eventually divorced on January 29, 1940, after which Esmond lived an exclusively gay life. Olivier made his film début in *Too Many Crooks* (1930). He starred in *Friends And Lovers* (1931) as Lieutenant Nichols and *Westward Passage* (1932) as Nicholas Allen for RKO before being cast opposite Garbo in *Queen Christina* (1933) only to be replaced by John Gilbert. He returned to Blighty to appear in Alexander Korda's *Moscow Nights* (1935) as Captain Ignatoff. The following year he starred in *Fire Over England* (1937) as Michael Ingolby, in which he starred opposite his future wife Vivien Leigh. He opened in a production of *Hamlet* at the Old Vic on January 5, 1937; at one point during a performance he swung the poisoned sword rather too enthusiastically and ended up almost impaling one of the governors of the theatre. Olivier was mortified as the audience giggled none too quietly. The man who had almost been stabbed was too shocked to retrieve the offending

weapon, as were those sitting near him. Eventually, it came down to *la grande dame* of the Old Vic Lilian Baylis herself, who shouted, "Oh, come on, dears – won't someone give him back his sword so we can get on with the play and go home?" Back in Hollywood he appeared as Heathcliffe in *Wuthering Heights* (1939), for which he received his first Oscar nomination. At Ranch San Ysidro, Santa Barbara, California, on August 31, 1940, he married Vivien Leigh and that year consolidated his cinematic success with *Pride And Prejudice* (1940) as Mr Fitzwilliam Darcy, *Rebecca* (1940) as George Fortescu Maximillian de Winter, for which he was again nominated for an Oscar, and *21 Days* (1940) as Larry Durrant. He appeared as Lord Horatio Nelson opposite Leigh's Lady Hamilton in *That Hamilton Woman* (1941). Many regard Olivier's *Henry V* (1944) as his masterpiece. He starred as King Henry V and was nominated for an Oscar for his performance, as well as producing and directing the film and co-writing the screenplay. Four years later, he turned his attention to *Hamlet* (1948), which he starred in, directed and produced, and won Oscars for Best Film (the first wholly British movie to win the prize), Best Actor and a nomination as Best Director. Olivier cast Eileen Herlie to play his mother Gertrude – in fact, she was 13 years younger than him. He was relatively quiet on the cinema front after that. He played George Hurstwood in *Carrie* (1952) and Captain MacHeath in *The Beggar's Opera* (1953). He was nominated for an Oscar for his portrayal of *Richard III* (1954), a style later lampooned by Peter Sellers. On April 12, 1955, a John Gielgud-produced version of *Twelfth Night* opened at Stratford starring Olivier and Vivien Leigh. The critics absolutely hated it. One of the kinder reviewers was Olivier's friend Kenneth Tynan, who called Leigh's Viola "dazzlingly monotonous".

Gielgud was horrified. "Good Heavens. After this no one will ever work with me again except Edith [Evans] at a pinch," he moaned. The following year Olivier appeared with Marilyn Monroe in the movie version of Terence Rattigan's *The Prince And The Showgirl* (1956). On April 10, 1957, he opened at the Royal Court Theatre, London, in John Osborne's *The Entertainer*. Olivier was fêted for his portrayal of Archie Rice (based on Max Miller) and when the film version was made in 1959 Olivier was nominated for a Best Actor Oscar. (It was his second favourite role, after Macbeth.) On the home front, Olivier's marriage to Vivien Leigh was crumbling and they divorced on December 2, 1960. That year he played Marcus Licinius Crassus in *Spartacus* (1960). In Wilton, Connecticut, on March 17, 1961, he married actress Joan Plowright (b. Grigg, near Scunthorpe, October 28, 1929) and had three children by her: Richard Kerr (b. Whitehaven Nursing Home, Wilbury Road, Hove, December 3, 1961), Tamsin Agnes Margaret (b. January 10, 1963) and Julie-Kate (b. Brighton, July 27, 1966, as Julianne Rose Henrietta Katherine). In 1980 the Oliviers separated, though they never divorced. In 1965 Olivier picked up another Best Actor nomination for the title role in *Othello*. In the last 20 years of his life Olivier gave some marvellous performances; he also starred in some films such as *The Jazz Singer* (1979) that were less satisfactory vehicles for his talent. His films during this period included *Uncle Vanya* (1963) as Astrov, *Khartoum* (1966) as the Mahdi, *The Shoes Of The Fisherman* (1968) as Premier Piotr Ilyich Kamenev, *Battle Of Britain* (1969) as Air Chief Marshal Sir Hugh Dowding, *Oh! What A Lovely War* (1969) as Field Marshal Sir John French, *Nicholas And Alexandra* (1971) as Count Witte, *Lady Caroline Lamb* (1972) as the Duke of Wellington (the film starred his former lover Sarah

Miles), *Sleuth* (1972) as Andrew Wyke, for which he was nominated for an Oscar, *The Seven-Per-Cent Solution* (1976) as Professor Moriarty, *Marathon Man* (1976) as Dr Szell, for which he was nominated for yet another Oscar (when Dustin Hoffman, an apostle of the 'Method' school of acting, stayed up all night to portray a character who hadn't slept, Olivier asked: "Why don't you just act?"), *A Bridge Too Far* (1977) as Doctor Spaander, *The Boys From Brazil* (1978) as Ezra Lieberman, for which he received his final Oscar nod, *The Betsy* (1978) as Loren Hardeman, *Dracula* (1979) as Professor Abraham Van Helsing, *Clash Of The Titans* (1981) as Zeus, *Inchon* (1982) as General Douglas MacArthur, *The Bounty* (1984) as Admiral Hood and *Wild Geese II* (1985) as Rudolf Hess. He became the first theatrical Lord elevated to a Baron in 1970, having been knighted in 1947. A *leitmotif* of many biographies of Olivier has been that he was bisexual and slept with several men including Danny Kaye, Sir Noël Coward and Kenneth Tynan. Biographer Donald Spoto even wrote that Lady Olivier, Joan Plowright, made him remove details of his homosexual experiences to avoid embarrassment to his family. Lady Olivier denies she did anything of the sort and referral to Olivier's papers bears out her claim. It seems likely that the only homosexual affair Olivier had was with the actor Henry Ainley in 1936–37. Olivier believed sex damaged the memory and once abstained to learn the part of Iago – the feat took him four days. Despite his success he considered acting not quite the occupation of an adult. "It is a masochistic form of exhibitionism, doing silly things well enough to be effective."
CAUSE: Olivier developed cancer and was told to cut down on booze. When his daughter, Julie-Kate, refused him a whisky top-up, he cursed her, "I can't believe a sperm from my testicle ever

created such a cunt." On July 1, 1989, Olivier's kidneys began to fail. He died ten days later at his home, the Malthouse, Ashurst, Sussex, aged 82. He left £1,352,383.
FURTHER READING: *Love Scene* – Jesse Lasky, Jr. & Pat Silver (London: Sphere, 1980); *Olivier: The Life Of Laurence Olivier* – Thomas Kiernan (London: Sidgwick & Jackson, 1981); *Confessions Of An Actor* – Laurence Olivier (London: Coronet, 1984); *Olivier* – Anthony Holden (London: Sphere, 1989); *Laurence Olivier: A Biography* – Donald Spoto (London: HarperCollins, 1991); *The Real Life Of Laurence Olivier* – Roger Lewis (London: Century, 1996); *Olivier: The Authorised Biography* – Terry Coleman (London: Bloomsbury, 2005).

Gary Olsen

Born November 3, 1957
Died September 12, 2000
Big likeable lad. Born in London, Olsen's parents died before he was 11 and he and a sister were raised by an aunt and uncle. When he reached the age of 15, he attended workshops at an arts centre in south London, and soon afterwards left home to pursue an acting career. For most of the Seventies Olsen was a jobbing actor who made his film début in *Birth Of The Beatles* (1979) playing Rory Storm, the troubled individual who led The Hurricanes, the first beat group to play at Liverpool's Cavern club, the first to back Cilla Black and whose life ended in tragedy with an overdose in 1972. He was also in *Outland* (1981), *The Sender* (1982), *The Wall* (1982, as a Pink Floyd roadie), *Party, Party* (1983), *Winter Flight* (1984), *Underworld* (1985) and Spangler in *The Cook, The Thief, His Wife & Her Lover* (1989). His first big break was playing Pc Dave Litton in the first series of the cop show *The Bill* (1984–1985). It was not until years later that Olsen achieved real recognition as Ben Porter in the BBC sitcom *2point4 Children* (from

September 3, 1991 until 1999). The show's creator Andrew Marshall remembered, "I still have the cast list I compiled years earlier, when we were starting, in which not only is his name the sole one on the list beneath the character of Ben, but it is ringed three times, just in case there should be any doubt in anyone's mind. I was surprised to find when he arrived to chat with us that he was in fact physically smaller than the character I [had seen] on the stage. This, I think, seems to summarise his essential quality as an actor; bursting with energy and somehow occupying more space than his actual body through sheer exuberance of performance." Playing Bill to Olsen's Ben was Belinda Lang (b. London, December 23, 1955), the daughter of Jeremy Hawk whose death is noticed in this book. Olsen was married twice. In 1985 he married the actress Candy Davis (b. Essex, January 2, 1962 as Clare Damaris Bastin) who won Miss Nude UK 1982 and later became a stripper to support them when his acting work dried up. She was best known as Miss Belfridge, Mr Rumbold's sexy secretary in *Are Y ou Being Served?*. The marriage did not survive. Olsen married, secondly, Australian-born Jane Anthony and by her had a son and a daughter.

CAUSE: Olsen died of cancer in Melbourne, Victoria, Australia, where he had gone to spend his last months with his in-laws following his diagnosis in December 1999.

Orry-Kelly
(JOHN KELLY)
Born December 31, 1897
Died February 27, 1964
Costumier par excellence. Born in Kiama, New South Wales, Australia, Kelly studied at art college in Sydney before going to London and then New York where, after an unsuccessful attempt at becoming an actor, he settled down to design costumes for Broadway plays and films. Short, effeminate, stocky and with large blue eyes, he lived with Cary Grant, with whom he ran a speakeasy, in 1921, before both were successful. In 1931 he joined Warner Bros and stayed there until 1946, working on costumes for all their big films, including Ingrid Bergman's gowns in *Casablanca* (1942) and Bette Davis' in *Jezebel* (1938). He designed for, among others, the following films: *Tiger Shark* (1932), *They Call It Sin* (1932), *I Am A Fugitive From A Chain Gang* (1932), *20,000 Years In Sing Sing* (1932), *Voltaire* (1933), *Frisco Jenny* (1933), *Female* (1933), *42nd Street* (1933), *Gold Diggers Of 1933* (1933), *Midnight Alibi* (1934), *Mandalay* (1934), *Dames* (1934), *I Found Stella Parish* (1935), *The Irish In Us* (1935), *Gold Diggers Of 1935* (1935), *Cain And Mabel* (1936), *Kid Galahad* (1937), *That Certain Woman* (1937), *Angels With Dirty Faces* (1938), *Dark Victory* (1939), *The Private Lives Of Elizabeth And Essex* (1939), *The Sea Hawk* (1940), *Million Dollar Baby* (1941), *The Bride Came C.O.D.* (1941), *The Maltese Falcon* (1941), *Kings Row* (1942), *Now, Voyager* (1942), *Mr Skeffington* (1944), *Arsenic And Old Lace* (1944), *Mother Wore Tights* (1947), *An American In Paris* (1951) for which he won his first Oscar, *Oklahoma!* (1955), *Les Girls* (1957) for which he won a second Oscar, *Some Like It Hot* (1959) for which he won his third and final Oscar, *Gypsy* (1962), *Irma La Douce* (1963) and many, many more.

CAUSE: He died in Hollywood, California, aged 66, of natural causes.

P

Hugh Paddick

Born August 22, 1915
Died November 9, 2000
'Straight actor gone wrong'. Hugh
Paddick was born at Hoddesdon,
Hertfordshire, the son of a farmer.
Destined for a career in the law,
Paddick failed his bar exams and
decided to move into acting, much
to the dismay of his family. He joined
the Liverpool repertory company and
played mainly leading roles. In January
1954 he was cast in the part of
Percival Brown in Sandy Wilson's
Twenties musical pastiche *The Boy
Friend*. The show was to run for five
years although Paddick left to appear in
other plays and revues. On July 1,
1958, he appeared in the first edition of
"a sort of radio show" entitled *Beyond
Our Ken*. Written by Eric Merriman
and the often uncredited Barry Took,
it starred Kenneth Horne with a
supporting cast of Kenneth Williams,
Betty Marsden, Ron Moody, Stanley
Unwin and Patricia Lancaster. The
show was lucky to air at all. After
making a pilot Horne suffered a stroke
that left his speech impaired.
Thankfully, he made a fullish recovery.
The second series saw the departure of
Moody and Unwin and the arrival of
Bill Pertwee. *Beyond Our Ken* ran for
six years and 122 episodes until
February 16, 1964. It introduced
several notable characters such as the
effeminate duo Rodney and Charles
(Paddick and Williams), teenage pop
idol Ricky Livid (Paddick), comedian
Hankie Flowered (Pertwee), TV cook
Fanny Haddock (Marsden), roving
reporter Cecil Snaith (Paddick), old
coots Ambrose and Felicity (Williams
and Marsden), pompous Cockney
Arthur Figley (Williams), sibilant
Stanley Birkenshaw (Paddick) and
Somerset farmer Arthur Fallowfield
(Williams) for whom "the answer lies
in the soil". In 1959 Paddick played
Colonel Pickering in *My Fair Lady* at
Drury Lane. He made his film début in
School For Scoundrels (1960) playing an
instructor. From November 9, 1963
until August 22, 1964, he played
Osbert Rigby-Soames in the television
series *The Larkins* which starred Peggy
Mount and David Kossoff. He played
Connell in *We Shall See* (1964). It was
in the replacement for *Beyond Our Ken*,
Round The Horne (from March 7,
1965), that Paddick shone despite the
stridency of Kenneth Williams. They
played the camp chorus boys Julian and
Sandy (named after Julian Slade and
Sandy Wilson) to perfection. In his
posthumously published diaries
Williams was often scathing about his
colleagues but for Paddick he has only
unqualified praise. The characters
created for the show also included
Rambling Syd Rumpo (Williams), J.
Peasmould Gruntfuttock (Williams),
Colonel Brown-Horrocks of MI5
(Paddick), Chou-en Ginsberg, MA
(Failed) (Williams), Lotus Blossom
the geisha girl (Paddick), Daphne
Whitethigh (Marsden), Madame Osiris
Gnomeclencher (Paddick), Seamus
Android (Pertwee), and Dame Celia
Molestrangler and aging juvenile Binkie
Huckaback (Marsden and Paddick).
The show ran until June 9, 1968 and
ended completely in February 1969
when Horne died of a massive heart
attack at the BAFTA Awards. Paddick
did not let the success of *Round The
Horne* stop him from working in other
media. In June 1966, he appeared on
stage with Fenella Fielding in *Let's Get
A Divorce* at the Mermaid Theatre. He
was a tourist in the film *San Ferry Ann*
(1966) and took various parts in the
television series *Beryl Reid Says Good
Evening* (March 4–April 8, 1968),
and was Sydney Jelliot, the lead role
in the sitcom *Wink To Me Only*
(Comedy Playhouse, May 3, 1968;

series June 11–July 16, 1969). His other films included: *The Killing Of Sister George* (1968) as Freddie, *Up The Chastity Belt* (1971) as Robin Hood, a priest in *Up Pompeii!* (1971) and a window dresser in *That's Your Funeral* (1972). He was also Mr Pettigrew in *Can We Get On Now, Please?* (June 2–July 7, 1980) (TV Series) and an anarchist in *Blackadder The Third* (1987). Paddick was an unassuming man who was embarrassed to be recognised in public, unlike his friend Kenneth Williams. Paddick recalled dining with Williams and the latter demanding a table away from the other patrons. Later, when Williams realised he was not being recognised his voice became louder until people turned round. He declared the "intrusion" intolerable and demanded that he and Paddick left, their meal unfinished. Paddick lived with his boyfriend, Francis, from the late Sixties until his death.
CAUSE: Hugh Paddick died aged 85 of natural causes.

Manuel Padilla, Jr

Born July 13, 1955
Died January 29, 2008
Tarzan's mate. Born in Los Angeles, California Padilla began acting at the age of six in *Dime With A Halo* (1963) as Rafael. He was usually cast as a Mexican or a Red Indian and usually much younger than his actual age, standing just 5′3″. Best known for playing Tarzan's little friend Jai in the television series opposite Ron Ely. Following *Tarzan*, he had a recurring role in *The Flying Nun* (1967) as Marcello. His films were: *The Young And The Brave* (1963) as Han, *4 For Texas* (shooting began on May 23, 1963), *Robin And The 7 Hoods* (released February 1964), *Sylvia* (1965) as Pancho, *Taffy And The Jungle Hunter* (1965) as Beau, *Black Spurs* (1965) as Manuel, *Tarzan And The Valley of Gold* (1966) as Ramel, *Tarzan And The Great River* (1967) as Pepe, *American Graffiti* (1973) as Carlos, *More American Graffiti* (1979) as Carlos and *Scarface* (1983). His parents and four children survived him.
CAUSE: Padilla died suddenly aged 52 after a public appearance at the Grand National Roadster Show in Pomona, California.

Lilli Palmer

(MARIA LILLIE PEISER)
Born May 24, 1911
Died January 28, 1986
Teutonic elegance. Born Posen, Germany, the daughter of a surgeon, she began appearing on stage on August 1, 1932, in Berlin. When the Nazis came to power she fled to Paris, arriving in London in 1935 to appear in films. She didn't make her London stage début until March 24, 1938. Her films included *Crime Unlimited* (1935), *A Girl Must Live* (1939), *The Rake's Progress* (1945), *Anastasia* (1956), *Mädchen In Uniform* (1958), *Operation Crossbow* (1965), *Sebastian* (1968), *De Sade* (1969) and *The Boys From Brazil* (1978). On January 25, 1943, in London she married Rex Harrison but the marriage came apart because of his affair with Kay Kendall. When Harrison discovered Kendall was seriously ill, Palmer agreed to give him a divorce so he could marry the sick woman on the understanding that when she died she and Harrison would remarry. They divorced in Juarez, Mexico, on February 6, 1957, but a remarriage never occurred and, instead, on September 21, of the same year, Palmer married Argentinean actor Carlos Thompson (b. Buenos Aires, June 7, 1916, as Juan Carlos Mundin Schafter, d. September, 1990, by his own hand). Not everyone liked Palmer. Noël Coward once stated: "The week has been hell, made entirely so by Lilli . . . I have never – with the possible exception of Claudette Colbert – worked with such a stupid bitch."
CAUSE: She died at home in Los Angeles, California, aged 74, from a heart attack.

FURTHER READING: *Change Lobsters And Dance* – Lilli Palmer (London: Star Books, 1977).

Bruce Paltrow

Born November 26, 1943
Died October 2, 2002

Gwynie's dad. For an accomplished director Bruce William Paltrow will probably be most remembered for the emotionally incontinent speech that his daughter, Gwyneth, made about him when she won an Oscar in 1999. In a performance that really had to be seen to be disbelieved, her voice breaking, seeming to cry but without tears, she told him, "I love you more than anything in the world," having told the assembled throng that she "understood love of a tremendous magnitude". 6'1" Paltrow was born in Brooklyn to a family of rabbis dating back to seventeenth-century Russia. He was educated at Tulane University in New Orleans. He moved back to New York where he began working in the theatre where in 1969 he met and later (1970) married the actress Blythe Katherine Danner (b. Philadelphia, Pennsylvania, February 3, 1943). They were to have two children: Gwyneth (b. September 28, 1972) and Jake (b. 1975). Paltrow's big break came with the television movie *Shirts/Skins* (1973). He worked for Mary Tyler Moore Productions and later won two Emmy nominations for *The White Shadow*. His first film with MTMP was *A Little Sex* (1982) but it was not a success. He then worked on the television series *St Elsewhere* and *Homicide: Life On The Streets*. He spent some time working on the film *Duets* (2000) only for its stars – Brad Pitt and Gwyneth Paltrow – to split in 1997, causing the film to lose much of its commercial appeal.

CAUSE: In January 1999 just before he was due to begin filming *Duets* Paltrow was diagnosed with throat cancer. He underwent radical surgery and radiation treatment and was back on-set in 13 days. In September 2002, he set out to travel Europe with his daughter to celebrate her 30th birthday. He was taken ill in Rome and died aged 58 from complications of pneumonia and throat cancer.

Hermes Pan

(HERMES PANAGIOTOPOULOS)
Born December 10, 1909
Died September 19, 1990

The hoofer's hoofer. Born in Memphis, Tennessee, Hermes Pan became a Hollywood choreographer nonpareil. He worked on over 50 Hollywood movies including 10 with his close friend Fred Astaire. In fact, he and Astaire were so close that Pan was able to double for Astaire in certain films, performing moves that Fred was unable to do himself. Pan had begun his life working in bars, where he was paid 10¢ a dance. On Broadway he met Ginger Rogers and she introduced him to Astaire. His films included: *Flying Down To Rio* (1933), *The Gay Divorcee* (1934), *Top Hat* (1935), *Follow The Fleet* (1936), *Swing Time* (1936), *Shall We Dance?* (1937), *A Damsel In Distress* (1937) for which he won an Oscar for the *Fun House* number, *The Story Of Vernon And Irene Castle* (1939), *Blood And Sand* (1941), *Song Of The Islands* (1942), *My Gal Sal* (1942), *Coney Island* (1943), *Diamond Horseshoe* (1945), *That Lady In Ermine* (1948), *The Barkleys Of Broadway* (1949), *Kiss Me Kate* (1953), *The Student Prince* (1954), *Silk Stockings* (1957), *Pal Joey* (1957), *Can-Can* (1960), *Flower Drum Song* (1961), *Cleopatra* (1963), *My Fair Lady* (1964), *The Great Race* (1965), *Finian's Rainbow* (1968), *Darling Lili* (1970) and *Lost Horizon* (1973).

CAUSE: He died aged 80 from a stroke in Beverly Hills, California.

Louella O. Parsons

(LOUELLA ROSE OETTINGER)
Born August 6, 1881
Died December 9, 1972

The reel wicked witch of the West. Like her rival Hedda Hopper, the

'Paganini of Piffle' Louella O. Parsons utilised obfuscation when it came to her origins. Hedda changed the year and month of her birth but only attempted to make herself five years younger than she really was. Louella practised a chronological deceit that even the Gabors would have to admire. She knocked a staggering 12 years off her true age and even reputable, usually thoroughly researched, tomes like Katz accept, wrongly, that she was born in 1893. She was born the oldest of five children, three of whom died in infancy, in Freeport, Illinois. On May 26, 1890, further tragedy entered her life when her father died, aged 31, of 'brain congestion', thereby making her claimed date of birth impossible. At school she reviewed musicals and social events for various publications. She landed a job on a newspaper and met John Dement Parsons. They married on Hallowe'en 1905. He was 32 and she gave her age as 24. Had her natal day really occurred in 1893 she would have married for the first time aged 12 and, no doubt, her husband would have ended up in prison on a charge of paedophilia. On August 23, 1906 (not 1911 as Katz has it), she gave birth to their daughter, Harriet Oettinger Parsons, later to become a film producer. (She died in 1983.) Louella was employed by Essanay in Chicago when her husband left her for his secretary. A mysterious second husband came into her life in the early part of the second decade of the twentieth century. Captain Jack McCaffery (b. Le Claire, Iowa, March 21, 1873) and Louella were married *circa* 1915, although no marriage certificate has ever surfaced. Louella had risen from script reader to scenarist at Essanay on a salary of $45 a week when she was made redundant in an economy drive. She found a job working on the *Chicago Record-Herald* revealing movie gossip, although exactly when is impossible to determine because very few copies of the newspaper exist in Chicago public libraries and the copies in Louella's scrapbook are undated thanks to her judicious wielding of a pair of scissors. Her early columns show an eye for the cynical and an eagerness to reveal manipulation by press agents. That soon disappeared as Louella realised that the truth was not what the public wanted to hear. A move to the *New York Morning Telegraph* followed on June 9, 1918, when the motion-picture editor received his call-up papers. Louella began to network, cultivating people she believed would be useful to her. On November 19, 1923, she joined William Randolph Hearst's *New York American* as motion picture editor. For the next 30 or so years she rose to become one of the most feared columnists in American journalism. One wrong word from Louella could wreck a career, a puff piece in her column could raise the stock of any actor. She often feuded with Hedda Hopper and canny stars were careful not to show favouritism to either. Parsons married Dr Harry Watson 'Docky' Martin (b. Redfield, South Dakota, January 16, 1890, d. Cedars of Lebanon Hospital, Los Angeles, June 24, 1951) on January 5, 1930. Martin, a hopeless drunk, had a sideline. He was the unofficial doctor at Madame Lee Frances' brothel and Hollywood's most popular 'clap doctor', an 'in' that Louella exploited to the max. Louella was aboard Hearst's yacht, the *Oneida*, when film director Thomas Ince was mortally shot and she became part of the cover-up that ensued. Parsons would also plug Hearst's mistress, Marion Davies, in her column whenever the need arose. Louella appeared as herself in a number of films including *Hollywood Hotel* (1937) and *Starlift* (1951). Her column may have been essential reading but she also exposed her own prejudices in it, referring to black actors as 'pickaninnies' and revealing that her all-time hero was Mussolini.

CAUSE: In September 1964 Louella fell and broke her hip and was hospitalised for 15 days. That year she retired from writing her column and moved from her mansion at 619 Maple Drive, Beverly Hills, into a nursing home. She died, senile and incontinent, of generalised arteriosclerosis aged 91. She was buried in Holy Cross Cemetery & Mausoleum, 5835 West Slauson Avenue, Culver City, California 90230.

FURTHER READING: *Hedda And Louella* – George Eells (London: W.H. Allen, 1972).

Pier Paolo Pasolini
Born March 5, 1922
Died November 2, 1975
A thorn in Italy's side. Born in Bologna, Italy, Pasolini was a film maker, a poet, a novelist, a Marxist and a proselytising homosexual. He began writing films in 1955, his first being *Prigioniero Della Montagna* (1955) and *La Donna Del Fiume* (1955). However, he really caused a stir when he began directing six years later. His first film was *Accattone* (1961) on which Bernardo Bertolucci was assistant director. The film was a look at the dark side of the Italian capital. Many of his films were blatant in their use of blasphemy, sex and violence to make a point. He followed *Accattone* up with *Mamma Roma* (1962), *La Rabbia* (1963), *Comizi D'Amore* (1964), *Il Vangelo Secondo Matteo/The Gospel According To St Matthew* (1964), in which he cast his mother as the Virgin Mary, and a Marxist lorry driver as Jesus, *Il Padre Selvaggio* (1965), *Edipo Re/Oedipus Rex* (1967), which was filmed in Morocco, *Teorema* (1968), *Porcile/Pigsty* (1969), *Il Decameron* (1970), *I Racconti Di Canterbury/The Canterbury Tales* (1971) in which he also played Geoffrey Chaucer and the most violent *Salò O Le 120 Giornate Di Sodoma/The 120 Days Of Sodom* (1975).

CAUSE: Pasolini was murdered, aged 53, by a 17-year-old boy whom he had propositioned in Ostia, Italy. The teenager bludgeoned the director to death and then ran him over with his own Alfa Romeo. However, some, including Bertolucci, believe Pasolini was killed for political reasons.

Charles Pathé
Born December 25, 1863
Died December 25, 1957
The news man. The son of a pork butcher and a cook, Pathé was born in Chevry-Cossigny, France, and quickly rose to become one of the early giants of cinema. In 1894 he bought and exhibited an Edison phonograph and began selling them. Two years later, he founded Pathé Frères with his brothers and they began selling projectors. In 1901 he bought a studio and produced documentaries. He expanded the business to include film stock, processing laboratories and cinemas. He launched the world's first newsreel for general distribution, *Pathé-Journal*, in 1908 in Paris under the directorship of Albert Gaveau. By 1908 Pathé was the world's largest film producer with interests in London, New York, Moscow and many other cities. He sold more films to America than America produced. Following the end of World War I, America began to assert itself as a film-maker and Pathé began to sell off parts of his empire. In 1929 he sold the last remnants and retired to the Riviera.

CAUSE: He died on his 94th birthday in Monte Carlo, Monaco, of natural causes.

Lee Payant
Born 1924
Died December 14, 1976
Beautiful voice. Born in Seattle, Washington, actor/singer/guitarist Payant is best known as the dubbed voice of Robinson Crusoe in the 1960s television programme. His films as an actor included *Nødlanding* (1952), *Bridge To The Sun* (1961) and

L'Évasion (1963). He directed *Astérix Et Cléopâtre* (1968) and *Blutiger Freitag* (1972) but preferred his life as a café proprietor with his black boyfriend Gordon Heath (b. New York, September 20, 1918, d. Paris, France, August 27, 1991 of AIDS), an actor, director, and folk-singer, on the Left Bank in Paris. The two men ran L'Abbaye which they bought in 1949, three years after they had met, having fled the racism and homophobia of America. They performed together at the café and in 1957 the couple released an album of their duets, *An Evening At L'Abbaye*. Heath appeared on British television quite often and narrated John Halas and Joy Batchelor's cartoon version of George Orwell's *Animal Farm* in 1956. CAUSE: He died aged 51 of cancer in Paris, France.

Laurence Payne

Born June 5, 1919
Died February 23, 2009
"Larry Two". Known as Larry Two in deference to Larry Olivier, Laurence Stanley Payne was born in north London, the son of a carpenter who died when Payne was three. Their mother, a Wesleyan Methodist, in Wood Green, raised Payne, his elder brother and sister in a strict fashion. A conscientious objector, he was exempted from service on condition that he went on tour with the Old Vic during the war. In 1945 he toured Germany for three months with ENSA. Payne apparently never worked in the West End because he rebuffed an invitation from powerful producer Binkie Beaumont to appear in a 1946 production of *The Brothers Karamazov*. In 1954 he played D'Artagnan in *The Three Musketeers* on television. He played *Sexton Blake* in 60 episodes on ITV between 1967 and 1971. On the big screen he was in *Ben-Hur* (1959), *The Singer Not The Song* (1960) and the Hammer horror flick *Vampire Circus* (1971). In 1961 he began writing crime

novels and published eleven commencing with *The Nose On My Face*, filmed as *Girl In The Headlines* (1963) starring Ian Hendry as a policeman trying to solve the murder of a model. In 1944 he married the actress Sheila Burrell (b. Blackheath, London May 9, 1922) but they divorced. Another marriage (in 1955) to another actress, Pamela Alan, also ended in divorce. In 1974 he married the equestrian journalist Judith Draper. CAUSE: In the Nineties Payne contracted septicaemia resulting in brain damage. Suffering from vascular dementia, he spent his last three years in a nursing home near Berwick-upon-Tweed. He died aged 89.

Barbara Payton

(BARBARA REDFIELD)
Born November 16, 1927
Died May 8, 1967
Flamboyant blonde. Born in Cloquet, Minnesota (also the birthplace of Jessica Lange), Barbara Payton was a beautiful, leggy teenager who shocked her parents by marrying when she was still in junior high school. That marriage was quickly annulled but on February 10, 1945, she married again, this time to air force pilot John Payton. Their honeymoon was spent in Hollywood where Barbara wangled a screen test with RKO. However, before the test she discovered she was pregnant. She later suffered a miscarriage though a son, John Lee, would be born in 1947. In 1948, with her marriage over, she travelled back to RKO but found that the studio was no longer interested in her, so she signed for Universal-International at a rate of $100 a week. She made a few films and began to date lawyer Greg Bautzer but the affair ended when she was cast as Meg Dixon, alias Laurie Fredericks in *Trapped* (1949). Her film *Kiss Tomorrow Goodbye* (1950) in which she played Holiday Carleton was well received. She began to date Franchot Tone and they announced their

engagement at New York's Stork Club, despite opposition from many of his friends and ex-wife Joan Crawford. She was Flo in *Dallas* (1950) and had an affair with leading man Gary Cooper. Maintaining her track record of sleeping with the leading man, she made *Only The Valiant* (1951) playing Cathy Eversham and bedded the star Gregory Peck. That year she was chosen as one of the six most promising starlets by the Hollywood Press Association. She also became involved in an unsavoury court case that displeased Warner Bros. She made *Drums In The Deep South* (1951) as Kathy Summers and, true to form, became romantically involved with the married star Guy Madison. Franchot Tone, still deeply in love with Barbara, had hired a private detective to keep track of her movements and he discovered her and Madison in flagrante at her second-floor home at 7456 Hollywood Boulevard. She then met actor Tom Neal and dumped Tone for him and then changed her mind and went back to Tone. On September 13, 1951, she and Tone were together at her new apartment, 1803 Courtney Terrace, when Neal burst in and gave Tone a good hiding. As a result of the assault, Tone suffered a broken nose, fractured cheekbone and concussion, spent a fortnight in the California Lutheran Hospital and later had to undergo plastic surgery. Fifteen days later, Barbara and Tone were married in Cloquet. She was 23 years old and on her third marriage. After a 72-hour honeymoon Barbara began work on *Lady In The Iron Mask* but was sacked and replaced by Patricia Medina (Joseph Cotten's wife). After 53 days, she and Tone called it a day and she went back to the thuggish Tom Neal. Mindful of Neal's temper, she went back to Tone briefly, but left him again. In March 1952 she attempted suicide but was found in time by Tone. Despite this they divorced in May 1952, due to her 'extreme mental cruelty'. She appeared in *Bride Of The Gorilla* (1951) as Mrs Dina Van Gelder, though this time she didn't have a fling with her leading man (Raymond Burr) because he was gay. She also didn't have a contract when Warner Bros decided not to pick up her option. In October 1952 she became involved in yet another imbroglio. "I became good friends with Ava Gardner and Lana Turner. We three were in Palm Springs together," remembered Barbara. "We were drinking and lying around with not many clothes on and talking about things. Ava was married to Frank Sinatra in those days. He was screaming crazy about her. Well, he didn't approve of the way we were carrying on like that, and one night he came in and caught us all together. Well, I jumped out of the window and into the bushes but he caught Lana and Ava together and he was mad as hell. It got into the gossip columns and contributed to the end of their marriage." For *The Great Jesse James Raid* (1953), in which she portrayed Kate, it was okay for her to sleep with her leading man for it was Tom Neal. She moved to England where she made *Four-Sided Triangle* (1953), playing the dual role of Lena Maitland and her duplicate Helen. Her second film was *The Flanagan Boy* (1953) as Lorna Vecchi before she returned to America. Her last film, *Murder Is My Beat* (1955) as Eden Lane, was probably one of her best. Then it all went horribly wrong. In October 1955 she was arrested for passing rubber cheques to buy alcohol. She married furniture salesman George A. Provas and moved to Nogales, Arizona, but they divorced in August 1958. She moved back to Hollywood and was arrested for drunkenness and prostitution. In her last years she worked washing hair in a hairdresser's and as a waitress in downmarket clubs before moving to Nevada.
CAUSE: She married for the fifth time, to Jess Rawley but that, too, failed and,

in April 1967, she went to stay with her parents at their home, 1901 Titus Street, San Diego, California. By this time her liver had failed, her skin was yellow and blotchy, she had put on weight and some of her front teeth had fallen out. Her father discovered her corpse on the bathroom floor. She had died of heart and liver failure. She was 39.

Gregory Peck
Born April 5, 1916
Died June 12, 2003
Rangy good guy. In 1880 Catherine Ashe, a 16-year-old from Dingle, County Kerry, emigrated to Rochester, New York, where she met and married Samuel Peck, who was of English descent. He died young of diphtheria and Catherine took her 11-month-old son Gregory back to Ireland. When Gregory was 10 he and his mother went back to America where the determined woman made a fortune selling corsets. She gave her son $10,000 to set up a chemist's in La Jolla, California. He married Bernice 'Bunny' Ayres, a girl from St Louis who became a Roman Catholic. Their son Eldred Gregory Peck was born at La Jolla in the spring of 1916. His unusual Christian name was chosen at random by his mother from the phone book. Not long after his birth the chemist's went bust, the marriage failed and his mother took him back to St Louis. (His mother was to marry a salesman called Joseph Maysuch né Masucci.) Returning to La Jolla, he was brought up by his father and grandmother and educated at San Diego High School and St John's Military Academy, Los Angeles, where he later recalled, "I was laminated with virtue by tough Irish nuns and square-jawed army officers. I was lonely, withdrawn and full of self-doubt. I could never remember a time when I sat down to dinner with my mother and my father. What I decided to do – what I had to do – was

to run my own life because there was no one else to do it for me. I grew like corn in the moonlight." He got his first job at 18 driving an oil lorry in nearby San Diego, before going to the University of California at Berkeley to read medicine. At university he changed his course and took a degree in English. His free time was divided between rowing (at which he represented the university) and acting. In 1939 Peck moved to New York to train at the Playhouse School of Dramatics. In 1941 he joined the Cape Playhouse at Cape Cod. The following year he played on Broadway opposite Jill Esmond (Laurence Olivier's lesbian first wife) in Emlyn Williams' *Morning Star* with the New York Neighborhood Playhouse. In the spring of 1941 he took a screen test at the Fox studios on 10th Avenue and 57th Street but it was not successful. Said David O. Selznick, "He photographs like Abe Lincoln but if he has a great personality, I don't think it comes through in the tests." Peck decided his future lay in the theatre but when America belatedly entered the Second World War, Peck was turned down for military service because of a spinal injury supposedly suffered as a student during a rowing accident. However, at the Neighborhood Playhouse, he was taught movement by Martha Graham, who, he insisted, gave him the back injury that kept him out of uniform. Later, 20th Century Fox claimed that the cause was a rowing injury. "In Hollywood, they didn't think a dance class was macho enough, I guess. I've been trying to straighten out that story for years," Peck explained. With many of his contemporaries fighting overseas he was cast as Vladimir, a Russian partisan, in Casey Robinson's *Days Of Glory* (1944), opposite the Russian ballerina Tamara Toumanova, Robinson's fiancée, for $1,000 a week. Toumanova had such a thick Russian accent that the only way to make any sense of the dialogue was to have the entire cast speak in a similar fashion. His next film saw him play Father Francis Chisholm in *The Keys Of The Kingdom* (1944) in a 20th Century Fox adaptation of A.J. Cronin's novel about a Scottish Roman Catholic priest in China. It won him his first Best Actor Oscar nomination. Soon everyone wanted a piece of Gregory Peck. He was Paul Scott, a handsome steel magnate, in *The Valley Of Decision* (1945) opposite Greer Garson.

Then he played John Ballantine, the amnesiac head of a mental hospital cured by Ingrid Bergman's psychiatrist in Alfred Hitchcock's *Spellbound* (1945). In King Vidor's *Duel In The Sun* (1946) he was Lewton McCanles, the leering and sarcastic seducer of Jennifer Jones. In *The Yearling* (1946) he was Pa Baxter, a father who has to kill his son's pet deer. The part won him his second Best Actor Oscar nomination. In *Gentleman's Agreement* (1947) Peck played Phil Green, a journalist who pretended to be Jewish to root out racial prejudice for a series of magazine articles. He took the role although his agent warned him, "You're just establishing yourself and a lot of people will resent the picture. Anti-semitism runs deep in this country." The film garnered him his third Best Actor Oscar nomination and made him one of America's Top 10 box office stars and the recipient of a prodigious amount of fan mail, said to be 3,000 letters a week. "Please let me spend the night with you," women would write. "You can do what you will with me. It would make my dreams come true." "I'm all booked up," his secretary would reply. *The Paradine Case* (1947) found Peck as Anthony Keene, once again working for Alfred Hitchcock as a British barrister, whose judgement is disastrously warped by his beautiful client (Alida Valli), on trial for murdering her husband. Peck disappointed and it is regarded as Hitchcock's worst film. In *The Great Sinner* (1949), a film inspired at some

remove by Dostoevsky, he appeared as Fedja, a young writer who becomes a compulsive gambler. His fourth Academy Award nomination came for playing the dithering General Frank Savage, the commander of an American bomber unit who is obliged to send his crews to their deaths over Nazi Germany in *Twelve O'Clock High* (1949), his third 20th Century Fox role to be so appreciated. Still with the armed forces, he took the lead in *Captain Horatio Hornblower RN* (1951) and stayed at sea in Raoul Walsh's *The World In His Arms* (1952), this time as Jonathan Clark, a seal pirate in Alaska. He was Commander Dwight Lionel Towers of the USS Sawfish, a submarine commander on the brink of nuclear war with Ava Gardner in *On The Beach* (1959). Back on dry land he was Lieutenant Joe Clemons, a platoon commander with a conscience, in *Pork Chop Hill* (1959), and the honourable Captain Keith Mallory in *The Guns Of Navarone* (1961). Peck certainly had versatility. In *Yellow Sky* (1948) he played James 'Stretch' Dawson, the leader of a gang of robbers who are chased into a salt flat after holding up a bank. In *The Gunfighter* (1950) he was brilliant as Johnny Ringo, simultaneously weary of shooting upstarts slower on the draw and haunted by the eventual certainty of death at the hands of a younger man. He played the lead opposite Susan Hayward in *David And Bathsheba* (1951), a film which, according to one critic, gained "hardly a single intentional laugh". He was cast because Darryl F. Zanuck thought he had "a biblical face". He was Harry Street, an injured hunter contemplating his lot, in *The Snows Of Kilimanjaro* (1952), a popular film based on various writings by Ernest Hemingway. In *Roman Holiday* (1953) Peck was at his most beguiling as Joe Bradley, an American journalist who determines to get a story from Audrey Hepburn's princess. Although his contract stipulated that his name should appear on its own above the title, he cabled the studio in Hollywood, saying, "Audrey Hepburn is going to be a big star. Put her name alongside mine. That is where it belongs." In *The Purple Plain* (1954) Peck was Squadron Leader Bill Forrester whose plane had crashed in the Burmese jungle. He made a respectable fist of playing Captain Ahab in John Huston's *Moby Dick* (1956). In *The Man In The Gray Flannel Suit* (1956) Peck was Tom Rath, a New York executive who looks back on his wartime adultery before deciding that his first loyalty lies with wife and children. Then came Vincente Minnelli's *Designing Woman* (1957), a comedy in which he played Mike Hagen, where Lauren Bacall (Marilla Brown Hagen) tipped a plate of spaghetti in his lap. In Willie Wyler's *The Big Country* (1958) Peck was James McKay, a retired, wealthy sea captain who rose above all sorts of provocation before he finally became involved in a savage fight with Charlton Heston (Steve Leech). The plot of the film turned on a battle for land – a subject dear to the heart of Peck, who owned no fewer than seven cattle ranches. Not all of his films were successful. He once commented, "When I'm wrongly cast I sink with the ship." 6′3″ Peck was one of the first actors to take on the studio system in Hollywood and win. Peck was taken to the office of Louis B. Mayer to be flattered into signing a contract. Mayer told him what he had done for the careers of Mickey Rooney, Spencer Tracy, Robert Montgomery, Judy Garland and many more. Peck stood firm, and told him he had no intention of signing an exclusive contract for anyone. As Mayer went on, Peck remembered, a strong note of emotion entered his voice. "He pulled out a handkerchief and began to weep to think I wouldn't allow him to make me the greatest star of all time. My refusal to sign was portrayed as an offence to American motherhood,

patriotism and family decency. It was an extraordinary performance." Fortunately, Peck had an instinct for a good script. The one film he regretted turning down was *High Noon*. Other, less remarkable Westerns in which he appeared were *Only The Valiant* (1951) as Captain Richard Lance, *The Bravados* (1958) as Jim Douglass with Joan Collins, *How The West Was Won* (1962) as Cleve Van Valen, *Mckenna's Gold* (1969) as Mckenna, John Frankenheimer's *I Walk The Line* (1970) as Sheriff Harry Tawes opposite Tuesday Weld, *Shoot Out* (1971) as Clay Lomax and *Billy Two Hats* (1974) as Arch Deans. He attempted, disastrously, to impersonate Scott Fitzgerald in *Beloved Infidel* (1959) before getting back on track as Sam Bowden being threatened by Robert Mitchum in the original *Cape Fear* (1962). Robert Mulligan's *To Kill A Mockingbird* (1962), based on Harper Lee's best-selling novel, which won him his only Oscar for playing Atticus Finch, a white lawyer defending a black man against rape charges in Thirties Alabama, was Peck's last great film. The comedy *Captain Newman MD* (1963), in which he played Captain Josiah J. Newman opposite Tony Curtis, failed to light up the screen. *Behold A Pale Horse* (1964) presented him, rather unconvincingly, as Manuel Artiguez, a Spanish loyalist. The comedy thrillers, *Mirage* (1965) in which he played David Stillwell and *Arabesque* (1966) as David Pollock with Sophia Loren, represented some improvement, but *The Chairman* (1969), in which Peck played John Hathaway, a scientist on a mission to Red China, was a feeble offering. *Marooned* (1970), which found him as Charles Keith, a space mission controller, was an even bigger flop. In the mid-Seventies Peck turned unsuccessfully to producing. It was perhaps in desperation that he accepted a part that Charlton Heston had declined in *The Omen* (1976). As

Robert Thorn, the American ambassador in London, he is persuaded that he has to stab to death his (adopted) son, who is demonically possessed, on a sacrificial altar with a special set of daggers. In *MacArthur The Rebel General* (1977), Peck played the soldier who loses his command rather than conform to presidential orders; he caught MacArthur's intelligence but not the general's overwhelming pride and lunacy. In *The Boys From Brazil* (1978) Peck was evil scientist Josef Mengele, a Nazi in hiding from Jewish revenge but still harbouring schemes of world domination. Peck tried a British accent as Colonel Lewis Pugh in *The Sea Wolves* (1980), directing a raid by fellow army veterans on a German spy ship. In *Amazing Grace And Chuck* (1987) he played the American president, while in *Old Gringo* (1989) he attempted a portrait of the American satirist Ambrose Bierce, who vanished in New Mexico during the Revolution of 1914. Having avoided television for much of his career he turned up as President Abraham Lincoln in *The Blue And The Gray* (1982) and *The Scarlet And The Black* (1983) as Monsignor Hugh Flaherty. He appeared again in *The Portrait* (1993) as Gardner Church and in 1998 he returned to *Moby Dick*, playing the part of Father Mapple in a television adaptation of the novel that won him a Golden Globe. On the big screen his late appearances included the modern version of Martin Scorsese's *Cape Fear* (1991), this time playing a shady lawyer called Lee Heller; the same year he appeared as Andrew Jorgenson in *Other People's Money*. Two years later, he resumed the part of Atticus Finch in the short film *Passage A L'Acte*, which dealt with an American family warring at the breakfast table. From 1967 to 1970 Peck was President of the Academy of Motion Picture Arts and Sciences. He insisted that the 1968 Oscars be delayed as a mark of respect to the recently assassinated Dr Martin Luther King, Jr. When Richard M. Nixon was in the White House Peck found himself on the president's enemies list. He was also chairman of the trustees of the American Film Institute, which he had helped to found, and in 1966 served as chairman of the American Cancer Society. Gregory Peck married first, in a Lutheran church on Fifth Avenue, New York, in October 1942, Greta Konen Rice, a petite Finnish-born blonde divorcée four years his senior, who served as hairdresser in the touring company in which he acted. They had three sons, Jonathan (b. July 20, 1944), Stephen (b. August 16, 1946) and Carey Paul (b. June 17, 1949). Jonathan looked and sounded like his father. Rather than acting he became a television and radio journalist. He killed himself with a shotgun aged 30 in June 1975 in Santa Barbara, California. Peck was later to say, "When that happens, you blame yourself. What went wrong? Was I responsible? Jonathan had a failed love affair [with a missionary's wife who was an ardent fan of his father's, only for her to call out "Gregory" at the moment of climax], he had been ill and was depressed from overwork, but you never get over a thing like that. I still think – what would Jonathan be doing now?" Peck and Greta divorced on December 30, 1954, amid allegations of "extreme cruelty" and "grievous mental suffering". When Greta Peck appeared before Los Angeles Superior Court, she accused Peck of causing her "anguish, embarrassment and humiliation" and of treating her in a "cruel and inhuman manner". The statement went on, "He has pursued a course of conduct towards his wife of such character as to constitute extreme cruelty. He has caused her to endure grievous mental suffering, extreme nervousness, and she can no longer live with him as his wife." Peck denied the cruelty charge but did not contest the divorce, and Greta was awarded one of the largest settlements in Hollywood history. As well as custody of their sons, she received half their property – including Peck's beloved house in the Pacific Palisades – and substantial financial interests in three of his films, including *Roman Holiday* and *Moby Dick*. She was also awarded 20 per cent of the first $100,000 he earned annually for the next ten years, 12.5 per cent on the second $100,000, and so on through a complicated and generous sliding scale. Even after the ten years were up, she was to receive five per cent of his earnings until she remarried (which she never did) along with monthly cheques for each child. Peck married secondly, on December 31, 1955, Veronique Passani, whom he had met when she interviewed him for *France Soir*. When he telephoned her at Paris Presse a few months later to suggest a visit to the races, she abandoned an interview with Albert Schweitzer to accept. She was supposed to be interviewing Schweitzer, who was lunching with French intellectual Jean-Paul Sartre. She calculated that she could fit in the interview and arrive to join Peck at the fourth race. But Schweitzer and Sartre lingered over lunch so long that finally, as she put it, "Dr Schweitzer and my career lost." They had a son and a daughter, Anthony (b. October 24, 1956) and Cecilia (b. May 1958), both actors. On November 23, 1990, Tony Peck married the beautiful 5'10" model Cheryl Tiegs (b. Breckinridge, Minnesota, September 25, 1947), nine years his senior (he was her third husband), and had one son Zachary who was born on October 1, 1991. The couple were divorced in 1994. Tony Peck suffered from drinking problems. The modern films Hollywood was producing did not appeal to Gregory Peck. "People don't believe in heroes of the sort I used to play. They don't believe in someone who can be depended upon. This is

not the age for good guys." CAUSE: In early June 2003 the American Film Institute voted Peck's Atticus Finch as the greatest Hollywood hero of all time. (Indiana Jones was second and James Bond third.) He died later that month aged 87 peacefully during the night at his Los Angeles home with his wife at his side. Monroe Friedman, Peck's spokesman, said, "[Veronique] said she was holding his hand and he just closed his eyes and went to sleep and he was gone. He had just been getting older and more fragile. He wasn't really ill. He just sort of ran his course and died of old age." Peck was buried on June 16, 2003, and the actor Brock Peters (who played the black man defended by Atticus Finch) delivered the eulogy. FURTHER READING: *Gregory Peck: A Biography* – Michael Freedland (London: W.H. Allen, 1980).

Sam Peckinpah
Born February 21, 1925
Died December 28, 1984
Violent director. David Samuel Peckinpah's adolescence was filled with boozing and brawling. He fought and drank in school, in military college and especially when he joined the marines. It should therefore, come as no surprise to anyone that his films were notable because of their violence. Born in Fresno, California, he studied drama and then landed a number of minor jobs in television, occasionally working with Don Siegel. His first theatrical directorial job was *The Deadly Companions* (1961), a western. His next film was *Ride The High Country* (1962), which starred Joel McCrea and Randolph Scott. There followed a three-year hiatus before Peckinpah came back with the film that was to make his name, *Major Dundee* (1965). The film, which starred Charlton Heston, Richard Harris, Jim Hutton and James Coburn, was about cavalry officers who intend to massacre Native Americans. It was the first film in

which Peckinpah espoused the link, as he saw it, between masculinity and a predisposition to violence. Four years later came the film that established Peckinpah's reputation: *The Wild Bunch* (1969). The movie, set against the background of the Mexican Revolution, was condemned for its bloodthirstiness, although Peckinpah claimed it was a film about violence rather than one that was violent just for the sake of it. It was said that more blanks were fired during filming than real bullets were used in the actual Mexican Revolution. *The Ballad Of Cable Hogue* (1970) followed and then Peckinpah once again fell foul of the censor. He travelled to England and shot *Straw Dogs* (1971). It starred Dustin Hoffman as David Sumner, a mathematician who, looking for somewhere peaceful to do some research, travels to Cornwall and rents a cottage with his beautiful blonde wife, Amy (Susan George). They are taunted by the locals and soon bloody violence erupts, including the rape of Amy Sumner. Regarded by Halliwell as "totally absurd, poorly contrived", by reviewer Simon Rose as "risible, unpleasant nonsense", it is given a four-star rating by Mick Martin and Marsha Porter in their *Video Movie Guide 2000*. It is also memorable, in a way, for being the first film in which Susan George bares her breasts. After that Peckinpah made *The Getaway* (1972) with Steve McQueen and Ali MacGraw as amoral villains. *Pat Garrett And Billy The Kid* (1973), starring James Coburn and Kris Kristofferson in the lead roles, is often regarded as Peckinpah's most thoughtful movie. *Bring Me The Head Of Alfredo Garcia* (1974) is the only film over which Peckinpah claims he had total control. Whether that is a good thing or a bad one can only be judged by viewing the film. Critic John Simon commented: "Peckinpah clearly doesn't lack talent – what he lacks is brains." His last directing job was

working on music videos for Julian Lennon.
CAUSE: Peckinpah died of a stroke in Mexico. He was 59.

Pina Pellicer
Born April 3, 1935
Died December 4, 1964
Latin tragedy. Born in Mexico 5'1" Roman Catholic Pina Pellicer made her name on Mexican television in a version of *The Diary Of Anne Frank*. She made few films but showed a talent that suggested she could go far. However, she was shy and neurotic and her lack of English probably pushed her further into her shell. She appeared in *Macario* (1960). When she arrived in America to star as Louisa opposite Marlon Brando in *One-Eyed Jacks* (1961) she broke down at the airport when she was asked her business in America by customs officers. Nonetheless, she gave a memorable performance. Brando was so entranced by her that they began a brief affair although he also slept with other women during filming. She starred in *Rogelia* (1962) and *Dias De Otoño* (1962), which won her the Best Actress Award at the San Sebastian Film Festival.
CAUSE: She found work hard to come by after that high and became very bitter. When she was 17 she had attempted suicide by slashing her wrists. She died by her own hand in Mexico City, aged 29. It may have been in the aftermath of the end of a lesbian affair.

George Peppard
Born October 1, 1926
Died May 8, 1994
Prima donna. Born in Detroit, Michigan, the son of a building contractor, Peppard was a struggling taxi driver until he became a struggling actor, a state of affairs that continued until 1956 when he landed a role on Broadway in *The Beautiful Changes* which led to a succession of television

parts. He was a staple on TV until the early Sixties when he was taken by film and began to appear in movies such as *Breakfast At Tiffany's* (1961), *How The West Was Won* (1962), *The Carpetbaggers* (1964), *Operation Crossbow* (1965), *The Blue Max* (1966), *Tobruk* (1967) and *Cannon For Cordoba* (1970). On September 13, 1972, he began starring in the NBC private eye series *Banacek* playing the lead, Thomas Banacek. The series ran for two years until September 3, 1974, when Peppard left because the producer had also departed. From 1975 until 1976 he played Dr Jake Goodwin in *Doctors' Hospital* but left that show as well. Peppard was well known for being difficult to work with and this presented him with career difficulties when no one wanted to employ him. Most of the films he appeared in in the Seventies flopped, although sanctuary seemed to be on the horizon when was offered the plum role of Blake Carrington in a new series to be called *Dynasty*. Never knowing when to keep his mouth shut, Peppard fell out with the producers over his interpretation of the part and he was sacked after just 16 days. Luckily, he was saved by an action series called *The A-Team* in which he took the part of Colonel John 'Hannibal' Smith. The NBC series ran from January 23, 1983, until June 14, 1987, after which Peppard didn't work very much. He married five times. His first wife was actress Helen Bradford Davies whom he married in 1954 and by whom he had a son, Bradford Davies (b. 1955), and a daughter, Julie Louise (b. 1956). They divorced in January 1965. On April 17, 1966, he married actress Elizabeth Ashley at the Bel-Air Hotel. A son, Christian Moore, was born on March 12, 1968. They divorced on April 30, 1972. On January 30, 1975, he married Sherry Boucher. In December 1984 he married actress Alexis Adams. His final wife was Laura Taylor and they married on September 10, 1992.

CAUSE: He died of pneumonia after suffering from lung cancer. He was 67.

Anthony Perkins
Born April 4, 1932
Died September 12, 1992
One role man. Born in New York City, Perkins was the son of successful stage actor James Osgood Ripley Perkins (b. West Newton, Massachusetts, May 16, 1892, d. Washington, September 21, 1937, of heart failure). Perkins was an only child and spoiled rotten by his parents. However, he was just five when his father died and his mother enveloped him in love. (She did, however, try to force the naturally left-handed Perkins to use his right hand, causing the boy to stammer. The same thing happened to King George VI with the same result.) Psychologists believe that a child brought up by an overbearing mother and without a counterbalancing male figure can turn out to be homosexual. Was this the root cause of Perkins' homosexuality? Perkins seemed to be often cast in sexually ambiguous or ambivalent roles. One of his earliest successes was as Tom Lee, the confused schoolboy in *Tea And Sympathy* (Ethel Barrymore Theater, West 47th Street, from September 30, 1953, although Perkins didn't join the cast until May 31, 1954). Perkins was spotted by director William Wyler, who cast him as Josh Birdwell in *Friendly Persuasion* (1956). The performance won Perkins his only Oscar nomination. He also supposedly romanced star Gary Cooper's daughter, Maria, during production. Cooper wasn't overly impressed with Perkins, believing he wasn't fully developed. He would have been even less impressed if he had known that the 6'2" Perkins' real romantic interest was in actor Tab Hunter who, aged 19, in October 1950 had been arrested at an all-male pyjama party in Tinseltown. (Hunter's career never recovered from the scandal.) Hollywood wasn't quite sure what to make of Perkins either and

when James Dean died, Perkins was seen as a potential replacement for the moody rebel without a cause. His next film was the first made under contract to Paramount Pictures, a Western called *The Lonely Man* (1957) with Perkins playing Riley Wade, Jack Palance's son. This was followed by the biopic *Fear Strikes Out* (1957) in which Perkins played pro baseball player Jim Piersall, who suffered a breakdown after striving unsuccessfully to gain his father's approval. Perkins put so much energy into the film that he lost weight (from his already lean frame) and had to be hospitalised. In his next film, *The Tin Star* (1957), he played a green sheriff, Ben Owens, opposite Henry Fonda. Perkins appeared in half a dozen more films, *Desire Under The Elms* (1958) as Eben Cabot, *The Matchmaker* (1958) as Cornelius Hackel, *This Angry Age* (1958) as Joseph Dufresne, *Green Mansions* (1959) as Abel, *On The Beach* (1959) as Peter Holmes and *Tall Story* (1960) as Ray Blent before he made the film with which he will be forever associated – Alfred Hitchcock's chilling *Psycho* (1960). The story of psychopathic mummy's boy Norman Bates became one of the most popular horror films of all time. The music, the atmosphere, the black-and-white photography and especially Perkins' superb acting all make for a film that gets better with every viewing. The character of Norman Bates was based on notorious Wisconsin killer Ed Gein (b. Plainfield, August 27, 1906, d. Mendota, July 26, 1984, of respiratory failure) who also inspired *The Texas Chainsaw Massacre* (1974) and the character Buffalo Bill in *The Silence Of The Lambs* (1991). Edward Theodore Gein (pronounced geen) lived with his mother, Augusta, and brother, Henry (b. Plainfield, January 17, 1902) on a farm in Plainfield and had the virtues of hard work and sexual abstinence drilled into him. His brother died on May 16, 1944, and his mother 18 months

later, on December 29, 1945, at the Wild Rose Hospital of a cerebral haemorrhage. Without any kind of socialising presence in his life, Gein became a recluse and took to studying anatomy from textbooks. Eventually, the theoretical side bored him and he began to dig up corpses from the local cemetery to put into practice what he had learned from the books. He would skin the corpses and then drape the flesh over himself. From 1954 Gein began murdering, although he wasn't caught until November 16, 1957; he confessed all the next day. On November 23, 1957, he was sentenced to an asylum for the criminally insane and four months later, on March 27, 1958, his farm was razed to the ground in a mysterious fire. His trial had begun on January 6, 1958, but was abandoned because of his insanity and did not resume until November 6, 1968. He died still, thankfully, incarcerated. Novelist Robert Bloch wrote a story about Gein that was seen by Hitchcock, who turned it into *Psycho*. Hitchcock, possessor of a black sense of humour, told the press he was considering both Judith Anderson and Helen Hayes for the role of Mrs Bates. The film was mauled by critics when it opened but went on to take $14 million in its first year alone, having cost $780,000 to make. The shower scene lasts just 45 seconds, yet took a week to shoot and Perkins wasn't even on set when the dirty deed is done. Trivia note: after she has been murdered and is lying on the shower floor Marion Crane (Janet Leigh) gulps – twice. (The blood is really chocolate sauce.) Leigh was paid $25,000 for the film as opposed to Perkins' remuneration of $40,000. *Psycho* made Tony Perkins, but also haunted him for the rest of his life. During his next film, *Goodbye Again* (1961), he played Philip Van der Bersh opposite Ingrid Bergman, who tried to seduce Perkins by luring him to her dressing room to 'rehearse' a scene. He didn't fall for her ruse, and kept the dressing room door open to 'protect' himself. In 1960 Perkins had an affair with an actor-dancer who wishes to remain anonymous with whom he indulged in some most peculiar behaviour. Of one incident his partner said: "We were doing things that [Perkins] liked, not the normal gay sex. Anything that got sloppy and messy was fine. Tony became like an animal. He loved being pissed on . . . There was some S&M. We had sex in leather. He wore jeans. He liked inventiveness." Perkins was in regular employment in both film and theatre. In 1970 he played Chaplain Tappman in Mike Nichols' *Catch-22* and two years later appeared in *The Life And Times Of Judge Roy Bean* as Reverend LaSalle. Co-star Ava Gardner had made a play for Perkins before but he was terrified by her and kept his distance. She later recalled: "Tony Perkins was shy about everything but attacking his plate." However, for the first time, one woman supposedly did manage to penetrate Perkins' defences. He claimed he had sex with future *Dallas* star Victoria Principal (b. Fukuoka, Japan, January 3, 1946) and then proceeded to tell everyone about it via an interview with *People* magazine. According to one source Principal denied sleeping with Perkins although she did tell *People*: "It was, for both of us, a special time in our lives." (Actress Cynthia Rogers would later claim it was she, and not Principal, who relieved Perkins of his heterosexual virginity.) Now he knew that he could have penetrative sex with a woman, Perkins was more confident about his desire to marry and raise a family despite his homosexuality. In a 1971 interview he claimed that he had had a homosexual encounter, but said "that kind of sex" was "unsatisfying". On August 9, 1973, in Wellsfleet, Massachusetts, he married Catholic Berinthia Berenson, whose death is noticed in this book, the younger sister of actress Marisa Berenson and granddaughter of Elsa Schiaparelli.

They were to have two sons, Osgood Robert (b. New York, February 2, 1974) and Elvis (b. February 9, 1976). Perkins went on to appear in *Murder On The Orient Express* (1974) as McQueen, *Remember My Name* (1978) as Neil Curry, *The Black Hole* (1980) as Dr Alex Durant and *Double Negative* (1980) as Lawrence Miles before being persuaded to recreate the role of Norman Bates for *Psycho II* (1983). The story picked up 22 years from where the original left off, with Norman Bates freed from the asylum to return to the Bates Motel. After *Psycho II* Perkins appeared in Ken Russell's *Crimes Of Passion* (1984), playing the disturbed Reverend Peter Shayne. The film flopped because of cuts made to avoid an X-rating in the States. On January 29, 1984, Perkins was arrested at Heathrow and charged with possession of "eight grams of marijuana" and LSD. On February 2, he was fined £100. Then it was back to the Bates Motel for the third time. *Psycho III* (1986) both starred and was directed by Perkins, but it flopped. On June 26, 1989, Perkins was again arrested in Britain for possession of marijuana and fined £200. In 1990 *Psycho IV: The Beginning* was made. It was a prequel that explained how, if not why, Norman became a killer and obsessed with his mother. Of his most famous role Perkins said: "I couldn't believe that all the other films I had done previously had been forgotten, and that I was being narrowed into this one image that other people had of me."

CAUSE: In early 1990 Perkins visited his doctor, worried about a case of Bell's Palsy, a facial paralysis caused by the herpes simplex virus. A few weeks passed and then, on March 27, 1990, the *National Enquirer* ran a story headlined "*Psycho* Star Battling AIDS Virus". The story goes that neither Perkins nor his wife knew he was HIV+. He was urged to sue the tabloid for libel but decided to have a blood

test just to make his case watertight. When the results came back from the doctor the Perkinses were horrified to learn that he was indeed stricken with the disease. Apparently, a minion at the first doctor's surgery had gotten hold of a sample of the star's blood and had it tested secretly. When he learned he had the disease, Perkins made a statement that was only released after his death. It read: "I chose not to go public because, to misquote *Casablanca,* 'I'm not much at being noble, but it doesn't take much to see the problems of one old actor don't amount to a hill of beans in this crazy world.' There are many who believe this disease is God's vengeance, but I believe it was sent to teach people how to love and understand and have compassion for each other. I have learned more about love, selflessness, and human understanding from the people I have met in this great adventure in the world of AIDS, than I ever did in the cut-throat, competitive world in which I spent my life." Perkins died aged 60 at 4.06pm at his home, 2840 Seattle Drive, Los Angeles, California 90046. His death was caused by gram negative bacteremia, due to bilateral pneumonitis, due to AIDS. Five days later, he was cremated. A memorial service was held on September 19, and lasted two and a half hours. It was attended by 150 people including his former boyfriend Grover Dale and his wife Anita Morris, gay mogul David Geffen, Sandy Gallin, Barry Diller, Janet Leigh, Buck Henry, Sophia Loren, Mike Nichols and Dan Aykroyd.
FURTHER READING: *Anthony Perkins: A Haunted Life* – Ronald Bergan (London: Little, Brown, 1995); *Split Image: The Life Of Anthony Perkins* – Charles Winecoff (New York: Dutton, 1996).

Jon Pertwee
Born July 7, 1919
Died May 20, 1996
The *only* Dr Who. Born in Chelsea, south-west London, John (after the apostle) Devon (after the county) Roland (after his father) Pertwee came from a theatrical family. His father was the playwright, novelist and director Roland Pertwee (b. Brighton, May 17, 1885, d. London, April 26, 1963); his brother was the playwright Michael Pertwee (b. London, April 24, 1916, d. London, April 17, 1991) and his cousin, the actor Bill Pertwee (b. July 21, 1926), was a radio stalwart with Kenneth Horne and plagued Captain Mainwaring as Chief ARP Warden Hodges in the TV and film versions of *Dad's Army*. The family name was Huguenot in origin, Perthuis de Laillavault. "Just the job for a variety act. Here he comes your own Happy Perthuis! No wonder our family changed it. I get called Peewit, Pee Wee – and a New York stage door man once told me seriously, 'There is an urgent message for you, Mr Putrid.' " He pronounced it P'twee. Pertwee had problems with authority as a young man. He was thrown out of his Eastbourne prep school, Aldro, for swinging on a lavatory chain, he was expelled from public school, Sherborne, in Dorset, and then was thrown out of RADA for refusing to portray "a Greek wind". He went into repertory theatre and was sacked for his habit of shaking hands with the leading man while holding a raw egg. Despite these setbacks he enjoyed life in other rep companies and also the people he met, including on one occasion Emperor Haile Selassie of Ethiopia. In 1939 he joined the Royal Navy and met his lifelong friend, the broadcaster David Jacobs. Following demob he appeared in several radio shows including *Waterlogged Spa* (began September 17, 1948) and *Up The Pole* (1947–1952). In 1958 he recorded the pilot of the sitcom *The Navy Lark* which then ran for 18 years. In 1936 he made his movie début in *Dinner At The Ritz* and followed that with *A Yank At Oxford* (1937), eventually appearing in over 40 films. He played a soothsayer

in *Carry On Cleo* (1964), Sheriff Albert
Earp in *Carry On Cowboy* (1965), Dr
Fettle in *Carry On Screaming* (1966)
and also appeared in *A Funny Thing
Happened On The Way To The Forum*
(1966), *The House That Dripped Blood*
(1970), *One Of Our Dinosaurs Is
Missing* (1975), *Adventures Of A Private
Eye* (1977), Cannon & Ball's execrable
The Boys In Blue (1983) and the
equally appalling *Carry On Columbus*
(1992) in which he was the Duke of
Costa Brava. However, it was his
performance (from 1970 until 1974)
as the dandified, short-tempered third
Dr Who that won him instant
recognition and lasting fame. He
regarded his mortal enemies the Daleks
as "ridiculous – put together with a
sink plunger, an egg whisk and 24
tennis balls." Most actors have just one
creation with which they are usually
associated or identified. Rarely do they
have two, as with 6'2" Pertwee. To a
second generation of children he was
the scarecrow Worzel Gummidge in
the Southern TV series of the same
name (31 episodes between February
25, 1979 and December 12, 1981.
A further 22 episodes made in New
Zealand were broadcast on Channel 4
between October 4, 1987 and April 16,
1989). "Worzel," he said, "is much
more like me than Dr Who ever was."
Pertwee was difficult to work with,
eccentric, egocentric and possessed of a
quick temper, although he was equally
fast to apologise. On April 2, 1955, he
married the actor Jean Lyndsay Torren
Marsh (b. Stoke Newington, London,
July 1, 1934) but the relationship
didn't last and they separated after only
a year and divorced in March 1960.
On August 13 of that year in Bourne,
Buckinghamshire, he married fashion
designer Ingeborg Rhoesa. They had
two children, both actors Sean (b.
London, June 4, 1964) and Dariel.
CAUSE: In 1992 he collapsed with
pneumonia in a Leeds shopping centre
and was hospitalised. In the months
leading up to his death he suffered

coronary problems. He died of a heart
attack, aged 76, in Connecticut. He left
£420,149.

Jean Peters
Born October 15, 1926
Died October 13, 2000
Mrs Howard Hughes. Born in Canton,
Ohio, Elizabeth Jean Peters intended
to become a teacher but instead chose
the cinema and made her film début in
Captain From Castile (1947) as Catana
Perez. The previous year on July 4 she
had met the film producer Howard
Hughes at a party at the home of
Bill Cagney, James' brother. He was
enchanted by her and not discouraged
by the fact that she was in the throes of
a passionate affair with Audie Murphy.
On July 7, 1946 while attempting
to impress Peters, Hughes crashed
his XF-11 aeroplane near Beverly
Hills. Not long after, he began a
non-exclusive affair with Peters,
non-exclusive for him that is. He kept
a harem of women including the
actress Terry Moore. Peters,
meanwhile, was forbidden from seeing
other men. Still, she tired of Hughes'
eccentricities and on May 29, 1954 she
married Stuart Cramer III in
Washington, D.C. Hughes assigned a
private detective to dig up any and all
dirt on Cramer. In the intervening
years since meeting Hughes, Peters
had appeared in the following films:
Deep Waters (1948) as Ann Freeman,
It Happens Every Spring (1949) as
Deborah Greenleaf, *Love That Brute*
(1950) as Ruth Manning, *Take Care
Of My Little Girl* (1951) as Dallas, *As
Young As You Feel* (1951) as Alice
Hodges, *Anne Of The Indies* (1951) as
Captain Anne Providence, *Wait Till
The Sun Shines, Nellie* (1952) as Nellie
Halper, *Lure Of The Wilderness* (1952)
as Laurie Harper, *O. Henry's Full
House* (1952) as Susan, *Viva Zapata!*
(1952) as Josefa Zapata, *A Blueprint
For Murder* (1953) as Lynne Cameron,
Niagara (1953) as Polly Cutler, *Vicki*
(1953) as Vicki Lynn, *Pickup On South*

Street (1953) as Candy, *Apache* (1954) as Nalinle, *Three Coins In The Fountain* (1954) as Anita Hutchins, *Broken Lance* (1954) as Barbara and *A Man Called Peter* (1955) as Catherine Wood Marshall which was to be her last cinematic release. Not long after the marriage Cramer was summoned to see Howard Hughes, his wife conveniently forgetting to mention her involvement with him. Hughes told Cramer that he was in love with his wife and she with him and he would like them to divorce. Back home, Cramer confronted Peters but she assured him that she did not want a divorce. Still Hughes would not give up. He rang Cramer and told him that if he truly loved Peters he would let her go. The millionaire Cramer later remarked, "If your wife is going to get a divorce, you might as well let her marry someone who can afford to support her. It's the cheapest way out." (In 1959 Cramer married Terry Moore.) Once he had her back in his clutches Hughes installed her in a bungalow in Los Angeles where she was watched around the clock by a team of aides and maids. He told her he was too busy to marry her and carried on romancing other women. Eventually, Peters and Hughes were married in secrecy on January 12, 1957 in the Mizpah Hotel, Main Street, Culver City, California. Hughes told his people to pretend they were going duck hunting. The couple even used fake names: he was G.A. Johnson and she Marian Evans. Hughes and Peters remained married, although often apart, until June 15, 1971. Five years earlier, she studied for a BA at UCLA. Jean Peters appeared in two television films and a mini series but to all intents and purposes her career was over the moment she married Howard Hughes. In August 1971, she married Stanley Hough, an executive at 20th Century Fox.
CAUSE: She died in Carlsbad, California, aged 74 from leukeamia.

Gérard Philipe
(GÉRARD PHILIP)
Born December 4, 1922
Died November 25, 1959
Handsome romantic Gall. Born in Cannes, Alpes-Maritimes, France, Philipe was the son of a hotel manager and intended to become a doctor until the lure of the stage became too much for him to ignore. He appeared in various stage roles before making his film début as Jérôme in *Les Petites Du Quai Aux Fleurs* (1944). His reputation was made with his portrayal of Prince Muichkine in *L'Idiot* (1946). The following year he played François Jaubert, a lovestruck 17-year-old schoolboy in *Le Diable Au Corps/Devil In The Flesh* (1947). The film caused an uproar but made Philipe an international star. He was propelled into being the most popular French romantic star of his era. His later films included: *Tous Les Chemins Mènent A Rome* (1949), *La Beauté Du Diable* (1950), *Fanfan La Tulipe* (1952), *Monsieur Ripois* (1954), *Pot-Bouille* (1957) as Octave Mouret and *Les Liaisons Dangereuses* (1959) as Vicomte de Valmont.
CAUSE: He died aged 36 in Paris of a heart attack.

Julia Phillips
(JULIA MILLER)
Born April 7, 1944
Died January 1, 2002
Tell-all producer. Julia Phillips was completely unknown to the general public until she decided to publish her revelatory autobiography *You'll Never Eat Lunch In This Town Again*. In the industry she was well known having in 1973 become the first woman to win a best picture Oscar for *The Sting*. Born in New York, the daughter of Jewish intellectuals, she grew up in Brooklyn and Great Neck, Long Island. She graduated from Mount Holyoke College in Massachusetts, where she won prestigious awards for her short-story writing. She married

Michael Phillips on July 31, 1966 and had one daughter, Kate. After working in magazine publishing, Phillips joined Paramount Pictures in 1969 as its East Coast story editor. Later, Phillips became president of her own company, Ruthless Productions. Following the success of *The Sting*, she went on to co-produce Martin Scorsese's *Taxi Driver* in 1976, followed by director Steven Spielberg's *Close Encounters Of The Third Kind* (1977), although by this time she was a drug addict. "He essentially kicked her off the movie," said one insider. "It pretty much ended her career." In 1990 she wrote her autobiography which wasn't like the usual anodyne Tinseltown tales. She named names and revealed the petty indiscretions and vindictiveness among the town's upper echelons. She revealed that Warren Beatty once asked if she wanted to have a threesome with him and her 12-year-old daughter. Julia replied, "Warren, we're both too old for you." She once said, "You always have to pay your dues. I paid them backwards – starting at the top and going to the bottom."

CAUSE: She was diagnosed with cancer in August 2001. She died at her West Hollywood home. She was 57.

River Phoenix

(RIVER JUDE BOTTOM)
Born August 23, 1970
Died October 31, 1993

Tragic waste. River Phoenix seemed to have it all going for him: a successful career, a well-known family, money, dashing good looks, a beautiful girlfriend, adoration of countless females around the globe, but it wasn't enough. The son of John and Arlyn Bottom, a new age couple with dubious beliefs, 5'11" River was one of five children, all of whom were saddled with strange names: Rainbow Joan of Arc (b. Crockett, Texas, March 31, 1973), Leaf Joaquin Raphael (b. San Juan, Puerto Rico, October 28, 1974),

5'4" Liberty Mariposa (b. Caracas, Venezuela, July 5, 1976) and 5'7" Summer Joy (b. Winter Park, Florida, December 10, 1978 at 2.34am). River was born in a log cabin in Metolius near Madras, Oregon, but his family moved to Venezuela in 1972 to serve David Berg's Children of God, a bizarre religious sect who believe in sex with children. In fact, River was sexually molested when he was eight years old. When his parents became disenchanted with the Children of God the family moved to Caracas where River and his sister Rainbow would sing songs to raise money from passers-by. The family returned to America where they settled in Gainesville, Florida. (Gainesville was where a lady called Gladys Eley lived out her final years. She was the mother of Marilyn Monroe.) For some time River was shrouded in mystery. His birthday was kept secret and, for more obvious reasons, his real name wasn't revealed until after his death. He was named River after The River of Life in Herman Hesse's *Siddartha*. He appeared in some adverts and his first TV appearance was playing a guitar on the NBC gameshow *Fantasy*. On September 19, 1982, he made his first appearance in the CBS show *Seven Brides For Seven Brothers* playing Guthrie McFadden. He made his film début in *Explorers* (1985), a film about children trying to build a spaceship. He beat off 4,000 contenders for the part of Wolfgang Muller, a bespectacled baby Einstein. He next appeared in the slow moving *Stand By Me* (1986) and *The Mosquito Coast* (1986) (playing Harrison Ford's son) before taking on the title role in *Jimmy Reardon* (1988). It was a decision he was to regret. The film dealt with drinking, fast driving and indiscriminate sex. "Morally, I have problems with it. I'm more of the monogamous type. I can see that there could be a stage in my life where I'd be free with sex – and there's nothing wrong with that. But the circumstance is so important, and how it's portrayed." He dated actress Martha Plimpton, Keith Carradine's daughter, who played his girlfriend in *The Mosquito Coast* and *Running On Empty* (1988). His movie *Little Nikita* (1988) was so bad it was never released theatrically in Britain. In February 1989, he was nominated for a Best Supporting Actor Oscar for his role as Danny Pope in Sidney Lumet's *Running On Empty*. The film echoed aspects of Phoenix's own life in that he played a prodigy whose parents were Sixties hippies. (He lost out to Kevin Kline in *A Fish Called Wanda*.) He again appeared with Harrison Ford (although they didn't obviously appear in the same scenes) in *Indiana Jones & The Last Crusade* (1989) when he played the young Indy. The following year he appeared in the flop *I Love You To Death* (1990), a film which features a 'Pizza Consultant' on the credits. *Dogfight* (1991) was no more successful. His next film was one that shocked his fans. He played Mike Waters, a narcoleptic, homosexual hustler in Gus Van Sant's *My Own Private Idaho* (1992). In America the movie won him the prestigious National Society of Film Critics' Award for Best Actor. He was offered the part that eventually went to Matt Dillon on *A Kiss Before Dying* (1990), rejecting it eight times. Instead he chose *Sneakers* (1992), a spy film which starred Robert Redford and Dan Aykroyd. His penultimate film was *Silent Tongue* (1993), a strange Western, in which he played Richard Harris' unbalanced son. His last film was Peter Bogdanovich's *The Thing Called Love* (1993) during which he met actress Samantha Mathis who was to become his girlfriend. An announcement was made heralding River's new film, John Boorman's *Broken Dreams*. Before that could happen he began work on *Dark Blood* with Jonathan Pryce and Judy Davis. During filming he was hired to work

with Tom Cruise on *Interview With The Vampire* (1994). With three weeks left to shoot on *Dark Blood*, River Phoenix died. Phoenix, who disliked flying and travelled everywhere by car or train, was paid around $400,000 per movie but was also a keen musician with his own band, Aleka's Attic.

CAUSE: River Phoenix was a fitting role model for young people. He read the Bible every day, was a strict vegan, didn't smoke and abhorred drugs. It was all a façade. He began taking cocaine in 1989 and progressed onto other drugs. Paul Petersen was a child actor (Jeff Stone on *The Donna Reed Show*) who founded a therapy group for child actors and heard rumours of Phoenix's drug taking in June 1992. He went to see the star but was assured that the rumours were wrong. "Oh no, you must have the wrong person. That wasn't me. I don't even eat meat." In the six months before his death River's boozing and drug taking increased. On October 30, 1993, he booked into the £400-a-night Suite 328 of the Niko Hotel in Hollywood. With him was his girlfriend Samantha Mathis, brother Leaf and sister Rain. The party began at 7pm and by 10.30 the floor of the suite was littered with empty beer bottles. Then the group adjourned to The Viper Room, a trendy Hollywood nightspot, part-owned by Johnny Depp and located at 8852 Sunset Boulevard. Phoenix had to be helped into the car that took them clubbing. At the Viper the group hooked up with blonde actress Christina Applegate, the slutty Kelly Bundy from *Married . . . with Children*. Depp was due to perform there and asked Phoenix if he wanted to jam with the band. Phoenix was barely able to stand let alone play music. A waiter was unable to understand Phoenix when he asked for bottle after bottle of a German liqueur called Jaegermeister. Twice Phoenix slipped under the table before throwing up. He was taken to the gents and cleaned up but by this time he had lost almost all control of his muscles, his arms and legs jerking spasmodically. Put back in his chair, Phoenix again slumped down where his friends left him. It was only when he began having spasms again that the group realised something might be seriously wrong. With a bouncer's help, Samantha Mathis and Leaf helped him out of the club around 1am. He collapsed on the pavement and began having more seizures. Rain threw herself on her brother's body in an attempt to stop the spasms. The doorman, Ed, yelled for someone to call 911 but Leaf said his brother "was fine. He's fine." An ambulance was eventually called and CPR was administered. The paramedics were told by someone that River was diabetic (he wasn't) and his brother didn't tell them what River had taken. River Phoenix died at 1.51am around forty minutes after being admitted to Cedars-Sinai Medical Center. An autopsy revealed Phoenix had died of "acute multiple drug intoxications" and that Valium, marijuana, cocaine, heroin and ephedrine had been found in his body. On November 18, a memorial service was held for Phoenix on the Paramount Lot. Attendees included: Richard Benjamin, Peter Bogdanovich, John Boorman, Christine Lahti, Sidney Poitier and Rob Reiner. Paul Petersen bitterly commented: "They were living the lie. Can't possibly have River Phoenix in trouble with a drug problem. He doesn't even eat meat. Well, he doesn't eat anything now." Aware of the ephemeral nature of Hollywood, River Phoenix once stated, "I could die tomorrow and the world would go on."

Mary Pickford

(GLADYS LOUISE SMITH)
Born April 8, 1892
Died May 29, 1979
America's Sweetheart. Born at 175 University Avenue, Toronto, Ontario, Canada, 5′ Mary Pickford began her career on the stage and then began making films for D.W. Griffith. Her early movies included: *Mrs Jones Entertains* (1908), *Two Memories* (1909), *Her First Biscuits* (1909), *The Mexican Sweethearts* (1909), *Tender Hearts* (1909), *Sweet And Twenty* (1909), *They Would Elope* (1909), *Oh, Uncle!* (1909), *Getting Even* (1909), *In Old Kentucky* (1909), *Wanted, A Child* (1909), *To Save Her Soul* (1909), *All On Account Of The Milk* (1910), *His Last Dollar* (1910), *Love Among The Roses* (1910), *In the Season Of Buds* (1910), *Ramona* (1910) as Ramona, *In The Border States* (1910), *Wilful Peggy* (1910), *Muggsy Becomes A Hero* (1910), *Examination Day At School* (1910), *Sunshine Sue* (1910), *Science* (1911), *Love Heeds Not The Showers* (1911), *Her Darkest Hour* (1911), *For Her Brother's Sake* (1911), *Back To The Soil* (1911), *When A Man Loves* (1911), *Their First Misunderstanding* (1911), *Just Like A Woman* (1912), *Home Folks* (1912), *Friends* (1912), *Caprice* (1913) as Mercy Baxter, *Fate* (1913) and dozens more. She became one of America's highest-paid actresses, once telling a producer, "I can't afford to work for less than $10,000 a week." She also negotiated her own contracts. She kept her persona, that of a little girl in ringlets, until she was nearly middle aged. Pickford was made an honorary US Army colonel during World War I. In 1919 she co-founded United Artists. Pickford became popular the world over. When one of her films played Scotland, the local cinema didn't bother to mention the title. It simply advertised: "What happened to Mary – twice nightly." Some uncertainty arose as to the validity of the divorce (March 2, 1920) from first husband Owen Moore when she married swashbuckling actor Douglas Fairbanks, Sr on March 27, 1920. The press wondered whether, in the event of Pickford becoming pregnant, the baby would be called Pickford, Moore or Fairbanks? On April 16, Leonard

Fowler, Nevada's Attorney-General, claimed there had been 'collusion' in the divorce and only a clever lawyer saved Pickford. Her marriage to Fairbanks was seen as a romantic ideal for all America. They were both firm believers in astrology and had their charts read every morning. However, the marriage was not to last and following their divorce, Mary remarried and gradually drifted away from films. By the time of her death she was still living in the 42-room Pickford-Fairbanks Hollywood mansion – Pickfair, 1143 Summit Drive, Beverly Hills – hidden away upstairs and hitting the bottle quite regularly every day. Her preferred method of communication, even with visitors to Pickfair, was by telephone. Eventually, actress-singer Pia Zadora and her then husband, Mehshulam Riklis, bought the house in 1990 and knocked it down to build a bigger house on the grounds. They, too, fell victim to the curse of Pickfair and subsequently divorced. On a visit to the Soviet Union in 1926 Pickford was followed by a film director posing as a news cameraman. He used all the footage and cut it into a film called *The Kiss Of Mary Pickford*. To this day no one knows how he contrived the kiss. Her later films included: *Through The Back Door* (1921) as Jeanne, *Little Lord Fauntleroy* (1921) as both Little Lord Fauntleroy and his mother, *Rosita* (1923) as Rosita, *Little Annie Rooney* (1925) as Little Annie Rooney, *Sparrows* (1926) as Molly, *My Best Girl* (1927) as Maggie Johnson, *Coquette* (1929) as Norma Besant, for which she won an Oscar and became the first recipient to cry when receiving the prize, *The Taming Of The Shrew* (1929) as Katherine, *Kiki* (1931) as Kiki and *Secrets* (1933) as Mary Carlton/Mary Marlow.

CAUSE: She died in Santa Monica Hospital, California, aged 87, of a cerebral haemorrhage. She was buried in Forest Lawn Memorial-Parks, 1712 Glendale Avenue, Glendale, California 91209.

FURTHER READING: *Sweetheart: The Story Of Mary Pickford* – Robert Windeler (London: W.H. Allen, 1973); *Mary Pickford* – Scott Eyman (London: Robson Books, 1992).

Molly Picon

(MARGARET PYCKOON)
Born February 28, 1898
Died April 5, 1992
"The Jewish Charlie Chaplin". Born in New York, the daughter of shirt maker Louis Pyckoon and Clara Ostrow, a wardrobe mistress, and raised in Philadelphia, Picon began her career aged five when she won $5 in a talent contest at the Bijou Theatre. In 1915, on leaving school, she joined a vaudeville troupe that travelled America until the influenza epidemic halted the tour in Boston in 1918. The only theatre that remained open in the city was a Yiddish playhouse and the director Yonkel "Jacob" Kalich (b. Rymanów, Galicia, Austria-Hungary November 18, 1891, d. Lake Mahopac, New York March 16, 1975 following a long illness) gave her a job. The following year on June 29 they married. Their only child was stillborn. In an early version of The Krankies, Kalich wrote plays for his 4'11" wife in which she dressed as a boy. She began touring Europe appearing in Yiddish plays. She made her first film in Austria *Das Judenmadel* (1921). The earliest surviving of her Yiddish films, *Ost Und West*, dates from the same year. In 1930 she opened the Molly Picon Theatre in New York. Her most successful film was *Yidl Mitn Fidl* (1937, *Yiddle With His Fiddle*), the story of a Jewish girl who disguises herself as a boy so she can tour with her musician father. She also appeared in *Mamele* (1938), the last Jewish film made in Poland. In 1945 she began touring Europe again, playing to Jewish survivors of the Holocaust. In 1948 she raised money for Jewish bonds to help the state of Israel. It was in that decade that she began gravitating to

English-language movies and in 1963 she appeared in her first Hollywood movie *Come Blow Your Horn*, with Frank Sinatra for which she was nominated for an Oscar. She played Yente the matchmaker in Norman Jewison's *Fiddler On The Roof* (released November 3, 1971) and was honoured by the Congress of Jewish Culture in 1985. Her last film was *Cannonball Run II* (1984) in which she reprised her role of Mrs Goldfarb that she had played in *The Cannonball Run* (1981). CAUSE: Picon died aged 93 of Alzheimer's disease at her sister's home in Lancaster, Pennsylvania. She was interred in the Yiddish theatre section of Mount Hebron Cemetery, 130-04 Horace Harding Expressway, Flushing, New York NY11352.

Walter Pidgeon

Born September 23, 1897
Died September 25, 1984
Canadian second lead. Born in East St John and educated at the University of New Brunswick and the New England Conservatory of Music in Boston, Massachusetts, pipe-smoking, 6'2" Pidgeon served in the Canadian Army during the First World War (having lied about his age to gain admittance) but was wounded in France. On his return to New York he worked in a bank, singing on the side, but decided to become an actor and began appearing in the theatre. In 1922 he married Edna Pickles but she died the following year giving birth to their daughter, Edna Verne. He travelled west in the mid-Twenties, making his film début in *Mannequin* (1926) playing Martin Innesbrook. With the advent of talkies Pidgeon's resonant baritone ensured that his career would not be harmed. On December 12, 1931, he married Ruth Walker. In 1937 he was put under contract by MGM but the studio seemed unable to find suitable starring roles for him, so he usually ended up playing second fiddle in such films as *Saratoga* (1937),

playing Hartley Madison opposite Jean Harlow and Clark Gable, and *The Girl Of The Golden West* (1938) as Sheriff Jack Rance opposite Jeanette MacDonald and Nelson Eddy. He was loaned out to 20th Century Fox for his first starring role in *How Green Was My Valley* (1941) as Mr Gruffydd. Back at MGM he was cast opposite Greer Garson in *Mrs Miniver* (1942) as Clem Miniver, for which he was nominated for an Oscar. He appeared opposite Garson in several films including *Madame Curie* (1943) as Pierre Curie, which also won him an Oscar nomination. That year he also became an American citizen. In 1956 he retired from film-making, preferring to concentrate on stage work. Five years later, he was back in harness and worked until his stroke-induced retirement in 1977. His films included: *Clothes Make The Woman* (1928) as Victor Trent, *Turn Back The Hours* (1928) as Philip Drake, *Her Private Life* (1929) as Ned Thayer, *Kiss Me Again* (1931) as Paul de St Cyr, *Fatal Lady* (1936) as David Roberts, *My Dear Miss Aldrich* (1937) as Ken Morley, *As Good As Married* (1937) as Fraser James, *Too Hot To Handle* (1938) as Bill Dennis, *Listen, Darling* (1938) as Richard Thurlow, *Stronger Than Desire* (1939) as Tyler Flagg, *Nick Carter – Master Detective* (1939) as Nick Carter/Robert Chalmers, *Flight Command* (1940) as Squadron Commander Bill Gary, *Blossoms In The Dust* (1941) as Sam Gladney, *White Cargo* (1942) as Harry Witzel, *Mrs Parkington* (1944) as Major August Parkington, *Holiday In Mexico* (1946) as Jeffrey Evans, *If Winter Comes* (1947) as Mark Sabre, *Julia Misbehaves* (1948) as William Sylvester Packett, *That Forsyte Woman* (1949) as Young Joslyn Forsyte, *The Miniver Story* (1950) as Clem Miniver, *Quo Vadis?* (1951) as the narrator, *Calling Bulldog Drummond* (1951) as Major Hugh 'Bulldog' Drummond, *Million Dollar Mermaid* (1952) as Frederick Kellerman, *Dream Wife* (1953) as

Walter McBride, *Deep In My Heart* (1954) as J.J. Shubert, *Forbidden Planet* (1956) as Dr Edward Morbius, *Voyage To The Bottom Of The Sea* (1961) as Admiral Harriman Nelson, *Funny Girl* (1968) as Florenz Ziegfeld, *Won Ton Ton, The Dog Who Saved Hollywood* (1976) as Grayson's butler and *Sextette* (1978) as the Chairman, which was also Mae West's last film. Oddly, Pidgeon had a superb memory for faces but a lousy one for names, with the result that he called everyone, apart from close friends, Joe.

CAUSE: He died aged 87 years and 2 days of a stroke in Santa Monica, California. His body was donated to UCLA Medical School for medical research.

ZaSu Pitts

Born January 3, 1898
Died June 7, 1963
Comedic *ingénue*. Born in Parsons, Kansas, ZaSu Pitts' unusual first name came from amalgamating the Christian names of her maternal aunts Eliza and Susan. The family moved to Santa Cruz, California, where ZaSu became star-struck, hoping for a career in movies herself. Her chance arrived in 1917 when Mary Pickford was filming *Rebecca Of Sunnybrook Farm* and spotted ZaSu, whom she employed as Becky in her next film, *The Little Princess* (1917). Over the course of her career ZaSu would appear in over 200 films, progressing from the innocent naïf to a fine comedienne. Probably her best roles were in the Erich von Stroheim-directed *Greed* (1925) as Trina Sieppe and *The Wedding March* (1928) as Cecilia Schweiser. Movie writer and historian Herman Weinberg believed ZaSu gave "two of the most beautiful performances ever given by an actress in the annals of the screen." Her high-pitched voice made her unsuitable for sound dramas but she worked well in humorous roles. She played Mrs Baumer in *All Quiet On The Western Front* (1930) but preview

audiences laughed when she appeared on screen so her part was reshot with Beryl Mercer replacing her. For the rest of her career ZaSu played a succession of nervous ninnies, although Erich von Stroheim remarked: "One looks at ZaSu Pitts and sees pathos, even tragedy, and a wistfulness that craves for something she had never had or hopes to have. Yet she is one of the happiest and most contented women I have ever known." ZaSu was married twice. On July 23, 1920, she married sportsman Thomas S. Gallery, by whom she had a daughter, Ann (b. 1923). In 1923 they adopted the son of ZaSu's late friend, Barbara La Marr. The couple separated in 1926 and was divorced on April 26, 1932. On October 8, 1933, ZaSu married estate agent John Edward Woodall, who survived her.

CAUSE: She died of cancer in Hollywood, California. She was 65 years old. ZaSu was buried in Grave 1 of Lot 195, in the Grotto section of Holy Cross Cemetery, 5835 West Slauson Avenue, Culver City, California 90230.

Dana Plato

Born November 7, 1964
Died May 8, 1999
Diff'rent stroke. Beautiful Dana Michelle Plato was born in Maywood, California, the illegitimate daughter of 16-year-old Linda Strain who already had an 18-month-old baby. The new baby was adopted by Dean and Florine Plato of California in June 1965. Growing to 5'2", the blue-green-eyed blonde became an actress who started her career aged six in TV ads. Her first film was the TV movie *Beyond The Bermuda Triangle* (1975), where she played Wendy. She appeared in *Exorcist II: The Heretic* (1977) as Sandra, *Return To Boggy Creek* (1978) as Evie Jo and *California Suite* (1978) as Jenny before her big break came in April 1979 when she landed the role of Kimberley Drummond in the hit sitcom *Diff'rent*

Strokes. She was paid $22,000 (£13,600) per week and worked in films when the show was not in production. She was Daisy Dallenger in *Schoolboy Father* (1980) and Cara Ames in *High School U.S.A.* (1983). She owned two homes in the San Fernando Valley and two boats docked in Marina del Rey. After falling pregnant, she left the series in 1984 and married Lanny Lambert in April of that year. Their son, Tyler Edward, was born three months later on July 2. Dana subsequently found acting work hard to come by. Her estranged father sued her for support, her marriage broke up (she was divorced in March 1990), she gave her son to her husband and was swindled out of her money by unscrupulous accountants. In 1989 she was cast as Diana Masters in *Prime Suspect* (1989) and posed for the June 1989 edition of *Playboy* in the hope that it would boost her career but the only offer of work she received was "for a triple X-rated hardcore adult film". Following the death of her adoptive mother in January 1988 Dana had moved in with her grandmother in Las Vegas. The older woman soon threw her out and Dana moved in with a warehouse worker boyfriend, his best friend and 11 cats and went through a series of jobs ending up working in a dry cleaners for $5.75 (£3) per hour. She was fired from that job following a dispute with a fellow employee. On February 28, 1991, she applied for a job clearing up the rubbish and cleaning toilets in the building where she lived. Plato didn't get it and, in desperation, she donned a black hat, coat and sunglasses and held up a video store with a starting pistol and stole $164. After Plato left, the shop assistant, Heather Dailey, rang the police at 10.25am and told them, "I've just been robbed by the girl who played Kimberley on *Diff'rent Strokes*." Plato was arrested because she went back to the shop 15 minutes later to collect the glasses she had left there. She was taken to Clark County Detention Center and held for five days. She was only allowed to leave after singer Wayne Newton posted the $13,000 bail because, he said, he knew "the trauma of being a child star". After pleading guilty to a charge of attempted robbery, she was put on probation for five years and ordered to perform 400 hours of community service. In January 1992 Plato was again arrested for forging a prescription for 400 Valium tablets. She was charged with four counts of obtaining a controlled substance by fraud and four counts of burglary with intent to commit a crime. Plato, in jail for 31 days before she made bail, threw herself on the mercy of the court. The judge showed leniency, giving her a suspended sentence and another five years' probation. That same year, Plato confessed to a tabloid that she was an alcoholic. From 1992 until 1994 she lived with David Schwartz, a Phoenix entrepreneur, who owned a swingers' club. Schwartz later said of their relationship: "Dana and I lived at the club for two years with three other women. Dana was more into women than men." He added, "We did a porno film called *Different, Different Strokes*. It involved sex scenes with Dana and a smaller black guy who resembled Gary Coleman. Most of the film was lesbian scenes with Dana but the film was confiscated by police when the club was raided." With dreams of stardom fading fast, Dana became a prostitute and was beaten up by several of her johns. She appeared in *The Sounds Of Silence* (1992), *Night Trap* (1992) as Kelli Medd and JD in *Bikini Beach Race* (1992), also known as *The Sex Puppets*. In October 1994 she underwent breast augmentation surgery and landed two more films: *Millennium Day* (1995) and *Compelling Evidence* (1995) playing a character called Dana Fields. In October 1996 she appeared as Jill Martin in a film called *Different Strokes* (*Kiss* in the UK). She appeared nude in several scenes and was also seen participating in lesbian activities; off-camera she had a lesbian affair with Jennifer Wejbe. She dated several men in the last years of her life, keeping them all secret from each other. In January 1999 she met Robert Menchacha in Tulsa, Oklahoma, and they became engaged. On May 7, 1999, she appeared on Howard Stern's radio show and denied she was on drugs. (In 1998 she had to cancel a photographic shoot for *Celebrity Sleuth* magazine five times because she was so strung out on drugs.) She broke down when callers to the Stern show criticised her. Twenty-four hours later, she was dead.

CAUSE: Dana died of an overdose of the painkiller Loritab in a caravan in Moore, Oklahoma, which was parked outside the home of Menchacha's mother. On May 21, 1999, the coroner ruled her death a suicide because of the high level of drugs in her system and her previous attempts to kill herself. She was just 34 years old. In a sickening attempt to raise money Menchacha offered to sell pictures of Dana's body and what he claimed were her dying breaths over the internet.

Louise Platt

Born August 3, 1915
Died September 6, 2003

The last passenger. Born in Stamford, Connecticut, the daughter of a high-ranking naval doctor, Louise Platt spent most of her childhood in Annapolis near the navy academy. She was educated in New York, Manila and Hong Kong and then joined a repertory company. On August 25, 1936 she made her Broadway début at the Empire Theater in Philip Barry's short-lived comedy *Spring Dance*. The play closed after 23 performances, although it was made into a film as *Spring Madness* in 1938, starring Maureen O'Sullivan, Lew Ayres, Burgess Meredith, Ruth Hussey and

Frank Albertson. *Spring Dance* was produced and directed by the libidinous Jed Harris (b. Vienna, Austria, February 25, 1900 as Jacob Horowitz, d. New York, November 14, 1979) who numbered Katharine Hepburn and Margaret Sullavan among his bedmates. Soon Louise Platt was to join their number. Perhaps she was bedazzled by Harris' undoubted genius – he became a Broadway legend when, at the age of 28, he produced four straight smash hits (*Broadway*, *Coquette*, *The Royal Family* and *The Front Page*) in the space of 18 months, a feat never again matched on the Great White Way – but probably not by his temperament: he was misogynistic, angry, bitter and held grudges. Whatever the attraction they were married in Mexico City in 1939. On the way back to California, however, he told her that he was sorry he had married her. "When we did *Spring Dance* he was even-tempered, really brilliant," she recalled. "He could control his temper, he could deal with people. But when things began to dry up and more people turned against him, that was when his quest for power over people became frightening." It was a violent marriage and Platt was terrified of her husband but his animus was usually directed at objects, hurling ashtrays or kicking out windows. When Platt gave birth to their daughter, Abigail, on April 27, 1941 they were already divorced. The birth of the child reunited them for a time. "Louise adored Jed," remembered her friend Doris Johnson, the wife of the writer Nunnally Johnson. "She was almost worshipful." Time was not a healer and her memories of Harris were so traumatic that she cut him out of all the pictures in her photo albums. She played Brenda, a wealthy and selfish student in her first film, *I Met My Love Again* (1937), which starred Henry Fonda and Joan Bennett. Her love for Fonda was not reciprocated. In *Spawn Of The North* (1938), she was Dian

Turlon, a newspaper editor's daughter, who was chased by Fonda. Her next film was playing the prim and pregnant Lucy Mallory in John Ford's classic Western *Stagecoach* (filmed November–December 1938, released in 1939). Of all the passengers on the vehicle, she was the last survivor. Lucy was on her way to rejoin her cavalry officer husband and did not take kindly to the friendship advances from Dallas the prostitute (Claire Trevor). Her fellow passengers were the alcoholic Doctor Josiah Boone (Thomas Mitchell for which he won a Best Supporting Actor Oscar), an absconding banker called Henry Gatewood (Berton Churchill), the gambler Mr Hatfield (John Carradine), Samuel Peacock, the timid whiskey salesman (Donald Meek) and Marshal Curly Wilcox (George Bancroft). John Wayne, as Henry the Ringo Kid, joined the group near the start of their journey. After *Stagecoach* Jed Harris asked his friend, the writer Ed Chodorov, to use his influence at MGM to get Platt work. She was hired as Ellen Frazier to star opposite Melvyn Douglas in *Tell No Tales* (1939), a fast-paced melodrama in which she was the witness to a kidnapping. The plan to propel her to stardom was unsuccessful and she made just three more films – the appropriately entitled *Forgotten Girls* (1940) as Judy Wingate, *Captain Caution* (1940) as Corunna and *Street Of Chance* (1942), generally regarded as her best film, in which she played Virginia Thompson opposite Burgess Meredith. She returned to Broadway and appeared in *Five Alarm Waltz* which opened at the Playhouse Theatre on March 13, 1941 and closed four performances later. Directed by Jed Harris, it told the tale of what might have happened had the writers William Saroyan and Claire Booth Luce married. Apart from the very short run, it was notable only as Elia Kazan's last performance as an actor. Platt retired to raise her daughter, returning in Maxwell Anderson's *Anne*

Of The Thousand Days at the Shubert Theatre on December 8, 1948. She played Mary Carey, Anne Boleyn's sister who was the king's mistress for several years before he married Anne. The affair ended in the mid-1520s but she was favoured enough for Henry to name a ship after her. Platt's final play, Herman Wouk's Cold War thriller *The Traitor*, was produced and directed by Harris and opened at the 48 Street Theater on April 4, 1949. It ran for only 67 performances despite being lauded by *Variety* as "tautly written, superbly produced, and convincingly performed". Platt moved to the small screen and played Ruth Jennings Holden in the soap opera *The Guiding Light* from 1958 to 1959. *The Saxon Charm*, a 1947 Frederic Wakeman novel, is said to be based on Harris and one of the female characters is thought to be an amalgam of Platt and Rosamond Pinchot (b. New York, October 26, 1904), an actor and former socialite who killed herself on January 24, 1938 in Old Brookville, New York, because of him. Following her divorce from Harris, Platt married Stanley Gould, a thoughtful academic who was Jed Harris' stage manager. She gave birth to another daughter.

CAUSE: She died, aged 88, in Greenport, New York, and was cremated.

Donald Pleasence, OBE

Born October 5, 1919
Died February 2, 1995

Sinister star. Born in Worksop, Nottinghamshire, 5'7" Pleasence worked for the railways at Swinton, South Yorkshire, when he left Ecclesfield Grammar School but dreamed of acting. His first stage performance came in May 1939 at the Playhouse, Jersey, where he was stage manager, as Hareton in *Wuthering Heights*. His London début came three years and a month later, in June 1942, as Curio in *Twelfth Night*. That same year he joined the RAF only to be captured two years later, spending two years in a POW camp. His first post-war job was in June 1946 at the Hammersmith Theatre playing Mavriky in *The Brothers Karamazov*. Five and a half years later, in December 1951, he made his Broadway début, appearing with Laurence Olivier's company in *Shakespeare's Rome*. His film début came in *The Beachcomber* (1954) as Tromp. Pleasence was to appear in almost 200 films and television movies but seemed to be most at home in villainous roles or in horror films such as the *Halloween* series. His movies included: *1984* (1956) as R. Parsons, *Barnacle Bill* (1957) as a bank clerk, *Look Back In Anger* (1958) as Hurst, *The Flesh And The Fiends* (1959) as William Hare, *Killers Of Kilimanjaro* (1959) as Captain, *Circus Of Horrors* (1960) as Vanet, *Hell Is A City* (1960) as Gus Hawkins, *Sons And Lovers* (1960) as Mr Puppleworth, *Spare The Rod* (1961) as Mr Jenkins, *What A Carve Up!* (1962) as Everett Sloane, *Dr Crippen* (1962) as Dr Hawley Harvey Crippen, *The Great Escape* (1963) as Colin Blythe, *The Caretaker* (1964) as Mac Davies/Bernard Jenkins, *The Greatest Story Ever Told* (1965) as the Dark Hermit/Satan, *Cul-De-Sac* (1966) as George, *Fantastic Voyage* (1966) as Dr Michaels, *The Night Of The Generals* (1967) as General Kahlenberge, *You Only Live Twice* (1967) as Ernst Stavro Blofeld, *The Madwoman Of Chaillot* (1969) as the prospector, *THX 1138* (1970) as SEN 5241, *Soldier Blue* (1970) as Isaac Q. Cumber, *Kidnapped* (1971) as Ebenezer Balfour, *The Mutations* (1973) as Professor Nolter, *Henry VIII And His Six Wives* (1973) as Thomas Cromwell, *Escape To Witch Mountain* (1975) as Lucas Deranian, *The Last Tycoon* (1976) as Boxley, *The Eagle Has Landed* (1976) as Heinrich Himmler, *Sgt. Pepper's Lonely Hearts Club Band* (1978) as B.D. Brockhurst, *Tomorrow Never Comes* (1978) as Dr Todd, *Halloween* (1978) as Dr Sam Loomis, *Dracula* (1979) as Dr Jack Seward, *Halloween II* (1981) as Dr Sam Loomis, *Nosferatu A Venezia* (1986) as Don Alvise, *Prince Of Darkness* (1987) as Father Loomis, *Halloween 4: The Return Of Michael Myers* (1988) as Dr Sam Loomis, *Ten Little Indians* (1989) as Judge Wargrave, *Halloween 5: The Revenge Of Michael Myers* (1989) as Dr Sam Loomis and *Halloween: The Curse Of Michael Myers* (1995) as Dr Sam Loomis. He was awarded the OBE in 1993. Pleasence, who eschewed alcohol, was married four times. His first wife, on August 7, 1941, was the actor Miriam Raymond by whom he had two daughters, the actor Angela Daphne Pleasence and Jean Denise Pleasence. They divorced in 1958. Number two on May 15, 1959 was the actor-singer Josephine Crombie by whom he had a further two daughters, Lucy Alice Maria (b. May 14, 1961) and Polly Jo Alexis Helena Pleasence. The couple were divorced in 1970. That year, on October 10, he married the singer Meira Shore by whom he had daughter Miranda (b. Chapeltown, Yorkshire, 1969). They divorced in 1988. Finally in January 1989 he married the red-headed Linda Woollen (b. 1947) with whom he had begun an affair in 1970 after meeting her in a Manchester bar. She had a daughter, blonde, blue-eyed Nikola (b. 1967), by a previous relationship.

CAUSE: Donald Pleasence died aged 75 at 6.20am at his home in St Paul de Vence, France, from a heart complaint. Each of his daughters wrote a letter which they placed in his coffin. He left £213,536. In May 1998 his stepdaughter Nikola admitted that she was an alcoholic. On June 12, 1989, her estranged husband tried to run her down and she ended up in a coma for a fortnight and then a further two years in hospital. Eighteen months in a wheelchair followed and 32 operations before her final discharge in September 1997. Pleasence paid for her surgery.

Suzanne Pleshette

Born January 31, 1937
Died January 19, 2008

Husky-voiced star. Born in New York City, she attended the High School of the Performing Arts, later popularised in the film and television series *Fame*. She began acting soon after, often cast for her looks and throaty voice, which began early. "When I was four, I was answering the phone, and [callers] thought I was my father. So I often got quirky roles because I was never the conventional ingénue." She played serious theatre roles before making her film debut with Jerry Lewis in 1958 in *The Geisha Boy*. She appeared in innumerable television episodes before landing a role as Bob Newhart's sarcastic wife for six years on *The Bob Newhart Show*. Her films included *Rome Adventure* (released March 15, 1962), *The Birds* (released March 28, 1963), *A Distant Trumpet* (released May 27, 1964), *Youngblood Hawke* (released November 4, 1964), *Fate Is The Hunter* (released November 8, 1964), *The Ugly Dachshund* (premièred February 4, 1966) and *Blackbeard's Ghost* (released February 8, 1968). On January 4, 1964 she married Troy Donahue but they divorced eight months later on September 8. From March 16, 1968 until his death on January 21, 2000 5'4" Pleshette was married to Texas oilman Tim Gallagher. On May 11, 2001 she married actor Tom Poston (b. Columbuso, Ohio 17 October 1921, d. Los Angeles, California, April 30, 2007), 41 years after they first had an affair. Of her career, she said, "I'm an actress, and that's why I'm still here. Anybody who has the illusion that you can have a career as long as I have and be a star is kidding themselves."

CAUSE: Pleshette underwent chemotherapy for lung cancer in 2006. She died of respiratory failure on the evening of January 19, 2008 at her Los Angeles home.

Sydney Pollack

Born July 1, 1934
Died May 26, 2008

Multi-talent. Born in Lafayette, Indiana, Sydney Irwin Pollack spent his time at school acting and playing football despite an ocular disability. "I was lousy because I wore glasses and couldn't see," he said. After leaving school, he joined the Neighbourhood Playhouse School of Theatre in New York where he met and befriended Sanford Meisner, the head of the acting department, whom he praised as his main mentor. After two years' national service Pollack became Meisner's assistant. Pollack divided his work between teaching and acting. He was dialogue coach for John Frankenheimer's *The Young Savages* (1961) where Burt Lancaster befriended him and recommended him to Universal Television as a director. He worked on programmes such as *The Defenders*, *Ben Casey* and *Dr Kildare*. Pollack's directorial movie debut came with *The Slender Thread* (released December 23, 1965), which starred Sidney Poitier and Anne Bancroft. The film that made his name was *They Shoot Horses, Don't They?* (released December 10, 1969), a story of the Great Depression told through a dance contest for which Gig Young won an Oscar and Jane Fonda was nominated. Pollack often worked with Robert Redford. They were together on *Jeremiah Johnson* (released December 21, 1972), the CIA thriller *Three Days Of The Condor* (released September 24, 1975), *The Electric Horseman* (released December 21, 1979), *Out Of Africa* (premièred December 10, 1985), *Havana* (released December 12, 1990) and the most successful, *The Way We Were* (released October 17, 1973) with Barbra Streisand. Of his work Pollack said, "I am a traditionalist. I think that my films are conventional in form, but not necessarily in point of view. I don't consider myself an *avant garde* or particularly original film-maker. I enjoy the challenge of working within the strict parameters of a given film genre and then striving to find some new voice within it." Not all Pollack's films were hits – his movie about the Japanese mafia *The Yakuza* (released March 19, 1975 in New York) with Robert Mitchum was a flop as were *Bobby Deerfield* (released September 29, 1977) with Al Pacino and *Absence Of Malice* (released December 18, 1981) with Paul Newman. Pollack bounced back immediately with *Tootsie* (premièred December 1, 1982) in which, at Dustin Hoffman's suggestion, he also acted, playing the part of George Fields, the agent of Michael Dorsey/Dorothy Michaels (Hoffman). The movie won a Best Supporting Actress Oscar for Jessica Lange and received nine other nominations including Best Film, Best Actor (Hoffman) and Best Director (Pollack). That situation was remedied the following year when his 1985 production *Out Of Africa*, based on the life of Isak Dinesen, was named Best Film in the Oscars and earned him a personal award as Best Director. *The Firm* (released June 30, 1993), the film version of John Grisham's novel about a corrupt law firm, starred Tom Cruise and Holly Hunter, who won an Oscar. Nominated twice in the same year, she also took the Best Actress gong for Jane Campion's *The Piano*. Two years later, Pollack's remake of Billy Wilder's *Sabrina* (released December 15, 1995) flopped and 6' tall Pollack acted in Stanley Kubrick's last film, *Eyes Wide Shut* (premièred July 13, 1999). *Random Hearts* (released October 8, 1999) starring Harrison Ford and Kristin Scott Thomas also flopped after which it seemed that Pollack had lost interest in filmmaking. After six years, he came back with *The Interpreter* (released April 22, 2005), a political thriller, starring Nicole Kidman and Sean Penn. His last film was a documentary about his architect friend *Sketches Of Frank Ghery* (released

May 12, 2006). On September 22, 1958 Sydney Pollack married the pregnant Claire Griswold, one of his former acting students, who survives him. They had a son, Steven (b. February 7, 1959, k. November 26, 1993 in a plane crash in Los Angeles) and two daughters, Rebecca Pollack (b. 1963) and Rachel (b. 1969). CAUSE: Pollack died from stomach cancer at his home in Pacific Palisades, California. He was 73.

Cole Porter
Born June 9, 1891
Died October 15, 1964
Gay songsmith. One of the most popular composers and lyricists of the twentieth century was born in Peru, Indiana, the son of a pharmacist. As with Anthony Perkins, Cole Albert Porter grew up in a household dominated by his mother where his father (alive, unlike Perkins') played little or no part. Porter's mother was wealthy, probably the cause of her husband's emasculation, and she spared her son no luxury or indulgence. In 1902 a waltz written by Porter was published and distributed by his mother at her own expense. After a grand tour of Europe he entered Yale where he excelled in socialising rather than academia. After gaining a BA there, he entered Harvard Law School but dropped out after 12 months to concentrate on songwriting. *See America First* was his first Broadway musical but it closed after just 15 performances in 1916. In 1917 he moved to France but, contrary to his own claims, he neither served in the French army nor the Foreign Legion. He met socialite Linda Lee Thomas and they married on December 18, 1919. However, it was a marriage of convenience. Her first husband had been sexually demanding, unlike Porter, whose demands for sex didn't include her. It seems unlikely, as some have suggested, that Mrs Porter was a lesbian. It is more probable that she

was asexual. Porter would indulge his tastes by going cruising with gay actor Monty Woolley and picking up rough trade. One of Porter's lovers was actor Jack Cassidy. Nine years later, Porter had his first major hit on his hands with 'Let's Do It, Let's Fall In Love'. The following year he began writing for films and his work appeared in *The Battle Of Paris* (1929). After that came *Paree, Paree* (1934), *The Gay Divorcee* (1934), *Anything Goes* (1936), *Broadway Melody Of 1940* (1940), *Du Barry Was A Lady* (1943), *Kiss Me Kate* (1953), *High Society* (1956), *Anything Goes* (1956), *Silk Stockings* (1957), *Les Girls* (1957) and *Can-Can* (1960). After finishing work on *Rosalie* (1937) in the autumn of 1937 he went out riding and was thrown by his horse, breaking his legs so badly that amputation seemed likely. He eventually learned to walk again, albeit with the help of callipers, crutches and sticks.

CAUSE: In April 1958 osteomyelitis forced doctors to amputate Porter's right leg at the hip. Depression set in and he stopped composing. His weight dropped to just over 5st and he was unable to fight off simple infections. He had to be carried everywhere, though he still insisted on using a sun lamp to keep his tan topped up. He died aged 73 in Santa Monica, California, of pneumonia following surgery for a kidney stone. He was buried in Mount Hope Cemetery, West 12th Street, Peru, Indiana 46970.

FURTHER READING: *Genius And Lust: The Creativity And Sexuality Of Cole Porter And Noël Coward* – Joseph Morella & George Mazzei (London: Robson Books, 1996).

Nyree Dawn Porter, OBE

(NGAIRE PORTER)
Born January 22, 1936
Died April 10, 2001
Kiwi beauty. Nyree Dawn Porter was born in Napier, New Zealand, the first daughter and first child of Kenneth Norman Porter, a master butcher and property developer, and Edna May Porter. Her original forename was a Maori word meaning "little white flower". Kenneth Porter walked out on his family in 1944 and he rarely saw them afterwards. Porter trained at the New Zealand Royal Academy of Ballet before joining the New Zealand Players Trust. In 1958 she won the title Miss Cinema New Zealand, a competition organised by the Rank Organisation, and moved to London with her new husband Bryon O'Leary. She began appearing on the stage and made her film début in 1960 playing Betty in *Sentenced For Life*, then moved to television playing the lead in *Madame Bovary* (1964). From January 7 until July 1, 1967 she appeared in the BBC2 drama *The Forsyte Saga* as Irene Forsyte née Heron. The role made her "the first romantic sex symbol of the television era" and when it was later shown on BBC1 attracted 18 million viewers. The role won Porter the Best Television Actress Award from the Society of Film and Television Arts. She played Blanche in the film *Jane Eyre* (1970) but found she was typecast by Irene. In 1970 her husband died from an accidental drugs overdose after a nervous breakdown. Another television role, Contessa Caroline di Contini in *The Protectors* (September 29, 1972–March 15, 1974), gave Porter another lease of professional life. On August 15, 1975 she married the actor Robin Bernard Halstead, seven months after the birth of their daughter Natalya (b. January 10, 1975), known as Tassy. The girl was to suffer from anorexia for many years. The marriage to Halstead ended in 1987 in divorce. Porter appeared on television game shows and her last film was playing Margot Fonteyn in *Hilary And Jackie* (1998).

CAUSE: Nyree Dawn Porter who lived at 118 Ravensbury Road, Earlsfield, south London, died of a stroke at St George's Hospital, Tooting, south London.

Eric Portman

Born July 13, 1903
Died December 7, 1969
Brit stalwart. Eric Harrison Portman
was born in Halifax, Yorkshire, the
son of Matthew Portman, a wool
merchant, and Alice Harrison. He
went to Rishworth School in Yorkshire
and then became an apprentice in his
father's firm. His spare time was spent
with the Halifax Opera Society. In
1923 he became a professional actor
and made his London début as
Antipholus of Syracuse in *The Comedy
Of Errors*, on September 1, 1924 at the
Savoy Theatre. In February 1927 he
joined the Old Vic playing a number of
Shakespearean leads. He made his film
début in *The Girl From Maxim's* (1933)
and his Broadway début in November
1937, as Rodolphe Boulanger in
Madame Bovary. He also appeared in
*Maria Marten, Or The Murder In The
Red Barn* (1935) as Carlos, *Hyde Park
Corner* (1935) as Edward Chester,
Hearts Of Humanity (1936) as Jack
Clinton, *The Prince And The Pauper*
(1937) and *Moonlight Sonata* (1937) as
Mario de la Costa. Portman had a
good war appearing in patriotic fare
such as *Forty-Ninth Parallel* (1941) as
Lieutnant Hans Hirth, *One Of Our
Aircraft Is Missing* (1942) as Tom
Earnshaw, *Squadron Leader X* (1943)
as Erich Kohler, *We Dive At Dawn*
(1943), *Escape To Danger* (1943) as
Arthur Lawrence and *Millions Like Us*
(1943) as Charlie Forbes. His post-war
movies included *Wanted For Murder*
(1946) as Victor James Colebrooke,
alias Tom Maren, *The Colditz Story*
(1955) as Colonel Richmond, *The
Deep Blue Sea* (1955) as Miller, *The
Good Companions* (1957) as Jess
Oakroyd, *Freud* (1962) as Dr
Theodore Meynert, *The Bedford
Incident* (1965) as Commodore
Wolfgang Schrepke and *The Whisperers*
(1966) as Archie.
CAUSE: He died of a heart ailment at
his home, Penpol, St Veet, Lostwithiel,
Cornwall. He was 66. He left £14,377.

Dick Powell

Born November 14, 1904
Died January 2, 1963
Diverse actor. Born in Mountain View,
Arkansas, Richard Ewing Powell began
life working for a telephone company
emptying coins from public phone
boxes and singing in the evenings. He
also was a singer and played the banjo
with a band before making his film
début in the Warner Bros flick *Blessed
Event* (1932) as Bunny Harmon. He so
impressed the studio that it signed him
to a long contract and he spent around
ten years playing the all-American boy
before moving into tough guy roles in
the Forties following his release from
Warners at the start of the decade. The
following decade saw him make yet
another transition, this time to behind
the cameras where he produced and
directed. Like many of the cast and
crew of *The Conqueror* (1956), which
Powell produced and directed, he was
stricken with cancer. His films
included: *Blessed Event* (1932) as
Bunny Harmon, *Convention City*
(1933) as Jerry Ford, *42nd Street*
(1933) as Billy Lawler, *Gold Diggers Of
1933* (1933), *Footlight Parade* (1933) as
Scott Blair, *Wonder Bar* (1934) as
Tommy, *Dames* (1934) as Jimmy
Higgins, *Twenty Million Sweethearts*
(1934) as Buddy Clayton, *Thanks A
Million* (1935) as Eric Land, *Broadway
Gondolier* (1935) as Richard Purcell,
Page Miss Glory (1935) as Bingo
Nelson, *A Midsummer Night's Dream*
(1935) as Lysander, *Gold Diggers Of
1935* (1935) as Dick Curtis, *Stage
Struck* (1936) as George Randall,
Colleen (1936) as Donald Ames III,
Hearts Divided (1936) as Captain
Jerome Bonaparte, *Gold Diggers Of
1937* (1936) as Rosmer Peck, *On
The Avenue* (1937) as Gary Blake,
Hollywood Hotel (1938) as Ronnie
Bowers, *Naughty But Nice* (1939) as
Professor Donald Hardwick, *Model
Wife* (1941) as Fred Chambers, *Riding
High* (1943) as Steve Baird, *Happy Go
Lucky* (1943) as Pete Hamilton,

Murder, My Sweet (1944) as Philip Marlowe, *It Happened Tomorrow* (1944) as Larry Stevens, *Cornered* (1945) as Gerard, *Rogues' Regiment* (1948) as Whit Corbett, *Pitfall* (1948) as John Forbes, *To The Ends Of The Earth* (1948) as Commissioner Michael Barrows, *The Reformer And The Redhead* (1950) as Andrew Rockton Hale, *Cry Danger* (1951) as Rocky Mulloy and *Susan Slept Here* (1954) as Mark Christopher. In 1925 Powell married model Maude Maund but the marriage was over by 1927. On September 19, 1936, he married actress Joan Blondell. On July 1, 1938, their daughter, Ellen, was born. The Powells divorced on July 14, 1944. On August 19, 1945, he married actress June Allyson. Their son, Richard Keith, was born on December 24, 1950. The Powells separated but were reconciled before the divorce was finalised.

CAUSE: Powell died of cancer in West Los Angeles, California. He was 58. He was buried in the Columbarian of Honor at Forest Lawn Memorial-Parks, 1712 Glendale Avenue, Glendale, California 91209.

Michael Powell

Born September 30, 1905
Died February 19, 1990
British original. Born in Bekesbourne, near Canterbury, Kent, Michael Latham Powell was educated at King's School, Canterbury, and joined the National Provincial Bank in 1922. He took three years before deciding the financial world wasn't for him and entering the world of film-making in 1925. Powell worked for British International Pictures and in 1927 married an American dancer from whom he split after just three weeks, although their divorce didn't become final until 1936. Powell's film *The Edge Of The World* (1937) won Best Direction of Foreign Film award at the 1938 Venice Film Festival, which led to a contract with Sir Alexander Korda. It was thanks to Korda that Powell first

teamed up with Emeric Pressburger on *The Spy In Black* (1939). It was to be the first of 21 films they collaborated on. Their film *The Life And Death Of Colonel Blimp* (1943) came in for criticism from Prime Minister Churchill and the Ministry of Information for its portrayal of the military. In 1943 Powell married Frances Reidy (d. 1983) by whom he had two sons. That year he and Pressburger adopted the partnership title The Archers and in 1944 they were offered a contract by the Rank Organisation. Powell's favourite of his own films was the fantastical *A Matter Of Life And Death* (1946). The Archers made films that were inventive, different . . . and expensive. Too expensive for Rank, and the two parted company until they were reunited to make *The Battle Of The River Plate* (1956). That year also saw the end of The Archers' partnership. Powell's later films included: *Peeping Tom* (1959), *They're A Weird Mob* (1966) and *Age Of Consent* (1969). In the Eighties Powell moved to America to teach and work at Frances Ford Coppola's Zoetrope Studio. In 1984 he married Thelma Schoonmaker, who survived him.

CAUSE: Powell died aged 84 at his home, 1 Lee Cottages, Avening, Gloucestershire, from cancer. He left £26,261.

William Powell

Born July 29, 1892
Died March 5, 1984
Light comic. Between 1922 and his retirement 33 years later, 6′ William Horatio Powell appeared in almost 100 films. He was born in Pittsburgh, Pennsylvania, made his Broadway début when he was 20 and made his first film, *Sherlock Holmes* (1922) as Foreman Wells, when he was 30. During the silent era Powell usually played villains, before moving into comedies and light drama when the talkies arrived. He played detective

Philo Vance in *The Canary Murder Case* (1929), *The Greene Murder Case* (1929), *The Benson Murder Case* (1930) and *The Kennel Murder Case* (1933) and was super sleuth Nick Charles in *The Thin Man* series, encompassing *The Thin Man* (1934), for which he was nominated for an Oscar, *After The Thin Man* (1936), *Another Thin Man* (1939), *Shadow Of The Thin Man* (1941), *The Thin Man Goes Home* (1945) and *Song Of The Thin Man* (1947). He was also lauded as Florenz Ziegfeld in *The Great Ziegfeld* (1936) and *My Man Godfrey* (1936) as Godfrey Parke, playing opposite his then wife Carole Lombard, which resulted in another Oscar nomination. Powell was engaged to Jean Harlow at the time of her untimely death. He was also nominated for an Academy Award for playing Clarence Day in *Life With Father* (1947). His last films were *How To Marry A Millionaire* (1953) as J.D. Hanley and *Mister Roberts* (1955) as Doc.
CAUSE: Powell died aged 91 in Palm Springs, California, of natural causes. He was cremated.

Tyrone Power

Born May 5, 1914
Died November 15, 1958
Pretty boy. Born at 2112 Fulton Avenue, Cincinnati, Ohio, at 5.30pm on May 5, 1914, 5′8″ Tyrone Edmund Power III came from a long line of thespians. As with so many actors, Power's mother, Patia Reaume, was a dominating force in her son's life. She also outlived him, dying in 1959 aged 77. Power's father, Frederick Tyrone Edmund II (b. London, May 2, 1869, d. Los Angeles, December 30, 1931), was sent to America (from Ireland) to learn about the citrus fruit business. He later became an actor when the first crop failed, going on to tour with Beerbohm Tree, the father of Sir Carol Reed. Both Tyrone Powers died of a heart attack on movie sets – father in 1931 and son in 1958. In 1929 Tyrone III joined Tyrone II in New York,

where the latter was appearing in *The Merchant Of Venice*. TIII landed a walk-on part. The Powers travelled to Hollywood two years later, where TII was due to star in *The Miracle Man* (1932), but he died four days into the shoot. His son decided to stay in Tinseltown and was signed up by Darryl F. Zanuck at 20th Century Fox. After seeing Power's first screen test Zanuck exclaimed: "My God, he looks like a chimp." The problem was Power's eyebrows or, rather, eyebrow. When that was shaved, however, he looked like a different man. With the public Power was an almost instantaneous hit, overtaking box-office giants such as Clark Gable and Spencer Tracy and appearing in films including *Lloyds Of London* (1936) as Jonathan Blake, *In Old Chicago* (1937) as Dion O'Leary, *Alexander's Ragtime Band* (1937) as Roger Grant aka Alexander, *Marie Antoinette* (1938) as Count Axel de Fersen and *Suez* (1938) as Ferdinand de Lesseps. It was on the set of *Suez* that Power met actress Annabella who was to become his first wife. She had lost her virginity to Errol Flynn . . . who was also Power's lover. They were married on St George's Day 1939 at her home on St Pierre Road, Bel Air. Actor Don Ameche was best man and Pat Peterson (Mrs Charles Boyer) was maid of honour. Producer Darryl F. Zanuck had tried to prevent the wedding, believing it would harm his star's box-office draw if he was married. He was wrong. Power subsequently made films for Fox that were even more successful, including the lead role in *Jesse James* (1939), *The Rains Came* (1939) as Major Rama Safti and *The Mark Of Zorro* (1940) as Don Diego Vega, a.k.a. Zorro, which was among his favourite of his own films, *Blood And Sand* (1941) as Juan Gallardo, *A Yank In The RAF* (1941) as Tim Baker and *Son Of Fury* (1942) as Benjamin Blake. On August 24, 1942, Power enrolled in the Marines. Following the war he resumed his career with *The Razor's Edge* (1946) as Larry Darrell and had affairs with Judy Garland and Lana Turner, which led to the break-up of his marriage. On January 7, 1949, he and Annabella were divorced. The affair with the tempestuous Turner led nowhere and in Rome on June 27, 1949, he married MGM starlet Linda Christian (b. Tampico, Mexico, November 13, 1923, as Blanca Rosa Welter). They had two daughters: Romina Francesca (b. Rome, October 2, 1951) who twice represented Italy in the Eurovision Song Contest and finished seventh both times, and Taryn Stephanie (b. Hollywood, September 13, 1953). Thereafter his career began to slump and he moved to London where he appeared in the stage version of *Mister Roberts*, although it wasn't a success. Returning to Hollywood, he appeared in mediocre movies and divorced Linda Christian. In 1952 his contract with 20th Century Fox wasn't renewed. His comeback film was the hit *The Eddie Duchin Story* (1956). On May 7, 1958, Power married for the third time. The bride was Deborah Jean Minardos (née Smith), but they were together for just six months. As with many stars, numerous allegations have been levelled at Power, including his being a coprophiliac and bisexual. It is said that he had affairs with both Howard Hughes and Errol Flynn. Alice Faye once said: "I did consider marrying Tyrone Power. But I decided he was too fond of the boys for it to work out." Fox publicist Harry Brand said: "When Ty died, he was 44 but looked over 50. His looks had coarsened due to the drinking that helped him ease the worries and fears about being exposed as queer . . . Rock Hudson, for example, had an easier time of it . . . being younger and not spending most of his adult life with marriages or kids he didn't genuinely want." Comedian Bob Monkhouse revealed in his best-selling autobiography that Power had attempted to seduce him in a bath

in Birmingham at the opening of ATV. CAUSE: He died of a heart attack in Madrid while making *Solomon & Sheba* (1959). He was 44 years old. Tyrone Power was a practising Roman Catholic but because of his two divorces was banned from having a Catholic ceremony at his burial in section 8 of Hollywood Memorial Park, 6000 Santa Monica Boulevard, Hollywood, California 90038. His only son, Tyrone IV, was born posthumously in Hollywood on January 22, 1959. FURTHER READING: *The Secret Life Of Tyrone Power* – Hector Arce (New York: Bantam Books, 1979); *Tyrone Power: The Last Idol* – Fred Lawrence Guiles (London: Granada, 1982).

Otto Preminger
Born December 5, 1906
Died April 23, 1986
Rude director. Born in Vienna, the son of a lawyer who became Attorney-General of the Austria-Hungary Empire, Otto Ludwig Preminger followed in his father's legal briefs and studied to become a lawyer but deviated from the law to direct *Die Große Liebe* (1932). Four years later, he was in Hollywood but his egocentric manner didn't make him many friends and Darryl F. Zanuck sacked him from *Kidnapped* (1938). It looked like Preminger's career was going nowhere until Zanuck was called up for war service. Preminger used the opportunity to direct *Margin For Error* (1943) and *Laura* (1944), which earned him an Oscar nomination and established his power base at Fox. Thereafter, he left 20th Century Fox and freelanced. His film *The Moon Is Blue* (1953) caused controversy by utilising the words 'virgin' and 'pregnant', previously unheard on the legitimate screen. He directed Marilyn Monroe (whom he described as "a vacuum with nipples") in *River Of No Return* (1954), an all-black version of Bizet's opera *Carmen Jones* (1954) and a film about drugs *The Man With The*

Golden Arm (1955). His film, *Saint Joan* (1957), was supposed to launch the career of Jean Seberg, but it flopped. He later commented: "Barbra Streisand's mother once scolded me for not picking her daughter to star in my film *Saint Joan*. I chose another unknown, Jean Seberg. So I told the lady: 'Look at Jean Seberg's career. You should *thank* me for not picking your Barbra.'" His later films included: *Bonjour Tristesse* (1958), *Porgy And Bess* (1959), *Anatomy Of A Murder* (1959), *Exodus* (1960) (which caused Jewish comedian Mort Sahl to beg "Otto, let my people go"), *Advise And Consent* (1962), *The Cardinal* (1963) for which he was nominated for an Oscar, *Bunny Lake Is Missing* (1965) and *Rosebud* (1975). Michael Caine commented on Preminger: "O.P. is only happy if everybody else is miserable. Still, if you can keep his paranoia from beating you down, you can learn a lot from the guy." Perhaps as an in-joke to his icy temperament, Preminger was cast as Mr Freeze in *Batman*. His Caped Crusader co-star Adam West was no big fan either, opining: "The man insisted on enhancing his reputation as one of the meanest bastards who ever walked a sound stage. Otto was crude. Though most men have been guilty of looking on women as sex objects . . . Otto was the only man I ever met who did that on his *good* days. The rest of them he treated them like dirt. He would swear at them, insult them, comment on their weight, the size of their nose (if it was too big) or their breasts (if they were too small), say anything that might hurt them." CAUSE: Preminger died of cancer in New York. He was 79.

Elvis Presley
Born January 8, 1935
Died August 16, 1977
'The King Of Rock'n'Roll'. Born in Tupelo, Mississippi, Elvis Aron Presley was a twin. His brother Jesse Garon Presley died at birth. His great-great-great-grandmother was a full-blooded Cherokee Indian named Morning White Dove. His mother walked him to school everyday until he was 15 and once remarked, "I can't understand all the fuss over Elvis. I think I have a better voice than he does." His father, Vernon, added, "I never knew a guitar player worth a damn." His grandmother, Minnie Mae, outlived both Elvis and his parents. A former truck driver, Elvis was the biggest music sensation of the Fifties. He was described early on as a white boy with a black voice. Under the influence of the shady Colonel Tom Parker, Presley took America by storm. "I don't like them to call me 'Elvis the Pelvis'," he complained. "It is the most childish expression I have heard from an adult." He was not always the impressive stage presence he later became. On September 25, 1954, Presley made his début at the Grand Ole Opry and was sacked after just one performance. Talent office manager Jim Denny told him, "Listen, son, you ain't going nowhere. You oughtta go back to driving a truck." To add insult to injury a suitcase of Elvis' clothes was left behind at a garage and the future King of Rock'n'Roll cried all the way home. Presley's recording of 'That's Alright, Mama' was rejected by a black radio station in Tennessee, with the line: "This boy is a country rooster crowin' who shouldn't be allowed to sing after the sun comes up in the morning." The song was also turned down by a white radio station – one of its DJs complained: "If I play this they'll run me out of town. I gotta play pure and simple white country music." Two years later, the East German magazine *Youth World* weighed in with its own opinion: "This is a weapon of the American psychological war aimed at infecting part of the population with a new philosophical outlook of inhumanity . . . in order to prepare for war." The same year comedian Jackie Gleason stated, "He can't last. I tell you

flatly, he can't last." Ed Sullivan refused to put Presley on his show, asserting: "Nothing in this great, free continent is going to make me put that boy on my programme." Just seven days later, Sullivan paid $17,000 for the privilege of changing his mind. Music critic Jack Payne of the *Daily Mail* said in 1956, "Any form of singing is alien to Elvis." Critic D.W. Brogan wrote in the *Manchester Guardian* in 1956, "Who will sing 'Blue Suede Shoes' ten years from now?" Comedian Steve Allen commented, "The fact that someone with so little ability became the most popular singer in history says something significant about our cultural standards." Bing Crosby damned the young pretender with the line, "He never contributed a damn thing to music." Gossip columnist Hedda Hopper was no fan either: "He may be the kingpin, but in Hollywood he is a square in a peg." She added, "I consider him a menace to young girls" and "He is the most obscene, vulgar influence on America today." The Chairman of the Board, Frank Sinatra, was positively vitriolic in his criticism: "His kind of music is deplorable, a rancid-smelling aphrodisiac . . . It fosters almost totally negative and destructive reactions in people." What did they know. In the 1957 *Billboard* charts Elvis spent 24 weeks at number one. His songs 'Jailhouse Rock', 'It's Now Or Never' and 'Surrender' were three of the first four records ever to début at number one. (Today, records regularly go straight in at number one, but readers should be aware in the first 30 years of the hit parade this happened just 15 times. Compare this to 1998 when 27 songs went straight to the top.) By 1999 he had spent an incredible 1,155 weeks on the British charts, 73 of them at the top of the pile. Unlike his music, Elvis' film career was less than satisfactory. He made his début in the American civil war drama *Love Me Tender* (1956) as Clint Reno and went on to appear in *Loving You*

(1957) as Jimmy Tompkins a.k.a. Deke Rivers (Elvis' beloved mother, Gladys, appears as an extra towards the end of the film. After her death on August 14, 1958, he refused to watch the film) and *Jailhouse Rock* (1957) as Vince Everett (another film Elvis didn't like to watch because his co-star Judy Tyler died in a car crash shortly before the film was released). (Continuity blip: in the film Elvis is seen in the warden's office wearing the number 6239 on his prison garb. Later on, he has been 'promoted' to 6240.) He went on to star in *King Creole* (1958) as high school dropout Danny Fisher, *G.I. Blues* (1960) as Tulsa McLean, which features the song 'Wooden Heart' sung to a puppet, *Flaming Star* (1960) as Pacer Burton, a half-breed, and directed by Don Siegel, *Wild In The Country* (1961) as Glenn Tyler, in the last serious film he made, *Blue Hawaii* (1961) as Chad Gates (one of the year's five most popular films; Elvis had been signed to a five-year contract with Hal Wallis), *Follow That Dream* (1962) as Toby Kwimper, *Kid Galahad* (1962) as Walter Gulick, *Girls! Girls! Girls!* (1962) as Ross Carpenter, *It Happened At The World's Fair* (1963) as Mike Edwards, *Fun In Acapulco* (1963) as Mike Windgren, *Kissin' Cousins* (1964) as Josh Morgan & Jodie Tatum, *Viva Las Vegas* (1964) as Lucky Jackson, *Roustabout* (1964) as Charlie Rogers, *Girl Happy* (1965) as Rusty Wells, *Tickle Me* (1965) as Lonnie Beale, *Harum Scarum* (1965) as Johnny Tyronne in a cheap and dreadful flick, *Frankie And Johnny* (1966) as Johnny, *Paradise, Hawaiian Style* (1966) as Rick Richards, *Spinout* (1966) as Mike McCoy, *Double Trouble* (1967) as Guy Lambert, *Easy Come, Easy Go* (1967) as Ted Jackson, *Clambake* (1967) as Scott Hayward, *Stay Away, Joe* (1968) as Joe Lightcloud, *Speedway* (1968) as Steve Grayson, *Live A Little, Love A Little* (1968) as Greg Nolan, *Charro!* (1969) as Jess Wade (one of the worst films Elvis ever made; some distributors refused to take it), *The Trouble With*

Girls (1969) as Walter Hale and *Change Of Habit* (1969) as Dr John Carpenter. CAUSE: Elvis was found dead or close to death aged 42 at a house called Graceland, located at 3764 Elvis Presley Boulevard, Memphis, Tennessee 38116. He was pronounced dead at 3.30pm in Trauma Room 2 of Baptist Memorial Hospital. That much is certain. The pathologist who performed the autopsy announced Elvis had died of "cardiac arrhythmia". Yet for years stories have circulated about how Elvis really died, including a report that 14 drugs were discovered in his corpse. One writer even suggested suicide, citing Elvis' 1967 attempt, depression, tax bill, impotence, failing health and career as evidence for this supposition.
FURTHER READING: *My Life With Elvis* – Becky Yancey & Cliff Lindecker (London: Mayflower, 1978); *Elvis: Portrait Of A Friend* – Marty Lacker, Patsy Lacker & Leslie S. Smith (New York: Bantam, 1980); *Elvis* – Albert Goldman (London: Penguin, 1982); *Elvis And Gladys* – Elaine Dundy (London: Weidenfeld & Nicolson, 1985); *Elvis And Me* – Priscilla Beaulieu Presley (London: Century Hutchinson, 1985); *Life With Elvis* – David Stanley With David Wimbish (Bromley: Marc Europe, 1986); *Are You Lonesome Tonight? The Untold Story Of Elvis Presley's One True Love And The Child He Never Knew* – Lucy De Barbin And Dary Matera (London: Century, 1987); *Elvis And The Colonel* – Dirk Vellenga With Mick Farren (New York: Dell, 1988); *Elvis: His Life From A–Z* – Fred L. Worth & Steve D. Tamerius (Chicago: Contemporary Books, 1988); *Priscilla, Elvis And Me* – Michael Edwards (New York: St Martin's Press, 1988); *The Elvis Files: Was His Death Faked?* – Gail Brewer-Giorgio (Lancaster: Impala Books, 1990); *Elvis: The Last 24 Hours* – Albert Goldman (New York: St Martin's Press, 1991); *The Death Of Elvis: What Really Happened* – Charles C. Thompson II & James P. Cole

(London: Orion, 1993); *The Ultimate Elvis* – Patricia Jobe Pierce (New York: Simon & Schuster, 1994); *Elvis Meets The Beatles* – Chris Hutchins & Peter Thompson (London: Smith Gryphon, 1994); *Last Train To Memphis: The Rise Of Elvis Presley* – Peter Guralnick (London: Little, Brown, 1994); *Down At The End Of Lonely Street: The Life And Death Of Elvis Presley* – Peter Harry Brown and Pat H. Broeske (London: William Heinemann, 1997); *Careless Love: The Unmaking Of Elvis Presley* – Peter Guralnick (London: Little, Brown, 1999).

Emeric Pressburger
(IMRE JOSEF PRESSBURGER)
Born December 5, 1902
Died February 5, 1988
One half of The Archers. Born at 3 St Peter's Street, Miskolc, Hungary, Pressburger studied maths and engineering at the Universities of Prague and Stuttgart before the death of his father prevented him from continuing his studies. A move to Berlin in 1926 saw him work as a journalist and short story writer for films. He joined Ufa where his first screen credit emerged as *Abschied* (1930). He worked uncredited on *Emil Und Die Detektive* (1931). In Germany he changed his name to Emmerich and then moved to France and then London where he worked for Sir Alexander Korda. In London he changed his name once again, becoming Emeric. In 1938 he worked on *The Challenge* (1938) and that year also met his future collaborator Michael Powell. Their first projects were *The Spy In Black* (1939) and *Contraband* (1940). In 1943 they christened their partnership The Archers and established a logo of nine arrows hitting a target. Pressburger's foreign eye helped The Archers' films become fantastical and unique. In 1946 Pressburger became a British subject and a devoted fan of Arsenal. His and Powell's films were not always

appreciated by their contemporaries and they split after *Ill Met By Moonlight* (1956). They resumed their partnership briefly in 1972, working for the Children's Film Foundation. After this, Pressburger virtually retired. He was married twice. Wife number one (1938–1941) was Agnes Anderson. His second wife was Gwynneth May Zillah 'Wendy' Greenbaum (née Orme) by whom he had two daughters, one of whom died in infancy. They married in 1947 and were divorced twice, once in Reno, Nevada, in 1953 and again in England in 1971.

CAUSE: Pressburger died of bronchial pneumonia, aged 85, in Saxstead, Suffolk.

Harve Presnell

Born September 14, 1933
Died June 30, 2009
Born too late. Born at 2.10am at Modesto, California, George Harvey Presnell went to Modesto High School before winning a place at the University of Southern California on a sports scholarship but after three weeks, changed to a music scholarship after the head of the music department heard him sing. Presnell dropped out and went to Europe where he spent three years singing for his supper. In Berlin composer Meredith Willson heard Presnell and wrote the part of Leadville Johnny Brown for him in *The Unsinkable Molly Brown*, which opened on November 3, 1960 at the Winter Garden Theatre with Tammy Grimes as Molly. 6'4" Presnell made his film debut reprising the part in the June 11, 1964 released movie in which Debbie Reynolds took the title role. In 1965 he appeared in the Western *The Glory Guys* (released July 7, 1965) as Sol Rogers but wanted to sing and was cast in the Connie Francis film *When The Boys Meet The Girls* (released October 10, 1965) as Danny Churchill. His next role was as Rotten Luck Willie in the flop Paramount musical *Paint Your Wagon* (released October 15, 1969),

although he did sing the remarkable ballad 'They Call The Wind Maria'. One of the patrons who saw the film was pregnant Long Island housewife Patricia Carey who named her baby daughter born on March 27, 1970 after the song, albeit with a slight change of spelling to Mariah. After playing Rotten Luck Willie, it seemed that Presnell's Hollywood career was at an end. The era of the big musical was over and audiences did not want to hear fine baritones like Presnell on screen. In 1972 at the Theatre Royal, Drury Lane, London, he played a singing Rhett Butler in a musical version of *Gone With The Wind* (adapted by Horton Foote who is noticed in this book) and with a score by Harold Rome. From 1979 until 1981 he played Oliver "Daddy" Warbucks in a nationwide tour of *Annie*, despite initially thinking that the title was an abbreviation for *Annie, Get Your Gun* in which he had played Frank Butler, a sharpshooter. Presnell said, "It was a question of saying, 'I'm no longer Frank Butler or Rhett Butler or Leadville Johnny Brown.' And they were paying good money." He then went into the role on Broadway replacing John Schuck and was still there when the show closed on January 2, 1983. He also reprised his role in January 1990 in the flop *Annie 2: Miss Hannigan's Revenge*. Another version, entitled *Annie Warbucks*, ran for four months off-Broadway at the Variety Arts Theatre from August 9, 1993 with Presnell again in his usual role. Three years later, the Coen brothers cast Presnell as Wade Gustafson, William H. Macy's father-in-law, in *Fargo* (1996) and the part rejuvenated his career. He appeared in several network television shows as well as *Face/Off* (1997) as Victor Lazarro, *Julian Po* (1997) as Mayor Henry Leech, *Saving Private Ryan* (1998) as General George C. Marshall, *Patch Adams* (1998) as Dean Anderson, *The Legend Of Bagger Vance* (2000) as John Invergordon,

The Family Man (2000) as Big Ed,
Mr Deeds (2002) as Preston Blake,
Old School (2003) as Mr Springbrook,
Flags Of Our Fathers (2006) as Dave
Severance and *Evan Almighty* (2007)
as Congressman Burrows. Presnell
married twice. His first wife, Sherri,
bore him three children as did his
second wife, Veeva Suzanne Hamblen,
whom he married on May 6, 1966.
CAUSE: Presnell died aged 75 of
pancreatic cancer at St. John's Health
Center, Santa Monica, California.

Robert Preston

(ROBERT PRESTON MESERVEY)
Born June 8, 1918
Died March 21, 1987
Reliable B star. Born in Newton
Highlands, Massachusetts, 6′1″
Preston looked as if he was on the
way to becoming a huge star when he
was awarded a Paramount Pictures
contract just two years after leaving
school. He had made his professional
début in a play directed by Tyrone
Power's mum. He never quite fulfilled
his promise, seemingly happy to drift
along until he won the part of Harold
Hill in *The Music Man* on Broadway. It
won him a Tony and made him a star.
When the play was made into a film in
1962, Preston reprised his role and
then shone in *All The Way Home*
(1963) and *Junior Bonner* (1972) as
Ace Bonner. A lull followed until the
Eighties when Blake Edwards rescued
Preston from obscurity and cast
him in *S.O.B.* (1981) as Dr Irving
Finegarten and in drag in *Victor/Victoria*
(1982) as Toddy for which he was
nominated for his only Oscar. He
opined: "I was disappointed not to
win. But actors never win in gay roles.
The Academy pats you on the back
with a nomination; it's as if they're
saying, 'How brave of you,' and 'Quite
a stretch.' But they can't help
wondering about you if you play the
role too well . . ." On November 9,
1940, he married actress Catherine
Craig (b. 1918), who survived him.

CAUSE: He died aged 78 in Santa
Barbara, California, from lung cancer.

Marie Prevost

(MARY BICKFORD DUNN)
Born November 8, 1893
Died January 21, 1937
Beautiful coquette with a poor mental
attitude. The 5′4″ Marie Prevost began
her showbiz life in 1916 as a Mack
Sennett Bathing Beauty and went on to
make almost 100 films. She was born
in Sarnia, Ontario, Canada, and
educated in Montreal in a convent
before moving to Los Angeles. She
worked as a typist for a legal firm for a
brief while and then joined Sennett
where she stayed for five years when
she joined Universal. Her best films
there were with Ernst Lubitsch: *The
Marriage Circle* (1924) as Mizzi Stock,
Three Women (1924) as Harriet and
Kiss Me Again (1925) as LouLou
Fleury. In 1926 she transferred to PDC
where she starred in several bedroom
farces such as *Up In Mabel's Room*
(1926) as Mabel Ainsworth and *Getting
Gertie's Garter* (1927) as Gertie
Darling. She was married twice, the
first time at 19, but both marriages
ended in divorce.
CAUSE: Marie made a successful
transition to the talkies. Her problem
wasn't her voice, it was her weight. She
went on a diet and eventually stopped
eating altogether, resulting in her death
due to extreme malnutrition, drug
addiction and alcoholism at the age of
43. Her body lay undiscovered for two
days at her home, 6230 Afton Place,
Hollywood. Her pet dachshund howled
continuously until she was found and
had begun eating Marie's arm and legs
in a bid to survive.

Dennis Price

Born June 23, 1915
Died October 6, 1973
Devious-looking smoothie. Born in
Ruscombe, Berkshire, Dennistoun John
Franklin Rose Price was the son of a
Brigadier-General and the official

referee of the Supreme Court of Judicature. After education at Radley College and Worcester College, Oxford, he made his West End stage début on September 6, 1937, at the Queen's Theatre as Green and Exton's servant in *Richard II*. Two years later, he married and went on to father two daughters but his real first loves were men and alcohol. Invalided out of the army, he joined Noël Coward's troupe and made his leading film début in *A Canterbury Tale* (1944). Price rose to become a leading figure in British films appearing in *The Bad Lord Byron* (1948), *The Dancing Years* (1948) and *Kind Hearts And Coronets* (1949). In 1950 he was divorced and his career went into a steep decline. On April 19, 1954, he tried to gas himself in his Egerton Gardens, Knightsbridge, home. The resulting publicity boosted his career and he appeared in *Private's Progress* (1955), *The Naked Truth* (1957), *I'm All Right, Jack* (1959) and *Tamahine* (1963). In 1966 he fell into trouble with the Inland Revenue and did a bunk from his London home, 16 Curzon Street, W1, to Sark. The following year he was declared bankrupt.

CAUSE: Price died of cirrhosis of the liver at the Princess Elizabeth Hospital, Guernsey. He was 58.

Vincent Price

Born May 27, 1911
Died October 25, 1993

Horror giant. Born in St. Louis, Missouri, Vincent Leonard Price made his name originally playing romantic leads on the West End and Broadway stages, yet it is his consummate portrayal of villains for which he is best known. He made his film début in *Service De Luxe* (1938) as Robert Wade and then went on to appear in a number of period dramas such as *The Private Lives Of Elizabeth And Essex* (1939) as Sir Walter Raleigh, *Tower Of London* (1939) as the Duke of Clarence, *Hudson's Bay* (1940) as King Charles II and *Brigham Young –*

Frontiersman (1940) as Joseph Smith. He didn't make a horror film until he was in his forties but then became synonymous with the genre. His films included: *House Of Wax* (1953) as Professor Henry Jarrod, *The Fly* (1958) as François Delambre, *House On Haunted Hill* (1958) as Frederick Loren, *House of Usher* (1960) as Roderick Usher, *Pit And The Pendulum* (1961) as Nicholas Medina, *Tales Of Terror* (1962) as Fortunato/Valdemar/Locke, *The Masque Of The Red Death* (1964) as Prospero, *The Tomb Of Ligeia* (1965) as Verden Fell, *Dr Goldfoot And The Bikini Machine* (1965) as Dr Goldfoot, in which he sent up his image, *Scream And Scream Again* (1969) as Dr Browning, *More Dead Than Alive* (1969) as Dan Ruffalo, *Cry Of The Banshee* (1970) as Lord Edward Whitman, *The Abominable Dr Phibes* (1971) as Dr Anton Phibes, *Dr Phibes Rises Again* (1972) as Dr Anton Phibes, *Theatre Of Blood* (1973) as Edward Lionheart, *Journey Into Fear* (1975) as Dervos, *The Monster Club* (1980) as Eramus and the fantastical *Edward Scissorhands* (1990) as the Inventor. To television viewers Price was probably best known as Egghead in the Sixties *Batman* series, while to music fans, he was the voice of the rap in Michael Jackson's 1983 hit 'Thriller'. Away from the screen Price was a talented cook and published several recipe books. He was married three times.

CAUSE: He died of emphysema caused by lung cancer at 7.30pm, aged 82, at his home, 9255 Swallow Drive, Los Angeles, California 90069. Four days later, he was cremated and his ashes scattered at sea three miles from Santa Monica.

Bryan Pringle

Born January 19, 1935
Died May 15, 2002

Craggy-faced character actor. Born in Glascote, Staffordshire, the son of the Reverend Craster Pringle, Bryan Pringle did not get on well with his mother and was raised mostly by a family friend. Pringle was to become a household face if not a household name. Raised in Lancashire he was educated at St Bees, a public school in Cumbria where he was told by a master that he had better become an actor because he had no chance of attaining any O levels. Pringle took his advice and went to RADA where he won the Bancroft Gold Medal in 1954 and joined the Old Vic the following year where he stayed until 1957. He made his film début playing Jack in *Saturday Night And Sunday Morning* (1960). He often played policemen or soldiers. "I don't particularly like playing nasty characters. I was just born with a face that nobody could think well of," he once commented. He was a sergeant in *The Challenge* (1960) with Jayne Mansfield. He also appeared in *HMS Defiant* (1962) as Sergeant Kneebone, *Lawrence Of Arabia* (1962) as a driver, the ambitious milkman Austin in *The Early Bird* (1965) opposite Norman Wisdom, PC Bradford in *Berserk!* (1967) with Joan Crawford, *Diamonds For Breakfast* (1968) as a police sergeant, *The Boy Friend* (1971) as Percy Parkhill/Percy Browne, *The Old Curiosity Shop* (1975) as Mr Garland, *Jabberwocky* (1977) as a security guard, a waiter in *Bullshot* (1983), *Brazil* (1985), Jake in *Drowning By Numbers* (1988), a gatekeeper in *Consuming Passions* (1988), *3 Men And A Little Lady* (1990) as an Englishman, *American Friends* (1991) as Haskell, *Snow White: A Tale Of Terror* (1997) as Father Gilbert and Stepan in *All Forgotten* (2000). He played Cheese and Egg in the sitcom *The Dustbinmen* (1969) and another policeman, Sergeant Flagg, in the sitcom *The Growing Pains Of PC Penrose* (1975). He was also Felix Norman, the pathologist, in the first *Prime Suspect* (1991). In 1958 he married Anne Jameson (who predeceased him in 1999) by whom he had one son,

Craster, and one daughter, Kate.
CAUSE: Pringle died in London, aged 67.

Freddie Prinze
(FREDERICK KARL PRUETZEL)
Born June 22, 1954
Died January 29, 1977
Hispanic heartbreaker. Born at 4.09am weighing just over 9lb at St Claire's Hospital, New York, Freddie Prinze was a bright young star in the firmament of American television. His starring vehicle, *Chico & The Man*, regularly topped the viewing charts. Despite his phenomenal success (he was a millionaire) Prinze was a deeply unhappy man whose only real solace came in the shape of his wife, Kathy, and infant son, Fred (b. March 9, 1976). He didn't like having to live in California, preferring the grittier New York. It was not unusual for his telephone bill to run into thousands of dollars as he spent hours ringing his mother, Maria. He was even threatened by real-life Chicanos who believed the role in *Chico & The Man* should have gone to an authentic Mexican. Like many stars, Prinze developed an unfortunate liking for drugs. His habit caused the break-up of his marriage. Allegedly, he took so much cocaine, he burned a hole in his nose and had to ingest it anally. In January 1977 Prinze, living at 216/10300 Wilshire Boulevard, began divorce proceedings and attempted to kick drugs. He took up karate as a way of redirecting his energies. That same month he began an engagement at Caesar's Palace in Las Vegas, commuting between there and Los Angeles where he was filming *Chico & The Man* during the day. His producer, James Komack, warned Prinze that he was burning the candle at both ends, but the star swore he could manage the arduous schedule. He couldn't and soon Prinze went to his doctor to ask for some Quaaludes to enable him to cope. Unsurprisingly, the medic said no, so Prinze simply bought them off a

dealer on the street. During a visit Komack noticed a gun in one of the drawers in Prinze's house. He confiscated it but the next day Prinze rang to ask for its return saying he needed it for protection. Komack demurred but eventually relented, realising that Prinze could easily purchase a gun almost anywhere. CAUSE: At 865-75 Comstock, Beverly Hills, on January 28, 1977, Freddie Prinze fatally shot himself in the temple. He died at UCLA Medical Center, 10833 LeConte Avenue, Los Angeles, the next day at 1pm. He was just 22 years old. A note was found in his room that read: *"I must end it. There's no hope left. I'll be at peace. No one had anything to do with this. My decision totally – Freddie Prinze P.S. I'm sorry. Forgive me. Dusty's here. He's innocent. He cared."* Dusty was Marvin 'Dusty' Snyder, Freddie's business manager, who was in the same room when Prinze shot himself. In January 1983 his death was ruled an accident by a jury who concluded that he was acting under the influence of drugs and was not responsible for his actions. His life insurers paid out. FURTHER READING: *The Freddie Prinze Story* – Maria Pruetzel And John A. Barbour (Kalamazoo: Master's Press, 1978).

Edmund Purdom

Born December 19, 1924
Died January 1, 2009
The replacement. Born in Welwyn Garden City, Hertfordshire, Edmund Anthony Cutlar Purdom was educated at Douai, St Ignatius and Downside schools. He began acting on stage in 1945 before making his film debut as an uncredited extra playing Second Officer Lightoller in *Titanic* (1953). He achieved a measure of celebrity in 1954 when he replaced Mario Lanza as Prince Karl Franz, the lead role in *The Student Prince* (1954) after the singer grew too fat. Purdom lip-synched to Lanza's singing. Purdom replaced original choice Marlon Brando as Sinuhe, the lead in *The Egyptian* (1954) after the mumbler chose to play Napoleon in *Desirée* (1954). Purdom moved to Italy settling in Rome where he earned a good living dubbing European films into English. His films included: *Agguato A Tangeri* (1957) as John Milwood, *Erode Il Grande* (1959) as Herod, *The Diary Of Anne Frank* (1959) as British radio announcer, *Les Nuits De Raspoutine* (1960) as Rasputin, *I Cosacchi* (1960) as Shamil, *Salambò* (1960) as Narr Havas, *Moment Of Danger* (1960) as Peter Carran, *La Furia Dei Barbari* (1960) as Toryok, *Das Große Wunschkonzert* (1960) as Harry Mell, *Solimano Il Conquistatore* (1961) as Ibrahim Pascià, *La Fayette* (1961) as Silas Deane, *L'Ultimo Dei Vikinghi* (1961) as King Sveno, *Nefertiti, Regina Del Nilo* (1961) as Tumos, *L'Ammutinamento* (1961) as Dr Bradley, *The Beauty Jungle* (1964) as Rex Carrick, *Der Letzte Ritt Nach Santa Cruz* (1964) as Rex Kelly, *The Comedy Man* (1964) as Julian Baxter, *The Yellow Rolls-Royce* (1964) as Fane, *L'Uomo Che Ride* (1966) as Caesar Borgia, *Il Corsaro Nero* (1971) as The Viceroy, *Giornata Nera Per L'Ariete* (1971) as Edouard Vermont, *Karzan, Il Favoloso Uomo Della Jungla* (1972) as Lord Carter, *Terror! Il Castello Delle Donne Maledette* (1974) as Prefect Ewing, the doctor in *Il Medaglione Insanguinato* (1975), *I Padroni Della Città* (1976) as Luigi Cherico, *Concorde Affaire '79* (1979) as Danker, *Ator L'Invincibile* (1982) as Griba, *Horror Safari* (1982) as Rex Larson, *Fracchia Contro Dracula* (1985) as Count Dracula and *Funny Boy* (1987) as Samuel. He married four times, leaving his second wife Anita Philips and their two children for Linda Christian, his co-star in the MGM musical *Athena* (1954). Their marriage lasted just a year. Of his work, he said, "One of the symptoms of an approaching nervous breakdown is the belief that one's work is terribly important."
CAUSE: Purdom died aged 84 in Rome of natural causes.

Q

Sir Anthony Quayle
Born September 7, 1913
Died October 20, 1989
Stiff upper-lipped Englishman. John
Anthony Quayle was born at
2 Delamere Road, Ainsdale, Sefton,
an only child. 6'1" Quayle's childhood
was rather solitary until he went to
Rugby and then RADA. During a
holiday from RADA he made his first
stage appearance – albeit unpaid – in
1931 in *The Ghost Train*. The following
year he worked as a comic's stooge
before moving to more traditional
theatre. He was much influenced by Sir
Tyrone Guthrie and Sir John Gielgud.
He made his film début just before the
outbreak of war in *Pygmalion* (1938) as
Eliza's Hairdresser. During the Second
World War Quayle served as a major in
the Royal Artillery and then worked
with Albanian patriots behind German
lines. Quayle would not appear on film
again until 1948 with roles in *Saraband
For Dead Lovers* (1948) as Durer and
Hamlet (1948) as Marcellus. It would
be eight more years before Quayle
made another film. He spent much of
his career in the theatre but he made
some memorable films including: *The
Battle Of The River Plate* (1956) as
Commodore Harwood, *No Time For
Tears* (1957) as Dr Seagrave, *Ice Cold
In Alex* (1958) as Captain van der Poel,
Tarzan's Greatest Adventure (1959) as
Slade, *The Guns Of Navarone* (1961)
as Major Roy Franklin, *Lawrence Of
Arabia* (1962) as Colonel Harry
Brighton, *The Fall Of The Roman
Empire* (1964) as Verulus, *A Study In
Terror* (1965) as Dr Murray, *Anne Of
The Thousand Days* (1969) as Cardinal
Wolsey for which he was nominated for
an Oscar, *The Eagle Has Landed* (1976)
as Admiral Canaris and *Murder By*

Decree (1979) as Sir Charles Warren.
He was married twice, firstly on
March 3, 1935 to the actress Hermione
Hannen (b. London, January 26, 1913,
d. Shrewsbury, October 1, 1983), the
daughter of the actor Nicholas James
Hannen (b. London, May 1, 1881,
d. London, June 25, 1972) and
stepdaughter of Athene Seyler, but they
divorced in 1943. On June 3, 1947 he
was married to another actress Dorothy
Wardell Finlayson (b. Chicago, Illinois,
December 24, 1914 as Dorothy
Wardell Hyson; m. firstly 1935 the
actor Robert Douglas Finlayson;
d. London, May 23, 1996 of a stroke),
the daughter of yet another actress,
Dorothy Dickson (b. Kansas City,
Missouri, July 25, 1893, d. London,
September 25, 1995, aged 102) who
was a friend of Queen Elizabeth the
Queen Mother, and Carl Constantine
Hyson. By her, Quayle had a son and
two daughters, one of whom, Jenny,
followed in her parents' footsteps.
A dazzling beauty, her "perfect
heart-shaped face, vivid cornflower
blue eyes and translucent halo of
blonde hair" inspired the Rodgers &
Hart song, 'The Most Beautiful Girl In
The World'. Quayle was appointed
CBE in 1952 and knighted in 1985.
CAUSE: Quayle died of cancer at his
home, 49B Elystan Place, Chelsea,
south west London. He was 76.

Anthony Quinn
(ANTONIO RUDOLFO OAXACA QUINN)
Born April 21, 1915
Died June 3, 2001
Irish-Latin heartthrob. Born in
Chihuahua, Mexico, Quinn was told
by his father that he had been adopted
after being discovered in a pigsty. After
dropping out of high school Quinn
became an actor and after a few stage
appearances he made his début in
Parole (1936) as Zingo Browning.
Despite marrying the daughter of Cecil
B. DeMille Quinn continued to
play supporting roles because his
father-in-law did not approve of him.

In the Fifties he gave his career a boost playing Stanley Kowalski in *A Streetcar Named Desire* on Broadway. On March 19, 1953, he won the Best Supporting Actor Oscar for his performance as Eufemio in *Viva Zapata!* (1952). Four years later, on March 27, 1957, he picked up another Best Supporting Actor Oscar for his portrayal of Paul Gauguin in *Lust For Life* (1956). He was also nominated for *Wild Is The Wind* (1957) as Gino and *Zorba The Greek* (1964). His other films included: *The Plainsman* (1936) as Northern Cheyenne Warrior, *Swing High, Swing Low* (1937) as The Don, *Waikiki Wedding* (1937) as Kimo, *The Last Train From Madrid* (1937) as Captain Ricardo Alvarez, *Partners In Crime* (1937) as Nicholas Mazaney, *Daughter Of Shanghai* (1937) as Harry Morgan, *The Buccaneer* (1938) as Beluche, *Dangerous To Know* (1938) as Nicholas 'Nicki' Kusnoff, *Tip-Off Girls* (1938) as Marty, *Hunted Men* (1938) as Legs, *Bulldog Drummond In Africa* (1938) as Fordine, *King Of Alcatraz* (1938) as Lou Gedney, *Union Pacific* (1939) as Jack Cordray, *Television Spy* (1939) as Forbes, *King Of Chinatown* (1939) as Mike Gordon, *Island Of Lost Men* (1939) as Chang Tai, *Emergency Squad* (1940) as Nick Buller, *Road To Singapore* (1940) as Caesar, *The Ghost Breakers* (1940) as Ramon/Francisco Mederos, *Parole Fixer* (1940) as Francis 'Big Boy' Bradmore, *City For Conquest* (1940) as Murray Burns, *The Texas Rangers Ride Again* (1940) as Joe Yuma, *The Perfect Snob* (1941) as Alex Moreno, *Bullets For O'Hara* (1941) as Tony Van Dyne aka Millard, *Knockout* (1941) as Mr Harry Trego, *Thieves Fall Out* (1941) as Chic Collins, *Blood And Sand* (1941) as Manola de Palma, *They Died With Their Boots On* (1941) as Chief Crazy Horse, *Larceny, Inc.* (1942) as Leo Dexter, *Road To Morocco* (1942) as Mullay Kassim, *The Black Swan* (1942) as Wogan, *Guadalcanal Diary* (1943) as Private Jesus 'Soose' Alvarez, *The Ox-Bow Incident* (1943) as Juan Martinez/Francisco Morez, *Roger Touhy, Gangster* (1944) as George Carroll, *Ladies Of Washington* (1944) as Michael Romanescue, *Irish Eyes Are Smiling* (1944) as Al Jackson, *Buffalo Bill* (1944) as Yellow Hand, *Where Do We Go From Here?* (1945) as Chief Badger, *China Sky* (1945) as Chen-Ta, *Back To Bataan* (1945) as Captain Andres Bonifacio, *California* (1946) as Don Luis Rivera y Hernandez, *Sinbad The Sailor* (1947) as Emir, *The Imperfect Lady* (1947) as Jose Martinez, *Black Gold* (1947) as Charley Eagle, *Tycoon* (1947) as Enrique 'Ricky' Vargas, *Mask Of The Avenger* (1951) as Viovanni Larocca, *The Brave Bulls* (1951) as Raul Fuentes, *The Brigand* (1952) as Prince Ramon, *Against All Flags* (1952) as Captain Roc Brasiliano, *The World In His Arms* (1952) as Portugee, *Seminole* (1953) as Osceola/John Powell, *Donne proibite* (1953) as Francesco Caserto, *Cavalleria Rusticana* (1953) as Alfio, *Blowing Wild* (1953) as Ward 'Paco' Conway, *City Beneath The Sea* (1953) as Tony Bartlett, *Ride, Vaquero!* (1953) as Jose Esqueda, *East Of Sumatra* (1953) as Kiang, *Ulisse* (1954) as Antinoos, *La Strada* (1954) as Zampanò, *Attila* (1954) as Attila, *The Long Wait* (1954) as Johnny McBride, *Seven Cities Of Gold* (1955) as Captain Gaspar de Portola, *The Magnificent Matador* (1955) as Luis Santos, *The Naked Street* (1955) as Phil Regal, *The Wild Party* (1956) as Tom Kupfen, *Man From Del Rio* (1956) as Dave Robles, *Notre Dame De Paris* (1956) as Quasimodo, *The River's Edge* (1957) as Ben Cameron, *The Ride Back* (1957) as Bob Kallen, *Hot Spell* (1958) as John Henry 'Jack' Duval, *The Black Orchid* (1958) as Frank Valente, *The Savage Innocents* (1959) as Inuk, *Last Train From Gun Hill* (1959) as Craig Belden, *Warlock* (1959) as Tom Morgan, *Portrait In Black* (1960) as Dr David Rivera, *Heller In Pink Tights* (1960) as Tom Healy, *The Guns Of Navarone* (1961) as Colonel Andrea Stavros,

Lawrence Of Arabia (1962) as Auda abu Tayi, *Requiem For A Heavyweight* (1962) as Mountain Rivera, *Barabbas* (1962) as Barabbas, *Behold A Pale Horse* (1964) as Vinolas, *The Visit* (1964) as Serge Miller, *Marco The Magnificent* (1965) as Kublai Khan, *A High Wind In Jamaica* (1965) as Captain Chavez, *Lost Command* (1966) as Lieutenant Colonel Pierre Raspeguy, *L'Avventuriero* (1967) as Peyrol, *La Vingt-Cinquième Heure* (1967) as Johann Moritz, *The Happening* (1967) as Roc Delmonico, *La Bataille De San Sebastian* (1968) as Leon Alastray, *The Shoes Of The Fisherman* (1968) as Kiril Lakota, *The Magus* (1968) as Maurice Conchis, *The Secret Of Santa Vittoria* (1969) as Italo Bombolini, *A Dream Of Kings* (1969) as Matsoukas, *R.P.M.* (1970) as Professor F.W.J. 'Paco' Perez, *Walk In The Spring Rain* (1970) as Will Cade, *Flap* (1970) as Flapping Eagle, *Los Amigos* (1972) as Erastus 'Deaf' Smith, *Across 110th Street* (1972) as Captain Mattelli, *The Don Is Dead* (1973) as Don Angelo, *The Destructors* (1974) as Steve Ventura, *Target Of An Assassin* (1976) as Ernest Hobday, *The Message* (1976) as Hamza, *L'Eredità Ferramonti* (1976) as Gregorio Ferramonti, *Bluff Storia Di Truffe E Di Imbroglioni* (1976) as Philip Bang, *The Children Of Sanchez* (1978) as Jesus Sanchez, *The Greek Tycoon* (1978) as Theo Tomasis, *Caravans* (1978) as Zulffiqar, *The Passage* (1979) as The Basque, *Lion Of The Desert* (1980) as Omar Mukhtar, *High Risk* (1981) as Mariano, *Crosscurrent* (1981), *Regina Roma* (1982), *Valentina* (1982) as Mosen Joaquin, *Stradivari* (1989) as Antonio Stradivari, *Revenge* (1990) as Tiburon 'Tibby' Mendez, *Ghosts Can't Do It* (1990) as Scott, *A Star For Two* (1991), *Only The Lonely* (1991) as Nick, *Jungle Fever* (1991) as Lou Carbone, *Mobsters* (1991) as Don Giuseppe 'Joe the Boss' Masseria, *Last Action Hero* (1993) as Tony Vivaldi, *Somebody To Love* (1994) as Emillio, *A Walk In The Clouds* (1995) as Don Pedro Aragón, *Il Sindaco* (1996), *Seven Servants* (1996) as Archie, *Oriundi* (1999) as Giuseppe Padovani, and *Avenging Angelo* (2002) as Angelo. On October 5, 1937, Quinn married Katherine DeMille, the daughter of Cecil, at All Saints Church in Los Angeles. Quinn had a shock on his wedding night. He discovered she wasn't a virgin so he punched her in the face. Despite this ignominious start they had five children: Christopher (b. 1939, d. 1941); Christina (b. 1941); Kathleen (b. 1942); Duncan (b. 1945) and Valentina (b. 1952). They divorced in Juarez, Mexico, on January 21, 1965. On January 2, 1966, he married Yolande Addolari. They had two sons born prior to the marriage and one more four months after. In 1977 Quinn had a son by Ferdel Dunbar. In 1993 Quinn fathered a daughter by Kathy Benvin, his former secretary, at which time his eldest daughter was 52.
CAUSE: Anthony Quinn died in Boston, Massachusetts, of pneumonia and respiratory complications during his battle with throat cancer.

R

George Raft

(GEORGE RANFT)
Born September 26, 1895
Died November 24, 1980

Screen tough-guy. Born in Hell's Kitchen, New York, bisexual Raft, whose most celebrated role was in *Scarface* (1932), began working as a boxer before becoming a dancer in nightclubs. He won a tango contest in the Twenties and was labelled 'the fastest dancer in the world'. He made his film début in 1932 in *Taxi* but, according to respected film critic Leonard Maltin, there was one problem that stopped Raft becoming a major star – "he couldn't act". He also was an extremely bad judge of material. He turned down the leading parts in both *High Sierra* (1941) and *The Maltese Falcon* (1941) the film that made Humphrey Bogart a star. Sometimes he took his 'acting' too far, assuming the role of a tough guy off screen and associating with known villains. Home Secretary Roy Jenkins refused him admittance to Britain on February 24, 1967, on the grounds that he was an undesirable. His wife, Grayce Mulroney, whom he married in 1932, no doubt found him undesirable as well, but put up with him. Although he romanced many women (including Betty Grable) she refused to give him a divorce and they stayed 'married' until her death in 1969. Asked who was the greatest lover in Hollywood, Carole Lombard said: "George Raft . . . or did you just mean on the screen?"

CAUSE: Raft died in Hollywood from leukaemia and emphysema. He was 85.

Claude Rains

Born November 10, 1889
Died May 30, 1967

Ironic Englishman. Born in Camberwell, London, William Claude Rains made his stage début aged ten, on August 31, 1900, in *Sweet Nell Of Old Drury* at the Haymarket Theatre, but it was not until he was in his forties that he made his film début as Jack Griffin in *The Invisible Man* (1933). (Trivia note: in the film, when the naked but invisible hero runs through the snow, the footprints he leaves are of shoes, not of feet.) Oddly, he became a star wrapped in bandages for the role, the very reason Boris Karloff, who had starred in *The Mummy* the previous year, turned down the part. Rains rose to the rank of captain during World War I and after demob he taught at RADA. Among his pupils was Sir John Gielgud, who said, "He was a great influence on me. I don't know what happened to him. I think he failed and went to America", and Charles Laughton. A small man who wore lifts in his shoes, Rains also overcame a lisp and an appalling Cockney accent (Beerbohm Tree paid for his elocution lessons) to pursue a career in acting. He excelled in *Anthony Adverse* (1936), *The Prince And The Pauper* (1937), *Adventures Of Robin Hood* (1938) as Prince John, *Mr Smith Goes To Washington* (1939) as Senator Joseph Paine, for which he was nominated for an Oscar, *The Sea Hawk* (1940) as Don Jose, *Kings Row* (1942) as Dr Alexander Tower, *Now Voyager* (1942) as Dr Jaquity, *The Phantom Of The Opera* (1943), *Mr Skeffington* (1944) as Job Skeffington, for which he was again nominated for an Oscar, *Cleopatra* (1945), Alfred Hitchcock's *Notorious* (1946) as Alexander Sebastian, for which he was nominated for an Oscar for the third time, David Lean's *Lawrence Of Arabia* (1962) as Dryden and *The Greatest Story Ever Told* (1965) but it was for his Oscar-nominated role as the wily Captain Louis Renault in

Casablanca (1942) that he is probably best remembered. Modestly, Rains once said of his craft: "I learn my lines and pray to God." He was married six times. He said of Hollywood: "God felt sorry for actors, so he gave them a place in the sun and lots of money. All they had to sacrifice was their talent."
CAUSE: He died of an intestinal haemorrhage in Laconia, New Hampshire, aged 77.

Jane Randolph
(JANE ROEMER)
Born October 30, 1915
Died May 4, 2009
Willowy beauty. Born in Youngstown, Ohio, and raised in Kokomo, Indiana, the daughter of George Roemer, a steel mill designer, Randolph moved to Hollywood in 1939 to study at director Max Reinhardt's acting school. In June 1942 she was the first glamour pin-up in the magazine *Yank*. That year, she made her first film but it was in *Cat People* (1942) that she did her best work. Randolph played Alice Moore, a self-confident Manhattanite, whose flirtation with a married colleague becomes dangerous because of the neurotic behaviour of his wife (Simone Simon). The RKO Radio Pictures film was very successful and earned more than $4 million. (The remake in 1982 was a poor imitation.) She appeared in *Curse Of The Cat People* (1944) but it had little do with the original. One of the last of her 20 films was *Abbott And Costello Meet Frankenstein* (1948), in which she danced with horror actor Bela Lugosi. "He was dressed in full vampire costume, but he moved very well," she later remembered. Her other films included: *Jealousy* (1945) and *Railroaded!* (1947) and she was a human model for the ice-skating sequence with Bambi and Thumper in *Bambi* (1942). Jane Randolph retired in 1948 to marry the wealthy businessman Jaime del Amo.

CAUSE: She died aged 93 in hospital near Gstaad, Switzerland, after breaking her hip.

J. Arthur Rank, 1st Baron Rank of Sutton Scotney
Born December 22, 1888
Died March 29, 1972
British film mogul. The money made by the Rank family didn't originate in films. Their wealth came from a successful flour business. It is ironic that Hull-born Joseph Arthur Rank's name has become rhyming slang for self-abuse, since he was a devout Methodist and it was religious films that got Rank interested in the cinema in the Thirties. In 1933 he founded the Religious Film Society. In 1936 he built Pinewood Film Studios, bought the chain of Odeon cinemas, established a film magazine and opened the Rank Charm School to breed young actresses for the screen. He wanted to rival Hollywood, and for a time it looked as if he would succeed. Films such as *Henry V* (1944), *Brief Encounter* (1945) and *Great Expectations* (1946) were world beaters and the symbol of a semi-naked man bashing a large gong that heralded the start of each Rank film became famous. However, the company expanded too quickly and was only saved from extinction by tight fiscal management. In October 1962 Rank was 'promoted' and became life president. He married Laura Ellen Brooks Marshall on October 18, 1917 (she predeceased him by a year), and had two daughters by her.
CAUSE: He died, aged 83, of a ruptured abdominal aneurysm at Royal Hampshire County Hospital, when his barony became extinct. He left £5,993,323.

Basil Rathbone, MC
Born June 13, 1892
Died July 21, 1967
Forever Sherlock Holmes. To millions of viewers the world over there was only one man who could ever have played Sir Arthur Conan Doyle's

immortal quintessentially English detective – and that man, the aquilined-featured Philip St John Basil Rathbone, was born in Johannesburg, South Africa! The son of Edgar Philip Rathbone (d. June 13, 1924), a mining engineer, the family travelled to England in 1895 to escape the Boers after Rathbone's father was accused of being a British spy. Rathbone was educated at Repton. He worked for the Liverpool, London, and Globe Insurance Company before getting an audition with his cousin Sir Frank Benson's No 2 Company. On April 22, 1911, he made his stage *début* as Hortensio in *The Taming Of The Shrew* at the Theatre Royal, Ipswich. After gaining experience in a succession of small parts, Benson took Rathbone to America with him in October 1913. Rathbone's London *début* came on July 9, 1914 playing Finch in *The Sin Of David* at the Savoy Theatre. During the First World War Rathbone served with the London Scottish as a private before becoming a lieutenant in the Liverpool Scottish. His brother, John, was killed in action. Following demobilisation, he joined the New Shakespeare Company in 1919. After a number of stage successes he went to America in 1923, having made his film *début* two years earlier in *The Fruitful Vine* (1921). He was a tremendous success on Broadway in both modern and Shakespearean roles and also built up a reputation as a baddie on the screen. On September 29, 1926 he opened at the Empire Theatre, New York City as Jacques Virieu in *The Captive*, based on Marcel Proust's novel and the first Broadway play to deal with the subject of lesbianism. His co-stars were Helen Menken, Humphrey Bogart's first wife, Ann Trevor, Winifred Fraser, Minna Phillips, Arthur Wontner, Norman Trevor, Arthur Lewis and Ann Andrews. On February 9, 1927 in a fit of morality the producers and cast were arrested along with the companies of the plays *Sex*, the Mae West vehicle,

and *The Virgin Man*. A plea bargain was arrived at and the producers and cast agreed to drop the play from Broadway in return for no obscenity charges being filed. 6′1½″ Rathbone was furious at what he saw as "a hideous betrayal, this most infamous example of the imposition of political censorship on a democratic society ever known in the history of responsible creative theatre; this cold-blooded unscrupulous sabotage of an important contemporary work of art; this cheap political expedient to gain votes by humiliating and despoiling the right of public opinion to express itself and act upon its considered judgment as respected and respectable citizens". Rathbone's films included: *The Loves Of Mary, Queen Of Scots* (released October 1923), *The Great Deception* (released July 25, 1926) as Rizzio, *The Last Of Mrs Cheyney* (1929) as Lord Arthur Dilling, *The Bishop Murder Case* (released January 3, 1930) as Philo Vance, *A Notorious Affair* (1930) as Paul Gherardi, *The Lady Of Scandal* (1930) as Edward, Duke of Warrington, *One Precious Year* (1933) as Derek Nagel, *After The Ball* (1933) as Jack Harrowby, *Anna Karenina* (released August 30, 1935) as Alexei Karenin, *The Personal History, Adventures, Experience, And Observation Of David Copperfield The Younger* (premièred January 8, 1935) as Mr Murdstone, *The Last Days Of Pompeii* (released October 18, 1935) as Pontius Pilate, *Captain Blood* (premièred December 19, 1935) as Captain Levasseur, *A Tale Of Two Cities* (released December 25, 1935) as Marquis St Evremonde, *Romeo And Juliet* (premièred August 20, 1936) as Tybalt in the only film he won a screen duel and for which he was nominated for a Best Supporting Actor Oscar, *The Garden Of Allah* (released October 15, 1936) as Count Anteoni, *Love From A Stranger* (1937) as Gerald Lovell, *The Adventures Of Marco Polo* (released April 7, 1938) as Ahmed,

The Adventures Of Robin Hood (released May 14, 1938) as Sir Guy of Gisbourne, If I Were King (released September 28, 1938) as King Louis XI for which he received his second Best Supporting Actor Oscar nomination, The Dawn Patrol (1938) as Major Brand, Son Of Frankenstein (released January 13, 1939) as Baron Wolf von Frankenstein, Tower Of London (1939) as Duke of Gloucester, The Mark Of Zorro (premièred November 1, 1940) as Captain Esteban Pasquale, Fingers At The Window (1942) as Cesar Ferrari, alias Dr Santelle, Frenchman's Creek (1944) as Lord Rockingham, Voyage To The Prehistoric Planet (1965) as Professor Hartman, Hillbillys In A Haunted House (1967) as Gregor and Autopsia De Un Fantasma (1967) as Canuto Perez. It was as Sherlock Holmes whom he also played on radio (from October 1939–1946) that Rathbone will be forever associated. The role came to him after meeting either Darryl F. Zanuck or Gene Markey at a party and one of them suggesting his perfection for the part. He played the consulting detective in: The Hound Of The Baskervilles (released March 24, 1939) and received second billing to Richard Greene, The Adventures Of Sherlock Holmes (released September 1, 1939), Sherlock Holmes And The Voice of Terror (released September 18, 1942), Sherlock Holmes And The Secret Weapon (released January 4, 1943), Sherlock Holmes In Washington (released April 30, 1943), Sherlock Holmes Faces Death (released September 17, 1943), Sherlock Holmes And The Spider Woman (released January 21, 1944), The Scarlet Claw (released May 26, 1944), The Pearl Of Death (released August 1, 1944), The House Of Fear (released March 16, 1945), The Woman In Green (released June 15, 1945), Pursuit To Algiers (released October 26, 1945), Terror By Night (released February 1, 1946) and Dressed To Kill (released May 24, 1946). Rathbone tired of playing Holmes – especially when people requested the detective's autograph rather than the actor's. When his Holmes radio and film contracts came up for renewal almost simultaneously Rathbone renewed neither. He relocated to New York hoping for stage success that never really materialised. Rathbone married twice. On October 13, 1914 he married actress Ethel Marion Foreman and their son, Rodion, was born on July 21, 1915. He died in Brooklyn, New York on August 22, 1996. The Rathbones divorced in 1926 and on April 18 of the same year, he married Ouida Bergére (b. Spain, December 14, 1886, d. New York City, 29 November 1974, of complications from a broken hip). In September 1939, they adopted an 8-month-old girl, Cynthia (b. January 1939, d. 1969).

CAUSE: After appearing in his one-man show An Evening With Basil Rathbone on July 20, 1967, Rathbone returned to his New York home at 135 Central Park West. He was tired and upset by the death of a close friend. The next day his doctor examined the actor and gave him a clean bill of health. Rathbone went into his study to listen to a record he had recently bought. After five minutes his wife wanted to ask him something but when she pushed open the door, Rathbone was lying dead on the floor from a heart attack. He was 75.

FURTHER READING: In And Out Of Character: An Autobiography – Basil Rathbone (New York: Doubleday, 1962)

Andrew Ray

(ANDREW OLDEN)
Born May 31, 1939
Died August 20, 2003

Ted Ray's film star son. Andrew Ray was the only male member of his family who was not sensitive about his age. Born in London while his father, the radio and stage comedian Ted Ray, was making his first broadcast, Andrew

Ray became an actor when he was 10 but it was only by chance that he took to the boards. In bed recovering from an attack of mumps, the casting director for 20th Century Fox, Ben Lyon, called his parents to see if Andrew's older brother Robin would be tested for a film part. But Robin was too tall, and Andrew was cast in the role. Andrew left Franklin House prep school in north London at the age of 11. "My education," he said, "really stopped at 10. How can you go back to school and remain unchanged when you've suddenly become a film star?" The film that made him a star was *The Mudlark* (1950) and Ray played Wheeler, an orphan boy who earns a miserable living beachcombing on the lower Thames and sneaks into Windsor Castle. Critics acclaimed the film and Ray's performance. He followed up his success with other films, notably *The Yellow Balloon* (1953), the story of Frankie Palmer, a child who gets mixed up with London gangsters; *Escapade* (1955), about three boys who steal an aeroplane – he played Max Hampden and *Woman In A Dressing Gown* (1957) in which he was Brian Preston. Ted Ray put his son's earnings into a trust fund accessible at 17. When he got his hands on the money Ray went, in his own words, "a bit mad". He bought sports cars and wrote off two in six months in near-fatal crashes. At 19, he became engaged to the Rhodesian-born actress Susan Burnet. His father did not approve but the couple was married in 1959. They had a son and a daughter and although separated in 1970 they never divorced and remained close friends. Ray went to work on Broadway but when he returned to Britain he found that he was no longer an instantly recognisable star. On April 16, 1965, feeling that he was "washed up" at 25, he attempted suicide and was taken unconscious to the Middlesex Hospital. Recovering, he returned to the stage in a West End production of *Howard's End* (1967).

In 1980 he played King George VI in the television serial *Edward And Mrs Simpson*. From 1992 to 1994 he played Dr John Reginald in the drama series *Peak Practice*. At the time of his death he was planning to write a biography of the Ray family.

CAUSE: He died of a heart attack in London (as did his father) at the age of 64.

Gene Anthony Ray

Born May 24, 1962
Died November 14, 2003

Always Leroy. Gene Anthony Ray was born in Harlem, New York, and attended Julia Richmond High School. He lived on West 153rd Street and was 17 when he was cast as Leroy Johnson, the rebellious teen, in Alan Parker's film *Fame* (1980), a role he reprised in the television series of the same name (1982–1984). In fact, Ray actually attended the High School of the Performing Arts where the show and film were set for a year before he was thrown out. His mother, Jean E. Ray, recalled, "It was too disciplined for this wild child of mine." Ray was to claim that he won the role of Leroy with his eyes as much if not more than his dancing skill. "The eyes had as much to do with obtaining the role of Leroy as the dance. A flash from those babies followed by a routine and I had them all hooked." *Fame* choreographer Louis Falco said, "Gene uncovered something inside me that I hadn't witnessed before. He was just incredible. I felt like I was in the same shoes as the person who had maybe seen Fred Astaire for the first time." Leroy was one of the most popular characters in the television series and he received a rapturous reception when he and the other cast members toured the UK in 1982 including a concert at the Royal Albert Hall. Although the girls screamed for Ray, it was the boys that interested him. He ignored warnings to keep his homosexuality secret lest he alienate his fan base. In

1984, he was sacked from the show after his mother was jailed for running a drug ring, and he failed to turn up for work 100 times. "For five months I sat at home in front of the TV and stuffed my face with junk food," he recalled. "Then one day I looked in the mirror and thought, 'Man, you are the fattest pig on Earth.' I couldn't believe it was my reflection. So I bought a new pair of pants in my usual size – 28in waist – and couldn't even get them over my thighs. Man, I was shocked! I ate like a bird on salad and worked out for two months until those pants fitted like a glove." He landed a job dancing with The Weather Girls in their video for 'It's Raining Men'. Despite being newly svelte, he found it impossible to stay off the party circuit and to curb his fondness for drink and drugs. His life fell apart once again and he resorted to sleeping on park benches. His attempts to found a school for the performing arts in Milan flopped and he shared a flat with a porn actress. Back in America, one of his last projects was a documentary that reunited the cast of the TV series (apart from Lori Singer and P.R. Paul). His other films included *Out Of Sync* (1995) which was directed by his *Fame* co-star Debbie Allen and *Eddie* (1996) which starred Whoopi Goldberg. He never married.

CAUSE: Gene Anthony Ray was diagnosed with HIV in 1996. In June 2003, he suffered a stroke and never recovered. He died in Manhattan of the effects of the embolism. He was 41.

Ted Ray

(CHARLES OLDEN)
Born November 21, 1905
Died November 8, 1977
Multi-skilled comic. Born at 110 Great George Street, Wigan, Lancashire, the son of the comedian Charles Olden and Margaret Ellen Kenyon (two previous babies had died in infancy and there was a younger sister, Lena), Ray was educated at Liverpool Collegiate

School and harboured ambitions to be a footballer. He was remarkably secretive about his age, leaving a gap for his birthday in both his *Who's Who* and *Who's Who On Television* entries. His son, Robin, a TV presenter, who was born at 630 Fulham Road, Fulham, London, on September 17, 1934, also suffered from the same reticence, never publicly revealing his birthday. Ray began his entertainment career in the mid-Twenties and was half of the musical duo Wardle and Olden. In 1927 he went solo as Hugh Neek (Unique) and then Nedlo (Olden reversed) the Gypsy Fiddler. Dropping the gypsy character, he added jokes to his act and made his debut in London in 1930. He adopted the name of the British winner of the 1920 American Open golf championship – Ted Ray – as his stage name after an agent refused to represent him if he kept his original name. Ray made his debut at the London Palladium in 1932 and was a hit. He appeared in numerous radio (*Ray's A Laugh*, from 1949 until January 1961, *Calling All Forces*, *Joker's Wild* and *Does The Team Think?*) and television shows and films including *Elstree Calling* (1930), *A Ray Of Sunshine* (1947), *Meet Me Tonight* (1952) as George Pepper, *Escape By Night* (1953) as Mr Weston, *The Crowning Touch* (1957) as Bert, *Please Turn Over* (1959) as Edward Haillday and *Carry On Teacher* (1959) as the headmaster of Maudlin Street School, William Wakefield. Ray was due to star in the next Carry On... film *Carry On Constable* (1960) but the powers-that-be at Associated British for whom Ray had once been under contract but never made a film didn't like his success in *Carry On Teacher* and pressurised ABC Cinemas to threaten to drop the *Carry On* . . . series unless Ray was dropped. He was, to be replaced by Sid James. In 1975 Ray was badly hurt in a car crash and was convicted of dangerous driving while under the influence of alcohol. On July 11, 1933 he married dancer Dorothy Sybil Stevens (b. June 29, 1909) at Croydon register office. She died in November 2002. Ray's other son, Andrew (1939–2003), was also an actor and is noticed above. CAUSE: Ray died of heart failure aged 71 at Highlands Hospital, Enfield, Middlesex. He left £192,199.

Martha Raye
(MARGARET TERESA YVONNE REED)
Born August 27, 1916
Died October 29, 1994
'The Mother Of The Troops'. Born in Butte, Montana, she was celebrated both for her ability to belt out a song and for her brash comedy. She entertained soldiers during Korea and Vietnam and appeared in, among others, *Hideaway Girl* (1936) as Helen Flint, *The Big Broadcast Of 1937* (1936) as Patsy, *College Holiday* (1936) as Daisy Schloggenheimer, *Mountain Music* (1937) as Mary Beamish, *Waikiki Wedding* (1937) as Myrtle Finch, *The Big Broadcast Of 1938* (1938) as Martha Bellows, *The Boys From Syracuse* (1940) as Luce, *Hellzapoppin* (1941) as Betty Johnson, *Navy Blues* (1941) as Lilibelle Bolton, *Four Jills In A Jeep* (1944) as herself, *Monsieur Verdoux* (1947) as Annabella Bonheur, *Billy Rose's Jumbo* (1962) as Lulu and *The Concorde: Airport '79* (1979) as Loretta. To television audiences she was probably best known for playing Rock Hudson's housekeeper, Agatha, on *McMillan And Wife*. Away from the screen, she married seven times, the last one (on September 25, 1991) being to homosexual Mark Harris (b. 1939), and was estranged from her only daughter, Melodye Condos (b. February 22, 1943). Melodye was to later claim that the only reason Martha Raye didn't abort her was because she was terrified of what then-husband Nick Condos might do when he found out.
CAUSE: She died aged 78 after a long illness in Los Angeles, California.

Ronald Reagan
Born February 6, 1911
Died June 5, 2004
The acting president. If Ronald Reagan had not made the decision to go into politics (as a Democrat), he would be remembered, if at all, as a poor B-movie actor who was acted off the screen by a chimpanzee in *Bedtime For Bonzo* (1951) in which he played Professor Peter Boyd. Born, weighing 10lb, in a five-room rented flat above a bakery on Main Street, Tampico, Illinois, Ronald Wilson Reagan was the second son of John Edward 'Jack' Reagan (b. Fulton, Illinois, July 13, 1883, d. West Hollywood, California, May 18, 1941), an alcoholic shoe salesman, and his wife Nelle Clyde Wilson (b. Fulton, Illinois, July 24, 1885, d. Santa Monica, California, July 25, 1962) whom he married in a Roman Catholic ceremony at the Church of the Immaculate Conception in Fulton, Illinois on November 8, 1904. Reagan was nicknamed 'Dutch' by his father because Jack Reagan thought his son looked like "a fat little Dutchman". On June 21, 1922 Reagan and his brother, Neil known as Moon, were baptised at the Christian Church at 123 Hennepin Avenue, Dixon. He was educated at Filas Willard School (February 1916–1918), Central School, Monmouth (1918–1919), Tampico Grade School (1919– December 1920), South Central Grammar School (December 1920–1923), South Dixon High School (1923–1927), North Dixon High School (1927–1928) and Eureka College, Illinois from September 1928 until he obtained a BA in sociology and economics on June 7, 1932. During the summers from 1926 until 1933 he worked as a lifeguard at Lowell Park riverside beach near Dixon, Illinois and saved 77 people from drowning. One man he rescued gave Reagan a $10 tip for retrieving his false teeth from the riverbed. The town put up a plaque in his honour. Later that year he began

work as a sports announcer on the wireless station WOC. On March 15, 1937 he had a screen test with Warner Bros and read from Philip Barry's play *Holiday*, which Katharine Hepburn had also used for her tryout with RKO five years earlier. On April 20, 1937 he signed a seven-year contract at a salary of $200 a week to commence from June 1 and made his début in *Love Is On The Air* (opened on November 12, 1937) as Andy McLeod, a newsreader with a conscience. Reagan got the part because Ross Alexander, the actor originally cast, shot himself. (The story of Ross Alexander is elsewhere in this book.) The film began shooting on June 7, 1937 with a budget of $119,000. Filming took three weeks and the film-makers quickly learned that Reagan could not find the marks on the studio floor to see where he should stand. Twenty years later, he had the same problem and on election day 1980 he refused to speak to reporters until he had positioned himself squarely on the marked "RR" on the ground. In the 1940 film *Knute Rockne – All American*, in which he played the terminally ill George Gipp and beat off John Wayne, Robert Young and a host of others for the part, he uttered the words, "Someday, when things are tough maybe you can ask the boys to go out there and win just once for the Gipper", a phrase that he was to utilise in the White House. In 1941 Warner Bros announced that Reagan was getting more fan mail than any of their other stars apart from Errol Flynn. In the film *King's Row* (1942) he played Drake McHugh, the victim of a sadistic surgeon who amputated his legs. When he awoke, legless, he cried out, "Where's the rest of me?" Bette Davis called it "the only passable performance Ronald Reagan ever gave". Then the Second World War intervened. On April 14, 1942 he joined the army as a second lieutenant of cavalry but never saw active service because of poor eyesight. Before his

demob with the rank of captain on December 9, 1945 he spent three years making training films. In 1946 Reagan signed a seven-year contract with Warner Bros worth $2,500 a week (it lapsed on January 28, 1952) and became active in politics, having joined the board of the Screen Actors' Guild (SAG) in July 1941. On November 17, 1947 he became SAG's president and held the position for five terms until November 1952 when he was elected to a three-year term on the board. Further three-year terms followed in November 1955 and November 1958. In November 1959 he was again elected president, a position he held until his resignation on June 6, 1960. On July 9, 1960 he resigned from the SAG board. In 1947 he was a friendly witness before the House Un-American Activities Committee. During the Forties Reagan was an FBI informant, code-named T-10, and gave up the names of actors he believed were Communists or had Communist sympathies. Reagan referred to himself as "the Errol Flynn of B pictures" and his work included: *Sergeant Murphy* (1937) as Private Dennis Riley, *Swing Your Lady* (1938) as Jack Miller, *Accidents Will Happen* (1938) as Eric Gregg, *Cowboy From Brooklyn* (1938) as Pat Dunn, a radio announcer in *The Amazing Dr Clitterhouse* (1938), *Boy Meets Girl* (1938), *Girls On Probation* (1938) as Neil Dillon, *Brother Rat* (1938) as Dan Crawford, *Going Places* (1938) as Jack Withering, *Secret Service Of The Air* (1939) as Lieutenant 'Brass' Bancroft, *Dark Victory* (1939) as Alec Hamm, *Code Of The Secret Service* (1939) as Lieutenant 'Brass' Bancroft, *Naughty But Nice* (1939) as Eddie Clark, *Hell's Kitchen* (1939) as Jim Donohue, *The Angels Wash Their Faces* (1939) as Deputy District Attorney Pat Remson, *Smashing The Money Ring* (1939) as Lieutenant 'Brass' Bancroft, *Brother Rat And A Baby* (1940) as Dan Crawford, *An Angel From Texas* (1940) as Marty Allen, *Murder In The Air*

(1940) as Lieutenant 'Brass' Bancroft, *Tugboat Annie Sails Again* (1940) as Eddie Kent, *Santa Fe Trail* (1940) as George Armstrong Custer, *The Bad Man* (1941) as Gil Jones, *Million Dollar Baby* (1941) as Pete Rowan, *International Squadron* (1941) as Jimmy Grant, *Nine Lives Are Not Enough* (1941) as Matt Sawyer, *Juke Girl* (1942) as Steve Talbot, *Desperate Journey* (1942) as Flying Officer Johnny Hammond, the Irving Berlin written and produced *This Is The Army* (1943) as Johnny Jones, *For God And Country* (1943) as Father Michael O'Keefe, *Stallion Road* (1947) as Larry Hanrahan, *That Hagen Girl* (1947) as Tom Bates opposite Shirley Temple in her first adult role, *The Voice Of The Turtle* (1947) as Sergeant Bill Page, *Night Unto Night* (1948) as John Galen, *John Loves Mary* (1949) as John Lawrence, *The Girl From Jones Beach* (1949) as Bob Randolph, *The Hasty Heart* (1949) as Yank, *Louisa* (1950) as Hal Norton, *Storm Warning* (1951) as Burt Rainey, *The Last Outpost* (1951) as Captain Vance Britten, *Hong Kong* (1952) as Jeff Williams, *The Winning Team* (1952) as Grover Cleveland Alexander, *She's Working Her Way Through College* (1952) as Professor John Palmer, *Tropic Zone* (1953) as Dan McCloud, *Law And Order* (1953) as Frame Johnson, *Prisoner Of War* (1954) as Webb Sloane, *Law And Order* (1954), *Cattle Queen Of Montana* (1954) as Farrell, a cowpoke in *Tennessee's Partner* (1955), *Hellcats Of The Navy* (1957) as Commander Casey Abbott and *The Killers* (1964) as Jack Browning. In 1948 he campaigned for Harry S Truman but gradually moved to the right and in 1962 switched allegiance to the Republicans. In 1964 he campaigned for the arch-conservative Senator Barry Goldwater (1909–1998) against incumbent President Lyndon Baines Johnson (1908–1973) but was on the losing side as the Texan won in a landslide on November 3, 1964 – 538

electoral college votes to 52. From 1965 until 1966 Reagan was host of the television series *Death Valley Days* and in 1965 published his autobiography *Where's The Rest Of Me?* On January 4, 1966 Reagan announced his candidature for the governorship of California promising to cut taxes and spending. He won the gubernatorial contest on November 8, 1966 beating the popular and experienced Democrat Pat Brown (1905–1996). Reagan was sworn in a few minutes past midnight on January 2, 1967. Jack Warner is said to have remarked, "All wrong. Jimmy Stewart for governor, Reagan for best friend." Four years later, on January 4, 1971, he was sworn in for a second term having defeated Jesse Unruh. In 1968 and 1976 Reagan tried for the Republican nomination for the presidency but lost to Richard Nixon (Reagan came third with just 182 votes) and Gerald Ford (Reagan was only narrowly defeated – 1,187 votes to 1,070). Undeterred Reagan stood again in 1980 and was adopted on July 16, 1980 in Detroit. The campaign was clumsy and many people registered anti-votes rather than actively voting for a candidate. Reagan spoke of renewing ties with Taiwan while his vice presidential nominee George Bush was in Peking trying to cultivate good relations. Reagan blamed trees not cars for the smog that crippled Los Angeles. At a later meeting one wag tied a sign to a tree that read, "Chop me down before I kill again". He claimed that air pollution was under control only for his plane to be diverted a few days later because LAX was closed due to smog. On November 13, 1979 Reagan appeared on television and told interviewer Tom Brokaw that, even at 68, he would be younger than many of the leaders he would be dealing with. Brokaw mentioned Valery Giscard d'Estaing, then French president and 15 years Reagan's junior. "Who?" said Reagan. Brokaw repeated the name and Reagan admitted that yes he was a bit older than the Frenchman. Reporters were amazed at Reagan's ignorance but his press secretary replied that the candidate had not heard Brokaw. Reporter Lou Cannon suggested, "We could run a correction. The good news is that Ronald Reagan knows who the president of France is. The bad news is that he can't hear." Reagan's flack said, "We'd rather you say he was too ignorant than too old." Reagan's people stole President Jimmy Carter's briefing book. Amazingly, the public didn't seem to mind that Reagan constantly engaged mouth before brain and on November 4, 1980 he beat President Carter in a landslide, winning 489 electoral college votes to 49. When he left the Pacific Palisades polling booth Reagan was asked who he voted for and replied, "Nancy." Reagan was inaugurated on January 20, 1981 at 11.57am and gave a 20-minute speech calling for "an era of national renewal". As he finished the speech the Iranian government released the 52 American hostages that had been captured in Teheran on November 4, 1979 during the Carter presidency. It is believed that a deal was done so that the hostages would be released during Reagan's term of office despite the efforts of President Carter. The Reagan inauguration cost $8 milllion, the most expensive ever at that time. Reagan's presidency was an exceptionally right wing one. On March 6, 1981 Reagan held his second press conference and the first in history in which the questioners' names were chosen from a jellybean jar. The event was boycotted by many of the major networks and the idea was quickly abandoned. Reagan was the first divorcé to occupy 1600 Pennsylvania Avenue; the first president to have been born in Illinois; the first to have been head of a union; the first to address a meeting of the combined Houses of Parliament (on June 6, 1982) and the oldest president at 69 years, 349 days. At 2.35pm on March 30, 1981, his seventieth day in

office, after addressing the American Enterprise Institute at the Washington Hilton hotel, Reagan became the eighth president to be the subject of an assassination attempt while in office. The would-be assassin was John Warnock Hinckley, Jr (b. Ardmore, Oklahoma, May 29, 1955), a mentally disturbed man, who thought that by shooting the president he could win the affections of the actor Jodie Foster. Reagan survived the attempt and left hospital on April 11, 1981. As he was wheeled into the operating theatre he is said to have asked if all the medical staff were Republicans. On discharge he said, "If I had got this much attention in Hollywood, I would never have left." The Academy Awards were postponed for 24 hours because of the shooting. On June 21, 1982 Hinckley was acquitted on the grounds of insanity but sent to St Elizabeth's Hospital, an asylum. On December 22, 1981 Reagan authorised the distribution of 30 million lbs of surplus cheese to the poor. Officials admitted that the cheese was more than a year old and was in a "critical inventory situation" – in other words it was mouldy. On March 1, 1982 a member of Reagan's own party – Senator Bob Packwood from Oregon – criticised the president for passing off entirely fictional anecdotes as if they were real events. On December 12, 1983, addressing a meeting of the Congressional Medal of Honor Society, he told a story of airborne heroism in the Second World War that resulted in the posthumous award of a Congressional Medal of Honor. A search among all 434 recipients during the war failed to trace Reagan's story and a journalist reported that the tale was very similar to one that appeared in the 1944 film *Wing And A Prayer* and also the April 1944 issue of *Reader's Digest*. President Carter commented, "President Reagan doesn't always check the facts before he makes statements and the press accepts this as kind of amusing." On April 5, 1982 Reagan refused to back the UK task force as it sailed for the Falkland Islands to retake the dependency from the Argentine invaders. "We're friends of both sides," he said. Ten days later, he told an audience that "England was always very proud of the fact that the police did not have to carry guns . . . In England if a criminal carried a gun, even though he didn't use it, he was tried not for burglary or theft or whatever he was doing, he was tried for first-degree murder and hung if he was found guilty." The next day Larry Speakes, the White House press secretary, admitted that the president was talking rubbish. Incredibly, Reagan repeated the fiction on March 21, 1986. On May 27, 1983, the night before a world economic summit in Williamsburg, Reagan eschewed his briefing notes and instead watched *The Sound Of Music* on television. On June 29, 1983 Reagan blamed poor student grades on the schools' efforts to comply with racial desegregation. He sought to destabilise governments he disagreed with and broke the law by sending aid to the Nicaraguan contras, rebels who were attempting to overthrow the government of Sandanista. Reagan clashed with the Senate which disagreed with his policy. On March 1, 1985 Reagan called the contra leaders the "moral equivalent of our founding fathers" only to be rebuffed by historical novelist Howard Fast who said the comment was "an explosion of such incredible ignorance that . . . he is not fit for public office of any kind". Reagan despatched $155 million of aid – food and guns – to the contras. He denied that secret funds were being sent: "Nothing of that kind could take place without the knowledge of Congress." He sent aid to the Afghans fighting the Soviet troops and invaded Grenada on October 25, 1983 without informing the head of state (the Queen, by the way). Reagan claimed that it was "a rescue mission"

rather than an invasion. Despite all this he was re-elected on November 6, 1984 in yet another landslide, winning 525 electoral college votes to the Democrat Walter Mondale's paltry 13. It was the biggest number of electoral college votes ever won. When some Democrats drew attention to Reagan's age, he came up with a nice response on October 21, 1984: "I will not make age an issue of this campaign. I'm not going to exploit for political purposes my opponent's youth and inexperience." Reagan's second inauguration, on January 20, 1985, took place in the foyer of the White House because it was too cold outside for the president. The inaugural parade was also cancelled, only the second time ever in history. Andrew Jackson's in 1833 was the first. On April 18, 1985 Reagan visited the Bitburg concentration camp and appalled many by claiming that the German guards "were victims, just as surely as the victims in the camps". On November 13, 1986 Reagan admitted that his administration had been secretly selling arms to Iran in exchange for freeing the hostages. This arms-for-hostages contravened Reagan's public declaration of never dealing with hostages. Later that month it emerged that the Iranians had been overcharged for the weapons and the profits – between $10 and $30 million – had been sent to the contras by members of the National Security Council. Reagan claimed not to know about the deals. A commission led by Senator John Tower was set up to investigate the misdemeanours. It discovered that Lieutenant-Colonel Oliver North had been leading a shadow government from inside the NSC and Reagan was heavily criticised. When Rear Admiral John Poindexter, head of the NSC, testified before the Iran-Contra hearings on July 15, 1987 he said that he had made the decisions to send the money and kept Reagan in the dark. However, he added that *if* Reagan had known, which of course, he didn't, he would have approved. In five days of testimony, Poindexter said, "I can't recall" or variations thereof 184 times. During his candidature Reagan promised to resign at the first sign of senility but on February 20, 1987 he told the Tower Commission that he did not remember if he had authorised material shipments. (For more examples of Reagan's "forgetfulness" see below.) Later when questioned by reporters Reagan on two occasions pretended to be unable to speak due to laryngitis. Despite claiming to save money, Reagan spent more on military expansion during peacetime than at any other time in American history. The country spent $148 million in 1980 and under Reagan more than $300 million. Incredibly, Reagan believed that money spent on the armed forces did not add to the national deficit because it employed companies who hired American labourers who then "paid" the money back in taxes. During Reagan's presidency the national debt soared (as indeed it did during the presidency of George W. Bush. President Clinton balanced the budget). He also sponsored tax cuts for the wealthiest in society. Following his retirement Reagan moved into a house at 666 St Cloud Road, Bel Air, bought for them by grateful friends. Superstitious Nancy Reagan changed the number to 668 in April 1987 before their move but city ordnance plans continued to refer to it as 666. Reagan was married twice. On January 24, 1940 at the Wee Kirk o'Heather wedding chapel in Glendale, California, Reagan married the actor Jane Wyman by whom he had a daughter Maureen (b. Los Angeles, California, January 4, 1941, d. Granite Bay, California, August 8, 2001 of cancer) and an adopted son, Michael (b. March 14, 1945). A second daughter died the day after her premature birth at the Queen of Angels hospital in Los Angeles on June 24,

1947. Reagan and Wyman separated in May 1948 and divorced on June 28, 1948 becoming final on July 19, 1949 after nine years and 176 days of marriage. Reagan refused to discuss the break-up but Wyman said that it was due to his increasing political ambitions and her failure to show interest in them. On March 4, 1952 at the Little Brown Church in Los Angeles he married the actor Nancy Davis (b. Sloane Hospital, New York, July 6, 1921 as Anne Frances Robbins) who was pregnant at the time with their daughter. Patricia Ann Reagan who would adopt the professional name Patti Davis was born at the Cedars of Lebanon Hospital in Los Angeles on October 21, 1952 weighing 7lb. She would later embarrass her parents by writing *Home Front* (published February 1986), a novel about a heartless mother and a staid father who happens to be president, and posing for full-frontal nude shots for *Playboy*. Nancy Reagan suffered two miscarriages between 1953 and 1957. A son, Ronald Prescott Reagan (b. Cedars of Lebanon Hospital, Los Angeles, California, May 20, 1958 at 8.04am weighing 8lb 8oz), worked for several years as a ballet dancer with the Joffrey Ballet until he left on January 17, 1983.

CAUSE: It is believed that 6'1" Reagan was diagnosed with the degenerative Alzheimer's disease while he was still in office but that the diagnosis was covered up until November 1994. Indeed his forgetfulness became legendary. At the White House on September 23, 1981 he introduced the boxer Sugar Ray Leonard and his wife as "Sugar Ray and Mrs Ray". On August 17, 1982 he called President Samuel K. Doe of Liberia "Chairman Moe". On October 9, 1982 during a sound check for his weekly radio address, he called the Polish government "a bunch of no-good lousy bums". Two days later addressing a meeting in Texas, he said, "You can't drink yourself sober, you can't spend yourself rich, and you can't pump the prime without priming the pump. You know something? I said that backwards . . . You can't prime the pump without pumping the prime . . ." On December 1, 1982 he proposed a toast to Brazilian president "João Figueiredo and the people of Bolivia". On January 14, 1983 he called his chief arms negotiator Paul H. Nitze "Ed Nitze". On January 20, 1984 he constantly referred to environmentalist William Ruckelshaus as "Don" until his chief of staff told him to stop. On April 10, 1984 he called Secretary of Agriculture John Block "John Black". On May 8, 1985 he failed to recognise Portuguese Prime Minister Maria Soares, whom he had met previously, and walked right past him. On October 8, 1985 he welcomed the President of Singapore Lee Kuan Yew and his wife Mrs Lee to the White House with the words, "It gives me great pleasure to welcome Prime Minister Lee Kuan Yew and Mrs Yew to Singapore." He mistook one of his own cabinet for an out of town mayor and on November 9, 1985, when the Prince and Princess of Wales dined at the White House, Reagan called them the "Prince of Wales and his lovely lady Princess David". On October 22, 1986 he signed his tax reform bill "Reagan Ronald" and explained, "I was in a hurry." Campaigning for Oklahoma Senator Don Nickles, on October 24, 1986, Reagan called him "Don Rickles" and five days later referred to Republican Party Chairman Jennifer Dunn as "Dunn Jennifer". On March 27, 1987 he greeted Denis Healey, then deputy Labour leader, with the words "Nice to see you, Mr Ambassador" while the real diplomat stood nearby. On October 22, 1987 he called George Schultz his Secretary of State "the Secretary General". During his time in office Reagan had 15 polyps removed from his colon, cancerous growths excised from his nose, and minor

prostate surgery on January 4, 1987. Reagan died at 1.09pm aged 93 at his home in Bel Air, California, from complications caused by pneumonia. His wife and son Ron and daughter Patti were at his bedside. Son Michael arrived shortly afterwards. Reagan was the longest-lived American president, beating John Adams (90) and Herbert Hoover (also 90). Reagan was also the first president to survive the dreaded Zero Factor – every American president who was elected in a year ending in zero since 1840 had died in office: William Henry Harrison (1840, died of pneumonia 32 days after taking office), Abraham Lincoln (1860, assassinated), James A. Garfield (1880, assassinated 199 days after taking office), William McKinley (1900, assassinated), Warren Harding (1920, died of apoplexy, pneumonia, high blood pressure and coronary enlargement), Franklin D. Roosevelt (1940, cerebral haemorrhage) and John F. Kennedy (1960, assassinated). FURTHER READING: *Reagan* – Lou Cannon (New York: Putnam, 1982); *Early Reagan* – Anne Edwards (London: Hodder & Stoughton, 1987); *On The Outside Looking In* – Michael Reagan with Joe Hyams (New York: Zebra Books, 1988); *Facts About The Presidents* – Joseph Nathan Kane (New York: H.W. Wilson, 1989); *First Father, First Daughter* – Maureen Reagan (New York: Little, Brown, 1989); *The Complete Book Of US Presidents* – William A. DeGregorio (New York: Gramercy Books, 2002).

Sir Michael Redgrave

Born March 20, 1908
Died March 21, 1985
Actor with a double life. Michael Scudamore Redgrave had an inauspicious start to life. He never knew his father who was a bigamist and promiscuous womaniser who married three times. His mother was an alcoholic. Michael was born in theatrical lodgings above a tobacconist

at Horfield Road, St Michael's Mount, Bristol, the son of actors George Ellsworthy 'Roy' Redgrave (b. London, January 11, 1873, d. Sydney, Australia, May 25, 1922) and his second wife, Daisy Bertha Scudamore (b. Portsmouth, 1880, d. October 5, 1958). His first stage appearance came in July 1921 in a walk-on part in *Henry IV, Part 2*. Redgrave was educated at Clifton College (beginning in 1922) where his love of acting quickly became evident and he appeared in both male and female roles (including Lady Macbeth in June 1925). In 1927 he went up to Magdalene College, Cambridge, where he acted and wrote for the university magazine. He also lost his virginity (to a woman) and had affairs with men. He got a job teaching modern languages at Cranleigh School, Surrey, and also worked semi-professionally in the Guildford Repertory Company. 6'3" and strikingly handsome, Redgrave resigned from Cranleigh and successfully auditioned for Lilian Baylis at the Old Vic, taking home £3 per week. However, before he accepted, he also tried out for the Liverpool Playhouse and that's where he spent 1934–1936. At the Royal Naval College Chapel, Dartmouth, on July 18, 1935, he married the actress Rachel Kempson and by her had three enormously successful children. Vanessa, CBE (1967), was born in London on January 30, 1937, during the afternoon matinee of a run of *Hamlet* where Redgrave was playing Laertes and having an affair with his much older co-star, Edith Evans. In 1941, and again later, he had an affair with Noël Coward. Vanessa went on to marry the film director Cecil Antonio 'Tony' Richardson and have a son, Carlo (b. 1969), out of wedlock by actor Franco Nero (b. Italy, November 23, 1941), whose birth was announced in *The Times*. Vanessa's younger siblings were Corin (after the character in *As You Like It*) William (b. Clifton

Hill, St John's Wood, London, July 16, 1939) and Lynn Rachel (b. London Clinic, London, March 8, 1943). Both Vanessa and Corin became leading lights in the Socialist Workers' Revolutionary Party after discovering their middle-class father was, in fact, a secret bisexual. (Oddly, Redgrave's entry in *The Dictionary Of National Biography 1981–1985* totally omits any mention of this most important facet of his life.) Their mother found solace in an affair with the actor-director Glencairn Alexander Byam Shaw, CBE (b. December 13, 1904, d. Goring-on-Thames, April 29, 1986) who was himself bisexual (he had had an affair with Siegfried Sassoon) and was married to the actress Angela Baddeley. In 1936 Redgrave made his film début in *Secret Agent* playing an army captain. He appeared in *A Stolen Life* (1939) as Alan MacKenzie opposite Elisabeth Bergner, *The Stars Look Down* (1939) as Davey Fenwick, *Lady In Distress* (1939) as Peter, *Climbing High* (1939) as Nicky Brooke and *Kipps* (1941) as Arthur Kipps before he was called up in June 1941. Discharged on medical grounds a year later, he resumed his stage and film careers appearing in, among others: *Thunder Rock* (1942) as David Charleston, *The Way To The Stars* (1945) as Flight Lieutenant David Archdale, *Fame Is The Spur* (1946) as Hamer Radshaw, *Mourning Becomes Electra* (1947) as Orin Mannon for which he was nominated for an Oscar, *The Magic Box* (1951) as Mr Lege, Anthony Asquith's *The Browning Version* (1951) as Andrew Crocker-Harris, *The Importance Of Being Earnest* (1952) as Jack (née Ernest) Worthing, *The Dam Busters* (1954) as Dr Barnes Wallis, *1984* (1956) as General O'Connor, *The Quiet American* (1958) as Thomas Fowler, *No My Darling Daughter* (1961) as Sir Matthew Carr, *Uncle Vanya* (1963) as Vanya, *The Heroes Of Telemark* (1965) as Uncle, *Battle Of Britain* (1969) as Air Vice Marshal Evill,

Goodbye, Mr Chips (1969) as the Headmaster, Nicholas And Alexandra (1971) as Sazonov and Rime Of The Ancient Mariner (1976) as The Ancient Mariner. Redgrave worked occasionally with his talented family. He appeared with his wife in Jeannie (1941) as Stanley Smith, The Captive Heart (1946) and The Sea Shall Not Have Them (1954) as Air Commodore Waltby. He appeared with his son on television in David Copperfield (1969), his daughter Vanessa in Behind The Mask (1958) and with Corin and Vanessa in Oh! What A Lovely War (1969) as General Sir Henry Wilson. He was directed by his son-in-law Tony Richardson in The Loneliness Of The Long Distance Runner (1962) in which he played the governor of the borstal. Towards the end of his life, Redgrave suffered from Parkinson's disease but still continued acting as best he could. For his performance in John Mortimer's autobiographical A Voyage Round My Father at the Haymarket Theatre, Redgrave was fitted with an ear piece linked to a microphone through which his lines were fed to him. This worked well at first until the frequency on which the lines were broadcast was interrupted by a taxi firm relaying details of fares to their drivers. CAUSE: Redgrave died the day after his 77th birthday in a nursing home in Denham, Buckinghamshire, from Parkinson's disease with Corin by his side. He was cremated at Mortlake Crematorium. He left £111,244. FURTHER READING: In My Mind's Eye – Michael Redgrave (London: Coronet, 1984); Secret Dreams: A Biography Of Michael Redgrave – Alan Strachan (London: Weidenfeld & Nicolson, 2004).

Sir Carol Reed

Born December 30, 1906
Died April 25, 1976
Dedicated technocrat. Born in Wandsworth, south London, the illegitimate son of actor-manager Sir Herbert Beerbohm Tree (b. 2 Pembridge Villas, Kensington, London, January 28, 1852, d. 1 All Souls' Place, Portland Place, London W1, July 2, 1917) and (Beatrice) May Pinney (b. Ramsgate, Kent, May 23, 1871) who had taken the name Reed by deed poll two years before her son's birth. Upon leaving school Reed travelled to America, where he learned about chicken farming. Back in England he came under the wing of Dame Sybil Thorndike and then worked as Basil Dean's assistant director on Autumn Crocus (1934) before making his own directorial début with Midshipman Easy (1935) and then Laburnum Grove (1936). His reputation was made with Bank Holiday (1938) and A Girl Must Live (1939). He also worked on Night Train To Munich (1940) and Kipps (1941). His apotheosis came in the late Forties with James Mason's IRA man on the run in Odd Man Out (1947), Graham Greene's The Fallen Idol (1948), for which both Greene and Reed were nominated for Oscars, and Greene's thriller The Third Man (1949), for which Reed was again nominated for an Oscar. His output declined in the Fifties, his most prominent films being A Kid For Two Farthings (1955) and Our Man In Havana (1959). His most commercially successful feature came towards the end of the Sixties. Oliver! (1968) won Reed an Oscar for Best Director and picked up four other gongs, including Best Picture, and four other nominations. It also co-starred his rambunctious nephew, Oliver. The director would make only two more films subsequently. Considering his background, which he kept secret until his death (he listed neither parent in Who's Who), it was not surprising that he rarely gave interviews and shunned publicity. He was married on two occasions. His first wife was beautiful blonde actress Diana Wynyard (b. Forest Hill, London, January 16, 1906, as Dorothy Isabel Cox, d. London, May 13, 1964) whom he

married in 1943 and divorced four years later. In 1948 he married actress Penelope 'Pempey' Dudley Ward (b. 1919, d. 1982), the former daughter-in-law of Fay Compton. There was a son from this marriage, which ended only with his death. Penelope's daughter by her first marriage to Anthony Pelissier, Tracy (b. 1942), married actor Edward Fox at Haywards Heath Registry Office, Sussex in October 1959. Reed also had an affair with novelist Daphne Du Maurier. CAUSE: He died in London, aged 69. He left £10,113.

Donna Reed

(DONNA BELLE MULLENGER)
Born January 27, 1921
Died January 14, 1986
Steady wife or girlfriend. Born on a farm in Denison, Iowa, Donna Reed wanted to be a great secretary and nothing more, but then she was given a screen test by MGM and made her début in *The Get-Away* (1941) as Maria Theresa O'Reilly. Her career developed with her portraying reliable women, so it came as something of a shock when she won an Oscar for playing a prostitute, Alma, in *From Here To Eternity* (1953). In 1951 she joined Columbia hoping to escape from her stereotyped roles but to no avail. On September 24, 1958, *The Donna Reed Show* began on ABC and for the next eight years she played a wholesome reliable wife on television. In 1984 she joined the cast of *Dallas* as Miss Ellie to replace the ailing Barbara Bel Geddes, but was replaced after one season when Geddes became well enough to resume her role. Reed was married three times. CAUSE: She died in Beverly Hills, California, from pancreatic cancer. She was a little short of her 65th birthday. Her family blamed the illness on her disappointment at being sacked from *Dallas*. She had launched a lawsuit against the producers who paid her off with $1 million.

Oliver Reed

Born February 13, 1938
Died May 2, 1999
Hell-raiser extraordinaire. Born in Wimbledon, the middle of three sons (David, b. 1936, and the sports commentator Simon, b. Sutton, Surrey, August 5, 1947) and nephew of film director Sir Carol Reed, Robert Oliver Reed made his film début in *The League Of Gentlemen* (1959) playing a flamboyant homosexual. In April 1964 Reed's career almost came to an end in a London nightclub. He was in the gents of The Crazy Elephant in Jermyn Street when he was bottled by two men he had upset. The cuts on his face needed 38 stitches. Although he was England's biggest film star in the Sixties, when many other big names made the move across the Atlantic, the agnostic and dyslexic Reed never became an international star because he refused to live in America. He was in love with his house, the 63-bedroomed Broome Hall, which he had bought for £85,000. He appeared in, among others, *The Bulldog Breed* (1960), *The Rebel* (1961), *The Pirates Of Blood River* (1962) as Brocaire, *The Crimson Blade* (1963) as Captain Tom Sylvester, *Paranoiac* (1963) as Simon Ashby, *The Brigand Of Kandahar* (1965) as Ali Khan, *The Jokers* (1966) as David Tremayne, *I'll Never Forget What's 'Is Name* (1967) as Andrew Quint, *Oliver!* (1968) as the villainous Bill Sikes and *Women In Love* (1969) as Gerald Crich, in which he wrestled naked with an equally unclothed Alan Bates. Both men were reticent to perform in the scene, worrying about how they would 'measure up' to each other. One night they went to a pub and got drunk and then went to the toilets together, where they cautiously eyed each other up. Upon seeing that they were of virtually equal dimensions, they agreed to do the scene. Reed's other films included *The Assassination Bureau* (1969) as Ivan Dragomiloff, the title role in *Hannibal Brooks* (1969),

Take A Girl Like You (1970) as Patrick Standish, *The Devils* (1971) as Urbain Grandier, *Blue Blood* (1973) as Tom, *Days Of Fury* (1973) as Palizyn, *The Three Musketeers* (1973) as Athos, *And Then There Were None* (1974) as Hugh Lombard, *The Four Musketeers* (1974) as Athos, *Lisztomania* (1975), *Tommy* (1975) as Frank Hobbs, *Royal Flash* (1975) as Otto von Bismarck, *Ransom* (1977) as Nick McCormick, *Tomorrow Never Comes* (1978) as Jim Wilson, *The Big Sleep* (1978) as Eddie Mars, *Venom* (1982) as Dave, *Fanny Hill* (1983) as Mr Widdlecome, *The House Of Usher* (1988) as Roderick Usher, *The Return Of The Musketeers* (1989) as Athos, *Funny Bones* (1995) as Dolly Hopkins and *Gladiator* (2000) as Proximo. Reed became legendary in show business folklore for his drinking. On January 27, 1991, he was booked to appear on the Channel 4 chat show *After Dark*, an open-ended discussion that went out late on Saturday nights and ended when the participants or producer got fed up and went home. The subject under discussion was feminism and before and during the show Reed had imbibed too deeply and too often. He took umbrage at the views expressed by feminist lesbian Kate Millett. Reed grabbed Millett and planted an unwanted smacker on her cheek before walking off the set. Ollie Reed was married twice. His first wife, on January 1, 1961, at Kensington Registry Office, was model Kate Byrne. She was only 19 and forged her father's signature on the wedding licence. They had one son, Mark. He had a daughter, Sarah, by Jacquie Daryl and on September 7, 1985, he married Josephine Burge, whom he had begun dating when she was just 16. They remained devoted to each other until his death.

CAUSE: He died aged 61 from a heart attack in Valletta, Malta, after a lengthy drinking session. He was buried in Churchtown, County Cork, Eire, 50 yards from his local pub. Very few celebrities attended the service. Film director Michael Winner cried even though he hadn't shed tears at either his mother or father's interments.

FURTHER READING: *Reed All About Me* – Oliver Reed (London: W.H. Allen, 1979).

Robert Reed

(JOHN ROBERT RIETZ)
Born October 19, 1932
Died May 12, 1992
All-American father. Here's the story of a handsome fellow, trying to come to terms with his sexuality; he played the doting father but that for him wasn't reality. To millions of Americans Robert Reed *was* the perfect dad. His role as architect Michael Paul Brady in the television series *The Brady Bunch* and subsequent spin-off films saw him idolised. Yet Reed wasn't happy with the show and had numerous arguments with its creator, Sherwood Schwartz. The disagreements would usually end with Reed storming off and drowning his sorrows in a local bar. He later admitted: "I should have tried to get out of the show, rather than inflict my views on [the cast]." Born in Highland Park, Illinois, he moved to Muskogee, Oklahoma, when he was six and became interested in drama at secondary school. By the age of 17 he was working for his local radio station. He attended Northwestern University and RADA. Shortly before coming to London, he married Marilyn Rosenberg and had a daughter, Karen (b. 1957). The marriage ended in 1959 because of Reed's homosexuality. He was extremely closeted and his fellow cast members professed shock when it was revealed he was gay. Back in America, he studied method acting and appeared in several Shakespearean plays and television shows. His big break came in 1959 playing a lawyer on *Father Knows Best*. As well as playing Mike Brady he also played Lieutenant Adam Tobias in the TV

show *Mannix*. Reed's other films included: *The Hunters* (1958), *Bloodlust* (1959), *Star!* (1968) and *The Maltese Bippy* (1969). Unlike many actors, Reed never legally changed his name: "I think of vanilla pudding or tapioca when I think of Reed," he once said.

CAUSE: Reed died aged 59 of colon lymphoma in Huntington Memorial Hospital, 100 West California, Pasadena, California. He was also infected with the AIDS virus. His corpse was cremated and his ashes buried in Memorial Park Cemetery, Skokie, Illinois.

Walter Reed

(WALTER REED SMITH)
Born March 16, 1916
Died August 20, 2001
Smooth heavy. Born in Fort Ward, on Bainbridge Island, Washington, he was the son of an army officer. As such the family often moved to keep up with the father's posting and they went first to Honolulu then Los Angeles where he attended the notorious Beverly Hills High School. He began making films – the first of his more than 150 – in the late Twenties with *Redskin* (1929), a silent picture that starred Richard Dix and Jane Novak. He later recalled, "Jane was the prettiest girl I ever saw, big eyes and the sweetest smile. I knew that if working in movies meant meeting women like Jane I was going to have a darn good time." In March 1932, he took $20 and hitched to the East Coast where he appeared in off-Broadway shows and in repertory. It was the day that he met Joel McCrea at the Santa Monica Beach Club that changed his career. He began working as McCrea's stand-in during the day while treading the boards at night. One day McCrea and his wife, Frances Dee, went backstage to congratulate Reed, much to the amazement of other members of the cast. Ten days after their initial meeting Reed was signed to RKO. He was cast as a juvenile lead in

many films such as *Mexican Spitfire's Elephant* (1942) and *Mexican Spitfire's Blessed Event* (1943) as Dennis Lindsay, opposite the unbalanced Lupe Velez. The Second World War intervened and he served in the army. Back home in civvy street and married (1946) to Peggy Shaw (one son, two daughters) he returned to Hollywood but became a second lead. "I started out as leading man then I came back from the service, looked in the mirror and decided to become a second man. They don't pay as much, but you last longer. I enjoyed character work." He appeared in *Banjo* (1947), *Fighter Squadron* (1948), *The Torch* (1948), *Captain China* (1949) and *Young Man With A Horn* (1949). The advent of regular television in the Fifties also opened up a new front for him and he appeared in early episodes of *Superman, Dragnet* and *The Lone Ranger*. He also began to get lots of fan mail, all of which received a personal reply. "It was a full-time job, but one that was rewarding and on occasion quite touching." For much of the Fifties and Sixties Reed worked on a horse or wearing a stetson, often with John Ford. He retired in 1968 after making *The Destructors* because of heart problems. He took the occasional role but spent his time dealing in real estate. On July 14, 2001, his home town of Santa Cruz declared a Walter Reed Day. He said at the time, "If I hadn't gone to RKO I'm told by friends that I could have been a matinée idol. That's as maybe. I liked riding horses, getting all dirty and enjoyed being a part of Hollywood."

CAUSE: He died aged 85 in Santa Cruz, California, of kidney failure.

Christopher Reeve

Born September 25, 1952
Died October 10, 2004
Tragic Superman. Christopher Reeve was the all-American cinematic hero – tall, handsome, a talented sportsman and then it all went horribly wrong. In

May 1995, Reeve had planned to fly to Dublin to appear in an adaption of Robert Louis Stevenson's *Kidnapped*, but at the last minute he decided to compete in a three-day event at Culpeper, Virginia. On May 27 after the initial dressage competition, he and his horse Buck were placed fourth out of 27, and Reeve thought that they could win. In the cross-country, at the comparatively straightforward third fence, Buck began to jump gracefully and then suddenly stopped. Reeve was thrown forward and landed headfirst on the top rail of the jump. He broke his neck and was paralysed from the neck down and confined to an electric wheelchair, which he operated by blowing through a straw. His subsequent determination not to give up and to walk again inspired millions and he was even mentioned in the 2004 US Presidential debates between Senator John Kerry and President George W. Bush. Reeve announced that he hoped to stand on his own two feet by the age of 50 and he spent £270,000 a year on his treatment. He founded the Christopher Reeve Paralysis Foundation, which funds research and hands out grants to individuals; he wrote a best-selling autobiography and even resumed his screen career, both as an actor and a director. Reeve was born in Manhattan, New York, the elder son of the novelist, poet and academic Franklin D. Reeve and the journalist Barbara Johnson. His parents split up when he was four, and his mother moved with Reeve and his brother, Benjamin (b. 1953), to Princeton, New Jersey, where she married a banker. The children grew up in an intellectually rarefied atmosphere and continued to spend much time with their father and his circle of friends, who included the poet Robert Frost. Reeve's interest in acting began when he attended the Princeton Day School. Aged nine, he had a small role in a professional production of Gilbert &

Sullivan's *The Yeoman Of The Guard*. He also excelled at sport, playing goalminder for the school's ice hockey team. He made a decision that would affect the rest of his life and concentrated on acting rather than sport. In his gap year he starred with Celeste Holm in a touring production of *The Irregular Verb To Love*. At Cornell University he studied English and music theory and continued to act. He spent a semester in London helping actors with American accents. He then enrolled in Juilliard School in New York where he studied under John Houseman. To fund his education 6'4" Reeve took the role of Ben Harper in the daytime soap *Love Of Life* in 1974 and played the role for two years. In 1976 Reeve made his Broadway début as Nicky, the doting grandson in Enid Bagnold's *A Matter Of Gravity*, with Katharine Hepburn, and his film début in a small role in *Gray Lady Down*, a naval adventure that starred Charlton Heston. In 1977 he auditioned for two jobs – one was for a washing powder advertisement. The other was for a film called *Superman*. The producers seriously considered 200 actors and gave screen tests to 10 before casting Reeve. To ensure that he looked the part of the Man of Steel Reeve worked in the gym with Dave Prowse, the bodybuilder who played Darth Vader in *Star Wars*, and put on 30lbs of muscle. The movie went vastly over budget, costing a reputed $40 million to make, but it eventually grossed $250 million. It also made Reeve an overnight star. His characterisation was, he said, based on Cary Grant. *Superman* was the top movie in North America in 1979, and the sequel *Superman II* was beaten only by *Raiders Of The Lost Ark* two years later. Two more sequels followed in 1983 and 1987, he directed and co-wrote the last one. In 1980 he played Richard Collier in *Somewhere In Time*, a quirky romance about a Chicago playwright who falls in love with a woman in an old painting and wills himself back in time to meet her. Two years later he starred as Clifford Anderson, a psychopathic homosexual, in Sidney Lumet's *Deathtrap* with Michael Caine. Audiences were probably shocked to see Reeve kissing another man on the lips. Caine later revealed, "I said to Chris, 'If you open your mouth I will kill you.'" In *Monsignor* (1982) he played Father Flaherty, a priest who flirts with the Mafia. Neither made much impact on audiences or critics. In 1984 he played Basil Ransome in the Merchant Ivory adaptation of Henry James' *The Bostonians* (1984), in a cast that included Vanessa Redgrave and Jessica Tandy. Other films included: *Street Smart* (1987), *Switching Channels* (1988), *The Remains Of The Day* (1993), *Speechless* (1994) as Bob 'Bagdad' Freed and *Village Of The Damned* (1995) as Dr Alan Chaffee. Reeve was said to have turned down starring roles in *The Bounty* (1984), *The Running Man* (1987) and *Total Recall* (1990). In a twist of irony worthy of Hollywood, in one of his last roles before his accident he played Dempsey Cain, a paralysed policeman in the cable TV movie *Above Suspicion* (1995). In 1998 he returned to acting in a television remake of the Alfred Hitchcock classic *Rear Window*, in which the hero is confined to a wheelchair. Reeve appeared before a Senate subcommittee and spoke in favour of federal funding for stem-cell research. He also directed two television movies on health-related themes. *In The Gloaming* (1997) was about a man dying of AIDS, and *The Brooke Ellison Story* was the true account of an 11-year-old girl who is almost killed in a car crash, survives as a quadriplegic and goes on to become an honours graduate at Harvard. While filming *Superman* Reeve met and fell in love with Gae Exton (b. 1952), a British models' agent. They had a son Matthew (b. 1979) and a daughter Alexandra (b. 1982). They split

after ten years in January 1987. In Williamstown in April 1992 he married the seven months pregnant Dana Morosini (b. Teaneck, New Jersey, March 17, 1961, d. Manhattan, New York, March 6, 2006, of lung cancer), whom he had met on June 30, 1987 in Williamstown, at a nightclub where Morosini was singing. They had one son, Will (b. North Adams, Massachusetts June 7, 1992, weighing 6 lb 14 oz). Reeve also led a bisexual life in New York and would reward his male lovers with a signed photograph as a memento.

CAUSE: Reeve died of a heart attack after a pressure sore caused an infection that affected his heart in Northern Westchester Hospital, Mount Kisco, New York aged 52.

George Reeves
(GEORGE BREWER)
Born January 5, 1914
Died June 16, 1959
The Original Man of Steel. Long before Christopher Reeve took to wearing his underpants on the outside, Superman was played by George Reeves, a burly ex-boxer and wrestler who appeared in *Gone With The Wind* (opened on December 15, 1939). *The Adventures Of Superman* was one of the most popular programmes on television in Fifties America. Reeves had been born in Woolstock, Iowa. His career was interrupted by the Second World War. At the cessation of hostilities he found that he had lost momentum. Major roles were still going to the established stars like Clark Gable and Humphrey Bogart while the newer upstarts like Gregory Peck and Burt Lancaster hogged the romantic leads. Reeves was reduced to appearing in children's serials and playing opposite starlets during their screen tests. Although his friends knew Reeves was bitterly disappointed at being passed over for stardom, never once was he unprofessional and always did his best to put the starlets at ease for their big

chance. In 1951 the producers of the *Superman* TV series began casting around for a new actor to don the mantle. The current incumbent, Kirk Alyn, wanted to do serious work on the New York stage and also wanted more money than the producers were prepared to pay. In late 1951 6'2" Reeves was sent along to audition by his agent. He had been preceded by more than 200 hopefuls but as soon as producer Robert Maxwell and director Tommy Carr saw Reeves they knew their search was at an end. Not only did Reeves look the part he was a good actor to boot. Despite Reeves' muscular physique it was necessary to pad his costume with foam muscles. Over the next six years, Reeves played the title role in 104 episodes of the serial. To keep costs down each episode was shot in just two-and-a-half days. To escape continuity problems the characters wore the same costume in every scene. Off-set Reeves hated making personal appearances. He would always sign his real name for autograph hunters, never 'Superman' which must have been rather confusing for the young fans. One incident required all of his tact and patience. A boy pointed his father's Luger pistol at Reeves because he wanted a souvenir bullet that had been flattened by the Man of Steel's mighty chest. Reeves told the boy that although he obviously would survive others nearby might be hurt by the ricocheting slug. Reeves had no illusions about his work but if he felt anger he relied upon his wide circle of friends to remind him of his good fortune. His good fortune was being seen by more people in a week than most actors in a year. His financial remuneration from the series was $2,500 per week for the thirteen weeks the show was in production. However, he was paid no money for the other 39 weeks of the year and, thanks to Ronald Reagan, then president of the Screen Actors' Guild, the cast earned no residuals. In 1949 Reeves had started an affair with Toni Mannix, the wife of the all-powerful MGM studio executive Eddie Mannix. He knew about his wife's relationship with Superman but did nothing to stop it. The affair progressed until 1958 when Reeves met and fell for Leonore Lemmon. Thanks to Toni Mannix's largesse, Reeves spent money whenever he felt like it making his home, 1579 Benedict Canyon Road, a regular drop-in for all sorts of characters. Reeves was sensible enough to make sure his hell-raising lifestyle was kept a secret from the ladies and gentlemen of the fourth estate. His career depended upon it. An arrest would have seen the series cancelled quicker than a producer could say charge sheet. However, Reeves' drinking became more and more serious with the result that the crew would take lunch very late in the afternoon and then allow Reeves to sleep off the booze. During one off-season, Reeves appeared in the hit movie *From Here To Eternity* (opened August 5, 1953) which won Best Supporting Academy Awards for Frank Sinatra and Donna Reed. However, Reeves' role was pared to virtually nothing when test audiences wondered aloud what Superman was doing in Hawaii. Following the cancellation of *The Adventures Of Superman* Reeves turned down the chance to star in a series about that square-jawed all-American hero Dick Tracy. He also rejected the opportunity of a nationwide tour on which, dressed as Superman, he would have sparred with boxer Archie Moore. The tour would have garnered Reeves $20,000 for just six weeks' work. Like many actors Reeves wanted to direct and had been behind the camera for the last three episodes of *The Adventures Of Superman*. He had also bought the rights to two scripts, intending to direct and star in both himself. In May 1959 he was offered a feature role in a film to be made in Spain. Despite stories to the contrary Reeves could not have been happier and to add to his joy the producers of *The Adventures Of Superman* approached him about reprising his role, a job Reeves was happy to accept. Moreover, he was engaged to Leonore Lemmon and the happy couple was due to marry on 19 June 1959.

CAUSE: Three days beforehand, Reeves retired early only for his front doorbell to ring. According to the story that did the rounds at the time and for many years subsequently his fiancée answered the door to two friends, Carol von Ronkel and William Bliss. Reeves got up and went downstairs where he shouted at his chums to go away. A short while afterwards, he apologised for his uncharacteristic outburst and invited them in. The pals sat and chatted for a while until Reeves went upstairs. The talk continued until Lemmon suddenly said, "He's going to shoot himself." The other friends were puzzled, especially when they heard a drawer slide open. "He's opening it to get a gun," explained the future Mrs Reeves. Within seconds a shot rang out and William Bliss raced up the stairs to find a naked Reeves with blood oozing from his left temple. The official autopsy listed the cause of death as suicide although Reeves' mother discounted this, having received a telephone call from the actor three days before his death in which she described his mood as "splendid". Some of his colleagues also refused to believe the coroner's verdict. Two unexplained bullet holes were discovered and there were some unexplained bruises on Reeves' head. His mother hired the famous Hollywood lawyer Jerry Giesler to look into her son's death, refusing to allow his cremation for three years. Was George Reeves' death suicide? Was it a mistake, a dreadful blunder? Or, was it something far more sinister? It would take almost 40 years for the full truth to come to light. In October 1996 the truth was finally revealed. Hell hath no fury like a woman scorned

and Toni Mannix did not take the end of the affair lying down. Reeves began to receive silent telephone calls at all hours of the day and night. He eventually invested in one of Los Angeles' first telephone answering machines, a large cumbersome device, to intercept the calls. On April 9, 1959 Reeves was involved in a car crash that could have killed him. Mysteriously, the brake lines on his Jaguar had been cut. Two months later, on June 12, 1959, Toni Mannix decided to kill what she loved. Her husband had a number of associates who were criminals or had underworld links. He kept their numbers under a glass lid on his desk. Toni went to the desk and retrieved a piece of paper and rang the number on it. Almost immediately, she regretted what she had done but there was no way to call off the hit. She knew that Reeves kept a Luger next to his bed because she had given him the weapon. The gunman was to quietly break in and shoot Reeves using his own weapon. If the gun could not be found, then the mission was to be abandoned. In her befuddled state Mannix believed that the world would accept that Reeves had killed himself if his own gun was the weapon used, or that Leonore Lemmon had done the foul deed. The hitman found Reeves' Luger but Superman did not go to his grave quietly. There was a struggle (hence the bruises) and a shot was fired (one of the mysterious bullet holes) before Reeves was overpowered and murdered. In June 1989, six months before her death, Leonore Lemmon, who had become a prostitute to support herself, told a journalist what really happened on the fateful night. Carol von Ronkel did not arrive with William Bliss. She was already at the residence because she was in bed with the houseguest Bobby Condon, with whom she was having an affair. Bliss arrived alone because Lemmon had switched on the porch light, usually a sign that drinks were being served. As

they spoke on the porch the gunman slipped in through the back door and shot Reeves. Lemmon joked, "That's just George shooting himself." Bliss ran up the stairs to discover Reeves' corpse. The commotion awakened the lovers and they came downstairs. With the help of madam Polly Adler, a friend of Condon, Carol von Ronkel was taken home and Lemmon's friend, Gwen Dailey, came over. When the police arrived Dailey pretended to be Carol von Ronkel. Lawyer Jerry Giesler was warned off the case by various interested parties and he warned Reeves' mother, Helen Bessolo, to drop the case. He died on January 1, 1962, some believe a mob murder victim. Eddie Mannix succumbed to his poor health on August 27, 1963. Toni Mannix died many years later, a sad recluse. Leonore Lemmon died on New Year's Day 1990. Truth will out, although for nearly 40 years the world believed that TV's Superman had killed himself.
FURTHER READING: *Hollywood Kryptonite* – Sam Kashner & Nancy Schoenberger (New York: St Martin's Paperbacks, 1996).

Beryl Reid, OBE

Born June 17, 1919
Died October 13, 1996
Comedic foil. Hereford-born Beryl Reid was probably best known on television for her numerous appearances on comedies and dramas. After working as a shop assistant in Manchester, she began her showbiz career on stage in 1936 but it was playing naughty schoolgirl Monica on the radio show *Educating Archie* (1952–1956) that made her famous. Her first West End appearance came in April 1951 in revue but she also showed her dramatic side, playing the lesbian radio actress June Buckridge in *The Killing Of Sister George* on stage in London and New York and in the 1968 film. Her first film was the 1940 George Formby comedy *Spare A*

Copper and that was followed by, among others, *The Belles Of St Trinian's* as Miss Dawn, *Two Way Stretch* (1960), *Inspector Clouseau* (1968), *Star!* (1968), *The Assassination Bureau* (1969), *Entertaining Mr Sloane* (1970), *No Sex Please, We're British* (1973), *Joseph Andrews* (1977) and *Carry On Emmanuelle* (1978) as Mrs Valentine. She won a BAFTA Best Actress award for her portrayal of Connie Sachs in *Smiley's People* (1982). She was married and divorced twice.
CAUSE: She died of severe osteoarthritis and kidney failure at the Thames Valley Nuffield Hospital, Wrexham, Buckinghamshire. She was 77. She left £420,219.

Wally Reid

Born April 15, 1891
Died January 18, 1923
Tragic heartthrob. Born in St Louis, Missouri, William Wallace Reid was the son of actor Hal Reid (b. 1860, d. May 22, 1920) and began acting at the age of four. Reid grew up to be a tall, exceptionally handsome man. His film début occurred in *The Phoenix* (1910) for the Selig Company. In 1913 he married actress Dorothy Davenport (b. 1895, d. August 17, 1977) but he was constantly surrounded by women who, ignoring his marital status, flung themselves at him. One day he found six girls hidden in his garage. Another flew 3,000 miles from New York and bribed his dresser $10,000 to let her hide in Reid's dressing room. By 1922 he was at the height of his popularity. He was also at the height of a drug addiction that was gradually killing him. Paramount found themselves between the proverbial rock and hard place. Reid earned them an absolute fortune but his drug habit was spiralling out of control. It began in 1920 while on location in New York for *Forever* (1921). He fell and hurt his head on a rock. The pain was excruciating and Reid was given

morphine shots to ease his agony. Shooting continued. Away from his family for the first time, he fell into a ceaseless round of partying. His input of alcohol was more than Prohibition Era bootleg suppliers could keep up with. To overcome exhaustion on the set, Reid turned to morphine. There is strong evidence that the authorities were aware of Reid's addiction and that his drugs were being delivered to him first class via the United States Postal Service. In 1922, in a desperate bid to break his habit, Reid went cold turkey. In fact, at the same time a secret enclave of movie executives met to discuss the drugs and sex scandals that were dogging the industry – actors, actresses and moguls. When Wally Reid came off drugs he fell into a deep depression. One day in early November 1922, Reid collapsed on the set. Finally, the public learned what was an open secret in Hollywood; Mrs Reid went public by telling the press about her husband's drug problems. The public was furious but when the police tried to investigate the studios they found their efforts blocked by strong political pressure. The moguls had leaned on friendly politicians fearing disclosures would fan the fires of scandal and ruin Hollywood as the movie capital of the world.

CAUSE: Wally Reid died aged 31 in a Los Angeles asylum from heroin addiction. He was buried in Forest Lawn-Memorial Parks, 1712 South Glendale Avenue, Glendale, California 91209. "Before he dozed into the sleep from which he never awakened," Dorothy Reid said, "Wally wanted the entire world to know he had won his fight against the drug habit. He died a martyr to prove he could kick the habit. Even though he is dead, I pray that his passing will accomplish a great purpose in helping to stamp out the horrors of narcotic peddling." Almost 80 years later, things in Hollywood haven't changed.

Karel Reisz

Born July 21, 1926
Died November 25, 2002

Sixties revolutionary. Born in Octava, Czechoslovakia, the son of a Jewish lawyer who died in Auschwitz along with his wife, Reisz came to England from Prague aged 12 as a refugee from the persecution of Jews in his Nazi-occupied country. He was educated at Leighton Park School, Reading, and then after seeing service in the Czech Royal Air Force during the Second World War he read chemistry at Emmanuel College, Cambridge, and taught for two years in a north London school. He wrote for the magazine *Sequence* along with Gavin Lambert and Lindsay Anderson and all were highly critical of the British film industry. From *Sequence* was born the Free Cinema movement, whose leading lights were Reisz, Anderson and Tony Richardson. The principal ideas of Free Cinema were that film directors should have the opportunities for personal expression; and that films should reflect the problems and issues of contemporary life. Reisz became a leading light in the rebirth of the British cinema that occurred in the early Sixties. His film *Saturday Night And Sunday Morning* (1960), an adaptation of Alan Sillitoe's novel of Midlands working-class life, starred Albert Finney as Arthur Seaton, a young factory worker, and was lauded by the critics. But not everyone was as accepting. Warwickshire County Council banned the film because of the (now tame) bedroom scenes but the production company refused to cut them. The film led to many of its ilk, such as *A Taste Of Honey* (1961) and *A Kind Of Loving* (1962). Reisz was a thorough worker and his films were planned meticulously. He preferred not to work on a film at all unless he could bring his sharp eye for detail to bear. Due entirely to this his output was less than prolific and he made only eight feature films over the next 30 years, the most popular being *Isadora* (1968) and *The French Lieutenant's Woman* (1981). In the Nineties Reisz became a successful stage director. In 1953 Reisz married Julia and was divorced ten years later, after three sons. In that same year he married the actress Betsy Blair (b. New York, December 11, 1923).

CAUSE: Reisz died in London from a blood disorder. He was 76.

Lee Remick

Born December 14, 1935
Died July 2, 1991

Horrific gentility. Born into wealth in Quincy, Massachusetts, Remick studied ballet and modern dance and appeared on stage and in television for a number of years before making her first film, *A Face In The Crowd*, as Betty Lou Fleckum, in 1957. She quickly revealed her versatility, appearing in everything from comedy to horror films and all genres in-between. Her films included: *Anatomy Of A Murder* (1959) as Laura Manion, *Wild River* (1960) as Carol Garth Baldwin, *Sanctuary* (1961) as Temple Drake, *Experiment In Terror* (1962) as Kelly Sherwood, *Days Of Wine And Roses* (1962) as Kirsten Arnesen Clay, for which she was nominated for an Oscar, *The Wheeler Dealers* (1963) as Molly Thatcher, *The Hallelujah Trail* (1965) as Cora Templeton Massingale, *No Way To Treat A Lady* (1968) as Kate Palmer, *Loot* (1970) as Fay and *The Omen* (1976) as Katherine Thorn. In 1970 she moved to Britain and appeared on television in the title role in *Jennie: Lady Randolph Churchill* (1975). Back in America, she became a regular in TV mini-series.

CAUSE: She died of kidney and lung cancer aged 55 at her Brentwood home, 570 North Bundy Drive, at 5.15pm on July 2, 1991. Remick was cremated at Westwood Memorial Park.

Brad Renfro

Born July 25, 1982
Died January 15, 2008

Junkie waster. Born in Knoxville, Tennessee, Bradley Barron Renfro was discovered, aged 10, by Joel Schumacher who cast him in his film *The Client* (1994) as Mark Sway opposite Susan Sarandon and Tommy Lee Jones. He impressed in *The Cure* (1995) as Erik and played Huckleberry Finn in *Tom And Huck* (1995). He was named *Hollywood Reporter*'s Young Star of the Year in 1995. His other films included *Sleepers* (1996), *Apt Pupil* (1998), *Deuces Wild* (2002) and *The Jacket* (2005). His offscreen antics kept him in the public eye. In June 1998 he was arrested in Knoxville after police found cocaine and marijuana in his trousers and socks. He plea-bargained to avoid prison. In August 2000 he and a friend tried to steal a 45-foot yacht in Florida. In court, 5ft 8″ Renfro was sentenced to two years' probation and ordered to pay more than $4,000 in damages to repair the yacht and the dock it had been moored to. On May 16, 2001, on probation, he was arrested for underage drinking. In March 2002 he was ordered to attend rehab. On December 23, 2005 he was arrested in downtown Los Angeles while trying to buy heroin. He was jailed for ten days in May 2006 for drunk driving and attempted heroin possession.

CAUSE: Renfro was found dead of a heroin overdose at a Los Angeles apartment. He was 25.

Jean Renoir

Born September 15, 1894
Died February 12, 1979

Poetic director. The son of famed painter Auguste Renoir, he was born in Paris and early on developed a passion for the cinema. He formed his own production company and directed his first film before he turned 30 – *La Fille De L'Eau* (1924). Eight years later, his

Boudu Sauvé Des Eaux (1932) was hailed as a comedy masterpiece. With *Le Crime De Monsieur Lange* (1936) he proved that he could direct political films but his *magnum opus* was *La Grande Illusion* (1937). His next most spectacular work, *La Règle Du Jeu* (1939), flopped when it was released but gained respect in later years. In the Forties he travelled to America and was put under contract at 20th Century Fox, but his films usually flopped, apart from *The Southerner* (1944) which earned him an Oscar nomination, and he was unable to recreate his Gallic glory.
CAUSE: He died in Beverly Hills, California, aged 84, from Parkinson's disease.

Tommy Rettig

Born December 10, 1941
Died February 15, 1996
Little boy lost. Born in Jackson Heights, New York, Thomas Noel Rettig was just five when he appeared in the stage version of *Annie Get Your Gun*, earning $60 a week. He made his film début playing Richard Widmark's son in *Panic In The Streets* (1950) and was signed to 20th Century Fox, where he appeared in *The 5,000 Fingers Of Dr T* (1953) and with Marilyn Monroe in *River Of No Return* (1954). That year he played Jeff Miller in the TV series *Lassie*, for which he was paid $500 a week, rising to $2,500 a week in the last season. When the series ended his work began to dry up and Rettig tried his hand at photography, tool salesman and managing a health club. He moved to California with his wife (Darlene Portwood, whom he had married in 1959 when she was just 15) and began to grow marijuana. In 1972 the 5'5" Rettig was arrested once again for growing marijuana, and sentenced to two years' probation but it wasn't a deterrent. Three years later, he was sentenced to five years for smuggling cocaine but the charge was later dropped on appeal. In 1976 he was divorced. He was arrested on drugs charges again in 1980.
CAUSE: Rettig died aged 54 in Marina Del Rey, apparently from natural causes.

Natasha Richardson

Born May 11, 1963
Died March 18, 2009
Heiress. Born in London, the daughter of Tony Richardson (see below) and Vanessa Redgrave, the sister of Joely Kim Richardson, the niece of Lynn Redgrave and of Corin Redgrave, the cousin of Jemma Redgrave and granddaughter of Sir Michael Redgrave and Rachel Kempson (who are both noticed in this book). Natasha Jane Richardson was educated at St Paul's Girls School, in London, and trained at the Central School of Speech and Drama. She made her first appearance in a film when she was just four, playing a bridesmaid at the wedding of her mother's character in *The Charge Of The Light Brigade* (1968), directed by her father. Her first real job was in an outdoor production of *A Midsummer Night's Dream*. 5'9" Richardson believed that she was not taken seriously in Britain because of her family connections and relocated to America. "I know the pressures of being the daughter of a great actress," she said four years before her death. "But it's inspiring. You learn so much that other people don't get to learn until later on. My father being a director, I [learned] a real work ethic. You think, 'One day, I'd like to be as good as that.' But when I was starting out professionally, I had a level of attention put on me that I didn't deserve or wasn't ready for. And it was hard, particularly in England, to make my way." In 1984 she met Liam Neeson on the set of the TV series *Ellis Island*. Ten years later, she left first husband Robert Fox for Neeson. In 1986 she played Mary Shelley in Ken Russell's *Gothic*. Following her move to America, in 1988 she played kidnapped

heiress Patty Hearst in Paul Schrader's film of that name. Two years later, she worked with Schrader again on *The Comfort Of Strangers* (1990) opposite Rupert Everett, a psychological drama written by Harold Pinter from a novel by Ian McEwan. The same year, she starred in *The Handmaid's Tale*, an adaptation of the novel by Margaret Atwood. In 1993 she appeared in two television films *Suddenly, Last Summer* in which she played Catherine Holly, the role played by Elizabeth Taylor in the original movie and the lunatic Zelda Fitzgerald in *Zelda*. Her later films included: *The Parent Trap* (1998) opposite Lindsay Lohan and Dennis Quaid, *Maid In Manhattan* (2002) with Jennifer Lopez, *Asylum* (2005), *The White Countess* (2005) opposite her mother and aunt, *Evening* (2007) and *Wild Child* (2008). She married Harrow-educated impresario Robert Fox (b. March 25, 1953) on December 15, 1990. Divorced on June 30, 1992, she married actor Liam Neeson (b. Ballymena, Northern Ireland, June 7, 1952) on July 3, 1994 and by him had two sons, Michael Richard Antonio (b. June 22, 1995) and Daniel Jack (b. August 27, 1996). During the marriage, Neeson had a facelift, which left him with a very unnatural looking physiognomy.
CAUSE: Richardson was taking a skiing lesson at the luxury Canadian resort of Mont Tremblant on March 16, 2009 when she fell on a "green" slope, suitable for novices in an area known as The Flats. She got to her feet and refused to see a doctor, even signing a medical form saying she did not need help. An hour later, she began to experience severe headaches and was taken to hospital. She was given emergency treatment at the Centre Hospitalier Laurentien, nearby, and was then transferred to Montreal's Sacre Coeur Hospital. From there she flew to New York and was admitted to the Lenox Hill Hospital, where she was put on a life support machine. She

died two days later from epidural haematoma. Her corpse was taken to her home near upstate Millbrook, New York where her grandmother had died in 2003. Richardson was buried at St Peter's Cemetery in Lithgow, New York.

Sir Ralph Richardson
Born December 19, 1902
Died October 10, 1983
Eccentric mummer. Ralph David Richardson was, by his own admission, "a mummy's boy". His parents separated when he was four and he was raised by his mother in Shoreham, Sussex, in a home made out of two disused railway carriages. (Trivia note: Profumo scandalite Christine Keeler also grew up in a converted railway carriage.) Richardson was born in Langsyne, Tivoli Road, Cheltenham, Gloucestershire, and intended to join the priesthood but ran away from the seminary. He joined the Liverpool & Victoria Insurance Company but left when an inheritance enabled him to enrol in an art college where, to his disappointment, he found he had no aptitude for art. After considering journalism for a while, he decided an actor's life was for him. At Hampstead Register Office on September 18, 1924, he married actress Muriel Bathia 'Kit' Hewitt (b. September 9, 1907, d. Sussex, October 4, 1942). He made his London stage début on July 10, 1926 playing the stranger in *Oedipus In Colonus*. In 1929 Kit Richardson fell victim to encephalitis lethargica. It left her in great pain and virtually crippled. Kit almost certainly died by her own hand by self-strangulation. She had spoken of suicide but the coroner recorded a verdict of "death by misadventure". Richardson had made his film début in *Friday The Thirteenth* (1933) as Horace Dawes and went on to appear in *Java Head* (1934) as William Ammidon, *Bulldog Jack* (1934) as Morelle, *The Return Of Bulldog Drummond* (1934) as Major Hugh

'Bulldog' Drummond, *The Man Who Could Work Miracles* (1937) as Colonel Winstanley, *South Riding* (1938) as Robert Carne, *The Divorce Of Lady X* (1938) as Lord Mere, *Q Planes* (1939) as Major Charles Hammond, *The Four Feathers* (1939) as Captain John Durrance, *The Lion Has Wings* (1939) as Wing Commander Richardson, *Anna Karenina* (1948) as Alexei Karenin, *The Fallen Idol* (1948) as Baines, *The Heiress* (1949) as Dr Austin Sloper, for which he was nominated for an Oscar, *Home At Seven* (1952) as David Preston, *Outcast Of The Islands* (1952) as Captain Lingard, *The Holly And The Ivy* (1952) as Reverend Martin Gregory, *Richard III* (1954) as Henry Stafford, Duke of Buckingham, *Oscar Wilde* (1959) as Sir Edward Carson, *Exodus* (1960) as General Sutherland, *Our Man In Havana* (1960) as 'C', *Long Day's Journey Into Night* (1962) as James Tyrone Sr, *Woman Of Straw* (1964) as Charles Richmond, *Doctor Zhivago* (1965) as Alexander Gromeko, *Battle Of Britain* (1969) as Sir David Kelly, *Oh! What A Lovely War* (1969) as Sir Edward Grey, *Lady Caroline Lamb* (1972) as King George III, *O Lucky Man!* (1973) as Monty/Sir James Burgess, *Time Bandits* (1981) as the Supreme Being/God, *Dragonslayer* (1981) as Ulrich, *Greystoke: The Legend Of Tarzan, Lord Of The Apes* (1984) as 6th Earl of Greystoke, for which he was nominated for an Oscar and *Give My Regards To Broad Street* (1984) as Jim. During the war he served with the Royal Naval Volunteer Reserve. He married for the second time on January 26, 1944, at Chelsea Register Office. The new Mrs Richardson was actress Meriel Forbes (b. London, September 13, 1913, d. April 7, 2000) by whom he had one son, Charles (b. London, January 1, 1945 dec.). Richardson was a regular in the theatre and casting him in *Macbeth* must have seemed a good idea at the time. However, Richardson had the utmost difficulty choreographing his

moves in time with his lines. He finally conquered his inability by saying out loud the lines "One, two, clash your swords, three, four, round we go." Unfortunately, on the opening night he spoke the line out loud, much to the amusement of the audience. Always eccentric, he was still riding his motorcycle into his seventies and had a penchant for pet parrots. He summed up his own profession rather well: "Actors never retire. They just get offered fewer parts", adding, "The art of acting lies in keeping people from coughing."

CAUSE: Richardson died, aged 80, in Marylebone, London, from a stroke and was buried in Highgate Cemetery, north London. He left £1,291,468.
FURTHER READING: *Ralph Richardson: An Actor's Life* – Garry O'Connor (London: Coronet, 1983).

Tony Richardson

Born June 5, 1928
Died November 14, 1991
Vanessa's gay ex. Born in Shipley, Yorkshire, and educated at Wadham College, Oxford, Cecil Antonio Richardson was a member of the Oxford University Debating Society before joining the Royal Court Theatre. On the screen he conjoined with Karel Reisz to form the Free Cinema group. On April 29, 1962 at Hammersmith, London, he married Vanessa Redgrave and fathered two daughters: Natasha Jane (see above) (b. London, May 11, 1963) who was formerly married to Harrow-educated impresario Robert Fox (b. March 25, 1953) and was subsequently wed to the actor Liam Neeson (b. Ballymena, Northern Ireland, June 7, 1952); and Joely Kim (b. London, January 11, 1965). Richardson and Redgrave were divorced on April 28, 1967 supposedly because of his adultery with Jeanne Moreau. The films Richardson directed included: *Look Back In Anger* (1958), *The Entertainer* (1960), *A Taste Of Honey* (1961) which he also wrote and

produced, *Sanctuary* (1961), *The Loneliness Of The Long Distance Runner* (1962) which he also produced, *Tom Jones* (1963) which he also produced and won Oscars for both disciplines, *The Charge Of The Light Brigade* (1968), *Hamlet* (1969) which he also wrote, *Ned Kelly* (1970) which he also wrote, *A Delicate Balance* (1973), *Joseph Andrews* (1977) which he also wrote, *The Hotel New Hampshire* (1984) which he also wrote and *Blue Sky* (1994) which was delayed for legal reasons. He produced *Saturday Night And Sunday Morning* (1960). Richardson directed seven actors to Oscar nominations – Diane Cilento, Dame Edith Evans, Albert Finney, Laurence Olivier, Joyce Redman and Jessica Lange, although only Lange triumphed. From the early Seventies until his death Richardson lived with Grizelda Jane Grimond, the only daughter of the former Liberal Party leader Jo Grimond. They had one daughter, Katherine (b. 1973). Sir Robert Stephens said of Richardson, "He convinced me (wrongly, of course) that anyone can make a movie. All Tony Richardson did was come in and ask his cameraman what he should do . . . He was a useless unpleasant creature."
CAUSE: Bisexual, Richardson was critical of Liberace for covering up his homosexuality and the fact that he had AIDS. "Interesting that Liberace, who created the phrase, 'I cried all the way to the bank,' chose to lie all the way to his grave," he said. Yet Richardson also kept secret both his sexuality and his own infection with HIV. Tony Richardson died of a neurological condition brought on by AIDS in Los Angeles, California, aged 63. Novelist Anthony Burgess commented: "I'm sorry . . . not actually. I'm sorry he died that way, but Tony Richardson was a terrible person. Not because he had AIDS, not because he was bisexual, not because he was hypocritical about it. Because he was a terrible person. Not a terrible director, just a terrible human being."

Shirley Jean Rickert
Born March 25, 1926
Died February 6, 2009
From child star to stripper. Born in Seattle, Rickert made her public debut winning a beauty contest when she was just 18-months-old. Her enthusiastic mother was convinced that she had a star on her hands and insisted on moving the family to Tinseltown. Aged four, she auditioned for a role in the Our Gang comedies and appeared in five of them in 1931. Of her time in films, she said, "We had fun. The mothers on the other hand, were awful. Stage mothers are just vile women, including my own." She left Our Gang and appeared in five Mickey McGuire comedies in 1933 and 1934 as Tomboy Taylor, playing opposite Mickey Rooney. She was an oil heiress in the John Wayne B-Western *'Neath The Arizona Skies* (1934). She never became a star and spent much of the rest of her career playing bit parts until she turned to stripping. Her manager called her Gilda and Her Crowning Glory. She stopped taking her clothes off in public in 1959 and became a barmaid, secretary and saleswoman.
CAUSE: She moved to upstate New York in 1997 to be close to her daughter but she lost much of her movie memorabilia in a house fire in Schoharie County. She died aged 82 of cardiovascular disease at Wesley Health Care Center, a nursing home in Saratoga Springs, New York.

Arnold Ridley, OBE
Born January 7, 1896
Died March 12, 1984
Aged gentleman. Born at 4 Pera Place, Bath, Somerset, the son of William Robert Ridley, a drill instructor, and Rosa Caroline Morrish, Arnold Ridley was educated at Clarendon School, Bath, and Bristol University where he began his acting career. Upon

graduation, he didn't know if he could make it in the high pressure world of acting and so turned to teaching before returning to tread the boards. In 1914 he made his professional début playing in *Prunella's* at the Theatre Royal, Bristol. At the outbreak of the First World War he tried to enlist with the Somerset Light Infantry but was rejected because he had a condition called hammer toe. He applied again in 1915 and was accepted but was invalided out, having been wounded at the Somme in 1916. Ridley twice went "over the top" during the battle. The first attack, at Delville Wood, was a horrible experience but he managed to come away unscathed. During the second occasion his unit was sent to attack the Gird trench near Gueudecourt. A German trench that was not marked on the map blocked their progress and many of Ridley's colleagues were killed by machine gun fire. Ridley and the other survivors made their way along the dugout using bayonets and grenades. During the fighting, a German solider hit him on the head with a rifle butt causing him to collapse. The Hun then lunged at him with a bayonet, but Ridley managed to deflect the blade into his groin rather than his stomach. Another soldier put a bayonet through his hand and wrist. It took 15 operations to save his hand and he was left without movement in three fingers. And it took him two years after the drama to realise that the rifle butt had cracked his skull – an injury that caused him to suffer blackouts for the rest of his life. In 1918 he returned to acting and joined the Birmingham Repertory Company but the injuries suffered in the war forced him to give up the stage in 1921. He turned his hand to writing plays and working in his father's boot shop in Bath. He wrote 35 plays in longhand. In 1923 his most celebrated play *The Ghost Train* was inspired by having to wait in Mangotsfield Junction, a remote country station, for several hours. In

1935 he formed Quality Films, his own film production company, with a partner but although their first production, *Royal Eagle* (1936), was a success, their financial backers went bankrupt during the second and left both Ridley and his partner in debt. It took 20 years to repay the money. The character of Charles Godfrey was a conscientious objector during the First World War but when the second conflict began Ridley signed up to the army and was commissioned as a major. However, he suffered severe shell-shock in France and was again discharged. Instead he joined ENSA, the army entertainment troupe – Entertainment National Service Association – that was cruelly dubbed "Every Night Something Awful". His first film was *The Interrupted Journey* (1949) in which he played Mr Saunders. He also appeared in *Green Grow The Rushes* (1951) as Tom Cuffley, *A Stolen Face* (1952) as Dr Russell, *Wings Of Mystery* (1963) as Mr Bell, *Crooks In Cloisters* (1964) as a newsagent, *Carry On Girls* (1973) as Alderman Pratt and a cinema attendant in *The Amorous Milkman* (1974). He also appeared in the television soaps *Coronation Street* playing Herbert Whittle (in 1967) and John Gilbert (in 1969), *Crossroads* in 1964 playing the Reverend Guy Atkins and the radio soap *The Archers* as Arthur 'Doughy' Hood, the baker. In 1968 he was approached by producer David Croft who offered him the role of the gentlemanly Charles Godfrey in a new television sitcom entitled *Dad's Army* about the Home Guard in Britain, a bunch of elderly and very young men who were unable to serve in the regular forces because of age or infirmity (or in the case of Joe Walker an allergy to corned beef). Croft warned Ridley, then in his seventies, that he would, on occasion, be required to run around and that he (Croft) would be unable to protect him. "I think I can manage," replied Ridley and manage he did. The show ran from July 31, 1968 until 80 episodes later on November 13, 1977 when Lance Corporal Jones married Mrs Fox. Ridley was the subject of some good-natured banter from his co-star John Laurie, the second oldest member of the cast. Laurie would stare at Ridley arriving each day and shake his head, "Poor old boy . . . look at him, he's falling apart." Ridley once underwent an operation after breaking his hip and arrived to film in a limousine lying flat on his back, his leg in plaster. Each member of the cast went to greet Ridley except John Laurie who hung back. David Croft went up and leaned into the car to shake Ridley's hand. All that was visible was Croft's arm going up and down. "Look," cried Laurie, "they're pumping him up! They're pumping him up!" The crew propped Ridley against a tree and photographed him looking left, right, up, down and worried and then sent him home. Whenever a reaction shot was needed the crew used one of those. He was awarded an OBE in the Queen's New Year's Honours List of 1982 for services to the theatre. He was married three times: firstly to Hilda Mary Cooke, then to Isola Strong and finally to Althea Parker by whom he had one son, Nick, born in 1947.

CAUSE: Arnold Ridley died, aged 88, of natural causes in hospital in Northwood, having been in poor health for some time. His funeral was held at St Anne's Church, Highgate, London, a week later. He left less than £4,000.

Dean Riesner

(DEAN FRANKLIN REISNER)
Born November 3, 1918
Died August 18, 2002
He made Clint feel lucky. Born in New York, Riesner was the son of silent film director Charles Reisner (b. Minneapolis, Minnesota, March 14, 1887, d. La Jolla, California, September 24, 1962) who was also credited as Charles F. Riesner, the version his son preferred, and began his professional life as a child actor before moving behind the typewriter. He made his film début aged five under the nom de screen Dinky Dean. He appeared in several Charlie Chaplin films including *The Pilgrim* (1923) in which his father also appeared. It was his mother's intervention that persuaded Dean's father to let him "have his life back" and he settled himself in front of a typewriter after being contracted to Warner Bros. His first screen credit – under the name Dean Franklin – was for co-writing *Code Of The Secret Service* (1939), a movie that featured Ronald Reagan. His second credit came for *The Fighting 69th* (1940), a First World War-based film starring James Cagney. Riesner joined the Coast Guard during the Second World War and saw service in the Pacific. After demob, he returned to Hollywood and wrote and directed *Bill And Coo* (1947), a film in which trained birds in hats and ties "acted" out the goings-on in a town called Chirpendale. It won a special Oscar for its creator, Ken Murray, for "artistry and patience". In the Fifties Riesner turned his hand to television and wrote scripts for *Ben Casey*, *The Outer Limits* and *Rawhide* among many others. It was while working on the last show that he met Clint Eastwood. Several years later, Eastwood and Don Siegel were working on the film *Coogan's Bluff* but were unable to find a scriptwriter who could convey what they wanted. Four had tried and failed when Siegel called upon Riesner. The film was a success and led to the television series *McCloud*. He worked with Eastwood on the *Dirty Harry* series and wrote the famous lines "Go ahead, punk, make my day" and "You've got to ask yourself one question: 'Do I feel lucky?' Well, do ya, punk?" He later worked on the English-dubbed version of *Das Boot* and *The Godfather III* (1990). He was married to Marie who predeceased him.

CAUSE: He died in Encino, California, aged 83, of natural causes.

Rin Tin Tin

Born 1916
Died August 8, 1932
Hollywood's first canine superstar. US soldier Lieutenant Lee Duncan found a litter of five Alsatian puppies in a trench during World War I. A dog lover, Duncan took one of the pups back to California and began the task of training him. Rin Tin Tin was to the manor born. He was a talented performer and it was his films that prevented Warner Bros from going bankrupt in their early days. He also made Lee Duncan around $5 million. He made his début in *The Man From Hell's River* (1922), but it was when he signed for Warners the following year that he became a superstar, appearing in films such as *Where The North Begins* (1923), *Below The Line* (1925), *A Hero Of The Big Snows* (1926), *The Night Cry* (1926), *Man Hunter* (1930) and even appeared in 'barkies' such as the 12-part serial *The Lone Defender* (1930). Many of Rin Tin Tin's adventures were written by Darryl F. Zanuck. Jack Warner commented: "The dog faced one hazard after another and was grateful to get an extra hamburger for a reward. He didn't ask for a raise, or a new press agent, or an air-conditioned dressing room, or more close-ups."
CAUSE: Rin Tin Tin died at 1352 Clubview, Beverly Hills, supposedly in Jean Harlow's arms, of natural causes, aged approximately 112 dog years old. He was buried in the back garden.

Martin Ritt

Born March 2, 1914
Died December 8, 1990
Methodic director. A talented university sportsman, Ritt was born in New York, the son of Jewish immigrants. He decided to become a lawyer but found himself distracted by his growing interest in drama occasioned by his friendship with Elia Kazan. A brief acting career decided that his place was on the other side of the camera. He worked on Broadway and directed early television broadcasts and taught at the Actors' Studio. His students included Paul Newman, Lee Remick, Rod Steiger and Joanne Woodward. The first film he directed was *Edge Of The City* (1957) and he went on to direct, among others, *The Long, Hot Summer* (1958), *The Black Orchid* (1959), *The Sound And The Fury* (1959), *Paris Blues* (1961), *Hud* (1963), for which he was nominated for an Oscar, *The Spy Who Came In From The Cold* (1965), *Hombre* (1967), *The Molly Maguires* (1970), *Pete'n'Tillie* (1972), *Norma Rae* (1979), *Murphy's Romance* (1985), *Nuts* (1987) and *Stanley & Iris* (1990).
CAUSE: He died of heart disease aged 76.

Tex Ritter

Born January 12, 1905
Died January 2, 1974
Singing cowboy. Born in Murvaul, Texas, hence his nickname (from 1931), Woodward Maurice Ritter was the son of a rancher and had no desire to go into showbiz. At the University of Texas at Austin, he studied political science and then law for two years before changing to music and becoming a relatively successful country and western singer. In 1931 he appeared in the Broadway play *Green Grow The Lilacs*. Five years later he made his first film, *Song Of The Gringo* (1936), as Tex. During the next nine years Ritter starred in 85 Westerns, including *Sing, Cowboy, Sing* (1937) as Tex Archer, *Mystery Of The Hooded Horsemen* (1937) as Tex Martin, *Tex Rides With The Boy Scouts* (1938) as Tex Collins, *Utah Trail* (1938) as Tex Stewart, *Starlight Over Texas* (1938) as Tex Newman, *Where The Buffalo Roam* (1938) as Tex Houston, *Down The Wyoming Trail* (1939) as Tex Yancey, *Take Me Back To Oklahoma* (1940) as

Tex Lawton, *The Cowboy From Sundown* (1940) as Tex Rockett, *King Of Dodge City* (1941) as Tex Rawlings, *Prairie Gunsmoke* (1942) as Tex Terrell and *Deep In The Heart Of Texas* (1942) as Brent Gordon often alongside Syd Sayler. In 1952 he sang 'Do Not Foresake Me, Oh My Darlin' ', the theme tune to *High Noon*, which won an Oscar. He was elected to the Country Music Hall Of Fame in 1964 and in the post-war period enjoyed 11 country Top 10 hits, including two number ones. In 1970, he ran unsuccessfully in Tennessee to become a senator (in the Republican favour against Al Gore, Sr) and three years later contested the gubernatorial election – both cost him financially. He married actress Dorothy Fay (b. Prescott, Arizona, April 4, 1915, as Dorothy Fay, Southworth, d. Woodland Hills, Los Angeles, California, November 5, 2003) on June 14, 1941. She appeared with him in four of his films. They had two sons – Tom (b. Burbank, California, January 8, 1947) who became a lawyer despite cerebral palsy and 5'11" Jonathan Southworth (b. Burbank, California, September 17, 1948, d. Burbank, California, September 11, 2003, of aortic dissection in the same hospital that he was born in) was an actor under the name John Ritter. He was best known for his television work.

CAUSE: Ritter died of a heart attack aged 68 at the jail in Nashville, Tennessee, where he had gone to help secure the release of a friend.

Thelma Ritter
Born February 14, 1905
Died February 5, 1969
Dependable support. Thelma Ritter was born in Brooklyn, New York, and was a huge success in the theatre before she deigned to set foot in front of a movie camera for *Miracle On 34th Street* (1947). When she did she showed just what had made her such a successful actress. She was nominated six times

for Oscars, although she never won. Her nominations were for: Bette Davis' maid Birdie in *All About Eve* (1950), Ellen McNulty in *The Mating Season* (1951), nurse Clancy in *With A Song In My Heart* (1952), Moe in *Pickup On South Street* (1953), the drunken daily woman Alma in *Pillow Talk* (1959) and Elizabeth Stroud in *Birdman Of Alcatraz* (1962).

CAUSE: Ritter died in New York aged 63 from a heart attack.

Hal Roach
Born January 14, 1892
Died November 2, 1992
Extraordinary director. Born in Elmira, New York, Hal Roach worked as a mule skinner and then became a gold prospector in Alaska before striking a rich seam in Hollywood. He arrived in the film capital in 1912, where he became a Universal stunt man and bit part player and met Harold Lloyd. Roach believed in Lloyd's comic potential and three years later, when Roach inherited $3,000, he formed his own studio and starred Lloyd in a comedy series called *Willie Work*. No, it didn't and Roach subsequently became a director for Essanay. A stroke of luck meant that Roach found a distributor and rehired Lloyd. They retitled the character 'Lonesome Luke' and had a hit on their hands. Roach and Lloyd made several films together, including *Ruses, Rhymes And Roughnecks* (1915), *Peculiar Patients' Pranks* (1915), *Lonesome Luke Leans To The Literary* (1916), *Luke Lugs Luggage* (1916), *Lonesome Luke Lolls In Luxury* (1916), *Luke, The Candy Cut-Up* (1916), *Luke Foils The Villain* (1916), *Luke And The Rural Roughnecks* (1916), *Luke Pipes The Pippins* (1916), *Lonesome Luke, Circus King* (1916), *Luke's Double* (1916), *Them Was The Happy Days!* (1916), *Luke And The Bomb Throwers* (1916), *Luke's Late Lunchers* (1916), *Luke Laughs Last* (1916), *Luke's Fatal Flivver* (1916), *Luke's Society Mixup* (1916), *Luke's Washful*

Waiting (1916), *Luke Rides Roughshod* (1916), *Luke, Crystal Gazer* (1916), *Luke's Lost Lamb* (1916), *Luke Does The Midway* (1916), *Luke Joins The Navy* (1916), *Luke And The Mermaids* (1916), *Luke's Speedy Club Life* (1916), *Luke And The Bang-Tails* (1916) and many more. Unlike his rival Mack Sennett, Roach made sure his films told a good story rather than just relying on slapstick. He worked with Charlie Chase, Edgar Kennedy, Will Rogers and, of course, Laurel & Hardy who signed with him on February 6, 1926. Their films included: *The Battle Of The Century* (1927), *Leave 'Em Laughing* (1928), *From Soup To Nuts* (1928), *Big Business* (1929), *Berth Marks* (1929), *Men O'War* (1929), *Brats* (1930), *The Laurel-Hardy Murder Case* (1930), *Pardon Us* (1931), *Be Big!* (1931), *Chickens Come Home* (1931), *Laughing Gravy* (1931), *Our Wife* (1931), *Come Clean* (1931), *One Good Turn* (1931), *Beau Hunks* (1931), *Helpmates* (1932), *The Music Box* (1932), *Pack Up Your Troubles* (1932), *Their First Mistake* (1932), *The Devil's Brother* (1933), *Busy Bodies* (1933), *Sons Of The Desert* (1933), *Oliver The Eighth* (1934), *Them Thar Hills* (1934), *Babes In Toyland* (1934), *Bonnie Scotland* (1935), *Way Out West* (1937), *Block-Heads* (1938), *The Flying Deuces* (1939) and *A Chump At Oxford* (1940). In the Twenties Roach's studio began diversifying from comedy, producing Westerns and action films. He also created the Our Gang series, later retitled the Little Rascals for television. His films were distributed by MGM to whom (in 1938) he sold the rights to the Our Gang series. In WWII Roach produced propaganda films, and was promoted to the rank of major by the US Government for his war services, but his fortunes declined afterwards. His company went bust in the late Fifties and his studio was demolished in 1963. Before the decade was out, Roach made the successful compilation film *The Crazy World Of Laurel &*

Hardy. He was awarded an honorary Oscar in 1984.

CAUSE: In 1992 he oversaw the colourisation of *Way Out West* and travelled world-wide promoting it. Roach died later that year, aged 100, of pneumonia in Los Angeles, California.

Jason Robards
Born July 22, 1922
Died December 26, 2000
Raspy, laconic actor. Jason Nelson Robards, Jr was born in Chicago, Illinois, the son of stage and silent screen actor Jason Robards, Sr (b. December 31, 1892, d. April 4, 1963) and Hope Maxine Glanville. After seeing service in the navy in the Second World War and studying at the American Academy of Dramatic Arts, Robards made his stage début at the Delyork Theater, Rehoboth Beach, Delaware, in July 1947 in *Out Of The Frying Pan*. Three months later, he made his first appearance in New York at the Children's World Theater playing the rear end of the cow in *Jack And The Beanstalk*. It was from this start that Robards began a lifelong love of the theatre. He received six Tony nominations in 14 years. He made films but only to pay his alimony and allow him to work treading the boards. He was often disparaging – in public at least – about the silver screen, liking to quote Spencer Tracy on the subject: "Be on time, know the jokes. Say them as fast as you can. Take the money and go home." He made his film début in *The Journey* (1959) as Paul Kedes in which he was billed as Jason Robards, Jr. His other films included *By Love Possessed* (1961) as Julius Penrose, *Long Day's Journey Into Night* (1962) as James 'Jamie' Tyrone, Jr, *Tender Is The Night* (1962) as Dr Dick Diver, *Act One* (1963) as George S. Kaufman (the first film in which he was not billed as Jason Robards, Jr), *A Thousand Clowns* (1965) as Murray Burns, *Any Wednesday* (1966) as John Cleves, *A Big Hand For The Little Lady* (1966) as

Henry Drummond, John Sturges'
Hour Of The Gun (1967) as Dr John
'Doc' Holliday, *Divorce American Style*
(1967) as Nelson Downes, *The St
Valentine's Day Massacre* (1967) as Al
Capone (which was shot in just 11
days), *Isadora* (1968) as Paris Singer,
The Night They Raided Minsky's (1968)
as Raymond Paine, *C'era Una Volta Il
West* (1969) as Manuel 'Cheyenne'
Gutierrez, *Rosolino Paternò: Soldato . . .*
(1970) as Sam Armstrong, *Julius
Caesar* (1970) as Brutus, *Fools*
(1970) as Matthew South, *The Ballad
Of Cable Hogue* (1970) as Cable
Hogue, *Tora! Tora! Tora!* (1970) as
Lieutenant-General Walter C. Short,
Murders In The Rue Morgue (1971) as
Cesar Charron, *Johnny Got His Gun*
(1971) as Joe's father, *The War Between
Men And Women* (1972) as Stephen
Kozlenko, *Tod Eines Fremden* (1973) as
Inspector Barkan, *Pat Garrett And Billy
The Kid* (1973) as Governor Lew
Wallace, *Mr Sycamore* (1974) as John
Gwilt, *A Boy And His Dog* (1975) as
Lou Craddock, Alan Pakula's *All The
President's Men* (1976) as Ben Bradlee,
the Executive Editor of the *Washington
Post* for which he won the Best
Supporting Actor Oscar, *Julia* (1977)
as Dashiell Hammett for which he won
the Best Supporting Actor Oscar for
the second year in a row, Alan Pakula's
Comes A Horseman (1978) as Jacob
'J.W.' Ewing, *Hurricane* (1979) as
Captain Bruckner, *Caboblanco* (1980)
as Gunther Beckdorff, *Raise The Titanic*
(1980) as Admiral James Sandecker,
Melvin And Howard (1980) as Howard
Hughes for which he was nominated
for a Best Supporting Actor Oscar, *The
Legend Of The Lone Ranger* (1981) as
President Ulysses S. Grant, *Burden Of
Dreams* (1982) as Fitzcarraldo, *Max
Dugan Returns* (1983) as Max Dugan,
Something Wicked This Way Comes
(1983) as Charles Halloway, *Square
Dance* (1987) as Grandpa Dillard,
Dream A Little Dream (1989) as
Coleman Ettinger, *Reunion* (1989)
as Henry Strauss, *Parenthood* (1989) as

Frank, *Black Rainbow* (1990) as Walter
Travis, *Quick Change* (1990) as Chief
Rotzinger, *Storyville* (1992) as Clifford
Fowler, *The Trial* (1993) as Doctor
Huld, *Philadelphia* (1993) as Charles
Wheeler, *The Paper* (1994) as Graham
Keighley, *Little Big League* (1994) as
Thomas Heywood, *A Thousand Acres*
(1997) as Larry Cook, *Heartwood*
(1998) as Logan Reeser, *The Real
Macaw* (1998) as Grandpa Ben Girdis,
Beloved (1998) as Mr Bodwin and
Magnolia (1999) as Earl Partridge.
Robards' gravitas and raspy voice
allowed him to carve a niche playing
American presidents on film and
television: he played Abraham Lincoln
three times on television, Ulysses S.
Grant twice, Franklin D. Roosevelt and
the fictional President Richard
Monckton in the 1977 television mini
series *Washington: Behind Closed Doors*.
He won an Emmy for the 1988
television movie *Inherit The Wind* in
which he played Henry Drummond.
On December 8, 1972, thanks in no
small part to his serious drink problem,
Robards was involved in a near fatal car
crash on a Californian motorway near
Malibu when he drove his Mercedes
into the side of a hill. When he arrived
at hospital he had no heartbeat, a
smashed up face and a partly severed
finger. It took three operations to repair
his injuries. On May 7, 1948 Robards
married the actress Eleanor Pitman and
fathered three children: Jason III (b.
1948), Sarah Louise (b. 1951) and
David (b. 1956). The couple was
divorced in 1958. In 1959 he married
the actress Rachel Taylor but they
divorced two years later in Mexico on
May 4, 1961. Wife number three was
Lauren Bacall, the widow of Humphrey
Bogart. They married on Independence
Day 1961 in Ensenada, Mexico. A son,
Sam, was born in New York City on
December 16, 1961. The couple
divorced in Juarez, Mexico, on
September 10, 1969 on the grounds of
incompatibility. On St Valentine's Day
1970, Robards married the actress

Lois O'Connor and by her had two children: Shannon (b. 1972) and Jake (b. August 15, 1974).
CAUSE: Robards died aged 78 of metastasised lung cancer in Bridgeport, Connecticut.

Lyda Roberti

Born May 20, 1906
Died March 12, 1938
Uninhibited screen man-chaser. Born in Warsaw, Poland, 5'3", platinum blonde Lyda was the daughter of a supposedly abusive German clown and a Polish trick rider. She was raised in the circus but left when they reached Shanghai, China, where she learned English. By 1927 she had relocated to California and landed a job in vaudeville. Three years later Broadway producer Lou Holtz cast her in his show *You Said It*, where she became an overnight sensation. In 1932 she signed for Paramount, working alongside Eddie Cantor and W.C. Fields. She appeared in three films for MGM and Columbia before retiring due to poor health. Her films included: *Dancers In The Dark* (1932) as Fanny Zabowolski, *Million Dollar Legs* (1932) as Mata Machree, *Three-Cornered Moon* (1933) as Jenny, *Torch Singer* (1933) as Dora, *George White's Scandals* (1935) as Manya, *The Big Broadcast Of 1936* (1936) as Countess Ysobel de Naigila, *Nobody's Baby* (1937) as Lena and *Wide Open Faces* (1938) as Kitty. She was married twice. Her first husband was R.A. Golden and on June 25, 1935, she married Hugh 'Bud' Ernst.
CAUSE: She died in Los Angeles, California, aged 31, from a heart attack suffered while bending over to tie a shoelace.

Peggy Robertson

(MARGARET SINGER)
Born September 13, 1916
Died February 6, 1998
Assistant to Mr Hitchcock. Born in London (on the same day as Roald Dahl, another master storyteller), Peggy Robertson was working at Denham studios as a script girl when she met Alfred Hitchcock in 1948. He hired her to work on *Under Capricorn* (1949) and it was her diplomacy that smoothed many arguments between Hitchcock and his leading lady, in this case Ingrid Bergman. It was Hitchcock's usual ploy – whenever things got tough on-set he left it to his minions to sort out the problems. On his next film *Stage Fright* (1949) Hitchcock ignored Jane Wyman to pay court to Marlene Dietrich. It was the invaluable Peggy who kept Wyman happy. Peggy left Hitchcock's employ for eight years and married Douglas Robertson, the Canadian film editor. She and Hitchcock were reunited for *Vertigo* (1957). Robertson allows us to dismiss a Hitchcock canard. He told the story of how Kim Novak had upset him, he enjoyed throwing her into the water of San Francisco bay (actually a tank in a studio) 24 times. In fact, she went into the water just four times – first because of a problem with star Jimmy Stewart's hair, second because of a hesitation on Stewart's part and the last two times because of continuity problems. It was during *North By Northwest* (1958) that she became Hitchcock's most trusted advisor. The following year he dismissed his recent films as "glossy technicolour baubles" and asked her to find a "typically un-Hitchcock picture". She suggested a novel by Robert Bloch called *Psycho*. To prevent too many members of the public learning the story, he then told her to go out and buy up as many copies of the novel as possible. She also worked on *The Birds* (1963), *Marnie* (1964), *Torn Curtain* (1966), *Topaz* (1969), *Frenzy* (1972) and *Family Plot* (1976). In 1979 Hitchcock tried and failed to make a film about George Blake, the spy. Consequently, he closed down his offices and made Peggy redundant. It was a mixed blessing for her. She had begun to find Hitchcock

irritating but she also was now without a salary. When Hitchcock died in 1980 he did not leave her anything in his will. She later worked as associate producer on *Mask* (1985) and *Illegally Yours* (1988).
CAUSE: She died aged 81 in Woodland Hills, California, of natural causes.

James Robertson Justice
Born June 15, 1907
Died July 2, 1975
Palpably British. Although red-bearded James Norval Harold Robertson-Justice appeared in numerous films, most memorably as Sir Lancelot Spratt in the *Doctor* series, you would never know from reading his entry in *Who's Who*, where he is more concerned with his invention of "the rocket propelled net method of catching wildfowl for marking". He admits to an "undistinguished but varied [career] comprising some three score jobs in different parts of the world". He is too modest. Born at 39 Baring Road, Lee, south London (not at Wigtown, Scotland as he claimed his whole life and two years later than he insisted), he was the only child of James Norval Justice (b. Aberdeen, May 25, 1876, d. Hillingbourne, near Maidstone, Kent, March 29, 1953), a mineral prospector, he was educated at Marlborough College and Bonn University although he dropped out after a year. Prior to acting he was a journalist for Reuter's in 1929 where he turned up for the nightshift in pyjamas and a dressing gown. On November 1, 1929 he emigrated to Canada where he spent two months in an insurance firm although he failed to sell one policy. He worked for a short while as a teacher at a prep school. After being sacked he worked as a lorry driver, gold miner and carpet layer and he claimed, untruthfully, a Mountie. By 1931 he was back in England and became involved in ice hockey and then motor racing (taking part in a race at Brooklands on May 16, 1932).

In the mid-Thirties he worked for Military Intelligence, his linguistic gifts coming in handy. He also worked for the League of Nations police force. In 1936 he fought for the International Brigade against Franco's fascists in the Spanish Civil War. In 1940 he joined the Royal Navy Volunteer Reserve, leaving injured in 1943. The following year he turned to acting and made his first screen appearance in *For Those In Peril* (1944). The possessor of a rich voice, he made his film début in *Fiddlers Three* (1944) as Centurion and went on to appear in, among others, *Scott Of The Antarctic* (1948) as Taff Evans, *My Brother Jonathan* (1948), *Whisky Galore!* (1949) as Dr McLaren, *Captain Horatio Hornblower* (1951), *David And Bathsheba* (1951), *The Story Of Robin Hood And His Merrie Men* (1952), *Miss Robin Hood* (1952), *The Sword And The Rose* (1953), *Doctor In The House* (1954), *Above Us The Waves* (1955), *Doctor At Sea* (1955), *Land Of The Pharaohs* (1955), *The Iron Petticoat* (1956), *Moby Dick* (1956), *Doctor At Large* (1957), *Doctor In Love* (1960), *Murder She Said* (1961), *The Guns Of Navarone* (1961) as Jensen, *Doctor In Clover* (1965), *The Face Of Fu Manchu* (1965), *Those Magnificent Men In Their Flying Machines* (1965), *Chitty Chitty Bang Bang* (1968) as Lord Scrumptious and *Doctor In Trouble* (1970). In 1946 he joined a select group of men who called themselves the Thursday Club, that being the day of the week on which they met for lunch in an upstairs room of Wheeler's Oyster Bar in Old Compton Street, Soho. They would eat oysters and lobster claws washed down with Champagne and Guinness. Each month the members elected one of their fellows 'Cunt of the Month', an honour that went to the chap who had made the biggest fool of himself since the last election. Other club members included Larry Adler, Iain Macleod M.P., Felix Topolski, Peter Ustinov, Gilbert Harding and sundry others. In

1950 he stood for Parliament in the Labour interest at North Angus and Mearns. He lost heavily to the Conservative. An expert naturalist, he taught Prince Charles falconry. Robertson Justice was married twice. In 1941 he married nurse Dilys Hayden at Chelsea. She gave birth to his son James Norval Robertson Justice (b. 1945). The boy tragically drowned on June 20, 1949, in the river at the end of the garden in Whitchurch, Hampshire. The marriage was never the same after the tragedy and they separated in 1958. The situation was not helped by his infidelities. In October 1961 Robertson Justice was named as co-respondent in a divorce case. The couple finally divorced in 1968. In 1960 he met and fell in love with the former actress Baroness Irina Margarethe Pauline Isabelle Caecilia von Meyendorff (b. Reval, Russia, June 6, 1916, d. 2001). Robertson Justice and the baroness married on 29 June 1975, only a few days before his death.

CAUSE: In 1967 Robertson Justice suffered a stroke and had to undergo two operations on his brain because the surgeons did not properly rectify the problem the first time. He recovered but he lost his short-term memory, no small problem for an actor. He continued to apply for roles but never got them because producers were unable to insure him. He suffered several more strokes. In 1970 he was made bankrupt after failing to keep up with £50-a-week maintenance payments to his ex-wife. He died aged 68 at his home, Top House, Ashley, Stockbridge, Hampshire, from heart failure. He died penniless. His corpse was cremated and his ashes placed in a cairn on Birichen Moor in the Highlands.

FURTHER READING: *James Robertson Justice: "What's The Bleeding Time?" A Biography* – James Hogg with Robert Sellers and Howard Watson (Sheffield: Tomahawk Press, 2008)

Paul Robeson
Born April 9, 1898
Died January 23, 1976
The first black hero. A star football player and lawyer, Paul Leroy Robeson was the sixth child of William Drew Robeson (b. Martin County, North Carolina, July 27, 1845, d. May 17, 1918), a Carolina cotton plantation slave who became a Presbyterian minister, and Maria Louisa Bustill (b. Philadelphia, Pennsylvania, November 8, 1853) who died on January 19, 1904, when Paul was five. Deciding against a career at the bar, he became a singer and actor. He appeared as Othello in Shakespeare's play in May 1930 opposite Peggy Ashcroft at the Savoy Theatre, but as a negro he was forbidden entrance to the hotel. It was Ashcroft's affair with Robeson that began the end of her first marriage. Robeson married Eslanda Cardozo 'Essie' Goode (b. 1897, d. New York City, December 13, 1965) in August 1921 but admitted he had no fatherly interest in his son Pauli (b. November 2, 1927) whom he sent to school in the Soviet Union. Eslanda wrote that Robeson was lazy, had no sense of loyalty to his friends and did not realise when he was being racially abused. He made his film début in *The Emperor Jones* (1933), although he was happier on stage, often performing in the United Kingdom. Later in the decade Robeson appeared in the films *Sanders Of The River* (1935) and *King Solomon's Mines* (1937). A left-winger, he was blacklisted in America for his views but his biggest 'crime' in US eyes came in December 1952 when he accepted the Stalin Peace Prize. His passport was revoked and he was unable to leave the States for six years. His final years were spent as a recluse. His signature tune was 'Ole Man River', which he performed in the film *Show Boat* (1936).

CAUSE: In January 1959 Robeson was treated in a Kremlin hospital suffering from flu and dizzy spells. Another illness in 1961 forced his retirement. He lived with wife Essie in Jumal Terrace, Harlem, until her death when he moved to live with his sister in Philadelphia. He suffered a stroke on December 28, 1975, and was admitted to the city's Presbyterian University Hospital where he died, aged 77.

FURTHER READING: *Paul Robeson: The Man And His Mission* – Ron Ramdin (London: Peter Owen, 1987).

Sir George Robey

(GEORGE EDWARD WADE)
Born September 20, 1869
Died November 29, 1954

'The Prime Minister of Mirth'. Robey was born at 334 Kennington Road, Herne Hill, London, the son of a civil engineer, which meant that the family moved about regularly. Studying at Leipzig University, Robey fought a duel in which he was wounded. At the end of his father's posting, the family returned to England where Robey began a clerical job working in Birmingham. A talented amateur singer, he regularly appeared in concerts, simultaneously discovering his comic talents. He began earning small amounts of money but since this caused friction at home he adopted the stage name Roby, later Robey – the name of a builder's business in Birmingham. He later changed his name by deed poll. He made his music hall début in June 1891 at Oxford. Although billed only as 'an extra', his talent shone through and his name was soon added to the publicity posters. Robey not only became a name but also a character. He wore a red nose but blackened his eyebrows and donned a long, black, frock coat and a top hat. (He later abandoned the topper in favour of a squashed bowler.) A masher's cane and the absence of a collar completed the ensemble. Robey pretended to scold his audience for seeing double meanings in his carefully delivered monologues: "Desist! Really, I meantersay! Let there be merriment

by all means, let there be merriment, but let it be tempered by dignity and the reserve which is compatible with the obvious refinement of our environment." He worked hard, often playing to several houses a night. At the turn of the century he made his first film, *The Rats* (1900). It would be 13 years before he stepped in front of a camera again, appearing in *And Very Nice Too, Good Queen Bess* (1913). At Christmas Robey was a favourite pantomime dame. Critics, usually the most cynical of audiences, flocked to his shows. One described his work as "finished like a cut jewel . . . the art within its limits, is not to be surpassed". When the popularity of the 'single turn' waned Robey became the comedian in large scale revues. During the First World War he appeared in a number of films including *George Robey Turns Anarchist* (1914), *£66.13.9 For Every Man Woman And Child* (1916), *Blood Tells* (1916), *Doing His Bit* (1917) and *George Robey's Day Off* (1918). Offered a knighthood after the war, he declined, accepting the CBE instead. In 1932 he moved to the world of operetta, appearing as Menelaus in A.P. Herbert's version of Offenbach's *La Belle Hélène* with Max Reinhardt as producer and C.B. Cochran as manager. It was an unusual role for Robey and he had to tone down his natural exuberance accordingly. He did so magnificently. James Agate commented, "A miracle of accommodation like that of a trombone player obliging with a pianissimo." He made more films in-between comedy and opera including *The Rest Cure* (1923), *One Arabian Night* (1923), *Don Quixote* (1923), *The Prehistoric Man* (1924), *The Barrister* (1928), *Safety First* (1928), *The Bride* (1928), *Mrs Mephistopheles* (1928), *The Temperance Fête* (1932), *Marry Me* (1932) and *Don Quixote* (1933) as Sancho Panza. On February 28, 1935, Robey opened as Falstaff in *Henry IV, Part I* at His Majesty's Theatre. First night nerves got to him, but although he stumbled over his lines, he won over the audience. It was agreed that the man from the music halls could play the classic character as well as the buffoon. Nine years later he appeared in Laurence Olivier's award-winning production of *Henry V* (1944). His last film was *The Pickwick Papers* (1952), a film described by the *Daily Mirror* "as welcome as the sun in the morning and as British as a cup of tea." He finally accepted a knighthood shortly before his death. Sadly, Robey never came to terms with retirement. Each evening he would sit before a mirror applying his make-up, just as if he had a show to perform.

CAUSE: He died of natural causes in Saltdean, Sussex.

Dany Robin

Born April 14, 1927
Died May 25, 1995
Beautiful *Carry On*ner. Born in Clamart, France, she began her career as a ballerina before making the move into movies and appeared in several films including *Les Portes De La Nuit* (1946), *Les Amoreux Sont Seuls Au Monde* (1948), *Le Soif Des Hommes* (1950), *Une Histoire D'Amour* (1951), *Les Amants De Minuit* (1953), *The Anatomy Of Love* (1953), *Un Acte D'Amour* (1954), *Paris Coquin* (1956), Jacqueline, the girlfriend of the Black Fingernail in *Carry On Don't Lose Your Head* (1966) and Hitchcock's *Topaz* (1969) after which she retired. Her pets included a donkey and five crocodiles. Formerly married to actor Georges Marchal, the Catholic Dany later (November 23, 1969) married showbiz agent Michael Sullivan (b. London, October 23, 1921). Sullivan represented Sid James, who twice clumsily tried to seduce Dany when he was staying *chez* Sullivan near Marbella. Sullivan's other clients included Dick Emery, Mike & Bernie Winters, Jon Pertwee, Shirley Bassey and Jack Douglas.

CAUSE: She died in a fire aged 68.

Coincidentally, her home had burned down shortly before she appeared in *Topaz*.

Edward G. Robinson
(EMANUEL GOLDENBERG)
Born December 12, 1893
Died January 26, 1973
Cinematic tough guy. Born at 671 Strada Cantemier, in the Jewish section of Bucharest, Rumania, the family moved to America in 1903 and young Manny grew up in New York on the lower East Side. He was torn between careers as a rabbi or an attorney but in the end the smell of the greasepaint and the roar of the crowd won out and he became an actor, making his stage début in late 1912 in *The Pillars Of Society*, a production put on by the American Academy of Dramatic Art where he was studying. His professional début came in April 1913 in Binghampton, New York, playing Sato in *Paid In Full* at a salary of $25 a week. His stage name came from a long since forgotten English play called *The Passerby*, in which one of the characters was called Robinson. The Edward came from King Edward VII and the G was a reminder of his real origins. On August 12, 1915, he made his début on Broadway, playing André Lemaire in a production of *Under Fire* at the Hudson Theater. Over the next 15 years Robinson was a regular on the Broadway stage. His early film experiences did not endear him to the new medium and he was sacked by Samuel Goldfish (who later changed his name to Goldwyn) for not being up to scratch. In 1923 he played Domingo Escobar, an OAP, in *The Bright Shawl*, but it wasn't until the advent of sound films that Robinson came into his own. In the meantime, he concentrated on the theatre. In Medina, Pennsylvania, on January 21, 1927, he married Gladys Lloyd (b. 1895, d. Culver City Hospital, June 6, 1971, from a stroke and a heart attack), a divorced gentile mother. The ceremony, performed by a justice of the peace, cost $25. On March 19, 1933, at

Doctors' Hospital, New York, their son, Edward G. Robinson, Jr, was born. He was to die, three wives and numerous problems later, just over a year after his father on February 26, 1974. Gladys Robinson suffered from mental problems and became a manic depressive who had electroshock therapy. On February 25, 1956, she filed for divorce from Robinson and on the same day Frances Chisholm Robinson also filed against Edward G. Robinson, Jr. The divorce settlement forced Robinson to sell his beloved art collection, one of the best in private hands anywhere in the world. On January 16, 1958, he married (taller) divorcée Jane Bodenheim Adler (b. 1921) in Arlington, Virginia. They were together when he died. In July 1930 Robinson began to shoot a gangster film for Warner Bros directed by Mervyn LeRoy. Originally cast as Otero, Robinson persuaded LeRoy to let him play Enrico Cesare 'Rico' Bandello. *Little Caesar* took 31 days to film, cost $250,000 and Robinson provided his own wardrobe. The most difficult scenes to shoot were those involving guns. Robinson was a pacifist who hated armoury and every time he fired a gun, he blinked. To get the shot he wanted, LeRoy taped Robinson's eyelid open. When it came for Rico to be shot, metal plates were taped to Robinson's stomach and blank, but still dangerous, machine bullets were fired at the actor. It was only the skill of George Daly, the special effects man, that stopped Robinson from really being shot. The actor couldn't, unsurprisingly, keep still and Daly compensated for his movements when he fired the machine gun. Following the première in New York on January 22, 1931, Robinson became the hottest star at Warner Bros. He set the standard by which cinematic gangsters would be measured and appeared in *Night Ride* (1930) as Tony Garotta, *A Lady To Love* (1930) as Tony, *Smart Money* (1931) as Nick 'The Barber' Venizelos,

Five Star Final (1931) as journalist Joseph Randall, *Two Seconds* (1932) as John Allen, *Tiger Shark* (1932) as Mike Mascarenhas, *Silver Dollar* (1932) as Yates Martin, *The Little Giant* (1933) as James Francis 'Bugs' Ahearn, *I Loved A Woman* (1933) as John Hayden, *The Man With Two Faces* (1934) as Damon Welles, *Barbary Coast* (1935) as Chamalis, *Bullets Or Ballots* (1936) as Johnny Blake, *Kid Galahad* (1937) as Nick Donati, *The Last Gangster* (1937) as Joe Krozac, *A Slight Case Of Murder* (1938) as Remy Marco, *The Amazing Dr Clitterhouse* (1938) as Dr T.S. Clitterhouse, *I Am The Law* (1938) as John Lindsay, *Confessions Of A Nazi Spy* (1939) as Ed Renard, *Dr Ehrlich's Magic Bullet* (1940) as Dr Paul Ehrlich, the German scientist who discovered a remedy for VD, *Brother Orchid* (1940) as Little John Sarto, *A Dispatch From Reuters* (1940) as Julius Reuter, *Tales Of Manhattan* (1942) as Avery 'Larry' L. Browne, *Flesh And Fantasy* (1943) as Marshall Tyler, *Mr Winkle Goes To War* (1944) as Wilbert Winkle, *Double Indemnity* (1944) as Barton Keyes, *The Woman In The Window* (1944) as Professor Richard Wanley and *Scarlet Street* (1945) as Christopher Cross. And then it all began to go wrong. On October 20, 1947, Robinson was filming *All My Sons* (1948) in which he played Joe Keller and learning his lines for *Key Largo* (1948) where he would be Johnny Rocco. At the same time, in Washington, DC, trouble was brewing at the House Un-American Activities Committee. Robinson was a paid-up member of the Democratic Party, an admirer of President Franklin D. Roosevelt and an unashamed liberal. When Adolphe Menjou testified before the committee he said he believed that in recent industrial disputes Robinson had favoured the 'communist' side, whatever that was. On October 20, former communist Howard Rushmore, who had been film critic of the *Daily Worker*, identified two actors that the newspaper 'knew' were sympathetic to their aims. One was Charlie Chaplin, the other Edward G. Robinson. (Rushmore would later go on to become editor-in-chief of the most notorious magazine ever published in Hollywood, *Confidential*. Not long after a libel trial, Rushmore and his wife were riding in a New York cab when he shot her before turning the gun on himself.) Damning testimony came from the simplistic president of the Screen Actors' Guild, a man who tried – and failed – to make himself look intellectual by donning a pair of spectacles. His name was Ronald Reagan. On October 27, Robinson testified that he had never been a communist or affiliated with communist organisations. He refused to drop anyone else in the mire, but was caught in a trap of smears and innuendo. Work began to dry up, but when he was offered the chance of signing a 26-page 'confession' admitting he had been duped by communist front organisations, Robinson told the messenger where to get off. He fell out with his friend J. Edgar Hoover over the smears. Robinson testified again on December 22, and again reiterated that he was not, nor had he ever been, a communist or fellow traveller. He was unable to leave America because his passport had expired and he could not get it renewed. Robinson found himself on what was unhumorously called a "gray (*sic*) list": he wasn't blacklisted, but he wasn't in the clear either. It all became too much for the diminutive actor. On April 30, 1952, Robinson appeared before the HUAC for the third time. He finally admitted that he had supported organisations, albeit unknowingly, that were communist fronts and named names. The HUAC then admitted that they had never had any evidence against Robinson, and thought he was a "well-meaning individual" but a "No 1 sucker". It had cost Robinson $100,000 to clear himself of all 'charges' and he was now desperate to get back to work. His post-Hearing films included: *Vice Squad*

(1953) as Captain Barnaby, *Big Leaguer* (1953) as John B. 'Hans' Lobert, *The Glass Web* (1953) as Henry Hayes, *The Violent Men* (1955) as Lew Wilkison, *Tight Spot* (1955) as Lloyd Hallett, *A Bullet For Joey* (1955) as Inspector Raoul Leduc, *Illegal* (1955) as Victor Scott, *Hell On Frisco Bay* (1956) as Victor Amat, *The Ten Commandments* (1956) as Dathan, *Seven Thieves* (1960) as Theo Wilkins, *My Geisha* (1962) as Sam Lewis, *The Prize* (1963) as Dr Max Stratman/Professor Walter Stratman, *Robin And The 7 Hoods* (1964) as Big Jim, *Cheyenne Autumn* (1964) as Carl Schurz and *Mackenna's Gold* (1969) as Old Adams. He was never even nominated for an Oscar.

CAUSE: Robinson died of cancer in Hollywood, California. He was 79. He was buried in Beth-El Cemetery, 80-12 Cypress Hills Street, Ridgewood, New York 11385. On March 27, 1973, he was awarded a posthumous Oscar. Too little, too late.

FURTHER READING: *Little Caesar: A Biography Of Edward G. Robinson* – Alan L. Gansberg (London: New English Library, 1985).

Dame Flora Robson

Born March 2 (Good Friday), 1902
Died July 7, 1984
Grande dame. Flora Robson was born in South Shields, Durham, the third of four daughters and sixth of seven children of marine engineer David Mather Robson and was educated at Palmer's Green High School in London where her father had been posted. She moved to RADA (where she won the bronze medal) and began performing on stage on November 17, 1921, when she appeared at the Shaftesbury Theatre as Queen Margaret in Clemence Dane's *Will Shakespeare*. She worked constantly for four years and then took a four-year break, during which she was unable to get theatrical work – producers rejected the 5'8½" Flora for not being pretty enough. She returned to the stage in

October 1929. In the intervening time she worked as welfare officer for Shredded Wheat although influenza chained her to her bed for a depressing month. Once she was back, at the behest of her fiancé Tyrone Guthrie, work came steadily and in October 1933 she joined the Old Vic–Sadler's Wells Company. Two years earlier, she had appeared in her first film, *Dance Pretty Lady* (1931). Her other films included *Catherine The Great* (1934), *Fire Over England* (1936) as Queen Elizabeth I, *Wuthering Heights* (1939) as Ellen Dean, *Romeo & Juliet* (1954), *55 Days At Peking* (1962), *Murder At The Gallop* (1963), *Those Magnificent Men In Their Flying Machines* (1964) and, bizarrely, *Clash Of The Titans* (1981). She was nominated for a Best Supporting Actress Academy Award for *Saratoga Trunk* (1946) but lost out to Anne Baxter for *The Razor's Edge* (1946). She had affairs with Robert Donat and Paul Robeson but never married.

CAUSE: She died in Brighton, Sussex, aged 82, of natural causes. She left £128,526.

FURTHER READING: *Flora Robson –* Janet Dunbar (London: George G. Harrap & Co. Ltd., 1960).

Patricia Roc

(FELICIA MIRIAM URSULA HEROLD)
Born June 7, 1915
Died December 30, 2003
"Goddess of the Odeons". London-born Patricia Roc was the daughter of a paper merchant but, while a baby, she was adopted by a Dutch-Belgian stockbroker, Andre Riese and grew up believing him to be her real father. She did not discover the truth until she was 34. She was educated at Francis Holland School at Regent's Park before moving to Bartram Gables School at Broadstairs, Kent and then for a while attended RADA. Then she travelled to France for a test at the Joinville studios but even though she spoke French fluently the studio decided not to go

ahead with the production. Bitterly disappointed, she returned to England and was spotted by the impresario Sydney Carroll which led to the West End play *Nuts In May*, where one of Alexander Korda's casting directors noticed her. It was to be her only stage experience. She made her film début in 1938 as Marina in *The Rebel Son*, based on *Taras Bulba*, and then as Mary Lenley in *The Gaunt Stranger*, based on Edgar Wallace's story *The Ringer*. In 1939 she married Dr Murray Laing, a Canadian osteopath 20 years her senior, but the match ended in divorce in 1944. Between 1939 and 1943 Patricia Roc appeared in more than a dozen films, including a version of Eden Philpotts' play *The Farmer's Wife* (1941) as Sibley, and *We'll Meet Again* (1943) with Vera Lynn, in which she played Ruth. Her big break came as Celia Crowson in *Millions Like Us* (1943), written and directed by Frank Launder and Sidney Gilliat and co-starring Anne Crawford and Joy Shelton. Critics generally regard it as the best film made during the war about the home front. 5'4" Roc played a young widow (her airman husband, Gordon Jackson, was killed in action) who worked in a factory to help the war effort. It made her a star overnight. Director Launder then made *Two Thousand Women* (1944), about an attempt to rescue British women from a concentration camp in France. The film starred Roc (as Rosemary Brown), Phyllis Calvert, Flora Robson, Renee Houston, Anne Crawford and Jean Kent. *Love Story* (1944) was the first of several pictures in which Roc played second fiddle to Margaret Lockwood. Roc was cast as Judy, the fiancée of Stewart Granger, a pilot losing his sight, who is stolen from under her nose by the terminally ill Lockwood. The film, featuring the popular 'Cornish Rhapsody', was a big hit, but Lockwood had the plum role. Patricia Roc was always the safe but sexy girl. "I was the bouncy, sexy girl next door that mothers would like their sons to marry and the sons wouldn't have minded, either." This was borne out by a fan letter she once received from a teenage boy who invited her down to Devon for a weekend. "If it's fine," he wrote, "we could cycle into Exeter on Saturday afternoon. It's only 15 miles." While Margaret Lockwood got the rampantly sexy roles Patricia Roc got the virginal ones. In both *The Wicked Lady* (1945) and *Jassy* (1947), American censors called for retakes to cover up her embonpoint. In *Madonna Of The Seven Moons* (1944), Phyllis Calvert took the honours. Patricia Roc was loaned to Ealing Studios for *Johnny Frenchman* (1945), a tale of the rivalry between Cornish and Breton fishermen, and to Hollywood for *Canyon Passage* (1946), neither of which was a popular or critical success. In Tinseltown she had a brief affair with Ronald Reagan. Under contract to J. Arthur Rank, Roc believed that the organisation did not really know what to do with her. She refused to make *Cardboard Cavalier*, fearing that she would have been a stooge to the comedian Sid Field. In 1947, she played Mary, an orphan girl, in *The Brothers*, a melodramatic tale of superstition and jealousy among Skye fishermen at the turn of the century, and Julie Morgan, a North country lass, in *So Well Remembered*. In 1948, there were thankless roles in *When The Bough Breaks* as Lily, a London shop girl, and Mary Santell in *One Night With You*. The following year she appeared as Penelope Belman in *The Perfect Woman* but after that her contract with Rank was terminated by mutual consent. She married the French cameraman Andre Thomas in 1949 and moved to France to try to kick-start her career. It did not work, and by 1952 and *Something Money Can't Buy*, her career in Britain was over. Thomas was infertile and during the filming of *Something Money Can't Buy* Roc had an affair with her co-star Anthony Steel and became pregnant by

him. Their son Michael was born and Thomas agreed to raise him but collapsed and died of a stroke when the boy was only two. In 1960 she made her last film *Bluebeard's Ten Honeymoons* opposite George Sanders. In 1964 she married Walter Reif, a Viennese businessman, and the couple moved to the Swiss resort of Minusio, overlooking Lake Maggiore, in 1976. Reif died in 1986.

CAUSE: She died, aged 88, in La Carita Hospital, Locarno, Switzerland of kidney failure.

Blossom Rock

(EDITH MARIE MACDONALD)
Born August 21, 1895
Died January 14, 1978
Multi-named sibling. Born in Philadelphia, Pennsylvania, Blossom Rock was the elder sister of Jeanette MacDonald. In 1926 she married Clarence Rock (d. 1960) and they toured vaudeville in an act called "Rock and Blossom". She signed a contract with MGM, making her film début in the Joan Crawford vehicle *Mannequin* (1937). Like many actors, she was superstitious and visited a numerologist who told her she would have more success if her Christian name and surname contained the same number of letters. Consequently, she changed her name to Marie Blake and it is under this monicker that she was usually known. From 1938 until the end of the series she played Sally the telephonist in the *Dr Kildare* films. From September 18, 1964, she was probably best known, although least recognised, as Grandmama on the hit TV show *The Addams Family*. To cope with her numerous names – Blossom MacDonald, Blossom Rock, Mrs Clarence W. Rock and Marie Blake – she legally became Blossom Rock in the Sixties. When the series ended, she retired.

CAUSE: In the Seventies she suffered a massive stroke that left her incoherent and prevented her from working on the

1977 Addams Family reunion film. She died aged 82 of acute myocardial infarction and cerebral arteriosclerosis at the Motion Picture And Television Hospital and Country Home, 23450 Calabasas Road, Woodland Hills, California.

Rodgers & Hammerstein

(RICHARD CHARLES RODGERS)
Born June 28, 1902
Died December 30, 1979
(OSCAR GREELEY CLENDENNING HAMMERSTEIN II)
Born July 12, 1895
Died August 23, 1960
They wrote several happy tunes. Oscar Hammerstein II (the first was his grandfather, an impresario) was born on 135th Street, New York and intended to become a lawyer. His first experience with the stage occurred in 1912 at Columbia College. He got a job as a process server but when he was refused what he thought was a much-deserved raise, he left the law, becoming an assistant stage manager for a musical and marrying Myra Finn, a distant relative of Richard Rodgers, in the summer of 1917. They divorced after two children and on May 14, 1929, he married Melbourne-born Dorothy Blanchard. Working on the musical *Sometime* in 1918 he had his first lines used in Broadway and wrote a play that closed before it reached New York. In 1920 he wrote the book and lyrics for *Always You*. In 1921 he wrote *Tickle Me* with Otto Harbach and Frank Mandel. It ran for 200 performances on Broadway. His next four efforts all flopped. Then he created *Wildflower* (1923), *Rose Marie* (1924), *Sunny* (1925) and *The Desert Song* (1926). It was after this that Hammerstein realised he was only confined by musicals because he allowed himself to be confined. With *Show Boat* (1927), he and Jerome Kern broke the mould of musicals, abandoning the big number, chorus girls and forced humour. In 1940 he wrote 'The Last Time I Saw Paris' which won an Oscar in *Lady Be Good* (1941). He began working with Richard Rodgers in 1943 and their first collaboration produced *Oklahoma!* It was a massive success, as was their *Carousel* (1945), *South Pacific* (1949), *The King And I* (1951), *Me And Juliet* (1953), *Pipe Dream* (1955), *Flower Drum Song* (1958) and *The Sound Of Music*. Richard Rodgers was born at Hammells Station, Arverne, Long Island, and became interested in music aged two, when his parents sang and played the piano. By the age of six he had taught himself to play. His parents scrimped and scraped to send him to Columbia and Juilliard. In spring 1919 he met Lorenz Milton Hart (b. New York, May 2, 1895, d. Doctors' Hospital, New York, November 22, 1943, at 9.30pm) who was to become his first major collaborator. Together they wrote their first published song, 'Any Old Place Of Mine', which was premièred on August 26, 1919. Their other works included *A Danish Yankee In King Tut's Court* (1923), *The Prisoner Of Zenda* (1924), *The Girl Friend* (1926), *A Connecticut Yankee* (1927), *The Melody Man* (1930), *America's Sweetheart* (1931), *Love Me Tonight* (1932), *Mississippi* (1935), *Billy Rose's Jumbo* (1935), *On Your Toes* (1936), *Babes In Arms* (1937), *Pal Joey* (1940) and *I Married An Angel* (1942). The partnership ended due to Hart's alcoholism. Several of the works of Rodgers and Hammerstein were turned into films and they won an Oscar for Best Song for 'It Might As Well Be Spring' from *State Fair* (1945). *Oklahoma!* (1955) won two Oscars, *The King And I* (1956) won five Oscars, *South Pacific* (1958) picked up a solitary Oscar and *The Sound Of Music* (1965) also picked up five trophies. CAUSE: On September 16, 1959, Hammerstein had his regular annual check-up with his doctor, but as he was leaving he mentioned he was waking in the middle of the night regularly feeling

hungry, although a glass of milk settled his hunger. To be on the safe side, his doctor sent the lyricist for a check-up. It was discovered that Hammerstein had cancer of the stomach. On September 19, an operation was performed but was tragically too late. Doctors removed three-quarters of his stomach but they knew Hammerstein would be dead within a year. Chemotherapy was discussed and then rejected. On October 4, Hammerstein was released from hospital and went to watch rehearsals for his latest show with Rodgers, a tale of a nun and Nazis called *The Sound Of Music*. On July 7, 1960, X-rays revealed that the disease was back with a vengeance and Hammerstein decided he wanted to die with dignity at home, Highland Farm, Doylestown, Pennsylvania, not surrounded by well-meaning strangers in a hospital. He died aged 65 just over six weeks later and was cremated before his ashes were interred in Ferncliff Cemetery & Mausoleum, Secor Road, Hartsdale, New York 10530. Richard Rodgers, too, suffered from cancer and in July 1969 he was felled by a cardiac arrest. In August 1974 he underwent a laryngectomy and had to learn to speak again. He died just over four years later. Despite their long and successful collaboration, Hammerstein said he didn't really know Rodgers and in 1975 Rodgers said that, although he cared about Hammerstein, he was never sure whether Hammerstein actually liked him.

FURTHER READING: *The Rodgers And Hammerstein Story* – Stanley Green (London: W.H. Allen, 1963); *The Sound Of Their Music: The Story Of Rodgers And Hammerstein* – Frederick Nolan (London: Unwin Paperbacks, 1979).

Estelita Rodriguez

Born July 2, 1913
Died March 12, 1966
'Cuban Fireball'. Born in Guanajay, Cuba, Rodriguez owed her career to Herbert J. Yates, who ran Republic Pictures. She appeared in *Mexicana* (1945) as Lupita, *Along The Navajo Trail* (1945), *On The Old Spanish Trail* (1947) as Lolita, *The Gay Ranchero* (1948) as Consuelo Belmonte, *Twilight In The Sierras* (1949) as Lola Chavez, *The Golden Stallion* (1949) as Pepe Valdez, *Sunset In The West* (1950) as Carmelita, *Belle Of Old Mexico* (1950) as Rosito, *In Old Amarillo* (1951) as Pepita, *Havana Rose* (1951) as Estelita DeMarco, *Cuban Fireball* (1951), *Tropical Heat Wave* (1952), *South Pacific Trail* (1952) as Lita Alvarez, *The Fabulous Senorita* (1952) as Estelita Rodriguez, *Rio Bravo* (1959) as Consuela and *Jesse James Meets Frankenstein's Daughter* (1966) as Juanita Lopez.

CAUSE: She died aged 52 on the kitchen floor of her home in Van Nuys, California, supposedly from influenza. At the time she had been negotiating to star in a biopic of Lupe Velez. Her mentor Yates had died in February 1966 and her ex-husband, Grant Withers, died by his own hand on March 27, 1959.

Charles "Buddy" Rogers

Born August 13, 1904
Died April 21, 1999
"America's Boyfriend". Born in Olathe, Kansas, Charles Rogers was the son of Bert Henry Rogers, a judge who edited the local paper, the *Mirror*. He began acting in school, before going to the University of Kansas where he played in a jazz band on the weekends – he was paid $10 for playing on a Friday and $12 for Saturdays. Spotted by a talent scout, he was put under contract at Paramount and attended their drama school at Astoria, Long Island, graduating in 1926 when he appeared in *Fascinating Youth* as Teddy Ward. Audience reaction was positive so he was put in *More Pay – Less Work* (1926) as Willia Hinchfield and *So's Your Old Man* (1926) as Kenneth Murchison opposite W.C. Fields.

He was cast in *Wings* (premièred August 12, 1927) as Jack Powell, opposite Clara Bow and Richard Arlen. The film later won the first Best Picture Oscar. His next film was *My Best Girl* (released October 31, 1927) as Joe Grant and his co-star later became his best girl off screen as well. On June 26, 1937 he became the third husband of America's Sweetheart Mary Pickford. It was the first film, in which Pickford kissed her leading man on screen and also her last silent film. It was a happy union and they were together until her death in 1979. They honeymooned in Hawaii with Jeanette MacDonald and her new husband Gene Raymond. Five thousand fans jammed the quayside at Honolulu to see the two couples. They lived a very private life in later years and when she became ill, Rogers attended Hollywood functions alone but he would never comment on his wife. A devout Christian Scientist, he was always positive about every subject. His other films included: *Get Your Man* (1927) as Robert deBellecontre, *Abie's Irish Rose* (1928) as Abie Levy, *Varsity* (1928) as Jimmy Duffy, *Close Harmony* (1929) as Al West, *Young Eagles* (1930) as Lieutenant Robert Banks, *Follow Thru* (1930) as Jerry Downes, *Heads Up* (1930) as Jack Mason, *Along Came Youth* (1930) as Larry Brooks, *The Road To Reno* (1931) as Tom Wood, *Working Girls* (1931) as Boyd Wheeler, *Best Of Enemies* (1933) as Jimmie Hartman, *Take A Chance* (1933) as Kenneth Raleigh, *Dance Band* (1935) as Buddy Milton, *Old Man Rhythm* (1935) as Johnny Roberts, *An Innocent Affair* (1948) as Claude Kimball and *The Parson And The Outlaw* (1957) as Reverend Jericho Jones. He also appeared as Dennis Lindsay in three Mexican Spitfire movies opposite Lupe Velez: *Mexican Spitfire's Baby* (1941), *Mexican Spitfire At Sea* (1942) and *Mexican Spitfire Sees A Ghost* (1942). Rogers and Pickford adopted two children – she was unable to have her own: Ronald Charles (b. 1937, adopted on May 2, 1943) and Roxanne (b. August 18, 1942, adopted in June 1944, d. April 17, 2001 from osteoporosis). However, the children turned out to be a disappointment and although financially provided for, Mary Pickford had no contact with them after they reached 21. In 1981 Rogers married estate agent Beverly Ricono (b. 1908, d. January 3, 2007) although he never really got over the loss of Mary Pickford. "I'll be talking to someone," he recalled, "and I'll overhear people saying 'He was married to Mary Pickford' and then someone else will say, 'Who was Mary Pickford?' And that hurts me."
CAUSE: Rogers died of natural causes aged 94 at Rancho Mirage, California. He was buried at Forest Lawn Memorial Park, 69855 East Ramon Road, Cathedral City, California CA92234.

Ginger Rogers

(VIRGINIA KATHERINE McMATH)
Born July 16, 1907 or 1911
Died April 25, 1995
Terpsichorean talent. To many people the Thirties were a time of hardship and financial worries. Not for Ginger Rogers: "It was a whole new life for me . . . It was happy and beautiful and gay and interesting. I was surrounded by marvellous people." On December 23, 1933, *Flying Down To Rio* (1933) opened with Ginger playing Honey Hale. It was her first big success and led to several other starring roles. Despite being forever linked with Fred Astaire in the public consciousness, they only made ten films together. Astaire wasn't initially keen on having a partner, saying: "I did not go into pictures with the thought of becoming a team." Like many showbiz stars, Ginger had a very pushy mother. Lela Rogers was born on Christmas Day 1891 as Lela Owens. She married at 18 and after an infant death, Ginger was born in Independence, Missouri. Her official date of birth and the one

listed on her death certificate is 1911 but some friends insist the year was 1908. She was nicknamed Ginger by a cousin. Her parents split up before Ginger was a year old and Lela took Ginger to Ennis, Texas. Her father, desperate to see his daughter, twice kidnapped Ginger and was eventually subjected to a court order. In 1916 Lela went to Hollywood to become a screenwriter, leaving Ginger with her parents. In 1919 she married John Rogers, who adopted Ginger. Seven years later, Ginger won a Charleston competition and she was on her way. Lela removed her from school and for the next two years Ginger toured the country in amateur dance challenges. In 1928, much to the annoyance of Rogers' overpowering mother, Ginger eloped to New Orleans with Jack Culpepper, a singer. They married and formed an act – Ginger and Pepper – but they were not a success and they split after ten months. They were divorced in 1931. That year Ginger and Lela travelled to Hollywood, where Ginger was spotted by Mervyn LeRoy who encouraged her to appear in *42nd Street* (1933). He also had a brief affair with her. She popularised the song 'We're In The Money' in *Gold Diggers Of 1933* (1933). In January 1934 she signed a long-term contract with RKO, who put her on the road to stardom with *Flying Down To Rio*. Ginger's first romantic feature with Astaire was *The Gay Divorcee* (1934). They then appeared in *Roberta* (1935), *Top Hat* (1935), *Follow The Fleet* (1936), *Swing Time* (1936), *Shall We Dance?* (1937), *Carefree* (1938), *The Story Of Vernon And Irene Castle* (1939) and *The Barkleys Of Broadway* (1949) (continuity blip: in one scene in this film, Fred and Ginger are in the back of a taxi when suddenly a lighted cigarette appears in his hand). On November 14, 1934, at the Little Church of the Flower in Glendale, California, Ginger married Lew Ayres. One Christmas she gave him a toy train set. However, it was not to be a happy match. RKO announced their separation on May 9, 1936, and the couple was divorced in 1941. That year Ginger won an Oscar for *Kitty Foyle* (1940). Then she engaged in an affair with director George Stevens, again much to the consternation of Lela, who played Ginger's on-screen mother in *The Major And The Minor* (1942). On January 16, 1943, Ginger married for the third time. Her new husband was Jack Calvin Briggs, a US marine. That year she was the highest paid actress in Hollywood. That didn't help her improve her private life and she was divorced in 1949. In the mid-Fifties Ginger's film appearances became fewer: *Monkey Business* (1952) as Edwina Fulton, *Dreamboat* (1952) as Gloria Marlowe, *We're Not Married!* (1952) as Ramona Gladwyn, *Forever Female* (1953) as Beatrice Page and *Black Widow* (1954) as Lottie. On February 7, 1953, she married the 18-years-younger lawyer-turned-actor Jacques Bergerac (b. Biarritz, France, May 26, 1927). They divorced in 1957 after MGM did not renew his contract. On March 16, 1961, Ginger married actor William Marshall (b. Chicago, Illinois, October 2, 1917) and that turned out to be her longest marriage, lasting ten years. Her last film was playing the mother of another Hollywood star in *Harlow* (1965). CAUSE: Ginger suffered two strokes and was confined to a wheelchair. She died at her home in Rancho Mirage, California, 40 230 Club View Drive, of acute myocardial infarction and arteriosclerosis cardiovascular disease after being in a diabetic coma. Reportedly the last words of the devoutly Christian Scientist Ginger were: "I've had a wonderful life. God's will will now be done. Praise to God." She was buried with her mother in Oakwood Memorial Park, 22601 Lassen, Chatsworth, California 91311. Coincidentally, that's also where Fred Astaire is interred.

Peter Rogers

Born February 20, 1914
Died April 14, 2009

Mr *Carry On*. Born in Rochester, Kent, the son of an amateur musician, Peter Rogers was educated at the King's School in Rochester from seven to 18. When he left school, he stayed at home writing plays supported by a small allowance from his father. He finally got his first job as a reporter on the *Kentish Express* when most of his plays flopped. In the late Thirties, he left to become Auriol Lee's assistant on West End productions such as JB Priestley's *People At Sea* and John Van Druten's *Gertie Maud* before returning to the written word initially on *Picture Post*, and then as a BBC radio scriptwriter. He had to find work. His father had remarried after his wife died, stopped the allowance and evicted his son. When cerebral spinal meningitis, which kept him in hospital for a year, ruled him out of military service in the war, he joined J. Arthur Rank's Religious Films in 1942. He wrote the *Sunday Thought For The Week*, which allowed him to know what audiences thought. "One night the audience at Edgware threw tomatoes at the screen," he recalled, "and they were rationed." After the war, he joined the Rank-owned Gainsborough Studios in Shepherd's Bush, west London as an assistant scenario editor. It was there he met his future wife, the producer Betty Box. They married on Christmas Eve 1948. They worked together on several films including *Marry Me* (1949) and *Don't Ever Leave Me* (released July 19, 1949) and when Rank moved its production department to Pinewood Studios, they continued their professional partnership on films such as *Appointment With Venus* (1951) and *Venetian Bird* (1952). Rogers began working with Gerald Thomas in the mid-Fifties and they produced children's films including: *The Dog And The Diamonds* (1953), which won the Venice Film Festival Award, *The Gay Dog* (released June 1954) which starred Wilfred Pickles as greyhound owner Jim Gay and *Circus Friends* (1956). In 1957 Rogers wrote and produced the thriller *Time Lock* (released August 27, 1957), which starred Robert Beatty. In 1958 Rogers produced the first of the 31 films that would make his name and, let it not be underestimated, his fortune. One day Rogers saw *The Bull Boys*, a script by R.F. Delderfield about the effect of army conscription on a pair of ballet dancers. It was not a comedy. The rights belonged to Rogers's fellow producer, and brother-in-law, Sydney Box, who had been unable to find the money for the project. Rogers thought the script unfilmable so he began to approach some well-known comedy writers. They all said no, one in dramatic fashion. When Rogers entered Spike Milligan's office he found Spike waving a loaded revolver around his head, shouting, "I can't see anybody just now. I'm just about to kill myself." John Antrobus did some work but Rogers was still not satisfied. He hired Norman Hudis to rewrite it and thus *Carry On Sergeant* (released August 1958) was born. The film began shooting on March 24, 1958, and starred William Hartnell, Bob Monkhouse, Kenneth Williams, Charles Hawtrey and Kenneth Connor and was made for less than £75,000. The film's critical response was lukewarm but the public flocked to the film and only *Dunkirk* (1958) and *Bridge On The River Kwai* (1957) beat it at the box office. Emboldened, Rogers decided to make a follow-up but dispensed with comedian Monkhouse preferring to work with comic actors (Ted Ray in *Teacher* being a rare exception and Phil Silvers who was brought in to encourage American sales). *Carry On Nurse* topped the box office charts in 1959. Just £475 was spent on costumes for the entire film. Rogers said that he conceived the title in his bath and then hired a scriptwriter

– first Hudis then Talbot Rothwell – to put his idea on paper. The format changed little over the years. Rogers told producer Hugh Stewart when the latter asked what he was working on, "Same story, different title." When the series started Rogers and Thomas released three *Carry On*s each year. They shot and edited them in less than six weeks so their stars could still do summer seasons and pantomimes. Most of the films were shot in and around Pinewood in part because Rogers did not want to spend money and also because he was loathe to be separated from his beloved Alsatians. "A tree is a tree anywhere," he said, "and it's only funny if someone falls out of it. It doesn't matter where it is. We went to Chobham for *Carry On Cowboy*, and sometimes as far as Windsor or Maidenhead." If Rogers did not want to spend money on locations, he was equally parsimonious when it came to his casts. He said he would "do anything for my actors except pay them." Kenneth Williams was paid £800 for *Sergeant*, which rose to £5,000 from *Carry On Cruising* (1962), the first colour film in the series. Sid James received the same amount but the women did not get parity of pay: £3,000 for Barbara Windsor, £2,500 for Joan Sims. The cast received no royalties or residuals. Rogers offered his stars the opportunity to take lower fees in exchange for a percentage of the profits after the success of *Carry On Nurse*, but they or their agents declined. Rogers and Thomas were paid £15,000 for each film, plus a reported one-third of profits, out of which Rogers treated himself to a new Rolls-Royce every year. Rogers said that the *Carry On* brand was more important than any one person. When Charles Hawtrey demanded top billing and a star on his dressing room door or he would not appear in the film, Rogers called his bluff and replaced him with another actor. The complete canon is: *Carry On*

Sergeant (1958), *Carry On Nurse* (1959), *Carry On Teacher* (1959), *Carry On Constable* (1960), *Carry On Regardless* (1961), *Carry On Cruising* (1962), *Carry On Cabby* (1963), *Carry On Spying* (1964), *Carry On Jack* (1964), *Carry On Cleo* (1964), *Carry On Cowboy* (1965), *Carry On Screaming* (1966), *Carry On Follow That Camel* (1967), *Carry On Don't Lose Your Head* (1967), *Carry On Up the Khyber* (1968), *Carry On Doctor* (1968), *Carry On Camping* (1969), *Carry On Again, Doctor* (1969), *Carry On Up The Jungle* (1970), *Carry On Loving* (1970), *Carry On Henry* (1971), *Carry On At Your Convenience* (1971), *Carry On Matron* (1972), *Carry On Abroad* (1972), *Carry On Girls* (1973), *Carry On Dick* (1974), *Carry On Behind* (1975), *Carry On England* (1976), *Carry On Emmannuelle* (1978) and *Carry On Columbus* (1992). The series began to lose its way by the Seventies and the death of Sid James in 1976 signalled the beginning of the end. *Carry On England* was the first to explicitly show bare breasts and most of the cast of *Carry On Emmannuelle* appeared out of loyalty. *Carry On Columbus* should never have been made. It featured Julian Clary, Peter Richardson, Richard Wilson and Alexei Sayle who either did not understand the *métier* or were just not funny in the first place. Execrable, it sank with all hands. Away from the *Carry On*s, Rogers also produced *Please Turn Over* (1959), *Twice Round The Daffodils* (1962) which starred Kenneth Williams and Joan Sims, and *Bless This House* (1972), the film version of the Sid James sitcom. Rogers was also in charge of *Ivanhoe*, with Roger Moore. In 1994 Rogers went bankrupt and while many blamed the failure of *Columbus*, he said it was due to a bad investment in a television company. That year, the Barbican put on a retrospective of all the *Carry On*'s and Rogers confessed that he had never sat through an entire screening with an audience and did not intend to do so.

Rogers watched *Carry On Up The Khyber*, his favourite, but did not view any others. "Even the Marquis de Sade couldn't have devised a worse torture," he said.

CAUSE: Rogers died of natural causes at Gerrards Cross, Buckinghamshire. He was 95.

Roy Rogers
(LEONARD SKYE)
Born November 5, 1911
Died July 6, 1998
'The King of the Cowboys'. Roy Rogers was born in Cincinnati, Ohio, and migrated to California in 1929 where he formed a singing duo with his cousin. Later changing his name to Dick Weston, he formed the group The Sons Of The Pioneers, which indirectly led him into films. In the Forties and Fifties he appeared regularly in films alongside his horse Trigger and, later, wife Dale Evans. When his film career came to an end, he moved onto the small screen. Away from showbiz, he was an astute businessman who came to be worth around $100 million.

CAUSE: He died of congestive heart failure in Apple Valley, California. He was 86.

Will Rogers
Born November 4, 1879
Died August 15, 1935
Homespun wit. William Penn Adair Rogers was a renaissance man of the twentieth century. Actor. Writer. Comic. Politician. Equestrian. Producer. Director. Journalist. Born in Oologah, Oklahoma, 5'11" Rogers began his career in South Africa before returning to America after the Boer War. He began appearing in silent films (the first being Samuel Goldfish's *Laughing Bill Hyde*) but lost money when he financed his own productions. His transition to sound films was seamless and he also began appearing on the wireless and writing for newspapers, where he was extremely influential as well as humorous. He once remarked: "You can't say civilisation doesn't advance, for in every war they kill you in a new way." He helped Franklin D. Roosevelt win the 1932 Presidential election and served as Mayor of Beverly Hills, where a park is named in his honour. (It was in the Will Rogers Memorial Park that singer George Michael was arrested for gross indecency on April 8, 1998.) Rogers' other pronouncements included: "I don't make jokes – I just watch the government and report the facts"; "The American people are generous and will forgive almost any weakness with the exception of stupidity"; "Nobody wants to be called common people, especially common people" and "A remark generally hurts in proportion to its truth." Rogers married Betty Blake (d. 1944) on November 25, 1908, and fathered four children: William Vann (b. October 20, 1911), Mary Amelia (b. May 18, 1913), James Blake (b. July 25, 1915) and Fred Stone (b. 1918, d. California 1919, of diphtheria).

CAUSE: After pulling out of a film, Rogers fulfilled a long-standing ambition to visit Alaska. His fellow traveller was aviator Wiley Post and they flew in a plane that can openly be described as a cut and shut – it was an amalgam of four separate aircraft. In Alaska they were warned not to continue their journey because of bad weather, but Rogers was impatient to visit Point Barrow. They took off from Fairbanks and followed the Trans Alaska Pipeline before heading west in near zero visibility. They landed in a lagoon and asked directions from some Inuits. They took off again but only reached an altitude of 50 feet when the engine cut out and the plane dived into the water. The fuselage split open and one of the wings came away before the plane exploded. It was exactly 3.18pm. Rogers, who "never met a man [he] didn't like", was 55. Originally buried at Forest Lawn Memorial-Parks,

Rogers was reinterred at Will Rogers Memorial, Box 157, Claremore, Oklahoma 74018.

Gilbert Roland

(LUIS ANTONIO DÁMASO DE ALONSO)
Born December 11, 1901
Died May 15, 1994
Latin lover. Born in Ciudad Juárez, or possibly Chihuahua, Mexico, the son of a bullfighter, he eschewed the life of a matador for the life of a thespian in Hollywood. His first major film was *The Plastic Age* (1925) as Carl Peters but it was as Armand Duval in *Camille* (1927) that he caught the public's attention. Hollywood had, and still has, an aversion to casting Latinos in leading roles in A pictures, so the handsome, moustachioed, 5'11" Roland was usually someone's friend or rival. His films included: *The Woman Disputed* (1928) as Paul Hartman, *New York Nights* (1929) as Fred Deverne, *Mephisto* (1930) as Robert d'Arbel, *No Living Witness* (1932) as Jerry Bennett, *The Passionate Plumber* (1932) as Tony Lagorce, *Call Her Savage* (1932) as Moonglow, *She Done Him Wrong* (1933) as Serge Stanieff, *After Tonight* (1933) as Captain Rudolph 'Rudy' Ritter, *Ladies Love Danger* (1935) as Ricardo Souchet, *Midnight Taxi* (1937) as Flash Dillon, *Thunder Trail* (1937) as Arizona Dick Ames, *Gambling On The High Seas* (1940) as Greg Morella, *My Life With Caroline* (1941) as Paco Del Valle, *Angels With Broken Wings* (1941) as Don Pablo Vicente, *Enemy Agents Meet Ellery Queen* (1942) as Paul Gillette, *The Desert Hawk* (1944) as The Hawk/Hassan, *Captain Kidd* (1945) as Jose Lorenzo, *The Gay Cavalier* (1946) as Chico Villa, *High Conquest* (1947) as Hugo Lanier, *Malaya* (1949) as Romano, *Crisis* (1950) as Gonzales, *Bullfighter And The Lady* (1951) as Manolo Estrada, *The Miracle Of Our Lady Of Fatima* (1952) as Hugo da Silva, *My Six Convicts* (1952) as Punch Pinero, *Thunder Bay* (1953) as Teche Bossier, *Underwater!*

(1955) as Dominic, *Around The World In 80 Days* (1956) as Achmed Abdullah, *Guns Of The Timberland* (1960) as Monty Walker, *Cheyenne Autumn* (1964) as Dull Knife, *Anche Nel West C'Era Una Volta Dio* (1968) as Juan Chasquisdo, *Islands In The Stream* (1977) as Captain Ralph and, his final film, *Barbarosa* (1982) as Don Branlio. He was married twice, the first time to Constance Bennett. His second wife, from December 12, 1954, was Guillermina Cantu.
CAUSE: Roland died aged 92 of cancer in Beverly Hills, California.

Ruth Roman

(NORMA ROMAN)
Born December 23, 1922
Died September 9, 1999
Reliable support who never quite made it. Born in Lynn, Massachusetts, Ruth Roman studied at the Bishop Lee Dramatic School in Boston, and appeared in various films in bit parts before landing her first starring role in an A picture in *Belle Starr's Daughter* (1948) as Rose of Cimarron. Prior to that she had starred as Lothel in the 1945 series *Jungle Queen* in which she fought Nazis in Africa! Her films included: *Dallas* (1950) as Tonia Robles (coincidentally, one of her last parts was as Sylvia Lean in TV series *Dallas* spin-off *Knots Landing* in 1986), *Colt .45* (1950) as Beth Donovan, *Barricade* (1950) as Judith Burns, Alfred Hitchcock's *Strangers On A Train* (1951) as Anne Morton, King Vidor's *Lightning Strikes Twice* (1951) as Shelley Carnes, *Mara Maru* (1952) as Stella Callahan, *Young Man With Ideas* (1952) as Julie Webster, *Invitation* (1952) as Maude Redwick, *Tanganyika* (1954) as Peggy Merion, *Joe MacBeth* (1955) as Lily MacBeth and *Impulse* (1974) as Julia Marstow. She was married three times. Towards the end of her career, she spent most of her time in television. She was a passenger on the *Andrea Doria* when it sank in the mid-Fifties.

CAUSE: She died in her sleep in Laguna Beach, California. She was 76.

"Prince" Michael Romanoff
(HERSHEL GEGUZIN or HARRY F. GERGUSON)
Born February 20, 1890 or 1895
Died September 1, 1971
Conman. Born in Vilnius, Lithuania, Geguzin may have emigrated to New York when he was around 10 but he claimed that he was born in the United States and travelled to Russia when he was young but then he also claimed that he was Prince Michael Dimitri Alexandrovich Obolensky-Romanoff, the nephew of Tsar Nicholas II. There is some evidence that he was born Harry F. Gerguson in Brooklyn in 1895 and spent time in orphanages in Texas, Illinois and New York. For his role in the Great War (if he had one at all) he let his imagination run riot – he was a Cossack colonel on the Eastern Front, served with General Allenby in Palestine or possibly spent time in prison after killing a German officer in a duel. The earliest definite sighting of him was in 1919 when he turned up in Paris claiming to be the tsar's nephew. He moved to London but was jailed after failing to pay his bills. In 1922 he arrived at Ellis Island but was refused admission because he could not prove his place of birth. Undaunted he escaped and made his way to Manhattan. He embarked on a lecture tour where he told how he had witnessed the murder of Rasputin, served in the French Foreign legion and escaped death from the Bolshevik agents who had been sent to kill him. On his tours he stole small but valuable items from his hosts and bounced cheques. In 1927 he moved to the fake capital of America, Hollywood, where he was welcomed with open arms. He opened the eponymous restaurant that made him famous in 1938 and even launched two more – one in San Franciso and one in Palm Springs – but they failed. Romanoff's was at 326 North Rodeo Drive and at 140 South Rodeo Drive in Beverly Hills. In 1951, it moved to a new location at 240 South Rodeo Drive. It was expensive and the place to be seen until its closure on December 31, 1962. In 1948 the American government gave up trying to deport him and he became a citizen although he had to forego his "titles". He appeared in a dozen or so films including two, *Von Ryan's Express* (1965) and *Tony Rome* (1967), with his friend Frank Sinatra. One day on the set of *Tony Rome*, a young actor tried to catch Romanoff out by speaking to him in Russian. Romanoff looked at him with hauteur: "The vulgarity of a stranger speaking to me in that tongue! We never spoke anything but French at court." (In fact, the tsar and tsarina usually spoke English at court.) In 1948 Romanoff married Gloria Lister and they lived on North Beverly Drive in Hollywood. Of himself he said, "No one has ever discovered the truth about me – not even myself."
CAUSE: He died aged 76 or 81 of a heart attack in Los Angeles, California.

Cesar Romero
Born February 15, 1907
Died January 1, 1994
Gay caballero. Despite spending 20 years as the archetypal Latin lover, Romero was actually born in New York. However, his parents were Cuban and his grandfather, José Martí, was the liberator of that country. Romero, who disliked being known as a Latin lover, was an exceptional dancer and that's how he began his career, being paid 10¢ for a dance in Manhattan. That led to Broadway shows and finally Hollywood, where he made his début in *The Shadow Laughs* (1933) as Tony Rico. He signed for MGM but the homophobic Louis B. Mayer didn't know what to do with him. In 1935 he signed for Paramount, where he was billed as "the new Valentino". When playing Marlene Dietrich's lover, Antonio Galvan, in

The Devil Is A Woman (1935) didn't win him acclaim, he moved to Fox. He went on to appear in over 100 films, including: *The Thin Man* (1934) as Chris Jorgenson, *British Agent* (1934) as Tito Del Val, *Metropolitan* (1935) as Niki Baroni, *Diamond Jim* (1935) as Jerry Richardson, *Cardinal Richelieu* (1935) as Andre de Pons, *Strange Wives* (1935) as Boris, *Rendezvous* (1935) as Captain Nicholas 'Nikki' Nieterstein, *Clive Of India* (1935) as Mir Jaffar, *Love Before Breakfast* (1936) as Bill Wadsworth, *Nobody's Fool* (1936) as Dizzy Rantz, *Wee Willie Winkie* (1937) as Khoda Khan, *My Lucky Star* (1938) as George Cabot, Jr, *Wife, Husband And Friend* (1939) as Hugo, *Charlie Chan At Treasure Island* (1939) as Fred Rhadini, *Return Of The Cisco Kid* (1939) as Lopez, *Viva Cisco Kid* (1940) as Cisco Kid, *The Gay Caballero* (1940) as Cisco Kid, *The Cisco Kid And The Lady* (1940) as Cisco Kid, *Tall, Dark And Handsome* (1941) as Shep Morrison, *Romance Of The Rio Grande* (1941) as Cisco Kid, *Ride On Vaquero* (1941) as Cisco Kid (thereafter the series was cancelled after complaints that Romero was playing the part in a 'gay' way), *Weekend In Havana* (1941) as Monte Blanca, *Tales Of Manhattan* (1942) as Harry Wilson, *Coney Island* (1943) as Joe Rocco, *Carnival In Costa Rica* (1947) as Pepe Castro, *Captain From Castile* (1947) as Hernando Cortez, *That Lady In Ermine* (1948) as Mario, *The Beautiful Blonde From Bashful Bend* (1949) as Blackie Jobero, *Love That Brute* (1950) as Pretty Willie, *FBI Girl* (1951) as Agent Glen Stedman, *Street Of Shadows* (1953) as Luigi, *Vera Cruz* (1954) as Marquis de Labordere, *Around the World In 80 Days* (1956) as a henchman, *Villa!* (1958) as Fierro, *Ocean's 11* (1960) as Duke Santos, *Donovan's Reef* (1963) as Marquis Andre de Lage, *A House Is Not A Home* (1964) as Mafioso Lucky Luciano in the story of madame Polly Adler, *Target: Harry* (1969) as Lieutenant George Duval, *The Computer Wore Tennis Shoes* (1970) as A.J. Arno, *Now You See Him, Now You Don't* (1972) as A.J. Arno, *The Spectre Of Edgar Allan Poe* (1974) as Doctor Grimalda, *Lust In The Dust* (1985) as Father Garcia and *Judgment Day* (1988). When his film roles began to dry up he turned to television and played The Joker in *Batman* (both the TV series and the spin-off 1966 film) and Peter Stavros in *Falcon Crest*. Romero was tall (6′3″), handsome, moustachioed, nicknamed 'Butch' by his friends and as gay as a goose. He had affairs with Tyrone Power and Desi Arnaz.
CAUSE: He died in Santa Monica, California, aged 86, of natural causes.

George Rose
Born February 19, 1920
Died May 5, 1988
Danger seeker. Stocky character actor. Born in Bicester, Oxfordshire, Rose became a secretary and then a farmer before studying at the Central School of Speech & Drama. He joined the Old Vic company and made his first stage appearance at the New Theatre on August 31, 1944. He continued to work in the theatre, appearing as Boanerges in Shaw's *The Apple Cart* opposite Noël Coward from May 7, 1953. Prior to the performance Rose had visited a trattoria and ate moules marinière and his breath stank of garlic. As he approached Coward (playing King Magnus) on stage to get his application papers, instead of handing the documentation over, Coward backed away, "Oh my dear, my dear, don't breathe out, you're scorching the furniture polish. We only need a loaf of bread and we can all have a meal." Rose corpsed and the Master was not impressed. "We can all do a bit of ad libbing during a long run, when it's getting rather dreary but I will not have corpsing." Rose had made his first film four years earlier in *Midnight Frolics* (1949) and appeared in several more films on both sides of the Atlantic. His

other films included: *The Square Ring* (1953) as Whitey Johnson, *Track The Man Down* (1954) as Rick Lambert, *The Sea Shall Not Have Them* (1954) as Tebbitt, *The Good Die Young* (1954) as Bunny, *The Shiralee* (1957) as Donny, *The Good Companions* (1957) as the theatre manager, *Barnacle Bill* (1957) as Bullen, *A Night To Remember* (1958) as Chief Baker Joughin, *Jack The Ripper* (1959) as Clarke, *Hawaii* (1966) as Captain Janders and *The Pirates Of Penzance* (1983) as Major-General Stanley. For his stage work, Rose received two Tonys and three other Tony nominations.

CAUSE: In late April 1988, Rose, 68, finished a three-week run in *The Mystery Of Edwin Drood* at Washington's Kennedy Center. On May 2, he flew to the Dominican Republic where four years earlier he had bought a large, three-bedroomed house near Sosua on the north coast, despite warning from friends that the country was dangerous. Perhaps it was the danger that attracted Rose. In 1986 Rose had adopted a 17-year-old Dominican boy named Domingo Antonio "Juan" Vásquez who, as a result of the action, stood to inherit Rose's estate valued at $2 million. Three days later, Rose's body was discovered in a ditch near his home, 120 miles north of Santo Domingo. His overturned red Suzuki was resting on its right side nearby and initial reports said that Rose had been killed in a car crash. The police stated that Rose had lost control of the car after suffering a heart attack or falling asleep at the wheel. In his wallet was a packet of white powder, believed to be cocaine. There was one problem. Rose hated driving. Another additional problem was the state of Rose's corpse: he had deep, five-inch wounds in the back of his head, and his left arm had been badly beaten and almost wrenched from its socket. In addition, the car's engine and headlights were off and it was in neutral. Domingo Vásquez arrived with his girlfriend but seemed unconcerned by his "father's" death. The local pathologist, Dr Sergio Santa Valdez, could not carry out a proper autopsy so tissue samples were flown to Miami where the Dade County coroner's report stated that Rose had been killed by massive blows to the head. Rose was buried in an unmarked grave in a tatty cemetery in Sosua. On May 12, the police charged Rose's adopted son, Juan Antonio Vásquez, the boy's natural father, Maximo Vásquez Padilla, an uncle, and Luis Manuel "El Gringo" Toribio with the actor's murder. They confessed that they had kidnapped Rose then tortured him for eight hours before killing him and faking a car crash. Domingo Vásquez said that he had been having a sexual relationship with Rose since the age of 13 and was jealous when Rose began flirting with another boy identified as Juli, aged 14. He planned the murder, he said, with his father who had hired the other two for $350. The father said that he "sought revenge on the American Rose because of his homosexual activities, since he was hurting a lot of boys . . . in addition to mine, whom he had already prostituted since the age of 13 to satisfy his sexual desires." The two men also said that they feared that Rose would disinherit the teenager. A year after the four men were charged, Domingo Vásquez was released on bail. None ever stood trial for George Rose's murder. When Rose's will went into probate Domingo Vásquez received the house in Sosua which he sold for $250,000 and then moved to America. He did not return to his homeland until 2006. The other three men remained in prison until March 1997 when they were released. The other beneficiary of the will is a tiny 12th century parish church at Bucknell, near Bicester where Rose's mother was born and where his grandparents are buried. A memorial service was held at New York's Shubert Theatre in June 1988.

Leonard Rosenman
Born September 7, 1924
Died March 4, 2008
Oscar winner. Born in Brooklyn, New York, Rosenman studied under composers Arnold Schoenberg, Roger Sessions and Luigi Dallapiccola. He became friendly with James Dean and was on the set of *East Of Eden* in 1954 when Dean introduced him to director Elia Kazan. Rosenman was asked to write the score and thus began his cinematic career. Rosenman next wrote the music for Dean's next film *Rebel Without A Cause* (1955). His other films included *The Cobweb* (1955), *Hell Is For Heroes* (1962), *The Chapman Report* (1962), *Fantastic Voyage* (1966), *A Man Called Horse* (1970), *Beneath The Planet Of The Apes* (1970), *Battle For The Planet Of The Apes* (1973), and *Barry Lyndon* (1975) and *Bound For Glory* (1976) for which he won back-to-back Oscars. He also won an Emmy for his television music and worked on shows such as *Marcus Welby, M.D.*, *Quincy, M.E.*, *The Virginian* and *The Defenders*.
CAUSE: Rosenman died of a heart attack at the Motion Picture & Television Country House and Hospital in Woodland Hills, California. He was 83.

Roberto Rossellini
Born May 8, 1906
Died June 3, 1977
'The father of Italian neo-realism'. Born in Rome, the son of an architect, Rossellini spent much of his childhood in a cinema designed by his father. His first film, *Dafne* (1936), was shot in a spare room of the family home. His second, *Prélude A L'Après-Midi D'Un Faune* (1937), was banned by the authorities for indecency. His reputation was made with *Roma, Città Aperta/Open City* (1946) and *Paisà/Paisan* (1946), which he co-wrote with Federico Fellini. Rossellini was never able to recapture his early form

and became notorious in 1949 when actress Ingrid Bergman left her husband for him. She became pregnant by Rossellini, news that was broken by gossip columnist Louella O. Parsons on December 12, 1949. Since it was impossible for the lovers to marry in Italy, they arranged a proxy ceremony in Mexico. Oddly, both proxies were men. Their son, Robertino, was born in Rome's Villa Margherita Clinic on February 2, 1950. They followed him with twin daughters – Isabella Fiorella Elettra Giovanna weighing 7lb 3oz and Isotta Ingrid Frieda Giuliana weighing 8lb 5oz, born in Rome on June 18, 1952. In 1957 Rossellini made another woman pregnant, Indian screenwriter Somali Das Gupta, and that led to the break-up of his marriage to Bergman. Crowds booed his *India* (1959) as a result of the affair and the film flopped.
CAUSE: He died aged 71 in Rome of a heart attack.

Norman Rossington
Born December 24, 1928
Died May 20, 1999
The dumb sidekick. Born in Liverpool, he began working on the docks as an office boy and then trained at the Bristol Old Vic. Rossington made a career out of playing the hero's thick friend or a stupid villain. He was Sergeant Cupcake in television's *The Army Game*. He was the perpetually incompetent Private Herbert Brown in *Carry On Sergeant* (1958), Norm in *Carry On Nurse* (1959) and a boxing referee in *Carry On Regardless* (1960). He was also in *The Long Haul* (1956), *A Night To Remember* (1958), *Saturday Night And Sunday Morning* (1960), *Lawrence Of Arabia* (1962), *The Longest Day* (1962), *A Hard Day's Night* (1964) and many more. Divorced, he numbered golf, skiing and languages among his hobbies.
CAUSE: He died aged 70 of natural causes.

Jean Rouch

Born May 31, 1917
Died February 18, 2004
'Exponent of cinéma vérité.' Born in
Paris, the son of Commander Jules
Rouch, a sailor and oceanographer,
Jean attended the Sorbonne where he
studied to become a civil engineer. In
1941 he left France to escape the Nazis
and settled in Niger. He developed an
interest in anthropology and sent
reports back to the Institut Français
d'Afrique Noir. After the war he
returned to France and studied
anthropology. Having graduated, he
turned his interest to film and began
with *Au Pays Des Mages* (1947). His
1957 film *Les Maîtres Fous* was banned
in British Africa as inflammatory after
it showed natives eating dogs and
speaking pidgin English. In 1958 he
made *Moi, Un Noir* about an Ivory
Coast tribe who adopted the names of
film stars. He made more than 120
films in all. In 1952 he married Jane
George.
CAUSE: He died in a car crash in Birni
N'Konni in Niger where he was
attending a festival of his work. He
was 86.

Patsy Rowlands

Born January 19, 1934
Died January 22, 2005
Comic support. Born in Palmers
Green, London, 5'4" Patricia
Rowlands was educated at the Convent
of the Sacred Heart, Whetstone and
then, aged 15, won a scholarship to the
Guildhall School of Music and Drama.
Her first professional appearance was
in the chorus for the touring version of
Annie Get Your Gun (1951). She made
her West End début playing Thetis
Cooke, Doris Hare's granddaughter, in
1959 at the Saville Theatre in Sandy
Wilson's classic musical *Valmouth*.
She then joined the Players Theatre
Company where she worked alongside
Hattie Jacques and Clive Dunn. In
1961 she appeared in David Turner's
Semi-Detached at the Saville Theatre

with Laurence Olivier. She made her
film début in *Over The Odds* (1961) as
Marilyn and her early films included
On The Fiddle (1961, with Alfred
Lynch and Sean Connery) as Evie,
In The Doghouse (1961) as a barmaid,
John Schlesinger's *A Kind Of Loving*
(1962) as Dorothy and *Ein Toter Sucht
Seinen Mörder* (1962). She had already
appeared in comedy when she was
signed to appear in the Norman
Wisdom Rank film *A Stitch In Time*
(1963) in which she played Amy.
It was the *Carry On . . .* films that
established her comic credentials. Her
first was *Carry On Again Doctor* (1969)
in which she played Miss Fosdick. Her
most memorable role in the series was
as Miss Dempsey, the lovelorn
housekeeper to Percival Snooper
(Kenneth Williams) in *Carry On
Loving* (1970). When Sophie Plummet
(Hattie Jacques) comes to dinner with
a view to romancing Snooper, Miss
Dempsey pulls out all the stops to show
her love rival that she will not give up
"her" man without a fight. She was also
in *Carry On Henry* (1970) as Queen,
Carry On At Your Convenience (1971)
as the long-suffering Hortense
Withering who has to test run the new
products of W.C. Boggs, *Carry On
Matron* (1972) as Evelyn Banks, *Carry
On Abroad* (1972) as Miss Dobbs,
Carry On Girls (1973) as Mildred
Bumble, *Carry On Dick* (1974) as Mrs
Giles, and *Carry On Behind* (1975)
as Linda Upmore. She did not think
much of *Carry On Columbus* (1992).
"The *Carry On*s have become a cult
because of the way they were done and
the people who were in them," she
said. "We couldn't recapture that sort
of spirit. These days we've got
alternative comedy and it's a
completely different type of humour.
That's progress and I wouldn't want to
stop it. But it wouldn't suit the *Carry
On*s." Patsy Rowlands also worked
with Sid James in *Bless This House* (TV
and film versions) as Betty Lewis, and
also appeared as Angela in the film

version of the sitcom *Please Sir!* (1971). Her other films included *Tom Jones* (1963) as Honor, *Dateline Diamonds* (1965) as Mrs Edgecomb, *Alice's Adventures In Wonderland* (1972) as the cook, *Sammy's Super T-Shirt* (1978) as Mum and *Tess* (1979) as the landlady. She married and divorced Malcolm Sircom and had one son, Alan.

CAUSE: While working as Mrs Pearce in the 2001 revival of *My Fair Lady* at the Theatre Royal, Drury Lane, she was diagnosed with breast cancer but she continued to appear in the show without telling her fellow performers. She died three days after her 71st birthday at her home in Hove, Sussex.

Alma Rubens

(ALMA SMITH)
Born February 19, 1897
Died January 21, 1931
Early victim of the drug culture. Born in San Francisco, where she was educated at the local convent, 5'7" Alma had talent and, with her jet black hair and black eyes, good looks. Before she turned 20 she was in films. She appeared opposite Douglas Fairbanks in *The Half-Breed* (1916) as Teresa and subsequently signed a contract with Triangle Pictures. In August of 1918 she married actor Franklyn Farnum (b. Boston, Massachusetts, 1876, d. Hollywood, California, July 4, 1961 of cancer), 42 to her 21. Within a month, the marriage was over and Alma made headlines for all the wrong reasons for the first time: she claimed that Farnum had been physically abusive towards her. Unlike many actresses Alma's career was not her reason for living and in the early Twenties she made just a few films each year: *Thoughtless Women* (1920) as Annie Marnet, *Humoresque* (1920) as Gina Berg, *The World and His Wife* (1920) as Teodora, *Find The Woman* (1922) as Sophie Carey, *The Valley Of Silent Men* (1922) as Marette Radison, *Under The Red*

Robe (1923) as Renee de Cocheforet, and *Enemies Of Women* (1923) as Alicia. On August 12, 1923, she married doctor and film producer Daniel Carson Goodman. They were divorced on January 28, 1925, after Alma alleged he hit her. Alma moved to Fox and then to MGM. On January 30, 1926, in Riverside, California, she married 6'1" actor Ricardo Cortez (b. Vienna, September 19, 1899, as Jacob Krantz, d. New York City, April 28, 1977). She was slated to star opposite her new husband in *The Torrent* (1926) but by this time she had already become a drug addict and the film went to Greta Garbo; it helped to make her a star. Soon, all Alma's earnings were going to fund her drug habit and MGM boss Louis B. Mayer ordered executives not to renew her contract. On January 26, 1929, Alma was spotted running down Hollywood Boulevard in a state of extreme agitation, hotly pursued by two men. She ran to a petrol station and the two men caught up with her, whereupon Alma pulled a knife and stabbed the younger man in the shoulder. The older man turned out to be her GP and Alma was committed to Alhambra Clinic. There, in April 1929, she stabbed a nurse and was taken to the psychiatric ward of Los Angeles General Hospital and thence to the California State Hospital for the Insane at Patton. She was released after six months and tried to resume her career on Broadway, unsuccessfully. She filed for divorce from Ricardo Cortez while in the Big Apple. Her next stop was a return to Hollywood. After a trip to Mexico, Alma was arrested on January 6, 1931, and charged with possession of 40 cubes of morphine. By this time Alma knew she was dying, and so gave an interview to the *Los Angeles Examiner* and berated the studio doctors who had prescribed her drugs to enable her to work after she had begun to suffer from blinding headaches.

CAUSE: Hopelessly addicted to heroin, she died of pneumonia in Hollywood aged 33.

Gail Russell

Born September 21, 1921
Died circa *August 26, 1961*
'The Hedy Lamarr of Santa Monica'. Born in Chicago, Illinois, Gail was raised mostly in Michigan on her uncle's farm. Her mother, Gladys, wanted to be famous but didn't have the necessary talent, so she channelled her energies into her daughter. Gail was a skilful artist and a very shy child who adored Ginger Rogers. When Gale was 12 the family moved to California and she went to school with Jane Russell who, although not related, became a close friend. On July 17, 1942, Gail signed a standard contract with Paramount Pictures. It paid $50 a week, rising in increments over a seven-year period. Her first film was *Henry Aldrich Gets Glamour* (1943) as high school *femme fatale* Virginia Lowry. Unbelievably, the film marked the first time Gail had ever worn high heels or danced with a member of the opposite sex. The studio also arranged dates for Gail. She was cast opposite her idol Ginger Rogers in *Lady In The Dark* (1944) as Barbara but Gail was so nervous it took nearly two days to shoot her two lines of dialogue. Nevertheless, she and Ginger Rogers became friends and the elder actress took a keen interest in the younger. *The Uninvited* (1944), in which she played Stella Meredith, established Gail as a film star, although again she suffered from stage fright and that led to a nervous breakdown. She spent three weeks recuperating in Mexico. *Our Hearts Were Young And Gay* (1944), in which she played Cornelia Otis Skinner, was another success for Gail. However, her nervousness increased, although she found it easier to cope with a little drink. She appeared in *The Unseen* (1945) as Elizabeth Howard, *Salty O'Rourke* (1945) as Barbara

Brooks, *Duffy's Tavern* (1945) and *Our Hearts Were Growing Up* (1946) again as Cornelia Otis Skinner. In 1945 Gail met actor Guy Madison and they fell in love. She was loaned to United Artists for *The Bachelor's Daughters* (1946) as Eileen. Her next move saw her at Republic, where she played John Wayne's girlfriend, Penelope Worth, in *Angel And The Badman* (1947). In *Calcutta* (1947) she played killer and jewel thief Virginia Moore. She almost certainly had an affair with the film's director John Farrow, who was known for his sadism towards actors. (Russell had a penchant for spending time with gay men.) Farrow also directed her as Jean Courtland in her next film, *Night Has A Thousand Eyes* (1948). In *Wake Of The Red Witch* (1949) she was Angelique Desaix opposite Duke Wayne again. In February 1949 Gail and Guy Madison went on a month-long holiday to get to know each other better and visit her relatives. On August 31, they married at the Biltmore Hotel in Santa Barbara. Gail's mother, father and brother were notable by their absence from the ceremony. Joseph Losey's *The Lawless* (1950), in which she starred as Mexican-American journalist Sunny Garcia, was her last film at Paramount. Losey later recalled Gail being absolutely terrified on set and unable to deliver a single line without a drink; once a drink arrived, she was word-perfect. Gail refused to make *Flaming Feather* and Paramount quietly dropped her contract. She made *Air Cadet* (1951) as Janet Page for Universal but it wasn't a happy experience. She was lonely (Madison was unable to visit her because of his own busy workload), depressed, tired and drinking. Back in her hotel room after shooting, she would drink herself into oblivion. Gail and Madison separated and then in October 1953 Gail was named as co-respondent by John Wayne's estranged wife, Esperanza 'Chata' Diaz Ceballos. Gail and Madison reconciled but it was never a love match. Gail entered a sanatorium in Seattle, Washington, to try and recover, but in November 1953 she was arrested for drink-driving. Madison bailed her out but on October 6, 1954, they were divorced. Gail continued to appear in films, but she put on weight and lost much of her beauty due to drink. In 1957 she began a two-year lesbian relationship with singer Dorothy Shay. In the summer of that year she was again arrested for drink-driving when she crashed her car through a shop window, pinning a man under the front wheels. She was sentenced to 30 days in prison suspended, fined $420 and put on probation for three years. The following year she made *No Place To Land* (1958) as Lynn Dillon but then was absent from the screen for three years until *The Silent Call* (1961) as Flore Brancato. It was to be her last film. She landed a job on *Perry Mason* but didn't turn up on the first day and was promptly sacked. She decided to take a drink to make up for the disappointment.

CAUSE: On August 27, 1961, she was discovered dead, surrounded by empty vodka bottles in her home, 1436 South Bentley Avenue, Brentwood, California. She was a month shy of her 40th birthday. Gail had died some time between August 24 and 26. Cause of death: alcoholism and cirrhosis of the liver.

Rosalind Russell

Born June 4, 1907
Died November 28, 1976

Stylish star. Rosalind Russell was born one of seven siblings into a Catholic family on Chestnut Avenue, Waterbury, Connecticut. She was educated at Marymount College, Tarrytown, New York, and the American Academy of Dramatic Arts in New York City. Her father, James Edward Russell (b. Waterbury, New Haven County, Connecticut, April 16,

1860, d. 1930), was a lawyer but Russell had no desire to repeat his successes and went into showbiz making her film début in *Evelyn Prentice* (1934) as Nancy Harrison. It starred Myrna Loy and William Powell. In the 1930s and 1940s she made several comedies before reverting back to dramatic roles in the 1950s. Her films included: *Forsaking All Others* (1934), *Craig's Wife* (1936), *Four's A Crowd* (1938), *The Citadel* (1938), George Cukor's *The Women* (1939) as gossipy Sylvia Fowler, *His Girl Friday* (1940), *The Feminine Touch* (1941), *Take A Letter Darling* (1942), murder mystery *The Velvet Touch* (1948), *The Girl Rush* (premièred August 18, 1955), *Picnic* (1955), *A Majority Of One* (1961), *Five Finger Exercise* (1962), *Gypsy* (1962), and *The Trouble With Angels* (1966). She was nominated for an Oscar four times: *My Sister Eileen* (1942) as Ruth Sherwood, *Sister Kenny* (1946) as Sister Elizabeth Kenny, *Mourning Becomes Electra* (1947) as Lavinia Mannon and *Auntie Mame* (1958) as Mame Dennis, an eccentric aunt whose orphaned nephew comes to stay. She received the Jean Hersholt Humanitarian Award at the Oscars in 1972. When she appeared as the Mystery Guest on *What's My Line?* on January 4, 1953, she disguised her voice so well that panellist Dorothy Killgallen thought Russell was a man. That year she won a Tony for her appearance on Broadway in *Wonderful Town*. She married Danish-American producer Frederick Brisson on October 25, 1941. They had one son, Lance, in 1943.

CAUSE: In 1943 she suffered a breakdown. In 1960 she underwent a mastectomy. Five years later, she underwent a second mastectomy and four years after that she was stricken with rheumatoid arthritis. In April 1975 she fell victim to pneumonia and in the autumn of that year, her cancer returned. In July 1976 she underwent a hip replacement operation. Four months later at 10.20am she died in Beverly Hills, California, from cancer. She was 69. She was buried in Holy Cross Catholic Cemetery in Culver City, California.

FURTHER READING: *Life Is A Banquet* – Rosalind Russell and Chris Chase (London: W.H. Allen, 1978).

Dame Margaret Rutherford, OBE

Born May 11, 1892
Died May 22, 1972

Endearing eccentric. On March 5, 1883, her father, William Rutherford Benn (b. 1855), murdered his father, the Rev. Julius Benn, by smashing him over the head with a chamber pot and then attempted to commit suicide by cutting his throat. On April 11, he was sent to Broadmoor. He was released after seven years, changed his name by deed poll to Rutherford and moved to Balham. There, at 15 Dornton Road, Margaret Taylor Rutherford was born, an only child. (One of her cousins was left-wing firebrand Rt. Hon. Anthony Wedgwood Benn.) In 1897 the family moved to India where Margaret's mother, Florence Rutherford, fell pregnant. Before she could give birth, she committed suicide by hanging herself from a tree. That sent William round the bend and in October 1902 he was admitted to the Northumberland House Asylum. In January 1904 he was readmitted to Broadmoor. He died there of pneumonia on August 4, 1921. Margaret was told her father had died years earlier. She became a music teacher but really wanted to act, an ambition that went unfulfilled until she was 33 and inherited some money from an aunt. She made her stage début at the Old Vic in December 1925. However, unable to get any more work, she returned to teaching for two years. A lucky break led to regular stage work and in January 1939 she appeared as Miss Prism in John Gielgud's production of *The Importance Of Being*

Earnest. In April 1940 she created the role of the spooky Mrs Danvers in *Rebecca*. She made her film début in 1936 in *Talk Of The Devil*, but her first real notable success was as the spiritualist Madame Arcati in *Blithe Spirit*. Worried about offending believers, she suffered the first of what would be many nervous breakdowns. Her other films included *Passport To Pimlico* (1948), *The Importance Of Being Earnest* (1952) as Miss Prism, *Trouble In Store* (1953), *I'm All Right Jack* (1959) as Aunt Dolly, *The VIPs* (1963) for which she won an Oscar and *A Countess From Hong Kong* (1967). For the present author (and also, although she was initially unsure, for Dame Agatha Christie) she was most memorable as Miss Marple in a short series of films: *Murder She Said* (1962), *Murder At The Gallop* (1963), *Murder Most Foul* (1963) and *Murder Ahoy* (1964) and a cameo appearance in *The Alphabet Murders* (1965). On March 26, 1945, she married her co-star, James Buckley Stringer Davis. In 1961 they adopted Dawn Langley Simmons (b. Sussex, October 16, 1937, as Gordon Langley Hall) who would become Dame Margaret's biographer. They adopted three other adults: Damaris Hayman, John Hibberd and another John.

CAUSE: Towards the end of her life Dame Margaret became rather vague but insisted on finishing any jobs she had been hired for. One day a cruel director humiliated her in front of the cast but she took the gross insult with characteristic good humour and extreme dignity. She died in Chalfont and Gerrard's Cross Hospital. She left £13,850. Just over a year later, on August 7, 1973, Stringer Davis followed her and they were buried together in St James Church, Gerrard's Cross.

FURTHER READING: *Margaret Rutherford: A Blithe Spirit* – Dawn Langley Simmons (London: Arthur Barker, 1983).

Robert Ryan

Born November 11, 1909
Died July 11, 1973
Screen heavy. Born in Chicago,
Illinois, Ryan was a college boxer,
which probably explains why he was so
believable in *The Set-Up* (1949), his
favourite own film. Appearing in films
from 1940 he was Oscar nominated for
playing Montgomery in *Crossfire*
(1947). He appeared in over 90 films
including: *Marine Raiders* (1944),
Caught (1949), *Beware My Lovely*
(1952), *The Naked Spur* (1953), *Bad
Day At Black Rock* (1955) as Reno
Smith, *King Of Kings* (1961) as John
the Baptist and *The Dirty Dozen*
(1967) as Colonel Everett
Dasher-Breed. He was politically left
wing, but was never targeted by nutty
Senator Joe McCarthy, possibly
because "my Irish name, my being a
Catholic and an ex-Marine sort of
softened the blow."
CAUSE: He died aged 63 of cancer in
New York.

S

Sabu

(SABU DASTAGIR)
Born January 27, 1924
Died December 2, 1963
Brown boy in the ring. Sabu was an unlikely film star. Born in Mysore, India, he was working as a stable boy in a maharajah's palace when he was noticed by Robert Flaherty who cast him as Toomai in *Elephant Boy* (1937). He played exotic roles in a number of British and Hollywood films before the fashion for eastern films ended and he went to Europe to salvage his career. He was not successful. During World War II he fought bravely and was rewarded with several medals. His films included: *The Drum* (1938) as Prince Azim, *The Thief Of Bagdad* (1940) as Abu, *Jungle Book* (1942) as Mowgli, *Arabian Nights* (1942) as Ali Ben Ali, *White Savage* (1943) as Orano, *Cobra Woman* (1944) as Kado, *Tangier* (1946) as Pepe, *Man-Eater Of Kumaon* (1948) as Narain, *Savage Drums* (1951) as Tipo Tairu, *Jungle Hell* (1956) as Jungle Boy, *Sabu And The Magic Ring* (1957) as Sabu, *Herrin Der Welt – Teil I* (1960) as Dr. Lin-Chor, *Rampage* (1963) as Talib and *A Tiger Walks* (1964) as Ram Singh.
CAUSE: Twice-married, 5′6″ Sabu died aged 39 of a heart attack in Chatsworth, California.

S.Z. Sakall

(EUGENE GERO SZAKALL)
Born February 2, 1884
Died February 12, 1955
'Cuddles'. Born in Budapest, Hungary, he began his career in Hungarian films in 1916 and often used the name Szoke Szakall, from where he got the S.Z. He moved to Germany where he appeared in talkies such as *Rutschbahn* (1928)

but the rise of the Nazis forced him to flee and he moved to Hungary and Austria where he appeared in films. The war necessitated another move and he landed in Hollywood, where he began a very successful film career. He became known for his thick Hungarian accent and appeared in films such as *Ball Of Fire* (1941) as Professor Magenbruch, *The Devil And Miss Jones* (1941) as George, *Casablanca* (1942) as Carl the head waiter, *Yankee Doodle Dandy* (1942) as Schwab, *Thank Your Lucky Stars* (1943) as Dr Schlenna, *Shine On Harvest Moon* (1944) as Poppa Carl, *San Antonio* (1945) as Sacha Bozic, *The Dolly Sisters* (1945) as Uncle Latzie, *Christmas In Connecticut* (1945) as Felix Bassenak, *Wonder Man* (1945) as Schmidt, *Cinderella Jones* (1946) as Gabriel Popik, *Embraceable You* (1948) as Sammy, *In The Good Old Summertime* (1949) as Otto Oberkugen, *Montana* (1950) as Poppa Schultz, *It's A Big Country* (1951) as Stefan Szabo and *The Student Prince* (1954) as Joseph Ruder, his final film role.
CAUSE: He died in Los Angeles, California of a heart attack. He was 10 days past his 71st birthday.

Albert Salmi

Born March 11, 1928
Died April 22, 1990
Suicidal murderer. Born in Brooklyn, New York to Finnish parents Salmi became an actor after military service in the Second World War. In 1948 he began to study with the Dramatic Workshop of the American Theatre Wing and the Actors Studio. He learned his trade before achieving recognition as Bo Decker in the 1955 Broadway production of *Bus Stop*. He turned down the film version, which made a star of Don Murray opposite Marilyn Monroe the following year. On May 16, 1956 he married the former child star Peggy Ann Garner (who is noticed elsewhere in this book). She was his co-star in *Bus Stop*. On March 30, 1957 she gave birth to her

only child, a daughter Catherine Ann. On May 17, 1995 she died of premature heart disease at the age of 38. Garner and Salmi were divorced on March 13, 1963. In 1958, he decided that perhaps Hollywood was a good career move and appeared as Smerdjakov in the MGM production of *The Brothers Karamazov*, with Yul Brynner, Lee J. Cobb, William Shatner, and Richard Basehart – a part for which Salmi turned down an Oscar-nomination. His other films included: *The Bravados* (1958) opposite Gregory Peck, *The Unforgiven* (1960), *Wild River* (1960), *The Flim-Flam Man* (1967), *The Ambushers* (1967), *Something Big* (1971), *Escape From The Planet Of The Apes* (1971), *Empire Of The Ants* (1977), *Love And Bullets* (1979), *Caddyshack* (1980), *Brubaker* (1980), *The Dragonslayer* (1981), *Love Child* (1982), and *Breaking In* (1989), his last theatrical film. He was a regular on television, appearing in more than 150 episodes of innumerable shows. In 1964 he married Roberta Pollock and fathered two daughters, Lizanne and Jennifer.

CAUSE: In February 1990 he and his wife separated due to his drinking and regular use of his fists. Unemployed, he was living in Spokane, Washington. Roberta Salmi feared enough for her life to hire a bodyguard but discharged him when her family suggested that she was overreacting. She wasn't. On April 23, 1990 a neighbour went to the family home having not seen Mrs Salmi for two days. Mrs Salmi was dead in a pool of blood on the kitchen floor. She had been shot to death with a .25-calibre pistol. Upstairs in the den, Salmi was dead by his own hand, having fired a .45-calibre handgun into his chest. He was 62. Salmi was cremated and his ashes interred at Greenwood Cemetery, Spokane.

George Sanders

Born July 3, 1906
Died April 25, 1972
Cinematic cynical cad. Born in St

Petersburg, Russia, the son of a rope manufacturer and a horticulturist, Sanders' family (his brother was the actor Tom Conway, b. St Petersburg, September 15, 1904, as Thomas Charles Sanders, d. Culver City, California, April 22, 1967, from cirrhosis of the liver) was uprooted at the time of the Russian Revolution and settled in Brighton. After jobs in textiles and tobacco, the 6'3" Sanders decided to become an actor. He made his first films in 1934 in *Love, Life And Laughter* before going to Hollywood in 1936 and appearing in four films that year: *Find The Lady* as Curly Randall, *Strange Cargo* as Roddy Burch, *Lloyds Of London* as Lord Everett Stacy and *Dishonour Bright* as Lisle. As with many talented people, Hollywood didn't quite know what to do with Sanders and he was placed in several unimaginative films or B movies. He appeared in two serials playing Simon Templar in *The Saint Strikes Back* (1939), *The Saint In London* (1939), *The Saint Takes Over* (1940), *The Saint's Double Trouble* (1940) and *The Saint In Palm Springs* (1941); and Gay Lawrence in *The Gay Falcon* (1941), *A Date With The Falcon* (1941), *The Falcon's Brother* (1942) and *The Falcon Takes Over* (1942). Sanders passed on the Falcon's mantle to his brother. "It bothered me that my brother physically resembled me," he once revealed. "Before he came out [to Hollywood], I asked that he not use my surname. He arrived in 1939, and anyone fleeing the war in Europe was not well viewed in England. Of the actors who left England for the States, they said they had 'gone with the wind up'. Tom took over the Falcon series when I'd tired of it, and I was amazed when he made a go of it — he had more luck with it than I did. But that was the acme of his career . . . His resemblance to me helped him at first; later, it was a handicap. Tom was a nice fellow; it's too bad for him that he was my brother." Sanders also played Nazis rather well but his first real major role was as Charles Strickland in *The Moon And Sixpence* (1942). He won an Oscar as Addison De Witt in *All About Eve* (1950) but after that seemed consigned to the sidelines of second banana. His last major part was as the voice of Shere Khan in *The Jungle Book* (1967). His 100-plus films included: *International Settlement* (1938) as Del Forbes, *Mr Moto's Last Warning* (1939) as Eric Norvel, *Confessions Of A Nazi Spy* (1939) as Schlager, *Nurse Edith Cavell* (1939) as Captain Heinrichs, *The Son Of Monte Cristo* (1940) as Gurko Lanen, *So This Is London* (1940) as Dr de Reseke, *The House Of The Seven Gables* (1940) as Jaffrey Pyncheon, *Rebecca* (1940) as Jack Favell, *Foreign Correspondent* (1940) as Scott Ffolliott, *Bitter Sweet* (1940) as Baron Von Tranisch, *Man Hunt* (1941) as Major Quive-Smith, *Sundown* (1941) as Major Coombes, *Quiet Please: Murder* (1942) as Fleg, *Her Cardboard Lover* (1942) as Tony Barling, *Tales Of Manhattan* (1942) as Williams, *Son Of Fury* (1942) as Sir Arthur Blake, *They Came To Blow Up America* (1943) as Carl Steelma, *Appointment In Berlin* (1943) as Keith Wilson, *This Land Is Mine* (1943) as George Lambert, *Summer Storm* (1944) as Fedor Mikhailovich Petroff, *The Lodger* (1944) as John Warwick, *Hangover Square* (1945) as Dr Allan Middleton, *The Picture Of Dorian Gray* (1945) as Lord Henry Wotton, *The Strange Affair Of Uncle Harry* (1945) as Harry Quincey, *A Scandal In Paris* (1946) as François Eugène Vidocq, *Lured* (1947) as Robert Fleming, *Forever Amber* (1947) as King Charles II, *The Ghost And Mrs Muir* (1947) as Miles Fairley, *The Private Affairs Of Bel Ami* (1947) as Georges Duroy aka Bel Ami, *The Fan* (1949) as Lord Darlington, *Samson And Delilah* (1949) as The Saran of Gaza, *Black Jack* (1950) as Mike Alexander, *Assignment: Paris* (1952) as Nick Strang, *Ivanhoe* (1952) as Sir Brian De Bois-Guilbert,

Call Me Madam (1953) as Cosmo Constantine, *Witness To Murder* (1954) as Albert Richter, *King Richard And The Crusaders* (1954) as King Richard I, *Moonfleet* (1955) as Lord Ashwood, *The King's Thief* (1955) again as King Charles II, *That Certain Feeling* (1956) as Larry Larkin, *Never Say Goodbye* (1956) as Victor, *Solomon And Sheba* (1959) as Adonijah, *Bluebeard's Ten Honeymoons* (1960) as Henri-Désiré Landru, *The Rebel* (1961) as Sir Charles Broward, *Operation Snatch* (1962) as Major Hobson, *Cairo* (1963) as Major Pickering, *A Shot In The Dark* (1964) as Benjamin Ballon, *The Amorous Adventures Of Moll Flanders* (1965) as the banker, *The Quiller Memorandum* (1966) as Gibbs, *The Candy Man* (1969) as Sidney Carter, *Psychomania* (1971) as Shadwell, *Endless Night* (1971) as Lippincott and *Doomwatch* (1972) as the Admiral. Sanders played Mr Freeze in the camp classic TV series *Batman* and hosted his own anthology series in 1957. Sanders' portrayal of unpleasant people may not have been too far from the truth of his real personality. His co-star on *All About Eve*, Celeste Holm, said of him: "George Sanders never spoke to anyone. He was a brilliant actor but he wasn't much fun." The bisexual Sanders married four times. On October 27, 1940, he wed the actress Susan Larson. They divorced in 1948. He once told some friends that he didn't bring his wife to parties because "She bores people." On April Fool's Day 1949 he married Zsa Zsa Gabor, who said of the match: "We were both in love with him . . . I fell out of love with him, but he didn't." The journalist Donald Zec recounts the time he saw Sanders and Gabor at a dinner and the actor managed only six words in the three hours: "Yes, darling" three times. They divorced exactly five years later. In February 1959 he married Benita Hume Colman, widow of Ronald Colman. She died on November 1, 1967, of cancer. Lastly, Sanders married his former sister-in-law Magda Gabor on December 4, 1970. "He just wanted to get back into the family. He missed me. I always liked George, but when a son-in-law comes back, I really like it," said the Gabor matriarch, Jolie. Sanders obviously didn't miss the Gabors that much because he and Magda were divorced after just six weeks. He later recalled: "Before I ever married two of the three Gabor sisters, I already knew that the words 'acting' and 'Gabor' are mutually exclusive terms." Even his close friend and biographer Brian Aherne opined: "He gossips, he attacks people viciously, he has no respect for man nor beast – but what an interesting man."

CAUSE: Sanders suffered a stroke in 1969 and was terrified of being unable to care for himself or, as he put it, "having someone to wipe my bum for me." He also suffered from vertigo and had to use a walking stick. In early 1972 he suffered a nervous breakdown and stayed with his sister, Margaret, in England to recuperate. Always in love with Spain, Sanders flew to Madrid in April 1972 to try and find himself a small house. On April 23, he arrived by himself at Castelldefels, 10 miles south of Barcelona, and booked into the Hotel Don Rey Jaime. The weather was unseasonably wet and cold and Sanders proceeded to get drunk. He asked for an early morning wake-up call and retired to his room. The next day he was discovered dead. Next to his body were five empty packets of Nembutal and a bottle of vodka. His suicide note read: "Dear World, I am leaving because I am bored. I feel I have lived long enough. I am leaving you with your worries in this sweet cesspool – good luck". He was 65.

Catya Sassoon

Born September 3, 1968
Died January 1, 2002
'Tuff Turf'. Born in New York, Catya Sassoon was the tall (5′8″), beautiful but rebellious daughter of celebrity hairdresser Vidal Sassoon (b. London, January 17, 1928) and the model Beverley Adams (b. Canada, November 7, 1945). Catya attended Beverly Hills High School (the school in *Beverly Hills 90210*) where she spent more time partying than studying. She once filled her father's swimming pool with so much of his own brand of shampoo that the suds covered the pool. When she was 14 Catya dropped out to pursue a modelling career in New York and signed with the Prestige Agency. Her parents seemed unable to control her and the following year, in August 1984, she got married to Luca Scalisi. Marriage did nothing to calm her wild ways. She developed a heavy drug problem. Her films included: *Tuff Turf* (1985) as Feather, *Inside Out* (1986), *Modern Girls* (1986), *Dance With Death* (1991) as Jodie, *Inside Out IV* (1992) as Pauline, *Bloodfist IV: Die Trying* (1992) as Lisa, *Secret Games* (1992) as Sandra in which she bared her silicone-enhanced breasts, *Angelfist* (1993) as Katara/Kat Lang, *Bloodfist VI: Ground Zero* (1994) as Tori. Her son, London Vidal Sassoon, was born in 1995 and in the spring of 2000 she gave birth to twin daughters, Mycca and Syke, by her second husband Joe Myers.

CAUSE: Catya died aged 33 of a heart attack at her Hollywood, California home. The coronary was almost certainly drug-related.

Ann Savage

(BERNICE MAXINE LYON)
Born February 19, 1921
Died December 25, 2008
Femme fatale. With a career that reached its peak in the 1940s Ann Savage was born in Columbia, South Carolina and moved to Los Angeles in 1930 with her mother and stepfather. She was a star struck fan when she joined Max Reinhardt's stage school. There she met Bert D'Armand who later (1947) became her second

husband and who worked as her agent. She was signed to a contract at Columbia Pictures but her work was mostly confined to B movies. She was not impressed. "They were mindless," she recalled years later. "The actresses were just scenery. The stories all revolved around the male actors; they really had the choice roles. All the actresses had to do was to look lovely, since the dialogue was ridiculous." She made her debut in 1943 in *One Dangerous Night* as Vivian and appeared in more than 30 films including *Saddles And Sagebrush* (1943) as Ann Parker, *Passport To Suez* (1943) as Valerie King, *Klondike Kate* (1943) as Kathleen O'Day, *Two-Man Submarine* (1944) as Pat Benson, *Ever Since Venus* (1944) as Janet Wilson, *Dancing In Manhattan* (1944) as Valerie Crawford, *Apology For Murder* (1945) as Toni Kirkland, *Jungle Flight* (1947) as Laurey Roberts and *Satan's Cradle* (1949) as Lil. It was Edgar G. Ulmer's 1945 B-movie *Detour* which made her name. She played Vera who ruthlessly blackmailed a stranger (Tom Neal). Savage said, "I had just come off a lot that kept me looking absolutely perfect but Vera was not a pretty woman: She was maniacal. Edgar objected to my hair looking so neat and had the hairdresser run cold cream through it to make it streaky and stringy. He even made sure my face stayed dirty . . . and shiny." She hoped to become a star on the back of *Detour* but it never happened and she virtually retired in the mid-Fifties. Her husband died in 1968 so she became a legal secretary. She made a brief comeback in *Fire With Fire* (1986) as Sister Harriet, more than 30 years after her last film. CAUSE: Savage died in her sleep at a nursing home in Hollywood from complications after a series of strokes.

Telly Savalas
Born January 21, 1922
Died January 22, 1994
Chrome dome. Aristoteles Savalas, the second son (there were four and one daughter) of Nicholas (who supposedly was the 24th of 27 children!) and Christina Savalas, a former Miss Greece beauty queen, was born, despite the Greek nomenclature, in Garden City, Long Island, New York. His bushy-haired younger brother, George (b. The Bronx, New York, December 5, 1926, d. October 2, 1985), was also an actor. Away from the screen, 6'1" Savalas, like the only other really successful bald actor, Yul Brynner, had an ego the size of Mount Olympus. He also told a different story every time he was interviewed, making the real story of Telly Savalas difficult to completely fathom. His first job was in the army and he received a Purple Heart after being wounded in action. How the wound occurred is a matter of some dispute. Some believe a shell did the damage, while others believe that it was a grenade. Savalas did have a mangled left index finger, but never revealed whether that was part of his wartime injuries. Following demob, he went to university where he married his first wife, Catherine, and then became a civil servant before joining ABC where he worked as a producer, winning a prize for one series he worked on. Just before he turned 40, he decided to give acting a shot and spent much of the Sixties playing a succession of evil men but also the occasional copper, good practice for the role that would make him internationally famous. His films included: *Mad Dog Coll* (1961) as Lieutenant Dawson, *The Young Savages* (1961) as Police Lt Gunderson, *Birdman Of Alcatraz* (1962) as Feto Gomez, for which he was nominated for an Oscar, *Cape Fear* (1962) as Charles Sievers, *Johnny Cool* (1963) as Vince Santangelo, *Love Is A Ball* (1963) as Dr Gump, *The Greatest Story Ever Told* (1965) as Pontius Pilate, *Genghis Khan* (1965) as Shan, *Battle Of The Bulge* (1965) as Guffy, *Beau Geste* (1966) as Sergeant Major Dagineau, *The Dirty Dozen* (1967) as

Archer Maggott, *The Karate Killers* (1967) as Count de Fanzini, *Buona Sera, Mrs Campbell* (1968) as Walter Braddock, *The Scalphunters* (1968) as Jim Howie, *Crooks And Coronets* (1969) as Herbie Haseler, *Mackenna's Gold* (1969) as Sergeant Tibbs, *The Assassination Bureau* (1969) as Lord Bostwick, *On Her Majesty's Secret Service* (1969) as Ernst Stavro Blofeld, *Città Violenta* (1970) as Webber, *Kelly's Heroes* (1970) as Big Joe, *Pretty Maids All In A Row* (1971) as Captain Sam Surcher, *Senza Ragione* (1972) as Memphis, *Una Ragione Per Vivere E Una Per Morire* (1972) as Ward and the lead in *Pancho Villa* (1972). He married for the second time in the early Sixties to Lynn, by whom he had two daughters. In England in 1966 filming *The Dirty Dozen* he indulged in a few extra curricular activities. He was seeing Sally Adams who would be the mother of his son, Nicholas, who would go out with Tori Spelling, the daughter of TV mogul Aaron Spelling who made *Starsky & Hutch* among many other successful US TV series. By 1973 Savalas was living with Sally Adams and Nicholas in London, accepting anything he was offered. His life changed when he was offered the role of a lollipop-sucking, cheroot-smoking Manhattan South, New York City police lieutenant called Theo Kojak. Oddly, Kojak was originally conceived to be Polish but Savalas' own ethnic background soon took over. His brother, George, was cast as Kojak's punch bag, Detective Stavros, although he was originally billed as Demosthenes (his real name). Savalas refused to share screen time with a young, good-looking actor to appeal to teenage girls, believing the show would appeal to a male audience. The show's producers were rather surprised when the teenage girl audience began tuning in to watch Telly Savalas. The first Kojak story was 'The Marcus-Nelson Murders', which aired on March 8, 1973 (although none of the characters appeared in the subsequent series), before the series proper took over on October 24 of the same year. *Kojak* ran until April 1978, before being revived in *The Belarus File* on February 16, 1985, and again in November 1989 with a different cast (including Savalas' daughter, Candace) in a series of TV movies: *Fatal Flaw* (1989), *Ariana* (1989), *None So Blind* (1990), *It's Always Something* (1990) and *Flowers For Matty* (1990).

CAUSE: Savalas died of prostate cancer one day after his 72nd birthday in Universal City, California.

FURTHER READING: *Telly Savalas* – Marsha Daly (London: Sphere, 1975).

Savannah

(SHANNON WILSEY)
Born October 9, 1970
Died July 11, 1994
Beautiful blonde rock groupie. Born in Laguna Beach, California, Savannah (the name came "from a movie called *Savannah Smiles* [1982] which was about a little blonde girl who looked exactly like me when I was little") began her love affair with sex and rock stars early. "I love sex and I love sex with rockers more than anything else," she once boasted. "I don't seem to go out with really normal people. I'm kind of on the wild side. I don't think I ever went out with anyone with short hair. I like musician types." She had a fling with Cher's ex-husband Gregg Allman while she was 16 and still in high school. Her subsequent rocker lovers included Billy Idol and Axl Rose of Guns N' Roses, whom she later called "a selfish, boring lover. Axl, despite his arrogance, was one of the world's worst lovers. He was rude, obnoxious and boring in bed" rating him a one on a scale of one to ten. She also dated Slash from Guns N' Roses, Danny Boy from rock group House of Pain, Vince Neil of Mötley Crüe and MTV personality Pauly Shore. In 1990 she began making pornographic films,

at one time calling herself Silver Kane. The 5'6", silicone-enhanced 34D-22-30 Savannah specialised in spanking and enema films for Prestige Video before signing a contract with Vivid Video in April 1991 and appearing in *America's Nastiest Home Videos 4* (1991), *Indian Summer* (1991), *Blonde Savage* (1991), *House Of Sleeping Beauties* (1992), *Sinderella* (1992), *Indian Summer 2: Sandstorm* (1992), *House Of Sleeping Beauties II* (1992) and many others. In 1992 she was named Best New Starlet by trade journal *Adult Video News*, much to the annoyance of many in the industry who didn't like her holier-than-thou attitude. "She is either loved or hated," said one reviewer. "Loved for her perfect beauty and hated for her lack of interest in matters sexual. She doesn't so much have sex, as let people perform sexual acts on her person." Her Vivid contract wasn't renewed, as she was considered "undependable and difficult to work with." In 1993 she was voted Worst Female in porn. She worked for various companies and performed in the first of Blackpool-born director John T. Bone's Starbangers gang bang series. The latter commented: "She was awesome. I think she felt her career was on the slide and she wanted to do something outrageous and shock the world. I met her one other time for about three minutes and had heard all the horror stories about her but, unlike her queen image, I found her to have a good, professional attitude. I think she had a secret sense of humour which Savannah didn't care to share with others — like she didn't want people to know she was having fun." Her mainstream films included: *Invisible Maniac* (1990) and *Ghoul School* (1990) and she also appeared in several music videos. In June 1994 she landed a job dancing at Club Paradise in Las Vegas, for which she was paid $9,000 plus tips. Before going on stage she would do a hit of cocaine. She was sacked after taking nights off to see David Lee Roth.

CAUSE: On July 10, 1994, on her way home after a night out clubbing, Savannah drove her white Corvette into a fence, breaking her nose in the process. She feared her looks and thus her career would be ruined. She had been booked for a dancing job at Goldfinger's nightclub in Nyack, New York. At 2.15am she called her manager Nancy Pera wailing about the crash: "Nancy, it's Savannah! I just got in a major fucking car accident! And I think my nose is broken, and my head. And my car is completely fucked, and I need you to come over here because I need to go to the hospital." At 2.40am Pera arrived at Savannah's Multiview Drive, North Hollywood, California, home to find a fire engine in the star's driveway. In the 25 minutes between the call and Pera's arrival, Savannah had gone to her garage and shot herself in the head with a .40 calibre Beretta. She was taken to St Joseph Medical Center in Burbank where she lay comatose until she died at 11.20pm the next day. Police found Valium in her handbag; doctors found cocaine in her body. Her funeral, attended by around 40 people, was held at the Faith Chapel at Forest Lawn Memorial-Parks, 1712 South Glendale Avenue, Glendale, California 91209 after which she was cremated and her ashes given to her father, Mike. After her death it was discovered that she was in debt, owing $2,540 to the IRS, $6,000 to American Express, $2,000 to other credit companies and sundry other borrowings.

Gia Scala

(GIOVANNA SGOGLIO)
Born March 3, 1934
Died April 30, 1972
Italian scouser. Despite her exotic name, 5'8" Gia Scala was born in Liverpool, although her father was a baron (her mother was Irish) and the family moved to Messina, Sicily, when

Gia was just three months old. She had a sister, Tina, and all four members of the family were incredibly close. Gia was a sensitive, some would say highly strung child. When she was 14, it was decided that Gia's education should be completed in America and she went to stay with her paternal aunt. She studied drama while attending Bayside High School in Queens. Upon leaving school, she began working for an insurance company and then an airline while studying at the Actors' Studio at night. Her mother moved to America to be with her and they lived on East 55th Street. At the Studio she was romanced by Steve McQueen, who proposed to her, but Gia turned him down. It was also at this time that Giovanna became Gia. She appeared on several quiz shows winning (for the time) tidy sums of money. In the winter of 1954 she was put under contract by Universal-International, who began to groom her and soften her still strong Italian accent. Her first film was a small part in *All That Heaven Allows* (1955). Her first featured film was as Nina Ferranti in *The Price Of Fear* (1956) and she also appeared as Vicki Dauray in *Four Girls In Town* (1956) for which she received critical acclaim. United Artists borrowed her to play Anita Ferrer in *The Big Boodle* (1957) opposite Errol Flynn. In October 1956 her contract was transferred jointly to Columbia and MGM. Socially, she was seen out and about with a series of young, handsome actors mostly, though not exclusively, homosexual. In 1958 she learned her mother was suffering from inoperable cancer and that night was involved in a drink-driving incident, although the charges were later dropped. That year she appeared in *The Tunnel Of Love* (1958) as Estelle Novick, *Ride A Crooked Trail* (1958) as Tessa Milotte, and became an American citizen. After a film in Greece (*The Angry Hills* [1959] as Eleftheria), she flew to England to star opposite Jack Hawkins

in *The Two-Headed Spy* (1959). Halfway during filming, suffering from depression, she flung herself off Waterloo Bridge, but was rescued by a taxi driver. She may have been saved from suicide but she subsequently began to drink heavily. On August 21, 1959, she married actor Don Burnett. Her last American film was *The Guns Of Navarone* (1961) playing Greek resistance fighter Anna. She filmed *Il Trionfo Di Robin Hood* (1963) in Czechoslovakia and *Operación Dalila* (1967) as Dalila in Spain. Around this time she also began appearing on television. In September 1970 she was divorced. Burnett obtained a restraining order against her, mainly because of her drinking. She travelled to Europe and settled into the Sunset Marquis Hotel-Apartments in Los Angeles when she returned to the States. On April 20, 1971, she and Larry Langston, a 21-year-old male friend, were arrested over a parking dispute and both received two years' probation. On May 19 she was sent for a psychiatric evaluation, having collapsed while in court on a drink-driving charge. On her release she moved in with Marlon Brando's ex-wife Anna Kashfi, but arguments soon forced her out. She was examined by another psychiatrist, who decided she was suicide prone. The Roman Catholic Gia had taken insecticide a few months earlier and was given the last rites. In July 1971, Gia, now aged 37 but looking nearer 50, was injured when her sports car turned over; she lost part of an index finger in the accident. Don Burnett's marriage to actress Barbara Anderson also played on her mind and caused her to drink more and more.

CAUSE: On April 30, 1972, Larry Langston summoned an ambulance to Gia's Hollywood Hills home at 7944 Woodrow Wilson Drive. She was lying dead on the second floor. Her death was listed as "possible accidental liquor and drug overdose." She was 38.

However, when 'Coroner to the Stars' Dr Thomas T. Noguchi performed the autopsy, he discovered that Gia was suffering from the early stages of arteriosclerosis, meaning the brain was not getting enough oxygen, which explained Gia's often irrational behaviour.

Roy Scheider

Born November 10, 1932
Died February 10, 2008
Streetwise actor. Born in Orange, New Jersey, the son of a Protestant father Roy Bernhard Scheider, and Catholic mother, Anna Crosson, Richard Roy Scheider was educated at Columbia High School in Maplewood, New Jersey, Rutgers University and Franklin and Marshall College where he developed an interest in acting. He spent three years in the air force and then appeared with the New York Shakespeare Festival, and won an Obie Award in 1968 for the play *Stephen D.* Scheider landed recurring roles on two television soaps, *Love Of Life* and *The Secret Storm.* 5'9" Scheider made his film debut in *Curse Of The Living Corpse* (1964), a horror film, where he was billed as Roy R. Sheider. His big break came eight years later, when he played a pimp in *Klute* (1971), and a policeman in *The French Connection* (1971), which garnered him his first Oscar nomination (for Best Supporting Actor). The film told the story of the largest haul of heroin ever captured in America. The cinematic depiction bore little resemblance to the actual events. The real as opposed to reel crime had no shoot-outs, no deaths and no car chases. The real cops – Eddie "Popeye" Egan (Gene Hackman as Popeye Doyle) and Sonny "Cloudy" Grosso (Scheider) – had bit parts in the film. In 1972 all 120lbs of heroin was stolen from a police locker and never recovered. Scheider commented on his professional persona, "I got inundated with cop scripts after that. It was the same role over and over, and every cop movie was a cheap imitation. I'd get this script and every one had a chase sequence, every scene was either set in a garage or a vacant lot or a warehouse with everybody getting gunned down." In 1973 he appeared in *The Seven-Ups*, a sort of follow-up to *The French Connection*, in which Scheider's character is once again based on Sonny Grosso. In 1975 Scheider appeared in one of the most successful films of all time, the Steven Spielberg-helmed *Jaws*. Scheider was cast as Chief Martin Brody, the head of police in the seaside resort of Amity when the area is terrorised by a giant shark. The co-stars were Robert Shaw and Richard Dreyfuss. Scheider's line to Shaw when he first sees the man-eater, "You're gonna need a bigger boat" was voted 35th on the American Film Institute's list of best movie quotes. It was actually ad-libbed by Scheider. The mechanical shark in the film was nicknamed Bruce after Spielberg's lawyer Bruce Ramer. The following year Scheider appeared in John Schlesinger's *Marathon Man*, with Dustin Hoffman (as his little brother) and Laurence Olivier. *Sorcerer* (1976), which reunited him with *French Connection* director William Friedkin, flopped. Scheider was originally scheduled to play the Robert De Niro role in *The Deer Hunter* but dropped out and was offered *Jaws 2* (1978) instead. It was not a happy set as Scheider constantly clashed with director Jeannot Szwarc. In 1979 he appeared in Bob Fosse's *All That Jazz* as the womanising choreographer Joe Gideon and received his second Oscar nomination, this time for Best Actor. He was in *Blue Thunder* (1983) and *2010* (1984), the sequel to *2001: A Space Odyssey* (1968). In 1993 he took the lead in the submarine drama *SeaQuest DSV* but left after criticising the production. His later films included: *Texas 46* (2002), *Citizen Verdict* (2003), *Dracula II: Ascension* (2003), *The Punisher* (2004), *Dracula III: Legacy* (2005), *Carrier: Arsenal Of*

The Sea (2005), *The Poet* (2007), *If I Didn't Care* (2007), *Dark Honeymoon* (2008) and *Iron Cross* (2010). On November 8, 1962 Scheider married film editor Cynthia Eddenfield Bebout and had one daughter, Maximillia, before their divorce. On February 11, 1989 he married documentary filmmaker Brenda King by whom he had two children: Christian (b. New York, January 1990) and Molly.
CAUSE: Scheider died from multiple myeloma (an illness diagnosed in 2004) also known as Kahler's disease (cancer of the white blood cells) at the University of Arkansas for Medical Sciences hospital in Little Rock, Arkansas. He was 75.

Joseph M. Schenck
Born Christmas Day, 1878
Died October 22, 1961
Movie mogul. Born in Rybinsk, Russia, Schenck travelled to the States in 1892 and began running errands for various shopkeepers, working his way up the commercial ladder until with his brother, Nicholas (b. Rybinsk, Russia, November 15, 1880, d. 1969), he eventually owned a couple of New York chemists. The brothers moved into the amusement arcade business in 1908 and opened their own amusement park four years later. They joined Marcus Loew in his chain of cinemas and the company that eventually became the parent of MGM. In 1917 Schenck branched out on his own and became an independent film producer. On October 20, 1916, he had married actress Norma Talmadge. They separated in 1928 and were divorced on April 14, 1934. He produced films starring his wife, her sister, Constance, and her brother-in-law, Buster Keaton. In 1924 Schenck became chairman of United Artists and nine years later co-founded Twentieth Century Pictures with Darryl F. Zanuck. Two years after that, he became chairman of the newly formed 20th Century Fox, a position he held until 1941. For a

number of years Schenck had paid off two gangsters, Willie Biof and George Browne, to the tune of $50,000 per annum. The two had complete control of the stage-hands' union and without their 'help' numerous productions would have been closed or run vastly over budget. The two men were eventually caught and jailed, thanks in no small part to Schenck. He served four months in prison for income tax evasion but was subsequently pardoned by President Harry S. Truman.
CAUSE: He died aged 82 in Beverly Hills, California, from the effects of a stroke.

Charles H. Schneer
Born May 5, 1920
Died January 21, 2009
Special FX producer. Charles Hirsh Schneer was born in Norfolk, Virginia, and educated at Columbia University before he joined Columbia Pictures. In the Second World War he produced training films as a member of the U.S. Army Signal Corps Photographic Unit stationed on Long Island. It is for his collaboration with Ray Harryhausen that Schneer is best known. Schneer produced 25 films including *Hellcats Of The Navy* (1957), the only film to star Ronald Reagan and Nancy Davis, and *Half A Sixpence* (1967) starring Tommy Steele. He worked with Harryhausen over four decades beginning in 1955 with the fantasy film *It Came From Beneath The Sea* about a giant octopus that destroys the Golden Gate Bridge. It was based on one of Schneer's ideas. "Charles and Ray were an ideal couple. They were both enthusiastic about doing fantasy films at a time when fantasy films were not being taken seriously by the studios," Arnold Kunert, Harryhausen's agent said. "Schneer, in his wisdom, believed in Ray's talent as a stop-motion animation artist." Their films included: *Jason And The Argonauts* (1963), *The 3 Worlds Of Gulliver* (1960), *The 7th Voyage Of Sinbad* (1958), *The Golden*

Voyage Of Sinbad (1974) and *Sinbad And The Eye Of The Tiger* (1977). Their last film together was *Clash Of The Titans* (1981). Of his friend, Harryhausen said, "He would supply the practical element . . . and always knew what would work and what wouldn't. Without his help and foresight, much of what we planned together would not have seen the light of day." He married Shirley in 1941 and they had three daughters: Lesley, Stacey and Bettine (b. January 9, 1954, d. March 15, 2001).

CAUSE: Schneer died at a hospice in Boca Raton, Florida after a long illness, thought to be Alzheimer's. He was 88.

B.P. Schulberg

Born January 19, 1892
Died February 25, 1957

Film pioneer. Benjamin Percival Schulberg was born in Bridgeport, Connecticut and began working as a reporter on the *New York Evening Mail* before joining the film industry in 1911 through Rex Films as a scriptwriter and PR. In 1912 he landed a job with Adolph Zukor's Famous Players. In 1919 he moved to Hollywood. In 1920 he founded Preferred Pictures Inc and began producing films starring the busty Katherine McDonald. Her embonpoint was the draw rather than the films. In 1921 he produced his first film, *Get Your Man* (released May 22, 1921) and was in charge of more than 100 productions. Schulberg had been renting space from Louis B. Mayer and the two companies merged with their first production being *Rich Men's Wives* (released September 15, 1922). He was responsible for making Clara Bow a star. Not long after, he and Mayer had a huge falling out. In 1925 Schulberg signed for Paramount Pictures and three years later he was appointed general manager of the company's West Coast operation. In 1932 he became freelance and signed short-term deals with various studios for staff jobs. He left Paramount in

1937 after a power struggle and did not work for three years until 1940. He was unable to find work after the Second World War. His last film was *City Without Men* (released January 14, 1943), which starred Linda Darnell and Edgar Buchanan. Schulberg's politics were to the left and he was described by one magazine as "a political liberal in the reactionary world of Mayer and Hearst". His films included: *The Woman Conquers* (1922), *White Man* (1924), *The Plastic Age* (1925), *Mantrap* (1926), *The Eagle Of The Sea* (1926), *Special Delivery* (1927), *Underworld* (1927), *Three-Cornered Moon* (1933), *Thirty Day Princess* (1934), *Little Miss Marker* (1934), *She Couldn't Take It* (1935), *Meet Nero Wolfe* (1936), *Wedding Present* (1936), *A Doctor's Diary* (1937), *John Meade's Woman* (1937), *Her Husband Lies* (1937), *The Great Gambini* (1937), *She's No Lady* (1937), *He Stayed For Breakfast* (1940), *Bedtime Story* (1941), *The Adventures Of Martin Eden* (1942), *The Wife Takes A Flyer* (1942) and *Flight Lieutenant* (1942). He was twice married: to Helen McHale Keebler and Adeline Jaffe, the agent sister of producer/talent agent Sam Jaffe. They had two children: Budd (see below) and writer-producer Stuart (b. November 17, 1922, d. New York June 28, 1979). Mrs Schulberg had a two-year affair with her husband's bitterest enemy Louis Mayer that began in 1932 after he promised to make her agency the most successful in Tinseltown.

CAUSE: Schulberg died at his home in Key Biscayne, Florida. He was a month past his 65th birthday.

Budd Schulberg

Born March 27, 1914
Died August 5, 2009

Stool pigeon. Seymour Wilson "Budd" Schulberg was born in New York, the son of Paramount Pictures chief B.P. Schulberg and was educated at Deerfield Academy and Dartmouth.

Following in his father's footsteps he joined the family business, becoming a publicist at 17 and a scriptwriter two years later. In 1939 he was sacked after a terrible collaboration with F. Scott Fitzgerald on *Winter Carnival*. (He used the experience in the best-selling 1950 novel *The Disenchanted*). Two years later, he had his revenge penning a savage novel about the inner workings of Hollywood, *What Makes Sammy Run?* which detailed the rise of Sammy Glick (né Shmelka Glickstein) as he steals, charms and backstabs his way from New York newspaper office boy to production chief at a major Hollywood studio. Many in Hollywood believed that they were the inspiration for Sammy Glick but Schulberg later admitted that the character was an amalgam of numerous hustlers he had met. The book was adapted for television and became a Broadway flop (a musical starring Steve Lawrence), but has never been made into a film. Some 55 years after publication, Schulberg said, "I have a feeling they're not going to do it. It's still a little tough for them." Some Jews believed that the book would stir up anti-Semitic feelings but Dorothy Parker came to its defence, "Those who hail us Jews as brothers must allow us to have our villains, the same, alas, as any other race." Some people began using the book as an instruction manual. "I grew up hating [Glick]," he said. "Now I'm being made to feel as if I'd written a how-to book: *How To Succeed In Business While Really Trying*." During the Second World War he worked with John Ford's film unit, spending three and a half years in Washington and Europe on duty with the Office of Strategic Services, forerunner of the CIA. After the war, he arrested the Nazi filmmaker Leni Riefenstahl. He wrote his father's last film *City Without Men* (released January 14, 1943), which starred Linda Darnell and Edgar Buchanan. In 1947, he published *The Harder They Fall*, a fictionalised exposé

of boxing. The 1955 screen version, which Schulberg also wrote, was Humphrey Bogart's last film. In 1951 he appeared before the House Un-American Activities Committee to confess that he had visited the Soviet Union in 1934 and had been a communist from 1936 until 1939 and named seventeen fellow travellers of the Thirties, including the screenwriter Ring Lardner, Jr and the director Herbert Biberman. Losing their livelihoods, Lardner served a year in prison and Biberman six months. "It didn't take a genius to tell you that something was vitally wrong with the country," he said of his decision to join the Communist Party. "The unemployment was all around us. The bread lines and the apple sellers. I couldn't help comparing that with my own family's status, with my father; at one point he was making $11,000 a week. And I felt a shameful contrast between the haves and the have-nots very early." Schulberg claimed that he had named names because the party represented a real threat to freedom of speech. "They say that you testified against your friends, but once they supported the party against me, even though I did have some personal attachments, they were really no longer my friends," he said. "And I felt that if they cared about real freedom of speech, they should have stood up for me when I was fighting the party." Three years later, he wrote *On The Waterfront*, about corruption on the New Jersey waterfront, which earned a dozen Oscar nominations and won eight Academy Awards including Best Film, Best Actor for Marlon Brando (as the failed boxer Terry Malloy) and Best Screenwriting for Schulberg. The writer continued to produce books, screenplays and television scripts but never again reached the heights of *On The Waterfront*. In 1965 Schulberg founded the Douglass House Watts Writers Workshop in Los Angeles to help black teenagers to write. He also

founded the Frederick Douglass Creative Arts Center in New York in 1971. "I didn't want to just hang back and complain about things," he said. "I thought that we should all do something. I found great poets, great hearts in the ashes of Watts."
Schulberg's 1936 marriage to Virginia Ray (d. 1960) by whom he had one daughter, Victoria (b. 1936), ended in divorce in 1942. His 1943 marriage to Virginia Anderson ended in divorce in 1964. They had two sons Stephen (b. 1944) and David (b. January 29, 1946, d. August 14, 2005). His third wife, the 5'2" actress Geraldine Brooks (b. New York, October 29, 1925), whom he married in 1964, died on June 19, 1977. On June 9, 1978 he married the actress and writer Betsy Ann Langman. They had two children: a son and daughter, Benjamin Stuart (b. 1979) and Jessica. He said a few years before his death, "I'd like to be remembered as someone who used their ability as a novelist or as a dramatist to say the things he felt needed to be said about the society [and was] as entertaining as possible. Because if you don't [entertain], nobody's listening."
CAUSE: Schulberg collapsed at his home in Westhampton Beach on Long Island and was rushed to hospital but doctors were unable to save him. He died aged 95 of natural causes.

Paul Scofield, CH, CBE
Born January 21, 1922
Died March 19, 2008
Actor for all seasons. David Paul Scofield was born in Hurstpierpoint, West Sussex, the son of Edward Harry Scofield (b. November 19, 1892, d. 1976), a schoolteacher, and Mary Wild, and made his professional acting debut in January 1940 in Eugene O'Neill's *Desire Under The Elms* at the Westminster Theatre, London.
Preferring the theatre – Richard Burton once said, "of the ten greatest moments in theatre, eight are Scofield's" – he did not make his first film until he was 33

when he appeared in *That Lady* (1955) as King Philip II of Spain. It would be three years before his second film the war drama *Carve Her Name With Pride* (1958) in which he played Tony Fraser and a further six years before he stepped in front of the cameras again for *The Train* (1964) as Von Waldheim. It was for his fourth film *A Man For All Seasons* (premièred December 12, 1966) – a part he also performed on stage – that Scofield won an Oscar for his portrayal of Sir Thomas More, King Henry VIII's Lord Chancellor. Five years earlier, Scofield had won a Tony for his performance in the role on Broadway. Scofield waited only two years for his next film, the drama-documentary *Tell Me Lies* (1968). His remaining few films were: *Bartleby* (1970), *King Lear* (1971) as King Lear, *Scorpio* (1973) as Zharkov, *A Delicate Balance* (1973) as Tobias, *Summer Lightning* (1984) as Old Robert Clarke, *1919* (1985) as Alexander Scherbatov, *When The Whales Came* (1989) as The Birdman, *Henry V* (1989) as King Charles VI of France, *Hamlet* (1990) as The Ghost, *Utz* (1992) as Doctor Vaclav Orlik, *Quiz Show* (1994) as Mark Van Doren and *The Crucible* (1996) as Judge Thomas Danforth. Awarded a CBE – "an honour with a hint of hard work about it" – in 1956, Scofield three times turned down a knighthood. In the 2001 New Year's Honours' List he was made a Companion of Honour. Scofield married actress Joy Mary Parker on May 15, 1943 and had two children: Martin (b. March 6, 1945) and Sarah (b. August 22, 1951).
CAUSE: Scofield died aged 86 from leukaemia in a Sussex hospital.

George C. Scott
Born October 18, 1927
Died September 20, 1999
Forceful arrogance. George Campbell Scott was born in Wise, Virginia, and graduated in journalism from the University of Missouri. After serving

four years in World War II he became an actor. He didn't make his film début until he was in his thirties in *The Hanging Tree* (1959) as Dr George Grubb. His films included: *Anatomy Of A Murder* (1959) as Claude Dancer, for which he was nominated for an Oscar, *The Hustler* (1961) as Bert Gordon, for which he was also nominated for an Oscar, *The List Of Adrian Messenger* (1963) as Anthony Gethryn, *Dr Strangelove Or: How I Learned To Stop Worrying And Love The Bomb* (1964) as General 'Buck' Turgidson, *The Flim-Flam Man* (1967) as Mordecai Jones, *They Might Be Giants* (1971) as Justin Playfair, *The Hospital* (1971) as Dr Herbert Bock, for which he was nominated for an Oscar, *The Last Run* (1971) as Harry Garmes, *The New Centurions* (1972) as Kilvinski, *The Day Of The Dolphin* (1973) as Dr Jake Terrell, *The Savage Is Loose* (1974) as John, *The Hindenburg* (1975) as Colonel Franz Ritter, *Hardcore* (1979) as Jake Van Dorn, *The Changeling* (1980) as John Russell, *Taps* (1981) as General Harlan Bache, *Firestarter* (1984) as John Rainbird and *Gloria* (1999) as Ruby. Most of his last films were television movies. From February to May 1969 he filmed *Patton* (1970) as General George S. Patton, after numerous actors including Burt Lancaster, Lee Marvin, Robert Mitchum and Rod Steiger turned down the role and it was decided John Wayne didn't have quite the right qualities, i.e. the ability to act. The film was made in 71 locations in three countries on three continents and President Richard M. Nixon said it was his favourite film. The director claimed that *Patton* was an anti-war film, but Republicans such as Nixon and Ronald Reagan applauded what they saw as its strong patriotic message. The film won seven Oscars, including Best Actor for Scott but he declined the award, somewhat ungraciously, saying the Academy was a "meaningless, self-serving meat parade." Scott was married five times:

his wives were Carolyn Hughes (August 31, 1951–1954); Patricia Reed (1954–1960); Colleen Dewhurst (1960–July 1965); Colleen Dewhurst again (July 4, 1967–February 3, 1972) and Trish Van Devere (September 13, 1972 onwards).

CAUSE: Scott died aged 71 from a ruptured abdominal aortic aneurysm in Westlake Village, California. He lay dead for two days (found at 3pm on September 22) before he was discovered by his housekeeper in his den in a house filled with empty bottles of booze.

Randolph Scott

(GEORGE RANDOLPH CRANE)
Born January 23, 1898
Died March 2, 1987
Cary Grant's husband. The quintessential movie cowboy Randy Scott was born in Orange County, Virginia. After fighting in World War I he studied at North Carolina University, obtaining an engineering degree before joining his father's textile mill. He went to Hollywood to work as an extra in various films including: *Sharp Shooters* (1928), *Weary River* (1929), *The Far Call* (1929), *The Black Watch* (1929), *Sailor's Holiday* (1929), *The Virginian* (1929), *Dynamite* (1929) and *Sky Bride* (1932), a part that he supposedly acquired due to his close friendship with bashful billionaire Howard Hughes. Scott was lean, over six feet tall, wore "an air of calculating laziness" and "disliked emotional commitments, indulging the attentions of both men and women while possessing the soul of a cash register." His long relationship with Cary Grant caused an enormous stir. He appeared with Grant in two films: *Hot Saturday* (1932) and *My Favorite Wife* (1940). It was after the first of these that the two men began living together, initially at 1129H North Sweetzer Avenue, West Hollywood, and then at 2177 West Live Oak Drive in Los Feliz. Grant moved out following his February 9,

1934 marriage to Virginia Cherrill. When he was divorced on March 26, 1935, he moved in again with Scott at 1019 (now 1039) Ocean Front Road in Santa Monica. They continued to live together until Scott married the mannish, tweed-suit-wearing Mariana du Pont Somerville on March 23, 1936. They separated in 1938 and Scott resumed living with Grant until Grant married Barbara Hutton on July 8, 1942, at Lake Arrowhead, California. When columnists began to enquire as to why two wealthy Hollywood actors were sharing a house, publicists explained it by saying that the two men were saving money! Hardly likely since both could easily have afforded separate residences if they wanted. The rent was around $75 a month and each man took home around $400 a week. Pictures appeared of the two of them doing the washing up wearing aprons, eating breakfast and sunbathing. Journalist Jimmie Fiddler opined that they were "carrying the buddy business a bit too far". Columnist Edith Gwynn went further than most in putting into print stories about Grant's sexual preferences. She suggested a game in which guests turned up to a party disguised as their favourite film. According to Gwynn, Marlene Dietrich would be *Male And Female*, Greta Garbo *The Son-Daughter* and Cary Grant *One Way Passage*. On March 3, 1944, Scott married heiress (Marie) Patricia Stillman. They adopted a son and a daughter. In the Fifties Scott set up his own production company, Ranown, with Harry Joe Brown. It was then that he produced and appeared in many of his best Westerns. His canon of work included: *Hello, Everybody!* (1933) as Hunt Blake, *Cocktail Hour* (1933) as Randolph Morgan, *The Thundering Herd* (1933) as Tom Doan, *Sunset Pass* (1933) as Jack Rock, *To The Last Man* (1933) as Lynn Hayden, *Broken Dreams* (1933) as Dr Robert Morley, *So Red The Rose* (1935) as Duncan Bedford, *Rocky Mountain Mystery* (1935) as Larry Sutton, *Roberta* (1935) as John Kent, *She* (1935) as Leo Vincey, *Follow The Fleet* (1936) as Bilge Smith, *The Last Of The Mohicans* (1936) as Hawkeye, *And Sudden Death* (1936) as Lieutenant James Knox, *Go West Young Man* (1936) as Bud Norton, *High, Wide, And Handsome* (1937) as Peter Cortlandt, *The Texans* (1938) as Kirk Jordan, *Rebecca Of Sunnybrook Farm* (1938) as Anthony Kent, *Paris Calling* (1941) as Nick, *Belle Starr* (1941) as Sam Starr, *Western Union* (1941) as Vance Shaw, *To The Shores of Tripoli* (1942) as Sergeant Dixie Smith, *Pittsburgh* (1942) as Cash Evans, *Gung Ho!* (1943) as Colonel Thorwald, *Corvette K-225* (1943) as Lieutenant Commander MacClain, *Bombardier* (1943) as Captain Buck Oliver, *Belle Of The Yukon* (1944) as Honest John Calhoun, *Captain Kidd* (1945) as Adam Mercy, *China Sky* (1945) as Dr Gay Thompson, *Home, Sweet Homicide* (1946) as Lieutenant Bill Smith, *Abilene Town* (1946) as Dan Mitchell, *Gunfighters* (1947) as Brazos Kane, *Christmas Eve* (1947) as Jonathan, *Trail Street* (1947) as William Barkley 'Bat' Masterson, *Albuquerque* (1948) as Cole Armin, *The Nevadan* (1950) as Andrew Barclay, which he also produced, *Colt .45* (1950) as Steve Farrell, *Santa Fe* (1951) as Britt Canfield, *Man In The Saddle* (1951) as Owen Merritt, which he also produced, *Fort Worth* (1951) as Ned Britt, *Sugarfoot* (1951) as Jackson 'Sugarfoot' Redan, *Hangman's Knot* (1952) as Matt Stewart, which he also produced, *Carson City* (1952) as Silent Jeff Kincaid, *Thunder Over The Plains* (1953) as Captain David Porter, *Riding Shotgun* (1954) as Larry Delong, *Tall Man Riding* (1955) as Larry Madden, *Ten Wanted Men* (1955) as John Stewart, which he also produced, *Rage At Dawn* (1955) as James Barlow, *7th Cavalry* (1956) as Captain Tom Benson, which he also produced, *Seven Men From Now* (1956) as Ben Stride,

Decision At Sundown (1957) as Bart Allison, which he also produced, *The Tall T* (1957) as Pat Brennan, which he also produced, *Shoot-Out At Medicine Bend* (1957) as Buck Devlin, *Westbound* (1958) as John Hayes, *Buchanan Rides Alone* (1958) as Tom Buchanan which he also produced, *Ride Lonesome* (1959) as Ben Brigade, which he also produced, *Comanche Station* (1960) as Jefferson Cody, which he also produced and his last film, *Ride The High Country* (1962) as Gil Westrum. CAUSE: A very wealthy man, Scott died aged 89 in Beverly Hills, California, of natural causes one day before his 43rd wedding anniversary.

Terry Scott

(OWEN JOHN SCOTT)
Born May 4, 1927
Died July 26, 1994
Overgrown cherub. Born in Watford in the shadow of Benskin's brewery, the son of a postman who retired to run a corner shop, Scott was educated at Watford Grammar School and wanted to be an entertainer and two years in the accountancy business did not deter him. Scott was a show business mainstay for more than 50 years appearing as a pantomime dame (some regarded him the best dame in the post-Clarkson Rose era), a West End comedian and a regular in clubs and summer shows. However, he was best known for his sitcoms alongside June Whitfield *Happy Ever After* (July 17, 1974–December 20, 1978) and *Terry & June* (October 24, 1979–August 31, 1988). The Second World War interrupted Terry Scott's career and he joined the Royal Navy. After being demobbed he became a stage manager, before making his professional début in rep at Grange-Over-Sands. He changed his name, deciding Owen was not a humorous moniker and became a stand-up in a pub at 25 shillings per night. In 1950 Terry Scott unveiled his schoolboy character based on his cousin Knocker, whom he remembered

as "a dreadful little tyke". The act would end with Scott singing 'My Brother', which became a hit and years later a regular on Radio 1's *Junior Choice* in the days when there was delineation between adults and children. From October 4, 1955 until December 20, 1956 he partnered Bill Maynard for the show *Great Scott, It's Maynard*. From July 17, 1962 until February 26, 1968 he made *Hugh And I* with Hugh Lloyd. It was said to be one of the Queen's favourite shows. Scott had made his film début in *Blue Murder At St Trinian's* (1957) playing a police sergeant and for some time after would nearly always be cast as a law officer. He appeared in *Too Many Crooks* (1958) as fire policeman Smith, *Carry On Sergeant* (1958) as Sergeant Paddy O'Brien, *I'm All Right Jack* (1959) as Crawley, *The Bridal Path* (1959) as PC Donald, *And The Same To You* (1960) as a police constable, *Mary Had A Little* (1961) as a police sergeant, *What A Whopper!* (1961) as the sergeant, *Nothing Barred* (1961) as a policeman, *No My Darling Daughter* (1961) as a constable, *The Night We Got The Bird* (1961) as PC Lovejoy, *Nearly A Nasty Accident* (1961) as Sam Stokes, *Double Bunk* (1961) as the second river policeman, *A Pair Of Briefs* (1962) as the policeman at the law courts and *Murder Most Foul* (1964) as PC Wells. He then went on to appear in the *Carry On . . .* series playing Sergeant Major MacNutt in *Carry On . . . Up The Khyber* (1968), Peter Potter in *Carry On Camping* (1969), Jungle Boy in *Carry On Up The Jungle* (1970) in which he woos a not unwilling Jacki Piper, Terence Philpot in *Carry On Loving* (1970) in which his attempts to seduce the sexy Jenny Grubb (Imogen Hassall) are frustrated by her flatmates, Cardinal Wolsey in *Carry On Henry* (1971), Mr Allcock in *Carry On At Your Convenience* (1971) although his scenes were deleted from the final edit and *Carry On Matron* (1972) as Dr Prodd. He also appeared

in the film version of another successful sitcom *Bless This House* (1972) in which he played Ronald Baines. In 1983 he began a long association with Ray Cooney's *Run For Your Wife* in the West End. But it was for his work with June Whitfield that Scott is most fondly remembered. He was twice married. He walked out on his first wife after their one-year-old son died after choking on food. He married again in 1957 to former ballet dancer Margaret Pollen, and had four daughters, Sarah, Nicola, Lindsay and Alexandra. Terry Scott was possessed of some rather strange views. He was a lay preacher and a fundamentalist Christian who was also a serial adulterer. He confessed to 24 adulterous relationships in his marriage. He insisted that his daughters never had boyfriends to stay. "I told the girls to go up to the woods if they wanted to mess about." Very right-wing, he was also in favour of the status quo in apartheid South Africa and believed that Communists had infiltrated all the important posts in Britain.
CAUSE: In 1980 he suffered a brain haemorrhage that almost killed him. In 1987 he was struck down by bladder cancer. Terry Scott died in Godalming, Surrey, aged 67 from cancer. His funeral took place on August 4, 1994 at his local parish church in Godalming and was followed by a private cremation.

Jean Seberg

Born November 13, 1938
Died August 30, 1979
Androgynous, easily led waif. Born in Marshalltown, Iowa, Seberg came to fame playing the title role in the 1957 Otto Preminger film *St Joan*. She was just 17 when Preminger discovered her, the result of a world-wide hunt for an actress to play the lead in his production of George Bernard Shaw's play. During the execution scene Jean was burned for real when the gas cylinders that were being used failed to work properly. The film was not a hit

and professional success; personal happiness was to elude Seberg for the rest of her life. Her second film was *Bonjour Tristesse* (1958) as Cecile, also for Preminger and also a failure. On September 5, 1958, she married Harvard-educated French lawyer François Moreuil (b. 1935). She also appeared in *The Mouse That Roared* (1959) as Helen Kokintz. It was filmed in England as a vehicle for Peter Sellers and in the film Jean gave him his first on-screen kiss. It, too, was not a great picture. Her career was rescued by Jean-Luc Godard, who cast her in *A Bout De Souffle* (1960) as Patricia Franchini. Shooting began on August 17, 1959, and Jean very nearly walked out on the first day because she didn't like her character. She refused to work until changes were made to the script. Bizarrely, the film was shot with no sound – it was dubbed in later. (The film was remade in 1983 with Richard Gere in Jean-Paul Belmondo's role and Valerie Kaprisky playing Jean's part.) The film was a success, making a star of Jean-Paul Belmondo and earning Godard his reputation as a leader of the New Wave film art. It also made Jean a hairdressing fashion icon, with thousands of teenage French girls asking for 'la coupe Seberg'. With her marriage on the rocks, Jean returned to Hollywood alone to play Barbara Holloway in *Let No Man Write My Epitaph* (1960). In December 1958 she met French novelist Romain Gary, a married womaniser, with whom she began an affair. In January 1960 columnist Dorothy Kilgallen reported that Jean and her husband had separated. They denied the report but it was, in fact, true and when they returned to France the Moreuils maintained separate residences. That year Jean appeared in quick succession in three monochrome films: *La Récréation* (1960), *Les Grandes Personnes* (1961) as Ann and the adultery comedy *L'Amant De Cinq Jours* (1961). On September 20, 1960, she and Moreuil were divorced. At the end of the year she moved in with Romain Gary at 108 Rue de Bac, Paris. In February 1961 her three films were all playing successfully (although they were not critically acclaimed) and one newspaper rather hyperbolically declared a "Jean Seberg Festival". During the filming of the Franco-Italian movie *Congo Vivo* (1962), she contracted a severe case of amoebic dysentery that left her lethargic and ill for months afterwards. The area was in the midst of political strife and the danger was increased on September 17, 1961, when United Nations Secretary-General Dag Hammarskjöld was killed in a plane crash in the Congo. Jean and Gary, who had joined her on location in October 1961, were pleased to get back to domesticity. Jean didn't make another film until *Lilith* (1964), during which time she gave birth to a son (Alexandre) Diego Gary in Barcelona on July 17, 1962. On October 16 she and Gary were married in Sarrola-Carcopino, Corsica. Her subsequent films were: *Les Plus Belles Escroqueries Du Monde* (1964) as Patricia Leacock, *Échappement Libre* (1964) as Olga Celan opposite Jean-Paul Belmondo, *Moment To Moment* (1965) as Kay Stanton, which flopped, *Diamantenbilliard* (1965), *A Fine Madness* (1966) as Lydia West in another film that flopped, Claude Chabrol's World War II French resistance film *La Ligne De Démarcation* (1966) as Mary, Comptesse de Grandville, *Estouffade A La Caraïbe* (1966) as Colleen O'Hara, Chabrol's *La Route De Corinthe* (1968) as Shanny, *Les Oiseaux Vont Mourir Au Pérou* (1968) as the frigid nymphomaniac Adriana in a story written and directed by Romain Gary (to many critics it was the most demeaning film Jean Seberg ever made and it was the first film to receive an X rating in America), and *Pendulum* (1968) as Adele Matthews, for which she was paid $100,000. In

the latter, she starred opposite George Peppard who tried unsuccessfully to seduce her and later claimed "there were two sides to her" when he was rebuffed. Then came another potentially big American film, just the thing to get her re-established in her native country. In March 1968 she screen-tested for the role of Elizabeth, Ben Rumson's wife, in the $15-million film version of the hit musical *Paint Your Wagon* (1969). She signed to do the film at $120,000 (compared to Lee Marvin's $1 million) and moved to Arden Drive, Beverly Hills. She also took singing lessons, even though she had just the one number to perform, 'A Million Miles Away Behind The Door', and that ended up being dubbed because Jean's nerves meant her singing wasn't good enough. Her marriage to Gary began to come apart and she had an affair with the equally married Clint Eastwood during filming. Her father would later say that Jean always sided with the underdog and when Dr the Reverend Martin Luther King, Jr was assassinated on April 4, 1968, she pronounced herself amazed at the apathy of white America at the event. Jean began to raise money for black causes such as Jim Brown's Negro Industrial Economic Union. The filming of *Paint Your Wagon* was not a happy experience for major cast or crew. Director Josh Logan clashed with lyricist Alan Jay Lerner. Some of the extras were drugged hippies whom Jean befriended. On September 17, 1968, she and Romain announced they were going their separate ways. The following month her affair with Eastwood was also over. She later confessed to writer Roderick Mann that the fling with Eastwood had been the major contributory factor to the break-up of her marriage. Following the critical mauling that *Paint Your Wagon* received, Jean's career began a steady decline. Personally, she began to identify more and more with black causes. She began a passionate affair with Hakim Abdullah Jamal (b. Roxbury, Massachusetts, March 28, 1931, as Allen Eugene Donaldson), a leading Black Muslim who was married to a distant cousin of Malcolm X. Jamal was an often delusional self-publicist who claimed that he was being persecuted for his Black Power views by all sorts of groups, including other blacks. Jean stayed with him in Lake Tahoe and became as paranoid as Jamal, believing they were under observation. Many young coloureds and whites supported the Black Panther movement although Jamal's ego never let him become totally subsumed in the culture. On November 17, 1968, Jamal introduced several Panthers to Jean and her house guest Vanessa Redgrave. The idea was to extract money for the Panthers' cause; they had received $10,000 from Marlon Brando. Some of the activists that night had no idea who either Jean or Redgrave were. They just knew that the two, some would say misguided, women were sympathetic to their cause. When Jean went back to Marshalltown for Thanksgiving she gave Jamal the run of her Coldwater Canyon home. Back at home she tried to persuade her family and friends of the validity of Jamal's cause. In December she flew to France to see Gary and their son. An estate agent management company went to check on the Coldwater Canyon house and were shocked to see how Jean's generosity had been abused. The place had been trashed and rubbish was strewn over the garden. Many of his white devotees soon tired of Jamal but Jean invited him to Paris and he flew there on January 24, 1969. When he spoke to a gathering of mostly African students, Jamal urged them to kill all whites, much to the consternation of the predominantly black audience, many of whom dismissed Jamal as a flake. Meanwhile, Jean's interest in the Black Panthers hadn't gone entirely unnoticed in the States and she was

placed under surveillance by the FBI. Jamal moved onto London, where he stayed with Vanessa Redgrave. Jean, in the meantime, was back in America filming her last US movie and, by all accounts, her worst – *Airport* (1970) in which she played public relations girl Tanya Livingston. She was paid $150,000 plus $1,000-a-week expenses for four months and was billed third in the cast; the film was lambasted by critics. The affair with Jamal moved into overdrive but Jean became more and more attuned to the message of the Black Panthers. He didn't. She paid for Panthers to hire cars but they usually totalled them. The FBI also increased their surveillance of Panthers and Panther supporters. Jamal was eventually renounced by fellow black activists for "talking black but sleeping white." By 1969 Jean was also sleeping with Raymond 'Masai' Hewitt, a leading Panther. It was around this time that J. Edgar Hoover announced the Black Panthers were the greatest threat to US internal security. The Bureau announced that Jean's bags were to be searched every time she went to an airport and her details were sent to every Bureau field station. In June 1969 she began to make *Ondata Di Calore* (1970) playing the schizophrenic Joyce Grasse. The film was lauded by critics and Jean later favoured it above her others. In the late summer of 1969 she split from Jamal, tired of his constant boasts and lies. He soon found another mug – 25-year-old divorcée Gale Benson was the daughter of a former MP. Jean discovered cancerous cysts in her breasts around the turn of the decade and travelled to Paris for an operation. She was paid $100,000 to appear as Confederate colonel's widow Alexandra Mountford in *Macho Callahan* (1970). On set she contracted a disease that caused her tongue to turn jet black. She would wander the locations jokingly asking if "anybody want[ed] to kiss the lady with the black tongue". The film was to give her the last of her big pay packets. She had earned a lot of money but had wasted much of it on her foolish attempts to ingratiate herself with the Black Panthers and other minority groups. In March 1970 Jean discovered she was pregnant. The father was Carlo Navarra, an extra on *Macho Callahan*, although Romain Gary subsequently acknowledged paternity. On July 1, Jean and Gary were divorced but announced they would remarry after the infant's birth. The FBI spread the rumour that the father was black, knowing full well that was not the case. On August 7, Jean tried to commit suicide with an overdose of sleeping pills. It all became academic when Nina Hart Gary was born, 63 days prematurely, in Geneva on August 23, 1970, weighing less than 4lb. The white baby died two days later at 6am. The following month on a flight to America, Jean drank heavily, disappeared to the toilet and came out completely naked and screaming that hijackers were attempting to take over the plane. Her bodyguard managed to make her return to her seat where she gobbled tranquillisers. By the time the flight landed in Chicago, Jean was out of it, barely able to stand. Her bodyguard put her into a luggage trolley and began wheeling her through the airport. Then she spotted a black policeman and began screaming at him that he was a traitor to his race, making a grab for his gun. Other officers joined their colleague and threatened to arrest the by now hysterical actress. Back home in Marshalltown on September 11, she wrote her resignation letter from the Black Panthers. She then rang columnist Joyce Haber, one of the leading critics of her affiliation with the Panthers, and berated her. Seberg had arranged for Nina to be buried in Marshalltown and the infant's tiny body was displayed in an open casket from September 16–18. Jean also put down a deposit on a farm and bought a house that she said would be

used to house black athletes visiting Marshalltown. That didn't please the mostly white locals. She spent most of November 1970 in a Parisian lunatic asylum. She managed to get out for one night with Jamal and Gale Benson and went to a club with them. There she stubbed a lit cigarette out on Jamal's hand before lighting another and burning three knuckles on her own hand. Jamal then proceeded to viciously beat her up, telling her that it was her suicide attempt that had killed Nina, not the press. In December she was released from care and was visited by Carlos Navarra. On December 29, she was placed on an FBI Security Index and listed as Priority 3. (If the President had declared a state of national emergency, all Priority 3s, including Jean Seberg, would have been arrested and interned for the duration.) In Spain and Tunisia in 1971 she filmed *Kill! Kill! Kill!* (1972) as Emily. Thereafter she moved to Italy, where she played the part of Giovanna in *Questa Specie D'Amore* (1972). She appeared in *Camorra* (1972) at the request of her lover Fabio Testi, with whom she was two-timing short, bearded wannabe film director Ricardo Franco (b. 1948). On January 2, 1972, Gale Benson was murdered by followers of Black Power leader Michael X (b. Trinidad, August 17, 1933, as Michael de Freitas) who later changed his name to Abdul Malik. He had been prosecuted in London in 1967 under the Race Relations Act by saying that any white man seen with a black woman should be shot. He spent a year in jail. In 1968 he was accused of a robbery and jumped bail. The sadly misguided Benson had been with Malik when his acolytes suddenly cut her throat with a cutlass and pushed her into a makeshift grave, where she was buried alive. Jamal returned to Boston alone, fearing for his own safety. On May 1, 1973, Jamal was shot dead in his home on Townsend Street, Roxbury, Massachusetts. On May 16,

1975, Malik was hanged for murder. Seberg began work on *L'Attentat* (1972) as wealthy social worker Edith Lemoine; the film was partially based on a true story of a left-wing Moroccan activist who was kidnapped and tortured by French police. Seberg was paid the equivalent of $40,000 for her work. The film was a commercial success but did nothing to lift the torpor of Jean's career. She met wannabe director Dennis Berry (b. 1944) whose father had been blacklisted during the McCarthy era. On March 12, 1972, they were married in Las Vegas' Chapel of the Bells. Next Jean played Ruth Miller in the Spanish thriller *La Corrupción De Chris Miller* (1973). The following year she made *Les Hautes Solitudes* (1974), a black-and-white improvised film about loneliness. In it Jean improvised a scene of suicide that so terrified the director Philippe Garrel by its realism, he warned Dennis Berry never to let her be alone. Even in company, she could still get into trouble and on one occasion, after drinking with Berry and Garrel, she smashed a tumbler and began slashing at her wrist. She starred in *Bianchi Cavalli D'Agosto*, which was released in 1975. Jean spent much of 1974 in various clinics and asylums drugged up to the eyeballs. Her next film *Die Große Ekstase* (1975) flopped. Her last film, *Die Wildente* (1976), saw her nearly 4st overweight. Back in Paris she received a letter from the US Department of Justice confirming that she had been under FBI surveillance. It resulted in another bout of paranoia. In May 1976 she and Berry separated but he collected her from a hotel where she had gone to visit Ricardo Franco. Her stomach bore the marks of self-inflicted burns. She was admitted to another asylum. In 1977 she really began to spiral downwards. She drank more and more, became hugely fat and had violent mood swings. She went back home to Marshalltown for the last time but was disgusted by what she saw as its small-mindedness. Back with her husband she began exhibiting signs of nymphomania, desperate to feel attractive despite being overweight or drugged out. She would have sex with almost any man who took her fancy. After that Christmas she stayed on in Europe while her husband flew to Los Angeles. She began sleeping with a young Moroccan student called Mohammed. Her paranoia increased but a weight loss clinic at least helped her to shed the extra weight she had put on. She left after six weeks as svelte as she was when she did *St Joan*. However, the shock of the sudden weight loss finally pushed her over the edge. Following the disintegration of the Black Panthers, she looked for another ethnic group she could identify with. France had and still has a large contingent of Algerians and Jean began a series of affairs with several of them. On January 3, 1979, she admitted herself to an asylum and then, ten days later, to a sanatorium. In February she was committed to a state mental institution. She was released in mid-March and met an Algerian called Ahmed Hasni (b. 1960) who moved in with her; she had already slept with his uncle. On May 31 they married, but since she was still legally hitched to Dennis Berry, the ceremony was neither legal nor legitimate. They flew to Palma, Majorca, on holiday but separated after an argument. On August 3, she flew to Guyana to film one day on *Le Légion Saute Sur Kolwezi* and returned to Paris the following Tuesday (August 7). She was not due to film again until September 6. On August 18, according to Hasni, Jean tried to throw herself into the path of an oncoming tube train. On August 29, the couple went to the pictures to see *Clair De Femme* (1979), a film by Romain Gary. It caused her to think back to the happier times with her second husband, rather than the bedsit she shared with a lover young enough to be her son. Within 24 hours she was dead.

CAUSE: At 6am on August 30, Jean rose naked, wrapped herself in a blanket, picked up two months' supply of barbiturates she had recently collected from the chemist, a bottle of mineral water and her car keys. She drove her white Renault (licence plate 334 APK 75) to the Rue du Général Appert, climbed into the back seat, swallowed the pills, pulled the blanket over her head and laid down to die. She was 40. On September 8, 1979, her decaying body was discovered by police. Jean's car had been parked around the corner from her home for ten days. One of the first journalists to arrive at the scene noted: "It wasn't a pretty sight. The car doors were the sort that close hermetically, so the body had literally baked in the sun for ten days. The odour was unimaginably foul. It just seemed to hang in the warm summer air for hours." It was only when her body was taken to a morgue that a note was discovered clutched in her hand. It was written in French and addressed to her son, Diego. It read:

Forgive me. I can no longer live with my nerves. Understand me. I know that you can and you know that I love you.
Be strong.
Your loving mother,
Jean

On September 14, she was buried in the Montparnasse Cemetery in Paris. By a strange coincidence, Romain Gary was also to die by his own hand. On December 2, 1980, he blew his brains out with a Smith & Wesson .38. A note was found by his body. It read in part: "No connection with Jean Seberg. Lovers of broken hearts are kindly asked to look elsewhere."

FURTHER READING: *Played Out: The Jean Seberg Story* – David Richards (New York: Playboy Paperbacks, 1982).

Sir Harry Secombe, CBE

Born September 8, 1921
Died April 11, 2001

'Sir Cumference'. Born in a council house near the Swansea docks Harry Donald Secombe had six brothers and sisters, was the son of a commercial traveller, and was constantly ill as a child and bullied. He compensated by finding humour in most things. In 1938 (adding two years to his age) he joined 132 Field Regiment, RA (a Territorial Regiment) and then in 1939 was called up to the Royal Artillery. In 1944 while serving, he met Lance Bombardier Spike Milligan on a battlefield in Italy. Secombe remembered, "A gun came flying over a cliff, missing us by a few feet. This man appeared and said, 'Has anyone seen a gun?' It was Spike Milligan." Following demob in April 1946, Secombe began working among the nudes at the Windmill. He then joined the BBC's *Variety Bandbox* on radio. On May 28, 1951, he, Peter Sellers (with whom he shared a birthday), Milligan and Michael Bentine created *The Goon Show*, a radio series that ran on the BBC for some seven years. Years later Bentine recalled being buttonholed by a customer who asked how they managed to formulate the "psychological and sociological" impact of the show. "We were all pissed," he replied. In 1963, at the Saville Theatre, Secombe created the title role in the musical *Pickwick*, which ran for two and a half years in London, with a further run in America. He began making films from the late-Forties but his first major role was a second-rate vaudeville comedian in the 1957 Ealing movie *Davy*. Secombe's films included *Svengali* (1954) and *Song Of Norway* (1970). In 1968 he played Mr Bumble the beadle in Carol Reed's *Oliver!*. He hosted the religious programme *Highway* for 10 years from 1983 on Sunday evenings. In 1948, Harry married Myra Atherton, a Swansea girl. They had two sons, Andrew and David, and two daughters, Katy and Jennifer. Harry's brother, the Rev Fred Secombe, conducted the wedding ceremony. CAUSE: Harry Secombe became a diabetic in 1980 after an operation for a perforated colon, caused by diverticulitis. He was found to have prostate cancer in 1998, and had a stroke in 1999. He died aged 79 in Guildford Hospital, Surrey, from the cancer.

Peter Sellers, CBE

(RICHARD HENRY SELLARS)
Born September 8, 1925
Died July 24, 1980
Troubled comedian. 5′8″ Peter Sellers was born, an only child, at 20 Southsea Terrace, Southsea, Hampshire, four years to the day after fellow Goon Sir Harry Secombe. One of his ancestors was the fighter Daniel Mendoza (b. Whitechapel, London, July 5, 1764, d. Horseshoe Alley, Petticoat Lane, London, September 3, 1836). Sellers was born a year after his brother died in infancy. The first child had been called Peter Sellars and when Richard Henry was born, virtually as a replacement, he was immediately named Peter. Sellers' mother was Jewish and his father, Bill Sellars (sic) (d. October 1962), a Protestant but he was educated at a Roman Catholic school, leaving at 14 to become a back room boy in various theatres. He then decided he wanted to be a drummer in a jazz band. Like most Jewish mothers, Agnes 'Peg' Sellers (b. 1895 as Agnes Doreen Marks, d. January 30, 1967) was extremely solicitous about her son's welfare (especially so since their first child, named Peter Sellars, was stillborn) and according to fellow Goon Spike Milligan she even tried to have him disqualified from military service on medical grounds. He joined the RAF in September 1943 as 2223033 Airman Second Class and was sent to the entertainment section where he appeared with Ralph Reader's Gang Show. Peg even followed him and cooked his meals convinced that NAAFI food was not good enough for her boy. When Sellers was posted overseas, she asked his friend David Lodge to keep an eye on him. Lodge recalled rescuing a drunk Sellers from a very lowlife French prostitute but in Germany the two men slept with hungry German girls using food as bait to bed them. Following demob Sellers landed a job in March 1948 appearing at the Windmill Theatre in the West End. That month he appeared on a television talent show, *New To You*, but lost in the final to a young comic called Benny Hill. He landed another slot by ringing a BBC producer, pretending to be Kenneth Horne, then starring in the popular wireless comedy *Much Binding In The Marsh*. On July 16, 1948 Sellers was initiated into Chelsea Lodge, Number 3098, of the Freemasons. He joined only so he could get on but spent so much time making secret signs and giving arcane handshakes that his brother masons tired of his antics. He appeared on a number of radio shows before the show that made his name, *The Goon Show*, which started on May 28, 1951, and ran for nine years. Fellow Goon Spike Milligan opined: "He was not a genius, Sellers, he was a freak." He also began making films in this period including *Penny Points To Paradise* (1951) as The Major/Arnold Fringe, *Let's Go Crazy* (1951) as Groucho/Giuseppe/Cedric/Izzy/Gozzunk/Crystal Jollibottom, *Down Among The Z Men* (1952) as Major Bloodnok, *Orders Are Orders* (1954) as Private Goffin and *Our Girl Friday* (1954) but came to fame in *The Ladykillers* (1955) as Harry – Mr Robinson. Then came another set of poor films such as *John And Julie* (1955) as Police Constable Diamond, *The Smallest Show On Earth* (1957) as Percy Quill, *The Naked Truth* (1957) as Sonny MacGregor, *Insomnia Is Good For You* (1957) as Hector Dimwiddle, *Up The Creek* (1958) as Chief Petty Officer Doherty, *tom thumb* (1958) as Tony and *The Mouse That Roared* (1959) as Tully Bascombe/Grand Duchess Gloriana XII/Prime Minister Count Mountjoy. Spike Milligan's award-winning *The Running Jumping &*

Standing Still Film (1959) brought Sellers a certain amount of praise but it was *I'm All Right Jack* (1959) as Fred Kite/Sir John Kennaway that won him international fame. Then came *Carlton-Browne Of The F.O.* (1959) as Prime Minister Amphibulos, *The Battle Of The Sexes* (1959) as Mr Martin, *Two Way Stretch* (1960) as Dodger Lane and *The Millionairess* (1960) as Dr Ahmed el Kabir during which time he had an affair (and a Top 5 hit – 'Goodness Gracious Me') with co-star Sophia Loren. He starred in and directed *Mr Topaze* (1961) as Auguste Topaze and played Pearly Gates in *The Wrong Arm Of The Law* (1962). He appeared in *Lolita* (1962) as Clare Quilty and *Waltz Of The Toreadors* (1962) as General Leo Fitzjohn but then his career took off meteorically with *The Pink Panther* (1963) in which he played the part of the bumbling, ineffectual Inspector Jacques Clouseau. A sequel, *A Shot In The Dark* (1964), proved almost as popular and then Sellers appeared in *Dr Strangelove Or: How I Learned To Stop Worrying And Love The Bomb* (1964) as Group Captain Lionel Mandrake/President Merkin Muffley/Dr Strangelove for which he was nominated for an Oscar and *What's New, Pussycat* (1965) as Dr Fritz Fassbender but then his career stalled. He appeared in a succession of duff or second-rate films including *The Wrong Box* (1966) as Doctor Pratt, *Casino Royale* (1967) as Evelyn Tremble, *I Love You, Alice B. Toklas!* (1968) as Harold Fine, *The Magic Christian* (1969) as Sir Guy Grand, *Hoffman* (1970) as Benjamin Hoffman, *There's A Girl In My Soup* (1970) as Robert Danvers, *Alice's Adventures In Wonderland* (1972) as the March Hare, *Where Does It Hurt?* (1972) as Albert T. Hopfnagel and *Soft Beds And Hard Battles* (1973) as General Latour/Major Robinson/Herr Schroeder/Adolf Hitler/The President/Prince Kyoto. It was only when he reprised the role of Inspector Clouseau in *The Return Of*

The Pink Panther (1974) that he hit gold again. He became a millionaire as a result of the success and appeared in *The Pink Panther Strikes Again* (1976), promoted to Chief Inspector Clouseau. He brought the character back again in *Revenge Of The Pink Panther* (1978). (Following Sellers' death, director Blake Edwards used unseen footage to make *Trail Of The Pink Panther* [1982] which, perhaps deservedly, was not a success.) Sellers appeared in *The Prisoner Of Zenda* (1979) as Rudolf IV/Rudolf V/Syd Frewin and co-wrote the flop *The Fiendish Plot Of Dr Fu Manchu* (1980) as Fu Manchu/Nayland Smith. His penultimate film is generally regarded to be his best. He played the bewildered Chance the gardener who achieves political greatness in Hal Ashby's *Being There* (1979) for which he was nominated for an Oscar. Sellers was married four times. On September 15, 1951, at Caxton Hall, Westminster, he married RADA-educated actress Anne Hayes (b. Australia, 1930, as Anne Howe) by whom he had two children, Michael (b. London Clinic, April 2, 1954, weighing 7lb 11oz, d. July 24, 2006 of heart failure – ironically, the same day as his father and of the same cause) and Sarah Jane (b. London Clinic, October 16, 1957), from whom he was often estranged. They divorced in March 1963. On February 19, 1964, at Guildford Registry Office, he married Swedish starlet Britt Ekland (b. Allmänna B.B., Stockholm, October 6, 1942, as Britt-Marie Eklund) who gave birth to his troubled daughter, Victoria (b. Welbeck Nursing Home, 27, Welbeck Street, St Marylebone, London, January 20, 1965). It was only the intercession of Bryan Forbes and Nanette Newman that stopped Sellers insisting on Ekland aborting Victoria. It was remarked, rather cruelly but probably accurately, that Victoria was blessed with her father's looks and her mother's talent, which might explain why her life became a tabloid headline involving, drugs, prostitution and even prison. Sellers and Ekland were divorced in 1968. Ten years later, Ekland sold her story to a newspaper and moaned: "I don't like very hairy men, which my ex-husband . . . is." On August 24, 1970, Sellers married Miranda Quarry (b. 1947) but they divorced in 1974. In Paris on February 18, 1977, he married Lynne Frederick but that marriage was also on the point of dissolution when Sellers died. Regarded by many as genius, an equal number thought him certifiable. Film director Roy Boulting commented: "As a man he was abject, probably his own worse enemy, although there was plenty of competition."

CAUSE: For the last 16 years of his life Sellers suffered from a heart condition. On April 5, 1964, he suffered a heart attack in Los Angeles and was admitted to the Cedars of Lebanon Medical Center the next day. At 4.32am Sellers' heart stopped beating and remained immobile for one and a half minutes. Restarted manually by a doctor, it stopped seven more times that day. In 1977 another heart attack necessitated the fitting of a pacemaker. Sellers collapsed in 1979. He needed a daily intake of between 50 and 60 pills to stay alive. He flew to London, alone, on July 21, 1980, and booked into the Dorchester Hotel, paying £200 a night for his sixth-floor suite. He had told his son that his marriage to Lynne Frederick was over. It therefore came as something of a shock when, on hearing the news of his collapse, Frederick flew over from America. On July 22, at 2pm he suffered another attack and was attended by the Dorchester medical staff. His pacemaker had failed. At 5pm he was taken to the Middlesex Hospital, Mortimer Street, London, where he died at 12.26am. Glenn Miller's 'In The Mood' was played, at his request, at his funeral.

FURTHER READING: *Peter Sellers* – Alexander Walker (London: Coronet, 1982); *P.S. I Love You Peter Sellers 1925–1980* – Michael Sellers with Sarah and Victoria Sellers (London: William Collins, 1981); *The Life And Death Of Peter Sellers* – Roger Lewis (London: Century, 1994); *Mr Strangelove: A Biography Of Peter Sellers* – Ed Sikov (London: Sidgwick & Jackson, 2002).

David O. Selznick
Born May 10, 1902
Died June 22, 1965

Legendary producer. Born in Pittsburgh, Pennsylvania, probably at 4743 Ben Venue Street, the son of film mogul Lewis Joseph Selznick (b. Kovno, Lithuania, May 5, 1869, d. Los Angeles, January 25, 1933, of a cerebral haemorrhage) a jeweller who made and lost a fortune in silent films and brother of agent Myron Charles Selznick (b. 44 Federal Street, Pittsburgh, Pennsylvania, October 8, 1898, d. Santa Monica Hospital, March 23, 1944, of an abdominal haemorrhage). Some time after his arrival in the United States the family name was shortened to the more familiar Selznick. In 1910 the family uprooted to New York City and Lewis' jewellery business went under. He began to make films and soon recouped his losses, but the victory was only temporary. In 1923 Lewis went bankrupt and David began to produce documentaries, but they were not commercial successes and three years later he upped sticks to Hollywood where he was taken under the wing of Louis B. Mayer, Lewis' former partner. He left MGM in 1928 and joined Paramount where he stayed until 1931. It was at Radio-Keith-Orpheum (RKO) that David began to create a name for himself with films such as *A Bill Of Divorcement* (1932), *What Price Hollywood* (1932) and *King Kong* (1933). He moved to MGM in early 1933, where he made *Dinner At Eight* (1933), *David Copperfield* (1935) and

A Tale Of Two Cities (1935). On October 15, 1935, he formed Selznick International Studios and bought the rights to Margaret Mitchell's epic Civil War novel *Gone With The Wind*. He had previously made *Little Lord Fauntleroy* (1936), *A Star Is Born* (1937), which earned eight Oscar nominations, *The Prisoner Of Zenda* (1937) and *The Adventures Of Tom Sawyer* (1938), but when he bought Mitchell's lengthy book, many people thought he had taken leave of his senses. Director Victor Fleming was not impressed. Rejecting a share of the profits in lieu of a fee, he told Selznick, "Don't be a damn fool, David. *Gone With The Wind* is going to be one of the biggest white elephants of all time." As the world knows, he proved them all wrong. The following year he hired Alfred Hitchcock to direct *Rebecca* (1940), which won 11 Academy Award nominations, but thereafter Selznick seemed to lose the magic touch. His *Spellbound* (1945), *Duel In The Sun* (1947) and *The Third Man* (1950) were all successes, but he struggled to recapture his early form. In the Fifties he worked with European producers but also failed to ignite the flames of success. His last film was *A Farewell To Arms* (1957). Incidentally, the 'O' in his name didn't stand for anything – he simply thought it sounded good. Selznick married twice. His first wife (on April 29, 1930) was Irene Mayer (b. 101 Russell Street, Greenpoint, April 2, 1907, d. Apartment 1007, Pierre Hotel, Los Angeles, October 10, 1990), the third daughter of Louis B. Mayer. His second wife was the actress Jennifer Jones (b. Tulsa, Oklahoma, March 2, 1919, as Phylis Isley) and she appeared in many of his later films.
CAUSE: Selznick was in a Beverly Hills office when at 12.30pm he suffered a heart attack. At 2.22pm he was pronounced dead at Cedars-Sinai Medical Center. He was 63.
FURTHER READING: *Showman: The Life Of David O. Selznick* – David Thomson (London: Andre Deutsch, 1993).

Mack Sennett

(MICHAEL SINNOTT)
Born January 17, 1880
Died November 5, 1960
The self-proclaimed king of silent comedy and the father of the casting couch. Born in Richmond, Quebec, Canada, the Catholic Sennett's family moved to East Berlin, Connecticut in 1897. He landed a job in an iron factory but was unhappy there and moved to Northampton, Massachusetts, where through the good offices of Calvin Coolidge (nicknamed 'Silent Cal', later 30th US President and the man about whom Dorothy Parker said, on being informed he was dead, "How can they tell?") he met actress Marie Dressler and she encouraged him to be an actor and so Sennett moved to New York. He appeared in minor roles in various musicals but never got his big break. On January 17, 1908, he signed with the Biograph and began working as an extra. He also worked on writing screenplays and in March 1911 directed his first film, *Comrades*. A disagreement on the direction of films led to Sennett leaving in 1912 to create the Keystone Film Company. The first Keystone Comedies premièred on September 23, 1912, and quickly became the industry standard by which others were measured. By 1915 Sennett was producing Fatty Arbuckle, Chester Conklin, Al St John and many others, but was bemused by the success of Charlie Chaplin, whom he found direly unfunny. He introduced the Bathing Beauties, having personally auditioned as many as he could find the energy for. As audience tastes became more sophisticated, Sennett moved with the times; although the Twenties were his most successful financial decade, they didn't produce his best films. In 1935, following a financial disaster that saw him lose

$15 million, he retired from making films. Sennett claimed he could only relax in hot water and had his best ideas in the bath. Ever mindful of star egos, a tub was installed in his office.
CAUSE: Sennett died aged 80 in Hollywood from natural causes.

Athene Seyler, CBE

Born May 31, 1889
Died September 12, 1990
Centenarian actress. Born at 18 Goulton Road, Hackney, east London, the seventh and youngest child by 10 years of Clarence Heinrici Seyler, secretary and financial adviser to a Greek millionaire, and Clara Thies, a baker's daughter, she studied at the Academy of Dramatic Art where she won a Gold Medal in 1908. Her stage début came on February 11, 1909, at the Kingsway Theatre, appearing as Pamela Grey in *The Truants*.
Twice-married, she was rarely out of work but didn't begin appearing in films until she was 34, when she appeared in *This Freedom* (1923) as Miss Keggs. It would be another eight years before she stepped in front of a camera again, in *The Perfect Lady* (1931) as Lady Westhaven. She eventually made over 50 films including: *Blossom Time* (1934) as the Archduchess, *The Private Life Of Don Juan* (1934) as Theresa, *Drake Of England* (1935) as Queen Elizabeth, *Royal Cavalcade* (1935) again as Queen Elizabeth, *Southern Roses* (1936) as Mrs Rowland, *It's Love Again* (1936) as Mrs Durland, *Moscow Nights* (1936) as Madame Sabline, *The Mill On The Floss* (1937) as Mrs Pullet, *Sailing Along* (1938) as Victoria Gulliver, *Jane Steps Out* (1938) as Grandma, *Young Man's Fancy* (1939) as Milliner, *Quiet Wedding* (1940) as Aunt Mary, *Dear Octopus* (1943) as Aunt Belle, *Nicholas Nickleby* (1947) as Miss la Creevy, *The Pickwick Papers* (1952) as Miss Witherfield, *Made In Heaven* (1952) as Miss Honeycroft, *The Beggar's Opera* (1953) as Mrs Trapes, *Yield To The Night* (1956) as Miss Bligh, *Campbell's Kingdom* (1957) as Miss Abigail, *Doctor At Large* (1957) as Lady Hawkins, *The Inn Of The Sixth Happiness* (1958) as Mrs Lawson, *Make Mine Mink* (1960) as Dame Beatrice, *Passport To China* (1961) as Mao Tai Tai and *Satan Never Sleeps* (1962) as Sister Agness. On February 14, 1914, Seyler married journalist James Bury Sterndale-Bennett (b. 1889, d. 1941), by whom she had one daughter. In 1922 she met the 5′8″ actor Nicholas James "Beau" Hannen (b. London, May 1, 1881, d. London, June 25, 1972), the son of Sir Nicholas James Hannen and Jessie Woodhouse. In 1928 she changed her name by deed poll to Hannen but they did not marry until 1960 when his wife who had refused to divorce him, died. It is thought that this living in sin was the reason that she never became Dame Athene.
CAUSE: She died at the Coach House, 26 Upper Mall, Hammersmith, west London of natural causes. She was 101.

Tupac Shakur

Born June 16, 1971
Died September 13, 1996
Gangsta rapper. Born in Brooklyn, New York, 5′10″ Tupac Amaru Shakur was raised in Oakland, California. He was named after Tupac Amaru, the Inca sentenced to death by the Spanish; Tupac Amaru means 'shining serpent' in Incan. In 1991 he came to public attention with the group Digital Underground and his solo album *2Pacalypse Now*. He was criticised for the references to sexual violence and killing policemen in his songs. He made his first film, *Nothing But Trouble* (1991), as a result of being in Digital Underground. His first acting film was *Juice* (1992), in which he played Bishop. The following year he starred opposite Janet Jackson as Lucky in *Poetic Justice* (1993). In 1994 he was

sentenced to 15 days in jail for assault and battery. That year he appeared in *Above The Rim* (1994) as Birdie. On April 29, 1995, he married Keisha Morris but the marriage was annulled the following year. That year he was accused of sexually assaulting a female fan. He was released after eight months pending an appeal. His last films were *Bullet* (1996) as Tank, *Gridlock'd* (1997) as Spoon and *Gang Related* (1997) as Rodriguez.

CAUSE: Following the Mike Tyson-Bruce Seldon fight in Las Vegas on September 7, 1996, Shakur was riding with Death Row Records chief executive Marion 'Suge' Knight when he was shot four times. Taken to hospital, his right lung was removed but doctors could do no more and after six days in a coma, he died. Amazingly, none of Shakur's 15-strong team of hangers-on was able to give police any details as to the crime. In spring of 1996 he told an interviewer: "All good niggers, all the niggers who change the world, die in violence. They don't die in regular ways."

Peggy Shannon

(WINONA SAMMON)
Born January 10, 1907
Died May 11, 1941
Alcoholic actress. Pine Bluff, Arkansas-born and Sacred Heart Convent-educated Shannon, 5′4″, was given a golden opportunity in Hollywood. She was cast as Wanda Kelly in *The Secret Call* (1931) opposite Richard Arlen, replacing It Girl Clara Bow. Paramount promoted her as a worthy successor to Bow but Peggy liked boozing better than making films and her drinking led to erratic behaviour, which eventually led to her being sacked. Her films included: *Touchdown* (1931) as Mary Gehring, *This Reckless Age* (1932) as Mary Burke, *Society Girl* (1932) as Judy Gelett, *The Painted Woman* (1932) as Kiddo opposite Spencer Tracy, *False*

Faces (1932) as Elsie Fryer, *Girl Missing* (1933) as Daisy Bradford, *Deluge* (1933) as Claire Arlington, *Fury Of The Jungle* (1934) as Joan, *Youth On Parole* (1937) as Peggy, *Fixer Dugan* (1939) as Aggie Moreno, *Adventures Of Jane Arden* (1939) as Lola Martin, *Blackwell's Island* (1939) as Pearl Murray and *The House Across The Bay* (1940) as Alice. She divorced actor Alan Davis in July 1940 after 14 years of marriage and in October of that year, married Warner Bros cameraman Albert Roberts (b. Los Angeles, California, October 11, 1902) in Mexico.

CAUSE: Albert Roberts discovered her corpse at their kitchen table at 4318 Irvine Avenue, North Hollywood as he returned from a fishing trip with a friend. She was dead at 34 from acute alcoholism. Her head was resting on her arms, a cigarette burned down to her fingertips on her right had, and an empty glass was in her other hand and empty bottles of booze strewn around. Nineteen days after her death, Roberts visited his wife's grave, number 4, plot 31, section 5 at Hollywood Memorial Park Cemetery, 6000 Santa Monica Boulevard, Hollywood, California. Returning to their home, he rang her sister Phoebe Genereux and said, "I'm going to join Peggy. I'm going to kill myself." She begged him to reconsider but heard a single gunshot ring out. When the police arrived they found Roberts sitting at the same chair that he had found his wife's body. He had shot himself in the head with a .22-calibre rifle. He had left three suicide notes. One read, "I am very much in love with my wife, Peggy Shannon. In this spot she passed away, so in reverence to her, you will find me in the same spot." In what was the final tragic chapter to the story, his family did not bury him with his wife but in space 3, lot 321 of the Wee Kirk Churchyard at Forest Lawn Memorial Park, 1712 South Glendale Avenue, Glendale, California.

Ray Sharkey

Born November 14, 1952
Died June 11, 1993
Evil bastard. Born in Brooklyn, New York, Sharkey may have been a friend of Sylvester Stallone and John Travolta, he may have appeared in films such as *Paradise Alley* (1978) as Legs, *Wise Guys* (1986) as Marco, *Wired* (1989) as Angel Velasquez and *Scenes From The Class Struggle In Beverly Hills* (1989) as Frank but he was also the man who callously disregarded the fact he had AIDS to sleep with and infect several women with the deadly disease. Twice-married Sharkey contracted AIDS through a £200-a-day heroin habit.
CAUSE: He died of AIDS aged 41 in New York.

Robert Shaw

Born August 9, 1927
Died August 28, 1978
Tough guy. Born in Westhoughton, Lancashire, the son of a doctor, RADA-trained (he paid his own fees after failing to get a scholarship) Shaw made his film début in *The Lavender Hill Mob* (1951), having made his stage début two years earlier. He then worked in television (he was Captain Dan Tempest in *The Buccaneers* from 1956 until 1957), wrote five novels and a play and was a stalwart support player in films such as *Operation Secret* (1952) as Jacques, *The Dam Busters* (1954) as Flight Sergeant Pulford, *A Hill In Korea* (1956) as Lance-Corporal Hodge, *Double Cross* (1956), *Sea Fury* (1958) as Gorman, *The Valiant* (1962) as Lieutenant Field, *From Russia With Love* (1963) as S.P.E.C.T.R.E. assassin Donald 'Red' Grant, *Tomorrow At Ten* (1964) as Marlowe and *Battle Of The Bulge* (1965) as Colonel Hessler. His rise to stardom began with his portrayal of King Henry VIII in *A Man For All Seasons* (1966) for which he was nominated for a Best Supporting Actor Oscar. He appeared in the lead or leading roles in *Custer Of The West* (1967) as General George Armstrong Custer, *The Royal Hunt Of The Sun* (1969) as Francisco Pizarro, *Battle Of Britain* (1969) as Squadron Leader Skipper and *Young Winston* (1972) as Lord Randolph Churchill, before his stardom was assured in *The Sting* (1973) as Doyle Lonnegan. He kept his profile high in hits such as *The Taking Of Pelham One Two Three* (1974) as Blue, *Jaws* (1975) as the maverick Quint, *Robin And Marian* (1976) as Sheriff of Nottingham, *The Scarlet Buccaneer* (1976) as Ned Lynch, *The Deep* (1977) as Romer Treece, *Force 10 From Navarone* (1978) as Mallory and *Avalanche Express* (1979) as General Marenkov. He was married three times: firstly in 1952 to Jennifer Bourke by whom he had four daughters, secondly, in 1963 to Mary Ure who predeceased him and by whom he had two sons and two daughters and finally in 1976 to Virginia Jansen.
CAUSE: He died of a sudden heart attack while driving his car near his home in Tourmakeady, Ireland, 19 days after his 51st birthday.

Norma Shearer

Born August 11, 1902
Died June 12, 1983
'The First Lady of the Screen'. Born in Montreal, Quebec, Canada (most sources list August 10, 1900 as her birthday but her assiduous biographer Gavin Lambert, who knew her, gives the above date), Edith Norma Shearer was the MGM movie queen of the Thirties, and wife of studio mogul 'Boy Wonder' Irving Thalberg. Her sister, Athole, married director Howard Hawks. Aged 14 Norma won a beauty contest (she was the first girl in her high school [Westmount High] to wear her hair in a bob) and when her father lost all his money she, her mother and sister moved to New York in the hope of becoming showgirls. Since money was tight the trip was partly paid for by selling the piano and family dog. She worked as a model after failing an

audition for the Ziegfeld Follies. (Both Florenz Ziegfeld and D.W. Griffith dismissed her as talentless.) Nonetheless, Griffith hired her as an extra in his films *Way Down East* (1920) and *The Flapper* (1920). Irving Thalberg spotted her in *The Stealers* (1920) in which she played Julie Martin. Her agent managed to wangle her a meeting with Thalberg who was then working for Carl Laemmle at Universal. It didn't get off to a good start – she mistook him for an office boy. When he moved to MGM Thalberg offered Shearer a five-year contract at $150 a week. Louis B. Mayer wasn't certain about the actress, but was persuaded by Thalberg to star her in their big-budget films. Shearer was a perfectionist when it came to her work, insisting her make-up, lighting, outfits and films be perfect. Before the five years were up, Thalberg offered her a different sort of contract and they married on September 29, 1927, at 9401 Sunset Boulevard. She had two children: Irving Jr (b. Good Samaritan Hospital, Los Angeles, August 25, 1930, d. 1987 of cancer) and Katharine (b. Good Samaritan Hospital, Los Angeles, June 13, 1935), who married in 1961, as her second husband, the actor Richard Anderson, who had previously been married to Alan Ladd's stepdaughter and who played Oscar Goldman in the TV series *The Six Million Dollar Man*. Not everyone liked Shearer. "How can I compete with Norma," moaned Joan Crawford, "when she sleeps with the boss?" Thalberg screened one of Shearer's pictures and awaited revered British actress Mrs Patrick Campbell's verdict. "Your wife is charming. Such a dainty creature, she. Such tiny hands, a tiny waist, and tiny, tiny eyes." Mrs Campbell's Hollywood career never materialised. Shearer's first talkie was *The Trial Of Mary Dugan* (1929) and the following year she won an Oscar for *The Divorcee* (1930). That year her salary was raised to $6,000 a week.

Two years later, she became an American citizen. The Thirties saw Shearer cut down on the number of films she was making and concentrate on blockbusters. Her subsequent movies included: *A Free Soul (*1931) as Jan Ashe, for which she was nominated for an Oscar, *Private Lives* (1931) as Amanda Chase Prynne, *Strange Interlude* (1932) as Nina Leeds, *The Barretts Of Wimpole Street* (1934) as Elizabeth Barrett, *Riptide* (1934) as Lady Mary Rexford, *Romeo And Juliet* (1936) as Juliet (aged 33!), for which she was nominated for an Oscar, and *Marie Antoinette* (1938), the last production Thalberg had arranged for her, as Marie Antoinette, for which she was nominated for yet another Oscar. Following Thalberg's untimely death, she signed a three-year contract at $150,000 per film. Her last film was *Her Cardboard Lover* (1942) as Consuelo Croyden. She retired from acting in 1942, married ski instructor Marti Arrougé (b. San Francisco, March 23, 1914) at the Church of the Good Shepherd, Beverly Hills, on August 23 of the same year, 'discovered' Janet Leigh and Robert Evans and lived happily until she fell victim to mental problems and failing eyesight.

CAUSE: Norma Shearer died aged 80 of bronchial pneumonia at the Motion Picture Country House and Hospital, 23450 Calabasas Road, Woodland Hills, San Fernando, California. She was buried in the Great Mausoleum of the Sanctuary of Benediction at Forest Lawn Memorial-Parks, 1712 South Glendale Avenue, Glendale, California 91209.

FURTHER READING: *Norma Shearer –* Gavin Lambert (New York: Alfred A. Knopf, 1990).

Ann Sheridan

(CLARA LOU SHERIDAN)
Born February 21, 1915
Died January 21, 1967
'The Oomph Girl'. Born in Denton,

Texas, Ann Sheridan's career was possibly harmed by her stupid nickname, which did nothing to highlight her undoubted intelligence and very obvious glamour. In 1933 she won a competition called 'Search For Beauty', the first prize being a bit part in a Paramount film of that name. She signed a contract with the studio and was cast in a succession of minor and/or mediocre films. She appeared in 27 of them in two years before moving to Warner Bros, who labelled her 'The Oomph Girl'. The parts and films improved (*San Quentin* [1937] as May Kennedy, *Little Miss Thoroughbred* [1938] as Madge Perry, *Angels With Dirty Faces* [1938] as Laury Ferguson, *The Angels Wash Their Faces* [1939] as Joy Ryan, *Naughty But Nice* [1939] as Zelda Manion), but it was *Kings Row* (1942), in which she played the part of Randy Monaghan, that made her a star. Her subsequent films included: *Shine On, Harvest Moon* (1944) as Nora Bayes, the title role in *Nora Prentiss* (1947), *I Was A Male War Bride* (1949) as Lieutenant Catherine Gates and the lead in *Stella* (1950). Her movie career was over by the end of the Fifties and she appeared for two years (1965–66) on the daytime soap *Another World* as Kathryn Corning. She was married on three occasions, each time to actors.

CAUSE: Ann Sheridan died of cancer aged 52 at the Motion Picture Country House and Hospital, 23450 Calabasas Road, Woodland Hills, San Fernando, California. Her remains are stored in the basement holding vault of the Chapel of the Pines Crematory, 1605 South Catalina, Los Angeles, California 90006.

Max Showalter

Born June 2, 1917
Died July 30, 2000

Steadfast support. Born in Kansas, he began his career in show business by playing the piano in cinemas for silent films. Between 1935 and 1938 he appeared in 92 shows at the Pasadena Playhouse before making his broadway début thanks to the patronage of Oscar Hammerstein II in *Knights of Song*. For two years he toured in the Irving Berlin musical *This Is the Army*. He made his film début in *Always Leave Them Laughing* (1949) as Comet Pen salesman. On screen he often worked under the name Casey Adams. His films included: *What Price Glory* (1952) (as Casey Adams) as Lieutenant Moore, *My Wife's Best Friend* (1952) as Pete Bentham, *With A Song In My Heart* (1952) as Harry Guild, *Dangerous Crossing* (1953) (as Casey Adams) as Jim Logcin, *Niagara* (1953) (as Casey Adams) as Ray Cutler, *Vicki* (1953) (as Casey Adams) as Larry Evans for which he also wrote the title song, *Destination Gobi* (1953) as Walter Landers, *Naked Alibi* (1954) (as Casey Adams) as Lieutenant Parks, *Night People* (1954) (as Casey Adams) as Frederick S. Hobart, *Down Three Dark Streets* (1954) (as Casey Adams) as Dave Milson, *The Return Of Jack Slade* (1955) (as Casey Adams) as Billy Wilcox, *Never Say Goodbye* (1956) (as Casey Adams) as Andy Leonard, *Indestructible Man* (1956) (as Casey Adams) as Lieutenant Richard Chasen, *Bus Stop* (1956) (as Casey Adams) as a reporter for *Life* magazine, *The Monster That Challenged The World* (1957) (as Casey Adams) as Dr Tad Johns, *The Female Animal* (1957) (as Casey Adams) as Charlie Grant, *Dragoon Wells Massacre* (1957) as Phillip Scott, *The Naked And The Dead* (1958) as Dalleson, *Voice In The Mirror* (1958) as Don Martin, *It Happened To Jane* (1959) (as Casey Adams) as Selwyn Harris, a deaf man in *Elmer Gantry* (1960), *Return To Peyton Place* (1961) as Nick Parker, *Summer And Smoke* (1961) as Roger Doremus, *Bon Voyage!* (1962) (as Casey Adams) as the tight suit, *My Six Loves* (1963) as B.J. Smith, a hotel desk clerk in *Move Over, Darling* (1963), *Fate Is The Hunter* (1964) as Dan Crawford, *Sex And The*

Single Girl (1964) as Holmes, *How To Murder Your Wife* (1965) as Tobey Rawlins, *Lord Love A Duck* (1966) as Howard Greene, *The Moonshine War* (1970) as Mr Worthman, *The Anderson Tapes* (1971) as Bingham, *Bonnie's Kids* (1973) as Frank, *10* (1979) as Reverend, *Racing With The Moon* (1984) as Mr Arthur and *Sixteen Candles* (1984) as Fred.

CAUSE: He died aged 83 in Middletown, Connecticut, of cancer. He spotted his home in Middletown while filming *It Happened To Jane* there.

Sylvia Sidney

(SOPHIA KOSSOW)
Born August 8, 1910
Died July 1, 1999

'Silently suffering Jewish actress'. Born in the Bronx, the daughter of a Russian father and a Rumanian mother, her parents soon separated and her mother married Sigmund Sidney, who adopted Sylvia. A career on the stage may have seemed an odd choice for a girl who was, by her own admission, shy but enrolled in the Theater Guild's School for Acting. An early production won favourable reviews from the *New York Times*. That led to a succession of plays and eventually Hollywood came a-knocking. Her film début came in *Broadway Nights* (1927), a film about the Great White Way, in which she played herself. It would be another two years before 5'4" Sylvia was again before the cameras and in the meantime she appeared in a succession of poor plays. Her return to films came in *Thru Different Eyes* (1929) as Valerie Briand and then *Five Minutes From The Station* (1930) as Carrie Adams. Paramount made her a star in *City Streets* (1931) as Nan. She knew that she was replacing Clara Bow but Sylvia grabbed her opportunity with both hands. Her films *Ladies Of The Big House* (1931) as wrongly accused Kathleen Storm and *Merrily We Go To Hell* (1932) as Joan Prentiss were critical and commercial hits. Then she appeared as geisha girl

Cho-Cho San in *Madame Butterfly* (1932). The film flopped but did have a residual effect. In Japan her picture adorned a packet of condoms and they quickly became known as 'Sylvia Sidneys'. She redeemed herself with the title role in *Jennie Gerhardt* (1933) as the poor pregnant widow. *Good Dame* (1934) as Lillie Taylor was a box-office flop. Her next film, *Mary Burns, Fugitive* (1935), in which she took the title role of a restaurateur who falls for a hoodlum, did good box office as did *Accent On Youth* (1935) as Linda Brown. Then came *Behold My Wife* (1935) as Tonita Storm, *Sabotage* (1936) as Mrs Verloc, *The Trail Of The Lonesome Pine* (1936) as June Tolliver, *Fury* (1936) as Katherine Grant and *You And Me* (1938) as Helen opposite George Raft. The film didn't do well and apart from a couple of films Sylvia was absent from the screen until *Blood On The Sun* (1945) as Iris Hilliard. *The Searching Wind* (1946) as Cassie Bowman was based on a Broadway play but flopped on the big screen. Her films became fewer and fewer and from 1946 until 1971 she made just seven films. In the Seventies and Eighties she appeared in several TV movies but her last big screen films were *Beetlejuice* (1988) as Juno and *Mars Attacks!* (1996) as Grandma Norris. She was married three times. Her husbands were Bennett Cerf (October 1, 1935–April 9, 1936), Luther Adler (August 13, 1938–1946) and Carleton W. Alsop (1947–March 22, 1951).

CAUSE: She died aged 88 of throat cancer in New York.

Don Siegel

Born October 26, 1912
Died April 20, 1991

Principled director. Born in Chicago, Illinois, and educated at Jesus College, Cambridge, Siegel is probably best known for his work with Clint Eastwood in films such as *Coogan's Bluff* (1968) in which he also played a passenger in a lift, *Two Mules For Sister*

Sara (1969), *Dirty Harry* (1971) in which he also played a pedestrian, *The Beguiled* (1971) and *Escape From Alcatraz* (1979) but there was much more to Siegel. He was head of montage at Warner Bros, a studio he got into by pretending to be related to Jack Warner. He won two Oscars for short films: *Hitler Lives* (1945) and *Star In The Night* (1945) before moving on to feature films with *The Verdict* (1946). Many of his films were violent, which brought him criticism from many quarters. His other films included: *The Big Steal* (1949), *No Time For Flowers* (1952), *China Venture* (1953), *Riot In Cell Block 11* (1954), *Private Hell 36* (1954), *Baby Face Nelson* (1957), *Spanish Affair* (1958), *Hound-Dog Man* (1959) and *Flaming Star* (1960) (one of Elvis Presley's better films), *Hell Is For Heroes* (1962) (one of Siegel's best), police drama *Madigan* (1968), *Death Of A Gunfighter* (1969) from which he removed his screen credit, with the film being credited to the famous fictional Allan Smithee, *Charley Varrick* (1973), John Wayne's last film *The Shootist* (1976), *Telefon* (1977), *Rough Cut* (1980) and the black comedy *Jinxed!* (1982). He was married to actress Viveca Lindfors from August 10, 1949 until April 29, 1953. They had one son, Christoper, born in September 1952. One of Siegel's most famous films was *Invasion Of The Body Snatchers* (1956) starring Kevin McCarthy and called by one critic "one of the most frightening films ever made". Despite popular belief, the film was not about a political take-over by either right- or left-wing politicians, it was about what Siegel saw as those who stopped him making the films he really wanted, "The front office" – the money men who really control Hollywood. He once said: "Most of my pictures, I'm afraid to say, are about nothing. Because I'm a whore. I work for money. It's the American way."
CAUSE: Siegel died aged 78 from cancer in Nipoma, California.

Simone Signoret
(SIMONE KAMINKA)
Born March 25, 1921
Died September 30, 1985
Cinematic good-time girl. Born in Wiesbaden, Germany, the daughter of a French Jew, Signoret was a star for almost 40 years and spent much of that time playing a succession of ladies of the night. She was also the long-suffering wife of Yves Montand. She made her film début in *Le Prince Charmant* (1941) and became one of the mainstays of French cinema in the Fifties. She married Yves Allegret in 1948 (they had a daughter, Catherine, born two years prior to the marriage while Allegret was still married to someone else) and became a star that year playing the title role of the prostitute Dédée D'Anvers. She also played a hooker in *La Ronde* (1950) as Leocadie. Her other films included: *Adieu Léonard* (1943), *Macadam* (1946) as Gisele, *Fantômas* (1947), *Impasse Des Deux Anges* (1948), *Against The Wind* (1948) as Michèle, *Swiss Tour* (1949) as Yvonne, *Manèges* (1949) as Dora, *Gunman In The Streets* (1950) as Denise Vernon, *Ombre Et Lumière* (1951) as Isabelle Leritz, the title role in *Thérèse Raquin* (1953), *Les Diaboliques* (1955) as Nicole Horner, *Les Sorcières De Salem* (1957) as Elisabeth Proctor, *Room At The Top* (1959) as Alice Aisgill, for which she won an Oscar, *Term Of Trial* (1962) as Anna, *Barabbas* (1962), *Dragées Au Poivre* (1963) as Genevieve, *Compartiment Tueurs* (1965) as Eliane Darres, *Ship Of Fools* (1965) as La Condesa, *Games* (1967) as Lisa Schindler, *The Deadly Affair* (1967) as Elsa Fennan, *The Sea Gull* (1968) as Arkadina, *Comptes A Rebours* (1970) as Léa, *Le Chat* (1971) as Clémence Bouin, *Les Granges Brulées* (1973) as Rose, *La Chair De L'Orchidée* (1974) as Lady Vamos, *Police Python 357* (1976) as Thérèse Ganay, the title role of the prostitute *Madame Rosa* (1977) for which she won a César, the French

equivalent of the Oscar, *L'Adolescente*
(1979) as Mamie, *Chère Inconnue*
(1980) as Louise and *L'Étoile Du Nord*
(1982) as Sylvie Baron. Following her
1949 divorce from Allegret, she married
Yves Montand on December 22, 1951,
standing by him despite his constant
philandering. As she became older, she
put on more and more weight,
commenting: "I got old the way that
women who aren't actresses grow old."
CAUSE: She died of cancer in
Normandy, France, aged 64.
FURTHER READING: *Nostalgia Isn't
What It Used To Be* – Simone Signoret
(London: Panther, 1979).

Ron Silver

Born July 2, 1946
Died March 15, 2009
Political activist. Born in Manhattan the
son of Irving Roy Silver, an executive in
the menswear business, and substitute
teacher May Zimelman, Ronald Arthur
Silver was raised on Manhattan's
Lower East Side. He was educated at
Stuyvesant High School, State
University of New York at Buffalo
(where he read Spanish), received a
master's degree in Asian studies at St
John's University in Queens and then
learned how to act at the Herbert
Berghof Studio after travelling to
Vietnam, Cambodia, India, Japan and
the Soviet Union. He also studied at
Lee Strasberg's Actors Studio. He made
his New York stage debut in 1971 and
four years later went west to appear in
films and television. He made his film
debut in *Tunnel Vision* (1976) and then
spent two years as Gary Levy on the
sitcom *Rhoda*. He played a psychopath
opposite Jamie Lee Curtis in *Blue Steel*
(1989). He was lawyer Alan Dershowitz
in *Reversal Of Fortune* (1990), based on
the trial of Claus von Bülow for the
attempted murder of his wife, Sunny.
His other films included: *Mr Saturday
Night* (1992), *Timecop* (1994), and *Ali*
(2001) as Angelo Dundee. He had two
stints (2001 to 2002 and 2005 to 2006)
as Bruno Gianelli on *The West Wing*,

which won him an Emmy nomination.
He once said, "I'm an actor by calling
but an activist by inclination," and
supported politicians from both sides of
the political divide. He was president
of Equity from 1991 until 2000. He
supported Ronald Reagan's Star Wars
initiative but also campaigned for Bill
Clinton and then Rudolphi Giuliani's
campaign for mayor of New York in
1994. In 2004 he spoke at the
Republican National Convention in
favour of a second term for President
George W. Bush, largely because of his
stance against Islamic terrorism. In
2008 he supported Giuliani for the
Republican presidential nomination. He
explained, "It sounds like a conversion
tale, but I was not reborn. It was fairly
consistent with my views in the past.
I've been a very aggressive liberal
interventionist in my foreign policy
feelings. I have felt for a long time that
the withdrawal of American power was
far more dangerous than getting
involved." He lost work because of his
support for the president: "In this
business, there are a million different
reasons people don't want to work with
you: you're too Jewish, you're not
Jewish enough, they want a bigger star,
they think you cost too much money.
Most people are very economical with
the truth out here, so it's very hard to
determine cause and effect." "Ron's
politics, as far as I know, were not
shared by anyone he knew, except for
the people he knew because of his
politics," his brother Mitchell Silver
said. "He told me that he did vote for
Barack Obama in the end." Silver
married once and had two children:
son, Adam, and a daughter, Alexandra.
CAUSE: Silver died at his Manhattan
home of oesophageal cancer, which had
been diagnosed in 2007. He was 62.

Jay Silverheels

(HAROLD J. SMITH)
Born May 26, 1912
Died March 5, 1980
Reliable Red Indian. Many actors are

irrevocably linked with one role – Robert Englund is Freddy Krueger, Basil Rathbone's name is rarely mentioned without the words Sherlock Holmes following rapidly, and Pat Phoenix will forever be identified with *Coronation Street*'s Elsie Tanner. The same is true of Jay Silverheels. Despite appearing in over 60 films, he will be forever associated with playing The Lone Ranger's trusted Red Indian buddy Tonto. Born on the Six Nations Reservation, Brantford, Ontario, Canada, he made his film début playing an Indian scout in *The Sea Hawk* (1940). He first played Tonto nine years later on television, beginning on September 15, 1949, and stayed with the show for the whole of its eight-year run (unlike Clayton Moore who was absent from 1952 for two years). Other films Silverheels appeared in were: *Too Many Girls* (1940), *Good Morning, Judge* (1943), *Song Of The Sarong* (1945), *Northwest Outpost* (1947), *Unconquered* (1947), *Captain From Castile* (1947), *Fury At Furnace Creek* (1948) as Little Dog, *Family Honeymoon* (1948), *Key Largo* (1948) as John Osceola, *The Feathered Serpent* (1948) as Diego, *Trail Of The Yukon* (1949) as Poleon, *Laramie* (1949) as Running Wolf, *The Cowboy And The Indians* (1949) as Lakohna, *Broken Arrow* (1950) as Geronimo, *Red Mountain* (1951) as Little Crow, *Yankee Buccaneer* (1952), *The Story Of Will Rogers* (1952) as Joe Arrow, *Last Of The Comanches* (1952), *Laramie Mountains* (1952) as Running Wolfe, *The Battle At Apache Pass* (1952) as Geronimo, *Brave Warrior* (1952) as Tecumseh, *War Arrow* (1953) as Satanta, *The Pathfinder* (1953) as Chingachgook, *Jack McCall Desperado* (1953) as Red Cloud, *Four Guns To The Border* (1954) as Yaqui, *Drums Across The River* (1954) as Taos, *Saskatchewan* (1954) as Cajou, *Masterson Of Kansas* (1954) as Yellow Hawk, *Walk The Proud Land* (1956) as Geronimo, *Indian Paint* (1963) as

Chief Hevatanu, *Smith!* (1969) as McDonald Lasheway, *True Grit* (1969), *Santee* (1973) as John Crow, *One Little Indian* (1973) as Jimmy Wolf and *The Man Who Loved Cat Dancing* (1973) as the Chief. He also played Tonto in two Lone Ranger films: *The Lone Ranger* (1956) and *The Lone Ranger And The Lost City Of Gold* (1958) plus the Bob Hope comedy: *Alias Jesse James* (1959). In later years Silverheels bred and raced horses. CAUSE: He died aged 67 following a stroke at the Motion Picture Country House and Hospital, 23450 Calabasas Road, Woodland Hills, San Fernando, California. He was cremated at the Chapel of the Pines Crematory, 1605 South Catalina, Los Angeles, California 90006.

Phil Silvers
(PHILIP SILVERSMITH)
Born May 11, 1911
Died November 1, 1985
Jewish wiseacre. Like the previous entrant, Phil Silvers is also predominantly known for one role – that of the fast-talking, scheming Master Sergeant Ernie Bilko in the variously named television series *You'll Never Get Rich*, *The Phil Silvers Show* and *Bilko*. Born in Brooklyn, Silvers was the youngest of eight children of a Russo-Jewish emigrant. He was an adept song-and-dance man who began his career in burlesque before appearing in a number of short films for Warner Bros. His feature début came in *Hit Parade Of 1941* (1940) as Charlie Moore. The unlikely portrayal of an ice-cream man in *Tom, Dick And Harry* (1941) brought him a measure of fame and established the style for which he was to become famous. He appeared in *You're In The Army Now* (1941) as Breezy Jones, *Footlight Serenade* (1942) as Slap, *All Through The Night* (1942) as Louie, *My Gal Sal* (1942) as Wiley, *Roxie Hart* (1942) as Babe, *Coney Island* (1943) as Frankie, *A Lady Takes A Chance* (1943) as

Smiley Lambert, *Something For The Boys* (1944) as Harry Hart, *Four Jills In A Jeep* (1944) as Eddie, *Don Juan Quilligan* (1945) as MacDenny, *Diamond Horseshoe* (1945) as Blinky Walker, *A Thousand And One Nights* (1945) as Abdullah, *Summer Stock* (1950) as Herb Blake, *Top Banana* (1953) as Jerry Biffle, *Lucky Me* (1954) as Hap, *Forty Pounds Of Trouble* (1963) as Bernie Friedman, *It's A Mad Mad Mad Mad World* (1963) as Otto Meyer, *A Funny Thing Happened On The Way To The Forum* (1966) as Lycus, *Buona Sera Mrs Campbell* (1968) as Phil Newman, *The Boatniks* (1970) as Harry Simmons, *The Strongest Man In The World* (1975) as Krinkle, *Won Ton Ton, The Dog Who Saved Hollywood* (1976) as Murray Fromberg and *The Happy Hooker Goes To Hollywood* (1980) as Warkoff. He was even a guest star in *Carry On . . . Follow That Camel* (1967) as the Foreign Legion's Sergeant Nocker. Silvers married twice. His first wife (on March 12, 1945, in Los Angeles) was former Miss America 1942 Jo-Carroll Dennison. They divorced in 1950. On October 21, 1956, he married actress Evelyn Patrick and had five daughters: Tracey (b. June 27, 1957), Nancey (b. January 19, 1959), Candy (b. May 27, 1961), Cathy (b. May 27, 1961) and Laury (b. January 19, 1964). The couple was divorced in 1965 amidst a certain amount of rancour. The first episode of *You'll Never Get Rich*, which later became *The Phil Silvers Show* and is known in Britain as *Bilko*, aired on CBS on September 20, 1955, and ended 142 episodes later on September 11, 1959. It, in turn, was the inspiration for the cartoon series *Top Cat*. CAUSE: Silvers suffered a stroke in 1973 and his health thereafter was 'shaky'. He died aged 74 in Century City, California, from natural causes. He was buried in Vault 1004 in the Heritage Gardens of Mount Sinai Memorial-Park, 5950 Forest Lawn Drive, Los Angeles, California 90068.

Alastair Sim, CBE
Born October 9, 1900
Died August 19, 1976
Eccentric Scot. Born in Lothian Road, Edinburgh, the youngest of four children of a tailor, Alastair George Bell Sim had various jobs when he left school before going to Edinburgh University, where he studied to become an analytical chemist. Deciding a life of academia wasn't for him, he joined the Officers' Training Corps but the war ended before he could be commissioned. For five years from 1925 he was an elocution teacher at New College, Edinburgh, where he founded his own drama school. He made his stage début in the Peggy Ashcroft–Paul Robeson version of *Othello* on May 19, 1930. He then worked at the Old Vic for two years before a back injury crippled him for a year. In 1932 he married Naomi Merlith and they had one daughter. He made his film début in *The Riverside Murder* (1935) as Sergeant McKay. He landed the role of Sergeant Bingham in the Inspector Hornleigh series: *Inspector Hornleigh On Holiday* (1939), *Inspector Hornleigh* (1939) and *Inspector Hornleigh Goes To It* (1941). In the Forties he made only rare forays into films, preferring to work on the stage. At the start of the Fifties he appeared as Charles Dickens' anti-hero Ebenezer Scrooge in *Scrooge* (1951). That decade also saw one of his best-known roles, that of Miss Fitton, the headmistress of St Trinian's, in a couple of films: *The Belles Of St Trinian's* (1954) and *Blue Murder At St Trinian's* (1957). His other films included: *Laughter In Paradise* (1951) as Deniston Russell, *Innocents In Paris* (1952) as Sir Norman Barker, *An Inspector Calls* (1954) as Inspector Poole, *The Green Man* (1956) as Hawkins, *The Doctor's Dilemma* (1959) as Cutler Walpole, *School For Scoundrels* (1960) as Mr S. Potter, *The Millionairess* (1960) as Sagamore and *Royal Flash* (1975) as Mr Greig. He was very close to the actor George

Cole, who was regarded as his unofficial adopted son. Sim refused the knighthood offered him by Premier Edward Heath.

CAUSE: He died in London aged 75 from cancer.

Jean Simmons, OBE

Born January 31, 1929
Died January 22, 2010
Ethereal beauty. Jean Merilyn Simmons was born at Cricklewood, north London, the daughter of Olympic gymnast Charles Simmons (d. 1945) and Winifred Ada Loveland. Evacuated to Somerset during the Second World War, the young Simmons hankered after a stage career and, at the age of 14, enrolled with the Ada Foster School of Dancing in London where her talent was spotted. She auditioned for the role of Margaret Lockwood's younger precocious teenage sister in the comedy *Give Us The Moon* (1944). In 1945, she was in *The Way To The Stars*, in *Meet Sexton Blake* (opposite David Farrar in the title role) and in *Caesar And Cleopatra*, playing a harpist in the film that marked her first appearance with her future husband, Stewart Granger. She also appeared as an Indian princess in Michael Powell and Emeric Pressburger's *Black Narcissus* (1947) and a castaway in *The Blue Lagoon* (1949). It was when David Lean gave her the role as the young Estella, companion to the reclusive Miss Havisham, in *Great Expectations* (1946) that she really came to attention and began to take acting seriously. In 1948 Laurence Olivier cast her as Ophelia in his film *Hamlet* and she received the first of two Academy Award nominations. Olivier believed that 5ft 6in Simmons would do her best work on the stage but she preferred to follow her heart and future husband, dashing screen idol Granger, to Hollywood. Her career was almost wrecked by Howard Hughes who developed an obsession with her. He bought her contract from J. Arthur Rank without consulting her or Granger, who foolishly agreed to let Hughes arrange his wedding to Simmons – supposedly to help them avoid an intrusive press. Simmons and Granger flew to Tucson, Arizona where they married on December 21, 1950 in the home of one of Hughes's lawyers. Granger's very close friend Michael Wilding was best man. The couple also enjoyed a honeymoon at Hughes's expense. Then Hughes's interference became oppressive. He refused to let her play in William Wyler's *Roman Holiday* so the part went to Audrey Hepburn. Her contract with Rank had committed her to three more films but Hughes wanted her to sign a seven-year contract with him or he threatened to put her "in three of the lousiest movies you've ever seen". At one stage Granger even contemplated killing Hughes. He abandoned the plan and instead resorted to a legal solution. They won an out-of-court settlement of $250,000, plus $35,000 costs. The bisexual Hughes did not try and get her into bed. "I was married to Jimmy, so Hughes remained at a distance," she remembered. "But those movies! So terrible they aren't even on videocassettes." During the 1950s and 1960s Simmons made more than 30 films including costume epics, romances, musicals and dramas. She played opposite Spencer Tracy in *The Actress* (1953). She was in *The Robe* (1953), with Richard Burton. She appeared with Marlon Brando in *Desirée* (1954), as Josephine to Brando's Napoleon, and was so awestruck by him that "I was sort of forgetting what I was supposed to do." She starred as Sarah Brown with Brando and Frank Sinatra in *Guys And Dolls* (1955) and actually sang her own songs rather than miming. She recalled that during rehearsal "Samuel Goldwyn came on the set one day and he heard us and said, 'I think it's better you do your own singing . . . Maybe you don't

sound so good, but at least it's you.'"
On August 12, 1960 she and Granger
divorced and on November 1, she
married Richard Brooks, who had just
directed her as the saintly evangelist in
Elmer Gantry (1960), based on the
Sinclair Lewis novel. In 1987, Brooks
said in an interview, "Every man I
would meet would say to me, 'I have
always loved your wife.'" They had one
daughter, Kate, named for Katharine
Hepburn. In 1960 Simmons launched
a thousand fantasies when she bared
her back in *Spartacus*. At the end of
the decade Brooks directed her in
The Happy Ending (1969) as a bored
Denver housewife who becomes a
suicidal alcoholic for which she
received her second Oscar nomination.
He later said that he wrote the
character as a way to tell his real-life
wife that she also had a drinking
problem. They split up in 1977 and
she later said, "It was simply that the
mixture of an alcoholic and a
workaholic just wasn't working." In
1986 she entered the Betty Ford
Center in Rancho Mirage. As her
screen roles dried up she turned to
television. "Every actress has to face
the facts there are younger, more
beautiful girls right behind you," she
said in 1988. "Once you've gone
beyond the vanity of the business,
you'll take on the tough roles." In 1983
she won an Emmy for her role in the
miniseries *The Thorn Birds*. "I didn't
have a dominant personality. It helped
me slip into character parts very
easily," she said. "I simply had to play
the mother in *The Thorn Birds*. I
understood her pain. I badgered the
producer until he gave in. He said it
wasn't a star part. That's why I wanted
it!" In 1989 she was in a remake of
Great Expectations as the miserable
recluse Miss Haversham. She still
received fan mail but some was
intended for the rock star Gene
Simmons. One day a letter arrived
from a 10-year-old. "It was the usual
fan letter, saying things like, 'I think

you're wonderful,'" she said. "Then I
got to the PS: 'I love it when you spit
blood!' That's when I realised the letter
wasn't for me." She summed up her
life and career. "It was extraordinary
for a Cockney kid from Cricklewood to
have this happen," she said in a 1989
interview. "If I hadn't gone to that
dancing school, I would have married
and had children like my mum and had
a normal life. My career has had a lot
of ups and downs," she said, "but
basically it has been wonderful."
CAUSE: Simmons died at her home in
Santa Monica, California, of lung
cancer. She was 80.

Charles Simon
Born February 4, 1909
Died May 19, 2002
Character actor with longevity. In a
business where much of the profession
is unemployed at any one time, Charles
Simon's career would be remarkable if
for no other reason than it spanned
79 years. Born in Tettenhall Wood,
Wolverhampton, the younger son of
three children in an army family, which
meant he had a peripatetic childhood,
Charles was raised in Tuffley,
Gloucestershire and left school aged
14. He enrolled in the Irving Academy
of Dramatic Art in Cheltenham and
while there made his professional début
in a cinema, reading "Back of the bar
in a solo game sat dangerous Dan
McGrew" three times a day to
accompany the film *The Shooting Of
Dan McGrew* (1924). In 1926, he wrote
and played all the roles in *The Tutor Of
Ratshorne*, which was broadcast on
BBC Birmingham. He joined Seymour
Hick's company but was sacked before
he could get to the West End. He
joined a tour of Ireland in 1930
appearing in plagiarised versions of
London shows and the following year
set up the Darlington Repertory
Company, befriending George Bernard
Shaw, a friendship that lasted until
GBS's death in 1950. During the
Fifties he made more than 1,000

broadcasts for the BBC. In March 1963 he joined the cast of the popular radio serial *Mrs Dale's Diary* as Dr Jim Dale when Jessie Matthews replaced the original incumbent Ellis Powell as Mary Dale and the show was renamed *The Dales*. The show ran in its new format until 25 April, 1969, when, at Simon's suggestion, it was killed off. In March 1970, a play written by Simon under the pseudonym Charles Henry, *At Home With The Dales*, flopped after just six of the 16-week tour. He made 20 films including *Shadowlands* (1983) and *Topsy Turvy* (1999). In 1986, he played George Adams in *The Singing Detective* and joined the National Theatre in 1989. In 1940, he had married Nancy McDermid by whom he had two daughters. She died in 1958 and seven years later in May 1965 he married Sheila Eves, an actress 24 years his junior, by whom he had a son. CAUSE: He died, aged 93, of pneumonia in Harrow, Middlesex.

Don Simpson
Born October 29, 1943
Died January 19, 1996
Mr Sicko. He was born in Swedish Hospital in Seattle, Washington, the son of a mechanic and a housewife. The family moved to Alaska before Simpson was two. In later years Simpson would boast to reporters of daring deeds, brushes with the law and numerous girlfriends. Pals from the time remember a shy Simpson who rarely got into trouble, came from a hard-working family and was obsessed with comics. To millions of cinema-goers world-wide, Donald Clarence Simpson was known, if his name was known at all, as the highly successful co-producer (with partner Jerry Bruckheimer) of Hollywood blockbusters such as *Flashdance* (1983), *Top Gun* (1986), *Beverly Hills Cop* (1984), *Beverly Hills Cop 2* (1987), *Bad Boys* (1995) and *The Rock* (1996). The 5'7" Simpson was one of the founders of the 'high concept' movie wherein the

basic premise of the film could be outlined in just a few words or, preferably, on the back of a book of matches. For example, *Alien* was '*Jaws* in a space ship' and *Under Siege* was '*Die Hard* on a boat'. Simpson's career really began in 1972 when he joined Warner Bros, but he failed to shine there and was sacked. He tried auditioning for acting jobs and sold one screenplay, *Cannonball* (1976), for $6,250. In 1976 Simpson joined Paramount Pictures and quickly began to rise up the corporate ladder. In 1977 he became Vice President of Creative Affairs and the following year Vice President of Production. Three years later, he became Senior Vice President of Worldwide Production and in 1981 was appointed president of the company. To Hollywood insiders he was known as a man who lived on the edge. Simpson could be both incredibly generous and horrifyingly abusive. He battled constantly with his weight and was obsessed with his appearance, having testosterone injections in his buttocks to increase his sex drive and wearing his black Levi's just once before he threw them away. His drug habits often raged out of control and his appetite for prostitutes never diminished. Horror tales are told of his peccadilloes in the kiss-all book *You'll Never Make Love In This Town Again* and its follow-up, *Once More With Feeling*. According to 5'11" call-girl Alexandra Datig (identified in the book as 'Tiffany'), Simpson 'auditioned' girls for parts in his films and "by the end of each interview, each actress ended up having sex with him". Each encounter was videoed by Simpson. On another occasion, said Datig, Simpson hired two whores and forced one, named Patricia Colombo, to penetrate the other, Afifa, anally with a 12" black dildo and another "specially designed tool". Another girl, a pale, redheaded newcomer to prostitution, was beaten bloody by Simpson for $1,000. On another occasion another call-girl, "Michelle", was told by Simpson to lick another girl's urine off his body. She refused but, after he took a shower, gave him oral sex, though Simpson failed to climax, even after an hour of such personal attention. "It was all the drugs I suppose," Michelle reflected. Simpson's drug use was indeed phenomenal. At one time he was spending $60,000 a month on prescription drugs and heaven knows how much on non-prescription ones. In the summer of 1995 he was having daily injections of Toradol for pain, Librium for his moods, Valium, Vistaril and lorazepam four times a day and Thorazine six times a day to counter his anxiety, Ativan also four times a day for agitation, Depakote four times a day to balance his 'acute mania', plus tablet forms of Valium, Vicodin, diphenoxylate, diphenhydramine, Colanadine, lithium carbonate, nystatin, Narcan, haloperidol, Promethazine, Benztropine, Unisom, Atarax, Compazine, Xanax, Desyrel, Tigan and phenobarbital. He also took heroin supplied by a shady character known only as 'Mr Brownstone'. Guns N' Roses wrote a song about him and the man himself believes that it was his smack that River Phoenix was taking on the night he died. Simpson and his partner were widely feared in the movie industry. Said one Hollywood insider: "Bruckheimer is the one to really watch for. He'll stab you in the back. Simpson at least will stab you in the chest."

CAUSE: The overweight (14st) 52-year-old Simpson "died of heart failure caused by a massive overdose of cocaine and prescription medicines" around 1am while sitting on the toilet at his home, 685 Stone Canyon Road, Bel Air, California. Rumours that he died while reading *You'll Never Make Love In This Town Again* are not true; he was engrossed in a biography of Oliver Stone. Simpson was later cremated.

FURTHER READING: *High Concept: Don Simpson And The Hollywood Culture Of Excess* – Charles Fleming (New York: Doubleday, 1998).

Joan Sims

Born May 9, 1930
Died June 28, 2001
'Queen of Puddings'. Irene Joan Marion Sims was born in Laindon, Essex, the daughter of John Henry Sims, a railway station master, and Gladys Marie Ladbrooke. She became interested in show business at an early age and played in the goods sheds pretending that they were stages. After schooling at St John's, Billericay, and Brentwood County High, she applied for RADA in 1946 with a rendition from *Winnie The Pooh* but failed the audition. Instead she was admitted to PARADA, the academy's preparatory school. It was her fourth attempt before she finally succeeded and was admitted to RADA. While there she won the £10 Mabel Temperley prize for grace and charm of movement. Graduating in 1950 she made her film début two years later in *Colonel March Investigates* playing Marjorie Dawson. She also appeared in Sir Norman Wisdom's film *Trouble In Store* (1953) as Edna, *The Square Ring* (1953) as Bunty, the Fairy Queen in *Meet Mr Lucifer* (1953), *Will Any Gentleman . . .?* (1953) as Beryl, *What Every Woman Wants* (1954) as Doll, a telephone operator in *To Dorothy A Son* (1954), *The Sea Shall Not Have Them* (1954) as Hilda Tebbitt, *Doctor In The House* (1954) as Rigor Mortis, *The Belles Of St Trinian's* (1954) as Miss Dawn, an ice cream girl in *Lost* (1955), *Doctor At Sea* (1955) as Wendy, *As Long As They're Happy* (1955) as Linda, *Keep It Clean* (1956) as Vi Tarbottom, *Dry Rot* (1956) as Beth, *The Silken Affair* (1957) as a lady barber, *No Time For Tears* (1957) as Sister O'Malley, *The Naked Truth* (1957) as Ethel Ransom, *Just My Luck* (1957) as Phoebe, a tea lady in *Davy* (1957), *Carry On Admiral* (1957) as

Mary and *Passport To Shame* (1958) as Marian. It was her appearance in *Doctor In The House* that led to her appearance in her first *Carry On* . . . She played Nurse Stella Dawson in *Carry On Nurse* (1958) and went on to appear in 23 more films finishing with *Carry On Emmannuelle* (1978) in which she played Mrs Dangle. Fortunately, she missed out on the execrable *Carry On Columbus* (1992). "I don't think it worked without us, dear. We were a unique formula." Joanie was the longest-serving female member of the team. She appeared in *Teacher* (1959) as Sarah Allcock (during filming she developed thrombophlebitis and had to have her leg propped up on off-camera cushions before being hospitalised for 10 days), *Constable* (1960) as Policewoman Gloria Passworthy and *Regardless* (1961) as Lily Duveen; she took a break for four films then returned in *Cleo* (1964) as Calpurnia, *Cowboy* (1965) as Belle Armitage, *Screaming!* (1966) as Emily Bung, *Follow That Camel* (1967) as Zig Zig, *Don't Lose Your Head* (1967) as Desiree Dubarry, *Up The Khyber* (1968) as Lady Joan Ruff-Diamond, *Doctor* (1968) as Chloe Gibson, *Camping* (1969) as Joan Fussey, *Again, Doctor* (1969) as Ellen Moore, *Up The Jungle* (1970) as Lady Evelyn Bagley, *Loving* (1970) as Esme Crowfoot, *Henry* (1971) as Queen Marie of Normandy, *At Your Convenience* (1971) as Chloe Moore, *Matron* (1972) as Mrs Tidey, *Abroad* (1972) as Cora Flange, *Girls* (1973) as Connie Philpotts, *Dick* (1974) as Madame Desiree, *Behind* (1975) as Daphne Barnes and *England* (1976) as Private Ffoukes Sharp. She was paid £2,500 per film, from the first to the last. Her other films included: *Upstairs And Downstairs* (1959) as Blodwen, *Please Turn Over* (1959) as Beryl, *Life In Emergency Ward 10* (1959) as Mrs Pryor, *The Captain's Table* (1959) as Maude Pritchett, *Watch Your Stern* (1960) as Ann Foster, *Doctor In Love* (1960) as Dawn,

Mr Topaze (1961) as Colette, *Twice Round The Daffodils* (1962) as Harriet, *The Iron Maiden* (1962) as Nellie Trotter, *A Pair Of Briefs* (1962) as Gale Tornado, *Strictly For The Birds* (1963) as Peggy Blessing, *Nurse On Wheels* (1963) as Deborah Walcott, *Doctor In Clover* (1966) as Matron, *Doctor In Trouble* (1970) as Russian Captain, a policewoman in *The Magnificent Seven Deadly Sins* (1971), *The Alf Garnett Saga* (1972) as Gran, *Not Now Darling* (1973) as Miss Tipdale, *Don't Just Lie There, Say Something* (1973) as Lady 'Birdie' Mannering-Brown, *One Of Our Dinosaurs Is Missing* (1975) as Emily and *The Fool* (1990) as Lady Daphne. She also appeared in numerous television series such as *Sykes*, *Till Death Us Do Part*, *Sam And Janet*, *Love Among The Ruins*, *Born And Bred*, *Worzel Gummidge*, *Deceptions*, *Farrington Of The F.O.*, *On The Up*, *Cluedo*, *As Time Goes By*, *Martin Chuzzlewit*, *Hetty Wainthropp Investigates*, *Only Fools And Horses*, *In Loving Memory* and *Dr Who*. In 1994 while filming *A Village Affair* she fell off a bicycle and fractured a rib. She was replaced on the show and also lost a BBC Schools programme contract because she was unwell. The actors' trade union, Equity, sued on her behalf but the court case took two years and the compensation she received was not enough to cover her lost earnings. In 1997 she fell at her home and fractured her spine. Her lack of self-esteem, paranoid shyness and intense loneliness turned her into an alcoholic and a depressive. "I've suffered from fears and nerves and painful shyness all my life. Loneliness, in itself, is one of the most terrible things to suffer from. In your heart of hearts you want friends but your body language is all wrong and you come across as unfriendly. Acting has been my only freedom. I've used acting as a substitute for all the joy and happiness that I've missed out on. That's the time when I can laugh and cry and be happy with other people. Then you go back home and find yourself becoming a recluse. Somebody would ring me up and invite me to a function and I would say I wasn't free but, really, it was because I was too shy to go on my own." Despite the sauciness of some of the *Carry On* films she had old school opinions about what she saw as the lowering of standards of decency. "I can get quite embarrassed seeing some of the things on television. I don't know whether things have to be quite as explicit as they are nowadays. *Carry On . . .* films were much more innocent." Yet, she also once said, "To be a comic woman, you have to put up with quite a bit of banter. But I didn't mind. I've got a dirty sense of humour and I never found those things really offensive." She was unmarried – "I don't think I've ever had anybody say the words, 'Will you marry me?' not even someone tight as a tick at a party" – although fellow *Carry On . . .* star Kenneth Williams did propose to her. He said, "I will give you a child if you want one but after that we wouldn't be sleeping together." She asked what was in it for her and he replied, "I would be frightfully amusing company and we would throw the most wonderful parties." However, she knew marriage to the homosexual Williams would never work.

CAUSE: She died after a long illness. She was 71.

Frank Sinatra

Born December 12, 1915
Died May 14, 1998

Ol' Blue Eyes. The Man. The Voice. The Chairman of the Board. Francis Albert Sinatra was never short of nicknames. His career spanned much of the twentieth century beginning with the dance bands, going solo and attracting the first teenage female music fans, called bobbysoxers. His management, ahead of their time when it came to hype, paid girls to scream at Sinatra. His renditions of songs such as

'My Way', 'Strangers In The Night', 'Come Fly With Me', 'My Kind Of Town', '(Theme From) New York, New York' among literally thousands of others send a chill down the spine decades after they were first recorded. Sinatra was born at 415 Monroe Street, Hoboken, New Jersey, the only child of Anthony Martin 'Marty' Sinatra (b. Catania, Italy, 1891, d. Methodist Hospital, Houston, Texas, January 24, 1969 at 7.55pm) and Natalie Della 'Dolly' Garavente (b. Genoa, Italy, December 25, 1894, k. San Gorgonio Mountains, January 6, 1977). Weighing 13lb 8oz, Sinatra was a breech birth and the midwife used forceps, leaving him with scars on the left side of his face and neck, a lacerated ear and a punctured eardrum. The eardrum meant he was turned down for military service. Sinatra's musical education began on his 15th birthday in 1930 when his maternal uncle, Domenico, bought him a ukulele and Frank began entertaining at family gatherings. On January 28, 1931 he entered Demarest High School where he arranged bands for school dances. To further his own ambitions, he dropped out of school but to please his mother he enrolled at Drake Business School, dropping out eleven months later. In 1932 he began offering his talents to local bands and supported himself by delivering the local rag. In 1933 he moved to New York where he sang for his supper or cigarettes. In 1935 he joined a group called The Hoboken Four and appeared on the wireless for the first time. In August 1937 after a disappointing two years he landed a job as house singer at the Rustic Cabin in Bergen County, Englewood Cliffs, New Jersey. On November 26, 1938 Sinatra was arrested on a morals charge following his affair with married 25-year-old brunette Antoinette Della Penta Francke. He was rearrested on December 22 and, on January 4, 1939, remanded to appear before a grand jury. On January 24 the case was dropped. It wasn't the first time the Sinatra name had appeared before the courts. His uncle Domenico had been charged with malicious mischief; his uncle Gus had been arrested several times for running numbers; another uncle, Babe, had been jailed after being implicated in a murder; his father was once charged with receiving stolen goods while his beloved mother was an illegal abortionist who was often arrested. The charges against Sinatra were dropped after he had spent sixteen hours in jail. On February 4, 1939 he married Nancy Barbato (b. 1917) at Our Lady Of Sorrows Church, Jersey City. They had three children: Nancy Sandra (b. Margaret Hague Maternity Hospital, Jersey City, June 8, 1940), the song 'Nancy With The Laughing Face' was written for her by Phil Silvers; Christina (b. Cedars of Lebanon Hospital, Hollywood, June 20, 1948) and Franklin Wayne Emmanuel (b. Margaret Hague Maternity Hospital, Jersey City, January 10, 1944). In July 1939 he received his first press attention: one line in *Metronome* which read "The very pleasing vocals of Frank Sinatra whose easy phrasing is especially commendable." On July 13 he recorded his first record, 'From The Bottom Of My Heart', with the Harry James Band. The bandleader supposedly wanted to change his vocalist's name to Frankie Satin. 5'7" Sinatra demurred. In December 1939 he joined the much bigger Tommy Dorsey Band. Sinatra was under a two-year contract with James when he left. "We dissolved with a handshake," reported James. "Frank's wife was expecting a baby and he needed the extra money. But I never did get around to tearing up the contract." Sinatra's first appearance with Dorsey came on January 26, 1940 and his first record, 'The Sky Fell Down', five days later. In August 1940 Sinatra made his film début in *Las Vegas Nights* (1941)

as a singer in Tommy Dorsey's band. On May 20, 1941 he was named as the best Male Band Vocalist in the States by *Billboard*. On January 19, 1942 he recorded his first solo songs 'The Night We Called It A Day', 'The Lamplighter's Serenade', 'The Song Is You' and 'Night And Day'. Later that year, on September 19, Sinatra and Dorsey went their separate ways. A persistent rumour has Sinatra's leaving facilitated by a mob friend, Willie Moretti, putting a gun to Dorsey's head for his acquiescence. In fact, two heavy friends of Sinatra did visit Dorsey but he was far from intimidated by them and one had to be restrained from asking the bandleader for his autograph. By this time, Sinatra was cheating regularly on Nancy. On December 30, 1942 Sinatra made his first solo appearance and soon "Sinatramania" was at its height. He made two films playing himself, *Show Business At War* (1943) and *Reveille With Beverly* (released February 4, 1941, re-released 1943). On October 22, 1943 he underwent a medical for the military and was declared 1-A but on December 9 was again examined and declared 4-F and unfit to serve because of his punctured eardrum. His acting début came with *Step Lively* (1944), as Glen Russell, in which he had his first on-screen kiss (with Gloria DeHaven). On June 15, 1944 he began shooting *Anchors Aweigh* (1945) as Clarence Doolittle with Gene Kelly. The experience was fraught. MGM had a policy of refusing to show actors dailies but Sinatra insisted and the studio relented. However, when he turned up with six friends they were refused admission and Sinatra walked off the film for a few days. He insisted on hiring Sammy Cahn to work with Jule Styne, overriding the objections of the studio and producer Joe Pasternak. Sinatra and Kelly got on well and Kelly led the nervous Sinatra through the dance routines, often to the detriment of his own performance. On March 7,

1946 Sinatra was awarded a special Oscar for his work on the charity short *The House I Live In* (released on September 11, 1945). In October 1946 he was named most popular actor by *Modern Screen*. On February 11, 1947 he attended, possibly unaware of the nature of the proceedings, the notorious Mafia Havana Conference (which began in December 1946) to legitimise the proceedings. In attendance and paying homage to Charles 'Lucky' Luciano (b. Lercara Friddi, Palermo, Sicily, November 24, 1897, d. Capodichino Airport, Naples, Italy, January 26, 1962 of a heart attack) were Anthony Joseph 'Joe Batters' Accardo (b. Chicago, Illinois, April 28, 1906, d. May 27, 1992 of heart failure), Joe Adonis (b. Montemarano, near Naples, Italy, November 22, 1902, d. Aucona, Italy, November 26, 1971 of a heart attack), Lord High Executioner Albert 'The Mad Hatter' Anastasia (b. Tropea, Italy, September 26, 1902, k. Park Sheraton Hotel, Manhattan, October 25, 1957 at 10.15am), Joe 'Bananas' Bonanno (b. January 18, 1905, d. May 11, 2002), Prime Minister of the Underworld Frank Costello (b. Calabria, Italy, January 26, 1891, d. New York, February 18, 1973 of natural causes), Meyer Lansky (b. Grodno, Poland, August 28, 1900, d. Miami Beach, Florida, January 15, 1983 of a heart attack), 5'2" Tommy 'Three-Finger Brown' Lucchese (b. Palermo, Sicily, 1900, d. July 13, 1967 following surgery for a brain tumour), Carlos Marcello (b. Tunis, February 6, 1910, d. March 2, 1993), Joe Profaci (b. 1896, d. Bay Shore, New York, June 6, 1962 of cancer), Santo Trafficante (b. November 15, 1914, d. Houston, Texas, March 17, 1987 of heart failure) and many others. For the first time the press raised questions about Sinatra's links with organised crime. However, later that year Hoboken named October 20 as Sinatra Day. The following year, he played

Father Paul in *The Miracle Of The Bells* (1948). Later that year, he re-teamed with Gene Kelly for *Take Me Out To The Ball Game* (1949) in which he played Dennis Ryan. On December 8, 1949 at the New York première of the musical *Gentlemen Prefer Blondes* he met the woman who was to have a profound and often disturbing effect on his life, Ava Gardner. The next day his latest film, *On The Town* (1949) in which he portrayed Chip, opened to favourable reviews. As the influence of Ava Gardner began to bite, he spent less time with Nancy and on St Valentine's Day 1950 she announced their separation. On July 12, 1950 he opened at the London Palladium to a tumultuous reception. On October 7 he began *The Frank Sinatra Show* on television, a programme that was to last two years. May 1951 was named "Frank Sinatra Record Month" by 1,500 American DJs. In Santa Monica, California, on October 30, 1951, he and Nancy were divorced. She was awarded custody of the children, their Holmby Hills home, a 1950 Cadillac, an interest in Sinatra Music Corporation, a third of his gross income up to $150,000 and 10% of monies over that up to another $150,000. Just over a week later, on November 7, Sinatra married Gardner in Philadelphia, Pennsylvania. The weather at the time was appalling but was nothing compared to the storms ahead for the newlyweds. At the time her career was more successful than his and Ava paid for the honeymoon. Dolly disliked her new daughter-in-law. Sinatra felt his career was over and desperately needed a new vehicle. That came with James Jones' 850-page epic 1951 novel *From Here To Eternity*. Sinatra particularly identified with the character of the feisty Private Angelo Maggio. When Sinatra heard that Columbia had bought the film rights for $100,00 in March 1951 and were casting for the movie, he called everyone he knew to bombard Harry

Cohn with pleas to let him play Maggio. Ava Gardner, ignoring her husband's instructions not to use her influence, rang Cohn's wife and finally Cohn agreed to test Sinatra. Before that could happen he and Gardner had a massive fight. He supposedly walked in on her in bed with Lana Turner. On November 7, 1952, their first wedding anniversary, they flew out to Nairobi where Ava was due to film *Mogambo* (1953). One day Gardner was having dinner with the one-eyed director John Ford and the British Governor of Uganda, Sir Andrew Cohan, and his wife when Ford asked, "Ava, why don't you tell the Governor what you see in that 120lb runt you're married to?" "Well," said Ava, never one to miss an opportunity to be blunt, "there's only ten pounds of Frank but there's one hundred and ten pounds of cock." The Governor was amused, Ford wasn't. On another day, Gardner and co-star Grace Kelly were out walking when they came across a line of Watusi warriors. To Grace's shock but amusement, Gardner wandered over and pulled up the loincloth of one of the warriors. Kelly gasped. "Frank's is bigger," said Mrs Sinatra. While in Africa, Gardner discovered she was pregnant. On November 23, she aborted Sinatra's baby in London. Meanwhile, he flew back to America to test for *From Here To Eternity* (opened August 5, 1953) and then back to Africa to celebrate Christmas with his wife. On March 2, 1953 he began filming the role that would revitalise his career and win him an Oscar. Filming wasn't that happy an experience. Sinatra couldn't reach Ava Gardner on the telephone, author James Jones believed that the film wasn't true to his vision in the book and Montgomery Clift was agonising over his homosexuality. All three men would often drink themselves unconscious. His musical career also revived when he signed a seven-year contract with Capitol Records on April 2, 1953

but his personal life was far from satisfactory. He and Ava fought like cat and dog. On October 27, 1953, MGM announced their separation. His film *Suddenly* (1954) in which he played would-be Presidential assassin John Baron was also a hit. On January 14, 1954 at San Francisco's City Hall one of the greatest baseball stars of all time married the most potent sex symbol of the twentieth century when 'Joltin' Joe' DiMaggio took unto him the divorcée Norma Jeane Dougherty better known to the world as Marilyn Monroe. For luck DiMaggio wore the same dark suit and polka dot tie he had worn when they first met on a blind date. She wore a modest brown outfit because he had told her to keep "those low-cut things for the movies". It was a marriage that was to last only nine months. DiMaggio was an incredibly jealous man and this jealousy led to an infamous incident that became known as "the wrong-door raid". At 11.15pm on November 5, 1954, a month and a day after their divorce was announced, DiMaggio with his then friend Sinatra, Sinatra's manager Hank Sanicola (d. October 10, 1974), restaurateur Patsy D'Amore, maître d' Billy Karen and private detectives Phil Irwin and Barney Ruditsky, believing that Marilyn was inside with a lover (accounts vary as to whether it was supposed to be male or female), broke into the apartment of 50-year-old Florence Kotz at 8122 Waring Avenue on the corner of Kilkea Drive in Hollywood. Kotz sat up in bed, pulling the bedclothes around her, not surprisingly terrified as the men smashed down her door and began taking photographs. Marilyn was reportedly visiting her friends Sheila Stewart and Hal Schaefer in another apartment in the same block. Hearing the commotion the beautiful star slipped away without being seen. On June 1, 1957 Florence Kotz Ross (she had since married) filed suit against DiMaggio, Sinatra et al for $200,000.

DiMaggio fled to Florida to avoid the litigation. The case was dismissed by the California Superior Court after Sinatra's lawyer Milton 'Mickey' Rudin organised an out-of-court payment of $7,500. In December 1954 Sinatra was named top male singer by *Billboard*. *Guys And Dolls* (premièred November 3, 1955) in which he played Nathan Detroit was a smash although he was puzzled by Marlon Brando's method acting. During that year he anonymously helped Bela Lugosi and Lee J. Cobb when they fell ill. Later that year he played the drug addict Frankie Machine in *The Man With The Golden Arm* (1955) for which he was nominated for an Oscar, losing out to *Eternity* co-star Ernest Borgnine and *Marty* (1955). In December 1955 he began filming his first Western *Johnny Concho* (1956) in which he took the title role and also directed. Oddly, the film opened in England four months before its American première. In March 1957 his seminal *Songs For Swinging Lovers* was released. He also formed the notorious, hard-living Rat Pack with friends Dean Martin, Sammy Davis, Jr, Peter Lawford and Joey Bishop. In March 1957 he took the lead, Joey Evans, in the hit *Pal Joey* (1957). On July 5, 1957 in Mexico City, he and Ava Gardner were divorced. That year Sinatra also hit out at a new type of music that was sweeping the western world: "Rock and roll is phony and false and sung, written and played for the most part by cretinous goons." On May 8, 1959 he recorded the song 'High Hopes' which became the campaign theme tune for Senator John F. Kennedy's ultimately successful bid for the White House in 1960. On July 10 of that year Sinatra publicly came out in favour of the young Bostonian. On January 19, 1961 he arranged the Inaugural Gala but later fell out with JFK when the president stayed at the house of Republican Bing Crosby rather than Sinatra's (despite Sinatra having a

helipad fitted) because Kennedy was warned about the links with organised crime. (This was a tad hypocritical since rumours have long circulated that it was his father's various deals with the mob that saw Kennedy elected in the first place.) Despite the divorce from Gardner, Sinatra had never been short of female company. These are just some of the women linked to him over the years: Judy Campbell Exner (b. Pacific Palisades, California, January 11, 1934 as Judith Eileen Katherine Immoor, d. September 24, 1999 of cancer), the mistress of mobster Sam 'Momo' Giancana, who broke up with Sinatra because his tastes were "too kinky" for her; Marilyn Monroe; Toni Anderson, a brunette he dated in the Sixties who left him to marry Lake Tahoe Deputy Sheriff Richard E. Anderson (when Sinatra confronted his rival on June 30, 1962 he was beaten so badly he was unable to perform at the Cal-Neva Lodge for several days. At 10.26pm on July 17, 1962 the Andersons were involved in a car accident on Highway 28 that left him dead and her badly injured. Anderson's mother said, "My husband and I . . . think Frank Sinatra had something to do with Dick's death"); Lauren Bacall whom Sinatra dated and, some say, proposed to after the death of her husband Humphrey Bogart (in her autobiography she labelled Sinatra "a shit"); Dame Elizabeth Rosamund Taylor whom Sinatra supposedly impregnated and then paid for her abortion; Jacqueline Park who dumped Sinatra to become movie mogul Jack Warner's mistress (this was her assessment of the Chairman of the Board: "He's a little twisted sexually. He loved call girls for orgies and he liked to see women in bed for kicks . . . I didn't see him again because he wanted me to go to bed with another woman"); Judy Garland to whom Sinatra proposed and then ignored; Vanessa Brown, yet another actress to whom Sinatra proposed although she turned him down; Peggy Connelly to whom he gave a $20,000 grand piano following their break-up; Natalie Wood who had a brief fling with Sinatra before she met Robert Wagner; Joi Lansing, the blonde actress who remained friends with Ol' Blue Eyes after the affair ended; Victoria Principal (b. Fukouka, Japan, January 3, 1946); Marilyn Maxwell (b. Clarinda, Iowa, August 3, 1921, d. Beverly Hills, California, March 20, 1972), Sinatra was an honorary pallbearer at her funeral; Juliet Prowse (b. Bombay, India, September 25, 1936, d. September 14, 1996) who became engaged to him on January 9, 1962 but who refused to become Mrs Sinatra III because he wanted her to give up her acting career; Jacqueline Lee Bouvier Kennedy Onassis (b. Southampton, New York, July 28, 1929, weighing 8lb, d. New York, New York, May 19, 1994 of cancer) whom he dated after JFK's assassination; actress Melissa Weston; socialite Pamela Beryl Harriman (b. Farnborough, Kent, March 20, 1920 as Pamela Digby, d. February 5, 1997, the mother of Winston Churchill, MP and Bill Clinton's Ambassador to France) was another to whom he proposed; and gossip columnist Suzy (b. El Paso, Texas, June 10 as Aileen Mehle). In April 1961 Sinatra launched his own record label, Reprise. On December 8, 1963, Sinatra's soundalike son was kidnapped from his motel room at Harrah's Lake Tahoe Casino and held for $239,985 (£150,000) ransom. The FBI arrested the kidnappers and Frank, Jr was safely returned on December 11. The whole event was financed by singer Jan Torrence of the duo Jan & Dean. Rumours still exist that the kidnapping was a publicity stunt. Sinatra's film career began to include films shot with the Rat Pack: *Ocean's 11* (premièred on August 3, 1960) as Danny Ocean, *Sergeants 3* (1962) as Mike Merry, *4 For Texas* (shooting began on May 23,

1963) as Zack Thomas and *Robin And The 7 Hoods* (shooting began on October 31, 1963; released February 1964) as Robbo. His later films included: *The Manchurian Candidate* (1962) as Bennett Marco, Mark Robson's *Von Ryan's Express* (premièred June 25, 1965) as Colonel Joseph L. Ryan, *Marriage On The Rocks* (1965) as Dan Edwards, *Assault On A Queen* (location filming began on September 20, 1965, released on July 27, 1966) as Mark Brittain, *Cast A Giant Shadow* (1966) as Spence Talmadge, *The Naked Runner* (1967) as Sam Laker, *Tony Rome* (1967) as Tony Rome, *Lady In Cement* (1968) reprising his role as Tony Rome and *Dirty Dingus Magee* (1970) as Dingus Magee. On May 10, 1964 he was rescued from drowning by actor Brad Dexter (the one no one can remember in *The Magnificent Seven*). On July 19, 1966 at 5.30pm in Las Vegas, Nevada he married actress Mia Farrow, known for her role in the soap *Peyton Place*. Ava Gardner wasn't impressed: "I always knew Frank would end up in bed with a boy with a cunt." The marriage ended in divorce in Juarez, Mexico, on August 16, 1968. On September 11, 1967 Sinatra became involved in a brawl at Las Vegas Sands casino which resulted in the 250lb boss Carl Cohen punching the singer in the mouth, breaking two teeth. On December 30, 1968 Sinatra recorded the song that would be his theme tune for the rest of his life 'My Way'. On June 14, 1971 Sinatra announced: "This is my last concert. I have retired." It would become almost a standing joke. On July 18, 1972 he was ordered to testify before a Congressional committee on organised crime. Joe 'The Baron' Barboza claimed Sinatra had invested in two multi-million dollar hotels as a front for New England Mafia boss Raymond Patriarca and New York *capo* 'Three-Finger Brown' Lucchese. Sinatra claimed he had never heard of Patriarca but had met Lucchese "two or three times" although he had had no business dealings with him. When Italian police raided the home of Charles 'Lucky' Luciano they found a gold cigarette case inscribed "To my dear pal Lucky, from his friend, Frank Sinatra". Sinatra had it written into his contracts that no one, no matter how famous, was to be allowed backstage or even to approach him. It therefore seemed strange that members of one of America's most powerful Mafia family including Carlo Gambino, Jimmy 'The Weasel' Fratianno, 'Big Paulie' Castellano, Gregory De Palma, Salvatore Spatola and Joe Gambino managed to "breech" this security in 1976 to pose with the singer in his dressing room. The FBI file on Sinatra weighed a stone and Prince Charles once opined: "I was not impressed by the creeps and Mafia types he kept about him." On October 20, 1972 Sinatra came out of retirement to appear at a fund-raiser for Richard Nixon. In 1973 his comeback was made official when he began recording again. Sinatra married for the fourth and final time on July 11, 1976 at Sunnylands, Rancho Mirage, California, to Barbara Marx (b. Glendale, California, October 16, 1930 as Barbara Jane Blakeley). It was her third marriage and despite the occasional bust-up they were still together when he died. Not everyone was enamoured of Sinatra. Marlon Brando once said: "He's the kind of guy that when he dies he's going up to Heaven and give God a bad time for making him bald."

CAUSE: During a concert on March 6, 1994 in Richmond, Virginia, Sinatra fell off his stool while singing 'My Way' and hit his head on a speaker. Examined by a hospital, he was allowed home the same night. He played his last show on American soil at the Sands in Atlantic City, New Jersey on November 20, 1994. On November 1, 1996 he was admitted to room 8016 of the VIP wing at Cedars-Sinai Medical Center, 8700

Beverly Boulevard, where he was treated for a pinched nerve and a minor bout of pneumonia. He was released eight days later on November 9. In January 1997 he was hospitalised with a sudden heart attack. On January 23, 1998 he was taken from his home, 915 North Foothill Road, Beverly Hills 90210, and again taken to Cedars-Sinai and checked for high blood pressure. He was released the next day. He was readmitted three days before Valentine's Day for "tests" and again released. On May 14, he was at home with a nurse (his wife was out at dinner with friends) when he suffered another heart attack. He was taken to Cedars-Sinai at 9.18pm but died there at 10.35pm. He was 82. He was buried on May 20 at a funeral attended by, among others, Milton Berle, Diahann Carroll, Tony Curtis, Vic Damone, Tony Danza, Dom DeLuise, Kirk Douglas, Faye Dunaway, Bob Dylan, Mia Farrow, Larry King, Jack Lemmon, Jerry Lewis, Sophia Loren, Lorna Luft, Ed McMahon, Liza Minnelli, Wayne Newton, Jack Nicholson, Anthony Quinn, Nancy Reagan, Debbie Reynolds, Don Rickles, Jill St John, Tom Selleck, Bruce Springsteen, Gregory Peck, Connie Stevens, Marlo Thomas, Ben Vereen and Robert Wagner. Sinatra was buried in Desert Memorial Park Cemetery, 69920 Ramon Road, Cathedral City, California 92234. In January 2000 Frank, Jr announced he was dropping the junior from his name, even though, technically, he was never Frank, Jr in the first place. With Sinatra in his coffin were a number of items to help him on his way. They were a roll of dimes (from son Frank), a cigarette lighter (from his niece) and a packet of Camel cigarettes (from stepson Bobby), a bottle of Jack Daniel's, a ring (from Mia Farrow), and a packet of Tootsie Rolls (from daughter Nancy).

FURTHER READING: *Sinatra* – Arnold Shaw (London: Coronet 1970); *Sinatra* – Earl Wilson (London: W.H. Allen

1976); *The Revised Compleat Sinatra* – Albert I. Lonstein & Vito R. Marino (New York: Cameron Publications, 1979); *The Frank Sinatra Scrapbook* – Richard Peters (London: Pop Universal, 1982); *His Way The Unauthorised Biography Of Frank Sinatra* – Kitty Kelley (London: Bantam Press, 1986); *Frank Sinatra My Father* – Nancy Sinatra (London: Coronet, 1986); *Sinatra The Man And The Myth* – Bill Adler (New York: Signet, 1987); *All Or Nothing At All A Life Of Frank Sinatra* – Donald Clarke (London: Macmillan, 1997); *All The Way A Biography Of Frank Sinatra* – Michael Freedland (London: Weidenfeld & Nicolson, 1997); *Sinatra Behind The Legend* – J. Randy Taraborrelli (New York: Birch Lane Press, 1997); *Mr S The Last Word On Frank Sinatra* – George Jacobs and William Stadiem (London: Sidgwick & Jackson, 2003); *Sinatra* – Richard Havers (London: Dorling Kindersley, 2004).

Penny Singleton

(MARIANNA DOROTHY AGNES LETITIA McNULTY)
Born September 15, 1908
Died November 12, 2003

Forever Blondie. Penny Singleton had two claims to fame. She brought Chic Young's cartoon strip character Blondie Bumstead to life in a popular series of films and was the voice of the mother on the television cartoon series *The Jetsons*. Singleton was born the daughter of Benny McNulty, a Philadelphia journalist, and got her start in show business by winning an amateur contest and was touring in vaudeville in her early teens. After her Broadway début in the late-Twenties, she began appearing in films, at first under her real name. It was her portrayal of Blondie in 28 films made from 1938 to 1950 that sealed her fame. The series was about the misadventures of a small-town family.

Arthur Lake played Blondie's husband, the bumbling Dagwood Bumstead. Lake and Singleton also co-starred as the Bumsteads on radio. No one else ever played Blondie and Dagwood on the big screen. The films were *Blondie* (1938), *Blondie Meets The Boss* (1939), *Blondie Takes A Vacation* (1939), *Blondie Brings Up Baby* (1939), *Blondie On A Budget* (1940), *Blondie Has Servant Trouble* (1940), *Blondie Plays Cupid* (1940), *Blondie Goes Latin* (1941), *Blondie In Society* (1941), *Blondie Goes To College* (1942), *Blondie's Blessed Event* (1942), *Blondie For Victory* (1942), *It's A Great Life* (1943), *Footlight Glamour* (1943), *Leave It To Blondie* (1945), *Life With Blondie* (1945), *Blondie's Lucky Day* (1946), *Blondie Knows Best* (1946), *Blondie's Big Moment* (1947), *Blondie's Holiday* (1947), *Blondie In The Dough* (1947), *Blondie's Anniversary* (1947), *Blondie's Reward* (1948), *Blondie's Secret* (1948), *Blondie's Big Deal* (1949), *Blondie Hits The Jackpot* (1949), *Blondie's Hero* (1950) and *Beware Of Blondie* (1950). Commented Singleton, "I'm proud and grateful I was Blondie. She was dumb and shrewish sometimes. But she was real and sympathetic and warm, a real woman, a human being. And that's how I tried to play her." Oddly, Singleton was naturally a brunette and dyed her hair blonde to play the part and kept it that way. Singleton went on to do the voice of Jane Jetson in *The Jetsons*, Hanna-Barbera's futuristic counterpart to its highly successful *Flintstones* cartoon. The show ran in prime time for just one season, September 23, 1962– September 8, 1963, but has been widely seen in syndication. Singleton also appeared in the 1964 film *The Best Man* but her scenes were cut before release. She spent most of her time touring in nightclubs and in road shows of plays and musicals like *Call Me Madam*. In 1937 she married Lawrence Singleton, a dentist who predeceased her, and had one daughter, Dorothy. The couple was divorced in 1939. In 1941 she married the *Blondie* producer (Salathiel) Robert Sparks (b. Peebles, Adams County, Ohio, February 4, 1898, d. July 22, 1963) and had another daughter, Susan.

CAUSE: Penny Singleton died in Sherman Oaks, California, aged 95, of complications from a stroke.

Curt Siodmak
Born August 10, 1902
Died September 2, 2000

Teutonic horrormeister. Born in Dresden, Saxony, Germany, the younger of two sons of a banker, Siodmak became a journalist while brother Robert (b. Dresden, Saxony, Germany, August 8, 1900, d. Locarno, Ticino, Switzerland 1973) followed their father into finance. Siodmak married Henrietta in 1925 and two years later they were hired as extras on Fritz Lang's *Metropolis* (1927) to get a story on the director. Siodmak began to contribute to silent films in Germany. In 1929 both brothers worked on the documentary *People On Sunday*, as did Billy Wilder and Fred Zinnemann. Siodmak wrote several more films but with the rise of Hitler decided to move abroad in the Thirties. The Siodmaks moved to France where they made *La Crise Est Finie* (1935) and then Curt left to go to England while Robert Siodmak stayed in Paris until 1939. In England he worked on, among other films, *I, Claudius* (1937), the famously unfinished Charles Laughton masterpiece. In the same year he moved to New York where he began writing and directing. His films included *Her Jungle Love* (1938) which starred Dorothy Lamour, *The Invisible Man Returns* (1939), *The Wolf Man* (1941) starring Lon Chaney and *The Invisible Agent* (1942). In 1942 he published the horror novel *Donovan's Brain* which was filmed three times between 1943 (as *The Lady And The Monster* starring Erich von Stroheim)

and 1962 (as *Over My Dead Body*). He wrote a number of other novels and short stories that were filmed. Unlike Robert Siodmak, Curt Siodmak's directorial career never really took off and his films remained in the horror genre rather than moving to mainstream fare. However, those films were in themselves memorable. In particular *I Walked With A Zombie* (1943) and *The Beast With Five Fingers* (1946) starring Peter Lorre are fondly remembered by horror aficionados. He wrote a German version of *Sherlock Holmes And The Deadly Necklace* (1962) which starred Christopher Lee and was directed by Terence Fisher. In the Sixties and Seventies he found work difficult to come by but maintained his enthusiasm for the genre.

CAUSE: He died of natural causes aged 98.

Everett Sloane
Born October 1, 1909
Died August 6, 1965

Menacing actor. Born in New York into a Jewish family, Sloane became an actor quite early in his life, playing Puck in *A Midsummer Night's Dream* when he was seven and even dropping out of the University of Pennsylvania to concentrate on acting. He joined a rep company but when he received poor reviews he gave up acting and took a job working as a runner on Wall Street being paid $17 a week. Like so many, he lost his job when the Stock market crashed in October 1929 but he found work as an actor on the wireless. He made his Broadway debut in 1935 in *Boy Meets Girl*. He joined Orson Welles' Mercury Theatre and took part in the infamous *War Of The Worlds* broadcast that made Welles' name (see Welles entry for full details). Welles cast him as Mr Bernstein in *Citizen Kane* (1941) and he stayed with Welles until 1947 when he played Arthur Bannister in Welles' *The Lady From Shanghai*. Sloane played a ruthless businessman in the film and television

versions of Rod Serling's *Patterns* (1956). He received an Emmy nomination in 1956 for his portrayal which was described by one critic as "extraordinary . . . a figure of dimension, almost of stature. His interpretation of the closing confrontation speech was acting of rare insight and depth". Sloane was short and not an especially attractive man and he resented the fact that he was never leading man material. Orson Welles said of him and his casting in *The Lady From Shanghai*, "Everett Sloane was basically a radio actor; he'd never really learned to move. He was like a marionette. That was okay for Bernstein in *Kane*. But it didn't seem to me that a marionette would be a great criminal lawyer. So I made him an elaborate sort of cripple. And, of course, he loved it. All actors like to play cripples." Of his performance in *Citizen Kane*, Welles said, "Everett Sloane, who aged with me, never wore any make-up at all. We just shaved his head and put the white around it. And he couldn't have been more than 21. It had a profound effect on him. Because he thought, 'How can I represent a 75-year-old man without make-up? It must be that my nose is too big.' And he began bobbing it. He must have had 20 operations . . . He must have thought, 'If I could ever bob my nose right, then I'll be a leading man'." Sloane's other films included: *Journey Into Fear* (1943), *Prince Of Foxes* (1949), *The Men* (1950), *The Enforcer* (1951), *Sirocco* (1951), *The Big Knife* (1955), *Lust For Life* (1956), *Somebody Up There Likes Me* (1956), *The Gun Runners* (1958), *Home From The Hill* (1960) and *The Disorderly Orderly* (1964). He married Lillian Herman in 1933 and had two children.
CAUSE: Sloane feared that he was going blind because of glaucoma and killed himself aged 55 with an overdose of sleeping pills at 13043 Sunset Boulevard, his home in Los Angeles, California. He is buried at Angelus-Rosedale Cemetery, 1831 West Washington Boulevard, Los Angeles, California.

Alexis Smith
(GLADYS SMITH)
Born June 8, 1921
Died June 9, 1993
Shrewd performer. Born in Penticton, British Columbia, Canada, she became an actress while a student and was signed to a contract by Warner Bros in 1940. Her performances were acclaimed by her admirers but she never really became a star. She appeared in *Steel Against The Sky* (1941) as Helen Powers, *Passage From Hong Kong* (1941), *Affectionately Yours* (1941) as a bridesmaid, *Dive Bomber* (1941) as Linda Fisher, *The Smiling Ghost* (1941) as Elinor Bentley Fairchild, *Gentleman Jim* (1942) as Victoria Ware, *The Constant Nymph* (1943) as Florence Creighton, *The Doughgirls* (1944) as Nan Curtiss, *The Adventures of Mark Twain* (1944) as Olivia Langdon Clemens, *Conflict* (1945) as Evelyn Turner, *Rhapsody In Blue* (1945) as Christine Gilbert, *San Antonio* (1945) as Jeanne Starr, *Of Human Bondage* (1946) as Nora Nesbitt, *Night And Day* (1946) as Linda Lee Porter, *The Two Mrs Carrolls* (1947) as Cecily Latham, *Stallion Road* (1947) as Rory Teller, *The Woman In White* (1948) as Marian Halcombe, *Whiplash* (1948) as Laurie Durant, *The Decision Of Christopher Blake* (1948) as Mrs Blake, *One Last Fling* (1949) as Olivia Pearce, *Any Number Can Play* (1949) as Lon Kyng, *South Of St Louis* (1949) as Rouge de Lisle, *Undercover Girl* (1950) as Christine Miller, *Montana* (1950) as Maria Singleton, *Wyoming Mail* (1950) as Mary Williams, *Here Comes The Groom* (1951) as Winifred Stanley, *Split Second* (1953) as Kay Garven, *Beau James* (1957) as Allie Walker, *This Happy Feeling* (1958) as Nita Hollaway, and *The Young Philadelphians* (1959) as Carol Wharton, after which she retired

from movies to concentrate on theatre. It would be 16 years before she appeared in front of the cameras again when she played Deidre Milford Granger in Jacqueline Susann's *Once Is Not Enough* (1975). Her subsequent film appearances were sporadic as she concentrated on television and television films. She played Clayton Farlow's demented sister Jessica Montfort on *Dallas* in 1984 and again in 1990. On June 18, 1944, the bisexual Smith married actor Craig Stevens (b. Liberty, Missouri, July 8, 1918, as Gail Shikles, Jr, d. Los Angeles, California, May 10, 2000, from cancer) at the Church of the Recessional, Forest Lawn, Glendale, California. There were no children. CAUSE: She died of cancer in Los Angeles, California, one day after her 72nd birthday.

Sir C. Aubrey Smith, CBE

Born July 21, 1863
Died December 20, 1948
The only English Test cricketer to become a successful Hollywood actor. Charles Aubrey Smith was born in the City of London, the son of a doctor, and educated at Charterhouse and Cambridge. Unlike other thespians, Smith's entry in *Who's Who* was a paradigm of modesty. It listed his name, profession (Film Actor), date of birth, the names of his parents, the year of his marriage (1896) but not the name of his wife, the fact he had one daughter who is similarly unnamed, his education, his hobby (cricket), his address and his clubs. Prior to becoming an actor Smith was a fine cricketer, winning a Blue at Cambridge in 1882. That year he joined Sussex, where he played for the next 14 seasons, captaining the side from 1887 until 1889. In 1887–1888 he toured Australia, winning 14 and losing two of the 25 fixtures and the following winter captained the first English side (Major Warton's) to venture to South Africa.

The side won 13 and lost four of its 19 matches. On March 12–13, 1889, the tourists played South Africa at St George's Park, Port Elizabeth. This later became known as the first South African Test although it wasn't recognised as such at the time. In the Test Smith scored 3 and took 5 for 19 and 2 for 42 playing his part in England's victory. On the tour he took 134 wickets at a cost of 7.61 runs apiece. He stayed in South Africa after the tour to captain Transvaal against Kimberley in the first Currie Cup match on April 5, 7–8, 1890. A useful right-arm fast bowler, his best bowling performances were taking 5 for 8 for Sussex against Cambridge in 1885 and 7 for 16 against the MCC at Lord's in 1890. His highest innings was 142 for Sussex against Hampshire at Hove in 1888. He stood over six feet tall and had such a peculiar bowling action that he was known as "Round The Corner Smith". He played 99 First Class matches for Sussex scoring 2,315 runs, averaging 14.55, and taking 208 wickets for 5006 runs, averaging 24.06. A sporting all-rounder, he also played outside right at football for Old Carthusians and Corinthians. Following his retirement from the sporting arena, he moved into the theatrical one becoming an accomplished stage (début aged 30) and silent screen actor. He made his first film during World War I and was most adept at playing nobility or soldiers. He was twice the Duke of Wellington, in *The House Of Rothschild* (1934) and *Sixty Glorious Years* (1938), but was probably best known for Colonel Zapt in *The Prisoner Of Zenda* (1937). His other films included: *Red Pottage* (1918) as Lord Newhaven, the title role in *The Temptation Of Carlton Earle* (1923), *The Unwanted* (1924) as Colonel Carrington, *Such Is The Law* (1930) as Sir James Whittaker, *Surrender* (1931) as Count Reichendorf, *Son Of India* (1931) as Dr Wallace, *Never The Twain Shall Meet* (1931) as

Mr Pritchard, *The Man In Possession* (1931) as Mr Dabney, *Daybreak* (1931) as General von Hertz, *Contraband Love* (1931) as Paul Machin, JP, *The Bachelor Father* (1931) as Sir Basil Winterton, *Just A Gigolo* (1931) as Lord George Hampton, *Guilty Hands* (1931) as Reverend Hastings, *Polly Of The Circus* (1932) as Reverend James Northcott, *Tarzan The Ape Man* (1932) as James Parker, *Love Me Tonight* (1932) as Duke d'Artelines, *Trouble In Paradise* (1932) as Adolph Giron, *Queen Christina* (1933) as Aage, *Adorable* (1933) as The Prime Minister, *Bombshell* (1933) as Mr Middleton, *Curtain At Eight* (1934) as Jim Hanvey, *Cleopatra* (1934) as Enobarbus, *The Scarlet Empress* (1934) as Prince August, *Bulldog Drummond Strikes Back* (1934) as Captain Nielsen, *Jalna* (1935) as Uncle Nicholas, *The Gilded Lily* (1935) as Duke of Loamshire, *Clive Of India* (1935) as Prime Minister, *Little Lord Fauntleroy* (1936) as Earl of Dorincourt, *Romeo And Juliet* (1936) as Lord Capulet, *The Garden Of Allah* (1936) as Father Roubier, *Victoria The Great* (1937), *Thoroughbreds Don't Cry* (1937) as Sir Peter Calverton, *Wee Willie Winkie* (1937) as Colonel Williams, *The Hurricane* (1937) as Father Paul, *Kidnapped* (1938) as Duke of Argyle, *The Sun Never Sets* (1939) as Sir John Randolph, *The Four Feathers* (1939) as General Burroughs, *Another Thin Man* (1939) as Colonel MacFay, *Balalaika* (1939) as General Karagin, *Rebecca* (1940) as Colonel Julyan, *Dr Jekyll And Mr Hyde* (1941) as Bishop Manners, *Forever And A Day* (1943) as Admiral Eustace Trimble, *Madame Curie* (1943) as Lord Kelvin, *Secrets Of Scotland Yard* (1944) as Sir Christopher Belt, *And Then There Were None* (1945) as General Sir John Mandrake, *Rendezvous With Annie* (1946) as Sir Archibald Clyde, *Unconquered* (1947) as the Lord Chief Justice, *An Ideal Husband* (1947) as the Earl of Caversham and *Little Women* (1949) as Mr James Laurence. In 1938 he was awarded the CBE, becoming a knight six years later.

CAUSE: He died, aged 85, in Beverly Hills, California, from pneumonia. His home was called "The Corner House". He left £1,038 19s 2d.

Anna Nicole Smith
(VICKI LYNN HOGAN)
Born November 28, 1967
Died February 8, 2007
Gold digger. Born in Houston, Texas, the daughter of Donald Eugene Hogan and Virgie Mae Tabers, 5'11" Smith worked as a waitress at Jim's Krispy Fried Chicken restaurant in Mexia, Texas and aged 18, married one of the cooks Billy Smith by whom she had one son, Daniel Wayne (b. Limestone County, Texas January 22, 1986). She began modelling when she was 20 and became *Playboy* Playmate of the Month in May 1992, winning the Playmate of the Year the following year when she measured 39DD-27-39 thanks to surgery. On February 3, 1993 she and Smith were divorced. Two years previously she had met billionaire J. Howard Marshall II in a topless bar in Houston. They married on June 27, 1994 – she was 26, he was 89. He died on August 4, 1995 and a legal battle raged between her and his family over his money. In March 2002, Smith was awarded $88 million from the estate. She said, "I'm sick of being accused of gold-digging. It just so happens I get turned on by liver spots." On September 7, 2006, Smith gave birth to Dannielynn Hope by photographer Larry Birkhead. Three days later, her son died of an overdose of methadone and escitalopram while visiting his mother and newborn sister in their hospital room at Doctors Hospital in Nassau, the Bahamas. Smith appeared in the following films: *The Hudsucker Proxy* (1994) as Za-Za, *Naked Gun 33⅓: The Final Insult* (1994) as Tanya Peters, *To The Limit* (1995) as Colette Dubois/Vickie Linn, *Skyscraper* (1997) as Carrie Wisk, *Wasabi Tuna* (2003) as

herself, *Be Cool* (2005) as herself and *Illegal Aliens* (2007) as Lucy. The bisexual Smith, who had to pay her former maid Maria Cerrato $830,000 to settle a sexual harassment suit, once said, "I want to be the new Marilyn Monroe." She wasn't even the new Mamie Van Doren.

CAUSE: Smith was found unconscious in room 607 at the Seminole Hard Rock Hotel and Casino in Hollywood, Florida. She was taken to Memorial Regional Hospital at 2.10pm and pronounced dead on arrival at 2.49pm. She was 39. Her death was ruled an accidental prescription drug overdose. In her system were the sedative chloral hydrate, Clonazepam, Lorazepam, Oxazepam, Diazepam, Diphenhydramine, Toprimate, benzodiazepines and an anticonvulsant. FURTHER READING: *Sex Bomb: The Life And Death Of Anna Nicole Smith* – Eric and D'eva Redding (Wrea Green: Milo Books, 2007).

Jay R. Smith
Born August 29, 1915
Found dead October 5, 2002
Freckled Little Rascal. Born in Los Angeles, California, Jay R. Smith was a member of the troupe known now as The Little Rascals but in their heyday were called Our Gang and starred in a plethora of Hal Roach comedies. Smith appeared in 36 of the shorts; his first was *Boys Will Be Joys* (1925) when the series had already been running for three years. His freckled face gave rise to him being called 'Spec' or 'Speck'. Like the pop group Menudo, The Little Rascals were replaced when they became too old for the series. The original idea for Smith was for him to be a leading light in the series but he only ever seemed to play supporting roles except in one film *Rainy Days* (1928). Smith also appeared in *Forty-Five Minutes* (1926), which was distinguished only insofar as it was the first Hal Roach film to feature both Laurel and Hardy. Smith left the series

after the gang's sixth talkie *Moan And Groan, Inc* (1929). As he collected his last wage packet, he commented, "Well, I don't know what you're gonna do without me." He was only half-joking when he recalled the studio going bankrupt – albeit 30 years later. After seeing service in the Second World War, Smith opened a paintshop. He moved to Kailua, Hawaii, before settling in Las Vegas.

CAUSE: On October 1, 2002 he was seen by his family. Four days later, his corpse was discovered in the Nevada desert near Apex. A vagrant he had befriended was charged with his murder.

Carrie Snodgress
Born October 27, 1946
Died April 1, 2004
Unfulfilled promise. Caroline Snodgress was born in Park Ridge, Illinois, and educated initially at Northern Illinois University before switching to the Goodman Theater School in Chicago. She worked in television before making her film début in a bit part in *Easy Rider* (1969). Her first major part was as Janice Angstrom in *Rabbit, Run* (1970). Her third film, *Diary Of A Mad Housewife* (1970), garnered a Best Actress Academy Award nomination for her role as the frustrated housewife Tina Balser. She also won two Golden Globes (Best Actress and Best Newcomer) but gave it all up in 1971 to live with the musician Neil Young, by whom she had a son Zeke who was born in 1972 with cerebral palsy. For eight long years she eschewed acting and by that time the chance of stardom was gone. She commented, "I was never really a career woman, you see. My life always came first. When I got nominated for *Diary Of A Mad Housewife*, I didn't think, 'Aah, now I'll get more money.' My dream had always just been to do my work well, fall in love and build a life for myself." She returned with a small part in Brian DePalma's *The Fury*

(1978). She said, "When I came back, the industry didn't trust me. Rock'n'roll carries a heavy stigma. They didn't want to fool around with a dropout." In 1981 she made her first appearance on Broadway in *A Coupla White Chicks Sitting Around Talking*. Her other films included: *Love's Dark Ride* (1978) as Nancy Warren, *The Attic* (1979) as Louise, *Homework* (1982) as Dr Delingua, *Trick Or Treats* (1982) as Joan, *A Night In Heaven* (1983) as Mrs Johnson, *L.A. Bad* (1985) as Margot, *Pale Rider* (1985) as Sarah Wheeler, *Murphy's Law* (1986) as Joan Freeman, *Blueberry Hill* (1988) as Becca Dane, *Chill Factor* (1990) as Amy Carlisle, *Across The Tracks* (1991) as Rosemary Maloney, *The Ballad Of Little Jo* (1993) as Ruth Badger, *8 Seconds* (1994) as Elsie Frost, *Blue Sky* (1994) as Vera Johnson, *White Man's Burden* (1995) as Josine, *Stranger In The Kingdom* (1998) as Ruth Kinneson, *Wild Things* (1998) as Ruby, *In The Light Of The Moon* (2000) as Augusta, *Bartleby* (2001) as the book publisher and *The Forsaken* (2001) as Ina Hamm. In 1979, a well-known industry songwriter/producer ex-boyfriend Jack Nitzsche broke into her home while drunk and pistol-whipped her. Pleading guilty, he was fined and put on three years probation. In 1981 she married the painter Robert Jones but they separated after a short period.

CAUSE: Ill with liver disease, she died at the University of California Medical Center, Los Angeles from heart failure. Her son was by her side when she died. She was 57.

Sam Spiegel

Born November 11, 1903
Died December 31, 1985
Epic producer. Born in Jaroslau, Austria, and educated at the University of Vienna where he earned a degree in economics, Spiegel made his first foray into Hollywood in 1927 when he translated foreign films. He returned to Europe where he became a director of French and German versions of Universal films before fleeing Hitler in 1933. He settled permanently in the States in 1935 where he worked under the pseudonym S.P. Eagle before reverting to his real name in 1954. His most successful films were *The African Queen* (1952), *On The Waterfront* (1954), for which he won a Best Film Oscar, *The Bridge On The River Kwai* (1957), which cost $2.5 million and in three years took $30 million at the box office and for which he won a Best Film Oscar, *Suddenly Last Summer* (1959), *Lawrence Of Arabia* (1962), which took four years to make and for which he won a Best Film Oscar, *The Night Of The Generals* (1967), *Nicholas And Alexandra* (1971) and *The Last Tycoon* (1976). At the 1963 Oscars he was given the Irving Thalberg Memorial Award.

CAUSE: Spiegel died of natural causes while on holiday in the Caribbean aged 82.

Lili St Cyr

(WILLIS MARIE VAN SHAAK)
Born June 3, 1918
Died January 29, 1999
Queen of burlesque. Born in Minneapolis, Minnesota, she became a model while still a teenager. She became a dancer in the Florentine Gardens nightclub in Hollywood after accompanying her sister (who also became a stripper) to an audition. Her fellow hoofers included Yvonne De Carlo and Marie McDonald. She moved to a San Francisco club, where she earnt $27.50 a week; the nude dancers in the club pocketed around $500 a week. Becoming a stripper in 1940, she was fired from her first job for being so awful but the producer relented and sent her on an intensive training course. The 5'9", 36-24-35 Lili began touring America with her act and, on occasion, would come on stage naked apart from a G-string and proceed to get dressed! She began appearing at El Rancho Vegas, where

her act included taking a bath in a see-through tub. On October 18, 1951, she was arrested at Ciro's nightclub in Los Angeles for "lewd and lascivious behaviour". Lawyer Jerry Giesler defended Lili, who offered to take a bath in the courtroom to show how clean her act was. She was acquitted after an hour's deliberation. Although she appeared in three films that showcased her act – *Love Moods* (1952), *Strip-O-Rama* (1953) and *Bedroom Fantasy* (1954), she made her film début in *Carmenesque* (1954), the 3-D story of the match girl but without any music. Her other films included *The Miami Story* (1954), *Varietease* (1954), *Son Of Sinbad* (1955) as Nerissa, *Boudoir Secrets* (1955), *Josette Of New Orleans* (1958), *The Naked And The Dead* (1958), *I, Mobster* (1959) and *Runaway Girl* (1966) a film she described as "a lousy movie". She married six times. Her first husband was motorcyclist Cordy Milne. Number two was Richard Hubert, the head waiter at the Florentine Gardens nightclub. Then came ballet dancer Paul Valentine (1946–August 1949) and New York restaurateur Armando Orsini (1950–1953). Husband number five was actor Ted Jordan (1954–1958) and her final trip up the aisle was in 1959 to wed special effects wizard Joe Albert Zomar. They divorced in 1964. She never received nor asked for alimony from any of her husbands. On November 1, 1958, she attempted to kill herself in Las Vegas following her separation from Ted Jordan. It was one of several attempts she made, usually following a failed romance.
CAUSE: She died in Los Angeles, California, aged 80 from a heart attack.

Robert Stack
Born January 13, 1919
Died May 14, 2003
Square-jawed crime solver. Robert

Langford Modini Stack was born at 4.40pm on a winter's day in 1919 in Los Angeles, the son of James Langford Stack and his wife Elizabeth, an aspiring opera singer. Stack's great-grandfather had arrived in what was then the village of Los Angeles in 1849, and set up the community's first theatre. Both his grandparents had been Italian opera singers. Elizabeth Stack wanted to study opera so her son grew up in Paris and Rome. Learning to speak both French and Italian fluently, when, aged seven, the family returned to America, he was unable to speak English. As a teen, Stack showed considerable ability as a sportsman. He and his brother won the International Outboard Motor Championships in Venice, and held a title as speedboat racing champions in America for three years. When he was 16 Stack became a member of the All-American Skeet Rifle Team, setting two world records and becoming National Skeet Champion. In 1937 he briefly attended the University of Southern California (distinguishing himself on the polo team) before abandoning his formal education to study acting and singing. Stack attended the Henry Duffy School of Theater in California for six months, until he was offered his first film role. "My singing classes had been going badly," he recalled, "and my tutor told me to go down to Universal and listen to Deanna Durbin. I did, and while I was standing off to one side of the set, Joe Pasternak came over and offered me a role in the film." This was *First Love* (1939), a romantic musical starring Deanna Durbin. There was frenzied press interest at the time because Durbin, then aged 17, received her first screen kiss. As Stack was the one who delivered the kiss, he gained considerable publicity. Later in 1939 he joined the navy, serving as a gunnery instructor throughout the Second World War. In 1940 he signed a contract with MGM and continued to make films while serving. These included: *The Mortal Storm* (1940) as Otto von Rohn, *Badlands Of Dakota* (1941) as Jim Holliday, *To Be Or Not To Be* (1942) as Lieutenant Stanislav Sobinski and *Eagle Squadron* (1942) as Chuck Brewer. After the cessation of hostilities, 6′ Stack remained at MGM and appeared in *Fighter Squadron* (1948) as Captain Stu Hamilton, and *A Date With Judy* (1948) as Stephen Andrews, which starred Wallace Beery and Elizabeth Taylor. Throughout the Fifties Stack appeared in numerous B films, including *The Bullfighter And The Lady* (1951) which was not a biopic of Ava Gardner but in which he starred as Johnny Regan. He was also in the world's first 3-D movie *Bwana Devil* (1952) as Bob Hayward; *War Paint* (1953) as Lieutenant Billings and *Conquest Of Cochise* (1953) as Major Tom Burke. He was nominated for a Best Supporting Actor Academy Award for his performance as the alcoholic playboy Kyle Hadley in *Written On The Wind* (1956) opposite Lauren Bacall and Rock Hudson. He did not win the Oscar, losing out to Anthony Quinn for *Lust For Life*. In 1959 Desi Arnaz approached Stack with the idea of making a television series about Eliot Ness, the Internal Revenue Service agent. Stack was originally not enthusiastic about the idea because he believed that television was the cinema's poor relation. However, having read some of the scripts for *The Untouchables* he accepted the role of Ness. "I knew it would be a success," he later recalled. "The scripts were grim and based on real events, the gangsters were tough and Ness was an ordinary man in a cheap suit who was impassioned by his need to stamp out crime." Desilu Productions, Arnaz's company, was different from other television organisations in that it spent money on scripts as well as on stars. A determined attempt was made not to glamorise the gangsters, and Stack, as the central grey presence of Ness, proved totally credible. "I felt I had to

play him dull, almost a nonentity," he remembered. "Because the thugs were so colourful, so flashy, we needed a balance." The show débuted on ABC on October 15, 1959, and after the first season was rated 43 in the charts. Word of mouth spread and in season two it was the number eight rated show. The show ran for four years until September 10, 1963 but was criticised for its violence and historical inaccuracy. However, Stack's performance won the approval of Ness' widow, who endorsed the series and claimed that Stack captured her husband's "total commitment and anger". It did not impress the FBI. J. Edgar Hoover was infuriated that Ness was occasionally portrayed as solving crimes that the FBI had cleared up, such as the arrest of Ma Baker. Hoover also initiated an investigation of the show's scriptwriters to discover whether any of them were ex-FBI agents. In documents made available under the Freedom of Information Act, federal agents were described as "pressuring" Arnaz to change the scripts to show the FBI solving the crimes. The show also came in for criticism from the Italian American Organisation who objected to the "continued portrayal of Italian-Americans as hoodlums and members of the Mafia". (A similar criticism came from Arab groups in 2004 when they claimed that all the villains in the hit show *24* were Arabic.) When *The Untouchables* ended, Robert Stack returned to his film career. By this stage, however, the public so identified him with Eliot Ness that they found him unacceptable in non-police roles. He made two less than successful films – *The Caretakers* (1963) as Dr Donovan MacLeod and *Die Hölle Von Macao* (1967) as Cliff Wilder – before returning to television in *The Name Of The Game*. In this, Stack played Dan Farrell, a former FBI agent turned investigative journalist. Stack continued in the series for three years. He then made two more attempts at returning to the cinema, with roles in the French film *Day Of The Delinquent* (1970) and in the ill-fated melodrama *Storia Du Ina Donna* (1970) as David Frasier. Neither film proved popular. Stack accepted the role of Linc Evers in the unsuccessful police series *Most Wanted*, which was axed after only 20 episodes, running from October 16, 1976 until April 25, 1977. He took two years off before appearing in Steven Spielberg's wartime farce *1941*. The film was a box office flop, but gave Stack his first chance at playing a comedy role. He next appeared in the spoof disaster film *Airplane!* (1980) as Captain Rex Kramer, the humourless air traffic controller. Despite an excellent performance and a successful film, Stack was not offered any more comedy parts. Stack returned to playing policemen in the television series *Strike Force* (November 13, 1981–September 24, 1982) as Captain Frank Murphy. During the remainder of the decade, Stack accepted less and less work. He made two films – *Uncommon Valour* (1983) as MacGregor, and the forgettable comedy *Big Trouble* (1986), in which he starred as Winslow with his wife Rosemarie. He appeared as George Lancaster in the television mini-series *Hollywood Wives* in 1985, and made his theatrical début in a limited season of *La Cage Aux Folles* on Broadway. In 1989 Stack was approached about the possibility of recreating the role of Eliot Ness for television, but was doubtful about a second series. He had not rated Kevin Costner's portrayal of Ness in the 1987 film version, claiming that "too much was factually wrong. Ness was no wimp; he was a tough street kid." Stack was persuaded to make the TV film *The Return Of The Untouchables* (1991), which was set in the Forties. "Obviously we couldn't do it in modern times because Ness would have been too old," Stack recalled, "so we set it in the Forties, with Ness

coming out of retirement to fight crime for the second time." Later the same year Stack appeared as the host on the TV series *Unsolved Mysteries*. He married 5'5", 36-23-36 Rosemarie Bowe (b. Butte, Montana, September 17, 1932) in 1956, and had a son, Charles, and a daughter, Elizabeth. CAUSE: In November 2002, Robert Stack underwent treatment for prostate cancer. He died of a heart attack in Beverly Hills, California, aged 84.

Barbara Stanwyck
(RUBY KATHERINE STEVENS)
Born July 16, 1907
Died January 20, 1990
'Missy'. Born at 246 Clauson Street in Brooklyn, New York, the youngest of five children, 5'3" Stanwyck was a tomboy. Her mother, the devoutly Catholic Catherine McGee, died in 1910, a week after falling from a tram. A few weeks later, Byron Stevens, her father, did a bunk. Ruby and her brother Byron (b. 1904, d. 1964 of a coronary thrombosis), were placed in foster homes but Ruby ran away every afternoon to the family home at 246 Clauson Street. The siblings lived in several different homes. In 1912 they learned their father had died at sea. In 1920 Ruby left school and began a series of menial jobs, spending her spare time perfecting her dancing. When she was 15 she made her professional début in the chorus of the Ziegfeld Follies. On October 20, 1926, she played the lead at the Hudson Theater in the Broadway play *The Noose* directed by Willard Mack. The play ran until June 1927 but it had a far-reaching effect on her life. Mack renamed her Barbara Stanwyck after a character called Jane Stanwyck in the play *Barbara Frietchi*. She always spelled her name BarBara. Her film début came in *Broadway Nights* (1927). In St Louis on August 26, 1928, she married red-haired, twice-divorced, egotistical vaudevillian Frank Fay (b. San Francisco, November 17, 1894, as

Francis Anthony Donner, d. St John's Hospital, Santa Monica, California, September 25, 1961) known as 'Broadway's Favourite Son'. The newlyweds travelled to Hollywood, where he signed for Warner Bros and later she took non-exclusive contracts with Warner Bros and Columbia. Stanwyck was a journeyman actress but she worked very hard and was known for her dedication and professionalism. In fact, she sacrificed everything to her career. In 1944 the Internal Revenue Service announced that she was the highest female wage earner in the USA – to the tune of $323,333. Her films included: the lead in *Mexicali Rose* (1929), *Ladies Of Leisure* (1930) as party girl Kay Arnold, *Ten Cents A Dance* (1931) as taxi dancer Barbara O'Neill (the film was directed by Lionel Barrymore who was suffering from arthritis throughout filming and took medicine that sent him to sleep during much of the day), *Illicit* (1931) as Anne Vincent and *Night Nurse* (1931) as Lora Hart. On July 17, 1931, the day after her 24th birthday, she called Harry Cohn and told him she was unable to work because of her husband's professional commitments in New York but that if he wanted to raise her salary to $50,000 a film from the $30,000 she was receiving, she would reconsider her position. In September Columbia injuncted Stanwyck from working for any other studio. She returned to Tinseltown with her tail between her legs but Cohn was magnanimous and gave her the $50,000 she wanted. Her subsequent films included: *Forbidden* (1932) as murderess and adulteress Lulu Smith (during which she was injured falling from a horse), *Shopworn* (1932) as Kitty Lane, *So Big* (1932) as widowed teacher Selina Peake, *The Bitter Tea Of General Yen* (1933) as Megan Davis who falls for a Chinese warlord, *Ladies They Talk About* (1933) as gangster's moll Nan Taylor, *Baby Face* (1933) as gold digger Lily Powers, *The Secret Bride* (1934) as governor's

daughter Ruth Vincent, *The Woman In Red* (1935) as wealthy Shelby Barrett, *Red Salute* (1935) as Drue Van Allen (her first comedy), the title role in *Annie Oakley* (1935), *The Bride Walks Out* (1936) as spendthrift Carolyn Martin, *His Brother's Wife* (1936) as Rita Wilson in her first film opposite Robert Taylor, *Banjo On My Knee* (1936) as entertainer Pearl Holley, *Internes Can't Take Money* (1937) as Janet Haley, *This Is My Affair* (1937) as undercover agent Lil Duryea, the title role in *Stella Dallas* (1937), for which she was nominated for a Best Actress Oscar, *Always Goodbye* (1938) as fashion designer Margot Weston, *Union Pacific* (1939) as postmistress Mollie Monahan, *Golden Boy* (1939) as Lorna Moon, *Remember The Night* (1940) as convicted thief Lea Leander, *Meet John Doe* (1941) as reporter Ann Mitchell, *You Belong To Me* (1941) as Dr Helen Hunt, *Ball Of Fire* (1941) as Sugarpuss O'Shea, for which she was nominated for a second Best Actress Oscar, *The Great Man's Lady* (1942) as pioneer bride Hannah Sempler in one of Stanwyck's favourite films, *The Gay Sisters* (1942) as Fiona Gaylord, *Lady Of Burlesque* (1943) as stripper Dixie Daisy, *Flesh And Fantasy* (1943) as fugitive Joan Stanley, *Double Indemnity* (1944) as femme fatale Phyllis Dietrichson, for which she was nominated for her third Best Actress Oscar, *Christmas In Connecticut* (1945) as magazine journalist Elizabeth Lane, *My Reputation* (1946) as wartime widow Jessica Drummond, *The Bride Wore Boots* (1946) as horsewoman Sally Warren, *The Strange Love Of Martha Ivers* (1946) as wealthy, scheming Martha Ivers, *California* (1946) as Lily Bishop in her first colour film, *The Two Mrs Carrolls* (1947) as Sally Morton Carroll, *Cry Wolf* (1947) as Sandra Marshall, *Sorry, Wrong Number* (1948) as the bedridden, neurotic Leona Stevenson, for which she was nominated for her fourth and final Best Actress Oscar, *The Lady Gambles* (1949) as gambler Joan Boothe, *East Side, West*

Side (1949) as society hostess Jessie Bourne, *The File On Thelma Jordon* (1949) as murder suspect Thelma Jordon, *No Man Of Her Own* (1949) as Helen Ferguson, *The Furies* (1950) as Vance Jeffords, *To Please A Lady* (1950) as journalist Regina Forbes, *Clash By Night* (1952) as Mae Doyle D'Amato, *Jeopardy* (1953) as Helen Stilwin, *Titanic* (1953) as Julia Sturges, *Executive Suite* (1954) as Julia O. Treadway, *Witness To Murder* (1954) as Beverly Hills fashion designer Cheryl Draper, *Cattle Queen Of Montana* (1954) as Sierra Nevada Jones, *Escape To Burma* (1955) as plantation owner Gwen Moore, *There's Always Tomorrow* (1956) as Norma Miller Vale, *The Maverick Queen* (1956) as bandit Kit Banion and *Crime Of Passion* (1957) as Kathy Doyle, by which time her film career was grinding inexorably to an end. She moved to the small screen with the anthology *The Barbara Stanwyck Show* (September 19, 1960–September 11, 1961) for which she won an Emmy at the 1960–1 Emmys Award ceremony held at the Moulin Rouge in Hollywood and the Ziegfeld Theater in New York on May 16, 1961. Stanwyck was so eager to get onto the stage to accept her prize that she ripped her evening dress. Everyone ummed and ahhed as an associate helped her on with her coat. New York host Joey Bishop saved the situation by quipping, "The guy who helped Barbara Stanwyck on with her coat was on camera longer than I was." She was also a hit as Miss Barbara Stanwyck (billed as she had been in her films) in the ABC Western *The Big Valley* (September 15, 1965–May 19, 1969) in which she played Victoria Barkley. She appeared in a few TV movies in the Seventies but came back to the fore in the mini-series *The Thorn Birds* (1983) as Mary Carson, for which she won an Outstanding Lead Actress In A Limited Series Or Special Emmy on September 25, 1983, and camping it up as Constance Colby Patterson in *The Colbys* (1985–1986). On December 6,

1932, she and Fay adopted a son they named Anthony Dion Fay (b. February 5, 1932, as John Charles Greene). It was a strange occurrence, since neither had expressed the idea of wanting children and if social services had investigated their home life, they would almost certainly have been refused permission to adopt. The Fays spent little time with their son. She was at the studio during the day and the couple were out clubbing at night. They were also fighting physically on a regular basis. They had few friends and when someone was invited to their home they never saw Dion; he was locked in his room with his nanny, principally for his own safety. Once in a drunken rage, Fay threw him into the family swimming pool. Dion was estranged from his mother from 1952. In 1962 he was arrested for selling pornography. The Fays fought regularly in public. He would hit her when he thought she had drunk too much or for other reasons best known to himself. In early 1935 she told reporters: "I'll never divorce Frank Fay! Never! You can gossip all you want, but if I can't stay married, I'll get out of pictures." On December 31, 1935, she divorced Frank Fay. He sued for access to their son on December 27, 1937, claiming that Stanwyck prevented him from seeing the boy so he could become accustomed to the handsome matinée idol Robert Taylor, whom she had been discreetly seeing. Fay won his case in January 1938 and was allowed access. Barbara was not a doting mother. Young Dion was not the image of Hollywood perfection. He was tubby, freckled, bespectacled and very insular. Barbara dated George Brent and, for a time, was escorted by Byron Stevens, causing the press to comment on her new beau, until his identity became known. Three and a half years later, on May 14, 1939, she married Taylor. It did not get off to a happy start. Taylor's mother went on hunger strike to protest at the match and the groom spent his wedding night with her, not his wife.

The couple had little in common and on the rare occasions they had the same day off, Stanwyck wanted to spend it with her husband but he wasn't interested. He was bored by her life and wanted to escape the city and go to the country where he could go shooting. A brief separation ensued in 1941. The final straw came in August 1950 when Taylor had flown to Rome for six months to film *Quo Vadis* (1951) and began an affair with bit player Lia De Leo. When Stanwyck asked what her husband was doing with De Leo, he screamed: "At least I can get it up with her." Stanwyck flew (something she feared doing) back to the States and filed for divorce on December 16, 1950. They divorced in 1951. Both parties were subjected to rumours about their respective sexualities. Stanwyck's supposed lovers included Marlene Dietrich, Joan Crawford and her publicist Helen Ferguson (who charged her $400 a month for 27 years, never varying her price). On October 27, 1981, she was robbed when a masked intruder burst into her home, bashed her over the head with a gun, locked her in the closet (no comment) and stole $5,000 worth of jewellery. On March 29, 1982, she was awarded an honorary Oscar. In May 1984 cataracts were discovered in both eyes for which she underwent surgery in December of that year. On June 22, 1985, her Beverly Hills home, 1055 Loma Vista Drive, was gutted by fire.

CAUSE: Alone for much of her life, Stanwyck drank herself into a stupor and smoked herself to death. In June 1988 she was hospitalised with pneumonia at St John's Hospital, Santa Monica, California. She was released after three weeks. In May 1989 she was again in St John's with, among other illnesses, a bladder complaint. On January 9, 1990, she was admitted again to St John's where she died, aged 82 of congestive heart failure, coupled with pneumonia, lung disease and emphysema. Nancy

Sinatra, Sr was by her side when she died. She was cremated on 25 January, 1990.

FURTHER READING: *Stanwyck: The Untold Biography* – Jane Ellen Wayne (London: Robson Books, 1986); *Stanwyck* – Axel Madsen (New York: HarperCollins, 1994).

Ray Stark
Born October 3, 1914
Died January 17, 2004
'Funny' producer. Born in Chicago, Illinois, Ray Stark began his career as a journalist before turning to PR and then becoming a literary agent. For a time one of his clients was Raymond Chandler. He then became a talent agent and joined Famous Artists. In 1957 with Eliot Hyman he formed Seven Arts Productions and the company was a successful packager of made-for-television films. In 1966 he left to become an independent producer. Two years earlier he had produced the original Broadway production of *Funny Girl*, the fictionalised story of his mother-in-law Fanny Brice. He made the film version four years later and its sequel *Funny Lady* in 1975. Barbra Streisand was not his first choice for the lead. He wanted Anne Bancroft but she withdrew after deciding she wouldn't be comfortable with the songs. His next two choices, Eydie Gorme or Carol Burnett, also turned down the opportunity. Ever the driver of a hard bargain, Stark made Streisand sign a four film deal in return for starring in *Funny Girl*. He also produced her in *The Owl And The Pussycat* (1970) and *The Way We Were* (1973) before *Funny Lady*. When the latter picture finished shooting she gave Stark an antique mirror on which she had written in lipstick, "Paid in full". At the 1980 Oscars ceremony Stark received the Irving G. Thalberg Award. His other films included: *The World Of Suzie Wong* (1960), *The Night Of The Iguana* (1964), *This Property Is Condemned* (1966), *Drop Dead Darling*

(1966), *The Sunshine Boys* (1975), *Robin And Marian* (1976), *Murder By Death* (1976), *The Goodbye Girl* (1977), *California Suite* (1978), *The Electric Horseman* (1979), *Annie* (1982), *Biloxi Blues* (1988), *Steel Magnolias* (1989) and *The Night Of The Iguana* (2005). In 1939 he married Frances Brice (d. May 31, 1992) by whom he had two children.

CAUSE: He died in West Hollywood, California, of heart failure. He was 89.

Ray Dennis Steckler
Born January 25, 1938
Died January 7, 2009

Mondo bizarro. Raymond Dennis Steckler was born in Reading, Pennsylvania, and became a film fan from an early age, spending his Saturdays in the local cinema. His stepfather gave him an eight-millimetre movie camera when Steckler was 15-years-old and his career path was set. He persuaded his friends to appear in his first film, which was about pirates. They all nearly drowned on a handmade raft. He studied photography while drafted into the army and after being demobbed he drove to Hollywood with a friend in 1959. Their car broke down at the corner of Hollywood and Vine. Steckler was hired as a props man before finding work as a cameraman. His first work as a cinematographer was on *Wild Ones* (1962) in which he also acted but his first notable work was on *The World's Greatest Sinner* (released June 1962), the story of a bored insurance salesman who left his job to enter politics. It was directed by and starred Timothy Carey, with music by a young Frank Zappa. Two years later, he directed the film that made his name in weird movie circles. *The Incredibly Strange Creatures Who Stopped Living And Became Mixed-Up Zombies!!?* cost just $38,000 (the most he ever spent on a movie) and Steckler publicised it as "The World's Weirdest Movie". Steckler also starred in many of his films using the name Cash Flagg. The picture features a fairground fortune teller, disfigured zombies, trigger-happy policemen and acid thrown in people's faces, mixed up with Las Vegas-esque musical numbers. Steckler advertised the film with posters that boasted, "SEE: the hunchback of the midway fight a duel of death with the mixed-up zombies! SEE: the world's first monster musical!" Steckler was perhaps unique in his films – they had no scripts, he hired his relatives, used his car in some scenes, used empty buildings for shots, and he dubbed in sound afterwards. Steckler also did not pay his actors and even hired one who could not speak English and had to learn his lines phonetically. During one film Steckler was punched in the mouth accidentally and lost his front teeth. Rather than lose a day's shooting, he replaced the teeth with Styrofoam. In 1964 Steckler made *The Thrill Killers*, his answer to *Psycho* in which Mort "Mad Dog" Click stabs a prostitute to death in her dark hotel room, while outside a neon light flashes in counterpoint to the knife. In September 1966 he released *Rat Pfink A Boo Boo*, which was intended as a psychological thriller but then halfway through shooting Steckler decided to make the rest of the film as a superhero parody. In 1970 he relocated to Las Vegas where he enlarged his portfolio to include soft-core pornography. Steckler taught film classes at the University of Nevada and owned video shops. He said, "I don't think I'm allowed in Hollywood – I have to sneak in and out. I'm not saying I'm a great filmmaker or anything; I try to just be different, not to be like everybody else." Steckler was twice married: his first wife was actress Carolyn Brandt by whom he had two daughters Linda and Laura. His second wife was Katherine Steckler whom he married in 1986 and with whom he had two daughters Morgan and Bailey.

CAUSE: Steckler died of heart failure at Las Vegas, Nevada. He was 70.

Anthony Steel

Born May 21, 1920
Died March 21, 2001
Beefcake. Born in London (some sources say in 1919), the son of Edward Steel (b. 1897, d. October 18, 1965), Anthony Maitland Steel was educated at school in Ireland and then Cambridge, serving in the Grenadier Guards during the Second World War. He took up acting only after the war and fortuitously his then girlfriend introduced him to her uncle who happened to be J. Arthur Rank. Steel made his début in *Saraband For Dead Lovers* (1948) and was signed to the Rank Organisation. Groomed for stardom by Rank he had bit parts in *Poet's Pub* (1949), *Marry Me* (1949) as Jack Harris, *Don't Ever Leave Me* (1949) as Harris, *Helter Skelter* (1949), *The Mudlark* (1950) as Lieutenant Charles McHatten and was a policeman in *The Blue Lamp* (1950). He was never a serious rival to his contemporaries Stewart Granger and Kenneth More. He played heroic roles relying on his good looks rather than any talent. His first major part was as John in *The Wooden Horse* (1950). Jack Lee, the film's director, commented, "Tony Steel was fine to work with – just a physical type, a young chap who could do certain things, though he didn't have much acting to do in this." His stardom was assured in *Where No Vultures Fly* (1951) where he played Bob Payton, a gamekeeper on the trail of ivory poachers in Kenya. He injured his leg, requiring an operation on his knee, after colliding with a tree during filming. He was presented to the Queen as *Where No Vultures Fly* was the movie chosen as the Royal Command Performance film. It was also the top British moneymaker of 1952. He starred opposite Bette Davis in Val Guest's *Another Man's Poison* (1951) as Larry Stevens but was acted off the screen by Davis. He starred opposite Patricia Roc in the comedy *Something Money Can't Buy* (1952) as Captain Harry Wilding, a soldier who finds difficulty adjusting to civvy street. In *The Planter's Wife* (1952) he played Hugh Dobson opposite Jack Hawkins (in 1954 he was second only to Hawkins as the most popular British star) and Claudette Colbert. He was Henry Durie, Errol Flynn's little brother, in *The Master Of Ballantrae* (1953) although Flynn managed to run his sword through Steel's hand. He reprised the role of gamekeeper Bob Payton in *West Of Zanzibar* (1954). In *The Sea Shall Not Have Them* (1954) he played Flying Officer Treherne, an Air Sea Rescue officer who rescued four downed airmen adrift in a dinghy in the North Sea. His co-stars were Dirk Bogarde and Michael Redgrave. *Storm Over The Nile* (1955) was a remake of *The Four Feathers*, in which Steel played the central character Harry Faversham who was branded a coward by his fellow officers after he resigned his commission in 1895 rather than go to the Sudan. In December 1955 he met the pneumatic Anita Ekberg, a former Miss Universe, at a film première. On May 22, 1956 in Florence she became his second wife. He announced an intention to break Hollywood much to the annoyance of Sir John Davis, the head of the Rank Organisation. It never happened and he made headlines for all the wrong reasons. Steel was arrested twice for drunken driving, and he acquired a reputation as a hell-raiser who physically attacked paparazzi for photographing his wife. His time in Tinseltown generated just one film *Valerie* (1957) in which he played Reverend Blake and appeared with Sterling Hayden and Ekberg. Back in England he appeared in Hugo Fregonese's *Harry Black And The Tiger* (1958) as Desmond Tanner and Raymond Stross' *A Question Of Adultery* (1959) as Mark Loring, a

sterile husband whose wife resorts to artificial insemination. His last prestigious leading role was in Michael Powell's *Honeymoon* (1959). That year, on May 14, he and Ekberg were divorced. He moaned, "It was no fun being married to a glamour girl." With his star fading he moved to Rome and began to make continental films such as *Luna De Miel* (1959) as Kit Kelly, *Med Fara För Livet* (1959) as Mike Gibson, *La Vendetta Dei Barbari* (1960) as Consul Olympus, *Vacanze Alla Baia D'Argento* (1961) as Pietro, *La Tigre Dei Sette Mari* (1963) as William Scott, *Die Goldsucher Von Arkansas* (1964) as Lopez, *Ich Spreng' Euch Alle In Die Luft* (1968) as Arthur Baker, *I Diavoli Della Guerra* (1969) as Colonel James Steele and *Rappresaglia* (1973) as Major Domizlaf. His film *Histoire D'O* (1975) in which he played Sir Stephen was banned in the UK for a quarter of a century. Some of his later work was in seedy films such as *Let's Get Laid* (1977) as Moncrieff Dovecraft, *Hardcore* (1977) as Robert Charlton and *The World Is Full Of Married Men* (1979) as Conrad Lee. His other films included *Laughter In Paradise* (1951) as Roger Godfrey, *Emergency Call* (1952) as Dr Carter, *Malta Story* (1953) as Wing Commander Bartlett, *Albert R.N.* (1953) as Lieutenant Geoffrey Ainsworth, *Out Of The Clouds* (1955) as Gus Randall, *Passage Home* (1955) as First Mate Vosper, *Checkpoint* (1956) as Bill Fraser, *The Black Tent* (1956) as Captain David Holland, *The Switch* (1962) as Bill Craddock, *A Matter Of Choice* (1963) as John Crighton, *Anzio* (1968) as General Marsh, *Hell Is Empty* (1969) as Major Morton, *La Notte Dell'Alta Marea* (1977) as Richard Butler, *Indagine Su Un Delitto Perfetto* (1978) as Superintendent Jeff Hawks and *The Mirror Crack'd* (1980) as Sir Derek Ridgeley. He was married three times. His first wife was Juanita Forbes whom he married in 1949. They divorced in 1954. He married Johanna Melcher, a

former Miss Austria, in 1964. That marriage also ended in divorce. He had a son and two daughters.
CAUSE: When work was scarce he left his seedy Earls Court hotel to live in sheltered accommodation in a council flat in Northolt, west London. He did not even tell David Daly, his agent, where he was living. In the mid-Nineties Daly discovered his whereabouts from a tabloid newspaper but when he drove over to see his client Steel refused to open the door. Daly found him work as Dr Steven Hart in the television series *The Broker's Man* (1999). He also arranged to have him admitted to Denville Hall, a home for retired theatre folk at 62 Ducks Hill Road, Northwood, Middlesex. Daly said, "He was a very private man. He just decided that he would withdraw. He found a place to live and simply went into hiding. In some ways, it was not unlike him; if he decided that things weren't right, he would withdraw into himself and not contact anybody." Steel died at Denville Hall of heart failure, aged 80.

Rod Steiger
Born April 14, 1925
Died July 9, 2002
Method actor. Rodney Stephen Steiger was born in Westhampton, Long Island, the son of a peripatetic song and dance act. Steiger's ancestry was French, German and Scottish. His parents split up before he celebrated his first birthday. As a result he never knew his father and was raised by his mother, an alcoholic, in various parts of New Jersey. Educated at West Side High School in Newark, the young Steiger took an interest in acting. He left school at 16 and joined the US Navy by lying about his age. He served aboard the destroyer USS *Taussig* for four years before his demob. He then joined the civil service where he landed a job with the Office of Dependants and Beneficiaries of the Veterans Administration. Using a government

grant to help ex-servicemen, Steiger moved to New York where he began to study acting at the New School for Social Research, the Dramatic Workshop and the Actors' Studio. (The Method acting taught at the Actors' Studio – in which the actor used his own experiences in a role and invented a life for the character – was not always a resounding success. For his performances as Napoleon in *Waterloo* (1970) Steiger regarded the French emperor as a man ill with disease and dependent on drugs. "I believe that on the night before the battle, he bombed himself out on laudanum." Steiger also used his Method in Fred Zinnemann's film of *Oklahoma!* in 1955 in which he played the baddie Judd Fry. One reviewer stated that Steiger "loaded the part with so many psychological hang-ups that he undermined the prevailing tone of exuberance and optimism".) Steiger began working in television in 1947 and, four years later, made his Broadway début in a revival of Clifford Odets' *Night Music*. That same year saw his big screen début in Fred Zinnemann's *Teresa* (1951). In 1953 he was the original Marty in the television production of Paddy Chayefsky's play about a butcher from the Bronx who falls in love with Clara, a shy teacher. Steiger was offered the role when the inevitable Hollywood movie came to be made in the winter of 1954–1955 but turned it down. The film won an Oscar for Ernest Borgnine. (In the original the butcher was Jewish but he metamorphosed into an Italian for the film.) Another Odets vehicle saw Steiger give a winning performance as a film executive in *The Big Knife* (1955) as Stanley Shriner Hoff, directed by Robert Aldrich. He appeared in *The Court-Martial Of Billy Mitchell* (1955), *The Harder They Fall* (1956) as Nick Benko (Humphrey Bogart's last film), *Jubal* (1956) as Pinky and *Run Of The Arrow* (1957) as Private O'Meara. It was during the filming that Steiger

began to get the reputation of being difficult to work with. Director Samuel Fuller said, "He has lots of talent but he doesn't know how to use it . . . he gets carried away and needs to be closely directed." Steiger was closely directed in *On The Waterfront* (1954) by Elia Kazan, in which Steiger played Marlon Brando's gangster brother Charley "the Gent" Malloy – "a killer in a camel hair coat". Steiger appeared as Paul Hochen opposite Diana Dors making her Hollywood début in *The Unholy Wife* (1957). Dors was married to the mentally unstable and paranoically jealous - not to say psychopathically violent - Dennis Hamilton at the time but that didn't stop her falling for Steiger. She was to write in one of her autobiographies, "Rod made me feel like a woman, not a child, and in him . . . I saw a real man." Steiger ended the affair – by phone – after a few months. Steiger then visited Britain to make *Across The Bridge* (1957) as Carl Schaffner, which despite being based on a Graham Greene story was not a success. His next venture playing Al Capone in 1959 was more successful. Back in New York, Steiger appeared in the Broadway production of *Rashomon* playing the bandit in a production that ran for 159 performances. Its co-star was Claire Bloom, who became Steiger's second wife. Unlike many husbands and wives the Rod Steigers rarely worked together. They appeared in two films *The Illustrated Man* (he was Carl) and *Three Into Two Won't Go* (he was Steve Howard) (both 1969). In 1964 he played Sol Nazerman, a Jewish survivor of a Nazi concentration camp in *The Pawnbroker* for which he was honoured at the Berlin Film Festival and Oscar nominated (his second nod, the first coming for *On The Waterfront*). The following year he appeared in David Lean's *Doctor Zhivago* and Tony Richardson's *The Loved One* (1965) playing Mr Joyboy, the mother-loving mortician. He also appeared in *Le Mani Sulla Citta* (1963), *E Venne Un Uomo*

(1965) as the intermediary, *No Way To Treat A Lady* (1968) as Christopher Gill, *Duck, You Sucker* (1971), *Lucky Luciano* (1973) as Gene Giannini, *Les Innocents Aux Mains Sales* (1975), and Franco Zeffirelli's *Jesus Of Nazareth* (1977) as Pontius Pilate. What is generally regarded as Steiger's finest role and the one for which he won an Oscar, was as the intolerant Sparta police chief Bill Gillespie in the 1967 film *In The Heat Of The Night*. His co-star was Sidney Poitier. Steiger later turned down the lead in *Patton* because he thought it glorified war. The part – and an Oscar – went to George C. Scott. Steiger later called his refusal his most stupid career move. His later films included: *The Amityville Horror* (1979), *The January Man* (1989), *The Ballad Of The Sad Cafe* (1991) and *The Specialist* (1994), in all of which he over-acts terribly. 5'10" Rod Steiger was married five times. His first wife was the actress Sally Gracie (b. Little Rock, Arkansas, December 31, 1920, d. New York, New York, August 13, 2001) whom he married in 1952 and divorced six years later. Wife number two (in Los Angeles on September 19, 1959) was Claire Bloom (b. North Finchley, London, February 15, 1931), by whom he had a daughter, Anna Justine (b. February 13, 1960). That marriage lasted ten years. His third wife (from April 23, 1973 until the autumn of 1979) was Sherry Nelson. Wife number four was Paula Ellis, by whom he had a son. They married in 1986 and divorced in 1997. His fifth and final wife was Joan Benedict, another actress, whom he married on October 10, 2000.
CAUSE: Steiger's later life was marred by mental illness. The break-up of his marriages and heart surgery left him severely depressed for eight years. He would lie in bed, not speaking and not washing, and on two occasions contemplated suicide and murdering his wife. He died in Los Angeles, California, aged 77 of pneumonia and kidney failure.

Anna Sten
(ANNEL [ANJUSCHKA] STENSKAYA SUDAKEVICH)
Born December 3, 1908
Died November 12, 1993
'Goldwyn's Folly'. Born in Kiev, the beautiful daughter of a Ukrainian father and a Swedish mother, Sten began her working life as a waitress before making the transition to silent films including *Zluta Knizka* (1927) as Maria, *Moskva V Oktyabre* (1927) and *Moj Syn* (1928) as Olga Surina. She left to work in Germany where she was spotted by Samuel Goldwyn playing Gruschenka in *Der Mörder Dimitri Karamasoff* (1931). He contacted her agent with a view to taking her to America in the hope she would be another Marlene Dietrich or Greta Garbo. The agent omitted to mention that Sten didn't speak English. Goldwyn signed her anyway and then spent a fortune teaching her English, acting and deportment labelling her 'The Passionate Peasant'. The public didn't take to her and Goldwyn cancelled her contract after three films. She appeared in just over a dozen films in America, but also pursued a career as a painter. Her movies included: *Nana* (1934) as Nana, *We Live Again* (1934) as Katusha Maslova, *A Woman Alone* (1936) as Maria, *Exile Express* (1939) as Nadine Nikolas, *So Ends Our Night* (1941) as Lilo, *They Came To Blow Up America* (1943) as Frau Reiker, *Chetniks* (1943) as Lubitca Mihailovitch, *Three Russian Girls* (1944) as Natasha, *Runaway Daughters* (1956) as Ruth Barton and *The Nun And The Sergeant* (1962). She was married and divorced twice.
CAUSE: She died aged 84 from a heart attack in New York.

Sir Robert Stephens
Born July 14, 1931
Died November 12, 1995
Knight errant. Born in Bristol, Robert Graham Stephens was at one time considered the heir apparent to Lord

Olivier but his departure from the National Theatre in 1970, the break-up of his marriage to Maggie Smith and his heavy drinking wrecked what was once a promising career. He dragged himself back from the brink in the Eighties, winning an Olivier Award in 1991. Married four times, the final time to long-term girlfriend Patricia Quinn 10 months before his death, his films included: *War And Peace* (1956), *A Taste Of Honey* (1961) as Peter, *A Circle Of Deception* (1961) as Captain Stein, *Cleopatra* (1963) as Germanicus, *Morgan: A Suitable Case For Treatment* (1966) as Charles Napier, *The Prime Of Miss Jean Brodie* (1969) as Teddy Lloyd, *The Private Life Of Sherlock Holmes* (1970) as Sherlock Holmes, *Travels With My Aunt* (1972) as Mr Visconti, *Luther* (1973) as Johan Von Eck, *Empire Of The Sun* (1987) as Mr Lockwood, *The Fruit Machine* (1988) as Vincent, *Henry V* (1989) as Pistol, *The Bonfire Of The Vanities* (1990) as Sir Gerald Moore, *The Pope Must Die* (1991) as Carmelengo, *Chaplin* (1992) as Ted and *England My England* (1995) as Dryden.

CAUSE: He died of liver failure in the Royal Free Hospital, Hampstead, north London, aged 64. He left less than £145,000.

Jan Sterling
(JANE STERLING ADRIANCE)
Born April 3, 1921
Died March 26, 2004
Thin star. Born in Manhattan, New York, 5′6″ Jan Sterling never quite made the top echelon of stardom but she was a solid if svelte actress who could always be relied upon to give a good account of herself. Her parents separated when she was young and her mother took the family to Europe. She was educated in London and Paris and at 15 joined Fay Compton's drama school in London. She stayed only a short while, and by the age of 17 she was treading the boards on Broadway in *Bachelor Born*, playing a young

English lady. During the course of the next 11 years she cornered the Broadway market in playing Brits. When she was 21 she changed her name to Jan Sterling at the suggestion of Ruth Gordon whose first idea was Amethyst Adriance because "you should name yourself after a gem". 35C-23-35 Sterling made her first film, *Tycoon*, in 1947 but it was her second outing playing Stella McCormick in *Johnny Belinda* (1948) that she shone. On stage she nearly always played docile young ladies but on screen she was cast, much to her delight, as slags, bitches and manipulators. She impressed in bad girl roles in *Caged* (1950) as Smoochie, *Ace In The Hole* (1951), *Flesh And Fury* (1952) as Sonya Bartow, *The Human Jungle* (1954) as Mary Abbot and *Female On The Beach* (1955) as Amy Rawlinson.

She was also in *Sky Full Of Moon* (1952) as Dixie Delmar and was nominated for a Best Supporting Actress Oscar for *The High And The Mighty* (1954) in which she played Sally McKee. She was twice married. Her first husband in 1941 was the actor John Merivale. They divorced in 1948. Her second husband was another actor, Paul Douglas, who she married in 1950. Her son Adams was born in 1955. He died in 2003. Following her husband's death in 1959 she reappraised her career. In the Seventies she moved in with Sam Wanamaker and they were together at his death in 1993.

CAUSE: She died at the Motion Picture and Television Hospital in Woodland Hills, California, following a series of strokes. She was 82.

Miroslava Stern
(MIROSLAVA STERNOVA)
Born February 26, 1926
Died March 10, 1955
Almost made it. Born in Prague, Miroslava was raised in Mexico, where her parents had emigrated in the early Thirties. She became a star in Mexican films, making her début as Beatriz in

Cinco Rostros De Mujer (1946). After winning a beauty contest she moved to Hollywood, making her first American picture playing Linda de Calderon opposite Anthony Quinn in *The Brave Bulls* (1951). Her exotic look and accent limited her appeal and her only other major American film was *Stranger On Horseback* (1955) in which she appeared opposite Joel McCrea. She moved permanently to Mexico City and, in total, appeared in over 30 films. CAUSE: Unlucky in love, she killed herself over a failed affair with bullfighter Luis Miguel Dominguin. She was 29.

George Stevens

Born December 18, 1904
Died March 8, 1975
Giant director. Born in Oakland, California, George Cooper Stevens was the son of (John) Landers Stevens (b. San Francisco, California February 17, 1877, d. Hollywood, California December 19, 1940), a Shakespearean actor and theatre company owner, and actress Georgie Cooper (b. Battle Creek, Michigan, July 31, 1882, d. Hollywood, California, September 3, 1968). His grandfather, James Stevens, had been a flash lawyer in San Francisco during the Gold Rush while his grandmother, Georgie Woodthorpe (b. San Francisco, California, October 11, 1859, d. Glendale, California, August 25, 1927), played Ophelia to Edwin Booth's Hamlet. Stevens made his stage debut aged four in a production of *Sappho* by his father's company. In 1919 he left school to become his father's stage manager and then business manager. In 1921 the family moved to Hollywood so Landers Stevens could become a film actor. George Stevens became a cameraman for Hal Roach in 1921 and his name started appearing onscreen from 1924. From that year until 1930 he worked on a number of two-reelers including some with Laurel and Hardy. From 1930 until 1932 he

was involved in the Boyfriend and Our Gang series and contributed jokes to the films. In 1932 he left Hal Roach for Universal where he made three shorts in his first year. His first feature film in 1933 was a comedy, *The Cohens And Kellys In Trouble*, starring Maureen O'Sullivan. He followed that with *Kentucky Kernels* (1934) and *Bachelor Bait* (1934). He then moved to RKO where he was paid $2,250 a week and stayed until 1940. His film *The Nitwits* (1935) was the vehicle that introduced Betty Grable, albeit in a minor role, to the public. He received acclaim for his direction of Katharine Hepburn and Fred MacMurray in *Alice Adams* (premièred August 15, 1935) making him a much in demand talent. Stevens changed Booth Tarkington's ending to a happy one. He directed *Annie Oakley* (1935) starring Barbara Stanwyck and Melvyn Douglas, *Swing Time* (1936) with Fred Astaire and Ginger Rogers, *Quality Street* (1937) with Katharine Hepburn and Franchot Tone, *A Damsel In Distress* (1937) starring Fred Astaire, George Burns and Gracie Allen, and Joan Fontaine with music and lyrics by George and Ira Gershwin, *Vivacious Lady* (1938) with James Stewart and Ginger Rogers and which he also produced, and *Gunga Din* (released February 17, 1939) with Cary Grant, Victor McLaglen, Douglas Fairbanks, Jr, Sam Jaffe in the title role, Eduardo Ciannelli and Joan Fontaine. His 1940 film *Vigil In The Night* with Carole Lombard was unusual in that it had two endings – one for Europe and one for America. In 1941 Stevens signed a two-year contract with Columbia and his first film with them was *Penny Serenade* (1941). The following year at the insistence of Katharine Hepburn MGM hired Stevens from Columbia to direct her and Spencer Tracy in *Woman Of The Year* (released January 19, 1942), their first film together. The film won an Oscar for Best Writing, Original Screenplay (Michael Kanin and Ring

Lardner, Jr) and Hepburn was nominated as Best Actress. Back at Columbia Stevens helmed *The Talk Of The Town* (released August 20, 1942) with Cary Grant, Jean Arthur and Ronald Colman. His last film at Columbia was *The More The Merrier* (premièred March 26, 1943), a romantic comedy that earned Stevens a Best Director Academy Award nomination. Between 1933 and 1943 Stevens gave the public what they wanted, two hours or so of escapist entertainment and he pleased his studio bosses by ensuring a healthy box office return. Stevens little relied on scripts, preferring improvisation. He spent hours cutting and editing his films until he was satisfied. In the summer of 1943 Stevens was recruited by General Dwight D. Eisenhower to lead the Special Motion Picture Coverage Unit of the US Army Signal Corps. Stevens' task was to document the American army in the European theatre of war. He was the first American to document the horrors of the Dachau concentration camp. Some of his footage was used at the Nuremberg Trials. Stevens was demobbed in 1945 with the rank of lieutenant colonel. As with many others, Stevens found it difficult to come to terms with civilian life after the war. With Samuel J. Briskin and two other cinematic colonels, William Wyler and Frank Capra, he formed Liberty Films to make movies for "a better America". The company made just two films, *It's A Wonderful Life* (1946) and *State Of The Union* (1948). In 1948 Liberty loaned Stevens to RKO to direct Irene Dunne in *I Remember Mama*. It was the last film Stevens made that had comedy. In 1949 Liberty Films went broke and merged with Paramount. That year Stevens began work on what would become *A Place In The Sun* (1951) with Elizabeth Taylor, Montgomery Clift and Shelley Winters. The update of Theodore Dreiser's *An American*

Tragedy won him the Best Director Oscar and the production won four other Academy Awards. The time that Stevens had taken to make the film angered Paramount and Liberty Films was cast adrift. Thus the next film, *Something To Live For* (1952) with Ray Milland and Joan Fontaine, was made quickly with the result that it flopped and was quickly forgotten. Determined to return to the top of his game, Stevens saw how successful *High Noon* (1952) had been and decided to direct a Western. The film Stevens made between late July and mid-October 1951 was *Shane* (premièred April 23, 1953) starring Alan Ladd as a weary gunfighter who becomes a child's hero and Jean Arthur in her last cinematic role. The film won a Best Colour Cinematography Oscar (Loyal Griggs) and was nominated for five more including Best Picture and Best Director for Stevens. *Shane* was the third most successful film at the box office in 1953. The *New York Post* said the film was "only a Western in the sense that *Romeo And Juliet* is only a love story". It could have been a very different film. Stevens originally cast Montgomery Clift as Shane, and William Holden as Joe Starrett (played by Van Heflin). At the Oscars on March 25, 1954 David O. Selznick presented Stevens with the Irving G. Thalberg Memorial Award. *Shane* re-established Stevens's reputation so he took his time on his next project. *Giant* (premièred October 10, 1956) about two generations of Texan rivalry starred James Dean, Rock Hudson, Elizabeth Taylor, Carroll Baker, Jane Withers, Chill Wills, Mercedes McCambridge, Dennis Hopper and Sal Mineo. On the set Stevens encouraged a rivalry between Dean and Hudson and irritated Elizabeth Taylor by his constant retakes and loud utterances that he wished that his original choice Grace Kelly had been available. It won Stevens another Best Director Oscar. Stevens then made *The Diary Of Anne*

Frank (1959) starring the Catholic Millie Perkins as the teenage Jewish diarist who hid from the Germans in an Amsterdam attic. Stevens spent six years on his penultimate film *The Greatest Story Ever Told* (premièred February 15, 1965) and cast Max Von Sydow as Jesus and a pantheon of stars in cameo roles including John Wayne as a centurion! However, the film was a box office flop and Stevens lost confidence in his ability to discern what the public liked. In October 1965 Stevens sued NBC and Paramount for what he believed was a butchering of his *A Place In The Sun* when they edited it for television. Stevens was awarded $1 million in damages. His last film, *The Only Game In Town* (1970) starring Elizabeth Taylor and Warren Beatty, also tanked at the box office allowing critics to write Stevens off as a has-been. 5′11″ George Stevens married Yvonne Howell on New Year's Day 1930 but they separated in 1937. It took until 1947 for their court battles over alimony and child support to be settled. Their son George Stevens, Jr was born in Los Angeles, California on April 3, 1932. In June 1968 he married Joan Pauline McTavish.

CAUSE: Stevens died of a heart attack on his ranch at Lancaster, California. He was 68.

Inger Stevens

(INGER STENSLAND)
Born October 18, 1933
Died April 30, 1970
Swedish siren. Born in Stockholm, the daughter of a professor, Inger was abandoned aged five when her mother ran off with another man. Inger was raised by an aunt and uncle while her father continued his academia. In 1946 she moved to America to stay with her father who was studying at Harvard. She knew just two words of English, 'Yes' and 'No', but was too shy to admit to her ignorance. Reunited with her father and a new stepmother, Swedish was banned at home. She

finally learnt to speak English without an accent but ironically had to utilise a Swedish accent in the 1963 television show *The Farmer's Daughter* in which she played Katy Holstrum. In 1949 the family moved to Manhattan, Kansas, but Inger was unhappy and left home, landing a job in burlesque. Her father brought her back home and she returned to school, where she studied drama. In 1951 she moved to New York and worked in a variety of jobs, including modelling, to support herself. She auditioned for and was accepted by Lee Strasberg's Actors' Studio. That led to her first acting job, playing a tired housewife in a television advertisement. She met Anthony Soglio who became her manager and lover and changed her name to Stevens. On July 1, 1955, they were married but separated within six months and divorced in 1958. However, Soglio continued to take 5 per cent of her salary until 1966 under the contract she signed with him. She made her film début in *Man On Fire* (1957) playing Nina Wylie opposite Bing Crosby. They began an affair but he broke her heart when he married Kathryn Grant in October 1957. Although *Man On Fire* won good reviews, it would be one of just four films she made in the Fifties. She lost out to Kim Novak for Hitchcock's *Vertigo* (1958) and almost died playing Mrs Joan Molner in *Cry Terror* (1958) when a generator expelled noxious carbon monoxide fumes and she and 11 crew members were hospitalised. During filming of *The Buccaneer* (1958) in which she was Annette Claiborne she began a passionate affair with co-star Anthony Quinn; her affair with Crosby had turned her on to older men. During *The World, The Flesh And The Devil* (1959), in which she portrayed Sarah Crandall, she romanced Harry Belafonte. In December 1959 she moved back east. On New Year's Eve of that year following a party, she attempted suicide by taking 25 sleeping pills and drinking half a bottle of ammonia. Her unconscious body was found three days later and she was rushed to Columbus Hospital; blood clots were found under her left lung, she was blind and her legs were swollen to four times their normal size with phlebitis. After a fortnight, her eyesight gradually returned. In June 1961 she barely escaped from a burning aeroplane that crashed at Lisbon. She was Emmy nominated in 1962 for *The Price Of Tomatoes*. She wouldn't make another film until the hospital soap *The New Interns* (1964), in which she played Nancy Terman. That decade she appeared in *Hang 'Em High* (1967) as Rachel, *A Guide For The Married Man* (1967) as Ruth Manning, *A Time For Killing* (1967) as Emily Biddle, the cop drama *Madigan* (1968) as Julia Madigan, *Firecreek* (1968) as Evelyn Pittman, the Western *5 Card Stud* (1968) as Lily Langford, the thriller *House Of Cards* (1968) as Anne and her last film *A Dream Of Kings* (1969) as Anna. She made what was to be her last television movie, *Run, Simon, Run* as Carroll Rennard, in 1970 opposite Burt Reynolds, with whom she fell in love. However, when the film finished so did the romance.

CAUSE: Inger's body, clad in a negligee, was found face down in the kitchen of her home 8000 Woodrow Wilson Drive in the Hollywood Hills. She had taken Tedral washed down with alcohol and despite being rushed to Hollywood Receiving Hospital was pronounced dead on arrival at 10am. Following her death, it was revealed she had married black athlete-cum-producer Isaac Jones in Tijuana on November 18, 1961. She left no will and her body was cremated. She was 36.

James Stewart
Born May 20, 1908
Died July 2, 1997
Hollywood good guy. It is unusual for a man to live in Hollywood for so long and for no one to have a bad word to say about him. Such a man was the slow-speaking Jimmy Stewart. Born Indiana, Pennsylvania (population: 5,000), James Maitland Stewart was the eldest of three children; his mother played the organ at the local Presbyterian church. At Princeton University he studied architecture. It was film director Josh Logan who persuaded Stewart to give acting a try. As he struggled with bit parts on Broadway, Stewart shared a flat with Henry Fonda. When they ventured to Hollywood, they again shared a home. His first two roles were playing journalists. His wife in the second film was played by Margaret Sullavan, who later married Henry Fonda. The two actors later went their separate ways when divided by politics; Stewart was a staunch conservative. His early films included: *After The Thin Man* (1936) as David Graham, *Rose-Marie* (1936) as John Flower, *Small Town Girl* (1936) as Elmer, *Speed* (1936) as Terry Martin, *Born To Dance* (1936) as Ted Barker, *Seventh Heaven* (1937) as Chico, *Of Human Hearts* (1938) as Jason Wilkins, *The Shopworn Angel* (1938) as Private Bill Pettigrew, *You Can't Take It With You* (1938) as Tony Kirby, *It's A Wonderful World* (1939) as Guy Johnson, *Mr Smith Goes To Washington* (1939) as Jefferson Smith, for which he was nominated for an Oscar, *Destry Rides Again* (1939) as Thomas Jefferson Destry, *The Philadelphia Story* (1940) as Macaulay (Mike) Connor, which won him a Best Actor Oscar, and *Ziegfeld Girl* (1941) as Gilbert Young. During World War II he joined the air force and flew 20 missions over Germany, winning the Distinguished Flying Cross. (In 1968 he retired from Air Force Reserve with the rank of Brigadier General. He was awarded the Distinguished Service Medal, only the second time this honour has been conferred on a reserve officer.) Following the end of hostilities, he returned to Hollywood with a vengeance. He was nominated

for another Oscar for *It's A Wonderful Life* (1946) as George Bailey and appeared in *Call Northside 777* (1948) as P.J. McNeal, *Rope* (1948) as Rupert Cadell, *Winchester '73* (1950) as Lin McAdam, *Harvey* (1950) as Elwood P. Dowd, for which he was nominated for an Oscar, *Broken Arrow* (1950) as Tom Jeffords, *No Highway* (1951) as Theodore Honey, *The Greatest Show on Earth* (1952) as Buttons, *Bend Of The River* (1952) as Glyn McLyntock, *Rear Window* (1954) as L.B. 'Jeff' Jefferies, *The Glenn Miller Story* (1954) as Glenn Miller, *The Far Country* (1954) as Jeff Webster, *The Man From Laramie* (1955) as Will Lockhart, *The Man Who Knew Too Much* (1956) as Doctor Ben McKenna, *The Spirit Of St Louis* (1957) as Charles Augustus Lindbergh, *Vertigo* (1958) as John 'Scottie' Ferguson, *Bell, Book And Candle* (1958) as Shepherd Henderson, *Anatomy Of A Murder* (1959) as Paul Biegler, for which he was nominated for an Oscar, *The Man Who Shot Liberty Valance* (1962) as Ransom Stoddard, *Mr Hobbs Takes A Vacation* (1962) as Roger Hobbs, *How The West Was Won* (1962) as Linus Rawlings, *Cheyenne Autumn* (1964) as Wyatt Earp, *Shenandoah* (1965) as Charlie Anderson, *Dear Brigitte* (1965) as Professor Robert Leaf, *The Flight Of The Phoenix* (1965) as Frank Towns, *Bandolero!* (1968) as Mace Bishop, *The Shootist* (1976) as Doctor Hostetler, *Airport '77* (1977) as Philip Stevens, *The Magic Of Lassie* (1978) as Clovis Mitchell and *The Big Sleep* (1978) as General Sternwood. For many years he was one of Hollywood's most eligible bachelors. Lucille Ball once commented: "Jimmy Stewart is sort of square. Even in the early days he told me his idea of a romantic evening was soft lights, sweet music, champagne . . . no girl, just soft lights, sweet music and champagne." He finally married divorcee Gloria Hatrick McLean (b. Larchmont, New York, 1918, d. 918 Roxbury Drive, Beverly Hills,

February 16, 1994 of lung cancer) on August 9, 1949, and was a devoted husband. They had four children: Ronald (b. June 22, 1944) and Michael (b. 1945) from his wife's first marriage and non-identical twins, Kelly and Judy (b. May 7, 1951). Ronald was killed in Quang Tri province, Vietnam, on June 11, 1969, 11 days before his 25th birthday.

CAUSE: In December 1996 when the battery in his pacemaker was due to be changed, he told his children that he did not want the procedure carried out. Stewart simply lost the desire to live after the death of his beloved wife. On the last day of January 1997 he fell in his bedroom and gashed his head. Taken to St John's Hospital, Santa Monica, he was given a dozen stitches. Not long afterwards, he was readmitted to hospital suffering from a blood clot in his right knee and an irregular heartbeat. He spent his last months in bed watching television, refusing visitors and waiting to die. The passing came in Beverly Hills at 11.05am with a heart attack. He was 89 years old. On July 7, 1997, he was laid to rest next to his beloved wife in Forest Lawn Memorial-Parks, 1712 South Glendale Avenue, Glendale, California 91209. A 21-gun salute was fired in recognition of his war service. In October 1997 his house was bought for $5.6 million and razed to the ground.

FURTHER READING: *Everybody's Man: A Biography Of Jimmy Stewart* – Jhan Robbins (London: Robson Books, 1985); *James Stewart: A Biography* – Donald Dewey (Atlanta: Turner Publishing, 1996).

Major Nigel Stock
Born September 21, 1919
Died June 22, 1986
Mr Dependability. Born in Malta, the son of Captain W.H. Stock of the Royal Engineers and Margaret Marion Munro, Stock was raised in India until the family returned to England. Stock was educated at RADA where he won

the Leverhulme Exhibition, Northcliffe Scholarship, and the Principal's Medal. He made his debut stage appearance at the Savoy Theatre in 1931 at the age of 12 in a production of *The Traveller In The Dark*. The Second World War interrupted his career and he served with the London Irish Rifles (1939–1941) and then the Assam Regiment of the Indian Army between 1941 and 1945 in Burma, China and Kohima. He was demobbed as a major and in 1946 returned to the stage. He had made his film debut in *The Man Who Could Work Miracles* (1936) and after the war appeared regularly in films such as *Brighton Rock* (1947) as Cubitt, *Derby Day* (1952) as Jim Molloy, a pilot in *The Night My Number Came Up* (1955), *The Dam Busters* (1955) as Flying Officer F.M. Spafford, D.F.C., D.F.M., *The Silent Enemy* (1958) as Able Seaman Fraser, *Victim* (1961) as Phip, *H.M.S. Defiant* (1962) as Senior Midshipman Kilpatrick, *The Night Of The Generals* (1967) as Otto, *The Lion In Winter* (1968) as Captain William Marshall, *Cromwell* (1970) as Sir Edward Hyde and *Young Sherlock Holmes* (1985) as Waxflatter. From 1964 until 1968 he was Dr Watson to Peter Cushing's Sherlock Holmes on the BBC and appeared in most of the popular drama series of the Sixties and Seventies. He was married three times, firstly to Catherine Hodnett (from April 29, 1943 until 1947) and with whom he had one son, Robert (born 1947), then actress Sonia Williams with whom he had three children, and finally actress Richenda Carey.
CAUSE: Stock died aged 66 of a heart attack in London, a month after he had appeared on stage with his third wife.

Lee Strasberg

(ISRAEL STRASSBERG)
Born November 17, 1901
Died February 17, 1982
Methodologist. Born in Budzanów, Austria-Hungary, and raised in New York from the age of seven, Strasberg's reputation has become polarised. He is either demonised or worshipped. From 1948 he ran the infamous Actors' Studio in New York and numbered some of Hollywood's greats under his patronage, including Marlon Brando, Montgomery Clift, Robert De Niro, James Dean, Sally Field, Jane Fonda, Julie Harris, Steve McQueen, Paul Newman, Al Pacino, Geraldine Page, Maureen Stapleton and Rod Steiger. The 'Method' required actors to dredge up personal feelings in order to play a role. Some believed in it wholeheartedly; others, such as Laurence Olivier, dismissed it. Strasberg once opined that he had taught two great acting talents: Marilyn Monroe and Brando. When Marilyn married Arthur Miller it was Strasberg who gave the bride away. Six years later, he delivered the eulogy at her funeral. He turned to acting in later life, appearing in *The Godfather: Part II* (1974) as Hyman Roth, for which he was nominated for a Best Supporting Actor Oscar, *The Cassandra Crossing* (1976) as Herman Kaplan, *Going In Style* (1979) as Willie, *Boardwalk* (1979) as David Rosen, and *. . . And Justice For All* (1979) as Grandpa Sam. He was thrice married: firstly, to Nora Z. Krecaun, then to Paula Miller (b. 1911, d. April 1966 of heart failure exacerbated by cancer) by whom he had two children, Susan (see below) and John (b. May 20, 1941), and then to Anna Mizrahi, who survived him. CAUSE: He died in New York aged 80 of natural causes.

Susan Strasberg

Born May 22, 1938
Died January 21, 1999
Acting scion. Born in Sydenham Hospital, New York, at midday Susan Elizabeth Strasberg was the daughter of Method acting guru Lee Strasberg. She made her name in the 1955 Broadway production of *The Diary Of Anne Frank*. However, the Sixties were not

kind to her and she faded from view during the decade. She wrote two volumes of memoirs, *Bittersweet* and *Marilyn & Me*. Among Strasberg's films were *In Praise Of Older Women* (1978) in which she bared her breasts, *Rollercoaster* (1986) and *The Delta Force* (1989). On September 25, 1965, in Las Vegas she married Christopher Jones and their daughter, Jennifer Robin, was born six months later on March 14, 1966, at 4.43pm.

CAUSE: She died in New York, New York, of breast cancer. She was 60.

FURTHER READING: *Bittersweet* – Susan Strasberg (New York: Signet, 1980); *Marilyn & Me* – Susan Strasberg (London: Doubleday, 1992).

Dorothy Stratten

(DOROTHY RUTH HOOGSTRATEN)
Born February 28, 1960
Died August 14, 1980

The Unicorn. Blonde and beautiful 5'9" Dorothy Stratten was born in a Salvation Army Hospital in Vancouver, British Columbia, Canada and was working as a waitress at a snack bar when she was spotted by a pimp and small-time hustler called Paul Leslie Snider (b. April 15, 1951) in October 1977. Four months later, after a fight with her first boyfriend she began seeing Snider. He persuaded her to pose nude for him and, in August 1978, after forging her mother Nellie's signature on the model release, sent her pictures to *Playboy* for the magazine's 25th Anniversary Playmate Contest. The magazine was impressed and offered 36-24-36 Dorothy a pictorial. Snider saw the opportunity to make some money and he persuaded Dorothy to marry him at the Silver Bell Wedding Chapel in Las Vegas on June 1, 1979. She was an instant hit at Playboy Inc., becoming Miss August of 1979 and later Playmate of The Year. She also moved into the Playboy Mansion. Snider used the money she had earned ($200,000 as Playmate of the Year) to finance several unsuccessful business ventures. Soon afterwards she and Snider split up and Dorothy became involved with film director Peter Bogdanovich, moving into his house at 212 Copa de Oro, Bel Air. Snider, insane with jealousy, hired a private detective to follow his estranged wife. She had been cast in a number of films including *Autumn Born* (1979), *Skatetown USA* (1979), *Galaxina* (1980), and Bogdanovich's *They All Laughed* (1981) and looked to become *Playboy*'s first superstar. It was not to be. Two films professed to tell the story of Dorothy Stratten – *Death Of A Centerfold: The Dorothy Stratten Story* (1981) and *Star 80* (1983), which was filmed in the actual apartment in which Dorothy died.

CAUSE: Snider rang Dorothy and told her he needed to discuss a financial settlement with her. Dorothy, naïve and kind-hearted and with $1,000 to give to Snider in her handbag, went to the house she had shared with him at 10881 Clarkson Road, West Los Angeles. There Snider tied her up, raped, tortured and sodomised her before blowing her head and tip of her left index finger off with a 12-gauge Mossberg shotgun. He had intercourse with her corpse before turning the weapon on himself. Their bodies lay undiscovered until 11pm that night because the other people in the house, a doctor and two women, thought they wanted privacy. In her Playmate Data sheet, in which the models reveal their likes and dislikes, Dorothy listed her major turn-off as "jealous people". On August 19, Dorothy's remains were cremated and she was buried in Westwood Village Memorial Park, 1218 Glendon Avenue, Los Angeles 90024. A bizarre footnote: on January 1, 1989, Peter Bogdanovich married Dorothy Stratten's younger sister, Louise who was born on May 8, 1968, the year after Bogdanovich's own daughter.

FURTHER READING: *The Killing Of The Unicorn: Dorothy Stratten 1960–1980* –

Peter Bogdanovich (London: Futura 1985).

Margaret Sullavan
Born May 16, 1909
Died January 1, 1960
Suicidally depressed actress. Born in Norfolk, Virginia, the daughter of a wealthy stockbroker, Margaret Brooke Sullavan was a sickly infant who later attended private schools, where she gained a reputation as a wild child. She made her Broadway début in *A Modern Virgin* in 1931. On Christmas Day 1931 she married Henry Fonda at the Kernan Hotel in Baltimore, Maryland, but they quickly separated and were divorced in 1933, the year she signed with Universal. Her film début came in *Only Yesterday* (1933) as Mary Lane. On November 25, 1934, in Yuma, Arizona, she married director William Wyler but they divorced on March 13, 1936. On November 15 of that year she married agent Leland Hayward, by whom she had three children: Brooke (b. July 4, 1937), Bridget (b. 1938, d. New York, October 1960, by her own hand) and William Leland III (b. Los Angeles, California, March 27, 1941, d. shot himself at Castaic, California, March 9, 2008). Both Bridget and Bill would spend time confined in mental institutions. Sullavan's films included: *Little Man, What Now?* (1934) as Lammchen Pinneberg, *So Red The Rose* (1935) as Valette Bedford, *Next Time We Love* (1936) as Cicely Tyler, *Three Comrades* (1938) as Pat Hollmann, *The Shopworn Angel* (1938) as Daisy Heath, *The Shop Around The Corner* (1940) as Klara Novak, *Appointment For Love* (1941) as Jane Alexander, *So Ends Our Night* (1941) as Ruth Holland, *Back Street* (1941) as Rae Smith, *Cry Havoc* (1943) as Lieutenant Mary Smith and her final flick *No Sad Songs For Me* (1950) as Mary Scott. She and Hayward were divorced in 1948 and in 1950 she married British industrialist Kenneth Arthur Wagg.
CAUSE: She died of a barbiturate overdose aged 50 in New Haven, Connecticut. A coroner later ruled her death accidental.
FURTHER READING: *Haywire –* Brooke Hayward (New York: Bantam, 1978).

Gloria Swanson
(GLORIA JOSEPHINE MAE SWENSON)
Born March 27, 1898
Died April 4, 1983
Forever Norma Desmond. Born in Chicago, Illinois, Swanson was a silent screen actress who for a time successfully managed the transition to the talkies. She began her career as Mack Sennett's leading lady at his Keystone studio. It was thanks to Cecil B. DeMille that she became a star in *Male And Female* (1919). She came to her wedding bed on her 18th birthday with fellow actor Wallace Beery. A virgin on her wedding day, the night that followed left Swanson feeling brutalised and physically hurt. After intercourse, Beery fell asleep; Swanson passed the rest of her wedding night on the floor of the bathroom, using towels to ease her pain and to staunch the bleeding that Beery's aggression had caused. On December 13, 1918, Beery received a divorce on the grounds of desertion. In 1928 Swanson received her first Academy Award nomination for *Sadie Thompson*. The same year, bankrolled by her lover, Presidential father Joseph P. Kennedy, she made *Queen Kelly*. It was directed by Erich von Stroheim, who wasted immense amounts of money on the feature; it flopped. In 1934 she announced her retirement from the screen. She made a comeback in 1941 in *Father Takes A Wife* but it would be nine years again before she was back in movie houses. The wait was worthwhile, as it produced the superb *Sunset Blvd.* (1950), a film that earned her another Oscar nomination. (She didn't win.) She lapsed back into retirement, making the occasional foray into film-making and promoting health

foods. (She was a vegetarian.) It was Swanson's affair with Joe Kennedy (they met for the first time in Renaissance Room of the Savoy Plaza Hotel on 5th Avenue and 59th Street on November 11, 1927) that wrecked her third marriage, to Henri, Marquis de la Falaise. (He went on to marry Constance Bennett.) One day aboard the family yacht the two lovers were espied by the then 11-year-old Jack Kennedy. He was so horrified by what he had witnessed that he jumped overboard and his father had to rescue him. By 1929 Joe was tiring of his movie star mistress and ended the affair. Afterwards, she discovered that a fur coat he had given her had actually been paid for out of her money. Uniquely, Swanson played herself in two films 51 years apart! They were *Hollywood* in 1923 and *Airport 1975* (1974). Lapsing back into retirement she commented: "Since there is no more live television it's getting harder to prove you're not dead." She was a gifted sculptress and exhibited in London.

CAUSE: She died in her sleep aged 85 at The New York Hospital, 525 East 68th Street, New York City. She had been admitted on March 20, supposedly to treat a minor coronary. The following day she was cremated at Trinity Church Crematory and her ashes interred in the Church of Heavenly Rest, New York City.

FURTHER READING: *Swanson On Swanson* – Gloria Swanson (London: Michael Joseph, 1980).

Patrick Swayze

Born August 18, 1952
Died September 14, 2009
Dirty dancer. Patrick Wayne Swayze was born in Houston, Texas, the son of Jesse Wayne Swayze (b. September 20, 1925, d. November 1982 of a heart attack), an engineer and rodeo cowboy, and Patsy Swayze (b. 1927), a dance teacher and choreographer. He had four siblings: two brothers, 6′ actor

Donald Carl (born August 10, 1958) and teamster Sean Kyle (born 1962), and two sisters, dancer Vicky Lynn (b. June 8, 1949, d. Los Angeles, California, December 2, 1994 by her own hand) and Bambi (b. Korea 1967, who was adopted). After an education at San Jacinto, a community college in Texas, Swayze became a member of Eliot Feld Ballet in New York. He made his Broadway debut in 1975 as a dancer in *Goodtime Charley* before taking over the lead role in *Grease*. He made his film début as Ace in the roller-disco movie *Skatetown, U.S.A.* (1979). Kevin Thomas wrote in the *LA Times*, "Not since Valentino did his tango in *The Four Horsemen Of The Apocalypse* has there been such a confident display of male sexuality as when a lithe newcomer to films named Patrick Swayze hits the rink." Swayze later said, "I saw that with not too much trouble I could become a teenybopper star, but I knew if I accepted that, it would take years to win credibility as a serious actor." In 1982 after the death of his father, Swayze who smoked 60 cigarettes-a-day developed a drink problem. He blamed success (even though he wasn't that well-known when he began boozing). "[Fame] can make you feel you've somehow pulled off an enormous hoax and that your whole life is a lie. All the hype wound up making me cynical, and I turned into a not-very-pretty drunk." In 1989 he smashed up a hotel room and quit alcohol the next day. But the problem reoccurred especially after his sister Vicky killed herself with a drugs overdose and he went into rehab. "I have a wild-man edge," Swayze once said. "If my life looks good, I sabotage it." His first critically acclaimed film was Francis Ford Coppola's *The Outsiders* (1983), a drama about teenage gangs, which also featured other newcomers like Tom Cruise, Rob Lowe, Matt Dillon and Emilio Estevez. *Red Dawn* (1984) was a success as was the mini-series *North And South* (1985), in which he played Orry Main, a conflicted Confederate soldier. Two years later, Swayze found stardom in the low-budget *Dirty Dancing* (1987) as working class dance instructor Johnny Castle hired to work in a Catskills resort. The film had been intended for one weekend in cinemas before going to video. It was a surprise hit and when it did go to tape, it became the first film on VHS to sell one million copies. 5'10" Swayze thought that people relived "those wonderfully painful moments . . . when you just need to love somebody with all your heart and to be loved back . . . Plus, it was a pretty sexy movie." He added, "*Dirty Dancing* was what sent my career into hyper space. I've had mothers from all over the world happily say, 'You're the reason my daughter lost her virginity.'" After *Dirty Dancing*, Swayze's career was in the doldrums until he starred with Demi Moore in *Ghost* (1990). "I needed to do something that will affect the audience in a positive way, make them feel better about their lives and appreciate what they have," he said of the film. The following year he appeared as a bank-robbing surfer in *Point Break* and *People* named him the "Sexiest Man Alive". He played Vida Boheme, a drag queen, in *To Wong Foo, Thanks For Everything, Julie Newmar* (1995), which won him his third Golden Globe nomination. (The others were for *Dirty Dancing* and *Ghost*.) In 1998 Swayze broke both legs and detached four tendons in his shoulder after falling from a horse while filming HBO's *Letters From A Killer* near Ione, California. In 2000 he appeared in *Waking Up In Reno*, with

Billy Bob Thornton and Charlize Theron, and in *Forever Lulu*, with Melanie Griffith. He played a motivational speaker who happened to be a paedophile in *Donnie Darko* (2001). In 2004 Swayze played Allan Quatermain in *King Solomon's Mines* and had a bit part in the *Dirty Dancing* sequel, *Dirty Dancing: Havana Nights* as an unnamed dance teacher. From July 27, 2006 until November 25, 2006 he played Nathan Detroit in *Guys And Dolls*, his West End theatre début. The following year he appeared with younger brother Don in a film for the first time in *Powder Blue*. It was to be his last film. On June 12, 1975 he married Lisa Niemi (b. Houston, May 26, 1956). Of his acting, he said, "The only plan I have is that every time people think they have me pegged, I'm going to come out of left field and do something unexpected."

CAUSE: In January 2008 Swayze was diagnosed with pancreatic cancer. In April he was hospitalised with pneumonia but seemed to make a recovery, each time fighting off reports of his death. He was released after a week and went home to rest. Naturally, he was furious with tabloid reports that seemed to want to kill him off referring to such "reckless reporting" as "emotional cruelty when hope is so precious". In mind, he had magazines like the *National Enquirer*, which ran a headline, "Patrick Swayze Has 5 Weeks To Live". He died in Los Angeles twenty months after the initial diagnosis. He was 57.

FURTHER READING: *Patrick Swayze –* Mitchell Kreugel (New York: St Martin's Press, 1988).

T

Sydney Tafler
Born July 31, 1916
Died November 8, 1979
Working-class spiv. Born in London, Tafler made his stage début aged 20, appearing in his first film six years later in *The Young Mr Pitt* (1942). Although a stalwart of British films, Tafler never became a star. He carved a niche as a small-time villain, someone you wouldn't want to bump into down a dark alley. In 1941 he married RADA-trained actress Joy Shelton (b. London, June 3, 1922, d. January 28, 2000, from emphysema) who was groomed for stardom by Gainsborough Studios before being unceremoniously dumped. She concentrated on raising their three children and only really resurfaced once they were adults. She converted to Judaism when she married Tafler. She made her last film in 1962, *HMS Defiant*. Tafler's films included: *Uneasy Terms* (1948) as Maysin, *London Belongs To Me* (1948), *It Always Rains On Sunday* (1948) as Morry Hyams, *Passport To Pimlico* (1949) as Fred Cowan, *Once A Sinner* (1950) as Jimmy Smart, *Mystery Junction* (1951), *The Lavender Hill Mob* (1951) as Clayton, *Hotel Sahara* (1951) as Corporal Pullar, *The Galloping Major* (1951) as Mr Leon, *Assassin For Hire* (1951) as Antonio Riccardi, *Wide Boy* (1952) as Benny, *Venetian Bird* (1952) as Boldesca, *Time Gentlemen Please!* (1952) as Joseph Spink, *Emergency Call* (1952) as Brett, *Blind Man's Bluff* (1952) as Rikki Martin, *There Was A Young Lady* (1953) as Johnny, *Operation Diplomat* (1953) as Wade, *Johnny On The Run* (1953) as Harry, *The Sea Shall Not Have Them* (1954) as Corporal Robb, *The Saint's Return* (1954) as Max Lennar, *Dial 999* (1955) as Alf Cressett, *A Kid For Two Farthings* (1955) as Madame Rita, *The Cockleshell Heroes* (1955) as the policeman, *Reach For The Sky* (1956) as Robert Desoutter, *Fire Maidens Of Outer Space* (1956) as Dr Higgins, *Carve Her Name With Pride* (1958) as Potter, *No Kidding* (1960) as Mr Rockbottom, *Make Mine Mink* (1960) as Mr Spanager, *Let's Get Married* (1960) as Pendle, *The Bulldog Breed* (1960) as the owner of a speedboat, *Sink The Bismarck!* (1960), *Carry On Regardless* (1961) as a strip club manager, *Alfie* (1966) as Frank and *The Spy Who Loved Me* (1977) as Liparus Captain. Not long before his death he and his wife toured in a production of *Barefoot In The Park*.
CAUSE: He died of cancer in London aged 63.

Constance Talmadge
Born April 19, 1898
Died November 23, 1973
'Dutch'. Born in Brooklyn, New York, Constance Alice Talmadge was the youngest of the three Talmadge sisters. Their father, Fred (b. Plainville, Connecticut, May 1868), was an alcoholic gambler and their mother, Peg (b. Spain 1861), the archetypal stage mother. She believed in and practised the philosophy "Get the money and get comfortable", meaning that although love was fine and dandy, jewellery was more substantive. As a child 5'7" Talmadge was nicknamed 'Dutch' because she was very tubby. She began making films in 1914 and, after appearing in innumerable short comedies, came to prominence in D.W. Griffith's *Intolerance* (1916) as The Mountain Girl/Marguerite de Valois. With the help of her brother-in-law, Joseph Schenck, her career took off. She was placed in highly successful sophisticated comedies, which meant she was never a rival to her more famous sister, who specialised in melodramas. On Boxing Day 1920 she eloped to Greenwich,

Connecticut, with John T. Pialogiou who made tobacco. The ceremony was a double wedding with her best friend Dorothy Gish, who married her leading man James Rennie. Mrs Talmadge was furious when she learned of the wedding and so were the Gishes, who accused Constance of leading Dorothy on. Neither marriage was to last. On June 1, 1922, Constance divorced her husband on the grounds of mental cruelty. With the advent of sound films, she retired because her strong Brooklyn accent was unsuitable for audiences. She never made a talkie. Her films included: *Uncle Bill* (1914) as Gladys, *Our Fairy Play* (1914), *The Moonstone Of Fez* (1914) as Winifred Osborne, *The Mysterious Lodger* (1914) as Lucy Lane, *In The Latin Quarter* (1914) as Marion, *In Bridal Attire* (1914) as Connie, *Forcing Dad's Consent* (1914) as Connie, *Fixing Their Dads* (1914), *Buddy's First Call* (1914), *Buddy's Downfall* (1914), *The Young Man Who Figgered* (1915) as Connie, *A Study In Tramps* (1915) as Connie, *Spades Are Trumps* (1915) as Connie, *The Master Of His House* (1915) as Connie, the title role in *The Lady Of Shalott* (1915), *Captivating Mary Carstairs* (1915), *Can You Beat It?* (1915), *Burglarious Billy* (1915) as Connie, *Billy's Wager* (1915) as Connie, *Billy The Bear Tamer* (1915) as Connie, *Bertie's Stratagem* (1915) as Connie, *The Missing Links* (1916) as Laura Haskins, *The Microscope Mystery* (1916) as Jessie Barton, *The Matrimaniac* (1916) as Marna Lewis, *Scandal* (1917) as Beatrix, *Betsy's Burglar* (1917) as Betsy Harlow, *Up The Road With Sallie* (1918) as Sallie Waters, *Sauce For The Goose* (1918) as Kitty Constable, *Mrs Leffingwell's Boots* (1918) as Mrs Leffingwell, *Good Night, Paul* (1918) as Mrs Richard, *Romance And Arabella* (1919) as Arabella Cadenhouse, *Who Cares?* (1919) as Joan Ludlow, *Experimental Marriage* (1919) as Suzanne Ercoll, *Happiness A La Mode* (1919) as Barbara Townsend, *The Veiled Adventure* (1919) as

Geraldine Barker, *A Virtuous Vamp* (1919) as Gwendolyn Armitage, *Good References* (1920) as Mary Wayne, *Two Weeks* (1920) as Lillums, *In Search Of A Sinner* (1920) as Georgianna Chadbourne, *Dangerous Business* (1920) as Nancy Flavelle, *Wedding Bells* (1921) as Rosalie Wayne, *Lessons In Love* (1921) as Leila Calthorpe, *Mama's Affair* (1921) as Eve Orrin, *Polly Of The Follies* (1922) as Polly Meacham, *East Is West* (1922) as Ming Toy, *Dulcy* (1923) as Dulcy, *The Dangerous Maid* (1923) as Barbara Winslow, *Learning To Love* (1925) as Patricia Stanhope, *Her Sister From Paris* (1925) as Helen Weyringer, *Venus Of Venice* (1927) as Carlotta, *Breakfast At Sunrise* (1927) as Madeleine and *Venus* (1929) as Princess Beatrice Doriani. Following her divorce, she married three more times. In February 1926 she married Captain Alistair MacIntosh in California, divorcing him in Edinburgh on October 15, 1927, on the grounds of misconduct. On May 8, 1929, at the Beverly Hills home of her sister Natalie and brother-in-law Buster Keaton, she married Townsend Netcher, an heir to a Chicago department store. That marriage also ended in divorce. In 1939 she married a New York stockbroker called Walter Michael Giblin (d. New York, May 1, 1964).
CAUSE: She died aged 75 in Los Angeles, California, from pneumonia. She was buried alongside her sisters in Corridor G-7 of the Family Room, in the Abbey of the Psalms, of Hollywood Memorial Park, 6000 Santa Monica Boulevard, Hollywood, California 90038.

Norma Talmadge
Born May 26, 1895
Died December 24, 1957
'The lady of the great indoors'. Born in Jersey City, New Jersey, she was the eldest of the Talmadge sisters, all of whom their mother had tried to 'abort' by riding the dodgems at Coney Island.

When Norma was 17, her mother noticed an advertisement from a photographer who was paying girls $5 a day to pose for sheet music covers. Peg landed the job for her 5'4" daughter, whose age she dropped to 14, and then began hawking her picture around film studios. Within four years Norma was a star with her own production company in New York at 320 East 48th Street and taking home $1,000 a week. Her early films included: *The Household Pest* (1909), *Uncle Tom's Cabin* (1910), *In Neighboring Kingdoms* (1910), *Love Of Chrysanthemum* (1910), *Paola And Francesca* (1911), *A Tale Of Two Cities* (1911), *Forgotten* (1911), *Her Hero* (1911), *The Lovesick Maidens Of Cuddleton* (1912), *Fortunes Of A Composer* (1912), *Casey At The Bat* (1912), *Captain Barnacle's Messmate* (1912), *Mrs Carter's Necklace* (1912), *Mrs 'Enry 'Awkins* (1912), *Counsel For The Defense* (1912), *Captain Barnacle's Waif* (1912), *Captain Barnacle, Reformer* (1912), *Wanted, A Stronghand* (1913), *O'Hara, Squatter And Philosopher* (1913), *O'Hara As A Guardian Angel* (1913), *His Official Appointment* (1913), *Extremities* (1913), *'Arriet's Baby* (1913), *Just Show People* (1913), *O'Hara's Goldchild* (1913), *The Silver Cigarette Case* (1913), *The Doctor's Secret* (1913), *His Silver Bachelorhood* (1913), *Sunshine And Shadows* (1914), *Sawdust And Salome* (1914), *Politics And The Press* (1914), *Old Reliable* (1914), *His Little Page* (1914), *Goodbye Summer* (1914), *Miser Murray's Wedding Present* (1914), *Fogg's Millions* (1914), *Captivating Mary Carstairs* (1915) as Mary Carstairs, *Janet Of The Chorus* (1915), *Elsa's Brother* (1915), *Going Straight* (1916) as Grace Remington, *Fifty-Fifty* (1916) as Naomi and the film that made her a star, *Panthea* (1917), as Panthea Romoff. The producer, Joseph Schenck, was determined to get Norma into bed; her mother was equally determined that nothing of the sort should occur. On October 20, 1916, he persuaded Irving Berlin to take Mrs Talmadge to the theatre. In the meantime he and Norma eloped to Connecticut. When Mrs Talmadge saw a screening of *Panthea* she told Schenck that perhaps he wouldn't make such a bad son-in-law after all. "I'm glad you feel that way," he replied. "I've been your son-in-law for two months already." In 1922 Talmadge moved her studio to Hollywood. Her films were aimed predominantly at a female audience and included: *Poppy* (1917) as Poppy Destinn, *By Right Of Purchase* (1918) as Margot Hughes, *De Luxe Annie* (1918) as Julie Kendal, *Her Only Way* (1918) as Lucille Westbrook, *The New Moon* (1919) as Princess Marie Pavlovna, *The Way Of A Woman* (1919) as Nancy Lee, *She Loves And Lies* (1920) as Marie Callender, *The Branded Woman* (1920) as Ruth Sawyer, *Passion Flower* (1921) as Acacia, *The Wonderful Thing* (1921) as Jacqueline Laurentine Boggs, *Love's Redemption* (1921) as Jennie Dobson, *The Eternal Flame* (1922) as Duchesse de Langeais, *The Voice From The Minaret* (1923) as Lady Adrienne Carlyle, *Secrets* (1924) as Mary Carlton, *The Only Woman* (1924) as Helen Brinsley, *Graustark* (1925) as Princess Yetive, *Kiki* (1926) as Kiki, *Camille* (1927) as Marguerite Gautier (Camille), *The Dove* (1927) as Dolores, *The Woman Disputed* (1928) as Mary Ann Wagner, *New York Nights* (1929) as Jill Deverne and her final film, *Du Barry, Woman Of Passion* (1930) as Jeannette Vaubernier/Madame Du Barry. Her voice was not suitable for talkies and she retired from film-making when the silent era ended. Between 1922 and her retirement she earned an estimated $5 million. In 1927 hers were the first footprints enshrined at Grauman's Chinese Theater at 6925 Hollywood Boulevard, Central Hollywood. That same year, she and her sisters opened a real estate development in San Diego, California, called Talmadge Park. It is about a mile south-west of the San Diego State University campus and has streets named after each sister. On April 14, 1934, she divorced Schenck and married entertainer George Jessel nine days later. She joined the cast of Jessel's radio show, hoping the exposure would kick-start her film career. In fact, it had almost the opposite effect and the show was cancelled. She and Jessel were divorced on August 11, 1939. On December 4, 1946, she married Beverly Hills doctor Carvel James in Las Vegas. She has been commemorated in many ways. Talmadge Street in Hollywood is named after Norma and Constance. Norma Place in West Hollywood, California, is also named for her. CAUSE: Plagued with arthritis and confined to a wheelchair in the last years of her life, she died aged 62 of a stroke in Las Vegas, Nevada. She was buried alongside her sisters in Corridor G-7 of the Sanctuary of Eternal Love, in the Abbey of the Psalms, of Hollywood Memorial Park, 6000 Santa Monica Boulevard, Hollywood, California 90038.

Jessica Tandy

Born June 7, 1909
Died September 11, 1994
The second oldest Oscar winner. Born in London, and educated at the Ben Greet Academy of Acting, Jessica Tandy's career began on November 22, 1927, when she made her stage début as Sara Manderson in *The Manderson Girls* at Playroom Six. Her New York début came three years later and her first film role was two years after that, as a maid in *The Indiscretions Of Eve* (1932). She wouldn't make another film for eight years and she was to make less than 40 films during her career, preferring the stage. In 1932 she married actor Jack Hawkins in Winchmore Hill, London. Their daughter, Susan, was born in 1934 and they were divorced in 1940. She found

great happiness with her second husband, the actor Hume Cronyn, whom she married on September 27, 1942. They had two children: Christopher (b. 1946) and Tandy (b. 1947). Her films included: *Murder In The Family* (1938) as Ann Osborne, *The Seventh Cross* (1944) as Liesel Roeder, *The Valley Of Decision* (1945) as Louise Kane, *Dragonwyck* (1946) as Peggy O'Malley, *Forever Amber* (1947) as Nan Britton, *September Affair* (1950) as Catherine Lawrence, *Desert Fox* (1951) as Lucie Rommel, *Hemingway's Adventures Of A Young Man* (1962) as Mrs Adams, *The Birds* (1963) as Lydia Brenner, *Butley* (1974) as Edna Shaft, *Honky Tonk Freeway* (1981) as Carol, *Still Of The Night* (1982) as Grace Rice, *The World According To Garp* (1982) as Mrs Fields, *Cocoon* (1985) as Alma Finley, **batteries not included* (1987) as Faye Riley, *The House On Carroll Street* (1988) as Miss Venable, *Cocoon: The Return* (1988) reprising her role as Alma Finley and *Fried Green Tomatoes At The Whistle Stop Cafe* (1991) as the eccentric Ninny Threadgoode, for which she was nominated for a Best Supporting Actress Oscar. She lost out on the film version of *A Streetcar Named Desire*, having been the first to play Blanche DuBois on stage, because Warner Bros thought that at 5'4" she was too short. The part went to Vivien Leigh. Tandy was to win three Tonys, an Emmy and an Oscar for *Driving Miss Daisy* (1989) in which she portrayed Daisy Werthan. CAUSE: She died of ovarian cancer in Easton, Connecticut. She was 85.

Sharon Tate

Born January 24, 1943
Died August 9, 1969
Texas belle. Sharon Marie Tate vies with Dorothy Stratten for suffering the most horrible death in Hollywood history. Born in Dallas, Texas, she was the daughter of Colonel Paul Tate (b. June 23, 1922, d. May 18, 2005) of the US Army intelligence division and his

wife, Dorothy. When she was just six months old, Sharon became Miss Tiny Tot of Dallas, winning the title of Miss Autorama in Richmond, Washington in 1959. In 1963 she began appearing as Janet Trego on the television sitcom *The Beverly Hillbillies*. Attracted to dominant men, she started an affair with a French actor who once beat her up so badly she was hospitalised at UCLA Medical Center. In 1963 she met 5′6″ sadomasochistic hairdresser and drug pusher Jay Sebring (b. Fairfield, Alabama, October 10, 1933, as Thomas John Kummer; married model Cami October 1960, separated August 1963, divorced March 1965) and their relationship lasted until she met her 5′4″ future husband Roman Polanski in London in the summer of 1966. Sebring lived at 9820 Easton Drive, Beverly Hills, a house he had bought because of its 'far out' reputation. It was where Jean Harlow had lived with Paul Bern and where Bern died under mysterious circumstances in September 1932. Sebring and Sharon remained close friends to the end. In the meantime, she appeared in *The Wheeler Dealers* (1963), *The Americanization Of Emily* (1964), *The Sandpiper* (1965) and her first major role, as Odile, in *Eye Of The Devil* (1967) which was made in London. During filming she met Polanski and they were married at Chelsea Register Office in the King's Road on January 20, 1968. Among the people attending the wedding reception at the Playboy Club were David Bailey, Warren Beatty, Candice Bergen, Michael Caine, Joan Collins, Sean Connery, Mia Farrow, Brian Jones, John Mills, Rudolf Nureyev, Keith Richard, Vidal Sassoon, Peter Sellers, Terence Stamp and Kenneth Tynan. Despite the marriage Polanski saw no reason to give up his womanising. Sharon was furious at his behaviour, but didn't walk out of the marriage despite the urging of her friends. One, singer-turned-actress Michelle Phillips

of The Mamas And The Papas and later the TV soap *Knots Landing*, who herself had an affair with Polanski behind her pal's back, recalled: "Sharon had a sweetness about her that was rare. She just did not have any kind of mean-spiritedness in her. She was very open and genuine, not particularly intellectual, but people loved her because she was beautiful and because she made an effort to make everyone feel welcome and loved." Sharon had appeared in *Don't Make Waves* (1967) as Malibu, Polanski's *The Fearless Vampire Killers* (1967) as Sarah Shagal (he had taken semi-nude pictures of Sharon that appeared in the March 1967 edition of *Playboy* to promote the film), *Valley Of The Dolls* (1967) as breast cancer victim and actress Jennifer North, *The Wrecking Crew* (1969) as Freya Carlson and *12 Plus 1* (1970) as Pat. Sharon's career never really took off. She was beautiful and thus probably not taken as seriously as she could have been. As her character Jennifer North commented in *Valley Of The Dolls* in the act of taking a drug overdose: "I have no talent. All I have is a body." In 5′3″ Sharon's case, that wasn't strictly true, but it might just as well have been. In early 1969 the Polanskis learned that a house at 10050 Cielo Drive, in a secluded cul-de-sac, then occupied by Doris Day's son Terry Melcher, would be available to rent. On February 12, 1969, the couple signed a lease to rent the bungalow at $1,200 a month. They moved in three days later. Sharon was soon to discover she was pregnant and, despite Polanski's constant philandering, she put her marriage and her baby first, leaving her career on the back burner. She had been a regular pot smoker, had tried LSD and had indulged in kinky sex before and after she met Polanski. All of it stopped with the pregnancy. Sharon didn't tell Polanski she was pregnant until it was too late for her to have an abortion, but he was quickly enthused by the idea of becoming a father. (The novelty quickly wore off and he would return to constantly criticising his wife in front of others.) In April 1969 they moved to London. Sharon returned to America via the *QE2*, her pregnancy being too far advanced to fly. At Southampton, Polanski hugged his wife and began crying, telling her he would be with her as quickly as he could. However, once he left the ship he got into his Alfa Romeo, drove to London, rang his friend Victor Lownes and asked him to set him up with some girls. For the four months they were in London the Polanskis had leased the Cielo Drive house to his friend, 5'10" wannabe writer Wojiciech "Voytek" Frykowski (b. Łódź, Poland, December 22, 1936; m. Zakopane, Poland 1963 song writer and author Agnieszka Osiecka, divorced in 1964) and his girlfriend 5'5" coffee heiress and former volunteer social worker Abigail Anne 'Gibby' Folger (b. San Francisco, California, December 1943). They had moved in on April 1, 1969. During their tenancy they had operated an open house policy, with many people from the pornography industry and drug dealers dropping in. Sharon liked Gibby but hated Frykowski and suffered him only because he was a friend of Polanski. The losers and drop-outs continued to visit Cielo Drive, much to Sharon's vexation. She rang Polanski, who claimed he was working on a script and couldn't return to Bel Air just yet. To a friend he confined he couldn't stand the sight of a pregnant Sharon and decided to wait until after the birth in the hope she would return to her old self. She was also annoyed that Polanski had asked Frykowski to stay at Cielo Drive and look after her. Then she learned of her husband's affair with Michelle Phillips and considered divorce.

CAUSE: August 1969 was much like any other summer month in California, hot and humid. On Friday August 8, the temperature reached 92°. The heat wave had lasted for three days and the residents of Los Angeles were worried. The heat did strange things to many people. Four years earlier in August 1965, the black area of Watts had erupted into violence during one such heat wave. In the hills above the city in the enclave called Bel Air the temperature was around 80°. The house at 10050 Cielo Drive was festooned with Christmas tree lights, put there by a previous resident, the actress Candice Bergen. Sharon Tate rose around 9am and went for a swim. She then rang her husband in London at 11.30am. He told her he would be home on the twelfth in time for his 36th birthday six days later. She leaned heavily for emotional support on Jay Sebring but was still unhappy about the presence of Folger and Frykowski. About 12.30pm actress Joanna Pettet and Sharon's friend, Barbara Lewis, arrived for lunch, leaving three hours later. Around 6pm, 16-year-old Debbie Tate rang and asked her sister if she could visit but Sharon put her off and also cancelled a dinner party invitation she had for that night. Sebring later arrived to spend the evening with his friend. They went out to a Mexican restaurant, returning around 10.15pm. Folger went to her bedroom, took the stimulant MDA and began to read. Frykowski also took the drug and listened to music in the living room. At the opposite end of the house Sharon lay on her bed in a bikini chatting to Sebring. He drank beer and smoked a joint. Many people went to bed with their windows open during the warm weather and the windows were open at 10050 Cielo Drive that night. Outside the house preparing to butcher the occupants were four black clad members of 5'7" Charles Manson's so-called Family of hippies and drop-outs. They were former topless dancer, bar hustler and practising satanist Susan Denise 'Sadie' Atkins (b. Milbrea, California, May 7, 1948, d. Central California Women's facility,

Chowchilla, September 24, 2009 at 11.46pm of brain cancer), 6'2" Charles Denton 'Tex' Watson (b. Farmersville, Texas, December 2, 1945), former Sunday School teacher and insurance clerk Patricia Dianne 'Katie' Krenwinkel (b. December 3, 1947), and Linda Drouin Kasabian (b. 1949) who claimed she lost her nerve at the last minute and waited outside. She later became a prosecution witness. Believing the gate to be electrified, they scrambled onto the property over an embankment. Cutting the telephone lines, they first murdered 18-year-old Steven Parent, the caretaker. Watson levered open a window and climbed into the house letting his accomplices in via the front door. Watson shook awake Frykowski telling him: "I'm the devil. I'm here to do the devil's business." He then kicked Frykowski in the head. Atkins wandered around the house and saw Folger reading in bed. The coffee heiress looked up, smiled and waved. Atkins returned the greeting and then found Sharon's room before she went back to report to Watson. He gave Atkins a rope and she tied up Frykowski and then went to fetch Folger, Sharon and Sebring. Watson took another rope, tied Sebring's wrists and then put the rope around his neck before throwing the end over a ceiling beam. The other end he put around Sharon's neck. The four were ordered to lie face down and Sharon began to weep. Sebring protested at the treatment of his former lover and was shot in the left armpit by Watson for his troubles. He then tied Folger's hands with a length of the rope that bound Sharon's neck. He tied it around Sebring's neck and when he pulled it Sharon and Folger had to stand on their toes to avoid being strangled. When Sebring moaned, Watson rushed to him and began to stab and kick him until he made no more noise. Frykowski made a dash for freedom but was caught on the lawn where he was stabbed 51 times and

shot twice. As he finished off Sebring, Folger also made a run for it but eventually surrendered to Watson's mercies. He showed her none and she was stabbed 28 times, turning her nightie red. Her body was also discovered on the front lawn. Sharon pleaded for her life and that of her unborn baby. Susan Atkins screamed at her: "Look, bitch, I don't care about you! I don't care if you are going to have a baby! You had better be ready. You're going to die and I don't feel anything about it." Then Sharon suggested they take her with them until she gave birth in around a fortnight and then kill her but allow her baby to live. At this point Tex Watson lost it and ordered Atkins to kill Sharon but Atkins, herself the mother of a 10-month-old boy named Zezo-ce Zadfrak (b. Spahn Movie Ranch, California, October 7, 1968), hesitated. Krenwinkel urged her on, saying, "Either do, or let her go, or just bring her with us and let her have her fucking baby." The three argued while Sharon waited in silence. Then Watson slashed his knife towards Sharon's face and Atkins began a stabbing frenzy. She took hold of Sharon's limp body, cradled it in her arms, put her hand onto Sharon's breast and then licked the blood from her fingers. The four left but then remembered one of Manson's instructions. They drove back to the house and the word 'Pig' was daubed by Watson in Sharon's blood on the front door. When 'Coroner to the Stars' Thomas Noguchi did the autopsy on Sharon he reported that she had died of multiple stab wounds of the chest and back, penetrating the heart, lungs and liver, causing a massive haemorrhage. She had been stabbed 16 times, five of which would have been fatal in themselves. Incredibly, each stabbing had missed the foetus and it was removed intact from her womb. Doctors estimated the boy, named Richard Paul on his gravestone, lived around 20 minutes after his mother's murder. Around 8.30am the next morning the bodies were discovered by the Polanski housekeeper Winifred Chapman. The police were alerted at 9.14am. Rumours were rife about Sharon and Polanski, including suggestions that they had been involved in satanism, orgies and drug dealing and that the killings were a revenge for Polanski's film *Rosemary's Baby* (1968). All over the city celebrities flushed their stashes of drugs. "The entire Los Angeles sewer system is stoned," said one actor, only half jokingly. A rumour circulated that Polanski and Tate had filmed themselves making love and that tapes were found in the house. Tapes certainly did exist of Polanski and another woman in the marital bed. The following night the four killers plus Manson and Family member Leslie Sue Van Houten (b. Altadena, California, August 23, 1949) set off to create more mayhem in Los Angeles. That evening they butchered wealthy supermarket boss Pasqualino Antonio "Leno" LaBianca (b. Los Angeles, California August 6, 1925) and his wife, Rosemary (b. Arkansas, December 15, 1930), at their home 3301 Waverley Drive, near Griffith Park. Despite writing 'Death to Pigs' in Mr LaBianca's blood at the scene, police didn't link the two sets of murders. They believed the Tate murders were related to the burgeoning drug culture and the LaBianca killings the result of copycats. In mid-August the Family ranch was raided by police and 26 arrests made, but all were released the next day. Manson believed a ranch hand had alerted the authorities to the presence of himself and his acolytes and the man paid for this belief with his life. A lucky break finally led to the capture of the Family and they began to talk about the murders while in custody. On December 1, 1969, Watson, Krenwinkel and Kasabian were charged with murder. Later Manson, Atkins and Van Houten were similarly charged. Their trial began in 1970 and they were all sentenced to death on April 19, 1971. Before the sentences could be carried out the State of California abolished the death penalty and the punishments were commuted to life imprisonment. The lives of Paul and Doris Tate were wrecked by the tragedy. He took early retirement from the army, becoming a private investigator, and she opened a beauty parlour. It took the devoutly Catholic Mrs Tate six months before she could visit her daughter's grave. In 1982 she began to devote her life to ensuring that Sharon's killers never walked free. That year Leslie Van Houten's supporters arranged a petition containing 900 signatures demanding her release. Doris wrote a newspaper feature condemning the hearing and received 350,000 letters of support. She formed an organisation for victims' rights and was instrumental in the passing of the Victims' Rights Bill, which allows the family of those harmed to speak at the perpetrator's sentencing and subsequent parole hearings. In this position Mrs Tate attended parole hearings for Tex Watson and Susan Atkins. Watson, who has fathered three children since being incarcerated, was denied parole in 1985. Atkins, like Watson, claimed to have found God but Mrs Tate told her: "You're an excellent actress – the greatest since Sarah Bernhardt." Application denied. In 1990 Watson again applied for parole and again Mrs Tate turned up. Amazingly, one of those supporting his application was the daughter of Rosemary LaBianca. Doris reminded the hearing of the words spoken by Watson as he entered her daughter's home: "I'm the devil. I'm here to do the devil's business." "As far as I am concerned, Mr Watson," she went on, "you are still in business. What mercy, sir, did you show my daughter when she was begging for her life? For twenty-one years I have wanted to ask this prisoner 'Why?' He did not know my daughter. How can an individual, without any feelings, slice up this woman, eight-and-a-half months pregnant? What about my family? When will Sharon come up for parole? When will I come up for parole? Can you tell me that? Will the victims walk out of their graves if you get paroled?" Watson's application was denied. On July 11, 1992, aged 67, Doris Tate lost her battle against a brain tumour. Her youngest daughter Patti has taken on her mother's mantle and has successfully opposed parole applications from Atkins and Krenwinkel. Atkins wrote a self-serving book about her religious conversion, about which Patti commented: "I don't hear the words of someone who is rehabilitated. I hear the desperation of someone trying to get out of prison. She does not deserve to walk the free streets . . . ever." Patti Tate died of breast cancer on June 3, 2000 and her elder sister Debra (b. 1952) now campaigns to keep the Manson family behind bars.

FURTHER READING: *A Chronicle Of Death* – J.D. Russell (Woodbridge: Apollo, 1971); *Child of Satan, Child Of God* – Susan Atkins with Bob Slosser (London: Hodder & Stoughton, 1978); *Repulsion* – Thomas Kiernan (London: New English Library, 1981); *Helter Skelter* – Vincent Bugliosi with Curt Gentry (New York: Bantam, 1982); *Roman by Polanski* – Roman Polanski (London: William Heinemann, 1984); *The Family* – Ed Sanders (New York: Signet, 1989); *Sharon Tate And The Manson Murders* – Greg King (New York: Barricade Books, 2000).

Jacques Tati
(JACQUES TATISCHEFF)
Born October 9, 1908
Died November 5, 1982
Gallic comic. Born in Le Pecq, France, the son of an art restorer Tati joined the music hall as soon as he could and later moved into short films including

L'Ecole Des Facteurs (1947), which was later developed into the classic *Jour De Fête* (1949). He directed just six films in his 60-year career and is probably best known for creating the bumbling Monsieur Hulot; he was nominated for an Oscar for writing *Les Vacances De M. Hulot* (1952). Tati went bankrupt in his native France and often asked to be paid in Italian lire. He also did not rate fellow Frenchman Marcel Marceau at all and was mightily offended when writer Barry Took mentioned the mime artist once when talking to Tati. He won an Oscar for *Mon Oncle* (1958) but much of his later work was disappointing.
CAUSE: He died in Paris aged 73 from a pulmonary embolism.

Robert Taylor
(SPANGLER ARLINGTON BRUGH)
Born August 5, 1911
Died June 8, 1969
'The man with the perfect face'. Born in Filley, Nebraska, the son of a doctor, his mother, Ruth, was not expected to survive his birth. (Ironically, she would outlive him.) Nicknamed Arly, his original career plan was to be a concert cellist and he followed his music teacher to Pomona College, Claremont, California. There he began acting in college productions and was given a screen test by MGM, of which he later recalled: "It was awful. I could see they were disappointed." He was subsequently given a seven-year contract at the studio, paying $35 a week, making him among the lowest paid actors in Tinseltown history. He moved to Hollywood with his mother, whose health had rallied somewhat. Taylor was not impressed when the studio changed his name: "After having a distinguished name like Spangler Arlington Brugh, who could accept such a common name – Robert Taylor?" It wasn't until his eighth film, *Magnificent Obsession* (1935) in which he played Robert Merrick, that he became a star, earning $750 a week.

His very brief romantic entanglements came to nothing until he met Barbara Stanwyck. Opposite in almost every way, they nonetheless began discreetly seeing each other. In February 1939 they became engaged and three months later, on May 14, they married. The marriage came as something of a relief to MGM, who had been distinctly worried about Taylor's seeming lack of interest in women. Marriage to Stanwyck laid – at least publicly – his 'queer' image to rest; their million-dollar investment in him would not be threatened. Taylor's overbearing mother was not impressed and went on hunger strike to protest at the wedding, which she referred to as "it". Taylor spent his wedding night with his mother. He didn't enjoy spending time with his wife and claimed to have fallen in love with Lana Turner during the filming of *Johnny Eager* (1941). He went so far as to boast that their passion had been consummated, a claim she refuted. Taylor told Stanwyck he was in love with Turner and they had a brief break-up. In February 1943 he joined the US Navy, being discharged on November 5, 1945. The pair began to grow apart and when he befriended MGM worker Ralph Couser, Stanwyck became convinced the two men were having an affair. When Couser telephoned the Taylor home, Stanwyck would call out, "Hey, Bob, your wife wants to speak to you." Taylor became convinced he was gay and went to visit a psychologist. He was told that he saw Stanwyck as a mother figure and, therefore, could not become aroused by her. He later let it be known that he had an affair with Ava Gardner. In *The Conspirator* (1949) he gave Elizabeth Taylor her first screen kiss. Taylor later complained to his agent about the kiss but, at first, his co-star was ecstatic: "Today I grew up. No one can say I am a child in this picture, because I am playing Robert Taylor's wife! He is just as wonderful as everyone in Hollywood told me he

was. I have to admit I did get nervous when he took me in his arms and made love to me, but the director said I shouldn't be upset." Taylor, E.'s admiration for Taylor, R. soon turned to loathing. She claimed he went over the top in their love scenes and hurt her back when he bent her over to kiss her. She even went so far as to claim that he was responsible for the chronic back problems she suffered later in life. (In actual fact, they were caused by her falling off a horse while filming *National Velvet* [1944]). Taylor flew to Rome for six months to film *Quo Vadis* (1951) as Marcus Vinicius then, at $7 million, the biggest budget film in Hollywood history. The press reported rumours of Taylor's womanising but how much of this was invention is uncertain. Nonetheless, he and Stanwyck were divorced on February 21, 1951. On May 24, 1954, he married divorced actress Ursula Theiss (b. 1917) aboard a boat in Jackson Lake, Jackson, Wyoming. A son, Terrance, was born on June 18, 1955, followed on August 16, 1959, by daughter Theresa. Theiss already had two children: 10-year-old Emanuela and 9-year-old Michael (who in 1963 would be arrested in Munich for attempted murder and who committed suicide in May 1969). With Theiss he found a new lease of life and felt his attraction to men almost disappear. He once yelled at Stanwyck: "At least I can get it up with her." His career was not so successful. The large roles dwindled and he made the television series *The Detectives Starring Robert Taylor* (1959) playing Detective Captain Matt Holbrook. His films included: *Handy Andy* (1934) as Lloyd Burmeister, *West Point Of The Air* (1935) as Jaskerelli, *Times Square Lady* (1935) as Steve Gordon, *Murder In The Fleet* (1935) as Lieutenant Tom Randolph, *Society Doctor* (1935) as Dr Tommy 'Sprout' Ellis, *Broadway Melody Of 1936* (1935) as Bob Gordon, *Private Number* (1936) as Richard Winfield, *Small Town Girl*

(1936) as Dr Robert Dakin, *Camille* (1937) as Armand Duval, *Personal Property* (1937) as Raymond Dabney, *This Is My Affair* (1937) as Lieutenant Richard Perry, *Broadway Melody Of 1938* (1937) as Steve Raleigh, *A Yank At Oxford* (1938) as Lee Sheridan, *Three Comrades* (1938) as Erich Lohkamp, *Remember?* (1939) as Jeff Holland, *Lady Of The Tropics* (1939) as Bill Carey, *Lucky Night* (1939) as William Overton, *Stand Up And Fight* (1939) as Blake Cantrell, *Waterloo Bridge* (1940) as Roy Cronin, *Flight Command* (1940) as Ensign Alan Drake, *Escape* (1940) as Mark Preysing, *When Ladies Meet* (1941) as Jimmy Lee, *Johnny Eager* (1941) as Johnny Eager, *Billy The Kid* (1941) as William 'Billy the Kid' Bonney, *Her Cardboard Lover* (1942) as Terry Trindale, *Stand By For Action* (1943) as Lieutenant Gregg Masterson, *Song Of Russia* (1943) as John Meredith, *Bataan* (1943) as Sergeant Bill Dane, *Undercurrent* (1946) as Alan Garroway, *Conspirator* (1949) as Major Michael Currah, *Ambush* (1949) as Ward Kinsman, *Westward The Women* (1951) as Buck Wyat, *Ivanhoe* (1952) as Ivanhoe, *Above And Beyond* (1952) as Colonel Paul Tibbets, *Ride, Vaquero!* (1953) as Rio, *Knights Of The Round Table* (1953) as Sir Lancelot, *All The Brothers Were Valiant* (1953) as Joel Shore, *The Adventures Of Quentin Durward* (1955) as Quentin Durward, *Many Rivers To Cross* (1955) as Bushrod Gentry, *D-Day The Sixth Of June* (1956) as Captain Brad Parker, *Saddle The Wind* (1958) as Steve Sinclair, *Party Girl* (1958) as Thomas Farrell, *The House Of The Seven Hawks* (1959) as John Nordley, *Killers Of Kilimanjaro* (1959) as Robert Adamson, *Miracle Of The White Stallions* (1963) as Colonel Podhajsky, *Cattle King* (1963) as Sam Brassfield, *A House Is Not A Home* (1964) as Frank Costigan, *Savage Pampas* (1966) as Captain Martin and *Where Angels Go, Trouble Follows* (1968) as Mr Farraday.

Sal Mineo once said of him: "I'd always heard around town that Robert Taylor was bisexual, that his marriage to Barbara Stanwyck was arranged, and that she was also gay. So, when I met Taylor, I figured we'd have something in common, right? Wrong! I was open, he was not only closeted, he was rightwing and a witch hunter, not at all friendly or honest or even smiling." CAUSE: He died of lung cancer in St John's Hospital, Santa Monica, California. He was buried at Forest Lawn Memorial-Parks, 1712 Glendale Avenue, Glendale, California 91209. The eulogy was delivered by Ronald Reagan. FURTHER READING: *Robert Taylor* – Jane Ellen Wayne (London: Robson Books, 1987).

William Desmond Taylor

(WILLIAM CUNNINGHAM DEANE TANNER) *Born April 26, 1867* *Died February 1, 1922* Hollywood mystery. The film director whose death became one of Hollywood's most enduring riddles. Born in Carlow, County Waterford, Ireland, the son of a British army major, Taylor married Eva Shannon around 1883. The following year he was acting on the London stage. He travelled to America and worked at various jobs before landing one in the New York theatre. In 1901 he married Ethel May Harrison in New York's Little Church Around the Corner. Two years later, a daughter was born and named Ethel Daisy Deane Tanner. On October 23, 1908, he walked out of his family's life. Reputed to be something of a ladies' man, he also had a bisexual side and it is possible that the growing realisation of this stopped him living a heterosexual lie. He escorted numerous attractive film stars including Mabel Normand and Mary Miles Minter. With the patronage of Hollywood pioneer Allan Dwan, Taylor began working in Hollywood. By 1922 Taylor

had become president of the Motion Picture Directors Association and was head director at Famous Players-Lasky, a Paramount subsidiary. He lived in one of the Spanish-style stucco homes arranged in a U-shape near Westlake Park at 404 South Alvarado Street, Los Angeles. (Charlie Chaplin's leading lady Edna Purviance and actor Douglas MacLean were other film inhabitants of the cul de sac.) Taylor's bungalow was more than a home – it was where he entertained his procession of lovelies. It was also where he met his death.
CAUSE: On the evening of February 1, 1922, Mabel Normand visited an unhappy Taylor. The film director was annoyed because Edward F. Sands, his English former butler, had made free use of the house while Taylor was abroad. He pawned Taylor's jewellery, used his charge accounts, forged his signature to write cheques, wrote off two cars, and then ran away with almost all Taylor's wardrobe. Sands' replacement was Henry Peavey (d. Sacramento, California, 1937), a black man who spoke in a falsetto and whose hobbies included crochet and needlepoint. He gave Taylor and Normand drinks and left them to it at 6.30pm. One hour and fifteen minutes later, Normand was driven away by her chauffeur. At approximately 8.15pm a sound like a car backfiring was heard. Douglas MacLean's wife, Faith, looked out of her window and saw a man leaving Taylor's home through an alley next to the garage. She later recalled: "He was funny-looking because he walked like a woman and was built like a woman." The man's face was covered by a scarf and a cap was pulled down low on his forehead. At 7.30 next morning Peavey arrived and found Taylor lying on the floor, a dried streak of blood at the corner of his mouth (and two .38-calibre slugs in his body). He ran into the street shouting, "Dey've kilt Massa! Dey've kilt Massa!" according to the *Los Angeles Examiner*. Edna Purviance telephoned

Mabel Normand who alerted the studio who sent executives over to carry out a damage limitation exercise which included removing any and all alcohol from Taylor's vicinity. Prohibition was still in force. Mabel Normand rushed over to fetch some love letters she had sent Taylor and eventually the police were called when neighbours became fed up with Peavey's hysterics. They discovered a roaring fire in the grate and a frantic Mabel Normand still looking for her letters. (They were eventually found by the police inside one of Taylor's riding boots. District Attorney Thomas Lee Woolwine went through the letters then returned them to Mabel without revealing their content. His only comment was that they were irrelevant as far as the case was concerned.) Mabel Normand was the first to be questioned by murder detectives because she was the last known person to see Taylor alive. Edna Purviance also rang Mary Miles Minter, a beautiful blonde ingénue, whom Paramount was grooming to replace Mary Pickford. The young actress was out when the call came and Purviance spoke to her mother, Charlotte Shelby, who disapproved of her daughter's relationship with Taylor. She disapproved so much she visited Taylor and threatened him unless he stopped seeing the girl. (The Shelby family maid informed the authorities that Mrs Shelby had a gun and practised shooting regularly.) When Charlotte Shelby told her daughter, none too tactfully, what had happened, Mary rushed over to South Alvarado Street but was prevented from entering the house by police. The place was already swarming with reporters and movie executives. She was eventually taken to Mabel Normand's house. Woolwine told the press that a handkerchief bearing the initials MMM was discovered in Taylor's bedroom among a collection of silk lingerie and nightgowns. Discovered nearby was a love note with a letterhead in the shape of a butterfly. On the wings and body of the butterfly was written the by now familiar MMM. The note read: "Dearest – I love you – I love you – I love you – – –" Then followed a sequence of ten kisses in the shape of Xs. The note was signed, "Yours always! Mary". She admitted, "I did love William Desmond Taylor. I loved him deeply and tenderly, with all the admiration a young girl gives a man like Mr Taylor." Her mother confessed to owning a .38-calibre pistol, but insisted she obtained it for protection at home against burglars, not to use against Taylor. In fact, Mrs Shelby insisted that she had no objection to her daughter's infatuation with the director. Mary didn't confirm her mother's claims. "Mother's actions over Mr Taylor's attention to me were not inspired by a desire to protect me from him. She was really trying to shove me into the background so she could monopolise his attentions and, if possible, his love." Police investigated the possibility that Taylor's killer may have been in drag and interviewed his ex-butler but those avenues led nowhere. Taylor had been a vocal opponent of the drug culture that was then becoming prevalent in Hollywood and had reported a number of dealers to the authorities but police ruled out a vengeful drugs baron as ordering the hit. Bizarrely, some of the jewellery stolen by Sands was pawned in Fresno, California, by someone using Taylor's real name, William Deane Tanner. The murder ended Taylor's life and Mary Miles Minter's career. The public tarred her with guilt by association. For years the case remained unsolved. Film director King Vidor began to take a close interest in the murder in 1966 and spent much of the following year investigating the crime. His conclusion was that the murder was committed in a fit of jealousy by Charlotte Shelby. FURTHER READING: *A Cast Of Killers* – Sidney Kirkpatrick (Mysterious Press: London, 1987).

Lou Tellegen

(ISADORE LOUIS BERNARD VAN DOMMELEM)
Born November 26, 1881
Died October 29, 1934
Leading man. Born in St Oedenrode, Holland, he began appearing on the stage in 1903 and later caught the eye of Sarah Bernhardt, becoming her leading man in Paris six years later. He went with her when she toured America in 1910 and three years later returned to live in America permanently, first in New York, where he appeared on Broadway, and then in Hollywood. His films included: *The Unknown* (1915) as Richard Farquhar, *The Black Wolf* (1917) as The Black Wolf, *The Long Trail* (1917) as Andre Dubois, *Flame Of The Desert* (1919) as Sheik Essad, *Let Not Man Put Asunder* (1924) as Dick Lechmere, *Between Friends* (1924) as David Drene, *Single Wives* (1924) as Martin Prayle, *Those Who Judge* (1924) as John Dawson, *Greater Than Marriage* (1924) as John Masters, *Fair Play* (1925) as Bruce Elliot, *Borrowed Finery* (1925) as Harlan, *The Verdict* (1925) as Victor Ronsard, *After Business Hours* (1925) as John King, *Parisian Love* (1925) as Pierre Marcel, *With This Ring* (1925) as Rufus Van Buren, *The Silver Treasure* (1926) as Solito, *Siberia* (1926) as Egor Kaplan, *Womanpower* (1926) as the broker, *The Princess From Hoboken* (1927) as Prince Anton Balakrieff, *The Little Firebrand* (1927) as Harley Norcross, *Married Alive* (1927) as James Duxbury, *Enemies Of The Law* (1931) as Eddie Swan, *Caravane* (1934) and *Together We Live* (1935) as Bischofsky. He was married and divorced four times.
CAUSE: With his career over, Tellegen sat in his living room and read through his press cuttings. Then he took all his clothes off, resumed his position and committed hara-kiri with a pair of gold scissors inscribed with his name. He was 52.

Terry-Thomas

(THOMAS TERRY HOAR STEVENS)
Born July 14, 1911
Died January 8, 1990
Gap-toothed gagster. Born in Finchley, London, the 6' son of a businessman, he began his working life in Smithfield market as a clerk but the lure of the stage proved too much and he began appearing as an extra in films. According to the man himself, his name change was hyphenated to match the gap in his teeth. He was known for his monocle, gaudy waistcoat, red carnation and cigarette holder encrusted with diamonds. During World War II he appeared with ENSA, the entertainment vehicle for troops lovingly, if not totally inaccurately, dubbed 'Every Night Something Awful'. His career began to take off after demob and he appeared in the West End with Sid Field, on radio with his own shows and also on TV where he, again, had his own show. He became a massive star after being cast as Major Hitchcock in *Private's Progress* (1956). He went on to appear in *The Naked Truth* (1957) as Lord Henry Mayley, *Lucky Jim* (1957) as Bertrand Welch, *Blue Murder At St Trinian's* (1957) as Romney, *Too Many Crooks* (1958) as Billy Gordon, *tom thumb* (1958) as Ivan, *I'm All Right Jack* (1959), *Carlton-Browne Of The F.O.* (1959) as Cadogan deVere Carlton-Browne, *School For Scoundrels* (1960) as Raymond Delauney, *Make Mine Mink* (1960) as Major Rayne, *Bachelor Flat* (1961) as Professor Bruce Patterson, *Operation Snatch* (1962) as Lieutenant 'Piggy' Wigg, *Kill Or Cure* (1962) as J. Barker-Rynde, *The Mouse On The Moon*, (1963) as Spender, *It's A Mad Mad Mad Mad World* (1963) as J. Algernon Hawthorne, *You Must Be Joking!* (1965) as Major Foskett, *Those Magnificent Men In Their Flying Machines, Or How I Flew From London To Paris In 25 hours 11 minutes* (1965) as Sir Percy Ware-Armitage, *Munster, Go Home* (1966) as Freddie Munster,

Our Man In Marrakesh (1966) as El Caid, *Those Fantastic Flying Fools* (1967) as Sir Harry Washington-Smythe, *The Perils Of Pauline* (1967) as Sten Martin, *Don't Raise The Bridge, Lower The River* (1967) as H. William Homer, *Monte Carlo Or Bust* (1969) as Sir Cuthbert Ware-Armitage, *12 Plus 1* (1970) as Albert, *The Abominable Dr Phibes* (1971) as Dr Longstreet, *Dr Phibes Rises Again* (1972) as Lombardo, *The Bawdy Adventures Of Tom Jones* (1976) as Mr Square, *The Last Remake Of Beau Geste* (1977) as Governor and *The Hound Of The Baskervilles* (1978) as Dr Mortimer, after which ill-health forced him to retire. In 1938 he married dancer Ida Florence (d. 1983) and they were divorced in 1962. In 1963 he married Belinda Cunningham. They had two sons.
CAUSE: When he learned he had Parkinson's disease he moved to Ibiza but medical bills running at £40,000 per annum soon depleted his fortune and he returned to London where he ended up living in poverty in Barnes. A fund-raising concert in April 1989 enabled him to move to Busbridge Hall Nursing Home in Godalming, Surrey, where he succumbed to pneumonia. He was 78. At his funeral the organist played the main theme of *Those Magnificent Men In Their Flying Machines*. He left less than £100,000.

Irving Thalberg

Born May 30, 1899
Died September 14, 1936
'The Boy Wonder'. Born in Brooklyn, the son of German Jews, 5'6" Irving Grant Thalberg was an exceptionally precocious movie executive but also a very sick one. He was born with cyanosis and a weak heart and doctors told his parents he was unlikely to live beyond 30. He packed a lot into his short life, becoming secretary to movie mogul Carl Laemmle at a salary of $25 a week. In 1920 he appointed him an executive at Universal City, raising his salary to $60 a week, then General

Manager at $90 a week, a job suggested by Thalberg himself. His reputation was made by the way he handled temperamental director Erich von Stroheim, then filming *Foolish Wives* (1922). Laemmle and Thalberg had a father and son relationship but it ended on February 1923 when Laemmle refused to increase Thalberg's salary from the $450 a week he was paid by the end of 1922. He joined the Mayer Company at $600 a week, raised by $50 when the company became MGM (in April 1924) although he was also guaranteed 4% of the annual profits. For the next nine years the studio flourished, boasting of "more stars than there are in the heavens" and put out films such as *The Merry Widow* (1925), *Ben-Hur* (1926), *Flesh And The Devil* (1927), *Anna Christie* (1930), *Freaks* (1932), *The Barratts Of Wimpole Street* (1934), *Mutiny On The Bounty* (1935), *A Night At The Opera* (1935), *Romeo And Juliet* (1936) and the only film in which he received an on-screen credit, *The Good Earth* (1937). He married Norma Shearer on September 29, 1927, at 9401 Sunset Boulevard. Despite his almost total absence of interest in sex, they had two children: Irving Jr (b. Good Samaritan Hospital, Los Angeles, August 25, 1930, d. 1987 of cancer) and Katharine (b. Good Samaritan Hospital, Los Angeles June 13, 1935). In December 1932 he suffered a heart attack and travelled to Europe to recuperate. When he returned he found that his power base had diminished, although he retained his title and salary. He was the subject of F. Scott Fitzgerald's *The Last Tycoon*. Although he is regarded as having been astute when it comes to movies, not all of his judgments were sound. He once opined: "Novelty is always welcome, but talking pictures are just a fad."
CAUSE: He died of pneumonia at 10.15am on September 14, 1936, aged 37, in Santa Monica. He was buried on September 17 and MGM closed for the day in his honour. His body was interred in the Sanctuary of Benediction at Forest Lawn Memorial-Parks, 1712 Glendale Avenue, Glendale, California 91209.

John Thaw, CBE
Born January 2, 1942
Died February 21, 2002
Telly's decent tec. John Edward Thaw was born at 48 Stowell Street, West Gorton in Manchester, the son of John Edward Thaw (d. 1997), a miner who became a lorry driver, and Dorothy, known as 'Dolly', Ablott (b. 1921, d. St Anne's Hospice, Hill Green, Stockport, February 2, 1974 of stomach cancer). Two years later, brother Raymond was born. After a man dropped dead in the street, Dolly insisted that they move and the family uprooted to 4 Daneholme Road, Burnage. Then when young Thaw was seven Dolly left home and he was not to see his mother again for 12 years. "My mother went off with another man. It wasn't very nice," he remembered. When he was 12 Thaw won a talent contest singing 'I've Got A Lovely Bunch Of Coconuts'. Thaw's father became an ambulance driver in order to spend more time with his children, and Thaw was always grateful for the support he gave the two boys and his encouragement when Thaw said that he wanted to be an actor. "A lot of 15-year-old lads would have been laughed at if they had said they wanted to act. Dad just said, 'If it doesn't work, come back. We're here.'" After school in which he obtained a single O level, in English, 5'9" Thaw became a devout socialist. Even when he became one of the highest paid actors in Britain, he never lost his principles. He always refused to do adverts. After school he briefly worked as a market porter and apprentice baker where he made doughnuts before moving to London hoping to become an actor. Although under age, he was accepted

by the Royal Academy of Dramatic Art after auditioning by reading from *Othello*. He entered RADA on September 29, 1958 "dressed like a typical Teddy boy". His fellow students included Tom Courtenay (with whom he and Nicol Williamson were later to share a London flat) and Sarah Miles. He left on July 23, 1960 and landed a bit part in the television cop series *Z Cars* and made his film début playing Bosworth in *The Loneliness Of The Long Distance Runner* (1962). He was Alan Roper in *Five To One* (1964) before landing his first telly lead Sergeant John Mann in *Redcap* (October 17, 1964–June 25, 1966), about the military police. His other films included *Dead Man's Chest* (1965) as David Jones, *The Bofors Gun* (1968) as Featherstone, *Praise Marx And Pass The Ammunition* (1970) as Dom, *The Last Grenade* (1970) as Terry Mitchell and *Dr Phibes Rises Again* (1972) as Shavers. It was his casting as Detective Inspector Jack Regan in the film *Regan* (1974) that made Thaw famous. The film was the forerunner of the television series (and two films) about the Flying Squad, *The Sweeney* (Sweeney was cockney rhyming slang: Sweeney Todd = Flying Squad). The show, created by Ian Kennedy-Martin, whose brother Troy had conceived *Z Cars*, began the day before Thaw's 33rd birthday and ran for 54 episodes, ending on December 28, 1978. With the connivance of his sergeant George Carter (Dennis Waterman), the tough policeman used whatever means possible to bring crooks to justice, much to the despair of his boss Chief Inspector Frank Haskins (Garfield Morgan). When the series ended Thaw managed to avoid the typecasting problem that befalls so many actors associated with one role. In 1981 he went to Zambia to star in a film version of Doris Lessing's novel *The Grass Is Singing*. Directed by Michael Raeburn, it co-starred Karen Black, who played a lonely woman who marries a stolid, inarticulate farmer

(Thaw) but cannot adjust to life with him in the African woodland. Though he won praise for his performance, Thaw would later describe the film as one of his most miserable experiences. He described conditions in the Zambian bush as "pure hell", and did not get along with Black, who had an affair with the director. Thaw joined the Royal Shakespeare Company for the 1983 season at Stratford, where he played Toby Belch in *Twelfth Night* and Cardinal Wolsey in *King Henry VIII*. On April 19, 1985 until January 19, 1990, he played the grumpy Henry Willows whose peace and quiet is ruined by his son's unexpected return to the family nest in the sitcom *Home To Roost*. From January 6, 1987 and *The Dead Of Jericho*, Thaw was also the equally miserable *Inspector Morse* in the detective series based on Colin Dexter's books. The series ran for 14 years and one of the biggest mysteries amid all the murders was what was Morse's first name. The revelation in *Death Is Now My Neighbour* (1997) that it was the unlikely Endeavour made national news. Morse was once described by Thaw as "the nearest character to myself I have ever played," adding, "I'm very fond of the old bugger. He's not a cliché copper any more than Regan was. The guy's brain is working all the time. He has a mind like an intellectual grasshopper, which made him challenging to play." However, Thaw insisted on some changes before he agreed to play the role. "I didn't like the seedy side of Morse in the early books," he said. "He was a bit of a dirty old man. I didn't like that and I wouldn't play it. I hated the fact that he was sometimes rude to women and I told the writers I wanted that changed. I wanted him to be more sensitive." His portrayal of Morse won Thaw two BAFTA awards as Best Actor in a Television Series, in 1989 and 1992. Not everything Thaw touched was a success – the BBC series, *A Year In Provence* (1993), was

a critical and ratings disaster, but it did him no harm. "I had a disaster with that, but we're all allowed one. I was saddened, because we all worked hard and hoped it would be enjoyed, and I won't accept that it was bad." Thaw then played *Kavanagh QC*, a bluff northern barrister, based in London, whose cases tended to have an unexpected twist at the end. The series, for which he was able to command a fee of £250,000 an episode, ran until 1999 and the following year on November 15 Thaw played Morse for the last time, in an episode where the character dies of a heart attack. It was watched by 13 million people. His last major television project saw him portraying the boss of a double-glazing firm in *The Glass*. He was teamed with Sarah Lancashire but they failed to lift a trite series. Thaw had cameos in Richard Attenborough's films *Cry Freedom* (1987), for which he won a BAFTA nomination as Best Supporting Actor for his chilling portrayal of a member of the South African secret service and *Chaplin* (1992) in which he played Fred Karno. In 2001 Thaw was awarded a fellowship by the British Academy of Film and Television Arts, having previously won two BAFTAs for his portrayal of Morse. John Thaw was twice married. In 1964 he married Sally Alexander, later a history professor at University College London, but they separated in 1966 and were divorced after four years. In Cirencester on Christmas Eve, 1973, he married the actress Sheila Hancock, a union which survived well-publicised difficulties including a six-month separation in 1988 after she had breast cancer diagnosed. He had daughters, Abigail (b. 1965) and Joanna (b. 1974), from each marriage and adopted Hancock's daughter, Melanie known as 'Elly Jane' (b. 1964), from her first marriage.
CAUSE: Thaw died of cancer of the oesophagus aged 60 in Luckington,

Wiltshire. His agent had made the announcement that Thaw was ill a few weeks after the actor received the BAFTA fellowship. Thaw was buried on February 25, 2002 near his family home in Wiltshire. Only his wife, Sheila Hancock, and their daughters, Melanie, Abigail and Joanna, were at the private funeral.

Ernest Thesiger, CBE

Born January 15, 1879
Died January 14, 1961

Camp old queen. Ernest Frederic Graham Thesiger was born in London, the third of the four children (three sons and one daughter) of the Honourable Sir Edward Peirson Thesiger, KCB (b. London, December 19, 1842, d. November 11, 1928) and Georgina Mary Stopford (d. 1906). He was the grandson of Frederick Thesiger, the 1st Baron Chelmsford, KC, Lord Chancellor of Great Britain (b. 1 Fowkes Buildings, Tower Street, London, April 15, 1794, d. 7 Eaton Square, south-west London, October 5, 1878). Educated at a private school at Weybridge, Surrey, and then Marlborough, he persuaded his father to let him enrol as a painter at the Slade School of Art. He spent four years at Slade and, in 1909, made his stage début in *Colonel Smith* at the St James's Theatre. Five years later he joined the army hoping to be sent to a Scottish regiment because he fancied himself in a kilt but joined the Queen Victoria Rifles. On New Year's Day, 1915 he was wounded in action and invalided out four months later. Asked what it was like in the trenches, he put his hand to his forehead and declaimed, "My dear, the noise! And the people!" Back in Blighty he appeared from October 27, 1915 as Bertram Tully more than 1,300 times in Walter W. Ellis' farce *A Little Bit Of Fluff* at the Criterion Theatre. In 1916 he made his first film playing a witch in *The Real Thing At Last* but he did not take film acting too seriously, commenting,

"Anyone with a modicum of intelligence and the right kind of physique ought to make a film actor, if they are lucky enough to be told exactly what to do, and I cannot see that the actor for the screen deserves any more credit than a schoolboy who is good at dictation should have for writing admirable prose." In 1918 he played William Pitt in *Nelson* and was Joseph Chamberlain in *The Life Story Of David Lloyd George*. He created the role of the Dauphin in *St Joan* (1924). He once moaned to Somerset Maugham that he never wrote any parts for him. "But I am always writing parts for you, Ernest," protested Maugham. "The trouble is that somebody called Gladys Cooper will insist on playing them." In 1930 he was summoned to Hollywood by his old friend James Whale and given the part of the skeletal Horace Femm in *The Old Dark House* (1932). He stole the show with his campness and sinister quips. At one point he tells his guests, "We make our own electric light here" – the lights go out – "but we're not very good at it." He returned to England to appear in *The Ghoul* (1933) with Boris Karloff. He was again summoned to Hollywood by Whale and cast as Dr Septimus Pretorius in *Bride Of Frankenstein* (1935). His performance was a *tour de force* "camp, shrill, frightening and oozing malevolent bitterness from every pore". Like Rock Hudson, he would sit on the set doing embroidery when not needed. His other films included the movie version of *A Little Bit Of Fluff* (1919), *The Bachelor's Club* (1921) as Israfel Mondego, *The Man Who Could Work Miracles* (1936) as Mr Maydig, *Henry V* (1944) as Duke of Bern, *Caesar And Cleopatra* (1945) as Theodotus, *The Winslow Boy* (1948) as Ridgeley Pierce, *The Robe* (1953) as the Emperor Tiberius, *Quentin Durward* (1955) as Lord Crawford, *Doctor At Large* (1957), *Sons And Lovers* (1960) as Henry Hadlock and *The Roman Spring Of Mrs Stone* (1961) as Stefano.

On May 29, 1917 (the day President Kennedy was born in Brookline, Massachusetts) he married Janette Mary Fernie Ranken (d. 1970). There were no children, mainly because the marriage was never consummated. She was the sister of Willie Ranken, his lifelong friend who he had met at Slade and who shaved off all his hair when he heard of the wedding. It was a lavender marriage to hide his flamboyant homosexuality and her lesbianism. Mrs Thesiger was in love with the poet Margaret Jourdain. He once stopped a party dead by loudly announcing, "Anyone fancy a spot of buggery?" At dinner parties he would take off his shoes and socks to display his green painted toenails. He would lay lilies at the feet of a handsome Ritz doorman with whom he had fallen in love. In later life he became a friend of Queen Mary and modelled himself on her appearance. They would sit together doing embroidery and Thesiger published *Adventures In Embroidery* in 1941.

CAUSE: Ernest Thesiger died in his sleep the day before his 82nd birthday at his home, 8 St George's Court, Gloucester Road, south-west London where he had lived since 1939. From 1917 until 1939 he resided at 6 Montpelier Terrace, south-west London. He was buried in the Brompton Cemetery alongside his father, mother and sister. He left £46,525 1s.

Gerald Thomas

Born December 10, 1920
Died November 9, 1993

Comedic director. With his partner, Peter Rogers, Gerald Thomas was responsible for some of the best-loved films in English cinematic history – the *Carry On* series. Born at 139 Coltman Street, Hull, the younger son (his brother was the director Ralph) of Samuel Thomas, a petrol company inspector, and Freda Cohen, Gerald Thomas intended to join the medical

profession but the war put paid to that and after being demobbed he landed a job as a film cutter at Denham Studios. That led to work as an assistant editor and then editor before teaming up with Rogers. Their first film, *Circus Friends* (1956), was not a great success but the second, *Time Lock* (1957), starring Robert Beatty, was. It is the low budget, high farce *Carry On* series for which Thomas is remembered. His films included: *Chain Of Events* (1957), *Carry On Sergeant* (1958), *Carry On Nurse* (1959), *Please Turn Over* (1959), *Carry On Teacher* (1959), *Watch Your Stern* (1960), *No Kidding* (1960), *Carry On Constable* (1960), *Raising The Wind* (1961), *Carry On Regardless* (1961), *Twice Round The Daffodils* (1962), *Carry On Cruising* (1962), *Nurse On Wheels* (1963), *Carry On Cabby* (1963), *Carry On Spying* (1964), *Carry On Jack* (1964), *Carry On Cleo* (1964), *Carry On Cowboy* (1965), *The Big Job* (1965), *Carry On Screaming* (1966), *Carry On Follow That Camel* (1967), *Carry On Don't Lose Your Head* (1967), *Carry On Up The Khyber* (1968), *Carry On Doctor* (1968), *Carry On Camping* (1969), *Carry On Again, Doctor* (1969), *Carry On Up The Jungle* (1970), *Carry On Loving* (1970), *Carry On Henry* (1971), *Carry On At Your Convenience* (1971), *Carry On Matron* (1972), *Carry On Abroad* (1972), *Bless This House* (1972), *Carry On Girls* (1973), *Carry On Dick* (1974), *Carry On Behind* (1975), *Carry On England* (1976), *Carry On Emmannuelle* (1978), *The Second Victory* (1986) and *Carry On Columbus* (1992).
CAUSE: He died, aged 72, of coronary thrombosis at his home, 16 Burnham Avenue in Beaconsfield, Buckinghamshire. He left £280,091.

Olive Thomas

(OLIVERETTA ELAINE DUFFY)
Born October 29, 1884
Died September 10, 1920
'The world's most beautiful girl'. The name of Olive Thomas has

been enshrined in Hollywood myth because of the manner of her death (Hollywood's first scandal) and because of her supposed youthfulness. In fact she was born, 14 years earlier than is usually reported, in Charleroi, Pennsylvania, and married Bernard Krug Thomas while still in her teens. She ran away to escape the poverty and her husband landing in New York where she found herself a job working in a shop in Harlem. She entered a beauty contest run by a newspaper and, to her surprise, won. That led to a career as a dancer with the Ziegfeld Follies and as a nude model for Peruvian artist Alberto Vargas. Films were next and she appeared in *Beatrice Fairfax* (1916) as Rita Malone after being signed by Triangle Pictures. That year, on October 20, she married Mary Pickford's brother, Jack, but the marriage was punctuated by fighting. She went on to appear in *A Girl Like That* (1917) as Fannie Brooks, *Madcap Madge* (1917) as Betty, *Broadway Arizona* (1917) as Fritzi Carlyle, *Indiscreet Corinne* (1917) as Corinne Chilvers, *Betty Takes A Hand* (1918) as Betty Marshall, *Limousine Life* (1918) as Minnie Wills, *Heiress For A Day* (1918) as Helen Thurston, *Toton* (1919) as Toton/Yvonne, *Upstairs And Down* (1919) as Prudence, *Love's Prisoner* (1919) as Nancy, *Prudence On Broadway* (1919) as Prudence, *Out Yonder* (1919) as Flotsam, *Footlights And Shadows* (1920) as Gloria Dawn, *Darling Mine* (1920) as Kitty McCarthy and *Everybody's Sweetheart* (1920) as Mary.
CAUSE: In a bid to save their marriage the Pickfords travelled to France for a second honeymoon. Versions of Olive's death are varied. According to one on September 5, 1920 (a year to the day before the Fatty Arbuckle affair), she was discovered nude in her room at the Hotel Crillon on the Place de la Concorde, Paris, having taken an overdose of mercury bichloride tablets washed down with booze. She was taken to the American Hospital in

Neuilly where she died, aged 35. Another has her in the Ritz Hotel on September 6, after a night of clubbing in Montmartre and screaming in the bathroom, whereupon her husband rushed in and caught her before she hit the ground. She lingered for four days before succumbing. The most likely version is that she committed suicide after learning that Pickford had given her syphilis. She left $36,875.

J. Lee Thompson

Born August 1, 1914
Died August 30, 2002
Underappreciated Brit. Born in Bristol John Lee Thompson attended Dover College and became a bantamweight boxer after leaving school before turning his fists to the stage. He found he could write plays and had two performed in the West End before he was 20. The first was bought by a film studio and he was asked to write the screenplay. When the second was snapped up, he was asked to direct. His clipped British accent also gave him work as a dialogue coach on Alfred Hitchcock films including *Jamaica Inn* (1939). As with many of his generation, his career was interrupted by the Second World War and he became a tailgunner in a B-29. After the war he directed *Murder Without Crime* (1950) and wrote *No Place For Jennifer* (1950). In February 1954, *The Weak And The Wicked* which starred Glynis Johns and Diana Dors was released. It was written and directed by Thompson and was the true story of Joan Henry who became his second wife. The film was based on the book *Who Lie In Gaol* written by Henry. During the filming, she told Dors that she was writing another book about a condemned woman's last days in the death cell. That film, supposedly based on the last days of Ruth Ellis, was *Yield To The Night* (1956) and it allowed Diana Dors to be taken seriously as a dramatic actress, although critic Leslie Halliwell described it as a "gloomy

melodrama". It was the only British film that year at the Cannes Film Festival. *The Weak And The Wicked* was a smash hit and set Thompson off on the journey that was to peak with *The Guns Of Navarone* (1961). His other films included: *For Better, For Worse* (1954), *An Alligator Named Daisy* (1955), *Woman In A Dressing Gown* (1957), *The Good Companions* (1957), *No Trees In The Street* (1958), *Ice-Cold In Alex* (1958) (for the film Sir John Mills was required to down a glass of beer in one gulp. At first the drink was ginger ale but Thompson decided that it did not look right and so a real pint of lager was substituted. Unfortunately, it took eight takes to get the scene right by which time Mills was in his own words "drunk as a Lord". He spent the rest of the day knocking over scenery and props), *Tiger Bay* (1959) and *North West Frontier* (1959), about an Allied plan to destroy German artillery. Alexander McKendrick was slated to direct the film but was sacked for "creative differences" 10 days before filming was due to begin. The film starred Gregory Peck, Anthony Quinn, David Niven, Anthony Quayle, Stanley Baker and Richard Harris. During shooting the crew managed to accidentally sink a Greek Navy ship and the captain was court-martialled. Thompson appeared as a witness for the captain and said "that it was entirely my fault. It was quite a debacle." The film was almost destroyed by the weather when the rain washed away much of the plaster set. It took three weeks to rebuild. The film was nominated for seven Academy Awards including Best Picture and Best Director but only won one for Best Visual Effects. *The Guns Of Navarone* brought him to the attention of Hollywood and he was given *Cape Fear* (1962). He stayed in Hollywood where he worked on *Taras Bulba* (1962), *Kings Of The Sun* (1963), *What A Way To Go!* (1964), *Return From The Ashes* (1965), *Eye Of The Devil* (1967),

Mackenna's Gold (1969), *Before Winter Comes* (1969), *Conquest Of The Planet Of The Apes* (1972), *Battle For The Planet Of The Apes* (1973), *Huckleberry Finn* (1974), *The Greek Tycoon* (1978), *Happy Birthday To Me* (1981), *10 To Midnight* (1983), *The Evil That Men Do* (1984), *King Solomon's Mines* (1985), *Murphy's Law* (1986), *Death Wish 4: The Crackdown* (1987), *Messenger Of Death* (1988) and *Kinjite: Forbidden Subjects* (1989). Thompson never retired but found work difficult to come by because of his age. He was the microphone boom operator on the 1998 slasher film *Bride Of Chucky*. J. Lee Thompson was married four times: Lucille Kelly, Joan Henry, Florence known as 'Bill' Bailey, by whom he had two children Lesley and Peter (who predeceased him), and finally Penny. CAUSE: Thompson died in Sooke, British Columbia, Canada, of congestive heart failure. He was 88.

Marshall Thompson

Born November 27, 1925
Died May 18, 1992
Nice TV vet. Born in Peoria, Illinois, James Marshall Thompson was known to millions of television viewers as Dr Marsh Tracy in the children's serial *Daktari* (Swahili for doctor) from January 11, 1966 until January 15, 1969. His nice guy persona on the show was no act – his co-stars called him "the original boy scout". In fact it was as nice guys that Thompson was nearly always cast. He made his film début in *Henry Aldrich, Boy Scout* (1944) playing, of all things, a boy scout patrol leader. His other films included: *The Purple Heart* (1944) as a crewman of the *Mrs Murphy*, *Reckless Age* (1944) as Roy Connors, *Blonde Fever* (1944) as Freddie Bilson, *The Clock* (1945) as Bill, *The Valley Of Decision* (1945) as Ted Scott, *Twice Blessed* (1945) as Jimmy, *They Were Expendable* (1945) as Ensign Snake Gardner, *The Cockeyed Miracle* (1946) as Jim Griggs, *Bad Bascomb* (1946) as

Jimmy Holden, *The Show-Off* (1946) as Joe Fisher, *The Secret Heart* (1946) as Brandon Reynolds, *Gallant Bess* (1947) as Tex Barton, *The Romance Of Rosy Ridge* (1947) as Ben Mac Bean, *B.F.'s Daughter* (1948) as the sailor, *Homecoming* (1948) as Staff Sergeant 'Mac' McKeen, *Words And Music* (1948) as Herbert Fields, *Command Decision* (1948) as Captain George Washington Bellpepper Lee, *Roseanna McCoy* (1949) as Tolbert McCoy, *Battleground* (1949) as Private Jim Layton, the narrator in *Stars In My Crown* (1950), *Mystery Street* (1950) as Henry Shanway, *Devil's Doorway* (1950) as Rod MacDougall, *Dial 1119* (1950) as Gunther Wyckoff, *The Tall Target* (1951) as Lance Beaufort, *The Basketball Fix* (1951) as Johnny Long, *My Six Convicts* (1952) as Blivens Scott, *The Rose Bowl Story* (1952) as Steve Davis, *The Caddy* (1953) as Bruce Reeber, *Port Of Hell* (1954) as Marshall 'Marsh' Walker, *Crashout* (1955) as Billy Lang, *Cult Of The Cobra* (1955) as Tom Markel, *To Hell And Back* (1955) as Johnson, *Battle Taxi* (1955) as 2nd Lieutenant Tim Vernon, *Good Morning, Miss Dove* (1955) as Wilfred Banning Pendleton III, *Down Liberty Road* (1957), *Lure Of The Swamp* (1957) as Simon Lewt, *La Grande Caccia* (1957) as Marsh Connors, *Fiend Without A Face* (1958) as Major Jeff Cummings, *The Secret Man* (1958) as Dr Cliff Mitchell, *It! The Terror From Beyond Space* (1958) as Colonel Edward Carruthers, *First Man Into Space* (1959) as Commander Charles Ernest 'Chuck' Prescott, *Flight Of The Lost Balloon* (1962) as Doctor Farady, *No Man Is An Island* (1962) as Jonn Sonnenberg, *A Yank In Vietnam* (1964) as Major Benson, *The Mighty Jungle* (1964) as Marsh Connors, Clarence, *The Cross-Eyed Lion* (1965) as Doctor Marsh Tracy, the shaving man in *Zebra In The Kitchen* (1965), *Around The World Under The Sea* (1966) as Dr Orin Hillyard, *To The Shores Of Hell* (1966) as Major Greg Donahue, *George*

(1972) as Jim Paulsen which spawned a television series of the same name, *The Turning Point* (1977) as Carter, a geologist in *The Formula* (1980), a director in *White Dog* (1982) and *Bog* (1983) as Dr Brad Wednesday. He also appeared in a number of TV movies including *Dallas: The Early Years* (1986) as Dr Ted Johnson. His brother-in-law was the actor Richard Long.
CAUSE: He died of congestive heart failure in Royal Oak, Michigan, aged 66.

June Thorburn

Born June 8, 1931
Died November 4, 1967
Tragic beauty. Born in Karachi, India, the eldest of three children of an Indian army colonel, she made her film debut in *The Pickwick Papers* (1952) as Arabella Allen the year after she had arrived in London determined to forge a career in showbusiness. She worked regularly on films and television and looked set for a bright future. She appeared in *The Triangle* (1953) as Mitzi, *The Cruel Sea* (1953) as Doris Ferraby, *Fast And Loose* (1954) as Barbara "Babsie" Wickham, *Delayed Action* (1954) as Anne Curlew, *Orders Are Orders* (1954) as Veronica Bellamy, *Children Galore* (1955) as Milly Ark, *Rooney* (1958) as Doreen O'Flynn, *Escort For Hire* (1960) as Terry, *The Spanish Sword* (1962) as Lady Eleanor, *Design For Loving* (1962) as Barbara Winters and *Master Spy* (1964) as Leila. In 1952 she married Aldon Richard Bryse-Harvey and in 1953 gave birth to a daughter named Heather-Louise June. The marriage ended in divorce and Thorburn moved back to Hampshire where her father had retired. After a break of two years she decided to resume her career and in 1957, returned to London where she met and married Morten Smith-Petersen. She had a daughter, Inger-Sheleen Christabel, by him.
CAUSE: Five months pregnant with her

third child and 36-years-old, she was aboard Iberia Airlines Flight 062, a twin-engined Sud Aviation Caravelle en route to Heathrow from Malaga when the aeroplane crashed at 10.02pm into the side of Black Down Hill, West Sussex. All 37 people – seven crew and 30 passengers – on the aeroplane died.

Ingrid Thulin

Born January 27, 1926
Died January 7, 2004
Aloof blonde. Born in Sollefteå, Ångermanland, Sweden, the daughter of a fisherman, Ingrid Thulin trained at the Royal Dramatic Theatre in Stockholm. She appeared in pantomime and in 1948 made her début with a small role in Ake Ohberg's *Dit Vindarna Bar*. But it was her work with Ingmar Bergman at the Malmo Theatre from the mid-Fifties that assured her reputation as one of her country's finest dramatic actors. It was her first film for Bergman, *Smultronstället* (1957), that put her in the public eye. She won jointly (with fellow Swedes Bibi Andersson and Eva Dahlbeck) the Best Actress Award at Cannes in 1958 for *Brink Of Life*. Hollywood beckoned and she appeared opposite Robert Mitchum in *Foreign Intrigue* (1956) and then with Glenn Ford in Vincente Minnelli's remake of the Valentino flick *Four Horsemen Of The Apocalypse* (1962) as Marguerite Laurier but both movies flopped. It was not helped by the fact that her thick Swedish accent proved impossible for Americans to understand and her voice was dubbed (by Angela Lansbury) before the film could be released. She made only one more film in Tinseltown, the ironically named *Return From The Ashes* in 1965 playing Dr Michele Wolf but this, too, was a failure. Her other films included: *Känn Dej Som Hemma* (1948) as Elsa Carlsson, *Havets Son* (1949) as Gudrun, *Kärleken Segrar* (1949) as Margit Dahlman, *Hjärter Knekt* (1950)

as Gunvor Ranterud, *När Kärleken Kom Till Byn* (1950) as Agneta, *Leva På "Hoppet"* (1951) as Yvonne, *Möte Med Livet* (1952) as Viola, *Kalle Karlsson Från Jularbo* (1952) as Elsa, *En Skärgårdsnatt* (1953) as Ingrid, *Göingehövdingen* (1953) as Anna Ryding, *Aldrig I Livet* (1957) as Lily, *Nattlek* (1966) as Irene, *Domani Non Siamo Più Qui* (1967) as Gioia, *Adélaïde* (1968) as Elisabeth Hermann, *La Caduta Degli Dei* (1969) as Sophie Von Essenbeck, *Malastrana* (1971) as Jessica, *Monismanien* (1975), *Salon Kitty* (1976) as Kitty Kellermann, *The Cassandra Crossing* (1976) as Dr Elena Stradner, *En Och En* (1978) as Ylva, *Il Giorno Prima* (1987) as Mrs Havemeyer and *Il Cuore Di Mamma* (1988) as Eloisa. Her last film was *La Casa Del Sorriso* (1988). She also directed three films – a short and two features – *Hängivelse* (1965), *En Och En* (1978) and *Brusten Himmel* (1982), which she also wrote. In 1951 Ingrid Thulin married Claes Sylvander. After they divorced in 1955 she married Harry Scheim, founder of the Swedish Film Institute, the following year. They divorced in 1989.

CAUSE: She died, aged 77, of cancer in Stockholm.

Carol Thurston

Born September 27, 1921
Died December 31, 1969

Youthful bloom. Born in Forsyth, Montana, Carol Thurston fought off competition from Simone Simon and Yvonne De Carlo to land the part of Tremartini in *The Story Of Dr. Wassell* (1944). She found a niche playing *naïfs* in *The Conspirators* (1944) as Rosa, *China Sky* (1945) as Siu-Mei, *Swamp Fire* (1946) as Toni Rousseau, *The Last Round Up* (1947) as Lydia Henry, *Jewels Of Brandenburg* (1947) as Carmelita Mendoza, *Arctic Manhunt* (1949) as Narana, *Apache Chief* (1949) as Watona, *Killer Ape* (1953) as Shari, *Conquest Of Cochise* (1953) as Terua and *Yukon Vengeance* (1954) as Yellow

Flower. Her career began to grind inexorably to a halt in the mid-Fifties when she was too old to play *ingénues*. Her last film was *The Hypnotic Eye* (1960), in which she played Doris Scott.

CAUSE: She died by her own hand aged 48.

Gene Tierney

Born November 20, 1920
Died November 6, 1991

JFK's squeeze. Born in Brooklyn, New York, Gene Eliza Tierney came from a wealthy background and appeared on Broadway before making her film début opposite Henry Fonda in *The Return Of Frank James* (1940) as Eleanor Stone at 20th Century Fox. It was at Fox that she spent most of her career although it seemed that the studio didn't really know what to do with her and she was often miscast. She was linked romantically with playboys John F. Kennedy (for whom, she claimed, she spurned the advances of Tyrone Power) and Aly Khan and was described by one critic as "a woman of exotic and quite unusual beauty". Her films included: *Hudson's Bay* (1940) as Barbara Hall, *Belle Starr* (1941) as Belle Starr, *Tobacco Road* (1941) as Ellie May Lester, *Sundown* (1941) as Zia, *Thunder Birds* (1942) as Kay Saunders, *China Girl* (1942) as Miss Young, *Son Of Fury* (1942) as Eve, *Heaven Can Wait* (1943) as Martha, *Laura* (1944) as Laura Hunt, *Leave Her To Heaven* (1945) as Ellen Berent for which she was nominated for an Oscar, *Dragonwyck* (1946) as Miranda Wells, *The Ghost And Mrs Muir* (1947) as Lucy Muir, *That Wonderful Urge* (1948) as Sara Farley, *Whirlpool* (1949) as Ann Sutton, *Where The Sidewalk Ends* (1950) as Morgan Taylor, *Night And The City* (1950) as Mary Bristol, *On The Riviera* (1951) as Lilli, *Way Of A Gaucho* (1952) as Teresa, *Plymouth Adventure* (1952) as Dorothy Bradford, *Personal Affair* (1953) as Kay Barlow, *Never Let Me Go* (1953) as Marva

Lamarkins, *Black Widow* (1954) as Iris, *The Egyptian* (1954) as Baketamon and *The Left Hand Of God* (1955) as Anne Scott following which she retired. She suffered a nervous breakdown and became a voluntary inmate of a mental institution. Otto Preminger tempted her out of retirement to play Washington hostess Dolly Harrison in *Advise And Consent* (1962) but although she made a handful of films and appeared in the television series *Scruples*, she preferred a quiet retirement in Texas. On June 1, 1941, she married designer Oleg Cassini after eloping with him to Las Vegas. They had two daughters: Daria (b. prematurely in Columbia Hospital, Washington, October 14, 1943, weighing 2½lb) and Christina (b. New York, November 18, 1948). Daria was born blind and severely retarded and today lives in an institution. Her disabilities may have been caused by a fan of her mother's, who though infected with German measles and quarantined, was determined to meet and shake her hand. The couple divorced in Santa Monica on February 28, 1952, when Tierney claimed Cassini was more interested in playing tennis than their marriage. On July 11, 1960, she married Houston oilman Howard Lee who was previously married to Hedy Lamarr. He died in 1980 and she never remarried. CAUSE: She died aged 70 in Houston, Texas, from emphysema.

Lawrence Tierney

Born March 15, 1919
Died February 26, 2002
'The handsome bad man of the screen'. Born to Irish parents and educated in Brooklyn, New York, Lawrence Tierney achieved real fame late in life when he played the gangster who arranged the heist in *Reservoir Dogs* (1992). Tierney was one of three sons of a policeman, who all became actors. The others were Scott Brady (b. Brooklyn, New York, September 13,

1924, d. Los Angeles, California, April 16, 1985 from emphysema) and Ed Tracy (b. Brooklyn, New York, May 13, 1928, d. Orange, California, December 18, 1985) from whom he was estranged. Tierney often played thugs and his off-screen life was fodder for the gossip columns. Tierney was an outstanding athlete and gained an athletics scholarship to Manhattan College, but left to become a labourer on the New York aqueduct. He worked briefly as a model for Sears-Roebuck but eventually took to acting and his talent was soon recognised. In 1943 he signed a contract with RKO. It was when he played the title role in *Dillinger* in 1945 while on loan to the independent producers Maurice and Frank King that he first established himself. Returning to RKO he appeared in *Kill Or Be Killed* (1946) and *The Devil Thumbs A Ride* (1947). During this period, Tierney also appeared in *Born To Kill* (1947), *San Quentin* (1950) and *The Greatest Show On Earth* (1952). Off screen Tierney gained a reputation as a bad boy. His offences included hitting a waiter in the face with a sugar bowl. In 1961 he was convicted of breaking a student's jaw when he kicked him in the face. The same year he gatecrashed a party hosted by Elizabeth Taylor and was sent to jail for disturbing the peace. He had violated his probation, having been arrested the previous year for drunken driving. In 1963 he was arrested on a charge of drunkenness after a woman claimed that he had driven her around for hours, having kidnapped her, and the following year he was found guilty of attempting to throttle a taxi driver. In January 1973 he was stabbed in a brawl outside a bar near the hotel where he lived in on 9th Avenue, New York. In June 1975 he was questioned by the police in connection with the apparent suicide of Bonnie Jones, a 24-year old woman, who fell out of her fourth floor window. Tierney said that he "had just gotten there, and she just went out the window". He also had a serious alcohol problem. He gave up the demon drink in the late Eighties. "I finally wised up," he said. "I threw away about seven careers through drink." He made a serious attempt to return to acting as a character actor. In 1987 he appeared in *Tough Guys Don't Dance*, which told the story of a writer who drinks so much that he cannot remember if he committed a murder. Romantically, he was linked with Dorothy Lovett, Betsy von Furstenburg, Shelley Winters and Yvonne De Carlo. His nephew Michael said, "The people who knew Larry knew that wasn't all that there was to Larry. He was a wacky, kind of quirky, comical guy, and a very nice man to a lot of people."

CAUSE: Tierney died from pneumonia. in Los Angeles, California, aged 82.

Ann Todd

Born January 24, 1909
Died May 6, 1993

Cool and refined. Born in Hartford, Cheshire, she was educated at St Winifred's School in Eastbourne before being trained at the Central School of Speech Training and Dramatic Art in London and making her stage début at the Arts Theatre on January 28, 1928, as a Faery Child in *The Land Of Heart's Desire*. Her first film came three years later, *Keepers Of Youth* (1931) as Millicent, but it would be almost another decade and a half before she became a star as a result of her performance as Francesca Cunningham in *The Seventh Veil* (1945). Her films included: *These Charming People* (1931) as Pamela Crawford, *The Return Of Bulldog Drummond* (1934) as Phyllis Drummond, *Things To Come* (1936) as Mary Gordon, *South Riding* (1938) as Madge Carne, *Action For Slander* (1938) as Ann Daviot, *Poison Pen* (1939) as Ann Rider, *Granny Get Your Gun* (1940) as Charlotte Westcott, *Little Orvie* (1940) as Patsy Balliser, *Ships With Wings* (1941) as Kay

Gordon, *Danny Boy* (1941) as Jane Kaye, *On The Sunny Side* (1942) as Betty, *Dixie Dugan* (1943) as Imogene Dugan, *Perfect Strangers* (1945) as Elena, *Gaiety George* (1946) as Kathryn Davis, *Daybreak* (1947) as Frankie, *So Evil My Love* (1948) as Olivia Harwood, *Madeleine* (1950) as Madeleine Smith, *Time Without Pity* (1956) as Honor Stanford, *Taste Of Fear* (1961) as Jane Appleby, *Ninety Degrees In The Shade* (1965) as Mrs Kurka, *The Fiend* (1971) as Birdie Wemyss and *The Human Factor* (1980) as Mrs Castle. Towards the end of her life Todd directed documentaries. Her autobiography was entitled *The Eighth Veil*, a reference to the film that made her famous; she also wrote two novels. She was married and divorced three times. Her husbands were Victor Malcolm by whom she had one son, Nigel Tangye by whom she had one daughter and Sir David Lean, who directed her in a number of films.

CAUSE: She died aged 84 in London from a stroke.

Bob Todd

Born December 15, 1921
Died October 20, 1992

Comedic stooge. Born in Faversham, Kent, he is best known as one of Benny Hill's straight men yet he actually began his working life breeding cattle. It was only when that business failed in 1962 that he turned to acting, making his television début in *Citizen James* and his film début in *Postman's Knock* (1962) as the district superintendent. He soon became a stalwart of British comedy, working with Michael Bentine, Dick Emery, Marty Feldman and Des O'Connor. His films included: *Carry On Again, Doctor* (1969), *Scars Of Dracula* (1970) as Burgomaster, *She'll Follow You Anywhere* (1971), *Adolf Hitler – My Part In His Downfall* (1972) as Referee, *Digby, The Biggest Dog In The World* (1973) as The Great Manzini, *The Ups And Downs Of A Handyman* (1975) as

Squire Bullsworthy, *Confessions Of A Pop Performer* (1975) as Mr Barnwell, *Come Play With Me* (1977) as the Vicar, *Rosie Dixon – Night Nurse* (1978) as Mr Buchanan, *Superman III* (1983) and *The Return Of The Musketeers* (1989).

CAUSE: He died aged 70 of natural causes.

Mike Todd

(AVRAM HIRSCH GOLDBOGEN)
Born June 22, 1907
Died March 22, 1958
Flamboyant producer. Born in Minneapolis, Minnesota, the son of Rabbi Chaim Goldbogen, he earned his first money as a boy shining shoes for a nickel and stealing cigars to sell at 3¢ each. He later sold worthless watches for $5. He began producing musicals, burlesque and strip shows. On February 14, 1927, he married Bertha Freshman by whom he had a son, Mike Jr (see below). After 20 years he wanted a divorce, which she refused to give him. He was seeing Joan Blondell and stripper Gypsy Rose Lee at the time. Shortly after the divorce papers were issued Mike and Bertha fought and she cut herself on a kitchen knife, severing the tendons in her hand. Todd suggested she needed hospital treatment. He drove her there but she died under anaesthesia, reportedly from shock. Todd was cleared of any malfeasance in her death, despite rumours that he had bribed the anaesthetist. In July 1947 he married actress Joan Blondell at the El Rancho Vegas Hotel in Las Vegas. He spent her money, went bankrupt for a second time and they divorced on June 8, 1950. He also broke her arm during a fight. He began romancing Evelyn Keyes but dumped her for Elizabeth Taylor, whom he married on February 2, 1957. He gave Taylor a 29.5 carat engagement ring that cost him $92,000. Their daughter, Elizabeth Frances 'Liza' Todd, was born in New York six months later, on August 6,

1957. All this despite the fact that Todd once proclaimed: "I'll never marry an actress. To live with an actress ya gotta be able to worry about her hair. And when their bosoms start to drop they get panicky and run to head shrinkers." Todd developed a widescreen camera system called Todd-AO to enhance viewing pleasure. It was shown to advantage in *Around The World In 80 Days* (1956), for which Todd wanted to include 50 stars, 68,894 extras filmed in 13 countries and wearing 74,685 costumes. Todd, already wealthy, became a very rich man indeed following the success of *Around The World In 80 Days*. He spent $3,000 a month renting a Lockheed Lodestar that he nicknamed *The Liz* and another $5,000 to put a phone on board. He also had cigars made especially for him, rented a yacht, bought two cinemas and rented mansions in Beverly Hills, Palm Springs and Westport, Connecticut. And as if that wasn't enough, he also gave Taylor amazing amounts of jewellery every Saturday night to mark the 'anniversary' of the day of the week they met. Perhaps Todd had some prescience. He told a friend: "I'm aware that this is the best time of my life. But I'm so happy it almost scares me. Being a gambling man, I know the law of averages and I get spooked I'll have to lose something to compensate for being so damn lucky." What he lost was his life.

CAUSE: In March 1958 Todd was elected Showman of the Year by the Friars Club of New York. He decided to fly in *The Liz* to New York, stopping off in Chicago to watch Sugar Ray Robinson fight Carmen Basilio before the return flight to Hollywood. Todd invited Joseph Mankiewicz, Kirk Douglas, publicist Warren Cowan, agent Kurt Frings and journalist James Bacon to accompany him. All declined, Bacon because of the bad weather. At 10.11pm on March 21, the plane took off, with pilots William S. Verner and

Thomas Barclay, Todd and his biographer Art Cohn aboard. Todd kissed Taylor six times before he drove to Burbank airport and promised to call her when the plane refuelled in Tulsa, Oklahoma. As it approached Tulsa the plane encountered a storm and the pilots asked traffic control for permission to climb to 13,000 feet and above the turbulence. However, the storm raged just as fiercely at that altitude and at 2.40pm, with its wings frozen, *The Liz* crashed into the Zuni Mountains in New Mexico. All aboard were burned to death and only dental records enabled the bodies to be identified. Todd had been married to Taylor for 414 days. He had spent $25,000 to put a bedroom aboard the plane but just $2,000 to improve the de-icing equipment. According to the manufacturer the plane's payload should have been no more than 18,605lb. With the additions Todd had put on board, it now weighed 20,757lb – a weight that proved fatal.

Mike Todd, Jr

Born October 8, 1929
Died May 5, 2002
Creator of Smell-o-Vision. The only son of legendary Broadway and film producer Mike Todd and his first wife, Bertha Freshman (d. 1946), Todd Jr is best known as the producer of *Scent Of Mystery*, the first, and thankfully the only, film to use "Smell-o-Vision", a technique of piping scents into a cinema to synchronise with the action on screen. The film premièred in Chicago in 1960, and with an all-star cast including Denholm Elliott, Peter Lorre, Elizabeth Taylor and Diana Dors, the publicity was overwhelming. "First they moved (1895)! Then they talked (1927)! Now they smell!" The film featured 30 different smells, released via tiny pipes connected to the back of each seat. The smells were produced by a New Jersey-based company that was founded by Raoul Pantaleone, an Italian immigrant, who

claimed that Pope Urban VI was one of his ancestors. The whiffs included baking bread, pipe tobacco, grass and clover, cheap perfume (for Diana Dors). The film flopped in America because the cinema was unable to synchronise smells and on-screen action. *Time* magazine wrote: "Customers will probably agree that the smell they liked best was the one they got during the intermission: fresh air." In Britain the film flopped for another reason. Cinemas could not afford the expensive "Smell-o-Vision" equipment and without the pongs the film took on a surreal quality, since there was no reason why, for example, a loaf of bread should be lifted from the oven and thrust into the camera for what seemed to be an unconscionably long time. Born in Los Angeles, Todd quickly joined his father in the entertainment business and worked with him on his 1956 blockbuster *Around The World In 80 Days*. It was Todd Sr who developed Smell-o-Vision but died before he could develop the project. The system Mike Todd, Sr had used for his Cinerama productions was named "Todd AO"; the system Todd Jr employed for the first smelly fiction film was unkindly dubbed "Todd-BO". Todd, who never made a successful film, emigrated to Ireland in 1973. In 1953 he married Sarah Weaver, who died in 1972. They had three sons, Cyrus, Daniel and Oliver, and three daughters, Susan, Sarah and Eliza. In 1972 he married Susan McCarthy and he had two more sons, Del and James. CAUSE: Todd died aged 72 of lung cancer at his home in Borris, County Carlow, Ireland.

Richard Todd, OBE

(RICHARD ANDREW PALETHORPE-TODD)
Born June 11, 1919
Died December 3, 2009
Real and reel life hero. Born in Dublin, Ireland, the son of a doctor who was an international Irish rugby player, Richard Todd was raised in India

where his father was in the Army. When the family moved to West Devon Todd attended Shrewsbury School before going to Sandhurst, but decided a military career was not for him and enrolled at the Italia Conti Academy. His mother was unhappy with the change of her son's career and committed suicide. Todd began his acting career at the Open Air Theatre, Regent's Park in 1936 in a production of *Twelfth Night*. In 1939 he co-founded the Dundee Repertory Theatre but his career was interrupted by the outbreak of war and he enlisted in the Army on September 4, 1939. Commissioned in 1941, he served in the King's Own Yorkshire Light Infantry before joining the Parachute Regiment and being assigned to the 7th (Light Infantry) Parachute Battalion as part of the British 6th Airborne Division. On D-Day, June 6, 1944 Todd was one of the first British officers to be parachuted into Normandy as part of Operation Overlord. He landed near Pegasus Bridge near Caen and he and his men along with Major John Howard played an important part in fighting off German counter attacks. On demob, Todd returned to acting and rep. "I have no idea why but acting was in my blood. God knows how I managed it, but none of it was spilled in the war," he said. In 1948 he was offered a film contract with Associated British. After playing the role on stage in London, he was cast as the dour young Corporal Lachlan McLachlan in Warner Bros' *The Hasty Heart* (1949) and was nominated for a Best Actor Oscar. In 1952 he played in his first Disney film *The Story Of Robin Hood And His Merrie Men* as the outlaw. He also appeared in *The Sword And The Rose* (1953) and *Rob Roy, The Highland Rogue* (1954) (chosen as the Royal Command Film performance) for the same studio. Todd remembered, "My image was all daring deeds, until my swash began to buckle a bit." In 1953 he played Heathcliff in the BBC television production of *Wuthering Heights* after he expressed an interest in the part. In 1955 he played Wing Commander Guy Gibson in *The Dam Busters* although subsequent broadcasts of the film have run into problems because of the name Gibson gave to his black Labrador, the decidedly politically incorrect Nigger. Of the role Todd said, "It was a most wonderful part. I wasn't the highest-earning matinee idol of the period. But it was much better than being shot at, for God's sake. I always reminded myself of that whenever I was in danger of feeling hard done by." His other films included *A Man Called Peter* (1955) as Peter Marshall, *The Virgin Queen* (1955) as Sir Walter Raleigh opposite Bette Davis as Queen Elizabeth I (the film flopped and Todd later rued, "Maybe if I'd played the queen") *D-Day The Sixth Of June* (1956), *Marie-Antoinette Reine De France* (1956) as Comte Axel von Fersen, *Yangtse Incident* (1957) as Commander John Kerans, *Saint Joan* (1957), *Danger Within* (1958) and *The Long And The Short And The Tall* (1961). In the last, he appeared with Laurence Harvey and Richard Harris who one lunchtime made fun of 5ft 8in Todd's diminutive stature by digging a hole for him to stand in to make him appear even shorter than his two tall co-stars. He took the "joke" in good stead saying, "How can you take seriously a bunch of actors playing silly buggers? If the prank amused them, it was fine with me. Elstree Studios isn't exactly war-torn France, is it?" It never occurred to him to mention that neither of his co-stars had ever served in a war. Always self-effacing, he said, "'I wish I had half the courage of some of those chaps I've played on the screen. That was wartime. You behave quite differently in war. You don't have much time to dwell on what you're doing when the bullets are zipping around. I put all that stuff behind me once the war ended." Todd was Ian

Fleming's choice to play James Bond in *Dr No* (1962) but producer Harry Saltzman thought him too short and cast Sean Connery instead. In the 1962 film *The Longest Day*, Todd played Major John Howard, the man with whom he had served on D-Day. His later films included *The Boys* (1962), *Death Drums Along The River* (1963), *Operation Crossbow* (1965), *The Love-Ins* (1967), *Subterfuge* (1968), *The Big Sleep* (1978) as Commander Barker and *House Of The Long Shadows* (1983) as Sam Allyson. In 1982 Todd guest-starred in four episodes of *Doctor Who*. Todd was married twice. On August 13, 1949 he married Catherine Stewart Crawford Grant-Bogle, whom he met in Dundee Repertory. Before their divorce in 1970 they had a son Peter (b. 1952) and a daughter Fiona. On September 21, 2005, Peter killed himself with a shotgun in East Malling, Kent, following the break-up of his marriage. In 1970 Todd married model Virginia Mailer; they divorced in 1992. They had two sons Andrew and Seamus (b. 1977). In 1997 Seamus shot himself in the head in the family home in Lincolnshire. A shotgun from the family gun cupboard was beside his bed. He had been taking a drug to combat his severe acne and an inquest ruled that it may have left him suicidally depressed. Todd said, "When I went to see his body I gave him a kiss and told him he had been a silly boy. It was such an appalling waste. None of us can understand why he did it. He was so popular and loved." Todd believed that the death may have been caused by an argument that he had had with his son after he crashed a car. "'I will never forgive myself. I was too hard on him. I gave Seamus an awful rollicking for crashing a little car I'd bought him. But I was too gruff, too military. He left a note saying he'd never be able to cope. In reality, he was a dazzling boy. He appeared to have the world at his feet . . . [I think that he did because he found himself in the] predicament that so many young people find themselves in nowadays, forced to live miserably, unhealthily, and in debt in order to achieve a university degree that is no longer even a fairly sure guarantee of employment at any level." Todd was a womaniser and on one occasion was almost caught out. He had been chosen as the guest of honour on *This Is Your Life* and had been brought to London on a ruse. So he decided to use the opportunity to see his girlfriend at his London *pied-a-terre* while his wife stayed in Lincolnshire. However, his wife knew about the show and had also decided to stay at the London flat. Todd was rescued in the nick of time by a friend. Todd, who was made an OBE in 1993, was never a great actor. He said, "I let myself become a willing workhorse. The roles were good, bad and indifferent, but I always gave a part my best shot and tried to enjoy it." CAUSE: Todd died aged 90 of cancer in his sleep at his Little Humby home.

Thelma Todd

Born July 29, 1906
Died December 16, 1935
'The ice cream blonde'. Born in Lawrence, Massachusetts, the daughter of a police lieutenant, 5'4" Thelma was an adorable baby with an overly protective mother. As a teenager Thelma shocked her neighbours by rarely wearing a bra and dressing in very short shorts. However, although she teased and flirted with men, often making suggestive remarks, she didn't actually go to bed with any of them. She kept men at a distance because of the remoteness from her own father, whom she idolised. In 1923 she enrolled in Lowell State Normal School, a teacher training college. Thelma wanted to be a schoolteacher but was inept at chemistry until she began seeing the class hunk, who helped her to get through her course, to the detriment of his own ambitions. He spent so much time helping Thelma he

failed his own exams. Thelma worked as a model to pay for her schooling. In the summer of 1925 the Todd family holidayed on a farm in northern Massachusetts. During the break, Thelma's brother, William, was killed when he fell into a grain silo and was suffocated and then crushed to death. His body was never found. In August of that year, Thelma learned she was a finalist in the Miss Massachusetts beauty contest. A beau had entered her picture without telling her. Thelma ignored the first telegram from the organisers and so they sent a second. Her mother intercepted the letter, and substituted one of her own, saying Thelma would be thrilled to enter. Unsurprisingly, Thelma won the competition. That resulted in a call from Hollywood and Thelma made her film début in *Fascinating Youth* (1926) as Lorraine Lane opposite Buddy Rogers and Josephine Dunn. That led to a highly successful movie career working as a foil for virtually every comedian in pictures. She appeared with Ed Wynn in *Rubber Heels* (1927) as Princess Aline, Charley Chase in *Snappy Sneezer* (1929), *Crazy Feet* (1929), *Stepping Out* (1929), Harry Langdon in *Sky Boy* (1929), *The Shrimp* (1930) and *All Teed Up* (1930) among others, with the Marx Brothers in *Monkey Business* (1931) as Lucille and *Horse Feathers* (1932) as Connie Bailey, and with Laurel & Hardy in *Unaccustomed As We Are* (1929) as Mrs Kennedy, *Chickens Come Home* (1931) as Mrs Hardy and *On The Loose* (1931). By 1935 she was receiving 500 fan letters a week. Four years earlier, in May 1931, she met Pasquale DiCicco (b. 1909, d. New York, 1980 of natural causes) known as Pat. DiCicco was a handsome playboy who supposedly made his money from being an agent, though friendships with various hoodlums made this claim somewhat suspect. He also had a fearsome temper. On July 18, 1932, the couple eloped to Prescott, Arizona. Thelma confessed to a friend that she wasn't in love with her new husband but that she needed a friend. Hollywood columnist Sidney Skolsky wrote of the newlyweds: "His pet name for her is Lambie. She never argues with him. He says she hasn't sense enough to argue . . ." Within weeks of the marriage they were living separate lives with DiCicco spending much of his time in New York. Whenever Thelma asked where he had been and with whom she received a punch in the face for her troubles; she quickly learned not to ask. She had had an alcohol problem before her marriage but her husband's cruelty and indifference pushed her back into the bottle and she began taking drugs as well to numb the pain of her loveless match. One day DiCicco came home to find his wife doubled up in pain and assumed that she was high, drunk or both. Luckily, he realised she was ill and she was taken to hospital where she underwent an emergency appendectomy. The stay in hospital gave her time to once again wean herself off her addictions and DiCicco also became more attentive for the first time since their wedding. It didn't last long and soon DiCicco was off on another of his jaunts. Thelma found solace with recently separated producer and director Roland West (b. Cleveland, Ohio, 1887, d. 1952). He became Thelma's financial manager, and together they opened Thelma Todd's Sidewalk Cafe at 17575 Pacific Coast Highway, north of Santa Monica. Thelma and DiCicco were divorced on March 2, 1934. That year she began an affair with gangster Charles 'Lucky' Luciano (b. Lercara Friddi, Palermo, Sicily, November 24, 1897, d. Capodichino Airport, Naples, Italy, January 26, 1962, of a heart attack) who 'arranged' for her to become hooked on diet pills, knowing he could use them to keep her subservient. Luciano began pressing Thelma to let him use a room at the Sidewalk Cafe for a gambling den but she refused, screaming at him in the Brown Derby restaurant "Over my dead body" to which the man they called Charley Lucifer responded: "That can be arranged."

CAUSE: On December 14, 1935, Thelma attended a party at the Cafe Trocadero in Hollywood. Roland West had told her to be home before 2am or he would lock her out. DiCicco had wangled an invitation. Actress Ida Lupino, a friend of Thelma, recalled: "Pat had asked especially for an invitation to the party at which Thelma was a guest of honour. He was to be seated by her side at the dinner. This was at his request and Thelma's. Instead, he came with [actress] Margaret Lindsay and they did not join her party. He and Thelma spoke, but she was very indignant. She berated him bitterly for slighting me and herself." At 12.15am DiCicco made a telephone call. An hour later, he and Margaret Lindsay left the gathering. Thelma had told Lupino: "I'm right in the middle of the loveliest romance I've ever had." She didn't name anyone but said the man was in San Francisco. Lupino asked if West knew and Thelma said she thought he probably did. At the end of the evening, recounted Lane: "Thelma stood facing the entrance of the Trocadero, just before she got into her car, and with an extravagant gesture of salute said: 'Goodbye!' This struck members of the party as very strange. It seemed a salute of farewell." Before she left the Trocadero at 2.45am, Thelma was told by a waiter that a man was waiting to see her. He was an acolyte of Lucky Luciano, but Thelma refused his 'invitation' to the beach where the gangster was waiting. Thelma had invited some of the party-goers to her cafe for an informal Sunday evening social. She had also let it be known she'd be attending a Sunday afternoon party that actor Wallace Ford's wife was giving at home. Thelma had arrived at the Trocadero alone and

left that way. She had had a few drink-driving incidents and was 'advised' not to drive, especially at night, so she hired a chauffeur, Ernest Peters, to drive her around. Back in the car Thelma urged Peters to put his foot to the floor until they got back to the Sidewalk Cafe at 3.30am. Peters didn't walk his employer to the door as was his custom. Breathing heavily, Thelma watched her car drive away. Then she heard another, a brown Packard, driving slowly through fog towards her. The headlights were off. As it stopped by her, a door opened and a voice told her to get in. It belonged to Lucky Luciano. For six hours they drove around until the car stopped in front of a tobacconists where Thelma rushed in and asked the owner, W.F. Persson, to dial a number for her but as he did so she vanished. At 10.30am on Monday December 16, Thelma's body was found by her maid, May Whitehead, slumped on the front seat of her Packard convertible in her garage at 17531 Posetano Road, the sliding doors slightly opened. According to Dr A.F. Wagner, Los Angeles County's autopsy surgeon, Thelma Todd died at the hands of that silent assassin, carbon monoxide. It billowed from her car to smother her moans and turn her into the cherry-red corpse of asphyxiation. Dr Wagner fixed the time of death at between 6 and 8am Sunday – 24 hours before the maid said she found the body. As related above, Thelma was alive at 9am on the Sunday, an hour after she had, according to the coroner, shook off this mortal coil. What did Dr Wagner make of the patches of blood on Thelma's face and on the seat and running board of the car? He suggested Thelma's head struck the steering wheel when asphyxia set in and she lapsed into the coma preceding death. What did he make of the later findings in the autopsy analysis of her stomach contents – undigested peas and beans? Peas and beans weren't served at the

Trocadero on Saturday night. How did they find their way into Thelma's digestive tract? Had she stopped off somewhere for a bite after Peters dropped her off? No answers to those questions. While there was no evidence of a struggle – her make-up and tinted nails, first casualties of modern woman in distress, suffered no damage – the blood left a lot to be accounted for despite Dr Wagner's implausible explanation. Certainly it was a more than reasonable assumption that someone could have quarrelled with Thelma, then struck her and thrown her half-dazed into the car, started the motor, and sneaked away into the darkness. A simple bang on the head after lapsing into unconsciousness would not have dislodged a dental filling in her mouth, nor bruised Thelma's lip. The investigation quickly focussed on what had been headline reading only 10 months before. Thelma had received notes threatening her life unless she paid $10,000. She had been uneasy about it until six weeks before her death, when the would-be extortioner was arrested in the Astoria section of Queens, the New York City borough. The day after her body was found, the note-writer was committed to a hospital for the insane and was subsequently ruled out as a suspect in her death. Roland West commanded a big share of the spotlight of suspicion. He told police that he waited up for Thelma until 2am on the Sunday, then had gone to bed after locking the door. He said Todd had no key, so in effect, "I locked her out." It was suggested that when she couldn't get into the apartment, Thelma went to the garage, got into the car, and tried to sleep. But being December, it was cold. In a bid to keep warm Thelma turned the motor on for the warmth of the heater – and carbon monoxide poisoning killed her. But those deadly fumes would surely have escaped through the partly open garage doors and we know they were open because the maid said

so. The coroner's jury returned a verdict of suicide but that was overturned by a grand jury order. At that hearing the maid May Whitehead revealed that she had given Thelma a key to the apartment, which ruled out West's story that he had locked Thelma out. The key and valuable jewellery were found in Thelma's handbag. Ida Lupino testified and said that although outwardly happy, Thelma was "one of the unhappiest persons who ever lived". The Jury foreman, George Rochester, added his two pennyworth: "I and other members of the jury believe a plot is afoot to show that Thelma Todd had a suicide complex, even though she had youth, health, wealth, fame, admiration, love, and happy prospects. It looks as if they are trying to build up this case as a suicide, but in the actual evidence, I have found nothing to support this theory definitely. I suggest the possibility strongly exists this was a monoxide murder!" For the benefit of the grand jury, authorities even recreated Thelma's so-called 'death walk' – the stroll she had to have taken to reach the scene of her death. A policewoman about the size of Thelma Todd climbed the 270 steps to the garage where the body was found. The slippers she wore in the test were considerably scuffed and caked in dirt. The dainty sandal slippers Thelma had on her feet when found behind the wheel of the car were spotless. She could not have made that long climb herself. That left unanswered the question of how she reached the garage from the street. Was she carried? Who was strong enough to haul her amplitudinous body all that distance? The cafe treasurer, Charles H. Smith, who slept above the garage, told investigators he heard no car engine running that early Sunday morning. Moreover, the touring car in which Thelma was found dead still had two gallons of petrol left in its tank. Why did the engine stop running? The ignition was on, but had someone turned it on to fake a carbon monoxide poisoning death? Mrs Wallace Ford lent the crowning touch to the mystery when she told the grand jury that she received a call at 4pm on Sunday from a voice that sounded "exactly like Thelma's". The message from Thelma was: "You're going to be surprised at the person I am bringing to your party." But how could she have spoken on the phone to Wallace Ford's wife at four in the afternoon when Miss Todd was supposed to have died between six and eight that morning? The most surprising advocate of suicide came from a very strange quarter. Alice Todd, Thelma's widowed mother, had travelled 3,300 miles from Massachusetts to put down the inquiry into her daughter's strange death. She said: "This investigation and the manner in which it is being conducted is the work of cheap politicians looking for jobs at the expense of my daughter's name. She is dead and is not able to defend herself. But I am here and I will defend her good name. I certainly am convinced that Thelma's death was an accident. If I am satisfied, I don't see why anyone else is interested." On December 21 – five days after her body was found – the LAPD formally dropped their investigation into Thelma's death. Captain Bert Wallis and Chief of Detectives Joe Taylor agreed with the county autopsy surgeon's report and coroner's jury verdict that the actress died "apparently accidentally". Yet Deputy District Attorney George Johnson, who was in charge of the investigation for the prosecutor's office, not only discounted the murder theory but also shied away from the idea Thelma's death was an accident. "It seems too difficult to believe Miss Todd went to that garage and started the motor of her car to keep warm. I believe it was suicide." The grand jury probe also came to nothing. Several weeks after her death, Mayor Hermon Peery of Ogden, Utah, attempted

to reopen the case. He said a black-haired, well-dressed, middle-aged woman called from a pay phone and dictated a message to the Western Union office there, addressed to the Los Angeles police. She claimed a man, a resident of a local hotel since January, was Thelma Todd's killer. She not only identified him but told police where he could be found. The message was relayed to Ogden Police Chief Rial Moore, who also wanted to begin an all-out investigation. The reply from the Los Angeles police: "No one is being sought in connection with Thelma Todd's death. The case is closed." So what happened? After interrogating Thelma to try and find out what she knew of his various scams and rackets, Luciano dropped her off at the Cafe. Thinking she was safe, Thelma made to go to her home but was grabbed by two men, one of whom punched her in the face, breaking her nose. The other carried her to her car and placed her on the front seat. He switched on the ignition and closed the garage door, but did not lock it. Some hours later, the door would open about six inches; unless it was locked, it always did. Weak from the beating, heady from champagne and tired, Thelma did not have the strength to open the car door, nor turn off the ignition. She died shortly after midnight on December 16, 1935. She was just 29 years old.

FURTHER READING: *Hot Toddy: The True Story Of Hollywood's Most Sensational Murder* – Andy Edmonds (London: Macdonald, 1989).

Sidney Toler

Born April 28, 1874
Died February 12, 1947
Charlie Chan No 2. Born in Warrensburg, Missouri, Toler was a heavy-set stage actor who had an undistinguished film career until he became the second non-Oriental to take on the mantle of the famous detective Charlie Chan, following the

death of Warner Oland. Toler's competitors to play Chan included Noah Beery and Leo Carillo. His early films included: *In The Nick Of Time* (1929), *Madame X* (1929) as Dr Merivel, *White Shoulders* (1931) as William Sothern, *Strictly Dishonorable* (1931) as Officer Mulligan, *Radio Patrol* (1932) as Sergeant Keogh, *Is My Face Red?* (1932) as Tony Mugatti, *Blondie Of The Follies* (1932) as Pete, *Tom Brown Of Culver* (1932) as Major Wharton, *Blonde Venus* (1932), *King Of The Jungle* (1933) as Neil Forbes, *Billion Dollar Scandal* (1933) as Carter B. Moore, *Upperworld* (1934) as Officer Moran, *Spitfire* (1934) as Mr Sawyer, *Operator 13* (1934) as Major Allen, *Massacre* (1934) as Thomas Shanks, *Dark Hazard* (1934) as John Bright, *Registered Nurse* (1934) as Frankie Sylvestrie, *Here Comes The Groom* (1934) as Detective Weaver, *This Is The Life* (1935) as Professor Breckenridge, *Orchids To You* (1935) as Nick Corsini, *Three Godfathers* (1936) as Professor Snape, *The Gorgeous Hussy* (1936) as Daniel Webster, *That Certain Woman* (1937) as Detective Lieutenant Neely, *Double Wedding* (1937) as Keough, *Up The River* (1938) as Jeffrey Mitchell, *One Wild Night* (1938) as Lawton and *Gold Is Where You Find It* (1938) as Harrison McCooey. He played the inscrutable detective in 22 films. Like Oland, Toler eschewed elaborate make-up for his portrayals of the sleuth. His films in the series were: *Charlie Chan In Honolulu* (1938), *City In Darkness* (1939), *Charlie Chan At Treasure Island* (1939), *Charlie Chan In Reno* (1939), *Murder Over New York* (1940), *Charlie Chan's Murder Cruise* (1940), *Charlie Chan In Panama* (1940), *Charlie Chan At The Wax Museum* (1940), *Dead Men Tell* (1941), *Charlie Chan In Rio* (1941), *Castle In The Desert* (1942), *Charlie Chan In The Secret Service* (1944), *The Chinese Cat* (1944), *Charlie Chan In Black Magic* (1944), *The Shanghai Cobra* (1945), *The Scarlet Clue* (1945), *The Red*

Dragon (1945), *The Jade Mask* (1945), *Shadows Over Chinatown* (1946), *Dark Alibi* (1946), *Dangerous Money* (1946) and *The Trap* (1947). On Toler's death Chan was played by yet another Caucasian, Roland Winters. Toler was married to supporting actress Viva Tattersall.

CAUSE: He died of intestinal cancer in Beverly Hills, aged 72.

David Tomlinson

Born May 7, 1917
Died June 24, 2000

Every child's favourite uncle. David Cecil MacAlister Tomlinson was born in Henley-on-Thames, Oxfordshire, the son of Florence Elizabeth Sinclair-Thomson and Clarence Samuel Tomlinson, a highly respected London lawyer who led a secret double life. Tomlinson found out by accident that, instead of living for 40 years at the Junior Carlton Club from Monday to Friday and spending weekends with his family in Folkestone, his father had lived during the week in Chiswick with a mistress by whom he had seven children. The secret only came to light when Tomlinson's brother, Peter, was travelling on the top of a double-decker bus through west London and saw his father in an upstairs room taking tea in his pyjamas. His father also "never gave up his search for the perfect piece of beef. This was the only perfection he ever sought." Tomlinson was educated at Tonbridge School but left without any qualifications. For 16 months from 1935 until 1936 he saw service with the Grenadier Guards. "The Foreign Legion would have been a holiday camp compared to life in the Guards," he later said. His father then secured for him a job as a clerk at Shell House in London. Tomlinson, who then had a stammer, was horrified. "But I'd like to be an actor," he stuttered. "Be an actor?" expostulated his father. "Good God, you can't even speak!" Over the coming years Tomlinson acted in amdram in Folkestone in his spare time. "Everyone in the business talked posh," he later explained, "and it was an advantage to have been to one of those terrible public schools." Tomlinson made his West End stage début at the Queen's on April 21, 1938 playing a walk-on part in *The Merchant Of Venice*. He was playing the bridegroom in a tour of *Quiet Wedding* when he was spotted by Anthony Asquith who cast him as John Royd, the best man, in *Quiet Wedding* (1940) opposite Margaret Lockwood. His early films included *Garrison Follies* (1940), *Pimpernel Smith* (1941) as Steve, *Name Rank And Number* (1941) and *My Wife's Family* (1941) as Willie Bagshott. However, almost as soon as his career had got off the ground than he joined the RAF in 1941 where he served during the Second World War, achieving the rank of Flight Lieutenant. Following demob in 1947, he returned to the stage and films where he mostly specialised in light comedies opining, "Personally I wouldn't want to go near *Hamlet*. Far too serious." He had his celebrity fans. Noel Coward once observed, "He looks like a very old baby." Tomlinson also eschewed the small screen claiming, "Television is all so rushed." He explained, "It's run by civil servants, you see – and all they know about the business is one line that goes, 'It'll be all right on the night.' They've no idea how to deal with nervous actors like me." He was Henry in *The Little Hut*, which ran at the Lyric Theatre for three years, starred in the film version of *Three Men In A Boat* (1956) as J and appeared with Peter Sellers in *Up The Creek* (1958) as Lieutenant Fairweather, a role he reprised in *Further Up The Creek* (1958). His other films included *I See A Dark Stranger* (1946) as an intelligence officer, *Master Of Bankdam* (1947) as Lancelot Handel Crowther, *Warning To Wantons* (1948) as Count Max Kardak, *Sleeping Car To Trieste* (1948) as Tom Bishop, *Love In Waiting* (1948) as Robert Clitheroe, *Here*

Come The Huggetts (1948) as Harold Hinchley, *Easy Money* (1948) as Martin, *My Brother's Keeper* (1948) as Ronnie Waring, *Miranda* (1948) as Charles, *Broken Journey* (1948) as Jimmy Marshall, *Vote For Huggett* (1949) as Harold, *Marry Me* (1949) as David Haig, *Landfall* (1949) as Binks, *Helter Skelter* (1949) as Nick Martin, *The Chiltern Hundreds* (1949) as Lord Tony Pym, *So Long At The Fair* (1950) as Johnny Barton, *The Wooden Horse* (1950) as Phil, *The Magic Box* (1951) as laboratory assistant, *Calling Bulldog Drummond* (1951) as Algy Longworth, *Hotel Sahara* (1951) as Captain Puffin Cheyne, *Made In Heaven* (1952) as Basil Topham, *Is Your Honeymoon Really Necessary?* (1952) as Frank Betterton, *Castle In The Air* (1952) as Earl of Locharne, *All For Mary* (1955) as Humpy Miller, *Carry On Admiral* (1957) as Tom Baker, *Follow That Horse!* (1960) as Dick Lanchester, *Tom Jones* (1963) as Lord Fellamar, *The Truth About Spring* (1964) as Skelton, *The Liquidator* (1965) as Quadrant, *City Under The Sea* (1965) as Harold Tiffin-Jones, *The Love Bug* (1968) as Peter Thorndyke, *Bons Baisers De Hong Kong* (1975) as Sir John MacGregor, *Wombling Free* (1977) as Roland Frogmorton, *The Water Babies* (1978) as Sir John, a lawyer in *Dominique* (1978) and *The Fiendish Plot Of Dr Fu Manchu* (1980) as Sir Roger Avery. There are two roles for which Tomlinson is most remembered. He played the ordered and orderly bank manager George W. Banks who lives with his two children, Jane and Michael, in Cherry Tree Lane in the smash hit *Mary Poppins* (1964) opposite Julie Andrews. Based on the 1934 book by P.L. Travers, *Mary Poppins* combined live action with artful animation winning five Oscars, including Best Song for 'Chim-Chim-Cher-ee'. Tomlinson was a huge fan of Disney: "They pay you well, and treat you like the Aga Khan." However when Tomlinson saw the rough cut of *Mary Poppins*, he was convinced the film would be a flop. "I thought it was appallingly sentimental and very nearly said, 'Well, Walt, you can't win them all.'" Oddly enough, Tomlinson was once involved in an argument with a real-life chimneysweep who, having arrived at Tomlinson's Buckinghamshire home to clean the chimneys, discovered that Tomlinson wanted to use the equipment himself. A heated stand-off ensued until the police were called and the situation was calmed. The second role was as Emelius Browne in *Bedknobs And Broomsticks* (1971). He always told children he was chosen as Emelius Browne because he was the only actor who could sing under water. A keen amateur pilot, in 1957 he crashed his red and silver Tiger Moth ten yards from his own back garden, watched by his wife and their two sons. One witness claimed to have seen him looping-the-loop and pretending to dive-bomb his own house. Responding to a "Don't fly again" petition organised by his neighbours, Tomlinson vowed to keep both feet on the ground in the future – until a jury at Aylesbury Quarter Sessions acquitted him on four charges of dangerous and low flying. He became a keen ornithologist and wrote several letters to the *Daily Telegraph* on the dangers to jet planes of birds nesting too close to runways. He also contributed valuable information on the nesting habits of the stork. He once opined, "I may look like a disappointed spaniel, but by nature I am cheerful." He enjoyed lunching in Boodle's, always shod in brightly polished shoes. He married the actress Audrey Freeman in 1953. They had four sons.

CAUSE: David Tomlinson died in his sleep, aged 83, at the King Edward VII Hospital, Buckinghamshire, following a series of strokes. He was buried in a cardboard coffin in his back garden in Mursley, near Milton Keynes, Buckinghamshire. He left £2,595,981.

Franchot Tone
Born February 27, 1905
Died September 18, 1968
Dashing society sophisticate. Stanislas Pascal Franchot Tone was born in Niagara Falls, New York, an indirect descendant of the Irish patriot Wolfe Tone (b. June 20, 1763, d. by his own hand, November 19, 1798). After being expelled from school "for being a subtle influence for disorder" Tone went to Cornell University, where he became President of the Drama Society. He began acting on stage in 1927 and signed a contract with MGM in 1932. He made his first film, *The Wiser Sex* (1932) as Phil Long, but loathed Hollywood, preferring the theatre, and always returned to the stage between movie assignments. His portrayal of midshipman Roger Byam in *Mutiny On The Bounty* (1935) earned him an Oscar nomination, but Tone was wont to make more headlines for his off-screen life rather than his on-. On October 11, 1935, he married Joan Crawford following her divorce from Douglas Fairbanks, Jr. They were together for less than four years, but Crawford was to later say that Tone was "an extremely loving, intelligent, considerate man . . . I wasn't as nice to him, as considerate, as I should have been . . . I didn't realise his insecurities and dissatisfactions ran so deeply. His sex life diminished considerably, which didn't help matters." His next wife, Jean Wallace (October 18, 1941–September 30, 1949) provided him with two sons: Pascal Franchot (b. Beverly Hills, California, July 29, 1943) and Thomas Jefferson (b. September 16, 1945). Following their divorce Tone took up with actress Barbara Payton and they announced their engagement at New York's Stork Club, despite opposition from many of his friends and ex-wife Joan Crawford. However, Payton was unable to remain faithful. Tone hired a private detective to keep track of her movements and discovered his wife

and Guy Madison in flagrante at her second floor home at 7456 Hollywood Boulevard. She then met thuggish actor Tom Neal and left Tone for him. Changing her mind, she went back to Tone. On September 13, 1951, she and Tone were together at her new apartment, 1803 Courtney Terrace, when Neal burst in and beat up Tone, who suffered a broken nose, fractured cheekbone and concussion and spent a fortnight in the California Lutheran Hospital and later had to undergo plastic surgery. Fifteen days later, she and Tone were married in Cloquet. Their honeymoon lasted just 72 hours before she began work on *Lady In The Iron Mask*. Shortly thereafter she was sacked. After 53 days of marital unbliss, Payton and Tone called it a day and she went back to Neal. Then she had second, or was it third or fourth, thoughts and, remembering Neal's temper, she went back to Tone briefly . . . but then left him again. In March 1952 she attempted suicide but was found in time by Tone. Despite his role in saving her life they divorced in May 1952, due to her "extreme mental cruelty". Tone married for the fourth and final time on May 14, 1956, to actress Dolores Dorn-Heft but the marriage was kept secret until 1958. A year later they divorced. His films included: *Stage Mother* (1933) as Warren Foster, *Midnight Mary* (1933) as Tom Mannering, *Bombshell* (1933) as Gifford Middleton, *Dancing Lady* (1933) as Tod Newton, *Gentlemen Are Born* (1934) as Bob Bailey, *One New York Night* (1935) as Foxhall, *The Lives Of A Bengal Lancer* (1935) as Lieutenant John Forsythe, *Reckless* (1935) as Bob Harrison, *Exclusive Story* (1936) as Dick Barton, *Suzy* (1936) as Terry Moore, *The Gorgeous Hussy* (1936) as John H. Eaton, *Quality Street* (1937) as Dr Valentine Brown, *Man-Proof* (1938) as Jimmy Kilmartin, *Three Comrades* (1938) as Otto Koster, *Fast And Furious* (1939) as Joel Sloane, *Trail Of The Vigilantes* (1940) as

Kansas, *She Knew All The Answers* (1941) as Mark Willows, *Five Graves To Cairo* (1943) as Corporal John J. Bramble, *Dark Waters* (1944) as Dr George Grover, *Phantom Lady* (1944) as Jack Marlow, *Because Of Him* (1946) as Paul Taylor, *Every Girl Should Be Married* (1948) as Roger Sanford, *I Love Trouble* (1948) as Stuart Bailey, *Jigsaw* (1949) as Howard Malloy, *Without Honor* (1950) as Dennis Williams, *Uncle Vanya* (1958) as Dr Mikhail Lvovich Astroff, which he also directed and produced, and *Nobody Runs Forever* (1968) as Ambassador Townsend.
CAUSE: Tone died aged 63 in New York, from lung cancer.

Regis Toomey
Born August 13, 1898
Died October 12, 1991
Stalwart actor. Born in Pittsburgh, Pennsylvania, 5'11" Toomey was in amdram for five years before trying his hand at the professional game. He went on to appear in over 170 films as well as making several regular appearances on television shows. His films included: *Alibi* (1929) as Danny McGann, *Illusion* (1929) as Eric, *Rich People* (1929) as Jef MacLean, *Framed* (1930) as Jimmy McArthur, *Crazy That Way* (1930) as Robert Metcalf, *Good Intentions* (1930) as Richard Holt, *Under Eighteen* (1931) as Jimmie, *Scandal Sheet* (1931) as Regan, *Other Men's Women* (1931) as Jack, *24 Hours* (1931) as Tony Bruzzi, *Finn And Hattie* (1931) as Collins, *Touchdown* (1931) as Tom Hussey, *Shopworn* (1932) as David Livingston, *State Trooper* (1933) as Michael Rolph, *She Had To Say Yes* (1933) as Tommy Nelson, *Redhead* (1934) as Scoop, *Murder On The Blackboard* (1934) as Detective Smiley North, *Skull And Crown* (1935) as Bob Franklin, *Red Morning* (1935) as John Hastings, *Great God Gold* (1935) as Phil Stuart, *One Frightened Night* (1935) as Tom Dean, *Manhattan Moon* (1935) as

Eddie, *Bulldog Edition* (1936) as Hardy, *Midnight Taxi* (1937) as Hilton, *Back In Circulation* (1937) as Buck, *Hunted Men* (1938) as Donovan, *Thunder Afloat* (1939) as Ives, *Street Of Missing Men* (1939) as Parker, *Smashing The Spy Ring* (1939) as Ted Hall, *Union Pacific* (1939) as Paddy O'Rourke, *His Girl Friday* (1940) as Sanders, *Northwest Passage* (1940) as Webster, *North West Mounted Police* (1940) as Constable Jerry Moore, *Arizona* (1940) as Grant Oury, *Meet John Doe* (1941) as Bert Hansen, *Dive Bomber* (1941) as Tim Griffin, *You're In The Army Now* (1941) as Captain Joe Radcliffe, *They Died With Their Boots On* (1941) as Fitzhugh Lee, *Tennessee Johnson* (1942) as McDaniel, *Bullet Scars* (1942) as Dr Steven Bishop, *I Was Framed* (1942) as Bob Leeds, *Jack London* (1943) as Scratch Nelson, *Destroyer* (1943) as Lieutenant Commander Clark, *Murder In The Blue Room* (1944) as Inspector McDonald, *Dark Mountain* (1944) as Steve Downey, *Strange Illusion* (1945) as Dr Vincent, *Spellbound* (1945) as Sergeant Gillespie, *Follow That Woman* (1945) as Barney Manners, *Mysterious Intruder* (1946) as James Summers, *The Big Sleep* (1946) as Bernie Ohls, *The Big Fix* (1947) as Lieutenant Brenner, *I Wouldn't Be In Your Shoes* (1948) as Judd, *Station West* (1948) as Goddard, *Mighty Joe Young* (1949) as John Young, *Undercover Girl* (1950) as Hank Miller, *Frenchie* (1950) as Carter, *My Pal Gus* (1952) as Farley Norris, *My Six Convicts* (1952) as Dr Gordon, *Son Of Belle Starr* (1953) as Tom Wren, *Island In The Sky* (1953) as Sergeant Harper, *Drums Across The River* (1954) as Sheriff Jim Beal, *Top Gun* (1955) as Jim O'Hara, *Guys And Dolls* (1955) as Arvide Abernathy, *Warlock* (1959) as Skinner, *Johnny Shiloh* (1963), *Cover Me Babe* (1970) as Michael, *Won Ton Ton, The Dog Who Saved Hollywood* (1976) as a burlesque stage-hand and *C.H.O.M.P.S.* (1979) as Chief Patterson.

CAUSE: Toomey died aged 93 of natural causes in the Motion Picture Country House and Hospital, 23450 Calabasas Road, Woodland Hills, San Fernando, California.

Spencer Tracy
Born April 5, 1900
Died June 10, 1967
'A man's man'. Spencer Bonaventure Tracy was born in Milwaukee, Wisconsin, and, following a Jesuit upbringing, intended to become a priest. On January 11, 1921 he matriculated at Ripon College, Wisconsin, where he first became interested in acting. He had a superb memory and was the only student to audition without reference to the script. On April 16, 1922 he changed tack and enrolled in New York's Academy of Dramatic Arts. The following year, on September 12, 1923, he married Louise Treadwell (b. 1896, d. November 13, 1983). They were still together at his death almost 44 years later although they lived separate lives. The devoutly Catholic Tracy would never consider a divorce. On June 26, 1924 son John was born totally deaf. He was to suffer ill-health throughout his life and was confined to a nursing home. Daughter Susie was born eight years later on July 1, 1932. He made his film début in *Up The River* (1930) with Humphrey Bogart who commented: "Spencer does it, that's all. Feels it. Says it. Talks. Listens. He means what he says when he says it, and if you think that's easy, try it." Tracy was a heavy drinker and had a fiery temper when roused. Publicists had successfully managed to keep his behaviour out of the press. In 1933 he began an affair with Loretta Young while filming *A Man's Castle* (1933). The romance lasted a year and was featured in fan magazines but ended when Tracy refused to get a divorce. Tracy's drinking led him into trouble. One night he was so drunk that Fox stagehands locked him in the studio. The next day, he woke and began

smashing up the set of *Dante's Inferno* (1935), his last film for Fox. When he passed out again studio guards entered the set and put him in a straitjacket and frogmarched him away. Accountants estimated he did about $100,000 worth of damage. During filming on March 11, 1935 he was arrested in Yuma, Arizona, for drunken behaviour in a hotel and wrecking furniture. Tracy joined MGM where he spent the next 24 years. During the filming of *Mannequin* (1938) he was rumoured to be romancing co-star Joan Crawford but this time he didn't leave Louise and the children. He won consecutive Oscars for his portrayal of Manuel in *Captains Courageous* (1937) and Father Edward J. Flanagan in *Boys Town* (1938), an achievement that wouldn't be equalled until Tom Hanks in 1993 and 1994. Tracy was Oscar nominated for *San Francisco* (1936) as Father Tim Mullin, *Father Of The Bride* (1950) as Stanley T. Banks, *Bad Day At Black Rock* (1955) as John J. Macreedy, *The Old Man And The Sea* (1958) as The Old Man, *Inherit The Wind* (1960) as Henry Drummond, *Judgment At Nuremberg* (1961) as Judge Dan Haywood and for his final film *Guess Who's Coming To Dinner?* (1967) as Matt Drayton. In 1942 he began filming *Woman Of The Year* (1942) as Sam Craig playing opposite Katharine Hepburn. It was to be the start of one of Hollywood's greatest romances lasting until his death. She said of Tracy: "To most men I'm a nuisance because I'm so busy I get to be a pest but Spencer is so masculine that once in a while he rather smashes me down, and there's something nice about me, when I'm smashed down." However, the affair didn't get off to a great start as evidenced by their first encounter when Joseph L. Mankiewicz introduced Kate to Tracy. She commented on their height disparity, "I'm afraid I'm a little tall for you. Mr Tracy." "Don't worry, Kate," Mankiewicz said, "he'll soon cut you down to size." They were

to make just nine films together. Said writer Garson Kanin: "It was always Tracy and Hepburn. I chided him once about his insistence on first billing. 'Why not?' he asked. 'Well, after all,' I argued, 'she's the lady. You're the man. Ladies first.' He said, 'This is a movie, chowderhead, not a lifeboat.'"
CAUSE: Fifteen days after the wrap of *Guess Who's Coming To Dinner?* Tracy died of heart failure aged 67 at home in Beverly Hills, California. The official version has him found by his housekeeper slumped over the kitchen table at 6am. Hepburn claims he died at 3am which probably means she was with him. She did not attend his funeral at the Immaculate Heart of Mary Church in Hollywood and was not mentioned in his will.
FURTHER READING: *Tracy And Hepburn* – Garson Kanin (New York: Bantam, 1972); *Spencer Tracy* – Bill Davidson (London: Sphere, 1989); *An Affair To Remember The Remarkable Love Story Of Katharine Hepburn And Spencer Tracy* – Christopher Andersen (New York: William Morrow & Co., 1997).

June Travis
(JUNE DOROTHEA GRABINER)
Born August 7, 1914
Died April 14 2008
B-movie starlet. Born in Chicago, Illinois, Travis was the daughter of Harry Grabiner, the vice-president of the Chicago White Sox baseball team. A petite and spirited brunette, Travis studied at the University of California and the University of Illinois where she was talent spotted by a Warner Bros scout while watching her dad's team in spring training. In her first year at the studio she made eight films, the most notable was playing Dublin, a gangster's moll, in William Dieterle's *Dr Socrates* (released October 19, 1935). She appeared in 30 films in just three years including *Love Is On The Air* (1937), Ronald Reagan's first movie. They became close friends. She appeared with several B-movie heroes

including Ricardo Cortez, Dick Foran, Robert Livingston and Dick Purcell. Her biggest picture was Howard Hawks' *Ceiling Zero* (released January 16, 1936), in which she played Tommy Thomas, a young aviatrix, and was billed third behind James Cagney and Pat O'Brien. To prepare for the role, she was tutored in flying, navigating and parachuting by aviation pioneer Amelia Earhart. Travis did a fine job in the film and many wonder why she was not offered meatier roles. She retired in 1938 but often said that had she stayed at Warner Bros for two more years, she would have been a major star. On January 3, 1940 she married Chicago businessman Fred Friedlob (d. May 1979) and they had two daughters, Kathy and June. She acted in local theatre productions but only made two more films: *The Star* (released December 11, 1952) as Phyllis Stone and the horror schlock *Monster A Go-Go* (released July 1965) as Ruth. CAUSE: She died aged 93 in a Chicago hospital of complications from a stroke she had suffered some weeks earlier.

Claire Trevor
(CLAIRE WEMLINGER)
Born March 8, 1909
Died April 8, 2000
'The Queen of Film Noir'. Born in New York City, her mother came from Northern Ireland and her father from France. Her father ran a clothing business but was ruined by the Great Depression and Trevor went out to work to help support the family. She also enrolled at Columbia University and then the American Academy of Dramatic Arts. After being spotted on Broadway in 1932 she was given a five-year contract by 20th Century Fox in 1933. In *Baby Takes A Bow* (1934) she played Shirley Temple's mother, then appeared opposite Spencer Tracy in *Dante's Inferno* (1935) and made six films with Allan Dwan. None of these films were particularly satisfactory

and she left Fox. She was signed by Samuel Goldwyn and cast as Francey, Humphrey Bogart's prostitute ex-girlfriend in William Wyler's *Dead End* (1937). She was on screen for less than five minutes but that was still enough for her to receive a Best Supporting Actress Oscar nomination. She then set off on a career of playing wanton women in films such as *The Amazing Dr Clitterhouse* (1938), *I Stole A Million* (1939), *Street Of Chance* (1942), *Murder My Sweet* (1944) and *Born To Kill* (1947). In 1948 she played Gaye Dawn in *Key Largo* (1948) and won the Best Supporting Actress Oscar for her portrayal of the alcoholic former nightclub singer lover of Johnny Rocco, a sadistic gangster (Edward G. Robinson). Six years later, she was again nominated by the academy for *The High And The Mighty*. She also appeared on television and radio winning an Emmy for *Dodsworth*. She was married three times. On July 27, 1938, she married radio producer Clark Andrews (b. November 21, 1908, d. Los Angeles, California, January 18, 1985). The couple was divorced on July 13, 1942 (the birthday of actor Harrison Ford), with the decree absolute being issued on July 24, 1943. In April 1943, she had married Lieutenant Cylos William Dunsmoore in Tijuana, Mexico, but they did not announce the marriage until her divorce from Andrews was finalised. They divorced in 1947. On November 14, 1948 (the birthday of Prince Charles), she married Milton H. Bren (b. Missouri, June 14, 1904), a producer. She was widowed on December 14, 1979 when Bren died in Los Angeles of a brain tumour. She had one son, Charles Cyclos (b. 1944), from the second marriage but he was killed in an aeroplane crash in 1978. In 1987 5'3" Trevor retired from acting.
CAUSE: She died aged 91 in Newport Beach, California from respiratory problems.

Marie Trintignant

Born January 21, 1962
Died August 1, 2003

Talented scion. Marie Joséphine Innocente Trintignant was born the daughter of the actors Nadine Marquand (b. Nice, France, November 11, 1934) and Jean-Louis Trintignant (b. Piolenc, France, December 11, 1930) in Boulogne-Billancourt, Paris, France, and the sister of Vincent Trintignant (b. September 3, 1973). She was also the niece of Serge Marquand (b. France, March 12, 1930, d. Paris, France, September 4, 2004 of leukaemia) and Christian Marquand (b. Marseille, France, March 15, 1927, d. near Paris, France, November 22, 2000 of Alzheimer's disease). She began her career aged five in the film *Mon Amour, Mon Amour* (1967) which was directed by her mother. Her other films included: *Ça N'Arrive Qu'Aux Autres* (1971), *Défense De Savoir* (1973), *Le Voyage De Noces* (1976), *Série Noire* (1979) as Mona, *Premier Voyage* (1980) as Marie Lambert, *Un Matin Rouge* (1982) as Marie, *Les Îles* (1983) as Nathalie, *L'Été Prochain* (1985) as Sidonie, *Noyade Interdite* (1987) as Isabelle, *La Maison De Jeanne* (1988) as Martine, *Wings Of Fame* (1990) as Bianca, *Alberto Express* (1990) as Clara, *Les Marmottes* (1993) as Lucie, *Fugueuses* (1995) as Marina, *Les Apprentis* (1995) as Lorette, *Des Nouvelles Du Bon Dieu* (1996) as Evangile, *Portraits Chinois* (1996) as Nina, *Les Démons De Jésus* (1997) as Levrette, *Harrison's Flowers* (2000) as Cathy, *Petites Misères* (2002) as Nicole, *Una Lunga Lunga Lunga Notte D'Amore* (2001) as Irene, *Total Kheops* (2002) as Lole, *Les Marins Perdus* (2003) as Mariette, *Janis Et John* (2003) as Brigitte Sterni and *Ce Qu'Ils Imaginent* (2004) as Juliette. Her mother directed her last television work, *Colette*, a 2004 mini-series. In 1998 she married the actor-director Samuel Benchetrit (b. 1973) and had a son Jules by him. She also had a son Roman (b. Paris, France, September 16, 1986) by the musician Richard Kolinka and another son Paul by François Cluzet (b. Paris, September 21, 1955) and a fourth son, Léon, by Mathias Othnin-Girard. CAUSE: On August 1, 2003 5'6" Trintignant got into a fight with her boyfriend, the 6'2" rock star Bertrand Bruno Lucien Cantat (b. Pau, Pyrénées-Atlantique, France, April 5, 1964), in their hotel room in Vilnius, Lithuania, during which she suffered fatal head injuries. He claimed that the injury (a cerebral oedema) was accidental but authorities disbelieved him and he was charged with intentional homicide. In March 2004, Cantat was convicted and was sentenced to eight years in prison.

François Truffaut

Born February 6, 1932
Died October 21, 1984

French auteur. Born in Paris, Truffaut suffered an unhappy childhood and was then dishonourably discharged from the army before becoming a film critic for *Cahiers Du Cinema*, where he began networking. He idolised Alfred Hitchcock, publishing a book on interviews with him and even considered at one time marrying his daughter. Eventually, he fell in love with a wealthy woman who financed his early work. His best-known films were: *Les Quatre Cents Coups* (1959), *Jules Et Jim* (1961), *La Peau Douce* (1964), *Mata-Hari* (1965), *Fahrenheit 451* (1966), *L'Enfant Sauvage* (1969), *Les Deux Anglaises Et Le Continent* (1971) and *La Chambre Verte* (1978). CAUSE: He died of cancer aged 62 in Paris.

Lana Turner

(JULIA JEAN MILDRED FRANCES TURNER)
Born February 8, 1920
Died June 29, 1995

'The Sweater Girl'. Born in Wallace, Idaho, Turner may have been a year older than the above date suggests. She was discovered in the Top Hat Cafe aged 15 drinking a coke and bunking off school. (The canard that she was discovered in Schwab's drugstore is simply that.) Her father had been murdered on December 14, 1930 when she was 10 following a card game in which he won a lot of money. Turner signed a contract with Mervyn Le Roy at MGM. She shaved her eyebrows for one film; they never grew back and so for the rest of her life they had to be pencilled in. Lana went on to marry seven times (her husbands included bandleader Artie Shaw and Tarzan actor Lex Barker) and make innumerable films (including *A Star Is Born* [1937], *Calling Dr Kildare* [1939], *Ziegfeld Girl* [1940], *Johnny Eager* [1942], *The Postman Always Rings Twice* [1946] and *Peyton Place* [1957]) but it was the incident on Good Friday (April 4) 1958 that will forever be associated with her. According to a close confidant speaking in 1996, Turner let her lesbian daughter, Cheryl, take the rap for a crime she had committed – the murder of her gangster boyfriend Johnny Stompanato at her Beverly Hills mansion at 730 North Bedford Drive. (Previously, the volatile and jealous thug had flown to England to confront Lana's then co-star in *Another Time, Another Place* [1958], Sean Connery, over rumours the two were romantically linked. Connery dispatched him with a well-aimed punch in the mouth and Stompanato was deported soon afterwards.) Cheryl was arrested, tried and convicted of the murder but stories have long persisted that it was, in fact, Lana herself who plunged the knife into her lover's stomach. Two of the participants from that rainy day are now dead and in her autobiography (written while her mother was still alive) Cheryl Crane sticks to the story that she was the killer. We will never really know the full truth about the event. Stompanato's family believed

that Lana had killed him and sued her for $1 million but accepted $20,000. CAUSE: In 1981 Lana was diagnosed with cervical cancer. Eleven years later, she was stricken with throat cancer but after treatment announced the following year that she had beaten the disease. It was not to be, and the cancer spread to her oesophagus. In September 1994, by then wheelchair bound, she received a lifetime achievement award at the San Sebastian Film Festival in Spain. On March 6, 1995, she went into Cedars-Sinai Medical Center suffering from a severely swollen neck and jaw. Her weight was down to a little over 6st. She was sent home and Cheryl moved in with her. She died at just past 10pm at home, suite 2006, 2170 Century Park East, Century City, California. She was 75. Her body was cremated and her ashes were scattered in Oahu, Hawaii.
FURTHER READING: *Lana: The Public And Private Lives Of Miss Turner* – Joe Morella & Edward Z. Epstein (London: W.H. Allen, 1972); *Always, Lana* – Taylor Pero & Jeff Rovin (New York: Bantam, 1982); *Lana: The Lady, The Legend, The Truth* – Lana Turner (London: New English Library, 1984); *Detour, A Hollywood Tragedy: My Life With Lana Turner, My Mother* – Cheryl Crane with Cliff Jahr (London: Michael Joseph, 1988); *Lana: The Life And Loves Of Lana Turner* – Jane Ellen Wayne (New York: St Martin's Press, 1995).

Ben Turpin

(BERNARD TURPIN)
Born September 17, 1874
Died July 1, 1940
Cross-eyed comic. Born in New Orleans, Louisiana, his career began as a comedian in vaudeville and then he signed to Essanay Studios in 1909 but was unable to fulfil his potential in a company more used to producing Westerns. He returned to the stage but gave the company another try in 1914,

where he worked as a stooge for Charlie Chaplin. Again disappointed, he left in 1916 and the following year joined Mack Sennett, with whom he achieved his greatest fame. Turpin appeared in almost 180 films, most of them shorts, but as with many silent stars, found opportunities hard to come by with the advent of the talkies.
CAUSE: He died aged 75 in Santa Monica, California, from heart disease.

Dame Dorothy Tutin, CBE

Born April 8, 1930
Died August 6, 2001
Adaptable actress. Born in London, Dorothy Tutin became a hit in the show business world with a performance in Graham Greene's *The Living Room* that Kenneth Tynan, the critic, said was like being "ablaze like a diamond in a mine". Her films included *The Importance Of Being Earnest*, *The Beggar's Opera*, *A Tale Of Two Cities*, *Cromwell* and *The Shooting Party*. In 1972, she was given the Variety Club of Great Britain film actress award for her performance in *Savage Messiah*. On television, she played Anne Boleyn in the BBC's *Six Wives Of Henry VIII* and in the Nineties she starred in *Body And Soul*. She appeared with her husband and daughter in Radio 4's 1996 production of Somerset Maugham's *Before The Party*. "I find what I do abominable," she once said. "I pick away at myself because I am not as perfect as I'd like to be. I can't make sense of myself at all. I don't even like

my name. It just doesn't belong to me." She married the actor Derek Waring (b. London, April 26, 1930) in 1963 and had one son, Nick (b. 1966), and one daughter, Amanda (b. 1965). Of Dame Dorothy, Sir John Mills said, "She was such a wonderful woman and a brilliant actress. She was one of the best we ever had. She could play almost anything."
CAUSE: She died aged 71 of leukaemia in the Edward VII Hospital in Midhurst, West Sussex.

Judy Tyler

(JUDITH HESS)
Born October 9, 1933
Died July 4, 1957
What might have been. Born in Milwaukee, Wisconsin, the daughter of a big band trumpeter and a Ziegfeld Follies dancer, Judy won the Miss Stardust beauty pageant in 1949, which led to regular parts on television and the occasional stage show. In 1950 she married Colin Romoff but they divorced in 1956. She made her film début as Jo Thomas in *Bop Girl Goes Calypso* (1957). Her second and last film was the Elvis Presley vehicle *Jailhouse Rock* (1957) in which she played Peggy Van Alden. In May 1957 she married for the second time, to actor Greg Lafayette.
CAUSE: Three days after filming ended on *Jailhouse Rock* Judy and her husband were involved in a car accident outside Billy The Kid, Wyoming. He died instantly and she succumbed to her injuries the next day.

U

Stanley Unwin

Born June 7, 1911
Died January 12, 2002

'The Professor'. Born in Pretoria, South Africa, he moved to England with his widowed mother, when he was three. One day his mother tripped and fell heavily, explaining to the little boy that she had "falloloped over and grazed her kneeclapper". Due to a change in circumstances Unwin was placed in an orphanage and then he worked in a variety of menial jobs until he went to sea. In 1940 a case of *mal de mer* wrecked Unwin's career in the Merchant Navy and he became a sound engineer with the BBC. To entertain his colleagues Unwin began telling them the stories he told his children at bedtime. "Are you all sitting comfity-bold, two-square on your botties?" he would ask them. "Then I'll begin. Once a-ponny tight-o . . ." He would tell them with his own spin. *The Pied Piper Of Hamlyn* became The Pidey Pipeload of Hamling and *Goldilocks* was transformed into Goldyloppers and the Three Bearloaders, which began, "Goldyloppers trittly-how in the early mordy, and she falloped down the steps. Oh unfortunate for the cracking of the eggers and the sheebs and buttery full-falollop and graze the knee-clappers. So she had a vaselubrious, rub it on and a quick healy huff and that was that." While working for BBC Midlands, he was given his own show, in which he reduced sports commentating to gibberish, "There's a great gathering round one goal mode as the net is folloped flat: what a clean groyle there as they kicking it on the bocus and the mable . . . all these people doing a very

fine suffery in the cause of sport." Soon he was popping up all over the radio and accepting "after-dinner speaklode". He received fan letters from the likes of J.B. Priestley, Joyce Grenfell and Sean O'Casey. On television Unwin appeared on Eric Sykes' shows, *Tell Tarby* (1973), *The David Nixon Show*, *The Dickie Henderson Show*, *Lunch Box*, and his own starring series *Unwin Time*. In 1958 he was teamed with Kenneth Horne, Hugh Paddick and Kenneth Williams in *Beyond Our Ken*, but he left after the first series to work in television. He appeared in Cardew Robinson's school spoof *Fun At St Fanny's* (1956), and in *Inn For Trouble* (1960). He said his favourite film role was as the landlord in *Carry On Regardless* (1961), because it gave him the chance to appear with Kenneth Williams. In one scene, Williams speaks to him in fluent Unwinese, and "Kenny got the rhythm perfectly". He was also in *Press For Time* (1966) with Norman Wisdom and was the Chancellor of Vulgaria in *Chitty Chitty Bang Bang* (1968). In 1967, he conducted a hilarious interview with Alan Abel, the American hoaxer who had written the book, *Yours For Decency*, prompting a spoof organisation called the Society for Indecency to Naked Animals, which believed that all animals should wear clothes. Only Abel remained unaware that his leg was being pulled. Unwin narrated the Small Faces' record *Ogden's Nut Gone Flake* in 1968. He was also Father Stanley Unwin, a genial lookalike priest in Gerry Anderson's puppet series *The Secret Service* (1968–1969). Unwin wrote several books, the first of which was *The Miscillian Manuscript* (1961), a beautifully illustrated study of a fictitious island. Other literary efforts included *House And Garbidge* (1962), *Rock-A-Bye Babel And Two Fairly Stories* (1966) and, in 1984, his autobiography, *Deep Joy*. He answered the telephone with the greeting, "Who calls?" Acquaintances were met with "Deep Joy". Stanley Unwin was married to Frances for more than 50 years until her death in 1993. They had one son and two daughters.

CAUSE: Stanley Unwin died in hospital in Daventry, Northamptonshire, aged 90 from natural causes. Once asked if there was to be a suitable epitaph for him, he replied simply: "Professor Unlow recitely kindly. Delivering joyfull roundness on all gathering (sitting quietly-softly), hanging roundlow. Deep Joy. Goodly byelode."

Mary Ure

Born February 18, 1933
Died April 3, 1975

Sensitive actress. Mary Eileen Ure was born in Glasgow and educated at the Mount School in York (and like many actresses was sensitive about her age, omitting it from directories even in her thirties) and then trained at the Central School of Speech & Drama. Her first stage appearance was at the Opera House, Manchester, on August 30, 1954, with her London début coming four months later on December 2. She made ten films, beginning in 1955 with *Storm Over The Nile*. She was nominated for an Oscar for *Sons And Lovers* (1960) in which she played Clara Dawes. Her first husband (in 1957) was playwright John James Osborne, from whom she was divorced. Husband number two, by whom she had two sons and two daughters from 1963, was Robert Shaw, who survived her.

CAUSE: She died in London aged 42 from an accidental drug and booze overdose.

Robert Urich

Born December 16, 1946
Died April 16, 2002

Suave television actor. Born in Toronto, Ohio, the son of Slovak immigrants, Robert Urich was educated by the Sisters of St Cyril and Methodius and considered becoming a priest. "I used to sit outside," he recalled, "watching the barges float by, and dream about being an actor or an artist. But that wasn't something you told your boilermaker father." A keen sportsman, Urich's athletic skill led to a four-year football scholarship at Florida State University. There he studied for a BA in Radio and Television Communications and later moved to Michigan State University where he earned an MA in Broadcast Research and Management. He then worked for WGN radio in Chicago as a salesman and briefly became a TV weatherman. His big break came in 1972 when he appeared alongside his fellow Florida State graduate Burt Reynolds as his younger brother in a stage production of *The Rainmaker*. It was also Reynolds' influence that persuaded Urich to move to Los Angeles. Urich's television début came in the short-lived (September 26–November 7, 1973) sitcom *Bob & Carol & Ted & Alice*. In the same year, 1973, he made his first big-screen appearance as vigilante motorcycle policeman Officer Mike Grimes in *Magnum Force*, the sequel to *Dirty Harry*. Thanks to an economy with the *actualite*, 6′2″ Urich didn't tell the producers he had never ridden a motorbike. The end result was that in one scene he zoomed off a garage ramp and drove straight onto the other actors' bikes. He then appeared in *S.W.A.T.* as Officer Jim Sweet for 34 episodes from February 24, 1975 until June 29, 1976. He holds the US record for starring in 15 television shows, more than any other actor. They include *Soap, Tabitha, Gavilan, American Dreamer, The Lazarus Man, It Had To Be You, Love Boat: The Next Wave* and *Emeril*. His best known roles were as Las Vegas' suave, no-nonsense private detective Dan Tanna in *Vega$* (September 20, 1978–June 3, 1981), and later as Boston's equally smooth, but much more cultured, private investigator in *Spenser: For Hire* (September 20, 1985–September 3,

1988). Urich was twice married. His first wife (in 1968) was Barbara Rucker, the actress. They divorced in 1974. On November 21, 1975, he married the actress Heather Menzies (b. Toronto, Ontario, December 3, 1949) who played Louise von Trapp in the film *The Sound Of Music*. They adopted three children: Ryan (b. 1979), Emily (b. 1980) and Allison Grady (b. April 18, 1998).

CAUSE: In 1996 Robert Urich announced he was suffering from synovial cell sarcoma, a rare soft tissue cancer that attacks the body's joints. Then he became active in cancer research, establishing the Heather and Robert Urich Foundation for Sarcoma Research at the University of Michigan. Urich died of cancer in Thousand Oaks, California, aged 55. His wife has suffered from ovarian cancer.

Sir Peter Ustinov

Born April 16, 1921
Died March 28, 2004

Renaissance polyglot. Although he was born at 11am, an only child, in a nursing home in Adelaide Road, Swiss Cottage, London, Peter Alexander Ustinov was conceived in Leningrad and boasted of Russian, German, Spanish, Italian, French and Ethiopian blood in his veins. His great-great-great-grandfather had made a fortune at the end of the seventeenth century from Siberian salt. His grandfather, Platon Grigorievich, sold his Russian estates and moved to Württemberg, where he became Baron Plato Von Ustinow. The Württemberg connection resulted in his four sons, including Peter's father, Jona (b. December 2, 1892, d. December 1, 1962), fighting on the German side in the First World War. Peter's uncle, after whom he was named, joined the German air force and was shot down and killed on July 13, 1917. Peter's father, by all accounts, was a bigot and a snob as well as a compulsive womaniser, despite standing just 5'2".

He often sported a monocle and married Nadezhda Leontievna Benois, the designer daughter of Alexandre Benois, whose family had descended from Jules-César Benois (b. January 20, 1770 at 9am), a French pastry chef who fled to St Petersburg after the French Revolution, and became *maître de bouche* to Tsar Paul I. Ustinov recalled that "to be *maître de bouche* to Paul I was a little like being accredited food-taster to Nero. Both emperors spent their lives hovering on the edge of lunacy, yet were sane enough to be in constant fear of assassination, a fate which attended them both." Her father, Albert (d. 1928), was the St Petersburg designer of the first big Diaghilev ballets. Jona Ustinov who was nicknamed 'Klop' (Bedbug) bribed Ivan Maisky (later Soviet ambassador in London) to issue a passport to allow them to leave Russia. At the time of his son's birth Jona was the London representative of the German News Agency. He was to become press attaché at the German News Agency, the Wolff Büro, until 1935 when, disgusted by the Nazi regime, he took out British nationality and joined MI5. A precocious child, in 1924 at the age of three Peter performed his repertoire of impressions at a dinner for the Emperor Haile Selassie of Ethiopia. It sent the emperor to sleep. At Gibbs' Preparatory School at 134 Sloane Street, where he was named Peter von Ustinov, he made his stage début in the role of a pig. The headmaster wrote in his report, "He shows great originality which must be curbed at all costs." He then went to Westminster School but at 16 his mother enrolled him in La Compagnie Quinze, an avant-garde French troupe run by Michel Saint-Denis. It was there on July 18, 1938 that Ustinov made his début before a paying audience. He played Waffles in Chekhov's *Wood Demon* at the Barn Theatre, Shere. He played a variety of roles before joining Leonard Sachs (the future host of *The Good Old*

Days) and his Players' Theatre, where the company included Bernard Miles and Alec Clunes (father of *Men Behaving Badly* star Martin). With the Players' Theatre Ustinov made his London début on August 30, 1939 and began to appear in revue before moving to Aylesbury Repertory Theatre. In May 1940 he appeared in another revue, *Swinging The Gate*, at the Gate Theatre. In October 1940 and January 1941 during the blitz he appeared respectively in the revues *Diversion* and *Diversion No 2* at Wyndham's Theatre. In 1940 he married for the first time and began appearing in films. He played Van de Lubbe, the Dutchman blamed for the burning of the Reichstag, in *Mein Kampf – My Crimes*, a Dutch priest in Michael Powell's *One Of Our Aircraft Is Missing* (1941), a cameo role as an elderly Czechoslovak professor in J.B. Priestley's *Let The People Sing* (1942), and Krauss, a star pupil of a Nazi spy school, in Will Hay's and Basil Dearden's *The Goose Steps Out* (1942). Ustinov's first play, *House Of Regrets*, opened at the Arts Theatre in London to favourable reviews on October 6, 1942. Nine months earlier, on January 16, 1942, Ustinov was called up and posted to the Royal Sussex Regiment, which sent him to defend St Margaret's Bay, near Dover. Then he was seconded to the Directorate of Army Psychiatry in Glasgow where he worked with the director Carol Reed and the writer Eric Ambler. Ustinov suggested making a film for those who had just entered the Army and *The New Lot* (1943) was a success. Ustinov was appointed batman to Colonel David Niven, who issued him with a pass which announced that "This man may go anywhere, and do anything at his discretion in the course of duty." His next film *The Way Ahead* (1944), starred Niven and, written by Ambler and Ustinov (who also appeared in the film), was a worthy successor to *The New Lot*. In 1944 Ustinov suffered a nervous breakdown,

and was placed under observation in a military hospital. On his release, he joined Army entertainments and directed Edith Evans as Mrs Malaprop in *The Rivals* at Salisbury; he himself took the part of Sir Anthony Absolute. In 1945 Ustinov's play *The Tragedy Of Good Intentions*, about the First Crusade, was performed by the Old Vic company at the Liverpool Playhouse. Shortly before his demob in 1946 Ustinov wrote and directed *School For Secrets* (1946) starring Ralph Richardson and Richard Attenborough, about the development of radar. From June 26, 1946, at the New Theatre, Ustinov appeared as Porfiry Petrovich, the police chief who tracks down Raskolnikov, in Rodney Ackland's version of *Crime And Punishment*. Despite starring John Gielgud and Edith Evans, Ustinov stole the show. He wrote and directed a film version of F. Anstey's *Vice-Versa* (1948) which gave James Robertson-Justice his first break. On the small screen in America, Ustinov won an Emmy for his performance in *The Life Of Samuel Johnson* (1957). He would repeat the achievement as Socrates in *Barefoot In Athens* (November 11, 1966) and as Herman Washington, a Jewish merchant who becomes a reluctant foster father to a black child, in Buzz Kulik's *A Storm In Summer* (February 6, 1970). He also played Herod the Great in the all-star television series *Jesus Of Nazareth* (April 3 and 10, 1977). Ustinov made a number of television documentary series although they were not always well received. The critic Noel Malcolm said that *Peter Ustinov's Russia* (1987) showed "all the investigative inclinations of an Intourist guide with a coach party and a lobotomy". In the book *My Russia* (1983) his comment that Stalin had caused suffering "to thousands" could be seen as a touch naïve. In 1962 Ustinov directed three operas at Covent Garden (Puccini's *Gianni Schicchi*, Ravel's *L'Heure Espagnole* and

Schoenberg's *Erwartung*). Six years later he went to Hamburg to direct *The Magic Flute*. His version of Massanet's *Don Quixote* at the Paris Opera in 1973 was greeted with prolonged booing. In films Ustinov played a wide range of characters. He achieved international acclaim – and a Best Supporting Actor Oscar nomination – as a gloating Nero in *Quo Vadis* (1951). He lost to Karl Malden in *A Streetcar Named Desire*. He was a petulant Prince Regent to Stewart Granger's *Beau Brummel* (1954); Jules, an escaped convict, in *We're No Angels* (1954); a ring master in Max Ophüls' *Lola Montez* (1955); Lentulus Batiatus, a slave-trader, in *Spartacus* (1960) for which he won his first Best Supporting Actor Oscar; he was the adaptor, director and played the ineffective humanitarian Captain Vere in Herman Melville's *Billy Budd* (1962), which many believed was his best film; the lecherous Middle Eastern King Fawz in *John Goldfarb, Please Come Home* (1964); Arthur Simon Simpson, a tourist guide who gets mixed up with gangsters, in *Topkapi* (1964) for which he won his second Best Supporting Actor Oscar; and Pineda, a Latin American ambassador, in *The Comedians* (1968). Ustinov's script for *Hot Millions* (1968) was nominated for an Oscar but lost out to Mel Brooks' *The Producers*. Ustinov played Marcus Pendleton, alias Caesar Smith, a crook who is caught out by a computer that he then co-opted to build his crooked empire. He played the Mexican general Maximilian Rodrigues de Santos in *Viva Max* (1969), the villainous oriental Hnup Wan in *One Of Our Dinosaurs Is Missing* (1974), the sadistic Foreign Legion sergeant Markov in *Let's Remake Beau Geste* (1977), Suleiman the caliph in *Ashanti* (1979), the Chinese detective in the disappointing *Charlie Chan And The Curse Of The Dragon Queen* (1981) and Professor Gus Nikolais in *Lorenzo's Oil* (1992). He played Belgium's celebrated detective Hercule Poirot

several times: in *Death On The Nile* (1978), *Evil Under The Sun* (1981) and the television movies *Thirteen At Dinner* (1985), *Dead Man's Folly* (1986) and *Appointment With Death* (1988). He was often in demand for voice-over work in films and television and worked on *Clochemerle* (1972), *Robin Hood* (1973), *The Mouse And His Child* (1977), *Winds Of Change* (1978) and *Tarka The Otter* (1979). *Memed, My Hawk* (1984), the last film he directed, was an unsuccessful version of Yashar Kemal's novel of young love. He also found time to write two novels, *The Loser* (1961) about a young Nazi on the run in Italy, and *Krumnagel* (1971) about an American police chief who is sentenced to seven years in jail for the manslaughter of a Scottish trade unionist. In January 1963 the Mirisch Company sued him for pulling out of *The Pink Panther*, which was in production in Rome. Ustinov was replaced by Peter Sellers. Ustinov, who was Goodwill Ambassador for UNICEF from 1968 until his death, was appointed Commander of the Order of the British Empire in 1975 and knighted in 1990. He was fluent in English, French, German, Italian, Russian and Spanish and could get by in Turkish and Greek. 5'11" Ustinov was married three times. His first wife Isolde Denham was the daughter of Reginald Denham and Moyna MacGill and half-sister of Angela Lansbury. They married in 1940 in London and divorced in the same city in 1950. They had one daughter, Tamara (b. Woolavington wing of the Middlesex Hospital, July 25, 1945). On February 15, 1954 at Chelsea register office he married the actor Suzanne Cloutier. It was her second marriage, the first was not consummated and she left her husband during the wedding reception. She went on to play Desdemona in Orson Welles' film of *Othello*. They had a son Igor (b. London, April 30, 1956) and two daughters, Pavla (b. St John's Hospital, Santa Monica, California,

June 2, 1954 at 3.33pm) and Andrea
(b. Los Angeles, March 30, 1959). The
couple was divorced in 1971. The
following year on June 21, 1972, in
Corsica, he married Hélène du Lau
d'Allemans, a French press agent. He
once remarked, "I am a constitutional
gypsy, at home nowhere and absolutely
at home everywhere."

CAUSE: He died in Genolier,
Switzerland from heart failure. He was
82.

FURTHER READING: *Dear Me* – Peter
Ustinov (London: Heinemann, 1977).

V

Roger Vadim

(ROGER VADIM PLÉMIANNIKOV)
Born January 26, 1928
Died February 11, 2000
Director with an eye for the ladies.
Born in Paris, France, Vadim is
probably best known not as a film
director (his profession) but for his
relationships with beautiful women,
including Brigitte Bardot, Jane Fonda,
Catherine Deneuve and Annette
Stroyberg, his second wife. He directed
And God Created Woman (1956) with
Bardot and *Barbarella* (1967), starring
Fonda. Vadim began his life of love
when he was 16 after a girl took pity on
him. Her name was Françoise; she was
four years older than Vadim and a
fellow aspiring actor. One day in a
Normandy hayloft after a meal of
rabbit, and when their friends were
asleep, Françoise crept over to Vadim
and relieved him of his virginity. As
they coupled the walls began to shake
and the ceiling vibrated alarmingly.
Vadim had heard about the earth
moving but this was too much. He was
convinced it was the wrath of God and
he was being punished for his sin.
There was a slightly more prosaic
reason for the noise. The date was
June 6, 1944: D-Day. The day the
Allies began the invasion of France. As
Vadim said, "I have always had a sense
of history."
CAUSE: Vadim died aged 72 in Paris
after a long struggle with cancer.
FURTHER READING: *Memoirs Of The
Devil* – Roger Vadim (London: Arrow
Books, 1978); *Bardot, Deneuve And
Fonda: The Memoirs Of Roger Vadim* –
Roger Vadim (London: Weidenfeld &
Nicolson, 1986).

Rudolph Valentino

(RODOLFO ALFONZO RAFAELO
FILIBERT GUGLIELMI DI VALENTINO
D'ANTONGUOLLA)
Born May 8, 1895
Died August 23, 1926
'The Great Lover'. Valentino was the
first real sex symbol to be created by
the cinema. Millions of women lusted
after him, smaller numbers of men
envied him or were jealous of him and
sometimes the jealousy provoked them
to violence. In the twenty-first century,
most intelligent, sophisticated people
are aware that the image portrayed
in public by film and television
personalities bears little or no
resemblance to their true identity in
private, where promiscuity, sexual
deviancy, drug taking and boorish
behaviour is often the norm. In the
1920s no such sophistication existed
among the vast majority of the
cinema-going audience. Whereas
today's *cognoscenti* take press releases
with a pinch of salt, in the more
innocent days of the early twentieth
century, an eager public lapped up
every word. Such an atmosphere
allowed Rudolph Valentino to flourish,
and flourish he did in a career that
lasted just seven years. Born in
Castellaneta, Italy, a town of 6,000
people, the son of a vet, the young
Valentino was a troublesome boy
who was, occasionally, locked out of
his home by his mother. He responded
by throwing bricks at the front door.
He was also jailed for vagrancy. A trip
to Paris saw him lose his virginity to a
man called Claude Rambeau when
he was 18. On December 9, 1913,
he set off for America aboard the
liner *Cleveland*, his fare paid for by his
mother out of her meagre widow's
stipend, to seek fame and fortune.
Arriving in New York two days before
Christmas, he worked as a gardener
earning $6 a week working for
millionaire Cornelius Bliss before
being sacked for spending too much
time admiring Bliss' fine lady and

gentleman guests and not enough tending to the herbaceous borders. He landed another job gardening in Central Park but was again sacked and ended up homeless. After contemplating suicide on August 4, 1914, he became a 10¢-a-dance gigolo but would spend more time in his clients' beds than in their arms on a dance floor. He joined the high-class nightclub Maxim's and was soon taking home $70 a week. Despite his burgeoning wealth, it never occurred to Rudolph to send for his mother. At Maxim's Valentino began an affair with the wealthy but ignored socialite Bianca de Saulles (b. Valparíso, Chile, as Bianca Erraruiz). In Paris in December 1911 she was married to former star American football player Jack de Saulles. Valentino and Bianca's affair lasted a year and created a number of problems at work where Valentino refused to sleep with the other ladies who wanted his favours. Bianca suggested he become a professional dancer. He teamed up with brunette divorcée Bonnie Glass (née Helen Roche from Roxbury, Massachusetts) who paid him $50 a week to be her partner. They played at the Winter Gardens and Glass opened her own cabaret club, Chez Fisher on West 55th Street, paying Valentino $100 a week. Then she fell in love with Ben Ali Hagin, a multi-millionaire, closed her club and retired, leaving Valentino unemployed. Not for long. His dancing talent soon earned him a job on tour paying $150 a week. He disliked his new dancing partner, Joan Sawyer, and Bianca disliked her husband so the two contrived to set up de Saulles with Sawyer so that Bianca could have proof of her husband's adultery, the only possible grounds for divorce at the time. When Sawyer learned of Valentino's connivance she sacked him, but on September 15, 1916, Jack and Bianca de Saulles were divorced. Valentino was unable to celebrate with Bianca because ten days

earlier he had been arrested by the vice squad at the New York home of Georgia Thym at 909 Seventh Avenue between 57th and 58th Streets during an investigation into blackmail and white slave trafficking. Valentino protested his innocence (he had been framed by Jack de Saulles) but still spent three days in New York's Tombs prison. He was charged on the day Bianca won her divorce but charges were later dropped. Today there is a file on Valentino in NYPD headquarters but it is empty as is Georgia Thym's. A cynical mind would believe that when Valentino achieved fame, someone organised for the files to be mislaid. Valentino was still wary of Jack de Saulles' power and he stopped seeing Bianca. He took lowly paid work dancing at cinemas before a film and was advised to go to Hollywood and dance in films. On August 3, 1917, his mind was made up for him when Jack de Saulles was shot and killed by Bianca. Fearing that he would be caught up in the scandal and deported, Valentino took the advice of John Babsone Soule (not Horace Greeley) and went west. After a number of jobs as a male prostitute, he made his first film, ironically entitled *Alimony* (1917), for which he was paid $5 a day. His second film was also aptly titled: *A Society Sensation* (1918). He appeared in a few more films and began to get noticed around Hollywood although not by the non-trade press. On November 2, 1919, he met actress Jean Acker and three days later they were married at the home of Joseph Engle, Metro Films' treasurer on Hollywood Boulevard and Mariposa Hollywood. Six hours later, the marriage was over after she locked him out of her room at the Hollywood Hotel, 6811 Hollywood Boulevard, telling him she never loved him and that it had all been a terrible mistake. On December 6, newspapers carried the story of their separation. Valentino remained one of

Hollywood's less famous stars; at the time of his divorce one newspaper referred to him as "Rudolph Balentino". He took to wearing a corset and explained the scar on his right cheek as the result of a duel (which he, of course, won). In fact, it was the consequence of messing around with his father's razor when Rudy was five. He became a star as a result of his appearance as Julio Desnoyers in *The Four Horsemen Of The Apocalypse* (1921). By this time he had met Natacha Rambova (her real name was the more prosaic Winifred Shaughnessy and she was born on January 19, 1897, dying on June 5, 1966, from dietary complications), in late 1920 on the set of the film *Unchartered Seas* (1921) in which he played Frank Underwood. Rambova was the costumier and she was not impressed by her first impressions of Valentino. Rambova's mentor and lesbian lover Alla Nazimova unsubtly invited Valentino to take Rambova as his date for the Los Angeles opening of his film *The Four Horsemen Of The Apocalypse* (1921). Despite that inauspicious start, they met again. Both were interested in the supernatural and believed they had known each other in a previous life. This was one of their main topics of conversation on their 'dates', the first of which was during Christmas week 1920. Rambova insisted that 'true love' was spiritual rather than physical and Valentino, with his complete lack of interest in hetero sex, was more than happy to go along with that. They became engaged in May 1922. On the thirteenth of that month Valentino, now 27, married Rambova in Mexicali, Mexico, in Mayor Otto Moller's house. His Worship had arranged for a military band to play a Spanish wedding march. The wedding night passed, as had Valentino's first, with no passion displayed by either bride or groom. The couple intended to honeymoon for a month in Palm Springs and San Diego but two days

later a judge pointed out that Valentino hadn't waited for the statutory year to elapse after his interlocutory divorce decree. He was arrested for bigamy as the couple pulled up to their Whitley Heights home eight days later. He spent several hours in prison before the $10,000 bond money could be raised. Eventually, on June 5, 1922, the judge declared the Mexican match invalid but warned the couple not to remarry until the divorce was finalised. Back in Hollywood they organised the city's first séances. She insisted he refer to her as 'Boss'. They married legally in Crown Point, Indiana, on March 14, 1923, when she took over running every aspect of his career – badly. As well as being a lesbian, Rambova had some rather strange quirks: she believed she was a psychic and a spiritualist. She also travelled everywhere with a monkey. When the couple was divorced on January 19, 1926, she admitted the marriage had never been consummated. Valentino's star continued to soar with his films *The Sheik* (1921) and *Blood And Sand* (1922) as Juan Gallardo. Under Rambova's influence Valentino's image became less masculine and his demeanour off screen more surly. On September 14, 1922, Famous Players-Lasky took out an injunction to stop the temperamental star from working for another studio. While working on *The Young Rajah* (1922) as Amos Judd, Valentino came to the conclusion that the film was poor and that the scripts he was being offered were worse. He went to see studio boss Jesse Lasky to demand a raise, a better dressing room and better films. Requests denied. On August 30, Valentino announced to the press that he intended to seek a better deal elsewhere. At the resultant court case the judge found in favour of the studio and when it went to appeal on December 8, the appellant judge confirmed the findings of the lower court. The star was told to see out his contract with Famous Players-Lasky or not appear in public until February 1, 1924. Just as his career seemed back on track with *The Eagle* (1925) as Vladimir Dubrovsky and *The Son Of The Sheik* (1926) as Ahmed/The Sheik, the *Chicago Tribune* ran a story in July 1926 headlined "Pink Powder Puff" and calling Valentino "that painted pansy". He responded by challenging the journalist to a fight. A quick scrap followed with 6′1″ boxing correspondent Frank O'Neil taking the place of the journalist who had originally penned the insults. O'Neil pronounced 5′11″ Valentino to have "a punch like the kick of a mule". Back in New York on August 16, 1926, Valentino collapsed and was hospitalised.

CAUSE: Valentino died in Polyclinic Hospital, New York, at 12.10pm on August 23, 1926, as a result of "a perforated gastric ulcer and inflamed appendix with resultant peritonitis". He was just 31 and newspapers eulogised about the death of a man at the height of his powers who had just been reunited with his one true love, Pola Negri. In reality, Valentino's star was fading and he left an estate sinking in around half a million dollars of debt. Following his death, several women, including Peggy Scott in London, committed suicide as did one man. Valentino's corpse was taken to Frank Campbell's Funeral Church on Broadway at 66th Street where thousands queued to pay their last respects. As with all sudden deaths, rumours abounded that Valentino had been murdered – shot or poisoned by a jealous rival – or that it was a wax dummy and not a human corpse that was on display. United Artists decided to make the most of Valentino in death, so arranged for a mass at the Roman Catholic St Malachy's Church and Actors Chapel at 239 West 49th Street. However, there was a slight problem – Valentino's two marriages. This was overcome by a declaration from Rome,

no doubt aided by 'persuasion' from Hollywood, that since both Valentino's weddings had been civil affairs (in a manner of speaking), neither counted in the eyes of the Church and he was entitled to a Catholic service. On August 30, the service took place and shopkeepers on 49th Street sold vantage points from their premises to view the cortege. In attendance were Douglas Fairbanks, George Jessel, Marilyn Miller and Gloria Swanson. Crowds cheered as each star arrived! Pola Negri repeatedly fainted, usually in full view of the press. Following the Mass, Valentino was taken back to Frank Campbell's where he remained on view for 48 more hours. Special dispensation was given by NYC's Department of Health to allow the body to stay above ground for so long. This was allegedly to let Valentino's brother, Alberto Guglielmi, arrive from Italy to pay his respects. When this occurred the whole circus began again as Valentino was loaded onto a train for the five-day journey to Hollywood. There, on September 7, another star-studded Mass took place, this time at the Church of the Good Shepherd, Beverly Hills. Then, over a fortnight after his death, Valentino was finally laid to rest in Crypt 1205 off Corridor A of the Cathedral Mausoleum of Hollywood Memorial Park, 6000 Santa Monica Boulevard, Hollywood, California 90038. At the second funeral Pola Negri fainted yet again, only for a photographer to call out, "Pola, the light's not good on your face – will you do it again?" So she did. Said a stunned Joseph Hergesheimer: "It's the only time I ever saw a retake on mourning." As one wag would say of the death of Elvis Presley, also nearly broke when he died, Valentino's demise was a great career move. Crowds queued to see his films and the $500,000 deficit soon turned into a credit of $600,000.

FURTHER READING: *Valentino* – Irving Shulman (London: Leslie Frewin, 1968); *Valentino* – Brad Steiger &

Chaw Mank (New York: Manor Books, 1975); *Valentino: The Love God* – Noel Botham & Peter Donnelly (London: Everest, 1976); *Rudolph Valentino* – Alexander Walker (London: Sphere, 1977).

Rudy Vallee
(HUBERT Prior VALLEE)
Born July 28, 1901
Died July 3, 1986
'The Vagabond Lover'. Born in Island Point, Vermont, Vallee never intended a career in showbiz and it was assumed he would follow his father into the pharmacy business. One day he heard someone playing a saxophone and fell in love with the instrument. That led to the formation of his own band, nightclub appearances, a wireless spot and eventually films, where his method of 'crooning' a song rather than belting it out proved immensely popular. He went on to become a character actor. His films included: *The Vagabond Lover* (1929), *George White's Scandals* (1934), *Gold Diggers In Paris* (1934), *Second Fiddle* (1939), *The Fabulous Suzanne* (1946), *The Bachelor And The Bobby-Soxer* (1947), *The Beautiful Blonde From Bashful Bend* (1949), *The Helen Morgan Story* (1947) and *Won Ton Ton, The Dog Who Saved Hollywood* (1976). A tad vain, he tried to persuade the local council to rename the street on which he lived as Rue de Vallee. He was married four times: wife number one was Leonie Cauchois whom he married in 1928 and received an annulment from the same year. The marriage was never consummated. On July 6, 1931, he married Fay Webb. They divorced on May 20, 1936. On December 2, 1943, he married actress Jane Greer but they divorced, on July 27, 1944, after just eight months. On September 4, 1949, he married Eleanor Kathleen Norris. During the reception the bride's veil caught fire. Vallee grabbed the material and beat out the flames with his bare hands. They were still together when he died.

CAUSE: Vallee died from a heart attack in his Hollywood home shortly before his 85th birthday.

Lee Van Cleef
Born January 9, 1925
Died December 14, 1989
' . . .The Bad . . .'. It was perhaps fitting that one of Lee Van Cleef's best-known films labels him as the kind of character he was best at playing. Born in Somerville, New Jersey, he joined the navy and then became an accountant before turning to acting. He made his film début in *High Noon* (1952) as gunman Jack Colby. His squinty-eyed expression made him a natural movie bad guy and he appeared in, among others, *Untamed Frontier* (1952) as Dave Chittun, *Kansas City Confidential* (1952) as Tony Romano, *White Lightning* (1953) as Brutus, *Jack Slade* (1953) as Toby Mackay, *The Beast From 20,000 Fathoms* (1953) as Corporal Stone, *Arena* (1953) as Smitty, *Vice Squad* (1953) as Pete, *The Yellow Tomahawk* (1954) as Fireknife, *Gypsy Colt* (1954) as Hank, *Rails Into Laramie* (1954) as Ace Winton, *I Cover The Underworld* (1955) as Flash Logan, *Ten Wanted Men* (1955) as Al Drucker, *Tribute To A Bad Man* (1956) as Fat Jones, *Accused Of Murder* (1956) as Sergeant Emmett Lackey, *The Conqueror* (1956) as Chepei, *Joe Dakota* (1957) as Adam Grant, *Gunfight At The O.K. Corral* (1957) as Ed Bailey, *The Bravados* (1958) as Alfonso Parral, *Guns, Girls, And Gangsters* (1959) as Mike Bennett, *The Man Who Shot Liberty Valance* (1962) as Reese and *How The West Was Won* (1962) as Marty before becoming a star in spaghetti Westerns such as *Per Qualche Dollaro In Più/For A Few Dollars More* (1965) as bounty hunter Colonel Douglas Mortimer and *Il Buono, Il Brutto, Il Cattivo/The Good, The Bad And The Ugly* (1966) as Angel Eyes Setenza. Van Cleef wasn't keen to fly to Spain to play Mortimer but he was nearly broke and the job paid $17,000,

a third more than anything else he had earned. He was also recovering from a knee injury and a drink problem. These films were followed by others of the same ilk: *La Resa Dei Conti/The Big Gundown* (1966) as Jonathan Corbett, *I Giorni Dell'Ira/Day Of Anger* (1967) as Frank Talby, *Al Di Là Della Legge* (1967) as Cudlip, *Da Uomo A Uomo/ Death Rides A Horse* (1967) as Ryan and *Ehi Amico . . . C'è Sabata, Hai Chiuso!* (1970) as Sabata.

CAUSE: Lee Van Cleef died in Oxnard, California, from a heart attack. He was 64.

Jo Van Fleet
Born December 30, 1914
Died June 10, 1996

Terminal matriarch. Born in Oakland, California, it seemed she was destined never to play anyone her own age. She made her stage début in Washington, DC in 1944 at 29 playing a much older character, the spinster Miss Phipps in *Uncle Harry*, and this continued into films. She won an Oscar for playing James Dean's brothel-owning mother, Kate Trask, in *East Of Eden* (1955) even though she was 16 years his senior and she was Susan Hayward's mother in *I'll Cry Tomorrow* (1955) even though she was just three years older than Hayward! She was a 'Method' actress and appeared in a dozen films. She was married to William Bales who died in 1990.

CAUSE: She died aged 81 in New York City's Jamaica Hospital of undisclosed causes.

Conrad Veidt
Born January 22, 1893
Died April 3, 1943

German expressionist. Born in Berlin and educated at Berlin High School, 6′2″ Veidt studied under Max Reinhardt, making his stage début in 1913 and later working with Emil Jannings. He made his movie début in 1917 but the first film in which Veidt was really noticed was *Das Kabinett Des Dr Caligari* (1919), in which he played the part of Cesare. He later bemoaned this: "No matter what roles I play, I can't get *Caligari* out of my system." He travelled to Hollywood but returned to Germany when sound films became popular. In 1934 he left Germany with his Jewish wife following the rise of the Nazis and settled in England, becoming a British subject in 1939. A return visit to Germany in 1935 almost caused an international incident. The Nazis kidnapped him, claiming he was too ill to return to Britain, but Gaumont British sent their own medical experts to examine the actor in preparation for his journey. He played a number of Nazis on screen, most notably Major Heinrich Strasser in *Casablanca* (1942). Veidt, whose friends called him Connie and who was superstitious about the number 17, was married three times.

CAUSE: He died of a heart attack in Los Angeles, aged 50. He was buried in Ferncliff Cemetery & Mausoleum, Secor Road, Hartsdale, New York 10530.

Lupe Velez
(MARÍA GUADALUPE VÉLEZ DE VILLALOBOS)
Born July 18, 1908
Died December 14, 1944

'The Mexican Spitfire'. Born in San Luis Potosi, a suburb of Mexico City, the daughter of a soldier. According to some accounts her mother was a prostitute. As soon as she became a teenager, she was sent to the Our Lady of the Lake Convent in San Antonio, Texas. A less than enthusiastic student, she left after two years when her father died. She entered showbiz where she was popular with the audiences and the stage door johnnies who paid for her favours with dinner and other inducements. She also worked as a stripper for a time. In 1924 she made her film début and three years later she was in Hollywood. Her first five years were spent in dramatic roles before she switched to comedy. The 5' Velez received her nickname because of a 1939 film of that name. However, her off-screen antics more than made up for her on-screen ones. The 37-26-35 actress changed lovers as regularly as most people change their underwear. Although her bed partners included some of the best-known names in Hollywood, there was nothing snobbish about her attitude towards her lovers. Among her paramours were actors Tom Mix (whom she dumped when his star began to wane), Clark Gable (who dumped her because of her reputation for revealing the sexual prowess or otherwise of her lovers: "She'll be all over town telling everyone what a lousy lay I am"), Charlie Chaplin (in 1928), Russ Columbo, Victor Fleming and Gary Cooper. Velez and Cooper slept together the first night they met and their passion was so hot that he began to fall asleep on set. She spent $500 a month on telephone calls to him and they often practised phone sex. It was a tempestuous relationship and during one argument with Cooper at a railway station she tried to shoot him. Fortunately, her aim was poor. Her other paramours included John Gilbert (in 1931, although he went back to his ex-wife, who didn't want him), Randolph Scott (who left her for Cary Grant) and Johnny Weissmuller, whom she secretly married on October 8, 1933. Their first (of many) separations came on January 24, 1934. She filed for divorce on January 2, 1935, though they were reconciled, but she again filed in early 1938 and this time the divorce was granted. Velez also dated boxers Jack Dempsey and Jack Johnson and assorted producers, directors and stage-hands. In fact, it was pretty much a case of whoever took her fancy at the time. By 1943 Lupe's acting had become a parody of itself. *The New York Times* said of her appearance in *Ladies Day* (1943): "Miss Velez doesn't act too well, but she acts loud; her

display of Latin temperament resembles the law of molecular motion."

CAUSE: Always temperamental and always theatrical she decided to commit suicide and planned it with all the precision of a military campaign. Sadly, like the best-laid plans of mice and actresses, it went awry. On November 27, 1944, Lupe announced her engagement to her latest lover, a 27-year-old actor called Harald Ramond. However, she didn't tell Ramond either that they were engaged or that she was pregnant. She assumed he would be both honoured and delighted to marry her. He wasn't on either count. Lupe realised the scandal and shame of being an unwed mother in Hollywood would ruin her career. (When Loretta Young became pregnant by Clark Gable she took herself off for a year and returned with an 'adopted' daughter. It was only recently that the truth was revealed.) Lupe broke off the brief engagement. As a Catholic, abortion was unthinkable. The only way out was death. (Oddly, Catholics also believe suicide to be a mortal sin.) On December 14, 1944, Lupe had her hair and nails done and tidied her bedroom at 732 North Rodeo Drive, Beverly Hills. She ate a spicy Mexican meal before donning her favourite blue satin pyjamas and then swallowing 75 Seconal tablets, washed down with the finest brandy. She placed her hands across her chest and imagined how serene and beautiful she would look when discovered by her maid in the morning. Things didn't go quite according to plan. The effect of the spicy food, the booze and the pills made Lupe feel woozy and sick. She got up and staggered to the bathroom, leaving a trail of vomit on the bedroom floor. As she reached the bathroom she slipped and fell headfirst into the toilet. She drowned in her Egyptian Chartreuse Onyx Hush-Flush Model deluxe commode. Ironically her house was called the Casa Felicitas – the Happy Home.

FURTHER READING: *Lupe Velez And Her Lovers* – Floyd Conner (New York: Barricade Books, 1993).

Victor Vicas

Born March 25, 1918
Died December 9, 1985

Soviet auteur. Born in Moscow, USSR but raised in Paris, France Vicas became an assistant cameraman in the late Thirties. He joined the French army at the outbreak of the Second World War but was captured by the Germans. Managing to escape he fled to the United States in 1942 where he began to make documentaries. He moved into feature films and directed *The Wayward Bus* (released May 27, 1957) based on John Steinbeck's novel and starring Joan Collins and Jayne Mansfield and the wartime spy drama *Count Five And Die* (released December 23, 1957). In his latter years he worked in French television.

CAUSE: He died in Paris, France from complications after heart surgery. He was 67.

King Vidor

Born February 8, 1894
Died November 1, 1982

Creative director. Born in Galveston, Texas, 5′11½″ King Wallis Vidor became interested in cinema when still a small child and in order to be near his beloved films, he began working in a cinema collecting tickets and occasionally operating the projector. In 1915 he married actress Florence Arto, a 5′4½″ brunette (b. Houston, Texas, July 23, 1895, as Florence Cobb, d. Pacific Palisades, California, November 3, 1977) and they headed for Tinseltown to seek their fame and fortune, he behind the cameras, she in front. She landed a deal with Vitagraph Pictures and appeared in numerous silent films becoming very successful. She and Vidor separated in 1923 and were divorced two years later. On August 20, 1928, she married violinist Jascha Heifetz in New York. They divorced on January 3, 1946, after Heifetz claimed she had belittled his musical talent. On September 8, 1926, Vidor married actress Eleanor Boardman but they were divorced on April 11, 1933, because of his adultery. He later married writer Elizabeth Hill (b. 1901, d. August 21, 1978, of heart failure due to anorexia nervosa) but they, too, separated in 1966 and she left her house and its contents to her Alsatian. After directing shorts Vidor made his first feature film, *The Turn In The Road* (1919). Vidor formed his own production company and called it Vidor Village before joining MGM where his reputation was made with *The Big Parade* (1925). His next big success was *The Crowd* (1928) for which he received the first of his five Oscar nominations. From the mid-Thirties he made films for whichever commercial theme was in vogue. His last film was the flop *Solomon And Sheba* (1959). He busied himself in the last years of his life trying to solve the mystery of the death of fellow director William Desmond Taylor.

CAUSE: He died aged 88 of heart failure at Willow Creek Ranch, Paso Robles, California.

Herve Villechaize

Born April 23, 1943
Died September 4, 1993

TV's most famous dwarf. One of the most popular television shows of the Seventies was *Fantasy Island* starring Ricardo Montalban as Mr Roarke and Paris-born Herve Jean-Pierre Villechaize as Tattoo. After the pilot TV executives wanted to ditch 3′10″ Villechaize in favour of a sexy girl but producer Aaron Spelling fought for the little actor and the network honchos relented. However, Villechaize was not one for gratitude; he believed he was the star of the show because of his line, "The plane! The plane!" Villechaize's behaviour became increasingly bizarre. He brought a gun to the set and carried it everywhere. Outside his trailer he hung a sign that said "The Doctor Of Sex". When the trailer was occupied he turned the sign over and it read "The Doctor Is In". Eventually, his behaviour became too much and Villechaize was sacked in 1983 over a pay dispute. He also played Scaramanga's servant, Nick Nack, in the Bond film *The Man With The Golden Gun* (1974) and appeared as a king in the unfunny comedy *The Forbidden Zone* (1980).

CAUSE: Because of his size, Villechaize was often sick. Born with small lungs, in 1992 he almost died of pneumonia. He was also a martyr to ulcers and a spastic colon. His physical ailments wore him down and, on September 3, 1993, he shot himself in the chest at his home, 11537 West Killion Street, North Hollywood, California 91601. He was taken to Medical Center of North Hollywood at 12629 Riverside Drive, where he expired the next day at 3.40am. He was 50. His body was cremated and his ashes scattered at sea off Point Fermin on September 14, 1993.

Luchino Visconti

Born November 2, 1906
Died March 17, 1976
Noble director. Born in Milan, Italy, the son of a musician and a notable beauty. He grew up with visits to the pictures a regular outing. Indeed, his family had their own box in the cinema. Visconti had left-wing views, which put him at odds with Mussolini, and he joined the anti-Fascist movement. In 1937 he travelled to America but wasn't happy and returned to Italy, though he didn't make his first feature film until *Ossessione* (1942). He made films only rarely but his *Rocco E I Suoi Fratelli* (1960) made a star of Alain Delon. Nine years later, his film *La Caduta Degli Dei* (1969) was a success, so Hollywood agreed to finance his film of

Thomas Mann's tale of homosexuality *Morte A Venezia/Death In Venice* (1971), although initially the studios wanted to make the subject of the lead character's affections a girl rather than a boy.

CAUSE: In 1972 he suffered a stroke that left him paralysed down the left side. Taken to a Zurich sanatorium to recover, he refused to give up smoking (he was on 100 cigarettes a day) and recovered within a month to direct *Ludwig* (1972), walking with the aid of a stick, which he loathed. His last film, *L'Innocente* (1976), was directed from a wheelchair. Visconti died of influenza and a heart complaint in Rome aged 69. His funeral two days later was attended by various famous faces including the President of Italy and Burt Lancaster.

Erich von Stroheim

Born September 22, 1885
Died May 12, 1957
'The Man You Love To Hate'. The bullet-headed director and actor was born in Vienna, Austria, as Erich Oswald Stroheim. The 'von' was an affectation and, contrary to studio biographies, his real name wasn't Erich Oswald Hans Carl Maria Stroheim von Nordenwall and he wasn't the scion of an old Prussian family. In his pre-screen days he was a manager in a hat factory run by his Jewish father, not a dashing cavalry officer as often reported. In November 1909 he emigrated to America and worked at various menial jobs. In 1913 he married Margaret Knox but they divorced the following year. In 1915 he joined D.W. Griffith's outfit, playing a black extra in *The Birth Of A Nation* (1915). He married May Jones in 1917 but they were divorced the same year. He had one son by her. That year he played a Prussian officer for the first time, a role he was to reprise on several occasions, earning him his nickname. Following the end of World War I his career moved onto a different plane

and he began to direct films. Stroheim was a perfectionist down to the smallest detail, which meant that films could take as much as a year to produce. He spent so much money that the studio began referring to him as $troheim. In 1919 he married Valerie Germonprez and had a son by her. His film *Greed* (1925) would, in its original incarnation, have lasted seven or, according to some sources, nine hours! His next project was also so long it was released in two sections, three years apart – *The Merry Widow* (1925) and *The Honeymoon* (1928)! In 1926 he became an American citizen and was hailed as Best Director of the Year by his colleagues. He was hired by Gloria Swanson to direct her in *Queen Kelly* (1929), a film paid for by her lover,

Joseph P. Kennedy, the father of the future President. After Stroheim had spent $600,000 on the project he was unceremoniously sacked. He found it nigh on impossible to get anyone to hire him as a director so he returned to acting. In 1935 he went bankrupt and began writing as well as acting to earn money. His best-known role was probably playing opposite Swanson as Norma Desmond's faithful old butler and ex-lover Max Von Mayerling in *Sunset Blvd.* (1950), for which he was nominated for an Oscar. An excerpt from *Queen Kelly* appears in the film. During that decade Stroheim appeared in several French films and wrote three novels.

CAUSE: He died of cancer in Maurepas, Seine-et-Oise, France, aged 71.

W

Anton Walbrook

(ADOLPH ANTON WILHELM
WOHLBRÜCK)
Born November 19, circa 1896
Died August 9, 1967
Born in Vienna, Walbrook came from a
family of clowns but opted to try his
luck in legitimate theatre. He worked
with Max Reinhardt before plunging
into German films, beginning with
Mater Dolorosa (1922), *Salto Mortale*
(1931) as Robby, *Die Fünf Verfluchten
Gentlemen* (1931), *Melodie Der Liebe*
(1932) as Kapellmeister, *Drei Von Der
Stempelstelle* (1932) and *Walzerkrieg*
(1933). Like many, he fled the Nazis
and landed in Britain, becoming a
subject in 1947. His films included:
Viktor Und Viktoria (1933) as Robert,
Victoria The Great (1937) and *Sixty
Glorious Years* (1938) both as Prince
Albert, *Forty-Ninth Parallel* (1941) as
Peter, *Dangerous Moonlight* (1941) as
Stefan Radetzky, *The Life And Death Of
Colonel Blimp* (1943) as Theo
Kretschmar-Schuldorff, *The Red Shoes*
(1948) as Boris Lermontov, *La Ronde*
(1950), *Lola Montès* (1955) as Ludwig
I, *Saint Joan* (1957) as Cauchon and *I
Accuse!* (1958) as Major Esterhazy.
CAUSE: He died in Garatshausen,
Germany, of a heart attack, aged 70.

Malvin Wald

Born August 8, 1917
Died March 6, 2008
Realist. Malvin Daniel Wald was born
in Brooklyn and it was this background
that allowed him a verisimilitude to his
writing. To write *The Naked City*
(released March 4, 1948), he followed
real New York homicide detectives. He
said, "No one had done a film where
the real hero was a hardworking police
detective, like the ones I knew in
Brooklyn. We knew we were making a
new genre that became the police
procedural." The film, directed by
Jules Dassin, was about the murder of
blonde model Jean Dexter in the bath
of her New York home. It was filmed
on location in New York and ended
with the line, "There are eight million
stories in the naked city. This has been
one of them." Wald was nominated for
an Oscar and a Writers Guild of
America award for his script, which he
co-wrote with Albert Maltz who would
be blacklisted during the McCarthy
era. He later went on to write for
television shows including *Daktari*,
Peter Gunn and *Perry Mason*.
CAUSE: Wald died at Sherman Oaks
Hospital in California from age-related
causes. He was 90.

Helen Walker

Born July 17, 1920
Died March 10, 1968
Tragic starlet. Born in Worcester,
Massachusetts, she seemed destined for
stardom after playing opposite Alan
Ladd in *Lucky Jordan* (1942) as Jill
Evans. She also appeared in *The Good
Fellows* (1943) as Ethel Hilton, *The
Man In Half Moon Street* (1944) as Eve
Brandon, *Abroad With Two Yanks*
(1944) as Joyce Stuart, *Murder, He
Says* (1945) as Claire Matthews,
Brewster's Millions (1945) as Peggy
Gray, *Murder In The Music Hall* (1946)
as Millicent, *Her Adventurous Night*
(1946) as Constance, *People Are
Funny* (1946) as Corey Sullivan and
Nightmare Alley (1947) as psychologist
Lilith Ritter. Then it all went horribly
wrong. On New Year's Eve 1946 she
was driving a car that was involved in
an accident, resulting in the death of
a soldier. Walker was badly injured in
the incident and lost work, as a result
of which she took to the bottle and
became an alcoholic. As booze took
over her life she also became paranoid
and mentally unstable; in 1955 she
wrapped a friend's birthday present in
her old publicity photographs. Her

penultimate film was *Problem Girls* (1953).

CAUSE: She died of cancer aged 47, forgotten, in North Hollywood, California.

Kim Walker

Born June 19, 1968
Died March 6, 2001
The most ironic death in this book. Kim Anne Walker, the daughter of Herbert H. Walker and Ruth Mary Weigel, made her film début in *Deadly Weapon* (1989) playing Traci but it was her performance as Heather '#1' Chandler, the nastiest of the nasty Heathers in the 1989 film of that name that made her for a time well known. She dated co-star Christian Slater for two years. She also appeared in *Say Anything . . .* (1989) as Sheila, *Nervous Ticks* (1992) as Janice, *Somewhere In The City* (1998) as Molly and *Killing Cinderella* (2000) before retiring from acting. But it was her biting lines in *Heathers* such as "You're such a pillowcase!" and "Did you eat a brain tumour for breakfast?" for which she will be remembered. She was unmarried.

CAUSE: Ironically, it was to be a brain tumour that killed her. On January 10, 1999, she had a craniotomy to try and remove the tumour but without success. Kim died at 6.30am on March 6, 2001 aged only 32 of cerebral herniation and malignant glioma at her home in Studio City, Los Angeles, California 91604. On March 10, she was buried in Pinelawn Memorial Park, Farmingdale, New York 11735.

Robert Walker

Born October 13, 1918
Died August 28, 1951
Misjudged thespian? Born in Salt Lake City Hospital, Utah, Robert Hudson Walker was the son of an uncaring journalist father, Horace (b. 1882, d. January 13, 1964) and a distant mother, Zella (b. June 1886, d. July 9, 1976). At school Walker behaved badly, often getting into fights. He was also small for his age and had very bad eyesight. When he was 9 he was cheated out of 50¢ by a man whose lawn he offered to cut. It left him with a lifelong mistrust of older men. Two years later, he got his first taste of acting but also threatened suicide when he didn't get his own way. His parents arranged for him to see a child psychiatrist. However, his acting skills came to the fore and the shrink never got to the bottom of the boy's problem. In September 1932 he enrolled in the prestigious Davis San Diego Military and Naval Academy. After a while Walker's belligerent side resurfaced and he was often in trouble with his fellow cadets and the authorities. In January 1935, to his amazement and joy, he won an award as Best Actor in San Diego County for his performance in the play *The Other Side*. That led to an offer of a scholarship at the Pasadena Playhouse but he had to defer for a year when he failed to graduate because of his poor academic record. At the end of the year, he decided to try out for the American Academy of Dramatic Art in New York instead. He was accepted after auditioning five days after his 19th birthday. On January 2, 1938, he summoned up the courage to approach a girl he had fancied for some time. Her name was Phylis Lee Isley (b. Tulsa, Oklahoma, March 2, 1919), later to become world famous as Jennifer Jones and Mrs Robert Walker. They married exactly a year after they first met and, at first, seemed like the ideal couple. They had two sons: Robert Jr (b. Jamaica Hospital, Queens, New York, April 15, 1940 at 5am) and Michael (b. March 13, 1941). In 1939 the couple travelled west to seek their fame and fortune. Phylis was signed on June 25, 1939, to a six-month contract with Republic Pictures. Walker had no such luck and after intervention by Phylis' father they

returned to the Big Apple, where their first child was born. Walker was hired for $25 to appear in the NBC radio soap opera *Yesterday's Children*. That led to regular work in soaps. In 1941 the couple's happiness was wrecked – although they didn't yet know it – when mogul David O. Selznick started to take a very personal interest in Phylis. Walker was classified 4F for war service because of his poor eyesight. Meanwhile, on December 9, 1942, it was announced that Selznick had cast Walker's wife in *The Song Of Bernadette* (1944). Thereafter the studio boss began his seduction of Jennifer Jones in earnest. Walker was flourishing at MGM, where he had made a name for himself in *Bataan* (1943). Audiences took to his look, an idiosyncrasy created mainly by his inability to focus properly. As Jones became more and more ensconced with Selznick, Walker became more and more belligerent. MGM studio chief Dore Schary recalled: "Bob began drinking and asserting his vigour and masculinity by going into bars and brawling with men who were bigger and hit harder." Walker appeared in *Madame Curie* (1943), *See Here, Private Hargrove* (1944) and *Since You Went Away* (1944), which featured several love scenes with his estranged wife, much to the distress of them both. Selznick seemed to take a sadistic pleasure in their discomfiture. Walker's other features included *Thirty Seconds Over Tokyo* (1944), *The Clock* (1945), *What Next, Corporal Hargrove* (1945), *The Sailor Takes A Wife* (1946), *The Sea Of Grass* (1947), *Song Of Love* (1947), *One Touch Of Venus* (1948), *Vengeance Valley* (1951), *Strangers On A Train* (1951) and *My Son John* (1952). Walker and Jones were divorced on June 20, 1945. He hit the bottle with enthusiasm and was often arrested for drunken behaviour. Schary gave him an ultimatum: his career or the booze. Walker was subsequently admitted to the Menninger Clinic, where he stayed for 11 months. On July 8, 1948, Walker married Barbara Ford (b. December 16, 1922), the daughter of director John Ford. They separated five weeks later. Ford was granted a divorce on December 16, 1948, on the grounds of extreme cruelty. Rumours circulated that Walker had thumped his new wife and Ford's friends John Wayne and Ward Bond had to be restrained from beating him up. The actor knew what was wrong with him but was too scared to admit the truth. "I basically felt inadequate, unwanted, and unloved since I was born. I was always trying to make an escape from life. I was an aggressive little character, but what nobody knew but me was my badness was only a cover-up for a basic lack of self-confidence, that I really was more afraid than frightening."
CAUSE: Walker slept late on August 28, 1951, at his home 14238 Sunset Boulevard. Unlike most days in Beverly Hills, the weather was unseasonably cold. At 2pm Walker took a call from his business manager Charles Trezona. At 6pm his psychiatrist, Frederick Hacker, received a call from Walker's housekeeper saying he was out of control. However, Walker's friend Jim Heneghan had called in for a drink and tried to leave when the shrink turned up. Hacker asked Heneghan to stay and another doctor, Sidney Silver, turned up and told the friend that Walker needed a shot of sodium Amytal to calm him down. However, when the injection was administered Walker stopped breathing and died around 9pm. On September 1, Walker was buried at Forest Lawn Memorial-Parks, 1712 Glendale Avenue, Glendale, California 91209. Neither Jennifer Jones nor David O. Selznick ever publicly discussed Robert Walker.
FURTHER READING: *Star Crossed: The Story Of Robert Walker And Jennifer Jones* – Beverly Linet (New York: Berkley, 1988).

Beryl Wallace

(BERYL HEISCHUBER)
Born 1910
Died June 17, 1948
Busty babe. Born in the Brighton
Beach section of Brooklyn, New York,
the eldest of nine children of working
class Austrian-Jewish émigrés,
voluptuous Beryl Wallace began her
professional career as a dancer and
then auditioned for impresario Earl
Carroll (b. Pittsburgh, Pennsylvania,
September 16, 1893) who was much
taken with her – on and offstage. He
cast her in *Earl Carroll Vanities Of 1928*
and changed her name to Beryl
Wallace. She was in several other
shows, appearing frontally naked if the
part required it. She appeared on
Broadway in the musical comedy
Treasure Girl (1928), Carroll's *Murder
At The Vanities* (1932) and *The Women*
(1936), as well as of Carroll's *Vanities*
of 1930, 1931, 1932, 1935 and 1940.
The beautiful brunette Wallace
headlined at Earl Carroll Theatre and
Restaurant at 6230 Sunset Boulevard,
Los Angeles which opened on 1938.
She appeared on the big screen in
Murder At The Vanities (released May
18, 1934) as Beryl, *Thanks For
Listening* (1937) as Gloria, *Rough
Riding Rhythm* (released August 15,
1937) as Helen Hobart opposite
Kermit Maynard, *Romance Of The
Rockies* (released December 15, 1937)
as Betty with Western star Tom Keene,
Air Devils (1938) as Marcia Bradford,
Trade Winds (released December 28,
1938), *A Night At Earl Carroll's*
(released December 6, 1940) as Miss
DuBarry, *Johnny Eager* (released
January 17, 1942) as Mabel, *Sunset On
The Desert* (released April 1, 1942) as
Julie Craig opposite Roy Rogers, *I
Married An Angel* (released July 9,
1942) as Fifi, *The Woman Of The Town*
(released December 31, 1943) as
Louella O. Parsons and *Enemy Of
Women* (released November 10, 1944)
as Jenny Hartmann. Mostly, she was
used as decoration and because her
boyfriend was an important man.
During the Second World War she
entertained the troops at the Masquers
Club and danced at the Hollywood
Canteen.
CAUSE: In 1948 the ambitious Carroll
planned to build a large theatre in New
York to rival Radio City Music Hall.
He budgeted $15,000,000 for the
venue, which would hold 7,000 people.
On June 17, 1948 Wallace, Carroll and
41 other people boarded United
Airlines Flight 624 from San Diego,
California via Los Angeles and Chicago
en route to LaGuardia Airport, New
York. The plane, Mainliner Utah,
crashed over Mount Carmel, a small
town 135 miles from Philadelphia
where delegates were gathering for the
Republican National Convention, into
a 66,000-volt pylon and exploded.
There were no survivors. Also on board
the plane was Venita Varden, the
ex-wife of actor Jack Oakie. There has
been no satisfactory explanation as to
why the aeroplane crashed. It may have
been caused by a leak of carbon dioxide
from a fire extinguisher into the
cockpit, which knocked out the crew
leaving the aircraft pilotless. Wallace
and Carroll were cremated and their
ashes were buried with his brother
Major James H. Carroll (d. 1941) in
Forest Lawn Memorial-Parks, 1712
Glendale Avenue, Glendale, California
91209. A large cast of Carroll's
hand holding a full-sized woman
representing the curvy Wallace
surmounts their grave.

Irving Wallace

Born March 19, 1916
Died June 29, 1990
The novelist. Irving Wallace was born
in Chicago, Illinois, the only son (there
was a younger sister, Esther, born in
1923) of Alex Wallace (b. Vasilishki,
near Vilna, Russia, 1892, as Ilya
Wallechinsky, d. 1982) and Bessie Liss
(b. Narevka, near Bialystock, Russia,
1890, d. 1970s). The family moved

to Kenosha, Wisconsin, a largely industrial town on Lake Michigan in 1917, and the young Irving began submitting freelance articles to a Milwaukee newspaper. He and two friends travelled to Honduras in search of material. It was there, at the age of 18, that Wallace lost his virginity to a prostitute. She charged him $2. During the Second World War he joined the film unit of the US Army Air Force on October 6, 1942 where his commanding officer was Ronald Reagan and then served in the Signals until February 1946 where he also wrote magazine features. After the war Wallace wrote for newspapers and magazines covering sporting events, ghosting showbiz autobiographies and reporting on the quirkier side of life. He moved to Hollywood where he began writing films for $750 a week. His first film was *The West Point Story* (1950) which starred Doris Day and James Cagney. His other films included *Meet Me At The Fair* (1953), *Gun Fury* (1953), *Desert Legion* (1953), *Split Second* (1953), *Bad For Each Other* (1953), *The Gambler From Natchez* (1954), *Jump Into Hell* (1955), *Sincerely Yours* (1955), *The Burning Hills* (1956), *Bombers B-52* (1957) and *The Big Circus* (1959). But Wallace intensely disliked the grind of Hollywood and looked for a way out. In his spare time he wrote a book about the prototypes of literary figures such as Robinson Crusoe and Sherlock Holmes. *The Fabulous Originals*, published on October 17, 1955, was a minor success. His first novel, *The Sins Of Philip Fleming* (published on September 30, 1959), was not. A second non-fiction book, *The Square Pegs*, was published on July 22, 1957 and told the stories of some great eccentrics. His third non-fiction effort, *The Fabulous Showman* (published on November 16, 1959), the life of P.T. Barnum, was well received. However, Wallace hit the big time with his second novel. *The Chapman Report* (published May 23,

1960) was based on the researches of Alfred Kinsey, the sexologist. It was filmed in 1962 starring Shelley Winters, Glynis Johns, Claire Bloom and Efrem Zimbalist, Jr and was directed by George Cukor. The success of the novel allowed Wallace to escape Hollywood on March 30, 1959 and to concentrate on writing his novels. Wallace's career took off. He has sold more than 120,000,000 books in 31 languages and all his fiction has one thing in common - titles beginning with "The". His novel, *The Prize*, about the shenanigans behind the Nobel prizes, is banned in Sweden. (*The Prize* was filmed in 1963 and starred Paul Newman and Elke Sommer.) *The Seven Minutes*, his novel about "the dirtiest book ever written" made it onto the big screen in 1971. It was directed by Russ Meyer and starred Wayne Maunder, Marianne MacAndrew and Yvonne De Carlo. However, literary critics dismissed his prose as flat and his characters one-dimensional. Wallace's 900,000,000 readers would undoubtedly disagree with this analysis. On June 3, 1941 at the Santa Barbara courthouse he married Sylvia Kahn, a successful novelist in her own right, and they had two children, David who reverted to the original family name Wallechinsky (b. Los Angeles, California, February 5, 1948) and Amy (b. Los Angeles, California, July 3, 1955). At one time all four family members worked together on various reference books for pleasure such as *The People's Almanac, The Book Of Lists, The Intimate Sex Lives Of Famous People, The Book Of Predictions* and *Significa*.

CAUSE: He died of cancer of the pancreas in Los Angeles, California, aged 74. He is buried in Hillside Memorial Park, 6001 West Centinela Avenue, Los Angeles 90045.

FURTHER READING: *Irving Wallace A Writer's Profile* – John Leverence (Bowling Green: The Popular Press, 1974).

Kenneth Waller

Born November 5, 1927
Died February 1, 2000
Old before his time. Born in Huddersfield, Yorkshire, lifelong bachelor Waller made his first appearance on stage at the age of six in a concert party arranged by his mother. During his national service on the Isle of Man he formed a drama society with a friend. Demobbed, he worked at an estate agents and appeared in local amateur dramatics. Seizing the chance he turned professional and first appeared in the West End in 1960, two years after he made his first film *Room At The Top* (1958). He also appeared in *Chitty Chitty Bang Bang* (1968) as an inventor, *Scrooge* (1970) as a party guest, *The Love Pill* (1971) as Professor Edwards, *Fiddler On The Roof* (1971) and *Carry On Behind* (1975) as a barman. It was as Grandad on *Bread* and as Old Mr Grace on *Are You Being Served?* that he found fame. Strangely, he replaced Harold Bennett (Young Mr Grace) even though he was nearly 30 years his junior. Said Waller, "I've played old men since the age of 18." CAUSE: He died in London of natural causes. He was 72.

Hal B. Wallis

Born September 14, 1899
Died October 5, 1986
Producer extraordinary. Harold Brent Wallis was born in Chicago, Illinois, and began his film career as a publicist for Warner Bros. Following the advent of talking pictures he was promoted to production executive where he oversaw the making of films such as *Little Caesar* (1930), *Miss Pinkerton* (1932), *I Am A Fugitive From A Chain Gang* (1932), *42nd Street* (1933), *Captain Blood* (1935), *Anthony Adverse* (1936), *Gold Diggers Of 1937* (1936), *The Charge Of The Light Brigade* (1936), *Kid Galahad* (1937), *Ever Since Eve* (1937), *The Prince And The Pauper* (1937), *Jezebel* (1938), *The Roaring Twenties* (1939), *The Oklahoma Kid* (1939), *Dark Victory* (1939), *Each Dawn I Die* (1939), *Nancy Drew And The Hidden Staircase* (1939), *The Private Lives Of Elizabeth And Essex* (1939), *The Sea Hawk* (1940), *Santa Fe Trail* (1940), *Dr Ehrlich's Magic Bullet* (1940), *Million Dollar Baby* (1941), *Affectionately Yours* (1941), *High Sierra* (1941), *The Sea Wolf* (1941), *Sergeant York* (1941), *The Bride Came C.O.D.* (1941), *The Maltese Falcon* (1941), *They Died With Their Boots On* (1941), *Kings Row* (1942), *The Man Who Came To Dinner* (1942), *Yankee Doodle Dandy* (1942), *Now, Voyager* (1942) and *Casablanca* (1942). In 1944 he left the company to form his own production unit with films distributed through Paramount. His later work included: *Rhapsody In Blue* (1945), *Desert Fury* (1947), *My Friend Irma* (1949), *Come Back, Little Sheba* (1952), *Three Ring Circus* (1954), *Gunfight At The O.K. Corral* (1957), *King Creole* (1958), *G.I. Blues* (1960), *Blue Hawaii* (1961), *Girls! Girls! Girls!* (1962), *4 for Texas* (1963), *Fun In Acapulco* (1963), *Roustabout* (1964), *Becket* (1964), *Boeing Boeing* (1965), *The Sons Of Katie Elder* (1965), *Paradise, Hawaiian Style* (1966), *Barefoot In The Park* (1967), *5 Card Stud* (1968), *True Grit* (1969), *Anne Of The Thousand Days* (1969), *Mary, Queen Of Scots* (1971) and *Rooster Cogburn* (1975). CAUSE: He died aged 87 in Rancho Mirage, California, from natural causes.

Dermot Walsh

Born September 10, 1924
Died June 26, 2002
Professional Irishman. Born in Dublin, the son of a journalist and civil servant, Walsh was educated at St Mary's College, Rathmines. It was there he decided to become an actor but was warned by his parents of the precarious nature of the profession and so, in 1940, he began work in a Dublin solicitor's. He was also given day release to study law at University College,

Dublin but his heart was never in his studies. He spent his evenings at the Abbey Theatre School of Acting, taking part in amateur productions. His parents bowed to the inevitable and gave permission for him to appear in a small no-line part in a play at the Olympic Theatre. This led to a role in another production at the Gate Theatre, Dublin, where he had 10 lines to learn. Then he became an assistant stage manager with Lord Longford's repertory company (earning £2 a week). He worked hard and graduated to juvenile leads. Realising that he could not further his career in the backwater of Ireland, he moved to England in 1945. He worked his passage on board the ship looking after horses. In December 1945 he joined the Croydon Repertory for a short time before returning to the Gate company in Dublin where, playing in *A Midsummer Night's Dream*, he had a stroke of luck and was spotted by Brian Desmond Hurst, of J. Arthur Rank. Hurst was casting for *Hungry Hill* (1946), a film adaptation of Daphne du Maurier's novel of 1943 about an Irish family feud spanning three generations. Hurst hired Walsh, whose performance as Wild Johnnie – alongside Margaret Lockwood, Dennis Price, Cecil Parker, Jean Simmons and Michael Denison – led to the part of Barney Hatton in Sydney Box's *Jassy* (1947), the story of a gypsy servant girl who falls in love with her master and is accused of murder. He also appeared as the chauffeur in *Bedelia* (1946), *The Mark Of Cain* (1947) as Jerome Thorn, *My Sister And I* (1948) as Graham Forbes alongside Hazel Court (whom he was to marry in 1949), Martita Hunt, Barbara Mullen and Sally Ann Howes, *Third Time Lucky* (1948) as Lucky and *Torment* (1950) as Cliff Brandon. Following his marriage to Court (the first girl to be put under contract by Rank), Walsh became a father in 1950. He appeared alongside his wife in *The Frightened Man* (1952) as Julius Roselli,

The Ghost Ship (1952) as Guy Thornton and *Counterspy* (1953) as Manning. Fame was his but not always when he wanted it. Once he was standing on a railway platform in Manchester with Rank's publicity manager and he spotted a group of small boys heading his way. Noticing that the lads were clutching notebooks, Walsh asked the publicity man to lend him a pen because, he explained, autograph hunters always had pens that leaked. But the boys rushed past him on their way to collect engine numbers. He appeared in the theatre, often working with his wife. His late-Fifties films included *Sea Fury* (1958) as Kelso, *Sea Of Sand* (1958), *Make Mine A Million* (1959), as Martin Russell opposite Sid James and Arthur Askey and *The Challenge* (1960) with Jayne Mansfield, in which he played Detective Sergeant Willis. On the small screen he appeared in *Danger Man*, *Court Martial*, *The Invisible Man* and the title role in the series *Richard The Lionheart*, which lasted for 39 episodes. When 6' Walsh toured he eschewed hotels and guest houses and took his caravan instead. His hobbies included making lists, collecting menus and stamps. Following his divorce from Hazel Court in 1963, he married the actress Diana Scougall in 1968. They had a son and divorced in 1974. That same year he married Elizabeth Knox (née Scott), who predeceased him. They had two daughters, one of whom is the actress Elizabeth Dermot-Walsh (b. 1976). CAUSE: Walsh died in hospital in Tunbridge Wells, Kent. He was 77.

Raoul Walsh
Born March 11, 1887
Died December 31, 1980
The director's director. Born in New York, Walsh ran away to sea when he was still a boy and worked on a ranch before entering the film industry in 1909. He edited D.W. Griffith's *The Birth Of A Nation* (1915) before turning to directing. By the end of his

career in 1964 (caused by failing eyesight) he had directed over 120 films. Walsh also acted, appearing in *The Birth Of A Nation* as John Wilkes Booth. His last performance came in *Sadie Thompson* (1928) as Sergeant Tim O'Hara, a film that he also wrote and directed. During the filming of *In Old Arizona* (1929) he lost an eye and wore a black patch for the rest of his life. His films were popular with actors, directors and the public but studiously ignored by the Academy. They included: *The Thief Of Bagdad* (1924), *Me And My Gal* (1932), *The Bowery* (1933), *Going Hollywood* (1933), *Spendthrift* (1936), *Klondike Annie* (1936), *When Thief Meets Thief* (1937), *O.H.M.S.* (1937), *The Roaring Twenties* (1939), *The Strawberry Blonde* (1941), *High Sierra* (1941), *They Died With Their Boots On* (1941), *Objective, Burma!* (1945), *Cheyenne* (1947), *White Heat* (1949), *Along The Great Divide* (1951), *Captain Horatio Hornblower* (1951), *Distant Drums* (1951), *Blackbeard The Pirate* (1952), *Sea Devils* (1953), *Saskatchewan* (1954), *The Sheriff Of Fractured Jaw* (1958), *The Naked And The Dead* (1958), *Esther And The King* (1960) and *A Distant Trumpet* (1964).
CAUSE: He died aged 93 in Simi Valley, California, of natural causes.

Sam Wanamaker, CBE (Hon.)

Born June 14, 1919
Died December 18, 1993
Acting-director. Born in Chicago, Illinois, Wanamaker studied at the Goodman Theater in his home town before making his stage début aged 17. His first film didn't come until after World War II, *My Girl Tisa* (1948), in which he played Mark Denek. Wanamaker had definite left-wing tendencies and believed his cause would be better suited in England. As it turned out his name did not crop up in either the 1947 nor 1951 Senate Un-American Activities investigations. However, the tentacles of McCarthy's

insidious campaign were long and Wanamaker found himself blacklisted. Unable to work in films, he found gainful employment in the English theatre, not returning to film-making until the Sixties. He appeared in *Taras Bulba* (1962) as Filipenko, *Those Magnificent Men In Their Flying Machines, Or How I Flew From London To Paris In 25 Hours 11 Minutes* (1965) as George Gruber, *The Spy Who Came In From The Cold* (1965) as Peters, *The Day The Fish Came Out* (1967) as Elias, *Voyage Of The Damned* (1976) as Carl Rosen, *Private Benjamin* (1980) as Teddy Benjamin, *Irreconcilable Differences* (1984) as David Kessler, *Raw Deal* (1986) as Patrovita and *Superman IV: The Quest For Peace* (1987) as David Warfield. His directing was mostly confined to the theatre and television: he directed two *Columbo* TV movies. He was married in 1940 to Charlotte Holland and had three daughters, one of whom is the actress Zoë Wanamaker (b. New York, May 13, 1948).
CAUSE: Wanamaker died aged 74 from cancer in London.

Michael Ward

(GEORGE WILLIAM EVERARD WARD)
Born April 9, 1909
Died November 8, 1997
Camp foil. Born in Redruth, Cornwall, the only child of a clergyman, Ward led a peripatetic lifestyle as a youngster thanks to his father's job. In 1930 the family settled in Caddington, near Luton where Ward worked as a private tutor. During the Second World War he drove ambulances. In March 1946 he won a scholarship to the Central School of Speech and Drama in London. He made his first film the following year, a production of *An Ideal Husband* (released November 13, 1947), directed by Alexander Korda. It was to be the first of almost 70 films including five *Carry On*s (*Regardless, Cabbie, Cleo, Screaming* and *Don't Lose Your Head*) and four Norman Wisdom

pictures. On television his campness found favour on *The Two Ronnies, The Dick Emery Show* and *The Morecambe And Wise Show* where he played their fey neighbour, Adrian Fondle. He never married.

CAUSE: Shortly after he finished filming *Revenge Of The Pink Panther* (1978), he suffered a stroke that forced him to retire. From 1986 until his death, he was unable to walk unaided. 6′ Ward died at St Mary's Hospital, Ladbroke Grove, London. He was 88.

Warner Bros
Albert
(ALBERT EICHELBAUM)
Born July 23, 1883
Died November 26, 1967
Harry
(HARRY EICHELBAUM)
Born December 12, 1881
Died July 25, 1958
Jack L.
(JACK EICHELBAUM)
Born August 2, 1892
Died September 9, 1978
Sam
(SAM EICHELBAUM)
Born August 10, 1887
Died October 5, 1927

Cinematic siblings. The four brothers were four of the twelve children (only eight survived childhood) of Jewish Polish immigrants, Ben and Pearl Eichelbaum, who arrived in Baltimore in 1883. Ben worked as a shoe mender, hardware salesman and butcher to support his large brood. The family drifted to and from Canada (Sam was born in Baltimore, Maryland; Jack was born in London, Ontario) before moving to Youngstown, Ohio. In 1903 the four brothers ventured into the entertainment business in Newcastle, Pennsylvania. Harry had the imagination and vision and he persuaded his brothers to invest in a projector and show films to paying audiences. The family rented an empty shop at New Castle, Pennsylvania, named it the Pioneer, hired 99 chairs

from a local undertaker and opened for business. When the funeral director needed the chairs, the films were standing room only. Harry and Albert looked after the box office, Sam worked the projector and Jack was a gifted singer who kept the audience amused in the intervals. In 1905, adopting the name Warner, they opened a larger cinema called the Cascade Theatre. In 1912 they moved into film production with two short Westerns *Perils Of The Plains* (1912) and *Raiders Of The Mexican Border* (1912). Harry bought the rights to a book written by an ambassador and his dealings with Kaiser Wilhelm II. *My Four Years In Germany* (1918) became a successful 10-part serial. In 1918 Sam and Jack moved to the West Coast to open a studio. In 1923 they established Warner Bros. Harry as president and Albert as treasurer stayed in New York to look after the financial side of the business while Sam was appointed CEO and Jack in charge of production made the films out west. The company's first success was *Where The North Begins* (1923), the first film at the studio of Rin Tin Tin. The company knew that with the doggy capers that they had money in the bank. They also made the first of The Gold Diggers films at the same time and in 1924 signed John Barrymore to play Beau Brummell in the eponymously named film. At first the company ran short of money and they could only borrow at extortionate rates or from advances at adverse rates from local distributors. Leading banker Waddill Catchings saw a potential in the future of film and allowed the brothers to borrow at favourable terms. Harry negotiated the takeover of the Vitagraph Company and with it 50 film exchanges across Europe and North America allowing Warner Bros to distribute their own films. Sam became interested in the possibility of actors talking in films but Harry said, "I wouldn't be so foolish as to try and make talking pictures. That's what everybody has done and lost. No, we'll do better than that. We can film and record vaudeville and musical acts, and make up programmes for houses that can't afford the real thing or can't get big time acts." In 1926 Warners launched *Don Juan* with a pre-recorded musical score. It was such a success that they planned another, *The Jazz Singer* (1927). Al Jolson made cinematic history in the film as Jakie Rabinowitz (Jack Robin) when he uttered the immortal line, "You ain't heard nothin' yet!" Jolson ad-libbed his famous line. Warner Bros offered Jolson shares in their company in lieu of a salary. He turned down their offer preferring cash ($75,000) and passed on a fortune. Sam died the day before the film opened in New York. The first all-talkie was *Lights Of New York* (1928). In 1930 Warner Bros took control of its main rivals First National although a complete merger would not happen until 1940. The company that had assets of $5 million in 1925 was worth $230 million in 1930. In the Thirties Warner Bros began producing gangster films such as *Little Caesar* (1930) and *The Public Enemy* (1931), making stars of Edward G. Robinson and James Cagney respectively. The studio also enabled Busby Berkeley to stage huge musicals such as *42nd Street* (1933) – his musical numbers were said to cost $10,000 per minute of screen time. The way Jack ran the company wasn't to everyone's taste. Humorist Wilson Mizner opined: "Working for Warner Bros is like fucking a porcupine. It's a hundred pricks against one," while actress Simone Signoret said, "[Jack] bore no grudge against those he had wronged." Many saw Jack as a kind of Prince Philip of his day. When he met Madame Chiang Kai-Shek he told her that he had forgotten to bring his laundry. Bette Davis and Olivia de Havilland went to court to try and break what they saw as restrictive contracts. The studio made some notable films in the Thirties including: *Black Fury* (1935), *G Men*

(1935), *A Midsummer Night's Dream* (1935), *Captain Blood* (1935), *Boulder Dam* (1936), *Brides Are Like That* (1936), *The Singing Kid* (1936), *The Golden Arrow* (1936), *Bengal Tiger* (1936), *Anthony Adverse* (1936), *China Clipper* (1936), *Cain And Mabel* (1936), *The Charge Of The Light Brigade* (1936), *Gold Diggers Of 1937* (1936), *Black Legion* (1937), *The Prince And The Pauper* (1937), *Kid Galahad* (1937), *That Certain Woman* (1937), *The Adventures Of Robin Hood* (1938), *Men Are Such Fools* (1938), *The Amazing Dr Clitterhouse* (1938), *Angels With Dirty Faces* (1938), *Jezebel* (1938), *The Dawn Patrol* (1938), *Nancy Drew . . . Reporter* (1939), *Nancy Drew . . . Trouble Shooter* (1939), *The Private Lives Of Elizabeth And Essex* (1939) and *The Angels Wash Their Faces* (1939). In the Forties the studio produced *Casablanca* (1942), *Yankee Doodle Dandy* (1942), *To Have And Have Not* (1944), *Mildred Pierce* (1945) and *The Big Sleep* (1946). At the end of the decade stars like Bette Davis, Humphrey Bogart and Errol Flynn left the studio as did directors John Huston and Jean Negulesco. In May 1956 Albert and Harry sold their interest in the studio although Jack remained until 1967 before going independent selling his interest to the Canadian company Seven Arts.

CAUSE: Sam died aged 40 (the day before *The Jazz Singer* opened in New York) of a sinus infection coupled with a brain abscess and pneumonia. Harry died, aged 76, in Hollywood, California, of a cerebral occlusion. Albert died of natural causes aged 83. Jack succumbed to a pulmonary oedema and inflammation of the heart in Los Angeles, California. He was 86.

Jack Warner, OBE

(HORACE JOHN WATERS)
Born October 24, 1895
Died May 24, 1981
Dependable Brit. Born in Bromley, Kent, Warner was one of six children of an undertaker's warehouseman. His

sisters, Elsie and Doris, became famous on the radio as Gert and Daisy in the Thirties and Forties. For a time he studied to become a car engineer but left and found work with an undertaker in Balham. That didn't suit him and in August 1913, aged 17, he travelled to France where he landed a job as a mechanic in Paris. The First World War saw him serving in the Royal Flying Corps and earning a meritorious service medal. After the war on March 31, 1919, he resumed his career as a mechanic and added racing driver to his CV. He was almost 40 before he made his acting début in the West End. He altered his surname to avoid charges of living off his more famous sisters. His film début came in *Dummy Talks* (1942). His fourth film was the one that gained him most notice. He played Mr Huggett in *Holiday Camp* (1947) opposite Kathleen Harrison as Mrs Huggett. The film spawned three sequels and a radio show. A brief role as PC George Dixon in *The Blue Lamp* (1949) led to the part that Warner immortalised on television in *Dixon Of Dock Green* from July 9, 1955, until May 1, 1976, when the realism of cop shows such as *Z Cars* and *The Sweeney* forced his final retirement as, no doubt, the oldest copper in the Met. In 1933 he married Muriel Winifred 'Mollie' Peters at St Mark's Church, Albert Road, Regent's Park, London. There were no children from the marriage. CAUSE: He suffered a stroke in 1980 that forced his retirement. He died from pneumonia following another stroke aged 85 in the Royal Masonic Hospital, Ravenscourt Park, London. FURTHER READING: *'Evening All* – Jack Warner (London: Star, 1979).

Ruth Warrick
Born June 29, 1915
Died January 15, 2005
Soap matriarch. Born in St Joseph, Missouri, Ruth Warrick was educated at the University of Kansas City and moved to New York where she was hired by Orson Welles' Mercury Theater. Welles hand-picked her to make her début playing Emily Monroe Norton Kane in 1941's *Citizen Kane*. She made 19 films in the Forties such as *Song Of The South* (1946) as Sally but by the end of that decade she was nothing more than a supporting player. 5′6″ Ruth Warrick moved from the big screen to the small and found a niche in soap operas. It was her portrayal of Phoebe Tyler Wallingford in *All My Children* (from 1970) that won her acclaim, two Emmy nominations and a Daytime Emmy Lifetime Achievement Award. She was married four times. Her first husband (on April 15, 1938) was the actor Erik Rolf (b. Chicago, Illinois, June 1, 1911, d. San Diego County, California, May 28, 1957) by whom she had two children, Karen Elizabeth (b. March 13, 1941) and Jon (b. September 1942). They divorced in 1946. Her second marriage was to the actor Carl Neubert in 1949. In July 1953 she married Robert McNamara by whom she had a son, Timothy. Her fourth and final marriage was in 1975 to Jarvis Cushing. CAUSE: She died in Manhattan, New York, of complications from pneumonia. She was 89.

Richard Warwick
Born April 29, 1945
Died December 16, 1997
Rugged support. Born in Dartford, Kent, Warwick studied at RADA before making his film début in Lindsay Anderson's *if. . .* (1968) as Wallace and then appeared in *Romeo And Juliet* (1968) as Gregory. It seemed as if his bid for stardom would succeed, then he appeared in the disastrous *The Breaking Of Bumbo* (1970) and his career never really recovered. His films included: *Nicholas And Alexandra* (1971) as Grand Duke Dimitry, *Alice's Adventures In Wonderland* (1972) as the Seven of Spades, *Confessions Of A Pop Performer* (1975) as Kipper, *Sebastiane* (1976), *International Velvet* (1978) as

Tim, *The Tempest* (1979) as Antonio, a prisoner in *Johnny Dangerously* (1984), *Hamlet* (1990) as Bernardo, *White Hunter, Black Heart* (1990) as Basil Fields and *Jane Eyre* (1996) as John. He was unmarried.

CAUSE: Warwick died of AIDS aged 52.

Lew Wasserman

Born March 15, 1913
Died June 3, 2002
MCA mogul. One of the most influential executives in Hollywood, Lewis Robert Wasserman developed his company MCA – Music Corporation of America – into a huge conglomerate encompassing all forms of media. Unlike his predecessors such as Jack Warner, Sam Goldwyn, Lew Grade or Louis B. Mayer, Wasserman preferred to keep a low profile and work behind the scenes. Wasserman was born in Cleveland, Ohio, the son of orthodox Jewish-Russian immigrants. His father was a clerk and failed restaurateur. While attending Glenville High School, young Wasserman got a job as an usher at the Palace, a cinema in Cleveland, where he worked from 3pm until midnight. He later recalled, "It was usually 2am when I got home. Then I had to get up early enough to walk five miles to school." It was the start of a work ethic that saw him working 16-hour days, seven days a week at MCA. Because his parents were too poor, Wasserman was unable to go on to further education. (In 1998 he gave $8.75 million for scholarships to the University of California at Los Angeles.) On leaving school in 1930 Wasserman began marketing for the Mayfair Casino, a Cleveland nightclub, where he met Jules Stein, an agent, who had created MCA six years earlier. Stein was impressed with the youngster and in 1936 Wasserman became MCA's director of advertising and publicity at a salary of $60 a week. That year also saw him marry Edith Beckerman on July 5. They had one daughter, Lynne

Kay. Wasserman began to look after the careers of stars such as Bette Davis, Errol Flynn, John Garfield, Betty Grable, James Stewart and Jane Wyman. Wasserman negotiated with the studios to release actors from restrictive long-term contracts. However, he wasn't necessarily kind to all his clientele. He told Shirley Temple she was "washed up". She recalled, "I started to cry. 'Here,' he said, pushing a Kleenex box across the desk top. 'Have one on me.'" In 1946 Wasserman had risen to become company president. At the start of the next decade he had increased the company's portfolio to include production. In 1959 he bought the Universal Pictures lot in North Hollywood, and, three years later, Universal Studios, with its parent company, Decca Records. It was at this time that MCA was the subject of a US Justice Department investigation for possible breach of the anti-trust laws. Wasserman avoided legal action by disbanding the talent agency but he also expanded the film and television production side, opened Universal Studios' theme park, and invested in the musical side of the business. Wasserman also began to cultivate political contacts and became one of Hollywood's most successful and in-demand political fund-raisers. A Democrat, he became a confidant of Presidents Johnson, Carter and Clinton. Yet he was also close to Ronald Reagan when the former B-movie actor occupied 1600 Pennsylvania Avenue. Wasserman had been Reagan's first agent in Hollywood, and the men were close friends. Under Wasserman, MCA was responsible for Steven Spielberg's *Jaws, Jurassic Park, ET The Extra Terrestrial* and *Schindler's List*. It also produced *The Sting, Day Of The Jackal, Out Of Africa* and *American Graffiti*. On the small screen Wasserman's MCA made *Alfred Hitchcock Presents, Kojak, Miami Vice* and *Murder, She Wrote* among others. It was Wasserman who pioneered the made-for-television movie and the mini-series. In 1990 MCA was sold to the Matsushita Corporation of Japan for $6.1 billion. Wasserman, although sidelined by his new bosses, stayed on as chief executive and was estimated to receive $30 million a year in dividends in return for his five million shares in the company. In 1995 the company was taken over by Seagram and Wasserman retired with the title chairman emeritus. By 1998, he was said to be worth $500 million. In 1995 he was awarded the Presidential Medal of Freedom – America's highest civilian honour – by Bill Clinton.

CAUSE: Lew Wasserman died aged 89 at his home in Beverly Hills, California, of complications following a stroke. He is buried in Hillside Memorial Park, 6001 West Centinela Avenue, Los Angeles 90045.

Coy Watson, Jr

(JAMES CAUGHEY WATSON JR)
Born November 16, 1912
Died March 14, 2009

Silent child star. Born the eldest of six sons and three daughters, all of whom acted, Coy Watson made his first film when he was just nine months old. The other acting Watsons were: Gloria (b. Los Angeles, California, July 4, 1917, d. Los Angeles, California, USA, June 1, 1997); Vivian (b. Los Angeles, California February 19, 1915, d. Los Angeles, California, December 18, 1994); Louise (b. Los Angeles, California, November 22, 1919); Harry (b. Los Angeles, California, August 31, 1921 d. Tujunga, California, June 8, 2001 of complications from a stroke); Billy (b. Los Angeles, California December 25, 1923); (David) Delmar (b. Los Angeles, California, July 1, 1926, d. Glendale, California, October 26, 2008 of complications from prostate cancer); Garry (b. Los Angeles, California, September 27, 1928) and Robert S. "Bobs" (b. Los Angeles, California, November 16,

1930 d. Laguna Beach, California June 27, 1999 of prostate cancer). Coy Watson, Jr got into acting by complete accident; his family was living in Edendale near the Mack Sennett Studios and the studio needed a baby for a short film, *The Price Of Silence* (1913). He was paid $5 per day but because Edendale then had no electricity the scene was shot on a set built specially to take advantage of the sun. Watson appeared in so many Keystone Cops comedies that he was nicknamed The Keystone Kid. By the end of the Thirties the Watson family had featured in more than one thousand films. As he attained his majority Watson had appeared in 60 films, including *The Hunchback Of Notre Dame* (1923) with Lon Chaney, *Buttons* (1927) with Jackie Coogan and *Show People* (1928) with Marion Davies. "Acting to our family was not a business," he said. "It was our life. We never knew anything but the movies." Coy Watson Sr (b. California, April 14, 1890, d. Edendale, California, May 23, 1968) was a horse wrangler and special effects co-ordinator. He created the flying carpet Douglas Fairbanks used in *The Thief Of Bagdad* (premièred March 18, 1924). In time he found it more lucrative to manage his children rather than work himself. When a director would say, "I need a child for a movie. Do you have one?" he replied, "What size and what sex?" His wife, Golda, washed and ironed actors' costumes. 5'6" Coy's brother Delmar was Shirley Temple's goatherd friend in *Heidi* (1937). Delmar and three other Watsons played Jimmy Stewart's sons in *Mr Smith Goes To Washington* (1939). His brother Bobs, who had an MGM contract, was Pee Wee in *Boys Town* (1938) with Spencer Tracy. Watson began turning his back on films when sound began replacing silent pictures. "[Sound pictures] scared the dickens out of everybody," he said. "We used to have fun making pictures. But when sound came in you couldn't drop a pin." He turned his attentions to photography. In 1932, he covered the Olympics in Los Angeles for Acme and the same year photographed the visit of future president Franklin D. Roosevelt to the city. In 1939, he invented and made the Coy Watson Lite Beam Focuser, a built-in camera device that assured accurate still camera focusing in total darkness. During the Second World War he and three of his brothers ran a Coast Guard photography unit in San Diego. All six brothers became cameramen for the press, newsreels or television after the conflict. He was married with a son, James Caughey III, and a daughter, Pattie.

CAUSE: Coy Watson, Jr died aged 96 of complications from stomach cancer in Alpine, California.

Richard Wattis

Born February 25, 1912
Died February 1, 1975
Owlish prude. Although he was more often than not cast as an interfering busybody or supercilious prude, off screen Dicky Wattis was vastly different. Best remembered to television audiences as the snooty Mr Charles Fulbright Brown, next door neighbour to Eric and Hattie Sykes in the long-running sitcom, *Sykes*, he also appeared with Marilyn Monroe and Laurence Olivier in *The Prince And The Showgirl* (1957). According to diarist Colin Clark, Marilyn kept her distance from Wattis because of his homosexuality. Clark goes on to recall that for most of the time he spent with Wattis all the actor "wanted to do was pick up some gorgeous hunk of a man". Wattis was born in Wednesbury, Staffordshire, and following schooling in Birmingham and Worcestershire, he joined the family engineering firm before making his first stage appearance at the Royal Theatre, Brighton, in September 1935. His first West End performance came at the Aldwych on June 30, 1948, as Lord

Seymour Sangate, MP, in *Ambassador Extraordinary*. He entered films in 1937 with *A Yank At Oxford* and became a stalwart British supporting actor in films such as *The Happiest Days Of Your Life* (1950) as Arnold Billings, *Appointment With Venus* (1951) as Carruthers, *Lady Godiva Rides Again* (1951), *Top Secret* (1952) as Barnes, *Mother Riley Meets The Vampire* (1952) as Police Constable Freddie, *Colonel March Investigates* (1952) as Cabot, *The Importance Of Being Earnest* (1952) as Seaton, *Doctor In The House* (1954), *Hobson's Choice* (1954) as Albert Prosser, *The Belles Of St Trinian's* (1954) as Manton Bassett, *The Colditz Story* (1955) as Richard Gordon, *Blue Murder At St Trinian's* (1957) as Manton Bassett, *The Inn Of The Sixth Happiness* (1958) as Mr Muffin, *Dentist On The Job* (1961) as Macreedy, *The Longest Day* (1962), *The V.I.P.s* (1963) as Sanders, *Carry On Spying* (1964) as Cobley, *Operation Crossbow* (1965) as Sir Charles Sims, *The Amorous Adventures Of Moll Flanders* (1965), *The Great St Trinian's Train Robbery* (1966) as Manton Bassett, *Casino Royale* (1967), *Chitty Chitty Bang Bang* (1968) as the sweet factory secretary, *Monte Carlo Or Bust* (1969) as the golf club secretary, *Wonderwall: The Movie* (1969) as Perkins, *Games That Lovers Play* (1970) as Mr Lothran and *Confessions Of A Window Cleaner* (1974) as Carole's Father. He lived in unmarried splendour at 23 Cadogan Place, London SW1.

CAUSE: Dicky Wattis died of a heart attack, aged 62, in London.

Carol Wayne

Born September 6, 1942
Died January 13, 1985
Busty blonde beauty. Carol Wayne was born in Chicago, Illinois, the eldest of two acting sisters (sibling Nina Wayne [b. Chicago, Illinois, September 18, 1943] appeared in the television series *Camp Runamuck*). Carol and Nina began their careers as teenage skaters

with the Ice Capades before becoming topless dancers in Las Vegas. Carol was very keen to showcase her 39C-24-35 figure. She made her film début in *Gunn* (1967) and followed that up with *The Party* (1968) as June Warren. In 1968 she made the first of her 101 appearances as the Matinee Lady for the Tea Time Movie on *The Tonight Show With Johnny Carson*. Her other films included: a nurse in *Scavenger Hunt* (1979), *Savannah Smiles* (1982) as Doreen, *Heartbreakers* (1984) as Candy, which featured her first topless scene, and *Surf II* (1984) as Jocko's mother. In February 1984 she posed nude for *Playboy* and claimed to have had an orgasm during the shoot. She was married three times. Her first marriage lasted less than a year. Husband number two was photographer Barry Finkelstein (who was previously married to Mary Travers of Peter, Paul & Mary) by whom she had a son, Alex (b. 1969). Husband number three was TV producer Burt Sugarman. They were divorced in 1980.

CAUSE: On December 13, 1984, Carol filed for bankruptcy, listing her income as "$000.00". On January 4, 1985, suffering from drink and cocaine problems, she flew to the exclusive Las Hadas Resort in Manzanillo on Mexico's Gold Coast to "clear her head". Her companion was Edward Durston, a used car dealer from Los Angeles. However, on January 10, they missed their 7pm return flight. With no money, they had to book into the cheaper Playa de Santiago hotel. When they arrived, Carol screamed at Durston: "Why have you brought me to this dump?" She refused to get out of the taxi and go into reception. She stomped off, heading towards the beach while Durston took their luggage up to their room. Durston went to the bar and then left the hotel. At 2.30 the next morning he returned and asked if Carol "had showed up". When told she hadn't, Durston left and booked into

another hotel, leaving town the next afternoon with Carol still missing. He left her luggage at the airport, saying she would collect it later. On January 13, 1985, her body was discovered floating in four feet of water three hundred yards from shore in Santiago Bay, Manzanillo. She was wearing a black jumpsuit, leather jacket and red shoes. An autopsy disclosed that she had drowned 36 to 48 hours earlier. No drugs or alcohol were found in her body. The local police chief wanted to know why Durston had left town so quickly, especially when it was disclosed that he was also the last person with TV personality Art Linkletter's daughter, Diane, when she supposedly jumped out of her apartment window in Shoreham Towers, West Los Angeles, on October 4, 1969, after taking LSD. In 1990 Carol Wayne's death was reinvestigated and labelled accidental. Carol couldn't swim. The American Consulate opined: "I don't think it was a drowning. A drowning yes, of course, but there's more to it than that."

David Wayne
(WAYNE MCMEEKAN)
Born January 30, 1914
Died February 9, 1995
Reliable second lead. Born in Traverse City, Michigan, the son of an insurance executive, 5'7" Wayne's mother died when he was four. Following a degree at Western Michigan University he became a statistician in Cleveland, Ohio. In his spare time he joined a local repertory company that specialised in the Bard. In 1941 he married Jane Gordon (d. 1993), by whom he had twin daughters Kearney and Melinda. He was turned down by the army and so became an ambulance driver in North Africa instead. On demob he was a hit on Broadway, earning praise from both Eugene O'Neill and Arthur Miller. He won a Tony for Best Supporting Actor in a Musical for *Finian's Rainbow* the first

year they were presented for 1947. Seven years later he won a Best Actor in a Dramatic Role award for *The Teahouse Of The August Moon*. He made his film début in *Portrait Of Jennie* (1948) as Gus O'Toole and also appeared, among other features, in *Adam's Rib* (1949) as Kip Lurie, *Stella* (1950) as Carl Granger, *M* (1951) as Martin Harrow, *As Young As You Feel* (1951) as Joe Elliott, *O. Henry's Full House* (1952) as Horace, *We're Not Married!* (1952) as Jeff Norris, *Down Among The Sheltering Palms* (1953) as Lieutenant Carl Schmidt, *How To Marry A Millionaire* (1953) as Freddie Denmark, *Tonight We Sing* (1953) as Sol Hurok, *Hell And High Water* (1954) as Tugboat Walker, *The Three Faces Of Eve* (1957) as Ralph White, *The Andromeda Strain* (1971) as Dr Charles Burton, *Huckleberry Finn* (1974) as the Duke, *The Front Page* (1974) as Bensinger, *The Apple Dumpling Gang* (1975) as Colonel Clydesdale and *The Fence* (1994) as the foreman of the steel mill. On television he was best known as Inspector Richard Queen in *Ellery Queen* and the original Willard 'Digger' Barnes in *Dallas*.

CAUSE: Wayne died of lung cancer in Santa Monica, California. He was 81.

John Wayne

(MARION ROBERT MORRISON)
Born May 26, 1907
Died June 11, 1979

The Duke. One of the giants of the cinema in more ways than one, 6'4½" Duke Wayne was born in Winterset, Iowa. He was named after his grandfathers Marion Mitchell Morrison and Robert Emmett Brown. When he was four, following the birth of his brother, Robert Emmett Wayne (b. December 18, 1911, d. St Joseph's Hospital, Burbank, July 25, 1970), his middle name was changed to Mitchell. His middle name was never Michael although he did like to tease people by claiming it was. Duke Wayne – the nickname came from an Airedale dog

he owned as a boy – was the American hero who made the cinematic West safe for decent folks. Duke was raised in Glendale, California, from 1916 and, being a sporty lad, won a football scholarship to the University of Southern California where he was part of the famous 'Thundering Herd' side, the team that, legend has it, rampaged on Clara Bow's lawn and in her bedroom. During the summer holidays Wayne worked as a general handyman on the Fox lot where he came to the attention of director John Ford, who was to have a pivotal effect in making Duke Wayne a star. Wayne began appearing in films in 1925 as an uncredited extra in *Brown Of Harvard* (1925) playing a Yale footballer, *Bardelays The Magnificent* (1926) as a spear-carrying guard and *The Great K & A Train Robbery* (1926). Two years later, he began playing bit parts in Ford's films, usually billed as Duke Morrison. In 1930 Ford mentioned Wayne to his friend Raoul Walsh, resulting in him being cast in his first leading role in a film *The Big Trail* (1930) as Breck Coleman. However, Duke's career seemed to be over before it had really begun as the public didn't really take to him and although he appeared in over 60 films, stardom remained elusive. It was his role in John Ford's *Stagecoach* (1939) in which Wayne played Henry, the Ringo Kid, that made him a star. (Trivia note: if you look carefully you can see rubber tyre tracks on the salt flats during the Indian chase.) From then on, often in tandem with Ford, Wayne became one of the biggest stars ever seen in America. His films included: *Allegheny Uprising* (1939) as Jim Smith, *Dark Command* (1940) as Bob Seton, *Three Faces West* (1940) as John Phillips, *Seven Sinners* (1940) as Lieutenant Dan Brent, *Lady For A Night* (1941) as Jack Morgan, *Lady From Louisiana* (1941) as John Reynolds, *Reunion In France* (1942) as Pat Talbot, *Reap The Wild Wind* (1942) as Captain Jack

Stuart, *In Old California* (1942) as Tom Craig, *Flying Tigers* (1942) as Jim Gordon, *A Lady Takes A Chance* (1943) as Duke Hudkins, *In Old Oklahoma* (1943) as Dan Somers, *Tall In The Saddle* (1944) as Rocklin, *Back To Bataan* (1945) as Colonel Joseph Madden, *Dakota* (1945) as John Devlin, *Without Reservations* (1946) as Rusty Thomas, *Desert Command* (1946) as Tom Wayne (!), *Angel And The Badman* (1947) as Quirt Evans, which he also produced, *Tycoon* (1947) as Johnny Munroe, *Fort Apache* (1948) as Captain Kirby York, *Red River* (1948) as Thomas Dunson, *The Fighting Kentuckian* (1949) as John Breen, which he also produced, *She Wore A Yellow Ribbon* (1949) as Captain Nathan Brittles, *Sands Of Iwo Jima* (1949) as Sergeant John M. Stryker, *Rio Grande* (1950) as Lieutenant Colonel Kirby Yorke, *Flying Leathernecks* (1951) as Major Dan Kirby, the title role in *Big Jim McLain* (1952), *Trouble Along the Way* (1953) as Steve Williams, *Island In The Sky* (1953) as Captain Dooley, *Blood Alley* (1955) as Captain Tom Wilder, which he also produced, and *The Searchers* (1956) as Ethan Edwards, which prompted John Ford to quip, "I never knew the big son of a bitch could act." (Historical trivia point: in the film, Ethan Edwards gives a medal to his niece that he says was awarded him by the Confederate government. The Confederates didn't give medals.) *The Conqueror* (1956) is undoubtedly one of the silliest movies ever made. Wayne playing Moghul Emperor Genghis Khan was not the most sensible or inspired piece of casting ever to hit Tinseltown. (It could have been worse. The original choice was Marlon Brando!) The critics were unanimous in their condemnation of the film. Leonard Maltin described it as "the silliest role of John Wayne's career" while Leslie Halliwell called it, "[A] solemn pantomime [with] too many dull spots." Jack Smith in *The Los*

Angeles Times opined: "John Wayne as Genghis Khan – history's most improbable piece of casting unless Mickey Rooney were to play Jesus in *King Of Kings*." Robert Hatch of *The Nation* wrote, "A substandard horse opera featuring John Wayne as Genghis Khan, Susan Hayward as his hot but reluctant bride and almost all of the Utah beyond Salt Lake City as the Gobi Desert. History has not been served well and neither has the popcorn public." Duke himself said, "*The Conqueror* is a Western in some ways. The way the screenplay reads, it is a cowboy picture and that is how I'm going to play Genghis Khan. I see him as a gunfighter." One of Wayne's less forgettable lines was "I am Temujin – barbarian – I fight! I love! I conquer – like a barbarian . . . The world? I will take it! The woman? I will tame her!" Other classic lines include this from Agnes Moorhead as Temujin's mum: "My son has won the world; still he must conquer that redheaded Jezebel!" *The Conqueror* has to be seen to be disbelieved. The screenwriter Oscar Millard had been recommended to bashful billionaire producer Howard Hughes as being an expert on Genghis Khan. Millard later admitted, "I was such an authority on Genghis Khan that when I prudently looked him up in the *Encyclopaedia Britannica* in the half hour before the meeting I had trouble finding him because I couldn't spell his name." Hughes was so impressed by Millard's erudition he spent $6 million making *The Conqueror,* but the film was a flop in America (it returned just $4.5 million). The public may have hated the movie but Hughes loved it and watched the film again and again. He lashed out a further $12 million buying up all the prints. The film was not shown publicly for 17 years (1957–1974). This was not because it was so bad, but rather because Hughes owned all the copies. It was the last film he personally produced before he began to develop strange ideas about personal hygiene. It was also RKO's most expensive film up to that time. John Wayne came up with the inspiring idea of holding the première in Moscow. However, when it was shown to the Soviet Embassy not only did they nix the idea, but they also banned the film throughout the USSR. Filming of *The Conqueror* took place in Utah's Escalante Desert where three of the mountains were renamed Mount Wayne, Mount Hughes and Mount Powell (after director Dick Powell). Unfortunately, it was also very near the site of 11 atomic bomb tests that had taken place three years earlier. One of the bombs was almost four times as powerful as that which devastated Hiroshima. It was only later that the area was discovered to be still replete with radiation poisoning. To add fuel to an already smouldering fire, Howard Hughes arranged for the shipment to Hollywood of 60 tons of (radioactive) soil so that filming could be completed. Horribly, many members of the 220-strong cast and crew began to suffer illnesses as a result of filming *The Conqueror*. Over 100 of them suffered from cancer, including director Dick Powell, Wayne, Susan Hayward, Agnes Moorehead and Pedro Armendariz. Undeterred, Wayne marched on gallantly in *Jet Pilot* (1957) as Colonel Shannon, *The Barbarian And The Geisha* (1958) as Townsend Harris, *Rio Bravo* (1959) as Sheriff John T. Chance, *The Horse Soldiers* (1959) as Colonel John Marlowe, *The Alamo* (1960) as Colonel Davy Crockett, which he also produced and directed (watch out for caravans in the battle sequences and a stuntman falling onto a mattress), *North To Alaska* (1960) as Sam McCord, in which Duke's toupee falls off and then miraculously reappears, *The Comancheros* (1961) as Jake Cutter, *The Longest Day* (1962) as Lieutenant Colonel Benjamin Vandervoort, *The Man Who Shot Liberty Valance* (1962) as Tom Doniphon, *Hatari!* (1962) as Sean

Mercer, *How The West Was Won* (1962) as General William Tecumseh Sherman, *Donovan's Reef* (1963) as Michael Patrick 'Guns' Donovan, *Circus World* (1964) as Matt Masters, *The Greatest Story Ever Told* (1965) as The Centurion, *The Sons Of Katie Elder* (1965) as John Elder, *El Dorado* (1967) as Cole Thornton, *The Green Berets* (1968) as Colonel Mike Kirby (Wayne's directorial paean to the Vietnam War. At the end Wayne tells Hamchunk, the orphaned Vietnamese boy, "You're what this is all about" and walks off *east* into the setting sun!) and *True Grit* (1969) as one-eyed Western marshal Reuben J. 'Rooster' Cogburn. The film won Wayne his only Oscar and only his second nomination, the first being for *Sands Of Iwo Jima*. When he accepted the golden trophy, he joked: "Wow. If I'd known, I'd have put that eyepatch on thirty-five years earlier." He starred in *Rio Lobo* (1970) as Colonel Cord McNally, *Chisum* (1970) as John Simpson Chisum, *Big Jake* (1971) as Jacob McCandles, *Cahill: United States Marshal* (1973) as J.D. Cahill, *McQ* (1974) as Detective Lieutenant Lon McQ, *Rooster Cogburn* (1975) reprising the role that won him the Oscar as Rooster Cogburn, *Brannigan* (1975) as Jim Brannigan and he won great acclaim for playing yet another cowboy, this time one dying of cancer (a disease he was to succumb to in real life) in *The Shootist* (1976), his last film. On screen he was the embodiment of the all-American dream. Off screen Wayne was a hard-drinking right-wing conservative who saw pinko commies everywhere and publicly admired the barking mad Senator Joe McCarthy. He was married three times. His first wife, Josephine 'Josie' Saenz (June 24, 1933–December 25, 1945) accused him of cruelty and drunkenness. They had two sons (Michael Anthony, b. November 23, 1934, and Patrick John, b. July 15, 1939) and two daughters (Mary Antonia 'Toni', b. February 26, 1936, and Melinda Ann, b. December 3, 1940). On January 17, 1946, he married Esperanza Diaz Cellabos but they divorced on November 1, 1954. That same day he married Peruvian actress Pilar Palette Weldy and by her had three more children: Aissa (b. St Joseph's Hospital, Burbank, California, March 31, 1956), John Ethan (b. Encino, California, February 22, 1962) and Marisa Carmela (b. San Fernando, California, February 22, 1966). They separated six years before his death but they never divorced. Wayne found solace with his secretary, Pat Stacy. Some criticised the lack of diversity in Wayne's roles, but he rejoindered: "I play John Wayne in every picture regardless of the character, and I've been doing all right haven't I?"

CAUSE: In 1964 Wayne contracted cancer from smoking three or four packets of cigarettes a day but made a successful recovery after a relapse. The public were initially told he was having surgery for an old ankle injury, as the studio believed that announcing he was suffering from cancer would be bad for his image. (When Wayne contracted cancer, he told his eldest son he had "the big C"; his son thought he meant he had the clap.) On March 29, 1978, he flew to Boston and was admitted to Massachusetts General Hospital, where he underwent surgery to replace the mitral valve in his heart with one from a pig's heart. When he left hospital, Wayne joked he could "oink with the best of them". On April 9, 1979, he made his last public appearance at the Oscars. Nine days later, he was admitted to Hoag Hospital with pneumonia. He was discharged after a week on April 25. During his enforced stay in hospital Wayne asked his son Michael to bring his .38 pistol to the hospital. When Patrick refused, Duke asked Pat Stacy, his boon companion, but she also demurred. On May 1, he was taken to UCLA Medical Center where he underwent an operation for a blocked intestinal passage on May 2.

On May 23, 1979, Congress debated the awarding to Wayne of a special medal. Not long before his death Duke converted to Catholicism. On June 5, Wayne's doctors stopped feeding him intravenously. He died at 5.23pm in Los Angeles, California, aged 72. On June 15, he was buried in an unmarked grave in Pacific View Memorial Park, 3500 Pacific View Drive, Newport Beach, California 92663.

FURTHER READING: *The John Wayne Story* – George Carpozi, Jr (London: Coronet; 1977); *Duke: The Life And Times Of John Wayne* – Donald Shepherd And Robert Slatzer With Dave Grayson (New York: Doubleday, 1985); *Duke: A Love Story* – Pat Stacy With Beverly Linet (London: Corgi, 1985); *John Wayne: My Life With The Duke* – Pilar Wayne With Alex Thorleifson (London: New English Library, 1989).

Dennis Weaver

Born June 4, 1924
Died February 24, 2006

Cowboy cop. Born at 8am in Joplin, Missouri, the son of Walter Weaver (1890–1967) and Lena Prather (1892–1970), William Dennis Weaver began a degree in theatre arts at the University of Oklahoma after seeing service in the navy. In 1948 he finished sixth in the trial for the US Olympic decathlon team. With a university friend, Lonny Chapman, Weaver went to New York to seek his fame and fortune. After studying at the Actors Studio, he understudied Chapman as Turk Fisher in *Come Back, Little Sheba* on Broadway in 1950. When the play went on tour Weaver took over the role and starred with Shelley Winters in a Los Angeles production of *A Streetcar Named Desire*. It was Winters who helped 6'2" Weaver get jobs in Hollywood when he relocated there in 1952 and began appearing in television Westerns. He first came to the attention of the public as Chester Goode on *Gunsmoke* from 1955, a part he almost didn't get. He asked for a second audition at which he read the lines in a funny accent before the producers cast him. Before the cameras began rolling he decided to give the character a limp thinking that he would go unnoticed next to 6'6" James Arness unless he had some peculiar trait. In 1959 he won a Best Supporting Actor Emmy for his portrayal. His fee for the part was $300-a-week, rising to $9,000-a-week as his stint on the show ended after nine years. He left to take the title role in *Kentucky Jones* (1964–65) about a vet and then played Florida game warden Tom Wedloe whose son adopts a 300lb bear in *Gentle Giant* (1967–1969). In 1970 he was cast as Deputy Marshal Sam McCloud from Taos, New Mexico, who was seconded to New York in the series *McCloud*. He played the role for seven years during which time he served as president of Screen Actors Guild (1973–1975). The show began with the TV movie *Who Killed Miss U.S.A.?* (1970). He reprised the role in *The Return Of Sam McCloud* (1989). His films included: *Horizons West* (1952) as Dandy Taylor, *The Raiders* (1952) as Dick Logan, *The Redhead From Wyoming* (1953) as Matt Jessup, *The Lawless Breed* (1953) as Jim Clements, *The Mississippi Gambler* (1953) as Julian Conant, *It Happens Every Thursday* (1953) as Al, *Law And Order* (1953) as Frank Durling, *Column South* (1953) as Menguito, *The Man From The Alamo* (1953) as Reb, *The Golden Blade* (1953), *The Nebraskan* (1953) as Captain De Witt, *War Arrow* (1953) as Pino, *The Bridges At Toko-Ri* (1954), *Ten Wanted Men* (1955) as Sheriff Clyde Gibbons, *Chief Crazy Horse* (1955) as Major Carlisle, *Storm Fear* (1955) as Hank, *The Gallant Hours* (1960) as Lieutenant Commander Andy Lowe, *Mission Batangas* (1968) as Chip Corbett, *Two Bits And Pepper* (1995) as Sheriff Pratt and *Escape From Wildcat Canyon* (1998) as Grandpa Flint. Away from

the screen, Weaver was a committed environmentalist and a vegetarian from 1958. On October 20, 1945 he married Gerry Stowell and they had three sons: actor Robby (b. Los Angeles, California, 8 April 1953), actor/producer/director Rick (b. 1948) and Rusty (b. 1958).

CAUSE: Weaver died at Earthship, his home made from recycled rubbish, at Ridgway, Colorado from cancer. He was 81.

Johnny Weissmuller
(PETER JONAS WEISSMULLER)
Born June 2, 1904
Died January 20, 1984
Wet star – the *only* Tarzan. Born at 6.30pm in Freidorf, Rumania, the son of German Swabian parentage, he and his parents emigrated to America in 1908. (Later Weissmuller would tell people he was born in Windber, Pennsylvania, if anyone questioned his eligibility for the US national swimming team.) Weissmuller's father landed a job as a miner, a job that was eventually to kill him when he contracted tuberculosis. On July 9, 1922, Weissmuller became the first man to swim 100m in less than a minute, achieving the feat in 58.6secs. On February 17, 1924, he went one better and lowered his time to 57.4secs. This world record would last for ten years. On July 18, 1924, he won a gold medal at the Paris Olympics for 400m freestyle and two days later added the 100m freestyle and 4x200m relay golds and a bronze in the water polo to his collection. Four years later, in Amsterdam on August 11, 1928, he retained his 100m gold, the fourth of his five Olympic golds. In 1930 while training for the 1932 Olympics, 6'3" Weissmuller was spotted by the BVD Underwear Company who offered him $500 a week to model their male lines. One of his pictures was spotted by Cyril Hume, a Hollywood writer who was adapting Edgar Rice Burroughs' works for MGM and he was invited

to audition for the role of Tarzan. The rest is history. He had made a couple of films prior to donning the famous loincloth, but his generally acknowledged film début came with *Tarzan The Ape Man* (1932). Weissmuller was called "the only man in Hollywood who's natural in the flesh and can act without clothes" by MGM's publicity department. He was the sixth actor to play Tarzan, the first in talkies and the first of four Olympic medallists to assume the role (the others being Buster Crabbe, Herman Brix and Glenn Morris). Over the next 16 years, Weissmuller donned the Lord of the Jungle's loincloth 11 more times, in *Tarzan And His Mate* (1934), *Tarzan Escapes* (1936), *Tarzan Finds A Son!* (1939), *Tarzan's Secret Treasure* (1941), *Tarzan's New York Adventure* (1942), *Tarzan's Desert Mystery* (1943), *Tarzan Triumphs* (1943), *Tarzan And The Amazons* (1945), *Tarzan And The Leopard Woman* (1946), *Tarzan And The Huntress* (1947) and *Tarzan And The Mermaids* (1948). When he finally hung up his vine, Weissmuller took on the mantle of Jungle Jim in a series of films for Columbia: *Jungle Jim* (1948), *The Lost Tribe* (1949), *Pygmy Island* (1950), *Captive Girl* (1950), *Mark Of The Gorilla* (1950), *Jungle Manhunt* (1951), *Fury Of The Congo* (1951), *Voodoo Tiger* (1952), *Jungle Jim In The Forbidden Land* (1952), *Valley Of Head Hunters* (1953), *Killer Ape* (1953), *Savage Mutiny* (1953) and *Jungle Man-Eaters* (1954). His last movie job was playing a stage-hand in *Won Ton Ton, The Dog Who Saved Hollywood* (1976). Weissmuller was married five times. His first wife was actress Bobbe Arnst, whom he married on February 28, 1931, two weeks after they met. They were divorced on October 4, 1932, after she told the hearing that Weissmuller rarely went home for dinner. On October 8, 1933, he married Mexican Spitfire Lupe Velez. Theirs was a fiery match with many separations. They finally divorced on

August 15, 1938. On August 20, 1939, he married socialite Beryl Scott, by whom he had three children: John Scott (b. September 23, 1940), Wendy Ann (b. June 1, 1942) and Heidi Elizabeth (b. July 20, 1943, k. 1962 in a car accident). The couple was divorced on January 29, 1948. Five hours later, he married golfer Ailene Gates. They divorced after 14 years. On April 23, 1963, he married Maria Block at the Dunes Hotel in Las Vegas. CAUSE: He died at his home in Acapulco, Mexico, aged 79 following a series of strokes.

Orson Welles
Born May 6, 1915
Died October 10, 1985
Wunderkind. Born at 463½ Park Avenue, Kenosha, Wisconsin, George Orson Welles was the precocious *enfant terrible* of the American cinema and theatre. Raised a Roman Catholic, his parents separated in 1919. His father, Richard Head Welles (b. 1872, d. Bismarck Hotel, Chicago, Illinois, December 28, 1930, of chronic myocarditis and nephritis) married Beatrice Ives (b. 1882, d. Chicago, Illinois, May 10, 1924, of jaundice) on November 21, 1903 but due to his womanising and drinking the marriage was quickly in trouble. Their first son, Richard Ives (b. Chicago, Illinois, October 7, 1905, d. San Francisco, California, September 1975) was a shy boy who in 1927 was certified insane. Both Welles boys were educated at Todd School for Boys, an independent school in Woodstock, Illinois. On his father's death when Welles was 15, Dr Maurice Bernstein (1886–1965), a friend of his mother's, became his guardian. Welles went to Europe thanks to a small inheritance from his father. On October 13, 1931 Welles made his theatre debut at the Gate Theatre in Dublin as Duke Karl Alexander in the première of *Jew Suss*. Back in America, Welles appeared in three off-Broadway productions. In

1936 John Houseman hired Welles to direct a play for the Federal Theatre Project's Negro Theater Unit. Welles selected the Scottish play in a production that would become known as the *Voodoo Macbeth*, because Welles set it in the Haitian court of King Henri Christophe, with voodoo witch doctors for the three witches. When Maurice Evans who was playing Macbeth fell ill, Welles took over in blackface. In the 1930s he became a wireless star, his mellifluous voice being perfect for the medium. Welles had a distinguished reputation as an actor-writer-producer-director but nothing was able to prepare America for an Orson Welles radio production that took to the air on October 30, 1938. It made him a household name. The Mercury Theater On The Air produced a large number of classic shows, including adaptations of *Heart Of Darkness*, *Jane Eyre*, *Oliver Twist* and *Around The World In 80 Days*. Welles was a voracious reader of fiction, always on the lookout for a possible new production. He had prepared R.D. Blackmore's classic *Lorna Doone* for broadcast but as the show date approached he began to have his doubts about it. The only other piece that Mercury had bought the rights to was H.G. Wells' 1898 novel *The War Of The Worlds*. The original story took place in England around the turn of the century and the script retained those details. Welles decided the story needed modernisation. He changed the location to the United States and brought the chronology up to date. A second draft was prepared and still Welles made changes and more changes. The date scheduled for the broadcast – Hallowe'en Eve – was perfect for his plans. It should be remembered that world events at the time were in tumult. The Munich crisis was at its height. Jews were being systematically murdered and Hitler was claiming the Sudetenland while in the Far East Japanese behaviour was

disturbingly menacing. It was in this climate that Welles chose to broadcast what became the most famous radio show of all time. A final draft was sent to the bigwigs at CBS, who were horrified by the show's realism and insisted that 28 changes be made before it took to the air. At 7.58pm Welles took his place in the studio. He drank an entire bottle of pineapple juice, clamped his headphones in place, loosened his tie and gave the signal for the show to start at exactly 8pm. Announcer Dan Seymour made his usual introduction before Bernard Herrmann's Orchestra played the show's theme tune from Tchaikovsky's well-worn B-flat-minor piano concerto. The show was under way. A weather report was followed by dance music. Suddenly, the music was interrupted by a newsflash that a Professor Farrell of Mount Jennings Observatory, Chicago, Illinois, had noticed a series of gas explosions on Mars. The show went over live "to the world-famous astronomer" Professor Richard Pierson (played by Welles) in Princeton, New Jersey for up-to-the-minute information. As Pierson is being interviewed, he is told that an earthquake-sized shock has hit Grovers Mill, New Jersey, 22 miles from Trenton. A glowing object of yellowish-white metal 30 yards in diameter has been observed. Meanwhile, the programme returned to dance music courtesy of Bobby Millette and his orchestra. Next, the listener was taken to Wilmuth Farm in Grovers Mill where Carl Phillips, an "on-the-spot reporter", was waiting with the latest news. As the 'reporter' spoke, the object gave off a hissing sound. Said Phillips, "This end of the thing is beginning to flake off! The top is beginning to rotate like a screw! The thing must be hollow." Something crawls out of the top. "I can see peering out of that black hole two luminous disks . . . Are they eyes? It might be a face. It might be . . . good heavens, something's wriggling out of the shadow like a grey snake." Suddenly, the creatures are at large; 40 people are killed. Screams are heard and the broadcast stopped "due to circumstances beyond our control." It was estimated that approximately 12 per cent of the radio audience (six million people) were listening to the show at this point and many really believed the earth was being invaded by Martians. Soon CBS' switchboard lit up with concerned listeners wanting to know if the show was real or a dramatisation. Two policemen even turned up at the studio to seek verification and one tried to barge his way in for further information but was stopped by a burly actor. People began to panic. In Harlem many fled to churches to pray while others believed (hoped?) they would be safe from the Martians' deadly gas in the countryside. Many dug out the gas masks they had been issued during the First World War. The roads to Philadelphia and New York were jammed with cars. The Associated Press issued a bulletin: "Note to Editors: Queries to newspapers from radio listeners throughout the United States tonight, regarding a reported meteor fall which killed a number of New Jerseyites, are a result of a radio dramatisation. The A.P., 8.48pm." The panic was at its highest in Trenton itself where people believed they had just minutes before they were annihilated by Martians. In New York City two women who had heard the broadcast rang a cinema and demanded their husbands be alerted to the danger. This caused further panic and soon the place was empty. In Rhode Island people urged the power station to cut the state lights so the Martians wouldn't be able to see where they were going. Students at a North Carolina university jammed the city exchange ringing their parents and begging to be collected. In Pittsburgh a man returned home to allegedly find

his wife about to take poison saying, "I'd rather die this way than that." A small town called Concrete in Washington was unfortunate enough to suffer a power cut, which only served to further convince the townsfolk that the Martians were at hand. In Hillside, New Jersey, a frantic man dashed into the police station and begged for a gas mask as protection against "the terrible people spraying liquid gas all over the Jersey Meadows". In San Francisco volunteers poured into the local army headquarters ready to take up arms against the fiendish invaders. Even some members of the fourth estate were taken in. The photographers of the *New York Herald Tribune* donned gas masks in preparation for going into the streets to take pictures of the advancing invaders. As more police arrived at the CBS studios Welles was aware that the show had been noteworthy but didn't realise just how sensational had been its effect. At the end of the broadcast he read a statement: "This is Orson Welles, ladies and gentlemen, out of character to assure you that *The War Of The Worlds* has no further significance than as the holiday offering it was intended to be. The Mercury Theater's own radio version of dressing up in a sheet and jumping out of a bush and saying Boo! Starting now, we couldn't soap all your windows and steal all your garden gates, by tomorrow night . . . so we did the next best thing. We annihilated the world before your very ears, and utterly destroyed the CBS. You will be relieved, I hope, to learn that we didn't mean it, and that both institutions are still open for business. So goodbye everybody and, remember, please for the next day or so, the terrible lesson you learned tonight. That grinning, glowing, globular invader of your living room is an inhabitant of the pumpkin patch, and if your doorbell rings and nobody's there, that was no Martian . . . it's Hallowe'en." CBS were furious at Welles and the cast were locked in a back room at the station until every copy of the script was either destroyed or locked away. They were released in the early hours of the morning. After just a few hours' sleep, Welles was dragged before the press to explain his actions. Unsurprisingly for America, lawsuits worth $750,000 were issued against Welles and CBS by people who claimed to have suffered emotional distress and injuries. Cleverly, Welles had ensured beforehand that he was exempt from personal liability so CBS had to fight all the cases itself. The company settled many of them out of court, believing it cheaper than fighting the suits.

Over the next few days newspaper columnists wrote editorials criticising the "incredible stupidity" and "gullibility" of the American public. Oddly, the people least fooled by the broadcast were children, who recognised the voice of Orson Welles from his portrayal of their hero, The Shadow. On the stage Welles was fêted for his voodoo production of *Macbeth* in Harlem. RKO rushed to sign Welles up and promised him artistic and creative autonomy over his films. Welles' first major film was his biopic of William Randolph Hearst. It made his reputation but also nearly killed off his professional life. Welles' career stalled after *Citizen Kane* – most believe he was stymied by the power of Hearst but even Louis B. Mayer of MGM tried to buy the print and bury it, literally. The film was a critical but not a commercial success; it garnered just one Oscar for Best Screenplay. Welles directed but didn't appear in *The Magnificent Ambersons* (1942) supplying his voice for the narration. New bosses at RKO were not impressed by the film and had it recut without Welles' knowledge. With his contract at an end Welles found work difficult to come by. He appeared in *Jane Eyre* (1944) as Edward Rochester, *Tomorrow Is Forever* (1946) as John A. MacDonald/Erik Kessler which he also directed and

The Stranger (1946) as Charles Rankin/Franz Kindler. Following *The Lady From Shanghai* (1948) in which he played Michael O'Hara and co-starred with then wife Rita Hayworth. (Welles thought up the title because he was being hounded by studio bosses. In fact, there is no character from Shanghai in the movie.) He also made a low-budget version of *Macbeth* (1948), playing the title role himself. Believing his career in America to be over, Welles migrated to Europe where he appeared as Harry Lime in the massively successful *The Third Man* (1949). He began filming *Othello* but ran out of money and the film wasn't completed until 1955. In June of that year he played Captain Ahab in a production of *Moby Dick* at the Duke of York's Theatre in London. Welles so hated his own nose that he always wore a false one on stage. During a performance of the play the proboscis began to come loose during an integral part of the play. Co-star Kenneth Williams (Elijah) tried to warn Gordon Jackson (Ishmael) about the imminent fall, but it was too late and as Welles delivered the line "Get that white whale, men," the nose fell to the floor, where he neatly drop kicked it into the stalls. It was during rehearsals for the same production that Welles called out, when Jackson delivered the opening line, "Call me Ishmael", "And if a man answers, hang up!" In the Fifties Welles spent much of his time trying and failing to get various projects off the ground. One notable success was *Touch Of Evil* (1958), a brooding film noir thriller set in a Mexican border town; Welles directed and also played the part of maverick police chief Hank Quinlan. He also appeared in, among others, *Trent's Last Case* (1952) as Sigsbee Manderson, *Napoléon* (1955) as Sir Hudson Lowe, *Moby Dick* (1956) as Father Mapple, *Compulsion* (1959) as Jonathan Wilk, and *Ferry To Hong Kong* (1959) as Captain Hart aka Singapore Cecil. In the 1960s and later in his life, Welles began to balloon in size and was known to a new audience not for his work in the past but for advertising Paul Masson wine. His later films included: *Waterloo* (1970) as King Louis XVIII, *12 Plus 1* (1970) as Markan, *Catch-22* (1970) as General Dreedle, *Necromancy* (1972) as Mr Cato, *Treasure Island* (1973) as Long John Silver, *Voyage Of The Damned* (1976) as Estedes, *The Muppet Movie* (1979) as Lew Lord, *Butterfly* (1981) as Judge Rauch, *History Of The World: Part I* (1981), *Where Is Parsifal?* (1983) as Klingsor and *Someone To Love* (1987) as Danny's friend. 6′1½″ Welles was married three times. His first wife was Virginia Nicholson whom he married in secret on November 14, 1934. When her family accepted him they insisted that they have a proper ceremony and they married again on December 23, 1934. On March 27, 1938 she gave birth to their daughter, Christopher, at Presbyterian Hospital, New York. The couple separated on December 16, 1939 and divorced on February 1, 1940 at Reno, Nevada. Her second husband was Charles Lederer, the nephew of Marion Davies, the mistress of W.R. Hearst whom Welles portrayed in *Citizen Kane*. Welles married the actress Rita Hayworth on September 7, 1943. Their daughter, Rebecca, was born in Santa Monica, California, on December 17, 1944. She died in Tacoma, Washington on October 17, 2004. Welles and Hayworth divorced on December 1, 1948. On May 8, 1955 he married Italian actress Paola Mori (b. 1934) who was pregnant at the time. Their daughter, Beatrice, was born in New York on November 13, 1955. In 1962 Welles met actress Oja Kodar (b. Zagreb, Croatia 1941, as Olga Palinkaš) during the filming of *The Trial*. They became lovers until his death but he never divorced the third Mrs Welles and split his time between the two women. On August 12, 1986 Paola Welles was killed in a car crash,

two days before she was to settle a disagreement in Welles' will with Oja Kodar.
CAUSE: He died at his home in Los Angeles, California, from a massive heart attack. Clad in a dressing gown, he had been sitting at his desk working at his typewriter. He was 70. His ashes were buried in an unmarked grave in Spain.
FURTHER READING: *Orson Welles: The Rise And Fall Of An American Genius* – Charles Higham (New York: St Martin's Press, 1985); *Citizen Welles: A Biography Of Orson Welles* – Frank Brady (London: Coronet, 1991); *Orson Welles: The Road To Xanadu* – Simon Callow (London: Jonathan Cape, 1995); *Rosebud: The Story Of Orson Welles* – David Thomson (London: Abacus, 1997); *The Encylopedia Of Orson Welles* – Chuck Berg and Tom Erskine with John C. Tibbetts and James M. Welsh(New York: Facts On File, 2003); *Despite The System: Orson Welles Versus The Hollywood Studios* – Clinton Heylin (Edinburgh: Canongate, 2005); *Orson Welles: Hello Americans* – Simon Callow (London: Jonathan Cape, 2006).

Paul Wendkos
Born September 20, 1922
Died November 12, 2009
Small screen director. Born at Philadelphia, Pennsylvania Wendkos served in the US Navy during World War II. After demob, he went to Columbia University in New York and then read film history and aesthetics at the New School for Social Research. His first foray as a director was making the documentary *Dark Interlude* about blind people. He made his feature film debut with *The Burglar* (1957) with Jayne Mansfield. It would be the first of more than 100 credits that included *Gidget* (1959), *Because They're Young* (1960), *Gidget Goes Hawaiian* (1961), *Gidget Goes To Rome* (1963), *Guns Of The Magnificent Seven* (1969) and *The Mephisto Waltz* (1971). On television

he directed the pilot *Cocoon* (1968) that became the long-running series *Hawaii Five-O*. He was nominated for an Emmy for *The Taking Of Flight 847: The Uli Derickson Story* with Lindsay Wagner in 1988. From 1970 until he retired in 1999, Wendkos concentrated on made-for-television films. In 1953 he married Ruth Burnat (d. 1978) by whom he had one son, Jordan. He later married Lin Bolan who survived him. CAUSE: Wendkos died aged 87 at his home in Malibu of a lung infection that followed a stroke.

Mae West

(MARY JANE WEST)
Born August 17, 1893
Died November 22, 1980
Blonde bombshell who shook up America. Born on Bushwick Avenue in Brooklyn, New York, the daughter of a father who was a heavyweight boxer and a mother who modelled corsets. Mae began her career in burlesque and vaudeville. She wrote much of her own material and on April 19, 1927, was jailed for 10 days after her play *Sex* was deemed obscene. People probably assume that Mae appeared in dozens of movies but, in fact, she appeared in just 12 films and didn't make her movie début until she was aged 40. In that film, *Night After Night*, she wore particularly impressive jewels, causing a cloakroom attendant to remark, "Goodness, what lovely diamonds." Replied Mae: "Goodness had nothing to do with it." She became notorious/celebrated for her West-isms including: "I used to be Snow White – but I drifted" and "It's not the men in my life, it's the life in my men." Told that a 5'10" man was waiting to see her, she quipped "Never mind about the five foot, tell me about the ten inches." Unlike many Hollywood stars, who frequently change abodes, Mae lived in the same block of flats, Ravenswood at 570 North Rossmore Avenue, off Wilshire Boulevard just three blocks from Paramount Studios,

from 1932 until her death. Everything in her home was white with the occasional bit of gold. Cary Grant once admitted, "I learned everything from Mae West – well, nearly everything." Her films were: *She Done Him Wrong* (1933) as Lady Lou, *I'm No Angel* (1933) as Tira, *Belle Of The Nineties* (1934) as Ruby Carter, *Goin' To Town* (1935) as Cleo Borden, *Klondike Annie* (1936) as the Frisco Doll, *Go West Young Man* (1936) as Mavis Arden, *Every Day's A Holiday* (1937) as Peaches O'Day, *My Little Chickadee* (1940) as Flower Belle Lee, *The Heat's On* (1943) as Fay Lawrence, *Myra Breckinridge* (1970) as Leticia Van Allen and *Sextette* (1978) as Marlo Manners. The RAF nicknamed a life jacket a 'Mae West' because of her magnificent embonpoint. She remarked: "I've been in *Who's Who* and I know what's what, but this is the first time I've been in a dictionary."
CAUSE: In August 1980 she suffered a minor stroke that paralysed her tongue, leaving her unable to speak, and was admitted to the Good Samaritan Hospital. On September 18, she suffered another stroke that paralysed her right arm and leg. On November 3, she was discharged and returned home. Less than three weeks later, she died aged 87 having received the last rites from a Catholic priest.
FURTHER READING: *Mae West: The Lies The Legend The Truth* – George Eels And Stanley Musgrove (London: Robson Books, 1989); *Mae West: Empress Of Sex* – Maurice Leonard (London: HarperCollins, 1991).

James Whale

Born July 22, 1889
Died Memorial Day (May 29), 1957
Horror auteur. James Whale was born at 41 Brewery Street, Dudley, Worcestershire, the sixth of seven children of William Whale (1855–1936), a blast furnaceman, and Sarah Peters (1855–1937), a nurse. Three more children died in infancy. William

Whale kept pigs in his back garden and James Whale was acutely embarrassed about his working-class origins and quietly began to expunge all traces of it. Charles Laughton disparagingly referred to Whale as the "Would-Be Gentleman". Shortly before Whale's death, he learned that his brother had discovered documents that showed that seventeenth century Whales had been landowners and "gentlemen". Whale said, "I cannot help a feeling of comfort in my old age that I was born right." A thin, red-headed, fey child, Whale was educated at Bayliss' School in Tower Street and Dudley Bluecoat School until his mid-teens and then, rather than following his brothers down the mines, he became a cobbler's assistant. An odd job as a sign drawer earned Whale enough to enrol at the Dudley School of Arts and Crafts in 1910. It became immediately apparent to his contemporaries that Whale was "different". When the First World War broke out Whale did not join up, instead working for the YMCA at Whittington Barracks. In October 1915 he joined the Inns of Court regiment as an officer cadet. In the summer of 1916 he joined the 2nd Battalion of the 7th Worcestershire regiment as a second lieutenant at the time when the average life span of a subaltern was three weeks. He served at the Somme, Arras and Ypres. On August 25–26, 1917 he was captured as he led his men on an attack on the German lines in the Pommern Redoubt, Belgium. He was imprisoned at Holzminden, near Hanover, for fifteen months and spent his time designing and performing in troop shows. Back in Blighty after the Armistice, Whale decided upon a theatrical career. He made his professional acting début with Barry Jackson's Birmingham Repertory Company on August 30, 1919. That year he also met the flamboyantly homosexual Ernest Thesiger and Whale relaxed in his company. In 1920 Whale moved to Stratford-upon-Avon

where he immersed himself in Shakespeare. He joined a rep company in Liverpool and began to commute between that city and London. In 1922 he appeared in *The Insect Play*. Also in the cast were Elsa Lanchester, Claude Rains, Angela Baddeley, John Gielgud and a woman to whom Whale became engaged. Doris Clare Zinkeisen (b. Kilcreggan, Scotland, July 31, 1898, d. January 1991) was an exotic creature who beguiled Whale. The relationship was one of the mysteries of Whale's life. Was it a rare heterosexual interlude or a "beard"? Whatever the case, he continued to take male lovers during the betrothal. Whale preferred younger men throughout his life. Whale worked steadily but without external recognition for almost a decade. In late 1928 Whale was given the job of directing a new play that no one wanted by an unknown playwright, R.C. Sherriff, based on his own experiences in the trenches. *Journey's End* was to change his life. During the run he finished with his girlfriend and fell in love with a young amateur actor called Robert Barthe Offen. *Journey's End* opened on December 10, 1928. The lead was a young actor of promise named Laurence Olivier. The play was a hit and transferred (without Olivier) to the West End, where it ran for nearly 600 performances. Whale was asked to go to New York to stage the play's Broadway première. Hollywood beckoned in June 1929 and Whale met a handsome young man called David Lewis (b. Trinidad, Colorado, December 14, 1903 as David Levy, d. March 13, 1987), a producer at MGM and Warner Bros who would be nominated for two Oscars. The two men hit it off and dated until Whale had to return to England to direct *Badger's Green* in April 1930. Before he could begin work on *Journey's End* Whale worked on *The Love Doctor* (1929) which starred Richard Dix. He then worked as a dialogue director on Howard Hughes' *Hell's Angels* (1930) and received a $5,000 bonus from the bashful billionaire. Finally, his next project was the film version of *Journey's End* (premièred March 13, 1930), which was made by a team of British producers that included Michael Balcon and shot on Hollywood's Sunset Boulevard. Universal Studios offered Whale a contract and his first job was a weepy melodrama, *Waterloo Bridge* (shooting began May 23, 1931). His next film would make his name. Universal had just had a smash hit with *Dracula* (released February 14, 1931) starring Bela Lugosi and wanted something similar. They bought the rights to Mary Shelley's Gothic novel *Frankenstein, or The New Prometheus* (although kept little of the original story) and hired the Frenchman Robert Florey to direct. He was sacked and replaced by Whale whose star was in the ascendancy. The bisexual Colin Clive, who had starred in *Journey's End*, was given the job of playing the title role and the part of the monster, originally intended for Lugosi who turned it down, went to a little-known, bit-part player called Boris Karloff. To add mystery in the opening credits Karloff was billed as '?'. Whale designed the look of the monster and created an icon that lasts to today. *Frankenstein* (released on December 4, 1931 at a cost of $291,000) was a smash hit taking $53,000 in its first week and $12 million in total. In interviews to promote the film Whale conveniently shaved seven years off his age and invented an education at the hands of private tutors. Whale was to make films in many genres – his next was the romantic comedy *The Impatient Maiden* (1932) – but it was for horror films he is remembered, much to his annoyance. His next film was an adaptation of a J.B. Priestley novel, *The Old Dark House* (1932) which was followed by *The Kiss Before The Mirror* (1933). *The Invisible Man* (1933), taken from H.G. Wells' classic novel, heralded the screen début of Claude

Rains in the title role. His next films were *By Candlelight* (1933) and an adaptation of a John Galsworthy novel, *One More River* (1934). At the start of 1934 Whale and David Lewis moved in together at 788 South Amalfi drive in Pacific Palisades. It was a bold move in an age when open homosexuality was frowned upon even in Hollywood and could get you imprisoned in England. Nonetheless, while Whale continued to produce hits, Hollywood continued to turn a blind eye. Universal wanted a sequel to *Frankenstein* but Whale was not keen to repeat his triumph. Eventually, he allowed himself to be persuaded and created his magnum opus. He cast Ernest Thesiger and Elsa Lanchester in *The Bride Of Frankenstein* (made in 1935 at a cost of $397,000, $100,000 over budget and 10 days over schedule). Lanchester played a dual role – the bride and authoress Mary Shelley in the prologue. Whale's next effort was the screwball comedy, *Remember Last Night?* (1935). It starred Robert Young and Constance Cummings. In November 1935 Whale began work on the film version of the Jerome Kern-Oscar Hammerstein musical *Show Boat* (released in April 1936). Paul Robeson and Helen Morgan triumphantly repeated their Broadway roles and it is undoubtedly the best of the three versions filmed so far. (The other two were made in 1929 and 1951.) However, it was also expensive and although it would earn back the outlay, it did not happen quickly enough to save Universal Studios from financial crisis. Carl Laemmle, who had founded the studio in 1912, stepped down and Universal had new owners, J. Cheever Cowdin and Charles R. Rogers. It was pure bad luck that Whale's first flop coincided with the changeover at Universal. *The Road Back* (began filming in February 1937 with a budget of $770,000 that rose to more than $880,000) was adapted from Erich Maria Remarque's novel, a sequel to *All Quiet On The*

Western Front. Any hopes for a hit were dashed by poor casting and the busybody German consul in Los Angeles, Dr Georg Gyssling, who threatened a boycott if the film was not changed. Whale ignored him, but Universal buckled under the pressure and cut several scenes before bringing in Ted Sloman to shoot extra material, including a clumsy new ending. Unsurprisingly, the film did badly. It was the beginning of the end for James Whale. His next film, *The Great Garrick* (1937) for Warner Bros, was well-written, well-directed, well-performed and badly received by the public. At MGM, Whale directed *Port Of Seven Seas* (1938), an attempt to combine Marcel Pagnol's Marseilles trilogy (*Marius, Fanny* and *César*) into one film, with Wallace Beery. Back at Universal, Whale made two forgettable films, *Sinners In Paradise* (1938) and *Wives Under Suspicion* (1938) which was a remake of his own *The Kiss Before The Mirror*. He made a version of *The Man In The Iron Mask* (1939) for United Artists but was bored, paid little attention, smoked on set and let the smoke drift into camera range and was sacked. His final film for Universal, the studio that had been the scene of his greatest successes, was a jungle melodrama, *Green Hell* (made in 1940 at a cost of more than $700,000) starring Douglas Fairbanks, Jr. It would not be unfair to say that this was one of the worst films ever produced in Hollywood. An anti-Nazi oeuvre *They Dare Not Love* (1941) was Whale's next assignment at Columbia but he fell out with the studio's boss, Harry Cohn, and was once again sacked. He never made another feature film. Whale had an English reserve about him – perhaps as a shield for his homosexuality – so he never bothered to socialise or network. When he was a success this did not matter but when he began to produce flops, he needed friends and he did not have any. He had told one interviewer, "That they should pay

such fabulous salaries is beyond ordinary reasoning. Who's worth it? But why not take it? And the architecture! And the furnishings! . . . All the world's made of plaster of Paris!" Whale's last film was a 41-minute adaptation of a William Saroyan play, *Hello Out There*. Whale took to retirement easily, taking up painting; it was old age he feared.

CAUSE: Whale's penchant was for young men and David Lewis was in his forties when Whale's retirement was forced upon him. Too old, far too old. Lewis joined the air force during the Second World War leaving Whale alone and lonely. To combat the solitude, Whale directed a half-hour army training film in 1942. He travelled to Paris where he met a 25-year-old called Pierre Foegel. Whale was taken with the young man and hired him as his chauffeur. The two men lived together in America from January to June 1953 when he went back to France. Whale asked Lewis to move out to make room for Foegel. In January 1954 he moved to America permanently. In late 1956 Whale suffered a stroke and was admitted to St John's Hospital where, remarkably, he was treated for a nervous breakdown and given electric shock treatment. Allowed home in the spring of 1957, on Memorial Day, he gave his nurse the day off. He dressed and went to his studio in the garden where he wrote a long note. It ended: "The future is just old age and pain. Goodbye all and thank you all for your love. I must have peace and this is the only way." Shortly before 1pm Whale threw himself into the shallow end of his pool and struck his head. Foegel showed the note to David Lewis who kept it a secret for 30 years until his own death. Suicide and homosexuality was too much to be revealed. James Whale was cremated on June 6 (death certificate; other sources say June 3) at the Kingsley and Gates Mortuary Chapel, South Sepulveda Boulevard. His ashes were interred in plot 20076 of the Great Mausoleum in Forest Lawn, Glendale, California. He left more than $600,000. On his bedside table he had left a book. In his films and life Whale had often displayed a sardonic sense of humour. The book was called *Don't Go Near The Water*.

FURTHER READING: *James Whale: A Biography* – Mark Gatiss (London: Cassell, 1995).

Carol White

Born April 1, 1943
Died September 16, 1991
British blonde bombshell. Born in Hammersmith, London, at 12.06am, Carole Joan White was named after the actress Carole Lombard but dropped the 'e' because Carol White was symmetrical with ten letters. She attended the famous Corona Stage School. Her portrayal in the BBC plays of a good-time girl in *Up The Junction* (1965) and of a homeless, single mother in *Cathy Come Home* (1966) won her numerous critical plaudits. She was later fêted for her performance in the West End play *Steaming* in 1981 but by that time successes were few and far between. She fell into a downward spiral resulting in alcoholism, drug addiction, a conviction for shoplifting, various attempts at suicide, three marriages, numerous affairs and obscurity before her untimely death. Her films included: *The Belles Of St Trinian's* (1954), *Around The World In 80 Days* (1956), *Blue Murder At St Trinian's* (1957), *Carry On Teacher* (1959), *Linda* (1960), *Slave Girls* (1966), *Poor Cow* (1967), *I'll Never Forget What's 'Is Name* (1968), *The Man Who Had Power Over Women* (1970), *Dulcima* (1971) and *The Squeeze* (1977). Carol was married and divorced three times. Husband number one was Michael King on April 29, 1962, by whom she had two sons: Sean (b. November 4, 1962) and Stephen (b. January 20, 1964). She married Stuart Lerner in April 1972

and Michael Arnold on November 25, 1977.

CAUSE: She died in Miami, Florida, aged 48, as a result of her overindulgence in drink and drugs.

FURTHER READING: *Carol Comes Home* – Carol White With Clifford Thurlow (London: New English Library, 1982).

Arkie Whiteley

Born November 6, 1965
Died December 19, 2001
Down under beauty. The only child of the Australian artist Brett Whiteley, London-born Arkje Deya Whiteley spent a bohemian childhood travelling with her parents to Fiji, Bali, Paris and New York, where, according to legend, in the two years the family spent at the Chelsea Hotel, Janis Joplin was Arkie's babysitter. Arkie first came to public prominence aged 15 when she won the Australian Oscar for her performance in *A Town Like Alice* (1981). She also appeared in *Mad Max 2: The Road Warrior* (1981) and *Razorback* (1984) as Sarah Cameron before training at the Central School of Speech and Drama in London. Following graduation, she starred in David Hare's *The Secret Rapture* at the National Theatre, and in the West End alongside Peter O'Toole in *Jeffrey Bernard Is Unwell*. She was a regular face on television in shows such as *Kavanagh QC*, *The Last Musketeer* and *Natural Lies*. Gorgeous Arkie stripped for a sex scene with Bob Peck in the thriller *Natural Lies* (1992). "I was totally nude apart from my stockings and a tattoo I put on my bottom using a transfer. It was quite erotic and I was surprised at myself. It was a turn-on. I wished I had more to do. I thought the nudity was right for the part. This was my first full-frontal nude scene and took two hours to shoot." Arkie's previous experience was a shower scene with Adam Faith in *Love Hurts*. "That was hilariously unsexy. I was wearing a body stocking and he had these huge white knickers on and stood on a box

to look taller. The hot water from the shower kept steaming up the camera." Her films included *Scandal* (1989) as Vicky and *Princess Caraboo* (1994) as Betty.

CAUSE: She died of cancer aged 36 in Palm Beach, Sydney, New South Wales, Australia.

James Whitmore

Born October 1, 1921
Died February 6, 2009
All-rounder. Born in White Plains, New York, the youngest of four children, Whitmore began acting in school, appearing in Gilbert and Sullivan operettas, much to the disapproval of his strict Methodist family. An athletic youth, he won a football scholarship to Yale in 1939 but left after two knee injuries wrecked his chances. He decided to devote all of his energies to acting. After the Second World War, where he served in the Marine Corps, he studied at the American Theatre Wing under the same GI Bill that helped so many actors including Rod Steiger. Whitmore survived on $20 a week and lived with another aspiring actor, Jack Warden. In 1947 he made his Broadway debut as Sergeant Harold Evans in the air force drama, *Command Decision*, for which he won a Tony for outstanding performance by a newcomer. Whitmore made his film debut in *The Undercover Man* (released April 20, 1949) playing George Pappas. His second film, *Battleground* (released January 20, 1950), saw him nominated for an Oscar and winning a Golden Globe as Best Supporting Actor for his performance as the hard-bitten, tobacco-chewing Kinnie. He was a versatile actor appearing in all genres of film including comedies, dramas, musicals, science fiction and Westerns. He once said, "If you're going to be in this business, you better learn your craft." His own favourite film was *Black Like Me* (released May 20, 1964), the true story of journalist

John Howard Griffin (1920–1980), a white man who artificially blackened his skin to learn firsthand of racism in America. For some reason, Griffin's character in the film is renamed John Finley Horton. In the early 1950s 5′8″ Whitmore taught acting and one of his pupils was James Dean. He told *Seventeen* in 1955, "I owe a lot to Whitmore. One thing he said helped more than anything. He told me I didn't know the difference between acting as a soft job and acting as a difficult art." Whitmore's other films included: John Huston's *The Asphalt Jungle* (released August 1, 1950) as the hunchback diner owner and sometime criminal Gus Minissi, John J. Malone in *Mr O'Malley and Mrs Malone* (released December 8, 1950), the narrator in *The Red Badge Of Courage* (released March 16, 1951), *Kiss Me Kate* (released November 26, 1953) as Slug a light-footed thug who, with Keenan Wynn, dances and sings his way through *Brush Up Your Shakespeare*, *The Great Diamond Robbery* (released January 29, 1954), *Them!* (released June 19, 1954) as Police Sergeant Ben Peterson, *Oklahoma!* (released January 9, 1956) as Andrew Carnes, *Planet Of The Apes* (released April 3, 1968) as the president of the assembly, *Guns Of The Magnificent Seven* (released July 30, 1969) as Levi, *Tora! Tora! Tora!* (released October 8, 1970) as Admiral William F. Halsey, Michael Winner's *Chato's Land* (released June 30, 1972), as Joshua Everette, *The Harrad Experiment* (1973) as Philip Tenhausen, *Bully: An Adventure With Teddy Roosevelt* (1978) as the president and *The Shawshank Redemption* (released September 23, 1994) as Brooks Hatlen, the prison librarian. Whitmore made cinematic history with his one-man show *Give 'Em Hell, Harry* about Harry S Truman which was released as a film on September 18, 1975, resulting in Whitmore being nominated for an Academy Award as Best Actor, the only time in Oscar history that an actor has been nominated for a film in which he was the only cast member. Whitmore was also a regular on television appearing in *The Virginian*, *My Friend Tony*, *The Practice* for which he won an Emmy, *Gunsmoke*, *Bonanza*, *Cowboy In Africa* and his last acting job, *CSI: Crime Scene Investigation*, in 2007. Like many actors, he preferred the stage. "I find the process of making movies absolutely boring," he said in 1994. "It's so fragmented. You wait and wait and wait and then, look, as Jack Lemmon says, 'It's magic time.'" In the theatre, once the curtain goes up, the actor is in charge." He married Nancy Mygatt in 1947 by whom he had three sons, James, Steven and Daniel. After their divorce, he married the actress Audra Lindley in 1972. They divorced in 1979 and he remarried Nancy Mygatt on March 24, 1979. They redivorced after two years and on August 7, 2001 he married actress-writer Noreen Nash.

CAUSE: Whitmore died, aged 87, at his Malibu home. He had been diagnosed with lung cancer in November 2008.

Dame May Whitty

Born June 19, 1865
Died May 29, 1948

Refined dowager. Born in Liverpool, Dame May Whitty's stage career earned her several plaudits and she appeared in the West End and on Broadway before the start of the twentieth century. Although she made her film début in *The Little Minister* (1915) as Nanny Webster, she only made one more film in 21 years before becoming a semi-regular in the Thirties and Forties. Probably her best-known role is that of the titular Miss Froy in *The Lady Vanishes* (1938). She was twice nominated for Oscars for *Night Must Fall* (1937) as Mrs Bramson and as Lady Beldon in *Mrs Miniver* (1942).

CAUSE: She died of natural causes, aged 82, in Beverly Hills, California. She left £26,581 17s 1d.

Richard Widmark

Born Boxing Day 1914
Died March 24, 2008

Underrated actor. Born in Sunrise, Minnesota (a town so obscure that when he tried to retrace it as an adult, he gave up), the son of Carl H. Widmark, a travelling salesman of Swedish descent, and Ethel Mae Barr, Richard Weedt Widmark was raised in South Dakota, in Missouri and in Chicago. His Scottish grandfather took four-year-old Widmark to the pictures and his favourite star was Boris Karloff. Widmark read Law at Lake Forest College, Illinois but was more interested in acting and American football. He was also an eloquent debater and many years later on set attracted notice because he was the only Tinseltown star who did not immediately turn to the sports and showbiz pages in newspapers. He graduated in 1936 but stayed there for two years as a drama teacher. He went on a bicycle tour of Germany but his attempt to visit Dachau, then a camp for political prisoners, was barred. He did get into a youth camp where he saw a "ferocious old boy yelling Nazi doctrines at these little kids". He shot some film and on his return to America lectured on what he had witnessed. Widmark then became a highly successful radio actor and by the early Forties was earning $100,000 a year. He joked that he was the only actor who had to take a pay cut and give up his swimming pool to go west. Widmark was unable to serve in the Second World War due to a perforated eardrum even though he tried to join up three times. He made his Broadway debut in 1943 as the juvenile lead in the comedy *Kiss And Tell*. Four years later, his agent heard that the producer Henry Hathaway was looking to cast Tommy Udo, a cold, callous gunman, in *Kiss Of Death* (1947). The agent wangled an audition but before Widmark opened his mouth Hathaway declared that he was "too well-bred, too intellectual" to play the part. Widmark picked up the script to read to himself. "Read it aloud," said Hathaway, "then you'll see what I mean about the part being unsuitable." Widmark began reading and Hathaway was completely entranced. When, during the murder scene, Widmark threw in a macabre chuckle, Hathaway knew he had found Tommy Udo. On screen, Widmark laughed as he pushed an old lady (Mildred Dunnock) down a flight of stairs, commenting, "Dames are no good if you wanna have some fun." The film for which he received an Oscar nomination as Best Supporting Actor – his only Academy Award nod – made him an overnight star. "That damned laugh of mine," he said. "For two years after that picture, you couldn't get me to smile. I played the part the way I did because the script struck me as funny and the part I played made me laugh. The guy was such a ridiculous beast." Despite his reservations, he signed a seven-year contract for Twentieth Century Fox. *Kiss Of Death* had left him rather typecast. In his first seven films Widmark killed or was killed in all but one. He was to later say, "I know I've made kind of a half-assed career out of violence, but I abhor violence. I am an ardent supporter of gun control. It seems incredible to me that we are the only civilised nation that does not put some effective control on guns." He quickly established himself in films such as Jean Negulesco's *Road House* (1948), in which he played Jefferson T. "Jefty" Robbins, a small-town nightclub owner, and William Keighley's *The Street With No Name* (1948), in which he was Alec Stiles, a gangster with a fear of germs. Widmark played very human characters with great attention to detail. This was especially apparent in Jules Dassin's *film noir Night And The City* (1950) and in Joseph Mankiewicz's *No Way Out* (1950) in which he blames a black doctor (Sidney Poitier in his first film)

for his brother's death that nearly starts a race riot. No racist in real life, Widmark apologised to Poitier at the end of every scene. He usually played a villain in his early films but in Elia Kazan's *Panic In The Streets* (1950) Widmark was a health inspector looking for a man with bubonic plague. It was when he earned Hollywood clout that he began to play good guys as well. He was not always the best judge of films or his fellow thespians. Of Marilyn Monroe, his co-star in *Don't Bother To Knock* (1952), he said, "That broad will never make it. She's much too obvious." He later changed his mind, "She wanted to be this great star but acting just scared the hell out of her. That's why she was always late – couldn't get her on the set. She had trouble remembering lines. But none of it mattered. With a very few special people, something happens between the lens and the film that is pure magic. And she really had it." Widmark donned a military uniform for *Halls Of Montezuma* (1950), *Take The High Ground* (1953), *The Bedford Incident* (1965) and *Twilight's Last Gleaming* (1977). He was equally at home in the Wild West in films such as William Wellman's *Yellow Sky* (1949) as a bank robber, *The Last Wagon* (1956), Jim Bowie in *The Alamo* (1960), opposite John Wayne who was also directing – the two men did not see eye to eye off-set but it was not reflected in their onscreen chemistry – and with James Stewart in John Ford's *Two Rode Together* (1961) and again worked with Ford on *Cheyennne Autumn* (1964) – he suggested the idea for the film – and played an old rodeo rider in *When The Legends Die* (1972). Neither film was very good and it was a great sense of disappointment to Widmark who idolised Ford. Widmark was nothing if not versatile but not always with great results, especially after the end of his Fox contract in 1955 after which he could pick and choose his own roles. He was the ambitious head of a psychiatric clinic in *The Cobweb* (1955); he was disastrous as the Dauphin in Otto Preminger's *Saint Joan* (1957), so bad that he said that he was "scared to leave the house for two weeks. I wasn't worth five bucks"; Doris Day's husband in *The Tunnel Of Love* (1959), and an American army prosecutor in *Judgment At Nuremburg* (released December 19, 1961). In 1968 he played a tough cop in Don Siegel's *Madigan*, which became a short-lived television series four years later. Among his other films were *Death Of A Gunslinger* (1969), *Murder On The Orient Express* (1974), *Rollercoaster* (1977), *The Swarm* (1978), *Hanky Panky* (1982), *Who Dares Wins* (1982) *Against All Odds* (1983) and *Blackout* (1985). Like the film critic Leslie Halliwell, Widmark had little time for modern films. He said, "I could choose the director and my fellow actors. I could carry out projects, which I liked but the studios didn't want. The businessmen who run Hollywood today have no self-respect. What interests them is not movies but the bottom line. Look at *Dumb And Dumber*, which turns idiocy into something positive, or *Forrest Gump*, a hymn to stupidity. Intellectual has become a dirty word." Standing 5′10″, Widmark was very blonde – his eyebrows were so fair they had to be pencilled in on screen. Intensely private – "When I see people destroying their privacy – what they think, what they feel – by beaming it out to millions of viewers, I think it cheapens them as individuals" – Widmark was also a teetotal pipe smoker and very careful with his money. Politically, like many actors he favoured the Democrats. "I'm a lifelong liberal," he said in 2001. "I've never been a real activist – I just shoot my mouth off. When I knew Ronald Reagan, he was an affable, boring fellow. Now he's an icon. It's incredible. Like half of America, I'm doubly mystified by Reagan's spiritual heir, our current president." Widmark

married the former actress and screenwriter (Ora) Jean Hazlewood (b. Illinois August 4, 1916, d. Santa Barbara, California March 2, 1997 of Alzheimer's disease) on April 5, 1942. They had one daughter, Ann, who married baseball legend Sandy Koufax on January 1, 1969. They divorced in 1982. On September 27, 1999 he married Susan Blanchard (b. 1928), stepdaughter of Oscar Hammerstein II and third wife of Henry Fonda.
CAUSE: Widmark died at his home in Roxbury, Connecticut of complications following a fall. He was 93.

Collin Wilcox
Born February 4, 1935
Died October 14, 2009
Iconic non-victim. Born in Cincinnati, Ohio, and raised in Highlands, North Carolina, Wilcox was educated at the University of Tennessee and then studied at the Actors Studio in New York. She made her Broadway debut in 1958 in *The Day The Money Stopped*, a drama by Maxwell Anderson and Brendan Gill although the play closed after just four performances. Her best known film role was in her debut movie as Mayella Ewell, the young woman who falsely accuses a black man (Brock Peters) of rape in *To Kill A Mockingbird* (1962). Her other films included: *Catch-22* (1970), *Jaws 2* (1978) and *Marie* (1985). She was married three times: to Walter Beakel, to Geoffrey Horne by whom she had two children William and Kimberly; and, finally in 1979 to Scott Paxton by whom she had a son, Michael.
CAUSE: She died of brain cancer at her home in Highlands, North Carolina. She was 74.

Herbert Wilcox, CBE
Born April 19, 1890
Died May 15, 1977
Mr Elstree. Herbert Sydney Wilcox was born in Norwood, London, the son of Joseph Wilcox, a sculptor who also ran a billiard hall. Wilcox became a

professional billiards player when he left school before joining the army, the Royal Flying Corps, becoming a film salesman and, in 1922, a film producer. His first effort, *The Wonderful Story* (1922), was a critical hit but a box-office flop. Realising the public wanted escapism in films he also began directing, starting with *Chu Chin Chow* (1923). In 1926 he founded Elstree Studios and two years later, in 1928, he was appointed head of production for the British and Dominions Film Corporation, a position he held for seven years. Wilcox announced he was to make 30 films each year and signed Anna Neagle for one of them, *Goodnight Vienna* (1932). Over the next quarter of a century, he directed her in 32 films. He also personally financed her in the hit *Victoria The Great* (1937). Wilcox continued to make films with a 'Thirties' feel to them, even after the war and into the Fifties, by which time public tastes had changed. In 1959 he directed his last film, *The Heart Of A Man* (1959). Five years later, he went bankrupt. In 1965 he suffered a coronary thrombosis. Regaining his health, he was discharged in 1966 but was to make no more films. A Roman Catholic, he married three times: to Dorothy Brown in 1916 (divorced 1917); to Mrs Maude Clark in 1918 (divorced 1943), by whom he had a son and three daughters, one of whom, Pamela, wrote Michael Wilding's autobiography which is dedicated to Wilcox; and, in 1943 to Anna Neagle. CAUSE: Wilcox died aged 87 in London following a long illness.

Billy Wilder

Born June 22, 1906
Died March 27, 2002
Director extraordinaire. Billy Wilder was a small, compact, bespectacled, brown-eyed, acid-tongued, fast-talking, round-faced Viennese Jew who chain-smoked on the set. The son of a hotel and restaurant owner, Samuel Wilder was born in Sucha, Austria-Hungary,

100 miles east of Vienna, and intended to become a lawyer but left university after only one year of a law degree. He became a journalist on a Viennese newspaper reporting on sport and crime and interviewing celebrities. He once tried to interview Sigmund Freud, who hated newspapermen and showed him the door. In 1926 he applied for and got a job on Berlin's largest tabloid but boosted his income as a dancer-cum-gigolo in a city hotel. In 1929 he became a screenwriter on Robert Siodmak's *People On Sunday* (1929). In the following year he adapted Erich Kastne's novel, *Emil And The Detectives* and wrote scripts for several other German films until Hitler came to power in January, 1933. 5'10" Wilder fled Nazi Germany and arrived in Paris where he co-directed *Mauvaise Graine*, a story about car thieves with Danielle Darrieux. In 1934 he arrived, via Mexico, in Hollywood. His mother and other members of his family who stayed died in the concentration camps. In Hollywood he was to earn himself a reputation as a master film-maker from *Double Indemnity* in the mid-Forties through *Sunset Boulevard* and *Some Like It Hot* to *The Apartment* at the beginning of the Sixties. *Sunset Boulevard* caused Louis B. Mayer to snarl, "This Wilder should be horsewhipped!" Most of Wilder's best films were in collaboration with Charles Brackett and I.A.L. Diamond. He and Brackett met in 1936 when Wilder was put under contract to Paramount. Wilder and Brackett made their mark with sharp-edged comedies such as *Bluebeard's Eighth Wife* (1938) and *Ninotchka* (1939) starring Greta Garbo, *Midnight* (1939) for Mitchell Leisen and *Ball Of Fire* (1941) for Howard Hawks. On the back of these achievements they became two of the most highly paid writers in Hollywood. In 1942 Wilder became a director with *The Major And The Minor*, a Ginger Rogers comedy. Wilder later described it as a chaste version of *Lolita*. He next

turned to a Second World War spy story, *Five Graves To Cairo* (1943), with his Austrian compatriot, Eric von Stroheim. Wilder's star rose with his third and fourth films. *Double Indemnity* (1944), scripted by Raymond Chandler from the novel by James M. Cain, remains the archetypal Forties film noir. In *The Lost Weekend* (1945) Wilder offered Hollywood's first serious treatment of alcoholism and gave Ray Milland the best part of his career as the tragic victim. The film won four Oscars, including two for Wilder himself. His flair for cynical comedy was apparent in the political farce, *A Foreign Affair* (1948), set in post-war Berlin and starring Marlene Dietrich. Two years later, Wilder made *Sunset Boulevard*, the story of a faded Hollywood screen goddess and a screenwriting flop (played respectively by Gloria Swanson and William Holden). Wilder and Brackett won the Oscar for best screenplay – and made plenty of enemies in Hollywood itself. In 1955 Wilder made *The Seven Year Itch*. His female lead Marilyn Monroe had married baseball hero Joe DiMaggio seven months before filming began. The marriage was already in trouble due to his jealousy and readiness with his fists. At 1am on September 15, 1954 the crew filmed the famous skirt blowing scene at the Trans-Lux Theater on Lexington Avenue and 52nd Street. Fifteen times Marilyn's dress blew into the air and fifteen times the huge crowd (estimated at between 1,000 and 5,000 people) cheered. Joe DiMaggio watched the proceedings with his friend the journalist Walter Winchell before storming off, his hands thrust deep into his pockets. Although Marilyn wore two pairs of knickers, her friend Jim Haspiel says that her pubes were clearly visible. However, in the end the scenes shot that night were not useable in the film and what finally appears was shot on a Fox soundstage. Following the shoot Marilyn returned to suite 1105-6 of the St Regis Hotel, 2 East 55th Street & 5th Avenue, where she was staying with DiMaggio. They had a violent fight that night and the next day he flew back to California alone. On October 5, 1954, Marilyn announced their separation. They were divorced 22 days later. DiMaggio was back by her side for the première on her 29th birthday in 1955. "We're just good friends," said Marilyn to ward off press speculation of a reconciliation. The film ran 13 days over schedule and ten per cent over budget due in no small part to Marilyn's health. She caught a serious lung illness while filming the skirt scene on Lexington Avenue. Fox publicised the film by hanging an enormous (52 ft high) poster of Marilyn at Loew's State Theater in Time Square on Broadway at a cost of $1,500. It had to be replaced by a more circumspect version after complaints. Writing in the New York *Daily Mirror*, Philip Strassberg said, "This is the film that every red-blooded American male has been awaiting ever since the publication of the tease photos showing the wind lifting Marilyn Monroe's skirt above her shapely gams. It was worth waiting for. *The Seven Year Itch* is another example of cinema ingenuity in transplanting a stage success to celluloid . . . Tom Ewell, who reaped critical acclaim in the legit show and won over other contenders for the role in the movie and La Monroe deserve most of the credit for carrying off the comedy coup . . . her pouting delivery, puckered lips – the personification of this decade's glamour – make her one of Hollywood's top attractions, which again proves her as the not too bright model." Wilder's next encounter with Monroe occurred on *Some Like It Hot* (1959). In October 1958, by which time most of the strenuous shots had been filmed, Marilyn found herself pregnant again. Heartbreak was to follow as she miscarried the child on December 16 in her third month. Marilyn could not sit down between takes because her costumes were tight fitting so she had to rest standing up in what looked like an upright barber's chair. Curtis and Lemmon had their legs and chests shaved and a female impersonator called Barbette was brought onto the set to show them how women behave, carry themselves, etc. However, Barbette walked off because he did not get on with Jack Lemmon. Wilder's original choices to play the musicians were Tony Curtis and Jack Lemmon, United Artists wanted Frank Sinatra to play Jerry/Daphne. The choice for Sugar was Mitzi Gaynor. Sinatra agreed to play the role but then failed to keep an appointment to discuss the part and no more was heard from Ol' Blue Eyes. By this time, with Monroe on board, UA didn't much mind who was cast as Jerry/Daphne. Enter Jack Lemmon. Marilyn took 47 takes to deliver the line, "It's me, Sugar." She kept saying, "It's Sugar, me," or "Sugar, it's me." Following the thirtieth take, Wilder had the line written on a blackboard. Another line also caused her problems. It was "Where's the bourbon?" The scene required Marilyn to search through a chest of drawers and deliver the line. Forty times she said either, "Where's the bottle?", "Where's the whisky?" or "Where's the bonbon?" Wilder had the line written on a piece of paper and put in the drawer. Then Marilyn became puzzled as to the location of the paper so Wilder placed it in every drawer. Marilyn took 59 takes to film the scene. Marilyn was not happy with her opening scene. Remembered Billy Wilder, "She called me after the first daily rushes . . . I hung up and Diamond and I met and decided it was not good enough. She had just come on originally doing something with that ukulele. And we made up that new introduction with a new entrance [showing Sugar] coming down to the train through that puff of steam. She was absolutely right about that." Marilyn remembered it slightly

differently. "I'm not going back into that fucking film until Wilder reshoots my opening. When Marilyn Monroe comes into a room, nobody's going to be looking at Tony Curtis playing Joan Crawford. They're going to be looking at Marilyn Monroe." Monroe wanted the film to be shot in colour (as stipulated by her contract) but when the tests were shown, the make-up made the faces of Tony Curtis and Jack Lemmon look distinctly green. She agreed to let Billy Wilder shoot in monochrome. Wilder hated colour films. He only shot *The Seven Year Itch* in colour because of Monroe's contract. It wasn't until 1969 that he began making colour films because monochrome ones were unsellable to television. After filming wrapped, Wilder swore he would never direct Monroe again: "I have discussed this with my doctor and my psychiatrist and my accountant and they tell me I am too old and too rich to go through this again." The partnership with Lemmon continued over six more films. Among them was *The Apartment* (1960) which also starred Fred MacMurray and Shirley MacLaine. It brought two more Oscars for Wilder and one for the Romanian-born I.A.L. Diamond, who succeeded Brackett as his regular script collaborator. During the Sixties Wilder's inspiration appeared to wane. He made *One, Two, Three* (1961), *Irma La Douce* (1963), *Kiss Me Stupid* (1964) and *The Fortune Cookie* (1966). He returned to form in the Seventies with *The Private Life Of Sherlock Holmes* (1970) and *The Front Page* (1974) with Lemmon and Walter Matthau. Perhaps the best of Wilder's later films was *Fedora* (1978). *Buddy Buddy* (1981), the last and least successful teaming of Lemmon and Matthau, was an anticlimactic farewell. He officially retired in 1981 although continued to go into his office as much as possible. He was married twice. In May 1936, he eloped to Yuma, Arizona with Judith

Coppicus. They divorced in 1946. They had twins, Victoria and Vincent (born December 21, 1939). Vincent died shortly after birth. On June 30, 1949, he married Audrey Young. CAUSE: He died aged 95 in Beverly Hills, California, from pneumonia. FURTHER READING: *Billy Wilder In Hollywood* – Maurice Zolotow (London: W.H. Allen, 1977); *The Pocket Essential Billy Wilder* – Glenn Hopp (Harpenden: Pocket Essentials, 2001).

Michael Wilding

Born July 23, 1912
Died July 8, 1979
The Second Mr Elizabeth Taylor. Born in Leigh-on-Sea, Essex, the son of an *attaché* to the Russian army, Michael Charles Gauntlet Wilding was to become one of the leading cinematic idols of post-war British cinema. He was a talented actor but his undoubted good looks did him no harm. Although a matinée favourite, Wilding once admitted his ambition was "to be rich and not have to work too hard". He might have added that access to willing young ladies was also important to him. He married Kay Young in 1938, but that marriage floundered during the war because he couldn't keep his trousers up. He met Elizabeth Taylor in 1949 but their romance didn't begin until she was filming *Ivanhoe* (1952). At the time, Wilding was in the middle of an affair with Marlene Dietrich that began when they co-starred in Alfred Hitchcock's *Stagefright* (1950) in which he was Inspector Wilfred Smith. However, Taylor won him over (she proposed and even bought her own engagement ring) and on February 21, 1952 they were married in Westminster's Caxton Hall. She commented: "He enjoys sitting at home, smoking his pipe, reading, painting, and that's what I intend doing . . . This is, for me, the beginning of a happy end." Their honeymoon, taken in the French Alps, lasted eight

days and ended when Wilding returned to begin filming *Derby Day* (1952) in which he was cast as David Scott opposite Anna Neagle, their sixth film together. He was then released from his contract by Herbert Wilcox so he could become a star in America. Wilding was an easygoing man but he was exasperated by Taylor's tardiness (it hadn't improved by 2000 when she turned up very late for a dinner to commemorate her damehood) and her untidiness. He painted several portraits of his wife and took hundreds of photographs of her, many of which found their way onto the walls of their home. They had two children: Michael Howard (b. Santa Monica, California, January 6, 1953) and Christopher Edward (b. February 27, 1955) but by the time of the younger boy's first birthday the marriage was in serious trouble. They divorced in Acapulco, Mexico, on January 31, 1957. On February 12, 1958, Wilding married socialite Susan Nell in Nevada but they divorced on July 23, 1962. His fourth and final marriage was to actress Margaret Leighton on July 15, 1964. That ended with her death 12 years later. His films included: *Tilly Of Bloomsbury* (1940) as Percy Welwyn, *Spring Meeting* (1940) as Tony Fox-Collier, *Convoy* (1940) as Dot, *Secret Mission* (1942) as Private Nobby Clark, *In Which We Serve* (1942) as Flags, *Dear Octopus* (1943) as Nicholas Randolph, *English Without Tears* (1944) as Tom Gilbey, *Carnival* (1946) as Maurice Avery, *The Courtneys Of Curzon Street* (1947) as Sir Edward Courtney, *An Ideal Husband* (1947) as Viscount Goring, *Spring In Park Lane* (1948) as Richard, *Under Capricorn* (1949) as Charles Adare, *Maytime In Mayfair* (1949) as Michael Gore-Brown, *Into The Blue* (1950) as Nicholas Foster, *The Lady With A Lamp* (1951) as Sidney Herbert, *Trent's Last Case* (1952) as Philip Trent, *Derby Day* (1952) as David Scott, *Torch Song* (1953) as Tye

Graham, *Zarak* (1956) as Major Ingram, *Danger Within* (1959) as Major Charles Marquand, *The World Of Suzie Wong* (1960) as Ben Marlowe, *A Girl Named Tamiko* (1962) as Nigel Costairs, *Waterloo* (1970) as Sir William Ponsonby, and *Lady Caroline Lamb* (1972) as Lord Holland.

CAUSE: Wilding died, aged 66, following a fall at his home in Chichester, Sussex. He left £147,392.

FURTHER READING: *Apple Sauce: The Story Of My Life* – Michael Wilding As Told To Pamela Wilcox (London: George Allen & Unwin, 1982).

Kenneth Williams

Born February 22, 1926
Died April 15, 1988

Cult comic. Small, camp, bitchy, narcissistic, secretive, solitary, articulate, well read – Kenneth Charles Williams was all this and much more. He was born in Bingfield Street off the Caledonian Road in King's Cross, north London and moved soon after to Marchmont Street in Bloomsbury, remaining in or very near the area for the rest of his life, living alone for all but a few months. The son of hairdresser Charles George Williams (although the writer Barry Took believed Charlie was not Kenneth's father. Certainly his elder sister, Pat, was the product of their mother's prior relationship) and Louisa Alexandra 'Louie' Morgan (b. December 20, 1900, d. July 1991), father and son rarely saw eye to eye. Kenneth treated a present of boxing gloves with complete disdain. He showed a precocity as a child lauded in a school play (playing Princess Angelica in Thackeray's *The Rose And The Ring*) which did not impress Charlie: "Acting is no good. The women are all trollops and the men are nancies." (His father was to die in unusual circumstances on October 15, 1962, aged 62, after drinking from a bottle of cleaning fluid.) In 1940, Kenneth began training

as a draughtsman before he was called up on April 20, 1944. He was posted to the Royal Engineers before joining Combined Services Entertainment where he gained his first adult experience of show business. Among his contemporaries were playwright Peter Nichols, film director John Schlesinger and comedian Stanley Baxter. On December 4, 1947, he was demobbed and resumed his career as a cartographer but the pull of the theatre was too strong and, in 1948, he became a repertory actor. "The thing to do, in any circumstance, is to appear to know exactly what you are doing," he once said, "and at the same time convey casual doubts about the abilities of everybody else and undermine their confidence." He made his film début in *Trent's Last Case* (1952) which starred Michael Wilding, Margaret Leighton and Orson Welles in the tale of a journalist who was convinced a tycoon's death was, in fact, homicide. That same year he first appeared on television in *The Wonderful Visit*. On September 29, 1954 he opened in *St Joan* at the Arts Theatre and established his reputation with a quite brilliant Dauphin. On November 2, 1954, the first of *Hancock's Half Hour* was broadcast bringing him radio fame. In the late-Fifties he regularly appeared in comedy revues such as *Share My Lettuce* (from August 21, 1957, written by *University Challenge* chairman Bamber Gascoigne) and *Pieces Of Eight* (from September 23, 1959). In 1958 he was cast as the intellectually effete Private James Bailey in *Carry On Sergeant* (1958), the first of the long-running comedy series. He was paid £800 for each of the films until 1962 when his remuneration rose to £5,000. None of the cast received residuals. Over the next 21 years he was to appear in 24 more *Carry On* movies, creating such memorable characters as nuclear physicist Oliver Reckitt in *Carry On Nurse* (1959); English master Edwin Milton in *Carry*

On Teacher (1959); rooky policeman PC Stanley Benson in *Carry On Constable* (1960); "helping hand" Francis Courtenay in *Carry On Regardless* (1961); first officer Leonard Marjoribanks in *Carry On Cruising* (1962); Captain Fearless of HMS Venus in *Carry On Jack* (1963), originally entitled *Carry On Sailor*; espionage agent Desmond Simkins in *Carry On Spying* (1964); Julius Caesar in *Carry On Cleo* (1964) in which he utters the immortal line "Infamy! Infamy! They've all got it in for me!"; Judge Burke in *Carry On Cowboy* (1965) in which he does an impression of Hal Roach; mad scientist Dr Orlando Watt in *Carry On Screaming* (1966); terror of the aristocracy Citizen Camembert – The Big Cheese – in *Carry On Don't Lose Your Head* (1966); Foreign Legion chief Commander Burger in *Carry On Follow That Camel* (1967); Dr Kenneth Tinkle in *Carry On Doctor* (1967); Randy Lal, the Khazi of Kalabar, in *Carry On Up The Khyber* (1968); surgeon Dr Frederick Carver in *Carry On Again Doctor* (1969); citizens advisor Percival Snooper in *Carry On Loving* (1970); Thomas Cromwell in *Carry On Henry* (1970); lavatory manufacturer W.C. Boggs in *Carry On At Your Convenience* (1971); Sir Bernard Cutting in *Carry On Matron* (1971); holiday rep Stuart Farquhar in *Carry On Abroad* (1972), Captain Desmond Fancey in *Carry On Dick* (1974), the last script by Talbot Rothwell; archaeologist Professor Roland Crump in *Carry On Behind* (1975) and French ambassador to the Court of St James's, Emile Prevert, in *Carry On Emmanuelle* (1978). His non *Carry On . . .* films were *Innocents In Paris* (1952) as a London airport window dresser; *The Beggar's Opera* (1952) as Jack the pot boy; *Valley Of Song* (1953) as Lloyd the Haulage; *The Seekers* (1954) as Peter Wishart; *Misalliance* (1954) as Bentley Summerhayes; *Tommy The Toreador*

(1959) as the Vice-Consul; *Make Mine Mink* (1960) as Freddie Warrington; *Raising The Winds* (1961) as Harold Chesney; *His And Hers* (1961) as a policeman; Henry Halfpenny in *Twice Round The Daffodils* (1962) and Sir Henry Baskerville in *The Hound Of The Baskervilles* (1978). He left Hancock's radio show after Tony Hancock claimed that his characters were "cardboardian stereotypes" and joined the show *Beyond Our Ken* (July 1, 1958–February 16, 1964) which became *Round The Horne* (March 7, 1965–June 9, 1968) when the writer Eric Merriman fell out with the BBC and Barry Took and Marty Feldman took over. In *RTH* he was renowned for his vocal dexterity creating such legendary characters as Sandy (with Hugh Paddick playing Julian), Rambling Syd Rumpo, Chou En Ginsberg, M.A. (Failed) and J. Peasemould Gruntfuttock, the walking slum. In 1968 he joined the cast of the radio show *Just A Minute* in which contestants have to talk for sixty seconds without hesitation, deviation or repetition. He was a regular until his death. He also hosted *International Cabaret* on BBC2 from July 5, 1966 until 1968 and told BBC boss Bill Cotton that his fee was too big. But it is for the *Carry On . . .* films that the name of Kenneth Williams will always be associated and remembered. To see him at his best view a video or DVD of *An Audience With Kenneth Williams* (1983). "Ten thou for a night of my old tat," he said to his friend Gyles Brandreth.

CAUSE: Williams was never the most physically vigorous of men, forever in and out of hospital with various complaints, many to do with his rectum. He had considered suicide a number of times before he took an overdose of sleeping pills at his London home: 8, Marlborough House, Osnaburgh Street, London NW1. He was 62, the same age as the father he detested. Although towards the end of his life Williams worried that work was drying up and that he would run short of money, he nevertheless left £538,379 in his will. The coroner, Dr Christopher Pease, returned an open verdict but left no doubt as to his belief that Williams had indeed committed suicide. The final entry in Williams' diary certainly left a clue: "I felt so weak I wanted to flake out. The pain got worse and worse . . . oh, I'm so tired these days! No energy at all. Pain came back with a vengeance! Nothing seems to allay it now . . . Even if the op. don't work, I can't be worse than I am at the moment . . . By 6.30 pain in the back was pulsating as it's never done before . . . so this, plus the stomach trouble continues to torture me – oh – what's the bloody point?" FURTHER READING: *Just Williams: An Autobiography* – Kenneth Williams (London: Dent, 1985); *Kenneth Williams: A Biography* – Michael Freedland (London: Weidenfeld & Nicolson, 1990); *The Kenneth Williams Diaries* – Russell Davies (London: HarperCollins, 1993); *The Kenneth Williams Letters* – Russell Davies (London: HarperCollins, 1994).

Beverly Wills

Born August 6, 1933
Died October 24, 1963
Wisecracker. The daughter of rubber-face comedienne Joan Davis (b. St Paul, Minnesota, June 29, 1907, d. Palm Springs, California, May 23, 1961, of a heart attack), Beverly Wills made her film début in *Anaesthesia* (1938) playing a small girl before landing a role on her mother's series *I Married Joan*, playing Beverly Grossman. Like her mother, she had natural comic timing and it seemed as if she was a star in the making. She appeared in *Small Town Girl* (1953) as Deidre, *Some Like It Hot* (1959) as Dolores and *The Ladies' Man* (1961). CAUSE: Having just completed *Son Of Flubber* (1963) she lay in bed smoking when she fell asleep, causing a blaze

that also killed her grandmother and two young sons. It was the same house her mother had died in two years earlier.

Shelley Winters

(SHIRLEY SCHRIFT)
Born August 18, 1920
Died January 14, 2006
Hollywood's bad girl. Shelley Winters was born at 12.05am on Newstead Avenue, St Louis, Missouri, the daughter of clothing salesman and designer Jonas Schrift (b. Austria, d. Los Angeles, California, August 16, 1955 of a cerebral haemorrhage) and Rose Winter (b. St Louis, Missouri, d. 1966 of a heart attack) who were third cousins. The family moved to Brooklyn where Winters remembered her childhood as "pretty damn lousy". Things became lousier when her father was sent to prison for arson in 1930. "It just broke everything up totally," she said. "My mother was heartbroken." Rose Schrift enrolled her then three-year-old daughter in a talent competition after teaching her to sing 'Moonlight And Roses'. The tuition paid off because Winters won. When she left school she landed a job in a shop but the appointment was not to last very long. "I got fired from the store real fast," she recalled. "I was mad because they didn't think I was pretty enough for the candy counter, they put me in light bulbs, selling expensive German-made ones. I broke as many as I sold." When she was 15, Winters fell pregnant by a fellow actor and had an abortion. Winters applied to play Scarlett O'Hara in *Gone With The Wind* (1939) but managed only to make David O. Selznick laugh till director George Cukor silenced him. He advised her to study acting and become known on the New York stage. Winters took his advice and made her professional début in the flop *The Night Before Christmas* in 1941 and the following year appeared as a singer in the light operetta *Rosalinda* where she

was spotted by a talent scout. Rather than rush to the West Coast she continued to learn her trade in the New York theatre. She changed her name to Shelley Winter because she didn't want to be another Shirley and using her mother's maiden name. She made her film début as Norma in *There's Something About A Soldier* (released November 30, 1943) and followed that playing a secretary in *What A Woman!* (released December 28, 1943), which starred Rosalind Russell. Bit part followed bit part including being murdered by Ronald Colman in George Cukor's *A Double Life* (1947), the first time she was billed as Shelley Winters. Death at the hands of a celebrity almost became a *leitmotif* for Winters' early career. "I was drowned by Montgomery Clift, run over by both Alan Ladd and James Mason, knifed by Robert Mitchum and strangled by Ronald Colman," said 5′4″ Winters. After that she took leading female roles including *The Great Gatsby* (1949) as Myrtle Wilson and *Winchester 73* (1950) as Lola Manners, opposite James Stewart. It was her performance as Alice Tripp in *A Place In The Sun* (1951) that won her a first Oscar nomination as Best Actress. In the late Forties in New York Winters had met and befriended Marilyn Monroe. The two women shared a home briefly in 1951 at 8573 Holloway Drive, Hollywood when they both went west. One day she met Dylan Thomas who told her that his ambitions were "to touch the titties of a beautiful blonde starlet and to meet Charlie Chaplin". That night after he had "sterilised" his index finger in champagne Winters allowed him to touch each breast with that digit. The next night she and Monroe entertained him to dinner – loin of pork, mashed potatoes and salad – and he spent all night drinking before they took him to see "the greatest comic genius of our century". Her second marriage, to Vittorio Gassman, was punctuated by public rows and

"the bad behaviour that puts me in the headlines". She remembered, "He used to take me in his arms and tell me how wonderful he was." She began dating in earnest, numbering Sean Connery, Marlon Brando, Errol Flynn and Burt Lancaster among her conquests. Studios often suspended her because she preferred to tour the country in Shakespearean plays directed by Charles Laughton to appearing in films. In 1958 she was cast as Petronella Van Daan in *The Diary Of Anne Frank* (released March 18, 1959). The film was nominated for eight Academy Awards, winning three including one for Winters as Best Actress In A Supporting Role. She was also nominated for a Golden Globe but lost out to Susan Kohner for *Imitation Of Life* (1959). Director George Stevens had been part of the first film unit into Dachau concentration camp and he insisted that all the adult actors on set watched the footage his unit had taken of the horrors. Winters said that shooting the film "scarred me for life". She helped the 17-year-old model Millie Perkins, who is Catholic, to understand what it is like to be Jewish. The Franks wore their Judaism lightly and until the advent of Hitler regarded themselves as German first and Jewish second. Stevens asked Winters to put on twenty pounds to play Mrs Van Daan; ever helpful, she put on thirty. Ten years later, Winters gave her Oscar to the Anne Frank Museum in Amsterdam. At the time she was filming *The Diary Of Anne Frank* her third husband Anthony Franciosa was filming *The Naked Maja* (1958) with Ava Gardner in Rome and spending far too much time with her for Winters' liking. She disliked it so much that she threatened to hire a hitman to kill Gardner if she continued the affair with Franciosa. He had also been rather too friendly with Anna Magnani. Winters later said, "All my men cheated on me and that's kinda sad. All I ever got out of marriage, except my daughter, was

some jewellery and a recipe for ravioli."
The Sixties saw Winters playing a
variety of roles including the sex-starved
Charlotte Haze in *Lolita* (1962), Sarah
Garnell in the behind-the-scenes story
of a sex survey *The Chapman Report*
(released October 5, 1962) directed by
George Cukor and based on Irving
Wallace's best-selling novel, Madame
Irma, the owner of a brothel in *The
Balcony* (released March 21, 1963),
Fran Cabrell in the comedy *Wives And
Lovers* (released August 28, 1963),
another brothel owner, albeit the
factual not fictional Polly Adler in *A
House Is Not A Home* (1964), a woman
healed by Jesus in *The Greatest Story
Ever Told* (1965), the prostitute
Rose-Ann D'Arcey who accidentally
blinds her daughter in *A Patch Of Blue*
(released December 10, 1965) for
which she won her second Oscar, and
Ruby, one of Michael Caine's
conquests in *Alfie* (1966) – "I couldn't
understand a word Michael Caine said.
I just waited for the gaps and then said
my lines". In the autumn of 1966
Winters joined the pantheon of stars
portraying villains in *Batman* when she
played Ma Parker, and coincidentally
played the real-life gangster, Ma
Barker, on whom the parody was based
four years later in *Bloody Mama*
(1970). Two years later, she earned her
fourth Oscar nomination for her role as
former professional swimmer Belle
Rosen in *The Poseidon Adventure*
(released December 12, 1972). The
rest of Winters' career was spent
mainly on television with the occasional
film. In 1980 she published the first
volume of her autobiography *Shelley –
Also Known As Shirley*. It detailed her
vigorous love life resulting in the sale of
T-shirts bearing the legend "I haven't
slept with Shelley Winters". To
supplement her income she began to
teach acting. A second autobiography
appeared ten years later and Winters
promoted the book by greeting
journalists in her hotel room bed
wearing pink negligees. Asked if she

minded growing old, she said,
"Goddam right I do, I hate it. My back
hurts, I need glasses, I'm fat, I can't
dance like I used to. I'd give my soul to
be 30 again." One critic described the
books as "the seedy image of 'kiss and
tell' senior citizenship." Of herself
Winters said, "The only way I'll ever be
a lady is to marry a lord." Winters
married four times. On January 1, 1942
she married Captain (Mack) Paul
Mayer. They divorced on October 1,
1948. On April 26, 1952 she married
6′1½″ actor Vittorio Gassman (b.
Genoa, Liguria, Italy, September 1,
1922, d. Rome, Italy, June 29, 2000)
by whom she had her only child, a
daughter named Vittoria-Gina (b.
Cedars of Lebanon Hospital, Los
Angeles, California, February 14,
1953). It was a second marriage for
both of them. The marriage ended in
divorce on June 2, 1954. On May 4,
1957 she married, as his second wife,
the actor Anthony Franciosa (b. New
York, October 25, 1928 d. Los
Angeles, California, January 19, 2006
of a stroke). Orson Welles did not
understand the attraction and asked
Winters, "Why did you marry that
streak of linguine?" Winters replied,
with a twinkle in her eye, "It's not
linguine. More like an Italian salami."
They divorced on November 18, 1960.
One critic said, "Watching Shelley
Winters and Tony Franciosa act is like
watching two broken-hearted clowns."
Ten hours before she died, Winters
married Gerry DeFord. The ceremony
was conducted by the actor Sally
Kirkland, Winters' godmother. Winters
insisted that she only ever really loved
two men, her first husband and Burt
Lancaster. Perhaps food was her real
love. "I lose track of the guys I've
known," she said, "but I never forget
the meals."

CAUSE: Winters died of heart failure at
the Rehabilitation Centre of Beverly
Hills; she had suffered a heart attack on
October 14, 2005. She was 85.

FURTHER READING: *Shelley Also Known*

As Shirley – Shelley Winters (London: Granada, 1981); *Best Of Times, Worst Of Times* – Shelley Winters (London: Muller, 1990).

Robert Wise

Born September 10, 1914
Died September 14, 2005
Mr Musical. Robert Earl Wise was born in Winchester and raised at Connorsville, Indiana, the son of meatpacker Earl Wise and housewife Olive Longnecker. Early on, he developed an interest in films and dropped out of Franklin College in Franklin, Indiana where he was studying journalism to go to Hollywood. In 1933 he landed a job at RKO as a messenger in the studio's editing department thanks to his elder brother who already worked at the company in the accounts department. Wise worked his way up to become a sound and music editor. In 1937 he worked as an assistant editor on the film *Stage Door* before moving onto *Fifth Avenue Girl* (1939) and *The Hunchback Of Notre Dame* (1939). He received an Academy Award nomination for his editing of Orson Welles' *Citizen Kane* (1941) and edited Welles' second film, *The Magnificent Ambersons* (1942). On orders from RKO studio bigwigs, Wise cut 40 minutes from the film causing Welles to refer to it as a "mutilation". Thirty years later, 5′10″ Wise confessed, "In terms of a work of art, I grant you Orson's original film was better. But we were faced with the realities of what the studio was demanding." Wise directed his first film in 1944, the horror movie *The Curse Of The Cat People*. In 1949 his boxing film, *The Set-Up*, won the critics' award for best picture at the Cannes Film Festival. It was one of his three favourite own films. The other two were: *I Want To Live!* (released November 18, 1958), which won Susan Hayward a Best Actress Academy Award in 1959, and *The Haunting*, a 1963 horror film. When

Howard Hughes bought RKO, Wise's contract was allowed to expire and he moved to Twentieth Century Fox. Wise made the Western *Two Flags West* (1950), *The House On Telegraph Hill* (1951) and the sci-fi drama *The Day The Earth Stood Still* (1951). A flying saucer appears in Washington DC during the Cold War and out gets an alien Klaatu (Michael Rennie) with a 10 foot high robot called Gort. He carried a message of peace but the Americans believe that it is a Russian trick and shoot him. Gort raises him from the dead. The only words that could stop the robot were, "Klaatu, borada nikto!" From 1950 for three years Wise freelanced, working at a number of studios. He made *Three Secrets* (1950), with Patricia Neal, Ruth Roman and Eleanor Parker and *So Big* (1953) with Jane Wyman at Warner Bros, *The Desert Rats* (1953) and *Destination Gobi* (1953) for Fox before receiving acclaim for *Executive Suite* (1953) starring William Holden, Fredric March, Barbara Stanwyck and June Allyson at MGM. Wise produced his first film, *Return To Paradise* that same year. He wanted complete control of the production. "I had no idea what the release pattern would be, what the ads would look like . . . I decided that I wanted to be informed, and to work with the studios to plan the entire film, not just the shooting." Wise intended to cast James Dean in his next film, a biopic of the middleweight boxing champion Rocky Graziano but Dean's death in a car crash put paid to the plans. Instead against some opposition, Wise cast Paul Newman in *Somebody Up There Likes Me* (released July 3, 1956). The film also marked the débuts of Frank Campanella, Angela Cartwright, Dean Jones, Robert Loggia and Steve McQueen. Two years later he made *I Want To Live!*, the story of drug-addicted prostitute, Barbara Graham (b. Oakland, California, June 26, 1923 as Barbara Elaine Wood), who died in the San Quentin gas chamber on June 3, 1955 after she and three confederates broke into the Burbank home of elderly widow Mable Monohan on March 9, 1953 believing that she kept a large amount of money and jewellery on the premises. When the old lady cried out, Graham hit her over the head with a gun butt and then suffocated her. The gang left without their booty, which was not to be found in the house. In preparing for the production, Wise watched an execution. The film was regarded as too harrowing to be shown in Britain at the time. Wise co-directed *West Side Story* (1961), with Jerome Robbins. The deal was that Robbins would look after the musical numbers while Wise oversaw the rest of the film. However, Robbins was sacked when the film went over budget and over schedule and Wise took total responsibility. *West Side Story* won ten Oscars in all, including Best Picture and Best Director. Four years later, Wise helmed one of the most successful films of all time, *The Sound Of Music* (premièred March 2, 1965). The story of the 5'7" noviciate nun Maria Augusta Kutschera (b. on a train heading for Vienna, Austro-Hungarian Empire, January 26, 1905, d. Morrisville, Vermont, March 28, 1987) from Nonnberg Abbey who is hired to look after the seven children of the widowed Korvettenkapitän Georg Ludwig Ritter von Trapp (b. Zadar, Dalmatia, Austro-Hungarian Empire, April 4, 1880, d. Stowe, Vermont, May 30, 1947) became one of the most beloved films of all time. On January 10, 1911, Korvettenkapitän von Trapp had married the wealthy Agathe Whitehead, the niece of Tory politician William St John Fremantle Brodrick, 1st Earl of Midleton, and granddaughter of Robert Whitehead, the inventor of the torpedo. They had seven children: Rupert (b. Pola, Istria, Austria, November 1, 1911, d. Stowe, Vermont February 22, 1992), Friedrich on screen; 5'4" Agathe Johanna Erwina Gobertina (b.

Pola, Istria, Austria, March 12, 1913) who was Liesl in the film; 5'4" Maria Franziska (b. Erlhof, Zell am See, Salzburg, Austria, August 28, 1914), Louisa in the film; Werner (b. Erlhof, Zell am See, Salzburg, Austria, December 21, 1915, d. Waitsfield, Vermont, October 11, 2007) who was portrayed as Kurt; Hedwig Maria Adolphine Gobertina (b. Erlhof, Zell am See, Salzburg, Austria, July 28, 1917, d. Zell am See, Salzburg, Austria September 14, 1972 of asthma) – the character of Brigitta was based on her; Johanna Karolina (b. Erlhof, Zell am See, Salzburg, Austria, September 7, 1919, d. Vienna, Austria, November 25, 1994), Marta on screen; and Martina (b. Martinsschlösse, Klosterneuburg, Austria, February 17, 1921, d. Stowe, Vermont, February 25, 1951 in childbirth), Gretl on screen. On September 3, 1922, Agathe von Trapp died of scarlet fever that she had caught from her daughter, Agathe. In reality, Maria was asked to teach just one of the children, Maria, who missed school after falling ill. The nun and the sea captain fell in love and married on November 26, 1927. They had three more children: Rosemarie (b. Salzburg, Austria, January 8, 1929), Eleonore (b. Salzburg, Austria, May 14, 1931) and Johannes (b. Philadelphia, Pennsylvania, January 17, 1939). The reel version differed from the real version in a number of ways. Korvettenkapitän von Trapp was not forced to join the German navy after the Anschluss. He had married "Fraulein Maria" ten years before the German annexation. The family did not hide at Nonnberg Abbey before fleeing on foot to Switzerland. In 1938 they caught a train to Italy and then London and finally America. In any case Salzburg is too far from the Swiss border to walk. Had the family walked over the mountain they would probably have ended up in Germany near the Kehlsteinhaus, Hitler's mountain retreat in Berchtesgaden. In 1939 they toured Europe and even visited Salzburg for a few months. Maria von Trapp did not like Julie Andrews's portrayal of her, believing it to be too saccharine. Luckily, most people disagreed and she was nominated for a Best Actress Oscar. It won five Oscars: Best Picture, Best Director (Wise), Sound, Best Adapted Score and Film Editing and was nominated for five including Andrews, Best Supporting Actress (Peggy Wood), Best Cinematography, Best Art Direction (Boris Leven, Walter M. Scott, Ruby Levitt) and Best Costume Design. In 2001, the US Library of Congress chose the film for preservation in the National Film Registry as it was deemed "culturally, historically, or aesthetically significant". Wise's next collaboration with Julie Andrews on *Star!* (1968), a biopic of Gertrude Lawrence was less successful. His other films included: *The Body Snatcher* (1945) with Boris Karloff as a grave-robber in the fog-shrouded Edinburgh of 1831, *The Haunting* (1963), *The Sand Pebbles* (1966), *The Andromeda Strain* (1971), *Two People* (1973), *The Hindenburg* (1975), *Audrey Rose* (1977), *Star Trek: The Motion Picture* (1979), *Rooftops* (1989) which flopped and *A Storm in Summer* (2000). Much lauded, Wise won the Irving G. Thalberg Award at the Academy Awards in 1967. He was president of the Directors Guild of America from 1971 to 1974 and president of the Academy of Motion Picture Arts and Sciences from 1985 to 1987. In 1998 Wise received the American Film Institute's award for lifetime achievement. Wise was married twice. His first wife (on May 25, 1942) was Patricia Doyle (d. September 22, 1975) by whom he had one son. On January 29, 1977 he married Millicent Franklin who survived him.

CAUSE: Robert Wise died of heart failure at UCLA Medical Center, Los Angeles, California. He was 91.

Joseph Wiseman
Born May 15, 1918
Died October 19, 2009

Iconic villain. Born in Montreal, he began his Broadway career in the Thirties when he appeared in Shakespeare and Chekhov. He made his film debut in *With These Hands* (1950) playing Deleo and then played regularly on television and in films but did not make an impression. He appeared in *Detective Story* (1951), starring Kirk Douglas, *Viva Zapata!* (1952) as Fernando Aguirre, *Les Misérables* (1952) as Genflou, *The Silver Chalice* (1954) as Mijamin, *The Prodigal* (1955) as Carmish, *Three Brave Men* (1956) as Jim Barron, *The Unforgiven* (1960) as Abe Kelsey, *The Happy Thieves* (1962) as Jean Marie Calbert before the iconic film that made his face if not his name known. Of the role, he said, "I had no idea what I was letting myself in for. I had no idea it would achieve the success it did. I know nothing about mysteries. I don't take to them. As far as I was concerned, I thought it might be just another Grade-B Charlie Chan mystery." The role was Dr Julius No in the first Bond film *Dr No* (premièred October 5, 1962). Wiseman's post-Bond cinematic career featured: *Bye Bye Braverman* (1968) as Felix Ottensteen, *The Counterfeit Killer* (1968) as Rajeski, *The Night They Raided Minsky's* (1968) as Louis Minsky, *Stiletto* (1969) as Matteo, *Lawman* (1971) as Lucas, *The Valachi Papers* (1972) as Salvatore Maranzano, *Journey Into Fear* (1975) as Colonel Haki, *The Betsy* (1978) as Jake Weinstein, *Jaguar Lives!* (1979) as Ben Ashir and *Seize The Day* (1986) as Dr Adler. Following the death of Charles Gray on March 7, 2000, Wiseman was the last surviving main Bond villain of the films that Sean Connery appeared in for United Artists. Wiseman's first marriage, to Nell Kinard, ended in divorce. They had one daughter, Martha. His second wife was the choreographer Pearl Lang (b. Chicago, Illinois, May 22, 1921, d. February 24, 1909).

CAUSE: Wiseman died aged 91 at his home in Manhattan. He had been ill for some time.

Anna May Wong
(WONG LIU TSONG)
Born January 3, 1907
Died February 3, 1961
The first Oriental star. Born the daughter of a laundry man in the Chinatown section of Los Angeles, her real name means 'Frosted Yellow Willow'. She made her film début as an extra in *The Red Lantern* (1919) but it was two years before she again graced the sound stage with small parts in *The First Born* (1921) and *Dinty* (1921) and then larger roles in *Bits Of Life* (1921) and *Shame* (1921). At the age of 13 she worked as a photographer's model. In 1922 she appeared in the first full-length Technicolor film, *The Toll Of The Sea*. It was her portrayal of a Mongol slave girl opposite Douglas Fairbanks in *The Thief Of Bagdad* (1924) that made her a star. In public she always dressed in traditional Oriental clothes but in private she preferred jeans and jumpers. Wong had the looks and talent to be a major star but was hampered by the racism that was prevalent in Twenties and Thirties America, when Orientals and blacks were consigned to minor roles while the major ethnic parts were played by made-up Caucasians. A case in point is *The Crimson City* (1928) in which Wong had a supporting role while the lead part, that of a Chinese girl, was played by Myrna Loy. She still excelled in films about China and the Far East, appearing in *Mr Wu* (1927), *Old San Francisco* (1927), *The Chinese Parrott* (1927), *Chinatown Charlie* (1928) and *Across To Singapore* (1928). Eventually, Wong became so fed up with her lack of success in her native land that she travelled to Germany where she was accepted, appearing in

Song (1928). She became so fluent in German that her voice did not have to be dubbed by another actress. She also worked in England, playing opposite Laurence Olivier in the play *The Circle Of Chalk* in March 1929. In 1930 she appeared in *Elstree Calling* and the English, French and German versions of *The Flame Of Love*. That same year she worked in Austria before returning to America to appear in the Broadway play *On The Spot*, which opened on October 29, 1930. In 1931 she was signed to Paramount and starred in *Daughter Of The Dragon* (1931) which was based on Sax Rohmer's Fu Manchu tales. She then appeared in *Shanghai Express* (1931) as Hui Fei, *A Study In Scarlet* (1933), *Tiger Bay* (1933), *Chu Chin Chow* (1934), *Java Head* (1934), *Limelight Blues* (1934), *Daughter Of Shanghai* (1937), *Dangerous To Know* (1938), *King Of Chinatown* (1939), *Island Of Lost Men* (1939), *Ellery Queen's Penthouse Mystery* (1941), *Bombs Over Burma* (1942) and *Lady From Chunkging* (1942). Following World War II she found film work difficult to come by, appearing in only *Impact* (1949) and *Portrait In Black* (1960). She worked on the television series *Gallery Of Mme Lui-Tsong* playing Mme Lui-Tsong in 1951. She never married.

CAUSE: She died of a heart attack exactly a month after her 54th birthday in Santa Monica, California. She was buried in section 5 of Rosedale Cemetery, 1831 West Washington Boulevard, Los Angeles, California 90007.

Ed Wood, Jr
Born October 10, 1924
Died December 10, 1978
The world's worst film director. Born in Poughkeepsie, New York, the son of a post office worker, Edward D. Wood, Jr's name until recently was known only to hardcore film buffs and the cognoscenti of truly awful films, the best example of which is his execrable

Plan 9 From Outer Space (1959), which later became a stage show. Tim Burton's film *Ed Wood* (1994) starring Johnny Depp changed all that and brought Wood's work to a greater audience able to 'appreciate' his abilities. Raised around Niagara Falls, Wood joined the US Marines in 1942 and served with distinction until being injured and shipped home where he joined a carnival. Like many more worthy directors, Wood set out to make great movies but only succeeded in producing dross. His first film was *Glen Or Glenda* (1953) in which Bela Lugosi narrates the story of a man Glen (played by Wood but billed as Daniel Davis) who cannot understand why his fiancée is upset by his need to wear her clothes. In *Bride Of The Monster* (1953) Lugosi plays mad scientist Dr Eric Vornoff who tells one girl not to be scared of his large assistant played by Swedish wrestler Tor Johnson, "Don't be afraid of Lobo," intones Lugosi, "he's as harmless as kitchen." The original script said that he was "as harmless as a *kitten*" but the drug-addicted Lugosi blew the line and refused to do a retake. In another scene a girl picks up a phone that didn't ring and begins what therefore seemed to the audience to be an imaginary conversation. In fact, the sound of the phone trilling was supposed to have been dubbed in post-production but Wood simply forgot. The original peroration of the film is unintentionally hysterical. Lugosi is supposed to be crushed to death by a giant octopus and Wood decided to film a real life cephalopod and then cut that with Lugosi's terrified face. However, filming the creature through the glass of its aquarium didn't produce realistic footage, so Wood borrowed a dummy octopus from Columbia. That still didn't solve the problem, because no one knew how to work the engine to set the creature's tentacles flailing. Ever resourceful, Wood had a crew member throw Lugosi onto the octopus. The star then did his best to create the spectre of a fearful human battling with a fearsome sea creature. This he did by screaming a lot and pulling the octopus' lifeless tentacles about him. Then Wood ran into another problem. His financier wanted another end – a nuclear explosion. So, the film ends with Lugosi's life and death struggle, then a large mushroom cloud from the film stock library. Following the disaster that was *Plan 9 From Outer Space* (the feature had not been helped by Wood's star dropping dead during filming), he made *Night Of The Ghouls* (1960) which went unreleased for 23 years because of financial problems. Thereafter, perhaps not surprisingly, Wood found directorial jobs difficult to come by so he turned his hand to writing pornographic books, often about transvestites, his own particular fetish. Wood had the habit of turning up for work fetchingly clad in women's suits, tights, high heels and Angora jumpers. Oh, and he had a beard, a very deep voice and smoked cigarettes. He claimed he wore a bra and knickers under his marines uniform. His last film was the hardcore *Necromancy* (1972). He left a widow, Kathy. CAUSE: He died of heart failure at home in Yucca Street, Los Angeles, while watching an American football game on television.

Natalie Wood

(NATASHA NIKOLAEVNA ZACHARENKO)
Born July 20, 1938
Died November 29, 1981
Brunette bombshell. Born in San Francisco, California, the daughter of a Russian architect who later changed his name to Gurdin and a Siberian ballet dancer, Natalie Wood was one of the few actors to be equally successful as a child star and an adult one. Her busty (36D-24-35) 5'2" younger sister, Lana (b. Santa Rosa, California, March 1, 1946) was also an actress; she appeared as Plenty O'Toole in *Diamonds Are Forever* (1971) and was married to

producer Robert Evans. Natalie, two inches shorter than her sister and a more demure 32B-22-34, was a good pupil at school and excelled at maths, which made her money conscious in later life. She made her film début aged five in *Happy Land* (1943) and appeared in *Driftwood* (1947) as Jenny, during which she broke her left wrist, leaving her with a deformed hand for the rest of her life that she skilfully hid with sleeves or jewellery. It was her portrayal of Susan Walker in *Miracle On 34th Street* (1947) that won audiences' hearts worldwide. Natalie Wood grew up on screen in films such as *The Ghost And Mrs Muir* (1947) as Anna Muir, *Scudda Hoo! Scudda Hay!* (1948) as Bean McGill, *Chicken Every Sunday* (1948) as Ruth Hefferan, *Father Was A Fullback* (1949) as Ellen Cooper, *Never A Dull Moment* (1950) as Nan, *No Sad Songs For Me* (1950) as Polly Scott, *Our Very Own* (1950) as Penny, *Dear Brat* (1951) as Pauline, *Just For You* (1952) as Barbara Blake, *The Silver Chalice* (1954) as Helena and the film in which she was a graceful adult, *Rebel Without A Cause* (1955) as Judy for which she earned an Oscar nomination as Best Supporting Actress. She also appeared in *The Girl He Left Behind* (1956) as Susan Daniels, *The Searchers* (1956) as Debbie Edwards, *A Cry In The Night* (1956) as Liz Taggart, *Marjorie Morningstar* (1958) as Marjorie Morgenstern, *Kings Go Forth* (1958) as Monique Blair, *Cash McCall* (1959) as Lory Austen, *All The Fine Young Cannibals* (1960) as Salome Davis, *Splendor In The Grass* (1961) as Wilma Dean Loomis, for which she was nominated for a Best Actress Oscar, *West Side Story* (1961) as Maria, *Gypsy* (1962) as Louise Hovick aka Gypsy Rose Lee, *Love With The Proper Stranger* (1963) as Angie Rossini, *Sex And The Single Girl* (1964) as Helen Gurley Brown, *Inside Daisy Clover* (1965) as Daisy Clover, *The Great Race* (1965) as Maggie DuBois, *Bob & Carol & Ted & Alice* (1969) as

Carol Sanders, *Peeper* (1975) as Ellen Prendergast, *Meteor* (1979) as Tatiana Nikolaevna Donskaya and *The Last Married Couple In America* (1980) as Mari Thompson. After *Bob & Carol & Ted & Alice* she put her career on hold to raise a family with husband Robert 'RJ' Wagner, whom she had remarried at sea on July 16, 1972, having divorced him on April 27, 1962. They had originally married on December 28, 1957. Between marriages to Wagner she was married (May 30, 1969–August 4, 1971) to Richard Gregson. Praised by many, in 1966 the *Harvard Lampoon* nevertheless awarded a Natalie Wood Award for "the worst actress of this year, next year and the following year." Natalie turned up in person to collect the prize.

CAUSE: Despite three Oscar nominations it is because of the manner of her death that Natalie Wood is now most remembered. She was filming *Brainstorm* (1983) with Christopher Walken when she drowned off the coast of Catalina. She was 43. That much is certain but how she came to be in the water is still something of a mystery, since she suffered from hydrophobia. Prior to beginning *Brainstorm* she began a strict diet and exercise regimen. At the time Wagner had the successful television series *Hart To Hart* running and gossips linked him romantically to his co-star Stefanie Powers. Arriving on location in Raleigh, North Carolina, for her film, gossips then suggested that Wood had become interested in the equally married Christopher Walken. *Brainstorm* was supposed to be Walken's second attempt at becoming a major star after the critical and commercial disaster that was *Heaven's Gate* (1980). Walken's wife accompanied him on the shoot and RJ flew down twice to spend the weekend with his wife and she went to California for the other two weekends so if an affair/affairs were being conducted, all parties were remarkably relaxed about the situation. The film company returned to Los Angeles and the rumour mill went into overdrive. However, no one on the set ever reported hard facts linking Wood and Walken. During filming William Holden, lover of RJ's *Hart To Hart* co-star Stefanie Powers, was found dead in his home. He had died after falling over and gashing his head while drunk. On Thanksgiving (November 26) 1981 the Robert Wagners held a party. Christopher Walken was one of the guests and it is thought then that the couple invited him to spend the weekend on their boat, *Splendour*, in Catalina. Walken's wife had gone to Connecticut and he accepted the offer. At 1.15am on November 29, 1981, Wagner called the coast guard to alert them to a missing person in *Valiant*, an 11-foot dinghy. An air-sea rescue operation began but it wasn't until 7.44am that the 'missing person' was discovered near Blue Cavern Point. It was Natalie Wood and she was dead. Hollywood pathologist Thomas Noguchi explained that Natalie had fallen into the sea while trying to get into the dinghy. She was wearing a red jacket that had become waterlogged, leaving her unable to get into the craft and had tried to paddle it to shore but exhaustion and hypothermia overcame her and she drowned. But why was she trying to leave the boat? The theories are many and varied and ultimately unsatisfactory. One had it that Wagner had found his wife in a compromising situation with Walken and she had fled the yacht and fell into the sea where she drowned. Another, even more unlikely, had Wood catching Walken and Wagner together and the shock causing her to fall overboard. We are never likely to know for sure.

FURTHER READING: *Natalie: A Memoir By Her Sister* – Lana Wood (New York: Dell, 1984); *Natalie & RJ* – Warren G. Harris (London: Sphere, 1989).

Peggy Wood

Born February 9, 1892
Died March 18, 1978

Leather-lunged singer-actress. Born in Brooklyn, New York, the daughter of a journalist, Margaret Wood studied singing under Arthur Van der Linde and later under Madame Calvé before making her stage début on November 7, 1910, at the New York Theater in *Naughty Marietta*. It was the start of what would be a phenomenally long career that reached its apotheosis when she was nominated for a Best Supporting Actress Academy Award for her performance as the Mother Abbess singing 'Climb Ev'ry Mountain' in *The Sound Of Music* (1965). A stage regular, she made few films but they included *Almost A Husband* (1919) as Eva McElwyn, *Wonder Of Women* (1929) as Brigitte, *Handy Andy* (1934) as Ernestine Yates, *Jalna* (1935) as Meg, *A Star Is Born* (1937) as Miss Phillips, *Call It A Day* (1937) as Ethel Francis, *Magnificent Doll* (1946) as Mrs Payne and *Dream Girl* (1948) as Lucy Allerton. For eight years from 1949 she played Marta Hansen in the television series *Mama*. Peggy Wood was married twice – to John Van Alstyn Weaver, who predeceased her, and then to Lieutenant-Colonel William Henry Walling.

CAUSE: She died aged 86 from a stroke at her home, 1022 Sunset Road, Stamford, Connecticut.

Edward Woodward, OBE

Born June 1, 1930
Died November 16, 2009

Screen spy. Born at Croydon, Surrey, the only child of a chicken farmer-turned metal worker, Edward Albert Arthur Woodward – Teddy to his friends – won first prize in a talent contest at Wallington, Surrey when he was five. He thought he had won a silver penknife, until it began peeling to reveal a dull, base metal. It taught him a valuable lesson: "You start doing deals with Americans, particularly the big

Hollywood ones, and you'll appreciate the story about the silver penknife." At 16 he joined RADA (he was their youngest student), which allowed him to give up his job as a sanitation engineer, and that same year began his acting career on the stage. A versatile actor, he appeared in Shakespeare, musicals (in 1964 he starred as Charles Condomine in the Broadway musical *High Spirits*, which was based on the Nöel Coward play *Blithe Spirit* and directed by Coward himself) and recorded more than a dozen albums of songs, as well as three albums of poetry and 14 books. In 1962, he appeared in Charles Dyer's comedy *Rattle Of A Simple Man*, in which he played a sexually inhibited, effeminate man who spends an evening with a prostitute. The show was a hit but when it moved to Broadway in 1963, it flopped, but Woodward received rave reviews. "Mr Woodward's Percy is all but perfect," Howard Taubman of *The New York Times* wrote. "He seems so truly the troubled, fearful middle-aged mother's boy from Manchester that one forgets he is an actor. He speaks Mr Dyer's lines as if he had just invented them, and even the way he moves and wears his dull, respectable clothes are expressions of character." However, it was for his roles as disgruntled secret agents on television that he became celebrated on both sides of the Atlantic. From 1967 to 1972 he was the eponymous Callan, a counter-intelligence agent often hired for his skills as an assassin. From 1985 to 1989, a bewigged Woodward was Robert McCall, a former intelligence agency officer, who set himself up as the last resort to help people who have no one else to turn to. McCall placed advertisements in the newspaper: "Got a problem? Odds against you? Call the Equalizer." He received five Emmy nominations and won a Golden Globe (in February 1987) for his role as Robert McCall. "Edward was brilliant in his portrayal of Robert McCall," said Richard Lindheim, the co-creator of the series. "One of the reasons for it is you felt beneath what he was doing the sadness and the pain that had driven him to do this. The brilliance of his performance was not always what he said but the emotion in his eyes and in his behaviour. And that's the real mark of a wonderful actor: the ability to convey emotion and have you understand his feelings without having to say a line of dialogue." The role made Woodward a rich man but badly affected his health. He smoked 100 cigarettes a day to cope with the strain of working 20-hour days. It caused him to have a major heart attack. In 1973 he played Sergeant Neil Howie, a virgin policeman, who investigates the disappearance of a young girl on an island of pagans and is burned alive for his troubles in the cult horror film *The Wicker Man*, opposite Sir Christopher Lee and a naked Britt Ekland. Director Robin Hardy said, "He was one of the greatest actors of his generation, without any question, with a broad career on American television as well as British film. He was an absolute star of *The Wicker Man*. He was an extremely nice human being." The following year Woodward reprised his role as Callan in a film version. His other well-known film was Bruce Beresford's acclaimed *Breaker Morant* (1980) in which he played the lead. The film was the story of three Australian lieutenants on trial for murdering Boer prisoners during the Boer War. "He was sensational in that part," said Beresford. "He's an actor with a tremendous emotional range." In 1990–1991 Woodward played an English mystery writer and amateur sleuth in *Over My Dead Body*. He later appeared in *Common As Muck*, *The Bill* (2008) and *EastEnders* as Tommy Clifford for six episodes in 2009. On July 30, 1952 he married the actress Venetia Barrett by whom he had three children: Tim (b. London, April 24, 1953), Peter (b. London, January 24, 1956) and Sarah (b. April 3, 1963).

They divorced on December 1, 1986. His second wife (on January 17, 1987) was the actress Michele Dotrice, a daughter of the actor Roy Dotrice, by whom he had a daughter Emily Beth (b. 1983). All his children are actors. CAUSE: In 1996 5'9" Woodward underwent triple bypass surgery. Seven years later, he was diagnosed with prostate cancer in 2003. Woodward died at the Royal Cornwall Hospital, Truro, Cornwall from pneumonia, heart problems and other ailments. He was 79.

Monty Woolley

Born August 17, 1888
Died May 6, 1963
'The Beard'. Born in Manhattan's Bristol Hotel (which his father owned), Edgar Montillion Woolley was indulged materially as a child, riding ponies and wearing a Little Lord Fauntleroy suit. He was educated at Yale (1907–1911) and Harvard (1911–1914) and developed a cultured, refined voice that made him a natural on Broadway. However, before he moved to the Great White Way (in 1936 when he was in his late forties) he worked as a drama teacher, numbering Thornton Wilder among his students. He made his theatrical and cinematic débuts in the same year, appearing in *Ladies In Love* (1936). He made a name for himself playing gregarious or talkative characters. His best-known role on the stage and subsequently in film was that of acidic theatre critic Sheridan Whiteside (based on Alexander Woollcott) in *The Man Who Came To Dinner* (1942). However, the Academy ignored him, though he was Oscar nominated for *The Pied Piper* (1942) as Howard and Colonel Smollett in *Since You Went Away* (1944). His other films included: *Live, Love And Learn* (1937) as Mr Charles C. Bawltitude, *Nothing Sacred* (1937) (uncredited) as Dr Vunch, *Three Comrades* (1938) as Dr Jaffe, *Lord Jeff* (1938) as a jeweller, *Arsène Lupin*

Returns (1938) as Georges Bouchet, *Everybody Sing* (1938) as John Flemming, *Young Dr Kildare* (1938) as Dr Lane-Porteus, *Artists And Models Abroad* (1938) as Gantvoort, *Never Say Die* (1939) as Dr Schmidt, *Midnight* (1939) as Judge, *Man About Town* (1939) as Henri Dubois, *Dancing Co-Ed* (1939) as Professor Lange, *Life Begins At Eight-Thirty* (1942) as Madden Thomas, *Holy Matrimony* (1943) as Priam Farli, *Irish Eyes Are Smiling* (1944) as Edgar Brawley, *Molly And Me* (1945) as John Graham, the biopic of his close friend Cole Porter *Night And Day* (1946) in which he played himself, *Miss Tatlock's Millions* (1948) as Miles Tatlock, *As Young As You Feel* (1951) as John Hodges and *Kismet* (1955) as Omar. He grew his famous beard when he was 27 after meeting his hero, the writer George Bernard Shaw. "I am always mistaken for a Grand Duke or a Supreme Court Justice. My beard gets me the best service in the world. Waiters scurry at the wag of my whiskers. I am listened to with reverence. Everywhere, people stand aside to let a Great Man pass. Best of all, I never have to shave." He claimed to love loneliness, always living on his own and even dining alone in restaurants: "If anyone speaks to me, I bark." An unmarried homosexual, he would often go cruising for gay pick-ups with his close friend, Cole Porter. Woolley supposedly inspired the Porter song 'It's De-Lovely'. Sailing into Rio de Janeiro harbour with Porter and his wife, the composer said of the sunrise, "It's delightful." His wife added, "It's delicious", causing the naturally sarcastic Woolley to chime, "It's de-lovely." CAUSE: Woolley died aged 74 from kidney and heart problems in Saratoga Springs, New York.

Fay Wray

Born September 15, 1907
Died August 8, 2004
Hollywood's first 'Scream Queen'.

Despite making more than 90 films it is a scene in which she is held in King Kong's paw for which Fay Wray will be forever remembered. Vina Fay Wray, the fourth child in a family of six, was born on a ranch near Cardston, Alberta, in the foothills of the Canadian Rockies. Her mother, Vina Marguerite Jones, had married young to a man who was impotent. To escape the horror she ran away to Canada with Joseph Herbert Wray, an ingenious if feckless wanderer who had been born in Hull. Wray was full of ideas and enthusiasm but usually they failed to materialise into anything substantial. He established a sawmill that failed. The family moved back to America, first to Arizona, where a small farm was also unsuccessful, then to Salt Lake City, Utah. He invented a can-opener for condensed milk, but the factory making it went bust. Meanwhile, Fay made her first theatrical appearance as Mrs Santa Claus in the school play. Following another move, to the small Mormon town of Lark, Joseph Wray drifted off, looking for work elsewhere. The Mormon community rallied and provided for the family. Fay's mother, having already introduced her daughter to silent films, entered her in a newspaper competition. The prize was a screen test and Fay was the winner. Tragedy was to strike the family, however. Her eldest sister died in the flu epidemic of 1918 and, because Fay's own health was considered frail, she was somewhat recklessly sent, at the age of 14, to live in Los Angeles with a young photographer named William Mortensen, who was a friend of Willow, her second sister. At the local junior high school, and afterwards at Hollywood High, she excelled academically and performed in school productions at the Hollywood Bowl. Her mother, hearing that Mortensen had taken photographs of Fay, jumped to the wrong conclusions, travelled to Los Angeles, broke his glass negatives and whisked her daughter off to a boarding house. "My mother was ridiculously oppressive without meaning to be," Fay recalled. "She wanted me to have a career, but she wanted me to be untouched by it in any way." One of the film people to whom Mortensen had introduced her gave Fay the leading role in a small film. This was followed by a series of bit parts in silent films in which she was hired purely for her looks. When she left school, she applied to the Hal Roach Studio, and was given a six-month contract. She appeared in two-reel Westerns, sharing a dressing room with Janet Gaynor and she played opposite Stan Laurel, who had not yet teamed up with Oliver Hardy. In 1928 Fay Wray starred in what she always thought her best film, Erich von Stroheim's hugely expensive and uncompleted masterpiece, *The Wedding March*. She resisted the director's sexual advances without too much difficulty or subsequent ill feeling, and she learned a great deal from him. (Much later, she refused to watch *Sunset Boulevard* because she thought it disrespectful that he should play a butler.) In the same year she made *Legion Of The Condemned*, starring Gary Cooper, whom she liked but remembered as "very stiff, rather like part of the furniture". The film which featured out-takes from the earlier *Wings* (1927) was a box office success and Paramount hoped that Cooper and Wray would become their equivalent of Fox's popular team of Janet Gaynor and Charles Farrell. Despite promoting them as the "Glorious Young Lovers" it was not to be although, with four eventual appearances opposite him, she became his leading lady almost by default. Nor did they become an item off screen. Cooper was involved with Evelyn Brent and Wray was seeing the film's scriptwriter. John Monk Saunders (b. Hinckley, Minnesota, November 22, 1895) was a handsome, charming, former Rhodes Scholar who had been a flying instructor during the

First World War and had wept when he heard of the Armistice, because he would never now see action. Captivated by Wray's "Nefertiti eyes", he had a failed marriage behind him and was much more disturbed than Fay realised when she embarked on the relationship with him. While she was on location in Maryland, filming *The First Kiss* with Gary Cooper, two incidents occurred that changed her life. In the first she was filming in Chesapeake Bay when she fell overboard and only a fully clothed Gary Cooper diving in to save her prevented tragedy. The second was tragic. She learned that her brother Vivien had died, ostensibly by accident, probably by suicide. Saunders arrived to comfort her, and, with Cooper as witness, they were married on June 15, 1928 at Calvary Methodist Church in Easton, Maryland. For the first time she felt independent of her mother. In 1929 Fay Wray made *The Four Feathers*; in 1930 *The Texan* and in 1931 *Dirigible*. Although late in life she was to refer to the coming of talkies as "a kind of rudeness" which led to her being "tossed on to the commercial heap", she appeared to take the development in her stride. Wray went to New York to star in Saunders' musical play *Nikki*, which flopped (opening at the Longacre Theatre on September 29, 1931, it closed on October 31 after just 39 performances) but which introduced her to an actor called Archie Leach. At the suggestion of Wray and Saunders he contemplated changing his name to Cary Lockwood, the name of his character in the play. The studio was concerned that Lockwood was too long a name to fit on a marquee and there was already a Harold Lockwood working in films. They had a list of alternatives – short, snappy names – and he picked his new surname – Grant. By this time Wray had discovered that Saunders was a compulsive womaniser and a periodic drunk. On November 10, 1931 at the

Sala D'Oro at the Biltmore Hotel in Los Angeles, Saunders won an Oscar for Best Original Screenplay for *The Dawn Patrol* (1930). He was in the midst of a legal battle at the time. He said, "This is indeed a crazy business where I am being sued for plagiarism on one hand and given the statuette for originality on the other." She made 10 films in Hollywood, one of which was *King Kong* (1933), which had a 10-week shooting schedule spread between June 1932 and February 1933. It saved RKO from bankruptcy, although nobody then, including Fay Wray, had any idea of its potential impact. For the rest of her life, she was asked about the special effects. King Kong himself was just 18 inches high and made of rabbit fur and moulded sponge rubber on an aluminium frame. The parts of him that "interacted" with humans – a lower leg, a foot and a paw – were built on a large scale. The paw that lifted her ten feet above the studio floor was eight feet long and, when she felt that she was slipping, she was genuinely frightened. It is said that Wray had been one of a dozen actresses auditioned for the part of Ann Darrow, and that she had been selected because she produced the loudest scream. "*King Kong* director Merian C. Cooper called me into his office and showed me sketches of jungle scenes and told me, 'You're going to have the tallest, darkest leading man in Hollywood,'" she recalled. "Naturally, I thought Clark Gable. But then he showed me this sketch of a giant ape up the side of the Empire State Building. He said, 'There's your leading man.'" Wray originally believed that Cooper was joking. Her auburn hair was covered in a blonde wig and that image stayed with her. She remembered, "At the première I wasn't too impressed. I thought there was too much screaming. I didn't realise then that King Kong and I were going to be together for the rest of our lives and longer." The film was released on March 2, 1933. The set of Skull Island was originally used in *The King Of Kings* (1927) and again in *She* (1935) before being burned as Atlanta in *Gone With The Wind* (1939). Throughout 1933 and 1934 she began a new film every fourth Friday, which was how Hollywood then worked. Among the best was *The Bowery* with Wallace Beery and Jackie Cooper. Reflecting on her career eight years before her death, Wray lamented what she saw as the demise of romance in cinema. Of screen kissing, she remarked, "These days, they just chew each other. Today there is no such thing as a really wonderful embrace. You never saw Ronald Colman taking a great big bite out of someone." She herself, when kissing on screen, always kept her mouth closed. Of silent films, she said, "Every little movement by Charlie Chaplin or Mary Pickford was compelling and wonderful. They held us close to their hearts. Every time we saw a silent film, we were drawn by the fact that the caring was inherent." As for modern pictures, Wray seldom watched them, "I get put off by the previews I see on television. You seem to see nothing but gasoline explosions." Life with the volatile Saunders became desperately erratic: sometimes sweet, sometimes tormenting. In 1935 they travelled to England ("I really came to get away from horror films," Wray said), and she appeared with Jack Hulbert and Ralph Richardson in *Bulldog Jack* and with Claude Rains in *The Clairvoyant*. Saunders showed her Oxford and took her to the Boat Race (Cambridge won). She returned to Hollywood for the birth of her daughter, Susan Cary Saunders, on September 24, 1936; but in February 1938 she and Saunders separated. They divorced in December 1939. Wray busied herself with films and also with repertory productions in New England. On one occasion while she was away, Saunders took Susan away with him. Fay traced and recovered her daughter with the assistance of Colonel William Donovan, who was to create the Office of Strategic Services, which became the CIA. Theatrical work improved her skill and introduced her to intelligent new people. Sinclair Lewis fell for her heavily, and pursued her relentlessly; Howard Hughes courted her briefly. She had a protracted affair with Clifford Odets, which ended for reasons she never quite understood. On March 11, 1940 in Fort Myers, Florida, John Monk Saunders hanged himself. Her second, and much happier, marriage (on August 23, 1942 at the St Regis Hotel in New York) was to the distinguished screenwriter Robert Riskin (b. New York, March 30, 1897). His credits included *It Happened One Night*, *Mr Deeds Goes To Town*, *Lost Horizon* and *You Can't Take It With You*. "Be good to her," she overheard Cary Grant say to Riskin. "I was so in love with her." She and Riskin had a son, Bobby (b. New York, July 23, 1943), and a daughter, Vicki (b. Los Angeles, California, 1945). During the Second World War, while Fay found new openings in radio drama, Riskin was in Europe working for the Office of War Information. The tranquil post-war years ended when Riskin suffered a debilitating stroke in 1951. Wray tended him devotedly until his death on September 20, 1955 in Beverly Hills. In 1971 she married Dr Sanford Rothenburg, whom she had met in the hospital where Riskin was being treated. Her last film was *Summer Love* in 1958, but in the mid-Eighties she wrote a play about her parents, which was produced in New Hampshire with her daughter Susan playing the role of Fay's mother. Her last appearance was alongside Henry Fonda in the TV film *Gideon's Trumpet* in 1980.

CAUSE: Fay Wray died aged 96 from natural causes in Manhattan, New York. She lived in Trump Tower. She is buried in the Hollywood Forever Cemetery, California. A card that came with lilies read, "Fay – We will never forget you. From everyone at the Empire State Building." On September 26, 2004 about 100 people went to the West Village for a private tribute at the cinema on Houston Street.

Teresa Wright

Born October 27, 1918
Died March 8, 2005

Too principled. 5′3″ Muriel Teresa Wright was born in Harlem, New York, the daughter of Arthur Wright, an insurance salesman, and Margaret Epsy. Not long after her birth, her parents went their separate ways and relatives raised her. When she was eight, her father came back into her life and he encouraged her interest in the arts and she appeared as Little Eva in a production of *Uncle Tom's Cabin*. She was educated at Rose Haven School for Girls, near Tenafly, New Jersey, and Columbia High School in Maplewood, New Jersey. She spent the summers of 1937 and 1938 doing work experience at the Wharf Theatre in Provincetown, Massachusetts. In autumn 1938 she was hired as an understudy to Dorothy McGuire in the lead role of Emily for the Broadway opening of Thornton Wilder's *Our Town*. She changed her name taking her middle name because there was already a Muriel Wright in Equity. In the summer of 1939 she was selected as the ingénue in Broadway's *Life With Father*. Samuel Goldwyn saw her and signed to a five-year contract. He said, "I knew she was a great actress before the end of the first act." Wright insisted that a no-cheesecake clause be written into the deal. She would "not be required to pose for photographs in a bathing suit" or "running on a beach with her hair flying in the wind". She would not have "to assume an athletic stance while pretending to hit something with a bow and arrow" nor would she pose "in shorts, playing with a cocker spaniel, digging in a garden, or whipping up a meal". Wright was nominated for an Oscar for her performance as Alexandra

Giddens, the daughter of Bette Davis in William Wyler's *The Little Foxes* (1941). She was loaned to MGM where she reunited with Wyler in *Mrs Miniver* (1942) and won a Best Supporting Actress Oscar for the film. She played Eleanor, the wife of New York Yankees baseball legend Lou Gehrig who suffered from Motor Neurone disease, in *The Pride Of The Yankees* (1942). The role garnered her third Oscar nomination, the only actor ever nominated for an Oscar for their first three films. That August *Time* hailed her as "Hollywood's best young dramatic actress". The following year, she was loaned to Universal Pictures to play Charlie Newton, a small-town girl who learns her uncle has a chilling secret in Alfred Hitchcock's *Shadow Of A Doubt* (1943). She reteamed with Gary Cooper in *Casanova Brown* (1944) and again with Willie Wyler for *The Best Years Of Our Lives* (1946), which won eight Oscars. In 1948 Goldwyn sacked her for refusing to co-operate with his PR department. Her income dropped from $5,000 a week and $125,000 per film to $20,000 per film and no weekly income. The offers did not come in. "I was going to be Joan of Arc," she told one interviewer. "And all I did was prove that I was an actress who would work for less money." In the Fifties she began to appear on the new medium of television and returned to Broadway in 1957. She appeared sporadically in plays thereafter. On May 23, 1942 she married, as his second wife, scriptwriter Niven Busch (b. New York, April 26, 1903, d. San Francisco, California, August 25, 1991 of heart failure). They had two children – Niven Terrence Busch (b. December 2, 1944, weighing 7lbs 4oz) and Mary Kelly Busch (b. September 12, 1947, weighing 5lbs 3oz) – before their November 25, 1952 divorce. She married, also as his second wife, the playwright Robert Anderson (b. Manhattan, New York, April 28, 1917, d. Manhattan,

New York, February 9, 2009 of complications of pneumonia and Alzheimer's disease) on December 11, 1959. They later divorced in the early Seventies, remarried, and divorced again.

CAUSE: Wright died in New Haven, Connecticut, aged 86, from a heart attack.

William Wyler

Born July 1, 1902
Died July 28, 1981

Star director. Born in Muhlhausen, Germany, Wyler was a business student who didn't even consider a career in films until he was asked to visit the States by his relative Carl Laemmle. He began working at Universal as a publicist before moving behind the camera to become a highly successful director, winning Oscars for *Mrs Miniver* (1942), *The Best Years Of Our Lives* (1946) and *Ben-Hur* (1959). During World War II he served with the air force, making documentaries. After the war he worked on *Carrie* (1952), *Roman Holiday* (1953), *Friendly Persuasion* (1956), *Funny Girl* (1968), and *The Liberation Of L.B. Jones* (1970). In 1965 he was awarded the Irving G. Thalberg Award for lifetime achievement. Ten of his films earned Best Film nominations. Wyler was the love of Bette Davis' life. They met in 1931 when she auditioned unsuccessfully for one of his films, *A House Divided*. In 1938 Wyler was divorced from actress Margaret Sullavan (whom he had married on November 25, 1934) and began an affair with Davis during the filming of *Jezebel*. The affair ended in October 1938 when he sent her an ultimatum in a letter – divorce her husband, Ham Nelson, and marry him or he would marry someone else. The following week he married actress Margaret Tallichet. The next film Wyler and Davis made together was, ironically, entitled *The Letter* (1940).

CAUSE: Wyler died in Beverly Hills,

California, aged 79 from natural causes. He was buried at Forest Lawn Memorial-Parks, 1712 Glendale Avenue, Glendale, California 91209.

Jane Wyman

(SARAH JANE MAYFIELD)
Born January 5, 1917
Died September 10, 2007

The first Mrs Ronald Reagan. Jane Wyman was born in St Joseph, Missouri, the daughter of Manning Jefferies Mayfield (b. 1894, d. San Francisco, California, January 21, 1922 of pneumonia) and (Gladys) Hope Christian (1895–1960). The couple married at Kansas City on May 17, 1916 but filed for divorce in October 1921. The child was fostered by Richard D. Fulks (b. 1862, d. March 23, 1928), the chief of detectives in Saint Joseph, and his second wife Emma Weymann (b. Germany 1866, d. 1951). Her foster parents were in late middle age when she went to live with them and they were old-fashioned. "I was raised with such strict discipline that it was years before I could reason myself out of the bitterness I brought from my childhood," she said years later. For a long time, her date of birth was a matter of mystery. The most commonly given date was January 4, 1914 but when she went to infant school on September 10, 1923 her foster mother listed her birthday as January 28, 1917. In 1980 Wyman announced that her correct date of birth was January 5, 1914 making her one of the very few actors who actually added rather than subtracted years from their age. In fact, her birth certificate states that she was indeed born on January 5 but the natal year was 1917. In January 1922 Mrs Fulks and Sarah Jane visited California to see her natural father before he died. They stayed for three months. They returned in 1928 where they lived for two years. Around this time the youngster developed an interest in performing. In 1930 under the name Jane Durrell,

Wyman began singing on the radio, probably adding three years to her age so that she could work legally. By 1934 she was back in Hollywood landing bit parts in films. Warner Bros signed her on May 6, 1936 to a $60-a-week contract on condition that she changed her name and thus she became Jane Wyman. For two years Warners cast 5'2½" Wyman in only B-pictures but she was ambitious. On June 29, 1937 she married 35-year-old divorced Myron Futterman, the owner of a dress factory, but Wyman filed for divorce on November 10, 1938 citing mental cruelty. The divorce became final on December 5. In 1938 Wyman co-starred with an amiable but dim actor called Ronald Reagan in *Brother Rat* (1938), and its sequel *Brother Rat And A Baby* (1940). He asked her to accompany him to the premiere of *Second Fiddle* (released June 30, 1939), a Sonja Henie film and they began to date regularly. On October 4, 1939 Wyman was rushed to Hollywood Receiving Hospital with what was said to be a stomach complaint although years later Nancy Reagan claimed that it had been a suicide attempt to blackmail Reagan into marrying her. However it happened, they married on January 24, 1940 at the Wee Kirk o'Heather wedding chapel in Glendale, California. They had three children: Maureen (b. Los Angeles, California, January 4, 1941, d. Granite Bay, California, August 8, 2001 of cancer); an adopted son, Michael (b. March 14, 1945) and a third daughter who died the day after her premature birth at the Queen of Angels hospital in Los Angeles on June 24, 1947. Reagan and Wyman separated in May 1948 and divorced on June 28, 1948 becoming final on July 19, 1949 after nine years and 176 days of marriage. Reagan refused to discuss the break-up but Wyman said that it was due to his increasing political ambitions and her failure to show interest in them. In 1945 Wyman had appeared with Ray

Milland in *The Lost Weekend* and in 1946 she was nominated for a Best Actress Oscar for her role as Ma Baxter in *The Yearling* (1946). Two years later she won the Oscar for playing deaf-mute rape victim Belinda MacDonald in *Johnny Belinda* (1948). While preparing, Wyman studied at a school for the deaf for six months and learned sign language. She memorised the lines of the other actors and performed wearing earplugs. Her other films included: Alfred Hitchcock's *Stage Fright* (1950), *The Glass Menagerie* (1950), Frank Capra's *Here Comes The Groom* (1951), *The Blue Veil* (1951) for which she was nominated for an Oscar, Michael Curtiz's *The Story Of Will Rogers* (1952), *Just For You* (1952) opposite Bing Crosby, *So Big* (1953), *Magnificent Obsession* (1954) for which she received an Academy Award nomination, *Lucy Gallant* (1955), *All That Heaven Allows* (1955), *Miracle In The Rain* (1956), *Holiday For Lovers* (1959), *Pollyanna* (1960) and her last film, *How To Commit Marriage* (1969). In 1955 she had her own television show, *Jane Wyman Presents The Fireside Theatre*. In 1981 she began playing the matriarch Angela Channing Erikson Stavros Agretti in the soap *Falcon Crest*, a role she played for nine years. Wyman was nominated on six occasions for a *Soap Opera Digest* Award, and in 1984 she won a Golden Globe for Best Performance by an Actress in a TV Series Drama. After her divorce from Reagan, Wyman twice married Hollywood music director and composer Fred Karger (1916–1979). Their first marriage was at El Montecito Presbyterian Church in Santa Barbara on November 1, 1952. They split up almost exactly two years later on November 7, 1954. The decree nisi was issued on December 7, 1954 and the decree absolute on December 30, 1955. They remarried on March 11, 1961, and re-divorced on March 9, 1965. Wyman later converted to the Roman Catholic Church and spent many of her final years with her close friend Loretta Young.

CAUSE: Wyman died in her sleep after suffering from diabetes and arthritis at her home at the Rancho Mirage Country Club. She was 90. A member of the Dominican order of the Catholic Church, Wyman was buried in a nun's habit. She was buried at Forest Lawn Mortuary and Memorial, 69855 East Ramon Road, Cathedral City, California CA92234.

Ed Wynn

(ISAIAH EDWIN LEOPOLD)
Born November 9, 1886
Died June 19, 1966

'The Perfect Fool'. Born in Philadelphia, Pennsylvania, Wynn left home aged 15 to join a touring show and later (1914) worked at the Ziegfeld Follies and also wrote, directed and produced as well as performing. He made his film début in *Rubber Heels* (1927) playing a character with the unlikely name of Homer Thrush. In the Thirties he was a popular radio star but failed to translate that popularity to film in such movies as *Follow The Leader* (1930) as Crickets and *The Chief* (1933) as Henry Summers. It wasn't until the advent of television that he became a star with *The Ed Wynn Show* in 1949. His career was energised when he was cast opposite his son in the *Playhouse 90* episode *Requiem For A Heavyweight*. That led to work as a character actor in *The Great Man* (1956) as Paul Beaseley, *Marjorie Morningstar* (1958) as Uncle Sampson, *The Diary Of Anne Frank* (1959) as Mr Dussell, for which he was nominated for an Oscar, *The Absent Minded Professor* (1961) as the fire chief, *Babes In Toyland* (1961) as the toy maker, *Son Of Flubber* (1963) as A.J. Allen, *Mary Poppins* (1964) as Uncle Albert, *Those Calloways* (1965) as Ed Parker, *The Greatest Story Ever Told* (1965) as Old Aram, *Dear Brigitte* (1965) as the captain, *That Darn Cat!* (1965) as Mr

Hofstedder and *The Gnome-Mobile* (1967) as Rufus. Wynn was married three times. On September 5, 1914, he married Hilda Keenan, the daughter of a silent film star. They had one son. The couple was divorced on May 13, 1937. On June 15, of the same year, he married dancer Frieda Mierse in New York City. They divorced on December 12, 1939 (the day Douglas Fairbanks died). On July 31, 1946, he married Dorothy Elizabeth Nesbitt in the Little Church of the West in Las Vegas. They divorced on March 1, 1955.

CAUSE: The 79-year-old Wynn died in Beverly Hills, California, from cancer. He was buried at Forest Lawn Memorial-Parks, 1712 Glendale Avenue, Glendale, California 91209.

Keenan Wynn

(FRANCIS XAVIER ALOYSIUS WYNN)
Born July 27, 1916
Died October 14, 1986

Likable, gruff character. Born in New York, the son of Ed Wynn, Keenan (his mother's maiden name) was signed by MGM to a long-term contract in 1942 and found himself playing a veritable smorgasbord of roles in dramas, comedies, musicals and melodramas. He was probably most unforgettable as Lippy, one of the gangsters in *Kiss Me Kate* (1953), who sings 'Brush Up Your Shakespeare'. Following the end of his contract he moved to New York, where he found a niche on television including the memorable *Requiem For A Heavyweight*, which saw him cast opposite his father. A later generation will remember him as the second Willard 'Digger' Barnes on the glossy soap *Dallas*. Wynn's films included: *Northwest Rangers* (1942) as Slip O'Mara, *Somewhere I'll Find You* (1942) as Sergeant Tom Purdy, *For Me And My Gal* (1942) as Eddie Melton, *See Here, Private Hargrove* (1944) as Private Thomas Mulvehill, *Marriage Is A Private Affair* (1944) as Major Bob Wilton, *Between Two Women* (1944) as

Tobey, *Since You Went Away* (1944) as Lieutenant Solomon, *Without Love* (1945) as Quentin Ladd, *What Next, Corporal Hargrove?* (1945) reprising his role as Private Thomas Mulvehill, *Week-End At The Waldorf* (1945) as Oliver Webson, *No Leave, No Love* (1946) as Slinky, *Easy To Wed* (1946) as Warren Haggerty, *Song Of The Thin Man* (1947) as Clarence 'Clinker' Krause, *My Dear Secretary* (1948) as Ronnie Hastings, *The Three Musketeers* (1948) as Planchet, *Neptune's Daughter* (1949) as Joe Backett, *Annie Get Your Gun* (1950) as Charlie Davenport, *Love That Brute* (1950) as Bugs, *Kind Lady* (1951) as Edwards, *Angels In The Outfield* (1951) as Fred Bayles, *Texas Carnival* (1951) as Dan Sabinas, *Holiday For Sinners* (1952) as Joe Piavi, *All The Brothers Were Valiant* (1953) as Silva, *Battle Circus* (1953) as Sergeant Orvil Statt, *Tennessee Champ* (1954) as Willy Wurble, *Shack Out On 101* (1955) as George, *The Glass Slipper* (1955) as Kovin, *The Naked Hills* (1956) as Sam Wilkins, *The Man In The Gray Flannel Suit* (1956) as Caesar Gardella, *Johnny Concho* (1956) as Barney Clark, *Joe Butterfly* (1957) as Harold Hathaway, *The Deep Six* (1957) as Lieutenant Commander Mike Edge, *That Kind Of Woman* (1959) as Harry Corwin, *King Of The Roaring 20s – The Story Of Arnold Rothstein* (1961) as Tom Fowler, *The Absent Minded Professor* (1961) as Alonzo Hawk, *Bikini Beach* (1964) as Harvey Huntington Honeywagon III, *Dr Strangelove Or: How I Learned To Stop Worrying And Love The Bomb* (1964) as Colonel 'Bat' Guano, *The Patsy* (1964) as Harry Silver, *Honeymoon Hotel* (1964) as Mr Sampson, *The Great Race* (1965) as Hezekiah Sturdy, *Stagecoach* (1966) as Luke Plummer, *Promise Her Anything* (1966) as Angelo Carelli, *Around The World Under The Sea* (1966) as Hank Stahl, *The Night Of The Grizzly* (1966) as Jed Curry, *Run Like A Thief* (1967) as Willy Gore, *Warning Shot* (1967) as Sergeant Ed Musso, *Finian's Rainbow* (1968) as Senator Billboard Rawkins, *80 Steps To Jonah* (1969) as Barney Glover, *Pretty Maids All In A Row* (1971) as Chief John Poldaski, *Snowball Express* (1972) as Martin Ridgeway, *Jeremiah Of Jacob's Neck* (1975) as Jeremiah Starbuck, *The Shaggy D.A.* (1976) as John Slade, *Orca* (1977) as Novak, *Sunburn* (1979) as Mark Elmes, *Just Tell Me What You Want* (1980) as Seymour Berger, *Wavelength* (1983) as Dan and *Black Moon Rising* (1986) as Iron John. Wynn's hobby was riding a motorcycle fast and in March 1945 he was involved in a near fatal crash when he fractured his skull, sprained his back and broke his jaw in five places. Wynn was married several times. Firstly, he married Eve Abbott on September 30, 1938, and by her had two sons: Edmund known as Ned (b. New York, April 27, 1941) and screenwriter Tracy Keenan (b. Hollywood, California, February 28, 1945). They divorced on January 25, 1947, and four hours later she married Wynn's best friend, Van Johnson. Wynn, his ex-wife and Johnson had spent a lot of time with Peter Lawford, leading to speculation that all four were involved in some kind of sexual square. Wynn's ex-wife later stated that she had sex with Lawford but that her husband didn't. On January 11, 1949, Wynn married model Betty Jane Butler by proxy. They separated in 1952 and were divorced on June 29, 1953. She claimed Wynn was unconscionably close to his ex-wife. On January 8, 1954, Wynn married Shirley Jean Hudson in Puerto Rico. Six months later, they remarried at the Little Brown Church in the Valley in California. They had two daughters: Hilda (b. 1954) and Edwynna (b. February 2, 1960).

CAUSE: Wynn died aged 70 of cancer at his home in Brentwood, California. He was buried at Forest Lawn Memorial-Parks, 1712 Glendale Avenue, Glendale, California 91209.

Y

Gig Young
(BYRON ELSWORTH BARR)
Born November 4, 1913
Died October 19, 1978
Insecure hunk. Born in St. Cloud,
Minnesota, the son of a businessman
and an ex-schoolteacher, Young was the
third child. There was already a brother,
Donald, and a sister, Genevieve. In
1932 with the Depression ruining the
family venture, Young and his parents
moved to Washington DC. There
Young began acting with the Phil
Hayden Players and, to please his father,
unsuccessfully as it turned out, worked
for a local car firm. When he realised
that his father would remain stoically
unimpressed at whatever he did, Young
decided to give Hollywood a try.
Enrolling at the famous Pasadena
Playhouse he worked in a petrol station
amongst other jobs to keep his head
above water. He also auditioned for
studios whenever an open casting was
held. On August 2, 1940, he married
fellow Pasadena Playhouse student
Sheila Stapler and signed for Warner
Bros. He made his first film, credited
still as Byron Barr, playing a floor walker
in *Misbehaving Husbands* (1940). He
was later to claim that he excelled at
"corpses, unconscious bodies and
people snoring in spectacular epics".
The first of his roles to get him noticed
was in Barbara Stanwyck's *The Gay
Sisters* (1942) in which he played a
character called Gig Young. Taking the
good reviews to be an omen, he adopted
his character name as his own stage
name. The following year he worked
closely with another Hollywood great
when he appeared opposite Bette Davis
in *Old Acquaintance* (1943). They also
became acquainted off screen, having a
brief romantic interlude. It has been
suggested by some that Young had an
Oedipus complex and certainly he did
have affairs with a number of women
older than himself. (Perhaps it had
started early for he lost his virginity
when he was 16 years old to a
"slim-waisted, full-breasted"
28-year-old blonde, who followed him
home from basketball practice one
evening.) During World War II he
served with the US Coast Guard.
Following demob he returned to Warner
Bros but felt frustrated by what he saw
as the studio's lack of enthusiasm over
his career. Around this time he also
began an affair with another older
woman, drama teacher Sophie
Rosenstein (b. 1906). In 1947 his
contract was not renewed by Warner
Bros. A gulf had opened up between
Young and his wife and they divorced in
1949. The following year, he married
Sophie Rosenstein but she was to die of
cancer in November 1952. It was a
bittersweet year for Gig Young. Thanks
to Sophie's encouragement, he had
earned a role in *Come Fill The Cup*
(1951) as Boyd Copeland, which
earned him his first Academy Award
nomination. To help with his grief,
Young began to drink heavily. He had
affairs with stripper Sherry Britton and
actress Elaine Stritch and worked in
television and on Broadway. While
hosting *Warner Brothers Presents* on TV
he met actress Elizabeth Montgomery,
the daughter of actor Robert
Montgomery. Against her father's
express wishes, Elizabeth Montgomery
married Gig Young on 28 December,
1956. Two years later, he was Oscar
nominated again, for *Teacher's Pet*
(1958) but still felt he should be getting
leading roles not supporting ones.
Young returned to Broadway and to
alcohol with a vengeance as well as
infatuations with older women. It led to
his divorce in January 1963 from
Elizabeth Montgomery. He then turned
to the bottle with a vengeance. On
September 18, 1963, he married estate
agent Elaine Whitman (who would later

sell O.J. Simpson his infamous house at 360 Rockingham Avenue, Brentwood). Their daughter, Jennifer, was born in Los Angeles on April 21, 1964. Tall (5'7½"), blonde and beautiful, she grew up to be a singer and co-authored a book about Hollywood excesses. Her parents' marriage wasn't all sweetness and light. Gig spent heavily, drank heavily and began taking LSD. Elaine Young received a divorce on November 23, 1966. The last time Jennifer Young saw her father, she was one and a half years old. Alcohol took hold of Young and he began to put on weight. He went back to Broadway to appear in *There's A Girl In My Soup* and began an affair with actress Skye Aubrey (b. 1944) but when she proposed, he turned her down. It seemed as if there was no way for Young to go until his former agent wangled him the role of Rocky in *They Shoot Horses, Don't They?* (1969). It won Young an Oscar. Unfortunately, it turned out not to be the salvation of his career. His next part was playing the grandfather Hal Henderson in *Lovers And Other Strangers* (1970). He was often in court with Elaine Young over his failure to pay her their divorce settlement. He was sacked from *Blazing Saddles* (1974) and replaced by Gene Wilder and quickly gained a reputation, perhaps deserved, perhaps not, of unreliability. In 1977 he met German-born actress Kim Schmidt (b. 1947) on the set of *Game Of Death* (1978). They began a relationship and eventually married on September 27, 1978, at City Hall in New York.
CAUSE: Almost immediately after his fifth marriage, Young began to argue with his young wife. His career was at an end and his alcoholism was affecting his thought capacity. His will didn't leave everything to Kim, who taunted him about his inability to satisfy her in bed, and he was concerned about getting older. The Youngs lived at number 1BB in the trendy Osborne Apartments, 205 West 57th Street in New York. On October 18, 1978, he called a friend in Hollywood, bemoaned his fate and

asked her to collect him and take him back to the West Coast. She refused. The next day, Kim Young ordered some groceries from a local shop on the phone. At 2.30pm Gig Young loaded a .38 calibre Smith & Wesson gun, walked into the bedroom and shot his wife in the head. Then he turned the gun on himself, putting the barrel in his mouth and pulling the trigger. The corpses were discovered five hours later when the porter wondered why the groceries hadn't been collected. A diary in the apartment was open on September 27, 1978, and police found three more guns and 350 bullets secreted in the property. On October 26, 1978, Young's body was cremated in Beverly Hills.

Loretta Young
(GRETCHEN MICHAELA YOUNG)
Born January 6, 1913
Died August 12, 2000
'Attila the Nun'. 5'5" Loretta Young was born in Salt Lake City, Utah, one of three daughters of John Earl and Gladys Royal Young. There was also a son, Jackie. Another was the 5'4½" actress Sally Blane (b. Salida, Colorado, July 11, 1910 as Elizabeth Jane Young, d. Los Angeles, California, August 27, 1997 of cancer). The girls' parents' marriage fell apart in 1916 and Mrs Young relocated from Salt Lake City to Los Angeles, where she moved in with her sister, set up a theatrical boarding house and began to promote her daughters as juvenile performers in films. Mrs Young withdrew the children from work while they were being educated at the Ramona Convent in Alambra. John Young later joined his family but was caught in bed with the maid. Disgraced, he left the family and his daughters never saw him alive again. A half-sister, Georgiana Belzer (b. Los Angeles, September 30, 1923), would be born later from their mother's marriage to George Belzer. Gladys Young was the archetypal stage mother who lived her life vicariously through her daughters. All four were

soon appearing as extras in small roles, and a very youthful Loretta is to be seen briefly in *The Primrose Ring* (1917), *Sirens Of The Sea* (1917), *The Only Way* (1919), *White And Unmarried* (1921) and *The Sheik* (1921). According to showbiz legend, her big break came in 1927 when she answered a phone call from the director Mervyn LeRoy asking her 5'2" older sister Polly Ann (b. Denver, October 25, 1908, d. Los Angeles, California, January 21, 1997 of cancer) to audition for his film *Naughty But Nice* (1927). Loretta went along instead, got the role, and never looked back. That year Gretchen Young became Loretta Young thanks to Colleen Moore who said Loretta was the name of "the most beautiful doll I ever had". Her first real leading role was in *Laugh, Clown, Laugh* (1928) as Simonetta, a circus story in which she was the object of romantic rivalry between Lon Chaney and Nils Asther. The same year she successfully made the transition to talkies in *The Squall* (1929) as Irma, and signed a contract with Warners, where Darryl Zanuck saw her star potential as the screen's favourite innocent. She was regularly cast opposite Douglas Fairbanks, Jr in *The Careless Age* (1930) as Muriel, *Fast Life* (1929) as Patricia Mason Stratton, *The Forward Pass* (1929) as Patricia Carlyle, *Loose Ankles* (1930) as Ann Harper, *I Like Your Nerve* (1931) as Diane and again, four years later, in *The Life Of Jimmy Dolan* (1935) in which she played Peggy. Her other films around this time included *Her Wild Oat* (1927), *The Magnificent Flirt* (1928) as Denise Laverne, *The Head Man* (1928) as Carol Watts, *Scarlet Seas* (1928) as Margaret Barbour, *Seven Footprints To Satan* (1929), *The Man From Blankley's* (1930) as Margery Seaton, *The Second Floor Mystery* (1930) as Marion Ferguson, *Road To Paradise* (1930) as Mary Brennan/Margaret Waring, *Kismet* (1930) as Marsinah, *The Truth About Youth* (1930) as Phyllis Ericson, *The Devil To Pay!* (1930) as Dorothy Hope, *Beau Ideal* (1931) as Isobel Brandon, *The Right Of Way* (1931) as Rosalie Evantural, *Three Girls Lost* (1931) as Noreen McMann, *Too Young To Marry* (1931) as Elaine Bumpstead, *Big Business Girl* (1931) as Claire 'Mac' McIntyre and *Platinum Blonde* (1931) as Gallagher. She got good notices for her acting in *The Hatchet Man* (1932), in which she played Sun Toya San, a Chinese girl who marries Edward G. Robinson, also Chinese and the murderer of her father, and she looked her most beautiful in Rowland V. Lee's curious romance *Zoo In Budapest* (1933) as Eve. In 1933 she fell in love with Spencer Tracy, her leading man in Frank Borzage's *A Man's Castle*. She said of him, "I'd never met anyone like him. Such fire, the talent blazed at you. The story was a trifle but we really lived it. I proved I could really act with that one." Tracy, who was separated from his wife at the time, was involved in a fight with William Wellman over Young at the Trocadero Club but the affair ended on October 24, 1934 because of their shared Catholicism. "Since Spence and I are both Catholic and can never be married, we have agreed not to see each other again," she announced. Other boyfriends included: George Brent, Lyle Talbot, Gilbert Roland and the tennis star Fred Perry. Her films included *The Ruling Voice* (1931) as Gloria Bannister, *Taxi!* (1932) as Sue Reilly, *The Hatchet Man* (1932), *Play-Girl* (1932) as Buster 'Bus' Green, *Week-end Marriage* (1932) as Lola Davis, *Life Begins* (1932) as Mrs Grace Sutton, *They Call It Sin* (1932) as Marion Cullen, *Employees' Entrance* (1933) as Madeline Walters West, *Grand Slam* (1933) as Marcia Stanislavsky, *Heroes For Sale* (1933) as Ruth Loring Holmes, *Midnight Mary* (1933) as Mary Martin, *She Had To Say Yes* (1933) as Florence Denny and *The Devil's In Love* (1933) as Margot Lesesne. When Darryl Zanuck left

Warner to found Twentieth Century he took her with him. Here she appeared (and was not best pleased) in a series of costume pieces, such as *The House Of Rothschild* (1934) as Julie Rothschild, *Clive Of India* (1935) as Margaret Maskelyne Clive and (on loan to Cecil B. DeMille) in *The Crusades* (1935), her dark hair disguised under a waist-length blonde wig, as Richard the Lion-Heart's Queen Berengaria. After Twentieth Century amalgamated with Fox she got a new contract, taking account of her constantly improving status, and found herself teamed as a romantic duo with Tyrone Power in *Ladies In Love* (1936) as Susie Schmidt, *Love Is News* (1937) as Toni Gateson, *Cafe Metropole* (1937) as Laura Ridgeway, *Second Honeymoon* (1937) as Vicky Benton and *Suez* (1938) as Countess Eugenie de Montijo. She also appeared, though not to any particular advantage, in a film directed by John Ford, *Four Men And A Prayer* (1938) as Miss Lynn Cherrington. Despite the high hopes of Zanuck, her career seemed to be going nowhere, and after making *The Story Of Alexander Graham Bell* (1939) as Mabel Hubbard Bell, a biography of the inventor of the telephone (which she resented because she was not allowed to play Bell's wife as the deaf-mute she had in fact been, but merely as deaf) she refused to renew her contract with 20th Century Fox. Her other films at this period included *Born To Be Bad* (1934) as Letty Strong, *Bulldog Drummond Strikes Back* (1934) as Lola Field, *Caravan* (1934) as Countess Wilma, *The White Parade* (1934) as June Arden, *Shanghai* (1935) as Barbara Howard, *The Call Of The Wild* (1935) as Claire Blake, *The Unguarded Hour* (1936) as Lady Helen Dudley Dearden, *Private Number* (1936) as Ellen Neal, the title role in *Ramona* (1936), *Love Under Fire* (1937) as Myra Cooper, *Wife, Doctor And Nurse* (1937) as Ina Lewis, *Three Blind Mice* (1938) as Pamela Charters, *Kentucky* (1938) as Sally Goodwin, *Wife, Husband And Friend* (1939) as Doris Borland, and *Eternally Yours* (1939) as Anita. That same year Loretta Young went freelance, and was supposedly blacklisted by the Hollywood majors as too difficult to deal with. After a period of inactivity she signed a three picture contract with Columbia, at half her usual salary, and made a succession of minor comedies for various studios, incidentally co-starring with Alan Ladd in two films, *China* (1943) as Carolyn Grant and *And Now Tomorrow* (1944) as Emily Blair, the film which caused Bosley Crowther of the *New York Times* to remark, "Whatever it was that this actress never had, she still hasn't got it." Then she made one of her most interesting films, *The Stranger* (1946) as Mary Longstreet (Rankin), directed by and co-starring Orson Welles, who was under strict instructions to stick strictly to the agreed script, schedule and budget in order to prove that Hollywood could trust him. In Hollywood you are only as good as your last effort and so many critics began to say that Young was finished in Tinseltown. Then Dore Schary, RKO's new wunderkind offered her the role of Katrin Holstrom, a Swedish farm girl from Minnesota who goes to Washington and becomes a Congresswoman, in his film *The Farmer's Daughter* (1947). The part was originally intended for Ingrid Bergman. Young made the critics eat their words as she won the Oscar against such stiff competition as Joan Crawford in *Possessed*, Susan Hayward in *Smash-Up*, and Rosalind Russell in *Mourning Becomes Electra*. When Young got to the podium at the ceremony, all she could sigh was, "At long last!" Her other films included *The Doctor Takes A Wife* (1940) as June Cameron, *He Stayed For Breakfast* (1940) as Marianna Duval, *Bedtime Story* (1941) as Jane Drake, *The Lady From Cheyenne* (1941) as Annie Morgan, *The Men In Her Life* (1941) as Lina Varsavina,

A Night To Remember (1943) as Nancy Troy, *Ladies Courageous* (1944) as Roberta Harper, *Along Came Jones* (1945) as Cherry de Longpre, *The Perfect Marriage* (1946) as Maggie Williams, *The Bishop's Wife* (1947) as Julia Brougham (both she and Cary Grant insisted on being photographed from the left side, so that one scene had to be shot with them both looking out of a window. "If I can only use half your face, you only get half your salary," Samuel Goldwyn told her), *The Accused* (1948) as Wilma Tuttle, *Rachel And The Stranger* (1948) as Rachel Harvey, *Mother Is A Freshman* (1949) as Abigail Fortitude Abbott (director Richard Sale commented, "Loretta was delightful in the leading role. She was very vain, but you expect that from actors. Still, her wardrobe tests were longer than the picture"), *Come To The Stable* (1949) as Sister Margaret in a sentimental comedy drama for which she was nominated for an Oscar, *Key To The City* (1950) as Clarissa Standish, *Cause For Alarm!* (1951) as Ellen Jones, *Half Angel* (1951) as Nora, *Paula* (1952) as Paula Rogers, *Because Of You* (1952) as Christine Carroll and *It Happens Every Thursday* (1953) as Jane MacAvoy, her last major cinematic appearance. With her big screen career over, Loretta Young retired to the small screen. She said, "I was considered a traitor in Beverly Hills. Louis B. Mayer took it upon himself to phone me and said, 'Loretta, television is considered the enemy. You'll never make another picture, dear.' He was right, too. I've never done another movie." From September 20, 1953 until September 10, 1961, she presented *The Loretta Young Show*, a dramatic anthology on NBC. The show was a considerable success and won three Emmy awards – in 1954, 1956 and 1959. The show ended with her second marriage – he worked on the programme. *The New Loretta Young Show* ran for only six months on CBS from September 24,

1962 until March 18, 1963. She appeared in the straight-to-video film *Christmas Eve* (1986) as Amanda Kingsley and her last appearance was as magazine editor Grace Guthrie in *Lady In The Corner* (1989). A critic commented after seeing the film that Young never could act and seemed unlikely to learn now. A devout Roman Catholic, Young was married three times. On January 26, 1930, she eloped with 6′3″ actor Grant Withers (b. Pueblo, Colorado, January 17, 1904, d. North Hollywood, California, March 27, 1959 by his own hand). He called her 'The Steel Butterfly' because she obtained exactly what she wanted when it came to lighting, costume and make-up. On January 17, 1931, the marriage was annulled. After filming *The Call Of The Wild* (1935) with Clark Gable, Loretta announced that she was exhausted and would be going to Europe with her mother for a long holiday, expected to last at least a year. On November 30, 1936, Loretta suddenly reappeared in Hollywood apparently fit and well. On May 11, 1937, single Loretta "adopted" a 23-month-old girl, Judy. Californian law of the time forbade single people from adopting but somehow Loretta circumvented the legal niceties. In fact, Judy was the product of her mother's affair with Gable. Director William Wellman said, "All I know is that Loretta and Clark were very friendly during the picture, and it was very cold up there. When the film was finished, she disappeared for a while and later showed up with a daughter with the biggest ears I ever saw except on an elephant." Loretta later arranged for surgery on her daughter's ears. Judy who became a therapist in Los Angeles, was not told that Clark Gable was her father for more than 30 years, and the matter only became public knowledge in 1994. In 1939 Loretta was dating William Buckner who was later indicted and jailed for fraud. On July 31, 1940, writer-producer Tom

Lewis became her second husband. They had two sons, Christopher Paul (b. Los Angeles, California, August 1, 1944) and Peter (b. Los Angeles, California, July 15, 1945) and he adopted Judy. The Lewises divorced on October 21, 1969 in Los Angeles, California on the grounds of desertion. In 1973 Chris Lewis, 29, was arrested and charged with "lewd conduct with two 13-year-old boys". He pleaded no contest and was sentenced to five years' probation and a $500 fine. He had also made a kiddie porn film called *Genesis's Children*. Detective Lloyd Martin described Lewis and his co-defendants as "not homosexuals at all, but sick child molesters who bring discredit on the gay community". On September 10, 1993 Loretta married Columbia Pictures designer Jean Louis. He died on April 20, 1997. Loretta Young was known in Hollywood as something of a prude. In 1972, she won $600,000 from NBC, after claiming that they were ruining her image by broadcasting films in which she was shown in outmoded costumes. She campaigned to abolish swearing, pornography and immoral literature. On every one of her sets she had a swear box with the money going to St Anne's Maternity Hospital for Unmarried Mothers in Los Angeles. Some actors would put $10 in the box at the start of filming. Once when working with Robert Mitchum, he asked what her rates were. "Five cents for every 'damn', ten cents for 'hell' and 25 cents for 'goddamn'," she told him. "How much for 'fuck'?" he asked. Smiling, she told him, "That's free." CAUSE: She died aged 87 of ovarian and stomach cancer in Los Angeles, California. Loretta Young was buried with her mother in Grave 49, Tier 65, Section F of Holy Cross Cemetery, 5835 West Slauson Avenue, Culver City, California 90230.

Z

Darryl F. Zanuck

Born September 5, 1902
Died December 22, 1979
The last tycoon. Darryl Francis Zanuck
was born on the second floor of Le
Grande Hotel, an establishment
managed by his father on the corner of
Fifth Street and Broadway in Wahoo,
Nebraska. When he was eight years old
Zanuck played a Native American in
a silent Western and the experience
seemed to pique his interest in films.
To escape an unhappy home life he
joined the Nebraska National Guard
on September 4, 1916, and later served
in World War I. In Hollywood after the
war he screen-tested unsuccessfully for
the role of Oliver Twist. Having failed,
he decided to become a writer but first
had to support himself in a variety of
menial jobs. He wrote pulp fiction but
soon realised that the real money was
made by the screenwriters who adapted
works for the cinema. In 1923 he
wrote, or rather cobbled together from
four rejected articles, a book called
Habit. All four tales were sold to
Hollywood studios for £11,000. He
became a joke writer for, among others,
Mack Sennett, Harold Lloyd and
Charlie Chaplin. On January 24, 1924,
he married actress Virginia Fox.
He had also, by this time, joined
Warner Bros as a screenwriter and
subsequently wrote many films for
canine star Rin Tin Tin. He also
became Jack Warner's favourite writer,
because of his speed and inventiveness.
However, after writing 19 films in one
year he had to change his name and
began using three pseudonyms:
Melville Crossman, Mark Canfield and
Gregory Rogers, only occasionally
utilising Darryl F. Zanuck for special
events. Zanuck was bemused when
MGM tried to hire 'Melville
Crossman'. The 5'5" Zanuck gradually
moved up the pecking order at the
studios to become manager in 1928.
The only advice Jack Warner gave his
new head of production was to grow a
moustache and invest in a pair of
glasses, even if he didn't need them.
His salary was $260,000 a year. He
began a brief affair with attractive
blonde actress Dolores Costello.
Zanuck supervised the first all-talking
film *The Lights Of New York* (1928).
He also instigated a series of historical
biopics at Warner Bros, such as *Disraeli*
(1929) starring George Arliss. In
March 1933 Hollywood finally felt the
chill wind of the Depression that was
sweeping across America and the
studios suggested taking a 50%
reduction in staff salaries, or 25% if
they earned below a certain figure. The
technicians' union, IATSE, refused to
allow its members to face a wage slump
and threatened to strike. Harry Warner
wanted to call their bluff, so the whole
of Hollywood shut down on March 13,
1933. IATSE was not to be intimidated
and so the studios announced that only
the highest paid employees would face
the cut. (Certain stars – Constance
Bennett, Clara Bow and Maurice
Chevalier to name but three – went off
salary rather than accept the
reduction.) Harry and Jack Warner
petulantly announced they would not
take a cut in salary. Samuel Goldwyn
tried to act as a mediator, but Zanuck
was ready to act. He had taken a cut
and was furious at the high-handed way
the Warners were behaving. On
April 15, 1933, he walked out on his
$5,000-a-week job. Two days later, he
had a breakfast meeting with Joseph
M. Schenck and on April 27,
announced the formation of Twentieth
Century Pictures. On May 27,
1935, Twentieth Century Pictures
announced a merger with the Fox
Film Corporation to create 20th
Century Fox. Schenck became
chairman and Zanuck was head of

production at 32. It was at TCF that Zanuck really began to build his reputation as a mogul. He would stride around the Fox lot wearing riding boots and jodhpurs, carrying a crop that he would beat against his leg or on a desk to make a point. Zanuck insisted that none of his male stars have hairy chests. The bald-chested Tyrone Power was okay but hirsute hunks such as John Payne and William Holden had to shave their chests to comply. He demanded that one of the Fox actresses had sex with him in his office every afternoon and would often flash his penis at actresses. Once he took it out before Betty Grable and put it on the desk. "Isn't it beautiful?" he asked. "Yes," she said, "and you can put it away now." During World War II Zanuck made propaganda films but stayed at TCF until 1956 when he became an independent producer, though still working with the company. His biggest success was the war epic *The Longest Day* (1962) and the following year he was summoned back to 20th Century Fox to try and rescue the company from the financial mire that the film *Cleopatra* (1963) had landed them in. Displacing Spyros Skouras on July 25, he became President of the company, appointing his son, Richard, as Vice President with responsibility for production. On August 28, 1969, Richard became President while Darryl took over as Chairman and CEO. The following year, on December 29, 1970, he sacked his son and consolidated his position but only until May 18, 1971, when he became Chairman Emeritus. CAUSE: Zanuck suffered an inoperable brain tumour that left him incoherent and spent his last days in paranoid seclusion in Palm Springs.
FURTHER READING: *Darryl F. Zanuck: "Don't Say Yes Until I Finish Talking"* – Mel Gussow (London: W.H. Allen, 1971); *Zanuck: The Rise And Fall Of Hollywood's Tycoon* – Leonard Mosley (Boston: Little, Brown, 1984).

Howard Zieff

Born October 21, 1927
Died February 22, 2009

The ad-man. Born in Chicago, Illinois, he relocated with his family to the Boyle Heights section of East Los Angeles. After serving in the navy, he enrolled in the Art Center College of Design in Los Angeles before relocating once again to the East Cast where he began shooting still pictures for advertisements. He also directed television advertisements in which he cast the then unknowns Dustin Hoffman, Robert De Niro and Richard Dreyfuss. His first film was *Slither*, a 1973 comedy with James Caan and Peter Boyle. His other films included *Hearts Of The West* (1975), *House Calls* (1978), *The Main Event* (1979), *Private Benjamin* (1980), *Unfaithfully Yours* (1984), *The Dream Team* (1989), *My Girl* (1991) and *My Girl 2* (1994). He was forced to retire through ill-heath not long after the release of *My Girl 2*.
CAUSE: Zieff died of complications of Parkinson's disease at Cedars-Sinai Medical Center in Los Angeles. He was 81.

Fred Zinnemann

Born April 29, 1907
Died March 14, 1997

Master craftsman. Born in Vienna, Austria, Zinnemann studied law at the University of Vienna, but instead of becoming a lawyer, enrolled in a film school in Paris in 1927 inspired by the works of Erich von Stroheim and King Vidor. Two years later, he moved to Hollywood and began his career as an extra on *All Quiet On The Western Front* (1930). He then became a film cutter, gradually working his way up to director. In 1936 he married Renée Bartlett and had one son, Tim. In 1938 he won an Oscar for *That Mothers Might Live*. His first major directorial effort came 10 years later with *The Search* (1948), for which he was nominated for an Oscar. His biggest

films came in the early Fifties when he directed *High Noon* (1952), which won four Oscars and saw Zinnemann nominated, and *From Here To Eternity* (1953) which won eight Oscars, including Best Director for Zinnemann. He won Oscars for Best Film and Best Director on *A Man For All Seasons* (1966). He was also nominated for *The Nun's Story* (1958), *The Sundowners* (1960) and *Julia* (1977). He wrote an article on directing for the *Encyclopaedia Britannica*. Loathing Hollywood, Zinnemann moved to London permanently in 1963. He gave up making films in 1982 after *Five Days One Summer* was slated by critics. Towards the end of his career he was summoned by a young executive at a film studio who began the meeting with the words: "Tell me about a few things that you've done." Zinnemann responded dryly: "You first."
CAUSE: He died in London aged 89 of natural causes.

Vera Zorina
(EVA BRIGITTA HARTWIG)
Born January 2, 1917
Died April 9, 2003
Ballet beauty. Born in Berlin, Germany, her father, Fritz, was German and her mother, Billie, Norwegian and both were professional singers. She was given a pair of ballet slippers and refused to be parted from them, even taking them to bed. In 1929 Max Reinhardt cast her in his productions of *A Midsummer Night's Dream* and two years later in *Tales Of Hoffman*. In between she made her film debut as Jaqueline in *Seine Freundin Annette* (1930), billed in the credits under her real name. Joining the Ballet Russe de Monte Carlo in 1933 she changed her name to Vera Zorina. In 1935 she became involved in an open *ménage à trois* with Léonide Massine, then the world's best-known choreographer, and his wife, Eugenia Delarova. Two years later, she appeared in *On Your Toes* at London

where Samuel Goldwyn spotted her and offered her a contract. Her first film for him was *The Goldwyn Follies* (1938) in which she played Olga Samara. She reprised her role in *On Your Toes* (1939) as Vera Barnova and then appeared in *I Was An Adventuress* (1940) as Countess Tanya Vronsky and *Louisiana Purchase* (1941) as Marina Von Minden opposite Bob Hope. In 1943 she was cast as Maria in *For Whom The Bell Tolls* (1943) but after a fortnight she was sacked and replaced by Ingrid Bergman. Her cinematic career never really recovered and she made just two more films: *Follow The Boys* (1944) as Gloria Vance with George Raft and *Lover Come Back* (1946) as Madeline Laslo. She was married three times. In December 1938 she married George Balanchine, the choreographer. They went through an expensive (for him) divorce in 1946. That year she married Goddard Lieberson (b. April 5, 1911), the president of Columbia Records. He died on May 29, 1977. They had two sons, Peter Goddard Crespian, a composer, and Jonathan (d. 1989), a philosophy teacher. In 1991 she married the harpsichordist Paul Wolfe.
CAUSE: Vera Zorina died in Santa Fe, New Mexico of a cerebral haemorrhage. She was 86.

George Zucco
Born January 11, 1886
Died May 28, 1960
Mad scientist. Born in Manchester, his family moved to Canada when Zucco was still a baby and he made his first appearance on stage in 1908. His family were opposed to his entering the field of acting, believing it to be a risky profession, but Zucco was determined to prove them wrong. In 1914 he returned to England and joined the army where he met director James Whale and the two men became firm friends. His first major film was *The Dreyfus Case* (1931), in which he

played Cavaignac, and he soon found a niche playing mad scientists or other villains. He appeared in, among others, *After The Thin Man* (1936) as Dr Adolph Kammer, *Parnell* (1937) as Sir Charles Russell, *Saratoga* (1937) as Dr Harmsworth Bierd, *Madame X* (1937) as Dr LaFarge, *Charlie Chan In Honolulu* (1938) as Dr Cardigan, *The Hunchback Of Notre Dame* (1939) as the Procurator of the Parisian High Court, *Captain Fury* (1939) as Arnold Trist, *Arrest Bulldog Drummond* (1939) as Rolf Alferson, *The Adventures Of Sherlock Holmes* (1939) as Professor Moriarty, *The Mummy's Hand* (1940) as Andoheb, *The Monster And The Girl* (1941) as Dr Perry, *Ellery Queen And The Murder Ring* (1941) as Dr Jannery, *My Favorite Blonde* (1942) as Doctor Hugo Streger, *The Mummy's Tomb* (1942) reprising his role as Andoheb, *The Mad Monster* (1942) as Dr Lorenzo Cameron, *The Black Swan* (1942) as the former governor of Jamaica Lord Denby, *The Black Raven* (1943) as Amos Bradford, *Sherlock Holmes In Washington* (1943) as Richard Stanley, *Voodoo Man* (1944) as Nicholas, *The Mummy's Ghost* (1944) again as Andoheb, *House Of Frankenstein* (1944) as Professor Bruno Lampini, *Hold That Blonde* (1945) as Pavel Sorasky, *Fog Island* (1945) as Leo Grainger, *Scared To Death* (1947) as Dr Josef Van Ee, *Who Killed Doc Robbin?* (1948) as Doc Robbin, *Tarzan And The Mermaids* (1948) as Palanth and *David And Bathsheba* (1951). CAUSE: Critics of films claim that impressionable minds can be affected by what is portrayed on screen. It is rare for an actor to be so affected, yet that is what happened to George Zucco. Years of playing madmen finally warped his mind and he was committed to an asylum. To be close to him, his wife and daughter moved into the asylum as well. Zucco

died, hopelessly insane, in Hollywood, on May 28, 1960. The following day, his wife and daughter committed suicide.

Adolph Zukor
Born January 7, 1873
Died June 10, 1976
Centenarian mogul. Born in Ricse, Austria-Hungary, Zukor emigrated to the United States aged 15 and became a road sweeper, then a film salesman, a cinema owner and, in 1913, an independent producer. He formed Famous-Players, which, in 1916, merged with Jesse Lasky's organisation. Zukor was President and later the company took over a smaller one called Paramount. Later, it evolved into Paramount Pictures and Zukor was President until 1936 when he became Chairman.
CAUSE: Zukor died in Los Angeles, California, aged 103. He once quipped: "If I'd known I was going to live this long, I'd have taken better care of myself."

Zulu
(GILBERT FRANCIS LANI DAMIAN KAUHI)
Born October 17, 1937
Died May 3, 2004
Top cop. Hilo, Hawaii-born Zulu was one of the original cast of the hit cop show *Hawaii Five-O*. He was a popular beach boy on Waikiki when he joined the programme as Detective Kono Kalakaua. He spent four years as Steve McGarrett's burly sidekick until he was sacked following an argument with the show's publicist. After he left he became an entertainer in the clubs and bars of Waikiki. Zulu's death leaves only James MacArthur alive from the original cast.
CAUSE: He died, aged 66, in Hilo Medical Center, Honolulu, of complications from diabetes.